BUSINESS STATISTICS
OF THE
UNITED STATES

PATTERNS OF ECONOMIC CHANGE

17TH EDITION
2012

BUSINESS STATISTICS
OF THE UNITED STATES

PATTERNS OF ECONOMIC CHANGE

17TH EDITION
2012

Edited by Cornelia J. Strawser

Associate Editor
Mary Meghan Ryan

 **Bernan** Press

Lanham, Maryland

Published in the United States of America
by Bernan Press, a wholly owned subsidiary of
The Rowman & Littlefield Publishing Group, Inc.
4501 Forbes Boulevard, Suite 200
Lanham, Maryland 20706

Bernan Press
800-865-3457
www.bernan.com

Copyright © 2013 by Bernan Press

ISBN-13: 978-1-59888-528-6

ISSN: 1086-8488

∞™ The paper used in this publication meets the minimum requirements of
American National Standard for Information Sciences—Permanence of
Paper for Printed Library Materials, ANSI/NISO Z39.48-1992.
Manufactured in the United States of America.

CONTENTS

PREFACE

Business Statistics of the United States: Patterns of Economic Change, 17th Edition, 2012 is a basic desk reference for anyone requiring statistics on the U.S. economy. It contains about 3,500 economic time series in all, portraying the period since World War II in comprehensive detail. In the case of about 200 key series, the period from 1929 through 1948 is shown as well. And for three important statistical series that have been compiled monthly on a continuous basis, monthly and annual data are included going back to 1919 for industrial production and 1913 for consumer and producer prices. Data for the period up through December 2011 are presented, as revised and updated by source agencies through June 2012.

The data are predominantly from federal government sources. Of equal importance are the extensive background notes for each chapter, which help users to understand the data, use them appropriately, and, if desired, seek additional information from the source agencies.

Business Statistics of the United States brings together in one place all historical data back to the year 1929—and even earlier for three major indexes—for each of the major U.S. economic indicators, instead of showing recent data in one chapter and historical background in another. More than ever, *Business Statistics* will be the best place to find historical perspectives on the U.S. economy.

Earlier editions of this book followed a basic one- or two-page format for each major statistical series, displaying a few years of the latest monthly or quarterly values and as many year of annual values as could fit on the page. As the years went by, we added chapters at the end of the volume with historical data extending back to the beginning of the post-World-War II period. Later still, yet another chapter was added with data for the period from 1929 through the end of World War II. The result was a book that "just growed" into a rather inconvenient arrangement, in which the user looking for a consistent time series on gross domestic product or unemployment for an extended period might have to refer to two or three different chapters.

Now, all chapters are organized according to subject matter. For most time series, users will find an initial page displaying the latest two years of monthly data, or three years of quarterly data, for the most recent completed years, along with annual averages for the last completed 40, 50, or even 60 years.

For the most important series for which we have long-term historical data, this initial page will be labeled with "A" after the table number, and identified in the title by the additional words "Recent Data". It will be immediately followed by pages labeled with "B" after the table number

and identified by the words "Historical Data", which will show all available historical data annually back to 1929, and monthly or quarterly back to the earliest available postwar year. In some cases, additional tables of historical data will be added, but in all cases the historical data will be grouped with the current data for the series.

In addition, the monthly index of industrial production is shown all the way back to 1919, and monthly indexes of consumer and producer prices back to 1913. In both cases, these are the earliest dates for which the originating agencies (respectively, the Federal Reserve Board and the Bureau of Labor Statistics [BLS]) have compiled a continuous series.

Other important recent additions include:

- Expanded data from the BLS "Productivity and Costs" system, including indexes of the share of the value of business product being paid to workers.
- Annual data from the BLS on hours worked per person, from the Current Population Survey (CPS), going back as far as 1948. These differ significantly from the well-known "average workweek" statistics from the Current Employment Statistics survey (CES) that are reported monthly and have always been included in *Business Statistics*. The CES workweek is average hours per job, and is extremely important as a business cycle indicator and an input to productivity measurement. But it does not represent the workweek of the average worker, since one worker may have more than one job. As an indication of the difference, in 2010 the average nonfarm job in the CES survey was 34.1 hours long, but the CPS indicates that the average nonfarm worker worked 38.1 hours for pay, which was an average of 40.4 hours for men and 35.6 hours for women.
- Additional data for those who would like to compare inflation rates among major industrial countries. A new table includes "Harmonized Indexes of Consumer Prices" for the United States, the European Union, the Euro area, 12 European nations, and Japan, all converted to the same conceptual basis—representing both urban and rural households and excluding owner-occupied housing. The harmonized indexes are used by the European Central Bank for the conduct of monetary policy. As an example of what difference this can make in yearly inflation rates, these indexes show that in 2009, the official U.S. price index declined 0.4 percent while the "harmonized" index not including owner-occupied housing declined 0.9 percent. For the United Kingdom, official inflation in that year was minus 0.5, while the harmonized index rose 2.1 percent. Index levels as well as changes are also shown, so that the user can also calculate that over longer periods of time the differences are smaller.

The leading article "Business Cycle Perspectives" presents an updated comparison of the current recession-recovery period (extended through June 2012) with earlier business cycles. In addition, there are detailed comparisons among the economic characteristics of the last three completed peak-to-peak business cycle periods, and a new section analyzing the continued lag of worker pay behind productivity growth. Today, when alternative policies to restore and extend economic growth are being vigorously debated, it can be useful to compare past periods on a standardized basis, to ascertain which economic policies produced more favorable economic outcomes.

THE PLAN OF THE BOOK

The history of the U.S. economy is told in major U.S. government sets of statistical data: the national income and product accounts compiled by the Bureau of Economic Analysis (BEA); the data on labor force, employment, hours, earnings, and productivity compiled by the Bureau of Labor Statistics (BLS); the price indexes collected by BLS; and the financial market and industrial production data compiled primarily by the Board of Governors of the Federal Reserve System (FRB). All of these sets exist in annual and either monthly or quarterly form beginning in 1946, 1947, or 1948; many are available, at least annually, as far back as 1929; and three are available monthly back to the teens of the 20th century.

In Part A, *Business Statistics* presents the aggregate United States economy in a number of important dimensions. The presentations begin with the national income and product accounts, or NIPAs. The NIPAs comprise a comprehensive, thorough, and internally consistent body of data. They measure the value of the total output of the U.S. economy (the gross domestic product, or GDP) and they allocate that value between its quantity, or "real," and price components. They show how the value of aggregate demand is distributed among consumers, business investors, government, and foreign customers; how much of aggregate demand is supplied by imports and how much by domestic production; and how the income generated in domestic production is distributed between labor and capital.

Production estimates covering only the sectors of the economy that used to be labeled "industrial"—manufacturing, mining, and utilities—are shown in Chapter 2, after the presentation of the overall NIPAs in Chapter 1.

The distribution of personal income, median income—the best measure of the economic well-being of the "typical" American—and poverty statistics from a Census household survey are presented in Chapter 3.

Then, more detail from the NIPAs is presented for the demand components of economic activity. GDP by definition consists of the sum of consumption expenditures, business investment, government purchases of goods and services, and exports minus imports—the elementary economics blackboard identity "GDP = C + I + G + X − M." Chapters on each of these components—consumption, investment, government, and foreign trade—are presented in Part A.

Following these chapters, there are a chapter on prices, two chapters on the compensation of labor and capital inputs and the amount and productivity of labor input, one chapter on energy inputs into production and consumption, and one chapter on money and financial markets.

At the end of Part A, BLS comparisons of output, prices, and labor markets among major industrial countries are presented, along with statistics on the value of the dollar against other currencies.

While GDP is initially defined and measured by adding up its demand categories and subtracting imports, this output is produced in industries—some in the old-line heavy industries such as manufacturing, mining, and utilities, but an increasing share in the huge and heterogeneous group known as "service-providing" industries. Part A gives a number of summary measures of activity classified by industry or industrial sector: industrial production, profits, and employment-related data. Further industry information is provided in Part B.

Industry data collection is important because demands for goods and services are channeled into demands for labor and capital through the industries responsible for producing the requested goods and services. These data are reported using the North American Industry Classification System (NAICS). This system, introduced in 1997 to replace the older Standard Industrial Classification System (SIC), delineates industries that are better defined in relation to today's demands and more closely related to each other by technology. Notable examples include more detailed data available on service industries, a more rational grouping of the Computer and electronic product manufacturing subsector, and the creation of the Information sector. See the References at the end of this Preface.

NAICS industries are groupings of producing units—not of products as such—and are grouped according to similarity of production processes. This is done in order to collect consistent data on inputs and outputs, which are then used to measure important concepts, such as productivity and input-output parameters. Emphasis on the production process helps to explain a number of ways in which the NAICS differs from the SIC.

Manufacturing activities at retail locations, such as bakeries, have been classified separately from retail activity and put into the Food manufacturing industry.

Central administrative offices of companies have a new sector of their own, Management of companies and enterprises (sector 55). For example, the headquarters office of a food-producing corporation is considered part of the new sector instead of part of the Food manufacturing industry.

Reproduction of packaged software, which was classified as a business service in the SIC, is now classified in sector 334, Computer and electronic product manufacturing, as a manufacturing process.

Electronic markets and agents and brokers, formerly undifferentiated components of wholesale trade industries, have a sector of their own (425).

Retail trade in NAICS (sectors 44 and 45) now includes establishments such as office supply stores, computer and software stores, building materials dealers, plumbing supply stores, and electrical supply stores, that display merchandise and use mass-media advertising to sell to individuals as well as to businesses, which were formerly classified in wholesale trade.

In Part B, *Business Statistics* shows GDP, income, employment, hours, and earnings by industry, followed by statistics for key sectors such as petroleum, housing, manufacturing, retail trade, and services.

Part C, Regional and State Data, contains annual data by state and region on personal income and employment back to 1958, and annual values and quantity indexes for GDP by state and region back to 1977.

NOTES AND DEFINITIONS

Productive use of economic data requires accurate knowledge about the sources and meaning of the data. The notes and definitions for each chapter, shown immediately after that chapter's tables, contain definitions, descriptions of recent data revisions, and references to sources of additional technical information. They also include information about data availability and revision and release schedules, which helps users to readily access the latest current values if they need to keep up with the data month by month or quarter by quarter.

A NOTE ON THE IMPORTANCE OF ECONOMIC STATISTICS

While retrieving data for 1929-1948, the editor of *Business Statistics* encountered some inspiring prefatory words in the Federal Reserve Board volume *Banking and Monetary Statistics* (1943). Written by the Fed's longtime statistics chief E. A. Goldenweiser in the stately cadences of an earlier era, they were written to apply just to the financial statistics collected in that volume. But they well express the hope and expectation of statisticians and economists that their work can lead to better economic decisions:

> "These serried ranks of organized statistics on banking and finance, even though they may inspire awe, should also inspire confidence. They are an augury that credit policy can be based in the future, as in the past, on fact rather than on fancy."

THE HISTORY OF *BUSINESS STATISTICS*

The history of *Business Statistics* began with the publication, many years ago, of the first edition of a volume with the same name by the U.S. Department of Commerce's Bureau of Economic Analysis (BEA). After 27 periodic editions, the last of which appeared in 1992, BEA found it necessary, for budgetary and other reasons, to discontinue both the publication and the maintenance of the database from which the publication was derived.

The individual statistical series gathered together here are publicly available. However, the task of gathering them from the numerous different sources within the government and assembling them into one coherent database is impractical for most data users. Even when current data are readily available, obtaining the full historical time series is often time-consuming and difficult. Definitions and other documentation can also be inconvenient to find. Believing that a *Business Statistics* compilation was too valuable to be lost to the public, Bernan Press published the first edition of the present publication, edited by Dr. Courtenay M. Slater, in 1995. The first edition received a warm welcome from users of economic data. Dr. Slater, formerly chief economist of the Department of Commerce, continued to develop *Business Statistics* through four subsequent annual editions. The current editor worked with Dr. Slater on the fourth and fifth editions. In subsequent editions, she has continued in the tradition established by Dr. Slater of ensuring high-quality data, while revising and expanding the book's scope to include significant new aspects of the U.S. economy and longer historical background.

Nearly all of the statistical data in this book are from federal government sources and are available in the public domain. Sources are given in the applicable notes and definitions.

The data in this volume meet the publication standards of the federal statistical agencies from which they were obtained. Every effort has been made to select data that are accurate, meaningful, and useful. All statistical data are subject to error arising from sampling variability, reporting errors, incomplete coverage, imputation, and other causes. The responsibility of the editor and publisher of this volume is limited to reasonable care in the reproduction and presentation of data obtained from established sources.

The 2012 edition has been edited by Cornelia J. Strawser, in association with Mary Meghan Ryan, who prepared all the tables and graphs and whose ability and experience have been essential in producing a timely and accurate reference work.

Dr. Strawser is the senior economic consultant to Bernan Press. She edited the seventh through sixteenth editions and was the co-editor of two previous editions of *Business Statistics*. She was co-editor of *Foreign Trade of the United States, 2001,* and also worked on the *Handbook of U.S. Labor Statistics.* She was formerly a senior economist for the U.S. House of Representatives Budget Committee and has also served at the Senate Budget Committee, at the Congressional Budget Office, and on the Federal Reserve Board staff.

The editor assumes full responsibility for the interpretations presented in this volume.

References

The NAICS is explained and laid out in *North American Industry Classification System: United States, 2007*, from the Executive Office of the President, Office of Management and Budget. This presents the second five-year updating of the system, which was first introduced in 1997. Changes introduced in these updatings have been minor and have not affected the definitions of the industry divisions presented in *Business Statistics*.

Information on differences between NAICS and SIC can be found in *North American Industry Classification System: United States, 1997*, from the Executive Office of the President, Office of Management and Budget (which contains matches between the 1997 NAICS and the 1987 SIC); and *North American Industry Classification System: United States, 2002* (which contains matches that show the relatively few changes from the 1997 NAICS to the 2002 NAICS).

All three of these volumes are available from Bernan Press. These volumes fully describe the development and application of the new classification system and are the sources for the material presented in this volume. Information is also available on the NAICS Web site at <http://www.census.gov/naics>. Additional background information can also be found in Bernan Press's *Business Statistics of the United States: 2002* (8th edition), pp. xxiv–xxviii.

BUSINESS CYCLE PERSPECTIVES

This 17th edition of *Business Statistics of the United States* presents comprehensive and detailed data on U.S. economic performance through December 2011. These data span the full course of the 11th recession of the postwar period and the first 2 ½ years of recovery, according to the chronology maintained by the National Bureau of Economic Research (NBER), which has determined that the recession began in December 2007 and ended in June 2009.

The 2007–2009 recession lasted 18 months and was the longest of the postwar period: the two longest previous postwar recessions each lasted 16 months. By many measures—see, for example, Figure A–1, the chart of payroll employment that follows—it was more severe than any other postwar recession. It was pointed out in the 2010 Annual Report of the President's Council of Economic Advisers (Chapter 2) that the financial shocks that set off this recession were at least as severe as those that precipitated the Great Depression of the 1930s; indeed, "in 1929, household wealth declined only 3 percent—about one –seventh as much as in 2008." While the latest recession did not follow the path of the Great Contraction of 1929–1933—probably because the policy responses have been markedly different—it does not seem to be inappropriate that it is being called the Great Recession. And it is of additional concern that the recovery has been slow, and incommensurate with the depth of the recession. (See the article that follows this one, "The U.S. Economy 1929–1948," for more about the Great Depression.)

This article begins with a general discussion of business cycles in the United States economy, including a chronology of the cycles occurring in the years covered by this volume, and a discussion of the meaning of the term "The Great Depression".

- Following this is an example of the use of monthly data, such as those provided in this book, to track recession and recovery.
- Then, other examples are provided of important analytical techniques for extracting key information from statistical records, particularly for focusing on growth issues.
- Following that section, and illustrating the use of the techniques described, is a comparison of the latest completed cycle of recession, recovery, and growth—between 2000 and 2007—with two previous full cycles. The tables, A–3 and A–4, also include a column showing developments since 2007.
- A new section analyzes the failure of worker compensation to keep up with productivity growth.

- The last section of this article concerns measuring the standard of living.

BUSINESS CYCLES IN THE U.S. ECONOMY

The study of economic fluctuations in the United States was pioneered by Wesley C. Mitchell and Arthur F. Burns early in the twentieth century, and was carried on subsequently by other researchers affiliated with the National Bureau of Economic Research (NBER), an independent, nonpartisan research organization. These analysts observed that indicators of the general state of business activity tended to move up and down over periods that were longer than a year and were therefore not accounted for by seasonal variation. Although these periods of expansion and contraction were not uniform in length, and thus not "cycles" in any strict mathematical sense, their recurrent nature caused them to be called "business cycles." NBER has identified 32 complete peak-to-peak business cycles over the period beginning with December 1854.

The first NBER-established business cycle dates, identifying the monthly peaks and troughs in general economic activity, were published in 1929. Currently, the dates are established by the NBER Business Cycle Dating Committee, first formed in 1978. It consists of eight economists who are university professors, associated with research organizations, or both.

Business cycle dates are based on monthly data, and have been identified for periods long before the availability of quarterly data on real gross national product (GDP). It is important to understand that even in the recent period for which such data are available, the NBER identification of a recession does not always coincide with the frequently cited definition of recession as two consecutive quarters of decline in real GDP.

The NBER monthly and quarterly dates of the cycles from 1912 to the latest announced turning point—the June 2009 trough ending the recession that began in December 2007—are shown in Table A–1 below. The quarterly turning points are identified by Roman numerals. NBER considers that the trough month is both the end of the decline and the beginning of the recovery, based on the concept that the actual turning point was some particular day within that month. Thus, the latest recession ended in June 2009, and the recovery also began in June 2009.

For additional information on NBER and its business cycle studies, see the NBER Web site at <http://www.nber .org/cycles>.

Table A-1. BUSINESS CYCLE REFERENCE DATES 1912–2009

TROUGH	PEAK
JANUARY 1912 (IV)	JANUARY 1913 (I)
DECEMBER 1914 (IV)	AUGUST 1918 (III)
MARCH 1919 (I)	JANUARY 1920 (I)
JULY 1921 (III)	MAY 1923 (II)
JULY 1924 (III)	OCTOBER 1926 (III)
NOVEMBER 1927 (IV)	AUGUST 1929 (III)
MARCH 1933 (I)	MAY 1937 (II)
JUNE 1938 (II)	FEBRUARY 1945 (I)
OCTOBER 1945 (IV)	NOVEMBER 1948 (IV)
OCTOBER 1949 (IV)	JULY 1953 (II)
MAY 1954 (II)	AUGUST 1957 (III)
APRIL 1958 (II)	APRIL 1960 (II)
FEBRUARY 1961 (I)	DECEMBER 1969 (IV)
NOVEMBER 1970 (IV)	NOVEMBER 1973 (IV)
MARCH 1975 (I)	JANUARY 1980 (I)
JULY 1980 (III)	JULY 1981 (III)
NOVEMBER 1982 (IV)	JULY 1990 (III)
MARCH 1991 (I)	MARCH 2001 (I)
NOVEMBER 2001 (IV)	DECEMBER 2007 (IV)
JUNE 2009 (II)	

SOURCE: NATIONAL BUREAU OF ECONOMIC RESEARCH, HTTP://WWW.NBER.ORG/CYCLES.

WHAT WAS THE GREAT DEPRESSION?

Note that most of the 1930s, after the March 1933 trough, is identified as a period of expansion by NBER, in apparent conflict with the fact that the entire decade is often considered to be in the "Great Depression." The NBER does not identify "depressions;" the popular usage denotes a prolonged period of idle resources. People interested in the economics and politics of the 1930s may wish to distinguish, as NBER does, between that part of the period when output and employment declined precipitously—the 43-month collapse from August 1929 through March 1933, sometimes called The Great Contraction—and the subsequent period when output and employment, though still far below a likely trend line, were rising most of the time, before accepting at face value statements like "the New Deal failed to end the Depression."

The article that follows this one, "The U.S. Economy 1929–1948," includes five graphs depicting the economic course of the Depression and World War II periods, accompanied by some explanatory narration. The Notes and Definitions to Chapter 10 discuss the important issue of the statistical treatment of work relief employment during the Depression.

TRACKING RECESSION AND RECOVERY: TOTAL PAYROLL EMPLOYMENT

Figure A–1 shows how current data can be tracked month by month in comparison with earlier business cycles. The figure depicts proportional movements in total payroll employment (see Tables 10–8 and 10–9 and the associated Notes and Definitions), beginning with the cycle peak and continuing over the following 4 ½ years—incorporating preliminary data through mid–2012 that are not published in the tables that constitute the main body of this volume.

Many economists would prefer to track cycles monthly using a comprehensive measure of aggregate output, not employment. However, we do not have a satisfactory monthly measure of gross domestic product (GDP); attempts to estimate it have proved to be volatile, "noisy", and subject to excessive revision.

The reliable and long-established monthly index of industrial production is a narrower measure of output, limited to manufacturing, mining, and utilities. It is presented in Chapter 2 of this volume. Mining and utilities are of little significance in the business cycle process; in fact, short-term variation in the utility sector is mostly influenced not by cycles in demand but by unusual weather conditions. As a result, the cyclical movements of the industrial production index are dominated by the manufacturing sector. Because manufacturing now accounts for only about 10 percent of total nonfarm employment, the industrial production index is an imperfect general business cycle gauge, but it is still one of the major indicators monitored by the Business Cycle Dating Committee. Furthermore, it is the only such indicator that extends monthly all the way back to 1919; these historical data are now shown in *Business Statistics*.

The employment count—covering the entire nonfarm economy, based on a large and long-established sample of large and small businesses, and available shortly after the end of each month—is a widely accepted indicator, more reliable and less subject either to substantial revision or to excessive random variation than any available broad monthly production measure. It is viewed as "the most reliable comprehensive estimate of employment" by the Business Cycle Dating Committee.

For ease of comparing proportional effects in this graph, the employment totals for each recession period are converted to indexes with the cycle's peak month set at 100. For example, the line labeled "From July 1981" represents employment at the peak and in each of the 54 successive months, July 1981 through January 1986, divided by the July 1981 value and multiplied by 100. The line labeled "From December 2007" represents employment in each month, December 2007 through a preliminary value for June 2012, divided by the December 2007 value and multiplied by 100.

Looked at in this way, the similarities among the four recessions in the first 10 months of decline were striking: nearly a year after the peak, employment was down about 1 ½ percent in each case. Two months later, the four declines no longer looked similar. Employment had leveled off in 1991 and 2002, but lurched further downward in winter 2008–2009 as it did in mid–1982.

Figure A–1 shows that the slide in employment from the July 1981 peak continued for a year and a half and then began a brisk recovery. However, the downward turn in the latest period was deeper and much longer. The low point was not reached until February 2010, more than two years after the employment peak and eight months past the NBER cycle trough.

In comparing the end-of-recession and beginning-of-recovery periods 1982–1984 and 2009–2011, it should be noted that both periods saw fiscal stimulus enacted, but the monetary conditions are strikingly different. A look at Table 12–9B shows that the federal funds rate (the rate banks charge on overnight loans, set by Federal Reserve open market operations) was 19 percent in July 1981, fell to 13 percent in July 1982, and was 9 percent by July 1983. The Fed had maintained a very tight policy in early 1981 to break the back of inflation, but then had plenty of room to reduce rates once the recession was under way. The housing industry was not burdened then with a huge overhang of household debt and excess housing inventory, and was able to play its usual role in sparking the recovery.

In contrast, the federal funds rate was already close to zero at the cycle peak in December 2007, and the initial obstacles to renewed credit flows and construction activity were not high interest rates but deflation, an overbuilt housing inventory, and deteriorating financial balance sheets. Later, as some of these conditions improved, other obstacles including new problems overseas and policy debates at home are said to be impeding recovery. Furthermore, as will be seen in analysis later in this chapter, a declining share of the value of private-sector output

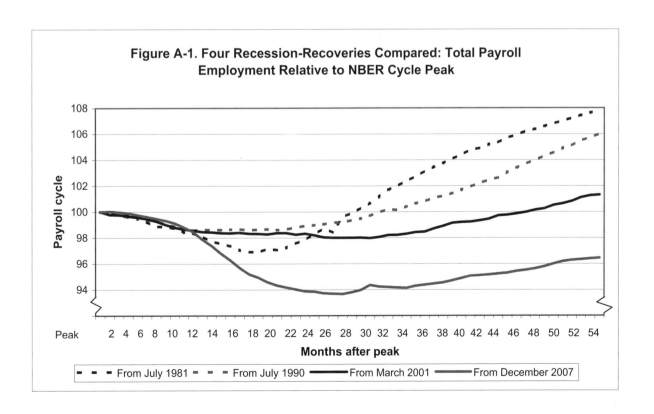

Figure A-1. Four Recession-Recoveries Compared: Total Payroll Employment Relative to NBER Cycle Peak

has been paid to workers and a rising share to profits, especially financial sector profits. This change in the flows of economic circulation may be hindering recovery as well.

ANALYTICAL TECHNIQUES FOR GROWTH ISSUES

In assessing the performance of an economy over longer periods of time, it is important to use analytical techniques that highlight the most important aspects of the series. In this article and in the graphs and text that accompany nearly every *Business Statistics* data chapter, the editor will frequently make use of three powerful tools: the ratio-scale graph, the calculation of compound annual growth rates, and the use of cyclically comparable years to estimate trends and to separate trend from cyclical behavior. Econometricians use more elaborate methods of statistical analysis to estimate relationships and construct models, but much can be discerned just by using these relatively simple techniques.

Ratio-scale graphs. At the beginning of Chapter 1 (Figure 1 –1) is a time series graph of output per capita from 1946 through 2011, drawn on a ratio scale. Output per capita is the constant-dollar value of each year's U.S. gross domestic product (GDP), divided by the size of that year's U.S. population.

The reader will quickly see that equal distances on the vertical scale of this graph do not represent equal differences in 2005-dollar values. However, equal vertical distances do represent equal <u>percent changes</u>. Any upward-sloping straight line plotted on this scale represents a constant percentage rate of growth over the period, and any downward-sloping straight line represents a constant percentage rate of decline.

This ratio-scale graph was produced by the following three steps: (1) The values to be graphed were converted into natural (base e) logarithms. (2) The natural logarithms were graphed. (3) For ease of interpretation, the vertical scale on this graph of the logarithms was re-labeled, replacing the numerical value of the logarithm that was plotted with the numerical value of its antilog—that is, the original value of per capita output.

This technique is only valid for data series that do not include zeroes or negative numbers, for which logarithms do not exist. Because percentage values such as the unemployment rate and percent changes such as the inflation rate are already in percentage terms, and because percent changes may include zero and/or negative values, they are not graphed in this fashion.

Compound annual growth rates. In the text of this article and in the highlights pages that precede and accompany each chapter, the editor often uses compound annual growth rates to summarize the history of important economic processes such as economic and demographic growth and inflation.

The compound annual growth rate is the percentage rate which, when compounded annually, would cause a quantity or price "X(t)" observed in a base period "t" to grow (or decline) to the observed quantity or price "X(t+i)" over a period of "i" years. Using this procedure, growth percentages for different periods spanning different numbers of years can be reduced to a common scale—the annual rate—for comparison. The formula for calculating such a growth rate, "r," is as follows:

$$ r = \left(\sqrt[i]{X(t+i) \Big/ X(t)} - 1 \right) x100 $$

When growth rates are functionally related to each other, such as the growth rates for output, hours worked, and output per hour worked (productivity), those rates will be arithmetically consistent as in the following formula, where "o" is the percentage growth rate for output, "h" the rate for hours worked, and "p" the growth rate for output per hour worked:

$$ p = \Big[\big[(100 + o)/(100 + h) \big] - 1 \Big] x100 $$

When the percentage growth rates are not very far from zero, relationships of this kind can be approximated or verified by simple addition or subtraction of the relevant percentage rates. For example, the productivity growth rate of 2.2 percent in output per hour at nonfarm business from 1948 to 2000 is approximately the difference between the output growth rate of 3.7 percent and the hours growth rate of 1.5 percent in that period.

Using cyclically comparable end points. For economic processes that have significant business-cycle components, such as output and employment, it is important to use comparable points in the business cycle for estimating underlying—that is, long-term sustainable—growth rates. One commonly used method is to calculate growth rates between years with similar, high rates of resource utilization. The broadest readily available measure of resource utilization is the unemployment rate—actually, of course, a measure of "un-utilization"—which was 3.8 percent in 1948, 5.8 in 1979, 5.6 percent in 1990, 4.0 percent in 2000, and 4.6 percent in 2007. These were all at or near the cycle low points. (See Tables 10–1A and B and Figure 10.2.) A narrower measure that focuses on capital rather than labor, namely capacity utilization in manufacturing, was 82.5 percent in 1948, 84.0 percent in 1979, 81.7 percent in 1990, 79.8 percent in 2000, and 78.5 percent in 2007. These rates were near their cycle highs. (See Tables 2–3 and 2–4A and Figure 2–1.)

ANALYSIS OF COMPLETED CYCLES

In the analysis that follows, the editor will compare the most recent full cycle with the two previous peak-to-peak periods. The analysis will use annual averages, because

End points that are not comparable: what difference does it make?

An interesting example of non-cyclically-comparable end points appeared in a commentary by Richard W. Rahn in *The Washington Times* (January 27, 2010). He wrote that "In the nine quarter-century periods since the American republic was founded in 1789, the one with highest economic growth and job creation was the period from 1983 through 2007." He showed an annual average growth rate of 3.33 percent during that period, which he measured from the year 1982 as a base.

However, November 1982 marked the trough of a deep recession, and December 2007 a cycle peak. If GDP growth is measured between the years of the two full cycle peaks nearest to this general time span, 1979 and 2007, it averages 2.95 percent; if it is measured between the two nearest troughs, 1982 and 2009, it averages 2.90 percent. This suggests that long-term growth in potential output was more like 3.0 percent than like 3 1/3 percent, although of course higher growth rates can—and should—be attained temporarily when starting from an under-utilization low.

Similarly, growth in payroll employment 1982–2007 averaged 1.73 percent; but between 1979 and 2007, it was 1.53 percent and between 1982 and 2009, 1.41 percent.

Furthermore, as will be seen in Tables A–2, A–3, and A–4 and subsequent analysis, the period between 1979 and 2007 includes three full cycles with somewhat different growth rates and other characteristics, including possible differences in potential labor input, capital input, and productivity—the determinants of long-term sustainable growth—as well as different economic policy settings.

All of these facts suggest that long-term growth rates using non-comparable end points will not provide a solid basis for policy analysis. Comparisons based on other artificial demarcation points, such as decades, may be subject to similar distortions.

they are less volatile, and also because it is thereby possible to include, in time-consistent comparisons, data that are only available annually from the Census Bureau's Current Population Survey of household income and earnings.

The three full cycles are: January 1980 to July 1990 (ignoring the brief and incomplete recovery between July 1980 and July 1981, which left unemployment and production far short of full utilization), July 1990 to March 2001, and March 2001 to December 2007. The measurements of economic developments over those cycles will be based on the high-utilization years 1979, 1990, 2000, and 2007 that are associated with the designated business cycle peaks.

It should be noted that the peak-to-peak definition used here includes the recessions themselves as part of the cycle, as well as the subsequent recoveries. The strength and speed of early cyclical recovery has often been roughly proportional to the depth and speed of the preceding recession. Hence, a comparison of recoveries that began with the cyclical troughs would tend to overestimate the underlying strength of the economy and the magnitude of sustainable increases in incomes in periods preceded by deep recessions.

Table A –2 presents a few summary descriptions of the last three completed peak-to-peak periods.

To begin with we show measures of the length, in months, of the cycles—the length of the full cycle and of its expansion phases. Although the recessions at the beginnings of the two later periods here compared were of equal length (8 months) and mildness, the full 2000–2007 cycle was markedly shorter than the 1990–2000 cycle. Also, the actual expansion in employment took longer to get started in the 2000s expansion, as can be seen by comparing the length of the NBER-designated output expansion phase with the length of the expansion in employment.

A further dimension is the "what happened next" question, since performance after a cycle is over can reflect imbalances that grew up during that cycle. For example, some think the Great Depression was shaped by the imbalances in income distribution and the speculative excesses of the 1920s. The relative severity of the recessions of 1973–1975 and the early 1980s had to do with inflationary buildups in the 1960s and 1970s. The recession following December 2007 was far more severe than the ones that followed July 1990 and March 2001, reflecting

Table A-2. Business Cycle Descriptions, Latest Three Completed Cycles

(Number, percent.)

Description	January 1980 to July 1990	July 1990 to March 2001	March 2001 to December 2007
Length of full cycle, peak to peak, months	126	128	81
Length of expansion phase, months	92	120	73
Length of payroll employment expansion	90	117	53
Length of following recession, months	8	8	18
Percent change in real GDP during the recession	-1.4	-0.3	-5.1

the pervasive buildup of debt and overbuilding problems during the expansion of the 2000s.

In the next table we turn to quantitative comparisons of economic performance over the three cycles, with a further column that highlights the weaker performance in the period of deep recession and partial recovery 2007–2011 (or in some cases 2010, where the 2011 data are not yet available).

Table A–3 demonstrates that the annual rates of growth in real GDP per capita, real disposable income per capita, and employment were all significantly slower in the full 2000–2007 cycle than in either of the two preceding cycles. Growth in the private nonresidential capital stock—generally considered the part of the capital stock most relevant to growth in economic productivity—was also much slower. Growth in the private residential capital stock was more rapid in the most recent full cycle period, reflecting the housing bubble.

Despite the slower growth in nonresidential capital in 2000–2007, private nonfarm productivity grew faster, perhaps as a delayed result of earlier investment. (In particular, it has been suggested that computer-related productivity gains are slow to be fully realized.) The faster productivity growth was associated with slower employment growth, as fewer workers were required to produce a given level of output. The faster productivity growth was not reflected in faster real earnings growth for the median full-time female worker, and the median full-time male worker did even worse, as his real earnings were essentially unchanged. Real median household income actually declined.

Finally, using data from the Federal Reserve Flow of Funds accounts in Chapter 12, Table A–3 shows ratios of domestic credit market borrowings to GDP over the course of the cycle. These are comprehensive measures of debt, including that owed by both financial and nonfinancial entities.

Both Federal and nonfederal debt grew relative to GDP in all three periods. In the 2000–2007 expansion, the ratio for Federal and related debt grew little more than in the 1990s and much less than in the 1980s. (This includes both the debt of the U.S. government and that associated with the government-sponsored enterprises supporting the mortgage market. See Table 12–5 and the associated notes and definitions for further information.) The growth in the nonfederal debt ratio in 2000–2007, however, far outstripped that of the previous two expansions. Although much attention is focused now on the rise in federal debt caused by the recession and by the policies undertaken to ameliorate and end it—as well as on the anticipated future borrowing increases resulting, under current policies, from an aging population with rising medical expenses—the debt buildup that preceded, precipitated, and deepened the recession was mainly in the private sector, by a ratio of 6 to 1.

PRODUCTIVITY, WAGES, AND THE SOURCES OF DIFFERENCE

Productivity growth is generally welcomed, and even sought as a policy goal, largely because it has theoretically and historically been associated with growth in real wages. Yet in recent periods, real wage growth has repeatedly fallen short of productivity growth. Table A–4 analyzes the relationship between productivity and wages.

Table A-3. Three Completed Cycles and Latest Period

(Number, percent.)

Description	1979–1990	1990–2000	2000–2007	2007–2011
Real GDP growth (percent change annual rate, Table 1-2)	2.92	3.40	2.36	0.21
Real per capita product and income (percent changes, annual rate, Table 1-3)				
Real gross domestic product per capita	1.93	2.16	1.26	-0.63
Real disposable (after-tax) personal income per capita	2.03	2.06	1.61	-0.09
Total civilian employment (CPS, 10-1)				
Change in employment, millions	20.0	18.1	9.2	-6.2
Percent change, annual rate	1.69	1.43	0.93	-1.07
Nonfarm payroll jobs (CES, Table 10-8)				
Change in jobs, millions	19.6	22.3	5.8	-6.2
Percent change, annual rate	1.80	1.87	0.62	-1.15
Capital stock growth (percent change, annual rate, in quantity index for net stock of fixed assets, Table 5-6)				
Private nonresidential	3.03	2.92	2.14	[1]1.1
Private residential	2.42	2.46	2.84	[1]0.6
Federal government	2.13	-0.10	0.36	[1]1.6
State and local government	2.09	2.47	2.49	[1]1.8
Productivity growth (percent change, annual rate, output per hour, nonfarm business, Table 9-3)	1.42	2.12	2.55	1.85
Growth in real median earnings, full-time year-round workers and household income (percent change, annual rate, Table 3-1)				
Earnings, men	-0.56	0.52	0.08	[1]0.2
Earnings, women	1.10	0.82	0.86	[1]0.02
Household income	0.45	0.94	-0.09	[1]-2.2
Credit market debt as a percent of GDP (Table 12-5 and 1-1)				
Federal and related: beginning of period	34.7	67.5	77.4	89.1
End	67.5	77.4	89.1	119.3
Domestic nonfederal: beginning of period	125.5	164.2	187.8	258.6
End	164.2	187.8	258.6	225.1

[1]Data refer to the years 2007–2010.

Table A-4. Productivity and Wage Growth in Private Nonfarm Business and Sources of Difference

(Percent change, annual rate.)

Description	1979–1990	1990–2000	2000–2007	2007–2011
Productivity, nonfarm business (Table 9-3)	1.42	2.12	2.55	1.85
Wages and salaries per hour, nonfarm private business, deflated with CPI-U-RS (Tables 9-1, 9-2, and 9-3)	-0.02	0.86	0.31	-0.21
Productivity-wage gap	1.44	1.26	2.24	2.06
Factors explaining the gap:				
Difference in deflators	0.71	0.68	0.56	0.53
Change in labor share	0.17	-0.09	0.79	1.07
Costs of supplements to wages and salaries	0.42	0.13	0.44	0.15
Inequality effect	0.14	0.54	0.45	0.31

Between the 1980s and the 1990s cycles, the productivity growth rate speeded up, from 1.42 to 2.12 percent, and real wage growth, though lower than productivity growth in both periods, speeded up by a comparable amount. In 2000–2007, however, productivity growth speeded up further while real wage and salary growth slipped back. The measure of wages and salaries per hour shown is from the Employment Cost Index (ECI) for private nonfarm business (Tables 9–1 and 9–2), deflated by the CPI-U-RS—the same deflator used by the Census Bureau to calculate real incomes and earnings (Table 8 –3).

Four principal factors, displayed in the table, explain the persistent and growing gap between growth in the productivity of America's private nonfarm business workers and growth in the real wages that they earn.

The first difference—in some sense, a technical one—is that different price indexes are used to calculate productivity and real earnings. Prices of the goods that workers buy have gone up more than prices of the goods that they produce, mainly because high-tech production—where many prices have actually declined—is a bigger proportion of U.S. production than of the typical worker's market basket. The result is that even if workers continued to share proportionately in the current-dollar value of sector output, their deflated earnings would not grow as fast. (Economists call this a change in the "terms of trade.") The effect of this difference on the productivity-wage gap is shown in the fourth line of Table A–4, calculated as the difference between the growth rates of the nonfarm business implicit deflator (Table 9–3) and the CPI-U-RS (Table 8–3).

But in recent years workers have not shared proportionately in current-dollar earnings—in contrast with the record for the 100 years of the 20th century. The labor share of the value of nonfarm business output, which fluctuated within a relatively narrow range before 2000, has declined since then to unprecedented low levels (Table 9–3). As shown in the fifth line of Table A–4, which is calculated as the difference between productivity and average compensation that is not accounted for by the deflator difference, this decline in labor's share is a major contributor to the wage-productivity gap after 2000.

Employers must pay the costs of total compensation, including employer social insurance taxes and health,

retirement, and other benefits. The benefit costs rise faster than wages and salaries. This portion of the productivity-wage gap is calculated as the difference between growth rates in total compensation and in wages and salaries for nonfarm private business as measured by the ECI (Tables 9–1 and 9–2).

ECI wages and salaries are measured using a fixed composition of employment. As the actual composition of employment shifts to higher-paid workers, and as disproportionate changes in compensation may accrue to such workers, a gap representing growing inequality appears between the rates of change shown in the actual, unweighted growth in compensation per hour as measured in the Productivity and Costs system (Table 9–3) and the weighted ECI for total compensation (Tables 9–1 and 9–2). This is the final line shown in Table A–4.

WHOSE STANDARD OF LIVING?

Some of the measures discussed in the preceding section are averages, such as GDP and personal income per capita and output per hour worked. Averages are calculated by dividing some aggregate measure (income or production, for example) by another aggregate measure (population or total hours worked, for example). It is important to note that such an average, known technically to statisticians as a "mean," is only one way of describing the central tendency of any set of statistical data, and for many purposes, is not necessarily the method that produces the most representative number.

To give an important example, most researchers who are interested in the economic well-being of a typical American family or household find that the best single number to characterize that well-being is the standard of living of the family or household situated at the middle of the income distribution. Half of all families or households have higher incomes and half have lower incomes. This is the measure known as the "median." Medians are not the same as averages or means, and in the case of income distributions, they are invariably lower.

This reason behind this difference is sometimes illustrated by calling up the image of a billionaire walking into a working-class bar. The "average income" (mean income) of each person in the bar would jump, as a billion dollars

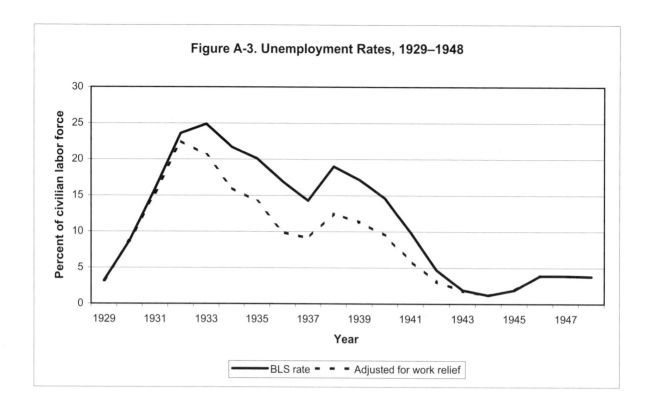

Figure A-3. Unemployment Rates, 1929–1948

that began in August 1929 and lasted until March 1933; a subsequent period of recovery, which failed to return many important economic indicators to their expected trend levels and was interrupted by a new, though less severe, recession; apprehension of coming war, then the outbreak of war in Europe in September 1939, leading to increased war-related production; United States participation in all-out war, beginning with the Japanese attack on Pearl Harbor on December 7, 1941, and ending in 1945, with supercharged production and employment rates; then, rapid demobilization, and return to a high peacetime rate of economic activity by 1948.

For a first overall view of the economy during these decades, Figure A-2 shows total U.S. employment as calculated by the Bureau of Economic Analysis, including all private and government jobs, both civilian and military. In this graph a "trend" line is shown connecting the two peacetime high employment levels of 1929 and 1948.

EMPLOYMENT, 1929–1948

- More than one-fifth of all the jobs held in the U.S. economy in 1929 were gone by 1932. In the subsequent recovery, total employment was back at the 1929 level by 1936, but only because of government employment, including over 3 ½ million work relief jobs; private industry employment would not recover to its 1929 level until 1941. (Table 10-21)
- Because the recovery was incomplete and economic activity did not recover to a trend level until after the decade's end, the entire decade of the 1930s is often described as "The Great Depression."
- During the war, men were drafted into the armed forces,

practically all of the unemployed were put back to work, and women were drawn into the labor force, resulting in a period of what might be called "super-employment." After the war, employment fell back to a more normal trend level. (Tables 10-1B and 10-21)

UNEMPLOYMENT RATES, 1929–1948

- The unemployment rates for the prewar period calculated by the Bureau of Labor Statistics, unlike the employment data used in Figure A-2, count people on government work relief programs as unemployed. By this reckoning, unemployment rose from 3.2 percent of the civilian labor force in 1929 to a peak of 24.9 percent in 1933, and got no lower than 14.3 percent for the rest of the 1930s, as shown in Figure A-3. (Table 10-1B)
- State and local governments started hiring people for work relief in 1930. The Federal government's programs began in 1933, and in 1936 and 1938 agencies such as the WPA and the CCC employed over 3 ½ million people. When workers in these programs are counted as employed rather than unemployed, the high point for unemployment was 22.5 percent in 1932, and it was reduced to 9.1 percent in 1937, as shown by the dashed line in Figure A-3. (Tables 10-1B and 10-21; see Notes and Definitions to Chapter 10 for further explanation.)
- By 1943, the economy reached a state of over-full employment, which would have been associated with runaway inflation if not for comprehensive price, wage, and production controls; the years of full wartime production, 1943 through 1945, all saw unemployment rates below 2 percent. After demobilization, the unemployment rate returned to just under 4 percent. (Table 10-1B)

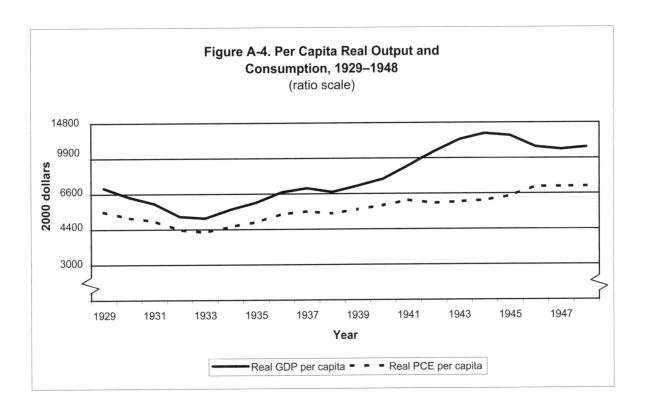

Figure A-4. Per Capita Real Output and Consumption, 1929–1948 (ratio scale)

PER CAPITA REAL OUTPUT AND CONSUMPTION, 1929–1948

- Real GDP declined 26.7 percent from 1929 to 1933—28.9 percent on a per capita basis. Per capita output recovered almost to the 1929 level in 1937 but fell back 4.1 percent in the 1938 recession. Output then nearly doubled from 1939 to the peak war production year, 1944; the per capita annual growth rate was 12.4 percent. Output fell back during the demobilization, but in 1948 was still at a per capita level representing a 4.9 percent growth rate since 1939. (Table 1-3B)
- Per capita personal consumption expenditures fell 20.9 percent from 1929 to 1933. The decline would have been greater if consumers had not dipped into their assets to keep their living standards from declining as steeply as their incomes; the personal saving rate was negative in 1932 and 1933. Real per capita consumption recovered to the 1929 level by 1937. Despite rationing and shortages, real per capita consumption spending declined little during the war years. In 1948, it was 29.3 percent above the 1939 level. (Table 1-3B)

INFLATION AND NOMINAL AND REAL INTEREST RATES, 1929–1948

- Why was the 1929–1933 contraction so deep and long-lasting? Often, blame is placed on U.S. government tax increases and imposition of new trade barriers (the Smoot-Hawley Tariff), which undoubtedly made their contribution. A substantial number of well-regarded economists, however, point primarily to deflation and its interaction with debt. The price index for personal con-sumption expenditures, whose rate of change is shown in Figure A-5, declined 27.2 percent from 1929 to 1933, for an annual average <u>deflation</u> rate of 7.6 percent. Current and prospective price declines make debt more burdensome and debtors more likely to default, as interest payments remain fixed while incomes and asset values decline. (Table 1-6B)
- Current and prospective price declines also make borrowing prohibitively expensive; a low nominal interest rate becomes high in real terms (since the real rate is the nominal rate <u>minus</u> the inflation rate, and subtraction means changing the sign and adding). A dollar in the hands of a prospective lender will be worth more in terms of purchasing power if he simply holds on to it than if he invests it in some real economic asset or activity whose price will be lower at the end of the year. There is no feasible way for a central bank to lower interest rates below zero in order to reduce real rates in the presence of deflation. As Figure A-5 shows, real rates were high from 1930 through 1933 despite near-zero market nominal rates on Treasury bills. (Tables 12-9B and 1-6B)

MONEY AND CREDIT GROWTH, 1930–1948

- Deflation was rooted in deep and sustained declines in the dollar volumes of money and credit, as shown in Tables 12-1B and 12-4B and illustrated in Figure A-6. The money stock (currency and demand deposits) declined 27 percent from June 30, 1929, to June 30, 1933. Loans and investments at all commercial banks declined 29 percent over the same period. Commercial paper outstanding plunged 76 percent between December

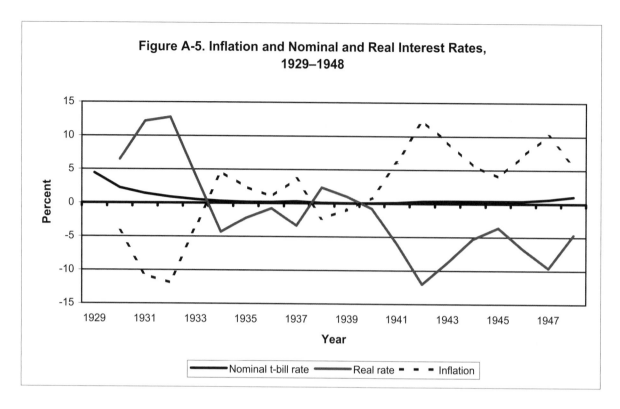

Figure A-5. Inflation and Nominal and Real Interest Rates, 1929–1948

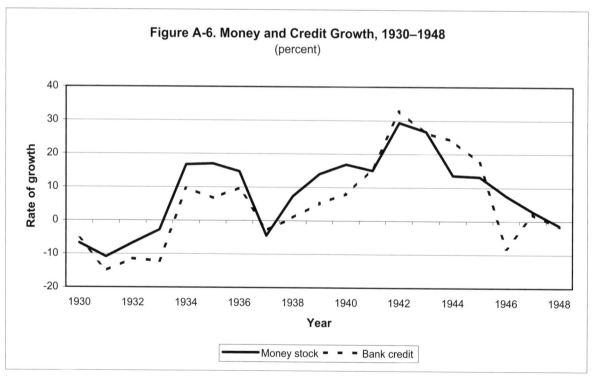

Figure A-6. Money and Credit Growth, 1930–1948
(percent)

1929 and December 1932, and bankers' acceptances were down 59 percent.

- Positive money and credit growth after 1933 was reflected in moderate rates of price increase and moderately negative—which means stimulative—real interest rates. As can be seen in Figures A-5 and A-6, there was a monetary component to the 1937-38 recession. There was also a premature federal budget retrenchment at that time (Table 6-14B).
- During the war, monetary policy was pre-empted by wartime needs. Interest rates were held low to facilitate the financing of huge federal deficits (Tables 6-14B and 12-9B).

- Worker incomes increased during the wartime boom as employment, average hours, and hourly wages all rose. But inflation and consumer spending were held down by price and production controls and rationing. Personal saving rates soared when there was little to buy and the government emphasized the sale of "war bonds"; the saving rate reached 26 percent in 1943 and 1944, then fell back to 4.2 percent in 1947, almost equal to its 1929 level. (Tables 1-6B, 4-1B, 8-1C, and 10-9)

GENERAL NOTES

These notes provide general information about the data in Tables 1-1 through 17-2. Specific notes with information about data sources, definitions, methodology, revisions, and sources of additional information follow the tables in each chapter.

MAIN DIVISIONS OF THE BOOK

The tables are divided into three main parts:

Part A (Tables 1-1 through 13-8) pertains to the U.S. economy as a whole. Generally, each table presents, on its initial page, annual averages as far back as data availability and space permit, and quarterly or monthly values for the most recent year or years. For many important series, this initial page is followed by full annual and quarterly or monthly histories as far back as they are available on a continuous, consistent basis. Some chapters present data for the United States only in aggregate, while others—such as the chapters concerning industrial production and capacity utilization (chapter 2), capital expenditures (chapter 5), profits (chapter 9), and employment, hours, and earnings (chapter 10)—also have detail for major industry groups.

Data by industry are classified using the new North American Industry Classification System (NAICS), as far back as such data are made available by the source agencies.

Part B focuses on the individual industries that together produce the gross domestic product (GDP).

- Chapter 14 contains data on the value of GDP, quantity production trends, and factor income by NAICS industry group.

- Chapter 15 provides further detail on payroll employment, hours, and earnings classified according to NAICS.

- Chapter 16 presents various data sets for key economic sectors. Some of the tables are based on definitions of products, rather than of producing establishments, and are valid for either classification system. This is the case for Tables 16-1, Petroleum and Petroleum Products; 16-2, New Construction; 16-3, Housing Starts and Building Permits, New House Sales, and Prices; and 16-8, Motor Vehicle Sales and Inventories. Tables 16-4 through 16-7 and 16-9, 16-11, and 16-12, which cover manufacturing and retail and wholesale trade, show data classified according to NAICS. Table 16-15 presents data for services industries classified according to NAICS.

Part C presents data by state and region, calculated by the Bureau of Economic Analysis. Table 17-1 contains data on

GDP and Table 17-2 shows data on personal income, population, and employment.

CHARACTERISTICS OF THE TABLES AND THE DATA

The subtitles or column headings for the data tables normally indicate whether the data are *seasonally adjusted, not seasonally adjusted,* or *at a seasonally adjusted annual rate.* These descriptions refer to the monthly or quarterly data, rather than the annual data. Annual data by definition require no seasonal adjustment. Annual values are normally calculated as totals or averages, as appropriate, of unadjusted data. Such annual values are shown in either or both adjusted or unadjusted data columns.

Seasonal adjustment removes from the time series the average impact of variations that normally occur at about the same time each year, due to occurrences such as weather, holidays, and tax payment dates.

A simplified example of the process of seasonal adjustment, or deseasonalizing, can indicate its importance in the interpretation of economic time series. Statisticians compare actual monthly data for a number of years with "moving average" trends of the monthly data for the 12 months centered on each month's data. For example, they may find that in November, sales values are usually about 95 percent of the moving average, while in December, usual sales values are 110 percent of the average. Suppose that actual November sales in the current year are $100 and December sales are $105. The seasonally adjusted value for November will be $105 ($100/0.95) while the value for December will be $95 ($105/1.10). Thus, an apparent increase in the unadjusted data turns out to be a decrease when adjusted for the usual seasonal pattern.

The statistical method used to achieve the seasonal adjustment may vary from one data set to another. Many of the data are adjusted by a computer method known as X-12-ARIMA, developed by the Census Bureau. A description of the method is found in "New Capabilities and Methods of the X-12-ARIMA Seasonal Adjustment Program," by David F. Findley, Brian C. Monsell, William R. Bell, Mark C. Otto and Bor-Chung Chen (*Journal of Business and Economic Statistics*, April 1998). This article can be downloaded from the Bureau of the Census Web site at <http://www.census.gov>.

Production and sales data presented at *annual rates*—such as NIPA data in dollars, or motor vehicle data in number of units—show values at their annual equivalents: the values that would be registered if the seasonally adjusted rate of activity measured during a particular month or quarter were maintained for a full year. Specifically, seasonally adjusted monthly values are multiplied by 12 and quarterly values by 4 to yield seasonally adjusted annual rates.

Percent changes at seasonally adjusted annual rates for quarterly time periods are calculated using a compound interest formula, by raising the quarter-to-quarter percent change in a seasonally adjusted series to the fourth power. See the preceding article for an explanation of compound annual growth rates.

Indexes. In many of the most important data sets presented in this volume, aggregate measures of prices and quantities are expressed in the form of indexes. The most basic and familiar form of index, the original Consumer Price Index, begins with a "market basket" of goods and services purchased in a base period, with each product category valued at its dollar prices—the amount spent on that category by the average consumer. The value weight ascribed to each component of the market basket is moved forward by the observed change in the price of the item selected to represent that component. These weighted component prices—which constitute the quantities in the base period repriced in the prices of subsequent periods—are aggregated, divided by the base period aggregate, and multiplied by 100 to provide an index number. An index calculated in this way is known as a *Laspeyres index*. In general, economists believe that Laspeyres price indexes have an upward bias, showing more price increase than they would if account were taken of consumers' ability to change spending patterns and maintain the same level of satisfaction in response to changing relative prices.

A *Paasche index* is one that uses the weights of the current period. Since the weights in the Paasche index change in each period, Paasche indexes only provide acceptable indications of change relative to the base period. Paasche indexes for two periods neither of which is the base period cannot be correctly compared: for example, a Paasche price index for a recent period might increase from the period just preceding even if no prices changed between those two periods, if there was a change in the composition of output toward prices that had previously increased more from the base period. When the national income and product account (NIPA) measures of real output were Laspeyres measures, using the weights of a single base year, the implicit deflators (current-dollar values divided by constant-dollar values) were Paasche indexes. Just as Laspeyres price indexes are upward-biased, Paasche price indexes are downward-biased because they overestimate consumers' ability to maintain the same level of satisfaction by changing spending patterns.

In recent years, government statisticians—with the aid of elaborate computer programs—have developed measures of real output and prices that minimize bias by using the weights of both periods and updating the weights for each period-to-period comparison. Such measures are described as chained indexes and are used in the NIPAs, the index of industrial production, and an experimental consumer price index. Chained measures are discussed more fully in the notes and definitions for Chapter 1, Chapter 2, and Chapter 8. The "Fisher Ideal" index, the "superlative" index, and the "Tornqvist formula" are all types of chained indexes that use weights for both periods under comparison.

Detail may not sum to totals due to rounding. Since annual data are typically calculated by source agencies as the annual totals or averages of not-seasonally-adjusted data, they therefore will not be precisely equal to the annual totals or averages of monthly seasonally-adjusted data. Also, seasonal adjustment procedures are typically multiplicative rather than additive, which may also prevent seasonally adjusted data from adding or averaging to the annual figure. Percent changes and growth rates may have been calculated using unrounded data and therefore differ from those using the published figures.

The data in this volume are from federal government sources and may be reproduced freely. A list of data sources is shown below.

The tables in this volume incorporate data revisions and corrections released by the source agencies through spring (April in some cases, May or June in others) of 2012.

DATA SOURCES

The source agencies for the data in this volume are listed below. The specific source or sources for each particular data set are identified at the beginning of the notes and definitions for the relevant data pages.

Board of Governors of the Federal Reserve System
20th Street & Constitution Avenue NW
Washington, DC 20551

Data Inquiries and Publication Sales:
    Publications Services
    Mail Stop 127
    Board of Governors of the Federal Reserve System
    Washington, DC 20551
    Phone: (202) 452-3245

Quarterly Publication:
As of 2006, the *Federal Reserve Bulletin* is available free of charge and only on the Federal Reserve Web site.

URL:
    http://www.federalreserve.gov

Census Bureau
U.S. Department of Commerce
4700 Silver Hill Road
Washington, DC 20233

URL:
http://www.census.gov

Ordering Data Products:
    Call Center: (301) 763-INFO (4636)

E-mail Questions:
    webmaster@census.gov

E-sales:
    http://www.census.gov/mp/www/censtore.html

Bureau of Economic Analysis
U.S. Department of Commerce
Washington, DC 20230

Data Inquiries:
    Public Information Office
    Phone: (202) 606-9900

Monthly Publication:
    Survey of Current Business
    Available online.

URL:
    http://www.bea.gov

Bureau of Labor Statistics
U.S. Department of Labor
2 Massachusetts Avenue NE
Washington, DC 20212-0001
(202) 691-5200

URL:
    http://www.bls.gov

Data Inquiries:
    Blsdata_staff@bls.gov

Monthly Publications available online:
    Monthly Labor Review
    Employment and Earnings
    Compensation and Working Conditions
    Producer Price Indexes
    CPI Detailed Report

Employment and Training Administration
U.S. Department of Labor
200 Constitution Avenue NW
Washington, DC 20210
(877) US2-JOBS

URL:
    http://www.doleta.gov
    http://www.itsc.state.md.us

Energy Information Administration
U.S. Department of Energy
1000 Independence Avenue SW
Washington, DC 20585

Data Inquiries and Publications:
    National Energy Information Center
    Phone: (202) 586-8800
    E-mail: infoctr@eia.doe.gov

Monthly Publication:
    Monthly Energy Review, as of 2007 available only on
the EIA Web site, free of charge.

URL:
    http://www.eia.doe.gov

Federal Housing Finance Agency
FHFAinfo@FHFA.gov
(202) 414-6921,6922
(202) 414-6376

URL:
    http://www.fhfa.gov/hpi

U.S. Department of the Treasury
Office of International Affairs
Treasury International Capital System

URL:
    http://www.treas.gov/tic

To order government publications
    Superintendent of Documents
    Government Printing Office
    Washington, DC 20402
    (202) 512-1800

URL:
    http://bookstore.gpo.gov

PART A

THE U.S. ECONOMY

CHAPTER 1: NATIONAL INCOME AND PRODUCT

Section 1a: Gross Domestic Product: Values, Quantities, and Prices

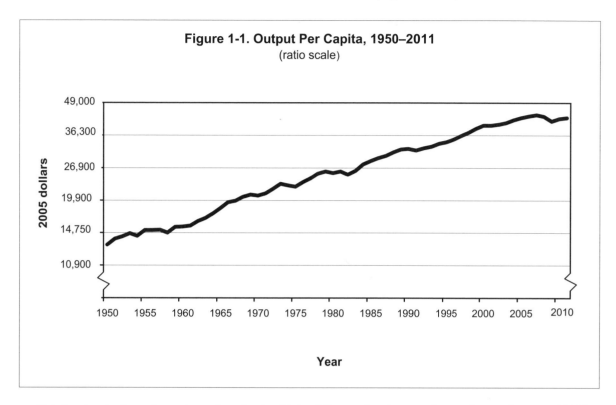

Figure 1-1. Output Per Capita, 1950–2011
(ratio scale)

- Total output of goods and services in the United States (real gross domestic product, or GDP), expressed in constant 2005-value dollars to remove the effect of inflation, rose from $2.00 trillion in 1950 to $13.32 trillion in 2011. This was a more than six-fold increase in real value over the 61-year period, with an annual average growth rate of 3.2 percent per year. (Table 1-2A)

- Real GDP per capita—the constant-dollar average value of production for each man, woman, and child in the population—rose from $13,213 (2005 dollars) in 1950 to a peak value of $43,774 in 2007, a growth rate of 2.1 percent per year. Reflecting the recession that began in December 2007, it declined 5.5 percent from 2007 to 2009. With the recovery that began in June 2009, a partial recovery in GDP per capita—3.2 percent from 2009 to 2011, or a meager 1.6 percent per year—was recorded. The history of per capita GDP is charted in Figure 1-1. It is graphed on a "ratio scale," with equal vertical distances signifying equal percent changes. (Table 1-3A)

- Measured in current dollars, the value of GDP has increased even faster, reflecting increases in the average price level. Current-dollar GDP rose from $294 billion in 1950 to over $15 trillion currently. (Table 1-1A) The price level in 2011 was more than 7 times that in 1950, reflecting an average inflation rate of 3.4 percent per year. (Table 1-6A) Annual changes in the chain-type price index for GDP ranged from inflation of 9 percent or more in 1947, 1974–1975, and 1980–1981 to changes of no more than 1.2 percent in 1949–1950, 1954, 1959, 1961, 1963, 1998, 2009, and 2010. Over the last 10 years, inflation averaged 2.2 percent per year; it was 2.1 percent in 2011. (Tables 1-6A and B)

Table 1-1A. Gross Domestic Product: Recent Data

(Billions of dollars, quarterly data are at seasonally adjusted annual rates.)   **NIPA Tables 1.1.5, 1.2.5**

| Year and quarter | Gross domestic product | Personal consumption expenditures | Gross private domestic investment | | | | | Exports and imports of goods and services | | | Government consumption expenditures and gross investment | | | Addendum: final sales of domestic product |
| | | | Total | Fixed investment | | Change in private inventories | Net exports | Exports | Imports | Total | Federal | State and local | |
				Nonresidential	Residential									
1950	293.7	192.2	54.1	27.8	20.5	5.8	0.7	12.4	11.6	46.7	26.0	20.7	288.0
1951	339.3	208.5	60.2	31.8	18.4	9.9	2.5	17.1	14.6	68.1	45.0	23.0	329.4
1952	358.3	219.5	54.0	31.9	18.6	3.5	1.2	16.5	15.3	83.6	59.1	24.4	354.8
1953	379.3	233.1	56.4	35.1	19.4	1.9	-0.7	15.3	16.0	90.5	64.4	26.1	377.4
1954	380.4	240.0	53.8	34.7	21.1	-1.9	0.4	15.8	15.4	86.1	57.2	28.9	382.3
1955	414.7	258.8	69.0	39.0	25.0	5.0	0.5	17.7	17.2	86.4	54.9	31.6	409.7
1956	437.4	271.7	72.0	44.5	23.6	4.0	2.4	21.3	18.9	91.4	56.7	34.7	433.5
1957	461.1	286.9	70.5	47.5	22.2	0.8	4.1	24.0	19.9	99.7	61.3	38.3	460.3
1958	467.2	296.2	64.5	42.5	22.3	-0.4	0.5	20.6	20.0	106.0	63.8	42.2	467.5
1959	506.6	317.7	78.5	46.5	28.1	3.9	0.4	22.7	22.3	110.0	65.3	44.7	502.7
1960	526.4	331.8	78.9	49.4	26.3	3.2	4.2	27.0	22.8	111.5	64.1	47.5	523.2
1961	544.8	342.2	78.2	48.8	26.4	3.0	4.9	27.6	22.7	119.5	67.9	51.6	541.8
1962	585.7	363.3	88.1	53.1	29.0	6.1	4.1	29.1	25.0	130.1	75.2	54.9	579.6
1963	617.8	382.7	93.8	56.0	32.1	5.6	4.9	31.1	26.1	136.4	76.9	59.5	612.1
1964	663.6	411.5	102.1	63.0	34.3	4.8	6.9	35.0	28.1	143.2	78.4	64.8	658.8
1965	719.1	443.8	118.2	74.8	34.2	9.2	5.6	37.1	31.5	151.4	80.4	71.0	709.9
1966	787.7	480.9	131.3	85.4	32.3	13.6	3.9	40.9	37.1	171.6	92.4	79.2	774.1
1967	832.4	507.8	128.6	86.4	32.4	9.9	3.6	43.5	39.9	192.5	104.6	87.9	822.6
1968	909.8	558.0	141.2	93.4	38.7	9.1	1.4	47.9	46.6	209.3	111.3	98.0	900.8
1969	984.4	605.1	156.4	104.7	42.6	9.2	1.4	51.9	50.5	221.4	113.3	108.2	975.3
1970	1 038.3	648.3	152.4	109.0	41.4	2.0	4.0	59.7	55.8	233.7	113.4	120.3	1 036.3
1971	1 126.8	701.6	178.2	114.1	55.8	8.3	0.6	63.0	62.3	246.4	113.6	132.8	1 118.6
1972	1 237.9	770.2	207.6	128.8	69.7	9.1	-3.4	70.8	74.2	263.4	119.6	143.8	1 228.8
1973	1 382.3	852.0	244.5	153.3	75.3	15.9	4.1	95.3	91.2	281.7	122.5	159.2	1 366.4
1974	1 499.5	932.9	249.4	169.5	66.0	14.0	-0.8	126.7	127.5	317.9	134.5	183.4	1 485.5
1975	1 637.7	1 033.8	230.2	173.7	62.7	-6.3	16.0	138.7	122.7	357.7	149.0	208.7	1 644.0
1976	1 824.6	1 151.3	292.0	192.4	82.5	17.1	-1.6	149.5	151.1	383.0	159.7	223.3	1 807.5
1977	2 030.1	1 277.8	361.3	228.7	110.3	22.3	-23.1	159.4	182.4	414.1	175.4	238.7	2 007.8
1978	2 293.8	1 427.6	438.0	280.6	131.6	25.8	-25.4	186.9	212.3	453.6	190.9	262.7	2 268.0
1979	2 562.2	1 591.2	492.9	333.9	141.0	18.0	-22.5	230.1	252.7	500.7	210.6	290.2	2 544.2
1980	2 788.1	1 755.8	479.3	362.4	123.2	-6.3	-13.1	280.8	293.8	566.1	243.7	322.4	2 794.5
1981	3 126.8	1 939.5	572.4	420.0	122.6	29.8	-12.5	305.2	317.8	627.5	280.2	347.3	3 097.0
1982	3 253.2	2 075.5	517.2	426.5	105.7	-14.9	-20.0	283.2	303.2	680.4	310.8	369.7	3 268.1
1983	3 534.6	2 288.6	564.3	417.2	152.9	-5.8	-51.7	277.0	328.6	733.4	342.9	390.5	3 540.4
1984	3 930.9	2 501.1	735.6	489.6	180.6	65.4	-102.7	302.4	405.1	796.9	374.3	422.6	3 865.5
1985	4 217.5	2 717.6	736.2	526.2	188.2	21.8	-115.2	302.0	417.2	878.9	412.8	466.1	4 195.6
1986	4 460.1	2 896.7	746.5	519.8	220.1	6.6	-132.5	320.3	452.9	949.3	438.4	510.9	4 453.5
1987	4 736.4	3 097.0	785.0	524.1	233.7	27.1	-145.0	363.8	508.7	999.4	459.5	539.9	4 709.2
1988	5 100.4	3 350.1	821.6	563.8	239.3	18.5	-110.1	443.9	554.0	1 038.9	461.6	577.3	5 081.9
1989	5 482.1	3 594.5	874.9	607.7	239.5	27.7	-87.9	503.1	591.0	1 100.6	481.4	619.2	5 454.5
1990	5 800.5	3 835.5	861.0	622.4	224.0	14.5	-77.6	552.1	629.7	1 181.7	507.5	674.2	5 786.0
1991	5 992.1	3 980.1	802.9	598.2	205.1	-0.4	-27.0	596.6	623.5	1 236.1	526.6	709.5	5 992.5
1992	6 342.3	4 236.9	864.8	612.1	236.3	16.3	-32.8	635.0	667.8	1 273.5	532.9	740.6	6 326.0
1993	6 667.4	4 483.6	953.3	666.6	266.0	20.8	-64.4	655.6	720.0	1 294.8	525.0	769.8	6 646.5
1994	7 085.2	4 750.8	1 097.3	731.4	302.1	63.8	-92.7	720.7	813.4	1 329.8	518.6	811.2	7 021.4
1995	7 414.7	4 987.3	1 144.0	810.0	302.9	31.2	-90.7	811.9	902.6	1 374.0	518.8	855.3	7 383.5
1996	7 838.5	5 273.6	1 240.2	875.4	334.1	30.8	-96.3	867.7	964.0	1 421.0	527.0	894.0	7 807.7
1997	8 332.4	5 570.6	1 388.7	968.6	349.1	71.0	-101.4	954.4	1 055.8	1 474.4	531.0	943.5	8 261.4
1998	8 793.5	5 918.5	1 510.8	1 061.1	385.9	63.7	-161.8	953.9	1 115.7	1 526.1	531.0	995.0	8 729.8
1999	9 353.5	6 342.8	1 641.5	1 154.9	425.8	60.8	-262.1	989.3	1 251.4	1 631.3	554.9	1 076.3	9 292.7
2000	9 951.5	6 830.4	1 772.2	1 268.7	449.0	54.5	-382.1	1 093.2	1 475.3	1 731.0	576.1	1 154.9	9 896.9
2001	10 286.2	7 148.8	1 661.9	1 227.8	472.4	-38.3	-371.0	1 027.7	1 398.7	1 846.4	611.7	1 234.7	10 324.5
2002	10 642.3	7 439.2	1 647.0	1 125.4	509.5	12.0	-427.2	1 003.0	1 430.2	1 983.3	680.6	1 302.7	10 630.3
2003	11 142.2	7 804.1	1 729.7	1 135.7	577.6	16.4	-504.1	1 041.0	1 545.1	2 112.6	756.5	1 356.1	11 125.8
2004	11 853.3	8 270.6	1 968.6	1 223.0	680.6	64.9	-618.7	1 180.2	1 798.9	2 232.8	824.6	1 408.2	11 788.3
2005	12 623.0	8 803.5	2 172.3	1 347.3	775.0	50.0	-722.7	1 305.1	2 027.8	2 369.9	876.3	1 493.6	12 573.0
2006	13 377.2	9 301.0	2 327.1	1 505.3	761.9	60.0	-769.3	1 471.0	2 240.3	2 518.4	931.7	1 586.7	13 317.3
2007	14 028.7	9 772.3	2 295.2	1 637.5	628.7	29.1	-713.1	1 661.7	2 374.8	2 674.2	976.3	1 697.9	13 999.6
2008	14 291.5	10 035.5	2 087.6	1 656.3	472.4	-41.1	-709.7	1 846.8	2 556.5	2 878.1	1 080.1	1 798.0	14 332.7
2009	13 939.0	9 866.1	1 546.8	1 353.0	354.7	-160.8	-391.5	1 583.0	1 974.6	2 917.5	1 142.7	1 774.8	14 099.8
2010	14 526.5	10 245.5	1 795.1	1 390.1	338.1	66.9	-516.9	1 839.8	2 356.7	3 002.8	1 222.8	1 780.0	14 459.6
2011	15 094.0	10 726.0	1 916.2	1 532.5	337.5	46.3	-578.7	2 085.5	2 664.2	3 030.6	1 232.9	1 797.7	15 047.7
2009													
1st quarter	13 893.7	9 781.7	1 620.1	1 430.6	369.0	-179.5	-383.5	1 522.2	1 905.7	2 875.5	1 105.3	1 770.1	14 073.3
2nd quarter	13 854.1	9 781.6	1 493.8	1 351.9	342.4	-200.5	-338.3	1 520.8	1 859.1	2 916.9	1 137.2	1 779.7	14 054.6
3rd quarter	13 920.5	9 911.1	1 481.2	1 324.3	353.9	-197.1	-406.7	1 590.3	1 997.0	2 935.0	1 157.7	1 777.3	14 117.6
4th quarter	14 087.4	9 990.0	1 592.2	1 305.1	353.2	-66.1	-437.6	1 699.0	2 136.5	2 942.7	1 170.6	1 772.1	14 153.5
2010													
1st quarter	14 277.9	10 103.7	1 702.3	1 318.7	339.3	44.3	-495.8	1 749.5	2 245.3	2 967.7	1 195.2	1 772.6	14 233.6
2nd quarter	14 467.8	10 184.8	1 809.7	1 377.1	354.5	78.1	-531.2	1 813.8	2 345.0	3 004.6	1 224.5	1 780.1	14 389.8
3rd quarter	14 605.5	10 276.6	1 850.5	1 416.5	327.3	106.7	-540.3	1 860.6	2 400.9	3 018.7	1 237.5	1 781.2	14 498.8
4th quarter	14 755.0	10 417.1	1 818.0	1 447.9	331.3	38.7	-500.2	1 935.3	2 435.5	3 020.2	1 234.3	1 786.0	14 716.3
2011													
1st quarter	14 867.8	10 571.7	1 853.1	1 460.5	330.6	62.0	-571.3	2 024.1	2 595.4	3 014.4	1 219.9	1 794.4	14 805.8
2nd quarter	15 012.8	10 676.0	1 895.3	1 506.0	335.7	53.6	-597.1	2 085.3	2 682.4	3 038.6	1 237.1	1 801.5	14 959.2
3rd quarter	15 176.1	10 784.5	1 906.6	1 568.7	337.0	0.8	-562.3	2 119.2	2 681.6	3 047.3	1 248.9	1 798.5	15 175.3
4th quarter	15 319.4	10 871.6	2 010.1	1 594.8	346.5	68.7	-584.3	2 113.2	2 697.4	3 021.9	1 225.5	1 796.5	15 250.7

Table 1-1B. Gross Domestic Product: Historical Data

(Billions of dollars, quarterly data are at seasonally adjusted annual rates.)   **NIPA Tables 1.1.5, 1.2.5**

Year and quarter	Gross domestic product	Personal consump-tion expen-ditures	Gross private domestic investment				Exports and imports of goods and services			Government consumption expenditures and gross investment			Addendum: Final sales of domestic product
			Total	Fixed investment		Change in private inventories	Net exports	Exports	Imports	Total	Federal	State and local	
				Nonresi-dential	Residential								
1929	103.6	77.4	16.5	11.0	4.0	1.5	0.4	5.9	5.6	9.4	1.7	7.6	102.1
1930	91.2	70.1	10.8	8.6	2.4	-0.2	0.3	4.4	4.1	10.0	1.8	8.2	91.4
1931	76.5	60.7	5.9	5.3	1.8	-1.1	0.0	2.9	2.9	9.9	1.9	8.0	77.6
1932	58.7	48.7	1.3	2.9	0.8	-2.4	0.0	2.0	1.9	8.7	1.8	6.9	61.1
1933	56.4	45.9	1.7	2.5	0.6	-1.4	0.1	2.0	1.9	8.7	2.3	6.4	57.8
1934	66.0	51.5	3.7	3.3	0.9	-0.6	0.3	2.6	2.2	10.5	3.3	7.2	66.6
1935	73.3	55.9	6.7	4.3	1.3	1.1	-0.2	2.8	3.0	10.9	3.4	7.5	72.2
1936	83.8	62.2	8.6	5.8	1.7	1.2	-0.1	3.0	3.2	13.1	5.6	7.5	82.6
1937	91.9	66.8	12.2	7.5	2.1	2.6	0.1	4.0	4.0	12.8	5.1	7.7	89.2
1938	86.1	64.3	7.1	5.5	2.1	-0.6	1.0	3.8	2.8	13.8	5.7	8.1	86.7
1939	92.2	67.2	9.3	6.1	3.0	0.2	0.8	4.0	3.1	14.8	6.0	8.8	92.0
1940	101.4	71.3	13.6	7.7	3.5	2.4	1.5	4.9	3.4	15.0	6.5	8.6	99.0
1941	126.7	81.1	18.1	9.7	4.1	4.3	1.0	5.5	4.4	26.5	18.0	8.6	122.4
1942	161.9	89.0	10.4	6.3	2.2	1.9	-0.3	4.4	4.6	62.7	54.1	8.6	160.0
1943	198.6	99.9	6.1	5.4	1.4	-0.7	-2.2	4.0	6.3	94.8	86.5	8.4	199.4
1944	219.8	108.7	7.8	7.4	1.4	-0.9	-2.0	4.9	6.9	105.3	96.9	8.4	220.7
1945	223.0	120.0	10.8	10.6	1.7	-1.5	-0.8	6.8	7.5	93.0	84.0	9.0	224.5
1946	222.2	144.3	31.1	17.3	7.8	6.0	7.2	14.2	7.0	39.6	28.8	10.8	216.2
1947	244.1	162.0	35.0	23.5	12.1	-0.6	10.8	18.7	7.9	36.3	22.6	13.7	244.6
1948	269.1	175.0	48.1	26.8	15.6	5.7	5.5	15.5	10.1	40.5	24.2	16.3	263.5
1949	267.2	178.5	36.9	24.9	14.6	-2.7	5.2	14.5	9.2	46.6	27.6	19.0	269.9
1947													
1st quarter	237.2	156.3	33.7	22.8	10.4	0.5	10.9	18.4	7.5	36.3	23.3	13.0	236.7
2nd quarter	240.4	160.2	32.4	23.2	10.4	-1.2	11.3	19.5	8.2	36.6	23.2	13.4	241.6
3rd quarter	244.5	163.7	32.7	23.3	12.3	-2.9	11.8	19.4	7.7	36.3	22.3	14.0	247.4
4th quarter	254.3	167.8	41.0	24.5	15.1	1.5	9.3	17.6	8.3	36.2	21.5	14.7	252.9
1948													
1st quarter	260.3	170.5	45.0	26.2	15.2	3.6	7.3	16.9	9.6	37.5	22.4	15.2	256.7
2nd quarter	267.3	174.3	48.1	26.0	16.3	5.9	5.2	15.2	10.0	39.7	23.7	15.9	261.4
3rd quarter	273.8	177.2	50.2	27.0	16.1	7.2	4.9	15.4	10.5	41.4	24.6	16.8	266.6
4th quarter	275.1	178.1	49.1	28.1	15.0	6.0	4.5	14.6	10.1	43.4	26.0	17.5	269.1
1949													
1st quarter	269.9	177.0	40.9	26.6	14.0	0.4	6.5	16.1	9.6	45.5	27.5	18.0	269.6
2nd quarter	266.2	178.6	34.0	25.5	13.7	-5.1	6.3	15.6	9.4	47.3	28.5	18.7	271.3
3rd quarter	267.6	178.0	37.3	24.1	14.5	-1.3	5.2	14.1	8.9	47.1	27.7	19.5	268.9
4th quarter	265.2	180.4	35.2	23.5	16.3	-4.7	3.0	12.1	9.1	46.6	26.9	19.7	269.9
1950													
1st quarter	275.2	183.1	44.4	24.2	18.1	2.0	2.2	11.7	9.5	45.5	25.5	20.0	273.2
2nd quarter	284.5	187.0	49.9	26.6	20.4	2.8	1.6	11.9	10.2	46.0	25.7	20.4	281.7
3rd quarter	301.9	200.7	56.1	29.6	22.3	4.2	-0.7	12.3	13.0	45.8	24.9	21.0	297.8
4th quarter	313.3	198.1	65.9	30.6	21.3	14.0	-0.2	13.5	13.7	49.5	27.8	21.6	299.3
1951													
1st quarter	329.0	209.4	62.1	30.9	20.8	10.4	0.2	15.0	14.9	57.3	35.2	22.1	318.6
2nd quarter	336.6	205.1	64.8	31.8	18.2	14.8	1.9	17.1	15.2	64.7	41.8	22.9	321.8
3rd quarter	343.5	207.8	59.4	32.5	17.2	9.7	3.7	18.1	14.3	72.6	49.1	23.4	333.8
4th quarter	347.9	211.8	54.4	32.2	17.5	4.7	4.2	18.2	14.0	77.6	53.9	23.7	343.2
1952													
1st quarter	351.2	213.1	55.2	32.4	18.0	4.7	3.7	18.7	15.0	79.1	55.3	23.8	346.5
2nd quarter	352.1	217.3	49.9	32.9	18.5	-1.5	2.0	16.6	14.6	83.0	58.4	24.6	353.7
3rd quarter	358.5	219.8	53.9	29.8	18.5	5.6	0.0	15.2	15.3	84.8	60.4	24.4	352.9
4th quarter	371.4	227.9	57.1	32.5	19.4	5.3	-1.0	15.3	16.3	87.3	62.4	25.0	366.1
1953													
1st quarter	378.4	231.5	57.9	34.3	19.7	3.9	-0.7	15.1	15.8	89.6	63.9	25.8	374.5
2nd quarter	382.0	233.3	58.1	34.8	19.8	3.6	-1.3	15.2	16.4	91.8	66.2	25.6	378.4
3rd quarter	381.1	234.0	57.4	35.9	19.2	2.3	-0.6	15.8	16.3	90.2	63.9	26.3	378.8
4th quarter	375.9	233.5	52.3	35.4	18.9	-2.0	-0.3	15.2	15.5	90.4	63.5	26.9	377.9
1954													
1st quarter	375.2	235.5	51.5	34.5	19.0	-2.0	-0.4	14.4	14.8	88.5	60.8	27.8	377.2
2nd quarter	376.0	238.3	51.2	34.3	20.3	-3.4	0.3	16.4	16.2	86.2	57.7	28.5	379.3
3rd quarter	380.8	240.7	54.7	35.0	21.8	-2.1	0.6	15.9	15.3	84.8	55.3	29.5	382.9
4th quarter	389.4	245.5	57.8	34.9	23.2	-0.3	1.1	16.6	15.5	85.0	55.2	29.8	389.7
1955													
1st quarter	402.6	251.8	64.2	35.4	25.0	3.8	1.1	17.3	16.2	85.4	54.6	30.8	398.8
2nd quarter	410.9	256.9	68.1	37.9	25.6	4.6	-0.2	16.9	17.1	86.0	54.7	31.3	406.3
3rd quarter	419.4	261.1	70.0	40.4	25.2	4.3	0.7	18.1	17.4	87.6	55.8	31.8	415.2
4th quarter	426.0	265.1	73.9	42.5	24.2	7.2	0.2	18.3	18.1	86.7	54.3	32.4	418.8
1956													
1st quarter	428.3	266.7	73.0	42.9	23.7	6.4	0.4	19.4	18.9	88.2	54.7	33.5	421.9
2nd quarter	434.2	269.4	71.4	43.9	23.9	3.6	1.9	20.9	19.0	91.4	57.1	34.4	430.6
3rd quarter	439.2	272.6	72.5	45.4	23.5	3.6	2.6	21.8	19.3	91.5	56.4	35.1	435.6
4th quarter	448.1	278.0	71.2	45.9	23.0	2.2	4.5	23.1	18.5	94.3	58.5	35.8	445.8
1957													
1st quarter	457.2	282.4	71.8	47.0	22.6	2.2	4.8	24.9	20.1	98.1	61.0	37.1	455.0
2nd quarter	459.2	284.7	71.9	47.1	22.2	2.7	4.1	24.4	20.3	98.4	60.4	38.0	456.5
3rd quarter	466.4	289.3	73.2	48.4	22.0	2.8	4.0	23.8	19.8	99.8	61.2	38.7	463.6
4th quarter	461.5	291.0	64.9	47.5	21.9	-4.5	3.4	23.0	19.6	102.3	62.7	39.6	466.0
1958													
1st quarter	453.9	290.5	60.5	43.6	20.9	-4.0	1.1	20.5	19.5	101.8	61.2	40.6	457.9
2nd quarter	458.0	293.4	58.7	42.0	21.0	-4.2	0.5	20.5	20.1	105.4	63.8	41.6	462.3
3rd quarter	471.7	298.5	65.5	41.4	22.5	1.5	0.9	20.6	19.7	106.9	64.2	42.7	470.2
4th quarter	485.0	302.3	73.2	43.1	24.9	5.2	-0.3	20.6	20.8	109.7	66.0	43.7	479.7

Table 1-1B. Gross Domestic Product: Historical Data—*Continued*

(Billions of dollars, quarterly data are at seasonally adjusted annual rates.)　　　　　　　　　　　　　NIPA Tables 1.1.5, 1.2.5

Year and quarter	Gross domestic product	Personal consumption expenditures	Gross private domestic investment				Exports and imports of goods and services			Government consumption expenditures and gross investment			Addendum: Final sales of domestic product
			Total	Fixed investment		Change in private inventories	Net exports	Exports	Imports	Total	Federal	State and local	
				Nonresidential	Residential								
1959													
1st quarter	495.5	310.1	76.2	44.5	27.8	3.9	0.4	21.8	21.4	108.8	64.3	44.5	491.6
2nd quarter	508.5	316.1	82.2	46.1	28.8	7.3	0.0	22.6	22.5	110.2	65.4	44.7	501.2
3rd quarter	509.3	321.3	76.4	47.8	28.3	0.4	0.6	23.5	22.9	111.0	66.2	44.8	508.9
4th quarter	513.2	323.4	79.3	47.7	27.5	4.1	0.6	23.1	22.5	110.0	65.4	44.6	509.1
1960													
1st quarter	527.0	326.9	89.1	49.5	28.4	11.2	2.7	26.0	23.3	108.2	62.4	45.8	515.8
2nd quarter	526.2	332.8	79.7	50.3	26.1	3.2	4.2	27.6	23.5	109.5	62.4	47.2	522.9
3rd quarter	529.0	332.8	78.7	49.0	25.3	4.3	4.2	27.0	22.9	113.3	65.3	48.1	524.6
4th quarter	523.7	334.7	68.1	48.6	25.3	-5.8	5.8	27.5	21.7	115.1	66.3	48.8	529.5
1961													
1st quarter	528.0	335.2	70.3	47.5	25.3	-2.5	5.8	27.5	21.7	116.7	66.0	50.7	530.5
2nd quarter	539.0	340.2	75.8	48.4	25.5	1.8	5.5	27.4	21.9	117.6	66.8	50.8	537.2
3rd quarter	549.5	343.1	82.4	48.8	26.9	6.7	3.9	27.2	23.3	120.1	68.6	51.6	542.8
4th quarter	562.6	350.3	84.2	50.4	27.8	6.0	4.4	28.3	23.9	123.6	70.2	53.4	556.6
1962													
1st quarter	576.1	355.6	89.4	51.6	28.4	9.4	4.0	28.3	24.3	127.1	73.4	53.7	566.6
2nd quarter	583.2	361.2	87.9	53.2	29.2	5.4	5.8	30.7	24.9	128.3	73.9	54.4	577.8
3rd quarter	590.0	365.1	89.3	53.9	29.2	6.2	3.8	29.0	25.1	131.8	76.6	55.2	583.8
4th quarter	593.3	371.4	86.0	53.5	29.1	3.4	2.8	28.4	25.6	133.2	77.0	56.1	590.0
1963													
1st quarter	602.5	375.0	90.5	53.4	30.2	6.9	3.9	29.1	25.2	133.1	75.5	57.6	595.6
2nd quarter	611.2	379.1	92.2	55.1	32.2	4.8	6.5	32.4	25.9	133.4	74.9	58.5	606.3
3rd quarter	623.9	386.1	95.0	56.8	32.5	5.7	3.9	30.6	26.7	139.0	78.8	60.2	618.2
4th quarter	633.5	390.7	97.4	58.7	33.7	5.1	5.4	32.2	26.8	139.9	78.4	61.5	628.4
1964													
1st quarter	649.6	400.4	100.7	60.1	35.4	5.1	7.3	34.2	27.0	141.3	78.6	62.7	644.5
2nd quarter	658.9	408.4	100.6	61.9	34.2	4.5	7.1	34.8	27.7	142.9	78.4	64.5	654.4
3rd quarter	670.5	417.3	102.5	64.1	33.7	4.7	6.4	34.8	28.4	144.4	78.9	65.5	665.8
4th quarter	675.6	419.8	104.6	65.7	33.8	5.0	6.9	36.2	29.3	144.3	77.8	66.5	670.6
1965													
1st quarter	695.7	430.5	115.7	70.3	33.9	11.5	4.6	33.1	28.5	144.9	77.1	67.8	684.1
2nd quarter	708.1	437.5	115.8	73.1	34.2	8.6	7.5	39.1	31.7	147.4	77.5	69.9	699.6
3rd quarter	725.2	446.6	119.7	76.1	34.3	9.3	4.9	36.9	32.0	154.0	81.5	72.5	715.9
4th quarter	747.5	460.6	121.8	79.7	34.5	7.6	5.5	39.5	33.9	159.6	85.5	74.1	739.9
1966													
1st quarter	770.8	471.0	131.7	83.0	34.8	13.9	4.4	39.4	35.0	163.6	87.6	76.0	756.9
2nd quarter	779.9	476.1	130.7	85.2	33.2	12.3	5.2	41.5	36.2	167.9	90.0	77.9	767.6
3rd quarter	793.1	485.3	130.2	86.4	31.9	11.9	2.2	40.4	38.2	175.5	95.6	79.9	781.3
4th quarter	806.9	491.1	132.7	87.0	29.2	16.5	3.6	42.4	38.8	179.6	96.5	83.0	790.4
1967													
1st quarter	817.8	495.4	129.3	85.6	28.3	15.4	4.6	44.0	39.4	188.5	103.0	85.4	802.3
2nd quarter	822.3	504.6	123.7	85.7	31.6	6.3	4.5	43.5	39.0	189.6	102.7	86.8	816.0
3rd quarter	837.0	511.8	128.5	85.8	33.4	9.3	2.9	42.4	39.5	193.8	105.4	88.3	827.7
4th quarter	852.7	519.4	132.9	88.4	36.0	8.4	2.2	43.9	41.7	198.2	107.3	90.9	844.3
1968													
1st quarter	879.8	537.3	137.2	91.9	36.9	8.4	1.1	45.5	44.4	204.1	110.1	94.0	871.3
2nd quarter	904.1	551.1	143.4	91.2	38.2	14.1	1.9	47.4	45.4	207.6	110.6	97.0	890.0
3rd quarter	919.3	567.3	139.7	93.2	38.9	7.7	1.3	49.5	48.2	210.9	111.7	99.2	911.6
4th quarter	936.2	576.2	144.4	97.4	40.9	6.0	1.1	49.2	48.2	214.6	112.6	102.0	930.2
1969													
1st quarter	960.9	588.4	155.7	101.0	43.2	11.5	0.2	44.0	43.8	216.5	112.1	104.4	949.4
2nd quarter	976.1	599.8	155.7	103.0	43.4	9.2	1.2	53.9	52.7	219.4	112.0	107.4	966.9
3rd quarter	996.3	610.1	160.3	106.9	43.2	10.2	1.0	53.3	52.4	224.9	115.4	109.5	986.1
4th quarter	1 004.5	622.1	154.1	107.6	40.7	5.8	3.3	56.5	53.1	224.9	113.6	111.3	998.7
1970													
1st quarter	1 017.1	633.2	150.7	108.1	40.7	1.8	3.4	56.9	53.5	229.8	115.0	114.9	1 015.3
2nd quarter	1 033.1	643.1	153.9	109.4	39.4	5.1	5.4	60.6	55.2	230.6	112.7	118.0	1 028.0
3rd quarter	1 050.5	655.1	156.1	110.6	40.4	5.1	3.8	60.3	56.4	235.5	112.7	122.7	1 045.4
4th quarter	1 052.7	661.8	148.9	107.9	45.0	-4.0	3.2	61.1	57.9	238.8	113.3	125.6	1 056.7
1971													
1st quarter	1 098.1	680.8	171.3	110.4	48.6	12.3	4.4	63.1	58.7	241.6	112.8	128.7	1 085.8
2nd quarter	1 118.8	694.9	178.8	113.4	54.6	10.9	-0.2	63.1	63.3	245.3	113.5	131.8	1 107.9
3rd quarter	1 139.1	707.3	183.4	114.8	58.3	10.2	-0.1	65.4	65.5	248.5	114.7	133.8	1 128.9
4th quarter	1 151.4	723.5	179.2	118.0	61.5	-0.3	-1.7	60.3	61.9	250.3	113.6	136.8	1 151.7
1972													
1st quarter	1 190.1	740.9	193.2	123.3	66.6	3.2	-3.5	68.6	72.2	259.6	119.7	139.9	1 186.9
2nd quarter	1 225.6	759.4	206.5	126.3	68.2	12.0	-4.3	67.2	71.4	263.9	122.6	141.3	1 213.6
3rd quarter	1 249.3	777.9	212.4	129.1	69.6	13.7	-2.6	71.5	74.1	261.6	116.8	144.8	1 235.6
4th quarter	1 286.6	802.7	218.4	136.6	74.3	7.5	-3.1	76.1	79.2	268.6	119.4	149.2	1 279.1
1973													
1st quarter	1 335.1	827.3	232.5	144.1	77.9	10.6	-1.4	84.0	85.4	276.7	123.3	153.4	1 324.5
2nd quarter	1 371.5	842.9	246.0	152.1	75.8	18.2	2.5	91.9	89.5	280.0	123.3	156.8	1 353.3
3rd quarter	1 390.7	861.4	241.8	157.0	75.0	9.8	6.4	97.6	91.1	281.1	120.3	160.8	1 380.9
4th quarter	1 431.8	876.5	257.6	159.9	72.7	25.0	9.0	107.6	98.7	288.8	122.8	165.9	1 406.8
1974													
1st quarter	1 446.5	894.7	244.1	162.6	69.0	12.5	6.4	116.7	110.3	301.4	128.6	172.8	1 434.0
2nd quarter	1 484.8	923.2	252.3	167.4	67.5	17.4	-2.7	126.7	129.4	312.0	131.1	181.0	1 467.4
3rd quarter	1 513.7	952.0	245.4	172.5	67.4	5.6	-7.0	126.6	133.6	323.2	136.1	187.1	1 508.1
4th quarter	1 552.8	961.8	255.8	175.4	60.0	20.4	0.0	136.6	136.6	335.1	142.5	192.6	1 532.3

Table 1-1B. Gross Domestic Product: Historical Data—*Continued*

(Billions of dollars, quarterly data are at seasonally adjusted annual rates.)   **NIPA Tables 1.1.5, 1.2.5**

Year and quarter	Gross domestic product	Personal consump-tion expen-ditures	Gross private domestic investment				Exports and imports of goods and services			Government consumption expenditures and gross investment			Addendum: Final sales of domestic product
			Total	Fixed investment		Change in private inventories	Net exports	Exports	Imports	Total	Federal	State and local	
				Nonresi-dential	Residential								
1975													
1st quarter	1 569.4	988.1	218.7	171.0	57.7	-10.0	16.5	141.4	124.9	346.2	144.0	202.2	1 579.5
2nd quarter	1 605.0	1 016.8	216.8	170.8	59.9	-14.0	21.6	136.8	115.2	349.8	144.9	204.9	1 618.9
3rd quarter	1 662.4	1 050.6	237.8	174.6	64.6	-1.4	12.0	134.1	122.1	362.0	151.3	210.7	1 663.8
4th quarter	1 713.9	1 079.6	247.6	178.6	68.7	0.3	13.8	142.5	128.7	372.9	156.0	216.9	1 713.6
1976													
1st quarter	1 771.9	1 113.4	274.8	183.9	76.2	14.7	4.7	143.6	138.9	379.1	156.3	222.8	1 757.2
2nd quarter	1 804.2	1 133.0	291.6	188.5	80.7	22.4	-0.5	146.6	147.1	380.1	157.8	222.3	1 781.8
3rd quarter	1 837.7	1 162.4	296.5	195.1	80.6	20.8	-4.1	151.8	155.8	382.8	159.8	223.0	1 816.9
4th quarter	1 884.5	1 196.2	304.9	201.9	92.5	10.5	-6.6	156.1	162.7	390.0	164.8	225.2	1 874.0
1977													
1st quarter	1 938.5	1 231.7	326.6	214.2	97.6	14.8	-21.1	155.4	176.4	401.3	169.8	231.5	1 923.7
2nd quarter	2 005.2	1 259.7	354.9	223.8	111.7	19.5	-21.1	161.9	183.0	411.8	174.8	237.0	1 985.8
3rd quarter	2 066.0	1 290.9	378.4	232.5	115.0	30.9	-20.6	162.3	182.9	417.3	176.5	240.8	2 035.1
4th quarter	2 110.8	1 329.1	385.5	244.5	116.9	24.1	-29.6	157.8	187.4	425.8	180.5	245.3	2 086.7
1978													
1st quarter	2 149.1	1 359.1	396.8	250.4	121.0	25.5	-38.7	164.6	203.3	431.9	182.9	249.0	2 123.6
2nd quarter	2 274.7	1 416.7	430.9	276.0	130.6	24.3	-22.6	186.2	208.8	449.7	189.2	260.6	2 250.5
3rd quarter	2 335.2	1 447.7	451.4	290.6	135.8	25.0	-23.8	191.3	215.1	459.9	192.4	267.4	2 310.3
4th quarter	2 416.0	1 487.0	472.8	305.3	139.0	28.5	-16.4	205.4	221.8	472.7	199.1	273.6	2 387.6
1979													
1st quarter	2 463.3	1 522.6	481.1	318.8	138.5	23.9	-18.2	211.7	229.8	477.8	202.2	275.5	2 439.5
2nd quarter	2 526.4	1 563.2	493.0	324.9	140.6	27.4	-22.2	220.9	243.1	492.5	207.9	284.6	2 499.0
3rd quarter	2 599.7	1 617.7	497.9	342.3	143.5	12.1	-23.0	234.3	257.3	507.2	211.7	295.5	2 587.6
4th quarter	2 659.4	1 661.2	499.5	349.6	141.4	8.6	-26.8	253.7	280.5	525.5	220.4	305.0	2 650.8
1980													
1st quarter	2 724.1	1 708.0	505.2	361.3	134.0	9.9	-35.8	268.5	304.3	546.7	231.6	315.1	2 714.2
2nd quarter	2 728.0	1 710.0	470.4	350.9	111.7	7.8	-15.2	277.4	292.6	562.7	243.0	319.8	2 720.3
3rd quarter	2 785.2	1 768.7	443.5	361.1	116.3	-33.9	5.5	284.7	279.2	567.5	243.6	324.0	2 819.0
4th quarter	2 915.3	1 836.6	497.9	376.2	130.8	-9.1	-6.7	292.5	299.2	587.5	256.7	330.7	2 924.4
1981													
1st quarter	3 051.4	1 892.4	563.1	393.1	131.3	38.8	-14.3	305.5	319.7	610.1	266.5	343.6	3 012.6
2nd quarter	3 084.3	1 924.0	551.4	410.8	128.9	11.7	-13.5	308.4	322.0	622.4	278.7	343.8	3 072.6
3rd quarter	3 177.0	1 963.4	592.8	428.4	120.4	44.0	-7.6	302.3	309.9	628.4	281.4	347.0	3 133.1
4th quarter	3 194.7	1 978.2	582.2	447.8	109.6	24.8	-14.8	304.7	319.4	649.0	294.1	354.8	3 169.9
1982													
1st quarter	3 184.9	2 016.2	526.5	443.2	104.8	-21.5	-16.3	293.2	309.5	658.5	298.7	359.9	3 206.4
2nd quarter	3 240.9	2 042.7	530.8	432.0	102.9	-4.2	-4.4	294.7	299.1	671.9	305.1	366.8	3 245.1
3rd quarter	3 274.4	2 090.7	528.7	419.4	103.5	5.8	-29.7	279.6	309.3	684.7	312.3	372.4	3 268.6
4th quarter	3 312.5	2 152.4	482.9	411.2	111.5	-39.8	-29.6	265.3	294.9	706.7	327.0	379.7	3 352.3
1983													
1st quarter	3 381.0	2 192.2	496.6	400.5	131.2	-35.1	-24.6	270.7	295.3	716.7	332.8	383.9	3 416.0
2nd quarter	3 482.2	2 256.4	542.2	402.9	147.0	-7.7	-45.4	272.5	318.0	729.1	342.1	387.0	3 489.9
3rd quarter	3 587.1	2 326.5	577.7	419.5	162.4	-4.2	-65.2	278.2	343.4	748.1	354.1	394.0	3 591.3
4th quarter	3 688.1	2 379.2	640.7	446.0	170.8	23.9	-71.4	286.6	358.0	739.7	342.4	397.3	3 664.2
1984													
1st quarter	3 807.4	2 425.5	709.7	460.1	176.6	73.0	-95.0	293.0	388.0	767.2	359.2	408.0	3 734.4
2nd quarter	3 906.3	2 484.1	735.1	484.4	181.4	69.3	-104.3	302.2	406.5	791.4	373.9	417.4	3 837.0
3rd quarter	3 976.0	2 522.8	753.5	500.7	181.4	71.3	-103.9	305.7	409.6	803.6	375.2	428.4	3 904.6
4th quarter	4 034.0	2 572.0	744.3	513.3	183.0	48.0	-107.8	308.6	416.4	825.5	388.8	436.7	3 986.0
1985													
1st quarter	4 117.2	2 643.4	720.0	520.5	183.3	16.2	-91.9	305.4	397.3	845.6	398.0	447.6	4 101.0
2nd quarter	4 175.7	2 687.4	735.3	528.5	185.1	21.6	-115.4	303.1	418.6	868.4	407.6	460.7	4 154.0
3rd quarter	4 258.3	2 755.9	727.2	522.2	188.8	16.3	-118.6	295.6	414.2	893.9	420.7	473.2	4 242.0
4th quarter	4 318.7	2 783.7	762.2	533.6	195.5	33.1	-134.9	304.0	438.9	907.7	424.6	483.0	4 285.6
1986													
1st quarter	4 382.4	2 827.2	763.8	527.2	206.3	30.3	-127.4	312.0	439.4	918.8	421.3	497.5	4 352.1
2nd quarter	4 423.2	2 859.2	753.0	517.5	219.8	15.7	-129.8	314.2	444.0	940.9	434.7	506.2	4 407.6
3rd quarter	4 491.3	2 930.6	732.5	513.5	226.1	-7.0	-139.3	320.2	459.4	967.4	451.9	515.5	4 498.3
4th quarter	4 543.3	2 969.9	736.7	521.2	228.3	-12.7	-133.6	335.0	468.6	970.2	445.8	524.4	4 556.0
1987													
1st quarter	4 611.1	3 004.8	765.0	506.8	230.1	28.0	-141.0	336.7	477.7	982.4	451.6	530.9	4 583.1
2nd quarter	4 686.7	3 071.9	767.6	518.2	232.9	16.5	-147.3	355.0	502.3	994.6	458.6	536.0	4 670.2
3rd quarter	4 764.5	3 138.3	769.5	534.2	234.2	1.0	-145.7	371.6	517.3	1 002.5	460.5	542.0	4 763.5
4th quarter	4 883.1	3 173.0	837.8	537.2	237.5	63.1	-145.7	391.8	537.5	1 018.1	467.5	550.6	4 820.0
1988													
1st quarter	4 948.6	3 253.5	797.6	546.2	234.4	17.0	-124.4	418.4	542.7	1 021.9	460.1	561.8	4 931.6
2nd quarter	5 059.3	3 313.0	820.4	562.3	238.4	19.7	-107.2	438.9	546.1	1 033.0	459.0	574.0	5 039.6
3rd quarter	5 142.8	3 380.4	825.7	567.5	240.0	18.2	-100.2	452.7	552.8	1 036.9	456.1	580.8	5 124.6
4th quarter	5 251.0	3 453.3	842.6	579.1	244.4	19.1	-108.7	465.6	574.3	1 063.8	471.1	592.7	5 231.9
1989													
1st quarter	5 360.3	3 507.7	884.1	591.3	244.6	48.2	-102.1	484.0	586.2	1 070.7	469.3	601.4	5 312.2
2nd quarter	5 453.6	3 570.0	878.2	601.9	240.2	36.0	-89.5	505.8	595.4	1 095.0	481.4	613.6	5 417.5
3rd quarter	5 532.9	3 626.8	870.3	621.9	238.4	10.0	-76.3	508.2	584.4	1 112.1	489.0	623.2	5 523.0
4th quarter	5 581.7	3 673.5	867.3	615.8	234.8	16.6	-83.6	514.5	598.2	1 124.6	486.1	638.5	5 565.1
1990													
1st quarter	5 708.1	3 758.7	880.0	626.9	239.2	13.9	-89.2	537.6	626.8	1 158.6	500.8	657.8	5 694.2
2nd quarter	5 797.4	3 811.8	882.5	617.9	230.9	33.7	-68.4	546.4	614.8	1 171.4	506.0	665.4	5 763.7
3rd quarter	5 850.6	3 875.2	866.8	626.1	218.8	21.9	-74.4	555.7	630.1	1 183.0	505.0	678.0	5 828.8
4th quarter	5 846.0	3 896.0	814.6	618.9	207.0	-11.3	-78.5	568.8	647.3	1 213.8	518.2	695.6	5 857.3

Table 1-1B. Gross Domestic Product: Historical Data—*Continued*

(Billions of dollars, quarterly data are at seasonally adjusted annual rates.) NIPA Tables 1.1.5, 1.2.5

Year and quarter	Gross domestic product	Personal consumption expenditures	Gross private domestic investment				Exports and imports of goods and services			Government consumption expenditures and gross investment			Addendum: Final sales of domestic product
			Total	Fixed investment		Change in private inventories	Net exports	Exports	Imports	Total	Federal	State and local	
				Nonresidential	Residential								
1991													
1st quarter	5 880.2	3 909.7	787.9	608.2	195.2	-15.5	-45.6	574.7	620.3	1 228.1	529.2	698.9	5 895.7
2nd quarter	5 962.0	3 963.3	784.1	601.4	200.7	-18.0	-21.6	592.3	613.9	1 236.2	531.7	704.5	5 980.0
3rd quarter	6 033.7	4 008.7	805.3	594.1	210.3	0.8	-19.5	602.2	621.7	1 239.2	526.0	713.2	6 032.8
4th quarter	6 092.5	4 038.6	834.3	589.0	214.2	31.1	-21.2	617.1	638.3	1 240.8	519.2	721.5	6 061.4
1992													
1st quarter	6 190.7	4 140.1	810.2	585.6	224.4	0.2	-18.5	627.3	645.8	1 258.8	525.7	733.1	6 190.5
2nd quarter	6 295.2	4 193.5	865.4	607.1	235.1	23.2	-31.1	627.9	659.0	1 267.3	528.9	738.4	6 272.0
3rd quarter	6 389.7	4 267.7	876.8	619.0	237.3	20.5	-36.5	641.4	677.9	1 281.7	538.6	743.1	6 369.2
4th quarter	6 493.6	4 346.2	906.7	636.7	248.6	21.4	-45.3	643.2	688.5	1 286.0	538.4	747.7	6 472.2
1993													
1st quarter	6 544.5	4 384.9	931.3	642.8	252.6	35.9	-54.3	645.0	699.3	1 282.6	526.8	755.8	6 508.6
2nd quarter	6 622.7	4 452.1	942.3	660.3	257.9	24.1	-62.0	654.3	716.3	1 290.3	522.9	767.4	6 598.6
3rd quarter	6 688.3	4 516.3	943.4	667.5	269.3	6.6	-67.9	651.4	719.3	1 296.6	522.4	774.2	6 681.7
4th quarter	6 813.8	4 581.1	996.4	695.7	284.1	16.6	-73.4	671.7	745.0	1 309.7	527.9	781.9	6 797.2
1994													
1st quarter	6 916.3	4 650.4	1 043.6	704.8	293.5	45.3	-80.7	681.2	761.8	1 302.9	512.0	791.0	6 871.0
2nd quarter	7 044.3	4 709.8	1 106.9	720.5	305.0	81.4	-91.3	706.3	797.6	1 318.8	515.0	803.7	6 962.9
3rd quarter	7 131.8	4 786.3	1 092.9	734.7	304.9	53.2	-96.7	737.1	833.8	1 349.3	529.1	820.2	7 078.6
4th quarter	7 248.2	4 856.7	1 145.7	765.6	304.9	75.2	-102.3	758.3	860.6	1 348.1	518.2	829.9	7 173.0
1995													
1st quarter	7 307.7	4 888.7	1 160.6	797.7	301.8	61.1	-106.2	780.7	886.9	1 364.6	523.1	841.5	7 246.5
2nd quarter	7 355.8	4 957.5	1 132.7	805.5	293.5	33.7	-110.6	797.7	908.3	1 376.3	521.7	854.6	7 322.1
3rd quarter	7 452.5	5 022.9	1 126.2	811.2	303.8	11.3	-75.4	830.5	905.8	1 378.8	520.1	858.7	7 441.2
4th quarter	7 542.5	5 080.1	1 156.7	825.8	312.4	18.5	-70.6	838.6	909.2	1 376.4	510.2	866.2	7 524.1
1996													
1st quarter	7 638.2	5 156.5	1 170.0	841.4	321.8	6.9	-89.1	847.6	936.7	1 400.7	527.9	872.8	7 631.3
2nd quarter	7 800.0	5 248.8	1 227.8	860.5	336.9	30.5	-93.8	859.0	952.8	1 417.1	530.9	886.2	7 769.5
3rd quarter	7 892.7	5 304.4	1 279.8	889.0	339.7	51.1	-114.0	859.7	973.8	1 422.6	523.6	898.9	7 841.6
4th quarter	8 023.0	5 384.7	1 283.1	910.6	337.9	34.6	-88.3	904.3	992.6	1 443.5	525.5	918.0	7 988.3
1997													
1st quarter	8 137.0	5 467.1	1 320.6	930.1	340.7	49.8	-108.1	919.1	1 027.2	1 457.4	523.6	933.7	8 087.2
2nd quarter	8 276.8	5 504.0	1 385.0	949.9	346.7	88.4	-84.7	955.0	1 039.7	1 472.4	533.5	939.0	8 188.4
3rd quarter	8 409.9	5 613.3	1 414.9	995.6	351.3	68.0	-96.2	974.7	1 070.9	1 477.9	532.4	945.6	8 341.9
4th quarter	8 505.7	5 698.1	1 434.1	998.8	357.5	77.8	-116.5	968.9	1 085.3	1 490.0	534.4	955.6	8 428.0
1998													
1st quarter	8 600.6	5 757.5	1 494.9	1 025.0	364.9	105.1	-134.5	963.8	1 098.2	1 482.6	519.5	963.1	8 495.5
2nd quarter	8 698.6	5 870.2	1 471.5	1 055.8	378.4	37.3	-161.8	947.8	1 109.6	1 518.7	534.8	983.9	8 661.3
3rd quarter	8 847.2	5 968.0	1 512.7	1 066.7	393.6	52.4	-173.9	936.0	1 109.9	1 540.4	531.8	1 008.6	8 794.8
4th quarter	9 027.5	6 078.2	1 564.0	1 097.1	406.8	60.0	-177.1	967.9	1 145.0	1 562.5	537.9	1 024.6	8 967.5
1999													
1st quarter	9 148.6	6 157.4	1 617.3	1 120.7	413.3	83.3	-212.0	958.7	1 170.6	1 585.8	541.2	1 044.6	9 065.3
2nd quarter	9 252.6	6 290.0	1 604.7	1 147.4	422.3	35.1	-250.9	971.2	1 222.2	1 608.8	544.3	1 064.5	9 217.5
3rd quarter	9 405.1	6 398.9	1 644.5	1 174.5	429.4	40.6	-282.9	998.8	1 281.7	1 644.6	558.9	1 085.7	9 364.5
4th quarter	9 607.7	6 524.9	1 699.5	1 177.0	438.1	84.3	-302.5	1 028.5	1 331.0	1 685.9	575.3	1 110.6	9 523.4
2000													
1st quarter	9 709.5	6 683.0	1 688.8	1 223.5	449.2	16.1	-357.9	1 052.8	1 410.7	1 695.6	562.4	1 133.2	9 693.5
2nd quarter	9 949.1	6 775.7	1 810.9	1 270.1	450.5	90.4	-364.4	1 089.2	1 453.6	1 726.9	583.2	1 143.7	9 858.7
3rd quarter	10 017.5	6 881.7	1 791.7	1 288.4	446.0	57.2	-395.9	1 119.1	1 515.0	1 740.0	579.4	1 160.6	9 960.2
4th quarter	10 129.8	6 981.1	1 797.4	1 292.7	450.2	54.5	-410.0	1 111.8	1 521.8	1 761.3	579.3	1 182.0	10 075.3
2001													
1st quarter	10 165.1	7 058.1	1 701.3	1 273.7	458.3	-30.7	-395.4	1 097.1	1 492.5	1 801.1	594.3	1 206.7	10 195.7
2nd quarter	10 301.3	7 118.7	1 699.4	1 240.6	470.4	-11.6	-363.8	1 056.6	1 420.3	1 846.9	608.7	1 238.2	10 312.9
3rd quarter	10 305.2	7 151.2	1 670.4	1 219.6	480.9	-30.1	-367.0	997.1	1 364.2	1 850.6	616.3	1 234.2	10 335.3
4th quarter	10 373.1	7 267.2	1 576.6	1 177.3	480.1	-80.8	-357.8	960.1	1 317.9	1 887.2	627.4	1 259.8	10 453.9
2002													
1st quarter	10 498.7	7 309.0	1 628.0	1 149.5	491.9	-13.4	-374.9	973.4	1 348.3	1 936.6	657.8	1 278.9	10 512.1
2nd quarter	10 601.9	7 403.4	1 648.1	1 128.3	506.6	13.2	-418.1	1 005.9	1 424.0	1 968.5	674.4	1 294.1	10 588.7
3rd quarter	10 701.7	7 491.2	1 650.4	1 120.6	511.5	18.3	-435.8	1 020.6	1 456.4	1 996.0	685.4	1 310.6	10 683.4
4th quarter	10 766.9	7 553.2	1 661.3	1 103.3	528.1	30.0	-479.9	1 012.2	1 492.1	2 032.3	705.0	1 327.3	10 737.0
2003													
1st quarter	10 887.4	7 645.9	1 671.5	1 097.7	545.2	28.6	-503.6	1 012.5	1 516.1	2 073.6	725.2	1 348.4	10 858.7
2nd quarter	11 011.6	7 727.4	1 678.5	1 123.8	557.8	-3.1	-504.3	1 011.6	1 515.9	2 110.0	762.1	1 347.8	11 014.7
3rd quarter	11 255.1	7 882.0	1 745.1	1 150.8	590.1	4.2	-499.5	1 041.4	1 540.8	2 127.5	765.2	1 362.3	11 250.9
4th quarter	11 414.8	7 961.2	1 823.6	1 170.4	617.4	35.8	-509.1	1 098.6	1 607.8	2 139.1	773.4	1 365.7	11 379.0
2004													
1st quarter	11 589.9	8 098.1	1 853.6	1 164.6	637.6	51.4	-546.3	1 138.8	1 685.1	2 184.5	805.1	1 379.4	11 538.5
2nd quarter	11 762.9	8 193.9	1 956.0	1 204.4	675.6	76.0	-606.1	1 170.8	1 776.9	2 219.0	819.9	1 399.2	11 686.9
3rd quarter	11 936.3	8 316.5	2 001.3	1 244.0	696.6	60.8	-635.9	1 185.4	1 821.3	2 254.4	839.1	1 415.3	11 875.6
4th quarter	12 123.9	8 473.8	2 063.3	1 279.1	712.7	71.5	-686.5	1 225.9	1 912.4	2 273.3	834.5	1 438.8	12 052.4
2005													
1st quarter	12 361.8	8 591.9	2 130.8	1 305.2	734.9	90.7	-677.4	1 262.4	1 939.8	2 316.5	862.0	1 454.6	12 271.1
2nd quarter	12 500.0	8 730.3	2 115.3	1 334.9	764.5	15.9	-690.2	1 298.5	1 988.7	2 344.6	867.2	1 477.3	12 484.1
3rd quarter	12 728.6	8 895.8	2 166.7	1 362.9	792.7	11.0	-734.0	1 308.2	2 042.1	2 400.1	894.1	1 506.0	12 717.6
4th quarter	12 901.4	8 996.1	2 276.3	1 386.3	807.9	82.2	-789.3	1 351.3	2 140.6	2 418.3	881.9	1 536.4	12 819.2
2006													
1st quarter	13 161.4	9 126.2	2 336.6	1 457.2	813.4	66.0	-775.8	1 414.0	2 189.8	2 474.5	928.5	1 546.1	13 095.5
2nd quarter	13 330.4	9 249.3	2 352.1	1 495.3	784.4	72.4	-781.4	1 456.0	2 237.4	2 510.5	930.3	1 580.2	13 258.0
3rd quarter	13 432.8	9 371.7	2 333.4	1 522.7	741.6	69.1	-805.7	1 476.0	2 281.7	2 533.3	932.2	1 601.2	13 363.7
4th quarter	13 584.2	9 456.8	2 286.5	1 546.1	708.0	32.3	-714.3	1 538.2	2 252.5	2 555.2	935.9	1 619.4	13 551.9

Table 1-1B. Gross Domestic Product: Historical Data—*Continued*

(Billions of dollars, quarterly data are at seasonally adjusted annual rates.)

NIPA Tables 1.1.5, 1.2.5

Year and quarter	Gross domestic product	Personal consump-tion expen-ditures	Gross private domestic investment				Exports and imports of goods and services			Government consumption expenditures and gross investment			Addendum: Final sales of domestic product
			Total	Fixed investment		Change in private inventories	Net exports	Exports	Imports	Total	Federal	State and local	
				Nonresi-dential	Residential								
2007													
1st quarter	13 758.5	9 601.7	2 277.4	1 579.6	680.7	17.0	-724.9	1 575.5	2 300.4	2 604.4	944.0	1 660.3	13 741.5
2nd quarter	13 976.8	9 720.9	2 329.6	1 624.9	657.2	47.5	-729.7	1 619.1	2 348.9	2 656.0	968.7	1 687.3	13 929.3
3rd quarter	14 126.2	9 817.7	2 313.4	1 660.7	613.4	39.4	-703.4	1 690.3	2 393.7	2 698.4	992.1	1 706.4	14 086.8
4th quarter	14 253.2	9 948.7	2 260.5	1 684.6	563.4	12.6	-694.3	1 761.8	2 456.1	2 738.2	1 000.6	1 737.6	14 240.6
2008													
1st quarter	14 273.9	10 018.5	2 185.7	1 689.3	515.9	-19.5	-742.3	1 819.3	2 561.6	2 812.0	1 042.7	1 769.3	14 293.4
2nd quarter	14 415.5	10 126.5	2 165.4	1 689.0	494.6	-18.3	-746.1	1 922.8	2 668.9	2 869.6	1 066.0	1 803.7	14 433.8
3rd quarter	14 395.1	10 135.8	2 086.3	1 665.9	464.6	-44.1	-756.9	1 933.8	2 690.6	2 929.8	1 100.6	1 829.2	14 439.2
4th quarter	14 081.7	9 861.3	1 913.0	1 580.9	414.6	-82.5	-593.7	1 711.1	2 304.8	2 901.1	1 111.2	1 789.9	14 164.2
2009													
1st quarter	13 893.7	9 781.7	1 620.1	1 430.6	369.0	-179.5	-383.5	1 522.2	1 905.7	2 875.5	1 105.3	1 770.1	14 073.3
2nd quarter	13 854.1	9 781.6	1 493.8	1 351.9	342.4	-200.5	-338.3	1 520.8	1 859.1	2 916.9	1 137.2	1 779.7	14 054.6
3rd quarter	13 920.5	9 911.1	1 481.2	1 324.3	353.9	-197.1	-406.7	1 590.3	1 997.0	2 935.0	1 157.7	1 777.3	14 117.6
4th quarter	14 087.4	9 990.0	1 592.2	1 305.1	353.2	-66.1	-437.6	1 699.0	2 136.5	2 942.7	1 170.6	1 772.1	14 153.5
2010													
1st quarter	14 277.9	10 103.7	1 702.3	1 318.7	339.3	44.3	-495.8	1 749.5	2 245.3	2 967.7	1 195.2	1 772.6	14 233.6
2nd quarter	14 467.8	10 184.8	1 809.7	1 377.1	354.5	78.1	-531.2	1 813.8	2 345.0	3 004.6	1 224.5	1 780.1	14 389.8
3rd quarter	14 605.5	10 276.6	1 850.5	1 416.5	327.3	106.7	-540.3	1 860.6	2 400.9	3 018.7	1 237.5	1 781.2	14 498.8
4th quarter	14 755.0	10 417.1	1 818.0	1 447.9	331.3	38.7	-500.2	1 935.3	2 435.5	3 020.2	1 234.3	1 786.0	14 716.3
2011													
1st quarter	14 867.8	10 571.7	1 853.1	1 460.5	330.6	62.0	-571.3	2 024.1	2 595.4	3 014.4	1 219.9	1 794.4	14 805.8
2nd quarter	15 012.8	10 676.0	1 895.3	1 506.0	335.7	53.6	-597.1	2 085.3	2 682.4	3 038.6	1 237.1	1 801.5	14 959.2
3rd quarter	15 176.1	10 784.5	1 906.6	1 568.7	337.0	0.8	-562.3	2 119.2	2 681.5	3 047.3	1 248.9	1 798.5	15 175.3
4th quarter	15 319.4	10 871.6	2 010.1	1 594.8	346.5	68.7	-584.3	2 113.2	2 697.4	3 021.9	1 225.5	1 796.5	15 250.7

Table 1-2A. Real Gross Domestic Product: Recent Data

(Billions of chained [2005] dollars, quarterly data are at seasonally adjusted annual rates.)   **NIPA Tables 1.1.6, 1.2.6**

Year and quarter	Gross domestic product	Personal consump-tion expen-ditures	Gross private domestic investment				Exports and imports of goods and services			Government consumption expen-ditures and gross investment			Residual	Adden-dum: final sales of domestic product
			Total	Fixed investment		Change in private inven-tories	Net exports	Exports	Imports	Total	Federal	State and local		
				Nonresi-dential	Resi-dential									
1950	2 004.2	1 282.7	252.3	...	...	19.3	...	54.7	65.7	492.4	...	...	-12.2	1 989.0
1951	2 159.3	1 302.8	253.0	...	...	26.7	...	67.0	68.3	672.7	...	...	-67.9	2 130.4
1952	2 242.0	1 343.9	228.8	...	...	10.8	...	64.1	74.3	810.0	...	...	-130.5	2 243.8
1953	2 345.2	1 408.1	239.6	...	...	6.7	...	59.8	81.3	868.0	...	...	-149.0	2 354.4
1954	2 330.4	1 437.7	228.5	...	...	-6.4	...	62.7	77.3	808.9	...	...	-130.1	2 361.0
1955	2 498.2	1 543.8	284.0	...	...	16.0	...	69.4	86.6	779.3	...	...	-91.7	2 494.0
1956	2 547.6	1 589.0	280.1	...	...	11.9	...	80.9	93.6	780.0	...	...	-88.8	2 551.1
1957	2 598.8	1 628.4	267.9	...	...	2.9	...	87.9	97.6	814.7	...	...	-102.5	2 616.7
1958	2 575.4	1 642.6	245.7	...	...	-0.7	...	76.0	102.2	840.9	...	...	-127.6	2 597.8
1959	2 760.1	1 735.9	295.5	...	...	13.9	...	83.9	113.0	869.5	...	...	-111.7	2 761.6
1960	2 828.5	1 783.6	295.4	...	...	11.8	...	98.4	114.5	871.0	...	...	-105.4	2 834.2
1961	2 894.4	1 820.3	293.5	...	...	10.6	...	99.0	113.7	914.8	...	...	-119.5	2 902.1
1962	3 069.8	1 910.3	330.8	...	...	21.9	...	104.0	126.6	971.1	...	...	-119.8	3 062.3
1963	3 204.0	1 989.0	353.0	...	...	20.3	...	111.4	130.0	996.1	...	...	-115.5	3 199.9
1964	3 389.4	2 107.5	382.1	...	...	17.3	...	124.5	136.9	1 018.0	...	...	-105.8	3 390.8
1965	3 607.0	2 240.8	435.7	...	...	32.9	...	128.0	151.5	1 048.7	...	...	-94.7	3 587.6
1966	3 842.1	2 367.9	474.1	...	...	47.1	...	136.9	174.0	1 141.1	...	...	-103.9	3 803.4
1967	3 939.2	2 438.8	452.4	240.6	225.7	33.9	...	140.0	186.7	1 228.7	...	...	-134.0	3 920.0
1968	4 129.9	2 579.6	478.7	251.3	256.4	30.8	...	151.0	214.5	1 267.2	...	...	-132.1	4 115.8
1969	4 258.2	2 676.2	506.6	270.4	264.0	30.3	...	158.3	226.7	1 264.3	...	...	-120.5	4 245.0
1970	4 266.3	2 738.9	473.4	269.0	248.2	5.6	...	175.3	236.4	1 233.7	...	...	-118.6	4 284.3
1971	4 409.5	2 843.3	527.3	269.0	316.3	25.0	...	178.3	249.0	1 206.9	...	...	-97.3	4 403.6
1972	4 643.8	3 018.1	589.8	293.7	372.5	25.7	...	191.7	277.0	1 198.1	...	...	-76.9	4 636.7
1973	4 912.8	3 167.7	658.9	336.4	370.1	39.0	...	227.8	289.9	1 193.9	...	...	-45.6	4 884.0
1974	4 885.7	3 141.4	610.3	339.2	293.7	29.1	...	245.8	283.3	1 224.0	...	...	-52.5	4 870.0
1975	4 875.4	3 212.6	502.2	305.7	255.6	-12.8	...	244.3	251.8	1 251.6	...	...	-83.5	4 922.1
1976	5 136.9	3 391.5	603.7	320.7	315.7	34.3	...	255.0	301.1	1 257.2	...	...	-69.4	5 115.9
1977	5 373.1	3 534.3	694.9	356.9	383.5	43.1	...	261.1	334.0	1 271.0	...	...	-54.2	5 340.3
1978	5 672.8	3 690.1	778.7	410.3	407.7	45.6	...	288.6	362.9	1 308.4	...	...	-30.1	5 634.9
1979	5 850.1	3 777.8	803.5	451.6	392.7	28.0	...	317.2	369.0	1 332.8	...	...	-12.2	5 836.2
1980	5 834.0	3 764.5	715.2	450.4	309.6	-9.3	...	351.4	344.5	1 358.8	...	...	-11.4	5 873.6
1981	5 982.1	3 821.6	779.6	476.0	284.8	39.0	...	355.7	353.5	1 371.2	...	...	7.5	5 954.4
1982	5 865.9	3 874.9	670.3	458.1	233.1	-19.7	...	328.5	349.1	1 395.3	...	...	-54.0	5 918.2
1983	6 130.9	4 096.4	732.8	452.2	329.6	-7.7	...	320.1	393.1	1 446.3	...	...	-71.6	6 167.6
1984	6 571.5	4 313.6	948.7	532.0	378.5	78.3	...	346.2	488.8	1 494.9	...	...	-43.1	6 490.0
1985	6 843.4	4 538.3	939.8	567.3	384.5	25.4	...	356.7	520.5	1 599.0	...	...	-69.9	6 833.1
1986	7 080.5	4 722.4	933.5	551.1	431.6	8.5	...	384.1	565.0	1 696.2	...	...	-90.7	7 092.7
1987	7 307.0	4 868.0	962.2	550.7	440.3	33.2	...	425.4	598.4	1 737.1	...	...	-87.3	7 289.9
1988	7 607.4	5 064.3	984.9	579.5	435.8	21.9	...	493.5	621.9	1 758.9	...	...	-72.3	7 601.3
1989	7 879.2	5 207.5	1 024.4	611.8	422.6	30.6	...	550.2	649.3	1 806.8	...	...	-60.4	7 860.8
1990	8 027.1	5 313.7	989.9	614.8	386.1	16.6	...	599.7	672.6	1 864.0	...	...	-67.6	8 025.8
1991	8 008.3	5 321.7	909.4	581.9	349.0	-1.4	...	639.5	671.6	1 884.4	...	...	-75.1	8 027.9
1992	8 280.0	5 503.2	983.1	600.4	397.3	17.9	...	683.5	718.7	1 893.2	...	...	-64.3	8 277.2
1993	8 516.2	5 698.6	1 070.9	652.9	429.7	22.3	...	705.9	780.8	1 878.2	...	...	-56.6	8 508.0
1994	8 863.1	5 916.2	1 216.4	712.9	471.5	69.3	...	767.4	873.9	1 878.0	...	...	-41.0	8 801.7
1995	9 086.0	6 076.2	1 254.3	787.9	456.1	32.1	-98.8	845.1	943.9	1 888.9	704.1	1 183.6	-179.2	9 065.4
1996	9 425.8	6 288.3	1 365.3	861.5	492.5	31.2	-110.7	915.3	1 026.0	1 907.9	696.0	1 211.1	-157.1	9 404.4
1997	9 845.9	6 520.4	1 535.2	965.5	501.8	77.4	-139.8	1 024.3	1 164.1	1 943.8	689.1	1 254.3	-121.3	9 774.2
1998	10 274.7	6 862.3	1 688.9	1 081.4	540.4	71.6	-252.5	1 047.7	1 300.2	1 985.0	681.4	1 303.8	-90.1	10 208.3
1999	10 770.7	7 237.6	1 837.6	1 194.3	574.2	68.5	-356.4	1 093.4	1 449.9	2 056.1	694.6	1 361.8	-51.2	10 706.5
2000	11 216.4	7 604.6	1 963.1	1 311.3	580.0	60.2	-451.3	1 187.4	1 638.7	2 097.8	698.1	1 400.1	-25.6	11 158.0
2001	11 337.5	7 810.3	1 825.2	1 274.8	583.3	-41.8	-471.8	1 120.8	1 592.6	2 178.3	726.5	1 452.3	-31.1	11 382.0
2002	11 543.1	8 018.3	1 800.4	1 173.7	613.8	12.8	-548.5	1 098.3	1 646.8	2 279.6	779.5	1 500.6	-22.2	11 533.6
2003	11 836.4	8 244.5	1 870.1	1 189.6	664.3	17.3	-603.7	1 116.0	1 719.7	2 330.5	831.1	1 499.7	-13.1	11 820.5
2004	12 246.9	8 515.8	2 058.2	1 263.0	729.5	66.3	-687.9	1 222.5	1 910.4	2 362.0	865.0	1 497.1	-3.7	12 181.3
2005	12 623.0	8 803.5	2 172.3	1 347.3	775.0	50.0	-722.7	1 305.1	2 027.8	2 369.9	876.3	1 493.6	-0.2	12 573.0
2006	12 958.5	9 054.5	2 231.8	1 455.5	718.2	59.4	-729.4	1 422.1	2 151.5	2 402.1	894.9	1 507.2	-1.8	12 899.3
2007	13 206.4	9 262.9	2 159.5	1 550.0	584.2	27.7	-648.8	1 554.4	2 203.2	2 434.2	906.1	1 528.1	-1.3	13 177.5
2008	13 161.9	9 211.7	1 939.8	1 537.6	444.4	-36.3	-494.8	1 649.3	2 144.0	2 497.4	971.1	1 528.1	16.3	13 200.5
2009	12 703.1	9 037.5	1 454.2	1 263.2	345.6	-144.9	-358.8	1 494.0	1 852.8	2 539.6	1 029.5	1 514.2	34.3	12 852.7
2010	13 088.0	9 220.9	1 714.9	1 319.2	330.8	58.8	-421.8	1 663.2	2 085.0	2 556.8	1 075.9	1 487.0	8.5	13 028.9
2011	13 315.1	9 421.3	1 797.3	1 435.5	326.3	34.6	-413.6	1 774.2	2 187.7	2 502.7	1 055.0	1 453.8	-25.8	13 284.6
2009														
1st quarter	12 663.2	9 040.9	1 490.4	1 312.9	354.9	-161.6	-404.2	1 451.1	1 855.3	2 509.6	995.2	1 517.2	35.5	12 836.0
2nd quarter	12 641.3	8 998.5	1 397.2	1 257.6	334.3	-183.0	-331.8	1 449.4	1 781.2	2 546.0	1 029.2	1 520.7	38.3	12 830.0
3rd quarter	12 694.5	9 050.3	1 407.3	1 247.0	348.2	-178.7	-352.4	1 497.3	1 849.7	2 554.2	1 043.9	1 514.9	32.5	12 875.1
4th quarter	12 813.5	9 060.2	1 522.0	1 235.2	344.8	-56.5	-346.9	1 578.3	1 925.2	2 548.5	1 049.6	1 503.9	31.6	12 869.5
2010														
1st quarter	12 937.7	9 121.2	1 630.0	1 253.3	330.8	39.9	-376.8	1 606.2	1 983.0	2 540.6	1 056.9	1 489.2	22.2	12 895.9
2nd quarter	13 058.5	9 186.9	1 728.3	1 308.0	348.2	64.6	-437.4	1 645.0	2 082.4	2 564.0	1 079.4	1 490.8	12.6	12 992.2
3rd quarter	13 139.6	9 247.1	1 766.8	1 343.6	321.1	92.3	-458.7	1 684.8	2 143.5	2 570.3	1 087.8	1 488.9	7.3	13 046.0
4th quarter	13 216.1	9 328.4	1 734.5	1 371.9	323.1	38.3	-414.2	1 716.8	2 131.0	2 552.1	1 079.6	1 478.9	-7.9	13 181.6
2011														
1st quarter	13 227.9	9 376.7	1 750.9	1 378.9	321.1	49.1	-424.4	1 749.6	2 173.9	2 513.9	1 053.3	1 466.4	-21.1	13 182.8
2nd quarter	13 271.8	9 392.7	1 778.4	1 413.2	324.4	39.1	-416.4	1 765.0	2 181.4	2 508.2	1 058.3	1 456.1	-17.6	13 236.2
3rd quarter	13 331.6	9 433.5	1 784.2	1 465.6	325.4	-2.0	-402.8	1 785.2	2 187.9	2 507.6	1 063.7	1 450.4	-27.7	13 340.9
4th quarter	13 429.0	9 482.1	1 875.7	1 484.2	334.5	52.2	-410.8	1 797.0	2 207.7	2 481.2	1 044.7	1 442.4	-37.4	13 378.3

Note: Chained (2005) dollar series are calculated as the product of the chain-type quantity index and the 2005 current-dollar value of the corresponding series, divided by 100. Because the formula for the chain-type quantity indexes uses weights from more than one period, the corresponding chained-dollar estimates are usually not additive. The residual column is the difference between the total and the sum of the most detailed components shown in the Bureau of Economic Analysis (BEA) published data.

. . . = Not available.

Table 1-2B. Real Gross Domestic Product: Historical Data

(Billions of chained [2005] dollars, quarterly data are at seasonally adjusted annual rates.)   **NIPA Tables 1.1.6, 1.2.6**

| Year and quarter | Gross domestic product | Personal consumption expenditures | Gross private domestic investment | | | | Exports and imports of goods and services | | | Government consumption expenditures and gross investment | | | Residual | Addendum: Final sales of domestic product |
| | | | Total | Fixed investment | | Change in private inventories | Net exports | Exports | Imports | Total | Federal | State and local | | |
				Nonresidential	Residential									
1929	976.1	736.3	101.4	...	...	10.3	...	37.9	49.1	146.5	...	...	3.1	986.8
1930	892.0	696.8	67.6	...	...	-4.6	...	31.3	42.7	161.4	...	...	-22.4	919.2
1931	834.2	674.9	42.5	...	...	-10.6	...	26.1	37.2	168.2	...	...	-40.3	865.2
1932	725.2	614.4	12.8	...	...	-23.8	...	20.4	30.9	162.6	...	...	-54.1	766.6
1933	715.8	600.8	18.9	...	...	-12.2	...	20.5	32.2	157.2	...	...	-49.4	743.2
1934	793.7	643.7	34.1	...	...	-5.8	...	22.8	32.9	177.3	...	...	-51.3	814.0
1935	864.2	683.0	63.1	...	...	7.6	...	24.1	43.1	182.2	...	...	-45.1	864.5
1936	977.0	752.5	80.9	...	...	7.8	...	25.3	42.6	212.6	...	...	-51.7	978.9
1937	1 027.1	780.4	101.1	...	...	13.0	...	31.9	47.9	203.6	...	...	-42.0	1 019.8
1938	991.8	767.8	66.8	...	...	-3.1	...	31.5	37.3	219.3	...	...	-56.3	1 005.2
1939	1 071.9	810.7	85.9	...	...	1.6	...	33.3	39.1	238.6	...	...	-57.5	1 079.5
1940	1 165.9	852.7	119.7	...	...	16.1	...	37.8	40.1	245.3	...	...	-49.5	1 152.8
1941	1 365.0	913.2	146.2	...	...	26.4	...	38.8	49.3	407.7	...	...	-91.6	1 337.8
1942	1 616.8	891.6	77.2	...	...	10.3	...	25.6	44.7	959.4	...	...	-292.3	1 616.7
1943	1 881.5	916.5	45.6	...	...	-3.6	...	21.6	56.4	1 427.2	...	...	-473.0	1 907.0
1944	2 033.5	942.6	56.3	...	...	-4.3	...	23.2	59.0	1 606.1	...	...	-535.7	2 061.4
1945	2 010.7	1 000.9	74.4	...	...	-8.1	...	32.5	62.8	1 402.2	...	...	-436.5	2 044.7
1946	1 790.7	1 125.4	190.7	...	...	25.4	...	70.2	52.0	482.1	...	...	-25.7	1 764.7
1947	1 774.6	1 147.0	183.2	...	...	-3.6	...	80.0	49.4	409.5	...	...	4.3	1 801.7
1948	1 852.7	1 172.9	234.1	...	...	19.3	...	63.0	57.6	439.4	...	...	0.9	1 835.7
1949	1 843.1	1 205.4	178.7	...	...	-10.2	...	62.5	55.6	491.9	...	...	-39.8	1 879.3
1947														
1st quarter	1 770.7	1 130.9	188.7	106.7	113.2	4.9	...	85.2	51.0	407.3	223.8	179.4	9.6	1 785.5
2nd quarter	1 768.0	1 149.7	173.5	105.0	107.6	-3.5	...	84.2	52.0	409.8	224.3	181.9	2.8	1 797.2
3rd quarter	1 766.5	1 153.4	167.9	102.9	124.1	-13.4	...	79.9	46.1	413.6	224.4	186.1	-2.2	1 811.7
4th quarter	1 793.3	1 153.8	202.7	106.2	148.1	-2.2	...	70.8	48.6	407.5	216.6	189.1	7.1	1 812.3
1948														
1st quarter	1 821.8	1 159.6	224.7	112.8	146.3	11.4	...	67.6	54.8	415.5	224.0	188.8	9.2	1 820.2
2nd quarter	1 855.3	1 173.0	239.5	108.9	154.8	21.4	...	61.3	56.9	435.5	237.6	194.3	2.9	1 833.4
3rd quarter	1 865.3	1 174.8	242.1	109.2	149.9	25.0	...	62.7	59.9	444.0	242.5	197.7	1.6	1 836.6
4th quarter	1 868.2	1 184.1	230.0	112.0	138.8	19.4	...	60.5	58.9	462.7	255.6	202.5	-10.2	1 852.4
1949														
1st quarter	1 842.2	1 186.0	194.2	106.7	128.4	-2.0	...	67.8	57.2	475.9	260.7	210.9	-24.5	1 860.0
2nd quarter	1 835.5	1 204.1	167.1	102.5	126.1	-17.4	...	67.2	56.3	497.4	270.5	222.9	-44.0	1 884.0
3rd quarter	1 856.1	1 206.9	181.7	97.4	136.9	-3.9	...	61.6	54.0	502.4	267.6	232.2	-42.5	1 883.2
4th quarter	1 838.7	1 224.5	171.8	95.7	153.8	-17.5	...	53.3	54.9	491.8	254.3	236.6	-47.8	1 890.0
1950														
1st quarter	1 913.0	1 244.9	214.9	98.4	171.2	7.4	...	52.4	56.4	483.5	242.2	242.5	-26.3	1 920.4
2nd quarter	1 971.2	1 265.4	238.9	107.2	187.8	10.8	...	53.1	59.5	491.4	247.6	244.6	-18.1	1 972.0
3rd quarter	2 048.4	1 330.3	260.4	116.8	198.1	14.1	...	54.4	73.4	482.0	238.8	244.8	-5.3	2 043.0
4th quarter	2 084.4	1 290.2	295.0	116.7	188.8	44.9	...	58.8	73.6	512.7	266.8	244.9	1.3	2 020.7
1951														
1st quarter	2 110.7	1 321.4	263.9	113.6	178.8	27.9	...	61.8	73.6	567.5	319.1	242.5	-30.3	2 080.4
2nd quarter	2 145.7	1 284.1	270.4	115.2	154.7	40.6	...	67.9	71.1	645.6	387.4	246.6	-51.2	2 090.3
3rd quarter	2 188.5	1 299.1	249.5	116.5	144.8	26.9	...	69.5	65.1	718.8	454.4	247.8	-83.3	2 159.5
4th quarter	2 192.2	1 306.7	228.3	114.1	146.2	11.6	...	68.9	63.4	758.9	492.0	247.4	-107.2	2 191.5
1952														
1st quarter	2 214.3	1 309.6	233.6	114.5	150.0	14.5	...	72.5	70.8	782.4	513.5	248.2	-113.0	2 209.5
2nd quarter	2 216.7	1 335.3	214.2	115.8	152.8	-3.6	...	64.6	70.4	808.9	533.8	253.4	-135.9	2 245.3
3rd quarter	2 231.6	1 341.8	225.6	105.4	151.2	16.0	...	59.5	74.7	817.0	547.6	246.6	-137.6	2 223.4
4th quarter	2 305.3	1 389.2	241.8	114.8	159.3	16.1	...	59.9	81.4	831.6	556.2	252.4	-135.8	2 297.1
1953														
1st quarter	2 348.4	1 405.7	246.6	121.1	161.8	13.0	...	58.9	79.4	859.8	577.8	257.8	-143.2	2 346.7
2nd quarter	2 366.2	1 414.2	247.5	122.0	162.3	12.8	...	59.2	83.5	878.7	596.0	257.4	-149.9	2 365.3
3rd quarter	2 351.8	1 411.0	241.7	124.7	156.1	7.7	...	61.6	83.2	868.1	579.8	264.3	-147.4	2 359.5
4th quarter	2 314.6	1 401.6	222.6	123.2	154.8	-6.7	...	59.6	79.1	865.4	571.4	270.7	-155.5	2 346.1
1954														
1st quarter	2 303.5	1 406.7	220.7	119.6	156.4	-5.9	...	56.9	74.5	842.2	541.0	280.4	-148.5	2 332.4
2nd quarter	2 306.4	1 425.0	220.0	118.3	166.6	-9.5	...	65.1	81.2	812.5	512.0	281.5	-135.0	2 341.9
3rd quarter	2 332.4	1 444.4	231.2	121.5	176.8	-7.6	...	63.0	76.3	792.9	486.5	289.4	-122.8	2 365.2
4th quarter	2 379.1	1 474.7	241.9	121.2	187.9	-2.7	...	65.9	77.1	788.0	480.8	290.7	-114.3	2 404.6
1955														
1st quarter	2 447.7	1 507.8	267.7	123.3	201.8	11.2	...	68.3	81.6	787.1	469.3	302.9	-101.6	2 450.5
2nd quarter	2 488.1	1 536.6	284.6	131.1	204.8	16.6	...	66.7	86.2	779.3	458.6	306.9	-92.9	2 482.6
3rd quarter	2 521.4	1 555.6	288.7	137.8	200.5	15.1	...	71.1	87.7	784.0	463.5	306.4	-90.3	2 518.8
4th quarter	2 535.5	1 575.2	294.9	141.6	191.9	20.8	...	71.4	90.9	767.0	446.1	308.2	-82.1	2 524.2
1956														
1st quarter	2 523.9	1 577.8	285.0	139.0	186.9	17.6	...	74.8	94.7	766.6	442.8	311.5	-85.6	2 518.6
2nd quarter	2 543.8	1 583.0	281.8	141.1	185.8	12.2	...	79.9	94.2	782.7	454.4	315.3	-89.4	2 546.6
3rd quarter	2 540.6	1 586.6	278.5	142.3	182.1	9.5	...	82.5	95.0	775.3	446.1	316.9	-87.3	2 547.6
4th quarter	2 582.1	1 608.4	275.2	141.9	179.3	8.4	...	86.2	90.7	795.4	462.1	320.1	-92.4	2 591.6
1957														
1st quarter	2 597.9	1 619.5	270.7	142.9	176.7	4.6	...	91.9	97.9	811.7	470.3	328.2	-98.0	2 614.3
2nd quarter	2 591.7	1 622.4	270.4	142.6	172.4	6.5	...	89.1	98.6	806.7	463.2	331.0	-98.3	2 604.7
3rd quarter	2 616.6	1 635.3	276.8	145.6	170.1	9.5	...	86.6	96.7	812.9	464.9	335.6	-98.3	2 624.2
4th quarter	2 589.1	1 636.1	253.7	141.8	169.9	-8.9	...	84.1	97.1	827.7	471.4	344.0	-115.4	2 623.6

Note: Chained (2005) dollar series are calculated as the product of the chain-type quantity index and the 2005 current-dollar value of the corresponding series, divided by 100. Because the formula for the chain-type quantity indexes uses weights from more than one period, the corresponding chained-dollar estimates are usually not additive. The residual column is the difference between the total and the sum of the most detailed components shown in the Bureau of Economic Analysis (BEA) published data.

. . . = Not available.

Table 1-2B. Real Gross Domestic Product: Historical Data—*Continued*

(Billions of chained [2005] dollars, quarterly data are at seasonally adjusted annual rates.)   **NIPA Tables 1.1.6, 1.2.6**

Year and quarter	Gross domestic product	Personal consumption expenditures	Gross private domestic investment Total	Fixed investment Nonresidential	Fixed investment Residential	Change in private inventories	Net exports	Exports	Imports	Government Total	Government Federal	Government State and local	Residual	Addendum: Final sales of domestic product
1958														
1st quarter	2 519.0	1 613.9	234.8	131.5	163.1	-11.1	...	75.7	98.5	818.4	454.5	353.7	-125.3	2 556.5
2nd quarter	2 534.5	1 627.1	229.3	125.9	163.6	-9.7	...	76.1	102.7	838.9	469.1	358.8	-134.2	2 569.8
3rd quarter	2 593.9	1 653.8	248.2	124.0	175.5	4.9	...	76.3	101.2	844.2	467.2	366.6	-127.4	2 607.2
4th quarter	2 654.3	1 675.6	270.6	128.6	194.2	13.0	...	76.1	106.5	862.2	478.2	373.3	-123.7	2 657.6
1959														
1st quarter	2 708.0	1 706.7	285.9	132.6	216.3	10.4	...	81.1	109.2	856.6	470.3	376.4	-113.1	2 712.4
2nd quarter	2 776.4	1 732.9	309.7	136.6	223.9	26.5	...	83.8	114.5	869.7	481.5	377.5	-105.2	2 759.1
3rd quarter	2 773.1	1 751.0	288.2	141.0	219.7	3.2	...	86.5	115.6	880.6	491.5	377.8	-117.6	2 792.7
4th quarter	2 782.8	1 752.9	298.3	140.4	213.3	15.6	...	84.1	112.6	871.0	484.3	375.8	-110.9	2 782.2
1960														
1st quarter	2 845.3	1 769.7	330.5	145.8	219.4	38.8	...	94.7	116.9	853.9	462.5	382.3	-86.6	2 812.6
2nd quarter	2 832.0	1 792.1	297.1	148.1	201.4	11.1	...	100.7	117.8	860.8	460.8	391.7	-100.9	2 839.4
3rd quarter	2 836.6	1 785.0	295.3	144.4	195.3	15.6	...	98.2	114.3	881.5	475.1	397.5	-109.1	2 835.4
4th quarter	2 800.2	1 787.4	258.8	143.6	195.0	-18.2	...	100.2	108.9	887.7	476.8	402.1	-125.0	2 849.3
1961														
1st quarter	2 816.9	1 786.9	265.4	140.6	195.8	-8.3	...	99.5	108.4	899.3	476.2	415.1	-125.8	2 851.6
2nd quarter	2 869.6	1 813.4	285.2	143.5	196.5	7.2	...	98.1	109.7	901.4	480.6	412.3	-118.8	2 882.2
3rd quarter	2 915.9	1 822.2	309.1	144.7	207.1	23.8	...	97.6	117.0	919.1	494.1	415.8	-115.1	2 904.4
4th quarter	2 975.3	1 858.7	314.3	149.5	214.0	19.8	...	100.6	119.7	939.3	502.8	427.3	-117.9	2 970.4
1962														
1st quarter	3 028.7	1 878.5	333.1	153.0	217.9	31.2	...	100.4	123.4	955.9	521.3	424.2	-115.8	3 006.7
2nd quarter	3 062.1	1 901.6	329.8	157.6	224.7	19.7	...	110.0	126.1	961.1	523.4	427.3	-114.3	3 057.9
3rd quarter	3 090.4	1 917.0	335.7	159.6	224.5	23.0	...	103.8	127.7	983.0	539.2	432.7	-121.4	3 081.6
4th quarter	3 097.9	1 944.2	324.5	158.5	224.2	13.6	...	101.6	129.2	984.4	536.3	437.4	-127.6	3 102.9
1963														
1st quarter	3 138.4	1 957.3	342.5	158.3	232.3	26.7	...	104.0	126.3	978.4	523.3	445.7	-117.5	3 123.5
2nd quarter	3 177.7	1 976.0	347.5	163.3	249.0	17.7	...	116.1	129.2	977.2	518.4	449.7	-109.9	3 176.5
3rd quarter	3 237.6	2 002.9	358.8	168.3	253.7	21.1	...	109.9	132.5	1 019.1	547.2	461.7	-120.6	3 232.9
4th quarter	3 262.2	2 019.6	363.2	173.8	261.4	15.4	...	115.5	132.1	1 009.8	532.6	468.2	-113.8	3 266.5
1964														
1st quarter	3 335.4	2 059.5	378.1	178.1	277.4	16.4	...	122.5	131.9	1 013.5	529.9	475.2	-106.3	3 337.9
2nd quarter	3 373.7	2 095.8	376.4	182.7	263.4	15.7	...	124.6	134.9	1 020.1	526.4	486.1	-108.3	3 377.6
3rd quarter	3 419.5	2 134.3	385.3	188.9	259.1	18.9	...	123.6	138.5	1 020.7	522.3	491.4	-105.9	3 419.4
4th quarter	3 429.0	2 140.2	388.5	192.8	254.4	18.0	...	127.3	142.3	1 017.8	514.9	496.6	-102.5	3 428.3
1965														
1st quarter	3 513.3	2 187.8	427.6	205.7	255.3	41.4	...	113.6	137.2	1 015.3	508.4	501.3	-93.8	3 482.6
2nd quarter	3 560.9	2 212.0	427.6	213.5	257.3	29.8	...	134.9	153.3	1 028.4	509.4	514.0	-88.7	3 545.5
3rd quarter	3 633.2	2 250.0	442.8	221.6	258.3	33.5	...	127.2	154.0	1 064.0	530.0	528.5	-96.8	3 612.1
4th quarter	3 720.8	2 313.2	444.9	231.0	252.7	26.9	...	136.4	161.5	1 086.9	544.7	536.1	-99.1	3 710.2
1966														
1st quarter	3 812.2	2 347.4	482.5	241.1	258.4	47.1	...	134.0	165.7	1 106.4	557.1	542.7	-92.4	3 772.1
2nd quarter	3 824.9	2 353.5	473.7	244.8	237.7	45.4	...	139.8	169.8	1 126.0	571.9	546.9	-98.3	3 789.2
3rd quarter	3 850.0	2 380.4	469.0	247.8	230.0	40.4	...	134.6	179.3	1 156.5	595.0	553.3	-111.2	3 820.7
4th quarter	3 881.2	2 390.3	471.2	247.2	205.9	55.6	...	139.0	181.3	1 175.3	600.0	567.5	-113.3	3 831.5
1967														
1st quarter	3 915.4	2 404.2	458.3	241.9	199.7	51.4	...	141.7	184.2	1 225.2	641.1	574.5	-129.8	3 870.3
2nd quarter	3 916.2	2 437.0	438.8	241.1	222.4	23.2	...	140.4	182.7	1 218.5	631.8	577.6	-135.8	3 911.6
3rd quarter	3 947.5	2 449.5	451.4	239.9	233.5	30.8	...	137.0	185.1	1 231.2	641.9	579.9	-136.5	3 931.6
4th quarter	3 977.6	2 464.6	461.1	244.8	247.1	30.1	...	140.9	194.8	1 239.6	640.5	590.0	-133.8	3 966.4
1968														
1st quarter	4 059.5	2 523.4	471.2	252.5	248.6	27.3	...	145.0	206.3	1 261.3	651.7	600.4	-135.1	4 049.4
2nd quarter	4 128.5	2 562.1	490.2	248.1	254.9	48.9	...	147.9	209.5	1 267.1	646.5	612.1	-129.3	4 090.1
3rd quarter	4 156.7	2 610.3	474.3	251.4	259.5	26.1	...	156.6	222.1	1 269.7	640.9	620.9	-132.1	4 148.7
4th quarter	4 174.7	2 622.3	479.2	258.9	262.7	21.0	...	154.6	220.2	1 270.8	637.0	626.2	-132.0	4 175.1
1969														
1st quarter	4 240.5	2 651.7	510.8	266.5	272.2	37.0	...	136.0	199.4	1 272.0	633.4	631.3	-130.6	4 218.2
2nd quarter	4 252.8	2 668.6	506.7	269.4	269.2	31.2	...	166.5	238.8	1 266.7	623.3	636.6	-116.9	4 239.0
3rd quarter	4 279.7	2 681.5	518.5	276.7	267.0	34.9	...	162.5	235.7	1 268.5	623.8	638.0	-115.6	4 260.9
4th quarter	4 259.6	2 702.9	490.5	275.0	247.5	18.0	...	168.2	233.1	1 249.8	607.1	636.6	-118.7	4 261.7
1970														
1st quarter	4 252.9	2 719.5	475.2	273.4	248.0	3.9	...	169.6	232.3	1 243.1	595.1	642.5	-122.2	4 273.3
2nd quarter	4 260.7	2 731.9	476.7	271.9	231.5	16.7	...	177.1	236.9	1 227.1	576.4	646.0	-115.2	4 265.1
3rd quarter	4 298.6	2 755.9	484.8	273.3	243.8	16.2	...	176.5	236.4	1 232.4	567.9	660.6	-114.6	4 303.3
4th quarter	4 253.0	2 748.4	456.7	263.1	269.5	-14.3	...	178.1	240.0	1 232.4	564.8	663.9	-122.6	4 295.3
1971														
1st quarter	4 370.3	2 800.9	516.0	265.5	283.9	38.5	...	178.8	237.2	1 212.4	542.8	666.9	-100.6	4 348.5
2nd quarter	4 395.1	2 826.6	532.0	269.5	312.6	33.0	...	178.5	255.1	1 208.5	535.0	671.4	-95.4	4 378.5
3rd quarter	4 430.2	2 849.1	539.0	270.5	328.0	31.5	...	185.8	260.7	1 207.8	532.8	673.1	-90.8	4 417.1
4th quarter	4 442.5	2 896.5	522.2	276.3	340.7	-3.0	...	170.2	243.1	1 198.8	516.3	681.7	-102.1	4 470.3
1972														
1st quarter	4 521.9	2 935.2	559.1	285.6	363.4	10.8	...	188.2	278.6	1 203.1	518.4	683.9	-85.1	4 532.4
2nd quarter	4 629.1	2 991.2	593.3	290.4	370.5	38.0	...	182.8	268.7	1 210.6	526.7	682.5	-80.1	4 607.7
3rd quarter	4 673.5	3 037.4	601.8	294.9	371.4	39.0	...	193.8	274.3	1 185.6	498.3	688.1	-70.8	4 649.2
4th quarter	4 750.5	3 108.6	604.9	310.3	384.6	14.9	...	202.0	286.6	1 193.1	496.6	697.8	-71.5	4 757.4

Note: Chained (2005) dollar series are calculated as the product of the chain-type quantity index and the 2005 current-dollar value of the corresponding series, divided by 100. Because the formula for the chain-type quantity indexes uses weights from more than one period, the corresponding chained-dollar estimates are usually not additive. The residual column is the difference between the total and the sum of the most detailed components shown in the Bureau of Economic Analysis (BEA) published data.

. . . = Not available.

Table 1-2B. Real Gross Domestic Product: Historical Data—*Continued*

(Billions of chained [2005] dollars, quarterly data are at seasonally adjusted annual rates.)   **NIPA Tables 1.1.6, 1.2.6**

| Year and quarter | Gross domestic product | Personal consumption expenditures | Gross private domestic investment | | | | Exports and imports of goods and services | | | Government consumption expenditures and gross investment | | | Residual | Addendum: Final sales of domestic product |
| | | | Total | Fixed investment | | Change in private inventories | Net exports | Exports | Imports | Total | Federal | State and local | | |
				Nonresidential	Residential									
1973														
1st quarter	4 872.0	3 165.5	643.3	324.8	397.6	23.1	. . .	216.8	299.9	1 204.8	504.8	700.9	-58.5	4 861.7
2nd quarter ...	4 928.4	3 163.9	673.4	338.1	377.3	52.9	. . .	227.3	291.2	1 197.6	497.0	702.1	-42.6	4 885.5
3rd quarter	4 902.1	3 175.3	647.0	343.7	361.3	23.2	. . .	228.0	283.2	1 182.3	475.9	709.5	-47.3	4 891.6
4th quarter	4 948.8	3 166.0	671.8	346.4	344.1	56.8	. . .	239.2	285.3	1 191.0	476.3	718.2	-33.9	4 897.2
1974														
1st quarter	4 905.4	3 138.3	628.9	346.1	318.8	26.4	. . .	242.3	275.6	1 215.9	491.3	727.6	-44.4	4 891.2
2nd quarter ...	4 918.0	3 149.2	625.8	345.3	304.9	37.0	. . .	254.1	290.2	1 224.1	490.5	736.9	-45.0	4 896.6
3rd quarter	4 869.4	3 162.2	590.5	341.3	294.9	12.7	. . .	240.4	285.1	1 225.9	493.0	736.1	-64.5	4 881.5
4th quarter	4 850.2	3 115.8	596.1	331.7	256.1	40.2	. . .	246.6	282.3	1 230.2	496.6	736.6	-56.2	4 810.6
1975														
1st quarter	4 791.2	3 142.0	491.4	311.4	240.3	-15.4	. . .	248.4	254.0	1 245.2	491.0	758.4	-81.8	4 848.2
2nd quarter ...	4 827.8	3 194.4	474.4	303.2	245.4	-29.6	. . .	241.2	233.7	1 235.7	487.1	752.8	-84.2	4 897.9
3rd quarter	4 909.1	3 239.9	514.5	306.0	262.5	-5.8	. . .	237.1	253.1	1 257.4	499.2	762.1	-86.7	4 941.9
4th quarter	4 973.3	3 274.2	528.7	308.9	274.0	-0.3	. . .	250.5	266.6	1 268.0	500.5	771.8	-81.5	5 000.3
1976														
1st quarter	5 086.3	3 339.6	583.4	314.5	302.0	31.8	. . .	248.8	283.3	1 271.2	495.9	780.2	-73.4	5 069.4
2nd quarter ...	5 124.6	3 370.3	608.3	318.3	310.7	47.1	. . .	251.3	295.6	1 257.3	494.8	766.8	-67.0	5 086.5
3rd quarter	5 149.7	3 405.9	609.4	325.3	305.6	43.9	. . .	258.6	307.6	1 250.7	493.4	761.5	-67.3	5 118.0
4th quarter	5 187.1	3 450.3	613.7	331.7	344.6	14.2	. . .	261.2	317.8	1 249.7	494.7	759.1	-70.0	5 189.5
1977														
1st quarter	5 247.3	3 489.7	643.8	344.6	355.0	24.0	. . .	257.0	332.9	1 261.0	498.8	766.4	-71.3	5 238.2
2nd quarter ...	5 351.6	3 509.0	693.6	354.6	395.6	40.2	. . .	263.9	335.9	1 274.1	507.0	770.9	-53.1	5 322.4
3rd quarter	5 447.3	3 542.5	731.4	362.0	394.4	71.1	. . .	266.0	331.2	1 276.5	509.9	770.1	-37.9	5 378.4
4th quarter	5 446.1	3 595.9	710.8	374.1	389.1	37.1	. . .	257.4	335.9	1 272.3	504.9	771.4	-54.4	5 422.3
1978														
1st quarter	5 464.7	3 616.9	724.9	377.8	391.1	43.2	. . .	263.5	358.5	1 274.4	506.7	771.5	-56.5	5 429.2
2nd quarter ...	5 679.7	3 694.2	774.6	409.7	409.9	42.5	. . .	291.0	359.6	1 308.8	518.8	794.2	-29.3	5 644.6
3rd quarter	5 735.4	3 709.7	798.5	424.3	415.6	44.8	. . .	294.2	364.3	1 319.3	520.6	803.1	-22.0	5 696.4
4th quarter	5 811.3	3 739.6	816.7	438.3	414.1	51.9	. . .	305.8	369.3	1 331.2	525.2	810.5	-12.7	5 769.5
1979														
1st quarter	5 821.0	3 758.5	816.6	447.8	404.4	39.8	. . .	306.1	368.3	1 319.2	525.9	797.2	-11.1	5 787.8
2nd quarter ...	5 826.4	3 756.3	814.7	446.5	396.9	44.9	. . .	306.9	370.3	1 333.2	532.4	804.6	-14.4	5 787.5
3rd quarter	5 868.3	3 793.2	798.8	460.4	392.2	17.0	. . .	317.9	364.6	1 335.1	531.6	807.5	-12.1	5 871.4
4th quarter	5 884.5	3 803.3	783.9	461.6	377.4	10.3	. . .	338.0	372.6	1 343.8	531.5	816.7	-11.9	5 898.2
1980														
1st quarter	5 903.4	3 796.7	778.3	466.6	348.5	13.4	. . .	347.4	372.9	1 365.4	548.5	820.5	-11.5	5 909.6
2nd quarter ...	5 782.4	3 710.5	708.1	442.9	284.0	11.4	. . .	353.9	345.8	1 369.7	562.3	809.8	-14.0	5 793.8
3rd quarter	5 771.7	3 750.3	654.1	446.3	288.9	-48.8	. . .	353.2	321.0	1 350.8	554.7	798.4	-15.7	5 869.3
4th quarter	5 878.4	3 800.3	720.6	455.7	317.1	-13.3	. . .	351.0	338.2	1 349.4	556.5	794.9	-4.7	5 921.8
1981														
1st quarter	6 000.6	3 821.1	792.2	463.0	311.4	55.4	. . .	357.7	352.6	1 367.3	568.1	800.9	14.9	5 950.9
2nd quarter ...	5 952.7	3 821.1	754.5	472.3	300.9	14.3	. . .	359.6	353.2	1 370.4	585.0	785.6	0.3	5 962.7
3rd quarter	6 025.0	3 836.6	801.3	483.8	277.7	57.9	. . .	352.0	349.1	1 367.3	584.4	783.0	16.9	5 969.6
4th quarter	5 950.0	3 807.6	770.2	495.5	249.2	28.3	. . .	353.6	359.1	1 379.9	590.7	789.3	-2.2	5 934.4
1982														
1st quarter	5 852.3	3 832.2	690.0	483.8	234.9	-27.2	. . .	338.3	348.9	1 378.5	591.6	786.8	-37.8	5 917.7
2nd quarter ...	5 884.0	3 845.9	689.4	466.5	227.4	-5.4	. . .	340.3	343.2	1 386.5	596.9	789.3	-34.9	5 915.2
3rd quarter	5 861.4	3 875.4	681.3	450.7	226.7	6.8	. . .	325.2	359.1	1 396.0	605.9	789.4	-57.4	5 876.5
4th quarter	5 866.0	3 946.1	620.7	441.7	243.3	-52.8	. . .	310.3	345.0	1 420.1	623.8	794.8	-86.2	5 963.5
1983														
1st quarter	5 938.9	3 984.8	642.8	433.4	284.8	-47.7	. . .	315.3	352.9	1 430.8	631.3	797.7	-81.9	6 026.5
2nd quarter ...	6 072.4	4 063.9	704.8	438.7	318.5	-6.7	. . .	316.3	380.1	1 443.0	644.7	795.8	-75.5	6 111.8
3rd quarter	6 192.2	4 135.7	752.2	458.5	350.1	-5.6	. . .	321.1	409.7	1 468.0	662.8	802.1	-75.1	6 225.2
4th quarter	6 320.2	4 201.3	831.4	488.2	364.9	29.4	. . .	327.5	429.8	1 443.2	639.6	801.6	-53.4	6 307.0
1984														
1st quarter	6 442.8	4 237.3	918.4	504.1	375.0	88.7	. . .	334.4	464.3	1 457.8	645.1	810.7	-40.8	6 349.2
2nd quarter ...	6 554.0	4 297.9	949.4	529.2	381.9	83.1	. . .	342.7	483.8	1 489.2	665.3	821.2	-41.4	6 465.6
3rd quarter	6 617.7	4 331.1	971.4	546.6	378.3	86.9	. . .	350.3	496.3	1 500.2	662.8	835.5	-39.0	6 525.2
4th quarter	6 671.6	4 388.1	955.5	559.8	378.7	54.4	. . .	357.4	510.8	1 532.3	684.8	844.9	-50.9	6 620.3
1985														
1st quarter	6 734.5	4 462.5	924.0	566.3	377.5	17.2	. . .	357.6	499.6	1 549.9	692.1	855.2	-59.9	6 732.5
2nd quarter ...	6 791.5	4 503.2	939.9	574.4	380.5	25.1	. . .	356.3	524.1	1 584.7	709.0	872.8	-68.5	6 783.8
3rd quarter	6 897.6	4 588.7	929.6	565.6	385.3	20.8	. . .	351.1	519.0	1 625.8	732.7	889.7	-78.6	6 894.0
4th quarter	6 950.0	4 598.8	965.9	575.3	394.5	38.6	. . .	361.7	539.4	1 635.5	732.5	900.0	-72.5	6 922.1
1986														
1st quarter	7 016.8	4 637.2	963.9	567.4	411.4	35.3	. . .	373.1	538.9	1 653.2	728.6	922.4	-71.7	6 993.4
2nd quarter ...	7 045.0	4 686.6	942.5	553.2	434.2	17.2	. . .	377.2	561.8	1 688.3	751.8	933.7	-87.8	7 046.1
3rd quarter	7 112.9	4 768.5	913.0	545.1	440.9	-9.5	. . .	385.8	577.4	1 726.6	780.2	942.7	-103.6	7 145.3
4th quarter	7 147.3	4 797.2	914.4	550.7	440.1	-9.2	. . .	400.2	581.9	1 716.6	768.1	945.3	-99.2	7 185.8
1987														
1st quarter	7 186.9	4 789.9	942.3	535.6	438.9	36.6	. . .	400.5	578.4	1 723.7	772.7	947.7	-91.1	7 166.6
2nd quarter ...	7 263.3	4 854.0	943.6	548.4	440.9	20.1	. . .	416.4	592.8	1 734.6	783.4	947.6	-92.5	7 262.2
3rd quarter	7 326.3	4 908.2	944.6	566.1	439.5	-0.7	. . .	434.3	604.3	1 734.6	784.3	946.8	-91.1	7 348.9
4th quarter	7 451.7	4 920.0	1 018.3	564.7	441.7	76.8	. . .	450.4	618.2	1 755.6	795.9	956.1	-74.4	7 382.0

Note: Chained (2005) dollar series are calculated as the product of the chain-type quantity index and the 2005 current-dollar value of the corresponding series, divided by 100. Because the formula for the chain-type quantity indexes uses weights from more than one period, the corresponding chained-dollar estimates are usually not additive. The residual column is the difference between the total and the sum of the most detailed components shown in the Bureau of Economic Analysis (BEA) published data.

. . . = Not available.

Table 1-2B. Real Gross Domestic Product: Historical Data—*Continued*

(Billions of chained [2005] dollars, quarterly data are at seasonally adjusted annual rates.)   **NIPA Tables 1.1.6, 1.2.6**

Year and quarter	Gross domestic product	Personal consumption expenditures	Gross private domestic investment				Exports and imports of goods and services			Government consumption expenditures and gross investment			Residual	Addendum: Final sales of domestic product
			Total	Fixed investment		Change in private inventories	Net exports	Exports	Imports	Total	Federal	State and local		
				Nonresidential	Residential									
1988														
1st quarter	7 490.2	5 002.2	960.9	569.1	432.1	17.9	. . .	475.3	615.3	1 747.1	774.3	969.7	-80.0	7 491.1
2nd quarter	7 586.4	5 038.5	984.3	583.1	435.6	22.9	. . .	488.5	608.3	1 751.7	766.4	982.4	-68.3	7 581.4
3rd quarter	7 625.6	5 078.3	990.6	586.1	435.8	20.7	. . .	497.5	622.6	1 750.7	760.7	987.2	-68.9	7 617.4
4th quarter	7 727.4	5 138.1	1 003.7	592.3	439.7	26.2	. . .	512.7	641.6	1 786.2	783.5	999.8	-71.7	7 715.3
1989														
1st quarter	7 799.9	5 156.9	1 042.2	602.3	436.8	54.4	. . .	527.8	644.6	1 775.2	767.5	1 005.0	-57.6	7 752.5
2nd quarter	7 858.3	5 180.0	1 030.0	610.9	423.8	41.0	. . .	550.8	647.6	1 802.8	784.8	1 015.1	-57.7	7 827.8
3rd quarter	7 920.6	5 233.7	1 017.9	628.4	419.2	10.8	. . .	556.8	646.7	1 819.7	792.3	1 024.5	-60.8	7 926.4
4th quarter	7 937.9	5 259.3	1 007.4	619.1	410.4	16.3	. . .	565.6	658.4	1 829.4	788.3	1 038.2	-65.4	7 936.3
1990														
1st quarter	8 020.8	5 300.9	1 017.3	627.3	414.6	15.1	. . .	590.3	679.3	1 857.6	800.2	1 054.6	-66.0	8 022.4
2nd quarter	8 052.7	5 318.4	1 017.6	616.5	398.6	37.0	. . .	598.3	678.2	1 860.4	801.1	1 056.4	-63.8	8 025.9
3rd quarter	8 052.6	5 338.6	993.7	620.4	376.0	24.9	. . .	602.7	675.4	1 859.8	794.0	1 063.0	-66.8	8 041.7
4th quarter	7 982.0	5 297.0	930.8	608.6	355.2	-10.8	. . .	607.7	657.3	1 878.3	800.9	1 074.5	-74.5	8 013.2
1991														
1st quarter	7 943.4	5 282.0	892.9	592.9	334.0	-17.2	. . .	612.1	649.8	1 885.9	807.2	1 075.8	-79.7	7 981.1
2nd quarter	7 997.0	5 322.2	888.5	587.2	341.9	-21.0	. . .	634.1	661.4	1 892.5	809.4	1 080.1	-78.9	8 038.5
3rd quarter	8 030.7	5 342.6	910.6	581.6	356.1	-0.5	. . .	648.6	680.0	1 883.5	794.4	1 086.3	-74.6	8 049.6
4th quarter	8 062.2	5 340.2	945.4	578.6	363.9	33.0	. . .	663.4	695.0	1 875.6	778.8	1 094.2	-67.4	8 042.3
1992														
1st quarter	8 150.7	5 432.0	924.4	576.0	382.5	2.7	. . .	675.2	700.1	1 889.9	779.0	1 108.3	-70.7	8 166.6
2nd quarter	8 237.3	5 464.2	985.3	598.8	397.1	23.9	. . .	675.3	711.6	1 887.6	778.2	1 106.8	-63.5	8 225.0
3rd quarter	8 322.3	5 524.6	995.5	610.9	398.0	21.1	. . .	689.9	722.8	1 897.3	787.1	1 107.5	-62.2	8 315.4
4th quarter	8 409.8	5 592.0	1 027.0	629.3	411.5	23.8	. . .	693.4	740.1	1 897.9	787.5	1 107.7	-60.4	8 401.9
1993														
1st quarter	8 425.3	5 614.7	1 051.1	633.3	413.4	40.3	. . .	695.0	756.1	1 877.9	763.3	1 112.2	-57.3	8 396.4
2nd quarter	8 479.2	5 668.6	1 059.4	650.1	418.3	26.8	. . .	703.5	771.8	1 876.5	752.5	1 121.8	-57.0	8 466.8
3rd quarter	8 523.8	5 730.1	1 058.6	657.4	432.7	6.3	. . .	701.2	781.9	1 874.6	744.6	1 128.0	-58.8	8 533.2
4th quarter	8 636.4	5 781.1	1 114.5	685.0	454.5	15.6	. . .	723.7	813.4	1 883.9	748.5	1 133.3	-53.4	8 635.4
1994														
1st quarter	8 720.5	5 845.5	1 162.6	691.8	464.2	50.5	. . .	730.6	832.3	1 859.9	721.7	1 136.5	-45.8	8 681.6
2nd quarter	8 839.8	5 888.8	1 230.4	705.8	479.5	90.5	. . .	754.7	863.3	1 867.7	717.6	1 148.5	-38.5	8 754.7
3rd quarter	8 896.7	5 936.0	1 208.2	719.0	474.3	56.0	. . .	783.5	887.6	1 900.5	737.3	1 161.4	-43.9	8 849.6
4th quarter	8 995.5	5 994.6	1 264.6	750.9	468.1	80.1	. . .	800.9	912.6	1 884.1	717.1	1 165.5	-36.1	8 920.7
1995														
1st quarter	9 017.6	6 001.6	1 277.4	777.3	457.7	65.9	-117.0	815.6	932.6	1 891.6	715.3	1 174.8	-182.8	8 958.7
2nd quarter	9 037.0	6 050.8	1 243.1	782.6	443.0	37.7	-114.6	826.8	941.5	1 897.9	712.5	1 184.1	-187.5	9 011.7
3rd quarter	9 112.9	6 104.9	1 231.1	787.9	456.7	8.2	-81.9	862.8	944.7	1 893.7	707.6	1 184.8	-179.6	9 119.0
4th quarter	9 176.4	6 147.8	1 265.8	803.8	467.0	16.5	-81.5	875.2	956.8	1 872.5	681.1	1 190.7	-166.4	9 172.2
1996														
1st quarter	9 239.3	6 204.0	1 282.4	823.7	479.3	3.2	-101.6	886.2	987.9	1 884.5	695.3	1 188.2	-170.2	9 251.4
2nd quarter	9 399.0	6 274.2	1 348.9	847.4	499.5	26.8	-108.9	901.1	1 010.0	1 911.6	705.2	1 205.4	-162.9	9 384.0
3rd quarter	9 480.8	6 311.8	1 416.9	875.6	498.2	62.0	-134.3	908.4	1 042.7	1 909.7	692.7	1 216.3	-150.7	9 425.0
4th quarter	9 584.3	6 363.2	1 413.0	899.3	493.0	32.8	-97.9	965.3	1 063.3	1 925.9	690.7	1 234.6	-144.1	9 557.2
1997														
1st quarter	9 658.0	6 427.3	1 446.0	922.2	494.7	43.2	-125.0	983.7	1 108.7	1 929.4	681.4	1 247.6	-138.4	9 624.4
2nd quarter	9 801.2	6 453.3	1 538.3	945.1	500.9	103.9	-123.2	1 022.7	1 145.9	1 946.0	693.5	1 252.1	-127.2	9 701.0
3rd quarter	9 924.2	6 563.0	1 565.7	993.3	503.2	75.4	-141.7	1 046.4	1 188.1	1 948.2	691.3	1 256.6	-111.8	9 854.1
4th quarter	10 000.3	6 638.1	1 590.7	1 001.3	508.4	87.0	-169.3	1 044.5	1 213.8	1 951.5	690.3	1 260.9	-108.0	9 917.5
1998														
1st quarter	10 094.8	6 704.1	1 666.6	1 035.9	517.5	117.2	-209.9	1 049.5	1 259.3	1 939.7	668.8	1 271.1	-96.2	9 979.8
2nd quarter	10 185.6	6 819.5	1 646.7	1 073.8	533.0	43.2	-250.8	1 037.4	1 288.2	1 981.9	687.2	1 294.7	-97.7	10 148.4
3rd quarter	10 320.0	6 909.9	1 693.9	1 090.0	549.0	60.6	-273.0	1 032.6	1 305.5	2 000.2	681.5	1 319.0	-93.8	10 265.5
4th quarter	10 498.6	7 015.9	1 748.4	1 126.0	562.2	65.5	-276.3	1 071.5	1 347.8	2 018.1	688.1	1 330.2	-73.8	10 439.6
1999														
1st quarter	10 592.1	7 085.1	1 803.4	1 152.1	565.5	89.4	-318.8	1 063.3	1 382.1	2 028.4	683.6	1 345.2	-69.6	10 508.3
2nd quarter	10 674.9	7 196.6	1 797.1	1 184.4	571.6	41.1	-350.7	1 075.5	1 426.1	2 036.9	683.6	1 353.7	-52.2	10 639.1
3rd quarter	10 810.7	7 283.1	1 842.2	1 218.4	576.4	44.6	-374.2	1 103.7	1 477.9	2 063.3	697.9	1 365.7	-41.9	10 770.5
4th quarter	11 004.8	7 385.8	1 907.6	1 222.2	583.4	99.1	-382.0	1 131.3	1 513.3	2 095.9	713.4	1 382.7	-42.3	10 908.1
2000														
1st quarter	11 033.6	7 497.8	1 880.9	1 267.6	588.0	18.7	-423.8	1 150.8	1 574.7	2 078.7	685.2	1 394.0	-25.9	11 018.2
2nd quarter	11 248.8	7 568.3	2 011.1	1 314.4	584.0	101.0	-439.2	1 183.5	1 622.7	2 106.4	712.6	1 394.2	-26.5	11 144.4
3rd quarter	11 258.3	7 642.4	1 979.7	1 329.0	573.7	63.1	-467.0	1 212.4	1 679.4	2 099.8	698.8	1 401.4	-25.1	11 196.8
4th quarter	11 325.0	7 710.0	1 980.7	1 334.2	574.2	58.1	-475.3	1 202.9	1 678.1	2 106.2	695.6	1 411.0	-25.5	11 268.5
2001														
1st quarter	11 287.8	7 740.8	1 876.1	1 321.7	576.8	-34.8	-466.6	1 187.1	1 653.7	2 137.3	710.4	1 427.3	-25.1	11 325.6
2nd quarter	11 361.7	7 770.0	1 870.0	1 286.9	584.9	-10.7	-456.1	1 148.3	1 604.4	2 181.7	725.6	1 456.5	-35.6	11 375.7
3rd quarter	11 330.4	7 804.2	1 830.3	1 265.5	588.1	-30.8	-476.3	1 089.2	1 565.6	2 177.8	730.5	1 447.7	-39.9	11 364.1
4th quarter	11 370.0	7 926.4	1 724.5	1 225.0	583.1	-90.7	-488.4	1 058.5	1 546.9	2 216.4	739.3	1 477.6	-23.4	11 462.6
2002														
1st quarter	11 467.1	7 953.7	1 781.9	1 195.8	598.7	-15.1	-510.2	1 075.4	1 585.7	2 250.4	756.9	1 494.0	-27.9	11 485.7
2nd quarter	11 528.1	7 994.1	1 803.4	1 176.6	613.4	13.4	-534.6	1 104.6	1 639.2	2 272.0	774.4	1 498.1	-24.0	11 518.2
3rd quarter	11 586.6	8 048.3	1 808.0	1 171.4	616.9	19.8	-553.9	1 112.3	1 666.2	2 290.4	786.7	1 504.2	-16.8	11 569.9
4th quarter	11 590.6	8 076.9	1 808.3	1 150.9	626.4	32.9	-595.2	1 101.0	1 696.2	2 305.7	800.0	1 506.3	-20.1	11 560.8

Note: Chained (2005) dollar series are calculated as the product of the chain-type quantity index and the 2005 current-dollar value of the corresponding series, divided by 100. Because the formula for the chain-type quantity indexes uses weights from more than one period, the corresponding chained-dollar estimates are usually not additive. The residual column is the difference between the total and the sum of the most detailed components shown in the Bureau of Economic Analysis (BEA) published data.

. . . = Not available.

Table 1-2B. Real Gross Domestic Product: Historical Data—*Continued*

(Billions of chained [2005] dollars, quarterly data are at seasonally adjusted annual rates.)   **NIPA Tables 1.1.6, 1.2.6**

Year and quarter	Gross domestic product	Personal consump- tion expen- ditures	Gross private domestic investment				Exports and imports of goods and services			Government consumption expenditures and gross investment			Residual	Adden- dum: Final sales of domestic product
			Total	Fixed investment		Change in private inventories	Net exports	Exports	Imports	Total	Federal	State and local		
				Nonresi- dential	Residential									
2003														
1st quarter	11 638.9	8 117.7	1 810.4	1 147.8	632.4	31.5	-584.9	1 090.8	1 675.7	2 300.9	800.2	1 501.2	-18.8	11 609.6
2nd quarter ...	11 737.5	8 198.1	1 821.8	1 179.5	646.8	-3.5	-612.4	1 087.3	1 699.6	2 335.1	838.8	1 496.6	-14.7	11 742.6
3rd quarter	11 930.7	8 308.5	1 888.4	1 206.8	679.7	3.0	-602.8	1 116.8	1 719.6	2 342.0	839.6	1 502.7	-11.0	11 928.6
4th quarter	12 038.6	8 353.7	1 959.9	1 224.1	698.2	38.3	-614.6	1 169.1	1 783.8	2 343.7	845.7	1 498.2	-8.1	12 001.1
2004														
1st quarter	12 117.9	8 427.6	1 970.1	1 214.3	704.5	52.4	-632.2	1 197.0	1 829.2	2 354.9	856.6	1 498.4	-6.9	12 066.5
2nd quarter ...	12 195.9	8 465.1	2 055.7	1 247.1	731.0	78.7	-686.9	1 215.7	1 902.6	2 363.5	861.4	1 502.2	-5.0	12 118.4
3rd quarter	12 286.7	8 539.1	2 082.1	1 281.2	738.4	62.7	-705.7	1 224.7	1 930.4	2 372.1	876.4	1 495.7	-2.4	12 224.2
4th quarter	12 387.2	8 631.3	2 124.9	1 309.3	744.2	71.6	-726.6	1 252.8	1 979.4	2 357.6	865.6	1 492.0	-0.4	12 316.1
2005														
1st quarter	12 515.0	8 700.1	2 170.0	1 321.1	757.8	91.4	-714.8	1 276.2	1 990.9	2 359.9	869.2	1 490.7	-1.1	12 424.1
2nd quarter ...	12 570.7	8 786.2	2 131.3	1 340.6	775.4	15.5	-709.3	1 303.6	2 012.9	2 362.4	870.0	1 492.4	0.0	12 555.2
3rd quarter	12 670.5	8 852.9	2 155.1	1 359.7	783.3	11.8	-721.4	1 303.9	2 025.3	2 383.9	890.4	1 493.5	0.1	12 658.5
4th quarter	12 735.6	8 874.9	2 232.8	1 367.9	783.5	81.0	-745.4	1 336.6	2 082.1	2 373.4	875.6	1 497.7	0.5	12 654.2
2006														
1st quarter	12 896.4	8 965.8	2 266.3	1 426.6	775.2	65.8	-732.8	1 388.7	2 121.5	2 397.1	900.5	1 496.6	-2.5	12 831.9
2nd quarter ...	12 948.7	9 019.8	2 263.1	1 452.4	740.0	72.5	-733.2	1 412.1	2 145.2	2 399.1	892.8	1 506.3	-2.1	12 877.3
3rd quarter	12 950.4	9 073.9	2 231.2	1 467.7	697.3	67.5	-756.8	1 414.2	2 170.9	2 402.7	892.0	1 510.8	-1.8	12 882.8
4th quarter	13 038.4	9 158.3	2 166.7	1 475.2	660.2	31.8	-694.7	1 473.5	2 168.2	2 409.4	894.4	1 515.0	-1.5	13 005.3
2007														
1st quarter	13 056.1	9 209.2	2 145.1	1 498.5	631.3	17.3	-703.2	1 496.5	2 199.8	2 406.7	883.6	1 522.9	-3.1	13 038.2
2nd quarter ...	13 173.6	9 244.5	2 193.0	1 537.5	611.4	44.9	-689.4	1 521.3	2 210.7	2 426.8	898.9	1 527.8	0.0	13 126.2
3rd quarter	13 269.8	9 285.2	2 176.3	1 571.4	570.7	36.1	-638.1	1 578.0	2 216.0	2 447.9	919.7	1 528.4	0.1	13 231.8
4th quarter	13 326.0	9 312.6	2 123.6	1 592.3	523.4	12.6	-564.6	1 621.9	2 186.5	2 455.3	922.2	1 533.3	-2.6	13 314.0
2008														
1st quarter	13 266.8	9 289.1	2 055.7	1 589.1	481.3	-12.5	-550.2	1 643.9	2 194.1	2 473.9	943.8	1 530.9	2.1	13 277.8
2nd quarter ...	13 310.5	9 285.8	2 024.0	1 580.0	462.8	-14.2	-486.2	1 693.9	2 180.1	2 484.5	955.1	1 530.5	7.0	13 325.9
3rd quarter	13 186.9	9 196.0	1 934.7	1 539.2	437.8	-38.1	-464.6	1 678.7	2 143.3	2 510.7	982.0	1 530.8	20.7	13 225.6
4th quarter	12 883.5	9 076.0	1 744.6	1 442.3	395.8	-80.3	-478.0	1 580.6	2 058.6	2 520.5	1 003.5	1 520.1	35.4	12 972.9
2009														
1st quarter	12 663.2	9 040.9	1 490.4	1 312.9	354.9	-161.6	-404.2	1 451.1	1 855.3	2 509.6	995.2	1 517.2	35.5	12 836.0
2nd quarter ...	12 641.3	8 998.5	1 397.2	1 257.6	334.3	-183.0	-331.8	1 449.4	1 781.2	2 546.0	1 029.2	1 520.7	38.3	12 830.0
3rd quarter	12 694.5	9 050.3	1 407.3	1 247.0	348.2	-178.7	-352.4	1 497.3	1 849.7	2 554.2	1 043.9	1 514.9	32.5	12 875.1
4th quarter	12 813.5	9 060.2	1 522.0	1 235.2	344.8	-56.5	-346.9	1 578.3	1 925.2	2 548.5	1 049.6	1 503.9	31.6	12 869.5
2010														
1st quarter	12 937.7	9 121.2	1 630.0	1 253.3	330.8	39.9	-376.8	1 606.2	1 983.0	2 540.6	1 056.9	1 489.2	22.2	12 895.9
2nd quarter ...	13 058.5	9 186.9	1 728.3	1 308.0	348.2	64.6	-437.4	1 645.0	2 082.4	2 564.0	1 079.4	1 490.8	12.6	12 992.2
3rd quarter	13 139.6	9 247.1	1 766.8	1 343.6	321.1	92.3	-458.7	1 684.8	2 143.5	2 570.3	1 087.8	1 488.9	7.3	13 046.0
4th quarter	13 216.1	9 328.4	1 734.5	1 371.9	323.1	38.3	-414.2	1 716.8	2 131.0	2 552.1	1 079.6	1 478.9	-7.9	13 181.6
2011														
1st quarter	13 227.9	9 376.7	1 750.9	1 378.9	321.1	49.1	-424.4	1 749.6	2 173.9	2 513.9	1 053.3	1 466.4	-21.1	13 182.8
2nd quarter ...	13 271.8	9 392.7	1 778.4	1 413.2	324.4	39.1	-416.4	1 765.0	2 181.4	2 508.2	1 058.3	1 456.1	-17.6	13 236.2
3rd quarter	13 331.6	9 433.5	1 784.2	1 465.6	325.4	-2.0	-402.8	1 785.2	2 187.9	2 507.6	1 063.7	1 450.4	-27.7	13 340.9
4th quarter	13 429.0	9 482.1	1 875.7	1 484.2	334.5	52.2	-410.8	1 797.0	2 207.7	2 481.2	1 044.7	1 442.4	-37.4	13 378.3

Note: Chained (2005) dollar series are calculated as the product of the chain-type quantity index and the 2005 current-dollar value of the corresponding series, divided by 100. Because the formula for the chain-type quantity indexes uses weights from more than one period, the corresponding chained-dollar estimates are usually not additive. The residual column is the difference between the total and the sum of the most detailed components shown in the Bureau of Economic Analysis (BEA) published data.

Table 1-3A. U.S. Population and Per Capita Product and Income: Recent Data

(Dollars, except as noted; quarterly data are at seasonally adjusted annual rates.)   NIPA Table 7.1

| Year and quarter | Population (mid-period, thousands) | Current dollars | | | | | | | Chained (2005) dollars | | | | | |
| | | Gross domestic product | Personal income | Disposable personal income | Personal consumption expenditures | | | | Gross domestic product | Disposable personal income | Personal consumption expenditures | | | |
					Total	Durable goods	Nondurable goods	Services			Total	Durable goods	Nondurable goods	Services
1950	151 684	1 937	1 509	1 384	1 267	214	556	497	13 213	9 236	8 456	480	2 990	4 912
1951	154 287	2 199	1 672	1 496	1 352	206	603	543	13 995	9 348	8 444	432	2 984	5 115
1952	156 954	2 283	1 753	1 550	1 399	199	621	578	14 284	9 487	8 563	416	3 044	5 254
1953	159 565	2 377	1 828	1 620	1 461	217	628	616	14 698	9 784	8 825	457	3 087	5 386
1954	162 391	2 342	1 812	1 627	1 478	208	628	642	14 350	9 744	8 853	447	3 081	5 477
1955	165 275	2 509	1 912	1 713	1 566	247	645	674	15 115	10 221	9 341	533	3 184	5 652
1956	168 221	2 600	2 018	1 800	1 615	239	666	710	15 144	10 531	9 446	504	3 238	5 819
1957	171 274	2 692	2 093	1 866	1 675	245	686	743	15 174	10 594	9 507	499	3 244	5 913
1958	174 141	2 683	2 119	1 897	1 701	227	701	773	14 789	10 521	9 433	454	3 233	6 005
1959	177 130	2 860	2 215	1 976	1 794	253	721	819	15 582	10 798	9 800	499	3 322	6 196
1960	180 760	2 912	2 275	2 020	1 836	252	727	856	15 648	10 860	9 867	499	3 309	6 309
1961	183 742	2 965	2 334	2 077	1 862	241	733	889	15 753	11 047	9 907	474	3 321	6 435
1962	186 590	3 139	2 446	2 170	1 947	265	748	934	16 452	11 408	10 238	520	3 371	6 637
1963	189 300	3 263	2 533	2 245	2 022	286	760	975	16 925	11 666	10 507	560	3 395	6 820
1964	191 927	3 458	2 680	2 408	2 144	310	796	1 038	17 660	12 336	10 980	604	3 505	7 127
1965	194 347	3 700	2 858	2 562	2 284	342	840	1 102	18 560	12 933	11 530	670	3 636	7 427
1966	196 599	4 007	3 071	2 733	2 446	365	905	1 176	19 543	13 460	12 044	717	3 794	7 706
1967	198 752	4 188	3 261	2 894	2 555	372	931	1 252	19 819	13 898	12 271	720	3 834	7 935
1968	200 745	4 532	3 545	3 112	2 780	423	995	1 362	20 573	14 386	12 850	792	3 956	8 276
1969	202 736	4 856	3 839	3 324	2 985	446	1 057	1 482	21 003	14 699	13 200	814	4 026	8 560
1970	205 089	5 063	4 089	3 586	3 161	439	1 116	1 607	20 802	15 151	13 355	783	4 068	8 792
1971	207 692	5 425	4 348	3 859	3 378	493	1 154	1 731	21 231	15 637	13 690	851	4 092	8 982
1972	209 924	5 897	4 729	4 140	3 669	555	1 226	1 888	22 121	16 221	14 377	946	4 213	9 400
1973	211 939	6 522	5 240	4 615	4 020	616	1 350	2 054	23 180	17 159	14 946	1 036	4 292	9 752
1974	213 898	7 010	5 716	5 010	4 362	609	1 502	2 251	22 841	16 871	14 686	960	4 150	9 848
1975	215 981	7 583	6 180	5 497	4 786	658	1 617	2 512	22 573	17 083	14 874	953	4 145	10 119
1976	218 086	8 366	6 762	5 972	5 279	773	1 732	2 774	23 555	17 592	15 551	1 062	4 300	10 452
1977	220 289	9 216	7 411	6 514	5 801	871	1 854	3 075	24 391	18 017	16 044	1 144	4 354	10 775
1978	222 629	10 303	8 250	7 220	6 413	958	2 022	3 432	25 481	18 662	16 575	1 191	4 464	11 158
1979	225 106	11 382	9 149	7 956	7 069	1 005	2 273	3 790	25 988	18 888	16 782	1 172	4 529	11 372
1980	227 726	12 243	10 107	8 794	7 710	994	2 518	4 198	25 618	18 855	16 531	1 066	4 469	11 414
1981	230 008	13 594	11 227	9 726	8 432	1 061	2 719	4 653	26 008	19 164	16 615	1 066	4 480	11 504
1982	232 218	14 009	11 915	10 390	8 938	1 090	2 783	5 065	25 260	19 397	16 686	1 055	4 483	11 616
1983	234 333	15 084	12 598	11 095	9 766	1 259	2 897	5 611	26 163	19 859	17 481	1 194	4 588	12 114
1984	236 394	16 629	13 828	12 232	10 580	1 447	3 052	6 080	27 799	21 096	18 247	1 353	4 736	12 478
1985	238 506	17 683	14 661	12 911	11 394	1 595	3 175	6 625	28 693	21 561	19 028	1 475	4 836	13 007
1986	240 683	18 531	15 356	13 540	12 036	1 751	3 217	7 068	29 418	22 073	19 621	1 602	4 963	13 273
1987	242 843	19 504	16 160	14 146	12 753	1 820	3 353	7 580	30 090	22 236	20 046	1 619	5 003	13 679
1988	245 061	20 813	17 266	15 206	13 670	1 939	3 519	8 213	31 043	22 986	20 665	1 696	5 088	14 131
1989	247 387	22 160	18 422	16 134	14 530	1 998	3 757	8 774	31 850	23 374	21 050	1 717	5 176	14 422
1990	250 181	23 185	19 373	17 004	15 331	1 987	3 974	9 370	32 085	23 557	21 240	1 690	5 178	14 684
1991	253 530	23 635	19 846	17 532	15 699	1 882	4 024	9 792	31 587	23 442	20 991	1 578	5 095	14 707
1992	256 922	24 686	20 813	18 436	16 491	1 978	4 107	10 406	32 228	23 947	21 420	1 647	5 125	15 030
1993	260 282	25 616	21 393	18 909	17 226	2 119	4 191	10 916	32 719	24 033	21 894	1 747	5 188	15 311
1994	263 455	26 893	22 299	19 678	18 033	2 305	4 325	11 403	33 642	24 505	22 456	1 864	5 325	15 578
1995	266 588	27 813	23 260	20 470	18 708	2 385	4 426	11 898	34 082	24 939	22 793	1 915	5 393	15 787
1996	269 714	29 062	24 439	21 355	19 553	2 507	4 603	12 443	34 948	25 463	23 315	2 034	5 484	16 060
1997	272 958	30 526	25 648	22 255	20 408	2 621	4 731	13 056	36 071	26 049	23 888	2 174	5 579	16 359
1998	276 154	31 843	27 251	23 534	21 432	2 825	4 816	13 791	37 207	27 287	24 850	2 410	5 722	16 882
1999	279 328	33 486	28 321	24 356	22 707	3 069	5 129	14 509	38 559	27 792	25 911	2 692	5 945	17 374
2000	282 398	35 239	30 310	25 946	24 187	3 243	5 465	15 479	39 718	28 888	26 929	2 897	6 071	18 037
2001	285 225	36 063	31 145	26 816	25 064	3 318	5 566	16 180	39 749	29 297	27 383	3 024	6 119	18 298
2002	287 955	36 958	31 464	27 816	25 835	3 445	5 618	16 771	40 087	29 981	27 846	3 222	6 182	18 470
2003	290 626	38 339	32 269	28 827	26 853	3 509	5 877	17 466	40 727	30 453	28 368	3 403	6 334	18 643
2004	293 262	40 419	33 885	30 312	28 202	3 658	6 204	18 340	41 761	31 211	29 038	3 618	6 454	18 968
2005	295 993	42 646	35 426	31 343	29 742	3 795	6 599	19 348	42 646	31 343	29 742	3 795	6 599	19 348
2006	298 818	44 767	37 709	33 183	31 126	3 865	6 926	20 334	43 366	32 303	30 301	3 930	6 710	19 663
2007	301 696	46 499	39 484	34 550	32 391	3 939	7 211	21 241	43 774	32 749	30 703	4 085	6 771	19 855
2008	304 543	46 928	40 914	36 200	32 953	3 641	7 463	21 849	43 219	33 229	30 248	3 848	6 630	19 757
2009	307 240	45 368	38 830	35 115	32 112	3 351	7 056	21 705	41 346	32 166	29 415	3 607	6 455	19 319
2010	309 774	46 894	39 944	36 090	33 074	3 504	7 430	22 140	42 250	32 481	29 767	3 836	6 590	19 343
2011	312 040	48 372	41 633	37 154	34 374	3 727	7 960	22 687	42 671	32 635	30 193	4 119	6 652	19 472
2009														
1st quarter	306 237	45 369	39 069	35 157	31 942	3 331	6 892	21 719	41 351	32 494	29 523	3 574	6 467	19 441
2nd quarter	306 866	45 147	38 923	35 272	31 876	3 290	6 955	21 632	41 195	32 448	29 324	3 530	6 429	19 320
3rd quarter	307 573	45 259	38 606	34 962	32 224	3 414	7 138	21 671	41 273	31 926	29 425	3 689	6 446	19 270
4th quarter	308 285	45 696	38 724	35 071	32 405	3 370	7 237	21 798	41 564	31 806	29 389	3 635	6 480	19 245
2010														
1st quarter	308 899	46 222	39 294	35 582	32 709	3 425	7 381	21 902	41 883	32 122	29 528	3 715	6 543	19 254
2nd quarter	309 457	46 752	39 830	36 032	32 912	3 463	7 330	22 118	42 198	32 501	29 687	3 778	6 562	19 338
3rd quarter	310 070	47 104	40 163	36 251	33 143	3 507	7 414	22 221	42 376	32 620	29 823	3 851	6 598	19 377
4th quarter	310 670	47 494	40 485	36 491	33 531	3 620	7 592	22 318	42 541	32 678	30 027	3 999	6 655	19 402
2011														
1st quarter	311 184	47 778	41 284	36 895	33 972	3 710	7 834	22 429	42 508	32 724	30 132	4 105	6 669	19 407
2nd quarter	311 717	48 162	41 561	37 082	34 249	3 669	7 952	22 627	42 577	32 625	30 132	4 043	6 662	19 463
3rd quarter	312 330	48 590	41 804	37 293	34 529	3 708	8 014	22 807	42 684	32 621	30 204	4 091	6 639	19 518
4th quarter	312 929	48 955	41 881	37 345	34 741	3 818	8 038	22 885	42 914	32 572	30 301	4 239	6 639	19 500

Table 1-3B. U.S. Population and Per Capita Product and Income: Historical Data

(Dollars, except as noted; quarterly data are at seasonally adjusted annual rates.)

NIPA Table 7.1

Year and quarter	Population (mid-period, thou-sands)	Current dollars							Chained (2005) dollars					
		Gross domestic product	Personal income	Dispos-able personal income	Personal consumption expenditures				Gross domestic product	Dispos-able personal income	Personal consumption expenditures			
					Total	Durable goods	Nondur-able goods	Services			Total	Durable goods	Nondur-able goods	Services
1929	121 878	850	697	683	635	81	278	276	8 009	6 495	6 041	283	2 278	3 545
1930	123 188	740	618	605	569	62	248	260	7 241	6 014	5 656	231	2 136	3 434
1931	124 149	616	525	517	489	48	208	233	6 719	5 755	5 436	198	2 096	3 321
1932	124 949	470	399	393	390	32	161	197	5 804	4 959	4 917	150	1 899	3 100
1933	125 690	449	372	366	366	30	159	177	5 695	4 784	4 780	145	1 880	2 967
1934	126 485	522	424	417	407	36	189	182	6 275	5 218	5 089	165	2 021	3 093
1935	127 362	576	474	465	439	43	205	191	6 786	5 682	5 363	198	2 124	3 179
1936	128 181	653	535	525	485	53	228	204	7 622	6 356	6 051	241	2 351	3 353
1937	128 961	712	574	559	518	57	240	221	7 964	6 532	6 051	252	2 394	3 489
1938	129 969	663	526	512	494	47	230	217	7 631	6 115	5 908	207	2 410	3 434
1939	131 028	703	556	545	513	55	235	223	8 181	6 571	6 187	243	2 499	3 539
1940	132 122	768	594	581	540	63	245	232	8 824	6 950	6 454	276	2 584	3 645
1941	133 402	950	720	703	608	77	279	252	10 232	7 915	6 845	316	2 714	3 825
1942	134 860	1 201	915	879	660	57	322	282	11 989	8 803	6 611	198	2 692	3 992
1943	136 739	1 452	1 112	990	731	55	357	319	13 760	9 083	6 703	176	2 672	4 251
1944	138 397	1 588	1 199	1 072	785	56	381	348	14 693	9 296	6 811	160	2 696	4 435
1945	139 928	1 594	1 227	1 088	857	65	418	374	14 369	9 074	7 153	176	2 832	4 622
1946	141 389	1 572	1 263	1 142	1 021	121	489	411	12 665	8 903	7 960	314	3 055	4 782
1947	144 126	1 694	1 324	1 187	1 124	151	538	434	12 313	8 405	7 958	361	2 979	4 711
1948	146 631	1 835	1 430	1 299	1 194	167	566	461	12 635	8 705	7 999	378	2 950	4 753
1949	149 188	1 791	1 387	1 275	1 196	178	546	472	12 354	8 611	8 080	402	2 942	4 784
1947														
1st quarter	143 156	1 657	1 310	1 176	1 092	145	523	424	12 369	8 509	7 900	350	2 964	4 703
2nd quarter	143 803	1 672	1 290	1 155	1 114	148	535	431	12 294	8 289	7 995	356	3 002	4 750
3rd quarter	144 462	1 692	1 340	1 203	1 133	151	544	438	12 228	8 480	7 984	359	3 002	4 718
4th quarter	145 135	1 752	1 357	1 213	1 156	162	551	443	12 356	8 342	7 950	381	2 949	4 672
1948														
1st quarter	145 761	1 786	1 387	1 241	1 170	162	559	449	12 499	8 442	7 955	377	2 946	4 701
2nd quarter	146 341	1 826	1 422	1 293	1 191	164	568	459	12 678	8 701	8 016	378	2 963	4 756
3rd quarter	146 973	1 863	1 457	1 333	1 206	172	568	466	12 692	8 836	7 993	383	2 932	4 761
4th quarter	147 659	1 863	1 451	1 326	1 206	169	567	470	12 652	8 820	8 019	376	2 956	4 787
1949														
1st quarter	148 298	1 820	1 404	1 284	1 193	165	558	471	12 423	8 602	7 997	367	2 955	4 796
2nd quarter	148 891	1 788	1 389	1 275	1 200	177	550	472	12 328	8 594	8 087	397	2 951	4 801
3rd quarter	149 529	1 790	1 378	1 269	1 190	183	537	471	12 413	8 608	8 071	415	2 912	4 771
4th quarter	150 211	1 765	1 377	1 272	1 201	189	539	473	12 241	8 630	8 152	429	2 946	4 764
1950														
1st quarter	150 852	1 824	1 468	1 358	1 214	194	540	479	12 681	9 233	8 252	444	2 971	4 802
2nd quarter	151 385	1 879	1 468	1 352	1 235	197	547	491	13 021	9 151	8 359	446	2 995	4 907
3rd quarter	152 039	1 986	1 520	1 396	1 320	246	570	505	13 473	9 253	8 750	549	3 034	4 961
4th quarter	152 724	2 052	1 575	1 427	1 297	218	567	512	13 648	9 296	8 448	479	2 953	4 970
1951														
1st quarter	153 336	2 145	1 627	1 468	1 366	232	600	533	13 765	9 262	8 618	492	2 996	5 085
2nd quarter	153 947	2 187	1 668	1 497	1 333	200	594	539	13 938	9 369	8 341	420	2 940	5 100
3rd quarter	154 655	2 221	1 681	1 501	1 344	195	602	546	14 151	9 386	8 400	410	2 988	5 140
4th quarter	155 389	2 239	1 708	1 517	1 363	196	614	553	14 108	9 359	8 409	407	3 009	5 128
1952														
1st quarter	156 033	2 251	1 714	1 516	1 366	197	607	561	14 191	9 314	8 393	408	2 972	5 170
2nd quarter	156 644	2 248	1 732	1 529	1 387	198	617	572	14 151	9 394	8 524	414	3 029	5 231
3rd quarter	157 324	2 279	1 768	1 562	1 397	187	626	584	14 184	9 539	8 529	388	3 069	5 277
4th quarter	158 043	2 350	1 798	1 589	1 442	213	635	594	14 586	9 683	8 790	453	3 100	5 328
1953														
1st quarter	158 648	2 385	1 821	1 610	1 459	222	634	604	14 803	9 775	8 861	466	3 107	5 362
2nd quarter	159 234	2 399	1 839	1 629	1 465	220	631	614	14 860	9 873	8 881	462	3 110	5 406
3rd quarter	159 963	2 382	1 831	1 624	1 463	216	624	623	14 702	9 789	8 821	457	3 067	5 415
4th quarter	160 713	2 339	1 818	1 613	1 453	210	622	621	14 402	9 681	8 721	442	3 057	5 349
1954														
1st quarter	161 389	2 325	1 811	1 623	1 459	204	627	628	14 273	9 696	8 716	426	3 074	5 377
2nd quarter	162 044	2 320	1 801	1 616	1 470	208	625	637	14 233	9 663	8 794	445	3 053	5 448
3rd quarter	162 792	2 339	1 805	1 621	1 479	204	628	647	14 328	9 727	8 872	445	3 077	5 517
4th quarter	163 585	2 381	1 830	1 644	1 501	214	632	654	14 544	9 872	9 015	470	3 114	5 557
1955														
1st quarter	164 266	2 451	1 858	1 666	1 533	234	636	663	14 901	9 977	9 179	510	3 133	5 598
2nd quarter	164 926	2 491	1 898	1 701	1 558	247	643	668	15 086	10 176	9 317	536	3 178	5 617
3rd quarter	165 674	2 532	1 934	1 733	1 576	256	645	675	15 219	10 321	9 390	551	3 185	5 649
4th quarter	166 481	2 559	1 955	1 749	1 593	249	655	689	15 230	10 390	9 462	533	3 234	5 734
1956														
1st quarter	167 190	2 562	1 978	1 767	1 595	237	661	697	15 096	10 453	9 437	507	3 257	5 764
2nd quarter	167 869	2 586	2 005	1 789	1 605	237	663	704	15 153	10 514	9 430	506	3 236	5 796
3rd quarter	168 654	2 604	2 025	1 806	1 616	235	667	715	15 064	10 509	9 407	494	3 223	5 830
4th quarter	169 497	2 644	2 060	1 836	1 640	245	671	725	15 234	10 624	9 489	508	3 232	5 876
1957														
1st quarter	170 218	2 686	2 075	1 848	1 659	250	678	731	15 262	10 597	9 514	515	3 238	5 874
2nd quarter	170 915	2 686	2 093	1 865	1 666	247	682	738	15 164	10 624	9 493	501	3 237	5 900
3rd quarter	171 684	2 717	2 108	1 880	1 685	244	695	746	15 241	10 627	9 525	495	3 267	5 917
4th quarter	172 463	2 676	2 096	1 871	1 687	240	690	756	15 013	10 519	9 487	487	3 231	5 955

Table 1-3B. U.S. Population and Per Capita Product and Income: Historical Data—*Continued*

(Dollars, except as noted; quarterly data are at seasonally adjusted annual rates.)   **NIPA Table 7.1**

Year and quarter	Population (mid-period, thousands)	Current dollars							Chained (2005) dollars					
		Gross domestic product	Personal income	Disposable personal income	Personal consumption expenditures				Gross domestic product	Disposable personal income	Personal consumption expenditures			
					Total	Durable goods	Nondurable goods	Services			Total	Durable goods	Nondurable goods	Services
1958														
1st quarter	173 116	2 622	2 091	1 870	1 678	228	692	758	14 551	10 390	9 323	453	3 190	5 927
2nd quarter	173 781	2 636	2 096	1 879	1 689	222	697	769	14 584	10 419	9 363	444	3 207	5 989
3rd quarter	174 535	2 703	2 134	1 911	1 710	226	705	779	14 862	10 588	9 475	451	3 251	6 043
4th quarter	175 340	2 766	2 150	1 926	1 724	232	708	784	15 138	10 673	9 556	466	3 281	6 052
1959														
1st quarter	176 045	2 815	2 178	1 946	1 761	248	716	797	15 383	10 713	9 694	489	3 310	6 105
2nd quarter	176 727	2 877	2 218	1 980	1 789	257	719	812	15 710	10 857	9 806	506	3 325	6 172
3rd quarter	177 481	2 870	2 221	1 980	1 810	261	722	827	15 625	10 792	9 866	513	3 323	6 229
4th quarter	178 268	2 879	2 243	1 998	1 814	247	726	840	15 610	10 828	9 833	487	3 329	6 276
1960														
1st quarter	179 694	2 933	2 261	2 009	1 819	253	721	845	15 834	10 877	9 849	498	3 311	6 283
2nd quarter	180 335	2 918	2 279	2 024	1 845	257	732	856	15 704	10 898	9 938	508	3 335	6 330
3rd quarter	181 094	2 921	2 282	2 025	1 837	254	727	857	15 664	10 861	9 857	502	3 302	6 296
4th quarter	181 915	2 879	2 279	2 023	1 840	246	728	866	15 393	10 805	9 825	487	3 289	6 328
1961														
1st quarter	182 634	2 891	2 292	2 038	1 835	231	730	874	15 424	10 861	9 784	458	3 296	6 367
2nd quarter	183 337	2 940	2 316	2 060	1 855	236	732	887	15 652	10 982	9 891	466	3 327	6 435
3rd quarter	184 103	2 984	2 344	2 087	1 863	242	731	890	15 839	11 086	9 898	475	3 316	6 427
4th quarter	184 894	3 043	2 382	2 121	1 895	252	736	906	16 092	11 256	10 053	496	3 346	6 512
1962														
1st quarter	185 553	3 105	2 409	2 143	1 916	257	743	917	16 322	11 322	10 124	505	3 362	6 551
2nd quarter	186 203	3 132	2 441	2 167	1 940	263	745	931	16 445	11 408	10 212	517	3 364	6 626
3rd quarter	186 926	3 156	2 456	2 176	1 953	265	749	939	16 533	11 427	10 255	519	3 377	6 657
4th quarter	187 680	3 161	2 477	2 192	1 979	275	754	950	16 506	11 475	10 359	539	3 382	6 714
1963														
1st quarter	188 299	3 199	2 496	2 209	1 991	279	757	955	16 667	11 533	10 395	548	3 389	6 718
2nd quarter	188 906	3 235	2 514	2 226	2 007	285	756	966	16 822	11 604	10 460	558	3 390	6 770
3rd quarter	189 631	3 290	2 541	2 253	2 036	288	766	982	17 073	11 690	10 562	563	3 408	6 862
4th quarter	190 362	3 328	2 580	2 290	2 053	293	763	997	17 137	11 838	10 609	570	3 391	6 929
1964														
1st quarter	190 954	3 402	2 622	2 340	2 097	304	778	1 015	17 467	12 037	10 785	590	3 438	7 019
2nd quarter	191 560	3 439	2 661	2 402	2 132	310	791	1 031	17 612	12 326	10 941	603	3 492	7 094
3rd quarter	192 256	3 487	2 700	2 432	2 170	319	806	1 045	17 786	12 440	11 101	621	3 548	7 161
4th quarter	192 938	3 502	2 736	2 460	2 176	308	808	1 061	17 773	12 539	11 093	600	3 542	7 233
1965														
1st quarter	193 467	3 596	2 783	2 488	2 225	336	815	1 074	18 159	12 644	11 309	654	3 566	7 295
2nd quarter	193 994	3 650	2 823	2 522	2 255	334	829	1 092	18 356	12 750	11 402	653	3 590	7 385
3rd quarter	194 647	3 726	2 885	2 592	2 295	343	843	1 109	18 665	13 057	11 559	673	3 632	7 461
4th quarter	195 279	3 828	2 942	2 644	2 359	354	873	1 131	19 054	13 278	11 846	699	3 755	7 564
1966														
1st quarter	195 763	3 937	2 997	2 683	2 406	369	889	1 147	19 473	13 370	11 991	731	3 772	7 623
2nd quarter	196 277	3 974	3 038	2 704	2 426	355	903	1 168	19 487	13 366	11 990	700	3 798	7 686
3rd quarter	196 877	4 029	3 096	2 751	2 465	367	913	1 184	19 555	13 494	12 091	721	3 814	7 726
4th quarter	197 481	4 086	3 153	2 795	2 487	368	913	1 206	19 654	13 606	12 104	718	3 792	7 786
1967														
1st quarter	197 967	4 131	3 198	2 839	2 503	359	921	1 222	19 778	13 776	12 145	703	3 825	7 839
2nd quarter	198 455	4 144	3 226	2 868	2 542	375	927	1 240	19 733	13 855	12 280	731	3 844	7 896
3rd quarter	199 012	4 206	3 285	2 914	2 572	375	933	1 263	19 835	13 948	12 308	723	3 830	7 981
4th quarter	199 572	4 273	3 333	2 952	2 602	379	941	1 282	19 931	14 011	12 349	723	3 836	8 026
1968														
1st quarter	199 995	4 399	3 422	3 029	2 687	404	968	1 315	20 298	14 225	12 617	766	3 903	8 134
2nd quarter	200 452	4 510	3 511	3 104	2 749	414	987	1 348	20 596	14 428	12 782	781	3 942	8 243
3rd quarter	200 997	4 574	3 591	3 133	2 822	436	1 009	1 378	20 680	14 418	12 987	814	3 994	8 327
4th quarter	201 538	4 645	3 656	3 181	2 859	436	1 017	1 406	20 714	14 474	13 011	807	3 984	8 397
1969														
1st quarter	201 955	4 758	3 719	3 211	2 914	446	1 034	1 434	20 997	14 468	13 130	820	4 020	8 454
2nd quarter	202 419	4 822	3 799	3 277	2 963	447	1 048	1 468	21 010	14 581	13 184	816	4 020	8 538
3rd quarter	202 986	4 908	3 889	3 376	3 006	446	1 064	1 495	21 084	14 836	13 210	812	4 024	8 582
4th quarter	203 584	4 934	3 949	3 430	3 056	446	1 079	1 530	20 923	14 901	13 277	806	4 039	8 663
1970														
1st quarter	204 086	4 984	3 991	3 478	3 103	439	1 100	1 564	20 839	14 938	13 325	792	4 063	8 733
2nd quarter	204 721	5 046	4 083	3 567	3 142	445	1 107	1 590	20 812	15 153	13 345	799	4 048	8 761
3rd quarter	205 419	5 114	4 128	3 638	3 189	448	1 118	1 623	20 926	15 305	13 416	799	4 063	8 830
4th quarter	206 130	5 107	4 153	3 661	3 211	424	1 138	1 649	20 633	15 202	13 333	743	4 097	8 844
1971														
1st quarter	206 763	5 311	4 233	3 757	3 293	474	1 141	1 678	21 137	15 457	13 546	820	4 101	8 877
2nd quarter	207 362	5 395	4 331	3 846	3 351	487	1 152	1 712	21 195	15 644	13 631	837	4 098	8 941
3rd quarter	208 000	5 476	4 380	3 889	3 400	497	1 156	1 747	21 299	15 665	13 698	856	4 077	8 998
4th quarter	208 642	5 519	4 447	3 942	3 468	514	1 168	1 786	21 292	15 782	13 883	890	4 093	9 111
1972														
1st quarter	209 142	5 691	4 572	3 999	3 542	529	1 181	1 832	21 621	15 843	14 034	908	4 096	9 245
2nd quarter	209 637	5 846	4 639	4 050	3 622	544	1 213	1 865	22 082	15 954	14 269	929	4 197	9 336
3rd quarter	210 181	5 944	4 750	4 159	3 701	559	1 237	1 904	22 236	16 238	14 451	950	4 244	9 438
4th quarter	210 737	6 105	4 952	4 348	3 809	586	1 272	1 951	22 542	16 840	14 751	998	4 313	9 581

Table 1-3B. U.S. Population and Per Capita Product and Income: Historical Data—Continued

(Dollars, except as noted; quarterly data are at seasonally adjusted annual rates.)

NIPA Table 7.1

Year and quarter	Population (mid-period, thousands)	Current dollars							Chained (2005) dollars					
		Gross domestic product	Personal income	Disposable personal income	Personal consumption expenditures				Gross domestic product	Disposable personal income	Personal consumption expenditures			
					Total	Durable goods	Nondurable goods	Services			Total	Durable goods	Nondurable goods	Services
1973														
1st quarter	211 192	6 322	5 040	4 442	3 917	624	1 304	1 989	23 069	16 994	14 989	1 059	4 329	9 684
2nd quarter	211 663	6 479	5 172	4 562	3 982	620	1 329	2 033	23 284	17 124	14 948	1 044	4 283	9 743
3rd quarter	212 191	6 554	5 289	4 657	4 059	616	1 366	2 077	23 102	17 167	14 964	1 033	4 292	9 784
4th quarter	212 708	6 731	5 457	4 799	4 121	603	1 399	2 118	23 266	17 334	14 884	1 006	4 265	9 797
1974														
1st quarter	213 144	6 787	5 526	4 856	4 197	594	1 449	2 154	23 015	17 034	14 724	980	4 199	9 762
2nd quarter	213 602	6 951	5 637	4 940	4 322	611	1 489	2 222	23 024	16 851	14 743	984	4 162	9 837
3rd quarter	214 147	7 068	5 799	5 076	4 446	637	1 530	2 279	22 738	16 861	14 766	987	4 161	9 860
4th quarter	214 700	7 232	5 902	5 168	4 480	592	1 541	2 346	22 591	16 741	14 513	891	4 076	9 933
1975														
1st quarter	215 135	7 295	5 968	5 233	4 593	613	1 563	2 417	22 271	16 642	14 605	908	4 076	10 006
2nd quarter	215 652	7 442	6 093	5 532	4 715	634	1 599	2 482	22 387	17 378	14 813	923	4 156	10 106
3rd quarter	216 289	7 686	6 249	5 543	4 858	679	1 646	2 533	22 697	17 092	14 979	978	4 184	10 125
4th quarter	216 848	7 904	6 409	5 678	4 979	707	1 659	2 613	22 934	17 221	15 099	1 004	4 163	10 240
1976														
1st quarter	217 314	8 154	6 559	5 813	5 123	751	1 691	2 681	23 405	17 437	15 368	1 052	4 239	10 338
2nd quarter	217 776	8 285	6 674	5 898	5 203	762	1 713	2 728	23 531	17 543	15 476	1 054	4 295	10 384
3rd quarter	218 338	8 417	6 831	6 026	5 324	778	1 743	2 803	23 586	17 656	15 599	1 063	4 316	10 483
4th quarter	218 917	8 608	6 982	6 149	5 464	801	1 780	2 883	23 694	17 736	15 761	1 077	4 350	10 600
1977														
1st quarter	219 427	8 834	7 109	6 250	5 613	838	1 807	2 968	23 914	17 709	15 904	1 114	4 337	10 702
2nd quarter	219 956	9 116	7 302	6 414	5 727	860	1 835	3 031	24 330	17 867	15 953	1 138	4 326	10 718
3rd quarter	220 573	9 366	7 489	6 590	5 852	879	1 858	3 114	24 696	18 085	16 060	1 151	4 336	10 803
4th quarter	221 201	9 543	7 741	6 800	6 009	907	1 915	3 186	24 621	18 397	16 256	1 172	4 416	10 876
1978														
1st quarter	221 719	9 693	7 894	6 939	6 130	894	1 944	3 292	24 647	18 467	16 313	1 138	4 425	11 024
2nd quarter	222 281	10 233	8 148	7 145	6 373	973	2 001	3 400	25 552	18 632	16 620	1 220	4 448	11 162
3rd quarter	222 933	10 475	8 368	7 309	6 494	972	2 044	3 478	25 727	18 728	16 641	1 200	4 469	11 209
4th quarter	223 583	10 806	8 588	7 483	6 651	994	2 099	3 557	25 992	18 820	16 726	1 206	4 513	11 235
1979														
1st quarter	224 152	10 989	8 818	7 688	6 793	996	2 162	3 635	25 969	18 978	16 767	1 189	4 522	11 320
2nd quarter	224 737	11 242	8 987	7 822	6 956	988	2 225	3 742	25 926	18 796	16 714	1 159	4 501	11 361
3rd quarter	225 418	11 533	9 256	8 037	7 176	1 024	2 317	3 835	26 033	18 847	16 827	1 188	4 540	11 372
4th quarter	226 117	11 761	9 532	8 272	7 347	1 013	2 385	3 948	26 024	18 938	16 820	1 154	4 550	11 435
1980														
1st quarter	226 754	12 013	9 772	8 519	7 532	1 023	2 469	4 039	26 034	18 938	16 744	1 132	4 535	11 415
2nd quarter	227 389	11 997	9 864	8 582	7 520	932	2 489	4 100	25 430	18 621	16 318	1 007	4 461	11 307
3rd quarter	228 070	12 212	10 168	8 846	7 755	988	2 528	4 239	25 307	18 756	16 444	1 049	4 437	11 398
4th quarter	228 689	12 748	10 618	9 227	8 031	1 033	2 585	4 413	25 705	19 092	16 618	1 078	4 442	11 537
1981														
1st quarter	229 155	13 316	10 856	9 414	8 258	1 074	2 680	4 505	26 186	19 009	16 675	1 106	4 473	11 492
2nd quarter	229 674	13 429	11 040	9 551	8 377	1 049	2 712	4 616	25 918	18 969	16 637	1 061	4 482	11 542
3rd quarter	230 301	13 795	11 443	9 896	8 525	1 094	2 732	4 700	26 162	19 337	16 659	1 090	4 480	11 501
4th quarter	230 903	13 836	11 565	10 041	8 567	1 026	2 753	4 788	25 768	19 326	16 490	1 009	4 485	11 480
1982														
1st quarter	231 395	13 764	11 678	10 158	8 713	1 065	2 765	4 883	25 292	19 307	16 561	1 039	4 484	11 498
2nd quarter	231 906	13 975	11 852	10 304	8 808	1 075	2 754	4 979	25 373	19 399	16 584	1 041	4 466	11 548
3rd quarter	232 498	14 083	11 988	10 484	8 992	1 084	2 795	5 113	25 210	19 434	16 669	1 046	4 474	11 627
4th quarter	233 074	14 212	12 139	10 612	9 235	1 134	2 818	5 283	25 168	19 455	16 930	1 091	4 509	11 792
1983														
1st quarter	233 546	14 477	12 266	10 766	9 387	1 151	2 813	5 422	25 429	19 568	17 062	1 100	4 514	11 923
2nd quarter	234 028	14 880	12 455	10 921	9 641	1 237	2 876	5 528	25 947	19 670	17 365	1 178	4 558	12 050
3rd quarter	234 603	15 290	12 674	11 204	9 917	1 289	2 934	5 694	26 394	19 917	17 629	1 220	4 616	12 193
4th quarter	235 153	15 684	12 995	11 485	10 118	1 358	2 962	5 798	26 877	20 280	17 866	1 278	4 661	12 288
1984														
1st quarter	235 605	16 160	13 371	11 840	10 295	1 407	2 998	5 889	27 346	20 684	17 985	1 323	4 664	12 325
2nd quarter	236 082	16 546	13 703	12 136	10 522	1 446	3 060	6 017	27 762	20 997	18 205	1 351	4 757	12 404
3rd quarter	236 657	16 801	14 012	12 391	10 660	1 445	3 062	6 153	27 963	21 273	18 301	1 348	4 749	12 535
4th quarter	237 232	17 004	14 223	12 556	10 842	1 492	3 089	6 261	28 123	21 423	18 497	1 389	4 774	12 647
1985														
1st quarter	237 673	17 323	14 452	12 636	11 122	1 548	3 124	6 450	28 335	21 331	18 776	1 434	4 794	12 852
2nd quarter	238 176	17 532	14 584	12 955	11 283	1 567	3 161	6 556	28 515	21 708	18 907	1 448	4 821	12 941
3rd quarter	238 789	17 833	14 687	12 923	11 541	1 660	3 185	6 696	28 886	21 519	19 217	1 537	4 848	13 082
4th quarter	239 387	18 041	14 917	13 128	11 629	1 603	3 231	6 795	29 032	21 687	19 211	1 480	4 879	13 154
1986														
1st quarter	239 861	18 271	15 128	13 353	11 787	1 633	3 249	6 905	29 253	21 902	19 333	1 508	4 931	13 173
2nd quarter	240 368	18 402	15 269	13 485	11 895	1 694	3 193	7 008	29 309	22 104	19 498	1 558	4 965	13 220
3rd quarter	240 962	18 639	15 443	13 622	12 162	1 850	3 200	7 113	29 519	22 165	19 789	1 686	4 963	13 294
4th quarter	241 539	18 810	15 583	13 698	12 296	1 826	3 225	7 244	29 590	22 125	19 861	1 656	4 991	13 405
1987														
1st quarter	242 009	19 053	15 798	13 937	12 416	1 729	3 295	7 392	29 697	22 218	19 792	1 554	4 988	13 537
2nd quarter	242 520	19 325	15 986	13 879	12 666	1 811	3 349	7 507	29 949	21 930	20 015	1 615	5 016	13 636
3rd quarter	243 120	19 597	16 247	14 238	12 908	1 894	3 376	7 638	30 135	22 268	20 188	1 677	5 007	13 719
4th quarter	243 721	20 036	16 607	14 529	13 019	1 846	3 392	7 780	30 575	22 528	20 187	1 628	5 001	13 825

Table 1-3B. U.S. Population and Per Capita Product and Income: Historical Data—*Continued*

(Dollars, except as noted; quarterly data are at seasonally adjusted annual rates.)   NIPA Table 7.1

Year and quarter	Population (mid-period, thou-sands)	Current dollars							Chained (2005) dollars					
		Gross domestic product	Personal income	Dispos-able personal income	Personal consumption expenditures				Gross domestic product	Dispos-able personal income	Personal consumption expenditures			
					Total	Durable goods	Nondur-able goods	Services			Total	Durable goods	Nondur-able goods	Services
1988														
1st quarter	244 208	20 264	16 859	14 807	13 323	1 926	3 433	7 963	30 671	22 766	20 483	1 702	5 045	13 964
2nd quarter	244 716	20 674	17 109	15 079	13 538	1 934	3 488	8 117	31 001	22 932	20 589	1 699	5 074	14 055
3rd quarter	245 354	20 961	17 403	15 342	13 778	1 917	3 549	8 311	31 080	23 048	20 698	1 672	5 096	14 205
4th quarter	245 966	21 349	17 690	15 591	14 040	1 977	3 603	8 460	31 417	23 198	20 889	1 711	5 136	14 298
1989														
1st quarter	246 460	21 749	18 163	15 927	14 232	1 974	3 662	8 597	31 648	23 415	20 924	1 700	5 149	14 343
2nd quarter	247 017	22 078	18 322	16 035	14 452	1 997	3 756	8 699	31 813	23 266	20 970	1 719	5 145	14 364
3rd quarter	247 698	22 337	18 483	16 182	14 642	2 041	3 780	8 821	31 977	23 352	21 129	1 753	5 183	14 435
4th quarter	248 374	22 473	18 719	16 391	14 790	1 980	3 830	8 980	31 960	23 467	21 175	1 695	5 227	14 545
1990														
1st quarter	248 936	22 930	19 059	16 727	15 099	2 070	3 913	9 115	32 220	23 590	21 294	1 763	5 209	14 575
2nd quarter	249 711	23 216	19 340	16 966	15 265	1 996	3 928	9 341	32 248	23 672	21 298	1 699	5 198	14 711
3rd quarter	250 595	23 347	19 524	17 135	15 464	1 970	4 003	9 492	32 134	23 605	21 304	1 676	5 188	14 772
4th quarter	251 482	23 246	19 566	17 184	15 492	1 912	4 051	9 529	31 740	23 364	21 063	1 624	5 118	14 679
1991														
1st quarter	252 258	23 310	19 587	17 294	15 499	1 870	4 020	9 609	31 489	23 363	20 939	1 575	5 105	14 644
2nd quarter	253 063	23 559	19 781	17 474	15 661	1 878	4 038	9 746	31 601	23 466	21 031	1 577	5 118	14 727
3rd quarter	253 965	23 758	19 897	17 582	15 784	1 907	4 034	9 844	31 621	23 432	21 037	1 596	5 109	14 711
4th quarter	254 835	23 908	20 115	17 775	15 848	1 874	4 005	9 969	31 637	23 504	20 955	1 565	5 048	14 747
1992														
1st quarter	255 585	24 222	20 426	18 131	16 199	1 941	4 060	10 197	31 890	23 789	21 253	1 621	5 108	14 910
2nd quarter	256 439	24 548	20 694	18 335	16 353	1 954	4 084	10 316	32 122	23 891	21 308	1 627	5 112	14 955
3rd quarter	257 386	24 825	20 866	18 481	16 581	1 990	4 122	10 469	32 334	23 924	21 464	1 656	5 124	15 066
4th quarter	258 277	25 142	21 260	18 794	16 828	2 025	4 161	10 641	32 561	24 181	21 651	1 683	5 157	15 188
1993														
1st quarter	259 039	25 264	20 925	18 553	16 928	2 038	4 166	10 724	32 525	23 756	21 675	1 694	5 147	15 207
2nd quarter	259 826	25 489	21 359	18 891	17 135	2 109	4 181	10 846	32 634	24 052	21 817	1 744	5 172	15 250
3rd quarter	260 714	25 654	21 453	18 933	17 323	2 135	4 191	10 997	32 694	24 022	21 978	1 757	5 206	15 367
4th quarter	261 547	26 052	21 829	19 255	17 515	2 194	4 226	11 095	33 020	24 298	22 103	1 794	5 225	15 421
1994														
1st quarter	262 250	26 373	21 761	19 202	17 733	2 245	4 259	11 229	33 253	24 136	22 290	1 832	5 281	15 499
2nd quarter	263 020	26 782	22 219	19 576	17 907	2 276	4 289	11 341	33 609	24 476	22 389	1 846	5 307	15 555
3rd quarter	263 870	27 028	22 442	19 817	18 139	2 309	4 357	11 473	33 716	24 577	22 496	1 859	5 336	15 618
4th quarter	264 678	27 385	22 770	20 114	18 349	2 387	4 394	11 568	33 987	24 827	22 649	1 919	5 376	15 640
1995														
1st quarter	265 388	27 536	23 012	20 299	18 421	2 341	4 397	11 683	33 979	24 921	22 614	1 874	5 381	15 673
2nd quarter	266 142	27 669	23 151	20 362	18 627	2 356	4 422	11 849	33 955	24 852	22 735	1 888	5 392	15 770
3rd quarter	267 000	27 912	23 335	20 534	18 812	2 407	4 433	11 972	34 131	24 958	22 865	1 935	5 394	15 831
4th quarter	267 820	28 163	23 541	20 682	18 968	2 435	4 449	12 083	34 263	25 029	22 955	1 962	5 405	15 872
1996														
1st quarter	268 487	28 449	23 939	20 972	19 206	2 458	4 511	12 237	34 412	25 232	23 107	1 979	5 426	15 987
2nd quarter	269 251	28 969	24 374	21 275	19 494	2 512	4 604	12 378	34 908	25 431	23 302	2 036	5 480	16 048
3rd quarter	270 128	29 218	24 588	21 485	19 637	2 515	4 614	12 507	35 097	25 565	23 366	2 044	5 502	16 081
4th quarter	270 991	29 606	24 851	21 683	19 870	2 545	4 680	12 645	35 367	25 623	23 481	2 077	5 528	16 124
1997														
1st quarter	271 709	29 947	25 231	21 932	20 121	2 597	4 715	12 809	35 545	25 784	23 655	2 127	5 547	16 213
2nd quarter	272 487	30 375	25 434	22 092	20 199	2 556	4 690	12 953	35 969	25 903	23 683	2 115	5 535	16 276
3rd quarter	273 391	30 762	25 756	22 335	20 532	2 644	4 747	13 142	36 300	26 113	24 006	2 202	5 605	16 415
4th quarter	274 246	31 015	26 164	22 656	20 777	2 688	4 770	13 319	36 465	26 393	24 205	2 251	5 627	16 531
1998														
1st quarter	274 950	31 281	26 724	23 123	20 940	2 684	4 755	13 502	36 715	26 924	24 383	2 264	5 654	16 672
2nd quarter	275 703	31 551	27 130	23 443	21 292	2 792	4 791	13 709	36 944	27 234	24 735	2 373	5 708	16 829
3rd quarter	276 564	31 990	27 445	23 695	21 579	2 842	4 830	13 907	37 315	27 435	24 985	2 434	5 732	16 980
4th quarter	277 400	32 543	27 699	23 870	21 911	2 979	4 889	14 044	37 846	27 553	25 292	2 570	5 793	17 047
1999														
1st quarter	278 103	32 896	27 907	24 046	22 141	2 953	4 983	14 205	38 087	27 669	25 477	2 570	5 885	17 148
2nd quarter	278 864	33 179	28 084	24 173	22 556	3 071	5 089	14 395	38 280	27 657	25 807	2 686	5 924	17 294
3rd quarter	279 751	33 620	28 369	24 379	22 873	3 121	5 152	14 600	38 644	27 747	26 034	2 743	5 934	17 446
4th quarter	280 592	34 241	28 920	24 823	23 254	3 131	5 290	14 833	39 220	28 098	26 322	2 769	6 037	17 607
2000														
1st quarter	281 304	34 516	29 788	25 506	23 757	3 283	5 312	15 162	39 223	28 616	26 654	2 917	5 970	17 828
2nd quarter	282 002	35 280	30 165	25 817	24 027	3 209	5 453	15 365	39 889	28 838	26 838	2 858	6 074	17 991
3rd quarter	282 769	35 426	30 570	26 172	24 337	3 236	5 519	15 582	39 814	29 065	27 027	2 899	6 099	18 108
4th quarter	283 518	35 729	30 712	26 287	24 623	3 243	5 576	15 804	39 944	29 031	27 194	2 913	6 142	18 219
2001														
1st quarter	284 169	35 771	31 175	26 609	24 838	3 276	5 545	16 016	39 722	29 182	27 240	2 955	6 092	18 263
2nd quarter	284 838	36 165	31 180	26 600	24 992	3 244	5 598	16 151	39 888	29 034	27 279	2 947	6 107	18 297
3rd quarter	285 584	36 085	31 096	27 211	25 041	3 252	5 586	16 203	39 674	29 696	27 327	2 975	6 121	18 299
4th quarter	286 311	36 230	31 128	26 840	25 382	3 499	5 537	16 347	39 712	29 275	27 685	3 216	6 158	18 333
2002														
1st quarter	286 935	36 589	31 290	27 567	25 473	3 420	5 535	16 517	39 964	29 999	27 720	3 173	6 169	18 412
2nd quarter	287 574	36 867	31 508	27 873	25 744	3 430	5 608	16 706	40 088	30 097	27 798	3 199	6 164	18 468
3rd quarter	288 303	37 120	31 476	27 847	25 984	3 505	5 625	16 855	40 189	29 918	27 916	3 284	6 165	18 486
4th quarter	289 007	37 255	31 580	27 976	26 135	3 427	5 705	17 004	40 105	29 915	27 947	3 233	6 228	18 513

Table 1-3B. U.S. Population and Per Capita Product and Income: Historical Data—*Continued*

(Dollars, except as noted; quarterly data are at seasonally adjusted annual rates.)   **NIPA Table 7.1**

Year and quarter	Population (mid-period, thousands)	Current dollars							Chained (2005) dollars					
		Gross domestic product	Personal income	Disposable personal income	Personal consumption expenditures				Gross domestic product	Disposable personal income	Personal consumption expenditures			
					Total	Durable goods	Nondurable goods	Services			Total	Durable goods	Nondurable goods	Services
2003														
1st quarter	289 609	37 593	31 748	28 221	26 401	3 389	5 844	17 168	40 188	29 963	28 030	3 236	6 270	18 550
2nd quarter	290 253	37 938	32 114	28 606	26 623	3 484	5 762	17 377	40 439	30 349	28 245	3 362	6 288	18 608
3rd quarter	290 974	38 681	32 370	29 121	27 088	3 586	5 932	17 571	41 003	30 697	28 554	3 495	6 382	18 682
4th quarter	291 669	39 136	32 840	29 353	27 295	3 578	5 971	17 747	41 275	30 800	28 641	3 520	6 393	18 731
2004														
1st quarter	292 237	39 659	33 123	29 669	27 711	3 619	6 095	17 997	41 466	30 877	28 838	3 562	6 435	18 845
2nd quarter	292 875	40 164	33 622	30 118	27 978	3 629	6 137	18 211	41 642	31 114	28 903	3 576	6 420	18 910
3rd quarter	293 603	40 655	34 056	30 430	28 326	3 664	6 206	18 455	41 848	31 245	29 084	3 638	6 455	18 993
4th quarter	294 334	41 191	34 733	31 026	28 790	3 721	6 376	18 693	42 086	31 603	29 325	3 694	6 508	19 125
2005														
1st quarter	294 957	41 911	34 712	30 765	29 129	3 747	6 427	18 955	42 430	31 152	29 496	3 725	6 567	19 205
2nd quarter	295 588	42 289	35 139	31 105	29 536	3 839	6 477	19 220	42 528	31 305	29 724	3 825	6 586	19 314
3rd quarter	296 340	42 953	35 694	31 563	30 019	3 855	6 697	19 468	42 757	31 411	29 874	3 869	6 595	19 410
4th quarter	297 086	43 426	36 154	31 934	30 281	3 740	6 796	19 745	42 868	31 504	29 873	3 761	6 649	19 461
2006														
1st quarter	297 736	44 205	37 035	32 597	30 652	3 864	6 820	19 968	43 315	32 024	30 113	3 899	6 671	19 544
2nd quarter	298 408	44 672	37 546	33 055	30 995	3 840	6 923	20 233	43 393	32 235	30 227	3 893	6 689	19 644
3rd quarter	299 180	44 899	37 893	33 366	31 325	3 867	7 016	20 442	43 286	32 306	30 329	3 941	6 705	19 685
4th quarter	299 946	45 289	38 356	33 710	31 528	3 889	6 947	20 692	43 469	32 646	30 533	3 985	6 774	19 777
2007														
1st quarter	300 609	45 769	38 968	34 116	31 941	3 911	7 056	20 974	43 432	32 721	30 635	4 025	6 780	19 833
2nd quarter	301 284	46 391	39 295	34 381	32 265	3 940	7 177	21 149	43 725	32 697	30 684	4 073	6 763	19 855
3rd quarter	302 062	46 766	39 576	34 618	32 502	3 954	7 231	21 317	43 931	32 741	30 740	4 114	6 776	19 860
4th quarter	302 829	47 067	40 093	35 081	32 853	3 952	7 378	21 522	44 005	32 837	30 752	4 127	6 766	19 872
2008														
1st quarter	303 494	47 032	40 909	35 848	33 011	3 832	7 445	21 734	43 714	33 238	30 607	4 016	6 696	19 901
2nd quarter	304 160	47 394	41 333	36 888	33 293	3 770	7 629	21 895	43 761	33 826	30 529	3 977	6 719	19 834
3rd quarter	304 902	47 212	41 040	36 343	33 243	3 629	7 706	21 908	43 250	32 974	30 160	3 840	6 610	19 700
4th quarter	305 616	46 077	40 378	35 722	32 267	3 335	7 075	21 857	42 156	32 878	29 698	3 560	6 496	19 596
2009														
1st quarter	306 237	45 369	39 069	35 157	31 942	3 331	6 892	21 719	41 351	32 494	29 523	3 574	6 467	19 441
2nd quarter	306 866	45 147	38 923	35 272	31 876	3 290	6 955	21 632	41 195	32 448	29 324	3 530	6 429	19 320
3rd quarter	307 573	45 259	38 606	34 962	32 224	3 414	7 138	21 671	41 273	31 926	29 425	3 689	6 446	19 270
4th quarter	308 285	45 696	38 724	35 071	32 405	3 370	7 237	21 798	41 564	31 806	29 389	3 635	6 480	19 245
2010														
1st quarter	308 899	46 222	39 294	35 582	32 709	3 425	7 381	21 902	41 883	32 122	29 528	3 715	6 543	19 254
2nd quarter	309 457	46 752	39 830	36 032	32 912	3 463	7 330	22 118	42 198	32 501	29 687	3 778	6 562	19 338
3rd quarter	310 070	47 104	40 163	36 251	33 143	3 507	7 414	22 221	42 376	32 620	29 823	3 851	6 598	19 377
4th quarter	310 670	47 494	40 485	36 491	33 531	3 620	7 592	22 318	42 541	32 678	30 027	3 999	6 655	19 402
2011														
1st quarter	311 184	47 778	41 284	36 895	33 972	3 710	7 834	22 429	42 508	32 724	30 132	4 105	6 669	19 407
2nd quarter	311 717	48 162	41 561	37 082	34 249	3 669	7 952	22 627	42 577	32 625	30 132	4 043	6 662	19 463
3rd quarter	312 330	48 590	41 804	37 293	34 529	3 708	8 014	22 807	42 684	32 621	30 204	4 091	6 639	19 518
4th quarter	312 929	48 955	41 881	37 345	34 741	3 818	8 038	22 885	42 914	32 572	30 301	4 239	6 639	19 500

Table 1-4A. Contributions to Percent Change in Real Gross Domestic Product: Recent Data

(Percent, percentage points.)   NIPA Table 1.1.2

Year and quarter	Percent change at seasonally adjusted annual rate, real GDP	Personal consump-tion expen-ditures	Gross private domestic investment				Exports and imports of goods and services			Government consumption expenditures and gross investment		
				Fixed investment		Change in private inventories						State and local
			Total	Nonresi-dential	Residential		Net exports	Exports	Imports	Total	Federal	
1950	8.7	4.29	5.74	0.86	2.03	2.84	-1.31	-0.66	-0.65	0.02	-0.56	0.58
1951	7.7	1.03	0.05	0.44	-1.14	0.75	0.81	0.98	-0.17	5.84	5.78	0.06
1952	3.8	1.95	-1.65	-0.18	-0.10	-1.37	-0.59	-0.22	-0.37	4.12	4.00	0.11
1953	4.6	2.93	0.70	0.80	0.18	-0.28	-0.70	-0.31	-0.39	1.67	1.33	0.34
1954	-0.6	1.29	-0.69	-0.20	0.42	-0.91	0.40	0.19	0.21	-1.64	-2.24	0.60
1955	7.2	4.63	3.45	1.01	0.90	1.54	-0.04	0.44	-0.48	-0.84	-1.39	0.55
1956	2.0	1.82	-0.23	0.55	-0.49	-0.29	0.37	0.71	-0.33	0.02	-0.23	0.25
1957	2.0	1.54	-0.71	0.16	-0.32	-0.54	0.25	0.43	-0.18	0.94	0.46	0.47
1958	-0.9	0.54	-1.25	-1.12	0.05	-0.18	-0.89	-0.69	-0.20	0.70	-0.01	0.70
1959	7.2	3.61	2.80	0.73	1.21	0.86	0.00	0.45	-0.45	0.76	0.42	0.34
1960	2.5	1.72	0.00	0.52	-0.39	-0.13	0.72	0.78	-0.06	0.04	-0.35	0.39
1961	2.3	1.30	-0.10	-0.06	0.01	-0.05	0.06	0.03	0.03	1.07	0.51	0.56
1962	6.1	3.10	1.81	0.78	0.46	0.57	-0.21	0.25	-0.47	1.36	1.07	0.29
1963	4.4	2.56	1.00	0.50	0.58	-0.08	0.24	0.35	-0.12	0.58	0.01	0.57
1964	5.8	3.69	1.25	1.07	0.30	-0.13	0.36	0.59	-0.23	0.49	-0.17	0.65
1965	6.4	3.91	2.16	1.65	-0.15	0.66	-0.30	0.15	-0.45	0.65	-0.01	0.66
1966	6.5	3.50	1.44	1.29	-0.43	0.58	-0.29	0.36	-0.65	1.87	1.24	0.63
1967	2.5	1.82	-0.76	-0.15	-0.13	-0.49	-0.22	0.12	-0.34	1.68	1.17	0.51
1968	4.8	3.51	0.90	0.46	0.53	-0.10	-0.30	0.41	-0.71	0.73	0.10	0.63
1969	3.1	2.29	0.90	0.78	0.13	0.00	-0.04	0.25	-0.29	-0.05	-0.42	0.37
1970	0.2	1.44	-1.04	-0.06	-0.26	-0.73	0.34	0.56	-0.22	-0.55	-0.86	0.31
1971	3.4	2.37	1.67	0.00	1.10	0.58	-0.19	0.10	-0.29	-0.50	-0.85	0.36
1972	5.3	3.81	1.87	0.93	0.89	0.06	-0.21	0.42	-0.63	-0.16	-0.42	0.26
1973	5.8	3.08	1.96	1.50	-0.04	0.50	0.82	1.12	-0.29	-0.08	-0.41	0.33
1974	-0.6	-0.52	-1.31	0.09	-1.13	-0.27	0.75	0.58	0.18	0.52	0.08	0.44
1975	-0.2	1.40	-2.98	-1.14	-0.57	-1.27	0.89	-0.05	0.94	0.48	0.03	0.45
1976	5.4	3.51	2.84	0.52	0.90	1.41	-1.08	0.37	-1.45	0.10	0.00	0.09
1977	4.6	2.66	2.43	1.19	0.99	0.25	-0.72	0.20	-0.92	0.23	0.19	0.04
1978	5.6	2.77	2.16	1.69	0.35	0.12	0.05	0.82	-0.78	0.60	0.22	0.38
1979	3.1	1.48	0.61	1.23	-0.21	-0.41	0.66	0.82	-0.16	0.37	0.20	0.17
1980	-0.3	-0.22	-2.12	-0.03	-1.17	-0.91	1.68	0.97	0.71	0.38	0.39	-0.01
1981	2.5	0.95	1.55	0.74	-0.35	1.16	-0.15	0.12	-0.27	0.19	0.42	-0.23
1982	-1.9	0.86	-2.55	-0.50	-0.71	-1.34	-0.60	-0.73	0.12	0.35	0.35	0.01
1983	4.5	3.65	1.45	-0.17	1.33	0.29	-1.35	-0.22	-1.13	0.76	0.63	0.13
1984	7.2	3.43	4.63	2.05	0.64	1.95	-1.58	0.63	-2.21	0.70	0.30	0.40
1985	4.1	3.32	-0.17	0.82	0.07	-1.06	-0.42	0.23	-0.65	1.41	0.74	0.67
1986	3.5	2.62	-0.12	-0.36	0.55	-0.32	-0.30	0.54	-0.84	1.27	0.55	0.71
1987	3.2	2.01	0.51	-0.01	0.10	0.42	0.16	0.77	-0.61	0.51	0.35	0.17
1988	4.1	2.64	0.39	0.58	-0.05	-0.14	0.82	1.24	-0.43	0.26	-0.16	0.42
1989	3.6	1.86	0.64	0.61	-0.14	0.17	0.52	0.99	-0.48	0.55	0.14	0.41
1990	1.9	1.34	-0.53	0.05	-0.37	-0.21	0.43	0.81	-0.38	0.64	0.18	0.46
1991	-0.2	0.10	-1.20	-0.57	-0.37	-0.26	0.64	0.63	0.02	0.22	-0.02	0.24
1992	3.4	2.27	1.07	0.31	0.47	0.29	-0.05	0.68	-0.72	0.10	-0.16	0.26
1993	2.9	2.37	1.21	0.83	0.31	0.07	-0.57	0.32	-0.90	-0.16	-0.33	0.17
1994	4.1	2.57	1.94	0.91	0.39	0.63	-0.43	0.85	-1.28	0.00	-0.30	0.30
1995	2.5	1.81	0.48	1.08	-0.14	-0.46	0.11	1.03	-0.92	0.11	-0.20	0.30
1996	3.7	2.35	1.35	1.01	0.33	0.02	-0.15	0.90	-1.04	0.19	-0.08	0.27
1997	4.5	2.48	1.95	1.33	0.08	0.54	-0.32	1.30	-1.62	0.34	-0.07	0.41
1998	4.4	3.50	1.65	1.38	0.32	-0.05	-1.18	0.26	-1.43	0.38	-0.07	0.45
1999	4.8	3.68	1.50	1.24	0.28	-0.02	-0.99	0.47	-1.45	0.63	0.12	0.51
2000	4.1	3.44	1.19	1.20	0.05	-0.05	-0.85	0.91	-1.76	0.36	0.03	0.33
2001	1.1	1.85	-1.24	-0.35	0.03	-0.92	-0.20	-0.61	0.41	0.67	0.24	0.43
2002	1.8	1.85	-0.22	-0.94	0.24	0.48	-0.65	-0.20	-0.46	0.84	0.44	0.40
2003	2.5	1.97	0.60	0.14	0.40	0.06	-0.45	0.15	-0.60	0.42	0.43	-0.01
2004	3.5	2.30	1.57	0.63	0.52	0.42	-0.66	0.90	-1.55	0.26	0.28	-0.02
2005	3.1	2.35	0.93	0.69	0.36	-0.13	-0.27	0.67	-0.95	0.06	0.09	-0.03
2006	2.7	1.98	0.47	0.86	-0.46	0.07	-0.06	0.93	-0.98	0.26	0.15	0.11
2007	1.9	1.60	-0.56	0.73	-1.05	-0.23	0.62	1.03	-0.40	0.25	0.09	0.17
2008	-0.3	-0.39	-1.66	-0.09	-1.05	-0.51	1.21	0.73	0.47	0.50	0.50	0.00
2009	-3.5	-1.32	-3.61	-2.05	-0.72	-0.84	1.11	-1.18	2.29	0.34	0.45	-0.11
2010	3.0	1.44	1.96	0.42	-0.11	1.64	-0.51	1.31	-1.82	0.14	0.37	-0.23
2011	1.7	1.53	0.60	0.84	-0.03	-0.21	0.05	0.86	-0.81	-0.44	-0.17	-0.28
2009												
1st quarter	-6.7	-1.02	-7.76	-3.90	-1.19	-2.66	2.44	-3.82	6.26	-0.33	-0.25	-0.08
2nd quarter	-0.7	-1.28	-2.84	-1.66	-0.60	-0.58	2.21	-0.02	2.24	1.21	1.09	0.12
3rd quarter	1.7	1.66	0.35	-0.29	0.42	0.21	-0.59	1.49	-2.08	0.28	0.48	-0.19
4th quarter	3.8	0.33	3.51	-0.33	-0.10	3.93	0.15	2.51	-2.36	-0.18	0.18	-0.37
2010												
1st quarter	3.9	1.92	3.25	0.56	-0.41	3.10	-0.97	0.86	-1.83	-0.26	0.23	-0.49
2nd quarter	3.8	2.05	2.92	1.62	0.50	0.79	-1.94	1.19	-3.13	0.77	0.71	0.05
3rd quarter	2.5	1.85	1.14	1.04	-0.76	0.86	-0.68	1.21	-1.89	0.20	0.26	-0.06
4th quarter	2.3	2.48	-0.91	0.82	0.06	-1.79	1.37	0.98	0.39	-0.58	-0.26	-0.33
2011												
1st quarter	0.4	1.47	0.47	0.20	-0.06	0.32	-0.34	1.01	-1.35	-1.23	-0.82	-0.41
2nd quarter	1.3	0.49	0.79	0.98	0.09	-0.28	0.24	0.48	-0.24	-0.18	0.16	-0.34
3rd quarter	1.8	1.24	0.17	1.49	0.03	-1.35	0.43	0.64	-0.21	-0.02	0.17	-0.19
4th quarter	3.0	1.47	2.59	0.53	0.25	1.81	-0.26	0.37	-0.63	-0.84	-0.58	-0.26

Table 1-4B. Contributions to Percent Change in Real Gross Domestic Product: Historical Data

(Percent; percentage points.)   NIPA Table 1.1.2

Year and quarter	Percent change at seasonally adjusted annual rate, real GDP	Personal consump-tion expen-ditures	Gross private domestic investment				Exports and imports of goods and services			Government consumption expenditures and gross investment		
			Total	Fixed investment		Change in private inventories	Net exports	Exports	Imports	Total	Federal	State and local
				Nonresi-dential	Residential							
1929	. . .	. . .	. . .	. . .	. . .	. . .	. . .	. . .	. . .	. . .	. . .	. . .
1930	-8.6	-4.01	-5.23	-1.86	-1.51	-1.86	-0.31	-0.97	0.66	0.93	0.18	0.75
1931	-6.5	-2.41	-4.32	-3.33	-0.42	-0.57	-0.22	-0.77	0.55	0.47	0.07	0.40
1932	-13.1	-7.09	-5.34	-2.79	-1.05	-1.49	-0.20	-0.81	0.62	-0.43	0.06	-0.49
1933	-1.3	-1.82	1.15	-0.48	-0.24	1.86	-0.11	0.02	-0.14	-0.50	0.75	-1.25
1934	10.9	5.78	2.79	1.22	0.41	1.16	0.33	0.41	-0.08	1.98	1.39	0.59
1935	8.9	4.78	4.51	1.35	0.56	2.61	-0.84	0.21	-1.05	0.44	0.09	0.35
1936	13.0	7.78	2.53	2.04	0.48	0.01	0.24	0.19	0.05	2.50	2.44	0.06
1937	5.1	2.75	2.57	1.39	0.19	1.00	0.46	0.95	-0.49	-0.66	-0.66	0.00
1938	-3.4	-1.18	-4.24	-2.22	0.01	-2.04	0.89	-0.05	0.94	1.09	0.59	0.50
1939	8.1	4.16	2.44	0.74	1.04	0.66	0.07	0.25	-0.17	1.41	0.48	0.93
1940	8.8	3.78	4.01	1.58	0.43	2.00	0.53	0.61	-0.08	0.45	0.76	-0.31
1941	17.1	4.99	2.93	1.36	0.22	1.36	-0.65	0.12	-0.77	9.80	10.34	-0.54
1942	18.5	-1.53	-6.54	-3.18	-1.58	-1.78	-1.21	-1.54	0.33	27.74	28.37	-0.63
1943	16.4	1.56	-2.59	-0.63	-0.56	-1.39	-1.18	-0.43	-0.75	18.58	19.07	-0.49
1944	8.1	1.45	0.75	0.90	-0.10	-0.05	0.01	0.16	-0.15	5.87	6.02	-0.15
1945	-1.1	3.08	1.16	1.36	0.11	-0.30	0.68	0.88	-0.20	-6.04	-6.17	0.13
1946	-10.9	6.48	7.45	2.24	2.37	2.84	3.82	3.25	0.57	-28.69	-29.08	0.39
1947	-0.9	1.24	-0.57	1.31	1.06	-2.94	1.08	0.91	0.17	-2.65	-3.32	0.67
1948	4.4	1.50	4.00	0.51	0.98	2.51	-2.18	-1.63	-0.55	1.08	0.71	0.37
1949	-0.5	1.80	-4.22	-0.93	-0.44	-2.85	0.08	-0.05	0.13	1.83	0.90	0.93
1947												
1st quarter	. . .	. . .	. . .	. . .	. . .	. . .	. . .	. . .	. . .	. . .	. . .	. . .
2nd quarter	-0.6	4.40	-4.78	-0.56	-0.88	-3.34	-0.71	-0.44	-0.27	0.47	0.16	0.31
3rd quarter	-0.3	0.96	-1.90	-0.67	2.71	-3.94	-0.17	-1.73	1.56	0.78	0.25	0.53
4th quarter	6.2	0.25	10.97	1.44	4.03	5.50	-4.33	-3.62	-0.72	-0.68	-1.07	0.39
1948												
1st quarter	6.5	1.55	6.45	2.65	-0.29	4.08	-3.06	-1.36	-1.70	1.57	1.56	0.01
2nd quarter	7.5	3.19	4.49	-1.23	1.41	4.31	-3.07	-2.43	-0.64	2.96	2.25	0.71
3rd quarter	2.2	0.38	0.93	0.20	-0.76	1.49	-0.33	0.49	-0.82	1.19	0.76	0.43
4th quarter	0.6	1.86	-3.09	1.04	-1.77	-2.35	-0.60	-0.81	0.21	2.44	1.86	0.58
1949												
1st quarter	-5.5	0.17	-10.06	-1.98	-1.68	-6.40	2.91	2.49	0.42	1.55	0.55	1.00
2nd quarter	-1.4	3.64	-8.00	-1.56	-0.34	-6.10	0.03	-0.16	0.19	2.88	1.41	1.47
3rd quarter	4.6	0.15	5.04	-1.82	1.76	5.10	-1.34	-1.90	0.56	0.70	-0.46	1.17
4th quarter	-3.7	3.34	-2.72	-0.50	2.71	-4.92	-2.92	-2.71	-0.20	-1.41	-1.98	0.57
1950												
1st quarter	17.2	4.11	14.27	1.26	2.95	10.06	-0.58	-0.21	-0.37	-0.62	-1.43	0.81
2nd quarter	12.7	4.11	7.70	3.34	2.68	1.69	-0.50	0.24	-0.75	1.43	1.15	0.28
3rd quarter	16.6	13.70	6.55	3.51	1.63	1.41	-2.83	0.45	-3.29	-0.83	-0.87	0.04
4th quarter	7.2	-7.89	9.83	-0.06	-1.38	11.27	1.27	1.31	-0.04	4.01	3.99	0.02
1951												
1st quarter	5.1	6.46	-9.01	-1.10	-1.45	-6.46	0.82	0.84	-0.01	6.88	7.16	-0.28
2nd quarter	6.8	-7.03	1.74	0.51	-3.44	4.66	2.38	1.82	0.57	9.72	9.25	0.46
3rd quarter	8.2	2.95	-5.75	0.48	-1.39	-4.85	2.00	0.51	1.49	9.02	8.88	0.14
4th quarter	0.7	1.34	-5.67	-0.68	0.17	-5.16	0.15	-0.18	0.33	4.85	4.89	-0.04
1952												
1st quarter	4.1	0.33	1.49	0.30	0.52	0.67	-0.78	1.16	-1.94	3.04	2.93	0.11
2nd quarter	0.4	4.59	-5.06	0.54	0.37	-5.97	-2.28	-2.25	-0.03	3.19	2.59	0.60
3rd quarter	2.7	1.10	3.13	-3.24	-0.22	6.59	-2.47	-1.39	-1.08	0.94	1.69	-0.74
4th quarter	13.9	8.84	4.49	3.16	1.14	0.19	-1.31	0.20	-1.52	1.86	1.19	0.67
1953												
1st quarter	7.7	2.94	1.20	1.94	0.34	-1.08	0.25	-0.18	0.43	3.32	2.72	0.59
2nd quarter	3.1	1.37	0.25	0.27	0.06	-0.09	-0.72	0.16	-0.88	2.16	2.20	-0.04
3rd quarter	-2.4	-0.72	-1.30	0.87	-0.78	-1.39	0.69	0.67	0.03	-1.09	-1.81	0.73
4th quarter	-6.2	-1.82	-4.44	-0.37	-0.17	-3.90	0.25	-0.54	0.79	-0.18	-0.87	0.69
1954												
1st quarter	-1.9	0.66	-0.21	-1.02	0.22	0.60	0.14	-0.75	0.88	-2.48	-3.52	1.03
2nd quarter	0.5	3.06	0.02	-0.30	1.33	-1.01	0.69	2.17	-1.49	-3.25	-3.38	0.12
3rd quarter	4.6	3.28	3.04	1.08	1.34	0.62	0.37	-0.60	0.97	-2.10	-2.96	0.86
4th quarter	8.3	5.24	2.89	-0.02	1.46	1.45	0.49	0.72	-0.23	-0.36	-0.52	0.16
1955												
1st quarter	12.0	5.71	6.51	0.74	1.80	3.97	-0.41	0.58	-0.98	0.22	-1.11	1.32
2nd quarter	6.8	4.76	4.05	2.26	0.35	1.45	-1.42	-0.45	-0.97	-0.61	-1.03	0.41
3rd quarter	5.5	3.04	0.94	1.90	-0.56	-0.41	0.71	1.06	-0.34	0.76	0.79	-0.03
4th quarter	2.2	3.16	1.37	1.03	-1.03	1.37	-0.58	0.05	-0.63	-1.70	-1.89	0.19
1956												
1st quarter	-1.8	0.39	-2.40	-0.84	-0.63	-0.93	0.07	0.82	-0.75	0.12	-0.23	0.35
2nd quarter	3.2	0.81	-0.79	0.57	-0.16	-1.20	1.28	1.23	0.05	1.88	1.48	0.40
3rd quarter	-0.5	0.53	-0.77	0.27	-0.45	-0.59	0.44	0.64	-0.20	-0.70	-0.86	0.16
4th quarter	6.7	3.43	-0.68	-0.11	-0.35	-0.22	1.68	0.91	0.77	2.27	1.93	0.34
1957												
1st quarter	2.5	1.69	-0.94	0.28	-0.30	-0.92	-0.01	1.36	-1.36	1.74	0.93	0.81
2nd quarter	-1.0	0.43	-0.08	-0.10	-0.48	0.51	-0.82	-0.63	-0.19	-0.49	-0.77	0.28
3rd quarter	3.9	2.00	1.41	0.90	-0.26	0.77	-0.26	-0.57	0.31	0.77	0.29	0.48
4th quarter	-4.1	0.14	-5.35	-1.03	-0.03	-4.28	-0.63	-0.57	-0.07	1.69	0.86	0.84

. . . = Not available.

Table 1-4B. Contributions to Percent Change in Real Gross Domestic Product: Historical Data—*Continued*

(Percent; percentage points.)

NIPA Table 1.1.2

Year and quarter	Percent change at seasonally adjusted annual rate, real GDP	Percentage points at seasonally adjusted annual rates										
		Personal consumption expenditures	Gross private domestic investment				Exports and imports of goods and services			Government consumption expenditures and gross investment		
			Total	Fixed investment		Change in private inventories	Net exports	Exports	Imports	Total	Federal	State and local
				Nonresidential	Residential							
1958												
1st quarter	-10.4	-3.31	-4.27	-2.82	-0.72	-0.72	-2.11	-1.89	-0.22	-0.71	-1.70	0.99
2nd quarter	2.5	2.18	-1.35	-1.63	0.05	0.24	-0.65	0.12	-0.77	2.30	1.78	0.52
3rd quarter	9.7	4.37	4.43	-0.53	1.34	3.62	0.29	0.10	0.19	0.63	-0.18	0.80
4th quarter	9.7	3.56	5.24	1.30	2.03	1.90	-1.00	-0.01	-0.99	1.86	1.19	0.67
1959												
1st quarter	8.3	4.86	3.78	1.07	2.33	0.38	0.55	1.16	-0.61	-0.84	-1.14	0.30
2nd quarter	10.5	4.08	5.47	1.09	0.80	3.59	-0.32	0.63	-0.94	1.25	1.15	0.11
3rd quarter	-0.5	2.69	-4.52	1.13	-0.43	-5.22	0.35	0.58	-0.23	1.00	0.97	0.03
4th quarter	1.4	0.33	2.06	-0.15	-0.64	2.85	-0.03	-0.48	0.45	-0.95	-0.77	-0.18
1960												
1st quarter	9.3	2.45	6.67	1.46	0.63	4.58	1.69	2.29	-0.60	-1.53	-2.15	0.62
2nd quarter	-1.9	3.14	-6.86	0.60	-1.76	-5.70	1.17	1.26	-0.09	0.70	-0.15	0.86
3rd quarter	0.7	-1.01	-0.40	-0.94	-0.60	1.14	0.02	-0.53	0.55	2.04	1.50	0.54
4th quarter	-5.0	0.36	-7.26	-0.18	-0.02	-7.06	1.25	0.43	0.82	0.62	0.20	0.42
1961												
1st quarter	2.4	-0.05	1.40	-0.76	0.07	2.08	-0.07	-0.14	0.07	1.12	-0.09	1.21
2nd quarter	7.7	3.82	4.12	0.76	0.07	3.29	-0.48	-0.28	-0.20	0.23	0.49	-0.25
3rd quarter	6.6	1.26	4.83	0.30	1.02	3.50	-1.18	-0.10	-1.07	1.72	1.39	0.32
4th quarter	8.4	5.05	1.17	1.20	0.66	-0.69	0.22	0.62	-0.40	1.95	0.89	1.05
1962												
1st quarter	7.4	2.67	3.67	0.82	0.36	2.49	-0.56	-0.05	-0.51	1.59	1.86	-0.27
2nd quarter	4.5	3.05	-0.54	1.06	0.62	-2.22	1.51	1.87	-0.37	0.48	0.21	0.27
3rd quarter	3.7	2.02	1.11	0.46	-0.02	0.66	-1.39	-1.17	-0.21	2.01	1.53	0.48
4th quarter	1.0	3.52	-2.04	-0.25	-0.03	-1.76	-0.63	-0.42	-0.21	0.13	-0.28	0.41
1963												
1st quarter	5.3	1.72	3.26	-0.04	0.71	2.59	0.86	0.45	0.40	-0.50	-1.23	0.72
2nd quarter	5.1	2.40	0.92	1.14	1.44	-1.66	1.88	2.26	-0.39	-0.09	-0.44	0.35
3rd quarter	7.7	3.42	2.08	1.10	0.39	0.58	-1.53	-1.11	-0.42	3.78	2.75	1.03
4th quarter	3.1	2.06	0.79	1.19	0.63	-1.03	1.04	0.98	0.06	-0.81	-1.35	0.54
1964												
1st quarter	9.3	4.94	2.68	0.93	1.31	0.44	1.29	1.26	0.03	0.38	-0.21	0.59
2nd quarter	4.7	4.35	-0.24	0.94	-1.10	-0.08	-0.02	0.35	-0.37	0.58	-0.31	0.89
3rd quarter	5.5	4.58	1.48	1.28	-0.34	0.54	-0.60	-0.16	-0.44	0.08	-0.35	0.43
4th quarter	1.1	0.71	0.47	0.81	-0.37	0.03	0.17	0.62	-0.45	-0.23	-0.65	0.42
1965												
1st quarter	10.2	5.63	6.32	2.68	0.08	3.57	-1.65	-2.29	0.65	-0.12	-0.51	0.39
2nd quarter	5.5	2.78	-0.02	1.54	0.15	-1.72	1.67	3.58	-1.91	1.12	0.12	1.00
3rd quarter	8.4	4.32	2.41	1.58	0.08	0.74	-1.31	-1.25	-0.07	2.95	1.82	1.13
4th quarter	10.0	7.03	0.45	1.80	-0.41	-0.94	0.64	1.49	-0.85	1.88	1.29	0.59
1966												
1st quarter	10.2	3.72	5.68	1.86	0.42	3.40	-0.82	-0.36	-0.45	1.61	1.10	0.51
2nd quarter	1.3	0.63	-1.22	0.65	-1.47	-0.40	0.44	0.89	-0.45	1.49	1.18	0.31
3rd quarter	2.7	2.79	-0.63	0.52	-0.55	-0.60	-1.82	-0.80	-1.02	2.33	1.86	0.46
4th quarter	3.3	1.02	0.35	-0.11	-1.70	2.16	0.48	0.67	-0.20	1.43	0.39	1.04
1967												
1st quarter	3.6	1.42	-1.77	-0.91	-0.43	-0.43	0.13	0.41	-0.28	3.78	3.27	0.52
2nd quarter	0.1	3.30	-2.68	-0.15	1.57	-4.11	-0.03	-0.20	0.17	-0.51	-0.74	0.23
3rd quarter	3.2	1.27	1.74	-0.21	0.77	1.18	-0.75	-0.51	-0.24	0.97	0.80	0.17
4th quarter	3.1	1.52	1.32	0.84	0.93	-0.45	-0.41	0.58	-0.99	0.65	-0.09	0.74
1968												
1st quarter	8.5	5.90	1.44	1.32	0.11	0.01	-0.54	0.60	-1.14	1.70	0.94	0.76
2nd quarter	7.0	3.80	2.57	-0.72	0.43	2.87	0.12	0.42	-0.31	0.48	-0.36	0.84
3rd quarter	2.8	4.60	-2.06	0.52	0.30	-2.88	0.01	1.22	-1.21	0.21	-0.41	0.62
4th quarter	1.7	1.13	0.63	1.18	0.21	-0.76	-0.10	-0.27	0.17	0.09	-0.29	0.37
1969												
1st quarter	6.5	2.77	4.13	1.22	0.64	2.28	-0.57	-2.52	1.95	0.12	-0.24	0.36
2nd quarter	1.2	1.56	-0.50	0.44	-0.19	-0.75	0.50	4.08	-3.58	-0.38	-0.74	0.36
3rd quarter	2.6	1.18	1.50	1.13	-0.14	0.51	-0.25	-0.53	0.28	0.12	0.03	0.09
4th quarter	-1.9	1.94	-3.45	-0.25	-1.27	-1.93	0.98	0.74	0.24	-1.34	-1.25	-0.10
1970												
1st quarter	-0.6	1.51	-1.89	-0.23	0.03	-1.68	0.26	0.19	0.07	-0.51	-0.92	0.41
2nd quarter	0.7	1.15	0.19	-0.24	-1.08	1.50	0.57	0.98	-0.41	-1.18	-1.42	0.24
3rd quarter	3.6	2.22	1.01	0.20	0.80	0.01	-0.02	-0.07	0.05	0.40	-0.64	1.04
4th quarter	-4.2	-0.61	-3.47	-1.60	1.62	-3.49	-0.12	0.22	-0.33	0.02	-0.23	0.24
1971												
1st quarter	11.5	4.97	7.51	0.36	0.94	6.22	0.39	0.12	0.27	-1.38	-1.63	0.24
2nd quarter	2.3	2.32	1.89	0.57	1.80	-0.48	-1.65	-0.04	-1.60	-0.28	-0.60	0.32
3rd quarter	3.2	2.01	0.85	0.18	0.97	-0.30	0.43	0.92	-0.49	-0.06	-0.18	0.12
4th quarter	1.1	4.13	-1.98	0.92	0.79	-3.70	-0.36	-1.93	1.57	-0.67	-1.27	0.60
1972												
1st quarter	7.3	3.36	4.54	1.49	1.43	1.63	-0.88	2.24	-3.12	0.32	0.16	0.16
2nd quarter	9.8	4.80	4.21	0.78	0.45	2.98	0.23	-0.67	0.90	0.59	0.68	-0.09
3rd quarter	3.9	3.81	1.04	0.69	0.05	0.30	0.82	1.30	-0.48	-1.78	-2.16	0.38
4th quarter	6.8	5.84	0.47	2.18	0.80	-2.52	-0.11	0.96	-1.07	0.56	-0.10	0.66
1973												
1st quarter	10.6	4.63	4.48	1.99	0.79	1.69	0.61	1.74	-1.13	0.91	0.69	0.22
2nd quarter	4.7	-0.13	3.35	1.75	-1.19	2.80	1.96	1.20	0.75	-0.47	-0.55	0.08
3rd quarter	-2.1	0.87	-2.73	0.73	-0.95	-2.51	0.78	0.06	0.71	-1.04	-1.52	0.48
4th quarter	3.9	-0.71	2.83	0.34	-1.03	3.52	1.16	1.38	-0.22	0.60	0.03	0.57

Table 1-4B. Contributions to Percent Change in Real Gross Domestic Product: Historical Data—*Continued*

(Percent; percentage points.)

NIPA Table 1.1.2

Year and quarter	Percent change at seasonally adjusted annual rate, real GDP	Personal consump-tion expen-ditures	Gross private domestic investment				Exports and imports of goods and services			Government consumption expenditures and gross investment		
			Total	Fixed investment		Change in private inventories	Net exports	Exports	Imports	Total	Federal	State and local
				Nonresi-dential	Residential							
1974												
1st quarter	-3.5	-2.13	-4.40	-0.06	-1.50	-2.84	1.39	0.38	1.01	1.68	1.07	0.61
2nd quarter	1.0	0.89	-0.29	-0.10	-0.83	0.64	-0.14	1.56	-1.70	0.57	-0.05	0.62
3rd quarter	-3.9	1.07	-3.88	-0.50	-0.59	-2.78	-1.26	-1.87	0.61	0.17	0.21	-0.05
4th quarter	-1.6	-3.61	0.48	-1.25	-2.31	4.04	1.23	0.87	0.36	0.33	0.29	0.04
1975												
1st quarter	-4.8	2.13	-11.84	-2.73	-0.94	-8.17	3.81	0.25	3.56	1.12	-0.36	1.49
2nd quarter	3.1	4.24	-2.03	-1.13	0.33	-1.23	1.52	-1.04	2.56	-0.63	-0.26	-0.37
3rd quarter	6.9	3.67	4.53	0.40	1.05	3.09	-2.88	-0.56	-2.32	1.60	0.95	0.65
4th quarter	5.3	2.69	1.62	0.37	0.68	0.57	0.26	1.81	-1.56	0.76	0.11	0.66
1976												
1st quarter	9.4	5.07	6.20	0.72	1.64	3.84	-2.11	-0.23	-1.89	0.25	-0.32	0.57
2nd quarter	3.0	2.29	2.74	0.47	0.49	1.77	-1.05	0.32	-1.37	-0.94	-0.08	-0.86
3rd quarter	2.0	2.66	0.14	0.90	-0.29	-0.47	-0.39	0.94	-1.33	-0.43	-0.09	-0.34
4th quarter	2.9	3.32	0.42	0.85	2.25	-2.68	-0.77	0.34	-1.11	-0.04	0.11	-0.15
1977												
1st quarter	4.7	2.98	3.09	1.70	0.61	0.78	-2.13	-0.52	-1.62	0.79	0.32	0.46
2nd quarter	8.2	1.49	5.23	1.32	2.34	1.57	0.57	0.88	-0.30	0.89	0.61	0.29
3rd quarter	7.4	2.44	3.97	1.00	-0.07	3.04	0.77	0.25	0.52	0.17	0.22	-0.05
4th quarter	-0.1	3.73	-1.99	1.56	-0.30	-3.25	-1.53	-1.03	-0.51	-0.29	-0.36	0.07
1978												
1st quarter	1.4	1.41	1.62	0.54	0.10	0.98	-1.75	0.67	-2.42	0.08	0.09	-0.01
2nd quarter	16.7	5.60	5.63	4.09	1.11	0.42	3.20	3.27	-0.07	2.25	0.86	1.39
3rd quarter	4.0	1.03	2.47	1.75	0.32	0.40	-0.14	0.34	-0.48	0.62	0.11	0.51
4th quarter	5.4	1.99	1.88	1.63	-0.08	0.33	0.81	1.31	-0.50	0.72	0.29	0.43
1979												
1st quarter	0.7	1.24	-0.01	1.04	-0.54	-0.51	0.14	0.03	0.10	-0.70	0.04	-0.74
2nd quarter	0.4	-0.16	-0.18	-0.21	-0.42	0.46	-0.10	0.09	-0.19	0.82	0.40	0.41
3rd quarter	2.9	2.41	-1.51	1.56	-0.27	-2.80	1.89	1.25	0.64	0.12	-0.05	0.16
4th quarter	1.1	0.62	-1.43	0.08	-0.84	-0.67	1.41	2.24	-0.83	0.50	-0.01	0.51
1980												
1st quarter	1.3	-0.48	-0.55	0.54	-1.65	0.56	1.07	1.03	0.04	1.26	1.06	0.20
2nd quarter	-7.9	-5.68	-6.63	-2.69	-3.63	-0.31	4.08	0.75	3.33	0.27	0.88	-0.61
3rd quarter	-0.7	2.67	-5.31	0.37	0.28	-5.96	3.04	-0.07	3.11	-1.14	-0.48	-0.67
4th quarter	7.6	3.43	6.55	1.09	1.64	3.82	-2.31	-0.19	-2.12	-0.06	0.14	-0.20
1981												
1st quarter	8.6	1.45	6.93	0.87	-0.30	6.37	-0.91	0.84	-1.75	1.09	0.74	0.36
2nd quarter	-3.2	0.02	-3.55	1.06	-0.58	-4.03	0.19	0.26	-0.07	0.19	1.04	-0.86
3rd quarter	4.9	1.04	4.42	1.33	-1.28	4.37	-0.35	-0.82	0.47	-0.16	-0.02	-0.14
4th quarter	-4.9	-1.85	-2.88	1.36	-1.55	-2.70	-0.92	0.18	-1.10	0.76	0.41	0.35
1982												
1st quarter	-6.4	1.62	-7.50	-1.25	-0.79	-5.47	-0.49	-1.65	1.16	-0.03	0.10	-0.13
2nd quarter	2.2	0.90	-0.05	-1.98	-0.42	2.35	0.84	0.20	0.63	0.50	0.36	0.14
3rd quarter	-1.5	1.92	-0.72	-1.82	-0.04	1.15	-3.31	-1.61	-1.69	0.57	0.57	0.00
4th quarter	0.3	4.64	-5.66	-1.09	0.92	-5.48	-0.10	-1.57	1.47	1.44	1.13	0.31
1983												
1st quarter	5.1	2.54	2.20	-1.02	2.28	0.94	-0.30	0.51	-0.81	0.63	0.47	0.15
2nd quarter	9.3	5.22	5.87	0.52	1.84	3.51	-2.54	0.11	-2.65	0.75	0.86	-0.11
3rd quarter	8.1	4.66	4.30	2.02	1.68	0.60	-2.32	0.48	-2.80	1.48	1.12	0.36
4th quarter	8.5	4.20	6.84	2.98	0.77	3.09	-1.17	0.65	-1.82	-1.35	-1.34	-0.02
1984												
1st quarter	8.0	2.35	7.15	1.55	0.52	5.07	-2.37	0.67	-3.04	0.86	0.35	0.51
2nd quarter	7.1	3.75	2.44	2.39	0.35	-0.30	-0.89	0.78	-1.67	1.79	1.22	0.56
3rd quarter	3.9	2.02	1.67	1.62	-0.17	0.21	-0.36	0.68	-1.05	0.62	-0.13	0.75
4th quarter	3.3	3.38	-1.26	1.22	0.02	-2.50	-0.58	0.62	-1.19	1.75	1.27	0.48
1985												
1st quarter	3.8	4.34	-2.38	0.62	-0.06	-2.94	0.91	0.01	0.90	0.95	0.43	0.52
2nd quarter	3.4	2.35	1.24	0.74	0.14	0.35	-2.01	-0.12	-1.88	1.85	0.95	0.90
3rd quarter	6.4	4.91	-0.68	-0.75	0.23	-0.16	-0.01	-0.44	0.43	2.18	1.32	0.85
4th quarter	3.1	0.54	2.72	0.85	0.42	1.45	-0.68	0.81	-1.49	0.50	-0.02	0.51
1986												
1st quarter	3.9	2.12	-0.08	-0.68	0.78	-0.17	0.95	0.85	0.10	0.90	-0.21	1.11
2nd quarter	1.6	2.72	-1.51	-1.22	1.04	-1.34	-1.37	0.28	-1.65	1.78	1.22	0.55
3rd quarter	3.9	4.52	-2.08	-0.70	0.31	-1.69	-0.47	0.63	-1.10	1.94	1.50	0.44
4th quarter	1.9	1.58	0.12	0.44	-0.04	-0.29	0.72	1.06	-0.33	-0.48	-0.60	0.13
1987												
1st quarter	2.2	-0.37	2.00	-1.29	-0.06	3.34	0.23	0.03	0.20	0.38	0.26	0.12
2nd quarter	4.3	3.52	0.12	1.03	0.09	-1.00	0.10	1.17	-1.08	0.58	0.58	0.00
3rd quarter	3.5	2.94	0.08	1.41	-0.06	-1.27	0.45	1.31	-0.86	0.04	0.08	-0.04
4th quarter	7.0	0.67	5.10	-0.09	0.10	5.09	0.18	1.18	-1.00	1.08	0.63	0.45
1988												
1st quarter	2.1	4.34	-3.87	0.35	-0.42	-3.80	1.99	1.78	0.20	-0.37	-1.01	0.64
2nd quarter	5.2	1.92	1.59	1.10	0.15	0.34	1.47	0.95	0.52	0.26	-0.34	0.60
3rd quarter	2.1	2.06	0.40	0.24	0.01	0.15	-0.36	0.64	-1.00	-0.02	-0.25	0.23
4th quarter	5.5	3.11	0.88	0.48	0.16	0.24	-0.21	1.07	-1.29	1.67	1.09	0.58
1989												
1st quarter	3.8	0.96	2.46	0.75	-0.12	1.84	0.86	1.04	-0.18	-0.48	-0.72	0.24
2nd quarter	3.0	1.18	-0.78	0.63	-0.54	-0.86	1.38	1.56	-0.19	1.25	0.80	0.45
3rd quarter	3.2	2.72	-0.76	1.26	-0.19	-1.83	0.48	0.41	0.07	0.77	0.35	0.42
4th quarter	0.9	1.29	-0.67	-0.67	-0.36	0.37	-0.18	0.58	-0.76	0.43	-0.17	0.60

Table 1-4B. Contributions to Percent Change in Real Gross Domestic Product: Historical Data—*Continued*

(Percent; percentage points.)

NIPA Table 1.1.2

Year and quarter	Percent change at seasonally adjusted annual rate, real GDP	Personal consump-tion expen-ditures	Gross private domestic investment				Exports and imports of goods and services			Government consumption expenditures and gross investment		
			Total	Fixed investment		Change in private inventories	Net exports	Exports	Imports	Total	Federal	State and local
				Nonresi-dential	Residential							
1990												
1st quarter	4.2	2.11	0.62	0.58	0.17	-0.13	0.26	1.61	-1.35	1.26	0.53	0.73
2nd quarter	1.6	0.87	0.03	-0.77	-0.64	1.44	0.58	0.51	0.07	0.12	0.04	0.08
3rd quarter	0.0	0.99	-1.41	0.26	-0.91	-0.76	0.44	0.28	0.16	-0.03	-0.31	0.29
4th quarter	-3.5	-2.08	-3.68	-0.83	-0.83	-2.02	1.50	0.33	1.17	0.81	0.31	0.50
1991												
1st quarter	-1.9	-0.79	-2.21	-1.11	-0.84	-0.26	0.75	0.28	0.46	0.33	0.27	0.06
2nd quarter	2.7	2.01	-0.23	-0.41	0.31	-0.12	0.65	1.40	-0.75	0.29	0.10	0.19
3rd quarter	1.7	1.01	1.32	-0.40	0.56	1.16	-0.25	0.91	-1.16	-0.39	-0.66	0.27
4th quarter	1.6	-0.11	2.02	-0.23	0.30	1.95	0.00	0.91	-0.91	-0.33	-0.67	0.34
1992												
1st quarter	4.5	4.61	-1.24	-0.20	0.72	-1.77	0.45	0.74	-0.29	0.65	0.03	0.62
2nd quarter	4.3	1.61	3.45	1.48	0.56	1.40	-0.67	0.01	-0.68	-0.07	-0.02	-0.05
3rd quarter	4.2	2.96	0.59	0.77	0.04	-0.22	0.21	0.87	-0.66	0.43	0.39	0.03
4th quarter	4.3	3.26	1.78	1.16	0.51	0.12	-0.80	0.21	-1.01	0.03	0.02	0.01
1993												
1st quarter	0.7	1.06	1.36	0.25	0.07	1.05	-0.83	0.08	-0.92	-0.85	-1.03	0.18
2nd quarter	2.6	2.56	0.48	1.04	0.18	-0.73	-0.40	0.48	-0.88	-0.06	-0.46	0.40
3rd quarter	2.1	2.92	-0.03	0.43	0.54	-1.00	-0.69	-0.13	-0.57	-0.07	-0.33	0.26
4th quarter	5.4	2.44	3.00	1.66	0.82	0.52	-0.45	1.26	-1.71	0.41	0.18	0.22
1994												
1st quarter	4.0	3.04	2.49	0.39	0.36	1.75	-0.62	0.39	-1.02	-0.96	-1.09	0.14
2nd quarter	5.6	2.04	3.53	0.81	0.57	2.16	-0.32	1.31	-1.63	0.34	-0.15	0.49
3rd quarter	2.6	2.16	-1.13	0.74	-0.19	-1.68	0.26	1.53	-1.27	1.32	0.80	0.51
4th quarter	4.5	2.66	2.89	1.80	-0.23	1.32	-0.39	0.91	-1.29	-0.65	-0.81	0.16
1995												
1st quarter	1.0	0.29	0.69	1.69	-0.38	-0.62	-0.28	0.74	-1.02	0.28	-0.08	0.36
2nd quarter	0.9	2.19	-1.69	0.27	-0.53	-1.43	0.12	0.58	-0.45	0.25	-0.12	0.36
3rd quarter	3.4	2.42	-0.59	0.27	0.49	-1.35	1.72	1.88	-0.16	-0.15	-0.18	0.03
4th quarter	2.8	1.91	1.68	0.85	0.37	0.45	0.03	0.65	-0.62	-0.81	-1.04	0.24
1996												
1st quarter	2.8	2.49	0.76	1.07	0.44	-0.74	-0.99	0.58	-1.57	0.50	0.59	-0.08
2nd quarter	7.1	3.13	3.18	1.26	0.72	1.20	-0.30	0.78	-1.08	1.09	0.42	0.67
3rd quarter	3.5	1.64	3.13	1.46	-0.05	1.72	-1.18	0.38	-1.56	-0.07	-0.47	0.40
4th quarter	4.4	2.22	-0.19	1.21	-0.18	-1.22	1.80	2.74	-0.94	0.60	-0.06	0.66
1997												
1st quarter	3.1	2.73	1.47	1.15	0.06	0.25	-1.19	0.87	-2.05	0.10	-0.35	0.45
2nd quarter	6.1	1.13	4.14	1.13	0.21	2.80	0.18	1.81	-1.63	0.61	0.47	0.15
3rd quarter	5.1	4.56	1.21	2.32	0.08	-1.19	-0.72	1.09	-1.81	0.08	-0.08	0.16
4th quarter	3.1	3.06	1.07	0.34	0.17	0.56	-1.16	-0.07	-1.08	0.12	-0.03	0.15
1998												
1st quarter	3.8	2.67	3.22	1.57	0.30	1.36	-1.66	0.22	-1.89	-0.40	-0.78	0.38
2nd quarter	3.6	4.62	-0.82	1.68	0.51	-3.02	-1.66	-0.51	-1.16	1.51	0.67	0.85
3rd quarter	5.4	3.61	1.96	0.69	0.53	0.75	-0.86	-0.19	-0.67	0.67	-0.19	0.86
4th quarter	7.1	4.19	2.24	1.56	0.43	0.25	0.02	1.61	-1.59	0.65	0.25	0.40
1999												
1st quarter	3.6	2.67	2.16	1.08	0.11	0.98	-1.59	-0.33	-1.27	0.36	-0.15	0.52
2nd quarter	3.2	4.26	-0.26	1.33	0.20	-1.79	-1.14	0.48	-1.62	0.30	0.01	0.29
3rd quarter	5.2	3.31	1.76	1.41	0.15	0.19	-0.80	1.11	-1.91	0.92	0.50	0.41
4th quarter	7.4	3.93	2.53	0.17	0.23	2.14	-0.22	1.08	-1.30	1.14	0.55	0.59
2000												
1st quarter	1.1	4.15	-0.99	1.83	0.14	-2.97	-1.53	0.74	-2.27	-0.58	-0.95	0.38
2nd quarter	8.0	2.67	4.91	1.89	-0.12	3.14	-0.50	1.26	-1.75	0.96	0.94	0.02
3rd quarter	0.3	2.67	-1.14	0.55	-0.32	-1.37	-0.98	1.07	-2.05	-0.22	-0.46	0.24
4th quarter	2.4	2.43	0.05	0.17	0.02	-0.14	-0.30	-0.34	0.04	0.22	-0.10	0.32
2001												
1st quarter	-1.3	1.08	-3.72	-0.52	0.08	-3.28	0.30	-0.56	0.86	1.04	0.49	0.55
2nd quarter	2.7	1.03	-0.19	-1.33	0.25	0.89	0.33	-1.39	1.72	1.48	0.50	0.97
3rd quarter	-1.1	1.20	-1.37	-0.80	0.10	-0.67	-0.79	-2.11	1.31	-0.13	0.16	-0.29
4th quarter	1.4	4.33	-3.71	-1.49	-0.16	-2.06	-0.48	-1.09	0.61	1.27	0.29	0.99
2002												
1st quarter	3.5	0.97	2.08	-1.03	0.49	2.62	-0.70	0.58	-1.28	1.12	0.58	0.54
2nd quarter	2.1	1.41	0.78	-0.69	0.46	1.01	-0.76	1.00	-1.76	0.71	0.58	0.13
3rd quarter	2.0	1.89	0.17	-0.21	0.11	0.26	-0.62	0.26	-0.88	0.60	0.40	0.20
4th quarter	0.1	0.99	-0.01	-0.79	0.30	0.48	-1.35	-0.39	-0.97	0.51	0.44	0.07
2003												
1st quarter	1.7	1.42	0.04	-0.18	0.19	0.03	0.36	-0.34	0.70	-0.14	0.02	-0.16
2nd quarter	3.4	2.80	0.37	1.06	0.46	-1.15	-0.89	-0.11	-0.77	1.15	1.30	-0.15
3rd quarter	6.7	3.84	2.27	0.94	1.04	0.29	0.39	1.01	-0.62	0.25	0.04	0.20
4th quarter	3.7	1.55	2.37	0.59	0.57	1.20	-0.30	1.74	-2.04	0.06	0.20	-0.14
2004												
1st quarter	2.7	2.49	0.36	-0.29	0.19	0.46	-0.54	0.92	-1.46	0.35	0.35	0.01
2nd quarter	2.6	1.26	2.80	1.11	0.83	0.86	-1.74	0.61	-2.35	0.27	0.15	0.12
3rd quarter	3.0	2.45	0.87	1.13	0.23	-0.49	-0.60	0.29	-0.89	0.28	0.48	-0.21
4th quarter	3.3	3.03	1.39	0.91	0.19	0.29	-0.65	0.91	-1.56	-0.46	-0.35	-0.11
2005												
1st quarter	4.2	2.25	1.46	0.37	0.43	0.66	0.40	0.76	-0.36	0.08	0.12	-0.04
2nd quarter	1.8	2.75	-1.23	0.61	0.56	-2.40	0.19	0.87	-0.68	0.08	0.02	0.06
3rd quarter	3.2	2.12	0.77	0.61	0.25	-0.09	-0.36	0.01	-0.37	0.68	0.65	0.04
4th quarter	2.1	0.68	2.48	0.27	0.00	2.21	-0.75	1.03	-1.78	-0.34	-0.47	0.13

Table 1-4B. Contributions to Percent Change in Real Gross Domestic Product: Historical Data—*Continued*

(Percent; percentage points.)

NIPA Table 1.1.2

Year and quarter	Percent change at seasonally adjusted annual rate, real GDP	Percentage points at seasonally adjusted annual rates										
		Personal consumption expenditures	Gross private domestic investment				Exports and imports of goods and services			Government consumption expenditures and gross investment		
			Total	Fixed investment		Change in private inventories	Net exports	Exports	Imports	Total	Federal	State and local
				Nonresidential	Residential							
2006												
1st quarter	5.1	2.85	1.11	1.87	-0.27	-0.50	0.44	1.64	-1.20	0.75	0.79	-0.04
2nd quarter	1.6	1.66	-0.10	0.81	-1.13	0.22	0.01	0.73	-0.71	0.06	-0.24	0.30
3rd quarter	0.1	1.66	-1.00	0.48	-1.36	-0.12	-0.72	0.06	-0.78	0.11	-0.03	0.14
4th quarter	2.7	2.60	-2.01	0.24	-1.18	-1.07	1.95	1.84	0.10	0.22	0.08	0.14
2007												
1st quarter	0.5	1.56	-0.68	0.72	-0.91	-0.49	-0.25	0.71	-0.96	-0.09	-0.34	0.25
2nd quarter	3.6	1.09	1.49	1.20	-0.62	0.90	0.42	0.76	-0.33	0.64	0.48	0.16
3rd quarter	3.0	1.24	-0.50	1.03	-1.25	-0.28	1.55	1.72	-0.17	0.67	0.64	0.02
4th quarter	1.7	0.83	-1.58	0.62	-1.43	-0.77	2.22	1.32	0.90	0.23	0.08	0.16
2008												
1st quarter	-1.8	-0.70	-2.02	-0.10	-1.26	-0.66	0.38	0.65	-0.28	0.58	0.66	-0.08
2nd quarter	1.3	-0.08	-0.94	-0.25	-0.55	-0.14	2.00	1.56	0.44	0.34	0.35	-0.01
3rd quarter	-3.7	-2.67	-2.63	-1.18	-0.73	-0.73	0.79	-0.47	1.25	0.85	0.84	0.01
4th quarter	-8.9	-3.53	-5.59	-2.84	-1.21	-1.54	-0.12	-2.97	2.84	0.35	0.69	-0.34
2009												
1st quarter	-6.7	-1.02	-7.76	-3.90	-1.19	-2.66	2.44	-3.82	6.26	-0.33	-0.25	-0.08
2nd quarter	-0.7	-1.28	-2.84	-1.66	-0.60	-0.58	2.21	-0.02	2.24	1.21	1.09	0.12
3rd quarter	1.7	1.66	0.35	-0.29	0.42	0.21	-0.59	1.49	-2.08	0.28	0.48	-0.19
4th quarter	3.8	0.33	3.51	-0.33	-0.10	3.93	0.15	2.51	-2.36	-0.18	0.18	-0.37
2010												
1st quarter	3.9	1.92	3.25	0.56	-0.41	3.10	-0.97	0.86	-1.83	-0.26	0.23	-0.49
2nd quarter	3.8	2.05	2.92	1.62	0.50	0.79	-1.94	1.19	-3.13	0.77	0.71	0.05
3rd quarter	2.5	1.85	1.14	1.04	-0.76	0.86	-0.68	1.21	-1.89	0.20	0.26	-0.06
4th quarter	2.3	2.48	-0.91	0.82	0.06	-1.79	1.37	0.98	0.39	-0.58	-0.26	-0.33
2011												
1st quarter	0.4	1.47	0.47	0.20	-0.06	0.32	-0.34	1.01	-1.35	-1.23	-0.82	-0.41
2nd quarter	1.3	0.49	0.79	0.98	0.09	-0.28	0.24	0.48	-0.24	-0.18	0.16	-0.34
3rd quarter	1.8	1.24	0.17	1.49	0.03	-1.35	0.43	0.64	-0.21	-0.02	0.17	-0.19
4th quarter	3.0	1.47	2.59	0.53	0.25	1.81	-0.26	0.37	-0.63	-0.84	-0.58	-0.26

Table 1-5A. Chain-Type Quantity Indexes for Gross Domestic Product and Domestic Purchases: Recent Data

(Index numbers, 2005 = 100.)

NIPA Tables 1.1.3, 1.4.3, 2.3.3

Year and quarter	Gross domestic product, total	Personal consumption expenditures		Private fixed investment			Exports and imports of goods and services		Government consumption expenditures and gross investment			Gross domestic purchases
		Total	Excluding food and energy	Total	Nonresidential	Residential	Exports	Imports	Total	Federal	State and local	
1950	15.9	14.6	12.0	11.4	8.1	24.1	4.2	3.2	20.8	28.4	16.3	15.2
1951	17.1	14.8	12.2	10.9	8.5	20.1	5.1	3.4	28.4	47.2	16.5	16.3
1952	17.8	15.3	12.6	10.7	8.3	19.8	4.9	3.7	34.2	61.4	16.7	17.0
1953	18.6	16.0	13.2	11.4	9.1	20.5	4.6	4.0	36.6	66.3	17.6	17.9
1954	18.5	16.3	13.4	11.6	8.9	22.2	4.8	3.8	34.1	57.6	19.1	17.8
1955	19.8	17.5	14.5	13.1	9.9	25.8	5.3	4.3	32.9	52.4	20.5	19.0
1956	20.2	18.0	14.9	13.2	10.4	23.7	6.2	4.6	32.9	51.5	21.2	19.3
1957	20.6	18.5	15.2	13.0	10.6	22.2	6.7	4.8	34.4	53.3	22.4	19.7
1958	20.4	18.7	15.3	12.1	9.4	22.5	5.8	5.0	35.5	53.3	24.3	19.7
1959	21.9	19.7	16.3	13.8	10.2	28.2	6.4	5.6	36.7	55.0	25.2	21.1
1960	22.4	20.3	16.8	13.9	10.7	26.2	7.5	5.6	36.8	53.5	26.3	21.5
1961	22.9	20.7	17.2	13.9	10.7	26.2	7.6	5.6	38.6	55.7	28.0	22.0
1962	24.3	21.7	18.2	15.1	11.6	28.8	8.0	6.2	41.0	60.5	28.8	23.4
1963	25.4	22.6	19.1	16.3	12.2	32.1	8.5	6.4	42.0	60.5	30.6	24.3
1964	26.9	23.9	20.4	17.9	13.7	34.0	9.5	6.8	43.0	59.7	32.6	25.7
1965	28.6	25.5	21.8	19.7	16.1	33.0	9.8	7.5	44.3	59.7	34.8	27.4
1966	30.4	26.9	23.1	20.8	18.1	30.1	10.5	8.6	48.1	66.3	37.0	29.3
1967	31.2	27.7	23.8	20.5	17.9	29.1	10.7	9.2	51.8	72.9	38.9	30.1
1968	32.7	29.3	25.3	21.9	18.7	33.1	11.6	10.6	53.5	73.5	41.2	31.6
1969	33.7	30.4	26.3	23.2	20.1	34.1	12.1	11.2	53.3	71.0	42.6	32.6
1970	33.8	31.1	26.8	22.8	20.0	32.0	13.4	11.7	52.1	65.7	43.7	32.6
1971	34.9	32.3	28.0	24.5	20.0	40.8	13.7	12.3	50.9	60.7	45.1	33.7
1972	36.8	34.3	30.0	27.4	21.8	48.1	14.7	13.7	50.6	58.2	46.1	35.6
1973	38.9	36.0	31.8	29.9	25.0	47.8	17.5	14.3	50.4	55.7	47.4	37.4
1974	38.7	35.7	31.8	28.1	25.2	37.9	18.8	14.0	51.6	56.2	49.2	36.9
1975	38.6	36.5	32.5	25.0	22.7	33.0	18.7	12.4	52.8	56.4	51.0	36.5
1976	40.7	38.5	34.4	27.5	23.8	40.7	19.5	14.8	53.0	56.5	51.3	38.9
1977	42.6	40.1	36.0	31.5	26.5	49.5	20.0	16.5	53.6	57.6	51.5	40.9
1978	44.9	41.9	38.0	35.3	30.5	52.6	22.1	17.9	55.2	59.1	53.2	43.1
1979	46.3	42.9	39.1	37.3	33.5	50.7	24.3	18.2	56.2	60.5	54.0	44.2
1980	46.2	42.8	39.1	34.8	33.4	39.9	26.9	17.0	57.3	63.4	54.0	43.3
1981	47.4	43.4	39.9	35.6	35.3	36.7	27.3	17.4	57.9	66.4	52.9	44.5
1982	46.5	44.0	40.5	33.1	34.0	30.1	25.2	17.2	58.9	69.0	52.9	43.9
1983	48.6	46.5	43.2	35.5	33.6	42.5	24.5	19.4	61.0	73.6	53.5	46.5
1984	52.1	49.0	45.8	41.5	39.5	48.8	26.5	24.1	63.1	75.8	55.4	50.5
1985	54.2	51.6	48.5	43.7	42.1	49.6	27.3	25.7	67.5	81.8	58.9	52.7
1986	56.1	53.6	50.6	44.2	40.9	55.7	29.4	27.9	71.6	86.4	62.7	54.7
1987	57.9	55.3	52.5	44.5	40.9	56.8	32.6	29.5	73.3	89.5	63.6	56.3
1988	60.3	57.5	54.7	45.9	43.0	56.2	37.8	30.7	74.2	88.0	65.9	58.1
1989	62.4	59.2	56.4	47.3	45.4	54.5	42.2	32.0	76.2	89.4	68.3	59.8
1990	63.6	60.4	57.7	46.3	45.6	49.8	46.0	33.2	78.7	91.2	71.1	60.7
1991	63.4	60.5	57.7	43.3	43.2	45.0	49.0	33.1	79.5	91.0	72.6	60.2
1992	65.6	62.5	60.0	45.9	44.6	51.3	52.4	35.4	79.9	89.4	74.2	62.2
1993	67.5	64.7	62.3	49.8	48.5	55.5	54.1	38.5	79.3	85.8	75.2	64.3
1994	70.2	67.2	64.9	54.5	52.9	60.8	58.8	43.1	79.2	82.6	77.2	67.2
1995	72.0	69.0	66.8	58.0	58.5	58.9	64.8	46.5	79.7	80.4	79.2	68.8
1996	74.7	71.4	69.4	63.2	63.9	63.6	70.1	50.6	80.5	79.4	81.1	71.4
1997	78.0	74.1	72.3	69.0	71.7	64.8	78.5	57.4	82.0	78.6	84.0	74.8
1998	81.4	78.0	76.5	76.5	80.3	69.7	80.3	64.1	83.8	77.8	87.3	78.9
1999	85.3	82.2	80.9	83.7	88.6	74.1	83.8	71.5	86.8	79.3	91.2	83.4
2000	88.9	86.4	85.4	89.8	97.3	74.8	91.0	80.8	88.5	79.7	93.7	87.5
2001	89.8	88.7	88.0	88.1	94.6	75.3	85.9	78.5	91.9	82.9	97.2	88.5
2002	91.4	91.1	90.5	84.4	87.1	79.2	84.2	81.2	96.2	89.0	100.5	90.6
2003	93.8	93.7	93.2	87.4	88.3	85.7	85.5	84.8	98.3	94.8	100.4	93.2
2004	97.0	96.7	96.6	93.9	93.7	94.1	93.7	94.2	99.7	98.7	100.2	96.9
2005	100.0	100.0	100.0	100.0	100.0	100.0	100.0	100.0	100.0	100.0	100.0	100.0
2006	102.7	102.9	103.2	102.4	108.0	92.7	109.0	106.1	101.4	102.1	100.9	102.6
2007	104.6	105.2	105.8	100.4	115.0	75.4	119.1	108.7	102.7	103.4	102.3	103.8
2008	104.3	104.6	105.5	93.2	114.1	57.3	126.4	105.7	105.4	110.8	102.3	102.3
2009	100.6	102.7	103.3	75.7	93.8	44.6	114.5	91.4	107.2	117.5	101.4	97.8
2010	103.7	104.7	105.4	77.7	97.9	42.7	127.4	102.8	107.9	122.8	99.6	101.2
2011	105.5	107.0	108.1	83.0	106.5	42.1	135.9	107.9	105.6	120.4	97.3	102.8
2009												
1st quarter	100.3	102.7	103.4	78.5	97.4	45.8	111.2	91.5	105.9	113.6	101.6	97.8
2nd quarter	100.1	102.2	102.8	74.9	93.3	43.1	111.1	87.8	107.4	117.4	101.8	97.1
3rd quarter	100.6	102.8	103.4	75.0	92.6	44.9	114.7	91.2	107.8	119.1	101.4	97.7
4th quarter	101.5	102.9	103.4	74.3	91.7	44.5	120.9	94.9	107.5	119.8	100.7	98.5
2010												
1st quarter	102.5	103.6	104.1	74.5	93.0	42.7	123.1	97.8	107.2	120.6	99.7	99.7
2nd quarter	103.5	104.4	105.0	77.9	97.1	44.9	126.0	102.7	108.2	123.2	99.8	101.1
3rd quarter	104.1	105.0	105.6	78.4	99.7	41.4	129.1	105.7	108.5	124.1	99.7	101.8
4th quarter	104.7	106.0	106.7	79.8	101.8	41.7	131.6	105.1	107.7	123.2	99.0	102.1
2011												
1st quarter	104.8	106.5	107.5	80.1	102.3	41.4	134.1	107.2	106.1	120.2	98.2	102.2
2nd quarter	105.1	106.7	107.7	81.8	104.9	41.9	135.2	107.6	105.8	120.8	97.5	102.5
3rd quarter	105.6	107.2	108.2	84.4	108.8	42.0	136.8	107.9	105.8	121.4	97.1	102.8
4th quarter	106.4	107.7	109.1	85.7	110.2	43.2	137.7	108.9	104.7	119.2	96.6	103.6

Table 1-5B. Chain-Type Quantity Indexes for Gross Domestic Product and Domestic Purchases: Historical Data

(Index numbers, 2005 = 100.)

NIPA Tables 1.1.3, 1.4.3, 2.3.3

Year and quarter	Gross domestic product											Gross domestic purchases
	Gross domestic product, total	Personal consumption expenditures		Private fixed investment			Exports and imports of goods and services		Government consumption expenditures and gross investment			
		Total	Excluding food and energy	Total	Nonresidential	Residential	Exports	Imports	Total	Federal	State and local	
1929	7.7	8.4	7.0	6.3	5.5	9.8	2.9	2.4	6.2	2.9	10.6	7.4
1930	7.1	7.9	6.5	4.8	4.5	5.9	2.4	2.1	6.8	3.2	11.7	6.8
1931	6.6	7.7	6.2	3.3	2.9	5.0	2.0	1.8	7.1	3.3	12.2	6.4
1932	5.7	7.0	5.6	1.9	1.8	2.6	1.6	1.5	6.9	3.3	11.6	5.6
1933	5.7	6.8	5.4	1.7	1.6	2.1	1.6	1.6	6.6	4.1	10.4	5.5
1934	6.3	7.3	5.7	2.2	2.0	2.9	1.8	1.6	7.5	5.5	11.0	6.1
1935	6.8	7.7	6.1	2.9	2.6	4.1	1.8	2.1	7.7	5.6	11.3	6.7
1936	7.7	8.5	6.7	3.8	3.5	5.2	1.9	2.1	9.0	8.5	11.4	7.5
1937	8.1	8.9	6.9	4.5	4.2	5.7	2.4	2.4	8.6	7.7	11.4	7.9
1938	7.9	8.7	6.7	3.6	3.0	5.7	2.4	1.8	9.3	8.5	12.0	7.5
1939	8.5	9.2	7.2	4.3	3.4	8.1	2.6	1.9	10.1	9.1	13.2	8.2
1940	9.2	9.7	7.6	5.1	4.2	9.1	2.9	2.0	10.4	10.2	12.8	8.8
1941	10.8	10.4	8.2	5.9	5.0	9.7	3.0	2.4	17.2	26.8	12.0	10.4
1942	12.8	10.1	8.0	3.3	2.9	4.9	2.0	2.2	40.5	82.4	10.9	12.5
1943	14.9	10.4	8.5	2.5	2.4	2.9	1.7	2.8	60.2	130.3	9.9	14.7
1944	16.1	10.7	8.7	3.1	3.2	2.5	1.8	2.9	67.8	148.7	9.5	15.9
1945	15.9	11.4	9.2	4.3	4.6	2.9	2.5	3.1	59.2	127.7	9.9	15.6
1946	14.2	12.8	10.3	7.9	6.7	12.3	5.4	2.6	20.3	34.3	10.8	13.3
1947	14.1	13.0	10.5	9.5	7.8	15.9	6.1	2.4	17.3	25.4	12.3	13.0
1948	14.7	13.3	10.8	10.5	8.2	19.0	4.8	2.8	18.5	27.4	13.1	13.9
1949	14.6	13.7	11.2	9.6	7.5	17.6	4.8	2.7	20.8	30.0	15.1	13.8
1947												
1st quarter	14.0	12.8	. . .	9.3	7.9	14.6	6.5	2.5	17.2	25.5	12.0	12.9
2nd quarter	14.0	13.1	. . .	9.0	7.8	13.9	6.5	2.6	17.3	25.6	12.2	12.9
3rd quarter	14.0	13.1	. . .	9.4	7.6	16.0	6.1	2.3	17.5	25.6	12.5	12.9
4th quarter	14.2	13.1	. . .	10.2	7.8	19.1	5.4	2.4	17.2	24.7	12.7	13.3
1948												
1st quarter	14.4	13.2	. . .	10.5	8.3	18.9	5.2	2.7	17.5	25.6	12.6	13.6
2nd quarter	14.7	13.3	. . .	10.5	8.0	20.0	4.7	2.8	18.4	27.1	13.0	14.0
3rd quarter	14.8	13.3	. . .	10.4	8.1	19.3	4.8	3.0	18.7	27.7	13.2	14.0
4th quarter	14.8	13.5	. . .	10.3	8.3	17.9	4.6	2.9	19.5	29.2	13.6	14.1
1949												
1st quarter	14.6	13.5	. . .	9.7	7.9	16.6	5.2	2.8	20.1	29.8	14.1	13.8
2nd quarter	14.5	13.7	. . .	9.4	7.6	16.3	5.1	2.8	21.0	30.9	14.9	13.7
3rd quarter	14.7	13.7	. . .	9.4	7.2	17.7	4.7	2.7	21.2	30.5	15.5	13.9
4th quarter	14.6	13.9	. . .	9.7	7.1	19.8	4.1	2.7	20.8	29.0	15.8	13.9
1950												
1st quarter	15.2	14.1	. . .	10.3	7.3	22.1	4.0	2.8	20.4	27.6	16.2	14.5
2nd quarter	15.6	14.4	. . .	11.3	7.9	24.2	4.1	2.9	20.7	28.3	16.4	15.0
3rd quarter	16.2	15.1	. . .	12.1	8.6	25.6	4.2	3.6	20.3	27.3	16.4	15.7
4th quarter	16.5	14.7	. . .	11.9	8.6	24.4	4.5	3.6	21.6	30.5	16.4	15.9
1951												
1st quarter	16.7	15.0	. . .	11.4	8.4	23.1	4.7	3.6	23.9	36.4	16.2	16.0
2nd quarter	17.0	14.6	. . .	10.9	8.5	20.0	5.2	3.5	27.2	44.2	16.5	16.2
3rd quarter	17.3	14.8	. . .	10.7	8.6	18.7	5.3	3.2	30.3	51.8	16.6	16.5
4th quarter	17.4	14.8	. . .	10.6	8.4	18.9	5.3	3.1	32.0	56.2	16.6	16.5
1952												
1st quarter	17.5	14.9	. . .	10.7	8.5	19.4	5.6	3.5	33.0	58.6	16.6	16.7
2nd quarter	17.6	15.2	. . .	10.9	8.6	19.7	4.9	3.5	34.1	60.9	17.0	16.8
3rd quarter	17.7	15.2	. . .	10.2	7.8	19.5	4.6	3.7	34.5	62.5	16.5	17.0
4th quarter	18.3	15.8	. . .	11.0	8.5	20.6	4.6	4.0	35.1	63.5	16.9	17.6
1953												
1st quarter	18.6	16.0	. . .	11.4	8.9	20.9	4.5	3.9	36.3	65.9	17.3	18.0
2nd quarter	18.7	16.1	. . .	11.5	9.0	20.9	4.5	4.1	37.1	68.0	17.2	18.1
3rd quarter	18.6	16.0	. . .	11.5	9.2	20.1	4.7	4.1	36.6	66.2	17.7	18.0
4th quarter	18.3	15.9	. . .	11.4	9.1	20.0	4.6	3.9	36.5	65.2	18.1	17.7
1954												
1st quarter	18.2	16.0	. . .	11.2	8.8	20.2	4.4	3.7	35.5	61.7	18.8	17.6
2nd quarter	18.3	16.2	. . .	11.4	8.7	21.5	5.0	4.0	34.3	58.4	18.8	17.6
3rd quarter	18.5	16.4	. . .	11.8	9.0	22.8	4.8	3.8	33.5	55.5	19.4	17.8
4th quarter	18.8	16.8	. . .	12.1	8.9	24.2	5.0	3.8	33.3	54.9	19.5	18.1
1955												
1st quarter	19.4	17.1	. . .	12.6	9.1	26.0	5.2	4.0	33.2	53.6	20.3	18.6
2nd quarter	19.7	17.5	. . .	13.1	9.7	26.4	5.1	4.3	32.9	52.3	20.5	19.0
3rd quarter	20.0	17.7	. . .	13.4	10.2	25.9	5.5	4.3	33.1	52.9	20.5	19.2
4th quarter	20.1	17.9	. . .	13.4	10.5	24.8	5.5	4.5	32.4	50.9	20.6	19.3

. . . = Not available.

Table 1-5B. Chain-Type Quantity Indexes for Gross Domestic Product and Domestic Purchases: Historical Data—*Continued*

(Index numbers, 2005 = 100.)   NIPA Tables 1.1.3, 1.4.3, 2.3.3

Year and quarter	Gross domestic product, total	Personal consumption expenditures		Private fixed investment			Exports and imports of goods and services		Government consumption expenditures and gross investment			Gross domestic purchases
		Total	Excluding food and energy	Total	Nonresidential	Residential	Exports	Imports	Total	Federal	State and local	
1956												
1st quarter	20.0	17.9	. . .	13.1	10.3	24.1	5.7	4.7	32.3	50.5	20.9	19.2
2nd quarter	20.2	18.0	. . .	13.3	10.4	24.0	6.1	4.6	33.0	51.9	21.1	19.3
3rd quarter	20.1	18.0	. . .	13.2	10.5	23.5	6.3	4.7	32.7	50.9	21.2	19.3
4th quarter	20.5	18.3	. . .	13.1	10.5	23.1	6.6	4.5	33.6	52.7	21.4	19.5
1957												
1st quarter	20.6	18.4	. . .	13.1	10.6	22.8	7.0	4.8	34.3	53.7	22.0	19.6
2nd quarter	20.5	18.4	. . .	13.0	10.5	22.3	6.8	4.9	34.0	52.9	22.2	19.6
3rd quarter	20.7	18.6	. . .	13.1	10.7	22.0	6.6	4.8	34.3	53.1	22.5	19.8
4th quarter	20.5	18.6	. . .	12.9	10.5	21.9	6.4	4.8	34.9	53.8	23.0	19.7
1958												
1st quarter	20.0	18.3	. . .	12.1	9.7	21.1	5.8	4.9	34.5	51.9	23.7	19.2
2nd quarter	20.1	18.5	. . .	11.8	9.3	21.1	5.8	5.1	35.4	53.5	24.0	19.4
3rd quarter	20.5	18.8	. . .	11.9	9.2	22.6	5.8	5.0	35.6	53.3	24.5	19.8
4th quarter	21.0	19.0	. . .	12.7	9.5	25.1	5.8	5.3	36.4	54.6	25.0	20.3
1959												
1st quarter	21.5	19.4	15.9	13.4	9.8	27.9	6.2	5.4	36.1	53.7	25.2	20.7
2nd quarter	22.0	19.7	16.3	13.9	10.1	28.9	6.4	5.6	36.7	55.0	25.3	21.2
3rd quarter	22.0	19.9	16.5	14.0	10.4	28.4	6.6	5.7	37.2	56.1	25.3	21.2
4th quarter	22.0	19.9	16.5	13.9	10.4	27.5	6.4	5.6	36.8	55.3	25.2	21.3
1960												
1st quarter	22.5	20.1	16.7	14.3	10.8	28.3	7.3	5.8	36.0	52.8	25.6	21.7
2nd quarter	22.4	20.4	16.9	14.1	10.9	26.0	7.7	5.8	36.3	52.6	26.2	21.5
3rd quarter	22.5	20.3	16.8	13.7	10.7	25.2	7.5	5.6	37.2	54.2	26.6	21.5
4th quarter	22.2	20.3	16.9	13.6	10.6	25.2	7.7	5.4	37.5	54.4	26.9	21.2
1961												
1st quarter	22.3	20.3	16.8	13.4	10.4	25.3	7.6	5.3	37.9	54.3	27.8	21.3
2nd quarter	22.7	20.6	17.1	13.6	10.6	25.4	7.5	5.4	38.0	54.8	27.6	21.7
3rd quarter	23.1	20.7	17.2	14.0	10.7	26.7	7.5	5.8	38.8	56.4	27.8	22.2
4th quarter	23.6	21.1	17.7	14.4	11.0	27.6	7.7	5.9	39.6	57.4	28.6	22.6
1962												
1st quarter	24.0	21.3	17.9	14.8	11.3	28.1	7.7	6.1	40.3	59.5	28.4	23.1
2nd quarter	24.3	21.6	18.2	15.2	11.6	29.0	8.4	6.2	40.6	59.7	28.6	23.2
3rd quarter	24.5	21.8	18.3	15.3	11.8	29.0	8.0	6.3	41.5	61.5	29.0	23.5
4th quarter	24.5	22.1	18.6	15.3	11.7	28.9	7.8	6.4	41.5	61.2	29.3	23.6
1963												
1st quarter	24.9	22.2	18.7	15.4	11.7	30.0	8.0	6.2	41.3	59.7	29.8	23.9
2nd quarter	25.2	22.4	19.0	16.1	12.1	32.1	8.9	6.4	41.2	59.2	30.1	24.1
3rd quarter	25.6	22.8	19.3	16.6	12.4	32.7	8.4	6.5	43.0	62.4	30.9	24.6
4th quarter	25.8	22.9	19.5	17.1	12.8	33.7	8.8	6.5	42.6	60.8	31.3	24.7
1964												
1st quarter	26.4	23.4	19.9	17.7	13.1	35.8	9.4	6.5	42.8	60.5	31.8	25.2
2nd quarter	26.7	23.8	20.3	17.7	13.5	34.0	9.5	6.7	43.0	60.1	32.5	25.5
3rd quarter	27.1	24.2	20.7	18.0	13.9	33.4	9.5	6.8	43.1	59.6	32.9	25.9
4th quarter	27.2	24.3	20.7	18.1	14.2	32.8	9.8	7.0	42.9	58.8	33.2	26.0
1965												
1st quarter	27.8	24.9	21.3	18.9	15.2	32.9	8.7	6.8	42.8	58.0	33.6	26.7
2nd quarter	28.2	25.1	21.5	19.5	15.8	33.2	10.3	7.6	43.4	58.1	34.4	27.0
3rd quarter	28.8	25.6	21.9	20.0	16.4	33.3	9.7	7.6	44.9	60.5	35.4	27.6
4th quarter	29.5	26.3	22.5	20.4	17.1	32.6	10.4	8.0	45.9	62.2	35.9	28.3
1966												
1st quarter	30.2	26.7	22.9	21.2	17.8	33.3	10.3	8.2	46.7	63.6	36.3	29.0
2nd quarter	30.3	26.7	22.9	20.9	18.1	30.7	10.7	8.4	47.5	65.3	36.6	29.1
3rd quarter	30.5	27.0	23.2	20.9	18.3	29.7	10.3	8.8	48.8	67.9	37.0	29.4
4th quarter	30.7	27.2	23.4	20.3	18.2	26.6	10.7	8.9	49.6	68.5	38.0	29.6
1967												
1st quarter	31.0	27.3	23.4	19.8	17.9	25.8	10.9	9.1	51.7	73.2	38.5	29.9
2nd quarter	31.0	27.7	23.8	20.3	17.8	28.7	10.8	9.0	51.4	72.1	38.7	29.9
3rd quarter	31.3	27.8	24.0	20.5	17.7	30.1	10.5	9.1	52.0	73.2	38.8	30.2
4th quarter	31.5	28.0	24.1	21.2	18.1	31.9	10.8	9.6	52.3	73.1	39.5	30.4
1968												
1st quarter	32.2	28.7	24.7	21.7	18.6	32.1	11.1	10.2	53.2	74.4	40.2	31.1
2nd quarter	32.7	29.1	25.1	21.6	18.3	32.9	11.3	10.3	53.5	73.8	41.0	31.6
3rd quarter	32.9	29.7	25.6	21.9	18.6	33.5	12.0	11.0	53.6	73.1	41.6	31.8
4th quarter	33.1	29.8	25.7	22.4	19.1	33.9	11.8	10.9	53.6	72.7	41.9	32.0

. . . = Not available.

Table 1-5B. Chain-Type Quantity Indexes for Gross Domestic Product and Domestic Purchases: Historical Data—*Continued*

(Index numbers, 2005 = 100.)

NIPA Tables 1.1.3, 1.4.3, 2.3.3

Year and quarter	Gross domestic product, total	Personal consumption expenditures		Private fixed investment			Exports and imports of goods and services		Government consumption expenditures and gross investment			Gross domestic purchases
		Total	Excluding food and energy	Total	Nonresidential	Residential	Exports	Imports	Total	Federal	State and local	
1969												
1st quarter	33.6	30.1	26.0	23.1	19.7	35.1	10.4	9.8	53.7	72.3	42.3	32.5
2nd quarter	33.7	30.3	26.2	23.2	19.9	34.7	12.8	11.8	53.5	71.1	42.6	32.6
3rd quarter	33.9	30.5	26.3	23.6	20.4	34.5	12.5	11.6	53.5	71.2	42.7	32.8
4th quarter	33.7	30.7	26.5	23.0	20.3	31.9	12.9	11.5	52.7	69.3	42.6	32.6
1970												
1st quarter	33.7	30.9	26.6	22.9	20.2	32.0	13.0	11.5	52.5	67.9	43.0	32.5
2nd quarter	33.8	31.0	26.8	22.4	20.1	29.9	13.6	11.7	51.8	65.8	43.3	32.5
3rd quarter	34.1	31.3	27.0	22.8	20.2	31.5	13.5	11.7	52.0	64.8	44.2	32.8
4th quarter	33.7	31.2	26.8	22.8	19.4	34.8	13.6	11.8	52.0	64.5	44.5	32.5
1971												
1st quarter	34.6	31.8	27.4	23.4	19.6	36.6	13.7	11.7	51.2	61.9	44.7	33.3
2nd quarter	34.8	32.1	27.7	24.3	19.9	40.3	13.7	12.6	51.0	61.1	45.0	33.7
3rd quarter	35.1	32.4	28.1	24.8	20.0	42.3	14.2	12.9	51.0	60.8	45.1	33.9
4th quarter	35.2	32.9	28.7	25.5	20.4	44.0	13.0	12.0	50.6	58.9	45.6	34.0
1972												
1st quarter	35.8	33.3	29.2	26.6	21.1	46.9	14.4	13.7	50.8	59.2	45.8	34.7
2nd quarter	36.7	34.0	29.6	27.1	21.4	47.8	14.0	13.3	51.1	60.1	45.7	35.5
3rd quarter	37.0	34.5	30.2	27.4	21.8	47.9	14.8	13.5	50.0	56.9	46.1	35.8
4th quarter	37.6	35.3	30.9	28.6	22.9	49.6	15.5	14.1	50.3	56.7	46.7	36.4
1973												
1st quarter	38.6	36.0	31.7	29.9	24.0	51.3	16.6	14.8	50.8	57.6	46.9	37.3
2nd quarter	39.0	35.9	31.8	30.1	25.0	48.7	17.4	14.4	50.5	56.7	47.0	37.5
3rd quarter	38.8	36.1	31.9	30.0	25.4	46.6	17.5	14.0	49.9	54.3	47.5	37.2
4th quarter	39.2	36.0	31.9	29.7	25.6	44.4	18.3	14.1	50.3	54.4	48.1	37.5
1974												
1st quarter	38.9	35.6	31.9	29.0	25.5	41.1	18.6	13.6	51.3	56.1	48.7	37.0
2nd quarter	39.0	35.8	31.9	28.6	25.5	39.3	19.5	14.3	51.7	56.0	49.3	37.1
3rd quarter	38.6	35.9	31.9	28.1	25.2	38.1	18.4	14.1	51.7	56.3	49.3	36.8
4th quarter	38.4	35.4	31.3	26.5	24.5	33.0	18.9	13.9	51.9	56.7	49.3	36.6
1975												
1st quarter	38.0	35.7	31.7	24.9	23.0	31.0	19.0	12.5	52.5	56.0	50.8	35.8
2nd quarter	38.2	36.3	32.2	24.5	22.4	31.7	18.5	11.5	52.1	55.6	50.4	36.0
3rd quarter	38.9	36.8	32.7	25.1	22.6	33.9	18.2	12.5	53.1	57.0	51.0	36.8
4th quarter	39.4	37.2	33.3	25.6	22.8	35.4	19.2	13.1	53.5	57.1	51.7	37.3
1976												
1st quarter	40.3	37.9	33.9	26.7	23.2	39.0	19.1	14.0	53.6	56.6	52.2	38.4
2nd quarter	40.6	38.3	34.1	27.1	23.5	40.1	19.3	14.6	53.1	56.5	51.3	38.7
3rd quarter	40.8	38.7	34.5	27.4	24.0	39.4	19.8	15.2	52.8	56.3	51.0	39.0
4th quarter	41.1	39.2	34.9	28.8	24.5	44.5	20.0	15.7	52.7	56.5	50.8	39.3
1977												
1st quarter	41.6	39.6	35.4	29.9	25.4	45.8	19.7	16.4	53.2	56.9	51.3	40.0
2nd quarter	42.4	39.9	35.8	31.5	26.2	51.0	20.2	16.6	53.8	57.9	51.6	40.7
3rd quarter	43.2	40.2	36.1	31.9	26.7	50.9	20.4	16.3	53.9	58.2	51.6	41.4
4th quarter	43.1	40.8	36.7	32.5	27.6	50.2	19.7	16.6	53.7	57.6	51.6	41.5
1978												
1st quarter	43.3	41.1	37.0	32.8	27.9	50.5	20.2	17.7	53.8	57.8	51.7	41.8
2nd quarter	45.0	42.0	38.1	35.2	30.2	52.9	22.3	17.7	55.2	59.2	53.2	43.1
3rd quarter	45.4	42.1	38.3	36.2	31.3	53.6	22.5	18.0	55.7	59.4	53.8	43.6
4th quarter	46.0	42.5	38.6	37.0	32.4	53.4	23.4	18.2	56.2	59.9	54.3	44.1
1979												
1st quarter	46.1	42.7	38.8	37.2	33.1	52.2	23.5	18.2	55.7	60.0	53.4	44.1
2nd quarter	46.2	42.7	38.9	36.9	33.0	51.2	23.5	18.3	56.3	60.8	53.9	44.2
3rd quarter	46.5	43.1	39.4	37.6	34.0	50.6	24.4	18.0	56.3	60.7	54.1	44.3
4th quarter	46.6	43.2	39.4	37.3	34.1	48.7	25.9	18.4	56.7	60.6	54.7	44.2
1980												
1st quarter	46.8	43.1	39.3	36.7	34.4	45.0	26.6	18.4	57.6	62.6	54.9	44.3
2nd quarter	45.8	42.1	38.3	33.5	32.7	36.6	27.1	17.1	57.8	64.2	54.2	43.0
3rd quarter	45.7	42.6	39.0	33.9	32.9	37.3	27.1	15.8	57.0	63.3	53.5	42.6
4th quarter	46.6	43.2	39.7	35.2	33.6	40.9	26.9	16.7	56.9	63.5	53.2	43.6
1981												
1st quarter	47.5	43.4	40.0	35.5	34.2	40.2	27.4	17.4	57.7	64.8	53.6	44.6
2nd quarter	47.2	43.4	39.9	35.7	34.9	38.8	27.6	17.4	57.8	66.8	52.6	44.2
3rd quarter	47.7	43.6	40.1	35.7	35.7	35.8	27.0	17.2	57.7	66.7	52.4	44.8
4th quarter	47.1	43.3	39.6	35.6	36.6	32.2	27.1	17.7	58.2	67.4	52.8	44.4

Table 1-5B. Chain-Type Quantity Indexes for Gross Domestic Product and Domestic Purchases: Historical Data—*Continued*

(Index numbers, 2005 = 100.)

NIPA Tables 1.1.3, 1.4.3, 2.3.3

Year and quarter	Gross domestic product, total	Personal consumption expenditures		Private fixed investment			Exports and imports of goods and services		Government consumption expenditures and gross investment			Gross domestic purchases
		Total	Excluding food and energy	Total	Nonresidential	Residential	Exports	Imports	Total	Federal	State and local	
1982												
1st quarter	46.4	43.5	39.9	34.5	35.7	30.3	25.9	17.2	58.2	67.5	52.7	43.7
2nd quarter	46.6	43.7	40.1	33.3	34.4	29.3	26.1	16.9	58.5	68.1	52.8	43.8
3rd quarter	46.4	44.0	40.5	32.4	33.3	29.3	24.9	17.7	58.9	69.1	52.9	44.0
4th quarter	46.5	44.8	41.4	32.3	32.6	31.4	23.8	17.0	59.9	71.2	53.2	44.1
1983												
1st quarter	47.0	45.3	41.9	33.0	32.0	36.7	24.2	17.4	60.4	72.0	53.4	44.7
2nd quarter	48.1	46.2	42.8	34.3	32.4	41.1	24.2	18.7	60.9	73.6	53.3	45.9
3rd quarter	49.1	47.0	43.6	36.4	33.8	45.2	24.6	20.2	61.9	75.6	53.7	47.1
4th quarter	50.1	47.7	44.4	38.5	36.0	47.1	25.1	21.2	60.9	73.0	53.7	48.2
1984												
1st quarter	51.0	48.1	45.0	39.7	37.2	48.4	25.6	22.9	61.5	73.6	54.3	49.4
2nd quarter	51.9	48.8	45.5	41.3	39.1	49.3	26.3	23.9	62.8	75.9	55.0	50.4
3rd quarter	52.4	49.2	46.0	42.2	40.3	48.8	26.8	24.5	63.3	75.6	55.9	50.9
4th quarter	52.9	49.8	46.7	43.0	41.3	48.9	27.4	25.2	64.7	78.1	56.6	51.4
1985												
1st quarter	53.4	50.7	47.5	43.3	41.8	48.7	27.4	24.6	65.4	79.0	57.3	51.7
2nd quarter	53.8	51.2	48.1	43.8	42.4	49.1	27.3	25.8	66.9	80.9	58.4	52.4
3rd quarter	54.6	52.1	49.1	43.5	41.7	49.7	26.9	25.6	68.6	83.6	59.6	53.2
4th quarter	55.1	52.2	49.1	44.3	42.5	50.9	27.7	26.6	69.0	83.6	60.3	53.7
1986												
1st quarter	55.6	52.7	49.6	44.4	41.9	53.1	28.6	26.6	69.8	83.1	61.8	54.1
2nd quarter	55.8	53.2	50.2	44.3	40.8	56.0	28.9	27.7	71.2	85.8	62.5	54.5
3rd quarter	56.3	54.2	51.3	44.0	40.2	56.9	29.6	28.5	72.9	89.0	63.1	55.0
4th quarter	56.6	54.5	51.5	44.3	40.7	56.8	30.7	28.7	72.4	87.7	63.3	55.2
1987												
1st quarter	56.9	54.4	51.5	43.4	39.5	56.6	30.7	28.5	72.7	88.2	63.4	55.4
2nd quarter	57.5	55.1	52.2	44.2	40.5	56.9	31.9	29.2	73.2	89.4	63.4	56.0
3rd quarter	58.0	55.8	53.0	45.1	41.8	56.7	33.3	29.8	73.2	89.5	63.4	56.4
4th quarter	59.0	55.9	53.1	45.1	41.7	57.0	34.5	30.5	74.1	90.8	64.0	57.3
1988												
1st quarter	59.3	56.8	54.0	45.1	42.0	55.8	36.4	30.3	73.7	88.4	64.9	57.3
2nd quarter	60.1	57.2	54.4	46.0	43.0	56.2	37.4	30.0	73.9	87.5	65.8	57.8
3rd quarter	60.4	57.7	54.8	46.1	43.3	56.2	38.1	30.7	73.9	86.8	66.1	58.2
4th quarter	61.2	58.4	55.5	46.6	43.7	56.7	39.3	31.6	75.4	89.4	66.9	59.0
1989												
1st quarter	61.8	58.6	55.7	47.1	44.5	56.4	40.4	31.8	74.9	87.6	67.3	59.4
2nd quarter	62.3	58.8	56.1	47.1	45.1	54.7	42.2	31.9	76.1	89.6	68.0	59.6
3rd quarter	62.7	59.5	56.8	48.0	46.4	54.1	42.7	31.9	76.8	90.4	68.6	60.0
4th quarter	62.9	59.7	56.8	47.2	45.7	53.0	43.3	32.5	77.2	90.0	69.5	60.2
1990												
1st quarter	63.5	60.2	57.7	47.7	46.3	53.5	45.2	33.5	78.4	91.3	70.6	60.8
2nd quarter	63.8	60.4	57.7	46.6	45.5	51.4	45.8	33.4	78.5	91.4	70.7	60.9
3rd quarter	63.8	60.6	57.9	46.1	45.8	48.5	46.2	33.3	78.5	90.6	71.2	60.9
4th quarter	63.2	60.2	57.5	44.8	44.9	45.8	46.6	32.4	79.3	91.4	71.9	60.1
1991												
1st quarter	62.9	60.0	57.3	43.3	43.8	43.1	46.9	32.0	79.6	92.1	72.0	59.7
2nd quarter	63.4	60.5	57.7	43.2	43.3	44.1	48.6	32.6	79.9	92.4	72.3	60.0
3rd quarter	63.6	60.7	57.9	43.4	42.9	45.9	49.7	33.5	79.5	90.7	72.7	60.3
4th quarter	63.9	60.7	58.1	43.5	42.7	47.0	50.8	34.3	79.1	88.9	73.3	60.6
1992												
1st quarter	64.6	61.7	59.2	43.9	42.5	49.4	51.7	34.5	79.7	88.9	74.2	61.2
2nd quarter	65.3	62.1	59.5	45.6	44.2	51.2	51.7	35.1	79.7	88.8	74.1	61.9
3rd quarter	65.9	62.8	60.3	46.3	45.1	51.4	52.9	35.6	80.1	89.8	74.2	62.5
4th quarter	66.6	63.5	61.1	47.8	46.5	53.1	53.1	36.5	80.1	89.9	74.2	63.3
1993												
1st quarter	66.7	63.8	61.4	48.0	46.7	53.3	53.3	37.3	79.2	87.1	74.5	63.5
2nd quarter	67.2	64.4	62.0	49.1	48.0	54.0	53.9	38.1	79.2	85.9	75.1	64.0
3rd quarter	67.5	65.1	62.7	50.0	48.5	55.8	53.7	38.6	79.1	85.0	75.5	64.4
4th quarter	68.4	65.7	63.3	52.2	50.6	58.6	55.5	40.1	79.5	85.4	75.9	65.4
1994												
1st quarter	69.1	66.4	64.0	52.9	51.1	59.9	56.0	41.0	78.5	82.4	76.1	66.1
2nd quarter	70.0	66.9	64.5	54.2	52.1	61.9	57.8	42.6	78.8	81.9	76.9	67.0
3rd quarter	70.5	67.4	65.1	54.7	53.1	61.2	60.0	43.8	80.2	84.1	77.8	67.4
4th quarter	71.3	68.1	65.9	56.2	55.4	60.4	61.4	45.0	79.5	81.8	78.0	68.2
1995												
1st quarter	71.4	68.2	66.0	57.5	57.7	59.1	62.5	46.0	79.8	81.6	78.7	68.4
2nd quarter	71.6	68.7	66.5	57.3	58.1	57.2	63.4	46.4	80.1	81.3	79.3	68.6
3rd quarter	72.2	69.3	67.2	58.0	58.5	58.9	66.1	46.6	79.9	80.8	79.3	68.8
4th quarter	72.7	69.8	67.7	59.2	59.7	60.3	67.1	47.2	79.0	77.7	79.7	69.3

Table 1-5B. Chain-Type Quantity Indexes for Gross Domestic Product and Domestic Purchases: Historical Data—*Continued*

(Index numbers, 2005 = 100.)   NIPA Tables 1.1.3, 1.4.3, 2.3.3

Year and quarter	Gross domestic product, total	Personal consumption expenditures		Private fixed investment			Exports and imports of goods and services		Government consumption expenditures and gross investment			Gross domestic purchases
		Total	Excluding food and energy	Total	Nonresidential	Residential	Exports	Imports	Total	Federal	State and local	
1996												
1st quarter	73.2	70.5	68.3	60.7	61.1	61.8	67.9	48.7	79.5	79.3	79.6	70.0
2nd quarter	74.5	71.3	69.2	62.7	62.9	64.5	69.0	49.8	80.7	80.5	80.7	71.2
3rd quarter	75.1	71.7	69.8	64.2	65.0	64.3	69.6	51.4	80.6	79.1	81.4	72.1
4th quarter	75.9	72.3	70.3	65.2	66.7	63.6	74.0	52.4	81.3	78.8	82.7	72.5
1997												
1st quarter	76.5	73.0	71.2	66.5	68.4	63.8	75.4	54.7	81.4	77.8	83.5	73.3
2nd quarter	77.6	73.3	71.5	67.9	70.1	64.6	78.4	56.5	82.1	79.1	83.8	74.3
3rd quarter	78.6	74.6	72.8	70.6	73.7	64.9	80.2	58.6	82.2	78.9	84.1	75.4
4th quarter	79.2	75.4	73.7	71.2	74.3	65.6	80.0	59.9	82.3	78.8	84.4	76.2
1998												
1st quarter	80.0	76.2	74.6	73.3	76.9	66.8	80.4	62.1	81.8	76.3	85.1	77.2
2nd quarter	80.7	77.5	75.9	75.9	79.7	68.8	79.5	63.5	83.6	78.4	86.7	78.2
3rd quarter	81.8	78.5	77.0	77.3	80.9	70.8	79.1	64.4	84.4	77.8	88.3	79.4
4th quarter	83.2	79.7	78.4	79.7	83.6	72.5	82.1	66.5	85.2	78.5	89.1	80.8
1999												
1st quarter	83.9	80.5	79.1	81.1	85.5	73.0	81.5	68.2	85.6	78.0	90.1	81.8
2nd quarter	84.6	81.7	80.4	83.0	87.9	73.8	82.4	70.3	86.0	78.0	90.6	82.7
3rd quarter	85.6	82.7	81.4	85.0	90.4	74.4	84.6	72.9	87.1	79.6	91.4	83.8
4th quarter	87.2	83.9	82.7	85.5	90.7	75.3	86.7	74.6	88.4	81.4	92.6	85.4
2000												
1st quarter	87.4	85.2	84.3	88.0	94.1	75.9	88.2	77.7	87.7	78.2	93.3	85.9
2nd quarter	89.1	86.0	84.9	90.2	97.6	75.3	90.7	80.0	88.9	81.3	93.3	87.6
3rd quarter	89.2	86.8	85.8	90.5	98.6	74.0	92.9	82.8	88.6	79.7	93.8	87.9
4th quarter	89.7	87.6	86.5	90.8	99.0	74.1	92.2	82.8	88.9	79.4	94.5	88.4
2001												
1st quarter	89.4	87.9	87.0	90.2	98.1	74.4	91.0	81.6	90.2	81.1	95.6	88.1
2nd quarter	90.0	88.3	87.5	88.8	95.5	75.5	88.0	79.1	92.1	82.8	97.5	88.6
3rd quarter	89.8	88.6	87.9	87.9	93.9	75.9	83.5	77.2	91.9	83.4	96.9	88.5
4th quarter	90.1	90.0	89.5	85.6	90.9	75.2	81.1	76.3	93.5	84.4	98.9	88.9
2002												
1st quarter	90.8	90.3	89.9	84.9	88.8	77.2	82.4	78.2	95.0	86.4	100.0	89.8
2nd quarter	91.3	90.8	90.2	84.5	87.3	79.1	84.6	80.8	95.9	88.4	100.3	90.4
3rd quarter	91.8	91.4	90.9	84.4	86.9	79.6	85.2	82.2	96.6	89.8	100.7	91.0
4th quarter	91.8	91.7	91.1	83.8	85.4	80.8	84.4	83.6	97.3	91.3	100.8	91.3
2003												
1st quarter	92.2	92.2	91.6	83.9	85.2	81.6	83.6	82.6	97.1	91.3	100.5	91.6
2nd quarter	93.0	93.1	92.7	86.1	87.5	83.5	83.3	83.8	98.5	95.7	100.2	92.6
3rd quarter	94.5	94.4	94.0	88.9	89.6	87.7	85.6	84.8	98.8	95.8	100.6	94.0
4th quarter	95.4	94.9	94.6	90.6	90.9	90.1	89.6	88.0	98.9	96.5	100.3	94.8
2004												
1st quarter	96.0	95.7	95.4	90.4	90.1	90.9	91.7	90.2	99.4	97.7	100.3	95.6
2nd quarter	96.6	96.2	95.9	93.2	92.6	94.3	93.2	93.8	99.7	98.3	100.6	96.5
3rd quarter	97.3	97.0	96.9	95.2	95.1	95.3	93.8	95.2	100.1	100.0	100.1	97.4
4th quarter	98.1	98.0	98.0	96.8	97.2	96.0	96.0	97.6	99.5	98.8	99.9	98.3
2005												
1st quarter	99.1	98.8	98.7	97.9	98.1	97.8	97.8	98.2	99.6	99.2	99.8	99.1
2nd quarter	99.6	99.8	99.8	99.7	99.5	100.1	99.9	99.3	99.7	99.3	99.9	99.5
3rd quarter	100.4	100.6	100.6	101.0	100.9	101.1	99.9	99.9	100.6	101.6	100.0	100.3
4th quarter	100.9	100.8	100.9	101.4	101.5	101.1	102.4	102.7	100.1	99.9	100.3	101.0
2006												
1st quarter	102.2	101.8	102.3	103.7	105.9	100.0	106.4	104.6	101.1	102.8	100.2	102.1
2nd quarter	102.6	102.5	102.8	103.3	107.8	95.5	108.2	105.8	101.2	101.9	100.9	102.5
3rd quarter	102.6	103.1	103.3	102.0	108.9	90.0	108.4	107.1	101.4	101.8	101.1	102.7
4th quarter	103.3	104.0	104.4	100.5	109.5	85.2	112.9	106.9	101.7	102.1	101.4	102.9
2007												
1st quarter	103.4	104.6	105.1	100.2	111.2	81.5	114.7	108.5	101.6	100.8	102.0	103.1
2nd quarter	104.4	105.0	105.6	101.1	114.1	78.9	116.6	109.0	102.4	102.6	102.3	103.9
3rd quarter	105.1	105.5	106.1	100.7	116.6	73.6	120.9	109.3	103.3	105.0	102.3	104.2
4th quarter	105.6	105.8	106.5	99.5	118.2	67.5	124.3	107.8	103.6	105.2	102.7	104.1
2008												
1st quarter	105.1	105.5	106.2	97.4	117.9	62.1	126.0	108.2	104.4	107.7	102.5	103.5
2nd quarter	105.4	105.5	106.3	96.1	117.3	59.7	129.8	107.5	104.8	109.0	102.5	103.4
3rd quarter	104.5	104.5	105.5	93.0	114.2	56.5	128.6	105.7	105.9	112.1	102.5	102.3
4th quarter	102.1	103.1	103.9	86.5	107.1	51.1	121.1	101.5	106.4	114.5	101.8	100.1

Table 1-6A. Chain-Type Price Indexes for Gross Domestic Product and Domestic Purchases: Recent Data

(Index numbers, 2005 = 100.)   NIPA Tables 1.1.4, 1.6.4, 2.3.4

Year and quarter	Gross domestic product, total	Personal consumption expenditures		Private fixed investment			Exports and imports of goods and services		Government consumption expenditures and gross investment			Gross domestic purchases
		Total	Excluding food and energy	Total	Nonresidential	Residential	Exports	Imports	Total	Federal	State and local	
1950	14.6	15.0	15.0	20.0	25.5	11.0	22.6	17.7	9.5	10.4	8.5	14.4
1951	15.6	16.0	16.0	21.7	27.9	11.8	25.5	21.4	10.1	10.9	9.4	15.4
1952	16.0	16.3	16.3	22.3	28.5	12.1	25.7	20.6	10.3	11.0	9.8	15.7
1953	16.2	16.6	16.6	22.4	28.8	12.2	25.6	19.7	10.4	11.1	10.0	15.9
1954	16.3	16.7	16.8	22.6	29.1	12.3	25.3	20.0	10.7	11.3	10.1	16.1
1955	16.6	16.8	17.0	23.0	29.5	12.5	25.5	19.9	11.1	11.9	10.3	16.3
1956	17.1	17.1	17.4	24.3	31.8	12.8	26.3	20.2	11.7	12.6	11.0	16.8
1957	17.7	17.6	17.9	25.2	33.4	12.9	27.3	20.4	12.2	13.1	11.5	17.4
1958	18.2	18.0	18.3	25.2	33.6	12.8	27.0	19.6	12.6	13.7	11.6	17.8
1959	18.4	18.3	18.7	25.5	34.0	12.9	27.1	19.8	12.7	13.6	11.9	18.0
1960	18.6	18.6	19.0	25.6	34.2	13.0	27.5	20.0	12.8	13.7	12.1	18.2
1961	18.8	18.8	19.3	25.5	34.0	13.0	27.9	20.0	13.1	13.9	12.4	18.4
1962	19.1	19.0	19.5	25.6	34.0	13.0	28.0	19.7	13.4	14.2	12.7	18.7
1963	19.3	19.3	19.8	25.5	34.0	12.9	27.9	20.1	13.7	14.5	13.0	18.9
1964	19.6	19.5	20.1	25.6	34.1	13.0	28.1	20.5	14.1	15.0	13.3	19.2
1965	19.9	19.8	20.3	26.1	34.5	13.4	29.0	20.8	14.4	15.4	13.7	19.5
1966	20.5	20.3	20.8	26.6	35.0	13.9	29.9	21.3	15.0	15.9	14.3	20.1
1967	21.1	20.8	21.4	27.4	35.9	14.3	31.0	21.4	15.7	16.4	15.1	20.7
1968	22.0	21.6	22.4	28.5	37.2	15.1	31.7	21.7	16.5	17.3	15.9	21.5
1969	23.1	22.6	23.4	29.9	38.7	16.1	32.8	22.3	17.5	18.2	17.0	22.6
1970	24.3	23.7	24.5	31.2	40.6	16.7	34.1	23.6	18.9	19.7	18.4	23.8
1971	25.6	24.7	25.7	32.7	42.5	17.6	35.3	25.0	20.4	21.4	19.7	25.0
1972	26.7	25.5	26.5	34.1	43.9	18.7	37.0	26.8	22.0	23.5	20.9	26.1
1973	28.1	26.9	27.5	36.0	45.6	20.4	41.8	31.4	23.6	25.1	22.5	27.6
1974	30.7	29.7	29.7	39.6	50.0	22.5	51.5	45.0	26.0	27.3	25.0	30.5
1975	33.6	32.2	32.2	44.5	56.9	24.5	56.8	48.7	28.6	30.2	27.4	33.3
1976	35.5	34.0	34.1	47.1	60.0	26.1	58.6	50.2	30.5	32.3	29.1	35.2
1977	37.8	36.2	36.3	50.8	64.2	28.8	61.0	54.6	32.6	34.7	31.0	37.6
1978	40.4	38.7	38.7	55.1	68.5	32.3	64.8	58.5	34.7	36.9	33.0	40.3
1979	43.8	42.1	41.6	60.1	74.0	35.9	72.5	68.5	37.6	39.7	36.0	43.8
1980	47.8	46.7	45.4	65.7	80.5	39.8	79.9	85.3	41.7	43.9	40.0	48.4
1981	52.3	50.8	49.3	71.8	88.3	43.0	85.8	89.9	45.8	48.2	44.0	52.9
1982	55.5	53.6	52.5	75.7	93.2	45.3	86.2	86.9	48.8	51.4	46.8	55.9
1983	57.7	55.9	55.2	75.6	92.4	46.4	86.5	83.6	50.7	53.2	48.9	57.9
1984	59.9	58.1	57.5	76.1	92.1	47.7	87.3	82.9	53.3	56.4	51.0	59.9
1985	61.7	60.0	59.7	77.0	92.9	48.9	84.7	80.2	55.0	57.6	53.0	61.6
1986	63.1	61.4	62.0	78.9	94.4	51.0	83.4	80.2	56.0	57.9	54.6	63.0
1987	64.8	63.6	64.3	80.3	95.3	53.1	85.5	85.0	57.5	58.6	56.8	65.0
1988	67.0	66.2	67.1	82.4	97.4	54.9	89.9	89.1	59.1	59.9	58.6	67.2
1989	69.6	69.0	69.9	84.4	99.4	56.7	91.4	91.0	60.9	61.5	60.7	69.8
1990	72.3	72.2	72.9	86.1	101.3	58.0	92.1	93.6	63.4	63.5	63.5	72.6
1991	74.8	74.8	75.7	87.4	102.9	58.8	93.3	92.8	65.6	66.1	65.4	75.0
1992	76.6	77.0	78.3	87.2	102.0	59.5	92.9	92.9	67.3	68.1	66.9	76.8
1993	78.3	78.7	80.1	88.2	102.1	61.9	92.9	92.2	68.9	69.8	68.5	78.4
1994	79.9	80.3	81.9	89.4	102.6	64.1	93.9	93.1	70.8	71.7	70.4	80.0
1995	81.6	82.1	83.8	90.4	102.8	66.4	96.1	95.6	72.8	73.7	72.3	81.7
1996	83.2	83.9	85.4	90.1	101.6	67.8	94.8	94.0	74.5	75.8	73.8	83.2
1997	84.6	85.4	87.0	89.9	100.3	69.6	93.2	90.7	75.9	77.0	75.2	84.5
1998	85.6	86.2	88.3	89.1	98.1	71.4	91.0	85.8	76.9	77.9	76.3	85.0
1999	86.8	87.6	89.6	89.0	96.7	74.2	90.5	86.3	79.3	79.9	79.0	86.4
2000	88.7	89.8	91.2	90.1	96.8	77.4	92.1	90.0	82.5	82.5	82.5	88.5
2001	90.7	91.5	92.8	90.9	96.3	81.0	91.7	87.8	84.8	84.2	85.0	90.2
2002	92.2	92.8	94.4	91.3	95.9	83.0	91.3	86.8	87.0	87.3	86.8	91.5
2003	94.1	94.7	95.8	92.4	95.5	87.0	93.3	89.9	90.7	91.0	90.4	93.6
2004	96.8	97.1	97.8	95.5	96.8	93.3	96.5	94.2	94.5	95.3	94.1	96.4
2005	100.0	100.0	100.0	100.0	100.0	100.0	100.0	100.0	100.0	100.0	100.0	100.0
2006	103.2	102.7	102.3	104.3	103.4	106.1	103.4	104.1	104.8	104.1	105.3	103.4
2007	106.2	105.5	104.6	106.4	105.6	107.6	106.9	107.8	109.9	107.8	111.1	106.4
2008	108.6	108.9	107.0	107.6	107.7	106.3	112.0	119.2	115.2	111.2	117.7	109.9
2009	109.7	109.2	108.7	106.3	107.1	102.6	106.0	106.6	114.9	111.0	117.2	109.8
2010	111.0	111.1	110.2	104.8	105.4	102.2	110.6	113.0	117.4	113.7	119.7	111.4
2011	113.3	113.8	111.8	106.2	106.7	103.4	117.6	121.8	121.1	116.9	123.7	114.2
2009												
1st quarter	109.7	108.2	107.9	108.1	109.0	104.0	104.9	102.8	114.6	111.1	116.7	109.3
2nd quarter	109.6	108.7	108.5	106.6	107.5	102.5	105.0	104.4	114.6	110.5	117.0	109.5
3rd quarter	109.7	109.5	108.9	105.4	106.2	101.6	106.2	108.0	114.9	110.9	117.3	109.9
4th quarter	110.0	110.3	109.5	105.2	105.7	102.4	107.7	111.0	115.5	111.5	117.8	110.5
2010												
1st quarter	110.4	110.8	109.8	104.8	105.2	102.6	109.0	113.3	116.8	113.1	119.0	111.1
2nd quarter	110.8	110.9	110.1	104.7	105.3	101.8	110.3	112.6	117.2	113.4	119.4	111.2
3rd quarter	111.2	111.1	110.4	104.8	105.4	101.9	110.5	112.0	117.4	113.8	119.6	111.5
4th quarter	111.7	111.7	110.5	105.0	105.5	102.6	112.8	114.3	118.3	114.3	120.8	112.0
2011												
1st quarter	112.4	112.7	111.0	105.4	105.9	103.0	115.7	119.4	119.9	115.8	122.4	113.1
2nd quarter	113.1	113.7	111.6	106.0	106.6	103.5	118.2	122.9	121.1	116.9	123.7	114.1
3rd quarter	113.8	114.3	112.2	106.4	107.0	103.6	118.7	122.5	121.5	117.4	124.0	114.6
4th quarter	114.1	114.7	112.5	106.8	107.4	103.6	117.6	122.2	121.8	117.3	124.5	115.0

Table 1-6B. Chain-Type Price Indexes for Gross Domestic Product and Domestic Purchases: Historical Data

(Index numbers, 2005 = 100.)   **NIPA Tables 1.1.4, 1.6.4, 2.3.4**

Year and quarter	Gross domestic product, total	Personal consumption expenditures		Private fixed investment			Exports and imports of goods and services		Government consumption expenditures and gross investment			Gross domestic purchases
		Total	Excluding food and energy	Total	Nonresidential	Residential	Exports	Imports	Total	Federal	State and local	
1929	10.6	10.5	10.6	11.3	15.0	5.3	15.7	11.3	6.4	6.9	4.8	10.4
1930	10.2	10.1	10.2	10.8	14.3	5.2	14.2	9.7	6.2	6.6	4.7	9.9
1931	9.2	9.0	9.4	10.0	13.4	4.7	11.2	7.8	5.9	6.6	4.4	9.0
1932	8.1	7.9	8.3	8.9	12.1	3.8	9.7	6.3	5.4	6.3	4.0	7.9
1933	7.9	7.7	7.9	8.7	11.9	3.8	9.7	6.0	5.5	6.3	4.1	7.7
1934	8.3	8.0	8.1	9.1	12.3	4.2	11.2	6.8	5.9	6.8	4.4	8.1
1935	8.5	8.2	8.2	9.2	12.4	4.1	11.5	6.9	6.0	6.8	4.5	8.2
1936	8.6	8.3	8.3	9.3	12.4	4.3	11.9	7.4	6.2	7.5	4.4	8.3
1937	8.9	8.6	8.7	10.1	13.4	4.7	12.7	8.3	6.3	7.6	4.5	8.6
1938	8.7	8.4	8.6	10.2	13.5	4.9	12.1	7.6	6.3	7.7	4.5	8.5
1939	8.6	8.3	8.5	10.2	13.4	4.9	11.9	8.0	6.2	7.6	4.4	8.4
1940	8.7	8.4	8.6	10.4	13.7	5.1	12.9	8.5	6.1	7.3	4.5	8.4
1941	9.2	8.9	9.1	11.2	14.6	5.5	14.1	9.0	6.5	7.7	4.8	9.0
1942	10.0	10.0	10.1	12.3	16.2	5.9	17.1	10.3	6.5	7.5	5.3	9.7
1943	10.6	10.9	10.9	12.8	16.7	6.4	18.7	11.1	6.6	7.6	5.7	10.2
1944	10.8	11.5	11.6	13.2	17.0	7.0	21.0	11.7	6.6	7.4	5.9	10.5
1945	11.1	12.0	12.2	13.7	17.4	7.5	20.9	12.0	6.6	7.5	6.1	10.8
1946	12.4	12.8	12.9	15.1	19.3	8.2	20.2	13.4	8.2	9.6	6.7	12.1
1947	13.7	14.1	14.0	17.7	22.4	9.8	23.4	16.1	8.9	10.2	7.5	13.4
1948	14.5	14.9	14.8	19.2	24.4	10.6	24.7	17.5	9.2	10.1	8.3	14.2
1949	14.5	14.8	14.8	19.6	24.9	10.7	23.2	16.6	9.5	10.5	8.4	14.2
1947												
1st quarter	13.4	13.8	. . .	16.9	21.5	9.2	21.5	14.7	8.9	10.4	7.2	13.1
2nd quarter	13.6	13.9	. . .	17.5	22.2	9.7	23.1	15.8	8.9	10.3	7.4	13.3
3rd quarter	13.8	14.2	. . .	18.0	22.8	10.0	24.2	16.6	8.8	10.0	7.5	13.5
4th quarter	14.1	14.6	. . .	18.3	23.2	10.2	24.8	17.2	8.9	9.9	7.8	13.8
1948												
1st quarter	14.3	14.7	. . .	18.5	23.4	10.4	25.0	17.6	9.0	10.0	8.0	13.9
2nd quarter	14.4	14.9	. . .	18.9	24.0	10.5	24.9	17.6	9.1	10.0	8.2	14.1
3rd quarter	14.7	15.1	. . .	19.5	24.9	10.7	24.6	17.5	9.3	10.1	8.5	14.4
4th quarter	14.7	15.0	. . .	19.8	25.3	10.8	24.2	17.2	9.4	10.2	8.6	14.4
1949												
1st quarter	14.6	14.9	. . .	19.7	25.1	10.9	23.8	16.8	9.6	10.6	8.5	14.3
2nd quarter	14.6	14.8	. . .	19.7	25.0	10.9	23.3	16.6	9.5	10.5	8.4	14.2
3rd quarter	14.4	14.8	. . .	19.5	24.9	10.6	23.0	16.5	9.4	10.3	8.4	14.1
4th quarter	14.4	14.7	. . .	19.4	24.8	10.6	22.7	16.6	9.5	10.6	8.3	14.1
1950												
1st quarter	14.4	14.7	. . .	19.4	24.8	10.6	22.3	16.9	9.4	10.5	8.3	14.1
2nd quarter	14.4	14.8	. . .	19.7	25.0	10.9	22.4	17.3	9.4	10.4	8.3	14.2
3rd quarter	14.7	15.1	. . .	20.3	25.6	11.3	22.6	17.8	9.5	10.4	8.6	14.5
4th quarter	15.0	15.4	. . .	20.7	26.4	11.3	23.0	18.7	9.7	10.4	8.8	14.7
1951												
1st quarter	15.5	15.9	. . .	21.4	27.4	11.6	24.4	20.2	10.1	11.0	9.1	15.3
2nd quarter	15.6	16.0	. . .	21.7	27.8	11.8	25.3	21.3	10.0	10.8	9.3	15.4
3rd quarter	15.6	16.0	. . .	21.8	28.1	11.8	26.0	21.9	10.1	10.8	9.5	15.4
4th quarter	15.8	16.2	. . .	22.1	28.4	11.9	26.4	22.0	10.2	11.0	9.6	15.6
1952												
1st quarter	15.9	16.3	. . .	22.2	28.5	12.0	25.8	21.1	10.1	10.8	9.6	15.6
2nd quarter	15.9	16.3	. . .	22.3	28.6	12.1	25.7	20.8	10.3	11.0	9.7	15.7
3rd quarter	16.0	16.4	. . .	22.3	28.5	12.2	25.6	20.4	10.4	11.1	9.9	15.8
4th quarter	16.1	16.4	. . .	22.3	28.5	12.2	25.6	20.1	10.5	11.2	9.9	15.8
1953												
1st quarter	16.1	16.5	. . .	22.3	28.5	12.2	25.7	19.9	10.4	11.1	10.0	15.8
2nd quarter	16.1	16.5	. . .	22.4	28.7	12.2	25.7	19.7	10.4	11.1	10.0	15.8
3rd quarter	16.2	16.6	. . .	22.6	29.0	12.3	25.6	19.6	10.4	11.0	10.0	15.9
4th quarter	16.3	16.7	. . .	22.5	28.9	12.2	25.5	19.6	10.4	11.1	9.9	16.0
1954												
1st quarter	16.3	16.8	. . .	22.5	29.0	12.2	25.3	19.8	10.5	11.2	9.9	16.0
2nd quarter	16.3	16.7	. . .	22.6	29.2	12.2	25.3	19.9	10.6	11.3	10.1	16.1
3rd quarter	16.3	16.7	. . .	22.6	29.0	12.3	25.2	20.0	10.7	11.4	10.2	16.1
4th quarter	16.4	16.7	. . .	22.7	29.0	12.3	25.2	20.1	10.8	11.5	10.3	16.1
1955												
1st quarter	16.4	16.7	. . .	22.7	28.9	12.4	25.3	19.8	10.8	11.6	10.2	16.1
2nd quarter	16.5	16.7	. . .	22.8	29.1	12.5	25.4	19.8	11.0	11.9	10.2	16.2
3rd quarter	16.6	16.8	. . .	23.1	29.6	12.6	25.5	19.9	11.2	12.0	10.4	16.3
4th quarter	16.7	16.8	. . .	23.4	30.2	12.6	25.7	19.9	11.3	12.2	10.5	16.4
1956												
1st quarter	16.9	16.9	. . .	23.9	31.1	12.7	25.9	20.0	11.5	12.4	10.8	16.6
2nd quarter	17.1	17.0	. . .	24.1	31.3	12.9	26.2	20.1	11.7	12.6	10.9	16.8
3rd quarter	17.3	17.2	. . .	24.6	32.1	12.9	26.5	20.3	11.8	12.6	11.1	16.9
4th quarter	17.4	17.3	. . .	24.8	32.6	12.9	26.8	20.5	11.9	12.7	11.2	17.0
1957												
1st quarter	17.6	17.5	. . .	25.0	33.1	12.8	27.1	20.5	12.1	13.0	11.3	17.2
2nd quarter	17.7	17.6	. . .	25.1	33.3	12.8	27.3	20.6	12.2	13.1	11.5	17.3
3rd quarter	17.8	17.7	. . .	25.3	33.5	12.9	27.4	20.4	12.3	13.2	11.5	17.5
4th quarter	17.9	17.8	. . .	25.4	33.8	12.9	27.4	20.2	12.4	13.3	11.5	17.6

. . . = Not available.

Table 1-6B. Chain-Type Price Indexes for Gross Domestic Product and Domestic Purchases: Historical Data—*Continued*

(Index numbers, 2005 = 100.)   NIPA Tables 1.1.4, 1.6.4, 2.3.4

Year and quarter	Gross domestic product											Gross domestic purchases
	Gross domestic product, total	Personal consumption expenditures		Private fixed investment			Exports and imports of goods and services		Government consumption expenditures and gross investment			
		Total	Excluding food and energy	Total	Nonresidential	Residential	Exports	Imports	Total	Federal	State and local	
1958												
1st quarter	18.1	18.0	. . .	25.1	33.4	12.8	27.1	19.7	12.4	13.5	11.5	17.7
2nd quarter	18.1	18.0	. . .	25.2	33.6	12.8	27.0	19.5	12.6	13.6	11.6	17.8
3rd quarter	18.2	18.1	. . .	25.3	33.6	12.8	27.0	19.5	12.7	13.7	11.7	17.8
4th quarter	18.2	18.1	. . .	25.3	33.7	12.8	27.0	19.6	12.7	13.8	11.7	17.8
1959												
1st quarter	18.3	18.2	18.5	25.4	33.8	12.9	26.9	19.6	12.7	13.7	11.8	17.9
2nd quarter	18.3	18.3	18.6	25.5	34.0	12.9	26.9	19.7	12.7	13.6	11.9	18.0
3rd quarter	18.4	18.4	18.8	25.5	34.1	12.9	27.1	19.8	12.6	13.5	11.9	18.0
4th quarter	18.5	18.5	18.9	25.6	34.2	12.9	27.4	20.0	12.6	13.5	11.9	18.1
1960												
1st quarter	18.5	18.5	18.9	25.6	34.2	12.9	27.5	19.9	12.7	13.5	12.0	18.1
2nd quarter	18.6	18.6	19.0	25.7	34.2	13.0	27.4	19.9	12.7	13.5	12.0	18.2
3rd quarter	18.7	18.7	19.1	25.6	34.2	13.0	27.5	20.0	12.9	13.8	12.1	18.3
4th quarter	18.7	18.7	19.1	25.6	34.1	13.0	27.5	20.0	13.0	13.9	12.1	18.4
1961												
1st quarter	18.8	18.8	19.2	25.5	34.0	12.9	27.6	20.0	13.0	13.9	12.2	18.4
2nd quarter	18.8	18.8	19.2	25.6	34.0	13.0	28.0	20.0	13.0	13.9	12.3	18.4
3rd quarter	18.9	18.8	19.3	25.5	33.9	13.0	27.9	19.9	13.1	13.9	12.4	18.4
4th quarter	18.9	18.9	19.4	25.5	34.0	13.0	28.1	19.9	13.2	14.0	12.5	18.5
1962												
1st quarter	19.0	18.9	19.4	25.6	34.0	13.0	28.2	19.7	13.3	14.1	12.7	18.6
2nd quarter	19.1	19.0	19.5	25.6	34.0	13.0	27.9	19.7	13.4	14.1	12.7	18.6
3rd quarter	19.1	19.1	19.6	25.6	34.0	13.0	27.9	19.7	13.4	14.2	12.8	18.7
4th quarter	19.2	19.1	19.6	25.5	34.0	13.0	27.9	19.8	13.5	14.4	12.8	18.8
1963												
1st quarter	19.2	19.2	19.7	25.6	34.0	13.0	28.0	20.0	13.6	14.4	12.9	18.8
2nd quarter	19.2	19.2	19.7	25.5	34.0	12.9	27.9	20.0	13.7	14.5	13.0	18.8
3rd quarter	19.3	19.3	19.8	25.4	34.0	12.8	27.8	20.2	13.6	14.4	13.0	18.9
4th quarter	19.4	19.4	19.9	25.5	34.0	12.9	27.9	20.3	13.9	14.7	13.1	19.0
1964												
1st quarter	19.5	19.5	20.0	25.4	34.0	12.8	27.9	20.4	13.9	14.8	13.2	19.1
2nd quarter	19.5	19.5	20.1	25.6	34.1	13.0	27.9	20.6	14.0	14.9	13.3	19.1
3rd quarter	19.6	19.6	20.1	25.6	34.1	13.0	28.2	20.5	14.1	15.1	13.3	19.2
4th quarter	19.7	19.6	20.2	25.9	34.3	13.3	28.5	20.6	14.2	15.1	13.4	19.3
1965												
1st quarter	19.8	19.7	20.3	25.9	34.4	13.3	29.1	20.8	14.3	15.2	13.5	19.4
2nd quarter	19.9	19.8	20.3	26.0	34.5	13.3	29.0	20.7	14.3	15.2	13.6	19.5
3rd quarter	20.0	19.9	20.4	26.0	34.6	13.3	29.0	20.8	14.5	15.4	13.7	19.6
4th quarter	20.1	19.9	20.4	26.3	34.7	13.6	28.9	21.0	14.7	15.7	13.8	19.7
1966												
1st quarter	20.2	20.1	20.5	26.2	34.7	13.5	29.4	21.1	14.8	15.7	14.0	19.8
2nd quarter	20.4	20.2	20.7	26.7	35.0	13.9	29.7	21.3	14.9	15.7	14.2	20.0
3rd quarter	20.6	20.4	20.9	26.7	35.1	13.9	30.0	21.3	15.2	16.1	14.4	20.2
4th quarter	20.8	20.6	21.1	27.0	35.4	14.2	30.5	21.4	15.3	16.1	14.6	20.3
1967												
1st quarter	20.9	20.6	21.2	27.1	35.6	14.2	31.0	21.4	15.4	16.1	14.9	20.4
2nd quarter	21.0	20.7	21.3	27.2	35.8	14.2	31.0	21.4	15.6	16.3	15.0	20.5
3rd quarter	21.2	20.9	21.5	27.4	36.0	14.3	31.0	21.4	15.7	16.4	15.2	20.7
4th quarter	21.4	21.1	21.7	27.7	36.4	14.6	31.1	21.4	16.0	16.8	15.4	20.9
1968												
1st quarter	21.7	21.3	22.0	28.0	36.6	14.8	31.4	21.5	16.2	16.9	15.7	21.2
2nd quarter	21.9	21.5	22.2	28.3	37.0	15.0	32.0	21.7	16.4	17.1	15.8	21.4
3rd quarter	22.1	21.8	22.5	28.5	37.3	15.0	31.6	21.7	16.6	17.4	16.0	21.6
4th quarter	22.4	22.0	22.7	29.1	37.9	15.6	31.9	21.9	16.9	17.7	16.3	21.9
1969												
1st quarter	22.7	22.2	23.0	29.4	38.2	15.9	32.3	22.0	17.0	17.7	16.5	22.1
2nd quarter	23.0	22.5	23.3	29.7	38.5	16.1	32.4	22.1	17.3	18.0	16.9	22.4
3rd quarter	23.3	22.8	23.5	30.0	38.9	16.2	32.8	22.2	17.7	18.5	17.2	22.7
4th quarter	23.6	23.0	23.8	30.4	39.4	16.4	33.6	22.8	18.0	18.7	17.5	23.0
1970												
1st quarter	23.9	23.3	24.1	30.6	39.8	16.4	33.6	23.0	18.5	19.3	17.9	23.4
2nd quarter	24.3	23.6	24.4	31.3	40.5	17.0	34.2	23.3	18.8	19.6	18.3	23.7
3rd quarter	24.5	23.8	24.6	31.2	40.7	16.6	34.2	23.9	19.1	19.9	18.6	23.9
4th quarter	24.8	24.1	25.0	31.6	41.3	16.7	34.3	24.1	19.4	20.1	18.9	24.2
1971												
1st quarter	25.1	24.3	25.3	32.1	41.8	17.1	35.3	24.7	19.9	20.8	19.3	24.6
2nd quarter	25.5	24.6	25.6	32.6	42.4	17.5	35.4	24.8	20.3	21.2	19.6	24.9
3rd quarter	25.7	24.8	25.8	33.0	42.7	17.8	35.2	25.1	20.6	21.5	19.9	25.2
4th quarter	25.9	25.0	26.0	33.3	43.0	18.1	35.4	25.5	20.9	22.0	20.1	25.4
1972												
1st quarter	26.4	25.3	26.2	33.7	43.5	18.3	36.5	25.9	21.6	23.1	20.5	25.8
2nd quarter	26.5	25.4	26.4	33.9	43.8	18.4	36.7	26.6	21.8	23.3	20.7	26.0
3rd quarter	26.8	25.6	26.6	34.2	44.1	18.7	36.9	27.0	22.1	23.5	21.0	26.2
4th quarter	27.1	25.8	26.8	34.7	44.3	19.3	37.7	27.6	22.5	24.0	21.4	26.5

. . . = Not available.

Table 1-6B. Chain-Type Price Indexes for Gross Domestic Product and Domestic Purchases: Historical Data—Continued

(Index numbers, 2005 = 100.)   NIPA Tables 1.1.4, 1.6.4, 2.3.4

Year and quarter	Gross domestic product, total	Personal consumption expenditures		Private fixed investment			Exports and imports of goods and services		Government consumption expenditures and gross investment			Gross domestic purchases
		Total	Excluding food and energy	Total	Nonresidential	Residential	Exports	Imports	Total	Federal	State and local	
1973												
1st quarter	27.4	26.2	26.9	35.1	44.7	19.6	38.8	28.4	23.0	24.4	21.9	26.9
2nd quarter	27.9	26.7	27.3	35.7	45.3	20.0	40.5	30.7	23.4	24.8	22.3	27.4
3rd quarter	28.4	27.1	27.7	36.4	46.0	20.7	42.9	32.1	23.8	25.3	22.7	27.9
4th quarter	28.9	27.7	28.1	36.9	46.5	21.1	45.1	34.5	24.2	25.8	23.1	28.4
1974												
1st quarter	29.5	28.5	28.6	37.6	47.3	21.6	48.2	40.0	24.8	26.2	23.8	29.2
2nd quarter	30.2	29.3	29.3	38.7	48.8	22.1	49.9	44.6	25.5	26.7	24.6	30.0
3rd quarter	31.1	30.1	30.1	40.2	50.8	22.8	52.7	46.9	26.4	27.6	25.4	30.9
4th quarter	32.1	30.9	30.8	41.8	53.2	23.4	55.4	48.4	27.2	28.7	26.1	31.8
1975												
1st quarter	32.8	31.5	31.4	43.3	55.3	24.0	56.9	49.2	27.8	29.4	26.7	32.5
2nd quarter	33.3	31.9	31.9	44.4	56.7	24.4	56.7	49.3	28.3	29.8	27.2	33.0
3rd quarter	33.9	32.5	32.4	44.9	57.4	24.7	56.6	48.2	28.8	30.3	27.6	33.6
4th quarter	34.5	33.0	32.9	45.6	58.2	25.1	56.9	48.3	29.4	31.2	28.1	34.2
1976												
1st quarter	34.9	33.4	33.4	46.0	58.9	25.2	57.7	49.1	29.8	31.5	28.5	34.6
2nd quarter	35.2	33.6	33.8	46.8	59.6	26.0	58.4	49.8	30.2	31.9	29.0	34.9
3rd quarter	35.7	34.2	34.4	47.4	60.4	26.4	58.7	50.7	30.6	32.4	29.3	35.4
4th quarter	36.3	34.7	34.9	48.2	61.3	26.9	59.8	51.2	31.2	33.3	29.7	36.0
1977												
1st quarter	36.9	35.3	35.5	49.2	62.6	27.5	60.4	53.0	31.8	34.1	30.2	36.7
2nd quarter	37.5	35.9	36.0	50.2	63.5	28.3	61.3	54.5	32.3	34.5	30.7	37.3
3rd quarter	38.0	36.5	36.6	51.3	64.7	29.2	61.0	55.2	32.7	34.6	31.3	37.9
4th quarter	38.7	37.0	37.2	52.4	65.8	30.1	61.3	55.8	33.5	35.8	31.8	38.6
1978												
1st quarter	39.3	37.6	37.8	53.4	66.8	31.0	62.5	56.7	33.9	36.1	32.3	39.2
2nd quarter	40.1	38.4	38.4	54.6	67.9	31.9	64.1	58.1	34.4	36.5	32.8	39.9
3rd quarter	40.8	39.1	39.1	55.6	69.0	32.7	65.1	59.1	34.9	37.0	33.3	40.6
4th quarter	41.6	39.8	39.8	56.7	70.2	33.6	67.3	60.1	35.5	37.9	33.8	41.4
1979												
1st quarter	42.4	40.5	40.3	57.9	71.7	34.2	69.2	62.4	36.2	38.5	34.6	42.2
2nd quarter	43.4	41.6	41.2	59.4	73.3	35.4	72.1	65.7	37.0	39.1	35.4	43.3
3rd quarter	44.3	42.7	42.0	60.9	74.8	36.5	73.8	70.6	38.0	39.9	36.6	44.4
4th quarter	45.2	43.7	42.8	62.1	76.2	37.4	75.1	75.2	39.1	41.5	37.3	45.5
1980												
1st quarter	46.2	45.0	43.9	63.5	77.9	38.4	77.3	81.5	40.0	42.3	38.4	46.7
2nd quarter	47.2	46.1	44.8	65.0	79.7	39.3	78.4	84.5	41.1	43.2	39.5	47.9
3rd quarter	48.3	47.2	45.8	66.4	81.4	40.2	80.6	86.8	42.0	43.9	40.6	49.0
4th quarter	49.6	48.4	47.0	67.9	83.1	41.2	83.3	88.4	43.5	46.2	41.6	50.3
1981												
1st quarter	50.9	49.6	48.0	69.7	85.5	42.1	85.4	90.6	44.6	47.0	42.9	51.6
2nd quarter	51.8	50.4	48.9	71.3	87.6	42.8	85.8	91.2	45.4	47.7	43.8	52.5
3rd quarter	52.8	51.3	49.8	72.5	89.2	43.3	85.9	88.8	46.0	48.2	44.3	53.3
4th quarter	53.7	52.0	50.7	73.9	91.0	44.0	86.2	89.0	47.0	49.8	45.0	54.2
1982												
1st quarter	54.5	52.7	51.4	74.9	92.2	44.6	86.7	88.7	47.8	50.5	45.7	55.0
2nd quarter	55.2	53.2	52.1	75.7	93.2	45.3	86.6	87.2	48.5	51.2	46.5	55.5
3rd quarter	55.9	54.0	52.9	76.1	93.6	45.6	86.0	86.1	49.1	51.6	47.2	56.3
4th quarter	56.5	54.6	53.7	76.2	93.7	45.9	85.5	85.5	49.8	52.5	47.8	56.9
1983												
1st quarter	57.0	55.1	54.4	75.9	93.0	46.1	85.9	83.7	50.1	52.8	48.1	57.2
2nd quarter	57.4	55.6	54.8	75.6	92.4	46.2	86.2	83.7	50.5	53.1	48.6	57.6
3rd quarter	58.0	56.3	55.7	75.5	92.1	46.4	86.7	83.8	51.0	53.5	49.1	58.2
4th quarter	58.4	56.7	56.1	75.6	91.9	46.8	87.5	83.3	51.3	53.6	49.6	58.5
1984												
1st quarter	59.1	57.3	56.7	75.6	91.9	47.1	87.6	83.5	52.6	55.7	50.3	59.2
2nd quarter	59.7	57.9	57.3	76.0	92.1	47.5	88.2	84.0	53.2	56.2	50.8	59.7
3rd quarter	60.2	58.3	57.9	76.2	92.2	47.9	87.3	82.5	53.6	56.7	51.3	60.2
4th quarter	60.5	58.7	58.3	76.4	92.3	48.3	86.3	81.5	53.9	56.8	51.7	60.5
1985												
1st quarter	61.2	59.3	59.0	76.7	92.5	48.6	85.4	79.5	54.6	57.6	52.3	61.1
2nd quarter	61.5	59.8	59.5	76.8	92.6	48.7	85.1	79.9	54.8	57.5	52.8	61.4
3rd quarter	61.8	60.1	60.0	77.1	92.9	49.0	84.2	79.8	55.0	57.4	53.2	61.7
4th quarter	62.2	60.6	60.5	77.6	93.3	49.6	84.0	81.4	55.5	58.0	53.7	62.2
1986												
1st quarter	62.5	61.1	61.1	77.9	93.5	50.2	83.6	81.5	55.6	57.9	53.9	62.6
2nd quarter	62.8	61.1	61.7	78.5	94.2	50.6	83.3	79.0	55.7	57.9	54.2	62.7
3rd quarter	63.2	61.5	62.3	79.2	94.8	51.3	83.0	79.5	56.0	58.0	54.7	63.1
4th quarter	63.7	62.0	62.8	79.8	95.2	51.9	83.7	80.5	56.5	58.1	55.5	63.6
1987												
1st quarter	64.2	62.7	63.4	80.0	95.2	52.4	84.1	82.6	57.0	58.5	56.0	64.2
2nd quarter	64.5	63.3	64.0	80.1	95.1	52.8	85.3	84.8	57.4	58.6	56.6	64.7
3rd quarter	65.0	63.9	64.6	80.3	95.0	53.3	85.6	85.6	57.8	58.8	57.2	65.2
4th quarter	65.5	64.5	65.3	80.9	95.8	53.8	87.1	87.0	58.0	58.8	57.6	65.7

Table 1-6B. Chain-Type Price Indexes for Gross Domestic Product and Domestic Purchases: Historical Data—*Continued*

(Index numbers, 2005 = 100.)   NIPA Tables 1.1.4, 1.6.4, 2.3.4

Year and quarter	Gross domestic product											Gross domestic purchases
	Gross domestic product, total	Personal consumption expenditures		Private fixed investment			Exports and imports of goods and services		Government consumption expenditures and gross investment			
		Total	Excluding food and energy	Total	Nonresidential	Residential	Exports	Imports	Total	Federal	State and local	
1988												
1st quarter	66.0	65.0	66.0	81.7	96.6	54.2	88.1	88.2	58.5	59.5	57.9	66.3
2nd quarter	66.7	65.8	66.8	82.2	97.1	54.7	89.9	89.8	59.0	59.9	58.4	66.9
3rd quarter	67.5	66.6	67.5	82.5	97.5	55.1	91.0	88.8	59.2	60.0	58.8	67.5
4th quarter	68.0	67.2	68.2	83.3	98.4	55.6	90.8	89.5	59.6	60.2	59.3	68.1
1989												
1st quarter	68.7	68.0	69.0	83.7	98.8	56.0	91.7	90.9	60.3	61.2	59.8	68.9
2nd quarter	69.4	68.9	69.6	84.3	99.2	56.7	91.8	91.9	60.8	61.4	60.4	69.6
3rd quarter	69.9	69.3	70.1	84.6	99.6	56.9	91.3	90.4	61.1	61.8	60.8	70.0
4th quarter	70.3	69.9	70.8	85.0	100.1	57.2	91.0	90.8	61.5	61.7	61.5	70.5
1990												
1st quarter	71.2	70.9	71.6	85.5	100.6	57.7	91.1	92.2	62.4	62.6	62.4	71.5
2nd quarter	72.0	71.7	72.6	85.8	100.9	57.9	91.3	90.6	63.0	63.2	63.0	72.1
3rd quarter	72.7	72.6	73.3	86.3	101.6	58.2	92.2	93.2	63.6	63.6	63.8	72.9
4th quarter	73.3	73.6	73.9	86.9	102.4	58.3	93.6	98.4	64.6	64.7	64.7	73.9
1991												
1st quarter	74.0	74.0	74.7	87.5	103.3	58.4	93.9	95.4	65.1	65.6	65.0	74.4
2nd quarter	74.6	74.5	75.3	87.5	103.1	58.7	93.4	92.8	65.3	65.7	65.2	74.7
3rd quarter	75.1	75.0	76.1	87.5	102.8	59.1	92.8	91.4	65.8	66.3	65.6	75.2
4th quarter	75.6	75.6	76.7	87.2	102.5	58.9	93.0	91.8	66.2	66.7	65.9	75.6
1992												
1st quarter	76.0	76.2	77.5	87.0	102.4	58.7	92.9	92.3	66.6	67.5	66.1	76.1
2nd quarter	76.4	76.8	78.0	87.0	102.1	59.2	93.0	92.6	67.1	68.0	66.7	76.6
3rd quarter	76.8	77.3	78.5	87.2	102.0	59.6	93.0	93.8	67.6	68.5	67.1	77.0
4th quarter	77.2	77.7	79.0	87.4	101.8	60.4	92.8	93.0	67.8	68.4	67.5	77.4
1993												
1st quarter	77.7	78.1	79.4	87.8	102.1	61.1	92.8	92.5	68.3	69.0	68.0	77.8
2nd quarter	78.1	78.5	80.0	88.1	102.1	61.7	93.0	92.8	68.8	69.5	68.4	78.3
3rd quarter	78.5	78.8	80.3	88.3	102.1	62.2	92.9	92.0	69.2	70.2	68.6	78.6
4th quarter	78.9	79.2	80.7	88.4	102.1	62.5	92.8	91.6	69.5	70.6	69.0	78.9
1994												
1st quarter	79.3	79.6	81.1	88.9	102.4	63.2	93.3	91.6	70.1	71.0	69.6	79.3
2nd quarter	79.7	80.0	81.6	89.2	102.6	63.6	93.6	92.4	70.6	71.8	70.0	79.8
3rd quarter	80.1	80.6	82.2	89.5	102.8	64.3	94.1	94.0	71.0	71.8	70.6	80.3
4th quarter	80.6	81.0	82.6	89.7	102.5	65.1	94.7	94.3	71.6	72.3	71.2	80.7
1995												
1st quarter	81.1	81.5	83.1	90.1	102.6	65.9	95.7	95.1	72.2	73.2	71.6	81.2
2nd quarter	81.4	81.9	83.6	90.4	102.9	66.3	96.5	96.5	72.5	73.3	72.2	81.6
3rd quarter	81.8	82.3	84.0	90.5	103.0	66.5	96.3	95.9	72.8	73.5	72.5	81.9
4th quarter	82.2	82.6	84.4	90.5	102.7	66.9	95.8	95.0	73.5	74.9	72.7	82.3
1996												
1st quarter	82.6	83.1	84.8	90.2	102.1	67.1	95.6	94.8	74.3	76.0	73.4	82.7
2nd quarter	82.9	83.7	85.1	90.0	101.5	67.4	95.3	94.3	74.1	75.3	73.5	83.0
3rd quarter	83.3	84.0	85.6	90.2	101.5	68.2	94.6	93.4	74.5	75.6	73.9	83.4
4th quarter	83.7	84.6	86.1	90.2	101.3	68.5	93.7	93.3	75.0	76.1	74.4	83.8
1997												
1st quarter	84.1	85.1	86.5	90.0	100.8	68.9	93.4	92.6	75.5	76.8	74.8	84.2
2nd quarter	84.5	85.3	86.9	89.9	100.5	69.2	93.4	90.7	75.7	76.9	75.0	84.3
3rd quarter	84.8	85.5	87.2	89.9	100.2	69.8	93.1	90.1	75.9	77.0	75.3	84.5
4th quarter	85.1	85.8	87.5	89.8	99.7	70.3	92.8	89.4	76.4	77.4	75.8	84.8
1998												
1st quarter	85.2	85.9	87.8	89.3	98.9	70.5	91.8	87.2	76.4	77.7	75.8	84.8
2nd quarter	85.4	86.1	88.1	89.1	98.3	71.0	91.4	86.1	76.6	77.8	76.0	84.9
3rd quarter	85.7	86.4	88.5	89.0	97.8	71.7	90.6	85.0	77.0	78.0	76.5	85.1
4th quarter	86.0	86.6	88.8	88.9	97.4	72.4	90.3	85.0	77.4	78.2	77.0	85.4
1999												
1st quarter	86.3	86.9	89.1	89.1	97.3	73.1	90.2	84.7	78.2	79.2	77.7	85.7
2nd quarter	86.7	87.4	89.4	89.1	96.9	73.9	90.3	85.7	79.0	79.6	78.6	86.2
3rd quarter	87.0	87.9	89.7	88.9	96.4	74.5	90.5	86.8	79.7	80.1	79.5	86.6
4th quarter	87.4	88.4	90.1	89.1	96.3	75.1	90.9	88.0	80.4	80.6	80.3	87.0
2000												
1st quarter	88.0	89.1	90.6	89.6	96.5	76.4	91.5	89.6	81.6	82.1	81.3	87.9
2nd quarter	88.5	89.5	90.9	89.9	96.6	77.1	92.0	89.6	82.0	81.8	82.0	88.2
3rd quarter	89.0	90.1	91.3	90.3	97.0	77.7	92.3	90.2	82.9	82.9	82.8	88.8
4th quarter	89.4	90.5	91.7	90.5	96.9	78.4	92.4	90.7	83.6	83.3	83.8	89.3
2001												
1st quarter	90.1	91.2	92.3	90.4	96.4	79.4	92.4	90.3	84.3	83.7	84.5	89.8
2nd quarter	90.7	91.6	92.7	90.8	96.4	80.4	92.0	88.6	84.7	83.9	85.0	90.2
3rd quarter	91.0	91.6	92.9	91.2	96.4	81.8	91.6	87.2	85.0	84.4	85.3	90.4
4th quarter	91.2	91.7	93.3	91.2	96.1	82.3	90.7	85.2	85.2	84.9	85.3	90.4
2002												
1st quarter	91.6	91.9	93.6	91.1	96.1	82.2	90.5	85.1	86.1	86.9	85.6	90.7
2nd quarter	92.0	92.6	94.2	91.1	95.9	82.6	91.1	86.9	86.6	87.1	86.4	91.3
3rd quarter	92.4	93.1	94.7	91.1	95.7	82.9	91.8	87.4	87.2	87.1	87.1	91.7
4th quarter	92.9	93.5	95.0	91.7	95.9	84.3	91.9	88.0	88.1	88.1	88.1	92.3

Table 1-6B. Chain-Type Price Indexes for Gross Domestic Product and Domestic Purchases: Historical Data—*Continued*

(Index numbers, 2005 = 100.)   NIPA Tables 1.1.4, 1.6.4, 2.3.4

Year and quarter	Gross domestic product											Gross domestic purchases
	Gross domestic product, total	Personal consumption expenditures		Private fixed investment			Exports and imports of goods and services		Government consumption expenditures and gross investment			
		Total	Excluding food and energy	Total	Nonresi-dential	Residential	Exports	Imports	Total	Federal	State and local	
2003												
1st quarter	93.5	94.2	95.2	92.2	95.6	86.2	92.8	90.5	90.1	90.6	89.8	93.2
2nd quarter	93.8	94.3	95.6	92.0	95.3	86.3	93.0	89.2	90.4	90.9	90.1	93.2
3rd quarter	94.3	94.9	96.0	92.3	95.4	86.8	93.3	89.6	90.8	91.1	90.7	93.7
4th quarter	94.8	95.3	96.4	93.0	95.6	88.5	94.0	90.1	91.3	91.5	91.2	94.2
2004												
1st quarter	95.6	96.1	97.0	94.0	95.9	90.5	95.2	92.2	92.8	94.0	92.1	95.2
2nd quarter	96.5	96.8	97.6	95.1	96.6	92.5	96.3	93.4	93.9	95.2	93.1	96.0
3rd quarter	97.2	97.4	98.1	96.1	97.1	94.4	96.8	94.4	95.0	95.8	94.6	96.8
4th quarter	97.9	98.2	98.5	97.0	97.7	95.8	97.9	96.7	96.4	96.4	96.4	97.7
2005												
1st quarter	98.8	98.8	99.2	98.2	98.8	97.0	98.9	97.5	98.2	99.2	97.6	98.6
2nd quarter	99.4	99.4	99.8	99.2	99.6	98.6	99.6	98.8	99.2	99.7	99.0	99.3
3rd quarter	100.5	100.5	100.2	100.6	100.2	101.2	100.3	100.9	100.7	100.4	100.8	100.5
4th quarter	101.3	101.4	100.8	102.0	101.4	103.1	101.1	102.8	101.9	100.7	102.6	101.6
2006												
1st quarter	102.1	101.8	101.3	103.1	102.2	104.9	101.8	103.2	103.2	103.1	103.3	102.3
2nd quarter	103.0	102.5	102.0	104.0	103.0	105.9	103.1	104.3	104.6	104.2	104.9	103.1
3rd quarter	103.7	103.3	102.6	104.6	103.8	106.3	104.4	105.1	105.4	104.5	106.0	103.9
4th quarter	104.2	103.3	103.1	105.7	104.8	107.2	104.4	103.9	106.1	104.6	106.9	104.1
2007												
1st quarter	105.4	104.3	103.9	106.3	105.4	107.8	105.3	104.6	108.2	106.8	109.0	105.3
2nd quarter	106.1	105.2	104.3	106.4	105.7	107.5	106.5	106.2	109.5	107.8	110.4	106.1
3rd quarter	106.5	105.7	104.8	106.4	105.7	107.5	107.2	108.0	110.2	107.9	111.6	106.6
4th quarter	107.0	106.8	105.6	106.4	105.8	107.7	108.7	112.3	111.5	108.5	113.3	107.6
2008												
1st quarter	107.6	107.9	106.2	106.7	106.3	107.3	110.7	116.8	113.7	110.5	115.6	108.7
2nd quarter	108.3	109.1	106.8	107.0	106.8	106.9	113.6	122.5	115.5	111.6	117.8	109.9
3rd quarter	109.1	110.2	107.4	107.9	108.2	106.2	115.3	125.6	116.7	112.1	119.5	111.0
4th quarter	109.2	108.7	107.6	108.7	109.6	104.8	108.3	112.0	115.1	110.7	117.8	109.9
2009												
1st quarter	109.7	108.2	107.9	108.1	109.0	104.0	104.9	102.8	114.6	111.1	116.7	109.3
2nd quarter	109.6	108.7	108.5	106.6	107.5	102.5	105.0	104.4	114.6	110.5	117.0	109.5
3rd quarter	109.7	109.5	108.9	105.4	106.2	101.6	106.2	108.0	114.9	110.9	117.3	109.9
4th quarter	110.0	110.3	109.5	105.2	105.7	102.4	107.7	111.0	115.5	111.5	117.8	110.5
2010												
1st quarter	110.4	110.8	109.8	104.8	105.2	102.6	109.0	113.3	116.8	113.1	119.0	111.1
2nd quarter	110.8	110.9	110.1	104.7	105.3	101.8	110.3	112.6	117.2	113.4	119.4	111.2
3rd quarter	111.2	111.1	110.4	104.8	105.4	101.9	110.5	112.0	117.4	113.8	119.6	111.5
4th quarter	111.7	111.7	110.5	105.0	105.5	102.6	112.8	114.3	118.3	114.3	120.8	112.0
2011												
1st quarter	112.4	112.7	111.0	105.4	105.9	103.0	115.7	119.4	119.9	115.8	122.4	113.1
2nd quarter	113.1	113.7	111.6	106.0	106.6	103.5	118.2	122.9	121.1	116.9	123.7	114.1
3rd quarter	113.8	114.3	112.2	106.4	107.0	103.6	118.7	122.5	121.5	117.4	124.0	114.6
4th quarter	114.1	114.7	112.5	106.8	107.4	103.6	117.6	122.2	121.8	117.3	124.5	115.0

Table 1-7. Final Sales

(Quarterly dollar data are at seasonally adjusted annual rates.)

NIPA Tables 1.4.4, 1.4.5, 1.4.6

Year and quarter	Final sales of domestic product			Final sales to domestic purchasers		
	Billions of dollars	Billions of chained (2005) dollars	Chain-type price index, 2005 = 100	Billions of dollars	Billions of chained (2005) dollars	Chain-type price index, 2005 = 100
1950	288.0	1 989.0	14.5	287.2	2 019.4	14.2
1951	329.4	2 130.4	15.5	326.8	2 146.3	15.2
1952	354.8	2 243.8	15.8	353.6	2 274.5	15.5
1953	377.4	2 354.4	16.0	378.1	2 403.2	15.7
1954	382.3	2 361.0	16.2	381.9	2 400.2	15.9
1955	409.7	2 494.0	16.4	409.3	2 536.6	16.1
1956	433.5	2 551.1	17.0	431.1	2 585.2	16.7
1957	460.3	2 616.7	17.6	456.2	2 645.6	17.2
1958	467.5	2 597.8	18.0	467.0	2 650.2	17.6
1959	502.7	2 761.6	18.2	502.3	2 817.4	17.8
1960	523.2	2 834.2	18.5	519.0	2 871.1	18.1
1961	541.8	2 902.1	18.7	536.9	2 938.8	18.3
1962	579.6	3 062.3	18.9	575.5	3 108.9	18.5
1963	612.1	3 199.9	19.1	607.2	3 242.0	18.7
1964	658.8	3 390.8	19.4	651.9	3 424.9	19.0
1965	709.9	3 587.6	19.8	704.3	3 636.4	19.4
1966	774.1	3 803.4	20.4	770.2	3 867.7	19.9
1967	822.6	3 920.0	21.0	819.0	3 995.6	20.5
1968	900.8	4 115.8	21.9	899.4	4 208.3	21.4
1969	975.3	4 245.0	23.0	973.8	4 342.0	22.4
1970	1 036.3	4 284.3	24.2	1 032.4	4 367.2	23.6
1971	1 118.6	4 403.6	25.4	1 117.9	4 497.6	24.9
1972	1 228.8	4 636.7	26.5	1 232.2	4 745.2	26.0
1973	1 366.4	4 884.0	28.0	1 362.3	4 958.0	27.5
1974	1 485.5	4 870.0	30.5	1 486.3	4 906.2	30.3
1975	1 644.0	4 922.1	33.4	1 628.0	4 914.7	33.1
1976	1 807.5	5 115.6	35.4	1 809.1	5 163.6	35.0
1977	2 007.8	5 340.3	37.6	2 030.9	5 427.0	37.4
1978	2 268.0	5 634.9	40.3	2 293.3	5 720.4	40.1
1979	2 544.2	5 836.2	43.6	2 566.8	5 884.2	43.6
1980	2 794.5	5 873.6	47.6	2 807.5	5 823.3	48.2
1981	3 097.0	5 954.4	52.1	3 109.6	5 911.7	52.6
1982	3 268.1	5 918.2	55.3	3 288.1	5 911.9	55.6
1983	3 540.4	6 167.6	57.5	3 592.0	6 239.3	57.6
1984	3 865.5	6 490.0	59.6	3 968.2	6 658.4	59.6
1985	4 195.6	6 833.1	61.5	4 310.9	7 029.3	61.3
1986	4 453.5	7 092.7	62.9	4 586.0	7 309.7	62.7
1987	4 709.2	7 289.9	64.6	4 854.2	7 495.3	64.8
1988	5 081.9	7 601.3	66.9	5 192.0	7 746.2	67.0
1989	5 454.5	7 860.8	69.4	5 542.3	7 965.8	69.6
1990	5 786.0	8 025.8	72.1	5 863.6	8 096.4	72.4
1991	5 992.5	8 027.9	74.7	6 019.4	8 047.1	74.8
1992	6 326.0	8 277.2	76.4	6 358.8	8 299.5	76.6
1993	6 646.5	8 508.0	78.1	6 710.9	8 577.3	78.2
1994	7 021.4	8 801.7	79.8	7 114.1	8 907.0	79.9
1995	7 383.5	9 065.4	81.4	7 474.2	9 160.6	81.6
1996	7 807.7	9 404.4	83.0	7 904.0	9 512.4	83.1
1997	8 261.4	9 774.2	84.5	8 362.7	9 912.5	84.4
1998	8 729.8	10 208.3	85.5	8 891.6	10 464.7	85.0
1999	9 292.7	10 706.5	86.8	9 554.7	11 067.7	86.3
2000	9 896.9	11 158.0	88.7	10 279.0	11 613.3	88.5
2001	10 324.5	11 382.0	90.7	10 695.4	11 860.9	90.2
2002	10 630.3	11 533.6	92.2	11 057.5	12 088.3	91.5
2003	11 125.8	11 820.5	94.1	11 630.0	12 429.0	93.6
2004	11 788.3	12 181.3	96.8	12 407.0	12 869.8	96.4
2005	12 573.0	12 573.0	100.0	13 295.7	13 295.7	100.0
2006	13 317.3	12 899.3	103.2	14 086.6	13 629.0	103.4
2007	13 999.6	13 177.5	106.2	14 712.6	13 826.4	106.4
2008	14 332.7	13 200.5	108.6	15 042.4	13 691.2	109.9
2009	14 099.8	12 852.7	109.7	14 491.3	13 200.0	109.8
2010	14 459.6	13 028.9	111.0	14 976.5	13 440.7	111.4
2011	15 047.7	13 284.6	113.3	15 626.5	13 688.7	114.2
2009						
1st quarter	14 073.3	12 836.0	109.6	14 456.8	13 228.5	109.3
2nd quarter	14 054.6	12 830.0	109.5	14 392.9	13 151.5	109.4
3rd quarter	14 117.6	12 875.1	109.7	14 524.3	13 215.0	109.9
4th quarter	14 153.5	12 869.5	110.0	14 591.1	13 204.8	110.5
2010						
1st quarter	14 233.6	12 895.9	110.4	14 729.4	13 261.7	111.1
2nd quarter	14 389.8	12 992.2	110.8	14 921.0	13 419.9	111.2
3rd quarter	14 498.8	13 046.0	111.1	15 039.1	13 495.4	111.4
4th quarter	14 716.3	13 181.6	111.6	15 216.6	13 585.9	112.0
2011						
1st quarter	14 805.8	13 182.8	112.3	15 377.1	13 598.4	113.1
2nd quarter	14 959.2	13 236.2	113.0	15 556.3	13 643.4	114.0
3rd quarter	15 175.3	13 340.9	113.8	15 737.6	13 733.4	114.6
4th quarter	15 250.7	13 378.3	114.0	15 834.9	13 779.4	114.9

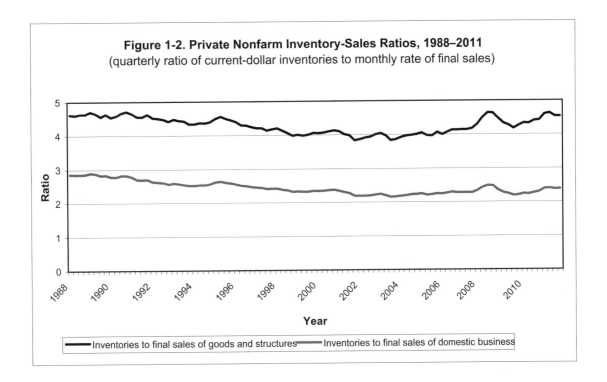

Figure 1-2. Private Nonfarm Inventory-Sales Ratios, 1988–2011
(quarterly ratio of current-dollar inventories to monthly rate of final sales)

- Inventories play a key role in the business cycle, since the change in inventories is a GDP component that, although small, can be volatile and even negative. When inventory change is positive, the economy is producing a little more than is sold; when it is negative, production has been reduced below the rate of sales in order to get rid of unwanted stocks. In 2009, inventories were reduced at a rate that contributed 0.84 percentage points to the 3.5 percent decline in GDP. In 2010, the return to inventory-building contributed 1.64 percentage points, more than half of the 3.0 percent GDP increase. This was the largest positive contribution since 1984. (Table 1-4A).

- Ratios of inventories to sales (I/S ratios) are important cyclical indicators. If sales take an unexpected dip, there can be "involuntary" inventory accumulation. In that case, I/S ratios rise; production then has to be cut back to get back to the desired ratio.

- In 2008 and early 2009, slowdowns and then declines in final sales (Table 1-1B) led to the increases in I/S ratios shown in Table 1-8B and Figure 1-2 above. Very large production cuts and inventory liquidation ensued. Later, in the second half of 2009, sales strengthened, contributing to a reduced rate of inventory liquidation even as I/S ratios stabilized or improved, and positive inventory growth resumed in 2010. But the decline in I/S ratios ended and they started to creep up again. As of the end of 2011, these ratios had increased enough to suggest that further inventory growth would be cautious in the absence of accelerated growth in sales. (Tables 1-7 and 1-8A and B)

Table 1-8A. Inventory Change and Inventory-Sales Ratios: Recent Data

(Quarterly dollar data are at seasonally adjusted annual rates.)   NIPA Tables 5.6.5A, 5.6.5B, 5.6.6.A, 5.6.6B, 5.7.5A, 5.7.5B, 5.7.6A, 5.7.6B

| Year and quarter | Change in private inventories | | | | Ratio, inventories at end of quarter to monthly rate of sales during the quarter | | | | | |
| | Billions of current dollars | | Billions of chained (2005) dollars | | Total private inventories to final sales of domestic business | | Nonfarm inventories to final sales of domestic business | | Nonfarm inventories to final sales of goods and structures | |
	Farm	Nonfarm	Farm	Nonfarm	Current dollars	Chained (2005) dollars	Current dollars	Chained (2005) dollars	Current dollars	Chained (2005) dollars
1950	-0.1	5.9	-0.3	22.8	5.81	3.67	3.04	2.30	3.94	3.97
1951	1.0	8.9	2.1	28.4	5.85	3.76	3.15	2.46	4.07	4.24
1952	1.4	2.1	3.1	7.4	5.24	3.74	3.06	2.45	3.98	4.23
1953	0.7	1.2	2.0	4.5	5.04	3.74	3.08	2.45	4.04	4.22
1954	0.2	-2.1	0.5	-7.5	4.74	3.52	2.88	2.28	3.81	3.94
1955	-0.6	5.6	-1.9	18.7	4.43	3.44	2.95	2.29	3.87	3.94
1956	-1.0	4.9	-3.2	15.6	4.47	3.45	3.03	2.35	4.00	4.07
1957	0.1	0.7	0.4	2.4	4.46	3.48	3.01	2.37	4.01	4.14
1958	2.0	-2.3	5.8	-7.7	4.50	3.44	2.90	2.30	3.88	4.00
1959	-1.6	5.5	-4.7	19.9	4.26	3.37	2.90	2.32	3.94	4.08
1960	0.6	2.7	1.7	9.9	4.22	3.37	2.89	2.34	3.93	4.10
1961	0.9	2.1	2.5	7.8	4.12	3.30	2.81	2.29	3.84	4.03
1962	0.6	5.5	1.7	20.4	4.14	3.32	2.82	2.34	3.87	4.11
1963	0.5	5.1	1.4	19.0	3.95	3.25	2.78	2.32	3.81	4.07
1964	-1.2	6.0	-3.8	21.8	3.79	3.17	2.75	2.31	3.79	4.07
1965	0.8	8.4	2.5	30.5	3.77	3.09	2.72	2.29	3.71	3.99
1966	-0.5	14.1	-1.4	50.2	3.92	3.26	2.92	2.50	4.01	4.38
1967	0.9	9.0	2.5	31.5	3.90	3.35	2.99	2.59	4.14	4.57
1968	1.4	7.7	4.1	26.5	3.79	3.33	2.90	2.58	4.03	4.56
1969	0.0	9.2	0.0	30.9	3.88	3.40	2.98	2.68	4.18	4.76
1970	-0.8	2.8	-2.4	8.6	3.81	3.39	2.96	2.68	4.23	4.83
1971	1.7	6.6	4.1	20.6	3.76	3.33	2.88	2.64	4.12	4.75
1972	0.3	8.8	0.4	26.7	3.74	3.18	2.77	2.55	3.94	4.53
1973	1.5	14.4	1.8	40.5	4.20	3.22	2.98	2.62	4.22	4.67
1974	-2.8	16.8	-4.4	39.0	4.52	3.46	3.54	2.88	5.11	5.26
1975	3.4	-9.6	5.8	-21.4	4.04	3.26	3.16	2.66	4.59	4.88
1976	-0.8	18.0	-1.6	37.6	3.95	3.23	3.19	2.68	4.68	4.92
1977	4.5	17.8	7.2	35.7	3.89	3.22	3.16	2.67	4.63	4.87
1978	1.4	24.4	2.1	44.9	3.98	3.14	3.15	2.63	4.54	4.73
1979	3.6	14.4	4.2	23.8	4.19	3.16	3.34	2.64	4.85	4.75
1980	-6.1	-0.2	-7.2	-0.4	4.24	3.13	3.44	2.65	5.08	4.82
1981	8.8	21.0	10.1	28.2	4.17	3.28	3.49	2.75	5.20	5.03
1982	5.8	-20.7	7.5	-27.4	3.97	3.23	3.30	2.68	5.10	4.99
1983	-15.4	9.6	-17.4	10.7	3.69	2.98	3.08	2.52	4.77	4.64
1984	5.7	59.7	6.3	72.3	3.72	3.05	3.16	2.60	4.89	4.72
1985	5.8	16.1	7.0	18.4	3.51	2.98	3.01	2.53	4.74	4.65
1986	-1.5	8.0	-2.3	10.4	3.25	2.90	2.82	2.47	4.49	4.53
1987	-6.4	33.6	-9.1	41.1	3.33	2.90	2.90	2.50	4.65	4.62
1988	-11.9	30.4	-13.1	35.4	3.29	2.81	2.86	2.47	4.63	4.55
1989	0.0	27.7	0.0	30.8	3.23	2.80	2.83	2.47	4.63	4.56
1990	2.4	12.2	2.5	14.0	3.22	2.83	2.82	2.49	4.71	4.66
1991	-1.3	0.9	-1.8	0.4	3.06	2.83	2.70	2.50	4.62	4.74
1992	6.3	10.1	7.1	11.0	2.92	2.73	2.56	2.39	4.41	4.53
1993	-6.2	27.0	-7.5	29.8	2.85	2.68	2.51	2.38	4.33	4.47
1994	12.0	51.8	13.7	55.9	2.89	2.72	2.56	2.40	4.39	4.47
1995	-11.1	42.2	-13.0	44.3	2.88	2.69	2.58	2.40	4.45	4.46
1996	8.6	22.1	8.3	23.2	2.76	2.62	2.47	2.33	4.24	4.28
1997	3.3	67.7	3.7	73.6	2.70	2.65	2.42	2.37	4.17	4.32
1998	1.3	62.5	1.6	69.5	2.55	2.62	2.32	2.35	3.98	4.22
1999	-2.7	63.5	-3.7	70.8	2.57	2.60	2.35	2.35	4.06	4.22
2000	-1.4	55.9	-1.8	61.2	2.59	2.60	2.37	2.36	4.13	4.26
2001	0.0	-38.3	0.1	-41.5	2.40	2.51	2.19	2.27	3.83	4.10
2002	-2.5	14.5	-3.1	15.6	2.45	2.53	2.22	2.30	4.01	4.21
2003	0.1	16.3	0.1	17.2	2.39	2.44	2.16	2.21	3.86	3.99
2004	8.8	56.1	7.9	58.3	2.46	2.46	2.23	2.23	4.01	4.04
2005	0.1	49.8	0.1	49.8	2.48	2.46	2.25	2.23	4.07	4.02
2006	-3.6	63.6	-3.7	63.2	2.49	2.45	2.28	2.24	4.13	4.05
2007	-0.7	29.8	-0.8	28.7	2.57	2.42	2.34	2.22	4.30	4.00
2008	1.6	-42.7	1.0	-37.6	2.59	2.49	2.35	2.27	4.47	4.20
2009	-1.8	-159.0	-1.5	-143.8	2.44	2.33	2.21	2.11	4.26	3.93
2010	-1.6	68.6	-1.4	60.7	2.57	2.33	2.30	2.12	4.42	3.91
2011	-7.7	54.0	-7.0	44.3	2.65	2.32	2.38	2.13	4.53	3.88
2009										
1st quarter	0.2	-179.7	0.2	-162.6	2.51	2.47	2.28	2.25	4.33	4.19
2nd quarter	-0.8	-199.8	-0.9	-182.7	2.47	2.42	2.24	2.20	4.27	4.09
3rd quarter	-5.5	-191.5	-4.9	-173.9	2.41	2.35	2.19	2.13	4.17	3.94
4th quarter	-0.9	-65.2	-0.3	-56.0	2.44	2.33	2.21	2.11	4.26	3.93
2010										
1st quarter	5.3	39.0	4.5	35.5	2.48	2.34	2.24	2.12	4.33	3.93
2nd quarter	1.0	77.1	0.8	64.0	2.46	2.34	2.23	2.12	4.32	3.94
3rd quarter	-6.2	112.9	-5.7	98.8	2.52	2.36	2.27	2.14	4.40	3.98
4th quarter	-6.5	45.2	-5.2	44.7	2.57	2.33	2.30	2.12	4.42	3.91
2011										
1st quarter	-9.4	71.4	-7.8	59.7	2.68	2.34	2.39	2.14	4.60	3.94
2nd quarter	-9.9	63.5	-8.7	51.0	2.68	2.34	2.40	2.15	4.63	3.96
3rd quarter	-5.6	6.4	-6.0	5.5	2.65	2.32	2.37	2.13	4.53	3.90
4th quarter	-5.8	74.5	-5.7	60.8	2.65	2.32	2.38	2.13	4.53	3.88

Table 1-8B. Inventory Change and Inventory-Sales Ratios: Historical Data

(Quarterly dollar data are at seasonally adjusted annual rates.)   **NIPA Tables 5.6.5A, 5.6.5B, 5.6.6A, 5.6.6B, 5.7.5A, 5.7.5B, 5.7.6A, 5.7.6B**

Year and quarter	Change in private inventories				Ratio, inventories at end of quarter to monthly rate of sales during the quarter					
	Billions of current dollars		Billions of chained (2005) dollars		Total private inventories to final sales of domestic business		Nonfarm inventories to final sales of domestic business		Nonfarm inventories to final sales of goods and structures	
	Farm	Nonfarm	Farm	Nonfarm	Current dollars	Chained (2005) dollars	Current dollars	Chained (2005) dollars	Current dollars	Chained (2005) dollars
1929	-0.1	1.7	-0.6	10.6	. . .	. . .	. . .	. . .	. . .	. . .
1930	-0.3	0.0	-1.7	-2.4	. . .	. . .	. . .	. . .	. . .	. . .
1931	0.5	-1.6	3.1	-13.4	. . .	. . .	. . .	. . .	. . .	. . .
1932	0.1	-2.5	0.8	-21.2	. . .	. . .	. . .	. . .	. . .	. . .
1933	-0.1	-1.3	-1.1	-9.4	. . .	. . .	. . .	. . .	. . .	. . .
1934	-0.8	0.2	-5.7	1.0	. . .	. . .	. . .	. . .	. . .	. . .
1935	0.7	0.4	4.0	2.5	. . .	. . .	. . .	. . .	. . .	. . .
1936	-0.9	2.0	-5.4	15.5	. . .	. . .	. . .	. . .	. . .	. . .
1937	0.9	1.7	4.1	7.9	. . .	. . .	. . .	. . .	. . .	. . .
1938	0.4	-1.0	2.8	-6.0	. . .	. . .	. . .	. . .	. . .	. . .
1939	-0.1	0.3	-1.1	2.7	. . .	. . .	. . .	. . .	. . .	. . .
1940	0.5	1.9	2.8	12.4	. . .	. . .	. . .	. . .	. . .	. . .
1941	0.4	3.9	1.9	24.3	. . .	. . .	. . .	. . .	. . .	. . .
1942	1.3	0.6	5.6	3.0	. . .	. . .	. . .	. . .	. . .	. . .
1943	-0.2	-0.5	-1.1	-2.3	. . .	. . .	. . .	. . .	. . .	. . .
1944	-0.3	-0.6	-1.5	-2.5	. . .	. . .	. . .	. . .	. . .	. . .
1945	-0.9	-0.6	-3.3	-3.8	. . .	. . .	. . .	. . .	. . .	. . .
1946	-0.2	6.2	-1.0	31.8	. . .	. . .	. . .	. . .	. . .	. . .
1947	-1.8	1.2	-4.5	4.4	. . .	. . .	. . .	. . .	. . .	. . .
1948	2.7	3.0	6.1	12.4	. . .	. . .	. . .	. . .	. . .	. . .
1949	-0.6	-2.1	-1.9	-8.6	. . .	. . .	. . .	. . .	. . .	. . .
1947										
1st quarter	-1.1	1.6	-0.4	6.6	5.93	3.88	2.82	2.27	3.71	3.99
2nd quarter	-2.7	1.5	-4.5	4.2	5.89	3.84	2.82	2.27	3.69	4.00
3rd quarter	-2.5	-0.4	-6.8	-3.7	6.02	3.76	2.76	2.23	3.61	3.93
4th quarter	-0.8	2.3	-6.3	10.5	6.30	3.74	2.81	2.25	3.65	3.93
1948										
1st quarter	1.3	2.4	1.6	11.7	6.00	3.76	2.87	2.27	3.71	3.96
2nd quarter	2.8	3.0	7.7	11.9	6.02	3.81	2.89	2.30	3.76	4.03
3rd quarter	3.4	3.7	8.3	15.0	5.88	3.88	2.97	2.34	3.85	4.10
4th quarter	3.1	2.9	6.6	11.1	5.74	3.91	3.00	2.36	3.90	4.13
1949										
1st quarter	-0.2	0.6	-1.2	-0.4	5.66	3.90	2.97	2.36	3.88	4.14
2nd quarter	-1.2	-4.0	-3.0	-15.1	5.38	3.82	2.83	2.30	3.70	4.02
3rd quarter	-0.9	-0.4	-2.3	-0.6	5.39	3.81	2.82	2.29	3.69	4.00
4th quarter	-0.2	-4.5	-0.9	-18.4	5.23	3.73	2.77	2.23	3.61	3.87
1950										
1st quarter	-0.1	2.2	-1.0	9.7	5.26	3.69	2.76	2.22	3.61	3.84
2nd quarter	-1.3	4.2	-2.5	16.2	5.27	3.62	2.75	2.20	3.57	3.79
3rd quarter	0.5	3.7	0.6	15.2	5.21	3.47	2.72	2.12	3.50	3.63
4th quarter	0.7	13.4	1.5	50.2	5.81	3.67	3.04	2.30	3.94	3.97
1951										
1st quarter	1.2	9.2	2.6	29.0	5.94	3.68	3.12	2.33	4.01	4.01
2nd quarter	0.9	13.8	2.5	44.3	5.99	3.81	3.25	2.45	4.23	4.28
3rd quarter	0.8	9.0	1.6	29.3	5.89	3.79	3.20	2.47	4.16	4.29
4th quarter	1.1	3.6	1.7	11.0	5.85	3.76	3.15	2.46	4.07	4.24
1952										
1st quarter	1.0	3.8	2.7	12.8	5.77	3.79	3.16	2.49	4.11	4.31
2nd quarter	1.9	-3.4	3.6	-10.5	5.63	3.75	3.08	2.44	4.01	4.24
3rd quarter	2.2	3.4	4.5	11.2	5.63	3.85	3.15	2.51	4.13	4.38
4th quarter	0.5	4.8	1.5	16.2	5.24	3.74	3.06	2.45	3.98	4.23
1953										
1st quarter	0.8	3.1	2.5	10.6	5.06	3.69	3.02	2.42	3.93	4.17
2nd quarter	-0.7	4.3	-0.2	14.1	5.00	3.69	3.06	2.43	3.99	4.20
3rd quarter	0.7	1.6	1.8	5.8	4.99	3.72	3.09	2.45	4.05	4.23
4th quarter	2.1	-4.1	3.8	-12.3	5.04	3.74	3.08	2.45	4.04	4.22
1954										
1st quarter	0.8	-2.8	2.1	-9.2	5.02	3.72	3.04	2.42	4.01	4.20
2nd quarter	-0.2	-3.2	0.5	-10.8	4.91	3.66	2.98	2.38	3.93	4.11
3rd quarter	0.7	-2.8	0.8	-9.1	4.85	3.59	2.93	2.32	3.89	4.04
4th quarter	-0.5	0.2	-1.5	-0.9	4.74	3.52	2.88	2.28	3.81	3.94
1955										
1st quarter	-0.1	3.9	-1.7	14.0	4.68	3.46	2.86	2.25	3.77	3.88
2nd quarter	-1.1	5.7	-2.1	20.0	4.57	3.44	2.87	2.26	3.73	3.83
3rd quarter	-1.3	5.6	-2.0	17.9	4.47	3.42	2.89	2.26	3.77	3.85
4th quarter	0.3	6.9	-1.6	22.7	4.43	3.44	2.95	2.29	3.87	3.94
1956										
1st quarter	0.0	6.4	-2.9	20.8	4.50	3.48	3.00	2.33	3.96	4.02
2nd quarter	-1.5	5.0	-3.4	16.2	4.57	3.48	3.03	2.35	3.99	4.04
3rd quarter	-0.8	4.3	-3.2	13.2	4.50	3.48	3.02	2.36	3.98	4.07
4th quarter	-1.6	3.9	-3.3	12.1	4.47	3.45	3.03	2.35	4.00	4.07
1957										
1st quarter	0.3	1.9	-0.9	5.7	4.44	3.44	3.02	2.35	3.97	4.05
2nd quarter	0.7	2.0	-0.2	6.8	4.48	3.48	3.04	2.38	4.00	4.11
3rd quarter	0.5	2.3	1.8	7.5	4.46	3.47	3.03	2.38	3.99	4.10
4th quarter	-1.0	-3.5	1.1	-10.2	4.46	3.48	3.01	2.37	4.01	4.14

. . . = Not available.

Table 1-8B. Inventory Change and Inventory-Sales Ratios: Historical Data—*Continued*

(Quarterly dollar data are at seasonally adjusted annual rates.)   NIPA Tables 5.6.5A, 5.6.5B, 5.6.6A, 5.6.6B, 5.7.5A, 5.7.5B, 5.7.6A, 5.7.6B

Year and quarter	Change in private inventories				Ratio, inventories at end of quarter to monthly rate of sales during the quarter					
	Billions of current dollars		Billions of chained (2005) dollars		Total private inventories to final sales of domestic business		Nonfarm inventories to final sales of domestic business		Nonfarm inventories to final sales of goods and structures	
	Farm	Nonfarm	Farm	Nonfarm	Current dollars	Chained (2005) dollars	Current dollars	Chained (2005) dollars	Current dollars	Chained (2005) dollars
1958										
1st quarter	2.2	-6.3	7.6	-20.4	4.67	3.56	3.04	2.41	4.06	4.20
2nd quarter	1.6	-5.8	6.9	-18.6	4.65	3.56	3.00	2.38	4.00	4.17
3rd quarter	2.2	-0.7	6.2	-2.5	4.58	3.48	2.92	2.32	3.92	4.07
4th quarter	1.8	3.4	2.5	10.6	4.50	3.44	2.90	2.30	3.88	4.00
1959										
1st quarter	-0.3	4.2	-3.5	14.9	4.37	3.35	2.83	2.25	3.79	3.93
2nd quarter	-1.9	9.2	-5.3	33.8	4.33	3.34	2.86	2.27	3.85	3.98
3rd quarter	-2.3	2.6	-5.4	9.6	4.25	3.31	2.84	2.27	3.82	3.96
4th quarter	-1.8	5.9	-4.6	21.1	4.26	3.37	2.90	2.32	3.94	4.08
1960										
1st quarter	0.6	10.6	0.4	39.0	4.29	3.37	2.93	2.35	3.96	4.10
2nd quarter	0.9	2.4	1.9	9.0	4.21	3.36	2.91	2.34	3.95	4.11
3rd quarter	1.0	3.3	3.1	12.1	4.27	3.41	2.95	2.38	3.99	4.15
4th quarter	-0.2	-5.6	1.5	-20.2	4.22	3.37	2.89	2.34	3.93	4.10
1961										
1st quarter	0.6	-3.1	2.5	-11.3	4.19	3.35	2.86	2.32	3.90	4.07
2nd quarter	0.6	1.2	2.2	4.7	4.12	3.33	2.83	2.30	3.89	4.07
3rd quarter	0.9	5.7	2.6	21.0	4.17	3.35	2.85	2.32	3.89	4.08
4th quarter	1.4	4.6	2.8	16.8	4.12	3.30	2.81	2.29	3.84	4.03
1962										
1st quarter	1.5	7.9	2.5	29.0	4.15	3.32	2.82	2.32	3.85	4.07
2nd quarter	0.2	5.2	0.8	19.2	4.09	3.29	2.80	2.31	3.84	4.06
3rd quarter	0.2	5.9	1.4	22.0	4.17	3.32	2.83	2.33	3.87	4.09
4th quarter	0.4	3.0	2.2	11.3	4.14	3.32	2.82	2.34	3.87	4.11
1963										
1st quarter	1.9	4.9	7.5	18.2	4.12	3.34	2.83	2.35	3.87	4.12
2nd quarter	0.1	4.8	0.7	17.4	4.04	3.29	2.79	2.32	3.83	4.08
3rd quarter	-0.6	6.4	-1.7	23.6	4.00	3.27	2.79	2.33	3.81	4.07
4th quarter	0.6	4.5	-0.8	16.7	3.95	3.25	2.78	2.32	3.81	4.07
1964										
1st quarter	-0.6	5.8	-3.9	21.1	3.85	3.19	2.74	2.29	3.75	4.01
2nd quarter	-1.2	5.7	-4.3	20.7	3.79	3.17	2.73	2.29	3.75	4.02
3rd quarter	-1.8	6.5	-4.2	23.8	3.78	3.15	2.73	2.29	3.74	4.00
4th quarter	-1.1	6.1	-3.1	21.7	3.79	3.17	2.75	2.31	3.79	4.07
1965										
1st quarter	0.3	11.2	0.9	40.8	3.81	3.17	2.76	2.33	3.79	4.08
2nd quarter	1.1	7.4	2.9	26.9	3.82	3.15	2.75	2.32	3.79	4.08
3rd quarter	0.8	8.5	3.1	30.5	3.78	3.14	2.76	2.32	3.78	4.06
4th quarter	1.0	6.6	3.2	23.7	3.77	3.09	2.72	2.29	3.71	3.99
1966										
1st quarter	0.6	13.2	1.1	46.8	3.80	3.09	2.73	2.31	3.71	4.00
2nd quarter	-1.7	14.0	-2.7	50.2	3.86	3.16	2.80	2.38	3.83	4.16
3rd quarter	-0.6	12.4	-1.7	43.7	3.91	3.19	2.84	2.42	3.88	4.22
4th quarter	-0.4	16.9	-2.3	59.9	3.92	3.26	2.92	2.50	4.01	4.38
1967										
1st quarter	1.7	13.7	3.4	48.6	3.94	3.32	2.98	2.55	4.11	4.50
2nd quarter	2.1	4.2	7.6	14.7	3.92	3.31	2.95	2.54	4.07	4.46
3rd quarter	0.5	8.7	1.4	29.7	3.92	3.34	2.97	2.57	4.10	4.52
4th quarter	-0.9	9.3	-2.2	33.1	3.90	3.35	2.99	2.59	4.14	4.57
1968										
1st quarter	3.0	5.4	7.3	19.1	3.87	3.32	2.94	2.57	4.08	4.51
2nd quarter	4.3	9.8	13.4	33.9	3.87	3.34	2.93	2.58	4.07	4.55
3rd quarter	0.2	7.5	1.2	25.1	3.81	3.32	2.90	2.56	4.03	4.51
4th quarter	-2.0	8.0	-5.5	27.8	3.79	3.33	2.90	2.58	4.03	4.56
1969										
1st quarter	1.8	9.7	3.9	33.0	3.79	3.32	2.90	2.59	4.02	4.54
2nd quarter	1.4	7.8	4.4	26.6	3.83	3.35	2.91	2.61	4.06	4.61
3rd quarter	-1.2	11.4	-2.5	38.6	3.83	3.38	2.94	2.64	4.10	4.67
4th quarter	-1.9	7.7	-5.8	25.5	3.88	3.40	2.98	2.68	4.18	4.76
1970										
1st quarter	1.6	0.2	3.4	0.0	3.86	3.38	2.96	2.66	4.18	4.74
2nd quarter	0.4	4.7	1.9	14.9	3.85	3.40	2.96	2.68	4.20	4.80
3rd quarter	-1.8	6.9	-4.4	21.9	3.84	3.39	2.97	2.67	4.22	4.79
4th quarter	-3.5	-0.5	-10.3	-2.2	3.81	3.39	2.96	2.68	4.23	4.83
1971										
1st quarter	2.5	9.7	6.6	31.3	3.83	3.38	2.95	2.68	4.21	4.81
2nd quarter	4.2	6.7	10.7	20.6	3.81	3.39	2.94	2.68	4.20	4.81
3rd quarter	2.3	7.9	5.8	25.2	3.80	3.38	2.93	2.68	4.18	4.80
4th quarter	-2.3	2.0	-6.8	5.4	3.76	3.33	2.88	2.64	4.12	4.75
1972										
1st quarter	-0.5	3.7	0.1	11.1	3.72	3.30	2.84	2.62	4.06	4.69
2nd quarter	2.0	10.0	6.8	30.6	3.75	3.27	2.83	2.60	4.03	4.64
3rd quarter	1.0	12.7	1.9	38.5	3.77	3.26	2.83	2.60	4.05	4.66
4th quarter	-1.4	8.9	-7.1	26.5	3.74	3.18	2.77	2.55	3.94	4.53

Table 1-8B. Inventory Change and Inventory-Sales Ratios: Historical Data—*Continued*

(Quarterly dollar data are at seasonally adjusted annual rates.)   NIPA Tables 5.6.5A, 5.6.5B, 5.6.6.A, 5.6.6B, 5.7.5A, 5.7.5B, 5.7.6A, 5.7.6B

| Year and quarter | Change in private inventories | | | | Ratio, inventories at end of quarter to monthly rate of sales during the quarter | | | | | |
| | Billions of current dollars | | Billions of chained (2005) dollars | | Total private inventories to final sales of domestic business | | Nonfarm inventories to final sales of domestic business | | Nonfarm inventories to final sales of goods and structures | |
	Farm	Nonfarm	Farm	Nonfarm	Current dollars	Chained (2005) dollars	Current dollars	Chained (2005) dollars	Current dollars	Chained (2005) dollars
1973										
1st quarter	-4.2	14.8	-10.7	42.9	3.86	3.11	2.79	2.52	3.92	4.45
2nd quarter	5.0	13.2	12.0	38.3	4.03	3.15	2.86	2.54	4.02	4.51
3rd quarter	2.6	7.2	3.5	20.0	4.11	3.16	2.87	2.56	4.05	4.55
4th quarter	2.8	22.2	2.3	60.9	4.20	3.22	2.98	2.62	4.22	4.67
1974										
1st quarter	-3.3	15.9	-5.2	39.7	4.26	3.27	3.13	2.68	4.42	4.76
2nd quarter	1.0	16.4	0.9	39.6	4.29	3.31	3.28	2.72	4.67	4.86
3rd quarter	-0.1	5.7	1.7	11.7	4.45	3.34	3.40	2.75	4.84	4.93
4th quarter	-8.7	29.2	-15.0	64.9	4.52	3.46	3.54	2.88	5.11	5.26
1975										
1st quarter	7.1	-17.1	16.4	-38.3	4.32	3.42	3.41	2.82	4.94	5.16
2nd quarter	3.1	-17.1	5.4	-38.6	4.26	3.35	3.30	2.75	4.81	5.06
3rd quarter	0.8	-2.2	-1.0	-5.0	4.18	3.31	3.24	2.71	4.69	4.95
4th quarter	2.5	-2.1	2.3	-3.7	4.04	3.26	3.16	2.66	4.59	4.88
1976										
1st quarter	-0.5	15.2	0.1	33.2	4.00	3.22	3.14	2.64	4.56	4.83
2nd quarter	-1.8	24.3	-1.9	51.8	4.07	3.26	3.21	2.69	4.67	4.91
3rd quarter	2.0	18.8	5.4	38.9	4.04	3.28	3.23	2.70	4.74	4.96
4th quarter	-3.0	13.6	-9.8	26.5	3.95	3.23	3.19	2.68	4.68	4.92
1977										
1st quarter	-1.3	16.1	-7.0	33.0	3.96	3.22	3.21	2.68	4.72	4.92
2nd quarter	5.3	14.2	11.3	27.8	3.88	3.19	3.16	2.65	4.62	4.84
3rd quarter	4.4	26.5	16.3	53.8	3.86	3.22	3.16	2.67	4.63	4.88
4th quarter	9.8	14.4	8.4	28.1	3.89	3.22	3.16	2.67	4.63	4.87
1978										
1st quarter	-0.6	26.1	-3.6	48.9	4.02	3.26	3.21	2.72	4.78	5.00
2nd quarter	0.4	23.9	0.2	44.2	3.92	3.14	3.12	2.62	4.55	4.75
3rd quarter	7.2	17.8	11.1	32.3	3.95	3.15	3.13	2.62	4.54	4.74
4th quarter	-1.5	30.0	0.5	54.1	3.98	3.14	3.15	2.63	4.54	4.73
1979										
1st quarter	4.2	19.6	6.6	33.0	4.15	3.17	3.22	2.65	4.66	4.78
2nd quarter	3.1	24.3	5.3	40.4	4.19	3.21	3.29	2.69	4.78	4.87
3rd quarter	6.6	5.5	7.0	8.2	4.16	3.16	3.28	2.64	4.74	4.73
4th quarter	0.3	8.3	-1.9	13.4	4.19	3.16	3.34	2.64	4.85	4.75
1980										
1st quarter	-0.6	10.5	-2.6	17.4	4.25	3.17	3.45	2.66	5.02	4.78
2nd quarter	-5.2	13.0	-5.9	19.3	4.40	3.28	3.57	2.76	5.26	5.02
3rd quarter	-12.5	-21.4	-14.2	-32.6	4.34	3.18	3.50	2.68	5.15	4.88
4th quarter	-6.1	-3.0	-6.0	-5.8	4.24	3.13	3.44	2.65	5.08	4.82
1981										
1st quarter	6.8	31.9	10.3	44.6	4.26	3.17	3.48	2.67	5.13	4.84
2nd quarter	9.9	1.8	10.9	1.7	4.24	3.18	3.47	2.67	5.15	4.87
3rd quarter	11.8	32.1	14.5	42.6	4.20	3.22	3.48	2.71	5.16	4.93
4th quarter	6.5	18.3	4.5	23.8	4.17	3.28	3.49	2.75	5.20	5.03
1982										
1st quarter	5.1	-26.5	6.7	-34.3	4.19	3.28	3.46	2.74	5.20	5.03
2nd quarter	4.3	-8.5	6.4	-12.2	4.15	3.28	3.42	2.74	5.17	5.04
3rd quarter	9.0	-3.2	12.0	-5.5	4.12	3.33	3.43	2.77	5.26	5.15
4th quarter	4.6	-44.4	4.9	-57.5	3.97	3.23	3.30	2.68	5.10	4.99
1983										
1st quarter	-7.3	-27.8	-10.4	-37.3	3.89	3.15	3.19	2.62	4.98	4.89
2nd quarter	-13.0	5.3	-12.6	6.5	3.81	3.09	3.14	2.58	4.89	4.80
3rd quarter	-32.4	28.2	-37.7	34.3	3.73	3.03	3.12	2.55	4.86	4.73
4th quarter	-8.8	32.7	-9.0	39.4	3.69	2.98	3.08	2.52	4.77	4.64
1984										
1st quarter	5.5	67.5	7.4	81.9	3.78	3.02	3.15	2.56	4.87	4.71
2nd quarter	5.6	63.7	6.4	77.2	3.76	3.03	3.16	2.57	4.88	4.69
3rd quarter	6.8	64.5	8.1	78.9	3.75	3.06	3.18	2.60	4.93	4.75
4th quarter	5.0	43.0	3.3	51.0	3.72	3.05	3.16	2.60	4.89	4.72
1985										
1st quarter	7.9	8.3	8.4	8.8	3.60	3.00	3.06	2.55	4.77	4.65
2nd quarter	4.2	17.4	4.8	20.3	3.55	2.99	3.04	2.55	4.76	4.66
3rd quarter	6.6	9.7	9.1	12.0	3.47	2.96	2.98	2.51	4.67	4.60
4th quarter	4.3	28.8	5.9	32.7	3.51	2.98	3.01	2.53	4.74	4.65
1986										
1st quarter	2.5	27.8	1.7	33.3	3.42	2.97	2.94	2.52	4.65	4.63
2nd quarter	-3.5	19.1	-5.9	22.3	3.37	2.97	2.92	2.53	4.63	4.65
3rd quarter	-3.1	-3.9	-4.3	-5.5	3.29	2.92	2.85	2.49	4.52	4.55
4th quarter	-1.8	-11.0	-0.6	-8.5	3.25	2.90	2.82	2.47	4.49	4.53
1987										
1st quarter	-7.7	35.6	-9.7	44.5	3.31	2.94	2.86	2.51	4.62	4.66
2nd quarter	-10.7	27.2	-14.5	33.1	3.30	2.90	2.86	2.49	4.60	4.60
3rd quarter	-4.0	5.0	-5.2	4.1	3.25	2.85	2.82	2.45	4.52	4.51
4th quarter	-3.3	66.4	-7.0	82.5	3.33	2.90	2.90	2.50	4.65	4.62

Table 1-8B. Inventory Change and Inventory-Sales Ratios: Historical Data—*Continued*

(Quarterly dollar data are at seasonally adjusted annual rates.)   NIPA Tables 5.6.5A, 5.6.5B, 5.6.6A, 5.6.6B, 5.7.5A, 5.7.5B, 5.7.6A, 5.7.6B

Year and quarter	Change in private inventories				Ratio, inventories at end of quarter to monthly rate of sales during the quarter					
	Billions of current dollars		Billions of chained (2005) dollars		Total private inventories to final sales of domestic business		Nonfarm inventories to final sales of domestic business		Nonfarm inventories to final sales of goods and structures	
	Farm	Nonfarm	Farm	Nonfarm	Current dollars	Chained (2005) dollars	Current dollars	Chained (2005) dollars	Current dollars	Chained (2005) dollars
1988										
1st quarter	-4.4	21.4	-7.6	25.1	3.30	2.86	2.86	2.47	4.61	4.56
2nd quarter	-12.2	31.9	-15.2	38.0	3.29	2.83	2.85	2.46	4.60	4.52
3rd quarter	-11.2	29.4	-11.4	32.6	3.30	2.83	2.85	2.47	4.63	4.57
4th quarter	-19.7	38.8	-18.3	45.9	3.29	2.81	2.86	2.47	4.63	4.55
1989										
1st quarter	7.2	41.0	7.8	46.6	3.32	2.83	2.89	2.48	4.70	4.58
2nd quarter	2.9	33.2	3.6	37.6	3.28	2.83	2.87	2.48	4.65	4.56
3rd quarter	-5.5	15.5	-5.8	16.9	3.21	2.79	2.82	2.45	4.55	4.49
4th quarter	-4.6	21.2	-5.6	22.3	3.23	2.80	2.83	2.47	4.63	4.56
1990										
1st quarter	1.8	12.1	1.7	13.3	3.18	2.78	2.78	2.45	4.53	4.50
2nd quarter	-1.5	35.3	-2.6	39.9	3.17	2.81	2.78	2.47	4.58	4.60
3rd quarter	4.0	17.9	4.4	20.3	3.20	2.82	2.82	2.48	4.67	4.63
4th quarter	5.2	-16.6	6.7	-17.7	3.22	2.83	2.82	2.49	4.71	4.66
1991										
1st quarter	0.0	-15.6	0.7	-18.1	3.18	2.85	2.78	2.51	4.65	4.71
2nd quarter	-0.7	-17.3	-0.5	-20.6	3.08	2.81	2.70	2.47	4.55	4.66
3rd quarter	-10.9	11.7	-13.8	13.1	3.04	2.81	2.69	2.48	4.54	4.67
4th quarter	6.4	24.7	6.1	27.1	3.06	2.83	2.70	2.50	4.62	4.74
1992										
1st quarter	8.0	-7.8	10.5	-7.5	3.00	2.78	2.63	2.44	4.52	4.64
2nd quarter	9.4	13.8	10.9	13.2	2.99	2.77	2.62	2.43	4.50	4.61
3rd quarter	5.1	15.4	4.7	16.6	2.96	2.75	2.60	2.41	4.47	4.57
4th quarter	2.5	18.9	2.4	21.6	2.92	2.73	2.56	2.39	4.41	4.53
1993										
1st quarter	-5.6	41.6	-6.2	46.5	2.95	2.75	2.58	2.42	4.47	4.60
2nd quarter	-4.9	29.0	-5.3	32.3	2.92	2.74	2.57	2.41	4.44	4.56
3rd quarter	-12.5	19.1	-14.2	20.6	2.89	2.72	2.54	2.40	4.42	4.55
4th quarter	-1.7	18.3	-4.1	19.9	2.85	2.68	2.51	2.38	4.33	4.47
1994										
1st quarter	16.5	28.8	19.4	31.1	2.87	2.69	2.51	2.38	4.33	4.48
2nd quarter	17.1	64.3	21.0	70.0	2.86	2.71	2.53	2.39	4.37	4.49
3rd quarter	10.7	42.5	10.6	46.1	2.86	2.71	2.53	2.39	4.36	4.48
4th quarter	3.7	71.5	3.7	76.3	2.89	2.72	2.56	2.40	4.39	4.47
1995										
1st quarter	-5.8	67.0	-5.9	71.2	2.93	2.75	2.62	2.43	4.49	4.52
2nd quarter	-13.7	47.4	-13.6	50.1	2.94	2.75	2.64	2.44	4.55	4.55
3rd quarter	-20.4	31.7	-26.4	32.8	2.90	2.71	2.60	2.41	4.49	4.50
4th quarter	-4.4	22.8	-6.2	22.9	2.88	2.69	2.58	2.40	4.45	4.46
1996										
1st quarter	1.1	5.8	-2.9	6.2	2.84	2.66	2.55	2.38	4.39	4.42
2nd quarter	11.8	18.6	7.4	19.8	2.81	2.63	2.51	2.35	4.30	4.35
3rd quarter	17.1	34.0	27.4	35.0	2.81	2.65	2.50	2.35	4.29	4.34
4th quarter	4.5	30.2	1.3	31.7	2.76	2.62	2.47	2.33	4.24	4.28
1997										
1st quarter	-0.5	50.3	-10.8	53.3	2.74	2.62	2.45	2.33	4.21	4.28
2nd quarter	0.8	87.6	8.2	95.7	2.73	2.65	2.44	2.36	4.21	4.33
3rd quarter	8.3	59.6	10.1	65.5	2.69	2.63	2.41	2.34	4.14	4.27
4th quarter	4.7	73.1	7.2	79.8	2.70	2.65	2.42	2.37	4.17	4.32
1998										
1st quarter	5.6	99.5	6.3	110.6	2.69	2.68	2.42	2.40	4.20	4.38
2nd quarter	-4.9	42.2	-3.0	45.6	2.64	2.65	2.38	2.38	4.13	4.32
3rd quarter	0.6	51.9	2.6	57.6	2.59	2.65	2.36	2.37	4.06	4.29
4th quarter	3.9	56.2	0.7	64.0	2.55	2.62	2.32	2.35	3.98	4.22
1999										
1st quarter	4.0	79.3	-2.1	90.0	2.56	2.64	2.33	2.37	4.01	4.27
2nd quarter	-0.3	35.3	1.4	39.3	2.54	2.61	2.32	2.35	3.98	4.22
3rd quarter	-9.1	49.6	-11.2	53.5	2.55	2.60	2.32	2.34	4.01	4.21
4th quarter	-5.6	90.0	-2.9	100.3	2.57	2.60	2.35	2.35	4.06	4.22
2000										
1st quarter	-17.8	33.9	-20.1	36.5	2.56	2.57	2.34	2.33	4.05	4.19
2nd quarter	5.9	84.5	7.2	93.7	2.56	2.58	2.35	2.34	4.07	4.22
3rd quarter	-1.1	58.4	-2.2	64.3	2.57	2.60	2.36	2.35	4.10	4.24
4th quarter	7.5	47.0	8.0	50.5	2.59	2.60	2.37	2.36	4.13	4.26
2001										
1st quarter	5.6	-36.2	5.9	-40.1	2.57	2.58	2.34	2.34	4.10	4.22
2nd quarter	-3.0	-8.6	-3.4	-7.4	2.52	2.57	2.30	2.33	4.02	4.20
3rd quarter	1.8	-31.9	2.7	-33.1	2.49	2.57	2.27	2.33	3.98	4.22
4th quarter	-4.2	-76.6	-4.9	-85.5	2.40	2.51	2.19	2.27	3.83	4.10
2002										
1st quarter	3.3	-16.7	5.1	-19.5	2.40	2.51	2.19	2.27	3.87	4.12
2nd quarter	-10.3	23.5	-13.3	25.5	2.40	2.51	2.19	2.27	3.91	4.16
3rd quarter	-2.3	20.6	-3.1	22.6	2.41	2.51	2.20	2.27	3.94	4.15
4th quarter	-0.7	30.7	-0.9	33.6	2.45	2.53	2.22	2.30	4.01	4.21

Table 1-8B. Inventory Change and Inventory-Sales Ratios: Historical Data—*Continued*

(Quarterly dollar data are at seasonally adjusted annual rates.)   **NIPA Tables 5.6.5A, 5.6.5B, 5.6.6A, 5.6.6B, 5.7.5A, 5.7.5B, 5.7.6A, 5.7.6B**

| Year and quarter | Change in private inventories | | | | Ratio, inventories at end of quarter to monthly rate of sales during the quarter | | | | | |
| | Billions of current dollars | | Billions of chained (2005) dollars | | Total private inventories to final sales of domestic business | | Nonfarm inventories to final sales of domestic business | | Nonfarm inventories to final sales of goods and structures | |
	Farm	Nonfarm	Farm	Nonfarm	Current dollars	Chained (2005) dollars	Current dollars	Chained (2005) dollars	Current dollars	Chained (2005) dollars
2003										
1st quarter	2.9	25.8	4.0	27.5	2.47	2.53	2.24	2.29	4.04	4.20
2nd quarter	-1.4	-1.7	-1.3	-2.3	2.42	2.50	2.20	2.27	3.97	4.13
3rd quarter	1.0	3.2	0.4	2.5	2.38	2.44	2.15	2.21	3.83	4.00
4th quarter	-2.1	37.9	-2.5	41.3	2.39	2.44	2.16	2.21	3.86	3.99
2004										
1st quarter	4.4	46.9	3.2	49.4	2.42	2.44	2.18	2.22	3.92	4.02
2nd quarter	18.4	57.6	17.7	60.2	2.45	2.46	2.20	2.23	3.96	4.04
3rd quarter	7.7	53.1	7.0	55.7	2.45	2.46	2.22	2.23	3.98	4.03
4th quarter	4.7	66.8	3.7	68.1	2.46	2.46	2.23	2.23	4.01	4.04
2005										
1st quarter	-6.5	97.2	-6.9	98.4	2.48	2.47	2.25	2.25	4.05	4.05
2nd quarter	0.3	15.5	0.2	15.3	2.43	2.44	2.21	2.22	3.97	3.98
3rd quarter	4.4	6.7	4.6	7.2	2.44	2.43	2.22	2.21	3.96	3.95
4th quarter	2.3	79.9	2.6	78.4	2.48	2.46	2.25	2.23	4.07	4.02
2006										
1st quarter	3.7	62.3	3.8	62.3	2.45	2.44	2.24	2.22	4.00	3.96
2nd quarter	-8.1	80.6	-8.2	80.4	2.47	2.45	2.27	2.23	4.07	4.00
3rd quarter	-6.3	75.4	-6.3	73.9	2.51	2.47	2.29	2.26	4.13	4.08
4th quarter	-3.6	36.0	-4.1	36.2	2.49	2.45	2.28	2.24	4.13	4.05
2007										
1st quarter	5.2	11.8	5.2	12.0	2.50	2.45	2.28	2.24	4.14	4.05
2nd quarter	-5.0	52.5	-5.0	50.3	2.50	2.44	2.28	2.24	4.14	4.04
3rd quarter	-2.3	41.6	-2.5	38.9	2.51	2.43	2.28	2.23	4.17	4.02
4th quarter	-0.8	13.4	-0.9	13.7	2.57	2.42	2.34	2.22	4.30	4.00
2008										
1st quarter	-6.5	-13.0	-6.9	-4.8	2.67	2.43	2.43	2.23	4.50	4.05
2nd quarter	4.0	-22.3	3.5	-18.1	2.75	2.42	2.49	2.21	4.64	4.00
3rd quarter	6.2	-50.3	5.1	-44.2	2.74	2.44	2.48	2.23	4.63	4.04
4th quarter	2.7	-85.2	2.3	-83.3	2.59	2.49	2.35	2.27	4.47	4.20
2009										
1st quarter	0.2	-179.7	0.2	-162.6	2.51	2.47	2.28	2.25	4.33	4.19
2nd quarter	-0.8	-199.8	-0.9	-182.7	2.47	2.42	2.24	2.20	4.27	4.09
3rd quarter	-5.5	-191.5	-4.9	-173.9	2.41	2.35	2.19	2.13	4.17	3.94
4th quarter	-0.9	-65.2	-0.3	-56.0	2.44	2.33	2.21	2.11	4.26	3.93
2010										
1st quarter	5.3	39.0	4.5	35.5	2.48	2.34	2.24	2.12	4.33	3.93
2nd quarter	1.0	77.1	0.8	64.0	2.46	2.34	2.23	2.12	4.32	3.94
3rd quarter	-6.2	112.9	-5.7	98.8	2.52	2.36	2.27	2.14	4.40	3.98
4th quarter	-6.5	45.2	-5.2	44.7	2.57	2.33	2.30	2.12	4.42	3.91
2011										
1st quarter	-9.4	71.4	-7.8	59.7	2.68	2.34	2.39	2.14	4.60	3.94
2nd quarter	-9.9	63.5	-8.7	51.0	2.68	2.34	2.40	2.15	4.63	3.96
3rd quarter	-5.6	6.4	-6.0	5.5	2.65	2.32	2.37	2.13	4.53	3.90
4th quarter	-5.8	74.5	-5.7	60.8	2.65	2.32	2.38	2.13	4.53	3.88

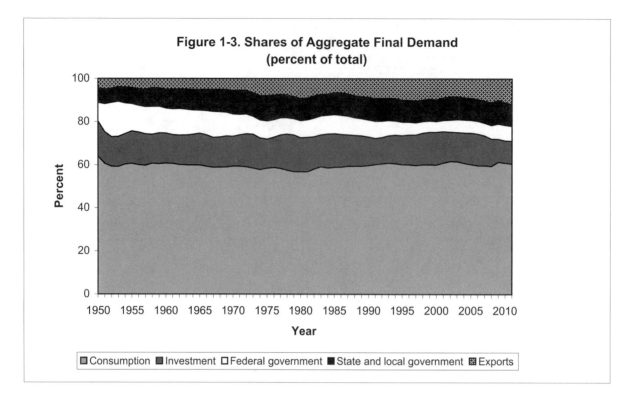

Figure 1-3. Shares of Aggregate Final Demand
(percent of total)

□ Consumption ■ Investment □ Federal government ■ State and local government ▨ Exports

- People often want to know how various sources of demand, especially consumption spending, affect GDP. It is often stated, in discussing such questions, that consumption "accounts for" about 70 percent of GDP. Such statements are based on a NIPA table showing the components of GDP as a percent of total GDP. On that basis, personal consumption expenditures (PCE) amounted to 71.1 percent of total GDP in 2011, up from a range of 60 to 65 percent earlier in the postwar period. (All such calculations must be made in current dollars, since for reasons stated in the notes and definitions, the 2005-dollar values do not sum to the total GDP.)

- Can this be interpreted as "accounting for" 71.1 percent of GDP? No, because the value of PCE includes imported goods and services—coffee, cocoa, and bananas; crude oil from the Middle East, transformed into gasoline; clothing, cars, and toys manufactured overseas—even the money that U.S. consumers spend when they travel. The imports included in PCE don't contribute to demand for U.S. GDP, which excludes imports; instead, they contribute to demand for GDP in China and other countries that export to us.

- It is not possible with NIPA data to precisely estimate and subtract out the import content of PCE, and so there is no way to precisely estimate PCE's contribution to GDP. What we can do is calculate PCE and the other sources of aggregate final demand for U.S. output as shares of total final demand; this is shown in Table 1-10 and Figure 1-3. These shares would approximate their contributions to GDP if each demand source had about the same percentage "import content" as total GDP.

- Consumption spending has been around 60 percent of final demand ever since 1951. (It was greater in 1946 through 1950, as consumers made up for wartime deprivations.) The shares of exports and state and local government spending have increased to more than 10 percent each, while the federal government direct spending share remains at less than half of its Korean War highs. (This measure of government spending does not include government financing of medical care and other consumption spending through transfer payment programs such as Social Security and Medicare.) Nonresidential and residential investment display the most cyclical variation in their shares. (Table 1-10)

- The share of imports in the total supply of goods and services in the U.S. market rose from around 4 percent in the 1950s to 15 percent in 2008. The recession and associated inventory liquidation reduced the import share to 12 percent in 2009, but it recovered to 15 percent in 2011. (Table 1-9)

Table 1-9. Shares of Aggregate Supply

(Billions of dollars, quarterly dollar data are at seasonally adjusted rates, percents.)   NIPA Table 1.1.5

Year and quarter	Aggregate supply (billions of dollars)			Shares of aggregate supply (percent)	
	Total	GDP	Imports	Domestic production (GDP)	Imports
1950	305.3	293.7	11.6	96.2	3.8
1951	353.9	339.3	14.6	95.9	4.1
1952	373.6	358.3	15.3	95.9	4.1
1953	395.3	379.3	16.0	96.0	4.0
1954	395.8	380.4	15.4	96.1	3.9
1955	431.9	414.7	17.2	96.0	4.0
1956	456.3	437.4	18.9	95.9	4.1
1957	481.0	461.1	19.9	95.9	4.1
1958	487.2	467.2	20.0	95.9	4.1
1959	528.9	506.6	22.3	95.8	4.2
1960	549.2	526.4	22.8	95.8	4.2
1961	567.5	544.8	22.7	96.0	4.0
1962	610.7	585.7	25.0	95.9	4.1
1963	643.9	617.8	26.1	95.9	4.1
1964	691.7	663.6	28.1	95.9	4.1
1965	750.6	719.1	31.5	95.8	4.2
1966	824.8	787.7	37.1	95.5	4.5
1967	872.3	832.4	39.9	95.4	4.6
1968	956.4	909.8	46.6	95.1	4.9
1969	1 034.9	984.4	50.5	95.1	4.9
1970	1 094.1	1 038.3	55.8	94.9	5.1
1971	1 189.1	1 126.8	62.3	94.8	5.2
1972	1 312.1	1 237.9	74.2	94.3	5.7
1973	1 473.5	1 382.3	91.2	93.8	6.2
1974	1 627.0	1 499.5	127.5	92.2	7.8
1975	1 760.4	1 637.7	122.7	93.0	7.0
1976	1 975.7	1 824.6	151.1	92.4	7.6
1977	2 212.5	2 030.1	182.4	91.8	8.2
1978	2 506.1	2 293.8	212.3	91.5	8.5
1979	2 814.9	2 562.2	252.7	91.0	9.0
1980	3 081.9	2 788.1	293.8	90.5	9.5
1981	3 444.6	3 126.8	317.8	90.8	9.2
1982	3 556.4	3 253.2	303.2	91.5	8.5
1983	3 863.2	3 534.6	328.6	91.5	8.5
1984	4 336.0	3 930.9	405.1	90.7	9.3
1985	4 634.7	4 217.5	417.2	91.0	9.0
1986	4 913.0	4 460.1	452.9	90.8	9.2
1987	5 245.1	4 736.4	508.7	90.3	9.7
1988	5 654.4	5 100.4	554.0	90.2	9.8
1989	6 073.1	5 482.1	591.0	90.3	9.7
1990	6 430.2	5 800.5	629.7	90.2	9.8
1991	6 615.6	5 992.1	623.5	90.6	9.4
1992	7 010.1	6 342.3	667.8	90.5	9.5
1993	7 387.4	6 667.4	720.0	90.3	9.7
1994	7 898.6	7 085.2	813.4	89.7	10.3
1995	8 317.3	7 414.7	902.6	89.1	10.9
1996	8 802.5	7 838.5	964.0	89.0	11.0
1997	9 388.2	8 332.4	1 055.8	88.8	11.2
1998	9 909.2	8 793.5	1 115.7	88.7	11.3
1999	10 604.9	9 353.5	1 251.4	88.2	11.8
2000	11 426.8	9 951.5	1 475.3	87.1	12.9
2001	11 684.9	10 286.2	1 398.7	88.0	12.0
2002	12 072.5	10 642.3	1 430.2	88.2	11.8
2003	12 687.3	11 142.2	1 545.1	87.8	12.2
2004	13 652.2	11 853.3	1 798.9	86.8	13.2
2005	14 650.8	12 623.0	2 027.8	86.2	13.8
2006	15 617.5	13 377.2	2 240.3	85.7	14.3
2007	16 403.5	14 028.7	2 374.8	85.5	14.5
2008	16 848.0	14 291.5	2 556.5	84.8	15.2
2009	15 913.6	13 939.0	1 974.6	87.6	12.4
2010	16 883.2	14 526.5	2 356.7	86.0	14.0
2011	17 758.2	15 094.0	2 664.2	85.0	15.0
2009					
1st quarter	15 799.4	13 893.7	1 905.7	87.9	12.1
2nd quarter	15 713.2	13 854.1	1 859.1	88.2	11.8
3rd quarter	15 917.5	13 920.5	1 997.0	87.5	12.5
4th quarter	16 223.9	14 087.4	2 136.5	86.8	13.2
2010					
1st quarter	16 523.2	14 277.9	2 245.3	86.4	13.6
2nd quarter	16 812.8	14 467.8	2 345.0	86.1	13.9
3rd quarter	17 006.4	14 605.5	2 400.9	85.9	14.1
4th quarter	17 190.5	14 755.0	2 435.5	85.8	14.2
2011					
1st quarter	17 463.2	14 867.8	2 595.4	85.1	14.9
2nd quarter	17 695.2	15 012.8	2 682.4	84.8	15.2
3rd quarter	17 857.7	15 176.1	2 681.6	85.0	15.0
4th quarter	18 016.8	15 319.4	2 697.4	85.0	15.0

Table 1-10. Shares of Aggregate Final Demand

(Billions of dollars, quarterly dollar data are at seasonally adjusted rates, percents.)   **NIPA Table 1.1.5**

Year and quarter	Aggregate final demand (billions of dollars)							Shares of aggregate final demand (percent)					
	Total	Consumption (PCE)	Nonresidential fixed investment	Residential investment	Exports	Government consumption and gross investment		PCE	Nonresidential investment	Residential investment	Exports	Federal government	State and local government
						Federal	State and local						
1950	299.6	192.2	27.8	20.5	12.4	26.0	20.7	64.2	9.3	6.8	4.1	8.7	6.9
1951	343.8	208.5	31.8	18.4	17.1	45.0	23.0	60.6	9.2	5.4	5.0	13.1	6.7
1952	370.0	219.5	31.9	18.6	16.5	59.1	24.4	59.3	8.6	5.0	4.5	16.0	6.6
1953	393.4	233.1	35.1	19.4	15.3	64.4	26.1	59.3	8.9	4.9	3.9	16.4	6.6
1954	397.7	240.0	34.7	21.1	15.8	57.2	28.9	60.3	8.7	5.3	4.0	14.4	7.3
1955	427.0	258.8	39.0	25.0	17.7	54.9	31.6	60.6	9.1	5.9	4.1	12.9	7.4
1956	452.5	271.7	44.5	23.6	21.3	56.7	34.7	60.0	9.8	5.2	4.7	12.5	7.7
1957	480.2	286.9	47.5	22.2	24.0	61.3	38.3	59.7	9.9	4.6	5.0	12.8	8.0
1958	487.6	296.2	42.5	22.3	20.6	63.8	42.2	60.7	8.7	4.6	4.2	13.1	8.7
1959	525.0	317.7	46.5	28.1	22.7	65.3	44.7	60.5	8.9	5.4	4.3	12.4	8.5
1960	546.1	331.8	49.4	26.3	27.0	64.1	47.5	60.8	9.0	4.8	4.9	11.7	8.7
1961	564.5	342.2	48.8	26.4	27.6	67.9	51.6	60.6	8.6	4.7	4.9	12.0	9.1
1962	604.6	363.3	53.1	29.0	29.1	75.2	54.9	60.1	8.8	4.8	4.8	12.4	9.1
1963	638.3	382.7	56.0	32.1	31.1	76.9	59.5	60.0	8.8	5.0	4.9	12.0	9.3
1964	687.0	411.5	63.0	34.3	35.0	78.4	64.8	59.9	9.2	5.0	5.1	11.4	9.4
1965	741.3	443.8	74.8	34.2	37.1	80.4	71.0	59.9	10.1	4.6	5.0	10.8	9.6
1966	811.1	480.9	85.4	32.3	40.9	92.4	79.2	59.3	10.5	4.0	5.0	11.4	9.8
1967	862.6	507.8	86.4	32.4	43.5	104.6	87.9	58.9	10.0	3.8	5.0	12.1	10.2
1968	947.3	558.0	93.4	38.7	47.9	111.3	98.0	58.9	9.9	4.1	5.1	11.7	10.3
1969	1 025.8	605.1	104.7	42.6	51.9	113.3	108.2	59.0	10.2	4.2	5.1	11.0	10.5
1970	1 092.1	648.3	109.0	41.4	59.7	113.4	120.3	59.4	10.0	3.8	5.5	10.4	11.0
1971	1 180.9	701.6	114.1	55.8	63.0	113.6	132.8	59.4	9.7	4.7	5.3	9.6	11.2
1972	1 302.9	770.2	128.8	69.7	70.8	119.6	143.8	59.1	9.9	5.3	5.4	9.2	11.0
1973	1 457.6	852.0	153.3	75.3	95.3	122.5	159.2	58.5	10.5	5.2	6.5	8.4	10.9
1974	1 613.0	932.9	169.5	66.0	126.7	134.5	183.4	57.8	10.5	4.1	7.9	8.3	11.4
1975	1 766.6	1 033.8	173.7	62.7	138.7	149.0	208.7	58.5	9.8	3.5	7.9	8.4	11.8
1976	1 958.7	1 151.3	192.4	82.5	149.5	159.7	223.3	58.8	9.8	4.2	7.6	8.2	11.4
1977	2 190.3	1 277.8	228.7	110.3	159.4	175.4	238.7	58.3	10.4	5.0	7.3	8.0	10.9
1978	2 480.3	1 427.6	280.6	131.6	186.9	190.9	262.7	57.6	11.3	5.3	7.5	7.7	10.6
1979	2 797.0	1 591.2	333.9	141.0	230.1	210.6	290.2	56.9	11.9	5.0	8.2	7.5	10.4
1980	3 088.3	1 755.8	362.4	123.2	280.8	243.7	322.4	56.9	11.7	4.0	9.1	7.9	10.4
1981	3 414.8	1 939.5	420.0	122.6	305.2	280.2	347.3	56.8	12.3	3.6	8.9	8.2	10.2
1982	3 571.4	2 075.5	426.5	105.7	283.2	310.8	369.7	58.1	11.9	3.0	7.9	8.7	10.4
1983	3 869.1	2 288.6	417.2	152.9	277.0	342.9	390.5	59.2	10.8	4.0	7.2	8.9	10.1
1984	4 270.6	2 501.1	489.6	180.6	302.4	374.3	422.6	58.6	11.5	4.2	7.1	8.8	9.9
1985	4 612.9	2 717.6	526.2	188.2	302.0	412.8	466.1	58.9	11.4	4.1	6.5	8.9	10.1
1986	4 906.2	2 896.7	519.8	220.1	320.3	438.4	510.9	59.0	10.6	4.5	6.5	8.9	10.4
1987	5 218.0	3 097.0	524.1	233.7	363.8	459.5	539.9	59.4	10.0	4.5	7.0	8.8	10.3
1988	5 636.0	3 350.1	563.8	239.3	443.9	461.6	577.3	59.4	10.0	4.2	7.9	8.2	10.2
1989	6 045.4	3 594.5	607.7	239.5	503.1	481.4	619.2	59.5	10.1	4.0	8.3	8.0	10.2
1990	6 415.7	3 835.5	622.4	224.0	552.1	507.5	674.2	59.8	9.7	3.5	8.6	7.9	10.5
1991	6 616.1	3 980.1	598.2	205.1	596.6	526.6	709.5	60.2	9.0	3.1	9.0	8.0	10.7
1992	6 993.8	4 236.9	612.1	236.3	635.0	532.9	740.6	60.6	8.8	3.4	9.1	7.6	10.6
1993	7 366.6	4 483.6	666.6	266.0	655.6	525.0	769.8	60.9	9.0	3.6	8.9	7.1	10.4
1994	7 834.8	4 750.8	731.4	302.1	720.7	518.6	811.2	60.6	9.3	3.9	9.2	6.6	10.4
1995	8 286.2	4 987.3	810.0	302.9	811.9	518.8	855.3	60.2	9.8	3.7	9.8	6.3	10.3
1996	8 771.8	5 273.6	875.4	334.1	867.7	527.0	894.0	60.1	10.0	3.8	9.9	6.0	10.2
1997	9 317.2	5 570.6	968.6	349.1	954.4	531.0	943.5	59.8	10.4	3.7	10.2	5.7	10.1
1998	9 845.4	5 918.5	1 061.1	385.9	953.9	531.0	995.0	60.1	10.8	3.9	9.7	5.4	10.1
1999	10 544.0	6 342.8	1 154.9	425.8	989.3	554.9	1 076.3	60.2	11.0	4.0	9.4	5.3	10.2
2000	11 372.3	6 830.4	1 268.7	449.0	1 093.2	576.1	1 154.9	60.1	11.2	3.9	9.6	5.1	10.2
2001	11 723.1	7 148.8	1 227.8	472.4	1 027.7	611.7	1 234.7	61.0	10.5	4.0	8.8	5.2	10.5
2002	12 060.4	7 439.2	1 125.4	509.5	1 003.0	680.6	1 302.7	61.7	9.3	4.2	8.3	5.6	10.8
2003	12 671.0	7 804.1	1 135.7	577.6	1 041.0	756.5	1 356.1	61.6	9.0	4.6	8.2	6.0	10.7
2004	13 587.2	8 270.6	1 223.0	680.6	1 180.2	824.6	1 408.2	60.9	9.0	5.0	8.7	6.1	10.4
2005	14 600.8	8 803.5	1 347.3	775.0	1 305.1	876.3	1 493.6	60.3	9.2	5.3	8.9	6.0	10.2
2006	15 557.6	9 301.0	1 505.3	761.9	1 471.0	931.7	1 586.7	59.8	9.7	4.9	9.5	6.0	10.2
2007	16 374.4	9 772.3	1 637.5	628.7	1 661.7	976.3	1 697.9	59.7	10.0	3.8	10.1	6.0	10.4
2008	16 889.1	10 035.5	1 656.3	472.4	1 846.8	1 080.1	1 798.0	59.4	9.8	2.8	10.9	6.4	10.6
2009	16 074.3	9 866.1	1 353.0	354.7	1 583.0	1 142.7	1 774.8	61.4	8.4	2.2	9.8	7.1	11.0
2010	16 816.3	10 245.5	1 390.1	338.1	1 839.8	1 222.8	1 780.0	60.9	8.3	2.0	10.9	7.3	10.6
2011	17 712.1	10 726.0	1 532.5	337.5	2 085.5	1 232.9	1 797.7	60.6	8.7	1.9	11.8	7.0	10.1
2009													
1st quarter	15 978.9	9 781.7	1 430.6	369.0	1 522.2	1 105.3	1 770.1	61.2	9.0	2.3	9.5	6.9	11.1
2nd quarter	15 913.6	9 781.6	1 351.9	342.4	1 520.8	1 137.2	1 779.7	61.5	8.5	2.2	9.6	7.1	11.2
3rd quarter	16 114.6	9 911.1	1 324.3	353.9	1 590.3	1 157.7	1 777.3	61.5	8.2	2.2	9.9	7.2	11.0
4th quarter	16 290.0	9 990.0	1 305.1	353.2	1 699.0	1 170.6	1 772.1	61.3	8.0	2.2	10.4	7.2	10.9
2010													
1st quarter	16 479.0	10 103.7	1 318.7	339.3	1 749.5	1 195.2	1 772.6	61.3	8.0	2.1	10.6	7.3	10.8
2nd quarter	16 734.8	10 184.8	1 377.1	354.5	1 813.8	1 224.5	1 780.1	60.9	8.2	2.1	10.8	7.3	10.6
3rd quarter	16 899.7	10 276.6	1 416.5	327.3	1 860.6	1 237.5	1 781.2	60.8	8.4	1.9	11.0	7.3	10.5
4th quarter	17 151.9	10 417.1	1 447.9	331.3	1 935.3	1 234.3	1 786.0	60.7	8.4	1.9	11.3	7.2	10.4
2011													
1st quarter	17 401.2	10 571.7	1 460.5	330.6	2 024.1	1 219.9	1 794.4	60.8	8.4	1.9	11.6	7.0	10.3
2nd quarter	17 641.6	10 676.0	1 506.0	335.7	2 085.3	1 237.1	1 801.5	60.5	8.5	1.9	11.8	7.0	10.2
3rd quarter	17 856.8	10 784.5	1 568.7	337.0	2 119.2	1 248.9	1 798.5	60.4	8.8	1.9	11.9	7.0	10.1
4th quarter	17 948.1	10 871.6	1 594.8	346.5	2 113.2	1 225.5	1 796.5	60.6	8.9	1.9	11.8	6.8	10.0

Section 1b: Income and Value Added

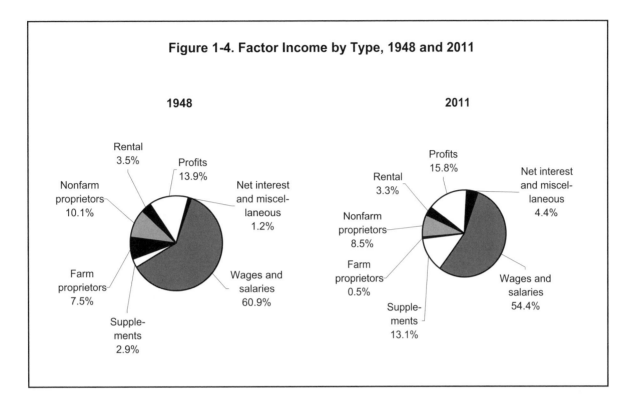

Figure 1-4. Factor Income by Type, 1948 and 2011

- The changing distribution of national income over the postwar period is shown in the figure above, based on data in Tables 1-13A and B. The total income concept whose distribution is shown in this graph is called "net national factor income," formerly known as simply "national income," and it is the sum of the income components identified in the graph.

- The share of labor compensation rose from 63.8 percent in 1948 to 67.5 percent in 2011. However, the wage and salary share declined from 60.9 to 54.4 percent. The increase in the total labor share is entirely accounted for by supplements to wages and salaries, which are the costs of fringe benefits—including health insurance—and taxes ("employer contributions") to pay for Social Security and Medicare. These rose from 2.9 to 13.1 percent of net national factor income. (Tables 1-13A and B)

- The farm proprietors' share dropped from 7.5 percent in 1948 to less than 1 percent in 2011, and the share going to nonfarm proprietors declined from 10.1 to 8.5 percent. Proprietors' income includes the return to their labor input as well as to their land and other capital, so it cannot be unequivocally attributed to either capital or labor. The rental income share, which includes the imputed net rent on owner-occupied houses, changed little. (Tables 1-13A and B)

- The share of capital incomes other than proprietors' and rental income—the sum of corporate profits and interest—rose from 15.1 percent in 1948 to 20.2 percent in 2011. The profit share alone in 2011 was higher than the share of profits and interest combined had been in 1948. (Tables 1-13A and B)

Table 1-11. Relation of Gross Domestic Product, Gross and Net National Product, National Income, and Personal Income

(Billions of dollars, quarterly data are at seasonally adjusted annual rates.)

NIPA Table 1.7.5

Year and quarter	Gross domestic product	Plus: Income receipts from the rest of the world	Less: Income payments to the rest of the world	Equals: Gross national product	Less: Consumption of fixed capital									Equals: Net national product
					Total	Private					Government			
						Total	Domestic business			House-holds and institutions	Total	General govern-ment	Govern-ment enter-prises	
							Total	Capital consump-tion allow-ances	Less: Capital consump-tion ad-justment					
1955	414.7	3.5	1.1	417.2	42.8	31.1	25.8	25.7	-0.2	5.2	11.7	11.0	0.8	374.4
1956	437.4	3.9	1.1	440.2	47.1	34.3	28.6	27.9	-0.7	5.7	12.8	11.9	0.9	393.1
1957	461.1	4.3	1.2	464.1	50.8	37.2	31.2	30.2	-1.0	6.1	13.6	12.7	0.9	413.3
1958	467.2	3.9	1.2	469.8	53.3	39.4	33.1	31.5	-1.5	6.3	13.9	12.9	1.0	416.5
1959	506.6	4.3	1.5	509.4	55.4	41.0	34.3	33.4	-0.9	6.7	14.5	13.4	1.0	454.0
1960	526.4	4.9	1.8	529.6	56.6	41.6	34.6	35.2	0.5	7.0	15.0	13.9	1.1	473.0
1961	544.8	5.3	1.8	548.3	58.2	42.6	35.4	36.6	1.2	7.2	15.6	14.4	1.2	490.1
1962	585.7	5.9	1.8	589.7	60.6	44.1	36.6	40.9	4.3	7.5	16.5	15.2	1.2	529.2
1963	617.8	6.5	2.1	622.2	63.3	45.9	38.1	43.3	5.3	7.8	17.5	16.1	1.3	558.9
1964	663.6	7.2	2.3	668.6	66.4	48.3	40.0	46.1	6.1	8.3	18.1	16.7	1.4	602.2
1965	719.1	7.9	2.6	724.4	70.7	51.9	42.9	49.4	6.4	8.9	18.9	17.4	1.5	653.7
1966	787.7	8.1	3.0	792.8	76.5	56.5	46.9	53.4	6.5	9.6	20.0	18.3	1.6	716.3
1967	832.4	8.7	3.3	837.8	82.9	61.6	51.2	57.8	6.6	10.4	21.4	19.6	1.8	754.9
1968	909.8	10.1	4.0	915.9	90.4	67.4	56.1	62.6	6.5	11.3	23.0	21.0	2.0	825.5
1969	984.4	11.8	5.7	990.5	99.2	74.5	61.9	68.8	6.9	12.6	24.7	22.5	2.2	891.4
1970	1 038.3	12.8	6.4	1 044.7	108.3	81.7	68.2	73.8	5.7	13.5	26.6	24.1	2.5	936.4
1971	1 126.8	14.0	6.4	1 134.4	117.8	89.5	74.6	79.4	4.8	14.9	28.2	25.5	2.8	1 016.6
1972	1 237.9	16.3	7.7	1 246.4	127.2	97.7	81.2	88.3	7.1	16.5	29.4	26.3	3.1	1 119.3
1973	1 382.3	23.5	10.9	1 394.9	140.8	109.5	90.6	96.8	6.2	18.8	31.3	27.8	3.5	1 254.1
1974	1 499.5	29.8	14.3	1 515.0	163.7	127.8	106.1	107.6	1.5	21.7	35.9	31.6	4.3	1 351.3
1975	1 637.7	28.0	15.0	1 650.7	190.4	150.4	125.8	118.4	-7.3	24.7	39.9	34.9	5.1	1 460.3
1976	1 824.6	32.4	15.5	1 841.4	208.2	165.5	138.5	128.5	-10.0	27.1	42.6	37.1	5.5	1 633.3
1977	2 030.1	37.2	16.9	2 050.4	231.8	186.1	155.5	146.1	-9.3	30.7	45.6	39.6	6.0	1 818.6
1978	2 293.8	46.3	24.7	2 315.3	261.4	212.0	176.4	165.5	-10.9	35.5	49.5	42.8	6.7	2 053.9
1979	2 562.2	68.3	36.4	2 594.2	298.9	244.5	203.5	189.7	-13.8	41.0	54.4	46.9	7.6	2 295.3
1980	2 788.1	79.1	44.9	2 822.3	344.1	282.3	235.4	216.9	-18.5	46.9	61.8	53.0	8.8	2 478.2
1981	3 126.8	92.0	59.1	3 159.8	393.3	323.2	271.2	269.3	-1.9	52.1	70.1	60.1	10.0	2 766.4
1982	3 253.2	101.0	64.5	3 289.7	433.5	356.4	300.7	309.4	8.7	55.8	77.1	66.2	10.9	2 856.2
1983	3 534.6	101.9	64.8	3 571.7	451.1	369.5	311.4	347.9	36.5	58.1	81.6	70.1	11.5	3 120.6
1984	3 930.9	121.9	85.6	3 967.2	474.3	387.5	326.0	393.5	67.5	61.5	86.9	74.7	12.2	3 492.8
1985	4 217.5	112.4	85.9	4 244.0	505.4	412.8	348.0	445.6	97.6	64.8	92.7	79.7	12.9	3 738.6
1986	4 460.1	111.0	93.4	4 477.7	538.5	439.1	369.9	458.5	88.6	69.2	99.4	85.6	13.8	3 939.2
1987	4 736.4	122.8	105.2	4 754.0	571.1	464.5	390.3	475.3	84.9	74.1	106.6	92.0	14.6	4 182.9
1988	5 100.4	151.6	128.3	5 123.8	611.0	497.1	417.6	501.3	83.7	79.5	113.9	98.3	15.6	4 512.8
1989	5 482.1	177.2	151.2	5 508.1	651.5	529.6	444.4	521.3	76.9	85.2	121.8	105.1	16.7	4 856.6
1990	5 800.5	188.5	154.1	5 835.0	691.2	560.4	469.8	521.2	51.4	90.6	130.8	112.9	17.9	5 143.7
1991	5 992.1	168.1	138.2	6 022.0	724.4	585.4	490.6	530.1	39.5	94.8	138.9	120.1	18.8	5 297.6
1992	6 342.3	151.8	122.7	6 371.4	744.4	599.9	500.9	541.3	40.4	99.0	144.5	124.7	19.8	5 627.1
1993	6 667.4	155.2	124.0	6 698.5	778.0	626.4	521.2	567.4	46.2	105.2	151.6	130.5	21.1	5 920.5
1994	7 085.2	184.1	160.0	7 109.2	819.2	661.0	549.4	605.1	55.7	111.5	158.2	135.8	22.4	6 290.1
1995	7 414.7	229.3	199.6	7 444.3	869.5	704.6	586.0	651.1	65.1	118.7	164.8	141.2	23.6	6 574.9
1996	7 838.5	245.8	214.2	7 870.1	912.5	743.4	619.2	697.4	78.2	124.2	169.2	144.5	24.6	6 957.6
1997	8 332.4	279.5	256.1	8 355.8	963.8	789.7	658.5	757.2	98.7	131.2	174.1	148.1	26.0	7 392.0
1998	8 793.5	286.2	268.9	8 810.8	1 020.5	841.6	702.1	810.6	108.5	139.5	179.0	151.9	27.1	7 790.3
1999	9 353.5	319.5	291.7	9 381.3	1 094.4	907.2	756.8	883.8	126.9	150.4	187.2	158.5	28.6	8 286.9
2000	9 951.5	380.5	342.8	9 989.2	1 184.3	986.8	824.3	945.3	121.0	162.5	197.5	166.8	30.7	8 804.9
2001	10 286.2	323.0	271.1	10 338.1	1 256.2	1 051.6	876.5	1 018.8	142.3	175.1	204.6	172.5	32.1	9 081.9
2002	10 642.3	313.5	264.4	10 691.4	1 305.0	1 094.0	908.5	1 110.9	202.4	185.5	210.9	177.3	33.7	9 386.4
2003	11 142.2	353.3	284.6	11 210.9	1 354.1	1 135.9	935.4	1 125.3	189.9	200.5	218.1	182.8	35.4	9 856.9
2004	11 853.3	448.6	357.4	11 944.5	1 432.8	1 200.9	978.7	1 138.8	160.1	222.2	231.9	193.4	38.5	10 511.7
2005	12 623.0	573.0	475.9	12 720.1	1 541.4	1 290.8	1 045.7	965.6	-80.1	245.1	250.6	208.7	41.9	11 178.7
2006	13 377.2	721.1	648.6	13 449.6	1 660.7	1 391.4	1 123.3	1 027.7	-95.6	268.1	269.3	224.7	44.6	11 789.0
2007	14 028.7	871.0	747.7	14 151.9	1 767.5	1 476.2	1 190.7	1 087.2	-103.6	285.5	291.3	243.2	48.1	12 384.4
2008	14 291.5	856.1	686.9	14 460.7	1 854.1	1 542.9	1 248.3	1 325.2	76.9	294.6	311.2	259.6	51.5	12 606.6
2009	13 939.0	639.8	487.5	14 091.2	1 866.2	1 542.4	1 249.9	1 289.5	39.5	292.5	323.7	270.5	53.2	12 225.0
2010	14 526.5	702.9	513.5	14 715.9	1 874.9	1 540.9	1 245.7	1 442.1	196.5	295.2	334.0	278.6	55.4	12 841.0
2011	15 094.0	779.3	533.8	15 339.5	1 950.1	1 597.9	1 294.4	1 622.2	327.7	303.4	352.2	293.2	59.1	13 389.4
2009														
1st quarter	13 893.7	624.6	491.9	14 026.4	1 885.2	1 562.6	1 267.2	1 290.9	23.8	295.4	322.6	269.3	53.3	12 141.2
2nd quarter	13 854.1	621.2	480.8	13 994.4	1 868.4	1 545.2	1 253.1	1 288.9	35.7	292.1	323.2	270.0	53.2	12 126.1
3rd quarter	13 920.5	636.9	473.2	14 084.2	1 854.1	1 530.5	1 240.6	1 288.1	47.5	289.9	323.6	270.5	53.1	12 230.1
4th quarter	14 087.4	676.5	504.2	14 259.8	1 857.1	1 531.4	1 238.8	1 289.9	51.1	292.6	325.6	272.2	53.4	12 402.7
2010														
1st quarter	14 277.9	674.0	504.6	14 447.4	1 858.6	1 529.6	1 235.6	1 303.3	67.7	294.0	329.0	274.8	54.2	12 588.8
2nd quarter	14 467.8	699.0	502.8	14 664.0	1 866.9	1 534.4	1 241.2	1 310.2	69.0	293.2	332.5	277.5	55.0	12 797.2
3rd quarter	14 605.5	708.9	501.6	14 812.8	1 878.2	1 542.6	1 247.2	1 445.8	198.6	295.4	335.5	279.6	55.9	12 934.7
4th quarter	14 755.0	729.4	545.0	14 939.4	1 896.1	1 557.0	1 258.7	1 709.2	450.5	298.4	339.1	282.5	56.6	13 043.3
2011														
1st quarter	14 867.8	752.1	525.0	15 094.9	1 914.3	1 570.5	1 270.1	1 607.9	337.8	300.4	343.8	286.4	57.4	13 180.6
2nd quarter	15 012.8	803.2	542.0	15 274.0	1 939.9	1 590.5	1 287.8	1 616.4	328.6	302.7	349.4	291.0	58.4	13 334.1
3rd quarter	15 176.1	792.2	524.9	15 443.4	1 962.8	1 607.6	1 303.2	1 626.5	323.3	304.4	355.2	295.6	59.6	13 480.5
4th quarter	15 319.4	769.7	543.4	15 545.6	1 983.4	1 622.9	1 316.7	1 637.9	321.1	306.2	360.5	299.8	60.7	13 562.2

Table 1-11. Relation of Gross Domestic Product, Gross and Net National Product, National Income, and Personal Income—*Continued*

(Billions of dollars, quarterly data are at seasonally adjusted annual rates.)

NIPA Table 1.7.5

Year and quarter	Net national product	Less: Statistical discrepancy	Equals: National income	Less: Corporate profits with IVA and CCAdj	Less: Taxes on production and imports less subsidies	Less: Contributions for government social insurance, domestic	Less: Net interest and miscellaneous payments on assets	Less: Business current transfer payments, net	Less: Current surplus of government enterprises	Less: Wage accruals less disbursements	Plus: Personal income receipts on assets	Plus: Personal current transfer receipts	Equals: Personal income	Addendum: Gross national income
1955	374.4	2.4	372.0	49.0	31.7	9.1	6.2	1.4	. . .	0.0	25.7	15.7	316.0	414.8
1956	393.1	-1.8	394.9	48.0	33.9	10.0	6.9	1.7	. . .	0.0	28.2	16.8	339.5	442.0
1957	413.3	-0.1	413.3	47.6	35.9	11.4	8.0	1.9	. . .	0.0	30.6	19.5	358.5	464.2
1958	416.5	1.0	415.6	42.5	36.8	11.4	9.5	1.8	. . .	0.0	31.9	23.5	368.9	468.8
1959	454.0	0.5	453.5	53.8	40.0	13.8	9.6	1.8	1.0	0.0	34.6	24.2	392.3	508.9
1960	473.0	-1.0	473.9	53.1	43.4	16.4	10.6	1.9	0.9	0.0	37.9	25.7	411.3	530.5
1961	490.1	-0.6	490.7	54.2	45.0	17.0	12.5	2.0	0.8	0.0	40.1	29.5	428.8	548.9
1962	529.2	0.3	528.9	62.3	48.1	19.1	14.2	2.2	0.9	0.0	44.1	30.4	456.4	589.4
1963	558.9	-0.8	559.7	68.3	51.2	21.7	15.2	2.7	1.4	0.0	47.9	32.2	479.5	623.1
1964	602.2	0.8	601.4	75.5	54.5	22.4	17.4	3.1	1.3	0.0	53.8	33.5	514.3	667.8
1965	653.7	1.5	652.2	86.5	57.7	23.4	19.6	3.6	1.3	0.0	59.4	36.2	555.5	722.9
1966	716.3	6.2	710.1	92.5	59.3	31.3	22.4	3.5	1.0	0.0	64.1	39.6	603.8	786.6
1967	754.9	4.5	750.4	90.2	64.1	34.9	25.5	3.8	0.9	0.0	69.0	48.0	648.1	833.3
1968	825.5	4.3	821.2	97.3	72.2	38.7	27.1	4.3	1.2	0.0	75.2	56.1	711.7	911.6
1969	891.4	2.9	888.5	94.5	79.3	44.1	32.7	4.9	1.0	0.0	84.1	62.3	778.3	987.7
1970	936.4	6.9	929.5	82.5	86.6	46.4	39.1	4.5	0.0	0.0	93.5	74.7	838.6	1 037.8
1971	1 016.6	11.0	1 005.6	96.1	95.8	51.2	43.9	4.3	-0.2	0.6	101.0	88.1	903.1	1 123.4
1972	1 119.3	8.9	1 110.3	111.4	101.3	59.2	47.9	4.9	0.5	0.0	109.6	97.9	992.6	1 237.5
1973	1 254.1	8.0	1 246.1	124.5	112.0	75.5	55.2	6.0	-0.4	-0.1	124.7	112.6	1 110.5	1 386.9
1974	1 351.3	9.8	1 341.5	115.1	121.6	85.2	70.8	7.1	-0.9	-0.5	146.4	133.3	1 222.7	1 505.2
1975	1 460.3	16.3	1 444.0	133.3	130.8	89.3	81.6	9.4	-3.2	0.1	162.2	170.0	1 334.9	1 634.4
1976	1 633.3	23.5	1 609.8	161.6	141.3	101.3	85.5	9.5	-1.8	0.1	178.4	184.0	1 474.7	1 818.0
1977	1 818.6	21.2	1 797.4	191.8	152.6	113.1	101.1	8.5	-2.7	0.1	205.3	194.2	1 632.5	2 029.2
1978	2 053.9	26.1	2 027.9	218.4	162.0	131.3	115.0	10.8	-2.2	0.3	234.8	209.6	1 836.7	2 289.3
1979	2 295.3	47.0	2 248.3	225.4	171.6	152.7	138.9	13.3	-2.9	-0.2	274.7	235.3	2 059.5	2 547.2
1980	2 478.2	45.3	2 433.0	201.4	190.5	166.2	181.8	14.7	-5.1	0.0	338.7	279.5	2 301.5	2 777.0
1981	2 766.4	36.6	2 729.8	223.3	224.2	195.7	232.3	17.9	-5.6	0.1	421.9	318.4	2 582.3	3 123.2
1982	2 856.2	4.8	2 851.4	205.7	225.9	208.9	271.1	20.6	-4.5	0.0	488.4	354.8	2 766.8	3 285.0
1983	3 120.6	49.7	3 070.9	259.8	242.0	226.0	285.3	22.6	-3.2	-0.4	529.6	383.7	2 952.2	3 522.0
1984	3 492.8	31.5	3 461.3	318.6	268.7	257.5	327.1	30.3	-1.9	0.2	607.9	400.1	3 268.9	3 935.6
1985	3 738.6	42.3	3 696.3	332.5	286.8	281.4	341.5	35.2	0.6	-0.2	653.2	424.9	3 496.7	4 201.7
1986	3 939.2	67.7	3 871.5	314.1	298.5	303.4	367.1	36.9	0.9	0.0	694.5	451.0	3 696.0	4 409.9
1987	4 182.9	32.9	4 150.0	367.8	317.3	323.1	366.7	34.1	0.2	0.0	715.8	467.6	3 924.4	4 721.1
1988	4 512.8	-9.5	4 522.3	426.6	345.0	361.5	385.3	33.6	2.6	0.0	767.0	496.5	4 231.2	5 133.3
1989	4 856.6	56.1	4 800.5	425.6	371.4	385.2	434.1	39.2	4.9	0.0	874.8	542.6	4 557.5	5 452.0
1990	5 143.7	84.2	5 059.5	434.4	398.0	410.1	444.2	40.1	1.6	0.1	920.8	594.9	4 846.7	5 750.8
1991	5 297.6	79.7	5 217.9	457.3	429.6	430.2	418.2	39.9	5.7	-0.1	928.6	665.9	5 031.5	5 942.3
1992	5 627.1	110.0	5 517.1	496.2	453.3	455.0	387.7	40.7	8.2	-15.8	909.7	745.8	5 347.3	6 261.5
1993	5 920.5	135.8	5 784.7	543.7	466.4	477.4	364.6	40.5	8.7	6.4	900.5	790.8	5 568.1	6 562.7
1994	6 290.1	108.8	6 181.3	628.2	512.7	508.2	362.2	41.9	9.6	17.6	947.7	826.4	5 874.8	7 000.4
1995	6 574.9	52.5	6 522.3	716.2	523.1	532.8	358.3	45.8	13.1	16.4	1 005.4	878.9	6 200.9	7 391.8
1996	6 957.6	25.9	6 931.7	801.5	545.5	555.1	371.1	53.8	14.4	3.6	1 080.7	924.1	6 591.6	7 844.2
1997	7 392.0	-14.0	7 406.0	884.8	577.8	587.2	407.6	51.3	14.1	-2.9	1 165.5	949.2	7 000.7	8 369.8
1998	7 790.3	-85.3	7 875.6	812.4	603.1	624.7	479.3	65.2	13.3	-0.7	1 269.2	977.9	7 525.4	8 896.1
1999	8 286.9	-71.1	8 358.0	856.3	628.4	661.3	481.4	69.0	14.1	5.2	1 246.8	1 021.6	7 910.8	9 452.4
2000	8 804.9	-134.0	8 938.9	819.2	662.7	705.8	539.3	87.0	9.1	0.0	1 360.7	1 083.0	8 559.4	10 123.2
2001	9 081.9	-103.4	9 185.2	784.2	669.0	733.2	544.4	101.3	4.0	0.0	1 346.0	1 188.1	8 883.3	10 441.4
2002	9 386.4	-22.1	9 408.5	872.2	721.4	751.5	506.4	82.4	6.3	0.0	1 309.6	1 282.1	9 060.1	10 713.5
2003	9 856.9	16.7	9 840.2	977.8	757.7	778.9	504.1	76.1	7.0	15.0	1 312.9	1 341.7	9 378.1	11 194.2
2004	10 511.7	-22.3	10 534.0	1 246.9	817.0	827.3	461.6	81.7	1.2	-15.0	1 408.5	1 415.5	9 937.2	11 966.8
2005	11 178.7	-95.1	11 273.8	1 456.1	869.3	872.7	543.0	95.9	-3.5	5.0	1 542.0	1 508.6	10 485.9	12 815.2
2006	11 789.0	-242.3	12 031.2	1 608.3	935.5	921.8	652.2	83.0	-4.2	1.3	1 829.7	1 605.0	11 268.1	13 691.9
2007	12 384.4	-12.0	12 396.4	1 510.6	972.6	959.5	731.6	103.3	-11.8	-6.3	2 057.0	1 718.5	11 912.3	14 163.9
2008	12 606.6	-2.4	12 609.1	1 248.4	985.7	987.3	870.1	123.0	-16.0	-5.0	2 165.4	1 879.2	12 460.2	14 463.1
2009	12 225.0	77.4	12 147.6	1 362.0	958.2	964.1	656.7	132.0	-14.9	5.0	1 707.7	2 138.1	11 930.2	14 013.8
2010	12 841.0	0.8	12 840.1	1 800.1	996.7	986.8	564.3	136.7	-15.7	0.0	1 721.2	2 281.2	12 373.5	14 715.1
2011	13 389.4	-31.8	13 421.2	1 942.8	1 035.1	924.4	535.1	134.1	-15.3	0.0	1 790.0	2 336.2	12 991.2	15 371.3
2009														
1st quarter	12 141.2	42.1	12 099.2	1 175.2	951.7	966.0	782.9	137.0	-16.8	20.0	1 851.5	2 029.8	11 964.4	13 984.3
2nd quarter	12 126.1	90.3	12 035.7	1 262.3	955.0	966.9	656.4	141.5	-15.3	0.0	1 707.5	2 167.7	11 944.1	13 904.1
3rd quarter	12 230.1	104.1	12 126.1	1 438.8	952.0	962.1	596.6	122.2	-14.0	0.0	1 635.7	2 170.1	11 874.1	13 980.2
4th quarter	12 402.7	73.2	12 329.5	1 571.6	974.2	961.5	591.0	127.5	-13.6	0.0	1 636.0	2 184.9	11 938.2	14 186.5
2010														
1st quarter	12 588.8	-7.2	12 595.9	1 724.2	984.5	976.0	589.1	134.6	-14.7	0.0	1 693.3	2 242.1	12 137.7	14 454.5
2nd quarter	12 797.2	-6.6	12 803.7	1 785.8	993.8	985.7	569.2	135.7	-15.5	0.0	1 724.5	2 252.1	12 325.6	14 670.6
3rd quarter	12 934.7	-7.4	12 942.1	1 833.1	1 002.0	991.5	550.1	140.9	-16.0	0.0	1 723.4	2 289.4	12 453.2	14 820.3
4th quarter	13 043.3	24.5	13 018.8	1 857.4	1 006.4	994.1	548.7	135.7	-16.5	0.0	1 743.5	2 341.2	12 577.6	14 914.9
2011														
1st quarter	13 180.6	-52.0	13 232.6	1 876.4	1 027.3	911.5	556.6	134.7	-15.6	0.0	1 777.2	2 328.1	12 846.9	15 146.9
2nd quarter	13 334.1	-10.0	13 344.1	1 937.6	1 038.5	917.4	525.6	133.9	-14.6	0.0	1 802.3	2 347.3	12 955.3	15 284.0
3rd quarter	13 480.5	-38.7	13 519.3	1 970.1	1 035.8	932.4	535.7	133.7	-14.5	0.0	1 794.2	2 336.6	13 056.8	15 482.1
4th quarter	13 562.2	-26.4	13 588.6	1 986.9	1 038.9	936.3	522.7	134.1	-16.7	0.0	1 786.3	2 333.1	13 105.7	15 572.0

. . . = Not available.

Table 1-12. Gross Domestic Income by Type of Income

(Billions of dollars, quarterly data are at seasonally adjusted annual rates.)   NIPA Tables 1.1.5, 1.10

Year and quarter	Gross domestic income	Compensation of employees, paid			Taxes on production and imports	Less: Subsidies	Net operating surplus					
		Total	Wage and salary accruals	Supplements to wages and salaries			Total	Private enterprises				
								Total	Net interest and miscellaneous payments, domestic industries	Business current transfer payments, net	Proprietors' income with IVA and CCAdj	Rental income of persons with CCAdj
1955	412.3	225.8	212.2	13.5	31.5	-0.2	112.1	112.1	6.1	1.4	44.3	13.8
1956	439.2	244.6	229.1	15.5	34.2	0.4	113.6	113.6	6.8	1.7	45.9	14.1
1957	461.1	257.6	240.0	17.6	36.6	0.7	116.7	116.7	8.0	1.9	47.8	14.5
1958	466.2	259.6	241.4	18.2	37.7	0.9	116.5	116.5	9.4	1.8	50.2	15.2
1959	506.1	281.1	259.9	21.1	41.1	1.1	129.7	128.7	9.5	1.8	50.3	16.0
1960	527.4	296.6	273.0	23.6	44.5	1.1	130.8	129.9	10.4	1.9	50.7	17.0
1961	545.3	305.4	280.7	24.8	47.0	2.0	136.8	135.9	12.1	2.0	53.2	17.7
1962	585.3	327.2	299.5	27.8	50.4	2.3	149.4	148.5	13.8	2.2	55.3	18.6
1963	618.6	345.3	314.9	30.4	53.4	2.2	158.8	157.5	14.7	2.7	56.5	19.3
1964	662.9	370.7	337.8	32.9	57.3	2.7	171.2	169.9	16.9	3.1	59.4	19.4
1965	717.6	399.5	363.8	35.7	60.7	3.0	189.7	188.3	19.1	3.6	63.9	19.9
1966	781.5	442.6	400.3	42.3	63.2	3.9	203.2	202.2	21.9	3.5	68.2	20.5
1967	827.9	475.1	429.0	46.1	67.9	3.8	205.8	204.9	24.9	3.8	69.8	20.9
1968	905.5	524.3	472.0	52.3	76.4	4.2	218.6	217.4	26.7	4.3	74.2	20.6
1969	981.6	577.6	518.3	59.3	83.9	4.5	225.5	224.4	33.2	4.9	77.5	20.9
1970	1 031.4	617.2	551.5	65.7	91.4	4.8	219.3	219.3	39.9	4.5	78.5	21.1
1971	1 115.8	658.9	584.5	74.4	100.5	4.7	243.3	243.6	44.2	4.3	84.7	22.2
1972	1 228.9	725.1	638.8	86.4	107.9	6.6	275.4	274.9	48.9	4.9	96.0	23.1
1973	1 374.3	811.2	708.8	102.5	117.2	5.2	310.2	310.6	57.5	6.0	113.6	23.9
1974	1 489.6	890.3	772.3	118.0	124.9	3.3	314.1	315.0	72.7	7.1	113.5	24.0
1975	1 621.4	949.2	814.9	134.3	135.3	4.5	351.0	354.3	83.2	9.4	119.6	23.4
1976	1 801.1	1 059.4	899.8	159.6	146.4	5.1	392.3	394.1	85.2	9.5	132.2	22.1
1977	2 008.9	1 180.6	994.2	186.4	159.7	7.1	444.0	446.7	99.8	8.5	146.0	19.6
1978	2 267.7	1 335.6	1 120.7	214.9	170.9	8.9	508.8	511.0	116.2	10.8	167.5	20.9
1979	2 515.3	1 498.4	1 253.4	245.0	180.1	8.5	546.4	549.3	141.5	13.3	181.1	22.6
1980	2 742.9	1 647.7	1 373.5	274.2	200.3	9.8	560.6	565.7	183.0	14.7	173.5	28.5
1981	3 090.3	1 819.8	1 511.5	308.3	235.6	11.5	652.9	658.5	228.9	17.9	181.6	36.5
1982	3 248.4	1 919.8	1 587.7	332.1	240.9	15.0	669.2	673.6	267.0	20.6	174.8	38.1
1983	3 484.9	2 035.7	1 677.7	358.0	263.3	21.3	756.1	759.3	283.1	22.6	190.7	38.2
1984	3 899.4	2 245.7	1 845.1	400.5	289.8	21.1	910.6	912.6	327.1	30.3	233.1	40.0
1985	4 175.2	2 412.0	1 982.8	429.2	308.1	21.4	971.0	970.4	352.8	35.2	246.1	41.9
1986	4 392.3	2 559.4	2 104.1	455.3	323.4	24.9	995.9	995.1	387.2	36.9	262.6	33.8
1987	4 703.5	2 737.0	2 257.6	479.4	347.5	30.3	1 078.1	1 078.0	395.7	34.1	294.2	34.2
1988	5 110.0	2 955.0	2 440.6	514.4	374.5	29.5	1 199.0	1 196.4	418.1	33.6	334.8	40.2
1989	5 426.0	3 132.6	2 584.3	548.3	398.9	27.4	1 270.6	1 265.6	474.0	39.2	351.6	42.4
1990	5 716.3	3 328.6	2 743.5	585.1	425.0	27.0	1 298.6	1 297.0	483.6	40.1	365.1	49.8
1991	5 912.4	3 441.1	2 817.2	623.9	457.1	27.5	1 317.3	1 311.6	462.0	39.9	367.3	61.6
1992	6 232.3	3 634.4	2 960.8	673.6	483.4	30.1	1 400.3	1 392.0	428.7	40.7	414.9	84.6
1993	6 531.6	3 800.4	3 086.4	714.1	503.1	36.7	1 486.7	1 478.0	407.0	40.5	449.6	114.1
1994	6 976.4	4 002.5	3 252.5	750.1	545.2	32.5	1 641.9	1 632.3	412.1	41.9	485.1	142.9
1995	7 362.1	4 199.3	3 438.5	760.8	557.9	34.8	1 770.3	1 757.2	417.5	45.8	516.0	154.6
1996	7 812.5	4 395.5	3 624.1	771.4	580.8	35.2	1 959.0	1 944.7	437.2	53.8	583.7	170.4
1997	8 346.3	4 670.0	3 878.0	792.0	611.6	33.8	2 134.7	2 120.6	487.3	51.3	628.2	176.5
1998	8 878.8	5 027.8	4 185.5	842.3	639.5	36.4	2 227.4	2 214.1	560.2	65.2	687.5	191.5
1999	9 424.6	5 359.2	4 470.4	888.8	673.6	45.2	2 342.6	2 328.5	569.9	69.0	746.8	208.2
2000	10 085.5	5 793.5	4 832.4	961.2	708.6	45.8	2 444.9	2 435.7	642.5	87.0	817.5	215.3
2001	10 389.5	5 984.5	4 957.4	1 027.1	727.7	58.7	2 479.8	2 475.7	656.9	101.3	870.7	232.4
2002	10 664.4	6 116.4	5 002.9	1 113.5	762.8	41.4	2 521.6	2 515.3	609.6	82.4	890.3	218.7
2003	11 125.5	6 388.3	5 160.3	1 228.0	806.8	49.1	2 625.4	2 618.5	595.5	76.1	930.6	204.2
2004	11 875.6	6 699.6	5 416.8	1 282.7	863.4	46.4	2 926.3	2 925.0	569.3	81.7	1 033.8	198.4
2005	12 718.0	7 071.5	5 712.4	1 359.1	930.2	60.9	3 236.0	3 239.4	678.9	95.9	1 069.8	178.2
2006	13 619.5	7 483.6	6 076.8	1 406.9	986.8	51.4	3 539.7	3 544.0	830.1	83.0	1 133.0	146.5
2007	14 040.7	7 863.0	6 422.6	1 440.4	1 027.2	54.6	3 437.5	3 449.3	952.1	103.3	1 090.4	143.7
2008	14 294.0	8 079.1	6 556.6	1 522.5	1 038.6	52.9	3 375.1	3 391.1	1 096.8	123.0	1 097.9	231.6
2009	13 861.5	7 815.4	6 284.4	1 531.1	1 017.9	59.7	3 221.7	3 236.6	855.8	132.0	941.2	305.9
2010	14 525.7	7 980.6	6 417.5	1 563.1	1 054.0	57.3	3 673.5	3 689.2	747.6	136.7	1 036.4	350.2
2011	15 125.8	8 285.6	6 677.2	1 608.4	1 097.9	62.8	3 854.9	3 870.3	709.7	134.1	1 108.9	403.9
2009												
1st quarter	13 851.7	7 839.4	6 309.8	1 529.6	1 008.0	56.4	3 175.4	3 192.1	1 001.0	137.0	960.2	278.8
2nd quarter	13 763.7	7 818.2	6 287.2	1 531.1	1 011.8	56.8	3 122.2	3 137.5	851.7	141.5	926.9	299.7
3rd quarter	13 816.5	7 790.7	6 260.2	1 530.6	1 020.4	68.4	3 219.7	3 233.6	786.6	122.2	929.3	319.3
4th quarter	14 014.2	7 813.4	6 280.4	1 533.0	1 031.3	57.1	3 369.5	3 383.1	784.0	127.5	948.5	325.9
2010												
1st quarter	14 285.1	7 861.7	6 310.8	1 550.9	1 040.9	56.4	3 580.3	3 595.0	779.3	134.6	981.7	344.1
2nd quarter	14 474.4	7 969.3	6 409.1	1 560.2	1 050.6	56.8	3 644.5	3 659.9	754.4	135.7	1 025.6	349.1
3rd quarter	14 612.9	8 031.5	6 463.8	1 567.7	1 059.0	57.0	3 701.2	3 717.1	728.7	140.9	1 057.0	352.8
4th quarter	14 730.5	8 059.9	6 486.2	1 573.7	1 065.5	59.1	3 768.1	3 784.6	728.0	135.7	1 081.5	354.8
2011												
1st quarter	14 919.8	8 181.5	6 587.2	1 594.4	1 087.4	60.0	3 796.7	3 812.2	731.3	134.7	1 095.6	385.0
2nd quarter	15 022.7	8 228.7	6 626.0	1 602.7	1 101.1	62.7	3 815.7	3 830.3	700.8	133.9	1 106.5	396.9
3rd quarter	15 214.8	8 347.3	6 733.3	1 614.0	1 100.0	64.2	3 868.9	3 883.3	710.3	133.7	1 113.7	406.3
4th quarter	15 345.8	8 384.9	6 762.3	1 622.6	1 103.3	64.4	3 938.6	3 955.2	696.6	134.1	1 119.7	427.2

Table 1-12. Gross Domestic Income by Type of Income—*Continued*

(Billions of dollars, quarterly data are at seasonally adjusted annual rates.)   **NIPA Tables 1.1.5, 1.10**

Year and quarter	Net operating surplus—*Continued*					Current surplus of government enterprises	Consumption of fixed capital			Statistical discrepancy	Gross domestic product
	Private enterprises—*Continued*						Total	Private	Government		
	Corporate profits with IVA and CCAdj, domestic industries										
	Total	Taxes on corporate income	Profits after tax								
			Total	Net dividends	Undistributed corporate profits						
1955	46.6	22.0	24.6	8.9	15.7	. . .	42.8	31.1	11.7	2.4	414.7
1956	45.2	22.0	23.2	9.5	13.7	. . .	47.1	34.3	12.8	-1.8	437.4
1957	44.5	21.4	23.1	9.9	13.3	. . .	50.8	37.2	13.6	-0.1	461.1
1958	39.9	19.0	21.0	9.8	11.1	. . .	53.3	39.4	13.9	1.0	467.2
1959	51.1	23.7	27.4	10.7	16.7	1.0	55.4	41.0	14.5	0.5	506.6
1960	50.0	22.8	27.2	11.4	15.8	0.9	56.6	41.6	15.0	-1.0	526.4
1961	50.9	22.9	28.0	11.5	16.5	0.8	58.2	42.6	15.6	-0.6	544.8
1962	58.6	24.1	34.5	12.4	22.1	0.9	60.6	44.1	16.5	0.3	585.7
1963	64.3	26.4	37.9	13.6	24.3	1.4	63.3	45.9	17.5	-0.8	617.8
1964	71.1	28.2	42.9	15.0	27.9	1.3	66.4	48.3	18.1	0.8	663.6
1965	81.8	31.1	50.8	16.9	33.9	1.3	70.7	51.9	18.9	1.5	719.1
1966	88.0	33.9	54.1	17.8	36.3	1.0	76.5	56.5	20.0	6.2	787.7
1967	85.4	32.9	52.5	18.3	34.2	0.9	82.9	61.6	21.4	4.5	832.4
1968	91.6	39.6	52.0	20.2	31.8	1.2	90.4	67.4	23.0	4.3	909.8
1969	87.9	40.0	47.9	20.4	27.5	1.0	99.2	74.5	24.7	2.9	984.4
1970	75.4	34.8	40.6	20.4	20.3	0.0	108.3	81.7	26.6	6.9	1 038.3
1971	88.2	38.2	50.1	20.3	29.7	-0.2	117.8	89.5	28.2	11.0	1 126.8
1972	101.9	42.3	59.6	21.9	37.6	0.5	127.2	97.7	29.4	8.9	1 237.9
1973	109.6	50.0	59.6	23.1	36.5	-0.4	140.8	109.5	31.3	8.0	1 382.3
1974	97.7	52.8	44.9	23.5	21.4	-0.9	163.7	127.8	35.9	9.8	1 499.5
1975	118.7	51.6	67.0	26.4	40.6	-3.2	190.4	150.4	39.9	16.3	1 637.7
1976	145.1	65.3	79.8	30.1	49.7	-1.8	208.2	165.5	42.6	23.5	1 824.6
1977	172.7	74.4	98.3	33.7	64.6	-2.7	231.8	186.1	45.6	21.2	2 030.1
1978	195.6	84.9	110.7	39.6	71.1	-2.2	261.4	212.0	49.5	26.1	2 293.8
1979	190.7	90.0	100.7	41.5	59.2	-2.9	298.9	244.5	54.4	47.0	2 562.2
1980	166.0	87.2	78.8	47.3	31.4	-5.1	344.1	282.3	61.8	45.3	2 788.1
1981	193.6	84.3	109.3	58.3	50.9	-5.6	393.3	323.2	70.1	36.6	3 126.8
1982	173.1	66.5	106.6	61.3	45.3	-4.5	433.5	356.4	77.1	4.8	3 253.2
1983	224.8	80.6	144.1	71.3	72.8	-3.2	451.1	369.5	81.6	49.7	3 534.6
1984	282.0	97.5	184.5	78.5	106.0	-1.9	474.3	387.5	86.9	31.5	3 930.9
1985	294.4	99.4	195.0	85.7	109.3	0.6	505.4	412.8	92.7	42.3	4 217.5
1986	274.7	109.7	165.0	88.3	76.7	0.9	538.5	439.1	99.4	67.7	4 460.1
1987	319.8	130.4	189.4	95.6	93.8	0.2	571.1	464.5	106.6	32.9	4 736.4
1988	369.6	141.6	228.0	98.0	130.0	2.6	611.0	497.1	113.9	-9.5	5 100.4
1989	358.4	146.1	212.4	126.4	86.0	4.9	651.5	529.6	121.8	56.1	5 482.1
1990	358.4	145.4	212.9	144.1	68.8	1.6	691.2	560.4	130.8	84.2	5 800.5
1991	380.8	138.6	242.2	156.4	85.9	5.7	724.4	585.4	138.9	79.7	5 992.1
1992	423.1	148.7	274.4	160.0	114.5	8.2	744.4	599.9	144.5	110.0	6 342.3
1993	466.8	171.0	295.7	182.3	113.4	8.7	778.0	626.4	151.6	135.8	6 667.4
1994	550.3	193.1	357.1	197.6	159.6	9.6	819.2	661.0	158.2	108.8	7 085.2
1995	623.2	217.8	405.4	221.6	183.8	13.1	869.5	704.6	164.8	52.5	7 414.7
1996	699.5	231.5	468.1	257.3	210.7	14.4	912.5	743.4	169.2	25.9	7 838.5
1997	777.3	245.4	531.9	284.0	247.9	14.1	963.8	789.7	174.1	-14.0	8 332.4
1998	709.7	248.4	461.3	309.2	152.1	13.3	1 020.5	841.6	179.0	-85.3	8 793.5
1999	734.8	258.8	476.0	295.7	180.3	14.1	1 094.4	907.2	187.2	-71.1	9 353.5
2000	673.6	265.1	408.5	348.5	60.1	9.1	1 184.3	986.8	197.5	-134.0	9 951.5
2001	614.5	203.3	411.2	330.1	81.1	4.0	1 256.2	1 051.6	204.6	-103.4	10 286.2
2002	714.3	192.3	522.0	351.2	170.8	6.3	1 305.0	1 094.0	210.9	-22.1	10 642.3
2003	812.0	243.8	568.3	392.8	175.5	7.0	1 354.1	1 135.9	218.1	16.7	11 142.2
2004	1 041.9	306.1	735.8	488.0	247.8	1.2	1 432.8	1 200.9	231.9	-22.3	11 853.3
2005	1 216.6	412.4	804.3	296.5	507.8	-3.5	1 541.4	1 290.8	250.6	-95.1	12 623.0
2006	1 351.5	473.3	878.2	626.9	251.3	-4.2	1 660.7	1 391.4	269.3	-242.3	13 377.2
2007	1 159.8	445.5	714.3	649.7	64.6	-11.8	1 767.5	1 476.2	291.3	-12.0	14 028.7
2008	841.8	309.0	532.8	606.3	-73.6	-16.0	1 854.1	1 542.9	311.2	-2.4	14 291.5
2009	1 001.6	272.4	729.2	516.4	212.8	-14.9	1 866.2	1 542.4	323.7	77.4	13 939.0
2010	1 418.2	411.1	1 007.1	615.3	391.8	-15.7	1 874.9	1 540.9	334.0	0.8	14 526.5
2011	1 513.7	416.2	1 097.5	639.6	457.9	-15.3	1 950.1	1 597.9	352.2	-31.8	15 094.0
2009											
1st quarter	815.2	208.8	606.3	571.7	34.6	-16.8	1 885.2	1 562.6	322.6	42.1	13 893.7
2nd quarter	917.7	244.8	672.9	536.9	136.0	-15.3	1 868.4	1 545.2	323.2	90.3	13 854.1
3rd quarter	1 076.3	301.6	774.7	446.4	328.3	-14.0	1 854.1	1 530.5	323.6	104.1	13 920.5
4th quarter	1 197.3	334.4	862.9	510.6	352.3	-13.6	1 857.1	1 531.4	325.6	73.2	14 087.4
2010											
1st quarter	1 355.3	409.7	945.6	581.7	363.9	-14.7	1 858.6	1 529.6	329.0	-7.2	14 277.9
2nd quarter	1 395.2	399.6	995.6	590.4	405.3	-15.5	1 866.9	1 534.4	332.5	-6.6	14 467.8
3rd quarter	1 437.8	430.3	1 007.5	629.3	378.2	-16.0	1 878.2	1 542.6	335.5	-7.4	14 605.5
4th quarter	1 484.5	404.7	1 079.8	659.8	420.0	-16.5	1 896.1	1 557.0	339.1	24.5	14 755.0
2011											
1st quarter	1 465.7	422.3	1 043.3	644.2	399.2	-15.6	1 914.3	1 570.5	343.8	-52.0	14 867.8
2nd quarter	1 492.2	420.5	1 071.7	664.1	407.6	-14.6	1 939.9	1 590.5	349.4	-10.0	15 012.8
3rd quarter	1 519.3	411.4	1 107.9	610.6	497.3	-14.5	1 962.8	1 607.6	355.2	-38.7	15 176.1
4th quarter	1 577.6	410.7	1 166.9	639.5	527.5	-16.7	1 983.4	1 622.9	360.5	-26.4	15 319.4

. . . = Not available.

Table 1-13A. National Income by Type of Income: Recent Data

(Billions of dollars, quarterly data are at seasonally adjusted annual rates.)   **NIPA Tables 1.7.5, 1.12**

Year and quarter	National income, total	Compensation of employees							Proprietors' income with IVA and CCAdj			Rental income of persons with CCAdj
		Total	Wage and salary accruals			Supplements to wages and salaries			Total	Farm	Nonfarm	
			Total	Government	Other	Total	Employer contributions for:					
							Employee pension and insurance funds	Government social insurance				
1950	263.9	155.3	147.3	22.6	124.6	8.0	4.7	3.4	37.5	12.9	24.6	9.1
1951	303.8	181.4	171.6	29.2	142.4	9.8	5.7	4.1	42.7	15.3	27.3	10.0
1952	321.3	196.2	185.6	33.4	152.3	10.5	6.4	4.1	43.1	14.3	28.8	11.2
1953	338.6	210.2	199.0	34.3	164.7	11.2	7.0	4.2	42.0	12.2	29.8	12.4
1954	338.7	209.2	197.3	34.9	162.4	11.9	7.3	4.6	42.3	11.7	30.5	13.4
1955	372.0	225.7	212.2	36.6	175.6	13.5	8.4	5.2	44.3	10.7	33.5	13.8
1956	394.9	244.5	229.0	38.8	190.2	15.5	9.8	5.7	45.9	10.6	35.3	14.1
1957	413.3	257.5	240.0	41.0	198.9	17.6	11.2	6.4	47.8	10.6	37.3	14.5
1958	415.6	259.5	241.3	44.1	197.2	18.2	11.9	6.3	50.2	12.4	37.8	15.2
1959	453.5	281.0	259.8	46.1	213.8	21.1	13.3	7.9	50.3	10.0	40.3	16.0
1960	473.9	296.4	272.9	49.2	223.7	23.6	14.3	9.3	50.7	10.6	40.1	17.0
1961	490.7	305.3	280.5	52.5	228.0	24.8	15.2	9.6	53.2	11.2	42.0	17.7
1962	528.9	327.1	299.4	56.3	243.0	27.8	16.6	11.2	55.3	11.2	44.1	18.6
1963	559.7	345.2	314.9	60.0	254.8	30.4	18.0	12.4	56.5	11.0	45.5	19.3
1964	601.4	370.7	337.8	64.9	272.9	32.9	20.3	12.6	59.4	9.8	49.6	19.4
1965	652.2	399.5	363.8	69.9	293.8	35.7	22.7	13.1	63.9	12.0	51.9	19.9
1966	710.1	442.7	400.3	78.4	321.9	42.3	25.5	16.8	68.2	13.0	55.2	20.5
1967	750.4	475.1	429.0	86.5	342.5	46.1	28.1	18.0	69.8	11.6	58.2	20.9
1968	821.2	524.3	472.0	96.7	375.3	52.3	32.4	20.0	74.2	11.7	62.5	20.6
1969	888.5	577.6	518.3	105.6	412.7	59.3	36.5	22.8	77.5	12.8	64.7	20.9
1970	929.5	617.2	551.6	117.2	434.3	65.7	41.8	23.8	78.5	12.9	65.6	21.1
1971	1 005.6	658.9	584.5	126.8	457.8	74.4	47.9	26.4	84.7	13.4	71.3	22.2
1972	1 110.3	725.1	638.8	137.9	500.9	86.4	55.2	31.2	96.0	17.0	79.0	23.1
1973	1 246.1	811.2	708.8	148.8	560.0	102.5	62.7	39.8	113.6	29.1	84.6	23.9
1974	1 341.5	890.2	772.3	160.5	611.8	118.0	73.3	44.7	113.5	23.5	90.0	24.0
1975	1 444.0	949.1	814.8	176.2	638.6	134.3	87.6	46.7	119.6	22.0	97.6	23.4
1976	1 609.8	1 059.3	899.7	188.9	710.8	159.6	105.2	54.4	132.2	17.2	115.0	22.1
1977	1 797.4	1 180.5	994.2	202.6	791.6	186.4	125.3	61.1	146.0	16.0	130.1	19.6
1978	2 027.9	1 335.5	1 120.6	220.0	900.6	214.9	143.4	71.5	167.5	19.9	147.6	20.9
1979	2 248.3	1 498.3	1 253.3	237.1	1 016.2	245.0	162.4	82.6	181.1	22.2	159.0	22.6
1980	2 433.0	1 647.6	1 373.4	261.5	1 112.0	274.2	185.2	88.9	173.5	11.7	161.8	28.5
1981	2 729.8	1 819.7	1 511.4	285.8	1 225.5	308.3	204.7	103.6	181.6	19.0	162.6	36.5
1982	2 851.4	1 919.6	1 587.5	307.5	1 280.0	332.1	222.4	109.8	174.8	13.3	161.5	38.1
1983	3 070.9	2 035.5	1 677.5	324.8	1 352.7	358.0	238.1	119.9	190.7	6.2	184.5	38.2
1984	3 461.3	2 245.4	1 844.9	348.1	1 496.8	400.5	261.5	139.0	233.1	20.9	212.1	40.0
1985	3 696.3	2 411.7	1 982.6	373.9	1 608.7	429.2	281.5	147.7	246.1	21.0	225.1	41.9
1986	3 871.5	2 557.7	2 102.3	397.2	1 705.1	455.3	297.5	157.9	262.6	22.8	239.7	33.8
1987	4 150.0	2 735.6	2 256.3	423.1	1 833.1	479.4	313.1	166.3	294.2	28.9	265.3	34.2
1988	4 522.3	2 954.2	2 439.8	452.0	1 987.7	514.4	329.7	184.6	334.8	26.8	308.0	40.2
1989	4 800.5	3 131.3	2 583.1	481.1	2 101.9	548.3	354.6	193.7	351.6	33.0	318.6	42.4
1990	5 059.5	3 326.3	2 741.2	519.0	2 222.2	585.1	378.6	206.5	365.1	32.2	333.0	49.8
1991	5 217.9	3 438.3	2 814.5	548.8	2 265.7	623.9	408.7	215.1	367.3	27.5	339.8	61.6
1992	5 517.1	3 631.4	2 957.8	572.0	2 385.8	673.6	445.2	228.4	414.9	35.8	379.1	84.6
1993	5 784.7	3 797.1	3 083.0	589.0	2 494.0	714.1	474.4	239.7	449.6	32.0	417.6	114.1
1994	6 181.3	3 998.5	3 248.5	609.5	2 639.0	750.1	495.9	254.1	485.1	35.6	449.5	142.9
1995	6 522.3	4 195.2	3 434.4	629.0	2 805.4	760.8	496.7	264.1	516.0	23.4	492.6	154.6
1996	6 931.7	4 391.4	3 620.0	648.1	2 971.9	771.4	496.6	274.8	583.7	38.4	545.2	170.4
1997	7 406.0	4 665.6	3 873.6	671.8	3 201.8	792.0	502.4	289.6	628.2	32.6	595.6	176.5
1998	7 875.6	5 023.2	4 180.9	701.2	3 479.7	842.3	535.1	307.2	687.5	28.9	658.7	191.5
1999	8 358.0	5 353.9	4 465.2	733.7	3 731.5	888.8	565.4	323.3	746.8	28.5	718.3	208.2
2000	8 938.9	5 788.8	4 827.7	779.7	4 048.0	961.2	615.9	345.2	817.5	29.6	787.8	215.3
2001	9 185.2	5 979.3	4 952.2	821.9	4 130.3	1 027.1	669.1	358.0	870.7	30.5	840.2	232.4
2002	9 408.5	6 110.8	4 997.3	873.1	4 124.2	1 113.5	747.4	366.1	890.3	18.5	871.8	218.7
2003	9 840.2	6 382.6	5 154.6	913.3	4 241.3	1 228.0	845.6	382.4	930.6	36.5	894.1	204.2
2004	10 534.0	6 693.4	5 410.7	952.8	4 457.9	1 282.7	874.6	408.1	1 033.8	49.7	984.1	198.4
2005	11 273.8	7 065.0	5 706.0	991.5	4 714.5	1 359.1	931.6	427.5	1 069.8	43.9	1 025.9	178.2
2006	12 031.2	7 477.0	6 070.1	1 035.2	5 035.0	1 406.9	960.1	446.7	1 133.0	29.3	1 103.6	146.5
2007	12 396.4	7 855.9	6 415.5	1 089.0	5 326.4	1 440.4	980.5	459.9	1 090.4	37.8	1 052.6	143.7
2008	12 609.1	8 068.3	6 545.9	1 144.1	5 401.8	1 522.5	1 052.4	470.1	1 097.9	51.8	1 046.1	231.6
2009	12 147.6	7 806.4	6 275.3	1 175.3	5 100.0	1 531.1	1 073.1	458.0	941.2	39.2	902.0	305.9
2010	12 840.1	7 971.4	6 408.2	1 190.8	5 217.4	1 563.1	1 089.9	473.2	1 036.4	52.2	984.2	350.2
2011	13 421.2	8 276.6	6 668.2	1 190.3	5 477.9	1 608.4	1 111.0	497.4	1 108.9	65.9	1 043.0	403.9
2009												
1st quarter	12 099.2	7 830.1	6 300.5	1 168.9	5 131.5	1 529.6	1 071.0	458.6	960.2	37.1	923.1	278.8
2nd quarter	12 035.7	7 809.2	6 278.2	1 175.9	5 102.2	1 531.1	1 071.7	459.4	926.9	38.7	888.2	299.7
3rd quarter	12 126.1	7 781.9	6 251.3	1 177.1	5 074.2	1 530.6	1 073.5	457.1	929.3	39.5	889.9	319.3
4th quarter	12 329.5	7 804.4	6 271.4	1 179.2	5 092.2	1 533.0	1 076.2	456.8	948.5	41.4	907.0	325.9
2010												
1st quarter	12 595.9	7 852.5	6 301.6	1 188.6	5 113.0	1 550.9	1 083.4	467.5	981.7	44.6	937.1	344.1
2nd quarter	12 803.7	7 960.0	6 399.8	1 196.3	5 203.5	1 560.2	1 087.6	472.6	1 025.6	45.8	979.7	349.1
3rd quarter	12 942.1	8 022.2	6 454.5	1 189.9	5 264.7	1 567.7	1 092.0	475.7	1 057.0	58.3	998.7	352.8
4th quarter	13 018.8	8 050.8	6 477.0	1 188.6	5 288.4	1 573.7	1 096.8	476.9	1 081.5	60.1	1 021.4	354.8
2011												
1st quarter	13 232.6	8 172.5	6 578.2	1 191.1	5 387.1	1 594.4	1 103.0	491.4	1 095.6	66.1	1 029.5	385.0
2nd quarter	13 344.1	8 219.7	6 617.1	1 191.9	5 425.2	1 602.7	1 108.7	494.0	1 106.5	67.3	1 039.2	396.9
3rd quarter	13 519.3	8 338.3	6 724.3	1 189.3	5 535.0	1 614.0	1 112.6	501.3	1 113.7	67.5	1 046.2	406.3
4th quarter	13 588.6	8 375.8	6 753.2	1 189.0	5 564.2	1 622.6	1 119.6	503.0	1 119.7	62.7	1 057.0	427.2

Table 1-13A. National Income by Type of Income: Recent Data—*Continued*

(Billions of dollars, quarterly data are at seasonally adjusted annual rates.)   **NIPA Tables 1.7.5, 1.12**

| Year and quarter | Corporate profits with IVA and CCAdj | | | | | Net interest and miscellaneous payments | Taxes on production and imports | Less: Subsidies | Business current transfer payments, net | | | Current surplus of government enterprises | Addendum: Net national factor income |
| | Total | Taxes on corporate income | Profits after tax | | | | | | Total 1 | To persons | To government | | |
			Total	Net dividends	Undistributed corporate profits								
1950	35.6	17.9	17.7	8.8	8.9	3.2	23.0	0.6	0.9	0.6	0.3	. . .	240.6
1951	40.8	22.6	18.2	8.6	9.7	3.7	24.7	0.7	1.2	0.9	0.3	. . .	278.6
1952	38.8	19.4	19.4	8.6	10.9	4.1	27.1	0.4	1.3	0.9	0.4	. . .	293.3
1953	39.1	20.3	18.8	8.9	9.9	4.7	29.1	0.1	1.2	0.8	0.4	. . .	308.4
1954	38.3	17.6	20.7	9.3	11.4	5.6	28.9	-0.1	1.0	0.6	0.4	. . .	308.8
1955	49.0	22.0	27.0	10.5	16.5	6.2	31.5	-0.2	1.4	0.9	0.4	. . .	339.0
1956	48.0	22.0	26.0	11.3	14.7	6.9	34.2	0.4	1.7	1.2	0.5	. . .	359.3
1957	47.6	21.4	26.2	11.7	14.5	8.0	36.6	0.7	1.9	1.4	0.5	. . .	375.5
1958	42.5	19.0	23.5	11.6	11.9	9.5	37.7	0.9	1.8	1.2	0.6	. . .	377.0
1959	53.8	23.7	30.1	12.6	17.5	9.6	41.1	1.1	1.8	1.3	0.4	1.0	410.8
1960	53.1	22.8	30.3	13.4	16.9	10.6	44.5	1.1	1.9	1.3	0.5	0.9	427.7
1961	54.2	22.9	31.3	13.9	17.4	12.5	47.0	2.0	2.0	1.4	0.7	0.8	442.9
1962	62.3	24.1	38.3	15.0	23.2	14.2	50.4	2.3	2.2	1.5	0.7	0.9	477.6
1963	68.3	26.4	42.0	16.2	25.7	15.2	53.4	2.2	2.7	1.9	0.8	1.4	504.6
1964	75.5	28.2	47.4	18.2	29.2	17.4	57.3	2.7	3.1	2.2	0.9	1.3	542.4
1965	86.5	31.1	55.5	20.2	35.3	19.6	60.7	3.0	3.6	2.3	1.4	1.3	589.5
1966	92.5	33.9	58.7	20.7	38.0	22.4	63.2	3.9	3.5	2.1	1.4	1.0	646.4
1967	90.2	32.9	57.3	21.5	35.8	25.5	67.9	3.8	3.8	2.3	1.5	0.9	681.6
1968	97.3	39.6	57.6	23.5	34.1	27.1	76.4	4.2	4.3	2.8	1.5	1.2	743.5
1969	94.5	40.0	54.5	24.2	30.3	32.7	83.9	4.5	4.9	3.3	1.6	1.0	803.2
1970	82.5	34.8	47.7	24.3	23.4	39.1	91.4	4.8	4.5	2.9	1.6	0.0	838.4
1971	96.1	38.2	57.9	25.0	32.9	43.9	100.5	4.7	4.3	2.7	1.6	-0.2	905.7
1972	111.4	42.3	69.1	26.8	42.2	47.9	107.9	6.6	4.9	3.1	1.8	0.5	1 003.6
1973	124.5	50.0	74.5	29.9	44.6	55.2	117.2	5.2	6.0	3.9	2.0	-0.4	1 128.5
1974	115.1	52.8	62.3	33.2	29.1	70.8	124.9	3.3	7.1	4.7	2.4	-0.9	1 213.7
1975	133.3	51.6	81.7	33.0	48.7	81.6	135.3	4.5	9.4	6.8	2.6	-3.2	1 307.1
1976	161.6	65.3	96.3	39.0	57.3	85.5	146.4	5.1	9.5	6.7	2.8	-1.8	1 460.8
1977	191.8	74.4	117.4	44.8	72.6	101.1	159.7	7.1	8.5	5.1	3.4	-2.7	1 639.1
1978	218.4	84.9	133.6	50.8	82.8	115.0	170.9	8.9	10.8	6.5	4.4	-2.2	1 857.3
1979	225.4	90.0	135.3	57.5	77.8	138.9	180.1	8.5	13.3	8.2	5.1	-2.9	2 066.3
1980	201.4	87.2	114.2	64.1	50.2	181.8	200.3	9.8	14.7	8.6	6.1	-5.1	2 232.8
1981	223.3	84.3	138.9	73.8	65.2	232.3	235.6	11.5	17.9	11.2	6.7	-5.6	2 493.3
1982	205.7	66.5	139.2	77.7	61.5	271.1	240.9	15.0	20.6	12.4	8.2	-4.5	2 609.4
1983	259.8	80.6	179.2	83.5	95.7	285.3	263.3	21.3	22.6	13.8	8.8	-3.2	2 809.5
1984	318.6	97.5	221.1	90.8	130.3	327.1	289.8	21.1	30.3	19.7	10.6	-1.9	3 164.2
1985	332.5	99.4	233.1	97.6	135.6	341.5	308.1	21.4	35.2	22.3	12.9	0.6	3 373.7
1986	314.1	109.7	204.5	106.2	98.3	367.1	323.4	24.9	36.9	22.9	13.9	0.9	3 535.3
1987	367.8	130.4	237.4	112.3	125.1	366.7	347.5	30.3	34.1	20.2	13.8	0.2	3 798.6
1988	426.6	141.6	285.0	129.9	155.1	385.3	374.5	29.5	33.6	20.6	13.0	2.6	4 141.1
1989	425.6	146.1	279.5	158.0	121.5	434.1	398.9	27.4	39.2	23.2	16.0	4.9	4 385.0
1990	434.4	145.4	289.0	169.1	120.0	444.2	425.0	27.0	40.1	22.2	17.9	1.6	4 619.9
1991	457.3	138.6	318.7	180.7	138.0	418.2	457.1	27.5	39.9	17.6	22.3	5.7	4 742.7
1992	496.2	148.7	347.5	188.0	159.5	387.7	483.4	30.1	40.7	16.3	24.5	8.2	5 014.9
1993	543.7	171.0	372.7	202.9	169.7	364.6	503.1	36.7	40.5	14.1	26.7	8.7	5 269.1
1994	628.2	193.1	435.1	235.7	199.4	362.2	545.2	32.5	41.9	13.3	29.1	9.6	5 617.0
1995	716.2	217.8	498.3	254.4	243.9	358.3	557.9	34.8	45.8	18.7	25.7	13.1	5 940.3
1996	801.5	231.5	570.0	297.7	272.3	371.1	580.8	35.2	53.8	22.9	31.8	14.4	6 318.1
1997	884.8	245.4	639.4	331.2	308.2	407.6	611.6	33.8	51.3	19.4	31.1	14.1	6 762.8
1998	812.4	248.4	564.1	351.5	212.6	479.3	639.5	36.4	65.2	26.0	35.4	13.3	7 194.0
1999	856.3	258.8	597.5	337.4	260.1	481.4	673.6	45.2	69.0	34.0	37.6	14.1	7 646.5
2000	819.2	265.1	554.1	377.9	176.3	539.3	708.6	45.8	87.0	42.4	43.6	9.1	8 180.1
2001	784.2	203.3	580.9	370.9	210.0	544.4	727.7	58.7	101.3	46.8	46.0	4.0	8 410.9
2002	872.2	192.3	679.9	399.3	280.6	506.4	762.8	41.4	82.4	34.2	47.9	6.3	8 598.4
2003	977.8	243.8	734.0	424.9	309.2	504.1	806.8	49.1	76.1	25.7	48.8	7.0	8 999.3
2004	1 246.9	306.1	940.8	550.3	390.5	461.6	863.4	46.4	81.7	16.9	52.5	1.2	9 634.1
2005	1 456.1	412.4	1 043.7	557.3	486.4	543.0	930.2	60.9	95.9	25.8	55.2	-3.5	10 312.2
2006	1 608.3	473.3	1 135.0	704.8	430.3	652.2	986.8	51.4	83.0	21.4	59.6	-4.2	11 017.0
2007	1 510.6	445.5	1 065.2	794.5	270.7	731.6	1 027.2	54.6	103.3	30.5	66.8	-11.8	11 332.3
2008	1 248.4	309.0	939.4	786.9	152.5	870.1	1 038.6	52.9	123.0	36.8	79.0	-16.0	11 516.3
2009	1 362.0	272.4	1 089.6	620.0	469.6	656.7	1 017.9	59.7	132.0	38.2	96.1	-14.9	11 072.3
2010	1 800.1	411.1	1 389.1	737.3	651.7	564.3	1 054.0	57.3	136.7	38.3	99.0	-15.7	11 722.4
2011	1 942.8	416.2	1 526.5	813.6	712.9	535.1	1 097.9	62.8	134.1	39.5	99.4	-15.3	12 267.2
2009													
1st quarter	1 175.2	208.8	966.4	671.9	294.5	782.9	1 008.0	56.4	137.0	37.8	96.7	-16.8	11 027.3
2nd quarter	1 262.3	244.8	1 017.5	600.9	416.6	656.4	1 011.8	56.8	141.5	38.2	106.1	-15.3	10 954.5
3rd quarter	1 438.8	301.6	1 137.3	584.1	553.1	596.6	1 020.4	68.4	122.2	38.4	88.1	-14.0	11 065.9
4th quarter	1 571.6	334.4	1 237.2	623.0	614.2	591.0	1 031.3	57.1	127.5	38.3	93.5	-13.6	11 241.3
2010													
1st quarter	1 724.2	409.7	1 314.5	684.8	629.7	589.1	1 040.9	56.4	134.6	38.0	96.2	-14.7	11 491.5
2nd quarter	1 785.8	399.6	1 386.3	729.3	657.0	569.2	1 050.6	56.8	135.7	38.0	97.9	-15.5	11 689.7
3rd quarter	1 833.1	430.3	1 402.8	760.5	642.3	550.1	1 059.0	57.0	140.9	37.9	101.8	-16.0	11 815.1
4th quarter	1 857.4	404.7	1 452.7	774.8	677.9	548.7	1 065.5	59.1	135.7	39.3	100.1	-16.5	11 893.3
2011													
1st quarter	1 876.4	422.3	1 454.1	793.8	660.3	556.6	1 087.4	60.0	134.7	39.5	99.1	-15.6	12 086.2
2nd quarter	1 937.6	420.5	1 517.1	807.4	709.6	525.6	1 101.1	62.7	133.9	39.4	99.0	-14.6	12 186.4
3rd quarter	1 970.1	411.4	1 558.7	821.4	737.3	535.7	1 100.0	64.2	133.7	39.4	99.3	-14.5	12 364.2
4th quarter	1 986.9	410.7	1 576.2	831.7	744.5	522.7	1 103.3	64.4	134.1	39.6	100.0	-16.7	12 432.3

1Includes net transfer payments to the rest of the world, not shown separately.
. . . = Not available.

Table 1-13B. National Income by Type of Income: Historical Data

(Billions of dollars, quarterly data are at seasonally adjusted annual rates.)

NIPA Tables 1.7.5, 1.12

Year and quarter	National income, total	Compensation of employees							Proprietors' income with IVA and CCAdj			Rental income of persons with CCAdj
		Total	Wage and salary accruals			Supplements to wages and salaries			Total	Farm	Nonfarm	
			Total	Government	Other	Total	Employer contributions for:					
							Employee pension and insurance funds	Government social insurance				
1929	93.9	51.1	50.5	5.0	45.5	0.7	0.7	0.0	14.1	5.7	8.4	6.2
1930	82.9	46.9	46.2	5.2	41.0	0.7	0.6	0.0	10.9	3.9	7.0	5.5
1931	67.4	39.8	39.2	5.3	33.9	0.6	0.6	0.0	8.4	3.0	5.3	4.5
1932	51.1	31.1	30.5	5.0	25.5	0.6	0.6	0.0	5.1	1.8	3.3	3.6
1933	48.8	29.6	29.0	5.2	23.9	0.5	0.5	0.0	5.3	2.2	3.1	2.9
1934	58.1	34.3	33.7	6.1	27.6	0.6	0.6	0.0	7.0	2.6	4.5	2.6
1935	66.0	37.4	36.7	6.5	30.2	0.7	0.6	0.0	10.1	4.9	5.2	2.6
1936	74.7	42.9	42.0	7.9	34.1	1.0	0.8	0.2	10.4	3.9	6.4	2.7
1937	83.3	48.0	46.1	7.5	38.6	1.8	0.8	1.0	12.5	5.6	6.9	3.0
1938	76.6	45.0	43.0	8.3	34.8	2.0	0.8	1.2	10.6	4.0	6.6	3.6
1939	82.0	48.1	46.0	8.2	37.7	2.2	0.9	1.3	11.1	4.0	7.1	3.8
1940	90.9	52.2	49.9	8.5	41.4	2.3	0.9	1.4	12.3	4.1	8.2	3.9
1941	115.8	64.8	62.1	10.2	51.9	2.7	1.0	1.7	16.6	6.0	10.6	4.5
1942	149.5	85.3	82.1	16.0	66.1	3.2	1.2	2.0	23.4	9.7	13.7	5.5
1943	184.2	109.6	105.8	26.6	79.2	3.8	1.5	2.3	28.3	11.5	16.7	6.1
1944	198.0	121.3	116.7	33.0	83.8	4.5	2.0	2.5	29.4	11.4	18.0	6.4
1945	198.3	123.3	117.5	34.9	82.6	5.8	2.3	3.5	30.8	11.8	19.0	6.7
1946	198.6	119.6	112.0	20.7	91.3	7.6	2.5	5.1	35.7	14.2	21.5	7.1
1947	216.3	130.1	123.1	17.5	105.6	7.0	3.0	3.9	34.5	14.3	20.1	7.2
1948	242.6	142.0	135.6	19.0	116.5	6.4	3.4	3.0	39.2	16.7	22.5	7.8
1949	237.5	141.9	134.7	20.8	113.9	7.1	3.8	3.3	34.6	12.0	22.6	8.1
1947												
1st quarter	211.8	127.2	119.7	17.9	101.7	7.5	2.9	4.7	36.6	16.0	20.6	6.9
2nd quarter	212.7	128.7	121.5	17.6	103.9	7.2	2.9	4.3	32.3	12.4	20.0	7.1
3rd quarter	216.1	130.1	123.4	17.0	106.4	6.6	3.1	3.5	33.8	14.1	19.7	7.3
4th quarter	224.6	134.3	127.8	17.5	110.3	6.5	3.3	3.2	35.2	14.9	20.3	7.5
1948												
1st quarter	233.0	137.9	131.4	17.9	113.5	6.5	3.3	3.2	36.0	14.5	21.5	7.6
2nd quarter	241.8	139.6	133.2	18.4	114.8	6.4	3.4	3.0	40.4	18.0	22.4	7.8
3rd quarter	246.9	144.5	138.1	19.5	118.6	6.4	3.4	2.9	40.9	17.9	23.0	7.9
4th quarter	248.7	145.9	139.5	20.3	119.2	6.4	3.5	2.9	39.6	16.4	23.2	7.9
1949												
1st quarter	241.5	144.1	137.0	20.4	116.6	7.1	3.6	3.5	35.4	12.7	22.7	7.8
2nd quarter	237.1	141.9	134.6	20.6	114.0	7.2	3.7	3.5	34.8	12.1	22.7	7.9
3rd quarter	237.5	141.0	133.9	20.9	113.0	7.1	3.8	3.3	34.2	11.6	22.5	8.2
4th quarter	233.9	140.5	133.4	21.4	112.1	7.0	4.0	3.0	34.2	11.5	22.7	8.4
1950												
1st quarter	243.6	144.6	137.1	21.5	115.6	7.5	4.2	3.3	35.6	12.2	23.4	8.7
2nd quarter	255.2	150.6	142.9	21.7	121.2	7.8	4.5	3.3	36.3	12.2	24.0	9.0
3rd quarter	272.8	159.0	150.8	22.8	128.0	8.2	4.8	3.4	38.7	13.1	25.6	9.1
4th quarter	283.8	166.9	158.3	24.7	133.6	8.6	5.1	3.6	39.4	13.9	25.5	9.4
1951												
1st quarter	295.5	175.0	165.5	26.8	138.8	9.4	5.4	4.0	42.0	15.0	27.0	9.6
2nd quarter	301.1	180.6	170.8	28.5	142.3	9.7	5.6	4.1	42.4	15.4	27.0	9.9
3rd quarter	306.2	183.7	173.8	30.5	143.3	9.9	5.8	4.1	42.6	15.1	27.5	10.2
4th quarter	312.3	186.5	176.2	31.1	145.1	10.2	6.1	4.1	43.5	15.7	27.9	10.5
1952												
1st quarter	314.3	191.5	181.2	32.5	148.7	10.3	6.2	4.1	41.8	13.7	28.1	10.7
2nd quarter	316.0	192.8	182.4	33.3	149.1	10.4	6.3	4.1	43.1	14.5	28.5	11.0
3rd quarter	321.7	196.3	185.7	33.8	151.9	10.6	6.5	4.1	44.8	16.0	28.8	11.3
4th quarter	332.9	204.1	193.3	34.0	159.3	10.8	6.6	4.2	42.6	13.0	29.5	11.6
1953												
1st quarter	339.0	208.0	196.9	34.2	162.7	11.1	6.9	4.2	43.0	13.0	30.0	11.9
2nd quarter	342.0	211.3	200.1	34.4	165.7	11.3	7.1	4.2	42.3	12.4	29.9	12.2
3rd quarter	340.8	211.5	200.3	34.4	165.9	11.2	7.0	4.3	41.5	11.7	29.8	12.5
4th quarter	332.7	210.0	198.7	34.4	164.3	11.3	7.2	4.2	41.3	11.5	29.8	12.8
1954												
1st quarter	334.5	208.1	196.4	34.4	162.0	11.7	7.1	4.6	42.6	12.9	29.7	13.1
2nd quarter	334.8	207.7	196.0	34.7	161.2	11.7	7.1	4.6	42.0	11.7	30.3	13.3
3rd quarter	338.3	208.3	196.3	35.1	161.2	11.9	7.3	4.6	42.3	11.8	30.5	13.5
4th quarter	347.3	212.6	200.4	35.4	165.0	12.2	7.6	4.6	42.2	10.7	31.5	13.6
1955												
1st quarter	359.3	217.1	204.2	35.6	168.6	12.9	7.8	5.0	43.4	10.9	32.5	13.7
2nd quarter	369.4	223.6	210.3	36.7	173.6	13.3	8.1	5.1	44.5	11.3	33.2	13.7
3rd quarter	376.4	228.6	214.7	36.8	177.8	13.9	8.6	5.2	44.7	10.7	34.0	13.8
4th quarter	382.9	233.6	219.5	37.3	182.2	14.1	8.9	5.3	44.5	10.0	34.6	13.9
1956												
1st quarter	386.6	238.0	223.3	37.8	185.4	14.8	9.2	5.6	44.9	10.2	34.7	14.0
2nd quarter	392.1	242.6	227.5	38.5	189.0	15.1	9.5	5.7	45.5	10.4	35.1	14.0
3rd quarter	396.3	245.7	230.0	39.2	190.8	15.8	10.1	5.7	46.2	10.9	35.3	14.1
4th quarter	404.5	251.6	235.4	39.7	195.7	16.2	10.4	5.8	46.9	10.9	36.0	14.2
1957												
1st quarter	411.1	255.3	238.3	40.2	198.0	17.1	10.7	6.4	46.9	9.9	37.0	14.3
2nd quarter	413.4	257.0	239.6	40.7	198.9	17.4	11.0	6.4	47.8	10.5	37.3	14.4
3rd quarter	417.4	259.7	241.8	41.5	200.3	17.8	11.4	6.4	48.7	11.0	37.6	14.5
4th quarter	411.5	258.1	240.1	41.6	198.5	18.1	11.7	6.3	47.9	10.7	37.2	14.7

Table 1-13B. National Income by Type of Income: Historical Data—*Continued*

(Billions of dollars, quarterly data are at seasonally adjusted annual rates.)

NIPA Tables 1.7.5, 1.12

Year and quarter	Corporate profits with IVA and CCAdj					Net interest and miscel-laneous payments	Taxes on production and imports	Less: Subsidies	Business current transfer payments, net			Current surplus of govern-ment enterprises	Addendum: Net national factor income
	Total	Taxes on corporate income	Profits after tax						Total [1]	To persons	To govern-ment		
			Total	Net dividends	Undis-tributed corporate profits								
1929	10.7	1.4	9.3	5.8	3.5	4.6	6.8	0.0	0.5	0.4	0.1	. . .	86.6
1930	7.4	0.8	6.5	5.5	1.0	4.8	7.0	0.0	0.5	0.4	0.1	. . .	75.5
1931	2.8	0.5	2.3	4.1	-1.7	4.8	6.7	0.1	0.5	0.4	0.1	. . .	60.3
1932	-0.3	0.4	-0.7	2.5	-3.2	4.5	6.6	0.1	0.6	0.5	0.1	. . .	44.0
1933	-0.3	0.5	-0.8	2.0	-2.8	4.0	6.9	0.1	0.5	0.4	0.1	. . .	41.5
1934	2.4	0.7	1.6	2.6	-0.9	4.0	7.6	0.4	0.5	0.4	0.1	. . .	50.3
1935	3.9	1.0	2.9	2.8	0.1	4.1	8.0	0.5	0.5	0.4	0.1	. . .	58.1
1936	6.0	1.4	4.6	4.5	0.1	3.8	8.5	0.2	0.5	0.4	0.1	. . .	65.9
1937	6.9	1.5	5.4	4.7	0.7	3.7	8.9	0.2	0.5	0.4	0.1	. . .	74.1
1938	4.8	1.0	3.8	3.2	0.6	3.6	8.9	0.4	0.4	0.3	0.2	. . .	67.6
1939	6.4	1.4	5.0	3.8	1.2	3.6	9.1	0.7	0.4	0.3	0.2	. . .	73.1
1940	9.6	2.8	6.8	4.0	2.8	3.3	9.8	0.6	0.5	0.3	0.2	. . .	81.3
1941	15.3	7.6	7.7	4.4	3.2	3.3	11.1	0.3	0.5	0.4	0.2	. . .	104.5
1942	20.4	11.4	9.0	4.3	4.8	3.2	11.5	0.4	0.5	0.3	0.2	. . .	137.8
1943	24.7	14.1	10.7	4.4	6.2	2.9	12.4	0.4	0.6	0.4	0.3	. . .	171.6
1944	24.8	12.9	11.8	4.6	7.2	2.4	13.7	0.9	0.8	0.4	0.4	. . .	184.3
1945	20.2	10.7	9.5	4.6	4.9	2.3	15.1	1.0	0.9	0.5	0.4	. . .	183.3
1946	17.9	9.1	8.8	5.6	3.3	1.9	16.8	1.2	0.7	0.4	0.3	. . .	182.2
1947	23.5	11.3	12.2	6.3	5.9	2.5	18.1	0.2	0.7	0.4	0.3	. . .	197.7
1948	30.9	12.4	18.5	7.0	11.4	2.6	19.7	0.3	0.7	0.4	0.4	. . .	222.4
1949	28.7	10.2	18.5	7.2	11.3	2.9	20.9	0.3	0.7	0.4	0.4	. . .	216.1
1947													
1st quarter	20.7	11.6	9.1	6.0	3.1	2.3	17.7	0.3	0.7	0.4	0.3	0.0	193.7
2nd quarter	23.9	10.9	13.0	6.3	6.7	2.4	17.7	0.2	0.7	0.4	0.3	0.0	194.4
3rd quarter	23.8	10.8	13.0	6.5	6.5	2.6	18.0	0.2	0.7	0.4	0.3	0.0	197.5
4th quarter	25.5	11.8	13.7	6.4	7.2	2.6	19.0	0.1	0.7	0.4	0.3	0.0	205.0
1948													
1st quarter	29.4	12.1	17.3	7.0	10.2	2.5	19.0	0.2	0.7	0.4	0.4	0.0	213.5
2nd quarter	31.2	12.8	18.4	6.7	11.7	2.6	19.7	0.1	0.7	0.4	0.4	0.0	221.5
3rd quarter	30.7	12.6	18.1	7.1	11.0	2.6	20.0	0.4	0.7	0.4	0.4	0.0	226.5
4th quarter	32.3	12.2	20.1	7.4	12.7	2.6	20.3	0.6	0.7	0.4	0.4	0.0	228.3
1949													
1st quarter	30.7	11.0	19.7	7.2	12.5	2.7	20.4	0.3	0.7	0.3	0.4	0.0	220.8
2nd quarter	28.3	9.7	18.6	7.2	11.4	2.8	20.8	0.2	0.7	0.3	0.4	0.0	215.8
3rd quarter	29.5	10.1	19.4	7.1	12.3	2.9	21.3	0.3	0.7	0.4	0.4	0.0	215.8
4th quarter	26.2	9.9	16.3	7.4	8.9	3.0	21.2	0.2	0.8	0.4	0.4	0.0	212.2
1950													
1st quarter	29.8	13.6	16.1	8.3	7.9	3.1	21.6	0.4	0.7	0.4	0.3	0.0	221.8
2nd quarter	33.4	16.3	17.1	8.4	8.7	3.2	22.5	0.6	0.8	0.5	0.3	0.0	232.4
3rd quarter	38.1	19.9	18.2	9.2	9.0	3.2	24.4	0.5	0.9	0.6	0.3	0.0	248.1
4th quarter	41.3	21.8	19.4	9.5	9.9	3.2	23.4	0.8	1.0	0.7	0.3	0.0	260.3
1951													
1st quarter	40.2	26.3	13.9	8.4	5.5	3.4	25.1	0.9	1.1	0.8	0.3	0.0	270.2
2nd quarter	40.2	22.3	17.9	8.6	9.3	3.6	24.1	0.8	1.2	0.9	0.3	0.0	276.7
3rd quarter	40.7	20.1	20.6	8.6	12.0	3.8	24.5	0.6	1.2	0.9	0.3	0.0	281.1
4th quarter	42.1	21.5	20.5	8.7	11.9	3.8	25.3	0.7	1.3	0.9	0.4	0.0	286.4
1952													
1st quarter	39.5	19.8	19.7	8.2	11.6	3.9	26.1	0.5	1.3	0.9	0.4	0.0	287.4
2nd quarter	37.4	18.7	18.8	8.7	10.1	4.0	26.9	0.4	1.3	0.9	0.4	0.0	288.3
3rd quarter	37.1	18.6	18.5	8.6	9.9	4.1	27.3	0.4	1.2	0.9	0.4	0.0	293.6
4th quarter	41.3	20.5	20.8	8.8	12.0	4.2	28.1	0.3	1.2	0.9	0.4	0.0	303.8
1953													
1st quarter	42.0	21.6	20.4	8.4	11.9	4.5	28.7	0.3	1.3	0.9	0.4	0.0	309.3
2nd quarter	41.2	21.7	19.5	9.2	10.3	4.6	29.2	0.1	1.3	0.9	0.4	0.0	311.7
3rd quarter	40.2	21.2	18.9	9.0	9.9	4.8	29.3	0.3	1.2	0.8	0.4	0.0	310.5
4th quarter	33.1	16.6	16.6	8.9	7.7	5.0	29.2	-0.2	1.1	0.8	0.4	0.0	302.2
1954													
1st quarter	35.5	16.4	19.0	9.4	9.6	5.2	28.7	-0.3	1.0	0.6	0.4	0.0	304.5
2nd quarter	36.8	16.9	19.9	8.9	11.0	5.5	28.8	0.3	1.0	0.5	0.4	0.0	305.3
3rd quarter	38.7	17.9	20.8	9.3	11.5	5.7	28.7	-0.1	1.0	0.5	0.4	0.0	308.5
4th quarter	42.4	19.3	23.1	9.5	13.6	6.0	29.3	-0.3	1.0	0.6	0.4	0.0	316.7
1955													
1st quarter	47.5	21.3	26.2	10.0	16.1	6.1	30.2	-0.2	1.2	0.7	0.4	0.0	327.8
2nd quarter	48.7	21.6	27.1	10.2	16.9	6.3	31.2	-0.1	1.3	0.9	0.4	0.0	336.8
3rd quarter	49.4	22.2	27.2	10.8	16.4	6.2	31.9	-0.4	1.5	1.0	0.4	0.0	342.6
4th quarter	50.4	23.1	27.4	10.9	16.5	6.3	32.5	-0.2	1.6	1.1	0.4	0.0	348.7
1956													
1st quarter	48.4	22.0	26.3	11.2	15.1	6.6	33.0	-0.1	1.7	1.2	0.5	0.0	351.9
2nd quarter	48.2	22.5	25.7	11.2	14.5	6.8	33.6	0.2	1.7	1.2	0.5	0.0	357.0
3rd quarter	47.4	21.1	26.2	11.2	15.1	7.1	34.6	0.5	1.8	1.3	0.5	0.0	360.5
4th quarter	48.1	22.3	25.8	11.6	14.2	7.0	35.7	0.8	1.8	1.3	0.5	0.0	367.7
1957													
1st quarter	49.7	22.8	26.8	11.6	15.2	7.7	36.1	0.9	1.9	1.4	0.5	0.0	373.9
2nd quarter	48.5	21.9	26.7	11.8	14.9	8.0	36.6	0.8	1.9	1.4	0.5	0.0	375.7
3rd quarter	48.0	21.4	26.6	11.9	14.7	8.2	37.0	0.6	1.9	1.4	0.5	0.0	379.1
4th quarter	44.3	19.6	24.7	11.7	13.1	8.2	36.7	0.5	1.9	1.4	0.5	0.0	373.3

[1]Includes net transfer payments to the rest of the world, not shown separately.
. . . = Not available.

Table 1-13B. National Income by Type of Income: Historical Data—*Continued*

(Billions of dollars, quarterly data are at seasonally adjusted annual rates.)   NIPA Tables 1.7.5, 1.12

Year and quarter	National income, total	Compensation of employees							Proprietors' income with IVA and CCAdj			Rental income of persons with CCAdj
		Total	Wage and salary accruals			Supplements to wages and salaries			Total	Farm	Nonfarm	
			Total	Government	Other	Total	Employer contributions for:					
							Employee pension and insurance funds	Government social insurance				
1958												
1st quarter	406.0	255.2	237.4	42.7	194.7	17.9	11.6	6.3	50.3	13.3	37.0	15.0
2nd quarter	407.5	254.8	236.9	43.7	193.2	17.9	11.7	6.3	50.4	13.0	37.4	15.2
3rd quarter	417.9	260.9	242.6	44.9	197.7	18.3	12.0	6.4	50.1	12.1	37.9	15.3
4th quarter	431.0	267.2	248.4	45.3	203.2	18.8	12.3	6.4	50.0	11.2	38.8	15.4
1959												
1st quarter	442.7	274.5	254.0	45.5	208.6	20.5	12.7	7.8	50.2	10.9	39.3	15.4
2nd quarter	457.3	281.6	260.6	45.8	214.7	21.1	13.2	7.9	50.4	9.9	40.5	15.9
3rd quarter	454.2	282.3	260.9	46.2	214.7	21.4	13.5	7.9	50.2	9.4	40.8	16.3
4th quarter	459.8	285.5	263.9	46.7	217.2	21.6	13.7	7.9	50.6	10.1	40.5	16.5
1960												
1st quarter	473.5	294.1	270.8	47.7	223.1	23.3	14.0	9.3	50.0	9.6	40.3	16.7
2nd quarter	473.8	296.9	273.4	48.6	224.8	23.5	14.2	9.3	50.8	10.6	40.2	16.9
3rd quarter	475.1	297.6	274.0	49.9	224.1	23.7	14.4	9.3	50.9	11.0	39.9	17.0
4th quarter	473.3	297.1	273.3	50.5	222.8	23.8	14.6	9.2	51.1	11.3	39.8	17.2
1961												
1st quarter	475.3	298.0	273.8	51.1	222.7	24.2	14.8	9.5	52.4	11.5	40.8	17.4
2nd quarter	484.9	302.2	277.6	51.8	225.8	24.6	15.0	9.6	52.6	10.9	41.7	17.6
3rd quarter	494.3	307.2	282.3	52.8	229.5	24.9	15.3	9.6	53.3	11.0	42.3	17.8
4th quarter	508.2	313.8	288.4	54.2	234.2	25.4	15.6	9.8	54.5	11.5	43.0	18.1
1962												
1st quarter	519.0	320.4	293.3	55.3	238.0	27.2	16.1	11.0	55.3	11.9	43.4	18.3
2nd quarter	525.6	326.4	298.7	56.0	242.8	27.6	16.4	11.2	55.1	11.1	44.0	18.5
3rd quarter	531.7	329.2	301.2	56.5	244.7	28.0	16.8	11.2	55.1	10.7	44.5	18.7
4th quarter	539.2	332.6	304.2	57.6	246.6	28.4	17.1	11.3	55.7	11.3	44.4	18.9
1963												
1st quarter	545.8	337.5	308.0	58.6	249.3	29.5	17.3	12.2	56.0	11.4	44.6	19.1
2nd quarter	555.3	342.4	312.4	59.4	253.0	30.0	17.7	12.3	55.9	10.8	45.1	19.3
3rd quarter	563.8	347.4	316.8	60.2	256.7	30.6	18.1	12.5	56.4	10.7	45.7	19.5
4th quarter	574.1	353.6	322.2	61.9	260.3	31.3	18.7	12.6	57.8	11.1	46.6	19.4
1964												
1st quarter	586.5	360.0	328.2	63.1	265.1	31.8	19.3	12.4	58.1	9.9	48.2	19.4
2nd quarter	596.2	367.4	334.8	64.2	270.7	32.5	20.0	12.6	59.0	9.5	49.5	19.4
3rd quarter	607.6	374.7	341.4	65.7	275.8	33.3	20.6	12.7	59.6	9.3	50.3	19.5
4th quarter	615.5	380.7	346.7	66.8	279.9	34.0	21.1	12.8	60.7	10.4	50.3	19.4
1965												
1st quarter	633.8	387.3	352.8	67.5	285.4	34.5	21.7	12.8	62.2	11.4	50.7	19.7
2nd quarter	644.8	394.1	358.9	68.5	290.3	35.2	22.3	13.0	63.4	12.0	51.4	19.9
3rd quarter	655.8	402.3	366.2	70.5	295.7	36.1	22.9	13.2	64.2	12.2	52.0	20.1
4th quarter	674.4	414.3	377.1	73.2	304.0	37.2	23.7	13.4	65.9	12.5	53.4	20.1
1966												
1st quarter	694.1	426.7	385.8	74.9	310.8	40.9	24.5	16.5	69.4	14.9	54.6	20.5
2nd quarter	703.8	437.8	395.9	76.9	319.0	41.9	25.1	16.7	67.5	12.7	54.9	20.4
3rd quarter	715.1	449.0	406.1	79.8	326.3	42.8	25.8	17.0	67.7	12.3	55.4	20.6
4th quarter	727.5	457.1	413.5	82.0	331.5	43.7	26.5	17.2	68.4	12.2	56.1	20.6
1967												
1st quarter	733.6	463.3	418.8	83.5	335.4	44.4	26.9	17.6	69.1	11.9	57.2	20.8
2nd quarter	740.5	469.0	423.6	85.0	338.6	45.4	27.6	17.8	68.9	11.1	57.7	20.9
3rd quarter	755.9	478.7	432.0	87.1	344.9	46.6	28.5	18.2	71.0	12.0	59.0	21.0
4th quarter	771.6	489.7	441.6	90.4	351.2	48.1	29.5	18.6	70.4	11.5	58.9	20.9
1968												
1st quarter	792.2	504.5	454.2	92.8	361.5	50.3	30.8	19.4	72.1	11.6	60.5	20.6
2nd quarter	813.0	517.6	465.9	95.2	370.7	51.7	31.9	19.8	73.4	11.2	62.2	20.6
3rd quarter	831.6	531.4	478.3	98.7	379.6	53.1	32.9	20.1	75.3	11.8	63.5	20.7
4th quarter	848.0	543.8	489.4	100.1	389.4	54.4	33.9	20.5	76.0	12.0	64.0	20.6
1969												
1st quarter	864.9	555.9	499.1	101.3	397.8	56.8	34.7	22.1	76.3	11.6	64.7	20.8
2nd quarter	881.0	569.8	511.4	103.1	408.3	58.4	35.9	22.5	77.6	12.5	65.0	20.9
3rd quarter	899.6	586.6	526.4	108.2	418.3	60.1	37.1	23.0	78.2	13.1	65.1	21.0
4th quarter	908.4	598.2	536.5	109.8	426.6	61.8	38.4	23.4	78.0	14.1	63.9	20.9
1970												
1st quarter	912.7	608.6	545.1	114.4	430.7	63.5	39.8	23.7	77.6	13.5	64.1	20.9
2nd quarter	924.4	614.2	549.1	116.5	432.6	65.1	41.2	23.9	77.1	12.4	64.7	20.6
3rd quarter	939.8	622.2	555.7	118.3	437.4	66.4	42.5	23.9	79.2	13.2	66.0	21.2
4th quarter	941.1	623.9	556.3	119.7	436.6	67.6	43.7	23.9	79.9	12.5	67.4	21.5
1971												
1st quarter	976.6	641.6	570.2	123.9	446.3	71.4	45.3	26.1	81.1	13.1	68.0	21.5
2nd quarter	996.4	653.7	580.3	125.6	454.6	73.4	47.0	26.4	83.7	13.3	70.5	22.0
3rd quarter	1 013.9	664.1	588.8	128.0	460.7	75.3	48.8	26.5	85.3	13.0	72.4	22.4
4th quarter	1 035.6	676.3	599.0	129.6	469.4	77.3	50.5	26.8	88.6	14.2	74.3	22.8
1972												
1st quarter	1 067.8	701.1	618.0	134.2	483.8	83.2	52.5	30.6	88.7	13.1	75.6	23.5
2nd quarter	1 088.6	715.8	630.5	135.7	494.8	85.3	54.3	31.0	92.2	15.4	76.7	20.5
3rd quarter	1 118.8	729.7	642.4	138.4	504.0	87.3	56.1	31.2	96.5	17.2	79.4	24.3
4th quarter	1 166.1	753.9	664.3	143.3	521.0	89.7	57.9	31.8	106.7	22.4	84.3	24.3

Table 1-13B. National Income by Type of Income: Historical Data—*Continued*

(Billions of dollars, quarterly data are at seasonally adjusted annual rates.)

NIPA Tables 1.7.5, 1.12

| Year and quarter | Corporate profits with IVA and CCAdj | | Profits after tax | | | Net interest and miscellaneous payments | Taxes on production and imports | Less: Subsidies | Business current transfer payments, net | | | Current surplus of government enterprises | Addendum: Net national factor income |
	Total	Taxes on corporate income	Total	Net dividends	Undistributed corporate profits				Total ¹	To persons	To government		
1958													
1st quarter	38.4	16.9	21.5	11.6	10.0	9.0	36.8	0.6	1.9	1.3	0.6	. . .	367.9
2nd quarter	39.2	17.2	21.9	11.7	10.2	9.5	37.3	0.8	1.8	1.3	0.6	. . .	369.1
3rd quarter	43.3	19.4	23.9	11.7	12.2	9.8	37.8	1.0	1.8	1.2	0.6	. . .	379.3
4th quarter	49.0	22.3	26.7	11.4	15.3	9.9	38.9	1.2	1.7	1.2	0.5	. . .	391.5
1959													
1st quarter	52.6	23.5	29.1	12.1	17.0	8.8	39.8	1.1	1.7	1.3	0.4	0.9	401.4
2nd quarter	57.6	25.7	31.9	12.5	19.4	9.8	40.3	0.9	1.8	1.3	0.4	0.9	415.3
3rd quarter	52.3	23.1	29.2	12.8	16.5	9.8	41.7	1.1	1.8	1.3	0.4	1.0	410.8
4th quarter	52.8	22.6	30.2	13.0	17.2	10.1	42.4	1.1	1.8	1.4	0.4	1.1	415.5
1960													
1st quarter	57.0	25.1	31.9	13.2	18.7	10.2	43.7	1.0	1.8	1.3	0.5	1.0	428.0
2nd quarter	53.2	23.1	30.1	13.2	16.8	10.1	44.3	1.3	1.8	1.3	0.5	1.0	427.9
3rd quarter	52.3	22.0	30.2	13.5	16.7	10.7	44.9	1.0	1.9	1.3	0.6	0.9	428.5
4th quarter	49.9	20.9	29.0	13.5	15.5	11.2	45.3	1.2	1.9	1.3	0.6	0.9	426.5
1961													
1st quarter	48.9	20.7	28.2	13.6	14.7	11.6	45.8	1.6	2.0	1.3	0.7	0.8	428.3
2nd quarter	53.2	22.1	31.1	13.6	17.4	12.2	46.5	2.0	2.0	1.3	0.7	0.8	437.7
3rd quarter	55.4	23.4	32.0	13.9	18.1	12.6	47.3	2.2	2.0	1.4	0.7	0.8	446.4
4th quarter	59.3	25.4	33.8	14.5	19.4	13.4	48.4	2.3	2.1	1.4	0.7	1.0	459.0
1962													
1st quarter	61.7	23.9	37.8	14.6	23.2	13.1	49.4	2.3	2.2	1.5	0.7	0.9	468.8
2nd quarter	61.0	23.7	37.3	15.0	22.3	14.1	49.9	2.4	2.2	1.5	0.7	0.9	475.0
3rd quarter	62.2	24.4	37.9	15.2	22.7	14.6	50.9	2.2	2.3	1.6	0.7	0.9	479.9
4th quarter	64.5	24.5	40.1	15.4	24.7	15.0	51.3	2.2	2.3	1.6	0.7	0.9	486.8
1963													
1st quarter	64.7	24.6	40.2	15.8	24.4	14.6	52.0	2.0	2.6	1.8	0.8	1.3	492.0
2nd quarter	68.1	26.3	41.9	16.1	25.8	14.8	52.9	2.2	2.6	1.8	0.8	1.3	500.6
3rd quarter	69.5	27.0	42.5	16.3	26.2	15.3	53.9	2.3	2.7	1.9	0.8	1.4	508.1
4th quarter	71.0	27.7	43.3	16.8	26.6	15.8	54.7	2.4	2.8	2.0	0.8	1.5	517.6
1964													
1st quarter	75.2	27.9	47.3	17.5	29.9	16.6	55.7	2.7	2.9	2.1	0.8	1.4	529.3
2nd quarter	75.1	28.0	47.2	18.0	29.2	17.1	56.7	2.9	2.9	2.2	0.7	1.4	538.0
3rd quarter	76.3	28.6	47.7	18.4	29.3	17.9	57.9	2.6	3.3	2.2	1.1	1.1	547.9
4th quarter	75.4	28.2	47.3	18.9	28.4	18.1	58.8	2.7	3.4	2.3	1.2	1.5	554.4
1965													
1st quarter	83.3	29.6	53.7	19.2	34.5	19.0	60.2	2.9	3.6	2.3	1.3	1.4	571.5
2nd quarter	85.4	30.5	54.9	19.9	35.0	19.5	60.3	3.0	3.6	2.3	1.3	1.5	582.3
3rd quarter	86.7	31.1	55.6	20.5	35.0	20.0	60.5	3.0	3.6	2.2	1.4	1.3	593.3
4th quarter	90.7	33.1	57.6	21.2	36.4	20.0	61.8	3.1	3.6	2.2	1.4	1.2	611.0
1966													
1st quarter	93.9	34.2	59.7	21.3	38.5	21.1	61.4	3.6	3.6	2.2	1.4	1.1	631.6
2nd quarter	92.8	34.2	58.6	20.9	37.7	21.9	62.8	3.9	3.5	2.1	1.4	1.0	640.3
3rd quarter	91.1	33.9	57.2	20.5	36.7	22.7	63.7	4.1	3.5	2.1	1.4	0.8	651.1
4th quarter	92.4	33.3	59.1	20.0	39.1	23.8	64.9	4.2	3.5	2.1	1.4	1.0	662.4
1967													
1st quarter	89.6	32.5	57.1	21.1	36.1	24.7	65.6	4.0	3.6	2.2	1.4	0.9	667.5
2nd quarter	88.5	32.2	56.2	21.7	34.6	25.5	66.8	3.9	3.7	2.2	1.5	1.1	672.7
3rd quarter	89.7	32.5	57.2	22.1	35.1	25.8	68.7	3.7	3.8	2.3	1.5	1.0	686.1
4th quarter	92.9	34.4	58.5	21.2	37.3	26.2	70.6	3.7	3.9	2.4	1.5	0.7	700.0
1968													
1st quarter	93.9	38.7	55.2	22.6	32.6	26.6	73.4	4.0	4.1	2.5	1.5	1.2	717.6
2nd quarter	97.7	39.5	58.2	23.4	34.8	27.0	75.4	4.2	4.3	2.7	1.5	1.2	736.3
3rd quarter	97.9	39.7	58.3	24.0	34.3	27.1	77.7	4.2	4.4	2.9	1.5	1.2	752.5
4th quarter	99.4	40.6	58.8	24.2	34.6	27.7	79.1	4.2	4.6	3.0	1.5	1.1	767.4
1969													
1st quarter	99.4	41.5	57.9	24.0	34.0	30.5	80.6	4.3	4.9	3.3	1.6	0.9	782.9
2nd quarter	96.4	40.4	55.9	24.1	31.8	32.1	82.9	4.5	5.0	3.4	1.6	1.0	796.6
3rd quarter	93.6	39.1	54.5	24.3	30.2	33.7	85.2	4.7	5.0	3.4	1.6	1.0	813.0
4th quarter	88.5	38.9	49.7	24.6	25.1	34.6	86.7	4.7	5.0	3.3	1.6	1.2	820.2
1970													
1st quarter	80.6	34.5	46.1	24.5	21.6	36.0	88.5	4.7	4.8	3.1	1.6	0.5	823.7
2nd quarter	84.4	34.7	49.8	24.3	25.5	38.1	90.5	4.8	4.6	3.0	1.7	-0.3	834.4
3rd quarter	84.6	35.7	48.9	24.2	24.6	40.5	92.5	4.7	4.4	2.8	1.5	-0.1	847.7
4th quarter	80.4	34.2	46.2	24.2	22.0	41.9	94.1	4.8	4.3	2.8	1.5	-0.2	847.8
1971													
1st quarter	92.7	37.8	54.9	25.0	29.9	43.1	97.7	4.8	4.3	2.7	1.6	-0.6	880.0
2nd quarter	94.6	38.6	56.0	25.0	31.0	44.0	98.9	4.8	4.3	2.7	1.6	0.0	898.0
3rd quarter	96.7	37.9	58.8	25.2	33.7	44.1	101.7	4.5	4.3	2.7	1.6	-0.3	912.7
4th quarter	100.2	38.4	61.9	24.9	37.0	44.3	103.7	4.6	4.4	2.8	1.6	-0.2	932.2
1972													
1st quarter	106.2	40.4	65.9	26.1	39.8	45.2	104.6	6.1	4.7	2.9	1.8	0.0	964.7
2nd quarter	107.9	40.7	67.2	26.4	40.8	46.5	106.8	6.2	4.8	3.0	1.8	0.4	982.8
3rd quarter	112.1	42.0	70.2	27.1	43.1	48.9	108.9	7.2	5.0	3.2	1.8	0.5	1 011.6
4th quarter	119.5	46.4	73.1	27.7	45.4	51.1	111.5	7.1	5.2	3.3	1.8	1.0	1 055.5

¹Includes net transfer payments to the rest of the world, not shown separately.
. . . = Not available.

Table 1-13B. National Income by Type of Income: Historical Data—*Continued*

(Billions of dollars, quarterly data are at seasonally adjusted annual rates.)

NIPA Tables 1.7.5, 1.12

Year and quarter	National income, total	Compensation of employees								Proprietors' income with IVA and CCAdj			Rental income of persons with CCAdj
		Total	Wage and salary accruals			Supplements to wages and salaries				Total	Farm	Nonfarm	
			Total	Government	Other	Total	Employer contributions for:						
							Employee pension and insurance funds	Government social insurance					
1973													
1st quarter	1 203.6	781.7	683.4	145.0	538.3	98.3	59.6	38.7		105.9	21.8	84.2	24.2
2nd quarter	1 228.6	800.8	700.1	147.2	552.9	100.7	61.4	39.3		111.7	27.6	84.1	24.1
3rd quarter	1 256.5	819.9	716.2	149.6	566.6	103.7	63.7	39.9		114.4	29.5	84.9	23.1
4th quarter	1 295.6	842.5	735.4	153.4	582.0	107.1	66.1	41.1		122.5	37.5	85.0	24.1
1974													
1st quarter	1 307.6	860.7	748.2	155.6	592.5	112.5	68.9	43.6		116.2	28.6	87.6	24.4
2nd quarter	1 328.7	881.4	765.3	158.2	607.1	116.1	71.6	44.5		109.3	20.1	89.2	23.8
3rd quarter	1 357.2	903.1	783.1	161.3	621.8	120.0	74.7	45.3		113.3	21.5	91.9	24.1
4th quarter	1 372.3	915.8	792.5	166.9	625.6	123.3	77.9	45.4		115.1	23.7	91.4	23.9
1975													
1st quarter	1 379.7	919.5	791.9	170.5	621.4	127.6	81.8	45.7		113.5	19.7	93.7	23.7
2nd quarter	1 411.2	931.7	800.4	174.5	625.9	131.4	85.4	46.0		115.5	20.1	95.4	23.5
3rd quarter	1 470.3	957.7	821.3	177.8	643.5	136.4	89.4	47.0		122.5	23.8	98.7	23.3
4th quarter	1 514.9	987.6	845.8	182.2	663.6	141.9	93.7	48.2		126.9	24.3	102.6	22.9
1976													
1st quarter	1 564.8	1 022.4	871.2	184.8	686.4	151.1	98.0	53.1		127.6	19.4	108.2	22.6
2nd quarter	1 591.4	1 046.1	889.4	187.3	702.1	156.8	102.8	53.9		130.0	17.0	113.0	21.7
3rd quarter	1 624.2	1 070.8	908.4	189.5	719.0	162.4	107.5	54.9		133.8	16.1	117.7	21.9
4th quarter	1 658.7	1 098.1	929.9	194.1	735.8	168.1	112.5	55.7		137.5	16.3	121.2	22.0
1977													
1st quarter	1 704.4	1 127.0	950.0	196.7	753.3	177.0	117.9	59.1		140.5	16.0	124.6	20.9
2nd quarter	1 774.2	1 164.4	980.9	199.7	781.2	183.5	122.9	60.6		141.9	14.1	127.9	19.9
3rd quarter	1 831.4	1 196.9	1 007.5	203.7	803.8	189.4	127.7	61.7		143.6	11.8	131.9	19.0
4th quarter	1 879.7	1 233.7	1 038.2	210.3	827.9	195.6	132.6	63.0		158.0	22.0	136.0	18.7
1978													
1st quarter	1 917.4	1 269.7	1 064.2	214.0	850.3	205.5	136.7	68.8		158.4	18.5	139.9	20.4
2nd quarter	2 012.6	1 317.9	1 106.0	217.2	888.8	212.0	141.0	71.0		168.1	20.9	147.2	19.8
3rd quarter	2 059.0	1 354.8	1 137.1	221.5	915.6	217.7	145.5	72.3		171.3	20.8	150.5	21.4
4th quarter	2 122.6	1 399.3	1 175.0	227.4	947.6	224.3	150.3	74.1		172.2	19.5	152.7	21.9
1979													
1st quarter	2 177.4	1 443.5	1 208.4	231.1	977.2	235.1	154.6	80.5		179.2	23.8	155.4	23.4
2nd quarter	2 216.8	1 475.2	1 234.0	233.1	1 000.9	241.2	159.6	81.6		179.3	21.8	157.4	21.1
3rd quarter	2 270.1	1 516.2	1 268.2	238.2	1 030.0	248.1	164.7	83.3		182.5	22.3	160.3	21.2
4th quarter	2 328.8	1 558.2	1 302.7	246.1	1 056.6	255.5	170.6	84.9		183.5	20.8	162.8	24.8
1980													
1st quarter	2 374.1	1 599.0	1 334.9	251.3	1 083.6	264.1	176.8	87.3		168.5	13.3	155.2	28.6
2nd quarter	2 367.7	1 621.3	1 351.0	257.7	1 093.3	270.3	182.6	87.7		162.2	3.1	159.1	24.1
3rd quarter	2 430.2	1 653.5	1 376.6	263.0	1 113.6	276.9	187.9	89.0		175.8	11.7	164.0	25.0
4th quarter	2 559.9	1 716.5	1 431.2	273.8	1 157.4	285.3	193.6	91.7		187.3	18.7	168.7	36.3
1981													
1st quarter	2 649.0	1 768.9	1 469.1	278.7	1 190.3	299.8	198.1	101.7		190.1	17.6	172.5	36.2
2nd quarter	2 690.8	1 801.9	1 496.2	282.1	1 214.1	305.7	202.7	102.9		177.9	18.2	159.7	35.1
3rd quarter	2 784.2	1 840.0	1 528.7	286.8	1 241.9	311.3	206.8	104.5		184.2	23.3	160.9	35.7
4th quarter	2 795.4	1 867.9	1 551.5	295.7	1 255.8	316.4	211.1	105.3		174.2	17.0	157.2	38.8
1982													
1st quarter	2 801.9	1 891.8	1 567.2	300.4	1 266.8	324.6	215.6	109.0		167.6	14.4	153.2	39.5
2nd quarter	2 851.2	1 911.1	1 580.9	304.6	1 276.3	330.2	220.6	109.6		173.0	12.8	160.3	36.2
3rd quarter	2 869.1	1 930.8	1 596.1	309.2	1 286.9	334.8	224.6	110.1		174.4	11.9	162.5	38.0
4th quarter	2 883.4	1 944.8	1 605.9	316.0	1 289.9	338.9	228.6	110.3		184.2	14.2	170.1	38.5
1983													
1st quarter	2 946.6	1 972.7	1 623.1	319.3	1 303.7	349.7	232.6	117.1		188.0	12.9	175.1	37.6
2nd quarter	3 026.5	2 010.5	1 655.1	323.0	1 332.1	355.4	236.7	118.7		188.2	7.9	180.3	37.8
3rd quarter	3 106.9	2 052.4	1 691.8	327.1	1 364.7	360.6	240.1	120.5		188.4	0.2	188.2	38.2
4th quarter	3 203.6	2 106.5	1 740.1	329.7	1 410.4	366.4	243.2	123.2		198.0	3.8	194.3	39.1
1984													
1st quarter	3 339.2	2 176.0	1 785.2	339.0	1 446.2	390.8	255.1	135.6		224.2	19.5	204.7	38.1
2nd quarter	3 436.9	2 225.7	1 828.2	344.8	1 483.4	397.5	259.3	138.2		234.9	21.3	213.7	36.7
3rd quarter	3 505.5	2 270.9	1 866.7	351.6	1 515.2	404.1	263.8	140.3		237.1	20.4	216.6	40.4
4th quarter	3 563.6	2 309.3	1 899.5	357.2	1 542.4	409.7	267.7	142.0		236.0	22.5	213.5	44.8
1985													
1st quarter	3 626.2	2 353.7	1 933.8	365.6	1 568.2	419.9	275.3	144.7		248.2	22.8	225.4	42.9
2nd quarter	3 669.2	2 389.2	1 963.2	370.0	1 593.2	426.0	279.5	146.4		244.6	20.4	224.2	41.7
3rd quarter	3 721.1	2 427.9	1 996.1	376.8	1 619.3	431.8	283.3	148.5		244.6	19.3	225.3	42.2
4th quarter	3 768.5	2 476.1	2 037.1	383.0	1 654.0	439.1	287.7	151.4		246.9	21.4	225.5	40.5
1986													
1st quarter	3 824.0	2 510.0	2 063.5	387.9	1 675.6	446.4	291.4	155.0		249.5	18.2	231.3	36.8
2nd quarter	3 841.8	2 533.3	2 081.8	393.6	1 688.3	451.5	295.1	156.4		257.2	19.7	237.5	35.6
3rd quarter	3 886.7	2 569.2	2 111.7	399.7	1 712.0	457.4	298.7	158.7		271.5	26.7	244.8	32.5
4th quarter	3 933.3	2 618.2	2 152.2	407.6	1 744.6	465.9	304.6	161.3		272.1	26.7	245.4	30.4
1987													
1st quarter	4 007.1	2 664.5	2 193.7	414.6	1 779.1	470.8	307.9	162.9		282.7	27.3	255.4	31.6
2nd quarter	4 100.7	2 706.2	2 230.1	420.1	1 810.0	476.1	311.4	164.7		289.7	29.1	260.7	30.5
3rd quarter	4 197.8	2 752.7	2 270.6	424.9	1 845.7	482.1	315.1	167.0		297.2	28.9	268.3	35.3
4th quarter	4 294.6	2 819.2	2 330.7	432.8	1 897.8	488.5	318.1	170.4		307.4	30.4	277.0	39.4

Table 1-13B. National Income by Type of Income: Historical Data—*Continued*

(Billions of dollars, quarterly data are at seasonally adjusted annual rates.)   **NIPA Tables 1.7.5, 1.12**

Year and quarter	Corporate profits with IVA and CCAdj					Net interest and miscel-laneous payments	Taxes on production and imports	Less: Subsidies	Business current transfer payments, net			Current surplus of govern-ment enterprises	Addendum: Net national factor income
	Total	Taxes on corporate income	Profits after tax						Total ¹	To persons	To govern-ment		
			Total	Net dividends	Undis-tributed corporate profits								
1973													
1st quarter	126.0	49.7	76.3	28.4	47.9	51.3	114.6	5.9	5.7	3.6	2.1	0.1	1 089.1
2nd quarter	122.8	50.2	72.6	29.3	43.3	52.8	116.2	5.7	6.1	3.9	2.2	-0.3	1 112.3
3rd quarter	123.2	48.6	74.6	30.4	44.2	56.8	118.4	4.7	5.9	4.1	1.8	-0.5	1 137.4
4th quarter	126.0	51.4	74.6	31.5	43.1	60.0	119.7	4.6	6.1	4.2	1.9	-0.8	1 175.2
1974													
1st quarter	118.8	49.7	69.1	32.5	36.5	64.4	120.8	3.6	6.6	4.3	2.3	-0.7	1 184.5
2nd quarter	117.4	52.2	65.2	33.3	31.9	69.1	124.1	2.9	6.9	4.5	2.4	-0.2	1 200.8
3rd quarter	114.1	57.3	56.8	33.6	23.2	72.4	127.1	3.2	7.3	4.9	2.4	-1.1	1 227.1
4th quarter	110.3	51.9	58.4	33.5	24.9	77.3	127.7	3.6	7.7	5.2	2.4	-1.8	1 242.3
1975													
1st quarter	111.8	43.8	68.0	32.9	35.0	80.7	128.8	4.2	8.7	6.1	2.6	-2.8	1 249.2
2nd quarter	124.5	46.8	77.7	32.7	45.0	80.8	133.0	4.3	9.5	6.9	2.6	-3.0	1 276.0
3rd quarter	144.8	57.2	87.6	32.9	54.8	82.2	138.2	4.6	9.7	7.1	2.6	-3.6	1 330.6
4th quarter	152.2	58.8	93.4	33.4	60.0	82.8	141.1	4.9	9.8	7.2	2.6	-3.6	1 372.4
1976													
1st quarter	164.9	66.6	98.2	36.2	62.1	82.5	141.7	5.1	9.9	7.0	2.9	-1.7	1 420.0
2nd quarter	160.3	65.2	95.2	38.1	57.1	85.2	144.9	4.8	9.8	7.0	2.8	-1.8	1 443.4
3rd quarter	160.9	64.9	96.0	39.9	56.1	86.6	147.7	5.1	9.4	6.7	2.8	-1.8	1 474.0
4th quarter	160.4	64.5	95.9	41.9	54.0	87.9	151.3	5.5	8.9	6.1	2.8	-2.0	1 505.9
1977													
1st quarter	170.3	68.8	101.5	42.7	58.8	90.5	154.8	5.8	8.5	5.5	3.1	-2.3	1 549.1
2nd quarter	191.5	74.4	117.1	43.9	73.1	98.6	158.0	5.9	8.2	5.0	3.2	-2.5	1 616.3
3rd quarter	206.2	76.7	129.4	45.6	83.8	105.1	161.5	6.4	8.4	4.9	3.6	-3.0	1 670.8
4th quarter	199.5	77.8	121.6	46.8	74.8	110.1	164.3	10.3	8.7	5.0	3.7	-3.0	1 720.1
1978													
1st quarter	192.5	72.5	120.0	48.3	71.7	111.3	166.9	8.7	9.8	5.6	4.1	-3.0	1 752.3
2nd quarter	220.2	86.6	133.6	49.5	84.1	113.9	173.1	8.4	10.5	6.2	4.3	-2.5	1 839.9
3rd quarter	225.1	87.4	137.7	51.8	85.9	115.3	169.7	8.3	11.2	6.7	4.4	-1.6	1 888.0
4th quarter	235.9	92.9	143.0	53.7	89.4	119.6	173.9	10.4	11.8	7.3	4.6	-1.8	1 949.0
1979													
1st quarter	226.1	90.1	136.0	55.4	80.5	126.6	176.4	8.4	12.8	7.9	4.9	-2.1	1 998.7
2nd quarter	228.0	90.9	137.1	56.9	80.2	132.8	178.5	8.8	13.2	8.2	5.0	-2.6	2 036.4
3rd quarter	226.2	90.6	135.6	58.0	77.6	140.8	180.9	8.1	13.6	8.4	5.2	-3.2	2 087.0
4th quarter	221.1	88.4	132.6	59.7	73.0	155.4	184.6	8.9	13.7	8.5	5.3	-3.7	2 143.1
1980													
1st quarter	216.5	97.0	119.5	61.8	57.7	171.3	189.5	9.2	13.9	8.2	5.7	-4.1	2 184.0
2nd quarter	186.3	77.2	109.1	64.3	44.8	176.9	196.9	9.6	14.1	8.3	5.8	-4.6	2 170.9
3rd quarter	192.6	83.2	109.5	64.7	44.8	180.1	204.3	10.1	14.5	8.7	5.7	-5.5	2 227.0
4th quarter	210.2	91.4	118.9	65.6	53.3	199.0	210.6	10.3	16.5	9.3	7.2	-6.2	2 349.3
1981													
1st quarter	221.0	91.1	129.9	68.7	61.2	201.9	230.8	10.6	17.2	10.4	6.9	-6.5	2 418.0
2nd quarter	217.2	82.6	134.5	72.7	61.8	221.4	235.5	10.7	17.4	11.0	6.5	-4.9	2 453.4
3rd quarter	235.4	86.2	149.2	75.9	73.3	251.0	237.5	11.1	18.2	11.5	6.7	-6.6	2 546.2
4th quarter	219.6	77.4	142.1	77.7	64.4	255.1	238.8	13.5	18.8	11.9	6.9	-4.3	2 555.6
1982													
1st quarter	197.3	65.7	131.5	77.7	53.8	266.4	237.4	14.0	20.0	12.0	8.0	-4.2	2 562.6
2nd quarter	211.6	68.4	143.2	76.5	66.6	278.3	238.3	13.6	20.6	12.3	8.3	-4.2	2 610.2
3rd quarter	210.1	68.6	141.5	77.1	64.4	271.4	241.8	13.0	20.8	12.5	8.3	-5.2	2 624.8
4th quarter	203.9	63.2	140.7	79.5	61.2	268.4	246.3	19.4	21.0	12.7	8.3	-4.3	2 639.8
1983													
1st quarter	225.2	64.2	161.0	81.0	80.0	274.8	250.7	19.9	21.2	12.8	8.5	-3.7	2 698.3
2nd quarter	256.1	79.2	176.9	82.1	94.8	275.6	261.2	21.6	21.8	13.2	8.6	-3.2	2 768.2
3rd quarter	273.3	88.3	185.1	84.3	100.7	290.0	267.5	22.2	22.8	14.0	8.8	-3.5	2 842.3
4th quarter	284.6	90.9	193.7	86.4	107.4	300.8	273.7	21.5	24.6	15.3	9.4	-2.3	2 929.1
1984													
1st quarter	311.5	103.9	207.6	88.6	119.0	303.3	281.6	21.2	27.7	17.6	10.1	-2.1	3 053.1
2nd quarter	323.2	102.9	220.3	90.9	129.5	321.7	287.7	21.0	29.8	19.2	10.5	-1.9	3 142.3
3rd quarter	316.6	91.1	225.5	91.1	134.5	340.0	292.2	20.9	31.3	20.6	10.7	-2.1	3 205.0
4th quarter	323.1	92.3	230.8	92.7	138.1	343.2	297.5	21.2	32.4	21.5	10.9	-1.6	3 256.5
1985													
1st quarter	325.6	98.7	226.9	95.4	131.5	343.0	301.0	21.1	33.4	21.9	11.5	-0.7	3 313.5
2nd quarter	327.4	97.0	230.4	97.0	133.4	341.3	305.7	21.0	39.3	22.1	17.2	0.9	3 344.2
3rd quarter	346.0	102.3	243.7	98.3	145.4	334.8	311.9	21.3	33.9	22.3	11.6	1.0	3 395.6
4th quarter	331.2	99.7	231.5	99.5	132.0	346.7	313.9	22.0	34.2	22.6	11.5	1.0	3 441.4
1986													
1st quarter	324.4	106.6	217.8	103.2	114.6	365.0	317.5	23.1	43.0	23.3	19.7	1.0	3 485.6
2nd quarter	315.1	106.3	208.8	106.4	102.4	368.9	319.5	24.2	35.4	23.5	12.0	1.0	3 510.0
3rd quarter	307.5	107.3	200.2	107.5	92.7	370.5	326.2	25.5	34.1	23.0	11.1	0.8	3 551.2
4th quarter	309.5	118.5	191.0	107.6	83.4	364.0	330.4	26.8	34.8	22.0	12.8	0.7	3 594.2
1987													
1st quarter	323.3	118.7	204.6	108.8	95.8	362.1	336.0	28.3	34.8	21.3	13.5	0.5	3 664.1
2nd quarter	363.1	132.8	230.3	109.8	120.5	361.9	344.4	30.4	35.1	20.6	14.5	0.2	3 751.4
3rd quarter	389.7	137.9	251.8	113.3	138.5	368.6	352.4	31.3	33.2	19.7	13.5	-0.1	3 843.5
4th quarter	395.2	132.4	262.9	117.2	145.6	374.0	357.4	31.1	33.1	19.3	13.8	0.0	3 935.2

¹Includes net transfer payments to the rest of the world, not shown separately.

Table 1-13B. National Income by Type of Income: Historical Data—*Continued*

(Billions of dollars, quarterly data are at seasonally adjusted annual rates.)

NIPA Tables 1.7.5, 1.12

Year and quarter	National income, total	Compensation of employees							Proprietors' income with IVA and CCAdj			Rental income of persons with CCAdj
		Total	Wage and salary accruals			Supplements to wages and salaries			Total	Farm	Nonfarm	
			Total	Government	Other	Total	Employer contributions for:					
							Employee pension and insurance funds	Government social insurance				
1988												
1st quarter	4 385.5	2 869.1	2 367.2	442.7	1 924.4	501.9	322.3	179.6	327.5	33.4	294.2	38.4
2nd quarter	4 476.5	2 932.3	2 422.2	449.1	1 973.0	510.1	326.7	183.4	333.8	27.4	306.3	36.9
3rd quarter	4 562.7	2 981.0	2 462.7	454.4	2 008.3	518.3	332.1	186.2	343.0	28.8	314.2	38.8
4th quarter	4 664.5	3 034.2	2 507.1	461.9	2 045.2	527.2	337.9	189.3	335.1	17.6	317.5	46.8
1989												
1st quarter	4 743.4	3 078.5	2 542.0	470.7	2 071.3	536.5	345.6	190.9	357.0	36.7	320.2	44.2
2nd quarter	4 771.9	3 107.8	2 563.3	476.7	2 086.6	544.5	352.1	192.4	348.4	32.4	316.0	43.5
3rd quarter	4 823.5	3 144.4	2 591.6	484.5	2 107.1	552.8	358.5	194.3	347.8	30.4	317.4	41.1
4th quarter	4 863.2	3 194.6	2 635.3	492.6	2 142.7	559.3	362.1	197.2	353.2	32.5	320.6	40.8
1990												
1st quarter	4 964.4	3 259.0	2 686.8	505.9	2 180.9	572.2	369.2	203.0	360.6	34.4	326.2	43.3
2nd quarter	5 059.7	3 317.4	2 735.9	515.8	2 220.1	581.5	375.2	206.2	364.3	32.7	331.6	48.2
3rd quarter	5 091.7	3 358.5	2 768.7	523.2	2 245.5	589.8	381.5	208.3	369.2	31.8	337.4	53.3
4th quarter	5 122.5	3 370.1	2 773.4	531.3	2 242.1	596.7	388.5	208.2	366.6	29.8	336.8	54.4
1991												
1st quarter	5 151.6	3 385.0	2 776.0	543.9	2 232.1	609.0	397.1	212.0	357.8	26.7	331.2	56.1
2nd quarter	5 190.0	3 419.4	2 801.2	547.1	2 254.1	618.2	404.4	213.8	365.2	28.5	336.6	58.1
3rd quarter	5 236.9	3 455.3	2 826.5	550.0	2 276.5	628.8	412.4	216.4	367.7	25.3	342.5	62.7
4th quarter	5 293.1	3 493.6	2 854.2	554.0	2 300.2	639.4	421.1	218.3	378.4	29.5	348.9	69.4
1992												
1st quarter	5 411.3	3 561.1	2 903.4	564.8	2 338.7	657.7	432.6	225.1	396.4	33.9	362.5	71.6
2nd quarter	5 492.0	3 612.7	2 942.8	570.6	2 372.2	669.9	442.1	227.8	410.4	36.4	374.0	81.3
3rd quarter	5 533.7	3 656.6	2 976.1	574.7	2 401.4	680.5	450.5	230.0	420.9	37.8	383.1	89.3
4th quarter	5 631.4	3 695.4	3 008.8	577.9	2 431.0	686.5	455.8	230.7	431.9	35.1	396.9	96.3
1993												
1st quarter	5 666.2	3 732.2	3 034.6	585.4	2 449.2	697.6	462.9	234.7	435.8	29.3	406.5	105.5
2nd quarter	5 755.2	3 777.3	3 067.4	585.7	2 481.8	709.8	471.0	238.9	450.1	35.6	414.5	113.5
3rd quarter	5 799.4	3 819.8	3 100.3	591.5	2 508.8	719.5	478.5	241.0	447.0	26.7	420.3	115.4
4th quarter	5 918.2	3 859.2	3 129.9	593.5	2 536.4	729.3	485.2	244.1	465.5	36.5	429.1	122.0
1994												
1st quarter	6 028.1	3 926.9	3 186.2	601.2	2 585.0	740.7	491.3	249.4	476.7	42.6	434.1	133.1
2nd quarter	6 129.3	3 978.6	3 229.3	608.4	2 620.8	749.3	496.0	253.3	481.8	37.5	444.3	141.6
3rd quarter	6 230.2	4 016.4	3 262.7	611.8	2 650.9	753.7	498.5	255.3	485.8	33.1	452.7	148.5
4th quarter	6 337.3	4 072.2	3 315.6	616.5	2 699.1	756.5	498.0	258.6	496.1	29.2	467.0	148.4
1995												
1st quarter	6 411.5	4 135.5	3 377.0	624.9	2 752.1	758.5	497.7	260.8	500.4	21.6	478.8	151.0
2nd quarter	6 468.6	4 171.3	3 411.6	627.6	2 784.1	759.7	496.8	262.9	506.3	19.8	486.5	153.0
3rd quarter	6 562.7	4 216.4	3 454.6	630.2	2 824.4	761.8	496.5	265.3	520.0	22.8	497.2	152.8
4th quarter	6 646.5	4 257.5	3 494.4	633.4	2 860.9	763.1	495.6	267.5	537.4	29.5	507.9	161.5
1996												
1st quarter	6 757.1	4 295.5	3 529.5	641.5	2 888.0	766.1	496.5	269.6	560.2	38.2	522.0	166.7
2nd quarter	6 886.9	4 364.3	3 594.2	646.3	2 947.9	770.1	496.7	273.4	586.5	45.4	541.1	168.4
3rd quarter	6 972.4	4 423.4	3 650.2	650.1	3 000.1	773.2	496.7	276.5	588.6	34.6	554.0	172.1
4th quarter	7 110.3	4 482.2	3 706.2	654.4	3 051.8	776.1	496.4	279.7	599.4	35.6	563.8	174.5
1997												
1st quarter	7 225.8	4 554.7	3 774.2	663.2	3 111.0	780.5	496.7	283.8	619.6	38.2	581.5	174.9
2nd quarter	7 333.4	4 617.9	3 832.3	667.8	3 164.6	785.6	498.5	287.1	619.4	28.3	591.1	175.9
3rd quarter	7 476.6	4 695.2	3 900.5	674.7	3 225.7	794.8	503.7	291.0	632.8	32.5	600.3	176.4
4th quarter	7 588.1	4 794.7	3 987.6	681.5	3 306.0	807.1	510.6	296.5	641.1	31.4	609.7	178.9
1998												
1st quarter	7 689.5	4 898.4	4 075.2	691.1	3 384.1	823.2	522.1	301.1	663.6	28.2	635.5	182.7
2nd quarter	7 815.4	4 982.0	4 145.2	698.0	3 447.2	836.8	531.6	305.2	677.0	26.8	650.2	188.6
3rd quarter	7 949.0	5 065.4	4 216.2	705.0	3 511.3	849.2	539.9	309.3	692.9	27.1	665.8	195.7
4th quarter	8 048.4	5 147.1	4 287.1	710.8	3 576.2	860.1	546.8	313.3	716.6	33.4	683.1	198.8
1999												
1st quarter	8 204.2	5 246.4	4 375.5	721.3	3 654.3	870.9	551.6	319.3	729.6	34.3	695.3	203.0
2nd quarter	8 284.0	5 297.9	4 417.9	728.0	3 689.9	880.0	559.0	321.0	738.9	28.7	710.1	206.9
3rd quarter	8 379.7	5 372.0	4 479.5	737.5	3 742.0	892.5	568.9	323.6	750.6	26.6	724.1	209.2
4th quarter	8 563.9	5 499.4	4 587.8	748.0	3 839.8	911.6	582.2	329.4	768.1	24.3	743.7	213.5
2000												
1st quarter	8 809.8	5 692.1	4 755.0	765.8	3 989.2	937.0	595.8	341.2	783.7	25.8	758.0	214.6
2nd quarter	8 896.0	5 731.4	4 781.9	778.6	4 003.4	949.5	607.9	341.6	819.4	31.6	787.8	212.1
3rd quarter	9 005.7	5 845.8	4 874.4	784.1	4 090.2	971.5	623.6	347.9	826.7	29.7	796.9	213.3
4th quarter	9 044.0	5 886.1	4 899.5	790.4	4 109.1	986.6	636.4	350.2	840.1	31.5	808.6	221.1
2001												
1st quarter	9 184.4	5 993.9	4 988.1	804.4	4 183.7	1 005.8	646.5	359.3	867.4	32.1	835.4	225.3
2nd quarter	9 209.9	5 979.9	4 961.4	815.4	4 146.0	1 018.5	660.1	358.4	871.6	30.8	840.8	230.6
3rd quarter	9 157.3	5 965.8	4 932.4	828.4	4 104.0	1 033.3	676.3	357.0	878.1	31.1	846.9	239.5
4th quarter	9 189.2	5 977.7	4 926.8	839.3	4 087.6	1 050.8	693.6	357.2	865.8	28.1	837.7	234.1
2002												
1st quarter	9 304.7	6 038.4	4 963.6	861.6	4 102.0	1 074.9	711.5	363.3	880.5	16.3	864.3	229.2
2nd quarter	9 380.5	6 101.3	5 003.0	870.4	4 132.6	1 098.4	731.9	366.5	884.2	11.6	872.6	231.7
3rd quarter	9 418.0	6 128.8	5 006.3	877.8	4 128.5	1 122.6	755.7	366.8	893.3	20.1	873.2	212.7
4th quarter	9 530.9	6 174.7	5 016.4	882.7	4 133.7	1 158.3	790.5	367.8	903.2	25.8	877.4	201.4

Table 1-13B. National Income by Type of Income: Historical Data—*Continued*

(Billions of dollars, quarterly data are at seasonally adjusted annual rates.)

NIPA Tables 1.7.5, 1.12

| Year and quarter | Corporate profits with IVA and CCAdj | | | | | Net interest and miscel- laneous payments | Taxes on production and imports | Less: Subsidies | Business current transfer payments, net | | | Current surplus of govern- ment enterprises | Addendum: Net national factor income |
| | Total | Taxes on corporate income | Profits after tax | | | | | | Total ¹ | To persons | To govern- ment | | |
			Total	Net dividends	Undis- tributed corporate profits								
1988													
1st quarter	405.1	129.3	275.8	121.7	154.0	379.4	365.1	30.4	31.9	19.6	12.3	-0.7	4 019.5
2nd quarter	421.4	136.6	284.7	126.4	158.3	373.6	372.6	29.8	32.5	20.1	12.4	3.3	4 097.9
3rd quarter	428.3	146.7	281.7	132.8	148.9	385.6	377.6	29.2	34.0	20.8	13.3	3.6	4 176.7
4th quarter	451.7	153.9	297.8	138.7	159.1	402.6	382.5	28.6	36.0	21.9	14.1	4.1	4 270.5
1989													
1st quarter	431.4	158.4	273.1	148.0	125.0	426.5	391.1	28.0	38.2	23.3	14.9	4.5	4 337.6
2nd quarter	423.9	145.0	278.8	155.7	123.1	434.7	397.4	27.4	38.6	23.1	15.5	5.0	4 358.3
3rd quarter	428.6	140.4	288.1	161.1	127.1	439.7	403.8	27.1	40.0	23.2	16.8	5.1	4 401.6
4th quarter	418.4	140.5	277.9	167.1	110.8	435.4	403.2	27.3	39.9	23.1	16.8	5.1	4 442.3
1990													
1st quarter	427.3	139.3	288.0	170.1	117.9	438.8	419.4	27.1	40.2	23.3	17.0	3.0	4 528.9
2nd quarter	452.4	144.9	307.5	169.9	137.6	443.5	419.5	26.9	39.9	22.9	16.9	1.5	4 625.7
3rd quarter	426.9	149.8	277.1	170.0	107.1	442.8	426.9	26.9	39.8	21.9	17.9	1.1	4 650.8
4th quarter	431.2	147.7	283.5	166.3	117.2	451.7	434.2	27.0	40.5	20.7	19.8	0.7	4 674.0
1991													
1st quarter	462.4	141.6	320.7	175.5	145.2	429.0	444.3	27.1	40.8	19.2	21.7	3.3	4 690.3
2nd quarter	455.8	136.8	319.0	180.5	138.5	421.5	451.6	27.2	39.7	17.9	21.8	5.9	4 720.0
3rd quarter	453.2	137.4	315.8	183.3	132.5	418.6	461.2	27.5	39.5	17.0	22.5	6.2	4 757.5
4th quarter	457.7	138.5	319.2	183.4	135.8	403.9	471.3	28.1	39.7	16.4	23.2	7.3	4 803.0
1992													
1st quarter	491.0	148.2	342.8	184.5	158.4	396.3	476.2	28.6	39.6	16.5	23.3	7.6	4 916.4
2nd quarter	498.7	149.8	348.9	186.9	162.0	389.6	481.1	29.2	39.3	16.5	23.0	8.2	4 992.6
3rd quarter	480.5	144.0	336.5	189.3	147.2	382.1	485.9	30.4	39.8	16.3	23.6	8.9	5 029.4
4th quarter	514.7	152.8	361.9	191.5	170.5	382.9	490.3	32.2	44.0	15.9	28.1	8.1	5 121.2
1993													
1st quarter	509.3	158.1	351.2	193.9	157.3	380.2	489.8	35.5	41.2	15.1	26.2	7.6	5 163.0
2nd quarter	533.6	170.1	363.6	198.3	165.2	370.5	497.9	37.6	40.4	14.4	26.2	9.4	5 245.1
3rd quarter	543.4	162.1	381.3	205.1	176.2	357.9	505.0	37.7	39.8	13.7	26.5	8.8	5 283.4
4th quarter	588.4	193.8	394.6	214.4	180.3	349.8	519.8	36.0	40.5	13.1	28.0	9.0	5 384.9
1994													
1st quarter	590.5	174.5	415.9	225.2	190.7	351.0	531.9	33.6	41.9	12.8	29.9	9.7	5 478.2
2nd quarter	610.0	183.6	426.4	234.1	192.3	354.7	544.2	32.4	40.9	12.8	28.9	9.8	5 566.8
3rd quarter	643.2	201.1	442.0	240.1	201.9	366.1	550.2	31.9	42.4	13.2	29.6	9.6	5 660.0
4th quarter	669.2	213.3	456.0	243.5	212.5	377.1	554.7	32.2	42.4	14.2	28.0	9.4	5 763.0
1995													
1st quarter	674.8	217.6	457.3	244.9	212.3	371.0	554.9	34.0	44.7	16.0	26.9	13.2	5 832.7
2nd quarter	702.2	214.8	487.4	248.9	238.5	358.1	553.7	34.6	45.7	17.8	25.9	13.0	5 890.9
3rd quarter	737.7	221.7	516.1	256.4	259.6	351.9	559.2	35.1	46.8	19.6	25.5	13.1	5 978.8
4th quarter	750.0	217.3	532.7	267.4	265.3	352.3	563.9	35.5	46.2	21.4	24.6	13.2	6 058.7
1996													
1st quarter	783.2	221.6	561.6	280.9	280.8	354.1	570.8	35.5	48.1	22.8	26.0	13.9	6 159.8
2nd quarter	795.9	233.4	562.5	293.4	269.1	366.4	577.7	35.4	49.2	23.5	26.8	14.0	6 281.4
3rd quarter	802.1	233.8	568.3	304.0	264.3	375.3	581.6	35.2	49.9	23.2	27.8	14.6	6 361.5
4th quarter	824.8	237.1	587.7	312.6	275.1	388.6	592.9	34.8	67.8	21.9	46.7	14.9	6 469.5
1997													
1st quarter	855.7	238.2	617.5	319.6	297.9	397.3	595.6	34.4	48.4	19.7	29.3	13.9	6 602.2
2nd quarter	878.8	242.9	635.8	327.0	308.8	401.6	610.3	33.6	48.6	18.7	29.7	14.7	6 693.6
3rd quarter	912.0	255.1	656.9	334.9	322.0	408.5	616.6	33.4	54.5	19.0	34.4	14.0	6 825.0
4th quarter	892.9	245.5	647.5	343.3	304.1	422.8	624.0	33.8	53.7	20.4	30.8	13.8	6 930.4
1998													
1st quarter	817.7	248.5	569.2	351.4	217.8	458.5	629.1	33.8	60.3	22.8	32.5	12.9	7 021.0
2nd quarter	811.5	245.5	566.0	355.1	210.9	480.8	635.5	35.0	61.4	25.1	31.4	13.5	7 140.0
3rd quarter	820.1	252.2	567.9	353.3	214.6	491.2	643.0	36.8	63.8	27.1	33.0	13.7	7 265.3
4th quarter	800.3	247.2	553.1	346.0	207.1	486.8	650.3	39.9	75.3	28.9	44.8	13.0	7 349.7
1999													
1st quarter	859.7	256.2	603.5	335.3	268.2	469.0	657.5	42.4	66.3	31.2	36.7	15.1	7 507.8
2nd quarter	859.4	254.1	605.4	331.0	274.3	477.0	667.1	45.0	67.2	32.8	37.0	14.7	7 580.1
3rd quarter	848.4	259.2	589.2	335.3	253.9	483.6	679.0	46.4	69.1	34.8	37.4	14.2	7 663.8
4th quarter	857.6	265.7	591.9	348.0	243.9	495.9	690.8	46.9	73.2	37.1	39.2	12.4	7 834.5
2000													
1st quarter	840.5	274.3	566.2	366.7	199.6	532.1	698.6	45.1	80.8	39.8	42.7	12.5	8 062.0
2nd quarter	831.7	273.1	558.6	379.5	179.1	543.9	707.3	45.5	84.6	41.5	43.2	11.0	8 138.5
3rd quarter	814.7	254.7	560.0	384.2	175.7	543.2	711.3	45.8	88.9	43.3	43.7	7.7	8 243.7
4th quarter	790.0	258.3	531.8	381.1	150.7	537.8	717.1	47.0	93.5	45.2	44.7	5.3	8 275.1
2001													
1st quarter	782.8	224.5	558.3	371.9	186.4	541.8	724.1	55.2	99.9	46.7	45.4	4.4	8 411.3
2nd quarter	812.3	216.6	595.6	366.9	228.8	547.7	724.1	62.0	102.8	48.0	45.8	3.0	8 442.1
3rd quarter	765.0	195.0	569.9	368.5	201.4	544.3	725.4	71.2	102.6	47.4	46.2	7.9	8 392.6
4th quarter	776.6	177.0	599.6	376.4	223.2	543.6	737.2	46.4	99.8	44.9	46.5	0.9	8 397.8
2002													
1st quarter	830.3	179.3	651.1	389.2	261.8	529.1	745.2	42.6	90.3	40.8	47.4	4.3	8 507.6
2nd quarter	852.0	186.0	666.0	399.0	267.0	505.7	756.9	39.8	84.2	36.1	47.8	4.4	8 574.9
3rd quarter	869.8	193.7	676.0	404.2	271.8	494.2	772.1	41.4	79.4	31.8	48.2	9.1	8 598.8
4th quarter	936.7	210.4	726.3	404.6	321.8	496.5	777.0	41.7	75.6	28.2	48.3	7.6	8 712.4

¹Includes net transfer payments to the rest of the world, not shown separately.

Table 1-13B. National Income by Type of Income: Historical Data—*Continued*

(Billions of dollars, quarterly data are at seasonally adjusted annual rates.)

NIPA Tables 1.7.5, 1.12

Year and quarter	National income, total	Compensation of employees								Proprietors' income with IVA and CCAdj			Rental income of persons with CCAdj
		Total	Wage and salary accruals			Supplements to wages and salaries				Total	Farm	Nonfarm	
			Total	Government	Other	Total	Employer contributions for:						
							Employee pension and insurance funds	Government social insurance					
2003													
1st quarter	9 614.2	6 255.8	5 061.0	904.8	4 156.1	1 194.9	819.3	375.6	889.6	29.9	859.7	209.7
2nd quarter	9 757.3	6 346.3	5 123.5	912.4	4 211.0	1 222.9	842.6	380.2	919.1	37.5	881.6	204.2
3rd quarter	9 899.4	6 425.6	5 184.6	915.6	4 269.0	1 241.0	856.9	384.1	945.8	38.3	907.4	186.2
4th quarter	10 089.8	6 502.6	5 249.4	920.4	4 328.9	1 253.2	863.4	389.7	968.1	40.4	927.7	216.6
2004													
1st quarter	10 281.2	6 539.8	5 275.9	941.9	4 334.0	1 263.9	863.1	400.8	1 002.1	54.2	947.9	204.2
2nd quarter	10 444.7	6 636.4	5 363.6	950.7	4 412.9	1 272.8	867.3	405.5	1 029.8	52.0	977.8	197.1
3rd quarter	10 641.6	6 756.3	5 468.9	955.8	4 513.1	1 287.4	876.4	411.0	1 040.1	44.0	996.1	196.8
4th quarter	10 768.7	6 841.2	5 534.4	962.7	4 571.6	1 306.8	891.7	415.1	1 063.1	48.5	1 014.6	195.4
2005													
1st quarter	11 019.6	6 921.1	5 584.2	982.4	4 601.7	1 336.9	914.3	422.6	1 046.8	43.7	1 003.1	190.7
2nd quarter	11 156.6	7 003.6	5 651.7	987.6	4 664.1	1 351.9	927.7	424.2	1 054.0	46.4	1 007.6	181.5
3rd quarter	11 360.2	7 128.4	5 758.3	994.5	4 763.9	1 370.1	939.7	430.4	1 082.6	45.6	1 037.0	168.4
4th quarter	11 559.0	7 207.1	5 829.7	1 001.4	4 828.3	1 377.4	944.6	432.8	1 095.8	39.9	1 055.9	172.3
2006													
1st quarter	11 838.2	7 353.7	5 958.9	1 019.0	4 939.9	1 394.8	950.7	444.1	1 126.9	28.4	1 098.5	161.3
2nd quarter	11 965.9	7 419.9	6 018.6	1 028.3	4 990.3	1 401.3	956.8	444.5	1 133.2	28.4	1 104.8	153.2
3rd quarter	12 093.0	7 484.1	6 075.4	1 041.0	5 034.5	1 408.7	962.7	445.9	1 131.2	28.4	1 102.8	140.3
4th quarter	12 227.9	7 650.3	6 227.6	1 052.3	5 175.4	1 422.6	970.4	452.2	1 140.6	32.2	1 108.4	131.2
2007													
1st quarter	12 261.4	7 756.4	6 328.1	1 076.4	5 251.8	1 428.3	970.2	458.0	1 103.0	36.2	1 066.8	122.4
2nd quarter	12 360.9	7 814.4	6 382.8	1 082.7	5 300.1	1 431.6	974.2	457.4	1 090.0	34.1	1 056.0	139.8
3rd quarter	12 407.1	7 868.5	6 427.6	1 092.6	5 335.0	1 441.0	982.0	459.0	1 079.3	35.0	1 044.3	146.8
4th quarter	12 556.3	7 984.3	6 523.4	1 104.5	5 418.9	1 460.9	995.6	465.2	1 089.1	45.9	1 043.3	165.9
2008													
1st quarter	12 693.9	8 099.0	6 600.5	1 127.6	5 472.9	1 498.5	1 026.7	471.8	1 113.7	60.5	1 053.1	188.9
2nd quarter	12 724.9	8 073.4	6 554.9	1 137.9	5 417.1	1 518.5	1 048.8	469.7	1 127.2	55.3	1 071.9	218.5
3rd quarter	12 733.1	8 084.7	6 550.6	1 151.0	5 399.6	1 534.1	1 063.5	470.6	1 104.0	46.6	1 057.4	243.5
4th quarter	12 284.4	8 016.1	6 477.4	1 160.0	5 317.4	1 538.7	1 070.5	468.3	1 046.7	44.6	1 002.1	275.6
2009													
1st quarter	12 099.2	7 830.1	6 300.5	1 168.9	5 131.5	1 529.6	1 071.0	458.6	960.2	37.1	923.1	278.8
2nd quarter	12 035.7	7 809.2	6 278.2	1 175.9	5 102.2	1 531.1	1 071.7	459.4	926.9	38.7	888.2	299.7
3rd quarter	12 126.1	7 781.9	6 251.3	1 177.1	5 074.2	1 530.6	1 073.5	457.1	929.3	39.5	889.9	319.3
4th quarter	12 329.5	7 804.4	6 271.4	1 179.2	5 092.2	1 533.0	1 076.2	456.8	948.5	41.4	907.0	325.9
2010													
1st quarter	12 595.9	7 852.5	6 301.6	1 188.6	5 113.0	1 550.9	1 083.4	467.5	981.7	44.6	937.1	344.1
2nd quarter	12 803.7	7 960.0	6 399.8	1 196.3	5 203.5	1 560.2	1 087.6	472.6	1 025.6	45.8	979.7	349.1
3rd quarter	12 942.1	8 022.2	6 454.5	1 189.9	5 264.7	1 567.7	1 092.0	475.7	1 057.0	58.3	998.7	352.8
4th quarter	13 018.8	8 050.8	6 477.0	1 188.6	5 288.4	1 573.7	1 096.8	476.9	1 081.5	60.1	1 021.4	354.8
2011													
1st quarter	13 232.6	8 172.5	6 578.2	1 191.1	5 387.1	1 594.4	1 103.0	491.4	1 095.6	66.1	1 029.5	385.0
2nd quarter	13 344.1	8 219.7	6 617.1	1 191.9	5 425.2	1 602.7	1 108.7	494.0	1 106.5	67.3	1 039.2	396.9
3rd quarter	13 519.3	8 338.3	6 724.3	1 189.3	5 535.0	1 614.0	1 112.6	501.3	1 113.7	67.5	1 046.2	406.3
4th quarter	13 588.6	8 375.8	6 753.2	1 189.0	5 564.2	1 622.6	1 119.6	503.0	1 119.7	62.7	1 057.0	427.2

Table 1-13B. National Income by Type of Income: Historical Data—*Continued*

(Billions of dollars, quarterly data are at seasonally adjusted annual rates.) NIPA Tables 1.7.5, 1.12

Year and quarter	Corporate profits with IVA and CCAdj					Net interest and miscel-laneous payments	Taxes on production and imports	Less: Subsidies	Business current transfer payments, net			Current surplus of govern-ment enterprises	Addendum: Net national factor income
	Total	Taxes on corporate income	Profits after tax						Total ¹	To persons	To govern-ment		
			Total	Net dividends	Undis-tributed corporate profits								
2003													
1st quarter	917.5	231.5	685.9	402.8	283.1	511.9	787.9	44.9	77.3	28.8	47.5	9.4	8 784.6
2nd quarter	950.1	227.0	723.1	409.8	313.3	511.5	799.5	57.1	75.8	26.8	48.3	7.9	8 931.2
3rd quarter	992.7	247.2	745.5	428.4	317.0	501.0	813.0	47.0	75.8	24.7	49.2	6.3	9 051.2
4th quarter	1 050.9	269.3	781.6	458.4	323.2	492.1	826.9	47.3	75.7	22.4	49.9	4.3	9 230.2
2004													
1st quarter	1 187.2	277.6	909.6	496.1	413.5	467.7	843.5	44.8	77.8	17.6	51.3	3.7	9 401.1
2nd quarter	1 226.9	298.2	928.7	524.4	404.3	460.6	855.7	43.6	80.0	16.2	52.3	1.9	9 550.7
3rd quarter	1 292.2	320.4	971.8	539.5	432.3	454.0	867.9	44.9	79.0	16.1	53.2	0.3	9 739.4
4th quarter	1 281.4	328.1	953.3	641.3	312.0	464.2	886.5	52.2	89.9	17.9	53.4	-0.9	9 845.3
2005													
1st quarter	1 408.2	405.1	1 003.1	534.1	469.0	509.4	905.6	56.9	96.5	23.8	53.9	-1.8	10 076.1
2nd quarter	1 429.0	395.6	1 033.3	538.8	494.5	528.0	925.1	61.0	99.6	26.5	55.2	-3.1	10 196.0
3rd quarter	1 454.7	403.1	1 051.6	559.7	492.0	558.0	939.6	62.1	95.2	27.3	55.4	-4.5	10 392.0
4th quarter	1 532.5	445.7	1 086.8	596.7	490.0	576.9	950.3	63.7	92.3	25.8	56.4	-4.5	10 584.6
2006													
1st quarter	1 590.9	460.7	1 130.2	646.4	483.9	608.9	971.5	55.6	82.8	21.7	57.8	-2.4	10 841.8
2nd quarter	1 597.7	475.1	1 122.6	691.1	431.5	654.4	983.3	51.4	79.3	19.8	58.9	-3.8	10 958.4
3rd quarter	1 655.1	496.6	1 158.5	727.1	431.4	661.6	991.6	49.8	83.6	20.6	60.1	-4.7	11 072.2
4th quarter	1 589.6	460.7	1 128.8	754.5	374.3	684.0	1 000.7	48.7	86.1	23.3	61.6	-6.0	11 195.7
2007													
1st quarter	1 515.5	474.1	1 041.4	756.5	284.9	703.9	1 014.7	50.0	105.6	26.7	64.8	-10.1	11 201.2
2nd quarter	1 565.3	467.9	1 097.4	804.4	293.0	693.7	1 023.9	58.1	102.9	29.6	65.1	-11.0	11 303.2
3rd quarter	1 501.0	431.0	1 070.0	809.7	260.2	743.3	1 030.7	55.7	104.4	32.0	66.6	-11.2	11 338.9
4th quarter	1 460.8	408.8	1 052.0	807.4	244.6	785.6	1 039.4	54.5	100.4	33.9	70.7	-14.8	11 485.7
2008													
1st quarter	1 360.0	355.2	1 004.8	835.9	168.9	843.7	1 035.0	51.9	120.8	36.8	74.0	-15.2	11 605.2
2nd quarter	1 333.7	344.1	989.7	803.4	186.3	875.1	1 047.3	51.9	117.3	36.6	74.4	-15.9	11 628.0
3rd quarter	1 328.6	312.5	1 016.1	780.5	235.5	878.0	1 046.7	52.5	116.1	36.7	74.4	-16.1	11 638.9
4th quarter	971.2	224.3	746.9	727.6	19.2	883.7	1 025.5	55.4	137.8	37.1	93.2	-16.8	11 193.4
2009													
1st quarter	1 175.2	208.8	966.4	671.9	294.5	782.9	1 008.0	56.4	137.0	37.8	96.7	-16.8	11 027.3
2nd quarter	1 262.3	244.8	1 017.5	600.9	416.6	656.4	1 011.8	56.8	141.5	38.2	106.1	-15.3	10 954.5
3rd quarter	1 438.8	301.6	1 137.3	584.1	553.1	596.6	1 020.4	68.4	122.2	38.4	88.1	-14.0	11 065.9
4th quarter	1 571.6	334.4	1 237.2	623.0	614.2	591.0	1 031.3	57.1	127.5	38.3	93.5	-13.6	11 241.3
2010													
1st quarter	1 724.2	409.7	1 314.5	684.8	629.7	589.1	1 040.9	56.4	134.6	38.0	96.2	-14.7	11 491.5
2nd quarter	1 785.8	399.6	1 386.3	729.3	657.0	569.2	1 050.6	56.8	135.7	38.0	97.9	-15.5	11 689.7
3rd quarter	1 833.1	430.3	1 402.8	760.5	642.3	550.1	1 059.0	57.0	140.9	37.9	101.8	-16.0	11 815.1
4th quarter	1 857.4	404.7	1 452.7	774.8	677.9	548.7	1 065.5	59.1	135.7	39.3	100.1	-16.5	11 893.3
2011													
1st quarter	1 876.4	422.3	1 454.1	793.8	660.3	556.6	1 087.4	60.0	134.7	39.5	99.1	-15.6	12 086.2
2nd quarter	1 937.6	420.5	1 517.1	807.4	709.6	525.6	1 101.1	62.7	133.9	39.4	99.0	-14.6	12 186.4
3rd quarter	1 970.1	411.4	1 558.7	821.4	737.3	535.7	1 100.0	64.2	133.7	39.4	99.3	-14.5	12 364.2
4th quarter	1 986.9	410.7	1 576.2	831.7	744.5	522.7	1 103.3	64.4	134.1	39.6	100.0	-16.7	12 432.3

¹Includes net transfer payments to the rest of the world, not shown separately.

Table 1-14. Gross and Net Value Added of Domestic Corporate Business

(Billions of dollars, quarterly data are at seasonally adjusted annual rates.)

NIPA Table 1.14

Year and quarter	Gross value added of corporate business, total	Consumption of fixed capital	Net value added											Gross value added of financial corporate business
						Net operating surplus								
									Corporate profits with IVA and CCAdj					
			Total	Compensation of employees	Taxes on production and imports less subsidies	Total	Net interest and miscellaneous payments	Business current transfer payments	Total	Taxes on corporate income	Profits after tax			
											Total	Net dividends	Undistributed	
1950	160.4	12.0	148.4	98.7	14.8	35.0	-0.1	0.7	34.4	17.9	16.4	7.9	8.6	7.3
1951	183.9	13.6	170.3	114.6	15.9	39.9	-0.2	1.1	39.1	22.6	16.5	7.4	9.1	8.2
1952	192.6	14.5	178.1	123.0	17.3	37.8	-0.2	1.1	37.0	19.4	17.6	7.5	10.1	9.2
1953	206.2	15.4	190.8	134.0	18.5	38.3	0.0	1.0	37.3	20.3	17.0	7.8	9.3	10.2
1954	203.6	16.2	187.5	132.2	17.9	37.3	0.2	0.8	36.4	17.6	18.7	7.9	10.9	10.8
1955	229.5	17.1	212.4	144.6	19.8	48.0	0.2	1.2	46.6	22.0	24.6	8.9	15.7	11.8
1956	245.6	19.2	226.4	158.2	21.5	46.7	0.0	1.5	45.2	22.0	23.2	9.5	13.7	12.9
1957	256.9	21.3	235.7	166.5	22.8	46.4	0.2	1.7	44.5	21.4	23.1	9.9	13.3	13.8
1958	251.8	22.7	229.1	164.0	23.1	42.0	0.6	1.5	39.9	19.0	21.0	9.8	11.1	14.7
1959	281.9	23.7	258.2	180.3	25.6	52.4	-0.2	1.5	51.1	23.7	27.4	10.7	16.7	15.9
1960	293.9	24.0	269.9	190.7	27.8	51.3	-0.2	1.6	50.0	22.8	27.2	11.4	15.8	17.5
1961	302.1	24.6	277.5	195.6	28.9	53.0	0.4	1.8	50.9	22.9	28.0	11.5	16.5	18.4
1962	329.0	25.5	303.5	211.0	31.2	61.3	0.7	2.0	58.6	24.1	34.5	12.4	22.1	19.3
1963	349.5	26.7	322.9	222.7	33.2	67.0	0.4	2.4	64.3	26.4	37.9	13.6	24.3	19.7
1964	377.7	28.2	349.5	239.2	35.6	74.7	0.8	2.9	71.1	28.2	42.9	15.0	27.9	21.6
1965	414.4	30.4	384.0	259.9	37.8	86.3	1.2	3.3	81.8	31.1	50.8	16.9	33.9	23.2
1966	454.1	33.4	420.7	288.5	38.9	93.3	2.3	3.0	88.0	33.9	54.1	17.8	36.3	25.1
1967	479.3	36.8	442.5	308.4	41.4	92.7	4.0	3.3	85.4	32.9	52.5	18.3	34.2	28.1
1968	529.1	40.6	488.5	341.3	47.8	99.4	3.9	3.8	91.6	39.6	52.0	20.2	31.8	31.3
1969	576.7	45.1	531.5	378.6	52.9	100.0	7.8	4.4	87.9	40.0	47.9	20.4	27.5	36.2
1970	597.8	50.0	547.7	400.2	57.0	90.6	11.3	3.9	75.4	34.8	40.6	20.4	20.3	39.4
1971	646.1	54.8	591.3	425.3	62.8	103.2	11.5	3.5	88.2	38.2	50.1	20.3	29.7	43.1
1972	716.7	59.7	657.0	472.5	67.3	117.2	11.3	4.0	101.9	42.3	59.6	21.9	37.6	47.3
1973	802.6	66.9	735.6	533.9	74.1	127.6	13.0	5.0	109.6	50.0	59.6	23.1	36.5	51.8
1974	869.9	78.8	791.0	587.4	78.6	125.0	20.7	6.6	97.7	52.8	44.9	23.5	21.4	60.0
1975	944.4	94.4	850.0	614.9	84.5	150.7	23.4	8.6	118.7	51.6	67.0	26.4	40.6	67.8
1976	1 062.9	104.5	958.4	695.2	91.4	171.7	18.8	7.9	145.1	65.3	79.8	30.1	49.7	73.2
1977	1 205.1	118.0	1 087.1	784.8	100.0	202.3	23.3	6.3	172.7	74.4	98.3	33.7	64.6	85.7
1978	1 376.1	134.2	1 241.9	901.8	108.7	231.3	27.5	8.2	195.6	84.9	110.7	39.6	71.1	103.4
1979	1 529.0	155.1	1 373.9	1 022.0	115.0	236.9	34.9	11.3	190.7	90.0	100.7	41.5	59.2	114.6
1980	1 663.0	179.8	1 483.2	1 120.1	128.6	234.5	55.9	12.6	166.0	87.2	78.8	47.3	31.4	128.5
1981	1 889.0	208.1	1 680.8	1 240.0	154.4	286.4	77.7	15.1	193.6	84.3	109.3	58.3	50.9	146.8
1982	1 967.3	231.4	1 736.0	1 293.8	161.3	280.8	90.0	17.7	173.1	66.5	106.6	61.3	45.3	164.7
1983	2 116.7	240.4	1 876.2	1 367.1	177.4	331.7	86.6	20.3	224.8	80.6	144.1	71.3	72.8	187.6
1984	2 371.3	252.9	2 118.4	1 513.9	195.6	408.9	98.8	28.0	282.0	97.5	184.5	78.5	106.0	209.9
1985	2 526.5	271.7	2 254.8	1 622.4	209.0	423.3	96.9	31.9	294.4	99.4	195.0	85.7	109.3	232.6
1986	2 640.6	289.8	2 350.8	1 720.4	219.6	410.8	106.3	29.9	274.7	109.7	165.0	88.3	76.7	257.4
1987	2 832.6	306.5	2 526.1	1 840.0	233.4	452.7	107.6	25.3	319.8	130.4	189.4	95.6	93.8	281.7
1988	3 065.5	328.8	2 736.7	1 980.4	252.0	504.3	107.8	26.9	369.6	141.6	228.0	98.0	130.0	300.1
1989	3 229.5	350.8	2 878.6	2 088.3	267.5	522.8	130.0	34.4	358.4	146.1	212.4	126.4	86.0	330.3
1990	3 377.0	373.0	3 003.9	2 200.6	284.5	518.9	125.8	34.8	358.4	145.4	212.9	144.1	68.8	341.8
1991	3 467.4	392.1	3 075.3	2 249.4	307.9	518.0	102.6	34.6	380.8	138.6	242.2	156.4	85.9	363.3
1992	3 642.2	402.0	3 240.2	2 375.5	325.9	538.8	80.6	35.1	423.1	148.7	274.4	160.0	114.5	401.1
1993	3 823.2	420.1	3 403.2	2 488.2	342.0	572.9	73.5	32.7	466.8	171.0	295.7	182.3	113.4	424.8
1994	4 110.5	444.9	3 665.7	2 634.8	372.4	658.5	75.0	33.2	550.3	193.1	357.1	197.6	159.6	433.0
1995	4 357.5	476.8	3 880.7	2 776.0	379.1	725.6	64.7	37.7	623.2	217.8	405.4	221.6	183.8	469.5
1996	4 625.0	506.0	4 119.0	2 914.9	390.7	813.4	69.3	44.6	699.5	231.5	468.1	257.3	210.7	505.6
1997	4 978.9	540.9	4 438.1	3 123.9	406.9	907.3	94.8	35.2	777.3	245.4	531.9	284.0	247.9	566.4
1998	5 299.3	578.3	4 720.9	3 396.8	418.4	905.7	142.2	53.8	709.7	248.4	461.3	309.2	152.1	630.9
1999	5 624.5	625.8	4 998.7	3 628.6	441.5	928.6	139.0	54.9	734.8	258.8	476.0	295.7	180.3	669.0
2000	6 016.4	685.1	5 331.4	3 950.7	466.6	914.1	166.6	73.8	673.6	265.1	408.5	348.5	60.1	737.0
2001	6 034.7	730.3	5 304.4	3 986.2	462.6	855.7	154.2	87.0	614.5	203.3	411.2	330.1	81.1	782.2
2002	6 122.7	755.9	5 366.8	3 980.7	492.2	893.9	116.2	63.5	714.3	192.3	522.0	351.2	170.8	815.0
2003	6 360.7	775.5	5 585.2	4 105.5	517.3	962.4	99.4	50.9	812.0	243.8	568.3	392.8	175.5	856.9
2004	6 774.2	809.2	5 965.0	4 265.9	553.7	1 145.4	48.6	54.9	1 041.9	306.1	735.8	488.0	247.8	896.7
2005	7 297.9	862.9	6 435.0	4 498.5	596.7	1 339.8	61.6	61.6	1 216.6	412.4	804.3	296.5	507.8	995.1
2006	7 823.3	925.9	6 897.4	4 743.4	633.7	1 520.3	120.4	48.4	1 351.5	473.3	878.2	626.9	251.3	1 083.0
2007	7 965.6	973.4	6 992.2	4 944.1	651.5	1 396.5	164.2	72.6	1 159.8	445.5	714.3	649.7	64.6	1 019.5
2008	7 999.0	1 028.5	6 970.5	5 025.9	661.0	1 283.7	338.7	103.2	841.8	309.0	532.8	606.3	-73.6	1 007.6
2009	7 686.0	1 030.4	6 655.7	4 721.7	632.6	1 301.4	204.5	95.3	1 001.6	272.4	729.2	516.4	212.8	1 094.0
2010	8 218.4	1 027.1	7 191.4	4 821.5	660.2	1 709.6	192.7	98.8	1 418.2	411.1	1 007.1	615.3	391.8	1 316.4
2011	8 597.7	1 068.7	7 529.0	5 044.3	686.4	1 798.3	189.0	95.6	1 513.7	416.2	1 097.5	639.6	457.9	1 348.6
2009														
1st quarter	7 619.8	1 045.3	6 574.5	4 750.8	629.4	1 194.3	277.2	102.0	815.2	208.8	606.3	571.7	34.6	969.5
2nd quarter	7 607.5	1 033.1	6 574.4	4 724.9	631.3	1 218.2	197.1	103.5	917.7	244.8	672.9	536.9	136.0	1 072.9
3rd quarter	7 678.0	1 022.5	6 655.5	4 699.4	626.7	1 329.4	167.4	85.7	1 076.3	301.6	774.7	446.4	328.3	1 144.6
4th quarter	7 838.9	1 020.6	6 818.3	4 711.9	642.8	1 463.6	176.3	90.1	1 197.3	334.4	862.9	510.6	352.3	1 189.1
2010														
1st quarter	8 053.3	1 018.0	7 035.3	4 736.8	653.1	1 645.5	193.1	97.1	1 355.3	409.7	945.6	581.7	363.9	1 242.3
2nd quarter	8 179.3	1 023.5	7 155.8	4 809.8	658.4	1 687.7	194.3	98.2	1 395.2	399.6	995.6	590.4	405.3	1 302.7
3rd quarter	8 281.8	1 028.5	7 253.3	4 859.7	663.1	1 730.4	189.7	102.9	1 437.8	430.3	1 007.5	629.3	378.2	1 327.9
4th quarter	8 359.3	1 038.3	7 321.0	4 879.8	666.3	1 774.9	193.6	96.8	1 484.5	404.7	1 079.8	659.8	420.0	1 392.8
2011														
1st quarter	8 451.8	1 048.0	7 403.8	4 967.7	680.2	1 755.9	194.0	96.2	1 465.7	422.3	1 043.3	644.2	399.2	1 373.5
2nd quarter	8 525.7	1 063.1	7 462.6	5 000.5	687.8	1 774.3	186.6	95.4	1 492.2	420.5	1 071.7	664.1	407.6	1 309.2
3rd quarter	8 659.6	1 076.2	7 583.4	5 091.8	687.8	1 803.8	189.3	95.3	1 519.3	411.4	1 107.9	610.6	497.3	1 337.5
4th quarter	8 753.7	1 087.6	7 666.2	5 117.2	689.7	1 859.3	186.1	95.5	1 577.6	410.7	1 166.9	639.5	527.5	1 374.3

Table 1-15. Gross Value Added of Nonfinancial Domestic Corporate Business in Current and Chained Dollars

(Billions of dollars, quarterly data are at seasonally adjusted annual rates.)

NIPA Table 1.14

Year and quarter	Current-dollar gross value added													Gross value added in billions of chained (2005) dollars
	Total	Consumption of fixed capital	Net value added											
			Total	Compensation of employees	Taxes on production and imports less subsidies	Net operating surplus								
						Total	Net interest and miscellaneous payments	Business current transfer payments	Corporate profits with IVA and CCAdj					
									Total	Taxes on corporate income	Profits after tax			
											Total	Net dividends	Undistributed	
1955	217.7	16.5	201.3	137.9	19.2	44.2	1.6	1.0	41.6	20.1	21.4	8.4	13.0	940.3
1956	232.7	18.5	214.2	150.8	20.8	42.6	1.8	1.1	39.8	19.9	19.8	9.0	10.8	970.1
1957	243.1	20.5	222.6	158.4	22.0	42.2	2.2	1.2	38.8	19.0	19.9	9.2	10.6	982.6
1958	237.1	21.8	215.3	155.2	22.3	37.8	2.8	1.2	33.8	16.1	17.7	9.1	8.6	944.0
1959	266.0	22.7	243.3	170.8	24.4	48.1	2.9	1.3	43.8	20.7	23.1	9.8	13.3	1 050.9
1960	276.4	23.1	253.3	180.4	26.6	46.3	3.2	1.4	41.7	19.1	22.6	10.5	12.1	1 086.0
1961	283.7	23.7	260.1	184.5	27.6	47.9	3.7	1.5	42.7	19.4	23.3	10.6	12.7	1 110.5
1962	309.8	24.5	285.2	199.3	29.9	56.1	4.3	1.7	50.1	20.6	29.5	11.6	17.9	1 205.5
1963	329.9	25.6	304.3	210.1	31.7	62.5	4.7	1.7	56.1	22.8	33.4	12.4	20.9	1 277.9
1964	356.1	27.0	329.0	225.7	33.9	69.5	5.2	2.0	62.4	23.9	38.5	14.0	24.5	1 368.1
1965	391.2	29.1	362.1	245.4	36.0	80.7	5.8	2.2	72.7	27.1	45.5	16.2	29.3	1 481.8
1966	429.0	31.9	397.1	272.9	37.0	87.2	7.0	2.7	77.5	29.5	48.0	16.8	31.2	1 588.1
1967	451.2	35.2	416.0	291.1	39.3	85.6	8.4	2.8	74.4	27.8	46.5	17.3	29.3	1 630.9
1968	497.8	38.7	459.1	321.9	45.5	91.7	9.7	3.1	78.9	33.5	45.4	19.0	26.4	1 736.7
1969	540.5	42.9	497.5	357.1	50.2	90.3	12.7	3.2	74.4	33.3	41.0	19.0	22.0	1 806.9
1970	558.3	47.5	510.8	376.5	54.2	80.1	16.6	3.3	60.2	27.3	32.9	18.3	14.6	1 792.4
1971	603.0	52.0	551.1	399.4	59.5	92.1	17.6	3.7	70.8	30.0	40.8	18.1	22.7	1 866.3
1972	669.4	56.5	613.0	443.9	63.7	105.4	18.6	4.0	82.8	33.8	49.0	19.7	29.3	2 009.0
1973	750.8	63.1	687.6	502.2	70.1	115.4	21.8	4.7	88.9	40.4	48.5	20.8	27.8	2 132.7
1974	809.8	74.2	735.7	552.2	74.4	109.1	27.5	4.1	77.5	42.8	34.6	21.5	13.1	2 099.0
1975	876.7	88.6	788.0	575.5	80.2	132.4	28.4	5.0	98.9	41.9	57.0	24.6	32.5	2 068.2
1976	989.7	97.8	892.0	651.4	86.7	153.9	26.0	7.0	121.0	53.5	67.5	27.8	39.7	2 237.2
1977	1 119.4	110.1	1 009.2	735.3	94.6	179.3	28.5	9.0	141.9	60.6	81.3	30.9	50.4	2 402.9
1978	1 272.7	125.1	1 147.5	845.1	102.7	199.7	33.4	9.5	156.8	67.6	89.2	35.9	53.3	2 560.2
1979	1 414.4	144.3	1 270.2	958.4	108.8	203.0	41.8	9.5	151.8	70.6	81.2	37.6	43.5	2 640.4
1980	1 534.5	166.7	1 367.8	1 047.2	121.5	199.1	54.2	10.2	134.7	68.2	66.5	44.7	21.9	2 613.4
1981	1 742.2	194.4	1 549.8	1 157.6	146.7	245.5	67.2	11.4	166.8	66.0	100.8	52.5	48.3	2 717.8
1982	1 802.6	212.8	1 589.8	1 200.4	152.9	236.5	77.4	8.8	150.2	48.8	101.5	54.1	47.4	2 653.0
1983	1 929.1	219.3	1 709.8	1 263.1	168.0	278.7	77.0	10.5	191.2	61.7	129.5	63.2	66.2	2 781.1
1984	2 161.4	228.8	1 932.6	1 400.0	185.0	347.5	86.0	11.7	249.8	75.9	173.9	67.2	106.7	3 027.7
1985	2 293.9	244.0	2 049.9	1 496.1	196.6	357.2	91.5	16.1	249.6	71.1	178.6	72.0	106.6	3 157.9
1986	2 383.2	258.0	2 125.2	1 575.4	204.6	345.2	98.5	27.3	219.5	76.2	143.2	72.9	70.4	3 235.5
1987	2 551.0	270.0	2 280.9	1 678.4	216.8	385.6	95.9	29.9	259.9	94.2	165.7	76.3	89.4	3 402.5
1988	2 765.4	287.3	2 478.1	1 804.7	233.8	439.6	107.9	27.4	304.3	104.0	200.3	82.2	118.2	3 599.1
1989	2 899.2	303.9	2 595.3	1 905.7	248.2	441.5	133.9	24.0	283.5	101.2	182.3	105.4	77.0	3 658.8
1990	3 035.2	321.0	2 714.2	2 005.5	263.5	445.2	143.1	25.4	276.7	98.5	178.3	118.3	60.0	3 713.1
1991	3 104.1	336.1	2 768.0	2 044.8	285.7	437.5	139.6	26.6	271.3	88.6	182.7	125.5	57.2	3 695.4
1992	3 241.1	344.1	2 897.0	2 152.9	302.5	441.6	114.2	31.3	296.1	94.4	201.7	134.3	67.4	3 804.9
1993	3 398.4	359.0	3 039.3	2 244.0	318.0	477.3	99.8	30.1	347.5	108.0	239.5	149.2	90.3	3 905.0
1994	3 677.6	380.1	3 297.5	2 382.1	347.8	567.5	98.8	35.3	433.5	132.4	301.1	158.0	143.1	4 155.3
1995	3 888.0	408.3	3 479.7	2 511.5	354.2	614.0	112.7	30.7	470.6	140.3	330.3	178.0	152.2	4 349.0
1996	4 119.4	435.1	3 684.4	2 631.3	365.6	687.5	112.1	38.0	537.4	152.9	384.5	197.6	186.9	4 588.6
1997	4 412.5	466.9	3 945.6	2 814.6	381.0	750.0	124.7	39.2	586.2	161.4	424.8	215.9	208.9	4 887.8
1998	4 668.3	499.9	4 168.5	3 049.7	393.1	725.7	146.8	35.2	543.7	158.7	385.1	241.0	144.0	5 167.3
1999	4 955.5	539.3	4 416.3	3 256.5	414.6	745.1	164.5	47.1	533.5	171.4	362.1	224.7	137.4	5 452.4
2000	5 279.4	590.1	4 689.4	3 541.8	439.4	708.2	192.8	47.9	467.5	170.2	297.3	251.3	46.0	5 745.7
2001	5 252.5	632.0	4 620.5	3 559.4	434.5	626.7	197.7	58.9	370.1	111.2	258.8	245.4	13.4	5 637.8
2002	5 307.7	654.5	4 653.1	3 544.2	461.9	647.1	163.7	56.3	427.2	97.1	330.1	254.8	75.3	5 675.5
2003	5 503.7	669.0	4 834.7	3 651.3	484.2	699.2	147.9	65.2	486.1	132.9	353.2	293.4	59.8	5 818.1
2004	5 877.5	695.6	5 181.9	3 786.7	517.7	877.5	134.4	65.5	677.5	187.0	490.6	364.5	126.1	6 085.1
2005	6 302.8	743.0	5 559.8	3 976.3	558.4	1 025.1	148.2	79.3	797.6	271.9	525.8	170.9	354.9	6 302.8
2006	6 740.3	800.9	5 939.4	4 182.3	593.3	1 163.7	164.0	75.8	923.9	307.6	616.2	471.1	145.1	6 543.2
2007	6 946.0	840.1	6 106.0	4 361.0	607.7	1 137.4	232.3	69.1	835.9	293.8	542.2	484.6	57.6	6 606.4
2008	6 991.4	864.3	6 127.1	4 441.2	615.2	1 070.8	257.7	58.1	755.0	227.4	527.7	474.1	53.5	6 515.9
2009	6 592.0	862.2	5 729.8	4 178.2	587.4	964.2	243.7	78.3	642.1	175.0	467.1	349.0	118.1	6 036.5
2010	6 902.0	856.8	6 045.2	4 263.0	614.3	1 167.8	130.9	85.4	951.5	229.3	722.3	398.8	323.5	6 329.5
2011	7 249.1	890.2	6 358.9	4 459.1	639.6	1 260.2	104.3	86.9	1 069.0	246.6	822.4	443.3	379.2	6 511.3
2009														
1st quarter	6 650.3	874.2	5 776.1	4 210.8	584.5	980.7	286.2	74.6	619.9	164.6	455.4	390.3	65.1	6 035.2
2nd quarter	6 534.6	864.5	5 670.1	4 178.9	586.5	904.7	255.2	83.4	566.1	156.7	409.4	374.7	34.7	5 966.1
3rd quarter	6 533.4	856.4	5 677.0	4 156.0	581.6	939.4	228.3	75.8	635.2	169.8	465.4	288.7	176.7	6 006.1
4th quarter	6 649.7	853.8	5 796.0	4 167.0	597.1	1 031.8	205.2	79.4	747.2	209.0	538.2	342.4	195.8	6 138.4
2010														
1st quarter	6 811.1	850.3	5 960.7	4 188.9	607.3	1 164.5	166.7	84.5	913.3	233.4	680.0	380.6	299.4	6 288.7
2nd quarter	6 876.6	853.9	6 022.6	4 247.5	612.3	1 162.8	135.5	84.8	942.5	232.0	710.5	376.2	334.3	6 329.3
3rd quarter	6 953.9	857.7	6 096.2	4 299.8	617.1	1 179.4	114.9	86.7	977.8	239.4	738.3	406.0	332.3	6 361.5
4th quarter	6 966.5	865.4	6 101.1	4 315.9	620.7	1 164.6	106.5	85.5	972.6	212.4	760.2	432.3	327.9	6 338.4
2011														
1st quarter	7 078.3	873.4	6 205.0	4 386.5	633.2	1 185.3	106.6	86.3	992.3	238.5	753.8	422.0	331.8	6 407.9
2nd quarter	7 216.5	885.4	6 331.1	4 426.3	641.2	1 263.6	103.0	87.5	1 073.1	252.2	821.0	459.2	361.7	6 504.1
3rd quarter	7 322.0	896.3	6 425.8	4 502.7	640.9	1 282.1	104.5	86.7	1 091.0	250.1	840.9	434.0	406.9	6 538.1
4th quarter	7 379.4	905.6	6 473.9	4 521.2	643.0	1 309.7	103.1	87.2	1 119.4	245.5	873.9	457.8	416.2	6 594.9

Table 1-16. Rates of Return and Related Data for Domestic Nonfinancial Corporations

Year	Rates of return (percent)					Shares of net value added (percent)					Value of produced assets (billions of dollars)	Tax liability as a percent of produced assets	Q3 ratio
	Net operating surplus		Corporate profits		Net interest	Net operating surplus		Corporate profits		Net interest			
	Before tax	After tax	Before tax	After tax		Before tax	After tax	Before tax	After tax				
1960	9.6	5.7	8.7	4.7	0.7	18.4	10.9	16.6	9.1	1.3	487.5	3.9	0.75
1961	9.7	5.8	8.7	4.8	0.7	18.6	11.1	16.6	9.1	1.4	498.3	3.9	0.89
1962	11.1	7.1	9.9	5.9	0.9	19.9	12.7	17.8	10.6	1.5	512.9	4.0	0.85
1963	11.9	7.6	10.6	6.4	0.9	20.7	13.2	18.6	11.1	1.5	530.9	4.3	0.92
1964	12.7	8.3	11.4	7.1	0.9	21.3	14.0	19.1	11.9	1.6	554.8	4.3	1.05
1965	13.8	9.2	12.4	7.8	1.0	22.4	15.0	20.2	12.7	1.6	590.3	4.6	1.12
1966	13.7	9.1	12.2	7.6	1.1	22.0	14.6	19.6	12.2	1.8	640.6	4.6	0.94
1967	12.4	8.4	10.8	6.8	1.2	20.7	14.1	18.0	11.4	2.0	697.6	4.0	1.10
1968	12.2	7.8	10.6	6.1	1.3	20.2	12.9	17.4	10.1	2.1	758.6	4.4	1.20
1969	10.9	6.9	9.0	5.0	1.5	18.2	11.5	15.0	8.4	2.6	831.7	4.0	0.95
1970	8.9	5.9	6.7	3.7	1.8	15.8	10.5	11.9	6.6	3.2	910.1	3.0	0.86
1971	9.4	6.4	7.3	4.3	1.8	16.9	11.5	13.1	7.6	3.2	991.1	3.0	0.92
1972	9.8	6.7	7.7	4.6	1.7	17.2	11.7	13.5	8.0	3.0	1 076.5	3.1	1.03
1973	9.7	6.3	7.5	4.1	1.8	16.8	11.0	13.0	7.1	3.2	1 198.5	3.4	0.74
1974	7.7	4.7	5.4	2.4	1.9	14.8	9.0	10.5	4.7	3.7	1 426.6	3.0	0.41
1975	8.1	5.5	6.1	3.5	1.7	16.9	11.6	12.6	7.3	3.6	1 645.7	2.6	0.57
1976	8.6	5.6	6.8	3.8	1.4	17.3	11.3	13.6	7.6	2.9	1 801.0	3.0	0.62
1977	9.0	5.9	7.1	4.1	1.4	17.7	11.7	14.0	8.0	2.8	1 991.8	3.0	0.53
1978	8.8	5.8	6.9	3.9	1.5	17.2	11.3	13.5	7.6	2.9	2 243.8	3.0	0.50
1979	7.8	5.0	5.8	3.0	1.6	15.8	10.2	11.7	6.2	3.3	2 577.1	2.7	0.52
1980	6.7	4.4	4.5	2.2	1.8	14.4	9.5	9.7	4.8	4.0	2 961.1	2.3	0.57
1981	7.4	5.4	5.0	3.0	2.0	15.9	11.6	10.8	6.5	4.3	3 350.5	2.0	0.48
1982	6.6	5.2	4.2	2.9	2.1	14.9	11.9	9.5	6.5	4.9	3 619.9	1.4	0.51
1983	7.5	5.8	5.2	3.5	2.1	16.4	12.8	11.3	7.7	4.5	3 744.6	1.7	0.55
1984	8.8	6.9	6.3	4.4	2.2	17.9	13.9	12.8	8.9	4.4	3 911.5	1.9	0.51
1985	8.6	6.9	6.0	4.3	2.2	17.2	13.8	12.0	8.5	4.5	4 119.3	1.7	0.60
1986	8.1	6.3	5.2	3.4	2.2	16.2	12.6	10.4	6.8	4.5	4 267.9	1.8	0.67
1987	8.7	6.6	5.9	3.7	2.2	16.9	12.7	11.3	7.2	4.2	4 440.9	2.1	0.65
1988	9.4	7.2	6.5	4.3	2.3	17.8	13.6	12.3	8.1	4.4	4 695.5	2.2	0.67
1989	9.0	7.0	5.7	3.7	2.9	17.2	13.3	10.8	7.0	5.4	4 967.2	2.0	0.78
1990	8.5	6.7	5.3	3.4	2.8	16.4	12.8	10.1	6.5	5.4	5 225.4	1.9	0.72
1991	7.9	6.2	4.9	3.2	2.5	15.4	12.2	9.5	6.3	4.9	5 391.8	1.6	0.89
1992	7.7	6.0	5.3	3.5	2.0	14.8	11.5	10.0	6.8	3.9	5 508.9	1.7	0.97
1993	8.2	6.4	5.9	4.0	1.8	15.5	12.0	11.2	7.6	3.4	5 716.9	1.9	1.01
1994	9.1	6.9	6.9	4.7	1.7	16.7	12.6	12.7	8.6	3.1	6 015.6	2.2	0.94
1995	9.4	7.2	7.1	4.9	1.8	17.3	13.2	13.1	9.0	3.3	6 371.1	2.2	1.12
1996	10.0	7.8	7.8	5.5	1.7	18.3	14.2	14.2	10.1	3.1	6 712.3	2.3	1.10
1997	10.4	8.1	8.1	5.8	1.8	18.7	14.6	14.6	10.5	3.2	7 056.0	2.3	1.29
1998	9.9	7.7	. . .	. . .	. . .	17.4	13.6	. . .	. . .	. . .	7 341.1	. . .	1.51
1999	9.6	7.4	. . .	. . .	. . .	16.9	13.0	. . .	. . .	. . .	7 729.9	. . .	1.83
2000	8.6	6.5	. . .	. . .	. . .	15.1	11.5	. . .	. . .	. . .	8 219.5	. . .	1.41
2001	7.2	5.9	. . .	. . .	. . .	13.6	11.2	. . .	. . .	. . .	8 648.3	. . .	1.17
2002	7.2	6.1	. . .	. . .	. . .	13.9	11.8	. . .	. . .	. . .	8 952.1	. . .	0.85
2003	7.5	6.1	. . .	. . .	. . .	14.5	11.7	. . .	. . .	. . .	9 238.2	. . .	1.09
2004	9.0	7.1	. . .	. . .	. . .	16.9	13.3	. . .	. . .	. . .	9 746.6	. . .	1.13
2005	9.7	7.1	. . .	. . .	. . .	18.4	13.5	. . .	. . .	. . .	10 550.8	. . .	1.01
2006	10.2	7.5	. . .	. . .	. . .	19.6	14.4	. . .	. . .	. . .	11 405.9	. . .	1.08
2007	9.4	6.9	. . .	. . .	. . .	18.6	13.8	. . .	. . .	. . .	12 155.1	. . .	1.10
2008	8.3	6.5	. . .	. . .	. . .	17.4	13.7	. . .	. . .	. . .	12 806.9	. . .	0.70
2009	7.5	6.1	. . .	. . .	. . .	16.8	13.8	. . .	. . .	. . .	12 919.5	. . .	0.83
2010	8.9	6.7	. . .	. . .	. . .	19.1	14.4	. . .	. . .	. . .	13 000.4	. . .	0.88

Note: See notes and definitions for explanation.
. . . = Not available.

NOTES AND DEFINITIONS, CHAPTER 1

TABLES 1-1 THROUGH 1-15
NATIONAL INCOME AND PRODUCT

SOURCE: U.S. DEPARTMENT OF COMMERCE, BUREAU OF ECONOMIC ANALYSIS (BEA)

All data in these tables are from the national income and product accounts (NIPAs). The data are as published in the 2009 comprehensive NIPA revision and continued through the fourth quarter of 2011 in the estimates released on May 31, 2012. Each table is notated, just above the table at the right-hand side, with the numbers of the NIPA tables from which the data are drawn.

NIPA data for recent years will be revised again in the 2012 annual revision, which will be released on July 27, 2012, along with the first estimate of GDP for the second quarter of 2012.

All the quarterly NIPA data published here, including indexes of quantity and price, are seasonally adjusted; this is not specifically noted on each table. All of the quarterly level values in current and constant dollars are also expressed at annual rates, which means that seasonally adjusted quarterly levels have been multiplied by 4 so that their scale will be comparable with the annual values shown, and this is noted on the pertinent *Business Statistics* tables. Where quarterly percent changes are shown, they are expressed as seasonally adjusted annual rates, which means that the quarter-to-quarter change in the level of GDP is calculated and then raised to the 4th power in order to express what that rate of change would be if continued over an entire year; this is noted in the column headings. For further information on these concepts see "General Notes" at the front of this volume.

The changes made in the 2009 revision are described in "Preview of the 2009 Comprehensive Revision of the NIPAs: Changes in Definitions and Presentations," *Survey of Current Business,* March 2009, available at <http://www.bea.gov>.

Definitions and notes on the data:
Basic concepts of total output and income (Tables 1-1, 1-11, and 1-12)

The NIPAs depict the U.S. economy in several different dimensions. The basic concept, and the measure that is now most frequently cited, is gross domestic product (GDP), which is the market value of all goods and services produced by labor and property located in the United States.

In principle, GDP can be measured by summing the values created by each industry in the economy. However, it can more readily be measured by summing all the final demands for the economy's output. This final-demand approach also has the advantage of depicting the origins of demand for economic production, whether from consumers, businesses, or government.

Since production for the market necessarily generates incomes equal to its value, there is also an income total that corresponds to the production value total. This income can be measured and its distribution among labor, capital, and other income recipients can be depicted.

The structure and relationships of several of these major concepts are illustrated in Table 1-11. The definitions of these concepts are as follows:

Gross domestic product (GDP), the featured measure of the value of U.S. output, is the market value of the goods and services produced by labor and property located in the United States. Market values represent output valued at the prices paid by the final customer, and therefore include taxes on production and imports, such as sales taxes, customs duties, and taxes on property.

The term "gross" in gross domestic product and gross national product is used to indicate that capital consumption allowances (economic depreciation) have not been deducted.

GDP is primarily measured by summing the values of all of the final demands in the economy, net of the demands met by imports; this is shown in Table 1-1. Specifically, GDP is the sum of personal consumption expenditures (PCE), gross private domestic investment (including change in private inventories and before deduction of charges for consumption of fixed capital), net exports of goods and services, and government consumption expenditures and gross investment. GDP measured in this way excludes duplication involving "intermediate" purchases of goods and services (goods and services purchased by industries and used in production), the value of which is already included in the value of the final products. Production of any intermediate goods that are not used in further production in the current period is captured in the measurement of inventory change.

In concept, GDP is equal to the sum of the economic value added by (formerly referred to as "gross product originating in") all industries in the United States. This, in turn, also makes it the conceptual equivalent of *gross domestic income (GDI),* a new concept introduced in the 2003 revision. GDI is the sum of the incomes earned in each domestic industry, plus the taxes on production and imports and less the subsidies that account for the difference between output value and factor input value. This derivation is shown in Table 1-12. Since the incomes and taxes can be measured directly, they can be summed to a total that is equivalent to GDP in concept but differs due to imperfections in measurement. The difference between the two is known as the *statistical discrepancy.* It is defined as GDP minus GDI, and is shown in Tables 1-11 and 1-12.

Gross national product (GNP) refers to all goods and services produced by labor and property supplied by U.S.

residents—whether located in the United States or abroad—expressed at market prices. It is equal to GDP, plus *income receipts from the rest of the world,* less *income payments to the rest of the world. Domestic* production and income refer to the <u>location</u> of the factors of production, with only factors located in the United States included; *national* production and income refer to the <u>ownership</u> of the factors of production, with only factors owned by United States residents included.

Before the comprehensive NIPA revisions that were made in 1991, GNP was the commonly used measure of U.S. production. However, GDP is clearly preferable to GNP when used in conjunction with indicators such as employment, hours worked, and capital utilized—for example, in the calculation of labor and capital productivity—because it is confined to production taking place within the borders of the United States. It is also the measure used by almost all other countries, thus facilitating international comparisons such as those shown in Chapter 13.

The income-side aggregate corresponding to GNP is *gross national income (GNI),* shown as an addendum to Table 1-11. It consists of gross domestic income plus income receipts from the rest of the world, less income payments to the rest of the world. It is used as the denominator for a national saving-income ratio, presented in Chapter 5. National income is the preferred measure for calculating and comparing saving, since it is the income aggregate from which that saving arises. As with GDP and gross domestic income, the statistical discrepancy indicates the difference between the product-side and income-side measurement of the same concept.

Net national product is the market value, net of depreciation, of goods and services attributable to the labor and property supplied by U.S. residents. It is equal to GNP minus the *consumption of fixed capital (CFC)*. CFC relates only to fixed capital located in the United States. (Investment in that capital is measured by private fixed investment and government gross investment.) As of the 2009 comprehensive revision, CFC represents only the normal using-up of capital in the process of production, and no longer includes extraordinary disaster losses such as those caused by Hurricane Katrina and the 9/11 attacks. These losses are still estimated and used to write down the estimates of the capital stock, but they no longer have negative effects on our calculation of current income from production.

National income has been redefined and now includes all net incomes (net of the consumption of fixed capital) earned in production. It now includes not only "factor incomes"—net incomes received by labor and capital as a result of their participation in the production process, but also "nonfactor charges"—taxes on production and imports, business transfer payments, and the current surplus of government enterprises, less subsidies. This change has been made to conform with the international guidelines for national accounts, *System of National Accounts (SNA) 1993.* According to *SNA 1993,* these charges cannot be eliminated from the input and output prices.

Since national income now includes the nonfactor charges, it is conceptually equivalent to *net national product* and differs only by the amount of the statistical discrepancy.

The concept formerly known as "national income," which excludes the nonfactor charges, is still included in the accounts as an addendum item, now called "net national factor income." It is shown in Table 1-13 and used as the denominator in Figure 1-4. *Net national factor income* consists of compensation of employees, proprietors' income with inventory valuation and capital consumption adjustments (IVA and CCadj, respectively), rental income of persons with capital consumption adjustment, corporate profits with inventory valuation and capital consumption adjustments, and net interest.

By definition, national income and its components exclude all income from capital gains (increases in the value of owned assets). Such increases have no counterpart on the production side of the accounts. This exclusion is partly accomplished by means of the inventory valuation and capital consumption adjustments, which will be described in the definitions of the components of product and income.

Definitions and notes on the data:
Imputation

The term *imputation* will appear from time to time in the definitions of product and income components. Imputed values are values estimated by BEA statisticians for certain important product and income components that are not explicitly valued in the source data, usually because a market transaction in money terms is not involved. Imputed values appear on both the product and income side of the accounts; they add equal amounts to income and spending, so that no imputed saving is created.

One important example is the imputed rent on owner-occupied housing. The building of such housing is counted as investment, yet in the monetary accounts of the household sector, there is no income from that investment nor any rental paid for it. In the NIPAs, the rent that each such dwelling would earn if rented is estimated and added to both national and personal income (as part of rental income receipts) and to personal consumption expenditures (as part of expenditures on housing services).

Another important example is imputed interest. For example, many individuals keep monetary balances in a bank or other financial institution, receiving either no interest or below-market interest, but receiving the institution's services, such as clearing checks and otherwise facilitating payments, with little or no charge. In this case, where is the product generated by the institution's workers and capital? In the NIPAs, the depositor is imputed a market-rate-based interest return on his or her balance, which is then imputed as a service charge received by the institution, and therefore included in the value of the institution's output.

**Definitions and notes on the data:
Components of product (Tables 1-1 through 1-6)**

Personal consumption expenditures (PCE) is goods and services purchased by persons residing in the United States. PCE consists mainly of purchases of new goods and services by individuals from businesses. It includes purchases that are financed by insurance, such as government-provided and private medical insurance. In addition, PCE includes purchases of new goods and services by nonprofit institutions, net purchases of used goods ("net" here indicates purchases of used goods from business less sales of used goods to business) by individuals and nonprofit institutions, and purchases abroad of goods and services by U.S. residents traveling or working in foreign countries. PCE also includes purchases for certain goods and services provided by government agencies. (See the notes and definitions for Chapter 4 for additional information.) In the 2009 revision, new detail has been provided on the allocation of PCE between the household and nonprofit sectors.

Gross private domestic investment consists of gross private fixed investment and change in private inventories.

Private fixed investment consists of both nonresidential and residential fixed investment. The term "residential" refers to the construction and equipping of living quarters for permanent occupancy. Hotels and motels are included in *nonresidential fixed investment*, as described subsequently in this section.

Private fixed investment consists of purchases of fixed assets, which are commodities that will be used in a production process for more than one year, including replacements and additions to the capital stock. It is measured "gross," before a deduction for consumption of existing fixed capital. It covers all investment by private businesses and nonprofit institutions in the United States, regardless of whether the investment is owned by U.S. residents. The residential component includes investment in owner-occupied housing; the homeowner is treated equivalently to a business in these investment accounts. (However, when GDP by sector is calculated, owner-occupied housing is no longer included in the business sector. It is allocated to the households and institutions sector.) Private fixed investment does not include purchases of the same types of equipment and structures by government agencies, which are included in government gross investment, nor does it include investment by U.S. residents in other countries.

Nonresidential fixed investment is the total of nonresidential structures and nonresidential equipment and software.

Nonresidential structures consists of new construction, brokers' commissions on sales of structures, and net purchases of used structures by private business and by nonprofit institutions from government agencies (that is, purchases of used structures from government minus sales of used structures to government). New construction also includes hotels and motels and mining exploration, shafts, and wells.

Nonresidential equipment and software consists of private business purchases on capital account of new machinery, equipment, and vehicles; purchases and in-house production of software; dealers' margins on sales of used equipment; and net purchases of used equipment from government agencies, persons, and the rest of the world (that is, purchases of such equipment minus sales of such equipment). It does not include the estimated personal-use portion of equipment purchased for both business and personal use, which is allocated to PCE.

Residential private fixed investment consists of both residential structures and residential producers' durable equipment (including such equipment as appliances owned by landlords and rented to tenants). Investment in structures consists of new units, improvements to existing units, purchases of manufactured homes, brokers' commissions on the sale of residential property, and net purchases of used residential structures from government agencies (that is, purchases of such structures from government minus sales of such structures to government). As noted above, it includes investment in owner-occupied housing.

Change in private inventories is the change in the physical volume of inventories held by businesses, with that change being valued at the average price of the period. It differs from the change in the book value of inventories reported by most businesses; an *inventory valuation adjustment (IVA)* converts book value change using historical cost valuations to the change in physical volume, valued at average replacement cost.

Net exports of goods and services is *exports of goods and services* less *imports of goods and services*. It does not include income payments or receipts or transfer payments to and from the rest of the world.

Government consumption expenditures is the estimated value of the services produced by governments (federal, state, and local) for current consumption. Since these are generally not sold, there is no market valuation and they are priced at the cost of inputs. The input costs consist of the compensation of general government employees; the estimated consumption of general government fixed capital, including software (CFC, or economic depreciation); and the cost of goods and services purchased by government less the value of sales to other sectors. The value of investment in equipment and structures produced by government workers and capital is also subtracted, and is instead included in government investment. Government sales to other sectors consist primarily of receipts of tuition payments for higher education and receipts of charges for medical care.

This definition of government consumption expenditures differs in concept—but not in the amount contributed to GDP—from the treatment in existence before the 2003 revision of the NIPAs. In the current definition, goods and services purchased by government are considered to be intermediate output. In the previous definition, they were considered to be final sales. Since their value is added to the other components to yield total government consumption expenditures, the dollar total contributed to GDP is the same. The only practical difference is that the goods purchased disappear from the goods account and appear in the services account instead. In the industry sector accounts, the value added by government is also unchanged. It continues to be measured as the sum of compensation and CFC, or equivalently as gross government output less the value of goods and services purchased. The new definition increases U.S. conformity with *SNA 1993*.

Gross government investment consists of general government and government enterprise expenditures for fixed assets (structures and equipment and software). Government inventory investment is included in government consumption expenditures.

Definitions and notes on the data:
Real values, quantity and price indexes (Tables 1-2 through 1-7)

Real, or chained (2005) dollar, estimates are estimates from which the effect of price change has been removed. Prior to the 1996 comprehensive revision, constant-dollar measures were obtained by combining real output measures for different goods and services using the relative prices of a single year as weights for the entire time span of the series. In the recent environment of rapid technological change, which has caused the prices of computers and electronic components to decline dramatically relative to other prices, this method distorts the measurement of economic growth and causes excessive revisions of growth rates at each benchmark revision. The current, chained-dollar measure changes the relative price weights each year, as relative prices shift over time. As a result, recent changes in relative prices do not change historical growth rates.

Chained-dollar estimates, although expressed for continuity's sake as if they had occurred according to the prices of a single year (currently 2005), are usually not additive. This means that because of the changes in price weights each year, the chained (2005) dollar components in any given table for any year other than 2005 usually do not add to the chained (2005) dollar total. The amount of the difference for the major components of GDP is called the *residual* and is shown in Table 1-2. In time periods close to the base year, the residual is usually quite small; over longer periods, the differences become much larger. For this reason, BEA no longer publishes chained-dollar estimates prior to 1995, except for selected aggregate series. For the more detailed components of GDP, historical trends and fluctuations in real volumes are represented by *chain-type quantity indexes,* which are presented in Tables 1-5, 4-3, 5-4, 5-6, 6-6, 6-7, 6-11, 6-16, 7-2, 7-5, and 15-2.

Chain-weighting leads to complexity in estimating the contribution of economic sectors to an overall change in output: it becomes difficult, for someone without access to the complicated statistical methods that BEA uses, to find the cor-

rect answers to questions such as "How much is the rise in defense spending contributing to GDP growth?" Because of this, BEA is now calculating and publishing estimates of the arithmetic contribution of each major component to the total change in real GDP. *Business Statistics* reproduces these calculations in Table 1-4. As will be explained later, these calculations are of limited analytical value because imports are treated as a negative contribution to GDP instead of being subtracted from the demand components that give rise to them. For further information, see J. Steven Landefeld, Brent R. Moulton, and Cindy M. Vojtech, "Chained-Dollar Indexes: Issues, Tips on Their Use, and Upcoming Changes," *Survey of Current Business* (November 2003); and J. Steven Landefeld and Robert P. Parker, "BEA's Chain Indexes, Time Series, and Measures of Long-Term Economic Growth," *Survey of Current Business* (May 1997).

GDP price indexes measure price changes between any two adjacent years (or quarters) for a fixed "market basket" of goods and services consisting of the average quantities purchased in those two years (or quarters). The annual measures are chained together to form an index with prices in 2005 set to equal 100. Using average quantities as weights and changing weights each period eliminates the substitution bias that arises in more conventional indexes, in which weights are taken from a single base period that usually takes place early in the period under measurement. Generally, using a single, early base period leads to an overstatement of price increase. (The CPI-U and the CPI-W are examples of such conventional indexes, technically known as "Laspeyres" indexes. See the "General Notes" at the beginning of this volume and the notes and definitions for Chapter 8 for further explanation.)

The chain-type formula guarantees that a GDP price index change will differ only trivially from the change in the implicit deflator (ratio of current-dollar to real value, expressed as a percent). Therefore, *Business Statistics* is no longer publishing a separate table of implicit deflators.

Definitions and notes on the data:
Aggregates of sales and purchases (Tables 1-1 and 1-5 through 1-7)

Final sales of domestic product is GDP minus change in private inventories. It is the sum of personal consumption expenditures, gross private domestic fixed investment, government consumption expenditures and gross investment, and net exports of goods and services.

Gross domestic purchases is the market value of goods and services purchased by U.S. residents, regardless of where those goods and services were produced. It is GDP minus net exports (that is, minus exports plus imports) of goods and services; equivalently, it is the sum of personal consumption expenditures, gross private domestic investment, and government consumption expenditures and gross investment. The price index for gross domestic purchases is therefore a measure of price change for goods and services purchased by (rather than produced by) U.S. residents.

Final sales to domestic purchasers is gross domestic purchases minus change in private inventories.

Definitions and notes on the data:
U.S. Population and per capita product and income estimates (Table 1-3)

In Table 1-3, annual and quarterly measures of product, income, and consumption spending are expressed in per capita terms—the aggregate dollar amount divided by the U.S. population. Population data from 1991 forward reflect the results of Census 2000.

National per capita totals, as shown in Table 1-3, are based on definitions of income and population that differ slightly from the sum of the states shown in Table 17-2. See the notes and definitions for Chapter 17 for further explanation.

Definitions and notes on the data:
Inventory-sales ratios (Table 1-8)

Inventories to sales ratios. The ratios shown in Table 1-8 are based on the inventory estimates underlying the measurement of inventory change in the NIPAs. They include data and estimates for not only the inventories held in manufacturing and trade (which are shown in Chapter 16), but also stocks held by all other businesses in the U.S. economy.

For the current-dollar ratios, inventories at the end of each quarter are valued in the prices that prevailed at the end of that quarter. For the constant-dollar ratios, they are valued in chained (2005) dollars. In both cases, the inventory-sales ratio is the value of the inventories at the end of the quarter divided by quarterly total sales at <u>monthly</u> rates (quarterly totals divided by 3). In other words, they represent how many months' supply businesses had on hand at the end of the period. This makes them comparable in concept and order of magnitude to the ratios shown in Chapter 16. Annual ratios are those for the fourth quarter.

Definitions and notes on the data:
Shares of aggregate supply and demand (Tables 1-9 and 1-10)

These tables, developed by the editor of *Business Statistics*, are not official NIPA calculations. They are components of current-dollar GDP rearranged in order to highlight relationships that are not always apparent in the official presentation of the NIPAs.

Aggregate supply combines the two sources that, between them, supply the goods and services demanded by consumers, businesses, and governments in the U.S. economy—domestic production (GDP) and imports. In this table the user can observe the growing share of imports that satisfy demands in the U.S. marketplace.

Aggregate final demand is the sum of all final (that is, excluding inventory change) demands for goods and serv-

ices in the U.S. market—consumption spending, fixed investment, exports, and government consumption and investment. It is different from *final sales of domestic product* (Tables 1-1 and 1-7) because imports are not subtracted; in this table, imports are considered a source of supply, not a negative element of demand. It is different from *gross domestic purchases* (Tables 1-5 and 1-6) because it includes exports, since they are a source of demand for U.S. output, but excludes inventory change. It is like *final sales to domestic purchasers* (Table 1-7) in excluding inventory change, but different because it includes exports.

Table 1-10 provides alternative data on the question of the relative importance of consumption spending and other final demands to the U.S. economy. NIPA statistics on PCE as a percent of GDP are frequently cited, but there is a problem with this, since PCE includes the value of imports while GDP does not.

Definitions and notes on the data:
Components of income (Tables 1-11, 1-12 and 1-13)

There are now two different presentations of aggregate income for the United States: *gross domestic income* (Table 1-12) and *national income* (Table 1-13). As noted above, domestic income refers to income generated from production within the United States, while national income refers to income received by residents of the United States. This means that some of the income components differ between the two tables. Domestic income payments include payments to the rest of the world from domestic industries. National income payments exclude payments to the rest of the world but include payments received by U.S. residents from the rest of the world. These differences are seen in employee compensation, interest, and corporate profits. Taxes on production and imports, taxes on corporate income, business transfer payments, subsidies, proprietors' income, rental income, and the current surplus of government enterprises are the same in both accounts.

A third important income aggregate is *personal income*. The derivation of this well-known statistic from national income is shown in Table 1-11. See Chapter 4 and its notes and definitions for more information.

Compensation of employees is the income accruing to employees as remuneration for their work. It is the sum of wage and salary accruals and supplements to wages and salaries. In the domestic income account, it is called "compensation of employees, paid." It refers to all payments generated by domestic production, including those to workers residing in the "rest of the world." In the national and personal income accounts, there is a different amount labeled "compensation of employees, received"—that is, received by U.S. residents—including from the rest of the world.

Wage and salary accruals consists of the monetary remuneration of employees, including the compensation of corporate officers; corporate directors' fees paid to directors who are also employees of the corporation; commissions, tips, and bonuses; voluntary employee contributions to certain deferred compensation plans, such as 401(k) plans; and receipts-in-kind that represent income. As of the 2003 revision, it also includes judicial fees to jurors and witnesses, compensation of prison inmates, and marriage fees to justices of the peace, all of which were formerly included in "other labor income."

In concept, wage and salary accruals include the value of the exercise by employees of "nonqualified stock options," in which an employee is allowed to buy stock for less than its current market price. (Actual measurement of these values involves a number of problems, particularly in the short run. Such stock options are not included in the monthly wage data from the Bureau of Labor Statistics, which are the main source for current extrapolations of wages and salaries, and are not consistently reported in corporate financial statements. They are, however, generally included in the unemployment insurance wage data that are used to correct the preliminary wage and salary estimates.) Another form of stock option, the "incentive stock option," leads to a capital gain only and is thus not included in the definition of wages and salaries.

Wage and salary accruals include retroactive wage payments for the period in which they were earned, not for the period in which they were paid. In the NIPAs, wages accrued is the appropriate measure for both domestic and national income, since the intent is to measure income associated with production. Wages disbursed is the appropriate measure for personal income, since the latter concept focuses on what individuals receive. The difference, *wage accruals less disbursements,* is shown in Table 1-11. Substantial entries appear for this item in 2003 and 2004 because there were 53 Fridays instead of 52 Fridays in the latter year. As a result, some of the wages disbursed in 2004 were actually accrued in 2003. In 2005 through 2009, this item reflects unusually large exercises of stock options and financial industry bonuses, paid in the year after they were earned.

Supplements to wages and salaries consists of *employer contributions for employee pension and insurance funds* and *employer contributions for government social insurance.*

Employer contributions for employee pension and insurance funds consists of employer payments (including payments-in-kind) to private pension and profit-sharing plans, private group health and life insurance plans, privately administered workers' compensation plans, government employee retirement plans, and supplemental unemployment benefit plans. This includes the major part of the former category "other labor income." The remainder of "other labor income" has been reclassified as wages and salaries, as noted above.

Employer contributions for government social insurance consists of employer payments under the following federal, state, and local government programs: old-age, survivors, and disability insurance (Social Security); hospital insurance (Medicare); unemployment insurance; railroad retirement; pension benefit guaranty; veterans' life insurance; publicly administered workers' compensation; military medical insurance; and temporary disability insurance.

Taxes on production and imports is included in the gross domestic income account to make it comparable in concept to gross domestic product. It consists of federal excise taxes and customs duties and of state and local sales taxes, property taxes (including residential real estate taxes), motor vehicle license taxes, severance taxes, special assessments, and other taxes. It is equal to the former "indirect business taxes and nontax liabilities" less most of the nontax liabilities, which have now been reclassified as "business transfer payments."

Subsidies (payments by government to business other than purchases of goods and services) are now presented separately from the current surplus of government enterprises, which is presented as a component of net operating surplus. However, for years before 1959, subsidies continue to be presented as net of the current surplus of government enterprises, since detailed data to separate the series for this period are not available.

Net operating surplus is a new aggregate introduced in the 2003 NIPA revision—a grouping of the business income components of the gross domestic income account. It represents the net income accruing to business capital. It is equal to gross domestic income minus compensation of employees, taxes on production and imports less subsidies (that is, the taxes are taken out of income and the subsidies are put in), and consumption of fixed capital (CFC). Net operating surplus consists of the surplus for private enterprises and the current surplus of government enterprises. The net operating surplus of private enterprises comprises net interest and miscellaneous payments, business current transfer payments, proprietors' income, rental income of persons, and corporate profits.

Net interest and miscellaneous payments, domestic industries consists of interest paid by domestic private enterprises and of rents and royalties paid by private enterprises to government, less interest received by domestic private enterprises. Interest received does not include interest received by noninsured pension plans, which are recorded as being directly received by persons in personal income. Both interest categories include monetary and imputed interest. In the *national* account, interest paid to the rest of the world is subtracted from the interest paid by domestic industries and interest received from the rest of the world is added. Interest payments on mortgage and home improvement loans and on home equity loans are included as net interest in the private enterprises account.

It should be noted that net interest does not include interest paid by federal, state, or local governments. In fact, government interest does not enter into the national and domestic income accounts, though it does appear as a component of personal income. The NIPAs draw a distinction between interest paid by government and that paid by business.

The reasoning behind this distinction is that interest paid by <u>business</u> is one of the income counterparts of the production side of the account. The value of business production (as measured by its output of goods and services) includes the value added by business capital, and interest paid by business to its lenders is part of the total return to business capital.

However, there is no product flow in the accounts that is a counterpart to the payment of interest by <u>government</u>. The output of government does not have a market value. For purposes of GDP measurement, BEA estimates the government contribution to GDP as the sum of government's compensation of employees, purchases of goods and services, and consumption of government fixed capital. (See above, and also the notes and definitions to Chapter 6.) This implies an estimate (described as "conservative" by BEA) that the <u>net</u> return to government capital is zero—that is, that the gross return is just sufficient to pay down the depreciation. Consequently, this assumption generates no income, imputed or actual, that might correspond to the government's interest payment.

Supporting the distinction between business and government interest payments, it may be noted that most federal government debt was not incurred to finance investment, but rather to finance wars, to avoid tax increases and spending cuts during recessions, or to stimulate the economy. Some of the largest and most productive government investments—investments for highways—are typically financed by taxes on a pay-as-you-go basis and not by borrowing.

Business current transfer payments, net consists of payments to persons, government, and the rest of the world by private business for which no current services are performed. Net insurance settlements—actual insured losses (or claims payable) less a normal level of losses—are treated as transfer payments. Payments to government consist of federal deposit insurance premiums, fines, regulatory and inspection fees, tobacco settlements, and other miscellaneous payments previously classified as "nontaxes." Taxes paid by domestic corporations to foreign governments, formerly classified as transfer payments, are now counted as taxes on corporate income.

In the NIPAs, capital income other than interest—corporate profits, proprietors' income, and rental income—is converted from the basis usually shown in the books of business, and reported to the Internal Revenue Service, to a basis that more closely represents income from current production. In the business accounts that provide the source data, depreciation of structures and equipment typically reflects a historical cost basis and a possibly arbitrary service life allowed by law to be used for tax purposes. BEA adjusts these values to reflect the average actual life of the capital goods and the cost of replacing them in the current period's prices. This conversion is done for all three forms

of capital income. In addition, corporate and proprietors' incomes also require an adjustment for inventory valuation to exclude any profits or losses that might appear in the books, should the cost of inventory acquisition not be valued in the current period's prices. These two adjustments are called the *capital consumption adjustment (CCAdj)* and the *inventory valuation adjustment (IVA)*. They are described in more detail below.

Proprietors' income with inventory valuation and capital consumption adjustments is the current-production income (including income-in-kind) of sole proprietorships and partnerships and of tax-exempt cooperatives. The imputed net rental income of owner-occupants of farm dwellings is included, but the imputed net rental income of owner-occupants of nonfarm dwellings is included in rental income of persons. Fees paid to outside directors of corporations are included. Proprietors' income excludes dividends and monetary interest received by nonfinancial business and rental incomes received by persons not primarily engaged in the real estate business; these incomes are included in dividends, net interest, and rental income of persons, respectively.

Rental income of persons with capital consumption adjustment is the net current-production income of persons from the rental of real property (except for the income of persons primarily engaged in the real estate business), the imputed net rental income of owner-occupants of nonfarm dwellings, and the royalties received by persons from patents, copyrights, and rights to natural resources. Consistent with the classification of investment in owner-occupied housing as business investment, the homeowner is considered to be paying himself or herself the rental value of the house (classified as PCE for services) and receiving as net income the amount of the rental that remains after paying interest and other costs.

Corporate profits with inventory valuation and capital consumption adjustments (often referred to as "economic profits") is the current-production income, net of economic depreciation, of organizations treated as corporations in the NIPAs. These organizations consist of all entities required to file federal corporate tax returns, including mutual financial institutions and cooperatives subject to federal income tax; private noninsured pension funds; nonprofit institutions that primarily serve business; Federal Reserve Banks, which accrue income stemming from the conduct of monetary policy; and federally sponsored credit agencies. This income is measured as receipts less expenses as defined in federal tax law, except for the following differences: receipts exclude capital gains and dividends received, expenses exclude depletion and capital losses and losses resulting from bad debts, inventory withdrawals are valued at replacement cost, and depreciation is on a consistent accounting basis and is valued at replacement cost.

Since *national* income is defined as the income of U.S. residents, its profits component includes income earned abroad by U.S. corporations and excludes income earned by the rest of the world within the United States.

Taxes on corporate income consists of taxes on corporate income paid to government and to the rest of the world.

Taxes on corporate income paid to government is the sum of federal, state, and local income taxes on all income subject to taxes. This income includes capital gains and other income excluded from profits before tax. These taxes are measured on an accrual basis, net of applicable tax credits.

Taxes on corporate income paid to the rest of the world consists of nonresident taxes, which are those paid by domestic corporations to foreign governments. These taxes were formerly classified as "business transfer payments to the rest of the world."

Profits after tax is total corporate profits with IVA and CCAdj less taxes on corporate income. It consists of dividends and undistributed corporate profits.

Dividends is payments in cash or other assets, excluding those made using corporations' own stock, that are made by corporations to stockholders. In the domestic account, these are payments by domestic industries to stockholders in the United States and abroad; in the national account, these are dividends received by U.S. residents from domestic and foreign industries. The payments are measured net of dividends received by U.S. corporations. Dividends paid to state and local government social insurance funds and general government are included.

Undistributed profits is corporate profits after tax with IVA and CCAdj less dividends.

The *inventory valuation adjustment (IVA)* is the difference between the cost of inventory withdrawals valued at replacement cost and the cost as valued in the source data used to determine profits before tax, which in many cases charge inventories at acquisition cost. It is calculated separately for corporate profits and for nonfarm proprietors' income. Its behavior is determined by price changes, especially for materials. When prices are rising, which has been typical of much of the postwar period, the business-reported value of inventory change will include a capital gains component, which needs to be removed from reported inventory change on the product side in order to correctly measure the change in the volume of inventories, and from reported profits on the income side of the accounts in order to remove the capital gains element. At such times, the IVA will be a negative figure, which is added to reported profits to yield economic profits. Occasionally, falling prices—especially for petroleum and products—will result in a positive IVA. No adjustment is needed for farm proprietors' income, as farm inventories are measured on a current-market-cost basis.

Consumption of fixed capital (CFC) is a charge for the using-up of private and government fixed capital located in the United States. It is not based on the depreciation schedules allowed in tax law, but instead on studies of prices of used equipment and structures in resale markets.

For general government and for nonprofit institutions that primarily serve individuals, CFC on their capital assets is recorded in government consumption expenditures and in personal consumption expenditures, respectively. It is considered to be the value of the current services of the fixed capital assets owned and used by these entities.

Private capital consumption allowances consists of tax-return-based depreciation charges for corporations and nonfarm proprietorships and of historical cost depreciation (calculated by BEA using a geometric pattern of price declines) for farm proprietorships, rental income of persons, and nonprofit institutions.

The *private capital consumption adjustment (CCAdj)* is the difference between private capital consumption allowances and private consumption of fixed capital. The CCAdj has two parts:

- The first component of CCAdj converts tax-return-based depreciation to consistent historical cost accounting based on actual service lives of capital. In the postwar period, this has usually been a large positive number, that is, a net addition to profits and subtraction from reported depreciation. This is the case because U.S. tax law typically allows depreciation periods shorter than actual service lives. Tax depreciation was accelerated even further for 2001 through 2004. This component is a reallocation of gross business saving from depreciation to profits; gross saving is unchanged, with exactly offsetting changes in capital consumption and net saving.

- The second component is analogous to the IVA: it converts reported business capital consumption allowances from the historical cost basis to a replacement cost basis. It is determined by the price behavior of capital goods. These prices have had an upward drift in the postwar period, which has been much more stable than the changes in materials prices. Hence, this component is consistently negative (serving to reduce economic profits relative to the reported data) but less volatile than the IVA.

In 1982 through 2004, positive values for the first component outweighed negative values for the second, resulting in a net positive CCAdj, an addition to profits. However, when the accelerated depreciation expired in 2005, there was a sharp decline in the consistent-accounting adjustment and it was outweighed by the price adjustment. This led to negative CCAdjs in 2005 through 2007, reducing profits from the reported numbers.

Definitions and notes on the data:
Gross value added of domestic corporate business (Tables 1-14 and 1-15)

Gross value added is the term now used for what was formerly called "gross domestic product originating." It represents the share of the GDP that is produced in the specified sector or industry. Tables 1-14 and 1-15 show the current-dollar value of gross value added for all domestic corporate business and its financial and nonfinancial components. For the total and for nonfinancial corporations, consumption of fixed capital and net value added are shown, as is the allocation of net value added among employee compensation, taxes and transfer payments, and capital income. Constant-dollar values are also shown for nonfinancial corporations.

The data for nonfinancial corporations are often considered to be somewhat sturdier than data for the other sectors of the economy, since they exclude sectors whose outputs are difficult to evaluate—households, institutions, general government, and financial business—as well as excluding all noncorporate business, in which the separate contributions of labor and capital are not readily measured.

Data availability and revisions

Annual data are available beginning with 1929. Quarterly data begin with 1946 for current-dollar values and 1947 for quantity and price measures such as real GDP and the GDP price index. Not all data are available for all time periods.

New data are normally released toward the end of each month. The "advance" estimate of GDP for each calendar quarter is released at the end of the month after the quarter's end. The "second" estimate, including more complete product data and the first estimates of corporate profits, is released at the end of the second month after the quarter's end, and a "third" estimate including still more complete data at the end of the third month. Wage and salary and related income-side components may be revised for previous quarters as well.

At the end of each July, there is an "annual" revision, incorporating more complete data and other improvements, affecting at least the previous 3 years. Every five years, there is a "comprehensive" revision, such as the 2009 revision incorporated in this volume, corresponding with updated statistics from the quinquennial benchmark input-output accounts and incorporating a revision of the base year for constant-price and index numbers.

The most recent data are published each month in the *Survey of Current Business*. Current and historical data may be obtained from the BEA Web site at <http://www.bea.gov> and the STAT-USA subscription Web site at <http://www .stat-usa.gov>.

References

The data shown in this edition of *Business Statistics* are as published in the 2009 comprehensive NIPA revision and continued through the fourth quarter of 2011 in the estimates released on May 31, 2012. The most recent annual revision is described in the August 2011 *Survey of Current Business*. These NIPA data for recent years will be revised again in the 2012 annual revision, which will be released on

July 27, 2012, along with the first estimate of GDP for the second quarter of 2012, and described in the August 2012 *Survey*.

The latest comprehensive revision is described in "Improved Estimates of the National Income and Product Accounts: Results of the 2009 Comprehensive Revision", *Survey of Current Business,* September 2009. Previous annual and comprehensive revisions are discussed in articles in earlier August issues.

Selected documentation available on the BEA Web site at <http://www.bea.gov> includes the following: "NIPA Handbook: Concepts and Methods of the U.S. National Income and Product Accounts, October 2009"; separate chapters from the Handbook on Personal Consumption Expenditures, Private Fixed Investment, and Change in Private Inventories; "Measuring the Economy: A Primer on GDP and the National Income and Product Accounts"; "An Introduction to the National Income and Product Accounts"; and "Taking the Pulse of the Economy: Measuring GDP," *Journal of Economic Perspectives*, Spring 2008.

The treatment of employee stock options is discussed in Carol Moylan, "Treatment of Employee Stock Options in the U.S. National Economic Accounts," available on the BEA Web site at <http://www.bea.gov>.

The data for 1929 through 1946 published here have been calculated after the fact and differ from the national income data that were currently available during the 1930s and 1940s. For an article on what was available at that time and the history of the NIPAs during that period, see Rosemary D. Marcuss and Richard E. Kane, "U.S. National Income and Product Statistics: Born of the Great Depression and World War II," *Survey of Current Business,* February 2007, pp. 32-46.

Definitions and notes on the data:
Rates of return and related data for domestic nonfinancial corporations (Table 1-16)

Table 1-16 shows various measures of the return to capital in nonfinancial corporate business. The measure of capital is the *value of produced assets,* which is the current-cost value of the net stock of equipment and software and structures and the replacement-cost value of inventories. The basic measure of the total return to capital is the *net operating surplus,* which is the sum of corporate profits, net interest paid, and net business transfer payments. Table 1-15 displays the same concept, but the numbers may not be exactly the same as those shown in Table 1-16, since the latter data set was compiled before the latest data revisions. (See below for the date of the Table 1-16 data.) In both cases, corporate profits are adjusted to an economic profits basis by including the inventory valuation and capital consumption adjustments.

Rates of return are total net operating surplus and its major components, before and after corporate taxes, as a percent of the value of produced assets. *Tax liability* is also shown as a percent of produced assets.

Shares of net value added are total net operating surplus and its major components, before and after corporate taxes, as a percent of net value added in nonfinancial domestic corporate business. Net value added, shown in Table 1-15, is the value of the industry's output after deducting the consumption of fixed capital, and is the sum of compensation of employees, the net operating surplus, and taxes on production and imports less subsidies.

A *Q ratio* (often known as "Tobin's Q" for the economist James Tobin, who originally proposed it) is the ratio of the valuation of assets in financial markets to the current-cost value of produced assets. A value of Q above 1 indicates that newly produced physical assets may be purchased more cheaply than the ownership claims to existing assets. Table 1-16 shows the BEA calculation of a ratio termed *Q3*.

The numerator is the sum of the market value of outstanding equity and an estimate of the market value of outstanding corporate bonds, minus net liquid assets. Previously published values also removed the estimated value of land from the numerator. BEA no longer makes this adjustment, and the entire series has consequently been revised from the values shown last year. The denominator is the value of the net stock of produced assets.

The rate of return data do not follow the general NIPA publication and revision schedule. They were presented and described in "Note on the Returns for Domestic Nonfinancial Corporations in 1960–2005," *Survey of Current Business* (May 2006), pp. 6–10. The rate of return for the net operating surplus before tax, the share of net value added, the value of produced assets, and the Q3 ratio were revised and updated most recently in "Returns for Domestic Nonfinancial Business," *Survey of Current Business* (June 2011), pp. 24-28.

CHAPTER 2: INDUSTRIAL PRODUCTION AND CAPACITY UTILIZATION

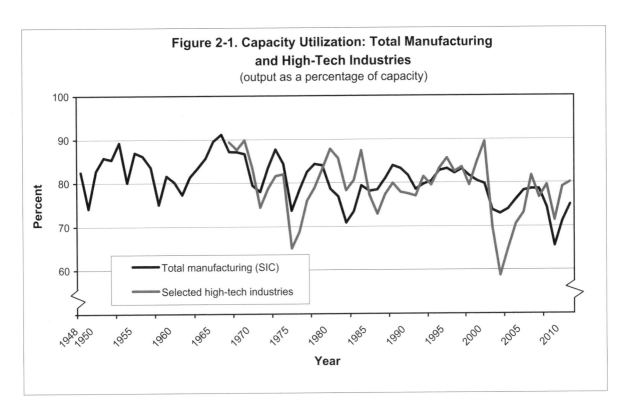

Figure 2-1. Capacity Utilization: Total Manufacturing and High-Tech Industries
(output as a percentage of capacity)

- Manufacturing capacity utilization is a key statistic for the U.S. economy, despite being limited to a sector that by some measures has diminished in importance. The Federal Reserve also provides measures of capacity utilization for "total industry"—manufacturing, mining, and utilities. However, mining and utilities are less significant in the context of business cycle analysis, and much of the variation in capacity use by utilities is a result of transitory weather variations, not economic factors. Manufacturing utilization is an important indicator of inflationary pressure and also measures an important element in the demand for new capital goods. (Tables 2-3 and 2-4A)

- Industrial production peaked at 100.7 percent of its 2007 average in December 2007 and fell to a low of 83.5 percent in June 2009—a decline of 17 percent. The preliminary index for May 2012, at 97.3 percent, was up nearly 17 percent from its low point—though still 3 percent below the previous high, as the increase is calculated from a lower base. (Table 2-4A and recent data)

- Manufacturing capacity utilization reached a high point of 79.7 percent in April 2007—lower than in previous periods of high activity—and then drifted down slightly for the rest of 2007, as capacity growth exceeded the increase in output. Then output plunged in 2008 and 2009, and utilization collapsed to 63.8 percent in June 2009, by far the lowest in the entire postwar period. The preliminary May 2012 reading was 77.6 percent. (Table 2-4A and recent data)

- Capacity utilization in the high-tech industries (computers and office equipment, communications equipment, and semiconductors and related electronic components) has been somewhat more volatile than in the rest of industry, as seen in Figure 2-1. (Table 2-4A)

Table 2-1. Industrial Production Indexes by Market Groups

(Seasonally adjusted, 2007 = 100.)

Year and month	Total industrial production	Final products and nonindustrial supplies							
		Total	Consumer goods						
			Total	Durable consumer goods					Nondurable consumer goods
				Total	Automotive products	Home electronics	Appliances, furniture, and carpeting	Miscellaneous durable goods	Total
1967	35.0	34.6	42.5	29.3	28.4	0.9	45.6	45.1	49.1
1968	37.0	36.3	45.1	32.7	33.8	1.0	49.0	48.1	51.0
1969	38.7	37.6	46.8	34.0	33.9	1.0	51.7	52.0	52.8
1970	37.4	36.5	46.2	31.4	28.6	0.9	51.1	50.2	53.7
1971	37.9	37.0	48.9	35.6	36.4	1.0	54.0	52.9	55.2
1972	41.6	40.4	52.8	39.8	39.3	1.1	63.4	59.5	58.7
1973	45.0	43.5	55.2	42.9	42.6	1.3	68.5	62.2	60.5
1974	44.9	43.3	53.6	39.0	36.9	1.2	62.4	59.9	60.6
1975	40.9	40.3	51.5	35.4	35.5	1.1	53.5	53.1	59.5
1976	44.1	43.2	55.7	39.9	40.4	1.2	60.4	59.2	63.2
1977	47.4	46.7	59.2	44.9	45.7	1.4	67.7	65.5	65.6
1978	50.1	49.5	61.0	45.9	45.4	1.6	71.3	67.8	67.9
1979	51.6	51.1	60.1	44.3	40.8	1.6	71.5	68.4	67.5
1980	50.3	50.5	57.9	38.5	31.5	1.7	66.6	62.7	67.6
1981	50.9	51.5	58.3	39.1	32.4	1.8	65.7	63.6	67.9
1982	48.3	50.2	58.1	36.9	31.5	1.5	59.5	60.2	69.1
1983	49.6	51.6	60.3	41.0	36.6	2.2	65.6	62.0	69.9
1984	54.1	55.9	63.1	45.8	40.9	2.7	73.1	68.5	71.3
1985	54.7	57.4	63.7	45.8	40.8	2.8	72.7	68.6	72.2
1986	55.3	58.5	65.9	48.8	43.9	3.7	76.2	70.8	73.9
1987	58.1	61.4	68.7	51.7	47.0	3.6	80.3	75.3	76.6
1988	61.1	64.4	71.3	54.3	49.2	4.8	81.7	78.6	79.1
1989	61.7	65.1	71.5	55.4	50.8	5.0	82.5	79.1	78.9
1990	62.3	65.8	71.9	54.0	47.8	5.9	80.4	78.4	80.2
1991	61.3	64.8	71.9	51.7	44.9	7.0	74.9	75.6	81.4
1992	63.0	66.4	74.0	56.5	52.1	7.6	79.3	78.0	82.0
1993	65.1	68.6	76.3	61.1	57.2	9.7	83.7	81.5	83.2
1994	68.5	71.6	79.4	66.6	62.8	12.6	89.6	86.0	85.2
1995	71.8	74.5	81.9	69.7	64.7	18.9	89.2	88.5	87.3
1996	75.0	77.4	83.4	72.0	65.8	23.0	90.2	91.5	88.5
1997	80.4	82.4	86.4	77.0	70.9	31.8	94.1	93.6	90.5
1998	85.1	87.1	89.6	83.0	76.2	43.3	100.3	96.8	92.5
1999	88.7	89.7	91.6	89.5	84.6	54.2	103.6	99.0	92.5
2000	92.3	92.6	93.3	92.1	86.1	61.3	106.6	101.8	93.9
2001	89.1	90.1	92.3	87.8	82.8	61.7	101.9	94.4	94.1
2002	89.3	89.7	94.1	93.0	90.9	62.6	104.4	96.8	94.6
2003	90.4	90.8	95.4	95.9	95.7	68.7	104.4	96.8	95.2
2004	92.5	92.5	96.5	97.4	95.7	76.3	107.6	98.7	96.1
2005	95.5	96.2	99.1	98.2	94.2	82.9	109.7	101.7	99.3
2006	97.6	98.4	99.6	98.4	93.0	95.6	106.5	103.3	99.9
2007	100.0	100.0	100.0	100.0	100.0	100.0	100.0	100.0	100.0
2008	96.5	95.8	95.1	88.8	84.8	110.2	87.4	92.4	97.2
2009	85.4	84.9	88.6	74.0	73.1	94.9	66.2	76.2	93.4
2010	90.1	87.5	89.6	80.1	83.5	75.0	66.0	81.5	92.7
2011	93.7	90.7	91.7	85.8	92.3	69.1	67.0	85.6	93.6
2010									
January	87.4	85.8	89.5	78.8	83.0	85.7	64.5	77.4	93.0
February	87.8	85.6	88.9	77.9	81.0	83.9	64.8	78.1	92.6
March	88.3	86.1	89.0	78.6	81.5	81.2	66.2	79.0	92.5
April	88.7	86.3	88.1	79.0	81.1	78.2	67.5	80.8	91.1
May	90.1	87.8	89.9	81.2	84.6	75.7	67.0	82.7	92.8
June	90.2	87.8	89.7	80.2	82.9	74.0	66.5	82.5	92.9
July	90.9	88.4	90.4	82.8	87.6	73.3	67.0	83.1	92.8
August	91.1	88.4	90.0	80.1	83.0	71.9	66.1	82.5	93.2
September	91.4	88.4	89.8	80.3	83.7	71.0	65.2	82.4	92.9
October	91.1	88.3	90.0	81.8	86.8	69.4	65.4	82.3	92.6
November	91.4	88.4	89.5	80.4	83.2	68.0	66.8	83.3	92.5
December	92.4	89.1	90.7	80.3	83.0	67.3	65.4	84.1	94.0
2011									
January	92.5	89.3	90.7	81.7	85.5	67.1	65.2	84.6	93.6
February	92.3	89.5	90.7	84.0	88.8	67.0	66.8	85.6	92.9
March	93.1	89.8	91.1	85.8	91.8	67.4	69.1	85.3	92.8
April	92.6	89.5	90.8	83.2	87.6	67.7	66.8	84.9	93.3
May	92.9	90.2	91.3	84.0	88.5	69.2	67.3	85.8	93.6
June	93.1	90.1	91.2	83.6	88.5	69.0	66.8	84.9	93.7
July	93.9	90.9	92.2	86.1	92.4	70.2	66.3	86.4	94.2
August	94.2	91.3	92.5	86.8	94.0	71.0	67.2	85.7	94.3
September	94.4	91.6	92.6	87.6	95.0	71.4	66.9	86.5	94.2
October	94.9	92.0	92.9	89.5	98.8	70.2	67.1	86.3	94.0
November	95.1	91.7	92.2	88.1	96.5	69.3	67.2	86.0	93.5
December	95.9	92.3	92.5	89.9	99.5	69.7	68.3	85.8	93.4

Table 2-1. Industrial Production Indexes by Market Groups—*Continued*

(Seasonally adjusted, 2007 = 100.)

Year and month	Final products and nonindustrial supplies—*Continued*												
	Consumer goods—*Continued*						Business equipment				Defense and space equipment	Construc-tion supplies	Business supplies
	Nondurable consumer goods—*Continued*						Total	Transit	Information processing	Industrial and other			
	Nondurable non-energy consumer goods					Consumer energy products							
	Total	Foods and tobacco	Clothing	Chemical products	Paper products								
1967	51.3	54.5	318.0	21.0	58.5	39.3	16.0	55.3	1.0	46.2	66.4	45.7	30.8
1968	53.1	55.9	329.5	22.9	57.9	42.1	16.7	61.7	1.1	46.1	66.5	48.1	32.7
1969	54.6	57.4	334.4	24.0	60.0	45.0	17.8	60.8	1.2	49.1	63.3	50.2	34.8
1970	55.2	58.2	324.7	26.1	57.8	47.6	17.1	53.3	1.3	47.4	53.6	48.4	34.9
1971	56.6	60.0	322.8	27.6	59.0	49.9	16.3	51.6	1.2	45.3	48.2	49.9	36.0
1972	60.3	63.4	351.3	30.2	59.5	52.6	18.6	56.3	1.4	51.5	46.9	56.7	39.6
1973	62.3	65.1	358.1	32.4	61.5	53.6	21.5	67.2	1.6	58.6	51.4	61.5	42.1
1974	62.0	65.4	335.7	34.2	60.6	55.0	22.7	65.5	2.0	61.1	53.1	60.0	41.9
1975	60.4	64.3	326.1	33.0	57.1	56.2	20.3	57.6	1.9	53.5	53.5	50.8	38.7
1976	64.3	68.5	343.5	35.9	59.4	59.1	21.6	59.6	2.2	55.7	51.9	54.7	41.2
1977	66.6	69.9	360.4	37.4	64.9	61.4	25.0	70.8	3.0	60.7	46.5	59.6	44.7
1978	69.2	72.5	369.0	39.7	68.1	62.6	28.2	82.1	3.8	65.0	47.4	63.0	47.1
1979	68.3	72.0	348.7	39.8	68.9	64.2	31.8	95.8	4.7	69.0	50.7	64.6	48.7
1980	69.1	73.1	355.0	39.6	69.7	61.8	32.5	90.3	5.9	66.7	60.3	59.8	47.6
1981	69.7	73.5	354.8	40.2	71.5	61.4	33.5	84.5	7.0	66.5	65.3	58.8	48.8
1982	71.0	75.8	353.8	40.3	73.3	61.8	30.6	64.8	8.0	57.6	78.0	53.4	48.2
1983	71.9	76.0	363.9	40.8	76.4	62.3	30.8	63.8	9.2	53.4	78.6	57.2	50.5
1984	73.2	76.9	365.5	41.7	80.3	64.2	35.4	65.8	11.3	60.9	90.0	62.2	54.9
1985	74.3	79.2	350.1	42.2	84.4	64.2	36.7	68.1	12.2	61.6	100.7	63.8	56.3
1986	76.2	80.5	349.9	45.4	85.6	65.5	36.2	62.3	12.3	61.3	107.0	65.9	58.1
1987	78.9	82.4	353.1	49.0	90.5	67.9	38.6	63.2	14.0	63.5	109.2	70.1	61.6
1988	81.2	84.7	347.9	51.9	93.0	71.4	42.6	70.5	15.8	69.0	110.2	71.8	63.9
1989	80.8	84.1	332.1	53.0	93.3	71.9	44.1	74.2	16.2	71.3	110.3	71.5	64.8
1990	82.6	86.5	325.7	54.9	95.1	71.4	45.6	79.4	17.5	70.8	106.4	70.9	66.3
1991	83.5	86.9	324.8	56.9	95.6	73.6	44.9	82.5	17.6	67.1	98.5	67.0	65.4
1992	84.5	88.1	332.1	56.7	96.8	72.6	46.7	80.6	19.8	68.2	91.3	69.8	66.9
1993	85.2	87.4	338.7	58.3	99.0	75.8	48.9	75.5	21.7	72.8	86.2	72.9	69.0
1994	87.5	90.9	344.9	59.5	98.0	76.7	52.2	73.1	24.4	77.7	80.9	78.1	71.8
1995	89.6	93.3	343.5	62.1	98.6	78.8	56.7	71.2	29.1	82.6	78.0	79.9	74.8
1996	90.2	93.0	334.5	65.1	98.3	82.3	62.3	75.3	35.6	85.5	76.0	83.4	77.7
1997	93.0	94.4	333.4	68.8	107.0	81.6	71.4	88.7	44.9	90.7	74.8	87.5	83.2
1998	95.4	96.8	313.5	72.2	112.0	81.7	79.0	104.1	53.0	93.5	78.0	92.1	87.9
1999	94.7	94.9	301.8	73.5	114.3	84.5	83.4	101.9	64.4	91.4	75.6	94.5	91.6
2000	96.0	96.4	289.4	76.2	113.8	86.3	89.6	90.2	78.1	96.8	67.2	96.5	95.3
2001	96.1	96.3	250.5	80.5	110.6	87.3	83.9	87.0	75.6	87.5	73.7	92.2	91.7
2002	95.8	94.6	192.9	87.1	109.0	91.1	78.2	80.0	65.3	86.1	74.5	92.2	91.9
2003	96.5	95.8	181.5	89.2	104.9	91.6	78.0	75.4	67.8	85.7	79.2	92.0	93.4
2004	97.3	97.1	150.8	91.4	105.6	92.9	81.7	79.6	73.2	88.0	77.2	94.2	95.1
2005	100.5	100.4	141.9	96.3	104.6	96.1	87.6	87.1	79.5	92.8	85.0	98.7	98.2
2006	101.4	100.5	132.1	99.6	104.5	95.8	95.7	101.1	91.0	96.4	84.1	101.1	99.2
2007	100.0	100.0	100.0	100.0	100.0	100.0	100.0	100.0	100.0	100.0	100.0	100.0	100.0
2008	96.4	96.5	88.4	96.4	95.4	99.8	97.6	92.5	100.8	98.0	107.0	90.7	95.9
2009	91.5	95.0	60.7	88.5	86.2	99.8	79.9	71.5	89.2	78.5	102.5	69.9	85.7
2010	90.0	95.1	61.4	84.2	83.3	102.2	86.5	83.4	91.0	85.0	106.7	72.6	87.6
2011	90.7	96.6	60.0	85.6	78.3	103.5	93.6	93.6	96.0	91.7	109.5	76.6	88.7
2010													
January	90.6	94.8	59.9	86.4	84.7	101.3	81.4	76.6	88.6	79.6	103.1	68.5	86.7
February	89.5	94.3	60.0	84.2	84.2	102.9	81.4	75.0	88.9	80.0	103.8	68.7	86.6
March	89.8	94.4	60.5	84.7	84.1	101.7	82.7	78.7	89.6	80.7	106.2	70.1	86.4
April	89.6	93.8	60.9	85.3	83.6	96.0	84.3	78.6	89.8	83.5	106.9	72.5	86.9
May	90.5	95.4	61.4	84.7	84.8	100.6	86.2	82.7	90.5	85.0	107.4	73.0	87.8
June	89.8	95.0	61.5	83.8	83.7	103.2	87.0	84.2	90.4	86.0	106.4	73.2	88.0
July	89.5	94.8	61.1	83.3	83.3	104.2	88.5	90.0	91.7	85.6	107.9	73.0	88.2
August	90.0	95.6	62.7	83.4	83.0	104.1	88.5	88.6	91.9	86.1	108.7	73.7	88.3
September	89.9	95.9	61.5	83.1	81.6	103.2	89.3	90.1	92.1	86.9	108.0	73.8	88.0
October	90.3	96.7	62.5	83.1	81.5	100.3	88.7	84.9	92.5	88.0	107.7	74.4	87.3
November	89.9	95.2	62.2	83.8	82.5	101.6	89.5	86.3	92.9	88.7	107.1	75.1	88.1
December	90.3	95.9	62.9	84.2	82.1	106.8	90.3	85.4	93.3	90.3	106.9	74.6	88.5
2011													
January	90.6	96.4	62.4	84.3	81.4	104.2	91.3	84.7	94.1	92.1	107.8	74.5	88.1
February	90.1	95.9	62.8	84.3	79.8	102.4	92.1	87.9	94.6	92.0	108.6	74.2	88.1
March	90.2	95.8	60.4	85.1	79.0	102.0	92.0	90.7	94.8	90.5	108.7	75.2	88.5
April	91.0	96.7	61.2	86.2	78.3	101.0	91.4	89.5	94.2	90.2	108.7	75.4	88.1
May	90.7	96.2	61.2	86.3	77.8	103.7	92.5	91.4	94.7	91.1	109.4	76.5	88.5
June	90.6	96.3	60.6	86.4	75.5	104.1	92.6	92.3	93.8	91.3	107.8	76.6	88.2
July	90.8	97.0	60.6	86.0	75.4	105.4	93.0	92.2	95.8	91.3	108.7	77.5	88.9
August	90.8	96.5	58.8	86.3	77.0	106.2	94.1	95.5	96.4	91.6	109.7	77.1	89.3
September	90.9	96.9	57.5	85.6	78.2	105.4	94.6	96.2	97.4	91.9	109.6	77.1	89.6
October	91.2	97.3	58.2	85.7	78.9	103.3	95.9	100.5	97.7	92.1	110.9	77.3	89.3
November	90.5	96.7	58.5	84.5	78.6	103.8	96.5	100.9	98.4	92.9	112.3	77.9	88.6
December	91.3	97.2	58.2	86.3	79.0	100.5	97.5	100.3	99.9	94.3	111.7	79.8	89.3

Table 2-1. Industrial Production Indexes by Market Groups—*Continued*

(Seasonally adjusted, 2007 = 100.)

Year and month		Materials										Energy materials
	Total	Non-energy materials										
		Total	Durable				Nondurable					
			Total	Consumer parts	Equipment parts	Other	Total	Textile	Paper	Chemicals		
1967	34.7	27.3	20.6	49.6	4.4	54.1	44.9	103.7	50.5	28.5		67.5
1968	37.0	29.3	21.8	55.9	4.5	56.9	49.3	114.5	52.8	33.1		70.6
1969	39.2	31.2	22.9	56.2	4.8	60.6	53.4	117.6	57.3	36.8		74.2
1970	37.8	29.3	20.8	47.2	4.4	56.6	53.7	113.3	56.8	37.6		77.9
1971	38.3	29.9	20.9	52.3	4.4	54.5	56.0	118.6	59.4	39.9		78.5
1972	42.2	33.5	23.6	58.1	5.1	61.6	61.7	124.9	63.3	46.4		81.5
1973	46.0	37.1	27.0	67.5	6.0	68.3	64.8	121.6	68.3	51.2		83.5
1974	45.9	37.0	26.7	59.7	6.3	68.1	65.7	113.7	71.7	52.6		83.2
1975	40.9	31.7	22.3	48.2	5.4	56.9	58.8	111.3	62.4	44.1		82.4
1976	44.4	35.3	24.9	61.5	5.8	61.1	65.2	123.9	68.6	50.5		84.2
1977	47.5	38.3	27.1	67.4	6.6	64.7	69.9	132.0	71.7	56.1		87.0
1978	49.9	40.8	29.3	71.2	7.4	69.0	72.5	130.6	75.2	59.6		88.0
1979	51.3	41.9	30.3	67.3	8.2	70.7	73.9	129.4	78.2	62.0		90.4
1980	49.3	39.4	28.0	51.9	8.4	65.4	71.5	126.5	78.8	57.4		91.1
1981	49.6	39.6	28.1	49.3	8.6	65.6	72.1	123.7	80.3	57.9		92.0
1982	45.8	35.6	24.5	42.0	7.9	55.4	68.3	113.1	81.0	51.9		88.0
1983	47.0	38.0	26.1	51.0	8.0	57.9	73.1	126.7	86.1	57.4		85.2
1984	51.5	42.4	30.3	60.6	9.7	64.1	76.3	126.3	91.5	61.0		90.6
1985	51.4	42.4	30.5	63.1	9.7	63.7	75.7	119.4	91.0	59.9		90.1
1986	51.3	43.3	30.9	62.5	9.8	64.9	78.1	124.3	94.9	62.8		86.6
1987	54.1	46.1	33.0	64.2	10.8	69.4	82.7	139.2	99.5	68.3		88.6
1988	57.1	49.1	35.7	69.4	11.8	74.4	85.8	137.8	102.8	72.4		91.7
1989	57.5	49.3	35.9	65.9	12.2	74.7	86.5	140.7	102.8	73.4		92.6
1990	57.9	49.4	35.9	61.4	12.6	75.0	86.8	133.6	103.1	74.2		94.5
1991	57.0	48.4	34.9	58.1	12.5	71.8	85.8	133.5	100.9	73.1		94.5
1992	58.9	50.7	37.2	65.2	13.2	75.6	87.9	141.2	103.4	74.9		93.7
1993	60.8	53.0	39.6	73.8	14.1	78.5	88.9	146.9	103.4	75.4		93.9
1994	64.7	57.2	44.1	85.2	16.0	84.3	91.6	155.8	107.3	77.7		95.4
1995	68.4	61.2	48.7	88.6	19.5	87.5	92.5	153.2	110.1	78.3		96.8
1996	71.9	65.0	53.8	91.0	24.0	90.1	91.6	148.9	106.6	78.7		98.3
1997	77.8	71.9	61.3	98.0	30.4	94.7	95.9	155.5	107.7	84.4		98.3
1998	82.4	77.3	68.0	101.5	37.5	97.3	97.2	154.1	108.8	84.6		98.5
1999	87.4	83.3	75.7	111.7	45.9	98.8	98.4	151.0	110.4	87.0		98.0
2000	91.9	88.4	83.2	111.8	57.2	99.7	97.8	144.6	108.6	87.2		99.6
2001	87.7	83.4	78.9	98.8	57.0	92.9	91.4	127.8	103.0	80.8		98.3
2002	88.7	84.7	80.0	103.7	57.7	92.9	93.1	129.6	103.3	83.6		98.0
2003	89.9	86.2	82.7	102.6	64.2	92.1	92.3	122.9	99.9	84.1		98.1
2004	92.4	89.8	87.3	102.7	71.1	95.8	94.1	117.5	101.1	88.5		97.9
2005	94.6	93.4	92.2	103.7	80.3	98.0	95.2	120.4	100.7	89.3		96.9
2006	96.5	95.7	95.7	100.9	88.0	100.1	95.6	109.3	99.9	91.2		98.1
2007	100.0	100.0	100.0	100.0	100.0	100.0	100.0	100.0	100.0	100.0		100.0
2008	97.3	95.2	96.8	84.3	104.7	95.3	92.7	86.9	95.5	89.1		100.6
2009	86.1	79.0	75.6	56.5	86.0	74.6	83.9	71.4	83.8	79.2		98.4
2010	93.3	87.7	86.9	75.0	98.1	82.8	88.8	78.5	85.3	87.9		102.5
2011	97.6	92.0	94.4	81.2	109.0	88.6	88.6	79.6	83.5	87.7		106.8
2010												
January	89.5	83.4	80.6	65.3	90.6	78.7	87.5	75.6	84.8	85.7		99.6
February	90.6	84.2	81.6	67.2	92.1	79.0	88.0	76.8	85.0	86.2		101.3
March	91.2	85.4	83.6	70.0	94.2	80.5	88.0	76.6	85.7	86.4		100.9
April	91.8	86.5	85.3	71.9	96.2	82.0	88.3	77.6	86.2	86.6		100.4
May	93.1	87.6	87.0	75.8	97.7	83.0	88.5	78.6	86.0	87.3		101.8
June	93.4	88.1	87.4	76.4	98.4	83.3	88.9	78.6	85.9	88.1		101.9
July	94.0	88.6	88.3	80.1	99.0	83.5	89.1	80.2	85.6	88.8		102.5
August	94.5	89.0	88.7	77.5	100.3	84.2	89.3	80.2	85.1	88.5		103.4
September	95.4	89.3	88.9	78.0	100.7	84.1	90.0	79.5	84.8	90.0		105.3
October	94.7	89.2	89.4	79.2	100.8	84.6	88.8	78.7	84.7	87.8		103.7
November	95.1	89.6	90.2	79.3	102.6	85.1	88.6	78.6	84.5	87.7		104.1
December	96.6	91.1	91.4	78.8	105.0	85.9	90.8	81.1	85.1	91.4		105.2
2011												
January	96.5	91.7	92.9	79.8	106.7	87.5	89.9	77.4	85.7	89.5		104.1
February	95.9	91.3	92.9	81.0	106.3	87.4	89.1	80.4	85.1	88.2		103.1
March	97.2	92.1	93.7	82.8	107.3	87.8	89.7	77.0	84.8	89.9		105.3
April	96.6	91.1	93.1	78.6	107.1	88.0	88.4	80.0	84.6	87.3		105.3
May	96.5	91.2	93.9	77.7	108.6	88.9	87.4	80.1	83.5	85.6		104.9
June	96.9	91.2	93.9	79.4	109.7	87.8	87.3	80.5	83.1	85.6		106.0
July	97.8	91.8	94.4	80.6	109.1	88.8	88.1	80.9	83.5	86.9		107.5
August	97.8	91.6	94.5	80.4	110.2	88.2	87.6	78.4	82.2	86.3		108.0
September	98.0	92.2	94.7	81.3	109.7	88.6	88.6	79.3	82.3	88.3		107.4
October	98.7	92.3	94.9	82.4	109.7	88.8	88.6	79.4	81.7	87.9		109.2
November	99.4	92.8	96.1	83.2	110.8	90.1	88.1	80.2	82.1	86.8		110.5
December	100.5	94.7	97.9	87.5	112.6	91.0	90.2	81.6	83.1	90.2		110.0

Table 2-1. Industrial Production Indexes by Market Groups—*Continued*

(Seasonally adjusted, 2007 = 100.)

Year and month	Special aggregates											
	Energy						Non-energy					Total non-energy, excluding high-tech
									Selected high-tech			
	Total	Consumer energy products	Commercial energy products	Oil and gas well drilling	Converted fuels	Primary energy	Total	Total	Computers and peripheral equipment	Communications equipment	Semiconductors and related components	
1967	54.4	39.3	26.7	. . .	52.0	80.5	31.6	0.1	. . .	. . .	. . .	48.6
1968	57.4	42.1	29.0	. . .	55.7	82.8	33.4	0.1	. . .	. . .	. . .	51.3
1969	60.4	45.0	30.5	. . .	59.6	85.6	34.9	0.1	. . .	. . .	. . .	53.4
1970	63.3	47.6	32.8	. . .	62.7	89.8	33.3	0.1	. . .	. . .	. . .	50.9
1971	64.5	49.9	34.5	. . .	64.4	89.1	33.8	0.1	. . .	. . .	. . .	51.8
1972	67.5	52.6	36.4	56.9	68.4	90.5	37.3	0.1	0.0	3.4	0.1	57.0
1973	69.2	53.6	38.4	59.9	71.1	91.6	40.7	0.2	0.1	3.7	0.1	61.9
1974	69.5	55.0	38.4	59.2	70.1	92.0	40.5	0.2	0.1	4.0	0.1	61.2
1975	69.8	56.2	39.8	54.8	67.6	92.8	36.2	0.2	0.1	3.9	0.1	54.6
1976	72.0	59.1	41.9	59.9	71.3	92.8	39.4	0.3	0.1	4.1	0.1	59.1
1977	74.8	61.4	43.3	63.5	74.0	95.5	42.7	0.3	0.2	5.0	0.2	63.6
1978	76.1	62.6	44.6	65.5	73.4	97.8	45.5	0.4	0.3	5.5	0.2	67.1
1979	78.3	64.2	46.7	66.6	76.1	100.0	46.9	0.5	0.4	6.5	0.2	68.4
1980	78.6	61.8	45.9	63.8	74.6	93.7	45.3	0.7	0.6	7.8	0.3	65.2
1981	79.9	61.4	47.1	63.8	73.6	95.7	45.9	0.8	0.8	8.4	0.3	65.3
1982	77.0	61.8	47.7	59.9	67.7	92.8	43.2	0.9	1.0	8.8	0.3	60.9
1983	74.7	62.3	48.7	63.1	67.6	96.7	45.3	1.1	1.4	9.4	0.4	63.1
1984	79.1	64.2	51.3	67.1	71.8	94.5	49.9	1.5	2.0	10.0	0.5	68.6
1985	78.8	64.2	53.2	66.6	71.5	93.9	50.7	1.5	2.4	9.7	0.5	69.6
1986	76.1	65.5	54.7	56.3	68.9	98.0	51.9	1.6	2.5	9.2	0.6	71.2
1987	78.3	67.9	57.6	54.3	72.4	98.7	54.8	1.9	3.3	10.3	0.7	74.5
1988	81.4	71.4	59.5	65.2	75.8	101.5	57.8	2.3	4.0	12.2	0.8	77.8
1989	82.3	71.9	61.7	56.8	78.6	100.8	58.3	2.4	4.2	12.7	0.9	78.2
1990	83.6	71.4	63.5	60.1	79.2	103.5	58.8	2.7	4.5	15.0	1.0	78.2
1991	84.0	73.6	64.4	46.8	79.3	103.6	57.6	3.0	4.7	15.6	1.1	76.2
1992	82.9	72.6	64.0	32.7	80.8	101.0	59.8	3.6	5.9	18.0	1.3	78.2
1993	84.4	75.8	65.9	45.5	82.3	100.2	61.9	4.2	7.3	20.6	1.5	80.3
1994	86.1	76.7	68.5	54.0	83.6	101.9	65.6	5.3	9.1	24.8	2.0	83.8
1995	87.9	78.8	70.9	52.6	84.8	103.5	69.0	7.5	12.6	30.3	3.0	86.0
1996	90.0	82.3	73.2	56.4	86.3	104.9	72.4	10.7	17.9	38.0	4.6	87.3
1997	90.5	81.6	76.2	64.7	87.6	103.9	78.5	15.8	25.4	52.0	7.2	91.6
1998	90.8	81.7	77.5	60.5	88.7	103.5	83.8	22.0	34.9	61.6	10.9	94.9
1999	91.4	84.5	80.5	47.4	90.3	101.5	87.9	31.6	45.9	78.7	17.3	96.1
2000	93.7	86.3	83.7	67.2	92.4	102.8	91.7	44.2	53.5	106.1	26.7	96.8
2001	93.7	87.3	85.1	81.4	89.2	102.5	87.9	45.1	54.1	97.9	29.0	92.1
2002	94.0	91.1	86.9	58.7	91.2	100.8	88.0	44.6	53.3	72.0	33.6	92.3
2003	95.1	91.6	91.2	68.2	91.8	100.7	89.1	53.4	57.7	74.0	44.9	92.3
2004	95.7	92.9	94.1	74.5	94.0	99.3	91.6	60.6	58.4	80.9	54.2	94.2
2005	96.3	96.1	96.7	83.7	95.3	97.4	95.2	71.1	69.5	81.1	67.5	97.1
2006	97.5	95.8	97.3	96.6	95.2	99.1	97.6	85.0	86.5	98.3	78.8	98.5
2007	100.0	100.0	100.0	100.0	100.0	100.0	100.0	100.0	100.0	100.0	100.0	100.0
2008	100.5	99.8	100.2	104.4	98.2	101.4	95.1	112.1	118.9	94.8	117.2	94.1
2009	97.7	99.8	98.5	61.4	92.9	100.2	81.5	96.0	104.0	79.2	100.4	80.6
2010	101.6	102.2	99.9	82.3	98.7	103.6	86.3	110.2	80.8	87.4	133.3	85.0
2011	105.2	103.5	100.7	99.2	98.2	109.5	90.0	116.9	75.6	84.6	149.3	88.5
2010												
January	99.2	101.3	99.3	69.9	97.8	100.0	83.6	103.2	92.1	85.7	116.2	82.5
February	100.8	102.9	100.3	75.2	99.4	101.7	83.6	106.0	90.4	86.7	121.8	82.3
March	100.2	101.7	98.7	79.9	97.4	101.9	84.4	108.2	87.4	87.3	126.9	83.2
April	98.8	96.0	98.7	82.9	96.2	101.6	85.3	109.9	83.5	87.6	131.7	84.0
May	100.8	100.6	99.3	83.5	99.7	102.4	86.5	111.0	80.2	87.8	134.9	85.2
June	101.4	103.2	100.7	80.5	100.0	102.4	86.5	110.3	78.2	88.2	134.3	85.2
July	102.1	104.2	100.6	81.6	100.1	103.1	87.2	110.5	77.3	88.5	134.9	85.9
August	102.7	104.1	100.3	84.8	99.8	104.4	87.2	111.4	76.9	88.6	136.6	85.9
September	103.7	103.2	100.5	86.2	99.1	107.2	87.4	111.5	76.5	88.1	137.2	86.1
October	101.9	100.3	98.4	86.9	95.5	106.3	87.5	110.8	76.1	87.4	136.3	86.2
November	102.7	101.6	100.7	87.4	97.7	106.1	87.6	112.8	75.6	86.8	140.5	86.3
December	104.7	106.8	101.7	89.2	101.2	106.4	88.4	116.5	75.0	86.7	147.9	86.9
2011												
January	103.3	104.2	100.0	90.3	98.4	105.9	88.9	117.9	74.5	86.5	150.7	87.4
February	102.1	102.4	99.4	91.0	96.2	105.2	89.0	116.8	74.5	85.9	149.0	87.5
March	103.7	102.0	101.3	91.8	97.5	107.7	89.5	115.5	75.0	84.5	146.8	88.1
April	103.5	101.0	99.7	94.4	98.2	107.6	89.0	116.3	76.0	83.0	148.8	87.6
May	104.0	103.7	101.0	97.3	98.8	106.8	89.3	117.5	77.0	82.0	151.1	87.8
June	104.8	104.1	101.1	98.5	99.6	108.1	89.2	118.2	77.7	82.3	151.9	87.7
July	106.1	105.4	101.5	100.9	101.7	109.3	89.9	118.0	77.9	83.3	151.0	88.4
August	106.8	106.2	102.4	103.2	99.5	110.7	90.0	119.2	77.3	84.5	153.0	88.5
September	106.3	105.4	102.6	104.5	97.5	110.6	90.4	117.4	76.0	85.4	149.6	89.0
October	107.0	103.3	101.6	106.2	96.9	113.2	91.0	114.6	74.2	85.7	145.0	89.6
November	107.7	103.8	99.7	106.0	97.8	114.6	91.0	115.0	73.4	85.9	145.9	89.7
December	106.5	100.5	98.3	106.6	96.2	114.4	92.4	116.7	73.3	86.5	148.9	91.1

. . . = Not available.

Table 2-2. Industrial Production Indexes by NAICS Industry Groups

(Seasonally adjusted, 2007 = 100.)

Year and month	Total industrial production	Manu- facturing (SIC)	Manufacturing (NAICS)										
			Total	Durable goods manufacturing									
				Total	Wood products	Nonmetallic mineral products	Primary metals	Fabricated metal products	Machinery	Computer and electronic products	Electrical equipment, appliances, and com- ponents	Motor vehicles and parts	Aerospace and miscel- laneous transport equipment
1967	35.0	31.7	. . .	. . .	. . .	. . .	. . .	. . .	. . .	. . .	. . .	. . .	. . .
1968	37.0	33.5	. . .	. . .	. . .	. . .	. . .	. . .	. . .	. . .	. . .	. . .	. . .
1969	38.7	34.9	. . .	. . .	. . .	. . .	. . .	. . .	. . .	. . .	. . .	. . .	. . .
1970	37.4	33.4	. . .	. . .	. . .	. . .	. . .	. . .	. . .	. . .	. . .	. . .	. . .
1971	37.9	33.9	. . .	. . .	. . .	. . .	. . .	. . .	. . .	. . .	. . .	. . .	. . .
1972	41.6	37.4	36.0	25.5	70.7	67.7	110.2	60.3	56.4	0.8	67.9	43.3	55.5
1973	45.0	40.8	39.4	28.7	68.4	72.6	119.9	66.6	65.2	0.9	76.4	49.5	63.3
1974	44.9	40.7	39.3	28.5	62.2	71.8	123.0	65.4	68.3	1.0	74.6	42.6	64.3
1975	40.9	36.4	35.1	24.7	57.7	64.3	93.5	56.5	59.5	0.9	59.9	37.1	61.1
1976	44.1	39.7	38.3	27.0	64.9	67.9	108.2	60.6	62.1	1.1	67.6	47.3	57.2
1977	47.4	43.1	41.6	29.7	70.0	72.3	109.3	65.7	67.8	1.3	74.5	53.8	57.6
1978	50.1	45.8	44.1	32.1	70.9	77.0	107.9	68.9	73.1	1.7	79.1	56.1	63.6
1979	51.6	47.2	45.5	33.6	68.6	76.9	110.6	72.0	77.1	2.0	82.3	51.4	74.0
1980	50.3	45.5	43.8	32.2	63.5	69.4	96.0	67.9	73.4	2.5	77.4	37.9	79.6
1981	50.9	46.0	44.3	32.5	62.1	66.4	96.2	67.4	72.7	2.9	76.4	36.9	75.8
1982	48.3	43.5	41.7	29.7	55.7	58.8	73.9	60.4	60.8	3.2	68.9	33.3	71.0
1983	49.6	45.6	43.8	31.2	64.6	63.3	75.7	60.8	54.9	3.7	71.2	42.5	67.8
1984	54.1	50.0	48.2	35.6	69.1	68.3	83.1	66.2	64.0	4.6	80.2	50.9	72.3
1985	54.7	50.9	48.9	36.4	70.0	69.6	76.7	67.2	64.2	4.9	78.9	52.9	77.3
1986	55.3	52.0	50.0	37.0	76.1	72.5	74.9	66.7	63.2	5.1	80.4	52.8	81.3
1987	58.1	54.9	52.8	39.2	82.9	76.5	80.7	68.0	64.5	5.8	81.5	54.7	84.3
1988	61.1	57.9	55.8	42.1	82.8	78.0	90.3	71.4	71.0	6.5	85.5	58.5	88.7
1989	61.7	58.3	56.3	42.6	81.6	77.4	88.2	70.9	73.7	6.6	84.2	57.9	94.0
1990	62.3	58.8	56.8	42.8	80.7	76.2	87.1	70.0	71.9	7.2	82.0	54.4	94.4
1991	61.3	57.6	55.8	41.4	75.5	70.2	81.8	66.8	67.5	7.5	77.8	52.0	91.1
1992	63.0	59.7	58.0	43.6	79.6	73.2	83.8	68.9	67.3	8.5	82.4	59.2	84.2
1993	65.1	61.8	60.1	46.0	80.5	74.8	87.9	71.5	72.3	9.3	87.6	65.4	78.5
1994	68.5	65.5	63.8	49.9	85.3	79.0	94.6	77.7	79.2	10.9	94.0	75.1	70.5
1995	71.8	68.9	67.3	54.1	87.3	81.3	95.6	82.5	84.8	14.1	96.2	77.3	67.0
1996	75.0	72.2	70.8	58.9	90.2	86.6	97.9	85.5	87.8	18.3	99.1	77.9	69.6
1997	80.4	78.3	76.7	66.0	92.8	89.4	102.0	89.4	92.6	24.5	102.8	84.0	77.7
1998	85.1	83.5	81.9	72.9	97.0	94.0	103.8	92.3	94.9	31.5	106.6	88.4	90.0
1999	88.7	87.6	86.0	79.1	100.6	94.9	103.7	92.9	93.0	41.3	108.4	98.1	86.6
2000	92.3	91.3	89.9	84.9	99.3	94.9	100.3	96.6	97.7	53.9	113.9	97.4	76.0
2001	89.1	87.6	86.3	80.9	93.1	91.4	91.3	89.6	86.4	54.6	102.5	88.8	80.8
2002	89.3	87.8	86.8	80.9	96.6	91.6	91.3	87.6	83.3	53.1	94.5	97.6	76.5
2003	90.4	88.9	88.1	82.9	96.6	92.4	89.8	86.6	82.8	60.3	92.1	101.1	73.1
2004	92.5	91.4	90.6	86.2	99.2	95.3	97.7	86.9	86.3	68.3	93.7	101.7	72.0
2005	95.5	95.0	94.4	91.2	105.9	99.4	95.2	90.9	91.6	77.0	95.3	102.3	80.2
2006	97.6	97.4	97.0	95.4	106.9	101.1	98.0	95.9	95.9	87.4	96.0	100.8	85.2
2007	100.0	100.0	100.0	100.0	100.0	100.0	100.0	100.0	100.0	100.0	100.0	100.0	100.0
2008	96.5	95.2	95.2	96.3	85.4	88.4	100.0	96.4	97.3	106.1	106.1	80.0	101.9
2009	85.4	82.0	82.1	78.0	65.3	66.6	74.0	74.2	75.8	92.9	75.6	58.6	92.8
2010	90.1	86.7	87.2	86.0	67.9	68.9	90.8	79.3	84.5	103.0	79.3	77.7	93.1
2011	93.7	90.5	91.4	92.6	69.5	70.9	96.8	87.2	94.3	111.1	81.9	86.9	97.7
2010													
January	87.4	83.9	84.2	81.2	67.1	64.9	86.6	73.8	77.3	96.8	75.6	72.1	91.0
February	87.8	84.0	84.4	81.5	65.7	65.0	88.5	74.2	78.3	98.7	75.3	70.4	91.4
March	88.3	84.9	85.3	83.0	66.7	65.7	91.7	75.3	79.1	100.5	76.5	72.8	92.7
April	88.7	85.8	86.3	84.5	69.6	69.0	91.3	76.8	82.2	101.9	78.5	73.5	92.9
May	90.1	87.0	87.5	86.3	70.3	69.0	92.3	78.3	84.5	103.3	78.4	78.6	92.9
June	90.2	87.0	87.5	86.5	68.2	69.4	92.9	79.6	85.6	102.9	79.2	78.3	93.0
July	90.9	87.6	88.1	87.7	67.6	70.2	89.2	80.7	85.7	103.8	79.5	84.6	94.0
August	91.1	87.6	88.2	87.5	67.1	70.6	90.0	81.7	86.2	104.4	80.7	79.9	95.0
September	91.4	87.8	88.4	87.8	66.7	70.8	90.3	82.1	86.6	104.6	80.3	81.4	94.5
October	91.1	87.9	88.5	88.1	67.9	71.5	89.1	82.1	88.0	104.6	82.0	81.6	94.0
November	91.4	88.0	88.7	88.6	68.5	71.6	92.2	83.1	89.2	106.0	82.8	79.8	93.3
December	92.4	88.9	89.6	89.3	69.1	69.4	95.3	83.6	91.2	108.4	82.4	79.6	92.5
2011													
January	92.5	89.2	90.0	90.3	70.0	67.5	95.6	84.1	94.1	109.9	82.5	81.4	92.4
February	92.3	89.4	90.3	91.1	69.7	69.8	95.1	84.1	94.2	109.9	82.8	85.1	92.8
March	93.1	90.0	90.9	91.8	71.3	69.9	96.5	85.0	93.6	109.4	83.1	88.6	93.4
April	92.6	89.5	90.4	90.9	69.4	70.7	96.0	85.9	92.5	109.6	81.5	82.8	94.9
May	92.9	89.7	90.6	91.6	70.0	71.8	95.5	86.7	93.4	110.8	81.4	83.2	95.9
June	93.1	89.7	90.7	91.7	68.3	71.6	94.3	88.0	94.4	110.2	81.4	83.3	96.6
July	93.9	90.4	91.5	92.5	68.2	72.2	95.2	88.6	94.3	111.5	79.8	85.9	97.5
August	94.2	90.7	91.6	93.1	67.4	72.5	95.8	88.3	93.8	112.6	80.4	87.6	99.1
September	94.4	91.1	92.0	93.5	69.5	72.3	96.7	87.9	94.1	112.4	81.3	88.3	100.0
October	94.9	91.5	92.5	94.3	69.8	71.3	97.2	88.4	94.6	111.3	83.4	92.1	102.1
November	95.1	91.5	92.5	94.8	70.0	70.8	100.4	89.4	95.4	112.0	82.2	90.6	103.7
December	95.9	92.9	93.9	96.2	71.0	71.1	103.0	90.3	98.0	114.0	82.0	93.6	103.2

. . . = Not available.

Table 2-2. Industrial Production Indexes by NAICS Industry Groups—*Continued*

(Seasonally adjusted, 2007 = 100.)

Year and month	Durable goods manufacturing—*Continued*		Manufacturing (NAICS)—*Continued* Nondurable goods manufacturing									Other manufacturing (non-NAICS)
	Furniture and related products	Miscellaneous manufacturing	Total	Food, beverage, and tobacco products	Textile and product mills	Apparel and leather	Paper	Printing and support	Petroleum and coal products	Chemicals	Plastics and rubber products	
1967	. . .	. . .	. . .	. . .	. . .	. . .	. . .	. . .	. . .	. . .	. . .	. . .
1968	. . .	. . .	. . .	. . .	. . .	. . .	. . .	. . .	. . .	. . .	. . .	. . .
1969	. . .	. . .	. . .	. . .	. . .	. . .	. . .	. . .	. . .	. . .	. . .	. . .
1970	. . .	. . .	. . .	. . .	. . .	. . .	. . .	. . .	. . .	. . .	. . .	. . .
1971	. . .	. . .	. . .	. . .	. . .	. . .	. . .	. . .	. . .	. . .	. . .	. . .
1972	55.7	37.6	57.2	62.0	104.6	276.1	68.1	49.4	65.5	41.1	34.7	75.3
1973	58.4	38.8	59.9	62.8	103.5	281.0	73.7	52.0	64.4	45.0	39.2	77.7
1974	53.8	37.9	60.1	63.6	94.6	263.3	76.9	50.4	69.5	46.8	37.8	78.2
1975	46.0	35.4	55.7	62.5	99.6	256.1	66.5	47.1	68.5	41.1	31.9	74.4
1976	51.2	38.5	60.8	66.8	102.4	270.2	73.4	50.5	75.9	46.0	35.2	76.7
1977	58.6	41.9	64.9	68.3	112.6	284.2	76.6	54.7	81.2	50.1	41.6	84.1
1978	63.1	42.8	67.3	70.7	112.3	290.8	80.1	57.9	82.1	52.6	43.5	87.0
1979	62.7	43.1	67.7	70.4	111.9	272.1	81.3	59.6	87.7	53.8	42.9	88.8
1980	60.5	40.8	65.7	71.5	107.1	277.8	81.1	60.0	77.7	50.9	38.4	91.9
1981	60.0	42.3	66.3	72.3	104.7	277.6	82.2	61.6	74.1	51.7	40.6	94.1
1982	56.6	42.8	65.3	74.4	96.7	275.8	80.8	66.2	70.8	48.4	40.0	95.1
1983	62.0	42.8	68.4	74.5	109.7	284.1	86.0	71.2	72.0	51.7	43.5	97.8
1984	69.5	46.3	71.5	75.5	112.5	284.0	90.4	77.5	73.5	54.8	50.2	102.3
1985	70.1	46.9	71.9	78.0	108.2	271.0	88.6	80.6	72.5	54.4	52.2	97.9
1986	73.3	48.0	74.0	79.0	121.1	286.6	92.3	84.7	72.1	56.8	54.4	108.4
1987	78.4	51.7	78.0	80.6	133.2	289.8	95.3	91.0	75.5	61.2	60.2	114.7
1988	77.6	56.5	80.6	82.8	131.9	284.9	99.1	93.9	77.8	64.8	62.9	114.2
1989	77.2	57.3	81.1	82.4	134.0	272.5	100.2	94.2	77.0	66.0	65.0	112.5
1990	75.6	60.1	82.4	84.7	128.5	266.5	100.1	97.8	77.1	67.5	66.8	111.2
1991	69.9	61.3	82.1	85.3	126.6	265.0	100.3	94.7	76.0	67.3	66.1	106.6
1992	75.5	63.9	84.2	86.4	133.4	272.4	102.8	99.9	75.7	68.3	71.1	104.5
1993	78.6	67.5	85.4	86.2	138.5	278.1	104.0	100.2	76.2	69.1	76.2	105.2
1994	81.3	68.0	88.4	89.1	145.9	281.5	108.5	101.3	78.3	70.9	82.5	104.3
1995	82.7	70.6	89.9	91.6	144.4	279.7	110.1	102.8	79.7	72.1	84.6	104.3
1996	83.4	74.1	90.2	90.9	141.0	273.3	106.6	103.5	81.6	73.6	87.4	103.4
1997	92.1	76.1	93.5	92.8	148.5	272.9	108.9	105.6	84.3	78.0	92.8	112.1
1998	98.6	80.5	94.9	95.6	147.3	257.1	109.8	106.8	82.7	79.2	96.1	118.8
1999	101.9	82.2	95.5	93.9	147.3	245.8	110.6	106.8	86.0	80.8	101.2	122.2
2000	103.6	86.8	95.9	95.3	144.2	235.2	107.7	107.8	85.2	81.9	102.3	121.9
2001	97.1	85.8	93.1	95.0	129.0	201.0	101.6	104.2	84.7	80.5	96.4	114.0
2002	100.8	90.6	94.2	94.1	129.3	158.8	102.9	102.1	89.3	85.1	99.8	110.2
2003	99.1	93.4	94.4	95.9	124.2	147.5	100.4	98.1	87.9	86.5	99.9	106.9
2004	101.8	93.4	95.9	96.3	122.7	129.3	101.2	98.5	93.1	90.0	101.1	107.8
2005	105.5	99.5	98.3	99.8	124.5	126.1	100.7	98.6	95.6	92.9	102.2	107.5
2006	103.9	102.6	98.8	99.9	113.0	123.1	99.6	97.8	97.3	95.2	102.8	106.2
2007	100.0	100.0	100.0	100.0	100.0	100.0	100.0	100.0	100.0	100.0	100.0	100.0
2008	90.3	101.6	94.1	97.2	87.9	80.6	95.8	93.8	95.6	92.5	90.6	93.6
2009	65.5	94.2	86.8	96.5	69.7	59.4	85.4	78.8	94.3	83.4	75.8	80.7
2010	64.3	98.0	88.7	96.5	74.8	61.2	87.2	78.9	93.6	86.3	82.5	76.5
2011	67.4	100.9	90.1	98.1	75.5	62.0	86.0	75.4	98.5	86.7	89.4	71.6
2010												
January	61.6	95.8	87.7	96.3	72.7	60.7	86.5	78.1	88.2	86.5	78.5	78.4
February	62.0	95.7	87.7	95.9	73.5	60.2	87.7	77.3	91.3	85.7	78.9	77.3
March	63.4	96.1	88.0	95.9	73.5	60.2	88.0	77.2	93.4	85.8	79.8	77.4
April	64.0	97.5	88.3	95.2	74.2	60.5	88.0	78.6	94.4	86.2	82.0	76.7
May	64.7	99.3	88.9	96.3	75.2	60.3	87.6	80.4	94.1	86.4	82.8	77.9
June	65.0	98.2	88.6	96.1	74.9	60.6	87.6	80.2	93.5	86.3	82.2	76.8
July	65.0	98.8	88.8	95.8	76.0	60.7	87.0	79.9	95.0	86.3	83.2	77.0
August	64.7	98.4	89.0	97.0	75.8	61.9	86.6	80.7	94.3	86.2	83.6	77.0
September	64.9	98.6	89.2	97.3	75.6	60.9	86.7	79.5	94.1	86.7	83.3	75.3
October	65.1	99.0	89.0	97.9	75.2	62.3	86.7	79.0	94.5	85.5	84.2	74.9
November	65.7	99.5	88.8	96.5	74.8	62.3	86.5	78.3	95.1	85.9	85.0	75.0
December	65.5	99.5	90.0	97.2	76.3	63.8	87.5	77.6	95.8	88.0	86.0	74.3
2011												
January	66.0	100.4	89.8	97.6	74.2	63.5	88.2	76.9	94.2	87.2	87.2	73.8
February	66.1	101.8	89.5	97.3	76.5	63.7	87.0	77.5	93.8	86.6	87.6	72.6
March	68.0	100.3	90.1	97.3	74.7	61.8	87.2	76.8	96.0	87.8	87.9	71.5
April	67.3	100.1	89.9	98.2	76.0	62.6	86.7	76.9	94.7	86.8	88.8	70.8
May	68.9	100.2	89.6	97.6	75.8	62.9	85.8	76.4	97.1	85.8	89.3	70.9
June	66.4	100.7	89.7	97.8	75.9	62.5	85.5	75.2	98.0	86.0	89.0	69.4
July	67.4	100.9	90.4	98.5	75.8	62.5	85.4	75.9	100.2	86.3	90.5	69.6
August	68.8	100.7	90.2	98.1	74.5	61.0	84.5	75.3	100.8	86.4	90.2	71.2
September	68.2	102.0	90.6	98.3	75.0	60.1	85.1	74.5	101.3	87.1	90.2	71.8
October	67.6	101.9	90.6	99.0	75.3	61.1	84.8	73.8	101.5	86.6	90.7	72.2
November	67.6	101.7	90.1	98.5	75.9	61.4	85.2	73.0	101.7	85.6	90.0	72.2
December	68.0	101.7	91.4	99.0	77.0	60.9	86.1	74.2	102.9	88.1	90.9	72.9

. . . = Not available.

Table 2-2. Industrial Production Indexes by NAICS Industry Groups—*Continued*

(Seasonally adjusted, 2007 = 100.)

Year and month	Mining	Utilities			Selected high-tech industries	Excluding selected high-tech industries	Stage-of-process groups		
		Total	Electric	Natural gas			Crude	Primary and semi-finished	Finished
1967	. . .	. . .	. . .	. . .	0.1	50.0	. . .	. . .	. . .
1968	. . .	. . .	. . .	. . .	0.1	52.7	. . .	. . .	. . .
1969	. . .	. . .	. . .	. . .	0.1	55.0	. . .	. . .	. . .
1970	. . .	. . .	. . .	. . .	0.1	53.1	. . .	. . .	. . .
1971	. . .	. . .	. . .	. . .	0.1	54.1	. . .	. . .	. . .
1972	98.0	46.4	37.0	103.9	0.1	59.1	82.5	. . .	34.7
1973	98.5	49.1	40.3	99.4	0.2	63.6	86.9	. . .	37.3
1974	97.0	48.9	40.5	95.8	0.2	63.0	88.0	. . .	36.8
1975	94.5	49.8	42.3	89.0	0.2	57.4	79.9	. . .	34.7
1976	95.3	52.1	45.0	88.0	0.3	61.6	84.5	. . .	38.1
1977	106.0	54.2	47.9	84.7	0.3	65.9	89.0	. . .	41.4
1978	109.3	55.6	49.4	85.5	0.4	69.0	90.7	. . .	44.0
1979	104.2	56.8	50.5	87.9	0.5	70.5	93.1	. . .	44.7
1980	106.3	57.3	51.3	85.9	0.7	67.9	92.5	. . .	43.9
1981	109.3	58.1	52.7	83.8	0.8	68.4	93.6	. . .	44.9
1982	103.5	56.2	51.4	78.2	0.9	64.3	87.3	. . .	44.1
1983	97.5	56.7	52.9	72.7	1.1	65.5	87.5	. . .	46.1
1984	104.4	60.0	55.9	77.7	1.5	70.6	93.3	. . .	50.3
1985	102.2	61.3	58.0	74.2	1.5	71.3	90.8	. . .	51.6
1986	102.5	61.8	59.2	78.4	1.6	72.0	88.3	50.5	53.5
1987	103.5	64.7	62.0	82.0	1.9	75.1	92.3	53.4	56.2
1988	106.1	68.4	65.5	87.0	2.3	78.4	95.9	56.2	59.4
1989	104.9	70.6	67.5	90.2	2.4	78.9	96.4	56.6	60.2
1990	106.4	71.9	69.4	87.1	2.7	79.1	98.3	56.7	61.3
1991	104.1	73.7	71.1	89.5	3.0	77.5	96.6	55.7	60.7
1992	101.8	73.6	70.7	92.0	3.6	79.0	97.5	58.0	62.1
1993	101.7	76.2	73.2	95.5	4.2	81.0	96.0	60.7	63.9
1994	104.1	77.7	74.8	96.1	5.3	84.2	97.9	64.9	66.5
1995	104.0	80.5	77.5	98.6	7.5	86.3	98.8	68.5	69.7
1996	105.7	82.8	79.5	103.3	10.7	87.7	98.0	72.4	72.5
1997	107.7	82.8	79.8	101.3	15.8	91.4	100.9	78.0	78.2
1998	105.7	84.9	83.1	94.7	22.0	94.2	99.3	83.0	83.6
1999	100.2	87.4	85.5	97.4	31.6	95.3	99.2	88.5	86.0
2000	102.9	89.9	87.9	100.3	44.2	96.3	97.9	92.9	89.1
2001	103.3	89.5	87.7	98.9	45.1	92.5	92.6	88.8	87.0
2002	98.4	92.3	90.5	101.8	44.6	92.7	93.3	90.3	86.0
2003	98.7	94.1	92.4	102.7	53.4	92.9	92.8	91.2	87.5
2004	98.1	95.3	94.2	100.5	60.6	94.5	95.8	93.5	89.6
2005	97.0	97.3	97.0	98.9	71.1	96.9	94.6	96.6	94.0
2006	99.4	96.7	97.5	93.0	85.0	98.3	96.4	97.8	97.2
2007	100.0	100.0	100.0	100.0	100.0	100.0	100.0	100.0	100.0
2008	101.0	99.9	99.4	102.3	112.1	95.8	96.0	95.7	96.3
2009	95.8	97.5	96.9	100.4	96.0	85.0	89.0	81.8	86.6
2010	100.7	100.9	100.7	101.8	110.2	89.3	96.8	87.6	88.9
2011	107.0	100.6	100.2	102.5	116.9	92.8	98.5	90.7	93.0
2010									
January	96.8	100.8	100.4	102.2	103.2	86.8	94.2	84.1	87.5
February	98.0	102.2	101.8	103.6	106.0	87.0	94.8	85.1	86.8
March	99.0	99.5	99.5	98.3	108.2	87.5	95.6	85.5	87.5
April	99.4	96.0	96.9	89.3	109.9	87.8	96.3	85.8	87.9
May	99.5	100.4	100.3	99.7	111.0	89.2	96.1	87.9	89.0
June	99.5	102.2	102.2	102.0	110.3	89.4	97.0	88.3	88.7
July	100.5	102.2	102.1	102.0	110.5	90.1	97.5	88.7	89.6
August	101.9	102.1	101.8	103.2	111.4	90.2	98.0	88.8	89.5
September	103.9	102.2	101.8	103.7	111.5	90.6	98.9	88.9	89.8
October	103.6	98.7	98.7	98.5	110.8	90.3	97.6	88.2	90.1
November	103.2	100.5	99.6	105.5	112.8	90.5	97.2	89.2	89.8
December	103.2	104.3	102.8	113.5	116.5	91.5	98.9	90.7	90.3
2011									
January	103.5	101.9	101.3	105.3	117.9	91.5	98.7	90.2	91.1
February	101.8	100.6	100.3	101.4	116.8	91.3	97.0	89.8	91.7
March	104.2	100.9	100.4	103.1	115.5	92.2	98.7	90.4	92.2
April	105.1	99.7	99.9	97.7	116.3	91.7	97.3	89.8	91.9
May	106.0	100.1	99.5	103.2	117.5	92.0	96.8	90.1	92.3
June	106.3	100.7	100.5	101.0	118.2	92.1	97.2	90.2	92.3
July	106.8	103.1	103.0	102.4	118.0	93.0	97.9	91.3	93.0
August	107.9	102.3	102.0	103.6	119.2	93.2	98.0	91.2	93.5
September	107.8	101.2	100.5	105.1	117.4	93.5	98.8	91.2	93.8
October	110.2	100.0	98.7	107.7	114.6	94.1	99.8	91.0	94.8
November	111.8	100.2	99.7	102.5	115.0	94.3	100.0	91.4	94.5
December	112.6	96.6	96.5	96.7	116.7	95.1	101.6	91.9	95.5

. . . = Not available.

Table 2-3. Capacity Utilization by NAICS Industry Groups

(Output as a percentage of capacity, seasonally adjusted.)

Year and month	Total industry	Total manufac- turing (SIC)	Manufacturing (NAICS) Total	Durable goods manufacturing Total	Wood products	Nonmetallic mineral products	Primary metals	Fabricated metal products	Machinery	Computer and electronic products	Electrical equipment, appliances, and components	Motor vehicles and parts	Aerospace and miscel- laneous transpor- tation equipment
1967	87.0	87.2	. . .	87.5	. . .	75.7	85.0	86.4	90.4	. . .	. . .	78.9	94.1
1968	87.3	87.1	. . .	87.4	. . .	78.4	84.8	87.3	85.1	. . .	. . .	90.1	90.2
1969	87.4	86.6	. . .	87.1	. . .	79.7	88.4	86.1	86.7	. . .	. . .	86.7	86.3
1970	81.3	79.4	. . .	77.8	. . .	73.8	79.5	78.4	79.7	. . .	. . .	66.3	75.2
1971	79.6	77.9	. . .	75.5	. . .	75.4	73.1	78.4	73.8	. . .	. . .	79.1	66.9
1972	84.7	83.4	83.3	82.1	92.2	79.4	82.9	85.0	83.1	80.7	89.8	84.3	65.6
1973	88.3	87.7	87.8	88.6	87.8	84.0	94.6	90.9	92.4	85.2	97.7	91.8	73.5
1974	85.1	84.4	84.5	84.7	77.9	81.6	96.5	86.1	91.9	83.1	91.6	76.7	74.4
1975	75.8	73.7	73.5	71.7	70.3	72.9	75.2	72.3	77.6	68.7	70.7	66.0	70.8
1976	79.8	78.3	78.3	76.4	79.5	77.6	78.6	75.8	79.9	72.1	78.8	81.8	66.1
1977	83.4	82.5	82.4	81.2	86.2	82.7	79.2	80.2	85.5	77.9	85.5	90.0	66.1
1978	85.1	84.4	84.3	83.8	84.8	86.5	84.2	81.0	88.6	80.4	87.8	90.7	72.3
1979	85.0	84.0	84.0	84.1	80.0	84.4	86.1	81.7	90.1	83.7	88.8	80.9	81.7
1980	80.7	78.6	78.4	77.5	72.4	75.3	75.9	75.1	83.4	86.8	81.8	59.8	84.4
1981	79.5	76.9	76.5	75.1	70.7	72.5	77.7	72.6	80.4	84.4	78.9	57.2	76.8
1982	73.6	70.8	70.3	66.4	63.7	64.8	56.9	64.4	66.6	81.0	69.7	50.7	69.7
1983	74.9	73.4	72.9	68.7	75.2	71.2	59.5	66.4	60.5	81.9	72.9	67.2	66.4
1984	80.4	79.3	78.9	76.9	81.0	76.6	69.0	73.3	70.9	87.5	82.4	81.7	69.7
1985	79.2	78.1	77.6	75.7	79.6	76.2	67.3	73.7	70.6	80.3	79.1	83.4	72.4
1986	78.7	78.4	78.0	75.4	83.5	78.5	69.5	73.4	70.1	77.5	80.2	79.5	74.0
1987	81.2	81.0	80.5	77.6	85.5	80.8	78.2	75.2	72.0	79.8	82.4	78.2	75.5
1988	84.3	84.0	83.8	82.1	84.1	81.8	88.9	80.1	80.4	81.5	87.2	82.6	79.9
1989	83.8	83.3	83.2	81.9	82.1	81.0	86.5	79.9	84.1	78.7	86.3	81.1	85.5
1990	82.5	81.7	81.6	79.6	80.6	79.2	85.3	78.0	81.7	78.8	83.9	72.2	85.1
1991	79.8	78.5	78.4	75.3	75.5	73.2	79.7	74.5	76.6	77.6	79.1	64.3	82.9
1992	80.6	79.6	79.6	77.2	78.1	77.1	81.2	76.8	75.4	79.6	82.2	72.4	77.5
1993	81.4	80.4	80.3	78.5	78.9	78.9	85.8	77.8	78.9	77.5	86.6	78.6	72.7
1994	83.6	82.8	82.9	81.6	82.9	81.6	91.0	82.4	83.5	80.3	91.8	85.9	66.6
1995	84.0	83.2	83.3	82.3	80.9	81.7	88.9	84.3	85.6	83.5	91.3	83.2	64.7
1996	83.4	82.2	82.3	81.6	81.6	84.9	88.8	83.8	84.6	81.1	90.0	80.4	67.5
1997	84.2	83.1	83.0	82.4	81.8	83.8	89.9	82.8	84.8	81.6	88.5	81.6	73.3
1998	82.8	81.6	81.3	80.6	82.1	83.4	86.4	80.6	81.6	77.9	86.1	78.7	81.2
1999	81.7	80.4	80.1	79.9	82.3	80.9	84.3	78.0	76.1	80.8	83.7	83.2	75.4
2000	81.5	79.8	79.4	79.4	78.1	77.9	82.1	78.8	77.2	84.7	86.4	81.5	65.2
2001	76.1	73.7	73.2	71.2	72.2	73.1	73.9	72.4	68.0	69.9	77.3	72.7	69.3
2002	74.9	72.9	72.5	69.9	74.7	73.1	75.7	71.2	67.1	60.9	73.7	78.6	65.9
2003	76.0	73.9	73.5	71.1	77.3	73.1	74.0	72.4	68.9	65.2	74.8	78.2	63.1
2004	77.9	76.2	75.8	73.7	81.4	73.5	81.7	74.4	72.7	71.0	77.3	76.8	62.5
2005	79.9	78.2	77.9	75.9	82.4	74.4	79.4	77.9	76.3	72.5	80.9	77.0	69.0
2006	80.3	78.5	78.4	77.1	78.7	73.0	79.2	82.5	79.4	77.0	82.8	71.9	72.2
2007	80.4	78.5	78.6	77.9	74.2	68.0	80.4	84.7	82.7	75.5	87.6	71.4	83.7
2008	77.3	74.3	74.1	74.2	66.7	59.0	77.1	79.9	80.6	76.3	85.5	58.0	82.7
2009	68.6	65.5	65.3	61.0	54.0	45.7	54.6	63.1	63.5	69.5	68.6	43.7	72.5
2010	73.7	71.2	71.4	68.4	59.1	49.9	68.5	70.4	71.2	76.8	74.5	58.9	71.0
2011	76.8	75.0	75.5	73.6	62.9	53.9	73.1	78.3	79.8	79.9	78.6	65.5	73.2
2010													
January	70.8	68.2	68.1	64.1	57.1	45.8	64.5	64.5	65.1	71.6	70.0	54.7	70.0
February	71.3	68.4	68.5	64.5	56.2	46.1	66.1	65.9	65.9	73.0	70.0	53.5	70.2
March	71.9	69.3	69.4	65.8	57.3	46.9	68.7	66.3	66.6	74.4	71.4	55.4	71.1
April	72.4	70.2	70.3	67.1	60.0	49.4	68.5	67.9	69.3	75.6	73.4	55.8	71.1
May	73.7	71.3	71.5	68.6	60.9	49.7	69.5	69.4	71.2	76.7	73.5	59.7	71.0
June	73.9	71.4	71.6	68.8	59.3	50.2	70.1	70.7	72.1	76.7	74.4	59.4	71.0
July	74.5	72.1	72.3	69.9	59.0	50.9	67.5	71.8	72.2	77.6	74.9	64.1	71.6
August	74.8	72.3	72.5	69.8	58.8	51.4	68.2	72.9	72.6	78.2	76.2	60.4	72.2
September	75.2	72.5	72.8	70.1	58.6	51.8	68.5	73.4	72.9	78.4	76.0	61.5	71.8
October	74.9	72.7	73.0	70.4	59.9	52.5	67.7	73.5	74.2	78.5	77.7	61.6	71.3
November	75.2	72.9	73.2	70.8	60.6	52.8	70.1	74.5	75.2	79.5	78.6	60.2	70.7
December	76.0	73.7	74.0	71.4	61.3	51.4	72.4	75.1	76.9	81.1	78.4	60.0	70.0
2011													
January	76.1	74.0	74.4	72.1	62.3	50.2	72.6	75.5	79.4	82.0	78.7	61.3	69.8
February	75.9	74.2	74.7	72.7	62.2	52.1	72.2	75.6	79.5	81.6	79.0	64.1	70.0
March	76.5	74.7	75.2	73.3	63.8	52.4	73.2	76.4	79.1	80.9	79.4	66.7	70.4
April	76.1	74.3	74.8	72.5	62.3	53.1	72.7	77.2	78.2	80.6	78.1	62.4	71.4
May	76.3	74.4	74.9	73.0	63.0	54.2	72.2	78.0	79.0	80.8	78.1	62.7	72.1
June	76.3	74.4	75.0	73.0	61.7	54.3	71.3	79.1	79.9	79.8	78.2	62.8	72.5
July	77.0	75.0	75.6	73.5	61.8	54.9	71.8	79.5	79.8	80.1	76.8	64.8	73.1
August	77.1	75.2	75.7	73.9	61.2	55.3	72.2	79.3	79.4	80.2	77.5	66.1	74.1
September	77.2	75.5	75.9	74.1	63.3	55.4	72.8	78.9	79.7	79.3	78.4	66.6	74.7
October	77.6	75.8	76.3	74.6	63.7	54.8	73.1	79.3	80.0	77.9	80.5	69.4	76.1
November	77.7	75.7	76.2	74.8	64.0	54.7	75.5	80.1	80.6	77.7	79.5	68.3	77.2
December	78.3	76.8	77.2	75.8	65.0	55.0	77.4	80.9	82.8	78.4	79.4	70.5	76.6

. . . = Not available.

Table 2-3. Capacity Utilization by NAICS Industry Groups—*Continued*

(Output as a percentage of capacity, seasonally adjusted.)

Year and month	Durable goods manufacturing—Continued		Manufacturing (NAICS)—Continued — Nondurable goods manufacturing									Other manufacturing (non-NAICS)
	Furniture and related products	Miscellaneous manufacturing	Total	Food, beverage, and tobacco products	Textile and product mills	Apparel and leather	Paper	Printing and support	Petroleum and coal products	Chemicals	Plastics and rubber products	
1967	91.9	. . .	86.3	85.0	. . .	. . .	89.7	. . .	94.9	78.9	88.3	. . .
1968	91.4	. . .	86.5	84.8	. . .	. . .	89.3	. . .	95.7	80.1	91.1	. . .
1969	92.8	. . .	86.1	85.1	. . .	. . .	91.1	. . .	96.0	79.1	90.3	. . .
1970	84.1	. . .	82.1	84.0	. . .	. . .	86.2	. . .	96.1	76.1	79.2	. . .
1971	85.0	. . .	81.7	84.0	. . .	. . .	86.9	. . .	94.8	75.4	79.8	. . .
1972	94.0	80.3	85.2	85.1	88.9	81.5	91.4	92.3	93.2	80.1	88.5	85.7
1973	95.4	79.5	86.6	84.8	86.3	82.1	94.9	94.0	90.4	83.7	92.5	84.7
1974	82.3	74.6	84.2	83.8	76.3	76.2	94.9	88.0	92.6	84.1	84.2	82.7
1975	68.2	67.7	76.1	80.1	72.5	74.5	80.4	79.6	83.7	71.8	70.1	77.3
1976	75.7	72.3	81.1	83.2	81.4	78.2	87.5	82.3	86.0	77.8	77.4	77.6
1977	83.8	77.6	84.3	82.8	88.6	81.6	90.1	86.1	87.7	81.3	88.4	83.2
1978	85.5	78.7	85.1	83.4	87.8	83.9	92.1	87.4	86.4	82.5	88.7	85.0
1979	80.2	78.4	83.8	81.0	87.3	78.9	90.7	86.0	88.6	82.9	83.8	85.6
1980	74.6	73.2	79.6	80.8	83.4	79.8	88.2	83.7	76.2	76.6	74.2	86.8
1981	71.6	75.7	78.8	80.3	80.6	78.6	86.8	81.2	72.9	76.0	77.5	87.5
1982	66.4	73.7	76.3	81.4	74.3	77.8	83.8	82.4	71.2	69.2	74.4	87.3
1983	72.2	70.8	79.4	80.9	83.9	81.1	88.9	84.3	74.4	72.9	81.4	87.9
1984	79.2	76.0	82.1	81.3	85.7	81.3	91.2	87.1	78.5	76.0	91.1	89.5
1985	77.3	74.1	80.5	82.6	81.4	77.9	87.9	85.2	80.1	73.4	86.8	90.4
1986	79.2	74.0	81.8	82.7	84.2	79.7	90.2	86.0	82.0	75.9	85.2	88.8
1987	82.8	77.2	84.7	83.7	91.4	81.9	90.2	89.6	82.4	80.9	89.3	90.6
1988	80.5	81.8	86.1	85.3	88.7	82.1	91.3	90.6	83.3	84.3	88.8	88.6
1989	79.0	79.8	85.0	83.7	88.5	80.3	90.4	89.3	84.3	83.3	86.8	85.4
1990	76.1	79.7	84.2	83.9	83.5	79.1	89.3	89.4	84.7	82.9	83.6	83.7
1991	70.7	78.3	82.3	82.8	81.7	80.5	87.7	84.3	82.7	81.1	78.5	80.7
1992	76.8	77.0	82.7	82.3	85.5	82.9	88.4	86.1	85.3	79.9	81.7	80.0
1993	79.4	77.1	82.7	81.0	87.9	84.1	89.0	84.3	89.1	79.2	86.2	81.3
1994	80.9	76.9	84.5	83.6	90.2	85.4	90.7	83.4	88.9	80.4	90.7	81.4
1995	80.3	79.3	84.6	85.1	86.4	85.1	89.4	82.5	89.5	80.7	88.9	82.2
1996	79.0	80.5	83.3	83.0	82.6	83.8	85.4	82.2	91.7	80.6	87.5	80.6
1997	83.3	78.7	83.9	83.0	84.7	83.7	87.3	80.6	95.0	81.6	88.1	85.6
1998	82.8	78.8	82.4	83.4	82.3	77.4	87.3	79.6	92.6	78.9	86.7	86.9
1999	80.5	76.3	80.4	79.3	81.7	76.8	86.7	78.7	90.3	77.4	85.1	87.1
2000	77.3	75.8	79.3	78.3	79.6	79.8	84.5	78.5	88.8	76.4	81.4	87.3
2001	70.6	72.0	75.9	76.8	71.9	74.6	80.1	76.7	87.9	72.1	76.3	82.6
2002	72.5	73.3	76.1	75.8	73.8	67.1	82.2	75.9	88.4	73.6	78.8	81.4
2003	71.3	74.6	76.7	77.4	72.9	70.1	82.0	73.5	89.6	73.5	80.1	81.4
2004	76.7	74.8	78.5	77.4	75.0	71.1	83.3	75.3	92.5	76.0	83.0	82.9
2005	80.2	77.5	80.3	79.3	78.4	76.5	83.8	78.7	92.7	76.4	84.6	82.8
2006	79.3	77.0	80.0	78.8	75.2	76.8	83.6	79.0	90.4	76.9	83.2	81.3
2007	75.9	73.3	79.4	78.5	71.8	74.8	83.9	77.9	88.0	77.9	78.9	77.4
2008	72.2	74.3	74.1	76.5	67.2	75.7	81.1	71.2	81.7	70.9	70.2	77.3
2009	59.4	69.8	70.5	76.2	56.7	62.0	76.0	61.7	78.2	68.0	60.3	70.0
2010	62.3	75.0	75.1	76.5	64.2	66.4	81.6	65.3	80.9	75.3	68.8	67.2
2011	67.1	77.6	77.7	78.4	66.9	69.3	81.9	65.1	84.7	77.5	76.2	63.8
2010												
January	58.6	72.1	73.0	76.1	61.1	64.9	79.6	63.2	74.0	73.6	64.4	68.5
February	59.3	72.3	73.2	75.9	62.1	64.6	81.0	62.9	77.0	73.3	65.1	67.6
March	60.9	72.9	73.8	75.9	62.3	64.7	81.7	63.1	79.3	73.8	66.0	67.7
April	61.7	74.1	74.3	75.4	63.2	65.2	82.0	64.5	80.6	74.5	68.1	67.2
May	62.5	75.8	75.0	76.4	64.2	65.1	81.8	66.2	80.8	75.1	68.9	68.3
June	62.9	75.2	75.0	76.2	64.2	65.6	82.0	66.3	80.9	75.3	68.6	67.4
July	63.1	75.9	75.3	76.1	65.4	65.8	81.7	66.3	82.6	75.6	69.6	67.7
August	62.9	75.7	75.8	77.0	65.4	67.4	81.5	67.3	82.3	75.8	70.1	67.7
September	63.3	76.1	76.1	77.4	65.4	66.5	81.7	66.5	82.4	76.4	70.0	66.2
October	63.6	76.5	76.1	77.9	65.3	68.1	81.8	66.3	82.9	75.5	70.9	66.0
November	64.3	77.0	76.1	76.9	65.1	68.3	81.9	65.9	83.5	76.1	71.7	66.1
December	64.2	77.0	77.2	77.5	66.5	70.1	82.8	65.5	84.1	78.1	72.7	65.7
2011												
January	64.8	77.7	77.1	77.9	64.9	70.0	83.6	65.2	82.6	77.5	73.8	65.3
February	65.1	78.8	77.0	77.6	67.0	70.4	82.6	65.9	82.1	77.2	74.3	64.3
March	67.0	77.6	77.5	77.7	65.7	68.5	82.9	65.6	83.8	78.3	74.7	63.4
April	66.5	77.3	77.5	78.4	66.9	69.6	82.4	65.8	82.3	77.5	75.6	62.9
May	68.3	77.3	77.2	78.0	66.9	70.0	81.7	65.5	84.0	76.6	76.1	63.1
June	65.9	77.5	77.3	78.2	67.2	69.7	81.4	64.7	84.5	76.9	75.9	61.8
July	67.0	77.5	78.0	78.8	67.2	69.9	81.4	65.6	86.0	77.2	77.3	62.1
August	68.6	77.2	77.8	78.5	66.2	68.4	80.6	65.2	86.1	77.3	77.1	63.7
September	68.2	78.0	78.1	78.6	66.7	67.5	81.1	64.6	86.2	77.9	77.2	64.3
October	67.7	77.7	78.2	79.2	67.2	68.8	80.9	64.2	86.1	77.6	77.6	64.7
November	67.8	77.3	77.7	78.8	67.8	69.3	81.4	63.7	86.1	76.6	77.0	64.8
December	68.3	77.1	78.9	79.2	69.0	68.9	82.3	64.8	86.9	78.8	77.8	65.6

. . . = Not available.

Table 2-3. Capacity Utilization by NAICS Industry Groups—*Continued*

(Output as a percentage of capacity, seasonally adjusted.)

| Year and month | Mining | Utilities | Selected high-tech industries | | | | Measures excluding selected high-tech industries | | Stage-of-process groups | | |
			Total	Computers and peripheral equipment	Communications equipment	Semiconductors and related electronic components	Total industry	Manufacturing	Crude	Primary and semi-finished	Finished
1967	81.2	94.5	89.4	. . .	. . .	. . .	86.9	86.8	81.1	85.0	88.2
1968	83.6	95.1	87.6	. . .	. . .	. . .	87.2	87.0	83.4	86.8	87.1
1969	86.7	96.8	89.8	. . .	. . .	. . .	87.1	86.4	85.6	88.1	85.6
1970	89.2	96.3	83.5	. . .	. . .	. . .	81.0	79.2	85.1	81.4	78.1
1971	87.8	94.7	74.4	. . .	. . .	. . .	80.0	78.3	84.3	81.6	75.7
1972	90.7	95.3	78.6	81.5	73.2	84.6	84.9	83.6	88.4	88.1	79.6
1973	91.6	93.3	81.6	82.0	75.1	91.1	88.5	87.9	90.0	92.1	83.3
1974	91.0	86.9	82.0	88.3	73.3	87.5	85.2	84.5	90.9	87.3	80.3
1975	89.3	85.1	65.0	68.9	62.1	64.8	76.2	74.0	83.9	75.2	73.7
1976	89.4	85.5	68.8	76.8	61.9	69.7	80.2	78.7	86.9	80.1	76.8
1977	89.5	86.6	75.9	77.8	72.4	78.3	83.7	82.8	89.1	84.6	79.9
1978	89.7	86.9	78.9	77.7	77.4	82.1	85.3	84.6	88.7	86.3	82.1
1979	91.3	87.0	83.2	78.3	85.6	87.2	85.1	84.0	89.9	85.9	81.7
1980	91.4	85.5	87.8	86.9	91.7	85.2	80.5	78.2	89.4	78.8	79.3
1981	90.9	84.4	85.7	85.2	89.2	83.3	79.3	76.4	89.3	77.2	77.4
1982	84.2	80.2	78.2	70.3	87.2	81.4	73.4	70.4	82.3	70.5	73.0
1983	79.8	79.6	80.5	75.7	85.8	81.6	74.6	73.0	79.9	74.5	73.0
1984	85.9	82.2	87.4	85.5	85.4	91.0	80.1	78.8	85.7	81.2	77.2
1985	84.4	81.9	77.2	76.4	78.7	76.9	79.3	78.2	83.8	79.9	76.6
1986	77.6	81.1	72.8	72.9	75.3	71.0	79.0	78.8	79.1	79.8	77.1
1987	80.3	83.6	77.3	73.8	79.5	79.4	81.4	81.2	82.8	82.8	78.7
1988	84.3	86.7	79.9	76.2	84.3	81.0	84.6	84.3	86.3	85.9	81.8
1989	85.0	86.9	77.8	74.8	79.9	79.3	84.2	83.7	86.7	84.7	81.7
1990	86.6	86.5	77.4	71.5	82.2	80.2	82.8	82.0	87.7	82.7	80.7
1991	85.0	87.9	76.9	73.7	78.0	78.7	80.0	78.6	85.2	79.9	78.2
1992	84.7	86.4	81.4	79.0	79.5	83.7	80.5	79.5	85.5	81.6	78.1
1993	85.5	88.3	79.4	79.3	81.7	78.1	81.6	80.4	85.7	83.3	78.2
1994	87.0	88.4	83.3	77.2	82.9	86.4	83.6	82.8	87.9	86.4	79.2
1995	87.6	89.4	85.6	82.4	79.3	89.9	83.9	83.0	88.8	86.4	80.0
1996	90.3	90.9	82.6	84.7	76.7	84.4	83.5	82.2	89.1	85.6	79.4
1997	91.5	90.4	83.6	81.4	80.5	86.3	84.2	83.1	90.6	86.1	80.4
1998	89.0	92.7	79.4	78.3	84.8	77.3	83.1	81.8	87.2	84.2	80.2
1999	85.8	94.2	84.8	83.3	88.7	83.3	81.4	80.0	86.1	84.1	78.0
2000	90.6	93.9	89.4	81.2	91.1	92.0	80.8	78.8	88.6	84.0	76.9
2001	90.2	89.6	69.7	71.5	69.5	69.2	76.6	74.1	85.6	77.3	72.4
2002	86.1	87.6	58.7	69.9	45.5	62.2	76.1	74.2	83.0	77.1	70.7
2003	88.1	85.7	65.0	73.2	46.4	73.9	76.7	74.6	84.8	78.1	71.5
2004	88.2	84.5	70.6	76.4	52.2	79.6	78.3	76.6	86.2	80.0	73.1
2005	88.5	85.1	73.2	75.8	55.5	82.1	80.3	78.5	86.3	81.8	75.2
2006	90.2	83.2	81.7	78.3	75.3	87.1	80.2	78.4	87.7	81.4	76.0
2007	89.2	85.7	76.6	75.8	76.8	76.2	80.6	78.7	88.2	80.8	76.9
2008	89.5	84.0	79.5	75.6	85.4	79.3	77.2	74.0	86.6	76.5	73.9
2009	80.3	80.8	71.3	83.0	78.1	65.0	68.4	65.2	78.0	65.9	68.4
2010	83.9	81.1	79.1	89.5	80.9	76.4	73.5	70.9	83.6	71.5	72.4
2011	87.4	77.7	80.1	85.8	76.5	80.1	76.7	74.8	85.8	74.2	76.0
2010											
January	80.4	82.7	73.8	91.7	80.4	67.4	70.7	67.9	80.5	68.3	70.5
February	81.4	83.6	75.6	92.6	81.0	70.0	71.1	68.0	81.4	69.2	70.2
March	82.4	81.1	77.1	91.9	81.1	72.6	71.7	68.9	82.3	69.5	70.9
April	82.9	78.0	78.4	90.0	81.1	75.1	72.1	69.8	82.8	69.9	71.4
May	83.0	81.2	79.3	88.2	81.1	76.9	73.4	70.9	82.9	71.7	72.4
June	83.0	82.4	79.0	87.6	81.4	76.7	73.7	71.1	83.3	72.1	72.3
July	83.9	82.0	79.4	87.9	81.6	77.2	74.4	71.8	84.0	72.5	73.2
August	85.1	81.6	80.2	88.5	81.6	78.3	74.6	71.9	84.7	72.7	73.2
September	86.6	81.3	80.5	89.0	81.1	78.7	75.0	72.1	85.9	72.8	73.5
October	86.2	78.2	80.0	89.1	80.4	78.3	74.7	72.3	85.0	72.2	73.8
November	85.8	79.3	81.4	88.8	79.8	80.5	75.0	72.5	84.6	73.1	73.6
December	85.6	82.0	83.9	88.2	79.6	84.5	75.8	73.2	85.3	74.3	74.1
2011											
January	85.7	79.8	84.6	87.6	79.3	85.7	75.8	73.5	85.2	73.9	74.7
February	84.0	78.5	83.4	87.3	78.6	84.2	75.7	73.8	83.9	73.6	75.2
March	85.7	78.5	81.9	87.5	77.2	82.2	76.3	74.4	85.2	74.1	75.6
April	86.3	77.4	81.9	88.1	75.6	82.5	75.9	73.9	84.9	73.6	75.3
May	86.8	77.5	81.9	88.5	74.5	82.8	76.1	74.1	84.8	73.8	75.6
June	86.8	77.7	81.5	88.6	74.5	82.2	76.2	74.1	85.0	73.9	75.5
July	87.0	79.4	80.5	88.1	75.2	80.6	76.9	74.8	85.3	74.7	76.1
August	87.7	78.6	80.5	86.7	76.1	80.5	77.0	74.9	85.7	74.6	76.4
September	87.5	77.6	78.3	84.6	76.6	77.7	77.2	75.3	86.0	74.6	76.5
October	89.3	76.6	75.7	82.0	76.7	74.3	77.7	75.8	87.3	74.3	77.2
November	90.4	76.6	75.1	80.5	76.7	73.8	77.8	75.7	87.7	74.7	76.8
December	91.0	73.7	75.5	80.0	77.0	74.4	78.4	76.8	88.6	75.1	77.5

. . . = Not available.

Table 2-4A. Industrial Production and Capacity Utilization, Historical Data, 1947–2011

(Seasonally adjusted.)

Year and month	Production indexes, 2007 = 100									Capacity utilization (output as percentage of capacity)	
	Total industry	Manufac-turing (SIC)	Market groups								
			Consumer goods			Business equipment	Defense and space equipment	Construction supplies	Business supplies	Materials	Total industry	Manufac-turing (SIC)
			Total	Durable	Nondurable							
1947	13.8	12.5	18.1	11.8	21.3	6.1	6.8	21.3	11.7	13.7	. . .	. . .
1948	14.4	13.0	18.6	12.4	21.9	6.3	8.0	22.8	12.1	14.3	. . .	82.5
1949	13.6	12.3	18.5	11.7	22.1	5.5	8.4	20.9	12.0	13.1	. . .	74.2
1950	15.8	14.3	21.2	15.6	23.9	5.9	9.8	25.2	13.4	15.7	. . .	82.8
1951	17.1	15.4	20.9	13.6	24.8	7.3	24.2	26.2	14.2	17.3	. . .	85.8
1952	17.7	16.1	21.4	13.2	25.8	8.2	34.0	26.0	14.1	17.6	. . .	85.4
1953	19.2	17.5	22.7	15.4	26.5	8.5	40.7	27.9	15.0	19.5	. . .	89.3
1954	18.2	16.4	22.5	14.3	26.8	7.5	35.8	27.5	15.2	18.0	. . .	80.1
1955	20.5	18.5	25.2	17.6	28.9	8.1	32.8	31.6	17.1	21.3	. . .	87.0
1956	21.4	19.2	26.1	17.1	30.8	9.4	32.1	32.5	18.1	21.9	. . .	86.1
1957	21.7	19.4	26.7	17.0	31.7	9.8	33.5	32.1	18.3	21.8	. . .	83.6
1958	20.3	18.1	26.5	15.1	32.7	8.3	33.6	31.0	18.1	19.7	. . .	75.0
1959	22.7	20.4	29.1	17.9	34.9	9.3	35.5	34.7	19.7	22.7	. . .	81.6
1960	23.2	20.8	30.2	18.9	36.0	9.5	36.4	33.9	20.4	23.0	. . .	80.1
1961	23.4	20.8	30.8	18.6	37.2	9.3	37.0	34.2	21.1	23.0	. . .	77.3
1962	25.3	22.7	32.9	21.1	39.0	10.1	42.9	36.3	22.4	25.1	. . .	81.4
1963	26.8	24.1	34.7	22.9	40.7	10.6	46.2	38.0	23.8	26.7	. . .	83.5
1964	28.7	25.7	36.6	24.6	42.7	11.8	44.8	40.3	25.5	28.8	. . .	85.6
1965	31.5	28.5	39.5	28.8	44.6	13.5	49.5	42.8	27.2	32.1	. . .	89.5
1966	34.3	31.1	41.5	30.5	46.7	15.7	58.2	44.6	29.3	35.0	. . .	91.1
1967	35.0	31.7	42.5	29.3	49.1	16.0	66.4	45.7	30.8	34.7	87.0	87.2
1968	37.0	33.5	45.1	32.7	51.0	16.7	66.5	48.1	32.7	37.0	87.3	87.1
1969	38.7	34.9	46.8	34.0	52.8	17.8	63.3	50.2	34.8	39.2	87.4	86.6
1970	37.4	33.4	46.2	31.4	53.7	17.1	53.6	48.4	34.9	37.8	81.3	79.4
1971	37.9	33.9	48.9	35.6	55.2	16.3	48.2	49.9	36.0	38.3	79.6	77.9
1972	41.6	37.4	52.8	39.8	58.7	18.6	46.9	56.7	39.6	42.2	84.7	83.4
1973	45.0	40.8	55.2	42.9	60.5	21.5	51.4	61.5	42.1	46.0	88.3	87.7
1974	44.9	40.7	53.6	39.0	60.6	22.7	53.1	60.0	41.9	45.9	85.1	84.4
1975	40.9	36.4	51.5	35.4	59.5	20.3	53.5	50.8	38.7	40.9	75.8	73.7
1976	44.1	39.7	55.7	39.9	63.2	21.6	51.9	54.7	41.2	44.4	79.8	78.3
1977	47.4	43.1	59.2	44.9	65.6	25.0	46.5	59.6	44.7	47.5	83.4	82.5
1978	50.1	45.8	61.0	45.9	67.9	28.2	47.4	63.0	47.1	49.9	85.1	84.4
1979	51.6	47.2	60.1	44.3	67.5	31.8	50.7	64.6	48.7	51.3	85.0	84.0
1980	50.3	45.5	57.9	38.5	67.6	32.5	60.3	59.8	47.6	49.3	80.7	78.6
1981	50.9	46.0	58.3	39.1	67.9	33.5	65.3	58.8	48.8	49.6	79.5	76.9
1982	48.3	43.5	58.1	36.9	69.1	30.6	78.0	53.4	48.2	45.8	73.6	70.8
1983	49.6	45.6	60.3	41.0	69.9	30.8	78.6	57.2	50.5	47.0	74.9	73.4
1984	54.1	50.0	63.1	45.8	71.3	35.4	90.0	62.2	54.9	51.5	80.4	79.3
1985	54.7	50.9	63.7	45.8	72.2	36.7	100.7	63.8	56.3	51.4	79.2	78.1
1986	55.3	52.0	65.9	48.8	73.9	36.2	107.0	65.9	58.1	51.3	78.7	78.4
1987	58.1	54.9	68.7	51.7	76.6	38.6	109.2	70.1	61.6	54.1	81.2	81.0
1988	61.1	57.9	71.3	54.3	79.1	42.6	110.2	71.8	63.9	57.1	84.3	84.0
1989	61.7	58.3	71.5	55.4	78.9	44.1	110.3	71.5	64.8	57.5	83.8	83.3
1990	62.3	58.8	71.9	54.0	80.2	45.6	106.4	70.9	66.3	57.9	82.5	81.7
1991	61.3	57.6	71.9	51.7	81.4	44.9	98.5	67.0	65.4	57.0	79.8	78.5
1992	63.0	59.7	74.0	56.5	82.0	46.7	91.3	69.8	66.9	58.9	80.6	79.6
1993	65.1	61.8	76.3	61.1	83.2	48.9	86.2	72.9	69.0	60.8	81.4	80.4
1994	68.5	65.5	79.4	66.6	85.2	52.2	80.9	78.1	71.8	64.7	83.6	82.8
1995	71.8	68.9	81.9	69.7	87.3	56.7	78.0	79.9	74.8	68.4	84.0	83.2
1996	75.0	72.2	83.4	72.0	88.5	62.3	76.0	83.4	77.7	71.9	83.4	82.2
1997	80.4	78.3	86.4	77.0	90.5	71.4	74.8	87.5	83.2	77.8	84.2	83.1
1998	85.1	83.5	89.6	83.0	92.5	79.0	78.0	92.1	87.9	82.4	82.8	81.6
1999	88.7	87.6	91.6	89.5	92.5	83.4	75.6	94.5	91.6	87.4	81.7	80.4
2000	92.3	91.3	93.3	92.1	93.9	89.6	67.2	96.5	95.3	91.9	81.5	79.8
2001	89.1	87.6	92.3	87.8	94.1	83.9	73.7	92.2	91.7	87.7	76.1	73.7
2002	89.3	87.8	94.1	93.0	94.6	78.2	74.5	92.2	91.9	88.7	74.9	72.9
2003	90.4	88.9	95.4	95.9	95.2	78.0	79.2	92.0	93.4	89.9	76.0	73.9
2004	92.5	91.4	96.5	97.4	96.1	81.7	77.2	94.2	95.1	92.4	77.9	76.2
2005	95.5	95.0	99.1	98.2	99.3	87.6	85.0	98.7	98.2	94.6	79.9	78.2
2006	97.6	97.4	99.6	98.4	99.9	95.7	84.1	101.1	99.2	96.5	80.3	78.5
2007	100.0	100.0	100.0	100.0	100.0	100.0	100.0	100.0	100.0	100.0	80.4	78.5
2008	96.5	95.2	95.1	88.8	97.2	97.6	107.0	90.7	95.9	97.3	77.3	74.3
2009	85.4	82.0	88.6	74.0	93.4	79.9	102.5	69.9	85.7	86.1	68.6	65.5
2010	90.1	86.7	89.6	80.1	92.7	86.5	106.7	72.6	87.6	93.3	73.7	71.2
2011	93.7	90.5	91.7	85.8	93.6	93.6	109.5	76.6	88.7	97.6	76.8	75.0
1947												
January	13.6	12.4	17.9	11.2	21.6	5.9	7.0	20.3	11.5	13.5	. . .	. . .
February	13.7	12.5	17.9	11.5	21.2	5.9	6.9	20.9	11.6	13.6	. . .	. . .
March	13.8	12.5	17.9	11.8	21.2	6.0	6.8	21.1	11.6	14.1	. . .	. . .
April	13.7	12.5	17.9	11.9	21.0	6.1	6.8	21.3	11.7	13.7	. . .	. . .
May	13.7	12.4	17.7	11.7	20.9	6.1	6.7	21.5	11.7	13.8	. . .	. . .
June	13.7	12.4	17.8	11.8	20.9	6.1	6.7	21.6	11.6	13.7	. . .	. . .
July	13.7	12.4	17.8	11.6	21.1	6.0	6.7	21.1	11.6	13.5	. . .	. . .
August	13.7	12.4	18.0	11.5	21.3	6.1	6.6	21.4	11.5	13.5	. . .	. . .
September	13.9	12.5	18.1	11.9	21.4	6.2	6.6	21.5	11.6	13.7	. . .	. . .
October	14.0	12.6	18.4	12.0	21.7	6.3	6.8	21.5	11.6	13.8	. . .	. . .
November	14.2	12.8	18.7	12.4	22.0	6.3	6.9	21.9	11.8	14.1	. . .	. . .
December	14.2	12.9	18.7	12.6	21.9	6.3	7.1	22.0	12.0	13.9	. . .	. . .

. . . = Not available.

Table 2-4A. Industrial Production and Capacity Utilization, Historical Data, 1947–2011—*Continued*

(Seasonally adjusted.)

Year and month	Total industry	Manufac- turing (SIC)	Consumer goods Total	Consumer goods Durable	Consumer goods Nondurable	Business equipment	Defense and space equipment	Construction supplies	Business supplies	Materials	Cap. util. Total industry	Cap. util. Manufac- turing (SIC)
1948												
January	14.3	12.9	18.6	12.4	21.8	6.4	7.2	23.0	12.0	14.0	. . .	84.4
February	14.3	12.9	18.7	12.3	22.0	6.3	7.4	22.7	12.1	14.1	. . .	84.0
March	14.2	12.9	18.5	12.4	21.7	6.4	7.6	22.8	12.1	13.9	. . .	83.4
April	14.2	12.9	18.6	12.3	22.0	6.3	7.8	22.7	12.0	13.8	. . .	82.8
May	14.4	13.0	18.6	12.0	22.0	6.3	7.6	22.8	12.1	14.6	. . .	83.3
June	14.6	13.1	18.9	12.5	22.2	6.4	7.9	22.6	12.2	14.6	. . .	83.6
July	14.6	13.2	18.8	12.8	21.9	6.4	8.0	23.2	12.1	14.7	. . .	83.4
August	14.6	13.1	18.7	12.6	21.8	6.4	8.2	23.1	12.3	14.5	. . .	82.7
September	14.5	13.0	18.6	12.3	21.8	6.4	8.4	22.8	12.1	14.5	. . .	81.5
October	14.6	13.1	18.8	12.7	21.9	6.3	8.6	23.3	12.2	14.6	. . .	81.7
November	14.4	12.9	18.6	12.2	22.0	6.3	8.7	22.6	12.2	14.4	. . .	80.2
December	14.3	12.8	18.3	11.7	21.8	6.2	8.7	22.4	12.2	14.3	. . .	79.3
1949												
January	14.1	12.7	18.1	11.4	21.7	6.1	8.6	21.8	12.0	14.1	. . .	77.9
February	14.0	12.5	18.1	11.2	21.8	6.0	8.6	21.4	11.8	14.0	. . .	76.9
March	13.7	12.4	18.2	11.2	22.0	5.9	8.6	21.1	11.9	13.4	. . .	75.9
April	13.6	12.2	18.2	11.2	21.9	5.8	8.4	20.8	11.8	13.3	. . .	74.2
May	13.5	12.1	18.2	11.1	22.0	5.7	8.6	20.5	11.9	12.9	. . .	73.2
June	13.4	12.1	18.4	11.4	22.0	5.6	8.6	20.5	11.9	12.7	. . .	73.1
July	13.4	12.1	18.6	11.8	22.1	5.5	8.6	20.3	11.9	12.6	. . .	73.1
August	13.5	12.3	18.7	12.0	22.3	5.4	8.4	20.4	12.0	12.9	. . .	73.6
September	13.7	12.5	19.0	12.4	22.4	5.4	8.3	21.1	12.1	13.1	. . .	74.8
October	13.2	12.0	19.1	12.6	22.5	5.2	8.0	20.4	12.3	11.7	. . .	71.7
November	13.5	12.1	18.8	11.9	22.4	5.0	8.0	21.1	12.2	12.8	. . .	72.0
December	13.7	12.4	18.6	11.7	22.2	5.0	7.9	22.0	12.3	13.4	. . .	73.6
1950												
January	14.0	12.7	19.4	13.1	22.6	5.1	7.9	21.7	12.4	13.5	. . .	74.9
February	14.0	12.8	19.4	13.1	22.6	5.3	7.9	22.6	12.7	13.3	. . .	75.4
March	14.5	13.0	19.8	13.6	23.0	5.3	8.0	23.1	12.8	14.2	. . .	76.4
April	15.0	13.6	20.4	14.6	23.3	5.5	8.1	24.3	13.0	14.8	. . .	79.2
May	15.3	13.9	20.8	15.4	23.5	5.7	8.4	24.6	13.1	15.2	. . .	81.0
June	15.8	14.3	21.4	16.7	23.7	5.9	8.7	25.4	13.2	15.8	. . .	83.1
July	16.3	14.8	22.0	17.3	24.2	6.1	9.2	26.1	13.5	16.2	. . .	85.5
August	16.8	15.3	22.7	17.9	25.1	6.5	10.1	26.6	13.9	16.7	. . .	88.4
September	16.7	15.2	22.2	17.1	24.7	6.3	11.1	26.6	13.8	16.9	. . .	87.2
October	16.8	15.3	22.0	16.7	24.6	6.4	12.0	26.9	14.0	17.1	. . .	87.5
November	16.8	15.3	21.9	16.4	24.6	6.5	12.8	26.9	14.0	16.9	. . .	87.0
December	17.1	15.5	22.2	16.2	25.3	6.6	13.9	26.9	14.2	17.2	. . .	88.1
1951												
January	17.1	15.6	22.4	15.9	25.7	6.7	15.4	27.2	14.4	17.0	. . .	88.3
February	17.2	15.7	22.3	16.0	25.6	6.8	17.8	26.9	14.2	17.1	. . .	88.3
March	17.3	15.7	22.0	15.9	25.1	6.9	20.2	27.0	14.5	17.5	. . .	88.4
April	17.3	15.8	21.6	15.1	25.0	7.0	22.1	26.9	14.8	17.6	. . .	88.2
May	17.3	15.7	21.2	14.4	24.8	7.1	22.9	26.7	14.6	17.7	. . .	87.4
June	17.2	15.6	20.9	13.7	24.7	7.2	24.1	26.5	14.4	17.8	. . .	86.6
July	16.9	15.3	20.3	12.2	24.5	7.3	25.5	25.9	14.2	17.5	. . .	84.9
August	16.8	15.1	19.8	11.4	24.3	7.4	26.3	25.8	14.1	17.2	. . .	83.6
September	16.9	15.2	20.0	11.9	24.3	7.5	27.1	25.7	14.0	17.3	. . .	83.7
October	16.9	15.1	19.9	11.8	24.2	7.6	28.3	25.5	13.6	17.1	. . .	83.1
November	17.0	15.3	20.2	12.0	24.6	7.8	29.9	25.3	13.7	17.1	. . .	83.6
December	17.1	15.4	20.4	12.2	24.7	7.9	30.6	25.3	13.8	17.1	. . .	83.9
1952												
January	17.3	15.6	20.5	12.1	25.0	8.1	31.1	25.7	13.8	17.5	. . .	84.4
February	17.4	15.7	20.7	12.1	25.3	8.2	31.4	25.9	13.8	17.4	. . .	84.6
March	17.5	15.7	20.8	12.4	25.3	8.2	31.5	25.7	13.9	17.4	. . .	84.7
April	17.3	15.6	20.8	12.3	25.3	8.2	31.8	25.3	13.8	17.1	. . .	83.6
May	17.1	15.6	20.7	12.6	25.1	8.3	32.9	24.9	13.7	16.8	. . .	83.1
June	17.0	15.4	21.3	12.8	25.9	8.3	33.9	24.8	14.0	15.9	. . .	81.9
July	16.7	15.1	20.9	11.5	26.0	7.9	34.1	24.7	14.1	15.5	. . .	79.8
August	17.8	16.1	21.4	12.7	26.1	8.0	34.6	26.4	14.2	17.5	. . .	85.1
September	18.4	16.7	21.9	14.0	26.1	8.2	35.2	26.7	14.4	18.6	. . .	87.7
October	18.6	16.9	22.3	14.4	26.3	8.3	36.3	27.1	14.6	18.5	. . .	88.8
November	19.0	17.3	22.7	15.4	26.6	8.4	37.1	27.5	14.7	19.1	. . .	90.2
December	19.1	17.4	22.7	15.4	26.6	8.5	38.2	27.6	14.7	19.1	. . .	90.5
1953												
January	19.1	17.5	22.9	16.0	26.5	8.6	38.8	28.1	14.5	19.0	. . .	90.5
February	19.3	17.6	23.1	16.2	26.7	8.6	39.6	28.5	14.8	19.5	. . .	91.1
March	19.4	17.7	23.1	16.3	26.6	8.7	40.4	28.6	15.1	19.7	. . .	91.4
April	19.5	17.8	23.1	16.2	26.7	8.7	40.9	28.7	15.1	19.9	. . .	91.5
May	19.6	17.9	23.2	16.3	26.8	8.6	41.6	28.1	15.2	20.3	. . .	91.7
June	19.5	17.8	22.8	15.6	26.7	8.6	41.9	27.9	15.2	20.3	. . .	90.7
July	19.8	17.9	22.9	15.5	26.6	8.7	42.2	28.3	15.3	20.6	. . .	91.0
August	19.7	17.9	22.7	15.4	26.5	8.7	41.9	28.2	15.3	20.0	. . .	90.6
September	19.3	17.5	22.4	14.8	26.4	8.6	41.9	27.6	15.2	19.5	. . .	88.3
October	19.1	17.3	22.4	14.7	26.5	8.6	41.5	27.7	15.0	18.9	. . .	87.2
November	18.6	16.9	22.1	14.1	26.3	8.3	38.8	27.2	15.0	18.4	. . .	84.7
December	18.2	16.4	21.7	13.6	26.0	8.1	39.1	26.6	14.8	18.0	. . .	82.3

. . . = Not available.

Table 2-4A. Industrial Production and Capacity Utilization, Historical Data, 1947–2011—*Continued*

(Seasonally adjusted.)

Year and month	Total industry	Manufac-turing (SIC)	Production indexes, 2007 = 100 — Market groups — Consumer goods — Total	Durable	Nondurable	Business equipment	Defense and space equipment	Construction supplies	Business supplies	Materials	Capacity utilization — Total industry	Manufac-turing (SIC)
1954												
January	18.0	16.3	21.8	13.4	26.3	7.9	38.3	27.1	14.8	17.8	. . .	81.3
February	18.1	16.3	22.1	13.7	26.5	7.8	38.0	27.2	14.9	17.8	. . .	80.8
March	18.0	16.2	22.1	13.7	26.5	7.7	37.5	27.0	14.9	17.6	. . .	80.2
April	17.9	16.1	22.1	13.9	26.4	7.5	36.9	27.0	15.0	17.5	. . .	79.4
May	18.0	16.2	22.2	14.2	26.4	7.5	36.3	27.3	15.0	17.8	. . .	79.8
June	18.0	16.3	22.4	14.3	26.5	7.4	35.8	26.7	15.1	18.0	. . .	79.9
July	18.1	16.2	22.4	14.1	26.8	7.4	35.6	26.6	14.9	18.1	. . .	79.4
August	18.0	16.1	22.5	14.2	26.8	7.4	34.9	26.5	15.0	18.0	. . .	78.8
September	18.1	16.3	22.7	14.3	27.0	7.3	34.5	27.8	15.5	17.8	. . .	79.2
October	18.3	16.4	22.7	14.5	27.1	7.3	34.2	28.7	15.6	18.2	. . .	79.7
November	18.6	16.7	23.2	14.9	27.6	7.4	34.0	29.0	15.8	18.6	. . .	80.9
December	18.8	17.0	23.7	15.5	27.8	7.4	33.5	29.3	16.0	18.9	. . .	81.8
1955												
January	19.3	17.4	24.2	16.6	27.9	7.5	33.3	29.7	16.2	19.5	. . .	83.5
February	19.5	17.6	24.3	16.8	27.9	7.6	33.3	30.1	16.4	20.0	. . .	84.1
March	20.0	18.0	24.7	17.2	28.4	7.7	33.1	31.1	16.8	20.6	. . .	85.8
April	20.2	18.2	24.9	17.5	28.6	7.9	33.1	31.3	16.7	21.0	. . .	86.7
May	20.5	18.5	25.2	18.0	28.8	8.0	33.1	31.4	17.0	21.4	. . .	87.9
June	20.5	18.6	25.0	17.6	28.7	8.1	32.7	32.0	17.1	21.4	. . .	87.6
July	20.7	18.6	25.1	17.9	28.7	8.2	32.7	32.0	17.1	21.7	. . .	87.7
August	20.7	18.6	25.2	17.8	28.7	8.2	32.5	32.0	17.0	21.6	. . .	87.3
September	20.8	18.7	25.3	17.9	29.0	8.3	32.5	32.2	17.4	21.9	. . .	87.5
October	21.2	19.0	25.8	18.0	29.7	8.7	32.4	32.2	17.5	22.1	. . .	88.4
November	21.2	19.1	25.9	17.8	29.9	8.7	32.4	32.6	17.8	22.0	. . .	88.3
December	21.3	19.3	26.0	17.8	30.2	8.8	32.5	32.8	17.6	22.2	. . .	89.0
1956												
January	21.4	19.2	26.0	17.6	30.3	8.9	32.1	33.3	17.8	22.3	. . .	88.2
February	21.2	19.1	26.0	17.3	30.4	9.0	31.8	33.2	17.8	21.9	. . .	87.4
March	21.2	19.1	25.9	17.3	30.4	9.1	31.1	33.1	18.0	21.8	. . .	87.0
April	21.4	19.3	26.0	17.6	30.4	9.4	31.3	33.0	18.2	21.9	. . .	87.8
May	21.2	19.1	25.9	17.1	30.5	9.4	31.4	32.5	18.0	21.5	. . .	86.3
June	21.0	19.0	25.8	16.7	30.6	9.4	31.4	32.2	18.0	21.2	. . .	85.3
July	20.4	18.2	25.9	16.8	30.7	9.4	31.4	30.5	18.0	19.5	. . .	81.5
August	21.2	19.0	26.0	16.8	30.9	9.5	31.8	32.0	18.1	21.3	. . .	84.9
September	21.7	19.3	26.0	16.5	31.0	9.6	32.1	32.9	18.1	22.5	. . .	86.0
October	21.9	19.5	26.2	16.7	31.2	9.6	32.9	32.6	18.2	22.8	. . .	86.5
November	21.7	19.5	26.1	16.5	31.1	9.8	33.4	32.4	18.2	22.3	. . .	85.8
December	22.0	19.7	26.3	17.2	31.0	9.9	34.2	33.0	18.3	22.7	. . .	86.8
1957												
January	21.9	19.7	26.5	17.2	31.2	10.0	34.3	32.5	18.4	22.3	. . .	86.2
February	22.2	19.9	26.8	17.5	31.5	10.3	34.5	33.5	18.4	22.4	. . .	87.0
March	22.1	19.9	26.8	17.4	31.7	10.2	34.4	32.9	18.3	22.3	. . .	86.4
April	21.8	19.6	26.6	16.9	31.6	10.0	34.5	32.2	18.4	22.0	. . .	85.0
May	21.8	19.5	26.6	16.8	31.7	9.8	34.0	32.1	18.5	21.9	. . .	84.2
June	21.8	19.6	26.7	17.1	31.7	9.9	34.2	32.3	18.3	22.0	. . .	84.6
July	21.9	19.6	26.8	17.0	32.0	9.9	33.8	32.4	18.4	22.2	. . .	84.3
August	21.9	19.7	27.0	17.4	31.9	9.9	33.9	32.1	18.4	22.2	. . .	84.2
September	21.8	19.5	27.0	17.4	32.0	9.8	33.2	31.9	18.4	21.9	. . .	83.2
October	21.4	19.1	26.6	16.7	31.7	9.5	32.4	31.5	18.2	21.6	. . .	81.4
November	20.9	18.7	26.5	16.7	31.6	9.3	31.3	31.2	18.0	20.8	. . .	79.4
December	20.5	18.3	26.3	16.0	31.9	9.0	31.1	30.7	18.0	20.1	. . .	77.5
1958												
January	20.1	17.9	26.0	15.3	31.8	8.8	31.4	30.3	17.9	19.5	. . .	75.7
February	19.7	17.5	25.8	14.8	31.8	8.5	31.7	29.3	17.8	18.9	. . .	73.8
March	19.5	17.3	25.6	14.3	31.8	8.3	32.3	29.1	17.9	18.4	. . .	72.7
April	19.1	17.1	25.3	13.7	31.8	8.1	32.8	28.8	17.7	18.0	. . .	71.3
May	19.3	17.2	25.7	14.2	32.1	7.9	33.2	29.8	17.7	18.2	. . .	71.9
June	19.8	17.8	26.2	14.6	32.6	7.9	34.1	30.9	17.9	19.0	. . .	73.9
July	20.1	17.9	26.6	14.8	33.0	8.0	34.2	30.7	17.9	19.4	. . .	74.3
August	20.5	18.3	26.7	15.1	33.0	8.1	34.5	32.1	18.2	20.0	. . .	75.7
September	20.7	18.5	26.4	14.1	33.2	8.2	34.7	32.2	18.4	20.5	. . .	76.2
October	21.0	18.6	26.6	14.8	33.2	8.3	34.7	32.2	18.7	20.9	. . .	76.4
November	21.6	19.3	27.9	17.3	33.6	8.5	34.9	33.4	18.8	21.5	. . .	79.1
December	21.6	19.3	28.1	17.4	33.6	8.5	35.0	33.0	18.7	21.5	. . .	79.0
1959												
January	21.9	19.7	28.4	17.4	34.1	8.7	35.1	33.6	19.2	21.9	. . .	80.2
February	22.4	20.0	28.6	17.5	34.4	8.8	34.8	34.5	19.4	22.6	. . .	81.4
March	22.7	20.3	28.6	17.9	34.3	8.9	34.9	35.4	19.5	23.2	. . .	82.5
April	23.2	20.8	29.0	18.0	34.8	9.1	35.2	36.4	19.5	23.8	. . .	84.0
May	23.5	21.0	29.2	18.3	34.8	9.4	35.5	36.7	19.5	24.4	. . .	84.9
June	23.6	21.1	29.0	18.5	34.6	9.6	35.5	36.6	19.7	24.3	. . .	84.8
July	23.0	20.7	29.4	18.8	34.9	9.7	35.7	35.2	20.0	22.8	. . .	83.0
August	22.2	19.9	29.4	18.3	35.3	9.6	35.5	32.9	19.9	21.1	. . .	79.5
September	22.2	19.8	29.3	17.8	35.5	9.5	35.7	32.6	20.0	21.1	. . .	79.0
October	22.0	19.7	29.2	18.2	35.0	9.4	35.6	32.7	20.0	20.8	. . .	78.2
November	22.2	19.8	28.6	15.9	35.5	9.3	35.6	33.8	20.0	21.7	. . .	78.5
December	23.5	21.1	29.5	18.0	35.6	9.4	35.9	36.4	20.1	24.0	. . .	83.6

. . . = Not available.

Table 2-4A. Industrial Production and Capacity Utilization, Historical Data, 1947–2011—*Continued*

(Seasonally adjusted.)

Year and month	Production indexes, 2007 = 100										Capacity utilization (output as percentage of capacity)	
	Total industry	Manufac-turing (SIC)	Market groups								Total industry	Manufac-turing (SIC)
			Consumer goods			Business equipment	Defense and space equipment	Construction supplies	Business supplies	Materials		
			Total	Durable	Nondurable							
1960												
January	24.1	21.7	30.4	19.9	35.8	9.8	36.1	36.2	20.4	24.7	. . .	85.6
February	23.9	21.6	30.1	19.7	35.4	9.8	36.3	35.8	20.4	24.4	. . .	84.6
March	23.7	21.3	30.1	19.3	35.8	9.9	36.5	34.7	20.4	24.0	. . .	83.2
April	23.5	21.1	30.3	19.2	36.1	9.8	36.3	34.7	20.6	23.4	. . .	82.3
May	23.5	21.0	30.5	19.4	36.3	9.8	36.7	34.4	20.8	23.2	. . .	81.5
June	23.2	20.8	30.3	19.2	36.1	9.7	35.8	33.7	20.5	22.8	. . .	80.2
July	23.1	20.7	30.0	18.5	36.1	9.5	36.7	34.1	20.6	22.8	. . .	79.7
August	23.1	20.6	30.1	18.7	36.1	9.4	36.8	33.2	20.4	22.7	. . .	79.1
September	22.9	20.4	30.0	18.5	36.0	9.3	36.7	32.9	20.3	22.4	. . .	77.9
October	22.8	20.4	30.3	18.7	36.4	9.3	36.4	33.0	20.4	22.3	. . .	77.5
November	22.5	20.0	29.7	18.1	36.0	9.2	36.5	32.6	20.4	21.7	. . .	75.8
December	22.1	19.7	29.5	17.4	36.0	9.0	36.0	32.2	20.0	21.1	. . .	74.3
1961												
January	22.1	19.7	29.3	16.8	36.1	9.1	36.3	31.9	20.3	21.3	. . .	74.1
February	22.1	19.6	29.4	16.7	36.3	9.0	36.1	31.8	20.4	21.1	. . .	73.5
March	22.2	19.7	29.4	16.7	36.3	9.0	36.0	32.6	20.6	21.3	. . .	73.9
April	22.7	20.2	30.1	17.9	36.7	9.1	36.1	33.4	20.7	22.0	. . .	75.4
May	23.0	20.5	30.5	18.5	36.9	9.1	36.1	33.5	20.8	22.6	. . .	76.4
June	23.3	20.8	30.8	19.1	37.1	9.2	36.1	34.2	20.9	23.0	. . .	77.3
July	23.6	21.1	31.1	19.5	37.2	9.2	36.3	34.8	21.2	23.3	. . .	78.1
August	23.8	21.4	31.3	19.5	37.6	9.3	36.5	35.2	21.3	23.8	. . .	79.0
September	23.8	21.2	30.8	18.4	37.4	9.4	37.3	35.5	21.2	23.8	. . .	78.2
October	24.2	21.6	31.6	19.4	38.0	9.4	38.1	35.8	21.5	24.2	. . .	79.6
November	24.6	22.0	32.2	20.3	38.4	9.6	39.1	35.5	21.7	24.6	. . .	80.8
December	24.8	22.3	32.3	20.7	38.4	9.7	39.8	35.8	21.9	24.9	. . .	81.6
1962												
January	24.6	22.0	32.0	20.2	38.2	9.6	40.2	34.1	21.9	24.7	. . .	80.2
February	25.0	22.4	32.2	20.3	38.5	9.8	40.9	36.1	22.1	25.1	. . .	81.4
March	25.2	22.6	32.5	20.6	38.7	9.9	41.5	36.5	22.0	25.1	. . .	81.9
April	25.2	22.6	32.7	21.1	38.7	10.0	41.8	36.0	22.0	25.1	. . .	81.7
May	25.2	22.5	32.9	21.3	39.0	10.0	42.1	36.0	22.4	24.8	. . .	81.3
June	25.1	22.5	32.7	20.9	38.9	10.1	42.5	36.3	22.4	24.7	. . .	80.9
July	25.4	22.7	33.3	21.3	39.4	10.2	43.4	36.1	22.3	24.9	. . .	81.5
August	25.4	22.8	32.9	21.1	39.0	10.3	44.0	36.7	22.5	25.0	. . .	81.4
September	25.6	22.9	33.1	21.3	39.2	10.2	44.1	37.2	22.7	25.2	. . .	81.8
October	25.6	22.9	33.0	21.4	39.1	10.3	44.2	36.6	22.6	25.2	. . .	81.4
November	25.7	23.1	33.2	21.4	39.2	10.3	44.7	36.7	22.8	25.4	. . .	81.8
December	25.7	23.1	33.4	21.6	39.4	10.2	44.8	37.0	22.6	25.2	. . .	81.7
1963												
January	25.9	23.2	33.8	21.8	40.0	10.2	46.9	36.1	22.8	25.4	. . .	81.9
February	26.2	23.4	34.2	22.1	40.4	10.3	46.6	36.2	23.0	25.7	. . .	82.4
March	26.3	23.6	34.3	22.1	40.6	10.3	46.3	36.6	22.8	26.1	. . .	82.6
April	26.6	23.9	34.4	22.3	40.7	10.4	46.3	37.9	23.6	26.3	. . .	83.5
May	26.9	24.1	34.5	22.7	40.6	10.3	46.3	38.7	23.8	27.0	. . .	84.0
June	27.0	24.2	34.7	23.0	40.7	10.4	46.2	38.5	23.7	27.1	. . .	83.9
July	26.9	24.1	34.6	23.0	40.5	10.5	45.8	38.4	23.9	26.8	. . .	83.3
August	26.9	24.2	34.9	23.1	40.9	10.8	45.9	38.5	24.0	26.6	. . .	83.5
September	27.2	24.4	35.0	23.5	40.8	10.7	46.1	38.2	24.2	27.1	. . .	83.8
October	27.4	24.6	35.2	23.5	41.1	10.9	46.1	38.8	24.4	27.2	. . .	84.3
November	27.5	24.7	35.3	23.7	41.1	11.0	45.9	39.3	24.7	27.4	. . .	84.3
December	27.5	24.7	35.5	23.8	41.5	11.0	46.1	38.7	24.5	27.2	. . .	84.0
1964												
January	27.7	24.9	35.8	23.8	41.9	11.3	45.6	38.9	24.8	27.5	. . .	84.5
February	27.9	25.0	35.8	24.0	41.7	11.2	45.2	39.9	24.9	27.9	. . .	84.7
March	27.9	25.0	35.6	23.8	41.6	11.4	45.1	40.1	25.1	27.9	. . .	84.4
April	28.4	25.5	36.5	24.4	42.6	11.6	45.0	40.2	25.4	28.2	. . .	85.6
May	28.5	25.6	36.8	24.6	43.0	11.8	44.2	40.4	25.6	28.4	. . .	85.6
June	28.6	25.6	36.7	24.8	42.7	11.8	44.0	40.1	25.7	28.6	. . .	85.4
July	28.8	25.8	37.2	25.2	43.3	12.0	43.9	40.9	25.7	28.7	. . .	85.9
August	29.0	26.0	37.1	25.4	43.0	11.9	44.1	40.5	25.6	29.3	. . .	86.1
September	29.1	26.1	36.7	24.8	42.7	12.1	44.4	40.2	25.6	29.7	. . .	86.2
October	28.7	25.7	36.0	22.2	43.3	12.0	44.7	40.3	25.6	29.2	. . .	84.6
November	29.6	26.5	37.3	25.3	43.4	12.4	45.2	41.3	25.8	30.1	. . .	86.8
December	29.9	27.0	38.1	26.8	43.7	12.6	45.5	40.7	26.1	30.4	. . .	88.0
1965												
January	30.2	27.3	38.7	27.2	44.3	12.6	46.0	41.0	26.3	30.8	. . .	88.6
February	30.4	27.5	38.8	27.6	44.2	12.8	46.5	42.1	26.4	30.9	. . .	88.7
March	30.8	27.8	39.1	28.3	44.2	12.9	47.3	42.5	26.7	31.4	. . .	89.3
April	31.0	28.0	39.0	28.3	44.1	13.1	47.9	41.8	26.7	31.7	. . .	89.3
May	31.2	28.2	39.3	28.5	44.4	13.2	49.0	42.3	27.0	31.8	. . .	89.4
June	31.4	28.4	39.4	28.8	44.4	13.4	49.6	42.3	27.1	32.2	. . .	89.5
July	31.7	28.8	39.4	29.0	44.3	13.7	50.3	43.5	27.1	32.5	. . .	90.3
August	31.9	28.8	39.3	28.7	44.4	13.7	50.8	43.1	27.4	32.8	. . .	89.9
September	32.0	28.9	39.9	29.2	45.0	13.9	50.8	42.7	27.4	32.6	. . .	89.6
October	32.3	29.1	40.1	29.5	45.1	14.1	51.5	43.3	27.7	32.9	. . .	89.8
November	32.4	29.3	40.3	29.7	45.4	14.4	52.0	43.9	27.9	32.8	. . .	89.6
December	32.8	29.7	40.6	30.3	45.3	14.7	52.5	44.9	28.3	33.1	. . .	90.5

. . . = Not available.

Table 2-4A. Industrial Production and Capacity Utilization, Historical Data, 1947–2011—*Continued*

(Seasonally adjusted.)

Year and month	Production indexes, 2007 = 100										Capacity utilization (output as percentage of capacity)	
	Total industry	Manufac-turing (SIC)	Market groups								Total industry	Manufac-turing (SIC)
			Consumer goods			Business equipment	Defense and space equipment	Construction supplies	Business supplies	Materials		
			Total	Durable	Nondurable							
1966												
January	33.1	30.0	40.8	30.4	45.6	15.0	53.6	44.8	28.3	33.6	. . .	90.9
February	33.4	30.2	40.9	30.3	45.8	15.0	54.4	44.4	28.6	34.0	. . .	90.9
March	33.8	30.6	41.2	30.6	46.2	15.3	54.9	45.3	28.9	34.6	. . .	91.6
April	33.9	30.8	41.3	31.1	46.1	15.4	56.0	45.3	28.6	34.5	. . .	91.5
May	34.2	31.0	41.3	30.6	46.4	15.6	57.0	45.5	29.0	34.9	. . .	91.6
June	34.3	31.1	41.5	30.6	46.6	15.7	57.9	44.8	29.4	35.1	. . .	91.5
July	34.5	31.3	41.4	30.1	46.9	16.0	58.7	45.3	29.7	35.2	. . .	91.4
August	34.6	31.4	41.3	29.6	47.0	16.0	59.4	43.9	29.6	35.5	. . .	91.1
September	34.9	31.6	41.4	29.8	47.1	16.2	60.2	43.9	29.8	35.8	. . .	91.2
October	35.1	31.9	42.3	31.3	47.5	16.2	61.2	44.0	29.8	36.0	. . .	91.6
November	34.9	31.6	42.1	30.4	47.7	15.9	62.3	44.0	29.9	35.5	. . .	90.1
December	35.0	31.7	42.0	30.0	47.8	16.2	62.9	43.9	29.9	35.5	. . .	90.0
1967												
January	35.1	31.8	42.4	29.3	48.9	16.0	64.0	45.1	30.5	35.3	89.4	89.8
February	34.7	31.5	41.8	28.5	48.5	16.1	64.7	44.7	30.3	34.6	88.0	88.4
March	34.5	31.3	41.9	28.7	48.5	16.0	65.4	44.8	30.4	34.0	87.1	87.5
April	34.9	31.5	42.7	29.0	49.5	16.0	66.1	44.7	30.6	34.3	87.5	87.7
May	34.6	31.3	41.8	28.5	48.5	16.1	66.5	45.4	30.1	33.9	86.4	86.6
June	34.6	31.2	42.0	28.2	48.9	16.0	66.4	45.6	30.3	33.9	86.0	86.1
July	34.5	31.1	41.9	28.6	48.5	15.7	66.7	45.8	30.4	33.9	85.4	85.3
August	35.1	31.7	42.3	28.9	49.0	16.0	66.9	46.3	31.2	34.9	86.6	86.5
September	35.1	31.7	42.4	28.9	49.2	15.9	67.1	46.7	31.3	34.6	86.1	86.1
October	35.4	31.9	43.0	29.4	49.7	15.7	67.6	46.4	31.5	35.1	86.4	86.4
November	35.9	32.5	43.9	31.0	50.1	16.2	67.7	46.8	31.6	35.5	87.3	87.5
December	36.3	32.9	44.6	32.3	50.5	16.3	67.7	46.7	31.6	35.9	87.8	88.0
1968												
January	36.2	32.8	44.0	31.3	50.1	16.4	67.4	47.0	31.7	36.1	87.4	87.4
February	36.3	32.9	44.2	31.8	50.2	16.4	68.2	47.5	31.9	36.1	87.3	87.4
March	36.5	33.0	44.5	31.7	50.7	16.5	66.9	47.6	32.0	36.2	87.3	87.2
April	36.5	33.0	44.4	31.8	50.6	16.5	65.5	47.9	32.2	36.5	87.1	86.9
May	36.9	33.4	44.6	32.2	50.7	16.7	66.4	48.1	32.5	37.1	87.7	87.6
June	37.1	33.5	44.9	32.5	50.9	16.7	66.8	48.1	32.7	37.2	87.7	87.4
July	37.0	33.4	44.8	32.2	50.9	16.5	66.8	48.1	32.6	37.3	87.2	86.7
August	37.1	33.6	45.3	32.6	51.5	16.7	66.9	48.3	33.0	37.0	87.1	86.8
September	37.2	33.6	45.5	33.0	51.6	16.8	66.9	48.0	33.1	37.1	87.1	86.5
October	37.3	33.8	45.8	33.4	51.7	17.0	65.1	47.9	33.3	37.2	86.9	86.6
November	37.8	34.3	46.4	34.2	52.2	17.0	65.8	49.1	33.7	37.8	87.7	87.5
December	37.9	34.3	46.2	34.5	51.5	17.2	65.5	50.0	33.9	38.0	87.7	87.1
1969												
January	38.1	34.5	46.4	34.4	52.0	17.4	65.6	50.3	34.0	38.1	87.9	87.3
February	38.4	34.8	46.8	34.4	52.6	17.4	65.1	50.8	33.9	38.6	88.1	87.7
March	38.7	35.0	47.1	34.6	53.0	17.6	65.3	51.0	35.0	38.7	88.5	88.0
April	38.6	34.9	46.4	33.7	52.5	17.8	64.8	50.5	34.5	38.9	87.8	87.3
May	38.4	34.7	46.1	33.2	52.2	17.6	64.7	50.1	34.8	38.8	87.2	86.6
June	38.8	35.0	46.6	34.3	52.3	17.8	63.8	50.4	35.1	39.3	87.7	86.8
July	39.0	35.2	47.4	34.3	53.6	18.0	63.6	50.0	34.9	39.3	87.9	87.1
August	39.1	35.3	47.3	34.7	53.2	17.9	62.6	49.9	35.0	39.7	87.8	86.9
September	39.1	35.2	47.0	34.4	52.9	18.1	62.3	49.9	35.0	39.8	87.4	86.5
October	39.1	35.2	47.0	34.5	52.8	18.2	61.7	50.1	35.1	39.8	87.2	86.2
November	38.7	34.9	46.6	33.1	53.1	17.7	60.6	49.8	34.9	39.6	86.0	85.0
December	38.6	34.7	46.6	32.9	53.3	17.7	59.8	49.5	35.3	39.4	85.5	84.2
1970												
January	37.9	33.9	45.9	31.2	53.2	17.4	59.0	48.0	35.3	38.5	83.7	82.1
February	37.9	34.0	46.3	31.6	53.6	17.5	58.0	47.8	35.0	38.2	83.3	81.9
March	37.8	33.9	46.3	31.9	53.3	17.5	56.7	48.2	35.2	38.1	83.0	81.4
April	37.7	33.7	46.4	31.9	53.6	17.5	55.5	48.7	35.0	37.9	82.5	80.9
May	37.7	33.7	46.7	32.0	54.0	17.5	54.3	48.8	34.9	37.8	82.1	80.4
June	37.6	33.6	46.8	32.6	53.8	17.4	53.3	48.5	34.9	37.6	81.6	80.0
July	37.6	33.7	46.9	32.6	53.9	17.4	52.4	49.1	35.0	37.8	81.6	80.0
August	37.6	33.4	46.1	31.7	53.3	17.3	52.0	48.9	34.7	38.2	81.2	79.2
September	37.3	33.2	46.0	30.8	53.6	16.9	51.5	48.8	34.9	38.0	80.4	78.3
October	36.6	32.4	45.4	29.0	53.9	16.4	50.8	48.3	34.8	37.0	78.5	76.3
November	36.4	32.2	45.1	29.1	53.4	16.3	50.4	47.7	34.9	36.7	77.8	75.6
December	37.2	33.1	47.0	32.4	54.3	16.5	49.8	48.2	34.9	37.6	79.4	77.3
1971												
January	37.5	33.3	47.7	33.7	54.5	16.2	50.2	48.3	35.1	38.1	79.7	77.8
February	37.4	33.4	47.7	34.5	54.0	16.2	49.0	48.6	35.5	37.9	79.4	77.6
March	37.4	33.3	47.8	34.5	54.2	16.1	48.6	48.4	35.1	37.9	79.1	77.2
April	37.6	33.5	48.2	34.8	54.7	16.0	48.6	48.8	35.5	38.2	79.3	77.4
May	37.8	33.7	48.3	35.3	54.4	15.9	49.2	49.1	35.6	38.6	79.5	77.8
June	37.9	33.8	48.6	35.6	54.8	16.0	48.5	49.6	35.4	38.8	79.7	77.8
July	37.8	33.8	49.4	36.2	55.5	16.0	48.1	50.1	36.3	37.9	79.2	77.7
August	37.6	33.4	48.8	35.9	54.9	16.2	48.1	49.2	35.9	37.7	78.6	76.6
September	38.2	34.1	49.3	35.8	55.6	16.6	47.6	51.0	36.5	38.4	79.7	77.9
October	38.5	34.6	49.9	36.5	56.3	16.8	47.3	51.7	36.7	38.5	80.1	78.9
November	38.6	34.7	50.3	36.8	56.7	16.8	46.9	51.9	37.1	38.6	80.2	79.0
December	39.1	35.1	50.7	37.0	57.1	16.9	46.2	52.8	37.3	39.4	80.9	79.5

. . . = Not available.

Table 2-4A. Industrial Production and Capacity Utilization, Historical Data, 1947–2011—*Continued*

(Seasonally adjusted.)

Year and month	Production indexes, 2007 = 100										Capacity utilization (output as percentage of capacity)	
	Total industry	Manufac-turing (SIC)	Market groups								Total industry	Manufac-turing (SIC)
			Consumer goods			Business equipment	Defense and space equipment	Construction supplies	Business supplies	Materials		
			Total	Durable	Nondurable							
1972												
January	40.0	36.0	51.4	38.1	57.6	17.5	46.2	54.2	37.9	40.6	82.7	81.4
February	40.4	36.2	51.7	38.3	57.9	17.7	46.3	54.4	38.6	41.0	83.2	81.7
March	40.7	36.5	51.7	38.0	58.2	18.0	46.7	54.8	39.0	41.4	83.7	82.1
April	41.1	36.9	52.3	39.1	58.4	18.3	46.9	55.5	39.0	41.8	84.3	82.9
May	41.1	37.0	52.1	38.8	58.2	18.2	46.5	55.7	39.2	41.9	84.1	82.7
June	41.2	37.1	52.1	38.8	58.3	18.3	46.5	56.2	39.6	42.0	84.1	82.8
July	41.2	37.1	52.5	39.6	58.3	18.3	46.5	57.0	39.5	41.7	83.8	82.6
August	41.8	37.6	53.1	40.0	59.0	18.7	46.4	57.4	40.0	42.3	84.7	83.5
September	42.1	37.9	53.3	40.4	59.2	18.8	46.7	57.9	40.0	42.7	85.1	83.9
October	42.6	38.4	54.2	41.3	59.9	19.2	46.8	58.8	40.7	43.2	86.0	84.9
November	43.1	38.9	54.6	42.3	59.8	19.6	48.1	59.2	40.8	43.8	86.8	85.7
December	43.6	39.5	55.0	43.1	60.0	19.9	48.9	59.0	40.9	44.5	87.5	86.6
1973												
January	43.9	39.7	54.9	43.0	59.9	20.2	49.5	59.7	41.2	44.9	87.8	86.9
February	44.6	40.4	55.6	43.8	60.5	20.6	50.6	60.9	41.7	45.6	88.8	88.1
March	44.6	40.5	55.7	43.8	60.6	20.8	50.4	61.2	41.7	45.4	88.6	87.9
April	44.5	40.4	55.2	43.1	60.2	20.9	50.1	61.0	41.7	45.5	88.1	87.5
May	44.8	40.6	55.5	43.0	60.8	21.2	50.4	61.3	41.9	45.8	88.4	87.8
June	44.8	40.6	55.1	42.9	60.3	21.3	50.9	61.4	42.0	45.9	88.1	87.4
July	45.0	40.8	55.0	42.9	60.1	21.6	52.0	61.9	42.2	46.1	88.2	87.5
August	45.0	40.7	54.5	41.6	60.2	21.7	52.1	62.0	42.2	46.1	87.8	87.0
September	45.4	41.1	55.4	43.0	60.7	22.1	52.0	62.0	42.3	46.3	88.3	87.5
October	45.7	41.4	55.6	42.7	61.2	22.3	53.2	61.8	42.7	46.7	88.6	87.9
November	45.9	41.7	55.7	42.6	61.5	22.5	52.7	62.3	42.7	47.0	88.8	88.3
December	45.8	41.7	54.7	41.8	60.4	22.6	52.4	62.8	42.3	47.2	88.3	88.1
1974												
January	45.5	41.4	54.0	39.7	60.7	22.6	52.2	62.9	42.4	46.8	87.4	87.1
February	45.3	41.2	53.8	39.5	60.5	22.5	52.7	62.1	42.2	46.7	86.9	86.5
March	45.3	41.2	53.9	39.6	60.6	22.7	52.6	62.3	42.2	46.6	86.6	86.1
April	45.2	41.0	53.7	39.3	60.5	22.4	52.5	61.7	42.3	46.5	86.2	85.6
May	45.5	41.3	54.2	39.4	61.2	22.8	52.7	62.0	42.5	46.8	86.6	85.9
June	45.5	41.4	54.5	40.0	61.3	22.8	52.0	61.6	42.7	46.6	86.4	85.8
July	45.5	41.3	54.3	39.8	61.1	22.8	52.5	60.4	42.3	46.8	86.2	85.4
August	45.1	40.9	54.3	39.8	61.1	22.8	53.6	59.7	42.2	46.0	85.2	84.5
September	45.1	41.0	53.9	39.7	60.4	23.3	53.7	59.3	42.0	46.1	85.1	84.4
October	44.9	40.7	53.9	39.2	60.8	23.3	54.5	58.2	41.7	45.8	84.6	83.6
November	43.4	39.5	52.3	37.3	59.6	22.9	54.2	56.4	40.8	43.8	81.6	80.9
December	41.9	37.7	50.7	34.3	59.0	21.9	53.6	53.7	40.0	42.1	78.6	77.1
1975												
January	41.4	36.9	49.6	32.9	58.0	21.5	54.0	53.6	39.4	41.8	77.4	75.5
February	40.4	35.9	48.9	31.9	57.6	20.8	51.2	51.9	38.6	40.8	75.5	73.2
March	40.0	35.4	49.0	32.3	57.5	20.5	51.7	49.9	38.1	40.2	74.6	72.1
April	40.0	35.4	50.0	33.5	58.4	20.3	51.4	49.4	38.2	39.9	74.5	71.8
May	39.9	35.4	50.3	34.4	58.2	20.0	53.8	49.5	38.0	39.7	74.2	71.7
June	40.2	35.7	51.0	34.8	59.2	19.8	54.7	49.2	38.1	40.0	74.6	72.2
July	40.6	36.2	52.3	36.5	60.1	20.0	54.0	50.0	38.5	40.2	75.2	73.2
August	41.0	36.5	52.6	37.0	60.2	19.8	53.6	50.5	38.8	40.8	75.8	73.7
September	41.5	37.1	53.3	37.8	60.9	20.1	55.2	51.1	38.9	41.3	76.6	74.7
October	41.6	37.3	53.4	37.6	61.1	20.2	55.1	51.3	39.1	41.5	76.7	74.9
November	41.8	37.4	53.6	37.6	61.5	20.1	52.9	51.6	39.2	41.7	76.8	75.0
December	42.3	37.9	54.1	38.3	61.7	20.5	54.5	51.6	39.6	42.3	77.6	75.8
1976												
January	42.9	38.4	54.8	39.0	62.5	20.7	54.4	52.9	40.0	43.0	78.6	76.7
February	43.3	38.9	55.0	39.4	62.4	20.9	54.4	53.7	40.2	43.6	79.1	77.6
March	43.3	39.0	54.8	39.4	62.2	21.0	54.4	52.9	40.3	43.8	79.0	77.6
April	43.6	39.3	55.0	39.4	62.5	21.2	53.3	53.6	40.5	44.1	79.3	77.9
May	43.8	39.5	55.5	39.4	63.2	21.4	52.8	54.3	40.7	44.2	79.5	78.2
June	43.8	39.5	55.2	39.2	63.0	21.4	52.2	54.7	40.5	44.3	79.4	78.0
July	44.1	39.8	55.6	39.4	63.4	21.6	50.7	55.9	41.1	44.4	79.6	78.4
August	44.4	40.1	55.7	40.0	63.2	21.9	50.8	55.3	41.2	44.9	80.0	78.8
September	44.5	40.2	55.7	39.8	63.4	21.9	50.3	55.6	42.1	45.0	80.1	78.7
October	44.5	40.2	56.2	40.3	63.8	22.0	50.3	55.7	42.3	44.7	80.0	78.6
November	45.2	40.7	57.2	41.5	64.5	22.7	50.0	55.9	42.5	45.3	81.0	79.4
December	45.6	41.1	57.7	42.5	64.8	23.1	49.1	56.2	42.9	45.8	81.6	80.0
1977												
January	45.4	41.0	57.6	42.4	64.7	23.1	48.4	55.3	42.8	45.4	80.9	79.6
February	46.1	41.7	58.3	42.9	65.5	23.6	48.3	56.5	43.3	46.1	81.9	80.7
March	46.6	42.3	58.3	44.1	64.8	24.0	47.3	57.7	43.6	47.0	82.8	81.7
April	47.1	42.8	58.7	44.4	65.2	24.4	47.5	59.2	44.1	47.4	83.4	82.4
May	47.5	43.1	58.8	44.7	65.1	24.9	47.5	60.0	44.5	47.7	83.8	82.9
June	47.8	43.5	59.2	45.5	65.2	25.4	47.4	60.5	44.9	47.9	84.2	83.3
July	47.9	43.5	59.4	45.5	65.4	25.6	47.3	60.5	45.1	47.9	84.1	83.1
August	47.9	43.7	59.4	45.6	65.5	25.6	47.0	61.0	45.4	47.8	84.0	83.3
September	48.2	43.8	59.5	45.8	65.5	25.8	47.0	60.8	45.5	48.2	84.1	83.1
October	48.3	43.9	60.1	45.8	66.4	25.7	42.9	60.8	45.5	48.4	84.1	83.1
November	48.3	44.0	60.1	45.7	66.4	25.7	42.5	61.1	45.5	48.5	83.9	83.0
December	48.4	44.4	60.6	46.0	67.1	26.1	45.4	61.7	45.9	48.0	83.7	83.6

Table 2-4A. Industrial Production and Capacity Utilization, Historical Data, 1947–2011—*Continued*

(Seasonally adjusted.)

Year and month	Production indexes, 2007 = 100										Capacity utilization (output as percentage of capacity)	
			Market groups									
	Total industry	Manufacturing (SIC)	Consumer goods			Business equipment	Defense and space equipment	Construction supplies	Business supplies	Materials	Total industry	Manufacturing (SIC)
			Total	Durable	Nondurable							
1978												
January	47.7	43.8	59.1	43.6	66.2	25.5	45.9	60.5	45.8	47.6	82.4	82.1
February	47.9	44.0	60.1	44.7	67.1	26.2	43.5	60.4	45.9	47.4	82.6	82.2
March	48.9	44.7	61.2	46.0	68.1	26.9	47.4	61.5	46.6	48.2	83.9	83.4
April	49.8	45.4	61.6	46.9	68.2	27.5	47.2	62.9	46.7	49.6	85.3	84.4
May	50.0	45.6	61.2	46.2	68.0	27.6	47.4	62.8	47.0	50.1	85.4	84.4
June	50.4	45.9	61.6	46.4	68.4	28.0	48.0	63.4	47.4	50.3	85.7	84.8
July	50.4	45.9	61.2	46.5	67.8	28.3	47.9	63.3	47.3	50.3	85.5	84.5
August	50.5	46.1	61.2	46.3	67.9	28.8	48.5	63.4	47.3	50.5	85.5	84.7
September	50.7	46.3	61.3	46.0	68.2	29.1	48.5	63.6	47.4	50.5	85.5	84.8
October	51.1	46.7	61.2	46.1	68.1	29.7	48.0	64.2	47.7	51.1	86.0	85.2
November	51.5	47.1	61.4	46.3	68.2	30.2	47.7	64.6	47.9	51.5	86.4	85.7
December	51.8	47.5	61.5	46.4	68.4	30.6	48.4	65.7	48.3	51.7	86.7	86.1
1979												
January	51.4	47.1	61.4	46.7	67.9	30.9	48.7	64.0	48.3	51.0	85.9	85.1
February	51.7	47.3	61.0	46.2	67.7	31.2	49.8	64.5	48.8	51.5	86.1	85.2
March	51.9	47.5	61.3	46.1	68.1	31.5	49.3	65.3	49.0	51.5	86.2	85.4
April	51.3	46.8	60.2	43.8	67.8	30.9	48.1	64.2	48.7	51.2	85.0	83.8
May	51.7	47.3	60.5	45.1	67.6	31.6	48.9	64.6	48.9	51.5	85.5	84.6
June	51.7	47.4	60.3	44.6	67.5	31.8	49.3	64.9	48.6	51.5	85.3	84.5
July	51.6	47.5	59.8	44.0	67.1	32.1	50.2	64.9	48.7	51.4	85.0	84.4
August	51.3	46.9	59.1	42.1	67.3	31.7	50.9	64.3	48.9	51.1	84.2	83.1
September	51.4	47.0	59.5	43.6	66.9	32.6	51.3	64.4	48.3	50.8	84.1	83.1
October	51.6	47.2	59.6	43.4	67.3	32.2	52.9	64.8	48.8	51.3	84.4	83.2
November	51.6	47.0	59.5	42.7	67.5	32.2	54.1	64.7	49.0	51.2	84.2	82.8
December	51.6	47.2	59.5	42.5	67.7	32.4	55.2	65.0	49.0	51.1	84.0	82.8
1980												
January	51.8	47.3	59.2	41.7	67.7	32.9	55.9	64.7	48.6	51.5	84.2	82.9
February	51.9	47.3	59.5	41.4	68.3	33.1	58.2	63.8	48.7	51.3	84.1	82.7
March	51.7	47.0	59.1	40.7	68.1	32.9	58.8	63.0	48.6	51.3	83.7	81.9
April	50.7	46.0	58.2	39.0	67.7	32.5	59.3	60.1	47.8	50.1	81.9	80.0
May	49.4	44.6	56.9	36.5	67.3	32.0	59.6	57.6	46.8	48.6	79.7	77.4
June	48.8	44.0	56.7	35.9	67.3	31.6	60.3	56.5	46.3	47.8	78.5	76.1
July	48.5	43.5	56.7	35.9	67.4	31.7	60.9	56.1	46.5	47.0	77.8	75.2
August	48.6	43.8	56.9	36.2	67.5	31.6	61.1	56.8	46.7	47.1	77.9	75.5
September	49.4	44.5	57.4	37.8	67.3	32.2	61.1	58.3	47.4	48.1	79.0	76.5
October	50.0	45.3	57.8	38.5	67.5	32.8	62.1	59.5	47.4	48.8	79.8	77.6
November	50.9	46.2	58.1	39.5	67.3	33.4	62.9	60.7	48.0	49.9	81.0	78.9
December	51.2	46.3	58.1	38.9	67.6	33.4	63.1	60.7	48.5	50.4	81.3	78.9
1981												
January	50.9	46.2	58.1	38.8	67.8	33.5	62.8	60.6	48.6	49.8	80.6	78.4
February	50.7	45.9	58.0	38.6	67.7	33.2	62.6	60.0	48.1	49.6	80.1	77.7
March	51.0	46.1	58.0	39.2	67.3	33.5	62.7	60.2	48.1	49.9	80.3	77.7
April	50.7	46.3	58.1	39.7	67.2	33.8	62.7	60.2	48.4	49.3	79.7	77.9
May	51.0	46.6	58.7	40.3	67.8	33.8	63.2	60.2	49.0	49.5	80.0	78.1
June	51.3	46.3	58.3	39.9	67.3	33.7	63.7	59.3	49.2	50.2	80.2	77.5
July	51.6	46.4	58.7	40.1	67.9	33.7	64.4	59.4	49.4	50.5	80.5	77.4
August	51.6	46.4	58.7	39.9	68.0	33.7	65.3	59.2	49.2	50.5	80.3	77.3
September	51.3	46.2	58.2	39.0	67.8	33.7	66.5	58.8	49.2	50.1	79.6	76.7
October	50.9	45.8	58.6	38.8	68.5	33.6	68.0	57.1	48.8	49.4	78.8	75.8
November	50.4	45.2	58.5	38.1	68.8	33.1	69.8	56.2	48.6	48.6	77.8	74.7
December	49.8	44.5	57.9	36.5	68.9	32.6	71.5	55.1	48.6	47.9	76.7	73.3
1982												
January	48.8	43.4	56.9	35.5	68.0	31.3	70.9	53.3	47.8	47.1	75.0	71.4
February	49.8	44.6	58.4	36.8	69.5	32.4	74.8	55.1	48.8	47.6	76.4	73.1
March	49.4	44.2	58.0	36.7	69.0	31.9	75.9	54.0	48.6	47.3	75.6	72.4
April	49.0	43.9	58.0	37.4	68.6	31.5	76.9	53.6	48.4	46.7	74.8	71.8
May	48.7	43.9	58.1	37.4	68.6	31.4	78.3	53.9	48.1	46.2	74.2	71.6
June	48.5	43.8	58.4	37.7	69.0	30.8	78.7	53.4	48.1	46.0	73.9	71.3
July	48.4	43.8	58.5	37.8	69.1	30.7	79.8	53.3	48.1	45.7	73.5	71.1
August	48.0	43.4	58.5	37.4	69.2	30.0	79.7	53.4	48.1	45.3	72.8	70.5
September	47.8	43.3	58.4	36.8	69.5	29.8	80.6	53.5	48.2	45.0	72.5	70.2
October	47.4	42.8	58.5	36.3	69.9	29.2	80.2	52.8	48.0	44.5	71.8	69.3
November	47.2	42.5	58.4	36.3	69.7	29.1	80.6	52.4	48.0	44.3	71.5	68.8
December	46.9	42.4	57.6	36.2	68.5	29.4	80.0	52.0	47.8	43.9	70.9	68.5
1983												
January	47.8	43.4	58.8	37.8	69.5	29.5	79.5	53.9	48.4	44.9	72.2	70.1
February	47.5	43.4	58.1	37.7	68.4	29.3	78.1	53.7	48.3	44.8	71.7	70.0
March	47.9	43.8	58.3	38.2	68.5	29.6	78.2	54.3	49.1	45.2	72.3	70.7
April	48.4	44.3	59.5	39.1	69.8	29.7	77.5	55.0	49.6	45.7	73.2	71.4
May	48.8	44.8	59.8	39.9	69.7	30.0	77.3	56.1	49.7	46.1	73.7	72.3
June	49.0	45.2	59.9	40.5	69.5	30.2	76.6	57.1	49.9	46.4	74.0	72.8
July	49.8	45.8	60.7	41.5	70.2	30.8	77.6	58.3	50.6	47.1	75.1	73.8
August	50.3	46.2	61.3	42.3	70.6	31.1	78.1	58.4	51.1	47.7	75.9	74.4
September	51.1	47.0	62.1	43.0	71.4	31.9	78.9	59.2	52.0	48.4	77.0	75.7
October	51.5	47.6	61.7	43.6	70.5	32.3	79.9	60.1	52.2	49.1	77.6	76.5
November	51.7	47.7	61.7	43.6	70.5	32.5	80.3	59.9	52.4	49.3	77.8	76.7
December	51.9	47.9	61.8	44.6	70.0	32.9	81.2	60.1	52.5	49.5	78.1	76.8

Table 2-4A. Industrial Production and Capacity Utilization, Historical Data, 1947–2011—*Continued*

(Seasonally adjusted.)

Year and month	Production indexes, 2007 = 100									Capacity utilization (output as percentage of capacity)	
	Total industry	Manufac-turing (SIC)	Market groups								Total industry	Manufac-turing (SIC)
			Consumer goods			Business equipment	Defense and space equipment	Construction supplies	Business supplies	Materials		
			Total	Durable	Nondurable							
1984												
January	53.0	48.7	63.1	45.6	71.4	33.7	83.5	60.5	53.5	50.6	79.6	78.1
February	53.2	49.3	62.9	45.8	71.1	34.0	85.2	62.0	53.6	50.9	79.9	78.9
March	53.5	49.5	63.2	45.9	71.4	34.3	85.6	61.5	54.1	51.1	80.2	79.1
April	53.8	49.8	63.4	45.8	71.7	34.6	87.8	61.9	54.1	51.4	80.5	79.4
May	54.1	49.9	63.1	45.4	71.6	34.8	88.6	62.1	54.8	51.8	80.8	79.4
June	54.3	50.1	63.0	45.5	71.4	35.2	89.8	62.5	55.1	51.9	80.9	79.6
July	54.5	50.4	63.1	46.0	71.1	35.7	89.0	62.3	55.3	52.1	81.0	79.8
August	54.5	50.4	62.7	46.3	70.4	36.1	91.9	62.6	55.4	52.0	80.9	79.7
September	54.4	50.3	62.6	45.6	70.6	36.3	94.0	62.8	55.3	51.8	80.6	79.4
October	54.3	50.5	63.1	45.3	71.6	36.5	94.7	62.5	55.6	51.3	80.3	79.4
November	54.5	50.7	63.3	46.0	71.5	36.8	94.0	62.5	55.9	51.5	80.4	79.5
December	54.6	50.9	63.6	46.5	71.7	37.1	95.8	63.1	55.5	51.4	80.3	79.5
1985												
January	54.5	50.7	63.2	45.9	71.3	36.9	96.2	62.0	55.6	51.4	79.9	79.0
February	54.7	50.5	63.6	45.5	72.3	36.6	97.1	62.1	56.1	51.6	80.0	78.5
March	54.8	50.9	63.5	46.0	71.9	37.0	98.6	63.8	56.0	51.5	79.9	78.9
April	54.7	50.8	63.2	45.4	71.7	36.7	98.9	63.8	56.3	51.5	79.5	78.4
May	54.7	50.8	63.3	45.4	71.8	36.8	99.4	64.0	56.5	51.5	79.4	78.2
June	54.7	50.9	63.5	45.3	72.3	36.9	100.8	64.4	56.2	51.4	79.3	78.2
July	54.4	50.6	63.2	45.3	71.8	36.6	99.9	64.1	55.7	51.0	78.6	77.5
August	54.6	50.9	63.5	45.8	72.0	36.7	101.6	64.2	56.3	51.1	78.7	77.8
September	54.8	51.0	63.9	45.8	72.6	36.6	102.3	64.2	56.7	51.4	78.9	77.7
October	54.6	50.8	63.8	45.6	72.6	36.5	103.3	64.3	56.2	51.1	78.5	77.4
November	54.8	51.1	64.1	46.7	72.4	36.9	104.6	64.3	56.4	51.2	78.6	77.7
December	55.4	51.4	64.9	46.8	73.5	36.8	105.6	64.1	57.2	51.9	79.3	78.0
1986												
January	55.6	51.9	65.6	48.0	73.9	36.8	106.3	65.5	57.6	51.9	79.6	78.8
February	55.2	51.6	65.0	47.6	73.2	36.4	104.8	64.8	57.1	51.7	78.9	78.2
March	54.9	51.5	64.8	47.7	72.9	36.4	105.8	65.1	56.9	51.2	78.4	77.9
April	54.9	51.7	65.2	47.6	73.5	36.2	106.0	65.7	57.4	51.1	78.4	78.2
May	55.0	51.8	65.6	47.7	74.0	36.1	106.4	66.1	57.8	51.1	78.4	78.3
June	54.8	51.6	65.6	48.3	73.8	35.7	106.9	65.3	58.3	50.8	78.1	77.9
July	55.2	51.9	66.1	48.9	74.2	35.9	107.9	65.8	58.3	51.2	78.5	78.3
August	55.1	52.0	66.0	49.1	73.9	36.0	107.7	66.4	58.3	50.9	78.3	78.4
September	55.2	52.1	66.1	49.5	73.8	36.0	107.4	66.5	58.4	51.1	78.3	78.4
October	55.4	52.3	66.3	49.5	74.2	35.9	107.7	66.4	58.8	51.4	78.6	78.6
November	55.7	52.6	66.8	50.2	74.6	36.0	108.3	66.6	58.9	51.6	78.9	78.9
December	56.2	53.0	67.4	51.1	75.0	36.4	108.4	67.0	59.7	52.0	79.4	79.4
1987												
January	56.0	52.8	66.8	50.8	74.1	36.5	108.8	67.8	59.3	51.9	79.0	79.0
February	56.7	53.6	67.6	51.7	74.9	37.3	109.3	69.0	59.7	52.5	79.9	79.9
March	56.8	53.7	67.8	51.4	75.4	37.2	109.2	68.6	60.1	52.7	79.9	79.8
April	57.2	54.0	67.7	51.1	75.5	37.5	109.3	69.0	60.7	53.1	80.2	80.0
May	57.5	54.4	68.2	51.4	76.1	37.8	109.0	69.5	61.4	53.4	80.6	80.4
June	57.8	54.6	68.4	50.9	76.6	38.2	108.6	69.8	61.7	53.8	80.8	80.5
July	58.2	55.0	68.8	50.7	77.3	38.3	108.2	70.0	62.1	54.2	81.2	80.8
August	58.6	55.2	69.2	51.2	77.7	38.8	109.3	70.5	62.3	54.5	81.6	81.1
September	58.8	55.6	68.9	51.7	76.9	39.4	109.5	70.8	62.5	54.8	81.7	81.4
October	59.7	56.5	70.1	53.4	77.9	40.3	109.2	71.9	63.0	55.5	82.8	82.5
November	60.0	56.8	70.2	53.3	78.0	40.7	109.8	71.9	63.0	56.1	83.1	82.9
December	60.3	57.1	70.3	52.9	78.4	41.1	110.6	72.5	63.1	56.3	83.4	83.3
1988												
January	60.3	57.0	70.7	52.7	79.0	41.2	113.0	71.3	63.4	56.1	83.4	83.0
February	60.5	57.2	71.0	52.7	79.5	41.4	111.3	71.9	63.8	56.3	83.6	83.1
March	60.7	57.3	70.9	53.2	79.2	41.8	110.5	72.2	63.8	56.5	83.8	83.3
April	61.0	57.8	71.4	54.4	79.2	42.3	109.5	72.0	63.8	56.9	84.2	84.0
May	61.0	57.8	71.1	54.4	78.8	42.5	109.5	72.1	63.3	56.9	84.1	83.9
June	61.1	57.8	71.1	54.6	78.7	42.9	108.6	71.6	63.5	57.1	84.3	84.0
July	61.2	57.9	71.1	53.3	79.3	42.6	109.9	71.7	63.8	57.3	84.4	84.0
August	61.5	57.9	71.6	53.9	79.9	42.7	109.7	71.2	64.4	57.5	84.7	84.0
September	61.2	58.1	71.1	54.9	78.5	43.1	110.0	71.4	63.9	57.2	84.3	84.2
October	61.6	58.4	71.7	55.4	79.2	43.4	110.2	71.7	64.2	57.4	84.7	84.6
November	61.7	58.5	71.7	56.0	78.9	43.5	110.0	72.0	64.2	57.6	84.8	84.7
December	61.9	58.8	72.1	56.6	79.1	43.6	110.5	72.1	64.4	57.9	85.1	85.0
1989												
January	62.1	59.2	72.1	58.0	78.4	44.1	110.6	73.3	64.4	58.0	85.2	85.6
February	61.8	58.7	72.1	57.3	78.8	43.9	110.5	71.5	64.6	57.6	84.7	84.6
March	62.0	58.6	72.3	56.4	79.6	43.7	109.7	71.7	65.3	57.8	84.8	84.4
April	62.0	58.7	72.1	56.8	79.1	44.4	111.3	71.7	64.8	57.8	84.7	84.4
May	61.6	58.2	71.4	55.5	78.7	43.7	111.7	71.1	64.5	57.6	84.0	83.5
June	61.7	58.4	71.5	54.9	79.1	44.4	111.5	71.2	64.8	57.3	83.9	83.5
July	61.1	57.7	69.9	53.1	77.7	43.9	112.0	71.2	64.3	57.1	82.9	82.4
August	61.6	58.2	71.1	55.1	78.4	44.5	112.5	71.2	64.5	57.3	83.4	82.8
September	61.4	58.0	70.8	55.0	78.0	44.4	111.8	71.1	64.7	57.2	83.0	82.5
October	61.4	58.0	71.0	54.0	78.9	43.7	107.7	71.3	64.8	57.3	82.8	82.1
November	61.5	58.0	71.3	54.4	79.1	43.9	106.1	71.4	65.1	57.4	82.8	82.0
December	61.9	58.1	72.5	55.0	80.6	44.6	108.5	70.5	65.5	57.3	83.1	81.9

Table 2-4A. Industrial Production and Capacity Utilization, Historical Data, 1947–2011—*Continued*

(Seasonally adjusted.)

Year and month	Production indexes, 2007 = 100										Capacity utilization (output as percentage of capacity)	
	Total industry	Manufac-turing (SIC)	Market groups								Total industry	Manufac-turing (SIC)
			Consumer goods			Business equipment	Defense and space equipment	Construction supplies	Business supplies	Materials		
			Total	Durable	Nondurable							
1990												
January	61.6	58.0	71.0	52.1	79.8	44.3	109.0	72.1	66.0	57.2	82.5	81.6
February	62.1	58.8	71.8	55.2	79.4	45.0	108.8	72.4	65.8	57.7	83.0	82.5
March	62.4	59.1	72.3	56.2	79.6	45.7	108.2	72.2	66.2	57.9	83.3	82.7
April	62.4	58.9	72.0	55.0	79.9	45.6	107.5	71.5	66.3	57.9	83.0	82.3
May	62.5	59.1	72.0	55.5	79.5	46.0	106.5	71.1	66.6	58.1	83.0	82.3
June	62.7	59.2	72.7	56.2	80.3	46.0	106.2	71.3	66.4	58.2	83.1	82.3
July	62.6	59.1	72.2	54.9	80.2	46.3	106.9	70.7	66.7	58.1	82.9	82.1
August	62.8	59.3	72.3	54.6	80.5	46.4	105.3	70.7	66.6	58.5	82.9	82.1
September	62.9	59.3	73.0	54.9	81.4	46.5	104.9	70.4	66.7	58.4	83.0	81.9
October	62.4	58.8	71.9	53.1	80.7	46.2	105.2	69.6	66.6	58.1	82.2	81.1
November	61.7	58.1	71.1	50.4	80.9	45.1	103.4	69.6	66.3	57.4	81.1	80.0
December	61.2	57.7	70.6	49.5	80.6	44.7	104.6	69.2	65.8	56.9	80.4	79.3
1991												
January	61.0	57.2	71.0	49.7	81.1	44.5	103.4	66.6	65.6	56.6	79.9	78.5
February	60.6	56.9	70.3	48.5	80.7	44.3	102.4	66.4	65.1	56.3	79.3	77.9
March	60.3	56.5	70.4	48.8	80.7	44.3	101.8	65.5	64.3	55.9	78.8	77.3
April	60.3	56.7	70.3	49.8	80.0	44.2	99.0	66.0	64.7	56.1	78.8	77.4
May	61.0	57.1	71.6	50.8	81.5	44.5	97.1	66.1	65.3	56.6	79.5	77.8
June	61.6	57.7	72.7	52.1	82.3	45.1	97.6	67.3	65.7	57.0	80.2	78.6
July	61.6	57.8	72.2	52.9	81.3	45.1	96.8	67.0	65.2	57.4	80.1	78.7
August	61.6	58.0	72.3	52.1	81.7	45.0	97.4	67.8	65.6	57.4	80.1	78.8
September	62.2	58.6	73.3	54.2	82.2	45.7	97.1	68.1	65.9	57.7	80.7	79.5
October	62.0	58.5	73.1	53.9	82.0	45.2	97.3	67.3	65.8	57.8	80.5	79.3
November	62.0	58.3	73.1	54.0	82.1	45.2	96.6	67.9	65.9	57.6	80.3	79.0
December	61.7	58.3	72.2	53.5	80.9	45.4	95.8	67.9	65.8	57.6	79.9	78.8
1992												
January	61.4	57.9	71.5	51.2	81.0	44.4	94.5	68.1	65.7	57.5	79.3	78.2
February	61.8	58.4	72.2	53.3	81.0	45.5	93.9	68.6	65.7	57.8	79.8	78.7
March	62.3	59.0	72.9	54.5	81.5	45.8	93.5	68.9	66.2	58.3	80.3	79.3
April	62.8	59.3	73.6	55.5	82.0	46.3	91.8	69.5	66.7	58.7	80.7	79.6
May	63.0	59.7	74.1	57.3	81.8	46.8	91.4	70.2	66.8	58.7	80.8	79.9
June	63.0	59.9	73.6	56.5	81.5	46.9	91.3	69.8	66.7	59.0	80.7	79.9
July	63.5	60.4	74.6	58.0	82.2	47.3	90.3	70.2	67.2	59.4	81.2	80.4
August	63.2	60.1	74.7	57.6	82.5	47.1	90.1	70.5	67.1	58.8	80.6	79.9
September	63.4	60.1	74.3	57.3	82.1	47.2	89.9	70.3	67.4	59.2	80.6	79.7
October	63.8	60.5	75.3	58.5	83.0	47.5	89.7	70.6	67.6	59.5	81.0	80.0
November	64.1	60.8	75.4	58.9	83.0	47.8	89.7	70.3	67.8	59.8	81.2	80.1
December	64.1	60.6	75.5	59.5	82.8	48.0	89.6	70.6	68.1	59.7	81.0	79.8
1993												
January	64.4	61.3	75.8	60.4	82.9	48.4	88.9	70.9	68.1	60.0	81.3	80.4
February	64.7	61.4	75.9	60.2	83.1	48.2	88.3	71.9	68.5	60.4	81.4	80.4
March	64.6	61.2	76.0	60.5	83.0	48.4	87.3	71.4	69.0	60.2	81.3	80.1
April	64.8	61.6	76.1	60.8	83.0	48.8	87.4	71.7	69.0	60.5	81.4	80.4
May	64.6	61.5	75.5	60.9	82.1	48.8	86.4	72.5	68.7	60.3	81.0	80.2
June	64.8	61.5	75.7	60.5	82.7	48.5	85.9	72.4	68.8	60.6	81.1	80.0
July	65.0	61.6	76.4	60.4	83.7	48.5	86.7	72.8	68.9	60.6	81.2	80.1
August	65.0	61.5	76.3	59.9	83.9	48.2	85.2	73.1	69.1	60.7	81.1	79.9
September	65.3	61.9	76.5	61.0	83.6	49.0	85.5	73.5	69.3	60.9	81.4	80.2
October	65.7	62.4	76.9	62.5	83.4	49.9	84.7	74.1	69.4	61.4	81.8	80.8
November	66.0	62.7	76.9	63.0	83.3	50.2	84.6	74.7	69.5	61.8	82.0	81.0
December	66.3	63.0	77.1	63.3	83.4	50.5	83.8	75.6	69.9	62.2	82.3	81.2
1994												
January	66.6	63.2	77.7	64.2	83.8	50.9	83.0	75.4	70.4	62.3	82.5	81.2
February	66.6	63.2	77.8	64.1	84.0	50.4	81.5	74.8	70.4	62.6	82.3	81.1
March	67.3	64.1	78.5	64.7	84.7	51.0	82.5	76.2	71.0	63.3	83.0	82.0
April	67.7	64.6	78.6	65.5	84.5	51.3	82.7	77.3	71.2	63.7	83.2	82.4
May	68.1	65.0	79.1	65.7	85.1	51.4	81.6	78.0	71.3	64.2	83.4	82.8
June	68.5	65.2	79.7	66.3	85.8	51.7	80.5	78.1	72.0	64.6	83.7	82.8
July	68.6	65.5	79.4	66.5	85.2	52.3	80.0	78.8	71.7	64.9	83.6	82.8
August	69.0	66.0	80.2	67.7	85.9	52.4	78.9	78.8	71.8	65.3	83.8	83.2
September	69.2	66.2	79.8	67.8	85.1	52.7	79.6	79.4	72.2	65.6	83.8	83.2
October	69.8	66.9	80.6	68.6	86.0	53.5	79.4	79.8	72.7	66.1	84.2	83.7
November	70.2	67.4	80.6	68.5	86.1	54.0	80.4	79.9	73.0	66.7	84.4	84.0
December	71.0	68.2	81.3	69.3	86.6	54.6	80.3	80.8	73.5	67.7	85.0	84.6
1995												
January	71.1	68.4	81.3	69.9	86.3	55.0	80.5	80.8	73.7	67.9	85.0	84.6
February	71.1	68.3	81.5	69.7	86.8	55.2	79.2	79.8	73.7	67.8	84.6	84.1
March	71.2	68.5	81.5	69.7	86.8	55.6	79.2	79.8	74.0	67.9	84.5	84.0
April	71.2	68.3	81.2	69.4	86.4	55.6	78.8	79.3	73.9	68.0	84.1	83.5
May	71.4	68.4	81.4	68.8	87.0	55.9	78.7	78.8	74.3	68.1	84.0	83.2
June	71.6	68.7	81.8	69.2	87.4	56.7	79.1	78.9	74.6	68.1	84.0	83.3
July	71.3	68.3	81.3	67.8	87.4	56.5	78.4	78.8	74.6	67.8	83.4	82.4
August	72.3	69.1	82.7	70.1	88.3	57.7	78.1	79.4	75.4	68.6	84.1	83.0
September	72.5	69.7	82.7	70.9	88.0	58.2	77.7	80.7	75.4	68.9	84.1	83.3
October	72.4	69.6	82.0	70.1	87.4	57.9	76.7	80.6	75.6	69.1	83.6	82.8
November	72.6	69.6	82.3	70.0	87.8	58.1	74.9	80.7	75.9	69.2	83.5	82.5
December	72.8	69.9	82.5	70.4	87.9	58.4	75.1	81.1	75.9	69.5	83.4	82.3

Table 2-4A. Industrial Production and Capacity Utilization, Historical Data, 1947–2011—*Continued*

(Seasonally adjusted.)

Year and month	Production indexes, 2007 = 100										Capacity utilization (output as percentage of capacity)	
	Total industry	Manufac-turing (SIC)	Market groups								Total industry	Manufac-turing (SIC)
			Consumer goods			Business equipment	Defense and space equipment	Construction supplies	Business supplies	Materials		
			Total	Durable	Nondurable							
1996												
January	72.4	69.3	81.6	68.5	87.4	57.6	74.2	79.8	75.6	69.4	82.5	81.3
February	73.5	70.4	82.9	70.4	88.5	59.2	76.4	80.8	76.5	70.3	83.5	82.2
March	73.4	70.3	82.4	68.2	88.8	59.1	76.6	81.7	76.6	70.3	83.0	81.6
April	74.1	71.1	83.1	71.4	88.4	60.6	76.4	82.2	76.4	70.9	83.4	82.0
May	74.6	71.6	83.3	71.8	88.4	61.5	76.5	82.9	77.2	71.4	83.6	82.2
June	75.3	72.4	84.0	73.5	88.7	62.5	76.0	84.3	77.4	72.1	84.0	82.7
July	75.2	72.6	83.4	74.1	87.5	63.2	76.4	83.8	77.4	72.1	83.5	82.5
August	75.7	73.1	83.3	73.4	87.7	63.8	76.3	84.6	78.2	72.7	83.6	82.6
September	76.1	73.5	84.0	73.4	88.6	64.2	76.3	84.9	78.5	73.0	83.7	82.7
October	76.1	73.5	83.5	72.1	88.6	64.1	75.9	85.0	78.7	73.2	83.3	82.1
November	76.7	74.0	84.5	73.0	89.6	65.0	75.3	85.7	79.4	73.6	83.6	82.3
December	77.2	74.7	84.7	74.2	89.4	66.2	75.3	85.3	79.8	74.1	83.7	82.6
1997												
January	77.2	74.7	84.4	73.7	89.2	66.5	74.2	84.4	80.4	74.4	83.4	82.1
February	78.2	75.7	84.9	74.8	89.3	67.5	74.8	86.0	81.2	75.5	83.9	82.8
March	78.8	76.6	85.5	75.8	89.8	68.7	74.5	87.0	81.5	75.9	84.2	83.3
April	78.8	76.5	84.6	73.7	89.5	69.0	74.6	86.6	81.8	76.3	83.8	82.6
May	79.3	77.2	85.2	74.6	89.9	69.9	74.5	87.2	82.3	76.8	83.9	82.9
June	79.7	77.7	85.3	76.2	89.3	71.0	74.4	87.1	82.6	77.2	83.8	82.9
July	80.2	78.0	85.6	74.9	90.4	71.0	74.9	87.2	83.3	77.9	83.9	82.8
August	81.3	79.3	86.9	78.4	90.7	73.1	75.0	87.8	83.5	78.8	84.5	83.5
September	82.0	80.0	87.7	79.4	91.3	73.5	75.0	88.3	84.5	79.5	84.7	83.7
October	82.5	80.5	88.9	79.7	92.9	74.3	75.2	88.7	85.4	79.6	84.7	83.6
November	83.3	81.4	89.2	81.7	92.4	75.8	74.8	89.1	85.7	80.5	84.9	83.9
December	83.6	81.7	88.7	81.5	91.8	76.2	75.8	90.2	86.0	81.1	84.7	83.6
1998												
January	84.0	82.4	89.1	82.0	92.2	77.1	76.3	90.8	85.9	81.5	84.5	83.7
February	84.0	82.4	88.9	81.8	92.0	77.3	76.8	91.1	86.1	81.5	84.0	83.1
March	84.1	82.3	89.2	82.1	92.2	77.6	76.3	90.5	86.6	81.4	83.5	82.4
April	84.4	82.7	89.6	82.3	92.8	77.8	76.3	90.9	86.9	81.6	83.3	82.2
May	85.0	83.2	90.0	83.0	93.1	78.3	77.2	92.0	87.7	82.3	83.3	82.1
June	84.5	82.6	89.1	79.2	93.4	78.3	77.5	91.8	87.8	81.7	82.4	80.9
July	84.1	82.2	88.2	75.8	93.6	77.7	78.6	92.2	88.3	81.4	81.5	80.0
August	85.9	84.3	90.9	85.3	93.4	80.4	78.9	92.5	88.9	82.9	82.8	81.6
September	85.7	84.0	90.1	84.8	92.3	80.3	78.3	92.2	88.9	82.9	82.1	80.8
October	86.3	84.8	90.5	86.5	92.2	81.3	80.0	93.4	89.1	83.6	82.4	81.1
November	86.3	85.0	89.9	86.2	91.5	81.2	79.9	93.4	89.4	83.7	81.9	80.8
December	86.6	85.4	89.9	86.9	91.1	81.3	79.3	94.6	89.3	84.4	81.8	80.8
1999												
January	86.9	85.6	90.9	87.0	92.5	81.4	79.1	94.0	90.0	84.5	81.8	80.6
February	87.3	86.3	91.1	87.7	92.6	82.0	79.8	94.0	90.1	85.0	81.8	80.8
March	87.5	86.2	91.0	87.4	92.5	81.9	79.5	93.1	90.5	85.6	81.6	80.4
April	87.7	86.6	90.9	88.4	92.0	82.1	78.6	93.3	90.7	86.0	81.5	80.3
May	88.4	87.4	91.8	89.2	92.9	83.3	77.7	93.7	91.2	86.5	81.8	80.7
June	88.2	87.1	90.9	88.7	91.8	83.1	76.5	93.7	91.2	86.9	81.4	80.1
July	88.8	87.5	90.5	88.8	91.3	83.8	76.0	94.4	91.8	88.0	81.6	80.1
August	89.2	88.1	91.7	90.9	92.1	84.2	75.4	94.3	91.9	88.1	81.7	80.3
September	88.9	87.8	91.1	89.8	91.7	84.0	72.9	94.4	91.9	88.0	81.1	79.7
October	90.1	89.1	92.8	92.6	93.0	84.7	72.2	95.5	92.7	89.0	81.9	80.6
November	90.5	89.7	92.7	91.8	93.1	84.6	70.5	96.1	93.2	90.1	82.0	80.7
December	91.2	90.3	93.6	91.9	94.4	85.2	69.4	97.0	93.9	90.7	82.3	80.9
2000												
January	91.3	90.5	92.6	93.7	92.1	86.6	69.4	97.5	94.2	91.1	82.1	80.8
February	91.6	90.7	93.1	93.3	93.1	87.3	67.8	97.7	94.3	91.3	82.1	80.6
March	92.0	91.3	92.8	93.2	92.8	88.1	67.4	97.8	95.0	91.9	82.2	80.8
April	92.6	91.9	93.7	94.2	93.5	89.2	66.3	98.2	96.0	92.2	82.4	81.0
May	92.7	91.7	93.8	93.9	93.8	89.8	65.8	96.6	96.0	92.4	82.2	80.5
June	92.8	91.9	93.9	93.6	94.1	89.9	66.5	96.3	95.8	92.6	82.0	80.3
July	92.6	91.9	93.2	91.2	94.1	90.6	68.0	96.8	95.9	92.1	81.6	80.0
August	92.3	91.3	92.9	91.6	93.5	90.2	66.4	96.1	95.6	92.0	81.1	79.2
September	92.8	91.7	93.9	92.3	94.6	91.4	63.5	96.2	95.5	92.3	81.2	79.3
October	92.3	91.4	93.0	91.3	93.7	91.0	66.7	95.8	95.1	92.0	80.6	78.7
November	92.3	91.0	93.3	89.1	95.0	90.8	68.7	95.5	95.4	91.7	80.4	78.2
December	92.0	90.5	93.8	87.8	96.2	89.9	69.3	94.2	95.1	91.1	79.9	77.4
2001												
January	91.4	89.9	93.1	86.2	95.8	89.7	71.1	94.5	94.8	90.1	79.1	76.7
February	90.8	89.4	92.4	86.1	94.9	89.2	70.8	93.6	93.6	89.7	78.4	76.0
March	90.6	89.1	92.3	87.9	94.0	88.8	72.7	93.7	93.0	89.3	77.9	75.5
April	90.3	88.9	92.7	88.4	94.4	86.8	73.4	93.5	92.5	89.1	77.5	75.1
May	89.6	88.1	92.5	89.0	93.9	85.2	73.6	93.0	91.8	88.3	76.8	74.3
June	89.1	87.5	92.3	88.2	94.0	84.4	74.7	92.3	91.4	87.5	76.1	73.7
July	88.7	87.2	92.1	89.1	93.3	83.6	75.6	92.3	91.4	86.9	75.6	73.2
August	88.4	86.7	92.1	87.6	93.8	82.1	74.6	91.2	91.0	87.0	75.2	72.7
September	88.2	86.5	91.7	87.0	93.5	80.9	75.2	91.2	91.1	86.9	74.8	72.4
October	87.7	86.0	92.1	86.3	94.3	79.3	74.9	90.1	90.5	86.4	74.2	71.8
November	87.2	85.7	91.9	87.6	93.6	78.8	74.1	89.9	89.7	85.8	73.7	71.5
December	87.3	86.0	92.4	89.6	93.6	78.2	73.9	90.7	90.0	85.6	73.6	71.6

Table 2-4A. Industrial Production and Capacity Utilization, Historical Data, 1947–2011—*Continued*

(Seasonally adjusted.)

Year and month	Production indexes, 2007 = 100										Capacity utilization (output as percentage of capacity)	
	Total industry	Manufac-turing (SIC)	Market groups								Total industry	Manufac-turing (SIC)
			Consumer goods			Business equipment	Defense and space equipment	Construction supplies	Business supplies	Materials		
			Total	Durable	Nondurable							
2002												
January	87.8	86.4	93.4	89.7	94.9	78.2	73.5	90.5	89.8	86.3	73.9	71.9
February	87.7	86.3	92.8	90.3	93.8	77.8	73.1	90.9	89.7	86.7	73.8	71.8
March	88.4	87.0	93.7	90.9	94.8	78.2	72.9	92.1	90.8	87.3	74.2	72.3
April	88.8	87.1	93.5	92.3	94.0	77.7	73.0	92.1	91.4	88.3	74.5	72.3
May	89.3	87.7	93.8	92.7	94.3	78.2	73.0	92.6	91.9	88.8	74.8	72.8
June	90.1	88.7	95.0	93.8	95.5	78.8	74.0	93.3	92.5	89.6	75.5	73.6
July	89.8	88.3	94.7	94.5	94.9	77.9	74.0	91.9	92.5	89.5	75.2	73.3
August	89.9	88.6	94.4	94.2	94.4	78.8	74.3	92.4	92.5	89.7	75.3	73.5
September	90.0	88.7	94.6	94.3	94.8	78.5	75.7	93.1	92.9	89.6	75.4	73.6
October	89.7	88.3	94.3	93.2	94.8	78.2	76.2	92.7	93.2	89.0	75.1	73.3
November	90.1	88.7	95.1	95.7	94.8	78.3	75.8	92.7	92.8	89.7	75.5	73.6
December	89.7	88.2	94.1	93.9	94.1	77.7	78.8	92.0	92.6	89.4	75.2	73.2
2003												
January	90.4	88.7	94.7	95.3	94.4	78.0	78.7	92.3	94.2	90.2	75.8	73.7
February	90.7	89.0	95.8	94.4	96.4	78.0	79.8	91.7	94.0	90.2	76.1	73.9
March	90.5	89.1	95.8	94.6	96.4	78.2	79.7	91.5	94.1	89.7	76.0	74.0
April	89.8	88.3	94.9	93.7	95.4	77.4	79.2	90.4	92.8	89.3	75.4	73.3
May	89.8	88.3	94.8	93.8	95.2	77.2	79.8	91.6	93.2	89.2	75.5	73.4
June	89.8	88.7	94.9	94.9	94.9	77.3	80.0	91.9	92.7	89.2	75.5	73.7
July	90.1	88.7	95.7	96.7	95.3	76.8	79.4	91.5	93.3	89.3	75.8	73.8
August	90.0	88.4	95.2	95.5	95.1	77.6	79.4	92.0	93.1	89.3	75.7	73.6
September	90.6	89.1	96.1	98.7	95.1	78.2	79.6	91.7	93.0	89.8	76.2	74.1
October	90.5	89.0	95.1	96.9	94.4	78.1	79.4	92.3	93.3	90.3	76.2	74.1
November	91.2	89.9	95.9	97.9	95.1	79.7	78.8	93.4	93.9	90.7	76.8	74.9
December	91.2	89.7	96.0	98.2	95.2	79.2	76.7	93.2	93.7	90.9	76.8	74.8
2004												
January	91.4	89.8	96.5	99.5	95.4	79.5	74.4	93.4	94.1	91.0	77.0	74.8
February	91.9	90.4	97.0	99.4	96.2	80.5	76.0	93.3	94.9	91.4	77.4	75.4
March	91.4	90.2	95.8	98.1	94.9	80.4	76.2	93.3	93.9	91.2	77.0	75.2
April	91.8	90.6	96.4	98.4	95.7	80.4	76.1	93.2	94.6	91.5	77.3	75.6
May	92.5	91.2	96.9	97.3	96.8	81.2	76.8	94.2	95.3	92.3	77.9	76.1
June	91.7	90.5	95.4	95.2	95.5	81.0	75.8	93.7	94.7	91.7	77.2	75.5
July	92.3	91.3	95.5	95.4	95.6	82.6	77.0	94.8	95.2	92.4	77.8	76.1
August	92.6	91.9	96.2	96.9	96.0	82.5	77.5	94.7	95.2	92.6	78.0	76.6
September	92.5	91.8	96.1	95.9	96.2	82.6	78.5	94.0	95.1	92.6	78.0	76.5
October	93.5	92.7	97.1	98.0	96.7	83.5	78.7	95.5	95.6	93.6	78.7	77.3
November	93.7	92.7	97.0	96.8	97.0	83.0	79.5	95.2	96.0	94.0	78.9	77.1
December	94.3	93.3	97.6	97.9	97.6	83.6	80.2	95.2	96.9	94.7	79.4	77.6
2005												
January	94.8	94.0	98.2	97.4	98.5	84.9	80.1	96.2	97.7	94.8	79.7	78.1
February	95.4	94.8	98.6	99.8	98.2	86.0	83.3	97.0	97.5	95.5	80.2	78.6
March	95.3	94.3	98.4	98.1	98.5	85.6	84.9	96.0	97.7	95.5	80.1	78.1
April	95.3	94.5	98.1	96.8	98.5	86.7	86.5	97.7	97.9	95.3	80.0	78.2
May	95.5	94.9	98.8	97.0	99.3	87.5	86.2	98.0	97.9	95.0	80.1	78.3
June	95.9	95.1	99.5	97.4	100.2	87.3	86.8	97.2	98.3	95.4	80.3	78.3
July	95.7	94.9	99.3	96.3	100.3	87.4	86.2	97.9	98.0	95.2	80.1	78.0
August	95.9	95.2	99.5	98.3	99.9	88.0	87.3	98.2	98.2	95.1	80.1	78.1
September	94.0	94.2	99.6	99.8	99.5	85.6	83.8	99.6	98.2	91.3	78.4	77.1
October	95.2	95.6	99.6	100.8	99.2	90.0	84.8	101.5	98.6	92.5	79.3	78.1
November	96.1	96.3	99.3	99.3	99.3	91.3	84.8	102.1	98.8	94.3	79.9	78.6
December	96.7	96.4	100.0	97.7	100.8	90.6	84.6	103.0	99.3	95.2	80.3	78.5
2006												
January	96.8	97.2	99.0	99.5	98.8	92.0	82.9	103.7	99.1	95.8	80.3	79.1
February	96.9	97.1	98.8	99.0	98.8	92.8	83.7	103.0	99.1	96.0	80.3	78.8
March	97.1	96.9	99.5	99.5	99.5	93.4	81.5	102.6	99.4	95.8	80.4	78.6
April	97.5	97.5	99.7	99.6	99.7	95.3	81.9	102.0	99.5	96.3	80.6	79.0
May	97.4	97.1	99.5	98.9	99.7	95.0	81.5	101.2	99.2	96.3	80.4	78.5
June	97.7	97.4	100.0	99.6	100.1	95.7	81.9	100.7	99.4	96.6	80.5	78.6
July	97.8	97.2	99.3	96.4	100.2	96.9	83.5	101.1	99.5	96.9	80.5	78.4
August	98.0	97.6	99.9	98.4	100.4	97.3	83.6	100.2	99.1	97.0	80.5	78.5
September	97.8	97.6	99.6	97.4	100.3	97.4	84.6	99.9	98.8	96.9	80.2	78.4
October	97.8	97.2	99.6	95.7	100.9	97.5	86.3	98.7	99.1	96.7	79.9	78.0
November	97.6	97.3	99.7	97.0	100.6	97.2	87.9	98.3	98.6	96.5	79.7	77.8
December	98.7	98.8	100.1	99.7	100.2	98.3	89.8	101.6	99.2	97.7	80.3	78.8
2007												
January	98.2	98.3	99.7	97.8	100.3	96.2	91.8	99.5	99.3	97.6	79.8	78.3
February	99.4	98.9	101.3	99.6	101.9	97.5	93.0	100.2	100.5	98.5	80.5	78.5
March	99.4	99.5	100.1	99.4	100.3	99.5	91.9	101.1	100.2	98.8	80.3	78.8
April	100.2	100.2	100.8	101.9	100.5	100.7	94.6	101.0	100.8	99.6	80.8	79.2
May	100.1	100.0	100.3	100.9	100.2	100.2	96.9	100.6	100.2	100.0	80.6	78.8
June	100.1	100.3	100.3	101.7	99.9	99.8	100.0	101.0	100.0	99.9	80.4	78.8
July	100.2	100.5	100.4	101.1	100.2	99.7	101.4	100.5	99.6	100.2	80.4	78.8
August	100.2	100.1	100.2	100.5	100.0	99.5	103.2	99.8	99.9	100.4	80.3	78.2
September	100.7	100.6	100.3	99.5	100.6	101.3	106.0	99.8	100.4	100.8	80.6	78.5
October	100.1	100.1	99.0	99.1	98.9	100.8	105.8	98.7	99.7	100.8	80.1	78.0
November	100.6	100.5	98.9	99.3	98.7	101.9	107.5	98.5	99.9	101.6	80.5	78.2
December	100.7	100.8	98.7	99.2	98.5	103.0	107.8	99.3	99.5	101.7	80.6	78.4

Table 2-4A. Industrial Production and Capacity Utilization, Historical Data, 1947–2011—*Continued*

(Seasonally adjusted.)

Year and month	Production indexes, 2007 = 100										Capacity utilization (output as percentage of capacity)	
			Market groups									
	Total industry	Manufac-turing (SIC)	Consumer goods			Business equipment	Defense and space equipment	Construction supplies	Business supplies	Materials	Total industry	Manufac-turing (SIC)
			Total	Durable	Nondurable							
2008												
January	100.4	100.4	98.4	96.7	98.9	103.4	108.2	98.9	99.5	101.2	80.4	78.0
February	100.3	99.9	98.2	95.8	99.0	104.4	107.7	97.3	99.5	100.9	80.3	77.6
March	99.9	99.5	97.3	94.5	98.2	104.0	107.9	95.8	99.1	101.0	80.1	77.4
April	99.1	98.4	96.7	92.5	98.0	102.0	107.6	94.2	98.1	100.4	79.5	76.5
May	98.6	97.9	96.2	91.8	97.7	102.2	107.1	93.5	97.4	99.8	79.1	76.2
June	98.4	97.3	96.0	91.9	97.4	101.9	108.8	92.4	96.8	99.5	78.9	75.8
July	97.9	96.2	95.0	88.5	97.1	101.4	107.0	92.1	96.1	99.4	78.6	75.1
August	96.2	94.9	93.6	85.9	96.1	97.9	107.6	90.0	95.2	97.7	77.2	74.1
September	92.3	91.6	93.2	85.7	95.6	89.8	105.6	87.8	94.0	91.6	74.0	71.7
October	93.0	91.0	93.4	83.6	96.6	87.1	106.4	86.3	93.6	93.9	74.6	71.4
November	91.9	88.9	92.7	81.2	96.5	88.3	105.7	82.0	91.9	92.5	73.6	69.9
December	89.4	86.0	91.0	77.9	95.4	89.1	104.5	77.7	89.1	89.1	71.6	67.7
2009												
January	87.4	83.6	88.9	70.1	95.1	84.3	104.0	74.8	88.2	87.7	69.9	65.9
February	86.9	83.5	89.1	71.6	94.9	84.1	103.9	73.6	87.1	87.0	69.5	66.0
March	85.4	81.8	88.7	71.7	94.3	81.8	102.1	71.0	85.9	85.3	68.3	64.8
April	84.7	81.2	88.4	72.3	93.7	79.9	101.4	69.5	85.4	84.8	67.7	64.5
May	83.8	80.2	87.1	69.0	93.1	77.9	101.3	69.2	84.8	84.2	67.1	63.9
June	83.5	80.0	86.8	68.6	92.8	77.2	101.3	69.1	84.9	83.8	66.8	63.8
July	84.3	80.9	87.9	74.6	92.3	77.6	102.6	69.1	84.8	84.8	67.5	64.8
August	85.1	81.8	88.7	76.3	92.8	78.6	103.1	69.2	85.2	85.9	68.3	65.6
September	85.7	82.4	89.6	79.0	93.0	78.7	103.9	68.7	85.0	86.6	68.9	66.2
October	85.9	82.3	89.8	77.5	93.8	79.2	102.9	67.7	85.6	86.7	69.1	66.4
November	86.2	83.1	89.2	79.3	92.4	78.9	102.1	68.9	85.5	87.8	69.5	67.2
December	86.6	83.2	89.1	78.3	92.7	80.3	101.3	67.6	86.7	88.3	70.0	67.4
2010												
January	87.4	83.9	89.5	78.8	93.0	81.4	103.1	68.5	86.7	89.5	70.8	68.2
February	87.8	84.0	88.9	77.9	92.6	81.4	103.8	68.7	86.6	90.6	71.3	68.4
March	88.3	84.9	89.0	78.6	92.5	82.7	106.2	70.1	86.4	91.2	71.9	69.3
April	88.7	85.8	88.1	79.0	91.1	84.3	106.9	72.5	86.9	91.8	72.4	70.2
May	90.1	87.0	89.9	81.2	92.8	86.2	107.4	73.0	87.8	93.1	73.7	71.3
June	90.2	87.0	89.7	80.2	92.9	87.0	106.4	73.2	88.0	93.4	73.9	71.4
July	90.9	87.6	90.4	82.8	92.8	88.5	107.9	73.0	88.2	94.0	74.5	72.1
August	91.1	87.6	90.0	80.1	93.2	88.5	108.7	73.7	88.3	94.5	74.8	72.3
September	91.4	87.8	89.8	80.3	92.9	89.3	108.0	73.8	88.0	95.4	75.2	72.5
October	91.1	87.9	90.0	81.8	92.6	88.7	107.7	74.4	87.3	94.7	74.9	72.7
November	91.4	88.0	89.5	80.4	92.5	89.5	107.1	75.1	88.1	95.1	75.2	72.9
December	92.4	88.9	90.7	80.3	94.0	90.3	106.9	74.6	88.5	96.6	76.0	73.7
2011												
January	92.5	89.2	90.7	81.7	93.6	91.3	107.8	74.5	88.1	96.5	76.1	74.0
February	92.3	89.4	90.7	84.0	92.9	92.1	108.6	74.2	88.1	95.9	75.9	74.2
March	93.1	90.0	91.1	85.8	92.8	92.0	108.7	75.2	88.5	97.2	76.5	74.7
April	92.6	89.5	90.8	83.2	93.3	91.4	108.7	75.4	88.1	96.6	76.1	74.3
May	92.9	89.7	91.3	84.0	93.6	92.5	109.4	76.5	88.5	96.5	76.3	74.4
June	93.1	89.7	91.2	83.6	93.7	92.6	107.8	76.6	88.2	96.9	76.3	74.4
July	93.9	90.4	92.2	86.1	94.2	93.0	108.7	77.5	88.9	97.8	77.0	75.0
August	94.2	90.7	92.5	86.8	94.3	94.1	109.7	77.1	89.3	97.8	77.1	75.2
September	94.4	91.1	92.6	87.6	94.2	94.6	109.6	77.1	89.6	98.0	77.2	75.5
October	94.9	91.5	92.9	89.5	94.0	95.9	110.9	77.3	89.3	98.7	77.6	75.8
November	95.1	91.5	92.2	88.1	93.5	96.5	112.3	77.9	88.6	99.4	77.7	75.7
December	95.9	92.9	92.5	89.9	93.4	97.5	111.7	79.8	89.3	100.5	78.3	76.8

Table 2-4B. Industrial Production: Historical Data, 1919–1947

(Seasonally adjusted, 2007 = 100.)

Year and month	January	February	March	April	May	June	July	August	September	October	Novemeber	December	Annual averages
1919													
Industrial production, total ...	4.9	4.6	4.5	4.6	4.6	4.9	5.2	5.3	5.2	5.1	5.0	5.1	4.9
Manufacturing	4.6	4.5	4.3	4.4	4.4	4.7	5.0	5.1	4.9	4.8	5.0	4.9	4.7
1920													
Industrial production, total ..	5.6	5.6	5.5	5.2	5.3	5.4	5.3	5.3	5.1	4.9	4.5	4.2	5.1
Manufacturing	5.4	5.4	5.3	4.9	5.1	5.1	4.9	4.9	4.8	4.6	4.1	3.8	4.9
1921													
Industrial production, total ..	4.0	3.9	3.8	3.8	3.9	3.9	3.8	4.0	4.0	4.2	4.2	4.2	4.0
Manufacturing	3.6	3.6	3.5	3.5	3.6	3.6	3.6	3.7	3.8	4.0	4.0	4.0	3.7
1922													
Industrial production, total ..	4.3	4.5	4.7	4.6	4.8	5.1	5.1	5.0	5.2	5.5	5.8	5.9	5.0
Manufacturing	4.1	4.2	4.3	4.5	4.8	5.0	5.0	4.9	5.0	5.2	5.4	5.6	4.8
1923													
Industrial production, total ..	5.8	5.9	6.1	6.2	6.3	6.2	6.2	6.1	5.9	5.9	5.9	5.8	6.0
Manufacturing	5.5	5.5	5.8	5.8	6.0	5.9	5.8	5.6	5.6	5.5	5.5	5.5	5.7
1924													
Industrial production, total ...	5.9	6.0	5.9	5.7	5.5	5.2	5.1	5.3	5.5	5.7	5.8	5.9	5.6
Manufacturing	5.5	5.7	5.6	5.4	5.2	4.9	4.8	5.0	5.2	5.3	5.5	5.6	5.3
1925													
Industrial production, total ..	6.1	6.1	6.1	6.2	6.1	6.1	6.2	6.1	6.1	6.3	6.4	6.5	6.2
Manufacturing	5.8	5.8	5.9	5.9	5.8	5.8	5.9	5.8	5.8	6.1	6.2	6.4	5.9
1926													
Industrial production, total ..	6.4	6.4	6.5	6.5	6.4	6.5	6.5	6.6	6.7	6.7	6.7	6.7	6.6
Manufacturing	6.2	6.2	6.2	6.2	6.1	6.2	6.2	6.3	6.4	6.3	6.3	6.3	6.2
1927													
Industrial production, total ..	6.6	6.7	6.8	6.6	6.7	6.6	6.6	6.6	6.5	6.3	6.3	6.4	6.6
Manufacturing	6.2	6.3	6.3	6.3	6.3	6.3	6.3	6.2	6.1	6.0	6.0	6.1	6.2
1928													
Industrial production, total ..	6.5	6.5	6.6	6.6	6.6	6.7	6.8	6.9	7.0	7.1	7.2	7.4	6.8
Manufacturing	6.2	6.3	6.3	6.3	6.4	6.4	6.5	6.7	6.7	6.8	7.0	7.1	6.6
1929													
Industrial production, total ..	7.5	7.4	7.5	7.6	7.7	7.8	7.9	7.8	7.8	7.6	7.3	6.9	7.6
Manufacturing	7.1	7.1	7.2	7.3	7.4	7.5	7.6	7.5	7.4	7.3	6.9	6.5	7.2
1930													
Industrial production, total ..	6.9	6.9	6.8	6.8	6.6	6.5	6.2	6.0	5.9	5.8	5.6	5.5	6.3
Manufacturing	6.6	6.5	6.3	6.4	6.3	6.1	5.8	5.6	5.6	5.4	5.2	5.1	5.9
1931													
Industrial production, total ..	5.5	5.5	5.6	5.6	5.5	5.4	5.3	5.1	4.9	4.7	4.7	4.6	5.2
Manufacturing	5.1	5.2	5.3	5.3	5.2	5.0	4.9	4.8	4.6	4.3	4.3	4.3	4.8
1932													
Industrial production, total ..	4.5	4.4	4.3	4.0	3.9	3.8	3.7	3.8	4.0	4.2	4.2	4.1	4.1
Manufacturing	4.2	4.1	3.9	3.7	3.6	3.5	3.4	3.5	3.7	3.8	3.8	3.7	3.7
1933													
Industrial production, total ..	4.0	4.0	3.8	4.0	4.7	5.4	5.9	5.7	5.4	5.1	4.8	4.9	4.8
Manufacturing	3.7	3.6	3.4	3.7	4.4	5.1	5.6	5.3	5.0	4.8	4.4	4.5	4.5
1934													
Industrial production, total ..	5.0	5.3	5.5	5.5	5.6	5.5	5.1	5.1	4.8	5.0	5.0	5.4	5.2
Manufacturing	4.6	4.9	5.1	5.2	5.3	5.1	4.7	4.7	4.4	4.6	4.7	5.0	4.9
1935													
Industrial production, total ..	5.8	5.9	5.9	5.8	5.8	5.8	5.8	6.1	6.2	6.4	6.5	6.6	6.0
Manufacturing	5.5	5.6	5.5	5.5	5.4	5.4	5.6	5.8	5.9	6.1	6.2	6.3	5.7
1936													
Industrial production, total ..	6.5	6.4	6.4	6.8	7.0	7.1	7.2	7.3	7.5	7.6	7.8	8.0	7.1
Manufacturing	6.2	6.0	6.1	6.5	6.7	6.8	6.9	7.1	7.2	7.3	7.5	7.7	6.8
1937													
Industrial production, total ..	8.0	8.1	8.3	8.3	8.3	8.2	8.3	8.2	8.0	7.4	6.6	6.1	7.8
Manufacturing	7.7	7.9	7.9	8.0	8.1	7.9	8.0	7.9	7.6	7.0	6.1	5.5	7.5
1938													
Industrial production, total ..	5.9	5.9	5.9	5.8	5.6	5.7	6.0	6.3	6.5	6.7	6.9	7.0	6.2
Manufacturing	5.4	5.4	5.4	5.2	5.2	5.2	5.5	5.9	6.1	6.3	6.6	6.6	5.7

Table 2-4B. Industrial Production: Historical Data, 1919–1947—*Continued*

(Seasonally adjusted, 2007 = 100.)

Year and month	January	February	March	April	May	June	July	August	September	October	Novemeber	December	Annual averages
1939													
Industrial production, total	7.0	7.1	7.1	7.1	7.0	7.2	7.4	7.5	8.0	8.4	8.6	8.6	7.6
Products	7.1	7.1	7.2	7.2	7.2	7.3	7.4	7.5	7.8	8.0	8.1	8.2	7.5
Consumer goods	10.6	10.6	10.7	10.7	10.8	10.9	11.0	11.1	11.2	11.3	11.4	11.5	11.0
Materials	6.7	6.8	6.8	6.6	6.6	6.9	7.2	7.3	8.1	8.9	9.0	9.0	7.5
Manufacturing	6.3	6.3	6.3	6.3	6.3	6.4	6.6	6.8	7.2	7.6	7.7	7.8	6.8
1940													
Industrial production, total	8.5	8.2	8.0	8.2	8.4	8.7	8.8	8.9	9.1	9.2	9.4	9.7	8.8
Products	8.1	8.0	7.9	8.0	8.1	8.3	8.3	8.4	8.7	8.8	9.0	9.3	8.4
Consumer goods	11.4	11.4	11.3	11.3	11.4	11.5	11.5	11.5	11.8	12.0	12.2	12.6	11.7
Materials	8.8	8.3	8.0	8.2	8.6	9.1	9.3	9.3	9.4	9.5	9.6	9.8	9.0
Manufacturing	7.7	7.5	7.3	7.4	7.7	8.0	8.1	8.2	8.4	8.5	8.7	9.0	8.0
1941													
Industrial production, total	10.0	10.3	10.6	10.6	11.1	11.2	11.3	11.4	11.4	11.5	11.6	11.8	11.1
Products	9.6	9.9	10.1	10.3	10.7	10.8	10.9	11.0	11.0	11.1	11.2	11.3	10.7
Consumer goods	12.9	13.2	13.6	13.8	14.2	14.3	14.3	14.3	14.2	14.2	14.3	14.3	14.0
Materials	10.3	10.5	10.9	10.7	11.3	11.5	11.5	11.7	11.7	11.7	11.8	11.9	11.3
Manufacturing	9.2	9.5	9.7	10.0	10.3	10.4	10.6	10.6	10.6	10.7	10.7	10.9	10.3
1942													
Industrial production, total	12.0	12.2	12.4	12.0	12.1	12.1	12.4	12.8	13.1	13.5	13.8	14.1	12.7
Products	11.7	12.0	12.1	11.3	11.4	11.4	11.7	12.1	12.5	13.0	13.4	13.8	12.2
Consumer goods	14.6	14.4	14.4	12.4	12.3	12.1	12.2	12.3	12.4	12.6	12.7	12.9	12.9
Materials	12.1	12.3	12.4	12.8	12.7	12.8	13.0	13.4	13.5	13.9	14.1	14.3	13.1
Manufacturing	11.1	11.4	11.6	11.2	11.3	11.3	11.7	12.1	12.4	12.9	13.3	13.6	12.0
1943													
Industrial production, total	14.3	14.6	14.7	14.9	15.0	15.0	15.4	15.7	16.1	16.4	16.6	16.4	15.4
Products	13.9	14.2	14.3	14.5	14.6	14.8	15.2	15.5	15.9	16.1	16.4	16.0	15.1
Consumer goods	12.5	12.7	12.7	12.8	13.0	13.2	13.4	13.5	13.6	13.5	13.5	13.2	13.1
Materials	14.5	14.9	15.0	15.1	15.1	14.8	15.3	15.6	16.0	16.3	16.4	16.4	15.4
Manufacturing	13.8	14.1	14.2	14.4	14.5	14.5	14.9	15.2	15.6	15.9	16.1	15.9	14.9
1944													
Industrial production, total	16.6	16.7	16.7	16.7	16.6	16.5	16.5	16.7	16.6	16.6	16.5	16.5	16.6
Products	16.2	16.4	16.4	16.4	16.4	16.5	16.6	16.8	16.7	16.7	16.5	16.3	16.5
Consumer goods	13.3	13.4	13.6	13.7	13.8	13.8	13.9	14.2	13.9	13.9	13.9	13.9	13.8
Materials	16.6	16.7	16.6	16.6	16.3	16.1	15.8	16.0	16.0	16.1	16.1	16.2	16.3
Manufacturing	16.1	16.2	16.2	16.2	16.1	16.0	16.0	16.3	16.2	16.2	16.1	16.1	16.1
1945													
Industrial production, total	16.3	16.2	16.1	15.8	15.4	15.1	14.7	13.2	12.0	11.5	12.0	12.0	14.2
Products	16.2	16.0	15.8	15.5	15.1	14.8	14.5	13.0	11.6	11.3	11.5	11.5	13.9
Consumer goods	14.1	14.0	14.0	14.1	14.1	14.2	14.2	13.6	14.2	14.4	14.8	15.0	14.2
Materials	16.0	16.1	16.2	15.9	15.5	15.1	14.5	13.2	12.2	11.5	12.3	12.5	14.3
Manufacturing	15.9	15.8	15.6	15.3	14.8	14.4	14.0	12.3	11.0	10.5	10.8	11.0	13.4
1946													
Industrial production, total	11.3	10.8	11.9	11.7	11.3	12.0	12.4	12.8	13.1	13.3	13.4	13.5	12.3
Products	11.4	11.3	11.5	11.7	11.6	11.7	12.0	12.4	12.7	12.9	13.1	13.2	12.1
Consumer goods	15.7	16.3	16.2	16.4	16.4	16.5	16.8	17.4	17.7	18.0	18.2	18.3	17.0
Materials	10.9	9.6	12.1	11.3	10.4	11.9	12.6	13.1	13.2	13.4	13.4	13.5	12.1
Manufacturing	10.2	9.6	10.8	10.8	10.3	10.9	11.2	11.7	12.0	12.2	12.4	12.4	11.2
1947													
Industrial production, total	13.6	13.7	13.8	13.7	13.7	13.7	13.6	13.7	13.8	14.0	14.1	14.2	13.8
Products	13.3	13.4	13.4	13.4	13.5	13.4	13.4	13.5	13.6	13.8	14.0	14.1	13.6
Consumer goods	17.9	17.8	17.9	17.8	17.7	17.7	17.8	18.0	18.1	18.4	18.7	18.7	18.1
Materials	13.5	13.6	14.1	13.7	13.8	13.6	13.5	13.5	13.7	13.8	14.1	13.9	13.7
Manufacturing	12.4	12.4	12.5	12.5	12.4	12.4	12.3	12.4	12.4	12.6	12.8	12.8	12.5

NOTES AND DEFINITIONS, CHAPTER 2

TABLES 2-1 THROUGH 2-4
INDUSTRIAL PRODUCTION AND CAPACITY UTILIZATION

SOURCE: BOARD OF GOVERNORS OF THE FEDERAL RESERVE SYSTEM

The *industrial production index* measures changes in the physical volume or quantity of output of manufacturing, mining, and electric and gas utilities. *Capacity utilization* is calculated by dividing a seasonally adjusted industrial production index for an industry or group of industries by a related index of productive capacity.

The index of industrial production is one of the oldest continuous statistical series maintained by the Federal government, and one of the few economic indicators for which monthly data are available before the post-World-War-II period. This edition of *Business Statistics* reprints monthly and annual values for total industrial production and its manufacturing component beginning with January 1919.

On March 25, 2011, a revision of the entire industrial production data system included rebasing all of the indexes from the previous comparison base, 2002 = 100, to 2007 = 100. This affected the levels of all current and historical production indexes, though not necessarily the changes that they record over time.

Around the 15th day of each month, the Federal Reserve issues estimates of industrial production and capacity utilization for the previous month. The production estimates are in the form of index numbers (2007 = 100) that reflect the monthly levels of total output of the nation's factories, mines, and gas and electric utilities expressed as a percent of the monthly average in the 2007 base year. Capacity estimates are expressed as index numbers, 2007 output = 100 (not 2007 capacity), and capacity utilization is measured by the production index as a percent of the capacity index. Since the bases of those two indexes are the same for each industry, this procedure yields production as a percent of capacity. Monthly estimates are subject to revision in subsequent months, as well as to annual and comprehensive revisions in subsequent years. Monthly series are seasonally adjusted using the Census X-12-ARIMA program.

Definitions and notes on the data

The index of industrial production measures a large portion of the goods output of the national economy on a monthly basis. That portion, together with construction, has also accounted for the bulk of the variation in output over the course of many historical business cycles. The substantial industrial detail included in the index illuminates structural developments in the economy.

The total industrial production index and the indexes for its major components are constructed from individual industry series (312 series for data from 1997 forward) based on the 2007 North American Industry Classification System (NAICS). See the Preface to this volume for information on NAICS.

The Federal Reserve has been able to provide a longer continuous historical series on the NAICS basis than some other government agencies. In a major research effort, the Fed and the Census Bureau's Center for Economic Studies re-coded data from seven Censuses of Manufactures, beginning in 1963, to establish benchmark NAICS data for output, value added, and capacity utilization. The resulting indexes are shown annually for the last 39 years (44 years for aggregate levels) in Tables 2-1 through 2-3.

The Fed's featured indexes for total industry and total manufacturing on the Standard Industrial Classification (SIC) basis do <u>not</u> observe the reclassifications under NAICS of the logging industry to the Agriculture sector and the publishing industry to the Information sector. (The reason cited by the Fed was to avoid "changing the scope or historical continuity of these statistics.") One advantage of the SIC index for capacity utilization is that it is a continuous series back to 1948 (shown in Table 2-4A). On the new NAICS basis, production and capacity utilization are shown back to 1972 in Tables 2-2 and 2-3.

The individual series components of the indexes are grouped in two ways: market groups and industry groups.

Market groups. For analyzing market trends and product flows, the individual series are grouped into two major divisions: *final products and nonindustrial supplies* and *materials*. *Final products* consists of products purchased by consumers, businesses, or government for final use. *Nonindustrial supplies* are expected to become inputs in nonindustrial sectors: the two major subgroups are *construction supplies* and *business supplies*. *Materials* comprises industrial output that requires further processing within the industrial sector. This twofold division distinguishes between products that are ready to ship outside the industrial sector and those that will stay within the sector for further processing.

Final products are divided into *consumer goods* and *equipment*, and *equipment* is divided into *business equipment* and *defense and space equipment*. Further subdivisions of each market group are based on type of product and the market destination for the product.

Industry groups are typically groupings by 3-digit NAICS industries and major aggregates of these industries—for example, *durable goods* and *nondurable goods manufacturing*, *mining*, and *utilities*. Indexes are also calculated for *stage-of-process* industry groups—*crude*, *primary and semi-finished*, and *finished* processing. The stage-of-process grouping was a new feature in the 2002 revision, replacing the two narrower and less well-defined "primary processing manufacturing" and "advanced processing manufacturing" groups that were previously published. *Crude processing* consists of logging, much of mining, and certain basic manufacturing activities in the chemical, paper, and metals industries. *Primary and semifinished processing* represents industries that produce materials and parts used as inputs by other industries. *Finished processing* includes industries that produce goods in their finished form for use by consumers, business investment, or government.

The indexes of industrial production are constructed with data from a variety of sources. Current monthly estimates of production are based on measures of physical output where possible and appropriate. For a few high-tech industries, the estimated value of nominal output is deflated by a corresponding price index. For industries in which such direct measurement is not possible on a monthly basis, output is inferred from production-worker hours, adjusted for trends in worker productivity derived from annual and benchmark revisions. (Between the 1960s and 1997, electric power consumption was used as a monthly output indicator for some industries instead of hours. However, the coverage of the electric power consumption survey deteriorated, and in the 2005 revision, the decision was made to resume the use of hours in those industries, beginning with the data for 1997.)

In annual and benchmark revisions, the individual indexes are revised using data from the quinquennial Censuses of Manufactures and Mineral Industries and the Annual Survey of Manufactures and Survey of Plant Capacity, prepared by the Census Bureau; deflators from the Producer Price Indexes and other sources; the *Minerals Yearbook*, prepared by the Department of the Interior; publications from the Department of Energy; and other sources.

The weights used in computing the indexes are based on Census value added—the difference between the value of production and the cost of materials and supplies consumed. Census value added differs in some respects from the economic concept of industry value added used in the national income and product accounts (NIPAs). Industry value added as defined in the NIPAs is not available in sufficient detail for the industrial production indexes. See Chapter 14 for data and a description of NIPA value added (equivalently, gross domestic product) by major industry group.

Before 1972, a linked-Laspeyres formula (base period prices) is used to compute the weighted individual indexes. Beginning with 1972, the index uses a version of the Fisher-ideal index formula—a chain-weighting (updated average price) system similar to that in the NIPAs. See the "General Notes" article at the front of this book and the notes and definitions for Chapter 1 for more information. Chain-weighting keeps the index from being distorted by the use of obsolete relative prices.

For the purpose of these value-added weights, value added per unit of output is based on data from the Censuses of Manufacturing and Mineral Industries, the Census Bureau's Annual Survey of Manufactures, and revenue and expense data reported by the Department of Energy and the Amer-

ican Gas Association, which are projected into recent years by using changes in relevant Producer Price Indexes.

To separate seasonal movements from cyclical patterns and underlying trends, each component of the index is seasonally adjusted by the Census X-12-ARIMA method.

The index does not cover production on farms, in the construction industry, in transportation, or in various trade and service industries. A number of groups and subgroups include data for individual series not published separately.

Capacity utilization is calculated for the manufacturing, mining, and electric and gas utilities industries. Output is measured by seasonally adjusted indexes of industrial production. The capacity indexes attempt to capture the concept of sustainable maximum output, which is defined as the greatest level of output that a plant can maintain within the framework of a realistic work schedule, taking account of normal downtime and assuming sufficient availability of inputs to operate the machinery and equipment in place. The 87 individual industry capacity indexes are based on a variety of data, including capacity data measured in physical units compiled by government agencies and trade associations, Census Bureau surveys of utilization rates and investment, and estimates of growth of the capital stock.

In its monthly release, the Federal Reserve includes the following "Perspective. Over the 1972–2011 period, the average total industry utilization rate is 80.3 percent; for manufacturing, the average factory operating rate has been 78.8 percent. Industrial plants usually operate at capacity utilization rates that are well below 100 percent: none of the broad aggregates has ever reached 100 percent. For total industry and total manufacturing, utilization rates have exceeded 90 percent only in wartime."

Revisions

Revisions normally occur annually. The data shown in this volume are as revised in the annual revision released March 30, 2012, and subsequent updates through May 2012. New data incorporated in this revision include information from the 2010 Annual Survey of Manufactures, new minerals data through 2010, and the Census Quarterly Survey of Plant Capacity through the fourth quarter of 2011.

Data availability

Data are available monthly in Federal Reserve release G.17. Current and historical data and background information are available on the Federal Reserve Web site at <http://www.federalreserve.gov>.

Chain-weighting makes it difficult for the user to analyze in detail the sources of aggregate output change. An "Explanatory Note," included in each month's index release, provides some assistance for the user, including a reference to a an Internet location with the exact contribution of a monthly change in a component index to the monthly change in the total index.

References

The G.17 release each month contains extensive explanatory material, as well as references for further detail.

An earlier detailed description of the industrial production index, together with a history of the index, a glossary of terms, and a bibliography is presented in *Industrial Production—1986 Edition*, available from Publication Services, Mail Stop 127, Board of Governors of the Federal Reserve System, Washington, DC 20551.

CHAPTER 3: INCOME DISTRIBUTION AND POVERTY

Section 3a: Household and Family Income

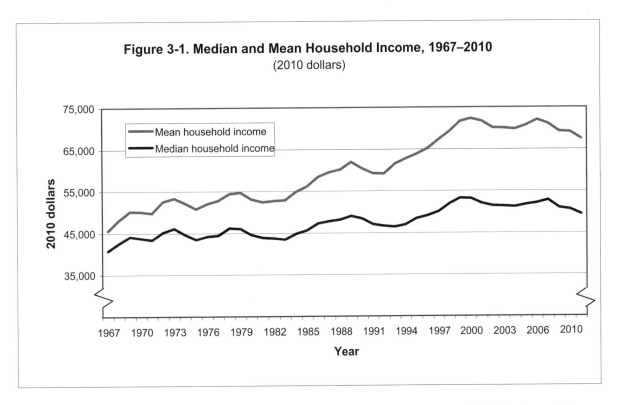

Figure 3-1. Median and Mean Household Income, 1967–2010
(2010 dollars)

- Measured as cash income before taxes, median household income in 2010 was $49,445—down 2.3 percent from the previous year, in constant (2010) dollars; 6.4 percent below 2007; and the lowest since 1996. Measured peak to peak over the latest completed business cycle, from 1999 to 2007, real median household income declined 0.8 percent. In contrast, between the 1969 business cycle peak and 1999, real median household income <u>rose</u> an average 0.6 percent <u>per year</u>. Median income is the income of the household at the middle of the income distribution. (Table 3-1)

- The Census Bureau also tabulates "mean income," which is the sum of all the reported household incomes divided by the number of households; this is also shown in Figure 3-1 above. Mean income is higher than median income when the distribution of income is skewed upward by very large incomes at the top of the distribution. (Table 3-1)

- Household income inequality, as measured by the "Gini coefficient," rose again in 2010 and was close to the postwar high reached in 2006. A new measure of inequality based on "equivalence-adjusted income," which takes account of the size and composition of the household, was down only slightly from 2009, which was an all-time postwar high; it is slightly lower in level than the raw "Gini" but has increased 24 percent since 1967, compared with 18 percent for the unadjusted measure. (Table 3-4)

- The ratio of women's to men's earnings for year-round, full-time workers increased from about 0.6 through 1981 to 0.778 in 2007, fell back somewhat in 2008 and 2009, and rose back to .774 in 2010. Men's median earnings at the cycle high in 2007 were 3.3 percent below their all-time high in 1973, in real terms. The men's median was actually higher in 2009 and 2010 than in 2007, as the number of full-time workers dropped sharply—apparently leaving proportionately more of the better-paid workers in their jobs. Women's real earnings in 2007 were up 32.8 percent since 1973, but were unchanged from 2007 to 2010. (Table 3-1)

Table 3-1. Median and Mean Household Income and Median Earnings

(2010 dollars, except as noted.)

Year	Number of households (thousands)	Average size of household (number of people)	Median household income — All races	Median household income — White — Total	Median household income — White — Not Hispanic	Median household income — Black	Median household income — Asian [1]	Median household income — Hispanic (any race)	Mean household income, all races	Median earnings — Male workers	Median earnings — Female workers	Ratio, female to male
1960	. . .	. . .	. . .	. . .	. . .	. . .	. . .	. . .	. . .	34 584	20 984	0.607
1961	. . .	. . .	. . .	. . .	. . .	. . .	. . .	. . .	. . .	35 688	21 145	0.592
1962	. . .	. . .	. . .	. . .	. . .	. . .	. . .	. . .	. . .	36 340	21 549	0.593
1963	. . .	. . .	. . .	. . .	. . .	. . .	. . .	. . .	. . .	37 253	21 959	0.589
1964	. . .	. . .	. . .	. . .	. . .	. . .	. . .	. . .	. . .	38 123	22 549	0.591
1965	. . .	. . .	. . .	. . .	. . .	. . .	. . .	. . .	. . .	38 666	23 171	0.599
1966	. . .	. . .	. . .	. . .	. . .	. . .	. . .	. . .	. . .	40 355	23 226	0.576
1967	60 813	. . .	40 770	42 516	. . .	24 686	. . .	. . .	45 599	40 992	23 687	0.578
1968	62 214	. . .	42 527	44 279	. . .	26 110	. . .	. . .	48 112	42 093	24 479	0.582
1969	63 401	. . .	44 108	46 032	. . .	27 824	. . .	. . .	50 180	44 455	26 168	0.589
1970	64 778	. . .	43 766	45 585	. . .	27 746	. . .	. . .	50 115	44 928	26 673	0.594
1971	66 676	. . .	43 340	45 332	. . .	26 778	. . .	. . .	49 845	45 121	26 850	0.595
1972	68 251	. . .	45 196	47 415	48 091	27 676	. . .	35 781	52 602	47 550	27 513	0.579
1973	69 859	. . .	46 109	48 324	48 749	28 445	. . .	35 722	53 324	49 065	27 787	0.566
1974	71 163	. . .	44 649	46 694	47 093	27 769	. . .	35 513	52 213	47 304	27 793	0.588
1975	72 867	2.89	43 479	45 469	45 812	27 296	. . .	32 665	50 771	47 009	27 650	0.588
1976	74 142	2.86	44 201	46 302	47 246	27 532	. . .	33 341	51 992	46 880	28 219	0.602
1977	76 030	2.81	44 481	46 775	47 702	27 602	. . .	34 894	52 766	47 935	28 244	0.589
1978	77 330	2.78	46 202	48 030	48 935	28 864	. . .	36 200	54 379	48 245	28 677	0.594
1979	80 776	2.76	46 074	48 307	48 987	28 362	. . .	36 504	54 731	47 621	28 412	0.597
1980	82 368	2.73	44 616	47 070	47 904	27 117	. . .	34 391	53 064	46 889	28 208	0.602
1981	83 527	2.72	43 876	46 358	47 027	26 014	. . .	35 194	52 417	46 604	27 606	0.592
1982	83 918	2.73	43 758	45 811	46 579	25 963	. . .	32 927	52 735	45 724	28 232	0.617
1983	85 407	2.71	43 453	45 569	. . .	25 859	. . .	33 094	52 849	45 525	28 951	0.636
1984	86 789	2.69	44 802	47 264	48 246	26 925	. . .	33 963	54 894	46 407	29 542	0.637
1985	88 458	2.67	45 640	48 132	49 215	28 636	. . .	33 750	56 167	46 755	30 192	0.646
1986	89 479	2.66	47 256	49 681	50 811	28 623	. . .	34 833	58 382	47 937	30 809	0.643
1987	91 124	2.64	47 848	50 413	51 799	28 774	59 167	35 501	59 505	47 637	31 049	0.652
1988	92 830	2.62	48 216	50 972	52 376	29 057	57 145	36 056	60 245	47 208	31 181	0.660
1989	93 347	2.63	49 076	51 622	52 733	30 701	61 293	37 217	62 003	46 402	31 866	0.687
1990	94 312	2.63	48 423	50 506	51 661	30 202	62 180	36 111	60 487	44 760	32 056	0.716
1991	95 669	2.62	47 032	49 285	50 462	29 361	56 904	35 425	59 203	45 932	32 087	0.699
1992	96 426	2.66	46 646	49 041	50 687	28 556	57 555	34 406	59 137	45 978	32 545	0.708
1993	97 107	2.67	46 419	48 974	50 776	29 023	56 978	34 005	61 556	45 180	32 313	0.715
1994	98 990	2.65	46 937	49 504	51 101	30 590	58 893	34 073	62 750	44 886	32 304	0.720
1995	99 627	2.65	48 408	50 809	52 815	31 811	57 696	32 475	63 838	44 743	31 959	0.714
1996	101 018	2.64	49 112	51 422	53 672	32 493	59 883	34 464	65 207	44 479	32 809	0.738
1997	102 528	2.62	50 123	52 787	54 961	33 930	61 289	36 067	67 307	45 611	33 826	0.742
1998	103 874	2.61	51 944	54 652	56 692	33 865	62 299	37 844	69 270	47 215	34 547	0.732
1999	106 434	2.60	53 252	55 384	57 781	36 521	66 683	40 232	71 626	47 619	34 436	0.722
2000	108 209	2.58	53 164	55 603	57 764	37 562	70 595	41 994	72 339	47 165	34 770	0.737
2001	109 297	2.58	52 005	54 824	57 026	36 293	66 054	41 337	71 685	47 137	35 979	0.763
2002	111 278	2.57	51 398	. . .	. . .	. . .	. . .	40 120	70 114	47 786	36 605	0.766
2003	112 000	2.57	51 353	. . .	. . .	. . .	. . .	39 118	70 023	48 211	36 423	0.755
2004	113 343	2.57	51 174	. . .	. . .	. . .	. . .	39 559	69 795	47 090	36 060	0.766
2005	114 384	2.57	51 739	. . .	. . .	. . .	. . .	40 170	70 746	46 222	35 581	0.770
2006	116 011	2.56	52 124	. . .	. . .	. . .	. . .	40 856	71 988	45 701	35 161	0.769
2007	116 783	2.56	52 823	. . .	. . .	. . .	. . .	40 673	71 095	47 439	36 912	0.778
2008	117 181	2.57	50 939	. . .	. . .	. . .	. . .	38 393	69 290	46 954	36 197	0.771
2009	117 538	2.59	50 599	. . .	. . .	. . .	. . .	38 667	69 098	47 905	36 877	0.770
2010	118 682	2.58	49 445	. . .	. . .	. . .	. . .	37 759	67 530	47 715	36 931	0.774
By race Race alone												
2002	. . .	. . .	. . .	54 642	56 841	35 178	63 781	. . .	. . .	. . .	. . .	. . .
2003	. . .	. . .	. . .	54 095	56 639	35 144	66 030	. . .	. . .	. . .	. . .	. . .
2004	. . .	. . .	. . .	53 857	56 456	34 738	66 376	. . .	. . .	. . .	. . .	. . .
2005	. . .	. . .	. . .	54 227	56 718	34 464	68 233	. . .	. . .	. . .	. . .	. . .
2006	. . .	. . .	. . .	54 797	56 690	34 571	69 466	. . .	. . .	. . .	. . .	. . .
2007	. . .	. . .	. . .	54 802	57 752	35 665	69 511	. . .	. . .	. . .	. . .	. . .
2008	. . .	. . .	. . .	52 974	56 232	34 651	66 467	. . .	. . .	. . .	. . .	. . .
2009	. . .	. . .	. . .	52 717	55 360	33 122	66 550	. . .	. . .	. . .	. . .	. . .
2010	. . .	. . .	. . .	51 846	54 620	32 068	64 308	. . .	. . .	. . .	. . .	. . .
Race alone or in combination												
2002	. . .	. . .	. . .	. . .	. . .	35 361	63 367	. . .	. . .	. . .	. . .	. . .
2003	. . .	. . .	. . .	. . .	. . .	35 196	65 512	. . .	. . .	. . .	. . .	. . .
2004	. . .	. . .	. . .	. . .	. . .	34 900	66 313	. . .	. . .	. . .	. . .	. . .
2005	. . .	. . .	. . .	. . .	. . .	34 571	68 181	. . .	. . .	. . .	. . .	. . .
2006	. . .	. . .	. . .	. . .	. . .	34 747	69 101	. . .	. . .	. . .	. . .	. . .
2007	. . .	. . .	. . .	. . .	. . .	35 849	69 273	. . .	. . .	. . .	. . .	. . .
2008	. . .	. . .	. . .	. . .	. . .	34 779	66 396	. . .	. . .	. . .	. . .	. . .
2009	. . .	. . .	. . .	. . .	. . .	33 291	66 147	. . .	. . .	. . .	. . .	. . .
2010	. . .	. . .	. . .	. . .	. . .	32 106	63 726	. . .	. . .	. . .	. . .	. . .

[1]For 1987 through 2001, Asian and Pacific Islander.
. . . = Not available.

Table 3-2. Median Income and Poverty Rates by Race and Hispanic Origin Using 3–Year Moving Averages

(Income in 2010 dollars; percent of population.)

Race and Hispanic origin	Median household income, 2010 dollars								
	2000–2002	2001–2003	2002–2004	2003–2005	2004–2006	2005–2007	2006–2008	2007–2009	2008–2010
All Races	52 189	51 585	51 308	51 422	51 679	52 229	51 962	51 454	50 328
White alone or in combination	. . .	. . .	. . .	. . .	. . .	. . .	. . .	. . .	. . .
White alone	55 023	54 520	54 198	54 060	54 294	54 609	54 191	53 498	52 512
Not Hispanic	57 210	56 835	56 645	56 604	56 621	57 053	56 891	56 448	55 404
Black alone or in combination	36 405	35 617	35 152	34 889	34 739	35 056	35 125	34 640	33 392
Black alone	36 344	35 538	35 020	34 782	34 591	34 900	34 962	34 479	33 280
American Indian and Alaskan Native alone or in combination	40 138	41 172	41 835	41 570	40 408	39 989	39 896	39 379	38 535
American Indian and Alaskan Native alone	39 614	39 138	38 157	37 561	36 436	36 742	36 020	36 086	34 416
Asian alone or in combination	66 672	64 978	65 064	66 669	67 865	68 852	68 257	67 272	65 423
Asian alone	66 810	65 288	65 396	66 880	68 025	69 070	68 481	67 509	65 775
Native Hawaiian and Other Pacific Islander alone or in combination ...	. . .	. . .	60 186	59 877	59 340	60 568	60 494	58 730	57 836
Native Hawaiian and Other Pacific Islander alone	. . .	. . .	59 612	60 671	59 466	59 179	58 877	58 157	57 894
Hispanic (any race)	41 150	40 192	39 599	39 616	40 195	40 566	39 974	39 244	38 273

Race and Hispanic origin	Poverty rates								
	2000–2002	2001–2003	2002–2004	2003–2005	2004–2006	2005–2007	2006–2008	2007–2009	2008–2010
All Races	11.7	12.1	12.4	12.6	12.5	12.5	12.7	13.4	14.2
White alone or in combination	9.9	10.3	10.6	10.7	10.7	10.5	10.8	11.5	12.3
White alone	9.9	10.2	10.5	10.6	10.6	10.4	10.7	11.3	12.2
Not Hispanic	7.7	8.0	8.3	8.4	8.4	8.2	8.3	8.7	9.3
Black alone or in combination	23.0	23.6	24.3	24.6	24.5	24.4	24.4	25.0	26.0
Black alone	23.1	23.7	24.4	24.7	24.6	24.6	24.5	25.0	26.0
American Indian and Alaskan Native alone or in combination	21.6	20.0	19.2	19.7	20.9	21.2	21.6	21.9	23.4
American Indian and Alaskan Native alone	23.1	23.3	24.3	25.3	27.2	26.6	26.7	26.1	27.6
Asian alone or in combination	10.0	10.7	10.5	10.8	10.3	10.4	10.6	11.4	12.0
Asian alone	10.1	10.7	10.6	10.9	10.4	10.5	10.8	11.5	12.1
Native Hawaiian and Other Pacific Islander alone or in combination ...	. . .	. . .	. . .	. . .	. . .	. . .	. . .	. . .	. . .
Native Hawaiian and Other Pacific Islander alone	. . .	. . .	. . .	. . .	. . .	. . .	. . .	. . .	. . .
Hispanic (any race)	21.6	21.9	22.1	22.0	21.4	21.3	21.8	23.3	25.0

. . . = Not available.

Table 3-3. Median Family Income by Type of Family

(2010 dollars, except as noted.)

Year	All families	Married couples			Male householder [1]	Female householder [1]	4-person families	Average size of family (number of people)
		Total	Wife in paid labor force	Wife not in paid labor force				
1947	25 881	26 547	. . .	. . .	25 070	18 546	28 109	3.64
1948	25 197	25 869	. . .	. . .	26 051	16 318	27 419	3.58
1949	24 872	25 576	30 875	24 479	22 582	16 835	27 041	3.54
1950	26 241	27 245	31 648	26 209	24 628	15 196	29 055	3.54
1951	27 177	28 115	33 932	26 627	25 294	16 266	30 203	3.54
1952	27 991	29 221	35 258	27 429	26 012	16 082	31 466	3.53
1953	30 319	31 241	38 631	29 426	29 397	17 547	. . .	3.59
1954	29 519	30 695	37 801	28 698	28 435	16 251	. . .	3.59
1955	31 437	32 724	40 004	30 782	29 814	17 583	35 001	3.58
1956	33 491	34 844	41 738	32 545	29 196	19 296	37 268	3.60
1957	33 689	34 985	41 660	32 787	31 077	18 744	37 230	3.64
1958	33 585	35 090	41 025	32 898	28 125	18 096	37 533	3.65
1959	35 471	37 075	43 905	34 816	30 206	18 099	39 747	3.67
1960	36 208	37 838	44 454	35 563	31 311	19 122	40 557	3.70
1961	36 581	38 507	45 849	35 668	32 333	19 091	41 058	3.67
1962	37 616	39 554	47 121	36 403	36 068	19 774	42 668	3.68
1963	38 929	41 072	48 522	37 620	35 571	20 003	44 467	3.70
1964	40 372	42 603	50 212	38 953	35 597	21 252	46 020	3.70
1965	42 110	43 975	52 037	39 901	37 213	21 379	47 213	3.69
1966	44 334	46 135	54 422	41 956	37 859	23 603	49 095	3.67
1967	45 279	48 178	56 826	43 441	38 892	24 509	51 335	3.63
1968	47 409	50 221	58 691	45 119	40 209	24 589	54 011	3.60
1969	49 597	52 583	61 143	46 684	43 850	25 353	55 854	3.58
1970	49 443	52 695	61 514	46 622	45 159	25 521	55 957	3.57
1971	49 374	52 759	61 702	46 777	41 871	24 550	55 812	3.53
1972	51 810	55 478	64 772	49 200	48 030	24 898	59 696	3.48
1973	52 859	57 145	66 834	50 083	47 118	25 427	60 136	3.44
1974	51 447	55 519	64 682	48 772	46 487	25 871	59 690	3.42
1975	50 550	54 780	63 513	46 987	47 883	25 218	58 395	3.39
1976	52 117	56 455	65 263	48 539	44 807	25 125	60 329	3.37
1977	52 468	57 734	66 426	49 367	47 581	25 449	61 362	3.33
1978	54 103	59 317	67 809	49 551	48 969	26 183	62 654	3.31
1979	54 823	59 979	69 585	49 558	47 045	27 654	63 010	3.29
1980	52 963	58 299	67 716	47 796	44 135	26 221	61 299	3.27
1981	51 499	57 657	67 277	46 753	45 750	25 211	60 438	3.25
1982	50 835	56 445	65 823	46 206	43 691	24 913	59 916	3.26
1983	51 140	56 770	66 801	45 544	45 450	24 528	60 719	3.24
1984	52 833	59 187	69 293	47 135	46 621	25 590	62 155	3.23
1985	53 595	60 098	70 400	47 452	43 715	26 397	63 339	3.21
1986	55 913	62 265	72 782	48 975	47 379	25 903	65 892	3.19
1987	56 861	64 038	74 819	48 911	46 282	26 958	68 090	3.17
1988	57 011	64 446	75 638	48 207	47 511	27 178	69 160	3.16
1989	58 086	65 444	76 851	48 806	47 278	27 915	69 206	3.17
1990	57 172	64 517	75 646	48 944	46 972	27 382	67 033	3.18
1991	56 108	64 001	75 201	46 953	44 261	26 059	67 219	3.17
1992	55 686	63 781	75 787	45 943	41 987	25 922	67 376	3.19
1993	54 915	63 899	76 081	44 899	39 326	25 918	67 102	3.20
1994	56 420	65 406	77 554	45 355	40 372	26 530	68 393	3.19
1995	57 691	66 856	79 301	45 991	43 126	27 973	70 585	3.20
1996	58 533	68 782	80 785	46 699	43 727	27 552	71 288	3.19
1997	60 367	69 879	82 175	48 798	44 644	28 475	72 262	3.18
1998	62 433	72 376	85 161	49 641	47 664	29 606	74 888	3.18
1999	63 897	73 934	86 989	50 353	48 860	31 094	78 192	3.15
2000	64 232	74 826	87 659	50 622	47 767	32 559	79 347	3.14
2001	63 310	74 305	87 235	50 225	45 062	31 706	77 929	3.15
2002	62 634	74 087	88 238	48 602	45 738	32 024	76 029	3.13
2003	62 451	73 833	89 113	48 750	45 086	31 475	77 167	3.13
2004	62 402	73 443	88 712	48 728	46 588	31 130	76 210	3.13
2005	62 760	73 607	87 957	49 652	45 915	30 427	78 528	3.13
2006	63 161	75 053	89 526	49 481	45 250	31 175	79 390	3.13
2007	64 518	76 332	90 892	49 769	46 645	31 858	79 577	3.15
2008	62 299	73 663	87 717	49 116	44 122	30 510	77 437	3.15
2009	61 080	72 809	87 367	48 436	42 186	30 261	75 634	3.16
2010	60 395	72 426	87 485	48 858	43 058	29 220	75 148	3.18

[1] No spouse present.
. . . = Not available.

Table 3-4. Shares of Aggregate Income Received by Each Fifth and Top 5 Percent of Households

Year	Money income							Equivalence-adjusted income						
	Share of aggregate income (percent)						Gini coefficient	Share of aggregate income (percent)						Gini coefficient
	Lowest fifth	Second fifth	Third fifth	Fourth fifth	Highest fifth	Top 5 percent		Lowest fifth	Second fifth	Third fifth	Fourth fifth	Highest fifth	Top 5 percent	
1967	4.0	10.8	17.3	24.2	43.6	17.2	0.397	5.2	11.9	17.1	23.3	42.5	. . .	0.370
1968	4.2	11.1	17.6	24.5	42.6	16.3	0.386	5.4	12.1	17.4	25.5	41.5	. . .	0.359
1969	4.1	10.9	17.5	24.5	43.0	16.6	0.391	5.4	12.0	17.4	23.6	41.6	. . .	0.361
1970	4.1	10.8	17.4	24.5	43.3	16.6	0.394	5.3	11.9	17.3	23.6	41.9	. . .	0.365
1971	4.1	10.6	17.3	24.5	43.5	16.7	0.396	5.2	11.8	17.2	23.6	42.1	. . .	0.367
1972	4.1	10.4	17.0	24.5	43.9	17.0	0.401	5.2	11.7	17.2	23.6	42.3	. . .	0.370
1973	4.2	10.4	17.0	24.5	43.9	16.9	0.400	5.3	11.8	17.2	23.6	42.0	. . .	0.367
1974	4.3	10.6	17.0	24.6	43.5	16.5	0.395	5.4	11.9	17.4	23.8	41.6	. . .	0.361
1975	4.3	10.4	17.0	24.7	43.6	16.5	0.397	5.3	11.7	17.3	23.8	42.0	. . .	0.367
1976	4.3	10.3	17.0	24.7	43.7	16.6	0.398	5.3	11.7	17.4	23.9	41.8	. . .	0.365
1977	4.2	10.2	16.9	24.7	44.0	16.8	0.402	5.2	11.6	17.3	23.9	42.1	. . .	0.369
1978	4.2	10.2	16.8	24.7	44.1	16.8	0.402	5.2	11.7	17.2	23.8	42.1	. . .	0.369
1979	4.1	10.2	16.8	24.6	44.2	16.9	0.404	5.0	11.6	17.3	23.9	42.2	. . .	0.371
1980	4.2	10.2	16.8	24.7	44.1	16.5	0.403	4.9	11.5	17.3	24.1	42.3	. . .	0.374
1981	4.1	10.1	16.7	24.8	44.3	16.5	0.406	4.6	11.2	17.2	24.2	42.9	. . .	0.384
1982	4.0	10.0	16.5	24.5	45.0	17.0	0.412	4.2	10.9	17.0	24.2	43.8	. . .	0.384
1983	4.0	9.9	16.4	24.6	45.1	17.0	0.414	4.1	10.7	16.9	24.2	44.2	. . .	0.396
1984	4.0	9.9	16.3	24.6	45.2	17.1	0.415	4.2	10.8	16.8	24.2	44.1	. . .	0.400
1985	3.9	9.8	16.2	24.4	45.6	17.6	0.419	4.1	10.7	16.6	23.9	44.7	. . .	0.404
1986	3.8	9.7	16.2	24.3	46.1	18.0	0.425	4.0	10.6	16.6	24.0	44.8	. . .	0.407
1987	3.8	9.6	16.1	24.3	46.2	18.2	0.426	4.3	10.7	16.7	23.8	44.4	. . .	0.400
1988	3.8	9.6	16.0	24.2	46.3	18.3	0.426	4.3	10.6	16.5	23.8	44.8	. . .	0.404
1989	3.8	9.5	15.8	24.0	46.8	18.9	0.431	4.3	10.5	16.3	23.4	45.5	. . .	0.410
1990	3.8	9.6	15.9	24.0	46.6	18.5	0.428	4.3	10.6	16.4	23.6	45.2	. . .	0.408
1991	3.8	9.6	15.9	24.2	46.5	18.1	0.428	4.2	10.5	16.5	23.7	45.1	. . .	0.408
1992	3.8	9.4	15.8	24.2	46.9	18.6	0.433	4.0	10.3	16.3	23.7	45.6	. . .	0.415
1993	3.6	9.0	15.1	23.5	48.9	21.0	0.454	3.8	9.8	15.6	23.1	47.7	. . .	0.438
1994	3.6	8.9	15.0	23.4	49.1	21.2	0.456	3.9	9.8	15.6	22.9	47.9	. . .	0.438
1995	3.7	9.1	15.2	23.3	48.7	21.0	0.450	4.0	9.9	15.6	22.9	47.6	. . .	0.435
1996	3.6	9.0	15.1	23.3	49.0	21.4	0.455	3.9	9.8	15.5	22.8	48.0	. . .	0.400
1997	3.6	8.9	15.0	23.2	49.4	21.7	0.459	3.8	9.8	15.4	22.6	48.4	. . .	0.443
1998	3.6	9.0	15.0	23.2	49.2	21.4	0.456	3.8	9.8	15.4	22.7	48.2	. . .	0.442
1999	3.6	8.9	14.9	23.2	49.4	21.5	0.458	3.9	9.7	15.3	22.7	48.5	. . .	0.443
2000	3.6	8.9	14.8	23.0	49.8	22.1	0.462	4.0	9.8	15.2	22.4	48.7	. . .	0.443
2001	3.5	8.7	14.6	23.0	50.1	22.4	0.466	3.9	9.6	15.2	22.4	49.0	. . .	0.448
2002	3.5	8.8	14.8	23.3	49.7	21.7	0.462	3.8	9.6	15.3	22.8	48.5	. . .	0.445
2003	3.4	8.7	14.8	23.4	49.8	21.4	0.464	3.7	9.5	15.2	22.9	48.6	. . .	0.447
2004	3.4	8.7	14.7	23.2	50.1	21.8	0.466	3.7	9.5	15.2	22.8	48.8	. . .	0.449
2005	3.4	8.6	14.6	23.0	50.4	22.2	0.469	3.7	9.5	15.1	22.7	49.1	. . .	0.452
2006	3.4	8.6	14.5	22.9	50.5	22.3	0.470	3.7	9.4	15.0	22.5	49.4	. . .	0.454
2007	3.4	8.7	14.8	23.4	49.7	21.2	0.463	3.7	9.6	15.3	22.9	48.5	. . .	0.445
2008	3.4	8.6	14.7	23.3	50.0	21.5	0.466	3.6	9.4	15.1	22.9	49.0	21.4	0.451
2009	3.4	8.6	14.6	23.2	50.3	21.7	0.468	3.4	9.2	15.0	22.9	49.4	21.7	0.458
2010	3.3	8.5	14.6	23.4	50.2	21.3	0.469	3.3	9.2	15.1	23.2	49.3	21.0	0.457

. . . = Not available.

Table 3-5. Shares of Aggregate Income Received by Each Fifth and Top 5 Percent of Families

Year	Number of families (thousands)	Share of aggregate income (percent)						Mean family income (2010 dollars)						Gini coefficient
		Lowest fifth	Second fifth	Third fifth	Fourth fifth	Highest fifth	Top 5 percent	Lowest fifth	Second fifth	Third fifth	Fourth fifth	Highest fifth	Top 5 percent	
1947	37 237	5.0	11.9	17.0	23.1	43.0	17.5	. . .	. . .	. . .	. . .	. . .	. . .	0.376
1948	38 624	4.9	12.1	17.3	23.2	42.4	17.1	. . .	. . .	. . .	. . .	. . .	. . .	0.371
1949	39 303	4.5	11.9	17.3	23.5	42.7	16.9	. . .	. . .	. . .	. . .	. . .	. . .	0.378
1950	39 929	4.5	12.0	17.4	23.4	42.7	17.3	. . .	. . .	. . .	. . .	. . .	. . .	0.379
1951	40 578	5.0	12.4	17.6	23.4	41.6	16.8	. . .	. . .	. . .	. . .	. . .	. . .	0.363
1952	40 832	4.9	12.3	17.4	23.4	41.9	17.4	. . .	. . .	. . .	. . .	. . .	. . .	0.368
1953	41 202	4.7	12.5	18.0	23.9	40.9	15.7	. . .	. . .	. . .	. . .	. . .	. . .	0.359
1954	41 951	4.5	12.1	17.7	23.9	41.8	16.3	. . .	. . .	. . .	. . .	. . .	. . .	0.371
1955	42 889	4.8	12.3	17.8	23.7	41.3	16.4	. . .	. . .	. . .	. . .	. . .	. . .	0.363
1956	43 497	5.0	12.5	17.9	23.7	41.0	16.1	. . .	. . .	. . .	. . .	. . .	. . .	0.358
1957	43 696	5.1	12.7	18.1	23.8	40.4	15.6	. . .	. . .	. . .	. . .	. . .	. . .	0.351
1958	44 232	5.0	12.5	18.0	23.9	40.6	15.4	. . .	. . .	. . .	. . .	. . .	. . .	0.354
1959	45 111	4.9	12.3	17.9	23.8	41.1	15.9	. . .	. . .	. . .	. . .	. . .	. . .	0.361
1960	45 539	4.8	12.2	17.8	24.0	41.3	15.9	. . .	. . .	. . .	. . .	. . .	. . .	0.364
1961	46 418	4.7	11.9	17.5	23.8	42.2	16.6	. . .	. . .	. . .	. . .	. . .	. . .	0.374
1962	47 059	5.0	12.1	17.6	24.0	41.3	15.7	. . .	. . .	. . .	. . .	. . .	. . .	0.362
1963	47 540	5.0	12.1	17.7	24.0	41.2	15.8	. . .	. . .	. . .	. . .	. . .	. . .	0.362
1964	47 956	5.1	12.0	17.7	24.0	41.2	15.9	. . .	. . .	. . .	. . .	. . .	. . .	0.361
1965	48 509	5.2	12.2	17.8	23.9	40.9	15.5	. . .	. . .	. . .	. . .	. . .	. . .	0.356
1966	49 214	5.6	12.4	17.8	23.8	40.5	15.6	13 803	30 643	43 845	58 695	100 174	153 820	0.349
1967	50 111	5.4	12.2	17.5	23.5	41.4	16.4	14 018	31 346	45 056	60 427	106 699	168 816	0.358
1968	50 823	5.6	12.4	17.7	23.7	40.5	15.6	15 109	32 954	47 080	62 964	107 588	165 850	0.348
1969	51 586	5.6	12.4	17.7	23.7	40.6	15.6	15 589	34 428	49 266	65 996	113 027	173 602	0.349
1970	52 227	5.4	12.2	17.6	23.8	40.9	15.6	15 354	33 949	49 087	66 215	113 864	173 384	0.353
1971	53 296	5.5	12.0	17.6	23.8	41.1	15.7	15 367	33 451	48 942	66 282	114 163	174 070	0.355
1972	54 373	5.5	11.9	17.5	23.9	41.4	15.9	16 038	34 994	51 400	70 192	121 737	186 630	0.359
1973	55 053	5.5	11.9	17.5	24.0	41.1	15.5	16 457	35 647	52 377	71 580	122 812	185 343	0.356
1974	55 698	5.7	12.0	17.6	24.1	40.6	14.8	16 748	35 354	51 615	70 715	119 156	173 801	0.355
1975	56 245	5.6	11.9	17.7	24.2	40.7	14.9	16 091	34 017	50 580	69 254	116 705	171 198	0.357
1976	56 710	5.6	11.9	17.7	24.2	40.7	14.9	16 480	34 877	52 026	71 085	119 641	175 107	0.358
1977	57 215	5.5	11.7	17.6	24.3	40.9	14.9	16 410	35 078	52 756	72 774	122 600	178 732	0.363
1978	57 804	5.4	11.7	17.6	24.2	41.1	15.1	16 642	36 090	54 192	74 664	126 697	185 661	0.363
1979	59 550	5.4	11.6	17.5	24.1	41.4	15.3	16 788	36 297	54 739	75 362	129 261	191 336	0.365
1980	60 309	5.3	11.6	17.6	24.4	41.1	14.6	16 151	35 159	53 114	73 689	124 069	176 375	0.365
1981	61 019	5.3	11.4	17.5	24.6	41.2	14.4	15 649	34 030	52 049	73 076	122 612	171 330	0.369
1982	61 393	5.0	11.3	17.2	24.4	42.2	15.3	14 763	33 495	51 145	72 555	125 370	179 373	0.380
1983	62 015	4.9	11.2	17.2	24.5	42.4	15.3	14 537	33 447	51 461	73 342	127 169	183 352	0.382
1984	62 706	4.8	11.1	17.1	24.5	42.5	15.4	15 033	34 419	53 103	75 937	131 976	190 813	0.383
1985	63 558	4.8	11.0	16.9	24.3	43.1	16.1	15 206	34 893	53 874	77 223	137 238	205 088	0.389
1986	64 491	4.7	10.9	16.9	24.1	43.4	16.5	15 636	36 103	55 932	79 917	143 944	218 588	0.392
1987	65 204	4.6	10.7	16.8	24.0	43.8	17.2	15 619	36 557	56 766	81 243	148 474	232 428	0.393
1988	65 837	4.6	10.7	16.7	24.0	44.0	17.2	15 753	36 685	57 087	81 986	150 430	235 042	0.395
1989	66 090	4.6	10.6	16.5	23.7	44.6	17.9	16 068	37 382	58 074	83 553	157 321	252 014	0.401
1990	66 322	4.6	10.8	16.6	23.8	44.3	17.4	15 902	37 090	57 122	82 147	152 667	239 542	0.396
1991	67 173	4.5	10.7	16.6	24.1	44.2	17.1	15 197	36 071	55 970	81 177	149 140	230 770	0.397
1992	68 216	4.3	10.5	16.5	24.0	44.7	17.6	14 596	35 204	55 616	80 840	150 435	236 849	0.404
1993	68 506	4.1	9.9	15.7	23.3	47.0	20.3	14 471	34 754	55 074	81 641	164 954	284 706	0.429
1994	69 313	4.2	10.0	15.7	23.3	46.9	20.1	15 111	35 752	56 458	83 456	168 186	288 538	0.426
1995	69 597	4.4	10.1	15.8	23.2	46.5	20.0	16 003	36 871	57 728	84 464	169 693	291 025	0.421
1996	70 241	4.2	10.0	15.8	23.1	46.8	20.3	15 758	37 150	58 764	85 865	173 836	300 765	0.425
1997	70 884	4.2	9.9	15.7	23.0	47.2	20.7	16 331	38 267	60 376	88 533	181 887	318 332	0.429
1998	71 551	4.2	9.9	15.7	23.0	47.3	20.7	16 733	39 383	62 333	91 411	188 147	329 310	0.430
1999	73 206	4.3	9.9	15.6	23.0	47.2	20.3	17 414	40 478	63 892	94 303	193 274	333 240	0.429
2000	73 778	4.3	9.8	15.4	22.7	47.7	21.1	17 880	40 882	64 251	94 694	198 677	352 059	0.433
2001	74 340	4.2	9.7	15.4	22.9	47.7	21.0	17 267	39 983	63 471	94 392	196 608	345 215	0.435
2002	75 616	4.2	9.7	15.5	23.0	47.6	20.8	16 988	39 414	62 863	93 497	193 063	337 883	0.434
2003	76 232	4.1	9.6	15.5	23.2	47.6	20.5	16 444	38 998	62 850	94 499	193 616	333 675	0.436
2004	76 866	4.0	9.6	15.4	23.0	47.9	20.9	16 390	39 012	62 612	93 545	194 686	339 173	0.438
2005	77 418	4.0	9.6	15.3	22.9	48.1	21.1	16 492	39 243	62 797	93 921	196 891	344 699	0.440
2006	78 454	4.0	9.5	15.1	22.9	48.5	21.5	16 804	39 762	63 245	95 589	202 641	358 700	0.444
2007	77 908	4.1	9.7	15.6	23.3	47.3	20.1	16 896	40 279	64 612	96 618	196 146	332 943	0.432
2008	78 874	4.0	9.6	15.5	23.1	47.8	20.5	16 107	38 607	62 361	93 326	192 809	331 064	0.438
2009	78 867	3.9	9.4	15.3	23.2	48.2	20.7	15 541	37 657	60 896	92 464	192 614	330 388	0.443
2010	78 633	3.8	9.5	15.4	23.5	47.8	20.0	14 991	37 066	60 363	91 991	187 395	313 298	0.440

. . . = Not available.

Table 3-6. Median Household Income by State

(2010 dollars.)

State	1990	1998	1999	2000	2001	2002	2003	2004	2005	2006	2007	2008	2009	2010
United States	48 423	51 944	53 252	53 164	52 005	51 398	51 353	51 174	51 739	52 124	52 823	50 939	50 599	49 445
Alabama	37 772	48 445	47 436	44 851	43 301	45 573	44 165	42 280	41 491	41 041	44 388	45 039	40 640	40 976
Alaska	63 552	67 716	67 254	66 910	70 645	63 960	61 452	63 559	62 422	61 010	66 241	64 798	62 621	58 198
Arizona	47 260	49 546	48 409	50 370	52 592	48 156	48 802	50 611	50 532	50 454	49 649	47 507	46 494	47 279
Arkansas	36 849	36 956	38 840	37 600	41 058	39 252	37 938	40 382	40 941	40 073	42 898	40 087	37 141	38 571
California	53 836	54 681	57 090	59 274	58 205	57 492	58 445	56 816	57 802	59 821	58 608	57 735	57 061	54 459
Colorado	49 701	62 249	63 042	61 077	60 834	58 530	59 203	58 737	56 344	60 230	64 293	61 714	56 853	60 442
Connecticut	62 859	62 127	66 203	63 523	65 699	64 703	65 160	63 601	63 476	67 483	67 448	65 500	65 922	66 452
Delaware	49 815	55 381	61 015	63 768	61 087	60 174	58 111	55 462	57 222	56 706	57 404	51 343	52 974	55 269
District of Columbia	44 298	44 661	50 601	52 192	50 701	47 351	53 399	50 155	50 250	52 423	49 394	48 155	56 293	55 528
Florida	43 154	46 633	46 886	49 196	44 854	46 084	46 201	46 789	48 013	49 394	48 155	45 424	46 384	44 243
Georgia	44 571	51 650	51 589	53 051	52 434	52 040	50 310	47 307	51 292	53 360	51 149	46 812	44 055	44 108
Hawaii	62 942	54 538	58 235	65 263	58 423	57 329	61 449	64 920	66 548	65 392	67 323	62 299	56 568	58 507
Idaho	40 923	48 998	46 846	47 620	47 095	45 709	50 231	51 202	49 338	49 974	51 720	48 020	47 550	47 014
Illinois	52 626	57 679	60 625	58 322	56 861	51 763	53 528	53 186	54 053	52 632	55 213	53 928	53 743	50 761
Indiana	43 547	53 074	53 438	51 740	49 728	49 747	50 294	48 860	47 396	49 103	49 900	47 108	45 036	46 322
Iowa	44 129	49 451	53 778	51 899	50 464	49 750	49 060	50 086	51 933	52 043	51 430	50 776	51 558	49 177
Kansas	48 381	49 040	48 871	51 985	51 004	51 653	52 436	47 402	46 938	49 260	50 998	48 483	45 455	46 229
Kentucky	40 074	48 427	44 148	45 916	47 337	44 554	43 787	41 104	40 987	42 699	41 486	41 669	43 368	41 236
Louisiana	36 233	42 393	42 729	38 892	41 037	41 216	39 722	42 050	41 587	39 458	43 443	40 063	46 183	39 443
Maine	44 414	47 609	50 853	47 183	45 089	44 664	43 997	47 706	49 055	49 357	50 363	47 825	48 286	48 133
Maryland	62 838	66 813	68 312	69 047	65 924	68 363	62 018	65 913	67 583	68 850	69 014	64 517	65 246	64 025
Massachusetts	58 618	56 566	57 582	59 195	64 352	60 422	60 406	60 045	62 562	59 833	61 477	61 083	60 353	61 333
Michigan	48 413	55 866	60 309	57 623	55 477	51 769	53 373	48 776	51 300	52 606	60 786	50 418	46 753	46 441
Minnesota	50 884	64 021	61 551	68 688	64 879	66 200	62 621	64 760	60 550	60 786	61 051	55 620	57 016	52 554
Mississippi	32 631	38 900	42 499	43 426	37 144	37 428	38 799	40 117	36 716	37 560	39 201	36 907	35 657	37 985
Missouri	44 201	53 702	54 151	57 098	50 911	51 843	51 879	48 638	48 009	48 207	48 377	46 620	49 574	46 184
Montana	37 801	42 182	40 614	41 499	39 564	42 219	40 435	39 195	41 673	44 451	45 906	43 443	41 105	41 467
Nebraska	44 443	48 642	50 544	52 860	53 809	50 829	51 867	52 131	50 542	53 523	52 064	51 709	50 414	52 728
Nevada	51 787	53 108	54 253	57 935	55 916	54 487	53 565	54 487	53 842	56 537	56 845	55 437	52 283	51 525
New Hampshire	65 989	60 057	60 265	64 478	63 216	67 047	65 874	65 581	63 642	67 014	71 060	67 013	65 190	66 707
New Jersey	62 640	66 559	65 079	63 818	63 758	66 134	66 441	63 803	70 772	73 598	63 628	66 132	65 846	63 540
New Mexico	40 492	42 136	42 624	44 432	40 793	42 972	41 617	45 666	43 498	43 286	46 643	42 635	44 261	45 098
New York	51 088	49 952	52 327	51 587	51 865	50 861	50 725	51 538	52 688	52 147	51 468	51 099	51 045	49 826
North Carolina	42 579	47 874	48 748	48 514	46 998	44 255	44 194	46 446	46 970	43 036	45 757	43 473	42 598	43 753
North Dakota	40 856	40 481	42 741	45 575	44 080	43 873	47 906	45 271	47 122	44 388	49 639	50 259	50 902	51 380
Ohio	48 536	51 997	51 673	54 395	51 460	51 731	51 592	49 698	49 368	49 636	51 631	47 528	46 636	46 093
Oklahoma	39 433	45 054	42 767	41 063	43 854	44 186	42 561	45 726	42 044	41 999	45 444	52 381	46 635	43 400
Oregon	47 352	52 187	53 152	53 809	50 829	50 662	49 361	47 319	49 319	50 924	52 826	52 381	49 909	50 526
Pennsylvania	46 906	52 118	49 408	53 400	53 571	51 506	50 897	50 911	51 710	52 423	50 934	52 052	48 967	48 460
Rhode Island	51 698	54 350	55 900	53 426	56 310	51 408	53 004	55 331	55 266	58 110	57 005	53 915	52 486	51 914
South Carolina	46 469	44 439	47 712	47 568	46 473	45 827	45 616	44 661	44 931	42 841	46 493	42 688	41 779	41 709
South Dakota	39 736	43 797	46 882	46 181	48 856	44 068	46 853	47 449	48 193	49 124	48 811	52 253	46 582	45 669
Tennessee	36 535	43 535	45 540	47 791	43 169	44 879	44 483	43 946	44 010	44 005	43 319	40 204	41 186	38 686
Texas	45 650	47 800	50 625	48 883	50 321	48 659	46 555	47 784	46 262	46 832	48 427	47 078	48 259	47 464
Utah	48 745	59 176	60 258	60 204	58 303	58 006	58 415	58 720	61 218	59 074	56 289	63 328	59 457	56 787
Vermont	50 291	52 595	54 414	50 130	50 239	52 113	51 285	54 631	56 629	56 212	49 833	51 347	53 182	55 942
Virginia	56 719	57 914	59 791	59 714	61 874	60 151	64 945	59 032	57 980	61 768	62 211	62 769	61 500	60 363
Washington	51 931	63 347	59 503	53 841	52 328	54 760	56 320	57 624	56 564	59 177	61 075	57 347	61 389	56 253
West Virginia	35 799	35 672	38 336	37 238	36 543	35 582	38 840	38 522	40 703	41 546	44 261	38 475	41 158	42 839
Wisconsin	49 665	55 206	59 757	57 087	55 845	55 633	54 851	52 788	49 867	55 899	53 921	51 848	52 083	50 522
Wyoming	47 642	47 088	48 741	50 175	48 915	48 191	50 448	52 401	49 943	50 870	51 257	54 012	53 336	52 359

Section 3b: Poverty

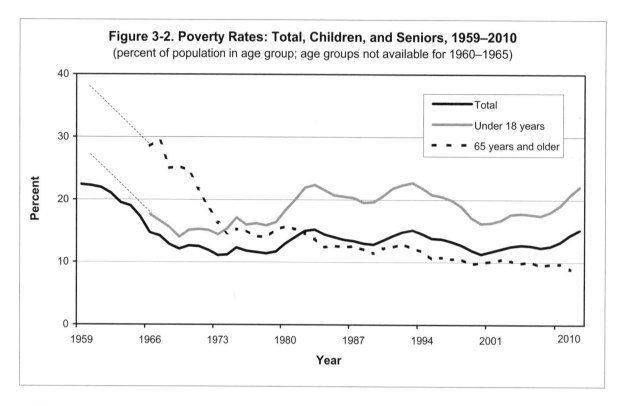

Figure 3-2. Poverty Rates: Total, Children, and Seniors, 1959–2010
(percent of population in age group; age groups not available for 1960–1965)

- The number of Americans with family money incomes below the poverty line rose to 15.1 percent of the population in 2010, which was the highest rate since 1993. (Table 3-8)

- Poverty affecting children continued to rise, with 22 percent living below the poverty threshold, while poverty for those 65 and older remained near an all-time low. In 1959, the first poverty rate calculations showed more than one-third of all seniors living in poverty, compared with 17 percent of working-age adults. Between 1959 and 1974, ad hoc legislative changes raised Social Security benefits by a cumulative 104 percent—exceeding the 69 percent increase in consumer prices—and since then, each year's benefits have been indexed to the rate of change in the Consumer Price Index, Urban Wage Earners and Clerical Workers (CPI-W). As a result, since the early 1980s, officially-measured senior poverty has been consistently lower than the population average. (Table 3-10)

- However, the official thresholds do not specifically include medical expenses or account for the disproportionate effect of medical price inflation on senior budgets. The new Supplemental Poverty Measure estimates the poverty rate for persons 65 and older to be close to the same level as the average for all ages. (Table 3-15)

- The poverty rate for children, on the other hand, has always been higher than the average, and remains so even in the Supplemental Poverty Measure, which takes account of government programs benefiting families with children. (Tables 3-10 and 3-15)

- Poverty among Hispanics (who may be of any race) was 26.6 percent in 2010, compared with 9.9 percent for non-Hispanic Whites. Poverty among Blacks was 27.4 percent and poverty among Asians was 12.1 percent. (Table 3-8)

Table 3-7. Weighted Average Poverty Thresholds by Family Size

(Dollars.)

Year	Unrelated individuals			Families of 2 people			Families, all ages								CPI-U, all items (1982–1984 = 100)
	All ages	Under 65 years	65 years and older	All ages	House-holder under 65 years	House-holder 65 years and older	3 people	4 people	5 people	6 people	7 people or more (before 1980)	7 people	8 people	9 people or more	
1959	1 467	1 503	1 397	1 894	1 952	1 761	2 324	2 973	3 506	3 944	4 849	. . .	. . .	. . .	29.2
1960	1 490	1 526	1 418	1 924	1 982	1 788	2 359	3 022	3 560	4 002	4 921	. . .	. . .	. . .	29.6
1961	1 506	1 545	1 433	1 942	2 005	1 808	2 383	3 054	3 597	4 041	4 967	. . .	. . .	. . .	29.9
1962	1 519	1 562	1 451	1 962	2 027	1 828	2 412	3 089	3 639	4 088	5 032	. . .	. . .	. . .	30.3
1963	1 539	1 581	1 470	1 988	2 052	1 850	2 442	3 128	3 685	4 135	5 092	. . .	. . .	. . .	30.6
1964	1 558	1 601	1 488	2 015	2 079	1 875	2 473	3 169	3 732	4 193	5 156	. . .	. . .	. . .	31.0
1965	1 582	1 626	1 512	2 048	2 114	1 906	2 514	3 223	3 797	4 264	5 248	. . .	. . .	. . .	31.5
1966	1 628	1 674	1 556	2 107	2 175	1 961	2 588	3 317	3 908	4 388	5 395	. . .	. . .	. . .	32.5
1967	1 675	1 722	1 600	2 168	2 238	2 017	2 661	3 410	4 019	4 516	5 550	. . .	. . .	. . .	33.4
1968	1 748	1 797	1 667	2 262	2 333	2 102	2 774	3 553	4 188	4 706	5 789	. . .	. . .	. . .	34.8
1969	1 840	1 893	1 757	2 383	2 458	2 215	2 924	3 743	4 415	4 958	6 101	. . .	. . .	. . .	36.7
1970	1 954	2 010	1 861	2 525	2 604	2 348	3 099	3 968	4 680	5 260	6 468	. . .	. . .	. . .	38.8
1971	2 040	2 098	1 940	2 633	2 716	2 448	3 229	4 137	4 880	5 489	6 751	. . .	. . .	. . .	40.5
1972	2 109	2 168	2 005	2 724	2 808	2 530	3 339	4 275	5 044	5 673	6 983	. . .	. . .	. . .	41.8
1973	2 247	2 307	2 130	2 895	2 984	2 688	3 548	4 540	5 358	6 028	7 435	. . .	. . .	. . .	44.4
1974	2 495	2 562	2 364	3 211	3 312	2 982	3 936	5 038	5 950	6 699	8 253	. . .	. . .	. . .	49.3
1975	2 724	2 797	2 581	3 506	3 617	3 257	4 293	5 500	6 499	7 316	9 022	. . .	. . .	. . .	53.8
1976	2 884	2 959	2 730	3 711	3 826	3 445	4 540	5 815	6 876	7 760	9 588	. . .	. . .	. . .	56.9
1977	3 075	3 152	2 906	3 951	4 072	3 666	4 833	6 191	7 320	8 261	10 216	. . .	. . .	. . .	60.6
1978	3 311	3 392	3 127	4 249	4 383	3 944	5 201	6 662	7 880	8 891	11 002	. . .	. . .	. . .	65.2
1979	3 689	3 778	3 479	4 725	4 878	4 390	5 784	7 412	8 775	9 914	12 280	. . .	. . .	. . .	72.6
1980	4 190	4 290	3 949	5 363	5 537	4 983	6 565	8 414	9 966	11 269	13 955	12 761	14 199	16 896	82.4
1981	4 620	4 729	4 359	5 917	6 111	5 498	7 250	9 287	11 007	12 449	. . .	14 110	15 655	18 572	90.9
1982	4 901	5 019	4 626	6 281	6 487	5 836	7 693	9 862	11 684	13 207	. . .	15 036	16 719	19 698	96.5
1983	5 061	5 180	4 775	6 483	6 697	6 023	7 938	10 178	12 049	13 630	. . .	15 500	17 170	20 310	99.6
1984	5 278	5 400	4 979	6 762	6 983	6 282	8 277	10 609	12 566	14 207	. . .	16 096	17 961	21 247	103.9
1985	5 469	5 593	5 156	6 998	7 231	6 503	8 573	10 989	13 007	14 696	. . .	16 656	18 512	22 083	107.6
1986	5 572	5 701	5 255	7 138	7 372	6 630	8 737	11 203	13 259	14 986	. . .	17 049	18 791	22 497	109.6
1987	5 778	5 909	5 447	7 397	7 641	6 872	9 056	11 611	13 737	15 509	. . .	17 649	19 515	23 105	113.6
1988	6 022	6 155	5 674	7 704	7 958	7 157	9 435	12 092	14 304	16 146	. . .	18 232	20 253	24 129	118.3
1989	6 310	6 451	5 947	8 076	8 343	7 501	9 885	12 674	14 990	16 921	. . .	19 162	21 328	25 480	124.0
1990	6 652	6 800	6 268	8 509	8 794	7 905	10 419	13 359	15 792	17 839	. . .	20 241	22 582	26 848	130.7
1991	6 932	7 086	6 532	8 865	9 165	8 241	10 860	13 924	16 456	18 587	. . .	21 058	23 582	27 942	136.2
1992	7 143	7 299	6 729	9 137	9 443	8 487	11 186	14 335	16 952	19 137	. . .	21 594	24 053	28 745	140.3
1993	7 363	7 518	6 930	9 414	9 728	8 740	11 522	14 763	17 449	19 718	. . .	22 383	24 838	29 529	144.5
1994	7 547	7 710	7 108	9 661	9 976	8 967	11 821	15 141	17 900	20 235	. . .	22 923	25 427	30 300	148.2
1995	7 763	7 929	7 309	9 933	10 259	9 219	12 158	15 569	18 408	20 804	. . .	23 552	26 237	31 280	152.4
1996	7 995	8 163	7 525	10 233	10 564	9 491	12 516	16 036	18 952	21 389	. . .	24 268	27 091	31 971	156.9
1997	8 183	8 350	7 698	10 473	10 805	9 712	12 802	16 400	19 380	21 886	. . .	24 802	27 593	32 566	160.5
1998	8 316	8 480	7 818	10 634	10 972	9 862	13 003	16 660	19 680	22 228	. . .	25 257	28 166	33 339	163.0
1999	8 499	8 667	7 990	10 864	11 213	10 075	13 289	17 030	20 128	22 730	. . .	25 918	28 970	34 436	166.6
2000	8 791	8 959	8 259	11 235	11 589	10 418	13 740	17 604	20 815	23 533	. . .	26 750	29 701	35 150	172.2
2001	9 039	9 214	8 494	11 569	11 920	10 715	14 128	18 104	21 405	24 195	. . .	27 517	30 627	36 286	177.1
2002	9 183	9 359	8 628	11 756	12 110	10 885	14 348	18 392	21 744	24 576	. . .	28 001	30 907	37 062	179.9
2003	9 393	9 573	8 825	12 015	12 384	11 133	14 680	18 810	22 245	25 122	. . .	28 544	31 589	37 656	184.0
2004	9 646	9 827	9 060	12 335	12 714	11 430	15 066	19 307	22 830	25 787	. . .	29 233	32 641	39 062	188.9
2005	9 973	10 160	9 367	12 755	13 145	11 815	15 577	19 971	23 613	26 683	. . .	30 249	33 610	40 288	195.3
2006	10 294	10 488	9 669	13 167	13 569	12 201	16 079	20 614	24 382	27 560	. . .	31 205	34 774	41 499	201.6
2007	10 590	10 787	9 944	13 540	13 954	12 550	16 530	21 203	25 080	28 323	. . .	32 233	35 816	42 739	207.3
2008	10 991	11 201	10 326	14 051	14 417	13 014	17 163	22 025	26 049	29 456	. . .	33 529	37 220	44 346	215.3
2009	10 956	11 161	10 289	13 991	14 366	12 968	17 098	21 954	25 991	29 405	. . .	33 372	37 252	44 366	214.5
2010	11 139	11 344	10 458	14 218	14 676	13 194	17 374	22 314	26 439	29 897	. . .	34 009	37 934	45 220	218.1

. . . = Not available.

Table 3-8. Poverty Status of People by Race and Hispanic Origin

(Thousands of people, percent of population.)

| Year | Number of people, all races | Below poverty level | | | | | | | | | | | |
| | | All races | | White | | White, not Hispanic | | Black | | Asian [1] | | Hispanic (any race) | |
		Number	Poverty rate (percent)	Number	Poverty rate (percent)	Number	Poverty rate (percent)	Number	Poverty rate (percent)	Number	Poverty rate (percent)	Number	Poverty rate (percent)
1959	176 557	39 490	22.4	28 484	18.1	...	...	9 927	55.1	...	...	...	...
1960	179 503	39 851	22.2	28 309	17.8	...	...	...	...	...	...	...	...
1961	181 277	39 628	21.9	27 890	17.4	...	...	...	...	...	...	...	...
1962	184 276	38 625	21.0	26 672	16.4	...	...	...	...	...	...	...	...
1963	187 258	36 436	19.5	25 238	15.3	...	...	...	...	...	...	...	...
1964	189 710	36 055	19.0	24 957	14.9	...	...	...	...	...	...	...	...
1965	191 413	33 185	17.3	22 496	13.3	...	...	...	...	...	...	...	...
1966	193 388	28 510	14.7	19 290	11.3	...	...	8 867	41.8	...	...	...	...
1967	195 672	27 769	14.2	18 983	11.0	...	...	8 486	39.3	...	...	...	...
1968	197 628	25 389	12.8	17 395	10.0	...	...	7 616	34.7	...	...	...	...
1969	199 517	24 147	12.1	16 659	9.5	...	...	7 095	32.2	...	...	...	...
1970	202 183	25 420	12.6	17 484	9.9	...	...	7 548	33.5	...	...	...	...
1971	204 554	25 559	12.5	17 780	9.9	...	...	7 396	32.5	...	...	...	...
1972	206 004	24 460	11.9	16 203	9.0	...	...	7 710	33.3	...	...	2 414	22.8
1973	207 621	22 973	11.1	15 142	8.4	12 864	7.5	7 388	31.4	...	...	2 366	21.9
1974	209 362	23 370	11.2	15 736	8.6	13 217	7.7	7 182	30.3	...	...	2 575	23.0
1975	210 864	25 877	12.3	17 770	9.7	14 883	8.6	7 545	31.3	...	...	2 991	26.9
1976	212 303	24 975	11.8	16 713	9.1	14 025	8.1	7 595	31.1	...	...	2 783	24.7
1977	213 867	24 720	11.6	16 416	8.9	13 802	8.0	7 726	31.3	...	...	2 700	22.4
1978	215 656	24 497	11.4	16 259	8.7	13 755	7.9	7 625	30.6	...	...	2 607	21.6
1979	222 903	26 072	11.7	17 214	9.0	14 419	8.1	8 050	31.0	...	...	2 921	21.8
1980	225 027	29 272	13.0	19 699	10.2	16 365	9.1	8 579	32.5	...	...	3 491	25.7
1981	227 157	31 822	14.0	21 553	11.1	17 987	9.9	9 173	34.2	...	...	3 713	26.5
1982	229 412	34 398	15.0	23 517	12.0	19 362	10.6	9 697	35.6	...	...	4 301	29.9
1983	231 700	35 303	15.2	23 984	12.1	19 538	10.8	9 882	35.7	...	...	4 633	28.0
1984	233 816	33 700	14.4	22 955	11.5	18 300	10.0	9 490	33.8	...	...	4 806	28.4
1985	236 594	33 064	14.0	22 860	11.4	17 839	9.7	8 926	31.3	...	...	5 236	29.0
1986	238 554	32 370	13.6	22 183	11.0	17 244	9.4	8 983	31.1	...	...	5 117	27.3
1987	240 982	32 221	13.4	21 195	10.4	16 029	8.7	9 520	32.4	1 021	16.1	5 422	28.0
1988	243 530	31 745	13.0	20 715	10.1	15 565	8.4	9 356	31.3	1 117	17.3	5 357	26.7
1989	245 992	31 528	12.8	20 785	10.0	15 599	8.3	9 302	30.7	939	14.1	5 430	26.2
1990	248 644	33 585	13.5	22 326	10.7	16 622	8.8	9 837	31.9	858	12.2	6 006	28.1
1991	251 192	35 708	14.2	23 747	11.3	17 741	9.4	10 242	32.7	996	13.8	6 339	28.7
1992	256 549	38 014	14.8	25 259	11.9	18 202	9.6	10 827	33.4	985	12.7	7 592	29.6
1993	259 278	39 265	15.1	26 226	12.2	18 882	9.9	10 877	33.1	1 134	15.3	8 126	30.6
1994	261 616	38 059	14.5	25 379	11.7	18 110	9.4	10 196	30.6	974	14.6	8 416	30.7
1995	263 733	36 425	13.8	24 423	11.2	16 267	8.5	9 872	29.3	1 411	14.6	8 574	30.3
1996	266 218	36 529	13.7	24 650	11.2	16 462	8.6	9 694	28.4	1 454	14.5	8 697	29.4
1997	268 480	35 574	13.3	24 396	11.0	16 491	8.6	9 116	26.5	1 468	14.0	8 308	27.1
1998	271 059	34 476	12.7	23 454	10.5	15 799	8.2	9 091	26.1	1 360	12.5	8 070	25.6
1999	276 208	32 791	11.9	22 169	9.8	14 735	7.7	8 441	23.6	1 285	10.7	7 876	22.7
2000	278 944	31 581	11.3	21 645	9.5	14 366	7.4	7 982	22.5	1 258	9.9	7 747	21.5
2001	281 475	32 907	11.7	22 739	9.9	15 271	7.8	8 136	22.7	1 275	10.2	7 997	21.4
2002	285 317	34 570	12.1	...	...	...	...	...	...	...	...	8 555	21.8
2003	287 699	35 861	12.5	...	...	...	...	...	...	...	...	9 051	22.5
2004	290 617	37 040	12.7	...	...	...	...	...	...	...	...	9 122	21.9
2005	293 135	36 950	12.6	...	...	...	...	...	...	...	...	9 368	21.8
2006	296 450	36 460	12.3	...	...	...	...	...	...	...	...	9 243	20.6
2007	298 699	37 276	12.5	...	...	...	...	...	...	...	...	9 890	21.5
2008	301 041	39 829	13.2	...	...	...	...	...	...	...	...	10 987	23.2
2009	303 820	43 569	14.3	...	...	...	...	...	...	...	...	12 350	25.3
2010	305 688	46 180	15.1	...	...	...	...	...	...	...	...	13 243	26.6
By race													
Race alone													
2002	...	...	...	23 466	10.2	15 567	8.0	8 602	24.1	1 161	10.1	...	...
2003	...	...	...	24 272	10.5	15 902	8.2	8 781	24.4	1 401	11.8	...	...
2004	...	...	...	25 327	10.8	16 908	8.7	9 014	24.7	1 201	9.8	...	...
2005	...	...	...	24 872	10.6	16 227	8.3	9 168	24.9	1 402	11.1	...	...
2006	...	...	...	24 416	10.3	16 013	8.2	9 048	24.3	1 353	10.3	...	...
2007	...	...	...	25 120	10.5	16 032	8.2	9 237	24.5	1 349	10.2	...	...
2008	...	...	...	26 990	11.2	17 024	8.6	9 379	24.7	1 576	11.8	...	...
2009	...	...	...	29 830	12.3	18 530	9.4	9 944	25.8	1 746	12.5	...	...
2010	...	...	...	31 650	13.0	19 599	9.9	10 675	27.4	1 729	12.1	...	...
Race alone or in combination													
2002	...	...	...	24 074	10.3	...	...	8 884	23.9	1 243	10.0	...	...
2003	...	...	...	24 950	10.6	...	...	9 108	24.3	1 527	11.8	...	...
2004	...	...	...	26 071	10.9	...	...	9 411	24.7	1 295	9.7	...	...
2005	...	...	...	25 631	10.7	...	...	9 517	24.7	1 501	10.9	...	...
2006	...	...	...	25 156	10.4	...	...	9 447	24.2	1 447	10.1	...	...
2007	...	...	...	25 864	10.6	...	...	9 668	24.4	1 467	10.2	...	...
2008	...	...	...	27 868	11.3	...	...	9 882	24.6	1 686	11.6	...	...
2009	...	...	...	...	...	...	...	10 575	25.9	1 901	12.4	...	...
2010	...	...	...	...	...	...	...	11 361	27.4	1 859	11.9	...	...

[1] For 1987 through 2001, Asian and Pacific Islander.
. . . = Not available.

Table 3-9. Poverty Status of Families by Type of Family

(Thousands of families, percent.)

Year	Married couple families				Families with no spouse present							Unrelated individuals	
	Number of families		Poverty rate (percent)		Male householder			Female householder					
						Poverty rate (percent)			Poverty rate (percent)				
	Total	Total below poverty level	Total	With children under 18 years	Families below poverty level	Total	With children under 18 years	Families below poverty level	Total	With children under 18 years	Below poverty level	Poverty rate
1959	39 335	...	...	...	...	...	...	1 916	42.6	59.9	4 928	46.1
1960	39 624	...	...	...	...	...	...	1 955	42.4	56.3	4 926	45.2
1961	40 405	...	...	...	...	...	...	1 954	42.1	56.0	5 119	45.9
1962	40 923	...	...	...	...	...	...	2 034	42.9	59.7	5 002	45.4
1963	41 311	...	...	...	...	...	...	1 972	40.4	55.7	4 938	44.2
1964	41 648	...	...	...	...	...	...	1 822	36.4	49.7	5 143	42.7
1965	42 107	...	...	...	...	...	...	1 916	38.4	52.2	4 827	39.8
1966	42 553	...	...	...	...	...	...	1 721	33.1	47.1	4 701	38.3
1967	43 292	...	...	...	...	...	...	1 774	33.3	44.5	4 998	38.1
1968	43 842	...	...	...	...	...	...	1 755	32.3	44.6	4 694	34.0
1969	44 436	...	...	...	...	...	...	1 827	32.7	44.9	4 972	34.0
1970	44 739	...	...	...	...	...	...	1 952	32.5	43.8	5 090	32.9
1971	45 752	...	...	...	...	...	...	2 100	33.9	44.9	5 154	31.6
1972	46 314	...	...	...	...	...	...	2 158	32.7	44.5	4 883	29.0
1973	46 812	2 482	5.3	...	154	10.7	...	2 193	32.2	43.2	4 674	25.6
1974	47 069	2 474	5.3	6.0	125	8.9	15.4	2 324	32.1	43.7	4 553	24.1
1975	47 318	2 904	6.1	7.2	116	8.0	11.7	2 430	32.5	44.0	5 088	25.1
1976	47 497	2 606	5.5	6.4	162	10.8	15.4	2 543	33.0	44.1	5 344	24.9
1977	47 385	2 524	5.3	6.3	177	11.1	14.8	2 610	31.7	41.8	5 216	22.6
1978	47 692	2 474	5.2	5.9	152	9.2	14.7	2 654	31.4	42.2	5 435	22.1
1979	49 112	2 640	5.4	6.1	176	10.2	15.5	2 645	30.4	39.6	5 743	21.9
1980	49 294	3 032	6.2	7.7	213	11.0	18.0	2 972	32.7	42.9	6 227	22.9
1981	49 630	3 394	6.8	8.7	205	10.3	14.0	3 252	34.6	44.3	6 490	23.4
1982	49 908	3 789	7.6	9.8	290	14.4	20.6	3 434	36.3	47.8	6 458	23.1
1983	50 081	3 815	7.6	10.1	268	13.2	20.2	3 564	36.0	47.1	6 740	23.1
1984	50 350	3 488	6.9	9.4	292	13.1	18.1	3 498	34.5	45.7	6 609	21.8
1985	50 933	3 438	6.7	8.9	311	12.9	17.1	3 474	34.0	45.4	6 725	21.5
1986	51 537	3 123	6.1	8.0	287	11.4	17.8	3 613	34.6	46.0	6 846	21.6
1987	51 675	3 011	5.8	7.7	340	12.0	16.8	3 654	34.2	45.5	6 857	20.8
1988	52 100	2 897	5.6	7.2	336	11.8	18.0	3 642	33.4	44.7	7 070	20.6
1989	52 317	2 931	5.6	7.3	348	12.1	18.1	3 504	32.2	42.8	6 760	19.2
1990	52 147	2 981	5.7	7.8	349	12.0	18.8	3 768	33.4	44.5	7 446	20.7
1991	52 457	3 158	6.0	8.3	392	13.0	19.6	4 161	35.6	47.1	7 773	21.1
1992	53 090	3 385	6.4	8.6	484	15.8	22.5	4 275	35.4	46.2	8 075	21.9
1993	53 181	3 481	6.5	9.0	488	16.8	22.5	4 424	35.6	46.1	8 388	22.1
1994	53 865	3 272	6.1	8.3	549	17.0	22.6	4 232	34.6	44.0	8 287	21.5
1995	53 570	2 982	5.6	7.5	493	14.0	19.7	4 057	32.4	41.5	8 247	20.9
1996	53 604	3 010	5.6	7.5	531	13.8	20.0	4 167	32.6	41.9	8 452	20.8
1997	54 321	2 821	5.2	7.1	507	13.0	18.7	3 995	31.6	41.0	8 687	20.8
1998	54 778	2 879	5.3	6.9	476	12.0	16.6	3 831	29.9	38.7	8 478	19.9
1999	56 290	2 748	4.9	6.4	485	11.8	16.3	3 559	27.8	35.7	8 400	19.1
2000	56 598	2 637	4.7	6.0	485	11.3	15.3	3 278	25.4	33.0	8 653	19.0
2001	56 755	2 760	4.9	6.1	583	13.1	17.7	3 470	26.4	33.6	9 226	19.9
2002	57 327	3 052	5.3	6.8	564	12.1	16.6	3 613	26.5	33.7	9 618	20.4
2003	57 725	3 115	5.4	7.0	636	13.5	19.1	3 856	28.0	35.5	9 713	20.4
2004	57 983	3 216	5.5	7.0	657	13.4	17.1	3 962	28.3	35.9	9 926	20.4
2005	58 189	2 944	5.1	6.5	669	13.0	17.6	4 044	28.7	36.2	10 425	21.1
2006	58 964	2 910	4.9	6.4	671	13.2	17.9	4 087	28.3	36.5	9 977	20.0
2007	58 395	2 849	4.9	6.7	696	13.6	17.5	4 078	28.3	37.0	10 189	19.7
2008	59 137	3 261	5.5	7.5	723	13.8	17.6	4 163	28.7	37.2	10 710	20.8
2009	58 428	3 409	5.8	8.3	942	16.9	23.7	4 441	29.9	38.5	11 678	22.0
2010	58 047	3 596	6.2	8.8	880	15.8	24.2	4 745	31.6	40.7	12 422	22.9

. . . = Not available.

Table 3-10. Poverty Status of People by Sex and Age

(Thousands of people, percent of population.)

Year	Poverty status of people by sex				Poverty status of people by age					
	Males below poverty level		Females below poverty level		Children under 18 years below poverty level		People 18 to 64 years below poverty level		People 65 years and older below poverty level	
	Number (thousands)	Poverty rate (percent)	Number (thousands)	Poverty rate (percent)	Number (thousands)	Poverty rate (percent)	Number (thousands)	Poverty rate (percent)	Number (thousands)	Poverty rate (percent)
1959	. . .	. . .	. . .	. . .	17 552	27.3	16 457	17.0	5 481	35.2
1966	12 225	13.0	16 265	16.3	12 389	17.6	11 007	10.5	5 114	28.5
1967	11 813	12.5	15 951	15.8	11 656	16.6	10 725	10.0	5 388	29.5
1968	10 793	11.3	14 578	14.3	10 954	15.6	9 803	9.0	4 632	25.0
1969	10 292	10.6	13 978	13.6	9 691	14.0	9 669	8.7	4 787	25.3
1970	10 879	11.1	14 632	14.0	10 440	15.1	10 187	9.0	4 793	24.6
1971	10 708	10.8	14 841	14.1	10 551	15.3	10 735	9.3	4 273	21.6
1972	10 190	10.2	14 258	13.4	10 284	15.1	10 438	8.8	3 738	18.6
1973	9 642	9.6	13 316	12.5	9 642	14.4	9 977	8.3	3 354	16.3
1974	10 313	10.2	13 881	12.9	10 156	15.4	10 132	8.3	3 085	14.6
1975	10 908	10.7	14 970	13.8	11 104	17.1	11 456	9.2	3 317	15.3
1976	10 373	10.1	14 603	13.4	10 273	16.0	11 389	9.0	3 313	15.0
1977	10 340	10.0	14 381	13.0	10 288	16.2	11 316	8.8	3 177	14.1
1978	10 017	9.6	14 480	13.0	9 931	15.9	11 332	8.7	3 233	14.0
1979	10 535	10.0	14 810	13.2	10 377	16.4	12 014	8.9	3 682	15.2
1980	12 207	11.2	17 065	14.7	11 543	18.3	13 858	10.1	3 871	15.7
1981	13 360	12.1	18 462	15.8	12 505	20.0	15 464	11.1	3 853	15.3
1982	14 842	13.4	19 556	16.5	13 647	21.9	17 000	12.0	3 751	14.6
1983	15 182	13.5	20 084	16.8	13 911	22.3	17 767	12.4	3 625	13.8
1984	14 537	12.8	19 163	15.9	13 420	21.5	16 952	11.7	3 330	12.4
1985	14 140	12.3	18 923	15.6	13 010	20.7	16 598	11.3	3 456	12.6
1986	13 721	11.8	18 649	15.2	12 876	20.5	16 017	10.8	3 477	12.4
1987	14 029	12.0	18 518	15.0	12 843	20.3	15 815	10.6	3 563	12.5
1988	13 599	11.5	18 146	14.5	12 455	19.5	15 809	10.5	3 481	12.0
1989	13 366	11.2	18 162	14.4	12 590	19.6	15 575	10.2	3 363	11.4
1990	14 211	11.7	19 373	15.2	13 431	20.6	16 496	10.7	3 658	12.2
1991	15 082	12.3	20 626	16.0	14 341	21.8	17 586	11.4	3 781	12.4
1992	16 222	12.9	21 792	16.6	15 294	22.3	18 793	11.9	3 928	12.9
1993	16 900	13.3	22 365	16.9	15 727	22.7	19 781	12.4	3 755	12.2
1994	16 316	12.8	21 744	16.3	15 289	21.8	19 107	11.9	3 663	11.7
1995	15 683	12.2	20 742	15.4	14 665	20.8	18 442	11.4	3 318	10.5
1996	15 611	12.0	20 918	15.4	14 463	20.5	18 638	11.4	3 428	10.8
1997	15 187	11.6	20 387	14.9	14 113	19.9	18 085	10.9	3 376	10.5
1998	14 712	11.1	19 764	14.3	13 467	18.9	17 623	10.5	3 386	10.5
1999	14 079	10.4	18 712	13.2	12 280	17.1	17 289	10.1	3 222	9.7
2000	13 536	9.9	18 045	12.6	11 587	16.2	16 671	9.6	3 323	9.9
2001	14 327	10.4	18 580	12.9	11 733	16.3	17 760	10.1	3 414	10.1
2002	15 162	10.9	19 408	13.3	12 133	16.7	18 861	10.6	3 576	10.4
2003	15 783	11.2	20 078	13.7	12 866	17.6	19 443	10.8	3 552	10.2
2004	16 399	11.5	20 641	13.9	13 041	17.8	20 545	11.3	3 453	9.8
2005	15 950	11.1	21 000	14.1	12 896	17.6	20 450	11.1	3 603	10.1
2006	16 000	11.0	20 460	13.6	12 827	17.4	20 239	10.8	3 394	9.4
2007	16 302	11.1	20 973	13.8	13 324	18.0	20 396	10.9	3 556	9.7
2008	17 698	12.0	22 131	14.4	14 068	19.0	22 105	11.7	3 656	9.7
2009	19 475	13.0	24 094	15.6	15 451	20.7	24 684	12.9	3 433	8.9
2010	21 012	14.0	25 167	16.2	16 401	22.0	26 258	13.7	3 520	9.0

. . . = Not available.

Table 3-11. Poor People Age 16 Years and Older by Work Experience

(Thousands of people, percent of population [poverty rate], percent of total poor people.)

| Year | Total number of poor people, 16 years and older | Worked | | | | | | | | | Did not work | | |
| | | Number | Percent of total poor | Worked year-round, full-time | | | Worked less than year-round or full-time | | | Number | Poverty rate (percent) | Percent of total poor |
				Number	Poverty rate (percent)	Percent of total poor	Number	Poverty rate (percent)	Percent of total poor			
1978	16 914	6 599	39.0	1 309	. . .	7.7	5 290	. . .	31.3	10 315	. . .	61.0
1979	16 803	6 601	39.3	1 394	. . .	8.3	5 207	. . .	31.0	10 202	. . .	60.7
1980	18 892	7 674	40.6	1 644	. . .	8.7	6 030	. . .	31.9	11 218	. . .	59.4
1981	20 571	8 524	41.4	1 881	. . .	9.1	6 643	. . .	32.3	12 047	. . .	58.6
1982	22 100	9 013	40.8	1 999	. . .	9.0	7 014	. . .	31.7	13 087	. . .	59.2
1983	22 741	9 329	41.0	2 064	. . .	9.1	7 265	. . .	31.9	13 412	. . .	59.0
1984	21 541	8 999	41.8	2 076	. . .	9.6	6 923	. . .	32.1	12 542	. . .	58.2
1985	21 243	9 008	42.4	1 972	. . .	9.3	7 036	. . .	33.1	12 235	. . .	57.6
1986	20 688	8 743	42.3	2 007	. . .	9.7	6 736	. . .	32.6	11 945	. . .	57.7
1987	20 546	8 258	40.2	1 821	2.4	8.9	6 436	12.5	31.3	12 288	21.6	59.8
1988	20 323	8 363	41.2	1 929	2.4	9.5	6 434	12.7	31.7	11 959	21.2	58.8
1989	19 952	8 376	42.0	1 908	2.4	9.6	6 468	12.5	32.4	11 576	20.8	58.0
1990	21 242	8 716	41.0	2 076	2.6	9.8	6 639	12.6	31.3	12 526	22.1	59.0
1991	22 530	9 208	40.9	2 103	2.6	9.3	7 105	13.4	31.5	13 323	22.8	59.1
1992	23 951	9 739	40.6	2 211	2.7	9.2	7 529	14.1	31.4	14 212	23.7	59.3
1993	24 832	10 144	40.8	2 408	2.9	9.7	7 737	14.6	31.2	14 688	24.2	59.1
1994	24 108	9 829	40.8	2 520	2.9	10.5	7 309	13.9	30.3	14 279	23.6	59.2
1995	23 077	9 484	41.1	2 418	2.7	10.5	7 066	13.7	30.6	13 593	22.3	58.9
1996	23 472	9 586	40.8	2 263	2.5	9.6	7 322	14.1	31.2	13 886	22.7	59.2
1997	22 753	9 444	41.5	2 345	2.5	10.3	7 098	13.8	31.2	13 310	21.7	58.5
1998	22 256	9 133	41.0	2 804	2.9	12.6	6 330	12.7	28.4	13 122	21.1	59.0
1999	21 762	9 251	42.5	2 559	2.6	11.8	6 692	13.2	30.8	12 511	19.9	57.5
2000	21 080	8 511	40.4	2 439	2.4	11.6	6 072	12.1	28.8	12 569	19.8	59.6
2001	22 245	8 530	38.3	2 567	2.6	11.5	5 964	11.8	26.8	13 715	20.6	61.7
2002	23 601	8 954	37.9	2 635	2.6	11.2	6 318	12.4	26.8	14 647	21.0	62.1
2003	24 266	8 820	36.3	2 636	2.6	10.9	6 183	12.2	25.5	15 446	21.5	63.7
2004	25 256	9 384	37.2	2 891	2.8	11.4	6 493	12.8	25.7	15 871	21.7	62.8
2005	25 381	9 340	36.8	2 894	2.8	11.4	6 446	12.8	25.4	16 041	21.8	63.2
2006	24 896	9 181	36.9	2 906	2.7	11.7	6 275	12.6	25.2	15 715	21.1	63.1
2007	25 297	9 089	35.9	2 768	2.5	10.9	6 320	12.7	25.0	16 208	21.5	64.1
2008	27 216	10 085	37.1	2 754	2.6	10.1	7 331	13.5	26.9	17 131	22.0	62.9
2009	29 625	10 680	36.1	2 641	2.7	8.9	8 039	14.5	27.1	18 944	22.7	63.9
2010	31 383	10 666	34.0	2 608	2.6	8.3	8 057	15.0	25.7	20 717	23.9	66.0

. . . = Not available.

Table 3-12. Poverty Rates by State

(Percent of population.)

State	1990	1997	1998	1999	2000	2001	2002	2003	2004	2005	2006	2007	2008	2009	2010
United States	13.5	13.3	12.7	11.9	11.3	11.7	12.1	12.5	12.7	12.6	12.3	12.5	13.2	14.3	15.1
Alabama	19.2	15.7	14.5	15.2	13.3	15.9	14.5	15.0	16.9	16.7	14.3	14.5	14.3	16.6	17.3
Alaska	11.4	8.8	9.4	7.6	7.6	8.5	8.8	9.6	9.1	10.0	8.9	7.6	8.2	11.7	12.4
Arizona	13.7	17.2	16.6	12.2	11.7	14.6	13.5	13.5	14.4	15.2	14.4	14.3	18.0	21.2	18.6
Arkansas	19.6	19.7	14.7	14.7	16.5	17.8	19.8	17.8	15.1	13.8	17.7	13.8	15.3	18.9	15.5
California	13.9	16.6	15.4	14.0	12.7	12.6	13.1	13.1	13.2	13.2	12.2	12.7	14.6	15.3	16.3
Colorado	13.7	8.2	9.2	8.5	9.8	8.7	9.8	9.7	10.0	11.4	9.7	9.8	11.0	12.3	12.2
Connecticut	6.0	8.6	9.5	7.2	7.7	7.3	8.3	8.1	10.1	9.3	8.0	8.9	8.1	8.4	8.3
Delaware	6.9	9.6	10.3	10.4	8.4	6.7	9.1	7.3	9.0	9.2	9.3	9.3	9.6	12.3	12.1
District of Columbia	21.1	21.8	22.3	14.7	15.2	18.2	17.0	16.8	17.0	21.3	18.3	18.0	16.5	17.9	19.9
Florida	14.4	14.3	13.1	12.4	11.0	12.7	12.6	12.7	11.6	11.1	11.5	12.5	13.1	14.6	16.0
Georgia	15.8	14.5	13.5	12.8	12.1	12.9	11.2	11.9	13.0	14.4	12.6	13.6	15.5	18.4	18.7
Hawaii	11.0	13.9	10.9	10.8	8.9	11.4	11.3	9.3	8.6	8.6	9.2	7.5	9.9	12.5	12.1
Idaho	14.9	14.7	13.0	14.1	12.5	11.5	11.3	10.2	9.9	9.9	9.5	9.9	12.2	13.7	14.0
Illinois	13.7	11.2	10.1	9.9	10.7	10.1	12.8	12.6	12.3	11.5	10.6	10.0	12.3	13.2	14.1
Indiana	13.0	8.8	9.4	6.7	8.5	8.5	9.1	9.9	11.6	12.6	10.6	11.8	14.3	16.1	16.3
Iowa	10.4	9.6	9.1	7.4	8.3	7.4	9.2	8.9	10.9	11.3	10.3	8.9	9.5	10.7	10.3
Kansas	10.3	9.7	9.6	12.3	8.0	10.1	10.1	10.8	11.4	12.5	12.8	11.7	12.7	13.7	14.3
Kentucky	17.3	15.9	13.5	12.1	12.6	12.6	14.2	14.4	17.8	14.8	16.8	15.5	17.1	17.0	17.7
Louisiana	23.6	16.3	19.1	19.2	17.2	16.2	17.5	17.0	16.8	18.3	17.0	16.1	18.2	14.3	21.6
Maine	13.1	10.1	10.4	10.6	10.1	10.3	13.4	11.6	11.6	12.6	10.2	10.9	12.0	11.4	12.5
Maryland	9.9	8.4	7.2	7.3	7.4	7.2	7.4	8.6	9.9	9.7	8.4	8.8	8.7	9.6	10.8
Massachusetts	10.7	12.2	8.7	11.8	9.8	8.9	10.0	10.3	9.3	10.1	12.0	11.2	11.3	10.8	10.6
Michigan	14.3	10.3	11.0	9.7	9.9	9.4	11.6	11.4	13.3	12.0	13.3	10.8	13.0	14.0	15.5
Minnesota	12.0	9.6	10.3	7.3	5.7	7.4	6.5	7.4	7.0	8.1	8.2	9.3	9.9	11.1	10.5
Mississippi	25.7	16.7	17.6	16.2	14.9	19.3	18.4	16.0	18.7	20.1	20.6	22.6	18.1	23.1	22.7
Missouri	13.4	11.8	9.8	11.7	9.2	9.7	9.9	10.7	12.2	11.6	11.4	12.8	13.3	15.5	14.8
Montana	16.3	15.6	16.6	15.8	14.1	13.3	13.5	15.1	14.2	13.8	13.5	13.0	12.9	13.5	14.0
Nebraska	10.3	9.8	12.3	11.0	8.6	9.4	10.6	9.8	9.5	9.5	10.2	9.9	10.6	9.9	10.2
Nevada	9.8	11.0	10.6	11.3	8.8	7.1	8.9	10.9	10.9	10.6	9.5	9.7	10.8	13.0	16.4
New Hampshire	6.3	9.1	9.8	7.6	4.5	6.5	5.8	5.8	5.5	5.6	5.4	5.8	7.0	7.8	6.6
New Jersey	9.2	9.3	8.6	7.8	7.3	8.1	7.9	8.6	8.0	6.8	8.8	8.7	9.2	9.3	10.7
New Mexico	20.9	21.2	20.4	20.9	17.5	18.0	17.9	18.1	16.5	17.9	16.9	14.0	19.3	19.3	18.6
New York	14.3	16.5	16.7	14.2	13.9	14.2	14.0	14.3	15.0	14.5	14.0	14.5	14.2	15.8	16.0
North Carolina	13.0	11.4	14.0	13.8	12.5	12.5	14.3	15.7	14.6	13.1	13.8	15.5	13.9	16.9	17.4
North Dakota	13.7	13.6	15.1	13.1	10.4	13.8	11.6	9.7	9.7	11.2	11.4	9.3	11.8	10.9	12.2
Ohio	11.5	11.0	11.2	12.0	10.0	10.5	9.8	10.9	11.6	12.3	12.1	12.8	13.7	13.3	15.3
Oklahoma	15.6	13.7	14.1	12.8	14.9	15.1	14.1	12.8	10.8	15.6	15.2	13.4	13.6	12.9	16.3
Oregon	9.2	11.6	15.0	12.6	10.9	11.8	10.9	12.5	11.8	12.0	11.8	12.8	10.6	13.4	14.2
Pennsylvania	11.0	11.2	11.3	9.3	8.6	9.6	9.5	10.5	11.4	11.2	11.3	10.4	11.0	11.1	12.2
Rhode Island	7.5	12.7	11.6	10.0	10.2	9.6	11.0	11.5	11.5	12.1	10.5	9.5	12.7	13.0	13.6
South Carolina	16.2	13.1	13.7	11.7	11.1	15.1	14.3	12.7	14.9	15.0	11.2	14.1	14.0	13.7	17.0
South Dakota	13.3	16.5	10.8	7.7	10.7	8.4	11.5	12.7	13.5	11.8	10.7	9.4	13.1	14.1	13.2
Tennessee	16.9	14.3	13.4	11.9	13.5	14.1	14.8	14.0	15.9	14.9	14.9	14.8	15.0	16.5	16.7
Texas	15.9	16.7	15.1	15.2	15.5	14.9	15.6	17.0	16.5	16.2	16.4	16.5	15.9	17.3	18.4
Utah	8.2	8.9	9.0	5.7	7.6	10.5	9.9	9.1	10.1	9.2	9.3	9.6	7.6	9.7	10.0
Vermont	10.9	9.3	9.9	9.6	10.0	9.7	9.9	8.5	7.8	7.6	7.8	9.9	9.0	9.4	10.8
Virginia	11.1	12.7	8.8	7.9	8.3	8.0	9.9	10.0	9.4	9.2	8.6	8.6	10.3	10.7	10.7
Washington	8.9	9.2	8.9	9.6	10.8	10.7	11.0	12.6	11.4	10.2	8.0	10.2	10.4	11.7	11.5
West Virginia	18.1	16.4	17.8	15.7	14.7	16.4	16.8	17.4	14.2	15.4	15.3	14.8	14.5	15.8	16.9
Wisconsin	9.3	8.2	8.8	8.6	9.3	7.9	8.6	9.8	12.4	10.2	10.1	11.0	9.8	10.8	9.9
Wyoming	11.0	13.5	10.6	11.6	10.8	8.7	9.0	9.8	10.0	10.6	10.0	10.9	10.1	9.2	9.6

Section 3c: Alternative Measures of Income and Poverty

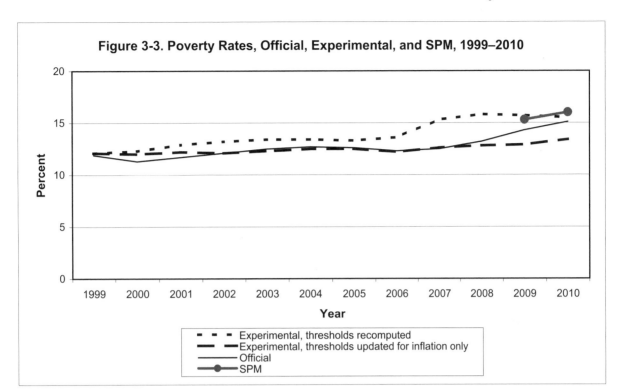

Figure 3-3. Poverty Rates, Official, Experimental, and SPM, 1999–2010

- A special panel of the National Academy of Sciences (NAS) has recommended a complete overhaul of poverty calculations, redefining both needs and resources. For the years 1999 forward, the Census Bureau has calculated experimental poverty measures according to several versions of the NAS recommendations; and for 2009 and 2010, the Bureau issued in 2011 a "Supplemental Poverty Measure," based on further refinement of the NAS recommendations. In Figure 3-3, two of the experimental measures are shown along with the official rate and the SPM. The SPM and all of the experimental measures use more comprehensive and realistic definitions of both needs and resources than the official rate. The SPM and the two experimental measures shown in the graph both include adjustment for geographic differences in the cost of living, and adjust for differing health care needs by excluding medical out-of-pocket expenses from the resources of the measurement unit. (Table 3-14)

- The thresholds for the experimental measures were initially based on needs estimated for the year 1999; in that year, the two experimental measures shown indicated a poverty rate of 12.1 percent, compared with 11.9 percent in the official rate. (Table 3-14)

- One of the experimental measures shown updates the thresholds for inflation only, using the CPI-U, as is the case with the official series. This measure tracks the official series fairly closely through 2007. In the recession years 2008 through 2010, it increases much less than the official measure, probably because resources are on an after-tax basis and include food aid and the Employment Tax Credit. (Table 3-14)

- The other experimental measure recomputes the thresholds each year using the percent increase in a 3-year average of <u>median</u> expenditures on necessities instead of the percent increase in the CPI. The poverty rate with this method of recomputing thresholds rises even in a year of economic expansion such as 2000, diverges even more sharply upward in 2007 and 2008, and then declines slightly in the next two recession years. (Table 3-14)

- The SPM indicates a poverty rate similar to the higher of the experimental rates in 2009, but it increases in 2010, like both the official and the CPI-based experimental rates. It also changes poverty incidence among demographic groups. Reflecting the inclusion of need-based benefits for families, child poverty is somewhat lower than in the official measure, though still above adult poverty rates. But reflecting the adjustment for out-of-pocket medical care spending, poverty for those 65 and older is considerably higher in the SPM, exceeding the rate for adults 18-64. (Tables 3-14 and 3-15)

Table 3-13. Poverty Rates and Income Distribution Coefficients for People, Based on Alternative Definitions of Income

Year	Definition 1, MI: Money income excluding capital gains (current official measure)			Definition 4: Money income before taxes and cash transfers, plus realized capital gains (losses) and health insurance supplements		
	Poverty rate (percent)		Gini coefficient [2]	Poverty rate (percent)		Gini coefficient
	Official threshold	CPI-U-RS threshold [1]		Official threshold	CPI-U-RS threshold [1]	
1979	11.7	10.6	0.403	18.8	17.8	0.460
1980	13.0	11.5	0.401	20.1	19.0	0.462
1981	14.0	12.2	0.404	21.1	19.8	0.466
1982	15.0	13.2	0.409	22.0	20.6	0.475
1983	15.2	13.7	0.412	21.8	20.6	0.478
1984	14.4	12.8	0.413	20.8	19.5	0.477
1985	14.0	12.5	0.418	20.4	19.1	0.486
1986	13.6	12.2	0.423	19.9	18.7	0.505
1987	13.4	12.1	0.424	19.7	18.7	0.488
1988	13.0	11.7	0.425	19.7	18.5	0.489
1989	12.8	11.3	0.429	19.4	18.1	0.492
1990	13.5	11.9	0.426	19.9	18.7	0.487
1991	14.2	12.4	0.425	21.1	19.7	0.490
1992	14.8	13.1	0.430	22.1	20.6	0.497
1993	15.1	13.4	0.448	22.6	21.1	0.514
1994	14.5	12.6	0.450	22.0	20.3	0.515
1995	13.8	11.7	0.444	21.1	19.5	0.509
1996	13.7	11.6	0.447	20.8	19.1	0.511
1997	13.3	11.3	0.448	20.3	18.7	0.513
1998	12.7	10.6	0.446	19.3	17.4	0.509
1999	11.9	9.9	0.445	18.7	16.9	0.508
2000	11.3	9.7	0.447	18.0	16.5	0.506
2001	11.7	9.9	0.450	18.5	16.9	0.510
2002	12.1	10.1	0.448	19.0	17.4	. . .
2003	12.5	10.5	0.450	19.5	17.8	. . .
2004	12.7	10.8	0.450	20.0	18.3	0.503
2005	12.6	10.8	0.450	19.7	18.1	0.501
2006	12.3	10.5	0.447	18.9	17.3	0.495
2007	12.5	11.0	0.443	19.3	18.0	0.492
2008 [4]	13.2	11.7	0.446	20.8	19.6	0.497
2009 [4]	14.3	12.8	0.447	23.0	21.6	0.505

Year	Definition 14, MI - Tx + NC: Income after all taxes and transfers			Definition 15, MI - Tx + NC + HE: Income after all taxes and transfers, plus net imputed return on equity in own home		
	Poverty rate (percent)		Gini coefficient [3]	Poverty rate (percent)		Gini coefficient [3]
	Official threshold	CPI-U-RS threshold [1]		Official threshold	CPI-U-RS threshold [1]	
1979	8.9	7.9	0.359	7.5	6.7	0.352
1980	10.1	8.6	0.354	8.2	7.0	0.347
1981	11.5	9.8	0.358	8.7	7.3	0.350
1982	12.3	10.6	0.366	9.9	8.5	0.359
1983	12.7	11.0	0.374	10.4	9.0	0.368
1984	12.0	10.4	0.378	9.9	8.6	0.372
1985	11.7	10.1	0.385	9.9	8.6	0.381
1986	11.3	9.8	0.409	10.1	8.6	0.404
1987	11.0	9.5	0.382	9.7	8.2	0.380
1988	10.8	9.4	0.385	9.4	8.2	0.384
1989	10.4	8.8	0.389	9.1	7.6	0.387
1990	10.9	9.3	0.382	9.8	8.3	0.381
1991	11.4	9.7	0.380	10.3	8.6	0.379
1992	11.9	10.2	0.385	10.7	9.1	0.381
1993	12.1	10.3	0.398	11.2	9.4	0.395
1994	11.1	9.2	0.400	10.0	8.3	0.395
1995	10.3	8.5	0.394	9.4	7.6	0.388
1996	10.2	8.4	0.398	9.3	7.6	0.392
1997	10.0	8.2	0.403	9.2	7.5	0.397
1998	9.5	7.7	0.405	8.8	7.1	0.399
1999	8.9	7.2	0.408	8.2	6.5	0.402
2000	8.8	7.2	0.410	8.0	6.5	0.402
2001	9.0	7.3	0.412	8.3	6.7	0.407
2002	9.3	7.7	0.394	8.6	7.1	0.388
2003	9.7	7.9	0.394	9.0	7.4	0.390
2004	9.6	7.9	0.404	8.8	7.2	0.398
2005	9.6	8.1	0.402	8.9	7.4	0.398
2006	9.3	7.9	0.405	8.7	7.4	0.400
2007	9.5	8.3	0.403	9.1	7.9	0.399
2008 [4]	9.8	8.4	0.392	9.2	7.9	0.389
2009 [4]	10.1	8.7	0.392	9.7	8.4	0.388

[1]Before 1987, threshold based on CPI-U-X1.
[2]Calculated for comparability by same method as the other coefficients in this table; differs from official calculation in Table 3-4.
[3]Earlier years not comparable with 2002 and subsequent years because of a change in tax estimating model.
[4]2008 and 2009 data do not include estimates of capital gains (losses).
. . . = Not available.

Table 3-14. Official and Experimental Poverty Rates and Supplemental Poverty Measure, 1999–2010

(Percent of population.)

Measurement method	Capital gains included in income								
	1999	2000	2001	2002 (new tax model)	2003	2004 (revised)	2005	2006	2007
Official measure	11.9	11.3	11.7	12.1	12.5	12.7	12.6	12.3	12.5
Experimental									
MSI-GA-CPI	12.1	12.0	12.2	12.1	12.3	12.5	12.5	12.2	12.6
MIT-GA-CPI	12.7	12.5	12.5	12.6	12.7	13.0	13.0	12.6	13.0
MSI-NGA-CPI	12.2	12.1	12.3	12.3	12.4	12.7	12.6	12.4	12.6
MIT-NGA-CPI	12.8	12.7	12.7	12.8	12.7	13.1	13.0	12.8	12.9
MSI-GA-CE	12.1	12.3	12.9	13.2	13.4	13.4	13.3	13.6	15.3
MIT-GA-CE	12.7	12.8	13.2	13.7	13.9	14.0	14.1	14.1	15.9
MSI-NGA-CE	12.2	12.5	13.0	13.4	13.5	13.4	13.5	13.7	15.1
MIT-NGA-CE	12.8	13.0	13.4	13.9	14.1	14.1	14.2	14.2	16.0
Supplemental poverty measure	...	...	...	...	...	...	...	...	...

Measurement method	Capital gains excluded from income			
	2007	2008	2009	2010
Official measure	12.5	13.2	14.3	15.1
Experimental				
MSI-GA-CPI	12.6	12.8	12.9	13.4
MIT-GA-CPI	13.0	13.2	13.2	13.8
MSI-NGA-CPI	12.6	12.8	12.8	13.5
MIT-NGA-CPI	13.0	13.1	13.3	14.0
MSI-GA-CE	15.3	15.8	15.7	15.5
MIT-GA-CE	15.9	16.9	17.3	17.2
MSI-NGA-CE	15.2	15.7	15.7	15.6
MIT-NGA-CE	16.1	17.1	17.3	17.3
Supplemental poverty measure	...	...	15.3	16.0

Note: The Census Bureau changed the way it modeled taxes, effective with the revised 2002 estimates. Consequently, comparisons of 2002 and later data with earlier years may be affected.

MSI means "Medical out-of-pocket expenses subtracted from income."
MIT means "Medical out-of-pocket expenses in the thresholds."
GA means "Geographic adjustment (of poverty thresholds)."
NGA means "No geographic adjustment (of poverty thresholds)."
CPI means "Thresholds were adjusted since 1999 using the Consumer Price Index for All Urban Consumers."
CE means "Thresholds were recomputed since 1999 using data from the Consumer Expenditure Survey."

See notes and definitions for further explanation.
... = Not available.

Table 3-15. Number and Percent of People in Poverty Using the Supplemental Poverty Measure, 2009–2010, and Comparison With Official Measures in 2010

(Numbers in thousands; percent of population.)

Characteristic	SPM 2009		SPM 2010		Official, 2010[1]	
	Number	Percent	Number	Percent	Number	Percent
All People	46 471	15.3	49 094	16.0	46 602	15.2
Age						
Under 18 years	12 951	17.3	13 622	18.2	16 823	22.5
18 to 64 years	27 537	14.4	29 235	15.2	26 258	13.7
65 years and older	5 984	15.5	6 237	15.9	3 520	9.0
Type of Unit						
In married-couple unit	17 677	9.5	18 295	9.9	14 200	7.6
In female householder unit	16 894	27.9	17 991	29.0	17 768	28.7
In male householder unit	6 960	21.9	7 317	22.7	5 927	18.4
In new SPM unit	4 940	19.4	5 490	21.0	8 690	33.2
Race and Hispanic Origin						
White	33 097	13.7	34 747	14.3	31 959	13.1
White, not Hispanic	20 696	10.5	21 876	11.1	19 819	10.0
Black	9 029	23.4	9 932	25.4	10 741	27.5
Asian	2 524	18.0	2 397	16.7	1 737	12.1
Hispanic, any race	13 485	27.6	14 088	28.2	13 346	26.7
Nativity						
Native born	37 010	13.9	39 329	14.7	38 965	14.5
Foreign born	9 462	25.2	9 765	25.5	7 636	20.0
Naturalized citizen	2 710	16.9	2 829	16.8	1 910	11.4
Not a citizen	6 752	31.3	6 936	32.4	5 727	26.7
Tenure						
Owner	19 895	9.5	20 205	9.7	16 529	8.0
Owner/mortgage	11 958	8.0	11 419	8.3	8 366	6.0
Owner/no-mortgage/rent-free	8 748	13.8	9 581	13.3	9 036	12.5
Renter	25 766	28.0	28 093	29.4	29 199	30.5
Residence						
Inside MSAs	40 000	15.6	42 979	16.6	38 650	15.0
Inside principal cities	19 227	19.6	20 748	21.0	19 584	19.8
Outside principal cities	20 773	13.1	22 231	13.9	19 066	11.9
Outside MSAs	6 471	13.5	6 114	12.8	7 951	16.6
Region						
Northeast	7 467	13.7	7 969	14.5	7 051	12.9
Midwest	7 995	12.1	8 678	13.1	9 246	14.0
South	17 697	15.8	18 503	16.3	19 210	17.0
West	13 312	18.7	13 944	19.4	11 904	15.4
Health Insurance Coverage						
With private insurance	13 498	6.9	14 631	7.5	9 336	4.8
With public, no private insurance	18 107	30.7	19 126	31.7	22 694	37.6
Not insured	14 866	30.3	15 337	30.7	14 571	29.2

[1]Differs from published official rates as unrelated individulas under 15 years of age are included in the universe.

NOTES AND DEFINITIONS, CHAPTER 3

TABLES 3-1 THROUGH 3-15
INCOME DISTRIBUTION AND POVERTY

SOURCE: U.S. DEPARTMENT OF COMMERCE, BUREAU OF THE CENSUS

All data in this chapter are derived from the Current Population Survey (CPS), which is also the source of the data on labor force, employment, and unemployment used in Chapter 10. (See the notes and definitions for Tables 10-1 through 10-5.) In March of each year (with some data also collected in February and April), the households in this monthly survey are asked additional questions concerning earnings and other income in the previous year. This additional information, informally known as the "March Supplement," is now formally known as the Current Population Survey Annual Social and Economic Supplement (CPS-ASEC). It was previously called the Annual Demographic Supplement.

The population represented by the survey is the civilian noninstitutional population of the United States and members of the armed forces in the United States living off post or with their families on post, but excluding all other members of the armed forces. (The armed forces households are not included in the basic CPS for purposes of collecting employment and unemployment data.) As it is a survey of households, homeless persons are not included.

Definitions: Racial classification and Hispanic origin

In 2002 and all earlier years, the CPS required respondents to report identification with only one race group. Since 2003, the CPS has allowed respondents to choose more than one race group. Income data for 2002 were collected in early 2003; thus, in the data for 2002 and all subsequent years, an individual could report identification with more than one race group. In the 2000 census, about 2.6 percent of people reported identification with more than one race.

Therefore, data from 2002 onward that are classified by race are not strictly comparable with race-classified data for 2001 and earlier years. As alternative approaches to dealing with this problem, the Census Bureau has tabulated two different race concepts for each racial category in a number of cases. In the case of Blacks, for example, this means there is one income measure for "Black alone," consisting of persons who report Black and no other race, and one for "Black alone or in combination," which includes all the "Black alone" reporters plus those who report Black in combination with any other race. The tables in this volume show both the "alone" and the "alone or in combination" values where available.

The race classifications now used in the CPS are *White, Black, Asian, American Indian and Alaska Native,* and *Native Hawaiian and Other Pacific Islander.* (Native Hawaiians and other Pacific Islanders were included in the "Asian" category in the data for 1987 through 2001.) The last two of these five racial groups are too small to provide reliable data for a single year, but in new Census Bureau tables available on the website, household income and poverty data for all five groups are presented in 2- and 3-year averages. Table 3-2 displays some of these data.

Hispanic origin is a separate question in the survey—not a racial classification—and Hispanics may be of any race. A subgroup of *White non-Hispanic* is shown in some tables. According to the Census Bureau, "Being Hispanic was reported by 13.2 percent of White householders who reported only one race, 3.1 percent of Black householders who reported only one race, and 1.9 percent of Asian householders who reported only one race…Data users should exercise caution when interpreting aggregate results for the Hispanic population or for race groups because these populations consist of many distinct groups that differ in socioeconomic characteristics, culture, and recency of immigration." ("Income, Poverty, and Health Insurance Coverage in the United States: 2010," footnote 2, p. 2)

Definitions: General

A *household* consists of all persons who occupy a housing unit. A household includes the related family members and all the unrelated persons, if any (such as lodgers, foster children, wards, or employees), who share the housing unit. A person living alone in a housing unit or a group of unrelated persons sharing a housing unit as partners is also counted as a household. The count of households excludes group quarters.

Earnings includes all income from work, including wages, salaries, armed forces pay, commissions, tips, piece-rate payments, and cash bonuses, before deductions such as taxes, bonds, pensions, and union dues. This category also includes net income from nonfarm self-employment and farm self-employment. Wage and salary supplements that are paid directly by the employer, such as the employer share of Social Security taxes and the cost of employer-provided health insurance, are not included.

Income, in the official definition used in the survey, is money income, including *earnings* from work as defined above; unemployment compensation; workers' compensation; Social Security; Supplemental Security Income; cash public assistance (welfare payments); veterans' payments; survivor benefits; disability benefits; pension or retirement income; interest income; dividends (but not capital gains); rents, royalties, and payments from estates or trusts; educational assistance, such as scholarships or grants; child support; alimony; financial assistance from outside of the household; and other cash income regularly received, such as foster child payments, military family allotments, and foreign government pensions. Receipts not counted as income include capital gains or losses, withdrawals of bank deposits, money borrowed, tax refunds, gifts, and lump-sum inheritances or insurance payments.

A *year-round, full-time worker* is a person who worked 35 or more hours per week and 50 or more weeks during the previous calendar year.

A *family* is a group of two or more persons related by birth, marriage, or adoption who reside together.

Unrelated individuals are persons 15 years old and over who are not living with any relatives. In the official poverty measure, the poverty status of unrelated individuals is determined independently of and is not affected by the incomes of other persons with whom they may share a household.

Median income is the amount of income that divides a ranked income distribution into two equal groups, with half having incomes above the median, and half having incomes below the median. The median income for persons is based on persons 15 years old and over with income.

Mean income is the amount obtained by dividing the total aggregate income of a group by the number of units in that group. In this survey, as in most surveys of incomes, means are higher than medians because of the skewed nature of the income distribution; see the section "Whose standard of living?" in the article at the beginning of this book.

Historical income figures are shown in constant *2010 dollars*. All constant-dollar figures are converted from current-dollar values using the *CPI-U-RS* (the Consumer Price Index, All Urban, Research Series), which measures changes in prices for past periods using the methodologies of the current CPI, and is similar in concept and behavior to the deflators used in the NIPAs for consumer income and spending. See Chapter 8 for CPI-U-RS data and the corresponding notes and definitions.

Definitions: Income distribution

Income distribution is portrayed by dividing the total ranked distribution of families or households into *fifths*, also known as *quintiles,* and also by separately tabulating the top 5 percent (which is included in the highest fifth). The households or families are arrayed from those with the lowest income to those with the highest income, then divided into five groups, with each group containing one-fifth of the total number of households. Within each quintile, incomes are summed and calculated as a share of total income for all quintiles, and are averaged to show the average (mean) income within that quintile.

A statistical measure that summarizes the dispersion of income across the entire income distribution is the *Gini coefficient* (also known as Gini ratio, Gini index, or index of income concentration), which can take values ranging from 0 to 1. A Gini value of 1 indicates "perfect" inequality; that is, one household has all the income and the rest have none. A value of 0 indicates "perfect" equality, a situation in which each household has the same income.

There are differences between the Gini coefficients for the official income measure presented in the report's main tables and those presented in Table 3-13. In the latter, the coefficients were recalculated, using a slightly different method, for comparability with the other income definitions.

A new "equivalence-adjusted" measure of household income inequality was introduced last year and is displayed in Table 3-4. For a Census-defined household, a given level of money income can have different implications for that household's well-being, depending on the size of the household and how many children, if any, are in the household. Since there have been substantial changes over past decades in the average size and composition of households, some have questioned the pertinence of standard income distribution tables. In response, the Census Bureau now also reports measures of income inequality for households using "equivalence-adjusted" income.

The equivalence adjustment is based on a three-parameter scale reflecting the size of the household and the facts that children consume less than adults; that as family size increases, expenses do not increase at the same rate; and that the increase in expenses is larger for the first child of a single-parent family than the first child of a two-adult family. The same concept is used in the poverty thresholds for the NAS-based alternative poverty estimates shown in Tables 3-14 and 3-15 and described later in these Notes.

As can be seen in Table 3-4, the equivalence-adjusted measures generally show somewhat less inequality than the raw money income measures, but they show a greater move toward inequality over the period 1967-2010. By 2010, the lowest fifth of the distribution has just 3.3 percent of total income by both measures.

Definitions: Poverty

The *number of people below poverty level,* or the number of poor people, is the number of people with family or individual incomes below a specified level that is intended to measure the cost of a minimum standard of living. These minimum levels vary by size and composition of family and are known as *poverty thresholds.*

The official poverty thresholds are based on a definition developed in 1964 by Mollie Orshansky of the Social Security Administration. She calculated food budgets for families of various sizes and compositions, using an "economy food plan" developed by the U.S. Department of Agriculture (the cheapest of four plans developed). Reflecting a 1955 Department of Agriculture survey that found that families of three or more persons spent about one-third of their after-tax incomes on food, Orshansky multiplied the costs of the food plan by 3 to arrive at a set of thresholds for poverty income for families of three or larger. For 2-person families, the multiplier was 3.7; for 1-person families, the threshold was 80 percent of the two-person threshold.

These poverty thresholds have been adjusted each year for price increases, using the percent change in the Consumer Price Index for All Urban Consumers (CPI-U).

For more information on the Orshansky thresholds (the description of which has been simplified here), see Gordon Fisher, "The Development of the Orshansky Thresholds and Their Subsequent History as the Official U.S. Poverty Measure" (May 1992), available on the Census Bureau Web site at <http://www.census.gov/hhes/poverty/povmeas/papers/orshansky.html>.

The *poverty rate* for a demographic group is the number of poor people or poor families in that group expressed as a percentage of the total number of people or families in the group.

Average poverty thresholds. The thresholds used to calculate the official poverty rates vary not only with the size of the family but with the number of children in the family. For example, the threshold for a three-person family in 2010 was $17,057 if there were no children in the family but $17,568 if the family consisted of 1 adult and 2 children. There are 48 different threshold values depending on size of household, number of children, and whether the householder is 65 years old or over (with lower thresholds for the older householders). The full matrix of thresholds is shown in the report referenced below. To give a general sense of the "poverty line," the Census Bureau also publishes the <u>average</u> threshold for each size family, based on the actual mix of family types in that year. These are the values shown in *Business Statistics* in Table 3-7 to represent the history of poverty thresholds. The <u>average</u> value for 3-person families in 2010, as shown in Table 3-7, was $17,374, a weighted average of the values actually used for the 3 different possible family compositions.

A person with *work experience* (Table 3-11) is one who, during the preceding calendar year and on a part-time or full-time basis, did any work for pay or profit or worked without pay on a family-operated farm or business at any time during the year. A *year-round* worker is one who worked for 50 weeks or more during the preceding calendar year. A person is classified as having worked *full time* if he or she worked 35 hours or more per week during a majority of the weeks worked. A *year-round, full-time worker* is a person who worked 35 or more hours per week and 50 or more weeks during the previous calendar year.

Toward better measures of income and poverty

The definition of the official poverty rate is established by the Office of Management of Budget in the Executive Office of the President and has not been substantially changed since 1969. Criticisms of the current definition are legion. In response to these criticisms, the Census Bureau has published extensive research work illustrating the effects of various ways of modifying income definitions and poverty thresholds. Some of the results of this work are published here in Tables 3-13 through 3-15 and explained in the notes and definitions below.

Improving the income concept

One type of criticism accepted the general concept of the Orshansky threshold but recommended making the income definition more realistic by including some or all of the following: capital gains; taxes and tax credits; noncash food,

housing, and health benefits provided by government and employers; and the value of homeownership. There is debate about whether it is appropriate to use income data augmented in this way in conjunction with the official thresholds. The original 1964 thresholds made no allowance for health insurance or other health expenses—in effect, they assumed that the poor would get free medical care, or at least that the poverty calculation was not required to allow for medical needs—and because of the imprecision of Orshansky's multiplier it is not clear to what extent they include housing expenses in a way that is comparable with the inclusion of a homeownership component in income. Nevertheless, the Census Bureau has calculated and published income and poverty figures based on broadened income definitions and either the official thresholds or thresholds that are closely related to the official ones. Some of these calculations are presented in Table 3-13 and described below.

Still accepting the validity of the basic Orshansky threshold concept, some critics have also argued that use of the CPI-U in the official measure to update the thresholds each year has overstated the price increase, and that an inflator such as the CPI-U-RS should be used instead. (See the notes and definitions for Chapter 8.) Use of the CPI-U-RS leads to lower poverty thresholds beginning in the late 1970s, when the CPI began to be distorted by housing and other biases subsequently corrected by new methods; these newer methods were not carried backward to revise the <u>official</u> CPI-U. Table 3-13 also shows poverty rates using the lower CPI-U-RS thresholds. Use of the CPI-U-RS, which does carry current methods back and thereby revises the CPI time series, eliminates a presumed upward bias in the poverty rate <u>relative to the poverty rates estimated before the bias emerged</u>. This is a bias in the behavior of the time series <u>given the concept of the Orshansky threshold</u>, not necessarily a bias in the current <u>level</u> of poverty, since all the other criticisms of the Orshansky thresholds need to be considered when assessing the general adequacy of today's poverty measurements.

Alternative definitions of income with Orshansky-type poverty thresholds—Table 3-13

The Census Bureau has calculated "alternative" income and poverty measures based on a number of different definitions of income. In many cases, these measures require simulation—use of data from sources other than the CPS to estimate elements of family and individual income and expenses. One system of income definition alternatives, shown in Table 3-13, was used for data through 2003 and has been selectively updated through 2009. The updated data for 2009 are shown on the website under the category "Effect of Benefits and Taxes on Income and Poverty." This system provides poverty rates including and excluding the effects of government tax and transfer programs, demonstrating the effects of these programs in alleviating poverty. In the most recent Census reports, these series have not been updated to 2010.

Table 3-13 shows household income distribution and poverty data through 2009 according to this system of alternative income definitions, which was last used in published reports for 2003 data, issued in June 2005.

Definition 1, also known as "MI," is the official Census Bureau definition of money income described above.

Definition 4 is Definition 1 income <u>minus</u> government cash transfers (Social Security, unemployment compensation, workers' compensation, veterans' payments, railroad retirement, Black Lung payments, government education assistance, Supplemental Security Income, and welfare payments), <u>plus</u> realized capital gains and employers' payments for health insurance coverage. Capital gains and health insurance were not collected in the CPS but were simulated using statistical data from the Internal Revenue Service and the National Medical Care Expenditure Survey. Definition 4 is the closest approach in this set of calculations to a measure of the income generated by the workings of the economy before government interventions in the form of taxes and transfer payments.

Definition 14, also known as "MI − Tx + NC," is income after all government income and earnings tax and transfer interventions. It consists of Definition 4 income minus payroll taxes and federal and state income taxes, plus the Earned Income Credit; plus all of the cash transfers listed above as being subtracted from money income to yield Definition 4; plus the "fungible" value of Medicare and Medicaid (see below for definition); plus the value of regular-price school lunches provided by government; and plus the value of noncash transfers, including food stamps, rent subsidies, and free and reduced-price school lunches. The tax information is not collected in the CPS but was simulated using statistical data from the Internal Revenue Service, Social Security payroll tax formulas, and a model of each state's income tax regulations.

The "fungible" value approach to medical benefits counts such benefits as income only to the extent that they free up resources that would have been spent on medical care. Therefore, if family income is not sufficient to cover the family's basic food and housing requirements, Medicare and Medicaid are treated as having no income value. Data on average Medicare and Medicaid outlays per enrollee are used in the valuation process. It appears that the inclusion of these estimates of fungible values makes little difference in the overall poverty rate, reducing it by just 0.2 percentage points in 2009.

Food stamp values are reported in the March CPS. Estimates of other government subsidy payments use data from the Department of Agriculture (for school lunches) and the 1985 American Housing Survey.

Definition 15 ("MI − Tx + NC + HE") is Definition 14 income plus the net imputed return on equity in owner-occupied housing—the calculated annual benefit of converting one's home equity into an annuity, net of property taxes. This concept can be thought of as measuring the extent to which equity in the home relieves the owner of the need for rental or mortgage payments. Information from the 1987 American Housing Survey is used to assign values of

home equity and amounts of property taxes. Since disposable personal income in the national income and product accounts (NIPAs) includes the imputed rent on owner-occupied housing plus most of the cash and in-kind transfers included in Definitions 14 and 15, Definition 15 is the Census Bureau income definition closest to the NIPA concept.

Improving the concepts of income and poverty together

Another type of criticism argues that the official thresholds are also no longer relevant to today's needs, and that the concepts of income (or "resources") and of the threshold level that depicts a minimum adequate standard of living need to be rethought together. These critics cite the availability of more up-to-date and detailed information about consumer spending at various income levels. The Consumer Expenditure Survey (CEX), originally designed to provide the weights for the Consumer Price Index, is now conducted quarterly and provides extensive data on consumer spending patterns. To give just one example of the information available now that was not available to Mollie Orshansky, the CEX indicates that food now accounts for one-sixth, not one-third, of total family expenditures, even among low-income families. (For data from, and notes on, the Consumer Expenditure Survey, see Bernan Press, *Handbook of U.S. Labor Statistics.*)

A special panel of the National Academy of Sciences (NAS) undertook a study that reconsidered both resources and thresholds. The Census Bureau has calculated and published experimental poverty rates for 1999 through 2010, developed following NAS recommendations, which are presented in Table 3-14. In November 2011 the Bureau issued "The Research Supplemental Poverty Measure" for 2009 and 2010, a further refinement of the NAS recommendations, which is presented in Tables 3-14 and 3-15.

Experimental measures based on NAS recommendations—Table 3-14

Several alternative poverty rates that redefined both resources and needs were presented in "Alternative Poverty Estimates in the United States: 2003" (see below for complete reference) and have been updated through 2010 on the Census Bureau Web site at <http://www.census.gov>, under the general heading "NAS-based Experimental Poverty Estimates."

To derive these estimates, a baseline set of poverty thresholds for the year 1999, based on data from the CEX for the years 1997–1999, was developed as follows:

- A reference family type was selected: a 2-adult, 2-child family.

- The definition of necessities for the purpose of the poverty threshold was expenditures on food, clothing, shelter, and utilities (FCSU), augmented by a multiplier of between 1.15 and 1.25 to include other needs such as household and personal supplies. The definition of food includes food away from home. Expenses on shelter include interest (but not principal repayment) for home-owners and rent for renters.

- The numerical estimates were derived as follows: FCSU expenditures for reference families falling between the 30th and 35th percentile of the distribution of expenditures in the CEX, based on 1997–1999 data but expressed in 1999 dollars, were calculated and expanded by the multiplier percentages. The midpoint of these estimates was then selected as the poverty threshold; it turned out to be 96.725 percent of FCSU expenditures by the median household.

- For health care, three different treatments were developed; these treatments are described below.

- Three-parameter equivalence scale adjustments were used to convert the threshold for the reference family to thresholds for other family sizes and compositions, accounting for the differing needs of adults and children and the economies of scale of living in larger families.

- For some of the experimental measures, thresholds were adjusted geographically to reflect differences in the cost of living (in practice, difference in housing costs) in different areas.

The family incomes to be compared with these poverty thresholds were defined and measured to include the effects of all taxes, tax credits, and in-kind benefits such as food stamps, but not the value of homeownership, and to allow for expenses such as child care that are necessary to hold a job.

The 8 experimental measures shown in Table 3-14 are as originally presented in Table B-3 in "Alternative Poverty Estimates in the United States: 2003," and most recently updated in the table "Official and National Academy of Sciences (NAS) Based Poverty Rates: 1999 to 2010" on the Census Bureau Web site. The following abbreviations are used to define the alternative definitions of poverty that are presented in this table.

- *MSI* indicates that in calculating the poverty rate, medical out-of-pocket expenses are subtracted from family income before comparing that income to the family's threshold.

- *MIT* indicates that poverty thresholds were increased to take the family's potential medical out-of-pocket expenses into account, using the CEX and the 1996 Medical Expenditures Panel Survey, with the amounts depending on family size, age, and health insurance coverage.

- *GA* indicates that the thresholds were adjusted for geographic differences in the cost of living. Measures labeled *NGA* were not.

- *CPI* indicates that the thresholds established for 1999 were updated to succeeding years using the percent change in the CPI-U. In effect, the thresholds for these measures have been held constant in real (inflation-

adjusted) terms since 1999, just as the official thresholds have been held constant in real terms—in intention, and in fact except for bias in the price indexes—since 1964.

- *CE* indicates that the thresholds were updated using the percent change in median FCSU expenditures from the latest available 12 quarters of CEX data. This means that if the actual real FCSU spending of middle-income families rises (or falls), the real standard of living represented by the poverty thresholds will rise (or fall) commensurately.

Supplemental Poverty Measure—Tables 3-14 and 3-15

In March of 2010, an Interagency Technical Working Group produced suggestions for a Supplemental Poverty Measure (SPM), which were implemented in the "Research Supplemental Poverty Measure: 2010" issued by the Census Bureau in November 2011. The resulting SPM goes beyond the experimental measures just described, and takes advantage of new data from questions introduced in the CPS-ASEC for 2009 and 2010 incomes. In the new SPM:

- The measurement unit now covers not just the family but "all related individuals who live at the same address, including any coresident unrelated children who are cared for by the family (such as foster children) and any cohabitors and their children." This redefinition adds unrelated individuals under the age of 15 to the universe measured by the official rate. The "official" measures shown in Table 3-15 have been adjusted to include these individuals, and are therefore slightly higher than the regular published official rates shown in Tables 3-8 through 3-14.

- The SPM thresholds are calculated separately for three housing status groups: owners with mortgages, owners without mortgages, and renters. For each of these three groups the basic threshold represents the 33rd percentile of expenditures on food, clothing, shelter, and utilities (FCSU), averaged over a five-year period, by consumer units with two children, multiplied by 1.2 to allow for other needs. (Before averaging, the expenditures are converted to their dollar values in the prices of the threshold year using the CPI-U.) The consumer units selected for calculating the threshold include not only two-adult two-child families but also other types with two children, such as single-parent families. But they are adjusted to a four-person basis, using the equivalence scales, before averaging them to determine the basic threshold appropriate to a two-adult two-child household. Then that threshold is used as the basis for calculating thresholds for other size measurement units, again using the three-parameter equivalence scales for family size and composition, and for geographic differences.

- The thresholds are updated each year, using an updated five-year moving average of FCSU at the 33rd percentile, expressed in the prices of the new threshold year. Thus the thresholds are adjusted for inflation, but in addition, the "real" (constant-dollar) purchasing power of the poverty threshold will change (gradually) over time as the real standard of FCSU spending in the 33rd percentile changes.

- Family resources include cash income, plus in-kind benefits that families can use to meet their FCSU needs (for example, the Supplemental Nutrition Assistance Program [SNAP] formerly known as food stamps), minus income and payroll taxes, plus tax credits, minus childcare and other work-related expenses, minus child support payments to another household, and minus out-of-pocket medical expenses.

The SPM is not intended to replace the official poverty measure and is not to be used in calculations affecting program eligibility and funding distribution. According to the report referenced above, it is "designed to provide information on aggregate levels of economic need at a national level or within large subpopulations or areas…providing further understanding of economic conditions and trends." Census Bureau presentation of the SPM has focused on the different distribution of the poverty population indicated by the new measures, as shown in Table 3-15.

Notes on the data

The following are the principal changes that may affect year-to-year comparability of all income and poverty data from the CPS.

- Beginning in 1952, the estimates are based on 1950 census population controls. Earlier figures were based on 1940 census population controls.

- Beginning in 1962, 1960 census–based sample design and population controls are fully implemented.

- With 1971 and 1972 data, 1970 census–based sample design and population controls were introduced.

- With 1983–1985 data, 1980 census–based sample design was introduced; 1980 population controls were introduced; and these were extended back to 1979 data.

- With 1993 data, there was a major redesign of the CPS, including the introduction of computer-assisted interviewing. The limits used to "code" reported income amounts were changed, resulting in reporting of higher income values for the highest-income families and, consequently, an exaggerated year-to-year increase in income inequality. (It is possible that this jump actually reflects in one year an increase that had emerged more gradually, so that the distribution measures for 1993 and later years may be properly comparable with data for decades earlier even if they should not be directly compared with 1992.) In addition, 1990 census–based population controls were introduced, and these were extended back to the 1992 data.

- With 1995 data, the 1990 census–based sample design was implemented and the sample was reduced by 7,000 households.

- Data for 2001 implemented population controls based on the 2000 census, which were carried back to 2000 and 1999 data as well. Data from 2000 forward also incorporate results from a 28,000-household sample expansion.

For more information on these and other changes that could affect comparability, see "Current Population Survey Technical Paper 63RV: Design and Methodology" (March 2002) and footnotes to CPS historical income tables, both available on the Census Bureau Web site at <http://www .census.gov/hhes/income>.

Data availability

Data embodying the official definitions of income and poverty are published annually in late summer or early fall by the Census Bureau, as part of a series with the general title *Current Population Reports: Consumer Income, P60.* Most of the data in this chapter were derived from report P60-239, "Income, Poverty, and Health Insurance Coverage in the United States: 2010" (September 2011), and from the "Historical Income Tables" and "Historical Poverty Tables" on the Census Web site (see below).

The data in Table 3-13 were first published in two reports, both issued in June 2005: P60-228, "Alternative Income Estimates in the United States: 2003," and P60-227, "Alternative Poverty Estimates in the United States: 2003." Updates available on the Web site are cited in the table description above. Corrections to the 2006 data on the Web site were obtained from Census Bureau staff.

The NAS-based experimental data used in Table 3-14 are from the Census Bureau Web site, as specified in the description above.

The SPM data in Tables 3-14 and 3-15 are from the report "The Research Supplemental Poverty Measure: 2010" (P60-241), available on the Census Web site.

All these reports and related data, including historical tabulations, used in *Business Statistics* are available on the Census Bureau Web site at <http://www.census.gov>, under the general headings of "Income" and "Poverty."

References

Definitions and descriptions of the concepts and data of all series are provided in the source documents listed above and in the references contained therein.

CHAPTER 4: CONSUMER INCOME AND SPENDING

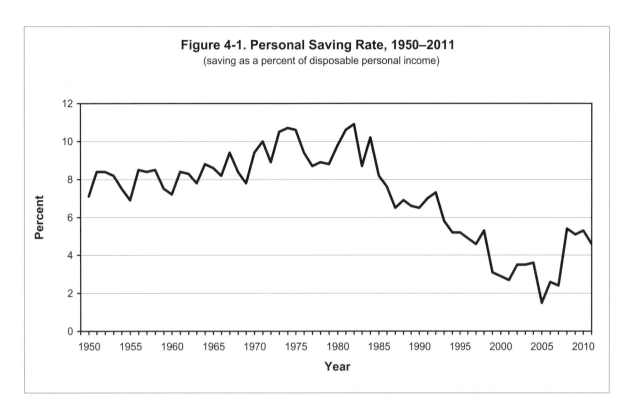

Figure 4-1. Personal Saving Rate, 1950–2011
(saving as a percent of disposable personal income)

- The personal saving rate—saving as a percent of disposable income—averaged 8 to 10 percent for much of the postwar period, but started to trend down around the mid-1980s. From 1999 through 2007, the saving rate ranged between 1.5 and 3.6 percent and averaged 2.9 percent. According to updated estimates, nonprofit institutions ("NPISHs"), which are included in the "personal" sector definition, actually dis-saved for much of this period—on net, borrowing and/or spending out of assets—and households saved less, borrowed more, and/or spent more out of assets than in earlier years. The personal saving rate rose back to a range of 4 ½ to 5 ½ percent, similar to the late 1990s, in 2008 through 2011, even while NPISHs increased their dis-saving. (Tables 4-1A and 4-6)

- It should be noted that personal income does not, by definition, include any capital gains. Despite that, taxes on realized capital gains are deducted from personal income to get after-tax income (along with all other income taxes). Capital gains, both realized and unrealized, can be a source of spending power in addition to current disposable income; during the housing price bubble they were converted into cash by asset sales, refinancing, and home equity loans, all of which were reflected in low saving rates. (Table 12-11)

- Labor compensation, excluding social insurance contributions, made up 53.0 percent of total personal income in 2011. This was down from 59.4 percent in 2000 and 65.4 percent in 1950. ("Contributions for social insurance," mainly Social Security taxes, are excluded from both the numerator and the denominator of this percentage.) Government social benefits rose from 5.9 percent in 1950 to 12.2 percent in 2000 and 17.7 percent in the high-unemployment economy of 2011. It should be understood that "consumption expenditures" in the national income and product accounts includes all spending financed by government health insurance programs such as Medicare and Medicaid, and personal income also includes the amount of that spending, in the government social benefits component. (Table 4-1)

Table 4-1A. Personal Income and Its Disposition: Recent Data

(Billions of current dollars, except as noted; quarterly data are at seasonally adjusted annual rates.) NIPA Table 2.1

Year and quarter	Total	Compensation of employees, received	Proprietors' income with IVA and CCAdj	Rental income of persons with CCAdj	Personal income receipts on assets		Personal current transfer receipts					
							Total	Government social benefits to persons				
					Personal interest income	Personal dividend income		Social Security and Medicare	Government unemployment insurance	Veterans	Medicaid	Other government benefits to persons
1950	228.9	155.3	37.5	9.1	9.7	8.8	13.4	1.0	1.5	7.7	. . .	3.3
1951	257.9	181.4	42.7	10.0	10.5	8.6	10.5	1.9	0.9	4.6	. . .	3.2
1952	275.2	196.2	43.1	11.2	11.3	8.6	11.0	2.2	1.1	4.3	. . .	3.4
1953	291.7	210.3	42.0	12.4	12.7	8.9	11.7	3.0	1.1	4.1	. . .	3.5
1954	294.3	209.2	42.3	13.4	14.0	9.3	13.7	3.6	2.3	4.1	. . .	3.7
1955	316.0	225.7	44.3	13.8	15.2	10.5	14.8	4.9	1.6	4.4	. . .	3.9
1956	339.5	244.5	45.9	14.1	16.9	11.3	15.6	5.7	1.6	4.3	. . .	4.0
1957	358.5	257.5	47.8	14.5	18.9	11.7	18.1	7.3	1.9	4.5	. . .	4.4
1958	368.9	259.5	50.2	15.2	20.3	11.6	22.2	8.5	4.2	4.6	. . .	4.9
1959	392.3	281.0	50.3	16.0	22.0	12.6	22.9	10.2	2.9	4.5	. . .	5.4
1960	411.3	296.4	50.7	17.0	24.5	13.4	24.4	11.1	3.1	4.5	. . .	5.7
1961	428.8	305.3	53.2	17.7	26.2	13.9	28.1	12.6	4.4	4.9	. . .	6.2
1962	456.4	327.1	55.3	18.6	29.1	15.0	28.8	14.3	3.2	4.6	. . .	6.8
1963	479.5	345.2	56.5	19.3	31.7	16.2	30.3	15.2	3.1	4.8	. . .	7.3
1964	514.3	370.7	59.4	19.4	35.6	18.2	31.3	16.0	2.8	4.6	. . .	7.9
1965	555.5	399.5	63.9	19.9	39.2	20.2	33.9	18.1	2.4	4.8	. . .	8.6
1966	603.8	442.7	68.2	20.5	43.4	20.7	37.5	20.8	1.9	4.8	1.9	8.1
1967	648.1	475.1	69.8	20.9	47.5	21.5	45.8	25.8	2.2	5.5	2.7	9.4
1968	711.7	524.3	74.2	20.6	51.6	23.5	53.3	30.5	2.2	5.9	4.0	10.8
1969	778.3	577.6	77.5	20.9	59.9	24.2	59.0	33.1	2.3	6.6	4.6	12.4
1970	838.6	617.2	78.5	21.1	69.2	24.3	71.7	38.7	4.2	7.5	5.5	16.0
1971	903.1	658.3	84.7	22.2	75.9	25.0	85.4	44.6	6.2	8.4	6.7	19.4
1972	992.6	725.1	96.0	23.1	82.8	26.8	94.8	49.7	6.0	9.4	8.2	21.4
1973	1 110.5	811.3	113.6	23.9	94.8	29.9	108.6	60.9	4.6	10.2	9.6	23.3
1974	1 222.7	890.7	113.5	24.0	113.2	33.2	128.6	70.3	7.0	11.6	11.2	28.4
1975	1 334.9	949.0	119.6	23.4	129.3	32.9	163.1	81.5	18.1	14.0	13.9	35.7
1976	1 474.7	1 059.2	132.2	22.1	139.5	39.0	177.3	93.3	16.4	13.8	15.5	38.4
1977	1 632.5	1 180.4	146.0	19.6	160.6	44.7	189.1	105.3	13.1	13.3	16.7	40.6
1978	1 836.7	1 335.2	167.5	20.9	184.0	50.7	203.2	116.9	9.4	13.6	18.6	44.6
1979	2 059.5	1 498.5	181.1	22.6	217.3	57.4	227.1	132.5	9.7	14.2	21.1	49.7
1980	2 301.5	1 647.6	173.5	28.5	274.7	64.0	270.8	154.8	16.1	14.7	23.9	61.4
1981	2 582.3	1 819.6	181.6	36.5	348.3	73.6	307.2	182.1	15.9	15.8	27.7	65.6
1982	2 766.8	1 919.6	174.8	38.1	410.8	77.6	342.4	204.6	25.2	16.3	30.2	66.1
1983	2 952.2	2 036.0	190.7	38.2	446.3	83.3	369.9	222.2	26.4	16.4	33.9	71.0
1984	3 268.1	2 245.2	233.1	40.0	517.2	90.6	380.4	237.7	16.0	16.3	36.6	73.8
1985	3 496.7	2 412.0	246.1	41.9	555.8	97.4	402.6	253.0	15.9	16.6	39.7	77.6
1986	3 696.0	2 557.7	262.6	33.8	588.4	106.0	428.0	268.9	16.5	16.6	43.6	82.4
1987	3 924.4	2 735.6	294.2	34.2	603.6	112.2	447.4	282.6	14.6	16.5	47.8	85.9
1988	4 231.2	2 954.2	334.8	40.2	637.3	129.7	475.9	300.2	13.3	16.7	53.0	92.6
1989	4 557.5	3 131.3	351.6	42.4	717.0	157.8	519.4	325.6	14.4	17.2	60.8	101.4
1990	4 846.7	3 326.2	365.1	49.8	751.9	168.8	572.7	351.7	18.2	17.7	73.1	111.9
1991	5 031.5	3 438.4	367.3	61.6	748.2	180.3	648.2	381.7	26.8	18.1	96.9	124.7
1992	5 347.3	3 647.2	414.9	84.6	722.2	187.6	729.5	414.4	39.6	18.6	116.2	140.6
1993	5 568.1	3 790.6	449.6	114.1	698.1	202.3	776.7	444.7	34.8	19.3	130.1	147.7
1994	5 874.8	3 980.9	485.1	142.9	712.7	235.0	813.1	476.6	23.9	19.7	139.4	153.5
1995	6 200.9	4 178.8	516.0	154.6	751.9	253.4	860.2	508.9	21.7	20.5	149.6	159.5
1996	6 591.6	4 387.7	583.7	170.4	784.4	296.4	901.2	536.9	22.3	21.4	158.2	162.4
1997	7 000.7	4 668.6	628.2	176.5	835.8	329.7	929.8	563.5	20.1	22.3	163.1	160.7
1998	7 525.4	5 023.9	687.5	191.5	919.3	349.8	951.9	574.8	19.7	23.3	170.2	164.0
1999	7 910.8	5 348.8	746.8	208.2	910.9	335.9	987.6	588.6	20.5	24.1	184.6	169.8
2000	8 559.4	5 788.8	817.5	215.3	984.2	376.5	1 040.6	620.5	20.7	25.0	199.5	174.8
2001	8 883.3	5 979.3	870.7	232.4	976.5	369.5	1 141.3	667.7	31.9	26.6	227.3	187.9
2002	9 060.1	6 110.8	890.3	218.7	911.9	397.7	1 247.9	706.1	53.5	29.5	250.1	208.8
2003	9 378.1	6 367.6	930.6	204.2	889.8	423.1	1 316.0	740.4	53.2	31.8	264.6	226.1
2004	9 937.2	6 708.4	1 033.8	198.4	860.2	548.3	1 398.6	790.2	36.4	34.0	289.7	248.3
2005	10 485.9	7 060.0	1 069.8	178.2	987.0	555.0	1 482.7	844.6	31.8	36.4	304.4	265.6
2006	11 268.1	7 475.7	1 133.0	146.5	1 127.5	702.2	1 583.6	943.3	30.4	38.9	299.0	272.1
2007	11 912.3	7 862.2	1 090.4	143.7	1 265.1	791.9	1 687.9	1 003.2	32.7	41.7	324.1	286.2
2008	12 460.2	8 073.3	1 097.9	231.6	1 382.0	783.4	1 842.4	1 067.1	50.9	45.0	338.2	341.1
2009	11 930.2	7 801.4	941.2	305.9	1 108.9	598.8	2 099.9	1 158.3	130.6	51.5	374.1	385.4
2010	12 373.5	7 971.4	1 036.4	350.2	1 003.4	717.7	2 242.9	1 208.6	138.7	57.9	405.4	432.4
2011	12 991.2	8 276.6	1 108.9	403.9	998.1	791.9	2 296.8	1 267.2	107.4	63.4	424.3	434.6
2009												
1st quarter	11 964.4	7 810.1	960.2	278.8	1 194.9	656.6	1 992.0	1 134.3	101.1	49.6	362.0	344.9
2nd quarter	11 944.1	7 809.2	926.9	299.7	1 129.7	577.8	2 129.4	1 154.1	127.9	50.5	373.3	423.6
3rd quarter	11 874.1	7 781.9	929.3	319.3	1 073.1	562.6	2 131.7	1 166.3	144.8	52.1	383.1	385.4
4th quarter	11 938.2	7 804.4	948.5	325.9	1 038.0	598.0	2 146.6	1 178.4	148.7	53.8	378.0	387.7
2010												
1st quarter	12 137.7	7 852.5	981.7	344.1	1 026.1	667.2	2 204.1	1 184.2	152.8	55.8	386.6	424.8
2nd quarter	12 325.6	7 960.0	1 025.6	349.1	1 014.1	710.4	2 214.1	1 199.8	137.4	57.3	389.8	429.9
3rd quarter	12 453.2	8 022.2	1 057.0	352.8	983.9	739.4	2 251.4	1 215.5	135.8	59.0	405.2	436.1
4th quarter	12 577.6	8 050.8	1 081.5	354.8	989.6	753.9	2 301.9	1 235.2	128.7	59.4	439.8	438.7
2011												
1st quarter	12 846.9	8 172.5	1 095.6	385.0	1 004.7	772.5	2 288.6	1 250.9	117.5	61.3	432.1	426.9
2nd quarter	12 955.2	8 219.7	1 106.5	396.9	1 015.9	786.4	2 307.9	1 266.1	108.8	62.8	437.4	432.7
3rd quarter	13 056.8	8 338.3	1 113.7	406.3	994.8	799.4	2 297.2	1 274.1	103.0	65.0	416.4	438.6
4th quarter	13 105.7	8 375.8	1 119.7	427.2	976.8	809.5	2 293.5	1 277.6	100.1	64.3	411.5	440.0

. . . = Not available.

Table 4-1A. Personal Income and Its Disposition: Recent Data—*Continued*

(Billions of current dollars, except as noted; quarterly data are at seasonally adjusted annual rates.)

NIPA Table 2.1

Year and quarter	Personal income —Continued: Personal current transfer receipts —Continued: From business, net	Less: Contributions for government social insurance, domestic	Less: Personal current taxes	Equals: Disposable personal income	Less: Personal outlays: Total	Personal consumption expenditures	Personal interest payments	Personal current transfer payments: Total	To government	To the rest of the world, net	Equals: Personal saving: Billions of dollars	Percent of disposable personal income	Billions of chained (2005) dollars: Percent income excluding current transfers	Disposable personal income
1950	0.6	5.5	18.9	209.9	195.0	192.2	2.0	0.8	0.3	0.4	14.9	7.1	1 433.9	1 400.9
1951	0.9	6.6	27.1	230.8	211.5	208.5	2.2	0.7	0.3	0.4	19.3	8.4	1 540.0	1 442.2
1952	0.9	6.9	32.0	243.2	222.9	219.5	2.6	0.8	0.4	0.4	20.3	8.4	1 612.2	1 489.0
1953	0.8	7.1	33.2	258.4	237.1	233.1	3.2	0.9	0.4	0.5	21.3	8.2	1 686.5	1 561.2
1954	0.6	8.1	30.2	264.1	244.3	240.0	3.4	0.9	0.4	0.5	19.8	7.5	1 677.2	1 582.3
1955	0.9	9.1	32.9	283.1	263.6	258.8	4.0	0.9	0.4	0.4	19.5	6.9	1 791.7	1 689.3
1956	1.2	10.0	36.6	302.9	277.2	271.7	4.6	1.0	0.5	0.5	25.6	8.5	1 887.1	1 771.5
1957	1.4	11.4	38.9	319.7	292.8	286.9	4.9	1.1	0.6	0.5	26.9	8.4	1 924.4	1 814.5
1958	1.2	11.4	38.5	330.4	302.2	296.2	5.0	1.0	0.6	0.4	28.2	8.5	1 915.8	1 832.1
1959	1.3	13.8	42.3	350.1	324.0	317.7	5.5	0.8	0.3	0.5	26.1	7.5	2 011.3	1 912.6
1960	1.3	16.4	46.1	365.2	338.9	331.8	6.2	0.8	0.3	0.5	26.3	7.2	2 072.3	1 963.1
1961	1.4	17.0	47.3	381.6	349.7	342.2	6.5	1.0	0.5	0.5	31.9	8.4	2 124.5	2 029.8
1962	1.5	19.1	51.6	404.9	371.4	363.3	7.0	1.1	0.5	0.6	33.5	8.3	2 239.9	2 128.6
1963	1.9	21.7	54.6	425.0	391.8	382.7	7.9	1.2	0.5	0.7	33.1	7.8	2 324.6	2 208.5
1964	2.2	22.4	52.1	462.3	421.7	411.5	8.9	1.3	0.6	0.7	40.5	8.8	2 462.7	2 367.6
1965	2.3	23.4	57.7	497.8	455.1	443.8	9.9	1.4	0.6	0.8	42.7	8.6	2 622.0	2 513.6
1966	2.1	31.3	66.4	537.4	493.1	480.9	10.7	1.6	0.8	0.8	44.3	8.2	2 777.9	2 646.1
1967	2.3	34.9	73.0	575.1	520.9	507.8	11.1	2.0	1.0	1.0	54.2	9.4	2 882.0	2 762.2
1968	2.8	38.7	87.0	624.7	572.2	558.0	12.2	2.0	1.0	1.0	52.5	8.4	3 030.7	2 887.9
1969	3.3	44.1	104.5	673.8	621.4	605.1	14.0	2.2	1.1	1.1	52.5	7.8	3 166.6	2 979.9
1970	2.9	46.4	103.1	735.5	666.1	648.3	15.2	2.6	1.3	1.3	69.4	9.4	3 227.4	3 107.3
1971	2.7	51.2	101.7	801.4	721.0	701.6	16.6	2.8	1.5	1.4	80.4	10.0	3 302.8	3 247.7
1972	3.1	59.2	123.6	869.0	791.5	770.2	18.1	3.2	1.8	1.4	77.5	8.9	3 505.9	3 405.2
1973	3.9	75.5	132.4	978.1	875.2	852.0	19.8	3.4	1.8	1.6	102.9	10.5	3 710.4	3 636.6
1974	4.7	85.2	151.0	1 071.7	957.5	932.9	21.2	3.4	2.1	1.4	114.2	10.7	3 668.4	3 608.6
1975	6.8	89.3	147.6	1 187.3	1 061.3	1 033.8	23.7	3.8	2.5	1.3	125.9	10.6	3 620.0	3 689.5
1976	6.7	101.3	172.3	1 302.3	1 179.6	1 151.3	23.9	4.4	3.0	1.4	122.8	9.4	3 802.3	3 836.6
1977	5.1	113.1	197.5	1 435.0	1 309.7	1 277.8	27.0	4.8	3.5	1.4	125.3	8.7	3 978.1	3 969.0
1978	6.5	131.3	229.4	1 607.3	1 465.0	1 427.6	31.9	5.4	3.9	1.6	142.4	8.9	4 205.7	4 154.6
1979	8.2	152.7	268.7	1 790.9	1 633.4	1 591.2	36.2	6.0	4.3	1.7	157.5	8.8	4 331.1	4 251.9
1980	8.6	166.2	298.9	2 002.7	1 806.4	1 755.8	43.6	6.9	5.0	2.0	196.3	9.8	4 335.2	4 293.7
1981	11.2	195.7	345.2	2 237.1	2 000.4	1 939.5	49.3	11.5	6.0	5.6	236.7	10.6	4 460.7	4 407.9
1982	12.4	208.9	354.1	2 412.7	2 148.8	2 075.5	59.5	13.8	7.1	6.7	263.9	10.9	4 503.1	4 504.4
1983	13.8	226.0	352.3	2 599.8	2 372.9	2 288.6	69.2	15.1	8.1	7.0	226.9	8.7	4 597.3	4 653.5
1984	19.7	257.5	377.4	2 891.5	2 595.2	2 501.1	77.0	17.1	9.2	7.9	296.3	10.2	4 947.7	4 986.9
1985	22.3	281.4	417.3	3 079.3	2 825.7	2 717.6	89.4	18.8	10.4	8.3	253.6	8.2	5 129.7	5 142.4
1986	22.9	303.4	437.2	3 258.8	3 012.4	2 896.7	94.5	21.1	12.0	9.1	246.5	7.6	5 290.2	5 312.6
1987	20.2	323.1	489.1	3 435.3	3 211.9	3 097.0	91.7	23.2	13.2	10.0	223.4	6.5	5 433.6	5 399.9
1988	20.6	361.5	504.9	3 726.3	3 469.7	3 350.1	94.0	25.6	14.8	10.8	256.6	6.9	5 645.8	5 633.0
1989	23.2	385.2	566.1	3 991.4	3 726.4	3 594.5	103.9	28.0	16.5	11.6	265.0	6.6	5 816.5	5 782.5
1990	22.2	410.1	592.7	4 254.0	3 977.3	3 835.5	111.3	30.6	18.4	12.2	276.7	6.5	5 890.6	5 893.6
1991	17.6	430.2	586.6	4 444.9	4 131.7	3 980.1	115.0	36.7	22.6	14.1	313.2	7.0	5 837.3	5 943.2
1992	16.3	455.0	610.5	4 736.7	4 388.7	4 236.9	111.3	40.5	26.0	14.5	348.1	7.3	5 976.8	6 152.5
1993	14.1	477.4	646.5	4 921.6	4 636.2	4 483.6	107.0	45.6	28.6	17.1	285.4	5.8	6 072.0	6 255.3
1994	13.3	508.2	690.5	5 184.3	4 913.6	4 750.8	113.0	49.8	30.9	18.9	270.7	5.2	6 286.8	6 456.0
1995	18.7	532.8	743.9	5 457.0	5 170.8	4 987.3	130.6	52.9	32.6	20.3	286.3	5.2	6 484.0	6 648.6
1996	22.9	555.1	832.0	5 759.6	5 478.5	5 273.6	147.3	57.6	34.9	22.6	281.1	4.9	6 758.0	6 867.8
1997	19.4	587.2	926.2	6 074.6	5 794.2	5 570.6	159.7	63.9	38.2	25.7	280.4	4.6	7 083.4	7 110.4
1998	26.0	624.7	1 026.4	6 498.9	6 157.5	5 918.5	169.5	69.5	39.9	29.7	341.5	5.3	7 591.6	7 535.4
1999	34.0	661.3	1 107.5	6 803.3	6 595.5	6 342.8	176.5	76.2	44.1	32.2	207.8	3.1	7 861.2	7 763.1
2000	42.4	705.8	1 232.3	7 327.2	7 114.1	6 830.4	200.3	83.4	48.8	34.6	213.1	2.9	8 324.0	8 157.8
2001	46.8	733.2	1 234.8	7 648.5	7 443.5	7 148.8	203.7	91.0	52.9	38.1	204.9	2.7	8 407.3	8 356.2
2002	34.2	751.5	1 050.4	8 009.7	7 727.5	7 439.2	191.3	97.0	56.4	40.6	282.2	3.5	8 383.4	8 633.2
2003	25.7	778.9	1 000.3	8 377.8	8 088.1	7 804.1	182.7	101.3	60.2	41.2	289.6	3.5	8 489.8	8 850.5
2004	16.9	827.3	1 047.8	8 889.4	8 571.2	8 270.6	190.3	110.3	66.7	43.6	318.2	3.6	8 774.3	9 152.9
2005	25.8	872.7	1 208.6	9 277.3	9 134.1	8 803.5	210.8	119.8	71.4	48.4	143.2	1.5	8 977.3	9 277.3
2006	21.4	921.8	1 352.4	9 915.7	9 659.1	9 301.0	230.1	128.0	76.4	51.6	256.6	2.6	9 406.9	9 652.8
2007	30.5	959.5	1 488.7	10 423.6	10 174.9	9 772.3	260.9	141.7	82.4	59.3	248.7	2.4	9 662.5	9 880.3
2008	36.8	987.3	1 435.7	11 024.5	10 432.2	10 035.5	245.6	151.0	84.9	66.2	592.3	5.4	9 712.3	10 119.5
2009	38.2	964.1	1 141.4	10 788.8	10 236.3	9 866.1	213.7	156.5	89.1	67.4	552.6	5.1	8 969.7	9 882.7
2010	38.3	986.8	1 193.9	11 179.7	10 586.9	10 245.5	173.4	168.0	95.1	72.9	592.8	5.3	9 083.0	10 061.6
2011	39.5	924.4	1 397.7	11 593.5	11 055.1	10 726.0	157.8	171.3	97.7	73.6	538.5	4.6	9 358.9	10 183.3
2009														
1st quarter	37.8	966.0	1 198.0	10 766.3	10 155.2	9 781.7	220.5	153.0	86.9	66.2	611.1	5.7	9 182.2	9 951.0
2nd quarter	38.2	966.9	1 120.3	10 823.8	10 153.4	9 781.6	217.6	154.2	88.3	66.0	670.3	6.2	8 993.8	9 957.3
3rd quarter	38.4	962.1	1 120.6	10 753.5	10 285.3	9 911.1	216.6	157.6	89.8	67.8	468.2	4.4	8 861.3	9 819.6
4th quarter	38.3	961.5	1 126.4	10 811.7	10 351.2	9 990.0	200.1	161.1	91.5	69.6	460.5	4.3	8 845.5	9 805.4
2010														
1st quarter	38.0	976.0	1 146.4	10 991.3	10 457.2	10 103.7	188.3	165.2	93.4	71.9	534.1	4.9	8 933.4	9 922.5
2nd quarter	38.0	985.7	1 175.4	11 150.2	10 527.0	10 184.8	174.4	167.8	94.8	72.9	623.3	5.6	9 086.5	10 057.8
3rd quarter	37.9	991.5	1 212.8	11 240.4	10 614.8	10 276.6	168.1	170.1	95.8	74.3	625.6	5.6	9 145.7	10 114.4
4th quarter	39.3	994.1	1 240.9	11 336.7	10 748.6	10 417.1	162.7	168.9	96.5	72.5	588.1	5.2	9 166.7	10 152.0
2011														
1st quarter	39.5	911.5	1 365.9	11 481.0	10 902.1	10 571.7	160.3	170.1	96.6	73.5	578.9	5.0	9 329.8	10 183.2
2nd quarter	39.4	917.4	1 396.2	11 559.2	11 002.6	10 676.0	155.9	170.7	97.1	73.5	556.5	4.8	9 332.9	10 169.7
3rd quarter	39.4	932.4	1 409.1	11 647.7	11 114.6	10 784.5	158.4	171.6	97.8	73.8	533.1	4.6	9 377.3	10 188.6
4th quarter	39.6	936.3	1 419.4	11 686.3	11 201.0	10 871.6	156.7	172.8	99.2	73.6	485.3	4.2	9 395.8	10 192.7

Table 4-1B. Personal Income and Its Disposition: Historical

(Billions of current dollars, except as noted; quarterly data are at seasonally adjusted annual rates.)   NIPA Table 2.1

Year and quarter	Personal income						Less: Contributions for government social insurance, domestic	Less: Personal current taxes	Equals: Disposable personal income	Less: Personal outlays	Equals: Personal saving		Billions of chained (2005) dollars	
	Total	Compensation of employees, received	Proprietors' income with IVA and CCAdj	Rental income of persons with CCAdj	Personal income receipts on assets	Personal current transfer receipts					Billions of dollars	Percent of disposable personal income	Personal income excluding current transfers	Disposable personal income
1929	84.9	51.1	14.1	6.2	12.5	1.2	0.1	1.7	83.2	79.6	3.6	4.3	797.2	792.0
1930	76.1	46.9	10.9	5.5	11.7	1.2	0.1	1.6	74.6	71.6	2.9	4.0	744.6	741.1
1931	65.2	39.8	8.4	4.5	10.3	2.3	0.1	1.0	64.2	61.8	2.4	3.7	699.9	714.9
1932	49.9	31.1	5.1	3.6	8.4	1.7	0.1	0.7	49.1	49.7	-0.5	-1.1	607.1	619.9
1933	46.8	29.6	5.3	2.9	7.4	1.7	0.1	0.8	46.0	46.8	-0.8	-1.7	590.1	601.6
1934	53.7	34.3	7.0	2.6	8.0	1.8	0.1	0.9	52.8	52.3	0.5	0.9	649.6	660.3
1935	60.3	37.4	10.1	2.6	8.3	2.0	0.1	1.1	59.3	56.7	2.5	4.2	712.8	723.9
1936	68.6	42.9	10.4	2.7	9.8	3.1	0.3	1.3	67.3	63.1	4.2	6.2	793.5	815.1
1937	74.1	48.0	12.5	3.0	10.0	2.0	1.5	1.9	72.2	67.9	4.3	5.9	842.2	842.8
1938	68.4	45.0	10.6	3.6	8.4	2.4	1.6	1.9	66.5	65.2	1.3	1.9	788.6	795.1
1939	72.9	48.1	11.1	3.8	9.1	2.5	1.8	1.5	71.4	68.2	3.2	4.4	848.9	861.4
1940	78.4	52.2	12.3	3.9	9.3	2.7	1.9	1.7	76.8	72.4	4.3	5.7	906.7	918.6
1941	96.0	64.8	16.6	4.5	9.8	2.7	2.3	2.3	93.7	82.3	11.4	12.2	1 052.4	1 056.3
1942	123.4	85.3	23.4	5.5	9.5	2.7	2.9	4.9	118.5	90.0	28.6	24.1	1 210.1	1 187.8
1943	152.1	109.4	28.3	6.1	9.7	2.5	3.8	16.7	135.4	100.8	34.6	25.5	1 373.4	1 242.6
1944	166.0	121.4	29.4	6.4	9.9	3.1	4.3	17.7	148.3	109.7	38.6	26.0	1 413.5	1 287.2
1945	171.6	123.2	30.8	6.7	10.6	5.6	5.3	19.4	152.2	121.2	31.0	20.4	1 385.4	1 270.2
1946	178.6	119.6	35.7	7.1	12.3	10.6	6.6	17.2	161.4	145.9	15.5	9.6	1 311.4	1 259.4
1947	190.9	130.1	34.5	7.2	13.9	10.8	5.6	19.8	171.1	163.8	7.3	4.2	1 275.4	1 211.9
1948	209.7	141.9	39.2	7.8	15.1	10.3	4.6	19.2	190.5	177.3	13.2	6.9	1 337.0	1 277.0
1949	207.0	141.9	34.6	8.1	16.0	11.2	4.9	16.7	190.2	180.9	9.4	4.9	1 322.5	1 285.2
1947														
1st quarter	187.5	127.2	36.6	6.9	13.4	9.7	6.3	19.2	168.3	158.1	10.2	6.1	1 286.4	1 218.1
2nd quarter ...	185.5	128.7	32.3	7.1	13.8	9.6	6.0	19.5	166.1	161.9	4.2	2.5	1 263.0	1 192.1
3rd quarter	193.6	130.0	33.8	7.3	14.2	13.5	5.2	19.7	173.8	165.6	8.3	4.8	1 269.2	1 225.1
4th quarter	196.9	134.3	35.2	7.5	14.2	10.5	4.8	20.8	176.1	169.7	6.4	3.6	1 281.4	1 210.7
1948														
1st quarter	202.1	137.8	36.0	7.6	14.9	10.7	4.8	21.2	180.9	172.7	8.3	4.6	1 302.0	1 230.5
2nd quarter ...	208.1	139.4	40.4	7.8	14.7	10.4	4.6	18.9	189.2	176.5	12.7	6.7	1 330.7	1 273.4
3rd quarter	214.2	144.6	40.9	7.9	15.2	10.1	4.6	18.2	195.9	179.5	16.5	8.4	1 352.6	1 298.7
4th quarter	214.3	145.8	39.6	7.9	15.6	9.8	4.5	18.4	195.9	180.4	15.5	7.9	1 359.9	1 302.3
1949														
1st quarter	208.2	143.9	35.4	7.8	15.7	10.5	5.2	17.8	190.4	179.2	11.1	5.8	1 324.7	1 275.6
2nd quarter ...	206.8	142.2	34.8	7.9	15.9	11.0	5.1	17.0	189.8	181.0	8.8	4.7	1 319.7	1 279.5
3rd quarter	206.1	141.0	34.2	8.2	16.0	11.5	4.8	16.3	189.8	180.4	9.4	5.0	1 319.4	1 287.1
4th quarter	206.8	140.5	34.2	8.4	16.5	11.8	4.5	15.8	191.0	183.0	8.0	4.2	1 323.8	1 296.4
1950														
1st quarter	221.5	144.6	35.6	8.7	17.7	20.2	5.3	16.6	204.9	185.7	19.1	9.3	1 368.4	1 392.8
2nd quarter ...	222.3	150.6	36.3	9.0	18.0	13.8	5.3	17.6	204.7	189.7	15.0	7.3	1 411.1	1 385.3
3rd quarter	231.1	159.0	38.7	9.1	19.0	10.8	5.5	18.9	212.2	203.6	8.7	4.1	1 460.5	1 406.7
4th quarter	240.5	166.8	39.4	9.4	19.6	11.1	5.8	22.5	218.0	201.1	16.9	7.8	1 494.1	1 419.7
1951														
1st quarter	249.5	174.8	42.0	9.6	18.6	11.1	6.6	24.4	225.1	212.4	12.7	5.6	1 504.4	1 420.2
2nd quarter ...	256.8	180.7	42.4	9.9	19.1	11.4	6.7	26.4	230.4	208.1	22.3	9.7	1 535.9	1 442.3
3rd quarter	260.0	183.0	42.6	10.2	19.2	11.6	6.6	27.8	232.2	210.8	21.4	9.2	1 553.0	1 451.6
4th quarter	265.3	187.0	43.5	10.5	19.5	11.6	6.7	29.6	235.7	214.8	20.9	8.9	1 565.8	1 454.3
1952														
1st quarter	267.4	191.3	41.8	10.7	19.1	11.4	6.9	30.9	236.5	216.2	20.3	8.6	1 572.9	1 453.2
2nd quarter ...	271.3	192.7	43.1	11.0	19.8	11.5	6.8	31.8	239.4	220.5	19.0	7.9	1 596.2	1 471.5
3rd quarter	278.1	196.6	44.8	11.3	20.0	12.3	6.9	32.3	245.8	223.2	22.6	9.2	1 622.9	1 500.8
4th quarter	284.1	204.1	42.6	11.6	20.5	12.3	7.1	33.1	251.1	231.5	19.5	7.8	1 656.6	1 530.3
1953														
1st quarter	288.8	208.0	43.0	11.9	20.6	12.4	7.1	33.4	255.4	235.3	20.1	7.9	1 678.7	1 550.8
2nd quarter ...	292.8	211.4	42.3	12.2	21.7	12.3	7.1	33.4	259.3	237.3	22.0	8.5	1 700.2	1 572.1
3rd quarter	292.9	211.6	41.5	12.5	21.9	12.5	7.2	33.2	259.7	238.2	21.5	8.3	1 690.5	1 565.8
4th quarter	292.1	210.1	41.3	12.8	22.1	12.9	7.1	32.9	259.2	237.7	21.5	8.3	1 676.2	1 555.9
1954														
1st quarter	292.2	208.1	42.6	13.1	23.0	13.5	8.1	30.2	262.0	239.7	22.3	8.5	1 664.6	1 564.9
2nd quarter ...	291.8	207.7	42.0	13.3	22.7	14.1	8.0	30.0	261.8	242.5	19.3	7.4	1 660.8	1 565.8
3rd quarter	293.9	208.3	42.3	13.5	23.4	14.5	8.1	30.0	263.9	245.2	18.7	7.1	1 676.6	1 583.4
4th quarter	299.3	212.6	42.2	13.6	23.9	15.2	8.1	30.5	268.9	249.9	19.0	7.1	1 706.6	1 614.9
1955														
1st quarter	305.1	216.9	43.4	13.7	24.7	15.3	8.9	31.4	273.7	256.3	17.4	6.4	1 735.3	1 638.8
2nd quarter ...	313.0	223.1	44.5	13.7	25.2	15.6	9.0	32.4	280.6	261.7	19.0	6.8	1 778.9	1 678.3
3rd quarter	320.4	229.1	44.7	13.8	26.1	15.9	9.2	33.4	287.0	266.1	20.9	7.3	1 814.2	1 710.0
4th quarter	325.4	233.6	44.5	13.9	26.7	16.0	9.3	34.2	291.2	270.3	20.9	7.2	1 838.3	1 729.8

Table 4-1B. Personal Income and Its Disposition: Historical—*Continued*

(Billions of current dollars, except as noted; quarterly data are at seasonally adjusted annual rates.)   NIPA Table 2.1

| Year and quarter | Personal income | | | | | | | Less: Personal current taxes | Equals: Disposable personal income | Less: Personal outlays | Equals: Personal saving | | Billions of chained (2005) dollars | |
	Total	Compen-sation of employees, received	Pro-prietors' income with IVA and CCAdj	Rental income of persons with CCAdj	Personal income receipts on assets	Personal current transfer receipts	Less: Contribu-tions for govern-ment social insurance, domestic				Billions of dollars	Percent of disposable personal income	Personal income excluding current transfers	Disposable personal income
1956														
1st quarter	330.8	238.0	44.9	14.0	27.4	16.3	9.9	35.4	295.4	272.1	23.3	7.9	1 860.2	1 747.6
2nd quarter ...	336.6	242.6	45.5	14.0	27.9	16.6	10.0	36.2	300.3	274.9	25.4	8.5	1 880.6	1 765.0
3rd quarter	341.5	245.7	46.2	14.1	28.3	17.1	10.0	36.9	304.6	278.2	26.3	8.6	1 887.8	1 772.4
4th quarter	349.1	251.6	46.9	14.2	29.2	17.3	10.1	37.9	311.2	283.7	27.5	8.9	1 919.5	1 800.7
1957														
1st quarter	353.1	255.3	46.9	14.3	29.8	18.2	11.4	38.6	314.6	288.3	26.3	8.4	1 920.5	1 803.7
2nd quarter ...	357.6	257.0	47.8	14.4	30.5	19.4	11.4	39.0	318.7	290.6	28.0	8.8	1 927.1	1 815.9
3rd quarter	362.0	259.7	48.7	14.5	31.0	19.6	11.5	39.2	322.8	295.3	27.5	8.5	1 935.0	1 824.4
4th quarter	361.4	258.1	47.9	14.7	31.1	20.8	11.3	38.8	322.6	297.0	25.6	7.9	1 915.2	1 814.1
1958														
1st quarter	362.0	254.6	50.3	15.0	31.3	22.1	11.3	38.2	323.8	296.6	27.2	8.4	1 887.9	1 798.7
2nd quarter ...	364.2	254.2	50.4	15.2	31.8	23.9	11.3	37.7	326.5	299.4	27.1	8.3	1 887.1	1 810.6
3rd quarter	372.5	262.2	50.1	15.3	32.1	24.2	11.4	38.9	333.5	304.4	29.1	8.7	1 929.7	1 848.0
4th quarter	377.0	267.2	50.0	15.4	32.2	23.7	11.5	39.4	337.6	308.3	29.3	8.7	1 958.5	1 871.4
1959														
1st quarter	383.4	274.5	50.2	15.4	33.0	24.0	13.7	40.8	342.6	316.0	26.7	7.8	1 978.1	1 885.9
2nd quarter ...	392.0	281.6	50.4	15.9	34.0	23.9	13.9	42.0	350.0	322.2	27.8	7.9	2 017.7	1 918.8
3rd quarter	394.1	282.3	50.2	16.3	35.1	24.2	13.9	42.7	351.5	327.6	23.8	6.8	2 016.2	1 915.4
4th quarter	399.9	285.5	50.6	16.5	36.3	24.8	13.9	43.7	356.1	330.0	26.1	7.3	2 032.8	1 930.3
1960														
1st quarter	406.4	294.0	50.0	16.7	37.4	24.6	16.4	45.3	361.1	333.7	27.4	7.6	2 066.3	1 954.5
2nd quarter ...	411.0	296.9	50.8	16.9	37.5	25.3	16.5	46.0	364.9	339.8	25.2	6.9	2 077.0	1 965.3
3rd quarter	413.2	297.6	50.9	17.0	38.1	26.0	16.5	46.5	366.7	339.9	26.7	7.3	2 076.7	1 966.8
4th quarter	414.5	297.1	51.1	17.2	38.5	27.0	16.4	46.4	368.1	342.0	26.1	7.1	2 069.4	1 965.7
1961														
1st quarter	418.6	298.0	52.4	17.4	38.7	28.8	16.7	46.5	372.1	342.6	29.5	7.9	2 077.8	1 983.6
2nd quarter ...	424.6	302.2	52.6	17.6	39.5	29.7	16.9	46.9	377.7	347.6	30.1	8.0	2 105.4	2 013.4
3rd quarter	431.6	307.2	53.3	17.8	40.5	29.9	17.1	47.4	384.2	350.6	33.7	8.8	2 134.0	2 040.9
4th quarter	440.4	313.8	54.5	18.1	41.9	29.4	17.3	48.1	392.2	358.0	34.3	8.7	2 180.5	2 081.1
1962														
1st quarter	447.1	320.4	55.3	18.3	42.0	30.0	18.9	49.4	397.7	363.3	34.4	8.6	2 203.3	2 100.8
2nd quarter ...	454.5	326.4	55.1	18.5	43.6	30.0	19.1	50.9	403.5	369.2	34.4	8.5	2 234.4	2 124.2
3rd quarter	459.1	329.2	55.1	18.7	44.9	30.4	19.2	52.3	406.8	373.3	33.5	8.2	2 251.0	2 136.0
4th quarter	465.0	332.6	55.7	18.9	45.9	31.2	19.3	53.6	411.4	379.8	31.6	7.7	2 271.0	2 153.7
1963														
1st quarter	470.1	337.5	56.0	19.1	46.1	32.6	21.3	54.1	416.0	383.6	32.4	7.8	2 283.6	2 171.6
2nd quarter ...	474.8	342.4	55.9	19.3	47.1	31.7	21.5	54.3	420.5	388.0	32.5	7.7	2 310.0	2 192.1
3rd quarter	481.9	347.4	56.4	19.5	48.4	32.0	21.8	54.6	427.3	395.4	31.9	7.5	2 334.2	2 216.8
4th quarter	491.2	353.6	57.8	19.4	49.9	32.5	22.0	55.2	436.0	400.3	35.7	8.2	2 370.6	2 253.5
1964														
1st quarter	500.6	360.0	58.1	19.4	51.5	33.6	22.0	53.8	446.8	410.1	36.7	8.2	2 402.4	2 298.6
2nd quarter ...	509.8	367.4	59.0	19.4	53.1	33.2	22.3	49.7	460.0	418.4	41.6	9.0	2 445.9	2 361.1
3rd quarter	519.1	374.6	59.6	19.5	54.6	33.5	22.5	51.6	467.6	427.7	39.8	8.5	2 484.0	2 391.6
4th quarter	527.8	380.8	60.7	19.4	55.8	33.7	22.7	53.2	474.6	430.5	44.0	9.3	2 518.6	2 419.3
1965														
1st quarter	538.4	387.3	62.2	19.7	57.1	35.0	22.9	57.0	481.4	441.3	40.1	8.3	2 557.7	2 446.3
2nd quarter ...	547.6	394.1	63.4	19.9	58.8	34.6	23.2	58.4	489.2	448.8	40.4	8.3	2 593.6	2 473.4
3rd quarter	561.5	402.3	64.2	20.1	60.3	38.1	23.6	57.0	504.5	458.2	46.3	9.2	2 636.5	2 541.4
4th quarter	574.6	414.3	65.9	20.1	61.4	36.9	24.0	58.3	516.3	472.3	44.0	8.5	2 700.2	2 592.8
1966														
1st quarter	586.7	426.7	69.4	20.5	62.6	37.8	30.4	61.5	525.2	482.9	42.3	8.1	2 735.3	2 617.3
2nd quarter ...	596.3	437.8	67.5	20.4	63.6	37.9	30.8	65.6	530.8	488.3	42.5	8.0	2 760.4	2 623.5
3rd quarter	609.5	449.0	67.7	20.6	64.5	39.6	31.9	67.9	541.6	497.7	43.9	8.1	2 795.2	2 656.6
4th quarter	622.6	457.2	68.4	20.6	65.5	43.1	32.2	70.6	552.1	503.7	48.4	8.8	2 820.4	2 686.9
1967														
1st quarter	633.1	463.3	69.1	20.8	67.5	46.1	33.6	71.2	562.0	508.3	53.7	9.6	2 849.0	2 727.2
2nd quarter ...	640.2	469.0	68.9	20.9	68.7	47.2	34.6	70.9	569.2	517.9	51.3	9.0	2 864.2	2 749.6
3rd quarter	653.8	478.7	71.0	21.0	69.8	48.7	35.2	73.8	580.0	525.0	55.0	9.5	2 896.2	2 775.9
4th quarter	665.1	489.7	70.4	20.9	70.1	50.0	36.0	75.9	589.2	532.6	56.6	9.6	2 918.9	2 796.2
1968														
1st quarter	684.3	504.5	72.1	20.6	72.4	52.4	37.6	78.6	605.8	550.9	54.9	9.1	2 967.6	2 844.9
2nd quarter ...	703.8	517.6	73.4	20.6	74.7	55.9	38.4	81.7	622.1	565.1	57.0	9.2	3 011.9	2 892.2
3rd quarter	721.7	531.4	75.3	20.7	76.0	57.3	39.1	91.9	629.8	581.8	48.0	7.6	3 056.8	2 898.0
4th quarter	736.9	543.8	76.0	20.6	77.6	58.7	39.7	95.9	641.0	591.1	49.9	7.8	3 086.2	2 917.1
1969														
1st quarter	751.0	555.9	76.3	20.8	80.5	60.4	42.9	102.6	648.4	603.8	44.6	6.9	3 112.0	2 922.0
2nd quarter ...	769.1	569.8	77.6	20.9	83.0	61.5	43.7	105.7	663.4	615.9	47.5	7.2	3 147.9	2 951.6
3rd quarter	789.4	586.6	78.2	21.0	85.3	62.9	44.6	104.1	685.2	626.6	58.6	8.6	3 192.8	3 011.6
4th quarter	803.9	598.2	78.0	20.9	87.7	64.3	45.3	105.6	698.2	639.1	59.1	8.5	3 212.9	3 033.5

Table 4-1B. Personal Income and Its Disposition: Historical—*Continued*

(Billions of current dollars, except as noted; quarterly data are at seasonally adjusted annual rates.)

NIPA Table 2.1

| Year and quarter | Personal income | | | | | | Less: Contributions for government social insurance, domestic | Less: Personal current taxes | Equals: Disposable personal income | Less: Personal outlays | Equals: Personal saving | | Billions of chained (2005) dollars | |
	Total	Compensation of employees, received	Proprietors' income with IVA and CCAdj	Rental income of persons with CCAdj	Personal income receipts on assets	Personal current transfer receipts					Billions of dollars	Percent of disposable personal income	Personal income excluding current transfers	Disposable personal income
1970														
1st quarter	814.4	606.1	77.6	20.9	89.6	66.1	46.0	104.6	709.8	650.5	59.3	8.4	3 213.9	3 048.6
2nd quarter ...	835.8	616.3	77.1	20.6	91.9	76.1	46.3	105.5	730.3	660.8	69.5	9.5	3 227.1	3 102.0
3rd quarter	848.0	622.5	79.2	21.2	95.4	76.3	46.7	100.7	747.4	673.0	74.4	9.9	3 246.2	3 144.0
4th quarter	856.1	623.9	79.9	21.5	97.1	80.1	46.5	101.5	754.6	680.0	74.6	9.9	3 222.6	3 133.7
1971														
1st quarter	875.2	641.6	81.1	21.5	99.5	82.0	50.5	98.3	776.8	699.4	77.4	10.0	3 263.0	3 195.9
2nd quarter ...	898.2	653.5	83.7	22.0	100.3	89.6	51.0	100.7	797.4	713.9	83.5	10.5	3 289.1	3 243.9
3rd quarter	911.1	663.5	85.3	22.4	101.7	89.6	51.3	102.3	808.8	726.9	81.9	10.1	3 309.6	3 258.3
4th quarter	927.9	674.8	88.6	22.8	102.4	91.3	51.9	105.5	822.5	743.7	78.8	9.6	3 349.6	3 292.7
1972														
1st quarter	956.1	702.6	88.7	23.5	105.2	94.3	58.1	119.8	836.4	761.5	74.9	9.0	3 414.3	3 313.5
2nd quarter ...	972.5	716.2	92.2	20.5	107.6	94.9	58.8	123.4	849.1	780.6	68.5	8.1	3 456.7	3 344.6
3rd quarter	998.4	729.9	96.5	24.3	111.1	96.0	59.5	124.3	874.1	799.5	74.7	8.5	3 523.2	3 413.0
4th quarter	1 043.5	751.9	106.7	24.3	114.6	106.4	60.4	127.1	916.4	824.6	91.8	10.0	3 629.1	3 548.8
1973														
1st quarter	1 064.4	781.6	105.9	24.2	117.2	109.1	73.6	126.4	938.0	849.5	88.5	9.4	3 655.5	3 589.1
2nd quarter ...	1 094.8	801.1	111.7	24.1	121.1	111.5	74.7	129.2	965.6	865.6	100.0	10.4	3 691.1	3 624.5
3rd quarter	1 122.3	819.9	114.4	23.1	127.6	113.3	76.1	134.1	988.2	884.5	103.7	10.5	3 719.4	3 642.8
4th quarter	1 160.7	842.5	122.5	24.1	132.6	116.5	77.6	140.0	1 020.8	901.2	119.5	11.7	3 772.0	3 687.2
1974														
1st quarter	1 177.8	860.7	116.2	24.4	137.7	121.9	83.1	142.8	1 035.0	918.3	116.7	11.3	3 704.0	3 630.6
2nd quarter ...	1 204.1	881.9	109.3	23.8	144.0	129.9	84.7	148.9	1 055.2	947.3	107.8	10.2	3 664.3	3 599.5
3rd quarter	1 241.9	904.6	113.3	24.1	149.1	137.1	86.4	154.9	1 087.0	976.9	110.1	10.1	3 669.8	3 610.7
4th quarter	1 267.1	915.7	115.1	23.9	154.7	144.3	86.6	157.6	1 109.6	987.5	122.1	11.0	3 637.5	3 594.4
1975														
1st quarter	1 283.9	919.4	113.5	23.7	159.0	155.9	87.6	158.0	1 125.9	1 015.0	110.9	9.8	3 587.0	3 580.3
2nd quarter ...	1 314.0	931.7	115.5	23.5	159.9	171.5	88.0	121.1	1 193.0	1 044.0	149.0	12.5	3 589.0	3 747.5
3rd quarter	1 351.7	957.6	122.5	23.3	163.1	174.8	89.8	152.8	1 198.8	1 078.5	120.3	10.0	3 629.1	3 696.9
4th quarter	1 389.9	987.5	126.9	22.9	166.7	177.6	91.8	158.5	1 231.3	1 107.7	123.6	10.0	3 676.4	3 734.3
1976														
1st quarter	1 425.4	1 022.3	127.6	22.6	170.4	181.4	98.9	162.1	1 263.3	1 141.2	122.1	9.7	3 731.5	3 789.3
2nd quarter ...	1 453.4	1 046.0	130.0	21.7	176.3	179.7	100.4	169.0	1 284.4	1 161.0	123.4	9.6	3 788.7	3 820.5
3rd quarter	1 491.4	1 070.7	133.8	21.9	180.8	186.4	102.2	175.8	1 315.7	1 190.8	124.9	9.5	3 823.8	3 854.9
4th quarter	1 528.4	1 098.0	137.5	22.0	186.2	188.5	103.8	182.4	1 346.1	1 225.2	120.9	9.0	3 865.0	3 882.6
1977														
1st quarter	1 559.9	1 126.9	140.5	20.9	190.2	190.6	109.3	188.4	1 371.4	1 262.0	109.5	8.0	3 879.6	3 885.8
2nd quarter ...	1 606.1	1 164.3	141.9	19.9	201.0	191.1	112.1	195.3	1 410.8	1 291.0	119.8	8.5	3 941.9	3 930.0
3rd quarter	1 651.8	1 196.8	143.6	19.0	210.5	196.2	114.3	198.2	1 453.6	1 323.2	130.4	9.0	3 994.4	3 989.0
4th quarter	1 712.2	1 233.7	158.0	18.7	219.5	199.0	116.7	208.1	1 504.1	1 362.5	141.6	9.4	4 094.2	4 069.4
1978														
1st quarter	1 750.3	1 269.6	158.4	20.4	224.9	203.1	126.2	211.7	1 538.6	1 394.1	144.4	9.4	4 117.5	4 094.5
2nd quarter ...	1 811.1	1 317.8	168.1	19.8	230.6	204.9	130.1	222.8	1 588.2	1 453.4	134.9	8.5	4 188.4	4 141.5
3rd quarter	1 865.4	1 354.3	171.3	21.4	237.4	213.6	132.8	236.0	1 629.3	1 485.9	143.5	8.8	4 232.6	4 175.1
4th quarter	1 920.1	1 398.9	172.2	21.9	246.2	216.9	136.0	247.0	1 673.2	1 526.4	146.8	8.8	4 283.4	4 207.9
1979														
1st quarter	1 976.7	1 443.3	179.2	23.4	257.1	222.5	148.8	253.4	1 723.3	1 562.8	160.5	9.3	4 330.2	4 253.9
2nd quarter ...	2 019.7	1 476.1	179.3	21.1	267.0	227.1	150.9	261.8	1 757.9	1 604.5	153.4	8.7	4 307.3	4 224.2
3rd quarter	2 086.4	1 516.4	182.5	21.2	277.7	242.7	154.2	274.6	1 811.8	1 660.5	151.3	8.4	4 323.0	4 248.3
4th quarter	2 155.4	1 558.1	183.5	24.8	297.2	248.9	157.1	285.0	1 870.4	1 705.8	164.6	8.8	4 364.9	4 282.3
1980														
1st quarter	2 216.0	1 599.2	168.5	28.6	324.0	258.7	163.1	284.2	1 931.8	1 758.2	173.6	9.0	4 350.8	4 294.3
2nd quarter ...	2 242.9	1 621.3	162.2	24.1	334.6	263.9	163.2	291.5	1 951.4	1 760.1	191.3	9.8	4 294.1	4 234.2
3rd quarter	2 319.0	1 652.9	175.8	25.0	336.0	295.9	166.6	301.5	2 017.5	1 818.4	199.1	9.9	4 289.7	4 277.8
4th quarter	2 428.2	1 717.0	187.3	36.3	360.1	299.3	171.8	318.2	2 110.0	1 888.7	221.3	10.5	4 405.1	4 366.1
1981														
1st quarter	2 487.6	1 768.9	190.1	36.2	378.2	305.9	191.6	330.3	2 157.4	1 949.0	208.3	9.7	4 405.4	4 356.1
2nd quarter ...	2 535.7	1 801.9	177.9	35.1	405.6	309.3	194.1	342.1	2 193.6	1 983.1	210.5	9.6	4 421.7	4 356.7
3rd quarter	2 635.3	1 839.8	184.2	35.7	445.5	327.9	197.7	356.3	2 279.1	2 025.9	253.2	11.1	4 508.8	4 453.3
4th quarter	2 670.4	1 867.9	174.2	38.8	458.5	330.4	199.4	352.0	2 318.4	2 043.4	275.0	11.9	4 503.9	4 462.3
1982														
1st quarter	2 702.3	1 892.0	167.6	39.5	474.7	335.7	207.2	351.9	2 350.4	2 084.9	265.6	11.3	4 498.3	4 467.5
2nd quarter ...	2 748.5	1 911.1	173.0	36.2	491.7	344.9	208.4	359.1	2 389.4	2 114.8	274.6	11.5	4 525.5	4 498.8
3rd quarter	2 787.1	1 930.8	174.4	38.0	492.3	361.5	209.8	349.5	2 437.6	2 165.5	272.1	11.2	4 496.2	4 518.5
4th quarter	2 829.2	1 944.7	184.2	38.5	494.7	377.3	210.2	355.9	2 473.3	2 229.9	243.4	9.8	4 495.3	4 534.4
1983														
1st quarter	2 864.6	1 972.8	188.0	37.6	506.4	380.2	220.4	350.3	2 514.3	2 272.3	242.0	9.6	4 515.8	4 570.1
2nd quarter ...	2 914.9	2 011.8	188.2	37.8	514.4	386.4	223.6	359.0	2 555.9	2 339.3	216.7	8.5	4 554.1	4 603.4
3rd quarter	2 973.4	2 052.8	188.4	38.2	539.3	381.9	227.2	344.9	2 628.5	2 412.6	216.0	8.2	4 606.6	4 672.5
4th quarter	3 055.7	2 106.6	198.0	39.1	558.2	386.5	232.6	355.1	2 700.6	2 467.5	233.1	8.6	4 713.5	4 768.9

Table 4-1B. Personal Income and Its Disposition: Historical—*Continued*

(Billions of current dollars, except as noted; quarterly data are at seasonally adjusted annual rates.)   **NIPA Table 2.1**

| Year and quarter | Personal income | | | | | | | Less: Personal current taxes | Equals: Disposable personal income | Less: Personal outlays | Equals: Personal saving | | Billions of chained (2005) dollars | |
	Total	Compensation of employees, received	Proprietors' income with IVA and CCAdj	Rental income of persons with CCAdj	Personal income receipts on assets	Personal current transfer receipts	Less: Contributions for government social insurance, domestic				Billions of dollars	Percent of disposable personal income	Personal income excluding current transfers	Disposable personal income
1984														
1st quarter	3 150.2	2 175.8	224.2	38.1	569.7	393.4	251.0	360.7	2 789.5	2 515.2	274.3	9.8	4 816.0	4 873.2
2nd quarter ...	3 235.1	2 225.5	234.9	36.7	596.0	397.8	255.8	369.9	2 865.1	2 576.8	288.3	10.1	4 908.9	4 957.1
3rd quarter	3 316.0	2 270.9	237.1	40.4	627.1	400.5	259.9	383.6	2 932.4	2 618.5	313.9	10.7	5 005.4	5 034.3
4th quarter	3 374.2	2 308.7	236.0	44.8	638.9	408.9	263.1	395.4	2 978.8	2 670.3	308.5	10.4	5 059.2	5 082.2
1985														
1st quarter	3 434.9	2 353.6	248.2	42.9	646.0	419.6	275.4	431.8	3 003.1	2 746.1	257.0	8.6	5 090.4	5 069.7
2nd quarter ...	3 473.6	2 390.2	244.6	41.7	653.7	422.1	278.8	388.1	3 085.6	2 795.2	290.3	9.4	5 113.3	5 170.4
3rd quarter	3 507.0	2 427.9	244.6	42.2	647.6	427.5	282.8	421.1	3 086.0	2 865.6	220.4	7.1	5 127.7	5 138.4
4th quarter	3 571.0	2 476.1	246.9	40.5	665.5	430.4	288.4	428.4	3 142.6	2 896.1	246.5	7.8	5 188.3	5 191.6
1986														
1st quarter	3 628.6	2 510.0	249.5	36.8	687.7	442.6	297.9	425.7	3 202.9	2 941.6	261.3	8.2	5 225.6	5 253.4
2nd quarter ...	3 670.2	2 533.3	257.2	35.6	694.4	448.5	300.7	428.8	3 241.4	2 974.5	266.8	8.2	5 280.8	5 313.0
3rd quarter	3 721.3	2 569.2	271.5	32.5	697.7	455.5	305.1	438.9	3 282.4	3 046.4	236.0	7.2	5 313.9	5 340.9
4th quarter	3 763.9	2 618.2	272.1	30.4	696.1	457.2	310.1	455.4	3 308.5	3 086.9	221.6	6.7	5 341.2	5 344.1
1987														
1st quarter	3 823.2	2 664.5	282.7	31.6	698.3	462.6	316.5	450.2	3 373.0	3 119.5	253.5	7.5	5 357.1	5 376.9
2nd quarter ...	3 877.0	2 706.2	289.7	30.5	703.3	467.6	320.2	511.1	3 365.9	3 186.1	179.7	5.3	5 387.4	5 318.6
3rd quarter	3 949.9	2 752.4	297.2	35.3	720.9	468.6	324.5	488.4	3 461.5	3 253.6	207.9	6.0	5 444.7	5 413.7
4th quarter	4 047.4	2 819.5	307.4	39.4	740.7	471.6	331.2	506.4	3 540.9	3 288.3	252.6	7.1	5 544.6	5 490.6
1988														
1st quarter	4 117.1	2 869.1	327.5	38.4	745.3	488.9	352.1	501.1	3 616.1	3 370.8	245.3	6.8	5 578.2	5 559.6
2nd quarter ...	4 186.8	2 932.3	333.8	36.9	750.4	492.5	359.1	496.8	3 690.0	3 431.8	258.1	7.0	5 618.3	5 611.8
3rd quarter	4 269.9	2 981.0	343.0	38.8	773.0	498.6	364.4	505.7	3 764.3	3 500.4	263.9	7.0	5 665.6	5 655.0
4th quarter	4 351.1	3 034.2	335.1	46.8	799.5	505.8	370.3	516.2	3 834.9	3 575.8	259.2	6.8	5 721.4	5 705.9
1989														
1st quarter	4 476.5	3 078.5	357.0	44.2	846.9	529.8	379.8	551.3	3 925.3	3 634.4	290.9	7.4	5 802.3	5 770.8
2nd quarter ...	4 525.9	3 107.8	348.4	43.5	871.8	537.2	382.8	565.0	3 960.8	3 700.3	260.5	6.6	5 787.5	5 747.1
3rd quarter	4 578.2	3 144.4	347.8	41.1	885.0	546.2	386.4	569.9	4 008.3	3 760.2	248.1	6.2	5 818.5	5 784.3
4th quarter	4 649.3	3 194.6	353.2	40.8	895.4	557.2	391.8	578.2	4 071.1	3 810.8	260.4	6.4	5 858.6	5 828.6
1990														
1st quarter	4 744.5	3 259.0	360.6	43.3	908.3	577.5	404.1	580.5	4 164.0	3 897.4	266.6	6.4	5 876.7	5 872.5
2nd quarter ...	4 829.3	3 317.4	364.3	48.2	919.3	588.5	408.3	592.6	4 236.7	3 952.1	284.6	6.7	5 916.9	5 911.1
3rd quarter	4 892.6	3 358.5	369.2	53.3	927.7	598.0	414.1	598.8	4 293.9	4 018.7	275.2	6.4	5 916.4	5 915.4
4th quarter	4 920.4	3 370.0	366.6	54.4	927.9	615.5	413.9	598.9	4 321.5	4 041.1	280.4	6.5	5 852.9	5 875.5
1991														
1st quarter	4 941.0	3 384.8	357.8	56.1	927.3	639.4	424.5	578.5	4 362.5	4 059.2	303.3	7.0	5 811.3	5 893.6
2nd quarter ...	5 005.8	3 419.8	365.2	58.1	931.3	659.1	427.7	583.7	4 422.1	4 114.3	307.8	7.0	5 837.1	5 938.3
3rd quarter	5 053.1	3 455.3	367.7	62.7	931.5	668.5	432.6	588.0	4 465.1	4 160.8	304.4	6.8	5 843.6	5 950.9
4th quarter	5 126.1	3 493.6	378.4	69.4	924.2	696.5	435.9	596.4	4 529.8	4 192.4	337.3	7.4	5 857.3	5 989.7
1992														
1st quarter	5 220.7	3 561.1	396.4	71.6	915.5	724.7	448.7	586.5	4 634.1	4 290.6	343.5	7.4	5 898.8	6 080.1
2nd quarter ...	5 306.8	3 612.7	410.4	81.3	912.8	743.3	453.7	604.9	4 701.9	4 344.2	357.7	7.6	5 946.3	6 126.7
3rd quarter	5 370.7	3 656.6	420.9	89.3	906.3	755.3	457.8	613.9	4 756.8	4 423.8	333.0	7.0	5 974.7	6 157.8
4th quarter	5 490.9	3 758.4	431.9	96.3	904.3	759.7	459.6	636.9	4 854.1	4 496.0	358.1	7.4	6 087.4	6 245.4
1993														
1st quarter	5 420.5	3 660.1	435.8	105.5	907.2	779.4	467.5	614.6	4 805.9	4 537.3	268.6	5.6	5 942.7	6 153.8
2nd quarter ...	5 549.7	3 775.3	450.1	113.5	902.5	783.8	475.6	641.3	4 908.4	4 604.9	303.4	6.2	6 068.0	6 249.5
3rd quarter	5 593.1	3 817.8	447.0	115.4	895.3	797.7	480.1	657.0	4 936.2	4 668.1	268.1	5.4	6 084.2	6 262.8
4th quarter	5 709.2	3 909.3	465.5	122.0	896.8	802.1	486.6	673.3	5 036.0	4 734.6	301.4	6.0	6 192.5	6 355.1
1994														
1st quarter	5 706.7	3 870.5	476.7	133.1	909.2	815.6	498.4	671.1	5 035.7	4 806.2	229.5	4.6	6 148.1	6 329.7
2nd quarter ...	5 844.1	3 973.9	481.8	141.6	932.8	820.3	506.4	695.3	5 148.8	4 870.1	278.7	5.4	6 281.3	6 437.7
3rd quarter	5 921.8	4 011.8	485.8	148.5	962.0	824.3	510.6	692.8	5 229.0	4 952.8	276.2	5.3	6 321.9	6 485.0
4th quarter	6 026.6	4 067.5	496.1	148.4	986.6	845.4	517.4	702.9	5 323.7	5 025.4	298.3	5.6	6 395.1	6 571.0
1995														
1st quarter	6 107.2	4 119.1	500.4	151.0	993.0	869.4	525.7	720.0	5 387.2	5 059.9	327.3	6.1	6 430.2	6 613.6
2nd quarter ...	6 161.3	4 155.0	506.3	153.0	998.3	879.0	530.1	742.2	5 419.1	5 138.1	281.0	5.2	6 447.3	6 614.2
3rd quarter	6 230.4	4 200.0	520.0	152.8	1 007.0	885.9	535.3	747.7	5 482.7	5 209.4	273.3	5.0	6 495.7	6 663.7
4th quarter	6 304.7	4 241.1	537.4	161.5	1 023.1	881.5	540.0	765.7	5 539.0	5 275.6	263.4	4.8	6 563.0	6 703.2
1996														
1st quarter	6 427.3	4 291.9	560.2	166.7	1 041.7	910.9	544.2	796.5	5 630.8	5 353.6	277.2	4.9	6 637.0	6 774.6
2nd quarter ...	6 562.7	4 360.6	586.5	168.4	1 067.9	931.3	552.1	834.4	5 728.3	5 451.3	277.0	4.8	6 731.7	6 847.4
3rd quarter	6 642.0	4 419.8	588.6	172.1	1 093.6	926.7	558.7	838.4	5 803.6	5 512.0	291.5	5.0	6 800.8	6 905.7
4th quarter	6 734.3	4 478.6	599.4	174.5	1 119.7	927.5	565.4	858.4	5 875.9	5 597.0	278.9	4.7	6 862.0	6 943.6
1997														
1st quarter	6 855.6	4 557.6	619.6	174.9	1 134.3	944.6	575.5	896.4	5 959.1	5 682.8	276.3	4.6	6 949.1	7 005.7
2nd quarter ...	6 930.4	4 620.9	619.4	175.9	1 152.2	944.3	582.2	910.5	6 019.9	5 725.2	294.7	4.9	7 018.6	7 058.3
3rd quarter	7 041.5	4 698.2	632.8	176.4	1 173.8	950.5	590.2	935.4	6 106.1	5 839.8	266.3	4.4	7 121.5	7 139.1
4th quarter	7 175.5	4 797.6	641.1	178.9	1 201.5	957.4	601.0	962.2	6 213.2	5 928.9	284.4	4.6	7 243.9	7 238.3

Table 4-1B. Personal Income and Its Disposition: Historical—*Continued*

(Billions of current dollars, except as noted; quarterly data are at seasonally adjusted annual rates.)   NIPA Table 2.1

| Year and quarter | Personal income | | | | | | | Less: Personal current taxes | Equals: Disposable personal income | Less: Personal outlays | Equals: Personal saving | | Billions of chained (2005) dollars | |
	Total	Compensation of employees, received	Proprietors' income with IVA and CCAdj	Rental income of persons with CCAdj	Personal income receipts on assets	Personal current transfer receipts	Less: Contributions for government social insurance, domestic				Billions of dollars	Percent of disposable personal income	Personal income excluding current transfers	Disposable personal income
1998														
1st quarter	7 347.7	4 899.1	663.6	182.7	1 245.4	968.7	611.8	990.1	6 357.6	5 987.2	370.4	5.8	7 427.8	7 402.9
2nd quarter ...	7 479.8	4 982.7	677.0	188.6	1 276.8	975.1	620.4	1 016.4	6 463.4	6 108.1	355.4	5.5	7 556.6	7 508.6
3rd quarter	7 590.4	5 066.1	692.9	195.7	1 286.2	978.5	629.0	1 037.2	6 553.2	6 210.3	342.9	5.2	7 655.5	7 587.5
4th quarter	7 683.6	5 147.8	716.6	198.8	1 268.3	989.4	637.4	1 062.0	6 621.6	6 324.3	297.2	4.5	7 726.9	7 643.1
1999														
1st quarter	7 760.9	5 241.3	729.6	203.0	1 229.5	1 010.0	652.5	1 073.5	6 687.4	6 400.9	286.5	4.3	7 768.0	7 694.9
2nd quarter ...	7 831.6	5 292.7	738.9	206.9	1 236.2	1 013.2	656.4	1 090.8	6 740.8	6 540.9	199.9	3.0	7 801.2	7 712.5
3rd quarter	7 936.2	5 366.9	750.6	209.2	1 245.4	1 026.3	662.2	1 116.2	6 819.9	6 653.9	166.0	2.4	7 864.7	7 762.4
4th quarter	8 114.7	5 494.3	768.1	213.5	1 276.0	1 036.8	674.1	1 149.6	6 965.1	6 786.4	178.7	2.6	8 011.8	7 884.1
2000														
1st quarter	8 379.6	5 692.1	783.7	214.6	1 334.3	1 052.4	697.5	1 204.7	7 174.9	6 955.1	219.9	3.1	8 220.6	8 049.8
2nd quarter ...	8 506.6	5 731.4	819.4	212.1	1 363.1	1 079.4	698.9	1 226.1	7 280.5	7 054.0	226.5	3.1	8 296.1	8 132.3
3rd quarter	8 644.2	5 845.8	826.7	213.3	1 375.9	1 093.7	711.2	1 243.6	7 400.6	7 171.5	229.0	3.1	8 385.1	8 218.6
4th quarter	8 707.3	5 886.1	840.1	221.1	1 369.4	1 106.5	715.8	1 254.6	7 452.7	7 275.7	177.0	2.4	8 394.5	8 230.9
2001														
1st quarter	8 859.0	5 993.9	867.4	225.3	1 357.8	1 150.0	735.5	1 297.6	7 561.4	7 353.2	208.2	2.8	8 454.7	8 292.7
2nd quarter ...	8 881.2	5 979.9	871.6	230.6	1 350.6	1 182.6	734.0	1 304.5	7 576.8	7 414.9	161.9	2.1	8 403.1	8 270.0
3rd quarter	8 880.6	5 965.8	878.1	239.5	1 340.6	1 188.2	731.5	1 109.5	7 771.1	7 448.1	323.0	4.2	8 394.8	8 480.6
4th quarter	8 912.3	5 977.7	865.8	234.1	1 334.8	1 231.7	731.7	1 227.7	7 684.6	7 557.9	126.7	1.6	8 377.3	8 381.7
2002														
1st quarter	8 978.3	6 038.4	880.5	229.2	1 319.1	1 257.7	746.6	1 068.4	7 909.9	7 596.2	313.7	4.0	8 401.6	8 607.6
2nd quarter ...	9 060.7	6 101.3	884.2	231.7	1 315.4	1 280.4	752.3	1 045.3	8 015.4	7 694.0	321.4	4.0	8 401.2	8 655.0
3rd quarter	9 074.6	6 128.8	893.3	212.7	1 303.8	1 288.6	752.7	1 046.3	8 028.3	7 781.3	247.0	3.1	8 365.0	8 625.3
4th quarter	9 126.8	6 174.7	903.2	201.4	1 300.0	1 301.9	754.2	1 041.7	8 085.1	7 838.5	246.7	3.1	8 367.5	8 645.7
2003														
1st quarter	9 194.5	6 244.4	889.6	209.7	1 299.2	1 318.1	766.7	1 021.3	8 173.2	7 922.2	250.9	3.1	8 362.4	8 677.5
2nd quarter ...	9 321.1	6 332.7	919.1	204.2	1 306.2	1 333.7	774.9	1 018.1	8 303.0	8 012.0	291.0	3.5	8 473.9	8 808.8
3rd quarter	9 418.7	6 400.6	945.8	186.2	1 312.4	1 355.6	781.8	945.2	8 473.5	8 166.7	306.9	3.6	8 499.5	8 932.1
4th quarter	9 578.3	6 492.6	968.1	216.6	1 333.8	1 359.6	792.3	1 016.8	8 561.5	8 251.6	309.9	3.6	8 623.9	8 983.5
2004														
1st quarter	9 679.8	6 543.3	1 002.1	204.2	1 350.0	1 392.5	812.3	1 009.3	8 670.5	8 387.7	282.8	3.3	8 624.6	9 023.4
2nd quarter ...	9 847.1	6 657.9	1 029.8	197.1	1 372.9	1 411.0	821.6	1 026.4	8 820.7	8 489.9	330.8	3.8	8 715.2	9 112.6
3rd quarter	9 999.1	6 781.3	1 040.1	196.8	1 395.5	1 418.5	833.1	1 064.7	8 934.4	8 621.1	313.3	3.5	8 810.2	9 173.5
4th quarter	10 223.1	6 851.2	1 063.1	195.4	1 515.5	1 440.1	842.2	1 090.9	9 132.1	8 786.0	346.1	3.8	8 946.2	9 301.8
2005														
1st quarter	10 238.6	6 921.1	1 046.8	190.7	1 459.7	1 481.3	861.0	1 164.2	9 074.3	8 914.8	159.5	1.8	8 867.5	9 188.5
2nd quarter ...	10 386.7	7 003.6	1 054.0	181.5	1 507.1	1 506.4	865.8	1 192.3	9 194.4	9 060.6	133.8	1.5	8 937.1	9 253.2
3rd quarter	10 577.5	7 128.4	1 082.6	168.4	1 560.4	1 516.7	879.0	1 224.0	9 353.5	9 230.2	123.3	1.3	9 017.1	9 308.4
4th quarter	10 740.8	7 187.1	1 095.8	172.3	1 640.8	1 529.8	885.0	1 253.8	9 487.1	9 331.0	156.1	1.6	9 087.0	9 359.3
2006														
1st quarter	11 026.7	7 373.7	1 126.9	161.3	1 711.1	1 569.0	915.4	1 321.5	9 705.2	9 471.4	233.7	2.4	9 291.4	9 534.6
2nd quarter ...	11 204.0	7 419.9	1 133.2	153.2	1 817.2	1 597.9	917.4	1 340.2	9 863.8	9 600.8	263.0	2.7	9 367.8	9 619.1
3rd quarter	11 336.9	7 484.1	1 131.2	140.3	1 881.3	1 620.7	920.8	1 354.3	9 982.5	9 734.8	247.7	2.5	9 407.4	9 665.3
4th quarter	11 504.8	7 625.3	1 140.6	131.2	1 909.0	1 632.4	933.8	1 393.5	10 111.2	9 829.2	282.0	2.8	9 560.7	9 792.0
2007														
1st quarter	11 714.3	7 781.4	1 103.0	122.4	1 959.2	1 701.6	953.4	1 458.7	10 255.5	9 983.8	271.7	2.6	9 603.3	9 836.3
2nd quarter ...	11 839.0	7 814.4	1 090.0	139.8	2 050.4	1 698.6	954.2	1 480.4	10 358.6	10 121.6	237.0	2.3	9 643.4	9 851.0
3rd quarter	11 954.4	7 868.5	1 079.3	146.8	2 098.7	1 719.8	958.7	1 497.5	10 456.9	10 234.1	222.8	2.1	9 679.5	9 889.7
4th quarter	12 141.4	7 984.3	1 089.1	165.9	2 119.8	1 753.8	971.6	1 518.0	10 623.4	10 360.1	263.3	2.5	9 723.4	9 944.1
2008														
1st quarter	12 415.6	8 099.0	1 113.7	188.9	2 205.0	1 798.9	989.8	1 536.0	10 879.6	10 424.5	455.0	4.2	9 843.7	10 087.4
2nd quarter ...	12 571.7	8 073.4	1 127.2	218.5	2 203.1	1 936.1	986.6	1 351.8	11 220.0	10 529.4	690.6	6.2	9 752.6	10 288.5
3rd quarter	12 513.3	8 084.7	1 104.0	243.5	2 197.5	1 872.2	988.7	1 432.1	11 081.2	10 538.4	542.8	4.9	9 654.4	10 053.7
4th quarter	12 340.0	8 036.1	1 046.7	275.6	2 056.0	1 909.7	984.2	1 422.8	10 917.3	10 236.3	680.9	6.2	9 599.7	10 047.9
2009														
1st quarter	11 964.4	7 810.1	960.2	278.8	1 851.5	2 029.8	966.0	1 198.0	10 766.3	10 155.2	611.1	5.7	9 182.2	9 951.0
2nd quarter ...	11 944.1	7 809.2	926.9	299.7	1 707.5	2 167.7	966.9	1 120.3	10 823.8	10 153.4	670.3	6.2	8 893.3	9 957.3
3rd quarter	11 874.1	7 781.9	929.3	319.3	1 635.7	2 170.1	962.1	1 120.6	10 753.5	10 285.3	468.2	4.4	8 861.3	9 819.6
4th quarter	11 938.2	7 804.4	948.5	325.9	1 636.0	2 184.9	961.5	1 126.4	10 811.7	10 351.2	460.5	4.3	8 845.5	9 805.4
2010														
1st quarter	12 137.7	7 852.5	981.7	344.1	1 693.3	2 242.1	976.0	1 146.4	10 991.3	10 457.2	534.1	4.9	8 933.4	9 922.5
2nd quarter ...	12 325.6	7 960.0	1 025.6	349.1	1 724.5	2 252.1	985.7	1 175.4	11 150.2	10 527.0	623.3	5.6	9 086.5	10 057.8
3rd quarter	12 453.2	8 022.2	1 057.0	352.8	1 723.4	2 289.4	991.5	1 212.8	11 240.4	10 614.8	625.6	5.6	9 145.7	10 114.4
4th quarter	12 577.6	8 050.8	1 081.5	354.8	1 743.5	2 341.2	994.1	1 240.9	11 336.7	10 748.6	588.1	5.2	9 166.7	10 152.0
2011														
1st quarter	12 846.9	8 172.5	1 095.6	385.0	1 777.2	2 328.1	911.5	1 365.9	11 481.0	10 902.1	578.9	5.0	9 329.8	10 183.2
2nd quarter ...	12 955.3	8 219.7	1 106.5	396.9	1 802.3	2 347.3	917.4	1 396.2	11 559.2	11 002.6	556.5	4.8	9 332.9	10 169.7
3rd quarter	13 056.8	8 338.3	1 113.7	406.3	1 794.2	2 336.6	932.4	1 409.1	11 647.7	11 114.6	533.1	4.6	9 377.3	10 188.6
4th quarter	13 105.7	8 375.8	1 119.7	427.2	1 786.3	2 333.1	936.3	1 419.4	11 686.3	11 201.0	485.3	4.2	9 395.8	10 192.7

Table 4-2. Personal Consumption Expenditures by Major Type of Product

(Billions of dollars, quarterly data are at seasonally adjusted rates.)   **NIPA Table 2.3.5**

| Year and quarter | Personal consumption expend-itures, total | Goods | | | | | | | | | | |
| | | Total goods | Durable goods | | | | | Nondurable goods | | | | |
			Durable goods, total	Motor vehicles and parts	Furnishings and household equipment	Recreational goods and vehicles	Other durable goods	Nondurable goods, total	Food and beverages off-premises	Clothing and footwear	Gasoline and other energy goods	Other nondurable goods
1950	192.2	116.8	32.4	13.7	11.8	4.1	2.9	84.4	41.4	18.9	8.9	15.2
1951	208.5	124.8	31.7	12.1	12.4	4.1	3.2	93.0	46.0	20.5	9.6	16.9
1952	219.5	128.8	31.2	11.4	12.2	4.3	3.4	97.5	48.4	21.2	10.2	17.8
1953	233.1	134.8	34.6	13.8	12.6	4.7	3.5	100.2	49.3	21.3	10.8	18.8
1954	240.0	135.8	33.7	12.7	12.5	4.9	3.6	102.1	50.6	21.4	11.3	18.8
1955	258.8	147.4	40.7	17.7	14.0	5.3	3.7	106.7	52.0	22.4	12.4	19.9
1956	271.7	152.2	40.2	15.7	14.8	5.7	4.0	112.0	54.2	23.4	13.3	21.1
1957	286.9	159.6	42.0	17.5	14.8	5.8	4.0	117.6	57.1	23.6	14.2	22.6
1958	296.2	161.6	39.5	15.0	14.6	5.9	4.1	122.0	59.8	23.9	14.7	23.6
1959	317.7	172.6	44.9	18.8	15.5	6.4	4.2	127.7	61.6	25.4	15.3	25.5
1960	331.8	177.0	45.6	19.6	15.4	6.4	4.3	131.4	62.6	25.9	15.8	27.1
1961	342.2	178.8	44.2	17.7	15.6	6.6	4.3	134.6	63.7	26.6	15.7	28.6
1962	363.3	189.0	49.5	21.4	16.4	6.9	4.7	139.5	64.7	27.9	16.3	30.7
1963	382.7	198.2	54.2	24.2	17.5	7.6	4.9	143.9	65.9	28.6	16.9	32.5
1964	411.5	212.3	59.6	25.8	19.5	8.8	5.5	152.7	69.5	31.1	17.7	34.5
1965	443.8	229.7	66.4	29.6	20.7	10.1	6.0	163.3	74.4	32.7	19.1	37.1
1966	480.9	249.6	71.7	29.9	22.6	12.3	6.9	177.9	80.6	35.8	20.7	40.8
1967	507.8	259.0	74.0	29.6	23.7	13.6	7.1	185.0	82.6	37.5	21.9	43.0
1968	558.0	284.6	84.8	35.4	26.1	15.3	8.0	199.8	88.8	41.3	23.2	46.5
1969	605.1	304.7	90.5	37.4	27.6	16.7	8.7	214.2	95.4	44.3	25.0	49.5
1970	648.3	318.8	90.0	34.5	28.2	17.9	9.4	228.8	103.5	45.5	26.3	53.6
1971	701.6	342.1	102.4	43.2	29.9	19.2	10.1	239.7	107.1	49.0	27.6	55.9
1972	770.2	373.8	116.4	49.4	33.5	22.6	11.0	257.4	114.5	53.5	29.4	60.0
1973	852.0	416.6	130.5	54.4	38.0	25.3	12.9	286.1	126.7	59.2	34.3	65.8
1974	932.9	451.5	130.2	48.2	40.9	26.6	14.5	321.4	143.0	62.4	43.8	72.1
1975	1 033.8	491.3	142.2	52.6	42.6	30.4	16.5	349.2	156.6	66.9	48.0	77.7
1976	1 151.3	546.3	168.6	68.2	47.2	34.2	19.1	377.7	167.3	72.2	53.0	85.2
1977	1 277.8	600.4	192.0	79.8	53.4	37.7	21.1	408.4	179.8	79.3	57.8	91.5
1978	1 427.6	663.6	213.3	89.2	59.0	41.7	23.5	450.2	196.1	89.3	61.5	103.3
1979	1 591.2	737.9	226.3	90.2	65.3	45.8	25.1	511.6	218.4	96.4	80.4	116.5
1980	1 755.8	799.8	226.4	84.4	67.8	46.5	27.6	573.4	239.2	103.0	101.9	129.3
1981	1 939.5	869.4	243.9	93.0	71.5	49.9	29.6	625.4	255.3	113.2	113.4	143.5
1982	2 075.5	899.3	253.0	100.0	71.8	51.3	29.9	646.3	267.1	116.7	108.4	154.0
1983	2 288.6	973.8	295.0	122.9	79.8	58.7	33.7	678.8	277.0	126.4	106.5	168.8
1984	2 501.1	1 063.7	342.2	147.2	88.8	67.8	38.3	721.5	291.1	137.6	108.2	184.6
1985	2 717.6	1 137.6	380.4	170.1	94.6	74.1	41.6	757.2	303.0	146.8	110.5	196.9
1986	2 896.7	1 195.6	421.4	187.5	103.5	83.0	47.5	774.2	316.4	157.2	91.2	209.4
1987	3 097.0	1 256.3	442.0	188.2	109.5	91.8	52.5	814.3	324.3	167.7	96.4	225.9
1988	3 350.1	1 337.3	475.1	202.2	115.2	99.9	57.8	862.3	342.8	178.2	99.9	241.4
1989	3 594.5	1 423.8	494.3	207.8	121.4	103.9	61.3	929.5	365.4	190.4	110.4	263.3
1990	3 835.5	1 491.3	497.1	205.1	120.9	105.6	65.5	994.2	391.2	195.2	124.2	283.6
1991	3 980.1	1 497.4	477.2	185.7	118.8	107.7	64.9	1 020.3	403.0	199.1	121.1	297.1
1992	4 236.9	1 563.3	508.1	204.8	124.3	111.0	68.0	1 055.2	404.5	211.2	125.0	314.5
1993	4 483.6	1 642.3	551.5	224.7	131.4	123.5	72.0	1 090.8	413.5	219.1	126.9	331.4
1994	4 750.8	1 746.6	607.2	249.8	140.5	140.3	76.5	1 139.4	432.1	227.4	129.2	350.6
1995	4 987.3	1 815.5	635.7	255.7	146.7	153.7	79.6	1 179.8	443.7	231.2	133.4	371.4
1996	5 273.6	1 917.7	676.3	273.5	153.5	164.9	84.3	1 241.4	461.9	239.5	144.7	395.2
1997	5 570.6	2 006.8	715.5	293.1	160.5	174.6	87.3	1 291.2	474.8	247.5	147.7	421.3
1998	5 918.5	2 110.0	780.0	320.2	173.6	192.1	94.2	1 330.0	486.5	257.8	133.4	452.3
1999	6 342.8	2 290.0	857.4	350.7	191.2	212.7	102.7	1 432.6	513.6	271.1	148.8	499.2
2000	6 830.4	2 459.1	915.8	363.2	208.1	234.1	110.4	1 543.4	537.5	280.8	188.8	536.2
2001	7 148.8	2 534.0	946.3	383.3	214.9	239.8	108.4	1 587.7	559.7	277.9	183.6	566.5
2002	7 439.2	2 610.0	992.1	401.3	225.9	251.5	113.4	1 617.9	569.6	278.8	174.6	594.9
2003	7 804.1	2 728.0	1 019.9	401.0	231.8	265.7	121.4	1 708.1	587.5	286.2	209.5	625.0
2004	8 270.6	2 892.1	1 072.9	403.9	247.0	290.5	131.5	1 819.3	613.0	298.7	249.4	658.2
2005	8 803.5	3 076.7	1 123.4	408.2	261.3	312.8	141.1	1 953.4	644.5	314.0	303.8	691.1
2006	9 301.0	3 224.7	1 155.0	394.8	271.5	334.1	154.6	2 069.8	674.2	327.3	335.2	733.0
2007	9 772.3	3 363.9	1 188.4	399.9	271.3	349.4	167.8	2 175.5	711.2	335.4	364.8	764.1
2008	10 035.5	3 381.7	1 108.9	339.3	257.9	344.0	167.7	2 272.8	746.4	330.9	410.5	785.1
2009	9 866.1	3 197.5	1 029.6	316.5	235.3	316.6	161.2	2 167.8	746.0	318.2	299.4	804.1
2010	10 245.5	3 387.0	1 085.5	340.1	243.8	329.8	171.8	2 301.5	766.4	334.3	354.1	846.7
2011	10 726.0	3 646.6	1 162.9	378.6	253.4	344.6	186.3	2 483.7	808.6	350.3	428.2	896.6
2009												
1st quarter	9 781.7	3 130.7	1 020.1	303.0	238.0	320.2	158.9	2 110.6	741.3	318.4	261.4	789.4
2nd quarter	9 781.6	3 143.6	1 009.5	303.5	234.2	311.2	160.7	2 134.1	743.8	314.1	275.5	800.7
3rd quarter	9 911.1	3 245.6	1 050.1	339.2	233.7	314.9	162.2	2 195.5	746.4	318.9	321.5	808.7
4th quarter	9 990.0	3 270.0	1 038.8	320.5	235.5	319.9	162.9	2 231.1	752.6	321.5	339.3	817.7
2010												
1st quarter	10 103.7	3 338.1	1 058.0	323.1	241.1	325.8	168.0	2 280.1	761.5	329.7	359.5	829.3
2nd quarter	10 184.8	3 340.1	1 071.7	330.6	244.5	327.6	169.1	2 268.3	759.4	332.3	337.0	839.7
3rd quarter	10 276.6	3 386.5	1 087.5	339.6	243.4	331.2	173.3	2 299.0	766.4	333.9	345.9	852.8
4th quarter	10 417.1	3 483.4	1 124.7	367.1	246.1	334.5	176.9	2 358.7	778.2	341.3	374.1	865.2
2011												
1st quarter	10 571.7	3 592.2	1 154.5	383.0	248.3	340.5	182.7	2 437.8	792.0	344.5	420.2	881.1
2nd quarter	10 676.0	3 622.7	1 143.8	363.4	251.2	342.5	186.7	2 478.9	806.7	348.6	431.5	892.1
3rd quarter	10 784.5	3 661.2	1 158.3	368.7	254.9	345.8	188.8	2 503.0	815.8	352.2	434.5	900.6
4th quarter	10 871.6	3 710.1	1 194.9	399.1	259.1	349.6	187.1	2 515.2	819.9	356.1	426.8	912.5

Table 4-2. Personal Consumption Expenditures by Major Type of Product—*Continued*

(Billions of dollars, quarterly data are at seasonally adjusted rates.)   **NIPA Table 2.3.5**

| Year and quarter | Services | Household consumption expenditures for services | | | | | | | | Nonprofit institutions serving households (NPISHs) | | |
		Household, total	Housing and utilities	Health care	Transportation services	Recreation services	Food services and accommodations	Financial services and insurance	Other services	Final consumption expenditures	Gross output	Less: receipts from sales of goods and services
1950	75.4	72.9	25.1	6.4	5.4	3.6	12.7	5.6	14.1	2.5	. . .	. . .
1951	83.8	81.1	28.1	6.9	6.0	3.8	15.0	6.3	15.1	2.6	. . .	. . .
1952	90.7	87.8	31.2	7.6	6.3	4.0	16.0	6.7	16.0	2.9	. . .	. . .
1953	98.2	95.2	34.5	8.4	6.8	4.2	16.5	7.8	17.1	3.1	. . .	. . .
1954	104.2	100.9	37.4	9.3	6.8	4.5	16.6	8.6	17.8	3.3	. . .	. . .
1955	111.4	107.9	40.0	9.9	7.1	4.8	17.0	9.6	19.4	3.5	. . .	. . .
1956	119.5	115.6	42.9	10.9	7.6	5.2	17.7	10.4	20.9	3.9	. . .	. . .
1957	127.3	123.1	45.9	12.0	8.0	5.2	18.5	11.1	22.4	4.2	. . .	. . .
1958	134.6	130.1	49.2	13.4	8.1	5.4	18.7	11.6	23.8	4.5	. . .	. . .
1959	145.1	140.0	52.8	14.8	8.7	5.9	19.7	12.5	25.5	5.1	14.1	9.0
1960	154.8	149.5	56.7	16.0	9.2	6.5	20.5	13.6	27.1	5.3	15.1	9.8
1961	163.4	157.9	60.3	17.1	9.6	6.9	21.0	14.8	28.3	5.5	16.0	10.5
1962	174.4	168.7	64.5	19.1	10.1	7.5	22.3	15.4	29.9	5.7	17.2	11.5
1963	184.6	178.6	68.2	21.0	10.6	7.9	23.3	15.9	31.6	6.0	18.6	12.6
1964	199.2	192.5	72.1	24.2	11.4	8.5	24.9	17.7	33.8	6.7	20.5	13.8
1965	214.1	206.9	76.6	26.0	12.1	9.0	27.2	19.4	36.6	7.2	22.3	15.1
1966	231.3	223.5	81.2	28.7	13.1	9.8	29.6	21.3	39.9	7.8	24.6	16.9
1967	248.8	240.4	86.3	31.9	14.3	10.5	31.0	22.8	43.6	8.4	27.4	18.9
1968	273.4	264.0	92.7	36.6	15.9	11.7	34.6	25.8	46.8	9.3	30.9	21.6
1969	300.4	290.4	101.0	42.1	18.0	12.9	37.5	28.5	50.5	10.1	34.6	24.6
1970	329.5	318.4	109.4	47.7	20.0	14.0	41.6	31.1	54.6	11.1	38.7	27.6
1971	359.5	347.2	120.0	53.7	22.4	15.1	43.8	34.1	58.1	12.3	43.4	31.1
1972	396.4	382.8	131.2	59.8	24.5	16.3	48.9	38.3	63.7	13.6	48.2	34.5
1973	435.4	420.7	143.5	67.2	26.1	18.3	54.8	41.5	69.3	14.6	52.7	38.1
1974	481.4	465.0	158.6	76.1	28.5	20.9	60.6	45.9	74.4	16.4	59.7	43.3
1975	542.5	524.4	176.5	89.0	32.0	23.7	68.8	54.0	80.3	18.1	68.2	50.2
1976	604.9	584.9	194.7	101.8	36.2	26.5	77.8	59.3	88.6	20.1	77.4	57.3
1977	677.4	655.6	217.8	115.7	41.4	29.6	85.7	67.8	97.7	21.8	86.3	64.5
1978	764.1	739.6	244.3	131.2	45.2	32.9	97.1	80.6	108.3	24.5	98.1	73.6
1979	853.2	825.4	273.4	148.8	50.7	36.7	110.9	87.6	117.2	27.8	111.0	83.2
1980	956.0	924.1	311.8	171.7	55.4	40.8	121.7	95.6	127.1	31.9	128.0	96.1
1981	1 070.1	1 033.9	352.0	201.9	59.8	47.1	133.9	102.0	137.2	36.3	147.8	111.5
1982	1 176.2	1 136.1	387.0	225.2	61.7	52.5	142.5	116.3	150.9	40.1	165.9	125.8
1983	1 314.8	1 271.9	421.2	253.1	68.9	59.4	153.6	145.9	169.8	42.9	181.4	138.5
1984	1 437.4	1 389.8	458.3	276.5	80.0	66.1	164.9	156.6	187.4	47.6	196.6	149.0
1985	1 580.0	1 529.7	500.7	302.2	90.1	74.0	174.3	180.5	207.9	50.3	211.7	161.4
1986	1 701.1	1 645.8	535.7	330.2	95.0	80.4	186.7	196.7	221.2	55.4	230.1	174.7
1987	1 840.7	1 782.1	571.8	366.0	103.1	87.3	204.4	207.1	242.4	58.5	249.7	191.2
1988	2 012.7	1 946.0	614.5	410.1	114.2	99.2	225.8	219.4	262.8	66.8	279.0	212.2
1989	2 170.7	2 099.0	655.6	451.2	121.8	110.7	242.6	235.7	281.3	71.7	304.9	233.2
1990	2 344.2	2 264.5	696.4	506.2	126.4	121.8	262.7	253.2	297.9	79.6	338.2	258.6
1991	2 482.6	2 398.4	735.5	555.8	123.7	127.2	273.4	282.0	300.9	84.2	367.0	282.8
1992	2 673.6	2 581.3	771.2	612.8	133.6	139.8	286.3	311.8	325.8	92.3	400.8	308.5
1993	2 841.2	2 746.6	814.5	648.8	146.1	153.4	298.6	341.0	344.2	94.6	423.3	328.7
1994	3 004.3	2 901.9	866.5	680.5	161.9	164.7	308.7	349.0	370.7	102.4	444.7	342.3
1995	3 171.7	3 064.6	913.8	719.9	177.9	181.1	316.7	364.7	390.5	107.2	463.4	356.2
1996	3 355.9	3 240.2	961.2	752.1	195.0	195.6	327.4	393.6	415.3	115.7	488.8	373.1
1997	3 563.9	3 451.6	1 009.9	790.9	214.3	208.3	344.6	431.3	452.3	112.2	509.3	397.0
1998	3 808.5	3 677.5	1 065.2	832.0	227.2	220.6	363.0	469.6	499.8	131.0	550.5	419.6
1999	4 052.8	3 907.4	1 125.0	863.6	243.3	238.8	381.6	514.2	540.9	145.4	585.3	439.9
2000	4 371.2	4 205.9	1 198.6	918.4	262.3	255.5	410.1	570.0	591.1	165.4	632.0	466.6
2001	4 614.8	4 428.6	1 287.7	996.6	262.7	263.6	421.2	562.8	634.0	186.2	688.0	501.8
2002	4 829.2	4 624.2	1 334.8	1 082.9	256.7	272.8	438.2	576.2	662.7	205.0	749.7	544.7
2003	5 076.1	4 864.8	1 393.9	1 148.2	263.2	290.1	464.2	602.5	702.8	211.3	785.9	574.7
2004	5 378.5	5 169.1	1 462.4	1 228.5	273.7	313.3	499.1	651.7	740.4	209.4	827.6	618.2
2005	5 726.8	5 515.1	1 582.6	1 308.9	286.0	328.2	533.9	698.4	777.1	211.7	874.3	662.6
2006	6 076.3	5 836.3	1 686.2	1 373.7	297.5	351.4	570.2	732.6	824.7	240.0	935.2	695.2
2007	6 408.3	6 154.4	1 756.2	1 457.7	307.0	375.4	600.5	790.3	867.4	253.9	989.4	735.5
2008	6 653.8	6 369.3	1 831.0	1 532.6	305.9	381.9	618.3	807.0	892.6	284.6	1 046.5	761.9
2009	6 668.7	6 388.4	1 871.6	1 604.2	287.1	371.2	610.3	747.8	896.2	280.3	1 078.2	797.9
2010	6 858.5	6 578.3	1 893.2	1 667.4	295.5	382.6	638.0	780.2	921.4	280.2	1 118.9	838.6
2011	7 079.4	6 794.9	1 921.3	1 730.4	305.1	400.5	680.1	804.8	952.7	284.5	1 157.6	873.2
2009												
1st quarter	6 651.0	6 366.9	1 867.2	1 571.8	290.4	373.3	612.8	753.8	897.6	284.1	1 065.0	780.9
2nd quarter	6 638.0	6 361.3	1 866.7	1 596.2	285.3	369.6	608.6	744.3	890.5	276.7	1 071.1	794.4
3rd quarter	6 665.5	6 386.7	1 872.1	1 615.4	285.0	370.0	608.2	741.9	894.1	278.8	1 082.7	803.9
4th quarter	6 720.1	6 438.7	1 880.3	1 633.5	287.6	372.0	611.6	751.2	902.6	281.4	1 093.8	812.5
2010												
1st quarter	6 765.6	6 484.0	1 883.6	1 632.9	291.2	374.2	624.2	770.5	907.4	281.6	1 094.5	813.0
2nd quarter	6 844.7	6 562.3	1 887.1	1 659.1	295.3	379.9	634.9	788.6	917.4	282.4	1 113.9	831.5
3rd quarter	6 890.1	6 610.9	1 900.8	1 677.1	297.0	388.6	642.8	779.2	925.4	279.2	1 125.3	846.1
4th quarter	6 933.7	6 656.0	1 901.1	1 700.4	298.5	387.7	650.1	782.7	935.5	277.6	1 141.6	864.0
2011												
1st quarter	6 979.4	6 700.0	1 901.7	1 708.1	302.1	387.9	663.7	795.7	940.7	279.4	1 143.5	864.0
2nd quarter	7 053.3	6 771.6	1 913.3	1 729.5	304.6	398.6	673.9	803.1	948.5	281.7	1 154.9	873.2
3rd quarter	7 123.2	6 834.4	1 937.7	1 734.4	305.6	407.3	685.6	811.9	952.0	288.8	1 159.8	871.0
4th quarter	7 161.5	6 873.5	1 932.6	1 749.3	308.3	408.2	697.0	808.7	969.4	288.0	1 172.3	884.3

. . . = Not available.

Table 4-3. Chain-Type Quantity Indexes for Personal Consumption Expenditures by Major Type of Product

(Index numbers, 2005 = 100.)   NIPA Table 2.3.3

Year and quarter	Personal consumption expenditures, total	Total goods	Goods									
			Durable goods					Nondurable goods				
			Durable goods, total	Motor vehicles and parts	Furnishings and household equipment	Recreational goods and vehicles	Other durable goods	Nondurable goods, total	Food and beverages off-premises	Clothing and footwear	Gasoline and other energy goods	Other nondurable goods
1955	17.5	17.8	7.8	16.4	12.0	1.1	8.6	26.9	43.5	14.1	39.5	16.5
1956	18.0	18.1	7.5	14.0	12.6	1.1	9.0	27.9	45.0	14.5	41.2	17.2
1957	18.5	18.4	7.6	14.6	12.4	1.1	9.0	28.4	46.1	14.4	42.2	17.9
1958	18.7	18.2	7.0	12.1	12.2	1.1	9.1	28.8	46.3	14.6	44.1	18.2
1959	19.7	19.4	7.9	14.4	13.0	1.2	9.4	30.1	48.2	15.3	45.1	19.3
1960	20.3	19.7	8.0	15.3	12.8	1.2	9.5	30.6	48.5	15.4	45.9	20.2
1961	20.7	19.8	7.8	13.8	12.9	1.2	9.7	31.2	49.2	15.7	45.6	21.3
1962	21.7	20.9	8.6	16.4	13.6	1.3	10.6	32.2	49.5	16.4	47.0	22.8
1963	22.6	21.7	9.4	18.4	14.5	1.4	11.0	32.9	49.9	16.7	48.7	23.8
1964	23.9	23.0	10.3	19.4	16.2	1.7	11.9	34.4	51.6	18.0	51.3	24.9
1965	25.5	24.6	11.6	22.5	17.2	2.0	13.1	36.2	54.2	18.8	53.7	26.4
1966	26.9	26.2	12.6	22.9	18.7	2.4	15.1	38.2	56.3	20.0	56.6	28.5
1967	27.7	26.7	12.7	22.3	19.2	2.7	15.2	39.0	57.6	20.2	58.1	29.3
1968	29.3	28.4	14.2	25.8	20.3	3.0	16.7	40.7	60.2	21.0	60.5	30.5
1969	30.4	29.2	14.7	26.8	20.8	3.2	17.4	41.8	61.8	21.4	63.2	31.4
1970	31.1	29.4	14.3	24.0	20.7	3.4	18.2	42.7	63.6	21.1	65.6	32.4
1971	32.3	30.7	15.7	28.6	21.7	3.5	19.0	43.5	64.3	22.0	67.9	32.5
1972	34.3	32.7	17.7	32.6	23.9	4.1	20.1	45.3	65.6	23.6	71.3	34.1
1973	36.0	34.4	19.5	35.7	26.4	4.5	22.8	46.6	64.4	25.3	75.4	36.4
1974	35.7	33.1	18.3	29.8	26.3	4.5	23.9	45.4	63.1	24.8	69.3	36.3
1975	36.5	33.3	18.3	29.7	25.0	4.8	25.3	45.8	64.3	25.4	70.9	35.1
1976	38.5	35.7	20.6	35.7	26.5	5.3	27.9	48.0	67.4	26.6	74.7	36.6
1977	40.1	37.2	22.4	39.5	28.9	5.6	29.5	49.1	68.4	28.0	76.0	37.2
1978	41.9	38.8	23.6	41.2	30.4	6.0	31.1	50.9	68.1	31.0	77.3	39.8
1979	42.9	39.4	23.5	38.8	31.7	6.3	30.7	52.2	69.1	32.8	75.0	42.1
1980	42.8	38.4	21.6	33.8	30.5	6.0	28.1	52.1	69.8	33.8	68.4	42.8
1981	43.4	38.8	21.8	34.6	29.9	6.2	28.5	52.8	69.6	36.0	67.5	43.8
1982	44.0	39.1	21.8	35.5	28.5	6.2	28.5	53.3	70.9	36.6	67.6	43.7
1983	46.5	41.6	24.9	42.3	31.0	7.2	31.1	55.0	72.7	39.1	69.1	44.8
1984	49.0	44.6	28.5	49.2	34.1	8.5	34.6	57.3	74.2	42.3	71.0	47.2
1985	51.6	46.9	31.3	55.6	35.9	9.4	37.2	59.0	76.4	44.2	72.3	48.5
1986	53.6	49.6	34.3	59.7	38.9	10.9	41.5	61.1	77.9	47.5	76.0	49.6
1987	55.3	50.4	35.0	57.3	40.5	12.2	43.0	62.2	77.4	49.3	77.5	51.4
1988	57.5	52.3	37.0	60.6	42.0	13.4	44.4	63.8	79.5	50.7	79.7	52.6
1989	59.2	53.6	37.8	60.5	44.1	13.9	45.0	65.6	80.5	53.4	81.0	54.3
1990	60.4	54.0	37.6	59.5	43.5	14.3	45.2	66.3	82.1	53.0	79.5	55.7
1991	60.5	52.9	35.6	52.4	42.5	14.8	43.3	66.1	82.0	53.1	78.9	55.4
1992	62.5	54.6	37.7	56.7	44.0	15.7	44.1	67.4	81.7	55.9	82.0	56.5
1993	64.7	56.8	40.5	59.9	46.2	18.1	46.4	69.1	82.4	58.2	84.1	58.6
1994	67.2	59.8	43.7	63.6	48.7	21.0	48.5	71.8	84.7	61.5	85.4	61.6
1995	69.0	61.6	45.4	62.6	50.9	24.0	49.6	73.6	85.1	64.0	87.0	64.1
1996	71.4	64.4	48.8	65.7	53.1	27.8	52.9	75.7	86.0	67.1	88.4	66.9
1997	74.1	67.5	52.8	70.1	55.6	32.1	55.6	78.0	86.7	69.4	90.2	70.6
1998	78.0	72.0	59.3	77.4	60.2	38.5	61.0	80.9	87.7	73.6	93.4	74.4
1999	82.2	77.7	66.9	84.5	67.2	46.8	68.3	85.0	91.1	78.4	96.3	79.0
2000	86.4	81.8	72.8	87.2	73.7	54.9	74.4	87.8	93.2	82.2	94.5	83.1
2001	88.7	84.4	76.8	91.7	77.4	60.4	72.8	89.4	94.3	83.0	95.2	85.8
2002	91.1	87.8	82.6	96.5	83.1	67.7	77.6	91.1	94.5	85.5	96.8	88.6
2003	93.7	91.9	88.1	99.2	87.7	76.3	84.4	94.2	95.7	90.0	99.4	92.9
2004	96.7	96.0	94.4	100.6	94.6	87.8	91.8	96.9	96.8	94.3	100.7	96.7
2005	100.0	100.0	100.0	100.0	100.0	100.0	100.0	100.0	100.0	100.0	100.0	100.0
2006	102.9	103.3	104.5	96.6	104.3	113.9	107.7	102.6	102.9	104.7	97.7	103.8
2007	105.2	106.4	109.7	98.3	105.0	128.2	112.7	104.6	104.5	108.3	96.9	106.7
2008	104.6	103.8	104.3	85.0	100.6	133.1	109.0	104.3	103.3	107.7	92.4	107.0
2009	102.7	100.7	98.7	79.0	92.1	130.8	103.5	101.5	102.0	102.7	92.5	105.0
2010	104.7	105.0	105.8	80.9	99.5	146.9	109.8	104.5	104.4	108.6	92.6	108.6
2011	107.0	108.9	114.4	87.4	105.0	164.7	115.6	106.3	106.0	111.9	88.5	113.2
2009												
1st quarter	102.7	100.2	97.4	77.5	92.3	128.4	102.5	101.4	100.4	103.3	93.8	105.4
2nd quarter	102.2	99.6	96.4	76.5	90.7	126.8	103.4	101.0	101.6	101.4	92.6	104.4
3rd quarter	102.8	101.4	101.0	84.4	91.8	131.6	104.3	101.5	102.5	102.4	91.9	104.7
4th quarter	102.9	101.6	99.8	77.6	93.6	136.5	103.8	102.3	103.5	103.5	91.9	105.6
2010												
1st quarter	103.6	103.1	102.1	77.4	96.7	141.3	107.9	103.5	104.2	106.5	92.8	106.7
2nd quarter	104.4	104.1	104.1	78.7	99.2	144.5	108.4	104.0	103.5	108.2	92.9	108.0
3rd quarter	105.0	105.3	106.3	80.4	100.1	148.9	110.9	104.7	104.4	108.3	93.1	109.2
4th quarter	106.0	107.5	110.6	87.0	102.2	153.0	112.1	105.8	105.6	111.5	91.7	110.6
2011												
1st quarter	106.5	108.7	113.7	90.2	103.1	158.5	114.4	106.2	105.8	112.3	90.3	112.1
2nd quarter	106.7	108.3	112.2	83.8	103.9	161.9	116.1	106.3	106.2	112.9	88.4	112.8
3rd quarter	107.2	108.6	113.7	84.1	105.3	166.6	116.9	106.2	106.1	110.7	88.1	113.5
4th quarter	107.7	110.1	118.1	91.3	107.6	171.6	114.8	106.4	105.8	111.6	87.5	114.4

Table 4-3. Chain-Type Quantity Indexes for Personal Consumption Expenditures by Major Type of Product—*Continued*

(Index numbers, 2005 = 100.) NIPA Table 2.3.3

Year and quarter	Services	Services — Household consumption expenditures for services — Household, total	Housing and utilities	Health care	Transportation services	Recreation services	Food services and accommodations	Financial services and insurance	Other services	NPISHs — Final consumption expenditures	Gross output	Less: receipts from sales of goods and services
1955	16.3	17.2	17.4	12.4	18.3	10.2	27.1	13.8	19.9	3.8	. . .	. . .
1956	17.1	18.0	18.4	13.2	18.8	10.7	27.8	14.5	20.7	4.1	. . .	. . .
1957	17.7	18.6	19.3	13.9	19.1	10.4	28.2	14.9	21.5	4.1	. . .	. . .
1958	18.3	19.2	20.3	15.0	18.8	10.3	27.7	15.4	22.2	4.4	. . .	. . .
1959	19.2	20.1	21.5	16.1	19.6	11.0	28.3	15.7	23.1	4.8	14.9	21.0
1960	19.9	20.8	22.6	16.3	20.2	11.6	28.6	16.3	23.9	5.4	15.5	21.1
1961	20.6	21.6	23.7	17.0	20.5	12.1	28.7	17.2	24.6	5.5	16.2	22.2
1962	21.6	22.7	25.1	18.6	21.2	12.7	29.8	17.2	25.6	5.7	17.1	23.7
1963	22.5	23.6	26.3	19.8	22.2	13.2	30.5	17.8	26.6	5.9	18.0	25.3
1964	23.9	25.0	27.5	22.0	23.4	13.8	32.1	19.0	27.7	6.5	19.4	26.8
1965	25.2	26.4	29.0	23.0	24.6	14.3	34.3	20.3	29.3	6.8	20.6	28.5
1966	26.5	27.7	30.3	24.3	26.0	15.2	36.1	21.0	31.1	7.1	21.9	30.8
1967	27.5	28.8	31.7	25.4	27.4	15.7	35.7	22.0	32.9	7.5	23.3	32.8
1968	29.0	30.3	33.3	27.4	29.1	16.7	37.9	23.2	33.8	8.0	25.0	35.3
1969	30.3	31.7	35.1	29.4	31.1	17.6	38.7	23.5	34.8	8.1	26.3	37.7
1970	31.5	33.0	36.4	31.0	32.1	18.3	40.1	24.3	35.9	8.5	27.6	39.5
1971	32.6	34.1	38.0	33.3	33.5	18.9	40.0	25.2	36.0	9.0	29.5	42.5
1972	34.5	36.0	40.0	35.5	35.4	19.9	43.1	26.7	37.6	9.6	31.3	45.0
1973	36.1	37.8	41.9	38.1	36.0	21.6	45.2	28.2	38.7	9.6	32.2	46.7
1974	36.8	38.6	43.9	39.4	36.2	23.1	44.8	28.9	37.4	9.5	32.6	47.8
1975	38.2	40.1	45.3	41.4	36.7	24.2	46.7	31.7	37.7	9.5	33.8	50.1
1976	39.8	41.8	46.6	43.2	38.5	25.9	49.5	33.4	39.2	10.1	35.6	52.7
1977	41.4	43.5	47.9	45.3	41.3	27.6	50.8	35.5	41.1	10.2	36.9	55.1
1978	43.4	45.5	50.2	47.4	42.3	28.9	53.0	37.3	43.3	10.8	39.0	58.3
1979	44.7	46.9	51.9	49.0	43.5	30.3	54.6	38.4	43.7	11.1	40.1	59.8
1980	45.4	47.6	53.6	50.4	40.9	31.3	54.6	38.9	43.4	11.7	41.3	61.2
1981	46.2	48.4	54.5	52.9	39.4	34.0	55.2	38.6	43.2	12.6	43.0	63.0
1982	47.1	49.1	54.9	53.0	38.6	35.6	55.5	41.6	44.1	14.6	44.8	63.4
1983	49.6	51.5	56.1	54.6	41.5	38.7	57.4	47.6	47.0	16.8	46.4	63.7
1984	51.5	53.3	58.1	55.5	46.3	41.2	59.0	48.1	49.3	19.4	48.0	63.6
1985	54.2	56.0	60.3	57.1	51.2	44.2	59.7	53.2	52.8	20.9	49.7	65.0
1986	55.8	57.5	61.6	58.9	53.4	46.3	61.5	54.8	53.3	23.7	52.2	66.6
1987	58.0	59.7	63.4	61.4	55.6	48.4	64.7	55.1	57.1	25.5	54.3	68.6
1988	60.5	62.1	65.6	63.8	58.8	53.0	68.5	55.0	59.4	29.3	57.3	70.5
1989	62.3	63.7	67.2	64.5	60.1	56.3	70.4	57.1	61.3	33.5	59.3	70.8
1990	64.2	65.3	68.5	66.7	60.1	58.7	72.9	58.4	62.3	40.3	62.8	72.1
1991	65.1	66.0	70.0	68.0	57.2	58.3	72.9	62.3	60.1	45.9	65.2	72.7
1992	67.4	68.0	71.4	70.0	60.1	62.2	74.8	64.1	62.4	55.0	68.7	73.8
1993	69.6	70.0	73.3	70.4	63.5	66.1	76.5	69.3	63.7	59.3	70.3	74.5
1994	71.7	72.0	76.0	70.9	69.5	69.4	77.7	69.8	66.2	64.2	71.8	74.8
1995	73.5	73.8	78.0	72.4	74.8	74.7	77.9	70.1	67.5	67.2	72.8	75.0
1996	75.6	75.9	79.7	73.9	80.9	78.1	78.4	72.8	69.7	71.3	74.7	76.3
1997	78.0	78.5	81.5	76.2	87.0	80.6	80.2	75.3	73.9	66.4	75.9	79.5
1998	81.4	81.8	84.0	78.7	90.6	83.3	82.3	80.1	80.0	72.7	79.7	82.4
1999	84.7	85.1	86.7	79.9	95.6	87.3	84.3	86.8	84.5	77.9	82.5	84.3
2000	88.9	89.2	89.3	82.6	100.1	90.0	88.1	95.4	90.6	84.0	85.7	86.5
2001	91.1	91.2	91.7	86.8	99.2	89.9	88.0	94.7	94.3	90.4	89.8	89.8
2002	92.9	92.7	92.4	91.9	96.5	90.4	89.4	94.3	94.8	98.7	95.1	94.0
2003	94.6	94.3	93.5	93.8	96.8	93.3	92.7	94.4	97.0	103.3	96.5	94.4
2004	97.1	96.9	95.6	96.8	99.2	98.1	96.5	96.7	98.9	102.8	98.4	97.0
2005	100.0	100.0	100.0	100.0	100.0	100.0	100.0	100.0	100.0	100.0	100.0	100.0
2006	102.6	102.3	102.2	101.8	99.8	103.6	103.3	102.6	102.6	111.1	103.2	100.7
2007	104.6	104.2	102.8	104.2	100.7	107.6	107.6	104.7	104.9	115.8	105.9	102.8
2008	105.1	104.2	103.5	106.7	95.1	106.2	103.7	104.9	103.6	128.9	109.2	103.1
2009	103.6	102.6	104.6	108.7	86.8	102.0	100.1	96.8	101.6	130.9	111.0	104.9
2010	104.6	103.6	105.5	110.2	87.5	104.0	103.2	95.6	101.9	132.3	113.1	107.2
2011	106.1	105.2	105.6	112.5	87.9	107.1	107.2	97.1	103.3	131.2	114.5	109.2
2009												
1st quarter	104.0	102.9	104.3	107.7	88.1	103.0	100.9	99.2	102.4	131.9	110.5	103.9
2nd quarter	103.5	102.6	104.3	108.6	86.9	102.1	99.9	97.3	101.4	129.1	110.7	105.0
3rd quarter	103.5	102.5	104.7	109.2	86.1	101.2	99.7	96.0	101.2	130.1	111.2	105.3
4th quarter	103.6	102.5	105.0	109.5	86.0	101.7	99.8	94.6	101.4	132.4	111.8	105.4
2010												
1st quarter	103.9	102.8	105.1	108.8	86.6	102.3	101.8	95.5	101.2	133.2	111.4	104.8
2nd quarter	104.5	103.4	105.3	109.9	87.4	103.4	102.9	96.0	101.6	134.4	113.0	106.5
3rd quarter	104.9	103.9	105.9	110.5	88.0	105.3	103.6	95.3	102.0	132.0	113.6	107.8
4th quarter	105.3	104.3	105.7	111.7	88.0	105.0	104.5	95.6	102.7	129.4	114.6	109.8
2011												
1st quarter	105.5	104.5	105.3	111.9	87.9	104.5	106.3	96.6	102.8	129.6	114.1	109.1
2nd quarter	105.9	105.0	105.5	112.7	87.9	106.8	106.6	96.9	103.2	129.8	114.4	109.5
3rd quarter	106.4	105.5	106.2	112.5	87.9	108.8	107.3	97.8	103.0	132.9	114.4	108.6
4th quarter	106.6	105.6	105.3	113.1	87.9	108.4	108.7	97.0	104.2	132.6	115.2	109.8

. . . = Not available.

Table 4-4. Chain-Type Price Indexes for Personal Consumption Expenditures by Major Type of Product

(Index numbers, 2005 =1000.)   NIPA Table 2.3.4

Year and quarter	Personal consumption expend- itures, total	Total goods	Goods									
			Durable goods					Nondurable goods				
			Durable goods, total	Motor vehicles and parts	Furnishings and household equipment	Recreational goods and vehicles	Other durable goods	Nondurable goods, total	Food and beverages off-premises	Clothing and footwear	Gasoline and other energy goods	Other nondurable goods
1955	16.8	26.9	46.3	26.4	44.5	162.8	31.0	20.3	18.5	50.4	10.3	17.5
1956	17.1	27.3	47.4	27.6	44.9	164.7	31.3	20.6	18.7	51.3	10.6	17.7
1957	17.6	28.2	49.2	29.3	45.6	170.5	31.5	21.2	19.2	52.1	11.1	18.3
1958	18.0	28.8	50.1	30.4	45.5	175.1	31.5	21.7	20.0	52.3	11.0	18.8
1959	18.3	29.0	50.9	31.9	45.6	170.1	31.7	21.7	19.8	52.8	11.1	19.1
1960	18.6	29.2	50.7	31.3	46.0	171.2	31.8	22.0	20.0	53.5	11.3	19.4
1961	18.8	29.3	50.8	31.5	46.1	170.3	31.7	22.1	20.1	53.8	11.4	19.4
1962	19.0	29.4	51.0	32.0	46.1	168.5	31.6	22.2	20.3	53.9	11.4	19.5
1963	19.3	29.7	51.2	32.3	46.1	168.1	31.7	22.4	20.5	54.4	11.4	19.7
1964	19.5	30.0	51.5	32.5	46.1	166.1	32.6	22.7	20.9	54.9	11.3	20.0
1965	19.8	30.3	51.0	32.3	45.8	163.8	32.4	23.1	21.3	55.4	11.7	20.3
1966	20.3	31.0	50.9	32.0	46.2	162.0	32.4	23.8	22.2	56.9	12.0	20.7
1967	20.8	31.5	51.7	32.5	47.3	163.0	33.2	24.3	22.2	59.3	12.4	21.2
1968	21.6	32.6	53.4	33.6	49.1	166.2	33.9	25.2	22.9	62.6	12.6	22.0
1969	22.6	33.9	54.9	34.3	50.9	170.0	35.6	26.2	23.9	66.0	13.0	22.9
1970	23.7	35.2	56.1	35.3	52.0	170.2	36.5	27.4	25.3	68.5	13.2	23.9
1971	24.7	36.3	58.0	37.0	52.9	176.3	37.5	28.2	25.8	70.9	13.4	24.8
1972	25.5	37.2	58.7	37.1	53.7	178.8	38.7	29.1	27.1	72.2	13.6	25.5
1973	26.9	39.4	59.5	37.3	54.9	181.6	40.0	31.5	30.5	74.6	15.0	26.2
1974	29.7	44.3	63.5	39.6	59.4	189.6	43.0	36.2	35.1	80.1	20.8	28.7
1975	32.2	47.9	69.1	43.5	65.3	202.2	46.3	39.0	37.8	83.7	22.3	32.0
1976	34.0	49.8	72.9	46.8	68.1	209.1	48.6	40.3	38.5	86.4	23.4	33.7
1977	36.2	52.4	76.2	49.5	70.6	215.1	50.7	42.6	40.8	90.1	25.0	35.6
1978	38.7	55.7	80.4	53.0	74.2	222.9	53.5	45.3	44.7	91.8	26.2	37.6
1979	42.1	60.9	85.8	57.0	78.8	232.8	57.9	50.2	49.0	93.6	35.3	40.0
1980	46.7	67.7	93.2	61.2	85.3	245.7	69.8	56.3	53.2	97.0	49.0	43.7
1981	50.8	72.8	99.5	65.9	91.6	256.7	73.6	60.7	57.0	100.2	55.3	47.4
1982	53.6	74.8	103.3	69.0	96.3	262.7	74.3	62.1	58.5	101.7	52.8	51.0
1983	55.9	76.1	105.4	71.2	98.5	259.5	76.7	63.1	59.1	103.1	50.7	54.6
1984	58.1	77.5	107.0	73.2	99.7	255.8	78.4	64.5	60.9	103.6	50.2	56.6
1985	60.0	78.8	108.1	74.9	100.8	251.3	79.2	65.7	61.6	105.9	50.3	58.8
1986	61.4	78.4	109.3	77.0	101.9	243.4	81.1	64.8	63.0	105.4	39.5	61.1
1987	63.6	80.9	112.4	80.5	103.5	240.3	86.6	67.0	65.0	108.5	40.9	63.6
1988	66.2	83.1	114.3	81.8	105.0	238.8	92.3	69.2	66.9	111.9	41.3	66.4
1989	69.0	86.3	116.4	84.2	105.3	238.1	96.5	72.6	70.5	113.6	44.9	70.1
1990	72.2	89.8	117.5	84.5	106.3	236.2	102.6	76.7	73.9	117.3	51.4	73.6
1991	74.8	92.0	119.3	86.8	106.9	233.2	106.4	79.0	76.2	119.5	50.6	77.6
1992	77.0	93.1	120.1	88.5	108.2	226.0	109.2	80.1	76.8	120.4	50.2	80.5
1993	78.7	93.9	121.3	92.0	108.8	217.9	110.1	80.8	77.9	119.8	49.7	81.8
1994	80.3	94.9	123.6	96.2	110.5	213.4	111.8	81.2	79.2	117.7	49.8	82.4
1995	82.1	95.8	124.5	100.0	110.3	204.4	113.7	82.1	80.9	115.0	50.5	83.9
1996	83.9	96.8	123.3	102.1	110.6	189.9	113.0	83.9	83.4	113.6	53.9	85.5
1997	85.4	96.7	120.6	102.4	110.4	174.0	111.4	84.8	85.0	113.6	53.9	86.4
1998	86.2	95.2	117.2	101.3	110.3	159.3	109.4	84.2	86.0	111.6	47.0	88.0
1999	87.6	95.7	114.0	101.6	108.9	145.4	106.6	86.3	87.4	110.1	50.9	91.4
2000	89.8	97.7	112.0	102.0	108.1	136.3	105.2	90.0	89.5	108.8	65.8	93.4
2001	91.5	97.6	109.7	102.4	106.3	127.0	105.6	91.0	92.1	106.6	63.5	95.6
2002	92.8	96.6	106.9	101.9	104.1	118.8	103.6	90.9	93.5	103.8	59.4	97.2
2003	94.7	96.5	103.1	99.1	101.2	111.3	101.9	92.8	95.3	101.2	69.4	97.3
2004	97.1	97.9	101.1	98.4	99.9	105.8	101.5	96.1	98.3	100.9	81.5	98.5
2005	100.0	100.0	100.0	100.0	100.0	100.0	100.0	100.0	100.0	100.0	100.0	100.0
2006	102.7	101.4	98.4	100.1	99.6	93.8	101.8	103.2	101.7	99.6	112.9	102.2
2007	105.5	102.8	96.4	99.6	98.9	87.2	105.5	106.5	105.6	98.6	123.9	103.6
2008	108.9	105.9	94.6	97.8	98.1	82.7	109.1	112.6	112.1	97.9	146.3	106.1
2009	109.2	103.2	92.9	98.2	97.8	77.4	110.4	109.3	113.5	98.7	106.5	110.8
2010	111.1	104.8	91.3	103.1	93.7	71.7	110.9	112.7	113.9	98.0	125.9	112.8
2011	113.8	108.8	90.4	106.2	92.4	66.9	114.3	119.7	118.4	99.7	159.2	114.6
2009												
1st quarter	108.2	101.6	93.2	95.9	98.6	79.7	109.9	106.6	114.6	98.2	91.7	108.4
2nd quarter	108.7	102.6	93.2	97.1	98.8	78.4	110.2	108.2	113.6	98.6	97.9	111.0
3rd quarter	109.5	104.0	92.5	98.5	97.5	76.4	110.2	110.7	112.9	99.2	115.0	111.7
4th quarter	110.3	104.7	92.7	101.2	96.3	74.9	111.3	111.7	112.9	98.9	121.5	112.1
2010												
1st quarter	110.8	105.2	92.2	102.3	95.4	73.7	110.4	112.8	113.4	98.6	127.5	112.5
2nd quarter	110.9	104.3	91.6	102.9	94.3	72.4	110.6	111.7	113.8	97.8	119.4	112.5
3rd quarter	111.1	104.5	91.1	103.5	93.1	71.1	110.8	112.4	113.9	98.2	122.3	113.0
4th quarter	111.7	105.4	90.5	103.5	92.1	69.9	111.9	114.1	114.3	97.5	134.3	113.2
2011												
1st quarter	112.7	107.4	90.4	104.0	92.2	68.6	113.2	117.5	116.1	97.6	153.2	113.8
2nd quarter	113.7	108.8	90.7	106.3	92.5	67.6	114.0	119.4	117.9	98.3	160.7	114.4
3rd quarter	114.3	109.5	90.6	107.4	92.6	66.3	114.5	120.7	119.3	101.3	162.4	114.8
4th quarter	114.7	109.5	90.1	107.1	92.1	65.1	115.5	121.1	120.3	101.6	160.6	115.4

Table 4-4.   Chain-Type Price Indexes for Personal Consumption Expenditures by Major Type of Product—*Continued*

(Index numbers, 2005 =1000.)   **NIPA Table 2.3.4**

Year and quarter	Services	Household consumption expenditures for services								Nonprofit institutions serving households (NPISHs)		
		Household, total	Housing and utilities	Health care	Transportation services	Recreation services	Food services and accommodations	Financial services and insurance	Other services	Final consumption expenditures	Gross output	Less: receipts from sales of goods and services
1955	11.9	11.4	14.5	6.1	13.7	14.5	11.8	10.2	12.4	43.3	. . .	. . .
1956	12.2	11.7	14.8	6.3	14.2	14.9	11.9	10.5	12.8	45.3	. . .	. . .
1957	12.6	12.0	15.0	6.6	14.7	15.5	12.3	10.8	13.2	47.4	. . .	. . .
1958	12.9	12.3	15.3	6.8	15.1	16.1	12.6	11.0	13.6	48.6	. . .	. . .
1959	13.2	12.6	15.6	7.0	15.5	16.5	13.1	11.6	14.0	49.5	10.8	6.5
1960	13.6	13.0	15.9	7.5	15.9	17.1	13.4	12.1	14.4	46.3	11.1	7.0
1961	13.8	13.3	16.1	7.7	16.4	17.6	13.7	12.6	14.5	46.8	11.3	7.2
1962	14.1	13.5	16.2	7.9	16.7	18.0	14.0	13.1	14.8	47.4	11.5	7.3
1963	14.3	13.7	16.4	8.1	16.8	18.4	14.3	13.1	15.1	48.2	11.8	7.5
1964	14.6	14.0	16.6	8.4	17.0	18.9	14.5	13.6	15.4	48.4	12.1	7.8
1965	14.8	14.2	16.7	8.6	17.3	19.3	14.8	14.0	15.8	49.8	12.4	8.0
1966	15.3	14.6	16.9	9.0	17.6	19.8	15.4	14.8	16.3	51.6	12.8	8.3
1967	15.8	15.1	17.2	9.6	18.3	20.5	16.3	15.2	16.8	53.3	13.4	8.7
1968	16.5	15.8	17.6	10.2	19.1	21.6	17.1	16.3	17.5	55.3	14.1	9.2
1969	17.3	16.6	18.2	10.9	20.3	22.5	18.1	17.7	18.4	58.7	15.1	9.8
1970	18.3	17.5	19.0	11.7	21.8	23.5	19.5	18.7	19.3	61.3	16.0	10.6
1971	19.3	18.5	19.9	12.3	23.4	24.5	20.5	19.8	20.4	64.7	16.8	11.0
1972	20.1	19.3	20.7	12.9	24.3	25.2	21.3	21.0	21.4	67.3	17.6	11.6
1973	21.1	20.2	21.6	13.5	25.3	26.1	22.7	21.5	22.7	71.6	18.7	12.3
1974	22.9	21.9	22.8	14.8	27.5	27.9	25.3	23.2	25.2	82.0	21.0	13.7
1975	24.8	23.7	24.6	16.4	30.5	29.9	27.6	24.9	27.0	89.5	23.1	15.1
1976	26.6	25.4	26.4	18.0	32.8	31.4	29.4	25.9	28.6	94.3	24.9	16.4
1977	28.6	27.3	28.7	19.5	35.1	32.9	31.6	27.9	30.1	100.8	26.8	17.7
1978	30.8	29.5	30.8	21.1	37.4	34.9	34.3	31.6	31.7	107.4	28.8	19.1
1979	33.4	31.9	33.3	23.2	40.7	37.2	38.0	33.3	34.0	118.0	31.7	21.0
1980	36.8	35.2	36.7	26.0	47.3	40.0	41.7	35.9	37.1	129.2	35.5	23.7
1981	40.6	38.9	40.8	29.2	53.0	42.5	45.5	38.6	40.9	136.0	39.3	26.7
1982	43.7	42.1	44.6	32.5	56.0	44.9	48.1	40.9	44.1	129.7	42.4	30.0
1983	46.4	44.9	47.5	35.4	58.1	46.8	50.1	44.8	46.5	120.7	44.7	32.8
1984	48.8	47.4	49.9	38.1	60.4	48.8	52.4	47.6	48.9	116.0	46.8	35.4
1985	51.0	49.6	52.5	40.4	61.6	50.9	54.7	49.7	50.7	113.7	48.7	37.5
1986	53.4	52.0	55.0	42.8	62.2	52.9	56.9	52.4	53.4	110.3	50.4	39.6
1987	55.4	54.1	57.0	45.6	64.8	55.0	59.2	53.8	54.6	108.5	52.6	42.1
1988	58.1	56.9	59.2	49.1	67.9	57.1	61.8	57.1	56.9	107.6	55.7	45.5
1989	60.8	59.7	61.6	53.4	70.9	59.9	64.5	59.1	59.1	101.1	58.8	49.7
1990	63.8	62.9	64.3	58.0	73.6	63.2	67.5	62.0	61.5	93.2	61.6	54.1
1991	66.6	65.9	66.4	62.5	75.6	66.5	70.2	64.8	64.4	86.7	64.4	58.7
1992	69.2	68.9	68.3	66.9	77.7	68.5	71.7	69.7	67.2	79.3	66.8	63.1
1993	71.3	71.1	70.2	70.4	80.4	70.7	73.1	70.4	69.5	75.3	68.8	66.6
1994	73.2	73.1	72.1	73.3	81.4	72.2	74.4	71.6	72.1	75.3	70.8	69.1
1995	75.4	75.3	74.0	76.0	83.2	73.8	76.1	74.4	74.5	75.3	72.8	71.7
1996	77.5	77.5	76.2	77.8	84.3	76.3	78.2	77.5	76.6	76.7	74.8	73.8
1997	79.8	79.8	78.3	79.3	86.1	78.8	80.5	82.0	78.8	79.9	76.7	75.4
1998	81.7	81.5	80.1	80.8	87.6	80.7	82.7	84.0	80.4	85.1	79.0	76.8
1999	83.5	83.3	82.0	82.6	88.9	83.3	84.8	84.8	82.4	88.2	81.2	78.7
2000	85.8	85.5	84.8	84.9	91.6	86.5	87.2	85.6	83.9	93.0	84.4	81.4
2001	88.4	88.1	88.7	87.8	92.6	89.4	89.6	85.1	86.5	97.3	87.6	84.3
2002	90.8	90.5	91.3	90.1	93.1	91.9	91.8	87.4	89.9	98.1	90.2	87.5
2003	93.7	93.6	94.2	93.5	95.1	94.8	93.8	91.4	93.2	96.6	93.1	91.9
2004	96.7	96.7	96.7	96.9	96.5	97.3	96.9	96.5	96.4	96.2	96.2	96.2
2005	100.0	100.0	100.0	100.0	100.0	100.0	100.0	100.0	100.0	100.0	100.0	100.0
2006	103.4	103.5	104.3	103.1	104.2	103.4	103.4	102.3	103.4	102.1	103.6	104.1
2007	107.0	107.1	108.0	106.9	106.6	106.3	107.4	106.8	106.4	103.5	106.8	108.0
2008	110.6	110.9	111.8	109.7	112.5	109.6	111.6	110.2	110.9	104.3	109.6	111.5
2009	112.4	112.9	113.1	112.7	115.7	110.9	114.2	110.6	113.5	101.1	111.1	114.8
2010	114.5	115.1	113.4	115.6	118.1	112.0	115.8	116.8	116.4	100.1	113.1	118.1
2011	116.5	117.2	115.0	117.5	121.4	113.9	118.8	118.7	118.7	102.4	115.6	120.7
2009												
1st quarter	111.7	112.2	113.2	111.5	115.3	110.4	113.8	108.7	112.7	101.7	110.3	113.5
2nd quarter	112.0	112.4	113.0	112.3	114.8	110.3	114.1	109.5	113.1	101.2	110.7	114.2
3rd quarter	112.5	113.0	113.0	113.0	115.8	111.4	114.3	110.6	113.6	101.3	111.4	115.2
4th quarter	113.3	113.9	113.2	114.0	117.0	111.4	114.8	113.6	114.6	100.4	112.0	116.3
2010												
1st quarter	113.8	114.4	113.2	114.7	117.6	111.4	114.9	115.5	115.4	99.8	112.3	117.1
2nd quarter	114.4	115.1	113.3	115.4	118.2	111.9	115.6	117.6	116.2	99.2	112.7	117.9
3rd quarter	114.7	115.4	113.5	115.9	118.0	112.4	116.2	117.0	116.8	99.9	113.4	118.5
4th quarter	115.0	115.7	113.7	116.3	118.6	112.5	116.5	117.3	117.2	101.3	114.0	118.8
2011												
1st quarter	115.6	116.2	114.1	116.7	120.2	113.1	116.9	117.9	117.8	101.9	114.7	119.6
2nd quarter	116.3	116.9	114.6	117.3	121.2	113.7	118.4	118.6	118.3	102.5	115.4	120.4
3rd quarter	116.9	117.5	115.3	117.8	121.5	114.1	119.7	118.9	119.0	102.7	116.0	121.1
4th quarter	117.4	118.0	115.9	118.2	122.6	114.7	120.1	119.3	119.7	102.6	116.4	121.6

. . . = Not available.

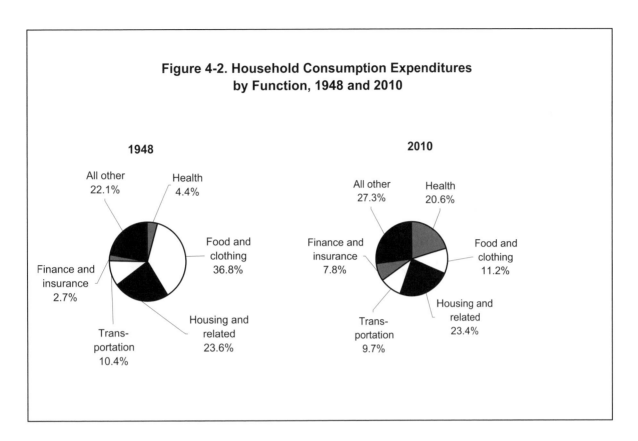

Figure 4-2. Household Consumption Expenditures by Function, 1948 and 2010

- Figure 4-2 compares the composition of household consumer spending (excluding the net spending of nonprofit institutions) in 1948 and 2010, the latest available data at the time *Business Statistics* went to press.

- Household spending on health in 2010 made up 20.6 percent of all household consumption spending—four and one/half times the percentage in 1948. It is important to recognize that household consumption spending, as presented in these data, includes (in health spending and in the total) medical care payments made by government and private insurance on behalf of individuals as well as out-of-pocket consumer payments. (Table 4-5)

- In 2010, a much smaller share was required for food and clothing than in 1948, as seen in Figure 4-2. The shares of housing-related spending and transportation were similar in the two years. The share of finance and insurance spending nearly tripled, and households also spent a larger share on the remaining category, here labeled "all other," which includes communication, recreation, education, food services, accommodations, and other miscellaneous goods and services. (Table 4-5)

Table 4-5. Household Consumption Expenditures by Function

(Billions of dollars.)   NIPA Table 2.5.5

Year	Household consumption expenditures, total	Food and beverages off-premises	Clothing, footwear, and related services	Housing, utilities, and fuels	Furnishings, household equipment, and maintenance	Health	Transportation	Communication	Recreation	Education	Food services and accommodations	Financial services and insurance	Other goods and services	Foreign travel and expenditures, net
1939	66.2	15.2	7.7	12.3	5.5	2.8	6.3	0.7	3.6	0.6	4.1	2.3	5.0	0.2
1940	70.2	15.9	8.1	12.8	6.0	3.0	7.0	0.7	3.9	0.6	4.4	2.4	5.3	0.1
1941	80.0	18.2	9.5	13.7	7.1	3.2	8.3	0.8	4.5	0.6	5.3	2.5	6.0	0.1
1942	87.7	21.6	11.8	14.8	7.4	3.6	5.4	1.0	4.9	0.7	6.9	2.6	6.8	0.2
1943	98.4	24.3	14.4	15.5	7.4	4.0	5.4	1.2	5.3	0.8	9.1	2.8	8.0	0.3
1944	107.0	26.0	15.7	16.2	8.0	4.5	5.7	1.3	5.8	0.9	10.9	3.0	8.5	0.6
1945	118.2	28.2	17.6	16.9	8.9	4.8	6.6	1.4	6.5	0.9	12.7	3.2	9.3	1.2
1946	142.3	34.9	19.7	18.8	12.7	5.9	12.1	1.6	9.0	1.0	12.7	3.8	10.3	-0.1
1947	159.9	40.2	20.4	21.2	15.5	6.6	15.4	1.7	9.8	1.2	12.5	4.2	11.1	0.0
1948	172.7	41.8	21.8	23.9	16.8	7.6	18.0	1.9	10.3	1.3	12.6	4.7	11.7	0.3
1949	176.1	40.4	21.1	25.6	16.3	7.9	21.2	2.1	10.6	1.4	12.4	4.9	11.8	0.6
1950	189.8	41.4	21.4	28.4	18.7	8.5	24.6	2.3	11.7	1.5	12.7	5.6	12.2	0.7
1951	205.9	46.0	23.1	31.6	19.7	9.3	24.2	2.6	12.3	1.6	15.0	6.3	13.3	0.9
1952	216.6	48.4	23.9	34.6	19.3	10.1	24.4	2.9	13.0	1.7	16.0	6.7	14.3	1.1
1953	230.0	49.3	24.2	37.9	20.0	11.0	28.0	3.2	13.8	1.8	16.5	7.8	15.0	1.5
1954	236.7	50.6	24.3	40.9	19.9	11.9	27.4	3.3	14.3	1.9	16.6	8.6	15.4	1.5
1955	255.3	52.0	25.4	43.8	22.3	12.8	33.4	3.6	15.4	2.1	17.0	9.6	16.3	1.6
1956	267.8	54.2	26.5	46.8	23.6	14.1	32.7	3.9	16.4	2.4	17.7	10.4	17.5	1.7
1957	282.7	57.1	26.8	50.0	23.9	15.5	35.7	4.3	16.8	2.6	18.5	11.1	18.8	1.7
1958	291.7	59.8	27.1	53.3	24.1	17.1	33.7	4.5	17.3	2.9	18.7	11.6	19.9	1.9
1959	312.6	61.6	28.6	56.9	25.6	18.8	38.8	4.8	18.8	3.1	19.7	12.5	21.4	2.0
1960	326.5	62.6	29.3	60.5	26.2	20.4	40.8	5.2	19.7	3.4	20.5	13.6	22.4	2.1
1961	336.7	63.7	29.9	64.0	26.8	21.8	39.3	5.6	20.5	3.6	21.0	14.8	23.7	2.0
1962	357.6	64.7	31.3	68.2	28.3	24.3	44.1	5.9	22.1	4.0	22.3	15.4	24.9	2.3
1963	376.7	65.9	32.1	72.2	29.8	26.4	47.8	6.4	23.9	4.3	23.3	15.9	26.2	2.5
1964	404.8	69.5	34.7	76.2	32.7	29.8	50.7	6.9	26.3	4.8	24.9	17.7	27.8	2.6
1965	436.6	74.4	36.5	81.0	34.7	32.0	56.5	7.5	28.9	5.5	27.2	19.4	30.2	2.9
1966	473.1	80.6	39.8	85.9	37.8	35.0	59.0	8.1	33.4	6.2	29.6	21.3	33.3	3.1
1967	499.4	82.6	41.7	91.1	39.7	38.4	61.0	8.9	35.8	6.9	31.0	22.8	35.8	3.8
1968	548.7	88.8	45.6	97.4	43.2	43.8	69.8	9.7	39.9	7.7	34.6	25.8	38.6	3.7
1969	595.0	95.4	48.8	105.5	45.4	50.0	75.9	10.7	43.7	8.7	37.5	28.5	41.0	4.0
1970	637.2	103.5	49.9	113.8	46.6	56.8	76.5	11.6	47.0	9.9	41.6	31.1	44.3	4.5
1971	689.3	107.1	53.4	124.5	48.8	63.4	88.7	12.8	50.1	10.9	43.8	34.1	47.0	4.8
1972	756.6	114.5	58.0	136.2	53.5	70.4	98.3	14.4	56.2	11.7	48.9	38.3	51.0	5.2
1973	837.4	126.7	63.7	149.7	59.9	78.7	108.6	16.1	63.0	13.0	54.8	41.5	56.9	4.7
1974	916.5	143.0	66.9	166.3	64.6	88.7	112.8	17.7	68.9	14.2	60.6	45.9	62.2	4.7
1975	1 015.7	156.6	71.4	184.8	67.8	102.7	124.4	20.0	77.1	15.9	68.8	54.0	67.8	4.4
1976	1 131.2	167.3	76.9	204.6	75.0	116.8	147.4	22.4	86.2	17.4	77.8	59.3	76.3	3.8
1977	1 256.0	179.8	84.3	228.7	84.0	131.6	168.1	24.3	94.9	18.8	85.7	67.8	83.8	4.3
1978	1 403.2	196.1	94.6	255.6	93.6	149.4	184.5	27.0	106.3	20.9	97.1	80.6	93.2	4.3
1979	1 563.4	218.4	101.9	287.5	104.3	169.9	207.1	29.4	118.9	22.9	110.9	87.6	100.4	4.1
1980	1 723.9	239.2	108.8	327.0	110.7	195.5	226.5	31.8	127.4	25.4	121.7	95.6	110.7	3.5
1981	1 903.2	255.3	119.1	367.5	118.3	228.9	250.7	36.0	141.6	28.3	133.9	102.0	121.2	0.4
1982	2 035.4	267.1	122.7	401.2	121.0	254.9	255.9	41.1	151.4	31.0	142.5	116.3	127.8	2.5
1983	2 245.7	277.0	132.9	434.5	132.3	287.1	284.9	44.8	169.3	34.3	153.6	145.9	143.4	5.4
1984	2 453.5	291.1	144.7	471.9	147.1	315.2	321.8	48.4	190.0	37.7	164.9	156.6	157.7	6.6
1985	2 667.3	303.0	154.3	514.0	156.0	345.3	357.4	53.1	207.2	41.2	174.3	180.5	173.3	7.7
1986	2 841.4	316.4	165.1	546.8	168.7	378.4	362.6	56.9	225.4	44.5	186.7	196.7	190.0	3.3
1987	3 038.4	324.3	176.4	582.8	176.9	419.9	376.6	60.0	247.0	48.8	204.4	207.1	208.2	6.1
1988	3 283.3	342.8	188.2	625.9	186.6	470.7	404.8	63.1	273.4	54.4	225.8	219.4	225.4	2.8
1989	3 522.8	365.4	201.4	667.3	197.5	519.0	428.3	67.3	295.7	60.6	242.6	235.7	245.7	-3.7
1990	3 755.8	391.2	207.0	709.1	200.6	583.7	442.9	70.1	314.7	66.0	262.7	253.2	262.3	-7.7
1991	3 895.8	403.0	210.4	747.8	199.1	638.4	418.3	73.9	326.3	70.6	273.4	282.0	268.0	-15.2
1992	4 144.5	404.5	223.0	783.3	209.4	700.4	451.3	81.1	346.8	76.4	286.3	311.8	290.1	-20.0
1993	4 389.0	413.5	231.0	826.9	221.9	741.7	485.3	85.8	378.4	81.1	298.6	341.0	304.5	-20.7
1994	4 648.4	432.1	239.7	879.2	238.6	779.9	528.2	93.3	414.0	86.4	308.7	349.0	316.9	-17.5
1995	4 880.1	443.7	244.1	926.8	251.7	826.0	554.1	98.9	449.8	92.3	316.7	364.7	332.7	-21.5
1996	5 157.9	461.9	252.7	975.5	263.7	868.3	598.9	108.3	481.5	99.6	327.4	393.6	350.8	-24.5
1997	5 458.4	474.8	262.0	1 023.1	277.3	919.9	641.8	120.1	509.5	107.1	344.6	431.3	368.4	-21.5
1998	5 787.5	486.5	273.0	1 076.8	296.8	979.7	669.2	130.6	546.0	115.2	363.0	469.6	394.8	-13.7
1999	6 197.4	513.6	287.1	1 137.4	319.7	1 033.3	730.5	144.7	593.6	123.9	381.6	514.2	431.6	-13.8
2000	6 665.0	537.5	297.3	1 214.5	342.5	1 109.6	798.4	162.1	639.9	134.3	410.1	570.0	462.3	-13.3
2001	6 962.6	559.7	294.3	1 303.2	351.1	1 209.4	814.1	171.3	655.7	143.6	421.2	562.8	483.5	-7.4
2002	7 234.2	569.6	295.2	1 349.1	363.5	1 317.1	818.4	177.5	680.9	149.5	438.2	576.2	504.3	-5.1
2003	7 592.9	587.5	301.7	1 410.6	374.7	1 405.7	857.0	182.9	715.5	159.9	464.2	602.5	531.2	-0.5
2004	8 061.2	613.0	314.6	1 480.2	397.0	1 507.5	909.1	189.1	770.6	169.8	499.1	651.7	558.9	0.6
2005	8 591.8	644.5	330.2	1 602.6	418.7	1 605.1	978.0	193.8	817.7	181.9	533.9	698.4	587.0	0.0
2006	9 061.0	674.2	344.2	1 706.8	436.5	1 694.5	1 007.0	206.8	872.0	194.6	570.2	732.6	617.9	3.8
2007	9 518.1	711.2	352.7	1 777.9	442.5	1 798.4	1 049.9	220.9	918.7	208.6	600.5	790.3	649.9	-3.2
2008	9 750.9	746.4	348.0	1 857.0	432.9	1 884.9	1 029.7	230.7	923.5	222.2	618.3	807.0	666.6	-16.3
2009	9 585.9	746.0	334.8	1 891.9	403.1	1 971.2	882.7	229.4	879.4	234.4	610.3	747.8	667.8	-13.0
2010	9 965.3	766.4	350.7	1 915.9	413.1	2 052.8	967.0	237.4	918.3	249.3	638.0	780.2	692.5	-16.3

Table 4-6. Personal Saving: Households and Nonprofit Institutions Serving Households (NPISHs)

(Billions of dollars, except as noted.)   **NIPA Table 2.9**

Year	Personal saving as a percentage of disposable personal income (percent)	Households				Nonprofit Institutions Serving Households (NPISHs)					
				Equals: household saving						Saving	
		Disposable income	Less: outlays	Billions of dollars	Percent of income	Income	Less: gross output	Plus: receipts from sales	Less: transfer payments	Billions of dollars	Percent of income and receipts from sales
1992	7.3	4 710.6	4 378.8	331.8	7.0	131.7	400.8	308.5	23.2	16.3	3.7
1993	5.8	4 896.4	4 625.5	270.9	5.5	135.3	423.3	328.7	26.2	14.5	3.1
1994	5.2	5 157.1	4 898.3	258.8	5.0	142.9	444.7	342.3	28.6	11.9	2.5
1995	5.2	5 423.1	5 152.3	270.8	5.0	151.3	463.4	356.2	28.7	15.5	3.0
1996	4.9	5 726.3	5 466.8	259.5	4.5	170.9	488.8	373.1	33.5	21.6	4.0
1997	4.6	6 039.8	5 799.2	240.6	4.0	188.8	509.3	397.0	36.7	39.9	6.8
1998	5.3	6 473.4	6 154.0	319.4	4.9	196.7	550.5	419.6	43.7	22.1	3.6
1999	3.1	6 776.2	6 596.0	180.1	2.7	221.8	585.3	439.9	48.8	27.6	4.2
2000	2.9	7 298.6	7 117.2	181.4	2.5	248.7	632.0	466.6	51.7	31.7	4.4
2001	2.7	7 630.3	7 421.5	208.9	2.7	241.0	688.0	501.8	58.7	-4.0	-0.5
2002	3.5	7 999.9	7 691.6	308.3	3.9	240.8	749.7	544.7	61.9	-26.1	-3.3
2003	3.5	8 370.9	8 047.3	323.5	3.9	243.0	785.9	574.7	65.6	-33.9	-4.1
2004	3.6	8 882.0	8 555.3	326.7	3.7	270.6	827.6	618.2	69.8	-8.5	-1.0
2005	1.5	9 262.2	9 125.4	136.9	1.5	294.7	874.3	662.6	76.7	6.3	0.7
2006	2.6	9 896.5	9 630.1	266.5	2.7	310.2	935.2	695.2	80.1	-9.8	-1.0
2007	2.4	10 404.5	10 130.3	274.2	2.6	315.0	989.4	735.5	86.5	-25.5	-2.4
2008	5.4	11 013.1	10 359.4	653.8	5.9	316.2	1 046.5	761.9	93.0	-61.4	-5.7
2009	5.1	10 781.1	10 165.1	616.1	5.7	314.2	1 078.2	797.9	97.4	-63.5	-5.7
2010	5.3	11 174.9	10 516.7	658.2	5.9	319.4	1 118.9	838.6	104.7	-65.4	-5.6

NOTES AND DEFINITIONS, CHAPTER 4

SOURCE: U.S. DEPARTMENT OF COMMERCE, BUREAU OF ECONOMIC ANALYSIS (BEA)

All personal income and personal consumption expenditure series are from the national income and product accounts (NIPAs). All quarterly series are shown at seasonally adjusted annual rates. Current and constant dollar values are in billions of dollars. Indexes of price and quantity are based on the average for the year 2005, which equals 100.

Tables 4-1 through 4-4 cover all income and spending by the personal sector, which includes nonprofit institutions serving households (NPISHs). In a new feature introduced in the 2009 comprehensive revision of the NIPAs, Tables 4-2, 4-3, and 4-4 show the services component of personal consumption expenditures broken down into separate aggregates for "household consumption expenditures for services" and "final consumption expenditures" by NPISHs. The last two tables give further details of the separate accounts for households and NPISHs that are only available annually. Table 4-5 shows a more detailed functional breakdown of household consumption expenditures, not including NPISHs. Table 4-6 shows income, spending, and saving data estimated separately for households and NPISHs.

In several cases, the notes and definitions below will refer to *imputations* or *imputed values*. See the notes and definitions to Chapter 1 for an explanation of imputation and the role it plays in national and personal income measurement.

TABLES 4-1 THROUGH 4-4
SOURCES AND DISPOSITION OF PERSONAL INCOME; PERSONAL CONSUMPTION EXPENDITURES BY MAJOR TYPE OF PRODUCT

Definitions

Personal income is the income received by persons residing in the United States from participation in production, from government and business transfer payments, and from government interest, which is treated similarly to a transfer payment rather than as income from participation in production. *Persons* denotes the total for individuals, *nonprofit institutions that primarily serve households (NPISHs)*, private noninsured welfare funds, and private trust funds. Personal income, outlays, and saving excluding NPISHs are referred to as *household* income, outlays, and saving. All proprietors' income is treated as received by individuals. Life insurance carriers and private noninsured pension funds are not counted as persons, but their saving is credited to persons.

Income from the sale of illegal goods and services is excluded by definition from national and personal income, and the value of purchases of illegal goods and services is not included in personal consumption expenditures.

Personal income is the sum of compensation received by employees, proprietors' income with inventory valuation and capital consumption adjustments (IVA and CCAdj), rental income of persons with capital consumption adjustment, personal receipts on assets, and personal current transfer receipts, less contributions for social insurance.

Personal income differs from national income in that it includes current transfer payments and interest received by persons, regardless of source, while it excludes the following national income components: employee and employer contributions for social insurance; business transfer payments, interest payments, and other payments on assets other than to persons; taxes on production and imports less subsidies; the current surplus of government enterprises; and undistributed corporate profits with IVA and CCAdj. The relationships of GDP, gross and net national product, national income, and personal income are displayed in Table 1-11.

Compensation of employees, received is the sum of wage and salary accruals and supplements to wages and salaries, as defined in the *national* income account (see Table 1-13 and the notes and definitions to Chapter 1), minus an adjustment item *wage accruals less disbursements*. By subtracting this adjustment, BEA puts retroactive wage payments back into the quarter <u>in which</u> the wages were received by workers rather than the quarter <u>for which</u> they were paid. This adjustment item is zero in most quarters but appears more frequently in recent years. There are substantial entries in 2003 and 2004 because 53 Friday paydays fell in 2004 instead of the usual 52. In other years there are entries for this item reflecting stock options and financial industry bonuses paid in a year different from the year of the activity with which they are associated. See the notes and definitions to Chapter 1. *Wage accruals less disbursements* is shown in Table 1-11, but is not shown separately in Table 4-1.

As in *national* income, the *compensation of employees* component of personal income refers to compensation received by residents of the United States, including compensation from the rest of the world, but excludes compensation from domestic industries to workers residing in the rest of the world.

Wage and salary disbursements consists of the monetary remuneration of employees, including wages and salaries as conventionally defined; the compensation of corporate officers; corporate directors' fees paid to directors who are also employees of the corporation; the value of employee exercise of "nonqualified stock options"; commissions, tips, and bonuses; voluntary employee contributions to certain deferred-compensation plans, such as 401(k) plans; and receipts in kind that represent income. This category also now includes judicial fees to jurors and witnesses, compensation of prison inmates, and marriage fees to justices of the peace, which before the latest comprehensive revision were classified as "other labor income".

Supplements to wages and salaries consists of employer contributions to employee pension and insurance funds and to government social insurance funds.

The following two categories, *proprietors' income* and *rental income,* are both measured net of depreciation of the capital (structures and equipment) involved. BEA calculates normal depreciation, based on the estimated life of the capital, and subtracts it from the estimated value of receipts to yield net income.

Proprietors' income with inventory valuation and capital consumption adjustments is the current-production income (including income-in-kind) of sole proprietors and partnerships and of tax-exempt cooperatives. The imputed net rental income of owner-occupants of farm dwellings is included. Dividends and monetary interest received by proprietors of nonfinancial business and rental incomes received by persons not primarily engaged in the real estate business are excluded. These incomes are included in personal income receipts on assets and rental income of persons, respectively. Fees paid to outside directors of corporations are included. The two valuation adjustments are designed to obtain income measures that exclude any element of capital gains: inventory withdrawals are valued at replacement cost, rather than historical cost, and charges for depreciation are on an economically consistent accounting basis and are valued at replacement cost.

Rental income of persons with capital consumption adjustment consists of the net current-production income of persons from the rental of real property (other than the incomes of persons primarily engaged in the real estate business), the imputed net rental income of owner-occupants of nonfarm dwellings, and the royalties received by persons from patents, copyrights, and rights to natural resources. The capital consumption adjustment converts charges for depreciation to an economically consistent accounting basis valued at replacement cost. Rental income is net of interest and other expenses, and hence is affected by changing indebtedness and interest payments on owner-occupied and other housing.

Personal income receipts on assets consists of personal interest income and personal dividend income.

Personal interest income is the interest income (monetary and imputed) of persons from all sources, including interest paid by government to government employee retirement plans as well as government interest paid directly to persons.

Personal dividend income is the dividend income of persons from all sources, excluding capital gains distributions. It equals net dividends paid by corporations (dividends paid by corporations minus dividends received by corporations) less a small amount of corporate dividends received by general government. Dividends received by government employee retirement systems are included in personal dividend income.

Personal current transfer receipts is income payments to persons for which no current services are performed. It consists of government social benefits to persons and net receipts from business.

Government social benefits to persons consists of benefits from the following categories of programs:

Social Security and Medicare, consisting of federal old-age, survivors, disability, and health insurance;
Medicaid, the federal-state means-tested program covering medical expenses for lower-income children and adults as well as nursing care expenses;

Unemployment insurance;

Veterans' benefits;

Other government benefits to persons, which includes pension benefit guaranty; workers' compensation; military medical insurance; temporary disability insurance; food stamps; Black Lung benefits; supplemental security income; family assistance, which consists of aid to families with dependent children and (beginning in 1996) assistance programs operating under the Personal Responsibility and Work Opportunity Reconciliation Act of 1996; educational assistance; and the earned income credit. Government payments to nonprofit institutions, other than for work under research and development contracts, also are included. Payments from government employee retirement plans are not included.

Note that the value of Medicare and Medicaid spending, though in practice it is usually paid directly from the government to the health care provider, is treated as if it were cash income to the consumer which is then expended in personal consumption expenditures; this value is not treated in the national accounts as a government purchase of medical services but as a government benefit paid to persons, which then finances personal consumption spending.

Contributions for government social insurance, domestic, which is subtracted to arrive at personal income, includes payments by U.S. employers, employees, self-employed, and other individuals who participate in the following programs: old-age, survivors, and disability insurance (Social Security); hospital insurance and supplementary medical insurance (Medicare); unemployment insurance; railroad retirement; veterans' life insurance; and temporary disability insurance. Contributions to government employee retirement plans are not included in this item.

In the 2009 comprehensive revision, most transactions between the U.S. government and economic agents in Guam, the U.S. Virgin Islands, American Samoa, Puerto Rico, and the Northern Mariana Islands are treated as government transactions with the rest of the world. Since the NIPAs only cover the 50 states and the District of Columbia, the *domestic* contributions to government social insurance funds are the only ones that need to be subtracted from NIPA payroll data to calculate personal income. The social insurance receipts of governments, shown in Chapter 6, will be somewhat larger than this personal income entry because they will include contributions from residents of those territories and commonwealths.

Personal current taxes is tax payments (net of refunds) by persons residing in the United States that are not chargeable to business expenses, including taxes on income, on realized net capital gains, and on personal property. As of the 1999 revisions, estate and gift taxes are classified as capital transfers and are not included in personal current taxes.

Disposable personal income is personal income minus personal current taxes. It is the income from current production that is available to persons for spending or saving. However, it is not the cash flow available, since it excludes realized capital gains. Disposable personal income in chained (2005) dollars represents the inflation-adjusted value of disposable personal income, using the implicit price deflator for personal consumption expenditures.

Personal income excluding current transfer receipts, also shown in chained (2005) dollars using the implicit price deflator for personal consumption expenditures, is an important business cycle indicator, to which particular attention is paid because it is calculated monthly as well as quarterly and annually, and thus can help establish monthly cycle turning point dates. As a pre-income-tax measure which excludes transfer payments, it is more directly related to the workings of the economy than alternative monthly income indicators such as total or disposable personal income.

Personal outlays is the sum of *personal consumption expenditures* (defined below), *personal interest payments,* and *personal current transfer payments.*

Personal interest payments is nonmortgage interest paid by households. As noted above in the definition of rental income, mortgage interest has been subtracted from gross rental or imputed rental receipts of persons to yield a net rental income estimate; hence, it is not included as an interest outlay in this category.

Personal current transfer payments to government includes donations, fees, and fines paid to federal, state, and local governments.

Personal current transfer payments to the rest of the world (net) is personal remittances in cash and in kind to the rest of the world less such remittances from the rest of the world.

Personal saving is derived by subtracting personal outlays from disposable personal income. It is the current net saving of individuals (including proprietors), nonprofit insti-

tutions that primarily serve individuals, life insurance carriers, retirement funds (including those of government employees), private noninsured welfare funds, and private trust funds. Conceptually, personal saving may also be viewed as the sum of the net acquisition of financial assets and the change in physical assets less the sum of net borrowing and consumption of fixed capital. In either case, it is defined to exclude both realized and unrealized capital gains.

Note that in the context of national income accounting, the term just defined is *saving,* not "savings." *Saving* refers to a <u>flow</u> of income during a particular time span (such as a year or a quarter) that is not consumed. It is therefore available to finance a commensurate <u>flow</u> of investment during that time span. Strictly defined, "savings" denotes an accumulated <u>stock</u> of monetary funds—possibly the cumulative effects of successive periods of *saving*—available to the owner in asset form, such as in a bank savings account.

Personal consumption expenditures (PCE) is goods and services purchased by persons residing in the United States. Persons are defined as individuals and nonprofit institutions that primarily serve individuals. PCE mostly consists of purchases of new goods and services by individuals from business, including purchases financed by insurance (such as both private and government medical insurance). In addition, PCE includes purchases of new goods and services by nonprofit institutions, net purchases of used goods by individuals and nonprofit institutions, and purchases abroad of goods and services by U.S. residents traveling or working in foreign countries. PCE also includes purchases for certain goods and services provided by the government, primarily tuition payments for higher education, charges for medical care, and charges for water and sanitary services. Finally, PCE includes imputed purchases that keep PCE invariant to changes in the way that certain activities are carried out. For example, to take account of the value of the services provided by owner-occupied housing, PCE includes an imputation equal to what (estimated) rent homeowners would pay if they rented their houses from themselves. (See the discussion of imputation in the notes and definitions to Chapter 1.) Actual purchases of residential structures by individuals are classified as gross private domestic investment.

In the 2009 comprehensive revision, the classification system used for breakdowns of PCE was revised, and new calculations were introduced separating the consumption spending of the household sector proper from that of nonprofit institutions serving households.

Goods is the sum of *Durable* and *Nondurable goods.*

The PCE category *Durable goods* now is subdivided into *Motor vehicles and parts, Furnishings and household equipment, Recreational goods and vehicles,* and *Other durable goods.*

Nondurable goods now encompasses *Food and beverages off-premises, Clothing and footwear, Gasoline and other energy goods,* and *Other nondurable goods.* This food and beverages category no longer includes meals and beverages purchased for consumption on the premises, which are now included in services, since they have a high service component and since their prices are much more stable than those of off-premises food and beverages.

Services, total is now subdivided into *Household services* and *Final consumption expenditures of nonprofit institutions serving households (NPISHs).* The latter is the difference between the *Gross output* of NPISHs and the amounts that they receive from sales of goods and services to households—for example, payments for services of a nonprofit hospital. Such sales of goods and services appear in the appropriate category of household expenditures—for example, *Health* in the case of the hospital services.

The components of *Household services* are *Housing and utilities, Health care, Transportation services, Recreation services, Food services and accommodations* (which includes meals and beverages purchased for consumption on premises, as well as payments for hotels and similar accommodations), *Financial services and insurance,* and *Other services.*

These are the categories used in the quarterly data presented in Tables 4-2, 4-3, and 4-4. This classification system is not particularly helpful with respect to the objective of spending. For example, the *Health care* component of services does not include drugs and medicines, which are included instead in nondurable goods. For a more precise classification of consumption spending by objective, see Table 4-5, Household Consumption Expenditures by Function, described in more detail below. This classification by type of expenditure is only available on an annual basis.

Data availability

Monthly data are made available in a BEA press release, usually distributed the first business day following the monthly release of the latest quarterly national income and product account (NIPA) estimates. Monthly and quarterly data are subsequently published each month in the BEA's *Survey of Current Business.* Current and historical data are available on the BEA Web site at <http://www.bea.gov>, and may also be obtained from the STAT-USA subscription Web site at <http://www.stat-usa.gov>.

References

References can be found in the notes and definitions to Chapter 1. A discussion of monthly estimates of personal income and its disposition appears in the November 1979 edition of the *Survey of Current Business.* Additional and more recent information can be found in the articles listed in the notes and definitions for Chapter 1.

TABLE 4-5
HOUSEHOLD CONSUMPTION EXPENDITURES BY FUNCTION

SOURCE: BUREAU OF ECONOMIC ANALYSIS (BEA)

In this table, also derived from the NIPAs, annual estimates of the current-dollar value of PCE by households—excluding the "final" consumption expenditures of nonprofit institutions serving households (NPISHs); see definition above—are presented by function.

Definitions

Food and beverages includes food and beverages (including alcoholic beverages) purchased for home consumption and food produced and consumed on farms.

Clothing, footwear, and related services includes purchases, rental, cleaning, and repair of clothing and footwear.

Housing, utilities, and fuels includes rents paid for rental housing, imputed rent of owner-occupied dwellings, and purchase of fuels and utility services.

Furnishings, household equipment, and routine household maintenance includes furniture, floor coverings, household textiles, appliances, tableware etc., tools, and other supplies and services.

Health includes drugs, other medical products and equipment, and outpatient, hospital, and nursing home services.

Transportation includes the purchase and operation of motor vehicles and public transportation services.

Communication includes telephone equipment, postal and delivery services, telecommunication services, and Internet access.

Recreation includes video and audio equipment, computers, and related services; sports vehicles and other sports goods and services; memberships and admissions; magazines, newspapers, books, and stationery; pets and related goods and services; photo goods and services; tour services; and legal gambling. (As noted earlier, purchases of goods and services that are illegal and the incomes from such purchases are outside the scope of the national income and product accounts.)

Education includes educational services and books.

Food services and accommodations includes meals and beverages purchased for consumption on the premises, food furnished to employees, and hotel and other accommodations including housing at schools.

Financial services and insurance consists of financial services and life, household, medical care, motor vehicle, and other insurance.

Other goods and services includes personal goods (such as cosmetics, jewelry, and luggage) and services, social services and religious activities, professional and other services, and tobacco.

Foreign travel and expenditures, net consists of foreign travel spending and other expenditures abroad by U.S. residents minus expenditures in the United States by nonresidents. A negative figure indicates that foreigners spent more here than U.S. residents spent abroad. Positive values for this foreign travel category, indicating that U.S. residents spent more abroad than foreigners spent here, appear in the 1980s when the dollar was strong against other major currencies. (The international value of the dollar is shown in Table 13-8.) Negative values in subsequent years have resulted in part from the weakening of the dollar, which discouraged U.S. residents' travel abroad and encouraged tourism by foreigners in the United States. The negative sign does not indicate a drain on GDP—these effects of a weaker dollar are in fact positive for GDP—but rather reflects the fact that the goods and services purchased by foreigners in the United States must be subtracted from the total consumer purchases recorded elsewhere in this table in order to be added to other exports and classified in the category of exports rather than in the consumption spending of U.S. residents.

Data availability and revisions

Data are updated once a year, after the general midyear revision of the NIPAs, and are available on the BEA Web site at <http://www.bea.gov>.

TABLE 4-6
PERSONAL SAVING: HOUSEHOLDS AND NONPROFIT INSTITUTIONS SERVING HOUSEHOLDS

Source: Bureau of Economic Analysis (BEA)

As noted above, the "personal" sector includes not only households but also "nonprofit institutions serving households" (NPISHs). This category comprises all nonprofit institutions except those that are considered to be serving government and business, such as chambers of commerce and trade associations. Those institutions are included in the business sector instead.

For annual (not quarterly) data beginning with 1992, BEA now compiles and makes available tables showing personal income and its disposition for households and NPISHs separately. Each major type of income and expenditure is estimated separately for the two groups. Household receipts from NPISHs, purchases from NPISHs, and contributions to NPISHs are identified separately instead of being netted out as they are in the quarterly accounts. Selected aggregates for households and NPISHs are shown in Table 4-6.

Data availability and references

These data and the data on income and outlays for the household and nonprofit sectors on which they are based become available about two months after the release of the midyear revision of the NIPAs. They are published in Table 2.9 in the NIPA tables on the BEA Web site at <http://www.bea.gov>. An article from the April 2003 *Survey,* "Income and Outlays of Households and of Nonprofit Institutions Serving Households," can also be found on the BEA Web site.

CHAPTER 5: SAVING AND INVESTMENT

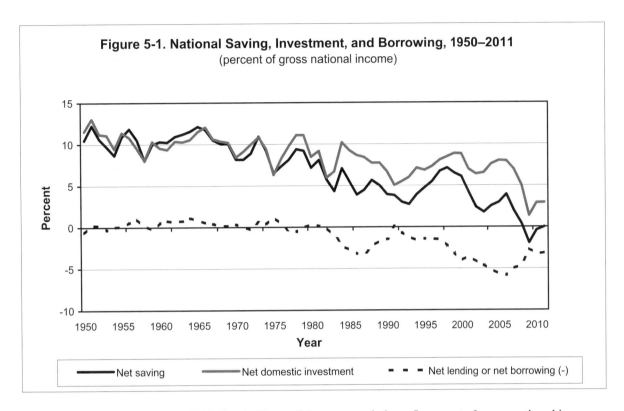

Figure 5-1. National Saving, Investment, and Borrowing, 1950–2011
(percent of gross national income)

Net saving ——— Net domestic investment ——— Net lending or net borrowing (-) - - -

- Net national saving—the middle line in Figure 5-1—averaged about 5 percent of gross national income (GNI) in the years 1984 through 2000, which was already lower than the rates seen in the 1950s and 1960s. Net saving is saving by U.S. persons, businesses, and governments, excluding the consumption of fixed capital—that is, saving available for investment over and above the replacement of the existing stock. In the years 2001–2007 the national saving rate fell even more, averaging 2.8 percent. In the recession that began at the end of 2007, national saving fell into negative territory for the first time since the depression years 1931 through 1934, and remained negative through early 2011. (Table 5-1)

- What accounted for the decline in the saving rate in the 2000s? Comparing 2007 with 2000, the biggest factor was the federal government's swing—in a prosperous economy, not in a recession—from a surplus of 1.8 percent of GNI to a deficit of 1.7 percent. Smaller declines in the personal saving rate and in state and local saving also contributed to the drop, while there was a small increase in domestic corporate business saving (undistributed corporate after-tax economic profits) relative to GNI. (Table 5-1)

- Net domestic investment (gross investment minus consumption of fixed capital) reached rates over 8 percent of GNI in the late 1990s. After the 2001 recession, it recovered to 8 percent in 2005 and 2006, before declining to 1.3 percent in 2009. This was the lowest investment rate in the entire postwar period—indeed, the lowest since net investment was negative (that is, gross investment was less than capital consumption) in the early 1930s. (Table 5-1)

- The excess of investment over saving in the 2000s was financed by a further increase in borrowing overseas (a larger negative entry for the lower line on the graph above), which reached a record 5.8 percent of GNI in 2006, then subsided somewhat as demand for foreign investment funds dwindled in the recession. (Table 5-1)

Table 5-1A. Saving and Investment: Recent Data

(Billions of dollars, except as noted; quarterly data are at seasonally adjusted annual rates.)

NIPA Tables 1.7.5, 5.1

Year and quarter	Total	Gross saving											
		Net saving						Consumption of fixed capital					
		Total	Private			Government		Total	Private			Government	
			Total ¹	Personal saving	Domestic corporate business	Federal	State and local		Total	Domestic business	House-holds and institutions	Federal	State and local
1955	88.0	45.2	36.0	19.5	16.5	5.7	3.5	42.8	31.1	25.8	5.2	8.6	3.1
1956	99.4	52.3	40.4	25.6	14.7	7.5	4.4	47.1	34.3	28.6	5.7	9.2	3.5
1957	99.6	48.8	41.3	26.9	14.5	3.3	4.2	50.8	37.2	31.2	6.1	9.7	3.9
1958	90.8	37.5	40.1	28.2	11.9	-5.4	2.9	53.3	39.4	33.1	6.3	9.9	4.0
1959	106.1	50.7	43.6	26.1	17.5	3.3	3.8	55.4	41.0	34.3	6.7	10.2	4.2
1960	111.3	54.7	43.3	26.3	16.9	7.1	4.3	56.6	41.6	34.6	7.0	10.6	4.4
1961	114.3	56.1	49.3	31.9	17.4	2.6	4.3	58.2	42.6	35.4	7.2	10.9	4.7
1962	124.9	64.3	56.7	33.5	23.2	2.4	5.2	60.6	44.1	36.6	7.5	11.5	5.0
1963	133.2	69.8	58.8	33.1	25.7	5.3	5.7	63.3	45.9	38.1	7.8	12.1	5.4
1964	143.4	77.0	69.7	40.5	29.2	0.9	6.4	66.4	48.3	40.0	8.3	12.3	5.7
1965	158.5	87.7	78.0	42.7	35.3	3.2	6.5	70.7	51.9	42.9	8.9	12.6	6.2
1966	168.7	92.3	82.3	44.3	38.0	2.3	7.8	76.5	56.5	46.9	9.6	13.1	6.9
1967	170.6	87.6	89.9	54.2	35.8	-9.3	7.0	82.9	61.6	51.2	10.4	13.9	7.5
1968	182.0	91.6	86.6	52.5	34.1	-2.4	7.5	90.4	67.4	56.1	11.3	14.7	8.3
1969	198.4	99.3	82.7	52.5	30.3	8.6	8.0	99.2	74.5	61.9	12.6	15.4	9.3
1970	192.8	84.5	92.9	69.4	23.4	-15.5	7.1	108.3	81.7	68.2	13.5	16.1	10.6
1971	209.2	91.5	113.7	80.4	32.9	-28.7	6.5	117.8	89.5	74.6	14.9	16.5	11.8
1972	237.3	110.1	119.4	77.5	42.2	-24.9	15.6	127.2	97.7	81.2	16.5	16.6	12.8
1973	292.2	151.4	147.5	102.9	44.6	-11.8	15.7	140.8	109.5	90.6	18.8	17.0	14.3
1974	301.8	138.1	143.3	114.2	29.1	-14.5	9.3	163.7	127.8	106.1	21.7	18.2	17.7
1975	296.9	106.5	174.6	125.9	48.7	-70.6	2.5	190.4	150.4	125.8	24.7	19.7	20.2
1976	342.0	133.8	180.1	122.8	57.3	-53.7	7.4	208.2	165.5	138.5	27.1	21.4	21.3
1977	396.7	164.9	197.9	125.3	72.6	-46.1	13.1	231.8	186.1	155.5	30.7	23.0	22.6
1978	476.3	214.9	225.2	142.4	82.8	-28.9	18.7	261.4	212.0	176.4	35.5	25.0	24.5
1979	533.2	234.3	235.3	157.5	77.8	-14.0	13.0	298.9	244.5	203.5	41.0	27.0	27.5
1980	542.7	198.6	246.5	196.3	50.2	-56.6	8.8	344.1	282.3	235.4	46.9	30.0	31.8
1981	646.1	252.7	301.9	236.7	65.2	-56.8	7.6	393.3	323.2	271.2	52.1	33.8	36.3
1982	621.5	187.9	325.4	263.9	61.5	-135.3	-2.2	433.5	356.4	300.7	55.8	37.6	39.5
1983	602.4	151.3	322.6	226.9	95.7	-176.2	4.9	451.1	369.5	311.4	58.1	40.7	40.9
1984	753.4	279.0	426.5	296.3	130.3	-171.5	23.9	474.3	387.5	326.0	61.5	44.5	42.3
1985	738.4	232.9	389.2	253.6	135.6	-178.6	22.4	505.4	412.8	348.0	64.8	48.0	44.6
1986	709.3	170.8	344.7	246.5	98.3	-194.6	20.7	538.5	439.1	369.9	69.2	51.6	47.8
1987	782.3	211.2	348.5	223.4	125.1	-149.3	12.0	571.1	464.5	390.3	74.1	55.2	51.4
1988	901.5	290.5	411.7	256.6	155.1	-138.4	17.2	611.0	497.1	417.6	79.5	59.1	54.8
1989	924.1	272.7	386.5	265.0	121.5	-133.9	20.1	651.5	529.6	444.4	85.2	63.3	58.5
1990	917.6	226.4	396.7	276.7	120.0	-176.4	6.2	691.2	560.4	469.8	90.6	67.7	63.0
1991	951.3	227.0	451.2	313.2	138.0	-218.4	-5.8	724.4	585.4	490.6	94.8	72.0	66.9
1992	932.3	187.9	491.8	348.1	159.5	-302.5	-1.4	744.4	599.9	500.9	99.0	74.6	69.9
1993	958.4	180.4	461.6	285.4	169.7	-280.2	-0.9	778.0	626.4	521.2	105.2	77.8	73.8
1994	1 094.7	275.5	487.7	270.7	199.4	-220.4	8.2	819.2	661.0	549.4	111.5	80.1	78.1
1995	1 219.0	349.6	546.6	286.3	243.9	-206.2	9.2	869.5	704.6	586.0	118.7	81.7	83.1
1996	1 344.4	431.8	557.1	281.1	272.3	-148.2	23.0	912.5	743.4	619.2	124.2	81.9	87.2
1997	1 525.7	561.9	585.7	280.4	308.2	-60.1	36.3	963.8	789.7	658.5	131.2	82.5	91.6
1998	1 654.4	633.9	553.4	341.5	212.6	33.6	46.9	1 020.5	841.6	702.1	139.5	82.8	96.2
1999	1 708.0	613.6	473.0	207.8	260.1	98.8	41.8	1 094.4	907.2	756.8	150.4	85.0	102.1
2000	1 800.1	615.8	389.4	213.1	176.3	185.2	41.3	1 184.3	986.8	824.3	162.5	87.8	109.7
2001	1 695.7	439.4	414.9	204.9	210.0	40.5	-15.9	1 256.2	1 051.6	876.5	175.1	88.6	116.0
2002	1 560.9	255.9	562.8	282.2	280.6	-252.8	-54.1	1 305.0	1 094.0	908.5	185.5	89.2	121.8
2003	1 552.6	198.6	613.8	289.6	309.2	-376.4	-38.8	1 354.1	1 135.9	935.4	200.5	90.8	127.3
2004	1 738.7	305.9	693.7	318.2	390.5	-379.5	-8.4	1 432.8	1 200.9	978.7	222.2	94.8	137.1
2005	1 918.8	377.5	634.5	143.2	486.4	-283.0	25.9	1 541.4	1 290.8	1 045.7	245.1	100.4	150.1
2006	2 196.1	535.4	688.1	256.6	430.3	-203.8	51.0	1 660.7	1 391.4	1 123.3	268.1	106.6	162.7
2007	2 047.7	280.2	513.2	248.7	270.7	-245.2	12.2	1 767.5	1 476.2	1 190.7	285.5	112.6	178.7
2008	1 908.2	54.1	739.8	592.3	152.5	-613.5	-72.2	1 854.1	1 542.9	1 248.3	294.6	120.0	191.2
2009	1 597.3	-268.8	1 027.1	552.6	469.6	-1 217.9	-78.0	1 866.2	1 542.4	1 249.9	292.5	124.7	199.0
2010	1 820.5	-54.5	1 244.5	592.8	651.7	-1 273.7	-25.3	1 874.9	1 540.9	1 245.7	295.2	130.0	204.0
2011	1 948.2	-1.9	1 251.4	538.5	712.9	-1 187.8	-65.5	1 950.1	1 597.9	1 294.4	303.4	137.9	214.3
2009													
1st quarter	1 698.7	-186.4	925.6	611.1	294.5	-993.9	-118.1	1 885.2	1 562.6	1 267.2	295.4	123.2	199.4
2nd quarter	1 577.0	-291.4	1 086.9	670.3	416.6	-1 303.0	-75.3	1 868.4	1 545.2	1 253.1	292.1	124.1	199.1
3rd quarter	1 496.1	-358.0	1 021.3	468.2	553.1	-1 305.4	-74.0	1 854.1	1 530.5	1 240.6	289.9	125.1	198.5
4th quarter	1 617.5	-239.5	1 074.7	460.5	614.2	-1 269.4	-44.8	1 857.1	1 531.4	1 238.8	292.6	126.4	199.2
2010													
1st quarter	1 718.4	-140.2	1 163.9	534.1	629.7	-1 271.8	-32.3	1 858.6	1 529.6	1 235.6	294.0	127.9	201.1
2nd quarter	1 840.9	-25.9	1 280.3	623.3	657.0	-1 278.0	-28.2	1 866.9	1 534.4	1 241.2	293.2	129.4	203.1
3rd quarter	1 883.2	5.0	1 267.9	625.6	642.3	-1 257.7	-5.2	1 878.2	1 542.6	1 247.2	295.4	130.5	205.0
4th quarter	1 839.3	-56.8	1 266.0	588.1	677.9	-1 287.3	-35.5	1 896.1	1 557.0	1 258.7	298.4	132.3	206.8
2011													
1st quarter	1 895.2	-19.1	1 239.2	578.9	660.3	-1 201.1	-57.2	1 914.3	1 570.5	1 270.1	300.4	134.6	209.2
2nd quarter	1 890.5	-49.4	1 266.2	556.5	709.6	-1 275.4	-40.2	1 939.9	1 590.5	1 287.8	302.7	136.8	212.6
3rd quarter	1 989.4	26.6	1 270.4	533.1	737.3	-1 160.7	-83.2	1 962.8	1 607.6	1 303.2	304.4	139.2	216.1
4th quarter	2 017.6	34.2	1 229.7	485.3	744.5	-1 114.1	-81.5	1 983.4	1 622.9	1 316.7	306.2	141.0	219.5

¹Includes wage accruals less disbursements, not shown separately.

Table 5-1A. Saving and Investment: Recent Data—*Continued*

(Billions of dollars, except as noted; quarterly data are at seasonally adjusted annual rates.)

NIPA Tables 1.7.5, 5.1

Year and quarter	Gross domestic investment, capital account transactions, and net lending, NIPAs						Statistical discrepancy	Net domestic investment	Gross national income	Gross saving as a percent of gross national income	Net saving as a percent of gross national income
	Total	Gross domestic investment			Capital account transactions, net	Net lending or net borrowing (-), NIPAs					
		Total	Private	Government							
1955	90.4	90.0	69.0	21.0	. . .	0.4	2.4	47.2	414.8	21.2	10.9
1956	97.6	94.9	72.0	22.9	. . .	2.7	-1.8	47.8	442.0	22.5	11.8
1957	99.5	94.8	70.5	24.4	. . .	4.7	-0.1	44.0	464.2	21.5	10.5
1958	91.8	91.0	64.5	26.5	. . .	0.8	1.0	37.7	468.8	19.4	8.0
1959	106.6	107.8	78.5	29.3	. . .	-1.3	0.5	52.4	508.9	20.8	10.0
1960	110.3	107.2	78.9	28.3	. . .	3.2	-1.0	50.6	530.5	21.0	10.3
1961	113.7	109.5	78.2	31.3	. . .	4.2	-0.6	51.3	548.9	20.8	10.2
1962	125.2	121.4	88.1	33.3	. . .	3.8	0.3	60.9	589.4	21.2	10.9
1963	132.3	127.4	93.8	33.6	. . .	4.9	-0.8	64.1	623.1	21.4	11.2
1964	144.2	136.7	102.1	34.6	. . .	7.5	0.8	70.3	667.8	21.5	11.5
1965	160.0	153.8	118.2	35.6	. . .	6.2	1.5	83.1	722.9	21.9	12.1
1966	174.9	171.1	131.3	39.8	. . .	3.8	6.2	94.6	786.6	21.5	11.7
1967	175.1	171.6	128.6	43.0	. . .	3.5	4.5	88.6	833.3	20.5	10.5
1968	186.4	184.8	141.2	43.6	. . .	1.5	4.3	94.4	911.6	20.0	10.1
1969	201.3	199.7	156.4	43.3	0.0	1.6	2.9	100.5	987.7	20.1	10.0
1970	199.7	196.0	152.4	43.6	0.0	3.7	6.9	87.6	1 037.8	18.6	8.1
1971	220.2	219.9	178.2	41.8	0.0	0.3	11.0	102.2	1 123.4	18.6	8.1
1972	246.2	250.2	207.6	42.6	0.0	-4.1	8.9	123.1	1 237.5	19.2	8.9
1973	300.2	291.3	244.5	46.8	0.0	8.8	8.0	150.6	1 386.9	21.1	10.9
1974	311.6	305.7	249.4	56.3	0.0	5.9	9.8	142.0	1 505.2	20.1	9.2
1975	313.2	293.3	230.2	63.1	0.1	19.8	16.3	102.9	1 634.4	18.2	6.5
1976	365.4	358.4	292.0	66.4	0.1	7.0	23.5	150.2	1 818.0	18.8	7.4
1977	417.9	428.8	361.3	67.5	0.1	-11.0	21.2	197.1	2 029.2	19.6	8.1
1978	502.4	515.0	438.0	77.1	0.1	-12.7	26.1	253.6	2 289.3	20.8	9.4
1979	580.2	581.4	492.9	88.5	0.1	-1.3	47.0	282.4	2 547.2	20.9	9.2
1980	588.0	579.5	479.3	100.3	0.1	8.4	45.3	235.4	2 777.0	19.5	7.2
1981	682.6	679.3	572.4	106.9	0.1	3.2	36.6	285.9	3 123.2	20.7	8.1
1982	626.2	629.5	517.2	112.3	0.1	-3.4	4.8	196.0	3 285.0	18.9	5.7
1983	652.1	687.2	564.3	122.9	0.1	-35.2	49.7	236.0	3 522.0	17.1	4.3
1984	784.9	875.0	735.6	139.4	0.1	-90.2	31.5	400.6	3 935.6	19.1	7.1
1985	780.7	895.0	736.2	158.8	0.1	-114.5	42.3	389.5	4 201.7	17.6	5.5
1986	777.1	919.7	746.5	173.2	0.1	-142.8	67.7	381.3	4 409.9	16.1	3.9
1987	815.1	969.2	785.0	184.3	0.1	-154.2	32.9	398.1	4 721.1	16.6	4.5
1988	892.0	1 007.7	821.6	186.1	0.1	-115.9	-9.5	396.7	5 133.3	17.6	5.7
1989	980.3	1 072.6	874.9	197.7	0.3	-92.7	56.1	421.2	5 452.0	17.0	5.0
1990	1 001.8	1 076.7	861.0	215.7	7.4	-82.3	84.2	385.5	5 750.8	16.0	3.9
1991	1 031.0	1 023.2	802.9	220.3	5.3	2.6	79.7	298.8	5 942.3	16.0	3.8
1992	1 042.3	1 087.9	864.8	223.1	-1.3	-44.3	110.0	343.5	6 261.5	14.9	3.0
1993	1 094.2	1 172.8	953.3	219.4	0.9	-79.4	135.8	394.8	6 562.7	14.6	2.7
1994	1 203.5	1 318.2	1 097.3	220.9	1.3	-116.0	108.8	499.0	7 000.4	15.6	3.9
1995	1 271.6	1 376.6	1 144.0	232.6	0.4	-105.5	52.5	507.2	7 391.8	16.5	4.7
1996	1 370.3	1 484.4	1 240.2	244.2	0.2	-114.4	25.9	571.9	7 844.2	17.1	5.5
1997	1 511.7	1 641.0	1 388.7	252.4	0.5	-129.8	-14.0	677.2	8 369.8	18.2	6.7
1998	1 569.1	1 773.6	1 510.8	262.9	0.2	-204.8	-85.3	753.1	8 896.1	18.6	7.1
1999	1 637.0	1 928.9	1 641.5	287.4	4.5	-296.4	-71.1	834.5	9 452.4	18.1	6.5
2000	1 666.2	2 076.5	1 772.2	304.3	0.3	-410.7	-134.0	892.2	10 123.2	17.8	6.1
2001	1 592.3	1 984.0	1 661.9	322.0	-12.9	-378.7	-103.4	727.7	10 441.4	16.2	4.2
2002	1 538.9	1 990.4	1 647.0	343.5	0.5	-452.1	-22.1	685.4	10 713.5	14.6	2.4
2003	1 569.3	2 085.4	1 729.7	355.8	2.1	-518.2	16.7	731.4	11 194.2	13.9	1.8
2004	1 716.3	2 340.9	1 968.6	372.4	-2.8	-621.8	-22.3	908.2	11 966.8	14.5	2.6
2005	1 823.8	2 564.3	2 172.3	392.0	-12.9	-727.7	-95.1	1 022.9	12 815.2	15.0	2.9
2006	1 953.8	2 752.2	2 327.1	425.1	2.1	-800.5	-242.3	1 091.5	13 691.9	16.0	3.9
2007	2 035.7	2 751.7	2 295.2	456.5	-0.1	-715.9	-12.0	984.2	14 163.9	14.5	2.0
2008	1 905.8	2 584.8	2 087.6	497.2	-5.4	-673.6	-2.4	730.7	14 463.1	13.2	0.4
2009	1 674.8	2 052.2	1 546.8	505.4	0.6	-378.0	77.4	186.0	14 013.8	11.4	-1.9
2010	1 821.3	2 300.4	1 795.1	505.3	0.7	-479.9	0.8	425.5	14 715.1	12.4	-0.4
2011	1 916.4	2 399.5	1 916.2	483.3	1.3	-484.4	-31.8	449.4	15 371.3	12.7	0.0
2009											
1st quarter	1 740.8	2 123.2	1 620.1	503.1	0.4	-382.8	42.1	238.0	13 984.3	12.1	-1.3
2nd quarter	1 667.3	2 005.0	1 493.8	511.2	0.5	-338.1	90.3	136.6	13 904.1	11.3	-2.1
3rd quarter	1 600.1	1 990.7	1 481.2	509.6	0.6	-391.2	104.1	136.6	13 980.2	10.7	-2.6
4th quarter	1 690.8	2 089.9	1 592.2	497.7	0.7	-399.9	73.2	232.8	14 186.5	11.4	-1.7
2010											
1st quarter	1 711.2	2 193.1	1 702.3	490.8	0.5	-482.4	-7.2	334.5	14 454.5	11.9	-1.0
2nd quarter	1 834.3	2 316.5	1 809.7	506.9	0.5	-482.7	-6.6	449.7	14 670.6	12.5	-0.2
3rd quarter	1 875.7	2 363.6	1 850.5	513.1	1.2	-489.1	-7.4	485.5	14 820.3	12.7	0.0
4th quarter	1 863.8	2 328.5	1 818.0	510.5	0.5	-465.3	24.5	432.4	14 914.9	12.3	-0.4
2011											
1st quarter	1 843.2	2 336.7	1 853.1	483.6	0.5	-494.0	-52.0	422.4	15 146.9	12.5	-0.1
2nd quarter	1 880.5	2 373.5	1 895.3	478.2	3.7	-496.7	-10.0	433.6	15 284.0	12.4	-0.3
3rd quarter	1 950.7	2 392.9	1 906.6	486.3	0.4	-442.7	-38.7	430.1	15 482.1	12.8	0.2
4th quarter	1 991.2	2 495.0	2 010.1	484.9	0.5	-504.2	-26.4	511.6	15 572.0	13.0	0.2

. . . = Not available.

Table 5-1B. Saving and Investment: Historical Data

(Billions of dollars, except as noted; quarterly data are at seasonally adjusted annual rates.)   **NIPA Tables 1.7.5, 5.1**

Year and quarter	Gross saving										Gross domestic investment and net lending, NIPAs				Net domestic invest-ment	Gross national income	Net saving as a percent-age of gross national income
	Total	Net saving			Consumption of fixed capital						Gross domestic investment			Net lending or net borrow-ing (-), NIPAs			
		Private	Government		Total	Private	Government				Total	Private	Govern-ment				
			Federal	State and local			Federal	State and local									
1929	19.3	7.1	1.0	1.5	9.7	8.7	0.2	0.7			19.3	16.5	2.8	0.8	9.6	103.6	9.3
1930	15.0	4.0	0.2	1.3	9.5	8.5	0.2	0.7			13.9	10.8	3.2	0.7	4.5	92.3	6.0
1931	8.3	0.7	-2.1	1.0	8.8	7.9	0.2	0.7			8.9	5.9	3.0	0.2	0.1	76.2	-0.6
1932	3.3	-3.7	-1.3	0.7	7.7	6.9	0.2	0.6			3.4	1.3	2.1	0.2	-4.3	58.8	-7.5
1933	3.3	-3.6	-0.9	0.4	7.4	6.5	0.2	0.7			3.7	1.7	1.9	0.2	-3.7	56.2	-7.4
1934	6.4	-0.4	-2.2	1.2	7.8	6.7	0.2	0.9			6.4	3.7	2.7	0.4	-1.4	65.9	-2.1
1935	9.6	2.6	-1.9	1.1	7.8	6.7	0.3	0.8			9.5	6.7	2.8	-0.1	1.7	73.9	2.5
1936	11.5	4.3	-3.2	2.3	8.1	6.9	0.3	0.9			12.8	8.6	4.1	-0.1	4.7	82.8	4.1
1937	16.2	5.0	0.2	2.0	9.0	7.7	0.4	1.0			15.9	12.2	3.8	0.2	7.0	92.3	7.8
1938	11.7	1.9	-1.3	2.0	9.2	7.8	0.4	1.0			11.3	7.1	4.2	1.2	2.0	85.8	2.9
1939	13.6	4.4	-2.1	2.0	9.3	7.8	0.4	1.0			13.8	9.3	4.5	1.0	4.6	91.2	4.7
1940	18.5	7.1	-0.3	2.0	9.7	8.1	0.5	1.1			18.0	13.6	4.4	1.5	8.3	100.6	8.7
1941	29.9	14.7	2.2	1.9	11.1	9.0	0.8	1.2			28.9	18.1	10.8	1.3	17.9	126.8	14.8
1942	39.8	33.3	-8.7	1.5	13.7	10.1	2.1	1.4			39.0	10.4	28.5	-0.1	25.3	163.2	16.0
1943	44.9	41.0	-14.1	1.5	16.5	10.3	4.8	1.5			45.2	6.1	39.1	-2.1	28.7	200.7	14.1
1944	39.9	45.6	-26.9	1.6	19.5	10.7	7.5	1.4			44.4	7.8	36.6	-2.0	24.9	217.5	9.4
1945	29.8	36.0	-28.9	1.6	21.1	11.0	8.7	1.4			35.0	10.8	24.1	-1.3	13.8	219.4	3.9
1946	38.4	18.8	-5.0	1.5	23.1	12.3	9.3	1.5			34.6	31.1	3.5	4.9	11.5	221.7	6.9
1947	46.6	13.2	5.3	1.4	26.6	16.1	8.8	1.8			39.6	35.0	4.6	9.3	12.9	242.9	8.2
1948	58.0	24.7	3.7	1.2	28.5	18.9	7.5	2.1			55.1	48.1	7.0	2.4	26.7	271.1	10.9
1949	45.6	20.6	-5.6	1.5	29.2	20.5	6.6	2.1			46.6	36.9	9.7	0.9	17.4	266.7	6.2
1950	60.6	23.8	5.6	1.3	29.9	22.0	5.8	2.1			63.9	54.1	9.8	-1.8	33.9	293.8	10.4
1951	75.1	29.0	9.7	2.6	33.8	25.2	6.1	2.6			77.8	60.2	17.6	0.9	44.0	337.6	12.2
1952	74.2	31.2	3.7	3.0	36.3	26.7	6.8	2.7			76.3	54.0	22.3	0.6	40.0	357.5	10.6
1953	75.1	31.2	1.8	3.5	38.6	28.2	7.6	2.8			80.4	56.4	24.0	-1.3	41.8	377.3	9.7
1954	73.4	31.2	-1.7	3.2	40.6	29.5	8.2	2.9			76.3	53.8	22.5	0.2	35.7	379.3	8.6
1947																	
1st quarter	46.6	13.4	6.0	1.6	25.6	14.6	9.3	1.7			38.0	33.7	4.3	9.4	12.4	237.3	8.8
2nd quarter	44.0	10.9	5.2	1.6	26.3	15.7	8.8	1.8			36.7	32.4	4.3	9.9	10.4	238.9	7.4
3rd quarter	45.1	14.8	2.0	1.1	27.1	16.6	8.6	1.9			37.4	32.7	4.7	10.1	10.3	243.2	7.4
4th quarter	50.6	13.7	8.0	1.3	27.6	17.4	8.3	1.9			46.2	41.0	5.1	7.8	18.5	252.3	9.1
1948																	
1st quarter	55.4	18.6	7.8	1.0	27.9	18.0	7.9	2.0			51.2	45.0	6.2	4.9	23.3	261.0	10.5
2nd quarter	59.1	24.5	5.1	1.2	28.3	18.6	7.6	2.1			54.8	48.1	6.7	3.0	26.5	270.1	11.4
3rd quarter	58.7	27.3	1.4	1.2	28.7	19.1	7.4	2.1			57.4	50.2	7.1	0.9	28.6	275.6	10.9
4th quarter	58.9	28.3	0.2	1.5	28.9	19.6	7.2	2.2			57.1	49.1	8.0	0.8	28.1	277.6	10.8
1949																	
1st quarter	51.1	23.7	-3.4	1.5	29.2	20.0	7.1	2.2			49.5	40.9	8.6	2.2	20.3	270.7	8.1
2nd quarter	44.1	19.9	-6.5	1.4	29.2	20.4	6.7	2.1			43.6	34.0	9.5	1.7	14.4	266.3	5.6
3rd quarter	46.0	21.7	-6.5	1.6	29.1	20.7	6.3	2.1			47.6	37.3	10.3	0.6	18.5	266.6	6.3
4th quarter	41.3	16.9	-6.1	1.3	29.2	21.0	6.1	2.1			45.5	35.2	10.4	-1.0	16.4	263.1	4.6
1950																	
1st quarter	48.7	27.0	-8.3	1.0	29.1	21.2	5.9	2.0			53.4	44.4	9.0	-1.0	24.3	272.7	7.2
2nd quarter	56.7	23.8	2.8	0.7	29.4	21.6	5.7	2.0			59.2	49.9	9.4	-1.3	29.8	284.5	9.6
3rd quarter	63.1	17.7	13.6	1.8	30.1	22.2	5.7	2.1			66.4	56.1	10.2	-2.7	36.3	302.9	10.9
4th quarter	74.1	26.9	14.2	1.8	31.2	23.1	5.9	2.3			76.5	65.9	10.6	-2.5	45.3	315.1	13.6
1951																	
1st quarter	70.8	18.4	17.3	2.7	32.5	24.1	6.0	2.4			75.0	62.1	13.0	-1.7	42.5	328.0	11.7
2nd quarter	77.5	31.5	10.1	2.5	33.5	24.9	6.0	2.5			81.1	64.8	16.2	0.3	47.6	334.6	13.2
3rd quarter	75.6	33.5	5.4	2.4	34.3	25.6	6.1	2.6			78.4	59.4	19.0	2.2	44.1	340.5	12.1
4th quarter	76.5	32.8	6.0	2.7	34.9	26.0	6.3	2.7			76.7	54.4	22.3	2.7	41.7	347.2	12.0
1952																	
1st quarter	77.1	31.9	6.9	2.9	35.4	26.3	6.5	2.6			77.1	55.2	21.9	3.5	41.7	349.7	11.9
2nd quarter	70.8	29.1	3.4	2.4	35.9	26.6	6.7	2.7			71.8	49.9	22.0	1.1	35.9	352.0	9.9
3rd quarter	73.2	32.1	1.1	3.3	36.6	26.9	6.9	2.8			76.4	53.9	22.5	-1.1	39.7	358.3	10.2
4th quarter	75.7	31.5	3.5	3.4	37.2	27.3	7.2	2.8			80.1	57.1	22.9	-1.2	42.9	370.1	10.4
1953																	
1st quarter	77.0	32.0	4.3	2.9	37.9	27.7	7.4	2.8			81.8	57.9	23.9	-1.4	43.9	376.9	10.4
2nd quarter	77.4	32.3	2.6	4.0	38.5	28.0	7.6	2.8			82.8	58.1	24.6	-1.8	44.3	380.5	10.2
3rd quarter	77.2	31.4	3.5	3.5	38.9	28.4	7.6	2.8			81.7	57.4	24.3	-1.2	42.8	379.6	10.1
4th quarter	68.9	29.1	-3.2	3.6	39.3	28.7	7.8	2.8			75.4	52.3	23.1	-0.9	36.1	372.1	7.9
1954																	
1st quarter	71.9	31.9	-3.4	3.6	39.8	29.0	8.0	2.8			75.3	51.5	23.8	-0.5	35.5	374.3	8.6
2nd quarter	72.0	30.3	-2.0	3.3	40.4	29.3	8.2	2.9			74.4	51.2	23.2	0.3	34.1	375.2	8.4
3rd quarter	72.6	30.2	-1.4	3.0	40.8	29.6	8.3	2.9			76.4	54.7	21.7	-0.1	35.5	379.1	8.4
4th quarter	77.0	32.6	0.0	3.1	41.4	29.9	8.5	3.0			79.2	57.8	21.4	0.9	37.8	388.7	9.2
1955																	
1st quarter	81.7	33.5	3.5	3.0	41.7	30.2	8.5	2.9			85.2	64.2	21.0	0.5	43.6	401.0	10.0
2nd quarter	88.1	35.9	6.7	3.3	42.2	30.7	8.5	3.0			90.0	68.1	21.9	-0.2	47.8	411.6	11.1
3rd quarter	89.1	37.4	4.8	3.8	43.1	31.3	8.7	3.2			90.7	70.0	20.7	0.8	47.6	419.5	11.0
4th quarter	93.1	37.3	7.7	3.9	44.2	32.1	8.8	3.2			94.1	73.9	20.3	0.4	49.9	427.1	11.5
1956																	
1st quarter	96.7	38.4	8.5	4.3	45.5	33.0	9.1	3.4			94.7	73.0	21.8	0.9	49.3	432.1	11.8
2nd quarter	97.7	39.9	6.6	4.5	46.6	34.0	9.2	3.5			93.7	71.4	22.2	2.2	47.0	438.8	11.6
3rd quarter	101.3	41.4	7.7	4.5	47.7	34.8	9.3	3.6			96.4	72.5	23.9	3.0	48.7	444.0	12.1
4th quarter	101.9	41.7	7.2	4.3	48.6	35.6	9.4	3.7			94.9	71.2	23.7	4.5	46.3	453.1	11.8

Table 5-1B. Saving and Investment: Historical Data—*Continued*

(Billions of dollars, except as noted; quarterly data are at seasonally adjusted annual rates.)   **NIPA Tables 1.7.5, 5.1**

Year and quarter	Gross saving Total	Net saving Private	Net saving Government Federal	Net saving Government State and local	Consumption of fixed capital Total	Consumption of fixed capital Private	Consumption of fixed capital Government Federal	Consumption of fixed capital Government State and local	Gross domestic investment Total	Gross domestic investment Private	Gross domestic investment Government	Net lending or net borrowing (-), NIPAs	Net domestic investment	Gross national income	Net saving as a percentage of gross national income
1957															
1st quarter	102.1	41.5	6.1	4.8	49.6	36.3	9.6	3.7	96.0	71.8	24.2	5.5	46.4	460.7	11.4
2nd quarter	102.0	42.9	4.3	4.3	50.5	37.0	9.7	3.9	95.8	71.9	23.9	4.8	45.3	463.9	11.1
3rd quarter	101.8	42.2	4.3	4.1	51.3	37.6	9.8	3.9	97.9	73.2	24.6	4.9	46.6	468.7	10.8
4th quarter	92.6	38.7	-1.6	3.6	51.9	38.2	9.9	3.9	89.6	64.9	24.7	3.6	37.7	463.4	8.8
1958															
1st quarter	88.8	37.2	-3.3	2.7	52.3	38.7	9.7	3.9	85.6	60.5	25.1	1.5	33.4	458.3	8.0
2nd quarter	84.4	37.3	-8.4	2.6	52.9	39.2	9.8	4.0	84.0	58.7	25.3	0.8	31.1	460.3	6.8
3rd quarter	91.0	41.3	-6.5	2.6	53.6	39.6	9.9	4.1	92.8	65.5	27.3	1.0	39.2	471.5	7.9
4th quarter	99.0	44.6	-3.6	3.6	54.2	40.1	10.0	4.1	101.5	73.2	28.2	-0.2	47.2	485.2	9.2
1959															
1st quarter	104.6	43.7	3.1	3.1	54.8	40.5	10.1	4.2	106.7	76.2	30.5	-1.5	51.9	497.5	10.0
2nd quarter	111.1	47.2	5.1	3.6	55.3	40.9	10.2	4.2	111.7	82.2	29.5	-2.1	56.5	512.6	10.9
3rd quarter	102.9	40.3	2.8	4.2	55.6	41.1	10.3	4.3	105.8	76.4	29.3	-0.6	50.1	509.9	9.3
4th quarter	105.7	43.4	2.0	4.3	55.9	41.3	10.4	4.3	107.1	79.3	27.8	-0.9	51.2	515.7	9.6
1960															
1st quarter	118.2	46.1	11.6	4.3	56.2	41.4	10.5	4.3	116.8	89.1	27.7	1.7	60.6	529.6	11.7
2nd quarter	110.8	42.0	8.2	4.2	56.4	41.5	10.5	4.4	107.2	79.7	27.5	2.5	50.8	530.2	10.3
3rd quarter	111.0	43.4	6.6	4.3	56.7	41.6	10.6	4.5	107.7	78.7	29.0	3.7	51.0	531.8	10.2
4th quarter	105.1	41.6	2.1	4.4	57.1	41.9	10.7	4.5	97.0	68.1	28.9	4.8	39.9	530.4	9.1
1961															
1st quarter	108.2	44.2	2.4	4.1	57.5	42.2	10.7	4.6	101.7	70.3	31.4	5.3	44.2	532.7	9.5
2nd quarter	110.2	47.5	0.7	4.0	57.9	42.5	10.8	4.6	105.7	75.8	30.0	4.0	47.8	542.9	9.6
3rd quarter	117.1	51.8	2.4	4.5	58.4	42.8	10.9	4.7	113.5	82.4	31.2	3.8	55.1	552.7	10.6
4th quarter	121.8	53.6	4.6	4.6	58.9	43.1	11.0	4.8	117.0	84.2	32.8	3.7	58.1	567.2	11.1
1962															
1st quarter	124.4	57.6	2.3	4.9	59.6	43.5	11.2	4.9	122.4	89.4	33.0	3.1	62.8	578.6	11.2
2nd quarter	123.9	56.7	2.1	5.0	60.1	43.9	11.3	5.0	120.6	87.9	32.7	4.8	60.4	585.8	10.9
3rd quarter	125.6	56.2	3.0	5.5	60.9	44.3	11.5	5.1	123.0	89.3	33.7	4.1	62.2	592.6	10.9
4th quarter	125.7	56.3	2.3	5.5	61.7	44.7	11.8	5.1	119.7	86.0	33.7	3.2	58.0	600.8	10.7
1963															
1st quarter	128.5	56.7	4.0	5.4	62.3	45.1	11.9	5.2	123.5	90.5	33.0	3.9	61.2	608.1	10.9
2nd quarter	133.1	58.3	6.2	5.5	63.0	45.6	12.1	5.3	125.0	92.2	32.8	5.3	62.0	618.3	11.3
3rd quarter	133.5	58.1	5.8	6.1	63.7	46.1	12.1	5.4	129.8	95.0	34.8	4.6	66.2	627.5	11.1
4th quarter	137.6	62.3	5.1	5.9	64.4	46.7	12.2	5.5	131.3	97.4	33.9	6.0	67.0	638.4	11.5
1964															
1st quarter	140.0	66.6	1.9	6.4	65.1	47.2	12.3	5.6	134.9	100.7	34.2	8.2	69.8	651.6	11.5
2nd quarter	140.3	70.8	-2.7	6.3	65.9	47.9	12.3	5.7	135.2	100.6	34.6	6.7	69.3	662.1	11.2
3rd quarter	143.6	69.1	1.2	6.5	66.8	48.6	12.3	5.8	137.2	102.5	34.8	7.6	70.5	674.3	11.4
4th quarter	149.7	72.4	3.1	6.4	67.7	49.4	12.4	5.9	139.5	104.6	34.9	7.3	71.7	683.2	12.0
1965															
1st quarter	157.2	74.6	7.5	6.2	68.8	50.3	12.5	6.0	149.9	115.7	34.2	5.7	81.1	702.6	12.6
2nd quarter	158.7	75.4	6.7	6.5	70.1	51.3	12.6	6.2	150.6	115.8	34.8	7.0	80.6	714.8	12.4
3rd quarter	158.8	81.4	-0.5	6.6	71.3	52.3	12.7	6.3	156.1	119.7	36.5	6.0	84.8	727.1	12.0
4th quarter	159.2	80.5	-0.7	6.8	72.7	53.5	12.7	6.4	158.5	121.8	36.7	5.9	85.9	747.1	11.6
1966															
1st quarter	167.5	80.8	4.9	7.7	74.1	54.7	12.8	6.6	170.4	131.7	38.7	4.7	96.3	768.2	12.2
2nd quarter	167.3	80.2	3.4	8.0	75.7	55.9	13.0	6.8	168.9	130.7	38.2	3.9	93.2	779.5	11.8
3rd quarter	167.3	80.6	1.5	8.0	77.2	57.1	13.2	7.0	170.4	130.2	40.3	2.7	93.2	792.3	11.4
4th quarter	172.8	87.5	-0.8	7.3	78.8	58.3	13.4	7.1	174.7	132.7	42.0	3.9	95.9	806.3	11.6
1967															
1st quarter	168.1	89.8	-9.6	7.5	80.4	59.6	13.5	7.3	172.8	129.3	43.4	4.4	92.4	814.0	10.8
2nd quarter	164.4	85.9	-10.4	6.9	82.0	60.9	13.7	7.4	165.7	123.7	42.0	3.6	83.7	822.5	10.0
3rd quarter	171.9	90.2	-8.5	6.4	83.8	62.2	14.0	7.6	171.7	128.5	43.2	3.2	87.9	839.7	10.5
4th quarter	177.9	93.9	-8.9	7.2	85.6	63.6	14.2	7.8	176.2	132.9	43.3	2.8	90.5	857.2	10.8
1968															
1st quarter	176.2	87.5	-6.0	7.2	87.5	65.1	14.4	8.1	180.3	137.2	43.1	1.7	92.8	879.8	10.1
2nd quarter	181.9	91.9	-7.5	8.2	89.4	66.6	14.6	8.2	187.4	143.4	44.0	2.2	98.1	902.4	10.3
3rd quarter	182.4	82.3	1.4	7.4	91.3	68.2	14.8	8.3	183.6	139.7	43.8	1.5	92.3	922.9	9.9
4th quarter	187.6	84.5	2.4	7.2	93.5	69.8	15.0	8.6	187.9	144.4	43.6	0.8	94.5	941.4	10.0
1969															
1st quarter	196.0	78.6	14.4	7.4	95.6	71.6	15.2	8.9	201.1	155.7	45.4	1.6	105.4	960.6	10.5
2nd quarter	196.4	79.3	11.4	7.8	98.0	73.4	15.3	9.2	199.1	155.7	43.4	0.6	101.1	979.0	10.1
3rd quarter	203.0	88.8	5.5	8.5	100.3	75.4	15.4	9.4	203.9	160.3	43.6	1.4	103.7	999.9	10.3
4th quarter	198.3	84.2	3.0	8.2	102.9	77.5	15.6	9.7	194.8	154.1	40.7	2.7	91.9	1 011.3	9.4
1970															
1st quarter	192.2	80.9	-2.5	8.2	105.6	79.8	15.8	10.0	193.5	150.7	42.8	3.8	87.9	1 018.3	8.5
2nd quarter	194.3	95.0	-16.2	7.7	107.8	81.4	16.0	10.4	196.5	153.9	42.6	5.2	88.7	1 032.2	8.4
3rd quarter	195.8	99.0	-19.7	7.1	109.4	82.5	16.2	10.7	200.1	156.1	44.1	3.5	90.7	1 049.2	8.2
4th quarter	189.0	96.6	-23.5	5.4	110.5	83.1	16.3	11.1	193.7	148.9	44.8	2.4	83.2	1 051.6	7.5
1971															
1st quarter	202.2	107.3	-23.9	5.0	113.8	86.0	16.5	11.4	212.9	171.3	41.7	4.3	99.1	1 090.4	8.1
2nd quarter	207.1	114.7	-30.4	6.0	116.7	88.5	16.5	11.7	220.6	178.8	41.8	0.1	103.9	1 113.1	8.1
3rd quarter	212.1	115.9	-29.5	6.5	119.2	90.8	16.5	11.9	225.7	183.4	42.3	-0.4	106.5	1 133.1	8.2
4th quarter	215.5	116.7	-31.0	8.4	121.3	92.8	16.4	12.2	220.5	179.2	41.3	-2.8	99.2	1 156.9	8.1

Table 5-1B. Saving and Investment: Historical Data—*Continued*

(Billions of dollars, except as noted; quarterly data are at seasonally adjusted annual rates.)   NIPA Tables 1.7.5, 5.1

Year and quarter	Gross saving Total	Net saving Private	Net saving Government Federal	Net saving Government State and local	Consumption of fixed capital Total	Consumption of fixed capital Private	Consumption of fixed capital Government Federal	Consumption of fixed capital Government State and local	Gross domestic investment Total	Gross domestic investment Private	Gross domestic investment Government	Net lending or net borrowing (-), NIPAs	Net domestic investment	Gross national income	Net saving as a percentage of gross national income
1972															
1st quarter	223.4	113.8	-22.9	9.1	123.5	94.5	16.6	12.4	235.5	193.2	42.3	-5.1	112.0	1 191.3	8.4
2nd quarter	225.2	109.1	-28.2	18.7	125.6	96.4	16.5	12.7	249.4	206.5	42.9	-4.8	123.8	1 214.2	8.2
3rd quarter	238.7	117.5	-17.1	10.1	128.2	98.7	16.6	12.9	253.5	212.4	41.1	-3.6	125.2	1 247.1	8.9
4th quarter	261.7	137.1	-31.4	24.6	131.3	101.3	16.8	13.3	262.7	218.4	44.3	-2.8	131.4	1 297.4	10.0
1973															
1st quarter	274.7	136.4	-15.2	18.9	134.6	104.1	16.8	13.7	280.0	232.5	47.5	2.2	145.4	1 338.2	10.5
2nd quarter	282.1	143.2	-15.2	15.7	138.4	107.4	17.0	14.1	292.8	246.0	46.7	5.4	154.3	1 367.0	10.5
3rd quarter	294.5	147.9	-10.6	14.6	142.7	111.1	17.1	14.5	287.4	241.8	45.6	12.4	144.7	1 399.2	10.8
4th quarter	317.4	162.7	-6.2	13.6	147.4	115.2	17.2	15.0	305.1	257.6	47.5	15.3	157.7	1 443.0	11.8
1974															
1st quarter	309.2	153.2	-8.9	11.8	153.1	119.8	17.4	15.9	295.6	244.1	51.5	16.5	142.5	1 460.7	10.7
2nd quarter	298.7	139.7	-11.4	10.6	159.7	124.8	17.8	17.1	308.8	252.3	56.5	2.6	149.1	1 488.4	9.3
3rd quarter	299.2	133.3	-11.3	10.0	167.2	130.4	18.5	18.4	303.4	245.4	58.0	0.3	136.2	1 524.4	8.7
4th quarter	300.2	147.0	-26.4	4.9	174.7	136.4	19.0	19.3	314.9	255.8	59.0	4.4	140.2	1 547.0	8.1
1975															
1st quarter	280.1	145.9	-48.5	0.6	182.1	143.0	19.2	19.9	281.3	218.7	62.6	17.8	99.2	1 561.8	6.3
2nd quarter	279.0	194.0	-105.7	2.6	188.1	148.6	19.4	20.1	274.8	216.8	58.1	21.4	86.7	1 599.3	5.7
3rd quarter	308.4	175.1	-63.7	3.6	193.4	153.3	19.9	20.3	301.7	237.8	63.9	18.3	108.3	1 663.7	6.9
4th quarter	320.0	183.6	-64.6	3.1	197.9	157.0	20.3	20.6	315.5	247.6	67.8	21.6	117.6	1 712.8	7.1
1976															
1st quarter	337.0	184.2	-54.3	5.7	201.4	159.7	20.8	20.9	345.2	274.8	70.4	13.1	143.8	1 766.2	7.7
2nd quarter	342.4	180.4	-50.0	6.5	205.5	163.2	21.1	21.2	357.4	291.6	65.8	8.9	151.9	1 796.9	7.6
3rd quarter	343.8	180.9	-53.6	6.3	210.2	167.3	21.6	21.3	361.8	296.5	65.3	2.4	151.7	1 834.4	7.3
4th quarter	344.7	174.9	-56.8	11.0	215.6	172.0	22.0	21.6	368.9	304.9	64.0	3.8	153.3	1 874.3	6.9
1977															
1st quarter	352.7	168.2	-47.2	9.6	222.1	177.5	22.6	22.0	393.5	326.6	66.9	-8.1	171.4	1 926.5	6.8
2nd quarter	391.8	192.9	-41.3	11.8	228.4	183.1	22.9	22.4	424.0	354.9	69.1	-8.9	195.6	2 002.6	8.2
3rd quarter	417.4	214.2	-47.3	15.7	234.8	189.0	23.0	22.8	446.0	378.4	67.6	-7.9	211.2	2 066.2	8.8
4th quarter	425.0	216.4	-48.7	15.5	241.8	195.0	23.6	23.2	452.0	385.5	66.5	-19.0	210.1	2 121.6	8.6
1978															
1st quarter	433.6	216.1	-48.6	16.9	249.2	201.3	24.3	23.6	463.2	396.8	66.4	-25.1	214.0	2 166.6	8.5
2nd quarter	471.2	219.0	-27.9	23.0	257.0	208.1	24.8	24.2	507.9	430.9	77.0	-12.9	250.8	2 269.6	9.4
3rd quarter	488.9	229.3	-21.9	16.1	265.4	215.3	25.3	24.8	532.0	451.4	80.7	-11.5	266.6	2 324.4	9.6
4th quarter	511.6	236.1	-17.2	18.7	274.0	223.1	25.6	25.4	557.0	472.8	84.2	-1.4	282.9	2 396.6	9.9
1979															
1st quarter	530.2	241.0	-8.7	14.5	283.3	231.3	25.9	26.1	560.2	481.1	79.1	-1.9	276.9	2 460.7	10.0
2nd quarter	530.0	233.6	-8.9	11.9	293.4	239.9	26.6	27.0	578.4	493.0	85.4	-2.8	285.0	2 510.2	9.4
3rd quarter	532.3	228.9	-14.6	13.9	304.0	248.7	27.4	27.9	591.6	497.9	93.7	2.3	287.5	2 574.1	8.9
4th quarter	540.4	237.6	-23.6	11.6	314.8	257.9	28.0	28.9	595.2	499.5	95.7	-2.7	280.4	2 643.7	8.5
1980															
1st quarter	534.2	231.3	-33.7	10.6	326.0	267.4	28.6	30.0	606.9	505.2	101.7	-10.8	281.0	2 700.0	7.7
2nd quarter	522.0	236.1	-57.6	5.5	337.9	277.1	29.7	31.1	570.3	470.4	99.9	9.7	232.4	2 705.6	6.8
3rd quarter	530.0	244.4	-71.8	7.5	349.9	287.2	30.4	32.4	541.3	443.5	97.9	28.0	191.4	2 780.1	6.5
4th quarter	584.7	274.1	-63.4	11.5	362.5	297.5	31.4	33.6	599.4	497.9	101.5	6.6	236.9	2 922.4	7.6
1981															
1st quarter	614.0	269.5	-42.6	11.7	375.3	308.1	32.4	34.8	670.7	563.1	107.6	1.5	295.4	3 024.4	7.9
2nd quarter	621.2	272.3	-46.9	8.0	387.7	318.4	33.4	35.9	656.9	551.4	105.5	0.0	269.2	3 078.4	7.6
3rd quarter	679.0	326.5	-54.6	7.7	399.5	328.4	34.3	36.8	698.0	592.8	105.2	6.9	298.5	3 183.7	8.8
4th quarter	670.1	339.4	-83.0	2.8	410.9	338.0	35.2	37.7	691.5	582.2	109.3	4.5	280.6	3 206.3	8.1
1982															
1st quarter	636.9	319.4	-103.9	-0.7	422.1	347.3	36.3	38.5	633.3	526.5	106.7	0.5	211.2	3 223.9	6.7
2nd quarter	661.7	341.2	-109.4	-1.4	431.3	354.7	37.3	39.3	643.6	530.8	112.8	17.3	212.3	3 282.5	7.0
3rd quarter	624.8	336.4	-147.2	-2.6	438.2	360.1	38.1	40.0	640.9	528.7	112.3	-14.2	202.8	3 307.3	5.6
4th quarter	562.5	304.6	-180.6	-4.0	442.6	363.6	38.7	40.3	600.4	482.9	117.4	-17.4	157.7	3 326.1	3.6
1983															
1st quarter	583.3	322.0	-176.4	-7.4	445.1	365.2	39.4	40.6	614.5	496.6	117.9	-8.0	169.3	3 391.8	4.1
2nd quarter	590.2	311.5	-172.6	3.0	448.4	367.6	40.1	40.7	662.0	542.2	119.7	-27.7	213.6	3 474.9	4.1
3rd quarter	590.5	316.7	-188.9	9.8	453.0	370.7	41.3	41.0	703.5	577.7	125.8	-48.0	250.5	3 559.9	3.9
4th quarter	645.5	340.5	-167.0	14.2	457.9	374.6	42.0	41.3	768.7	640.7	128.0	-56.9	310.8	3 661.5	5.1
1984															
1st quarter	722.9	393.3	-157.0	22.5	464.0	379.3	43.1	41.6	842.6	709.7	133.0	-78.6	378.6	3 803.2	6.8
2nd quarter	747.9	417.8	-167.3	26.7	470.6	384.4	44.1	42.1	872.2	735.1	137.1	-88.0	401.6	3 907.5	7.1
3rd quarter	771.9	448.4	-175.2	21.1	477.5	390.0	44.9	42.6	892.6	753.5	139.1	-90.5	415.0	3 983.1	7.4
4th quarter	770.8	446.6	-186.4	25.4	485.2	396.2	46.0	43.0	892.5	744.3	148.3	-103.5	407.3	4 048.9	7.1
1985															
1st quarter	755.8	388.5	-150.7	24.7	493.3	402.8	46.8	43.7	869.2	720.0	149.1	-89.6	375.9	4 119.5	6.4
2nd quarter	747.8	423.7	-201.0	24.0	501.1	409.4	47.4	44.3	893.3	735.3	157.9	-111.5	392.2	4 170.2	5.9
3rd quarter	719.0	365.8	-178.0	21.7	509.5	416.1	48.5	44.9	892.2	727.2	165.0	-121.4	382.7	4 230.6	5.0
4th quarter	730.8	378.6	-184.7	19.0	517.9	422.8	49.4	45.7	925.3	762.2	163.1	-135.3	407.4	4 286.5	5.0
1986															
1st quarter	744.5	375.9	-184.2	26.9	525.9	429.6	49.9	46.4	928.9	763.8	165.1	-128.4	403.0	4 349.9	5.0
2nd quarter	718.3	369.2	-205.7	20.2	534.5	436.1	51.1	47.4	923.5	753.0	170.5	-142.0	389.0	4 376.3	4.2
3rd quarter	683.1	328.7	-210.9	22.5	542.7	442.3	52.2	48.3	913.6	732.5	181.1	-150.3	370.9	4 429.5	3.2
4th quarter	691.4	305.0	-177.7	13.3	550.7	448.3	53.1	49.3	913.0	736.7	176.2	-150.4	362.3	4 484.0	3.1

Table 5-1B. Saving and Investment: Historical Data—*Continued*

(Billions of dollars, except as noted; quarterly data are at seasonally adjusted annual rates.)   **NIPA Tables 1.7.5, 5.1**

Year and quarter	Gross saving									Gross domestic investment and net lending, NIPAs				Net domestic invest-ment	Gross national income	Net saving as a percent-age of gross national income
	Total	Net saving			Consumption of fixed capital					Gross domestic investment			Net lending or net borrow-ing (-), NIPAs			
		Private	Government		Total	Private	Government			Total	Private	Govern-ment				
			Federal	State and local			Federal	State and local								
1987																
1st quarter	733.2	349.3	-181.9	7.4	558.4	454.0	54.2	50.1		943.8	765.0	178.9	-151.1	385.4	4 565.5	3.8
2nd quarter	758.5	300.2	-127.8	19.9	566.2	460.5	54.7	51.0		951.3	767.6	183.7	-154.5	385.1	4 666.9	4.1
3rd quarter	793.7	346.3	-139.0	11.2	575.1	467.7	55.5	51.9		957.4	769.5	187.9	-154.2	382.2	4 772.9	4.6
4th quarter	843.6	398.3	-148.7	9.4	584.6	475.7	56.3	52.6		1 024.4	837.8	186.7	-157.2	439.8	4 879.2	5.3
1988																
1st quarter	859.2	399.3	-147.9	12.3	595.5	484.4	57.5	53.5		979.1	797.6	181.5	-127.0	383.6	4 980.9	5.3
2nd quarter	896.6	416.4	-137.9	12.1	605.9	493.0	58.6	54.3		1 006.7	820.4	186.3	-110.1	400.8	5 082.4	5.7
3rd quarter	920.5	412.8	-130.0	21.6	616.2	501.4	59.5	55.2		1 012.0	825.7	186.3	-106.6	395.8	5 178.9	5.9
4th quarter	929.7	418.2	-137.8	22.9	626.5	509.6	60.8	56.1		1 033.1	842.6	190.4	-119.8	406.5	5 291.0	5.7
1989																
1st quarter	964.4	415.9	-115.4	27.4	636.4	517.6	61.8	57.0		1 075.2	884.1	191.1	-106.8	438.8	5 379.8	6.1
2nd quarter	921.3	383.6	-134.9	26.1	646.4	525.6	62.7	58.0		1 073.2	878.2	195.1	-93.7	426.9	5 418.3	5.1
3rd quarter	912.4	375.2	-140.8	21.6	656.5	533.6	63.8	59.1		1 072.5	870.3	202.2	-81.8	416.0	5 480.0	4.7
4th quarter	898.5	371.2	-144.7	5.4	666.6	541.6	64.9	60.1		1 069.6	867.3	202.3	-88.5	403.0	5 529.8	4.2
1990																
1st quarter	905.3	384.5	-171.3	15.3	676.8	549.5	66.1	61.2		1 092.4	880.0	212.4	-90.9	415.6	5 641.2	4.1
2nd quarter	941.1	422.2	-176.7	9.0	686.6	557.0	67.1	62.5		1 096.2	882.5	213.7	-73.0	409.7	5 746.2	4.4
3rd quarter	910.9	382.3	-172.0	4.4	696.1	564.2	68.2	63.8		1 082.6	866.8	215.8	-82.5	386.5	5 787.8	3.7
4th quarter	913.2	397.6	-185.8	-3.9	705.3	571.0	69.6	64.7		1 035.6	814.6	221.0	-82.7	330.3	5 827.7	3.6
1991																
1st quarter	998.2	448.5	-157.4	-6.6	713.8	577.4	70.8	65.6		1 004.4	787.9	216.4	42.1	290.5	5 865.4	4.8
2nd quarter	942.5	446.3	-217.1	-8.1	721.3	583.2	71.5	66.6		1 005.3	784.1	221.3	14.2	284.0	5 911.4	3.7
3rd quarter	922.1	436.8	-240.5	-2.4	728.3	588.3	72.6	67.4		1 027.2	805.3	222.0	-29.1	299.0	5 965.1	3.3
4th quarter	942.4	473.1	-258.7	-6.1	734.1	592.8	73.3	68.0		1 055.8	834.3	221.5	-17.0	321.8	6 027.1	3.5
1992																
1st quarter	944.1	501.9	-296.0	-0.5	738.7	596.6	73.6	68.5		1 037.3	810.2	227.1	-22.0	298.6	6 150.0	3.3
2nd quarter	960.3	519.7	-302.2	-0.4	743.2	599.4	74.3	69.5		1 090.0	865.4	224.6	-39.8	346.8	6 235.2	3.5
3rd quarter	908.6	480.2	-313.2	-4.8	746.3	601.3	74.8	70.2		1 098.1	876.8	221.3	-46.8	351.8	6 280.0	2.6
4th quarter	916.1	465.5	-298.6	0.1	749.2	602.3	75.7	71.2		1 126.1	906.7	219.4	-68.6	376.9	6 380.6	2.6
1993																
1st quarter	937.7	498.0	-312.1	-10.2	762.0	612.7	77.0	72.3		1 147.2	931.3	215.9	-59.2	385.3	6 428.1	2.7
2nd quarter	965.0	470.6	-275.3	-3.6	773.3	622.3	77.5	73.4		1 163.2	942.3	220.9	-73.9	390.0	6 528.4	2.9
3rd quarter	944.0	446.2	-282.2	-3.7	783.6	631.2	78.2	74.2		1 162.4	943.4	219.0	-77.0	378.8	6 583.0	2.4
4th quarter	987.0	431.4	-251.3	13.7	793.2	639.4	78.7	75.2		1 218.3	996.4	221.8	-107.6	425.0	6 711.4	2.9
1994																
1st quarter	1 047.8	476.6	-236.4	5.4	802.2	646.8	79.0	76.4		1 254.2	1 043.6	210.6	-92.3	452.0	6 830.4	3.6
2nd quarter	1 089.3	475.7	-202.9	3.7	812.7	655.4	79.9	77.4		1 324.3	1 106.9	217.3	-111.9	511.5	6 942.1	4.0
3rd quarter	1 101.7	482.8	-220.6	15.2	824.3	665.3	80.2	78.7		1 321.8	1 092.9	229.0	-121.9	497.6	7 054.5	3.9
4th quarter	1 139.8	515.5	-221.7	8.6	837.5	676.3	81.2	79.9		1 372.5	1 145.7	226.8	-137.9	535.1	7 174.8	4.2
1995																
1st quarter	1 196.8	556.0	-221.4	10.9	851.4	688.6	81.5	81.3		1 391.6	1 160.6	231.0	-118.7	540.2	7 262.9	4.8
2nd quarter	1 191.5	535.9	-206.2	-2.3	864.1	699.9	81.6	82.6		1 367.7	1 132.7	235.1	-118.4	503.6	7 332.8	4.5
3rd quarter	1 223.9	549.3	-210.3	9.3	875.7	710.3	81.7	83.7		1 357.6	1 126.2	231.4	-101.0	482.0	7 438.3	4.7
4th quarter	1 263.9	545.1	-186.7	18.9	886.7	719.8	82.0	84.9		1 389.6	1 156.7	233.0	-84.0	503.0	7 533.2	5.0
1996																
1st quarter	1 284.0	561.6	-194.3	20.5	896.2	728.3	82.0	85.9		1 409.3	1 170.0	239.3	-102.3	513.1	7 653.3	5.1
2nd quarter	1 325.0	549.7	-149.5	18.6	906.3	737.8	81.9	86.7		1 470.2	1 227.8	242.4	-108.7	563.9	7 793.2	5.4
3rd quarter	1 363.9	559.5	-138.3	25.1	917.7	748.1	81.9	87.7		1 525.7	1 279.8	245.9	-132.8	608.0	7 890.1	5.7
4th quarter	1 404.5	557.6	-110.8	27.8	929.9	759.3	81.9	88.7		1 532.4	1 283.1	249.3	-113.6	602.6	8 040.2	5.9
1997																
1st quarter	1 452.4	571.3	-92.4	30.0	943.5	771.4	82.4	89.8		1 574.4	1 320.6	253.8	-131.5	630.9	8 169.3	6.2
2nd quarter	1 519.8	600.6	-71.0	33.1	957.1	783.5	82.5	91.0		1 638.0	1 385.0	253.0	-101.7	680.9	8 290.6	6.8
3rd quarter	1 560.5	585.4	-35.6	40.4	970.3	795.8	82.5	92.0		1 668.8	1 414.9	253.9	-122.7	698.5	8 446.9	7.0
4th quarter	1 570.0	585.5	-41.5	41.7	984.3	808.1	82.7	93.5		1 682.9	1 434.1	248.8	-163.4	698.6	8 572.4	6.8
1998																
1st quarter	1 638.3	587.5	7.9	45.6	997.3	820.6	82.3	94.4		1 741.6	1 494.9	246.6	-164.3	744.3	8 686.8	7.4
2nd quarter	1 640.8	565.6	20.7	42.5	1 011.9	834.0	82.7	95.3		1 730.1	1 471.5	258.6	-195.5	718.2	8 827.4	7.1
3rd quarter	1 682.1	556.8	52.3	45.0	1 027.9	848.3	82.9	96.8		1 785.8	1 512.7	273.0	-224.1	757.8	8 977.0	7.3
4th quarter	1 656.4	503.6	53.4	54.4	1 045.0	863.5	83.3	98.2		1 837.1	1 564.0	273.2	-235.2	792.1	9 093.4	6.7
1999																
1st quarter	1 746.1	559.8	79.1	44.1	1 063.2	879.6	84.0	99.5		1 893.8	1 617.3	276.5	-244.0	830.7	9 267.3	7.4
2nd quarter	1 696.1	479.4	96.1	37.4	1 083.2	897.1	84.7	101.3		1 888.4	1 604.7	283.7	-279.3	805.2	9 367.2	6.5
3rd quarter	1 674.3	425.1	103.5	41.6	1 104.2	916.0	85.4	102.8		1 933.6	1 644.5	289.1	-313.4	829.4	9 483.9	6.0
4th quarter	1 715.6	427.8	116.6	44.2	1 127.1	936.2	86.1	104.8		1 999.6	1 699.5	300.2	-348.9	872.6	9 691.0	6.1
2000																
1st quarter	1 827.5	419.4	205.3	51.2	1 151.6	957.7	87.2	106.7		1 992.2	1 688.8	303.4	-386.0	840.6	9 961.4	6.8
2nd quarter	1 807.8	405.6	175.0	52.8	1 174.4	978.0	87.5	109.0		2 111.8	1 810.9	300.9	-391.3	937.4	10 070.5	6.3
3rd quarter	1 820.9	404.8	181.8	38.6	1 195.8	997.0	88.1	110.8		2 097.0	1 791.7	305.3	-430.1	901.1	10 201.6	6.1
4th quarter	1 744.5	327.6	178.8	22.6	1 215.4	1 014.7	88.3	112.4		2 105.1	1 797.4	307.8	-435.5	889.7	10 259.5	5.2
2001																
1st quarter	1 802.4	394.6	159.4	15.0	1 233.5	1 031.2	88.3	114.0		2 013.7	1 701.3	312.4	-423.1	780.3	10 417.8	5.5
2nd quarter	1 753.9	390.6	119.0	-5.7	1 250.0	1 045.9	88.7	115.4		2 030.3	1 699.4	330.9	-385.6	780.3	10 459.9	4.8
3rd quarter	1 661.5	524.4	-104.4	-22.9	1 264.4	1 059.0	88.8	116.6		1 984.7	1 670.4	314.2	-360.2	720.3	10 421.7	3.8
4th quarter	1 564.9	349.8	-12.0	-50.0	1 277.1	1 070.3	88.7	118.1		1 907.2	1 576.6	330.6	-345.9	630.1	10 466.3	2.7

Table 5-1B. Saving and Investment: Historical Data—*Continued*

(Billions of dollars, except as noted; quarterly data are at seasonally adjusted annual rates.)

NIPA Tables 1.7.5, 5.1

Year and quarter	Gross saving Total	Net saving Private	Net saving Government Federal	Net saving Government State and local	Consumption of fixed capital Total	Consumption of fixed capital Private	Consumption of fixed capital Government Federal	Consumption of fixed capital Government State and local	Gross domestic investment Total	Gross domestic investment Private	Gross domestic investment Government	Net lending or net borrowing (-), NIPAs	Net domestic investment	Gross national income	Net saving as a percentage of gross national income
2002															
1st quarter	1 602.6	575.6	-205.4	-55.9	1 288.3	1 079.8	88.8	119.6	1 965.8	1 628.0	337.9	-406.9	677.6	10 593.0	3.0
2nd quarter	1 580.3	588.4	-249.7	-57.9	1 299.5	1 089.4	88.9	121.2	1 988.9	1 648.1	340.7	-454.3	689.4	10 680.0	2.6
3rd quarter	1 519.4	518.8	-262.9	-47.0	1 310.5	1 098.8	89.1	122.6	1 997.2	1 650.4	346.8	-457.8	686.7	10 728.5	1.9
4th quarter	1 541.5	568.4	-293.0	-55.6	1 321.7	1 108.1	89.8	123.7	2 009.8	1 661.3	348.5	-489.4	688.2	10 852.6	2.0
2003															
1st quarter	1 495.3	544.0	-300.6	-81.3	1 333.2	1 117.4	90.2	125.5	2 020.4	1 671.5	349.0	-533.9	687.3	10 947.3	1.5
2nd quarter	1 537.9	619.3	-375.0	-52.3	1 345.9	1 128.6	90.7	126.6	2 030.1	1 678.5	351.6	-523.7	684.3	11 103.2	1.7
3rd quarter	1 532.3	648.9	-451.4	-25.5	1 360.4	1 141.5	91.1	127.8	2 106.8	1 745.1	361.8	-515.9	746.4	11 259.8	1.5
4th quarter	1 645.1	643.1	-378.5	3.8	1 376.8	1 156.2	91.4	129.1	2 184.4	1 823.6	360.8	-499.5	807.6	11 466.6	2.3
2004															
1st quarter	1 656.0	691.3	-409.3	-22.7	1 396.7	1 172.8	92.6	131.3	2 214.9	1 853.6	361.3	-536.8	818.3	11 677.9	2.2
2nd quarter	1 729.2	715.1	-384.4	-21.0	1 419.5	1 190.7	94.1	134.7	2 328.2	1 956.0	372.2	-614.7	908.7	11 864.2	2.6
3rd quarter	1 799.8	720.6	-361.6	-3.6	1 444.4	1 209.8	95.5	139.1	2 379.2	2 001.3	377.9	-620.0	934.8	12 086.1	2.9
4th quarter	1 769.8	648.1	-362.5	13.8	1 470.4	1 230.2	97.1	143.2	2 441.3	2 063.3	378.0	-715.7	970.8	12 239.1	2.4
2005															
1st quarter	1 860.5	628.5	-288.9	25.2	1 495.7	1 251.9	98.8	145.0	2 508.5	2 130.8	377.6	-703.5	1 012.8	12 515.3	2.9
2nd quarter	1 883.3	628.3	-288.1	18.9	1 524.2	1 276.1	99.7	148.3	2 502.7	2 115.3	387.4	-704.5	978.5	12 680.7	2.8
3rd quarter	1 909.2	615.3	-287.4	25.3	1 556.0	1 302.9	100.9	152.2	2 563.3	2 166.7	396.6	-673.5	1 007.3	12 916.2	2.7
4th quarter	2 022.5	666.1	-267.7	34.4	1 589.6	1 332.3	102.4	154.9	2 682.7	2 276.3	406.4	-829.3	1 093.1	13 148.6	3.3
2006															
1st quarter	2 170.9	697.6	-207.3	62.6	1 618.0	1 357.4	103.8	156.8	2 746.2	2 336.6	409.7	-794.7	1 128.3	13 456.2	4.1
2nd quarter	2 176.5	694.5	-229.4	63.2	1 648.2	1 381.1	106.0	161.2	2 779.5	2 352.1	427.4	-813.3	1 131.3	13 614.0	3.9
3rd quarter	2 181.2	679.1	-215.5	42.4	1 675.2	1 403.2	107.8	164.2	2 761.0	2 333.4	427.6	-853.6	1 085.8	13 768.2	3.7
4th quarter	2 255.6	681.3	-163.0	35.9	1 701.3	1 423.9	108.7	168.7	2 722.0	2 286.5	435.6	-740.3	1 020.7	13 929.2	4.0
2007															
1st quarter	2 093.8	531.6	-201.6	29.8	1 733.9	1 449.6	110.5	173.8	2 721.2	2 277.4	443.8	-794.2	987.2	13 995.4	2.6
2nd quarter	2 080.1	530.1	-237.4	29.8	1 757.6	1 468.6	112.0	177.0	2 784.7	2 329.6	455.0	-765.3	1 027.0	14 118.5	2.3
3rd quarter	2 006.0	483.0	-265.2	10.0	1 778.2	1 484.8	113.2	180.2	2 773.6	2 313.4	460.2	-682.5	995.4	14 185.3	1.6
4th quarter	2 010.8	507.9	-276.7	-20.7	1 800.3	1 501.8	114.9	183.6	2 727.3	2 260.5	466.8	-621.6	927.0	14 356.5	1.5
2008															
1st quarter	2 010.1	624.0	-388.8	-42.5	1 817.4	1 515.0	116.7	185.8	2 660.6	2 185.7	475.0	-709.7	843.2	14 511.3	1.3
2nd quarter	1 925.5	876.9	-764.4	-29.8	1 842.7	1 534.6	119.2	189.0	2 661.3	2 165.4	495.9	-707.1	818.5	14 567.6	0.6
3rd quarter	1 907.1	778.3	-639.1	-101.8	1 869.6	1 555.5	121.3	192.8	2 594.3	2 086.3	508.0	-672.1	724.7	14 602.7	0.3
4th quarter	1 790.1	680.2	-661.7	-114.9	1 886.5	1 566.5	122.7	197.3	2 422.8	1 913.0	509.8	-605.5	536.3	14 171.0	-0.7
2009															
1st quarter	1 698.7	925.6	-993.9	-118.1	1 885.2	1 562.6	123.2	199.4	2 123.2	1 620.1	503.1	-382.8	238.0	13 984.3	-1.3
2nd quarter	1 577.0	1 086.9	-1 303.0	-75.3	1 868.4	1 545.2	124.1	199.1	2 005.0	1 493.8	511.2	-338.1	136.6	13 904.1	-2.1
3rd quarter	1 496.1	1 021.3	-1 305.4	-74.0	1 854.1	1 530.5	125.1	198.5	1 990.7	1 481.2	509.6	-391.2	136.6	13 980.2	-2.6
4th quarter	1 617.5	1 074.7	-1 269.4	-44.8	1 857.1	1 531.4	126.4	199.2	2 089.9	1 592.2	497.7	-399.9	232.8	14 186.5	-1.7
2010															
1st quarter	1 718.4	1 163.9	-1 271.8	-32.3	1 858.6	1 529.6	127.9	201.1	2 193.1	1 702.3	490.8	-482.4	334.5	14 454.5	-1.0
2nd quarter	1 840.9	1 280.3	-1 278.0	-28.2	1 866.9	1 534.4	129.4	203.1	2 316.5	1 809.7	506.9	-482.7	449.7	14 670.6	-0.2
3rd quarter	1 883.2	1 267.9	-1 257.7	-5.2	1 878.2	1 542.6	130.5	205.0	2 363.6	1 850.5	513.1	-489.1	485.5	14 820.3	0.0
4th quarter	1 839.3	1 266.0	-1 287.3	-35.5	1 896.1	1 557.0	132.3	206.8	2 328.5	1 818.0	510.5	-465.3	432.4	14 914.9	-0.4
2011															
1st quarter	1 895.2	1 239.2	-1 201.1	-57.2	1 914.3	1 570.5	134.6	209.2	2 336.7	1 853.1	483.6	-494.0	422.4	15 146.9	-0.1
2nd quarter	1 890.5	1 266.2	-1 275.4	-40.2	1 939.9	1 590.5	136.8	212.6	2 373.5	1 895.3	478.2	-496.7	433.6	15 284.0	-0.3
3rd quarter	1 989.4	1 270.4	-1 160.7	-83.2	1 962.8	1 607.6	139.2	216.1	2 392.9	1 906.6	486.3	-442.7	430.1	15 482.1	0.2
4th quarter	2 017.6	1 229.7	-1 114.1	-81.5	1 983.4	1 622.9	141.0	219.5	2 495.0	2 010.1	484.9	-504.2	511.6	15 572.0	0.2

Table 5-2. Gross Private Fixed Investment by Type

(Billions of dollars, quarterly data are at seasonally adjusted annual rates.)   **NIPA Table 5.3.5**

Year and quarter	Total gross private fixed investment	Nonresidential									
		Total	Structures						Equipment and software		
			Total	Commercial and health care	Manufac-turing	Power and communi-cation	Mining exploration, shafts, and wells	Other non-residential structures	Total	Information processing equipment and software	
										Total	Computers and peripheral equipment
1955	64.0	39.0	15.2	3.4	2.3	3.3	2.5	3.7	23.9	2.8	. . .
1956	68.1	44.5	18.2	4.2	3.2	4.1	2.7	4.0	26.3	3.4	. . .
1957	69.7	47.5	19.0	4.1	3.6	4.5	2.6	4.1	28.6	4.0	. . .
1958	64.9	42.5	17.6	4.2	2.4	4.4	2.4	4.2	24.9	3.6	. . .
1959	74.6	46.5	18.1	4.6	2.1	4.3	2.5	4.7	28.4	4.0	0.0
1960	75.7	49.4	19.6	4.8	2.9	4.4	2.3	5.2	29.8	4.9	0.2
1961	75.2	48.8	19.7	5.5	2.8	4.1	2.3	5.0	29.1	5.3	0.3
1962	82.0	53.1	20.8	6.2	2.8	4.1	2.5	5.2	32.3	5.7	0.3
1963	88.1	56.0	21.2	6.1	2.9	4.4	2.3	5.6	34.8	6.5	0.7
1964	97.2	63.0	23.7	6.8	3.6	4.8	2.4	6.2	39.2	7.4	0.9
1965	109.0	74.8	28.3	8.2	5.1	5.4	2.4	7.2	46.5	8.5	1.2
1966	117.7	85.4	31.3	8.3	6.6	6.3	2.5	7.8	54.0	10.7	1.7
1967	118.7	86.4	31.5	8.2	6.0	7.1	2.4	7.8	54.9	11.3	1.9
1968	132.1	93.4	33.6	9.4	6.0	8.3	2.6	7.3	59.9	11.9	1.9
1969	147.3	104.7	37.7	11.7	6.8	8.7	2.8	7.8	67.0	14.6	2.4
1970	150.4	109.0	40.3	12.5	7.0	10.2	2.8	7.8	68.7	16.6	2.7
1971	169.9	114.1	42.7	14.9	6.3	11.0	2.7	7.9	71.5	17.3	2.8
1972	198.5	128.8	47.2	17.6	5.9	12.1	3.1	8.6	81.7	19.5	3.5
1973	228.6	153.3	55.0	19.8	7.9	13.8	3.5	9.9	98.3	23.1	3.5
1974	235.4	169.5	61.2	20.6	10.0	15.1	5.2	10.3	108.2	27.0	3.9
1975	236.5	173.7	61.4	17.7	10.6	15.7	7.4	10.1	112.4	28.5	3.6
1976	274.8	192.4	65.9	18.1	10.1	18.2	8.6	11.0	126.4	32.7	4.4
1977	339.0	228.7	74.6	20.3	11.1	19.3	11.5	12.5	154.1	39.2	5.7
1978	412.2	280.6	93.6	25.3	16.2	21.4	15.4	15.2	187.0	48.7	7.6
1979	474.9	333.9	117.7	33.5	22.0	24.6	19.0	18.5	216.2	58.5	10.2
1980	485.6	362.4	136.2	41.0	20.5	27.3	27.4	20.0	226.2	68.8	12.5
1981	542.6	420.0	167.3	48.3	25.4	30.0	42.5	21.2	252.7	81.5	17.1
1982	532.1	426.5	177.6	55.8	26.1	29.6	44.8	21.3	248.9	88.3	18.9
1983	570.1	417.2	154.3	55.8	19.5	25.8	30.0	23.3	262.9	100.1	23.9
1984	670.2	489.6	177.4	70.6	20.9	26.5	31.3	28.1	312.2	121.5	31.6
1985	714.4	526.2	194.5	84.1	24.1	26.5	27.9	31.8	331.7	130.3	33.7
1986	739.9	519.8	176.5	80.9	21.0	28.3	15.7	30.7	343.3	136.8	33.4
1987	757.8	524.1	174.2	80.8	21.2	25.4	13.1	33.7	349.9	141.2	35.8
1988	803.1	563.8	182.8	86.3	23.2	25.0	15.7	32.5	381.0	154.9	38.0
1989	847.3	607.7	193.7	88.3	28.8	27.5	14.9	34.3	414.0	172.6	43.1
1990	846.4	622.4	202.9	87.5	33.6	26.3	17.9	37.6	419.5	177.2	38.6
1991	803.3	598.2	183.6	68.9	31.4	31.6	18.5	33.2	414.6	182.9	37.7
1992	848.5	612.1	172.6	64.5	29.0	33.9	14.2	31.0	439.6	199.9	44.0
1993	932.5	666.6	177.2	69.4	23.6	33.2	16.6	34.5	489.4	217.6	47.9
1994	1 033.5	731.4	186.8	75.4	28.9	31.2	16.4	34.9	544.6	235.2	52.4
1995	1 112.9	810.0	207.3	83.1	35.5	33.1	15.0	40.6	602.8	263.0	66.1
1996	1 209.4	875.4	224.6	91.5	38.2	29.2	16.8	48.9	650.8	290.1	72.8
1997	1 317.7	968.6	250.3	104.3	37.6	28.8	22.4	57.2	718.3	330.3	81.4
1998	1 447.1	1 061.1	275.1	116.0	40.5	34.2	22.3	62.2	786.0	366.1	87.9
1999	1 580.7	1 154.9	283.9	125.4	35.1	40.4	18.3	64.7	871.0	417.1	97.2
2000	1 717.7	1 268.7	318.1	139.3	37.6	48.1	23.7	69.4	950.5	478.2	103.2
2001	1 700.2	1 227.8	329.7	137.3	37.8	51.1	34.6	68.9	898.1	452.5	87.6
2002	1 634.9	1 125.4	282.8	119.4	22.7	51.0	30.2	59.3	842.7	419.8	79.7
2003	1 713.3	1 135.7	281.9	115.1	21.4	48.1	38.4	58.9	853.8	430.9	77.6
2004	1 903.6	1 223.0	306.7	125.3	23.7	42.8	51.9	62.9	916.4	455.3	80.2
2005	2 122.3	1 347.3	351.8	135.9	29.9	45.2	77.1	63.7	995.6	475.3	78.9
2006	2 267.2	1 505.3	433.7	156.4	35.1	53.3	114.2	74.6	1 071.7	505.2	84.9
2007	2 266.1	1 637.5	524.9	181.9	43.7	77.6	130.9	90.7	1 112.6	536.6	87.0
2008	2 128.7	1 656.3	586.3	181.9	57.4	90.5	151.7	104.8	1 070.0	536.4	84.9
2009	1 707.6	1 353.0	449.9	126.8	61.2	90.1	87.9	83.8	903.0	504.0	75.6
2010	1 728.2	1 390.1	374.4	92.7	40.8	79.9	100.9	60.2	1 015.7	543.8	93.8
2011	1 870.0	1 532.5	409.5	90.4	38.4	90.4	133.5	56.8	1 123.0	567.9	103.1
2009											
1st quarter	1 799.6	1 430.6	527.4	150.5	69.1	89.9	123.9	94.0	903.2	491.9	71.3
2nd quarter	1 694.3	1 351.9	461.4	134.6	65.9	90.8	79.9	90.1	890.5	492.7	71.6
3rd quarter	1 678.3	1 324.3	424.8	117.5	58.4	93.4	75.1	80.5	899.5	507.3	74.6
4th quarter	1 658.3	1 305.1	386.1	104.5	51.5	86.5	72.9	70.7	918.9	524.2	84.9
2010											
1st quarter	1 658.0	1 318.7	361.2	96.3	46.6	73.0	81.7	63.6	957.5	528.4	86.6
2nd quarter	1 731.6	1 377.1	370.2	92.8	43.2	77.8	95.3	61.2	1 006.9	539.8	94.1
3rd quarter	1 743.8	1 416.5	376.6	91.7	38.5	77.6	109.6	59.2	1 039.9	548.0	95.3
4th quarter	1 779.3	1 447.9	389.6	90.1	34.8	91.1	117.1	56.6	1 058.3	559.3	99.3
2011											
1st quarter	1 791.1	1 460.5	379.5	85.6	32.8	83.4	122.6	55.2	1 081.0	557.9	95.6
2nd quarter	1 841.7	1 506.0	405.2	90.7	36.9	87.3	135.3	55.1	1 100.8	567.6	103.9
3rd quarter	1 905.8	1 568.7	424.8	93.8	40.3	92.3	140.9	57.5	1 143.9	567.4	105.1
4th quarter	1 941.4	1 594.8	428.3	91.4	43.5	98.7	135.2	59.6	1 166.5	578.7	107.8

. . . = Not available.

Table 5-2. Gross Private Fixed Investment by Type—*Continued*

(Billions of dollars, quarterly data are at seasonally adjusted annual rates.)   NIPA Table 5.3.5

Year and quarter	Nonresidential—*Continued* Equipment and software—*Continued*					Residential						
	Information processing equipment and software—*Continued*		Industrial equipment	Transportation equipment	Other nonresidential equipment	Total	Residential structures					Residential equipment
	Software [1]	Other information processing					Total	Permanent site			Other residential structures	
								Total	Single family	Multifamily		
1955	...	2.8	7.3	7.5	6.3	25.0	24.6	18.6	...	...	6.0	0.4
1956	...	3.4	8.8	7.4	6.7	23.6	23.1	16.5	...	...	6.6	0.5
1957	...	4.0	9.6	8.3	6.7	22.2	21.7	15.1	...	...	6.6	0.5
1958	...	3.6	8.2	6.1	6.9	22.3	21.9	15.4	13.1	2.3	6.4	0.5
1959	0.0	4.0	8.5	8.3	7.6	28.1	27.5	19.7	16.7	3.0	7.9	0.6
1960	0.1	4.6	9.4	8.5	7.1	26.3	25.8	17.5	14.9	2.6	8.3	0.5
1961	0.2	4.8	8.8	8.0	7.0	26.4	25.9	17.4	14.1	3.3	8.5	0.5
1962	0.2	5.1	9.3	9.8	7.5	29.0	28.4	19.9	15.1	4.8	8.5	0.5
1963	0.4	5.4	10.0	9.4	8.8	32.1	31.5	22.4	16.0	6.4	9.1	0.6
1964	0.5	5.9	11.4	10.6	9.9	34.3	33.6	24.1	17.6	6.4	9.5	0.6
1965	0.7	6.7	13.7	13.2	11.0	34.2	33.5	23.8	17.8	6.0	9.7	0.7
1966	1.0	8.0	16.2	14.5	12.7	32.3	31.6	21.8	16.6	5.2	9.8	0.7
1967	1.2	8.2	16.9	14.3	12.4	32.4	31.6	21.5	16.8	4.7	10.1	0.7
1968	1.3	8.7	17.3	17.6	13.0	38.7	37.9	26.7	19.5	7.2	11.1	0.9
1969	1.8	10.4	19.1	18.9	14.4	42.6	41.6	29.2	19.7	9.5	12.4	1.0
1970	2.3	11.6	20.3	16.2	15.6	41.4	40.2	27.1	17.5	9.5	13.2	1.1
1971	2.4	12.2	19.5	18.4	16.3	55.8	54.5	38.7	25.8	12.9	15.8	1.3
1972	2.8	13.2	21.4	21.8	19.0	69.7	68.1	50.1	32.8	17.2	18.0	1.5
1973	3.2	16.3	26.0	26.6	22.6	75.3	73.6	54.6	35.2	19.4	19.0	1.7
1974	3.9	19.2	30.7	26.3	24.3	66.0	64.1	43.4	29.7	13.7	20.7	1.9
1975	4.8	20.2	31.3	25.2	27.4	62.7	60.8	36.3	29.6	6.7	24.5	1.9
1976	5.2	23.1	34.1	30.0	29.6	82.5	80.4	50.8	43.9	6.9	29.6	2.1
1977	5.5	28.0	39.4	39.3	36.3	110.3	107.9	72.2	62.2	10.0	35.7	2.4
1978	6.3	34.8	47.7	47.3	43.2	131.6	128.9	85.6	72.8	12.8	43.3	2.7
1979	8.1	40.2	56.2	53.6	47.9	141.0	137.8	89.3	72.3	17.0	48.6	3.2
1980	9.8	46.4	60.7	48.4	48.3	123.2	119.8	69.6	52.9	16.7	50.2	3.4
1981	11.8	52.5	65.5	50.6	55.2	122.6	118.9	69.4	52.0	17.5	49.5	3.6
1982	14.0	55.3	62.7	46.8	51.2	105.7	102.0	57.0	41.5	15.5	45.0	3.7
1983	16.4	59.8	58.9	53.5	50.4	152.9	148.6	95.0	72.5	22.4	53.7	4.2
1984	20.4	69.6	68.1	64.4	58.1	180.6	175.9	114.6	86.4	28.2	61.3	4.7
1985	23.8	72.9	72.5	69.0	59.9	188.2	183.1	115.9	87.4	28.5	67.2	5.1
1986	25.6	77.7	75.4	70.5	60.7	220.1	214.6	135.2	104.1	31.0	79.4	5.5
1987	29.0	76.4	76.7	68.1	63.9	233.7	227.9	142.7	117.2	25.5	85.2	5.8
1988	34.2	82.8	84.2	72.9	69.0	239.3	233.2	142.4	120.1	22.3	90.9	6.1
1989	41.9	87.6	93.3	67.9	80.2	239.5	233.4	143.2	120.9	22.3	90.1	6.1
1990	47.6	90.9	92.1	70.0	80.2	224.0	218.0	132.1	112.9	19.3	85.8	6.0
1991	53.7	91.5	89.3	71.5	70.8	205.1	199.4	114.6	99.4	15.1	84.8	5.7
1992	57.9	98.1	93.0	74.7	72.0	236.3	230.4	135.1	122.0	13.1	95.3	5.9
1993	64.3	105.4	102.2	89.4	80.2	266.0	259.9	150.9	140.1	10.8	109.0	6.1
1994	68.3	114.6	113.6	107.7	88.1	302.1	295.9	176.4	162.3	14.1	119.5	6.2
1995	74.6	122.3	129.0	116.1	94.7	302.9	296.5	171.4	153.5	17.9	125.1	6.3
1996	85.5	131.9	136.5	123.2	101.0	334.1	327.7	191.1	170.8	20.3	136.6	6.3
1997	107.5	141.4	140.4	135.5	112.1	349.1	342.8	198.1	175.2	22.9	144.7	6.3
1998	126.0	152.2	147.4	147.1	125.4	385.9	379.2	224.0	199.4	24.6	155.3	6.7
1999	157.3	162.5	149.1	174.4	130.4	425.8	418.5	251.3	223.8	27.4	167.2	7.3
2000	184.5	190.6	162.9	170.8	138.6	449.0	441.2	265.0	236.8	28.3	176.1	7.8
2001	186.6	178.4	151.9	154.2	139.5	472.4	464.4	279.4	249.1	30.3	185.0	8.0
2002	183.0	157.0	141.7	141.6	139.6	509.5	501.3	298.8	265.9	33.0	202.4	8.2
2003	191.3	162.0	142.6	132.9	147.5	577.6	569.1	345.7	310.6	35.1	223.4	8.5
2004	205.7	169.4	142.0	161.1	157.9	680.6	671.4	417.5	377.6	39.9	253.9	9.2
2005	218.0	178.4	159.6	181.7	178.9	775.0	765.2	480.8	433.5	47.3	284.4	9.8
2006	229.8	190.6	178.4	198.2	189.8	761.9	751.6	468.8	416.0	52.8	282.8	10.3
2007	245.0	204.6	193.0	190.2	192.8	628.7	618.4	354.1	305.2	49.0	264.3	10.3
2008	257.2	194.3	194.5	146.9	192.2	472.4	462.7	230.1	185.8	44.3	232.5	9.8
2009	253.2	175.2	156.2	77.8	165.1	354.7	345.9	133.9	105.3	28.5	212.1	8.7
2010	257.9	192.1	168.6	122.7	180.5	338.1	329.2	127.2	112.6	14.7	202.0	8.9
2011	273.2	191.6	195.7	157.8	201.6	337.5	328.4	121.4	106.9	14.6	207.0	9.1
2009												
1st quarter	250.3	170.3	162.6	72.2	176.4	369.0	360.1	149.9	112.1	37.8	210.2	8.9
2nd quarter	252.3	168.8	155.2	79.0	163.6	342.4	333.8	124.1	92.9	31.2	209.7	8.6
3rd quarter	252.6	180.0	153.2	78.8	160.3	353.9	345.3	130.0	105.0	25.0	215.3	8.6
4th quarter	257.6	181.7	153.6	81.2	159.9	353.2	344.5	131.4	111.3	20.1	213.1	8.7
2010												
1st quarter	254.8	187.0	154.5	104.4	170.2	339.3	330.5	130.4	114.4	16.1	200.0	8.8
2nd quarter	255.1	190.5	169.1	120.7	177.4	354.5	345.5	133.1	118.7	14.5	212.4	8.9
3rd quarter	258.6	194.0	172.9	132.8	186.3	327.3	318.4	124.7	110.7	14.0	193.7	8.9
4th quarter	263.2	196.8	178.0	133.1	187.9	331.3	322.5	120.7	106.6	14.1	201.8	8.9
2011												
1st quarter	265.1	197.3	185.0	145.4	192.7	330.6	321.7	120.5	106.9	13.5	201.3	8.8
2nd quarter	270.4	193.3	186.5	152.0	194.6	335.7	326.7	119.0	105.2	13.9	207.7	8.9
3rd quarter	275.5	186.8	201.2	163.1	212.3	337.0	327.8	121.5	106.3	15.1	206.4	9.2
4th quarter	281.8	189.2	209.9	170.9	206.9	346.5	337.2	124.7	109.1	15.7	212.5	9.3

[1]Excludes software "embedded," or bundled, in computers and other equipment.
... = Not available.

Table 5-3. Real Gross Private Fixed Investment by Type

(Billions of chained [2005] dollars, quarterly data are at seasonally adjusted annual rates.)   **NIPA Table 5.3.6**

Year and quarter	Total gross private fixed investment	Nonresidential							Equipment and software		
		Total	Structures						Total	Information processing equipment and software	
			Total	Commercial and health care	Manufac- turing	Power and communi- cation	Mining exploration, shafts, and wells	Other non- residential structures		Total	Computers and peripheral equipment [1]
1995	1 231.2	787.9	342.0	126.7	51.7	45.4	52.6	59.2	489.4	147.3	. . .
1996	1 341.6	861.5	361.4	136.5	54.4	39.0	56.1	69.6	541.4	176.5	. . .
1997	1 465.4	965.5	387.9	150.8	51.9	37.6	66.0	79.0	615.9	217.6	. . .
1998	1 624.4	1 081.4	407.7	160.2	53.7	44.2	57.7	83.2	705.2	267.1	. . .
1999	1 775.5	1 194.3	408.2	166.1	44.8	52.1	48.8	83.3	805.0	327.2	. . .
2000	1 906.8	1 311.3	440.0	177.2	46.2	60.1	61.0	85.8	889.2	386.2	. . .
2001	1 870.7	1 274.8	433.3	168.6	44.9	62.0	71.9	81.7	860.6	384.5	. . .
2002	1 791.5	1 173.7	356.6	142.8	26.2	60.5	52.6	68.9	824.2	373.9	. . .
2003	1 854.7	1 189.6	343.0	133.8	24.3	55.7	60.0	66.5	850.0	403.7	. . .
2004	1 992.5	1 263.0	346.7	137.1	25.5	46.2	69.9	67.4	917.3	443.1	. . .
2005	2 122.3	1 347.3	351.8	135.9	29.9	45.2	77.1	63.7	995.6	475.3	. . .
2006	2 172.7	1 455.5	384.0	144.2	33.0	48.7	88.3	69.6	1 071.1	516.3	. . .
2007	2 130.6	1 550.0	438.2	158.6	39.0	67.8	93.6	80.3	1 106.8	558.2	. . .
2008	1 978.6	1 537.6	466.4	152.7	48.6	74.0	101.5	90.4	1 059.4	569.7	. . .
2009	1 606.3	1 263.2	367.3	105.9	50.8	74.5	65.8	73.5	889.7	548.3	. . .
2010	1 648.4	1 319.2	309.1	80.0	34.6	63.2	76.7	54.2	1 019.4	602.6	. . .
2011	1 761.0	1 435.5	323.2	76.6	32.0	67.7	93.6	50.5	1 125.7	639.7	. . .
2002											
1st quarter	1 801.1	1 195.8	381.4	151.5	30.4	68.9	51.8	71.3	826.0	369.6	. . .
2nd quarter	1 794.1	1 176.6	360.7	144.6	27.2	61.4	50.1	70.8	823.7	372.9	. . .
3rd quarter	1 791.9	1 171.4	344.7	139.5	23.9	55.3	54.5	67.2	831.3	380.3	. . .
4th quarter	1 778.9	1 150.9	339.6	135.6	23.4	56.3	53.9	66.4	815.9	372.7	. . .
2003											
1st quarter	1 781.4	1 147.8	336.2	130.8	22.6	60.7	54.1	64.3	815.8	383.7	. . .
2nd quarter	1 827.8	1 179.5	346.3	132.3	24.7	57.8	60.7	68.2	837.7	389.4	. . .
3rd quarter	1 887.2	1 206.8	345.6	135.6	24.9	53.1	62.6	67.3	864.3	411.2	. . .
4th quarter	1 922.5	1 224.1	343.9	136.6	25.0	51.1	62.7	66.5	882.1	430.5	. . .
2004											
1st quarter	1 918.7	1 214.3	341.9	134.6	24.4	50.3	65.8	65.7	874.5	431.4	. . .
2nd quarter	1 977.9	1 247.1	345.9	139.8	23.7	43.1	70.6	68.4	902.6	438.7	. . .
3rd quarter	2 019.6	1 281.2	349.4	139.5	24.9	44.5	71.7	68.5	932.5	446.6	. . .
4th quarter	2 053.7	1 309.3	349.7	134.6	28.9	47.0	71.4	67.3	959.6	455.4	. . .
2005											
1st quarter	2 078.8	1 321.1	356.0	136.9	30.1	46.5	76.6	65.6	965.2	461.6	. . .
2nd quarter	2 115.8	1 340.6	354.6	136.3	29.2	45.1	81.2	62.8	985.8	470.9	. . .
3rd quarter	2 143.1	1 359.7	347.2	134.5	29.8	44.1	76.1	62.6	1 012.5	481.5	. . .
4th quarter	2 151.6	1 367.9	349.3	136.0	30.4	44.9	74.4	63.9	1 018.8	487.0	. . .
2006											
1st quarter	2 201.9	1 426.6	364.8	139.1	30.9	48.6	80.5	65.7	1 062.5	507.4	. . .
2nd quarter	2 191.9	1 452.4	383.7	143.6	33.2	46.9	89.3	70.0	1 068.4	511.0	. . .
3rd quarter	2 163.8	1 467.7	393.2	147.5	34.8	48.8	90.9	70.7	1 073.8	522.1	. . .
4th quarter	2 133.4	1 475.2	394.6	146.5	32.8	50.3	92.3	72.0	1 079.9	524.8	. . .
2007											
1st quarter	2 127.1	1 498.5	404.8	153.5	33.9	56.1	89.9	71.6	1 092.4	546.0	. . .
2nd quarter	2 145.6	1 537.5	430.6	158.4	35.6	64.0	94.0	79.0	1 102.9	548.5	. . .
3rd quarter	2 138.2	1 571.4	454.6	161.0	41.6	71.9	97.5	83.5	1 109.8	558.5	. . .
4th quarter	2 111.5	1 592.3	462.9	161.3	44.7	79.1	93.0	87.1	1 121.9	579.7	. . .
2008											
1st quarter	2 066.4	1 589.1	463.8	159.8	45.1	79.6	92.8	89.0	1 117.2	583.0	. . .
2nd quarter	2 039.1	1 580.0	474.4	157.8	48.6	74.5	102.2	92.2	1 094.6	583.3	. . .
3rd quarter	1 973.5	1 539.2	469.9	153.1	49.8	69.6	105.4	92.2	1 056.8	571.7	. . .
4th quarter	1 835.4	1 442.3	457.5	140.2	50.9	72.1	105.6	88.3	969.0	540.7	. . .
2009											
1st quarter	1 665.5	1 312.9	415.3	122.2	55.5	72.5	86.6	80.3	883.7	529.9	. . .
2nd quarter	1 589.8	1 257.6	375.4	111.2	54.2	74.9	60.7	78.6	874.2	535.5	. . .
3rd quarter	1 592.6	1 247.0	354.9	100.4	49.7	78.2	58.5	71.7	888.0	553.7	. . .
4th quarter	1 577.5	1 235.2	323.7	89.7	43.7	72.2	57.3	63.4	912.9	574.1	. . .
2010											
1st quarter	1 582.0	1 253.3	301.5	83.0	39.7	59.6	63.6	57.2	958.8	581.2	. . .
2nd quarter	1 654.0	1 308.0	306.9	80.2	36.8	62.0	73.0	55.2	1 010.1	596.1	. . .
3rd quarter	1 663.5	1 343.6	310.1	79.2	32.6	60.8	83.0	53.5	1 044.1	608.5	. . .
4th quarter	1 693.9	1 371.9	318.0	77.5	29.4	70.6	87.2	50.9	1 064.5	624.5	. . .
2011											
1st quarter	1 699.0	1 378.9	305.9	73.4	27.8	63.8	88.9	49.4	1 086.9	625.0	. . .
2nd quarter	1 736.7	1 413.2	321.9	77.3	31.0	65.7	95.6	49.1	1 103.5	638.4	. . .
3rd quarter	1 790.4	1 465.6	332.9	79.3	33.5	68.8	97.4	51.0	1 145.7	640.2	. . .
4th quarter	1 817.9	1 484.2	332.1	76.5	35.7	72.6	92.5	52.5	1 166.6	655.1	. . .

[1] See notes and definitions.
. . . = Not available.

Table 5-3. Real Gross Private Fixed Investment by Type—Continued

(Billions of chained [2005] dollars, quarterly data are at seasonally adjusted annual rates.)

NIPA Table 5.3.6

Year and quarter	Nonresidential—Continued					Residential						
	Equipment and software—Continued					Total	Residential structures					Residential equipment
	Information processing equipment and software—Continued		Industrial equipment	Transportation equipment	Other nonresidential equipment		Total	Permanent site			Other residential structures	
	Software 2	Other information processing						Total	Single family	Multifamily		
1995	66.9	90.1	145.5	131.5	110.6	456.1	450.1	268.7	240.2	28.3	180.9	5.9
1996	78.5	98.7	150.9	136.8	114.8	492.5	486.8	293.9	262.4	31.3	192.6	5.9
1997	101.7	107.2	154.1	148.2	125.9	501.8	496.3	295.5	261.6	33.7	200.2	5.8
1998	122.8	120.7	160.8	162.0	138.8	540.4	534.5	323.5	290.1	33.4	210.6	6.2
1999	151.5	134.6	161.8	190.3	142.4	574.2	567.5	347.6	311.5	36.0	219.8	6.9
2000	172.4	162.0	175.8	186.2	150.4	580.0	572.6	350.4	315.0	35.4	222.1	7.4
2001	173.7	157.0	162.8	169.6	149.3	583.3	575.6	352.5	315.4	36.9	223.1	7.6
2002	173.4	142.7	151.9	154.2	148.2	613.8	605.9	366.6	327.7	38.9	239.0	7.9
2003	185.6	155.1	151.6	140.4	155.0	664.3	655.9	402.5	362.6	39.9	253.2	8.4
2004	204.6	168.1	147.4	162.3	164.4	729.5	720.1	449.1	406.1	43.0	271.0	9.4
2005	218.0	178.4	159.6	181.7	178.9	775.0	765.2	480.8	433.5	47.3	284.4	9.8
2006	227.1	192.8	172.9	196.5	185.5	718.2	708.1	438.8	391.1	47.6	269.3	10.1
2007	240.9	208.4	179.9	185.8	184.2	584.2	574.2	326.6	284.0	42.2	248.2	10.0
2008	250.8	202.4	172.9	142.7	177.8	444.4	434.9	216.8	178.4	37.1	218.8	9.7
2009	249.1	186.1	137.1	70.7	145.6	345.6	336.9	130.2	105.5	23.6	207.3	8.8
2010	256.1	207.3	146.6	119.3	162.6	330.8	321.5	125.2	114.7	12.0	196.8	9.5
2011	271.8	209.6	165.2	150.4	179.2	326.3	316.6	118.7	108.1	11.8	198.5	10.0
2002												
1st quarter	169.2	142.7	154.2	163.1	144.5	598.7	590.8	355.3	316.6	38.5	235.1	7.9
2nd quarter	173.7	143.2	150.2	155.1	149.6	613.4	605.4	366.6	327.2	39.3	238.5	7.9
3rd quarter	177.6	143.7	152.0	152.7	149.3	616.9	609.1	370.2	331.0	39.1	238.6	7.9
4th quarter	173.2	141.4	151.2	145.9	149.2	626.4	618.4	374.4	335.8	38.6	243.7	7.9
2003												
1st quarter	177.2	146.5	150.4	131.5	151.2	632.4	624.5	382.4	342.9	39.4	242.0	7.9
2nd quarter	179.1	150.1	156.2	142.5	151.5	646.8	638.5	387.5	348.2	39.3	250.8	8.2
3rd quarter	189.4	158.1	152.0	144.0	157.8	679.7	671.1	408.2	367.6	40.6	262.7	8.6
4th quarter	196.6	165.7	148.0	143.7	159.6	698.2	689.3	432.0	391.6	40.4	257.5	8.8
2004												
1st quarter	199.1	166.0	141.9	142.5	158.2	704.5	695.4	434.6	393.9	40.7	260.8	9.1
2nd quarter	200.4	170.0	145.2	156.8	161.7	731.0	721.7	448.9	406.5	42.4	272.8	9.3
3rd quarter	206.6	168.7	149.7	169.0	167.2	738.4	728.9	456.3	412.0	44.3	272.6	9.4
4th quarter	212.5	167.6	152.7	181.1	170.6	744.2	734.5	456.7	412.0	44.7	277.8	9.7
2005												
1st quarter	213.4	174.5	156.2	174.3	173.2	757.8	748.1	469.7	423.9	45.8	278.4	9.7
2nd quarter	218.6	176.1	154.4	180.1	180.3	775.4	765.6	477.6	430.2	47.3	288.1	9.8
3rd quarter	219.9	181.8	160.7	189.7	180.5	783.3	773.5	483.9	435.9	48.1	289.6	9.8
4th quarter	220.1	181.2	167.2	182.7	181.7	783.5	773.5	492.1	444.1	48.0	281.3	10.1
2006												
1st quarter	222.4	193.9	165.1	202.6	187.3	775.2	764.9	490.3	442.4	47.9	274.5	10.3
2nd quarter	224.8	191.9	176.2	194.1	187.0	740.0	730.0	456.9	409.4	47.5	273.0	10.1
3rd quarter	228.5	193.7	174.7	193.7	183.4	697.3	687.3	421.4	374.6	46.8	265.9	10.1
4th quarter	232.8	191.7	175.6	195.5	184.3	660.2	650.2	386.6	338.0	48.2	263.9	10.0
2007												
1st quarter	238.9	200.9	172.6	195.1	179.9	631.3	621.3	361.4	314.0	46.8	260.4	10.1
2nd quarter	239.2	204.1	185.0	184.1	185.8	611.4	601.5	345.2	301.8	43.0	256.9	10.0
3rd quarter	241.1	208.0	185.4	181.3	185.6	570.7	560.7	318.8	278.0	40.3	242.5	10.0
4th quarter	244.2	220.5	176.5	182.6	185.6	523.4	513.5	281.2	242.1	38.5	232.9	10.1
2008												
1st quarter	251.0	211.8	176.9	180.6	180.0	481.3	471.6	248.5	209.6	38.0	223.8	9.9
2nd quarter	251.4	209.8	175.6	158.2	181.1	462.8	453.0	232.7	193.2	38.3	221.1	10.0
3rd quarter	251.9	203.3	173.1	133.6	181.9	437.8	428.3	207.4	168.4	37.5	221.5	9.6
4th quarter	248.8	184.8	165.8	98.3	168.3	395.8	386.9	178.8	142.4	34.5	208.6	9.1
2009												
1st quarter	244.8	180.0	142.8	65.5	154.4	354.9	346.2	143.1	109.8	31.1	203.7	8.8
2nd quarter	247.8	179.8	136.5	69.8	143.5	334.3	325.9	121.0	93.3	25.9	205.4	8.6
3rd quarter	249.8	190.8	134.5	70.6	142.3	348.2	339.6	128.4	106.9	20.9	211.8	8.8
4th quarter	253.9	193.7	134.5	76.7	142.3	344.8	336.0	128.3	112.2	16.5	208.3	9.1
2010												
1st quarter	252.0	200.3	135.1	101.8	153.8	330.8	321.7	127.5	115.6	13.1	194.8	9.3
2nd quarter	252.9	204.8	147.3	117.6	160.5	348.2	338.9	132.0	121.8	11.9	207.4	9.6
3rd quarter	257.2	209.9	150.1	129.1	167.1	321.1	311.8	123.2	113.1	11.5	189.1	9.6
4th quarter	262.4	214.4	153.7	128.9	168.9	323.1	313.6	118.2	108.1	11.5	195.9	9.8
2011												
1st quarter	263.7	215.2	158.1	139.6	174.0	321.1	311.5	118.0	108.4	11.0	194.0	9.8
2nd quarter	268.9	211.5	157.7	144.6	173.8	324.4	314.8	116.6	106.7	11.3	198.6	9.9
3rd quarter	274.1	204.3	169.0	155.2	187.9	325.4	315.7	118.8	107.6	12.3	197.4	10.0
4th quarter	280.6	207.3	176.1	162.1	181.0	334.5	324.6	121.4	109.8	12.7	203.8	10.2

2Excludes software "embedded," or bundled, in computers and other equipment.

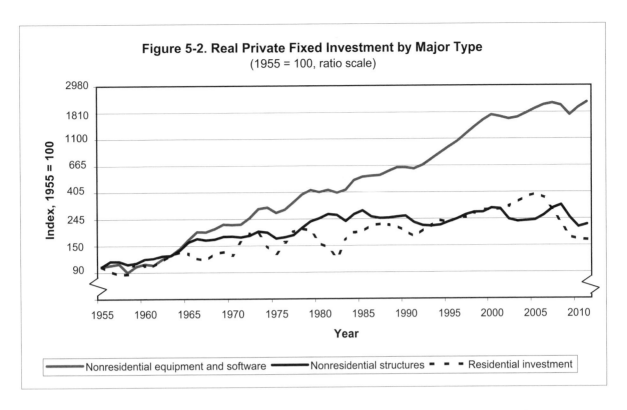

Figure 5-2. Real Private Fixed Investment by Major Type
(1955 = 100, ratio scale)

- Between 1955 and 2006, which was the recent high point for total real (constant-dollar) investment, the quantity of real gross private fixed investment increased nearly eightfold, with an average annual growth rate of 4.1 percent. Every major type of investment grew in real terms between those two years, but as Figure 5-2 indicates, by far the fastest-growing category has been nonresidential equipment and software, which includes computers, other information processing equipment, and computer software. By 2011, equipment and software purchases reached new highs, while residential investment continued to decline and nonresidential structures recovered modestly. (Table 5-4)

- Between 2006 and 2009, total investment fell 26 percent in real terms—a collapse unprecedented in the postwar period. As of 2011, only one-quarter of that aggregate loss had been recovered. In 2011, nonresidential structures were down 31 percent from their 2008 high, and residential investment was 58 percent below its volume in 2005, with home construction down 75 percent. (Table 5-4)

Table 5-4. Chain-Type Quantity Indexes for Private Fixed Investment by Type

(Index numbers, 2005 = 100, quarterly data are seasonally adjusted.) NIPA Table 5.3.3

Year and quarter	Total gross private fixed investment	Nonresidential									
		Total	Structures						Equipment and software		
			Total	Commercial and health care	Manufac-turing	Power and communi-cation	Mining exploration, shafts, and wells	Other non-residential structures	Total	Information processing equipment and software	
										Total	Computers and peripheral equipment
1955	13.1	9.9	42.0	22.9	66.8	53.8	62.3	51.1	5.2	0.2	. . .
1956	13.2	10.4	46.4	25.9	87.8	62.9	60.3	50.6	5.3	0.2	. . .
1957	13.0	10.6	46.4	24.6	93.1	65.3	56.9	50.6	5.5	0.3	. . .
1958	12.1	9.4	43.9	25.9	64.2	62.8	53.2	52.9	4.7	0.2	. . .
1959	13.8	10.2	44.9	28.1	57.2	60.2	54.6	58.5	5.2	0.3	0.0
1960	13.9	10.7	48.5	29.9	77.6	60.8	51.3	64.9	5.5	0.3	0.0
1961	13.9	10.7	49.2	34.1	75.9	57.0	52.2	63.4	5.4	0.4	0.0
1962	15.1	11.6	51.4	38.0	76.7	57.3	54.8	64.7	6.0	0.4	0.0
1963	16.3	12.2	52.0	36.8	76.9	61.1	51.4	68.5	6.5	0.5	0.0
1964	17.9	13.7	57.4	40.0	92.5	66.6	55.1	75.1	7.3	0.5	0.0
1965	19.7	16.1	66.6	46.9	127.9	73.6	54.4	84.5	8.6	0.6	0.0
1966	20.8	18.1	71.1	45.8	158.9	84.0	51.6	87.6	10.0	0.8	0.0
1967	20.5	17.9	69.3	44.0	139.8	91.9	49.3	85.8	10.0	0.9	0.0
1968	21.9	18.7	70.3	48.2	134.6	102.1	49.6	75.8	10.6	1.0	0.0
1969	23.2	20.1	74.1	55.6	141.6	102.1	51.7	75.2	11.5	1.2	0.0
1970	22.8	20.0	74.3	56.3	136.7	111.7	48.6	70.7	11.4	1.3	0.0
1971	24.5	20.0	73.1	61.5	112.9	112.6	45.0	66.3	11.5	1.4	0.0
1972	27.4	21.8	75.4	67.2	98.6	117.4	48.3	67.0	13.0	1.6	0.0
1973	29.9	25.0	81.5	70.3	122.2	125.0	51.5	72.2	15.4	1.9	0.0
1974	28.1	25.2	79.8	65.9	139.2	117.0	61.3	66.1	15.8	2.2	0.0
1975	25.0	22.7	71.4	51.3	133.5	107.6	71.5	58.3	14.3	2.2	0.0
1976	27.5	23.8	73.1	50.6	123.3	117.3	77.2	61.2	15.2	2.5	0.0
1977	31.5	26.5	76.1	53.3	126.6	115.5	87.2	64.5	17.4	3.0	0.1
1978	35.3	30.5	87.1	60.7	168.8	121.0	99.4	73.3	20.1	3.9	0.1
1979	37.3	33.5	98.1	72.4	207.4	125.6	105.9	80.5	21.9	4.7	0.2
1980	34.8	33.4	103.8	79.6	173.5	126.8	148.8	78.2	21.1	5.5	0.3
1981	35.6	35.3	112.2	86.2	197.0	130.0	173.0	75.7	22.0	6.3	0.5
1982	33.1	34.0	110.3	93.9	190.2	122.8	159.9	71.4	20.8	6.8	0.6
1983	35.5	33.6	98.4	91.1	137.6	105.6	132.4	75.4	22.0	7.9	0.9
1984	41.5	39.5	112.1	110.9	142.3	107.9	150.5	88.3	26.3	10.0	1.5
1985	43.7	42.1	120.1	128.1	159.2	106.7	134.1	97.2	28.0	11.2	1.8
1986	44.2	40.9	106.9	119.0	133.8	113.9	78.6	91.3	28.5	12.1	2.1
1987	44.5	40.9	103.9	114.6	130.4	101.3	76.8	96.8	28.9	12.8	2.7
1988	45.9	43.0	104.5	118.1	137.6	95.5	84.2	90.2	31.1	14.2	3.1
1989	47.3	45.4	106.6	116.6	164.9	99.2	76.2	92.1	33.4	16.2	3.7
1990	46.3	45.6	108.2	112.0	186.7	92.3	88.0	97.8	33.4	17.1	3.7
1991	43.3	43.2	96.2	87.0	172.0	109.6	86.1	84.8	32.5	18.0	4.0
1992	45.9	44.6	90.4	80.8	157.9	116.2	71.2	78.6	34.9	20.7	5.4
1993	49.8	48.5	89.8	84.1	124.0	108.6	82.8	84.8	39.2	23.5	7.0
1994	54.5	52.9	91.4	88.0	146.8	98.4	80.5	83.0	43.9	26.4	8.7
1995	58.0	58.5	97.2	93.2	173.1	100.5	68.3	92.9	49.2	31.0	13.1
1996	63.2	63.9	102.7	100.4	182.0	86.5	72.8	109.2	54.4	37.1	18.9
1997	69.0	71.7	110.3	111.0	173.8	83.3	85.6	123.9	61.9	45.8	27.4
1998	76.5	80.3	115.9	117.9	179.7	97.8	74.9	130.5	70.8	56.2	39.8
1999	83.7	88.6	116.0	122.2	149.9	115.4	63.4	130.7	80.9	68.8	56.6
2000	89.8	97.3	125.1	130.4	154.6	133.1	79.1	134.6	89.3	81.3	68.6
2001	88.1	94.6	123.2	124.0	150.3	137.3	93.3	128.2	86.4	80.9	70.3
2002	84.4	87.1	101.4	105.1	87.7	133.9	68.2	108.2	82.8	78.7	73.7
2003	87.4	88.3	97.5	98.4	81.3	123.3	77.9	104.4	85.4	84.9	80.3
2004	93.9	93.7	98.6	100.9	85.3	102.3	90.6	105.8	92.1	93.2	89.5
2005	100.0	100.0	100.0	100.0	100.0	100.0	100.0	100.0	100.0	100.0	100.0
2006	102.4	108.0	109.2	106.1	110.3	107.8	114.5	109.2	107.6	108.6	123.1
2007	100.4	115.0	124.6	116.7	130.3	150.1	121.5	126.0	111.2	117.4	140.4
2008	93.2	114.1	132.6	112.4	162.6	163.8	131.7	141.9	106.4	119.9	151.5
2009	75.7	93.8	104.4	77.9	169.9	164.9	85.4	115.3	89.4	115.4	146.6
2010	77.7	97.9	87.9	58.8	115.8	140.1	99.5	85.1	102.4	126.8	191.3
2011	83.0	106.5	91.9	56.4	107.0	150.0	121.4	79.3	113.1	134.6	223.6
2009											
1st quarter	78.5	97.4	118.1	89.9	185.7	160.6	112.3	126.0	88.8	111.5	133.7
2nd quarter	74.9	93.3	106.7	81.8	181.2	165.8	78.8	123.3	87.8	112.7	137.7
3rd quarter	75.0	92.6	100.9	73.9	166.3	173.3	75.9	112.5	89.2	116.5	146.1
4th quarter	74.3	91.7	92.0	66.0	146.3	159.9	74.4	99.5	91.7	120.8	169.1
2010											
1st quarter	74.5	93.0	85.7	61.0	132.7	132.1	82.5	89.8	96.3	122.3	173.8
2nd quarter	77.9	97.1	87.3	59.0	123.1	137.2	94.7	86.7	101.5	125.4	190.8
3rd quarter	78.4	99.7	88.2	58.3	109.2	134.7	107.7	83.9	104.9	128.0	195.1
4th quarter	79.8	101.8	90.4	57.0	98.4	156.3	113.2	79.9	106.9	131.4	205.5
2011											
1st quarter	80.1	102.3	87.0	54.0	92.9	141.2	115.4	77.6	109.2	131.5	202.0
2nd quarter	81.8	104.9	91.5	56.9	103.7	145.6	124.1	77.1	110.8	134.3	223.7
3rd quarter	84.4	108.8	94.6	58.3	111.9	152.3	126.3	80.1	115.1	134.7	230.2
4th quarter	85.7	110.2	94.4	56.2	119.3	160.8	120.0	82.4	117.2	137.8	238.6

. . . = Not available.

Table 5-4. Chain-Type Quantity Indexes for Private Fixed Investment by Type—*Continued*

(Index numbers, 2005 = 100, quarterly data are seasonally adjusted.)   **NIPA Table 5.3.3**

Year and quarter	Nonresidential—*Continued*					Residential						
	Equipment and software—*Continued*					Total	Residential structures					Residential equipment
	Information processing equipment and software—*Continued*		Industrial equipment	Transportation equipment	Other nonresidential equipment		Total	Permanent site			Other residential structures	
	Software [1]	Other information processing						Total	Single family	Multifamily		
1955	...	3.0	31.2	18.8	21.5	25.8	26.5	33.3	...	...	16.1	7.2
1956	...	3.4	34.4	16.9	22.2	23.7	24.3	28.8	...	...	17.3	8.0
1957	...	3.9	34.9	18.0	21.0	22.2	22.8	26.2	...	...	17.4	8.0
1958	...	3.5	29.1	13.1	21.3	22.5	23.0	26.9	25.1	38.8	17.0	8.5
1959	0.0	3.8	29.5	17.4	22.8	28.2	28.9	34.3	31.9	49.9	20.6	9.8
1960	0.0	4.4	31.8	17.9	21.0	26.2	26.8	30.3	28.2	43.9	21.5	9.2
1961	0.1	4.6	30.1	17.0	20.8	26.2	26.9	30.1	26.8	55.3	21.9	9.2
1962	0.1	4.9	31.6	20.9	22.1	28.8	29.5	34.3	28.5	80.4	22.0	9.8
1963	0.1	5.1	34.2	20.2	25.7	32.1	33.0	38.9	30.5	107.9	23.8	10.9
1964	0.2	5.6	38.6	22.9	28.5	34.0	34.9	41.6	33.4	107.2	24.6	11.7
1965	0.2	6.3	45.5	28.7	31.7	33.0	33.8	39.7	32.7	96.4	24.6	13.1
1966	0.4	7.5	52.4	31.6	35.6	30.1	30.7	34.9	29.1	80.8	24.2	13.4
1967	0.4	7.5	52.6	30.5	33.6	29.1	29.7	33.2	28.5	70.2	24.1	13.7
1968	0.5	7.7	51.5	36.7	34.1	33.1	33.7	39.1	31.3	101.4	25.3	16.3
1969	0.6	8.9	55.0	38.2	36.4	34.1	34.6	40.2	29.8	126.1	25.9	18.6
1970	0.8	9.6	55.8	31.3	37.9	32.0	32.4	36.3	25.9	123.4	26.2	20.3
1971	0.9	9.7	51.2	33.8	37.8	40.8	41.4	49.0	35.9	157.1	29.8	22.7
1972	1.0	10.3	55.2	39.3	42.9	48.1	48.7	59.3	42.7	196.7	32.7	27.2
1973	1.2	12.5	65.3	47.2	50.1	47.8	48.3	59.0	41.7	202.2	31.9	30.7
1974	1.3	13.8	70.3	42.8	49.4	37.9	38.1	42.7	32.0	130.2	31.1	31.2
1975	1.6	13.3	59.6	36.8	45.8	33.0	33.1	32.7	29.2	58.1	33.7	29.1
1976	1.7	14.5	59.9	41.0	46.2	40.7	41.0	42.9	40.7	56.3	38.2	30.6
1977	1.8	17.5	63.5	49.8	51.9	49.5	50.0	55.4	52.3	74.6	41.7	33.5
1978	2.1	20.8	70.6	55.0	57.2	52.6	53.1	57.9	54.0	84.0	45.8	36.4
1979	2.6	23.4	75.7	57.4	58.3	50.7	51.0	54.2	47.9	102.6	46.2	39.9
1980	3.1	25.1	72.4	46.9	52.4	39.9	40.0	38.1	31.5	91.9	43.1	39.9
1981	3.6	26.6	71.3	45.6	53.8	36.7	36.7	35.1	28.6	88.4	39.3	39.9
1982	4.2	26.8	65.1	40.4	46.6	30.1	29.8	27.4	22.0	72.0	33.9	38.3
1983	4.9	28.1	59.9	45.5	44.9	42.5	42.5	44.7	38.1	98.6	39.3	42.8
1984	6.2	32.0	68.6	54.2	50.8	48.8	48.9	52.6	44.3	120.5	43.4	47.4
1985	7.4	33.1	71.8	56.3	51.3	49.6	49.6	51.9	43.9	117.4	46.2	51.2
1986	8.3	34.4	71.4	54.2	50.4	55.7	55.7	57.9	50.2	120.9	52.6	55.4
1987	9.4	33.0	69.6	51.5	51.8	56.8	56.8	58.7	54.3	95.4	54.1	57.6
1988	11.2	35.3	73.1	54.3	54.3	56.2	56.2	56.6	53.6	81.4	55.7	59.6
1989	14.5	36.9	78.2	48.9	60.6	54.5	54.4	55.2	52.1	81.2	53.4	59.9
1990	17.1	37.8	73.7	48.6	58.3	49.8	49.6	49.9	47.3	70.8	49.5	58.1
1991	19.3	37.6	69.0	47.3	49.8	45.0	44.8	42.9	41.5	54.6	47.8	55.8
1992	22.7	39.9	70.3	48.2	49.6	51.3	51.1	50.1	50.4	46.4	53.0	57.6
1993	25.4	42.9	76.2	57.1	54.3	55.5	55.4	53.4	55.2	37.4	58.6	58.7
1994	27.9	46.9	83.0	66.9	58.6	60.8	60.9	59.8	61.0	48.3	62.7	59.1
1995	30.7	50.5	91.1	72.4	61.8	58.9	58.8	55.9	55.4	59.9	63.6	59.8
1996	36.0	55.4	94.5	75.3	64.2	63.6	63.6	61.1	60.5	66.2	67.7	59.6
1997	46.6	60.1	96.5	81.6	70.4	64.8	64.9	61.5	60.3	71.3	70.4	59.1
1998	56.3	67.7	100.7	89.2	77.5	69.7	69.9	67.3	66.9	70.5	74.1	63.4
1999	69.5	75.5	101.4	104.7	79.6	74.1	74.2	72.3	71.9	76.1	77.3	70.4
2000	79.1	90.8	110.1	102.5	84.1	74.8	74.8	72.9	72.7	74.8	78.1	75.3
2001	79.7	88.0	102.0	93.3	83.4	75.3	75.2	73.3	72.8	78.1	78.4	77.3
2002	79.6	80.0	95.1	84.9	82.8	79.2	79.2	76.3	75.6	82.2	84.0	80.4
2003	85.1	86.9	95.0	77.3	86.6	85.7	85.7	83.7	83.6	84.4	89.1	85.4
2004	93.9	94.2	92.3	89.3	91.9	94.1	94.1	93.4	93.7	90.9	95.3	95.2
2005	100.0	100.0	100.0	100.0	100.0	100.0	100.0	100.0	100.0	100.0	100.0	100.0
2006	104.2	108.1	108.3	108.1	103.7	92.7	92.5	91.3	90.2	100.7	94.7	102.8
2007	110.5	116.8	112.7	102.2	103.0	75.4	75.0	67.9	65.5	89.1	87.3	102.0
2008	115.0	113.5	108.3	78.5	99.4	57.3	56.8	45.1	41.2	78.4	76.9	98.2
2009	114.3	104.3	85.9	38.9	81.4	44.6	44.0	27.1	24.3	49.9	72.9	89.7
2010	117.5	116.2	91.8	65.7	90.9	42.7	42.0	26.0	26.4	25.4	69.2	97.0
2011	124.7	117.5	103.5	82.8	100.1	42.1	41.4	24.7	24.9	25.0	69.8	101.6
2009												
1st quarter	112.3	100.9	89.5	36.1	86.3	45.8	45.2	29.8	25.3	65.7	71.6	89.8
2nd quarter	113.7	100.8	85.5	38.4	80.2	43.1	42.6	25.2	21.5	54.8	72.2	87.4
3rd quarter	114.6	107.0	84.2	38.9	79.5	44.9	44.4	26.7	24.7	44.1	74.5	89.6
4th quarter	116.5	108.6	84.3	42.2	79.5	44.5	43.9	26.7	25.9	34.9	73.2	92.0
2010												
1st quarter	115.6	112.3	84.6	56.0	85.9	42.7	42.0	26.5	26.7	27.7	68.5	94.3
2nd quarter	116.0	114.8	92.2	64.7	89.7	44.9	44.3	27.5	28.1	25.2	72.9	97.3
3rd quarter	118.0	117.7	94.1	71.0	93.4	41.4	40.7	25.6	26.1	24.4	66.5	97.2
4th quarter	120.4	120.2	96.3	70.9	94.4	41.7	41.0	24.6	24.9	24.2	68.9	99.2
2011												
1st quarter	121.0	120.7	99.0	76.8	97.2	41.4	40.7	24.5	25.0	23.3	68.2	100.0
2nd quarter	123.3	118.6	98.8	79.6	97.1	41.9	41.1	24.3	24.6	23.8	69.8	100.8
3rd quarter	125.7	114.5	105.9	85.4	105.0	42.0	41.3	24.7	24.8	26.0	69.4	102.1
4th quarter	128.7	116.2	110.3	89.2	101.1	43.2	42.4	25.2	25.3	26.8	71.7	103.4

[1] Excludes software "embedded," or bundled, in computers and other equipment.
. . . = Not available.

Table 5-5A.   Current-Cost Net Stock of Fixed Assets: Recent Data

(Billions of dollars, year-end estimates.)

Year	Total	Private					Government				Private and government fixed assets			Government, by level	
		Total	Nonresidential			Resi-dential	Total	Nonresidential		Resi-dential	Nonresidential		Resi-dential	Federal	State and local
			Total	Equip-ment and software	Struc-tures			Equip-ment and software	Struc-tures		Equip-ment and software	Struc-tures			
1950	871.7	661.5	321.6	99.6	222.1	339.9	210.2	40.3	163.6	6.4	139.8	385.6	346.3	101.0	109.2
1951	955.8	719.7	350.7	109.7	241.0	369.0	236.1	44.1	184.1	7.9	153.8	425.1	376.9	113.2	122.8
1952	1 010.2	757.4	369.6	115.5	254.1	387.8	252.9	50.5	194.9	7.4	166.0	449.0	395.1	122.7	130.1
1953	1 046.3	787.6	385.4	125.0	260.4	402.2	258.7	57.3	193.5	7.8	182.3	454.0	410.0	130.0	128.8
1954	1 093.1	819.0	395.2	128.7	266.5	423.8	274.1	63.9	199.7	10.5	192.6	466.2	434.3	139.7	134.5
1955	1 187.7	891.9	435.4	141.7	293.7	456.5	295.8	69.4	218.8	7.6	211.2	512.5	464.1	146.5	149.3
1956	1 288.5	959.8	481.2	159.1	322.1	478.6	328.7	74.0	245.8	8.9	233.1	567.9	487.5	159.4	169.3
1957	1 351.1	1 008.4	513.8	173.4	340.4	494.6	342.7	76.1	257.2	9.4	249.5	597.6	504.0	165.3	177.4
1958	1 393.3	1 032.5	523.0	178.8	344.2	509.6	360.8	77.8	272.8	10.2	256.6	616.9	519.8	171.3	189.5
1959	1 447.4	1 076.3	544.6	187.3	357.3	531.7	371.1	82.4	277.6	11.1	269.7	634.9	542.8	175.3	195.7
1960	1 492.9	1 108.3	555.7	193.4	362.3	552.6	384.6	85.2	287.7	11.7	278.6	650.0	564.3	179.5	205.1
1961	1 547.5	1 143.5	570.8	196.9	373.9	572.7	404.0	89.1	302.3	12.5	286.0	676.2	585.3	186.5	217.4
1962	1 615.1	1 185.0	591.2	204.6	386.6	593.8	430.1	96.4	320.3	13.4	301.0	706.9	607.2	197.4	232.7
1963	1 671.7	1 220.8	612.4	213.4	399.0	608.4	450.9	99.1	338.1	13.7	312.5	737.1	622.1	202.9	248.1
1964	1 779.1	1 305.9	648.5	226.5	422.1	657.4	473.2	102.0	356.7	14.6	328.4	778.7	671.9	208.5	264.7
1965	1 895.6	1 392.2	694.2	244.3	449.9	698.0	503.4	104.6	383.6	15.3	348.8	833.4	713.3	215.4	288.0
1966	2 054.1	1 510.2	755.4	272.3	483.1	754.9	543.9	109.3	418.1	16.4	381.6	901.2	771.3	225.7	318.2
1967	2 210.2	1 622.5	816.3	298.5	517.8	806.2	587.7	116.1	454.4	17.3	414.6	972.2	823.4	240.0	347.7
1968	2 426.1	1 788.0	897.3	329.5	567.8	890.7	638.1	120.7	498.0	19.4	450.2	1 065.9	910.1	252.2	385.9
1969	2 643.2	1 940.9	988.0	363.8	624.1	952.9	702.4	124.9	555.9	21.6	488.8	1 180.0	974.5	266.6	435.8
1970	2 877.7	2 096.1	1 087.4	399.6	687.8	1 008.7	781.6	131.0	627.5	23.0	530.7	1 315.3	1 031.8	284.5	497.1
1971	3 177.5	2 331.0	1 197.2	428.3	768.9	1 133.8	846.4	131.9	688.7	25.8	560.2	1 457.6	1 159.7	298.5	547.9
1972	3 493.6	2 570.9	1 303.2	462.0	841.2	1 267.8	922.7	134.1	759.7	28.9	596.0	1 600.9	1 296.7	321.8	600.8
1973	3 959.3	2 921.4	1 468.8	515.2	953.6	1 452.6	1 037.9	136.2	869.0	32.7	651.3	1 822.7	1 485.3	348.6	689.3
1974	4 716.7	3 441.4	1 788.4	635.3	1 153.2	1 653.0	1 275.3	149.5	1 089.2	36.6	784.8	2 242.4	1 689.6	402.1	873.2
1975	5 102.5	3 762.5	1 970.4	727.4	1 243.0	1 792.1	1 340.0	164.5	1 135.4	40.1	891.8	2 378.4	1 832.2	425.5	914.4
1976	5 562.7	4 146.2	2 157.0	805.3	1 351.7	1 989.1	1 416.5	178.5	1 193.3	44.7	983.8	2 545.0	2 033.9	461.3	955.2
1977	6 225.1	4 719.6	2 398.1	904.1	1 494.0	2 321.5	1 505.5	194.9	1 259.1	51.5	1 099.0	2 753.1	2 372.9	484.2	1 021.3
1978	7 047.6	5 401.0	2 723.7	1 033.1	1 690.6	2 677.3	1 646.6	207.9	1 379.2	59.5	1 240.9	3 069.8	2 736.8	522.6	1 124.0
1979	8 126.3	6 251.6	3 143.2	1 199.7	1 943.5	3 108.4	1 874.7	225.0	1 579.0	70.8	1 424.6	3 522.5	3 179.2	581.7	1 293.0
1980	9 259.6	7 113.1	3 608.4	1 392.6	2 215.8	3 504.7	2 146.5	251.4	1 817.4	77.7	1 644.0	4 033.2	3 582.3	645.6	1 500.8
1981	10 209.7	7 851.6	4 081.8	1 553.6	2 528.1	3 769.8	2 358.1	282.7	1 990.3	85.1	1 836.4	4 518.5	3 854.9	694.7	1 663.5
1982	10 770.9	8 281.7	4 341.2	1 646.8	2 694.5	3 940.5	2 489.2	307.6	2 091.4	90.2	1 954.4	4 785.8	4 030.7	733.5	1 755.6
1983	11 121.6	8 573.3	4 474.1	1 702.6	2 771.5	4 099.2	2 548.3	337.3	2 110.3	100.7	2 039.9	4 881.8	4 200.0	769.9	1 778.4
1984	11 721.2	9 072.5	4 741.8	1 796.8	2 945.0	4 330.6	2 648.7	361.3	2 182.9	104.5	2 158.1	5 127.9	4 435.1	809.0	1 839.7
1985	12 334.2	9 570.4	5 007.4	1 903.8	3 103.6	4 563.0	2 763.8	383.6	2 274.5	105.6	2 287.5	5 378.1	4 668.6	840.4	1 923.4
1986	13 106.8	10 172.9	5 244.8	2 010.7	3 234.2	4 928.1	2 933.9	411.7	2 412.6	109.5	2 422.4	5 646.8	5 037.6	883.6	2 050.3
1987	13 864.0	10 774.8	5 528.1	2 112.2	3 415.9	5 246.7	3 089.2	436.4	2 533.4	119.4	2 548.5	5 949.3	5 366.1	918.8	2 170.4
1988	14 703.8	11 455.3	5 882.3	2 238.6	3 643.7	5 573.0	3 248.4	470.7	2 642.7	135.0	2 709.4	6 286.4	5 708.0	975.1	2 273.3
1989	15 539.4	12 113.9	6 234.3	2 374.7	3 859.5	5 879.6	3 425.5	507.9	2 773.4	144.2	2 882.7	6 633.0	6 023.8	1 028.9	2 396.6
1990	16 268.3	12 670.5	6 563.5	2 506.7	4 056.7	6 107.0	3 597.8	550.8	2 898.1	148.9	3 057.5	6 954.9	6 255.9	1 076.8	2 521.0
1991	16 656.7	12 937.2	6 694.0	2 577.7	4 116.2	6 243.2	3 719.6	583.7	2 985.8	150.0	3 161.5	7 102.1	6 393.2	1 120.6	2 599.0
1992	17 370.2	13 487.9	6 902.2	2 650.3	4 251.9	6 585.7	3 882.3	612.9	3 110.6	158.8	3 263.2	7 362.5	6 744.5	1 167.3	2 715.1
1993	18 267.0	14 204.1	7 214.1	2 761.4	4 452.8	6 990.0	4 062.9	637.2	3 255.7	170.0	3 398.5	7 708.5	7 160.0	1 208.7	2 854.2
1994	19 374.3	15 080.9	7 594.8	2 911.5	4 683.4	7 486.0	4 293.4	665.5	3 446.4	181.5	3 577.0	8 129.8	7 667.5	1 259.7	3 033.7
1995	20 314.7	15 810.6	7 989.8	3 099.5	4 890.3	7 820.8	4 504.1	675.2	3 640.8	188.1	3 774.7	8 531.1	8 008.9	1 291.5	3 212.6
1996	21 305.4	16 624.9	8 371.9	3 261.8	5 110.1	8 253.0	4 680.5	675.0	3 809.1	196.4	3 936.8	8 919.2	8 449.4	1 315.0	3 365.5
1997	22 429.2	17 542.6	8 828.2	3 418.1	5 410.2	8 714.4	4 886.6	670.6	4 021.5	194.5	4 088.7	9 431.7	8 908.8	1 335.8	3 550.8
1998	23 705.1	18 618.1	9 332.6	3 607.9	5 724.7	9 285.5	5 087.0	677.8	4 204.8	204.4	4 285.7	9 929.5	9 489.9	1 357.7	3 729.3
1999	25 244.6	19 857.6	9 883.1	3 853.2	6 029.9	9 974.6	5 386.9	699.3	4 470.2	217.3	4 552.5	10 500.2	10 191.9	1 403.7	3 983.2
2000	26 932.4	21 230.4	10 562.7	4 134.1	6 428.6	10 667.7	5 702.0	703.7	4 769.3	229.0	4 837.8	11 197.9	10 896.7	1 431.5	4 270.5
2001	28 535.4	22 575.0	11 114.1	4 283.0	6 831.1	11 460.9	5 960.5	703.8	5 012.8	243.8	4 986.9	11 843.9	11 704.7	1 449.3	4 511.2
2002	29 973.8	23 739.4	11 541.6	4 378.9	7 162.7	12 197.7	6 234.4	716.5	5 260.6	257.4	5 095.4	12 423.3	12 455.1	1 478.7	4 755.7
2003	31 665.4	25 170.6	11 932.8	4 495.6	7 437.3	13 237.7	6 494.8	731.6	5 487.6	275.7	5 227.1	12 924.9	13 513.4	1 513.6	4 981.3
2004	34 978.0	27 735.5	12 910.7	4 702.4	8 208.4	14 824.8	7 242.5	767.4	6 172.1	303.0	5 469.7	14 380.5	15 127.8	1 636.5	5 606.0
2005	38 511.9	30 593.2	14 063.3	4 936.7	9 126.6	16 529.9	7 918.7	802.3	6 784.5	331.8	5 739.0	15 911.2	16 861.7	1 743.8	6 174.9
2006	41 713.1	32 956.6	15 274.6	5 277.1	9 997.6	17 682.0	8 756.5	850.1	7 560.8	345.6	6 127.2	17 558.4	18 027.6	1 861.9	6 894.6
2007	43 563.5	34 080.8	16 124.7	5 513.4	10 611.3	17 956.2	9 482.7	895.4	8 244.5	342.8	6 408.8	18 855.8	18 299.0	1 947.5	7 535.2
2008	45 058.6	34 869.3	17 184.8	5 765.9	11 419.0	17 684.5	10 189.3	956.3	8 900.1	332.9	6 722.2	20 319.0	18 017.4	2 036.4	8 152.9
2009	44 083.2	33 886.9	16 540.9	5 685.6	10 855.3	17 346.0	10 196.3	992.3	8 878.8	325.2	6 677.9	19 734.1	17 671.2	2 024.3	8 172.0
2010	44 742.5	34 200.8	16 803.7	5 739.8	11 063.8	17 397.1	10 541.7	1 046.4	9 166.9	328.5	6 786.2	20 230.7	17 725.6	2 092.1	8 449.6

Table 5-5B. Current-Cost Net Stock of Fixed Assets: Historical Data

(Billions of dollars, year-end estimates.)

Year	Total	Private					Government				Private and government fixed assets			Government, by level	
		Total	Nonresidential			Resi-dential	Total	Nonresidential		Resi-dential	Nonresidential		Resi-dential	Federal	State and local
			Total	Equip-ment and software	Struc-tures			Equip-ment and software	Struc-tures		Equip-ment and software	Struc-tures			
1925	263.3	225.0	124.3	31.3	93.0	100.7	38.3	2.9	35.4	0.0	34.2	128.4	100.7	9.2	29.1
1926	272.3	233.2	128.8	33.1	95.6	104.5	39.1	2.8	36.3	0.0	35.9	132.0	104.5	9.0	30.1
1927	278.5	238.6	131.4	33.8	97.5	107.2	40.0	2.8	37.2	0.0	36.6	134.7	107.2	8.7	31.3
1928	291.1	250.5	134.8	34.5	100.3	115.7	40.6	2.6	38.0	0.0	37.1	138.3	115.7	8.3	32.3
1929	294.5	253.7	133.9	34.7	99.2	119.8	40.8	2.4	38.4	0.0	37.1	137.6	119.8	7.9	32.9
1930	280.9	241.2	126.9	33.0	93.9	114.3	39.6	2.3	37.3	0.0	35.3	131.2	114.3	7.4	32.2
1931	242.7	206.6	113.1	30.0	83.1	93.5	36.1	2.3	33.7	0.0	32.3	116.8	93.6	6.8	29.2
1932	224.2	188.5	104.6	27.0	77.6	84.0	35.6	2.3	33.3	0.0	29.2	111.0	84.0	6.7	29.0
1933	239.7	197.9	106.1	26.7	79.5	91.8	41.8	2.3	39.4	0.0	29.0	118.9	91.8	7.6	34.2
1934	245.8	200.0	107.3	26.7	80.6	92.7	45.8	2.6	43.2	0.0	29.4	123.8	92.7	8.7	37.2
1935	249.7	201.0	106.8	26.2	80.6	94.2	48.7	2.8	45.8	0.0	29.0	126.4	94.2	9.9	38.8
1936	276.3	222.2	117.5	28.2	89.3	104.7	54.1	2.9	51.1	0.1	31.1	140.4	104.8	11.4	42.7
1937	290.8	233.6	122.2	30.3	91.9	111.4	57.2	3.2	53.8	0.2	33.5	145.7	111.6	12.6	44.6
1938	293.0	233.9	120.7	30.3	90.4	113.2	59.2	3.3	55.6	0.2	33.6	146.0	113.4	13.3	45.9
1939	299.2	237.6	120.8	30.9	89.9	116.8	61.5	3.6	57.7	0.3	34.5	147.6	117.1	13.9	47.6
1940	324.1	256.5	128.3	33.2	95.1	128.2	67.5	4.0	63.0	0.5	37.2	158.1	128.7	15.7	51.8
1941	369.1	284.7	144.8	38.3	106.5	139.9	84.5	7.7	75.8	1.0	45.9	182.2	141.0	24.3	60.1
1942	421.2	304.2	153.6	39.2	114.4	150.7	117.0	20.9	94.4	1.7	60.1	208.8	152.4	49.6	67.4
1943	468.4	319.2	155.6	39.6	116.0	163.6	149.2	45.3	101.3	2.6	84.9	217.3	166.2	80.7	68.4
1944	501.2	331.6	156.7	39.5	117.2	174.9	169.6	65.2	101.5	2.8	104.7	218.8	177.7	102.7	66.9
1945	543.4	355.5	171.0	44.7	126.2	184.5	187.9	75.4	109.5	3.0	120.1	235.8	187.5	118.5	69.4
1946	637.8	438.4	211.1	54.5	156.7	227.3	199.3	70.2	125.2	4.0	124.7	281.8	231.3	121.6	77.8
1947	734.7	521.6	254.0	66.6	187.4	267.6	213.1	61.7	145.8	5.6	128.3	333.2	273.2	119.8	93.3
1948	780.3	567.0	278.8	81.3	197.5	288.3	213.3	51.9	156.5	5.0	133.1	353.9	293.2	111.8	101.5
1949	785.5	586.5	283.7	85.4	198.3	302.8	199.0	44.1	149.8	5.2	129.5	348.1	307.9	102.1	96.9

Table 5-6A. Chain-Type Quantity Indexes for Net Stock of Fixed Assets: Recent Data

(Index numbers, 2005 = 100.)

Year	Total	Private					Government				Private and government fixed assets			Government, by level	
		Total	Nonresidential			Resi-dential	Total	Nonresidential		Resi-dential	Nonresidential		Resi-dential	Federal	State and local
			Total	Equip-ment and software	Struc-tures			Equip-ment and software	Struc-tures		Equip-ment and software	Struc-tures			
1950	19.76	18.40	17.51	9.35	25.20	19.44	24.87	26.11	24.74	16.67	11.62	25.04	19.41	51.61	16.57
1951	20.50	19.08	18.12	9.88	25.84	20.20	25.86	27.93	25.51	17.92	12.32	25.74	20.18	53.76	17.20
1952	21.28	19.71	18.66	10.32	26.44	20.92	27.23	31.23	26.43	19.33	13.13	26.48	20.92	57.55	17.83
1953	22.12	20.39	19.29	10.84	27.13	21.67	28.68	34.72	27.42	20.60	14.03	27.30	21.68	61.43	18.54
1954	22.90	21.07	19.83	11.18	27.84	22.50	29.92	36.54	28.54	21.18	14.57	28.19	22.50	63.75	19.44
1955	23.78	21.89	20.51	11.70	28.63	23.48	30.96	37.30	29.68	21.64	15.13	29.12	23.48	64.94	20.43
1956	24.63	22.70	21.26	12.23	29.56	24.34	31.98	38.01	30.80	22.22	15.68	30.14	24.33	66.02	21.44
1957	25.44	23.45	22.00	12.76	30.46	25.12	33.01	38.47	31.96	23.28	16.20	31.15	25.11	66.88	22.52
1958	26.16	24.05	22.46	12.92	31.22	25.88	34.22	39.11	33.27	25.16	16.43	32.14	25.91	68.11	23.73
1959	27.06	24.82	23.00	13.21	32.00	26.93	35.63	40.78	34.57	27.28	16.89	33.14	26.97	70.16	24.95
1960	27.93	25.59	23.64	13.59	32.89	27.85	36.90	41.86	35.87	28.84	17.37	34.21	27.91	71.65	26.16
1961	28.83	26.33	24.24	13.89	33.78	28.76	38.40	43.58	37.29	30.74	17.86	35.32	28.84	73.78	27.48
1962	29.84	27.20	24.98	14.37	34.74	29.77	39.98	45.63	38.71	32.87	18.55	36.48	29.88	76.08	28.84
1963	30.91	28.17	25.77	14.95	35.68	30.95	41.47	46.89	40.28	33.97	19.22	37.69	31.05	77.63	30.33
1964	32.11	29.28	26.77	15.74	36.79	32.19	42.99	47.95	41.92	35.16	20.05	39.03	32.29	78.90	31.95
1965	33.43	30.54	28.11	16.89	38.19	33.37	44.49	48.44	43.67	36.43	21.11	40.58	33.47	79.69	33.68
1966	34.81	31.85	29.68	18.34	39.69	34.37	46.17	49.45	45.52	37.80	22.52	42.23	34.48	80.88	35.53
1967	36.10	33.02	31.06	19.55	41.09	35.30	47.94	50.81	47.39	39.34	23.76	43.84	35.42	82.04	37.49
1968	37.44	34.29	32.46	20.82	42.49	36.41	49.52	51.03	49.28	40.85	24.90	45.45	36.54	82.18	39.53
1969	38.79	35.63	33.99	22.23	44.00	37.55	50.86	50.74	50.96	42.76	26.09	47.03	37.70	81.84	41.41
1970	39.97	36.84	35.35	23.38	45.46	38.57	51.98	50.20	52.41	44.72	27.02	48.49	38.74	81.23	43.06
1971	41.19	38.16	36.59	24.38	46.85	40.01	52.80	48.18	53.78	46.61	27.62	49.87	40.18	79.69	44.59
1972	42.59	39.72	38.00	25.68	48.27	41.74	53.58	46.57	55.04	48.19	28.53	51.21	41.91	78.45	46.00
1973	44.13	41.45	39.76	27.56	49.83	43.44	54.42	45.34	56.26	49.70	29.97	52.62	43.60	77.54	47.39
1974	45.44	42.87	41.38	29.29	51.26	44.62	55.37	45.07	57.42	51.12	31.43	53.93	44.80	77.17	48.74
1975	46.44	43.88	42.47	30.30	52.39	45.55	56.33	45.06	58.53	52.82	32.31	55.04	45.74	77.02	50.02
1976	47.59	45.09	43.61	31.41	53.49	46.84	57.29	45.38	59.59	54.15	33.32	56.13	47.03	77.11	51.25
1977	48.99	46.65	45.04	33.00	54.66	48.55	58.12	45.63	60.51	55.41	34.73	57.19	48.73	77.23	52.31
1978	50.66	48.49	46.91	35.13	56.18	50.37	59.09	45.92	61.62	56.47	36.61	58.53	50.54	77.43	53.55
1979	52.42	50.41	49.04	37.45	58.03	52.07	60.20	46.86	62.76	57.48	38.76	60.08	52.23	77.87	54.86
1980	53.87	51.95	50.93	39.13	60.05	53.22	61.32	47.98	63.87	58.77	40.36	61.71	53.38	78.49	56.15
1981	55.28	53.45	52.94	40.76	62.33	54.19	62.32	49.27	64.79	60.30	41.96	63.40	54.36	79.39	57.18
1982	56.34	54.56	54.49	41.64	64.45	54.81	63.22	50.92	65.53	61.71	42.93	64.92	55.00	80.46	58.02
1983	57.55	55.82	55.78	42.56	66.04	56.04	64.24	54.46	66.22	63.41	44.08	66.12	56.25	82.07	58.87
1984	59.23	57.60	57.79	44.38	68.14	57.58	65.53	56.80	67.10	64.85	46.11	67.69	57.78	84.08	59.94
1985	61.03	59.45	59.94	46.16	70.57	59.11	67.13	61.17	68.15	66.62	48.23	69.53	59.32	86.69	61.23
1986	62.80	61.22	61.65	47.61	72.45	60.95	68.87	65.94	69.33	68.51	50.13	71.11	61.16	89.56	62.63
1987	64.52	62.93	63.19	48.79	74.27	62.82	70.65	70.76	70.56	70.49	51.77	72.67	63.03	92.57	64.04
1988	66.20	64.63	64.81	50.23	76.00	64.63	72.26	74.47	71.80	72.24	53.50	74.19	64.84	94.55	65.54
1989	67.86	66.30	66.49	51.83	77.69	66.28	73.89	78.51	73.01	73.78	55.41	75.67	66.49	96.36	67.11
1990	69.42	67.80	68.07	53.07	79.52	67.71	75.68	82.64	74.41	75.49	57.02	77.31	67.93	98.21	68.87
1991	70.64	68.90	69.11	53.86	80.77	68.87	77.35	85.68	75.85	76.97	58.09	78.65	69.10	99.57	70.65
1992	71.88	70.05	70.09	54.88	81.67	70.20	78.94	88.19	77.29	78.58	59.31	79.78	70.43	100.69	72.39
1993	73.35	71.56	71.48	56.66	82.66	71.84	80.28	89.30	78.65	79.98	61.00	80.93	72.07	101.07	74.02
1994	74.96	73.27	73.12	59.06	83.56	73.64	81.44	89.58	79.96	81.13	63.14	82.01	73.86	100.83	75.62
1995	76.75	75.20	75.21	62.05	84.82	75.40	82.72	89.70	81.44	82.54	65.75	83.37	75.62	100.68	77.35
1996	78.80	77.40	77.62	65.45	86.33	77.39	84.21	89.93	83.14	83.94	68.75	84.96	77.59	101.09	79.17
1997	80.98	79.79	80.41	69.49	88.06	79.38	85.56	89.74	84.73	89.93	72.23	86.63	79.58	100.37	81.17
1998	83.42	82.49	83.60	74.29	89.94	81.60	87.03	90.17	86.36	91.35	76.45	88.40	81.78	99.92	83.22
1999	86.06	85.37	87.02	79.80	91.78	83.97	88.72	91.26	88.15	92.73	81.36	90.22	84.13	99.68	85.49
2000	88.82	88.40	90.75	85.70	93.91	86.35	90.45	92.14	90.04	93.80	86.58	92.25	86.49	99.17	87.90
2001	91.19	90.91	93.43	89.50	95.81	88.70	92.26	92.81	92.03	95.10	89.96	94.18	88.82	98.63	90.40
2002	93.27	93.01	95.05	91.82	96.97	91.23	94.29	94.15	94.19	96.48	92.14	95.78	91.32	98.68	93.02
2003	95.41	95.17	96.49	93.91	97.99	94.03	96.34	95.65	96.35	97.80	94.15	97.29	94.10	98.94	95.59
2004	97.70	97.56	98.14	96.61	99.00	97.06	98.26	97.01	98.38	99.02	96.67	98.73	97.10	99.47	97.91
2005	100.00	100.00	100.00	100.00	100.00	100.00	100.00	100.00	100.00	100.00	100.00	100.00	100.00	100.00	100.00
2006	102.57	102.74	102.47	104.19	101.56	102.98	101.93	103.51	101.81	100.48	104.10	101.67	102.93	100.77	102.25
2007	104.87	105.15	105.24	108.20	103.71	105.06	103.83	107.17	103.59	101.13	108.06	103.65	104.98	101.67	104.43
2008	106.63	106.85	107.59	110.56	106.05	106.15	105.82	111.92	105.34	101.86	110.75	105.74	106.07	103.12	106.56
2009	107.44	107.32	108.01	109.50	107.21	106.68	107.72	116.25	107.03	102.76	110.45	107.13	106.60	104.71	108.54
2010	108.28	107.88	108.72	110.65	107.69	107.11	109.52	120.89	108.54	104.32	112.10	108.08	107.05	106.70	110.28

Table 5-6B. Chain-Type Quantity Indexes for Net Stock of Fixed Assets: Historical Data

(Index numbers, 2005 = 100.)

Year	Total	Private					Government				Private and government fixed assets			Government, by level	
		Total	Nonresidential			Resi-dential	Total	Nonresidential		Resi-dential	Nonresidential		Resi-dential	Federal	State and local
			Total	Equip-ment and software	Struc-tures			Equip-ment and software	Struc-tures		Equip-ment and software	Struc-tures			
1925	11.82	13.28	13.23	5.52	20.86	13.30	7.44	2.20	9.61	0.00	4.65	15.80	13.04	7.15	7.65
1926	12.26	13.78	13.67	5.73	21.52	13.88	7.72	2.17	10.02	0.00	4.80	16.34	13.61	7.04	8.07
1927	12.67	14.22	14.04	5.84	22.16	14.41	8.06	2.19	10.49	0.00	4.89	16.91	14.13	6.94	8.57
1928	13.07	14.64	14.40	5.96	22.77	14.88	8.44	2.20	11.01	0.00	4.99	17.47	14.59	6.88	9.10
1929	13.45	15.01	14.84	6.15	23.44	15.18	8.83	2.22	11.54	0.03	5.14	18.08	14.89	6.85	9.64
1930	13.69	15.19	15.09	6.17	23.95	15.29	9.32	2.23	12.23	0.05	5.16	18.66	14.99	6.90	10.29
1931	13.78	15.17	15.00	5.97	24.05	15.34	9.84	2.26	12.94	0.08	5.00	19.03	15.04	7.04	10.95
1932	13.71	14.97	14.69	5.62	23.88	15.27	10.25	2.25	13.52	0.10	4.73	19.18	14.98	7.27	11.43
1933	13.60	14.74	14.36	5.32	23.61	15.18	10.53	2.24	13.92	0.13	4.50	19.20	14.89	7.72	11.65
1934	13.57	14.60	14.14	5.14	23.38	15.13	10.90	2.38	14.38	0.15	4.38	19.30	14.84	8.35	11.94
1935	13.62	14.54	14.02	5.09	23.21	15.14	11.30	2.55	14.88	0.22	4.37	19.44	14.86	9.21	12.20
1936	13.82	14.61	14.08	5.21	23.16	15.21	11.95	2.65	15.73	0.63	4.48	19.80	14.93	10.03	12.80
1937	14.05	14.74	14.26	5.43	23.24	15.30	12.49	2.76	16.41	1.19	4.67	20.16	15.03	10.77	13.27
1938	14.20	14.76	14.22	5.41	23.19	15.39	13.10	2.93	17.19	1.41	4.68	20.49	15.12	11.49	13.86
1939	14.43	14.87	14.24	5.45	23.17	15.59	13.79	3.12	18.07	1.83	4.74	20.88	15.34	12.14	14.58
1940	14.72	15.08	14.40	5.66	23.22	15.85	14.43	3.30	18.83	3.06	4.93	21.25	15.61	13.13	15.10
1941	15.30	15.34	14.65	5.95	23.34	16.13	16.15	6.14	20.12	5.56	5.61	21.89	15.94	19.20	15.38
1942	16.24	15.29	14.52	5.86	23.19	16.18	20.65	17.96	22.56	8.30	7.27	22.92	16.04	62.38	15.28
1943	17.31	15.16	14.31	5.73	22.92	16.13	26.08	40.88	23.53	11.80	10.30	23.22	16.07	82.62	15.11
1944	18.18	15.11	14.26	5.76	22.76	16.07	30.50	62.85	23.82	12.64	13.25	23.27	16.03	89.91	14.98
1945	18.56	15.19	14.48	6.10	22.77	16.02	32.03	70.52	23.95	12.84	14.55	23.33	15.98	89.91	14.98
1946	18.49	15.69	15.07	6.70	23.26	16.45	29.62	57.86	23.73	14.24	13.43	23.51	16.43	79.20	14.99
1947	18.60	16.33	15.74	7.54	23.67	17.06	27.57	46.06	23.76	14.68	12.61	23.75	17.04	61.67	15.17
1948	18.89	17.05	16.43	8.33	24.18	17.80	26.07	36.24	24.00	14.95	12.02	24.14	17.78	61.67	15.47
1949	19.26	17.62	16.93	8.80	24.65	18.46	25.57	31.13	24.48	15.86	11.78	24.62	18.44	57.69	15.97

Table 5-7. Capital Expenditures

(Millions of dollars.)

Capital expenditures	All companies										
	2000	2001	2002	2003	2004	2005	2006	2007	2008	2009	2010
TOTAL	1 161 029	1 109 004	997 894	975 015	1 042 060	1 144 783	1 309 939	1 354 727	1 374 160	1 090 070	1 105 701
Structures	364 407	363 748	358 484	344 641	368 707	401 653	488 701	525 273	562 381	448 132	428 713
New	329 525	335 538	321 191	305 291	324 680	365 938	448 861	480 839	522 999	421 044	394 517
Used	34 882	28 210	37 293	39 350	44 028	35 715	39 840	44 434	39 382	27 088	34 196
Equipment	796 622	745 256	639 410	630 373	673 353	743 130	821 238	829 455	811 779	641 938	676 989
New	750 626	706 617	598 668	579 414	628 591	701 247	777 059	790 407	765 279	606 935	639 214
Used	45 996	38 639	40 741	50 960	44 762	41 884	44 179	39 048	46 501	35 003	37 775
Not distributed as structures or equipment	0	0	0	0	0	0	0	0	0	0	0
CAPITALIZED COMPUTER SOFTWARE [1]	. . .	. . .	. . .	. . .	. . .	. . .	. . .	. . .	. . .	. . .	. . .
Prepackaged	. . .	. . .	. . .	. . .	. . .	. . .	. . .	. . .	. . .	. . .	. . .
Vendor-customized	. . .	. . .	. . .	. . .	. . .	. . .	. . .	. . .	. . .	. . .	. . .
Internally-developed	. . .	. . .	. . .	. . .	. . .	. . .	. . .	. . .	. . .	. . .	. . .
CAPITAL LEASE AND CAPITALIZED INTEREST EXPENSES [1]											
Capital leases	19 545	15 529	15 334	15 641	17 996	18 103	24 442	20 210	20 169	17 410	15 780
Capitalized interest	. . .	. . .	. . .	. . .	. . .	. . .	. . .	. . .	. . .	. . .	. . .

Capital expenditures	Companies with employees										
	2000	2001	2002	2003	2004	2005	2006	2007	2008	2009	2010
TOTAL	1 089 862	1 052 344	917 490	886 846	953 171	1 062 536	1 217 107	1 270 522	1 294 491	1 014 698	1 036 162
Structures	338 120	346 221	325 168	314 021	335 405	368 791	453 893	490 779	529 393	412 638	395 531
New	309 541	323 871	299 941	281 892	300 371	341 223	420 090	457 233	500 474	393 286	366 853
Used	28 579	22 349	25 227	32 128	35 034	27 568	33 802	33 546	28 919	19 352	28 678
Equipment	751 742	706 123	592 321	572 825	617 766	693 745	763 215	779 744	765 098	602 060	640 631
New	718 227	679 090	564 218	540 611	588 110	664 648	734 160	750 353	728 322	577 410	612 441
Used	33 515	27 033	28 103	32 214	29 656	29 096	29 055	29 391	36 776	24 650	28 190
Not distributed as structures or equipment	0	0	0	0	0	0	0	0	0	0	0
CAPITALIZED COMPUTER SOFTWARE [1]	. . .	. . .	. . .	49 869	49 868	49 149	58 522	63 116	72 241	66 704	63 780
Prepackaged	. . .	. . .	. . .	17 307	17 306	17 630	21 181	21 777	26 260	21 407	21 749
Vendor-customized	. . .	. . .	. . .	15 554	15 553	13 876	16 912	17 990	19 259	18 610	17 264
Internally-developed	. . .	. . .	. . .	17 008	17 008	17 643	20 433	23 350	26 723	26 687	24 768
CAPITAL LEASE AND CAPITALIZED INTEREST EXPENSES [1]											
Capital leases	19 184	15 500	15 092	15 137	17 526	17 640	23 923	19 432	19 422	16 832	15 212
Capitalized interest	11 423	11 969	. . .	. . .	. . .	. . .	. . .	. . .	. . .	. . .	. . .

Capital expenditures	Companies without employees										
	2000	2001	2002	2003	2004	2005	2006	2007	2008	2009	2010
TOTAL	71 168	56 660	80 404	88 169	88 889	82 247	92 832	84 205	79 669	75 372	69 539
Structures	26 287	17 527	33 316	30 621	33 302	32 862	34 809	34 494	32 988	35 493	33 182
New	19 984	11 667	21 250	23 399	24 309	24 715	28 771	23 606	22 525	27 758	27 664
Used	6 303	5 860	12 066	7 222	8 993	8 146	6 038	10 888	10 463	7 735	5 518
Equipment	44 880	39 133	47 088	57 549	55 587	49 386	58 023	49 711	46 681	39 878	36 357
New	32 399	27 528	34 450	38 803	40 481	36 598	42 899	40 054	36 957	29 525	26 773
Used	12 481	11 605	12 638	18 746	15 106	12 787	15 124	9 657	9 724	10 353	9 585
Not distributed as structures or equipment	0	0	0	0	0	0	0	0	0	0	0
CAPITALIZED COMPUTER SOFTWARE [1]	. . .	. . .	. . .	. . .	. . .	. . .	. . .	. . .	. . .	. . .	. . .
Prepackaged	. . .	. . .	. . .	. . .	. . .	. . .	. . .	. . .	. . .	. . .	. . .
Vendor-customized	. . .	. . .	. . .	. . .	. . .	. . .	. . .	. . .	. . .	. . .	. . .
Internally-developed	. . .	. . .	. . .	. . .	. . .	. . .	. . .	. . .	. . .	. . .	. . .
CAPITAL LEASE AND CAPITALIZED INTEREST EXPENSES [1]											
Capital leases	361	29	242	504	469	463	519	778	747	577	568
Capitalized interest	. . .	. . .	. . .	. . .	. . .	. . .	. . .	. . .	. . .	. . .	. . .

[1]Included in structures and equipment data shown above.
. . . = Not available.

Table 5-8. Capital Expenditures for Structures and Equipment for Companies with Employees by Major NAICS Industry Sector

(Millions of dollars.)

Year and type of expenditure	Total	Forestry, fishing, and agricultural services (113–115)	Mining (21)	Utilities (22)	Construction (23)	Manufacturing (31–33) Total	Durable goods industries (321, 327, 33)	Nondurable goods industries (31, 322–326)	Wholesale trade (42)	Retail trade (44–45)	Transportation and warehousing (48–49)	Information (51)
1998												
Total expenditures	896 452	854	40 424	36 010	26 867	203 587	117 901	85 685	29 169	57 276	51 287	96 487
Structures, total	300 283	206	26 503	18 574	7 062	39 028	19 406	19 622	7 480	25 105	13 036	24 721
New	260 008	158	24 714	17 771	4 749	37 122	18 449	18 673	6 738	23 104	12 365	24 218
Used	40 275	49	1 789	804	2 313	1 906	957	949	742	2 001	671	503
Equipment, total	596 169	648	13 921	17 436	19 805	164 559	98 496	66 063	21 690	32 171	38 251	71 766
New	570 397	603	12 625	17 266	15 346	159 363	95 571	63 792	20 470	30 359	33 409	70 827
Used	25 773	46	1 296	170	4 458	5 196	2 925	2 271	1 220	1 812	4 842	939
1999												
Total expenditures	974 631	1 716	30 586	42 802	23 110	196 399	117 005	79 394	32 442	64 063	57 299	122 827
Structures, total	293 787	344	17 626	21 241	1 753	33 985	17 320	16 665	7 264	29 494	14 122	34 924
New	276 094	331	17 039	20 784	1 505	32 814	16 581	16 233	6 508	28 670	13 859	33 733
Used	17 693	13	587	457	248	1 171	739	432	756	824	263	1 191
Equipment, total	680 843	1 371	12 960	21 561	21 356	162 414	99 685	62 729	25 179	34 569	43 178	87 903
New	656 344	1 190	12 167	20 545	18 600	157 715	96 434	61 281	23 714	33 567	40 425	85 310
Used	24 499	182	793	1 016	2 756	4 699	3 251	1 448	1 465	1 002	2 752	2 593
2000												
Total expenditures	1 089 862	1 488	42 522	61 302	25 049	214 827	133 786	81 041	33 579	69 791	59 851	160 177
Structures, total	338 120	139	28 620	29 472	2 803	39 434	21 228	18 207	8 923	32 037	13 457	41 502
New	309 541	134	25 500	29 258	2 583	36 643	19 748	16 895	8 364	30 413	13 190	40 062
Used	28 579	5	3 120	214	220	2 791	1 480	1 312	559	1 624	267	1 440
Equipment, total	751 742	1 350	13 902	31 830	22 245	175 393	112 558	62 835	24 656	37 754	46 394	118 675
New	718 227	1 086	12 854	27 937	17 788	169 454	108 703	60 751	23 610	36 428	43 455	117 835
Used	33 515	264	1 048	3 893	4 458	5 939	3 856	2 083	1 046	1 326	2 938	841
2001												
Total expenditures	1 052 344	1 532	51 278	82 823	24 802	192 835	118 875	73 959	29 981	66 917	57 756	144 793
Structures, total	346 221	226	32 678	38 093	3 859	39 815	22 032	17 784	6 932	30 010	16 594	41 742
New	323 871	149	31 825	36 504	3 389	38 001	20 701	17 301	5 357	29 118	14 479	41 384
Used	22 349	77	853	1 588	470	1 814	1 331	483	1 575	892	2 116	358
Equipment, total	706 123	1 306	18 600	44 731	20 943	153 019	96 844	56 176	23 049	36 906	41 161	103 051
New	679 090	1 091	17 567	42 939	17 432	148 397	94 251	54 145	20 757	35 074	38 521	102 410
Used	27 033	215	1 033	1 792	3 511	4 623	2 592	2 030	2 292	1 833	2 640	641
2002												
Total expenditures	917 490	1 910	42 467	65 502	24 773	157 243	84 062	73 181	26 789	59 316	47 124	88 156
Structures, total	325 168	184	30 685	29 893	1 890	32 643	15 133	17 510	5 885	26 286	14 498	33 607
New	299 941	118	29 775	29 008	1 254	31 022	14 396	16 626	5 447	25 051	13 870	33 472
Used	25 227	66	910	886	456	1 622	737	885	438	1 234	628	135
Equipment, total	592 321	1 726	11 783	35 609	23 063	124 600	68 929	55 671	20 904	33 030	32 626	54 550
New	564 218	1 319	10 262	34 816	19 257	118 621	66 112	52 510	18 562	31 157	29 178	54 247
Used	28 103	407	1 520	793	3 806	5 978	2 817	3 161	2 342	1 873	3 447	303
2003												
Total expenditures	886 846	1 894	50 548	54 569	23 159	149 065	80 226	68 839	26 014	65 868	44 460	80 524
Structures, total	314 021	202	36 617	24 841	1 676	31 108	13 330	17 778	5 615	29 675	13 005	30 765
New	281 892	177	35 897	24 580	1 424	29 315	12 631	16 685	4 921	27 393	11 779	30 406
Used	32 128	25	720	261	251	1 793	700	1 093	694	2 282	1 226	358
Equipment, total	572 825	1 692	13 931	29 729	21 484	117 956	66 895	51 061	20 399	36 193	31 454	49 759
New	540 611	1 267	12 135	29 044	16 170	112 102	62 810	49 292	19 457	32 162	26 786	47 857
Used	32 214	425	1 796	685	5 313	5 855	4 086	1 769	942	4 031	4 668	1 902
2004												
Total expenditures	953 171	2 081	51 253	50 409	28 627	156 651	85 119	71 532	32 314	72 170	46 054	83 488
Structures, total	335 405	324	34 564	24 398	4 511	31 823	13 606	18 217	7 133	33 308	13 992	28 636
New	300 371	309	33 583	23 626	4 167	30 016	12 818	17 198	6 555	31 486	13 018	26 253
Used	35 034	15	982	772	345	1 807	788	1 019	578	1 822	975	2 384
Equipment, total	617 766	1 757	16 689	26 011	24 115	124 828	71 513	53 315	25 181	38 862	32 062	54 852
New	588 110	1 507	15 415	25 724	18 939	120 481	68 904	51 576	21 888	36 965	28 472	53 120
Used	29 656	250	1 274	286	5 176	4 347	2 609	1 738	3 293	1 897	3 590	1 732
2005												
Total expenditures	1 062 536	2 702	66 746	58 032	30 072	165 634	92 180	73 455	40 578	73 531	56 926	91 373
Structures, total	368 791	344	46 433	24 186	2 544	34 132	14 735	19 397	9 184	34 119	17 855	31 977
New	341 223	283	45 655	23 485	2 247	32 564	14 033	18 531	8 830	33 360	16 954	31 716
Used	27 568	61	777	701	297	1 569	703	866	355	759	901	262
Equipment, total	693 745	2 358	20 313	33 847	27 528	131 502	77 444	54 058	31 394	39 412	39 072	59 396
New	664 648	2 016	18 495	33 083	22 082	126 387	73 889	52 498	28 224	38 301	34 953	59 071
Used	29 096	341	1 818	764	5 446	5 115	3 555	1 560	3 169	1 111	4 119	325
2006												
Total expenditures	1 217 107	2 672	99 309	69 757	30 257	192 364	106 843	85 521	36 600	86 735	68 021	104 373
Structures, total	453 893	391	68 662	30 587	2 556	41 617	17 515	24 103	10 375	43 188	20 852	31 947
New	420 090	316	67 322	29 294	2 217	39 419	16 243	23 176	9 956	41 985	19 765	31 621
Used	33 802	75	1 340	1 293	338	2 198	1 272	926	419	1 203	1 087	326
Equipment, total	763 215	2 281	30 647	39 170	27 701	150 747	89 328	61 419	26 226	43 547	47 168	72 425
New	734 160	1 846	28 813	37 617	23 276	146 551	86 637	59 914	24 366	41 943	41 258	71 830
Used	29 055	435	1 833	1 553	4 425	4 196	2 692	1 504	1 860	1 604	5 911	595

Note: Detail may not sum to total because of rounding.

Table 5-8. Capital Expenditures for Structures and Equipment for Companies with Employees by Major NAICS Industry Sector—*Continued*

(Millions of dollars.)

Year and type of expenditure	Finance and insurance (52)	Real estate and rental and leasing (53)	Professional, scientific, and technical services (54)	Management of companies and enterprises (55)	Administrative and support and waste management (56)	Educational services (61)	Health care and social assistance (62)	Arts, entertainment, and recreation (71)	Accommodation and food services (72)	Other services, except public administration (81)	Structure and equipment expenditures serving multiple industries
1998											
Total expenditures	118 173	85 184	22 277	1 821	13 110	12 983	47 109	8 994	20 822	20 627	3 392
Structures, total	27 221	36 775	4 886	753	4 288	9 109	23 971	5 045	12 045	13 737	738
New	16 858	24 109	4 572	502	3 745	8 734	21 328	4 838	10 402	13 280	699
Used	10 362	12 666	314	251	543	374	2 643	206	1 643	457	39
Equipment, total	90 952	48 409	17 390	1 068	8 822	3 874	23 138	3 949	8 777	6 890	2 654
New	90 058	46 877	16 868	1 030	8 346	3 825	22 465	3 752	8 005	6 296	2 609
Used	894	1 532	522	38	476	49	672	197	772	594	46
1999											
Total expenditures	130 101	100 629	29 546	6 065	16 227	13 532	51 342	13 355	23 328	16 902	2 359
Structures, total	20 080	33 903	6 780	1 668	2 875	9 767	25 922	8 119	13 431	9 975	516
New	17 918	30 295	6 168	1 509	2 773	9 140	24 159	7 971	11 391	9 033	495
Used	2 162	3 608	613	159	102	627	1 763	148	2 040	941	21
Equipment, total	110 021	66 726	22 766	4 397	13 353	3 766	25 420	5 236	9 897	6 928	1 843
New	109 577	63 555	22 153	4 319	12 323	3 668	24 945	5 125	9 324	6 370	1 752
Used	444	3 171	613	78	1 029	97	475	111	573	558	91
2000											
Total expenditures	133 684	92 456	34 055	5 054	17 506	18 223	52 166	19 125	26 307	21 125	1 572
Structures, total	23 010	24 815	8 141	1 570	4 032	13 699	26 868	12 245	13 873	13 274	206
New	20 298	17 793	7 470	955	3 504	12 965	23 999	11 627	12 879	11 705	200
Used	2 712	7 022	671	615	528	735	2 869	618	993	1 569	6
Equipment, total	110 675	67 641	25 914	3 484	13 475	4 523	25 299	6 880	12 434	7 852	1 366
New	109 678	62 175	24 847	3 403	12 723	4 338	24 407	6 161	11 501	7 192	1 357
Used	997	5 466	1 067	81	752	186	892	719	933	659	10
2001											
Total expenditures	131 105	82 674	30 464	3 035	15 785	17 377	52 932	14 974	21 365	29 006	911
Structures, total	22 744	20 489	7 258	933	3 527	12 852	27 030	8 998	12 248	20 031	163
New	19 571	17 325	6 793	869	3 367	11 860	25 241	8 157	11 402	18 918	162
Used	3 173	3 164	465	64	160	991	1 789	841	846	1 112	0
Equipment, total	108 361	62 185	23 206	2 102	12 258	4 525	25 902	5 976	9 117	8 976	749
New	107 268	60 295	22 330	2 019	11 644	4 238	24 573	5 590	7 921	8 300	725
Used	1 093	1 891	876	83	613	287	1 329	386	1 196	676	24
2002											
Total expenditures	128 444	94 529	25 864	3 430	14 719	19 532	59 311	13 169	22 409	21 269	1 532
Structures, total	24 308	35 579	7 129	933	3 276	14 655	30 291	7 758	12 157	13 261	250
New	19 748	30 227	6 424	913	2 948	13 601	27 273	7 332	10 848	11 363	248
Used	4 739	5 352	706	21	328	1 055	3 018	425	1 309	1 899	2
Equipment, total	103 956	58 949	18 735	2 497	11 443	4 876	29 021	5 412	10 252	8 007	1 282
New	103 421	56 847	18 021	2 481	10 585	4 690	28 196	5 132	9 290	6 858	1 276
Used	535	2 102	714	16	857	186	825	280	962	1 149	6
2003											
Total expenditures	120 787	87 952	24 703	3 298	16 612	16 667	61 151	11 029	21 036	26 035	1 476
Structures, total	26 200	25 028	5 314	925	3 976	11 984	30 996	6 800	10 568	18 518	209
New	17 908	16 446	4 671	869	3 213	11 569	28 885	6 532	9 417	16 288	202
Used	8 292	8 583	643	56	763	415	2 111	268	1 151	2 230	7
Equipment, total	94 587	62 923	19 389	2 373	12 636	4 683	30 155	4 229	10 468	7 517	1 267
New	94 205	61 253	18 675	2 368	11 374	4 569	29 497	4 038	9 684	6 706	1 263
Used	383	1 671	714	5	1 262	114	658	192	783	811	4
2004											
Total expenditures	153 629	91 606	26 688	2 825	17 455	18 919	64 561	12 165	20 641	19 701	1 572
Structures, total	43 919	27 277	6 007	860	2 567	13 728	32 608	7 360	9 860	12 278	321
New	30 216	21 610	5 714	798	2 309	12 781	30 668	7 196	9 126	10 867	307
Used	13 703	5 667	293	62	259	947	1 939	164	734	1 411	13
Equipment, total	109 710	64 329	20 681	1 965	14 888	5 190	31 953	4 804	10 781	7 423	1 252
New	109 244	61 947	20 081	1 931	12 692	4 965	31 280	4 677	10 373	6 788	1 248
Used	466	2 382	600	34	2 196	225	673	128	408	635	3
2005											
Total expenditures	161 389	103 022	33 066	2 809	18 194	17 484	73 825	14 165	30 718	20 105	2 163
Structures, total	39 383	24 791	8 717	857	3 051	12 711	39 089	9 242	17 679	12 036	460
New	31 023	17 341	7 633	795	2 759	11 913	37 493	8 805	16 567	11 350	452
Used	8 360	7 450	1 084	62	292	798	1 597	436	1 112	686	8
Equipment, total	122 005	78 231	24 350	1 951	15 143	4 773	34 736	4 924	13 039	8 069	1 703
New	121 511	76 894	23 887	1 917	13 523	4 597	34 110	4 757	11 950	7 209	1 681
Used	494	1 337	463	34	1 620	176	626	166	1 089	861	22
2006											
Total expenditures	163 069	132 073	30 284	3 306	19 231	22 615	75 296	17 156	36 217	25 959	1 813
Structures, total	41 326	40 794	6 971	875	3 613	17 537	41 197	11 733	22 585	16 621	467
New	34 028	30 240	6 375	799	3 485	16 203	37 765	11 326	21 774	15 754	446
Used	7 298	10 554	596	76	128	1 334	3 433	406	811	866	21
Equipment, total	121 743	91 280	23 313	2 432	15 618	5 078	34 099	5 424	13 632	9 339	1 346
New	121 157	88 957	22 867	2 188	14 932	4 983	33 508	5 121	13 161	8 463	1 322
Used	586	2 323	446	244	686	95	591	303	472	875	24

Note: Detail may not sum to total because of rounding.

Table 5-8. Capital Expenditures for Structures and Equipment for Companies with Employees by Major NAICS Industry Sector—*Continued*

(Millions of dollars.)

Year and type of expenditure	Total	Forestry, fishing, and agricultural services (113–115)	Mining (21)	Utilities (22)	Construction (23)	Manufacturing (31–33)			Wholesale trade (42)	Retail trade (44–45)	Transportation and warehousing (48–49)	Information (51)
						Total	Durable goods industries (321, 327, 33)	Nondurable goods industries (31, 322–326)				
2007												
Total expenditures	1 270 522	2 149	120 681	85 354	36 692	197 298	107 664	89 633	30 776	82 511	67 351	106 084
Structures, total	490 779	469	85 242	40 178	3 529	42 458	17 879	24 579	7 526	41 527	23 712	29 081
New	457 233	320	83 206	37 647	2 704	41 247	17 431	23 816	7 091	40 471	22 808	28 304
Used	33 546	149	2 036	2 531	824	1 211	447	763	436	1 056	904	777
Equipment, total	779 744	1 681	35 440	45 176	33 164	154 840	89 786	65 054	23 250	40 983	43 639	77 003
New	750 353	1 368	33 095	44 107	27 325	150 333	87 020	63 313	21 690	39 668	39 238	76 143
Used	29 391	313	2 344	1 069	5 838	4 507	2 766	1 741	1 560	1 316	4 400	861
2008												
Total expenditures	1 294 491	2 337	149 272	98 668	40 838	213 117	103 022	110 095	32 370	73 234	79 617	103 327
Structures, total	529 393	421	109 683	43 515	11 129	49 346	18 896	30 450	8 387	36 147	30 078	27 376
New	500 474	417	105 064	41 746	10 525	48 184	18 168	30 015	7 958	35 342	29 214	27 080
Used	28 919	4	4 618	1 769	603	1 162	728	434	430	805	863	296
Equipment, total	765 098	1 917	39 590	55 154	29 709	163 771	84 125	79 645	23 982	37 087	49 539	75 951
New	728 322	1 610	35 928	53 486	22 404	158 104	80 690	77 414	22 554	36 328	41 877	75 342
Used	36 776	307	3 662	1 668	7 305	5 667	3 435	2 232	1 429	759	7 662	609
2009												
Total expenditures	1 015 322	2 168	100 564	103 024	19 751	155 153	76 039	79 114	25 252	58 428	55 702	88 373
Structures, total	414 051	460	72 255	45 973	4 556	13 054	13 054	22 680	5 485	28 205	22 088	21 764
New	395 022	453	69 942	45 168	4 215	34 537	12 273	22 264	5 131	27 220	21 128	21 410
Used	19 030	7	2 313	805	341	1 198	782	416	354	985	961	354
Equipment, total	601 270	1 708	28 308	57 051	15 195	119 418	62 985	56 434	19 767	30 223	33 614	66 609
New	577 051	1 428	26 790	54 848	11 815	115 470	60 699	54 772	18 512	29 063	30 182	65 879
Used	24 219	279	1 518	2 204	3 380	3 948	2 286	1 662	1 255	1 160	3 432	731
2010												
Total expenditures	1 036 162	3 244	114 995	94 580	17 856	159 621	85 274	74 347	31 197	66 263	58 948	97 445
Structures, total	395 531	678	84 719	43 128	2 633	31 608	14 044	17 564	6 879	29 171	23 287	21 822
New	366 853	670	81 654	42 084	2 361	30 515	13 432	17 084	5 710	27 555	22 507	20 747
Used	28 678	8	3 065	1 044	272	1 092	612	480	1 170	1 616	780	1 076
Equipment, total	640 631	2 566	30 276	51 451	15 223	128 013	71 230	56 783	24 317	37 092	35 660	75 623
New	612 441	1 969	28 568	49 560	11 377	124 375	69 437	54 938	21 877	35 351	30 023	74 900
Used	28 190	597	1 708	1 891	3 846	3 638	1 793	1 845	2 440	1 741	5 638	723

Note: Detail may not sum to total because of rounding.

Table 5-8. Capital Expenditures for Structures and Equipment for Companies with Employees by Major NAICS Industry Sector—Continued

(Millions of dollars.)

Year and type of expenditure	Finance and insurance (52)	Real estate and rental and leasing (53)	Professional, scientific, and technical services (54)	Management of companies and enterprises (55)	Administrative and support and waste management (56)	Educational services (61)	Health care and social assistance (62)	Arts, entertainment, and recreation (71)	Accommodation and food services (72)	Other services, except public administration (81)	Structure and equipment expenditures serving multiple industries
2007											
Total expenditures	172 894	117 969	31 804	4 542	18 167	23 238	84 160	18 769	38 021	29 680	2 380
Structures, total	45 159	41 222	7 453	1 472	3 859	17 910	45 361	12 589	22 211	19 165	656
New	36 507	34 026	6 944	1 404	3 677	17 322	43 522	11 894	21 226	16 264	650
Used	8 652	7 196	509	69	182	588	1 839	695	984	2 901	6
Equipment, total	127 735	76 747	24 351	3 070	14 308	5 328	38 799	6 180	15 810	10 515	1 725
New	126 763	74 735	23 931	2 943	13 599	5 253	38 258	5 916	14 671	9 593	1 724
Used	972	2 012	420	127	709	75	541	264	1 139	922	1
2008											
Total expenditures	132 913	106 910	32 980	4 567	16 552	27 426	90 248	17 109	40 519	28 312	4 175
Structures, total	25 058	45 929	8 836	1 304	4 133	21 698	50 105	11 594	24 947	18 673	1 035
New	22 640	36 532	8 481	1 241	3 789	20 632	47 205	11 224	24 271	17 899	1 030
Used	2 418	9 397	355	63	344	1 065	2 900	370	675	775	6
Equipment, total	107 855	60 981	24 144	3 264	12 420	5 728	40 143	5 515	15 572	9 638	3 139
New	107 108	59 117	23 349	3 146	11 687	5 672	39 161	5 340	14 012	8 974	3 124
Used	747	1 864	794	117	733	56	981	175	1 560	664	15
2009											
Total expenditures	99 466	72 902	28 163	4 719	19 234	28 018	79 370	16 265	26 439	29 296	3 034
Structures, total	21 825	26 564	6 669	1 371	5 876	22 388	44 375	11 035	14 735	22 054	641
New	20 419	22 350	5 975	1 334	5 361	21 577	42 188	10 804	13 607	21 564	639
Used	1 406	4 214	694	36	515	810	2 187	231	1 128	490	2
Equipment, total	77 641	46 339	21 494	3 349	13 359	5 630	34 994	5 230	11 704	7 243	2 393
New	77 169	44 594	20 980	3 311	12 471	5 403	34 271	5 073	10 858	6 545	2 389
Used	473	1 745	514	38	888	227	723	157	846	698	4
2010											
Total expenditures	102 715	81 305	29 213	4 549	16 891	23 365	78 525	12 118	19 915	20 951	2 468
Structures, total	16 206	32 375	5 736	1 557	3 520	17 672	42 887	7 709	9 765	13 605	572
New	13 649	23 085	5 395	1 506	3 434	16 677	40 139	7 546	9 051	11 999	568
Used	2 557	9 290	341	50	86	995	2 749	163	714	1 606	4
Equipment, total	86 509	48 929	23 477	2 992	13 371	5 693	35 638	4 409	10 151	7 346	1 896
New	86 026	47 615	22 894	2 972	12 676	5 550	34 925	4 158	8 856	6 879	1 890
Used	483	1 315	583	20	695	142	713	251	1 294	467	7

Note: Detail may not sum to total because of rounding.

NOTES AND DEFINITIONS, CHAPTER 5

TABLES 5-1 THROUGH 5-4
GROSS SAVING AND INVESTMENT ACCOUNTS

SOURCE: U.S. DEPARTMENT OF COMMERCE, BUREAU OF ECONOMIC ANALYSIS (BEA)

All of the data in these tables are from the National Income and Product Accounts, which are described in the Notes and Definitions to Chapter 1. All quarterly series are shown at seasonally adjusted annual rates. Current and constant dollar values are in billions of dollars. Indexes of quantity are based on the average for the year 2005, set to equal 100.

Definitions: Table 5-1

Gross saving is saving before the deduction of allowances for the consumption of fixed capital. It represents the amount of saving available to finance gross investment. *Net saving* is gross saving less allowances for fixed capital consumption. It represents the amount of saving available for financing expansion of the capital stock, and comprises net private saving (the sum of personal saving, undistributed corporate profits, and wage accruals less disbursements) and the net saving of federal, state, and local governments.

Personal saving is derived by subtracting personal outlays from disposable personal income. (See Chapter 4 for more information.) It is the current net saving of individuals (including proprietors of unincorporated businesses), nonprofit institutions that primarily serve individuals, life insurance carriers, retirement funds, private noninsured welfare funds, and private trust funds. Conceptually, personal saving may also be viewed as the sum for all persons (including institutions as previously defined) of the net acquisition of financial assets and the change in physical assets, less the sum of net borrowing and consumption of fixed capital. In either case, it is defined to exclude capital gains. That is, it excludes profits on the increase in the value of homes, securities, and other property—whether realized or unrealized—and therefore includes the noncorporate inventory valuation adjustment and the capital consumption adjustment (IVA and CCAdj, respectively). (See notes and definitions to Chapter 1.)

The net saving of *Domestic corporate business* is corporate profits after tax less dividends plus the corporate IVA and corporate CCAdj. (See notes and definitions for Chapter 1.)

Government net saving was formerly called "current surplus or deficit (-) of general government." (See Chapter 6 for further detail from the government accounts.) Where current receipts of government exceed current expenditures, government has a current surplus (indicated by a positive value) and saving is made available to finance investment by government or other sectors—for example, by the

repayment of debt, which can free up funds for private investment. Where current expenditures exceed current receipts, there is a government deficit (indicated by a negative value) and government must borrow, drawing on funds that would otherwise be available for private investment. In these accounts, current expenditures are defined to include a charge for the consumption of fixed capital.

Consumption of fixed capital is an accounting charge for the using-up of private and government fixed capital, including software, located in the United States. It is based on studies of prices of used equipment and structures in resale markets. For general government and nonprofit institutions that primarily serve individuals, consumption of fixed capital is recorded in government consumption expenditures and in personal consumption expenditures (PCE), respectively, and taken to be the value of the current services of the fixed capital assets owned and used by these entities. *Private consumption of fixed capital* consists of tax-return-based depreciation charges for corporations and nonfarm proprietorships and historical-cost depreciation (calculated by the Bureau of Economic Analysis [BEA] using a geometric pattern of price declines) for farm proprietorships, rental income of persons, and nonprofit institutions, minus the capital consumption adjustments. (In other words, in the NIPA treatment of saving, the amount of the CCAdj is taken out of book depreciation and added to income and profits—a reallocation from one form of gross saving to another.)

Gross private domestic investment consists of gross private fixed investment and change in private inventories. (See the notes and definitions for Chapter 1.)

Gross government investment consists of federal, state, and local general government and government enterprise expenditures for fixed assets (structures, equipment, and software). Government inventory investment is included in government consumption expenditures. For further detail, see Chapter 6.

Capital account transactions, net are the net cash or in-kind transfers between the United States and the rest of the world that are linked to the acquisition or disposition of assets rather than the purchase or sale of currently-produced goods and services. When positive, it represents a net transfer from the United States to the rest of the world; when negative, it represents a net transfer to the United States from the rest of the world. This is a definitional category that was introduced in the 1999 revision of the NIPAs. Estimates are available only from 1982 forward. With the new treatment of disaster losses and disaster insurance introduced in the 2009 revision, this line will include disaster-related insurance payouts to the rest of the world less what is received from the rest of the world.

Net lending or net borrowing (-), NIPAs is equal to the international balance on current account as measured in the NIPAs (see Chapter 7) less capital account transactions, net. When positive, this represents net investment by the United

States in the rest of the world; when negative, it represents net borrowing by the United States from the rest of the world. For data before 1982, net lending or net borrowing equals the NIPA balance on current account, because estimates of capital account transactions are not available.

By definition, gross national saving must equal the sum of gross domestic investment, capital account transactions, and net international lending (where net international borrowing appears as negative lending). In practice, due to differences in measurement, these two aggregates differ by the *statistical discrepancy* calculated in the product and income accounts. (See Chapter 1.) Gross saving is therefore equal to the sum of gross domestic investment, capital account transactions, and net international lending minus the statistical discrepancy. Where the statistical discrepancy is negative, it means that the sum of measured investment, capital transactions, and net international lending has fallen short of measured saving.

Net domestic investment is gross domestic investment minus consumption of fixed capital.

Gross national income is national income plus the consumption of fixed capital. (See Chapter 1 for further information.) This is a new concept introduced in the 2003 revision. It is conceptually equal to gross national product, but differs by the statistical discrepancy. Gross national income is an appropriate denominator for the national saving ratios. Saving was previously shown as a percentage of gross national product; in the revision, it is instead shown as a percentage of the income-side equivalent of gross national product. Since saving is measured as a residual from income, it is appropriate to involve consistent measurements—and consistent imperfections in those measurements— in both the numerator and the denominator of the fraction.

Definitions: Tables 5-2 through 5-4

Gross private fixed investment comprises both nonresidential and residential fixed investment. It consists of purchases of fixed assets, which are commodities that will be used in a production process for more than one year, including replacements and additions to the capital stock. It is "gross" in the sense that it is measured before a deduction for consumption of fixed capital. It covers all investment by private businesses and nonprofit institutions in the United States, regardless of whether the investment is owned by U.S. residents. It does not include purchases of the same types of equipment and structures by government agencies, which are included in government gross investment, or investment by U.S. residents in other countries.

Gross nonresidential fixed investment consists of structures, equipment, and software that are not related to personal residences.

Nonresidential structures consists of new construction, brokers' commissions on sales of structures, and net purchases (purchases less sales) of used structures by private business

and by nonprofit institutions from government agencies. New construction includes hotels, motels, and mining exploration, shafts, and wells.

Other nonresidential structures consists primarily of religious, educational, vocational, lodging, railroads, farm, and amusement and recreational structures, net purchases of used structures, and brokers' commissions on the sale of structures.

Nonresidential equipment and software consists of private business purchases—on capital account—of new machinery, equipment, and vehicles; purchases and in-house production of software; dealers' margins on sales of used equipment; and net purchases (purchases less sales) of used equipment from government agencies, persons, and the rest of the world. (However, it does not include the personal-use portion of equipment purchased for both business and personal use. This is included in PCE.)

Software excludes the value of software "embedded," or bundled, in computers and other equipment, which is instead included in the value of that equipment.

Other information processing includes communication equipment, nonmedical instruments, medical equipment and instruments, photocopy and related equipment, and office and accounting equipment.

Other nonresidential equipment consists primarily of furniture and fixtures, agricultural machinery, construction machinery, mining and oilfield machinery, service industry machinery, and electrical equipment not elsewhere classified.

Residential private fixed investment consists of both *structures* and residential producers' durable *equipment*—that is, equipment owned by landlords and rented to tenants. Investment in *structures* consists of new units, improvements to existing units, manufactured homes, brokers' commissions on the sale of residential property, and net purchases (purchases less sales) of used structures from government agencies.

Other residential structures consists primarily of manufactured homes, improvements, dormitories, net purchases of used structures, and brokers' commissions on the sale of residential structures.

Real gross private investment (Table 5-3) and *chain-type quantity indexes for private fixed investment* (Table 5-4) are defined and explained in the notes and definitions to Chapter 1. The chained-dollar (2005) estimates in Table 5-3 are constructed by applying the changes in the chain-type quantity indexes, as shown in Table 5-4, to the 2005 current-dollar values. Thus, they do not contain any information about time trends that is not already present in the quantity indexes.

In Table 5-4, the user may wish to distinguish between the use of the "not available" symbol (...) and the publication of zero values (0.0). The "not available" values shown for computers and software mean that BEA has no separate estimates of their values; they are included in total "information processing equipment and software." The zeroes indicate quantities so small relative to the 2005 base that they round to zero, but they do exist and are included in the higher-level aggregates.

As the quantity indexes are chain-weighted at the basic level of aggregation, chained constant-dollar components generally do not add to the chained constant-dollar totals. For this reason, BEA only makes available year-2005-dollar estimates back to 1995 (except for the very highest levels of aggregation of gross domestic product [GDP]), since the addition problem is less severe for years close to the base year. However, the addition problem is so severe for computers that BEA does not even publish recent year-2005-dollar values for this component. BEA notes that "The quantity index for computers can be used to accurately measure the real growth rate of this component. However, because computers exhibit rapid changes in prices relative to other prices in the economy, the chained-dollar estimates should not be used to measure the component's relative importance or its contribution to the growth rate of more aggregate series." (Footnote to BEA Table 5.3.6, *Survey of Current Business*, available on the BEA Web site at <http://www.bea.gov>.) Accurate estimates of these contributions are shown in BEA Table 5.3.2, which is published in the *Survey of Current Business* and can be found on the BEA Web site.

Data availability, revisions, and references

See the information on the NIPAs at the end of the notes and definitions to Chapter 1. All current and historical data are available on the BEA Web site at <http://www.bea.gov> or the STAT-USA subscription Web site at <http://www.stat-usa.gov>.

TABLES 5-5 AND 5-6
CURRENT-COST NET STOCK OF FIXED ASSETS; CHAIN-TYPE QUANTITY INDEXES FOR NET STOCK OF FIXED ASSETS

SOURCE: U.S. DEPARTMENT OF COMMERCE, BUREAU OF ECONOMIC ANALYSIS (BEA)

The Bureau of Economic Analysis (BEA) calculates measurements, integrated with the national income and product accounts (NIPAs), of the level of the stock of fixed assets in the U.S. economy, or what is commonly called the "capital stock." (The fixed investment component of the GDP is a flow, or the increment of new capital goods into the capital stock.) Data on consumer stocks of durable goods are also included in the accounts, but are not shown here. Historical data are available back to 1901, with detailed annual estimates of net stocks, depreciation, and investment by type and by NAICS (North American Industry Classification System) industry. This volume of *Business Statistics* presents time series data on the net stock of fixed assets

valued in current dollars and also as constant-dollar quantity indexes.

Definitions and methods

The definitions of capital stock categories are the same as used in GDP investment categories. (See the notes and definitions to Tables 5-2 through 5-4 for more information.)

The values of fixed capital and depreciation typically reported by businesses are inadequate for economic analysis and are not typically used in these measures. In business reports, capital is generally valued at historical costs—each year's capital acquisition in the prices of the year acquired—and the totals thus represent a mixture of pricing bases. Reported depreciation is generally based on historical cost and on depreciation rates allowable by federal income tax law, rather than on a realistic rate of economic depreciation.

In these data, the *net stock of fixed assets* is measured by a perpetual inventory method. In other words, net stock at any given time is the cumulative value of past gross investment less the cumulative value of past depreciation (measured by "consumption of fixed capital," the component of the NIPAs that is subtracted from GDP in order to yield net domestic product) and also less damages from disasters and war losses that exceed normal depreciation (such as Hurricane Katrina and the terrorist attacks of September 11, 2001).

The initial calculations using this perpetual inventory method are performed in real terms for each type of asset. They are then aggregated to higher levels using an annual-weighted Fisher-type index. (See the definition of *real or chained-dollar estimates* in the notes and definitions for Chapter 1.) This provides the *chain-type quantity indexes* shown in Table 5-6. Growth rates in these indexes measure real growth in the capital stock.

The real values are then converted to a *current-cost* basis to yield the values shown in Table 5-5. They are converted by multiplying the real values by the appropriate price index for the period under consideration. A major use of the current-cost net stock figures is comparison with the value of output in that year; for example, the current-cost net stock of fixed assets for the total economy divided by the current-dollar value of GDP yields a capital-output ratio for the entire economy. Growth rates in current-cost values will reflect both the real growth measured by the quantity indexes and the increase in the value at current prices of the existing stock.

Data availability and references

The latest comprehensive revision was presented and described in "Fixed Assets and Consumer Durable Goods for 1999–2008," *Survey of Current Business* (November 2009). Annual data are available on the BEA Web site at <www.bea.gov/national/FA2004/Index.asp>.

TABLES 5-7 AND 5-8
ANNUAL CAPITAL EXPENDITURES

SOURCE: U.S. DEPARTMENT OF COMMERCE, CENSUS BUREAU

These data are from the Census Bureau's Annual Capital Expenditures Survey (ACES). The survey provides detailed information on capital investment in new and used structures and equipment by nonfarm businesses.

The survey is based on a stratified random sample of approximately 47,000 companies with employees and 30,000 non-employer businesses (businesses with an owner but no employees). For companies with employees, the Census Bureau reports data for 132 separate industry categories from the North American Industry Classification System (NAICS); Table 5-8 shows these data for the major NAICS sectors. Total capital expenditures, with no industry detail, are reported for the nonemployer businesses and are shown in Table 5-7, where they can be compared with the totals for companies with employees. The 1999 ACES was the first to use NAICS, providing data for the years 1998 forward on that basis.

Definitions

Capital expenditures include all capitalized costs during the year for both new and used structures and equipment, including software, that were chargeable to fixed asset accounts for which depreciation or amortization accounts are ordinarily maintained. For projects lasting longer than one year, this definition includes gross additions to construction-in-progress accounts, even if the asset was not in use and not yet depreciated. For *capital leases*, the company using the asset (lessee) is asked to include the cost or present value of the leased assets in the year in which the lease was entered. Also included in capital expenditures are capitalized leasehold improvements and capitalized interest charges on loans used to finance capital projects.

Structures consist of the capitalized costs of buildings and other structures and all necessary expenditures to acquire, construct, and prepare the structures. The costs of any machinery and equipment that is integral to or built-in features of the structures are classified as structures. Also included are major additions and alterations to existing structures and capitalized repairs and improvements to buildings.

New structures include new buildings and other structures not previously owned, as well as buildings and other structures that have been previously owned but not used or occupied.

Used structures are buildings and other structures that have been previously owned and occupied.

Equipment includes machinery, furniture and fixtures, computers, and vehicles used in the production and distribution of goods and services. Expenditures for machinery and equipment that is housed in structures and can be removed or replaced without significantly altering the structure are classified as equipment.

New equipment consists of machinery and equipment purchased new, as well as equipment produced in the company for the company's own use.

Used equipment is secondhand machinery and equipment.

Capital leases consist of new assets acquired under capital lease arrangements entered into during the year. Capital leases are defined by the criteria in the Financial Accounting Standards (FASB) Number 13.

Capitalized computer software consists of costs of materials and services directly related to the development or acquisition of software; payroll and payroll-related costs for employees directly associated with software development; and interest cost incurred while developing the software. Capitalized computer software is defined by the criteria in Statement of Position 98-1, Accounting for the Costs of Computer Software Developed or Obtained for Internal Use.

Prepackaged software is purchased off-the-shelf through retailers or other mass-market outlets for internal use by the company and includes the cost of licensing fees and service/maintenance agreements.

Vendor-customized software is externally developed by vendors and customized for the company's use.

Internally-developed software is developed by the company's employees for internal use and includes loaded payroll (salaries, wages, benefits, and bonuses related to all software development activities).

Data availability and references

Current and historical data and references are available on the Census Bureau Web site at <http://www.census.gov/econ/aces>.

CHAPTER 6: GOVERNMENT

Section 6a: Federal Government in the National Income and Product Accounts

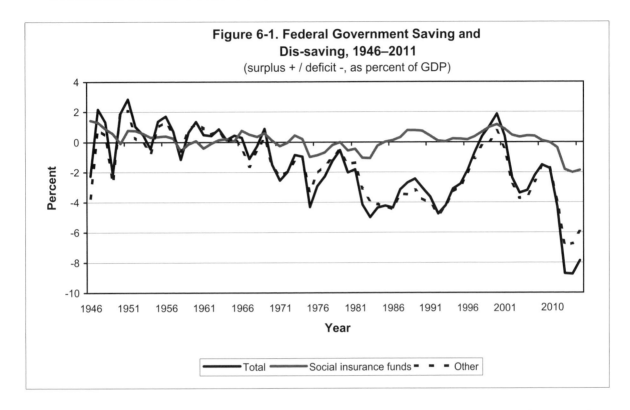

Figure 6-1. Federal Government Saving and
Dis-saving, 1946–2011
(surplus + / deficit -, as percent of GDP)

- In the recovery and economic expansion of the 2000s, the federal budget never got back to a surplus such as those achieved in 1999 and 2000. With the onset of the most severe recession of the postwar period beginning in December 2007, deficits grew rapidly as receipts fell while expenditures continued to rise. In calendar 2010, the total NIPA budget deficit peaked at 8.8 percent of GDP, including a 2.0 percent deficit in social insurance funds. This was not as great as World War II deficits but exceeded in scale the deficits of the 1930s. The calendar 2011 deficit was slightly lower in dollar terms, and significantly lower—7.9 percent—as a percent of GDP. (Tables 6-1, 1-1, and 6-14B)

- From 2007 to 2010 (calendar years), the deficit rose from 1.7 percent of GDP to 8.8 percent, an increase of 7.1 percentage points. The main contributors to this rise were a 2.5 percentage point drop in tax receipts, an 0.9 percent increase in defense program spending, an 0.6 percentage point increase in non-defense program spending, and a 2.9 percentage point rise in social benefits to persons such as Social Security and unemployment insurance. (Tables 6-1, 6-2, 6-3, and 1-1)

- Total federal government current expenditures increased from 17.6 percent of gross domestic product (GDP) in 1953—the peak for Korean War spending— to 25.5 percent of GDP in 2010, falling back a bit to 24.9 percent in 2011. The composition of current expenditures changed significantly over that period. "Consumption" spending on defense and nondefense programs fell from 72 percent of total spending to 29 percent, while social benefits to persons such as Social Security and Medicare rose from 13 percent to 46 percent. Grants to state and local governments increased from 3 percent to 13 percent. (Tables 6-1 and 1-1)

Table 6-1. Federal Government Current Receipts and Expenditures

(National income and product accounts, calendar years, billions of dollars, quarterly data are at seasonally adjusted annual rates.)

NIPA Table 3.2

Year and quarter	Total current receipts	Current tax receipts							Contributions for government social insurance	Income receipts on assets			Current transfer receipts	Current surplus of government enterprises
		Total tax receipts	Personal current taxes	Taxes on production and imports		Taxes on corporate income		Taxes from the rest of the world		Interest receipts	Dividends	Rents and royalties		
				Excise taxes	Customs duities	Federal Reserve banks	Other corporate taxes							
1955	71.1	62.0	30.5	9.8	0.7	0.3	20.8	. . .	8.8	. . .	. . .	. . .	0.3	. . .
1956	75.8	65.8	33.9	10.2	0.7	0.4	20.5	. . .	9.6	. . .	. . .	. . .	0.4	. . .
1957	79.3	67.9	36.0	10.7	0.8	0.5	19.9	. . .	11.0	. . .	. . .	. . .	0.4	. . .
1958	76.1	64.6	35.5	10.4	0.8	0.5	17.4	. . .	11.0	. . .	. . .	. . .	0.4	. . .
1959	87.0	73.2	38.5	11.2	1.0	0.9	21.6	0.1	13.5	. . .	. . .	0.0	0.4	-0.1
1960	93.9	76.5	41.8	12.0	1.1	0.9	20.6	0.1	16.0	1.3	. . .	0.0	0.4	-0.3
1961	95.5	77.5	42.7	12.1	1.0	0.7	20.8	0.1	16.6	1.4	. . .	0.1	0.5	-0.5
1962	103.6	83.3	46.5	12.9	1.2	0.8	21.7	0.1	18.6	1.6	. . .	0.1	0.5	-0.5
1963	111.8	88.6	49.1	13.5	1.2	0.9	23.7	0.2	21.1	1.7	. . .	0.1	0.6	-0.3
1964	111.8	87.7	46.0	14.1	1.3	1.6	24.6	0.2	21.8	1.7	. . .	0.1	0.7	-0.3
1965	121.0	95.6	51.1	13.8	1.6	1.3	27.6	0.2	22.7	1.8	. . .	0.1	1.1	-0.3
1966	138.0	104.7	58.6	12.6	1.9	1.6	29.8	0.2	30.6	2.0	. . .	0.1	1.2	-0.6
1967	146.9	109.8	64.4	13.3	1.9	1.9	28.1	0.2	34.1	2.3	. . .	0.2	1.1	-0.6
1968	171.3	129.7	76.4	14.6	2.3	2.5	33.6	0.3	37.9	2.7	. . .	0.2	1.1	-0.3
1969	192.7	146.0	91.7	15.4	2.4	3.0	33.0	0.4	43.3	2.5	. . .	0.2	1.1	-0.4
1970	186.1	137.9	88.9	15.6	2.5	3.5	27.1	0.4	45.5	2.8	. . .	0.2	1.1	-1.5
1971	191.9	138.6	85.8	15.9	3.1	3.4	30.1	0.4	50.3	3.1	. . .	0.3	1.1	-1.6
1972	220.3	158.2	102.8	15.5	3.0	3.2	33.4	0.4	58.3	3.3	. . .	0.4	1.3	-1.1
1973	250.8	173.0	109.6	16.5	3.3	4.3	38.9	0.4	74.5	3.4	. . .	0.4	1.3	-1.8
1974	280.0	192.1	126.5	16.4	3.7	5.6	39.6	0.4	84.1	3.6	. . .	0.5	1.4	-1.8
1975	277.6	186.8	120.7	16.2	5.9	5.4	38.2	0.5	88.1	4.3	. . .	0.6	1.5	-3.6
1976	323.0	217.9	141.2	16.8	4.6	5.9	48.7	0.7	99.8	5.2	. . .	0.7	1.6	-2.2
1977	364.0	247.2	162.2	17.3	5.4	5.9	55.7	0.7	111.1	5.8	. . .	0.9	2.0	-3.0
1978	424.0	286.6	188.9	18.2	7.1	7.0	64.4	1.0	128.7	7.4	. . .	1.1	2.7	-2.5
1979	486.9	325.9	224.6	18.2	7.5	9.3	65.1	1.1	149.8	9.2	. . .	1.5	3.1	-2.6
1980	532.8	355.5	250.0	26.5	7.2	11.7	58.6	1.6	163.6	11.3	. . .	2.3	3.9	-3.9
1981	619.9	407.7	290.6	41.3	8.6	14.0	51.7	1.5	193.0	14.8	. . .	3.5	4.1	-3.2
1982	617.4	386.3	295.0	32.3	8.6	15.2	33.8	1.4	206.0	18.3	. . .	3.8	5.7	-2.9
1983	643.3	393.2	286.2	35.3	9.1	14.2	47.1	1.2	223.1	20.4	. . .	3.5	6.1	-3.0
1984	710.0	425.2	301.4	35.4	11.9	16.1	59.2	1.3	254.1	22.8	. . .	3.9	7.4	-3.4
1985	774.4	460.2	336.0	33.9	12.2	17.8	58.5	1.9	277.9	25.7	. . .	3.5	9.7	-2.6
1986	816.0	479.2	350.0	30.0	13.7	17.8	66.0	1.7	298.9	28.8	. . .	2.4	8.5	-1.9
1987	896.5	543.6	392.5	30.4	15.5	17.7	85.4	2.0	317.4	25.1	. . .	2.3	11.0	-3.0
1988	958.5	566.2	402.8	33.4	16.4	17.4	93.8	2.4	354.8	27.4	. . .	2.0	10.5	-2.3
1989	1 038.0	621.2	451.5	32.3	17.5	21.6	95.6	2.7	378.0	25.9	. . .	2.1	12.7	-1.7
1990	1 082.8	642.2	470.1	33.4	17.5	23.6	94.5	3.0	402.0	27.0	. . .	2.6	14.2	-5.3
1991	1 101.9	635.6	461.3	44.9	16.8	20.8	89.2	2.6	420.6	26.3	. . .	2.8	18.2	-1.6
1992	1 148.0	659.9	475.2	45.0	18.3	16.8	102.0	2.6	444.0	22.2	. . .	2.6	19.4	0.0
1993	1 224.1	713.0	505.5	46.5	19.8	16.0	122.5	2.7	465.5	22.8	. . .	2.7	21.3	-1.3
1994	1 322.1	781.4	542.5	57.5	21.4	20.5	136.3	3.1	496.2	20.0	. . .	2.7	22.8	-0.9
1995	1 407.8	844.6	585.8	55.7	19.8	23.4	155.9	3.9	521.9	20.8	. . .	2.5	18.4	-0.3
1996	1 526.4	931.9	663.3	53.6	19.2	20.1	170.5	5.2	545.4	22.5	. . .	4.0	23.8	-1.2
1997	1 656.2	1 030.1	744.2	58.2	19.6	20.7	182.3	5.1	579.4	21.0	. . .	4.5	21.3	-0.1
1998	1 777.9	1 115.8	825.2	61.1	19.6	26.6	177.7	5.7	617.4	17.3	. . .	3.9	22.6	0.8
1999	1 895.0	1 195.4	893.0	64.3	19.2	25.4	187.6	5.9	654.8	17.1	. . .	3.5	23.4	0.8
2000	2 057.1	1 309.6	995.6	66.1	21.1	25.3	194.1	7.3	698.6	19.3	. . .	5.2	25.7	-1.2
2001	2 020.3	1 249.4	991.8	64.6	20.6	27.1	137.6	7.7	723.3	18.1	. . .	6.5	27.0	-4.0
2002	1 859.3	1 073.5	828.6	66.9	19.9	24.5	126.0	7.6	739.3	15.4	. . .	4.8	26.1	0.2
2003	1 885.1	1 070.2	774.2	67.9	21.4	22.0	175.8	9.0	762.8	16.4	. . .	6.4	25.6	3.7
2004	2 013.9	1 153.8	799.2	71.0	23.3	18.1	232.2	10.0	807.6	16.3	0.1	6.8	29.0	0.3
2005	2 290.1	1 383.7	931.9	73.5	25.3	21.5	319.5	12.1	852.6	16.4	0.2	7.0	33.6	-3.5
2006	2 524.5	1 558.3	1 049.9	72.7	26.7	29.1	366.0	14.0	904.6	18.2	0.3	7.7	38.3	-2.9
2007	2 654.7	1 637.6	1 165.6	65.7	28.8	34.6	328.2	14.7	945.3	22.2	0.2	7.3	44.8	-2.7
2008	2 502.2	1 447.7	1 101.3	64.8	29.2	31.7	202.0	18.8	973.1	20.1	0.6	10.0	54.4	-3.7
2009	2 232.5	1 170.2	856.6	74.2	23.1	47.4	154.3	14.7	948.9	24.5	18.7	4.8	69.8	-4.4
2010	2 429.6	1 340.7	896.4	72.9	28.6	79.3	250.3	13.3	970.9	29.9	17.0	6.2	69.7	-4.8
2011	2 564.8	1 536.7	1 072.0	79.1	31.7	77.2	261.0	15.7	907.3	30.3	18.5	6.5	67.4	-1.8
2009														
1st quarter	2 225.9	1 169.7	915.7	66.0	24.5	23.2	124.5	15.7	951.2	21.4	12.7	4.9	71.1	-5.1
2nd quarter	2 214.0	1 137.1	844.6	77.6	22.4	34.5	142.2	15.8	951.7	23.5	21.0	5.2	80.2	-4.7
3rd quarter	2 221.6	1 168.7	830.8	77.1	21.9	57.6	168.4	13.0	946.6	25.3	19.0	4.3	61.6	-4.0
4th quarter	2 268.5	1 205.4	835.2	76.2	23.5	74.4	181.9	14.3	945.9	27.7	22.3	4.9	66.1	-3.9
2010														
1st quarter	2 364.8	1 290.3	856.5	71.5	26.8	75.4	246.9	13.2	960.3	29.6	14.9	5.3	69.1	-4.7
2nd quarter	2 407.8	1 322.0	888.7	73.5	28.5	70.2	247.9	13.2	969.9	29.9	16.3	6.0	68.6	-4.9
3rd quarter	2 475.4	1 377.8	912.3	73.4	30.2	84.2	264.7	13.0	975.5	30.1	18.6	6.6	71.6	-4.8
4th quarter	2 470.5	1 372.8	927.8	73.1	28.8	87.4	241.7	13.9	977.9	30.0	18.2	6.8	69.7	-4.9
2011														
1st quarter	2 527.9	1 513.3	1 046.8	76.5	30.2	91.3	254.1	14.3	894.6	29.7	18.5	6.4	68.1	-2.7
2nd quarter	2 554.1	1 532.7	1 065.4	80.0	32.0	84.4	255.6	15.3	900.3	30.6	18.0	6.3	67.4	-1.2
3rd quarter	2 583.5	1 547.1	1 083.2	79.5	32.8	69.8	264.7	17.0	915.1	30.2	18.7	6.5	66.9	-1.1
4th quarter	2 593.8	1 553.6	1 092.4	80.5	31.7	63.3	269.4	16.3	919.0	30.8	18.9	6.6	67.2	-2.4

. . . = Not available.

Table 6-1. Federal Government Current Receipts and Expenditures—*Continued*

(National income and product accounts, calendar years, billions of dollars, quarterly data are at seasonally adjusted annual rates.)

NIPA Table 3.2

Year and quarter	Total current expenditures	Consumption expenditures	Government social benefits		Other current transfer payments		Interest payments			Subsidies	Net federal government saving, NIPA (surplus + / deficit -)		
			Benefits to persons	Benefits to the rest of the world	Grants-in-aid to state and local governments	Payments to the rest of the world	Total	To persons and business	To the rest of the world		Total	Social insurance funds	Other
1955	65.4	43.9	11.5	0.0	2.4	2.2	4.8	. . .	0.1	0.6	5.7	1.5	4.1
1956	68.3	45.0	12.3	0.0	2.5	2.0	5.2	. . .	0.2	1.2	7.5	1.7	5.8
1957	76.1	49.5	14.5	0.0	2.9	2.0	5.7	. . .	0.2	1.6	3.3	1.1	2.2
1958	81.5	50.9	18.2	0.0	3.3	2.0	5.4	. . .	0.1	1.8	-5.4	-2.7	-2.8
1959	83.7	49.9	18.6	0.0	3.8	4.0	6.3	. . .	0.3	1.1	3.3	-0.7	3.9
1960	86.8	49.7	19.9	0.2	4.0	3.5	8.4	8.0	0.3	1.1	7.1	0.4	6.7
1961	92.9	51.6	23.1	0.3	4.5	3.5	7.9	7.6	0.3	2.0	2.6	-2.3	4.9
1962	101.2	57.8	23.5	0.3	5.0	3.6	8.6	8.3	0.3	2.3	2.4	-0.6	3.0
1963	106.5	60.8	24.6	0.3	5.6	3.6	9.3	8.9	0.4	2.2	5.3	0.8	4.5
1964	110.9	62.8	25.2	0.3	6.5	3.4	10.0	9.6	0.5	2.7	0.9	1.3	-0.3
1965	117.7	65.7	27.3	0.5	7.2	3.6	10.6	10.1	0.5	3.0	3.2	0.4	2.8
1966	135.7	75.7	29.9	0.5	10.1	4.0	11.6	11.1	0.5	3.9	2.3	6.0	-3.7
1967	156.2	87.0	36.5	0.6	11.7	4.0	12.7	12.1	0.6	3.8	-9.3	4.1	-13.4
1968	173.7	95.3	41.9	0.6	12.7	4.5	14.6	13.9	0.7	4.1	-2.4	3.2	-5.6
1969	184.1	98.3	45.8	0.6	14.6	4.5	15.8	15.0	0.8	4.5	8.6	5.7	2.9
1970	201.6	98.6	55.6	0.7	19.3	4.8	17.7	16.7	1.0	4.8	-15.5	1.0	-16.4
1971	220.6	101.9	66.1	0.8	23.2	6.0	17.9	16.1	1.8	4.6	-28.7	-3.0	-25.7
1972	245.2	107.6	72.9	1.0	31.7	7.2	18.8	16.1	2.7	6.6	-24.9	-0.6	-24.3
1973	262.6	108.8	84.5	1.2	34.8	5.4	22.8	19.0	3.8	5.1	-11.8	5.9	-17.7
1974	294.5	117.9	103.3	1.3	36.3	6.0	26.0	21.7	4.3	3.2	-14.5	3.2	-17.7
1975	348.3	129.5	132.3	2.0	45.1	6.1	28.9	24.4	4.5	4.3	-70.6	-16.3	-54.4
1976	376.7	137.1	143.1	2.5	50.7	4.5	33.8	29.3	4.5	4.9	-53.7	-16.0	-37.6
1977	410.1	150.7	152.1	2.6	56.6	4.2	37.1	31.6	5.5	6.9	-46.1	-14.1	-32.1
1978	452.9	163.3	162.4	2.7	65.5	5.0	45.3	36.7	8.7	8.7	-28.9	-4.7	-24.2
1979	500.9	178.9	182.8	3.0	66.3	5.8	55.7	44.6	11.1	8.2	-14.0	0.0	-13.9
1980	589.5	207.4	219.6	3.5	72.3	7.3	69.7	57.0	12.7	9.4	-56.6	-15.8	-40.8
1981	676.7	238.3	250.1	4.3	72.5	6.7	93.9	76.6	17.3	11.1	-56.8	-14.3	-42.5
1982	752.6	263.3	281.2	4.1	69.5	8.1	111.8	92.5	19.3	14.6	-135.3	-34.4	-100.9
1983	819.5	286.4	303.0	3.6	71.6	8.9	124.6	105.6	19.0	20.9	-176.2	-37.9	-138.4
1984	881.5	309.9	309.2	3.7	76.7	11.2	150.3	129.1	21.2	20.7	-171.5	-9.4	-162.1
1985	953.0	338.3	325.4	4.0	80.9	13.8	169.4	146.3	23.1	21.0	-178.6	0.9	-179.5
1986	1 010.7	358.0	343.7	4.4	87.6	14.2	178.2	153.5	24.6	24.6	-194.6	5.7	-200.3
1987	1 045.9	373.7	356.7	4.3	83.9	12.7	184.6	158.4	26.2	30.0	-149.3	14.5	-163.8
1988	1 096.9	381.7	377.4	4.6	91.6	13.2	199.3	167.6	31.7	29.2	-138.4	39.1	-177.5
1989	1 172.0	398.5	410.1	5.1	98.3	13.5	219.3	181.0	38.4	27.1	-133.9	42.6	-176.6
1990	1 259.2	419.0	445.1	6.2	111.4	13.5	237.5	196.7	40.8	26.6	-176.4	42.4	-218.8
1991	1 320.3	438.3	491.7	6.3	131.6	-25.6	250.9	210.1	40.9	27.1	-218.4	24.7	-243.1
1992	1 450.5	444.1	549.5	6.2	149.1	20.6	251.3	212.2	39.1	29.7	-302.5	5.4	-307.8
1993	1 504.3	441.2	581.5	6.2	164.0	21.7	253.4	214.0	39.4	36.3	-280.2	2.8	-283.1
1994	1 542.5	440.7	606.4	6.8	175.1	19.9	261.3	217.1	44.2	32.2	-220.4	15.4	-235.7
1995	1 614.0	440.1	642.6	6.8	184.2	15.4	290.4	234.8	55.6	34.5	-206.2	15.6	-221.8
1996	1 674.7	446.5	676.9	7.6	191.1	20.4	297.3	230.6	66.6	34.9	-148.2	12.9	-161.2
1997	1 716.3	457.5	702.2	7.9	198.4	17.0	300.0	218.3	81.7	33.4	-60.1	28.9	-89.1
1998	1 744.3	454.6	716.1	8.2	212.6	18.0	298.8	214.7	84.2	35.9	33.6	58.3	-24.7
1999	1 796.2	473.3	735.3	8.5	232.9	18.7	282.7	202.1	80.5	44.8	98.8	92.5	6.3
2000	1 871.9	496.0	769.1	8.7	247.3	22.3	283.3	198.7	84.5	45.3	185.2	114.3	70.9
2001	1 979.8	530.2	836.3	9.4	276.1	18.2	258.6	180.2	78.4	51.1	40.5	88.1	-47.6
2002	2 112.1	590.5	914.9	9.7	304.2	23.3	229.1	154.2	74.9	40.5	-252.8	49.7	-302.5
2003	2 261.5	660.3	962.6	10.1	338.0	28.6	212.9	139.0	73.8	49.0	-376.4	37.6	-413.9
2004	2 393.4	721.4	1 014.3	10.6	349.2	30.9	221.0	138.4	82.5	46.0	-379.5	50.3	-429.7
2005	2 573.1	765.8	1 078.0	11.2	361.2	40.9	255.4	151.5	103.9	60.5	-283.0	49.0	-332.0
2006	2 728.3	811.0	1 180.7	12.4	359.0	34.9	279.2	144.2	135.0	51.0	-203.8	12.4	-216.1
2007	2 900.0	848.9	1 254.2	13.3	380.8	42.2	313.2	148.8	164.4	47.4	-245.2	-3.0	-242.3
2008	3 115.7	931.7	1 385.7	15.5	395.5	45.3	292.1	125.3	166.8	49.9	-613.5	-53.0	-560.5
2009	3 450.4	986.6	1 601.8	16.1	482.4	53.3	251.9	107.6	144.4	58.3	-1 217.9	-251.7	-966.2
2010	3 703.3	1 054.0	1 708.3	16.6	531.5	57.3	279.9	143.7	136.1	55.8	-1 273.7	-294.1	-979.5
2011	3 752.6	1 072.1	1 738.8	16.8	492.5	57.8	312.4	176.4	136.1	62.3	-1 187.8	-283.1	-904.7
2009													
1st quarter	3 219.8	955.2	1 507.7	15.2	438.4	44.8	204.1	48.4	155.7	54.4	-993.9	-193.9	-800.0
2nd quarter	3 516.9	981.2	1 632.8	16.9	503.4	57.3	269.8	124.3	145.5	55.6	-1 303.0	-241.4	-1 061.6
3rd quarter	3 527.0	997.8	1 624.0	16.0	486.4	63.5	272.1	132.4	139.6	67.2	-1 305.4	-276.6	-1 028.8
4th quarter	3 537.9	1 012.4	1 642.7	16.1	501.4	47.6	261.8	125.2	136.6	55.9	-1 269.4	-295.0	-974.4
2010													
1st quarter	3 636.6	1 033.9	1 690.2	16.3	514.8	61.7	264.9	129.1	135.8	54.8	-1 271.8	-292.5	-979.3
2nd quarter	3 685.8	1 056.0	1 695.7	16.6	524.2	52.6	286.2	149.5	136.7	54.7	-1 278.0	-284.9	-993.0
3rd quarter	3 733.1	1 066.6	1 716.0	17.0	542.1	56.9	279.1	142.4	136.7	55.4	-1 257.7	-294.5	-963.2
4th quarter	3 757.8	1 059.6	1 731.3	16.4	544.9	58.1	289.4	154.0	135.4	58.2	-1 287.3	-304.6	-982.6
2011													
1st quarter	3 729.0	1 059.1	1 725.1	16.4	514.5	56.8	298.0	162.7	135.4	59.2	-1 201.1	-289.2	-911.9
2nd quarter	3 829.5	1 077.5	1 737.5	16.8	527.7	64.9	342.8	207.5	135.4	62.2	-1 275.4	-290.5	-984.9
3rd quarter	3 744.2	1 084.9	1 745.6	17.1	470.6	55.8	306.6	170.6	136.0	63.8	-1 160.7	-278.1	-882.6
4th quarter	3 707.8	1 066.9	1 747.0	16.8	457.1	53.7	302.3	164.7	137.6	63.9	-1 114.1	-274.7	-839.4

. . . = Not available.

Table 6-2. Federal Government Consumption Expenditures and Gross Investment

(National income and product accounts, calendar years, billions of dollars, quarterly data are at seasonally adjusted annual rates.)

NIPA Tables 3.9.5, 3.10.5

| Year and quarter | Total | Consumption expenditures | | | | | Gross investment | | | | | | |
| | | Total | Compensation of general government employees | Consumption of general government fixed capital | Intermediate goods and services purchased [1] | Less: Own-account investment and sales to other sectors | Total | National defense | | | Nondefense | | |
								Total	Structures	Equipment and software	Total	Structures	Equipment and software
1955	54.9	43.9	19.0	8.6	17.7	1.3	10.9	10.1	2.1	8.0	0.9	0.6	0.2
1956	56.7	45.0	19.6	9.1	17.1	0.8	11.6	10.5	2.1	8.4	1.2	0.9	0.3
1957	61.3	49.5	20.2	9.6	20.8	1.3	11.9	10.5	2.3	8.2	1.4	1.1	0.2
1958	63.8	50.9	21.3	9.8	21.1	1.3	12.9	11.3	2.6	8.7	1.6	1.4	0.2
1959	65.3	49.9	21.7	10.1	19.3	1.2	15.4	13.7	2.5	11.2	1.7	1.5	0.2
1960	64.1	49.7	22.6	10.4	17.8	1.1	14.3	12.3	2.2	10.1	2.0	1.7	0.3
1961	67.9	51.6	23.7	10.7	18.2	1.0	16.3	13.9	2.4	11.5	2.4	1.9	0.6
1962	75.2	57.8	25.2	11.3	22.4	1.1	17.4	14.5	2.0	12.5	2.9	2.1	0.8
1963	76.9	60.8	26.5	11.9	23.5	1.2	16.1	12.6	1.6	11.0	3.5	2.3	1.2
1964	78.4	62.8	28.5	12.1	23.3	1.2	15.6	11.5	1.3	10.2	4.2	2.5	1.6
1965	80.4	65.7	30.0	12.4	24.6	1.3	14.7	10.0	1.1	8.9	4.7	2.8	1.9
1966	92.4	75.7	34.3	12.9	30.3	1.7	16.7	11.8	1.3	10.5	4.9	2.8	2.1
1967	104.6	87.0	37.9	13.6	36.8	1.3	17.7	13.5	1.2	12.3	4.2	2.2	1.9
1968	111.3	95.3	41.9	14.4	40.3	1.3	16.0	12.2	1.2	10.9	3.8	2.1	1.7
1969	113.3	98.3	44.9	15.1	39.8	1.4	15.0	11.3	1.5	9.9	3.6	1.9	1.7
1970	113.4	98.6	48.3	15.7	35.9	1.4	14.8	11.1	1.3	9.8	3.8	2.1	1.7
1971	113.6	101.9	51.7	16.1	35.7	1.5	11.7	7.5	1.8	5.7	4.2	2.5	1.7
1972	119.6	107.6	55.4	16.1	38.4	2.3	12.0	7.5	1.8	5.7	4.5	2.7	1.8
1973	122.5	108.8	57.4	16.5	37.7	2.8	13.6	8.7	2.1	6.6	4.9	3.1	1.8
1974	134.5	117.9	62.0	17.5	41.7	3.4	16.6	11.1	2.2	8.9	5.6	3.4	2.2
1975	149.0	129.5	68.4	18.9	45.2	3.0	19.5	13.0	2.3	10.7	6.5	4.1	2.4
1976	159.7	137.1	73.3	20.5	46.2	2.8	22.6	15.3	2.1	13.2	7.3	4.6	2.7
1977	175.4	150.7	79.9	22.1	52.4	3.8	24.7	16.7	2.4	14.4	8.0	5.0	3.0
1978	190.9	163.3	85.8	23.9	58.2	4.5	27.6	17.8	2.5	15.3	9.8	6.1	3.7
1979	210.6	178.9	91.8	25.8	66.9	5.6	31.6	21.4	2.5	18.9	10.2	6.3	4.0
1980	243.7	207.4	102.5	28.7	82.3	6.2	36.3	24.3	3.2	21.1	12.0	7.1	4.9
1981	280.2	238.3	115.1	32.3	97.0	6.2	41.9	28.9	3.2	25.7	13.0	7.7	5.3
1982	310.8	263.3	125.3	35.9	108.2	6.1	47.5	34.7	4.0	30.8	12.7	6.8	6.0
1983	342.9	286.4	132.3	38.9	121.3	6.1	56.4	41.9	4.8	37.1	14.5	6.7	7.8
1984	374.3	309.9	149.4	42.7	124.5	6.7	64.4	48.7	4.9	43.8	15.7	7.0	8.7
1985	412.8	338.3	159.0	46.1	140.2	6.9	74.4	57.5	6.2	51.3	16.9	7.3	9.6
1986	438.4	358.0	163.1	49.5	152.3	6.9	80.4	62.9	6.8	56.1	17.5	8.0	9.5
1987	459.5	373.7	170.3	53.0	158.3	7.9	85.8	66.4	7.7	58.8	19.4	9.0	10.4
1988	461.6	381.7	178.0	56.8	155.8	8.7	79.8	61.3	7.4	53.9	18.6	6.8	11.7
1989	481.4	398.5	185.7	60.7	161.5	9.4	83.0	62.7	6.4	56.3	20.3	6.9	13.4
1990	507.5	419.0	193.9	64.9	170.5	10.3	88.5	65.9	6.1	59.8	22.6	8.0	14.6
1991	526.6	438.3	205.9	69.0	174.8	11.3	88.2	63.4	4.6	58.8	24.8	9.2	15.7
1992	532.9	444.1	210.7	71.3	173.4	11.3	88.8	61.6	5.2	56.3	27.2	10.3	16.9
1993	525.0	441.2	210.9	74.2	167.0	11.0	83.8	55.5	5.3	50.1	28.3	11.2	17.0
1994	518.6	440.7	208.9	76.3	168.6	13.0	77.9	53.0	5.8	47.2	24.9	10.2	14.7
1995	518.8	440.1	205.8	77.8	167.2	10.6	78.6	51.8	6.7	45.1	26.8	10.8	16.0
1996	527.0	446.5	209.7	77.9	170.1	11.1	80.4	51.6	6.3	45.4	28.8	11.3	17.5
1997	531.0	457.5	212.1	77.9	176.6	9.1	73.4	45.3	6.1	39.2	28.1	9.9	18.2
1998	531.0	454.6	214.3	78.0	172.4	10.1	76.4	45.8	5.8	39.9	30.7	10.8	19.9
1999	554.9	473.3	220.6	79.8	181.4	8.5	81.6	48.2	5.4	42.8	33.4	10.7	22.7
2000	576.1	496.0	233.0	82.1	190.7	9.8	80.1	49.2	5.4	43.8	30.9	8.3	22.6
2001	611.7	530.2	242.1	82.8	214.4	9.1	81.5	50.9	5.3	45.6	30.6	8.1	22.5
2002	680.6	590.5	268.4	83.5	248.0	9.4	90.1	57.0	5.8	51.2	33.1	9.9	23.2
2003	756.5	660.3	297.8	85.2	287.2	9.9	96.2	62.8	7.3	55.4	33.5	10.3	23.1
2004	824.6	721.4	323.0	89.0	320.0	10.6	103.3	69.6	7.1	62.4	33.7	9.1	24.6
2005	876.3	765.8	344.4	94.3	340.8	13.7	110.5	74.2	7.5	66.8	36.3	8.3	28.0
2006	931.7	811.0	360.1	100.5	363.2	12.8	120.7	81.0	8.1	72.9	39.7	9.5	30.2
2007	976.3	848.9	379.7	106.3	374.8	11.9	127.4	86.9	10.1	76.9	40.5	11.1	29.4
2008	1 080.1	931.7	404.3	113.4	427.9	13.9	148.4	104.5	13.7	90.9	43.8	11.4	32.4
2009	1 142.7	986.6	435.2	118.1	448.2	14.8	156.1	110.8	17.3	93.5	45.3	12.4	32.9
2010	1 222.8	1 054.0	466.3	123.3	481.1	16.5	168.8	117.1	17.3	99.8	51.7	16.3	35.4
2011	1 232.9	1 072.1	477.5	130.9	482.6	19.0	160.8	108.1	14.8	93.3	52.7	15.6	37.1
2009													
1st quarter	1 105.3	955.2	427.4	116.6	425.6	14.3	150.1	105.7	16.9	88.9	44.4	12.1	32.3
2nd quarter	1 137.2	981.2	433.1	117.4	445.3	14.7	156.1	112.1	17.0	95.0	44.0	11.5	32.5
3rd quarter	1 157.7	997.8	437.4	118.5	457.1	15.2	159.8	114.4	17.9	96.5	45.4	12.5	32.9
4th quarter	1 170.6	1 012.4	442.8	119.8	465.0	15.2	158.3	110.9	17.4	93.5	47.4	13.6	33.8
2010													
1st quarter	1 195.2	1 033.9	459.6	121.3	468.6	15.7	161.3	112.6	16.6	96.0	48.7	14.2	34.6
2nd quarter	1 224.5	1 056.0	469.5	122.7	481.0	17.3	168.5	116.4	17.2	99.3	52.1	17.0	35.1
3rd quarter	1 237.5	1 066.6	467.6	123.7	493.4	18.1	170.8	118.2	18.0	100.2	52.6	16.7	35.8
4th quarter	1 234.3	1 059.6	468.3	125.5	481.1	15.4	174.7	121.2	17.5	103.7	53.5	17.1	36.3
2011													
1st quarter	1 219.9	1 059.1	474.1	127.7	471.5	14.3	160.9	108.0	15.5	92.6	52.8	16.4	36.4
2nd quarter	1 237.1	1 077.5	477.3	129.9	486.1	15.8	159.6	107.3	14.4	92.9	52.4	16.0	36.3
3rd quarter	1 248.9	1 084.9	478.8	132.1	503.1	29.2	164.0	110.9	15.9	94.9	53.1	15.2	37.9
4th quarter	1 225.5	1 066.9	479.8	133.9	469.6	16.4	158.5	106.1	13.4	92.7	52.4	14.7	37.7

[1] Includes general government intermediate inputs for goods and services sold to other sectors and for own-account investment.

Table 6-3. Federal Government Defense and Nondefense Consumption Expenditures by Type

(National income and product accounts, calendar years, billions of dollars, quarterly data are at seasonally adjusted annual rates.)

NIPA Table 3.10.5

Year and quarter	Defense consumption expenditures [1]						Nondefense consumption expenditures [1]					
	Total	Compensation of general government employees	Consumption of general government fixed capital	Intermediate goods and services purchased [2]			Total	Compensation of general government employees	Consumption of general government fixed capital	Intermediate goods and services purchased [2]		
				Durable goods	Nondurable goods	Services				Durable goods	Nondurable goods	Services
1950	17.1	8.0	5.2	1.7	0.9	1.5	4.9	3.1	0.6	0.1	0.5	0.9
1951	30.1	13.5	5.4	4.4	2.3	5.0	4.3	3.1	0.6	0.1	0.1	0.7
1952	38.9	16.1	6.1	8.0	2.8	6.1	5.3	3.2	0.6	0.1	0.5	1.3
1953	41.2	16.0	6.9	9.1	4.2	5.1	7.1	3.1	0.6	0.1	2.4	1.3
1954	37.1	15.4	7.5	6.8	3.2	4.2	6.9	2.9	0.6	0.1	2.2	1.4
1955	36.8	15.8	7.9	6.0	1.7	5.9	7.1	3.2	0.6	0.1	2.5	1.6
1956	38.7	16.1	8.5	6.1	1.7	6.7	6.3	3.5	0.6	0.1	0.8	1.7
1957	43.1	16.5	9.0	6.7	2.2	9.3	6.3	3.7	0.6	0.1	0.8	1.8
1958	44.0	17.0	9.1	7.1	2.1	9.5	6.8	4.3	0.7	0.0	0.7	1.7
1959	40.1	17.3	9.4	5.1	1.8	6.9	9.8	4.4	0.7	0.0	3.3	2.1
1960	41.0	17.7	9.8	4.4	1.9	7.7	8.7	5.0	0.7	0.1	1.1	2.5
1961	42.7	18.3	10.0	3.6	2.3	8.8	9.0	5.4	0.7	0.1	0.4	3.0
1962	46.6	19.4	10.6	4.6	2.9	9.6	11.3	5.8	0.8	0.2	1.5	3.6
1963	48.3	20.1	11.0	4.7	2.7	10.2	12.4	6.4	0.9	0.3	1.2	4.5
1964	48.8	21.6	11.1	4.0	2.9	9.7	14.0	7.0	1.0	0.4	1.1	5.3
1965	50.6	22.6	11.3	4.2	3.2	9.9	15.1	7.4	1.2	0.5	1.1	5.7
1966	59.9	26.3	11.5	6.2	4.7	12.2	15.9	8.0	1.4	0.5	0.4	6.4
1967	69.9	29.3	12.0	6.2	7.3	15.5	17.0	8.6	1.6	0.4	1.2	6.2
1968	77.1	32.4	12.7	7.5	8.4	16.4	18.2	9.5	1.7	0.4	1.9	5.7
1969	78.1	34.7	13.2	6.5	7.6	16.5	20.2	10.1	1.9	0.3	3.0	5.9
1970	76.5	36.6	13.6	6.1	5.4	15.2	22.1	11.7	2.1	0.3	2.0	7.1
1971	77.1	38.2	13.8	4.6	4.4	16.3	24.9	13.4	2.3	0.3	2.1	8.1
1972	79.5	40.5	13.8	5.7	4.7	15.5	28.2	14.8	2.4	0.3	2.4	9.9
1973	79.4	41.4	14.0	5.5	4.3	15.3	29.4	16.0	2.5	0.2	1.9	10.4
1974	84.5	44.1	14.7	5.2	5.2	16.9	33.4	18.0	2.8	0.2	2.6	11.7
1975	90.9	47.9	15.7	6.0	5.1	17.4	38.7	20.5	3.2	0.2	2.8	13.7
1976	95.8	50.3	17.1	5.8	4.5	18.8	41.4	23.1	3.4	0.3	3.5	13.3
1977	104.2	53.6	18.4	8.0	4.5	20.4	46.5	26.3	3.7	0.3	4.4	14.7
1978	112.7	57.5	19.9	9.6	4.9	21.7	50.6	28.3	4.0	0.4	4.9	16.7
1979	123.8	61.7	21.3	11.3	6.2	24.2	55.1	30.1	4.5	0.5	5.2	19.4
1980	143.7	68.6	23.5	12.8	10.0	30.2	63.8	34.0	5.2	0.7	7.4	21.3
1981	167.3	78.8	26.3	16.2	11.8	35.8	71.0	36.3	6.0	0.6	11.2	21.4
1982	191.1	87.4	29.2	19.6	11.5	45.4	72.1	37.9	6.7	0.6	9.1	22.1
1983	208.7	92.4	31.7	25.1	11.3	49.5	77.7	39.9	7.3	0.9	10.6	23.9
1984	232.8	107.5	34.8	27.1	10.4	54.7	77.1	41.8	7.9	0.9	6.4	24.9
1985	253.7	115.3	37.4	29.3	10.0	63.4	84.7	43.6	8.7	1.0	9.5	27.1
1986	267.9	118.8	40.2	31.9	10.2	68.7	90.1	44.3	9.3	1.0	12.4	28.1
1987	283.6	123.5	43.0	33.8	10.3	75.1	90.1	46.8	10.0	1.1	6.9	31.1
1988	293.5	126.9	45.9	33.5	10.6	79.0	88.3	51.1	10.9	1.2	-0.1	31.6
1989	299.4	131.7	49.0	32.0	10.8	78.3	99.1	54.0	11.8	1.3	5.7	33.3
1990	308.0	134.5	52.3	31.6	11.0	81.8	111.0	59.3	12.7	1.5	5.7	38.9
1991	319.7	141.8	55.3	31.0	10.7	84.3	118.6	64.0	13.6	1.6	6.3	41.0
1992	315.2	143.0	57.1	28.4	9.4	81.3	128.9	67.7	14.2	1.7	6.9	45.8
1993	307.5	137.7	59.4	26.4	8.5	79.8	133.7	73.3	14.8	1.7	8.3	42.4
1994	300.8	133.7	61.0	22.9	7.6	81.7	139.9	75.2	15.3	1.6	6.9	47.9
1995	297.0	129.8	61.7	20.9	6.3	81.9	143.2	76.1	16.0	1.5	8.6	47.9
1996	303.2	132.3	61.2	20.8	7.6	85.2	143.4	77.4	16.6	1.7	7.9	46.9
1997	304.5	131.9	60.4	20.9	7.6	87.3	153.0	80.2	17.6	1.7	9.7	49.4
1998	300.3	130.8	59.7	20.9	7.0	85.1	154.3	83.5	18.3	1.7	10.8	46.9
1999	313.0	132.7	60.0	22.2	8.2	92.9	160.3	87.9	19.8	1.8	7.9	48.5
2000	321.8	138.1	60.7	22.1	10.4	93.6	174.2	94.9	21.5	1.8	9.7	53.0
2001	342.0	144.8	60.5	22.3	10.3	107.8	188.1	97.3	22.4	1.9	12.7	59.4
2002	380.7	162.0	60.5	23.2	11.5	127.7	209.8	106.4	23.0	2.3	13.0	70.3
2003	435.2	182.1	61.7	25.7	13.4	156.8	225.1	115.6	23.5	2.2	14.9	74.3
2004	481.2	199.4	64.8	28.8	17.1	175.8	240.2	123.6	24.2	2.4	16.7	79.1
2005	514.8	215.7	68.7	29.5	20.9	185.4	251.0	128.7	25.6	2.8	19.7	82.5
2006	543.9	225.6	73.2	32.8	22.1	196.0	267.1	134.5	27.4	2.9	19.7	89.7
2007	575.4	238.3	77.4	36.1	24.1	204.7	273.5	141.4	28.9	2.9	19.1	87.9
2008	633.3	254.6	83.1	42.7	30.5	228.3	298.5	149.6	30.4	3.2	22.8	100.5
2009	664.1	273.9	86.5	45.5	24.6	239.6	322.5	161.3	31.6	3.4	25.8	109.2
2010	702.1	291.6	90.7	47.2	26.6	252.2	351.9	174.7	32.6	3.9	28.5	122.7
2011	716.9	301.2	96.8	44.4	33.2	247.7	355.2	176.3	34.1	3.8	29.0	124.5
2009												
1st quarter	641.9	269.2	85.2	41.4	22.3	229.8	313.3	158.2	31.3	3.3	24.9	103.9
2nd quarter	659.5	271.1	85.9	45.5	23.7	239.2	321.7	162.0	31.5	3.3	27.3	106.3
3rd quarter	674.6	275.5	86.9	48.8	25.8	243.6	323.2	161.9	31.6	3.5	24.6	110.8
4th quarter	680.5	279.9	87.9	46.3	26.7	245.7	331.9	163.0	31.9	3.6	26.6	116.0
2010												
1st quarter	691.0	288.7	89.1	44.6	27.0	247.6	342.9	170.9	32.1	3.7	27.0	118.6
2nd quarter	701.6	290.5	90.3	46.0	27.0	253.9	354.4	179.0	32.4	3.9	28.1	122.2
3rd quarter	713.1	292.6	91.0	48.1	25.5	262.0	353.6	175.0	32.7	3.9	29.1	124.7
4th quarter	702.7	294.5	92.5	50.2	26.8	245.2	356.9	173.9	33.0	3.9	29.7	125.4
2011												
1st quarter	701.0	298.1	94.4	42.4	31.4	241.1	358.1	176.1	33.3	3.9	29.1	123.7
2nd quarter	723.4	300.4	96.0	44.1	34.4	254.8	354.1	177.0	33.8	3.7	28.2	120.8
3rd quarter	733.2	302.6	97.8	45.1	33.6	260.4	351.7	176.2	34.4	4.0	30.5	129.5
4th quarter	709.9	303.8	99.0	45.8	33.5	234.3	357.0	176.1	34.9	3.7	28.4	123.9

[1]Excludes government sales to other sectors and government own-account investment (construction and software).
[2]Includes general government intermediate inputs for goods and services sold to other sectors and for own-account investment.

Table 6-4. National Defense Consumption Expenditures and Gross Investment: Selected Detail

(National income and product accounts, calendar years, billions of dollars, quarterly data are at seasonally adjusted annual rates.)

NIPA Table 3.11.5

Year and quarter	Compensation of general government employees		Consumption expenditures							Gross investment			
			Intermediate goods and services purchased [1]							Equipment and software			
			Durable goods	Nondurable goods		Services							
	Military	Civilian	Aircraft	Petroleum products	Ammunition	Research and development	Installation support	Weapons support	Personnel support	Aircraft	Missiles	Ships	Electronics and software
1972	27.0	13.5	2.7	1.8	2.0	5.1	4.4	1.6	1.7	2.6	1.5	1.8	0.8
1973	27.6	13.8	2.4	1.7	1.7	5.3	4.3	1.6	1.5	2.3	1.5	1.6	0.9
1974	29.1	15.0	2.0	2.8	1.4	5.7	4.7	1.8	1.8	2.3	1.7	2.2	1.0
1975	31.1	16.8	2.1	2.9	1.1	5.9	4.9	1.7	2.1	3.6	1.3	2.2	1.2
1976	32.4	17.8	2.0	2.5	0.6	6.4	5.4	1.9	2.3	3.4	1.4	2.4	1.3
1977	34.0	19.7	3.3	2.4	0.8	6.8	6.2	2.1	2.2	3.7	1.2	3.1	1.5
1978	36.2	21.3	3.5	2.5	1.0	7.1	6.3	2.4	2.6	3.7	1.1	3.9	1.8
1979	38.7	22.9	4.8	3.6	1.2	7.7	7.3	2.9	2.7	4.8	1.8	4.3	2.1
1980	43.5	25.1	5.6	6.8	1.4	10.2	8.5	4.4	3.0	6.1	2.3	4.1	2.6
1981	50.5	28.3	7.8	7.7	1.6	12.4	9.3	5.2	4.0	7.5	2.8	5.1	3.2
1982	56.6	30.8	10.2	6.8	2.1	14.1	13.7	6.0	5.8	8.4	3.4	6.2	3.8
1983	59.8	32.7	13.6	6.4	2.5	14.5	15.5	7.3	6.4	10.1	4.6	7.1	4.6
1984	72.8	34.8	14.0	5.9	2.2	16.2	17.0	8.6	6.7	10.9	5.7	8.0	5.6
1985	78.2	37.2	15.4	5.8	1.3	21.7	17.2	9.8	8.4	13.4	6.6	9.0	7.0
1986	80.6	38.1	17.2	3.6	3.6	23.8	18.5	10.4	9.4	17.9	7.9	8.9	7.8
1987	83.7	39.8	18.2	3.9	2.8	27.0	19.1	11.0	10.9	17.6	8.7	8.8	8.7
1988	85.2	41.7	17.9	3.5	3.5	31.5	19.0	9.8	11.4	13.5	7.8	8.6	9.2
1989	87.4	44.3	16.4	4.2	3.1	28.6	19.0	10.3	12.4	12.2	8.8	10.0	9.6
1990	89.1	45.4	14.8	5.3	2.8	26.1	22.1	11.7	13.0	12.0	11.2	10.8	9.9
1991	93.8	48.0	13.6	4.7	2.7	21.9	23.8	10.2	12.7	9.2	10.8	10.2	9.7
1992	93.2	49.8	12.2	3.5	2.6	23.7	23.2	8.5	14.4	8.3	10.6	10.1	9.8
1993	87.0	50.7	10.7	3.2	2.5	26.7	24.8	6.8	12.1	9.3	7.9	8.7	9.9
1994	83.2	50.5	9.2	3.0	1.8	25.6	26.1	7.8	13.8	10.5	5.7	8.1	9.3
1995	80.2	49.5	8.9	2.8	1.2	25.0	25.4	8.2	14.9	9.0	4.7	8.0	8.8
1996	82.9	49.4	8.8	3.4	1.4	27.4	25.9	7.4	15.9	9.2	4.1	6.8	9.0
1997	82.8	49.1	9.4	2.9	1.7	28.2	25.0	8.8	17.2	5.8	2.9	6.1	9.0
1998	82.5	48.2	9.9	2.1	1.9	26.9	23.9	8.5	17.2	5.8	3.3	6.4	9.1
1999	84.3	48.4	10.5	2.6	1.9	27.2	25.0	9.9	21.8	7.0	2.9	6.8	9.7
2000	88.5	49.6	9.8	4.1	1.8	27.0	25.2	10.1	22.2	7.8	2.7	6.6	10.1
2001	94.5	50.3	9.8	4.2	2.1	29.7	27.5	13.3	27.3	8.5	3.3	7.2	9.7
2002	107.6	54.4	9.8	4.6	2.5	36.8	30.5	16.5	33.8	9.4	3.3	8.7	9.9
2003	124.4	57.7	11.2	5.3	2.6	43.1	35.5	21.1	40.5	9.2	3.5	9.5	10.5
2004	135.1	64.3	11.9	7.0	3.6	50.6	35.8	21.5	51.0	11.1	4.1	10.0	11.5
2005	147.0	68.7	10.7	10.1	4.0	53.9	35.3	24.4	55.8	13.5	4.0	9.8	12.6
2006	153.8	71.8	11.0	11.2	4.2	58.0	36.7	25.5	60.8	13.6	4.5	10.5	14.3
2007	162.8	75.5	11.3	12.5	4.1	56.6	36.6	26.2	65.6	13.0	4.3	10.3	16.4
2008	175.7	78.9	12.7	17.6	4.5	60.3	41.3	28.7	77.4	13.7	4.4	11.0	20.3
2009	189.8	84.1	14.6	10.7	4.1	59.7	43.8	30.8	82.7	14.1	5.2	11.1	20.0
2010	198.1	93.5	15.7	13.4	4.3	59.5	46.3	32.5	89.4	17.4	6.0	11.8	20.4
2011	202.6	98.6	17.8	19.8	4.2	56.5	44.1	25.9	97.2	19.2	5.4	11.7	18.2
2005													
1st quarter	148.1	67.8	10.7	6.9	3.7	53.2	33.7	22.8	53.1	12.6	3.1	9.9	11.6
2nd quarter	146.6	68.3	10.7	10.4	4.0	56.8	34.0	22.7	52.4	13.5	4.5	9.5	12.4
3rd quarter	146.5	69.6	10.6	12.2	4.2	55.3	37.6	28.2	60.1	14.0	3.5	10.6	13.5
4th quarter	147.0	68.9	10.9	10.8	4.0	50.5	36.0	23.8	57.7	14.1	4.9	9.2	13.1
2006													
1st quarter	153.5	71.0	10.6	9.9	4.1	58.2	36.0	24.3	60.8	13.0	4.7	9.7	13.5
2nd quarter	153.1	71.7	10.3	11.2	4.1	58.4	37.3	26.8	63.7	15.2	4.7	11.1	13.9
3rd quarter	153.7	71.9	10.8	14.1	4.2	56.0	35.6	23.3	58.7	11.9	3.4	10.6	14.8
4th quarter	154.8	72.7	12.5	9.5	4.4	59.5	37.8	27.8	60.2	14.3	5.3	10.7	14.8
2007													
1st quarter	160.8	75.1	10.1	10.4	4.2	58.2	35.2	23.6	59.4	12.1	5.2	9.8	15.5
2nd quarter	162.2	75.5	10.9	12.3	3.7	57.5	36.0	25.3	63.2	13.9	4.3	10.2	16.1
3rd quarter	164.0	75.3	11.8	13.7	4.4	54.9	37.3	27.8	68.5	13.1	3.9	10.2	17.1
4th quarter	164.2	76.0	12.5	13.5	3.9	55.8	38.0	28.1	71.1	12.7	3.8	11.1	16.8
2008													
1st quarter	170.7	78.0	11.4	17.9	4.5	56.9	40.0	28.8	74.5	8.9	4.5	9.7	19.0
2nd quarter	174.0	78.8	12.2	20.2	4.1	58.4	39.3	25.8	73.2	14.5	4.7	11.0	20.2
3rd quarter	177.8	79.6	13.3	19.1	4.6	59.2	43.4	31.5	82.1	14.6	4.6	11.7	21.2
4th quarter	180.5	79.3	13.8	13.3	4.7	66.6	42.5	28.7	79.8	16.7	3.9	11.7	20.9
2009													
1st quarter	187.3	81.8	13.5	9.2	3.8	58.4	42.3	27.1	80.5	13.2	4.4	10.5	19.1
2nd quarter	189.3	81.8	14.3	9.2	4.3	61.0	43.4	29.9	82.7	15.8	4.8	10.9	20.3
3rd quarter	190.9	84.6	14.9	10.7	4.1	60.1	44.3	32.9	83.4	13.5	6.6	10.9	21.0
4th quarter	191.7	88.2	16.0	13.7	4.3	59.2	45.4	33.3	84.3	14.2	5.0	12.3	19.6
2010													
1st quarter	197.6	91.1	13.7	13.4	4.4	59.9	46.1	31.9	85.6	15.9	6.0	10.7	20.3
2nd quarter	198.1	92.5	15.1	13.6	4.5	60.0	46.9	33.8	88.8	18.5	5.7	11.3	20.0
3rd quarter	198.2	94.4	16.0	12.9	3.9	60.2	48.1	35.6	93.5	16.4	6.3	11.9	20.5
4th quarter	198.4	96.0	18.2	13.7	4.3	57.9	44.1	28.7	89.6	18.9	5.9	13.2	20.7
2011													
1st quarter	201.2	96.9	15.2	18.2	4.1	56.0	43.4	25.2	91.8	16.7	5.5	10.6	18.2
2nd quarter	202.5	97.8	17.6	21.0	4.0	55.8	45.8	29.4	99.4	18.1	5.8	11.5	18.2
3rd quarter	203.5	99.1	18.7	20.1	4.3	61.1	45.5	28.4	101.4	21.4	4.7	11.4	18.3
4th quarter	203.2	100.6	19.6	19.9	4.4	53.1	41.8	20.5	96.1	20.4	5.8	13.1	18.2

[1]Includes general government intermediate inputs for goods and services sold to other sectors and for own-account investment.

Table 6-5. Federal Government Output, Lending and Borrowing, and Net Investment

(National income and product accounts, calendar years, billions of dollars, quarterly data are at seasonally adjusted annual rates.)

NIPA Tables 3.2, 3.10.5

Year and quarter	Output						Net lending (net borrowing -)							Net investment
	Gross		Value added		Intermediate goods and services purchased ¹		Net saving, current (surplus +, deficit -)	Plus: capital transfer receipts	Minus			Plus: Consumption of fixed capital	Equals: Net lending (borrowing -)	
	Defense	Non-defense	Defense	Non-defense	Defense	Non-defense			Gross investment	Capital transfer payments	Net purchases of non-produced assets			
1960	41.5	9.3	27.4	5.6	14.0	3.7	7.1	1.8	14.3	2.6	0.5	10.6	2.0	3.7
1961	43.0	9.6	28.3	6.1	14.7	3.5	2.6	2.0	16.3	2.9	0.5	10.9	-4.3	5.4
1962	47.0	11.9	30.0	6.6	17.0	5.3	2.4	2.1	17.4	3.1	0.6	11.5	-5.1	5.9
1963	48.7	13.2	31.1	7.3	17.6	5.9	5.3	2.2	16.1	3.6	0.5	12.1	-0.6	4.0
1964	49.2	14.8	32.7	8.0	16.5	6.8	0.9	2.6	15.6	4.1	0.6	12.3	-4.5	3.3
1965	51.1	15.8	33.8	8.6	17.3	7.3	3.2	2.8	14.7	4.0	0.5	12.6	-0.5	2.1
1966	60.8	16.6	37.8	9.4	23.0	7.2	2.3	3.0	16.7	4.4	0.6	13.1	-3.3	3.6
1967	70.3	17.9	41.4	10.1	29.0	7.8	-9.3	3.1	17.7	4.3	-0.2	13.9	-14.1	3.8
1968	77.3	19.2	45.1	11.3	32.3	8.0	-2.4	3.1	16.0	6.0	-0.9	14.7	-5.7	1.3
1969	78.4	21.3	47.9	12.1	30.5	9.2	8.6	3.6	15.0	5.9	0.1	15.4	6.6	-0.4
1970	76.8	23.2	50.2	13.8	26.6	9.3	-15.5	3.7	14.8	5.3	-0.3	16.1	-15.6	-1.3
1971	77.3	26.1	52.0	15.7	25.3	10.4	-28.7	4.6	11.7	5.9	-0.4	16.5	-24.9	-4.8
1972	80.1	29.8	54.3	17.2	25.8	12.6	-24.9	5.4	12.0	6.1	-0.7	16.6	-20.3	-4.6
1973	80.5	31.2	55.4	18.6	25.1	12.6	-11.8	5.1	13.6	6.0	-3.2	17.0	-6.1	-3.4
1974	86.1	35.2	58.8	20.8	27.3	14.4	-14.5	4.8	16.6	7.9	-5.7	18.2	-10.4	-1.6
1975	92.1	40.4	63.6	23.7	28.5	16.8	-70.6	4.9	19.5	9.7	-0.4	19.7	-74.9	-0.2
1976	96.4	43.6	67.3	26.5	29.1	17.1	-53.7	5.6	22.6	10.6	-2.4	21.4	-57.5	1.2
1977	105.0	49.5	72.0	30.0	32.9	19.5	-46.1	7.2	24.7	11.2	-1.4	23.0	-50.4	1.7
1978	113.6	54.3	77.4	32.3	36.2	22.0	-28.9	5.2	27.6	12.0	-0.6	25.0	-37.7	2.6
1979	124.8	59.7	83.0	34.6	41.8	25.1	-14.0	5.5	31.6	14.5	-2.8	27.0	-24.9	4.6
1980	145.0	68.6	92.0	39.2	52.9	29.4	-56.6	6.5	36.3	16.7	-4.0	30.0	-69.1	6.3
1981	168.9	75.5	105.1	42.3	63.8	33.2	-56.8	6.9	41.9	15.7	-5.5	33.8	-68.2	8.1
1982	193.0	76.4	116.6	44.6	76.4	31.8	-135.3	7.5	47.5	14.7	-3.6	37.6	-148.7	9.9
1983	210.0	82.5	124.1	47.1	85.9	35.4	-176.2	5.8	56.4	15.6	-4.9	40.7	-196.9	15.7
1984	234.5	82.0	142.3	49.8	92.2	32.2	-171.5	6.0	64.4	17.8	-3.9	44.5	-199.2	19.9
1985	255.4	89.8	152.8	52.3	102.7	37.5	-178.6	6.4	74.4	19.6	-1.1	48.0	-217.0	26.4
1986	269.7	95.2	158.9	53.7	110.8	41.5	-194.6	7.0	80.4	20.1	-3.0	51.6	-233.6	28.8
1987	285.7	95.9	166.5	56.8	119.2	39.1	-149.3	7.2	85.8	19.1	-0.4	55.2	-191.5	30.6
1988	295.8	94.7	172.8	62.0	123.1	32.7	-138.4	7.6	79.8	19.8	-0.1	59.1	-171.2	20.7
1989	301.8	106.1	180.7	65.8	121.1	40.3	-133.9	8.9	83.0	20.2	-0.7	63.3	-164.2	19.7
1990	311.2	118.1	186.8	72.0	124.5	46.1	-176.4	11.6	88.5	28.2	-0.7	67.7	-213.1	20.8
1991	323.1	126.6	197.2	77.7	125.9	48.9	-218.4	11.0	88.2	26.5	0.2	72.0	-250.3	16.2
1992	319.2	136.2	200.2	81.8	119.1	54.4	-302.5	11.3	88.8	22.6	0.2	74.6	-328.2	14.2
1993	311.8	140.4	197.1	88.1	114.7	52.3	-280.2	12.9	83.8	24.3	0.2	77.8	-297.8	6.0
1994	306.8	147.0	194.6	90.5	112.2	56.4	-220.4	15.1	77.9	26.0	0.2	80.1	-229.3	-2.2
1995	300.7	150.1	191.5	92.1	109.2	58.0	-206.2	14.9	78.6	27.9	-7.4	81.7	-208.7	-3.1
1996	307.2	150.5	193.5	94.0	113.7	56.4	-148.2	17.5	80.4	28.4	-3.8	81.9	-153.9	-1.5
1997	308.0	158.6	192.2	97.8	115.8	60.8	-60.1	20.6	73.4	29.2	-7.6	82.5	-52.1	-9.1
1998	303.5	161.2	190.4	101.8	113.0	59.4	33.6	25.2	76.4	28.9	-5.8	82.8	42.0	-6.4
1999	316.0	165.8	192.7	107.7	123.3	58.1	98.8	28.8	81.6	36.3	-0.4	85.0	95.0	-3.4
2000	324.9	180.9	198.8	116.3	126.2	64.6	185.2	28.1	80.1	36.6	-0.2	87.8	184.7	-7.7
2001	345.6	193.7	205.2	119.7	140.3	74.0	40.5	28.0	81.5	42.0	-0.7	88.6	34.2	-7.1
2002	384.9	214.9	222.5	129.3	162.4	85.5	-252.8	25.3	90.1	49.2	0.3	89.2	-278.0	0.9
2003	439.7	230.4	243.8	139.1	195.9	91.3	-376.4	22.0	96.2	62.6	-0.2	90.8	-422.2	5.4
2004	485.8	246.2	264.2	147.8	221.6	98.3	-379.5	24.6	103.3	63.5	0.0	94.8	-426.8	8.5
2005	520.2	259.4	284.4	154.4	235.8	105.0	-283.0	25.0	110.5	84.8	-0.5	100.4	-352.4	10.1
2006	549.6	274.2	298.8	161.9	250.9	112.3	-203.8	27.8	120.7	70.5	-13.3	106.6	-247.2	14.1
2007	580.6	280.3	315.7	170.4	264.9	109.9	-245.2	26.5	127.4	82.8	-1.3	112.6	-315.0	14.8
2008	639.2	306.4	337.7	180.0	301.5	126.4	-613.5	28.3	148.4	161.8	-19.2	120.0	-756.2	28.4
2009	670.1	331.4	360.4	192.9	309.7	138.5	-1 217.9	20.6	156.1	224.7	-7.1	124.7	-1 446.3	31.4
2010	708.3	362.3	382.3	207.2	326.0	155.1	-1 273.7	15.0	168.8	164.6	0.2	130.0	-1 462.3	38.8
2011	723.2	367.8	398.0	210.4	325.2	157.4	-1 187.8	5.1	160.8	151.4	-0.1	137.9	-1 356.9	22.9
2009														
1st quarter	647.9	321.6	354.4	189.6	293.5	132.0	-993.9	22.7	150.1	309.8	-27.0	123.2	-1 281.0	26.9
2nd quarter	665.4	330.5	357.0	193.6	308.4	136.9	-1 303.0	20.9	156.1	233.0	-2.7	124.1	-1 544.4	32.0
3rd quarter	680.6	332.3	362.4	193.4	318.2	138.9	-1 305.4	20.7	159.8	161.4	1.8	125.1	-1 482.7	34.7
4th quarter	686.5	341.1	367.7	194.9	318.8	146.2	-1 269.4	18.1	158.3	194.6	-0.5	126.4	-1 477.2	31.9
2010														
1st quarter	697.0	352.5	377.8	203.1	319.2	149.4	-1 271.8	21.3	161.3	166.4	-0.2	127.9	-1 450.0	33.4
2nd quarter	707.7	365.5	380.8	211.3	326.9	154.1	-1 278.0	18.1	168.5	211.0	-0.8	129.4	-1 509.2	39.1
3rd quarter	719.3	365.4	383.7	207.7	335.7	157.7	-1 257.7	15.5	170.8	146.4	1.8	130.5	-1 430.8	40.3
4th quarter	709.1	365.9	387.0	206.8	322.1	159.0	-1 287.3	5.0	174.7	134.4	0.1	132.3	-1 459.2	42.4
2011														
1st quarter	707.3	366.1	392.5	209.4	314.9	156.7	-1 201.1	1.5	160.9	126.7	0.3	134.6	-1 352.8	26.3
2nd quarter	729.7	363.6	396.4	210.8	333.3	152.8	-1 275.4	5.7	159.6	157.0	-0.2	136.8	-1 449.4	22.8
3rd quarter	739.5	374.6	400.4	210.6	339.1	164.0	-1 160.7	1.5	164.0	151.3	-0.6	139.2	-1 334.7	24.8
4th quarter	716.3	367.0	402.8	210.9	313.5	156.0	-1 114.1	11.8	158.5	170.6	0.2	141.0	-1 290.6	17.5

¹Includes general government intermediate inputs for goods and services sold to other sectors and for own-account investment.

Table 6-6. Chain-Type Quantity Indexes for Federal Government Defense and Nondefense Consumption Expenditures and Gross Investment

(Seasonally adjusted, 2005 = 100.)

NIPA Tables 3.9.3, 3.10.3

| Year and quarter | Defense consumption expenditures [1] | | | | | | Defense gross investment | Nondefense consumption expenditures [1] | | | | | | Non-defense gross investment |
| | Total | Compensation of general government employees | Consumption of general government fixed capital | Intermediate goods and services purchased [2] | | | | Total | Compensation of general government employees | Consumption of general government fixed capital | Intermediate goods and services purchased [2] | | | |
				Durable goods	Non-durable goods	Services					Durable goods	Non-durable goods excluding CCC inventory change	Services	
1960	68.8	131.8	60.9	55.5	73.6	25.9	59.1	28.7	55.1	10.3	3.8	19.8	18.8	19.5
1961	70.5	134.5	62.1	45.5	90.8	28.4	65.6	28.4	56.5	10.5	6.9	23.1	22.3	23.5
1962	75.3	140.2	64.0	56.3	115.0	29.8	67.8	34.7	59.5	11.1	11.1	23.0	26.0	27.5
1963	76.2	137.8	65.6	56.8	107.0	32.0	58.6	37.7	63.0	12.3	15.4	25.6	32.6	32.3
1964	74.2	137.7	66.4	48.0	118.1	29.2	53.2	40.4	64.4	13.8	20.0	27.5	37.4	37.1
1965	74.4	137.9	66.3	49.7	127.6	28.9	46.4	42.3	65.7	15.7	25.6	27.6	38.6	42.3
1966	84.9	151.8	66.4	72.4	182.0	34.5	53.7	42.5	68.3	18.0	26.6	32.4	41.9	43.5
1967	96.1	165.2	67.8	71.4	280.0	41.0	60.6	44.4	71.6	19.7	23.3	34.9	38.7	35.4
1968	100.2	167.4	68.9	82.8	320.6	41.7	53.1	44.5	73.3	20.8	18.6	28.1	34.2	30.9
1969	96.3	167.6	68.8	69.1	284.5	39.5	47.0	46.8	74.0	21.6	16.2	35.3	33.4	28.1
1970	87.5	155.4	67.7	61.8	198.0	36.0	42.8	46.6	74.9	22.1	12.9	36.2	37.9	26.6
1971	80.7	143.6	64.9	44.5	161.9	36.0	27.3	48.8	77.4	22.4	12.4	34.4	41.3	27.9
1972	75.8	132.7	61.4	56.9	165.0	32.0	20.4	52.5	79.7	22.5	13.3	38.7	48.9	28.9
1973	70.3	125.8	58.5	52.6	122.6	30.0	23.0	51.9	79.9	22.8	10.5	33.4	49.1	29.7
1974	68.1	123.9	56.7	45.5	105.9	30.4	28.0	54.8	83.9	23.2	9.2	36.7	49.6	30.6
1975	66.4	122.2	55.9	47.2	87.7	28.5	31.1	56.7	85.3	23.7	9.8	27.8	52.3	31.8
1976	65.2	119.7	56.0	42.4	71.6	29.0	33.9	56.6	89.6	24.2	10.5	35.2	46.9	34.1
1977	65.9	118.6	56.2	53.7	66.9	29.4	34.6	59.0	91.6	24.9	12.1	40.2	49.7	35.8
1978	66.6	119.4	56.5	60.0	67.4	29.0	34.4	61.4	93.9	26.1	15.3	47.0	53.4	42.4
1979	67.5	118.5	57.0	64.8	69.5	30.0	39.3	62.5	93.8	27.5	18.4	47.1	57.1	41.4
1980	70.1	119.2	58.1	67.9	75.9	33.8	42.1	65.7	96.4	29.2	21.5	46.4	56.8	44.6
1981	74.1	122.8	59.5	79.2	80.3	37.2	46.4	66.8	93.5	31.0	19.1	77.0	51.7	44.5
1982	79.0	125.6	61.6	86.8	79.9	44.6	52.2	63.9	91.8	32.8	16.4	54.9	49.7	41.3
1983	83.3	127.6	64.5	102.7	83.7	47.2	61.2	66.2	93.1	35.1	25.0	57.5	52.2	46.9
1984	85.8	129.3	68.6	103.8	79.3	50.8	69.9	63.8	93.1	38.1	27.1	60.1	52.7	50.4
1985	91.0	131.8	74.1	111.4	77.9	57.7	84.2	67.5	93.3	41.2	27.7	52.7	55.1	53.8
1986	95.1	132.4	80.4	119.0	98.3	61.0	96.4	69.9	92.0	44.1	28.0	46.5	55.0	55.1
1987	98.6	133.6	86.6	126.4	96.3	64.8	105.3	68.6	93.6	47.0	31.3	53.0	59.9	60.5
1988	99.8	132.0	91.7	130.0	92.8	66.4	97.4	65.1	96.0	49.9	32.7	52.2	59.1	56.6
1989	99.0	131.9	95.8	124.8	89.9	64.3	98.0	70.7	96.5	52.7	35.9	46.3	60.0	60.4
1990	98.4	131.1	99.5	120.3	80.2	64.3	101.0	76.4	101.3	55.9	41.0	49.4	67.9	65.9
1991	98.3	130.6	102.4	114.8	81.7	64.1	95.2	77.2	101.0	59.0	42.2	42.1	69.6	71.3
1992	93.2	123.0	104.1	103.3	75.6	60.4	91.6	81.8	102.8	61.5	45.7	51.6	75.4	78.7
1993	89.5	117.7	104.6	93.9	69.3	58.1	80.4	80.6	102.8	63.7	45.5	57.9	68.0	81.0
1994	85.5	111.6	103.7	80.5	63.1	58.1	74.5	81.4	99.9	65.4	43.2	49.6	75.4	70.6
1995	82.5	105.5	102.2	73.4	51.6	57.0	71.1	80.2	95.9	67.1	42.4	57.4	73.5	74.8
1996	81.3	101.0	100.7	72.8	57.0	58.4	70.5	78.2	93.3	70.0	48.9	51.5	71.0	80.9
1997	80.1	97.4	99.2	73.1	57.4	58.6	63.0	80.9	92.7	73.3	51.9	60.7	73.1	80.0
1998	77.9	94.3	97.6	73.7	59.3	56.1	64.1	80.2	93.8	77.1	52.0	66.4	68.7	88.2
1999	79.2	92.0	96.5	78.3	66.3	60.3	66.4	80.8	94.0	82.5	56.9	47.2	70.2	95.9
2000	78.4	91.4	95.6	77.5	69.6	59.2	67.8	84.6	96.9	87.5	60.7	51.1	74.6	87.3
2001	81.3	92.1	94.9	78.1	71.5	66.1	71.1	89.3	96.9	90.8	65.3	68.0	81.1	86.4
2002	86.6	94.5	94.8	81.3	81.7	76.5	80.4	95.5	98.7	93.6	79.1	73.0	93.7	94.3
2003	94.0	97.9	95.7	89.2	86.3	90.6	88.0	98.5	101.2	95.5	77.5	82.2	96.6	95.4
2004	98.9	99.7	97.5	98.9	99.4	98.3	95.8	99.7	100.2	97.2	86.8	93.0	99.8	95.0
2005	100.0	100.0	100.0	100.0	100.0	100.0	100.0	100.0	100.0	100.0	100.0	100.0	100.0	100.0
2006	100.8	98.5	102.8	108.4	96.4	102.3	107.0	102.6	100.0	104.3	106.8	93.2	105.5	107.8
2007	102.6	98.1	106.2	119.2	99.9	103.9	113.2	101.5	100.6	108.6	107.6	88.2	100.4	109.1
2008	108.7	101.9	110.8	139.8	102.4	111.8	133.0	107.9	104.4	112.9	122.7	100.2	110.8	117.1
2009	114.9	108.6	116.1	148.0	107.7	117.2	141.3	115.4	110.1	117.9	134.2	117.2	119.1	121.6
2010	118.3	112.0	121.1	153.3	102.9	120.7	148.5	122.5	114.8	121.9	150.2	128.0	130.7	139.0
2011	117.0	113.0	126.2	143.4	106.9	114.6	134.2	120.7	113.6	127.0	149.6	124.7	128.8	140.4
2009														
1st quarter	110.9	105.6	114.1	134.5	102.1	112.9	134.5	112.5	108.1	116.1	128.1	114.1	114.1	118.4
2nd quarter	114.7	107.9	115.5	148.0	108.4	117.6	143.1	115.8	111.5	117.4	130.9	120.3	116.3	117.9
3rd quarter	116.9	110.0	116.8	159.0	111.5	119.0	146.2	115.5	110.2	118.5	137.4	114.9	120.5	122.6
4th quarter	117.1	111.0	118.1	150.5	108.7	119.4	141.3	118.0	110.4	119.5	140.5	119.5	125.4	127.5
2010														
1st quarter	117.1	111.5	119.3	144.9	103.8	119.6	143.1	120.0	112.8	120.4	145.2	122.9	127.5	131.2
2nd quarter	118.4	111.9	120.5	149.0	106.1	121.7	147.7	123.6	118.0	121.3	150.3	127.2	130.1	140.2
3rd quarter	120.1	112.2	121.7	156.0	101.5	125.1	150.1	122.8	114.6	122.4	152.3	130.4	132.6	141.2
4th quarter	117.6	112.5	122.9	163.1	100.3	116.3	153.0	123.6	113.8	123.5	152.9	131.5	132.6	143.4
2011														
1st quarter	115.4	112.7	124.1	137.5	102.8	112.8	135.2	122.9	114.6	124.8	150.5	127.4	129.2	141.5
2nd quarter	117.9	112.9	125.4	142.7	108.2	117.7	133.2	120.4	114.1	126.2	145.4	120.3	124.7	139.7
3rd quarter	119.1	113.1	126.9	145.8	107.5	119.9	137.0	118.9	112.9	127.7	155.9	130.1	133.4	141.1
4th quarter	115.5	113.5	128.5	147.5	109.1	108.2	131.4	120.6	112.7	129.5	146.6	121.2	127.7	139.1

[1]Excludes government sales to other sectors and government own-account investment (construction and software).
[2]Includes general government intermediate inputs for goods and services sold to other sectors and for own-account investment.

Table 6-7. Chain-Type Quantity Indexes for National Defense Consumption Expenditures and Gross Investment: Selected Detail

(Seasonally adjusted, 2005 = 100.)   NIPA Table 3.11.3

Year and quarter	Consumption expenditures									Gross investment			
	Compensation of general government employees		Intermediate goods and services purchased [1]							Equipment and software			
			Durable goods	Nondurable goods		Services							
	Military	Civilian	Aircraft	Petroleum products	Ammunition	Research and development	Installation support	Weapons support	Personnel support	Aircraft	Missiles	Ships	Electronics and software
1972	131.8	133.5	79.3	317.9	171.7	25.7	51.3	27.1	20.6	24.6	36.1	79.0	5.5
1973	124.3	128.0	66.3	201.2	133.9	25.7	46.8	25.5	16.7	21.6	37.8	66.6	6.1
1974	119.9	131.3	51.5	182.8	91.5	25.5	47.0	27.3	18.9	21.7	41.8	82.2	6.1
1975	117.3	131.3	47.4	153.9	63.7	24.5	44.8	23.7	18.9	32.8	30.5	73.5	7.0
1976	114.5	129.8	39.7	127.5	32.0	25.3	46.0	25.0	18.6	30.7	26.0	75.4	7.4
1977	113.5	128.5	60.7	108.5	43.7	26.2	48.4	24.9	16.4	32.1	20.4	88.0	8.2
1978	112.4	133.0	62.0	107.9	50.5	25.9	45.1	27.1	17.1	30.3	16.7	99.0	10.1
1979	110.6	133.6	77.2	109.8	56.2	26.7	48.2	29.8	16.4	37.9	33.8	101.9	11.1
1980	111.8	133.5	83.8	121.5	56.3	33.0	51.2	40.1	16.1	45.4	48.7	89.6	13.6
1981	115.4	137.2	108.0	119.3	63.6	38.2	52.6	42.9	19.8	52.5	56.5	102.1	16.1
1982	117.4	141.7	126.3	112.3	78.4	41.2	72.0	46.6	27.2	52.8	72.9	119.0	18.6
1983	119.4	143.4	153.7	120.3	91.9	40.7	78.8	54.1	29.0	60.0	92.3	132.3	22.7
1984	120.9	145.8	145.3	120.0	77.8	43.9	84.0	61.7	29.7	64.5	111.0	140.1	28.5
1985	122.7	149.8	156.1	122.0	46.4	58.0	82.4	68.3	36.3	88.0	126.5	154.0	36.5
1986	123.8	148.9	172.7	121.9	124.9	62.2	84.8	71.5	38.5	134.2	160.4	148.7	41.8
1987	125.4	149.4	184.9	125.2	94.8	70.0	84.6	74.0	41.9	154.0	182.5	144.6	47.7
1988	124.4	146.1	191.5	105.5	109.4	82.5	81.0	64.5	39.2	126.5	166.1	137.0	50.5
1989	123.8	147.5	180.6	115.8	91.5	73.6	80.3	65.2	40.0	115.7	190.2	152.1	52.8
1990	124.1	144.1	158.6	114.8	82.5	65.8	88.5	71.5	39.0	106.7	247.0	160.5	54.7
1991	125.5	139.6	141.9	113.4	77.8	54.3	93.7	59.6	35.7	76.8	248.4	144.0	53.9
1992	114.7	138.8	123.8	94.9	73.9	57.2	90.2	47.6	38.5	67.2	245.7	139.1	56.9
1993	108.8	135.0	107.3	91.2	73.4	63.5	95.3	36.8	31.3	72.4	178.4	117.4	57.3
1994	103.6	127.2	91.0	93.9	50.5	59.9	97.5	40.6	34.7	72.3	131.0	105.6	54.8
1995	98.2	119.7	86.8	85.2	32.3	58.4	91.7	42.1	35.8	58.4	110.3	99.4	52.5
1996	94.6	113.5	86.1	86.1	37.9	63.6	92.3	37.2	37.3	56.9	98.8	84.0	56.4
1997	92.1	107.6	92.0	77.3	46.5	63.8	88.9	42.9	39.4	39.5	73.1	74.5	59.2
1998	90.0	102.6	97.6	75.5	52.7	59.9	84.0	41.0	38.5	39.8	82.3	78.8	62.8
1999	88.4	99.0	103.1	83.4	53.6	59.6	86.5	46.9	47.3	41.5	74.7	83.5	69.0
2000	89.2	95.7	96.0	77.0	51.0	57.9	86.3	46.5	46.3	48.3	70.3	79.4	71.4
2001	91.0	94.1	94.7	90.0	58.2	62.7	91.4	59.4	54.9	56.5	88.3	87.1	70.6
2002	94.3	94.8	95.0	103.7	70.8	76.4	98.8	72.5	65.6	65.1	88.2	104.1	74.3
2003	99.5	94.6	106.7	94.4	73.3	86.9	110.0	90.9	76.2	64.6	90.9	112.8	80.4
2004	100.6	97.7	112.0	102.8	96.1	98.2	106.2	90.6	93.7	79.7	103.3	108.5	89.5
2005	100.0	100.0	100.0	100.0	100.0	100.0	100.0	100.0	100.0	100.0	100.0	100.0	100.0
2006	97.7	100.2	99.9	96.1	98.2	103.6	99.8	102.3	105.9	101.6	111.6	98.6	113.8
2007	96.9	100.8	103.5	99.8	92.0	98.3	96.6	102.9	110.3	96.8	105.3	91.8	132.7
2008	101.2	103.4	116.1	99.5	94.2	100.9	105.3	109.6	128.0	98.4	106.1	91.4	167.1
2009	109.0	107.7	133.6	101.7	88.9	98.9	112.8	115.5	134.8	100.6	123.4	97.6	167.9
2010	110.8	114.7	143.9	100.5	89.4	96.6	115.2	120.2	143.9	122.9	139.5	98.4	172.1
2011	110.3	118.9	162.9	108.2	83.9	88.9	104.1	93.9	153.7	129.3	121.4	92.4	155.1
2005													
1st quarter	101.0	99.1	99.9	83.8	94.6	99.9	95.9	94.4	95.8	91.1	79.3	101.0	91.2
2nd quarter	99.8	99.9	99.6	109.5	99.7	105.6	97.0	93.3	94.2	99.6	112.3	97.7	97.8
3rd quarter	99.4	100.7	98.6	111.5	106.3	102.1	106.3	115.3	107.4	104.4	86.8	109.4	106.7
4th quarter	99.7	100.3	102.0	95.2	99.4	92.5	100.9	96.9	102.6	104.9	121.6	92.0	104.4
2006													
1st quarter	97.6	99.6	97.3	91.9	100.7	105.3	99.3	98.4	107.2	97.4	116.5	94.6	107.7
2nd quarter	97.0	99.6	93.0	91.8	97.1	104.5	101.9	107.4	111.4	113.6	115.9	105.1	110.8
3rd quarter	98.2	100.2	97.2	113.2	95.4	99.4	96.1	93.1	101.6	87.4	83.3	97.2	118.3
4th quarter	97.8	101.3	112.0	87.3	99.7	105.0	101.8	110.4	103.6	107.9	130.9	97.5	118.3
2007													
1st quarter	96.7	100.4	91.3	98.4	96.7	102.2	94.0	93.1	100.9	91.5	129.0	89.1	124.7
2nd quarter	96.1	100.2	99.6	102.2	84.6	100.2	95.0	99.8	106.6	105.4	106.0	90.0	129.9
3rd quarter	97.5	100.7	108.3	108.8	100.1	95.0	98.1	108.8	114.9	97.5	95.0	90.1	138.8
4th quarter	97.3	101.8	114.9	90.0	86.6	96.0	99.2	109.7	118.8	92.7	91.3	98.1	137.3
2008													
1st quarter	98.6	101.3	104.8	100.7	98.3	96.6	103.3	111.2	124.1	64.5	108.2	84.3	156.2
2nd quarter	99.4	102.9	112.5	100.3	86.0	98.2	99.7	99.1	121.3	105.0	113.7	90.5	165.5
3rd quarter	102.2	104.5	121.4	92.7	94.4	98.3	109.2	120.1	135.2	105.7	109.6	92.8	174.3
4th quarter	104.6	104.7	125.8	104.3	97.9	110.5	109.0	107.9	131.4	118.5	92.8	97.9	172.4
2009													
1st quarter	106.1	104.5	122.1	97.7	81.9	96.6	110.4	101.7	131.7	93.6	104.7	92.1	159.4
2nd quarter	108.7	106.0	130.1	97.7	92.4	101.4	112.4	112.4	134.9	112.6	114.6	96.7	170.4
3rd quarter	110.7	108.3	136.3	99.4	89.1	99.7	113.2	123.3	135.7	95.5	156.6	95.4	176.7
4th quarter	110.6	111.8	145.9	112.0	92.3	97.8	115.0	124.7	137.0	100.8	117.6	106.2	164.9
2010													
1st quarter	111.1	112.3	124.7	98.2	93.2	97.9	115.6	118.7	138.6	113.0	141.7	90.4	171.0
2nd quarter	111.1	113.5	137.7	104.9	94.2	97.7	116.5	125.4	143.4	130.8	133.0	93.5	168.8
3rd quarter	110.6	115.5	146.1	102.1	81.7	97.5	120.1	131.4	150.1	116.5	147.3	99.7	172.9
4th quarter	110.2	117.5	167.0	96.8	88.6	93.0	108.7	105.4	143.4	131.6	135.7	109.9	175.6
2011													
1st quarter	110.2	118.0	139.8	101.4	83.6	89.2	103.8	92.3	146.0	113.5	124.0	85.5	154.5
2nd quarter	110.4	118.2	161.2	110.7	80.3	87.7	107.2	106.8	157.5	122.2	128.5	91.1	154.7
3rd quarter	110.4	118.9	171.6	109.2	84.3	95.6	106.5	102.6	160.0	142.9	105.1	89.4	155.7
4th quarter	110.3	120.4	178.9	111.4	87.4	82.8	99.1	73.8	151.3	138.7	128.0	103.8	155.4

[1]Includes general government intermediate inputs for goods and services sold to other sectors and for own-account investment.

Section 6b: State and Local Government in the National Income and Product Accounts

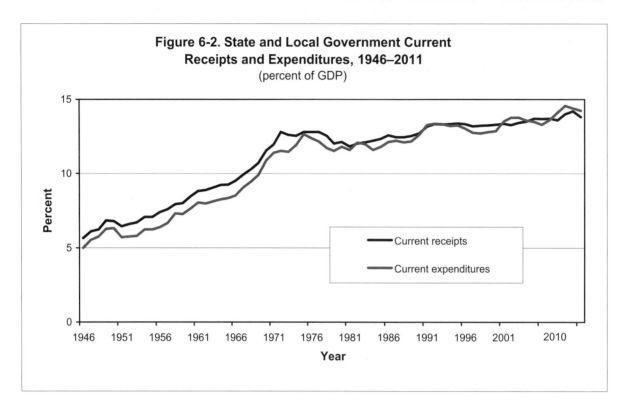

Figure 6-2. State and Local Government Current Receipts and Expenditures, 1946–2011
(percent of GDP)

- While the recession also reduced state and local tax revenues, most such governments are forced to attempt to balance their budgets, so they were required to limit revenue losses and restrain expenditure growth. Increases in federal grants during the period 2007–2010 helped maintain spending levels. In the aggregate, these governments nevertheless ran deficits. (Table 6-8)

- Both current receipts and current spending of state and local governments have increased as a share of gross domestic product (GDP) over the postwar period, but the growth slowed markedly after the early 1970s. (Tables 6-8 and 1-1)

- Despite the net saving typically registered in their current receipts and expenditures accounts during normal economic conditions, state and local governments on balance have not been suppliers of funds to the capital markets, even before the latest recession. Though they are constrained against deficits in their annual budgets, these governments can and do borrow—for investment, or just to cover short-falls in current accounts—by issuing bonds. (Usually, the permission of voters in the state or local juris-diction is required.) They have usually been net borrowers from the rest of the economy. This borrowing has allowed their net investment (gross investment minus estimated capital depreciation) usually to exceed the sum of their current surpluses (if any) and capital transfer receipts (which are mainly federal highway grants). (Table 6-10)

- State and local gross investment rose at an annual rate of 2.1 percent in real terms from 1960 to 2011, compared with 3.9 percent for federal nondefense investment. (Tables 6-6 and 6-11)

Table 6-8. State and Local Government Current Receipts and Expenditures

(National income and product accounts, calendar years, billions of dollars, quarterly data are at seasonally adjusted annual rates.)

NIPA Table 3.3

Year and quarter	Total current receipts	Current receipts										
		Current tax receipts						Taxes on corporate income	Contributions for government social insurance	Income receipts on assets		
		Total tax receipts	Personal current taxes		Taxes on production and imports					Interest receipts	Dividends	Rents and royalties
			Income taxes	Other personal taxes	Sales taxes	Property taxes	Other taxes on prod. and imports					
1950	20.0	16.5	0.8	0.7	4.8	7.1	2.3	0.8	0.2	0.3	. . .	0.2
1951	21.9	18.1	0.9	0.8	5.4	7.7	2.5	0.9	0.2	0.4	. . .	0.2
1952	23.7	19.7	1.0	0.8	5.8	8.4	2.8	0.8	0.3	0.4	. . .	0.2
1953	25.5	21.1	1.0	0.9	6.3	9.1	3.0	0.8	0.3	0.5	. . .	0.3
1954	26.9	22.2	1.1	1.0	6.5	9.7	3.2	0.8	0.3	0.5	. . .	0.3
1955	29.4	24.4	1.3	1.0	7.1	10.4	3.5	1.0	0.3	0.6	. . .	0.3
1956	32.4	27.0	1.6	1.1	8.0	11.5	3.8	1.0	0.4	0.7	. . .	0.3
1957	35.0	29.0	1.7	1.2	8.6	12.6	3.9	1.0	0.4	0.7	. . .	0.3
1958	37.1	30.6	1.8	1.2	10.0	13.8	2.8	1.0	0.4	0.8	. . .	0.4
1959	40.6	33.8	2.2	1.6	11.1	14.8	2.9	1.2	0.4	0.9	. . .	0.3
1960	44.5	37.0	2.5	1.7	12.2	16.2	3.1	1.2	0.5	1.0	. . .	0.3
1961	48.1	39.7	2.8	1.8	13.0	17.6	3.2	1.3	0.5	1.1	. . .	0.4
1962	52.0	42.8	3.2	1.8	14.0	19.0	3.3	1.5	0.5	1.1	. . .	0.4
1963	56.0	45.8	3.4	2.0	15.0	20.2	3.5	1.7	0.6	1.2	. . .	0.4
1964	61.3	49.8	4.0	2.1	16.5	21.7	3.7	1.8	0.7	1.5	. . .	0.4
1965	66.5	53.9	4.4	2.2	18.2	23.2	3.9	2.0	0.8	1.8	. . .	0.4
1966	74.9	58.8	5.4	2.4	20.0	24.5	4.3	2.2	0.8	2.1	. . .	0.5
1967	82.5	64.0	6.1	2.5	21.4	27.0	4.4	2.6	0.9	2.4	. . .	0.6
1968	93.5	73.4	7.8	2.7	25.1	29.9	4.6	3.3	0.9	2.8	. . .	0.7
1969	105.5	82.5	9.8	3.0	28.6	32.8	4.7	3.6	1.0	3.6	. . .	0.8
1970	120.1	91.3	10.9	3.3	31.6	36.7	5.0	3.7	1.1	4.3	. . .	0.8
1971	134.9	101.7	12.4	3.5	35.4	40.4	5.7	4.3	1.2	4.6	. . .	0.9
1972	158.4	115.6	17.2	3.7	39.8	43.2	6.4	5.3	1.3	4.9	. . .	1.0
1973	174.3	126.3	18.9	4.0	44.1	46.4	7.0	6.0	1.5	6.6	0.0	1.1
1974	188.1	136.0	20.4	4.2	48.2	49.0	7.7	6.7	1.7	8.9	0.0	1.3
1975	209.6	147.4	22.5	4.4	51.7	53.4	8.1	7.3	1.8	9.8	0.0	1.3
1976	233.7	165.7	26.3	4.8	57.8	58.2	9.0	9.6	2.2	9.0	0.0	1.3
1977	259.9	183.7	30.4	5.0	64.0	63.2	9.7	11.4	2.8	10.4	0.0	1.3
1978	287.6	198.2	35.0	5.5	71.0	63.7	10.9	12.1	3.4	13.3	0.1	1.3
1979	308.4	212.0	38.2	5.8	77.3	64.4	12.7	13.6	3.9	18.1	0.1	1.9
1980	338.2	230.0	42.6	6.3	82.9	68.8	15.0	14.5	3.6	23.1	0.1	3.1
1981	370.2	255.8	47.9	6.7	90.7	77.1	17.9	15.4	3.9	28.5	0.1	3.3
1982	391.4	273.2	51.9	7.3	96.2	85.3	18.5	14.0	4.0	33.1	0.2	3.5
1983	428.6	300.9	58.3	7.8	107.7	91.9	19.4	15.9	4.1	37.0	0.2	4.3
1984	480.2	337.3	67.5	8.6	121.0	99.7	21.8	18.8	4.7	42.6	0.2	4.9
1985	521.1	363.7	72.1	9.2	131.1	107.5	23.5	20.2	4.9	49.3	0.2	5.4
1986	561.6	389.5	77.4	9.8	139.9	116.2	23.7	22.7	6.0	52.0	0.2	6.2
1987	590.6	422.1	86.0	10.6	150.3	126.4	24.9	23.9	7.2	52.7	0.2	5.3
1988	635.5	452.8	90.6	11.5	162.4	136.5	25.7	26.0	8.4	55.9	0.2	4.4
1989	687.5	488.0	102.3	12.4	172.3	149.9	26.9	24.2	9.0	61.4	0.2	4.1
1990	738.0	519.1	109.6	13.0	184.3	161.5	28.3	22.5	10.0	64.1	0.2	4.2
1991	789.4	544.3	111.7	13.6	190.7	176.1	28.6	23.6	11.6	63.1	0.3	4.5
1992	846.2	579.8	120.4	14.9	204.3	184.7	31.1	24.4	13.1	59.6	0.5	4.8
1993	888.2	604.7	126.2	14.8	216.4	187.3	33.1	26.9	14.1	56.2	0.6	4.5
1994	944.8	644.2	132.2	15.7	231.4	199.4	35.5	30.0	14.5	58.0	0.8	4.5
1995	991.9	672.1	141.7	16.4	242.7	202.6	37.0	31.7	13.6	63.0	1.0	4.5
1996	1 045.1	709.6	152.3	16.3	256.2	212.4	39.4	33.0	12.5	67.5	1.4	4.6
1997	1 099.5	749.9	164.7	17.3	268.7	223.5	41.6	34.1	10.8	71.9	1.5	4.8
1998	1 164.5	794.9	183.0	18.2	283.9	231.0	43.9	34.9	10.4	75.2	1.6	4.6
1999	1 240.4	840.4	195.5	19.0	301.6	242.8	45.8	35.8	9.8	79.1	1.5	5.1
2000	1 322.6	893.2	217.4	19.4	316.8	254.7	49.8	35.2	10.8	86.7	1.4	6.3
2001	1 374.0	914.3	223.3	19.7	321.8	268.0	52.6	28.9	13.7	82.1	1.4	6.5
2002	1 412.7	928.7	201.3	20.5	331.1	289.4	55.5	30.9	15.9	71.5	1.6	6.6
2003	1 496.3	977.7	204.1	22.1	348.8	306.8	61.9	34.0	20.1	64.6	1.7	7.6
2004	1 601.0	1 059.4	224.7	23.8	370.7	326.7	71.7	41.7	24.1	66.7	2.0	8.5
2005	1 730.4	1 163.1	251.7	25.0	402.2	346.9	82.3	54.9	24.8	76.4	2.1	9.8
2006	1 829.7	1 249.0	276.1	26.4	430.4	370.1	86.9	59.2	21.8	90.9	2.3	10.3
2007	1 923.1	1 313.6	295.9	27.2	447.1	396.0	89.7	57.8	18.9	100.6	2.4	11.5
2008	1 944.8	1 326.4	307.7	26.7	444.0	408.3	92.3	47.4	19.0	91.9	2.9	12.0
2009	1 953.6	1 252.8	256.6	28.2	421.8	419.8	79.0	47.4	20.2	78.7	2.5	12.1
2010	2 064.7	1 307.9	266.9	30.6	438.3	430.6	83.6	57.9	20.8	75.0	2.6	13.4
2011	2 084.2	1 364.3	293.7	31.9	458.2	435.3	93.7	51.5	21.6	72.3	3.1	14.2
2009												
1st quarter	1 893.3	1 237.4	255.0	27.3	424.5	415.3	77.7	37.6	19.7	82.4	2.7	11.8
2nd quarter	1 952.8	1 232.5	248.0	27.7	416.7	418.3	76.8	45.0	20.1	79.3	2.2	11.9
3rd quarter	1 969.2	1 264.4	261.5	28.3	421.9	421.3	78.3	53.1	20.3	77.2	2.5	12.1
4th quarter	1 999.2	1 276.8	261.9	29.3	424.1	424.3	83.3	53.9	20.5	76.0	2.7	12.4
2010												
1st quarter	2 034.0	1 296.7	260.0	29.9	429.5	427.3	85.8	64.2	20.6	75.9	2.6	12.9
2nd quarter	2 043.3	1 293.4	256.1	30.5	434.7	429.9	84.0	58.2	20.7	75.7	2.5	13.3
3rd quarter	2 082.1	1 313.8	269.6	30.9	442.2	431.9	81.4	57.9	20.9	74.5	2.5	13.6
4th quarter	2 099.3	1 327.8	281.9	31.1	447.0	433.4	83.2	51.1	21.1	73.9	2.7	13.8
2011												
1st quarter	2 092.5	1 351.4	287.7	31.3	453.1	434.3	93.3	51.7	21.3	73.8	2.9	13.9
2nd quarter	2 128.0	1 374.2	299.1	31.7	459.9	435.1	94.0	54.4	21.6	72.0	3.0	14.1
3rd quarter	2 062.1	1 363.4	293.7	32.1	458.5	435.7	93.5	49.8	21.7	72.0	3.3	14.3
4th quarter	2 054.1	1 368.2	294.4	32.7	461.1	436.1	93.8	50.1	21.8	71.4	3.3	14.6

. . . = Not available.

Table 6-8. State and Local Government Current Receipts and Expenditures—*Continued*

(National income and product accounts, calendar years, billions of dollars, quarterly data are at seasonally adjusted annual rates.)

NIPA Table 3.3

| Year and quarter | Current receipts—Continued | | | | | Current expenditures | | | | | Net state and local government saving, NIPA (surplus + / deficit -) | | |
| | Current transfer receipts | | | | Current surplus of government enterprises | Total | Consumption expenditures | Government social benefits to persons | Interest payments | Subsidies | Total | Social insurance funds | Other |
	Total	Federal grants-in-aid	From business, net	From persons									
1950	2.3	1.9	0.1	0.3	0.4	18.6	14.9	3.2	0.6	. . .	1.3	0.1	1.2
1951	2.5	2.0	0.1	0.3	0.5	19.4	16.1	2.6	0.6	. . .	2.6	0.1	2.5
1952	2.6	2.2	0.1	0.3	0.5	20.7	17.1	2.9	0.7	. . .	3.0	0.1	2.9
1953	2.8	2.3	0.1	0.3	0.6	22.0	18.2	3.0	0.8	. . .	3.5	0.1	3.4
1954	2.9	2.3	0.2	0.4	0.7	23.7	19.7	3.1	0.9	. . .	3.2	0.1	3.1
1955	3.0	2.4	0.2	0.4	0.8	25.9	21.6	3.3	1.1	. . .	3.5	0.1	3.4
1956	3.2	2.5	0.2	0.4	0.9	28.0	23.4	3.3	1.2	. . .	4.4	0.1	4.3
1957	3.6	2.9	0.2	0.5	0.9	30.8	25.8	3.6	1.4	. . .	4.2	0.1	4.1
1958	4.1	3.3	0.2	0.5	0.9	34.2	28.6	4.0	1.5	. . .	2.9	0.0	2.8
1959	4.2	3.8	0.1	0.3	1.1	36.9	30.7	4.3	1.8	0.0	3.8	0.0	3.8
1960	4.5	4.0	0.2	0.3	1.2	40.2	33.5	4.6	2.1	0.0	4.3	0.0	4.3
1961	5.2	4.5	0.2	0.4	1.3	43.8	36.6	5.0	2.2	0.0	4.3	0.0	4.3
1962	5.8	5.0	0.2	0.5	1.4	46.8	39.0	5.3	2.4	0.0	5.2	0.0	5.2
1963	6.4	5.6	0.3	0.5	1.6	50.3	41.9	5.7	2.7	0.0	5.7	0.0	5.7
1964	7.3	6.5	0.3	0.5	1.6	54.9	45.8	6.2	2.9	0.0	6.4	0.0	6.3
1965	8.0	7.2	0.3	0.5	1.7	60.0	50.2	6.7	3.1	0.0	6.5	0.1	6.4
1966	11.1	10.1	0.3	0.7	1.6	67.2	56.1	7.6	3.4	0.0	7.8	0.1	7.6
1967	13.1	11.7	0.5	0.9	1.5	75.5	62.6	9.2	3.7	0.0	7.0	0.1	6.9
1968	14.2	12.7	0.5	1.0	1.5	86.0	70.4	11.4	4.2	0.0	7.5	0.1	7.3
1969	16.2	14.6	0.5	1.1	1.5	97.5	79.8	13.2	4.4	0.0	8.0	0.2	7.8
1970	21.1	19.3	0.6	1.2	1.5	113.0	91.5	16.1	5.3	0.0	7.1	0.2	6.9
1971	25.2	23.2	0.6	1.4	1.4	128.5	102.7	19.3	6.5	0.0	6.5	0.2	6.2
1972	34.0	31.7	0.7	1.7	1.6	142.8	113.2	22.0	7.5	0.1	15.6	0.3	15.4
1973	37.3	34.8	0.9	1.7	1.5	158.6	126.0	24.1	8.5	0.1	15.7	0.3	15.4
1974	39.3	36.3	1.1	2.0	0.9	178.7	143.7	25.3	9.6	0.1	9.3	0.4	9.0
1975	48.7	45.1	1.2	2.4	0.4	207.1	165.1	30.8	11.1	0.2	2.5	0.5	2.0
1976	55.0	50.7	1.4	2.9	0.4	226.3	179.5	34.1	12.5	0.2	7.4	0.6	6.8
1977	61.4	56.6	1.6	3.3	0.3	246.8	195.9	37.0	13.7	0.2	13.1	1.0	12.2
1978	71.1	65.5	1.9	3.7	0.3	268.9	213.2	40.8	14.9	0.2	18.7	1.5	17.2
1979	72.7	66.3	2.2	4.1	-0.3	295.4	233.3	44.3	17.2	0.3	13.0	1.8	11.2
1980	79.5	72.3	2.5	4.7	-1.2	329.4	258.4	51.2	19.4	0.4	8.8	1.3	7.5
1981	81.0	72.5	2.9	5.7	-2.4	362.7	282.3	57.1	22.8	0.4	7.6	1.3	6.3
1982	79.1	69.5	3.2	6.4	-1.6	393.6	304.9	61.2	27.1	0.5	-2.2	1.2	-3.4
1983	82.4	71.6	3.6	7.2	-0.2	423.7	324.1	66.9	32.3	0.4	4.9	1.2	3.7
1984	89.0	76.7	4.2	8.1	1.5	456.2	347.7	71.2	37.0	0.4	23.9	1.4	22.5
1985	94.5	80.9	4.4	9.2	3.2	498.7	381.8	77.3	39.4	0.3	22.4	1.3	21.0
1986	105.0	87.6	6.7	10.6	2.8	540.9	418.1	84.3	38.2	0.3	20.7	1.9	18.9
1987	100.0	83.9	4.9	11.2	3.1	578.6	441.4	90.7	46.2	0.3	12.0	2.2	9.8
1988	109.0	91.6	5.4	12.0	4.8	618.3	471.0	98.5	48.4	0.4	17.2	2.5	14.7
1989	118.1	98.3	6.4	13.4	6.7	667.4	504.5	109.3	53.2	0.4	20.1	2.3	17.8
1990	133.5	111.4	7.1	14.9	6.9	731.8	547.0	127.7	56.8	0.4	6.2	2.0	4.2
1991	158.2	131.6	7.9	18.7	7.3	795.2	577.5	156.5	60.8	0.4	-5.8	2.4	-8.2
1992	180.3	149.1	9.2	21.9	8.3	847.6	606.2	180.0	61.0	0.4	-1.4	3.1	-4.5
1993	198.1	164.0	10.5	23.5	9.9	889.1	634.2	195.2	59.4	0.4	-0.9	4.2	-5.1
1994	212.3	175.1	12.0	25.2	10.5	936.6	668.2	206.7	61.4	0.3	8.2	4.6	3.6
1995	224.2	184.2	13.5	26.5	13.5	982.7	701.3	217.6	63.5	0.3	9.2	4.0	5.1
1996	234.0	191.1	15.2	27.8	15.6	1 022.1	730.2	224.3	67.3	0.3	23.0	2.8	20.2
1997	246.4	198.4	17.7	30.3	14.2	1 063.2	764.5	227.6	70.6	0.4	36.3	1.2	35.1
1998	265.3	212.6	21.6	31.1	12.5	1 117.6	808.6	235.8	72.8	0.4	46.9	1.7	45.2
1999	291.1	232.9	24.0	34.2	13.3	1 198.6	870.6	252.3	75.2	0.4	41.8	1.7	40.1
2000	313.9	247.3	28.6	38.0	10.4	1 281.3	930.6	271.4	78.8	0.5	41.3	2.0	39.3
2001	348.0	276.1	29.8	42.0	8.0	1 389.9	994.2	305.1	83.0	7.7	-15.9	2.6	-18.5
2002	382.3	304.2	32.6	45.6	6.1	1 466.8	1 049.4	333.0	83.5	0.9	-54.1	1.5	-55.6
2003	421.3	338.0	33.8	49.5	3.3	1 535.1	1 096.5	353.4	85.1	0.1	-38.8	3.4	-42.2
2004	439.4	349.2	36.5	53.7	1.0	1 609.3	1 139.1	384.3	85.6	0.4	-8.4	6.9	-15.3
2005	454.3	361.2	36.5	56.5	0.1	1 704.5	1 212.0	404.8	87.3	0.4	25.9	7.4	18.5
2006	456.7	359.0	38.4	59.2	-1.3	1 778.6	1 282.3	402.9	93.0	0.4	51.0	4.7	46.4
2007	485.1	380.8	41.3	63.1	-9.1	1 910.8	1 368.9	433.7	101.1	7.1	12.2	1.9	10.4
2008	505.0	395.5	44.3	65.2	-12.3	2 017.0	1 449.2	456.7	108.1	3.0	-72.2	1.2	-73.4
2009	597.8	482.4	46.1	69.4	-10.5	2 031.7	1 425.5	498.1	106.7	1.4	-78.0	1.7	-79.7
2010	655.9	531.5	50.3	74.1	-10.8	2 090.0	1 443.5	534.6	110.4	1.6	-25.3	1.9	-27.3
2011	622.1	492.5	51.9	77.7	-13.5	2 149.7	1 475.2	558.0	116.0	0.5	-65.5	2.3	-67.8
2009													
1st quarter	550.9	438.4	45.0	67.4	-11.7	2 011.4	1 417.1	484.2	108.1	2.0	-118.1	1.5	-119.6
2nd quarter	617.5	503.4	45.4	68.7	-10.6	2 028.2	1 424.6	496.6	105.8	1.2	-75.3	1.6	-76.9
3rd quarter	602.7	486.4	46.2	70.0	-9.9	2 043.2	1 427.6	507.7	106.7	1.2	-74.0	1.7	-75.7
4th quarter	620.3	501.4	47.6	71.3	-9.7	2 044.0	1 432.7	503.8	106.2	1.2	-44.8	1.8	-46.6
2010													
1st quarter	635.4	514.8	48.0	72.6	-10.0	2 066.2	1 443.1	513.9	107.6	1.6	-32.3	1.8	-34.1
2nd quarter	648.3	524.2	50.4	73.7	-10.6	2 071.6	1 441.8	518.5	109.2	2.1	-28.2	1.9	-30.1
3rd quarter	668.1	542.1	51.3	74.7	-11.1	2 087.4	1 438.9	535.5	111.4	1.6	-5.2	2.0	-7.2
4th quarter	671.8	544.9	51.4	75.6	-11.6	2 134.8	1 450.1	570.6	113.2	1.0	-35.5	2.1	-37.6
2011													
1st quarter	642.1	514.5	51.3	76.3	-12.9	2 149.7	1 471.7	563.6	113.7	0.9	-57.2	2.2	-59.5
2nd quarter	656.4	527.7	51.5	77.2	-13.3	2 168.2	1 482.9	570.4	114.5	0.4	-40.2	2.4	-42.5
3rd quarter	600.8	470.6	52.0	78.2	-13.4	2 145.3	1 476.1	551.6	117.1	0.4	-83.2	2.4	-85.6
4th quarter	589.1	457.1	52.7	79.3	-14.3	2 135.6	1 470.1	546.5	118.6	0.5	-81.5	2.4	-83.8

. . . = Not available.

Table 6-9. State and Local Government Consumption Expenditures and Gross Investment

(National income and product accounts, calendar years, billions of dollars, quarterly data are at seasonally adjusted annual rates.)

NIPA Tables 3.9.5, 3.10.5

| Year and quarter | Total | Consumption expenditures [1] | | | | | Less | | | | Gross investment | | |
| | | Total | Compensation of general government employees | Consumption of general government fixed capital | Intermediate goods and services purchased [2] | Own-account investment | Sales to other sectors | | | Total | Structures | Equipment and software |
							Total [3]	Tuition and related educational charges	Health and hospital charges			
1960	47.5	33.5	25.5	3.5	8.9	0.8	3.5	0.4	1.0	13.9	12.7	1.2
1961	51.6	36.6	27.9	3.7	9.7	0.8	3.9	0.5	1.0	15.0	13.8	1.3
1962	54.9	39.0	30.2	3.9	10.1	0.9	4.4	0.6	1.3	15.9	14.5	1.3
1963	59.5	41.9	32.9	4.2	10.8	1.0	4.9	0.7	1.3	17.5	16.0	1.5
1964	64.8	45.8	35.9	4.5	11.9	1.0	5.5	0.8	1.5	19.0	17.2	1.8
1965	71.0	50.2	39.3	4.9	13.4	1.1	6.3	1.0	1.8	20.8	19.0	1.9
1966	79.2	56.1	44.1	5.5	14.9	1.2	7.2	1.2	2.1	23.1	21.0	2.1
1967	87.9	62.6	49.5	6.0	16.5	1.2	8.2	1.4	2.5	25.3	23.0	2.3
1968	98.0	70.4	55.9	6.6	18.7	1.3	9.5	1.6	3.2	27.7	25.2	2.4
1969	108.2	79.8	62.6	7.4	21.8	1.4	10.6	1.9	3.5	28.3	25.6	2.7
1970	120.3	91.5	71.1	8.4	25.4	1.5	11.8	2.4	3.8	28.7	25.8	3.0
1971	132.8	102.7	79.2	9.4	29.2	1.6	13.5	2.9	4.6	30.1	27.0	3.1
1972	143.8	113.2	87.7	10.2	32.2	1.7	15.2	3.2	5.6	30.6	27.1	3.5
1973	159.2	126.0	98.0	11.3	35.4	1.7	17.0	3.7	6.6	33.2	29.1	4.1
1974	183.4	143.7	107.7	14.1	42.7	2.1	18.7	4.0	7.4	39.6	34.7	4.9
1975	208.7	165.1	121.2	15.9	50.7	2.1	20.6	4.3	8.5	43.6	38.1	5.5
1976	223.3	179.5	133.0	16.6	55.2	2.0	23.3	4.7	9.9	43.8	38.1	5.7
1977	238.7	195.9	145.1	17.5	61.1	2.0	25.8	5.2	10.9	42.8	36.9	5.9
1978	262.7	213.2	158.9	18.9	66.9	2.3	29.2	5.8	12.7	49.5	42.8	6.6
1979	290.2	233.3	174.3	21.1	74.3	2.9	33.4	6.4	15.2	56.8	49.0	7.8
1980	322.4	258.4	193.0	24.3	82.0	3.3	37.6	7.2	17.3	64.0	55.1	8.9
1981	347.3	282.3	210.1	27.8	91.6	3.5	43.7	8.3	21.0	65.0	55.4	9.5
1982	369.7	304.9	227.4	30.3	100.6	3.7	49.7	9.4	24.5	64.8	54.2	10.6
1983	390.5	324.1	243.0	31.2	109.6	4.0	55.7	10.7	27.8	66.4	54.2	12.2
1984	422.6	347.7	261.1	32.0	119.0	4.6	59.8	11.7	29.4	75.0	60.5	14.4
1985	466.1	381.8	284.7	33.7	134.0	5.2	65.4	12.8	32.0	84.4	67.6	16.8
1986	510.9	418.1	307.6	36.2	151.6	5.7	71.5	13.9	34.8	92.8	74.2	18.6
1987	539.9	441.4	329.3	39.0	156.2	6.1	76.9	15.0	37.0	98.4	78.8	19.6
1988	577.3	471.0	354.3	41.5	166.0	6.7	84.1	16.6	40.3	106.3	84.8	21.5
1989	619.2	504.5	381.4	44.4	180.2	7.8	93.8	18.4	45.0	114.7	88.7	26.0
1990	674.2	547.0	415.9	48.0	195.2	8.6	103.5	20.3	50.0	127.2	98.5	28.7
1991	709.5	577.5	441.7	51.1	209.4	9.3	115.4	22.7	57.0	132.1	103.2	28.9
1992	740.6	606.2	466.6	53.4	224.9	9.5	129.1	25.5	65.3	134.3	104.2	30.1
1993	769.8	634.2	489.7	56.3	240.6	9.7	142.7	27.5	73.1	135.7	104.5	31.2
1994	811.2	668.2	515.2	59.5	256.8	10.1	153.3	29.4	78.8	143.0	108.7	34.3
1995	855.3	701.3	537.7	63.4	275.8	10.6	165.0	31.2	85.0	154.0	117.3	36.7
1996	894.0	730.2	557.1	66.7	290.6	11.0	173.2	33.0	86.6	163.8	126.8	36.9
1997	943.5	764.5	580.1	70.2	309.6	12.2	183.2	35.5	89.9	178.9	139.5	39.4
1998	995.0	808.6	606.4	73.9	332.8	12.6	191.9	38.0	93.5	186.4	143.6	42.9
1999	1 076.3	870.6	642.5	78.7	364.8	13.5	201.8	40.6	96.7	205.7	159.7	46.1
2000	1 154.9	930.6	679.0	84.7	400.0	14.9	218.2	43.7	104.0	224.3	176.0	48.3
2001	1 234.7	994.2	725.0	89.7	432.5	16.7	236.3	46.2	116.2	240.5	192.3	48.2
2002	1 302.7	1 049.4	765.8	93.8	454.1	17.0	247.3	49.4	120.8	253.3	205.8	47.5
2003	1 356.1	1 096.5	811.7	97.6	464.6	17.2	260.1	53.6	124.8	259.6	211.8	47.8
2004	1 408.2	1 139.1	842.9	104.4	485.2	18.1	275.4	56.9	130.9	269.1	220.2	48.9
2005	1 493.6	1 212.0	883.3	114.4	522.1	19.1	288.7	61.2	132.3	281.6	230.8	50.8
2006	1 586.7	1 282.3	927.1	124.2	556.2	20.5	304.7	65.8	137.8	304.4	249.9	54.5
2007	1 697.9	1 368.9	981.7	136.9	596.8	21.6	324.9	70.9	145.9	329.0	268.4	60.7
2008	1 798.0	1 449.2	1 034.1	146.2	631.2	22.9	339.3	75.9	153.3	348.8	285.0	63.8
2009	1 774.8	1 425.5	1 058.5	152.4	594.4	22.9	356.9	81.7	163.8	349.3	284.5	64.8
2010	1 780.0	1 443.5	1 064.2	155.3	623.7	21.4	378.3	87.8	173.3	336.5	270.8	65.7
2011	1 797.7	1 475.2	1 067.8	162.3	662.3	20.5	396.6	93.9	180.1	322.5	254.2	68.3
2009												
1st quarter	1 770.1	1 417.1	1 051.8	152.7	584.7	23.3	348.8	79.3	159.5	353.0	289.4	63.6
2nd quarter	1 779.7	1 424.6	1 059.1	152.6	590.1	23.4	353.8	80.7	162.3	355.1	290.7	64.5
3rd quarter	1 777.3	1 427.6	1 061.2	152.0	596.4	22.8	359.2	82.4	165.1	349.7	284.9	64.8
4th quarter	1 772.1	1 432.7	1 061.7	152.4	606.4	21.9	366.0	84.3	168.2	339.4	273.0	66.4
2010												
1st quarter	1 772.6	1 443.1	1 063.4	153.6	619.4	21.2	372.1	86.1	170.8	329.5	263.7	65.8
2nd quarter	1 780.1	1 441.8	1 064.9	154.8	621.1	21.6	377.5	87.5	172.9	338.3	272.8	65.6
3rd quarter	1 781.2	1 438.9	1 063.7	155.9	621.8	21.8	380.7	88.6	174.3	342.3	276.6	65.7
4th quarter	1 786.0	1 450.1	1 064.8	157.0	632.5	21.3	382.9	89.1	175.2	335.9	270.0	65.8
2011												
1st quarter	1 794.4	1 471.7	1 066.5	158.7	655.8	20.5	388.8	91.2	177.1	322.8	256.8	66.0
2nd quarter	1 801.5	1 482.9	1 067.8	161.1	668.0	20.3	393.8	92.9	179.2	318.6	250.6	68.0
3rd quarter	1 798.5	1 476.1	1 067.5	163.5	665.4	20.5	399.8	94.9	181.3	322.3	252.9	69.5
4th quarter	1 796.5	1 470.1	1 069.4	165.9	659.7	20.8	404.2	96.8	182.9	326.4	256.5	69.9

[1]Excludes government sales to other sectors and government own-account investment (construction and software).
[2]Includes general government intermediate inputs for goods and services sold to other sectors and for own-account investment.
[3]Includes components not shown separately.

Table 6-10. State and Local Government Output, Lending and Borrowing, and Net Investment

(National income and product accounts, calendar years, billions of dollars, quarterly data are at seasonally adjusted annual rates.)

NIPA Tables 3.3, 3.10.5

| Year and quarter | Output | | | Net lending (net borrowing -) | | | | | | | Net investment |
| | Gross | Value added | Intermediate goods and services purchased [1] | Net saving, current (surplus +, deficit -) | Plus: Capital transfer receipts | Minus | | | Plus: consumption of fixed capital | Equals: Net lending (borrowing -) | |
						Gross investment	Capital transfer payments	Net purchases of nonproduced assets			
1955	24.2	18.2	6.0	3.5	1.0	10.0	. . .	0.6	3.1	-3.1	6.9
1956	26.3	20.4	5.9	4.4	1.1	11.3	. . .	0.7	3.5	-2.9	7.8
1957	29.0	22.6	6.4	4.2	1.6	12.5	. . .	0.7	3.9	-3.5	8.6
1958	32.2	24.7	7.5	2.9	2.7	13.5	. . .	0.8	4.0	-4.7	9.5
1959	34.8	26.5	8.3	3.8	3.5	13.9	. . .	0.8	4.2	-3.2	9.7
1960	37.9	28.9	8.9	4.3	3.0	13.9	. . .	0.9	4.4	-3.1	9.5
1961	41.3	31.6	9.7	4.3	3.3	15.0	. . .	1.0	4.7	-3.8	10.3
1962	44.3	34.2	10.1	5.2	3.5	15.9	. . .	1.1	5.0	-3.2	10.9
1963	47.9	37.1	10.8	5.7	4.1	17.5	. . .	1.2	5.4	-3.5	12.1
1964	52.3	40.4	11.9	6.4	4.7	19.0	. . .	1.3	5.7	-3.4	13.3
1965	57.6	44.2	13.4	6.5	4.7	20.8	. . .	1.3	6.2	-4.6	14.6
1966	64.5	49.6	14.9	7.8	5.1	23.1	. . .	1.4	6.9	-4.7	16.2
1967	72.0	55.5	16.5	7.0	5.1	25.3	. . .	1.4	7.5	-7.1	17.8
1968	81.2	62.5	18.7	7.5	6.8	27.7	. . .	1.4	8.3	-6.4	19.4
1969	91.9	70.0	21.8	8.0	6.8	28.3	. . .	1.0	9.3	-5.1	19.0
1970	104.9	79.5	25.4	7.1	6.2	28.7	. . .	1.1	10.6	-6.0	18.1
1971	117.9	88.6	29.2	6.5	7.0	30.1	. . .	1.6	11.8	-6.4	18.3
1972	130.0	97.9	32.2	15.6	7.3	30.6	. . .	1.7	12.8	3.4	17.8
1973	144.7	109.3	35.4	15.7	7.3	33.2	. . .	1.7	14.3	2.4	18.9
1974	164.5	121.8	42.7	9.3	9.2	39.6	. . .	1.9	17.7	-5.3	21.9
1975	187.9	137.2	50.7	2.5	11.0	43.6	. . .	1.9	20.2	-11.9	23.4
1976	204.8	149.7	55.2	7.4	12.0	43.8	. . .	1.7	21.3	-4.9	22.5
1977	223.7	162.6	61.1	13.1	13.1	42.8	. . .	1.6	22.6	4.5	20.2
1978	244.7	177.8	66.9	18.7	13.7	49.5	. . .	1.6	24.5	5.8	25.0
1979	269.6	195.4	74.3	13.0	16.2	56.8	. . .	1.7	27.5	-1.8	29.3
1980	299.3	217.3	82.0	8.8	18.6	64.0	. . .	1.8	31.8	-6.6	32.2
1981	329.5	237.9	91.6	7.6	17.8	65.0	. . .	2.0	36.3	-5.3	28.7
1982	358.3	257.7	100.6	-2.2	16.9	64.8	. . .	2.0	39.5	-12.6	25.3
1983	383.7	274.1	109.6	4.9	18.0	66.4	. . .	2.2	40.9	-4.9	25.5
1984	412.1	293.1	119.0	23.9	20.1	75.0	. . .	2.6	42.3	8.8	32.7
1985	452.4	318.4	134.0	22.4	22.0	84.4	. . .	3.1	44.6	1.5	39.8
1986	495.3	343.7	151.6	20.7	23.0	92.8	. . .	3.7	47.8	-4.9	45.0
1987	524.4	368.2	156.2	12.0	22.3	98.4	. . .	4.2	51.4	-16.9	47.0
1988	561.8	395.8	166.0	17.2	23.1	106.3	. . .	4.3	54.8	-15.5	51.5
1989	606.0	425.8	180.2	20.1	23.4	114.7	0.0	4.9	58.5	-17.5	56.2
1990	659.0	463.9	195.2	6.2	25.0	127.2	0.0	5.7	63.0	-38.8	64.2
1991	702.2	492.8	209.4	-5.8	25.8	132.1	0.0	5.8	66.9	-51.0	65.2
1992	744.8	519.9	224.9	-1.4	26.9	134.3	0.0	5.9	69.9	-44.9	64.4
1993	786.6	546.0	240.6	-0.9	28.2	135.7	0.0	5.9	73.8	-40.5	61.9
1994	831.6	574.7	256.8	8.2	29.9	143.0	0.0	6.2	78.1	-33.0	64.9
1995	876.9	601.2	275.8	9.2	32.4	154.0	0.0	6.6	83.1	-35.9	70.9
1996	914.3	623.7	290.6	23.0	33.8	163.8	0.0	6.0	87.2	-25.7	76.6
1997	959.9	650.3	309.6	36.3	35.2	178.9	0.0	5.8	91.6	-21.7	87.3
1998	1 013.1	680.3	332.8	46.9	35.9	186.4	0.0	7.6	96.2	-15.1	90.2
1999	1 086.0	721.2	364.8	41.8	39.8	205.7	0.0	8.6	102.1	-30.6	103.6
2000	1 163.7	763.7	400.0	41.3	43.8	224.3	0.0	8.6	109.7	-38.1	114.6
2001	1 247.2	814.7	432.5	-15.9	51.2	240.5	0.0	10.1	116.0	-99.3	124.5
2002	1 313.7	859.6	454.1	-54.1	52.4	253.3	0.0	11.2	121.8	-144.4	131.5
2003	1 373.8	909.3	464.6	-38.8	51.5	259.6	0.0	11.4	127.3	-131.1	132.3
2004	1 432.6	947.3	485.2	-8.4	52.0	269.1	4.5	11.4	137.1	-104.2	132.0
2005	1 519.9	997.7	522.1	25.9	56.2	281.6	6.4	10.3	150.1	-66.0	131.5
2006	1 607.5	1 051.3	556.2	51.0	57.4	304.4	0.0	11.1	162.7	-44.3	141.7
2007	1 715.4	1 118.6	596.8	12.2	58.9	329.0	0.0	13.8	178.7	-93.1	150.3
2008	1 811.5	1 180.3	631.2	-72.2	62.8	348.8	0.0	14.1	191.2	-181.1	157.6
2009	1 805.3	1 210.9	594.4	-78.0	67.3	349.3	0.0	14.4	199.0	-175.4	150.3
2010	1 843.2	1 219.5	623.7	-25.3	78.3	336.5	0.0	14.5	204.0	-94.0	132.5
2011	1 892.3	1 230.1	662.3	-65.5	76.1	322.5	0.0	15.5	214.3	-113.1	108.2
2009											
1st quarter	1 789.2	1 204.6	584.7	-118.1	57.9	353.0	0.0	14.3	199.4	-228.1	153.6
2nd quarter	1 801.7	1 211.6	590.1	-75.3	62.5	355.1	0.0	14.4	199.1	-183.2	156.0
3rd quarter	1 809.7	1 213.3	596.4	-74.0	75.4	349.7	0.0	14.4	198.5	-164.2	151.2
4th quarter	1 820.6	1 214.2	606.4	-44.8	73.4	339.4	0.0	14.4	199.2	-126.0	140.2
2010											
1st quarter	1 836.4	1 217.0	619.4	-32.3	63.7	329.5	0.0	14.4	201.1	-111.4	128.4
2nd quarter	1 840.8	1 219.8	621.1	-28.2	78.0	338.3	0.0	14.4	203.1	-99.9	135.2
3rd quarter	1 841.4	1 219.6	621.8	-5.2	88.0	342.3	0.0	14.6	205.0	-69.0	137.3
4th quarter	1 854.3	1 221.8	632.5	-35.5	83.7	335.9	0.0	14.8	206.8	-95.7	129.1
2011											
1st quarter	1 881.0	1 225.2	655.8	-57.2	72.3	322.8	0.0	15.2	209.2	-113.7	113.6
2nd quarter	1 896.9	1 228.9	668.0	-40.2	75.7	318.6	0.0	15.5	212.6	-86.0	106.0
3rd quarter	1 896.4	1 231.0	665.4	-83.2	79.2	322.3	0.0	15.7	216.1	-125.9	106.2
4th quarter	1 895.0	1 235.3	659.7	-81.5	77.3	326.4	0.0	15.8	219.5	-126.9	106.9

[1] Includes general government intermediate inputs for goods and services sold to other sectors and for own-account investment.
. . . = Not available.

Table 6-11. Chain-Type Quantity Indexes for State and Local Government Consumption Expenditures and Gross Investment

(Seasonally adjusted, 2005 = 100.)   NIPA Tables 3.9.3, 3.10.3

Year and quarter	Total	State and local government consumption expenditures and gross investment										
		Consumption expenditures [1]								Gross investment		
						Less						
							Sales to other sectors					
		Total	Compen-sation of general government employees	Consump-tion of general government fixed capital	Intermediate goods and services purchased [2]	Own-account investment	Total [3]	Tuition and related educational charges	Health and hospital charges	Total	Structures	Equipment and software
1955	20.5	19.1	25.8	12.5	8.6	21.6	11.0	8.0	7.5	24.5	35.1	3.1
1956	21.2	19.8	27.4	13.2	8.2	24.2	11.4	9.1	8.5	25.1	35.6	3.5
1957	22.4	20.9	28.9	14.0	8.6	24.5	12.1	10.5	9.7	26.9	37.7	4.3
1958	24.3	22.5	30.7	14.9	9.9	26.2	13.5	11.9	12.2	29.5	41.8	4.3
1959	25.2	23.5	31.9	15.8	10.6	35.5	14.3	12.8	12.8	30.4	42.9	4.6
1960	26.3	24.8	33.6	16.7	11.2	33.3	14.8	14.2	11.9	30.8	43.1	5.2
1961	28.0	26.2	35.3	17.6	12.0	34.8	15.8	15.5	12.1	33.2	46.7	5.3
1962	28.8	26.9	36.5	18.6	12.4	37.0	17.6	17.5	14.2	34.4	48.2	5.7
1963	30.6	28.2	38.4	19.6	13.3	41.6	19.3	20.0	14.7	37.4	52.2	6.6
1964	32.6	30.1	40.7	20.9	14.5	41.1	21.1	23.4	15.9	40.2	55.6	7.4
1965	34.8	32.1	43.1	22.2	15.9	42.2	23.5	27.2	18.1	43.0	59.6	8.0
1966	37.0	34.0	45.7	23.6	17.2	44.5	25.7	30.8	20.7	45.9	63.3	8.8
1967	38.9	35.6	47.5	25.1	18.6	43.2	28.3	34.3	23.5	48.7	67.4	9.1
1968	41.2	37.9	50.3	26.6	20.4	45.5	31.0	38.6	27.4	50.9	70.4	9.5
1969	42.6	40.3	52.6	28.1	22.7	45.8	32.5	42.5	28.4	48.8	66.7	10.3
1970	43.7	42.7	54.9	29.4	25.0	46.3	34.0	49.5	28.9	45.7	61.7	10.7
1971	45.1	44.8	57.1	30.6	27.3	46.4	37.1	55.7	33.7	44.4	59.7	10.9
1972	46.1	46.5	59.1	31.7	28.9	45.2	39.8	59.2	38.6	43.0	56.7	12.1
1973	47.4	48.1	61.1	32.9	29.9	43.9	41.5	63.8	42.8	43.2	56.3	13.5
1974	49.2	50.3	63.3	34.0	31.5	46.7	41.5	63.6	44.1	43.6	56.1	14.8
1975	51.0	52.8	65.3	35.1	34.1	44.0	41.9	63.7	45.3	43.2	55.7	14.5
1976	51.3	53.5	66.0	36.1	35.0	38.9	44.3	65.8	48.2	42.4	54.7	14.3
1977	51.5	54.6	66.9	37.0	36.1	35.5	45.7	68.4	49.1	39.9	51.1	14.0
1978	53.2	55.7	68.5	37.8	37.0	38.2	47.8	72.2	52.5	43.5	55.9	14.8
1979	54.0	56.0	69.7	38.7	36.9	44.2	50.0	74.2	56.9	45.6	58.3	16.2
1980	54.0	55.9	70.5	39.7	35.7	46.0	50.8	76.7	57.4	45.8	58.0	17.3
1981	52.9	55.7	70.3	40.5	36.0	44.0	53.1	78.3	61.0	41.9	52.4	17.2
1982	52.9	56.5	70.6	41.3	37.6	44.3	54.7	78.2	62.8	39.4	48.1	18.2
1983	53.5	57.1	70.1	42.0	39.9	44.0	56.6	80.7	64.4	39.9	47.5	20.7
1984	55.4	58.2	70.4	43.1	41.7	48.9	56.5	80.6	62.9	44.8	52.8	24.3
1985	58.9	61.3	72.4	44.6	45.9	52.7	58.4	80.6	64.3	49.6	57.9	28.2
1986	62.7	65.1	74.4	46.4	52.0	56.5	60.3	81.2	66.0	53.0	61.5	30.9
1987	63.6	65.9	75.6	48.2	51.9	57.7	61.2	81.8	66.1	54.4	62.8	32.2
1988	65.9	68.1	78.1	50.2	53.2	60.3	62.4	84.3	66.1	57.2	65.6	34.9
1989	68.3	70.4	80.4	52.7	55.3	67.4	64.2	86.9	66.6	60.3	67.0	41.3
1990	71.1	72.6	82.5	55.5	57.0	70.5	65.4	88.8	67.3	65.1	72.0	45.1
1991	72.6	74.1	83.3	58.2	59.6	73.6	67.5	90.3	70.2	66.6	74.4	44.6
1992	74.2	75.8	84.4	60.7	62.5	72.9	70.6	92.0	74.2	67.5	74.7	46.8
1993	75.2	77.3	85.4	63.1	65.6	72.5	74.0	90.9	78.6	66.8	73.0	48.4
1994	77.2	79.3	86.7	65.3	68.8	73.1	76.5	90.9	81.7	68.7	73.5	53.3
1995	79.2	81.1	88.2	67.7	71.4	74.1	79.4	91.3	85.4	71.7	76.0	57.3
1996	81.1	82.6	89.4	70.3	73.2	75.0	80.9	91.5	85.0	75.0	79.9	59.0
1997	84.0	84.8	90.9	73.1	76.7	82.1	83.6	93.6	87.1	80.7	85.3	65.2
1998	87.3	88.3	92.6	76.6	82.7	83.8	86.2	96.2	89.6	83.0	85.1	74.3
1999	91.2	91.5	93.7	80.3	88.5	87.0	88.4	99.0	91.1	89.8	91.4	82.4
2000	93.7	93.5	95.4	84.1	92.0	91.9	92.7	102.4	95.6	94.7	96.3	87.3
2001	97.2	96.8	97.5	87.7	98.1	100.0	97.6	102.9	103.6	99.4	101.7	89.2
2002	100.5	99.9	99.3	91.0	102.5	100.0	98.8	103.0	104.1	102.8	105.8	90.3
2003	100.4	99.6	99.5	94.0	100.6	97.3	98.9	103.1	102.2	103.8	106.4	92.8
2004	100.2	99.6	99.6	97.4	100.2	99.1	99.7	99.9	102.5	102.9	104.6	95.7
2005	100.0	100.0	100.0	100.0	100.0	100.0	100.0	100.0	100.0	100.0	100.0	100.0
2006	100.9	100.7	100.6	102.7	100.6	103.0	100.9	100.9	100.0	101.7	100.3	108.6
2007	102.3	102.3	101.8	105.8	102.8	104.6	103.0	102.2	102.4	102.4	98.6	121.4
2008	102.3	102.1	103.0	108.0	100.0	106.1	103.0	103.1	104.6	103.3	98.8	126.8
2009	101.4	101.4	102.8	110.2	99.3	104.6	105.2	104.6	108.6	101.3	96.3	127.6
2010	99.6	100.1	101.4	112.5	99.5	96.2	108.2	106.9	111.8	97.4	91.3	130.2
2011	97.3	98.9	100.0	114.7	99.8	89.7	110.3	108.8	114.2	90.7	82.7	135.1
2009												
1st quarter	101.6	101.7	103.2	109.4	99.0	107.5	103.9	103.9	107.1	101.2	96.6	124.8
2nd quarter	101.8	101.6	103.0	109.9	99.4	107.1	104.7	104.3	108.1	102.6	98.0	126.6
3rd quarter	101.4	101.2	102.7	110.5	99.3	104.3	105.6	104.7	109.2	102.2	97.3	127.7
4th quarter	100.7	101.0	102.5	111.1	99.4	99.5	106.5	105.5	110.0	99.4	93.3	131.4
2010												
1st quarter	99.7	100.6	102.0	111.7	99.4	95.6	107.4	106.5	110.9	96.1	89.7	130.2
2nd quarter	99.8	100.2	101.7	112.3	99.5	97.0	108.1	106.9	111.6	98.2	92.2	129.7
3rd quarter	99.7	99.9	101.2	112.8	99.6	97.6	108.5	107.1	112.1	98.9	93.0	130.1
4th quarter	99.0	99.6	100.9	113.4	99.4	94.7	108.7	107.2	112.6	96.6	90.2	130.9
2011												
1st quarter	98.2	99.6	100.5	113.9	100.1	90.5	109.3	107.9	113.3	92.2	85.1	131.0
2nd quarter	97.5	99.3	100.0	114.4	100.2	88.6	110.0	108.5	113.9	90.1	82.0	134.5
3rd quarter	97.1	98.8	99.8	115.0	99.9	89.3	110.7	109.2	114.6	90.2	81.7	137.1
4th quarter	96.6	98.1	99.6	115.6	98.7	90.3	111.2	109.7	115.2	90.3	81.8	137.8

[1]Excludes government sales to other sectors and government own-account investment (construction and software).
[2]Includes general government intermediate inputs for goods and services sold to other sectors and for own-account investment.
[3]Includes components not shown separately.

Table 6-12. State Government Current Receipts and Expenditures

(National income and product accounts, calendar years, billions of dollars.)   NIPA Table 3.20

Year	Current receipts Total [1]	Current tax receipts Total	Personal current taxes Total [1]	Income taxes	Taxes on production and imports Total	Sales taxes	Property taxes	Other	Taxes on corporate income	Contributions for government social insurance	Income receipts on assets Total [1]	Interest receipts	Rents and royalties
1959	21.8	16.7	3.1	2.0	12.5	10.0	0.5	2.0	1.1	0.4	0.5	0.3	0.2
1960	23.5	18.1	3.4	2.3	13.5	10.8	0.5	2.2	1.2	0.5	0.5	0.4	0.2
1961	25.2	19.3	3.7	2.5	14.4	11.6	0.5	2.3	1.3	0.5	0.6	0.4	0.2
1962	27.5	21.0	4.0	2.8	15.4	12.6	0.6	2.3	1.5	0.5	0.6	0.4	0.2
1963	29.6	22.4	4.3	3.1	16.4	13.4	0.6	2.4	1.6	0.6	0.6	0.4	0.2
1964	32.3	24.5	4.9	3.6	17.7	14.5	0.6	2.6	1.8	0.7	0.7	0.4	0.2
1965	35.8	26.9	5.4	3.9	19.6	16.1	0.7	2.8	1.9	0.8	0.8	0.5	0.3
1966	42.3	30.2	6.4	4.8	21.7	18.0	0.7	3.0	2.2	0.8	0.9	0.6	0.3
1967	46.5	32.7	7.0	5.3	23.3	19.4	0.7	3.1	2.5	0.9	1.1	0.8	0.3
1968	54.7	38.6	8.8	6.9	26.7	22.8	0.8	3.2	3.1	0.9	1.7	1.4	0.3
1969	62.6	44.0	10.8	8.6	29.9	25.7	0.9	3.3	3.4	1.0	2.1	1.8	0.3
1970	70.1	48.1	12.0	9.6	32.7	28.2	0.9	3.6	3.5	1.1	2.5	2.2	0.3
1971	79.4	53.8	13.4	11.0	36.3	31.4	1.0	3.9	4.0	1.2	2.7	2.3	0.4
1972	96.3	63.5	17.9	15.2	40.7	35.2	1.1	4.4	5.0	1.3	2.9	2.5	0.4
1973	104.5	70.2	19.8	16.8	44.7	38.8	1.2	4.7	5.7	1.5	3.9	3.3	0.5
1974	113.5	75.9	21.1	18.0	48.4	42.0	1.1	5.3	6.3	1.7	5.0	4.4	0.6
1975	127.4	81.9	23.2	19.9	51.8	44.7	1.4	5.6	6.9	1.8	5.6	5.0	0.6
1976	143.4	93.8	27.0	23.4	57.7	49.9	1.5	6.3	9.1	2.2	5.3	4.7	0.6
1977	160.0	105.1	30.9	27.2	63.4	55.0	1.5	6.9	10.8	2.8	6.1	5.4	0.6
1978	179.3	117.4	35.6	31.6	70.3	60.8	1.9	7.6	11.5	3.4	7.4	6.7	0.6
1979	197.3	128.9	38.9	34.6	77.1	65.7	2.3	9.0	12.9	3.9	10.3	9.2	1.1
1980	218.7	140.9	43.7	39.1	83.4	70.0	2.6	10.8	13.7	3.6	13.4	11.2	2.0
1981	239.5	155.6	48.5	43.6	92.7	76.5	2.7	13.6	14.5	3.9	15.6	13.2	2.2
1982	247.9	162.3	52.3	47.0	97.0	80.3	2.8	13.9	13.1	4.0	17.5	15.3	2.1
1983	272.9	180.5	58.9	53.2	106.8	90.0	3.0	13.8	14.9	4.1	19.5	17.2	2.2
1984	308.2	205.4	68.2	61.9	119.7	100.9	3.4	15.5	17.4	4.7	22.4	19.8	2.5
1985	333.1	220.9	73.2	66.1	129.0	109.0	3.5	16.5	18.7	4.9	25.9	23.1	2.6
1986	359.1	234.0	78.3	70.7	134.9	115.8	3.6	15.6	20.7	6.0	27.3	24.5	2.7
1987	380.5	253.7	87.5	79.1	144.3	124.6	3.7	16.0	21.8	7.2	28.3	25.5	2.6
1988	408.8	269.4	90.4	81.5	155.2	135.1	3.8	16.3	23.8	8.4	30.5	27.7	2.7
1989	441.7	288.4	102.4	92.9	163.5	142.3	4.3	17.0	22.4	9.0	32.4	29.8	2.4
1990	476.7	305.6	109.6	99.6	175.4	152.5	4.6	18.3	20.5	10.0	33.9	31.4	2.3
1991	512.4	314.2	111.8	101.4	180.8	157.5	4.9	18.3	21.6	11.6	34.4	31.5	2.6
1992	559.9	338.8	120.6	109.0	195.9	169.7	6.1	20.1	22.2	13.1	33.9	30.8	2.7
1993	594.0	357.1	126.3	114.9	206.3	179.4	5.9	21.0	24.5	14.1	32.5	29.4	2.5
1994	630.6	380.4	132.1	120.2	220.8	191.7	7.0	22.1	27.5	14.5	33.8	30.5	2.5
1995	663.5	401.5	140.9	128.4	231.3	200.5	7.2	23.6	29.2	13.6	36.6	33.1	2.6
1996	696.8	425.9	150.9	138.6	245.0	211.8	8.2	25.0	29.9	12.5	39.3	35.2	2.7
1997	731.2	449.1	162.7	149.7	255.4	221.3	8.1	26.0	31.0	10.8	41.8	37.5	2.7
1998	777.3	480.7	180.4	166.8	268.8	233.3	8.5	27.0	31.6	10.4	43.4	39.3	2.4
1999	828.2	507.9	192.6	178.4	283.0	245.9	9.1	27.9	32.3	9.8	47.1	42.9	2.6
2000	884.1	540.1	213.5	199.2	294.8	255.5	7.8	31.6	31.7	10.8	49.5	44.5	3.6
2001	922.5	546.8	220.1	205.7	300.8	259.9	8.1	32.8	25.9	13.7	47.0	41.9	3.7
2002	940.6	536.4	199.1	184.2	309.6	267.9	7.7	34.0	27.7	15.9	43.0	37.7	3.7
2003	991.8	561.2	201.8	185.8	328.9	282.0	9.1	37.8	30.5	20.1	42.0	35.9	4.4
2004	1 072.2	610.8	221.4	204.4	352.3	300.5	8.3	43.5	37.1	24.1	44.6	37.5	5.1
2005	1 161.8	681.2	246.7	229.2	385.4	325.7	9.0	50.6	49.1	24.8	50.5	42.5	6.0
2006	1 220.0	732.1	271.2	252.9	408.9	346.3	9.7	52.9	52.0	21.8	59.5	50.7	6.4
2007	1 277.5	765.0	289.5	270.6	424.8	358.5	9.8	56.4	50.8	18.9	63.3	53.5	7.4
2008	1 299.0	769.6	301.1	282.3	427.1	355.1	9.7	62.4	41.5	19.0	59.9	49.2	7.8
2009	1 307.9	691.5	256.0	235.9	395.1	336.0	10.3	48.8	40.3	20.2	52.3	42.0	7.8
2010	1 393.5	730.5	267.2	245.0	413.6	350.8	11.1	51.7	49.7	20.8	51.5	40.0	8.9

[1]Includes components not shown separately.

Table 6-12. State Government Current Receipts and Expenditures—*Continued*

(National income and product accounts, calendar years, billions of dollars.)

Year	Current receipts—Continued					Current expenditures					Net state government saving, NIPA (surplus + / deficit -)		
	Current transfer receipts					Total [1]	Consumption expenditures	Government social benefits to persons	Grants-in-aid to local governments	Interest payments	Total	Social insurance funds	Other
	Total	Federal grants-in-aid	Local grants-in-aid	From business, net	From persons								
1959	3.8	3.4	0.2	0.0	0.1	20.8	8.6	3.6	7.7	0.8	1.0	0.0	1.0
1960	3.9	3.5	0.2	0.0	0.1	22.6	9.3	3.8	8.6	0.9	0.9	0.0	0.9
1961	4.4	4.0	0.3	0.0	0.1	24.5	9.9	4.1	9.4	0.9	0.8	0.0	0.8
1962	4.9	4.4	0.3	0.1	0.2	26.6	10.7	4.4	10.3	1.0	0.9	0.0	0.9
1963	5.4	4.9	0.3	0.1	0.2	28.9	11.6	4.7	11.3	1.1	0.7	0.0	0.6
1964	5.9	5.4	0.3	0.1	0.2	31.4	12.5	5.1	12.4	1.2	0.9	0.0	0.9
1965	6.7	6.1	0.3	0.1	0.3	35.1	13.9	5.5	14.3	1.3	0.6	0.1	0.5
1966	9.6	8.9	0.4	0.1	0.3	40.2	15.6	6.4	16.7	1.4	2.1	0.1	2.0
1967	11.1	10.3	0.5	0.1	0.3	46.4	17.9	7.7	19.1	1.6	0.0	0.1	-0.1
1968	12.6	11.6	0.6	0.1	0.3	53.6	20.2	9.5	22.0	1.8	1.0	0.1	0.9
1969	14.6	13.3	0.8	0.1	0.4	61.4	23.2	10.8	25.4	1.8	1.1	0.2	1.0
1970	17.6	16.2	0.9	0.1	0.4	71.3	26.7	12.9	29.2	2.2	-1.2	0.2	-1.3
1971	21.0	19.4	1.0	0.1	0.4	81.1	29.8	15.3	33.0	2.8	-1.7	0.2	-2.0
1972	27.6	25.8	1.1	0.2	0.5	90.6	32.6	17.5	36.9	3.2	5.8	0.3	5.5
1973	27.9	25.8	1.2	0.2	0.7	101.2	36.5	19.4	41.1	3.6	3.3	0.3	3.0
1974	30.0	27.6	1.3	0.2	0.8	114.3	43.6	19.9	45.9	4.1	-0.8	0.4	-1.1
1975	36.9	33.9	1.7	0.2	1.0	132.4	51.0	24.2	51.4	4.7	-5.0	0.5	-5.4
1976	40.8	37.1	2.3	0.3	1.2	145.1	55.6	26.9	56.2	5.3	-1.8	0.6	-2.4
1977	44.6	40.6	2.4	0.3	1.4	157.5	60.6	29.1	60.7	5.8	2.5	1.0	1.5
1978	49.5	45.2	2.5	0.3	1.5	171.8	64.7	32.0	67.3	6.3	7.5	1.5	6.0
1979	52.4	48.3	2.2	0.4	1.6	191.9	72.0	35.4	75.4	7.3	5.3	1.8	3.6
1980	59.2	54.7	2.3	0.4	1.7	216.5	81.2	41.3	83.8	8.2	2.2	1.3	0.9
1981	62.8	57.7	2.7	0.5	2.0	238.7	89.8	46.7	90.4	9.4	0.8	1.3	-0.5
1982	61.9	56.0	3.1	0.6	2.3	255.9	96.6	51.0	94.5	11.3	-8.0	1.2	-9.2
1983	66.0	58.6	4.2	0.6	2.6	273.7	102.6	55.9	99.0	13.5	-0.8	1.2	-2.0
1984	72.1	63.3	5.0	0.8	3.0	297.3	110.2	59.8	108.7	15.5	10.9	1.4	9.5
1985	76.9	67.3	5.2	0.9	3.6	323.6	118.8	65.2	120.0	16.3	9.5	1.3	8.2
1986	86.7	74.5	5.3	2.8	4.1	343.3	124.4	71.4	128.9	15.0	15.8	1.9	13.9
1987	85.8	74.9	5.5	0.9	4.5	372.6	135.6	77.4	137.8	17.6	7.9	2.2	5.7
1988	93.9	82.1	5.6	1.1	5.2	402.7	146.9	84.4	148.1	18.4	6.1	2.5	3.6
1989	104.6	91.5	5.8	1.3	5.9	436.1	157.9	94.4	159.5	19.2	5.5	2.3	3.2
1990	119.5	104.7	6.2	1.6	6.9	478.6	171.5	111.0	169.4	21.2	-1.9	2.0	-3.9
1991	144.2	124.6	7.6	2.0	10.0	528.1	179.6	137.6	181.9	23.1	-15.7	2.4	-18.0
1992	165.4	141.8	9.0	2.6	12.1	569.8	186.4	159.5	194.8	23.1	-9.9	3.1	-13.0
1993	181.0	155.9	10.1	2.9	12.1	603.8	195.7	173.6	206.0	22.6	-9.8	4.2	-14.0
1994	191.9	165.1	11.0	3.4	12.4	640.5	207.8	184.4	218.9	23.2	-9.9	4.6	-14.5
1995	201.0	173.6	11.1	4.1	12.2	674.2	217.1	194.8	231.6	24.0	-10.7	4.0	-14.8
1996	207.5	178.4	12.0	5.0	12.0	701.5	223.6	202.5	242.4	25.3	-4.7	2.8	-7.5
1997	217.3	184.3	13.5	6.6	13.0	731.9	235.3	206.8	255.1	26.2	-0.7	1.2	-1.9
1998	230.9	194.6	13.3	9.8	13.2	775.6	252.0	214.6	273.3	26.7	1.7	1.7	0.0
1999	251.8	212.7	12.9	11.4	14.9	844.3	280.5	230.3	296.4	27.8	-16.1	1.7	-17.8
2000	272.9	226.7	14.0	15.0	17.2	903.8	297.9	248.4	318.7	29.1	-19.7	2.0	-21.7
2001	304.4	253.6	14.9	16.1	19.8	985.3	319.0	281.0	336.7	31.1	-62.7	2.6	-65.3
2002	334.6	280.3	15.5	17.2	21.5	1 033.8	332.0	307.2	351.9	31.3	-93.2	1.5	-94.7
2003	356.9	301.5	16.4	16.6	22.3	1 068.1	333.5	326.1	366.7	31.3	-76.4	3.4	-79.8
2004	380.4	320.5	17.6	17.7	24.6	1 117.1	339.5	355.2	379.5	32.7	-44.9	6.9	-51.8
2005	392.1	330.2	16.6	18.4	26.9	1 177.7	360.7	373.9	397.8	34.9	-15.9	7.4	-23.3
2006	393.8	332.4	15.0	18.4	28.0	1 218.9	374.4	371.2	423.0	38.3	1.2	4.7	-3.5
2007	420.2	353.8	17.1	19.5	29.8	1 303.2	395.6	400.1	445.9	41.4	-25.7	1.9	-27.5
2008	441.3	370.8	17.1	21.7	31.6	1 358.3	417.0	421.2	459.6	43.7	-59.3	1.2	-60.5
2009	533.6	459.7	15.9	23.3	34.7	1 392.2	401.4	460.1	472.5	42.7	-84.2	1.7	-85.9
2010	579.7	499.2	16.1	26.3	38.0	1 443.6	403.3	494.2	485.8	44.4	-50.2	1.9	-52.1

[1] Includes components not shown separately.

Table 6-13. Local Government Current Receipts and Expenditures

(National income and product accounts, calendar years, billions of dollars.)   NIPA Table 3.21

Year	Current receipts Total [1]	Current tax receipts Total	Personal current taxes Total [1]	Personal current taxes Income taxes	Taxes on production and imports Total	Sales taxes	Property taxes	Other	Taxes on corporate income	Contributions for government social insurance	Income receipts on assets Total [1]	Interest receipts	Rents and royalties
1959	26.9	17.1	0.8	0.2	16.4	1.2	14.3	0.9	0.0	. . .	0.7	0.5	0.1
1960	29.9	18.8	0.8	0.3	18.0	1.3	15.7	0.9	0.0	. . .	0.8	0.7	0.1
1961	32.6	20.3	0.9	0.3	19.4	1.4	17.0	1.0	0.0	. . .	0.9	0.7	0.2
1962	35.2	21.8	1.0	0.3	20.8	1.5	18.4	1.0	0.0	. . .	1.0	0.8	0.2
1963	38.2	23.4	1.1	0.4	22.3	1.6	19.7	1.0	0.0	. . .	1.0	0.9	0.2
1964	41.8	25.3	1.2	0.5	24.1	1.9	21.1	1.1	0.0	. . .	1.3	1.1	0.2
1965	45.5	27.0	1.2	0.5	25.7	2.1	22.5	1.1	0.0	. . .	1.4	1.2	0.2
1966	49.9	28.5	1.4	0.6	27.1	2.0	23.8	1.3	0.0	. . .	1.7	1.4	0.3
1967	55.8	31.3	1.6	0.8	29.5	1.9	26.2	1.3	0.2	. . .	2.0	1.6	0.3
1968	61.7	34.8	1.7	0.9	32.8	2.3	29.1	1.4	0.3	. . .	1.7	1.4	0.4
1969	69.2	38.4	2.0	1.1	36.1	2.9	31.9	1.4	0.3	. . .	2.2	1.8	0.4
1970	80.3	43.2	2.3	1.3	40.6	3.5	35.7	1.5	0.2	. . .	2.6	2.2	0.5
1971	89.8	47.9	2.5	1.5	45.2	4.0	39.5	1.8	0.3	. . .	2.8	2.3	0.5
1972	100.5	52.0	3.0	2.0	48.8	4.6	42.2	2.0	0.3	. . .	3.0	2.4	0.6
1973	112.8	56.1	3.0	2.0	52.7	5.2	45.2	2.3	0.3	. . .	3.9	3.3	0.6
1974	122.6	60.2	3.4	2.3	56.4	6.1	47.9	2.4	0.3	. . .	5.2	4.5	0.7
1975	136.5	65.5	3.7	2.5	61.4	7.0	51.9	2.5	0.4	. . .	5.6	4.9	0.7
1976	150.1	71.9	4.1	2.8	67.3	7.9	56.7	2.7	0.5	. . .	5.1	4.4	0.7
1977	164.5	78.6	4.5	3.2	73.6	9.0	61.7	2.9	0.6	. . .	5.6	4.9	0.7
1978	179.6	80.8	4.9	3.4	75.3	10.2	61.8	3.3	0.6	. . .	7.2	6.5	0.7
1979	190.4	83.1	5.1	3.6	77.3	11.5	62.1	3.7	0.6	. . .	9.8	8.9	0.9
1980	207.6	89.1	5.1	3.5	83.3	12.8	66.2	4.2	0.7	. . .	12.9	11.8	1.1
1981	226.1	100.2	6.2	4.3	93.0	14.3	74.4	4.3	1.0	. . .	16.4	15.3	1.1
1982	243.7	110.8	6.9	4.9	103.0	15.9	82.5	4.6	1.0	. . .	19.2	17.8	1.4
1983	261.7	120.4	7.2	5.1	112.1	17.7	88.9	5.5	1.0	. . .	21.9	19.8	. 2.1
1984	288.9	131.9	7.8	5.6	122.7	20.1	96.3	6.3	1.4	. . .	25.2	22.8	2.4
1985	316.8	142.8	8.2	6.0	133.1	22.1	104.0	7.0	1.5	. . .	28.9	26.2	2.7
1986	341.0	155.6	8.9	6.8	144.7	24.1	112.6	8.1	2.0	. . .	31.1	27.5	3.5
1987	358.5	168.5	9.1	6.8	157.3	25.7	122.7	8.9	2.1	. . .	29.9	27.2	2.7
1988	386.1	183.3	11.7	9.1	169.4	27.2	132.7	9.4	2.3	. . .	30.0	28.3	1.7
1989	417.1	199.6	12.3	9.4	185.6	30.1	145.6	10.0	1.8	. . .	33.3	31.6	1.7
1990	443.3	213.6	12.9	10.0	198.7	31.8	157.0	9.9	2.0	. . .	34.5	32.7	1.8
1991	473.3	230.1	13.5	10.3	214.5	33.2	171.1	10.2	2.1	. . .	33.6	31.6	1.9
1992	497.1	241.0	14.7	11.4	224.2	34.6	178.6	11.0	2.1	. . .	30.9	28.8	2.0
1993	517.1	247.7	14.8	11.3	230.5	37.0	181.3	12.1	2.4	. . .	28.8	26.7	2.1
1994	551.4	263.8	15.9	12.0	245.4	39.7	192.4	13.3	2.5	. . .	29.5	27.5	2.0
1995	578.9	270.7	17.2	13.3	251.0	42.2	195.3	13.4	2.5	. . .	31.9	29.9	2.0
1996	611.5	283.7	17.8	13.7	262.9	44.4	204.2	14.4	3.1	. . .	34.2	32.2	2.0
1997	646.5	300.8	19.3	14.9	278.4	47.4	215.5	15.6	3.1	. . .	36.4	34.3	2.1
1998	683.8	314.2	20.9	16.2	290.0	50.6	222.5	16.9	3.4	. . .	38.1	35.9	2.2
1999	731.8	332.5	21.9	17.1	307.1	55.6	233.7	17.8	3.5	. . .	38.7	36.2	2.5
2000	782.0	353.1	23.2	18.1	326.5	61.3	246.9	18.3	3.5	. . .	44.8	42.1	2.7
2001	814.6	367.5	22.9	17.6	341.6	61.9	260.0	19.8	3.0	. . .	43.1	40.3	2.8
2002	851.7	392.3	22.7	17.1	366.4	63.2	281.7	21.5	3.1	. . .	36.7	33.8	2.9
2003	899.6	416.5	24.4	18.2	388.6	66.8	297.7	24.2	3.5	. . .	31.9	28.7	3.2
2004	937.2	448.6	27.2	20.3	416.8	70.2	318.4	28.2	4.6	. . .	32.6	29.2	3.4
2005	995.0	481.9	30.0	22.5	446.0	76.5	337.8	31.7	5.8	. . .	37.7	33.9	3.8
2006	1 061.5	517.0	31.3	23.1	478.6	84.2	360.3	34.1	7.2	. . .	44.0	40.1	3.9
2007	1 123.9	548.5	33.6	25.3	507.9	88.5	386.2	33.2	7.0	. . .	51.2	47.1	4.0
2008	1 138.4	556.7	33.3	25.4	517.5	88.9	398.7	29.9	5.9	. . .	46.9	42.7	4.2
2009	1 150.1	561.3	28.8	20.7	525.5	85.9	409.4	30.2	7.1	. . .	41.0	36.7	4.3
2010	1 189.5	577.4	30.3	21.9	538.9	87.5	419.5	31.9	8.2	. . .	39.5	35.0	4.5

[1] Includes components not shown separately.
. . . = Not available.

Table 6-13. Local Government Current Receipts and Expenditures—*Continued*

(National income and product accounts, calendar years, billions of dollars.)

NIPA Table 3.21

Year	Current receipts—Continued					Current expenditures					Net local government saving, NIPA (surplus + / deficit -)		
	Current transfer receipts					Total [1]	Consumption expenditures	Government social benefits to persons	Grants-in-aid to state governments	Interest payments	Total	Social insurance funds	Other
	Total	Federal grants-in-aid	State grants-in-aid	From business, net	From persons								
1959	8.3	0.4	7.7	0.1	0.1	24.1	22.1	0.7	0.2	1.0	2.8	...	2.8
1960	9.4	0.5	8.6	0.1	0.2	26.4	24.2	0.8	0.2	1.2	3.4	...	3.4
1961	10.4	0.6	9.4	0.2	0.3	29.1	26.6	0.9	0.3	1.3	3.5	...	3.5
1962	11.5	0.6	10.3	0.2	0.3	30.9	28.3	0.9	0.3	1.4	4.3	...	4.3
1963	12.6	0.8	11.3	0.2	0.3	33.2	30.4	1.0	0.3	1.5	5.0	...	5.0
1964	14.0	1.1	12.4	0.2	0.3	36.3	33.3	1.0	0.3	1.7	5.5	...	5.5
1965	15.9	1.1	14.3	0.3	0.3	39.6	36.3	1.1	0.3	1.8	5.9	...	5.9
1966	18.6	1.2	16.7	0.2	0.4	44.2	40.5	1.3	0.4	2.0	5.7	...	5.7
1967	21.6	1.5	19.1	0.4	0.6	48.9	44.7	1.6	0.5	2.1	7.0	...	7.0
1968	24.2	1.1	22.0	0.4	0.7	55.2	50.2	2.0	0.6	2.4	6.5	...	6.5
1969	27.7	1.3	25.4	0.4	0.7	62.4	56.6	2.4	0.8	2.5	6.9	...	6.9
1970	33.6	3.2	29.2	0.4	0.8	72.0	64.9	3.2	0.9	3.1	8.3	...	8.3
1971	38.2	3.8	33.0	0.5	0.9	81.6	72.9	4.0	1.0	3.8	8.2	...	8.2
1972	44.4	5.9	36.9	0.5	1.1	90.6	80.6	4.5	1.1	4.3	9.9	...	9.9
1973	51.8	9.0	41.1	0.7	1.0	100.4	89.5	4.7	1.2	4.9	12.4	...	12.4
1974	56.6	8.7	45.9	0.9	1.1	112.5	100.1	5.4	1.3	5.6	10.1	...	10.1
1975	65.0	11.2	51.4	1.0	1.4	129.1	114.1	6.6	1.7	6.4	7.4	...	7.4
1976	72.6	13.6	56.2	1.1	1.7	140.9	123.9	7.3	2.3	7.2	9.1	...	9.1
1977	79.9	16.0	60.7	1.3	1.9	153.9	135.3	8.0	2.4	7.9	10.6	...	10.6
1978	91.4	20.4	67.3	1.5	2.2	168.5	148.5	8.7	2.5	8.6	11.2	...	11.2
1979	97.8	18.1	75.4	1.8	2.6	182.8	161.3	8.9	2.2	9.9	7.7	...	7.7
1980	106.4	17.6	83.8	2.0	3.0	201.0	177.2	9.9	2.3	11.2	6.6	...	6.6
1981	111.3	14.8	90.4	2.4	3.7	219.4	192.5	10.4	2.7	13.4	6.8	...	6.8
1982	114.8	13.5	94.5	2.7	4.1	237.9	208.2	10.2	3.1	15.8	5.8	...	5.8
1983	119.5	13.0	99.0	3.0	4.5	256.0	221.5	11.0	4.2	18.8	5.7	...	5.7
1984	130.6	13.3	108.7	3.4	5.2	275.9	237.4	11.4	5.0	21.5	13.1	...	13.1
1985	142.7	13.6	120.0	3.5	5.7	304.0	263.0	12.1	5.2	23.0	12.8	...	12.8
1986	152.4	13.2	128.9	3.9	6.5	336.1	293.7	12.9	5.3	23.1	4.9	...	4.9
1987	157.4	9.0	137.8	4.0	6.7	354.4	305.8	13.4	5.5	28.6	4.1	...	4.1
1988	168.8	9.5	148.1	4.3	6.9	375.0	324.1	14.1	5.6	30.0	11.1	...	11.1
1989	178.8	6.8	159.5	5.1	7.5	402.5	346.5	15.0	5.8	34.0	14.6	...	14.6
1990	189.6	6.7	169.4	5.5	8.0	435.3	375.5	16.6	6.2	35.6	8.1	...	8.1
1991	203.5	7.0	181.9	5.9	8.7	463.4	397.9	18.9	7.6	37.7	9.9	...	9.9
1992	218.6	7.4	194.8	6.7	9.8	488.6	419.9	20.5	9.0	37.9	8.5	...	8.5
1993	233.1	8.1	206.0	7.7	11.4	508.3	438.4	21.6	10.1	36.8	8.8	...	8.8
1994	250.3	9.9	218.9	8.6	12.9	533.3	460.4	22.4	11.0	38.2	18.1	...	18.1
1995	265.9	10.6	231.6	9.4	14.3	559.0	484.2	22.9	11.1	39.4	19.9	...	19.9
1996	280.9	12.7	242.4	10.2	15.7	583.8	506.6	21.8	12.0	42.0	27.7	...	27.7
1997	297.6	14.1	255.1	11.1	17.3	609.5	529.3	20.8	13.5	44.5	37.0	...	37.0
1998	321.0	18.0	273.3	11.8	17.9	638.7	556.6	21.1	13.3	46.0	45.2	...	45.2
1999	348.6	20.2	296.4	12.7	19.3	674.0	590.1	22.1	12.9	47.4	57.9	...	57.9
2000	373.7	20.6	318.7	13.5	20.8	721.1	632.8	23.0	14.0	49.7	61.0	...	61.0
2001	395.2	22.5	336.7	13.7	22.3	767.8	675.3	24.0	14.9	51.9	46.8	...	46.8
2002	415.2	23.8	351.9	15.4	24.1	812.6	717.4	25.8	15.5	52.2	39.1	...	39.1
2003	447.5	36.5	366.7	17.2	27.1	862.0	763.0	27.3	16.4	53.8	37.6	...	37.6
2004	456.1	28.7	379.5	18.8	29.1	900.7	799.5	29.1	17.6	52.9	36.6	...	36.6
2005	476.6	31.1	397.8	18.1	29.6	953.2	851.4	30.9	16.6	52.4	41.9	...	41.9
2006	500.9	26.6	423.0	20.0	31.3	1 011.6	907.9	31.7	15.0	54.7	49.9	...	49.9
2007	528.0	27.0	445.9	21.7	33.4	1 086.0	973.3	33.6	17.1	59.7	37.9	...	37.9
2008	540.4	24.7	459.6	22.6	33.6	1 151.3	1 032.2	35.5	17.1	64.4	-12.9	...	-12.9
2009	552.7	22.7	472.5	22.8	34.6	1 143.9	1 024.1	38.0	15.9	64.0	6.2	...	6.2
2010	578.1	32.3	485.8	23.9	36.1	1 164.7	1 040.2	40.4	16.1	66.0	24.9	...	24.9

[1]Includes components not shown separately.

. . . = Not available.

Section 6c: Federal Government Budget Accounts

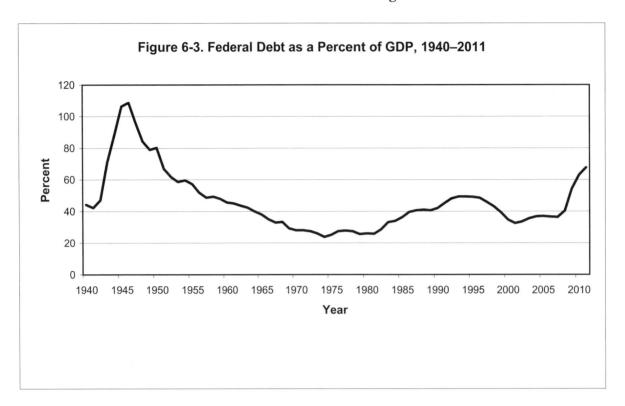

Figure 6-3. Federal Debt as a Percent of GDP, 1940–2011

- The "debt held by the public" is generally thought to be a more significant measure of the burden of the federal debt on credit markets than the gross debt, because it nets out the intragovernmental debt of the Social Security and other U.S. government trust funds. The ratio of this debt to GDP was reduced in the late 1990s, began to creep back upward after 2001, and then rose rapidly beginning in 2008, as the recession reduced revenues and increased spending, and taxes were reduced further. The spending increases were a result of both automatic stabilizer programs, such as unemployment insurance, and an unprecedented level of spending for stimulus and financial rescue programs. At the end of fiscal year 2011, the debt held by the public was 67.7 percent of GDP, the highest since 1950. (Tables 6-14 and 6-15)

- Further increases in the debt ratio are forecast under current budget policies, as a result of the slow recovery combined with increased demographic and cost pressures on federal retirement and medical care programs.

- From the end of fiscal year 2001 through the end of fiscal year 2011, foreign investors bought 54 percent of the Treasury debt sold to the public to finance the deficits of 2002 through 2011. At the end of 2011, foreign residents—including central banks—held $4.7 trillion of Treasury debt, 46 percent of the $10.1 trillion total debt held by the public. (Table 6-15)

Table 6-14A. Federal Government Receipts and Outlays by Fiscal Year [1]

(Budget accounts, millions of dollars.)

Year	Receipts, outlays, deficit, and financing							Receipts by source				
	Total receipts, net	Total outlays, net	Budget surplus or deficit (-)			Sources of financing, total		Individual income taxes	Corporate income taxes	Social insurance taxes and contributions		
			Total	On-budget	Off-budget	Borrowing from the public	Other financing			Employment taxes and contributions	Unemployment insurance	Other retirement contributions
1940	6 548	9 468	-2 920	-3 484	564	. . .	. . .	892	1 197	725	1 015	45
1941	8 712	13 653	-4 941	-5 594	653	5 451	-510	1 314	2 124	827	1 056	57
1942	14 634	35 137	-20 503	-21 333	830	19 530	973	3 263	4 719	1 064	1 299	89
1943	24 001	78 555	-54 554	-55 595	1 041	60 013	-5 459	6 505	9 557	1 338	1 477	229
1944	43 747	91 304	-47 557	-48 735	1 178	57 030	-9 473	19 705	14 838	1 557	1 644	272
1945	45 159	92 712	-47 553	-48 720	1 167	50 386	-2 833	18 372	15 988	1 592	1 568	291
1946	39 296	55 232	-15 936	-16 964	1 028	6 679	9 257	16 098	11 883	1 517	1 316	282
1947	38 514	34 496	4 018	2 861	1 157	-17 522	13 504	17 935	8 615	1 835	1 329	259
1948	41 560	29 764	11 796	10 548	1 248	-8 069	-3 727	19 315	9 678	2 168	1 343	239
1949	39 415	38 835	580	-684	1 263	-1 948	1 368	15 552	11 192	2 246	1 205	330
1950	39 443	42 562	-3 119	-4 702	1 583	4 701	-1 582	15 755	10 449	2 648	1 332	358
1951	51 616	45 514	6 102	4 259	1 843	-4 697	-1 405	21 616	14 101	3 688	1 609	377
1952	66 167	67 686	-1 519	-3 383	1 864	432	1 087	27 934	21 226	4 315	1 712	418
1953	69 608	76 101	-6 493	-8 259	1 766	3 625	2 868	29 816	21 238	4 722	1 675	423
1954	69 701	70 855	-1 154	-2 831	1 677	6 116	-4 962	29 542	21 101	5 192	1 561	455
1955	65 451	68 444	-2 993	-4 091	1 098	2 117	876	28 747	17 861	5 981	1 449	431
1956	74 587	70 640	3 947	2 494	1 452	-4 460	513	32 188	20 880	7 059	1 690	571
1957	79 990	76 578	3 412	2 639	773	-2 836	-576	35 620	21 167	7 405	1 950	642
1958	79 636	82 405	-2 769	-3 315	546	7 016	-4 247	34 724	20 074	8 624	1 933	682
1959	79 249	92 098	-12 849	-12 149	-700	8 365	4 484	36 719	17 309	8 821	2 131	770
1960	92 492	92 191	301	510	-209	2 139	-2 440	40 715	21 494	11 248	2 667	768
1961	94 388	97 723	-3 335	-3 766	431	1 517	1 818	41 338	20 954	12 679	2 903	857
1962	99 676	106 821	-7 146	-5 881	-1 265	9 653	-2 507	45 571	20 523	12 835	3 337	875
1963	106 560	111 316	-4 756	-3 966	-789	5 968	-1 212	47 588	21 579	14 746	4 112	946
1964	112 613	118 528	-5 915	-6 546	632	2 871	3 044	48 697	23 493	16 959	3 997	1 007
1965	116 817	118 228	-1 411	-1 605	194	3 929	-2 518	48 792	25 461	17 358	3 803	1 081
1966	130 835	134 532	-3 698	-3 068	-630	2 936	762	55 446	30 073	20 662	3 755	1 129
1967	148 822	157 464	-8 643	-12 620	3 978	2 912	5 731	61 526	33 971	27 823	3 575	1 221
1968	152 973	178 134	-25 161	-27 742	2 581	22 919	2 242	68 726	28 665	29 224	3 346	1 354
1969	186 882	183 640	3 242	-507	3 749	-11 437	8 195	87 249	36 678	34 236	3 328	1 451
1970	192 807	195 649	-2 842	-8 694	5 852	5 090	-2 248	90 412	32 829	39 133	3 464	1 765
1971	187 139	210 172	-23 033	-26 052	3 019	19 839	3 194	86 230	26 785	41 699	3 674	1 952
1972	207 309	230 681	-23 373	-26 068	2 695	19 340	4 033	94 737	32 166	46 120	4 357	2 097
1973	230 799	245 707	-14 908	-15 246	338	18 533	-3 625	103 246	36 153	54 876	6 051	2 187
1974	263 224	269 359	-6 135	-7 198	1 063	2 789	3 346	118 952	38 620	65 888	6 837	2 347
1975	279 090	332 332	-53 242	-54 148	906	51 001	2 241	122 386	40 621	75 199	6 771	2 565
1976	298 060	371 792	-73 732	-69 427	-4 306	82 704	-8 972	131 603	41 409	79 901	8 054	2 814
TQ	81 232	95 975	-14 744	-14 065	-679	18 105	-3 361	38 801	8 460	21 801	2 698	720
1977	355 559	409 218	-53 659	-49 933	-3 726	53 595	64	157 626	54 892	92 199	11 312	2 974
1978	399 561	458 746	-59 185	-55 416	-3 770	58 022	1 163	180 988	59 952	103 881	13 850	3 237
1979	463 302	504 028	-40 726	-39 633	-1 093	33 180	7 546	217 841	65 677	120 058	15 387	3 494
1980	517 112	590 941	-73 830	-73 141	-689	71 617	2 213	244 069	64 600	138 748	15 336	3 719
1981	599 272	678 241	-78 968	-73 859	-5 109	77 487	1 481	285 917	61 137	162 973	15 763	3 984
1982	617 766	745 743	-127 977	-120 593	-7 384	135 165	-7 188	297 744	49 207	180 686	16 600	4 212
1983	600 562	808 364	-207 802	-207 692	-110	212 693	-4 891	288 938	37 022	185 766	18 799	4 429
1984	666 438	851 805	-185 367	-185 269	-98	169 707	15 660	298 415	56 893	209 658	25 138	4 580
1985	734 037	946 344	-212 308	-221 529	9 222	200 285	12 023	334 531	61 331	234 646	25 758	4 759
1986	769 155	990 382	-221 227	-237 915	16 688	233 363	-12 136	348 959	63 143	255 062	24 098	4 742
1987	854 288	1 004 017	-149 730	-168 357	18 627	149 130	600	392 557	83 926	273 028	25 575	4 715
1988	909 238	1 064 416	-155 178	-192 265	37 087	161 863	-6 685	401 181	94 508	305 093	24 584	4 658
1989	991 105	1 143 744	-152 639	-205 393	52 754	139 100	13 539	445 690	103 291	332 859	22 011	4 546
1990	1 031 958	1 252 994	-221 036	-277 626	56 590	220 842	194	466 884	93 507	353 891	21 635	4 522
1991	1 054 988	1 324 226	-269 238	-321 435	52 198	277 441	-8 203	467 827	98 086	370 526	20 922	4 568
1992	1 091 208	1 381 529	-290 321	-340 408	50 087	310 738	-20 417	475 964	100 270	385 491	23 410	4 788
1993	1 154 335	1 409 386	-255 051	-300 398	45 347	248 659	6 392	509 680	117 520	396 939	26 556	4 805
1994	1 258 566	1 461 753	-203 186	-258 840	55 654	184 669	18 517	543 055	140 385	428 810	28 004	4 661
1995	1 351 790	1 515 742	-163 952	-226 367	62 415	171 313	-7 361	590 244	157 004	451 045	28 878	4 550
1996	1 453 053	1 560 484	-107 431	-174 019	66 588	129 695	-22 264	656 417	171 824	476 361	28 584	4 469
1997	1 579 232	1 601 116	-21 884	-103 248	81 364	38 271	-16 387	737 466	182 293	506 751	28 202	4 418
1998	1 721 728	1 652 458	69 270	-29 925	99 195	-51 245	-18 025	828 586	188 677	540 014	27 484	4 333
1999	1 827 452	1 701 842	125 610	1 920	123 690	-88 736	-36 874	879 480	184 680	580 880	26 480	4 473
2000	2 025 191	1 788 950	236 241	86 422	149 819	-222 559	-13 682	1 004 462	207 289	620 451	27 640	4 761
2001	1 991 082	1 862 846	128 236	-32 445	160 681	-90 189	-38 047	994 339	151 075	661 442	27 812	4 713
2002	1 853 136	2 010 894	-157 758	-317 417	159 659	220 812	-63 054	858 345	148 044	668 547	27 619	4 594
2003	1 782 314	2 159 899	-377 585	-538 418	160 833	373 016	4 569	793 699	131 778	674 981	33 366	4 631
2004	1 880 114	2 292 841	-412 727	-567 961	155 234	382 101	30 626	808 959	189 371	689 360	39 453	4 594
2005	2 153 611	2 471 957	-318 346	-493 611	175 265	296 668	21 678	927 222	278 282	747 664	42 002	4 459
2006	2 406 869	2 655 050	-248 181	-434 494	186 313	236 760	11 421	1 043 908	353 915	790 043	43 420	4 358
2007	2 567 985	2 728 686	-160 701	-342 153	181 452	206 157	-45 456	1 163 472	370 243	824 258	41 091	4 258
2008	2 523 991	2 982 544	-458 553	-641 848	183 295	767 921	-309 368	1 145 747	304 346	856 459	39 527	4 169
2009	2 104 989	3 517 677	-1 412 688	-1 549 681	136 993	1 741 657	-328 969	915 308	138 229	848 885	37 889	4 143
2010	2 162 724	3 456 213	-1 293 489	-1 370 494	77 005	1 474 175	-180 686	898 549	191 437	815 894	44 823	4 097
2011	2 303 466	3 603 061	-1 299 595	-1 366 777	67 182	1 109 324	190 271	1 091 473	181 085	758 516	56 241	4 035

[1] Fiscal years through 1976 are from July 1 through June 30. Beginning with October 1976 (fiscal year 1977), fiscal years are from October 1 through September 30. The period from July 1 through September 30, 1976, is a separate fiscal period known as the transition quarter (TQ) and is not included in any fiscal year.
. . . = Not available.

Table 6-14A. Federal Government Receipts and Outlays by Fiscal Year [1]—*Continued*

(Budget accounts, millions of dollars.)

Year	Receipts by source—*Continued*					Outlays by function						
	Excise taxes	Estate and gift taxes	Customs duties and fees	Miscellaneous receipts		National defense	International affairs	General science, space, and technology	Energy	Natural resources and environment	Agriculture	Commerce and housing credit
				Federal reserve deposits	All other							
1940	1 977	353	331	. . .	14	1 660	51	0	88	997	369	550
1941	2 552	403	365	. . .	14	6 435	145	0	91	817	339	398
1942	3 399	420	369	. . .	11	25 658	968	4	156	819	344	1 521
1943	4 096	441	308	. . .	50	66 699	1 286	1	116	726	344	1 521
1944	4 759	507	417	. . .	48	79 143	1 449	48	65	642	1 275	624
1945	6 265	637	341	. . .	105	82 965	1 913	111	25	455	1 635	-2 630
1946	6 998	668	424	. . .	109	42 681	1 935	34	41	482	610	-1 857
1947	7 211	771	477	15	69	12 808	5 791	5	18	700	814	-923
1948	7 356	890	403	100	68	9 105	4 566	1	292	780	69	306
1949	7 502	780	367	187	54	13 150	6 052	48	341	1 080	1 924	800
1950	7 550	698	407	192	55	13 724	4 673	55	327	1 308	2 049	1 035
1951	8 648	708	609	189	72	23 566	3 647	51	383	1 310	-323	1 228
1952	8 852	818	533	278	81	46 089	2 691	49	474	1 233	176	1 278
1953	9 877	881	596	298	81	52 802	2 119	49	425	1 289	2 253	910
1954	9 945	934	542	341	88	49 266	1 596	46	432	1 007	1 817	-184
1955	9 131	924	585	251	90	42 729	2 223	74	325	940	3 514	92
1956	9 929	1 161	682	287	140	42 523	2 414	79	174	870	3 486	506
1957	10 534	1 365	735	434	139	45 430	3 147	122	240	1 098	2 288	1 424
1958	10 638	1 393	782	664	123	46 815	3 364	141	348	1 407	2 411	930
1959	10 578	1 333	925	491	171	49 015	3 144	294	382	1 632	4 509	1 933
1960	11 676	1 606	1 105	1 093	119	48 130	2 988	599	464	1 559	2 623	1 618
1961	11 860	1 896	982	788	130	49 601	3 184	1 042	510	1 779	2 641	1 203
1962	12 534	2 016	1 142	718	125	52 345	5 639	1 723	604	2 044	3 562	1 424
1963	13 194	2 167	1 205	828	194	53 400	5 308	3 051	530	2 251	4 384	62
1964	13 731	2 394	1 252	947	139	54 757	4 945	4 897	572	2 364	4 609	418
1965	14 570	2 716	1 442	1 372	222	50 620	5 273	5 823	699	2 531	3 954	1 157
1966	13 062	3 066	1 767	1 713	163	58 111	5 580	6 717	612	2 719	2 447	3 245
1967	13 719	2 978	1 901	1 805	302	71 417	5 566	6 233	782	2 869	2 990	3 979
1968	14 079	3 051	2 038	2 091	400	81 926	5 301	5 524	1 037	2 988	4 544	4 280
1969	15 222	3 491	2 319	2 662	247	82 497	4 600	5 020	1 010	2 900	5 826	-119
1970	15 705	3 644	2 430	3 266	158	81 692	4 330	4 511	997	3 065	5 166	2 112
1971	16 614	3 735	2 591	3 533	325	78 872	4 159	4 182	1 035	3 915	4 290	2 366
1972	15 477	5 436	3 287	3 252	380	79 174	4 781	4 175	1 296	4 241	5 227	2 222
1973	16 260	4 917	3 188	3 495	425	76 681	4 149	4 032	1 237	4 775	4 821	931
1974	16 844	5 035	3 334	4 845	523	79 347	5 710	3 980	1 303	5 697	2 194	4 705
1975	16 551	4 611	3 676	5 777	935	86 509	7 097	3 991	2 916	7 346	2 997	9 947
1976	16 963	5 216	4 074	5 451	2 576	89 619	6 433	4 373	4 204	8 184	3 109	7 619
TQ	4 473	1 455	1 212	1 500	111	22 269	2 458	1 162	1 129	2 524	972	931
1977	17 548	7 327	5 150	5 908	623	97 241	6 353	4 736	5 770	10 032	6 734	3 093
1978	18 376	5 285	6 573	6 641	778	10 449	7 482	4 926	7 991	10 983	11 301	6 254
1979	18 745	5 411	7 439	8 327	925	11 634	7 459	5 234	9 179	12 135	11 176	4 686
1980	24 329	6 389	7 174	11 767	981	13 399	12 714	5 831	10 156	13 858	8 774	9 390
1981	40 839	6 787	8 083	12 834	956	15 751	13 104	6 468	15 166	13 568	11 241	8 206
1982	36 311	7 991	8 854	15 186	975	18 530	12 300	7 199	13 527	12 998	15 866	6 256
1983	35 300	6 053	8 655	14 492	1 108	20 990	11 848	7 934	9 353	12 672	22 814	6 681
1984	37 361	6 010	11 370	15 684	1 328	22 741	15 869	8 311	7 073	12 586	13 526	6 959
1985	35 992	6 422	12 079	17 059	1 460	25 274	16 169	8 622	5 608	13 345	25 477	4 337
1986	32 919	6 958	13 327	18 374	1 574	27 337	14 146	8 962	4 690	13 628	31 368	5 058
1987	32 457	7 493	15 085	16 817	2 635	28 199	11 645	9 200	4 072	13 355	26 513	6 434
1988	35 227	7 594	16 198	17 163	3 031	29 036	10 466	10 820	2 296	14 601	17 137	19 163
1989	34 386	8 745	16 334	19 604	3 639	30 355	9 583	12 821	2 705	16 169	16 859	29 709
1990	35 345	11 500	16 707	24 319	3 647	29 932	13 758	14 426	3 341	17 055	11 804	67 599
1991	42 402	11 138	15 949	19 158	4 412	27 328	15 846	16 092	2 436	18 544	15 054	76 270
1992	45 569	11 143	17 359	22 920	4 293	29 834	16 090	16 389	4 499	20 001	15 087	10 918
1993	48 057	12 577	18 802	14 908	4 491	29 108	17 218	17 006	4 319	20 224	20 245	-21 853
1994	55 225	15 225	20 099	18 023	5 081	28 164	17 067	16 189	5 218	21 000	14 914	-4 228
1995	57 484	14 763	19 301	23 378	5 143	27 206	16 429	16 692	4 936	21 889	9 671	-17 808
1996	54 014	17 189	18 670	20 477	5 048	26 574	13 487	16 684	2 839	21 503	9 035	-10 478
1997	56 924	19 845	17 928	19 636	5 769	27 050	15 173	17 136	1 475	21 201	8 889	-14 640
1998	57 673	24 076	18 297	24 540	8 048	26 819	13 054	18 172	1 270	22 278	12 077	1 007
1999	70 414	27 782	18 336	25 917	9 010	27 476	15 239	18 084	911	23 943	22 879	2 641
2000	68 865	29 010	19 914	32 293	10 506	29 436	17 213	18 594	-761	25 003	36 458	3 207
2001	66 232	28 400	19 369	26 124	11 576	30 473	16 485	19 753	9	25 532	26 252	5 731
2002	66 989	26 507	18 602	23 683	10 206	34 845	22 315	20 734	475	29 426	21 965	-407
2003	67 524	21 959	19 862	21 878	12 636	404 744	21 199	20 831	-736	29 667	22 496	727
2004	69 855	24 831	21 083	19 652	12 956	455 833	26 870	23 029	-167	30 694	15 439	5 265
2005	73 094	24 764	23 379	19 297	13 448	495 308	34 565	23 597	429	27 980	26 565	7 566
2006	73 961	27 877	24 810	29 945	14 632	521 827	29 499	23 584	782	33 021	25 969	6 187
2007	65 069	26 044	26 010	32 043	15 497	551 271	28 482	24 407	-860	31 716	17 662	487
2008	67 334	28 844	27 568	33 598	16 399	616 073	28 857	26 772	628	31 817	18 387	27 870
2009	62 483	23 482	22 453	34 318	17 799	661 049	37 529	28 417	4 749	35 568	22 237	291 535
2010	66 909	18 885	25 298	75 845	20 987	693 586	45 195	30 098	11 613	43 662	21 356	-82 298
2011	72 381	7 399	29 519	82 546	20 271	705 625	45 685	29 466	12 174	45 470	20 661	-12 575

[1]Fiscal years through 1976 are from July 1 through June 30. Beginning with October 1976 (fiscal year 1977), fiscal years are from October 1 through September 30. The period from July 1 through September 30, 1976, is a separate fiscal period known as the transition quarter (TQ) and is not included in any fiscal year.
. . . = Not available.

Table 6-14A. Federal Government Receipts and Outlays by Fiscal Year [1]—*Continued*

(Budget accounts, millions of dollars.)

Year	Transportation	Community and regional development	Education, employment, and social services	Health	Medicare	Income security	Social Security	Veterans benefits and services	Administration of justice	General government	Net interest
1940	392	285	1 972	55	0	1 514	28	570	81	274	899
1941	353	123	1 592	60	0	1 855	91	560	92	306	943
1942	1 283	113	1 062	71	0	1 828	137	501	117	397	1 052
1943	3 220	219	375	92	0	1 739	177	276	154	673	1 529
1944	3 901	238	160	174	0	1 503	217	-126	192	900	2 219
1945	3 654	243	134	211	0	1 137	267	110	178	581	3 112
1946	1 970	200	85	201	0	2 384	358	2 465	176	825	4 111
1947	1 130	302	102	177	0	2 820	466	6 344	176	1 114	4 204
1948	787	78	191	162	0	2 499	558	6 457	170	1 045	4 341
1949	916	-33	178	197	0	3 174	657	6 599	184	824	4 523
1950	967	30	241	268	0	4 097	781	8 834	193	986	4 812
1951	956	47	235	323	0	3 352	1 565	5 526	218	1 097	4 665
1952	1 124	73	339	347	0	3 655	2 063	5 341	267	1 163	4 701
1953	1 264	117	441	336	0	3 823	2 717	4 519	243	1 209	5 156
1954	1 229	100	370	307	0	4 434	3 352	4 613	257	799	4 811
1955	1 246	129	445	291	0	5 071	4 427	4 675	256	651	4 850
1956	1 450	92	591	359	0	4 734	5 478	4 891	302	1 201	5 079
1957	1 662	135	590	479	0	5 427	6 661	5 005	303	1 360	5 354
1958	2 334	169	643	541	0	7 535	8 219	5 350	325	655	5 604
1959	3 655	211	789	685	0	8 239	9 737	5 443	356	926	5 762
1960	4 126	224	968	795	0	7 378	11 602	5 441	366	1 184	6 947
1961	3 987	275	1 063	913	0	9 683	12 474	5 705	400	1 354	6 716
1962	4 290	469	1 241	1 198	0	9 207	14 365	5 619	429	1 049	6 889
1963	4 596	574	1 458	1 451	0	9 311	15 788	5 514	465	1 230	7 740
1964	5 242	933	1 555	1 788	0	9 657	16 620	5 675	489	1 518	8 199
1965	5 763	1 114	2 140	1 791	0	9 469	17 460	5 716	536	1 499	8 591
1966	5 730	1 105	4 363	2 543	64	9 678	20 694	5 916	564	1 603	9 386
1967	5 936	1 108	6 453	3 351	2 748	10 261	21 725	6 735	618	1 719	10 268
1968	6 316	1 382	7 634	4 390	4 649	11 816	23 854	7 032	659	1 757	11 090
1969	6 526	1 552	7 548	5 162	5 695	13 076	27 298	7 631	766	1 939	12 699
1970	7 008	2 392	8 634	5 907	6 213	15 655	30 270	8 669	959	2 320	14 380
1971	8 052	2 917	9 849	6 843	6 622	22 946	35 872	9 768	1 307	2 442	14 841
1972	8 392	3 423	12 529	8 674	7 479	27 650	40 157	10 720	1 684	2 960	15 478
1973	9 066	4 605	12 745	9 356	8 052	28 276	49 090	12 003	2 174	9 774	17 349
1974	9 172	4 229	12 457	10 733	9 639	33 713	55 867	13 374	2 505	10 032	21 449
1975	10 918	4 322	16 022	12 930	12 875	50 176	64 658	16 584	3 028	10 374	23 244
1976	13 739	5 442	18 910	15 734	15 834	60 799	73 899	18 419	3 430	9 706	26 727
TQ	3 358	1 569	5 169	3 924	4 264	14 985	19 763	3 960	918	3 878	6 949
1977	14 829	7 021	21 104	17 302	19 345	61 060	85 061	18 022	3 701	12 791	29 901
1978	15 521	11 841	26 710	18 524	22 768	61 505	93 861	18 961	3 923	11 961	35 458
1979	18 079	10 480	30 223	20 494	26 495	66 376	104 073	19 914	4 286	12 241	42 633
1980	21 329	11 252	31 843	23 169	32 090	86 557	118 547	21 169	4 702	12 975	52 533
1981	23 379	10 568	33 152	26 866	39 149	100 299	139 584	22 973	4 908	11 373	68 766
1982	20 625	8 347	26 612	27 445	46 567	108 155	155 964	23 938	4 842	10 861	85 032
1983	21 334	7 564	26 197	28 641	52 588	123 031	170 724	24 824	5 246	11 181	89 808
1984	23 669	7 673	26 920	30 417	57 540	113 352	178 223	25 575	5 811	11 746	111 102
1985	25 838	7 676	28 592	33 541	65 822	128 979	188 623	26 251	6 426	11 515	129 478
1986	28 113	7 233	29 776	35 933	70 164	120 633	198 757	26 314	6 735	12 491	136 017
1987	26 222	5 049	28 921	39 964	75 120	124 088	207 352	26 729	7 715	7 487	138 611
1988	27 272	5 293	30 931	44 483	78 878	130 377	219 341	29 367	9 397	9 399	151 803
1989	27 608	5 362	35 328	48 380	84 964	137 426	232 542	30 003	9 644	9 316	168 981
1990	29 485	8 531	37 171	57 699	98 102	148 668	248 623	29 034	10 185	10 460	184 347
1991	31 099	6 810	41 235	71 168	104 489	172 462	269 015	31 275	12 486	11 566	194 448
1992	33 332	6 836	42 741	89 486	119 024	199 562	287 584	34 037	14 650	12 881	199 344
1993	35 004	9 146	47 380	99 401	130 552	209 969	304 585	35 642	15 193	12 943	198 713
1994	38 066	10 620	43 286	107 107	144 747	217 166	319 565	37 559	15 516	11 159	202 932
1995	39 350	10 746	51 027	115 399	159 855	223 799	335 846	37 862	16 508	13 799	232 134
1996	39 565	10 741	48 321	119 365	174 225	229 736	349 671	36 956	17 898	11 755	241 053
1997	40 767	11 049	48 975	123 832	190 016	235 032	365 251	39 283	20 617	12 547	243 984
1998	40 343	9 771	50 512	131 425	192 822	237 750	379 215	41 741	23 359	15 544	241 118
1999	42 532	11 865	50 605	141 048	190 447	242 478	390 037	43 155	26 536	15 363	229 755
2000	46 853	10 623	53 764	154 504	197 113	253 724	409 423	46 989	28 499	13 013	222 949
2001	54 447	11 773	57 094	172 233	217 384	269 774	432 958	44 974	30 201	14 358	206 167
2002	61 833	12 981	70 566	196 497	230 855	312 720	455 980	50 929	35 061	16 951	170 949
2003	67 069	18 850	82 587	219 541	249 433	334 632	474 680	56 984	35 340	23 164	153 073
2004	64 627	15 820	87 974	240 122	269 360	333 059	495 548	59 746	45 576	22 338	160 245
2005	67 894	26 262	97 555	250 548	298 638	345 847	523 305	70 120	40 019	16 997	183 986
2006	70 244	54 465	118 482	252 739	329 868	352 477	548 549	69 811	41 016	18 177	226 603
2007	72 905	29 567	91 656	266 382	375 407	365 975	586 153	72 818	42 362	17 425	237 109
2008	77 616	23 952	91 287	280 599	390 758	431 313	617 027	84 653	48 097	20 323	252 757
2009	84 289	27 650	79 749	334 335	430 093	533 224	682 963	95 429	52 581	22 017	186 902
2010	91 972	23 804	127 710	369 054	451 636	622 210	706 737	108 384	54 385	23 031	196 194
2011	92 965	23 816	101 233	372 500	485 653	597 352	730 811	127 189	56 055	25 507	229 968

[1]Fiscal years through 1976 are from July 1 through June 30. Beginning with October 1976 (fiscal year 1977), fiscal years are from October 1 through September 30. The period from July 1 through September 30, 1976, is a separate fiscal period known as the transition quarter (TQ) and is not included in any fiscal year.

Table 6-14B. The Federal Budget and GDP

(Billions of dollars; percent.)

Year	Fiscal year GDP	Billions of dollars						Percent of GDP					
		Receipts			Outlays		Budget surplus or deficit	Receipts			Outlays		Budget surplus or deficit
		Total	Individual income taxes	Corporate income taxes	Total	National defense		Total	Individual income taxes	Corporate income taxes	Total	National defense	
1929	...	3.9	...	...	3.1	...	0.7	...	...	...	...	...	...
1930	97.4	4.1	...	...	3.3	...	0.7	4.2	...	...	3.4	...	0.8
1931	83.9	3.1	...	...	3.6	...	-0.5	3.7	...	...	4.3	...	-0.6
1932	67.6	1.9	...	...	4.7	...	-2.7	2.8	...	...	6.9	...	-4.0
1933	57.6	2.0	...	...	4.6	...	-2.6	3.5	...	...	8.0	...	-4.5
1934	61.2	3.0	0.4	0.4	6.5	...	-3.6	4.8	0.7	0.6	10.7	...	-5.9
1935	69.6	3.6	0.5	0.5	6.4	...	-2.8	5.2	0.8	0.8	9.2	...	-4.0
1936	78.5	3.9	0.7	0.7	8.2	...	-4.3	5.0	0.9	0.9	10.5	...	-5.5
1937	87.8	5.4	1.1	1.0	7.6	...	-2.2	6.1	1.2	1.2	8.6	...	-2.5
1938	89.0	6.8	1.3	1.3	6.8	...	-0.1	7.6	1.4	1.4	7.7	...	-0.1
1939	89.1	6.3	1.0	1.1	9.1	...	-2.8	7.1	1.2	1.3	10.3	...	-3.2
1940	96.8	6.5	0.9	1.2	9.5	1.7	-2.9	6.8	0.9	1.2	9.8	1.7	-3.0
1941	114.1	8.7	1.3	2.1	13.7	6.4	-4.9	7.6	1.2	1.9	12.0	5.6	-4.3
1942	144.3	14.6	3.3	4.7	35.1	25.7	-20.5	10.1	2.3	3.3	24.3	17.8	-14.2
1943	180.3	24.0	6.5	9.6	78.6	66.7	-54.6	13.3	3.6	5.3	43.6	37.0	-30.3
1944	209.2	43.7	19.7	14.8	91.3	79.1	-47.6	20.9	9.4	7.1	43.6	37.8	-22.7
1945	221.4	45.2	18.4	16.0	92.7	83.0	-47.6	20.4	8.3	7.2	41.9	37.5	-21.5
1946	222.6	39.3	16.1	11.9	55.2	42.7	-15.9	17.7	7.2	5.3	24.8	19.2	-7.2
1947	233.2	38.5	17.9	8.6	34.5	12.8	4.0	16.5	7.7	3.7	14.8	5.5	1.7
1948	256.6	41.6	19.3	9.7	29.8	9.1	11.8	16.2	7.5	3.8	11.6	3.5	4.6
1949	271.3	39.4	15.6	11.2	38.8	13.2	0.6	14.5	5.7	4.1	14.3	4.8	0.2
1950	273.1	39.4	15.8	10.4	42.6	13.7	-3.1	14.4	5.8	3.8	15.6	5.0	-1.1
1951	320.2	51.6	21.6	14.1	45.5	23.6	6.1	16.1	6.8	4.4	14.2	7.4	1.9
1952	348.7	66.2	27.9	21.2	67.7	46.1	-1.5	19.0	8.0	6.1	19.4	13.2	-0.4
1953	372.5	69.6	29.8	21.2	76.1	52.8	-6.5	18.7	8.0	5.7	20.4	14.2	-1.7
1954	377.0	69.7	29.5	21.1	70.9	49.3	-1.2	18.5	7.8	5.6	18.8	13.1	-0.3
1955	395.9	65.5	28.7	17.9	68.4	42.7	-3.0	16.5	7.3	4.5	17.3	10.8	-0.8
1956	427.0	74.6	32.2	20.9	70.6	42.5	3.9	17.5	7.5	4.9	16.5	10.0	0.9
1957	450.9	80.0	35.6	21.2	76.6	45.4	3.4	17.7	7.9	4.7	17.0	10.1	0.8
1958	460.0	79.6	34.7	20.1	82.4	46.8	-2.8	17.3	7.5	4.4	17.9	10.2	-0.6
1959	490.2	79.2	36.7	17.3	92.1	49.0	-12.8	16.2	7.5	3.5	18.8	10.0	-2.6
1960	518.9	92.5	40.7	21.5	92.2	48.1	0.3	17.8	7.8	4.1	17.8	9.3	0.1
1961	529.9	94.4	41.3	21.0	97.7	49.6	-3.3	17.8	7.8	4.0	18.4	9.4	-0.6
1962	567.8	99.7	45.6	20.5	106.8	52.3	-7.1	17.6	8.0	3.6	18.8	9.2	-1.3
1963	599.2	106.6	47.6	21.6	111.3	53.4	-4.8	17.8	7.9	3.6	18.6	8.9	-0.8
1964	641.5	112.6	48.7	23.5	118.5	54.8	-5.9	17.6	7.6	3.7	18.5	8.5	-0.9
1965	687.5	116.8	48.8	25.5	118.2	50.6	-1.4	17.0	7.1	3.7	17.2	7.4	-0.2
1966	755.8	130.8	55.4	30.1	134.5	58.1	-3.7	17.3	7.3	4.0	17.8	7.7	-0.5
1967	810.0	148.8	61.5	34.0	157.5	71.4	-8.6	18.4	7.6	4.2	19.4	8.8	-1.1
1968	868.4	153.0	68.7	28.7	178.1	81.9	-25.2	17.6	7.9	3.3	20.5	9.4	-2.9
1969	948.1	186.9	87.2	36.7	183.6	82.5	3.2	19.7	9.2	3.9	19.4	8.7	0.3
1970	1 012.7	192.8	90.4	32.8	195.6	81.7	-2.8	19.0	8.9	3.2	19.3	8.1	-0.3
1971	1 080.0	187.1	86.2	26.8	210.2	78.9	-23.0	17.3	8.0	2.5	19.5	7.3	-2.1
1972	1 176.5	207.3	94.7	32.2	230.7	79.2	-23.4	17.6	8.1	2.7	19.6	6.7	-2.0
1973	1 310.6	230.8	103.2	36.2	245.7	76.7	-14.9	17.6	7.9	2.8	18.7	5.9	-1.1
1974	1 438.5	263.2	119.0	38.6	269.4	79.3	-6.1	18.3	8.3	2.7	18.7	5.5	-0.4
1975	1 560.2	279.1	122.4	40.6	332.3	86.5	-53.2	17.9	7.8	2.6	21.3	5.5	-3.4
1976	1 738.1	298.1	131.6	41.4	371.8	89.6	-73.7	17.1	7.6	2.4	21.4	5.2	-4.2
1977	1 973.5	355.6	157.6	54.9	409.2	97.2	-53.7	18.0	8.0	2.8	20.7	4.9	-2.7
1978	2 217.5	399.6	181.0	60.0	458.7	104.5	-59.2	18.0	8.2	2.7	20.7	4.7	-2.7
1979	2 501.4	463.3	217.8	65.7	504.0	116.3	-40.7	18.5	8.7	2.6	20.1	4.7	-1.6
1980	2 724.2	517.1	244.1	64.6	590.9	134.0	-73.8	19.0	9.0	2.4	21.7	4.9	-2.7
1981	3 057.0	599.3	285.9	61.1	678.2	157.5	-79.0	19.6	9.4	2.0	22.2	5.2	-2.6
1982	3 223.7	617.8	297.7	49.2	745.7	185.3	-128.0	19.2	9.2	1.5	23.1	5.7	-4.0
1983	3 440.7	600.6	288.9	37.0	808.4	209.9	-207.8	17.5	8.4	1.1	23.5	6.1	-6.0
1984	3 844.4	666.4	298.4	56.9	851.8	227.4	-185.4	17.3	7.8	1.5	22.2	5.9	-4.8
1985	4 146.3	734.0	334.5	61.3	946.3	252.7	-212.3	17.7	8.1	1.5	22.8	6.1	-5.1
1986	4 403.9	769.2	349.0	63.1	990.4	273.4	-221.2	17.5	7.9	1.4	22.5	6.2	-5.0
1987	4 651.4	854.3	392.6	83.9	1 004.0	282.0	-149.7	18.4	8.4	1.8	21.6	6.1	-3.2
1988	5 008.5	909.2	401.2	94.5	1 064.4	290.4	-155.2	18.2	8.0	1.9	21.3	5.8	-3.1
1989	5 399.5	991.1	445.7	103.3	1 143.7	303.6	-152.6	18.4	8.3	1.9	21.2	5.6	-2.8
1990	5 734.5	1 032.0	466.9	93.5	1 253.0	299.3	-221.0	18.0	8.1	1.6	21.9	5.2	-3.9
1991	5 930.5	1 055.0	467.8	98.1	1 324.2	273.3	-269.2	17.8	7.9	1.7	22.3	4.6	-4.5
1992	6 242.0	1 091.2	476.0	100.3	1 381.5	298.3	-290.3	17.5	7.6	1.6	22.1	4.8	-4.7
1993	6 587.3	1 154.3	509.7	117.5	1 409.4	291.1	-255.1	17.5	7.7	1.8	21.4	4.4	-3.9
1994	6 976.6	1 258.6	543.1	140.4	1 461.8	281.6	-203.2	18.0	7.8	2.0	21.0	4.0	-2.9

. . . = Not available.

Table 6-14B. The Federal Budget and GDP—*Continued*

(Billions of dollars; percent.)

Year	Fiscal year GDP	Billions of dollars						Percent of GDP					
		Receipts			Outlays		Budget surplus or deficit	Receipts			Outlays		Budget surplus or deficit
		Total	Individual income taxes	Corporate income taxes	Total	National defense		Total	Individual income taxes	Corporate income taxes	Total	National defense	
1995	7 341.1	1 351.8	590.2	157.0	1 515.7	272.1	-164.0	18.4	8.0	2.1	20.6	3.7	-2.2
1996	7 718.3	1 453.1	656.4	171.8	1 560.5	265.7	-107.4	18.8	8.5	2.2	20.2	3.4	-1.4
1997	8 211.7	1 579.2	737.5	182.3	1 601.1	270.5	-21.9	19.2	9.0	2.2	19.5	3.3	-0.3
1998	8 663.0	1 721.7	828.6	188.7	1 652.5	268.2	69.3	19.9	9.6	2.2	19.1	3.1	0.8
1999	9 208.4	1 827.5	879.5	184.7	1 701.8	274.8	125.6	19.8	9.6	2.0	18.5	3.0	1.4
2000	9 821.0	2 025.2	1 004.5	207.3	1 789.0	294.4	236.2	20.6	10.2	2.1	18.2	3.0	2.4
2001	10 225.3	1 991.1	994.3	151.1	1 862.8	304.7	128.2	19.5	9.7	1.5	18.2	3.0	1.3
2002	10 543.9	1 853.1	858.3	148.0	2 010.9	348.5	-157.8	17.6	8.1	1.4	19.1	3.3	-1.5
2003	10 980.2	1 782.3	793.7	131.8	2 159.9	404.7	-377.6	16.2	7.2	1.2	19.7	3.7	-3.4
2004	11 676.0	1 880.1	809.0	189.4	2 292.8	455.8	-412.7	16.1	6.9	1.6	19.6	3.9	-3.5
2005	12 428.6	2 153.6	927.2	278.3	2 472.0	495.3	-318.3	17.3	7.5	2.2	19.9	4.0	-2.6
2006	13 206.5	2 406.9	1 043.9	353.9	2 655.1	521.8	-248.2	18.2	7.9	2.7	20.1	4.0	-1.9
2007	13 861.4	2 568.0	1 163.5	370.2	2 728.7	551.3	-160.7	18.5	8.4	2.7	19.7	4.0	-1.2
2008	14 334.4	2 524.0	1 145.7	304.3	2 982.5	616.1	-458.6	17.6	8.0	2.1	20.8	4.3	-3.2
2009	13 937.5	2 105.0	915.3	138.2	3 517.7	661.0	-1 412.7	15.1	6.6	1.0	25.2	4.7	-10.1
2010	14 359.7	2 162.7	898.5	191.4	3 456.2	693.6	-1 293.5	15.1	6.3	1.3	24.1	4.8	-9.0
2011	14 958.6	2 303.5	1 091.5	181.1	3 603.1	705.6	-1 299.6	15.4	7.3	1.2	24.1	4.7	-8.7

Table 6-15. Federal Government Debt by Fiscal Year

(Billions of dollars, except as noted.)

| Year | Federal government debt held by the public at end of fiscal year | | Gross federal debt at end of fiscal year held by: | | | | | | |
| | Debt held by the public | Debt/GDP ratio (percent) | Total | Social Security funds | Other U.S. government accounts | Federal Reserve System | Private investors | | |
							Total	Foreign residents	Domestic investors
1940	43	44.2	51	2	6	2	40	. . .	. . .
1941	48	42.3	58	2	7	2	46	. . .	. . .
1942	68	47.0	79	3	8	3	65	. . .	. . .
1943	128	70.9	143	4	11	7	121	. . .	. . .
1944	185	88.3	204	5	14	15	170	. . .	. . .
1945	235	106.2	260	7	18	22	213	. . .	. . .
1946	242	108.7	271	8	21	24	218	. . .	. . .
1947	224	96.2	257	9	24	22	202	. . .	. . .
1948	216	84.3	252	10	26	21	195	. . .	. . .
1949	214	79.0	253	11	27	19	195	. . .	. . .
1950	219	80.2	257	13	25	18	201	. . .	. . .
1951	214	66.9	255	15	26	23	191	. . .	. . .
1952	215	61.6	259	17	28	23	192	. . .	. . .
1953	218	58.6	266	18	29	25	194	. . .	. . .
1954	224	59.5	271	20	26	25	199	. . .	. . .
1955	227	57.2	274	21	27	24	203	. . .	. . .
1956	222	52.0	273	23	28	24	198	. . .	. . .
1957	219	48.6	272	23	30	23	196	. . .	. . .
1958	226	49.2	280	24	29	25	201	. . .	. . .
1959	235	47.9	287	23	30	26	209	. . .	. . .
1960	237	45.6	291	23	31	27	210	. . .	. . .
1961	238	45.0	293	23	31	27	211	. . .	. . .
1962	248	43.7	303	22	33	30	218	. . .	. . .
1963	254	42.4	310	21	35	32	222	. . .	. . .
1964	257	40.0	316	22	37	35	222	. . .	. . .
1965	261	37.9	322	22	39	39	222	12	210
1966	264	34.9	328	22	43	42	222	12	210
1967	267	32.9	340	26	48	47	220	11	209
1968	290	33.3	369	28	51	52	237	11	226
1969	278	29.3	366	32	56	54	224	10	214
1970	283	28.0	381	38	60	58	225	14	211
1971	303	28.1	408	41	64	66	238	32	206
1972	322	27.4	436	44	70	71	251	49	202
1973	341	26.0	466	44	81	75	266	59	207
1974	344	23.9	484	46	94	81	263	57	206
1975	395	25.3	542	48	99	85	310	66	244
1976	477	27.5	629	45	107	95	383	70	313
1977	549	27.8	706	40	118	105	444	96	348
1978	607	27.4	777	35	134	115	492	121	371
1979	640	25.6	829	33	156	116	525	120	405
1980	712	26.1	909	32	165	121	591	122	469
1981	789	25.8	995	27	178	124	665	131	534
1982	925	28.7	1 137	19	193	134	790	141	649
1983	1 137	33.1	1 372	32	202	156	982	160	822
1984	1 307	34.0	1 565	32	225	155	1 152	176	976
1985	1 507	36.4	1 817	40	270	170	1 337	223	1 114
1986	1 741	39.5	2 121	46	334	191	1 550	266	1 284
1987	1 890	40.6	2 346	65	391	212	1 678	280	1 398
1988	2 052	41.0	2 601	104	445	229	1 822	346	1 476
1989	2 191	40.6	2 868	157	520	220	1 971	395	1 576
1990	2 412	42.1	3 206	215	580	234	2 177	464	1 713
1991	2 689	45.3	3 598	268	641	259	2 430	506	1 924
1992	3 000	48.1	4 002	319	683	296	2 703	563	2 140
1993	3 248	49.3	4 351	366	737	326	2 923	619	2 304
1994	3 433	49.2	4 643	423	788	355	3 078	682	2 396
1995	3 604	49.1	4 921	483	833	374	3 230	820	2 410
1996	3 734	48.4	5 181	550	898	391	3 343	993	2 350
1997	3 772	45.9	5 369	631	966	425	3 348	1 231	2 117
1998	3 721	43.0	5 478	730	1 027	458	3 263	1 224	2 039
1999	3 632	39.4	5 606	855	1 118	497	3 136	1 281	1 855
2000	3 410	34.7	5 629	1 007	1 212	511	2 898	1 039	1 859
2001	3 320	32.5	5 770	1 170	1 280	534	2 785	1 006	1 779
2002	3 540	33.6	6 198	1 329	1 329	604	2 936	1 201	1 735
2003	3 913	35.6	6 760	1 485	1 362	656	3 257	1 454	1 803
2004	4 296	36.8	7 355	1 635	1 424	700	3 595	1 799	1 796
2005	4 592	36.9	7 905	1 809	1 504	736	3 856	1 930	1 926
2006	4 829	36.6	8 451	1 994	1 628	769	4 060	2 025	2 035
2007	5 035	36.3	8 951	2 181	1 735	780	4 255	2 235	2 020
2008	5 803	40.5	9 986	2 366	1 817	491	5 312	2 802	2 510
2009	7 545	54.1	11 876	2 504	1 827	769	6 776	3 571	3 205
2010	9 019	62.8	13 529	2 585	1 925	812	8 207	4 324	3 883
2011	10 128	67.7	14 764	2 653	1 982	1 665	8 464	4 660	3 803

. . . = Not available.

Section 6d: Government Output and Employment

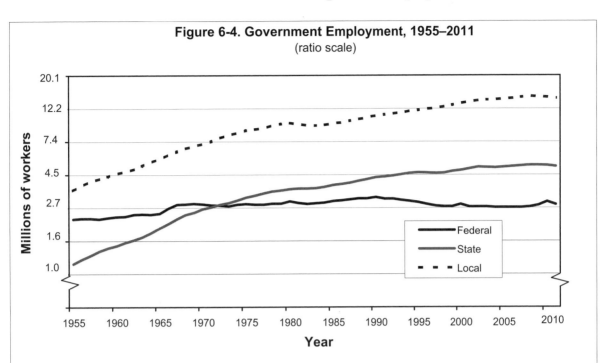

- Since 1955, total reported employment of civilians by all levels of government has increased 215 percent—an annual rate of 2.1 percent per year—and government's proportion of total nonfarm payroll employment has risen from 13.8 percent to 16.8 percent. Federal employment rose 25 percent; state government employment rose 335 percent, with 53 percent of this increase due to education; and local government rose 298 percent, with 58 percent of this increase due to education. (Tables 6-17 and 10-8B)

- Contracting and outsourcing of federal government spending can be seen in comparisons between government purchases and government value added. From 1955 to 2011, the volume (measured by the quantity index) of "intermediate" goods and services purchased for nondefense purposes rose more than twice as fast as real nondefense value added by government itself. (Real value added comprises the input of government employees and government-owned capital, valued in constant dollars). For defense, government value added was unchanged over that period, while purchases of goods and services rose 248 percent in real terms. (Table 6-16)

- A similar process has occurred at state and local governments, where real value added increased 326 percent while goods and services purchased rose 1,060 percent. (Table 6-16)

Table 6-16. Chain-Type Quantity Indexes for Government Output

(Seasonally adjusted, 2005 = 100.)   NIPA Table 3.10.3

Year and quarter	Federal government									State and local government		
	Gross output of general government			Value added			Intermediate goods and services purchased [1]			Gross output of general government	Value added	Intermediate goods and services purchased [1]
	Total	Defense	Nondefense	Total	Defense	Nondefense	Total	Defense	Nondefense			
1950	32.1	37.3	22.9	61.8	72.2	44.9	10.4	12.0	7.9	15.4	19.7	8.0
1951	48.5	64.1	19.2	81.4	103.0	42.0	21.7	31.4	4.7	15.3	20.2	7.4
1952	61.3	81.9	22.5	90.7	117.6	41.2	33.4	47.4	9.0	15.6	20.9	7.2
1953	65.9	85.6	28.8	91.2	119.7	38.3	39.2	51.2	18.1	16.1	21.8	7.2
1954	58.4	74.7	27.9	89.0	117.1	36.6	30.6	37.9	17.8	16.8	22.8	7.5
1955	55.9	70.3	28.9	86.9	113.9	36.9	28.3	33.8	18.9	18.0	23.9	8.6
1956	54.3	70.3	24.1	86.1	112.2	37.6	26.7	34.7	12.4	18.6	25.3	8.2
1957	57.7	75.2	24.4	85.8	111.4	38.4	31.3	41.7	12.4	19.6	26.7	8.6
1958	56.6	73.8	23.9	83.4	107.2	39.5	31.1	42.1	11.1	21.2	28.4	9.9
1959	56.1	67.8	34.1	82.7	106.1	39.6	31.0	34.2	25.5	22.3	29.6	10.6
1960	55.3	68.7	29.7	84.3	107.1	42.3	28.7	34.9	17.4	23.4	31.1	11.2
1961	56.2	70.3	29.5	86.1	109.3	43.3	28.9	35.8	16.4	24.7	32.7	12.0
1962	61.5	75.2	35.5	89.6	113.5	45.7	34.5	40.5	24.0	25.7	33.9	12.4
1963	63.1	75.9	38.8	90.4	113.2	48.6	36.4	41.7	27.1	27.1	35.7	13.3
1964	62.7	74.1	41.1	91.3	113.7	50.3	35.2	38.6	29.6	28.9	37.8	14.5
1965	63.6	74.5	42.8	91.9	113.7	52.0	36.2	39.2	31.1	30.9	40.1	15.9
1966	70.8	85.4	43.1	98.0	121.5	54.8	43.2	51.0	29.6	32.9	42.5	17.2
1967	78.2	95.6	45.3	104.4	129.7	57.8	50.5	61.5	30.9	34.6	44.3	18.6
1968	80.8	99.5	45.5	106.1	131.5	59.5	53.3	66.3	30.0	36.9	47.0	20.4
1969	79.1	95.6	47.8	106.5	131.6	60.3	50.3	60.1	33.0	39.2	49.1	22.7
1970	73.4	87.0	47.6	101.9	124.0	61.2	44.4	51.4	32.0	41.4	51.3	25.0
1971	69.8	80.2	49.7	97.2	115.7	63.0	41.9	46.3	34.2	43.6	53.4	27.3
1972	68.4	75.8	53.9	92.5	107.6	64.7	43.4	45.3	40.2	45.4	55.2	28.9
1973	64.7	70.7	53.1	89.0	102.1	64.9	39.8	40.6	38.6	47.0	57.2	29.9
1974	64.3	68.7	55.9	88.8	100.2	67.9	39.3	38.7	40.9	48.9	59.2	31.5
1975	63.5	66.6	57.5	88.3	98.8	69.1	38.3	36.2	42.8	51.0	61.0	34.1
1976	62.6	65.0	57.8	88.4	97.3	72.3	36.5	34.6	40.5	51.9	61.8	35.0
1977	64.0	65.8	60.6	88.7	96.8	73.9	38.9	36.4	44.2	52.9	62.8	36.1
1978	65.4	66.5	63.4	89.8	97.4	76.0	40.4	37.2	47.4	54.2	64.2	37.0
1979	66.5	67.3	65.0	89.7	97.0	76.5	42.4	38.9	50.0	54.9	65.4	36.9
1980	69.2	70.1	67.6	91.1	97.9	78.9	45.9	42.8	52.5	54.9	66.3	35.7
1981	72.1	74.1	68.1	92.5	100.8	77.5	49.8	47.4	54.7	55.0	66.2	36.0
1982	74.4	79.1	65.0	94.0	103.4	76.9	52.6	53.9	49.6	55.9	66.7	37.6
1983	77.9	83.0	67.7	96.2	105.8	78.6	57.0	58.7	52.9	56.7	66.4	39.9
1984	79.0	85.6	65.5	98.4	108.6	79.7	57.1	61.1	47.8	57.7	66.8	41.7
1985	83.7	90.7	69.2	101.2	112.2	80.9	63.1	67.2	53.7	60.5	68.7	45.9
1986	87.3	94.9	71.7	103.0	114.9	80.8	68.3	72.5	58.4	64.1	70.7	52.0
1987	89.4	98.5	70.7	105.7	117.9	82.9	69.7	76.4	54.5	64.9	72.1	51.9
1988	89.2	99.6	67.6	107.0	118.6	85.5	68.1	77.9	45.9	67.0	74.5	53.2
1989	90.5	98.9	73.2	108.3	119.9	86.8	69.3	75.3	55.8	69.2	76.8	55.3
1990	91.9	98.5	78.5	110.3	120.7	91.2	70.1	73.8	61.9	71.2	79.1	57.0
1991	92.3	98.3	79.9	110.9	121.3	91.9	70.2	72.9	63.9	72.8	80.1	59.6
1992	90.2	93.4	83.7	108.6	116.7	94.0	68.4	67.9	69.4	74.8	81.5	62.5
1993	87.2	89.8	81.9	106.5	113.3	94.5	64.5	64.2	65.3	76.6	82.6	65.6
1994	85.1	86.3	82.7	103.1	108.9	92.6	64.0	61.7	69.1	78.7	84.0	68.8
1995	82.2	82.6	81.4	99.2	104.4	90.0	62.2	58.9	69.4	80.7	85.7	71.4
1996	80.8	81.5	79.4	96.4	100.9	88.6	62.3	60.3	66.6	82.2	87.0	73.2
1997	80.5	80.2	81.2	94.6	97.9	88.9	63.6	60.6	70.2	84.5	88.8	76.7
1998	79.0	77.9	81.2	93.5	95.3	90.6	61.7	58.8	68.1	87.9	90.7	82.7
1999	79.7	79.1	80.9	92.8	93.3	91.9	64.0	63.2	65.9	90.9	92.2	88.5
2000	80.6	78.4	85.0	93.6	92.7	95.2	65.1	62.4	71.0	93.4	94.1	92.0
2001	83.9	81.3	89.0	93.9	92.9	95.8	71.6	68.1	79.4	96.9	96.4	98.1
2002	89.3	86.6	94.6	95.8	94.6	97.9	81.4	77.5	90.0	99.7	98.3	102.5
2003	95.2	94.0	97.6	98.4	97.3	100.2	91.2	90.1	93.7	99.5	98.9	100.6
2004	98.9	98.8	98.9	99.3	99.1	99.7	98.2	98.5	97.7	99.6	99.3	100.2
2005	100.0	100.0	100.0	100.0	100.0	100.0	100.0	100.0	100.0	100.0	100.0	100.0
2006	101.2	100.8	101.9	99.9	99.5	100.7	102.8	102.5	103.6	100.8	100.9	100.6
2007	101.8	102.4	100.6	100.7	100.0	101.9	103.3	105.4	98.6	102.5	102.3	102.8
2008	108.2	108.6	107.3	104.6	104.0	105.8	112.8	114.3	109.4	102.3	103.6	100.0
2009	114.7	114.7	114.8	110.8	110.4	111.4	120.0	120.0	119.9	102.1	103.7	99.3
2010	119.4	118.1	122.1	114.8	114.2	116.0	125.5	122.9	131.2	101.6	102.7	99.5
2011	118.2	116.8	121.1	116.0	116.1	115.7	121.1	117.5	129.1	101.0	101.7	99.8
2009												
1st quarter	111.1	110.7	111.8	108.3	107.6	109.5	114.7	114.5	115.2	102.2	103.9	99.0
2nd quarter	114.7	114.5	115.1	110.7	109.7	112.5	119.9	120.4	118.9	102.3	103.8	99.4
3rd quarter	116.1	116.7	114.9	111.6	111.6	111.6	122.0	123.1	119.8	102.1	103.6	99.3
4th quarter	117.1	116.9	117.3	112.4	112.7	111.9	123.2	122.2	125.5	102.0	103.5	99.4
2010												
1st quarter	117.7	116.9	119.4	113.6	113.4	114.0	123.1	121.2	127.4	101.8	103.1	99.4
2nd quarter	120.0	118.2	123.4	115.6	113.9	118.6	125.7	123.5	130.5	101.7	102.9	99.5
3rd quarter	120.9	119.9	122.9	114.9	114.4	115.9	128.7	126.6	133.4	101.5	102.6	99.6
4th quarter	119.2	117.4	122.7	115.1	114.9	115.4	124.5	120.4	133.7	101.3	102.3	99.4
2011												
1st quarter	117.3	115.2	121.6	115.7	115.4	116.2	119.5	114.9	129.7	101.4	102.0	100.1
2nd quarter	118.4	117.7	119.7	115.9	115.8	116.0	121.6	120.0	125.1	101.2	101.7	100.2
3rd quarter	120.2	118.9	122.8	115.9	116.3	115.3	125.7	122.0	133.9	100.9	101.5	99.9
4th quarter	117.0	115.3	120.3	116.4	117.0	115.3	117.6	113.2	127.6	100.5	101.5	98.7

[1]Includes general government intermediate inputs for goods and services sold to other sectors and for own-account investment.

Table 6-17. Government Employment

(Calendar years, payroll employment in thousands.)

Year and month	Total government employment	Federal			State			Local		
		Total	Department of Defense	Postal Service	Total	Education	State government hospitals	Total	Education	Local government hospitals
1950	6 120	2 023	533	516	. . .	. . .	. . .	. . .	. . .	. . .
1951	6 502	2 415	797	521	. . .	. . .	. . .	. . .	. . .	. . .
1952	6 727	2 539	868	542	. . .	. . .	. . .	. . .	. . .	. . .
1953	6 758	2 418	818	530	. . .	. . .	. . .	. . .	. . .	. . .
1954	6 858	2 295	744	533	. . .	. . .	. . .	. . .	. . .	. . .
1955	7 021	2 295	744	534	1 168	308	. . .	3 558	1 751	. . .
1956	7 386	2 318	749	539	1 249	334	. . .	3 819	1 884	. . .
1957	7 724	2 326	729	555	1 328	363	. . .	4 071	2 026	. . .
1958	7 946	2 298	695	567	1 415	389	. . .	4 232	2 115	. . .
1959	8 192	2 342	699	578	1 484	420	. . .	4 366	2 198	. . .
1960	8 464	2 381	681	591	1 536	448	. . .	4 547	2 314	. . .
1961	8 706	2 391	683	601	1 607	474	. . .	4 708	2 411	. . .
1962	9 004	2 455	697	601	1 669	511	. . .	4 881	2 522	. . .
1963	9 341	2 473	687	603	1 747	557	. . .	5 121	2 674	. . .
1964	9 711	2 463	676	604	1 856	609	. . .	5 392	2 839	. . .
1965	10 191	2 495	679	619	1 996	679	. . .	5 700	3 031	. . .
1966	10 910	2 690	741	686	2 141	775	. . .	6 080	3 297	. . .
1967	11 525	2 852	802	719	2 302	873	. . .	6 371	3 490	. . .
1968	11 972	2 871	801	729	2 442	958	. . .	6 660	3 649	. . .
1969	12 330	2 893	815	737	2 533	1 042	. . .	6 904	3 785	. . .
1970	12 687	2 865	756	741	2 664	1 104	. . .	7 158	3 912	. . .
1971	13 012	2 828	731	731	2 747	1 149	. . .	7 437	4 091	. . .
1972	13 465	2 815	720	703	2 859	1 188	459	7 790	4 262	467
1973	13 862	2 794	696	698	2 923	1 205	472	8 146	4 433	477
1974	14 303	2 858	698	710	3 039	1 267	483	8 407	4 584	483
1975	14 820	2 882	704	699	3 179	1 323	503	8 758	4 722	489
1976	15 001	2 863	693	676	3 273	1 371	518	8 865	4 786	492
1977	15 258	2 859	676	657	3 377	1 385	538	9 023	4 859	494
1978	15 812	2 893	661	660	3 474	1 367	541	9 446	4 958	535
1979	16 068	2 894	649	673	3 541	1 378	538	9 633	4 989	571
1980	16 375	3 000	645	673	3 610	1 398	530	9 765	5 090	604
1981	16 180	2 922	655	675	3 640	1 420	515	9 619	5 095	622
1982	15 982	2 884	690	684	3 640	1 433	494	9 458	5 049	635
1983	16 011	2 915	699	685	3 662	1 450	471	9 434	5 020	644
1984	16 159	2 943	716	706	3 734	1 488	459	9 482	5 076	623
1985	16 533	3 014	738	750	3 832	1 540	449	9 687	5 221	608
1986	16 838	3 044	736	792	3 893	1 561	438	9 901	5 358	601
1987	17 156	3 089	736	815	3 967	1 586	439	10 100	5 469	606
1988	17 540	3 124	719	835	4 076	1 621	446	10 339	5 590	619
1989	17 927	3 136	735	838	4 182	1 668	442	10 609	5 740	632
1990	18 415	3 196	722	825	4 305	1 730	426	10 914	5 902	646
1991	18 545	3 110	702	813	4 355	1 768	417	11 081	5 994	653
1992	18 787	3 111	702	800	4 408	1 799	419	11 267	6 076	665
1993	18 989	3 063	670	793	4 488	1 834	414	11 438	6 206	673
1994	19 275	3 018	657	821	4 576	1 882	407	11 682	6 329	673
1995	19 432	2 949	627	850	4 635	1 919	395	11 849	6 453	669
1996	19 539	2 877	597	867	4 606	1 911	376	12 056	6 592	648
1997	19 664	2 806	588	866	4 582	1 904	360	12 276	6 759	632
1998	19 909	2 772	550	881	4 612	1 922	346	12 525	6 921	630
1999	20 307	2 769	525	890	4 709	1 983	344	12 829	7 120	626
2000	20 790	2 865	510	880	4 786	2 031	343	13 139	7 294	622
2001	21 118	2 764	504	873	4 905	2 113	345	13 449	7 479	628
2002	21 513	2 766	499	842	5 029	2 243	349	13 718	7 654	642
2003	21 583	2 761	486	809	5 002	2 255	348	13 820	7 709	651
2004	21 621	2 730	473	782	4 982	2 238	348	13 909	7 765	656
2005	21 804	2 732	488	774	5 032	2 260	350	14 041	7 856	655
2006	21 974	2 732	493	770	5 075	2 293	357	14 167	7 913	647
2007	22 218	2 734	491	769	5 122	2 318	360	14 362	7 987	654
2008	22 509	2 762	496	747	5 177	2 354	361	14 571	8 084	659
2009	22 555	2 832	519	703	5 169	2 360	359	14 554	8 079	661
2010	22 490	2 977	545	659	5 137	2 373	354	14 376	8 013	650
2011	22 104	2 858	561	631	5 082	2 384	347	14 165	7 893	649

. . . = Not available.

NOTES AND DEFINITIONS, CHAPTER 6

TABLES 6-1 THROUGH 6-13 AND 6-16
FEDERAL, STATE, AND LOCAL GOVERNMENT IN THE NATIONAL INCOME AND PRODUCT ACCOUNTS

SOURCE: U.S. DEPARTMENT OF COMMERCE, BUREAU OF ECONOMIC ANALYSIS (BEA)

These data are from the national income and product accounts (NIPAs), as published in the 2009 comprehensive NIPA revision and as updated through June 2012. For general information about the NIPAs and the 2009 revision, see the notes and definitions for Chapter 1.

The framework for the government accounts

In the 2003 revision, a new framework was introduced for government consumption expenditures—federal, state, and local—that explicitly recognizes the services produced by general government. Governments serve several functions in the economy. Three of these functions are recognized in the NIPAs: the production of nonmarket services; the consumption of these services, as the value of services provided to the general public is treated as government consumption expenditures; and the provision of transfer payments. These functions are financed through taxation, through contributions to social insurance funds, and in the world's capital markets.

In the new framework, the value of the government services produced and consumed (most of which are not sold in the market) is measured as the sum of the costs of the three major inputs: compensation of government employees, consumption of fixed capital (CFC), and intermediate goods and services purchased. The purchase from the private sector of goods and services by government, classified as final sales to government before the 2003 revision, was reclassified as intermediate purchases.

The value of government final purchases of consumption expenditures and gross investment, which constitutes the contribution of government demand to the gross domestic product (GDP), was not changed by this reclassification, since the previous definition of that contribution was the sum of compensation, CFC, and goods and services purchased. However, the distribution of GDP by type of product was changed—final sales of goods were reduced by the amount of goods purchased by government, and services were increased by the same amount.

In addition to this change in the conceptual framework, a number of the categories of government receipts and expenditures were redefined to make more precise distinctions. For example, items that used to be called "nontax payments" and included with taxes are now classified as transfer or fee payments and not included in taxes.

Finally, the concept previously known as "current surplus or deficit (-), national income and product accounts" was renamed "net government saving." This recognizes, in part, the role of government in the capital markets. When government runs a current surplus, net government saving is positive and funds are made available (for example, by repayment of outstanding debt) to finance investment—both private-sector capital spending and government investment. When government runs a current deficit, or "dis-saves," it must borrow funds that would otherwise be available to finance investment.

However, this definition of net government saving does not give a complete picture of governments' role in capital markets, because it is based on current receipts and expenditures alone and does not include government investment activity.

In the NIPAs, the capital spending of all levels of government is treated the same way as the accounts treat private investment spending. A depreciation, or more precisely "consumption of fixed capital" (CFC), entry for existing capital is calculated, using estimated replacement costs and realistic depreciation rates. In the government accounts this CFC value is entered as one element of current expenditures and output. Capital spending is excluded from government current expenditures but appears in the account for "net lending or borrowing (-)."

The basic concept expressed in the net lending section of the NIPAs is that when CFC exceeds actual investment expenditures, governments have a positive net cash flow and can lend (or repay debt); if gross investment exceeds CFC, government must borrow to finance the difference, indicating negative net cash flow and requiring borrowing. (As will be seen below in the definitions, capital transfer and purchase accounts also enter into the calculation of net lending.)

The federal *budget* accounts (see Tables 6-14 and 6-15) do not draw a distinction between current and capital spending. The budget accounts of individual state and local governments typically separate capital from current spending and allow capital spending to be financed by borrowing—even when deficit financing of current spending is constitutionally forbidden. However, neither federal nor state and local government budget accounts typically show depreciation as a current expense in the way that is standard to private-sector accounting or in the way adopted in the NIPAs.

Notes on the data

Government receipts and expenditures data are derived from the U.S. government accounts and from Census Bureau censuses and surveys of the finances of state and local governments. However, BEA makes a number of adjustments to the data to convert them from fiscal year to calendar year and quarter bases and to agree with the concepts of national income accounting. Data are converted from the cash basis usually found in financial statements to the timing bases required for the NIPAs. In the NIPAs, receipts from businesses are generally on an accrual basis, purchases of goods and services are recorded when delivered, and receipts from and transfer payments to persons are on a cash basis. The federal receipts and expenditure data from the NIPAs in Table 6-1 therefore differ from the federal receipts and outlay data in Table 6-14. Among other differences, the latter are by fiscal year and are on a modified cash basis.

The NIPA data on government receipts and expenditures record transactions of governments (federal, state, and local) with other U.S. residents and foreigners. Each entry in the government receipts and expenditures account has a corresponding entry elsewhere in the NIPAs. Thus, for example, the sum of personal current taxes received by federal and state and local governments (Tables 6-1 and 6-8) is equal to personal current taxes paid, as shown in personal income (Table 4-1).

Definitions: general

In the 2003 revision of the NIPAs, several items appear separately that were previously treated as "negative expenditures" and netted against other items on the expenditures side. This grossing-up of the accounts raises both receipts and outlays and has no effect on net saving. Grossing-up has been applied to taxes from the rest of the world, interest receipts (back to 1960 for the federal government and back to 1946 for state and local governments), dividends, and subsidies and the current surplus of government enterprises (back to 1959).

Definitions: current receipts

Current tax receipts includes personal current taxes, taxes on production and imports, taxes on corporate income and (for the federal government only) taxes from the rest of the world. The category *total tax receipts* does not include *contributions for government social insurance,* which are the taxes levied to finance Social Security, unemployment insurance, and Medicare, and are included in *receipts* in the budget accounts (Table 6-14). Analysts using NIPA data to analyze tax burdens as they are usually understood should add *contributions for government social insurance* to *tax receipts* for this purpose.

Personal current taxes is personal tax payments from residents of the United States that are not chargeable to business expense. Personal taxes consist of taxes on income, including on realized net capital gains, and on personal property. Personal contributions for social insurance are not included in this category. As of the 1999 revisions, estate and gift taxes are classified as capital transfers and are no longer included in personal current taxes. However, estate and gift taxes continue to be included in federal government receipts in Table 6-14.

Taxes on production and imports in the case of the federal government consists of *excise taxes* and *customs duties.* In the case of state and local governments, these taxes include *sales taxes, property taxes* (including residential real estate taxes), and *Other* taxes such as motor vehicle licenses, severance taxes, and special assessments. Before the 2003 revision, these taxes were a component of "indirect business tax

and nontax liabilities."

Taxes on corporate income covers federal, state, and local government taxes on all corporate income subject to taxes. This taxable income includes capital gains and other income excluded from NIPA profits. The taxes are measured on an accrual basis, net of applicable tax credits. Federal corporate income tax receipts in the NIPAs include receipts from *Federal Reserve Banks* that represent the return of their surplus earnings. (In the budget accounts in Table 6-14, these are included under "Miscellaneous receipts.")

Contributions for social insurance includes employer and personal contributions for Social Security, Medicare, unemployment insurance, and other government social insurance programs. As of the 1999 revisions, contributions to government employee retirement plans are no longer included in this category; these plans are now treated the same as private pension plans.

Income receipts on assets consists of *interest, dividends* and *rents and royalties.*

Interest receipts (1960 to the present for federal government; 1946 to the present for state and local governments) consists of monetary and imputed interest received on loans and investments. In the NIPAs, this no longer includes interest received by government employee retirement plans, which is now credited to personal income. However, such interest received is still deducted from interest paid in the budget accounts that are shown in Table 6-14. Before the indicated years, receipts are deducted from aggregate interest payments in the NIPAs. Hence, they are not shown as receipts, and net interest is presented on the expenditure side. In the federal budget accounts in Table 6-14, net interest (total interest expenditures minus interest receipts) is the interest "expenditure" concept used throughout the period covered.

Current transfer receipts includes receipts in categories other than those specified above from persons and business. In the case of state and local government accounts (Table 6-8), it also includes *federal grants-in-aid,* a component of federal expenditures. Receipts from *business* and *persons* were previously included with income taxes in "tax and nontax payments." They consist of federal deposit insurance premiums and other nontaxes (largely fines and regulatory and inspection fees), state and local fines and other nontaxes (largely donations and tobacco settlements), and net insurance settlements paid to governments as policyholders.

The *current surplus of government enterprises* is the current operating revenue and subsidies received from other levels of government by such enterprises less their current expenses. No deduction is made for depreciation charges or net interest paid. Before 1959, this category of receipts is treated as a deduction from subsidies. In the federal NIPA accounts before 1959, there is no entry shown for the current surplus on the receipts side, and on the expenditure side, there is an entry for subsidies, which is net of the current surplus. (Subsidies are usually a larger amount than the enterprise surplus in the federal accounts.) In the state and local NIPA accounts before 1959, there is an entry for the surplus on the receipts side, which is net of subsidies. (Subsidies are typically smaller than the enterprise surplus in state and local finance.)

Definitions: consumption expenditures, saving, and gross investment

Government consumption expenditures is expenditures by governments (federal or state and local) on services for current consumption. It includes *compensation of general government employees* (including employer contributions to government employee retirement plans, as of the 1999 revision); an allowance for *consumption of general government fixed capital (CFC),* including software (depreciation); and *intermediate goods and services purchased.* (See the general discussion above for an explanation.) The estimated value of *own-account investment*—investment goods, including software, produced by government resources and purchased inputs—is subtracted here, and added to *government gross investment. Sales to other sectors*—primarily tuition payments received from individuals for higher education and charges for medical care to individuals—are also deducted.

Government social benefits consists of payments to individuals for which the individuals do not render current services. Examples are Social Security benefits, Medicare, Medicaid, unemployment benefits, and public assistance. Retirement payments to retired government employees from their pension plans are no longer included in this category.

Government social benefits to persons consists of payments to persons residing in the United States (with a corresponding entry of an equal amount in the personal income receipts accounts). Government social benefits to the *rest of the world* appear only in the federal government account, and are transfers, mainly retirement benefits, to former residents of the United States.

Other current transfer payments (federal account only) includes *grants-in-aid to state and local governments* and *grants to the rest of the world*—military and nonmilitary grants to foreign governments.

Federal grants-in-aid comprises net payments from federal to state and local governments that are made to help finance programs such as health (Medicaid), public assistance (the old Aid to Families with Dependent Children and the new Temporary Assistance for Needy Families), and education. Investment grants to state and local governments for highways, transit, air transportation, and water treatment plants are now classified as capital transfers and are no longer included in this category. However, such investment grants continue to be included as federal government outlays in Table 6-14.

Interest payments is monetary interest paid to U.S. and foreign persons and businesses and to foreign governments for public debt and other financial obligations. As noted above, from 1960 forward for the federal government and from 1946 forward for state and local governments, this represents gross total (not net) interest payments. Before those dates in the NIPAs, and throughout the federal budget accounts presented in Table 6-14, net instead of aggregate interest is shown; that is, gross total interest paid less interest received.

Subsidies are monetary grants paid by government to business, including to government enterprises at another level of government. Subsidies no longer include federal maritime construction subsidies, which are now classified as a capital transfer. For years prior to 1959, subsidies continue to be presented net of the *current surplus of government enterprises,* because detailed data to separate the series are not available for this period. See the entry for *current surplus of government enterprises,* described above, for explanation of the pre-1959 treatment of this item in the federal accounts in *Business Statistics,* which differs from the treatment in the state and local accounts.

Net saving, NIPA (surplus+/deficit-), is the sum of current receipts less the sum of current expenditures. This is shown separately for *social insurance funds* (which, in the case of the federal government, include Social Security and other trust funds) and *other* (all other government). As of the 1999 revision, net government saving—particularly that of state and local governments—is measured as being significantly smaller than before that revision, as the net accumulations of government employee retirement plans (not Social Security) are now classified as personal saving rather than in the government sector.

Gross government investment consists of general government and government enterprise expenditures for fixed assets—structures, equipment, and software. The expenditures include the compensation of government employees producing the assets and the purchase of goods and services as intermediate inputs to be incorporated in the assets. Government inventory investment is included in government consumption expenditures.

Capital consumption. Consumption of fixed capital (CFC; economic depreciation) is included in government consumption expenditures as a partial measure of the value of the services of general government fixed assets, including structures, equipment, and software.

Definitions: output, lending and borrowing, and net investment

In Tables 6-5 and 6-10, current-dollar values of gross output and value added of government are presented, as described in the general discussion above. *Gross output* of government is the sum of the *intermediate goods and services purchased* by government and the value added by government as a producing industry. *Value added* consists of compensation of general government employees and consumption of general government fixed capital. Since this depreciation allowance is the only entry on the product side of the accounts measuring the output associated with such capital, a zero net return on these assets is implicitly assumed.

Gross output minus own-account investment and sales to other sectors (see the previous description) yields *government consumption expenditures*, which represents the contribution of government consumption spending to final demands in GDP.

Net lending (net borrowing -) consists of current *net saving* as defined above, plus the *consumption of fixed capital* (CFC, from the current expenditure account), minus *gross investment*, plus *capital transfer receipts*, and minus *capital transfer payments* and *net purchases of non-produced assets*.

Capital transfer receipts and *payments* include grants between levels of government, or between government and the private sector, associated with acquisition or disposal of assets rather than with current consumption expenditures. Examples are federal grants to state and local government for highways, transit, air transportation, and water treatment plants; federal shipbuilding subsidies and other subsidies to businesses; and lump-sum payments to amortize the unfunded liability of the Uniformed Services Retiree Health Care Fund. Government capital transfer receipts include estate and gift taxes, which are no longer included in personal tax receipts. (Federal estate and gift taxes are shown in Table 6-14 and, although they are reported on a fiscal year basis, are almost identical to the calendar year values for federal capital transfer receipts in Table 6-5.)

Non-produced assets are land and radio spectrum. Unusually large negative entries for net purchases of non-produced assets in recent years result from the negative purchase–that is, the sale–of spectrum.

The values of *net investment* shown in these tables are calculated by the editor, as gross investment minus the consumption of fixed capital.

Definitions: chain-type quantity indexes

Chain-type quantity indexes represent changes over time in real values, removing the effects of inflation. Indexes for key categories in the government expenditure accounts, as well as for government gross output, value added, and intermediate goods and services purchased, use the chain formula described in the notes and definitions for Chapter 1 and are expressed as index numbers, with the average for the year 2005 equal to 100.

Data availability

The most recent data are published each month in the *Survey of Current Business*. Current and historical data may be obtained from the BEA Web site at <http://www.bea.gov> and the STAT-USA subscription Web site at <http://www.stat-usa.gov>.

References

See the references regarding the 2009 comprehensive revision of the NIPAs in the notes and definitions for Chapter

1. NIPA concepts and their differences from the budget estimates are discussed in "NIPA Estimates of the Federal Sector and the Federal Budget Estimates," *Survey of Current Business*, March 2007, p. 11.

For information about the classification of government expenditures into current consumption and gross investment, first undertaken in the 1996 comprehensive revisions, see the *Survey of Current Business* article, "Preview of the Comprehensive Revision of the National Income and Product Accounts: Recognition of Government Investment and Incorporation of a New Methodology for Calculating Depreciation" September 1995. Other sources of information about the NIPAs are listed in the notes and definitions for Chapter 1.

TABLES 6-12 AND 6-13
STATE GOVERNMENT CURRENT RECEIPTS AND EXPENDITURES; LOCAL GOVERNMENT CURRENT RECEIPTS AND EXPENDITURES

SOURCE: BUREAU OF ECONOMIC ANALYSIS (BEA)

In the standard presentation of the state and local sector of the national income and product accounts (NIPAs) such as in Tables 6-8 through 6-11 above, state and local governments are combined. Annual measures for aggregate state governments and aggregate local governments are now available on the BEA Web site. These measures are shown in Tables 6-12 and 6-13. The definitions are the same as in the other NIPA tables described above.

Two new categories appear in each table, detailing intergovernmental flows that are consolidated in Table 6-8. State government receipts include not only *federal grants-in-aid* but also *local grants-in-aid*, and state government expenditures include *grants-in-aid to local governments*. Local government receipts include not only *federal grants-in-aid* but also *state grants-in-aid*, and local government expenditures include *grants-in-aid to state governments*. To make room for these columns, the components *current surplus of government enterprises* and *subsidies* are not shown, though they are included in total current receipts and total current expenditures respectively.

These measures are described in "Receipts and Expenditures of State Governments and of Local Governments," *Survey of Current Business*, October 2005. Data back to 1959 are available on the BEA Web site at <http://www.bea.gov>.

TABLES 6-14A AND 6-14B
FEDERAL GOVERNMENT RECEIPTS AND OUTLAYS BY FISCAL YEAR; THE FEDERAL BUDGET AND GDP

SOURCE: U.S. OFFICE OF MANAGEMENT AND BUDGET

These data on federal government receipts and outlays are on a modified cash basis and are from the *Budget of the United States Government: Historical Tables*. The data are by federal fiscal years, which are defined as July 1 through June 30 through 1976 and October 1 through September 30 for 1977 and subsequent years. They are identified by the end year—i.e., the year from July 1, 1975, through June 30, 1976, is identified as Fiscal 1976. The period July 1 through September 30, 1976, is a separate fiscal period known as the transition quarter (TQ) and is not included in any fiscal year.

There are numerous differences in both timing and definition between these estimates and the NIPA estimates in Tables 6-1 through 6-7. See the notes and definitions for those tables for the definitional differences that were introduced with the 1999 comprehensive revision of the NIPAs.

Definitions

The definitions for these tables are not affected by the 2003 or 1999 changes in the government sectors of the NIPAs.

Table references will be given indicating the source of each item in the *Historical Tables*; for example, "HT Table 1.1."

Receipts consist of gifts and of taxes or other compulsory payments to the government. Other types of payments to the government are netted against outlays. (HT Table 1.1)

Outlays occur when the federal government liquidates an obligation through a cash payment or when interest accrues on public debt issues. Beginning with the data for 1992, outlays include the subsidy cost of direct and guaranteed loans made. Before 1992, the costs and repayments associated with such loans are recorded on a cash basis. As noted previously, various types of nontax receipts are netted against cash outlays. These accounts do not distinguish between investment outlays and current consumption and do not include allowances for depreciation. (HT Table 1.1)

The *total surplus (deficit-)* is receipts minus outlays. (HT Table 1.1)

On-budget and off-budget. By law, two government programs that are included in the federal receipts and outlays totals are "off-budget"—old-age, survivors, and disability insurance (Social Security) and the Postal Service. The former accounts for nearly all of the off-budget activity. The *surplus (deficit-)* not accounted for by these two programs is the on-budget surplus or deficit. (HT Table 1.1)

Sources of financing is the means by which the total deficit is financed or the surplus is distributed. By definition, sources of financing sum to the total deficit or surplus with the sign reversed. The principal source is *borrowing from the public*, shown as a positive number, that is, the increase in the debt held by the public. (This entry is calculated by the editors as the change in the debt held by the public as shown in HT Table 7.1.) When there is a budget surplus, as in fiscal years 1998 to 2001, this provides resources for debt reduction, which is indicated by a minus sign in this column. *Other financing* includes drawdown (or buildup, shown here with a minus sign) in Treasury cash balances, seigniorage on coins, direct and guaranteed loan account cash transactions, and miscellaneous other transactions. Large negative "financ-

ing" in 2008 through 2010 resulted from direct loans and asset purchases under TARP and other emergency financial procedures; in other words, the government borrowed from the public to undertake these loans and asset purchases, but they are not included in budget expenditures or the budget deficit. *Other financing* is calculated by the editors, by reversing the sign of the surplus/deficit—so that the deficit becomes a positive number—and subtracting the value of borrowing from the public.

Some of the categories of *receipts by source* are self-explanatory. *Employment taxes and contributions* includes taxes for old-age, survivors, and disability insurance (Social Security), hospital insurance (Medicare), and railroad retirement funds. *Other retirement contributions* includes the employee share of payments for retirement pensions, mainly those for federal employees. *Excise taxes* includes federal taxes on alcohol, tobacco, telephone service, and transportation fuels, as well as taxes funding smaller programs such as black lung disability and vaccine injury compensation. *Miscellaneous receipts* includes deposits of earnings by the Federal Reserve system and all other receipts. (HT Tables 2.1, 2.4, and 2.5)

Outlays by function presents outlays according to the major purpose of the spending. Functional classifications cut across departmental and agency lines. Most categories of offsetting receipts are netted against cash outlays in the appropriate function, which explains how recorded outlays in *energy* and *commerce and housing credit* (which, as its name suggests, includes loan programs) can be negative. There is also a category of "undistributed offsetting receipts" (not shown), always with a negative sign, that includes proceeds from the sale or lease of assets and payments from federal agencies to federal retirement funds and the Social Security and Medicare trust funds. Note that *Social Security* is recorded separately from other *income security* outlays, and *Medicare* separately from other *health* outlays. (HT Table 3.1) For further explanation, consult the *Budget of the United States Government*.

In order to provide authoritative comparisons of these budget values with the overall size of the economy, a special calculation of gross domestic product by fiscal year is supplied to the Office of Management and Budget by the BEA, and is shown in Table 6-14B. That table also displays selected budget aggregates in dollar values and as a percent of GDP. (HT Tables 1.2, 1.3, 2.3, and 3.1)

Data availability and references

Definitions, budget concepts, and historical data are from *Budget of the United States Government for Fiscal Year 2032: Historical Tables*, available on the Office of Management and Budget Web site at <http://www.whitehouse.gov/omb/Budget/historicals>

Similarly defined data for the latest month, the year-ago month, and the current and year-ago fiscal year to date are published in the *Monthly Treasury Statement* prepared by the Financial Management Service, U.S. Department of the Treasury. For those who need up-to-date budget information, this publication is available on the Financial Management Service Web site at <http://www.fms.treas.gov>. As these monthly figures are never revised to agree with the final annual data, they are not published in this volume.

TABLE 6-15
FEDERAL GOVERNMENT DEBT BY FISCAL YEAR

SOURCE: U.S. OFFICE OF MANAGEMENT AND BUDGET

Debt outstanding at the end of each fiscal year is from the *Budget of the United States Government.* Most securities are recorded at sales price plus amortized discount or less amortized premium.

Definitions

Federal government debt held by the public consists of all federal debt held outside the federal government accounts—by individuals, financial institutions (including the Federal Reserve Banks), and foreign individuals, businesses, and central banks. It does not include federal debt held by federal government trust funds such as the Social Security trust fund. The level and change of the ratio of this debt to the value of gross domestic product (GDP) provide proportional measures of the impact of federal borrowing on credit markets. (HT Table 7.1) This measure of debt held by the public is very similar in concept and scope to the total federal government credit market debt outstanding in the flow-of-funds accounts, shown in Business Statistics in Table 12-5; however, it is not identical, being priced somewhat differently, and is shown here in Chapter 6 on a fiscal year rather than calendar year basis.

Gross federal debt—total. This is the total debt owed by the U.S. Treasury. It includes a small amount of matured debt. (HT Table 7.1)

Debt held by Social Security funds is the sum of the end-year trust fund balances for old age and survivors insurance and disability insurance. The separate disability trust fund begins in 1957. (HT Table 13.1)

Debt held by other U.S. government accounts is calculated by the editors by subtracting the Social Security debt holdings from the total debt held by federal government accounts, which is shown in HT Table 7.1. It includes the balances in all the other trust funds, including the Medicare funds, federal employee retirement funds, and the highway trust fund.

Debt held by the Federal Reserve System is the total value of Treasury securities held by the 12 Federal Reserve Banks, which are acquired in open market operations that carry out monetary policy. (HT Table 7.1)

Debt held by private investors is calculated by subtracting the Federal Reserve debt from the total debt held by the public, and is shown as "Debt Held by the Public: Other" in HT Table 7.1.

Debt held by foreign residents is based on surveys by the Treasury Department. (Table 6-7, *Budget of the United States for Fiscal Year 2012: Analytical Perspectives,* p. 73.)

Debt held by domestic investors is calculated by the editors by subtracting the foreign-held debt from the total debt held by private investors.

The "debt subject to statutory limitation," not shown here, is close to the gross federal debt in concept and size, but there are some relatively minor definitional differences specified by law. The debt limit can only be changed by an Act of Congress. For information about the debt subject to limit and other debt subjects, see the latest *Budget of the United States Government: Historical Statistics* and *Analytical Perspectives.*

Data availability and references

For the end-of-fiscal-year data, see *Historical Tables* and *Analytical Perspectives* in the *Budget of the United States Government,* which is available on the OMB Web site at <http://www.whitehouse.gov/omb/Budget>. In the *Analytical Perspectives,* debt analysis and data are included in the "Economic and Budget Analysis" section.

Recent quarterly data, measured on a somewhat different basis, are found in the *Treasury Bulletin* in the chapter on "Ownership of Federal Securities (OFS)," in Tables OFS-1 and OFS-2. The *Treasury Bulletin* can be accessed on the Internet at <http://www.fms.treas.gov/bulletin>. Holdings by Social Security funds are also available in the *Bulletin* in the chapter on "Federal Debt," Table FD-3. The Disability Fund is listed separately from the Old-Age and Survivors Fund.

TABLE 6-17
GOVERNMENT EMPLOYMENT

SOURCE: U.S. DEPARTMENT OF LABOR, BUREAU OF LABOR STATISTICS (SEE NOTES AND DEFINITIONS FOR TABLE 10-8).

Government payroll employment includes federal, state, and local activities such as legislative, executive, and judicial functions, as well as all government-owned and government-operated business enterprises, establishments, and institutions (arsenals, navy yards, hospitals, etc.), and government force account construction. The figures relate to civilian employment only. The Bureau of Labor Statistics (BLS) considers regular full-time teachers (private and governmental) to be employed during the summer vacation period, regardless of whether they are specifically paid in those months.

Employment in federal government establishments reflects employee counts as of the pay period containing the 12th of the month. Federal government employment excludes employees of the Central Intelligence Agency and the National Security Agency.

CHAPTER 7: U.S. FOREIGN TRADE AND FINANCE

Section 7a: Foreign Transactions in the National Income and Product Accounts

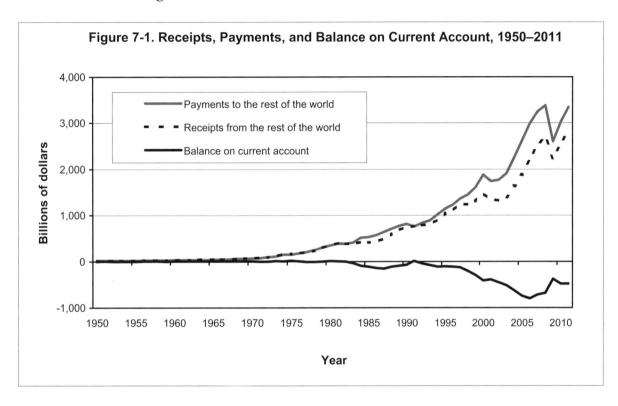

Figure 7-1. Receipts, Payments, and Balance on Current Account, 1950–2011

- Beginning in 1983, chronic current-account deficits in U.S. transactions with the rest of the world have emerged and increased, requiring increasing net capital inflows from abroad to finance them. The only current-account surplus since then occurred in 1991, when payments from other countries financed most of the cost of the first Gulf War. In 2006 the NIPA deficit reached a record $798 billion, 6.0 percent of GDP. (Tables 7-1 and 1-1A)

- U.S. current-account deficits typically diminish somewhat during recessions, as receipts hold up somewhat better than payments. The deficit diminished to $377 billion, 2.7 percent of GDP, in 2009, the recession's low point. Recovery has increased the gap to $483 billion in 2011, 3.2 percent of GDP. (Tables 7-1 and 1-1A)

- The NIPA current-account deficit of $483 billion in 2011 comprised a deficit of $765 billion on goods, a surplus of $186 billion on services, net income receipts of $246 billion, and net payments of $150 billion in taxes and transfer payments. (Table 7-1)

- Looking at quarterly data on the real volume flows of goods and services in U.S. trade, the quantity index for exports of goods and services reached a high point in the second quarter of 2008 and fell 14 percent over the next year. By the end of 2010, the volume of exports recovered fully to the level in 2008:II, and by the end of 2011 were 6 percent past the 2008 peak. Imports of goods and services, also in real terms, peaked earlier—in the third quarter of 2007—and plunged 20 percent between then and the second quarter of 2009. At the end of 2011, imports were about the same as at their 2007 peak. (Table 7-2)

Table 7-1. Foreign Transactions in the National Income and Product Accounts

(Billions of dollars, quarterly data are at seasonally adjusted annual rates.)

NIPA Table 4.1

Year and quarter	Current receipts from the rest of the world					Current payments to the rest of the world						Balance on current account, NIPAs	Net lending or net borrowing (-), NIPAs
	Total	Exports of goods and services			Income receipts	Total	Imports of goods and services			Income payments	Current taxes and transfer payments, net		
		Goods 1		Services 1			Goods 1		Services 1				
		Durable	Nondurable				Durable	Nondurable					
1950	14.5	5.1	5.1	2.1	2.2	16.4	3.0	6.1	2.5	0.7	4.0	-1.8	-1.8
1951	19.9	6.6	7.6	2.9	2.8	19.0	3.8	7.4	3.4	0.9	3.5	0.9	0.9
1952	19.3	6.9	6.5	3.0	2.9	18.7	4.1	6.7	4.5	0.9	2.6	0.6	0.6
1953	18.2	6.9	5.5	2.9	2.8	19.5	4.1	6.9	5.0	0.9	2.5	-1.3	-1.3
1954	18.9	7.1	5.8	2.9	3.0	18.7	3.6	6.7	5.1	0.9	2.3	0.2	0.2
1955	21.2	8.2	6.2	3.3	3.5	20.8	4.5	7.1	5.7	1.1	2.6	0.4	0.4
1956	25.2	9.8	7.8	3.7	3.9	22.5	5.2	7.6	6.1	1.1	2.5	2.7	2.7
1957	28.3	10.9	8.6	4.5	4.3	23.6	5.3	8.0	6.7	1.2	2.4	4.7	4.7
1958	24.4	9.0	7.4	4.1	3.9	23.6	5.0	8.0	7.1	1.2	2.4	0.8	0.8
1959	27.0	8.9	7.5	6.3	4.3	28.3	6.6	8.7	7.0	1.5	4.4	-1.3	-1.3
1960	31.9	11.3	9.2	6.6	4.9	28.8	6.4	8.9	7.6	1.8	4.1	3.2	3.2
1961	32.9	11.5	9.4	6.7	5.3	28.7	6.0	9.0	7.6	1.8	4.2	4.2	4.2
1962	35.0	12.0	9.7	7.4	5.9	31.2	6.9	9.9	8.1	1.8	4.4	3.8	3.8
1963	37.6	12.7	10.7	7.7	6.5	32.7	7.4	10.3	8.4	2.1	4.5	4.9	4.9
1964	42.3	14.7	12.0	8.3	7.2	34.8	8.4	11.0	8.7	2.3	4.4	7.5	7.5
1965	45.0	15.8	12.0	9.4	7.9	38.9	10.4	11.8	9.3	2.6	4.7	6.2	6.2
1966	49.0	17.5	13.2	10.2	8.1	45.2	13.3	13.1	10.7	3.0	5.1	3.8	3.8
1967	52.1	18.4	13.7	11.3	8.7	48.7	14.5	13.2	12.2	3.3	5.5	3.5	3.5
1968	58.0	21.0	14.3	12.6	10.1	56.5	18.8	15.1	12.6	4.0	5.9	1.5	1.5
1969	63.7	23.7	14.6	13.7	11.8	62.1	20.8	16.1	13.7	5.7	5.9	1.6	1.6
1970	72.5	27.1	17.4	15.2	12.8	68.8	22.8	18.1	14.9	6.4	6.6	3.7	3.7
1971	77.0	27.5	18.0	17.4	14.0	76.7	26.6	19.9	15.8	6.4	7.9	0.3	0.3
1972	87.1	31.0	20.8	19.0	16.3	91.2	33.3	23.6	17.3	7.7	9.2	-4.0	-4.1
1973	118.8	41.4	32.6	21.3	23.5	109.9	40.8	31.0	19.3	10.9	7.9	8.9	8.8
1974	156.5	56.5	44.5	25.7	29.8	150.5	50.3	54.2	22.9	14.3	8.7	6.0	5.9
1975	166.7	63.8	45.8	29.1	28.0	146.9	45.6	53.4	23.7	15.0	9.1	19.8	19.8
1976	181.9	69.0	48.7	31.7	32.4	174.8	56.8	67.8	26.5	15.5	8.1	7.1	7.0
1977	196.6	72.0	51.6	35.7	37.2	207.5	69.2	83.4	29.8	16.9	8.1	-10.9	-11.0
1978	233.1	85.3	60.1	41.5	46.3	245.8	89.0	88.4	34.8	24.7	8.8	-12.6	-12.7
1979	298.5	108.0	76.0	46.1	68.3	299.6	100.4	112.3	39.9	36.4	10.6	-1.2	-1.3
1980	359.9	133.3	92.5	55.0	79.1	351.4	111.9	136.6	45.3	44.9	12.6	8.5	8.4
1981	397.3	140.1	99.0	66.1	92.0	393.9	126.0	141.8	49.9	59.1	17.0	3.4	3.2
1982	384.2	124.7	90.3	68.2	101.0	387.5	125.1	125.4	52.6	64.5	19.8	-3.3	-3.4
1983	378.9	120.4	86.9	69.7	101.9	413.9	147.3	125.4	56.0	64.8	20.5	-35.1	-35.2
1984	424.2	132.4	93.2	76.7	121.9	514.3	192.4	143.9	68.8	85.6	23.6	-90.1	-90.2
1985	414.5	137.2	85.0	79.8	112.4	528.8	204.2	139.1	73.9	85.9	25.7	-114.3	-114.5
1986	431.3	142.6	83.4	94.3	111.0	574.0	238.8	131.2	82.9	93.4	27.8	-142.7	-142.8
1987	486.6	162.9	94.6	106.2	122.8	640.7	264.2	150.6	93.9	105.2	26.8	-154.1	-154.2
1988	595.5	208.8	117.0	118.1	151.6	711.2	294.8	157.3	101.9	128.3	29.0	-115.7	-115.9
1989	680.3	239.8	129.5	133.8	177.2	772.7	310.3	174.5	106.2	151.2	30.4	-92.4	-92.7
1990	740.6	262.0	134.7	155.5	188.5	815.6	314.5	193.5	121.7	154.1	31.7	-74.9	-82.3
1991	764.7	282.3	141.3	173.0	168.1	756.9	315.5	185.2	122.8	138.2	-4.9	7.9	2.6
1992	786.8	300.5	147.4	187.0	151.8	832.4	346.7	198.2	122.9	122.7	41.9	-45.6	-44.3
1993	810.8	314.0	146.0	195.7	155.2	889.4	386.4	206.4	127.2	124.0	45.4	-78.6	-79.4
1994	904.8	349.6	160.4	210.6	184.1	1 019.5	454.0	222.8	136.6	160.0	46.1	-114.7	-116.0
1995	1 041.1	394.0	189.3	228.6	229.3	1 146.2	510.8	246.7	145.1	199.6	44.1	-105.1	-105.5
1996	1 113.5	421.1	197.2	249.3	245.8	1 227.6	533.4	274.1	156.5	214.2	49.5	-114.1	-114.4
1997	1 233.9	482.3	205.4	266.7	279.5	1 363.3	588.5	297.1	170.1	256.1	51.4	-129.3	-129.8
1998	1 240.1	486.6	194.3	273.0	286.2	1 444.6	637.7	293.0	184.9	268.9	60.0	-204.5	-204.8
1999	1 308.8	503.3	193.9	292.1	319.5	1 600.7	716.7	331.0	203.7	291.7	57.6	-291.9	-296.4
2000	1 473.7	569.2	215.1	308.9	380.5	1 884.1	823.6	422.9	228.8	342.8	66.1	-410.4	-410.7
2001	1 350.8	521.1	210.1	296.5	323.0	1 742.4	758.3	413.4	227.0	271.1	72.6	-391.6	-378.7
2002	1 316.5	488.5	211.8	302.7	313.5	1 768.1	774.5	419.3	236.3	264.4	73.5	-451.6	-452.1
2003	1 394.4	497.3	229.5	314.2	353.3	1 910.5	806.6	482.6	255.9	284.6	80.7	-516.1	-518.2
2004	1 628.8	561.2	255.8	363.2	448.6	2 253.4	936.3	565.4	297.3	357.4	97.1	-624.6	-621.8
2005	1 878.1	624.9	281.2	399.0	573.0	2 618.6	1 025.4	682.6	319.8	475.9	115.0	-740.5	-727.7
2006	2 192.1	709.1	315.3	446.6	721.1	2 990.5	1 130.2	754.7	355.4	648.6	101.5	-798.4	-800.5
2007	2 532.7	781.6	380.5	499.7	871.0	3 248.7	1 172.5	828.2	374.0	747.7	126.2	-716.0	-715.9
2008	2 702.9	829.4	468.1	549.3	856.1	3 381.9	1 162.0	984.3	410.1	686.9	138.4	-679.0	-673.6
2009	2 222.8	671.8	392.9	518.4	639.8	2 600.3	892.9	694.3	387.3	487.5	138.2	-377.4	-378.0
2010	2 542.7	800.7	477.1	562.0	702.9	3 021.8	1 105.7	841.6	409.4	513.5	151.6	-479.2	-479.9
2011	2 864.8	897.4	576.0	612.1	779.3	3 347.9	1 236.4	1 001.6	426.3	533.8	149.9	-483.1	-484.4
2009													
1st quarter	2 146.7	651.4	362.1	508.7	624.6	2 529.1	867.9	653.8	384.0	491.9	131.5	-382.4	-382.8
2nd quarter	2 142.0	630.6	380.7	509.5	621.2	2 479.6	827.8	650.4	380.8	480.8	139.7	-337.7	-338.1
3rd quarter	2 227.2	673.8	401.1	515.5	636.9	2 617.7	896.7	711.6	388.6	473.2	147.6	-390.6	-391.2
4th quarter	2 375.5	731.3	427.8	539.9	676.5	2 774.6	979.1	761.5	395.8	504.2	133.9	-399.1	-399.9
2010													
1st quarter	2 423.5	755.0	453.7	540.8	674.0	2 905.4	1 022.5	821.5	401.3	504.6	155.5	-481.9	-482.4
2nd quarter	2 512.9	797.2	462.4	554.2	699.0	2 995.0	1 102.5	837.2	405.3	502.8	147.2	-482.2	-482.7
3rd quarter	2 569.5	814.3	474.7	571.6	708.9	3 057.4	1 137.4	845.3	418.2	501.6	155.0	-487.9	-489.1
4th quarter	2 664.7	836.4	517.4	581.5	729.4	3 129.4	1 160.6	862.2	412.7	545.0	148.9	-464.7	-465.3
2011													
1st quarter	2 776.2	869.1	561.9	593.2	752.1	3 269.7	1 214.2	962.0	419.3	525.0	149.3	-493.5	-494.0
2nd quarter	2 888.5	893.0	580.6	611.7	803.2	3 381.5	1 223.7	1 033.6	425.1	542.0	157.1	-493.0	-496.7
3rd quarter	2 911.5	917.0	579.6	622.6	792.2	3 353.7	1 246.2	1 005.7	429.7	524.9	147.2	-442.2	-442.7
4th quarter	2 882.8	910.5	582.0	620.7	769.7	3 386.6	1 261.4	1 005.0	431.1	543.4	145.8	-503.8	-504.2

1 Exports and imports of certain goods, primarily military equipment purchased and sold by the federal government, are included in services. Beginning with 1986, repairs and alterations of equipment are reclassified from goods to services.

Table 7-2. Chain-Type Quantity Indexes for Exports and Imports of Goods and Services

(Index numbers, 2005 = 100; quarterly indexes are seasonally adjusted.)   NIPA Table 4.2.3

| Year and quarter | Exports of goods and services | | | | | Imports of goods and services | | | | |
| | Total | Goods [1] | | | Services [1] | Total | Goods [1] | | | Services [1] |
		Total	Durable	Nondurable			Total	Durable	Nondurable	
1967	10.73	9.92	6.98	19.04	12.93	9.21	7.47	4.06	16.43	19.96
1968	11.57	10.70	7.64	20.15	13.93	10.58	9.01	5.17	18.61	20.32
1969	12.13	11.26	8.26	20.34	14.44	11.18	9.50	5.52	19.30	21.60
1970	13.44	12.55	9.03	23.32	15.73	11.66	9.87	5.67	20.35	22.72
1971	13.66	12.50	8.97	23.35	16.94	12.28	10.70	6.24	21.61	22.08
1972	14.69	13.84	9.91	25.96	16.84	13.66	12.16	7.18	24.14	23.01
1973	17.46	17.02	12.34	31.34	18.03	14.30	13.02	7.65	26.03	22.24
1974	18.84	18.37	14.25	31.06	19.43	13.97	12.65	7.68	24.41	22.21
1975	18.72	17.94	13.95	30.23	20.63	12.42	11.06	6.27	22.65	21.25
1976	19.54	18.80	14.15	33.14	21.24	14.85	13.56	7.69	27.79	22.71
1977	20.01	19.04	14.12	34.30	22.61	16.47	15.21	8.70	30.95	23.85
1978	22.12	21.17	15.74	37.98	24.50	17.90	16.58	10.05	31.96	25.55
1979	24.31	23.67	17.92	41.40	25.25	18.20	16.86	10.28	32.33	25.90
1980	26.93	26.49	19.98	46.57	26.83	16.99	15.61	10.36	27.83	25.32
1981	27.26	26.21	19.27	47.79	29.68	17.43	15.93	11.23	27.00	26.78
1982	25.17	23.84	16.74	46.34	28.86	17.21	15.53	11.35	25.42	28.21
1983	24.52	23.15	16.40	44.48	28.38	19.39	17.64	13.68	27.08	30.48
1984	26.53	24.98	18.17	46.24	30.91	24.11	21.91	18.21	30.84	38.13
1985	27.33	25.90	19.63	45.03	31.28	25.67	23.28	20.03	31.21	41.03
1986	29.43	27.23	20.78	46.83	35.82	27.86	25.67	21.89	34.89	41.49
1987	32.59	30.25	23.73	49.63	39.39	29.51	26.86	22.85	36.65	46.38
1988	37.82	35.95	29.43	54.70	42.94	30.67	27.94	23.81	38.05	47.95
1989	42.16	40.24	33.58	59.13	47.38	32.02	29.15	24.86	39.60	50.28
1990	45.95	43.62	37.17	61.61	52.37	33.17	30.00	25.52	40.93	53.56
1991	49.01	46.63	39.94	65.20	55.51	33.12	30.13	25.66	41.05	52.17
1992	52.37	50.12	43.11	69.46	58.50	35.44	32.97	28.35	44.19	50.77
1993	54.09	51.76	45.36	68.97	60.44	38.51	36.27	31.71	47.16	52.12
1994	58.80	56.79	50.85	72.23	64.28	43.10	41.11	36.95	50.66	54.90
1995	64.76	63.44	58.10	76.88	68.32	46.55	44.82	41.18	52.74	56.56
1996	70.13	69.03	64.78	79.45	73.10	50.60	49.02	45.59	56.28	59.51
1997	78.49	78.96	76.49	84.60	77.44	57.41	56.08	53.12	62.13	64.69
1998	80.28	80.72	78.96	84.47	79.30	64.12	62.73	60.12	67.81	71.72
1999	83.79	83.79	82.73	85.63	83.86	71.50	70.55	68.87	73.27	76.57
2000	90.99	93.08	93.41	91.20	86.10	80.81	80.02	79.36	80.46	84.96
2001	85.88	87.32	85.63	90.74	82.53	78.54	77.46	74.45	82.65	84.29
2002	84.16	84.18	80.78	92.13	84.12	81.21	80.34	77.57	85.00	85.84
2003	85.51	85.69	82.22	93.81	85.11	84.81	84.30	80.91	90.13	87.47
2004	93.68	93.00	91.33	96.77	95.24	94.21	93.64	92.12	96.07	97.25
2005	100.00	100.00	100.00	100.00	100.00	100.00	100.00	100.00	100.00	100.00
2006	108.97	109.43	110.74	106.54	107.94	106.10	105.92	108.80	101.74	107.06
2007	119.11	120.09	121.01	118.02	116.89	108.65	108.67	111.30	104.85	108.54
2008	126.38	127.69	127.36	127.95	123.40	105.73	104.50	107.21	100.59	112.49
2009	114.48	112.42	105.66	124.90	119.04	91.37	88.17	84.91	91.74	108.58
2010	127.44	128.56	123.49	137.67	125.03	102.82	101.25	103.94	96.96	111.74
2011	135.95	138.14	135.57	142.97	131.11	107.89	107.06	113.73	98.01	112.94
2005										
1st quarter	97.79	97.03	95.53	100.39	99.51	98.18	98.07	97.20	99.42	98.82
2nd quarter	99.89	100.23	99.01	102.92	99.09	99.27	99.23	99.07	99.47	99.44
3rd quarter	99.91	99.96	100.46	98.82	99.80	99.88	99.90	100.30	99.29	99.73
4th quarter	102.42	102.78	105.01	97.87	101.60	102.68	102.80	103.44	101.82	102.01
2006										
1st quarter	106.41	107.07	108.55	103.86	104.90	104.62	104.38	107.61	99.79	105.89
2nd quarter	108.20	109.02	110.14	106.59	106.34	105.79	105.68	108.19	102.06	106.36
3rd quarter	108.36	109.08	110.19	106.65	106.73	107.06	107.12	108.95	104.40	106.72
4th quarter	112.90	112.53	114.08	109.06	113.77	106.92	106.50	110.45	100.73	109.28
2007										
1st quarter	114.67	115.96	116.46	114.74	111.75	108.48	108.67	111.09	105.08	107.51
2nd quarter	116.57	118.10	119.10	115.84	113.11	109.02	109.13	111.01	106.28	108.47
3rd quarter	120.91	121.70	122.79	119.27	119.13	109.28	109.21	112.33	104.71	109.64
4th quarter	124.28	124.60	125.69	122.21	123.55	107.83	107.69	110.74	103.30	108.54
2008										
1st quarter	125.97	127.39	127.20	127.42	122.72	108.20	107.52	111.73	101.84	111.89
2nd quarter	129.79	131.67	132.05	130.69	125.54	107.51	106.91	111.46	100.91	110.70
3rd quarter	128.63	130.88	131.51	129.42	123.54	105.70	104.40	108.00	99.47	112.91
4th quarter	121.11	120.83	118.67	124.29	121.77	101.52	99.18	97.64	100.12	114.46
2009										
1st quarter	111.19	108.53	103.06	118.54	117.04	91.49	88.34	82.78	95.04	108.49
2nd quarter	111.06	107.72	100.07	122.09	118.39	87.84	84.08	79.27	89.77	107.82
3rd quarter	114.73	113.06	105.88	126.35	118.43	91.22	87.92	85.18	90.70	108.94
4th quarter	120.94	120.35	113.63	132.61	122.30	94.94	92.36	92.41	91.45	109.06
2010										
1st quarter	123.07	123.84	116.90	136.51	121.46	97.79	95.52	96.23	93.75	110.30
2nd quarter	126.05	127.34	122.90	135.24	123.26	102.70	101.20	103.40	97.51	111.20
3rd quarter	129.10	130.10	125.84	137.64	126.96	105.71	104.21	107.22	99.47	114.28
4th quarter	131.55	132.98	128.32	141.29	128.43	105.09	104.06	108.90	97.10	111.18
2011										
1st quarter	134.06	136.36	132.24	143.73	128.98	107.21	106.46	112.68	97.88	111.80
2nd quarter	135.24	137.21	134.98	141.44	130.93	107.57	106.88	112.28	99.15	111.92
3rd quarter	136.79	138.87	137.91	141.08	132.20	107.90	107.02	114.00	97.63	113.24
4th quarter	137.69	140.12	137.14	145.65	132.33	108.87	107.89	115.94	97.37	114.80

[1]Exports and imports of certain goods, primarily military equipment purchased and sold by the federal government, are included in services. Beginning with 1986, repairs and alterations of equipment are reclassified from goods to services.

Table 7-3. Chain-Type Price Indexes for Exports and Imports of Goods and Services

(Index numbers, 2005 = 100; quarterly indexes are seasonally adjusted.) **NIPA Table 4.2.4**

Year and quarter	Exports of goods and services					Imports of goods and services				
	Total	Goods [1]			Services [1]	Total	Goods [1]			Services [1]
		Total	Durable	Nondurable			Total	Durable	Nondurable	
1967	31.05	35.81	42.27	25.66	21.89	21.38	21.77	34.98	11.79	19.04
1968	31.72	36.37	43.98	25.18	22.76	21.70	22.06	35.55	11.90	19.41
1969	32.80	37.49	45.90	25.48	23.71	22.27	22.68	36.68	12.19	19.81
1970	34.05	39.19	48.04	26.57	24.16	23.59	24.23	39.17	13.02	20.51
1971	35.31	40.23	49.15	27.43	25.75	25.04	25.47	41.55	13.52	22.37
1972	36.96	41.30	50.14	28.42	28.36	26.79	27.42	45.20	14.35	23.48
1973	41.82	47.94	53.62	36.94	29.68	31.45	32.32	52.04	17.47	27.16
1974	51.52	60.67	63.42	50.98	33.11	44.99	48.36	63.93	32.53	32.30
1975	56.78	67.43	73.19	53.90	35.33	48.73	52.41	70.95	34.52	34.92
1976	58.65	69.15	78.09	52.29	37.47	50.20	53.81	72.10	35.75	36.50
1977	61.03	71.67	81.66	53.51	39.58	54.62	58.74	77.60	39.50	39.09
1978	64.75	75.80	86.69	56.30	42.45	58.48	62.66	86.38	40.52	42.65
1979	72.55	85.81	96.49	65.29	45.75	68.48	73.89	95.28	50.91	48.16
1980	79.90	94.06	106.78	70.60	51.38	85.30	93.23	105.35	71.92	55.89
1981	85.81	100.70	116.40	73.65	55.85	89.89	98.43	109.51	76.92	58.32
1982	86.20	99.55	119.16	69.31	59.23	86.86	94.45	107.49	72.26	58.36
1983	86.54	98.82	117.48	69.47	61.55	83.60	90.50	105.00	67.82	57.40
1984	87.35	99.68	116.58	71.71	62.23	82.88	89.88	103.08	68.35	56.42
1985	84.67	94.69	111.87	67.11	63.93	80.16	86.34	99.41	65.31	56.35
1986	83.41	91.59	109.84	63.31	66.01	80.15	84.41	106.40	55.09	62.45
1987	85.52	93.96	109.91	67.79	67.59	85.01	90.43	112.74	60.20	63.34
1988	89.95	100.01	113.52	76.06	68.94	89.07	94.74	120.76	60.58	66.42
1989	91.44	101.31	114.30	77.91	70.78	91.02	97.39	121.71	64.57	66.07
1990	92.06	100.35	112.80	77.72	74.41	93.63	99.17	120.20	69.27	71.02
1991	93.28	100.24	113.12	77.05	78.13	92.85	97.30	119.93	66.09	73.61
1992	92.90	98.63	111.55	75.48	80.13	92.92	96.77	119.28	65.72	75.67
1993	92.88	98.08	110.78	75.25	81.14	92.21	95.69	118.84	64.10	76.31
1994	93.91	99.12	110.03	78.99	82.14	93.08	96.38	119.86	64.41	77.81
1995	96.07	101.48	108.54	87.54	83.87	95.63	98.95	120.95	68.52	80.24
1996	94.80	98.86	104.04	88.26	85.49	93.96	96.44	114.10	71.34	82.23
1997	93.17	96.13	100.91	86.32	86.34	90.69	92.46	108.06	70.06	82.23
1998	91.04	93.09	98.61	81.79	86.29	85.81	86.88	103.46	63.31	80.63
1999	90.48	91.83	97.35	80.53	87.31	86.31	86.95	101.49	66.19	83.19
2000	92.07	93.00	97.53	83.87	89.92	90.03	91.21	101.21	77.00	84.21
2001	91.70	92.42	97.39	82.33	90.04	87.82	88.56	99.33	73.27	84.22
2002	91.32	91.82	96.79	81.73	90.20	86.85	87.00	97.38	72.27	86.09
2003	93.28	93.62	96.81	86.99	92.53	89.85	89.54	97.23	78.45	91.47
2004	96.54	96.96	98.34	93.98	95.60	94.16	93.90	99.12	86.21	95.57
2005	100.00	100.00	100.00	100.00	100.00	100.00	100.00	100.00	100.00	100.00
2006	103.44	103.32	102.47	105.23	103.72	104.13	104.19	101.31	108.67	103.81
2007	106.90	106.79	103.36	114.63	107.15	107.79	107.79	102.75	115.72	107.75
2008	111.98	112.14	104.22	130.09	111.57	119.24	120.25	105.71	143.36	114.01
2009	105.96	104.52	101.75	111.86	109.15	106.57	105.40	102.56	110.87	111.54
2010	110.62	109.69	103.77	123.22	112.67	113.03	112.61	103.76	127.15	114.56
2011	117.57	117.75	105.93	143.35	117.01	121.76	122.35	106.02	149.69	118.02
2005										
1st quarter	98.93	99.15	99.86	97.60	98.43	97.48	97.30	100.20	92.92	98.41
2nd quarter	99.62	99.77	99.94	99.38	99.27	98.83	98.67	100.27	96.23	99.68
3rd quarter	100.34	100.20	99.92	100.79	100.67	100.86	100.84	99.72	102.49	101.01
4th quarter	101.11	100.88	100.27	102.24	101.62	102.83	103.20	99.81	108.35	100.91
2006										
1st quarter	101.83	101.55	101.10	102.51	102.49	103.24	103.39	100.17	108.34	102.45
2nd quarter	103.13	102.92	102.20	104.50	103.61	104.31	104.41	101.06	109.61	103.82
3rd quarter	104.39	104.30	103.05	107.13	104.60	105.10	105.22	101.89	110.43	104.51
4th quarter	104.41	104.50	103.54	106.78	104.19	103.88	103.76	102.13	106.29	104.46
2007										
1st quarter	105.31	105.22	103.48	109.24	105.50	104.56	104.43	102.14	108.05	105.19
2nd quarter	106.46	106.40	103.59	112.86	106.60	106.23	106.10	102.54	111.69	106.93
3rd quarter	107.16	106.98	103.13	115.77	107.57	108.01	107.89	102.99	115.55	108.66
4th quarter	108.68	108.58	103.26	120.65	108.92	112.34	112.75	103.33	127.60	110.22
2008										
1st quarter	110.73	110.91	103.93	126.64	110.36	116.79	117.82	104.15	139.38	111.60
2nd quarter	113.58	114.43	104.87	135.86	111.63	122.49	123.99	106.63	151.45	114.96
3rd quarter	115.26	116.03	105.46	139.83	113.46	125.62	127.44	107.30	159.34	116.50
4th quarter	108.32	107.21	102.61	118.04	110.85	112.05	111.77	104.77	123.26	112.97
2009										
1st quarter	104.94	103.13	101.20	108.72	108.94	102.79	100.96	102.29	100.71	110.67
2nd quarter	104.97	103.66	100.89	110.97	107.88	104.44	103.03	101.89	106.05	110.45
3rd quarter	106.25	104.97	101.88	112.96	109.11	108.03	107.19	102.70	114.85	111.55
4th quarter	107.67	106.33	103.03	114.79	110.66	111.02	110.40	103.37	121.90	113.49
2010										
1st quarter	108.96	107.76	103.37	118.26	111.62	113.25	113.05	103.64	128.32	113.76
2nd quarter	110.30	109.22	103.83	121.65	112.70	112.61	112.22	103.99	125.74	113.98
3rd quarter	110.46	109.39	103.56	122.69	112.87	111.99	111.38	103.46	124.47	114.43
4th quarter	112.76	112.40	104.32	130.27	113.49	114.27	113.78	103.94	130.08	116.07
2011										
1st quarter	115.72	115.86	105.19	139.07	115.28	119.37	119.65	105.09	143.97	117.26
2nd quarter	118.18	118.57	105.87	146.03	117.12	122.95	123.63	106.28	152.71	118.75
3rd quarter	118.75	118.98	106.41	146.16	118.06	122.54	123.17	106.60	150.90	118.64
4th quarter	117.63	117.60	106.26	142.15	117.58	122.16	122.95	106.10	151.19	117.42

[1] Exports and imports of certain goods, primarily military equipment purchased and sold by the federal government, are included in services. Beginning with 1986, repairs and alterations of equipment are reclassified from goods to services.

Table 7-4. Exports and Imports of Selected NIPA Types of Product

(Billions of dollars, quarterly data are at seasonally adjusted annual rates.)   **NIPA Table 4.2.5**

Year and quarter	Exports — Goods					Exports — Services		Imports — Goods						Imports — Services	
	Foods, feeds, and beverages	Industrial supplies and materials	Capital goods, except automotive	Automotive vehicles, engines, and parts	Consumer goods, except automotive	Travel	Other private services (financial, professional, etc.)	Foods, feeds, and beverages	Industrial supplies and materials, except petroleum and products	Petroleum and products	Capital goods, except automotive	Automotive vehicles, engines, and parts	Consumer goods, except automotive	Travel	Other private services (financial, professional, etc.)
1967	5.0	10.0	9.9	2.8	2.1	1.6	0.7	4.6	9.9	2.1	2.5	2.4	4.2	3.2	0.4
1968	4.8	11.0	11.1	3.5	2.3	1.8	0.8	5.3	12.0	2.4	2.8	4.0	5.4	3.0	0.5
1969	4.7	11.7	12.4	3.9	2.6	2.0	0.9	5.2	11.7	2.6	3.4	5.1	6.5	3.4	0.6
1970	5.9	13.8	14.7	3.9	2.8	2.3	1.0	6.1	12.2	2.9	4.0	5.7	7.4	4.0	0.6
1971	6.1	12.6	15.4	4.7	2.9	2.5	1.3	6.4	13.6	3.7	4.3	7.6	8.4	4.4	0.7
1972	7.5	13.9	16.9	5.5	3.6	2.8	1.5	7.3	16.0	4.7	5.9	9.0	11.1	5.0	0.8
1973	15.2	19.7	22.0	7.0	4.8	3.4	1.7	9.1	19.2	8.4	8.3	10.7	12.9	5.5	0.9
1974	18.6	29.9	30.9	8.8	6.4	4.0	3.0	10.6	27.0	26.6	9.8	12.4	14.4	6.0	1.9
1975	19.2	29.3	36.6	10.8	6.6	4.7	3.7	9.6	23.6	27.0	10.2	12.1	13.2	6.4	2.3
1976	19.8	31.6	39.1	12.2	8.0	5.7	4.5	11.5	28.5	34.6	12.3	16.8	17.2	6.9	2.9
1977	19.7	33.2	39.8	13.5	8.9	6.2	4.9	14.0	33.4	45.0	14.0	19.4	21.8	7.5	3.2
1978	25.7	38.4	47.5	15.2	11.4	7.2	6.2	15.8	39.3	42.6	19.3	25.0	29.4	8.5	3.9
1979	30.5	53.3	60.2	17.9	14.0	8.4	7.3	18.0	45.0	60.4	24.6	26.6	31.3	9.4	4.6
1980	36.3	68.0	76.3	17.4	17.8	10.6	8.6	18.6	47.3	79.5	31.6	28.3	34.3	10.4	5.1
1981	38.8	65.7	84.2	19.7	17.7	12.9	13.2	18.6	52.0	78.4	37.1	31.0	38.4	11.5	6.3
1982	32.2	61.8	76.5	17.2	16.1	12.4	16.9	17.5	45.4	62.0	38.4	34.3	39.7	12.4	7.4
1983	32.1	57.1	71.7	18.5	14.9	10.9	17.6	18.8	51.1	55.1	43.7	43.0	47.3	13.2	7.3
1984	32.2	61.9	77.0	22.4	15.1	17.2	18.6	21.9	62.6	58.1	60.4	56.5	61.1	22.9	8.2
1985	24.6	59.4	79.3	24.9	14.6	17.8	19.4	21.8	59.2	51.4	61.3	64.9	66.3	24.6	9.4
1986	23.5	59.0	82.8	25.1	16.7	20.4	28.3	24.4	62.5	34.3	72.0	78.1	79.4	25.9	13.8
1987	25.2	67.4	92.7	27.6	20.3	23.6	29.6	24.8	66.1	42.9	85.1	85.2	88.8	29.3	17.3
1988	33.8	84.2	119.1	33.4	27.0	29.4	31.4	24.9	76.6	39.6	102.2	87.9	96.4	32.1	18.4
1989	36.3	95.4	136.9	35.1	35.9	36.2	37.0	24.9	78.8	50.9	112.3	87.4	103.6	33.4	19.9
1990	35.1	101.9	153.0	36.2	43.5	43.0	40.6	26.4	78.2	62.3	116.4	88.2	105.0	37.4	23.3
1991	35.7	106.2	166.6	39.9	46.6	48.4	48.1	26.2	75.7	51.7	121.1	85.5	107.7	35.3	26.8
1992	40.3	105.2	176.4	46.9	51.2	54.7	50.3	27.6	82.4	51.6	134.8	91.5	122.4	38.6	25.4
1993	40.5	102.9	182.7	51.6	54.5	57.9	53.5	27.9	88.7	51.5	153.2	102.1	133.7	40.7	27.8
1994	42.4	115.4	205.7	57.5	59.7	58.4	60.8	31.0	105.0	51.3	185.0	118.1	145.9	43.8	31.6
1995	50.8	141.0	234.4	61.4	64.2	63.4	65.0	33.2	119.6	56.0	222.1	123.7	159.7	44.9	35.2
1996	56.0	141.3	254.0	64.4	69.3	69.8	73.3	35.7	124.6	72.7	228.4	128.7	172.5	48.1	39.7
1997	52.0	153.0	295.8	73.4	77.0	73.4	83.9	39.7	134.7	71.8	253.6	139.4	195.2	52.1	43.2
1998	46.8	143.3	299.8	72.5	79.4	71.3	91.8	41.3	142.2	50.9	269.8	148.6	218.5	56.5	47.6
1999	46.0	142.4	311.2	75.3	80.9	74.8	103.9	43.6	148.3	67.8	295.7	179.0	243.5	59.0	55.5
2000	47.9	166.6	357.0	80.4	89.4	82.4	107.9	46.0	173.6	120.3	347.0	195.9	284.2	64.7	60.5
2001	49.4	155.3	321.7	75.4	88.3	71.9	113.9	46.6	165.8	103.6	298.4	189.8	286.5	60.2	66.0
2002	49.6	153.5	290.4	78.9	84.4	66.6	122.2	49.7	159.6	103.5	283.9	203.7	310.7	58.7	72.6
2003	55.0	168.3	293.7	80.6	89.9	64.4	131.6	55.8	175.7	133.1	296.4	210.1	337.7	57.4	79.8
2004	56.6	199.5	327.5	89.2	103.2	74.5	149.3	62.1	226.4	180.5	344.5	228.2	377.1	65.8	90.3
2005	59.0	227.5	358.4	98.4	115.3	81.8	160.0	68.1	266.0	251.9	380.7	239.4	411.5	69.0	97.8
2006	66.0	267.3	404.0	107.3	129.1	85.8	186.0	74.9	291.4	302.4	420.0	256.6	446.1	72.1	125.5
2007	84.3	316.2	433.0	121.3	146.0	96.9	222.4	81.7	295.7	346.7	446.0	256.7	478.2	76.3	151.9
2008	108.3	386.9	457.7	121.5	161.3	110.4	232.0	90.4	318.9	476.1	458.7	233.2	486.7	80.5	172.5
2009	93.9	293.7	390.5	81.7	150.0	94.2	234.9	82.8	197.1	267.7	372.7	159.2	432.5	74.1	174.3
2010	107.7	388.7	446.6	112.0	165.9	103.5	250.3	92.5	250.4	353.7	450.0	225.6	486.6	75.5	180.6
2011	125.4	485.6	491.6	132.6	176.2	115.2	273.1	108.6	296.2	461.5	513.9	255.8	518.6	77.8	187.8
2006															
1st quarter	61.9	250.1	391.6	106.7	123.9	83.2	179.4	73.6	288.0	291.4	407.7	256.6	430.6	70.5	120.5
2nd quarter	64.5	267.8	403.2	105.6	127.0	85.0	181.8	73.1	288.5	312.9	416.2	256.5	437.3	71.8	124.6
3rd quarter	67.8	271.6	403.8	106.6	129.6	86.4	183.1	75.3	300.0	331.8	426.0	251.6	449.7	72.1	126.0
4th quarter	69.7	279.7	417.6	110.2	135.8	88.6	199.7	77.8	289.1	273.7	429.9	261.8	466.9	74.0	130.8
2007															
1st quarter	74.5	293.3	420.4	114.9	141.3	87.8	211.1	80.4	286.9	296.8	439.1	253.1	482.9	74.1	143.4
2nd quarter	77.1	310.5	424.3	122.3	144.1	92.3	218.5	80.3	302.7	326.5	443.3	255.8	474.2	75.3	148.4
3rd quarter	87.9	320.2	439.5	124.1	147.9	100.8	228.6	82.7	300.7	345.0	450.4	264.0	472.7	77.0	156.5
4th quarter	97.6	340.8	447.8	123.8	150.6	106.6	231.6	83.4	292.4	418.5	451.3	253.6	483.0	79.0	159.3
2008															
1st quarter	108.9	371.1	454.4	122.2	157.6	109.3	226.7	87.8	309.5	469.0	465.0	257.9	490.9	82.6	163.8
2nd quarter	116.5	418.1	470.8	126.4	164.7	112.6	235.9	91.2	334.6	520.2	476.6	252.5	499.7	80.9	170.1
3rd quarter	115.3	430.8	473.3	130.3	167.8	115.5	232.6	92.8	347.6	554.2	466.5	229.2	498.3	79.8	176.7
4th quarter	92.6	327.7	432.2	106.9	155.0	104.4	232.9	89.9	283.7	361.1	426.7	193.2	457.9	78.7	179.5
2009															
1st quarter	86.8	263.6	392.7	69.0	145.6	94.8	234.8	83.0	210.4	220.1	371.1	131.3	428.8	76.4	167.9
2nd quarter	95.8	273.7	375.8	67.8	145.0	92.6	232.0	82.4	176.0	240.2	351.4	128.8	423.1	71.3	172.7
3rd quarter	92.9	308.4	383.7	88.6	150.5	93.9	230.9	82.3	188.6	292.3	369.7	174.9	426.9	74.2	176.9
4th quarter	100.2	329.3	409.7	101.5	159.0	95.4	241.8	83.8	213.4	318.2	398.5	201.6	451.0	74.6	179.8
2010															
1st quarter	104.8	357.1	422.2	107.2	162.3	100.8	238.3	88.2	239.8	353.0	409.4	206.8	459.2	76.3	174.8
2nd quarter	97.8	388.2	441.5	111.2	161.4	101.6	244.4	91.9	252.6	356.3	446.1	224.9	484.7	73.2	180.2
3rd quarter	105.9	388.1	456.4	113.7	165.3	104.8	255.2	94.1	255.1	347.6	464.8	236.3	501.7	76.3	185.1
4th quarter	122.4	421.2	466.3	115.8	174.6	106.8	263.4	95.7	254.2	358.0	479.5	234.3	500.6	76.2	182.3
2011															
1st quarter	128.2	469.8	470.4	128.2	169.5	110.2	267.3	103.5	283.9	445.5	493.6	256.1	514.9	75.8	185.1
2nd quarter	128.2	489.2	488.9	128.7	176.3	116.2	272.9	109.7	306.5	479.8	514.1	232.8	525.5	77.8	186.3
3rd quarter	122.7	494.4	502.4	137.9	178.0	119.1	275.6	108.6	306.8	457.7	516.5	267.1	515.1	79.0	188.6
4th quarter	122.4	489.0	504.8	135.8	180.9	115.4	276.6	112.6	287.7	463.1	531.6	267.2	519.0	78.9	191.2

Table 7-5. Chain-Type Quantity Indexes for Exports and Imports of Selected NIPA Types of Product

(Index numbers, 2005 = 100; quarterly indexes are seasonally adjusted.)   NIPA Table 4.2.3

| Year and quarter | Exports | | | | | | | Imports | | | | | | | |
| | Goods | | | | | Services | | Goods | | | | | | Services | |
	Foods, feeds, and beverages	Industrial supplies and materials	Capital goods, except automotive	Automotive vehicles, engines, and parts	Consumer goods, except automotive	Travel	Other private services (financial, professional, etc.)	Foods, feeds, and beverages	Industrial supplies and materials, except petroleum and products	Petroleum and products	Capital goods, except automotive	Automotive vehicles, engines, and parts	Consumer goods, except automotive	Travel	Other private services (financial, professional, etc.)
1967	26.08	21.44	3.93	14.60	6.16	10.98	1.84	27.20	19.47	16.55	0.64	7.11	4.04	20.07	1.24
1968	25.67	24.39	4.05	17.99	6.70	11.35	1.91	30.86	23.18	19.06	0.73	11.06	5.10	18.19	1.40
1969	25.13	25.51	4.29	19.44	7.17	12.39	2.09	29.25	21.93	21.26	0.85	13.51	6.02	19.73	1.56
1970	30.33	28.56	4.80	19.00	7.60	13.37	2.24	31.24	22.16	22.97	0.89	13.82	6.47	22.76	1.64
1971	29.53	25.82	5.01	21.53	7.62	13.95	2.60	32.25	24.16	26.27	0.88	16.86	6.81	22.74	1.81
1972	34.85	27.50	5.49	24.16	8.91	14.99	2.90	34.33	26.51	32.08	1.13	18.26	8.30	24.60	1.86
1973	45.12	33.83	6.97	28.37	10.87	17.22	3.16	35.21	26.68	44.57	1.39	18.84	8.51	23.20	2.08
1974	40.44	34.82	8.70	31.65	13.52	18.74	5.16	32.57	25.99	43.87	1.48	20.02	7.66	20.83	4.19
1975	42.78	30.46	8.83	33.32	12.46	20.26	5.99	28.81	21.89	43.15	1.41	15.88	5.94	20.09	4.73
1976	48.54	32.90	8.71	34.84	14.05	23.08	6.93	32.79	26.66	52.03	1.70	21.05	7.66	21.37	5.69
1977	48.50	33.17	8.57	35.09	15.20	23.13	7.14	32.46	28.69	62.59	1.82	22.30	9.26	22.02	5.96
1978	59.92	36.66	9.78	36.03	17.55	24.85	8.46	36.45	31.41	59.18	2.35	24.13	11.37	22.75	6.96
1979	63.56	41.98	11.75	36.26	18.45	26.63	9.43	37.41	30.18	59.86	2.87	23.33	11.46	22.19	7.89
1980	71.65	47.64	13.71	30.53	22.36	29.75	10.07	32.56	26.34	48.34	3.38	23.11	11.54	22.17	8.05
1981	73.16	44.44	13.77	30.18	21.44	32.84	14.40	33.88	28.59	42.36	3.99	22.37	12.64	23.45	9.48
1982	68.73	43.09	12.17	24.73	19.30	29.28	17.37	34.53	25.92	36.43	4.34	23.94	13.21	27.79	10.75
1983	65.70	41.00	11.74	25.59	17.65	24.72	17.16	37.48	30.78	36.05	5.25	29.31	15.90	31.49	10.07
1984	63.93	43.10	13.00	30.20	17.56	36.87	17.40	42.46	38.17	38.08	7.85	37.65	20.07	57.55	11.29
1985	55.33	43.35	14.29	32.86	17.04	36.50	17.37	44.30	38.39	35.76	8.24	42.19	21.91	63.52	12.58
1986	57.08	45.28	15.59	32.32	18.85	40.73	24.60	45.34	40.43	44.21	10.04	45.67	24.27	59.05	17.99
1987	61.09	46.41	18.00	34.83	22.17	44.94	24.66	46.48	40.03	46.18	11.46	46.87	25.06	70.02	20.57
1988	67.13	52.32	22.89	41.35	28.32	54.22	25.81	44.63	40.47	51.08	13.21	45.69	25.43	71.95	21.96
1989	69.83	58.19	26.55	42.50	36.31	64.81	29.83	45.64	39.55	55.23	14.94	44.53	26.61	74.14	25.62
1990	72.04	61.62	30.71	42.56	42.60	73.10	31.36	47.38	40.17	55.82	16.14	44.59	26.14	79.21	27.78
1991	73.42	65.80	33.61	45.65	44.14	77.45	35.69	45.24	39.43	55.92	17.36	41.58	26.59	71.73	30.92
1992	83.22	67.03	36.81	52.62	47.54	85.92	36.32	47.76	43.34	58.13	20.11	43.71	29.36	73.85	28.98
1993	82.80	65.25	39.23	57.37	49.94	90.13	37.86	48.32	47.02	63.68	23.46	48.04	31.79	77.47	30.75
1994	83.66	68.64	45.26	63.42	54.57	90.57	42.46	49.43	54.02	67.99	28.77	53.86	34.45	80.22	34.67
1995	92.41	74.05	53.93	66.84	57.84	97.11	44.47	50.67	56.56	66.76	35.41	54.79	37.16	80.85	38.16
1996	90.94	77.81	62.51	69.31	61.69	104.44	49.14	55.73	59.78	72.39	41.62	56.65	40.01	84.02	41.80
1997	91.51	84.59	76.63	78.46	68.04	107.42	55.56	61.38	64.71	75.38	52.23	61.23	45.83	91.27	44.84
1998	90.58	83.66	79.88	77.39	70.10	103.17	60.83	65.87	71.86	80.58	60.06	65.19	52.00	103.17	50.10
1999	93.22	84.39	84.30	79.83	71.72	105.37	70.10	71.98	75.35	81.23	68.85	77.95	58.38	105.17	58.55
2000	98.65	92.66	97.15	84.53	78.89	110.86	72.45	76.91	80.44	85.73	82.70	84.73	68.60	117.09	65.14
2001	101.35	88.95	87.54	79.09	78.25	96.20	76.80	80.43	77.66	88.25	73.28	82.15	69.72	111.52	71.47
2002	99.31	89.22	79.95	82.35	75.11	89.86	82.48	84.67	79.88	86.18	72.10	87.93	76.42	104.66	76.05
2003	101.00	91.48	81.84	83.52	79.60	85.09	87.31	91.23	81.15	91.94	76.30	90.20	83.24	95.40	82.08
2004	94.74	97.42	91.60	91.68	90.55	95.22	96.53	96.50	93.77	98.03	89.84	96.30	92.47	101.80	92.69
2005	100.00	100.00	100.00	100.00	100.00	100.00	100.00	100.00	100.00	100.00	100.00	100.00	100.00	100.00	100.00
2006	107.95	107.51	111.94	107.69	110.56	100.49	112.03	106.06	104.27	98.12	111.19	106.76	108.00	100.58	121.42
2007	117.34	118.32	120.97	120.35	122.45	109.53	129.62	107.41	100.19	100.82	118.58	105.71	114.22	98.50	143.16
2008	125.11	131.22	128.22	119.08	132.46	119.44	131.49	107.69	93.39	96.92	121.45	93.67	113.42	97.02	157.38
2009	119.52	122.24	109.46	79.70	122.95	106.31	134.16	101.68	70.81	89.77	100.55	63.44	101.16	93.10	157.02
2010	131.91	141.25	124.76	108.66	134.49	113.36	139.91	103.93	81.17	90.10	122.18	89.33	113.83	93.01	160.35
2011	129.53	150.69	137.84	126.56	140.89	119.93	148.30	106.47	87.15	88.39	139.16	98.32	119.31	93.51	164.30
2006															
1st quarter	104.46	104.60	109.24	107.73	107.06	98.56	109.25	105.68	104.33	96.93	107.99	107.23	104.58	100.87	118.56
2nd quarter	108.75	107.97	111.94	106.15	109.00	99.25	109.97	104.85	104.46	98.11	110.34	106.87	106.21	100.90	121.14
3rd quarter	110.12	106.60	111.61	106.72	110.40	100.04	109.44	106.01	106.31	103.14	112.74	104.46	108.68	99.41	120.84
4th quarter	108.48	110.89	114.94	110.15	115.74	104.12	119.45	107.70	101.99	94.30	113.68	108.50	112.53	101.13	125.15
2007															
1st quarter	109.87	114.79	116.32	114.35	119.56	101.84	124.27	109.21	99.61	100.61	116.37	104.79	115.82	100.26	137.40
2nd quarter	112.11	116.81	118.20	121.51	121.01	104.87	128.31	107.01	102.40	102.94	117.96	105.77	113.66	98.16	140.89
3rd quarter	121.85	119.04	123.18	123.08	123.84	113.24	132.73	107.68	102.55	99.65	119.70	108.81	112.71	98.10	146.56
4th quarter	125.55	122.63	126.20	122.47	125.37	118.15	133.19	105.76	96.20	100.07	120.30	103.47	114.71	97.50	147.78
2008															
1st quarter	128.63	128.60	127.98	120.44	130.33	119.29	128.92	107.98	95.27	97.93	124.03	104.14	115.53	100.03	151.33
2nd quarter	128.89	135.24	131.96	124.08	135.04	120.96	133.81	107.36	94.38	95.66	125.67	101.45	116.08	94.39	155.00
3rd quarter	124.94	134.89	132.25	127.57	137.16	121.53	130.56	106.99	95.85	93.43	122.80	91.80	115.45	94.77	159.04
4th quarter	117.98	126.15	120.71	104.24	127.32	115.98	132.69	108.43	88.07	100.66	113.29	77.31	106.62	98.91	164.17
2009															
1st quarter	113.12	114.40	110.16	67.20	119.49	108.15	134.85	102.31	74.25	98.21	99.63	52.53	100.24	97.83	153.57
2nd quarter	119.38	117.13	105.81	66.16	119.61	105.88	134.09	101.36	65.45	89.10	94.94	51.59	99.02	89.90	156.50
3rd quarter	117.42	126.94	107.66	86.53	123.00	105.29	131.61	101.66	69.68	86.86	99.87	69.68	99.95	92.45	158.34
4th quarter	128.18	130.49	114.21	98.93	129.72	105.92	136.09	101.39	73.88	84.92	107.77	79.98	105.43	92.21	159.68
2010															
1st quarter	133.25	136.01	117.65	104.04	132.44	111.36	133.94	103.38	77.97	87.11	111.00	82.28	107.19	94.31	155.18
2nd quarter	125.38	141.58	123.01	108.12	131.27	111.70	136.55	104.68	81.94	92.27	121.19	89.34	113.05	90.70	160.19
3rd quarter	131.12	141.81	127.58	110.40	134.19	114.41	142.92	105.79	83.85	92.93	126.32	93.43	117.50	94.27	164.88
4th quarter	137.89	145.60	130.79	112.06	140.07	115.98	146.21	101.86	80.93	88.09	130.22	92.25	117.59	92.77	161.14
2011															
1st quarter	134.45	150.89	132.35	123.63	136.23	117.26	146.34	103.98	84.75	90.88	133.77	100.38	120.03	91.43	162.27
2nd quarter	131.90	148.51	137.26	123.33	141.14	120.99	147.96	104.96	89.35	88.19	139.07	89.17	121.46	92.61	162.46
3rd quarter	124.93	150.12	140.61	131.17	141.68	122.47	148.83	106.19	88.80	86.88	139.72	101.91	117.95	94.41	164.52
4th quarter	126.84	153.25	141.13	128.10	144.51	119.00	150.08	110.73	85.68	87.62	144.08	101.80	117.80	95.61	167.93

Section 7b: U.S. International Transactions Accounts

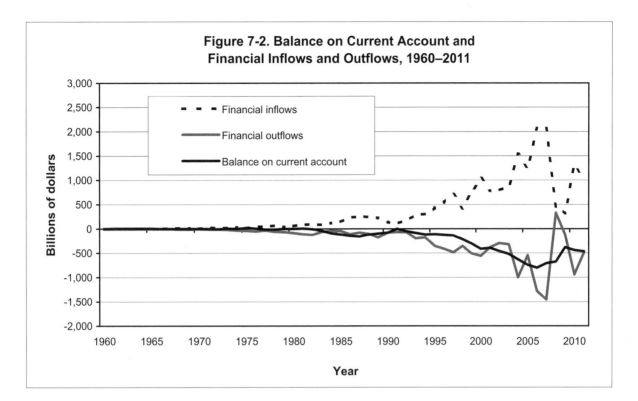

Figure 7-2. Balance on Current Account and Financial Inflows and Outflows, 1960–2011

- The U.S. current-account international balance is also recorded in the International Transactions Accounts (ITAs). The definitional differences between this balance and the balance in the NIPAs are minor, and the trends in the two measures are similar. The ITAs measure the current account surplus or deficit (commonly known as the "balance of payments") and directly measure the financial flows required to finance it. (Table 7-6A and B)

- Figure 7-2 above shows the current-account balance since 1960, culminating in a $466 billion deficit in 2011, and the corresponding estimated financial flows. U.S. net investment in assets abroad contributed a further outflow, amounting to $484 billion, in 2011. Financing the sum of these was a financial inflow, that is a net increase in foreign-owned assets in the United States, estimated at $1,001 billion. The net of the estimated financial flows does not equal the current-account balance because of small capital transactions, a net derivatives balance of $39 billion, and a negative $89 billion ITA statistical discrepancy. (Table 7-6A)

- Large quarterly and annual variations during the last several years in many types of financial flows, including those involving official assets, are evidence of an extreme amount of international financial turbulence and official intervention. (Table 7-6A and B)

- Before the 1980s, the United States was a net creditor with respect to the rest of the world. In other words, the value of the stock of U.S.-owned assets abroad exceeded the value of foreign-owned assets in the United States. Since then, the persistent net financial inflows associated with current-account deficits have cumulated, resulting in a growing net debtor status, with the value of foreign-owned assets in the United States exceeding the value of U.S.-owned assets abroad by $4.0 trillion as of the end of 2011. (Table 7-8)

Table 7-6A. U.S. International Transactions: Recent Data

(Millions of dollars, seasonally adjusted.)

Year and quarter	Current account									
	Exports of goods and services and income receipts									
					Income receipts					
						Income receipts on U.S.-owned assets abroad				
	Total	Exports of goods and services	Exports of goods	Exports of services	Total	Total	Direct investment receipts	Other private receipts	U.S. government receipts	Compensation of employees
1960	30 556	25 940	19 650	6 290	4 616	4 616	3 621	646	349	. . .
1961	31 402	26 403	20 108	6 295	4 999	4 999	3 823	793	383	. . .
1962	33 340	27 722	20 781	6 941	5 618	5 618	4 241	904	473	. . .
1963	35 776	29 620	22 272	7 348	6 157	6 157	4 636	1 022	499	. . .
1964	40 165	33 341	25 501	7 840	6 824	6 824	5 106	1 256	462	. . .
1965	42 722	35 285	26 461	8 824	7 437	7 437	5 506	1 421	510	. . .
1966	46 454	38 926	29 310	9 616	7 528	7 528	5 260	1 669	599	. . .
1967	49 353	41 333	30 666	10 667	8 021	8 021	5 603	1 781	636	. . .
1968	54 911	45 543	33 626	11 917	9 367	9 367	6 591	2 021	756	. . .
1969	60 132	49 220	36 414	12 806	10 913	10 913	7 649	2 338	925	. . .
1970	68 387	56 640	42 469	14 171	11 748	11 748	8 169	2 671	907	. . .
1971	72 384	59 677	43 319	16 358	12 707	12 707	9 160	2 641	906	. . .
1972	81 986	67 222	49 381	17 841	14 765	14 765	10 949	2 949	866	. . .
1973	113 050	91 242	71 410	19 832	21 808	21 808	16 542	4 330	936	. . .
1974	148 484	120 897	98 306	22 591	27 587	27 587	19 157	7 356	1 074	. . .
1975	157 936	132 585	107 088	25 497	25 351	25 351	16 595	7 644	1 112	. . .
1976	172 090	142 716	114 745	27 971	29 375	29 375	18 999	9 043	1 332	. . .
1977	184 655	152 301	120 816	31 485	32 354	32 354	19 673	11 057	1 625	. . .
1978	220 516	178 428	142 075	36 353	42 088	42 088	25 458	14 788	1 843	. . .
1979	287 965	224 131	184 439	39 692	63 834	63 834	38 183	23 356	2 295	. . .
1980	344 440	271 834	224 250	47 584	72 606	72 606	37 146	32 898	2 562	. . .
1981	380 928	294 398	237 044	57 354	86 529	86 529	32 549	50 300	3 680	. . .
1982	366 983	275 236	211 157	64 079	91 747	91 747	29 469	58 160	4 118	. . .
1983	356 106	266 106	201 799	64 307	90 000	90 000	31 750	53 418	4 832	. . .
1984	399 913	291 094	219 926	71 168	108 819	108 819	35 325	68 267	5 227	. . .
1985	387 612	289 070	215 915	73 155	98 542	98 542	35 410	57 633	5 499	. . .
1986	407 098	310 033	223 344	86 689	97 064	96 156	36 938	52 806	6 413	908
1987	457 053	348 869	250 208	98 661	108 184	107 190	46 288	55 592	5 311	994
1988	567 862	431 149	320 230	110 919	136 713	135 718	58 445	70 571	6 703	995
1989	648 290	487 003	359 916	127 087	161 287	160 270	61 981	92 638	5 651	1 017
1990	706 975	535 233	387 401	147 832	171 742	170 570	65 973	94 072	10 525	1 172
1991	727 557	578 344	414 083	164 261	149 214	147 924	58 718	81 186	8 019	1 290
1992	750 648	616 883	439 631	177 252	133 766	131 970	57 538	67 316	7 115	1 796
1993	778 920	642 863	456 943	185 920	136 057	134 237	67 246	61 865	5 126	1 820
1994	869 775	703 254	502 859	200 395	166 521	164 578	77 344	83 106	4 128	1 943
1995	1 004 631	794 387	575 204	219 183	210 244	208 065	95 260	108 092	4 713	2 179
1996	1 077 731	851 602	612 113	239 489	226 129	223 948	102 505	116 852	4 591	2 181
1997	1 191 257	934 453	678 366	256 087	256 804	254 534	115 323	135 652	3 559	2 270
1998	1 194 993	933 174	670 416	262 758	261 819	259 382	103 963	151 818	3 601	2 437
1999	1 262 431	967 008	698 218	268 790	295 423	291 177	131 626	156 354	3 197	4 246
2000	1 425 260	1 072 782	784 781	288 002	352 478	348 083	151 839	192 398	3 846	4 395
2001	1 300 156	1 007 725	731 189	276 537	292 430	287 918	128 665	155 692	3 561	4 512
2002	1 263 580	980 879	697 439	283 440	282 701	278 131	145 590	129 238	3 303	4 570
2003	1 345 930	1 023 519	729 816	293 703	322 411	317 740	186 417	126 529	4 794	4 671
2004	1 578 939	1 163 146	821 986	341 160	415 793	411 059	250 606	157 313	3 140	4 734
2005	1 824 780	1 287 441	911 686	375 755	537 339	532 542	294 538	235 120	2 884	4 796
2006	2 144 443	1 459 823	1 039 406	420 417	684 620	679 608	324 816	352 122	2 670	5 012
2007	2 488 394	1 654 561	1 163 957	490 604	833 834	828 732	370 758	455 436	2 538	5 102
2008	2 656 585	1 842 682	1 307 499	535 183	813 903	808 721	413 739	389 881	5 101	5 182
2009	2 180 553	1 578 945	1 069 733	509 212	601 609	596 131	357 793	233 546	4 792	5 478
2010	2 518 767	1 842 485	1 288 882	553 603	676 282	670 641	444 044	225 103	1 494	5 641
2011	2 847 988	2 103 367	1 497 406	605 961	744 621	738 810	480 238	256 649	1 923	5 811
2008										
1st quarter	670 832	455 042	323 357	131 685	215 789	214 491	107 490	106 229	772	1 298
2nd quarter	692 907	478 774	342 620	136 154	214 133	212 835	112 619	99 424	792	1 299
3rd quarter	691 564	483 210	346 910	136 300	208 354	207 055	108 316	97 371	1 368	1 298
4th quarter	601 284	425 657	294 612	131 044	175 627	174 341	85 314	86 857	2 170	1 286
2009										
1st quarter	525 222	378 471	254 092	124 379	146 751	145 387	78 005	64 906	2 476	1 364
2nd quarter	522 332	379 076	253 850	125 225	143 257	141 888	83 131	57 640	1 117	1 369
3rd quarter	546 847	397 070	270 106	126 964	149 776	148 403	91 929	55 735	739	1 373
4th quarter	586 153	424 328	291 685	132 643	161 825	160 452	104 727	55 265	460	1 372
2010										
1st quarter	599 298	437 334	304 032	133 302	161 964	160 556	105 412	54 706	438	1 408
2nd quarter	617 954	451 663	315 478	136 184	166 292	164 880	108 759	55 771	350	1 412
3rd quarter	636 778	465 468	325 198	140 271	171 310	169 898	113 421	56 122	355	1 412
4th quarter	664 736	488 020	344 175	143 845	176 716	175 307	116 452	58 504	351	1 409
2011										
1st quarter	689 593	508 811	360 917	147 894	180 781	179 328	118 621	60 262	445	1 453
2nd quarter	713 499	524 000	372 160	151 839	189 499	188 047	123 417	64 123	506	1 452
3rd quarter	724 800	537 351	382 161	155 190	187 449	185 994	119 106	66 361	527	1 455
4th quarter	720 095	533 204	382 167	151 037	186 891	185 441	119 094	65 903	444	1 450

. . . = Not available.

Table 7-6A. U.S. International Transactions: Recent Data—*Continued*

(Millions of dollars, seasonally adjusted.)

Year and quarter	Current account—*Continued*									
	Imports of goods and services and income payments [1]									
					Income payments					
						Income payments on foreign-owned assets in the U.S.				
	Total	Imports of goods and services	Imports of goods	Imports of services	Total	Total	Direct investment payments	Other private payments	U.S. government payments	Compensation of employees
1960	-23 670	-22 432	-14 758	-7 674	-1 238	-1 238	-394	-511	-332	. . .
1961	-23 453	-22 208	-14 537	-7 671	-1 245	-1 245	-432	-535	-278	. . .
1962	-25 676	-24 352	-16 260	-8 092	-1 324	-1 324	-399	-586	-339	. . .
1963	-26 970	-25 410	-17 048	-8 362	-1 560	-1 560	-459	-701	-401	. . .
1964	-29 102	-27 319	-18 700	-8 619	-1 783	-1 783	-529	-802	-453	. . .
1965	-32 708	-30 621	-21 510	-9 111	-2 088	-2 088	-657	-942	-489	. . .
1966	-38 468	-35 987	-25 493	-10 494	-2 481	-2 481	-711	-1 221	-549	. . .
1967	-41 476	-38 729	-26 866	-11 863	-2 747	-2 747	-821	-1 328	-598	. . .
1968	-48 671	-45 293	-32 991	-12 302	-3 378	-3 378	-876	-1 800	-702	. . .
1969	-53 998	-49 129	-35 807	-13 322	-4 869	-4 869	-848	-3 244	-777	. . .
1970	-59 901	-54 386	-39 866	-14 520	-5 515	-5 515	-875	-3 617	-1 024	. . .
1971	-66 414	-60 979	-45 579	-15 400	-5 435	-5 435	-1 164	-2 428	-1 844	. . .
1972	-79 237	-72 665	-55 797	-16 868	-6 572	-6 572	-1 284	-2 604	-2 684	. . .
1973	-98 997	-89 342	-70 499	-18 843	-9 655	-9 655	-1 610	-4 209	-3 836	. . .
1974	-137 274	-125 190	-103 811	-21 379	-12 084	-12 084	-1 331	-6 491	-4 262	. . .
1975	-132 745	-120 181	-98 185	-21 996	-12 564	-12 564	-2 234	-5 788	-4 542	. . .
1976	-162 109	-148 798	-124 228	-24 570	-13 311	-13 311	-3 110	-5 681	-4 520	. . .
1977	-193 764	-179 547	-151 907	-27 640	-14 217	-14 217	-2 834	-5 841	-5 542	. . .
1978	-229 870	-208 191	-176 002	-32 189	-21 680	-21 680	-4 211	-8 795	-8 674	. . .
1979	-281 657	-248 696	-212 007	-36 689	-32 961	-32 961	-6 357	-15 481	-11 122	. . .
1980	-333 774	-291 241	-249 750	-41 491	-42 532	-42 532	-8 635	-21 214	-12 684	. . .
1981	-364 196	-310 570	-265 067	-45 503	-53 626	-53 626	-6 898	-29 415	-17 313	. . .
1982	-355 975	-299 391	-247 642	-51 749	-56 583	-56 583	-2 114	-35 187	-19 282	. . .
1983	-377 488	-323 874	-268 901	-54 973	-53 614	-53 614	-4 120	-30 501	-18 993	. . .
1984	-473 923	-400 166	-332 418	-67 748	-73 756	-73 756	-8 443	-44 158	-21 155	. . .
1985	-483 769	-410 950	-338 088	-72 862	-72 819	-72 819	-6 945	-42 745	-23 129	. . .
1986	-530 142	-448 572	-368 425	-80 147	-81 571	-78 893	-6 856	-47 412	-24 625	-2 678
1987	-594 443	-500 552	-409 765	-90 787	-93 891	-91 553	-7 676	-57 659	-26 218	-2 338
1988	-663 741	-545 715	-447 189	-98 526	-118 026	-116 179	-12 150	-72 314	-31 715	-1 847
1989	-721 607	-580 144	-477 665	-102 479	-141 463	-139 177	-7 045	-93 768	-38 364	-2 286
1990	-759 290	-616 097	-498 438	-117 659	-143 192	-139 728	-3 450	-95 508	-40 770	-3 464
1991	-734 563	-609 479	-491 020	-118 459	-125 084	-121 058	2 266	-82 452	-40 872	-4 026
1992	-765 626	-656 094	-536 528	-119 566	-109 531	-104 779	-2 189	-63 509	-39 081	-4 752
1993	-823 914	-713 173	-589 394	-123 779	-110 741	-105 609	-7 943	-58 290	-39 376	-5 132
1994	-951 122	-801 747	-668 690	-133 057	-149 375	-143 423	-22 150	-77 081	-44 192	-5 952
1995	-1 080 124	-890 771	-749 374	-141 397	-189 353	-183 090	-30 318	-97 149	-55 623	-6 263
1996	-1 159 478	-955 667	-803 113	-152 554	-203 811	-197 511	-33 093	-97 800	-66 618	-6 300
1997	-1 286 921	-1 042 726	-876 794	-165 932	-244 195	-237 529	-42 950	-112 878	-81 701	-6 666
1998	-1 356 868	-1 099 314	-918 637	-180 677	-257 554	-250 560	-38 418	-127 988	-84 154	-6 994
1999	-1 513 659	-1 230 168	-1 034 389	-195 779	-283 492	-272 082	-53 437	-138 120	-80 525	-11 410
2000	-1 782 832	-1 449 532	-1 230 568	-218 964	-333 300	-322 345	-56 910	-180 918	-84 517	-10 955
2001	-1 632 198	-1 369 496	-1 152 464	-217 032	-262 702	-250 989	-12 783	-159 825	-78 381	-11 713
2002	-1 655 837	-1 398 311	-1 171 930	-226 381	-257 526	-245 164	-43 244	-127 012	-74 908	-12 362
2003	-1 793 223	-1 514 503	-1 270 225	-244 278	-278 721	-266 743	-73 750	-119 051	-73 942	-11 978
2004	-2 119 214	-1 768 502	-1 485 492	-283 010	-350 712	-337 691	-99 754	-155 266	-82 671	-13 021
2005	-2 464 813	-1 996 065	-1 692 416	-303 649	-468 748	-453 800	-121 333	-228 408	-104 059	-14 948
2006	-2 853 549	-2 213 111	-1 875 095	-338 016	-640 438	-624 912	-150 770	-338 897	-135 245	-15 526
2007	-3 083 637	-2 351 288	-1 982 843	-368 446	-732 349	-717 623	-126 174	-426 796	-164 653	-14 725
2008	-3 207 834	-2 541 020	-2 137 608	-403 413	-666 814	-650 880	-129 447	-354 609	-166 824	-15 934
2009	-2 439 990	-1 958 099	-1 575 491	-382 608	-481 891	-468 579	-104 828	-219 396	-144 355	-13 312
2010	-2 829 645	-2 337 222	-1 934 006	-403 216	-492 423	-479 624	-146 149	-196 354	-137 121	-12 799
2011	-3 180 861	-2 663 247	-2 235 819	-427 428	-517 614	-503 796	-158 559	-212 506	-132 731	-13 817
2008										
1st quarter	-814 329	-637 577	-539 441	-98 135	-176 752	-172 687	-34 823	-95 814	-42 050	-4 065
2nd quarter	-836 822	-662 620	-562 565	-100 055	-174 203	-170 234	-38 814	-88 522	-42 898	-3 969
3rd quarter	-833 469	-669 345	-565 850	-103 495	-164 124	-160 196	-28 913	-89 978	-41 305	-3 928
4th quarter	-723 214	-571 479	-469 752	-101 727	-151 735	-147 763	-26 897	-80 295	-40 571	-3 972
2009										
1st quarter	-594 817	-471 903	-376 641	-95 262	-122 913	-119 327	-16 363	-64 040	-38 924	-3 587
2nd quarter	-578 983	-458 818	-364 901	-93 917	-120 165	-116 749	-26 094	-54 277	-36 378	-3 416
3rd quarter	-609 608	-494 515	-398 962	-95 553	-115 093	-111 872	-26 230	-50 734	-34 908	-3 221
4th quarter	-656 583	-532 862	-434 986	-97 876	-123 721	-120 632	-36 142	-50 345	-34 145	-3 089
2010										
1st quarter	-675 611	-555 285	-456 570	-98 716	-120 325	-117 166	-34 257	-48 953	-33 956	-3 159
2nd quarter	-697 957	-579 349	-480 118	-99 231	-118 607	-115 346	-32 183	-49 003	-34 160	-3 261
3rd quarter	-718 137	-594 605	-492 068	-102 536	-123 532	-120 296	-37 515	-48 152	-34 629	-3 236
4th quarter	-737 941	-607 983	-505 250	-102 733	-129 958	-126 816	-42 194	-50 246	-34 376	-3 143
2011										
1st quarter	-774 367	-646 036	-542 276	-103 761	-128 330	-124 863	-39 891	-51 501	-33 471	-3 467
2nd quarter	-798 839	-665 549	-559 344	-106 205	-133 290	-129 835	-43 855	-53 193	-32 787	-3 455
3rd quarter	-801 143	-672 173	-562 778	-109 395	-128 971	-125 508	-38 261	-54 157	-33 090	-3 463
4th quarter	-806 512	-679 489	-571 421	-108 068	-127 022	-123 590	-36 552	-53 655	-33 383	-3 433

[1]A minus sign indicates imports of goods and services or payments of incomes.
. . . = Not available.

Table 7-6A. U.S. International Transactions: Recent Data—*Continued*

(Millions of dollars, seasonally adjusted.)

Year and quarter	Current account—*Continued*				Capital account transactions, net [2]	Financial account					
	Unilateral current transfers, net [2]					U.S.-owned assets abroad, net, excluding financial derivatives [2]					
		U.S. government		Private remittances and other transfers			U.S. official reserve assets, net				
	Total	Grants	Pensions and other transfers			Total	Total	Gold	Special drawing rights	Reserve position in the IMF	Foreign currencies
1960	-4 062	-3 367	-273	-423	. . .	-4 099	2 145	1 703	0	442	0
1961	-4 127	-3 320	-373	-434	. . .	-5 538	607	857	0	-135	-115
1962	-4 277	-3 453	-347	-477	. . .	-4 174	1 535	890	0	626	19
1963	-4 392	-3 479	-339	-575	. . .	-7 270	378	461	0	29	-112
1964	-4 240	-3 227	-399	-614	. . .	-9 560	171	125	0	266	-220
1965	-4 583	-3 444	-463	-677	. . .	-5 716	1 225	1 665	0	-94	-346
1966	-4 955	-3 802	-499	-655	. . .	-7 321	570	571	0	537	-538
1967	-5 294	-3 844	-571	-879	. . .	-9 757	53	1 170	0	-94	-1 023
1968	-5 629	-4 256	-537	-836	. . .	-10 977	-870	1 173	0	-870	-1 173
1969	-5 735	-4 259	-537	-939	. . .	-11 585	-1 179	-967	0	-1 034	822
1970	-6 156	-4 449	-611	-1 096	. . .	-9 337	2 481	787	-851	389	2 156
1971	-7 402	-5 589	-696	-1 117	. . .	-12 475	2 349	866	-249	1 350	382
1972	-8 544	-6 665	-770	-1 109	. . .	-14 497	-4	547	-703	153	-1
1973	-6 913	-4 748	-915	-1 250	. . .	-22 874	158	0	9	-33	182
1974	-9 249	-7 293	-939	-1 017	. . .	-34 745	-1 467	0	-172	-1 265	-30
1975	-7 075	-5 101	-1 068	-906	. . .	-39 703	-849	0	-66	-466	-317
1976	-5 686	-3 519	-1 250	-917	. . .	-51 269	-2 558	0	-78	-2 212	-268
1977	-5 226	-2 990	-1 378	-859	. . .	-34 785	-375	-118	-121	-294	158
1978	-5 788	-3 412	-1 532	-844	. . .	-61 130	732	-65	1 249	4 231	-4 683
1979	-6 593	-4 015	-1 658	-920	. . .	-66 054	-1 133	-65	-1 136	-189	257
1980	-8 349	-5 486	-1 818	-1 044	. . .	-86 967	-8 155	0	-16	-1 667	-6 472
1981	-11 702	-5 145	-2 041	-4 516	. . .	-114 147	-5 175	*	-1 823	-2 491	-861
1982	-16 544	-6 087	-2 251	-8 207	. . .	-127 882	-4 965	0	-1 371	-2 552	-1 041
1983	-17 310	-6 469	-2 207	-8 635	. . .	-66 373	-1 196	0	-66	-4 434	3 304
1984	-20 335	-8 696	-2 159	-9 479	. . .	-40 376	-3 131	0	-979	-995	-1 156
1985	-21 998	-11 268	-2 138	-8 593	. . .	-44 752	-3 858	0	-897	908	-3 869
1986	-24 132	-11 883	-2 372	-9 877	. . .	-111 723	312	0	-246	1 501	-942
1987	-23 265	-10 309	-2 409	-10 548	. . .	-79 296	9 149	0	-509	2 070	7 588
1988	-25 274	-10 537	-2 709	-12 028	. . .	-106 573	-3 912	0	127	1 025	-5 064
1989	-26 169	-10 860	-2 775	-12 534	-207	-175 383	-25 293	0	-535	471	-25 229
1990	-26 654	-10 359	-3 224	-13 070	-7 220	-81 234	-2 158	0	-192	731	-2 697
1991	9 904	29 193	-3 775	-15 514	-5 130	-64 388	5 763	0	-177	-367	6 307
1992	-36 636	-16 320	-4 043	-16 273	1 449	-74 410	3 901	0	2 316	-2 692	4 277
1993	-39 812	-17 036	-4 104	-18 672	-714	-200 552	-1 379	0	-537	-44	-797
1994	-40 265	-14 978	-4 556	-20 731	-1 111	-178 937	5 346	0	-441	494	5 293
1995	-38 074	-11 190	-3 451	-23 433	-222	-352 264	-9 742	0	-808	-2 466	-6 468
1996	-43 017	-15 401	-4 466	-23 150	-7	-413 409	6 668	0	370	-1 280	7 578
1997	-45 062	-12 472	-4 191	-28 399	-256	-485 475	-1 010	0	-350	-3 575	2 915
1998	-53 187	-13 270	-4 305	-35 612	-8	-353 829	-6 783	0	-147	-5 119	-1 517
1999	-50 428	-13 774	-4 406	-32 248	-4 176	-504 062	8 747	0	10	5 484	3 253
2000	-58 767	-16 836	-4 705	-37 226	-1	-560 523	-290	0	-722	2 308	-1 876
2001	-64 561	-11 591	-5 798	-47 172	13 198	-382 616	-4 911	0	-630	-3 600	-681
2002	-64 990	-17 139	-5 125	-42 726	-141	-294 646	-3 681	0	-475	-2 632	-574
2003	-71 796	-22 175	-5 341	-44 280	-1 821	-325 424	1 523	0	601	1 494	-572
2004	-88 243	-23 704	-6 264	-58 275	3 049	-100 087	2 805	0	-398	3 826	-623
2005	-105 741	-33 615	-6 303	-65 822	13 116	-546 631	14 096	0	4 511	10 200	-615
2006	-91 515	-27 767	-6 508	-57 240	-1 788	-128 572	2 374	0	-223	3 331	-734
2007	-115 061	-34 567	-7 323	-73 170	384	-145 360	-122	0	-154	1 021	-989
2008	-125 885	-36 461	-8 390	-81 034	6 010	332 109	-4 848	0	-106	-3 473	-1 269
2009	-122 459	-42 699	-8 874	-70 886	-140	-119 535	-52 256	0	-48 230	-3 357	-669
2010	-131 074	-42 736	-9 581	-78 757	-157	-939 484	-1 834	0	-31	-1 293	-510
2011	-133 053	-47 350	-8 947	-76 756	-1 212	-483 653	-15 877	0	1 752	-18 079	450
2008											
1st quarter	-33 735	-10 442	-2 082	-21 211	-8	-238 333	-276	0	-29	112	-359
2nd quarter	-31 347	-8 012	-2 097	-21 238	-18	177 984	-1 267	0	-22	-955	-290
3rd quarter	-31 703	-8 711	-2 100	-20 892	6 043	113 445	-179	0	-30	256	-405
4th quarter	-29 103	-9 296	-2 113	-17 694	-7	279 012	-3 126	0	-25	-2 886	-215
2009											
1st quarter	-28 905	-8 932	-2 180	-17 793	-20	119 562	-982	0	-15	-754	-213
2nd quarter	-30 331	-11 184	-2 222	-16 925	-29	57 395	-3 632	0	-8	-3 485	-139
3rd quarter	-32 935	-13 315	-2 233	-17 387	-36	-297 502	-49 021	0	-47 720	-1 098	-203
4th quarter	-30 289	-9 267	-2 241	-18 780	-56	1 010	1 379	0	-487	1 980	-114
2010											
1st quarter	-34 681	-11 772	-2 352	-20 557	-3	-269 433	-773	0	-7	-581	-185
2nd quarter	-31 710	-9 479	-2 394	-19 838	-2	-154 408	-165	0	-6	-77	-82
3rd quarter	-33 216	-10 560	-2 420	-20 236	-146	-294 523	-1 096	0	-8	-956	-132
4th quarter	-31 466	-10 925	-2 415	-18 126	-7	-221 120	200	0	-10	321	-111
2011											
1st quarter	-35 223	-11 136	-2 202	-21 884	-29	-372 944	-3 619	0	1 961	-6 428	848
2nd quarter	-33 777	-13 486	-2 227	-18 064	-829	7 418	-6 267	0	-159	-5 974	-134
3rd quarter	-31 815	-11 176	-2 250	-18 389	-300	-91 896	-4 079	0	-27	-3 909	-143
4th quarter	-32 240	-11 551	-2 269	-18 419	-55	-26 231	-1 912	0	-23	-1 768	-121

[2]A minus sign indicates increases in U.S. official assets or financial outflows.
. . . = Not available.
* = Less than $500,000 (+/-).

Table 7-6A. U.S. International Transactions: Recent Data—*Continued*

(Millions of dollars, seasonally adjusted.)

Year and quarter	Financial account—*Continued* U.S.-owned assets abroad, net, excluding financial derivatives [3]—*Continued* U.S. government assets other than official reserve assets, net Total	U.S. credits and other long-term assets	Repayments on U.S. credits and other long-term assets	U.S. foreign currency holdings and short-term assets, net	U.S. private assets, net Total	Direct investment	Foreign securities	U.S. claims On unaffiliated foreigners reported by U.S. nonbanking concerns	Reported by U.S. banks, and securities brokers
1960	-1 100	-1 214	642	-528	-5 144	-2 940	-663	-394	-1 148
1961	-910	-1 928	1 279	-261	-5 235	-2 653	-762	-558	-1 261
1962	-1 085	-2 128	1 288	-245	-4 623	-2 851	-969	-354	-450
1963	-1 662	-2 204	988	-447	-5 986	-3 483	-1 105	157	-1 556
1964	-1 680	-2 382	720	-19	-8 050	-3 760	-677	-1 108	-2 505
1965	-1 605	-2 463	874	-16	-5 336	-5 011	-759	341	93
1966	-1 543	-2 513	1 235	-265	-6 347	-5 418	-720	-442	233
1967	-2 423	-3 638	1 005	209	-7 386	-4 805	-1 308	-779	-495
1968	-2 274	-3 722	1 386	62	-7 833	-5 295	-1 569	-1 203	233
1969	-2 200	-3 489	1 200	89	-8 206	-5 960	-1 549	-126	-570
1970	-1 589	-3 293	1 721	-16	-10 229	-7 590	-1 076	-596	-967
1971	-1 884	-4 181	2 115	182	-12 940	-7 618	-1 113	-1 229	-2 980
1972	-1 568	-3 819	2 086	165	-12 925	-7 747	-618	-1 054	-3 506
1973	-2 644	-4 638	2 596	-602	-20 388	-11 353	-671	-2 383	-5 980
1974	366	-5 001	4 826	541	-33 643	-9 052	-1 854	-3 221	-19 516
1975	-3 474	-5 941	2 475	-9	-35 380	-14 244	-6 247	-1 357	-13 532
1976	-4 214	-6 943	2 596	133	-44 498	-11 949	-8 885	-2 296	-21 368
1977	-3 693	-6 445	2 719	33	-30 717	-11 890	-5 460	-1 940	-11 427
1978	-4 660	-7 470	2 941	-131	-57 202	-16 056	-3 626	-3 853	-33 667
1979	-3 746	-7 697	3 926	25	-61 176	-25 222	-4 726	-5 014	-26 213
1980	-5 162	-9 860	4 456	242	-73 651	-19 222	-3 568	-4 023	-46 838
1981	-5 097	-9 674	4 413	164	-103 875	-9 624	-5 699	-4 377	-84 175
1982	-6 131	-10 063	4 292	-360	-116 786	-4 556	-7 983	6 823	-111 070
1983	-5 006	-9 967	5 012	-51	-60 172	-12 528	-6 762	-10 954	-29 928
1984	-5 489	-9 599	4 490	-379	-31 757	-16 407	-4 756	533	-11 127
1985	-2 821	-7 657	4 719	117	-38 074	-18 927	-7 481	-10 342	-1 323
1986	-2 022	-9 084	6 089	973	-110 014	-23 995	-4 271	-21 773	-59 975
1987	1 006	-6 506	7 625	-113	-89 450	-35 034	-5 251	-7 046	-42 119
1988	2 967	-7 680	10 370	277	-105 628	-22 528	-7 980	-21 193	-53 927
1989	1 233	-5 608	6 725	115	-151 323	-43 447	-22 070	-27 646	-58 160
1990	2 317	-8 410	10 856	-130	-81 393	-37 183	-28 765	-27 824	12 379
1991	2 924	-12 879	16 776	-974	-73 075	-37 889	-45 673	11 097	-610
1992	-1 667	-7 408	5 807	-66	-76 644	-48 266	-49 166	-387	21 175
1993	-351	-6 311	6 270	-310	-198 822	-83 950	-146 253	766	30 615
1994	-390	-5 383	5 088	-95	-183 893	-80 167	-63 190	-36 336	-4 200
1995	-984	-4 859	4 125	-250	-341 538	-98 750	-122 394	-45 286	-75 108
1996	-989	-5 025	3 930	106	-419 088	-91 885	-149 315	-86 333	-91 555
1997	68	-5 417	5 438	47	-484 533	-104 803	-116 852	-121 760	-141 118
1998	-422	-4 678	4 111	145	-346 624	-142 644	-130 204	-38 204	-35 572
1999	2 750	-6 175	9 559	-634	-515 559	-224 934	-122 236	-97 704	-70 685
2000	-941	-5 182	4 265	-24	-559 292	-159 212	-127 908	-138 790	-133 382
2001	-486	-4 431	3 873	72	-377 219	-142 349	-90 644	-8 520	-135 706
2002	345	-5 251	5 701	-105	-291 310	-154 460	-48 568	-50 022	-38 260
2003	537	-7 279	7 981	-165	-327 484	-149 564	-146 722	-18 184	-13 014
2004	1 710	-3 044	4 716	38	-1 005 385	-316 223	-170 549	-152 566	-366 047
2005	5 539	-2 255	5 603	2 191	-566 266	-36 235	-251 199	-71 207	-207 625
2006	5 346	-2 992	8 329	9	-1 293 449	-244 922	-365 129	-181 299	-502 099
2007	-22 273	-2 475	4 104	-23 902	-1 431 209	-414 039	-366 512	-928	-649 730
2008	-529 615	-2 202	2 354	-529 766	866 571	-329 081	197 347	456 177	542 128
2009	541 342	-4 069	2 133	543 278	-608 622	-289 451	-227 024	153 695	-245 842
2010	7 540	-4 976	2 408	10 108	-945 189	-327 877	-138 984	32 969	-511 297
2011	-103 666	-7 307	3 333	-99 692	-364 110	-419 332	-146 797	-11 608	213 627
2008									
1st quarter	3 268	-179	490	2 957	-241 325	-92 199	-11 990	120 047	-257 183
2nd quarter	-41 592	-1 106	497	-40 983	220 844	-95 140	-4 820	75 492	245 312
3rd quarter	-225 997	-475	695	-226 217	339 621	-66 710	115 406	121 264	169 661
4th quarter	-265 293	-442	672	-265 523	547 432	-75 031	98 751	139 374	384 338
2009									
1st quarter	244 102	-240	484	243 858	-123 559	-67 510	-36 497	18 234	-37 786
2nd quarter	193 750	-1 947	432	195 265	-132 723	-56 711	-94 166	36 979	-18 825
3rd quarter	57 736	-616	534	57 818	-306 217	-74 759	-54 256	84 760	-261 962
4th quarter	45 754	-1 266	683	46 337	-46 122	-90 470	-42 105	13 722	72 731
2010									
1st quarter	9 433	-1 247	399	10 281	-278 092	-109 091	-42 124	45 003	-171 880
2nd quarter	-2 441	-1 835	783	-1 389	-151 802	-65 020	-15 728	6 596	-77 650
3rd quarter	788	-1 027	679	1 136	-294 215	-90 647	-39 329	2 067	-166 306
4th quarter	-240	-867	547	80	-221 080	-63 119	-41 803	-20 697	-95 461
2011									
1st quarter	-547	-1 307	610	150	-368 778	-104 404	-85 472	-92 203	-86 699
2nd quarter	-1 358	-2 337	1 259	-279	15 042	-133 397	-57 195	6 147	199 487
3rd quarter	-1 137	-1 396	812	-553	-86 679	-70 323	-40 110	9 326	14 428
4th quarter	-100 624	-2 267	653	-99 010	76 305	-111 208	35 980	65 122	86 411

[3]A minus sign indicates increases in U.S. official assets or financial outflows.

Table 7-6A. U.S. International Transactions: Recent Data—*Continued*

(Millions of dollars, seasonally adjusted.)

Year and quarter	Total	Foreign-owned assets in the United States, net, excluding financial derivatives [4]											
		Foreign official assets in the United States, net							Other foreign assets in the United States, net				
		Total	U.S. government securities			Other U.S. govern-ment liabilities	U.S. liabilities reported by U.S. banks and securities brokers	Other foreign official assets	Total	Direct investment	U.S. Treasury securities	U.S. securities other than Treasury securities	U.S. currency
			Total	U.S. Treasury securities	Other								
1960	2 294	1 473	655	655	0	215	603	0	821	315	-364	282	. . .
1961	2 705	765	233	233	0	25	508	0	1 939	311	151	324	. . .
1962	1 911	1 270	1 409	1 410	-1	152	-291	0	641	346	-66	134	. . .
1963	3 217	1 986	816	803	12	429	742	0	1 231	231	-149	287	. . .
1964	3 643	1 660	432	434	-2	298	930	0	1 983	322	-146	-85	. . .
1965	742	134	-141	-134	-7	65	210	0	607	415	-131	-358	. . .
1966	3 661	-672	-1 527	-1 548	21	113	742	0	4 333	425	-356	906	. . .
1967	7 379	3 451	2 261	2 222	39	83	1 106	0	3 928	698	-135	1 016	. . .
1968	9 928	-774	-769	-798	29	-15	10	0	10 703	807	136	4 414	. . .
1969	12 702	-1 301	-2 343	-2 269	-74	251	792	0	14 002	1 263	-68	3 130	. . .
1970	7 226	7 775	9 439	9 411	28	411	-2 075	0	-550	1 464	81	2 189	. . .
1971	23 687	27 596	26 570	26 578	-8	207	819	0	-3 909	367	-24	2 289	. . .
1972	22 171	11 185	8 470	8 213	257	892	1 638	185	10 986	949	-39	4 507	. . .
1973	18 388	6 026	641	59	582	936	4 126	323	12 362	2 800	-216	4 041	. . .
1974	35 227	10 546	4 172	3 270	902	301	5 818	254	24 682	4 760	697	378	986
1975	16 870	7 027	5 563	4 658	905	1 517	-2 158	2 104	9 843	2 603	2 590	2 503	1 200
1976	37 839	17 693	9 892	9 319	573	4 627	969	2 205	20 147	4 347	2 783	1 284	1 321
1977	52 770	36 816	32 538	30 230	2 308	1 400	773	2 105	15 954	3 728	534	2 437	1 451
1978	66 275	33 678	24 221	23 555	666	2 476	5 551	1 430	32 597	7 897	2 178	2 254	2 239
1979	40 693	-12 526	-21 972	-22 435	463	1 099	7 213	1 135	53 218	11 877	4 060	1 351	1 702
1980	62 037	16 649	11 895	9 708	2 187	1 767	-159	3 145	45 388	16 918	2 645	5 457	2 773
1981	85 684	6 053	6 322	5 019	1 303	755	-3 670	2 646	79 631	25 195	2 927	6 905	1 559
1982	95 056	3 593	5 085	5 779	-694	605	-1 747	-350	91 464	12 635	7 027	6 085	2 467
1983	87 399	5 845	6 496	6 972	-476	602	545	-1 798	81 554	10 372	8 689	8 164	4 105
1984	116 048	3 140	4 703	4 690	13	739	555	-2 857	112 908	24 468	23 001	12 568	2 396
1985	144 231	-1 119	-1 139	-838	-301	844	645	-1 469	145 349	19 742	20 433	50 962	3 316
1986	228 330	35 648	33 150	34 364	-1 214	2 195	1 187	-884	192 681	35 420	3 809	70 969	2 421
1987	247 100	45 387	44 802	43 238	1 564	-2 326	3 918	-1 007	201 713	58 470	-7 643	42 120	3 866
1988	244 833	39 758	43 050	41 741	1 309	-467	-319	-2 506	205 075	57 735	20 239	26 353	4 111
1989	222 777	8 503	1 532	149	1 383	160	4 976	1 835	214 274	68 274	29 618	38 767	3 749
1990	139 357	33 910	30 243	29 576	667	1 868	3 385	-1 586	105 447	48 494	-2 534	1 592	16 586
1991	108 221	17 389	16 147	14 846	1 301	1 367	-1 484	1 359	90 833	23 171	18 826	35 144	12 813
1992	168 349	40 477	22 403	18 454	3 949	2 191	16 571	-688	127 872	19 823	37 131	30 043	11 086
1993	279 758	71 753	53 014	48 952	4 062	1 313	14 841	2 585	208 005	51 362	24 381	80 092	16 618
1994	303 174	39 583	36 827	30 750	6 077	1 564	3 665	-2 473	263 591	46 121	34 274	56 971	20 585
1995	435 102	109 880	72 712	68 977	3 735	-105	34 008	3 265	325 222	57 776	91 544	77 249	8 840
1996	547 885	126 724	120 679	115 671	5 008	-982	5 704	1 323	421 161	86 502	147 022	103 272	14 151
1997	704 452	19 036	-2 161	-6 690	4 529	-881	22 286	-208	685 416	105 603	130 435	161 409	22 425
1998	420 794	-19 903	-3 589	-9 921	6 332	-3 326	-9 501	-3 487	440 697	179 045	28 581	156 315	13 847
1999	742 210	43 543	32 527	12 177	20 350	-2 863	12 964	915	698 667	289 444	-44 497	298 834	24 407
2000	1 038 224	42 758	35 710	-5 199	40 909	-1 825	5 746	3 127	995 466	321 274	-69 983	459 889	-3 357
2001	782 870	28 059	54 620	33 700	20 920	-2 309	-29 978	5 726	754 811	167 021	-14 378	393 885	23 794
2002	795 161	115 945	90 971	60 466	30 505	137	21 221	3 616	679 216	84 372	100 403	283 299	18 861
2003	858 303	278 069	224 874	184 931	39 943	-723	48 643	5 275	580 234	63 750	91 455	220 705	10 591
2004	1 533 201	397 755	314 941	273 279	41 662	-134	69 245	13 703	1 135 446	145 966	93 608	381 493	13 301
2005	1 247 347	259 268	213 334	112 841	100 493	-421	26 260	20 095	988 079	112 638	132 300	450 386	8 447
2006	2 065 169	487 939	428 401	208 564	219 837	2 816	22 365	34 357	1 577 230	243 151	-58 229	683 245	2 227
2007	2 064 642	481 043	269 897	98 432	171 465	5 436	109 019	96 691	1 583 599	221 166	66 845	605 414	-10 675
2008	431 406	554 634	591 381	548 653	42 728	9 029	-149 676	103 900	-123 228	310 092	162 944	-165 639	29 187
2009	314 390	480 286	437 324	569 893	-132 569	58 206	-68 848	53 604	-165 896	150 442	-15 451	1 855	12 632
2010	1 308 279	398 188	353 294	442 012	-88 718	12 321	-7 967	40 540	910 091	205 831	297 797	139 316	28 319
2011	1 000 990	211 826	158 735	171 179	-12 444	9 063	30 010	14 018	789 164	233 988	240 878	-56 442	54 996
2008													
1st quarter	456 245	216 229	185 239	106 005	79 234	1 779	-16 724	45 935	240 016	88 544	14 415	-15 059	-6 750
2nd quarter	-19 863	181 419	169 365	76 220	93 145	2 565	-27 230	36 719	-201 282	66 637	18 801	20 240	230
3rd quarter	72 116	142 224	129 263	151 979	-22 716	1 602	4 145	7 214	-70 108	62 738	66 153	-123 022	5 845
4th quarter	-77 093	14 762	107 514	214 449	-106 935	3 083	-109 867	14 032	-91 855	92 172	63 575	-47 798	29 862
2009													
1st quarter	-119 117	109 442	145 512	163 809	-18 297	2 455	-43 319	4 794	-228 559	-2 335	45 873	-67 748	11 816
2nd quarter	-38 011	129 253	120 776	149 213	-28 437	926	-4 555	12 106	-167 264	30 243	-30 093	-279	-1 935
3rd quarter	335 302	109 204	69 961	126 593	-56 632	53 415	-33 650	19 478	226 098	54 849	-28 060	48 758	4 179
4th quarter	136 217	132 387	101 075	130 278	-29 203	1 410	12 676	17 226	3 830	67 686	-3 171	21 124	-1 428
2010													
1st quarter	311 935	89 961	84 837	97 364	-12 527	4 063	-15 851	16 912	221 974	40 375	84 046	4 582	2 265
2nd quarter	170 919	65 838	43 553	30 077	13 476	2 517	4 545	15 223	105 081	23 478	83 488	-16 364	2 100
3rd quarter	512 515	168 611	151 633	220 891	-69 258	1 789	9 981	5 208	343 904	79 097	74 630	92 957	10 514
4th quarter	312 910	73 778	73 271	93 680	-20 409	3 952	-6 642	3 197	239 132	62 881	55 633	58 141	13 440
2011													
1st quarter	578 972	72 974	67 719	56 274	11 445	2 714	-3 090	5 631	505 998	33 365	55 054	4 338	12 576
2nd quarter	98 554	121 822	97 184	104 363	-7 179	2 236	15 764	6 638	-23 268	61 281	-17 613	-5 108	13 989
3rd quarter	266 397	19 889	11 249	28 115	-16 866	2 287	5 121	1 232	246 508	63 222	120 918	-20 396	9 614
4th quarter	57 067	-2 859	-17 417	-17 573	156	1 826	12 215	517	59 926	76 120	82 519	-35 276	18 817

[4]A minus sign indicates financial outflows or a decrease in foreign official assets in the United States.
. . . = Not available.

Table 7-6A. U.S. International Transactions: Recent Data—*Continued*

(Millions of dollars, seasonally adjusted.)

Year and quarter	Financial account—*Continued*					Balance on goods	Balance on services	Balance on goods and services	Balance on income	Balance on goods, services, and income	Unilateral current transfers, net	Balance on current account
	Foreign-owned assets in the United States, net 4—*Cont.*		Financial derivatives, net	Statistical discrepancy 5								
	Other foreign assets in the United States, net—*Cont.*			Total	Seasonal adjustment discrepancy							
	U.S. liabilities											
	To unaffiliated foreigners reported by U.S. nonbanking concerns	Reported by U.S. banks and securities brokers										
1960	-90	678	. . .	-1 019	0	4 892	-1 385	3 508	3 379	6 887	-4 062	2 824
1961	226	928	. . .	-989	0	5 571	-1 376	4 195	3 755	7 950	-4 127	3 822
1962	-110	336	. . .	-1 124	0	4 521	-1 151	3 370	4 294	7 664	-4 277	3 387
1963	-37	898	. . .	-360	0	5 224	-1 014	4 210	4 596	8 806	-4 392	4 414
1964	75	1 818	. . .	-907	0	6 801	-779	6 022	5 041	11 063	-4 240	6 823
1965	178	503	. . .	-457	0	4 951	-287	4 664	5 350	10 014	-4 583	5 431
1966	476	2 882	. . .	629	0	3 817	-877	2 940	5 047	7 987	-4 955	3 031
1967	584	1 765	. . .	-205	0	3 800	-1 196	2 604	5 274	7 878	-5 294	2 583
1968	1 475	3 871	. . .	438	0	635	-385	250	5 990	6 240	-5 629	611
1969	792	8 886	. . .	-1 516	0	607	-516	91	6 044	6 135	-5 735	399
1970	2 014	-6 298	. . .	-219	0	2 603	-349	2 254	6 233	8 487	-6 156	2 331
1971	369	-6 911	. . .	-9 779	0	-2 260	957	-1 303	7 272	5 969	-7 402	-1 433
1972	815	4 754	. . .	-1 879	0	-6 416	973	-5 443	8 192	2 749	-8 544	-5 795
1973	1 035	4 702	. . .	-2 654	0	911	989	1 900	12 153	14 053	-6 913	7 140
1974	1 844	16 017	. . .	-2 444	0	-5 505	1 213	-4 292	15 503	11 211	-9 249	1 962
1975	319	628	. . .	4 717	0	8 903	3 501	12 404	12 787	25 191	-7 075	18 116
1976	-578	10 990	. . .	9 134	0	-9 483	3 401	-6 082	16 063	9 981	-5 686	4 295
1977	1 086	6 719	. . .	-3 650	0	-31 091	3 845	-27 246	18 137	-9 109	-5 226	-14 335
1978	1 889	16 141	. . .	9 997	0	-33 927	4 164	-29 763	20 408	-9 355	-5 788	-15 143
1979	1 621	32 607	. . .	25 647	0	-27 568	3 003	-24 565	30 873	6 308	-6 593	-285
1980	6 852	10 743	. . .	22 613	0	-25 500	6 093	-19 407	30 073	10 666	-8 349	2 317
1981	917	42 128	. . .	23 433	0	-28 023	11 852	-16 172	32 903	16 731	-11 702	5 030
1982	-2 383	65 633	. . .	38 362	0	-36 485	12 329	-24 156	35 164	11 008	-16 544	-5 536
1983	-118	50 342	. . .	17 666	0	-67 102	9 335	-57 767	36 386	-21 381	-17 310	-38 691
1984	16 626	33 849	. . .	18 672	0	-112 492	3 419	-109 073	35 063	-74 010	-20 335	-94 344
1985	9 851	41 045	. . .	18 677	0	-122 173	294	-121 880	25 723	-96 157	-21 998	-118 155
1986	3 325	76 737	. . .	30 570	0	-145 081	6 543	-138 538	15 494	-123 044	-24 132	-147 197
1987	18 363	86 537	. . .	-7 149	0	-159 557	7 874	-151 684	14 293	-137 391	-23 265	-160 655
1988	32 893	63 744	. . .	-17 107	0	-126 959	12 393	-114 566	18 687	-95 879	-25 274	-121 153
1989	22 086	51 780	. . .	52 299	0	-117 749	24 607	-93 142	19 824	-73 318	-26 169	-99 486
1990	45 133	-3 824	. . .	28 066	0	-111 037	30 173	-80 864	28 550	-52 314	-26 654	-78 968
1991	-3 115	3 994	. . .	-41 601	0	-76 937	45 802	-31 135	24 130	-7 005	9 904	2 898
1992	13 573	16 216	. . .	-43 775	0	-96 897	57 685	-39 212	24 234	-14 978	-36 636	-51 613
1993	10 489	25 063	. . .	6 314	0	-132 451	62 141	-70 310	25 316	-44 994	-39 812	-84 806
1994	1 302	104 338	. . .	-1 514	0	-165 831	67 338	-98 493	17 146	-81 347	-40 265	-121 612
1995	59 637	30 176	. . .	30 951	0	-174 170	77 786	-96 384	20 891	-75 493	-38 074	-113 567
1996	53 736	16 478	. . .	-9 705	0	-191 000	86 935	-104 065	22 318	-81 747	-43 017	-124 764
1997	116 518	149 026	. . .	-77 995	0	-198 428	90 155	-108 273	12 609	-95 664	-45 062	-140 726
1998	23 140	39 769	. . .	148 105	0	-248 221	82 081	-166 140	4 265	-161 875	-53 187	-215 062
1999	76 247	54 232	. . .	67 684	0	-336 171	73 011	-263 159	11 931	-251 228	-50 428	-301 656
2000	170 672	116 971	. . .	-61 361	0	-445 787	69 038	-376 749	19 178	-357 571	-58 767	-416 338
2001	66 110	118 379	. . .	-16 849	0	-421 276	59 505	-361 771	29 728	-332 043	-64 561	-396 603
2002	95 871	96 410	. . .	-43 126	0	-474 491	57 059	-417 432	25 175	-392 257	-64 990	-457 248
2003	96 526	97 207	. . .	-11 969	0	-540 409	49 425	-490 984	43 691	-447 293	-71 796	-519 089
2004	165 872	335 206	. . .	93 138	0	-663 507	58 150	-605 356	65 081	-540 275	-88 243	-628 519
2005	69 572	214 736	. . .	31 942	0	-780 730	72 106	-708 624	68 591	-640 033	-105 741	-745 774
2006	244 793	462 043	29 710	-6 742	0	-835 689	82 402	-753 288	44 182	-709 106	-91 515	-800 621
2007	183 221	517 628	6 222	92 660	0	-818 886	122 158	-696 728	101 485	-595 243	-115 061	-710 303
2008	-31 475	-428 337	-32 947	-59 443	0	-830 109	131 770	-698 338	147 089	-551 249	-125 885	-677 135
2009	8 956	-324 330	44 816	142 365	0	-505 758	126 603	-379 154	119 717	-259 437	-122 459	-381 896
2010	62 957	175 871	14 076	59 237	0	-645 124	150 387	-494 737	183 859	-310 878	-131 074	-441 951
2011	6 567	309 177	39 010	-89 208	0	-738 413	178 533	-559 880	227 007	-332 873	-133 053	-465 926
2008												
1st quarter	72 442	86 424	-7 966	-32 706	7 650	-216 084	33 550	-182 535	39 037	-143 498	-33 735	-177 232
2nd quarter	-61 088	-246 102	-2 355	19 513	-5 317	-219 945	36 099	-183 846	39 931	-143 915	-31 347	-175 262
3rd quarter	85 846	-167 668	-4 886	-13 110	-28 736	-218 940	32 805	-186 135	44 229	-141 906	-31 703	-173 608
4th quarter	-128 675	-100 991	-17 740	-33 139	26 404	-175 139	29 317	-145 822	23 893	-121 929	-29 103	-151 032
2009												
1st quarter	-7 776	-208 389	7 146	90 929	13 241	-122 549	29 117	-93 432	23 838	-69 594	-28 905	-98 500
2nd quarter	15 644	-180 844	7 561	60 065	-6 823	-111 051	31 308	-79 743	23 092	-56 651	-30 331	-86 982
3rd quarter	20 559	125 813	10 645	47 288	-22 750	-128 856	31 411	-97 445	34 684	-62 761	-32 935	-95 697
4th quarter	-19 471	-60 910	19 464	-55 916	16 334	-143 301	34 767	-108 534	38 104	-70 430	-30 289	-100 719
2010												
1st quarter	17 312	73 394	16 152	52 342	16 062	-152 538	34 587	-117 952	41 639	-76 313	-34 681	-110 994
2nd quarter	12 728	-349	9 980	85 224	-8 819	-164 640	36 953	-127 687	47 685	-80 002	-31 710	-111 713
3rd quarter	10 923	75 783	-11 893	-91 379	-22 075	-166 871	37 734	-129 137	47 778	-81 359	-33 216	-114 574
4th quarter	21 994	27 043	-163	13 051	14 832	-161 075	41 112	-119 962	46 758	-73 204	-31 466	-104 671
2011												
1st quarter	40 688	359 977	2 927	-88 930	17 684	-181 358	44 133	-137 225	52 451	-84 774	-35 223	-119 997
2nd quarter	25 538	-101 355	7 419	6 555	-11 134	-187 184	45 634	-141 549	56 209	-85 340	-33 777	-119 117
3rd quarter	-19 670	92 820	-3 949	-62 094	-26 771	-180 617	45 795	-134 822	58 478	-76 344	-31 815	-108 158
4th quarter	-39 989	-42 265	32 613	55 263	20 223	-189 254	42 969	-146 286	59 869	-86 417	-32 240	-118 656

4A minus sign indicates financial outflows or a decrease in foreign official assets in the United States.
5Sum of credits and debits with the sign reversed.
. . . = Not available.

Table 7-6B. U.S. International Transactions: Historical Data

(Millions of dollars, seasonally adjusted.)

Year and quarter	Exports of goods, services, and income				Imports of goods, services, and income [1]				Unilateral current transfers, net [2]	U.S.-owned assets abroad, net, excluding financial derivatives [3]			U.S. private assets, net		
	Total	Goods	Services	Income receipts	Total	Goods	Services	Income payments		Total	U.S. official reserve assets, net	U.S. government assets other than official reserve assets, net	Total	Direct investment	Foreign securities
1960															
1st quarter	7 355	4 685	1 543	1 127	-6 050	-3 812	-1 907	-331	-955	-1 066	159	-237	-988	-664	-266
2nd quarter	7 762	4 916	1 715	1 131	-6 078	-3 858	-1 906	-314	-1 154	-1 156	175	-339	-992	-586	-166
3rd quarter	7 650	5 031	1 453	1 166	-5 925	-3 648	-1 970	-307	-889	-956	740	-160	-1 536	-754	-111
4th quarter	7 791	5 018	1 580	1 193	-5 619	-3 440	-1 892	-287	-1 064	-923	1 071	-365	-1 629	-936	-120
1961															
1st quarter	7 827	5 095	1 481	1 251	-5 599	-3 394	-1 912	-293	-989	-1 320	371	-381	-1 310	-774	-135
2nd quarter	7 773	4 806	1 758	1 209	-5 659	-3 438	-1 922	-299	-1 208	-1 029	-320	471	-1 180	-551	-246
3rd quarter	7 757	5 038	1 468	1 251	-6 026	-3 809	-1 900	-317	-887	-1 928	-212	-486	-1 230	-737	-124
4th quarter	8 047	5 169	1 590	1 288	-6 171	-3 896	-1 939	-336	-1 043	-1 260	768	-513	-1 515	-592	-257
1962															
1st quarter	8 015	5 077	1 666	1 272	-6 256	-3 966	-1 971	-319	-1 113	-1 301	427	-406	-1 322	-545	-196
2nd quarter	8 719	5 336	2 004	1 379	-6 402	-4 080	-1 992	-330	-1 272	-1 461	-163	-381	-917	-716	-308
3rd quarter	8 295	5 331	1 567	1 397	-6 455	-4 116	-2 005	-334	-879	-279	881	8	-1 168	-811	-87
4th quarter	8 315	5 037	1 709	1 569	-6 567	-4 098	-2 126	-343	-1 016	-1 134	390	-306	-1 218	-779	-378
1963															
1st quarter	8 428	5 063	1 849	1 516	-6 478	-4 064	-2 057	-357	-1 107	-1 922	32	-482	-1 472	-980	-522
2nd quarter	9 244	5 599	2 150	1 495	-6 674	-4 226	-2 066	-382	-1 371	-2 631	124	-654	-2 101	-874	-536
3rd quarter	8 832	5 671	1 620	1 541	-6 893	-4 372	-2 122	-399	-918	-887	227	-86	-1 028	-721	-100
4th quarter	9 275	5 939	1 731	1 605	-6 926	-4 386	-2 118	-422	-999	-1 831	-5	-440	-1 386	-908	53
1964															
1st quarter	9 885	6 242	1 922	1 721	-6 982	-4 416	-2 140	-426	-993	-2 086	-51	-288	-1 747	-822	20
2nd quarter	9 975	6 199	2 088	1 688	-7 179	-4 598	-2 142	-439	-1 269	-2 018	303	-386	-1 935	-970	-206
3rd quarter	10 009	6 423	1 851	1 735	-7 349	-4 756	-2 153	-440	-935	-2 255	70	-414	-1 911	-1 018	2
4th quarter	10 299	6 637	1 982	1 680	-7 594	-4 930	-2 186	-478	-1 043	-3 200	-151	-592	-2 457	-949	-494
1965															
1st quarter	9 689	5 768	2 047	1 874	-7 395	-4 711	-2 187	-497	-1 037	-1 576	843	-374	-2 045	-1 606	-198
2nd quarter	11 263	6 876	2 448	1 939	-8 208	-5 428	-2 269	-511	-1 478	-1 270	69	-536	-803	-1 250	-147
3rd quarter	10 625	6 643	2 120	1 862	-8 307	-5 516	-2 263	-528	-1 013	-1 454	42	-254	-1 242	-1 030	-209
4th quarter	11 149	7 174	2 212	1 763	-8 802	-5 855	-2 393	-554	-1 058	-1 416	271	-441	-1 246	-1 125	-205
1966															
1st quarter	11 190	7 242	2 124	1 824	-9 068	-6 012	-2 483	-573	-1 140	-1 465	424	-321	-1 568	-1 115	-437
2nd quarter	11 726	7 169	2 705	1 852	-9 390	-6 195	-2 601	-594	-1 547	-1 967	68	-504	-1 531	-1 373	-115
3rd quarter	11 470	7 290	2 301	1 879	-9 912	-6 576	-2 693	-643	-1 073	-1 681	83	-339	-1 425	-1 314	-115
4th quarter	12 068	7 609	2 487	1 972	-10 098	-6 710	-2 717	-671	-1 194	-2 208	-5	-380	-1 823	-1 616	-53
1967															
1st quarter	12 439	7 751	2 731	1 957	-10 248	-6 708	-2 866	-674	-1 315	-1 203	1 027	-643	-1 587	-1 186	-265
2nd quarter	12 275	7 693	2 666	1 916	-10 136	-6 475	-2 986	-675	-1 472	-2 339	-419	-543	-1 377	-964	-261
3rd quarter	12 134	7 530	2 540	2 064	-10 262	-6 526	-3 059	-677	-1 309	-3 155	-375	-551	-2 229	-1 359	-419
4th quarter	12 506	7 692	2 731	2 083	-10 833	-7 157	-2 955	-721	-1 199	-3 060	-180	-685	-2 195	-1 297	-363
1968															
1st quarter	13 016	7 998	2 816	2 202	-11 571	-7 796	-2 997	-778	-1 249	-1 299	912	-706	-1 505	-981	-449
2nd quarter	13 577	8 324	2 936	2 317	-11 885	-8 051	-2 990	-844	-1 363	-2 427	-135	-632	-1 660	-1 172	-283
3rd quarter	14 195	8 745	3 039	2 411	-12 611	-8 612	-3 129	-870	-1 445	-3 447	-572	-568	-2 307	-1 573	-318
4th quarter	14 126	8 559	3 129	2 438	-12 604	-8 532	-3 185	-887	-1 573	-3 803	-1 075	-368	-2 360	-1 568	-519
1969															
1st quarter	12 921	7 468	2 884	2 569	-11 622	-7 444	-3 174	-1 004	-1 177	-2 595	-45	-406	-2 144	-1 556	-366
2nd quarter	15 492	9 536	3 283	2 673	-13 978	-9 527	-3 303	-1 148	-1 645	-3 428	-298	-632	-2 498	-1 663	-498
3rd quarter	15 439	9 400	3 245	2 794	-14 072	-9 380	-3 368	-1 324	-1 319	-3 361	-685	-703	-1 973	-1 548	-546
4th quarter	16 279	10 010	3 394	2 875	-14 329	-9 456	-3 481	-1 392	-1 593	-2 199	-151	-459	-1 589	-1 192	-139
1970															
1st quarter	16 461	10 258	3 235	2 968	-14 458	-9 587	-3 449	-1 422	-1 383	-3 478	-386	-399	-2 693	-1 958	-306
2nd quarter	17 419	10 744	3 645	3 030	-14 861	-9 766	-3 690	-1 405	-1 586	-1 725	1 025	-348	-2 402	-2 144	80
3rd quarter	17 267	10 665	3 625	2 977	-15 141	-10 049	-3 715	-1 377	-1 611	-2 146	802	-423	-2 525	-1 718	-517
4th quarter	17 241	10 802	3 666	2 773	-15 443	-10 464	-3 668	-1 311	-1 576	-1 989	1 040	-419	-2 610	-1 771	-333
1971															
1st quarter	17 980	10 920	4 048	3 012	-15 551	-10 600	-3 724	-1 227	-1 746	-3 464	151	-573	-3 042	-2 033	-408
2nd quarter	18 163	10 878	4 087	3 198	-16 764	-11 614	-3 867	-1 283	-1 808	-2 534	839	-567	-2 806	-1 949	-368
3rd quarter	18 676	11 548	3 972	3 156	-17 460	-12 171	-3 861	-1 428	-1 752	-3 390	1 377	-387	-4 380	-2 308	-346
4th quarter	17 564	9 973	4 251	3 340	-16 639	-11 194	-3 948	-1 497	-2 098	-3 084	-18	-355	-2 711	-1 327	9
1972															
1st quarter	19 757	11 833	4 473	3 451	-19 153	-13 501	-4 173	-1 479	-2 297	-4 295	-90	-212	-3 993	-2 187	-476
2nd quarter	19 427	11 618	4 233	3 576	-19 105	-13 254	-4 228	-1 623	-2 011	-2 125	-60	-271	-1 794	-1 481	-318
3rd quarter	20 788	12 351	4 634	3 803	-19 767	-14 022	-4 095	-1 650	-2 306	-3 952	96	-518	-3 530	-2 435	203
4th quarter	22 015	13 579	4 503	3 933	-21 212	-15 020	-4 371	-1 821	-1 933	-4 125	50	-566	-3 609	-1 644	-28
1973															
1st quarter	24 681	15 474	4 579	4 628	-23 000	-16 285	-4 613	-2 102	-1 536	-7 886	213	-572	-7 527	-3 785	55
2nd quarter	27 127	17 112	4 828	5 187	-24 301	-17 168	-4 741	-2 392	-1 953	-4 154	11	-423	-3 742	-2 691	-86
3rd quarter	29 329	18 271	5 145	5 913	-24 841	-17 683	-4 640	-2 518	-1 751	-3 189	-23	-608	-2 558	-2 159	-196
4th quarter	31 912	20 553	5 279	6 080	-26 855	-19 363	-4 849	-2 643	-1 674	-7 646	-43	-1 042	-6 561	-2 718	-445

[1] A minus sign indicates imports of goods or services or income payments.
[2] A minus sign indicates net unilateral transfers to foreigners.
[3] A minus sign indicates financial outflows or increases in U.S. official assets.

Table 7-6B. U.S. International Transactions: Historical Data—*Continued*

(Millions of dollars, seasonally adjusted.)

Year and quarter	U.S.-owned assets abroad, net [3] —Continued		Foreign-owned assets in the United States, net, excluding financial derivatives [4]								Statistical discrep-ancy [5]	Balance on goods and services	Balance on current account
	U.S. private assets, net—Continued		Total	Foreign official assets in the United States, net	Other foreign assets in the United States, net								
	U.S. claims				Total	Direct invest-ment	U.S. Treasury securities and U.S. currency flows	U.S. securities other than U.S. Treasury securities	U.S. liabilities				
	On unaffiliated foreigners reported by U.S. nonbanking concerns	Reported by U.S. banks and securities brokers							To unaffiliated foreigners reported by U.S. nonbanking concerns	Reported by U.S. banks and securities brokers			
1960													
1st quarter	38	-96	926	380	546	89	-100	170	-1	388	-210	509	350
2nd quarter	-100	-140	912	435	477	102	-143	118	-50	450	-286	867	530
3rd quarter	-51	-620	381	283	98	93	-99	5	-11	110	-261	866	836
4th quarter	-281	-292	77	377	-300	31	-22	-11	-28	-270	-262	1 266	1 108
1961													
1st quarter	-117	-284	435	438	-3	68	-82	104	73	-166	-354	1 270	1 239
2nd quarter	-164	-219	620	-307	927	86	-38	152	72	655	-497	1 204	906
3rd quarter	-149	-220	934	673	261	58	83	3	14	103	150	797	844
4th quarter	-128	-538	715	-41	756	99	188	66	67	336	-288	924	833
1962													
1st quarter	-186	-395	737	. . .	737	89	193	145	-14	324	-82	806	646
2nd quarter	-5	112	675	503	172	130	-51	7	-64	150	-259	1 268	1 045
3rd quarter	-181	-89	-277	178	-455	59	-109	-23	16	-398	-405	777	961
4th quarter	17	-78	779	591	188	68	-99	6	-47	260	-377	522	732
1963													
1st quarter	-27	57	1 191	946	245	40	25	14	-36	202	-112	791	843
2nd quarter	-108	-583	1 527	910	617	108	-109	119	69	430	-95	1 457	1 199
3rd quarter	47	-254	205	56	149	105	1	52	11	-20	-339	797	1 021
4th quarter	245	-776	295	75	220	-22	-66	102	-80	286	186	1 166	1 350
1964													
1st quarter	-206	-739	462	393	69	87	32	-42	0	-8	-286	1 608	1 910
2nd quarter	-166	-593	630	227	403	109	-108	14	19	369	-139	1 547	1 527
3rd quarter	-532	-363	769	275	494	56	-65	-30	37	496	-239	1 365	1 725
4th quarter	-204	-810	1 781	763	1 018	70	-5	-27	19	961	-243	1 503	1 662
1965													
1st quarter	286	-527	208	-202	410	184	60	57	3	106	111	917	1 257
2nd quarter	165	429	-330	-194	-136	-21	64	-243	63	1	23	1 627	1 577
3rd quarter	-19	16	587	115	472	147	-149	-227	49	652	-438	984	1 305
4th quarter	-91	175	280	421	-141	104	-106	54	63	-256	-153	1 138	1 289
1966													
1st quarter	-159	143	458	-164	622	143	-102	173	68	340	25	871	982
2nd quarter	-68	25	961	-57	1 018	133	-316	518	78	605	217	1 078	789
3rd quarter	-105	109	909	-342	1 251	-37	66	107	195	920	287	322	485
4th quarter	-110	-44	1 332	-111	1 443	187	-4	108	135	1 017	100	669	776
1967													
1st quarter	-107	-29	401	708	-307	169	-6	133	219	-822	-74	908	876
2nd quarter	-69	-83	1 884	1 100	784	174	-61	329	66	276	-212	898	667
3rd quarter	-40	-411	2 513	548	1 965	127	-36	520	164	1 190	79	485	563
4th quarter	-563	28	2 584	1 098	1 486	228	-32	34	135	1 121	2	311	474
1968													
1st quarter	-231	156	1 374	-533	1 907	367	22	855	207	456	-271	21	196
2nd quarter	-567	362	2 192	-2 007	4 199	133	86	1 122	478	2 380	-94	219	329
3rd quarter	-213	-203	2 809	442	2 367	148	-8	1 124	315	788	499	43	139
4th quarter	-191	-82	3 550	1 321	2 229	160	36	1 312	474	247	304	-29	-51
1969													
1st quarter	-132	-90	3 664	-1 117	4 781	359	-125	1 388	90	3 069	-1 191	-266	122
2nd quarter	-21	-316	3 896	-766	4 662	267	-35	365	181	3 884	-337	-11	-131
3rd quarter	141	-20	3 833	1 256	2 577	261	79	396	345	1 496	-520	-103	48
4th quarter	-114	-144	1 311	-672	1 983	376	13	981	176	437	531	467	357
1970													
1st quarter	-366	-63	3 027	3 697	-670	592	16	304	222	-1 804	-169	457	620
2nd quarter	-73	-265	848	694	154	212	-35	374	534	-931	-95	933	972
3rd quarter	-157	-133	1 940	1 411	529	357	1	720	510	-1 059	-309	526	515
4th quarter	0	-506	1 413	1 975	-562	303	99	792	748	-2 504	354	336	222
1971													
1st quarter	-355	-246	3 809	5 895	-2 086	196	179	559	-62	-2 958	-1 028	644	683
2nd quarter	-131	-358	5 154	5 630	-476	140	1 862	196	-34	-2 640	-2 211	-516	-409
3rd quarter	-337	-1 389	8 726	10 367	-1 641	-293	-795	626	79	-1 258	-4 800	-512	-536
4th quarter	-406	-987	5 997	5 704	293	324	-1 270	908	386	-55	-1 740	-918	-1 173
1972													
1st quarter	-248	-1 082	5 077	3 472	1 605	-136	-3	1 059	-14	699	911	-1 368	-1 693
2nd quarter	-185	190	4 277	1 103	3 174	373	-83	961	250	1 673	-463	-1 631	-1 689
3rd quarter	-241	-1 057	6 382	4 740	1 642	310	-12	718	216	410	-1 145	-1 132	-1 285
4th quarter	-380	-1 557	6 437	1 871	4 566	403	59	1 769	363	1 972	-1 182	-1 309	-1 130
1973													
1st quarter	-809	-2 988	10 743	9 937	806	631	-119	1 718	246	-1 670	-3 002	-845	145
2nd quarter	-202	-763	3 056	-403	3 458	835	-185	489	54	2 265	225	31	873
3rd quarter	-502	299	2 168	-772	2 940	539	-205	1 173	454	979	-1 716	1 093	2 737
4th quarter	-870	-2 528	2 423	-2 736	5 159	795	293	662	281	3 128	1 840	1 620	3 383

[3] A minus sign indicates financial outflows or increases in U.S. official assets.
[4] A minus sign indicates financial outflows or decreases in foreign official assets in the United States.
[5] Sum of credits and debits with the sign reversed.
. . . = Not available.

Table 7-6B. U.S. International Transactions: Historical Data—*Continued*

(Millions of dollars, seasonally adjusted.)

Year and quarter	Exports of goods, services, and income				Imports of goods, services, and income [1]				Unilateral current transfers, net [2]	U.S.-owned assets abroad, net, excluding financial derivatives [3]					
										Total	U.S. official reserve assets, net	U.S. government assets other than official reserve assets, net	U.S. private assets, net		
	Total	Goods	Services	Income receipts	Total	Goods	Services	Income payments					Total	Direct invest-ment	Foreign securities
1974															
1st quarter	34 698	22 614	5 189	6 895	-29 643	-21 952	-4 985	-2 706	-3 443	-5 914	-246	1 389	-7 057	900	-600
2nd quarter	37 295	24 500	5 691	7 104	-34 710	-26 346	-5 359	-3 005	-2 475	-10 318	-358	267	-10 227	-1 790	-272
3rd quarter	37 385	24 629	5 633	7 123	-36 004	-27 368	-5 360	-3 276	-1 676	-7 694	-1 002	-354	-6 338	-4 385	-282
4th quarter	39 105	26 563	6 078	6 464	-36 918	-28 145	-5 675	-3 098	-1 656	-10 818	139	-938	-10 019	-3 776	-699
1975															
1st quarter	40 047	27 480	6 454	6 113	-33 797	-24 980	-5 580	-3 237	-2 043	-10 576	-327	-877	-9 372	-4 022	-1 931
2nd quarter	38 675	25 866	6 807	6 002	-31 284	-22 832	-5 309	-3 143	-2 377	-9 591	-28	-875	-8 688	-3 990	-985
3rd quarter	38 347	26 109	5 886	6 352	-33 078	-24 487	-5 379	-3 212	-1 189	-5 099	-333	-745	-4 021	-1 495	-938
4th quarter	40 868	27 633	6 351	6 884	-34 588	-25 886	-5 729	-2 973	-1 467	-14 436	-161	-977	-13 298	-4 736	-2 393
1976															
1st quarter	41 183	27 575	6 556	7 052	-37 464	-28 176	-5 883	-3 405	-1 153	-12 364	-777	-749	-10 838	-3 923	-2 467
2nd quarter	42 309	28 256	6 660	7 393	-39 494	-30 182	-5 980	-3 332	-1 167	-11 701	-1 580	-914	-9 207	-2 017	-1 405
3rd quarter	43 818	29 056	7 311	7 451	-41 737	-32 213	-6 231	-3 293	-2 165	-10 618	-408	-1 428	-8 782	-3 327	-2 751
4th quarter	44 780	29 858	7 444	7 478	-43 416	-33 657	-6 478	-3 281	-1 201	-16 588	207	-1 124	-15 671	-2 682	-2 262
1977															
1st quarter	44 916	29 668	7 494	7 754	-46 360	-36 585	-6 676	-3 099	-1 243	-1 198	-420	-1 062	284	-1 880	-749
2nd quarter	46 796	30 852	7 901	8 043	-48 401	-38 063	-6 940	-3 398	-1 426	-12 182	-24	-885	-11 273	-3 783	-1 784
3rd quarter	47 125	30 752	7 991	8 382	-48 511	-38 005	-6 894	-3 612	-1 371	-6 297	112	-1 001	-5 408	-2 762	-2 177
4th quarter	45 818	29 544	8 098	8 176	-50 495	-39 254	-7 133	-4 108	-1 185	-15 109	-43	-746	-14 320	-3 466	-749
1978															
1st quarter	48 847	30 470	8 704	9 673	-54 471	-42 487	-7 612	-4 372	-1 396	-15 219	187	-1 009	-14 397	-4 771	-1 115
2nd quarter	54 213	35 674	8 772	9 767	-56 513	-43 419	-7 768	-5 326	-1 477	-5 606	248	-1 257	-4 597	-3 720	-1 094
3rd quarter	56 058	36 523	9 203	10 332	-58 300	-44 422	-8 248	-5 630	-1 425	-9 703	115	-1 394	-8 424	-2 753	-510
4th quarter	61 399	39 408	9 673	12 318	-60 587	-45 674	-8 561	-6 352	-1 491	-30 601	182	-999	-29 784	-4 812	-907
1979															
1st quarter	64 530	41 475	9 664	13 391	-63 492	-47 582	-8 649	-7 261	-1 462	-8 980	-3 585	-1 094	-4 301	-5 465	-908
2nd quarter	68 445	43 885	9 713	14 847	-67 584	-50 778	-8 960	-7 846	-1 552	-15 565	322	-970	-14 917	-7 220	-492
3rd quarter	74 411	47 104	9 936	17 371	-71 856	-54 002	-9 329	-8 525	-1 632	-27 156	2 779	-779	-29 156	-7 166	-2 331
4th quarter	80 577	51 975	10 378	18 224	-78 726	-59 645	-9 751	-9 330	-1 949	-14 353	-649	-904	-12 800	-5 370	-995
1980															
1st quarter	85 274	54 237	10 997	20 040	-86 559	-65 815	-10 335	-10 409	-2 174	-13 814	-3 268	-1 441	-9 105	-5 188	-787
2nd quarter	83 441	55 967	11 491	15 983	-82 734	-62 274	-10 106	-10 354	-1 648	-24 724	502	-1 159	-24 067	-2 659	-1 387
3rd quarter	86 148	55 830	12 543	17 775	-79 906	-59 010	-10 292	-10 604	-1 909	-19 666	-1 109	-1 382	-17 175	-4 156	-944
4th quarter	89 578	58 216	12 554	18 808	-84 577	-62 651	-10 760	-11 166	-2 618	-28 761	-4 279	-1 178	-23 304	-7 219	-450
1981															
1st quarter	94 665	60 317	13 684	20 664	-91 024	-67 004	-11 360	-12 660	-2 678	-23 015	-4 529	-1 361	-17 125	-2 044	-473
2nd quarter	96 294	60 141	14 392	21 761	-92 303	-67 181	-11 447	-13 675	-2 763	-24 158	-905	-1 491	-21 762	-5 709	-1 564
3rd quarter	95 013	58 031	14 835	22 147	-89 787	-64 407	-11 236	-14 144	-3 145	-17 945	-4	-1 268	-16 673	-1 124	-697
4th quarter	94 958	58 555	14 446	21 957	-91 082	-66 475	-11 460	-13 147	-3 117	-49 028	262	-976	-48 314	-745	-2 966
1982															
1st quarter	94 006	55 163	16 032	22 811	-90 336	-63 502	-12 749	-14 085	-3 955	-36 335	-1 089	-800	-34 446	-2 695	-628
2nd quarter	96 060	55 344	16 187	24 529	-88 318	-60 580	-13 096	-14 642	-3 953	-42 754	-1 132	-1 727	-39 895	1 074	-471
3rd quarter	90 925	52 089	16 003	22 833	-90 938	-63 696	-12 794	-14 448	-4 027	-23 547	-794	-2 524	-20 229	903	-3 397
4th quarter	85 993	48 561	15 857	21 575	-86 379	-59 864	-13 109	-13 406	-4 611	-25 246	-1 949	-1 080	-22 217	-3 838	-3 488
1983															
1st quarter	86 146	49 198	16 239	20 709	-85 097	-59 757	-12 951	-12 389	-3 566	-28 890	-787	-1 136	-26 967	-862	-1 549
2nd quarter	87 214	49 340	16 093	21 781	-91 096	-64 783	-13 557	-12 756	-3 951	-2 974	16	-1 263	-1 727	-1 842	-2 813
3rd quarter	89 919	50 324	16 308	23 287	-98 481	-70 370	-14 133	-13 978	-4 339	-12 191	529	-1 171	-11 549	-4 861	-1 308
4th quarter	92 831	52 937	15 671	24 223	-102 822	-73 991	-14 337	-14 494	-5 453	-22 318	-953	-1 436	-19 929	-4 962	-1 093
1984															
1st quarter	96 000	52 991	17 353	25 656	-112 576	-79 740	-16 131	-16 705	-4 354	-8 338	-657	-2 033	-5 648	-1 837	758
2nd quarter	100 257	54 626	18 045	27 586	-119 220	-83 798	-16 885	-18 537	-4 476	-25 718	-565	-1 342	-23 811	-1 967	-764
3rd quarter	102 296	55 893	17 936	28 467	-120 533	-83 918	-17 168	-19 447	-5 147	15 298	-799	-1 392	17 489	-3 209	-1 106
4th quarter	101 361	56 416	17 834	27 111	-121 591	-84 962	-17 564	-19 065	-6 359	-21 618	-1 109	-720	-19 789	-9 396	-3 644
1985															
1st quarter	97 794	54 866	18 227	24 701	-116 249	-80 319	-17 707	-18 223	-5 064	-5 491	-233	-760	-4 498	-2 783	-2 474
2nd quarter	97 437	54 154	18 214	25 069	-120 891	-84 565	-18 276	-18 050	-5 235	-2 340	-356	-1 053	-931	-4 374	-2 219
3rd quarter	94 771	52 836	17 961	23 974	-120 285	-83 909	-18 151	-18 225	-5 789	-5 776	-121	-453	-5 202	-4 698	-1 572
4th quarter	97 612	54 059	18 756	24 797	-126 349	-89 295	-18 732	-18 322	-5 911	-31 146	-3 147	-555	-27 444	-7 073	-1 217
1986															
1st quarter	100 332	53 536	21 052	25 744	-129 342	-89 220	-19 855	-20 267	-5 199	-17 406	-115	-266	-17 025	-9 781	-5 930
2nd quarter	102 206	56 828	20 912	24 466	-131 690	-91 743	-19 066	-20 881	-6 208	-24 945	16	-230	-24 731	-7 298	-1 051
3rd quarter	101 288	55 645	21 969	23 674	-132 879	-92 801	-20 448	-19 630	-6 458	-32 615	280	-1 554	-31 341	-4 975	181
4th quarter	103 275	57 335	22 761	23 179	-136 232	-94 661	-20 778	-20 793	-6 269	-36 753	132	29	-36 914	-1 938	2 529
1987															
1st quarter	104 750	56 696	23 602	24 452	-138 887	-96 023	-21 273	-21 591	-5 128	8 177	1 956	-5	6 226	-6 547	-1 749
2nd quarter	111 642	60 202	24 740	26 700	-146 125	-100 648	-22 537	-22 940	-5 502	-26 738	3 419	-168	-29 989	-7 541	-287
3rd quarter	116 688	64 217	24 986	27 485	-151 111	-104 412	-22 833	-23 866	-5 706	-27 791	32	310	-28 133	-8 795	-1 159
4th quarter	123 968	69 093	25 329	29 546	-158 324	-108 682	-24 146	-25 496	-6 926	-32 943	3 742	868	-37 553	-12 150	-2 056

[1] A minus sign indicates imports of goods or services or income payments.
[2] A minus sign indicates net unilateral transfers to foreigners.
[3] A minus sign indicates financial outflows or increases in U.S. official assets.

Table 7-6B. U.S. International Transactions: Historical Data—Continued

(Millions of dollars, seasonally adjusted.)

Year and quarter	U.S.-owned assets abroad, net [3] —Continued / U.S. private assets, net—Continued / U.S. claims — On unaffiliated foreigners reported by U.S. nonbanking concerns	Reported by U.S. banks and securities brokers	Foreign-owned assets in the United States, net, excluding financial derivatives [4] — Total	Foreign official assets in the United States, net	Other foreign assets in the United States, net — Total	Direct investment	U.S. Treasury securities and U.S. currency flows	U.S. securities other than U.S. Treasury securities	U.S. liabilities — To unaffiliated foreigners reported by U.S. nonbanking concerns	Reported by U.S. banks and securities brokers	Statistical discrepancy [5]	Balance on goods and services	Balance on current account
1974													
1st quarter	-2 113	-5 244	6 444	-1 138	7 582	1 784	266	712	354	4 466	-2 142	866	1 612
2nd quarter	-588	-7 577	9 897	4 434	5 463	539	-5	363	390	4 176	311	-1 514	110
3rd quarter	273	-1 944	9 310	3 062	6 248	1 610	407	227	239	3 765	-1 321	-2 466	-295
4th quarter	-793	-4 751	9 577	4 188	5 389	828	1 015	-925	861	3 610	710	-1 179	531
1975													
1st quarter	353	-3 772	2 701	3 419	-718	278	805	344	359	-2 504	3 668	3 374	4 207
2nd quarter	112	-3 825	4 307	2 244	2 063	870	-54	385	55	807	270	4 532	5 014
3rd quarter	-939	-649	2 934	-1 731	4 665	86	2 367	737	-163	1 638	-1 915	2 129	4 080
4th quarter	-883	-5 286	6 929	3 095	3 834	1 369	672	1 038	68	687	2 694	2 369	4 813
1976													
1st quarter	-747	-3 701	7 709	3 699	4 010	1 471	677	1 036	154	672	2 089	72	2 566
2nd quarter	-999	-4 786	8 425	4 039	4 386	1 086	-119	134	-231	3 516	1 628	-1 246	1 648
3rd quarter	616	-3 320	9 062	2 958	6 104	999	3 267	64	-184	1 958	1 640	-2 077	-84
4th quarter	-1 166	-9 561	12 644	6 997	5 647	790	279	51	-317	4 844	3 781	-2 833	163
1977													
1st quarter	-771	3 684	2 968	5 554	-2 586	980	1 087	749	-98	-5 304	917	-6 099	-2 687
2nd quarter	-1 124	-4 582	14 673	7 888	6 785	965	-907	589	-102	6 240	540	-6 250	-3 031
3rd quarter	1 310	-1 779	14 585	8 257	6 328	1 023	1 560	337	768	2 640	-5 531	-6 156	-2 757
4th quarter	-1 355	-8 750	20 547	15 117	5 430	761	245	763	518	3 143	424	-8 745	-5 862
1978													
1st quarter	-2 241	-6 270	18 461	15 448	3 013	1 356	1 158	396	507	-404	3 778	-10 925	-7 020
2nd quarter	315	-98	1 412	-5 113	6 525	2 313	1 354	1 082	304	1 472	7 971	-6 741	-3 777
3rd quarter	-29	-5 132	17 390	4 903	12 487	2 620	-560	296	912	9 219	-4 020	-6 944	-3 667
4th quarter	-1 898	-22 167	29 013	18 440	10 573	1 608	2 465	480	166	5 854	2 267	-5 154	-679
1979													
1st quarter	-3 854	5 926	3 472	-7 558	11 030	1 554	2 590	409	-296	6 773	5 932	-5 092	-424
2nd quarter	716	-7 921	7 379	-9 775	17 154	3 354	459	524	799	12 018	8 877	-6 140	-691
3rd quarter	-1 826	-17 833	25 063	6 036	19 027	3 382	2 116	166	210	13 153	1 170	-6 291	923
4th quarter	-50	-6 385	4 780	-1 228	6 008	3 588	597	252	908	663	9 671	-7 043	-98
1980													
1st quarter	-1 927	-1 203	10 180	-6 261	16 441	3 321	3 746	2 435	340	6 599	7 093	-10 916	-3 459
2nd quarter	144	-20 165	10 994	7 731	3 264	5 756	-150	496	1 671	-4 509	14 671	-4 922	-941
3rd quarter	365	-12 440	14 599	7 564	7 035	4 713	-109	263	1 252	916	734	-929	4 333
4th quarter	-2 605	-13 030	26 263	7 614	18 649	3 128	1 931	2 263	3 590	7 737	115	-2 641	2 383
1981													
1st quarter	-2 944	-11 664	10 303	6 595	3 708	3 146	1 877	2 357	121	-3 793	11 749	-4 363	963
2nd quarter	513	-15 002	14 906	-3 159	18 065	5 294	1 183	3 512	13	8 063	8 024	-4 095	1 228
3rd quarter	458	-15 310	17 212	-5 992	23 204	5 505	-567	704	1 084	16 478	-1 348	-2 777	2 081
4th quarter	-2 404	-42 199	43 264	8 609	34 655	11 251	1 993	332	-301	21 380	5 005	-4 934	759
1982													
1st quarter	2 220	-33 343	26 797	-3 265	30 062	2 154	854	1 263	-65	25 856	9 823	-5 056	-285
2nd quarter	-1 095	-39 403	34 995	1 534	33 461	2 945	3 928	2 486	-2 023	26 125	3 970	-2 145	3 789
3rd quarter	3 670	-21 405	18 267	2 694	15 573	2 849	1 695	555	-282	10 756	9 320	-8 398	-4 040
4th quarter	2 028	-16 919	14 995	2 629	12 366	4 685	3 017	1 781	-13	2 896	15 248	-8 555	-4 997
1983													
1st quarter	-4 253	-20 303	15 870	-38	15 908	1 254	3 317	2 873	-2 763	11 227	15 537	-7 271	-2 517
2nd quarter	-590	3 518	16 049	1 612	14 437	3 287	4 340	2 470	-64	4 404	-5 242	-12 907	-7 833
3rd quarter	-1 764	-3 616	20 106	-2 689	22 795	4 059	1 994	1 777	1 311	13 654	4 986	-17 871	-12 901
4th quarter	-4 347	-9 527	35 373	6 960	28 413	1 771	3 143	1 044	1 398	21 057	2 389	-19 720	-15 444
1984													
1st quarter	-3 012	-1 557	22 780	-2 956	25 736	4 858	1 928	1 333	6 092	11 525	6 488	-25 527	-20 930
2nd quarter	-934	-20 146	42 415	-156	42 571	8 625	7 762	362	4 232	21 590	6 742	-28 012	-23 439
3rd quarter	3 987	17 817	7 158	-884	8 042	4 432	5 693	1 447	1 662	-5 192	928	-27 257	-23 384
4th quarter	492	-7 241	43 694	7 136	36 558	6 552	10 014	9 426	4 640	5 926	4 513	-28 276	-26 589
1985													
1st quarter	475	284	17 783	-10 962	28 745	4 913	2 831	9 615	-720	12 106	11 227	-24 933	-23 519
2nd quarter	2 337	3 325	28 903	8 502	20 401	4 376	6 457	7 194	1 724	650	2 126	-30 473	-28 689
3rd quarter	-2 779	3 847	37 802	2 506	35 296	4 839	8 675	11 669	2 801	7 312	-723	-31 263	-31 303
4th quarter	-10 375	-8 779	59 746	-1 165	60 911	5 618	5 786	22 484	6 046	20 977	6 048	-35 212	-34 648
1986													
1st quarter	-6 230	4 916	40 898	2 712	38 186	3 431	5 829	18 730	696	9 500	10 717	-34 487	-34 209
2nd quarter	-2 722	-13 660	53 279	15 918	37 361	5 520	4 189	22 752	1 635	3 265	7 358	-33 069	-35 692
3rd quarter	-7 638	-18 909	70 490	15 789	54 701	8 746	-1 240	17 107	1 947	28 141	174	-35 635	-38 049
4th quarter	-5 183	-32 322	63 662	1 229	62 433	17 723	-2 548	12 380	-953	35 831	12 317	-35 343	-39 226
1987													
1st quarter	-5 715	20 237	41 667	14 199	27 468	12 883	-2 906	18 372	6 151	-7 032	-10 579	-36 998	-39 265
2nd quarter	712	-22 873	57 020	10 444	46 576	8 593	-1 042	15 960	5 595	17 470	9 703	-38 243	-39 985
3rd quarter	-1 319	-16 860	82 791	764	82 027	20 763	-2 189	12 676	6 656	44 121	-14 871	-38 042	-40 129
4th quarter	-724	-22 623	65 621	19 980	45 641	16 230	2 360	-4 888	-39	31 978	8 604	-38 406	-41 282

[3] A minus sign indicates financial outflows or increases in U.S. official assets.
[4] A minus sign indicates financial outflows or decreases in foreign official assets in the United States.
[5] Sum of credits and debits with the sign reversed.

Table 7-6B. U.S. International Transactions: Historical Data—Continued

(Millions of dollars, seasonally adjusted.)

| Year and quarter | Exports of goods, services, and income | | | | Imports of goods, services, and income [1] | | | | Unilateral current transfers, net [2] | U.S.-owned assets abroad, net, excluding financial derivatives [3] | | | | | |
| | | | | | | | | | | | | | U.S. private assets, net | | |
	Total	Goods	Services	Income receipts	Total	Goods	Services	Income payments		Total	U.S. official reserve assets, net	U.S. government assets other than official reserve assets, net	Total	Direct invest-ment	Foreign securities
1988															
1st quarter	134 932	75 655	26 598	32 679	-161 810	-109 963	-24 503	-27 344	-6 074	2 892	1 502	-1 597	2 987	-5 037	-4 504
2nd quarter	139 984	79 542	27 567	32 875	-163 265	-110 836	-28 147	-28 147	-5 615	-23 428	39	-854	-22 613	-2 594	1 318
3rd quarter	143 879	80 941	28 453	34 485	-165 901	-110 901	-24 588	-30 412	-5 902	-49 965	-7 380	1 960	-44 545	-7 791	-1 500
4th quarter	149 068	84 092	28 302	36 674	-172 770	-115 489	-25 157	-32 124	-7 685	-36 074	1 925	3 457	-41 456	-7 105	-3 294
1989															
1st quarter	155 853	86 322	30 576	38 955	-178 297	-118 709	-25 140	-34 448	-6 048	-53 703	-4 000	961	-50 664	-12 136	-2 225
2nd quarter	163 435	91 482	31 110	40 843	-182 850	-121 012	-25 241	-36 597	-5 753	-8 202	-12 095	-306	4 199	-7 686	-6 192
3rd quarter	163 560	90 743	32 316	40 501	-178 980	-117 459	-25 792	-35 729	-6 630	-51 678	-5 996	489	-46 171	-8 704	-9 149
4th quarter	165 444	91 369	33 087	40 988	-181 480	-120 485	-26 306	-34 689	-7 739	-61 803	-3 202	87	-58 688	-14 922	-4 504
1990															
1st quarter	171 856	95 070	35 016	41 770	-188 962	-124 947	-28 173	-35 842	-6 540	37 828	-3 177	-756	41 761	-10 391	-8 580
2nd quarter	174 266	96 273	35 988	42 005	-186 146	-121 782	-28 764	-35 600	-7 644	-37 204	371	-796	-36 779	-4 651	-11 037
3rd quarter	176 466	97 227	37 402	41 837	-190 664	-124 132	-29 923	-36 609	-7 339	-43 716	1 739	-338	-45 117	-17 898	-1 037
4th quarter	184 389	98 831	39 428	46 130	-193 514	-127 577	-30 795	-35 142	-5 133	-38 142	-1 092	4 205	-41 255	-4 240	-8 111
1991															
1st quarter	181 296	101 258	37 891	42 147	-186 167	-122 326	-29 801	-34 040	14 828	-10 570	-353	549	-10 766	-14 318	-9 960
2nd quarter	180 627	102 674	37 208	37 208	-181 695	-120 103	-29 660	-31 932	3 593	745	1 014	-423	154	-1 230	-12 021
3rd quarter	181 647	104 238	41 860	35 549	-182 800	-122 448	-29 200	-31 152	-3 033	-15 900	3 878	3 256	-23 034	-9 356	-12 550
4th quarter	183 993	105 913	43 766	34 314	-183 906	-126 143	-29 799	-27 964	-5 488	-38 664	1 226	-459	-39 431	-12 987	-11 142
1992															
1st quarter	186 444	108 062	44 164	34 218	-185 468	-127 962	-29 762	-27 744	-7 210	-11 428	-1 057	-259	-10 112	-20 695	-8 668
2nd quarter	186 873	107 941	44 133	34 799	-190 414	-132 484	-29 443	-28 487	-8 349	-16 235	1 464	-302	-17 397	-10 268	-8 196
3rd quarter	188 127	110 847	44 609	32 671	-193 313	-136 048	-30 175	-27 090	-9 517	-13 570	1 952	-392	-15 130	-5 157	-13 059
4th quarter	189 201	112 781	44 343	32 077	-196 427	-140 034	-30 182	-26 211	-11 561	-33 177	1 542	-715	-34 004	-12 145	-19 243
1993															
1st quarter	191 422	112 099	45 984	33 339	-197 860	-142 331	-29 996	-25 533	-8 339	-21 491	-983	487	-20 995	-14 982	-28 208
2nd quarter	193 169	113 257	46 457	33 455	-204 737	-146 800	-30 661	-27 276	-9 111	-45 843	822	-304	-46 361	-23 264	-29 833
3rd quarter	194 153	112 982	46 707	34 464	-205 549	-147 763	-30 922	-26 864	-9 906	-52 975	-544	-194	-52 237	-13 155	-51 940
4th quarter	200 170	118 605	46 766	34 799	-215 772	-152 500	-32 202	-31 070	-12 456	-80 243	-673	-340	-79 230	-32 550	-36 272
1994															
1st quarter	204 240	118 833	48 362	37 045	-220 726	-156 303	-32 809	-31 614	-8 495	-39 740	-59	399	-40 080	-28 554	-19 540
2nd quarter	211 812	122 251	49 978	39 583	-231 476	-163 200	-33 023	-35 253	-8 914	-45 677	3 537	477	-49 691	-14 932	-11 834
3rd quarter	222 795	128 947	50 667	43 181	-244 319	-171 342	-33 624	-39 353	-10 084	-31 948	-165	-323	-31 460	-17 316	-13 368
4th quarter	230 930	132 828	51 391	46 711	-254 602	-177 845	-33 603	-43 154	-12 773	-61 574	2 033	-943	-62 664	-19 367	-18 448
1995															
1st quarter	241 117	138 370	52 173	50 574	-263 108	-183 966	-34 426	-44 716	-9 443	-64 771	-5 318	-553	-58 900	-19 325	-8 596
2nd quarter	248 705	142 520	53 163	53 022	-271 587	-189 910	-35 097	-46 580	-9 131	-118 089	-2 722	-225	-115 142	-15 078	-27 964
3rd quarter	255 495	146 536	56 436	52 523	-272 929	-187 685	-35 604	-49 640	-9 543	-47 311	-1 893	252	-45 670	-21 772	-42 116
4th quarter	259 310	147 778	57 408	54 124	-272 501	-187 813	-36 272	-48 416	-9 956	-122 091	191	-458	-121 824	-42 573	-43 718
1996															
1st quarter	263 221	150 552	57 442	55 227	-279 419	-194 445	-37 090	-47 884	-11 242	-80 431	17	-210	-80 238	-23 759	-43 538
2nd quarter	266 995	152 861	59 360	54 784	-287 312	-200 070	-37 606	-49 636	-9 523	-68 123	-523	-568	-67 032	-15 096	-30 579
3rd quarter	266 854	151 856	58 664	56 334	-293 261	-202 367	-38 836	-52 058	-9 651	-91 580	7 489	105	-99 174	-23 129	-33 178
4th quarter	280 655	156 844	64 029	59 782	-299 487	-206 231	-39 023	-54 233	-12 603	-173 272	-315	-316	-172 641	-29 898	-42 020
1997															
1st quarter	287 279	162 670	62 515	62 094	-313 391	-214 209	-40 405	-58 777	-9 967	-152 729	4 480	-76	-157 133	-29 544	-24 352
2nd quarter	299 679	170 249	64 292	65 138	-318 210	-217 296	-40 879	-60 035	-10 267	-93 152	-236	-298	-92 618	-24 883	-31 275
3rd quarter	303 542	173 155	64 855	65 532	-325 593	-220 974	-42 078	-62 541	-10 666	-119 387	-730	377	-119 034	-21 217	-51 401
4th quarter	300 762	172 292	64 429	64 041	-329 728	-224 315	-42 571	-62 842	-14 160	-120 209	-4 524	65	-115 750	-29 161	-9 824
1998															
1st quarter	302 195	171 060	64 690	66 445	-334 146	-227 667	-43 304	-63 175	-12 053	-74 438	-444	-80	-73 914	-41 844	-19 451
2nd quarter	298 846	165 559	66 174	67 113	-337 834	-228 497	-44 627	-64 710	-12 361	-138 628	-1 945	-483	-136 200	-44 689	-42 961
3rd quarter	293 115	164 054	64 786	64 275	-338 864	-227 854	-45 784	-65 226	-13 140	-58 520	-2 025	188	-56 683	-20 479	7 783
4th quarter	300 835	169 743	67 106	63 986	-346 026	-234 619	-46 965	-64 442	-15 633	-82 245	-2 369	-47	-79 829	-35 634	-75 575
1999															
1st quarter	301 005	167 904	65 610	67 491	-352 302	-239 650	-47 020	-65 632	-11 885	-84 623	4 068	118	-88 809	-68 498	2 696
2nd quarter	307 938	170 270	66 299	71 370	-367 809	-251 046	-48 469	-68 295	-12 260	-182 426	1 159	-392	-183 193	-50 190	-69 682
3rd quarter	320 396	176 349	67 896	76 150	-389 266	-265 660	-49 755	-73 850	-11 987	-123 490	1 951	-686	-124 755	-64 062	-39 790
4th quarter	333 095	183 695	68 984	80 416	-404 283	-278 033	-50 536	-75 714	-14 295	-113 524	1 569	3 710	-118 803	-42 185	-15 460
2000															
1st quarter	342 570	188 447	70 444	83 680	-428 360	-295 126	-53 154	-80 080	-12 843	-207 606	-554	-127	-206 925	-34 934	-32 542
2nd quarter	356 151	194 625	72 372	89 154	-442 215	-303 191	-54 038	-84 985	-13 348	-107 301	2 020	-570	-108 751	-52 029	-38 171
3rd quarter	361 296	201 770	72 323	87 202	-454 812	-314 280	-56 082	-84 450	-14 387	-84 847	-346	114	-84 615	-39 618	-32 363
4th quarter	365 246	199 939	72 864	92 443	-457 448	-317 971	-55 693	-83 784	-18 191	-160 771	-1 410	-358	-159 003	-32 633	-24 832
2001															
1st quarter	351 600	196 761	72 512	82 327	-443 696	-311 066	-55 215	-77 415	-15 151	-216 194	190	77	-216 461	-35 381	-25 355
2nd quarter	335 986	188 487	71 249	76 250	-417 491	-291 757	-56 449	-69 285	-15 782	-86 702	-1 343	-783	-84 576	-26 783	-50 200
3rd quarter	313 257	175 917	68 065	69 275	-401 351	-279 565	-53 587	-68 199	-16 265	32 858	-3 559	77	36 340	-44 327	11 639
4th quarter	299 313	170 023	64 711	64 580	-369 660	-270 077	-51 779	-47 804	-17 356	-112 577	-199	143	-112 521	-35 857	-26 728

[1] A minus sign indicates imports of goods or services or income payments.
[2] A minus sign indicates net unilateral transfers to foreigners.
[3] A minus sign indicates financial outflows or increases in U.S. official assets.

Table 7-6B. U.S. International Transactions: Historical Data—*Continued*

(Millions of dollars, seasonally adjusted.)

Year and quarter	U.S.-owned assets abroad, net [3] —Continued — U.S. private assets, net—Continued — U.S. claims — On unaffiliated foreigners reported by U.S. nonbanking concerns	Reported by U.S. banks and securities brokers	Foreign-owned assets in the United States, net, excluding financial derivatives [4] — Total	Foreign official assets in the United States, net	Other foreign assets in the United States, net — Total	Direct investment	U.S. Treasury securities and U.S. currency flows	U.S. securities other than U.S. Treasury securities	U.S. liabilities — To unaffiliated foreigners reported by U.S. nonbanking concerns	Reported by U.S. banks and securities brokers	Statistical discrepancy [5]	Balance on goods and services	Balance on current account
1988													
1st quarter	-3 454	15 982	31 524	24 925	6 599	8 425	6 007	2 423	12 593	-22 849	-1 464	-32 213	-32 952
2nd quarter	-9 954	-11 383	74 187	6 006	68 181	13 717	7 329	9 702	6 742	30 691	-21 863	-28 009	-28 896
3rd quarter	-5 217	-30 037	52 329	-1 974	54 303	13 778	4 275	7 464	6 399	22 387	25 560	-26 095	-27 924
4th quarter	-2 568	-28 489	86 793	10 801	75 992	21 815	6 739	6 764	7 159	33 515	-19 332	-28 252	-31 387
1989													
1st quarter	-9 293	-27 010	66 021	7 700	58 321	18 584	10 316	8 544	6 637	14 240	16 174	-26 951	-28 492
2nd quarter	-5 767	23 844	10 571	-5 114	15 685	15 325	4 380	9 365	12 000	-25 385	22 799	-23 661	-25 168
3rd quarter	-5 924	-22 394	73 526	13 060	60 466	11 519	12 202	10 270	-1 121	27 596	202	-20 192	-22 050
4th quarter	-6 662	-32 600	72 660	-7 142	79 802	22 846	6 469	10 588	4 570	35 329	13 125	-22 335	-23 775
1990													
1st quarter	3 019	57 713	-23 477	-6 421	-17 056	15 774	1 056	1 311	12 904	-48 101	9 467	-23 034	-23 646
2nd quarter	-5 069	-16 022	40 868	6 207	34 661	13 773	5 910	2 114	6 713	6 151	15 860	-18 285	-19 524
3rd quarter	-15 514	-10 668	62 621	13 937	48 684	8 313	5 434	-2 874	16 838	20 973	2 632	-19 426	-21 537
4th quarter	-10 260	-18 644	59 345	20 186	39 159	10 635	1 652	1 041	8 678	17 153	104	-20 113	-14 258
1991													
1st quarter	-40	13 552	7 590	5 569	2 021	4 076	8 782	5 023	-586	-15 274	-5 909	-12 978	9 957
2nd quarter	7 902	5 503	12 016	-4 913	16 929	13 378	14 999	14 872	-2 549	-23 771	-15 187	-6 344	2 525
3rd quarter	3 341	-4 469	32 574	3 854	28 720	-1 354	2 342	10 310	4 761	12 661	-8 528	-5 550	-4 186
4th quarter	-106	-15 196	56 043	12 879	43 164	7 072	5 516	4 939	-4 741	30 378	-11 976	-6 263	-5 401
1992													
1st quarter	7 562	11 689	30 212	20 988	9 224	2 086	1 119	4 569	5 689	-4 239	-12 537	-5 498	-6 234
2nd quarter	-6 620	7 687	49 732	20 879	28 853	5 916	10 759	10 467	3 954	-2 243	-21 545	-9 853	-11 890
3rd quarter	-3 737	6 823	34 931	-7 524	42 455	2 898	10 470	2 531	4 854	21 702	-8 187	-10 767	-14 703
4th quarter	2 408	-5 024	53 472	6 133	47 339	8 922	25 869	12 476	-924	996	-1 503	-13 092	-18 787
1993													
1st quarter	-6 130	28 325	24 531	10 937	13 594	8 060	15 795	9 694	-215	-19 740	12 359	-14 244	-14 777
2nd quarter	-725	7 461	58 599	17 466	41 133	11 386	5 169	15 205	6 531	2 842	7 936	-17 747	-20 679
3rd quarter	5 896	6 962	84 967	19 073	65 894	11 688	8 931	17 782	288	27 205	-10 622	-18 996	-21 302
4th quarter	1 725	-12 133	111 662	24 277	87 385	20 229	11 104	37 411	3 885	14 756	-3 350	-19 331	-28 058
1994													
1st quarter	-2 215	10 229	89 488	10 568	78 920	5 883	14 620	21 070	5 856	31 491	-24 759	-21 917	-24 981
2nd quarter	-20 966	-1 959	56 279	9 455	46 824	5 767	-1 361	12 352	4 269	25 797	18 842	-23 994	-28 578
3rd quarter	-960	184	81 239	19 358	61 881	13 709	9 666	13 389	-1 620	26 737	-17 455	-25 352	-31 608
4th quarter	-12 195	-12 654	76 168	202	75 966	20 762	31 934	10 160	-7 203	20 313	21 861	-27 229	-36 445
1995													
1st quarter	-2 631	-28 348	96 842	21 956	74 886	9 924	33 337	12 400	17 764	1 461	-629	-27 849	-31 434
2nd quarter	-24 580	-47 520	121 385	37 072	84 313	11 888	29 574	15 851	11 864	15 136	28 598	-29 324	-32 013
3rd quarter	13 729	4 489	115 499	39 302	76 197	16 764	36 327	26 218	13 493	-16 605	-40 767	-20 317	-26 977
4th quarter	-31 804	-3 729	101 376	11 550	89 826	19 200	1 146	22 780	16 516	30 184	43 751	-18 899	-23 147
1996													
1st quarter	-15 210	2 269	84 335	51 771	32 564	28 518	12 726	20 356	4 350	-33 386	23 538	-23 541	-27 440
2nd quarter	-22 000	643	100 610	13 503	87 107	16 184	28 719	24 686	15 259	2 259	-2 645	-25 465	-29 840
3rd quarter	-9 090	-33 777	143 269	23 020	120 249	15 257	43 276	29 719	28 925	3 072	-15 630	-30 683	-36 058
4th quarter	-40 033	-60 690	219 670	38 430	181 240	26 542	76 452	28 511	5 202	44 533	-14 962	-24 381	-31 435
1997													
1st quarter	-38 112	-65 125	172 247	27 763	144 484	28 626	31 779	38 490	25 055	20 534	16 577	-29 429	-36 079
2nd quarter	-9 885	-26 575	140 222	-6 019	146 241	23 150	38 253	45 651	6 461	32 726	-18 184	-23 634	-28 798
3rd quarter	-22 173	-24 243	166 609	23 474	143 135	17 865	42 095	52 544	25 550	5 081	-14 392	-25 042	-32 717
4th quarter	-51 590	-25 175	225 372	-26 182	251 554	35 960	40 733	24 724	59 452	90 685	-61 998	-30 165	-43 126
1998													
1st quarter	-7 822	-4 797	78 365	11 072	67 293	19 759	-6 594	63 237	39 833	-48 942	40 079	-35 221	-44 004
2nd quarter	-20 363	-28 187	154 539	-10 235	164 774	20 391	23 647	56 146	30 722	33 868	35 435	-41 391	-51 349
3rd quarter	-15 658	-28 329	75 193	-46 640	121 833	23 490	1 425	6 628	14 976	75 314	42 229	-44 798	-58 889
4th quarter	5 639	25 741	112 697	25 900	86 797	115 405	23 950	30 304	-62 391	-20 471	30 369	-44 735	-60 824
1999													
1st quarter	-47 211	24 204	108 317	4 381	103 936	28 759	-11 853	49 157	51 307	-13 434	39 495	-53 156	-63 182
2nd quarter	-27 021	-36 300	247 211	-757	247 968	140 759	-9 004	70 205	16 928	29 080	7 347	-62 946	-72 131
3rd quarter	-13 663	-7 240	156 060	12 625	143 435	50 758	7 584	86 202	-8 777	7 668	48 290	-71 170	-80 857
4th quarter	-9 809	-51 349	230 623	27 294	203 329	69 169	-6 817	93 270	16 789	30 918	-27 451	-75 890	-85 483
2000													
1st quarter	-79 800	-59 649	242 782	22 542	220 240	52 094	-23 776	129 306	72 433	-9 817	63 456	-89 389	-98 633
2nd quarter	-25 287	6 736	246 564	6 952	239 612	91 669	-22 889	88 189	28 796	53 847	-39 853	-90 232	-99 412
3rd quarter	-14 121	1 487	245 064	11 354	233 710	79 979	-13 777	122 138	16 914	28 456	-52 304	-96 268	-107 903
4th quarter	-19 582	-81 956	303 816	1 910	301 906	97 534	-12 898	120 256	52 529	44 485	-32 658	-100 862	-110 394
2001													
1st quarter	-46 769	-108 956	330 767	21 333	309 434	59 145	-16 736	129 474	112 097	25 454	-7 326	-97 007	-107 247
2nd quarter	-7 507	-86	206 867	-19 965	226 832	59 338	-10 143	108 537	-173	69 273	-22 881	-88 469	-97 287
3rd quarter	1 824	67 204	24 226	15 653	8 573	13 783	1 495	60 748	-23 171	-44 282	34 087	-89 170	-104 359
4th quarter	43 932	-93 868	221 010	11 038	209 972	34 755	34 800	95 126	-22 643	67 934	-20 736	-87 123	-87 703

[3] A minus sign indicates financial outflows or increases in U.S. official assets.
[4] A minus sign indicates financial outflows or decreases in foreign official assets in the United States.
[5] Sum of credits and debits with the sign reversed.

Table 7-6B. U.S. International Transactions: Historical Data—*Continued*

(Millions of dollars, seasonally adjusted.)

| Year and quarter | Exports of goods, services, and income | | | | Imports of goods, services, and income [1] | | | | Unilateral current transfers, net [2] | U.S.-owned assets abroad, net, excluding financial derivatives [3] | | | U.S. private assets, net | | |
	Total	Goods	Services	Income receipts	Total	Goods	Services	Income payments		Total	U.S. official reserve assets, net	U.S. government assets other than official reserve assets, net	Total	Direct investment	Foreign securities
2002															
1st quarter	304 361	168 672	68 817	66 873	-389 616	-274 648	-55 048	-59 920	-18 540	-84 841	390	133	-85 364	-48 155	-9 012
2nd quarter	316 088	175 682	70 205	70 201	-416 300	-293 046	-55 358	-67 896	-14 988	-139 712	-1 843	42	-137 911	-36 163	-20 735
3rd quarter	323 800	178 288	71 214	74 298	-424 236	-299 078	-56 700	-68 457	-15 089	892	-1 416	-27	2 335	-33 165	4 884
4th quarter	319 332	174 798	73 201	71 333	-425 684	-305 157	-59 275	-61 252	-16 374	-70 987	-812	197	-70 372	-36 979	-23 705
2003															
1st quarter	323 717	177 427	71 007	75 283	-440 022	-312 374	-59 171	-68 477	-18 252	-82 315	83	53	-82 451	-22 656	-31 947
2nd quarter	326 636	178 414	70 185	78 038	-438 819	-312 830	-58 113	-67 876	-17 634	-157 427	-170	310	-157 567	-46 512	-32 734
3rd quarter	337 118	182 186	74 061	80 871	-448 830	-316 082	-61 970	-70 778	-17 676	-755	-611	483	-627	-40 597	-27 677
4th quarter	358 454	191 790	78 449	88 215	-465 553	-328 938	-65 024	-71 591	-18 234	-84 924	2 221	-309	-86 836	-39 796	-54 364
2004															
1st quarter	377 095	197 823	82 584	96 687	-490 218	-346 942	-67 807	-75 469	-22 941	-353 976	557	727	-355 260	-77 283	-36 045
2nd quarter	388 727	203 914	84 259	100 554	-522 894	-367 207	-70 074	-85 613	-21 367	-170 502	1 122	-2	-171 622	-75 377	-44 702
3rd quarter	398 132	207 198	85 066	105 868	-535 296	-375 876	-71 209	-88 211	-21 121	-169 462	429	484	-170 375	-51 998	-53 988
4th quarter	414 985	213 050	89 252	112 684	-570 807	-395 467	-73 921	-101 419	-22 815	-306 929	697	501	-308 127	-111 564	-35 814
2005															
1st quarter	436 444	219 215	92 045	125 184	-581 819	-402 362	-73 974	-105 483	-28 741	-129 175	5 331	2 591	-137 097	-58 799	-59 599
2nd quarter	449 101	227 630	92 471	129 000	-602 553	-415 019	-75 446	-112 088	-25 175	-222 397	-797	989	-222 589	-41 548	-57 317
3rd quarter	458 956	228 111	94 195	136 650	-618 933	-425 357	-76 524	-117 053	-24 618	-204 361	4 766	1 501	-210 628	12 163	-66 383
4th quarter	480 278	236 730	97 045	146 503	-661 508	-449 679	-77 705	-134 124	-27 206	9 302	4 796	459	4 047	51 948	-67 900
2006															
1st quarter	505 587	249 307	100 482	155 798	-682 915	-457 330	-82 820	-142 765	-20 516	-387 689	513	1 049	-389 251	-58 801	-75 689
2nd quarter	532 230	257 793	104 386	170 051	-709 192	-466 998	-83 931	-158 262	-23 610	-223 953	-560	1 765	-225 158	-35 160	-80 203
3rd quarter	542 555	261 991	104 380	176 183	-731 811	-479 860	-84 183	-167 768	-25 141	-295 389	1 006	1 570	-297 965	-72 149	-72 552
4th quarter	564 073	270 314	111 170	182 588	-729 632	-470 908	-87 082	-171 642	-22 248	-378 698	1 415	962	-381 075	-78 812	-136 685
2007															
1st quarter	582 062	276 492	114 690	190 880	-747 524	-478 769	-89 109	-179 645	-32 211	-487 524	-72	445	-487 897	-101 224	-122 024
2nd quarter	610 791	285 624	118 426	206 741	-771 861	-490 289	-91 488	-190 084	-26 481	-563 522	26	-596	-562 951	-88 737	-107 067
3rd quarter	638 132	295 342	125 337	217 453	-779 067	-498 775	-93 861	-186 431	-28 092	-189 912	-54	623	-190 481	-77 349	-113 821
4th quarter	657 411	306 499	132 152	218 760	-785 184	-515 009	-93 986	-176 189	-28 279	-212 647	-22	-22 744	-189 880	-146 729	-23 600
2008															
1st quarter	670 832	323 357	131 685	215 789	-814 329	-539 441	-98 135	-176 752	-33 735	-238 333	-276	3 268	-241 325	-92 199	-11 990
2nd quarter	692 907	342 620	136 154	214 133	-836 822	-562 565	-100 055	-174 203	-31 347	177 984	-1 267	-41 592	220 844	-95 140	-4 820
3rd quarter	691 564	346 910	136 300	208 354	-833 469	-565 850	-103 495	-164 124	-31 703	113 445	-179	-225 997	339 621	-66 710	115 406
4th quarter	601 284	294 612	131 044	175 627	-723 214	-469 752	-101 727	-151 735	-29 103	279 012	-3 126	-265 293	547 432	-75 031	98 751
2009															
1st quarter	525 222	254 092	124 379	146 751	-594 817	-376 641	-95 262	-122 913	-28 905	119 562	-982	244 102	-123 559	-67 510	-36 497
2nd quarter	522 332	253 850	125 225	143 257	-578 983	-364 901	-93 917	-120 165	-30 331	193 750	-3 632	193 750	-132 723	-56 711	-94 166
3rd quarter	546 847	270 106	126 964	149 776	-609 608	-398 962	-95 553	-115 093	-32 935	-297 502	-49 021	57 736	-306 217	-74 759	-54 256
4th quarter	586 153	291 685	132 643	161 825	-656 583	-434 986	-97 876	-123 721	-30 289	1 010	1 379	45 754	-46 122	-90 470	-42 105
2010															
1st quarter	599 298	304 032	133 302	161 964	-675 611	-456 570	-98 716	-120 325	-34 681	-269 433	-773	9 433	-278 092	-109 091	-42 124
2nd quarter	617 954	315 478	136 184	166 292	-697 957	-480 118	-99 231	-118 607	-31 710	-154 408	-165	-2 441	-151 802	-65 020	-15 728
3rd quarter	636 778	325 198	140 271	171 310	-718 137	-492 068	-102 536	-123 532	-33 216	-294 523	-1 096	788	-294 215	-90 647	-39 329
4th quarter	664 736	344 175	143 845	176 716	-737 941	-505 250	-102 733	-129 958	-31 466	-221 120	200	-240	-221 080	-63 119	-41 803
2011															
1st quarter	689 593	360 917	147 894	180 781	-774 367	-542 276	-103 761	-128 330	-35 223	-372 944	-3 619	-547	-368 778	-104 404	-85 472
2nd quarter	713 499	372 160	151 839	189 499	-798 839	-559 344	-106 205	-133 290	-33 777	7 418	-6 267	-1 358	15 042	-133 397	-57 195
3rd quarter	724 800	382 161	155 190	187 449	-801 143	-562 778	-109 395	-128 971	-31 815	-91 896	-4 079	-1 137	-86 679	-70 323	-40 110
4th quarter	720 095	382 167	151 037	186 891	-806 512	-571 421	-108 068	-127 022	-32 240	-26 231	-1 912	-100 624	76 305	-111 208	35 980

[1] A minus sign indicates imports of goods or services or income payments.
[2] A minus sign indicates net unilateral transfers to foreigners.
[3] A minus sign indicates financial outflows or increases in U.S. official assets.

Table 7-6B. U.S. International Transactions: Historical Data—*Continued*

(Millions of dollars, seasonally adjusted.)

Year and quarter	U.S. private assets, net—Continued / U.S. claims — On unaffiliated foreigners reported by U.S. nonbanking concerns	Reported by U.S. banks and securities brokers	Total	Foreign official assets in the United States, net	Total	Direct investment	U.S. Treasury securities and U.S. currency flows	U.S. securities other than U.S. Treasury securities	To unaffiliated foreigners reported by U.S. nonbanking concerns	Reported by U.S. banks and securities brokers	Statistical discrepancy [5]	Balance on goods and services	Balance on current account
2002													
1st quarter	-27 798	-399	173 225	12 801	160 424	24 485	13 964	73 750	57 788	-9 563	15 403	-92 207	-103 794
2nd quarter	-13 680	-67 333	231 325	53 312	178 013	7 194	26 042	99 689	17 805	27 283	23 589	-102 518	-115 200
3rd quarter	-7 443	38 059	160 335	18 328	142 007	13 929	55 166	43 282	7 515	22 115	-45 634	-106 277	-115 524
4th quarter	-1 101	-8 587	230 275	31 504	198 771	38 763	24 092	66 578	12 763	56 575	-36 484	-116 434	-122 727
2003													
1st quarter	1 757	-29 605	240 908	50 531	190 377	37 169	10 894	52 209	68 460	21 645	-23 953	-123 112	-134 558
2nd quarter	-15 089	-63 232	217 732	66 877	150 855	-5 460	48 179	81 187	15 129	11 820	70 763	-122 344	-129 817
3rd quarter	21 261	46 386	129 177	64 397	64 780	-1 574	36 749	15 354	9 137	5 114	1 458	-121 805	-129 388
4th quarter	-26 113	33 437	270 487	96 264	174 223	33 616	6 224	71 955	3 800	58 628	-60 235	-123 723	-125 334
2004													
1st quarter	-67 088	-174 844	459 483	147 636	311 847	26 000	29 034	47 862	61 265	147 686	30 614	-134 342	-136 065
2nd quarter	-11 754	-39 789	331 630	79 949	251 681	32 658	73 376	87 270	21 013	37 364	-5 594	-149 108	-155 534
3rd quarter	-9 235	-55 154	274 147	76 120	198 027	34 113	-3 198	86 577	29 957	50 578	50 427	-154 821	-158 286
4th quarter	-64 489	-96 260	467 941	94 050	373 891	53 195	7 697	159 784	53 637	99 578	17 692	-167 087	-178 636
2005													
1st quarter	-64 051	45 352	234 182	25 052	209 130	38 871	76 819	75 631	86 298	-68 489	71 269	-165 077	-174 116
2nd quarter	59 260	-182 984	304 880	81 292	223 588	-9 004	-13 197	107 694	-26 159	164 254	96 227	-170 364	-178 627
3rd quarter	-69 527	-86 881	425 404	54 736	370 668	38 016	26 597	141 900	51 727	112 428	-51 809	-179 575	-184 595
4th quarter	3 111	16 888	282 881	98 188	184 693	44 755	50 528	125 161	-42 294	6 543	-83 746	-193 608	-208 435
2006													
1st quarter	-41 792	-212 969	545 648	130 427	415 221	44 357	-25 884	167 589	66 064	163 095	39 472	-190 361	-197 845
2nd quarter	-48 226	-61 569	407 652	127 303	280 349	65 611	-26 369	139 681	59 820	41 606	3 270	-188 750	-200 572
3rd quarter	-57 478	-95 786	525 441	121 843	403 598	55 495	-23 914	197 877	69 975	104 165	-30 787	-197 671	-214 397
4th quarter	-33 803	-131 775	586 428	108 366	478 062	77 688	20 165	178 098	48 934	153 177	-18 697	-176 504	-187 807
2007													
1st quarter	-36 540	-228 109	726 910	165 888	561 022	49 999	35 962	183 458	83 177	208 426	-56 508	-176 696	-197 673
2nd quarter	-156 215	-210 932	717 694	88 383	629 311	65 513	-15 072	310 289	124 643	143 938	33 943	-177 727	-187 551
3rd quarter	88 737	-88 048	269 827	47 707	222 120	86 233	17 528	-9 826	78 299	49 886	83 228	-171 958	-169 028
4th quarter	103 090	-122 641	350 211	179 065	171 146	19 421	17 752	121 493	-102 898	115 378	31 997	-170 344	-156 052
2008													
1st quarter	120 047	-257 183	456 245	216 229	240 016	88 544	7 665	-15 059	72 442	86 424	-32 706	-182 535	-177 232
2nd quarter	75 492	245 312	-19 863	181 419	-201 282	66 637	19 031	20 240	-61 088	-246 102	19 513	-183 846	-175 262
3rd quarter	121 264	169 661	72 116	142 224	-70 108	62 738	71 998	-123 022	85 846	-167 668	-13 110	-186 135	-173 608
4th quarter	139 374	384 338	-77 093	14 762	-91 855	92 172	93 437	-47 798	-128 675	-100 991	-33 139	-145 822	-151 032
2009													
1st quarter	18 234	-37 786	-119 117	109 442	-228 559	-2 335	57 689	-67 748	-7 776	-208 389	90 929	-93 432	-98 500
2nd quarter	36 979	-18 825	-38 011	129 253	-167 264	30 243	-32 028	-279	15 644	-180 844	60 065	-79 743	-86 982
3rd quarter	84 760	-261 962	335 302	109 204	226 098	54 849	-23 881	48 758	20 559	125 813	47 288	-97 445	-95 697
4th quarter	13 722	72 731	136 217	132 387	3 830	67 686	-4 599	21 124	-19 471	-60 910	-55 916	-108 534	-100 719
2010													
1st quarter	45 003	-171 880	311 935	89 961	221 974	40 375	86 311	4 582	17 312	73 394	52 342	-117 952	-110 994
2nd quarter	6 596	-77 650	170 919	65 838	105 081	23 478	85 588	-16 364	12 728	-349	85 224	-127 687	-111 713
3rd quarter	2 067	-166 306	512 515	168 611	343 904	79 097	85 144	92 957	10 923	75 783	-91 379	-129 137	-114 574
4th quarter	-20 697	-95 461	312 910	73 778	239 132	62 881	69 073	58 141	21 994	27 043	13 051	-119 962	-104 671
2011													
1st quarter	-92 203	-86 699	578 972	72 974	505 998	33 365	67 630	4 338	40 688	359 977	-88 930	-137 225	-119 997
2nd quarter	6 147	199 487	98 554	121 822	-23 268	61 281	-3 624	-5 108	25 538	-101 355	6 555	-141 549	-119 117
3rd quarter	9 326	14 428	266 397	19 889	246 508	63 222	130 532	-20 396	-19 670	92 820	-62 094	-134 822	-108 158
4th quarter	65 122	86 411	57 067	-2 859	59 926	76 120	101 336	-35 276	-39 989	-42 265	55 263	-146 286	-118 656

[3] A minus sign indicates financial outflows or increases in U.S. official assets.
[4] A minus sign indicates financial outflows or decreases in foreign official assets in the United States.
[5] Sum of credits and debits with the sign reversed.

Table 7-7. Foreigners' Transactions in Long-Term Securities with U.S. Residents

(Billions of dollars, not seasonally adjusted.)

Year and month	Gross purchases from U.S. residents	Gross sales to U.S. residents	Transactions in U.S. domestic securities between foreigners and U.S. residents — Net purchases						Official	
			Total	Private — Total	Treasury bonds and notes	Government agency bonds	Corporate bonds	Equities	Total	Treasury bonds and notes
1977	60.7	30.1	30.6	. . .	. . .	. . .	. . .	. . .	5.8	. . .
1978	60.5	51.1	9.4	3.6	1.0	0.6	0.3	1.7	3.2	3.7
1979	72.9	67.2	5.7	2.5	1.2	0.1	0.2	1.1	3.2	1.7
1980	106.9	91.1	15.8	6.6	1.0	0.4	0.9	4.3	9.2	3.9
1981	126.5	100.5	26.0	10.2	3.3	0.3	1.9	4.8	15.6	11.7
1982	159.5	136.8	22.7	9.2	2.8	0.3	2.5	3.6	13.5	14.6
1983	223.4	211.7	11.7	13.2	4.6	0.5	1.7	6.4	-1.5	0.8
1984	335.5	304.0	31.5	33.8	21.0	1.2	12.5	-0.9	-2.4	0.5
1985	667.2	588.9	78.3	71.9	21.1	4.6	41.4	4.8	6.3	8.1
1986	1 355.4	1 266.9	88.5	76.4	5.2	8.2	45.1	18.0	12.1	14.2
1987	1 692.1	1 623.0	69.1	37.5	-5.5	3.5	22.7	16.8	31.7	31.1
1988	1 827.9	1 753.1	74.8	49.4	22.2	5.4	21.3	0.4	25.4	26.6
1989	2 431.7	2 335.2	96.5	66.5	27.4	13.7	17.5	7.9	30.0	26.8
1990	2 111.2	2 092.4	18.8	-3.6	-5.3	5.6	9.8	-13.7	22.5	23.3
1991	2 382.1	2 324.0	58.1	54.3	18.7	8.9	16.5	10.1	3.8	1.2
1992	2 677.8	2 604.6	73.2	63.1	32.4	14.3	20.0	-3.7	10.1	6.9
1993	3 212.5	3 101.4	111.1	103.2	22.2	31.4	29.9	19.6	7.9	1.3
1994	3 351.1	3 210.7	140.4	94.9	37.0	15.6	38.0	4.3	45.4	41.8
1995	3 737.6	3 505.7	231.9	185.3	94.5	25.0	57.6	8.2	46.5	39.6
1996	4 667.6	4 297.4	370.2	278.1	146.4	36.7	82.2	12.7	92.1	85.8
1997	6 573.3	6 185.3	388.0	339.7	140.2	45.3	82.8	71.3	48.3	44.0
1998	7 633.5	7 355.7	277.8	270.8	44.9	50.5	121.7	53.7	6.9	4.1
1999	7 483.5	7 133.3	350.2	338.8	-0.1	71.9	158.8	108.2	11.4	-9.9
2000	8 684.1	8 226.3	457.8	420.1	-47.7	111.9	182.1	173.8	37.7	-6.3
2001	10 261.8	9 740.9	520.8	494.2	15.0	146.6	218.2	114.4	26.7	3.5
2002	13 022.9	12 475.4	547.6	508.3	112.8	166.6	176.7	52.2	39.3	7.1
2003	13 526.0	12 806.1	719.9	585.0	159.7	129.9	260.3	35.0	134.9	103.8
2004	15 178.9	14 262.4	916.5	680.9	150.9	205.7	298.0	26.2	235.6	201.1
2005	17 157.5	16 145.9	1 011.6	891.1	269.4	187.6	353.1	81.0	120.4	68.7
2006	21 077.1	19 933.9	1 143.2	946.6	125.9	193.8	482.2	144.6	196.6	69.6
2007	29 730.6	28 724.8	1 005.8	818.1	195.0	99.9	342.8	180.4	187.8	3.0
2008	30 724.9	30 310.0	414.9	311.9	238.7	-7.4	59.2	21.4	103.0	76.2
2009	20 479.7	19 840.9	638.9	511.0	377.0	31.4	-38.4	141.1	127.9	161.4
2010	25 017.0	24 108.7	908.3	776.1	531.6	146.2	-14.0	112.3	132.2	172.1
2011	27 818.8	27 325.5	493.4	322.6	288.4	57.6	-44.0	20.6	170.7	144.2
2009										
January	1 337.4	1 346.7	-9.3	-0.7	12.9	-7.7	-7.7	1.8	-8.6	-1.9
February	1 457.0	1 434.5	22.6	27.6	23.7	5.3	3.0	-4.3	-5.1	-2.0
March	1 757.8	1 696.1	61.7	35.5	26.2	-12.9	8.2	14.0	26.2	29.0
April	1 485.4	1 451.2	34.1	18.2	24.8	1.1	-10.8	3.0	16.0	17.1
May	1 548.3	1 539.0	9.3	32.6	-0.8	13.7	1.8	18.0	-23.4	-21.8
June	2 040.7	1 915.3	125.4	107.0	78.0	13.7	-2.4	17.7	18.4	22.5
July	1 649.6	1 603.8	45.8	33.9	15.5	2.7	-9.6	25.2	11.9	15.7
August	1 744.0	1 704.8	39.2	27.6	14.9	6.2	-5.5	12.1	11.6	13.2
September	1 815.1	1 758.9	56.2	45.4	25.7	6.7	-2.5	15.4	10.9	19.0
October	1 992.4	1 949.3	43.0	28.4	23.9	-3.9	-1.4	9.7	14.6	15.0
November	1 894.3	1 765.4	128.9	95.6	86.7	3.5	-4.3	9.8	33.3	31.2
December	1 757.8	1 675.9	81.9	60.0	45.5	3.0	-7.2	18.7	22.0	24.3
2010										
January	1 709.0	1 672.6	36.4	40.6	61.0	-1.3	-24.9	5.8	-4.2	0.6
February	1 899.6	1 848.4	51.3	52.4	47.1	5.0	-12.2	12.6	-1.2	1.1
March	2 308.4	2 152.8	155.6	122.8	79.4	18.0	13.7	11.8	32.7	28.3
April	1 998.0	1 890.8	107.2	89.4	62.5	9.7	8.1	9.1	17.7	14.7
May	2 321.5	2 293.8	27.7	19.6	8.8	22.9	-13.2	1.0	8.1	6.1
June	2 085.0	2 055.5	29.5	12.9	20.3	14.6	-17.5	-4.7	16.6	11.4
July	1 694.4	1 621.6	72.7	68.5	21.9	28.7	5.5	12.4	4.3	8.2
August	2 125.0	1 989.5	135.5	112.9	87.4	13.3	7.7	4.5	22.6	30.6
September	2 154.2	2 075.3	79.0	69.4	35.8	7.8	4.4	21.4	9.6	41.4
October	2 043.4	1 995.1	48.4	55.5	24.0	7.0	7.4	17.2	-7.2	-0.7
November	2 537.2	2 444.8	92.4	72.1	44.0	10.0	3.5	14.5	20.3	16.6
December	2 141.2	2 068.5	72.8	60.0	39.3	10.5	3.6	6.7	12.7	13.7
2011										
January	2 197.1	2 121.1	76.0	46.3	30.6	2.1	-0.2	13.9	29.6	18.2
February	2 281.1	2 247.6	33.4	13.6	17.0	-6.8	-3.3	6.6	19.9	15.7
March	2 663.5	2 606.2	57.2	46.8	21.9	9.2	1.2	14.6	10.4	7.4
April	2 030.8	1 985.5	45.3	13.8	-4.4	5.1	-3.6	16.6	31.5	29.6
May	2 481.4	2 427.8	53.6	30.3	27.1	-9.2	4.5	7.9	23.3	21.6
June	2 574.2	2 581.2	-7.0	-16.1	-9.4	2.1	-11.8	2.9	9.1	11.3
July	2 099.4	2 075.5	23.9	9.4	1.2	6.4	2.3	-0.5	14.5	14.2
August	3 201.9	3 132.9	69.0	77.6	76.7	8.6	-1.2	-6.5	-8.6	-9.7
September	2 343.7	2 267.2	76.5	39.6	55.9	8.2	-5.2	-19.4	36.9	38.4
October	2 172.2	2 153.8	18.4	22.5	27.5	4.1	-10.9	1.8	-4.0	-6.0
November	2 121.7	2 057.1	64.6	47.0	37.1	11.5	3.5	-5.2	17.7	23.7
December	1 652.0	1 669.5	-17.6	-8.1	7.2	16.4	-19.3	-12.3	-9.5	-20.3

. . . = Not available.

Table 7-7. Foreigners' Transactions in Long-Term Securities with U.S. Residents—*Continued*

(Billions of dollars, not seasonally adjusted.)

Year and month	Transactions in U.S. domestic securities between foreigners and U.S. residents—Continued			Transactions in foreign securities between foreigners and U.S. residents					Net long-term securities transactions	Other acquisitions of long-term securities, net	Net foreign acquisition of long-term securities
	Net purchases—Continued			Gross purchases from U.S. residents	Gross sales to U.S. residents	Net purchases¹					
	Official—Continued					Total	Bonds	Equities			
	Government agency bonds	Corporate bonds	Equities								
1977	. . .	. . .	. . .	10.3	15.8	-5.5	-5.1	-0.4	25.1	. . .	. . .
1978	0.7	0.7	0.7	14.8	18.5	-3.7	-4.2	0.5	5.7	. . .	. . .
1979	0.5	0.4	0.6	17.3	22.1	-4.8	-4.0	-0.8	0.9	0.1	1.0
1980	2.2	2.0	1.1	25.0	28.1	-3.1	-1.0	-2.1	12.7	-1.6	11.0
1981	1.3	1.6	1.0	26.9	32.6	-5.7	-5.5	-0.2	20.3	-5.2	15.0
1982	-0.7	-0.7	0.3	34.3	42.3	-8.0	-6.6	-1.3	14.7	-5.4	9.3
1983	-0.5	-0.8	-1.0	49.6	56.6	-7.0	-3.2	-3.8	4.7	-3.2	1.5
1984	0.0	-0.8	-2.1	70.8	75.9	-5.1	-3.9	-1.1	26.4	-1.5	24.9
1985	-0.3	-1.6	0.1	102.1	110.0	-7.9	-4.0	-3.9	70.4	-2.3	68.1
1986	-1.2	-1.6	0.7	216.1	221.7	-5.6	-3.7	-1.9	82.9	-2.3	80.8
1987	1.6	-0.4	-0.6	294.5	301.4	-6.9	-8.0	1.1	62.2	-1.0	61.3
1988	1.3	-0.1	-2.4	293.9	303.3	-9.4	-7.4	-2.0	65.4	0.2	65.6
1989	1.4	-0.2	2.0	344.6	363.2	-18.6	-5.5	-13.1	77.9	0.0	78.0
1990	0.7	-0.1	-1.4	437.7	468.9	-31.2	-21.9	-9.2	-12.4	3.9	-8.5
1991	1.3	0.4	0.9	450.9	497.7	-46.8	-14.8	-32.0	11.3	0.4	11.7
1992	3.9	0.8	-1.5	663.6	711.5	-47.9	-15.6	-32.3	25.3	-0.3	25.0
1993	4.0	0.6	2.0	991.4	1 134.5	-143.1	-80.4	-62.7	-32.0	1.1	-30.8
1994	6.1	0.0	-2.5	1 234.5	1 291.8	-57.3	-9.2	-48.1	83.1	0.5	83.5
1995	3.7	0.2	3.0	1 235.1	1 333.8	-98.7	-48.4	-50.3	133.2	0.4	133.6
1996	5.0	1.5	-0.2	1 564.4	1 675.0	-110.6	-51.4	-59.3	259.6	-0.5	259.1
1997	4.5	1.5	-1.7	2 207.7	2 296.8	-89.1	-48.1	-40.9	298.9	0.0	298.9
1998	6.3	0.2	-3.7	2 257.8	2 269.0	-11.2	-17.3	6.2	266.6	0.1	266.7
1999	20.4	1.5	-0.6	1 975.6	1 965.6	10.0	-5.7	15.6	360.2	0.0	360.2
2000	40.9	2.0	1.1	2 761.1	2 778.3	-17.1	-4.1	-13.1	440.7	-59.8	380.8
2001	17.4	3.8	2.0	2 557.8	2 577.4	-19.6	30.5	-50.1	501.2	-41.5	459.8
2002	28.6	5.6	-2.0	2 640.0	2 613.0	27.0	28.5	-1.5	574.6	-39.3	535.2
2003	25.9	5.4	-0.3	2 761.8	2 818.4	-56.5	32.0	-88.6	663.3	-138.9	524.5
2004	20.8	11.5	2.2	3 123.1	3 276.0	-152.8	-67.9	-85.0	763.6	-38.8	724.8
2005	31.6	19.1	1.0	3 700.0	3 872.4	-172.4	-45.1	-127.3	839.2	-143.0	696.2
2006	92.6	28.6	5.8	5 515.9	5 766.8	-250.9	-144.5	-106.5	892.3	-174.6	717.7
2007	119.1	50.6	15.1	8 189.1	8 418.3	-229.2	-133.9	-95.3	776.6	-235.2	541.4
2008	-31.3	34.7	23.4	7 714.9	7 640.7	74.2	53.9	20.2	489.1	-197.9	291.2
2009	-42.9	-2.3	11.7	5 121.4	5 308.3	-186.8	-127.5	-59.4	452.0	-205.1	246.9
2010	-38.2	0.8	-2.5	7 323.8	7 439.1	-115.3	-54.6	-60.6	793.0	-234.7	558.3
2011	23.3	-1.2	4.5	7 499.3	7 623.6	-124.3	-52.6	-71.7	369.0	-172.2	196.8
2009											
January	-7.9	0.3	1.0	350.6	374.4	-23.8	-26.9	3.1	-33.1	-16.5	-49.6
February	-3.2	0.0	0.1	314.9	313.4	1.5	-0.1	1.6	24.1	-17.1	6.9
March	-2.7	-0.9	0.7	380.3	381.2	-0.9	-0.3	-0.6	60.8	-20.3	40.5
April	-3.5	1.4	0.9	381.9	404.6	-22.7	-13.8	-8.9	11.4	-21.2	-9.7
May	-0.6	-0.9	-0.1	400.0	426.9	-26.9	-16.1	-10.8	-17.6	-19.2	-36.8
June	-5.8	-0.4	2.2	485.3	518.7	-33.4	-19.5	-13.9	92.0	-21.6	70.3
July	-7.2	-1.2	4.6	438.5	466.9	-28.4	-14.2	-14.2	17.4	-19.9	-2.5
August	-1.6	-0.1	0.2	389.8	392.6	-2.9	10.0	-12.9	36.4	-16.1	20.2
September	-8.3	0.0	0.2	490.2	505.2	-15.0	-15.5	0.5	41.2	-13.6	27.6
October	-1.5	0.5	0.6	555.4	579.1	-23.7	-19.4	-4.3	19.3	-12.3	7.0
November	2.4	-0.3	0.0	482.0	484.5	-2.5	-5.1	2.6	126.4	-14.1	112.4
December	-3.0	-0.7	1.3	452.5	460.7	-8.2	-6.6	-1.6	73.7	-13.2	60.5
2010											
January	-3.8	0.3	-1.2	589.9	611.3	-21.4	-16.0	-5.4	15.0	-16.1	-1.1
February	-2.4	-0.3	0.4	619.0	621.0	-1.9	-0.5	-1.4	49.4	-6.1	43.3
March	2.6	1.6	0.3	770.8	786.6	-15.9	-13.0	-2.8	139.7	-20.2	119.5
April	2.8	-0.4	0.7	713.1	742.6	-29.5	-16.2	-13.3	77.6	-20.9	56.7
May	3.3	-0.4	-1.0	675.1	670.9	4.2	14.2	-10.0	31.9	-21.6	10.3
June	4.9	0.0	0.4	583.0	569.6	13.5	9.4	4.1	43.0	-21.4	21.6
July	-4.2	-0.1	0.3	513.5	526.8	-13.3	-7.1	-6.2	59.4	-17.7	41.7
August	-8.2	-0.2	0.4	487.7	496.7	-9.0	-16.0	6.9	126.5	-28.1	98.4
September	-31.3	0.3	-0.8	607.0	610.5	-3.5	2.0	-5.5	75.4	-21.0	54.4
October	-5.3	-0.2	-1.0	611.7	630.6	-19.0	-9.0	-10.0	29.4	-20.8	8.6
November	4.0	0.9	-1.2	602.3	610.3	-8.0	0.6	-8.6	84.4	-20.0	64.3
December	-0.4	-0.7	0.1	550.8	562.2	-11.5	-3.0	-8.5	61.3	-20.8	40.5
2011											
January	9.9	-0.5	2.1	592.3	619.7	-27.4	-8.5	-18.9	48.6	-20.7	27.8
February	5.8	-1.1	-0.5	636.3	648.1	-11.8	1.6	-13.4	21.7	-14.9	6.8
March	2.7	0.4	-0.1	781.8	825.2	-43.3	-29.4	-13.9	13.9	-12.0	1.9
April	1.8	-1.0	1.2	639.1	662.7	-23.5	-10.4	-13.1	21.7	-11.0	10.8
May	0.6	-0.4	1.4	649.0	681.2	-32.2	-25.8	-6.4	21.4	-15.3	6.1
June	-2.4	-0.7	0.8	698.2	688.9	9.3	7.6	1.6	2.3	-11.5	-9.3
July	1.4	-0.4	-0.6	590.7	612.6	-21.9	-6.0	-15.9	2.0	-16.8	-14.8
August	-0.9	2.0	0.0	631.1	642.1	-11.1	-7.9	-3.2	57.9	-10.6	47.4
September	-1.8	0.3	0.0	575.2	575.3	0.0	-2.0	2.0	76.4	-12.5	63.9
October	0.7	0.4	0.9	574.2	578.3	-4.1	-1.9	-2.2	14.3	-14.2	0.1
November	-5.3	1.3	-2.0	588.1	584.8	3.3	2.0	1.4	68.0	-16.1	51.9
December	10.8	-1.4	1.3	543.4	504.9	38.5	28.2	10.3	20.9	-16.7	4.2

¹(-) indicates net U.S. acquisitions of foreign securities.
. . . = Not available.

Table 7-8. International Investment Position of the United States at Year-End

(Millions of dollars.)

Year	U.S. net international investment position	U.S.-owned assets abroad									
		Total	Financial derivatives	Official reserve assets	Other U.S. government assets	Direct investment		Foreign bonds	Foreign corporate stocks	U.S. nonbank claims	U.S. bank claims
						Current cost	Market value				
1980	360 347	929 806	...	171 412	65 573	388 072	...	43 524	18 930	38 429	203 866
1981	340 385	1 001 667	...	124 568	70 893	407 804	...	45 675	16 467	42 752	293 508
1982	331 373	1 108 436	...	143 445	76 903	374 059	226 638	56 604	17 442	35 405	404 578
1983	302 404	1 210 974	...	123 110	81 664	355 643	274 342	58 569	26 154	131 329	434 505
1984	166 747	1 204 900	...	105 040	86 945	348 342	270 574	62 810	25 994	130 138	445 631
1985	61 739	1 287 396	...	117 930	89 792	371 036	386 352	75 020	44 383	141 872	447 363
1986	-27 759	1 469 396	...	139 875	91 850	404 818	530 074	85 724	72 399	167 392	507 338
1987	-70 919	1 646 527	...	162 370	90 681	478 062	590 246	93 889	94 700	177 368	549 457
1988	-167 458	1 829 665	...	144 179	87 892	513 761	692 461	104 187	128 662	197 757	653 227
1989	-246 232	2 070 868	...	168 714	86 643	553 093	832 460	116 949	197 345	234 307	713 817
1990	-230 375	2 178 978	...	174 664	84 344	616 655	731 762	144 717	197 596	265 315	695 687
1991	-291 754	2 286 456	...	159 223	81 422	643 364	827 537	176 774	278 976	256 295	690 402
1992	-411 021	2 331 696	...	147 435	83 022	663 830	798 630	200 817	314 266	254 303	668 023
1993	-284 460	2 753 648	...	164 945	83 382	723 526	1 061 299	309 666	543 862	242 022	686 245
1994	-298 458	2 987 118	...	163 394	83 908	786 565	1 114 582	310 391	626 762	322 980	693 118
1995	-430 194	3 486 272	...	176 061	85 064	885 506	1 363 792	413 310	790 615	367 567	768 149
1996	-463 338	4 032 307	...	160 739	86 123	989 810	1 608 340	481 411	1 006 135	450 578	857 511
1997	-786 174	4 567 906	...	134 836	86 198	1 068 063	1 879 285	543 396	1 207 787	545 524	982 102
1998	-858 363	5 095 546	...	146 006	86 768	1 196 021	2 279 601	594 400	1 474 983	588 322	1 009 046
1999	-731 068	5 974 394	...	136 418	84 227	1 414 355	2 839 639	548 233	2 003 716	704 517	1 082 928
2000	-1 337 014	6 238 785	...	128 400	85 168	1 531 607	2 694 014	572 692	1 852 842	836 559	1 231 517
2001	-1 875 032	6 308 681	...	129 961	85 654	1 693 131	2 314 934	557 062	1 612 673	839 303	1 390 897
2002	-2 044 631	6 649 079	...	158 602	85 309	1 867 043	2 022 588	702 742	1 373 980	901 946	1 559 457
2003	-2 093 794	7 638 086	...	183 577	84 772	2 054 464	2 729 126	868 948	2 079 422	594 004	1 772 899
2004	-2 253 026	9 340 634	...	189 591	83 062	2 498 494	3 362 796	984 978	2 560 418	793 556	2 230 535
2005	-1 932 149	11 961 552	1 190 029	188 043	77 523	2 651 721	3 637 996	1 011 554	3 317 705	1 018 462	2 506 515
2006	-2 191 653	14 428 137	1 238 995	219 853	72 189	2 948 172	4 470 343	1 275 515	4 328 960	1 184 073	3 160 380
2007	-1 796 005	18 399 676	2 559 332	277 211	94 471	3 553 095	5 274 991	1 587 089	5 247 990	1 233 341	3 847 147
2008	-3 260 158	19 464 717	6 127 450	293 732	624 099	3 748 512	3 102 418	1 237 284	2 748 428	930 909	3 754 303
2009	-2 321 770	18 511 691	3 489 779	403 804	82 774	4 029 457	4 287 203	1 570 341	3 995 295	930 337	4 009 904
2010	-2 473 599	20 298 413	3 652 313	488 673	75 235	4 306 843	4 766 730	1 689 462	4 646 908	874 762	4 564 217
2011	-4 030 250	21 132 370	4 704 666	536 036	178 901	4 681 569	4 499 962	1 763 754	4 158 247	796 827	4 312 370

Year	Foreign-owned assets in the United States										
	Total	Financial derivatives	Foreign official assets	Direct investment in the United States		U.S. Treasury securities	Corporate and other bonds	Corporate stocks	U.S. currency	U.S. nonbank liabilities	U.S. bank liabilities
				Current cost	Market value						
1980	569 459	...	181 217	127 105	...	16 113	9 545	64 569	19 415	30 426	121 069
1981	661 282	...	186 128	164 623	...	18 505	10 694	64 391	20 974	30 606	165 361
1982	777 063	...	194 514	184 842	130 428	25 758	16 709	76 279	23 441	27 532	227 988
1983	908 570	...	199 598	193 708	153 318	33 846	17 454	96 357	27 546	61 731	278 330
1984	1 038 153	...	204 481	223 538	172 377	62 121	32 421	96 056	29 942	77 415	312 179
1985	1 225 657	...	207 864	247 223	219 996	87 954	82 290	125 578	33 258	86 993	354 497
1986	1 497 155	...	247 219	284 701	272 966	96 078	140 863	168 940	35 679	90 703	432 972
1987	1 717 446	...	290 009	334 552	316 200	82 588	166 089	175 643	39 545	110 187	518 833
1988	1 997 123	...	328 629	401 766	391 530	100 877	191 314	200 978	43 656	144 548	585 355
1989	2 317 100	...	348 185	467 886	534 734	166 541	231 673	251 191	47 405	167 093	637 126
1990	2 409 353	...	380 263	505 346	539 601	152 452	238 903	221 741	63 991	213 406	633 251
1991	2 578 210	...	405 546	533 404	669 137	170 295	274 136	271 872	76 804	208 908	637 245
1992	2 742 717	...	444 000	540 270	696 177	197 739	299 287	300 160	87 890	220 666	652 705
1993	3 038 108	...	516 152	593 313	768 398	221 501	355 822	340 627	104 508	229 038	677 147
1994	3 285 576	...	542 380	617 982	757 853	235 684	368 077	371 618	125 093	239 817	784 925
1995	3 916 466	...	690 156	680 066	1 005 726	326 995	459 080	510 769	133 933	300 424	815 043
1996	4 495 645	...	827 868	745 619	1 229 118	433 903	539 308	625 805	148 084	346 810	828 248
1997	5 354 080	...	880 327	824 136	1 637 408	538 137	618 837	893 888	170 509	459 407	968 839
1998	5 953 909	...	903 073	920 044	2 179 035	543 323	724 619	1 178 824	184 356	485 675	1 013 995
1999	6 705 462	...	957 813	1 101 709	2 798 193	440 685	825 175	1 526 116	208 763	578 046	1 067 155
2000	7 575 799	...	1 037 092	1 421 017	2 783 235	381 630	1 068 566	1 554 448	205 406	738 904	1 168 736
2001	8 183 713	...	1 115 229	1 518 473	2 560 294	375 059	1 343 071	1 478 301	229 200	798 314	1 326 066
2002	8 693 710	...	1 257 638	1 499 952	2 021 817	473 503	1 530 982	1 248 085	248 061	897 335	1 538 154
2003	9 731 880	...	1 569 845	1 580 994	2 454 877	527 223	1 710 787	1 712 069	258 652	450 884	1 921 426
2004	11 593 660	...	2 019 508	1 742 716	2 717 383	561 610	2 035 149	1 960 357	271 953	600 161	2 402 206
2005	13 893 701	1 132 114	2 313 295	1 905 979	2 817 970	643 793	2 243 135	2 109 863	280 400	658 177	2 606 945
2006	16 619 790	1 179 159	2 832 999	2 154 062	3 293 053	567 861	2 824 871	2 547 468	282 627	799 471	3 431 272
2007	20 195 681	2 487 860	3 411 831	2 345 923	3 551 307	639 755	3 289 070	2 900 948	271 952	863 140	3 985 202
2008	22 724 875	5 967 815	3 943 862	2 397 396	2 486 446	852 458	2 770 606	1 850 055	301 139	740 553	3 900 991
2009	20 833 461	3 363 444	4 402 809	2 398 208	2 995 459	790 985	2 825 638	2 494 310	313 771	706 387	3 537 909
2010	22 772 012	3 541 931	4 912 727	2 597 707	3 397 411	1 101 828	2 915 698	3 018 260	342 090	643 618	3 698 153
2011	25 162 620	4 578 414	5 250 792	2 908 791	3 509 359	1 418 050	2 909 962	3 058 215	397 086	629 728	4 011 582

. . . = Not available.

Section 7c: Exports and Imports

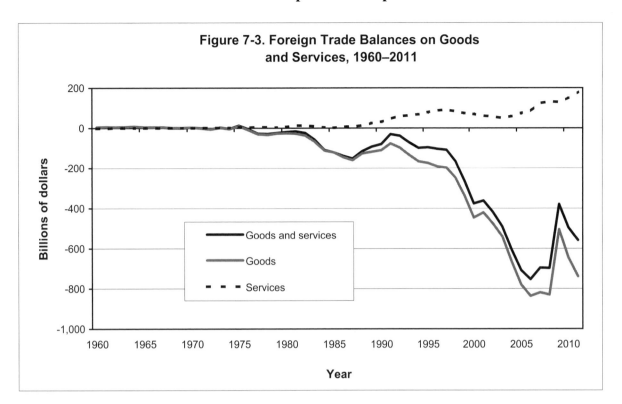

Figure 7-3. Foreign Trade Balances on Goods and Services, 1960–2011

- U.S. imports of goods and services exceeded exports by a record $753 billion in 2006, setting yet another new record. This negative "trade balance" (to differentiate it from the more comprehensive "current account deficit" shown in earlier pages) diminished to $379 billion in 2009 but rose back to $559 billion in 2011. (Table 7-9)

- By 2011, all major U.S. goods export categories had recovered to match or surpass pre-recession values. The value of imports of food, capital goods, nonautomotive consumer goods, and advanced technology (which is also included in other categories, especially capital goods) also recovered to above pre-recession levels in 2011. (Tables 7-10 and 7-11)

- Canada and Mexico are the principal trading partners of the United States, with relations governed by the North American Free Trade Agreement (NAFTA). In 2011, U.S. exports to those two countries brought in $479 billion, compared with $268 billion in exports to the European Union and $307 billion in exports to China, Japan, and the newly industrialized countries of Asia (the NICS—Hong Kong, South Korea, Singapore, and Taiwan). (Table 7-13)

- U.S. imports from Canada and Mexico in 2011 amounted to $578 billion, more than the $368 billion imported from the European Union but somewhat less than the $650 billion from China, Japan, and the Asian NICS. (Table 7-14)

- The value of imports from China, which grew by an average 23 percent per year from 2001 to 2006, slowed to a 7 percent increase between 2006 and 2011. (Table 7-14)

- For U.S. services trade, "other private services" is the largest single category among both exports and imports. This includes such activities as education, financial services, and many other types of business and professional services. The United States had a surplus of $78 billion on "other private services" in 2010, continuing to account for a substantial share of the total surplus on services. (Tables 7-9, 7-15 and 7-16)

Table 7-9. U.S. Exports and Imports of Goods and Services

(Balance of payments basis; millions of dollars, seasonally adjusted.)

Year and month	Goods and services			Goods			Services		
	Exports	Imports	Balance	Exports	Imports	Balance	Exports	Imports	Balance
1970	56 640	54 386	2 254	42 469	39 866	2 603	14 171	14 520	-349
1971	59 677	60 979	-1 302	43 319	45 579	-2 260	16 358	15 400	958
1972	67 222	72 665	-5 443	49 381	55 797	-6 416	17 841	16 868	973
1973	91 242	89 342	1 900	71 410	70 499	911	19 832	18 843	989
1974	120 897	125 190	-4 293	98 306	103 811	-5 505	22 591	21 379	1 212
1975	132 585	120 181	12 404	107 088	98 185	8 903	25 497	21 996	3 501
1976	142 716	148 798	-6 082	114 745	124 228	-9 483	27 971	24 570	3 401
1977	152 301	179 547	-27 246	120 816	151 907	-31 091	31 485	27 640	3 845
1978	178 428	208 191	-29 763	142 075	176 002	-33 927	36 353	32 189	4 164
1979	224 131	248 696	-24 565	184 439	212 007	-27 568	39 692	36 689	3 003
1980	271 834	291 241	-19 407	224 250	249 750	-25 500	47 584	41 491	6 093
1981	294 398	310 570	-16 172	237 044	265 067	-28 023	57 354	45 503	11 851
1982	275 236	299 391	-24 156	211 157	247 642	-36 485	64 079	51 749	12 329
1983	266 106	323 874	-57 767	201 799	268 901	-67 102	64 307	54 973	9 335
1984	291 094	400 166	-109 072	219 926	332 418	-112 492	71 168	67 748	3 420
1985	289 070	410 950	-121 880	215 915	338 088	-122 173	73 155	72 862	294
1986	310 033	448 572	-138 538	223 344	368 425	-145 081	86 689	80 147	6 543
1987	348 869	500 552	-151 684	250 208	409 765	-159 557	98 661	90 787	7 874
1988	431 149	545 715	-114 566	320 230	447 189	-126 959	110 919	98 526	12 393
1989	487 003	580 144	-93 141	359 916	477 665	-117 749	127 087	102 479	24 607
1990	535 233	616 097	-80 864	387 401	498 438	-111 037	147 832	117 659	30 173
1991	578 344	609 479	-31 135	414 083	491 020	-76 937	164 261	118 459	45 802
1992	616 882	656 094	-39 212	439 631	536 528	-96 897	177 251	119 566	57 685
1993	642 863	713 174	-70 311	456 943	589 394	-132 451	185 920	123 780	62 141
1994	703 254	801 747	-98 493	502 859	668 690	-165 831	200 395	133 057	67 338
1995	794 387	890 771	-96 384	575 204	749 374	-174 170	219 183	141 397	77 786
1996	851 602	955 667	-104 065	612 113	803 113	-191 000	239 489	152 554	86 935
1997	934 453	1 042 726	-108 273	678 366	876 794	-198 428	256 087	165 932	90 155
1998	933 174	1 099 314	-166 140	670 416	918 637	-248 221	262 758	180 677	82 081
1999	967 008	1 230 168	-263 160	698 218	1 034 389	-336 171	268 790	195 779	73 011
2000	1 072 783	1 449 532	-376 749	784 781	1 230 568	-445 787	288 002	218 964	69 038
2001	1 007 726	1 369 496	-361 771	731 189	1 152 464	-421 276	276 537	217 032	59 505
2002	980 879	1 398 311	-417 432	697 439	1 171 930	-474 491	283 440	226 381	57 059
2003	1 023 519	1 514 503	-490 984	729 816	1 270 225	-540 409	293 703	244 278	49 425
2004	1 163 146	1 768 502	-605 357	821 986	1 485 492	-663 507	341 160	283 010	58 150
2005	1 287 441	1 996 065	-708 624	911 686	1 692 416	-780 730	375 755	303 649	72 106
2006	1 459 823	2 213 111	-753 288	1 039 406	1 875 095	-835 689	420 417	338 016	82 401
2007	1 654 561	2 351 289	-696 728	1 163 957	1 982 843	-818 886	490 604	368 446	122 158
2008	1 842 682	2 541 020	-698 338	1 307 499	2 137 608	-830 109	535 183	403 413	131 770
2009	1 578 945	1 958 099	-379 154	1 069 733	1 575 491	-505 758	509 212	382 608	126 603
2010	1 842 485	2 337 222	-494 737	1 288 882	1 934 006	-645 124	553 603	403 216	150 387
2011	2 103 367	2 663 247	-559 880	1 497 406	2 235 819	-738 413	605 961	427 428	178 533
2009									
January	124 956	162 685	-37 729	83 572	130 573	-47 002	41 384	32 111	9 272
February	127 334	154 606	-27 272	86 044	123 019	-36 975	41 291	31 587	9 704
March	126 181	154 612	-28 431	84 476	123 049	-38 572	41 705	31 563	10 141
April	124 322	153 378	-29 056	82 490	121 785	-39 295	41 833	31 593	10 239
May	126 049	150 904	-24 855	84 433	119 795	-35 362	41 616	31 109	10 507
June	128 704	154 535	-25 832	86 927	123 321	-36 394	41 776	31 214	10 562
July	130 454	162 872	-32 417	88 657	131 096	-42 439	41 798	31 776	10 022
August	130 992	161 982	-30 990	88 781	130 269	-41 488	42 211	31 713	10 498
September	135 623	169 661	-34 038	92 668	137 597	-44 929	42 955	32 065	10 891
October	139 683	173 252	-33 569	95 857	140 834	-44 977	43 826	32 418	11 408
November	140 579	177 622	-37 043	96 197	144 986	-48 789	44 382	32 636	11 746
December	144 066	181 989	-37 923	99 631	149 166	-49 535	44 435	32 823	11 612
2010									
January	143 735	180 813	-37 078	99 354	148 209	-48 855	44 381	32 604	11 777
February	144 639	185 319	-40 679	100 417	152 072	-51 654	44 222	33 247	10 975
March	148 960	189 153	-40 194	104 260	156 289	-52 028	44 699	32 865	11 835
April	147 605	189 023	-41 418	103 403	156 677	-53 274	44 202	32 346	11 856
May	152 195	192 781	-40 586	106 463	159 672	-53 208	45 731	33 109	12 622
June	151 863	197 546	-45 682	105 612	163 770	-58 158	46 251	33 776	12 476
July	154 711	195 129	-40 418	108 186	161 074	-52 888	46 525	34 055	12 469
August	154 941	200 053	-45 112	108 386	165 923	-57 536	46 555	34 130	12 425
September	155 816	199 422	-43 606	108 625	165 072	-56 446	47 191	34 350	12 841
October	160 332	200 757	-40 425	112 715	166 351	-53 636	47 617	34 405	13 211
November	162 190	201 050	-38 860	114 139	166 841	-52 703	48 051	34 209	13 843
December	165 499	206 176	-40 677	117 321	172 057	-54 736	48 177	34 119	14 059
2011									
January	168 098	215 621	-47 523	119 050	180 995	-61 946	49 048	34 626	14 422
February	166 545	211 346	-44 801	117 651	177 012	-59 361	48 894	34 334	14 560
March	174 169	219 071	-44 902	124 217	184 268	-60 051	49 952	34 803	15 149
April	175 662	219 218	-43 556	125 586	184 143	-58 557	50 076	35 075	15 001
May	175 673	223 343	-47 669	124 910	187 948	-63 038	50 763	35 394	15 369
June	172 664	222 988	-50 324	121 664	187 253	-65 588	51 000	35 736	15 264
July	178 339	223 919	-45 580	126 585	187 474	-60 889	51 754	36 445	15 309
August	178 382	223 157	-44 775	126 523	186 728	-60 205	51 859	36 429	15 431
September	180 629	225 096	-44 467	129 053	188 575	-59 522	51 576	36 521	15 056
October	178 742	224 445	-45 703	127 920	188 446	-60 526	50 822	35 999	14 823
November	176 710	225 545	-48 835	126 385	189 678	-63 293	50 325	35 867	14 458
December	177 751	229 499	-51 748	127 862	193 297	-65 436	49 890	36 202	13 688

Table 7-10. U.S. Exports of Goods by End-Use and Advanced Technology Categories

(Census basis, except as noted; billions of dollars; seasonally adjusted, except as noted.)

Year and month	Total exports of goods			Principal end-use category							Advanced technology products [1]
	Total, balance of payments basis	Net adjustments	Total, Census basis	Foods, feeds, and beverages	Industrial supplies and materials		Capital goods, except automotive	Automotive vehicles, engines, and parts	Consumer goods, except automotive	Other goods	
					Total	Petroleum and products					
1980	224.25	3.55	220.70	36.28	72.09	3.57	76.28	17.44	17.75	. . .	. . .
1981	237.04	3.31	233.74	38.84	70.19	4.56	84.17	19.69	17.70	. . .	. . .
1982	211.16	-1.12	212.28	32.20	64.05	6.87	76.50	17.23	16.13	. . .	. . .
1983	201.80	0.09	201.71	32.09	58.94	5.59	71.66	18.46	14.93	. . .	. . .
1984	219.93	1.18	218.74	32.20	64.12	5.43	77.01	22.42	15.09	. . .	. . .
1985	215.92	3.29	212.62	24.57	61.16	5.71	79.32	24.95	14.59	. . .	. . .
1986	223.34	-3.13	226.47	23.52	64.72	4.43	82.82	25.10	16.73	. . .	. . .
1987	250.21	-3.70	253.90	25.23	70.05	4.63	92.71	27.58	20.31	. . .	. . .
1988	320.23	-3.11	323.34	33.77	90.02	4.48	119.10	33.40	26.98	. . .	. . .
1989	359.92	-3.08	363.00	36.34	98.36	6.46	136.94	35.05	36.01	. . .	. . .
1990	387.40	-5.57	392.97	35.18	105.55	8.36	153.07	36.07	43.60	20.73	. . .
1991	414.08	-7.77	421.85	35.79	109.69	8.40	166.72	39.72	46.65	23.66	. . .
1992	439.63	-8.54	448.17	40.34	109.59	7.62	176.50	46.71	51.31	24.39	. . .
1993	456.94	-7.92	464.86	40.59	111.89	7.49	182.85	51.35	54.56	23.89	. . .
1994	502.86	-9.77	512.63	41.96	121.55	6.97	205.82	57.31	59.86	26.50	. . .
1995	575.20	-9.54	584.74	50.47	146.37	8.10	234.46	61.26	64.31	28.72	. . .
1996	612.11	-12.96	625.08	55.53	147.98	9.63	253.99	64.24	70.11	33.85	. . .
1997	678.37	-10.82	689.18	51.51	158.32	10.42	295.87	73.30	77.96	33.51	. . .
1998	670.42	-11.72	682.14	46.40	148.31	8.08	299.87	72.39	80.29	35.44	. . .
1999	683.97	-11.83	695.80	45.98	147.52	8.62	310.79	75.26	80.92	35.32	. . .
2000	771.99	-9.92	781.92	47.87	172.62	12.01	356.93	80.36	89.38	34.77	227.39
2001	718.71	-10.39	729.10	49.41	160.10	10.64	321.71	75.44	88.33	34.11	199.63
2002	682.42	-10.68	693.10	49.62	156.81	10.34	290.44	78.94	84.36	32.94	178.57
2003	713.42	-11.36	724.77	55.03	173.04	12.69	293.67	80.63	89.91	32.49	180.21
2004	807.52	-11.26	818.78	56.57	203.96	17.08	331.56	89.21	103.08	34.40	201.42
2005	894.63	-11.35	905.98	58.96	233.05	22.66	363.32	98.41	115.29	36.96	216.06
2006	1 015.81	-10.16	1 025.97	66.00	276.00	31.57	404.00	107.30	129.10	43.60	252.71
2007	1 138.38	-9.82	1 148.20	84.30	316.40	37.76	433.00	121.30	146.00	47.30	264.88
2008	1 307.50	20.06	1 287.44	108.35	388.03	67.18	457.66	121.45	161.28	50.67	270.13
2009	1 069.73	13.69	1 056.04	93.91	296.51	49.18	391.24	81.72	149.46	43.22	244.71
2010	1 288.88	10.62	1 278.26	107.71	391.54	70.87	447.50	111.99	165.19	54.34	273.34
2011	1 497.41	16.97	1 480.43	126.22	500.34	113.24	492.99	133.12	174.96	52.81	286.82
2009											
January	83.57	1.16	82.42	7.04	22.12	3.35	32.84	5.41	11.37	3.62	18.73
February	86.04	1.14	84.90	7.20	22.10	3.09	33.30	5.87	12.70	3.74	18.85
March	84.48	0.98	83.50	7.26	22.46	3.10	32.35	5.79	12.24	3.40	20.76
April	82.49	1.40	81.09	7.62	21.21	3.16	31.21	5.82	11.87	3.37	18.70
May	84.43	1.06	83.37	7.99	23.14	3.97	31.14	5.57	12.14	3.39	19.15
June	86.93	1.19	85.74	8.29	24.37	4.28	31.92	5.60	12.10	3.46	20.74
July	88.66	0.82	87.83	8.09	24.79	4.51	31.99	6.84	12.48	3.65	20.00
August	88.78	1.02	87.77	7.82	25.84	4.63	30.95	7.47	12.33	3.36	18.52
September	92.67	1.00	91.67	7.46	27.27	4.95	32.93	7.77	12.64	3.60	20.59
October	95.86	1.03	94.83	7.86	27.66	4.87	33.75	8.03	13.56	3.97	23.69
November	96.20	1.56	94.64	8.58	27.11	4.57	33.78	8.63	12.86	3.67	21.00
December	99.63	1.34	98.29	8.71	28.45	4.70	35.07	8.92	13.16	3.99	23.98
2010											
January	99.35	0.96	98.40	8.86	28.98	4.58	34.60	8.72	13.50	3.73	21.31
February	100.42	0.99	99.42	8.55	29.56	4.91	35.22	9.01	13.14	3.94	19.86
March	104.26	0.74	103.53	8.55	31.41	5.57	36.11	8.79	13.82	4.84	23.95
April	103.40	0.92	102.48	8.16	31.81	6.05	36.01	9.20	13.04	4.27	21.19
May	106.46	0.99	105.47	8.10	32.66	6.00	37.54	9.30	13.58	4.30	21.80
June	105.61	0.88	104.73	8.00	32.10	5.52	37.09	9.41	13.53	4.61	23.36
July	108.19	0.84	107.35	8.23	32.63	6.06	38.61	9.17	13.67	5.03	23.95
August	108.39	0.94	107.44	9.03	33.34	5.76	37.43	9.51	13.69	4.45	21.93
September	108.63	0.66	107.96	9.37	32.61	5.99	37.93	9.58	13.71	4.78	22.88
October	112.72	0.58	112.14	10.16	34.56	6.65	38.53	9.89	13.93	5.08	23.73
November	114.14	1.07	113.07	10.29	35.21	7.08	38.60	9.56	14.89	4.53	23.23
December	117.32	1.05	116.27	10.40	36.68	6.70	39.85	9.87	14.68	4.80	26.15
2011											
January	119.05	1.44	117.61	10.36	39.38	8.28	39.01	10.61	13.95	4.31	21.11
February	117.65	1.71	115.94	10.39	38.61	7.75	39.12	10.15	13.90	3.77	20.99
March	124.22	1.67	122.55	11.10	41.26	7.97	40.16	11.07	14.41	4.56	25.36
April	125.59	1.44	124.15	10.86	42.67	9.70	41.02	10.69	14.66	4.26	23.03
May	124.91	1.45	123.46	10.86	41.48	9.27	41.23	10.90	14.36	4.63	23.38
June	121.66	1.43	120.23	10.20	39.83	8.70	40.23	10.93	14.88	4.17	24.70
July	126.59	1.49	125.09	10.39	42.16	9.89	41.95	11.82	14.46	4.32	23.56
August	126.52	1.34	125.18	10.47	42.89	10.27	41.67	11.14	14.65	4.37	23.82
September	129.05	1.55	127.51	10.44	44.31	9.97	41.80	11.41	15.18	4.37	24.22
October	127.92	1.22	126.70	10.36	42.93	10.27	42.40	11.39	14.76	4.86	25.69
November	126.39	1.15	125.24	10.31	42.08	10.35	42.23	11.26	14.92	4.44	24.75
December	127.86	1.08	126.78	10.47	42.76	10.83	42.19	11.76	14.84	4.77	26.22

[1] Not seasonally adjusted.
. . . = Not available.

Table 7-11. U.S. Imports of Goods by End-Use and Advanced Technology Categories

(Census basis, except as noted; billions of dollars; seasonally adjusted, except as noted.)

Year and month	Total, balance of payments basis	Net adjustments	Total, Census basis	Foods, feeds, and beverages	Industrial supplies and materials Total	Petroleum and products	Capital goods, except automotive	Automotive vehicles, engines, and parts	Consumer goods, except automotive	Other goods	Advanced technology products [1]
1980	249.75	4.23	245.52	18.55	124.96	. . .	30.72	28.13	34.22	. . .	. . .
1981	265.07	3.76	261.31	18.53	131.10	. . .	36.86	30.80	38.30	. . .	. . .
1982	247.64	3.70	243.94	17.47	107.82	. . .	38.22	34.26	39.66	. . .	. . .
1983	268.90	7.18	261.72	18.56	105.63	. . .	42.61	42.04	46.59	. . .	. . .
1984	332.42	1.91	330.51	21.92	122.72	. . .	60.15	56.77	61.19	. . .	. . .
1985	338.09	1.71	336.38	21.89	112.48	. . .	60.81	65.21	66.43	. . .	. . .
1986	368.43	2.75	365.67	24.40	101.37	. . .	71.86	78.25	79.43	. . .	. . .
1987	409.77	3.48	406.28	24.81	110.67	. . .	84.77	85.17	88.82	. . .	. . .
1988	447.19	5.26	441.93	24.93	118.06	. . .	101.79	87.95	96.42	. . .	. . .
1989	477.37	3.72	473.65	25.08	132.40	. . .	112.45	87.38	102.26	. . .	. . .
1990	498.34	2.36	495.98	26.65	143.41	62.16	116.04	87.69	105.29	16.09	. . .
1991	490.98	2.53	488.45	26.21	131.38	51.78	120.80	84.94	107.78	15.94	. . .
1992	536.46	3.80	532.66	27.61	138.64	51.60	134.25	91.79	122.66	17.71	. . .
1993	589.44	8.78	580.66	27.87	145.61	51.50	152.37	102.42	134.02	18.39	. . .
1994	668.59	5.33	663.26	27.87	145.61	51.28	152.37	102.42	134.02	18.39	. . .
1995	749.57	6.03	743.54	33.18	181.85	56.16	221.43	123.80	159.91	23.39	. . .
1996	803.33	8.04	796.77	35.74	204.43	72.75	228.07	128.95	172.00	26.11	. . .
1997	876.37	6.66	869.70	39.69	213.77	71.77	253.28	139.81	193.81	29.34	. . .
1998	917.18	5.28	911.90	41.24	200.14	50.90	269.56	149.05	216.52	35.39	. . .
1999	1 029.99	5.37	1 024.62	43.60	221.39	67.81	295.72	178.96	241.91	43.04	. . .
2000	1 224.42	6.40	1 218.02	45.98	298.98	120.28	347.03	195.88	281.83	48.33	222.08
2001	1 145.90	4.90	1 141.00	46.64	273.87	103.59	297.99	189.78	284.29	48.42	195.18
2002	1 164.72	3.35	1 161.37	49.69	267.69	103.51	283.32	203.74	307.84	49.08	195.15
2003	1 260.72	3.60	1 257.12	55.83	313.82	133.10	295.87	210.14	333.88	47.59	207.03
2004	1 477.09	7.39	1 469.70	62.14	412.83	180.46	343.49	228.20	372.94	50.11	238.28
2005	1 681.78	8.33	1 673.46	68.09	523.77	251.86	379.33	239.45	407.24	55.57	290.76
2006	1 861.38	7.44	1 853.94	74.94	601.99	302.43	418.26	256.63	442.64	59.49	290.76
2007	1 969.38	12.41	1 956.96	81.68	634.75	330.98	444.49	258.92	474.89	62.23	326.81
2008	2 137.61	33.97	2 103.64	89.00	779.48	453.28	453.74	231.24	481.64	68.54	331.18
2009	1 575.49	15.87	1 559.63	81.62	462.38	253.69	370.48	157.65	427.33	60.17	300.89
2010	1 934.01	20.85	1 913.16	91.74	602.55	336.10	449.29	225.09	483.21	61.27	354.20
2011	2 235.82	28.00	2 207.82	107.46	755.81	439.34	510.74	254.61	514.06	65.15	386.43
2009											
January	130.57	1.46	129.12	6.91	38.30	18.23	31.81	11.21	35.85	5.04	20.74
February	123.02	1.21	121.81	6.77	34.44	16.66	30.22	10.49	34.49	5.40	20.27
March	123.05	1.16	121.89	6.74	34.51	17.57	30.06	10.39	35.37	4.82	23.40
April	121.79	1.21	120.57	6.71	33.46	17.71	29.17	10.62	35.82	4.79	23.42
May	119.80	1.06	118.74	6.70	33.21	17.91	28.91	10.21	34.77	4.94	22.77
June	123.32	1.17	122.16	6.79	36.77	21.18	29.11	11.12	33.61	4.75	25.33
July	131.10	1.18	129.91	6.83	38.58	22.32	30.40	13.32	35.45	5.33	26.59
August	130.27	1.50	128.77	6.72	38.29	21.91	30.11	14.14	34.79	4.72	24.15
September	137.60	1.33	136.27	6.74	41.67	24.35	31.38	15.76	35.45	5.27	26.61
October	140.83	1.53	139.31	6.91	42.23	23.93	32.21	16.22	36.67	5.07	29.32
November	144.99	1.51	143.48	6.83	44.73	25.53	32.82	16.51	37.69	4.89	29.33
December	149.17	1.55	147.62	6.97	46.19	26.39	34.28	17.66	37.37	5.16	28.97
2010											
January	148.21	1.19	147.02	7.21	47.98	27.40	33.57	16.66	36.49	5.11	24.38
February	152.07	1.70	150.38	7.20	48.87	28.08	34.19	16.69	38.19	5.24	23.62
March	156.29	1.74	154.55	7.43	50.68	29.09	34.75	17.59	38.92	5.17	28.65
April	156.68	1.76	154.91	7.39	51.52	29.90	36.09	17.55	37.75	4.62	26.98
May	159.67	1.64	158.03	7.59	50.13	28.12	37.09	18.89	39.64	4.70	27.50
June	163.77	1.85	161.92	7.69	48.94	26.25	37.79	19.88	42.43	5.20	31.64
July	161.07	1.54	159.53	7.65	49.23	26.78	37.53	19.17	41.00	4.96	30.67
August	165.92	1.61	164.31	7.82	50.29	28.17	38.56	20.00	42.35	5.31	30.69
September	165.07	1.74	163.34	7.90	49.35	26.92	40.04	19.45	41.55	5.05	32.32
October	166.35	1.78	164.57	7.77	50.08	27.20	39.20	19.81	42.37	5.34	32.38
November	166.84	1.76	165.09	7.98	50.87	27.44	40.37	19.60	40.98	5.28	33.77
December	172.06	2.54	169.51	8.11	54.62	30.76	40.13	19.82	41.55	5.30	31.61
2011											
January	181.00	2.14	178.85	8.43	60.83	35.91	41.67	21.22	41.73	4.98	28.32
February	177.01	2.22	174.80	8.58	57.40	32.85	39.89	20.32	43.64	4.96	27.01
March	184.27	2.17	182.10	8.59	63.59	37.36	41.27	21.25	41.98	5.43	32.12
April	184.14	2.26	181.89	8.86	62.96	36.45	41.81	19.10	43.70	5.46	30.15
May	187.95	2.44	185.51	9.02	66.22	39.15	42.72	19.37	42.75	5.44	31.41
June	187.25	2.48	184.77	9.10	64.53	37.83	42.46	19.61	43.16	5.92	33.47
July	187.47	2.37	185.10	8.86	62.98	36.16	42.93	22.32	43.00	5.02	32.50
August	186.73	2.34	184.39	8.90	62.89	35.88	42.84	21.49	42.41	5.86	33.01
September	188.58	2.53	186.04	9.15	63.90	36.23	42.97	22.37	42.31	5.35	32.68
October	188.45	2.56	185.89	9.43	62.24	35.72	43.73	21.80	43.38	5.32	36.14
November	189.68	2.26	187.42	9.32	63.50	37.48	43.59	22.57	42.65	5.79	35.62
December	193.30	2.22	191.07	9.23	64.78	38.32	44.87	23.21	43.36	5.63	34.00

[1]Not seasonally adjusted.
. . . = Not available.

Table 7-12. U.S. Exports and Imports of Goods by Principal End-Use Category in Constant Dollars

(Census basis; billions of 2005 chain-weighted dollars, except as noted; seasonally adjusted.)

Year and month	Exports							Imports						
	Total	Foods, feeds, and beverages	Industrial supplies and materials	Capital goods, except automotive	Automotive vehicles, engines, and parts	Consumer goods, except automotive	Other goods	Total	Foods, feeds, and beverages	Industrial supplies and materials	Capital goods, except automotive	Automotive vehicles, engines, and parts	Consumer goods, except automotive	Other goods
1986[1]	227.20	22.30	57.30	75.80	21.70	. . .	. . .	365.40	24.40	101.30	71.80	78.20	79.40	. . .
1987[1]	254.10	24.30	66.70	86.20	24.60	. . .	. . .	406.20	24.80	111.00	84.50	85.00	88.70	. . .
1988[1]	322.40	32.30	85.10	109.20	29.30	. . .	. . .	441.00	24.80	118.30	101.40	87.70	95.90	. . .
1989[1]	363.80	37.20	99.30	138.80	34.80	. . .	. . .	473.20	25.10	132.30	113.30	86.10	102.90	. . .
1990[1]	393.60	35.10	104.40	152.70	37.40	39.22	18.70	495.30	26.60	146.20	116.40	87.30	105.70	14.46
1991[1]	421.70	35.70	109.70	166.70	40.00	40.42	21.11	488.50	26.50	131.60	120.70	85.70	108.00	14.15
1992[1]	448.20	40.30	109.10	175.90	47.00	43.60	21.71	532.70	27.60	138.60	134.30	91.80	122.70	15.46
1993[1]	471.17	40.19	111.08	190.02	51.93	54.03	23.91	591.45	28.03	151.26	160.16	100.73	132.92	18.35
1994[1]	522.29	40.43	114.17	225.76	56.54	58.97	26.41	675.05	29.52	168.80	199.56	112.13	144.22	20.82
1994	518.88	51.73	159.76	161.08	62.39	64.22	31.39	681.66	32.83	308.46	108.44	129.07	143.21	22.95
1995	572.02	57.09	170.57	187.07	66.03	67.94	32.24	740.59	33.68	317.51	130.75	131.28	154.15	24.23
1996	632.65	55.26	181.03	222.06	68.72	72.92	37.64	817.86	37.28	336.85	157.72	135.76	165.09	27.05
1997	717.11	55.11	195.90	272.04	77.54	80.09	37.39	931.43	40.86	360.07	197.50	146.77	187.96	30.60
1998	734.04	54.77	195.16	284.07	75.68	83.21	40.49	1 041.17	43.97	394.68	226.53	155.94	213.08	37.71
1999	757.64	56.64	196.57	299.44	78.37	83.80	40.45	1 166.52	48.01	400.97	259.84	186.25	239.26	46.02
2000	841.15	59.80	216.28	346.52	82.87	91.98	38.94	1 321.24	51.13	425.98	311.79	202.48	281.43	50.89
2001	789.15	61.38	206.54	312.53	77.48	90.95	38.25	1 277.44	53.11	423.88	275.21	196.27	286.07	51.38
2002	752.23	60.00	203.17	284.74	80.76	87.14	36.80	1 323.75	56.61	426.38	269.97	210.09	312.57	52.99
2003	773.76	61.01	212.05	292.27	82.07	91.90	35.41	1 398.24	61.84	443.69	289.33	215.52	339.48	50.64
2004	841.56	56.34	226.35	328.30	90.15	104.62	35.91	1 562.89	65.65	498.32	340.87	230.48	376.52	51.83
2005	901.08	58.96	233.05	358.43	98.41	115.29	36.96	1 673.46	68.09	523.77	379.33	239.45	407.24	55.57
2006	992.07	63.21	250.85	403.39	106.13	126.76	41.69	1 773.29	72.04	525.88	424.00	255.45	439.96	58.10
2007	1 070.80	67.20	267.87	434.47	118.75	139.83	43.06	1 808.12	72.65	510.22	451.70	252.93	464.71	61.60
2008	1 147.41	71.10	300.23	461.81	117.63	151.23	43.59	1 755.39	71.04	486.22	461.78	222.58	459.32	61.92
2009	993.86	69.29	267.18	396.42	78.77	139.39	39.18	1 480.09	66.50	407.34	383.94	150.81	408.76	56.73
2010	1 142.20	76.05	306.26	452.97	107.46	150.72	46.45	1 698.22	69.01	430.34	469.52	214.04	461.81	56.10
2011	1 228.14	74.60	332.85	499.96	125.80	156.56	41.46	1 802.84	71.09	438.02	531.85	235.41	483.49	56.91
2008														
January	94.52	5.87	23.95	38.56	9.96	12.68	3.55	150.61	6.06	42.38	38.62	20.48	38.34	5.15
February	96.53	5.86	25.33	38.38	10.37	12.58	3.85	153.21	6.06	42.12	39.52	21.66	39.82	4.97
March	93.64	5.84	24.69	38.00	9.39	11.99	3.52	146.75	5.85	39.32	39.39	19.69	38.70	5.26
April	97.62	6.16	25.30	39.78	9.84	12.75	3.66	150.90	6.02	41.06	40.06	20.59	38.98	5.35
May	97.77	6.12	25.88	38.96	10.11	12.68	3.73	149.09	6.03	39.98	40.07	20.04	39.26	5.21
June	101.44	6.28	27.29	40.04	10.68	13.16	3.63	148.01	5.79	40.05	39.31	19.64	39.31	5.17
July	101.10	5.90	26.76	40.13	11.32	13.58	3.43	150.62	5.77	42.07	39.38	19.34	38.90	5.38
August	101.51	6.30	27.07	40.96	10.19	12.98	3.74	147.87	5.92	40.96	38.51	18.03	39.69	5.18
September	94.26	5.73	24.43	38.11	10.01	12.57	3.43	142.11	5.86	37.96	39.07	17.19	38.33	5.12
October	93.97	5.89	24.59	37.72	9.68	12.34	3.60	146.01	5.98	42.28	37.89	16.37	37.87	5.08
November	91.00	5.74	23.77	36.41	8.75	12.29	3.85	137.17	6.05	38.88	35.67	15.68	35.40	5.18
December	84.06	5.41	21.19	34.77	7.33	11.64	3.62	133.05	5.65	39.15	34.30	13.88	34.73	4.87
2009														
January	78.32	5.19	20.67	33.19	5.20	10.60	3.32	127.09	5.57	38.77	32.61	10.74	34.21	4.71
February	80.93	5.38	20.80	33.68	5.65	11.78	3.44	120.67	5.57	35.34	31.10	10.06	32.93	5.07
March	80.69	5.65	21.66	32.85	5.58	11.49	3.17	121.19	5.60	35.38	31.16	9.98	33.89	4.57
April	77.92	5.71	20.21	31.71	5.61	11.21	3.12	118.76	5.52	33.26	30.20	10.22	34.30	4.56
May	79.51	5.80	21.75	31.65	5.37	11.41	3.11	116.11	5.50	32.18	29.97	9.80	33.28	4.70
June	80.53	5.76	22.10	32.47	5.40	11.32	3.13	116.22	5.51	32.46	30.23	10.67	32.15	4.51
July	82.98	5.86	22.66	32.53	6.61	11.63	3.32	123.00	5.64	33.38	31.57	12.76	33.95	5.07
August	81.95	5.68	22.77	31.42	7.21	11.47	3.02	120.83	5.48	32.24	31.27	13.52	33.32	4.47
September	85.73	5.63	23.97	33.37	7.49	11.74	3.24	126.09	5.47	33.57	32.58	15.06	33.96	4.97
October	88.42	6.01	24.04	34.14	7.74	12.60	3.56	127.91	5.57	33.26	33.48	15.47	35.07	4.76
November	87.03	6.34	22.87	34.05	8.31	11.92	3.25	129.81	5.49	33.67	34.11	15.74	36.00	4.56
December	89.84	6.29	23.69	35.34	8.59	12.20	3.51	132.41	5.60	33.82	35.67	16.81	35.70	4.79
2010														
January	89.51	6.37	23.75	35.00	8.40	12.47	3.25	130.32	5.77	33.87	34.99	15.88	34.82	4.71
February	90.97	6.43	24.45	35.59	8.65	12.08	3.46	133.51	5.67	34.74	35.66	15.90	36.46	4.83
March	94.10	6.35	25.58	36.45	8.44	12.69	4.22	136.52	5.73	35.53	36.37	16.79	37.09	4.76
April	92.33	6.11	25.19	36.32	8.84	11.94	3.69	136.72	5.67	36.11	37.77	16.72	35.92	4.24
May	94.68	5.99	25.63	37.87	8.93	12.45	3.70	140.45	5.72	36.03	38.78	18.01	37.71	4.29
June	94.69	5.93	25.61	37.56	9.03	12.44	3.99	145.79	5.85	36.52	39.56	18.96	40.43	4.78
July	97.15	6.06	26.20	39.10	8.81	12.52	4.36	143.89	5.83	36.85	39.32	18.25	39.18	4.56
August	96.18	6.38	26.15	37.93	9.13	12.54	3.81	147.59	5.83	37.27	40.35	19.01	40.55	4.87
September	96.00	6.50	25.26	38.44	9.18	12.44	4.06	146.16	5.85	36.25	41.84	18.46	39.76	4.62
October	98.57	6.89	26.06	39.08	9.48	12.56	4.26	146.11	5.67	35.82	40.90	18.77	40.79	4.88
November	98.00	6.56	25.91	39.19	9.14	13.38	3.73	144.63	5.72	35.11	42.14	18.54	39.29	4.79
December	100.01	6.52	26.48	40.46	9.43	13.22	3.93	146.53	5.72	36.24	41.85	18.75	39.82	4.78
2011														
January	100.57	6.34	27.99	39.71	10.14	12.64	3.50	151.41	5.89	38.12	43.48	20.03	39.83	4.45
February	97.69	6.16	26.58	39.78	9.70	12.55	3.01	146.55	5.87	35.29	41.45	19.15	41.49	4.40
March	102.10	6.52	27.69	40.79	10.53	12.95	3.60	149.94	5.60	37.36	42.84	19.91	40.02	4.79
April	102.83	6.38	28.21	41.64	10.16	13.15	3.34	147.53	5.67	35.79	43.46	17.70	41.41	4.78
May	101.96	6.40	27.26	41.74	10.34	12.88	3.62	149.62	5.83	37.13	44.38	17.84	40.44	4.74
June	99.09	5.91	26.23	40.64	10.35	13.29	3.25	149.56	6.01	36.57	44.11	17.98	40.67	5.16
July	103.18	6.19	27.68	42.41	11.17	12.86	3.37	150.96	5.78	36.59	44.64	20.52	40.38	4.36
August	102.61	6.08	27.88	42.13	10.49	13.02	3.38	149.21	5.86	35.77	44.53	19.74	39.72	5.07
September	103.91	5.93	28.46	42.35	10.73	13.48	3.36	150.50	6.01	36.39	44.68	20.53	39.52	4.62
October	105.23	6.27	28.57	43.03	10.67	13.17	3.81	151.46	6.25	36.08	45.81	20.01	40.31	4.62
November	103.61	6.12	27.76	42.94	10.54	13.33	3.47	152.10	6.17	36.44	45.64	20.70	39.58	5.03
December	105.37	6.30	28.54	42.82	11.01	13.25	3.74	153.99	6.16	36.50	46.83	21.31	40.14	4.90

[1]Data on the 2005 chain-weighted dollar basis are only available from 1994 forward. To provide more historical range, values in 1992 dollars are shown for the years 1986–1994.
. . . = Not available.

Table 7-13. U.S. Exports of Goods by Selected Regions and Countries

(Census f.a.s. basis; millions of dollars, not seasonally adjusted.)

Year and month	Total, all countries	Selected regions [1]					Selected countries				
		European Union, 15 countries	European Union	Euro area	Asian NICS	OPEC	Brazil	Canada	China	Japan	Mexico
1978	. . .	32 051	. . .	. . .	. . .	16 655	2 981	30 540	824	12 885	6 680
1979	. . .	42 582	. . .	. . .	. . .	15 051	3 442	37 599	1 724	17 581	9 847
1980	. . .	53 679	. . .	. . .	. . .	17 759	4 344	40 331	3 755	20 790	15 145
1981	. . .	52 363	. . .	. . .	. . .	21 533	3 798	44 602	3 603	21 823	17 789
1982	. . .	47 932	. . .	. . .	. . .	22 863	3 423	37 887	2 912	20 966	11 817
1983	201 708	44 311	. . .	. . .	. . .	16 905	2 557	43 345	2 173	21 894	9 082
1984	218 743	46 976	. . .	. . .	. . .	14 387	2 640	51 777	3 004	23 575	11 992
1985	212 621	48 994	. . .	. . .	16 918	12 478	3 140	47 251	3 856	22 631	13 635
1986	226 471	53 154	. . .	. . .	18 290	10 844	3 885	45 333	3 106	26 882	12 392
1987	254 122	60 575	. . .	. . .	23 547	11 057	4 040	59 814	3 497	28 249	14 582
1988	322 426	75 755	. . .	. . .	34 816	13 994	4 266	71 622	5 022	37 725	20 629
1989	363 812	86 331	. . .	. . .	38 429	13 196	4 804	78 809	5 755	44 494	24 982
1990	393 592	98 027	. . .	. . .	40 734	13 703	5 048	83 674	4 806	48 580	28 279
1991	421 730	103 123	. . .	. . .	45 628	19 054	6 148	85 150	6 278	48 125	33 277
1992	448 165	102 958	. . .	. . .	48 592	21 960	5 751	90 594	7 419	47 813	40 592
1993	465 090	96 973	. . .	. . .	52 501	19 500	6 058	100 444	8 763	47 892	41 581
1994	512 625	102 818	. . .	. . .	59 595	17 868	8 102	114 439	9 282	53 488	50 844
1995	584 740	123 671	. . .	. . .	74 234	19 533	11 439	127 226	11 754	64 343	46 292
1996	625 073	127 710	. . .	. . .	75 768	22 275	12 718	134 210	11 993	67 607	56 792
1997	689 180	140 773	. . .	. . .	78 225	25 525	15 915	151 767	12 862	65 549	71 389
1998	682 139	149 035	. . .	. . .	63 269	25 154	15 142	156 604	14 241	57 831	78 773
1999	695 797	151 814	. . .	. . .	70 989	20 166	13 203	166 600	13 111	57 466	86 909
2000	781 918	165 065	. . .	116 212	84 624	19 078	15 321	178 941	16 185	64 924	111 349
2001	729 101	158 768	. . .	112 903	71 981	20 052	15 879	163 424	19 182	57 452	101 297
2002	693 101	143 691	. . .	105 838	69 770	18 812	12 376	160 923	22 128	51 449	97 470
2003	724 771	151 731	. . .	113 132	71 601	17 279	11 211	169 924	28 368	52 004	97 412
2004	814 875	168 572	171 230	127 158	82 997	22 256	13 886	189 880	34 428	53 569	110 731
2005	901 082	. . .	185 166	137 497	86 003	31 641	15 372	211 899	41 192	54 681	120 248
2006	1 025 967	. . .	211 887	155 735	96 496	38 658	18 887	230 656	53 673	58 459	133 722
2007	1 148 199	. . .	244 166	180 232	105 751	48 485	24 172	248 888	62 937	61 160	135 918
2008	1 287 442	. . .	271 810	199 986	108 947	64 880	32 299	261 150	69 733	65 142	151 220
2009	1 056 043	. . .	220 599	162 002	90 380	49 857	26 095	204 658	69 497	51 134	128 892
2010	1 278 263	. . .	239 583	176 587	120 477	54 294	35 425	249 105	91 881	60 486	163 473
2011	1 480 432	. . .	268 474	195 904	136 975	64 620	42 944	280 890	103 939	65 706	198 378
2009											
January	78 151	. . .	17 667	12 930	5 896	3 925	2 118	14 734	4 160	3 975	9 781
February	80 349	. . .	18 679	13 889	5 942	4 315	1 836	15 508	4 662	4 200	9 263
March	87 848	. . .	19 834	14 224	6 853	4 950	1 963	16 924	5 579	4 440	10 025
April	80 822	. . .	17 764	13 205	6 556	4 077	1 849	16 151	5 161	3 825	9 571
May	83 651	. . .	17 916	13 627	7 131	3 717	2 000	16 090	5 256	4 271	9 398
June	86 830	. . .	18 672	13 422	7 380	3 774	2 089	16 817	5 549	3 993	10 547
July	85 635	. . .	17 089	12 266	7 696	3 512	2 242	16 454	5 269	4 145	11 131
August	87 315	. . .	16 652	12 046	7 840	3 693	2 318	17 639	5 518	4 048	11 072
September	91 458	. . .	18 056	13 292	8 499	4 187	2 339	18 392	5 764	4 437	11 577
October	100 005	. . .	20 591	15 234	9 103	4 503	2 578	18 831	6 879	4 637	12 731
November	94 607	. . .	18 708	13 855	8 149	4 403	2 268	18 586	7 374	4 235	12 014
December	99 372	. . .	18 972	14 013	9 334	4 801	2 496	18 533	8 325	4 928	11 783
2010											
January	92 601	. . .	18 558	13 673	8 725	3 758	2 266	17 226	6 899	4 846	11 518
February	93 854	. . .	17 851	12 770	8 882	4 349	2 360	18 540	6 841	4 626	11 711
March	110 511	. . .	20 956	14 852	10 736	4 627	3 086	22 184	7 400	5 073	14 194
April	102 443	. . .	18 945	13 958	9 567	4 504	2 758	20 963	6 600	4 493	13 237
May	105 477	. . .	19 428	14 449	9 760	4 704	2 912	21 367	6 753	5 193	13 267
June	107 202	. . .	20 335	15 018	10 041	4 589	3 025	22 342	6 733	5 008	13 881
July	104 057	. . .	18 785	13 672	10 449	4 368	3 366	19 633	7 338	5 130	13 185
August	106 846	. . .	19 359	14 324	9 941	4 571	3 424	21 210	7 210	4 923	14 149
September	107 644	. . .	20 310	15 084	10 460	4 324	2 980	21 784	7 131	4 959	13 929
October	117 104	. . .	21 811	16 178	10 277	4 879	3 200	22 148	9 388	5 554	14 874
November	113 046	. . .	21 003	15 837	10 268	4 622	3 025	21 055	9 450	5 182	14 889
December	117 480	. . .	22 241	16 771	11 370	4 999	3 022	20 652	10 137	5 499	14 639
2011											
January	110 179	. . .	20 218	14 804	10 346	4 320	3 225	20 644	8 022	4 996	14 847
February	109 647	. . .	19 911	14 994	10 130	4 233	2 866	20 493	8 379	5 275	14 025
March	131 728	. . .	24 397	17 586	12 018	5 280	3 606	25 657	9 565	5 924	17 322
April	123 959	. . .	23 437	17 117	11 886	5 340	3 436	23 799	7 999	5 188	16 024
May	124 107	. . .	22 713	16 377	11 170	5 467	3 618	24 453	7 843	5 631	16 843
June	123 039	. . .	22 727	16 419	11 055	5 208	3 540	24 259	7 727	5 380	16 595
July	120 239	. . .	21 409	15 548	11 353	5 276	3 722	22 229	8 158	5 315	16 052
August	126 633	. . .	22 350	16 389	11 406	5 252	3 967	24 960	8 422	5 415	17 709
September	127 107	. . .	23 200	16 543	12 891	5 894	4 069	23 958	8 370	5 459	17 064
October	131 058	. . .	23 350	17 387	11 340	6 357	3 932	24 539	9 744	6 142	17 621
November	125 899	. . .	22 007	16 303	11 661	5 484	3 579	23 240	9 986	5 562	17 913
December	126 837	. . .	22 755	16 438	11 720	6 510	3 385	22 659	9 724	5 419	16 361

[1]See notes and definitions for definitions of regions.
. . . = Not available.

Table 7-14. U.S. Imports of Goods by Selected Regions and Countries

(Census Customs basis; millions of dollars, not seasonally adjusted.)

Year and month	Total, all countries	Selected regions [1]					Selected countries				
		European Union, 15 countries	European Union	Euro area	Asian NICS	OPEC	Brazil	Canada	China	Japan	Mexico
1978	. . .	29 009	. . .	. . .	. . .	. . .	2 826	33 525	. . .	24 458	6 094
1979	. . .	33 295	. . .	. . .	. . .	. . .	3 118	38 046	. . .	26 248	8 800
1980	. . .	35 958	. . .	. . .	. . .	. . .	3 715	41 455	. . .	30 701	12 520
1981	. . .	41 624	. . .	. . .	. . .	. . .	4 475	46 414	. . .	37 612	13 765
1982	. . .	42 509	. . .	. . .	. . .	. . .	4 285	46 477	. . .	37 744	15 566
1983	261 723	43 892	. . .	. . .	. . .	. . .	4 946	52 130	. . .	41 183	16 776
1984	330 510	57 360	. . .	. . .	. . .	. . .	7 621	66 478	. . .	57 135	18 020
1985	336 383	67 822	. . .	. . .	39 066	22 801	7 526	69 006	3 862	68 783	19 132
1986	365 672	75 736	. . .	. . .	46 136	19 751	6 813	68 253	4 771	81 911	17 302
1987	406 241	81 188	. . .	. . .	57 663	23 952	7 865	71 085	6 294	84 575	20 271
1988	440 952	84 939	. . .	. . .	63 030	22 962	9 294	81 398	8 511	89 519	23 260
1989	473 211	85 153	. . .	. . .	62 774	30 611	8 410	87 953	11 990	93 553	27 162
1990	495 311	91 868	. . .	. . .	60 573	38 052	7 898	91 380	15 237	89 684	30 157
1991	488 453	86 481	. . .	. . .	59 276	32 644	6 717	91 064	18 969	91 511	31 130
1992	532 662	93 993	. . .	. . .	62 384	33 200	7 609	98 630	25 728	97 414	35 211
1993	580 656	97 941	. . .	. . .	64 572	31 739	7 479	111 216	31 540	107 246	39 918
1994	663 252	110 875	. . .	. . .	71 388	31 685	8 683	128 406	38 787	119 156	49 494
1995	743 545	131 871	. . .	. . .	82 008	35 606	8 833	144 370	45 543	123 479	62 100
1996	795 287	142 947	. . .	. . .	82 770	44 285	8 773	155 893	51 513	115 187	74 297
1997	869 703	157 528	. . .	. . .	86 164	44 025	9 625	167 234	62 558	121 663	85 938
1998	911 897	176 380	. . .	. . .	85 960	33 925	10 102	173 256	71 169	121 845	94 629
1999	1 024 616	195 227	. . .	. . .	95 103	41 977	11 314	198 711	81 788	130 864	109 721
2000	1 218 023	220 019	. . .	163 520	111 438	67 090	13 853	230 838	100 018	146 479	135 926
2001	1 140 998	220 057	. . .	166 373	93 202	59 754	14 466	216 268	102 278	126 473	131 338
2002	1 161 366	225 771	. . .	172 573	91 850	53 245	15 781	209 088	125 193	121 429	134 616
2003	1 257 121	244 826	. . .	187 204	92 818	68 344	17 910	221 595	152 436	118 037	138 060
2004	1 469 705	272 439	281 959	209 606	105 476	92 099	21 160	256 360	196 682	129 805	155 902
2005	1 673 454	298 879	309 628	228 881	102 609	127 169	24 436	290 384	243 470	138 004	170 109
2006	1 853 938	319 590	330 482	246 667	109 730	150 758	26 367	302 438	287 774	148 181	198 253
2007	1 956 961	. . .	354 409	266 074	111 260	165 651	25 644	317 057	321 443	145 463	210 714
2008	2 103 641	. . .	367 617	277 658	106 763	242 579	30 453	339 491	337 773	139 262	215 942
2009	1 559 625	. . .	281 801	212 557	86 854	111 602	20 070	226 248	296 374	95 804	176 654
2010	1 913 160	. . .	319 195	242 215	106 444	149 893	23 958	277 647	364 944	120 545	229 908
2011	2 207 824	. . .	368 355	284 943	121 581	191 504	31 736	315 347	399 362	128 925	262 864
2009											
January	122 415	. . .	21 188	16 391	7 550	7 983	1 811	17 553	24 743	8 165	12 465
February	109 012	. . .	21 978	16 231	5 968	6 363	1 342	17 262	18 845	6 409	12 380
March	121 359	. . .	24 116	18 582	7 041	7 302	1 591	17 895	21 225	7 246	13 930
April	118 896	. . .	23 217	17 471	6 837	7 632	1 400	17 211	21 921	6 932	13 716
May	116 341	. . .	20 749	15 676	6 890	7 847	1 540	16 399	22 734	6 145	13 318
June	127 173	. . .	23 137	17 527	6 987	9 626	1 784	18 549	23 973	7 792	14 011
July	135 696	. . .	25 180	19 076	7 404	10 476	1 926	18 763	25 671	8 168	14 082
August	131 272	. . .	22 372	16 584	7 211	10 054	1 612	19 230	25 798	8 165	15 060
September	141 004	. . .	23 529	17 413	7 726	11 908	1 759	19 913	27 894	8 588	16 130
October	147 027	. . .	25 692	19 136	7 877	10 344	1 637	21 229	29 558	9 198	17 290
November	143 324	. . .	25 271	19 025	7 672	10 480	1 815	20 395	27 542	9 478	17 186
December	146 106	. . .	25 372	19 445	7 690	11 588	1 853	21 848	26 470	9 518	17 087
2010											
January	136 725	. . .	21 293	16 532	7 293	10 966	1 942	21 654	25 216	8 341	16 089
February	133 898	. . .	23 124	17 016	6 601	10 781	1 432	21 233	23 343	8 776	16 459
March	157 728	. . .	28 264	21 892	7 970	13 657	1 958	24 316	24 292	10 485	20 089
April	153 163	. . .	24 770	18 807	8 412	13 838	2 002	23 657	25 920	9 442	18 594
May	156 124	. . .	25 734	19 786	8 904	12 495	1 884	23 658	29 052	8 641	19 419
June	168 321	. . .	27 708	20 800	9 452	13 518	2 217	24 772	32 842	10 218	20 040
July	163 861	. . .	28 483	21 587	9 414	12 405	2 400	21 295	33 266	10 091	18 213
August	170 966	. . .	27 551	20 775	9 440	13 549	2 082	23 452	35 375	10 729	20 252
September	167 078	. . .	26 628	19 984	9 768	13 312	1 707	23 529	35 195	10 056	19 909
October	170 239	. . .	28 691	22 040	9 880	10 495	2 088	23 441	35 082	11 281	21 002
November	168 765	. . .	28 190	21 413	10 210	11 579	1 875	22 902	34 563	11 091	20 504
December	166 293	. . .	28 760	21 585	9 100	13 297	2 370	24 239	30 798	11 396	19 336
2011											
January	167 048	. . .	26 134	19 961	9 401	14 358	2 206	24 793	31 377	9 885	19 606
February	156 315	. . .	26 833	21 206	8 613	13 499	1 984	23 215	27 245	10 567	19 054
March	185 975	. . .	33 504	25 810	9 645	16 045	2 055	28 306	27 600	11 807	23 270
April	178 293	. . .	31 133	24 277	10 407	14 848	2 495	25 936	29 580	8 829	21 360
May	188 953	. . .	31 677	24 123	11 211	16 916	2 909	26 965	32 788	8 317	22 970
June	191 579	. . .	32 343	25 135	10 982	18 833	2 820	26 857	34 374	9 421	22 714
July	187 263	. . .	30 175	23 222	10 943	17 190	2 922	25 446	35 152	10 859	21 091
August	196 321	. . .	31 354	24 212	10 365	18 515	2 349	27 147	37 378	11 829	23 152
September	189 562	. . .	29 526	22 900	10 282	16 420	2 892	27 235	36 418	10 858	22 302
October	191 811	. . .	31 508	24 487	10 377	14 423	2 583	26 725	37 819	12 386	22 848
November	190 263	. . .	31 709	24 530	10 022	14 734	3 095	26 172	36 763	12 123	23 146
December	184 443	. . .	32 458	25 080	9 333	15 723	3 427	26 548	32 869	12 043	21 351

[1]See notes and definitions for definitions of regions.
. . . = Not available.

Table 7-15. U.S. Exports of Services

(Balance of payments basis, millions of dollars, seasonally adjusted.)

Year and month	Total	Travel	Passenger fares	Other transportation	Royalties and license fees	Other private services (financial, professional, etc.)	Transfers under U.S. military sales contracts [1]	U.S. government miscellaneous services
1960	6 290	919	175	1 607	837	570	2 030	153
1961	6 295	947	183	1 620	906	607	1 867	164
1962	6 941	957	191	1 764	1 056	585	2 193	195
1963	7 348	1 015	205	1 898	1 162	613	2 219	236
1964	7 840	1 207	241	2 076	1 314	651	2 086	265
1965	8 824	1 380	271	2 175	1 534	714	2 465	285
1966	9 616	1 590	317	2 333	1 516	814	2 721	326
1967	10 667	1 646	371	2 426	1 747	951	3 191	336
1968	11 917	1 775	411	2 548	1 867	1 024	3 939	353
1969	12 806	2 043	450	2 652	2 019	1 160	4 138	343
1970	14 171	2 331	544	3 125	2 331	1 294	4 214	332
1971	16 358	2 534	615	3 299	2 545	1 546	5 472	347
1972	17 841	2 817	699	3 579	2 770	1 764	5 856	357
1973	19 832	3 412	975	4 465	3 225	1 985	5 369	401
1974	22 591	4 032	1 104	5 697	3 821	2 321	5 197	419
1975	25 497	4 697	1 039	5 840	4 300	2 920	6 256	446
1976	27 971	5 742	1 229	6 747	4 353	3 584	5 826	489
1977	31 485	6 150	1 366	7 090	4 920	3 848	7 554	557
1978	36 353	7 183	1 603	8 136	5 885	4 717	8 209	620
1979	39 692	8 441	2 156	9 971	6 184	5 439	6 981	520
1980	47 584	10 588	2 591	11 618	7 085	6 276	9 029	398
1981	57 354	12 913	3 111	12 560	7 284	10 250	10 720	517
1982	64 079	12 393	3 174	12 317	5 603	17 444	12 572	576
1983	64 307	10 947	3 610	12 590	5 778	18 192	12 524	666
1984	71 168	17 177	4 067	13 809	6 177	19 255	9 969	714
1985	73 155	17 762	4 411	14 674	6 678	20 035	8 718	878
1986	86 689	20 385	5 582	15 438	8 113	28 027	8 549	595
1987	98 661	23 563	7 003	17 027	10 174	29 263	11 106	526
1988	110 919	29 434	8 976	19 311	12 139	31 111	9 284	664
1989	127 087	36 205	10 657	20 526	13 818	36 729	8 564	587
1990	147 832	43 007	15 298	22 042	16 634	40 251	9 932	668
1991	164 261	48 385	15 854	22 631	17 819	47 748	11 135	690
1992	177 252	54 742	16 618	21 531	20 841	50 292	12 387	841
1993	185 920	57 875	16 528	21 958	21 695	53 510	13 471	883
1994	200 395	58 417	16 997	23 754	26 712	60 841	12 787	887
1995	219 183	63 395	18 909	26 081	30 289	65 048	14 643	818
1996	239 489	69 809	20 422	26 074	32 470	73 340	16 446	928
1997	256 087	73 426	20 868	27 006	33 228	83 929	16 675	955
1998	262 758	71 325	20 098	25 604	35 626	91 774	17 405	926
1999	281 919	74 801	19 785	26 916	39 670	103 934	15 928	885
2000	298 603	82 400	20 687	29 803	43 233	107 904	13 790	786
2001	286 184	71 893	17 926	28 442	40 696	113 857	12 539	831
2002	292 299	66 605	17 046	29 195	44 508	122 207	11 943	795
2003	302 681	64 348	15 693	31 512	46 988	130 561	12 769	810
2004	349 734	74 546	18 851	36 957	54 490	148 149	15 781	959
2005	389 122	81 799	20 970	41 281	64 395	160 051	19 539	1 087
2006	435 873	85 789	22 036	46 225	70 727	186 028	23 913	1 155
2007	488 299	96 896	25 646	40 315	84 580	222 434	17 216	1 212
2008	535 183	110 423	30 957	44 016	102 125	232 019	14 711	933
2009	509 212	94 187	26 103	36 087	98 406	237 348	16 013	1 069
2010	553 603	103 481	30 983	40 817	107 165	255 293	14 752	1 112
2011	605 961	116 115	36 631	43 064	120 836	270 193	17 946	1 176
2010								
January	44 381	8 348	2 276	3 222	9 044	20 158	1 194	139
February	44 222	8 332	2 364	3 346	8 667	20 176	1 211	126
March	44 699	8 546	2 491	3 345	8 557	20 460	1 195	105
April	44 202	8 056	2 314	3 408	8 657	20 439	1 240	87
May	45 731	8 594	2 659	3 404	8 823	20 900	1 273	78
June	46 251	8 690	2 748	3 533	8 928	21 001	1 277	74
July	46 525	8 755	2 769	3 375	8 966	21 275	1 304	81
August	46 555	8 591	2 605	3 377	8 972	21 620	1 308	82
September	47 191	8 830	2 697	3 386	8 982	21 926	1 287	83
October	47 617	8 881	2 769	3 391	9 033	22 281	1 180	82
November	48 051	8 931	2 712	3 512	9 160	22 502	1 149	85
December	48 177	8 927	2 578	3 517	9 377	22 555	1 133	90
2011								
January	49 048	9 210	2 808	3 526	9 631	22 429	1 339	104
February	48 894	8 953	2 698	3 454	9 831	22 500	1 351	107
March	49 952	9 244	2 868	3 540	9 943	22 820	1 431	106
April	50 076	9 573	2 926	3 596	10 010	22 392	1 489	90
May	50 763	9 784	3 077	3 649	10 095	22 554	1 516	88
June	51 000	9 903	3 077	3 515	10 238	22 638	1 540	89
July	51 754	10 079	3 291	3 677	10 375	22 686	1 545	102
August	51 859	10 005	3 313	3 584	10 404	22 894	1 555	104
September	51 576	10 110	3 285	3 695	10 276	22 543	1 564	104
October	50 822	9 964	3 154	3 628	10 082	22 357	1 538	99
November	50 325	9 765	3 103	3 631	9 958	22 236	1 535	97
December	49 890	9 525	3 030	3 568	9 994	22 143	1 542	88

[1] Contains goods that cannot be separately identified.

Table 7-16. U.S. Imports of Services

(Balance of payments basis, millions of dollars, seasonally adjusted.)

Year and month	Total	Travel	Passenger fares	Other transportation	Royalties and license fees	Other private services (financial, professional, etc.)	Direct defense expenditures [1]	U.S. government miscellaneous services
1960	7 674	1 750	513	1 402	74	593	3 087	254
1961	7 671	1 785	506	1 437	89	588	2 998	268
1962	8 092	1 939	567	1 558	100	528	3 105	296
1963	8 362	2 114	612	1 701	112	493	2 961	370
1964	8 619	2 211	642	1 817	127	527	2 880	415
1965	9 111	2 438	717	1 951	135	461	2 952	457
1966	10 494	2 657	753	2 161	140	506	3 764	513
1967	11 863	3 207	829	2 157	166	565	4 378	561
1968	12 302	3 030	885	2 367	186	668	4 535	631
1969	13 322	3 373	1 080	2 455	221	751	4 856	586
1970	14 520	3 980	1 215	2 843	224	827	4 855	576
1971	15 400	4 373	1 290	3 130	241	956	4 819	592
1972	16 868	5 042	1 596	3 520	294	1 043	4 784	589
1973	18 843	5 526	1 790	4 694	385	1 180	4 629	640
1974	21 379	5 980	2 095	5 942	346	1 262	5 032	722
1975	21 996	6 417	2 263	5 708	472	1 551	4 795	789
1976	24 570	6 856	2 568	6 852	482	2 006	4 895	911
1977	27 640	7 451	2 748	7 972	504	2 190	5 823	951
1978	32 189	8 475	2 896	9 124	671	2 573	7 352	1 099
1979	36 689	9 413	3 184	10 906	831	2 822	8 294	1 239
1980	41 491	10 397	3 607	11 790	724	2 909	10 851	1 214
1981	45 503	11 479	4 487	12 474	650	3 562	11 564	1 287
1982	51 749	12 394	4 772	11 710	795	8 159	12 460	1 460
1983	54 973	13 149	6 003	12 222	943	8 001	13 087	1 568
1984	67 748	22 913	5 735	14 843	1 168	9 040	12 516	1 534
1985	72 862	24 558	6 444	15 643	1 170	10 203	13 108	1 735
1986	80 147	25 913	6 505	17 766	1 401	13 146	13 730	1 686
1987	90 787	29 310	7 283	19 010	1 857	16 485	14 950	1 893
1988	98 526	32 114	7 729	20 891	2 601	17 667	15 604	1 921
1989	102 479	33 416	8 249	22 172	2 528	18 930	15 313	1 871
1990	117 659	37 349	10 531	24 966	3 135	22 229	17 531	1 919
1991	118 459	35 322	10 012	24 975	4 035	25 590	16 409	2 116
1992	119 566	38 552	10 603	23 767	5 161	25 386	13 835	2 263
1993	123 779	40 713	11 410	24 524	5 032	27 760	12 086	2 255
1994	133 057	43 782	13 062	26 019	5 852	31 565	10 217	2 560
1995	141 397	44 916	14 663	27 034	6 919	35 199	10 043	2 623
1996	152 554	48 078	15 809	27 403	7 837	39 679	11 061	2 687
1997	165 932	52 051	18 138	28 959	9 161	43 154	11 707	2 762
1998	180 677	56 483	19 971	30 363	11 235	47 591	12 185	2 849
1999	199 190	58 963	21 315	34 139	13 107	55 510	13 335	2 821
2000	223 748	64 705	24 274	41 425	16 468	60 520	13 473	2 883
2001	221 791	60 200	22 633	38 682	16 538	66 021	14 835	2 882
2002	231 069	58 715	19 969	38 407	19 353	72 604	19 101	2 920
2003	250 276	57 444	20 957	44 705	19 033	79 710	25 296	3 131
2004	292 247	65 750	24 718	54 161	23 274	91 267	29 299	3 778
2005	313 540	68 970	26 149	61 937	24 612	97 818	30 075	3 979
2006	348 972	72 104	27 501	65 318	23 518	125 478	31 032	4 021
2007	367 206	76 331	28 437	53 513	24 931	151 894	27 917	4 184
2008	403 413	80 494	31 841	56 696	29 623	172 543	28 311	3 905
2009	382 608	74 132	25 117	42 601	31 297	174 573	30 474	4 415
2010	403 216	75 510	27 256	51 258	33 434	180 586	30 391	4 781
2011	427 428	78 651	31 109	54 711	36 620	191 973	29 510	4 854
2010								
January	32 604	6 379	2 068	3 798	2 789	14 623	2 571	376
February	33 247	6 293	2 020	3 926	3 505	14 562	2 574	368
March	32 865	6 296	2 141	4 144	2 682	14 660	2 576	365
April	32 346	5 796	2 095	4 131	2 584	14 828	2 539	374
May	33 109	6 131	2 325	4 279	2 532	14 932	2 529	381
June	33 776	6 250	2 351	4 506	2 739	15 016	2 523	391
July	34 055	6 380	2 379	4 514	2 672	15 155	2 539	416
August	34 130	6 311	2 290	4 588	2 723	15 256	2 538	425
September	34 350	6 402	2 353	4 523	2 753	15 359	2 532	428
October	34 405	6 471	2 422	4 388	2 765	15 438	2 499	422
November	34 209	6 424	2 427	4 245	2 802	15 403	2 489	420
December	34 119	6 377	2 385	4 216	2 888	15 354	2 483	415
2011								
January	34 626	6 433	2 535	4 576	2 978	15 175	2 520	409
February	34 334	6 343	2 470	4 378	3 005	15 210	2 525	403
March	34 803	6 481	2 537	4 486	2 938	15 440	2 525	396
April	35 075	6 519	2 514	4 545	2 839	15 756	2 525	377
May	35 394	6 533	2 591	4 612	2 806	15 959	2 517	376
June	35 736	6 576	2 593	4 579	2 899	16 201	2 503	385
July	36 445	6 670	2 634	4 666	3 105	16 477	2 471	422
August	36 429	6 559	2 624	4 550	3 197	16 620	2 448	431
September	36 521	6 666	2 688	4 551	3 201	16 559	2 424	432
October	35 999	6 615	2 606	4 558	3 211	16 225	2 372	413
November	35 867	6 538	2 636	4 563	3 214	16 160	2 348	408
December	36 202	6 718	2 681	4 648	3 228	16 191	2 332	404

[1]Contains goods that cannot be separately identified.

Table 7-17. U.S. Export and Import Price Indexes by End-Use Category

(2000 = 100, not seasonally adjusted.)

Year and month	Exports			Imports		
	All commodities	Agricultural	Nonagricultural	All commodities	Petroleum [1]	Nonpetroleum
1990	95.5	105.1	94.4	94.0	75.5	97.1
1991	96.3	103.4	95.4	94.2	67.3	98.7
1992	96.3	102.5	95.7	94.9	62.9	100.0
1993	96.9	104.4	96.2	94.6	57.7	100.6
1994	98.9	109.4	98.0	96.2	54.3	103.2
1995	103.9	119.0	102.5	100.6	59.8	107.2
1996	104.5	132.6	101.6	101.6	71.1	106.4
1997	103.1	120.6	101.3	99.1	66.0	104.1
1998	99.7	108.8	98.8	93.1	44.8	100.4
1999	98.4	101.1	98.2	93.9	60.1	99.0
2000	100.0	100.0	100.0	100.0	100.0	100.0
2001	99.2	101.2	99.0	96.5	82.8	98.5
2002	98.2	103.2	97.8	94.1	85.3	96.2
2003	99.7	112.3	98.8	96.9	103.2	97.3
2004	103.6	123.4	102.1	102.3	134.6	99.8
2005	106.9	121.0	105.9	110.0	185.1	102.5
2006	110.7	125.8	109.6	115.4	223.3	104.2
2007	116.1	150.9	113.6	120.2	249.1	107.0
2008	123.1	183.5	118.8	134.1	343.2	112.7
2009	117.4	160.0	114.3	118.6	219.9	108.0
2010	123.1	172.6	119.6	126.8	282.2	111.0
2011	133.0	211.0	127.5	140.6	385.1	115.9
2008						
January	120.7	177.5	116.6	129.2	319.6	109.7
February	121.8	185.6	117.3	129.5	315.6	110.4
March	123.8	194.3	118.8	133.5	347.5	111.6
April	124.4	190.5	119.6	137.3	375.8	113.1
May	124.8	190.8	120.1	141.2	412.2	113.9
June	126.1	195.2	121.2	145.5	450.3	114.9
July	128.0	208.2	122.3	147.5	465.0	115.6
August	125.9	188.2	121.5	143.0	419.5	115.1
September	124.9	188.3	120.4	137.8	371.5	114.0
October	122.3	172.5	118.7	129.6	288.9	113.0
November	118.4	160.6	115.4	120.0	201.6	111.1
December	115.8	150.8	113.2	114.5	150.8	109.9
2009						
January	116.6	159.7	113.5	113.0	143.8	109.0
February	116.3	157.0	113.3	113.0	151.6	108.2
March	115.5	151.6	112.9	113.6	168.5	107.3
April	116.1	157.2	113.1	114.8	185.5	107.1
May	116.6	162.8	113.4	116.8	206.1	107.3
June	117.8	169.7	114.1	120.0	241.5	107.4
July	117.4	161.3	114.2	119.3	235.8	107.2
August	118.1	161.6	115.0	121.1	253.7	107.6
September	117.9	156.9	115.1	121.3	252.2	107.9
October	117.9	155.8	115.2	122.3	258.3	108.4
November	118.9	161.8	115.8	124.1	272.2	109.1
December	119.7	164.7	116.5	124.4	269.3	109.7
2010						
January	120.7	166.8	117.3	125.9	279.6	110.3
February	120.3	160.2	117.4	125.8	277.4	110.4
March	121.2	163.3	118.1	126.3	284.2	110.3
April	122.5	162.7	119.6	127.7	294.5	110.8
May	123.1	165.3	120.0	126.7	278.9	111.2
June	122.2	165.3	119.1	125.2	267.4	110.7
July	122.0	165.0	118.9	125.2	269.6	110.5
August	123.0	172.0	119.5	125.7	273.4	110.7
September	123.7	176.1	120.0	125.7	269.8	111.0
October	124.7	181.0	120.7	127.1	282.4	111.3
November	126.6	194.7	121.7	129.2	296.6	112.2
December	127.5	198.5	122.4	131.0	313.0	112.6
2011						
January	129.1	204.7	123.6	133.0	324.7	113.6
February	130.8	214.1	124.8	135.3	342.5	114.4
March	132.7	218.8	126.5	139.3	380.2	115.0
April	133.8	217.8	127.7	142.9	410.7	115.9
May	134.3	215.5	128.4	143.1	407.6	116.4
June	134.5	217.2	128.6	142.2	397.8	116.4
July	134.0	208.5	128.7	142.4	399.2	116.5
August	134.6	211.9	129.1	141.9	390.0	116.8
September	135.3	216.0	129.5	141.7	386.5	117.0
October	132.6	201.9	127.7	141.2	385.5	116.6
November	132.7	205.3	127.5	142.2	398.8	116.3
December	132.0	201.0	127.0	142.0	397.0	116.0

[1] Petroleum and petroleum products.

NOTES AND DEFINITIONS, CHAPTER 7

This chapter presents data from two different data systems on international flows of goods, services, income payments, and financial transactions as they affect the U.S. economy. Tables 7-1 through 7-5 present data on the value, quantities, and prices of foreign transactions in the national income and product accounts (NIPAs). Tables 7-6 through 7-8 show foreign transactions and investment positions in current-dollar values as depicted in the U.S. international transactions accounts (ITAs). Both sets of accounts are prepared by the Bureau of Economic Analysis (BEA) and draw on the same original source data. The Census Bureau source data for goods and services are presented in somewhat greater detail in Tables 7-9 through 7-16. Table 7-17 shows selected summary values for export and import price indexes compiled by the Bureau of Labor Statistics (BLS).

Due to a few differences in concept, scope, and definitions, the aggregate values of international transactions in the NIPAs (shown in Tables 7-1 and 7-4) are not exactly equal to the values for similar concepts in the ITAs or the Census values that serve as their sources, shown in Tables 7-6 through 7-16. The principal sources of differences are as follows:

- The NIPAs cover only the 50 states and the District of Columbia. The ITAs include the U.S. territories and Puerto Rico as part of the U.S. economy.

- Gold is treated differently.

- Services without payment by financial intermediaries except life insurance carriers (imputed interest) is treated differently.

A reconciliation of the two sets of international accounts is published from time to time. As of the time of writing, the most up-to-date reconciliation was Reconciliation Table 1, "Relation of Net Exports of Goods and Services and Net Receipts of Income in the NIPAs to Balance on Goods and Services and Income in the ITAs," which can be found in the Appendixes to the *Survey of Current Business*, July 2012, page D-81.

In addition, certain conventions of presentation differ between the two sets of international accounts. In the NIPAs (Tables 7-1 through 7-5) and in Census tables of exports and imports of goods and services (Tables 7-9 through 7-16), values of imports are shown as positive values, even though they are in fact subtracted in the calculation of gross domestic product (GDP). In the ITA balance of payments (Table 7-6), however, values of imports of goods and services and of all other transactions that result in a payment to the rest of the world—income payments to foreigners, net transfers to foreigners, and net acquisition of assets from abroad—are presented with a minus sign.

TABLES 7-1 AND 7-4
FOREIGN TRANSACTIONS IN THE NATIONAL INCOME AND PRODUCT ACCOUNTS

SOURCE: U.S. DEPARTMENT OF COMMERCE, BUREAU OF ECONOMIC ANALYSIS

See the notes and definitions to Chapter 1 for an overview of the national income and product accounts (NIPAs).

In the 2003 comprehensive revision, the NIPA foreign transactions account was split into two accounts—the current account and the capital account. (This change had already been made in the ITAs.) Most international transactions fall into the current account, but occasionally there are substantial flows in the capital account when major already-existing assets are transferred. An example of this is the U.S. government's transfer of the Panama Canal to the Republic of Panama in 1999.

Definitions

In accordance with the split between current and capital account, there are now two NIPA measures of the balance of international transactions.

The *balance on current account, national income and product accounts* is *current receipts from the rest of the world* minus *current payments to the rest of the world*. A negative value indicates that current payments exceed current receipts.

Net lending or net borrowing (-), national income and product accounts is equal to the balance on current account less capital account transactions with the rest of the world (net). Capital account transactions with the rest of the world (net) is not shown separately in Table 7-1 (for space reasons) but can be calculated from that table as the difference between net lending/borrowing and the current account balance. (A similar measure, a component of the ITAs, is shown explicitly in Table 7-6.) Capital account transactions with the rest of the world are cash or in-kind transfers linked to the acquisition or disposition of an existing, nonproduced, nonfinancial asset. In contrast, the current account is limited to flows associated with current production of goods and services.

Net lending or net borrowing provides an indirect measure of the net acquisition of foreign assets by U.S. residents less the net acquisition of U.S. assets by foreign residents. These asset flows are measured directly in the ITAs. See Table 7-6 and its notes and definitions for a more extensive discussion of the relationship between the balances on current and capital account and international asset flows.

Current receipts from the rest of the world is *exports of goods and services* plus *income receipts*.

Current payments to the rest of the world is *imports of goods and services* plus *income payments* plus *current taxes and transfer payments (net).*

Exports and imports of goods and services. Goods, in general, are products that can be stored or inventoried. *Services*, in general, are products that cannot be stored and are consumed at the place and time of their purchase. Goods imports include expenditures abroad by U.S. residents, except for travel. Services include foreign travel by U.S. residents, expenditures in the United States by foreign travelers, and exports and imports of certain goods—primarily military equipment purchased and sold by the federal government. See the following paragraph for the definition of *travel*.

Table 7-4 shows values for selected components of total goods and services; the components shown will not add to the total because of omitted items. In the case of goods, a miscellaneous "other" category is not shown. In the case of services, only two components are shown in this table. One is *travel*, which does not include passenger fares but includes as exports spending by foreign tourists in the United States, and includes as imports all other spending abroad by tourists from the United States. The other component shown here is a category called *other private services*, which includes the professional and financial services (for example, computer services) that have accounted for a large part of the long-term growth in the service category. The remaining components of total services are transfers under U.S. military agency sales contracts; passenger fares; other transportation; royalties and license fees; and a miscellaneous, smaller *other* category. They are shown separately in Tables 7-15 and 7-16.

Income receipts and payments. Income receipts—receipts from abroad of factor (labor or capital) income by U.S. residents—are analogous to exports and are combined with them to yield total *current receipts from the rest of the world. Income payments* by U.S. entities of factor income to entities abroad are analogous to imports.

Current taxes and transfer payments (net) consists of net payments between the United States and abroad that do not involve payment for the services of the labor or capital factors of production, purchase of currently-produced goods and services, or transfer of an existing asset. It includes net flows from persons, government, and business. The types of payments included are personal remittances from U.S. residents to the rest of the world, net of remittances from foreigners to U.S. residents; government grants; and transfer payments from businesses. Only the net payment to the rest of the world is shown. It usually appears in these accounts as a positive value, with transfers from the United States to abroad exceeding the reverse flow. An exception came in 1991, when U.S. allies in the Gulf War reimbursed the United States for the cost of the war. This resulted in net payments to the United States from the rest of the world and appears as a negative entry in the net transfer payments column of the NIPA accounts. (Note that these signs are reversed in the ITAs, because of the differing measurement conventions described above.)

TABLES 7-2, 7-3 AND 7-5
CHAIN-TYPE QUANTITY AND PRICE INDEXES FOR NIPA FOREIGN TRANSACTIONS

These indexes represent the separation of the current-dollar values in Tables 7-1 and 7-4 into their real quantity and price trends components. (See the notes and definitions to Chapter 1 for a general explanation of chained-dollar estimates of real output and prices.) As those notes explain, quantity indexes are shown instead of constant-dollar estimates, because BEA no longer publishes its real output estimates before 1995 in any detail in the constant-dollar form. Therefore, quantity indexes are the only comprehensive source of information about longer-term trends in real volumes.

TABLE 7-6A
U.S. INTERNATIONAL TRANSACTIONS: RECENT DATA

SOURCE: U.S. DEPARTMENT OF COMMERCE, BUREAU OF ECONOMIC ANALYSIS

The U.S. international transactions accounts (ITAs), or "balance of payments accounts," provide a comprehensive view of economic and financial transactions between the United States and foreign countries, measured in current dollars only—unlike the NIPAs, in which price and quantity trends are also estimated. Direct measurement of the values of financial asset flows further distinguishes this set of accounts from the NIPAs.

The ITAs are subdivided into three sets of accounts, with each comprising credit and debit items. In concept, all of these items together provide a complete accounting for U.S. international transactions and should therefore sum to zero. In practice, there are substantial discrepancies due to measurement problems. See the definitions below for an explanation of the *statistical discrepancy* in these accounts, which is different from the measure of the same name in the NIPAs.

The *balance on current account* is the most frequently quoted statistic from these accounts, and is often, but imprecisely, called the "trade balance." (See the definitions below for the correct definitions of "trade balance" and "merchandise trade balance," both of which differ from the current account balance.) The current account includes exports and imports of goods and of travel, transportation, and other services; receipts and payments of income between U.S. and foreign residents; and foreign aid and other current transfers. The *financial account* covers most international flows of private and official capital, including direct investment. The *capital account*, which is small relative to the other two accounts, includes certain transactions in existing assets.

More detailed data on exports and imports of goods and services as measured in these accounts are shown in Tables 7-9 through 7-16.

Definitions

Unlike the practice in the NIPA accounts, each category of transaction in the ITAs is presented either as a *credit*, with an implicit plus sign, or as a *debit*, with a clearly marked minus sign. The signs indicate the direction of the ultimate impact on the overall balance.

Credits (+): The following items are treated as credits in the international transactions accounts: exports of goods and services and income receipts; unilateral current transfers to the United States; capital account transactions receipts; and financial inflows, which are increases in foreign-owned assets (U.S. liabilities) and decreases in U.S.-owned assets (U.S. claims). Credits represent payments of funds to U.S. entities, whether earned (as with exports), received as gifts, received in payment for assets, or received in exchange for a claim, such as a stock, bond, or loan agreement, on a U.S. entity.

Debits (-): The following items are treated as debits in the international transactions accounts, indicated by minus signs in the data cells: imports of goods and services and income payments; unilateral current transfers to foreigners; capital accounts transactions payments; financial outflows, which are decreases in foreign-owned assets (U.S. liabilities) and increases in U.S.-owned assets (U.S. claims). Debits represent requirements for U.S. entities to make payments to foreigners, whether for imports, as gifts, or as payments for the acquisition of real or financial assets.

This convention of credits and debits is used only in the ITAs in Table 7-6. In Table 7-6, import values all have a negative sign. Import values are shown without negative signs both in the NIPA tables (Tables 7-1 and 7-4) and in the detailed tables from the Census Bureau on exports and imports of goods and services (Tables 7-9 through 7-16).

The *balance on goods* is the excess of exports of goods over imports of goods—the algebraic sum of the two, in ITA transactions accounting. A minus sign indicates an excess of imports over exports. A similar concept, which appears in monthly trade reports, is called the "merchandise trade balance."

The *balance on services* is the excess of service exports over service imports. A minus sign indicates an excess of imports over exports.

The *balance on goods and services* is the sum of the balance on goods and the balance on services. This concept is accurately described as the "balance of trade."

The *balance on income* is the excess of income receipts from abroad over income payments to foreigners. A minus sign indicates an excess of payments over receipts.

The *balance on goods, services, and income* is the excess of exports of goods and services and income receipts over imports of goods and services and income payments. It is equal to the sum of the balance on goods and services and the balance on income. A minus sign indicates an excess of imports and payments over exports and receipts.

Unilateral current transfers, net is equal to unilateral transfers to the United States minus transfers from the United States. This category includes U.S. government grants, pensions, and other transfers, and private remittances and other transfers. In the July 2009 revision, insurance payments for extraordinary disaster losses were shifted from this account to the *capital account.*

The *balance on current account* is equal to the sum of the balance on goods, services, and income and the net balance on unilateral transfers. It is the featured measure of the U.S. balance of payments.

The *capital account* covers net capital transfers and the acquisition and disposal of nonproduced nonfinancial assets.

The major type of *capital transfers* is debt forgiveness. As of the 2010 comprehensive revision, and beginning with the data for 1982, migrants' transfers—the net worth of individuals who immigrate or emigrate during a period—are excluded from the capital account, as they do not generate transactions between a resident and a nonresident. This change is in accordance with international guidelines. Migrants' investments in their country of origin will continue to be recorded in the international investment position accounts (shown in Table 7-8) when migration changes the status of these investments from domestic to international, but they will enter the position as "other changes in value."

Nonproduced nonfinancial assets include rights to natural resources, patents, copyrights, trademarks, franchises, and leases. In the July 2009 revision, insurance payments for extraordinary disaster losses such as those caused by major hurricanes and the 2001 terror attack were shifted to the capital account from the current unilateral transfers account.

The *financial account* includes all other inflows and outflows of capital, or changes in U.S.-owned assets abroad and foreign-owned assets in the United States, including official reserve assets, direct investment, securities, currency, and bank deposits. Most of the categories are self-explanatory.

U.S. government assets other than official reserve assets, net and its component *U.S. foreign currency holdings and short-term assets, net* include the initiation and reversal of large swap positions under temporary reciprocal currency arrangements between the U.S. Federal Reserve System and foreign central banks, undertaken in order to deal with the international financial crisis in late 2008. The accounts indicate creation of a half-trillion dollars' worth of swaps in 2008 (because a minus sign in these accounts indicates increases in U.S. official assets) and the reversal of about the same amount in 2009.

Direct investment financial flows are those associated with the acquisition of a significant interest (10 percent or more) in a business enterprise in one country by a resident of another country.

U.S. claims reported by U.S. banks and securities brokers, a component of *U.S. private assets, net*. Beginning with 2003, these entries include securities brokers' claims on their foreign affiliates. Prior to 2003, such claims are included in the claims of nonbanking concerns.

U.S. liabilities reported by U.S. banks and securities brokers, components of *Foreign official assets in the United States, net* and *Other foreign assets in the United States, net*. Beginning with 2003, these entries include securities brokers' liabilities to their foreign affiliates. Prior to 2003, such liabilities are included in the liabilities of nonbanking concerns.

Foreign official assets in the United States. U.S. Treasury securities includes bills, certificates, marketable bonds and notes, and nonmarketable convertible and nonconvertible bonds and notes. *Other U.S. government securities* consists of U.S. Treasury and Export-Import Bank obligations, not included elsewhere, and of debt securities of U.S. government corporations and agencies. *Other U.S. government liabilities* primarily includes U.S. government liabilities to foreign official authorities associated with military agency sales contracts and other transactions arranged with or through foreign official agencies. *Other foreign official assets* consists of official investments in U.S. corporate stocks and in debt securities of private corporations and state and local governments.

In concept, the balance on current account is exactly offset by the net financial and capital inflow or outflow. For example, a U.S. current account deficit results in more dollars held by foreigners, which <u>must</u> be reflected in additional claims on the United States held by foreigners, whether in the form of U.S. currency, dollar bank accounts, securities, loans, or other forms of ownership or obligation. However, because of different and incomplete data sources, the measured financial and capital accounts do not exactly offset the measured current account. The *statistical discrepancy* in the U.S. international accounts—the sum of all credits and debits, with the sign reversed—measures the amount by which the measured net financial and capital flow would have to be augmented (or diminished, in the case of a negative discrepancy) to exactly offset the current account balance. In the quarterly accounts, a part of this discrepancy, the *seasonal adjustment discrepancy*, results from separate seasonal adjustments of the components of the accounts. The statistical discrepancy in the international accounts is not the same as the statistical discrepancy in the national income and product accounts, which arises from measurement differences between domestic output and domestic income.

Notes on the data

There are "breaks" (discontinuities) in the historical series for several of the components of the balance of payments

accounts. See Technical Notes in the June 1989–1990, 1992–1995, and July 1996–2007 issues of the *Survey of Current Business*.

Exports and imports of goods. In the 2010 comprehensive revision, and beginning with the statistics for 1999, new adjustments were introduced to reclassify goods transactions by the U.S. military and by air and ocean carriers from services, where they had previously been included due to data deficiencies, to the goods categories. The goods data also reflect various other adjustments (for valuation, coverage, and timing) of Census Bureau statistics to a balance-of-payments basis. See the notes and definitions to Tables 7-9 through 7-16 for further information.

U.S. government grants includes transfers of goods and services under U.S. military grant programs. The positive value in 1991 reflects net grants to the United States from other countries.

Beginning in 1982, *private remittances and other transfers* includes taxes paid by U.S. private residents to foreign governments and taxes paid by private nonresidents to the U.S. government.

At the present time, all U.S. Treasury-owned *gold* is held in the United States.

Repayments on U.S. credits and other long-term assets includes sales of foreign obligations to foreigners. The data for 1974 include extraordinary U.S. government transactions with India, as described in "Special U.S. Government Transactions," *Survey of Current Business*, June 1974, page 27.

Beginning with the data for 1982, *direct investment income payments* and the reinvested earnings component of *direct investment* financial flows are measured on a current-cost (replacement-cost) basis after adjustment to reported depreciation, depletion, and expensed exploration and development costs. For prior years, depreciation is valued in terms of the historical cost of assets and reflects a mix of prices for the various years in which capital investments were made. See *Survey of Current Business*, July 1999, pages 65–67, and *Survey of Current Business*, June 1992, pages 72ff.

The *U.S. Treasury securities* component of *other foreign assets in the United States* includes foreign-currency denominated notes sold to private residents abroad for 1978 through 1983.

Estimates of *U.S. currency flows abroad* were introduced for the first time as part of the July 1997 revisions. Data for 1974 and subsequent years were affected (see *Survey of Current Business*, July 1997). Beginning with the 1998 revisions, currency flows are published separately from U.S. Treasury securities.

Financial derivatives, net are estimated for the first time for 2006. (Previously, they were partly measured in other financial flow components and in part contributed to the statistical discrepancy.) They are reported on a net basis only. See "References," below, for more explanation.

Data availability

Quarterly estimates are reported in a press release around the middle of the third month of each quarter, available on the BEA Web site at <http://www.bea.gov>. The data published here were released on June 14, 2012. Complete historical data are available on the BEA Web site at <http://www.bea.gov/>.

References

Discussions of the impact of changes in methodology and incorporation of new data sources when they occur are found in July issues (the June issues for 1995 and earlier years) of the *Survey of Current Business*, with the most recent such article entitled "Annual Revision of the U.S. International Transactions Accounts" (July 2012). A similarly titled article in the July 2007 *Survey* includes an extensive discussion of the new data on financial derivatives and their role in the ITA financial account and investment position data.

The Balance of Payments of the United States: Concepts, Data Sources, and Estimating Procedures (May 1990), available on the BEA Web site or from the National Technical Information Service (Accession No. PB 90-268715), describes the methodology in detail and provides a list of data sources.

TABLE 7-6B
U.S. INTERNATIONAL TRANSACTIONS: HISTORICAL

For space reasons, the amounts for *U.S. Treasury securities and U.S. currency flows* under the heading *Other foreign assets in the United States, net*, which are separate columns in Table 7-6A, are combined in Table 7-6B.

The *Balance on current account* as shown in the final column of Table 7-6B includes some items not shown separately, which are displayed in Table 7-6A. They are *Capital account transactions, net* and *Financial derivatives, net*.

TABLE 7-7
FOREIGNERS' TRANSACTIONS IN LONG-TERM SECURITIES WITH U.S. RESIDENTS

SOURCE: U.S. DEPARTMENT OF THE TREASURY

Some of the transactions that go into the ITA financial account are collected monthly. Since December 2003, these transactions have been reported by the Treasury Department in a monthly press release. They are presented in Table 7-7.

These data cover transactions in long-term securities, measured at market value plus or minus commissions and fees, between foreigners and U.S. residents. They have more reporting gaps than the more comprehensive quarterly cur-

rent account data in Table 7-6. These monthly data do not include direct investment, currency flows, changes in bank accounts, or transactions in short-term securities. They may be distorted by inappropriate reporting of repurchases and securities lending transactions. The data are more timely but less detailed than other information sources and are not reliable for country-by-country detail. They are based on a reporting panel of some 250 banks, securities dealers, and other enterprises with cross-border transactions of at least $50 million. This survey was designed to provide timely information for the balance of payments accounts, and its use for other applications—particularly those involving country detail—is less appropriate.

Definitions and notes on the data

U.S. residents includes any individual, corporation, or organization located in the United States (including branches, subsidiaries, and affiliates of foreign entities located in the United States) and any corporation incorporated in the United States, even if it has no physical presence in the country.

Gross purchases minus *gross sales* equals *net purchases*. Positive values for net purchases of U.S. securities by foreigners indicate capital inflows from foreigners to U.S. residents (and increased liabilities to foreigners on the part of the U.S. residents). Negative values for net purchases of foreign securities from U.S. residents indicate a capital outflow from U.S. residents to foreigners (and increased liabilities to U.S. residents on the part of foreigners). The algebraic sum of the two net purchases components gives *net long-term securities transactions*. When positive, this indicates that the net capital inflows on U.S. securities exceed the net U.S. acquisitions of foreign securities.

Other acquisitions of long-term securities, net consists of estimated foreign acquisitions of U.S. equity through stock swaps, plus the increase in nonmarketable treasury bonds and notes issued to official institutions and other residents of foreign countries, minus estimated unrecorded principal payments to foreigners on domestic corporate and agency asset-backed securities, minus estimated U.S. acquisitions of foreign equity through stock swaps.

Net foreign acquisition of long-term securities is the sum of *net long-term securities transactions* and *other acquisitions of long-term securities*.

Revisions

The monthly and annual data are revised frequently, when quarterly and annual benchmark data become available. The June release usually includes the final results from an annual survey of foreign holding of U.S. securities.

Data availability and references

Data for the latest month and recent historical data are published in a press release available around the middle of the second following month. The press release, supporting descriptions, references, and other relevant information concerning the Treasury International Capital System (TIC) can be found online at <http://www.treas.gov/tic>.

TABLE 7-8
INTERNATIONAL INVESTMENT POSITION OF THE UNITED STATES

SOURCE: U.S. DEPARTMENT OF COMMERCE, BUREAU OF ECONOMIC ANALYSIS

The data presented in Tables 7-1 through 7-7 all represent <u>flows</u> of goods, services, and money over the designated time periods. Table 7-8, in contrast, is a measure of <u>stocks</u>, or total holdings of money and other claims. The data on the international investment position of the United States measure the extent to which the United States and its residents hold claims of ownership on foreigners or are creditors of foreigners; the extent to which foreigners, including foreign governments, hold claims of ownership on assets located in the United States or are creditors of U.S. residents and entities; and the net difference between the two amounts. This difference measures the amount by which the United States is a net creditor of the rest of the world or a net debtor to the rest of the world. A position of net U.S. indebtedness is represented by a minus sign in the net international investment position.

Changes in the net investment position can arise in two principal ways:

- The first way is through inflows or outflows of capital. A net inflow of capital increases U.S. indebtedness to foreigners, while a net outflow increases foreigners' indebtedness to the United States. A deficit in the U.S. international current account requires an equivalent inflow of foreign capital, while a surplus would require an equivalent outflow of U.S. capital; see notes for Table 7-6 for further explanation.

- The second way is through valuation adjustments, which are of several kinds: changes in market prices of assets; changes in exchange rates, which can cause revaluation of foreign-currency-denominated assets; and miscellaneous other adjustments due to changes in coverage, statistical discrepancies, and the like. Valuation adjustments are shown separately from financial flows in the *Survey of Current Business* articles accompanying each annual update (see below for reference). They were particularly sharp in 2008 and 2009, far exceeding the actual net volume of financial flows in both years.

Two new features were introduced into the investment position accounts with the 2007 revision.

- First, only one version of the net position is now published, the one in which direct investment is measured at current cost. (See definitions below.) However, alternative measures of direct investment measured at market prices are also published, so that the user can calculate the position with market valuation of direct investment.

- Second, for the years 2005 forward, assets and the net position include financial derivatives, which introduces a break in the series. The values for financial derivatives are shown separately so that the user can eliminate them from the calculation if desired. The net value of derivatives was reported to be $126 billion at the end of 2011. Without including derivatives, the U.S. international investment position would have been net indebtedness of $4.16 trillion instead of the net indebtedness of $4.03 trillion shown in Table 7-8.

Definitions: direct investment, current cost, and market value

Direct investment occurs when an individual or business in one country (the parent) obtains a lasting interest in, and a degree of influence over the management of, a business enterprise in another country (the affiliate). The U.S. data define this degree of interest to be ownership of at least 10 percent of the voting securities of an incorporated business enterprise or the equivalent interest in an unincorporated business enterprise.

When direct investment positions are valued at the historical costs carried on the books of the affiliated companies, much of the investment will reflect the price levels of earlier time periods. Therefore, before calculating the overall U.S. position, BEA re-estimates the <u>aggregate</u> direct investment totals using two alternative valuation bases. <u>Detailed</u> direct investment data by country and industry are available only on a historical cost basis.

At *current cost*, the portion of the direct investment position representing the parents' shares of their affiliates' tangible assets (property, plant, equipment, and inventories) is revalued to replacement cost in today's money, using a perpetual inventory model, appropriate price indexes, and appropriate depreciation allowances. (The same methodology is used for the U.S. stock of fixed assets; see the notes and definitions to Tables 5-5 and 5-6 for further information.) This is an adjustment made to the asset side of the balance sheet and reflects prices of tangible assets only.

The *market value* method revalues the owners' equity portion of the direct investment positions using general country indexes of stock market prices. This adjustment is made on the liability and owner's equity side of the balance sheet. Stock price changes reflect changes not only in the value of tangible assets, but also in the value of intangible assets and in the outlook for a country or industry.

Market values are more volatile than current cost, reflecting the nature of stock markets and the additional uncertainties concerning the intangibles included in the valuation. Typically, the total market value of direct investment is greater than the current replacement cost, though by varying proportions. However, in 1982 through 1984 and in 2008, aggregate market values fell below the estimated replacement cost.

Definitions: net international investment position

U.S. net international investment position is defined as the value of *U.S.-owned assets abroad* minus the value of *foreign-owned assets in the United States*.

U.S.-owned assets abroad is the sum of *financial derivatives, official reserve assets, other U.S. government assets, direct investment at current cost, foreign bonds, foreign corporate stocks, U.S. nonbank claims,* and *U.S. bank claims*.

As a component of U.S.-owned assets, the *financial derivatives* category is the sum of derivatives positions with a positive "fair value" to U.S. residents. The fair value of a derivatives contract is the amount for which the contract could be exchanged between willing parties. A derivatives contract between a U.S. and a foreign resident with a positive fair value represents the amount that the foreign resident would have to pay to the U.S. resident if the contract was terminated.

U.S. official reserve assets includes gold, valued at the current market price; special drawing rights; the U.S. reserve position in the International Monetary Fund; and official holdings of foreign currencies.

Other U.S. government assets includes other U.S. government claims on foreigners and holdings of foreign currency and short-term assets.

U.S. nonbank claims includes U.S. claims on affiliated foreigners reported by U.S. nonbanking concerns.

U.S. bank claims consists of claims on foreigners, such as loans and commercial paper, held by U.S. banks and not reported elsewhere in the accounts.

Foreign-owned assets in the United States includes *financial derivatives, foreign official assets, direct investment in the United States at current cost, U.S. Treasury securities, U.S. currency, corporate and other bonds, corporate stocks, U.S. nonbank liabilities,* and *U.S. bank liabilities*.

As a component of foreign-owned assets in the United States, *financial derivatives* consists of derivatives positions with a negative "fair value" to U.S. residents. A contract with a negative fair value represents the amount that the U.S. resident would have to pay to the foreign resident if the contract was terminated.

Foreign official assets includes foreign government holdings of claims on the United States, including U.S. government securities and other liabilities and deposits held by such governments in U.S. banks.

Foreign-owned assets in the United States, other than official assets, also include *U.S. Treasury securities, U.S. cur-rency, corporate and other bonds, corporate stocks, U.S. liabilities (to foreigners) reported by U.S. nonbanking concerns,* and *U.S. bank liabilities to foreigners* (such as deposits).

Data availability

The annual (year-end) data, along with revisions for earlier years, are released around the middle of the following year; the data shown in this edition of *Business Statistics* were released June 26, 2012, and are available on the BEA Web site at <http://www.bea.gov>.

References

"The International Investment Position of the United States at Yearend 2011" is published in the July 2012 *Survey of Current Business*. Comparable articles each July describe and analyze the estimates, and the article in the July 2007 *Survey* includes extensive data and discussion of the new coverage of financial derivatives. For background on the valuation of direct investment and other components, see "Valuation of the U.S. Net International Investment Position," *Survey of Current Business*, May 1991. Also see the references for Table 7-6.

TABLES 7-9 THROUGH 7-16
EXPORTS AND IMPORTS OF GOODS AND SERVICES

SOURCES: U.S. DEPARTMENT OF COMMERCE, CENSUS BUREAU AND BUREAU OF ECONOMIC ANALYSIS

These tables present the source data used to build up the aggregate measures of goods and services flows shown in Tables 7-1 through 7-6. These data are compiled and published monthly, making trends evident before the publication of the quarterly aggregate estimates. They also provide more detail than the quarterly aggregates.

Monthly and annual data on exports and imports of *goods* are compiled by the Census Bureau from documents collected by the U.S. Customs Service. The Bureau of Economic Analysis (BEA) makes certain adjustments to these data (as described below) to place the estimates on a *balance of payments* basis—a basis consistent with the national and international accounts.

Data on exports and imports of *services* are prepared by BEA from a variety of sources. Monthly data on services are available from January 1992. Annual and quarterly data for earlier years are available as part of the international transactions accounts. Current data on goods and services are available each month in a joint Census Bureau-BEA press release.

In the case of some of the detailed breakdowns of exports and imports, such as by end-use categories, monthly data may not sum exactly to annual totals. This is due to later revisions, which are made only to annual data and are not allocated to monthly data. Also, the constant-dollar figures expressed in 2005 dollars are now calculated using chain weights. Therefore, the 2005-dollar detail will not add to the 2005-dollar totals.

In addition, monthly and annual data on exports and imports of goods for individual countries and various country groupings do not reflect subsequent revisions of annual total data. These country data are compiled by the Census Bureau for all countries, although this volume includes only a selection of the most significant countries and areas. The full set of data can be accessed on the Census Web site at <http://www.census.gov>.

Definitions: Goods

Goods: Census basis. The Census basis goods data are compiled from documents collected by the U.S. Customs Service. They reflect the movement of goods between foreign countries and the 50 states, the District of Columbia, Puerto Rico, the U.S. Virgin Islands, and U.S. Foreign Trade Zones. They include government and nongovernment shipments of goods, and exclude shipments between the United States and its territories and possessions; transactions with U.S. military, diplomatic, and consular installations abroad; U.S. goods returned to the United States by its armed forces; personal and household effects of travelers; and in-transit shipments. The general import values reflect the total arrival of merchandise from foreign countries that immediately enters consumption channels, warehouses, or Foreign Trade Zones.

For *imports,* the value reported is the U.S. Customs Service appraised value of merchandise (generally, the price paid for merchandise for export to the United States). Import duties, freight, insurance, and other charges incurred in bringing merchandise to the United States are excluded.

Exports are valued at the f.a.s. (free alongside ship) value of merchandise at the U.S. port of export, based on the transaction price including inland freight, insurance, and other charges incurred in placing the merchandise alongside the carrier at the U.S. port of exportation.

Goods: balance of payments (BOP) basis. Goods on a Census basis are adjusted by BEA to goods on a BOP basis to bring the data in line with the concepts and definitions used to prepare the international and national accounts. In general, the adjustments include changes in ownership that occur without goods passing into or out of the customs territory of the United States. These adjustments are necessary to supplement coverage of the Census basis data, to eliminate duplication of transactions recorded elsewhere in the international accounts, and to value transactions according to a standard definition.

The *export* adjustments include the following: (1) The deduction of *U.S. military sales contracts.* The Census Bureau has included these contracts in the goods data, but BEA includes them in the service category "Transfers Under U.S. Military Sales Contracts." BEA's source material for these contracts is more comprehensive but does not distinguish

between goods and services. (2) The addition of *private gift parcels* mailed to foreigners by individuals through the U.S. Postal Service. Only commercial shipments are covered in Census goods exports. (3) The addition to *nonmonetary gold exports* of gold purchased by foreign official agencies from private dealers in the United States and held at the Federal Reserve Bank of New York. The Census data include only gold that leaves the customs territory. (4) *Smaller adjustments* includes deductions for repairs of goods, exposed motion picture film, and military grant aid, and additions for sales of fish in U.S. territorial waters, exports of electricity to Mexico, and vessels and oil rigs that change ownership without export documents being filed.

The *import* adjustments include the following: (1) On *inland freight in Canada,* the customs value for imports for certain Canadian goods is the point of origin in Canada. BEA makes an addition for the inland freight charges of transporting these Canadian goods to the U.S. border. (2) An addition is made to *nonmonetary gold imports* for gold sold by foreign official agencies to private purchasers out of stock held at the Federal Reserve Bank of New York. The Census Bureau data include only gold that enters the customs territory. (3) A deduction is made for *imports by U.S. military agencies.* The Census Bureau has included these contracts in the goods data, but BEA includes them in the service category "Direct Defense Expenditures." BEA's source material is more comprehensive but does not distinguish between goods and services. (4) *Smaller adjustments* includes deductions for repairs of goods and for exposed motion picture film and additions for imported electricity from Mexico, conversion of vessels for commercial use, and repairs to U.S. vessels abroad.

Definitions: Services

The statistics are estimates of service transactions between foreign countries and the 50 states, the District of Columbia, Puerto Rico, the U.S. Virgin Islands, and other U.S. territories and possessions. Transactions with U.S. military, diplomatic, and consular installations abroad are excluded because they are considered to be part of the U.S. economy. Services are shown in the broad categories described below. For six of these categories, the definitions are the same for imports and exports. For the seventh, the export category is "Transfers under U.S. Military Sales Contracts," while for imports, the category is "Direct Defense Expenditures."

Travel includes purchases of services and goods by U.S. travelers abroad and by foreign visitors to the United States. A traveler is defined as a person who stays for a period of less than one year in a country where the person is not a resident. Included are expenditures for food, lodging, recreation, gifts, and other items incidental to a foreign visit. Not included are the international costs of the travel itself, which are covered in *passenger fares* (see below).

Passenger fares consists of fares paid by residents of one country to residents in other countries. Receipts consist of fares received by U.S. carriers from foreign residents for travel between the United States and foreign countries and between two foreign points. Payments consist of fares paid by U.S. residents to foreign carriers for travel between the United States and foreign countries.

Break in series: travel and passenger fares. Beginning with data for 1984, these items incorporate results from a survey administered by the U.S. Travel and Tourism Administration. See *Survey of Current Business,* June 1989, pages 57ff.

Other transportation includes charges for the transportation of goods by ocean, air, waterway, pipeline, and rail carriers to and from the United States. Included are freight charges, operating expenses that transportation companies incur in foreign ports, and payments for vessel charter and aircraft and freight car rentals. (*Break in series*: Estimates of freight charges for the transportation of goods by truck between the United States and Canada are included in the data beginning with 1986. Reliable estimates for earlier years are not available. See *Survey of Current Business*, June 1994, pages 70ff.)

Royalties and license fees consists of transactions with foreign residents involving intangible assets and proprietary rights, such as the use of patents, techniques, processes, formulas, designs, know-how, trademarks, copyrights, franchises, and manufacturing rights. The term *royalties* generally refers to payments for the utilization of copyrights or trademarks, and the term *license fees* generally refers to payments for the use of patents or industrial processes.

Other private services includes transactions with "affiliated" foreigners for which no identification by type is available and transactions with unaffiliated foreigners.

The term "affiliated" refers to a direct investment relationship, which exists when a U.S. person has ownership or control (directly or indirectly) of 10 percent or more of a foreign business enterprise, or when a foreign person has a similar interest in a U.S. enterprise.

Transactions with "unaffiliated" foreigners in this "other private services" category consist of education services, financial services, insurance services, telecommunications services, and business, professional, and technical services. Included in the last group are advertising services; computer and data processing services; database and other information services; research, development, and testing services; management, consulting, and public relations services; legal services; construction, engineering, architectural, and mining services; industrial engineering services; installation, maintenance, and repair of equipment; and other services, including medical services and film and tape rental.

The insurance component of "other private services" was measured before the July 2003 revision as premiums less actual losses paid or recovered. Furthermore, catastrophic losses were entered immediately when the loss occurred, rather than when the insurance claim was actually paid out. This led to sharp swings for any month in which catastrophic losses occurred, such as Hurricane Katrina in August 2005 or the September 11, 2001, terror attacks. In the accounts as revised in July 2003 and presented here, insurance services are now measured as premiums less "normal" losses. Normal losses consist of a measure of expected regularly occurring losses based on six years of past experience <u>plus</u> an additional allowance for catastrophic loss. Catastrophic losses, when they occur, are added in equal increments to the estimate of regularly occurring losses over the 20 years following the occurrence. As adoption of this methodology introduces a difference between actual and normal losses, an amount equal to the difference is entered in the international accounts as a capital account transaction.

BEA conducts surveys of international transactions in financial services and "selected services" (largely business, professional, and technical services). Beginning with data for 1986, *other private services* includes estimates of business, professional, and technical services from the BEA surveys of selected services. (See *Survey of Current Business*, June 1989, pages 57ff.)

Breaks in series: royalties and license fees and other private services. These items are presented on a gross basis beginning in 1982. The definition of exports is revised to exclude U.S. parents' payments to foreign affiliates and to include U.S. affiliates' receipts from foreign parents. The definition of imports is revised to include U.S. parents' payments to foreign affiliates and to exclude U.S. affiliates' receipts from foreign parents.

Transfers under U.S. military sales contracts (exports only) includes exports of goods and services in which U.S. government military agencies participate. This category includes both goods, such as equipment, and services, such as repair services and training, that cannot be separately identified. Transfers of goods and services under U.S. military grant programs are included.

Direct defense expenditures (imports only) consists of expenditures incurred by U.S. military agencies abroad, including expenditures by U.S. personnel, payments of wages to foreign residents, construction expenditures, payments for foreign contractual services, and procurement of foreign goods. Included are both goods and services that cannot be separately identified.

U.S. government miscellaneous services includes transactions of U.S. government nonmilitary agencies with foreign residents. Most of these transactions involve the provision of services to, or purchases of services from, foreigners. Transfers of some goods are also included.

Services estimates are based on quarterly, annual, and benchmark surveys and partial information generated from monthly reports. Service transactions are estimated at market prices. Estimates are seasonally adjusted when statistically significant seasonal patterns are present.

Definitions: Area groupings

The Census trade statistics for groups of countries present "groups as they were at the time of reporting", which means that as multinational organizations such as the European Union expand, the statistics for trade with that group include the added country only beginning with the year it entered the group. The European Union was expanded from 15 to 25 nations on May 1, 2004, and data for that year are available for both the new and the old group; to provide historical perspective, they are both shown here, along with the historical data back to 1974 for the original group.

The *European Union* now includes Austria, Belgium, Bulgaria, Cyprus, Czech Republic, Denmark, Estonia, Finland, France, Germany, Greece, Hungary, Ireland, Italy, Latvia, Lithuania, Luxembourg, Malta, Netherlands, Poland, Portugal, Romania, Slovakia, Slovenia, Spain, Sweden, and the United Kingdom.

The *Euro area* now includes Austria, Belgium, Cyprus, Estonia, Finland, France, Germany, Greece, Ireland, Italy, Luxembourg, Malta, the Netherlands, Portugal, Slovakia, Slovenia, and Spain. See the notes and definitions to Table 13-8 for further information about the euro.

The *Asian Newly Industrialized Countries (NICS)* includes Hong Kong SAR, South Korea, Singapore, and Taiwan.

The *Organization of Petroleum Exporting Countries (OPEC)* currently consists of Algeria, Angola, Ecuador, Iran, Iraq, Kuwait, Libya, Nigeria, Qatar, Saudi Arabia, the United Arab Emirates, and Venezuela. Indonesia is no longer a member as of January 2009.

Notes on the data

U.S./Canada data exchange and substitution. The data for U.S. exports to Canada are derived from import data compiled by Canada. The use of Canada's import data to produce U.S. export data requires several alignments in order to compare the two series.

- *Coverage*: Canadian imports are based on country of origin. U.S. goods shipped from a third country are included, but U.S. exports exclude these foreign shipments. U.S. export coverage also excludes certain Canadian postal shipments.

- *Valuation*: Canadian imports are valued at their point of origin in the United States. However, U.S. exports are valued at the port of exit in the United States and include

inland freight charges, making the U.S. export value slightly larger. Canada requires inland freight to be reported.

- *Reexports*: U.S. exports include re-exports of foreign goods. Again, the aggregate U.S. export figure is slightly larger.

- *Exchange Rate*: Average monthly exchange rates are applied to convert the published data to U.S. currency.

End-use categories and seasonal adjustment of trade in goods. Goods are initially classified under the Harmonized System, which describes and measures the characteristics of goods traded. Combining trade into approximately 140 export and 140 import end-use categories makes it possible to examine goods according to their principal uses. These categories are used as the basis for computing the seasonal and working-day adjusted data. Adjusted data are then summed to the six end-use aggregates for publication.

The seasonal adjustment procedure is based on a model that estimates the monthly movements as percentages above or below the general level of each end-use commodity series (unlike other methods that redistribute the actual series values over the calendar year). Imports of petroleum and petroleum products are adjusted for the length of the month.

Data availability

Data are released monthly in a joint Census Bureau-BEA press release (FT-900), which is published about six weeks after the end of the month to which the data pertain. The release and historical data are available on the Census Bureau Web site at <http://www.census.gov/foreign-trade/www/>.

Revisions

Data for recent years are normally revised annually. In some cases, revisions to annual totals are not distributed to monthly data; therefore, monthly data may not sum to the revised total shown. Data on trade in services may be subject to extensive revision as part of BEA's annual revision of the international transactions accounts (ITAs), usually released in July.

References

Discussion of the impact of changes in methodology and incorporation of new data sources are found in the discussions of annual revisions of the ITAs in the July issues of BEA's *Survey of Current Business*. The most recent pertinent article is "Annual Revision of the U.S. International Accounts" (July 2012).

TABLE 7-17
EXPORT AND IMPORT PRICE INDEXES

SOURCE: U.S. DEPARTMENT OF LABOR, BUREAU OF LABOR STATISTICS

The International Price Program of the Bureau of Labor Statistics (BLS) collects price data for nonmilitary goods traded between the United States and the rest of the world and for selected transportation services in international markets. BLS aggregates the goods price data into export and import price indexes. Summary values of these price indexes for goods are presented in *Business Statistics.* For product and locality detail on international prices for both goods and services, see the *Handbook of U.S. Labor Statistics,* also published by Bernan Press.

Definitions

The *export* price index provides a measure of price change for all goods sold by U.S. residents (businesses and individuals located within the geographic boundaries of the United States, whether or not owned by U.S. citizens) to foreign buyers.

The *import* price index provides a measure of price change for goods purchased from other countries by U.S. residents.

Notes on the data

Published index series use a base year of 2000 = 100 whenever possible.

The product universe for both the import and export indexes includes raw materials, agricultural products, and manufactures. Price data are primarily collected by mail questionnaire, and directly from the exporter or importer in all but a few cases.

To the greatest extent possible, the data refer to prices at the U.S. border for exports and at either the foreign border or the U.S. border for imports. For nearly all products, the prices refer to transactions completed during the first week of the month and represent the actual price for which the product was bought or sold, including discounts, allowances, and rebates.

For the export price indexes, the preferred pricing basis is f.a.s. (free alongside ship) U.S. port of exportation. Where necessary, adjustments are made to reported prices to place them on this basis. An attempt is made to collect two prices for imports: f.o.b. (free on board) at the port of exportation and c.i.f. (cost, insurance, and freight) at the U.S. port of importation. Adjustments are made to account for changes in product characteristics in order to obtain a pure measure of price change.

The indexes are weighted indexes of the Laspeyres type. (See "General Notes" at the beginning of this volume for further explanation.) The values assigned to each weight category are based on trade value figures compiled by the Census Bureau. They are reweighted annually, with a two-year lag (as concurrent value data are not available) in revisions.

The merchandise price indexes are published using three different classification systems: the Harmonized System, the Bureau of Economic Analysis End-Use System, and the Standard International Trade Classification (SITC) system. The aggregate indexes shown here are from the End-Use System.

Data availability

Indexes are published monthly in a press release and a more detailed report. Indexes are published for detailed product categories, as well as for all commodities. Aggregate import indexes by country or region of origin also are available, as are indexes for selected categories of internationally traded services. Additional information is available from the Division of International Prices in the Bureau of Labor Statistics. Complete historical data are available on the BLS Web site at <http://www.bls.gov>.

References

The indexes are described in "BLS to Produce Monthly Indexes of Export and Import Prices," *Monthly Labor Review* (December 1988), and Chapter 15, "International Price Indexes," *BLS Handbook of Methods* Bulletin 2490 (April 1997).

CHAPTER 8: PRICES

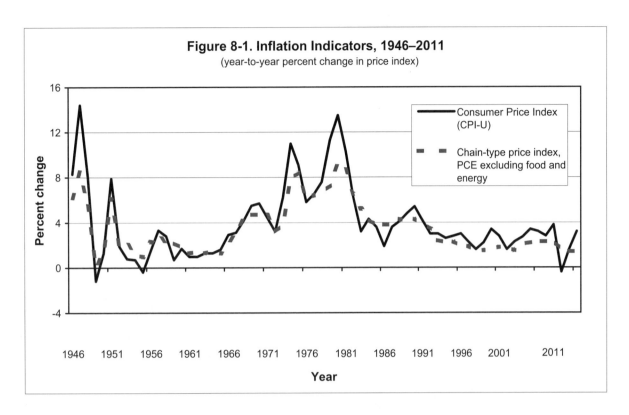

Figure 8-1. Inflation Indicators, 1946–2011
(year-to-year percent change in price index)

- Figure 8-1 shows annual rates of change in the Consumer Price Index for All Urban Consumers (CPI-U), the most widely used measure of the general price level. It also shows changes in the chain-type price index for personal consumption expenditures (PCE) excluding food and energy, which provides one widely used measure of the "core" or underlying rate of inflation. (Tables 8-1, 8-4, and 1-6)

- Sharp swings in energy prices caused the all-items CPI to drop 0.4 percent in 2009—the first year-to-year deflation registered since 1955—and then swing back to 3.1 percent inflation by 2011. (Table 8-4)

- The core PCE inflation rate strips out volatile food and energy prices, in order to try to isolate the "underlying" rate of inflation, and is based on a concept slightly different from the CPI (see Notes and definitions for details). It shows a deceleration of inflation from 2.3 percent in 2008 to about 1 1/2 percent in 2009 through 2011, similar to previous lows in 1998-1999 and 2003. (Table 8-4)

- From 1965 to 2011, commodity prices in the CPI-U rose at an average rate of 3.6 percent per year, but services prices increased at an average annual rate of 5.0 percent. (Table 8-1A)

- The Producer Price Index (PPI) measures prices at the point of production, rather than at the consumer level. The most widely used product of the PPI system—the PPI for Finished Goods—only covers commodities, whereas the CPI covers both commodities and services. For these reasons, the PPI for Finished Goods fluctuates more (both up and down) than the aggregate CPI-U, but has had a less inflationary long-term trend. The total finished goods PPI dropped 2.6 percent in 2009 and then rose 10.4 percent from 2009 to 2011. The core PPI for finished goods excluding foods and energy did not decline, rising at an average 2.4 percent annual rate from 2007 to 2011. (Table 8-1A)

- The PPI data set also includes prices for intermediate materials, supplies, and components and crude materials for further processing. Intermediate materials prices fluctuate more than those of finished goods, and crude materials prices fluctuate most of all. From 2008 to 2009, and then from 2009 to 2011, respectively, core intermediate goods fell 4 percent and rebounded 11 percent; core crude materials plunged 23 percent and rebounded 57 percent. (Table 8-1A)

Table 8-1A. Summary Consumer and Producer Price Indexes: Recent Data

(Seasonally adjusted.)

Year and month	Urban wage earners and clerical workers (CPI-W), all items	Consumer Price Index, 1982–1984 = 100 — All urban consumers (CPI-U)						Producer Price Index, 1982 = 100 — Finished goods		Intermediate materials, supplies, and components		Crude materials for further processing	
		All items	Food	Energy	All items less food and energy	Commodities	Services	Total	Less food and energy	Total	Less food and energy	Total	Crude nonfood less energy
1965	31.7	31.5	32.2	22.9	32.7	35.2	26.6	34.1	...	31.2	...	31.1	...
1966	32.6	32.4	33.8	23.3	33.5	36.1	27.6	35.2	...	32.0	...	33.1	...
1967	33.6	33.4	34.1	23.8	34.7	36.8	28.8	35.6	...	32.2	...	31.3	...
1968	35.0	34.8	35.3	24.2	36.3	38.1	30.3	36.6	...	33.0	...	31.8	...
1969	36.9	36.7	37.1	24.8	38.4	39.9	32.4	38.0	...	34.1	...	33.9	...
1970	39.0	38.8	39.2	25.5	40.8	41.7	35.0	39.3	...	35.4	...	35.2	...
1971	40.7	40.5	40.4	26.5	42.7	43.2	37.0	40.5	...	36.8	...	36.0	...
1972	42.1	41.8	42.1	27.2	44.0	44.5	38.4	41.8	...	38.2	...	39.9	...
1973	44.7	44.4	48.2	29.4	45.6	47.8	40.1	45.6	48.1	42.4	44.3	54.5	70.8
1974	49.6	49.3	55.1	38.1	49.4	53.5	43.8	52.6	53.6	52.5	54.0	61.4	83.3
1975	54.1	53.8	59.8	42.1	53.9	58.2	48.0	58.2	59.7	58.0	60.2	61.6	69.3
1976	57.2	56.9	61.6	45.1	57.4	60.7	52.0	60.8	63.1	60.9	63.8	63.4	80.2
1977	60.9	60.6	65.5	49.4	61.0	64.2	56.0	64.7	66.9	64.9	67.6	65.5	79.8
1978	65.6	65.2	72.0	52.5	65.5	68.8	60.8	69.8	71.9	69.5	72.5	73.4	87.8
1979	73.1	72.6	79.9	65.7	71.9	76.6	67.5	77.6	78.3	78.4	80.7	85.9	106.2
1980	82.9	82.4	86.8	86.0	80.8	86.0	77.9	88.0	87.1	90.3	90.3	95.3	113.1
1981	91.4	90.9	93.6	97.7	89.2	93.2	88.1	96.1	94.6	98.6	97.7	103.0	111.7
1982	96.9	96.5	97.4	99.2	95.8	97.0	96.0	100.0	100.0	100.0	100.0	100.0	100.0
1983	99.8	99.6	99.4	99.9	99.6	99.8	99.4	101.6	103.0	100.6	101.6	101.3	105.3
1984	103.3	103.9	103.2	100.9	104.6	103.2	104.6	103.7	105.5	103.1	104.7	103.5	111.7
1985	106.9	107.6	105.6	101.6	109.1	105.4	109.9	104.7	108.1	102.7	105.2	95.8	104.9
1986	108.6	109.6	109.0	88.2	113.5	104.4	115.4	103.2	110.6	99.1	104.9	87.7	103.1
1987	112.5	113.6	113.5	88.6	118.2	107.7	120.2	105.4	113.3	101.5	107.8	93.7	115.7
1988	117.0	118.3	118.2	89.3	123.4	111.5	125.7	108.0	117.0	107.1	115.2	96.0	133.0
1989	122.6	124.0	125.1	94.3	129.0	116.7	131.9	113.6	122.1	112.0	120.2	103.1	137.9
1990	129.0	130.7	132.4	102.1	135.5	122.8	139.2	119.2	126.6	114.5	120.9	108.9	136.3
1991	134.3	136.2	136.3	102.5	142.1	126.6	146.3	121.7	131.1	114.4	121.4	101.2	128.2
1992	138.2	140.3	137.9	103.0	147.3	129.1	152.0	123.2	134.2	114.7	122.0	100.4	128.4
1993	142.1	144.5	140.9	104.2	152.2	131.5	157.9	124.7	135.8	116.2	123.8	102.4	140.2
1994	145.6	148.2	144.3	104.6	156.5	133.8	163.1	125.5	137.1	118.5	127.1	101.8	156.2
1995	149.8	152.4	148.4	105.2	161.2	136.4	168.7	127.9	140.0	124.9	135.2	102.7	173.6
1996	154.1	156.9	153.3	110.1	165.6	139.9	174.1	131.3	142.0	125.7	134.0	113.8	155.8
1997	157.6	160.5	157.3	111.5	169.5	141.8	179.4	131.8	142.4	125.6	134.2	111.1	156.5
1998	159.7	163.0	160.7	102.9	173.4	141.9	184.2	130.7	143.7	123.0	133.5	96.8	142.1
1999	163.2	166.6	164.1	106.6	177.0	144.4	188.8	133.0	146.1	123.2	133.1	98.2	135.2
2000	168.9	172.2	167.8	124.6	181.3	149.2	195.3	138.0	148.0	129.2	136.6	120.6	145.2
2001	173.5	177.1	173.1	129.3	186.1	150.7	203.4	140.7	150.0	129.7	136.4	121.0	130.7
2002	175.9	179.9	176.2	121.7	190.5	149.7	209.8	138.9	150.2	127.8	135.8	108.1	135.7
2003	179.8	184.0	180.0	136.5	193.2	151.2	216.5	143.3	150.5	133.7	138.5	135.3	152.5
2004	184.5	188.9	186.2	151.4	196.6	154.7	222.8	148.5	152.7	142.6	146.5	159.0	193.0
2005	191.0	195.3	190.7	177.1	200.9	160.2	230.1	155.7	156.4	154.0	154.6	182.2	202.4
2006	197.1	201.6	195.2	196.9	205.9	164.0	238.9	160.4	158.7	164.0	163.8	184.8	244.5
2007	202.8	207.3	202.9	207.7	210.7	167.5	246.8	166.6	161.7	170.7	168.4	207.1	282.6
2008	211.1	215.3	214.1	236.7	215.6	174.8	255.5	177.1	167.2	188.3	180.9	251.8	324.4
2009	209.6	214.5	218.0	193.1	219.2	169.7	259.2	172.5	171.5	172.5	173.4	175.2	248.4
2010	214.0	218.1	219.6	211.4	221.3	174.6	261.3	179.8	173.6	183.4	180.8	212.2	329.1
2011	221.6	224.9	227.8	243.9	225.0	183.9	265.8	190.5	177.8	199.8	192.0	249.4	390.4
2010													
January	213.4	217.5	218.4	213.7	220.5	174.8	259.9	179.3	172.7	180.5	177.0	219.0	305.2
February	213.3	217.4	218.5	211.7	220.6	174.5	260.0	178.2	172.7	180.3	178.4	215.7	305.8
March	213.3	217.4	218.9	210.6	220.8	174.2	260.4	179.1	173.0	181.1	179.6	213.4	321.4
April	213.2	217.4	219.1	208.8	220.9	173.8	260.7	178.9	173.1	182.5	181.5	208.6	330.7
May	212.9	217.2	219.3	204.9	221.0	173.2	260.9	178.5	173.6	182.9	181.9	204.5	326.5
June	212.9	217.2	219.2	202.9	221.3	173.0	261.2	178.2	173.8	181.9	181.1	199.5	315.3
July	213.5	217.6	219.2	206.4	221.5	173.6	261.4	178.6	174.1	181.4	180.4	203.2	313.0
August	213.9	218.1	219.5	209.3	221.6	174.2	261.6	179.9	174.4	182.5	180.6	209.0	324.7
September	214.3	218.4	220.3	210.7	221.7	174.6	261.8	180.6	174.7	183.4	181.1	210.1	336.4
October	215.1	219.0	220.6	216.7	221.8	175.7	262.0	182.0	174.4	185.6	182.1	220.2	348.4
November	215.5	219.4	221.1	218.4	222.1	176.2	262.4	182.7	174.3	186.9	183.2	221.1	357.9
December	216.6	220.4	221.4	227.3	222.2	177.7	262.8	184.4	174.7	189.2	184.2	235.0	367.9
2011													
January	217.3	221.0	222.4	229.1	222.6	178.6	263.2	185.8	175.5	191.7	186.6	242.5	382.4
February	218.4	222.0	223.6	234.4	223.1	180.0	263.8	187.9	175.9	195.0	188.8	251.3	391.2
March	219.7	223.2	225.2	242.2	223.4	182.0	264.2	188.9	176.4	197.4	190.2	248.8	384.3
April	220.7	224.0	226.0	246.6	223.8	183.3	264.6	190.2	176.9	200.0	192.5	257.5	393.2
May	221.3	224.6	226.8	247.3	224.4	184.0	265.0	190.3	177.2	201.4	193.7	250.3	389.1
June	221.5	224.8	227.4	244.2	224.9	184.1	265.3	190.4	177.8	201.9	193.9	251.0	396.0
July	222.2	225.5	228.4	246.4	225.4	185.0	265.8	191.4	178.7	202.8	194.4	250.5	401.1
August	223.0	226.3	229.6	248.3	225.9	185.8	266.4	191.8	179.0	201.8	194.3	248.3	403.6
September	223.7	226.9	230.6	251.9	226.1	186.5	267.0	193.6	179.5	203.0	194.3	252.4	403.7
October	223.6	226.8	231.1	247.4	226.5	185.9	267.5	193.0	179.5	200.9	193.1	248.0	386.2
November	223.7	227.0	231.3	246.0	226.9	185.8	267.9	193.2	179.6	200.6	192.3	252.6	378.5
December	223.7	227.0	231.8	242.7	227.2	185.3	268.5	193.1	180.0	200.1	191.2	251.0	376.3

. . . = Not available.

Table 8-1B. Summary Consumer and Producer Price Indexes: Historical Data, 1946–2010

(Seasonally adjusted.)

Year and month	Urban wage earners and clerical workers (CPI-W), all items	Consumer Price Index, 1982–1984 = 100						Producer Price Index, 1982 = 100					
		All urban consumers (CPI-U)						Finished goods		Intermediate materials, supplies, and components		Crude materials for further processing	
		All items	Food	Energy	All items less food and energy	Commodities	Services	Total	Less food and energy	Total	Less food and energy	Total	Crude nonfood less energy
1946	19.6	19.5	19.8	...	...	22.9	14.1	...	...	23.3	...	...	...
1947	22.5	22.3	24.1	...	...	27.6	14.7	26.4	...	23.3	...	31.7	...
1948	24.2	24.1	26.1	...	...	29.6	15.6	28.5	...	25.2	...	34.7	...
1949	24.0	23.8	25.0	...	...	28.8	16.4	27.7	...	24.2	...	30.1	...
1950	24.2	24.1	25.4	...	...	29.0	16.9	28.2	...	25.3	...	32.7	...
1951	26.1	26.0	28.2	...	...	31.6	17.8	30.8	...	28.4	...	37.6	...
1952	26.7	26.5	28.7	...	...	32.0	18.6	30.6	...	27.5	...	34.5	...
1953	26.9	26.7	28.3	...	...	31.9	19.4	30.3	...	27.7	...	31.9	...
1954	27.0	26.9	28.2	...	...	31.6	20.0	30.4	...	27.9	...	31.6	...
1955	26.9	26.8	27.8	...	...	31.3	20.4	30.5	...	28.4	...	30.4	...
1956	27.3	27.2	28.0	...	...	31.6	20.9	31.3	...	29.6	...	30.6	...
1957	28.3	28.1	28.9	21.5	28.9	32.6	21.8	32.5	...	30.3	...	31.2	...
1958	29.1	28.9	30.2	21.5	29.6	33.3	22.6	33.2	...	30.4	...	31.9	...
1959	29.3	29.1	29.7	21.9	30.2	33.3	23.3	33.1	...	30.8	...	31.1	...
1960	29.8	29.6	30.0	22.4	30.6	33.6	24.1	33.4	...	30.8	...	30.4	...
1961	30.1	29.9	30.4	22.5	31.0	33.8	24.5	33.4	...	30.6	...	30.2	...
1962	30.4	30.2	30.6	22.6	31.4	34.1	25.0	33.5	...	30.6	...	30.5	...
1963	30.8	30.6	31.1	22.6	31.8	34.4	25.5	33.4	...	30.7	...	29.9	...
1964	31.2	31.0	31.5	22.5	32.3	34.8	26.0	33.5	...	30.8	...	29.6	...
1947													
January	21.6	21.5	22.8	...	...	...	...	...	...	...	...	...	...
February	21.7	21.6	23.1	...	...	...	...	...	...	...	...	...	...
March	22.1	22.0	23.8	...	...	...	...	...	...	...	...	...	...
April	22.1	22.0	23.5	...	...	...	...	26.0	...	23.1	...	30.7	...
May	22.1	22.0	23.4	...	...	...	...	26.1	...	23.0	...	30.4	...
June	22.2	22.1	23.5	...	...	...	...	26.2	...	23.2	...	30.6	...
July	22.4	22.2	23.8	...	...	...	...	26.2	...	23.2	...	31.0	...
August	22.5	22.4	24.1	...	...	...	...	26.3	...	23.3	...	31.6	...
September	23.0	22.8	24.8	...	...	...	...	26.7	...	23.7	...	32.4	...
October	23.0	22.9	24.9	...	...	...	...	26.8	...	24.0	...	33.7	...
November	23.2	23.1	25.2	...	...	...	...	27.1	...	24.3	...	33.9	...
December	23.5	23.4	25.7	...	...	...	...	27.7	...	24.5	...	35.3	...
1948													
January	23.8	23.7	26.1	...	...	...	...	28.1	...	25.0	...	36.2	...
February	23.8	23.7	25.9	...	...	...	...	27.9	...	24.7	...	34.4	...
March	23.6	23.5	25.3	...	...	...	...	28.0	...	24.8	...	33.5	...
April	24.0	23.8	26.0	...	...	...	...	28.1	...	25.1	...	34.2	...
May	24.1	24.0	26.3	...	...	...	...	28.4	...	25.1	...	35.3	...
June	24.3	24.2	26.5	...	...	...	...	28.6	...	25.4	...	36.2	...
July	24.5	24.4	26.7	...	...	...	...	28.8	...	25.4	...	36.1	...
August	24.6	24.4	26.5	...	...	...	...	28.9	...	25.5	...	35.5	...
September	24.5	24.4	26.3	...	...	...	...	28.8	...	25.5	...	34.9	...
October	24.4	24.3	26.1	...	...	...	...	28.7	...	25.5	...	33.8	...
November	24.3	24.2	25.7	...	...	...	...	28.5	...	25.4	...	33.5	...
December	24.2	24.1	25.5	...	...	...	...	28.5	...	25.2	...	33.0	...
1949													
January	24.2	24.0	25.4	...	...	...	...	28.3	...	25.2	...	32.0	...
February	24.1	23.9	25.3	...	...	...	...	28.0	...	24.8	...	30.9	...
March	24.0	23.9	25.3	...	...	...	...	28.0	...	24.7	...	30.8	...
April	24.1	23.9	25.3	...	...	...	...	27.9	...	24.5	...	30.2	...
May	24.0	23.9	25.2	...	...	...	...	27.8	...	24.3	...	30.1	...
June	24.1	23.9	25.3	...	...	...	...	27.7	...	24.1	...	29.7	...
July	23.8	23.7	24.8	...	...	...	...	27.5	...	24.1	...	29.2	...
August	23.8	23.7	24.8	...	...	...	...	27.4	...	23.9	...	29.2	...
September	23.9	23.8	25.0	...	...	...	...	27.4	...	23.9	...	29.5	...
October	23.8	23.7	24.8	...	...	...	...	27.3	...	23.8	...	29.5	...
November	23.8	23.7	24.8	...	...	...	...	27.2	...	23.7	...	29.6	...
December	23.8	23.6	24.5	...	...	...	...	27.2	...	23.8	...	29.6	...
1950													
January	23.6	23.5	24.3	...	...	...	...	27.2	...	23.8	...	29.6	...
February	23.7	23.6	24.7	...	...	...	...	27.2	...	23.9	...	30.5	...
March	23.8	23.6	24.6	...	...	...	...	27.3	...	24.1	...	30.3	...
April	23.8	23.7	24.6	...	...	...	...	27.3	...	24.2	...	30.5	...
May	23.9	23.8	24.8	...	...	...	...	27.5	...	24.6	...	31.6	...
June	24.0	23.9	25.1	...	...	...	...	27.6	...	24.7	...	32.1	...
July	24.2	24.1	25.6	...	...	...	...	28.0	...	25.3	...	33.3	...
August	24.3	24.2	25.8	...	...	...	...	28.6	...	25.6	...	34.0	...
September	24.5	24.3	25.8	...	...	...	...	28.9	...	26.2	...	34.5	...
October	24.6	24.5	26.0	...	...	...	...	29.0	...	26.7	...	34.5	...
November	24.7	24.6	26.1	...	...	...	...	29.4	...	26.9	...	35.4	...
December	25.1	25.0	26.9	...	...	...	...	30.0	...	27.8	...	36.7	...

. . . = Not available.

Table 8-1B. Summary Consumer and Producer Price Indexes: Historical Data, 1946–2010—*Continued*

(Seasonally adjusted.)

Year and month	Consumer Price Index, 1982–1984 = 100							Producer Price Index, 1982 = 100					
	Urban wage earners and clerical workers (CPI-W), all items	All urban consumers (CPI-U)						Finished goods		Intermediate materials, supplies, and components		Crude materials for further processing	
		All items	Food	Energy	All items less food and energy	Commodities	Services	Total	Less food and energy	Total	Less food and energy	Total	Crude nonfood less energy
1951													
January	25.5	25.4	27.6	...	...	...	...	30.5	...	28.5	...	38.2	...
February	26.0	25.8	28.5	...	...	...	...	30.8	...	28.7	...	39.6	...
March	26.0	25.9	28.4	...	...	...	...	30.9	...	28.8	...	39.1	...
April	26.1	25.9	28.2	...	...	...	...	30.9	...	28.8	...	39.1	...
May	26.1	26.0	28.3	...	...	...	...	31.1	...	28.8	...	38.4	...
June	26.1	25.9	28.0	...	...	...	...	31.0	...	28.7	...	38.1	...
July	26.1	25.9	27.9	...	...	...	...	30.8	...	28.4	...	36.8	...
August	26.0	25.9	27.8	...	...	...	...	30.7	...	28.0	...	36.2	...
September	26.2	26.0	27.9	...	...	...	...	30.6	...	28.0	...	35.9	...
October	26.3	26.2	28.4	...	...	...	...	30.8	...	27.9	...	36.7	...
November	26.5	26.3	28.6	...	...	...	...	30.9	...	27.9	...	36.4	...
December	26.6	26.5	28.9	...	...	...	...	30.9	...	27.8	...	36.6	...
1952													
January	26.6	26.5	28.9	...	...	...	...	30.8	...	27.8	...	35.8	...
February	26.6	26.4	28.6	...	...	...	...	30.7	...	27.7	...	35.5	...
March	26.5	26.4	28.5	...	...	...	...	30.9	...	27.6	...	35.0	...
April	26.6	26.5	28.7	...	...	...	...	30.7	...	27.5	...	34.9	...
May	26.6	26.5	28.7	...	...	...	...	30.7	...	27.5	...	34.8	...
June	26.7	26.5	28.6	...	...	...	...	30.7	...	27.6	...	34.6	...
July	26.8	26.7	28.9	...	...	...	...	30.8	...	27.5	...	34.6	...
August	26.8	26.7	28.9	...	...	...	...	30.7	...	27.6	...	34.7	...
September	26.8	26.6	28.7	...	...	...	...	30.6	...	27.6	...	33.8	...
October	26.8	26.7	28.8	...	...	...	...	30.5	...	27.5	...	33.8	...
November	26.8	26.7	28.8	...	...	...	...	30.4	...	27.4	...	33.7	...
December	26.9	26.7	28.6	...	...	...	...	30.2	...	27.3	...	32.9	...
1953													
January	26.8	26.6	28.4	...	...	...	...	30.3	...	27.4	...	32.5	...
February	26.7	26.6	28.3	...	...	...	...	30.2	...	27.4	...	32.4	...
March	26.8	26.6	28.3	...	...	...	...	30.3	...	27.5	...	32.4	...
April	26.8	26.7	28.1	...	...	...	...	30.2	...	27.5	...	31.6	...
May	26.9	26.7	28.2	...	...	...	...	30.3	...	27.6	...	31.8	...
June	26.9	26.8	28.4	...	...	...	...	30.4	...	27.7	...	31.4	...
July	26.9	26.8	28.2	...	...	...	...	30.5	...	28.0	...	32.3	...
August	27.0	26.9	28.3	...	...	...	...	30.4	...	27.9	...	31.8	...
September	27.0	26.9	28.4	...	...	...	...	30.4	...	27.9	...	32.0	...
October	27.1	27.0	28.4	...	...	...	...	30.4	...	27.9	...	31.4	...
November	27.0	26.9	28.1	...	...	...	...	30.3	...	27.8	...	31.2	...
December	27.0	26.9	28.3	...	...	...	...	30.4	...	27.8	...	31.7	...
1954													
January	27.1	26.9	28.5	...	...	...	...	30.5	...	27.9	...	32.0	...
February	27.1	27.0	28.5	...	...	...	...	30.4	...	27.9	...	32.0	...
March	27.1	26.9	28.4	...	...	...	...	30.4	...	27.9	...	32.1	...
April	27.0	26.9	28.4	...	...	...	...	30.6	...	27.9	...	32.2	...
May	27.1	26.9	28.4	...	...	...	...	30.6	...	27.9	...	32.1	...
June	27.1	26.9	28.4	...	...	...	...	30.4	...	27.8	...	31.5	...
July	27.0	26.9	28.4	...	...	...	...	30.5	...	27.9	...	31.4	...
August	27.0	26.9	28.3	...	...	...	...	30.4	...	27.9	...	31.3	...
September	27.0	26.8	28.0	...	...	...	...	30.3	...	27.8	...	31.5	...
October	26.9	26.7	27.9	...	...	...	...	30.2	...	27.8	...	31.2	...
November	26.9	26.8	27.9	...	...	...	...	30.3	...	27.9	...	31.4	...
December	26.9	26.8	27.8	...	...	...	...	30.3	...	27.9	...	30.8	...
1955													
January	26.9	26.8	27.8	...	...	...	...	30.4	...	27.9	...	31.1	...
February	27.0	26.8	28.0	...	...	...	...	30.5	...	28.0	...	31.0	...
March	26.9	26.8	28.0	...	...	...	...	30.3	...	28.0	...	30.7	...
April	26.9	26.8	28.0	...	...	...	...	30.4	...	28.1	...	31.0	...
May	26.9	26.8	27.9	...	...	...	...	30.4	...	28.1	...	30.2	...
June	26.9	26.7	27.7	...	...	...	...	30.5	...	28.2	...	30.7	...
July	26.9	26.8	27.7	...	...	...	...	30.4	...	28.4	...	30.4	...
August	26.9	26.7	27.6	...	...	...	...	30.4	...	28.5	...	30.1	...
September	27.0	26.9	27.8	...	...	...	...	30.5	...	28.8	...	30.4	...
October	27.0	26.8	27.7	...	...	...	...	30.6	...	28.9	...	30.4	...
November	27.0	26.9	27.6	...	...	...	...	30.6	...	28.9	...	29.4	...
December	27.0	26.9	27.6	...	...	...	...	30.7	...	29.0	...	29.5	...
1956													
January	27.0	26.8	27.5	...	...	31.2	20.7	30.7	...	29.1	...	29.4	...
February	27.0	26.9	27.5	...	...	31.1	20.7	30.8	...	29.2	...	29.9	...
March	27.1	26.9	27.5	...	...	31.2	20.7	30.9	...	29.4	...	29.8	...
April	27.1	26.9	27.6	...	...	31.3	20.8	31.0	...	29.5	...	30.3	...
May	27.2	27.0	27.8	...	...	31.4	20.8	31.2	...	29.6	...	30.7	...
June	27.3	27.2	28.1	...	...	31.5	20.9	31.4	...	29.6	...	30.5	...
July	27.4	27.3	28.4	...	...	31.8	20.9	31.3	...	29.4	...	30.5	...
August	27.5	27.3	28.2	...	...	31.7	21.0	31.4	...	29.7	...	31.0	...
September	27.5	27.4	28.2	...	...	31.8	21.1	31.6	...	29.8	...	31.0	...
October	27.7	27.5	28.3	...	...	32.0	21.1	31.8	...	30.0	...	31.0	...
November	27.7	27.5	28.4	...	...	32.0	21.2	31.9	...	30.0	...	31.1	...
December	27.8	27.6	28.5	...	...	32.1	21.3	31.9	...	30.1	...	31.7	...

. . . = Not available.

Table 8-1B. Summary Consumer and Producer Price Indexes: Historical Data, 1946–2010—*Continued*

(Seasonally adjusted.)

Year and month	Urban wage earners and clerical workers (CPI-W), all items	Consumer Price Index, 1982–1984 = 100 — All urban consumers (CPI-U)						Producer Price Index, 1982 = 100 — Finished goods		Intermediate materials, supplies, and components		Crude materials for further processing	
		All items	Food	Energy	All items less food and energy	Commodities	Services	Total	Less food and energy	Total	Less food and energy	Total	Crude nonfood less energy
1957													
January	27.8	27.7	28.4	21.3	28.5	32.1	21.4	32.1	. . .	30.3	. . .	31.3	. . .
February	28.0	27.8	28.7	21.4	28.6	32.3	21.4	32.2	. . .	30.3	. . .	31.0	. . .
March	28.0	27.9	28.6	21.5	28.7	32.3	21.6	32.1	. . .	30.3	. . .	30.9	. . .
April	28.1	27.9	28.6	21.6	28.8	32.4	21.6	32.3	. . .	30.2	. . .	30.8	. . .
May	28.2	28.0	28.7	21.6	28.8	32.4	21.7	32.3	. . .	30.2	. . .	30.7	. . .
June	28.3	28.1	28.9	21.6	28.9	32.5	21.8	32.5	. . .	30.3	. . .	31.5	. . .
July	28.4	28.2	29.1	21.5	29.0	32.6	21.8	32.6	. . .	30.3	. . .	32.0	. . .
August	28.4	28.3	29.4	21.4	29.0	32.8	21.9	32.6	. . .	30.4	. . .	32.0	. . .
September	28.5	28.3	29.2	21.4	29.1	32.8	22.0	32.6	. . .	30.4	. . .	31.2	. . .
October	28.5	28.3	29.2	21.4	29.2	32.7	22.1	32.7	. . .	30.3	. . .	31.0	. . .
November	28.6	28.4	29.2	21.5	29.3	32.8	22.2	32.9	. . .	30.4	. . .	31.1	. . .
December	28.6	28.5	29.2	21.5	29.3	32.9	22.2	33.0	. . .	30.4	. . .	31.5	. . .
1958													
January	28.8	28.6	29.8	21.6	29.3	33.1	22.3	33.2	. . .	30.4	. . .	31.4	. . .
February	28.9	28.7	29.9	21.3	29.4	33.2	22.4	33.2	. . .	30.3	. . .	31.9	. . .
March	29.0	28.9	30.5	21.4	29.5	33.4	22.4	33.4	. . .	30.3	. . .	32.3	. . .
April	29.1	28.9	30.6	21.4	29.5	33.5	22.5	33.2	. . .	30.2	. . .	31.8	. . .
May	29.1	28.9	30.5	21.5	29.5	33.5	22.6	33.2	. . .	30.3	. . .	32.4	. . .
June	29.1	28.9	30.3	21.5	29.6	33.4	22.6	33.3	. . .	30.3	. . .	32.0	. . .
July	29.1	28.9	30.2	21.6	29.6	33.3	22.7	33.2	. . .	30.3	. . .	32.1	. . .
August	29.1	28.9	30.1	21.7	29.6	33.3	22.7	33.2	. . .	30.4	. . .	31.9	. . .
September	29.1	28.9	30.0	21.7	29.7	33.3	22.8	33.2	. . .	30.4	. . .	31.6	. . .
October	29.1	28.9	30.0	21.7	29.7	33.2	22.8	33.2	. . .	30.4	. . .	31.9	. . .
November	29.1	29.0	30.0	21.4	29.8	33.3	22.8	33.2	. . .	30.5	. . .	32.1	. . .
December	29.1	29.0	29.9	21.4	29.9	33.3	22.8	33.1	. . .	30.6	. . .	31.6	. . .
1959													
January	29.2	29.0	30.0	21.4	29.9	33.3	22.9	33.1	. . .	30.6	. . .	31.6	. . .
February	29.2	29.0	29.8	21.6	29.9	33.3	23.0	33.2	. . .	30.7	. . .	31.4	. . .
March	29.1	29.0	29.7	21.7	30.0	33.2	23.0	33.2	. . .	30.7	. . .	31.5	. . .
April	29.1	29.0	29.5	21.8	30.0	33.2	23.1	33.2	. . .	30.7	. . .	31.7	. . .
May	29.2	29.0	29.5	21.8	30.1	33.3	23.2	33.3	. . .	30.9	. . .	31.5	. . .
June	29.3	29.1	29.7	21.9	30.2	33.3	23.2	33.2	. . .	30.9	. . .	31.3	. . .
July	29.3	29.2	29.6	21.8	30.2	33.3	23.3	33.1	. . .	30.8	. . .	31.0	. . .
August	29.3	29.2	29.6	21.9	30.2	33.3	23.4	33.0	. . .	30.8	. . .	30.7	. . .
September	29.4	29.3	29.7	21.9	30.3	33.5	23.5	33.4	. . .	30.8	. . .	30.9	. . .
October	29.5	29.4	29.7	22.2	30.4	33.5	23.6	33.1	. . .	30.8	. . .	30.7	. . .
November	29.5	29.4	29.7	22.2	30.4	33.5	23.6	33.0	. . .	30.9	. . .	30.5	. . .
December	29.6	29.4	29.6	22.3	30.5	33.5	23.7	33.0	. . .	30.9	. . .	30.3	. . .
1960													
January	29.5	29.4	29.6	22.3	30.5	33.5	23.7	33.1	. . .	30.8	. . .	30.4	. . .
February	29.6	29.4	29.5	22.2	30.6	33.4	23.8	33.1	. . .	30.9	. . .	30.4	. . .
March	29.6	29.4	29.6	22.3	30.6	33.5	23.9	33.4	. . .	30.9	. . .	30.7	. . .
April	29.7	29.5	30.0	22.4	30.6	33.6	23.9	33.4	. . .	30.8	. . .	30.8	. . .
May	29.7	29.6	30.0	22.3	30.6	33.6	24.0	33.4	. . .	30.8	. . .	30.8	. . .
June	29.8	29.6	30.0	22.4	30.7	33.6	24.0	33.4	. . .	30.9	. . .	30.4	. . .
July	29.7	29.6	29.9	22.5	30.6	33.5	24.1	33.5	. . .	30.8	. . .	30.4	. . .
August	29.8	29.6	30.0	22.5	30.6	33.6	24.1	33.4	. . .	30.8	. . .	29.8	. . .
September	29.8	29.6	30.1	22.6	30.6	33.6	24.2	33.4	. . .	30.8	. . .	30.0	. . .
October	29.9	29.8	30.3	22.5	30.8	33.7	24.2	33.7	. . .	30.8	. . .	30.2	. . .
November	30.0	29.8	30.5	22.7	30.8	33.8	24.3	33.7	. . .	30.7	. . .	30.2	. . .
December	30.0	29.8	30.5	22.6	30.7	33.9	24.3	33.6	. . .	30.7	. . .	30.3	. . .
1961													
January	30.0	29.8	30.5	22.7	30.8	33.8	24.4	33.6	. . .	30.6	. . .	30.4	. . .
February	30.0	29.8	30.5	22.6	30.8	33.8	24.4	33.7	. . .	30.7	. . .	30.5	. . .
March	30.0	29.8	30.5	22.6	30.9	33.8	24.4	33.6	. . .	30.8	. . .	30.3	. . .
April	30.0	29.8	30.4	22.2	30.9	33.8	24.5	33.4	. . .	30.7	. . .	30.2	. . .
May	30.0	29.8	30.3	22.4	30.9	33.8	24.5	33.3	. . .	30.6	. . .	29.9	. . .
June	30.0	29.8	30.2	22.5	31.0	33.8	24.5	33.3	. . .	30.5	. . .	29.5	. . .
July	30.1	29.9	30.3	22.5	31.0	33.9	24.5	33.3	. . .	30.5	. . .	29.7	. . .
August	30.1	29.9	30.3	22.5	31.1	33.9	24.6	33.4	. . .	30.5	. . .	30.5	. . .
September	30.2	30.0	30.3	22.6	31.1	33.9	24.6	33.3	. . .	30.5	. . .	30.3	. . .
October	30.2	30.0	30.3	22.4	31.1	33.9	24.7	33.3	. . .	30.4	. . .	30.3	. . .
November	30.2	30.0	30.3	22.5	31.2	33.8	24.7	33.4	. . .	30.5	. . .	30.2	. . .
December	30.2	30.0	30.3	22.4	31.2	33.9	24.8	33.4	. . .	30.6	. . .	30.6	. . .
1962													
January	30.2	30.0	30.4	22.4	31.2	33.9	24.8	33.5	. . .	30.5	. . .	30.6	. . .
February	30.3	30.1	30.5	22.6	31.2	34.0	24.8	33.6	. . .	30.6	. . .	30.5	. . .
March	30.4	30.2	30.6	22.4	31.3	34.0	24.9	33.5	. . .	30.6	. . .	30.5	. . .
April	30.4	30.2	30.7	22.7	31.3	34.1	24.9	33.5	. . .	30.6	. . .	30.1	. . .
May	30.4	30.2	30.6	22.7	31.4	34.1	25.0	33.4	. . .	30.6	. . .	30.1	. . .
June	30.4	30.2	30.5	22.5	31.4	34.1	25.0	33.4	. . .	30.6	. . .	29.9	. . .
July	30.4	30.2	30.4	22.3	31.4	34.0	25.1	33.4	. . .	30.6	. . .	30.2	. . .
August	30.5	30.3	30.6	22.4	31.5	34.1	25.1	33.5	. . .	30.6	. . .	30.5	. . .
September	30.6	30.4	30.9	22.8	31.5	34.3	25.1	33.8	. . .	30.6	. . .	31.2	. . .
October	30.6	30.4	30.8	22.7	31.5	34.2	25.1	33.6	. . .	30.5	. . .	30.8	. . .
November	30.6	30.4	30.9	22.7	31.5	34.3	25.2	33.6	. . .	30.5	. . .	31.0	. . .
December	30.6	30.4	30.7	22.8	31.6	34.2	25.2	33.5	. . .	30.5	. . .	30.6	. . .

. . . = Not available.

Table 8-1B. Summary Consumer and Producer Price Indexes: Historical Data, 1946–2010—*Continued*

(Seasonally adjusted.)

Year and month	Urban wage earners and clerical workers (CPI-W), all items	Consumer Price Index, 1982–1984 = 100						Producer Price Index, 1982 = 100					
		All urban consumers (CPI-U)						Finished goods		Intermediate materials, supplies, and components		Crude materials for further processing	
		All items	Food	Energy	All items less food and energy	Commodities	Services	Total	Less food and energy	Total	Less food and energy	Total	Crude nonfood less energy
1963													
January	30.6	30.4	31.0	22.8	31.5	34.3	25.3	33.4	...	30.5	...	30.3	...
February	30.7	30.5	31.1	22.7	31.6	34.3	25.3	33.4	...	30.5	...	30.0	...
March	30.7	30.5	31.0	22.7	31.7	34.3	25.3	33.3	...	30.5	...	29.6	...
April	30.7	30.5	30.9	22.6	31.7	34.3	25.4	33.3	...	30.5	...	29.8	...
May	30.7	30.5	30.9	22.6	31.7	34.3	25.4	33.4	...	30.7	...	29.6	...
June	30.8	30.6	31.0	22.5	31.8	34.4	25.5	33.5	...	30.7	...	29.9	
July	30.9	30.7	31.2	22.7	31.8	34.5	25.5	33.4	...	30.7	...	30.0	...
August	30.9	30.8	31.2	22.6	31.9	34.6	25.6	33.4	...	30.7	...	29.9	...
September	30.9	30.7	31.1	22.5	31.9	34.5	25.6	33.4	...	30.7	...	29.8	...
October	30.9	30.8	31.0	22.7	32.0	34.5	25.6	33.5	...	30.8	...	29.9	...
November	31.0	30.8	31.2	22.6	32.0	34.6	25.7	33.5	...	30.8	...	30.2	...
December	31.1	30.9	31.3	22.6	32.1	34.7	25.8	33.4	...	30.8	...	29.4	...
1964													
January	31.1	30.9	31.4	22.8	32.2	34.7	25.8	33.5	...	30.8	...	29.8	...
February	31.1	30.9	31.4	22.2	32.2	34.7	25.8	33.5	...	30.8	...	29.4	...
March	31.1	30.9	31.4	22.6	32.2	34.7	25.8	33.4	...	30.8	...	29.5	...
April	31.1	31.0	31.4	22.5	32.2	34.7	25.9	33.5	...	30.8	...	29.5	...
May	31.2	31.0	31.4	22.5	32.2	34.7	25.9	33.5	...	30.7	...	29.4	...
June	31.2	31.0	31.4	22.6	32.3	34.7	26.0	33.5	...	30.6	...	29.0	...
July	31.2	31.0	31.5	22.5	32.3	34.7	26.0	33.5	...	30.7	...	29.2	...
August	31.2	31.1	31.4	22.6	32.3	34.7	26.0	33.6	...	30.6	...	29.4	...
September	31.3	31.1	31.6	22.5	32.3	34.8	26.0	33.6	...	30.7	...	30.1	...
October	31.3	31.1	31.6	22.5	32.4	34.8	26.1	33.6	...	30.8	...	29.8	...
November	31.4	31.2	31.7	22.5	32.5	34.9	26.2	33.6	...	30.8	...	29.9	...
December	31.4	31.3	31.7	22.6	32.5	35.0	26.2	33.6	...	30.9	...	29.8	...
1965													
January	31.5	31.3	31.6	22.8	32.6	35.0	26.3	33.6	...	30.9	...	29.5	...
February	31.5	31.3	31.5	22.7	32.6	34.9	26.4	33.7	...	30.9	...	29.9	...
March	31.5	31.3	31.7	22.6	32.6	35.0	26.4	33.7	...	31.0	...	30.0	...
April	31.6	31.4	31.8	22.9	32.7	35.0	26.5	34.0	...	31.1	...	30.4	...
May	31.7	31.5	32.1	23.0	32.7	35.1	26.5	34.1	...	31.1	...	30.8	...
June	31.8	31.6	32.6	23.1	32.7	35.3	26.5	34.2	...	31.2	...	31.6	...
July	31.8	31.6	32.5	23.0	32.7	35.3	26.6	34.1	...	31.2	...	31.2	...
August	31.7	31.6	32.4	23.0	32.7	35.2	26.6	34.2	...	31.3	...	31.5	...
September	31.8	31.6	32.3	23.1	32.8	35.2	26.7	34.3	...	31.3	...	31.4	...
October	31.8	31.7	32.5	23.0	32.8	35.3	26.8	34.4	...	31.3	...	31.8	...
November	31.9	31.8	32.6	23.1	32.9	35.4	26.9	34.5	...	31.4	...	32.1	...
December	32.0	31.9	32.8	23.1	33.0	35.5	26.9	34.7	...	31.4	...	32.7	...
1966													
January	32.1	31.9	33.0	23.1	33.0	35.6	27.0	34.7	...	31.4	...	33.1	...
February	32.3	32.1	33.5	23.2	33.1	35.8	27.0	35.0	...	31.6	...	33.7	...
March	32.4	32.2	33.8	23.2	33.1	35.9	27.1	35.0	...	31.7	...	33.5	...
April	32.5	32.3	33.8	23.2	33.3	36.0	27.3	35.1	...	31.8	...	33.3	...
May	32.5	32.4	33.7	23.2	33.4	36.0	27.4	35.1	...	32.0	...	33.0	...
June	32.6	32.4	33.7	23.3	33.5	36.0	27.5	34.9	...	32.0	...	33.0	...
July	32.6	32.5	33.5	23.4	33.6	36.1	27.7	35.1	...	32.2	...	33.4	...
August	32.8	32.7	34.0	23.3	33.7	36.2	27.7	35.4	...	32.3	...	33.5	...
September	32.9	32.8	34.1	23.4	33.8	36.4	27.9	35.6	...	32.2	...	33.4	...
October	33.0	32.9	34.2	23.4	34.0	36.4	28.0	35.5	...	32.1	...	32.9	...
November	33.1	32.9	34.1	23.5	34.0	36.4	28.2	35.5	...	32.2	...	32.3	...
December	33.1	32.9	34.0	23.5	34.1	36.4	28.2	35.4	...	32.2	...	32.1	...
1967													
January	33.1	32.9	33.9	23.6	34.2	36.4	28.3	35.4	...	32.2	...	32.2	...
February	33.2	33.0	33.8	23.7	34.2	36.4	28.4	35.3	...	32.1	...	31.5	...
March	33.2	33.0	33.8	23.6	34.3	36.4	28.5	35.3	...	32.1	...	31.1	...
April	33.3	33.1	33.7	23.9	34.4	36.4	28.6	35.3	...	32.1	...	30.7	...
May	33.3	33.1	33.7	23.9	34.5	36.5	28.6	35.4	...	32.1	...	31.1	...
June	33.5	33.3	34.0	23.8	34.6	36.6	28.8	35.7	...	32.2	...	31.4	...
July	33.6	33.4	34.1	23.8	34.7	36.8	28.8	35.7	...	32.2	...	31.3	...
August	33.7	33.5	34.3	23.9	34.9	37.0	28.9	35.8	...	32.2	...	31.3	...
September	33.8	33.6	34.3	24.0	35.0	37.0	29.0	35.8	...	32.3	...	31.2	...
October	33.9	33.7	34.4	23.9	35.1	37.1	29.2	35.9	...	32.3	...	31.3	...
November	34.0	33.9	34.5	24.0	35.2	37.2	29.2	35.9	...	32.4	...	31.1	...
December	34.1	34.0	34.6	23.9	35.4	37.4	29.4	36.0	...	32.6	...	31.5	...
1968													
January	34.3	34.1	34.6	24.0	35.5	37.5	29.5	36.1	...	32.6	...	31.4	...
February	34.4	34.2	34.8	24.1	35.7	37.6	29.6	36.2	...	32.7	...	31.5	...
March	34.5	34.3	34.9	24.1	35.8	37.7	29.8	36.3	...	32.8	...	31.6	...
April	34.6	34.4	35.0	24.0	35.9	37.8	29.9	36.5	...	32.8	...	31.7	...
May	34.7	34.5	35.1	24.1	36.0	37.8	30.0	36.5	...	32.8	...	31.5	...
June	34.9	34.7	35.2	24.2	36.2	38.0	30.2	36.6	...	32.9	...	31.3	...
July	35.0	34.9	35.3	24.2	36.4	38.1	30.4	36.7	...	33.0	...	31.6	...
August	35.2	35.0	35.4	24.3	36.5	38.3	30.6	36.8	...	33.0	...	31.7	...
September	35.3	35.1	35.6	24.3	36.7	38.4	30.7	37.0	...	33.1	...	31.9	...
October	35.5	35.3	35.9	24.3	36.9	38.6	30.9	37.0	...	33.2	...	32.1	...
November	35.6	35.4	35.9	24.4	37.1	38.7	31.0	37.1	...	33.2	...	32.8	...
December	35.8	35.6	36.0	24.3	37.2	38.8	31.2	37.1	...	33.4	...	32.4	...

. . . = Not available.

Table 8-1B. Summary Consumer and Producer Price Indexes: Historical Data, 1946–2010—*Continued*

(Seasonally adjusted.)

Year and month	Urban wage earners and clerical workers (CPI-W), all items	Consumer Price Index, 1982–1984 = 100 — All urban consumers (CPI-U)						Producer Price Index, 1982 = 100 — Finished goods		Intermediate materials, supplies, and components		Crude materials for further processing	
		All items	Food	Energy	All items less food and energy	Commodit-ies	Services	Total	Less food and energy	Total	Less food and energy	Total	Crude nonfood less energy
1969													
January	35.9	35.7	36.1	24.4	37.3	38.9	31.4	37.2	. . .	33.6	. . .	32.6	. . .
February	36.0	35.8	36.1	24.4	37.6	39.0	31.5	37.2	. . .	33.7	. . .	32.3	. . .
March	36.3	36.1	36.2	24.7	37.8	39.3	31.8	37.4	. . .	33.9	. . .	32.7	. . .
April	36.5	36.3	36.4	24.9	38.1	39.4	32.0	37.6	. . .	33.8	. . .	33.1	. . .
May	36.6	36.4	36.6	24.8	38.1	39.5	32.2	37.8	. . .	33.9	. . .	34.0	. . .
June	36.8	36.6	37.0	25.0	38.3	39.8	32.3	38.0	. . .	34.0	. . .	34.5	. . .
July	37.0	36.8	37.3	24.9	38.5	39.9	32.5	38.1	. . .	34.0	. . .	34.1	. . .
August	37.1	36.9	37.5	24.9	38.7	40.1	32.7	38.2	. . .	34.2	. . .	34.4	. . .
September	37.3	37.1	37.7	25.0	38.9	40.2	33.0	38.3	. . .	34.2	. . .	34.4	. . .
October	37.5	37.3	37.8	25.0	39.1	40.4	33.1	38.5	. . .	34.4	. . .	34.8	. . .
November	37.7	37.5	38.2	25.0	39.2	40.6	33.3	38.8	. . .	34.6	. . .	35.2	. . .
December	37.9	37.7	38.6	25.1	39.4	40.8	33.5	38.9	. . .	34.7	. . .	35.1	. . .
1970													
January	38.1	37.9	38.7	25.1	39.6	41.0	33.8	39.1	. . .	35.0	. . .	35.1	. . .
February	38.3	38.1	38.9	25.1	39.8	41.2	34.0	39.0	. . .	35.0	. . .	35.2	. . .
March	38.5	38.3	38.9	25.0	40.1	41.2	34.4	39.1	. . .	34.9	. . .	35.6	. . .
April	38.7	38.5	39.0	25.5	40.4	41.4	34.6	39.1	. . .	35.1	. . .	35.5	. . .
May	38.8	38.6	39.2	25.4	40.5	41.5	34.8	39.1	. . .	35.2	. . .	35.0	. . .
June	39.0	38.8	39.2	25.3	40.8	41.6	35.0	39.2	. . .	35.3	. . .	35.0	. . .
July	39.1	38.9	39.2	25.5	40.9	41.7	35.2	39.2	. . .	35.5	. . .	35.1	. . .
August	39.2	39.0	39.2	25.4	41.1	41.8	35.4	39.2	. . .	35.5	. . .	34.7	. . .
September	39.4	39.2	39.4	25.6	41.3	42.0	35.6	39.6	. . .	35.6	. . .	35.5	. . .
October	39.6	39.4	39.5	25.9	41.5	42.2	35.8	39.6	. . .	35.8	. . .	35.5	. . .
November	39.8	39.6	39.5	26.0	41.8	42.3	36.0	39.8	. . .	35.9	. . .	35.1	. . .
December	40.0	39.8	39.5	26.2	42.0	42.5	36.2	39.8	. . .	35.9	. . .	34.5	. . .
1971													
January	40.1	39.9	39.4	26.3	42.1	42.5	36.4	39.9	. . .	36.0	. . .	34.8	. . .
February	40.2	39.9	39.5	26.2	42.2	42.6	36.5	40.1	. . .	36.1	. . .	35.9	. . .
March	40.2	40.0	39.8	26.2	42.2	42.7	36.5	40.2	. . .	36.3	. . .	35.4	. . .
April	40.4	40.1	40.1	26.1	42.4	42.9	36.6	40.3	. . .	36.3	. . .	36.0	. . .
May	40.5	40.3	40.3	26.2	42.6	43.1	36.7	40.5	. . .	36.5	. . .	36.0	. . .
June	40.7	40.5	40.5	26.3	42.8	43.2	37.0	40.6	. . .	36.7	. . .	36.2	. . .
July	40.9	40.6	40.6	26.3	42.9	43.3	37.1	40.4	. . .	36.9	. . .	35.9	. . .
August	41.0	40.7	40.6	26.8	43.0	43.4	37.3	40.7	. . .	37.2	. . .	35.8	. . .
September	41.0	40.8	40.6	26.9	43.0	43.4	37.4	40.7	. . .	37.2	. . .	35.7	. . .
October	41.1	40.9	40.7	27.0	43.1	43.5	37.5	40.7	. . .	37.1	. . .	36.4	. . .
November	41.2	41.0	40.9	26.9	43.2	43.5	37.6	40.8	. . .	37.2	. . .	37.0	. . .
December	41.4	41.1	41.3	27.0	43.3	43.8	37.7	41.1	. . .	37.4	. . .	37.2	. . .
1972													
January	41.5	41.2	41.1	27.0	43.5	43.8	37.9	41.0	. . .	37.5	. . .	37.8	. . .
February	41.6	41.4	41.7	26.8	43.6	44.0	38.0	41.3	. . .	37.7	. . .	38.1	. . .
March	41.7	41.4	41.6	26.9	43.6	44.0	38.1	41.3	. . .	37.8	. . .	38.1	. . .
April	41.7	41.5	41.6	26.9	43.8	44.1	38.2	41.3	. . .	37.9	. . .	38.7	. . .
May	41.8	41.6	41.7	27.0	43.9	44.2	38.3	41.5	. . .	38.0	. . .	39.3	. . .
June	41.9	41.7	41.9	27.0	44.0	44.3	38.4	41.7	. . .	38.0	. . .	39.4	. . .
July	42.1	41.8	42.1	27.1	44.1	44.5	38.5	41.8	. . .	38.1	. . .	40.0	. . .
August	42.2	41.9	42.2	27.3	44.3	44.5	38.6	42.0	. . .	38.2	. . .	40.3	. . .
September	42.3	42.1	42.5	27.6	44.3	44.8	38.7	42.2	. . .	38.5	. . .	40.5	. . .
October	42.5	42.2	42.8	27.7	44.4	44.9	38.8	42.0	. . .	38.7	. . .	40.9	. . .
November	42.6	42.4	43.0	27.9	44.4	45.1	38.9	42.3	. . .	39.0	. . .	42.0	. . .
December	42.8	42.5	43.2	27.8	44.6	45.2	39.0	42.7	. . .	39.6	. . .	43.8	. . .
1973													
January	43.0	42.7	44.0	27.9	44.6	45.5	39.1	43.0	. . .	39.8	. . .	45.0	. . .
February	43.2	43.0	44.6	28.2	44.8	45.9	39.2	43.5	. . .	40.4	. . .	47.1	. . .
March	43.6	43.4	45.8	28.3	45.0	46.4	39.4	44.4	. . .	41.1	. . .	49.3	. . .
April	43.9	43.7	46.5	28.6	45.1	46.8	39.5	44.7	. . .	41.3	. . .	50.1	. . .
May	44.2	43.9	47.1	28.8	45.3	47.2	39.6	45.0	. . .	42.2	. . .	52.5	. . .
June	44.4	44.2	47.6	29.2	45.4	47.5	39.8	45.5	. . .	43.0	. . .	55.0	. . .
July	44.5	44.2	47.7	29.2	45.5	47.5	39.9	45.4	. . .	42.3	. . .	52.5	. . .
August	45.3	45.0	50.5	29.4	45.7	48.7	40.2	47.0	. . .	43.5	. . .	64.1	. . .
September	45.4	45.2	50.4	29.4	46.0	48.7	40.5	46.9	. . .	43.0	. . .	60.9	. . .
October	45.8	45.6	50.7	30.3	46.3	49.0	41.0	46.8	. . .	43.4	. . .	58.5	. . .
November	46.2	45.9	51.4	31.5	46.5	49.5	41.3	47.2	. . .	43.8	. . .	59.0	. . .
December	46.5	46.3	51.9	32.5	46.7	49.9	41.5	47.6	. . .	44.8	. . .	59.1	. . .
1974													
January	47.0	46.8	52.5	34.1	46.9	50.5	41.8	48.8	49.7	45.9	47.5	63.3	86.3
February	47.6	47.3	53.6	35.4	47.2	51.3	42.0	49.7	50.0	46.8	48.1	64.3	86.5
March	48.1	47.8	54.2	36.9	47.6	51.9	42.4	50.2	50.5	48.1	49.5	62.3	88.3
April	48.3	48.1	54.1	37.6	47.9	52.1	42.6	50.7	51.1	49.0	50.9	60.6	89.7
May	48.8	48.6	54.5	38.3	48.5	52.7	43.1	51.3	52.2	50.6	52.5	58.3	83.8
June	49.2	49.0	54.5	38.6	49.0	53.1	43.5	51.3	53.1	51.5	53.7	55.4	82.9
July	49.6	49.3	54.3	38.9	49.5	53.3	44.0	52.7	54.0	53.4	55.2	59.8	84.2
August	50.2	49.9	55.1	39.2	50.2	54.1	44.5	53.7	55.0	55.8	57.0	62.9	85.5
September	50.9	50.6	56.2	39.3	50.7	54.8	45.0	54.3	55.7	55.9	57.6	60.9	82.5
October	51.3	51.0	56.8	39.2	51.2	55.3	45.4	55.3	56.7	57.2	58.2	63.2	80.6
November	51.8	51.5	57.5	39.4	51.6	55.8	45.8	56.4	57.4	57.8	58.8	64.2	77.6
December	52.2	51.9	58.2	39.6	52.0	56.3	46.2	56.4	57.9	57.8	59.1	61.5	71.6

. . . = Not available.

Table 8-1B. Summary Consumer and Producer Price Indexes: Historical Data, 1946–2010—*Continued*

(Seasonally adjusted.)

Year and month	Urban wage earners and clerical workers (CPI-W), all items	All urban consumers (CPI-U)						Finished goods		Intermediate materials, supplies, and components		Crude materials for further processing	
		All items	Food	Energy	All items less food and energy	Commodities	Services	Total	Less food and energy	Total	Less food and energy	Total	Crude nonfood less energy
1975													
January	52.6	52.3	58.4	40.0	52.3	56.7	46.5	56.7	58.3	58.0	59.6	59.6	69.8
February	52.9	52.6	58.5	40.3	52.8	56.9	46.9	56.6	58.7	57.8	59.8	57.9	69.2
March	53.1	52.8	58.4	40.6	53.0	57.1	47.0	56.6	59.0	57.4	59.7	57.1	68.2
April	53.3	53.0	58.3	41.0	53.3	57.2	47.3	57.1	59.2	57.5	59.7	59.5	67.7
May	53.4	53.1	58.6	41.3	53.5	57.5	47.5	57.4	59.3	57.3	59.7	61.2	68.8
June	53.8	53.5	59.2	41.7	53.8	57.9	47.8	57.9	59.5	57.3	59.8	61.5	66.5
July	54.3	54.0	60.3	42.5	54.0	58.6	48.0	58.4	59.8	57.5	59.9	62.4	66.5
August	54.5	54.2	60.3	42.8	54.2	58.7	48.3	58.9	59.9	58.0	60.1	63.0	67.7
September	54.9	54.6	60.7	43.2	54.5	59.0	48.7	59.3	60.2	58.2	60.3	64.5	71.2
October	55.2	54.9	61.3	43.5	54.8	59.4	49.0	59.8	60.6	58.8	61.0	65.1	71.5
November	55.6	55.3	61.7	43.9	55.2	59.7	49.6	60.0	61.0	59.0	61.4	64.4	71.9
December	55.9	55.6	62.1	44.1	55.5	59.9	49.9	60.1	61.4	59.2	61.8	64.0	73.1
1976													
January	56.2	55.8	61.9	44.5	55.9	60.0	50.5	60.0	61.7	59.4	62.1	63.0	72.4
February	56.2	55.9	61.3	44.4	56.2	59.9	50.8	59.9	61.9	59.6	62.3	62.1	73.8
March	56.3	56.0	60.9	44.1	56.5	59.8	51.1	60.0	62.2	59.8	62.6	61.5	74.5
April	56.5	56.1	60.9	43.9	56.7	59.9	51.3	60.3	62.3	60.0	62.8	63.9	78.1
May	56.7	56.4	61.1	44.1	57.0	60.2	51.4	60.4	62.4	60.3	63.2	63.6	80.6
June	57.0	56.7	61.3	44.4	57.2	60.4	51.7	60.5	62.8	60.8	63.6	65.2	82.8
July	57.3	57.0	61.6	44.8	57.6	60.7	52.1	60.7	63.1	61.1	63.9	64.8	87.3
August	57.6	57.3	61.8	45.2	57.9	61.0	52.4	60.9	63.5	61.3	64.3	63.6	84.1
September	57.9	57.6	62.1	45.7	58.2	61.3	52.8	61.1	63.9	61.9	64.7	63.4	84.4
October	58.2	57.9	62.4	46.1	58.5	61.6	53.1	61.4	64.1	62.0	65.0	63.0	82.2
November	58.4	58.1	62.3	46.8	58.7	61.7	53.4	61.9	64.6	62.4	65.3	63.4	81.8
December	58.7	58.4	62.5	47.5	58.9	62.0	53.7	62.4	64.9	62.8	65.6	64.5	81.1
1977													
January	59.1	58.7	62.7	48.1	59.3	62.3	54.1	62.5	65.1	63.0	65.8	64.3	78.7
February	59.6	59.3	63.9	48.1	59.7	63.0	54.4	63.2	65.4	63.3	65.9	65.7	79.7
March	59.9	59.6	64.2	48.4	60.0	63.2	54.8	63.7	65.7	63.9	66.4	66.6	81.5
April	60.3	60.0	65.0	48.6	60.3	63.7	55.2	64.0	65.9	64.4	66.7	68.3	82.1
May	60.6	60.2	65.3	48.9	60.6	63.9	55.4	64.4	66.1	64.9	67.1	67.6	82.5
June	60.9	60.5	65.7	48.9	61.0	64.2	55.8	64.6	66.5	64.9	67.4	65.5	79.7
July	61.2	60.8	65.9	49.1	61.2	64.4	56.3	64.8	66.8	65.1	67.9	64.7	78.8
August	61.4	61.1	66.2	49.5	61.5	64.6	56.6	65.2	67.3	65.4	68.2	63.9	79.2
September	61.7	61.3	66.4	49.8	61.8	64.8	56.9	65.5	67.8	65.7	68.7	63.7	79.2
October	61.9	61.6	66.6	50.5	62.0	65.0	57.2	65.9	68.2	65.8	68.8	64.0	78.5
November	62.3	62.0	67.1	51.3	62.3	65.5	57.6	66.4	68.8	66.3	69.1	65.4	78.4
December	62.6	62.3	67.4	51.6	62.7	65.7	57.9	66.7	69.0	66.6	69.4	66.4	80.1
1978													
January	63.0	62.7	67.9	51.1	63.1	66.1	58.3	67.0	69.2	66.9	69.8	67.3	80.3
February	63.3	63.0	68.6	50.6	63.4	66.4	58.7	67.5	69.5	67.4	70.3	68.4	80.6
March	63.8	63.4	69.5	51.0	63.8	66.8	59.1	67.8	69.9	67.8	70.6	69.8	80.3
April	64.2	63.9	70.6	51.4	64.3	67.4	59.6	68.6	70.6	68.1	71.1	72.1	82.2
May	64.8	64.5	71.6	51.7	64.7	68.0	60.0	69.1	71.1	68.7	71.6	72.8	84.6
June	65.3	65.0	72.7	51.9	65.2	68.6	60.5	69.7	71.7	69.2	72.2	74.6	87.4
July	65.8	65.5	73.0	52.1	65.6	69.1	61.0	70.3	72.3	69.4	72.5	74.2	89.6
August	66.2	65.9	73.3	52.6	66.1	69.4	61.5	70.4	72.8	69.9	73.2	73.7	90.4
September	66.7	66.5	73.6	53.2	66.7	70.0	62.1	71.1	73.5	70.5	73.7	75.1	92.3
October	67.4	67.1	74.2	54.1	67.2	70.6	62.6	71.4	73.4	71.3	74.5	77.0	94.7
November	67.8	67.5	74.7	54.9	67.6	71.1	63.1	72.0	74.1	71.9	75.2	77.4	96.3
December	68.3	67.9	75.1	55.9	68.0	71.6	63.3	72.8	74.7	72.4	75.6	78.0	96.8
1979													
January	68.8	68.5	76.4	55.8	68.5	72.2	63.8	73.7	75.3	73.1	76.3	80.1	96.4
February	69.6	69.2	77.7	55.9	69.2	72.9	64.4	74.4	75.9	73.7	77.0	82.1	99.6
March	70.3	69.9	78.4	57.4	69.8	73.8	64.9	75.0	76.4	74.6	77.8	83.8	104.2
April	71.1	70.6	79.0	59.5	70.3	74.7	65.5	75.8	77.0	75.7	78.9	84.4	105.1
May	71.9	71.4	79.7	62.0	70.8	75.6	66.2	76.2	77.4	76.6	79.6	84.7	106.7
June	72.7	72.2	80.0	64.7	71.3	76.4	66.8	76.6	78.0	77.5	80.1	85.6	111.6
July	73.5	73.0	80.5	67.3	71.9	77.2	67.6	77.4	78.5	78.7	81.1	86.5	109.4
August	74.2	73.7	80.4	69.7	72.7	77.9	68.5	78.2	78.8	79.8	81.8	85.5	106.4
September	75.0	74.4	80.9	71.9	73.3	78.6	69.2	79.5	79.7	81.1	82.7	87.9	106.5
October	75.7	75.2	81.5	73.5	74.0	79.3	70.1	80.4	80.4	82.4	83.9	88.8	108.9
November	76.5	76.0	82.0	74.8	74.8	80.0	71.1	81.4	81.0	83.2	84.5	90.0	111.3
December	77.3	76.9	82.8	76.8	75.7	80.8	72.0	82.2	81.7	84.0	85.2	91.2	111.3
1980													
January	78.5	78.0	83.3	79.1	76.7	82.0	73.1	83.4	83.3	86.0	87.2	90.9	112.6
February	79.4	79.0	83.4	81.9	77.5	82.8	74.1	84.6	84.2	87.6	88.2	92.6	115.3
March	80.6	80.1	84.1	84.5	78.6	83.9	75.4	85.5	84.7	88.2	88.6	90.8	111.7
April	81.4	80.9	84.7	85.4	79.5	84.4	76.6	86.2	85.5	88.5	88.8	88.3	109.9
May	82.2	81.7	85.2	86.4	80.1	84.9	77.6	86.6	85.7	89.0	89.1	89.5	107.2
June	83.0	82.5	85.7	86.5	81.0	85.3	79.0	87.3	86.6	89.8	89.8	90.1	106.1
July	83.1	82.6	86.6	86.7	80.8	85.9	78.5	88.7	87.7	90.5	90.3	94.6	109.6
August	83.7	83.2	88.0	87.2	81.3	86.9	78.5	89.7	88.4	91.5	91.1	99.0	112.4
September	84.4	83.9	89.1	87.5	82.1	87.8	79.0	90.1	88.8	91.9	91.4	100.4	116.2
October	85.3	84.7	89.8	88.0	83.0	88.5	80.0	90.8	89.6	92.8	92.1	102.2	118.2
November	86.2	85.6	90.8	88.8	83.9	89.2	81.1	91.4	90.1	93.5	92.6	103.5	119.8
December	87.0	86.4	91.3	90.7	84.9	89.7	82.2	91.8	90.4	94.4	93.7	102.7	119.3

Table 8-1B. Summary Consumer and Producer Price Indexes: Historical Data, 1946–2010—*Continued*

(Seasonally adjusted.)

Year and month	Urban wage earners and clerical workers (CPI-W), all items	Consumer Price Index, 1982–1984 = 100						Producer Price Index, 1982 = 100					
		All urban consumers (CPI-U)						Finished goods		Intermediate materials, supplies, and components		Crude materials for further processing	
		All items	Food	Energy	All items less food and energy	Commodities	Services	Total	Less food and energy	Total	Less food and energy	Total	Crude nonfood less energy
1981													
January	87.7	87.2	91.6	92.1	85.4	90.4	83.0	92.8	91.4	95.6	94.7	103.4	113.3
February	88.6	88.0	92.1	95.2	85.9	91.4	83.7	93.6	92.0	96.1	94.9	104.2	106.2
March	89.1	88.6	92.6	97.4	86.4	91.9	84.4	94.7	92.6	97.1	95.6	103.8	108.9
April	89.6	89.1	92.8	97.6	87.0	92.0	85.3	95.7	93.5	98.3	96.6	104.2	111.9
May	90.2	89.7	92.8	97.9	87.8	92.4	86.4	96.0	94.0	98.7	97.1	103.8	113.7
June	90.9	90.5	93.2	97.3	88.6	92.9	87.5	96.5	94.6	99.0	97.7	104.9	115.5
July	92.0	91.5	93.9	97.3	89.8	93.6	88.9	96.7	94.8	99.2	98.4	105.0	116.4
August	92.7	92.2	94.4	97.8	90.7	94.0	89.9	96.8	95.3	99.7	98.9	104.0	115.5
September	93.5	93.1	94.8	98.6	91.8	94.6	91.2	97.2	95.9	99.7	99.3	102.7	112.6
October	93.8	93.4	95.0	99.2	92.1	94.7	91.7	97.6	96.5	99.8	99.5	101.2	110.8
November	94.2	93.8	95.1	100.5	92.5	94.9	92.5	97.9	97.0	99.9	99.7	99.7	107.5
December	94.5	94.1	95.3	101.5	93.0	95.1	93.0	98.3	97.6	100.0	99.8	98.8	106.0
1982													
January	94.8	94.4	95.6	100.6	93.3	95.2	93.5	98.9	98.1	100.4	99.9	99.7	101.2
February	95.1	94.7	96.3	98.0	93.8	95.4	93.9	98.8	98.1	100.3	100.0	100.0	100.7
March	95.0	94.7	96.2	96.6	93.9	95.3	94.0	98.8	98.7	99.9	99.9	99.7	100.0
April	95.3	95.0	96.4	94.2	94.7	95.1	94.9	99.0	99.0	99.7	99.8	100.2	101.1
May	96.1	95.9	97.2	95.7	95.4	96.0	95.7	99.0	99.4	99.7	100.1	101.9	102.2
June	97.3	97.0	98.1	98.4	96.1	97.4	96.5	99.8	99.9	99.8	100.0	101.8	101.0
July	97.8	97.5	98.2	99.3	96.7	97.9	97.0	100.2	100.1	100.0	99.8	100.7	101.4
August	98.1	97.7	98.0	99.8	97.1	97.9	97.6	100.6	100.6	99.9	99.7	99.8	100.0
September	98.1	97.7	98.2	100.3	97.2	97.8	97.6	100.7	100.8	100.0	100.2	99.2	98.9
October	98.5	98.1	98.2	101.7	97.5	98.2	97.9	101.0	101.3	99.9	100.2	98.7	97.7
November	98.4	98.0	98.2	102.5	97.3	98.3	97.7	101.4	101.6	100.1	100.2	99.2	96.3
December	98.1	97.7	98.2	102.8	97.2	98.3	96.9	101.8	102.2	100.1	100.3	98.8	95.9
1983													
January	98.2	97.9	98.1	99.6	97.6	98.3	97.5	101.0	101.8	99.8	100.3	98.8	97.3
February	98.2	98.0	98.2	97.7	98.0	98.1	97.9	101.1	102.2	100.0	100.8	100.0	99.8
March	98.5	98.1	98.8	96.8	98.2	98.2	98.1	101.0	102.5	99.7	100.8	100.5	102.2
April	99.1	98.8	99.2	98.9	98.6	98.9	98.7	101.1	102.4	99.5	100.9	101.2	102.1
May	99.5	99.2	99.5	100.4	98.9	99.5	98.9	101.4	102.6	99.8	101.0	100.9	103.4
June	99.7	99.4	99.6	100.6	99.2	99.8	99.2	101.6	102.8	100.2	101.3	100.5	104.8
July	100.0	99.8	99.6	100.9	99.8	100.2	99.6	101.6	103.1	100.5	101.8	99.5	106.2
August	100.5	100.1	99.7	101.2	100.1	100.5	99.8	101.9	103.5	100.9	102.0	102.2	108.4
September	100.7	100.4	100.0	101.0	100.5	100.7	100.2	102.2	103.5	101.6	102.3	103.3	109.0
October	101.0	100.8	100.3	100.8	101.0	101.0	100.7	102.2	103.6	101.7	102.5	103.2	109.1
November	101.2	101.1	100.3	100.5	101.5	101.1	101.3	102.0	103.8	101.8	102.8	102.3	109.9
December	101.3	101.4	100.6	100.0	101.8	101.2	101.6	102.3	104.1	101.9	103.1	103.5	111.2
1984													
January	101.8	102.1	102.0	100.2	102.5	101.9	102.1	103.0	104.5	102.1	103.4	104.6	111.5
February	102.0	102.6	102.7	101.4	102.8	102.4	102.6	103.4	104.7	102.5	103.8	103.8	113.8
March	102.0	102.9	102.9	101.4	103.2	102.6	103.0	103.8	105.2	103.0	104.4	105.7	114.8
April	102.2	103.3	102.9	101.7	103.7	102.9	103.5	103.9	105.3	103.2	104.5	105.2	115.1
May	102.5	103.5	102.7	101.6	104.1	103.0	103.9	103.8	105.3	103.4	104.6	104.5	115.7
June	102.7	103.7	103.1	100.8	104.5	103.1	104.2	103.8	105.5	103.6	104.8	103.3	114.1
July	103.2	104.1	103.3	100.5	105.0	103.2	104.9	104.0	105.7	103.4	104.9	104.0	112.0
August	104.1	104.4	103.9	100.1	105.4	103.4	105.4	103.8	105.9	103.2	105.1	103.3	109.6
September	104.5	104.7	103.8	100.6	105.8	103.6	105.9	103.8	106.2	103.1	105.0	102.8	110.5
October	104.7	105.1	104.0	101.1	106.2	103.9	106.3	103.6	105.9	103.2	105.1	101.5	108.5
November	104.8	105.3	104.1	100.8	106.4	103.9	106.7	104.0	106.2	103.3	105.3	101.9	107.7
December	104.9	105.5	104.5	100.1	106.8	103.9	107.1	104.0	106.3	103.2	105.3	101.4	107.3
1985													
January	105.2	105.7	104.7	100.3	107.1	104.1	107.4	104.0	106.9	103.1	105.3	99.9	107.4
February	105.7	106.3	105.2	100.3	107.7	104.7	107.9	104.1	107.3	102.8	105.3	99.4	107.2
March	106.1	106.8	105.5	101.3	108.1	105.1	108.4	104.1	107.6	102.7	105.2	97.6	107.0
April	106.4	107.0	105.4	102.3	108.4	105.4	108.7	104.6	107.6	102.9	105.2	96.7	107.4
May	106.6	107.2	105.2	102.2	108.8	105.2	109.4	104.9	107.8	103.2	105.3	95.8	105.3
June	106.9	107.5	105.5	102.2	109.1	105.3	109.8	104.6	108.2	102.6	105.5	95.2	103.6
July	107.0	107.7	105.5	102.2	109.4	105.3	110.3	104.7	108.4	102.3	105.3	94.9	104.3
August	107.1	107.9	105.6	101.2	109.8	105.2	110.7	104.5	108.5	102.3	105.3	92.9	103.6
September	107.3	108.1	105.8	101.2	110.0	105.4	111.0	103.8	107.9	102.2	105.2	91.8	103.3
October	107.7	108.5	105.8	101.2	110.5	105.6	111.5	104.9	108.9	102.3	105.1	94.1	103.7
November	108.2	109.0	106.5	101.8	111.1	106.1	112.1	105.5	109.1	102.5	105.1	95.7	103.0
December	108.7	109.5	107.3	102.4	111.4	106.6	112.5	106.0	109.1	102.9	105.1	95.5	102.4
1986													
January	109.1	109.9	107.5	102.6	111.9	106.9	113.1	105.5	109.3	102.4	105.0	94.2	103.6
February	108.8	109.7	107.3	99.5	112.2	106.0	113.5	104.1	109.5	101.2	104.9	90.5	103.5
March	108.1	109.1	107.5	92.6	112.5	104.5	114.1	102.8	109.6	99.9	105.0	88.2	103.8
April	107.7	108.7	107.7	87.2	112.9	103.3	114.6	102.3	110.1	98.9	104.7	85.6	103.9
May	107.8	109.0	108.2	87.2	113.1	103.5	114.8	102.8	110.2	98.7	104.6	86.5	104.1
June	108.3	109.4	108.3	88.8	113.4	103.8	115.5	103.1	110.5	98.6	104.7	86.2	104.7
July	108.3	109.5	109.1	85.6	113.8	103.7	115.7	102.3	110.7	98.0	104.8	86.4	105.3
August	108.4	109.6	110.1	83.6	114.2	103.6	116.1	102.7	110.8	98.0	104.9	86.7	99.7
September	108.8	110.0	110.2	84.4	114.6	104.0	116.5	102.9	110.7	98.5	105.1	86.6	100.3
October	108.9	110.2	110.5	82.8	115.0	104.0	116.9	103.5	111.8	98.3	105.1	87.4	102.0
November	109.2	110.4	111.1	82.1	115.3	104.2	117.2	103.4	112.0	98.3	105.2	87.6	102.8
December	109.5	110.8	111.4	82.5	115.6	104.5	117.5	103.6	112.1	98.5	105.3	86.9	104.1

Table 8-1B. Summary Consumer and Producer Price Indexes: Historical Data, 1946–2010—*Continued*

(Seasonally adjusted.)

Year and month	Consumer Price Index, 1982–1984 = 100							Producer Price Index, 1982 = 100					
	Urban wage earners and clerical workers (CPI-W), all items	All urban consumers (CPI-U)						Finished goods		Intermediate materials, supplies, and components		Crude materials for further processing	
		All items	Food	Energy	All items less food and energy	Commodities	Services	Total	Less food and energy	Total	Less food and energy	Total	Crude nonfood less energy
1987													
January	110.2	111.4	111.8	85.4	115.9	105.5	117.9	104.1	112.5	99.0	105.6	89.3	105.4
February	110.7	111.8	112.2	87.4	116.2	106.1	118.3	104.4	112.3	99.8	105.9	90.2	106.2
March	111.1	112.2	112.4	87.6	116.6	106.5	118.6	104.5	112.4	99.9	106.2	90.5	106.5
April	111.6	112.7	112.6	87.6	117.3	106.9	119.2	105.1	112.9	100.3	106.5	92.5	107.5
May	111.9	113.0	113.2	87.1	117.7	107.2	119.6	105.2	113.0	100.8	107.0	93.8	110.0
June	112.4	113.5	113.9	88.5	117.9	107.7	120.0	105.5	113.1	101.4	107.5	94.5	113.2
July	112.7	113.8	113.7	89.2	118.3	108.0	120.3	105.7	113.3	101.9	107.9	95.6	115.9
August	113.2	114.3	113.9	90.5	118.7	108.5	120.9	105.9	113.6	102.4	108.3	96.5	119.1
September	113.6	114.7	114.3	90.3	119.2	108.8	121.4	106.2	113.9	102.6	108.9	96.0	122.8
October	113.9	115.0	114.5	89.6	119.8	109.0	121.8	106.0	114.0	103.1	109.6	95.8	126.6
November	114.2	115.4	114.5	90.0	120.1	109.3	122.2	106.0	114.2	103.5	110.1	95.1	127.5
December	114.4	115.6	115.1	89.5	120.4	109.3	122.6	105.8	114.3	103.8	110.7	94.9	127.9
1988													
January	114.7	116.0	115.6	88.8	120.9	109.5	123.0	106.4	115.0	104.1	111.8	94.2	129.4
February	114.9	116.2	115.6	88.7	121.2	109.5	123.5	106.3	115.3	104.4	112.2	95.2	131.7
March	115.2	116.5	115.8	88.4	121.7	109.8	123.9	106.6	115.6	104.8	112.8	94.1	133.0
April	115.8	117.2	116.4	88.8	122.3	110.5	124.4	107.0	115.9	105.5	113.6	95.4	132.1
May	116.2	117.5	116.9	88.5	122.7	110.7	124.8	107.2	116.2	106.2	114.3	95.8	130.7
June	116.6	118.0	117.6	88.9	123.2	111.2	125.4	107.5	116.6	107.4	114.9	97.0	131.1
July	117.3	118.5	118.8	89.4	123.6	111.9	125.8	108.4	117.2	108.3	115.8	96.7	133.2
August	117.7	119.0	119.4	90.1	124.0	112.2	126.4	108.8	117.7	108.5	116.3	97.0	134.3
September	118.2	119.5	120.1	89.8	124.7	112.8	126.9	109.0	118.1	108.7	116.8	97.0	133.3
October	118.6	119.9	120.3	89.8	125.2	113.0	127.5	109.2	118.4	108.6	117.3	96.6	133.6
November	118.9	120.3	120.5	89.8	125.6	113.3	127.9	109.6	118.7	108.8	118.0	95.2	136.0
December	119.3	120.7	121.1	89.6	126.0	113.5	128.4	110.0	119.2	109.4	118.6	98.1	137.6
1989													
January	119.9	121.2	121.6	90.3	126.5	114.1	128.9	111.1	119.9	110.8	119.5	102.0	140.6
February	120.3	121.6	122.5	90.8	126.9	114.5	129.4	111.9	120.5	111.3	119.9	101.7	140.3
March	120.9	122.2	123.2	91.8	127.4	115.1	130.0	112.3	120.7	111.9	120.2	102.9	140.6
April	121.9	123.1	123.9	96.6	127.8	116.5	130.5	113.1	120.8	112.5	120.5	104.1	140.3
May	122.5	123.7	124.7	97.4	128.3	117.1	131.1	114.0	121.6	112.6	120.6	104.5	139.8
June	122.8	124.1	125.1	96.9	128.8	117.2	131.6	114.0	122.2	112.5	120.6	103.2	137.9
July	123.2	124.5	125.6	96.7	129.2	117.3	132.3	113.8	122.1	112.2	120.3	103.5	135.9
August	123.2	124.5	125.9	94.9	129.5	117.0	132.8	113.4	122.7	111.8	120.2	101.2	136.8
September	123.4	124.8	126.3	93.8	129.9	117.2	133.1	114.0	123.1	112.1	120.2	102.5	137.5
October	123.9	125.4	126.8	94.4	130.6	117.8	133.7	114.6	123.5	112.2	120.3	102.7	137.9
November	124.4	125.9	127.4	93.9	131.1	118.1	134.3	114.8	123.9	112.0	120.0	103.5	134.9
December	124.9	126.3	127.8	94.2	131.6	118.4	134.9	115.5	124.2	112.2	119.8	105.1	132.8
1990													
January	126.1	127.5	129.7	98.9	132.1	120.2	135.4	117.7	124.5	113.7	120.0	106.7	132.7
February	126.6	128.0	130.8	98.2	132.7	120.7	136.0	117.6	124.9	112.8	119.9	106.8	131.6
March	127.0	128.6	131.0	97.6	133.5	120.9	136.8	117.5	125.3	112.9	120.2	105.1	133.9
April	127.3	128.9	130.8	97.5	134.0	121.0	137.4	117.4	125.5	113.1	120.5	102.7	137.0
May	127.5	129.1	131.1	96.7	134.4	121.0	137.9	117.5	126.0	113.1	120.6	103.1	138.0
June	128.2	129.9	132.1	97.3	135.1	121.6	138.8	117.6	126.4	112.9	120.4	100.6	137.3
July	128.8	130.5	132.8	97.1	135.8	122.0	139.6	117.9	126.6	112.8	120.6	101.0	138.0
August	129.9	131.6	133.2	101.6	136.6	123.2	140.6	119.2	127.1	114.0	120.8	110.5	140.1
September	130.9	132.5	133.6	106.5	137.1	124.5	141.1	120.7	127.7	115.8	121.5	115.8	139.9
October	131.7	133.4	134.1	110.8	137.6	125.8	141.6	121.9	128.0	117.4	122.1	125.8	138.4
November	132.1	133.7	134.5	111.2	138.0	126.0	142.2	122.6	128.4	117.7	122.3	117.8	135.7
December	132.5	134.2	134.6	111.0	138.6	126.3	142.7	122.0	128.6	116.9	122.1	110.8	133.8
1991													
January	132.9	134.7	135.0	108.5	139.5	126.3	143.7	122.6	129.5	116.9	122.4	113.3	134.2
February	132.9	134.8	135.1	104.5	140.2	125.9	144.4	121.8	129.8	115.9	122.1	104.1	133.7
March	133.0	134.8	135.3	101.9	140.5	125.5	144.7	121.3	130.1	114.7	121.7	100.5	131.8
April	133.3	135.1	136.1	101.2	140.9	126.0	144.9	121.3	130.4	114.2	121.5	100.2	131.7
May	133.8	135.6	136.6	102.1	141.3	126.4	145.4	121.6	130.6	114.1	121.3	100.9	130.4
June	134.1	136.0	137.4	101.1	141.8	126.7	145.9	121.4	130.7	113.9	121.3	99.2	126.1
July	134.3	136.2	136.7	100.7	142.3	126.6	146.5	121.1	131.0	113.6	121.1	99.4	125.4
August	134.6	136.6	136.2	101.1	142.9	126.8	146.9	121.3	131.3	113.8	121.0	99.1	125.8
September	135.0	137.0	136.4	101.5	143.4	127.0	147.6	121.5	131.8	114.0	121.0	98.4	125.7
October	135.2	137.2	136.2	101.6	143.7	127.0	148.0	121.9	132.3	114.0	121.1	100.8	125.4
November	135.8	137.8	136.7	102.4	144.2	127.6	148.5	122.4	132.5	114.1	121.1	100.7	124.4
December	136.2	138.2	137.0	103.1	144.7	127.9	149.2	122.3	132.6	114.0	121.1	98.2	123.4
1992													
January	136.2	138.3	136.6	101.5	145.1	127.6	149.6	122.0	133.0	113.4	121.0	97.2	123.4
February	136.5	138.6	137.1	101.2	145.4	127.8	149.9	122.3	133.1	113.8	121.3	98.6	125.2
March	136.9	139.1	137.6	101.2	145.9	128.2	150.4	122.4	133.4	113.9	121.5	97.1	127.7
April	137.2	139.4	137.5	101.4	146.3	128.3	150.9	122.5	133.8	114.1	121.7	98.1	128.4
May	137.5	139.7	137.2	102.0	146.8	128.6	151.3	122.9	134.3	114.5	121.8	100.3	129.1
June	138.0	140.1	137.6	103.3	147.1	129.1	151.7	123.4	134.1	115.1	122.0	101.6	128.8
July	138.4	140.5	137.4	103.7	147.6	129.3	152.2	123.3	134.3	115.2	122.1	101.6	129.6
August	138.7	140.8	138.4	103.5	147.9	129.6	152.6	123.4	134.3	115.1	122.3	100.7	130.4
September	139.0	141.1	138.9	103.6	148.1	129.9	152.9	123.7	134.6	115.3	122.4	102.8	130.4
October	139.5	141.7	138.9	104.3	148.8	130.2	153.7	124.2	134.9	115.3	122.4	102.8	128.9
November	139.8	142.1	138.7	105.1	149.2	130.3	154.3	124.1	135.1	115.1	122.4	102.5	128.2
December	140.1	142.3	138.8	105.3	149.6	130.5	154.7	124.2	135.2	115.1	122.5	101.3	130.5

Table 8-1B. Summary Consumer and Producer Price Indexes: Historical Data, 1946–2010—*Continued*

(Seasonally adjusted.)

Year and month	Urban wage earners and clerical workers (CPI-W), all items	Consumer Price Index, 1982–1984 = 100						Producer Price Index, 1982 = 100					
		All urban consumers (CPI-U)						Finished goods		Intermediate materials, supplies, and components		Crude materials for further processing	
		All items	Food	Energy	All items less food and energy	Commodities	Services	Total	Less food and energy	Total	Less food and energy	Total	Crude nonfood less energy
1993													
January	140.5	142.8	139.1	105.0	150.1	130.7	155.3	124.4	135.6	115.4	122.9	101.7	135.0
February	140.8	143.1	139.6	104.3	150.6	131.1	155.6	124.7	135.9	115.9	123.5	101.2	136.8
March	141.0	143.3	139.6	104.9	150.8	131.1	156.0	125.0	136.1	116.3	123.8	101.7	137.0
April	141.4	143.8	140.0	104.9	151.4	131.4	156.7	125.7	136.5	116.6	124.0	103.2	138.4
May	141.8	144.2	141.0	104.3	151.8	131.6	157.3	125.7	136.6	116.3	123.7	105.6	140.3
June	142.0	144.3	140.6	103.9	152.1	131.3	157.8	125.2	136.4	116.3	123.7	103.8	140.3
July	142.1	144.5	140.6	103.4	152.3	131.3	158.1	125.1	136.6	116.3	123.7	101.6	142.1
August	142.4	144.8	141.1	103.4	152.8	131.6	158.6	123.9	134.9	116.2	123.9	100.8	140.4
September	142.5	145.0	141.4	103.0	152.9	131.3	159.0	124.1	134.9	116.3	124.0	101.2	140.7
October	143.2	145.6	142.0	105.3	153.4	132.2	159.4	124.2	135.0	116.4	124.0	103.7	142.6
November	143.4	146.0	142.3	104.4	153.9	132.4	159.9	124.4	135.3	116.5	124.3	103.0	144.1
December	143.7	146.3	142.8	103.7	154.3	132.4	160.5	124.4	135.7	116.2	124.5	101.7	145.3
1994													
January	143.8	146.3	142.9	102.8	154.5	132.3	160.8	124.8	136.3	116.5	124.7	103.8	148.3
February	144.0	146.7	142.7	104.1	154.8	132.4	161.4	125.0	136.3	116.9	124.9	102.1	151.0
March	144.3	147.1	142.7	104.3	155.3	132.5	162.0	125.1	136.4	117.1	125.1	103.8	151.5
April	144.5	147.2	143.0	103.7	155.5	132.6	162.2	125.1	136.6	117.1	125.3	103.8	150.7
May	144.8	147.5	143.3	102.8	155.9	132.9	162.4	125.1	137.0	117.2	125.6	102.2	149.7
June	145.3	147.9	143.8	103.1	156.4	133.5	162.8	125.2	137.2	117.8	126.3	102.7	151.2
July	145.9	148.4	144.6	104.5	156.7	134.1	163.1	125.7	137.3	118.3	126.7	101.7	155.5
August	146.5	149.0	145.1	106.7	157.1	134.7	163.8	126.2	137.6	119.1	127.4	101.6	158.8
September	146.8	149.3	145.3	106.1	157.5	134.8	164.1	125.9	137.7	119.6	128.4	99.7	160.5
October	146.9	149.4	145.3	105.7	157.8	134.8	164.5	125.5	137.4	120.1	129.3	98.6	161.3
November	147.3	149.8	145.6	106.1	158.2	135.0	165.0	126.1	137.6	121.0	130.3	99.8	166.6
December	147.6	150.1	146.8	105.9	158.3	135.4	165.2	126.6	137.9	121.5	131.0	101.1	169.9
1995													
January	148.0	150.5	146.7	105.7	159.0	135.4	166.0	126.9	138.4	122.8	132.6	102.1	174.5
February	148.4	150.9	147.3	105.8	159.4	135.6	166.5	127.2	138.7	123.7	133.7	102.9	176.5
March	148.6	151.2	147.1	105.5	159.9	135.6	167.1	127.4	139.0	124.3	134.3	102.3	177.8
April	149.2	151.8	148.1	105.6	160.4	136.2	167.7	127.7	139.3	125.0	135.2	103.7	180.2
May	149.5	152.1	148.2	105.8	160.7	136.4	168.1	127.8	139.7	125.2	135.5	102.4	179.6
June	149.8	152.4	148.3	106.7	161.1	136.6	168.5	127.8	139.8	125.5	135.7	103.0	179.5
July	149.9	152.6	148.5	105.8	161.4	136.6	168.9	128.0	140.2	125.6	136.1	101.6	176.4
August	150.2	152.9	148.6	105.6	161.8	136.8	169.3	127.9	140.2	125.6	136.1	99.7	173.4
September	150.4	153.1	149.1	104.1	162.2	136.8	169.7	128.1	140.2	125.5	136.2	102.0	170.9
October	150.8	153.5	149.5	104.4	162.7	137.1	170.3	128.4	141.0	125.4	135.8	101.9	166.6
November	150.9	153.7	149.6	103.4	163.0	137.0	170.7	128.7	141.3	125.2	135.5	104.1	163.6
December	151.3	153.9	149.9	104.4	163.1	137.3	170.9	129.3	141.5	125.4	135.2	106.5	162.3
1996													
January	152.0	154.7	150.4	106.9	163.7	138.2	171.5	129.7	141.5	125.5	134.8	109.8	162.6
February	152.3	155.0	150.8	107.1	164.0	138.3	172.0	129.7	141.6	125.0	134.4	111.6	162.1
March	152.9	155.5	151.4	108.3	164.4	139.0	172.4	130.5	141.6	125.3	134.1	109.8	158.2
April	153.4	156.1	152.0	111.2	164.6	139.6	172.8	130.9	141.6	125.7	133.8	114.2	156.7
May	153.8	156.4	151.9	112.0	165.0	139.7	173.4	130.9	142.0	126.2	134.0	114.6	157.6
June	154.0	156.7	152.9	110.3	165.4	139.8	173.8	131.3	142.2	125.8	133.9	112.2	154.6
July	154.3	157.0	153.4	110.1	165.7	139.8	174.4	131.2	142.2	125.5	133.6	114.6	152.2
August	154.5	157.2	153.9	109.7	166.0	139.8	174.9	131.6	142.3	125.6	133.6	115.3	152.5
September	154.9	157.7	154.6	109.8	166.5	140.3	175.4	131.7	142.2	126.1	134.0	112.7	153.5
October	155.4	158.2	155.5	110.5	166.8	140.8	175.8	132.4	142.3	126.0	133.7	111.9	153.3
November	155.9	158.7	156.1	111.8	167.2	141.4	176.3	132.5	142.1	125.8	133.7	115.7	153.0
December	156.3	159.1	156.3	113.9	167.4	141.7	176.7	132.9	142.3	126.4	133.9	122.5	153.6
1997													
January	156.6	159.4	155.9	115.2	167.8	141.8	177.3	133.0	142.5	126.6	134.1	127.5	156.2
February	156.9	159.7	156.5	115.0	168.1	142.1	177.6	132.7	142.4	126.5	134.1	116.6	157.6
March	156.9	159.8	156.6	113.0	168.4	141.8	178.0	132.6	142.6	126.1	134.2	107.5	158.7
April	157.0	159.9	156.5	111.0	168.9	141.6	178.4	131.8	142.6	125.6	134.1	107.8	155.8
May	157.0	159.9	156.6	108.8	169.2	141.4	178.7	131.5	142.4	125.4	134.2	109.1	157.0
June	157.3	160.2	156.9	110.0	169.4	141.5	179.2	131.3	142.4	125.4	134.2	106.2	156.9
July	157.4	160.4	157.2	109.1	169.7	141.4	179.7	130.9	142.2	125.1	134.2	106.2	155.7
August	157.8	160.8	157.7	110.9	169.8	141.9	179.9	131.4	142.3	125.3	134.3	106.8	156.8
September	158.2	161.2	158.0	112.4	170.2	142.2	180.4	131.6	142.6	125.5	134.3	108.4	155.8
October	158.4	161.5	158.3	111.8	170.6	142.2	180.9	131.9	142.6	125.4	134.3	113.4	156.7
November	158.6	161.7	158.6	111.4	170.8	142.1	181.4	131.6	142.4	125.6	134.4	115.8	156.5
December	158.6	161.8	158.7	109.8	171.2	142.1	181.7	131.4	142.3	125.4	134.4	108.8	154.2
1998													
January	158.8	162.0	159.5	107.5	171.6	142.0	182.1	130.7	142.4	124.6	134.3	102.8	150.4
February	158.7	162.0	159.4	105.1	171.9	141.8	182.3	130.6	142.6	124.2	134.2	100.8	150.1
March	158.7	162.0	159.7	103.3	172.2	141.4	182.8	130.5	143.3	123.7	134.1	99.5	148.7
April	158.8	162.2	159.7	102.4	172.5	141.3	183.3	130.7	143.4	123.6	134.0	100.6	147.3
May	159.3	162.6	160.3	103.2	172.9	141.7	183.7	130.5	143.5	123.5	133.9	99.6	146.2
June	159.5	162.8	160.2	103.6	173.2	141.8	184.0	130.4	143.5	123.1	133.6	97.1	145.9
July	159.8	163.2	160.6	103.3	173.5	142.1	184.3	130.7	143.8	123.0	133.5	97.4	143.4
August	160.0	163.4	161.0	102.1	174.0	142.2	184.7	130.4	143.8	122.7	133.4	93.6	139.4
September	160.1	163.5	161.1	101.3	174.2	142.0	185.1	130.4	144.0	122.3	133.1	91.4	137.6
October	160.5	163.9	162.0	101.5	174.4	142.3	185.5	130.9	144.2	122.2	132.7	93.9	134.0
November	160.7	164.1	162.2	101.1	174.8	142.2	186.0	130.8	144.3	122.0	132.5	93.6	131.6
December	161.1	164.4	162.4	100.1	175.4	142.5	186.4	131.3	145.8	121.3	132.2	90.2	129.4

Table 8-1B. Summary Consumer and Producer Price Indexes: Historical Data, 1946–2010—*Continued*

(Seasonally adjusted.)

Year and month	Urban wage earners and clerical workers (CPI-W), all items	Consumer Price Index, 1982–1984 = 100						Producer Price Index, 1982 = 100					
		All urban consumers (CPI-U)						Finished goods		Intermediate materials, supplies, and components		Crude materials for further processing	
		All items	Food	Energy	All items less food and energy	Commodities	Services	Total	Less food and energy	Total	Less food and energy	Total	Crude nonfood less energy
1999													
January	161.4	164.7	163.0	99.7	175.6	142.8	186.6	131.7	145.6	121.2	132.0	91.0	128.7
February	161.3	164.7	163.3	99.2	175.6	142.4	186.9	131.2	145.7	120.8	131.8	89.0	130.5
March	161.4	164.8	163.3	100.4	175.7	142.4	187.4	131.5	145.7	121.1	131.9	89.6	129.6
April	162.4	165.9	163.5	105.5	176.3	144.0	187.9	132.1	145.7	121.9	132.0	91.3	128.7
May	162.6	166.0	163.8	104.9	176.5	143.9	188.1	132.3	145.7	122.2	132.4	96.8	130.5
June	162.6	166.0	163.7	104.5	176.6	143.8	188.3	132.4	145.8	122.6	132.8	97.0	131.6
July	163.3	166.7	163.9	106.7	177.1	144.5	188.9	132.7	145.8	123.4	133.3	97.3	133.6
August	163.8	167.1	164.2	109.5	177.3	145.0	189.3	133.5	145.7	124.1	133.6	102.4	136.3
September	164.6	167.8	164.6	111.8	177.8	145.9	189.8	134.5	146.5	124.6	133.9	106.4	138.8
October	164.9	168.1	165.0	112.0	178.1	146.1	190.2	134.4	146.9	124.9	134.3	103.8	142.5
November	165.1	168.4	165.3	111.5	178.4	145.9	190.9	134.9	146.9	125.4	134.5	109.7	144.4
December	165.6	168.8	165.5	113.8	178.7	146.5	191.2	135.2	147.0	125.8	134.7	104.4	147.6
2000													
January	166.0	169.3	165.6	115.0	179.3	146.7	192.0	135.2	146.8	126.4	135.1	106.8	150.5
February	166.7	170.0	166.2	118.8	179.4	147.6	192.5	136.6	147.3	127.5	135.5	111.0	151.3
March	167.8	171.0	166.5	124.3	180.0	149.1	193.1	137.3	147.4	128.4	136.0	113.2	150.5
April	167.6	170.9	166.7	120.9	180.3	148.5	193.5	136.9	147.4	128.3	136.5	111.3	148.8
May	167.9	171.2	167.3	120.0	180.7	148.5	194.0	137.0	147.8	128.2	136.6	115.1	147.8
June	169.0	172.2	167.4	126.8	181.1	149.6	194.9	138.1	147.8	129.3	136.9	124.8	145.1
July	169.5	172.7	168.3	127.3	181.5	149.8	195.7	138.2	148.1	129.6	137.1	122.1	142.8
August	169.3	172.7	168.7	123.8	181.9	149.2	196.3	137.9	148.2	129.3	136.9	117.6	141.2
September	170.3	173.6	168.9	129.2	182.3	150.4	196.9	139.0	148.6	130.3	137.0	125.6	142.9
October	170.5	173.9	169.0	129.6	182.6	150.1	197.7	139.5	148.5	130.7	137.1	130.2	142.1
November	170.8	174.2	169.2	129.2	183.1	150.3	198.1	140.2	148.7	130.7	136.9	129.1	139.6
December	171.2	174.6	170.0	130.1	183.3	150.4	198.8	140.5	148.9	131.3	136.9	141.1	139.5
2001													
January	172.2	175.6	170.3	135.0	183.9	150.6	200.6	141.7	149.5	132.1	137.1	165.6	138.7
February	172.5	176.0	171.2	134.1	184.4	150.8	201.2	141.9	149.2	131.8	137.3	141.7	136.5
March	172.6	176.1	171.7	131.7	184.7	150.5	201.6	141.2	149.5	131.0	137.4	132.4	135.0
April	173.0	176.4	172.1	132.3	185.1	150.9	202.0	142.0	149.8	130.9	137.3	133.0	131.3
May	174.0	177.3	172.4	138.4	185.3	151.9	202.7	142.3	150.1	131.1	137.3	130.5	130.9
June	174.2	177.7	173.1	136.9	186.0	151.9	203.5	141.8	150.2	130.9	137.1	119.9	129.7
July	173.8	177.4	173.6	129.6	186.4	150.9	203.8	140.1	150.5	129.4	136.4	113.3	130.6
August	173.8	177.4	174.0	127.3	186.7	150.4	204.4	140.7	150.5	129.1	135.9	112.3	128.4
September	174.7	178.1	174.2	130.9	187.1	151.6	204.5	141.3	150.7	129.3	135.9	107.2	128.8
October	173.9	177.6	174.8	122.9	187.4	150.3	204.8	139.0	149.8	127.6	135.4	97.4	126.5
November	173.7	177.5	174.9	116.9	188.1	149.2	205.6	138.5	150.2	127.0	135.1	102.7	126.2
December	173.4	177.4	174.7	113.9	188.4	148.3	206.1	138.0	150.4	126.1	134.8	95.5	125.7
2002													
January	173.7	177.7	175.3	114.2	188.7	148.3	206.8	137.7	150.0	125.7	134.7	99.8	126.2
February	173.9	178.0	175.7	113.5	189.1	148.3	207.5	138.0	150.1	125.5	134.6	98.4	127.5
March	174.5	178.5	176.1	117.6	189.2	149.0	207.9	138.8	150.0	126.4	135.0	103.8	128.1
April	175.4	179.3	176.4	121.5	189.7	150.0	208.5	138.7	150.3	127.2	135.3	108.1	130.8
May	175.5	179.5	175.8	121.9	190.0	149.7	209.0	138.4	150.2	127.1	135.3	109.0	134.2
June	175.7	179.6	175.9	121.6	190.2	149.7	209.3	138.8	150.5	127.3	135.6	105.1	138.2
July	176.1	180.0	176.1	122.4	190.5	149.9	209.9	138.6	150.0	127.7	136.0	106.5	140.8
August	176.6	180.5	176.1	123.1	191.1	150.2	210.6	138.7	149.9	128.0	136.2	108.3	140.0
September	176.8	180.8	176.5	123.7	191.3	150.2	211.1	139.2	150.3	128.9	136.5	110.8	140.2
October	177.2	181.2	176.4	126.9	191.5	150.5	211.7	140.0	150.5	129.8	136.7	112.6	140.0
November	177.5	181.5	176.9	126.7	191.9	150.5	212.4	140.0	150.3	129.9	136.8	116.6	141.0
December	177.7	181.8	177.1	127.1	192.1	150.3	213.0	139.7	149.5	130.0	136.7	118.9	141.3
2003													
January	178.6	182.6	177.1	133.5	192.4	151.3	213.7	141.1	149.8	131.4	137.2	128.0	143.3
February	179.7	183.6	178.1	140.8	192.5	152.7	214.2	142.7	149.9	133.8	138.1	134.3	148.1
March	180.1	183.9	178.4	143.9	192.5	152.6	215.0	144.0	150.7	136.3	138.6	152.2	147.5
April	179.2	183.2	178.5	136.5	192.5	151.1	215.1	142.2	149.9	133.1	138.3	128.2	145.9
May	178.7	182.9	178.8	129.4	192.9	149.4	216.0	141.9	150.1	132.4	138.4	129.9	146.0
June	178.9	183.1	179.7	129.8	193.0	149.7	216.2	142.7	150.1	133.1	138.4	135.5	145.7
July	179.4	183.7	179.8	132.2	193.4	150.3	216.8	142.8	150.3	133.3	138.2	131.9	148.5
August	180.3	184.5	180.5	137.8	193.6	151.4	217.2	143.7	150.5	133.9	138.4	130.8	152.1
September	180.9	185.1	180.9	142.9	193.7	152.1	217.8	144.0	150.4	133.8	138.8	134.4	156.2
October	180.6	184.9	181.6	137.8	194.0	151.1	218.4	144.8	151.1	134.2	139.1	138.2	160.2
November	180.6	185.0	182.6	136.9	194.0	151.1	218.6	144.6	151.0	134.2	139.3	137.9	165.6
December	181.0	185.5	183.5	138.8	194.2	151.6	219.0	145.1	151.0	135.0	139.6	142.4	171.0
2004													
January	181.9	186.3	183.4	143.9	194.6	152.5	219.7	145.9	151.4	136.6	140.5	148.7	179.7
February	182.4	186.7	183.9	145.8	194.9	153.1	220.1	145.8	151.3	137.8	141.8	150.8	190.0
March	182.7	187.1	184.2	145.1	195.5	153.3	220.8	146.2	151.8	138.4	142.9	153.2	195.0
April	182.8	187.4	184.6	143.4	195.9	153.0	221.4	147.2	151.9	140.1	144.6	156.2	187.1
May	183.8	188.2	186.1	147.6	196.2	154.2	221.9	148.4	152.3	141.7	145.7	160.6	177.6
June	184.4	188.9	186.4	151.5	196.6	154.9	222.7	148.4	152.8	142.2	146.2	161.5	176.3
July	184.6	189.1	186.8	151.1	196.8	154.6	223.2	148.2	152.5	142.9	146.9	161.3	195.7
August	184.7	189.2	187.0	151.5	196.9	154.4	223.7	148.6	152.9	144.4	148.4	161.7	201.6
September	185.3	189.8	186.9	152.9	197.5	154.9	224.2	148.8	153.2	144.8	149.6	154.0	198.3
October	186.4	190.8	187.8	158.6	197.9	156.7	224.6	151.2	153.7	146.6	150.2	161.0	204.6
November	187.4	191.7	188.4	163.8	198.3	157.8	225.4	152.1	154.1	147.9	150.7	172.7	208.9
December	187.4	191.7	188.4	162.3	198.6	157.4	225.8	151.4	154.5	147.7	151.3	167.2	206.0

Table 8-1B. Summary Consumer and Producer Price Indexes: Historical Data, 1946–2010—*Continued*

(Seasonally adjusted.)

Year and month	Urban wage earners and clerical workers (CPI-W), all items	Consumer Price Index, 1982–1984 = 100						Producer Price Index, 1982 = 100					
		All urban consumers (CPI-U)						Finished goods		Intermediate materials, supplies, and components		Crude materials for further processing	
		All items	Food	Energy	All items less food and energy	Commodities	Services	Total	Less food and energy	Total	Less food and energy	Total	Crude nonfood less energy
2005													
January	187.2	191.6	188.7	157.2	199.0	156.8	226.2	151.9	155.4	148.5	152.4	164.2	203.7
February	188.0	192.4	188.6	161.8	199.4	157.5	226.9	152.7	155.3	149.5	153.2	162.9	200.2
March	188.6	193.1	189.1	163.5	200.1	157.9	228.0	153.7	155.6	150.7	153.8	170.5	199.6
April	189.3	193.7	190.4	166.7	200.2	158.6	228.5	154.2	156.0	151.3	153.9	175.0	203.5
May	189.1	193.6	190.6	163.3	200.5	158.1	228.9	153.9	156.4	150.6	153.5	169.1	196.6
June	189.3	193.7	190.5	163.7	200.6	158.0	229.1	153.9	156.2	151.1	153.3	165.5	188.9
July	190.6	194.9	190.9	172.8	200.9	159.6	229.9	155.0	156.8	152.3	153.5	174.4	190.5
August	192.0	196.1	191.1	183.5	201.1	161.5	230.4	156.3	156.9	153.2	153.4	181.5	200.9
September	195.1	198.8	191.5	208.2	201.3	166.0	231.4	158.8	157.1	157.2	155.0	200.3	211.3
October	195.2	199.1	192.0	205.9	202.0	164.8	233.1	160.5	156.8	162.3	157.2	212.7	207.7
November	193.7	198.1	192.6	191.0	202.5	161.8	234.2	158.7	156.8	160.3	157.9	209.9	214.0
December	193.7	198.1	192.9	187.6	202.8	161.5	234.4	159.6	156.8	160.2	158.5	202.0	216.7
2006													
January	195.1	199.3	193.6	196.6	203.2	162.9	235.5	160.5	157.5	162.4	159.9	203.2	216.7
February	195.0	199.4	193.7	194.1	203.6	162.5	235.9	158.7	158.0	161.6	160.4	186.6	224.0
March	195.3	199.7	194.0	192.0	204.3	162.6	236.5	159.3	158.4	161.5	161.1	179.6	227.1
April	196.4	200.7	193.8	198.5	204.8	164.1	237.1	160.6	158.5	163.0	162.0	182.9	238.2
May	197.0	201.3	194.1	199.8	205.4	164.6	237.8	160.6	158.9	164.4	163.7	184.4	259.1
June	197.4	201.8	194.7	199.8	205.9	164.8	238.5	161.4	159.0	165.2	164.7	178.5	255.3
July	198.6	202.9	195.2	207.9	206.3	166.4	239.2	161.0	158.1	165.5	165.6	180.5	259.5
August	199.5	203.8	195.7	211.9	206.8	167.2	239.9	162.1	158.7	166.5	166.3	187.0	251.7
September	198.3	202.8	196.3	198.1	207.2	164.6	240.7	160.2	159.2	164.7	166.2	182.7	255.2
October	197.1	201.9	196.9	184.1	207.6	162.5	241.0	158.7	158.5	163.0	166.2	168.6	249.7
November	197.2	202.0	197.0	184.1	207.8	162.0	241.7	160.0	159.9	163.8	165.5	189.4	249.8
December	198.4	203.1	197.1	192.7	208.1	163.4	242.4	161.1	160.0	164.7	165.6	195.4	253.7
2007													
January	198.6	203.4	198.4	190.3	208.6	163.3	243.2	160.9	160.2	164.1	165.6	184.9	257.2
February	199.4	204.2	199.7	192.3	209.1	164.1	244.1	162.7	160.9	165.3	165.6	201.6	265.9
March	200.7	205.3	200.4	200.2	209.4	165.6	244.7	164.1	160.9	166.7	166.3	203.6	282.7
April	201.3	205.9	201.0	203.3	209.7	166.2	245.3	165.3	161.0	168.3	167.7	204.0	285.1
May	202.3	206.8	201.7	208.6	210.1	167.3	245.9	166.0	161.4	169.7	168.6	204.8	280.3
June	202.7	207.2	202.6	209.8	210.4	167.5	246.6	166.1	161.7	170.4	169.0	205.9	280.7
July	203.0	207.6	203.2	209.6	210.8	167.8	247.1	167.2	162.1	171.8	169.6	203.7	283.0
August	203.0	207.7	204.0	206.4	211.1	167.5	247.5	166.0	162.3	170.1	168.9	198.6	284.2
September	204.0	208.5	205.0	210.7	211.6	168.5	248.2	167.6	162.3	171.4	169.0	203.2	290.8
October	204.7	209.2	205.7	212.4	212.1	169.0	249.1	169.3	162.9	172.7	169.7	214.4	295.0
November	206.5	210.8	206.5	223.8	212.7	171.5	249.8	172.4	163.4	176.7	171.0	229.5	293.4
December	207.1	211.4	206.9	225.6	213.2	172.0	250.5	171.7	163.4	176.9	171.2	235.6	294.7
2008													
January	207.9	212.2	208.2	227.1	213.8	172.7	251.4	173.4	164.1	179.2	172.6	243.7	309.5
February	208.4	212.6	208.9	229.2	213.9	173.0	251.9	173.8	164.8	180.7	173.8	253.9	320.0
March	209.2	213.4	209.3	233.3	214.4	173.7	252.9	175.2	165.0	184.6	175.9	264.6	329.5
April	209.8	214.0	211.2	235.0	214.6	174.1	253.6	175.9	165.8	186.5	178.3	273.1	362.1
May	211.1	215.2	212.0	243.9	214.9	175.5	254.6	178.2	166.3	191.2	181.2	287.8	369.0
June	213.7	217.5	213.3	262.0	215.4	178.8	255.8	181.2	166.5	195.3	183.8	294.4	372.4
July	215.5	219.1	215.4	271.6	216.0	180.7	257.0	183.6	167.5	200.9	187.5	302.6	384.7
August	215.0	218.7	216.5	262.8	216.4	179.6	257.5	182.1	168.3	197.9	188.7	269.6	373.5
September	215.1	218.9	217.8	260.1	216.7	179.8	257.5	182.7	168.9	197.9	188.9	254.3	338.5
October	212.7	217.0	218.7	238.0	216.8	175.8	257.7	178.2	170.4	189.5	185.0	216.0	278.6
November	207.9	213.1	219.1	194.5	216.9	168.0	257.9	172.8	170.3	179.6	180.5	187.0	226.9
December	205.9	211.4	219.1	176.8	216.9	164.5	258.1	169.7	170.7	172.4	176.2	176.8	222.7
2009													
January	206.5	212.0	219.2	179.1	217.3	165.2	258.6	171.2	171.0	172.1	174.8	173.8	225.6
February	207.4	212.8	219.0	185.1	217.8	166.7	258.7	170.7	171.1	170.5	173.5	164.2	224.4
March	207.1	212.6	218.5	179.1	218.3	166.2	258.8	169.2	171.4	168.0	172.7	161.0	221.1
April	207.4	212.7	218.2	177.4	218.7	166.6	258.7	170.0	171.5	168.2	171.8	162.9	221.6
May	207.8	213.0	217.7	179.5	218.9	167.3	258.5	170.2	171.4	169.1	171.6	168.2	232.2
June	209.9	214.7	217.8	196.2	219.2	170.6	258.6	173.5	172.0	171.3	171.9	175.4	240.6
July	210.0	214.7	217.3	195.5	219.3	170.6	258.6	171.5	171.6	170.7	172.4	168.0	246.8
August	210.9	215.5	217.4	201.7	219.5	171.5	259.2	174.2	172.1	173.6	173.3	175.9	264.0
September	211.3	215.9	217.3	202.9	219.9	172.0	259.5	173.8	171.9	174.0	174.3	174.0	269.5
October	211.9	216.5	217.5	204.6	220.5	172.7	260.0	174.5	171.6	174.8	174.6	187.9	274.4
November	212.7	217.1	217.6	209.8	220.6	173.7	260.2	176.8	172.2	176.5	175.0	195.7	274.6
December	213.0	217.3	218.0	210.2	220.8	174.0	260.4	177.5	172.2	177.7	176.0	201.9	287.8
2010													
January	213.4	217.5	218.4	213.7	220.5	174.8	259.9	179.3	172.7	180.5	177.0	219.0	305.2
February	213.3	217.4	218.5	211.7	220.6	174.5	260.0	178.2	172.7	180.3	178.4	215.7	305.8
March	213.3	217.4	218.9	210.6	220.8	174.2	260.4	179.1	173.0	181.1	179.6	213.4	321.4
April	213.2	217.4	219.1	208.8	220.9	173.8	260.7	178.9	173.1	182.5	181.5	208.6	330.7
May	212.9	217.2	219.3	204.9	221.0	173.2	260.9	178.5	173.6	182.9	181.9	204.5	326.5
June	212.9	217.2	219.2	202.9	221.3	173.0	261.2	178.2	173.8	181.9	181.1	199.5	315.3
July	213.5	217.6	219.2	206.4	221.5	173.6	261.4	178.6	174.1	181.4	180.4	203.2	313.0
August	213.9	218.1	219.5	209.3	221.6	174.2	261.6	179.9	174.4	182.5	180.6	209.0	324.7
September	214.3	218.4	220.3	210.7	221.7	174.6	261.8	180.6	174.7	183.4	181.1	210.1	336.4
October	215.1	219.0	220.6	216.7	221.8	175.7	262.0	182.0	174.4	185.6	182.1	220.2	348.4
November	215.5	219.4	221.1	218.4	222.1	176.2	262.4	182.7	174.3	186.9	183.2	221.1	357.9
December[1]	216.6	220.4	221.4	227.3	222.2	177.7	262.8	184.4	174.7	189.2	184.2	235.0	367.9

[1]Data are preliminary.

Table 8-1C. Consumer and Producer Price Indexes: Historical Data, 1913–1949

(Not seasonally adjusted.)

Year and month	Consumer price indexes, 1982–1984 =100				Producer Price Index, 1982 = 100			
	All urban consumers (CPI-U)		Urban wage earners and clerical workers (CPI-W)		All commodities		Farm products	Industrial commodities
	Index	Percent change	Index	Percent change	Index	Percent change		
1913	9.9	. . .	10.0	. . .	12.0	. . .	18.0	11.9
1914	10.0	1.0	10.1	1.0	11.8	-1.7	17.9	11.3
1915	10.1	1.0	10.2	1.0	12.0	1.7	18.0	11.6
1916	10.9	7.9	11.0	7.8	14.7	22.5	21.3	15.0
1917	12.8	17.4	12.9	17.3	20.2	37.4	32.6	19.5
1918	15.1	18.0	15.1	17.1	22.6	11.9	37.4	21.1
1919	17.3	14.6	17.4	15.2	23.9	5.8	39.8	22.0
1920	20.0	15.6	20.1	15.5	26.6	11.3	38.0	27.4
1921	17.9	-10.5	18.0	-10.4	16.8	-36.8	22.3	17.8
1922	16.8	-6.1	16.9	-6.1	16.7	-0.6	23.7	17.4
1923	17.1	1.8	17.2	1.8	17.3	3.6	24.9	17.8
1924	17.1	0.0	17.2	0.0	16.9	-2.3	25.2	17.0
1925	17.5	2.3	17.6	2.3	17.8	5.3	27.7	17.5
1926	17.7	1.1	17.8	1.1	17.2	-3.4	25.3	17.0
1927	17.4	-1.7	17.5	-1.7	16.5	-4.1	25.1	16.0
1928	17.1	-1.7	17.2	-1.7	16.7	1.2	26.7	15.8
1929	17.1	0.0	17.2	0.0	16.4	-1.8	26.4	15.6
1930	16.7	-2.3	16.8	-2.3	14.9	-9.1	22.4	14.5
1931	15.2	-9.0	15.3	-8.9	12.6	-15.4	16.4	12.8
1932	13.7	-9.9	13.7	-10.5	11.2	-11.1	12.2	11.9
1933	13.0	-5.1	13.0	-5.1	11.4	1.8	13.0	12.1
1934	13.4	3.1	13.5	3.8	12.9	13.2	16.5	13.3
1935	13.7	2.2	13.8	2.2	13.8	7.0	19.8	13.3
1936	13.9	1.5	13.9	0.7	13.9	0.7	20.4	13.5
1937	14.4	3.6	14.4	3.6	14.9	7.2	21.8	14.5
1938	14.1	-2.1	14.2	-1.4	13.5	-9.4	17.3	13.9
1939	13.9	-1.4	14.0	-1.4	13.3	-1.5	16.5	13.9
1940	14.0	0.7	14.1	0.7	13.5	1.5	17.1	14.1
1941	14.7	5.0	14.8	5.0	15.1	11.9	20.8	15.1
1942	16.3	10.9	16.4	10.8	17.0	12.6	26.7	16.2
1943	17.3	6.1	17.4	6.1	17.8	4.7	30.9	16.5
1944	17.6	1.7	17.7	1.7	17.9	0.6	31.2	16.7
1945	18.0	2.3	18.1	2.3	18.2	1.7	32.4	17.0
1946	19.5	8.3	19.6	8.3	20.8	14.3	37.5	18.6
1947	22.3	14.4	22.5	14.8	25.6	23.1	45.1	22.7
1948	24.1	8.1	24.2	7.6	27.7	8.2	48.5	24.6
1949	23.8	-1.2	24.0	-0.8	26.3	-5.1	41.9	24.1
1913								
January	9.8	. . .	9.9	. . .	12.1	. . .	17.6	12.3
February	9.8	0.0	9.8	-1.0	12.0	-0.8	17.5	12.2
March	9.8	0.0	9.8	0.0	12.0	0.0	17.6	12.1
April	9.8	0.0	9.9	1.0	12.0	0.0	17.5	12.0
May	9.7	-1.0	9.8	-1.0	11.9	-0.8	17.4	11.9
June	9.8	1.0	9.8	0.0	11.9	0.0	17.6	11.8
July	9.9	1.0	9.9	1.0	12.0	0.8	18.1	11.8
August	9.9	0.0	10.0	1.0	12.0	0.0	18.2	11.7
September	10.0	1.0	10.0	0.0	12.2	1.7	18.8	11.8
October	10.0	0.0	10.1	1.0	12.2	0.0	18.8	11.8
November	10.1	1.0	10.1	0.0	12.1	-0.8	18.9	11.7
December	10.0	-1.0	10.1	0.0	11.9	-1.7	18.5	11.6
1914								
January	10.0	0.0	10.1	0.0	11.8	-0.8	18.4	11.5
February	9.9	-1.0	10.0	-1.0	11.8	0.0	18.3	11.5
March	9.9	0.0	10.0	0.0	11.7	-0.8	18.2	11.5
April	9.8	-1.0	9.9	-1.0	11.7	0.0	18.0	11.5
May	9.9	1.0	9.9	0.0	11.6	-0.9	18.0	11.4
June	9.9	0.0	10.0	1.0	11.6	0.0	18.1	11.3
July	10.0	1.0	10.1	1.0	11.6	0.0	18.0	11.2
August	10.2	2.0	10.2	1.0	12.0	3.4	18.3	11.2
September	10.2	0.0	10.3	1.0	12.1	0.8	17.9	11.3
October	10.1	-1.0	10.2	-1.0	11.7	-3.3	17.2	11.0
November	10.2	1.0	10.2	0.0	11.7	0.0	17.6	11.0
December	10.1	-1.0	10.2	0.0	11.6	-0.9	17.4	11.0
1915								
January	10.1	0.0	10.2	0.0	11.8	1.7	18.1	11.1
February	10.0	-1.0	10.1	-1.0	11.8	0.0	18.4	11.0
March	9.9	-1.0	10.0	-1.0	11.8	0.0	17.9	11.0
April	10.0	1.0	10.1	1.0	11.8	0.0	18.2	11.1
May	10.1	1.0	10.1	0.0	11.9	0.8	18.2	11.2
June	10.1	0.0	10.2	1.0	11.8	-0.8	17.7	11.4
July	10.1	0.0	10.2	0.0	11.9	0.8	18.1	11.5
August	10.1	0.0	10.2	0.0	11.8	-0.8	17.9	11.5
September	10.1	0.0	10.2	0.0	11.8	0.0	17.5	11.7
October	10.2	1.0	10.3	1.0	12.1	2.5	18.1	11.9
November	10.3	1.0	10.4	1.0	12.3	1.7	18.0	12.3
December	10.3	0.0	10.4	0.0	12.8	4.1	18.4	12.9

. . . = Not available.

Table 8-1C. Consumer and Producer Price Indexes: Historical Data, 1913–1949—*Continued*

(Not seasonally adjusted.)

Year and month	Consumer price indexes, 1982–1984 =100				Producer Price Index, 1982 = 100			
	All urban consumers (CPI-U)		Urban wage earners and clerical workers (CPI-W)		All commodities		Farm products	Industrial commodities
	Index	Percent change	Index	Percent change	Index	Percent change		
1916								
January	10.4	1.0	10.5	1.0	13.3	3.9	19.4	13.6
February	10.4	0.0	10.5	0.0	13.5	1.5	19.4	14.0
March	10.5	1.0	10.6	1.0	13.9	3.0	19.4	14.4
April	10.6	1.0	10.7	0.9	14.1	1.4	19.6	14.6
May	10.7	0.9	10.7	0.0	14.2	0.7	19.8	14.7
June	10.8	0.9	10.9	1.9	14.3	0.7	19.7	14.8
July	10.8	0.0	10.9	0.0	14.4	0.7	20.3	14.6
August	10.9	0.9	11.0	0.9	14.7	2.1	21.7	14.6
September	11.1	1.8	11.2	1.8	15.0	2.0	22.6	14.8
October	11.3	1.8	11.3	0.9	15.7	4.7	23.7	15.5
November	11.5	1.8	11.5	1.8	16.8	7.0	25.3	16.8
December	11.6	0.9	11.6	0.9	17.1	1.8	25.0	17.7
1917								
January	11.7	0.9	11.8	1.7	17.6	2.9	26.2	18.3
February	12.0	2.6	12.0	1.7	18.0	2.3	27.2	18.6
March	12.0	0.0	12.1	0.8	18.5	2.8	28.6	18.8
April	12.6	5.0	12.6	4.1	19.7	6.5	31.6	19.0
May	12.8	1.6	12.9	2.4	20.8	5.6	33.6	19.8
June	13.0	1.6	13.0	0.8	21.0	1.0	33.8	20.4
July	12.8	-1.5	12.9	-0.8	21.2	1.0	34.0	20.7
August	13.0	1.6	13.1	1.6	21.5	1.4	34.6	20.7
September	13.3	2.3	13.3	1.5	21.3	-0.9	34.3	20.1
October	13.5	1.5	13.6	2.3	21.1	-0.9	35.2	19.1
November	13.5	0.0	13.6	0.0	21.2	0.5	36.0	19.2
December	13.7	1.5	13.8	1.5	21.2	0.0	35.6	19.5
1918								
January	14.0	2.2	14.0	1.4	21.6	1.9	37.0	19.9
February	14.1	0.7	14.2	1.4	21.1	-2.3	37.1	19.0
March	14.0	-0.7	14.1	-0.7	21.8	3.3	37.3	20.2
April	14.2	1.4	14.3	1.4	22.1	1.4	36.6	20.7
May	14.5	2.1	14.5	1.4	22.1	0.0	35.4	21.0
June	14.7	1.4	14.8	2.1	22.2	0.5	35.4	21.3
July	15.1	2.7	15.2	2.7	22.7	2.3	37.0	21.5
August	15.4	2.0	15.4	1.3	23.2	2.2	38.6	21.7
September	15.7	1.9	15.8	2.6	23.7	2.2	39.6	22.1
October	16.0	1.9	16.1	1.9	23.5	-0.8	38.2	22.1
November	16.3	1.9	16.3	1.2	23.5	0.0	38.0	22.1
December	16.5	1.2	16.6	1.8	23.5	0.0	38.1	21.8
1919								
January	16.5	0.0	16.6	0.0	23.2	-1.3	38.9	21.1
February	16.2	-1.8	16.2	-2.4	22.4	-3.4	37.5	20.6
March	16.4	1.2	16.5	1.9	22.6	0.9	38.5	20.1
April	16.7	1.8	16.8	1.8	22.9	1.3	40.0	20.0
May	16.9	1.2	17.0	1.2	23.3	1.7	40.9	20.2
June	16.9	0.0	17.0	0.0	23.4	0.4	39.6	21.1
July	17.4	3.0	17.5	2.9	24.3	3.8	41.5	22.1
August	17.7	1.7	17.8	1.7	24.9	2.5	41.3	23.1
September	17.8	0.6	17.9	0.6	24.3	-2.4	38.7	23.2
October	18.1	1.7	18.2	1.7	24.4	0.4	38.5	23.5
November	18.5	2.2	18.6	2.2	24.9	2.0	40.3	23.8
December	18.9	2.2	19.0	2.2	26.0	4.4	41.8	24.7
1920								
January	19.3	2.1	19.4	2.1	27.2	4.6	43.0	26.1
February	19.5	1.0	19.6	1.0	27.1	-0.4	41.2	27.1
March	19.7	1.0	19.8	1.0	27.3	0.7	41.5	27.7
April	20.3	3.0	20.4	3.0	28.5	4.4	42.5	28.7
May	20.6	1.5	20.7	1.5	28.8	1.1	42.8	29.0
June	20.9	1.5	21.0	1.4	28.7	-0.3	42.3	29.0
July	20.8	-0.5	20.9	-0.5	28.6	-0.3	40.5	29.5
August	20.3	-2.4	20.4	-2.4	27.8	-2.8	37.8	29.7
September	20.0	-1.5	20.1	-1.5	26.8	-3.6	36.4	28.5
October	19.9	-0.5	20.0	-0.5	24.9	-7.1	32.2	26.9
November	19.8	-0.5	19.9	-0.5	23.0	-7.6	30.0	24.5
December	19.4	-2.0	19.5	-2.0	20.8	-9.6	26.4	22.7
1921								
January	19.0	-2.1	19.1	-2.1	19.6	-5.8	25.6	21.1
February	18.4	-3.2	18.5	-3.1	18.1	-7.7	23.4	19.4
March	18.3	-0.5	18.4	-0.5	17.7	-2.2	22.7	18.7
April	18.1	-1.1	18.2	-1.1	17.0	-4.0	20.9	18.4
May	17.7	-2.2	17.8	-2.2	16.6	-2.4	21.0	17.9
June	17.6	-0.6	17.7	-0.6	16.1	-3.0	20.3	17.4
July	17.7	0.6	17.8	0.6	16.1	0.0	21.8	16.9
August	17.7	0.0	17.8	0.0	16.1	0.0	22.5	16.5
September	17.5	-1.1	17.6	-1.1	16.1	0.0	22.7	16.5
October	17.5	0.0	17.6	0.0	16.2	0.6	22.7	17.0
November	17.4	-0.6	17.5	-0.6	16.2	0.0	22.1	17.3
December	17.3	-0.6	17.4	-0.6	16.0	-1.2	22.2	17.0

Table 8-1C. Consumer and Producer Price Indexes: Historical Data, 1913–1949—*Continued*

(Not seasonally adjusted.)

Year and month	Consumer price indexes, 1982–1984 =100				Producer Price Index, 1982 = 100			
	All urban consumers (CPI-U)		Urban wage earners and clerical workers (CPI-W)		All commodities		Farm products	Industrial commodities
	Index	Percent change	Index	Percent change	Index	Percent change		
1922								
January	16.9	-2.3	17.0	-2.3	15.7	-1.9	22.2	16.7
February	16.9	0.0	17.0	0.0	16.0	1.9	24.0	16.6
March	16.7	-1.2	16.8	-1.2	16.0	0.0	23.6	16.5
April	16.7	0.0	16.8	0.0	16.1	0.6	23.4	16.6
May	16.7	0.0	16.8	0.0	16.6	3.1	23.8	17.4
June	16.7	0.0	16.8	0.0	16.6	0.0	23.4	17.4
July	16.8	0.6	16.9	0.6	17.1	3.0	24.1	18.1
August	16.6	-1.2	16.7	-1.2	17.0	-0.6	23.0	18.2
September	16.6	0.0	16.7	0.0	17.1	0.6	23.3	18.2
October	16.7	0.6	16.8	0.6	17.2	0.6	23.8	17.9
November	16.8	0.6	16.9	0.6	17.3	0.6	24.7	17.7
December	16.9	0.6	17.0	0.6	17.3	0.0	25.0	17.7
1923								
January	16.8	-0.6	16.9	-0.6	17.6	1.7	25.1	18.2
February	16.8	0.0	16.9	0.0	17.8	1.1	25.3	18.6
March	16.8	0.0	16.9	0.0	18.0	1.1	25.3	18.8
April	16.9	0.6	17.0	0.6	17.9	-0.6	24.8	18.7
May	16.9	0.0	17.0	0.0	17.5	-2.2	24.4	18.3
June	17.0	0.6	17.1	0.6	17.3	-1.1	24.2	17.9
July	17.2	1.2	17.3	1.2	17.0	-1.7	23.7	17.6
August	17.1	-0.6	17.2	-0.6	16.9	-0.6	24.2	17.4
September	17.2	0.6	17.3	0.6	17.2	1.8	25.3	17.3
October	17.3	0.6	17.4	0.6	17.1	-0.6	25.4	17.1
November	17.3	0.0	17.4	0.0	17.0	-0.6	25.7	16.9
December	17.3	0.0	17.4	0.0	16.9	-0.6	25.5	16.9
1924								
January	17.3	0.0	17.4	0.0	17.2	1.8	25.6	17.4
February	17.2	-0.6	17.3	-0.6	17.2	0.0	25.0	17.6
March	17.1	-0.6	17.2	-0.6	17.0	-1.2	24.2	17.5
April	17.0	-0.6	17.1	-0.6	16.7	-1.8	24.6	17.3
May	17.0	0.0	17.1	0.0	16.5	-1.2	24.0	17.0
June	17.0	0.0	17.1	0.0	16.4	-0.6	23.8	16.7
July	17.1	0.6	17.2	0.6	16.5	0.6	24.9	16.6
August	17.0	-0.6	17.1	-0.6	16.7	1.2	25.7	16.6
September	17.1	0.6	17.2	0.6	16.7	0.0	25.3	16.6
October	17.2	0.6	17.3	0.6	16.9	1.2	26.0	16.6
November	17.2	0.0	17.3	0.0	17.1	1.2	26.2	16.8
December	17.3	0.6	17.4	0.6	17.5	2.3	27.3	17.1
1925								
January	17.3	0.0	17.4	0.0	17.7	1.1	28.7	17.3
February	17.2	-0.6	17.3	-0.6	17.9	1.1	28.4	17.7
March	17.3	0.6	17.4	0.6	17.9	0.0	28.5	17.5
April	17.2	-0.6	17.3	-0.6	17.5	-2.2	27.1	17.2
May	17.3	0.6	17.4	0.6	17.5	0.0	27.1	17.3
June	17.5	1.2	17.6	1.1	17.7	1.1	27.6	17.5
July	17.7	1.1	17.8	1.1	18.0	1.7	28.3	17.6
August	17.7	0.0	17.8	0.0	17.9	-0.6	28.1	17.4
September	17.7	0.0	17.8	0.0	17.8	-0.6	27.7	17.4
October	17.7	0.0	17.8	0.0	17.8	0.0	27.0	17.5
November	18.0	1.7	18.1	1.7	18.0	1.1	27.3	17.6
December	17.9	-0.6	18.0	-0.6	17.8	-1.1	26.6	17.6
1926								
January	17.9	0.0	18.0	0.0	17.8	0.0	27.1	17.5
February	17.9	0.0	18.0	0.0	17.6	-1.1	26.5	17.3
March	17.8	-0.6	17.9	-0.6	17.3	-1.7	25.7	17.1
April	17.9	0.6	18.0	0.6	17.3	0.0	26.0	17.0
May	17.8	-0.6	17.9	-0.6	17.3	0.0	25.8	17.0
June	17.7	-0.6	17.8	-0.6	17.3	0.0	25.5	17.0
July	17.5	-1.1	17.6	-1.1	17.1	-1.2	24.9	16.9
August	17.4	-0.6	17.5	-0.6	17.1	0.0	24.6	16.9
September	17.5	0.6	17.6	0.6	17.2	0.6	25.1	16.9
October	17.6	0.6	17.7	0.6	17.1	-0.6	24.7	16.9
November	17.7	0.6	17.8	0.6	17.0	-0.6	23.9	16.9
December	17.7	0.0	17.8	0.0	16.9	-0.6	24.0	16.7
1927								
January	17.5	-1.1	17.6	-1.1	16.4	-3.0	24.3	16.4
February	17.4	-0.6	17.5	-0.6	16.6	1.2	24.1	16.3
March	17.3	-0.6	17.4	-0.6	16.5	-0.6	23.8	16.1
April	17.3	0.0	17.4	0.0	16.3	-1.2	23.8	15.9
May	17.4	0.6	17.5	0.6	16.2	-0.6	24.3	15.9
June	17.6	1.1	17.7	1.1	16.2	0.0	24.3	15.9
July	17.3	-1.7	17.4	-1.7	16.2	0.0	24.6	15.9
August	17.2	-0.6	17.3	-0.6	16.4	1.2	25.8	15.9
September	17.3	0.6	17.4	0.6	16.6	1.2	26.7	16.0
October	17.4	0.6	17.5	0.6	16.7	0.6	26.5	15.9
November	17.3	-0.6	17.4	-0.6	16.6	-0.6	26.3	15.8
December	17.3	0.0	17.4	0.0	16.6	0.0	26.3	15.9

Table 8-1C. Consumer and Producer Price Indexes: Historical Data, 1913–1949—*Continued*

(Not seasonally adjusted.)

| Year and month | Consumer price indexes, 1982–1984 =100 | | | | Producer Price Index, 1982 = 100 | | | |
| | All urban consumers (CPI-U) | | Urban wage earners and clerical workers (CPI-W) | | All commodities | | Farm products | Industrial commodities |
	Index	Percent change	Index	Percent change	Index	Percent change		
1928								
January	17.3	0.0	17.4	0.0	16.6	0.0	26.8	15.8
February	17.1	-1.2	17.2	-1.1	16.5	-0.6	26.4	15.8
March	17.1	0.0	17.2	0.0	16.5	0.0	26.1	15.8
April	17.1	0.0	17.2	0.0	16.7	1.2	27.1	15.8
May	17.2	0.6	17.3	0.6	16.8	0.6	27.7	15.8
June	17.1	-0.6	17.2	-0.6	16.7	-0.6	26.9	15.8
July	17.1	0.0	17.2	0.0	16.8	0.6	27.4	15.8
August	17.1	0.0	17.2	0.0	16.8	0.0	27.0	15.8
September	17.3	1.2	17.4	1.2	17.0	1.2	27.5	15.8
October	17.2	-0.6	17.3	-0.6	16.7	-1.8	26.1	15.8
November	17.2	0.0	17.3	0.0	16.5	-1.2	25.7	15.8
December	17.1	-0.6	17.2	-0.6	16.5	0.0	26.2	15.8
1929								
January	17.1	0.0	17.2	0.0	16.5	0.0	26.7	15.7
February	17.1	0.0	17.2	0.0	16.4	-0.6	26.6	15.6
March	17.0	-0.6	17.1	-0.6	16.6	1.2	27.1	15.7
April	16.9	-0.6	17.0	-0.6	16.5	-0.6	26.5	15.6
May	17.0	0.6	17.1	0.6	16.3	-1.2	25.8	15.6
June	17.1	0.6	17.2	0.6	16.4	0.6	26.1	15.6
July	17.3	1.2	17.4	1.2	16.6	1.2	27.1	15.6
August	17.3	0.0	17.4	0.0	16.6	0.0	27.1	15.5
September	17.3	0.0	17.4	0.0	16.6	0.0	26.9	15.6
October	17.3	0.0	17.4	0.0	16.4	-1.2	26.2	15.6
November	17.3	0.0	17.4	0.0	16.1	-1.8	25.5	15.5
December	17.2	-0.6	17.3	-0.6	16.1	0.0	25.7	15.4
1930								
January	17.1	-0.6	17.2	-0.6	15.9	-1.2	25.5	15.2
February	17.0	-0.6	17.1	-0.6	15.7	-1.3	24.7	15.1
March	16.9	-0.6	17.0	-0.6	15.5	-1.3	23.9	15.0
April	17.0	0.6	17.1	0.6	15.5	0.0	24.2	15.0
May	16.9	-0.6	17.0	-0.6	15.3	-1.3	23.5	14.9
June	16.8	-0.6	16.9	-0.6	15.0	-2.0	22.5	14.6
July	16.6	-1.2	16.7	-1.2	14.5	-3.3	21.0	14.4
August	16.5	-0.6	16.6	-0.6	14.5	0.0	21.4	14.2
September	16.6	0.6	16.7	0.6	14.5	0.0	21.5	14.2
October	16.5	-0.6	16.6	-0.6	14.3	-1.4	20.8	14.0
November	16.4	-0.6	16.5	-0.6	14.0	-2.1	20.0	13.8
December	16.1	-1.8	16.2	-1.8	13.7	-2.1	19.0	13.6
1931								
January	15.9	-1.2	16.0	-1.2	13.5	-1.5	18.4	13.4
February	15.7	-1.3	15.7	-1.9	13.2	-2.2	17.7	13.3
March	15.6	-0.6	15.6	-0.6	13.1	-0.8	17.8	13.1
April	15.5	-0.6	15.5	-0.6	12.9	-1.5	17.7	12.9
May	15.3	-1.3	15.4	-0.6	12.6	-2.3	16.9	12.8
June	15.1	-1.3	15.2	-1.3	12.4	-1.6	16.5	12.6
July	15.1	0.0	15.2	0.0	12.4	0.0	16.4	12.6
August	15.1	0.0	15.1	-0.7	12.4	0.0	16.1	12.6
September	15.0	-0.7	15.1	0.0	12.3	-0.8	15.3	12.6
October	14.9	-0.7	15.0	-0.7	12.1	-1.6	14.8	12.4
November	14.7	-1.3	14.8	-1.3	12.1	0.0	14.8	12.5
December	14.6	-0.7	14.7	-0.7	11.8	-2.5	14.1	12.3
1932								
January	14.3	-2.1	14.4	-2.0	11.6	-1.7	13.3	12.2
February	14.1	-1.4	14.2	-1.4	11.4	-1.7	12.8	12.1
March	14.0	-0.7	14.1	-0.7	11.4	0.0	12.7	12.0
April	13.9	-0.7	14.0	-0.7	11.3	-0.9	12.4	12.0
May	13.7	-1.4	13.8	-1.4	11.1	-1.8	11.8	11.9
June	13.6	-0.7	13.7	-0.7	11.0	-0.9	11.6	11.9
July	13.6	0.0	13.7	0.0	11.1	0.9	12.1	11.8
August	13.5	-0.7	13.5	-1.5	11.2	0.9	12.4	11.9
September	13.4	-0.7	13.5	0.0	11.3	0.9	12.4	11.9
October	13.3	-0.7	13.4	-0.7	11.1	-1.8	11.8	11.9
November	13.2	-0.8	13.3	-0.7	11.0	-0.9	11.8	11.9
December	13.1	-0.8	13.2	-0.8	10.8	-1.8	11.1	11.7
1933								
January	12.9	-1.5	13.0	-1.5	10.5	-2.8	10.8	11.4
February	12.7	-1.6	12.8	-1.5	10.3	-1.9	10.3	11.2
March	12.6	-0.8	12.7	-0.8	10.4	1.0	10.8	11.2
April	12.6	0.0	12.6	-0.8	10.4	0.0	11.2	11.1
May	12.6	0.0	12.7	0.8	10.8	3.8	12.7	11.3
June	12.7	0.8	12.8	0.8	11.2	3.7	13.4	11.7
July	13.1	3.1	13.2	3.1	11.9	6.3	15.2	12.3
August	13.2	0.8	13.3	0.8	12.0	0.8	14.6	12.6
September	13.2	0.0	13.3	0.0	12.2	1.7	14.4	13.0
October	13.2	0.0	13.3	0.0	12.3	0.8	14.1	13.1
November	13.2	0.0	13.3	0.0	12.3	0.0	14.3	13.1
December	13.2	0.0	13.2	-0.8	12.2	-0.8	14.0	13.2

Table 8-1C. Consumer and Producer Price Indexes: Historical Data, 1913–1949—*Continued*

(Not seasonally adjusted.)

Year and month	Consumer price indexes, 1982–1984 =100				Producer Price Index, 1982 = 100			
	All urban consumers (CPI-U)		Urban wage earners and clerical workers (CPI-W)		All commodities		Farm products	Industrial commodities
	Index	Percent change	Index	Percent change	Index	Percent change		
1934								
January	13.2	0.0	13.3	0.8	12.4	1.6	14.8	13.3
February	13.3	0.8	13.4	0.8	12.7	2.4	15.5	13.4
March	13.3	0.0	13.4	0.0	12.7	0.0	15.5	13.4
April	13.3	0.0	13.4	0.0	12.7	0.0	15.1	13.4
May	13.3	0.0	13.4	0.0	12.7	0.0	15.1	13.4
June	13.4	0.8	13.4	0.0	12.9	1.6	16.0	13.3
July	13.4	0.0	13.4	0.0	12.9	0.0	16.3	13.3
August	13.4	0.0	13.5	0.7	13.2	2.3	17.6	13.3
September	13.6	1.5	13.7	1.5	13.4	1.5	18.5	13.3
October	13.5	-0.7	13.6	-0.7	13.2	-1.5	17.8	13.3
November	13.5	0.0	13.5	-0.7	13.2	0.0	17.8	13.3
December	13.4	-0.7	13.5	0.0	13.3	0.8	18.2	13.3
1935								
January	13.6	1.5	13.7	1.5	13.6	2.3	19.6	13.2
February	13.7	0.7	13.8	0.7	13.7	0.7	20.0	13.2
March	13.7	0.0	13.8	0.0	13.7	0.0	19.7	13.2
April	13.8	0.7	13.9	0.7	13.8	0.7	20.3	13.1
May	13.8	0.0	13.8	-0.7	13.8	0.0	20.3	13.2
June	13.7	-0.7	13.8	0.0	13.8	0.0	19.8	13.3
July	13.7	0.0	13.7	-0.7	13.7	-0.7	19.5	13.3
August	13.7	0.0	13.7	0.0	13.9	1.5	20.0	13.3
September	13.7	0.0	13.8	0.7	13.9	0.0	20.1	13.2
October	13.7	0.0	13.8	0.0	13.9	0.0	19.7	13.3
November	13.8	0.7	13.9	0.7	13.9	0.0	19.6	13.4
December	13.8	0.0	13.9	0.0	14.0	0.7	19.8	13.4
1936								
January	13.8	0.0	13.9	0.0	13.9	-0.7	19.7	13.4
February	13.8	0.0	13.8	-0.7	13.9	0.0	20.1	13.4
March	13.7	-0.7	13.8	0.0	13.7	-1.4	19.3	13.4
April	13.7	0.0	13.8	0.0	13.7	0.0	19.4	13.4
May	13.7	0.0	13.8	0.0	13.5	-1.5	19.0	13.4
June	13.8	0.7	13.9	0.7	13.7	1.5	19.7	13.4
July	13.9	0.7	14.0	0.7	13.9	1.5	20.5	13.5
August	14.0	0.7	14.1	0.7	14.0	0.7	21.2	13.5
September	14.0	0.0	14.1	0.0	14.0	0.0	21.2	13.5
October	14.0	0.0	14.1	0.0	14.0	0.0	21.2	13.6
November	14.0	0.0	14.1	0.0	14.2	1.4	21.5	13.8
December	14.0	0.0	14.1	0.0	14.5	2.1	22.4	14.0
1937								
January	14.1	0.7	14.2	0.7	14.8	2.1	23.1	14.2
February	14.1	0.0	14.2	0.0	14.9	0.7	23.1	14.3
March	14.2	0.7	14.3	0.7	15.1	1.3	23.8	14.5
April	14.3	0.7	14.4	0.7	15.2	0.7	23.3	14.7
May	14.4	0.7	14.4	0.0	15.1	-0.7	22.7	14.7
June	14.4	0.0	14.5	0.7	15.0	-0.7	22.3	14.6
July	14.5	0.7	14.5	0.0	15.2	1.3	22.6	14.7
August	14.5	0.0	14.6	0.7	15.1	-0.7	21.8	14.6
September	14.6	0.7	14.7	0.7	15.1	0.0	21.7	14.6
October	14.6	0.0	14.6	-0.7	14.7	-2.6	20.3	14.5
November	14.5	-0.7	14.5	-0.7	14.4	-2.0	19.1	14.3
December	14.4	-0.7	14.5	0.0	14.1	-2.1	18.4	14.2
1938								
January	14.2	-1.4	14.3	-1.4	14.0	-0.7	18.1	14.2
February	14.1	-0.7	14.2	-0.7	13.8	-1.4	17.6	14.1
March	14.1	0.0	14.2	0.0	13.7	-0.7	17.7	14.1
April	14.2	0.7	14.2	0.0	13.5	-1.5	17.2	14.0
May	14.1	-0.7	14.2	0.0	13.5	0.0	17.0	13.9
June	14.1	0.0	14.2	0.0	13.5	0.0	17.3	13.8
July	14.1	0.0	14.2	0.0	13.6	0.7	17.5	13.9
August	14.1	0.0	14.2	0.0	13.4	-1.5	17.0	13.9
September	14.1	0.0	14.2	0.0	13.5	0.7	17.2	13.9
October	14.0	-0.7	14.1	-0.7	13.4	-0.7	16.8	13.8
November	14.0	0.0	14.1	0.0	13.4	0.0	17.1	13.7
December	14.0	0.0	14.1	0.0	13.3	-0.7	17.0	13.6
1939								
January	14.0	0.0	14.0	-0.7	13.3	0.0	17.0	13.6
February	13.9	-0.7	14.0	0.0	13.3	0.0	16.9	13.6
March	13.9	0.0	13.9	-0.7	13.2	-0.8	16.6	13.7
April	13.8	-0.7	13.9	0.0	13.1	-0.8	16.1	13.7
May	13.8	0.0	13.9	0.0	13.1	0.0	16.1	13.7
June	13.8	0.0	13.9	0.0	13.0	-0.8	15.7	13.6
July	13.8	0.0	13.9	0.0	13.0	0.0	15.8	13.6
August	13.8	0.0	13.9	0.0	12.9	-0.8	15.4	13.6
September	14.1	2.2	14.2	2.2	13.6	5.4	17.3	14.0
October	14.0	-0.7	14.1	-0.7	13.7	0.7	16.9	14.2
November	14.0	0.0	14.1	0.0	13.6	-0.7	17.0	14.3
December	14.0	0.0	14.0	-0.7	13.7	0.7	17.1	14.3

Table 8-1C. Consumer and Producer Price Indexes: Historical Data, 1913–1949—*Continued*

(Not seasonally adjusted.)

| Year and month | Consumer price indexes, 1982–1984 =100 | | | | Producer Price Index, 1982 = 100 | | | |
| | All urban consumers (CPI-U) | | Urban wage earners and clerical workers (CPI-W) | | All commodities | | Farm products | Industrial commodities |
	Index	Percent change	Index	Percent change	Index	Percent change		
1940								
January	13.9	-0.7	14.0	0.0	13.7	0.0	17.4	14.3
February	14.0	0.7	14.1	0.7	13.6	-0.7	17.3	14.2
March	14.0	0.0	14.1	0.0	13.5	-0.7	17.1	14.1
April	14.0	0.0	14.1	0.0	13.5	0.0	17.5	14.0
May	14.0	0.0	14.1	0.0	13.5	0.0	17.1	14.0
June	14.1	0.7	14.1	0.0	13.4	-0.7	16.7	14.0
July	14.0	-0.7	14.1	0.0	13.4	0.0	16.8	14.0
August	14.0	0.0	14.1	0.0	13.4	0.0	16.5	14.0
September	14.0	0.0	14.1	0.0	13.4	0.0	16.7	14.0
October	14.0	0.0	14.1	0.0	13.6	1.5	16.8	14.2
November	14.0	0.0	14.1	0.0	13.7	0.7	17.2	14.3
December	14.1	0.7	14.2	0.7	13.8	0.7	17.6	14.3
1941								
January	14.1	0.0	14.2	0.0	13.9	0.7	18.1	14.3
February	14.1	0.0	14.2	0.0	13.9	0.0	17.7	14.3
March	14.2	0.7	14.2	0.0	14.0	0.7	18.1	14.4
April	14.3	0.7	14.4	1.4	14.4	2.9	18.8	14.6
May	14.4	0.7	14.5	0.7	14.6	1.4	19.3	14.9
June	14.7	2.1	14.7	1.4	15.0	2.7	20.7	15.1
July	14.7	0.0	14.8	0.7	15.3	2.0	21.7	15.2
August	14.9	1.4	14.9	0.7	15.6	2.0	22.1	15.5
September	15.1	1.3	15.2	2.0	15.8	1.3	23.0	15.6
October	15.3	1.3	15.4	1.3	15.9	0.6	22.7	15.9
November	15.4	0.7	15.5	0.6	15.9	0.0	22.9	15.9
December	15.5	0.6	15.5	0.0	16.2	1.9	23.9	15.9
1942								
January	15.7	1.3	15.7	1.3	16.5	1.9	25.5	16.1
February	15.8	0.6	15.9	1.3	16.7	1.2	25.6	16.1
March	16.0	1.3	16.1	1.3	16.8	0.6	26.0	16.2
April	16.1	0.6	16.2	0.6	17.0	1.2	26.4	16.2
May	16.3	1.2	16.3	0.6	17.0	0.0	26.3	16.3
June	16.3	0.0	16.4	0.6	17.0	0.0	26.3	16.3
July	16.4	0.6	16.5	0.6	17.0	0.0	26.6	16.3
August	16.5	0.6	16.6	0.6	17.1	0.6	26.8	16.2
September	16.5	0.0	16.6	0.0	17.2	0.6	27.2	16.2
October	16.7	1.2	16.8	1.2	17.2	0.0	27.5	16.2
November	16.8	0.6	16.9	0.6	17.3	0.6	27.9	16.3
December	16.9	0.6	17.0	0.6	17.4	0.6	28.7	16.3
1943								
January	16.9	0.0	17.0	0.0	17.5	0.6	29.5	16.4
February	16.9	0.0	17.0	0.0	17.7	1.1	30.0	16.4
March	17.2	1.8	17.3	1.8	17.8	0.6	31.0	16.4
April	17.4	1.2	17.5	1.2	17.9	0.6	31.2	16.5
May	17.5	0.6	17.6	0.6	17.9	0.0	31.7	16.5
June	17.5	0.0	17.6	0.0	17.9	0.0	31.9	16.5
July	17.4	-0.6	17.5	-0.6	17.8	-0.6	31.5	16.5
August	17.3	-0.6	17.4	-0.6	17.8	0.0	31.2	16.5
September	17.4	0.6	17.5	0.6	17.8	0.0	31.0	16.5
October	17.4	0.0	17.5	0.0	17.8	0.0	30.9	16.5
November	17.4	0.0	17.5	0.0	17.7	-0.6	30.6	16.6
December	17.4	0.0	17.5	0.0	17.8	0.6	30.7	16.6
1944								
January	17.4	0.0	17.5	0.0	17.8	0.0	30.7	16.6
February	17.4	0.0	17.5	0.0	17.8	0.0	30.9	16.7
March	17.4	0.0	17.5	0.0	17.9	0.6	31.2	16.7
April	17.5	0.6	17.6	0.6	17.9	0.0	31.1	16.7
May	17.5	0.0	17.6	0.0	17.9	0.0	31.0	16.7
June	17.6	0.6	17.7	0.6	18.0	0.6	31.5	16.7
July	17.7	0.6	17.8	0.6	17.9	-0.6	31.3	16.7
August	17.7	0.0	17.8	0.0	17.9	0.0	30.9	16.8
September	17.7	0.0	17.8	0.0	17.9	0.0	31.0	16.8
October	17.7	0.0	17.8	0.0	17.9	0.0	31.2	16.8
November	17.7	0.0	17.8	0.0	18.0	0.6	31.4	16.8
December	17.8	0.6	17.9	0.6	18.0	0.0	31.6	16.8
1945								
January	17.8	0.0	17.9	0.0	18.1	0.6	31.9	16.8
February	17.8	0.0	17.9	0.0	18.1	0.0	32.1	16.9
March	17.8	0.0	17.9	0.0	18.1	0.0	32.1	16.9
April	17.8	0.0	17.9	0.0	18.2	0.6	32.5	16.9
May	17.9	0.6	18.0	0.6	18.3	0.5	32.8	16.9
June	18.1	1.1	18.2	1.1	18.3	0.0	32.9	16.9
July	18.1	0.0	18.2	0.0	18.3	0.0	32.5	17.0
August	18.1	0.0	18.2	0.0	18.2	-0.5	32.0	17.0
September	18.1	0.0	18.2	0.0	18.1	-0.5	31.4	17.0
October	18.1	0.0	18.2	0.0	18.2	0.6	32.1	17.0
November	18.1	0.0	18.2	0.0	18.4	1.1	33.1	17.0
December	18.2	0.6	18.3	0.5	18.4	0.0	33.2	17.1

Table 8-1C. Consumer and Producer Price Indexes: Historical Data, 1913–1949—*Continued*

(Not seasonally adjusted.)

Year and month	Consumer price indexes, 1982–1984 =100				Producer Price Index, 1982 = 100			
	All urban consumers (CPI-U)		Urban wage earners and clerical workers (CPI-W)		All commodities		Farm products	Industrial commodities
	Index	Percent change	Index	Percent change	Index	Percent change		
1946								
January	18.2	0.0	18.3	0.0	18.4	0.0	32.7	17.1
February	18.1	-0.5	18.2	-0.5	18.5	0.5	33.0	17.2
March	18.3	1.1	18.4	1.1	18.8	1.6	33.6	17.4
April	18.4	0.5	18.5	0.5	19.0	1.1	34.1	17.5
May	18.5	0.5	18.6	0.5	19.1	0.5	34.7	17.7
June	18.7	1.1	18.8	1.1	19.4	1.6	35.4	18.0
July	19.8	5.9	19.9	5.9	21.5	10.8	39.6	18.6
August	20.2	2.0	20.3	2.0	22.2	3.3	40.6	19.0
September	20.4	1.0	20.5	1.0	21.4	-3.6	39.0	19.1
October	20.8	2.0	20.9	2.0	23.1	7.9	41.7	19.7
November	21.3	2.4	21.5	2.9	24.1	4.3	42.8	20.6
December	21.5	0.9	21.6	0.5	24.3	0.8	42.4	21.2
1947								
January	21.5	0.0	21.6	0.0	24.5	0.8	41.6	21.8
February	21.5	0.0	21.6	0.0	24.7	0.8	42.6	22.0
March	21.9	1.9	22.1	2.3	25.3	2.4	45.5	22.3
April	21.9	0.0	22.1	0.0	25.1	-0.8	44.0	22.4
May	21.9	0.0	22.0	-0.5	25.0	-0.4	43.6	22.3
June	22.0	0.5	22.2	0.9	25.0	0.0	43.8	22.4
July	22.2	0.9	22.4	0.9	25.3	1.2	44.3	22.5
August	22.5	1.4	22.6	0.9	25.6	1.2	44.8	22.8
September	23.0	2.2	23.1	2.2	26.1	2.0	46.6	23.1
October	23.0	0.0	23.1	0.0	26.4	1.1	47.4	23.3
November	23.1	0.4	23.3	0.9	26.7	1.1	47.7	23.6
December	23.4	1.3	23.6	1.3	27.2	1.9	50.1	23.9
1948								
January	23.7	1.3	23.8	0.8	27.7	1.8	51.2	24.3
February	23.5	-0.8	23.6	-0.8	27.2	-1.8	47.7	24.1
March	23.4	-0.4	23.6	0.0	27.2	0.0	47.6	24.1
April	23.8	1.7	23.9	1.3	27.4	0.7	48.3	24.3
May	23.9	0.4	24.1	0.8	27.5	0.4	49.4	24.3
June	24.1	0.8	24.2	0.4	27.7	0.7	50.4	24.4
July	24.4	1.2	24.5	1.2	28.0	1.1	50.2	24.6
August	24.5	0.4	24.6	0.4	28.2	0.7	49.6	24.9
September	24.5	0.0	24.6	0.0	28.1	-0.4	48.8	25.0
October	24.4	-0.4	24.5	-0.4	27.8	-1.1	46.9	25.0
November	24.2	-0.8	24.4	-0.4	27.8	0.0	46.3	25.1
December	24.1	-0.4	24.2	-0.8	27.6	-0.7	45.2	25.1
1949								
January	24.0	-0.4	24.2	0.0	27.3	-1.1	43.8	24.9
February	23.8	-0.8	23.9	-1.2	26.8	-1.8	42.0	24.7
March	23.8	0.0	24.0	0.4	26.8	0.0	42.7	24.6
April	23.9	0.4	24.0	0.0	26.5	-1.1	42.7	24.3
May	23.8	-0.4	24.0	0.0	26.3	-0.8	42.7	24.0
June	23.9	0.4	24.0	0.0	26.0	-1.1	41.8	23.8
July	23.7	-0.8	23.8	-0.8	26.0	0.0	41.7	23.7
August	23.8	0.4	23.9	0.4	26.0	0.0	41.7	23.8
September	23.9	0.4	24.0	0.4	26.1	0.4	41.8	23.8
October	23.7	-0.8	23.9	-0.4	26.0	-0.4	41.0	23.8
November	23.8	0.4	23.9	0.0	26.0	0.0	40.9	23.8
December	23.6	-0.8	23.8	-0.4	25.9	-0.4	40.3	23.8

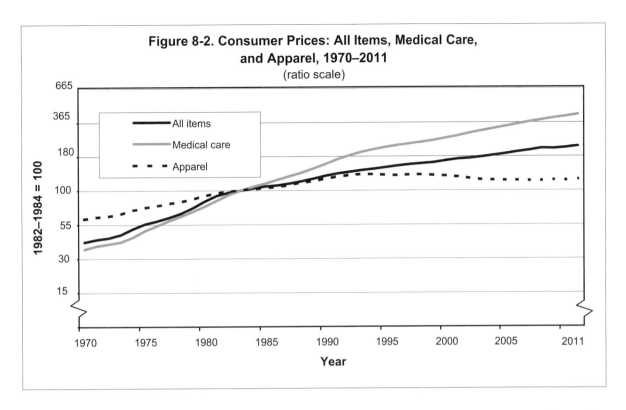

Figure 8-2. Consumer Prices: All Items, Medical Care, and Apparel, 1970–2011
(ratio scale)

- Figure 8-2 charts two components of the Consumer Price Index for All Urban Consumers (CPI-U) along with the all-items total. Since all three indexes have the base years 1982–1984, they converge around 100 in those years. However, over the entire postwar period, the trends of the two components are very different. (Table 8-2)

- Apparel has been one of the areas most subject to international competition, and the apparel index shows far less growth than the overall average of prices.

- Medical care, on the other hand, has little price competition from producers in other countries. It is often paid for by third-party insurers, both government and private, rather than directly by consumers. Furthermore, it is characterized by trend growth in demand, due to rising income and expectations and to technological progress. All of these economic factors cause medical care prices to rise faster than the general price level.

- Medical care has arguably been overstated in the CPI due to the difficulties of making quality adjustments. Quality adjustments in the indexes have been much improved in recent years, although such improvements are not retroactively introduced into the official CPIs. But even since 1997, when a major improvement was introduced into the hospital cost component of the CPI, measured medical care prices have increased at a 3.9 percent annual rate, while the total CPI rose at a 2.4 percent average annual rate. (Table 8-2)

Table 8-2. Consumer Price Indexes and Purchasing Power of the Dollar

(1982–1984 = 100, seasonally adjusted, except as noted.)

| Year and month | CPI-U, All items | | | CPI-U, Food and beverages | | | | | | | | | | |
| | Not seasonally adjusted | Seasonally adjusted | | Total | Total food | Food at home | | | | | | | Food away from home [1] | Alcoholic beverages |
		Index	Percent change from previous period			Total	Cereals and bakery products	Meats, poultry, fish, and eggs	Dairy and related products[1]	Fruits and vegetables	Non-alcoholic beverages	Other food at home		
1970	38.8	38.8	5.7	40.1	39.2	39.9	37.1	44.6	44.7	37.8	27.1	32.9	37.5	52.1
1971	40.5	40.5	4.4	41.4	40.4	40.9	38.8	44.1	46.1	39.7	28.1	34.3	39.4	54.2
1972	41.8	41.8	3.2	43.1	42.1	42.7	39.0	48.0	46.8	41.6	28.0	34.6	41.0	55.4
1973	44.4	44.4	6.2	48.8	48.2	49.7	43.5	60.9	51.2	47.4	30.1	36.7	44.2	56.8
1974	49.3	49.3	11.0	55.5	55.1	57.1	56.5	62.2	60.7	55.2	35.9	47.8	49.8	61.1
1975	53.8	53.8	9.1	60.2	59.8	61.8	62.9	67.0	62.6	56.9	41.3	55.4	54.5	65.9
1976	56.9	56.9	5.8	62.1	61.6	63.1	61.5	68.0	67.7	58.4	49.4	56.4	58.2	68.1
1977	60.6	60.6	6.5	65.8	65.5	66.8	62.5	67.4	69.5	63.8	74.4	68.4	62.6	70.0
1978	65.2	65.2	7.6	72.2	72.0	73.8	68.1	77.6	74.2	70.9	78.7	73.6	68.3	74.1
1979	72.6	72.6	11.3	79.9	79.9	81.8	74.9	89.0	82.8	76.6	82.6	79.0	75.9	79.9
1980	82.4	82.4	13.5	86.7	86.8	88.4	83.9	92.0	90.9	82.1	91.4	88.4	83.4	86.4
1981	90.9	90.9	10.3	93.5	93.6	94.8	92.3	96.0	97.4	92.0	95.3	94.9	90.9	92.5
1982	96.5	96.5	6.2	97.3	97.4	98.1	96.5	99.6	98.8	97.0	97.9	97.3	95.8	96.7
1983	99.6	99.6	3.2	99.5	99.4	99.1	99.6	99.2	100.0	97.3	99.8	99.5	100.0	100.4
1984	103.9	103.9	4.3	103.2	103.2	102.8	103.9	101.3	101.3	105.7	102.3	103.1	104.2	103.0
1985	107.6	107.6	3.6	105.6	105.6	104.3	107.9	100.1	103.2	108.4	104.3	105.7	108.3	106.4
1986	109.6	109.6	1.9	109.1	109.0	107.3	110.9	104.5	103.3	109.4	110.4	109.4	112.5	111.1
1987	113.6	113.6	3.6	113.5	113.5	111.9	114.8	110.5	105.9	119.1	107.5	110.5	117.0	114.1
1988	118.3	118.3	4.1	118.2	118.2	116.6	122.1	114.3	108.4	128.1	107.5	113.1	121.8	118.6
1989	124.0	124.0	4.8	124.9	125.1	124.2	132.4	121.3	115.6	138.0	111.3	119.1	127.4	123.5
1990	130.7	130.7	5.4	132.1	132.4	132.3	140.0	130.0	126.5	149.0	113.5	123.4	133.4	129.3
1991	136.2	136.2	4.2	136.8	136.3	135.8	145.8	132.6	125.1	155.8	114.1	127.3	137.9	142.8
1992	140.3	140.3	3.0	138.7	137.9	136.8	151.5	130.9	128.5	155.4	114.3	128.8	140.7	147.3
1993	144.5	144.5	3.0	141.6	140.9	140.1	156.6	135.5	129.4	159.0	114.6	130.5	143.2	149.6
1994	148.2	148.2	2.6	144.9	144.3	144.1	163.0	137.2	131.7	165.0	123.2	135.6	145.7	151.5
1995	152.4	152.4	2.8	148.9	148.4	148.8	167.5	138.8	132.8	177.7	131.7	140.8	149.0	153.9
1996	156.9	156.9	3.0	153.7	153.3	154.3	174.0	144.8	142.1	183.9	128.6	142.9	152.7	158.5
1997	160.5	160.5	2.3	157.7	157.3	158.1	177.6	148.5	145.5	187.5	133.4	147.3	157.0	162.8
1998	163.0	163.0	1.6	161.1	160.7	161.1	181.1	147.3	150.8	198.2	133.0	150.8	161.1	165.7
1999	166.6	166.6	2.2	164.6	164.1	164.2	185.0	147.9	159.6	203.1	134.3	153.5	165.1	169.7
2000	172.2	172.2	3.4	168.4	167.8	167.9	188.3	154.5	160.7	204.6	137.8	155.6	169.0	174.7
2001	177.1	177.1	2.8	173.6	173.1	173.4	193.8	161.3	167.1	212.2	139.2	159.6	173.9	179.3
2002	179.9	179.9	1.6	176.8	176.2	175.6	198.0	162.1	168.1	220.9	139.2	160.8	178.3	183.6
2003	184.0	184.0	2.3	180.5	180.0	179.4	202.8	169.3	167.9	225.9	139.8	162.6	182.1	187.2
2004	188.9	188.9	2.7	186.6	186.2	186.2	206.0	181.7	180.2	232.7	140.4	164.9	187.5	192.1
2005	195.3	195.3	3.4	191.2	190.7	189.8	209.0	184.7	182.4	241.4	144.4	167.0	193.4	195.9
2006	201.6	201.6	3.2	195.7	195.2	193.1	212.8	186.6	181.4	252.9	147.4	169.6	199.4	200.7
2007	207.3	207.3	2.8	203.3	202.9	201.2	222.1	195.6	194.8	262.6	153.4	173.3	206.7	207.0
2008	215.3	215.3	3.8	214.2	214.1	214.1	244.9	204.7	210.4	278.9	160.0	184.2	215.8	214.5
2009	214.5	214.5	-0.4	218.2	218.0	215.1	252.6	203.8	197.0	272.9	163.0	191.2	223.3	220.8
2010	218.1	218.1	1.6	220.0	219.6	215.8	250.4	207.7	199.2	273.5	161.6	191.1	226.1	223.3
2011	224.9	224.9	3.2	227.9	227.8	226.2	260.3	223.2	212.7	284.7	166.8	197.4	231.4	226.7
2010														
January	216.7	217.5	0.1	218.8	218.4	214.6	251.1	201.7	198.9	273.4	162.5	191.2	224.9	222.4
February	216.7	217.4	0.0	218.9	218.5	214.7	251.2	202.8	198.8	272.3	162.1	191.4	225.1	222.1
March	217.6	217.4	0.0	219.2	218.9	215.4	250.8	203.2	198.8	279.0	162.0	190.8	225.0	222.2
April	218.0	217.4	0.0	219.5	219.1	215.6	250.4	205.5	197.3	278.0	162.1	190.8	225.3	222.4
May	218.2	217.2	-0.1	219.6	219.3	215.6	250.4	206.2	197.7	276.3	161.2	191.2	225.6	222.4
June	218.0	217.2	0.0	219.6	219.2	215.4	249.5	208.1	197.9	273.1	160.9	190.7	225.8	222.6
July	218.0	217.6	0.2	219.6	219.2	215.4	249.1	208.8	199.0	269.4	161.4	191.0	225.7	223.7
August	218.3	218.1	0.2	219.9	219.5	215.4	249.4	208.5	198.7	270.3	161.5	191.1	226.4	223.7
September	218.4	218.4	0.1	220.6	220.3	216.2	250.5	210.4	199.0	271.0	161.7	191.3	227.1	224.1
October	218.7	219.0	0.3	221.0	220.6	216.7	250.1	211.7	201.3	271.7	161.1	191.1	227.3	224.4
November	218.8	219.4	0.2	221.4	221.1	217.3	250.9	213.0	201.3	271.5	162.3	191.3	227.5	224.6
December	219.2	220.4	0.4	221.7	221.4	217.7	252.0	212.2	202.1	276.4	160.4	191.5	227.7	224.7
2011														
January	220.2	221.0	0.3	222.7	222.4	219.2	253.7	214.1	202.3	279.8	162.8	191.7	228.2	225.0
February	221.3	222.0	0.4	223.8	223.6	220.8	254.0	216.7	203.5	283.8	163.2	192.9	228.6	225.4
March	223.5	223.2	0.5	225.3	225.2	223.1	255.3	219.3	206.2	288.0	164.3	194.6	229.3	225.5
April	224.9	224.0	0.4	226.1	226.0	224.0	256.0	221.1	209.7	284.4	166.0	195.1	230.1	226.2
May	226.0	224.6	0.3	227.0	226.8	225.1	258.2	223.8	211.3	282.3	166.1	195.9	230.5	226.9
June	225.7	224.8	0.1	227.5	227.4	225.6	259.9	223.1	212.3	281.9	166.8	197.0	231.1	227.1
July	225.9	225.5	0.3	228.4	228.4	227.0	259.9	224.2	214.8	285.8	168.0	197.6	231.6	227.0
August	226.5	226.3	0.3	229.5	229.6	228.4	262.7	225.3	216.7	287.3	168.0	199.1	232.5	227.3
September	226.9	226.9	0.3	230.5	230.6	229.8	264.6	226.3	219.4	289.1	168.1	200.3	233.0	227.3
October	226.4	226.8	0.0	230.9	231.1	230.3	265.6	227.5	219.5	286.1	168.9	201.1	233.5	227.3
November	226.2	227.0	0.1	231.1	231.3	230.3	266.5	227.6	218.8	284.8	169.4	201.2	234.0	227.5
December	225.7	227.0	0.0	231.6	231.8	230.8	267.4	229.1	218.5	283.3	169.8	202.0	234.4	227.8

[1]Not seasonally adjusted.

Table 8-2. Consumer Price Indexes and Purchasing Power of the Dollar—*Continued*

(1982–1984 = 100, seasonally adjusted, except as noted.)

Year and month	CPI-U, Housing												
	Total	Shelter						Fuels and utilities				Household furnishings and operations	
		Total	Rent of shelter[2]	Rent of primary residence	Lodging away from home[3]	Owners' equivalent rent of primary residence[2]	Tenants' and household insurance[1,3]	Total	Fuels		Water and sewer and trash collection services[3]	Total	Household operations[1,3]
									Fuel oil and other fuels	Energy services			
1970	36.4	35.5	. . .	46.5	. . .	. . .	. . .	29.1	17.0	25.4	. . .	46.8	. . .
1971	38.0	37.0	. . .	48.7	. . .	. . .	. . .	31.1	18.2	27.1	. . .	48.6	. . .
1972	39.4	38.7	. . .	50.4	. . .	. . .	. . .	32.5	18.3	28.5	. . .	49.7	. . .
1973	41.2	40.5	. . .	52.5	. . .	. . .	. . .	34.3	21.1	29.9	. . .	51.1	. . .
1974	45.8	44.4	. . .	55.2	. . .	. . .	. . .	40.7	33.2	34.5	. . .	56.8	. . .
1975	50.7	48.8	. . .	58.0	. . .	. . .	. . .	45.4	36.4	40.1	. . .	63.4	. . .
1976	53.8	51.5	. . .	61.1	. . .	. . .	. . .	49.4	38.8	44.7	. . .	67.3	. . .
1977	57.4	54.9	. . .	64.8	. . .	. . .	. . .	54.7	43.9	50.5	. . .	70.4	. . .
1978	62.4	60.5	. . .	69.3	. . .	. . .	. . .	58.5	46.2	55.0	. . .	74.7	. . .
1979	70.1	68.9	. . .	74.3	. . .	. . .	. . .	64.8	62.4	61.0	. . .	79.9	. . .
1980	81.1	81.0	. . .	80.9	. . .	. . .	. . .	75.4	86.1	71.4	. . .	86.3	. . .
1981	90.4	90.5	. . .	87.9	. . .	. . .	. . .	86.4	104.6	81.9	. . .	93.0	. . .
1982	96.9	96.9	. . .	94.6	. . .	. . .	. . .	94.9	103.4	93.2	. . .	98.0	. . .
1983	99.5	99.1	102.7	100.1	. . .	102.5	. . .	100.2	97.2	101.5	. . .	100.2	. . .
1984	103.6	104.0	107.7	105.3	. . .	107.3	. . .	104.8	99.4	105.4	. . .	101.9	. . .
1985	107.7	109.8	113.9	111.8	. . .	113.2	. . .	106.5	95.9	107.1	. . .	103.8	. . .
1986	110.9	115.8	120.2	118.3	. . .	119.4	. . .	104.1	77.6	105.7	. . .	105.2	. . .
1987	114.2	121.3	125.9	123.1	. . .	124.8	. . .	103.0	77.9	103.8	. . .	107.1	. . .
1988	118.5	127.1	132.0	127.8	. . .	131.1	. . .	104.4	78.1	104.6	. . .	109.4	. . .
1989	123.0	132.8	138.0	132.8	. . .	137.4	. . .	107.8	81.7	107.5	. . .	111.2	. . .
1990	128.5	140.0	145.5	138.4	. . .	144.8	. . .	111.6	99.3	109.3	. . .	113.3	. . .
1991	133.6	146.3	152.1	143.3	. . .	150.4	. . .	115.3	94.6	112.6	. . .	116.0	. . .
1992	137.5	151.2	157.3	146.9	. . .	155.5	. . .	117.8	90.7	114.8	. . .	118.0	. . .
1993	141.2	155.7	162.0	150.3	. . .	160.5	. . .	121.3	90.3	118.5	. . .	119.3	. . .
1994	144.8	160.5	167.0	154.0	. . .	165.8	. . .	122.8	88.8	119.2	. . .	121.0	. . .
1995	148.5	165.7	172.4	157.8	. . .	171.3	. . .	123.7	88.1	119.2	. . .	123.0	. . .
1996	152.8	171.0	178.0	162.0	. . .	176.8	. . .	127.5	99.2	122.1	. . .	124.7	. . .
1997	156.8	176.3	183.4	166.7	. . .	181.9	. . .	130.8	99.8	125.1	. . .	125.4	. . .
1998	160.4	182.1	189.6	172.1	109.0	187.8	99.8	128.5	90.0	121.2	101.6	126.6	101.5
1999	163.9	187.3	195.0	177.5	112.3	192.9	101.3	128.8	91.4	120.9	104.0	126.7	104.5
2000	169.6	193.4	201.3	183.9	117.5	198.7	103.7	137.9	129.7	128.0	106.5	128.2	110.5
2001	176.4	200.6	208.9	192.1	118.6	206.3	106.2	150.2	129.3	142.4	109.6	129.1	115.6
2002	180.3	208.1	216.7	199.7	118.3	214.7	108.7	143.6	115.5	134.4	113.0	128.3	119.0
2003	184.8	213.1	221.9	205.5	119.3	219.9	114.8	154.5	139.5	145.0	117.2	126.1	121.8
2004	189.5	218.8	227.9	211.0	125.9	224.9	116.2	161.9	160.5	150.6	124.0	125.5	125.0
2005	195.7	224.4	233.7	217.3	130.3	230.2	117.6	179.0	208.6	166.5	130.3	126.1	130.3
2006	203.2	232.1	241.9	225.1	136.0	238.2	116.5	194.7	234.9	182.1	136.8	127.0	136.6
2007	209.6	240.6	250.8	234.7	142.8	246.2	117.0	200.6	251.5	186.3	143.7	126.9	140.6
2008	216.3	246.7	257.2	243.3	143.7	252.4	118.8	220.0	334.4	202.2	152.1	127.8	147.5
2009	217.1	249.4	259.9	248.8	134.2	256.6	121.5	210.7	239.8	193.6	161.1	128.7	150.3
2010	216.3	248.4	258.8	249.4	133.7	256.6	125.7	214.2	275.1	192.9	170.9	125.5	150.3
2011	219.1	251.6	262.2	253.6	137.4	259.6	127.4	220.4	337.1	194.4	179.6	124.9	151.8
2010													
January	216.3	248.1	258.8	248.7	131.2	256.6	124.4	213.5	280.9	193.1	166.6	127.3	149.5
February	216.2	248.1	258.5	248.7	131.8	256.5	124.4	213.2	277.3	192.6	167.6	126.8	149.7
March	216.3	248.0	258.2	248.9	132.4	256.3	124.4	215.2	276.0	194.8	168.4	126.4	150.0
April	216.1	248.0	258.3	248.9	133.2	256.2	124.9	215.1	278.1	194.4	169.3	125.7	150.1
May	216.1	248.0	258.5	249.0	134.4	256.2	125.0	214.3	272.6	193.4	170.1	125.7	150.6
June	216.0	248.2	258.5	249.2	134.9	256.3	125.3	213.0	265.5	192.0	170.6	125.3	150.6
July	216.1	248.3	258.5	249.5	134.7	256.4	125.9	213.4	261.3	192.6	171.3	125.2	150.7
August	216.2	248.4	258.5	249.3	134.3	256.5	126.5	214.2	263.2	193.2	171.9	125.1	150.6
September	216.1	248.5	258.9	249.6	134.0	256.6	126.6	213.8	265.8	192.3	172.6	124.8	150.3
October	216.3	248.7	259.2	249.7	134.2	256.8	127.1	214.4	276.6	192.3	173.3	124.7	150.2
November	216.5	249.0	259.7	250.3	133.4	257.2	127.5	214.2	286.4	191.3	174.1	124.5	150.2
December	216.9	249.4	260.2	250.7	134.7	257.4	126.2	216.1	298.0	192.7	174.9	124.4	150.6
2011													
January	217.2	249.7	260.2	251.1	134.7	257.8	126.2	216.2	314.1	191.9	175.5	124.4	151.2
February	217.6	250.0	260.4	251.5	135.0	258.1	126.5	218.0	326.9	193.0	176.7	124.5	151.4
March	218.0	250.2	260.6	251.9	136.0	258.3	125.9	219.5	341.9	193.8	177.5	124.4	150.5
April	218.2	250.4	260.9	252.1	135.8	258.4	126.6	220.6	348.7	194.5	178.1	124.6	151.3
May	218.5	250.7	261.2	252.5	137.0	258.6	126.8	221.4	347.0	195.4	178.8	124.8	151.7
June	218.7	251.2	261.6	252.9	139.1	259.0	127.2	220.3	340.8	194.1	179.5	124.8	151.7
July	219.2	251.8	262.2	253.3	140.6	259.6	127.3	220.4	336.9	194.3	179.9	124.9	151.9
August	219.6	252.3	262.7	254.3	138.8	260.2	127.6	220.9	336.0	194.9	180.2	125.2	152.1
September	220.0	252.6	263.2	254.9	138.3	260.4	127.9	222.4	334.7	196.4	181.4	125.2	152.0
October	220.4	253.2	263.8	255.7	137.5	261.0	128.4	221.8	335.1	195.5	181.9	125.4	152.4
November	220.7	253.6	264.4	256.3	137.8	261.5	128.8	221.5	342.8	194.6	182.4	125.5	152.6
December	221.0	254.1	265.0	256.9	137.5	262.0	129.5	221.3	340.5	194.2	183.2	125.6	152.7

[1]Not seasonally adjusted.
[2]December 1982 = 100.
[3]December 1997 = 100.
. . . = Not available.

Table 8-2. Consumer Price Indexes and Purchasing Power of the Dollar—*Continued*

(1982–1984 = 100, seasonally adjusted [preliminary], except as noted.)

Year and month	CPI-U, Apparel					CPI-U, Transportation								
							Private transportation						Motor vehicle parts and equipment	Motor vehicle mainte-nance and repair [1]
								New and used motor vehicles			Motor fuel			
	Total	Men's and boys' apparel	Women's and girls' apparel	Infants' and toddlers' apparel	Footwear	Total	Total	Total [3]	New vehicles	Used cars and trucks	Total	Gasoline (all types)		
1970	59.2	62.2	71.8	39.2	56.8	37.5	37.5	. . .	53.1	31.2	27.9	27.9	. . .	36.6
1971	61.1	63.9	74.4	40.0	58.6	39.5	39.4	. . .	55.3	33.0	28.1	28.1	. . .	39.3
1972	62.3	64.7	76.2	41.1	60.3	39.9	39.7	. . .	54.8	33.1	28.4	28.4	. . .	41.1
1973	64.6	67.1	78.8	42.5	62.8	41.2	41.0	. . .	54.8	35.2	31.2	31.2	. . .	43.2
1974	69.4	72.4	83.5	54.2	66.6	45.8	46.2	. . .	58.0	36.7	42.2	42.2	. . .	47.6
1975	72.5	75.5	85.5	64.5	69.6	50.1	50.6	. . .	63.0	43.8	45.1	45.1	. . .	53.7
1976	75.2	78.1	87.9	68.0	72.3	55.1	55.6	. . .	67.0	50.3	47.0	47.0	. . .	57.6
1977	78.6	81.7	90.6	74.6	75.7	59.0	59.7	. . .	70.5	54.7	49.7	49.7	. . .	61.9
1978	81.4	83.5	92.4	77.4	79.0	61.7	62.5	. . .	75.9	55.8	51.8	51.8	77.6	67.0
1979	84.9	85.4	94.0	79.0	85.3	70.5	71.7	. . .	81.9	60.2	70.1	70.2	85.1	73.7
1980	90.9	89.4	96.0	85.5	91.8	83.1	84.2	. . .	88.5	62.3	97.4	97.5	95.3	81.5
1981	95.3	94.2	97.5	92.9	96.7	93.2	93.8	. . .	93.9	76.9	108.5	108.5	101.0	89.2
1982	97.8	97.6	98.5	96.3	99.1	97.0	97.1	. . .	97.5	88.8	102.8	102.8	103.6	96.0
1983	100.2	100.3	100.2	101.1	99.8	99.3	99.3	. . .	99.9	98.7	99.4	99.4	100.7	100.3
1984	102.1	102.1	101.3	102.6	101.1	103.7	103.6	. . .	102.6	112.5	97.9	97.8	95.6	103.8
1985	105.0	105.0	104.9	107.2	102.3	106.4	106.2	. . .	106.1	113.7	98.7	98.6	95.9	106.8
1986	105.9	106.2	104.0	111.8	101.9	102.3	101.2	. . .	110.6	108.8	77.1	77.0	95.4	110.3
1987	110.6	109.1	110.4	112.1	105.1	105.4	104.2	. . .	114.4	113.1	80.2	80.1	96.1	114.8
1988	115.4	113.4	114.9	116.4	109.9	108.7	107.6	. . .	116.5	118.0	80.9	80.8	97.9	119.7
1989	118.6	117.0	116.4	119.1	114.4	114.1	112.9	. . .	119.2	120.4	88.5	88.5	100.2	124.9
1990	124.1	120.4	122.6	125.8	117.4	120.5	118.8	. . .	121.4	117.6	101.2	101.0	100.9	130.1
1991	128.7	124.2	127.6	128.9	120.9	123.8	121.9	. . .	126.0	118.1	99.4	99.2	102.2	136.0
1992	131.9	126.5	130.4	129.3	125.0	126.5	124.6	. . .	129.2	123.2	99.0	99.0	103.1	141.3
1993	133.7	127.5	132.6	127.1	125.9	130.4	127.5	91.8	132.7	133.9	98.0	97.7	101.6	145.9
1994	133.4	126.4	130.9	128.1	126.0	134.3	131.4	95.5	137.6	141.7	98.5	98.2	101.4	150.2
1995	132.0	126.2	126.9	127.2	125.4	139.1	136.3	99.4	141.0	156.5	100.0	99.8	102.1	154.0
1996	131.7	127.7	124.7	129.7	126.6	143.0	140.0	101.0	143.7	157.0	106.3	105.9	102.2	158.4
1997	132.9	130.1	126.1	129.0	127.6	144.3	141.0	100.5	144.3	151.1	106.2	105.8	101.9	162.7
1998	133.0	131.8	126.0	126.1	128.0	141.6	137.9	100.1	143.4	150.6	92.2	91.6	101.1	167.1
1999	131.3	131.1	123.3	129.0	125.7	144.4	140.5	100.1	142.9	152.0	100.7	100.1	100.5	171.9
2000	129.6	129.7	121.5	130.6	123.8	153.3	149.1	100.8	142.8	155.8	129.3	128.6	101.5	177.3
2001	127.3	125.7	119.3	129.2	123.0	154.3	150.0	101.3	142.1	158.7	124.7	124.0	104.8	183.5
2002	124.0	121.7	115.8	126.4	121.4	152.9	148.8	99.2	140.0	152.0	116.6	116.0	106.9	190.2
2003	120.9	118.0	113.1	122.1	119.6	157.6	153.6	96.5	137.9	142.9	135.8	135.1	107.8	195.6
2004	120.4	117.5	113.0	118.5	119.3	163.1	159.4	94.2	137.1	133.3	160.4	159.7	108.7	200.2
2005	119.5	116.1	110.8	116.7	122.6	173.9	170.2	95.6	137.9	139.4	195.7	194.7	111.9	206.9
2006	119.5	114.1	110.7	116.5	123.5	180.9	177.0	95.6	137.6	140.0	221.0	219.9	117.3	215.6
2007	119.0	112.4	110.3	113.9	122.4	184.7	180.8	94.3	136.3	135.7	239.1	238.0	121.6	223.0
2008	118.9	113.0	107.5	113.8	124.2	195.5	191.0	93.3	134.2	134.0	279.7	277.5	128.7	233.9
2009	120.1	113.6	108.1	114.5	126.9	179.3	174.8	93.5	135.6	127.0	202.0	201.6	134.1	243.3
2010	119.5	111.9	107.1	114.2	128.0	193.4	188.7	97.1	138.0	143.1	239.2	238.6	137.0	248.0
2011	122.1	114.7	109.2	113.6	128.5	212.4	207.6	99.8	141.9	149.0	302.6	301.7	143.9	253.1
2010														
January	120.1	112.1	108.4	114.5	128.9	192.7	188.3	96.6	137.7	140.2	243.3	243.2	135.3	245.6
February	120.0	111.9	108.4	114.5	128.7	192.3	188.0	96.9	137.8	141.1	239.9	239.5	135.6	246.0
March	119.9	111.8	108.3	114.8	127.8	191.7	187.3	97.1	137.9	141.9	235.5	235.0	135.5	246.6
April	119.2	111.1	107.2	114.7	127.8	191.2	186.6	97.0	137.9	142.4	231.9	231.4	135.7	247.4
May	119.4	111.4	107.2	114.7	127.6	189.9	185.1	97.0	137.8	142.7	225.0	224.1	136.1	247.3
June	119.8	113.1	106.9	114.8	128.0	189.6	184.7	97.1	137.9	143.3	222.6	221.7	136.7	247.6
July	119.7	112.7	107.3	116.4	127.9	191.4	186.7	97.3	138.0	144.1	229.5	228.9	137.2	247.5
August	119.5	112.3	106.9	114.6	127.7	192.9	188.3	97.6	138.2	145.2	235.0	234.4	137.6	248.4
September	119.3	112.1	106.2	113.3	128.1	193.9	189.2	97.5	138.3	144.6	238.6	237.9	137.8	249.2
October	119.0	111.9	105.9	112.2	128.7	196.8	192.2	97.3	138.3	144.0	250.6	250.0	138.3	249.8
November	118.9	111.4	106.0	112.7	127.5	198.0	193.3	97.2	138.2	143.8	254.7	254.0	138.8	249.9
December	119.1	111.3	106.1	112.6	127.2	202.0	197.2	97.2	138.1	144.0	271.6	271.4	139.2	250.1
2011														
January	120.1	112.4	107.3	111.3	127.9	203.2	198.2	97.1	137.9	143.8	275.2	274.7	140.5	250.7
February	119.5	111.5	106.8	110.6	127.8	205.9	201.0	97.6	139.1	143.9	284.6	283.7	140.9	250.9
March	119.3	111.0	106.4	110.6	127.9	210.1	205.2	98.4	140.1	145.4	299.3	298.2	140.7	250.8
April	119.5	111.0	106.8	110.8	127.0	212.8	208.0	99.2	141.2	147.1	307.5	306.7	141.6	251.5
May	120.7	112.5	107.9	111.6	128.5	213.7	209.0	100.1	142.6	148.6	308.2	307.4	143.3	252.4
June	122.0	114.8	108.9	111.9	128.8	213.2	208.6	100.9	143.5	150.4	303.4	302.4	144.6	252.5
July	123.3	117.0	110.0	114.8	128.8	214.4	209.9	101.0	143.4	151.6	307.9	307.0	145.0	252.8
August	124.3	116.4	111.9	115.7	129.5	215.5	211.0	101.1	143.4	152.7	311.4	310.6	145.5	253.3
September	123.4	116.5	110.2	115.4	129.6	217.1	212.5	100.9	143.3	152.0	317.6	316.8	145.6	255.2
October	124.0	117.2	110.8	115.6	128.7	215.1	210.4	100.6	143.0	151.4	308.9	308.0	145.3	255.8
November	124.6	118.4	111.6	116.4	128.5	214.4	209.7	100.3	142.7	150.9	306.6	305.2	146.3	255.7
December	124.5	117.8	111.3	117.8	128.8	212.9	208.1	100.0	142.5	149.9	300.1	298.8	147.5	255.6

[1]Not seasonally adjusted.
[3]December 1997 = 100.
. . . = Not available.

Table 8-2. Consumer Price Indexes and Purchasing Power of the Dollar—*Continued*

(1982–1984 = 100, seasonally adjusted [preliminary], except as noted.)

Year and month	CPI-U, Transportation—*Continued*		CPI-U, Medical care					CPI-U, Recreation		CPI-U, Education and communication				
					Medical care services						Education			
	Public transportation	Transportation services	Medical care, total	Medical care commodities	Total	Professional services	Hospital and related services	Total [3]	Video and audio [3]	Total [3]	Total [3]	Educational books and supplies	Tuition, other school fees, and childcare
1970	35.2	40.2	34.0	34.0	32.3	37.0	. . .	. . .	. . .	. . .	. . .	38.8	. . .
1971	37.8	43.4	36.1	36.1	34.7	39.4	. . .	. . .	. . .	. . .	. . .	41.4	. . .
1972	39.3	44.4	37.3	37.3	35.9	40.8	. . .	. . .	. . .	. . .	. . .	44.2	. . .
1973	39.7	44.7	38.8	38.8	37.5	42.2	. . .	. . .	. . .	. . .	. . .	45.6	. . .
1974	40.6	46.3	42.4	42.4	41.4	45.8	. . .	. . .	. . .	. . .	. . .	47.2	. . .
1975	43.5	49.8	47.5	47.5	46.6	50.8	. . .	. . .	. . .	. . .	. . .	50.3	. . .
1976	47.8	56.9	52.0	52.0	51.3	55.5	. . .	. . .	. . .	.,.	. . .	53.7	. . .
1977	50.0	61.5	57.0	57.0	56.4	60.0	. . .	. . .	. . .	. . .	. . .	56.9	. . .
1978	51.5	64.4	61.8	61.8	61.2	64.5	55.1	. . .	. . .	. . .	. . .	61.6	59.8
1979	54.9	69.5	67.5	67.5	67.2	70.1	61.0	. . .	. . .	. . .	. . .	65.7	64.7
1980	69.0	79.2	74.9	74.9	74.8	77.9	69.2	. . .	. . .	. . .	. . .	71.4	71.2
1981	85.6	88.6	82.9	82.9	82.8	85.9	79.1	. . .	. . .	. . .	. . .	80.3	79.9
1982	94.9	96.1	92.5	92.5	92.6	93.2	90.3	. . .	. . .	. . .	. . .	91.0	90.5
1983	99.5	99.1	100.6	100.6	100.7	99.8	100.5	. . .	. . .	. . .	. . .	100.3	99.7
1984	105.7	104.8	106.8	106.8	106.7	107.0	109.2	. . .	. . .	. . .	. . .	108.7	109.8
1985	110.5	110.0	113.5	113.5	113.2	113.5	116.1	. . .	. . .	. . .	. . .	118.2	119.7
1986	117.0	116.3	122.0	122.0	121.9	120.8	123.1	. . .	. . .	. . .	. . .	128.1	129.6
1987	121.1	121.9	130.1	130.1	130.0	128.8	131.6	. . .	. . .	. . .	. . .	138.1	140.0
1988	123.3	128.0	138.6	138.6	138.3	137.5	143.9	. . .	. . .	. . .	. . .	148.1	151.0
1989	129.5	135.6	149.3	149.3	148.9	146.4	160.5	. . .	. . .	. . .	. . .	158.0	162.7
1990	142.6	144.2	162.8	162.8	162.7	156.1	178.0	. . .	. . .	. . .	. . .	171.3	175.7
1991	148.9	151.2	177.0	177.0	177.1	165.7	196.1	. . .	. . .	. . .	. . .	180.3	191.4
1992	151.4	155.7	190.1	190.1	190.5	175.8	214.0	. . .	. . .	. . .	. . .	190.3	208.5
1993	167.0	162.9	201.4	201.4	202.9	184.7	231.9	90.7	96.5	85.5	78.4	197.6	225.3
1994	172.0	168.6	211.0	211.0	213.4	192.5	245.6	92.7	95.4	88.8	83.3	205.5	239.8
1995	175.9	175.9	220.5	220.5	224.2	201.0	257.8	94.5	95.1	92.2	88.0	214.4	253.8
1996	181.9	180.5	228.2	228.2	232.4	208.3	269.5	97.4	96.6	95.3	92.7	226.9	267.1
1997	186.7	185.0	234.6	234.6	239.1	215.4	278.4	99.6	99.4	98.4	97.3	238.4	280.4
1998	190.3	187.9	242.1	242.1	246.8	222.2	287.5	101.1	101.1	100.3	102.1	250.8	294.2
1999	197.7	190.7	250.6	250.6	255.1	229.2	299.5	102.0	100.7	101.2	107.0	261.7	308.4
2000	209.6	196.1	260.8	260.8	266.0	237.7	317.3	103.3	101.0	102.5	112.5	279.9	324.0
2001	210.6	201.9	272.8	272.8	278.8	246.5	338.3	104.9	101.5	105.2	118.5	295.9	341.1
2002	207.4	209.1	285.6	285.6	292.9	253.9	367.8	106.2	102.8	107.9	126.0	317.6	362.1
2003	209.3	216.3	297.1	297.1	306.0	261.2	394.8	107.5	103.6	109.8	134.4	335.4	386.7
2004	209.1	220.6	310.1	310.1	321.3	271.5	417.9	108.6	104.2	111.6	143.7	351.0	414.3
2005	217.3	225.7	323.2	323.2	336.7	281.7	439.9	109.4	104.2	113.7	152.7	365.6	440.9
2006	226.6	230.8	336.2	336.2	350.6	289.3	468.1	110.9	104.6	116.8	162.1	388.9	468.1
2007	230.0	233.7	351.1	351.1	369.3	300.8	498.9	111.4	102.9	119.6	171.4	420.4	494.1
2008	250.5	244.1	364.1	364.1	384.9	311.0	534.0	113.3	102.6	123.6	181.3	450.2	522.1
2009	236.3	251.0	375.6	375.6	397.3	319.4	567.9	114.3	101.3	127.4	190.9	482.1	549.0
2010	251.4	259.8	388.4	388.4	411.2	328.2	607.7	113.3	99.1	129.9	199.3	505.6	573.2
2011	269.4	268.0	400.3	400.3	423.8	335.7	641.5	113.4	98.4	131.5	207.8	529.5	597.2
2010													
January	245.8	256.1	382.7	310.5	405.0	324.5	588.4	113.6	100.5	128.9	195.5	498.8	561.8
February	244.7	256.8	384.5	312.9	406.5	325.0	593.7	113.4	99.6	129.1	196.4	501.4	564.3
March	245.5	257.6	385.9	314.0	407.9	325.4	599.9	113.2	99.6	129.4	197.3	501.5	567.3
April	248.8	258.5	386.8	314.5	409.0	326.3	601.5	113.6	99.5	129.7	198.2	502.5	570.0
May	252.6	259.5	387.2	314.9	409.4	326.6	603.8	113.6	99.2	129.8	198.8	504.8	571.5
June	252.8	259.8	388.3	314.9	410.9	327.7	607.6	113.7	99.5	130.0	199.6	508.1	573.7
July	251.7	260.0	388.1	314.1	411.0	328.6	605.8	113.6	99.0	130.2	200.3	507.8	575.8
August	250.6	260.1	389.0	314.9	412.0	329.4	608.5	113.5	98.8	130.3	200.3	503.3	576.3
September	252.0	260.9	391.4	315.8	414.9	330.6	617.7	113.1	98.7	130.4	200.6	505.9	577.2
October	253.2	261.9	391.8	316.1	415.4	330.7	620.7	113.0	98.7	130.3	200.8	508.3	577.6
November	257.7	263.1	392.3	316.8	415.8	331.6	620.2	113.0	98.6	130.5	201.8	510.1	580.3
December	261.5	263.7	393.2	317.2	416.8	332.0	624.7	112.6	97.7	130.4	202.6	514.5	582.6
2011													
January	264.7	264.9	393.9	318.9	417.1	332.0	626.0	112.9	97.9	130.5	203.7	520.2	585.4
February	268.1	265.8	395.6	321.2	418.5	333.3	628.3	113.2	98.3	130.7	204.4	519.1	587.6
March	270.8	266.9	396.4	322.7	419.1	333.9	630.2	113.2	98.4	130.9	205.1	522.1	589.5
April	271.3	267.6	397.8	324.2	420.4	334.2	633.6	113.2	98.4	131.0	205.7	523.9	591.4
May	270.2	267.9	398.8	324.4	421.7	334.6	637.7	113.5	98.4	131.1	206.5	526.1	593.6
June	267.2	267.7	399.6	324.1	422.9	335.2	640.9	113.5	98.1	131.3	207.2	527.3	595.6
July	267.2	267.6	400.5	324.2	424.2	335.9	643.4	113.4	98.4	131.5	208.2	529.0	598.5
August	269.0	268.2	401.5	324.4	425.4	336.5	646.5	113.5	98.2	131.7	209.0	529.5	600.9
September	270.8	269.3	402.4	325.1	426.4	336.9	648.2	113.4	98.5	131.8	209.6	536.0	602.4
October	271.4	269.9	404.0	326.0	428.3	337.9	651.3	113.3	98.7	132.1	210.5	538.4	604.8
November	271.3	270.0	405.5	326.6	430.1	338.4	654.5	113.4	98.7	132.4	211.4	541.6	607.3
December	271.3	270.3	406.9	327.3	431.8	339.3	657.4	113.8	98.8	132.6	212.1	541.5	609.5

[3]December 1997 = 100.
. . . = Not available.

Table 8-2. Consumer Price Indexes and Purchasing Power of the Dollar—*Continued*

(1982–1984 = 100, seasonally adjusted [preliminary], except as noted.)

Year and month	CPI-U, Education and communication—*Continued* — Communication					CPI-U, Other goods and services					CPI-W, All items, not seasonally adjusted	Purchasing power of the dollar, CPI-U, 1982–1984 = $1.00
	Total 3	Information and information processing				Total	Tobacco and smoking products 1	Personal care				
		Total 3	Telephone services 1,3	Information technology, hardware, and services				Total	Personal care products 1	Personal care services 1		
				Total 1,4	Personal computers and peripheral equip- ment 1,5							
1970	. . .	. . .	. . .	. . .	. . .	40.9	43.1	43.5	42.7	44.2	39.0	2.574
1971	. . .	. . .	. . .	. . .	. . .	42.9	44.9	44.9	44.0	45.7	40.7	2.466
1972	. . .	. . .	. . .	. . .	. . .	44.7	47.4	46.0	45.2	46.8	42.1	2.391
1973	. . .	. . .	. . .	. . .	. . .	46.4	48.7	48.1	46.4	49.7	44.7	2.251
1974	. . .	. . .	. . .	. . .	. . .	49.8	51.1	52.8	51.5	53.9	49.6	2.029
1975	. . .	. . .	. . .	. . .	. . .	53.9	54.7	57.9	58.0	57.7	54.1	1.859
1976	. . .	. . .	. . .	. . .	. . .	57.0	57.0	61.7	61.3	61.9	57.2	1.757
1977	. . .	. . .	. . .	. . .	. . .	60.4	59.8	65.7	64.7	66.4	60.9	1.649
1978	. . .	. . .	. . .	. . .	. . .	64.3	63.0	69.9	68.2	71.3	65.6	1.532
1979	. . .	. . .	. . .	. . .	. . .	68.9	66.8	75.2	72.9	77.2	73.1	1.380
1980	. . .	. . .	. . .	. . .	. . .	75.2	72.0	81.9	79.6	83.7	82.9	1.215
1981	. . .	. . .	. . .	. . .	. . .	82.6	77.8	89.1	87.8	90.2	91.4	1.098
1982	. . .	. . .	. . .	. . .	. . .	91.1	86.5	95.4	95.1	95.7	96.9	1.035
1983	. . .	. . .	. . .	. . .	. . .	101.1	103.4	100.3	100.7	100.0	99.8	1.003
1984	. . .	. . .	. . .	. . .	. . .	107.9	110.1	104.3	104.2	104.4	103.3	0.961
1985	. . .	. . .	. . .	. . .	. . .	114.5	116.7	108.3	107.6	108.9	106.9	0.928
1986	. . .	. . .	. . .	. . .	. . .	121.4	124.7	111.9	111.3	112.5	108.6	0.913
1987	. . .	. . .	. . .	. . .	. . .	128.5	133.6	115.1	113.9	116.2	112.5	0.880
1988	. . .	. . .	. . .	. . .	. . .	137.0	145.8	119.4	118.1	120.7	117.0	0.846
1989	. . .	. . .	. . .	96.3	. . .	147.7	164.4	125.0	123.2	126.8	122.6	0.807
1990	. . .	. . .	. . .	93.5	. . .	159.0	181.5	130.4	128.2	132.8	129.0	0.766
1991	. . .	. . .	. . .	88.6	. . .	171.6	202.7	134.9	132.8	137.0	134.3	0.734
1992	. . .	. . .	. . .	83.7	. . .	183.3	219.8	138.3	136.5	140.0	138.2	0.713
1993	96.7	97.7	. . .	78.8	. . .	192.9	228.4	141.5	139.0	144.0	142.1	0.692
1994	97.6	98.6	. . .	72.0	. . .	198.5	220.0	144.6	141.5	147.9	145.6	0.675
1995	98.8	98.7	. . .	63.8	. . .	206.9	225.7	147.1	143.1	151.5	149.8	0.656
1996	99.6	99.5	. . .	57.2	. . .	215.4	232.8	150.1	144.3	156.6	154.1	0.638
1997	100.3	100.4	. . .	50.1	. . .	224.8	243.7	152.7	144.2	162.4	157.6	0.623
1998	98.7	98.5	100.7	39.9	875.1	237.7	274.8	156.7	148.3	166.0	159.7	0.614
1999	96.0	95.5	100.1	30.5	598.7	258.3	355.8	161.1	151.8	171.4	163.2	0.600
2000	93.6	92.8	98.5	25.9	459.9	271.1	394.9	165.6	153.7	178.1	168.9	0.581
2001	93.3	92.3	99.3	21.3	330.1	282.6	425.2	170.5	155.1	184.3	173.5	0.565
2002	92.3	90.8	99.7	18.3	248.4	293.2	461.5	174.7	154.7	188.4	175.9	0.556
2003	89.7	87.8	98.3	16.1	196.9	298.7	469.0	178.0	153.5	193.2	179.8	0.544
2004	86.7	84.6	95.8	14.8	171.2	304.7	478.0	181.7	153.9	197.6	184.5	0.530
2005	84.7	82.6	94.9	13.6	143.2	313.4	502.8	185.6	154.4	203.9	191.0	0.512
2006	84.1	81.7	95.8	12.5	120.9	321.7	519.9	190.2	155.8	209.7	197.1	0.496
2007	83.4	80.7	98.2	10.6	108.4	333.3	554.2	195.6	158.3	216.6	202.8	0.482
2008	84.2	81.4	100.5	10.1	94.9	345.4	588.7	201.3	159.3	223.7	211.1	0.465
2009	85.0	81.9	102.4	9.7	82.3	368.6	730.3	204.6	162.6	227.6	209.6	0.466
2010	84.7	81.5	102.4	9.4	76.4	381.3	807.3	206.6	161.1	229.6	214.0	0.459
2011	83.3	80.0	101.2	9.0	68.9	387.2	834.8	208.6	160.5	230.8	221.6	0.445
2010												
January	84.9	81.8	102.7	9.4	78.1	377.9	786.9	205.9	161.6	228.6	212.6	0.461
February	84.9	81.7	102.3	9.5	77.5	378.0	785.7	206.1	162.0	228.1	212.5	0.461
March	84.9	81.7	102.3	9.5	77.6	378.5	787.3	206.4	162.4	228.4	213.5	0.459
April	84.8	81.7	102.4	9.5	77.1	378.2	788.1	206.1	161.6	229.6	214.0	0.459
May	84.7	81.6	102.4	9.5	76.2	379.5	798.2	206.1	160.4	230.0	214.1	0.458
June	84.7	81.5	102.3	9.4	76.1	380.9	806.2	206.4	160.1	230.2	213.8	0.459
July	84.7	81.6	102.5	9.4	76.2	383.4	819.2	207.1	161.4	230.5	213.9	0.459
August	84.7	81.6	102.5	9.4	76.4	384.4	822.7	207.5	161.3	230.4	214.2	0.458
September	84.7	81.6	102.6	9.4	76.4	384.0	823.8	207.1	161.0	230.3	214.3	0.458
October	84.6	81.4	102.5	9.3	75.8	382.8	821.5	206.5	160.0	229.3	214.6	0.457
November	84.5	81.3	102.3	9.3	75.2	383.6	820.9	207.1	160.4	229.6	214.8	0.457
December	84.0	80.8	101.7	9.2	73.9	384.5	827.7	207.2	160.7	230.2	215.3	0.456
2011												
January	83.8	80.4	101.4	9.2	72.8	384.9	828.1	207.5	160.9	229.9	216.4	0.454
February	83.7	80.4	101.3	9.2	72.3	385.4	829.5	207.7	161.3	230.2	217.5	0.452
March	83.7	80.3	101.3	9.2	71.4	385.3	830.7	207.5	161.0	230.0	220.0	0.447
April	83.6	80.2	101.2	9.1	70.9	385.5	827.3	207.9	161.4	230.4	221.7	0.445
May	83.4	80.0	101.2	9.1	70.5	385.3	825.7	208.0	159.5	230.5	223.0	0.443
June	83.4	80.0	101.2	9.0	69.4	386.2	828.9	208.3	160.2	230.6	222.5	0.443
July	83.2	79.8	101.0	9.0	69.0	386.7	833.1	208.3	159.8	230.5	222.7	0.443
August	83.1	79.7	101.0	9.0	67.3	387.7	837.4	208.7	159.0	230.8	223.3	0.441
September	83.1	79.7	101.1	8.9	66.5	388.9	843.1	209.1	160.2	231.0	223.7	0.441
October	83.1	79.7	101.3	8.9	65.8	389.2	842.8	209.3	160.7	231.2	223.0	0.442
November	83.1	79.6	101.3	8.9	66.0	390.7	843.6	210.3	161.6	232.2	222.8	0.442
December	83.1	79.6	101.4	8.8	64.6	391.0	847.1	210.2	160.8	232.3	222.2	0.443

[1]Not seasonally adjusted.
[3]December 1997 = 100.
[4]December 1988 = 100.
[5]December 2007 = 100.
. . . = Not available.

Table 8-3. Alternative Measures of Total and Core Consumer Prices: Index Levels

(Various bases; monthly data seasonally adjusted, except as noted.)

Year and month	CPIs, all items						CPIs, all items less food and energy			Chain-type price indexes for personal consumption expenditures (PCE), 2005 = 100			
												Excluding food and energy	
	CPI-U, 1982–1984 = 100	CPI-W, 1982–1984 = 100	CPI-U-X1, 1982–1984 = 100	CPI-E, Dec. 1982 = 100, not seasonally adjusted	CPI-U-RS, Dec. 1977 = 100, not seasonally adjusted	C-CPI-U, Dec. 1999 = 100, not seasonally adjusted	CPI-U, 1982–1984 = 100	CPI-U-RS, Dec. 1977 = 100, not seasonally adjusted	C-CPI-U, Dec. 1999 = 100, not seasonally adjusted	PCE, total	PCE, market-based	PCE, total	PCE, market-based
1960	29.6	29.8	32.2	. . .	. . .	. . .	30.6	. . .	. . .	18.6	. . .	19.0	. . .
1961	29.9	30.1	32.5	. . .	. . .	. . .	31.0	. . .	. . .	18.8	. . .	19.3	. . .
1962	30.2	30.4	32.8	. . .	. . .	. . .	31.4	. . .	. . .	19.0	. . .	19.5	. . .
1963	30.6	30.8	33.3	. . .	. . .	. . .	31.8	. . .	. . .	19.3	. . .	19.8	. . .
1964	31.0	31.2	33.7	. . .	. . .	. . .	32.3	. . .	. . .	19.5	. . .	20.1	. . .
1965	31.5	31.7	34.2	. . .	. . .	. . .	32.7	. . .	. . .	19.8	. . .	20.3	. . .
1966	32.4	32.6	35.2	. . .	. . .	. . .	33.5	. . .	. . .	20.3	. . .	20.8	. . .
1967	33.4	33.6	36.3	. . .	. . .	. . .	34.7	. . .	. . .	20.8	. . .	21.4	. . .
1968	34.8	35.0	37.7	. . .	. . .	. . .	36.3	. . .	. . .	21.6	. . .	22.4	. . .
1969	36.7	36.9	39.4	. . .	. . .	. . .	38.4	. . .	. . .	22.6	. . .	23.4	. . .
1970	38.8	39.0	41.3	. . .	. . .	. . .	40.8	. . .	. . .	23.7	. . .	24.5	. . .
1971	40.5	40.7	43.1	. . .	. . .	. . .	42.7	. . .	. . .	24.7	. . .	25.7	. . .
1972	41.8	42.1	44.4	. . .	. . .	. . .	44.0	. . .	. . .	25.5	. . .	26.5	. . .
1973	44.4	44.7	47.2	. . .	. . .	. . .	45.6	. . .	. . .	26.9	. . .	27.5	. . .
1974	49.3	49.6	51.9	. . .	. . .	. . .	49.4	. . .	. . .	29.7	. . .	29.7	. . .
1975	53.8	54.1	56.2	. . .	. . .	. . .	53.9	. . .	. . .	32.2	. . .	32.2	. . .
1976	56.9	57.2	59.4	. . .	. . .	. . .	57.4	. . .	. . .	34.0	. . .	34.1	. . .
1977	60.6	60.9	63.2	. . .	. . .	. . .	61.0	. . .	. . .	36.2	. . .	36.3	. . .
1978	65.2	65.6	67.5	. . .	104.4	. . .	65.5	103.6	. . .	38.7	. . .	38.7	. . .
1979	72.6	73.1	74.0	. . .	114.4	. . .	71.9	111.0	. . .	42.1	. . .	41.6	. . .
1980	82.4	82.9	82.3	. . .	127.1	. . .	80.8	120.9	. . .	46.7	. . .	45.4	. . .
1981	90.9	91.4	90.1	. . .	139.2	. . .	89.2	132.2	. . .	50.8	. . .	49.3	. . .
1982	96.5	96.9	95.6	. . .	147.6	. . .	95.8	142.4	. . .	53.6	. . .	52.5	. . .
1983	99.6	99.8	99.6	102.1	153.9	. . .	99.6	150.4	. . .	55.9	. . .	55.2	. . .
1984	103.9	103.3	103.9	106.5	160.2	. . .	104.6	157.9	. . .	58.1	. . .	57.5	. . .
1985	107.6	106.9	107.6	110.5	165.7	. . .	109.1	164.8	. . .	60.0	. . .	59.7	. . .
1986	109.6	108.6	109.6	113.3	168.7	. . .	113.5	171.4	. . .	61.4	. . .	62.0	. . .
1987	113.6	112.5	113.6	117.7	174.4	. . .	118.2	178.1	. . .	63.6	64.5	64.3	65.5
1988	118.3	117.0	118.3	122.7	180.8	. . .	123.4	185.2	. . .	66.2	67.0	67.1	68.3
1989	124.0	122.6	124.0	128.9	188.6	. . .	129.0	192.6	. . .	69.0	70.1	69.9	71.4
1990	130.7	129.0	130.7	136.6	198.0	. . .	135.5	201.4	. . .	72.2	73.6	72.9	74.6
1991	136.2	134.3	136.2	143.0	205.1	. . .	142.1	209.9	. . .	74.8	76.4	75.7	77.8
1992	140.3	138.2	140.3	147.6	210.3	. . .	147.3	216.4	. . .	77.0	78.6	78.3	80.4
1993	144.5	142.1	144.5	152.2	215.5	. . .	152.2	222.5	. . .	78.7	80.4	80.1	82.5
1994	148.2	145.6	148.2	156.6	220.1	. . .	156.5	227.7	. . .	80.3	82.0	81.9	84.2
1995	152.4	149.8	152.4	161.2	225.4	. . .	161.2	233.4	. . .	82.1	83.7	83.8	86.0
1996	156.9	154.1	156.9	166.1	231.4	. . .	165.6	239.1	. . .	83.9	85.3	85.4	87.4
1997	160.5	157.6	160.5	170.1	236.4	. . .	169.5	244.4	. . .	85.4	86.6	87.0	88.7
1998	163.0	159.7	163.0	173.2	239.7	. . .	173.4	249.7	. . .	86.2	87.1	88.3	89.7
1999	166.6	163.2	166.6	177.3	244.7	. . .	177.0	254.8	. . .	87.6	88.4	89.6	90.8
2000	172.2	168.9	172.2	183.5	252.9	102.0	181.3	260.8	101.4	89.8	90.5	91.2	92.1
2001	177.1	173.5	177.1	189.2	260.0	104.3	186.1	267.8	103.5	91.5	92.2	92.8	93.8
2002	179.9	175.9	179.9	192.7	264.2	105.6	190.5	273.9	105.4	92.8	93.2	94.4	95.2
2003	184.0	179.8	184.0	197.4	270.1	107.8	193.2	277.9	106.6	94.7	95.0	95.8	96.4
2004	188.9	184.5	188.9	203.3	277.4	110.5	196.6	282.9	108.4	97.1	97.3	97.8	98.1
2005	195.3	191.0	195.3	210.4	286.7	113.7	200.9	289.0	110.4	100.0	100.0	100.0	100.0
2006	201.6	197.1	201.6	217.3	296.1	117.0	205.9	296.2	112.9	102.7	102.7	102.3	102.2
2007	207.3	202.8	207.3	223.8	304.5	120.0	210.7	303.1	115.0	105.5	105.3	104.6	104.3
2008	215.3	211.1	215.3	232.4	316.2	124.4	215.6	310.1	117.3	108.9	108.9	107.0	106.7
2009	214.5	209.6	214.5	231.9	315.0	123.9	219.2	315.4	119.1	109.2	109.2	108.7	108.6
2010	218.1	214.0	218.1	235.0	320.2	125.6	221.3	318.4	120.0	111.1	110.9	110.2	109.8
2011	224.9	221.6	224.9	241.8	330.3	¹129.1	225.0	323.7	¹121.8	113.8	113.7	111.8	111.3
2010													
January	217.5	213.4	217.5	233.6	318.2	125.0	220.5	316.6	119.5	110.7	110.5	109.7	109.4
February	217.4	213.3	217.4	233.8	318.3	125.0	220.6	317.3	119.7	110.7	110.6	109.8	109.4
March	217.4	213.3	217.4	234.6	319.6	125.4	220.8	318.0	119.9	110.9	110.7	110.0	109.5
April	217.4	213.2	217.4	234.9	320.1	125.6	220.9	318.1	120.0	111.0	110.7	110.0	109.5
May	217.2	212.9	217.2	235.1	320.4	125.7	221.0	318.2	119.9	110.9	110.6	110.2	109.7
June	217.2	212.9	217.2	235.0	320.1	125.5	221.3	318.3	119.9	110.7	110.4	110.2	109.8
July	217.6	213.5	217.6	235.1	320.1	125.5	221.5	318.3	120.0	111.0	110.7	110.3	109.9
August	218.1	213.9	218.1	235.3	320.6	125.8	221.6	318.7	120.2	111.2	110.9	110.4	110.0
September	218.4	214.3	218.4	235.4	320.8	125.8	221.7	319.2	120.3	111.3	111.1	110.4	110.0
October	219.0	215.1	219.0	235.6	321.2	126.0	221.8	319.5	120.4	111.5	111.2	110.5	110.0
November	219.4	215.5	219.4	235.7	321.3	125.9	222.1	319.5	120.3	111.6	111.3	110.6	110.0
December	220.4	216.6	220.4	236.1	321.9	126.1	222.2	319.0	120.2	111.9	111.6	110.6	110.1
2011													
January	221.0	217.3	221.0	237.2	323.4	¹126.7	222.6	319.6	¹120.4	112.3	112.0	110.8	110.2
February	222.0	218.4	222.0	238.3	325.0	¹127.3	223.1	320.8	¹120.8	112.7	112.5	111.0	110.4
March	223.2	219.7	223.2	240.3	328.2	¹128.4	223.4	321.8	¹121.2	113.2	113.0	111.1	110.5
April	224.0	220.7	224.0	241.5	330.3	¹129.1	223.8	322.4	¹121.4	113.6	113.4	111.3	110.8
May	224.6	221.3	224.6	242.5	331.8	¹129.5	224.4	323.0	¹121.6	113.8	113.6	111.6	111.0
June	224.8	221.5	224.8	242.5	331.5	¹129.5	224.9	323.5	¹121.8	113.6	113.5	111.8	111.3
July	225.5	222.2	225.5	242.8	331.8	¹129.6	225.4	323.9	¹121.9	114.1	113.9	112.0	111.5
August	226.3	223.0	226.3	243.3	332.7	¹130.0	225.9	324.9	¹122.2	114.4	114.2	112.2	111.7
September	226.9	223.7	226.9	243.6	333.2	¹130.2	226.1	325.5	¹122.4	114.6	114.5	112.2	111.8
October	226.8	223.6	226.8	243.3	332.5	¹130.0	226.5	326.2	¹122.7	114.6	114.5	112.4	111.9
November	227.0	223.7	227.0	243.1	332.2	¹129.9	226.9	326.3	¹122.7	114.7	114.6	112.5	112.0
December	227.0	223.7	227.0	242.8	331.4	¹129.6	227.2	326.2	¹122.6	114.7	114.6	112.7	112.2

¹Interim values.
. . . = Not available.

Table 8-4. Alternative Measures of Total and Core Consumer Prices: Inflation Rates

(Percent changes from year earlier, except as noted; monthly data seasonally adjusted, except as noted.)

Year and month	CPIs, all items						CPIs, all items less food and energy			Chain-type price indexes for personal consumption expenditures (PCE), 2000 = 100			
	CPI-U, 1982–1984 = 100	CPI-W, 1982–1984 = 100	CPI-U-X1, 1982–1984 = 100	CPI-E, Dec. 1982 = 100, not seasonally adjusted	CPI-U-RS, Dec. 1977 = 100, not seasonally adjusted	C-CPI-U, Dec. 1999 = 100, not seasonally adjusted	CPI-U, 1982–1984 = 100	CPI-U-RS, Dec. 1977 = 100, not seasonally adjusted	C-CPI-U, Dec. 1999 = 100, not seasonally adjusted	PCE, total	PCE, market-based	Excluding food and energy	
												PCE, total	PCE, market-based
1960	1.7	1.7	1.9	. . .	. . .	. . .	1.3	. . .	. . .	1.6	. . .	1.7	. . .
1961	1.0	1.0	0.9	. . .	. . .	. . .	1.3	. . .	. . .	1.0	. . .	1.3	. . .
1962	1.0	1.0	0.9	. . .	. . .	. . .	1.3	. . .	. . .	1.2	. . .	1.4	. . .
1963	1.3	1.3	1.5	. . .	. . .	. . .	1.3	. . .	. . .	1.2	. . .	1.3	. . .
1964	1.3	1.3	1.2	. . .	. . .	. . .	1.6	. . .	. . .	1.5	. . .	1.5	. . .
1965	1.6	1.6	1.5	. . .	. . .	. . .	1.2	. . .	. . .	1.4	. . .	1.3	. . .
1966	2.9	2.8	2.9	. . .	. . .	. . .	2.4	. . .	. . .	2.5	. . .	2.3	. . .
1967	3.1	3.1	3.1	. . .	. . .	. . .	3.6	. . .	. . .	2.5	. . .	3.1	. . .
1968	4.2	4.2	3.9	. . .	. . .	. . .	4.6	. . .	. . .	3.9	. . .	4.3	. . .
1969	5.5	5.4	4.5	. . .	. . .	. . .	5.8	. . .	. . .	4.5	. . .	4.7	. . .
1970	5.7	5.7	4.8	. . .	. . .	. . .	6.3	. . .	. . .	4.7	. . .	4.7	. . .
1971	4.4	4.4	4.4	. . .	. . .	. . .	4.7	. . .	. . .	4.3	. . .	4.7	. . .
1972	3.2	3.4	3.0	. . .	. . .	. . .	3.0	. . .	. . .	3.4	. . .	3.2	. . .
1973	6.2	6.2	6.3	. . .	. . .	. . .	3.6	. . .	. . .	5.4	. . .	3.8	. . .
1974	11.0	11.0	10.0	. . .	. . .	. . .	8.3	. . .	. . .	10.4	. . .	7.9	. . .
1975	9.1	9.1	8.3	. . .	. . .	. . .	9.1	. . .	. . .	8.4	. . .	8.4	. . .
1976	5.8	5.7	5.7	. . .	. . .	. . .	6.5	. . .	. . .	5.5	. . .	6.1	. . .
1977	6.5	6.5	6.4	. . .	. . .	. . .	6.3	. . .	. . .	6.5	. . .	6.4	. . .
1978	7.6	7.7	6.8	. . .	. . .	. . .	7.4	. . .	. . .	7.0	. . .	6.7	. . .
1979	11.3	11.4	9.6	. . .	9.6	. . .	9.8	7.1	. . .	8.9	. . .	7.3	. . .
1980	13.5	13.4	11.2	. . .	11.1	. . .	12.4	8.9	. . .	10.7	. . .	9.2	. . .
1981	10.3	10.3	9.5	. . .	9.5	. . .	10.4	9.3	. . .	8.9	. . .	8.7	. . .
1982	6.2	6.0	6.1	. . .	6.0	. . .	7.4	7.7	. . .	5.5	. . .	6.5	. . .
1983	3.2	3.0	4.2	. . .	4.3	. . .	4.0	5.6	. . .	4.3	. . .	5.2	. . .
1984	4.3	3.5	4.3	4.3	4.1	. . .	5.0	5.0	. . .	3.8	. . .	4.2	. . .
1985	3.6	3.5	3.6	3.8	3.4	. . .	4.3	4.4	. . .	3.3	. . .	3.8	. . .
1986	1.9	1.6	1.9	2.5	1.8	. . .	4.0	4.0	. . .	2.4	. . .	3.8	. . .
1987	3.6	3.6	3.6	3.9	3.4	. . .	4.1	3.9	. . .	3.6	. . .	3.8	. . .
1988	4.1	4.0	4.1	4.2	3.7	. . .	4.4	4.0	. . .	4.0	3.9	4.3	4.3
1989	4.8	4.8	4.8	5.0	4.3	. . .	4.5	4.0	. . .	4.3	4.6	4.1	4.4
1990	5.4	5.2	5.4	6.0	5.0	. . .	5.0	4.6	. . .	4.6	4.9	4.3	4.6
1991	4.2	4.1	4.2	4.7	3.6	. . .	4.9	4.2	. . .	3.6	3.8	3.9	4.2
1992	3.0	2.9	3.0	3.2	2.5	. . .	3.7	3.1	. . .	2.9	2.8	3.4	3.3
1993	3.0	2.8	3.0	3.2	2.5	. . .	3.3	2.8	. . .	2.2	2.4	2.4	2.6
1994	2.6	2.5	2.6	2.9	2.1	. . .	2.8	2.3	. . .	2.1	1.9	2.2	2.1
1995	2.8	2.9	2.8	2.9	2.4	. . .	3.0	2.5	. . .	2.2	2.0	2.3	2.1
1996	3.0	2.9	3.0	3.1	2.7	. . .	2.7	2.4	. . .	2.2	1.9	1.9	1.6
1997	2.3	2.3	2.3	2.4	2.2	. . .	2.4	2.2	. . .	1.9	1.5	1.9	1.5
1998	1.6	1.3	1.6	1.8	1.4	. . .	2.3	2.2	. . .	1.0	0.6	1.5	1.1
1999	2.2	2.2	2.2	2.3	2.1	. . .	2.1	2.0	. . .	1.6	1.4	1.5	1.2
2000	3.4	3.5	3.4	3.5	3.4	. . .	2.4	2.4	. . .	2.5	2.4	1.7	1.5
2001	2.8	2.7	2.8	3.1	2.8	2.3	2.6	2.7	2.1	1.9	1.9	1.8	1.8
2002	1.6	1.4	1.6	1.8	1.6	1.2	2.4	2.3	1.8	1.4	1.1	1.7	1.5
2003	2.3	2.2	2.3	2.5	2.2	2.1	1.4	1.5	1.1	2.0	2.0	1.5	1.4
2004	2.7	2.6	2.7	3.0	2.7	2.5	1.8	1.8	1.7	2.6	2.4	2.1	1.7
2005	3.4	3.5	3.4	3.5	3.4	2.9	2.2	2.2	1.8	3.0	2.8	2.2	1.9
2006	3.2	3.2	3.2	3.3	3.3	2.9	2.5	2.5	2.3	2.7	2.7	2.3	2.2
2007	2.8	2.9	2.8	3.0	2.8	2.5	2.3	2.3	1.8	2.7	2.5	2.3	2.0
2008	3.8	4.1	3.9	3.8	3.8	3.7	2.3	2.3	2.0	3.3	3.4	2.3	2.3
2009	-0.4	-0.7	-0.4	-0.2	-0.4	-0.5	1.7	1.7	1.5	0.2	0.3	1.6	1.9
2010	1.6	2.1	1.6	1.4	1.7	1.4	1.0	1.0	0.7	1.8	1.5	1.4	1.0
2011	3.2	3.6	3.1	2.9	3.2	¹2.8	1.7	1.7	¹1.5	2.5	2.5	1.4	1.4
Percent change, annual rate:													
1978–2011	3.8	3.8	3.7	. . .	3.6	. . .	3.8	3.5	. . .	3.3	. . .	3.3	. . .
1983–2011	3.0	2.9	3.0	3.1	2.8	. . .	3.0	2.8	. . .	2.6	. . .	2.5	. . .
2000–2011	2.5	2.5	2.5	2.5	2.5	2.2	2.0	2.0	1.7	2.2	2.1	1.9	1.7
2011													
January	1.6	1.8	1.6	1.5	1.6	¹1.4	1.0	0.9	¹0.7	1.5	1.3	1.0	0.8
February	2.1	2.4	2.1	2.0	2.1	¹1.9	1.1	1.1	¹0.9	1.8	1.7	1.1	0.9
March	2.6	3.0	2.6	2.4	2.7	¹2.3	1.2	1.2	¹1.0	2.0	2.1	1.0	1.0
April	3.1	3.5	3.1	2.8	3.2	¹2.7	1.3	1.4	¹1.2	2.4	2.5	1.2	1.1
May	3.4	4.0	3.4	3.2	3.6	¹3.1	1.5	1.5	¹1.4	2.6	2.7	1.3	1.3
June	3.5	4.0	3.5	3.2	3.6	¹3.2	1.6	1.6	¹1.5	2.6	2.8	1.4	1.4
July	3.6	4.1	3.6	3.3	3.7	¹3.3	1.7	1.8	¹1.6	2.8	2.9	1.6	1.5
August	3.8	4.3	3.8	3.4	3.8	¹3.4	1.9	1.9	¹1.7	2.9	3.0	1.7	1.6
September	3.9	4.4	3.9	3.5	3.9	¹3.5	2.0	2.0	¹1.8	2.9	3.1	1.6	1.6
October	3.6	4.0	3.6	3.2	3.5	¹3.2	2.1	2.1	¹1.9	2.7	2.9	1.7	1.7
November	3.5	3.8	3.5	3.2	3.4	¹3.1	2.2	2.1	¹2.0	2.7	2.9	1.8	1.8
December	3.0	3.3	3.0	2.8	3.0	¹2.7	2.2	2.3	¹2.0	2.5	2.7	1.9	2.0

¹Interim values.
. . . = Not available.

Table 8-5. Producer Price Indexes by Stage of Processing

(1982 = 100, seasonally adjusted.)

Year and month	Finished goods		Finished consumer goods	Finished consumer foods			Finished consumer goods, except foods			Capital equipment		
	Total	Percent change from previous period	Total	Total	Crude	Processed	Total	Durable goods	Nondurable goods less foods	Total	Manufacturing industries	Nonmanufacturing industries
1965	34.1	1.8	34.2	36.8	39.0	36.8	33.6	43.2	28.8	33.8	31.5	35.4
1966	35.2	3.2	35.4	39.2	41.5	39.2	34.1	43.4	29.3	34.6	32.5	36.0
1967	35.6	1.1	35.6	38.5	39.6	38.8	34.7	44.1	30.0	35.8	33.8	37.0
1968	36.6	2.8	36.5	40.0	42.5	40.0	35.5	45.1	30.6	37.0	35.0	38.2
1969	38.0	3.8	37.9	42.4	45.9	42.3	36.3	45.9	31.5	38.3	36.2	39.5
1970	39.3	3.4	39.1	43.8	46.0	43.9	37.4	47.2	32.5	40.1	38.1	41.3
1971	40.5	3.1	40.2	44.5	45.8	44.7	38.7	48.9	33.5	41.7	39.6	43.0
1972	41.8	3.2	41.5	46.9	48.0	47.2	39.4	50.0	34.1	42.8	40.5	44.2
1973	45.6	9.1	46.0	56.5	63.6	55.8	41.2	50.9	36.1	44.2	42.2	45.3
1974	52.6	15.4	53.1	64.4	71.6	63.9	48.2	55.5	44.0	50.5	48.8	51.2
1975	58.2	10.6	58.2	69.8	71.7	70.3	53.2	61.0	48.9	58.2	56.5	58.9
1976	60.8	4.5	60.4	69.6	76.7	69.0	56.5	63.7	52.4	62.1	60.3	62.9
1977	64.7	6.4	64.3	73.3	79.5	72.7	60.6	67.4	56.8	66.1	64.5	66.8
1978	69.8	7.9	69.4	79.9	85.8	79.4	64.9	73.6	60.0	71.3	70.1	71.8
1979	77.6	11.2	77.5	87.3	92.3	86.8	73.5	80.8	69.3	77.5	77.1	77.7
1980	88.0	13.4	88.6	92.4	93.9	92.3	87.1	91.0	85.1	85.8	86.0	85.7
1981	96.1	9.2	96.6	97.8	104.4	97.2	96.1	96.4	95.8	94.6	94.9	94.4
1982	100.0	4.1	100.0	100.0	100.0	100.0	100.0	100.0	100.0	100.0	100.0	100.0
1983	101.6	1.6	101.3	101.0	102.4	100.9	101.2	102.8	100.5	102.8	102.3	103.0
1984	103.7	2.1	103.3	105.4	111.4	104.9	102.2	104.5	101.1	105.2	104.9	105.4
1985	104.7	1.0	103.8	104.6	102.9	104.8	103.3	106.5	101.7	107.5	107.4	107.6
1986	103.2	-1.4	101.4	107.3	105.6	107.4	98.5	108.9	93.3	109.7	109.7	109.7
1987	105.4	2.1	103.6	109.5	107.1	109.6	100.7	111.5	94.9	111.7	111.8	111.6
1988	108.0	2.5	106.2	112.6	109.8	112.7	103.1	113.8	97.3	114.3	115.5	113.9
1989	113.6	5.2	112.1	118.7	119.6	118.6	108.9	117.6	103.8	118.8	120.3	118.2
1990	119.2	4.9	118.2	124.4	123.0	124.4	115.3	120.4	111.5	122.9	124.5	122.2
1991	121.7	2.1	120.5	124.1	119.3	124.4	118.7	123.9	115.0	126.7	127.8	126.3
1992	123.2	1.2	121.7	123.3	107.6	124.4	120.8	125.7	117.3	129.1	129.3	129.0
1993	124.7	1.2	123.0	125.7	114.4	126.5	121.7	128.0	117.6	131.4	131.2	131.4
1994	125.5	0.6	123.3	126.8	111.3	127.9	121.6	130.9	116.2	134.1	133.2	134.3
1995	127.9	1.9	125.6	129.0	118.8	129.8	124.0	132.7	118.8	136.7	135.8	137.0
1996	131.3	2.7	129.5	133.6	129.2	133.8	127.6	134.2	123.3	138.3	137.2	138.6
1997	131.8	0.4	130.2	134.5	126.6	135.1	128.2	133.7	124.3	138.2	137.7	138.4
1998	130.7	-0.8	128.9	134.3	127.2	134.8	126.4	132.9	122.2	137.6	137.9	137.4
1999	133.0	1.8	132.0	135.1	125.5	135.9	130.5	133.0	127.9	137.6	138.5	137.3
2000	138.0	3.8	138.2	137.2	123.5	138.3	138.4	133.9	138.7	138.8	139.5	138.6
2001	140.7	2.0	141.5	141.3	127.7	142.4	141.4	134.0	142.8	139.7	140.4	139.4
2002	138.9	-1.3	139.4	140.1	128.5	141.0	138.8	133.0	139.8	139.1	140.0	138.7
2003	143.3	3.2	145.3	145.9	130.0	147.2	144.7	133.1	148.4	139.5	139.9	139.3
2004	148.5	3.6	151.7	152.7	138.2	153.9	150.9	135.0	156.6	141.4	142.4	141.0
2005	155.7	4.8	160.4	155.7	140.2	156.9	161.9	136.6	172.0	144.6	146.0	144.1
2006	160.4	3.0	166.0	156.7	151.3	157.1	169.2	136.9	182.6	146.9	149.2	145.9
2007	166.6	3.9	173.5	167.0	170.2	166.7	175.6	138.3	191.7	149.5	152.5	148.3
2008	177.1	6.3	186.3	178.3	175.5	178.6	189.1	141.2	210.5	153.8	157.3	152.5
2009	172.5	-2.6	179.1	175.5	157.8	177.3	179.4	144.3	194.1	156.7	159.2	155.8
2010	179.8	4.2	189.1	182.4	172.6	183.3	190.4	144.9	210.1	157.3	159.6	156.4
2011	190.5	6.0	203.3	193.9	182.3	195.0	205.5	147.4	231.5	159.7	162.5	158.7
2010												
January	179.3	0.9	188.4	180.5	174.5	180.6	190.1	144.7	209.4	157.2	159.2	156.4
February	178.2	-0.6	186.7	181.3	180.4	180.9	187.7	144.6	205.8	157.2	159.2	156.3
March	179.1	0.5	188.1	185.6	225.2	180.6	188.0	144.9	206.2	157.2	159.4	156.3
April	178.9	-0.1	187.7	184.5	204.6	181.7	187.9	144.7	206.0	157.3	159.6	156.3
May	178.5	-0.2	187.1	183.7	185.4	183.0	187.3	145.1	204.9	157.6	159.8	156.6
June	178.2	-0.2	186.6	179.4	152.4	181.9	188.2	145.0	206.4	157.5	159.9	156.6
July	178.6	0.2	187.2	181.2	167.7	182.1	188.3	145.2	206.4	157.8	160.0	156.8
August	179.9	0.7	188.8	180.6	160.7	182.3	190.7	145.6	209.8	158.0	160.2	157.1
September	180.6	0.4	189.8	182.1	158.6	184.2	191.4	145.8	210.8	158.2	160.2	157.3
October	182.0	0.8	191.9	183.4	157.6	185.8	193.9	144.9	214.9	157.6	160.0	156.7
November	182.7	0.4	193.1	185.2	170.6	186.3	194.8	144.7	216.4	157.5	159.9	156.5
December	184.4	0.9	195.4	186.6	185.2	186.2	197.4	144.7	220.2	157.6	160.2	156.6
2011												
January	185.8	0.8	197.1	187.4	187.9	186.8	199.5	145.0	223.2	158.1	160.8	157.0
February	187.9	1.1	200.1	194.0	232.4	189.1	201.1	145.4	225.4	158.5	161.3	157.4
March	188.9	0.5	201.3	193.0	201.3	191.5	203.1	146.1	228.1	158.9	161.7	157.8
April	190.2	0.7	202.9	193.1	189.7	192.9	205.2	146.6	230.9	159.4	162.3	158.2
May	190.3	0.1	203.0	190.8	170.7	192.4	206.1	146.8	232.3	159.5	162.4	158.4
June	190.4	0.1	202.9	192.4	178.6	193.4	205.5	147.5	230.9	160.1	162.9	159.0
July	191.4	0.5	204.2	194.4	176.5	195.8	206.5	148.2	232.0	160.6	163.4	159.5
August	191.8	0.2	204.6	196.3	178.3	197.7	206.5	148.5	231.8	160.6	163.4	159.5
September	193.6	0.9	207.1	197.3	183.7	198.3	209.3	148.9	235.9	161.0	163.6	159.9
October	193.0	-0.3	206.2	197.4	183.8	198.3	208.1	148.8	234.2	160.9	163.4	159.8
November	193.2	0.1	206.5	199.3	189.6	199.8	207.9	148.8	233.9	160.9	163.4	159.9
December	193.1	-0.1	206.2	197.9	176.2	199.7	208.0	149.0	233.9	161.3	163.6	160.3

Table 8-5. Producer Price Indexes by Stage of Processing—*Continued*

(1982 = 100, seasonally adjusted.)

Year and month	Total	Materials and components for manufacturing					Materials and components for construction	Processed fuels and lubricants			Containers, nonreturnable	Supplies	
		Total	Materials for food manufacturing	Materials for nondurable manufacturing	Materials for durable manufacturing	Components for manufacturing		Total	Manufacturing industries	Nonmanufacturing industries		Total	Manufacturing industries
1965	31.2	33.6	38.3	35.2	31.2	34.2	32.8	16.5	19.6	14.4	33.5	35.0	36.1
1966	32.0	34.3	40.0	35.4	31.8	35.4	33.6	16.8	19.9	14.7	34.5	36.5	37.1
1967	32.2	34.5	39.2	35.2	32.3	36.5	34.0	16.9	20.1	14.8	35.0	36.8	37.6
1968	33.0	35.3	39.8	35.6	33.4	37.3	35.7	16.5	19.8	14.2	35.9	37.1	38.7
1969	34.1	36.5	42.0	36.0	35.2	38.5	37.7	16.6	20.0	14.4	37.2	37.8	39.8
1970	35.4	38.0	44.3	36.5	37.0	40.6	38.3	17.7	21.5	15.2	39.0	39.7	41.4
1971	36.8	38.9	45.7	37.0	38.1	41.9	40.8	19.5	23.6	16.6	40.8	40.8	42.5
1972	38.2	40.4	47.0	38.5	39.9	42.9	43.0	20.1	24.5	16.9	42.7	42.5	43.3
1973	42.4	44.1	57.2	42.6	43.1	44.3	46.5	22.2	26.4	19.4	45.2	51.7	45.6
1974	52.5	56.0	82.0	54.6	55.4	51.1	55.0	33.6	35.5	32.7	53.3	56.8	53.3
1975	58.0	61.7	82.1	61.4	60.8	57.8	60.1	39.4	41.9	38.0	60.0	61.8	59.4
1976	60.9	64.0	70.6	64.8	64.8	60.8	64.1	42.3	44.8	41.1	63.1	65.8	62.6
1977	64.9	67.4	71.9	66.8	70.2	64.5	69.3	47.7	51.0	46.2	65.9	69.3	66.6
1978	69.5	72.0	81.0	69.2	76.2	69.2	76.5	49.9	53.7	48.1	71.0	72.9	71.2
1979	78.4	80.9	89.9	78.3	87.3	75.8	84.2	61.6	64.3	60.4	79.4	80.2	78.1
1980	90.3	91.7	103.7	91.2	97.1	84.6	91.3	85.0	85.5	84.7	89.1	89.9	87.2
1981	98.6	98.7	102.1	100.5	100.7	94.7	97.9	100.6	100.2	101.0	96.7	96.9	95.2
1982	100.0	100.0	100.0	100.0	100.0	100.0	100.0	100.0	100.0	100.0	100.0	100.0	100.0
1983	100.6	101.2	101.3	98.5	103.0	102.4	102.8	95.4	96.2	94.9	100.4	101.8	101.5
1984	103.1	104.1	106.3	102.1	104.9	105.0	105.6	95.7	97.1	94.6	105.9	104.1	105.0
1985	102.7	103.3	101.5	100.5	103.3	106.4	107.3	92.8	93.8	92.0	109.0	104.4	107.3
1986	99.1	102.2	98.4	98.1	101.2	107.5	108.1	72.7	75.1	71.2	110.3	105.6	108.3
1987	101.5	105.3	100.8	102.2	106.2	108.8	109.8	73.3	75.9	71.7	114.5	107.7	110.0
1988	107.1	113.2	106.0	112.9	118.7	112.3	116.1	71.2	73.3	69.9	120.1	113.7	114.8
1989	112.0	118.1	112.7	118.5	123.6	116.4	121.3	76.4	78.3	75.3	125.4	118.1	119.8
1990	114.5	118.7	117.9	118.0	120.7	119.0	122.9	85.9	87.3	85.0	127.7	119.4	122.1
1991	114.4	118.1	115.3	116.7	117.2	121.0	124.5	85.3	88.4	83.4	128.1	121.4	124.4
1992	114.7	117.9	113.9	115.4	117.2	122.0	126.5	84.5	87.5	82.6	127.7	122.7	125.9
1993	116.2	118.9	115.6	115.5	119.1	123.0	132.0	84.7	88.1	82.6	126.4	125.0	128.5
1994	118.5	122.1	118.5	119.2	125.2	124.3	136.6	83.1	86.1	81.1	129.7	127.0	130.7
1995	124.9	130.4	119.5	135.1	135.6	126.5	142.1	84.2	87.1	82.3	148.8	132.1	137.0
1996	125.7	128.6	125.3	130.5	131.3	126.9	143.6	90.0	92.4	88.4	141.1	135.9	138.7
1997	125.6	128.3	123.2	129.6	132.8	126.4	146.5	89.3	92.0	87.6	136.0	135.9	139.4
1998	123.0	126.1	123.2	126.7	128.0	125.9	146.8	81.1	85.8	78.1	140.8	134.8	140.6
1999	123.2	124.6	120.8	124.9	125.1	125.7	148.9	84.6	87.9	82.5	142.5	134.2	140.7
2000	129.2	128.1	119.2	132.6	129.0	126.2	150.7	102.0	100.9	102.3	151.6	136.9	143.5
2001	129.7	127.4	124.3	131.8	125.1	126.4	150.6	104.5	105.7	103.5	153.1	138.7	145.4
2002	127.8	126.1	123.2	129.2	124.7	126.1	151.3	96.3	98.7	94.8	152.1	138.9	144.7
2003	133.7	129.7	134.4	137.2	127.9	125.9	153.6	112.6	116.0	110.5	153.7	141.5	146.5
2004	142.6	137.9	145.0	147.8	146.6	127.4	166.4	124.3	125.1	123.8	159.3	146.7	149.2
2005	154.0	146.0	146.0	163.2	158.3	129.9	176.6	150.0	148.6	150.9	167.1	151.9	155.7
2006	164.0	155.9	146.2	175.0	180.5	134.5	188.4	162.8	158.1	165.7	175.0	157.0	161.1
2007	170.7	162.4	161.4	184.0	189.8	136.3	192.5	173.9	172.6	175.0	180.3	161.7	162.9
2008	188.3	177.2	180.4	214.3	203.3	140.3	205.4	206.2	199.4	209.6	191.8	173.8	170.5
2009	172.5	162.7	165.1	191.6	168.9	141.0	202.9	161.9	165.7	160.9	195.8	172.2	168.0
2010	183.4	174.0	174.4	215.4	186.6	142.2	205.7	185.2	184.8	185.8	201.2	175.0	172.2
2011	199.8	189.8	193.4	249.2	204.2	145.8	212.8	215.0	213.2	216.2	205.4	184.2	180.5
2010													
January	180.5	169.6	169.9	207.6	179.8	141.1	202.6	184.6	178.6	187.7	194.3	172.9	168.3
February	180.3	171.1	170.4	211.9	180.8	141.2	203.7	179.3	174.1	182.1	196.3	173.0	169.0
March	181.1	172.6	170.2	215.0	183.4	141.5	204.6	179.1	175.3	181.4	199.1	173.2	170.3
April	182.5	174.9	171.8	217.9	189.1	142.1	206.0	179.2	175.0	181.5	200.4	173.7	171.5
May	182.9	175.2	173.0	217.1	190.5	142.3	207.2	179.2	176.9	180.8	201.9	174.3	172.4
June	181.9	173.6	171.7	213.0	188.2	142.4	206.5	177.9	176.9	179.0	203.9	174.2	172.8
July	181.4	172.6	172.2	211.7	185.1	142.4	206.2	177.7	175.5	179.3	204.4	174.4	172.9
August	182.5	173.1	173.7	213.2	184.7	142.6	206.2	181.5	178.9	183.3	204.8	174.8	173.2
September	183.4	174.1	176.9	214.8	186.1	142.6	206.0	183.1	179.7	185.1	201.9	175.4	173.4
October	185.6	175.8	179.3	218.1	188.9	142.6	206.3	188.7	185.0	190.9	202.1	176.6	173.7
November	186.9	177.4	181.9	221.9	190.9	142.6	206.7	189.9	186.7	192.0	202.5	177.7	174.1
December	189.2	178.8	180.9	225.8	192.3	142.9	207.5	196.7	191.3	199.5	202.9	178.3	174.8
2011													
January	191.7	181.8	181.5	232.2	196.5	143.7	208.6	200.2	194.3	203.4	203.5	179.5	176.0
February	195.0	185.4	187.0	238.7	202.2	144.2	209.7	205.8	198.5	209.5	204.2	180.8	176.7
March	197.4	187.7	190.2	244.3	204.0	144.7	210.8	210.4	202.4	214.4	204.9	182.2	178.2
April	200.0	190.9	192.0	252.0	207.7	145.3	212.0	213.1	205.2	217.1	205.2	183.7	179.8
May	201.4	192.4	190.6	257.5	207.4	145.7	212.6	215.9	208.1	219.8	206.7	184.1	181.1
June	201.9	192.3	192.4	256.6	206.7	146.1	213.6	217.2	212.6	220.0	206.5	184.8	182.4
July	202.8	193.4	195.4	258.1	207.9	146.4	214.6	218.3	215.7	220.3	207.0	185.3	182.5
August	201.8	192.8	198.5	255.4	207.2	146.5	214.7	214.3	212.6	215.8	205.6	185.8	182.0
September	203.0	192.9	198.7	256.6	206.2	146.5	214.7	218.9	215.9	221.0	205.6	186.5	182.3
October	200.9	190.9	197.6	251.8	202.7	146.7	214.8	213.9	209.0	216.7	205.3	185.9	182.3
November	200.6	189.9	198.7	248.1	202.1	146.8	214.7	215.2	209.8	218.2	205.3	185.6	181.9
December	200.1	188.1	197.4	242.7	200.7	146.9	214.7	217.2	214.1	219.3	205.6	185.1	181.5

Table 8-5. Producer Price Indexes by Stage of Processing—*Continued*

(1982 = 100, seasonally adjusted.)

Year and month	Intermediate materials, supplies, and components—*Continued*			Crude materials for further processing								
	Supplies—*Continued*											
	Nonmanufacturing industries			Total	Foodstuffs and feedstuffs	Crude nonfood materials					Crude fuel [3]	
							Crude nonfood materials except fuel [2]					
	Total	Feeds	Other supplies			Total	Total [2]	Manu-facturing [2]	Construc-tion	Total	Manu-facturing industries	Nonmanu-facturing industries
1965	34.5	45.9	33.0	31.1	39.2	. . .	27.7	27.2	36.1	10.6	9.0	11.9
1966	36.2	50.0	33.8	33.1	42.7	. . .	28.3	27.8	36.3	10.9	9.3	12.3
1967	36.3	48.3	34.5	31.3	40.3	21.1	26.5	25.8	37.0	11.3	9.7	12.8
1968	36.4	46.5	35.4	31.8	40.9	21.6	27.1	26.3	38.4	11.5	9.9	13.1
1969	36.9	46.4	36.0	33.9	44.1	22.5	28.4	27.6	39.8	12.0	10.2	13.8
1970	38.9	49.9	37.6	35.2	45.2	23.8	29.1	28.3	42.1	13.8	11.3	16.6
1971	39.9	50.4	38.9	36.0	46.1	24.7	29.4	28.4	44.1	15.7	12.6	19.3
1972	42.0	56.1	39.8	39.9	51.5	27.0	32.3	31.5	45.0	16.8	13.5	20.6
1973	54.7	97.3	42.7	54.5	72.6	34.3	42.9	42.7	46.2	18.6	14.8	22.9
1974	58.4	90.2	50.5	61.4	76.4	44.1	54.5	55.0	50.0	24.8	19.1	31.8
1975	62.9	84.0	58.9	61.6	77.4	43.7	50.0	49.7	55.9	30.6	24.4	38.0
1976	67.3	95.1	62.0	63.4	76.8	48.2	54.9	54.7	59.6	34.5	29.0	40.5
1977	70.7	99.3	65.2	65.5	77.5	51.7	56.3	56.0	63.1	42.0	37.2	47.4
1978	73.8	95.5	69.7	73.4	87.3	57.5	61.9	61.5	68.7	48.2	43.1	53.8
1979	81.2	106.9	76.3	85.9	100.0	69.6	75.5	75.6	76.6	57.3	53.1	62.0
1980	91.1	110.6	87.5	95.3	104.6	84.6	91.8	92.3	87.9	69.4	66.7	72.5
1981	97.8	111.3	95.4	103.0	103.9	101.8	109.8	110.9	96.8	84.8	83.6	86.2
1982	100.0	100.0	100.0	100.0	100.0	100.0	100.0	100.0	100.0	100.0	100.0	100.0
1983	102.0	109.1	101.0	101.3	101.8	100.7	98.8	98.6	100.1	105.1	105.8	104.4
1984	103.7	104.2	103.7	103.5	104.7	102.2	101.0	100.8	103.1	105.1	105.6	104.6
1985	103.0	86.6	105.3	95.8	94.8	96.9	94.3	93.1	105.7	102.7	102.7	102.5
1986	104.2	90.5	106.2	87.7	93.2	81.6	76.0	72.6	106.5	92.2	91.1	93.6
1987	106.6	94.6	108.3	93.7	96.2	87.9	88.5	84.7	114.8	84.1	82.1	86.3
1988	113.2	115.0	112.7	96.0	106.1	85.5	85.9	81.5	126.5	82.1	80.1	84.5
1989	117.2	114.4	117.5	103.1	111.2	93.4	95.8	91.0	136.9	85.3	83.9	87.0
1990	118.0	102.8	120.2	108.9	113.1	101.5	107.3	102.5	145.2	84.8	82.9	87.0
1991	119.9	101.3	122.5	101.2	105.5	94.6	97.5	92.2	147.5	82.9	82.3	84.1
1992	121.1	103.0	123.7	100.4	105.1	93.5	94.2	87.9	162.1	84.0	83.1	85.2
1993	123.2	105.4	125.8	102.4	108.4	94.7	94.1	85.6	193.6	87.1	85.9	88.6
1994	125.1	105.8	127.9	101.8	106.5	94.8	97.0	88.3	199.1	82.4	81.7	83.6
1995	129.5	103.4	133.2	102.7	105.8	96.8	105.8	97.3	201.7	72.1	72.5	72.9
1996	134.4	133.1	134.6	113.8	121.5	106.5	105.7	97.6	195.7	92.6	90.7	94.3
1997	134.1	129.1	134.8	111.1	112.2	106.4	103.5	95.0	201.4	101.3	98.4	103.3
1998	132.2	100.2	136.2	96.8	103.9	88.4	84.5	76.7	196.0	86.7	84.8	88.5
1999	131.4	89.2	136.5	98.2	98.7	94.3	91.1	83.0	195.7	91.2	90.0	92.9
2000	134.1	94.6	138.8	120.6	100.2	130.4	118.0	108.7	193.4	136.9	136.9	139.3
2001	135.8	96.8	140.5	121.0	106.1	126.8	101.5	93.2	181.7	151.4	150.2	154.2
2002	136.3	98.1	140.9	108.1	99.5	111.4	101.0	92.5	181.4	117.3	113.4	119.8
2003	139.0	106.6	143.1	135.3	113.5	148.2	116.9	107.5	180.8	185.7	176.4	189.9
2004	144.9	119.1	148.4	159.0	127.0	179.2	149.2	137.7	191.8	211.4	200.5	216.2
2005	149.7	107.4	154.9	182.2	122.7	223.4	176.7	163.4	199.3	279.7	263.9	286.3
2006	154.7	110.9	160.1	184.8	119.3	230.6	210.0	194.5	201.1	241.5	229.2	247.0
2007	160.1	138.4	163.2	207.1	146.7	246.3	238.7	221.6	201.7	236.8	224.9	242.2
2008	173.2	182.4	173.4	251.8	163.4	313.9	308.5	287.3	199.0	298.3	283.5	305.0
2009	171.4	170.7	173.0	175.2	134.5	197.5	211.1	197.1	200.5	166.3	185.0	169.0
2010	174.0	166.6	176.2	212.2	152.4	249.3	280.8	265.0	203.0	188.0	202.3	191.3
2011	183.3	203.2	183.3	249.4	188.4	284.0	342.0	324.6	206.6	181.5	206.0	184.3
2010												
January	172.2	170.8	174.0	219.0	143.6	269.9	287.0	270.6	199.9	231.5	226.1	236.3
February	172.2	165.4	174.4	215.7	142.6	264.7	285.5	269.2	200.4	221.1	219.0	225.6
March	172.2	162.2	174.7	213.4	147.4	255.8	284.8	268.5	200.5	200.5	205.7	204.3
April	172.6	157.7	175.5	208.6	148.3	246.0	287.1	270.7	200.5	173.6	189.0	176.5
May	173.2	158.4	176.1	204.5	149.3	237.3	268.5	252.6	201.4	179.6	194.0	182.7
June	173.0	158.8	175.9	199.5	142.1	235.1	263.3	247.5	201.7	181.9	196.6	185.0
July	173.2	159.5	176.0	203.2	147.0	237.2	257.5	241.8	201.9	195.7	206.0	199.2
August	173.6	162.1	176.3	209.0	151.3	243.8	268.4	252.3	204.0	195.7	207.5	199.2
September	174.3	164.3	176.8	210.1	159.8	237.6	277.8	261.5	203.1	166.9	187.8	169.4
October	175.6	173.1	177.5	220.2	164.9	251.5	299.4	282.5	203.8	168.7	189.8	171.3
November	176.8	181.6	178.1	221.1	166.0	252.2	308.6	291.6	203.6	156.8	182.6	159.0
December	177.5	186.5	178.4	235.0	166.7	277.4	332.5	314.8	204.8	182.8	200.5	185.8
2011												
January	178.6	189.6	179.4	242.5	173.1	285.3	343.6	325.6	204.3	185.6	203.2	188.6
February	180.0	194.6	180.5	251.3	184.6	290.7	350.3	332.2	203.9	188.7	206.3	191.9
March	181.3	200.2	181.4	248.8	186.4	284.2	348.9	330.8	204.2	175.3	198.1	178.0
April	182.8	207.9	182.4	257.5	192.1	294.8	359.1	340.8	204.4	185.9	205.2	188.9
May	183.1	208.5	182.7	250.3	185.7	287.6	345.1	327.1	204.8	188.9	207.5	192.0
June	183.7	209.7	183.3	251.0	189.1	285.6	340.8	322.8	206.4	190.5	209.1	193.6
July	184.2	205.0	184.2	250.5	188.9	284.9	339.2	321.2	206.7	191.1	210.4	194.2
August	184.9	207.8	184.7	248.3	195.4	274.4	322.4	304.9	206.3	190.5	211.0	193.5
September	185.7	213.9	185.1	252.4	194.1	283.5	345.0	326.9	206.4	179.2	204.7	181.9
October	185.0	205.7	185.0	248.0	190.5	278.8	341.8	323.7	206.8	172.5	200.3	174.9
November	184.7	200.0	185.1	252.6	192.8	285.0	357.1	338.7	207.0	165.1	196.1	167.3
December	184.2	196.8	184.9	251.0	187.2	287.5	362.9	344.3	207.9	162.5	195.1	164.6

[2]Includes crude petroleum.
[3]Excludes crude petroleum.
. . . = Not available.

Table 8-6. Producer Price Indexes by Major Commodity Groups

(1982 = 100.)

Year and month	All commodities	Farm products	Processed foods and feeds	Industrial commodities Total	Textile products and apparel	Hides, leather, and related products	Fuels and related products and power	Chemicals and allied products	Rubber and plastics products	Lumber and wood products	Pulp, paper, and allied products	Metals and metal products	Machinery and equipment	Furniture and household durables	Nonmetallic mineral products	Transportation equipment	Miscellaneous products
1950	27.3	44.0	33.2	25.0	50.2	32.9	12.6	30.4	35.6	31.4	25.7	22.0	22.6	40.9	23.5	. . .	28.6
1951	30.4	51.2	36.9	27.6	56.0	37.7	13.0	34.8	43.7	34.1	30.5	24.5	25.3	44.4	25.0	. . .	30.3
1952	29.6	48.4	36.4	26.9	50.5	30.5	13.0	33.0	39.6	33.2	29.7	24.5	25.3	43.5	25.0	. . .	30.2
1953	29.2	43.8	34.8	27.2	49.3	31.0	13.4	33.4	36.9	33.1	29.6	25.3	25.9	44.4	26.0	. . .	31.0
1954	29.3	43.2	35.4	27.2	48.2	29.5	13.2	33.8	37.5	32.5	29.6	25.5	26.3	44.9	26.6	. . .	31.3
1955	29.3	40.5	33.8	27.8	48.2	29.4	13.2	33.7	42.4	34.1	30.4	27.2	27.2	45.1	27.3	. . .	31.3
1956	30.3	40.0	33.8	29.1	48.2	31.2	13.6	33.9	43.0	34.6	32.4	29.6	29.3	46.3	28.5	. . .	31.7
1957	31.2	41.1	34.8	29.9	48.3	31.2	14.3	34.6	42.8	32.8	33.0	30.2	31.4	47.5	29.6	. . .	32.6
1958	31.6	42.9	36.5	30.0	47.4	31.6	13.7	34.9	42.8	32.5	33.4	30.0	32.1	47.9	29.9	. . .	33.3
1959	31.7	40.2	35.6	30.5	48.1	35.9	13.7	34.8	42.6	34.7	33.7	30.6	32.8	48.0	30.3	. . .	33.4
1960	31.7	40.1	35.6	30.5	48.6	34.6	13.9	34.8	42.7	33.5	34.0	30.6	33.0	47.8	30.4	. . .	33.6
1961	31.6	39.7	36.2	30.4	47.8	34.9	14.0	34.5	41.1	32.0	33.0	30.5	33.0	47.5	30.5	. . .	33.7
1962	31.7	40.4	36.5	30.4	48.2	35.3	14.0	33.9	39.9	32.2	33.4	30.2	33.0	47.2	30.5	. . .	33.9
1963	31.6	39.6	36.8	30.3	48.2	34.3	13.9	33.5	40.1	32.8	33.1	30.3	33.1	46.9	30.3	. . .	34.2
1964	31.6	39.0	36.7	30.5	48.5	34.4	13.5	33.6	39.6	33.5	33.0	31.1	33.3	47.1	30.4	. . .	34.4
1965	32.3	40.7	38.0	30.9	48.8	35.9	13.8	33.9	39.7	33.7	33.3	32.0	33.7	46.8	30.4	. . .	34.7
1966	33.3	43.7	40.2	31.5	48.9	39.4	14.1	34.0	40.5	35.2	34.2	32.8	34.7	47.4	30.7	. . .	35.3
1967	33.4	41.3	39.8	32.0	48.9	38.1	14.4	34.2	41.4	35.1	34.6	33.2	35.9	48.3	31.2	. . .	36.2
1968	34.2	42.3	40.6	32.8	50.7	39.3	14.3	34.1	42.8	39.8	35.0	34.0	37.0	49.7	32.4	. . .	37.0
1969	35.6	45.0	42.7	33.9	51.8	41.5	14.6	34.2	43.6	44.0	36.0	36.0	38.2	50.7	33.6	40.4	38.1
1970	36.9	45.8	44.6	35.2	52.4	42.0	15.3	35.0	44.9	39.9	37.5	38.7	40.0	51.9	35.3	41.9	39.8
1971	38.1	46.6	45.5	36.5	53.3	43.4	16.6	35.6	45.2	44.7	38.1	39.4	41.4	53.1	38.2	44.2	40.8
1972	39.8	51.6	48.0	37.8	55.5	50.0	17.1	35.6	45.3	50.7	39.3	40.9	42.3	53.8	39.4	45.5	41.5
1973	45.0	72.7	58.9	40.3	60.5	54.5	19.4	37.6	46.6	62.2	42.3	44.0	43.7	55.7	40.7	46.1	43.3
1974	53.5	77.4	68.0	49.2	68.0	55.2	30.1	50.2	56.4	64.5	52.5	57.0	50.0	61.8	47.8	50.3	48.1
1975	58.4	77.0	72.6	54.9	67.4	56.5	35.4	62.0	62.2	62.1	59.0	61.5	57.9	67.5	54.4	56.7	53.4
1976	61.1	78.8	70.8	58.4	72.4	63.9	38.3	64.0	66.0	72.2	62.1	65.0	61.3	70.3	58.2	60.5	55.6
1977	64.9	79.4	74.0	62.5	75.3	68.3	43.6	65.9	69.4	83.0	64.6	69.3	65.2	73.2	62.6	64.6	59.4
1978	69.9	87.7	80.6	67.0	78.1	76.1	46.5	68.0	72.4	96.9	67.7	75.3	70.3	77.5	69.6	69.5	66.7
1979	78.7	99.6	88.5	75.7	82.5	96.1	58.9	76.0	80.5	105.5	75.9	86.0	76.7	82.8	77.6	75.3	75.5
1980	89.8	102.9	95.9	88.0	89.7	94.7	82.8	89.0	90.1	101.5	86.3	95.0	86.0	90.7	88.4	82.9	93.6
1981	98.0	105.2	98.9	97.4	97.6	99.3	100.2	98.4	96.4	102.8	94.8	99.6	94.4	95.9	96.7	94.3	96.1
1982	100.0	100.0	100.0	100.0	100.0	100.0	100.0	100.0	100.0	100.0	100.0	100.0	100.0	100.0	100.0	100.0	100.0
1983	101.3	102.4	101.8	101.1	100.3	103.2	95.9	100.3	100.8	107.9	103.3	101.8	102.7	103.4	101.6	102.8	104.8
1984	103.7	105.5	105.4	103.3	102.7	109.0	94.8	102.9	102.3	108.0	110.3	104.8	105.1	105.7	105.4	105.2	107.0
1985	103.2	95.1	103.5	103.7	102.9	108.9	91.4	103.7	101.9	106.6	113.3	104.4	107.2	107.1	108.6	107.9	109.4
1986	100.2	92.9	105.4	100.0	103.2	113.0	69.8	102.6	101.9	107.2	116.1	103.2	108.8	108.2	110.0	110.5	111.6
1987	102.8	95.5	107.9	102.6	105.1	120.4	70.2	106.4	103.0	112.8	121.8	107.1	110.4	109.9	110.0	112.5	114.9
1988	106.9	104.9	112.7	106.3	109.2	131.4	66.7	116.3	109.3	118.9	130.4	118.7	113.2	113.1	111.2	114.3	120.2
1989	112.2	110.9	117.8	111.6	112.3	136.3	72.9	123.0	112.6	126.7	137.8	124.1	117.4	116.9	112.6	117.7	126.5
1990	116.3	112.2	121.9	115.8	115.0	141.7	82.3	123.6	113.6	129.7	141.2	122.9	120.7	119.2	114.7	121.5	134.2
1991	116.5	105.7	121.9	116.5	116.3	138.9	81.2	125.6	115.1	132.1	142.9	120.2	123.0	121.2	117.2	126.4	140.8
1992	117.2	103.6	122.1	117.4	117.8	140.4	80.4	125.9	115.1	146.6	145.2	119.2	123.4	122.2	117.3	130.4	145.3
1993	118.9	107.1	124.0	119.0	118.0	143.7	80.0	128.2	116.0	174.0	147.3	119.2	124.0	123.7	120.0	133.7	145.4
1994	120.4	106.3	125.5	120.7	118.3	148.5	77.8	132.1	117.6	180.0	152.5	124.8	125.1	126.1	124.2	137.2	141.9
1995	124.7	107.4	127.0	125.5	120.8	153.7	78.0	142.5	124.3	178.1	172.2	134.5	126.6	128.2	129.0	139.7	145.4
1996	127.7	122.4	133.3	127.3	122.4	150.5	85.8	142.1	123.8	176.1	168.7	131.0	126.5	130.4	131.0	141.7	147.7
1997	127.6	112.9	134.0	127.7	122.6	154.2	86.1	143.6	123.2	183.8	167.9	131.8	125.9	130.8	133.2	141.6	150.9
1998	124.4	104.6	131.6	124.8	122.9	148.0	75.3	143.9	122.6	179.1	171.7	127.8	124.9	131.3	135.4	141.2	156.0
1999	125.5	98.4	131.1	126.5	121.1	146.0	80.5	144.2	122.5	183.6	174.1	124.6	124.3	131.7	138.9	141.8	166.6
2000	132.7	99.5	133.1	134.8	121.4	151.5	103.5	151.0	125.5	178.2	183.7	128.1	124.0	132.6	142.5	143.8	170.8
2001	134.2	103.8	137.3	135.7	121.3	158.4	105.3	151.8	127.2	174.4	184.8	125.4	123.7	133.2	144.3	145.2	181.3
2002	131.1	99.0	136.2	132.4	119.9	157.6	93.2	151.9	126.8	173.3	185.9	125.9	122.9	133.5	146.2	144.6	182.4
2003	138.1	111.5	143.4	139.1	119.8	162.3	112.9	161.8	130.1	177.4	190.0	129.2	121.9	133.9	148.2	145.7	179.6
2004	146.7	123.3	151.2	147.6	121.0	164.5	126.9	174.4	133.8	195.6	195.7	149.6	122.1	135.1	153.2	148.6	183.2
2005	157.4	118.5	153.1	160.2	122.8	165.4	156.4	192.0	143.8	196.5	202.6	160.8	123.7	139.4	164.2	151.0	195.1
2006	164.7	117.0	153.8	168.8	124.5	168.4	166.7	205.8	153.8	194.4	209.8	181.6	126.2	142.6	179.9	152.6	205.6
2007	172.6	143.4	165.1	175.1	125.8	173.6	177.6	214.8	155.0	192.4	216.9	193.5	127.3	144.7	186.2	155.0	210.3
2008	189.6	161.3	180.5	192.3	128.9	173.1	214.6	245.5	165.9	191.3	226.8	213.0	129.7	148.9	197.1	158.6	216.6
2009	172.9	134.6	176.2	174.8	129.5	157.0	158.7	229.4	165.2	182.8	225.6	186.8	131.3	153.1	202.4	162.2	217.5
2010	184.7	151.0	182.3	187.0	131.7	181.4	185.8	246.6	170.7	192.7	236.9	207.6	131.1	153.2	201.8	163.4	221.5
2011	201.0	186.7	197.5	202.0	141.7	199.9	215.9	275.1	182.7	194.7	245.1	225.9	132.7	156.4	205.0	166.1	229.2

. . . = Not available.

Table 8-7. Producer Price Indexes for the Net Output of Selected NAICS Industry Groups

(Various index bases, not seasonally adjusted.)

Year and month	Mining		Manufacturing (Dec. 1984 = 100)									
	Total (Dec. 1984 = 100)	Oil and gas extraction (Dec. 1985 = 100)	Total	Food manu- facturing	Leather and products	Petroleum and coal products	Chemicals	Plastics and rubber products	Nonmetallic mineral products	Primary metals	Fabricated metal products	Furniture and related products
1990	81.8	82.7	114.5	116.2	122.6	91.4	121.0	111.3	110.0	116.5	115.1	119.1
1991	78.4	77.9	115.9	116.5	124.8	83.1	124.4	113.7	112.3	113.1	116.6	121.6
1992	76.9	76.5	117.4	116.9	127.0	80.3	125.8	114.2	112.8	111.7	117.2	122.9
1993	76.4	76.2	119.1	118.7	129.0	77.6	127.2	115.4	115.4	111.4	118.2	125.4
1994	73.3	71.1	120.7	120.1	130.6	74.8	130.0	117.1	119.6	117.0	120.3	129.7
1995	71.0	66.6	124.2	121.7	134.1	77.2	143.4	123.3	124.3	128.2	124.8	133.3
1996	84.4	84.8	127.1	127.1	134.7	87.4	145.8	123.1	125.8	123.7	126.2	136.2
1997	86.1	87.5	127.5	127.9	137.1	85.6	147.1	122.8	127.4	124.7	127.6	138.2
1998	70.8	68.3	126.2	126.3	137.1	66.3	148.7	122.1	129.3	120.9	128.7	139.7
1999	78.0	78.5	128.3	126.3	136.5	76.8	149.7	122.2	132.6	115.8	129.1	141.3
2000	113.5	126.8	133.5	128.5	137.9	112.8	156.7	124.6	134.7	119.8	130.3	143.3
2001	114.3	127.5	134.6	132.8	141.3	105.3	158.4	125.9	136.0	116.1	131.0	145.1
2002	96.6	107.0	133.7	132.0	141.1	98.8	157.3	125.5	137.1	116.2	131.7	146.3
2003	131.3	160.1	137.1	137.4	142.8	122.0	164.6	128.4	138.0	118.4	132.9	147.4
2004	153.4	192.7	142.9	144.3	143.6	149.9	172.8	131.7	142.7	142.8	141.3	151.5
2005	201.0	262.0	150.8	146.1	144.5	200.4	187.3	141.2	152.0	156.3	149.5	157.8
2006	208.7	252.5	156.9	146.8	146.6	235.5	196.8	149.7	163.4	179.3	155.7	162.5
2007	220.1	267.1	162.9	158.6	149.7	260.3	203.3	150.6	166.8	190.5	162.3	165.7
2008	274.7	347.5	175.8	173.8	153.5	329.2	228.2	161.3	170.9	211.9	174.4	171.7
2009	178.2	187.3	167.1	169.5	153.8	218.8	224.7	161.3	174.0	172.5	175.2	176.6
2010	214.4	240.5	175.4	175.5	156.2	285.8	233.7	166.1	172.5	196.1	176.5	177.1
2011	242.6	274.6	189.1	191.3	164.0	374.4	252.1	176.3	174.9	217.2	182.8	181.0
2011												
January	232.7	261.7	181.1	181.1	160.5	321.1	242.6	170.6	173.0	208.0	178.7	178.2
February	232.4	259.7	183.3	184.6	161.6	335.4	245.0	171.6	173.7	215.7	179.8	178.9
March	241.7	275.0	187.3	187.8	162.0	371.4	247.6	173.0	174.3	218.1	180.9	179.9
April	256.6	297.6	190.2	190.8	162.7	393.8	250.2	174.4	174.3	223.0	182.1	180.2
May	251.0	289.1	191.9	191.2	163.8	409.3	252.8	176.4	174.4	221.8	182.9	180.5
June	247.2	281.9	191.1	191.8	164.9	396.6	253.4	178.4	174.9	220.2	183.5	180.8
July	251.2	286.8	191.7	193.4	166.2	396.1	255.1	178.8	175.5	221.6	184.0	181.5
August	237.4	264.3	190.7	195.5	166.3	379.6	255.2	178.4	175.5	220.6	184.1	181.7
September	241.6	270.8	191.5	196.4	166.1	385.7	256.7	178.6	175.3	219.1	184.4	182.2
October	235.1	262.9	190.2	194.4	165.7	368.9	255.9	178.7	175.2	214.2	184.3	182.4
November	245.6	278.0	190.6	194.8	164.8	372.6	255.6	178.3	175.7	213.1	184.2	182.7
December	238.6	267.7	189.6	194.2	163.9	362.4	254.7	178.2	176.8	211.5	184.2	183.0

Year and month	Transportation and warehousing					Health care and social assistance			Other services industries (Dec. 1996 = 100)			
	Air transpor- tation (Dec. 1992 = 100)	Rail transpor- tation (Dec. 1996 = 100)	Pipeline transportation (June 1986 = 100) Crude oil	Pipeline transportation (June 1986 = 100) Refined petr. products	Postal service (June 1989 = 100)	Offices of physicians (Dec. 1996 = 100)	Home health care (Dec. 1996 = 100)	Hospitals (Dec. 1992 = 100)	Legal services	Architec- tural, engineering, and related services	Employment services	Accom- modation
1990	. . .	. . .	94.2	100.8	100.0	. . .	. . .	. . .	. . .	. . .	. . .	. . .
1991	. . .	. . .	94.4	101.1	117.9	. . .	. . .	. . .	. . .	. . .	. . .	. . .
1992	. . .	. . .	94.8	101.2	119.8	. . .	. . .	. . .	. . .	. . .	. . .	. . .
1993	105.6	. . .	95.0	101.3	119.8	. . .	. . .	102.5	. . .	. . .	. . .	. . .
1994	108.5	. . .	102.5	103.4	119.8	. . .	. . .	106.2	. . .	. . .	. . .	. . .
1995	113.7	. . .	113.4	104.6	132.2	. . .	. . .	110.0	. . .	. . .	. . .	. . .
1996	121.1	. . .	104.7	104.3	132.3	. . .	. . .	112.6	. . .	. . .	. . .	. . .
1997	125.3	100.5	96.0	105.3	132.3	101.0	103.3	113.6	102.5	102.2	101.0	104.2
1998	124.5	101.7	96.8	104.8	132.3	103.2	106.2	114.4	106.1	105.1	103.2	108.1
1999	130.8	101.3	95.5	104.9	135.3	105.5	107.1	116.4	108.7	108.5	105.2	112.7
2000	147.7	102.6	101.0	105.3	135.2	107.3	111.1	119.4	112.5	111.8	107.3	116.2
2001	157.2	104.5	111.1	108.5	143.4	110.4	114.0	123.0	117.9	115.9	108.2	121.3
2002	157.8	106.6	112.3	111.0	150.2	110.3	116.6	127.5	121.7	121.1	108.9	121.3
2003	162.1	108.8	111.1	112.7	155.0	112.1	117.0	134.9	125.6	124.3	111.4	122.0
2004	162.3	113.4	115.2	116.0	155.0	114.3	119.8	141.5	131.8	126.8	113.9	125.2
2005	171.0	125.2	125.5	120.3	155.0	116.4	121.1	146.9	138.5	129.2	116.3	131.9
2006	180.4	135.9	135.3	123.8	164.7	117.5	121.8	153.3	145.2	134.4	119.2	136.7
2007	183.7	140.9	138.9	131.7	171.9	122.3	124.0	158.6	153.6	140.0	121.7	142.9
2008	203.8	157.3	152.0	139.2	178.9	123.6	126.1	163.4	161.6	141.0	123.2	146.0
2009	188.5	148.5	156.3	147.3	185.0	126.6	128.0	168.3	166.2	142.9	123.5	141.5
2010	202.9	156.2	203.3	153.1	187.7	129.7	129.5	173.3	171.9	143.5	124.9	140.6
2011	218.3	169.8	204.7	157.1	190.6	131.6	129.5	177.0	177.9	145.5	125.5	142.8
2011												
January	208.0	161.6	200.6	152.7	188.5	130.6	129.8	175.2	176.6	144.3	125.5	140.0
February	211.0	162.8	200.6	152.7	188.5	131.1	129.5	175.7	177.1	144.5	125.6	140.9
March	220.2	165.6	200.6	152.7	188.5	131.2	129.6	176.1	177.3	144.7	125.6	143.6
April	219.6	168.9	198.7	152.9	188.5	131.3	129.5	176.2	177.8	144.8	125.4	142.5
May	218.9	172.2	198.7	152.9	191.6	131.3	129.5	176.3	177.8	144.8	125.3	142.6
June	219.5	173.3	202.5	153.0	191.6	131.5	129.5	176.5	178.0	145.3	125.4	141.9
July	220.0	173.2	209.1	161.4	191.6	131.6	129.5	176.8	178.2	145.8	125.1	143.4
August	224.0	172.3	209.1	161.4	191.6	131.9	129.6	177.1	178.4	145.9	125.3	143.5
September	216.2	172.3	209.1	161.4	191.6	132.0	129.5	177.5	178.4	146.2	125.2	143.6
October	220.2	171.9	209.1	161.4	191.6	132.3	129.8	178.7	178.4	146.3	125.6	145.2
November	220.0	171.8	209.1	161.4	191.6	132.4	128.9	178.8	178.6	146.4	125.6	144.1
December	221.8	171.7	209.1	161.5	191.6	132.5	129.0	179.4	178.7	146.4	125.9	142.9

. . . = Not available.

NOTES AND DEFINITIONS, CHAPTER 8

TABLES 8-1 THROUGH 8-4
CONSUMER PRICE INDEXES

SOURCES: U.S. DEPARTMENT OF LABOR, BUREAU OF LABOR STATISTICS (BLS) AND U.S. DEPARTMENT OF COMMERCE, BUREAU OF ECONOMIC ANALYSIS (BEA)

The Consumer Price Index (CPI), which is compiled by the Bureau of Labor Statistics (BLS), was originally conceived as a statistical measure of the average change in the cost to consumers of a market basket of goods and services purchased by urban wage earners and clerical workers. In 1978, its scope was broadened to also provide a measure of the change in the cost of the average market basket for all urban consumers. There was still a demand for a wage-earner index, so both versions have been calculated and published since then. The most commonly cited measure in this system is the Consumer Price Index for All Urban Consumers (CPI-U). The wage-earner alternative, used for calculating cost of living adjustments in many government programs, including Social Security, and in wage contracts, is called the Consumer Price Index for Urban Wage Earners and Clerical Workers (CPI-W). Both are presented by the BLS back to 1913, and reproduced in *Business Statistics*; however, the movements (percent changes) in the two indexes before 1978 are identical and are based on the wage-earner market basket.

These CPIs have typically been called "cost-of-living" indexes, even though the original fixed market basket concept does not correspond to economists' definition of a cost-of-living index. In recent years, the concept measured in practice in the CPI has developed into something intended to be closer to the theoretical definition of a cost-of-living index—that is, the cost of maintaining a constant standard of living or level of satisfaction rather than the cost of a fixed market basket. In addition, a new variation of the CPI—the Chained Consumer Price Index for All Urban Consumers (C-CPI-U)—is intended to provide an even closer approximation of a cost-of-living index.

The reference base for the total BLS Consumer Price Index and most of its components is currently 1982–1984 = 100. However, new products that have been introduced into the index since January 1982 are shown on later reference bases, as is the entire C-CPI-U.

Price indexes for personal consumption expenditures (PCE) are calculated and published by the Bureau of Economic Analysis (BEA) as a part of the national income and product accounts (NIPAs). (See Chapters 1 and 4 and their notes and definitions.) The reference base for these indexes is the average in the NIPA base year, 2005. These indexes differ in a number of other respects from the CPIs, and are often emphasized by the Federal Reserve in its analyses of the nation's economy. NIPA data are also available monthly; four important NIPA aggregate price indexes are shown in Tables 8-3 and 8-4 for convenient comparison with the CPIs. See the definitions for those tables for more information.

The CPI-U and the CPI-W

The *CPI-U*, which is displayed in Tables 8-1 through 8-4 and also provides all of the component category sub-indexes shown in Table 8-2, uses the consumption patterns for all urban consumers, who comprise about 88 percent of the population.

A slightly different index that is widely used for adjusting wages and government benefits is the *CPI-W*, of which the all-items total is shown in each of Tables 8-1 through 8-4. It represents the buying habits of only urban wage earners and clerical workers, who comprise about 29 percent of the population. The weights are derived from the same Consumer Expenditure Surveys (CES) used for the CPI-U weights, and are changed on the same schedule. However, they include only consumers from the specified categories instead of all urban consumers.

Beginning with January 2012, the weights in both indexes are based on consumer expenditures in the 2009–2010 period. From January 2010 to December 2011, 2007–2008 weights were used; from January 2008 to December 2009, 2005–2006 weights; from January 2006 to December 2007, 2003–2004 weights; from January 2004 to December 2005, 2001–2002 weights; from January 2002 to December 2003, 1999–2000 weights; and from January 1998 to December 2001, 1993–1995 weights. The weights will continue to be updated at two-year intervals, with new weights introduced in the January indexes of each even-numbered year. Previously, new weights were introduced only at the time of a major revision, which translated into a lag of a decade or more.

Specifically, the CPI weights for 1964 through 1977 were derived from reported expenditures of a sample of wage-earner and clerical-worker families and individuals in 1960–1961 and adjusted for price changes between the survey dates and 1963. Weights for the 1978–1986 period were derived from a survey undertaken during the 1972–1974 period and adjusted for price change between the survey dates and December 1977. For 1987 through 1997, the spending patterns reflected in the CPI were derived from a survey undertaken during the 1982–1984 period. The reported expenditures were adjusted for price change between the survey dates and December 1986.

The CPI was overhauled and updated in the latest major revision, which took effect in January 1998. In addition, new products and improved methods are regularly introduced into the index, usually in January.

The latest change in methods was the introduction of a geometric mean formula for calculating many of the basic components of the index. Beginning with the index for January 1999, this formula is used for categories comprising approximately 61 percent of total consumer spending. The new formula allows for the possibility that some consumers may react to changing relative prices within a category by substituting items whose relative prices have declined for products whose relative prices have risen, while maintaining their overall level of satisfaction. The geometric mean formula is not used for a few categories in which consumer substitution in the short term is not feasible, currently housing rent and utilities.

The CPI-U was introduced in 1978. Before that time, only CPI-W data were available. The movements of the CPI-U before 1978 are therefore based on the changes in the CPI-W. However, the index <u>levels</u> are different because the two indexes differed in the 1982–1984 base period.

Because the official CPI-U and CPI-W are so widely used in "escalation"—the calculation of cost-of-living adjustments for wages and other private contracts, and for government payments and tax parameters—these price indexes are not retrospectively revised to incorporate new information and methods. (An exception is occasionally made for outright error, which happened in September 2000 and affected the data for January through August of that year.) Instead, the new information and methods of calculation are introduced in the current index and affect future index changes only. In Tables 8-3 and 8-4, PCE indexes, which are subject to routine revision, and special CPI indexes that have been retrospectively revised are presented. These indexes can be used by researchers to provide more consistent historical information.

Notes on the CPI data

The CPI is based on prices of food, clothing, shelter, fuel, utilities, transportation, medical care, and other goods and services that people buy for day-to-day living. The quantity and quality of these priced items are kept essentially constant between revisions to ensure that only price changes will be measured. All taxes directly associated with the purchase and use of these items, such as sales and property taxes, are included in the index; the effects of income and payroll tax changes are not included.

Data are collected from about 26,000 retail and service establishments and about 4,000 housing units in 87 urban areas across the country. These data are used to develop the U.S. city average.

Periodic major revisions of the indexes update the content and weights of the market basket of goods and services; update the statistical sample of urban areas, outlets, and unique items used in calculating the CPI; and improve the statistical methods used. In addition, retail outlets and items are resampled on a rotating 5-year basis. Adjustments for changing quality are made at times of major product changes, such as the annual auto model changeover. Other methodological changes are introduced from time to time.

The CES provides the weights—that is, the relative importance—used to combine the individual price changes into subtotals and totals. This survey is composed of two separate surveys: an interview survey and a diary survey, both of which are conducted by the Census Bureau for BLS. Each expenditure reported in the two surveys is classified into a series of detailed categories, which are then combined into expenditure classes and ultimately into major expenditure groups. CPI data as of 1998 are grouped into eight such categories: (1) food and beverages, (2) housing, (3) apparel, (4) transportation, (5) medical care, (6) recreation, (7) education and communication, and (8) other goods and services.

Seasonally adjusted national CPI indexes are published for selected series for which there is a significant seasonal pattern of price change. The factors currently in use were derived by the X-12-ARIMA seasonal adjustment method. Some series with extreme or sharp movements are seasonally adjusted using X-12-ARIMA Intervention Analysis Seasonal Adjustment. Seasonally adjusted indexes and seasonal factors for the preceding five years are updated annually based on data through the previous December. Due to these revisions, BLS advises against the use of seasonally adjusted data for escalation. Detailed descriptions of seasonal adjustment procedures are available upon request from BLS.

BLS estimates the "standard error"—the error due to collecting data from a sample instead of the universe—of the one-month percent change in the not-seasonally-adjusted U.S. all-items index at 0.03 percentage point. Monthly percent changes in the seasonally adjusted indexes, in contrast, are often revised by 0.1 percentage point and occasionally even more.

CPI Definitions

Definitions of the major CPI groupings were modified beginning with the data for January 1998. These modifications were carried back to 1993. The following definitions are the current definitions currently used for the CPI components.

The *food and beverage index* includes both food at home and food away from home (restaurant meals and other food bought and eaten away from home).

The *housing index* measures changes in rental costs and expenses connected with the acquisition and operation of a home. The CPI-U, beginning with data for January 1983, and the CPI-W, beginning with data for January 1985, reflect a change in the methodology used to compute the homeownership component. A rental equivalence measure replaced an asset-price approach, which included purchase prices and interest costs. The intent of the change was to separate shelter costs from the investment component of homeownership, so that the index would only reflect the cost of the shelter services provided by owner-occupied homes. In addition to measures of the cost of shelter, the housing category includes insurance, fuel, utilities, and household furnishings and operations.

The *apparel index* includes the purchase of apparel and footwear.

The *private transportation index* includes prices paid by urban consumers for such items as new and used automobiles and other vehicles, gasoline, motor oil, tires, repairs and maintenance, insurance, registration fees, driver's licenses, parking fees, and the like. Auto finance charges, like mortgage interest payments, are considered to be a cost of asset acquisition, not of current consumption. Therefore, they are no longer included in the CPI. City bus, streetcar, subway, taxicab, intercity bus, airplane, and railroad coach fares are some of the components of the *public transportation index*.

The *medical care index* includes prices for professional medical services, hospital and related services, prescription and nonprescription drugs, and other medical care commodities. The weight for the portion of health insurance premiums that is used to cover the costs of these medical goods and services is distributed among the items; the weight for the portion of health insurance costs attributable to administrative expenses and profits of insurance providers constitutes a separate health insurance item. Effective with the January 1997 data, the method of calculating the hospital cost component was changed from the pricing of individual commodities and services to a more comprehensive cost-of-treatment approach.

Recreation includes components formerly listed in housing, apparel, entertainment, and "other goods and services."

Education and communication is a new group including components formerly categorized in housing and "other goods and services," such as telephone services and computers.

Other goods and services now includes tobacco, personal care, and miscellaneous.

TABLE 8-2
PURCHASING POWER OF THE DOLLAR

SOURCE: U.S. DEPARTMENT OF LABOR, BUREAU OF LABOR STATISTICS (BLS)

The purchasing power of the dollar measures changes in the quantity of goods and services a dollar will buy at a particular date compared with a selected base date. It must be defined in terms of the following: (1) the specific commodities and services that are to be purchased with the dollar; (2) the market level (producer, retail, etc.) at which they are purchased; and (3) the dates for which the comparison is to be made. Thus, the purchasing power of the dollar for a selected period, compared with another period, may be measured in terms of a single commodity or a large group of commodities such as all goods and services purchased by consumers at retail.

The purchasing power of the dollar is computed by dividing the price index number for the base period by the price index number for the comparison date and expressing the result in dollars and cents. The base period is the period in which the price index equals 100; the average purchasing power in that base period—1982–1984 in the case of the measure shown here—is therefore $1.00.

Purchasing power estimates in terms of both the CPI-U and the CPI-W are calculated by BLS, based on indexes not adjusted for seasonal variation, and published in the CPI press release. The CPI-U version is shown here.

Alternative price measures in Tables 8-3 and 8-4

Table 8-3 shows the all-items CPI-U and CPI-W, along with a number of other indexes that various analysts of price trends have preferred as measures of the price level. Table 8-4 shows the inflation rates (percent changes in price levels) implied by each of the indexes in Table 8-3.

As food and energy prices are volatile and frequently determined by forces separate from monetary aggregate demand pressures, many analysts prefer an index of prices excluding those components. Indexes *excluding food and energy* are known as *core* indexes, and inflation rates calculated from them are known as *core inflation rates*.

The *CPI-U-X1* is a special experimental version of the CPI that researchers have used to provide a more historically consistent series. As explained above, the official CPI-U treated homeownership on an asset-price basis until January 1983. It then changed to a rental equivalence method. The CPI-U-X1 incorporates a rental equivalence approach to homeowners' costs for the years 1967–1982 as well. It is rebased to the December 1982 value of the CPI-U (1982–1984 = 100); thus, it is identical to the CPI-U in December 1982 and all subsequent periods, as can be seen in Table 8-3. For this reason, it is not updated or published in the CPI news release or on the BLS Web site. We continue to present it here because it provides the only available data before 1978 on changes in an improved and more consistent CPI.

The *CPI-E* is an experimental re-weighting of components of the CPI-U to represent price change for the goods and services purchased by Americans age 62 years and over, who accounted for 16.5 percent of the total number of urban consumer units in the 2001–2002 CES.

BLS does not consider the CPI-E to be an ideal measure of price change for older Americans. Because the sample is small, the sampling error in the weights is greater than the error in the all-urban index. The products and outlets sampled are those characteristic of the general urban population rather than older residents. In addition, senior discounts are not included in the prices collected. Such discounts are included—appropriately—in the weights, which are based on the expenditures reported by the older consumers' households. Therefore, such discounts are only a problem if they do not move proportionately to general prices.

The *CPI-U-RS* is a "research series" CPI that retroactively incorporates estimates of the effects of most of the methodological changes implemented since 1978, including the rental equivalence method, new or improved quality adjustments, and improvement of formulas to eliminate bias and allow for some consumer substitution within categories. This index is calculated from 1977 onward. Its reference base is December 1977 = 100. Thus, although it generally shows less <u>increase</u> than the official index, its current <u>levels</u> are considerably higher because the earlier reference base period had lower prices. Unlike the official CPIs and the CPI-U-X1, its historical values will be revised each time a significant change is made in the calculation of the current index. This index is not seasonally adjusted and is not included in the CPI news release. It is available on the BLS Web site, along with an explanation and background material. The CPI-U-RS is used by BLS in the calculation of historical trends in real compensation per hour in its Productivity and Costs system; see Table 9-3 and its notes and definitions. It is also now used by the Census Bureau to convert household incomes into constant dollars, as seen in Chapter 3. And it is used by the editor in some analytical calculations in this volume.

The *C-CPI-U* (Chained Consumer Price Index for All Urban Consumers) is a new, supplemental index that has been published in the monthly CPI news release since August 2002. It is available only from December 1999 to date and is calculated with the base December 1999 = 100; it is not seasonally adjusted. It is designed to be a still-closer approximation to a true cost-of-living index than the CPI-U and the CPI-W, in that it assumes that consumers substitute between as well as within categories as relative prices change, in order to maintain a fixed basket of "consumer satisfaction."

The C-CPI-U is technically a "superlative" index, using a method known as the "Tornqvist formula" to incorporate the composition of consumer spending in the current period as well as in the earlier base period. (All of the other Consumer Price Indexes use a "Laspeyres" formula; see the General Notes at the beginning of this volume.) As it requires consumer expenditure data for the current as well as the earlier period, its final version can only be calculated after the expenditure data become available—about two years later—and is approximated in more recent periods by making more extensive use of the geometric mean formula (see above). With the release of January 2012 data, the indexes for 2010 were revised to their final form, and the initial indexes for 2011 were revised to "interim" levels, shown in Tables 8-3 and 8-4.

Personal consumption expenditure (PCE) chain-type price indexes are calculated by the Bureau of Economic Analysis (BEA) in the framework of the national income and product accounts (NIPAs). (See the notes and definitions for Chapters 1 and 4.) The scope of NIPA PCE is broader than the scope of the CPI. PCE includes the rural as well as the urban population and also covers the consumption spending of nonprofit entities. The CPI includes only consumer out-of-pocket cash spending, whereas PCE includes some imputed services and includes expenditures financed by government and private insurance, particularly in the medical care area. For this reason, there is a large difference between the relatively small weight of medical care spending in the CPI and the markedly greater percentage of PCE that is accounted for by total medical care spending. Housing, on the other hand, has a somewhat smaller weight in PCE while all non-housing components have a higher weight. The reason for this is that the CES—the survey on which the CPI weights are based—tends to report housing expenditures accurately and somewhat underestimate other spending. This suggests that the weight of housing relative to all other products may be overestimated in the CPI but measured more correctly in the PCE price index.

PCE chain-type indexes use the expenditure weights of both the earlier and the later period to determine the aggregate price change between the two periods. (See the notes and definitions for Chapter 1, as well as the General Notes on index number formulas.) Thus, they are subject to revision as improved data on the composition of consumption spending become available, and in this respect resemble the C-CPI-U.

For a large share of PCE, the price movements for basic individual spending categories are determined by CPI components. Hence, the differences between the rates of change in the aggregate CPI and PCE indexes are largely the result of the different weights, but also reflect some alternative methodologies and the previously mentioned differences in scope.

Market-based PCE indexes are based on household expenditures for which there are observable price measures. They exclude most implicit prices (for example, the services furnished without payment by financial intermediaries) and they exclude items not deflated by a detailed component of either the Consumer Price Index (CPI) or the Producer Price Index (PPI). This means that the price observations that make up these new aggregate measures are all based on observed market transactions, making them "market-based price indexes." The imputed rent for owner-occupied housing is included in the market-based price index, since it is based on observed rentals of comparable homes. Household insurance premiums are also included in the market-based index, since they are deflated by the CPI for tenants' and household insurance. Excluded are services furnished without payment by financial intermediaries, most insurance purchases, expenses of NPISHs (nonprofit institutions serving households), legal gambling (illegal gambling is excluded from all measures), margins on used light motor vehicles, and expenditures by U.S. residents working and traveling abroad. Also excluded are medical, hospitalization, and income loss insurance; expense of handling life insurance; motor vehicle insurance; and workers' compensation.

The *inflation rates* shown in Table 8-4 are percent changes in the price indexes introduced in Table 8-3. For annual indexes, the rate is the percent change from the previous year. For monthly indexes, the rate is the percent change from the same month a year earlier. To give an indication of the longer-run implications of these different price indicators, comparisons of compound annual inflation rates, calculated by the editor, are also shown for the 1978–2011, 1983–2011, and 2000–2011 periods, using the growth rate formula presented in the article at the beginning of this volume.

Data availability and references

The CPI-U, CPI-W, and C-CPI-U are initially issued in a press release two to three weeks after the end of the month for which the data were collected. This release and detailed and complete current and historical data on the CPI and its variants and components, along with extensive documentation, are available on the BLS Web site at <http://www.bls.gov/cpi>. Seasonal factors and seasonally adjusted indexes are revised once a year with the issuance of the January index.

Information available on the BLS Web site includes "Common Misconceptions about the Consumer Price Index: Questions and Answers;" another fact sheet on frequently asked questions; a fact sheet on seasonal adjustment; Chapter 17 of the *BLS Handbook of Methods*, entitled "The Consumer Price Index"; a section entitled "Note on Chained Consumer Price Index for All Urban Consumers"; and a number of explanatory CPI fact sheets on specific subjects.

As previously indicated, the CPI-U-X1 is not currently published because its recent values are identical to the CPI-U. The CPI-E is presented in articles in the CPI section of the BLS Web site, the most recent of which is "Experimental Consumer Price Index for Americans 62 Years of Age and Older, 1998-2005"; recent values are available by request from BLS. The CPI-U-RS is updated each month in a report entitled "CPI Research Series Using Current Methods" on the site. In both cases, the reports describe the indexes and provide references.

The monthly PCE indexes are included in the personal income report issued by BEA, which is published near the end of the following month. These indexes are revised month-by-month to reflect new information and annually to reflect the annual and quinquennial benchmarking of the NIPAs. The complete historical record can be found on the BEA Web site at <http://www.bea.gov> in the Personal Income and Outlays section of the NIPA tables, in tables entitled "Price Indexes for Personal Consumption Expenditures by Major Type of Product."

Two special editions of the *Monthly Labor Review* were devoted to CPI issues. The December 1996 issue describes the subsequently implemented 1997 and 1998 revisions in a series of articles, and the December 1993 issue, entitled *The Anatomy of Price Change*, includes the following articles: "The Consumer Price Index: Underlying Concepts and Caveats"; "Basic Components of the CPI: Estimation of Price Changes"; "The Commodity Substitution Effect in CPI Data, 1982–1991"; and "Quality Adjustment of Price Indexes."

The new formula for calculating basic components is described in "Incorporating a Geometric Mean Formula into the CPI," *Monthly Labor Review* (October 1998). For a detailed discussion of the treatment of homeownership, see "Changing the Homeownership Component of the Consumer Price Index to Rental Equivalence," *CPI Detailed Report* (January 1983).

For a comprehensive professional review of CPI concepts and methodology, see Charles Schultze and Christopher Mackie, ed., *At What Price? Conceptualizing and Measuring Cost-of-Living and Price Indexes* (Washington, DC: National Academy Press, 2001). Earlier references include: "Using Survey Data to Assess Bias in the Consumer Price Index," *Monthly Labor Review* (April 1998); Joel Popkin, "Improving the CPI: The Record and Suggested Next Steps," *Business Economics*, Vol. XXXII, No. 3 (July 1997), pages 42–47; *Measurement Issues in the Consumer Price Index* (Bureau of Labor Statistics, U.S. Department of Labor, June 1997); *Toward a More Accurate Measure of the Cost of Living* (Final Report to the Senate Finance Committee from the Advisory Commission to Study the Consumer Price Index, December 4, 1996)—also known as the "Boskin Commission" report; and *Government Price Statistics* (U.S. Congress Joint Economic Committee, 87th Congress, 1st Session, January 24, 1961)—also known as the "Stigler Committee" report.

For an explanation of the differences between the CPI-U and the PCE index, see Clinton P. McCully, Brian C. Moyer, and Kenneth J. Stewart, "Comparing the Consumer Price Index and the Personal Consumption Expenditures Price Index," *Survey of Current Business*, November 2007, pp. 26-33.

**TABLES 8-1 AND 8-5 THROUGH 8-7
PRODUCER PRICE INDEXES**

SOURCE: U.S. DEPARTMENT OF LABOR, BUREAU OF LABOR STATISTICS (BLS)

Producer Price Indexes (PPI) measure average changes in prices received by domestic producers. The prices of individual commodities are organized into three different, separate systems: stage of processing, commodity group, and industry. Most of the indexes currently are published on a base of 1982 = 100. However, there are a number of exceptions for products and industries introduced into the index system since 1982. In this book, alternative base periods are identified in the column headings for the individual series.

Tables 8-1A, 8-1B, and 8-5 present price indexes for commodities by stage of processing. Table 8-6 and 8-1C presents data by major commodity groups; these are the groupings that have the longest continuous history. In recent years, the major commodity groups—particularly the totals for all commodities and industrial commodities—have been de-emphasized, as they aggregate successive stages of processing and thus often exaggerate price trends. This effect was particularly acute in the energy price crisis of the early 1970s. To avoid this problem, the stage-of-processing groups were introduced in 1978, and the finished goods components, in total and minus food and energy, have been the headline Producer Price Indexes. However, the individual commodity groups (for example, textile products and apparel) provide a much longer historical perspective on individual industrial sectors than the current industry groupings; annual indexes for these groups are presented in Table 8-6 for that reason.

Table 8-7 presents PPIs for the net output of selected industry groups. As the coverage of the PPI is expanded, indexes for additional industries are frequently introduced, and new industries may only go back to December of the most recent year. This volume includes only those industry groupings with 15 years or more of historical data.

Definitions

The *stage-of-processing* PPI indexes (Tables 8-1 and 8-5) organize commodities by class of buyer and degree of fabrication. These have been the featured measures since 1978. The three major indexes are: (1) *finished goods*, or commodities that will not undergo further processing and are ready for sale to the ultimate user (such as automobiles, meats, apparel, and machine tools, and also unprocessed foods such as eggs and fresh vegetables, that are ready for the consumer); (2) *intermediate materials, supplies, and components*, or commodities that have been processed but require further processing before they become finished goods (such as steel mill products, cotton yarns, lumber, and flour), as well as physically complete goods that are purchased by business firms as inputs for their operations (such as diesel fuel and paper boxes); and (3) *crude materials* for further processing, or products entering the market for the first time that have not been manufactured or fabricated and are not sold directly to consumers (such as ores, scrap metals, crude petroleum, raw cotton, and livestock).

PPIs for the *net output* of industries and their products (Table 8-7) are grouped according to the North American Industry Classification System (NAICS). For each industry, they include both measures of price change for the products "primary" to that industry (products made primarily but not necessarily exclusively by that industry), and measures of changes in prices received by establishments classified in the industry for products or services chiefly made in some other industry. Thus, they are designed to be compatible with other economic time series organized by industry, such as data on shipments, employment, wages, and productivity.

Notes on the data

The probability sample used for calculating the PPI provides more than 100,000 price quotations per month,

selected to represent the movement of prices of all commodities produced in the manufacturing; agriculture, forestry, and fishing; mining; and gas, electricity, and public utility sectors.

In addition, new PPIs are gradually being introduced for the products and services produced by industries in the construction, transportation, trade, finance, and services sectors. These are only used for industry indexes and are not incorporated in the commodity indexes or the published commodity by stage of processing indexes. In February 2011, BLS announced the development of an experimental aggregation system that will incorporate new services and construction data in an experimental aggregation system for the different portions of final and intermediate demand. For further information, see <http://www.bls.gov/ppi/experimentalaggregation.htm>.

To the greatest extent possible, prices used in calculating the PPI represent prices received by domestic producers in the first important commercial transaction for each commodity. These indexes attempt to measure only price changes (changes in receipts per unit of measurement not influenced by changes in quality, quantity sold, terms of sale, or level of distribution). Most quotations are the selling prices of selected manufacturers or other producers, although a few prices are those quoted on organized exchanges or markets. Transaction prices are sought instead of list or book prices.

Price data are generally collected monthly, primarily by mail questionnaire. Most prices are obtained directly from producing companies on a voluntary and confidential basis. Prices are generally reported for the Tuesday of the week containing the 13th day of the month.

The name "Producer Price Index" became effective with the release of March 1978 data and replaced the term "Wholesale Price Index." The change was made to more accurately reflect the coverage of the data. At the same time, there was a shift in analytical emphasis from the All Commodities Index and other traditional commodity grouping indexes (as shown in Table 8-6) to the Finished Goods Index and other stage-of-processing indexes.

The BLS revises the PPI weighting structure when data from economic censuses become available. Beginning with data for January 2012, the weights used to construct the PPI reflect 2007 shipments values as measured by the 2002 Economic Censuses. Data for January 2007 through December 2011 used 2002 values; 2002 through 2006, 1997 shipments values; 1996 through 2001, 1992 values; 1992 through 1995, 1987 values; 1987 through 1991, 1982 values; 1976 through 1986, 1972 values; and 1967 through 1975, 1963 values.

BLS has been working for a number of years on a comprehensive overhaul of the theory, methodology, and procedures used to construct the PPI. One aspect of this overhaul was the previously mentioned shift in emphasis to the stage-of-processing measures, which began in 1978.

Other changes phased in since 1978 include the replacement of judgment sampling with probability sampling techniques; expansion to systematic coverage of the net output of virtually all industries in the mining and manufacturing sectors; introduction of measures for selected services industries, including retail trade; a shift from a commodity to an industry orientation; and the exclusion of imports from, and the inclusion of exports in, the survey universe.

The commodity components of the stage-of-processing indexes, in addition to being available in unadjusted form, are also adjusted for seasonal variation using the X-12-ARIMA method. Since January 1988, BLS has also used X-12-ARIMA Intervention Analysis Seasonal Adjustment for a small number of series to remove unusual values that might distort seasonal patterns before calculating the seasonal adjustment factors. Seasonal factors for the PPI are revised annually to take into account the most recent 12 months of data. Seasonally adjusted data for the previous 5 years are subject to these annual revisions. The industry net output indexes are not seasonally adjusted.

Data availability and references

The indexes are initially issued in a press release two to three weeks after the end of the month for which the data were collected. Data are subsequently published in greater detail in a monthly BLS publication, *PPI Detailed Report*. Each month, data for the fourth previous month (both unadjusted and seasonally adjusted) are revised to reflect late reports and corrections.

The press release, the *PPI Detailed Report*, detailed and complete current and historical data, and extensive documentation are available at <http://www.bls.gov/ppi>. The items available on this Web site include Chapter 14 of the *BLS Handbook of Methods*, "Producer Price Indexes"; a selection of *Monthly Labor Review* articles on the PPI; and fact sheets on a number of issues and index components.

CHAPTER 9: EMPLOYMENT COSTS, PRODUCTIVITY, AND PROFITS

Section 9a: Employment Cost Indexes

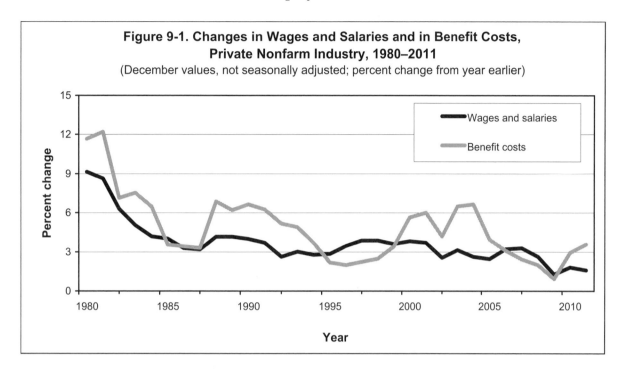

Figure 9-1. Changes in Wages and Salaries and in Benefit Costs, Private Nonfarm Industry, 1980–2011
(December values, not seasonally adjusted; percent change from year earlier)

- Through 2005, benefit costs in private nonfarm industry usually rose faster than wages and salaries, driven by the rising costs of medical benefits. The late 1990s were an exception, and so were the years 2006 through 2009. In 2009, both increased by the smallest amount ever recorded in this survey, which has been collected since 1979. In 2010 and 2011, however both rose faster than in 2009 and benefit growth again exceeded wage and salary growth. (Tables 9-1 and 9-2)

- Between December 2001 and December 2011, total private nonfarm compensation per hour (wages, salaries, and benefits combined) as measured in the ECI—which holds the composition of employment constant in order to isolate increases in compensation for individual workers and excludes stock options—rose at an average annual rate of 2.8 percent. (Table 9-1) The CPI-U-RS (see Table 8-3 and its notes and definitions) rose at a 2.3 percent annual rate from 2001 to 2010, implying an increase in average real worker compensation per hour of about 0.6 percent per year.

- Real worker compensation is said to track worker productivity—but over the same 9-year period, the output per hour of nonfarm industry workers rose 2.6 percent per year (Table 9-3), exceeding the rate of real compensation increase by 2.0 percentage points. Of this gap, 0.4 percentage points reflects a difference between the CPI-U-RS and the price index used in calculating productivity, leaving a real gap between productivity growth and compensation growth of 1.6 percentage points per year. These differences are discussed in more detail in the article introducing this volume, "Business Cycle Perspectives." (Tables 9-3 and 8-3)

Table 9-1. Employment Cost Indexes, NAICS Basis

(December 2005 [not seasonally adjusted] = 100; annual values are for December, not seasonally adjusted; quarterly values, seasonally adjusted, except as noted.)

Year and month	All civilian workers [1]	State and local government workers	Private industry workers												Union [2]	Non-union [2]
			All private industry workers	Excluding incentive paid occupations [2]	By occupational group					By industry					
					Management, professional, and related	Sales and office	Natural resources, construction, and maintenance	Production, transportation, and material moving	Service occupations	Goods-producing industries		Service-providing			
										Total	Manufacturing				
TOTAL COMPENSATION															
2001	87.1	86.2	87.3	. . .	87.4	86.9	86.6	87.4	89.4	86.0	85.5	87.8		84.8	87.8
2002	90.0	89.7	90.0	. . .	89.7	89.8	89.7	90.3	92.0	89.0	88.7	90.4		88.2	90.3
2003	93.5	92.8	93.6	. . .	93.8	93.1	93.3	93.6	95.0	92.6	92.4	94.0		92.3	93.9
2004	97.0	96.1	97.2	. . .	97.1	96.8	97.1	97.8	97.7	96.9	96.9	97.3		97.3	97.2
2005	100.0	100.0	100.0	100.0	100.0	100.0	100.0	100.0	100.0	100.0	100.0	100.0		100.0	100.0
2006	103.3	104.1	103.2	103.2	103.5	102.9	103.6	102.3	103.1	102.5	101.8	103.4		103.0	103.2
2007	106.7	108.4	106.3	106.4	106.8	106.1	106.7	104.5	107.0	105.0	103.8	106.7		105.1	106.5
2008	109.5	111.6	108.9	109.5	109.9	107.9	109.6	106.9	109.8	107.5	105.9	109.4		108.0	109.1
2009	111.0	114.2	110.2	110.8	110.7	109.2	111.2	108.9	111.8	108.6	107.0	110.8		111.1	110.1
2010	113.2	116.2	112.5	113.1	113.0	111.6	113.3	111.5	113.5	111.1	110.0	113.0		114.8	112.1
2011	115.5	117.7	115.0	115.5	115.4	114.2	115.8	114.2	115.4	113.8	113.1	115.3		117.9	114.5
2001															
March	84.7	83.6	85.0	. . .	. . .	. . .	. . .	. . .	. . .	84.0	83.7	85.3		82.0	85.5
June	85.5	84.5	85.8	. . .	. . .	. . .	. . .	. . .	. . .	84.7	84.4	86.1		82.9	86.3
September	86.4	85.5	86.7	. . .	. . .	. . .	. . .	. . .	. . .	85.4	84.9	87.1		83.7	87.2
December	87.2	86.1	87.5	. . .	. . .	. . .	. . .	. . .	. . .	86.2	85.8	87.9		84.8	87.8
2002															
March	87.9	86.8	88.2	. . .	88.2	87.8	87.6	88.5	90.3	87.1	86.8	88.6		85.7	88.7
June	88.8	87.5	89.1	. . .	89.0	88.9	88.6	89.1	90.7	87.7	87.5	89.6		86.5	89.6
September	89.5	88.7	89.6	. . .	89.4	89.3	89.3	89.8	91.6	88.2	88.0	90.1		87.5	90.0
December	90.1	89.6	90.2	. . .	90.0	90.1	90.2	90.5	92.1	89.2	89.0	90.5		88.2	90.3
2003															
March	91.2	90.4	91.4	. . .	91.5	90.9	91.0	91.6	93.0	90.6	90.6	91.7		89.5	91.8
June	92.0	91.3	92.2	. . .	92.2	91.7	92.0	92.4	93.5	91.4	91.3	92.4		90.7	92.5
September	92.9	92.0	93.2	. . .	93.2	92.8	92.8	93.2	94.4	92.1	92.0	93.5		91.6	93.5
December	93.6	92.7	93.8	. . .	94.1	93.4	93.7	93.7	95.1	92.8	92.6	94.1		92.3	93.9
2004															
March	94.6	93.5	94.9	. . .	94.7	94.5	95.0	95.4	95.9	94.5	94.6	95.0		94.5	95.0
June	95.5	94.4	95.8	. . .	95.5	95.5	95.9	96.5	96.7	95.4	95.6	96.0		95.9	95.9
September	96.4	95.1	96.7	. . .	96.4	96.5	96.4	97.4	97.2	96.4	96.7	96.8		96.7	96.7
December	97.1	95.9	97.3	. . .	97.4	97.0	97.3	97.9	97.8	97.1	97.1	97.4		97.3	97.2
2005															
March	98.0	97.0	98.2	. . .	98.4	97.9	98.0	98.5	98.4	98.0	98.2	98.3		97.9	98.3
June	98.6	97.8	98.8	. . .	99.0	98.4	98.7	99.0	99.0	98.9	99.0	98.8		98.8	98.9
September	99.3	98.7	99.5	. . .	99.6	99.2	99.4	99.6	99.6	99.7	99.7	99.4		99.6	99.5
December	100.1	99.8	100.2	. . .	100.3	100.1	100.2	100.1	100.1	100.2	100.2	100.2		100.0	100.0
2006															
March	100.7	100.5	100.8	100.9	101.0	100.6	100.9	100.4	100.8	100.3	99.9	100.9		100.5	100.9
June	101.6	101.5	101.6	101.7	101.8	101.5	102.0	101.0	101.5	101.2	100.9	101.8		101.8	101.7
September	102.6	102.8	102.5	102.5	102.9	102.2	102.9	101.7	102.2	101.9	101.4	102.7		102.4	102.6
December	103.4	103.9	103.3	103.2	103.8	103.0	103.7	102.4	103.2	102.7	102.0	103.5		103.0	103.2
2007															
March	104.2	105.1	103.9	104.0	104.5	103.8	104.1	102.5	104.4	102.8	101.9	104.3		102.7	104.2
June	105.1	106.2	104.8	105.0	105.5	104.5	104.9	103.3	105.2	103.8	102.8	105.2		103.9	105.1
September	105.9	107.2	105.6	105.8	106.3	105.2	105.8	103.9	106.3	104.4	103.2	106.0		104.4	105.9
December	106.8	108.2	106.5	106.4	107.1	106.2	106.8	104.7	107.2	105.2	104.0	106.9		105.1	106.5
2008															
March	107.6	109.0	107.2	107.6	108.0	106.8	107.7	105.4	107.8	106.0	104.5	107.6		105.9	107.5
June	108.3	109.9	108.0	108.3	108.8	107.4	108.2	106.0	108.7	106.7	105.0	108.4		106.7	108.3
September	109.1	110.9	108.6	109.0	109.6	107.8	109.0	106.5	109.3	107.2	105.6	109.1		107.4	108.9
December	109.6	111.5	109.1	109.5	110.2	108.0	109.8	107.1	109.9	107.7	106.1	109.5		108.0	109.1
2009															
March	109.9	112.4	109.3	110.0	110.2	108.1	109.9	107.6	110.6	107.8	106.3	109.8		109.1	109.4
June	110.3	113.2	109.5	110.2	110.4	108.2	110.2	108.1	111.0	108.1	106.6	110.0		109.8	109.6
September	110.6	113.4	109.9	110.6	110.6	108.8	110.8	108.5	111.6	108.3	106.8	110.5		110.5	109.9
December	111.1	114.0	110.4	110.8	111.0	109.3	111.4	109.1	112.0	108.8	107.4	110.9		111.1	110.1
2010															
March	111.8	114.5	111.1	111.8	111.6	109.9	112.2	109.8	112.3	109.6	108.2	111.5		112.8	110.9
June	112.3	115.2	111.6	112.3	112.2	110.6	112.6	110.4	112.7	110.2	109.0	112.1		113.7	111.4
September	112.8	115.5	112.1	112.8	112.7	111.1	113.0	111.2	113.1	110.9	109.9	112.5		114.6	111.8
December	113.3	116.1	112.7	113.1	113.3	111.6	113.4	111.8	113.7	111.3	110.4	113.1		114.8	112.1
2011															
March	114.0	116.7	113.3	114.0	113.9	112.2	113.8	112.2	114.5	111.9	111.1	113.8		115.6	113.0
June	114.8	117.2	114.2	114.9	114.7	113.2	114.8	113.5	114.7	113.2	112.6	114.6		117.1	113.8
September	115.1	117.2	114.6	115.1	115.1	113.8	115.5	113.7	114.8	113.3	112.8	115.0		117.4	114.2
December	115.6	117.5	115.1	115.5	115.7	114.2	116.0	114.5	115.6	114.1	113.5	115.5		117.9	114.5

[1]Excludes farm workers, private household workers, and federal government employees.
[2]Not seasonally adjusted.
. . . = Not available.

Table 9-1. Employment Cost Indexes, NAICS Basis—*Continued*

(December 2005 [not seasonally adjusted] = 100; annual values are for December, not seasonally adjusted; quarterly values, seasonally adjusted, except as noted.)

Year and month	All civilian workers [1]	State and local government workers	All private industry workers	Excluding incentive paid occupations [2]	Management, professional, and related	Sales and office	Natural resources, construction, and maintenance	Production, transportation, and material moving	Service occupations	Goods-producing industries Total	Manufacturing	Service-providing	Union [2]	Non-union [2]
WAGES AND SALARIES														
2001	89.9	90.2	89.9	. . .	89.5	89.1	90.0	91.0	91.7	90.0	90.2	89.8	89.6	89.9
2002	92.4	93.0	92.2	. . .	91.7	91.7	92.6	93.3	93.9	92.6	92.8	92.1	92.6	92.2
2003	95.1	95.0	95.1	. . .	95.3	94.3	95.2	95.4	96.1	94.9	95.1	95.2	94.9	95.1
2004	97.5	97.0	97.6	. . .	97.8	97.2	97.5	97.8	97.9	97.2	97.4	97.7	97.6	97.6
2005	100.0	100.0	100.0	100.0	100.0	100.0	100.0	100.0	100.0	100.0	100.0	100.0	100.0	100.0
2006	103.2	103.5	103.2	103.2	103.6	103.0	103.4	102.4	102.9	102.9	102.3	103.3	102.3	103.3
2007	106.7	107.1	106.6	106.7	107.2	106.2	107.1	105.0	107.1	106.0	104.9	106.8	104.7	106.9
2008	109.6	110.4	109.4	110.1	110.5	108.0	110.5	107.8	110.1	109.0	107.7	109.6	108.1	109.6
2009	111.2	112.5	110.8	111.6	111.5	109.4	112.0	109.6	112.3	110.0	108.9	111.1	110.9	110.9
2010	113.0	113.8	112.8	113.4	113.7	111.5	113.3	111.3	113.5	111.6	110.7	113.1	112.9	112.7
2011	114.6	114.9	114.6	115.2	115.5	113.6	115.4	112.8	115.1	113.5	112.7	114.9	114.9	114.6
2001														
March	87.6	87.6	87.6	. . .	. . .	. . .	. . .	. . .	. . .	87.9	88.2	87.4	86.5	87.7
June	88.4	88.4	88.4	. . .	. . .	. . .	. . .	. . .	. . .	88.7	89.0	88.3	87.4	88.6
September	89.2	89.4	89.2	. . .	. . .	. . .	. . .	. . .	. . .	89.3	89.5	89.1	88.3	89.3
December	90.0	90.0	90.0	. . .	. . .	. . .	. . .	. . .	. . .	90.1	90.3	90.0	89.6	89.9
2002														
March	90.7	90.5	90.7	. . .	90.4	90.1	90.7	91.9	. . .	90.8	91.2	90.7	90.2	90.8
June	91.5	91.2	91.6	. . .	91.2	91.1	91.6	92.4	. . .	91.3	91.7	91.6	91.1	91.7
September	92.0	92.1	92.0	. . .	91.5	91.3	92.2	92.8	. . .	91.8	92.2	92.0	91.9	92.0
December	92.4	92.8	92.3	. . .	91.9	92.0	92.8	93.3	. . .	92.7	93.0	92.2	92.6	92.2
2003														
March	93.3	93.5	93.3	. . .	93.3	92.5	93.4	94.1	. . .	93.3	93.8	93.2	93.0	93.3
June	93.9	94.1	93.8	. . .	93.9	93.2	94.0	94.6	. . .	94.0	94.4	93.8	93.8	94.0
September	94.6	94.4	94.7	. . .	94.8	94.1	94.6	95.1	. . .	94.5	94.8	94.7	94.4	94.9
December	95.1	94.9	95.2	. . .	95.4	94.5	95.3	95.4	. . .	95.0	95.3	95.2	94.9	95.1
2004														
March	95.7	95.5	95.7	. . .	95.9	95.2	95.9	96.0	. . .	95.6	95.7	95.8	95.6	95.8
June	96.3	96.0	96.4	. . .	96.4	96.0	96.5	96.7	. . .	96.2	96.4	96.5	96.4	96.5
September	97.0	96.3	97.2	. . .	97.2	97.0	97.0	97.6	. . .	97.2	97.4	97.2	97.1	97.3
December	97.5	96.9	97.7	. . .	98.0	97.3	97.6	97.9	. . .	97.4	97.6	97.8	97.6	97.6
2005														
March	98.2	97.7	98.3	. . .	98.6	98.0	98.0	98.4	. . .	97.9	98.2	98.4	97.9	98.3
June	98.7	98.3	98.8	. . .	99.1	98.4	98.6	98.9	. . .	98.6	98.8	98.9	98.7	98.9
September	99.3	98.8	99.4	. . .	99.5	99.2	99.3	99.5	. . .	99.4	99.6	99.4	99.5	99.5
December	100.1	99.8	100.1	. . .	100.2	100.1	100.1	100.1	. . .	100.2	100.2	100.1	100.0	100.0
2006														
March	100.7	100.4	100.8	100.8	101.0	100.6	100.8	100.6	100.6	100.7	100.6	100.8	100.3	100.8
June	101.5	101.2	101.6	101.7	101.9	101.5	101.8	101.1	101.3	101.7	101.6	101.6	101.2	101.8
September	102.5	102.4	102.5	102.5	102.9	102.2	102.7	101.7	101.9	102.2	101.8	102.6	101.7	102.7
December	103.3	103.4	103.3	103.2	103.8	103.0	103.4	102.5	103.0	103.0	102.5	103.4	102.3	103.3
2007														
March	104.3	104.2	104.3	104.3	104.8	104.0	104.3	103.2	104.6	103.9	103.2	104.4	102.8	104.5
June	105.1	105.0	105.1	105.2	105.7	104.7	105.0	103.8	105.3	104.6	103.8	105.2	103.7	105.3
September	105.9	106.0	105.9	106.1	106.6	105.2	106.1	104.4	106.4	105.4	104.4	106.1	104.4	106.2
December	106.8	107.0	106.7	106.7	107.4	106.2	107.1	105.0	107.2	106.1	105.1	106.9	104.7	106.9
2008														
March	107.6	107.8	107.6	107.9	108.4	106.9	108.2	106.0	107.9	107.1	105.9	107.7	105.5	107.9
June	108.4	108.6	108.4	108.7	109.2	107.5	108.9	106.8	108.9	107.9	106.7	108.6	106.7	108.7
September	109.2	109.7	109.0	109.5	110.1	107.9	109.7	107.4	109.6	108.5	107.3	109.2	107.4	109.4
December	109.7	110.3	109.5	110.1	110.7	108.0	110.5	107.9	110.2	109.1	107.9	109.7	108.1	109.6
2009														
March	110.0	111.0	109.8	110.6	110.9	108.1	110.7	108.4	111.0	109.2	108.0	110.0	108.8	110.0
June	110.4	111.8	110.1	110.8	111.1	108.2	111.0	108.8	111.3	109.4	108.3	110.3	109.6	110.2
September	110.8	111.9	110.5	111.3	111.3	108.9	111.5	109.2	112.0	109.7	108.6	110.7	110.2	110.6
December	111.2	112.4	110.9	111.6	111.7	109.4	112.1	109.7	112.4	110.2	109.1	111.2	110.9	110.9
2010														
March	111.7	112.8	111.4	112.2	112.3	109.9	112.6	109.9	112.6	110.4	109.4	111.7	111.5	111.4
June	112.2	113.3	111.9	112.6	112.9	110.5	112.8	110.3	112.8	110.9	109.9	112.2	112.1	111.9
September	112.5	113.2	112.3	113.1	113.4	110.8	113.1	110.9	113.1	111.4	110.5	112.6	112.7	112.4
December	113.0	113.7	112.8	113.4	113.9	111.5	113.3	111.3	113.6	111.7	110.9	113.2	112.9	112.7
2011														
March	113.4	114.1	113.2	114.0	114.3	111.8	113.7	111.7	114.2	112.1	111.4	113.5	113.6	113.2
June	113.9	114.5	113.8	114.4	114.8	112.5	114.5	112.1	114.3	112.7	112.0	114.1	114.0	113.8
September	114.2	114.3	114.2	114.8	115.3	113.2	115.2	112.3	114.4	113.1	112.5	114.6	114.6	114.3
December	114.7	114.7	114.7	115.2	115.8	113.6	115.4	112.9	115.2	113.6	112.9	115.0	114.9	114.6

[1] Excludes farm workers, private household workers, and federal government employees.
[2] Not seasonally adjusted.
. . . = Not available.

Table 9-1. Employment Cost Indexes, NAICS Basis—*Continued*

(December 2005 [not seasonally adjusted] = 100; annual values are for December, not seasonally adjusted; quarterly values, seasonally adjusted, except as noted.)

Year and month	All civilian workers [1]	State and local government workers	All private industry workers	Excluding incentive paid occupations [2]	Management, professional, and related	Sales and office	Natural resources, construction, and maintenance	Production, transportation, and material moving	Service occupations	Goods-producing industries Total	Goods-producing industries Manufacturing	Service-providing	Union [2]	Non-union [2]
TOTAL BENEFITS														
2001	80.6	78.1	81.3	...	82.0	81.1	79.8	80.7	82.5	78.5	77.2	82.4	77.3	82.2
2002	84.3	83.0	84.7	...	84.7	84.7	84.1	84.5	86.5	82.3	81.3	85.8	81.2	85.5
2003	89.7	88.2	90.2	...	90.1	90.0	89.8	90.2	91.7	88.2	87.3	91.0	88.1	90.6
2004	95.7	94.1	96.2	...	95.4	95.8	96.4	97.7	97.0	96.3	96.0	96.1	96.8	96.0
2005	100.0	100.0	100.0	...	100.0	100.0	100.0	100.0	100.0	100.0	100.0	100.0	100.0	100.0
2006	103.6	105.2	103.1	...	103.4	102.9	104.0	102.0	103.6	101.7	100.8	103.7	104.2	102.9
2007	106.8	111.0	105.6	...	106.0	106.0	105.9	103.7	106.7	103.2	101.7	106.6	105.8	105.6
2008	109.1	114.2	107.7	...	108.5	107.8	107.7	105.1	108.8	104.7	102.5	108.9	107.8	107.6
2009	110.7	117.7	108.7	...	108.8	108.7	109.5	107.4	110.5	105.8	103.6	109.9	111.4	108.2
2010	113.9	121.1	111.9	...	111.2	111.8	113.2	112.0	113.5	110.1	108.8	112.6	117.9	110.6
2011	117.5	123.6	115.9	...	115.2	115.5	116.8	117.0	116.4	114.4	113.9	116.4	122.8	114.4
2001														
March	78.0	75.2	78.8	...	...	...	...	...	...	76.5	75.4	79.7	74.8	79.9
June	78.8	76.3	79.5	...	...	...	...	...	...	77.0	75.8	80.5	75.7	80.5
September	79.9	77.4	80.6	...	...	...	...	...	...	77.8	76.4	81.7	76.6	81.6
December	80.8	78.0	81.5	...	...	...	...	...	...	78.7	77.4	82.6	77.3	82.2
2002														
March	81.5	78.8	82.3	...	82.7	81.8	81.2	81.8	83.5	79.9	78.8	83.2	78.6	83.2
June	82.5	79.9	83.3	...	83.7	83.2	82.1	82.7	84.4	80.6	79.7	84.4	79.3	84.3
September	83.5	81.4	84.1	...	84.2	84.2	83.3	83.7	86.0	81.2	80.3	85.2	80.5	84.9
December	84.6	82.9	85.0	...	85.2	85.1	84.6	84.8	86.8	82.5	81.5	86.0	81.2	85.5
2003														
March	86.3	84.1	87.0	...	87.1	86.6	86.0	86.7	88.5	85.2	84.7	87.7	83.9	83.2
June	87.5	85.4	88.1	...	88.0	88.0	87.6	88.1	89.4	86.5	85.7	88.8	85.7	84.3
September	88.9	86.9	89.4	...	89.5	89.3	88.7	89.4	90.8	87.5	86.8	90.2	87.2	84.9
December	90.0	88.0	90.5	...	90.7	90.4	90.3	90.4	92.0	88.4	87.5	91.4	88.1	85.5
2004														
March	92.1	89.5	92.9	...	91.9	92.5	92.9	94.4	94.3	92.4	92.7	93.0	92.8	93.0
June	93.7	91.1	94.4	...	93.4	94.2	94.5	96.0	95.9	93.8	94.1	94.6	95.0	94.5
September	94.8	92.5	95.4	...	94.5	95.2	95.4	97.1	96.7	95.0	95.4	95.5	96.0	95.2
December	95.9	93.9	96.5	...	95.9	96.1	96.9	98.0	97.3	96.5	96.1	96.5	96.8	96.0
2005														
March	97.5	95.6	98.0	...	97.9	97.5	98.0	98.7	98.0	98.3	98.2	97.9	98.0	98.2
June	98.4	96.8	98.8	...	98.8	98.4	98.9	99.2	98.8	99.5	99.4	98.6	98.9	99.0
September	99.4	98.4	99.7	...	99.8	99.3	99.7	99.9	99.5	100.3	100.1	99.4	99.8	99.6
December	100.2	99.9	100.3	...	100.4	100.2	100.4	100.1	100.3	100.2	100.1	100.3	100.0	100.0
2006														
March	100.8	100.8	100.8	...	101.0	100.7	101.1	100.0	101.3	99.4	98.6	101.3	100.8	101.0
June	101.7	102.0	101.6	...	101.7	101.5	102.4	100.8	102.1	100.3	99.6	102.2	102.7	101.5
September	102.7	103.5	102.5	...	102.8	102.1	103.4	101.6	103.0	101.3	100.7	103.0	103.4	102.3
December	103.7	105.1	103.4	...	103.8	103.0	104.4	102.3	103.9	102.0	101.1	104.0	104.2	102.9
2007														
March	103.9	107.1	103.1	...	103.5	103.3	103.5	101.0	104.0	100.8	99.3	104.0	102.4	103.4
June	105.2	108.7	104.2	...	104.8	104.2	104.4	102.3	105.0	102.1	100.8	105.1	104.1	104.3
September	106.0	109.7	105.0	...	105.6	105.2	105.2	102.8	106.0	102.4	100.8	106.0	104.3	105.1
December	106.9	110.9	105.9	...	106.4	106.1	106.3	104.0	107.0	103.5	102.0	106.8	105.8	105.6
2008														
March	107.5	111.5	106.4	...	107.0	106.4	106.5	104.2	107.4	103.9	102.0	107.4	106.6	106.5
June	108.1	112.4	106.9	...	107.8	107.0	106.7	104.4	108.4	104.3	102.1	108.0	106.6	107.1
September	108.8	113.3	107.5	...	108.5	107.6	107.4	104.8	108.7	104.6	102.4	108.7	107.2	107.6
December	109.2	114.0	107.9	...	108.9	108.0	108.1	105.5	109.1	105.1	102.9	109.1	107.8	107.6
2009														
March	109.6	115.3	108.0	...	108.5	107.9	108.2	106.1	109.5	105.2	103.1	109.2	109.5	107.9
June	110.0	116.3	108.3	...	108.8	108.1	108.5	106.6	109.9	105.5	103.5	109.4	110.3	108.0
September	110.4	116.8	108.6	...	108.9	108.6	109.2	107.2	110.4	105.6	103.5	109.9	110.9	108.2
December	110.9	117.6	109.0	...	109.2	108.9	109.9	107.9	110.8	106.3	104.2	110.1	111.4	108.2
2010														
March	112.0	118.2	110.3	...	109.9	110.1	111.5	109.5	111.5	108.0	106.1	111.2	114.8	109.5
June	112.7	119.2	110.9	...	110.4	111.0	112.1	110.6	112.4	108.8	107.3	111.8	116.2	110.0
September	113.5	120.2	111.6	...	110.9	111.7	112.9	111.8	113.2	110.0	108.7	112.3	117.6	110.4
December	114.1	121.0	112.2	...	111.6	112.0	113.7	112.7	113.8	110.7	109.6	112.8	117.9	110.6
2011														
March	115.4	122.1	113.5	...	113.1	113.3	114.0	113.1	115.3	111.4	110.6	114.4	119.0	112.6
September	116.9	122.7	115.3	...	114.7	115.0	115.6	116.3	116.0	114.0	113.8	115.8	122.3	113.9
December	117.0	123.1	115.4	...	114.7	115.3	116.2	116.3	115.9	113.8	113.4	116.0	122.0	114.0
December	117.7	123.5	116.2	...	115.6	115.7	117.3	117.6	116.8	115.1	114.7	116.6	122.8	114.4

[1]Excludes farm workers, private household workers, and federal government employees.
[2]Not seasonally adjusted.
. . . = Not available.

Table 9-2. Employment Cost Indexes, SIC Basis

(Not seasonally adjusted, December 2005 = 100; annual values are for December.)

Year	All civilian workers [1,2]	State and local government workers [2]	All private industry workers [2]	Private industry workers excluding sales occupations	Production and nonsupervisory occupations	White-collar occupations	Blue-collar occupations	Service occupations [2]	Total [2]	Construction [2]	Manufacturing [2]	Total [2]	Transportation and utilities	Wholesale trade	Retail trade	Finance, insurance, and real estate [2]	Services
TOTAL COMPENSATION																	
1979	...	...	32.8	32.5	...	31.2	35.0	33.9	33.7	...	33.1	32.0	...	...	...	...	...
1980	...	...	35.9	35.9	...	34.2	38.5	37.1	37.0	...	36.4	35.1	...	...	...	...	...
1981	39.0	36.8	39.5	39.4	40.1	37.6	42.2	40.5	40.7	...	40.0	38.6	...	...	...	...	...
1982	41.5	39.4	42.0	42.0	42.8	40.1	44.7	43.9	43.2	...	42.4	41.1	...	...	...	...	...
1983	43.9	41.8	44.4	44.4	45.2	42.7	47.0	46.3	45.3	...	44.6	43.8	...	...	...	...	...
1984	46.2	44.6	46.6	46.7	47.3	44.8	49.0	49.4	47.4	...	46.9	46.0	...	...	...	...	...
1985	48.2	47.1	48.4	48.3	49.1	47.0	50.5	50.9	49.0	50.8	48.4	48.1	50.6	...	52.4	44.7	46.1
1986	49.9	49.6	49.9	49.9	50.5	48.6	51.9	52.4	50.5	52.3	50.0	49.6	51.8	48.5	53.5	46.1	48.1
1987	51.7	51.8	51.6	51.7	52.2	50.4	53.5	53.7	52.1	54.2	51.5	51.4	53.3	50.4	54.8	47.0	50.5
1988	54.2	54.7	54.1	54.1	54.8	52.9	55.9	56.5	54.4	56.5	53.8	54.0	54.9	52.5	58.0	50.0	53.5
1989	56.9	58.1	56.7	56.5	57.6	55.7	58.2	59.0	56.7	59.0	56.3	56.8	56.9	57.1	59.9	52.7	56.4
1990	59.7	61.5	59.3	59.3	60.1	58.4	60.7	61.8	59.4	60.9	59.1	59.4	59.1	58.2	62.5	54.9	59.9
1991	62.3	63.7	61.9	62.0	62.7	61.0	63.4	64.7	62.1	63.3	61.9	61.9	61.7	60.7	65.2	57.2	62.5
1992	64.4	66.0	64.1	64.2	64.9	63.1	65.6	66.7	64.5	65.6	64.3	63.9	63.9	62.5	66.9	57.9	65.2
1993	66.7	67.9	66.4	66.6	67.3	65.4	68.1	68.8	67.0	67.1	66.9	66.2	66.1	64.4	68.9	60.5	67.5
1994	68.7	69.9	68.5	68.6	69.2	67.5	70.0	70.8	69.0	69.6	69.0	68.1	68.7	66.4	70.8	61.8	69.4
1995	70.6	72.0	70.2	70.4	71.0	69.4	71.7	72.1	70.7	71.1	70.8	70.0	71.2	69.4	72.3	64.0	70.9
1996	72.6	73.9	72.4	72.4	73.1	71.7	73.6	74.2	72.7	72.9	72.9	72.3	73.4	71.5	75.1	65.5	73.1
1997	75.0	75.6	74.9	74.9	75.4	74.4	75.5	77.2	74.5	74.8	74.6	75.1	75.5	73.8	77.7	69.9	75.9
1998	77.6	77.8	77.5	77.2	78.1	77.3	77.6	79.4	76.5	77.4	76.6	78.0	78.4	78.0	80.0	74.1	78.2
1999	80.2	80.5	80.2	80.0	80.4	79.9	80.2	82.1	79.1	79.9	79.2	80.6	80.1	81.1	83.0	77.1	80.9
2000	83.6	82.9	83.6	83.6	84.0	83.6	83.6	85.3	82.6	84.6	82.3	84.2	83.5	84.4	86.4	81.0	84.5
2001	87.0	86.4	87.1	87.0	87.4	87.1	86.7	89.1	85.7	88.2	85.3	87.8	87.5	87.2	90.3	83.9	88.3
2002	90.0	89.9	90.0	89.9	90.2	89.9	89.8	92.0	88.9	91.0	88.5	90.5	91.0	91.1	91.9	87.6	90.7
2003	93.5	92.9	93.6	93.6	93.6	93.6	93.4	94.9	92.4	94.1	92.2	94.2	94.0	94.0	94.9	94.1	94.0
2004	96.9	96.1	97.1	97.2	97.2	96.9	97.5	97.7	96.8	96.4	96.7	97.3	97.6	96.5	97.1	96.7	97.5
2005	100.0	100.0	100.0	100.0	100.0	100.0	100.0	100.0	100.0	100.0	100.0	100.0	100.0	100.0	100.0	100.0	100.0
WAGES AND SALARIES																	
1979	...	...	36.1	36.1	36.8	34.1	39.4	37.9	38.2	41.4	37.5	34.9	39.1	33.7	39.7	32.8	31.7
1980	...	...	39.4	39.3	40.3	37.1	43.1	41.0	41.8	45.0	41.0	38.0	43.5	37.1	42.5	35.2	34.5
1981	42.3	40.1	42.8	42.9	43.9	40.4	46.8	44.4	45.4	49.0	44.5	41.4	47.1	40.0	45.6	38.8	38.1
1982	45.0	42.7	45.5	45.6	46.7	43.1	49.4	48.2	48.0	51.5	47.0	44.2	50.5	42.5	47.5	41.3	41.2
1983	47.3	45.0	47.8	47.9	48.9	45.7	51.3	50.4	49.9	53.0	49.2	46.7	53.0	45.1	49.5	44.3	43.9
1984	49.4	47.7	49.8	50.1	50.8	47.6	53.1	53.5	51.8	53.7	51.2	48.7	54.8	47.6	52.0	43.9	46.7
1985	51.5	50.3	51.8	51.9	52.9	50.0	55.0	54.8	53.6	55.3	53.0	51.0	56.9	49.7	54.5	47.9	48.4
1986	53.3	53.0	53.5	53.6	54.3	51.7	56.4	56.2	55.3	56.7	54.8	52.5	57.9	51.5	55.7	49.2	50.3
1987	55.2	55.2	55.2	55.5	56.0	53.6	58.1	57.6	57.1	58.6	56.6	54.3	59.1	53.6	57.2	49.8	53.0
1988	57.5	57.9	57.5	57.5	58.4	56.1	59.9	60.1	58.9	60.7	58.3	56.9	60.6	55.6	60.1	52.9	55.6
1989	60.1	61.0	59.9	59.8	61.0	58.7	62.0	62.3	61.2	62.8	60.6	59.5	62.2	60.7	62.0	55.7	58.3
1990	62.6	64.2	62.3	62.4	63.2	61.2	64.2	64.8	63.4	64.1	63.1	61.8	64.3	61.2	64.2	57.6	61.6
1991	64.9	66.4	64.6	64.7	65.4	63.5	66.4	67.4	65.8	66.0	65.6	64.1	66.6	63.6	66.6	59.6	63.8
1992	66.6	68.4	66.3	66.5	67.2	65.2	68.1	68.8	67.6	67.3	67.6	65.7	68.7	65.5	68.2	59.5	66.0
1993	68.7	70.2	68.3	68.5	69.2	67.4	70.0	70.3	69.6	68.6	69.7	67.8	70.9	67.1	70.2	62.1	68.0
1994	70.6	72.4	70.2	70.5	71.1	69.3	72.0	72.4	71.7	70.8	71.8	69.6	73.5	69.1	71.9	62.8	70.0
1995	72.7	74.7	72.2	72.5	73.0	71.3	74.1	74.0	73.7	72.5	73.9	71.7	76.0	72.4	73.6	65.1	71.7
1996	75.1	76.8	74.7	74.9	75.5	73.8	76.3	76.6	76.0	74.6	76.3	74.2	78.1	74.7	76.8	67.2	74.2
1997	77.9	78.9	77.6	77.7	78.3	77.0	78.8	79.9	78.3	77.1	78.6	77.4	80.7	77.0	79.7	71.8	77.5
1998	80.8	81.3	80.6	80.4	81.4	80.3	81.3	82.4	81.1	79.9	81.3	80.5	83.0	81.5	82.2	76.9	80.1
1999	83.6	84.2	83.5	83.4	83.8	83.1	84.0	85.1	83.8	82.5	84.1	83.4	84.8	84.5	85.2	79.8	83.0
2000	86.7	87.0	86.7	86.7	87.1	86.4	87.1	88.3	87.1	86.9	87.1	86.6	87.5	87.4	88.6	83.4	86.3
2001	90.0	90.2	90.0	90.0	90.4	89.6	90.5	91.8	90.2	90.4	90.2	89.9	91.7	89.3	91.9	85.8	90.0
2002	92.6	93.1	92.4	92.5	92.6	92.0	93.0	94.1	92.9	92.8	93.0	92.3	94.7	92.8	93.2	89.4	92.0
2003	95.2	95.0	95.2	95.4	95.1	95.2	95.2	96.2	95.1	95.1	95.2	95.3	96.2	95.3	95.5	95.9	94.8
2004	97.5	97.0	97.5	97.8	97.5	97.5	97.6	97.9	97.4	97.0	97.5	97.7	98.6	96.6	97.2	97.7	97.8
2005	100.0	100.0	100.0	100.0	100.0	100.0	100.0	100.0	100.0	100.0	100.0	100.0	100.0	100.0	100.0	100.0	100.0

[1]Excludes farm workers, private household workers, and federal government employees.
[2]Roughly continuous and comparable with new NAICS-based series. See notes and definitions for more information.
. . . = Not available.

Table 9-2. Employment Cost Indexes, SIC Basis—*Continued*

(Not seasonally adjusted, December 2005 = 100; annual values are for December.)

Year	All civilian workers [1,2]	State and local government workers [2]	All private industry workers [2]	Private industry workers excluding sales occupations	By occupational group				By industry division								
									Goods-producing industries			Service-providing industries					
					Production and nonsupervisory occupations	White-collar occupations	Blue-collar occupations	Service occupations [2]	Total [2]	Construction [2]	Manufacturing [2]	Total [2]	Transportation and utilities	Wholesale trade	Retail trade	Finance, insurance, and real estate [2]	Services
TOTAL BENEFITS																	
1979 ...	...	...	25.7	...	...	24.7	27.4	...	26.0	...	25.8	25.4	...	...	...	...	...
1980 ...	...	...	28.7	...	...	27.7	30.4	...	28.8	...	28.5	28.6	...	...	...	...	...
1981 ...	31.8	...	32.2	...	...	31.1	34.0	...	32.4	...	32.1	31.9	...	...	...	...	...
1982 ...	34.2	...	34.5	...	...	33.3	36.5	...	34.8	...	34.4	34.1	...	...	...	...	...
1983 ...	36.8	...	37.1	...	...	35.8	39.1	...	37.2	...	36.9	36.8	...	...	...	...	...
1984 ...	39.3	...	39.5	...	...	38.3	41.4	...	39.6	...	39.3	39.4	...	...	...	...	...
1985 ...	40.8	...	40.9	...	...	40.0	42.5	41.2	40.8	...	40.4	40.9	...	...	...	...	...
1986 ...	42.4	...	42.3	...	...	41.4	43.8	42.9	42.0	...	41.6	42.5	...	...	...	...	...
1987 ...	44.0	...	43.7	...	...	42.9	45.3	43.9	43.2	...	42.7	44.2	...	...	...	...	...
1988 ...	47.0	...	46.7	...	...	45.6	48.6	47.4	46.3	...	46.0	47.1	...	...	...	...	...
1989 ...	50.1	52.2	49.6	...	...	48.6	51.2	50.5	48.8	...	48.7	50.2	...	...	...	...	...
1990 ...	53.5	55.8	52.9	...	...	52.0	54.4	53.8	52.3	...	52.1	53.4	...	...	...	...	...
1991 ...	56.5	58.0	56.2	...	...	55.2	57.8	57.7	55.5	...	55.2	56.7	...	...	...	...	...
1992 ...	59.5	61.1	59.1	...	...	57.8	61.0	61.0	58.7	...	58.3	59.4	...	...	...	...	...
1993 ...	62.2	62.9	62.0	...	...	60.5	64.4	64.4	62.0	...	61.8	62.0	...	...	...	...	...
1994 ...	64.4	64.6	64.3	...	...	63.2	66.2	66.0	64.1	...	63.9	64.4	...	...	...	...	...
1995 ...	65.8	66.3	65.7	...	...	64.8	67.2	66.6	65.2	...	65.0	66.0	...	...	...	...	...
1996 ...	67.1	67.8	67.0	...	...	66.2	68.4	67.3	66.4	...	66.5	67.3	...	...	...	...	...
1997 ...	68.5	68.6	68.5	...	...	68.0	69.4	69.6	67.3	...	67.4	69.2	...	...	...	...	...
1998 ...	70.3	70.7	70.2	...	...	69.9	70.7	70.9	68.1	...	67.9	71.4	...	...	...	...	...
1999 ...	72.6	72.7	72.6	...	...	72.3	73.0	73.4	70.5	...	70.3	73.8	...	...	...	...	...
2000 ...	76.2	74.4	76.7	...	...	76.5	76.9	76.6	74.3	...	73.6	78.1	...	...	...	...	...
2001 ...	80.2	78.5	80.6	...	...	81.1	79.5	81.3	77.3	...	76.3	82.5	...	...	...	...	...
2002 ...	84.2	83.3	84.4	...	...	84.6	83.8	85.7	81.3	...	80.4	86.1	...	...	...	...	...
2003 ...	89.5	88.4	89.8	...	...	89.7	89.8	91.3	87.4	...	86.7	91.2	...	...	...	...	...
2004 ...	95.7	94.3	96.0	...	...	95.3	97.3	97.1	95.7	...	95.3	96.2	...	...	...	...	...
2005 ...	100.0	100.0	100.0	...	...	100.0	100.0	100.0	100.0	...	100.0	100.0	...	...	...	...	...

[1]Excludes farm workers, private household workers, and federal government employees.
[2]Roughly continuous and comparable with new NAICS-based series. See notes and definitions for more information.
. . . = Not available.

Section 9b: Productivity and Related Data

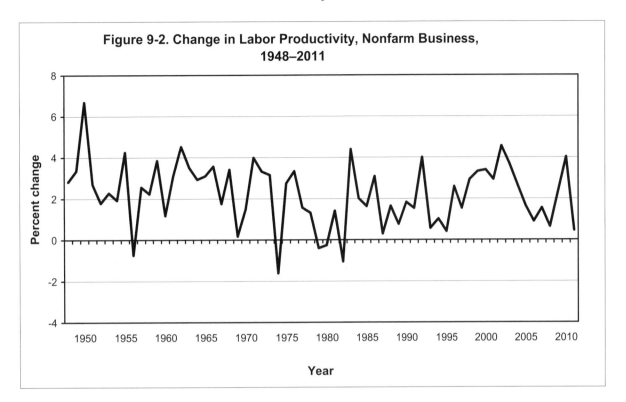

Figure 9-2. Change in Labor Productivity, Nonfarm Business, 1948–2011

- As Figure 9-2 demonstrates, the rate of change in U.S. nonfarm labor productivity has often been quite variable from year to year. Up through the 1980s, productivity tended to decline (growth rates were less than zero) in recession years but rebound sharply in recovery. One explanation of this was that firms expected that declines in demand would be temporary, and therefore held on to their experienced workers in order to be prepared for the recovery. (Table 9-3)

- On average, measuring between cyclically high growth years, productivity grew at a 2.8 percent annual rate from 1948 to 1973. Productivity growth slowed between 1973 and 1989, averaging just 1.3 percent. From 1989 to 2011, however, productivity growth has speeded up to an average of 2.2 percent per year. (Table 9-3)

- In the 1990s and 2000s, productivity growth rates were still variable, but output per hour no longer declined in recession years—in fact, in the recession year 2009 when output plunged 5.0 percent, firms reduced labor input 7.2 percent and productivity grew 2.3 percent. This suggests that the steepness of this decline in demand was not regarded as temporary. (Table 9-3)

- The productivity accounts for nonfinancial corporations allow us to identify separately the cost pressures and profits trends in this sector. From 2000 to 2011, unit labor costs rose at an annual rate of only 1.0 percent, as a 3.1 percent rate of rise in compensation per hour was largely offset by a 2.1 percent rate of productivity growth. Unit non-labor costs (depreciation, interest, and indirect taxes) rose at a 1.6 percent rate. Unit profits rose at a 6.6 percent annual rate. (Table 9-3)

Table 9-3A. Productivity and Related Data: Recent Data

(2005 = 100, seasonally adjusted.)

Year and quarter	Output per hour of all persons	Output	Hours of all persons	Employment	Average weekly hours	Unit labor costs	Compensation per hour	Real hourly compensation	Labor share	Unit nonlabor payments	Implicit price deflator	Current dollar output	Compensation per hour	Nonlabor payments	Output per person
1950	27.3	14.5	53.0	46.3	114.6	18.5	5.1	37.3	104.9	16.3	17.7	2.6	2.7	2.4	31.3
1951	28.1	15.4	54.7	47.5	115.2	19.7	5.5	37.9	103.5	18.0	19.0	2.9	3.0	2.8	32.4
1952	28.9	15.9	54.8	47.7	114.9	20.3	5.9	39.5	105.5	17.6	19.2	3.1	3.2	2.8	33.3
1953	30.0	16.7	55.5	48.4	114.7	20.9	6.3	41.7	107.5	17.2	19.4	3.2	3.5	2.9	34.4
1954	30.6	16.4	53.7	47.2	113.7	21.1	6.5	42.7	108.1	17.1	19.5	3.2	3.5	2.8	34.8
1955	31.9	17.8	55.7	48.6	114.6	20.7	6.6	44.0	105.0	18.2	19.7	3.5	3.7	3.2	36.6
1956	32.0	18.1	56.5	49.6	114.0	22.1	7.1	46.2	108.3	17.8	20.4	3.7	4.0	3.2	36.4
1957	33.0	18.4	55.7	49.5	112.6	22.8	7.5	47.6	108.3	18.3	21.0	3.9	4.2	3.4	37.1
1958	33.9	18.0	53.2	47.6	111.8	23.1	7.8	48.3	108.1	18.7	21.4	3.9	4.2	3.4	37.9
1959	35.2	19.5	55.4	49.1	113.0	23.2	8.2	50.0	107.5	19.1	21.6	4.2	4.5	3.7	39.8
1960	35.8	19.9	55.5	49.3	112.6	23.7	8.5	51.2	108.9	18.8	21.8	4.3	4.7	3.7	40.3
1961	37.1	20.3	54.7	48.8	112.1	23.8	8.8	52.6	108.5	19.1	22.0	4.5	4.8	3.9	41.6
1962	38.8	21.6	55.7	49.4	112.6	23.8	9.2	54.4	107.2	19.7	22.2	4.8	5.1	4.3	43.7
1963	40.3	22.6	56.1	49.7	112.8	23.7	9.6	55.6	106.3	20.2	22.3	5.0	5.4	4.6	45.5
1964	41.7	24.0	57.7	50.6	113.9	23.8	9.9	57.0	105.5	20.7	22.6	5.4	5.7	5.0	47.4
1965	43.1	25.7	59.6	52.1	114.5	23.9	10.3	58.2	104.1	21.5	22.9	5.9	6.1	5.5	49.4
1966	44.9	27.5	61.2	53.6	114.1	24.5	11.0	60.4	104.2	22.0	23.5	6.4	6.7	6.0	51.2
1967	45.9	28.0	61.0	54.4	112.2	25.3	11.6	61.9	104.8	22.3	24.1	6.8	7.1	6.3	51.5
1968	47.4	29.4	61.9	55.4	111.7	26.4	12.5	64.2	105.4	23.0	25.1	7.4	7.8	6.8	53.0
1969	47.7	30.3	63.5	57.2	111.1	28.1	13.4	65.1	107.3	23.3	26.2	7.9	8.5	7.1	53.0
1970	48.6	30.3	62.2	57.0	109.2	29.7	14.5	66.3	108.5	23.8	27.4	8.3	9.0	7.2	53.1
1971	50.6	31.4	62.1	57.1	108.7	30.3	15.4	67.5	106.3	25.8	28.5	9.0	9.5	8.1	55.0
1972	52.3	33.5	64.0	58.8	108.9	31.2	16.3	69.6	105.7	27.0	29.6	9.9	10.5	9.0	56.9
1973	53.9	35.8	66.5	61.3	108.4	32.9	17.7	71.0	105.7	28.4	31.1	11.1	11.8	10.2	58.4
1974	53.0	35.3	66.6	62.3	106.9	36.6	19.4	70.1	107.4	30.2	34.1	12.0	12.9	10.7	56.6
1975	54.8	34.9	63.7	60.4	105.5	39.0	21.4	70.8	104.2	35.0	37.4	13.1	13.6	12.2	57.8
1976	56.6	37.2	65.8	62.3	105.7	41.1	23.2	72.7	104.2	36.8	39.4	14.7	15.3	13.7	59.8
1977	57.5	39.3	68.3	65.0	105.2	43.6	25.1	73.7	104.4	39.0	41.8	16.4	17.1	15.3	60.5
1978	58.2	41.8	71.8	68.5	104.8	46.9	27.3	74.9	104.8	41.4	44.7	18.7	19.6	17.3	61.0
1979	58.1	43.2	74.3	71.2	104.3	51.4	29.9	74.9	105.9	44.1	48.5	21.0	22.2	19.1	60.6
1980	58.0	42.7	73.6	71.4	103.1	57.0	33.1	74.6	107.8	46.6	52.9	22.6	24.3	19.9	59.8
1981	59.2	43.9	74.1	72.1	102.8	61.1	36.2	74.5	105.8	52.6	57.8	25.4	26.8	23.1	60.9
1982	58.7	42.6	72.5	70.9	102.2	66.1	38.8	75.4	108.2	53.3	61.1	26.0	28.1	22.7	60.0
1983	60.8	44.8	73.7	71.5	103.1	66.4	40.4	75.3	105.2	58.1	63.1	28.3	29.8	26.1	62.7
1984	62.5	48.7	78.0	75.1	103.8	67.4	42.1	75.4	103.8	61.2	65.0	31.7	32.9	29.8	64.9
1985	63.9	51.0	79.8	77.0	103.7	69.0	44.1	76.3	103.8	62.7	66.5	33.9	35.2	32.0	66.2
1986	65.7	52.9	80.5	78.3	102.8	70.5	46.4	78.8	104.3	63.1	67.6	35.8	37.3	33.4	67.6
1987	65.9	54.6	82.9	80.4	103.1	72.9	48.0	79.0	105.2	63.7	69.2	37.8	39.8	34.8	68.0
1988	66.9	57.0	85.2	82.9	102.8	75.5	50.5	80.1	105.7	65.1	71.4	40.7	43.0	37.1	68.8
1989	67.6	59.1	87.4	84.7	103.3	76.7	51.9	78.9	103.7	69.9	74.0	43.8	45.4	41.3	69.8
1990	69.0	60.0	86.9	85.2	102.0	80.0	55.2	80.0	101.9	71.6	76.7	46.0	48.0	43.0	70.4
1991	70.1	59.5	84.9	83.9	101.2	82.8	58.0	81.1	104.6	73.6	79.2	47.1	49.3	43.8	70.9
1992	73.0	61.8	84.7	83.4	101.5	83.7	61.1	83.3	103.7	76.1	80.7	49.9	51.7	47.0	74.1
1993	73.4	63.8	86.9	85.2	102.1	85.1	62.5	83.1	103.5	77.9	82.3	52.5	54.3	49.7	74.9
1994	74.1	67.0	90.4	88.0	102.7	85.6	63.4	82.6	102.3	80.7	83.7	56.0	57.3	54.1	76.0
1995	74.1	68.8	92.9	90.5	102.6	87.4	64.7	82.4	102.5	81.9	85.2	58.7	60.1	56.4	76.0
1996	76.3	72.0	94.4	92.5	102.0	87.8	66.9	82.9	101.4	84.7	86.6	62.3	63.2	61.0	77.8
1997	77.6	75.7	97.5	95.0	102.7	89.1	69.1	83.8	101.3	86.2	87.9	66.6	67.4	65.3	79.7
1998	79.9	79.5	99.4	97.0	102.6	91.7	73.3	87.7	103.6	83.6	88.5	70.4	72.9	66.4	82.0
1999	82.7	83.9	101.4	98.5	102.9	92.6	76.6	89.8	103.8	84.0	89.2	74.9	77.7	70.5	85.2
2000	85.6	87.7	102.4	100.2	102.2	96.1	82.3	93.3	105.7	82.9	90.9	79.7	84.3	72.7	87.5
2001	88.2	88.4	100.3	99.4	100.9	97.7	86.1	95.0	105.6	84.5	92.5	81.8	86.4	74.7	89.0
2002	92.2	90.2	97.8	97.2	100.7	96.4	88.8	96.4	103.4	88.4	93.2	84.0	86.9	79.7	92.8
2003	95.7	93.0	97.2	97.0	100.2	97.2	93.0	98.7	102.9	90.3	94.5	87.8	90.4	83.9	95.9
2004	98.4	96.7	98.3	98.2	100.1	97.8	96.2	99.5	101.0	95.4	96.9	93.7	94.6	92.3	98.5
2005	100.0	100.0	100.0	100.0	100.0	100.0	100.0	100.0	100.0	100.0	100.0	100.0	100.0	100.0	100.0
2006	100.9	103.0	102.1	101.9	100.2	102.8	103.8	100.5	100.0	103.0	102.9	106.0	106.0	106.1	101.2
2007	102.4	105.1	102.6	102.6	100.0	105.5	108.1	101.8	100.0	105.6	105.6	110.9	110.9	111.0	102.4
2008	103.2	103.7	100.5	101.1	99.4	108.2	111.7	101.2	100.7	106.3	107.5	111.4	112.2	110.2	102.6
2009	105.7	98.7	93.3	95.3	97.9	107.4	113.5	103.3	99.2	109.6	108.3	106.8	105.9	108.1	103.5
2010	109.9	102.5	93.3	94.2	99.0	105.2	115.7	103.6	96.0	116.3	109.6	112.4	107.9	119.3	108.8
2011	110.1	104.7	95.1	95.6	99.5	107.4	118.2	102.6	95.6	119.9	112.3	117.6	112.4	125.6	109.6
2009															
1st quarter	102.9	98.3	95.5	97.2	98.3	108.5	111.7	102.6	100.1	108.2	108.4	106.6	106.7	106.4	101.2
2nd quarter	105.0	98.1	93.4	95.5	97.8	108.1	113.6	103.9	100.1	108.0	108.1	106.0	106.0	105.9	102.8
3rd quarter	106.8	98.5	92.2	94.6	97.5	107.0	114.3	103.6	98.9	109.9	108.1	106.5	105.4	108.3	104.2
4th quarter	108.1	99.7	92.2	94.1	98.0	105.9	114.6	103.1	97.7	112.3	108.4	108.1	105.6	112.0	106.0
2010															
1st quarter	109.3	101.0	92.4	93.9	98.4	105.1	114.9	103.1	96.5	114.7	108.9	110.0	106.2	115.8	107.5
2nd quarter	109.6	102.1	93.2	94.2	99.0	105.5	115.6	103.9	96.4	115.5	109.4	111.8	107.7	118.0	108.5
3rd quarter	110.2	103.1	93.5	94.2	99.3	105.4	116.1	104.0	96.0	116.5	109.7	113.1	108.6	120.0	109.4
4th quarter	110.5	103.9	94.0	94.6	99.4	105.0	116.1	103.2	95.2	118.5	110.4	114.7	109.1	123.2	109.9
2011															
1st quarter	110.1	104.0	94.5	95.2	99.3	106.8	117.5	103.3	96.0	117.9	111.2	115.6	111.0	122.6	109.3
2nd quarter	110.0	104.4	94.9	95.4	99.5	106.8	117.5	102.2	95.4	119.9	111.9	116.9	111.5	125.1	109.4
3rd quarter	110.4	105.1	95.2	95.7	99.5	107.8	119.0	102.7	95.7	120.1	112.7	118.4	113.3	126.3	109.9
4th quarter	110.7	106.1	95.8	96.1	99.7	107.4	118.9	102.3	95.2	121.1	112.8	119.7	113.9	128.5	110.4

Table 9-3A. Productivity and Related Data: Recent Data—*Continued*

(2005 = 100, seasonally adjusted.)

Year and quarter	Nonfarm business sector														
	Output per hour of all persons	Output	Hours of all persons	Employment	Average weekly hours	Unit labor costs	Compensation per hour	Real hourly compensation	Labor share	Unit nonlabor payments	Implicit price deflator	Current dollar output	Compensation	Nonlabor payments	Output per person
1950	30.8	14.2	45.9	39.5	116.1	17.7	5.4	40.2	104.7	15.6	16.9	2.4	2.5	2.2	35.8
1951	31.7	15.2	48.1	41.3	116.3	18.7	5.9	40.5	104.0	16.8	18.0	2.7	2.8	2.6	36.9
1952	32.2	15.7	48.6	41.8	116.2	19.4	6.2	42.0	105.7	16.7	18.3	2.9	3.0	2.6	37.5
1953	33.0	16.4	49.8	43.1	115.7	20.0	6.6	44.0	107.0	16.6	18.7	3.1	3.3	2.7	38.2
1954	33.6	16.2	48.1	41.9	114.9	20.2	6.8	45.0	107.4	16.7	18.8	3.0	3.3	2.7	38.6
1955	35.0	17.5	50.1	43.2	116.0	20.1	7.1	46.9	104.9	17.7	19.2	3.4	3.5	3.1	40.6
1956	34.8	17.8	51.3	44.4	115.6	21.5	7.5	49.0	108.4	17.3	19.9	3.5	3.8	3.1	40.2
1957	35.7	18.2	51.0	44.6	114.3	22.2	7.9	50.2	108.3	17.9	20.5	3.7	4.0	3.2	40.8
1958	36.5	17.8	48.9	43.1	113.5	22.6	8.2	50.7	108.6	18.0	20.8	3.7	4.0	3.2	41.4
1959	37.9	19.4	51.1	44.6	114.6	22.6	8.6	52.3	107.3	18.7	21.0	4.1	4.4	3.6	43.4
1960	38.3	19.7	51.4	45.1	114.1	23.3	8.9	53.7	109.4	18.2	21.3	4.2	4.6	3.6	43.7
1961	39.5	20.1	50.9	44.8	113.7	23.3	9.2	54.9	108.7	18.6	21.5	4.3	4.7	3.7	44.9
1962	41.3	21.5	52.0	45.6	114.1	23.2	9.6	56.5	107.2	19.3	21.7	4.7	5.0	4.1	47.1
1963	42.7	22.5	52.6	46.1	114.1	23.2	9.9	57.7	106.3	19.7	21.8	4.9	5.2	4.4	48.8
1964	44.0	24.0	54.5	47.2	115.4	23.2	10.2	58.7	105.2	20.3	22.1	5.3	5.6	4.9	50.8
1965	45.4	25.7	56.6	48.9	115.8	23.3	10.6	59.7	104.0	21.0	22.4	5.8	6.0	5.4	52.5
1966	47.0	27.5	58.6	50.8	115.3	23.8	11.2	61.5	104.0	21.5	22.9	6.3	6.6	5.9	54.2
1967	47.8	28.0	58.6	51.7	113.4	24.8	11.8	63.1	104.9	21.9	23.6	6.6	6.9	6.1	54.2
1968	49.4	29.5	59.6	52.9	112.7	25.8	12.8	65.3	105.2	22.6	24.6	7.2	7.6	6.7	55.7
1969	49.5	30.4	61.3	54.8	111.9	27.5	13.6	66.2	107.3	22.8	25.7	7.8	8.4	6.9	55.4
1970	50.2	30.3	60.4	54.8	110.1	29.1	14.6	67.1	108.5	23.3	26.8	8.1	8.8	7.1	55.3
1971	52.3	31.5	60.2	55.0	109.6	29.8	15.5	68.4	106.4	25.2	28.0	8.8	9.4	7.9	57.2
1972	54.0	33.6	62.2	56.6	109.8	30.7	16.6	70.5	106.3	26.0	28.8	9.7	10.3	8.7	59.3
1973	55.7	36.0	64.7	59.2	109.4	32.2	17.9	71.8	107.7	26.3	29.9	10.8	11.6	9.5	60.9
1974	54.8	35.5	64.8	60.1	107.8	35.9	19.7	71.0	108.9	28.4	32.9	11.7	12.7	10.1	59.0
1975	56.3	34.9	62.0	58.4	106.3	38.4	21.6	71.6	105.3	33.5	36.5	12.7	13.4	11.7	59.8
1976	58.2	37.4	64.2	60.4	106.4	40.3	23.5	73.4	104.7	35.7	38.5	14.4	15.1	13.3	61.9
1977	59.1	39.5	66.8	63.1	105.8	42.9	25.4	74.5	104.9	37.8	40.9	16.1	16.9	14.9	62.5
1978	59.9	42.1	70.3	66.6	105.4	46.1	27.6	75.8	105.6	39.9	43.7	18.4	19.4	16.8	63.1
1979	59.6	43.4	72.8	69.5	104.7	50.7	30.2	75.7	106.9	42.3	47.4	20.6	22.0	18.4	62.4
1980	59.5	42.9	72.2	69.7	103.6	56.2	33.4	75.4	108.2	45.3	51.9	22.3	24.1	19.5	61.6
1981	60.3	43.8	72.7	70.5	103.2	60.8	36.7	75.5	106.8	50.9	56.9	24.9	26.6	22.3	62.2
1982	59.7	42.4	71.1	69.3	102.5	65.8	39.3	76.3	108.9	52.1	60.4	25.6	27.9	22.1	61.2
1983	62.3	45.1	72.5	70.0	103.5	65.7	40.9	76.2	105.3	57.2	62.4	28.1	29.6	25.8	64.5
1984	63.5	48.9	76.9	73.8	104.2	67.0	42.6	76.2	104.5	59.7	64.1	31.3	32.7	29.2	66.2
1985	64.6	51.0	78.9	75.9	104.0	68.9	44.5	76.9	104.4	61.5	66.0	33.6	35.1	31.3	67.1
1986	66.6	52.9	79.5	77.2	103.0	70.3	46.8	79.5	104.8	62.1	67.1	35.5	37.2	32.9	68.5
1987	66.8	54.7	81.9	79.4	103.2	72.7	48.5	79.7	105.7	62.7	68.7	37.6	39.7	34.3	68.9
1988	67.9	57.2	84.3	81.9	102.9	75.1	50.9	80.8	106.0	64.2	70.8	40.5	42.9	36.7	69.8
1989	68.4	59.2	86.6	83.8	103.4	76.4	52.2	79.4	104.1	68.7	73.4	43.5	45.2	40.7	70.7
1990	69.6	60.1	86.3	84.4	102.2	79.7	55.5	80.3	104.7	70.5	76.1	45.7	47.9	42.4	71.2
1991	70.7	59.5	84.2	83.0	101.4	82.6	58.4	81.6	104.9	72.8	78.7	46.9	49.1	43.3	71.7
1992	73.5	61.8	84.0	82.5	101.8	83.7	61.5	83.9	104.2	75.1	80.3	49.6	51.7	46.4	74.8
1993	73.9	63.9	86.4	84.5	102.3	84.9	62.7	83.5	103.6	77.3	81.9	52.3	54.2	49.4	75.6
1994	74.7	66.9	89.6	87.2	102.7	85.5	63.9	83.2	102.6	80.1	83.4	55.8	57.2	53.6	76.7
1995	75.0	69.0	92.0	89.7	102.6	86.9	65.2	82.9	102.5	81.6	84.8	58.6	60.0	56.3	76.9
1996	76.9	72.1	93.7	91.8	102.0	87.5	67.4	83.4	101.8	83.7	86.0	62.0	63.1	60.3	78.5
1997	78.1	75.7	96.9	94.4	102.7	88.9	69.4	84.2	101.5	85.6	87.6	66.3	67.3	64.8	80.2
1998	80.4	79.6	99.0	96.5	102.6	91.5	73.6	88.0	103.7	83.3	88.3	70.3	72.9	66.3	82.5
1999	83.1	84.1	101.2	98.2	103.0	92.4	76.8	88.9	103.6	84.1	89.1	74.9	77.7	70.7	85.6
2000	85.9	87.8	102.2	100.0	102.2	96.0	82.5	93.5	105.6	83.0	90.9	79.8	84.3	72.8	87.8
2001	88.4	88.6	100.2	99.3	100.9	97.5	86.2	95.0	105.5	84.6	92.4	81.8	86.3	74.9	89.2
2002	92.4	90.3	97.6	97.0	100.6	96.2	88.9	96.5	103.2	88.7	93.2	84.2	86.8	80.1	93.0
2003	95.8	93.0	97.1	96.9	100.1	97.1	93.1	98.8	102.9	90.1	94.4	87.8	90.4	83.9	96.0
2004	98.4	96.7	98.3	98.2	100.1	97.8	96.2	99.4	101.2	94.8	96.6	93.5	94.6	91.7	98.5
2005	100.0	100.0	100.0	100.0	100.0	100.0	100.0	100.0	100.0	100.0	100.0	100.0	100.0	100.0	100.0
2006	100.9	103.1	102.2	101.9	100.3	102.8	103.8	100.5	99.9	103.2	103.0	106.2	106.0	106.2	101.2
2007	102.5	105.3	102.7	102.7	100.0	105.3	107.9	101.6	100.0	105.4	105.4	110.9	110.9	111.0	102.5
2008	103.1	103.7	100.6	101.1	99.5	108.2	111.6	101.2	100.9	105.8	107.3	111.3	112.3	109.7	102.5
2009	105.5	98.5	93.3	95.3	97.9	107.5	113.5	103.3	99.2	109.8	108.4	106.8	105.9	108.1	103.3
2010	109.8	102.4	93.3	94.2	99.0	105.4	115.7	103.6	96.2	116.1	109.6	112.2	107.9	118.9	108.7
2011	110.2	104.8	95.1	95.5	99.5	107.3	118.3	102.6	95.9	119.1	111.9	117.3	112.4	124.8	109.7
2009															
1st quarter	102.8	98.2	95.5	97.2	98.3	108.6	111.7	102.6	100.0	108.5	108.6	106.6	106.6	106.5	101.0
2nd quarter	104.9	97.9	93.3	95.4	97.8	108.3	113.6	103.9	100.1	108.1	108.2	105.9	106.0	105.8	102.6
3rd quarter	106.5	98.2	92.2	94.5	97.5	107.2	114.2	103.5	98.9	110.3	108.4	106.5	105.3	108.3	103.9
4th quarter	107.9	99.6	92.3	94.1	98.0	106.1	114.5	103.0	97.7	112.3	108.5	108.1	105.6	111.8	105.8
2010															
1st quarter	109.1	100.8	92.4	93.9	98.4	105.3	114.9	103.1	96.6	114.7	109.0	109.9	106.1	115.7	107.4
2nd quarter	109.5	102.0	93.1	94.1	98.9	105.6	115.6	103.9	96.4	115.6	109.5	111.7	107.7	117.8	108.3
3rd quarter	110.0	102.9	93.5	94.2	99.3	105.6	116.1	103.9	96.2	116.2	109.7	112.9	108.6	119.5	109.2
4th quarter	110.5	103.8	94.0	94.5	99.4	105.1	116.1	103.2	95.4	118.0	110.2	114.4	109.1	122.5	109.8
2011															
1st quarter	110.2	104.0	94.4	95.1	99.3	106.7	117.6	103.3	96.3	117.1	110.8	115.2	111.0	121.8	109.4
2nd quarter	110.1	104.5	94.9	95.4	99.5	106.7	117.4	102.1	95.7	119.0	111.5	116.5	111.5	124.3	109.5
3rd quarter	110.6	105.2	95.2	95.6	99.5	107.7	119.1	102.7	96.0	119.1	112.2	118.1	113.3	125.4	110.1
4th quarter	110.9	106.2	95.8	96.1	99.7	107.3	119.0	102.3	95.4	120.3	112.4	119.3	113.9	127.8	110.5

Table 9-3A. Productivity and Related Data: Recent Data—*Continued*

(2005 = 100, seasonally adjusted.)

Year and quarter	Nonfinancial corporations										Manufacturing					
	Output per hour of all persons	Output	Employee hours	Compensation per hour	Real compensation per hour	Unit costs Total	Labor costs	Nonlabor costs	Unit profits	Implicit price deflator	Output per hour of all persons	Output	Hours of all persons	Compensation per hour	Real compensation per hour	Unit labor costs
1950	30.1	11.5	38.1	6.2	46.0	19.3	20.7	15.6	34.2	21.2	...	...	...	...	...	...
1951	29.8	12.1	40.6	6.8	46.5	21.0	22.8	16.3	36.8	23.0	...	...	...	...	...	...
1952	30.5	12.6	41.2	7.2	48.3	21.8	23.6	17.1	32.8	23.2	...	...	...	...	...	...
1953	31.7	13.5	42.5	7.6	50.6	22.0	24.0	17.0	30.5	23.1	...	...	...	...	...	...
1954	33.0	13.3	40.3	7.9	52.0	22.0	23.8	17.4	29.7	23.0	...	...	...	...	...	...
1955	35.0	14.9	42.6	8.1	54.0	21.5	23.2	16.8	34.9	23.2	...	...	...	...	...	...
1956	35.1	15.4	43.8	8.6	56.6	22.8	24.6	17.9	32.4	24.0	...	...	...	...	...	...
1957	35.8	15.6	43.5	9.2	58.0	23.8	25.6	19.2	31.2	24.7	...	...	...	...	...	...
1958	36.5	15.0	41.0	9.5	58.7	24.7	26.1	21.0	28.3	25.1	...	...	...	...	...	...
1959	38.4	16.7	43.5	9.9	60.5	24.2	25.8	20.2	33.0	25.3	...	...	...	...	...	...
1960	39.0	17.2	44.2	10.3	61.8	24.7	26.3	20.6	30.4	25.4	...	...	...	...	...	...
1961	40.3	17.6	43.8	10.6	63.2	24.8	26.3	21.0	30.4	25.6	...	...	...	...	...	...
1962	42.1	19.1	45.5	11.0	65.0	24.7	26.2	20.7	32.8	25.7	...	...	...	...	...	...
1963	43.6	20.3	46.5	11.4	66.1	24.5	26.1	20.5	34.7	25.8	...	...	...	...	...	...
1964	44.3	21.7	49.0	11.6	66.5	24.6	26.1	20.5	36.0	26.0	...	...	...	...	...	...
1965	45.4	23.5	51.8	11.9	67.3	24.6	26.3	20.4	38.7	26.4	...	...	...	...	...	...
1966	46.2	25.2	54.6	12.6	69.1	25.3	27.2	20.4	38.6	27.0	...	...	...	...	...	...
1967	46.9	25.9	55.1	13.3	70.8	26.5	28.3	21.7	36.0	27.7	...	...	...	...	...	...
1968	48.6	27.6	56.7	14.3	73.1	27.6	29.4	23.0	35.9	28.7	...	...	...	...	...	...
1969	48.7	28.7	58.9	15.3	74.0	29.5	31.3	24.9	32.5	29.9	...	...	...	...	...	...
1970	49.0	28.4	58.0	16.3	74.9	31.8	33.3	28.0	26.5	31.1	...	...	...	...	...	...
1971	51.1	29.6	57.9	17.3	76.3	32.6	33.9	29.3	30.0	32.3	...	...	...	...	...	...
1972	52.2	31.9	61.1	18.3	77.9	33.4	35.0	29.3	32.6	33.3	...	...	...	...	...	...
1973	52.7	33.8	64.2	19.7	78.9	35.5	37.3	30.9	32.9	35.2	...	...	...	...	...	...
1974	51.7	33.3	64.5	21.5	77.8	39.9	41.7	35.4	29.2	38.6	...	...	...	...	...	...
1975	53.6	32.8	61.2	23.7	78.3	43.1	44.1	40.3	37.8	42.4	...	...	...	...	...	...
1976	55.5	35.5	64.0	25.6	80.1	44.5	46.2	40.1	42.7	44.2	...	...	...	...	...	...
1977	56.9	38.1	66.9	27.6	81.2	46.6	48.5	41.6	46.6	46.6	...	...	...	...	...	...
1978	57.7	40.6	70.4	30.2	82.9	49.9	52.3	43.6	48.4	49.7	...	...	...	...	...	...
1979	57.2	41.9	73.2	32.9	82.5	54.8	57.5	47.5	45.4	53.6	...	...	...	...	...	...
1980	57.0	41.5	72.7	36.2	81.7	61.3	63.5	55.6	40.7	58.7	...	...	...	...	...	...
1981	58.5	43.1	73.8	39.5	81.3	66.4	67.5	63.4	48.5	64.1	...	...	...	...	...	...
1982	58.6	42.1	71.8	42.1	81.7	71.3	71.7	70.2	44.7	67.9	...	...	...	...	...	...
1983	60.6	44.1	72.8	43.6	81.3	71.5	72.0	70.4	54.3	69.4	...	...	...	...	...	...
1984	62.0	48.0	77.5	45.4	81.3	72.3	73.3	69.7	65.2	71.4	...	...	...	...	...	...
1985	63.2	50.1	79.3	47.5	82.1	74.1	75.1	71.6	62.5	72.6	...	...	...	...	...	...
1986	64.6	51.3	79.5	49.8	84.7	76.6	77.2	75.0	53.6	73.7	...	...	...	...	...	...
1987	65.8	54.0	82.0	51.5	84.6	77.1	78.2	74.2	60.4	75.0	51.0	62.9	123.2	49.4	81.2	96.8
1988	67.5	57.1	84.6	53.7	85.1	78.3	79.5	75.2	66.8	76.8	52.1	66.1	126.9	51.2	81.1	98.2
1989	66.6	58.1	87.2	55.0	83.6	81.8	82.6	80.0	61.2	79.2	52.6	67.2	127.7	52.7	80.1	100.1
1990	67.3	58.9	87.5	57.6	83.4	85.1	85.6	83.6	58.9	81.7	53.8	67.0	124.5	55.2	80.0	102.7
1991	69.0	58.6	85.0	60.5	84.6	87.8	87.7	87.9	58.0	84.0	55.2	65.8	119.3	58.5	81.8	106.0
1992	70.7	60.4	85.4	63.4	86.5	88.6	89.7	85.8	61.5	85.2	57.3	68.0	118.7	61.3	83.5	106.9
1993	70.9	62.0	87.4	64.6	85.9	89.4	91.1	85.2	70.3	87.0	58.8	70.7	120.3	62.7	83.4	106.6
1994	72.3	65.9	91.1	65.7	85.6	89.4	90.9	85.5	82.4	88.5	60.8	74.9	123.1	64.2	83.7	105.6
1995	73.1	69.0	94.4	66.9	85.1	90.0	91.5	85.9	85.5	89.4	63.6	78.8	123.9	65.2	83.0	102.6
1996	75.7	72.8	96.1	68.9	85.3	89.4	90.9	85.4	92.5	89.8	65.9	81.5	123.6	66.4	82.2	100.7
1997	77.7	77.6	99.8	71.0	86.0	89.6	91.3	85.3	94.8	90.3	69.5	87.4	125.9	68.0	82.4	97.8
1998	80.4	82.0	102.0	75.2	90.0	91.4	93.5	85.8	83.1	90.3	73.3	92.1	125.5	72.2	86.3	98.4
1999	83.0	86.5	104.3	78.6	92.0	92.9	94.7	88.1	77.3	90.9	76.9	95.9	124.7	75.4	88.3	97.9
2000	86.4	91.2	105.6	84.4	95.6	95.9	97.7	91.1	64.3	91.9	80.4	98.9	123.1	81.2	92.0	101.0
2001	87.1	89.4	102.7	87.1	96.1	99.1	100.1	96.7	51.9	93.2	81.9	94.2	115.0	84.3	92.9	102.9
2002	90.4	90.0	99.6	89.5	97.1	98.5	99.0	97.1	59.5	93.5	87.8	93.9	106.9	88.9	96.5	101.2
2003	94.4	92.3	97.8	93.9	99.7	98.7	99.5	96.8	66.0	94.6	93.3	94.9	101.7	96.0	101.9	102.9
2004	97.8	96.5	98.7	96.5	99.7	97.8	98.6	95.7	88.0	96.6	95.4	96.5	101.1	96.8	100.0	101.4
2005	100.0	100.0	100.0	100.0	100.0	100.0	100.0	100.0	100.0	100.0	100.0	100.0	100.0	100.0	100.0	100.0
2006	101.9	103.8	101.9	103.3	100.0	101.8	101.3	103.0	111.6	103.0	100.9	101.6	100.7	102.0	98.8	101.1
2007	102.6	104.8	102.2	107.3	101.0	105.9	104.6	109.2	100.0	105.1	104.8	103.8	99.1	105.3	99.1	100.4
2008	102.9	103.4	100.5	111.2	100.8	109.6	108.0	113.6	91.6	107.3	104.3	99.2	95.1	109.8	99.6	105.2
2009	103.4	95.8	92.6	113.5	103.3	112.8	109.7	121.0	84.1	109.2	104.9	86.8	82.7	114.8	104.5	109.4
2010	108.2	100.4	92.8	115.6	103.5	107.6	106.8	109.9	118.8	109.0	111.8	92.5	82.7	116.6	104.4	104.3
2011	108.5	103.3	95.2	117.8	102.2	108.7	108.6	109.0	129.7	111.3	114.6	97.0	84.6	118.3	102.7	103.2
2009																
1st quarter	100.7	95.8	95.1	111.4	102.4	114.4	110.6	124.3	81.2	110.2	101.6	87.3	86.0	112.7	103.6	111.0
2nd quarter	102.3	94.7	92.6	113.5	103.8	114.5	111.0	123.7	75.0	109.5	103.4	85.1	82.3	115.1	105.3	111.3
3rd quarter	104.2	95.3	91.4	114.3	103.6	112.4	109.7	119.6	83.6	108.8	106.5	86.7	81.4	115.4	104.6	108.3
4th quarter	106.6	97.4	91.4	114.7	103.2	110.1	107.6	116.6	96.2	108.3	108.4	88.1	81.3	116.2	104.5	107.2
2010																
1st quarter	108.9	99.8	91.7	114.9	103.2	107.4	105.6	112.0	114.8	108.3	109.7	89.8	81.9	115.4	103.6	105.2
2nd quarter	108.5	100.4	92.6	115.4	103.7	107.3	106.4	109.9	117.7	108.6	111.9	92.3	82.5	116.6	104.8	104.2
3rd quarter	108.3	100.9	93.2	116.1	103.9	107.6	107.1	108.6	121.5	109.3	112.3	93.6	83.3	116.9	104.7	104.1
4th quarter	107.3	100.6	93.7	115.8	103.0	108.3	107.9	109.1	121.2	109.9	113.4	94.3	83.2	117.5	104.5	103.6
2011																
1st quarter	107.8	101.7	94.3	117.0	102.8	108.7	108.5	109.3	122.4	110.5	114.2	95.9	83.9	118.6	104.3	103.8
2nd quarter	108.6	103.2	95.0	117.1	101.9	108.1	107.9	108.8	130.4	111.0	113.7	96.1	84.5	118.0	102.6	103.8
3rd quarter	108.6	103.7	95.5	118.6	102.3	109.1	109.2	109.0	131.9	112.0	115.2	97.3	84.4	118.9	102.6	103.2
4th quarter	109.0	104.6	96.0	118.4	101.9	108.7	108.7	108.7	134.1	111.9	115.4	98.6	85.4	117.8	101.4	102.1

. . . = Not available.

Table 9-3B. Productivity and Related Data: Historical Data

(2005 = 100, seasonally adjusted.)

Year and quarter	Business sector								Nonfarm business sector							
	Output per hour of all persons	Output	Hours of all persons	Compensation per hour	Real compensation per hour	Unit labor costs	Unit nonlabor payments	Implicit price deflator	Output per hour of all persons	Output	Hours of all persons	Compensation per hour	Real compensation per hour	Unit labor costs	Unit nonlabor payments	Implicit price deflator
1947	23.5	12.6	53.6	4.3	34.3	18.2	14.1	16.6	27.2	12.4	45.5	4.6	36.7	16.9	13.3	15.5
1948	24.6	13.3	54.0	4.7	34.4	18.9	14.6	17.6	28.0	12.9	46.3	5.0	36.9	17.9	14.5	16.5
1949	25.2	13.2	52.3	*4.7	35.3	18.7	15.5	17.4	28.9	12.9	44.5	5.1	38.5	17.8	14.9	16.7
1947																
1st quarter	23.5	12.5	53.4	4.2	34.2	17.7	13.6	16.1	26.8	12.2	45.4	4.5	36.6	16.6	12.5	15.0
2nd quarter	23.6	12.6	53.3	4.3	34.5	18.1	13.6	16.3	27.5	12.5	45.4	4.5	36.7	16.5	13.2	15.2
3rd quarter	23.4	12.6	53.7	4.3	34.0	18.3	14.3	16.7	26.7	12.1	45.5	4.6	36.7	17.4	13.6	15.9
4th quarter	23.7	12.8	54.1	4.5	34.3	18.8	14.7	17.2	27.8	12.8	45.9	4.8	36.6	17.1	13.9	15.8
1948																
1st quarter	24.2	13.1	53.9	4.5	34.1	18.7	15.3	17.3	27.9	12.9	46.2	4.9	36.7	17.4	14.1	16.1
2nd quarter	24.8	13.4	53.9	4.6	34.0	18.5	15.9	17.5	27.9	12.9	46.2	4.9	36.7	17.7	14.3	16.4
3rd quarter	24.7	13.4	54.4	4.7	34.4	19.1	15.8	17.8	27.9	13.0	46.5	5.1	36.9	18.1	14.6	16.7
4th quarter	24.8	13.4	54.0	4.8	35.5	19.4	15.4	17.8	28.1	12.9	46.1	5.1	37.7	18.2	15.0	16.9
1949																
1st quarter	24.7	13.2	53.3	4.7	35.1	19.1	15.5	17.7	28.4	12.9	45.3	5.1	38.2	18.1	14.8	16.8
2nd quarter	24.8	13.1	52.8	4.7	34.7	18.7	15.5	17.5	28.7	12.8	44.6	5.1	38.2	17.9	14.8	16.7
3rd quarter	25.6	13.3	51.9	4.7	35.5	18.5	15.6	17.4	29.4	13.0	44.1	5.1	38.7	17.5	15.2	16.6
4th quarter	25.6	13.1	51.3	4.8	36.0	18.7	15.2	17.3	29.2	12.8	43.9	5.1	38.7	17.6	14.9	16.5
1950																
1st quarter	26.8	13.8	51.4	5.0	37.4	18.5	15.4	17.3	30.2	13.4	44.3	5.3	39.8	17.5	15.3	16.6
2nd quarter	27.1	14.2	52.6	5.0	37.4	18.4	15.7	17.4	30.5	13.9	45.4	5.4	40.3	17.6	15.3	16.7
3rd quarter	27.5	14.8	53.9	5.1	37.4	18.5	16.7	17.7	31.2	14.6	46.8	5.5	40.3	17.5	15.8	16.9
4th quarter	27.7	15.0	54.2	5.2	37.4	18.8	17.2	18.2	31.3	14.8	47.2	5.6	40.6	18.0	16.0	17.2
1951																
1st quarter	27.7	15.2	54.8	5.4	37.2	19.4	17.9	18.8	31.4	15.1	48.0	5.8	40.0	18.4	16.6	17.7
2nd quarter	27.8	15.3	55.1	5.5	37.8	19.8	17.7	19.0	31.3	15.1	48.4	5.9	40.4	18.8	16.5	17.9
3rd quarter	28.6	15.6	54.4	5.6	38.5	19.6	18.0	19.0	32.0	15.3	47.9	6.0	41.0	18.7	17.0	18.0
4th quarter	28.5	15.6	54.6	5.7	38.3	19.9	18.2	19.2	32.0	15.4	47.9	6.1	41.0	18.9	17.0	18.1
1952																
1st quarter	28.6	15.7	54.9	5.7	38.5	20.0	17.8	19.1	32.2	15.5	48.2	6.1	41.4	19.1	16.8	18.2
2nd quarter	28.8	15.7	54.3	5.8	39.2	20.2	17.4	19.1	32.1	15.4	48.0	6.2	41.6	19.3	16.5	18.2
3rd quarter	28.9	15.8	54.5	5.9	39.5	20.4	17.6	19.3	32.0	15.5	48.4	6.2	41.7	19.5	16.6	18.4
4th quarter	29.3	16.4	55.8	6.1	40.4	20.6	17.4	19.3	32.6	16.2	49.7	6.4	42.7	19.6	16.8	18.5
1953																
1st quarter	29.8	16.7	56.1	6.2	41.2	20.7	17.3	19.3	32.9	16.5	50.2	6.5	43.3	19.7	16.7	18.5
2nd quarter	30.1	16.8	56.0	6.2	41.5	20.7	17.2	19.3	32.9	16.6	50.3	6.6	43.7	19.9	16.7	18.6
3rd quarter	30.1	16.7	55.5	6.3	41.9	21.0	16.9	19.4	33.1	16.5	49.8	6.6	44.0	20.0	16.6	18.7
4th quarter	30.0	16.4	54.6	6.3	41.8	21.1	17.0	19.4	33.0	16.2	49.0	6.7	44.3	20.3	16.3	18.7
1954																
1st quarter	29.9	16.2	54.2	6.4	42.0	21.2	16.9	19.5	33.0	16.0	48.3	6.8	44.6	20.5	16.3	18.8
2nd quarter	30.4	16.2	53.5	6.4	42.7	21.2	16.7	19.4	33.3	16.0	48.0	6.8	44.7	20.3	16.5	18.8
3rd quarter	30.8	16.4	53.3	6.5	42.9	20.9	17.2	19.5	33.9	16.2	47.8	6.8	45.2	20.1	16.8	18.8
4th quarter	31.3	16.8	53.7	6.6	43.6	20.9	17.2	19.5	34.3	16.6	48.4	6.9	45.8	20.1	17.0	18.9
1955																
1st quarter	31.8	17.4	54.7	6.5	43.4	20.5	18.1	19.6	34.9	17.2	49.2	6.9	46.1	19.9	17.6	19.0
2nd quarter	32.1	17.7	55.2	6.6	44.0	20.6	18.0	19.6	35.0	17.4	49.8	7.0	46.6	20.0	17.5	19.0
3rd quarter	32.0	18.0	56.1	6.6	44.0	20.7	18.3	19.7	35.1	17.7	50.3	7.1	47.2	20.2	17.8	19.2
4th quarter	31.8	18.0	56.7	6.7	44.4	21.1	18.2	19.9	35.0	17.8	50.9	7.2	47.6	20.5	17.7	19.4
1956																
1st quarter	31.7	17.9	56.6	6.9	45.6	21.7	17.7	20.1	34.6	17.7	51.2	7.3	48.3	21.1	17.3	19.6
2nd quarter	31.8	18.0	56.7	7.0	46.2	22.0	17.5	20.2	34.7	17.8	51.4	7.4	48.9	21.4	17.1	19.7
3rd quarter	31.8	18.0	56.5	7.1	46.2	22.3	17.8	20.5	34.7	17.8	51.2	7.5	49.2	21.7	17.2	20.0
4th quarter	32.5	18.3	56.3	7.2	46.8	22.3	17.9	20.6	35.1	18.0	51.4	7.7	49.6	21.9	17.3	20.1
1957																
1st quarter	32.7	18.4	56.3	7.4	47.4	22.6	18.2	20.9	35.5	18.3	51.5	7.8	49.9	21.9	17.8	20.3
2nd quarter	32.7	18.3	56.0	7.5	47.4	22.8	18.2	21.0	35.3	18.2	51.4	7.9	50.0	22.2	17.7	20.4
3rd quarter	33.1	18.5	55.9	7.5	47.5	22.8	18.5	21.1	35.9	18.3	51.1	8.0	50.2	22.2	17.9	20.5
4th quarter	33.4	18.2	54.6	7.7	48.1	23.0	18.2	21.1	36.0	18.0	50.1	8.1	50.6	22.4	17.7	20.6
1958																
1st quarter	33.1	17.6	53.2	7.7	48.0	23.4	18.1	21.3	35.4	17.3	48.9	8.1	50.2	22.9	17.3	20.7
2nd quarter	33.6	17.7	52.7	7.8	47.8	23.1	18.5	21.3	36.1	17.4	48.2	8.2	50.3	22.6	17.7	20.7
3rd quarter	34.2	18.2	53.1	7.9	48.7	23.1	18.9	21.4	36.8	18.0	48.8	8.3	51.0	22.5	18.1	20.8
4th quarter	34.6	18.7	53.9	8.0	49.0	23.0	19.2	21.5	37.4	18.5	49.5	8.4	51.5	22.4	18.6	20.9
1959																
1st quarter	34.9	19.1	54.7	8.1	49.6	23.1	19.0	21.5	37.5	18.9	50.5	8.4	51.8	22.5	18.6	20.9
2nd quarter	35.1	19.7	56.0	8.1	49.6	23.0	19.2	21.5	38.0	19.6	51.5	8.5	52.3	22.4	18.7	21.0
3rd quarter	35.3	19.6	55.5	8.2	50.0	23.2	19.0	21.6	38.0	19.5	51.3	8.6	52.3	22.6	18.6	21.0
4th quarter	35.4	19.6	55.5	8.3	50.4	23.5	18.8	21.6	37.9	19.4	51.3	8.7	52.5	22.9	18.5	21.1
1960																
1st quarter	36.4	20.1	55.3	8.5	51.6	23.4	19.1	21.7	38.8	20.0	51.6	8.8	53.6	22.8	18.6	21.2
2nd quarter	35.7	19.9	55.9	8.5	51.1	23.8	18.7	21.8	38.2	19.8	51.7	8.9	53.6	23.3	18.1	21.2
3rd quarter	35.7	19.9	55.8	8.5	51.0	23.7	18.9	21.8	38.3	19.7	51.4	8.9	53.9	23.4	18.2	21.3
4th quarter	35.5	19.6	55.1	8.6	51.2	24.1	18.4	21.8	37.8	19.3	51.0	9.0	53.7	23.8	17.7	21.4

Table 9-3B. Productivity and Related Data: Historical Data—*Continued*

(2005 = 100, seasonally adjusted.)

Year and quarter	Business sector								Nonfarm business sector							
	Output per hour of all persons	Output	Hours of all persons	Compensation per hour	Real compensation per hour	Unit labor costs	Unit nonlabor payments	Implicit price deflator	Output per hour of all persons	Output	Hours of all persons	Compensation per hour	Real compensation per hour	Unit labor costs	Unit nonlabor payments	Implicit price deflator
1961																
1st quarter	35.8	19.7	54.8	8.6	51.5	24.1	18.5	21.9	38.3	19.4	50.7	9.1	54.1	23.7	17.9	21.4
2nd quarter	37.1	20.1	54.2	8.8	52.7	23.8	19.0	21.9	39.4	19.9	50.5	9.2	54.9	23.3	18.5	21.4
3rd quarter	37.5	20.5	54.6	8.9	52.9	23.7	19.3	22.0	39.9	20.3	50.8	9.3	55.1	23.2	18.8	21.5
4th quarter	37.9	20.9	55.1	9.0	53.4	23.7	19.4	22.0	40.3	20.8	51.5	9.3	55.4	23.1	18.9	21.5
1962																
1st quarter	38.2	21.3	55.7	9.1	53.7	23.8	19.7	22.1	41.0	21.2	51.7	9.5	56.1	23.1	19.1	21.6
2nd quarter	38.5	21.5	56.0	9.2	54.2	23.9	19.5	22.2	40.9	21.4	52.3	9.5	56.2	23.3	19.0	21.6
3rd quarter	39.0	21.7	55.7	9.3	54.4	23.7	19.8	22.2	41.4	21.6	52.2	9.6	56.5	23.2	19.3	21.7
4th quarter	39.3	21.8	55.3	9.4	55.0	23.8	19.7	22.2	41.7	21.6	51.9	9.7	56.9	23.2	19.3	21.7
1963																
1st quarter	39.6	22.1	55.7	9.4	55.1	23.8	19.8	22.2	42.0	21.9	52.2	9.8	57.2	23.3	19.3	21.7
2nd quarter	39.9	22.4	56.1	9.5	55.3	23.7	20.0	22.2	42.4	22.2	52.5	9.8	57.4	23.2	19.5	21.8
3rd quarter	40.7	22.8	56.1	9.6	55.7	23.6	20.3	22.3	43.2	22.8	52.6	9.9	57.7	23.0	19.9	21.8
4th quarter	40.9	23.0	56.4	9.7	56.1	23.8	20.3	22.4	43.3	23.0	53.1	10.1	58.2	23.2	19.8	21.9
1964																
1st quarter	41.4	23.6	57.0	9.8	56.3	23.6	20.7	22.4	43.7	23.6	54.0	10.1	57.9	23.0	20.3	21.9
2nd quarter	41.5	23.9	57.6	9.9	56.6	23.7	20.6	22.5	44.0	23.9	54.3	10.2	58.4	23.1	20.3	22.0
3rd quarter	41.9	24.3	57.9	10.0	57.2	23.8	20.7	22.6	44.3	24.2	54.6	10.3	59.1	23.2	20.4	22.1
4th quarter	41.7	24.3	58.2	10.1	57.5	24.1	20.4	22.7	43.9	24.2	55.2	10.4	59.2	23.6	20.0	22.2
1965																
1st quarter	42.4	25.0	59.0	10.2	57.8	23.9	21.0	22.8	44.5	24.9	56.0	10.4	59.3	23.4	20.6	22.3
2nd quarter	42.4	25.3	59.7	10.2	57.7	24.0	21.1	22.9	44.8	25.3	56.6	10.5	59.3	23.4	20.6	22.3
3rd quarter	43.4	25.9	59.6	10.3	58.3	23.8	21.6	22.9	45.6	25.8	56.7	10.6	59.7	23.2	21.1	22.4
4th quarter	44.1	26.6	60.2	10.5	58.6	23.7	22.0	23.0	46.4	26.6	57.2	10.8	60.3	23.2	21.4	22.5
1966																
1st quarter	44.9	27.3	60.8	10.7	59.5	23.8	22.1	23.2	47.1	27.3	58.1	10.9	60.8	23.2	21.4	22.5
2nd quarter	44.7	27.4	61.3	10.9	60.0	24.4	21.7	23.3	46.8	27.4	58.6	11.1	61.2	23.8	21.3	22.8
3rd quarter	44.7	27.5	61.4	11.1	60.4	24.7	21.8	23.6	46.8	27.6	58.9	11.3	61.5	24.1	21.2	23.0
4th quarter	45.1	27.6	61.2	11.3	60.9	24.9	22.0	23.8	47.1	27.7	58.7	11.4	61.9	24.2	21.7	23.2
1967																
1st quarter	45.5	27.9	61.2	11.3	61.3	24.9	22.2	23.9	47.5	27.9	58.7	11.6	62.5	24.4	21.8	23.3
2nd quarter	45.9	27.8	60.6	11.6	62.0	25.2	22.1	23.9	47.7	27.8	58.3	11.8	63.2	24.7	21.6	23.5
3rd quarter	45.9	28.0	61.0	11.7	62.1	25.4	22.3	24.2	47.9	28.0	58.5	11.9	63.4	24.9	21.8	23.7
4th quarter	46.0	28.2	61.3	11.8	62.2	25.7	22.4	24.4	48.0	28.2	58.8	12.1	63.6	25.2	21.9	23.9
1968																
1st quarter	47.0	28.8	61.3	12.2	63.5	25.9	22.8	24.7	49.1	28.9	58.9	12.4	64.8	25.3	22.4	24.2
2nd quarter	47.5	29.4	61.8	12.4	64.0	26.1	23.1	24.9	49.6	29.5	59.5	12.6	65.2	25.5	22.7	24.4
3rd quarter	47.6	29.6	62.1	12.7	64.4	26.6	22.9	25.1	49.5	29.6	59.9	12.9	65.4	26.0	22.5	24.6
4th quarter	47.5	29.7	62.5	12.9	64.8	27.2	22.9	25.5	49.4	29.8	60.2	13.1	65.9	26.5	22.5	24.9
1969																
1st quarter	47.6	30.2	63.4	13.0	64.3	27.2	23.6	25.8	49.8	30.3	60.8	13.3	66.0	26.7	23.0	25.2
2nd quarter	47.6	30.2	63.5	13.3	65.0	27.9	23.3	26.1	49.4	30.3	61.4	13.5	66.0	27.3	22.7	25.5
3rd quarter	47.7	30.4	63.7	13.6	65.5	28.4	23.2	26.4	49.5	30.5	61.7	13.7	66.3	27.8	22.7	25.8
4th quarter	47.6	30.2	63.4	13.9	65.8	29.1	22.9	26.7	49.2	30.3	61.5	14.0	66.5	28.5	22.3	26.0
1970																
1st quarter	47.8	30.2	63.1	14.1	66.1	29.5	22.9	26.9	49.4	30.2	61.2	14.3	66.7	28.9	22.3	26.3
2nd quarter	48.4	30.2	62.4	14.3	66.0	29.6	23.7	27.3	50.1	30.3	60.4	14.5	66.9	28.9	23.3	26.7
3rd quarter	49.2	30.5	62.0	14.6	66.5	29.6	24.1	27.4	50.9	30.6	60.1	14.8	67.3	29.0	23.5	26.8
4th quarter	49.0	30.1	61.4	14.8	66.4	30.2	24.1	27.8	50.5	30.1	59.7	14.9	67.1	29.6	23.6	27.2
1971																
1st quarter	50.4	31.1	61.7	15.1	67.1	29.9	25.3	28.1	52.0	31.2	59.9	15.2	67.9	29.3	24.8	27.5
2nd quarter	50.4	31.3	62.1	15.2	67.3	30.2	25.7	28.4	52.1	31.4	60.1	15.5	68.3	29.7	25.1	27.8
3rd quarter	51.0	31.6	61.9	15.5	67.8	30.4	26.1	28.7	52.6	31.6	60.1	15.7	68.6	29.8	25.5	28.1
4th quarter	50.6	31.7	62.6	15.6	67.9	30.9	25.7	28.8	52.2	31.7	60.8	15.8	68.7	30.3	25.0	28.2
1972																
1st quarter	51.1	32.4	63.4	16.0	68.9	31.3	26.0	29.2	52.9	32.5	61.5	16.2	69.8	30.6	25.5	28.6
2nd quarter	52.3	33.3	63.7	16.2	69.3	30.9	26.9	29.3	54.0	33.4	62.0	16.4	70.2	30.4	26.1	28.7
3rd quarter	52.5	33.7	64.2	16.4	69.5	31.2	27.2	29.6	54.3	33.8	62.3	16.6	70.6	30.6	26.2	28.9
4th quarter	53.0	34.4	64.8	16.7	70.4	31.6	27.4	29.9	54.7	34.4	63.0	17.0	71.4	31.0	26.0	29.1
1973																
1st quarter	54.0	35.5	65.6	17.2	71.3	31.9	27.7	30.2	56.0	35.8	63.9	17.4	72.1	31.1	26.3	29.2
2nd quarter	54.2	36.0	66.4	17.5	70.9	32.3	28.3	30.7	56.0	36.2	64.6	17.7	71.7	31.6	26.4	29.5
3rd quarter	53.5	35.7	66.7	17.9	71.0	33.4	28.1	31.3	55.5	36.1	65.0	18.0	71.7	32.5	25.9	29.9
4th quarter	53.7	36.0	67.1	18.2	70.6	33.9	29.0	32.0	55.1	36.0	65.3	18.4	71.5	33.4	26.3	30.6
1974																
1st quarter	52.9	35.5	67.1	18.6	69.9	35.1	28.9	32.7	55.0	35.8	65.1	18.9	71.1	34.3	26.7	31.3
2nd quarter	53.1	35.1	67.0	19.1	70.2	36.1	29.6	33.5	54.9	35.8	65.2	19.4	71.0	35.3	28.1	32.4
3rd quarter	52.6	35.1	66.6	19.7	70.4	37.5	30.1	34.6	54.3	35.3	65.0	19.9	71.1	36.7	28.5	33.5
4th quarter	53.1	34.8	65.6	20.2	69.9	38.1	31.9	35.6	54.8	35.0	63.9	20.4	70.7	37.3	30.1	34.5
1975																
1st quarter	53.8	34.2	63.5	20.8	70.5	38.7	33.2	36.5	55.2	34.2	61.9	21.0	71.2	38.0	31.9	35.6
2nd quarter	54.7	34.5	63.0	21.2	71.1	38.8	34.3	37.0	56.2	34.5	61.3	21.4	71.8	38.2	33.0	36.1
3rd quarter	55.3	35.2	63.7	21.5	70.7	38.9	35.8	37.7	56.8	35.2	61.9	21.8	71.6	38.4	34.1	36.7
4th quarter	55.4	35.8	64.6	22.0	70.9	39.7	36.1	38.3	56.8	35.8	63.0	22.2	71.6	39.1	34.4	37.3

Table 9-3B. Productivity and Related Data: Historical Data—*Continued*

(2005 = 100, seasonally adjusted.)

Year and quarter	Business sector								Nonfarm business sector							
	Output per hour of all persons	Output	Hours of all persons	Compensation per hour	Real compensation per hour	Unit labor costs	Unit nonlabor payments	Implicit price deflator	Output per hour of all persons	Output	Hours of all persons	Compensation per hour	Real compensation per hour	Unit labor costs	Unit nonlabor payments	Implicit price deflator
1976																
1st quarter	56.2	36.8	65.5	22.5	71.8	40.1	36.4	38.6	57.7	36.9	64.0	22.7	72.4	39.4	35.1	37.7
2nd quarter	56.6	37.1	65.7	23.0	72.6	40.6	36.5	39.0	58.2	37.3	64.0	23.2	73.2	39.8	35.4	38.1
3rd quarter	56.6	37.3	66.0	23.4	72.8	41.4	36.7	39.5	58.3	37.5	64.3	23.7	73.6	40.7	35.5	38.6
4th quarter	56.9	37.6	66.1	24.0	73.5	42.2	37.3	40.2	58.4	37.8	64.6	24.2	74.1	41.4	36.1	39.3
1977																
1st quarter	57.2	38.2	66.8	24.4	73.5	42.7	38.1	40.9	58.7	38.4	65.3	24.6	74.1	41.9	36.9	39.9
2nd quarter	57.3	39.1	68.3	24.8	73.4	43.3	38.6	41.4	59.0	39.3	66.6	25.1	74.2	42.5	37.6	40.6
3rd quarter	58.1	40.0	68.8	25.3	73.9	43.6	39.2	41.9	59.6	40.1	67.3	25.6	74.7	42.9	38.3	41.1
4th quarter	57.4	39.9	69.5	25.8	74.1	44.9	39.4	42.7	58.8	40.0	67.9	26.1	74.9	44.3	38.1	41.9
1978																
1st quarter	57.2	39.9	69.9	26.7	75.5	46.6	38.8	43.5	58.9	40.2	68.3	27.0	76.4	45.9	37.4	42.5
2nd quarter	58.3	41.9	71.9	27.0	74.6	46.2	41.3	44.3	60.0	42.2	70.2	27.3	75.6	45.5	39.6	43.2
3rd quarter	58.4	42.3	72.4	27.4	74.5	46.9	42.0	44.9	60.0	42.5	70.8	27.7	75.4	46.2	40.4	43.9
4th quarter	58.6	42.9	73.2	28.0	74.8	47.8	43.0	45.9	60.4	43.3	71.7	28.4	75.6	47.0	41.4	44.8
1979																
1st quarter	58.2	42.9	73.7	28.9	75.3	49.6	42.5	46.8	59.8	43.2	72.2	29.2	76.1	48.8	40.6	45.6
2nd quarter	58.1	43.0	74.0	29.5	75.0	50.8	43.9	48.1	59.6	43.2	72.5	29.8	75.8	50.0	42.1	46.9
3rd quarter	58.1	43.3	74.6	30.2	74.7	52.0	44.7	49.1	59.5	43.5	73.1	30.5	75.5	51.2	42.8	47.9
4th quarter	58.0	43.4	74.8	30.9	74.6	53.3	44.9	50.0	59.4	43.5	73.3	31.3	75.5	52.6	43.1	48.9
1980																
1st quarter	58.3	43.4	74.5	31.8	74.5	54.6	45.6	51.1	59.7	43.6	73.1	32.2	75.2	53.9	44.3	50.1
2nd quarter	57.6	42.2	73.2	32.7	74.6	56.7	45.3	52.2	59.0	42.4	71.8	33.0	75.3	55.9	44.8	51.5
3rd quarter	57.7	42.1	72.9	33.5	74.6	58.0	46.3	53.4	59.2	42.3	71.5	33.8	75.5	57.1	45.0	52.4
4th quarter	58.3	43.0	73.9	34.3	74.7	58.8	48.4	54.7	59.8	43.3	72.4	34.7	75.6	58.0	46.5	53.5
1981																
1st quarter	59.4	44.1	74.3	35.2	74.5	59.2	51.5	56.2	60.8	44.2	72.8	35.6	75.5	58.6	49.8	55.2
2nd quarter	58.9	43.6	74.1	35.8	74.6	60.9	51.6	57.2	60.0	43.7	72.8	36.3	75.5	60.5	49.9	56.3
3rd quarter	59.6	44.2	74.2	36.6	74.7	61.4	53.5	58.3	60.5	44.0	72.8	37.1	75.6	61.3	51.6	57.5
4th quarter	58.8	43.5	73.9	37.2	74.5	63.2	53.1	59.2	59.7	43.3	72.5	37.6	75.4	63.0	51.7	58.5
1982																
1st quarter	58.4	42.5	72.7	38.1	75.5	65.3	51.8	59.9	59.4	42.3	71.3	38.6	76.4	65.0	50.5	59.3
2nd quarter	58.6	42.7	72.9	38.5	75.4	65.7	52.8	60.6	59.5	42.6	71.6	38.9	76.2	65.4	51.6	60.0
3rd quarter	58.6	42.5	72.4	39.1	75.2	66.6	53.5	61.4	59.6	42.3	71.1	39.5	76.1	66.3	52.1	60.7
4th quarter	59.2	42.5	71.8	39.6	75.4	66.8	54.5	62.0	60.1	42.3	70.4	40.0	76.3	66.6	53.4	61.4
1983																
1st quarter	59.7	43.1	72.2	39.9	75.6	66.8	55.7	62.4	60.8	43.1	70.8	40.4	76.5	66.5	54.4	61.7
2nd quarter	60.8	44.3	72.9	40.3	75.4	66.2	57.4	62.7	62.2	44.6	71.6	40.8	76.3	65.5	56.4	61.9
3rd quarter	61.0	45.4	74.3	40.4	75.0	66.2	58.9	63.4	62.8	45.9	73.0	41.0	76.0	65.3	58.4	62.6
4th quarter	61.6	46.5	75.5	41.0	75.3	66.6	59.4	63.8	63.1	46.9	74.4	41.4	76.0	65.6	58.7	62.9
1984																
1st quarter	61.8	47.6	77.0	41.5	75.1	67.1	60.0	64.3	63.0	47.8	75.8	41.9	75.9	66.5	58.5	63.3
2nd quarter	62.4	48.6	78.0	41.8	75.1	67.1	61.1	64.7	63.4	48.7	76.8	42.3	75.9	66.7	59.5	63.9
3rd quarter	62.7	49.1	78.4	42.4	75.5	67.7	61.3	65.1	63.7	49.2	77.2	42.9	76.4	67.3	59.9	64.4
4th quarter	62.8	49.5	78.8	42.7	75.5	68.0	61.5	65.5	63.8	49.6	77.7	43.2	76.3	67.7	60.0	64.7
1985																
1st quarter	63.1	50.1	79.4	43.3	75.8	68.6	62.2	66.1	63.9	50.1	78.3	43.7	76.5	68.4	60.8	65.4
2nd quarter	63.3	50.5	79.8	43.6	75.7	68.9	62.4	66.3	64.1	50.5	78.9	44.0	76.4	68.7	61.1	65.7
3rd quarter	64.4	51.5	79.9	44.3	76.4	68.8	63.0	66.5	64.9	51.3	79.1	44.7	77.0	68.8	62.0	66.1
4th quarter	64.6	51.8	80.2	45.1	77.1	69.8	62.3	66.8	65.2	51.8	79.4	45.5	77.6	69.7	61.2	66.3
1986																
1st quarter	65.3	52.4	80.3	45.6	77.5	69.9	62.8	67.1	66.1	52.4	79.3	46.1	78.2	69.7	62.0	66.7
2nd quarter	65.7	52.6	80.1	46.1	78.7	70.1	63.1	67.3	66.5	52.7	79.1	46.5	79.4	69.9	62.2	66.9
3rd quarter	66.0	53.2	80.5	46.6	79.1	70.5	63.2	67.6	66.8	53.2	79.5	47.0	79.9	70.4	62.1	67.1
4th quarter	65.8	53.4	81.1	47.1	79.6	71.6	62.4	68.0	66.7	53.4	80.1	47.6	80.4	71.4	61.3	67.4
1987																
1st quarter	65.4	53.7	82.0	47.4	79.1	72.5	62.6	68.6	66.2	53.7	81.1	47.9	79.8	72.3	61.6	68.0
2nd quarter	65.8	54.3	82.5	47.7	78.8	72.5	63.3	68.9	66.7	54.4	81.6	48.2	79.5	72.3	62.3	68.3
3rd quarter	65.9	54.7	83.1	48.2	78.9	73.2	63.7	69.4	66.7	54.8	82.1	48.7	79.6	73.0	62.7	69.0
4th quarter	66.5	55.8	83.9	48.8	79.1	73.4	64.1	69.7	67.3	55.8	83.0	49.2	79.9	73.2	63.1	69.2
1988																
1st quarter	66.7	56.0	84.0	49.7	80.0	74.5	64.0	70.4	67.5	56.0	83.1	50.1	80.7	74.3	62.8	69.8
2nd quarter	66.8	56.9	85.1	50.3	80.2	75.3	64.2	70.9	67.7	57.0	84.2	50.7	80.8	74.9	63.3	70.3
3rd quarter	67.0	57.1	85.3	50.9	80.3	76.1	65.2	71.8	67.9	57.3	84.5	51.3	80.9	75.6	64.2	71.1
4th quarter	67.1	57.9	86.3	51.2	80.0	76.3	66.1	72.3	68.2	58.3	85.4	51.6	80.6	75.6	65.6	71.7
1989																
1st quarter	67.2	58.5	87.1	51.4	79.4	76.5	68.0	73.1	67.9	58.6	86.3	51.8	80.1	76.2	66.5	72.4
2nd quarter	67.5	58.9	87.3	51.6	78.6	76.4	69.9	73.8	68.2	59.0	86.6	51.9	79.1	76.1	68.7	73.2
3rd quarter	67.8	59.4	87.6	52.0	78.6	76.6	70.6	74.2	68.6	59.5	86.8	52.3	79.1	76.3	69.6	73.6
4th quarter	67.9	59.5	87.6	52.6	78.9	77.6	70.2	74.6	68.6	59.6	86.8	53.0	79.5	77.2	69.0	74.0
1990																
1st quarter	68.5	60.1	87.7	53.8	79.4	78.5	71.0	75.5	69.2	60.2	87.0	54.0	79.8	78.1	69.8	74.8
2nd quarter	69.1	60.3	87.2	55.0	80.4	79.5	71.5	76.3	69.7	60.4	86.6	55.2	80.7	79.1	70.4	75.7
3rd quarter	69.5	60.2	86.5	55.9	80.4	80.3	71.8	77.0	70.0	60.2	86.0	56.1	80.7	80.1	70.7	76.4
4th quarter	68.9	59.4	86.2	56.3	79.8	81.7	71.1	77.5	69.4	59.4	85.6	56.6	80.2	81.5	70.2	77.0

Table 9-3B. Productivity and Related Data: Historical Data—*Continued*

(2005 = 100, seasonally adjusted.)

Year and quarter	Business sector								Nonfarm business sector							
	Output per hour of all persons	Output	Hours of all persons	Compensation per hour	Real compensation per hour	Unit labor costs	Unit nonlabor payments	Implicit price deflator	Output per hour of all persons	Output	Hours of all persons	Compensation per hour	Real compensation per hour	Unit labor costs	Unit nonlabor payments	Implicit price deflator
1991																
1st quarter	69.0	58.9	85.3	56.8	80.0	82.3	72.3	78.3	69.6	58.9	84.7	57.1	80.4	82.0	71.5	77.9
2nd quarter	70.0	59.4	84.8	57.8	81.1	82.6	73.1	78.8	70.6	59.4	84.1	58.2	81.6	82.4	72.1	78.3
3rd quarter	70.4	59.7	84.7	58.5	81.5	83.0	73.9	79.4	71.1	59.7	84.0	58.8	82.0	82.8	73.2	79.0
4th quarter	70.8	59.9	84.6	59.1	81.9	83.5	74.1	79.8	71.4	59.9	83.9	59.5	82.4	83.3	73.2	79.3
1992																
1st quarter	72.2	60.7	84.1	60.3	83.0	83.6	74.6	80.0	72.6	60.6	83.5	60.6	83.5	83.5	73.6	79.6
2nd quarter	72.6	61.4	84.6	60.7	83.0	83.6	75.6	80.4	73.1	61.3	83.9	61.1	83.6	83.6	74.5	80.0
3rd quarter	73.4	62.1	84.7	61.6	83.8	84.0	75.8	80.8	73.8	62.0	84.0	62.0	84.3	84.0	74.7	80.3
4th quarter	73.8	63.0	85.3	61.9	83.5	83.8	77.3	81.2	74.4	62.9	84.6	62.3	84.0	83.7	76.4	80.8
1993																
1st quarter	73.3	62.9	85.9	62.1	83.3	84.7	77.0	81.6	73.9	63.0	85.3	62.4	83.7	84.4	76.5	81.3
2nd quarter	73.1	63.4	86.8	62.4	83.1	85.3	77.0	82.0	73.5	63.5	86.3	62.6	83.4	85.1	76.3	81.6
3rd quarter	73.2	63.8	87.2	62.6	83.1	85.6	77.4	82.4	73.8	64.0	86.7	62.9	83.4	85.2	77.0	82.0
4th quarter	73.9	65.0	87.9	62.9	82.9	85.1	79.1	82.7	74.3	65.0	87.4	63.1	83.2	84.9	78.3	82.3
1994																
1st quarter	74.2	65.7	88.6	63.5	83.5	85.6	79.1	83.0	74.8	65.6	87.8	63.9	84.0	85.4	78.2	82.6
2nd quarter	74.1	66.8	90.1	63.3	82.8	85.5	80.1	83.3	74.7	66.7	89.3	63.8	83.4	85.4	79.3	83.0
3rd quarter	73.7	67.2	91.2	63.3	82.2	86.0	80.7	83.9	74.2	67.1	90.3	63.7	82.7	85.9	80.1	83.6
4th quarter	74.2	68.1	91.7	63.6	82.2	85.7	81.9	84.2	74.9	68.1	90.9	64.1	82.8	85.6	81.4	83.9
1995																
1st quarter	73.8	68.2	92.4	64.2	82.4	86.9	81.0	84.6	74.7	68.3	91.5	64.6	82.9	86.5	80.9	84.3
2nd quarter	73.8	68.3	92.5	64.4	82.1	87.3	81.4	84.9	74.8	68.5	91.5	65.0	82.8	86.8	81.3	84.7
3rd quarter	74.0	69.0	93.3	64.9	82.3	87.7	81.7	85.3	74.9	69.3	92.5	65.3	82.9	87.2	81.3	84.9
4th quarter	74.6	69.7	93.4	65.5	82.7	87.7	82.3	85.6	75.5	69.9	92.6	65.9	83.2	87.4	81.7	85.1
1996																
1st quarter	75.4	70.3	93.2	66.1	82.8	87.7	83.3	85.9	76.1	70.4	92.4	66.6	83.4	87.4	82.3	85.4
2nd quarter	76.3	71.7	93.9	66.7	82.9	87.5	84.7	86.4	77.0	71.7	93.2	67.2	83.5	87.3	83.3	85.7
3rd quarter	76.6	72.4	94.6	67.3	83.2	87.9	84.4	86.5	77.2	72.5	93.9	67.7	83.6	87.6	83.6	86.1
4th quarter	76.6	73.4	95.7	67.6	82.8	88.2	85.1	87.0	77.3	73.5	95.1	67.9	83.3	87.9	84.3	86.5
1997																
1st quarter	76.4	74.0	96.8	68.0	82.9	89.0	85.3	87.5	77.0	74.0	96.2	68.4	83.4	88.8	84.3	87.0
2nd quarter	77.3	75.3	97.3	68.5	83.3	88.6	86.2	87.7	77.9	75.3	96.7	68.9	83.8	88.5	85.8	87.4
3rd quarter	78.1	76.4	97.8	69.3	83.9	88.8	86.6	87.9	78.5	76.4	97.2	69.6	84.3	88.6	86.2	87.7
4th quarter	78.4	77.0	98.2	70.6	85.1	90.0	85.4	88.2	78.9	77.0	97.7	70.9	85.3	89.9	85.0	87.9
1998																
1st quarter	78.9	77.8	98.7	72.0	86.6	91.3	83.7	88.3	79.3	77.9	98.3	72.2	86.9	91.1	83.3	88.0
2nd quarter	79.3	78.6	99.2	72.9	87.4	92.0	82.7	88.3	79.8	78.7	98.7	73.2	87.8	91.7	82.5	88.1
3rd quarter	80.4	79.8	99.3	74.0	88.4	92.1	83.0	88.5	80.9	79.9	98.8	74.4	88.8	91.9	82.8	88.3
4th quarter	81.0	81.5	100.6	74.4	88.4	91.8	83.7	88.6	81.5	81.7	100.2	74.6	88.7	91.6	83.3	88.3
1999																
1st quarter	82.0	82.3	100.4	75.8	89.8	92.5	83.3	88.8	82.3	82.5	100.3	75.9	89.9	92.3	82.9	88.6
2nd quarter	82.1	83.0	101.2	76.0	89.3	92.6	83.5	89.0	82.4	83.1	100.9	76.1	89.5	92.4	83.6	88.9
3rd quarter	82.7	84.2	101.8	76.6	89.4	92.6	84.1	89.3	83.0	84.4	101.6	76.7	89.5	92.4	84.3	89.2
4th quarter	84.1	86.0	102.3	78.1	90.5	92.9	84.1	89.4	84.5	86.1	101.9	78.3	90.7	92.7	84.4	89.5
2000																
1st quarter	83.8	86.1	102.7	80.9	92.9	96.5	80.5	90.2	84.2	86.2	102.3	81.2	93.2	96.5	80.6	90.3
2nd quarter	85.8	88.1	102.6	81.3	92.6	94.7	84.4	90.6	86.1	88.2	102.4	81.5	92.8	94.7	84.4	90.6
3rd quarter	85.8	88.1	102.6	83.0	93.6	96.7	82.5	91.1	86.1	88.2	102.4	83.2	93.9	96.6	82.6	91.1
4th quarter	86.8	88.6	102.1	83.6	93.7	96.3	84.1	91.5	87.0	88.7	102.0	83.7	93.8	96.3	84.2	91.5
2001																
1st quarter	86.5	88.1	101.9	85.5	94.9	98.9	81.2	91.9	86.7	88.3	101.8	85.6	95.0	98.8	81.3	91.9
2nd quarter	88.0	88.7	100.9	85.9	94.6	97.6	84.8	92.5	88.2	88.9	100.8	85.9	94.6	97.3	85.0	92.5
3rd quarter	88.5	88.2	99.7	86.2	94.7	97.4	85.4	92.6	88.8	88.4	99.6	86.2	94.7	97.1	85.5	92.5
4th quarter	89.9	88.6	98.6	87.0	95.7	96.8	86.4	92.7	90.0	88.7	98.5	87.0	95.7	96.7	86.6	92.7
2002																
1st quarter	91.5	89.5	97.9	87.8	96.3	96.0	87.6	92.7	91.9	89.8	97.6	87.9	96.4	95.6	88.0	92.6
2nd quarter	91.8	89.9	98.0	88.7	96.4	96.6	87.6	93.1	92.1	90.0	97.8	88.8	96.6	96.4	88.1	93.2
3rd quarter	92.7	90.6	97.6	89.2	96.5	96.1	89.0	93.3	92.9	90.6	97.5	89.2	96.6	96.0	89.3	93.4
4th quarter	92.7	90.7	97.8	89.6	96.3	96.6	89.1	93.7	92.9	90.7	97.6	89.7	96.4	96.6	89.3	93.7
2003																
1st quarter	93.6	91.0	97.2	91.0	96.9	97.3	89.1	94.0	93.7	91.0	97.1	91.1	97.0	97.2	89.3	94.1
2nd quarter	95.1	92.0	96.7	92.7	98.9	97.5	89.0	94.2	95.0	91.9	96.8	92.7	98.8	97.6	88.9	94.2
3rd quarter	97.0	94.1	97.1	93.8	99.3	96.7	91.4	94.6	97.2	94.2	96.9	93.9	99.4	96.7	91.2	94.5
4th quarter	97.2	94.8	97.6	94.5	99.7	97.3	91.5	95.0	97.5	95.0	97.4	94.7	99.9	97.1	91.1	94.7
2004																
1st quarter	97.7	95.6	97.9	94.3	98.6	96.5	94.7	95.8	97.7	95.6	97.8	94.3	98.6	96.5	94.0	95.5
2nd quarter	98.3	96.3	98.0	95.5	99.1	97.2	95.6	96.6	98.5	96.4	97.9	95.6	99.2	97.1	94.8	96.2
3rd quarter	98.5	97.1	98.6	97.0	100.0	98.5	95.1	97.2	98.6	97.1	98.4	97.1	100.1	98.5	94.7	97.0
4th quarter	99.0	97.9	98.9	98.1	100.0	99.1	96.2	97.9	98.8	97.9	99.1	97.9	99.8	99.1	95.8	97.8
2005																
1st quarter	99.8	99.1	99.2	98.8	100.2	98.9	98.5	98.7	99.8	99.1	99.3	98.6	100.1	98.9	98.4	98.7
2nd quarter	99.5	99.5	100.0	99.2	100.0	99.7	98.9	99.4	99.6	99.5	99.9	99.3	100.1	99.7	98.9	99.4
3rd quarter	100.3	100.4	100.1	100.7	100.0	100.3	100.7	100.5	100.3	100.4	100.1	100.7	100.0	100.4	100.7	100.5
4th quarter	100.4	101.0	100.6	101.4	99.8	101.0	101.9	101.3	100.3	101.0	100.7	101.3	99.7	101.0	102.0	101.4

Table 9-3B. Productivity and Related Data: Historical Data—*Continued*

(2005 = 100, seasonally adjusted.)

Year and quarter	Business sector								Nonfarm business sector							
	Output per hour of all persons	Output	Hours of all persons	Compensation per hour	Real compensation per hour	Unit labor costs	Unit nonlabor payments	Implicit price deflator	Output per hour of all persons	Output	Hours of all persons	Compensation per hour	Real compensation per hour	Unit labor costs	Unit nonlabor payments	Implicit price deflator
2006																
1st quarter	101.0	102.5	101.5	102.8	100.6	101.8	101.9	101.8	100.9	102.6	101.7	102.7	100.5	101.7	102.3	101.9
2nd quarter	101.1	103.0	101.8	103.1	100.0	102.0	103.7	102.6	101.0	102.9	101.9	103.1	100.0	102.0	104.0	102.8
3rd quarter	100.5	102.8	102.3	103.5	99.4	102.9	104.0	103.4	100.5	102.9	102.4	103.4	99.4	102.9	104.3	103.5
4th quarter	101.1	103.8	102.7	105.8	102.1	104.7	102.2	103.7	101.1	103.9	102.7	105.9	102.1	104.7	102.2	103.7
2007																
1st quarter	100.9	103.7	102.8	106.8	102.0	105.8	103.5	104.8	101.1	103.9	102.7	106.8	102.1	105.7	103.3	104.7
2nd quarter	102.0	104.9	102.8	107.5	101.5	105.4	105.8	105.6	101.9	105.1	103.1	107.2	101.3	105.2	105.8	105.4
3rd quarter	103.2	105.7	102.4	108.3	101.7	104.9	107.0	105.8	103.2	105.9	102.7	108.0	101.4	104.7	106.8	105.5
4th quarter	103.6	106.0	102.4	109.8	101.8	106.0	106.3	106.1	103.6	106.2	102.5	109.7	101.7	105.8	105.8	105.8
2008																
1st quarter	103.0	105.2	102.1	111.3	102.1	108.0	104.1	106.5	103.0	105.2	102.2	111.2	102.1	108.0	103.3	106.2
2nd quarter	103.6	105.3	101.6	111.0	100.6	107.1	107.4	107.2	103.6	105.3	101.7	110.9	100.5	107.1	106.8	107.0
3rd quarter	103.4	103.8	100.4	111.9	99.8	108.3	108.0	108.2	103.4	103.9	100.5	111.9	99.8	108.2	107.6	108.0
4th quarter	102.6	100.5	98.0	112.4	102.7	109.6	105.6	108.0	102.5	100.4	98.0	112.4	102.7	109.7	105.4	108.0
2009																
1st quarter	102.9	98.3	95.5	111.7	102.6	108.5	108.2	108.4	102.8	98.2	95.5	111.7	102.6	108.6	108.5	108.6
2nd quarter	105.0	98.1	93.4	113.6	103.9	108.1	108.1	108.1	104.9	97.9	93.3	113.6	103.9	108.3	108.1	108.2
3rd quarter	106.8	98.5	92.2	114.3	103.6	107.0	109.9	108.1	106.5	98.2	92.2	114.2	103.5	107.2	110.3	108.4
4th quarter	108.1	99.7	92.2	114.6	103.1	105.9	112.3	108.4	107.9	99.6	92.3	114.5	103.0	106.1	112.3	108.5
2010																
1st quarter	109.3	101.0	92.4	114.9	103.1	105.1	114.7	108.9	109.1	100.8	92.4	114.9	103.1	105.3	114.7	109.0
2nd quarter	109.6	102.1	93.2	115.6	103.9	105.5	115.5	109.4	109.5	102.0	93.1	115.6	103.9	105.6	115.6	109.5
3rd quarter	110.2	103.1	93.5	116.1	104.0	105.4	116.5	109.7	110.0	102.9	93.5	116.1	103.9	105.6	116.2	109.7
4th quarter	110.5	103.9	94.0	116.1	103.2	105.0	118.5	110.4	110.5	103.8	94.0	116.1	103.2	105.1	118.0	110.2
2011																
1st quarter	110.1	104.0	94.5	117.5	103.3	106.8	117.9	111.2	110.2	104.0	94.4	117.6	103.3	106.7	117.1	110.8
2nd quarter	110.0	104.4	94.9	117.5	102.2	106.8	119.9	111.9	110.1	104.5	94.9	117.4	102.1	106.7	119.0	111.5
3rd quarter	110.4	105.1	95.2	119.0	102.7	107.8	120.1	112.7	110.6	105.2	95.2	119.1	102.7	107.7	119.1	112.2
4th quarter	110.7	106.1	95.8	118.9	102.3	107.4	121.1	112.8	110.9	106.2	95.8	119.0	102.3	107.3	120.3	112.4

Section 9c: Returns and Profits by Industry

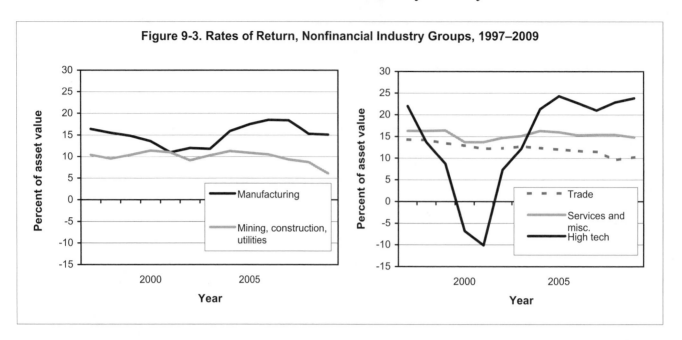

Figure 9-3. Rates of Return, Nonfinancial Industry Groups, 1997–2009

- Corporate profits reached a high point in 1997 and began to decline well before the business cycle peak in early 2001. However, by 2003, aggregate dollar profits recovered to surpass their 1997 highs, and they continued to increase through 2006. Measuring between the high points for profits, profits of domestic industries as a share of gross domestic income increased from 9.3 percent in 1997 to 9.9 percent in 2006. Profits plunged 38 percent from 2006 to 2008, then recovered to a new high of 10.0 percent of domestic income in 2011. (Table 1-12)

- Rates of return on physical capital in nonfinancial industry groups are shown in Figure 9-3. The rate of return is the net operating surplus—the sum of corporate profits, net interest, transfer payments, and proprietors' income—as a percentage of the value of the net stock of capital plus inventories. The net operating surplus is a more comprehensive measure of the return to capital than corporate profits. As the figure indicates, rates of return generally declined from 1997 through 2001, rose into the mid-2000s, and declined again as recession set in; only in trade and high-tech ("ICT") industries was there some recovery as of 2009. (Table 9-4)

- The "ICT-producing" industries—a small group of industries, one of which is a component of manufacturing and the rest of which are components of the services and miscellaneous group ("other" in BEA terminology)—went from a 22 percent rate of return in 1997 to a loss in 2001, but returned to surpass previous highs in the mid-2000s and again by 2009. (Table 9-4)

- Comparable rate of return data are not available for financial industries, presumably because of greater difficulty in identifying and measuring the capital base. Aggregate profits of financial industries (leaving out the Federal Reserve System) rose an average 15.2 percent per year from 1998 to 2006, much faster than aggregate profits of nonfinancial industries, which rose at a 10.8 percent rate. Financial profits dropped precipitously from 2006 to 2008, but then recovered to mid-2000s levels; for the full 13-year period from 1998 to 2011, the rate of financial profits growth at 8.5 percent per year still outstripped the 5.4 percent growth rate for nonfinancial profits. (Table 9-5)

Table 9-4. Rates of Return and Related Data for Major Nonfinancial Industry Groups, NAICS Basis

Year	Nonfinancial corporations	Nonfinancial industries					
		Total	Mining, construction, and utilities	Manufacturing	Wholesale and retail trade	Other industries [1]	ICT-producing industries [2]
NET OPERATING SURPLUS BEFORE TAX (Billions of dollars)							
1997	736.3	1 278.1	164.0	320.1	202.9	591.1	71.3
1998	725.7	1 305.2	153.9	313.7	213.2	624.4	47.1
1999	745.1	1 367.5	173.1	311.8	215.2	667.4	32.1
2000	708.2	1 320.1	197.9	298.8	219.4	604.0	-28.2
2001	626.7	1 310.4	204.5	248.7	215.2	642.1	-45.3
2002	647.1	1 395.6	181.6	272.3	221.8	719.9	33.2
2003	699.2	1 492.3	215.9	269.5	237.8	769.1	55.5
2004	877.5	1 756.4	257.0	373.7	248.6	877.1	98.9
2005	1 025.1	1 900.9	279.1	432.9	260.9	928.0	118.3
2006	1 163.7	2 017.5	303.7	482.7	273.5	957.7	115.9
2007	1 137.4	2 109.5	293.7	507.4	285.9	1 022.5	112.2
2008	1 061.1	2 055.6	298.0	443.6	246.0	1 068.0	128.6
2009	962.5	1 958.5	215.3	443.8	259.1	1 040.3	136.3
2010	1 156.1	...	...	...	...	...	...
PRODUCED ASSETS, AVERAGE OF YEAR-END VALUES (Billions of dollars)							
1997	7 056.0	8 580.9	1 584.2	1 951.6	1 422.5	3 622.8	323.7
1998	7 341.4	8 968.6	1 613.5	2 028.6	1 498.4	3 828.1	344.0
1999	7 729.9	9 438.4	1 658.6	2 111.9	1 591.1	4 076.8	371.2
2000	8 219.5	10 036.4	1 736.4	2 200.7	1 698.8	4 400.6	413.4
2001	8 648.3	10 574.7	1 859.1	2 253.4	1 760.8	4 701.5	448.0
2002	8 952.1	10 973.8	1 989.1	2 275.2	1 802.9	4 906.7	455.9
2003	9 238.2	11 360.3	2 096.4	2 290.4	1 877.3	5 096.3	453.6
2004	9 746.6	12 019.3	2 267.4	2 350.2	2 007.0	5 394.8	464.1
2005	10 550.8	13 030.7	2 565.9	2 474.8	2 179.7	5 810.3	486.0
2006	11 405.9	14 101.2	2 884.9	2 610.7	2 339.4	6 266.3	510.3
2007	12 155.1	15 048.0	3 161.3	2 762.1	2 477.4	6 647.2	534.1
2008	12 806.9	15 864.2	3 442.3	2 908.3	2 567.9	6 945.7	562.8
2009	12 919.5	16 002.0	3 529.0	2 937.1	2 530.4	7 006.3	573.2
2010	13 000.4	...	...	...	...	...	...
RATES OF RETURN BEFORE TAX (Percent)							
1997	10.4	14.9	10.4	16.4	14.3	16.3	22.0
1998	9.9	14.6	9.5	15.5	14.2	16.3	13.7
1999	9.6	14.5	10.4	14.8	13.5	16.4	8.7
2000	8.6	13.2	11.4	13.6	12.9	13.7	-6.8
2001	7.2	12.4	11.0	11.0	12.2	13.7	-10.1
2002	7.2	12.7	9.1	12.0	12.3	14.7	7.3
2003	7.5	13.1	10.3	11.8	12.7	15.1	12.2
2004	9.0	14.6	11.3	15.9	12.4	16.3	21.3
2005	9.7	14.6	10.9	17.5	12.0	16.0	24.3
2006	10.2	14.3	10.5	18.5	11.7	15.3	22.7
2007	9.4	14.0	9.3	18.4	11.5	15.4	21.0
2008	8.3	13.0	8.7	15.3	9.6	15.4	22.9
2009	7.5	12.2	6.1	15.1	10.2	14.8	23.8
2010	8.9	...	...	...	...	...	...
NET OPERATING SURPLUS BEFORE TAX AS A SHARE OF NET VALUE ADDED (Percent)							
1997	18.7	20.2	32.1	28.1	19.7	16.2	22.7
1998	17.4	22.7	29.1	26.6	19.1	21.3	14.1
1999	16.9	22.4	29.9	25.8	18.6	21.1	8.9
2000	15.1	20.4	30.9	23.9	17.9	18.1	-7.9
2001	13.6	20.0	30.5	21.3	17.4	18.4	-14.0
2002	13.9	20.7	27.6	23.1	17.6	19.8	9.1
2003	14.5	21.1	30.3	22.5	18.1	20.1	14.5
2004	16.9	23.1	32.8	28.6	18.0	21.3	22.6
2005	18.4	23.5	32.7	31.2	17.9	21.2	24.8
2006	19.6	23.7	32.5	34.1	17.8	20.7	23.3
2007	18.6	23.6	30.8	34.9	18.0	20.7	21.8
2008	17.4	22.8	30.4	31.9	15.9	20.9	23.9
2009	16.8	22.8	26.2	33.5	17.4	20.9	25.8
2010	19.1	...	...	...	...	...	...

[1] Consists of agriculture, forestry, fishing and hunting; transportation and warehousing; information; rental and leasing services and lessors of intangible assets; professional, scientific, and technical services; administrative and waste management services; educational services; health care and social assistance; arts, entertainment, and recreation; accommodation and food services; and "other services, except government."
[2] Information-communication-technology (ICT) producing industries consists of computer and electronic products; publishing industries (includes software); information and data processing services; and computer systems design and related services. Computer and electronic products are included in manufacturing; the other ICT-producing industries are included in "other" industries.
. . . = Not available.

Table 9-5. Corporate Profits with Inventory Valuation Adjustment by Industry Group, NAICS Basis

(Billions of dollars, quarterly data are at seasonally adjusted annual rates.)   **NIPA Table 6.16D**

Year and quarter	Total	Domestic industries — Financial Total	Federal Reserve banks	Other financial	Nonfinancial Total	Utilities	Manufacturing Total	Fabricated metal products	Machinery	Computer and electronic products	Electrical equipment, appliances, and components	Motor vehicles, bodies and trailers, and parts	Other durable goods
1998	738.6	635.9	25.6	133.9	476.4	33.5	155.8	16.4	15.3	4.2	6.2	6.4	34.2
1999	776.6	655.0	26.7	162.6	465.7	33.7	148.8	16.4	11.7	-6.8	6.4	7.7	35.9
2000	755.7	610.0	31.2	158.4	420.4	25.6	143.9	15.8	7.7	4.2	5.9	-0.7	27.1
2001	720.8	551.1	28.9	199.1	323.1	25.2	49.7	9.8	2.0	-48.6	1.9	-8.9	16.8
2002	762.8	604.9	23.5	241.7	339.7	12.3	47.7	9.1	1.4	-34.4	0.0	-4.5	20.7
2003	892.2	726.4	20.1	291.8	414.6	12.4	69.4	8.0	1.0	-14.7	2.2	-11.7	10.8
2004	1 195.1	990.1	20.0	342.3	627.8	19.4	154.1	12.2	7.1	-4.3	0.6	-6.8	31.9
2005	1 609.5	1 370.0	26.6	417.0	926.4	29.8	247.2	18.1	14.5	9.0	-1.4	1.1	54.2
2006	1 784.7	1 527.8	33.8	414.1	1 079.9	54.4	304.5	18.7	19.2	17.4	11.5	-6.8	58.9
2007	1 691.1	1 340.2	36.0	309.5	994.7	50.3	271.3	20.5	22.1	11.0	-1.2	-16.4	60.2
2008	1 315.5	908.9	35.1	87.1	786.7	30.7	195.5	15.8	16.6	12.2	4.6	-33.1	40.7
2009	1 456.3	1 095.9	47.3	354.5	694.1	22.2	125.2	10.5	7.8	15.4	8.4	-45.1	23.6
2010	1 780.4	1 398.5	71.6	423.2	903.7	25.0	217.1	11.7	15.3	39.5	7.0	-12.7	34.1
2011	1 836.2	1 407.1	76.8	387.7	942.6	15.2	253.8	17.0	23.3	36.0	2.6	-11.4	42.3
2009													
1st quarter	1 285.7	925.7	27.1	214.2	684.4	18.2	109.2	16.2	10.1	7.0	8.8	-64.1	22.2
2nd quarter	1 359.7	1 015.1	43.3	351.7	620.1	21.6	107.4	11.4	6.7	15.2	7.7	-53.6	20.4
3rd quarter	1 525.0	1 162.5	54.2	427.0	681.2	15.5	130.8	8.6	5.9	17.0	7.9	-37.1	19.9
4th quarter	1 654.6	1 280.3	64.7	425.0	790.6	33.4	153.4	5.9	8.3	22.3	9.0	-25.5	31.7
2010													
1st quarter	1 797.0	1 428.0	71.5	408.3	948.2	46.5	216.2	11.4	13.3	39.5	8.8	-14.9	41.7
2nd quarter	1 859.9	1 469.3	73.9	416.7	978.7	18.2	237.3	9.3	14.3	37.4	9.3	-6.9	36.9
3rd quarter	1 812.6	1 417.3	71.4	416.4	929.5	28.0	227.2	12.5	16.8	39.0	7.6	-9.9	29.2
4th quarter	1 652.2	1 279.3	69.5	451.3	758.5	7.1	187.7	13.5	16.9	41.9	2.4	-19.1	28.8
2011													
1st quarter	1 761.1	1 350.3	72.7	418.8	858.8	14.9	217.6	14.6	20.0	29.0	4.3	-12.0	34.8
2nd quarter	1 830.2	1 384.9	80.7	358.3	945.9	15.2	249.9	15.6	20.3	34.5	2.0	-12.2	36.8
3rd quarter	1 867.4	1 416.6	77.6	371.0	967.9	10.7	268.2	17.5	24.5	35.4	1.9	-10.9	45.1
4th quarter	1 886.0	1 476.7	76.2	402.5	998.0	19.9	279.2	20.5	28.3	45.1	2.3	-10.3	52.3

Domestic industries—Continued / Nonfinancial—Continued / Manufacturing—Continued

Year and quarter	Nondurable goods Total	Food and beverage and tobacco products	Petroleum and coal products	Chemical products	Other nondurable goods	Wholesale trade	Retail trade	Transportation and warehousing	Information	Other nonfinancial	Rest of the world, net
1998	73.1	22.1	5.3	25.0	20.7	52.8	67.3	21.3	21.9	123.7	102.8
1999	77.6	30.9	2.2	22.8	21.7	54.8	65.7	16.5	12.5	133.6	121.5
2000	83.9	26.0	27.6	13.8	16.5	58.7	60.7	15.2	-15.5	131.8	145.6
2001	76.6	28.2	29.7	11.6	7.1	51.3	72.6	1.2	-24.4	147.4	169.7
2002	55.4	25.3	1.3	17.8	11.0	49.1	81.6	-0.1	-3.8	153.0	157.9
2003	73.8	24.0	23.5	18.9	7.4	54.8	88.9	7.4	4.9	176.7	165.8
2004	113.4	24.3	49.1	24.7	15.3	75.6	93.4	14.4	45.6	225.2	205.0
2005	151.7	27.3	79.4	25.7	19.3	92.2	122.6	29.0	81.3	324.3	239.4
2006	185.7	32.5	76.6	52.5	24.0	103.7	133.2	42.1	92.4	349.6	256.8
2007	175.2	30.7	73.5	48.3	22.7	99.9	117.8	27.7	93.6	334.2	350.9
2008	138.6	29.9	77.8	23.9	7.1	86.3	81.6	31.9	75.1	285.7	406.6
2009	104.7	41.5	9.4	38.3	15.5	83.3	106.0	23.5	81.2	252.8	360.4
2010	122.1	37.8	36.0	34.7	13.7	85.8	122.6	34.4	87.7	331.2	381.9
2011	143.9	33.6	55.6	37.1	17.5	84.4	116.6	31.2	101.3	340.1	429.1
2009											
1st quarter	109.1	39.2	29.5	29.6	10.8	102.7	101.6	24.4	75.7	252.5	360.1
2nd quarter	99.5	44.1	-4.5	43.2	16.6	77.4	103.8	13.6	70.8	225.6	344.6
3rd quarter	108.6	43.6	3.3	44.6	17.1	73.0	107.7	27.0	80.2	247.1	362.6
4th quarter	101.7	39.1	9.5	35.6	17.5	79.9	110.9	29.2	97.9	285.8	374.3
2010											
1st quarter	116.5	41.1	31.3	28.8	15.3	93.4	128.6	32.5	91.4	339.6	368.9
2nd quarter	136.9	40.8	52.8	29.4	13.9	111.0	125.4	37.7	93.5	355.6	390.6
3rd quarter	132.0	39.6	31.7	45.5	15.2	89.4	119.0	39.3	86.6	340.0	395.3
4th quarter	103.2	29.6	28.4	35.0	10.2	49.5	117.3	28.2	79.1	289.6	372.9
2011											
1st quarter	126.9	33.5	37.9	36.1	19.3	71.6	120.2	23.5	98.9	312.0	410.8
2nd quarter	152.9	34.7	71.3	32.4	14.4	90.8	112.7	26.8	103.6	346.9	445.4
3rd quarter	154.7	28.5	72.2	38.0	16.0	85.6	110.6	33.5	97.1	362.2	450.8
4th quarter	141.0	37.8	41.1	41.9	20.2	89.7	122.8	41.2	105.7	339.4	409.3

Table 9-6. Corporate Profits with Inventory Valuation Adjustment by Industry Group, SIC Basis

(Billions of dollars, quarterly data are at seasonally adjusted rates.)   **NIPA Tables 6.16B, 6.16C**

Classification basis, year, and quarter	Total	Domestic industries										
		Financial			Nonfinancial							
							Manufacturing					
								Durable goods				
		Total	Federal Reserve banks	Other financial	Total	Total	Primary metal industries	Fabricated metal products	Industrial machinery and equipment	Electronic and other electric equipment	Motor vehicles and equipment	Other durable goods
1972 SIC Basis												
1948	33.7	32.5	0.2	2.5	29.7	17.5	1.6	0.8	1.3	0.6	1.4	1.8
1949	31.5	30.3	0.2	3.1	27.0	16.2	1.5	0.7	1.3	0.8	2.1	1.7
1950	38.3	37.0	0.2	3.1	33.7	21.0	2.3	1.1	1.6	1.2	3.1	2.6
1951	43.6	41.8	0.3	3.4	38.1	24.7	3.1	1.3	2.3	1.3	2.4	2.8
1952	41.2	39.3	0.3	4.1	34.9	21.7	1.9	1.0	2.3	1.5	2.4	2.6
1953	40.7	38.9	0.4	4.4	34.0	22.0	2.5	1.0	1.9	1.4	2.6	2.6
1954	39.0	37.1	0.3	4.8	32.0	19.9	1.7	0.9	1.7	1.2	2.1	2.9
1955	48.1	45.8	0.3	5.0	40.5	26.1	2.9	1.1	1.7	1.1	4.1	3.5
1956	47.8	44.9	0.5	5.2	39.3	24.8	3.0	1.1	2.1	1.2	2.2	3.1
1957	47.5	44.4	0.6	5.4	38.5	24.1	3.1	1.1	2.0	1.5	2.6	3.1
1958	42.7	40.2	0.6	5.9	33.7	19.5	1.9	0.9	1.5	1.3	0.9	2.9
1959	53.5	50.8	0.7	6.9	43.2	26.5	2.3	1.1	2.2	1.7	3.0	3.5
1960	51.5	48.3	0.9	7.5	39.9	23.8	2.0	0.8	1.8	1.3	3.0	2.7
1961	51.8	48.5	0.8	7.6	40.2	23.4	1.6	1.0	1.9	1.3	2.5	2.9
1962	57.0	53.3	0.9	7.7	44.7	26.3	1.6	1.2	2.4	1.5	4.0	3.4
1963	62.1	58.1	1.0	7.3	49.8	29.7	2.0	1.3	2.6	1.6	4.9	4.0
1964	68.6	64.1	1.1	7.6	55.4	32.6	2.5	1.5	3.3	1.7	4.6	4.4
1965	78.9	74.2	1.3	8.0	64.9	39.8	3.1	2.1	4.0	2.7	6.2	5.2
1966	84.6	80.1	1.7	9.1	69.3	42.6	3.6	2.4	4.6	3.0	5.2	5.2
1967	82.0	77.2	2.0	9.2	66.0	39.2	2.7	2.5	4.2	3.0	4.0	4.9
1968	88.8	83.2	2.5	10.3	70.4	41.9	1.9	2.3	4.2	2.9	5.5	5.6
1969	85.5	78.9	3.1	10.5	65.3	37.3	1.4	2.0	3.8	2.3	4.8	4.9
1970	74.4	67.3	3.5	11.9	52.0	27.5	0.8	1.1	3.1	1.3	1.3	2.9
1971	88.3	80.4	3.3	14.3	62.8	35.1	0.8	1.5	3.1	2.0	5.2	4.1
1972	101.2	91.7	3.3	15.8	72.6	41.9	1.7	2.2	4.5	2.9	6.0	5.6
1973	115.3	100.4	4.5	16.0	79.9	47.2	2.3	2.7	4.9	3.2	5.9	6.2
1974	109.5	92.1	5.7	14.5	71.9	41.4	5.0	1.8	3.3	0.6	0.7	4.0
1975	135.0	120.4	5.6	14.6	100.2	55.2	2.8	3.3	5.1	2.6	2.3	4.7
1976	165.6	149.0	5.9	19.1	124.1	71.3	2.1	3.9	6.9	3.8	7.4	7.3
1977	194.7	175.6	6.1	25.8	143.7	79.3	1.0	4.5	8.6	5.9	9.4	8.5
1978	222.4	199.6	7.6	31.9	160.0	90.5	3.6	5.0	10.7	6.7	9.0	10.5
1979	231.8	197.2	9.4	30.9	156.8	89.6	3.5	5.3	9.5	5.6	4.7	8.5
1980	211.4	175.9	11.8	22.2	141.9	78.3	2.7	4.4	8.0	5.2	-4.3	2.7
1981	219.1	189.4	14.4	14.7	160.3	91.1	3.1	4.5	9.0	5.2	0.3	-2.6
1982	191.0	158.5	15.2	10.8	132.4	67.1	-4.7	2.7	3.1	1.7	0.0	2.1
1983	226.5	191.4	14.6	20.9	155.9	76.2	-4.9	3.1	4.0	3.5	5.3	8.4
1984	264.6	228.1	16.4	18.0	193.7	91.8	-0.4	4.7	6.0	5.1	9.2	14.6
1985	257.5	219.4	16.3	29.5	173.5	84.3	-0.9	4.9	5.7	2.6	7.4	10.1
1986	253.0	213.5	15.5	41.2	156.8	57.9	0.9	5.2	0.8	2.7	4.6	12.1
1987	301.4	253.4	15.7	44.1	193.5	86.3	2.6	5.5	5.4	5.9	3.7	17.6
1987 SIC Basis												
1987	301.4	253.4	15.7	44.1	193.5	86.3	2.6	5.5	5.4	5.9	3.7	17.6
1988	363.9	306.9	17.6	51.1	238.2	121.2	6.0	6.5	11.1	7.7	6.2	16.5
1989	367.4	300.3	20.2	57.8	222.3	110.9	6.4	6.4	12.2	9.3	2.7	14.2
1990	396.6	320.5	21.4	73.0	226.1	113.1	3.5	6.0	11.8	8.5	-1.9	15.9
1991	427.9	351.4	20.3	103.9	227.3	98.0	1.5	5.3	5.7	10.0	-5.4	17.3
1992	458.3	385.2	17.8	111.9	255.4	99.5	0.0	6.2	7.5	10.4	-1.0	17.4
1993	513.1	436.1	16.2	120.6	299.3	115.6	0.4	7.4	7.5	15.2	6.0	19.4
1994	564.6	487.6	18.1	101.8	367.7	147.0	2.3	11.1	9.1	22.8	7.8	21.3
1995	656.0	563.2	22.5	139.7	401.0	173.7	7.1	11.8	14.8	21.5	0.0	25.8
1996	736.1	634.2	22.1	150.5	461.6	188.8	5.6	14.5	16.9	20.1	4.2	29.2
1997	812.3	701.4	23.8	169.2	508.4	209.0	6.3	17.0	16.7	25.3	4.8	33.0
1998	738.5	635.5	25.2	140.7	469.6	173.5	6.5	16.4	19.5	8.9	5.9	30.1
1999	776.8	655.3	26.3	170.1	458.9	175.2	2.4	16.2	12.4	5.3	7.3	35.3
2000	759.3	613.6	30.8	173.0	409.8	166.3	1.2	15.4	16.3	4.7	-1.5	28.8
1998												
1st quarter	752.0	643.1	25.0	147.9	470.2	178.5	6.9	14.9	14.4	12.2	6.4	28.8
2nd quarter	732.5	626.3	25.2	136.4	464.7	170.1	6.2	16.7	19.5	8.3	3.5	27.4
3rd quarter	743.5	647.3	25.4	136.9	485.0	176.6	6.1	18.5	20.4	6.6	4.5	31.3
4th quarter	725.9	625.3	25.1	141.8	458.4	168.8	6.8	15.7	23.7	8.3	9.3	32.9
1999												
1st quarter	771.3	657.3	24.9	163.0	469.5	175.0	3.8	15.9	9.8	4.3	8.9	33.9
2nd quarter	773.2	656.5	25.5	157.8	473.2	182.5	3.1	15.7	12.8	4.9	6.1	37.8
3rd quarter	766.8	648.3	26.2	175.3	446.8	174.2	1.5	16.2	12.3	6.9	7.3	34.3
4th quarter	796.1	659.1	28.6	184.5	446.0	169.1	1.2	17.1	14.7	4.9	6.7	35.3
2000												
1st quarter	766.8	635.7	30.0	179.5	426.2	172.6	2.1	18.8	12.6	2.5	1.2	33.3
2nd quarter	773.5	634.9	30.5	164.5	440.0	186.1	2.0	16.2	16.1	8.7	0.3	33.7
3rd quarter	756.3	611.7	31.1	171.1	409.5	164.9	0.5	15.2	18.1	3.4	-2.4	27.3
4th quarter	740.7	572.1	31.7	176.8	363.6	141.6	0.3	11.3	18.1	4.1	-5.2	21.0

Table 9-6. Corporate Profits with Inventory Valuation Adjustment by Industry Group, SIC Basis —Continued

(Billions of dollars, quarterly data are at seasonally adjusted rates.)

NIPA Tables 6.16B, 6.16C

Classification basis, year, and quarter	Manufacturing—Continued Nondurable goods Total	Food and kindred products	Chemicals and allied products	Petroleum and coal products	Other nondurable goods	Transportation and public utilities Total	Transportation	Communications	Electric, gas, and sanitary services	Wholesale trade	Retail trade	Other nonfinancial	Rest of the world
1972 SIC Basis													
1948	10.0	1.9	1.7	2.8	3.7	3.0	1.5	0.4	1.1	2.4	3.2	3.5	1.3
1949	8.1	1.6	1.8	1.9	2.8	3.0	1.2	0.5	1.4	1.9	2.8	3.1	1.1
1950	9.0	1.6	2.3	2.3	2.7	4.1	1.9	0.7	1.5	2.1	3.0	3.5	1.3
1951	11.4	1.4	2.8	2.8	4.4	4.7	1.9	1.0	1.8	2.6	2.6	3.6	1.7
1952	10.0	1.8	2.3	2.3	3.6	5.0	1.9	1.1	2.0	2.3	2.7	3.3	1.9
1953	10.0	1.8	2.2	2.7	3.3	5.0	1.6	1.2	2.2	1.8	2.3	3.0	1.8
1954	9.5	1.6	2.2	2.8	2.9	4.7	1.0	1.3	2.4	1.7	2.3	3.3	2.0
1955	11.8	2.2	3.0	3.0	3.6	5.7	1.5	1.7	2.5	2.4	2.9	3.5	2.4
1956	12.0	1.8	2.8	3.3	4.1	5.9	1.4	1.8	2.7	2.2	2.6	3.9	2.8
1957	10.8	1.8	2.8	2.6	3.6	5.9	1.1	2.0	2.7	2.2	2.6	3.8	3.1
1958	10.2	2.1	2.5	2.1	3.4	5.9	0.9	2.3	2.7	2.2	2.6	3.5	2.5
1959	12.9	2.5	3.5	2.6	4.3	7.1	1.1	2.8	3.1	2.9	3.3	3.4	2.7
1960	12.2	2.2	3.1	2.6	4.2	7.5	0.9	3.0	3.6	2.5	2.8	3.3	3.1
1961	12.1	2.4	3.3	2.3	4.2	7.9	1.0	3.2	3.7	2.5	3.0	3.4	3.3
1962	12.3	2.4	3.2	2.2	4.4	8.5	1.0	3.6	3.9	2.8	3.4	3.6	3.8
1963	13.3	2.7	3.7	2.2	4.7	9.5	1.4	3.9	4.2	2.8	3.6	4.1	4.1
1964	14.5	2.7	4.1	2.4	5.3	10.2	1.6	4.0	4.6	3.4	4.5	4.7	4.5
1965	16.5	2.9	4.6	2.9	6.1	11.0	2.1	4.3	4.6	3.8	4.9	5.4	4.7
1966	18.6	3.3	4.9	3.4	6.9	12.0	2.3	4.8	4.9	4.0	4.9	5.9	4.5
1967	18.0	3.3	4.3	4.0	6.4	10.9	1.3	4.8	4.8	4.1	5.7	6.1	4.8
1968	19.4	3.2	5.3	3.8	7.1	11.0	1.0	5.1	4.9	4.6	6.4	6.6	5.6
1969	18.1	3.1	4.6	3.4	7.0	10.7	0.7	5.4	4.6	4.9	6.4	6.1	6.6
1970	17.0	3.2	3.9	3.7	6.1	8.3	-0.1	4.8	3.6	4.4	6.0	5.8	7.1
1971	18.5	3.6	4.5	3.8	6.6	8.9	0.7	4.1	4.1	5.2	7.2	6.4	7.9
1972	19.2	3.0	5.3	3.3	7.6	9.5	1.5	3.9	4.0	6.9	7.4	7.0	9.5
1973	22.0	2.5	6.2	5.4	7.9	9.1	1.3	4.3	3.4	8.2	6.6	8.7	14.9
1974	26.1	2.6	5.3	10.9	7.3	7.6	2.0	4.1	1.5	11.5	2.3	9.1	17.5
1975	34.5	8.6	6.4	10.1	9.5	11.0	1.0	4.3	5.7	13.8	8.2	12.0	14.6
1976	39.9	7.1	8.2	13.5	11.1	15.3	3.0	5.7	6.5	12.9	10.5	14.0	16.5
1977	41.4	6.9	7.8	13.1	13.6	18.6	3.7	6.6	8.3	15.6	12.4	17.8	19.1
1978	45.1	6.2	8.3	15.8	14.8	21.8	4.1	8.6	9.1	15.6	12.3	19.8	22.9
1979	52.5	5.8	7.2	24.8	14.7	17.0	3.5	7.5	6.0	18.8	9.8	21.6	34.6
1980	59.5	6.1	5.7	34.7	13.1	18.4	2.7	7.7	8.0	17.2	6.2	21.8	35.5
1981	71.6	9.2	8.0	40.0	14.5	20.3	1.7	8.6	10.0	22.4	9.9	16.7	29.7
1982	62.1	7.3	5.1	34.7	15.0	23.1	-0.1	8.6	14.6	19.6	13.4	9.2	32.6
1983	56.7	6.3	7.4	23.9	19.1	29.5	3.2	9.9	16.4	21.0	18.7	10.4	35.1
1984	52.6	6.8	8.2	17.6	20.1	40.1	6.1	12.8	21.3	29.5	21.1	11.1	36.6
1985	54.6	8.8	6.6	18.7	20.5	33.8	1.8	14.2	17.8	23.9	22.2	9.2	38.1
1986	31.7	7.5	7.5	-4.7	21.3	35.8	3.4	17.6	14.7	24.1	23.5	15.5	39.5
1987	45.6	11.4	14.4	-1.5	21.3	41.9	3.4	19.4	19.1	18.6	23.4	23.4	48.0
1987 SIC Basis													
1987	45.6	11.4	14.4	-1.5	21.3	41.9	3.4	19.4	19.1	18.6	23.4	23.4	48.0
1988	67.1	12.0	18.6	12.7	23.7	48.4	7.9	19.5	21.1	20.1	20.3	28.3	57.0
1989	59.7	11.1	18.2	6.5	23.9	43.3	1.3	18.2	23.9	21.8	20.8	25.5	67.1
1990	69.2	14.3	16.8	16.4	21.7	44.2	-0.4	20.1	24.5	19.2	20.7	29.0	76.1
1991	63.6	18.1	16.2	7.3	22.0	53.3	2.3	23.5	27.5	21.7	26.7	27.5	76.5
1992	59.0	18.2	16.0	-0.9	25.6	58.4	2.3	27.7	28.4	25.1	32.6	39.7	73.1
1993	59.7	16.4	15.9	2.7	24.7	69.5	7.0	32.9	29.6	26.3	39.1	48.9	76.9
1994	72.6	19.9	23.2	1.2	28.3	83.2	10.5	36.7	36.1	30.9	46.2	60.4	77.1
1995	92.8	27.1	27.9	7.1	30.6	85.8	11.5	33.6	40.8	27.3	43.1	71.2	92.8
1996	98.2	22.1	26.4	15.0	34.7	91.3	15.7	35.0	40.7	39.8	51.9	89.7	101.9
1997	105.9	24.6	32.3	17.3	31.7	84.2	19.0	25.5	39.7	47.6	64.2	103.4	110.9
1998	86.2	21.9	26.5	6.7	31.1	78.9	21.6	21.4	35.8	52.3	73.4	91.5	103.0
1999	96.4	28.1	25.2	4.3	38.9	56.8	15.8	4.6	36.3	52.6	74.6	99.7	121.5
2000	101.5	25.7	16.0	29.1	30.7	43.8	15.2	1.3	27.3	56.9	70.1	72.8	145.7
1998													
1st quarter	94.9	23.6	30.5	9.4	31.3	76.8	20.6	22.1	34.1	50.2	71.3	93.4	108.8
2nd quarter	88.5	24.6	22.9	8.9	32.1	81.0	21.5	24.0	35.5	52.6	72.5	88.6	106.2
3rd quarter	89.2	25.8	24.9	7.3	31.3	86.7	24.2	25.1	37.4	57.5	73.8	90.4	96.2
4th quarter	72.0	13.6	27.6	1.3	29.6	71.0	20.3	14.5	36.3	48.8	76.0	93.8	100.5
1999													
1st quarter	98.5	28.5	31.8	0.6	37.6	62.6	16.8	9.2	36.6	54.8	79.4	97.7	113.9
2nd quarter	102.1	28.6	31.8	4.0	37.7	52.1	16.0	3.4	32.8	53.1	79.0	106.6	116.6
3rd quarter	95.8	27.0	22.1	8.2	38.5	52.5	13.5	1.3	37.6	49.3	69.6	101.2	118.5
4th quarter	89.1	28.2	14.9	4.4	41.6	59.9	17.0	4.5	38.4	53.3	70.5	93.2	137.0
2000													
1st quarter	102.1	28.3	20.0	15.3	38.6	47.5	14.7	-0.3	33.0	52.4	75.5	78.3	131.1
2nd quarter	109.2	25.4	17.4	33.8	32.7	42.4	19.4	-3.4	26.4	63.2	70.8	77.4	138.5
3rd quarter	102.8	28.2	13.3	33.9	27.4	43.2	15.7	0.4	27.1	62.9	70.3	68.3	144.6
4th quarter	91.9	21.0	13.2	33.4	24.3	42.2	11.2	8.4	22.6	48.9	63.9	67.0	168.6

NOTES AND DEFINITIONS, CHAPTER 9

GENERAL NOTE ON DATA ON COMPENSATION PER HOUR

This chapter includes two data series with similar names— the Employment Cost Index for total compensation and the index of compensation per hour—that often display different behavior. Both are compiled and published by the Bureau of Labor Statistics (BLS), but the definitions, sources, and methods of compilation are different. Users should be aware of these differences and of the consequent differences in the appropriate uses and interpretations for each of the two series.

The *Employment Cost Index (ECI)* (Tables 9-1 and 9-2) measures changes in hourly compensation for "all civilian workers", which is not quite as broad as it sounds, as it excludes federal government workers, farm workers, and private household workers. Indexes are also published for subgroups including state and local workers, "all private industry" (again excluding farm and private household workers), and a number of industry and occupational subgroups.

The ECI is calculated and published separately for *total compensation* and for the two components of hourly compensation, *wages and salaries* and the employer cost of employee *benefits*. It is constructed by analogy with the Consumer Price Index (CPI); that is, it holds the composition of employment constant in order to isolate hourly compensation trends that take place for individual occupations, which are then aggregated, using fixed relative importance weights. The ECI is based on a sample survey and may be revised from time to time, due to updated classification, weighting, and seasonal adjustments. However, it is not subject to major benchmark revision of the underlying wage, salary, and benefit rate observations. By design, it excludes any representation of employee stock options. As it is based on a sample survey, the ECI is measured "from the bottom up," aggregating from individual employers' reports to higher levels. The ECI is frequently and appropriately used as the best available measure of the general trend of wages and of the extent of inflationary pressure exerted on prices by labor costs.

The *compensation per hour* component of the report on "Productivity and Costs" (Table 9-3) is calculated and published for total compensation in total business, nonfarm business, nonfinancial corporations, and manufacturing. The nonfarm business category is similar in scope to the "all private industry" category in the ECI. The measures in Table 9-3, however, are compiled "from the top down," starting with aggregate estimates of compensation and hours, then dividing the former by the latter. Compensation per hour is affected by changes in the composition of employment. If the composition of employment shifts toward a larger proportion of higher-paid employees and/or industries, compensation per hour will rise even if there is no increase in hourly compensation for any individual worker.

In addition, *compensation per hour* includes the value of exercised stock options as expensed by companies. Also included are other transitory payments, many of which may be of little relevance to the typical worker or to ongoing production costs. These values are not reported immediately. Instead, they are incorporated when later, more comprehensive reports are received. This process can lead to dramatic revisions in compensation per hour and in the unit labor costs index, which is based on compensation. For example, the fourth-quarter 2004 increase in compensation per hour in nonfarm business was initially reported at an annual rate of 3.1 percent. Four months later, the reported rate for the same time period was 10.2 percent. The rate of increase from a year earlier was revised from 3.6 to 5.9 percent. According to then-Federal Reserve Chairman Alan Greenspan, in testimony before the Joint Economic Committee on June 9, 2005, this reflected "a large but apparently transitory surge in bonuses and the proceeds of stock option exercises," not a potentially inflationary acceleration in the rate of labor compensation increase. More recently, it was reported in August 2009 that "first-quarter unit labor costs were revised to negative 2.7% from positive 3%." (*Wall Street Journal,* August 12, 2009, p. A2.)

These characteristics suggest that *compensation per hour* should not be considered a reliable or appropriate indicator of wage or compensation trends for typical workers. It is useful in conjunction with the productivity series, because aggregate productivity is subject to the same composition shifts—higher-productivity industries also tend to have higher-paid employees. Hence, the measure of *unit labor costs* (derived by dividing compensation per hour by output per hour in this system) is not distorted when the composition of output shifts toward higher-productivity industries. The shift affects the numerator and denominator of the ratio similarly. However, both compensation and unit labor costs can still be distorted by transitory payments, such as those discussed above.

There are other, probably less important differences between the two measures. Compensation per hour refers to the entire quarter, while the ECI is observed in the terminal month of each quarter. Tips and other forms of compensation not provided by employers are included in hourly compensation but not in the ECI. The ECI excludes persons working for token wages, business owners and others who set their own wage, and family workers who do not earn a market wage; all of these workers are included in the productivity and cost accounts. Hourly compensation excludes employees of nonprofit institutions serving individuals—about 10 percent of private workers (mostly in education and medical care) who are within the scope of the ECI. Hourly compensation measures include an estimate for the unincorporated self-employed, who are assumed to earn the same hourly compensation as other employees in the sector. Implicitly, unpaid family workers also are included in the hourly compensation measures with the assumption that their hourly compensation is zero. Both of these groups are also excluded from the ECI.

TABLES 9-1 AND 9-2
EMPLOYMENT COST INDEXES

SOURCE: U.S. DEPARTMENT OF LABOR, BUREAU OF LABOR STATISTICS (BLS)

The Employment Cost Index (ECI) is a quarterly measure of the change in the cost of labor, independent of the influence of employment shifts among occupations and industries. It uses a fixed market basket of labor—similar in concept to the Consumer Price Index's fixed market basket of goods and services—to measure changes over time in employer costs of employing labor. Data are quarterly in all cases and are reported for the final month of each quarter. These measures are expressed as indexes, with the not-seasonally-adjusted value for December 2005 set at 100.

Care should be used in comparing the ECI with other data sets. The "all private industry" category in the ECI excludes farm and household workers (it is sometimes, and more precisely, called "private nonfarm industry"), and the "all civilian workers" category excludes federal government, farm, and household workers.

The data for 1979 through 2005, which are presented in Table 9-2 and are the official ECI measures for that time period, were based on the 1987 Standard Industrial Classification (SIC) and 1990 Occupational Classification System (OCS).

Currently the ECI is compiled based on the 2007 North American Industry Classification System (NAICS) and the 2000 Standard Occupational Classification Manual (SOC). These data, along with comparable data for 2001 through 2005, are shown in Table 9-1.

For certain broad categories shown in this volume—indicated by footnote 2 in Table 9-2—the old SIC categories are roughly comparable and continuous with the data for 2006 and subsequent years. (However, they differ slightly on overlap dates, and should be "linked" if a continuous time series is desired; see the article at the beginning of this volume.) Many of the new industry and occupational categories are not continuous with the old series shown here, and some of the old categories are not being continued because BLS finds them obsolete and no longer meaningful.

Definitions

Total compensation comprises wages, salaries, and the employer's costs for employee benefits. Excluded from wages and salaries and employee benefits are the value of stock option exercises and items such as payment-in-kind, free room and board, and tips.

Wages and salaries consists of straight-time earnings per hour before payroll deductions, including production bonuses, incentive earnings, commissions, and cost-of-living adjust-

ments. These wage rates exclude premium pay for overtime and for work on weekends and holidays, shift differentials, and nonproduction bonuses such as lump-sum payments provided in lieu of wage increases. According to BLS, wages and salaries are about 70 percent of total compensation.

Benefits includes the cost to employers for paid leave—vacations, holidays, sick leave, and other leave; for supplemental pay—premium pay for work in addition to the regular work schedule (such as overtime, weekends, and holidays), shift differentials, and nonproduction bonuses (such as referral bonuses and lump-sum payments provided in lieu of wage increases); for insurance benefits—life, health, short-term disability, and long-term disability; for retirement and savings benefits—defined benefit and defined contribution plans; and for legally required benefits—Social Security, Medicare, federal and state unemployment insurance, and workers' compensation. Severance pay and supplemental unemployment benefit (SUB) plans are included in the data through December 2005 but were dropped beginning with the March 2006 data. The combined cost of these two benefits accounted for less than one-tenth of one percent of compensation, and according to BLS, dropping these benefits has had virtually no impact on the index. According to BLS, benefit costs are about 30 percent of total compensation.

Civilian workers are private industry workers, as defined below, and workers in state and local government. Federal workers are not included.

Private industry workers are paid workers in private industry excluding farms and private households. To be included in the ECI, employees in occupations must receive cash payments from the establishment for services performed and the establishment must pay the employer's portion of Medicare taxes on that individual's wages. Major exclusions from the survey are the self-employed, individuals who set their own pay (for example, proprietors, owners, major stockholders, and partners in unincorporated firms), volunteers, unpaid workers, family members being paid token wages, individuals receiving long-term disability compensation, and U.S. citizens working overseas.

Private industry workers excluding incentive paid occupations is a new category introduced in the 2006 revision to eliminate the quarter-to-quarter variability related to the way workers (for example, salespersons working on commission) are paid. (The category *private industry workers excluding sales occupations* was intended to serve a similar purpose in the previous SIC-based classification system, but was much less accurate in separately identifying workers with highly variable compensation.)

Goods-producing industries include mining, construction, and manufacturing.

Service-providing industries include the following NAICS industries: wholesale trade; retail trade; transportation and warehousing; utilities; information; finance and insurance; real estate and rental and leasing; professional, scientific, and technical services; management of companies and enterprises; administrative and support and waste management and remediation services; education services; health care and social assistance; arts, entertainment, and recreation; accommodation and food services; and other services, except public administration.

Notes on the data

Employee benefit costs are calculated as cents per hour worked.

The December 2011 data were collected from probability samples of approximately 48,200 occupational observations in about 9,400 sample establishments in private industry, and approximately 9,300 occupations within about 1,400 establishments in state and local governments. The private industry sample is rotated over approximately five years. The state and local government sample is replaced less frequently; the latest sample was introduced in September 2007.

Currently, the sample establishments are classified in industry categories based on the NAICS. Within an establishment, specific job categories are selected and classified into approximately 800 occupational classifications according to the SOC. Similar procedures were followed under the previous classification systems. Data are collected each quarter for the pay periods including the 12th day of March, June, September, and December.

Aggregate indexes are calculated using fixed employment weights. Beginning with March 2006, ECI weights are based on fixed employment counts for 2002 from the BLS Occupational Employment Statistics survey. ECI measures were based on 1990 employment counts from March 1995 through December 2005 and 1980 census employment counts from June 1986 through December 1994. Prior to June 1986, they were based on 1970 census employment counts. Use of fixed weights ensures that changes in the indexes reflect only changes in hourly compensation, not employment shifts among industries or occupations with different levels of wages and compensation. This feature distinguishes the ECI from other compensation series such as average hourly earnings (see Chapter 10 and its notes and definitions) and the compensation per hour component of the productivity series (see Table 9-3 and its notes and definitions, and the general note above), each of which is affected by such employment shifts.

Data availability

Data for wages and salaries for the private nonfarm economy are available beginning with the data for 1975; data for compensation begin with the 1980 data. The series for state and local government and for the civilian nonfarm economy begin with the 1981 data. All series are available on the BLS Web site at <http://www.bls.gov>.

Wage and salary change and compensation cost change data also are available by major occupational and industry groups, as well as by region and collective bargaining status. Information on wage and salary change is available from 1975 to the present for most of these series. Compensation cost change data are available from 1980 to the present for most series. For 10 occupational and industry series, benefit cost change data are available from the early 1980s to the present. For state and local governments and the civilian economy (state and local governments plus private industry), wage and salary change and compensation cost change data are available for major occupational and industry series. BLS provides data for all these series from June 1981 to the present.

Updates are available about four weeks after the end of the reference quarter. Reference quarters end in March, June, September, and December. Seasonal adjustment factors and seasonally adjusted indexes are released in late April.

References

Explanatory notes, including references, are included in a Technical Note in each quarter's ECI news release, and can be found on the BLS Web site, in the PDF version of the release.

More detailed information on the ECI is available from Chapter 8, "National compensation measures," (www.bls.gov/opub/hom/pdf/homch8.pdf) from the BLS Handbook of Methods, and several articles published in the *Monthly Labor Review* and *Compensation and Working Conditions*. The articles and other descriptive pieces are available at www.bls.gov/ect/#publications, by calling (202) 691-6199, or sending e-mail to NCSinfo@bls.gov.

TABLE 9-3A AND 9-3B
PRODUCTIVITY AND RELATED DATA

These series have been completely revised and rebased to 2005 = 100. Previously, the index base was 1992.

Productivity measures relate real physical output to real input. They encompass a family of measures that includes single-factor input measures, such as output per unit of labor input or output per unit of capital input, as well as measures of multifactor productivity—that is, output per unit of combined labor and capital inputs. The indexes published in this book are indexes of labor productivity expressed in terms of output per hour of labor input. (A larger group of BLS productivity measures can be found in Bernan Press's *Handbook of U.S. Labor Statistics*.) Data are provided here for four sectors of the economy: business, nonfarm business, the nonfinancial corporate sector, and manufacturing. All data are presented as indexes with a base of 2005= 100.

Definitions

Current dollar output is the current-dollar value of the goods and services produced in the specified sector. *Output* is the constant-dollar value of the same goods and services, derived as current-dollar output divided by the sector *implicit price deflator*. All these data are derived from components of the NIPAs; see Notes on the data below, and for general information on the NIPAs, see the Notes and Definitions to Chapter 1.

Output per hour of all persons (labor productivity) is the value of goods and services in constant dollars produced per hour of labor input. By definition, nonfinancial corporations include no self-employed persons. Productivity in this sector is expressed as *output per hour of all employees. Output per person* is output divided by the index for employment instead of by the index for hours of all persons.

Compensation is the total value of the wages and salaries of employees, plus employers' contributions for social insurance and private benefit plans, plus wages, salaries, and supplementary payments for the self-employed. *Compensation per hour* is compensation divided by *hours of all persons.* Included in compensation is the value of exercised stock options that companies report as a charge against earnings. Stock option values are reported with a delay; consequently, recent values are estimated based on extrapolation. They are revised to actual values when the data become available; sometimes the revisions are very large. The labor compensation of proprietors cannot be explicitly identified and must be estimated. This is done by assuming that proprietors have the same hourly compensation as employees in the same sector. The quarterly labor productivity and cost measures do not contain estimates of compensation for unpaid family workers.

Real compensation per hour is compensation per hour deflated by the Consumer Price Index Research Series (CPI-U-RS) for the period 1978 through 2011. (For current quarters, before the CPI-U-RS becomes available, changes in the CPI-U are used.) Changes in the Consumer Price Index for Urban Wage Earners and Clerical Workers (CPI-W) are used for data before 1978, as there was no CPI-U for that period. See the Notes and Definitions to Chapter 8 for explanation of the CPI-U, the CPI-W, and the CPI-U-RS.

Unit labor costs are the current-dollar labor costs expended in the production of a unit of output. They are derived by dividing compensation by output.

Unit nonlabor payments include profits, depreciation, interest, rental income of persons, and indirect taxes per unit of output. They are computed by subtracting current-dollar compensation of all persons from current-dollar value of output, providing the data for the index of total *nonlabor payments,* which is then divided by output.

Unit nonlabor costs are available for nonfinancial corporations only. They contain all the components of unit nonlabor payments except unit profits (and rental income of persons, which is zero by definition for nonfinancial corporations).

Unit profits, the other component of unit nonlabor payments, are also only available for nonfinancial corporations.

Hours of all persons (labor input) consists of the total hours at work (*employment* multiplied by *average weekly hours*) of payroll workers, self-employed persons, and unpaid family workers. For the nonfinancial corporations data, there are no self-employed persons; the data represent *employee hours.*

Labor share is the total dollar amount of labor compensation divided by the total current-dollar value of output.

Notes on the data

Output for the business sector is equal to constant-dollar gross domestic product minus: the rental value of owner-occupied dwellings, the output of nonprofit institutions, the output of paid employees of private households, and general government output. The measures are derived from national income and product account (NIPA) data supplied by the U.S. Department of Commerce's Bureau of Economic Analysis (BEA). For manufacturing, BLS produces annual estimates of sectoral output. Quarterly manufacturing output indexes derived from the Federal Reserve Board of Governors' monthly indexes of industrial production (see Chapter 2) are adjusted to these annual measures by the BLS, and are also used to project the quarterly values in the current period. The business sector accounted for 75 percent of the value of GDP in 2011; nonfarm business, for 74 percent.

Nonfinancial corporate output excludes unincorporated businesses and financial corporations from business sector output and accounted for approximately 48 percent of the value of GDP in 2011. Unit profits and unit nonlabor costs can be calculated separately for this sector and are shown in this table.

Compensation and hours data are developed from BLS and BEA data. The primary source for hours and employment is BLS's Current Employment Statistics (CES) program (see the notes and definitions for Chapter 10). Other data sources are the Current Population Survey (CPS) and the National Compensation Survey (NCS). Weekly paid hours are adjusted to hours at work using the NCS. For paid employees, hours at work differ from hours paid, in that they exclude paid vacation and holidays, paid sick leave, and other paid personal or administrative leave.

Although the labor productivity measures relate output to labor input, they do not measure the contribution of labor or any other specific factor of production. Instead, they reflect the joint effect of many influences, including changes in technology; capital investment; level of output; utilization of capacity, energy, and materials; the organization of production; managerial skill; and the characteristics and efforts of the work force.

Revisions

Data for recent years are revised frequently to take account of revisions in the output and labor input measures that underlie the estimates. Customarily, all revisions to source data are reflected in the release following the source data revision. Data in this volume were released June 6, 2012, and reflect the midyear 2011 revisions to the NIPAs and all revisions in labor input and compensation available up to that release date, including the annual benchmark revision of the CES and updated seasonal factors.

Data availability

Series are available quarterly and annually. Quarterly measures are based entirely on seasonally adjusted data. For some detailed manufacturing series (not shown here), only annual averages are available. Productivity indexes are published early in the second and third months of each quarter, reflecting new data for preceding quarters. Complete historical data are available on the BLS Web site at <http://www.bls.gov>.

BLS also publishes productivity estimates for a number of individual industries. A release entitled "Productivity and Costs by Industry" is available on the BLS Web site at <http://www.bls.gov>.

References

Further information is available in the Technical Notes and footnotes on the most current monthly release, available on the Web site, and from the following sources: Chapter 10, "Productivity Measures: Business Sector and Major Subsectors," *BLS Handbook of Methods*—Bulletin 2490 (April 1997) and the following *Monthly Labor Review* articles: "Alternative Measures of Supervisory Employee Hours and Productivity Growth" (April 2004); "Possible Measurement Bias in Aggregate Productivity Growth" (February 1999); "Improvements to the Quarterly Productivity Measures" (October 1995); "Hours of Work: A New Base for BLS Productivity Statistics" (February 1990); and "New Sector Definitions for Productivity Series" (October 1976).

TABLE 9-4
RATES OF RETURN AND RELATED DATA FOR MAJOR NONFINANCIAL INDUSTRY GROUPS

SOURCE: U.S. DEPARTMENT OF COMMERCE, BUREAU OF ECONOMIC ANALYSIS

This table presents data on the net operating surplus and rate of return for five major nonfinancial industry groups from 1997 through 2009, based on the NAICS. The industry groups include both corporations and proprietors. Therefore, their data differ from the data for nonfinancial corporations alone, which are available through 2010 and shown for comparison purposes in the first column of this table. (Nonfinancial corporation rates of return and related data can also be found in Table 1-16.)

Definitions

Net operating surplus for the nonfinancial industries includes corporate profits, net interest, business current transfer payments, and proprietors' income (mainly the income of unincorporated self-employed workers).

Produced assets is the average of the end-year values for the current and previous year of the net stock of capital plus inventories, valued at current cost.

Rate of return is net operating surplus as a percent of the average value of produced assets at the beginning and end of the year.

Share of net value added is the net operating surplus as a percent of total value added in the industry. Value added is the portion of total national gross domestic product (GDP) produced in the industry and includes the net operating surplus, compensation of employees, taxes on production and imports less subsidies, and consumption of fixed capital.

Data availability, revisions, and references

These data were presented for the first time and described in "Returns for Domestic Nonfinancial Business," *Survey of Current Business,* May 2007, pp. 6-10. The data were revised and updated in the May 2009, August 2010, and June 2011 *Surveys of Current Business.*

TABLE 9-5 AND 9-6
CORPORATE PROFITS WITH INVENTORY VALUATION ADJUSTMENT BY INDUSTRY GROUP

SOURCE: U.S. DEPARTMENT OF COMMERCE, BUREAU OF ECONOMIC ANALYSIS

These profits measures are derived from the NIPAs. See the notes and definitions to Chapter 1 for definitions, data availability, and references. Note that this industry breakdown of profits incorporates the inventory valuation adjustment (IVA), which eliminates any capital gain element in profits arising from changes in the prices at which inventories are valued, but does not incorporate the capital consumption adjustment (CCAdj), which adjusts historical costs of fixed capital to replacement costs and uses actual rather than tax-based service lives. This is because the CCAdj is calculated by BEA at an aggregate level, whereas the IVA is calculated at an industry level.

Beginning with 1998, data are compiled on the NAICS basis, as shown in Table 9-5. Data for earlier years based on the December 2003 revision—including an overlap for the years 1998 through 2000—are based on the older Standard Industrial Classification system (SIC) and are shown back to 1948 in Table 9-6 on that basis; these have not been revised and are as shown in previous years' *Business Statistics.*

CHAPTER 10: EMPLOYMENT, HOURS, AND EARNINGS

Section 10a: Labor Force, Employment, and Unemployment

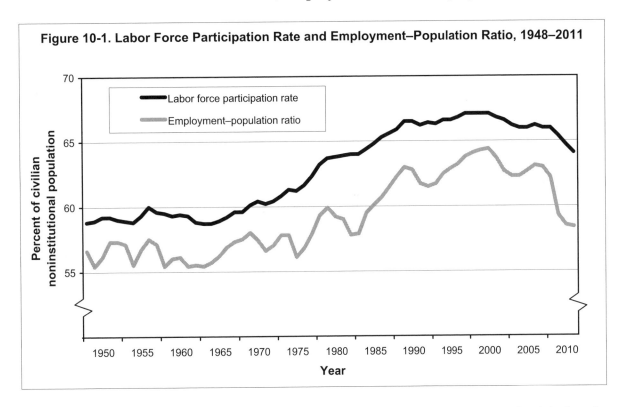

Figure 10-1. Labor Force Participation Rate and Employment–Population Ratio, 1948–2011

- From a high point in November 2007 to a low in December 2009, 8.6 million Americans lost jobs, based on total civilian employment smoothed for population adjustments. (Table 10-6) The employment/population ratio, charted in Figure 10-1 above, registered the steepest plunge of the postwar period. (Tables 10-1A and B) However, this 5.9 percent employment decline during 2008 and 2009 was far less than the length and scale of job loss in the Great Depression, when jobs dropped 22 percent from 1929 to 1932. (Table 10-21)

- By June 2012—the latest month available as this was written—there were 4.3 million more employed than at the December 2009 low, using the December 2009 figure in Table 10-6, which is based on population controls consistent with the current estimates. The employment/population ratio, which got as low as 58.2 percent in some months during 2009 through 2011, moved up to 58.6 percent by June 2012. (Tables 10-1A, 10-6, and recent data)

- The labor force participation rate, already in a downtrend since the late 1990s, declined more rapidly through 2011, but seemed to stabilize at 63.8 percent in early 2012. (Tables 10-1, 10-2, and recent data)

Table 10-1A. Summary Labor Force, Employment, and Unemployment: Recent Data

(Thousands of persons, percent, seasonally adjusted, except as noted.)

Year and month	Civilian noninstitutional population [1]	Civilian labor force Thousands of persons	Civilian labor force Participation rate (percent)	Employment Total	By age and sex Men, 20 years and over	By age and sex Women, 20 years and over	By age and sex Both sexes, 16 to 19 years	By industry Agricultural	By industry Nonagricultural	Employment-population ratio, percent	Unemployment Total	Unemployment Unemployed 15 weeks and over	Rate (percent)
1965	126 513	74 455	58.9	71 088	43 422	22 630	5 036	4 361	66 726	56.2	3 366	755	4.5
1966	128 058	75 770	59.2	72 895	43 668	23 510	5 721	3 979	68 915	56.9	2 875	526	3.8
1967	129 874	77 347	59.6	74 372	44 294	24 397	5 682	3 844	70 527	57.3	2 975	448	3.8
1968	132 028	78 737	59.6	75 920	44 859	25 281	5 781	3 817	72 103	57.5	2 817	412	3.6
1969	134 335	80 734	60.1	77 902	45 388	26 397	6 117	3 606	74 296	58.0	2 832	375	3.5
1970	137 085	82 771	60.4	78 678	45 581	26 952	6 144	3 463	75 215	57.4	4 093	663	4.9
1971	140 216	84 382	60.2	79 367	45 912	27 246	6 208	3 394	75 972	56.6	5 016	1 187	5.9
1972	144 126	87 034	60.4	82 153	47 130	28 276	6 746	3 484	78 669	57.0	4 882	1 167	5.6
1973	147 096	89 429	60.8	85 064	48 310	29 484	7 271	3 470	81 594	57.8	4 365	826	4.9
1974	150 120	91 949	61.3	86 794	48 922	30 424	7 448	3 515	83 279	57.8	5 156	955	5.6
1975	153 153	93 775	61.2	85 846	48 018	30 726	7 104	3 408	82 438	56.1	7 929	2 505	8.5
1976	156 150	96 158	61.6	88 752	49 190	32 226	7 336	3 331	85 421	56.8	7 406	2 366	7.7
1977	159 033	99 009	62.3	92 017	50 555	33 775	7 688	3 283	88 734	57.9	6 991	1 942	7.1
1978	161 910	102 251	63.2	96 048	52 143	35 836	8 070	3 387	92 661	59.3	6 202	1 414	6.1
1979	164 863	104 962	63.7	98 824	53 308	37 434	8 083	3 347	95 477	59.9	6 137	1 241	5.8
1980	167 745	106 940	63.8	99 303	53 101	38 492	7 710	3 364	95 938	59.2	7 637	1 871	7.1
1981	170 130	108 670	63.9	100 397	53 582	39 590	7 225	3 368	97 030	59.0	8 273	2 285	7.6
1982	172 271	110 204	64.0	99 526	52 891	40 086	6 549	3 401	96 125	57.8	10 678	3 485	9.7
1983	174 215	111 550	64.0	100 834	53 487	41 004	6 342	3 383	97 450	57.9	10 717	4 210	9.6
1984	176 383	113 544	64.4	105 005	55 769	42 793	6 444	3 321	101 685	59.5	8 539	2 737	7.5
1985	178 206	115 461	64.8	107 150	56 562	44 154	6 434	3 179	103 971	60.1	8 312	2 305	7.2
1986	180 587	117 834	65.3	109 597	57 569	45 556	6 472	3 163	106 434	60.7	8 237	2 232	7.0
1987	182 753	119 865	65.6	112 440	58 726	47 074	6 640	3 208	109 232	61.5	7 425	1 983	6.2
1988	184 613	121 669	65.9	114 968	59 781	48 383	6 805	3 169	111 800	62.3	6 701	1 610	5.5
1989	186 393	123 869	66.5	117 342	60 837	49 745	6 759	3 199	114 142	63.0	6 528	1 375	5.3
1990	189 164	125 840	66.5	118 793	61 678	50 535	6 581	3 223	115 570	62.8	7 047	1 525	5.6
1991	190 925	126 346	66.2	117 718	61 178	50 634	5 906	3 269	114 449	61.7	8 628	2 357	6.8
1992	192 805	128 105	66.4	118 492	61 496	51 328	5 669	3 247	115 245	61.5	9 613	3 408	7.5
1993	194 838	129 200	66.3	120 259	62 355	52 099	5 805	3 115	117 144	61.7	8 940	3 094	6.9
1994	196 814	131 056	66.6	123 060	63 294	53 606	6 161	3 409	119 651	62.5	7 996	2 860	6.1
1995	198 584	132 304	66.6	124 900	64 085	54 396	6 419	3 440	121 460	62.9	7 404	2 363	5.6
1996	200 591	133 943	66.8	126 708	64 897	55 311	6 500	3 443	123 264	63.2	7 236	2 316	5.4
1997	203 133	136 297	67.1	129 558	66 284	56 613	6 661	3 399	126 159	63.8	6 739	2 062	4.9
1998	205 220	137 673	67.1	131 463	67 135	57 278	7 051	3 378	128 085	64.1	6 210	1 637	4.5
1999	207 753	139 368	67.1	133 488	67 761	58 555	7 172	3 281	130 207	64.3	5 880	1 480	4.2
2000	212 577	142 583	67.1	136 891	69 634	60 067	7 189	2 464	134 427	64.4	5 692	1 318	4.0
2001	215 092	143 734	66.8	136 933	69 776	60 417	6 740	2 299	134 635	63.7	6 801	1 752	4.7
2002	217 570	144 863	66.6	136 485	69 734	60 420	6 332	2 311	134 174	62.7	8 378	2 904	5.8
2003	221 168	146 510	66.2	137 736	70 415	61 402	5 919	2 275	135 461	62.3	8 774	3 378	6.0
2004	223 357	147 401	66.0	139 252	71 572	61 773	5 907	2 232	137 020	62.3	8 149	3 072	5.5
2005	226 082	149 320	66.0	141 730	73 050	62 702	5 978	2 197	139 532	62.7	7 591	2 619	5.1
2006	228 815	151 428	66.2	144 427	74 431	63 834	6 162	2 206	142 221	63.1	7 001	2 266	4.6
2007	231 867	153 124	66.0	146 047	75 337	64 799	5 911	2 095	143 952	63.0	7 078	2 303	4.6
2008	233 788	154 287	66.0	145 362	74 750	65 039	5 573	2 168	143 194	62.2	8 924	3 188	5.8
2009	235 801	154 142	65.4	139 877	71 341	63 699	4 837	2 103	137 775	59.3	14 265	7 272	9.3
2010	237 830	153 889	64.7	139 064	71 230	63 456	4 378	2 206	136 858	58.5	14 825	8 786	9.6
2011	239 618	153 617	64.1	139 869	72 182	63 360	4 327	2 254	137 615	58.4	13 747	8 077	8.9
2010													
January	236 832	153 454	64.8	138 500	70 529	63 542	4 430	2 121	136 464	58.5	14 953	8 924	9.7
February	236 998	153 704	64.9	138 665	70 645	63 541	4 479	2 295	136 459	58.5	15 039	8 924	9.8
March	237 159	153 964	64.9	138 836	70 929	63 426	4 481	2 202	136 702	58.5	15 128	9 051	9.8
April	237 329	154 528	65.1	139 306	71 352	63 453	4 501	2 247	137 026	58.7	15 221	9 070	9.9
May	237 499	154 216	64.9	139 340	71 416	63 491	4 432	2 205	137 074	58.7	14 876	8 898	9.6
June	237 690	153 653	64.6	139 137	71 338	63 533	4 266	2 120	136 968	58.5	14 517	8 915	9.4
July	237 890	153 748	64.6	139 139	71 403	63 399	4 337	2 188	136 776	58.5	14 609	8 695	9.5
August	238 099	154 073	64.7	139 338	71 538	63 406	4 394	2 182	137 080	58.5	14 735	8 407	9.6
September	238 322	153 918	64.6	139 344	71 545	63 540	4 259	2 184	137 233	58.5	14 574	8 394	9.5
October	238 530	153 709	64.4	139 072	71 410	63 352	4 311	2 373	136 816	58.3	14 636	8 666	9.5
November	238 715	154 041	64.5	138 937	71 128	63 400	4 409	2 206	136 686	58.2	15 104	8 747	9.8
December	238 889	153 613	64.3	139 220	71 494	63 429	4 297	2 173	137 036	58.3	14 393	8 613	9.4
2011													
January	238 704	153 250	64.2	139 330	71 593	63 403	4 334	2 252	137 156	58.4	13 919	8 458	9.1
February	238 851	153 302	64.2	139 551	71 901	63 351	4 299	2 247	137 388	58.4	13 751	8 208	9.0
March	239 000	153 392	64.2	139 764	71 918	63 515	4 332	2 244	137 619	58.5	13 628	8 122	8.9
April	239 146	153 420	64.2	139 628	71 942	63 431	4 255	2 090	137 505	58.4	13 792	7 919	9.0
May	239 313	153 700	64.2	139 808	72 161	63 385	4 262	2 244	137 508	58.4	13 892	8 197	9.0
June	239 489	153 409	64.1	139 385	71 981	63 088	4 316	2 224	137 125	58.2	14 024	8 137	9.1
July	239 671	153 358	64.0	139 450	71 930	63 257	4 262	2 250	136 993	58.2	13 908	8 134	9.1
August	239 871	153 674	64.1	139 754	72 098	63 322	4 333	2 373	137 290	58.3	13 920	8 218	9.1
September	240 071	154 004	64.1	140 107	72 340	63 406	4 362	2 268	137 932	58.4	13 897	8 227	9.0
October	240 269	154 057	64.1	140 297	72 379	63 520	4 398	2 257	138 167	58.4	13 759	7 869	8.9
November	240 441	153 937	64.0	140 614	72 846	63 352	4 416	2 262	138 304	58.5	13 323	7 766	8.7
December	240 584	153 887	64.0	140 790	73 080	63 323	4 387	2 349	138 411	58.5	13 097	7 628	8.5

[1]Not seasonally adjusted.

Table 10-1B. Summary Labor Force, Employment, and Unemployment: Historical

(Thousands of persons, percent, seasonally adjusted, except as noted.)

Year and month	Civilian noninstitutional population [1]	Civilian labor force — Thousands of persons	Civilian labor force — Participation rate (percent)	Employment — Total	Men, 20 years and over	Women, 20 years and over	Both sexes, 16 to 19 years	Agricultural	Nonagricultural	Employment-population ratio, percent	Unemployment Total	Unemployed 15 weeks and over	Rate (percent)
14 Years and Over													
1929	...	49 180	...	47 630	...	...	...	10 450	37 180	...	1 550	...	3.2
1930	...	49 820	...	45 480	...	...	...	10 450	37 180	...	4 340	...	8.7
1931	...	50 420	...	42 400	...	...	...	10 450	37 180	...	8 020	...	15.9 (15.3)
1932	...	51 000	...	38 940	...	...	...	10 450	37 180	...	12 060	...	23.6 (22.5)
1933	...	51 590	...	38 760	...	...	...	10 450	37 180	...	12 830	...	24.9 (20.6)
1934	...	52 230	...	40 890	...	...	...	10 450	37 180	...	11 340	...	21.7 (16.0)
1935	...	52 870	...	42 260	...	...	...	10 450	37 180	...	10 610	...	20.1 (14.2)
1936	...	53 440	...	44 410	...	...	...	10 450	37 180	...	9 030	...	16.9 (9.9)
1937	...	54 000	...	46 300	...	...	...	10 450	37 180	...	7 700	...	14.3 (9.1)
1938	...	54 610	...	44 220	...	...	...	10 450	37 180	...	10 390	...	19.0 (12.5)
1939	...	55 230	...	45 750	...	...	...	10 450	37 180	...	9 480	...	17.2 (11.3)
1940	99 840	55 640	55.7	47 520	...	...	...	10 450	37 180	47.6	8 120	...	14.6 (9.5)
1941	99 900	55 910	56.0	50 350	...	...	...	10 450	37 180	50.4	5 560	...	9.9 (6.0)
1942	98 640	56 410	57.2	53 750	...	...	...	10 450	37 180	54.5	2 660	...	4.7 (3.1)
1943	94 640	55 540	58.7	54 470	...	...	...	10 450	37 180	57.6	1 070	...	1.9 (1.8)
1944	93 220	54 630	58.6	53 960	...	...	...	10 450	37 180	57.9	670	...	1.2
1945	94 090	53 860	57.2	52 820	...	...	...	10 450	37 180	56.1	1 040	...	1.9
1946	103 070	57 520	55.8	55 250	...	...	...	10 450	37 180	53.6	2 270	...	3.9
1947	106 018	60 168	56.8	57 812	...	...	...	8 256	49 557	54.5	2 356	...	3.9
16 Years and Over													
1947	101 827	59 350	58.3	57 038	...	...	...	7 890	49 148	56.0	2 311	...	3.9
1948	103 068	60 621	58.8	58 343	39 382	14 936	4 026	7 629	50 714	56.6	2 276	309	3.8
1949	103 994	61 286	58.9	57 651	38 803	15 137	3 712	7 658	49 993	55.4	3 637	684	5.9
1950	104 995	62 208	59.2	58 918	39 394	15 824	3 703	7 160	51 758	56.1	3 288	782	5.3
1951	104 621	62 017	59.2	59 961	39 626	16 570	3 767	6 726	53 235	57.3	2 055	303	3.3
1952	105 231	62 138	59.0	60 250	39 578	16 958	3 719	6 500	53 749	57.3	1 883	232	3.0
1953	107 056	63 015	58.9	61 179	40 296	17 164	3 720	6 260	54 919	57.1	1 834	210	2.9
1954	108 321	63 643	58.8	60 109	39 634	17 000	3 475	6 205	53 904	55.5	3 532	812	5.5
1955	109 683	65 023	59.3	62 170	40 526	18 002	3 642	6 450	55 722	56.7	2 852	702	4.4
1956	110 954	66 552	60.0	63 799	41 216	18 767	3 818	6 283	57 514	57.5	2 750	533	4.1
1957	112 265	66 929	59.6	64 071	41 239	19 052	3 778	5 947	58 123	57.1	2 859	560	4.3
1958	113 727	67 639	59.5	63 036	40 411	19 043	3 582	5 586	57 450	55.4	4 602	1 452	6.8
1959	115 329	68 369	59.3	64 630	41 267	19 524	3 838	5 565	59 065	56.0	3 740	1 040	5.5
1960	117 245	69 628	59.4	65 778	41 543	20 105	4 129	5 458	60 318	56.1	3 852	957	5.5
1961	118 771	70 459	59.3	65 746	41 342	20 296	4 108	5 200	60 546	55.4	4 714	1 532	6.7
1962	120 153	70 614	58.8	66 702	41 815	20 693	4 195	4 944	61 759	55.5	3 911	1 119	5.5
1963	122 416	71 833	58.7	67 762	42 251	21 257	4 255	4 687	63 076	55.4	4 070	1 088	5.7
1964	124 485	73 091	58.7	69 305	42 886	21 903	4 516	4 523	64 782	55.7	3 786	973	5.2
1948													
January	102 603	60 095	58.6	58 061	39 386	14 556	4 119	8 077	49 984	56.6	2 034	311	3.4
February	102 698	60 524	58.9	58 196	39 480	14 621	4 095	7 696	50 500	56.7	2 328	283	3.8
March	102 771	60 070	58.5	57 671	39 098	14 481	4 092	7 333	50 338	56.1	2 399	292	4.0
April	102 831	60 677	59.0	58 291	39 157	15 001	4 133	7 557	50 734	56.7	2 386	324	3.9
May	102 923	59 972	58.3	57 854	39 139	14 712	4 003	7 141	50 713	56.2	2 118	329	3.5
June	102 992	60 957	59.2	58 743	39 392	15 213	4 138	7 591	51 152	57.0	2 214	322	3.6
July	103 216	61 181	59.3	58 968	39 607	15 348	4 013	7 602	51 366	57.1	2 213	295	3.6
August	103 240	60 806	58.9	58 456	39 510	14 994	3 952	7 562	50 894	56.6	2 350	332	3.9
September	103 291	60 815	58.9	58 513	39 324	15 207	3 982	7 865	50 648	56.6	2 302	298	3.8
October	103 361	60 646	58.7	58 387	39 522	14 956	3 909	7 626	50 761	56.5	2 259	324	3.7
November	103 424	60 702	58.7	58 417	39 459	15 054	3 904	7 624	50 793	56.5	2 285	282	3.8
December	103 468	61 169	59.1	58 740	39 539	15 137	4 064	7 984	50 756	56.8	2 429	305	4.0
1949													
January	103 529	60 771	58.7	58 175	39 233	14 991	3 951	7 790	50 385	56.2	2 596	315	4.3
February	103 559	61 057	59.0	58 208	39 117	15 117	3 974	8 022	50 186	56.2	2 849	374	4.7
March	103 665	61 073	58.9	58 043	39 015	15 069	3 959	8 008	50 035	56.0	3 030	414	5.0
April	103 739	61 007	58.8	57 747	38 993	14 978	3 776	7 911	49 836	55.7	3 260	483	5.3
May	103 845	61 259	59.0	57 552	38 701	15 066	3 785	8 067	49 485	55.4	3 707	602	6.1
June	103 930	60 948	58.6	57 172	38 632	15 003	3 537	7 802	49 370	55.0	3 776	705	6.2
July	104 042	61 301	58.9	57 190	38 405	15 244	3 541	8 021	49 169	55.0	4 111	848	6.7
August	104 121	61 590	59.2	57 397	38 610	15 181	3 606	7 604	49 793	55.1	4 193	917	6.8
September	104 219	61 633	59.1	57 584	38 744	15 129	3 711	7 297	50 287	55.3	4 049	973	6.6
October	104 338	62 185	59.6	57 269	38 394	15 260	3 615	6 814	50 455	54.9	4 916	1 000	7.9
November	104 421	62 005	59.4	58 009	38 860	15 422	3 727	7 497	50 512	55.6	3 996	1 056	6.4
December	104 524	61 908	59.2	57 845	38 908	15 300	3 637	7 379	50 466	55.3	4 063	961	6.6

[1] Not seasonally adjusted.
[2] In 1930 through 1943, the official BLS data count persons on work relief as unemployed. The unemployment rates for those years shown in parentheses count persons on work relief as employed, which is more consistent with the postwar practice. See notes and definitions.
. . . = Not available.

Table 10-1B. Summary Labor Force, Employment, and Unemployment: Historical—Continued

(Thousands of persons, percent, seasonally adjusted, except as noted.)

Year and month	Civilian noninstitutional population [1]	Civilian labor force Thousands of persons	Civilian labor force Participation rate (percent)	Total	Men, 20 years and over	Women, 20 years and over	Both sexes, 16 to 19 years	Agricultural	Nonagricultural	Employment-population ratio, percent	Total	Unemployed 15 weeks and over	Rate (percent)
1950													
January	104 619	61 661	58.9	57 635	38 780	15 255	3 600	7 065	50 570	55.1	4 026	947	6.5
February	104 737	61 687	58.9	57 751	38 818	15 339	3 594	7 057	50 694	55.1	3 936	947	6.4
March	104 844	61 604	58.8	57 728	38 851	15 366	3 511	7 116	50 612	55.1	3 876	912	6.3
April	104 943	62 158	59.2	58 583	39 100	15 831	3 652	7 264	51 319	55.8	3 575	920	5.8
May	105 014	62 083	59.1	58 649	39 416	15 628	3 605	7 277	51 372	55.8	3 434	890	5.5
June	105 104	62 419	59.4	59 052	39 476	15 953	3 623	7 285	51 767	56.2	3 367	868	5.4
July	105 194	62 121	59.1	59 001	39 517	15 793	3 691	7 126	51 875	56.1	3 120	769	5.0
August	105 282	62 596	59.5	59 797	39 879	16 124	3 794	7 248	52 549	56.8	2 799	633	4.5
September	105 269	62 349	59.2	59 575	39 865	15 902	3 808	6 992	52 583	56.6	2 774	648	4.4
October	105 096	62 428	59.4	59 803	39 737	16 175	3 891	7 371	52 432	56.9	2 625	545	4.2
November	104 979	62 286	59.3	59 697	39 668	16 195	3 834	7 163	52 534	56.9	2 589	507	4.2
December	104 872	62 068	59.2	59 429	39 536	16 149	3 744	6 760	52 669	56.7	2 639	482	4.3
1951													
January	104 844	61 941	59.1	59 636	39 595	16 279	3 762	6 828	52 808	56.9	2 305	438	3.7
February	104 604	61 778	59.1	59 661	39 695	16 257	3 709	6 738	52 923	57.0	2 117	386	3.4
March	104 629	62 526	59.8	60 401	40 013	16 557	3 831	6 858	53 543	57.7	2 125	355	3.4
April	104 541	61 808	59.1	59 889	39 804	16 426	3 659	6 722	53 167	57.3	1 919	294	3.1
May	104 491	62 044	59.4	60 188	39 752	16 581	3 855	6 752	53 436	57.6	1 856	269	3.0
June	104 488	61 615	59.0	59 620	39 538	16 368	3 714	6 529	53 091	57.1	1 995	258	3.2
July	104 504	62 106	59.4	60 156	39 483	16 898	3 775	6 601	53 555	57.6	1 950	260	3.1
August	104 536	61 927	59.2	59 994	39 508	16 665	3 821	6 790	53 204	57.4	1 933	249	3.1
September	104 588	61 780	59.1	59 713	39 416	16 504	3 793	6 558	53 155	57.1	2 067	223	3.3
October	104 690	62 204	59.4	60 010	39 555	16 674	3 781	6 636	53 374	57.3	2 194	269	3.5
November	104 740	62 014	59.2	59 836	39 504	16 669	3 663	6 699	53 137	57.1	2 178	316	3.5
December	104 810	62 457	59.6	60 497	39 691	16 946	3 860	7 065	53 432	57.7	1 960	269	3.1
1952													
January	104 862	62 432	59.5	60 460	39 714	17 001	3 745	7 148	53 312	57.7	1 972	282	3.2
February	104 868	62 419	59.5	60 462	39 772	16 935	3 755	7 020	53 442	57.7	1 957	248	3.1
March	104 860	61 721	58.9	59 908	39 580	16 627	3 701	6 468	53 440	57.1	1 813	234	2.9
April	104 906	61 720	58.8	59 909	39 542	16 659	3 708	6 525	53 384	57.1	1 811	242	2.9
May	104 996	62 058	59.1	60 195	39 588	16 844	3 763	6 334	53 861	57.3	1 863	219	3.0
June	105 118	62 103	59.1	60 219	39 558	16 837	3 824	6 529	53 690	57.3	1 884	210	3.0
July	105 246	61 962	58.9	59 971	39 496	16 778	3 697	6 334	53 637	57.0	1 991	194	3.2
August	105 346	61 877	58.7	59 790	39 289	16 867	3 634	6 174	53 616	56.8	2 087	211	3.4
September	105 436	62 457	59.2	60 521	39 386	17 477	3 658	6 537	53 984	57.4	1 936	249	3.1
October	105 591	61 971	58.7	60 132	39 451	17 032	3 649	6 363	53 769	56.9	1 839	230	3.0
November	105 706	62 491	59.1	60 748	39 549	17 450	3 749	6 509	54 239	57.5	1 743	216	2.8
December	105 812	62 621	59.2	60 954	40 011	17 181	3 762	6 361	54 593	57.6	1 667	238	2.7
1953													
January	106 594	63 439	59.5	61 600	40 256	17 482	3 862	6 642	54 958	57.8	1 839	268	2.9
February	106 678	63 520	59.5	61 884	40 546	17 321	4 017	6 463	55 421	58.0	1 636	208	2.6
March	106 744	63 657	59.6	62 010	40 648	17 397	3 965	6 420	55 590	58.1	1 647	213	2.6
April	106 826	63 167	59.1	61 444	40 346	17 242	3 856	6 362	55 082	57.5	1 723	180	2.7
May	106 910	62 615	58.6	61 019	40 323	16 983	3 713	5 937	55 082	57.1	1 596	176	2.5
June	106 978	63 063	58.9	61 456	40 358	17 301	3 797	6 361	55 095	57.4	1 607	213	2.5
July	107 034	63 057	58.9	61 397	40 378	17 341	3 678	6 267	55 130	57.4	1 660	168	2.6
August	107 132	62 816	58.6	61 151	40 352	17 108	3 691	6 319	54 832	57.1	1 665	177	2.7
September	107 253	62 727	58.5	60 906	40 192	17 063	3 651	6 198	54 708	56.8	1 821	178	2.9
October	107 383	62 867	58.5	60 893	40 155	17 236	3 502	6 096	54 797	56.7	1 974	190	3.1
November	107 504	62 949	58.6	60 738	40 163	16 974	3 601	6 345	54 393	56.5	2 211	259	3.5
December	107 623	62 795	58.3	59 977	39 885	16 599	3 493	5 929	54 048	55.7	2 818	309	4.5
1954													
January	107 763	63 101	58.6	60 024	39 834	16 574	3 616	6 073	53 951	55.7	3 077	372	4.9
February	107 880	63 994	59.3	60 663	39 899	17 162	3 602	6 590	54 073	56.2	3 331	532	5.2
March	107 987	63 793	59.1	60 186	39 497	17 022	3 667	6 395	53 791	55.7	3 607	765	5.7
April	108 080	63 934	59.2	60 185	39 613	17 015	3 557	6 142	54 043	55.7	3 749	774	5.9
May	108 184	63 675	58.9	59 908	39 467	16 975	3 466	6 210	53 698	55.4	3 767	879	5.9
June	108 267	63 343	58.5	59 792	39 476	16 894	3 422	6 162	53 630	55.2	3 551	880	5.6
July	108 344	63 302	58.4	59 643	39 467	16 777	3 399	6 222	53 421	55.0	3 659	932	5.8
August	108 440	63 707	58.7	59 853	39 582	16 868	3 403	6 087	53 766	55.2	3 854	1 002	6.0
September	108 546	64 209	59.2	60 282	39 702	17 133	3 447	6 453	53 829	55.5	3 927	1 017	6.1
October	108 668	63 936	58.8	60 270	39 618	17 209	3 443	6 242	54 028	55.5	3 666	1 009	5.7
November	108 798	63 759	58.6	60 357	39 745	17 213	3 399	5 934	54 423	55.5	3 402	975	5.3
December	108 892	63 312	58.1	60 116	39 763	17 121	3 232	5 848	54 268	55.2	3 196	827	5.0

[1]Not seasonally adjusted.
[2]In 1930 through 1943, the official BLS data count persons on work relief as unemployed. The unemployment rates for those years shown in parentheses count persons on work relief as employed, which is more consistent with the postwar practice. See notes and definitions.

Table 10-1B. Summary Labor Force, Employment, and Unemployment: Historical—*Continued*

(Thousands of persons, percent, seasonally adjusted, except as noted.)

Year and month	Civilian noninsti- tutional popu- lation [1]	Civilian labor force		Employment, thousands of persons						Employ- ment- population ratio, percent	Unemployment [2]		
		Thousands of persons	Participa- tion rate (percent)	Total	By age and sex			By industry			Thousands of persons		Rate (percent)
					Men, 20 years and over	Women, 20 years and over	Both sexes, 16 to 19 years	Agri- cultural	Nonagri- cultural		Total	Unem- ployed 15 weeks and over	
1955													
January	109 059	63 910	58.6	60 753	39 937	17 375	3 441	6 113	54 640	55.7	3 157	882	4.9
February	109 078	63 696	58.4	60 727	39 964	17 413	3 350	5 854	54 873	55.7	2 969	826	4.7
March	109 254	63 882	58.5	60 964	40 111	17 415	3 438	6 242	54 722	55.8	2 918	816	4.6
April	109 377	64 564	59.0	61 515	40 120	17 867	3 528	6 363	55 152	56.2	3 049	811	4.7
May	109 544	64 381	58.8	61 634	40 410	17 665	3 559	6 327	55 307	56.3	2 747	734	4.3
June	109 680	64 482	58.8	61 781	40 444	17 837	3 500	6 243	55 538	56.3	2 701	668	4.2
July	109 792	65 145	59.3	62 513	40 751	18 123	3 639	6 438	56 075	56.9	2 632	640	4.0
August	109 882	65 581	59.7	62 797	40 747	18 377	3 673	6 575	56 222	57.1	2 784	535	4.2
September	109 977	65 628	59.7	62 950	40 920	18 285	3 745	6 819	56 131	57.2	2 678	558	4.1
October	110 085	65 821	59.8	62 991	40 858	18 327	3 806	6 728	56 263	57.2	2 830	572	4.3
November	110 177	66 037	59.9	63 257	40 936	18 422	3 899	6 655	56 602	57.4	2 780	564	4.2
December	110 296	66 445	60.2	63 684	41 063	18 630	3 991	6 653	57 031	57.7	2 761	581	4.2
1956													
January	110 390	66 419	60.2	63 753	41 203	18 691	3 859	6 590	57 163	57.8	2 666	561	4.0
February	110 478	66 124	59.9	63 518	41 175	18 582	3 761	6 457	57 061	57.5	2 606	545	3.9
March	110 582	66 175	59.8	63 411	41 199	18 496	3 716	6 221	57 190	57.3	2 764	521	4.2
April	110 650	66 264	59.9	63 614	41 289	18 629	3 696	6 460	57 154	57.5	2 650	476	4.0
May	110 810	66 722	60.2	63 861	41 166	18 844	3 851	6 375	57 486	57.6	2 861	506	4.3
June	110 903	66 702	60.1	63 820	41 196	18 748	3 876	6 335	57 485	57.5	2 882	516	4.3
July	111 019	66 752	60.1	63 800	41 216	18 718	3 866	6 320	57 480	57.5	2 952	523	4.4
August	111 099	66 673	60.0	63 972	41 265	18 864	3 843	6 280	57 692	57.6	2 701	543	4.1
September	111 222	66 714	60.0	64 079	41 221	19 019	3 839	6 375	57 704	57.6	2 635	577	3.9
October	111 335	66 546	59.8	63 975	41 261	18 928	3 786	6 137	57 838	57.5	2 571	530	3.9
November	111 432	66 657	59.8	63 796	41 208	18 846	3 742	5 997	57 799	57.3	2 861	575	4.3
December	111 526	66 700	59.8	63 910	41 192	18 859	3 859	5 806	58 104	57.3	2 790	567	4.2
1957													
January	111 626	66 428	59.5	63 632	41 168	18 740	3 724	5 790	57 842	57.0	2 796	509	4.2
February	111 711	66 879	59.9	64 257	41 341	19 115	3 801	6 125	58 132	57.5	2 622	530	3.9
March	111 824	66 913	59.8	64 404	41 500	19 066	3 838	5 963	58 441	57.6	2 509	514	3.7
April	111 933	66 647	59.5	64 047	41 345	18 937	3 765	5 836	58 211	57.2	2 600	516	3.9
May	112 031	66 695	59.5	63 985	41 334	18 897	3 754	5 999	57 986	57.1	2 710	538	4.1
June	112 172	67 052	59.8	64 196	41 411	18 973	3 812	6 002	58 194	57.2	2 856	526	4.3
July	112 317	67 336	60.0	64 540	41 472	19 262	3 806	6 401	58 139	57.5	2 796	535	4.2
August	112 421	66 706	59.3	63 959	41 243	19 020	3 696	5 898	58 061	56.9	2 747	542	4.1
September	112 554	67 064	59.6	64 121	41 213	19 116	3 792	5 728	58 393	57.0	2 943	559	4.4
October	112 710	67 066	59.5	64 046	41 069	19 160	3 817	5 875	58 171	56.8	3 020	650	4.5
November	112 874	67 123	59.5	63 669	40 853	19 082	3 734	5 686	57 983	56.4	3 454	674	5.1
December	113 013	67 398	59.6	63 922	40 884	19 285	3 753	6 037	57 885	56.6	3 476	731	5.2
1958													
January	113 138	67 095	59.3	63 220	40 617	19 035	3 568	5 831	57 389	55.9	3 875	879	5.8
February	113 234	67 201	59.3	62 898	40 336	18 951	3 611	5 654	57 244	55.5	4 303	1 005	6.4
March	113 337	67 223	59.3	62 731	40 180	18 968	3 583	5 561	57 170	55.3	4 492	1 128	6.7
April	113 415	67 647	59.6	62 631	40 129	18 969	3 533	5 602	57 029	55.2	5 016	1 387	7.4
May	113 534	67 895	59.8	62 874	40 253	18 978	3 643	5 647	57 227	55.4	5 021	1 493	7.4
June	113 647	67 674	59.5	62 730	40 208	19 008	3 514	5 510	57 220	55.2	4 944	1 677	7.3
July	113 727	67 824	59.6	62 745	40 270	19 039	3 436	5 525	57 220	55.2	5 079	1 796	7.5
August	113 835	68 037	59.8	63 012	40 343	19 103	3 566	5 673	57 339	55.4	5 025	1 888	7.4
September	113 977	68 002	59.7	63 181	40 564	19 033	3 584	5 453	57 728	55.4	4 821	1 795	7.1
October	114 138	68 045	59.6	63 475	40 699	19 091	3 685	5 563	57 912	55.6	4 570	1 708	6.7
November	114 283	67 658	59.2	63 470	40 684	19 157	3 629	5 571	57 899	55.5	4 188	1 570	6.2
December	114 429	67 740	59.2	63 549	40 666	19 170	3 713	5 521	58 028	55.5	4 191	1 490	6.2
1959													
January	114 582	67 936	59.3	63 868	40 769	19 292	3 807	5 481	58 387	55.7	4 068	1 396	6.0
February	114 712	67 649	59.0	63 684	40 699	19 167	3 818	5 429	58 255	55.5	3 965	1 277	5.9
March	114 849	68 068	59.3	64 267	41 079	19 379	3 809	5 677	58 590	56.0	3 801	1 210	5.6
April	114 986	68 339	59.4	64 768	41 419	19 498	3 851	5 893	58 875	56.3	3 571	1 039	5.2
May	115 144	68 178	59.2	64 699	41 355	19 565	3 779	5 792	58 907	56.2	3 479	965	5.1
June	115 287	68 278	59.2	64 849	41 387	19 658	3 804	5 712	59 137	56.3	3 429	963	5.0
July	115 429	68 539	59.4	65 011	41 596	19 595	3 820	5 564	59 447	56.3	3 528	889	5.1
August	115 555	68 432	59.2	64 844	41 485	19 568	3 791	5 442	59 402	56.1	3 588	889	5.2
September	115 668	68 545	59.3	64 770	41 351	19 531	3 888	5 447	59 323	56.0	3 775	895	5.5
October	115 798	68 821	59.4	64 911	41 362	19 702	3 847	5 355	59 556	56.1	3 910	883	5.7
November	115 916	68 533	59.1	64 530	41 062	19 594	3 874	5 480	59 050	55.7	4 003	982	5.8
December	116 040	68 994	59.5	65 341	41 651	19 717	3 973	5 458	59 883	56.3	3 653	920	5.3

[1] Not seasonally adjusted.
[2] In 1930 through 1943, the official BLS data count persons on work relief as unemployed. The unemployment rates for those years shown in parentheses count persons on work relief as employed, which is more consistent with the postwar practice. See notes and definitions.

Table 10-1B. Summary Labor Force, Employment, and Unemployment: Historical—*Continued*

(Thousands of persons, percent, seasonally adjusted, except as noted.)

Year and month	Civilian noninsti-tutional popu-lation [1]	Civilian labor force		Employment, thousands of persons						Employ-ment-population ratio, percent	Unemployment [2]		
		Thousands of persons	Participa-tion rate (percent)	Total	By age and sex			By industry			Thousands of persons		Rate (percent)
					Men, 20 years and over	Women, 20 years and over	Both sexes, 16 to 19 years	Agri-cultural	Nonagri-cultural		Total	Unem-ployed 15 weeks and over	
1960													
January	116 594	68 962	59.1	65 347	41 637	19 686	4 024	5 458	59 889	56.0	3 615	915	5.2
February	116 702	68 949	59.1	65 620	41 729	19 765	4 126	5 443	60 177	56.2	3 329	841	4.8
March	116 827	68 399	58.5	64 673	41 320	19 388	3 965	4 959	59 714	55.4	3 726	959	5.4
April	116 910	69 579	59.5	65 959	41 641	20 110	4 208	5 471	60 488	56.4	3 620	896	5.2
May	117 033	69 626	59.5	66 057	41 668	20 186	4 203	5 359	60 698	56.4	3 569	797	5.1
June	117 167	69 934	59.7	66 168	41 553	20 290	4 325	5 416	60 752	56.5	3 766	854	5.4
July	117 281	69 745	59.5	65 909	41 490	20 257	4 162	5 542	60 367	56.2	3 836	921	5.5
August	117 431	69 841	59.5	65 895	41 503	20 316	4 076	5 520	60 375	56.1	3 946	927	5.6
September	117 521	70 151	59.7	66 267	41 604	20 493	4 170	5 755	60 512	56.4	3 884	982	5.5
October	117 643	69 884	59.4	65 632	41 464	20 076	4 092	5 436	60 196	55.8	4 252	1 189	6.1
November	117 829	70 439	59.8	66 109	41 543	20 384	4 182	5 513	60 596	56.1	4 330	1 223	6.1
December	118 001	70 395	59.7	65 778	41 416	20 332	4 030	5 622	60 156	55.7	4 617	1 142	6.6
1961													
January	118 155	70 447	59.6	65 776	41 363	20 325	4 088	5 422	60 354	55.7	4 671	1 328	6.6
February	118 250	70 420	59.6	65 588	41 177	20 392	4 019	5 472	60 116	55.5	4 832	1 416	6.9
March	118 358	70 703	59.7	65 850	41 273	20 459	4 118	5 406	60 444	55.6	4 853	1 463	6.9
April	118 503	70 267	59.3	65 374	41 206	20 145	4 023	5 037	60 337	55.2	4 893	1 598	7.0
May	118 638	70 452	59.4	65 449	41 139	20 261	4 049	5 099	60 350	55.2	5 003	1 686	7.1
June	118 767	70 878	59.7	65 993	41 349	20 446	4 198	5 220	60 773	55.6	4 885	1 651	6.9
July	118 889	70 536	59.3	65 608	41 245	20 252	4 111	5 153	60 455	55.2	4 928	1 830	7.0
August	119 006	70 534	59.3	65 852	41 362	20 279	4 211	5 366	60 486	55.3	4 682	1 649	6.6
September	119 107	70 217	59.0	65 541	41 400	20 112	4 029	5 021	60 520	55.0	4 676	1 531	6.7
October	119 202	70 492	59.1	65 919	41 509	20 338	4 072	5 203	60 716	55.3	4 573	1 481	6.5
November	119 153	70 376	59.1	66 081	41 556	20 330	4 195	5 090	60 991	55.5	4 295	1 388	6.1
December	119 214	70 077	58.8	65 900	41 534	20 287	4 079	4 992	60 908	55.3	4 177	1 361	6.0
1962													
January	119 300	70 189	58.8	66 108	41 547	20 501	4 060	5 094	61 014	55.4	4 081	1 235	5.8
February	119 360	70 409	59.0	66 538	41 745	20 693	4 100	5 289	61 249	55.7	3 871	1 244	5.5
March	119 476	70 414	58.9	66 493	41 696	20 567	4 230	5 157	61 336	55.7	3 921	1 162	5.6
April	119 702	70 278	58.7	66 372	41 647	20 567	4 158	5 009	61 363	55.4	3 906	1 122	5.6
May	119 813	70 551	58.9	66 688	41 847	20 558	4 283	4 964	61 724	55.7	3 863	1 134	5.5
June	119 943	70 514	58.8	66 670	41 761	20 547	4 362	4 943	61 727	55.6	3 844	1 079	5.5
July	120 128	70 302	58.5	66 483	41 671	20 592	4 220	4 840	61 643	55.3	3 819	1 049	5.4
August	120 323	70 981	59.0	66 968	41 900	20 841	4 227	4 866	62 102	55.7	4 013	1 081	5.7
September	120 653	71 153	59.0	67 192	42 020	20 982	4 190	4 867	62 325	55.7	3 961	1 096	5.6
October	120 856	70 917	58.7	67 114	42 086	20 856	4 172	4 816	62 298	55.5	3 803	1 022	5.4
November	121 045	70 871	58.5	66 847	41 985	20 794	4 068	4 831	62 016	55.2	4 024	1 051	5.7
December	121 236	70 854	58.4	66 947	41 934	20 831	4 182	4 647	62 300	55.2	3 907	1 068	5.5
1963													
January	121 463	71 146	58.6	67 072	41 938	20 933	4 201	4 882	62 190	55.2	4 074	1 122	5.7
February	121 633	71 262	58.6	67 024	41 876	21 046	4 102	4 652	62 372	55.1	4 238	1 137	5.9
March	121 824	71 423	58.6	67 351	42 047	21 162	4 142	4 696	62 655	55.3	4 072	1 087	5.7
April	121 986	71 697	58.8	67 642	42 131	21 281	4 230	4 670	62 972	55.5	4 055	1 071	5.7
May	122 162	71 832	58.8	67 615	42 145	21 225	4 245	4 729	62 886	55.3	4 217	1 157	5.9
June	122 352	71 626	58.5	67 649	42 268	21 185	4 196	4 642	63 007	55.3	3 977	1 067	5.6
July	122 521	71 956	58.7	67 905	42 427	21 268	4 210	4 694	63 211	55.4	4 051	1 070	5.6
August	122 667	71 786	58.5	67 908	42 400	21 185	4 323	4 604	63 304	55.4	3 878	1 114	5.4
September	122 821	72 131	58.7	68 174	42 500	21 317	4 357	4 650	63 524	55.5	3 957	1 069	5.5
October	123 014	72 281	58.8	68 294	42 437	21 456	4 401	4 702	63 592	55.5	3 987	1 071	5.5
November	123 192	72 418	58.8	68 267	42 415	21 553	4 299	4 694	63 573	55.4	4 151	1 054	5.7
December	123 360	72 188	58.5	68 213	42 427	21 481	4 305	4 629	63 584	55.3	3 975	1 007	5.5
1964													
January	123 560	72 356	58.6	68 327	42 510	21 462	4 355	4 603	63 724	55.3	4 029	1 057	5.6
February	123 707	72 683	58.8	68 751	42 579	21 652	4 520	4 563	64 188	55.6	3 932	1 015	5.4
March	123 857	72 713	58.7	68 763	42 600	21 685	4 478	4 366	64 397	55.5	3 950	1 039	5.4
April	124 019	73 274	59.1	69 356	42 885	22 110	4 361	4 414	64 942	55.9	3 918	934	5.3
May	124 204	73 395	59.1	69 631	43 025	22 103	4 503	4 603	65 028	56.1	3 764	975	5.1
June	124 386	73 032	58.7	69 218	42 760	21 995	4 463	4 556	64 662	55.6	3 814	1 047	5.2
July	124 567	73 007	58.6	69 399	42 998	21 846	4 555	4 591	64 808	55.7	3 608	1 002	4.9
August	124 731	73 118	58.6	69 463	42 963	22 002	4 498	4 573	64 890	55.7	3 655	934	5.0
September	124 920	73 290	58.7	69 578	43 009	21 863	4 706	4 619	64 959	55.7	3 712	917	5.1
October	125 108	73 308	58.6	69 582	43 023	21 984	4 575	4 550	65 032	55.6	3 726	903	5.1
November	125 291	73 286	58.5	69 735	43 171	21 954	4 610	4 496	65 239	55.7	3 551	922	4.8
December	125 468	73 465	58.6	69 814	43 109	22 136	4 569	4 322	65 492	55.6	3 651	873	5.0

[1] Not seasonally adjusted.
[2] In 1930 through 1943, the official BLS data count persons on work relief as unemployed. The unemployment rates for those years shown in parentheses count persons on work relief as employed, which is more consistent with the postwar practice. See notes and definitions.

Table 10-1B. Summary Labor Force, Employment, and Unemployment: Historical—*Continued*

(Thousands of persons, percent, seasonally adjusted, except as noted.)

Year and month	Civilian noninsti-tutional popu-lation [1]	Civilian labor force		Employment, thousands of persons						Employ-ment-population ratio, percent	Unemployment [2]		
					By age and sex			By industry			Thousands of persons		
		Thousands of persons	Participa-tion rate (percent)	Total	Men, 20 years and over	Women, 20 years and over	Both sexes, 16 to 19 years	Agri-cultural	Nonagri-cultural		Total	Unem-ployed 15 weeks and over	Rate (percent)
1965													
January	125 647	73 569	58.6	69 997	43 237	22 282	4 478	4 271	65 726	55.7	3 572	793	4.9
February	125 810	73 857	58.7	70 127	43 279	22 276	4 572	4 322	65 805	55.7	3 730	919	5.1
March	125 985	73 949	58.7	70 439	43 370	22 373	4 696	4 318	66 121	55.9	3 510	796	4.7
April	126 155	74 228	58.8	70 633	43 397	22 416	4 820	4 424	66 209	56.0	3 595	796	4.8
May	126 320	74 466	59.0	71 034	43 579	22 494	4 961	4 724	66 310	56.2	3 432	736	4.6
June	126 499	74 412	58.8	71 025	43 487	22 759	4 779	4 444	66 581	56.1	3 387	786	4.6
July	126 573	74 761	59.1	71 460	43 489	22 841	5 130	4 390	67 070	56.5	3 301	683	4.4
August	126 756	74 616	58.9	71 362	43 447	22 783	5 132	4 355	67 007	56.3	3 254	733	4.4
September	126 906	74 502	58.7	71 286	43 371	22 684	5 231	4 271	67 015	56.2	3 216	732	4.3
October	127 043	74 838	58.9	71 695	43 461	22 819	5 415	4 418	67 277	56.4	3 143	672	4.2
November	127 171	74 797	58.8	71 724	43 447	22 829	5 448	4 093	67 631	56.4	3 073	645	4.1
December	127 294	75 093	59.0	72 062	43 513	22 983	5 566	4 159	67 903	56.6	3 031	659	4.0
1966													
January	127 394	75 186	59.0	72 198	43 495	23 098	5 605	4 077	68 121	56.7	2 988	623	4.0
February	127 514	74 954	58.8	72 134	43 528	23 089	5 517	4 078	68 056	56.6	2 820	594	3.8
March	127 626	75 075	58.8	72 188	43 576	23 109	5 503	4 069	68 119	56.6	2 887	583	3.8
April	127 744	75 338	59.0	72 510	43 679	23 227	5 604	4 108	68 402	56.8	2 828	575	3.8
May	127 879	75 447	59.0	72 497	43 710	23 282	5 505	3 930	68 567	56.7	2 950	534	3.9
June	127 983	75 647	59.1	72 775	43 662	23 359	5 754	3 967	68 808	56.9	2 872	475	3.8
July	128 102	75 736	59.1	72 860	43 574	23 422	5 864	3 920	68 940	56.9	2 876	427	3.8
August	128 240	76 046	59.3	73 146	43 636	23 605	5 905	3 921	69 225	57.0	2 900	464	3.8
September	128 359	76 056	59.3	73 258	43 718	23 881	5 659	3 952	69 306	57.1	2 798	488	3.7
October	128 494	76 199	59.3	73 401	43 776	23 881	5 744	3 912	69 489	57.1	2 798	494	3.7
November	128 627	76 610	59.6	73 840	43 804	24 130	5 906	3 945	69 895	57.4	2 770	464	3.6
December	128 730	76 641	59.5	73 729	43 820	24 025	5 884	3 906	69 823	57.3	2 912	488	3.8
1967													
January	128 909	76 639	59.5	73 671	44 029	23 872	5 770	3 890	69 781	57.1	2 968	489	3.9
February	129 032	76 521	59.3	73 606	43 997	23 919	5 690	3 723	69 883	57.0	2 915	459	3.8
March	129 190	76 328	59.1	73 439	43 922	23 832	5 685	3 757	69 682	56.8	2 889	436	3.8
April	129 344	76 777	59.4	73 882	44 061	24 161	5 660	3 748	70 134	57.1	2 895	428	3.8
May	129 515	76 773	59.3	73 844	44 100	24 172	5 572	3 658	70 186	57.0	2 929	417	3.8
June	129 722	77 270	59.6	74 278	44 230	24 303	5 745	3 689	70 589	57.3	2 992	422	3.9
July	129 918	77 464	59.6	74 520	44 364	24 416	5 740	3 833	70 687	57.4	2 944	412	3.8
August	130 187	77 712	59.7	74 767	44 410	24 600	5 757	3 963	70 804	57.4	2 945	441	3.8
September	130 392	77 812	59.7	74 854	44 535	24 683	5 636	3 851	71 003	57.4	2 958	448	3.8
October	130 582	78 194	59.9	75 051	44 610	24 802	5 639	4 008	71 043	57.5	3 143	472	4.0
November	130 754	78 191	59.8	75 125	44 625	24 914	5 586	3 933	71 192	57.5	3 066	490	3.9
December	130 936	78 491	59.9	75 473	44 719	25 104	5 650	4 076	71 397	57.6	3 018	485	3.8
1968													
January	131 112	77 578	59.2	74 700	44 606	24 581	5 513	3 908	70 792	57.0	2 878	503	3.7
February	131 277	78 230	59.6	75 229	44 659	24 881	5 689	3 959	71 270	57.3	3 001	468	3.8
March	131 412	78 256	59.6	75 379	44 663	25 019	5 697	3 904	71 475	57.4	2 877	447	3.7
April	131 553	78 270	59.5	75 561	44 753	25 072	5 736	3 875	71 686	57.4	2 709	393	3.5
May	131 712	78 847	59.9	76 107	44 841	25 513	5 753	3 814	72 293	57.8	2 740	395	3.5
June	131 872	79 120	60.0	76 182	44 914	25 466	5 802	3 806	72 376	57.8	2 938	405	3.7
July	132 053	78 970	59.8	76 087	44 935	25 347	5 805	3 820	72 267	57.6	2 883	426	3.7
August	132 251	78 811	59.6	76 043	44 897	25 201	5 945	3 736	72 307	57.5	2 768	393	3.5
September	132 446	78 858	59.5	76 172	44 893	25 445	5 834	3 758	72 414	57.5	2 686	375	3.4
October	132 617	78 913	59.5	76 224	44 884	25 475	5 865	3 741	72 483	57.5	2 689	386	3.4
November	132 903	79 209	59.6	76 494	44 996	25 674	5 824	3 758	72 736	57.6	2 715	357	3.4
December	133 120	79 463	59.7	76 778	45 262	25 712	5 804	3 746	73 032	57.7	2 685	351	3.4
1969													
January	133 324	79 523	59.6	76 805	45 154	25 777	5 874	3 704	73 101	57.6	2 718	339	3.4
February	133 465	80 019	60.0	77 327	45 339	26 092	5 896	3 770	73 557	57.9	2 692	358	3.4
March	133 639	80 079	59.9	77 367	45 305	26 115	5 947	3 668	73 699	57.9	2 712	353	3.4
April	133 821	80 281	60.0	77 523	45 262	26 233	6 028	3 629	73 894	57.9	2 758	386	3.4
May	134 027	80 125	59.8	77 412	45 278	26 283	5 851	3 706	73 706	57.8	2 713	387	3.4
June	134 213	80 696	60.1	77 880	45 313	26 429	6 138	3 663	74 217	58.0	2 816	368	3.5
July	134 414	80 827	60.1	77 959	45 305	26 516	6 138	3 548	74 411	58.0	2 868	377	3.5
August	134 597	81 106	60.3	78 250	45 513	26 556	6 181	3 613	74 637	58.1	2 856	373	3.5
September	134 774	81 290	60.3	78 250	45 447	26 572	6 231	3 551	74 699	58.1	3 040	391	3.7
October	135 012	81 494	60.4	78 445	45 488	26 658	6 299	3 517	74 928	58.1	3 049	374	3.7
November	135 239	81 397	60.2	78 541	45 505	26 652	6 384	3 477	75 064	58.1	2 856	392	3.5
December	135 489	81 624	60.2	78 740	45 577	26 832	6 331	3 409	75 331	58.1	2 884	413	3.5

[1]Not seasonally adjusted.
[2]In 1930 through 1943, the official BLS data count persons on work relief as unemployed. The unemployment rates for those years shown in parentheses count persons on work relief as employed, which is more consistent with the postwar practice. See notes and definitions.

Table 10-1B. Summary Labor Force, Employment, and Unemployment: Historical—*Continued*

(Thousands of persons, percent, seasonally adjusted, except as noted.)

Year and month	Civilian noninstitutional population¹	Civilian labor force Thousands of persons	Civilian labor force Participation rate (percent)	Employment Total	By age and sex Men, 20 years and over	By age and sex Women, 20 years and over	By age and sex Both sexes, 16 to 19 years	By industry Agricultural	By industry Nonagricultural	Employment-population ratio, percent	Unemployment² Total	Unemployed 15 weeks and over	Rate (percent)
1970													
January	135 713	81 981	60.4	78 780	45 654	26 908	6 218	3 422	75 358	58.0	3 201	431	3.9
February	135 957	82 151	60.4	78 698	45 627	26 828	6 243	3 439	75 259	57.9	3 453	470	4.2
March	136 179	82 498	60.6	78 863	45 668	26 933	6 262	3 499	75 364	57.9	3 635	534	4.4
April	136 416	82 727	60.6	78 930	45 679	27 114	6 137	3 568	75 362	57.9	3 797	602	4.6
May	136 686	82 483	60.3	78 564	45 666	26 739	6 159	3 547	75 017	57.5	3 919	591	4.8
June	136 928	82 484	60.2	78 413	45 554	26 904	5 955	3 555	74 858	57.3	4 071	657	4.9
July	137 196	82 901	60.4	78 726	45 516	27 083	6 127	3 517	75 209	57.4	4 175	662	5.0
August	137 455	82 880	60.3	78 624	45 495	27 011	6 118	3 418	75 206	57.2	4 256	705	5.1
September	137 717	82 954	60.2	78 498	45 535	26 784	6 179	3 451	75 047	57.0	4 456	788	5.4
October	137 988	83 276	60.4	78 685	45 508	27 058	6 119	3 337	75 348	57.0	4 591	771	5.5
November	138 264	83 548	60.4	78 650	45 540	27 020	6 090	3 372	75 278	56.9	4 898	871	5.9
December	138 529	83 670	60.4	78 594	45 466	27 038	6 090	3 380	75 214	56.7	5 076	1 102	6.1
1971													
January	138 795	83 850	60.4	78 864	45 527	27 173	6 164	3 393	75 471	56.8	4 986	1 113	5.9
February	139 021	83 603	60.1	78 700	45 455	27 040	6 205	3 288	75 412	56.6	4 903	1 068	5.9
March	139 285	83 575	60.0	78 588	45 520	26 967	6 101	3 356	75 232	56.4	4 987	1 098	6.0
April	139 566	83 946	60.1	78 987	45 789	26 984	6 214	3 574	75 413	56.6	4 959	1 149	5.9
May	139 826	84 135	60.2	79 139	45 917	27 056	6 166	3 449	75 690	56.6	4 996	1 173	5.9
June	140 090	83 706	59.8	78 757	45 879	27 013	5 865	3 334	75 423	56.2	4 949	1 167	5.9
July	140 343	84 340	60.1	79 305	46 000	27 054	6 251	3 386	75 919	56.5	5 035	1 251	6.0
August	140 596	84 673	60.2	79 539	46 041	27 171	6 327	3 395	76 144	56.6	5 134	1 261	6.1
September	140 869	84 731	60.1	79 689	46 090	27 390	6 209	3 367	76 322	56.6	5 042	1 239	6.0
October	141 146	84 872	60.1	79 918	46 132	27 538	6 248	3 405	76 513	56.6	4 954	1 268	5.8
November	141 393	85 458	60.4	80 297	46 209	27 721	6 367	3 410	76 887	56.8	5 161	1 277	6.0
December	141 666	85 625	60.4	80 471	46 280	27 791	6 400	3 371	77 100	56.8	5 154	1 283	6.0
1972													
January	142 736	85 978	60.2	80 959	46 471	27 956	6 532	3 366	77 593	56.7	5 019	1 257	5.8
February	143 017	86 036	60.2	81 108	46 600	28 016	6 492	3 358	77 750	56.7	4 928	1 292	5.7
March	143 263	86 611	60.5	81 573	46 821	28 126	6 626	3 438	78 135	56.9	5 038	1 232	5.8
April	143 483	86 614	60.4	81 655	46 863	28 114	6 678	3 382	78 273	56.9	4 959	1 203	5.7
May	143 760	86 809	60.4	81 887	46 950	28 184	6 753	3 412	78 475	57.0	4 922	1 168	5.7
June	144 033	87 006	60.4	82 083	47 147	28 175	6 761	3 402	78 681	57.0	4 923	1 141	5.7
July	144 285	87 143	60.4	82 230	47 244	28 225	6 761	3 461	78 769	57.0	4 913	1 154	5.6
August	144 522	87 517	60.6	82 578	47 321	28 382	6 875	3 603	78 975	57.1	4 939	1 156	5.6
September	144 761	87 392	60.4	82 543	47 394	28 417	6 732	3 568	78 975	57.0	4 849	1 131	5.5
October	144 988	87 491	60.3	82 616	47 354	28 438	6 824	3 634	78 982	57.0	4 875	1 123	5.6
November	145 211	87 592	60.3	82 990	47 529	28 567	6 894	3 517	79 473	57.2	4 602	1 040	5.3
December	145 446	87 943	60.5	83 400	47 747	28 698	6 955	3 596	79 804	57.3	4 543	1 006	5.2
1973													
January	145 720	87 487	60.0	83 161	47 701	28 596	6 864	3 456	79 705	57.1	4 326	947	4.9
February	145 943	88 364	60.5	83 912	47 884	28 995	7 033	3 415	80 497	57.5	4 452	894	5.0
March	146 230	88 846	60.8	84 452	48 117	29 110	7 225	3 469	80 983	57.8	4 394	889	4.9
April	146 459	89 018	60.8	84 559	48 098	29 304	7 157	3 407	81 152	57.7	4 459	809	5.0
May	146 719	88 977	60.6	84 648	48 068	29 432	7 148	3 376	81 272	57.7	4 329	816	4.9
June	146 981	89 548	60.9	85 185	48 244	29 505	7 436	3 509	81 676	58.0	4 363	779	4.9
July	147 233	89 604	60.9	85 299	48 452	29 592	7 255	3 540	81 759	57.9	4 305	756	4.8
August	147 471	89 509	60.7	85 204	48 353	29 578	7 273	3 425	81 779	57.8	4 305	788	4.8
September	147 731	89 838	60.8	85 488	48 408	29 710	7 370	3 342	82 146	57.9	4 350	785	4.8
October	147 980	90 131	60.9	85 987	48 631	30 071	7 471	3 424	82 563	58.1	4 144	793	4.6
November	148 219	90 716	61.2	86 320	48 764	30 071	7 485	3 593	82 727	58.2	4 396	832	4.8
December	148 479	90 890	61.2	86 401	48 902	29 991	7 508	3 658	82 743	58.2	4 489	767	4.9
1974													
January	148 753	91 199	61.3	86 555	49 107	29 893	7 555	3 756	82 799	58.2	4 644	799	5.1
February	148 982	91 485	61.4	86 754	49 057	30 146	7 551	3 824	82 930	58.2	4 731	829	5.2
March	149 225	91 453	61.3	86 819	48 986	30 293	7 540	3 726	83 093	58.2	4 634	849	5.1
April	149 478	91 287	61.1	86 669	48 853	30 376	7 440	3 582	83 087	58.0	4 618	889	5.1
May	149 750	91 596	61.2	86 891	49 039	30 424	7 428	3 529	83 362	58.0	4 705	880	5.1
June	150 012	91 868	61.2	86 941	48 946	30 512	7 483	3 386	83 555	58.0	4 927	926	5.4
July	150 248	92 212	61.4	87 149	48 883	30 869	7 397	3 436	83 713	58.0	5 063	924	5.5
August	150 493	92 059	61.2	87 037	48 950	30 662	7 425	3 429	83 608	57.8	5 022	960	5.5
September	150 753	92 488	61.4	87 051	48 978	30 569	7 504	3 460	83 591	57.7	5 437	1 021	5.9
October	151 009	92 518	61.3	86 995	48 959	30 570	7 466	3 431	83 564	57.6	5 523	1 072	6.0
November	151 256	92 766	61.3	86 626	48 833	30 424	7 369	3 405	83 221	57.3	6 140	1 128	6.6
December	151 494	92 780	61.2	86 144	48 458	30 431	7 255	3 361	82 783	56.9	6 636	1 326	7.2

¹Not seasonally adjusted.
²In 1930 through 1943, the official BLS data count persons on work relief as unemployed. The unemployment rates for those years shown in parentheses count persons on work relief as employed, which is more consistent with the postwar practice. See notes and definitions.

Table 10-1B. Summary Labor Force, Employment, and Unemployment: Historical—*Continued*

(Thousands of persons, percent, seasonally adjusted, except as noted.)

Year and month	Civilian noninstitutional population [1]	Civilian labor force		Employment, thousands of persons						Employment-population ratio, percent	Unemployment [2]		
		Thousands of persons	Participation rate (percent)	Total	By age and sex			By industry			Thousands of persons		Rate (percent)
					Men, 20 years and over	Women, 20 years and over	Both sexes, 16 to 19 years	Agricultural	Nonagricultural		Total	Unemployed 15 weeks and over	
1975													
January	151 755	93 128	61.4	85 627	48 086	30 343	7 198	3 401	82 226	56.4	7 501	1 555	8.1
February	151 990	92 776	61.0	85 256	47 927	30 215	7 114	3 361	81 895	56.1	7 520	1 841	8.1
March	152 217	93 165	61.2	85 187	47 776	30 334	7 077	3 358	81 829	56.0	7 978	2 074	8.6
April	152 443	93 399	61.3	85 189	47 759	30 410	7 020	3 315	81 874	55.9	8 210	2 442	8.8
May	152 704	93 884	61.5	85 451	47 835	30 483	7 133	3 560	81 891	56.0	8 433	2 643	9.0
June	152 976	93 575	61.2	85 355	47 754	30 618	6 983	3 368	81 987	55.8	8 220	2 843	8.8
July	153 309	94 021	61.3	85 894	48 050	30 794	7 050	3 457	82 437	56.0	8 127	2 943	8.6
August	153 580	94 162	61.3	86 234	48 239	30 966	7 029	3 429	82 805	56.1	7 928	2 862	8.4
September	153 848	94 202	61.2	86 279	48 126	30 979	7 174	3 508	82 771	56.1	7 923	2 906	8.4
October	154 082	94 267	61.2	86 370	48 165	31 121	7 084	3 397	82 973	56.1	7 897	2 689	8.4
November	154 338	94 250	61.1	86 456	48 203	31 135	7 118	3 331	83 125	56.0	7 794	2 789	8.3
December	154 589	94 409	61.1	86 665	48 266	31 268	7 131	3 259	83 406	56.1	7 744	2 868	8.2
1976													
January	154 853	94 934	61.3	87 400	48 592	31 595	7 213	3 387	84 013	56.4	7 534	2 713	7.9
February	155 066	94 998	61.3	87 672	48 721	31 680	7 271	3 304	84 368	56.5	7 326	2 519	7.7
March	155 306	95 215	61.3	87 985	48 836	31 842	7 307	3 296	84 689	56.7	7 230	2 441	7.6
April	155 529	95 746	61.6	88 416	49 097	31 951	7 368	3 438	84 978	56.8	7 330	2 210	7.7
May	155 765	95 847	61.5	88 794	49 193	32 147	7 454	3 367	85 427	57.0	7 053	2 115	7.4
June	156 026	95 885	61.5	88 563	49 010	32 267	7 286	3 310	85 253	56.8	7 322	2 332	7.6
July	156 276	96 583	61.8	89 093	49 236	32 334	7 523	3 358	85 735	57.0	7 490	2 316	7.8
August	156 525	96 741	61.8	89 223	49 417	32 437	7 369	3 380	85 843	57.0	7 518	2 378	7.8
September	156 779	96 553	61.6	89 173	49 485	32 390	7 298	3 278	85 895	56.9	7 380	2 296	7.6
October	156 993	96 704	61.6	89 274	49 524	32 412	7 338	3 316	85 958	56.9	7 430	2 292	7.7
November	157 235	97 254	61.9	89 634	49 561	32 753	7 320	3 263	86 371	57.0	7 620	2 354	7.8
December	157 438	97 348	61.8	89 803	49 599	32 914	7 290	3 251	86 552	57.0	7 545	2 375	7.8
1977													
January	157 688	97 208	61.6	89 928	49 738	32 872	7 318	3 185	86 743	57.0	7 280	2 200	7.5
February	157 913	97 785	61.9	90 342	49 838	32 997	7 507	3 222	87 120	57.2	7 443	2 174	7.6
March	158 131	98 115	62.0	90 808	50 031	33 246	7 531	3 212	87 596	57.4	7 307	2 057	7.4
April	158 371	98 330	62.1	91 271	50 185	33 470	7 616	3 313	87 958	57.6	7 059	1 936	7.2
May	158 657	98 665	62.2	91 754	50 280	33 851	7 623	3 432	88 322	57.8	6 911	1 928	7.0
June	158 928	99 093	62.4	91 959	50 544	33 678	7 737	3 340	88 619	57.9	7 134	1 918	7.2
July	159 185	98 913	62.1	92 084	50 597	33 749	7 738	3 247	88 837	57.8	6 829	1 907	6.9
August	159 430	99 366	62.3	92 441	50 745	33 809	7 887	3 260	89 181	58.0	6 925	1 836	7.0
September	159 674	99 453	62.3	92 702	50 825	34 218	7 659	3 201	89 501	58.1	6 751	1 853	6.8
October	159 915	99 815	62.4	93 052	51 046	34 187	7 819	3 272	89 780	58.2	6 763	1 789	6.8
November	160 129	100 576	62.8	93 761	51 316	34 536	7 909	3 375	90 386	58.6	6 815	1 804	6.8
December	160 376	100 491	62.7	94 105	51 492	34 668	7 945	3 320	90 785	58.7	6 386	1 717	6.4
1978													
January	160 617	100 873	62.8	94 384	51 542	34 948	7 894	3 434	90 950	58.8	6 489	1 643	6.4
February	160 831	100 837	62.7	94 519	51 578	35 118	7 823	3 320	91 199	58.8	6 318	1 584	6.3
March	161 038	101 092	62.8	94 755	51 635	35 310	7 810	3 351	91 404	58.8	6 337	1 531	6.3
April	161 263	101 574	63.0	95 394	51 912	35 546	7 936	3 349	92 045	59.2	6 180	1 502	6.1
May	161 518	101 896	63.1	95 769	52 050	35 597	8 122	3 325	92 444	59.3	6 127	1 420	6.0
June	161 794	102 371	63.3	96 343	52 240	35 828	8 275	3 483	92 860	59.5	6 028	1 352	5.9
July	162 034	102 399	63.2	96 090	52 190	35 764	8 136	3 441	92 649	59.3	6 309	1 373	6.2
August	162 259	102 511	63.2	96 431	52 228	35 856	8 347	3 401	93 030	59.4	6 080	1 242	5.9
September	162 502	102 795	63.3	96 670	52 284	36 274	8 112	3 400	93 270	59.5	6 125	1 308	6.0
October	162 783	103 080	63.3	97 133	52 448	36 525	8 160	3 409	93 724	59.7	5 947	1 319	5.8
November	163 017	103 562	63.5	97 485	52 802	36 559	8 124	3 284	94 201	59.8	6 077	1 242	5.9
December	163 272	103 809	63.6	97 581	52 807	36 686	8 088	3 396	94 185	59.8	6 228	1 269	6.0
1979													
January	163 516	104 057	63.6	97 948	53 072	36 697	8 179	3 305	94 643	59.9	6 109	1 250	5.9
February	163 726	104 502	63.8	98 329	53 233	36 904	8 192	3 373	94 956	60.1	6 173	1 297	5.9
March	164 027	104 589	63.8	98 480	53 120	37 159	8 201	3 368	95 112	60.0	6 109	1 365	5.8
April	164 162	104 172	63.5	98 103	53 085	36 944	8 074	3 291	94 812	59.8	6 069	1 272	5.8
May	164 459	104 171	63.3	98 331	53 178	37 134	8 019	3 272	95 059	59.8	5 840	1 239	5.6
June	164 720	104 638	63.5	98 679	53 309	37 221	8 149	3 331	95 348	59.9	5 959	1 171	5.7
July	164 970	105 002	63.6	99 006	53 384	37 514	8 108	3 335	95 671	60.0	5 996	1 123	5.7
August	165 198	105 096	63.6	98 776	53 336	37 548	7 892	3 374	95 402	59.8	6 320	1 203	6.0
September	165 431	105 530	63.8	99 340	53 510	37 798	8 032	3 371	95 969	60.0	6 190	1 172	5.9
October	165 813	105 700	63.7	99 404	53 478	37 931	7 995	3 325	96 079	59.9	6 296	1 219	6.0
November	166 051	105 812	63.7	99 574	53 435	38 065	8 074	3 436	96 138	60.0	6 238	1 239	5.9
December	166 300	106 258	63.9	99 933	53 555	38 259	8 119	3 400	96 533	60.1	6 325	1 277	6.0

[1]Not seasonally adjusted.
[2]In 1930 through 1943, the official BLS data count persons on work relief as unemployed. The unemployment rates for those years shown in parentheses count persons on work relief as employed, which is more consistent with the postwar practice. See notes and definitions.

Table 10-1B. Summary Labor Force, Employment, and Unemployment: Historical—*Continued*

(Thousands of persons, percent, seasonally adjusted, except as noted.)

Year and month	Civilian noninstitutional population [1]	Civilian labor force		Employment, thousands of persons						Employment-population ratio, percent	Unemployment [2]		
		Thousands of persons	Participation rate (percent)	Total	By age and sex			By industry			Thousands of persons		Rate (percent)
					Men, 20 years and over	Women, 20 years and over	Both sexes, 16 to 19 years	Agricultural	Nonagricultural		Total	Unemployed 15 weeks and over	
1980													
January	166 544	106 562	64.0	99 879	53 501	38 367	8 011	3 316	96 563	60.0	6 683	1 353	6.3
February	166 759	106 697	64.0	99 995	53 686	38 389	7 920	3 397	96 598	60.0	6 702	1 358	6.3
March	166 984	106 442	63.7	99 713	53 353	38 406	7 954	3 418	96 295	59.7	6 729	1 457	6.3
April	167 197	106 591	63.8	99 233	53 035	38 427	7 771	3 326	95 907	59.4	7 358	1 694	6.9
May	167 407	106 929	63.9	98 945	52 915	38 335	7 695	3 382	95 563	59.1	7 984	1 740	7.5
June	167 643	106 780	63.7	98 682	52 712	38 312	7 658	3 296	95 386	58.9	8 098	1 760	7.6
July	167 932	107 159	63.8	98 796	52 733	38 374	7 689	3 319	95 477	58.8	8 363	1 995	7.8
August	168 103	107 105	63.7	98 824	52 815	38 511	7 498	3 234	95 590	58.8	8 281	2 162	7.7
September	168 297	107 098	63.6	99 077	52 866	38 595	7 616	3 443	95 634	58.9	8 021	2 309	7.5
October	168 503	107 405	63.7	99 317	53 094	38 620	7 603	3 372	95 945	58.9	8 088	2 306	7.5
November	168 695	107 568	63.8	99 545	53 210	38 795	7 540	3 396	96 149	59.0	8 023	2 329	7.5
December	168 883	107 352	63.6	99 634	53 333	38 737	7 564	3 492	96 142	59.0	7 718	2 406	7.2
1981													
January	169 104	108 026	63.9	99 955	53 392	39 042	7 521	3 429	96 526	59.1	8 071	2 389	7.5
February	169 280	108 242	63.9	100 191	53 445	39 280	7 466	3 345	96 846	59.2	8 051	2 344	7.4
March	169 453	108 553	64.1	100 571	53 662	39 464	7 445	3 365	97 206	59.4	7 982	2 276	7.4
April	169 641	108 925	64.2	101 056	53 886	39 628	7 542	3 529	97 527	59.6	7 869	2 231	7.2
May	169 829	109 222	64.3	101 048	53 879	39 759	7 410	3 369	97 679	59.5	8 174	2 221	7.5
June	170 042	108 396	63.7	100 298	53 576	39 682	7 040	3 334	96 964	59.0	8 098	2 250	7.5
July	170 246	108 556	63.8	100 693	53 814	39 683	7 196	3 296	97 397	59.1	7 863	2 166	7.2
August	170 399	108 725	63.8	100 689	53 718	39 723	7 248	3 379	97 310	59.1	8 036	2 241	7.4
September	170 593	108 294	63.5	100 064	53 625	39 342	7 097	3 361	96 703	58.7	8 230	2 261	7.6
October	170 809	109 024	63.8	100 378	53 482	39 843	7 053	3 412	96 966	58.8	8 646	2 303	7.9
November	170 996	109 236	63.9	100 207	53 335	39 908	6 964	3 415	96 792	58.6	9 029	2 345	8.3
December	171 166	108 912	63.6	99 645	53 149	39 708	6 788	3 227	96 418	58.2	9 267	2 374	8.5
1982													
January	171 335	109 089	63.7	99 692	53 103	39 821	6 768	3 393	96 299	58.2	9 397	2 409	8.6
February	171 489	109 467	63.8	99 762	53 172	39 859	6 731	3 375	96 387	58.2	9 705	2 758	8.9
March	171 667	109 567	63.8	99 672	53 054	39 936	6 682	3 372	96 300	58.1	9 895	2 965	9.0
April	171 844	109 820	63.9	99 576	53 081	39 848	6 647	3 351	96 225	57.9	10 244	3 086	9.3
May	172 026	110 451	64.2	100 116	53 234	40 121	6 761	3 434	96 682	58.2	10 335	3 276	9.4
June	172 190	110 081	63.9	99 543	52 933	40 219	6 391	3 331	96 212	57.8	10 538	3 451	9.6
July	172 364	110 342	64.0	99 493	52 896	40 228	6 369	3 402	96 091	57.7	10 849	3 555	9.8
August	172 511	110 514	64.1	99 633	52 797	40 336	6 500	3 408	96 225	57.8	10 881	3 696	9.8
September	172 690	110 721	64.1	99 504	52 760	40 275	6 469	3 385	96 119	57.6	11 217	3 889	10.1
October	172 881	110 744	64.1	99 215	52 624	40 105	6 486	3 489	95 726	57.4	11 529	4 185	10.4
November	173 058	111 050	64.2	99 112	52 537	40 111	6 464	3 510	95 602	57.3	11 938	4 485	10.8
December	173 199	111 083	64.1	99 032	52 497	40 164	6 371	3 414	95 618	57.2	12 051	4 662	10.8
1983													
January	173 354	110 695	63.9	99 161	52 487	40 268	6 406	3 439	95 722	57.2	11 534	4 668	10.4
February	173 505	110 634	63.8	99 089	52 453	40 336	6 300	3 382	95 707	57.1	11 545	4 641	10.4
March	173 656	110 587	63.7	99 179	52 615	40 368	6 196	3 360	95 819	57.1	11 408	4 612	10.3
April	173 794	110 828	63.8	99 560	52 814	40 542	6 204	3 341	96 219	57.3	11 268	4 370	10.2
May	173 953	110 796	63.7	99 642	52 922	40 538	6 182	3 328	96 314	57.3	11 154	4 538	10.1
June	174 125	111 879	64.3	100 633	53 515	40 695	6 423	3 462	97 171	57.8	11 246	4 470	10.1
July	174 306	111 756	64.1	101 208	53 835	41 041	6 332	3 481	97 727	58.1	10 548	4 329	9.4
August	174 440	112 231	64.3	101 608	53 837	41 314	6 457	3 502	98 106	58.2	10 623	4 070	9.5
September	174 602	112 298	64.3	102 016	53 983	41 650	6 383	3 347	98 669	58.4	10 282	3 854	9.2
October	174 779	111 926	64.0	102 039	54 146	41 597	6 296	3 303	98 736	58.4	9 887	3 648	8.8
November	174 951	112 228	64.1	102 729	54 499	41 788	6 442	3 291	99 438	58.7	9 499	3 535	8.5
December	175 121	112 327	64.1	102 996	54 662	41 852	6 482	3 332	99 664	58.8	9 331	3 379	8.3
1984													
January	175 533	112 209	63.9	103 201	54 975	41 812	6 414	3 293	99 908	58.8	9 008	3 254	8.0
February	175 679	112 615	64.1	103 824	55 213	42 196	6 415	3 353	100 471	59.1	8 791	2 991	7.8
March	175 824	112 713	64.1	103 967	55 281	42 328	6 358	3 233	100 734	59.1	8 746	2 881	7.8
April	175 969	113 098	64.3	104 336	55 373	42 512	6 451	3 291	101 045	59.3	8 762	2 858	7.7
May	176 123	113 649	64.5	105 193	55 661	43 071	6 461	3 343	101 850	59.7	8 456	2 884	7.4
June	176 284	113 817	64.6	105 591	55 996	42 944	6 651	3 383	102 208	59.9	8 226	2 612	7.2
July	176 440	113 972	64.6	105 435	55 921	42 979	6 535	3 344	102 091	59.8	8 537	2 638	7.5
August	176 583	113 682	64.4	105 163	55 930	42 885	6 348	3 286	101 877	59.6	8 519	2 604	7.5
September	176 763	113 857	64.4	105 490	56 095	42 967	6 428	3 393	102 097	59.7	8 367	2 538	7.3
October	176 956	114 019	64.4	105 638	56 183	43 052	6 403	3 194	102 444	59.7	8 381	2 526	7.4
November	177 135	114 170	64.5	105 972	56 274	43 244	6 454	3 394	102 578	59.8	8 198	2 438	7.2
December	177 306	114 581	64.6	106 223	56 313	43 472	6 438	3 385	102 838	59.9	8 358	2 401	7.3

[1]Not seasonally adjusted.
[2]In 1930 through 1943, the official BLS data count persons on work relief as unemployed. The unemployment rates for those years shown in parentheses count persons on work relief as employed, which is more consistent with the postwar practice. See notes and definitions.

Table 10-1B. Summary Labor Force, Employment, and Unemployment: Historical—*Continued*

(Thousands of persons, percent, seasonally adjusted, except as noted.)

| Year and month | Civilian noninsti-tutional popu-lation [1] | Civilian labor force | | Employment, thousands of persons | | | | | | Employ-ment-population ratio, percent | Unemployment [2] | | |
| | | Thousands of persons | Participa-tion rate (percent) | Total | By age and sex | | | By industry | | | Thousands of persons | | Rate (percent) |
					Men, 20 years and over	Women, 20 years and over	Both sexes, 16 to 19 years	Agri-cultural	Nonagri-cultural		Total	Unem-ployed 15 weeks and over	
1985													
January	177 384	114 725	64.7	106 302	56 184	43 589	6 529	3 317	102 985	59.9	8 423	2 284	7.3
February	177 516	114 876	64.7	106 555	56 216	43 787	6 552	3 317	103 238	60.0	8 321	2 389	7.2
March	177 667	115 328	64.9	106 989	56 356	44 035	6 598	3 250	103 739	60.2	8 339	2 394	7.2
April	177 799	115 331	64.9	106 936	56 374	44 000	6 562	3 306	103 630	60.1	8 395	2 393	7.3
May	177 944	115 234	64.8	106 932	56 531	43 905	6 496	3 280	103 652	60.1	8 302	2 292	7.2
June	178 096	114 965	64.6	106 505	56 288	43 958	6 259	3 161	103 344	59.8	8 460	2 310	7.4
July	178 263	115 320	64.7	106 807	56 435	43 975	6 397	3 143	103 664	59.9	8 513	2 329	7.4
August	178 405	115 291	64.6	107 095	56 655	44 103	6 337	3 121	103 974	60.0	8 196	2 258	7.1
September	178 572	115 905	64.9	107 657	56 845	44 395	6 417	3 064	104 593	60.3	8 248	2 242	7.1
October	178 770	116 145	65.0	107 847	56 969	44 565	6 313	3 051	104 796	60.3	8 298	2 295	7.1
November	178 940	116 135	64.9	108 007	56 972	44 617	6 418	3 062	104 945	60.4	8 128	2 207	7.0
December	179 112	116 354	65.0	108 216	56 995	44 889	6 332	3 141	105 075	60.4	8 138	2 208	7.0
1986													
January	179 670	116 682	64.9	108 887	57 637	44 944	6 306	3 287	105 600	60.6	7 795	2 089	6.7
February	179 821	116 882	65.0	108 480	57 269	44 804	6 407	3 083	105 397	60.3	8 402	2 308	7.2
March	179 985	117 220	65.1	108 837	57 353	44 960	6 524	3 200	105 637	60.5	8 383	2 261	7.2
April	180 148	117 316	65.1	108 952	57 358	45 081	6 513	3 153	105 799	60.5	8 364	2 162	7.1
May	180 311	117 528	65.2	109 089	57 287	45 289	6 513	3 150	105 939	60.5	8 439	2 232	7.2
June	180 503	118 084	65.4	109 576	57 471	45 621	6 484	3 193	106 383	60.7	8 508	2 320	7.2
July	180 682	118 129	65.4	109 810	57 514	45 837	6 459	3 141	106 669	60.8	8 319	2 269	7.0
August	180 828	118 150	65.3	110 015	57 597	45 926	6 492	3 082	106 933	60.8	8 135	2 276	6.9
September	180 997	118 395	65.4	110 085	57 630	45 972	6 483	3 171	106 914	60.8	8 310	2 318	7.0
October	181 186	118 516	65.4	110 273	57 660	46 046	6 567	3 128	107 145	60.9	8 243	2 188	7.0
November	181 363	118 634	65.4	110 475	57 941	46 070	6 464	3 220	107 255	60.9	8 159	2 202	6.9
December	181 547	118 611	65.3	110 728	58 185	46 132	6 411	3 148	107 580	61.0	7 883	2 161	6.6
1987													
January	181 827	118 845	65.4	110 953	58 264	47 862	6 470	3 143	107 810	61.0	7 892	2 168	6.6
February	181 998	119 122	65.5	111 257	58 279	47 919	6 534	3 208	108 049	61.1	7 865	2 117	6.6
March	182 179	119 270	65.5	111 408	58 362	48 090	6 497	3 214	108 194	61.2	7 862	2 070	6.6
April	182 344	119 336	65.4	111 794	58 503	48 147	6 545	3 246	108 548	61.3	7 542	2 091	6.3
May	182 533	120 008	65.7	112 434	58 713	47 946	6 669	3 345	109 089	61.6	7 574	2 104	6.3
June	182 703	119 644	65.5	112 246	58 581	48 146	6 563	3 216	109 030	61.4	7 398	2 087	6.2
July	182 885	119 902	65.6	112 634	58 740	48 186	6 665	3 235	109 399	61.6	7 268	1 921	6.1
August	183 002	120 318	65.7	113 057	58 810	48 467	6 925	3 112	109 945	61.8	7 261	1 878	6.0
September	183 161	120 011	65.5	112 909	58 964	48 511	6 660	3 189	109 720	61.6	7 102	1 866	5.9
October	183 311	120 509	65.7	113 282	59 073	48 859	6 676	3 219	110 063	61.8	7 227	1 794	6.0
November	183 470	120 540	65.7	113 505	59 210	49 254	6 673	3 145	110 360	61.9	7 035	1 797	5.8
December	183 620	120 729	65.7	113 793	59 217	49 257	6 795	3 213	110 580	62.0	6 936	1 767	5.7
1988													
January	183 822	120 969	65.8	114 016	59 346	49 529	6 808	3 247	110 769	62.0	6 953	1 714	5.7
February	183 969	121 156	65.9	114 227	59 535	49 497	6 773	3 201	111 026	62.1	6 929	1 738	5.7
March	184 111	120 913	65.7	114 037	59 393	49 503	6 554	3 169	110 868	61.9	6 876	1 744	5.7
April	184 232	121 251	65.8	114 650	59 832	49 565	6 671	3 224	111 426	62.2	6 601	1 563	5.4
May	184 374	121 071	65.7	114 292	59 644	49 583	6 702	3 121	111 171	62.0	6 779	1 647	5.6
June	184 562	121 473	65.8	114 927	59 751	49 542	7 030	3 111	111 816	62.3	6 546	1 531	5.4
July	184 729	121 665	65.9	115 060	59 888	49 693	6 986	3 060	112 000	62.3	6 605	1 601	5.4
August	184 830	122 125	66.1	115 282	59 877	49 804	6 938	3 119	112 163	62.4	6 843	1 639	5.6
September	184 962	121 960	65.9	115 356	59 980	50 015	6 865	3 165	112 191	62.4	6 604	1 569	5.4
October	185 114	122 206	66.0	115 638	60 023	49 871	6 756	3 231	112 407	62.5	6 568	1 562	5.4
November	185 244	122 637	66.2	116 100	60 042	50 221	6 804	3 241	112 859	62.7	6 537	1 468	5.3
December	185 402	122 622	66.1	116 104	60 059	50 116	6 788	3 194	112 910	62.6	6 518	1 490	5.3
1989													
January	185 644	123 390	66.5	116 708	60 477	50 436	6 702	3 287	113 421	62.9	6 682	1 480	5.4
February	185 777	123 135	66.3	116 776	60 588	50 438	6 691	3 234	113 542	62.9	6 359	1 304	5.2
March	185 897	123 227	66.3	117 022	60 795	50 463	6 724	3 198	113 824	62.9	6 205	1 353	5.0
April	186 024	123 565	66.4	117 097	60 764	50 457	6 768	3 162	113 935	62.9	6 468	1 397	5.2
May	186 181	123 474	66.3	117 099	60 795	50 646	6 721	3 125	113 974	62.9	6 375	1 348	5.2
June	186 329	123 995	66.5	117 418	61 054	50 550	6 822	3 068	114 350	63.0	6 577	1 300	5.3
July	186 483	123 967	66.5	117 472	60 947	50 514	6 832	3 227	114 245	63.0	6 495	1 435	5.2
August	186 598	124 166	66.5	117 655	60 915	50 635	6 936	3 284	114 371	63.1	6 511	1 302	5.2
September	186 726	123 944	66.4	117 354	60 668	50 587	6 671	3 219	114 135	62.8	6 590	1 360	5.3
October	186 871	124 211	66.5	117 581	60 958	50 616	6 752	3 215	114 366	62.9	6 630	1 392	5.3
November	187 017	124 637	66.6	117 912	60 958	50 541	6 733	3 132	114 780	63.0	6 725	1 418	5.4
December	187 165	124 497	66.5	117 830	61 068	50 530	6 646	3 188	114 642	63.0	6 667	1 375	5.4

[1]Not seasonally adjusted.
[2]In 1930 through 1943, the official BLS data count persons on work relief as unemployed. The unemployment rates for those years shown in parentheses count persons on work relief as employed, which is more consistent with the postwar practice. See notes and definitions.

Table 10-1B. Summary Labor Force, Employment, and Unemployment: Historical—Continued

(Thousands of persons, percent, seasonally adjusted, except as noted.)

Year and month	Civilian noninsti-tutional popu-lation [1]	Civilian labor force Thousands of persons	Civilian labor force Participa-tion rate (percent)	Employment Total	Men, 20 years and over	Women, 20 years and over	Both sexes, 16 to 19 years	Agri-cultural	Nonagri-cultural	Employ-ment-population ratio, percent	Unemployment Total	Unem-ployed 15 weeks and over	Rate (percent)
1990													
January	188 413	125 833	66.8	119 081	61 742	50 472	6 903	3 210	115 871	63.2	6 752	1 412	5.4
February	188 516	125 710	66.7	119 059	61 805	50 523	6 816	3 188	115 871	63.2	6 651	1 350	5.3
March	188 630	125 801	66.7	119 203	61 832	50 422	6 908	3 260	115 943	63.2	6 598	1 331	5.2
April	188 778	125 649	66.6	118 852	61 579	50 760	6 816	3 231	115 621	63.0	6 797	1 376	5.4
May	188 913	125 893	66.6	119 151	61 778	50 457	6 727	3 266	115 885	63.1	6 742	1 415	5.4
June	189 058	125 573	66.4	118 983	61 762	50 585	6 671	3 245	115 738	62.9	6 590	1 436	5.2
July	189 188	125 732	66.5	118 810	61 683	50 636	6 613	3 192	115 618	62.8	6 922	1 534	5.5
August	189 342	125 990	66.5	118 802	61 715	50 601	6 452	3 197	115 605	62.7	7 188	1 607	5.7
September	189 528	125 892	66.4	118 524	61 608	50 864	6 329	3 206	115 318	62.5	7 368	1 695	5.9
October	189 710	125 995	66.4	118 536	61 606	50 811	6 314	3 270	115 266	62.5	7 459	1 689	5.9
November	189 872	126 070	66.4	118 306	61 545	50 759	6 220	3 189	115 117	62.3	7 764	1 831	6.2
December	190 017	126 142	66.4	118 241	61 506	50 728	6 205	3 245	114 996	62.2	7 901	1 804	6.3
1991													
January	190 163	125 955	66.2	117 940	61 383	51 095	6 085	3 208	114 732	62.0	8 015	1 866	6.4
February	190 271	126 020	66.2	117 755	61 117	51 033	6 115	3 270	114 485	61.9	8 265	1 955	6.6
March	190 381	126 238	66.3	117 652	61 144	51 204	6 086	3 177	114 475	61.8	8 586	2 137	6.8
April	190 517	126 548	66.4	118 109	61 280	51 323	6 069	3 241	114 868	62.0	8 439	2 206	6.7
May	190 650	126 176	66.2	117 440	61 052	51 245	5 931	3 275	114 165	61.6	8 736	2 252	6.9
June	190 800	126 331	66.2	117 639	61 147	51 383	5 907	3 300	114 339	61.7	8 692	2 533	6.9
July	190 946	126 154	66.1	117 568	61 179	51 458	5 753	3 319	114 249	61.6	8 586	2 388	6.8
August	191 116	126 150	66.0	117 484	61 122	51 386	5 761	3 313	114 171	61.5	8 666	2 460	6.9
September	191 302	126 650	66.2	117 928	61 279	51 359	5 785	3 319	114 609	61.6	8 722	2 497	6.9
October	191 497	126 642	66.1	117 800	61 174	51 373	5 815	3 289	114 511	61.5	8 842	2 638	7.0
November	191 657	126 701	66.1	117 770	61 201	51 535	5 810	3 296	114 474	61.4	8 931	2 718	7.0
December	191 798	126 664	66.0	117 466	61 074	51 524	5 664	3 146	114 320	61.2	9 198	2 892	7.3
1992													
January	191 953	127 261	66.3	117 978	61 116	51 505	5 767	3 155	114 823	61.5	9 283	3 060	7.3
February	192 067	127 207	66.2	117 753	61 062	51 573	5 658	3 239	114 514	61.3	9 454	3 182	7.4
March	192 204	127 604	66.4	118 144	61 363	51 808	5 577	3 236	114 908	61.5	9 460	3 196	7.4
April	192 354	127 841	66.5	118 426	61 468	51 732	5 635	3 245	115 181	61.6	9 415	3 130	7.4
May	192 503	128 119	66.6	118 375	61 513	51 996	5 617	3 213	115 162	61.5	9 744	3 444	7.6
June	192 663	128 459	66.7	118 419	61 537	52 183	5 499	3 297	115 122	61.5	10 040	3 758	7.8
July	192 826	128 563	66.7	118 713	61 641	52 088	5 614	3 285	115 428	61.6	9 850	3 614	7.7
August	193 018	128 613	66.6	118 826	61 681	52 294	5 759	3 279	115 547	61.6	9 787	3 579	7.6
September	193 229	128 501	66.5	118 720	61 663	52 241	5 698	3 274	115 446	61.4	9 781	3 504	7.6
October	193 442	128 026	66.2	118 628	61 550	52 379	5 705	3 254	115 374	61.3	9 398	3 505	7.3
November	193 621	128 441	66.3	118 876	61 644	52 531	5 697	3 207	115 669	61.4	9 565	3 397	7.4
December	193 784	128 554	66.3	118 997	61 721	52 813	5 752	3 259	115 738	61.4	9 557	3 651	7.4
1993													
January	193 962	128 400	66.2	119 075	61 895	51 505	5 675	3 222	115 853	61.4	9 325	3 346	7.3
February	194 108	128 458	66.2	119 275	61 963	51 573	5 739	3 125	116 150	61.4	9 183	3 190	7.1
March	194 248	128 598	66.2	119 542	62 007	51 808	5 727	3 119	116 423	61.5	9 056	3 115	7.0
April	194 398	128 584	66.1	119 474	62 032	51 732	5 710	3 074	116 400	61.5	9 110	3 014	7.1
May	194 549	129 264	66.4	120 115	62 309	51 996	5 810	3 100	117 015	61.7	9 149	3 101	7.1
June	194 719	129 411	66.5	120 290	62 409	52 183	5 698	3 108	117 182	61.8	9 121	3 141	7.0
July	194 882	129 379	66.4	120 467	62 497	52 088	5 882	3 126	117 341	61.8	8 930	3 046	6.9
August	195 063	129 619	66.4	120 856	62 634	52 294	5 928	3 026	117 830	62.0	8 763	3 026	6.8
September	195 259	129 268	66.2	120 554	62 437	52 241	5 876	3 174	117 380	61.7	8 714	3 042	6.7
October	195 444	129 573	66.3	120 823	62 614	52 379	5 830	3 084	117 739	61.8	8 750	3 029	6.8
November	195 625	129 711	66.3	121 169	62 732	52 531	5 906	3 157	118 012	61.9	8 542	2 986	6.6
December	195 794	129 941	66.4	121 464	62 760	52 813	5 891	3 116	118 348	62.0	8 477	2 968	6.5
1994													
January	195 953	130 596	66.6	121 966	62 798	53 052	6 116	3 302	118 664	62.2	8 630	3 060	6.6
February	196 090	130 669	66.6	122 086	62 708	53 266	6 112	3 339	118 747	62.3	8 583	3 118	6.6
March	196 213	130 400	66.5	121 930	62 780	53 099	6 051	3 354	118 576	62.1	8 470	3 055	6.5
April	196 363	130 621	66.5	122 290	62 906	53 274	6 110	3 428	118 862	62.3	8 331	2 921	6.4
May	196 510	130 779	66.6	122 864	63 116	53 624	6 124	3 409	119 455	62.5	7 915	2 836	6.1
June	196 693	130 561	66.4	122 634	63 041	53 393	6 200	3 299	119 335	62.3	7 927	2 735	6.1
July	196 859	130 652	66.4	122 706	63 034	53 531	6 141	3 333	119 373	62.3	7 946	2 822	6.1
August	197 043	131 275	66.6	123 342	63 294	53 744	6 304	3 451	119 891	62.6	7 933	2 750	6.0
September	197 248	131 421	66.6	123 687	63 631	53 991	6 065	3 430	120 257	62.7	7 734	2 746	5.9
October	197 430	131 744	66.7	124 112	63 818	54 071	6 223	3 490	120 622	62.9	7 632	2 955	5.8
November	197 607	131 891	66.7	124 516	64 080	54 168	6 268	3 574	120 942	63.0	7 375	2 666	5.6
December	197 765	131 951	66.7	124 721	64 359	54 054	6 308	3 577	121 144	63.1	7 230	2 488	5.5

[1]Not seasonally adjusted.
[2]In 1930 through 1943, the official BLS data count persons on work relief as unemployed. The unemployment rates for those years shown in parentheses count persons on work relief as employed, which is more consistent with the postwar practice. See notes and definitions.

Table 10-1B. Summary Labor Force, Employment, and Unemployment: Historical—*Continued*

(Thousands of persons, percent, seasonally adjusted, except as noted.)

Year and month	Civilian noninsti-tutional popu-lation [1]	Civilian labor force		Employment, thousands of persons						Employ-ment-population ratio, percent	Unemployment [2]		
		Thousands of persons	Participa-tion rate (percent)	Total	By age and sex			By industry			Thousands of persons		Rate (percent)
					Men, 20 years and over	Women, 20 years and over	Both sexes, 16 to 19 years	Agri-cultural	Nonagri-cultural		Total	Unem-ployed 15 weeks and over	
1995													
January	197 753	132 038	66.8	124 663	64 185	54 087	6 391	3 519	121 144	63.0	7 375	2 396	5.6
February	197 886	132 115	66.8	124 928	64 378	54 226	6 324	3 620	121 308	63.1	7 187	2 345	5.4
March	198 007	132 108	66.7	124 955	64 321	54 141	6 493	3 634	121 321	63.1	7 153	2 287	5.4
April	198 148	132 590	66.9	124 945	64 165	54 366	6 414	3 566	121 379	63.1	7 645	2 473	5.8
May	198 286	131 851	66.5	124 421	63 829	54 272	6 320	3 349	121 072	62.7	7 430	2 577	5.6
June	198 452	131 949	66.5	124 522	63 992	54 020	6 510	3 461	121 061	62.7	7 427	2 266	5.6
July	198 615	132 343	66.6	124 816	63 962	54 476	6 378	3 379	121 437	62.8	7 527	2 311	5.7
August	198 801	132 336	66.6	124 852	63 875	54 434	6 543	3 374	121 478	62.8	7 484	2 391	5.7
September	199 005	132 611	66.6	125 133	64 179	54 507	6 447	3 285	121 848	62.9	7 478	2 306	5.6
October	199 192	132 716	66.6	125 388	64 272	54 692	6 424	3 438	121 950	62.9	7 328	2 272	5.5
November	199 355	132 614	66.5	125 188	63 931	54 850	6 407	3 338	121 850	62.8	7 426	2 339	5.6
December	199 508	132 511	66.4	125 088	64 041	54 674	6 373	3 352	121 736	62.7	7 423	2 331	5.6
1996													
January	199 634	132 616	66.4	125 125	64 180	54 580	6 365	3 483	121 642	62.7	7 491	2 371	5.6
February	199 772	132 952	66.6	125 639	64 398	54 844	6 397	3 547	122 092	62.9	7 313	2 307	5.5
March	199 921	133 180	66.6	125 862	64 506	54 994	6 362	3 489	122 373	63.0	7 318	2 454	5.5
April	200 101	133 409	66.7	125 994	64 481	55 067	6 446	3 406	122 588	63.0	7 415	2 455	5.6
May	200 278	133 667	66.7	126 244	64 683	55 034	6 527	3 473	122 771	63.0	7 423	2 403	5.6
June	200 459	133 697	66.7	126 602	64 940	55 177	6 485	3 424	123 178	63.2	7 095	2 355	5.3
July	200 641	134 284	66.9	126 947	65 068	55 362	6 517	3 433	123 514	63.3	7 337	2 297	5.5
August	200 847	134 054	66.7	127 172	65 216	55 525	6 431	3 395	123 777	63.3	6 882	2 267	5.1
September	201 060	134 515	66.9	127 536	65 169	55 669	6 698	3 448	124 088	63.4	6 979	2 220	5.2
October	201 273	134 921	67.0	127 890	65 460	55 750	6 680	3 463	124 427	63.5	7 031	2 268	5.2
November	201 463	135 007	67.0	127 771	65 320	55 896	6 555	3 356	124 415	63.4	7 236	2 159	5.4
December	201 636	135 113	67.0	127 860	65 435	55 849	6 576	3 445	124 415	63.4	7 253	2 124	5.4
1997													
January	202 285	135 456	67.0	128 298	65 679	56 024	6 595	3 449	124 849	63.4	7 158	2 162	5.3
February	202 388	135 400	66.9	128 298	65 758	55 955	6 585	3 353	124 945	63.4	7 102	2 140	5.2
March	202 513	135 891	67.1	128 891	65 974	56 270	6 647	3 419	125 472	63.6	7 000	2 110	5.2
April	202 674	136 016	67.1	129 143	66 092	56 347	6 704	3 462	125 681	63.7	6 873	2 176	5.1
May	202 832	136 119	67.1	129 464	66 328	56 446	6 690	3 437	126 027	63.8	6 655	2 121	4.9
June	203 000	136 211	67.1	129 412	66 308	56 573	6 531	3 409	126 003	63.7	6 799	2 085	5.0
July	203 166	136 477	67.2	129 822	66 422	56 785	6 615	3 422	126 400	63.9	6 655	2 119	4.9
August	203 364	136 618	67.2	130 010	66 508	56 852	6 650	3 359	126 651	63.9	6 608	2 004	4.8
September	203 570	136 675	67.1	130 019	66 483	56 931	6 605	3 392	126 627	63.9	6 656	2 074	4.9
October	203 767	136 633	67.1	130 179	66 511	56 982	6 686	3 312	126 867	63.9	6 454	1 950	4.7
November	203 941	136 961	67.2	130 653	66 765	57 039	6 849	3 386	127 267	64.1	6 308	1 817	4.6
December	204 098	137 155	67.2	130 679	66 643	57 219	6 817	3 405	127 274	64.0	6 476	1 901	4.7
1998													
January	204 238	137 095	67.1	130 726	66 750	56 941	7 035	3 299	127 389	64.0	6 368	1 833	4.6
February	204 400	137 112	67.1	130 807	66 856	56 992	6 959	3 284	127 522	64.0	6 306	1 809	4.6
March	204 546	137 236	67.1	130 814	66 721	57 080	7 014	3 146	127 650	64.0	6 422	1 772	4.7
April	204 731	137 150	67.0	131 209	67 151	57 074	6 985	3 334	127 852	64.1	5 941	1 476	4.3
May	204 899	137 372	67.0	131 325	67 164	57 155	7 007	3 360	127 959	64.1	6 047	1 490	4.4
June	205 085	137 455	67.0	131 244	67 054	57 156	7 033	3 380	127 874	64.0	6 212	1 613	4.5
July	205 270	137 588	67.0	131 329	67 119	57 192	7 018	3 455	127 913	64.0	6 259	1 577	4.5
August	205 479	137 570	67.0	131 390	66 985	57 332	7 074	3 509	127 970	63.9	6 179	1 626	4.5
September	205 699	138 286	67.2	131 986	67 254	57 520	7 212	3 500	128 399	64.2	6 300	1 688	4.6
October	205 919	138 279	67.2	131 999	67 433	57 529	7 036	3 593	128 389	64.1	6 280	1 582	4.5
November	206 104	138 381	67.1	132 280	67 591	57 638	7 052	3 375	128 897	64.2	6 100	1 590	4.4
December	206 270	138 634	67.2	132 602	67 548	57 840	7 214	3 246	129 320	64.3	6 032	1 559	4.4
1999													
January	206 719	139 003	67.2	133 027	67 679	58 256	7 092	3 233	129 802	64.4	5 976	1 490	4.3
February	206 873	138 967	67.2	132 856	67 498	58 129	7 229	3 246	129 647	64.2	6 111	1 551	4.4
March	207 036	138 730	67.0	132 947	67 660	58 132	7 155	3 238	129 656	64.2	5 783	1 472	4.2
April	207 236	138 959	67.1	132 955	67 542	58 260	7 153	3 336	129 615	64.2	6 004	1 480	4.3
May	207 427	139 107	67.1	133 311	67 539	58 440	7 331	3 335	129 937	64.3	5 796	1 505	4.2
June	207 632	139 329	67.1	133 378	67 700	58 641	7 037	3 386	129 982	64.2	5 951	1 624	4.3
July	207 828	139 439	67.1	133 414	67 731	58 490	7 193	3 346	130 146	64.2	6 025	1 513	4.3
August	208 038	139 430	67.0	133 591	67 768	58 707	7 117	3 234	130 366	64.2	5 838	1 455	4.2
September	208 265	139 622	67.0	133 707	67 882	58 735	7 090	3 173	130 434	64.2	5 915	1 449	4.2
October	208 483	139 771	67.0	133 993	67 840	58 921	7 232	3 229	130 758	64.3	5 778	1 438	4.1
November	208 666	140 025	67.1	134 309	68 094	59 018	7 198	3 343	130 989	64.4	5 716	1 378	4.1
December	208 832	140 177	67.1	134 523	68 217	59 056	7 251	3 260	131 257	64.4	5 653	1 375	4.0

[1]Not seasonally adjusted.
[2]In 1930 through 1943, the official BLS data count persons on work relief as unemployed. The unemployment rates for those years shown in parentheses count persons on work relief as employed, which is more consistent with the postwar practice. See notes and definitions.

Table 10-1B. Summary Labor Force, Employment, and Unemployment: Historical—*Continued*

(Thousands of persons, percent, seasonally adjusted, except as noted.)

| Year and month | Civilian noninstitutional population [1] | Civilian labor force | | Employment, thousands of persons | | | | | | Employment-population ratio, percent | Unemployment [2] | | |
| | | Thousands of persons | Participation rate (percent) | Total | By age and sex | | | By industry | | | Thousands of persons | | Rate (percent) |
					Men, 20 years and over	Women, 20 years and over	Both sexes, 16 to 19 years	Agricultural	Nonagricultural		Total	Unemployed 15 weeks and over	
2000													
January	211 410	142 267	67.3	136 559	69 419	59 842	7 298	2 613	133 863	64.6	5 708	1 380	4.0
February	211 576	142 456	67.3	136 598	69 505	59 887	7 206	2 731	133 912	64.6	5 858	1 300	4.1
March	211 772	142 434	67.3	136 701	69 482	59 977	7 241	2 579	134 022	64.6	5 733	1 312	4.0
April	212 018	142 751	67.3	137 270	69 519	60 358	7 393	2 505	134 806	64.7	5 481	1 261	3.8
May	212 242	142 388	67.1	136 630	69 399	59 951	7 280	2 480	134 144	64.4	5 758	1 325	4.0
June	212 466	142 591	67.1	136 940	69 629	60 027	7 284	2 445	134 528	64.5	5 651	1 242	4.0
July	212 677	142 278	66.9	136 531	69 525	60 011	6 995	2 408	134 196	64.2	5 747	1 343	4.0
August	212 916	142 514	66.9	136 662	69 823	59 719	7 120	2 433	134 311	64.2	5 853	1 394	4.1
September	213 163	142 518	66.9	136 893	69 700	60 083	7 110	2 384	134 489	64.2	5 625	1 290	3.9
October	213 405	142 622	66.8	137 088	69 762	60 238	7 088	2 319	134 808	64.2	5 534	1 337	3.9
November	213 540	142 962	66.9	137 322	69 910	60 269	7 143	2 330	134 921	64.3	5 639	1 315	3.9
December	213 736	143 248	67.0	137 614	69 939	60 503	7 172	2 389	135 194	64.4	5 634	1 329	3.9
2001													
January	213 888	143 800	67.2	137 778	70 064	60 609	7 104	2 360	135 304	64.4	6 023	1 372	4.2
February	214 110	143 701	67.1	137 612	69 959	60 615	7 038	2 370	135 291	64.3	6 089	1 491	4.2
March	214 305	143 924	67.2	137 783	69 881	60 902	7 001	2 350	135 372	64.3	6 141	1 521	4.3
April	214 525	143 569	66.9	137 299	69 916	60 523	6 860	2 336	135 036	64.0	6 271	1 499	4.4
May	214 732	143 318	66.7	137 092	69 865	60 509	6 717	2 353	134 735	63.8	6 226	1 502	4.3
June	214 950	143 357	66.7	136 873	69 690	60 371	6 812	2 082	134 755	63.7	6 484	1 532	4.5
July	215 180	143 654	66.8	137 071	69 808	60 480	6 784	2 295	134 858	63.7	6 583	1 653	4.6
August	215 420	143 284	66.5	136 241	69 585	60 301	6 356	2 305	133 944	63.2	7 042	1 861	4.9
September	215 665	143 989	66.8	136 846	69 933	60 265	6 649	2 322	134 558	63.5	7 142	1 950	5.0
October	215 903	144 086	66.7	136 392	69 621	60 168	6 602	2 327	134 098	63.2	7 694	2 082	5.3
November	216 117	144 240	66.7	136 238	69 444	60 174	6 620	2 203	133 955	63.0	8 003	2 318	5.5
December	216 315	144 305	66.7	136 047	69 551	60 095	6 400	2 293	133 751	62.9	8 258	2 444	5.7
2002													
January	216 506	143 883	66.5	135 701	69 308	60 032	6 361	2 385	133 233	62.7	8 182	2 578	5.7
February	216 663	144 653	66.8	136 438	69 534	60 479	6 425	2 397	134 127	63.0	8 215	2 608	5.7
March	216 823	144 481	66.6	136 177	69 480	60 190	6 507	2 368	133 816	62.8	8 304	2 719	5.7
April	217 006	144 725	66.7	136 126	69 574	60 204	6 349	2 371	133 833	62.7	8 599	2 852	5.9
May	217 198	144 938	66.7	136 539	69 981	60 226	6 332	2 260	134 278	62.9	8 399	2 967	5.8
June	217 407	144 808	66.6	136 415	69 769	60 297	6 348	2 161	134 135	62.7	8 393	3 023	5.8
July	217 630	144 803	66.5	136 413	69 806	60 290	6 317	2 324	134 107	62.7	8 390	2 966	5.8
August	217 866	145 009	66.6	136 705	69 937	60 560	6 208	2 127	134 593	62.7	8 304	2 887	5.7
September	218 107	145 552	66.7	137 302	70 207	60 679	6 416	2 285	135 102	63.0	8 251	2 971	5.7
October	218 340	145 314	66.6	137 008	69 948	60 663	6 397	2 471	134 580	62.7	8 307	3 042	5.7
November	218 548	145 041	66.4	136 521	69 615	60 697	6 209	2 261	134 171	62.5	8 520	3 062	5.9
December	218 741	145 066	66.3	136 426	69 620	60 667	6 139	2 352	134 071	62.4	8 640	3 271	6.0
2003													
January	219 897	145 937	66.4	137 417	69 919	61 406	6 091	2 337	135 045	62.5	8 520	3 166	5.8
February	220 114	146 100	66.4	137 482	70 262	61 159	6 060	2 234	135 306	62.5	8 618	3 161	5.9
March	220 317	146 022	66.3	137 434	70 243	61 317	5 874	2 263	135 232	62.4	8 588	3 161	5.9
April	220 540	146 474	66.4	137 633	70 311	61 374	5 948	2 150	135 561	62.4	8 842	3 348	6.0
May	220 768	146 500	66.4	137 544	70 215	61 393	5 936	2 183	135 370	62.3	8 957	3 318	6.1
June	221 014	147 056	66.5	137 790	70 159	61 747	5 884	2 185	135 419	62.3	9 266	3 552	6.3
July	221 252	146 485	66.2	137 474	70 190	61 437	5 847	2 187	135 242	62.1	9 011	3 633	6.2
August	221 507	146 445	66.1	137 549	70 237	61 442	5 870	2 313	135 200	62.1	8 896	3 557	6.1
September	221 779	146 530	66.1	137 609	70 631	61 119	5 860	2 349	135 355	62.0	8 921	3 486	6.1
October	222 039	146 716	66.1	137 984	70 685	61 451	5 848	2 479	135 571	62.1	8 732	3 451	6.0
November	222 279	147 000	66.1	138 424	70 935	61 494	5 995	2 373	136 003	62.3	8 576	3 420	5.8
December	222 509	146 729	65.9	138 411	71 170	61 396	5 845	2 243	136 145	62.2	8 317	3 366	5.7
2004													
January	222 161	146 842	66.1	138 472	71 318	61 183	5 971	2 196	136 228	62.3	8 370	3 364	5.7
February	222 357	146 709	66.0	138 542	71 122	61 514	5 906	2 210	136 362	62.3	8 167	3 248	5.6
March	222 550	146 944	66.0	138 453	71 155	61 534	5 764	2 180	136 302	62.2	8 491	3 314	5.8
April	222 757	146 850	65.9	138 680	71 121	61 647	5 912	2 241	136 474	62.3	8 170	2 971	5.6
May	222 967	147 065	66.0	138 852	71 180	61 762	5 911	2 300	136 556	62.3	8 212	3 103	5.6
June	223 196	147 460	66.1	139 174	71 562	61 793	5 819	2 237	136 748	62.4	8 286	3 130	5.6
July	223 422	147 692	66.1	139 556	71 780	61 884	5 891	2 222	137 354	62.5	8 136	2 918	5.5
August	223 677	147 564	66.0	139 573	71 808	61 836	5 930	2 333	137 230	62.4	7 990	2 846	5.4
September	223 941	147 415	65.8	139 487	71 744	61 859	5 884	2 251	137 323	62.3	7 927	2 910	5.4
October	224 192	147 793	65.9	139 732	71 860	61 942	5 931	2 216	137 598	62.3	8 061	3 041	5.5
November	224 422	148 162	66.0	140 231	72 110	62 088	6 033	2 206	137 978	62.5	7 932	2 960	5.4
December	224 640	148 059	65.9	140 125	72 058	62 136	5 931	2 171	137 947	62.4	7 934	2 927	5.4

[1] Not seasonally adjusted.
[2] In 1930 through 1943, the official BLS data count persons on work relief as unemployed. The unemployment rates for those years shown in parentheses count persons on work relief as employed, which is more consistent with the postwar practice. See notes and definitions.

Table 10-1B. Summary Labor Force, Employment, and Unemployment: Historical—*Continued*

(Thousands of persons, percent, seasonally adjusted, except as noted.)

| Year and month | Civilian noninsti-tutional popu-lation [1] | Civilian labor force | | Employment, thousands of persons | | | | | | Employ-ment-population ratio, percent | Unemployment [2] | | |
| | | Thousands of persons | Participa-tion rate (percent) | Total | By age and sex | | | By industry | | | Thousands of persons | | Rate (percent) |
					Men, 20 years and over	Women, 20 years and over	Both sexes, 16 to 19 years	Agri-cultural	Nonagri-cultural		Total	Unem-ployed 15 weeks and over	
2005													
January	224 837	148 029	65.8	140 245	72 063	62 260	5 922	2 112	138 111	62.4	7 784	2 851	5.3
February	225 041	148 364	65.9	140 385	72 299	62 253	5 832	2 129	138 267	62.4	7 980	2 896	5.4
March	225 236	148 391	65.9	140 654	72 478	62 222	5 954	2 180	138 462	62.4	7 737	2 817	5.2
April	225 441	148 926	66.1	141 254	72 860	62 483	5 912	2 248	138 992	62.7	7 672	2 678	5.2
May	225 670	149 261	66.1	141 609	73 133	62 557	5 920	2 225	139 379	62.8	7 651	2 683	5.1
June	225 911	149 238	66.1	141 714	73 223	62 516	5 975	2 302	139 276	62.7	7 524	2 405	5.0
July	226 153	149 432	66.1	142 026	73 337	62 691	5 999	2 308	139 789	62.8	7 406	2 449	5.0
August	226 421	149 779	66.2	142 434	73 513	62 844	6 077	2 183	140 277	62.9	7 345	2 569	4.9
September	226 693	149 954	66.1	142 401	73 333	63 035	6 033	2 181	140 276	62.8	7 553	2 537	5.0
October	226 959	150 001	66.1	142 548	73 445	63 127	5 976	2 191	140 435	62.8	7 453	2 492	5.0
November	227 204	150 065	66.0	142 499	73 341	63 127	6 031	2 174	140 299	62.7	7 566	2 486	5.0
December	227 425	150 030	66.0	142 752	73 467	63 209	6 076	2 094	140 635	62.8	7 279	2 429	4.9
2006													
January	227 553	150 214	66.0	143 150	73 892	63 151	6 106	2 164	140 933	62.9	7 064	2 270	4.7
February	227 763	150 641	66.1	143 457	73 972	63 304	6 182	2 178	141 254	63.0	7 184	2 546	4.8
March	227 975	150 813	66.2	143 741	74 228	63 353	6 160	2 153	141 604	63.1	7 072	2 373	4.7
April	228 199	150 881	66.1	143 761	74 204	63 413	6 144	2 249	141 388	63.0	7 120	2 353	4.7
May	228 428	151 069	66.1	144 089	74 229	63 656	6 204	2 194	141 859	63.1	6 980	2 303	4.6
June	228 671	151 354	66.2	144 353	74 261	63 866	6 226	2 256	142 019	63.1	7 001	2 127	4.6
July	228 912	151 377	66.1	144 202	74 011	64 030	6 162	2 278	142 066	63.0	7 175	2 289	4.7
August	229 167	151 716	66.2	144 625	74 384	64 139	6 102	2 240	142 440	63.1	7 091	2 293	4.7
September	229 420	151 662	66.1	144 815	74 866	63 922	6 026	2 182	142 661	63.1	6 847	2 231	4.5
October	229 675	152 041	66.2	145 314	74 833	64 298	6 183	2 183	143 222	63.3	6 727	2 062	4.4
November	229 905	152 406	66.3	145 534	74 962	64 328	6 244	2 164	143 350	63.3	6 872	2 159	4.5
December	230 108	152 732	66.4	145 970	75 232	64 518	6 220	2 233	143 716	63.4	6 762	2 083	4.4
2007													
January	230 650	153 144	66.4	146 028	75 238	64 621	6 169	2 214	143 785	63.3	7 116	2 156	4.6
February	230 834	152 983	66.3	146 057	75 239	64 750	6 068	2 295	143 741	63.3	6 927	2 211	4.5
March	231 034	153 051	66.2	146 320	75 386	64 928	6 006	2 178	144 153	63.3	6 731	2 255	4.4
April	231 253	152 435	65.9	145 586	75 342	64 366	5 877	2 069	143 385	63.0	6 850	2 281	4.5
May	231 480	152 670	66.0	145 903	75 386	64 724	5 793	2 081	143 773	63.0	6 766	2 231	4.4
June	231 713	153 041	66.0	146 063	75 327	64 788	5 948	1 946	144 112	63.0	6 979	2 281	4.6
July	231 958	153 054	66.0	145 905	75 247	64 766	5 892	2 016	144 041	62.9	7 149	2 364	4.7
August	232 211	152 749	65.8	145 682	75 195	64 838	5 649	1 863	143 865	62.7	7 067	2 333	4.6
September	232 461	153 414	66.0	146 244	75 273	65 086	5 885	2 095	144 148	62.9	7 170	2 355	4.7
October	232 715	153 183	65.8	145 946	75 146	64 842	5 958	2 121	143 926	62.7	7 237	2 300	4.7
November	232 939	153 835	66.0	146 595	75 683	64 985	5 927	2 148	144 413	62.9	7 240	2 366	4.7
December	233 156	153 918	66.0	146 273	75 510	64 910	5 853	2 219	144 018	62.7	7 645	2 501	5.0
2008													
January	232 616	154 075	66.2	146 397	75 554	65 074	5 768	2 204	144 187	62.9	7 678	2 541	5.0
February	232 809	153 648	66.0	146 157	75 454	65 023	5 680	2 188	143 965	62.8	7 491	2 444	4.9
March	232 995	153 925	66.1	146 108	75 299	65 092	5 717	2 172	143 946	62.7	7 816	2 489	5.1
April	233 198	153 761	65.9	146 130	75 182	65 116	5 832	2 109	143 902	62.7	7 631	2 685	5.0
May	233 405	154 325	66.1	145 929	74 965	65 141	5 824	2 113	143 748	62.5	8 395	2 779	5.4
June	233 627	154 316	66.1	145 738	74 969	65 172	5 597	2 121	143 631	62.4	8 578	2 916	5.6
July	233 864	154 480	66.1	145 530	74 939	65 104	5 487	2 138	143 467	62.2	8 950	3 115	5.8
August	234 107	154 646	66.1	145 196	74 651	65 003	5 541	2 151	143 066	62.0	9 450	3 422	6.1
September	234 360	154 559	65.9	145 059	74 453	65 069	5 537	2 238	142 814	61.9	9 501	3 620	6.1
October	234 612	154 875	66.0	144 792	74 264	65 088	5 440	2 207	142 691	61.7	10 083	3 991	6.5
November	234 828	154 622	65.8	144 078	73 933	64 870	5 274	2 212	141 836	61.4	10 544	3 928	6.8
December	235 035	154 626	65.8	143 328	73 319	64 769	5 240	2 202	141 107	61.0	11 299	4 556	7.3
2009													
January	234 739	154 236	65.7	142 187	72 734	64 238	5 216	2 143	140 069	60.6	12 049	4 771	7.8
February	234 913	154 521	65.8	141 660	72 279	64 206	5 176	2 124	139 558	60.3	12 860	5 449	8.3
March	235 086	154 143	65.6	140 754	71 658	64 053	5 043	2 027	138 756	59.9	13 389	5 871	8.7
April	235 271	154 450	65.6	140 654	71 597	64 045	5 011	2 124	138 484	59.8	13 796	6 364	8.9
May	235 452	154 800	65.7	140 294	71 437	63 825	5 032	2 149	138 075	59.6	14 505	7 022	9.4
June	235 655	154 730	65.7	140 003	71 316	63 735	4 952	2 150	137 839	59.4	14 727	7 842	9.5
July	235 870	154 538	65.5	139 891	71 239	63 765	4 887	2 135	137 719	59.3	14 646	7 837	9.5
August	236 087	154 319	65.4	139 458	71 080	63 628	4 750	2 099	137 318	59.1	14 861	7 829	9.6
September	236 322	153 786	65.1	138 775	70 819	63 314	4 641	2 046	136 755	58.7	15 012	8 370	9.8
October	236 550	153 822	65.0	138 401	70 701	63 245	4 455	2 058	136 446	58.5	15 421	8 678	10.0
November	236 743	153 833	65.0	138 607	70 765	63 371	4 471	2 111	136 481	58.5	15 227	8 792	9.9
December	236 924	153 091	64.6	137 968	70 491	63 035	4 442	2 078	135 877	58.2	15 124	8 878	9.9

[1]Not seasonally adjusted.
[2]In 1930 through 1943, the official BLS data count persons on work relief as unemployed. The unemployment rates for those years shown in parentheses count persons on work relief as employed, which is more consistent with the postwar practice. See notes and definitions.

Table 10-2. Labor Force and Employment by Major Age and Sex Groups

(Thousands of persons, percent, seasonally adjusted.)

Year and month	Civilian labor force (thousands)			Participation rate (percent)			Employment (thousands)			Employment-population ratio, percent		
	Men, 20 years and over	Women, 20 years and over	Both sexes, 16 to 19 years	Men, 20 years and over	Women, 20 years and over	Both sexes, 16 to 19 years	Men, 20 years and over	Women, 20 years and over	Both sexes, 16 to 19 years	Men, 20 years and over	Women, 20 years and over	Both sexes, 16 to 19 years
1965	44 857	23 686	5 910	83.9	39.4	45.7	43 422	22 630	5 036	81.2	37.6	38.9
1966	44 788	24 431	6 558	83.6	40.1	48.2	43 668	23 510	5 721	81.5	38.6	42.1
1967	45 354	25 475	6 521	83.4	41.1	48.4	44 294	24 397	5 682	81.5	39.3	42.2
1968	45 852	26 266	6 619	83.1	41.6	48.3	44 859	25 281	5 781	81.3	40.0	42.2
1969	46 351	27 413	6 970	82.8	42.7	49.4	45 388	26 397	6 117	81.1	41.1	43.4
1970	47 220	28 301	7 249	82.6	43.3	49.9	45 581	26 952	6 144	79.7	41.2	42.3
1971	48 009	28 904	7 470	82.1	43.3	49.7	45 912	27 246	6 208	78.5	40.9	41.3
1972	49 079	29 901	8 054	81.6	43.7	51.9	47 130	28 276	6 746	78.4	41.3	43.5
1973	49 932	30 991	8 507	81.3	44.4	53.7	48 310	29 484	7 271	78.6	42.2	45.9
1974	50 879	32 201	8 871	81.0	45.3	54.8	48 922	30 424	7 448	77.9	42.8	46.0
1975	51 494	33 410	8 870	80.3	46.0	54.0	48 018	30 726	7 104	74.8	42.3	43.3
1976	52 288	34 814	9 056	79.8	47.0	54.5	49 190	32 226	7 336	75.1	43.5	44.2
1977	53 348	36 310	9 351	79.7	48.1	56.0	50 555	33 775	7 688	75.6	44.8	46.1
1978	54 471	38 128	9 652	79.8	49.6	57.8	52 143	35 836	8 070	76.4	46.6	48.3
1979	55 615	39 708	9 638	79.8	50.6	57.9	53 308	37 434	8 083	76.5	47.7	48.5
1980	56 455	41 106	9 378	79.4	51.3	56.7	53 101	38 492	7 710	74.6	48.1	46.6
1981	57 197	42 485	8 988	79.0	52.1	55.4	53 582	39 590	7 225	74.0	48.6	44.6
1982	57 980	43 699	8 526	78.7	52.7	54.1	52 891	40 086	6 549	71.8	48.4	41.5
1983	58 744	44 636	8 171	78.5	53.1	53.5	53 487	41 004	6 342	71.4	48.8	41.5
1984	59 701	45 900	7 943	78.3	53.7	53.9	55 769	42 793	6 444	73.2	50.1	43.7
1985	60 277	47 283	7 901	78.1	54.7	54.5	56 562	44 154	6 434	73.3	51.0	44.4
1986	61 320	48 589	7 926	78.1	55.5	54.7	57 569	45 556	6 472	73.3	52.0	44.6
1987	62 095	49 783	7 988	78.0	56.2	54.7	58 726	47 074	6 640	73.8	53.1	45.5
1988	62 768	50 870	8 031	77.9	56.8	55.3	59 781	48 383	6 805	74.2	54.0	46.8
1989	63 704	52 212	7 954	78.1	57.7	55.9	60 837	49 745	6 759	74.5	54.9	47.5
1990	64 916	53 131	7 792	78.2	58.0	53.7	61 678	50 535	6 581	74.3	55.2	45.3
1991	65 374	53 708	7 265	77.7	57.9	51.6	61 178	50 634	5 906	72.7	54.6	42.0
1992	66 213	54 796	7 096	77.7	58.5	51.3	61 496	51 328	5 669	72.1	54.8	41.0
1993	66 642	55 388	7 170	77.3	58.5	51.5	62 355	52 099	5 805	72.3	55.0	41.7
1994	66 921	56 655	7 481	76.8	59.3	52.7	63 294	53 606	6 161	72.6	56.2	43.4
1995	67 324	57 215	7 765	76.7	59.4	53.5	64 085	54 396	6 419	73.0	56.5	44.2
1996	68 044	58 094	7 806	76.8	59.9	52.3	64 897	55 311	6 500	73.2	57.0	43.5
1997	69 166	59 198	7 932	77.0	60.5	51.6	66 284	56 613	6 661	73.7	57.8	43.4
1998	69 715	59 702	8 256	76.8	60.4	52.8	67 135	57 278	7 051	73.9	58.0	45.1
1999	70 194	60 840	8 333	76.7	60.7	52.0	67 761	58 555	7 172	74.0	58.5	44.7
2000	72 010	62 301	8 271	76.7	60.6	52.0	69 634	60 067	7 189	74.2	58.4	45.2
2001	72 816	63 016	7 902	76.5	60.6	49.6	69 776	60 417	6 740	73.3	58.1	42.3
2002	73 630	63 648	7 585	76.3	60.5	47.4	69 734	60 420	6 332	72.3	57.5	39.6
2003	74 623	64 716	7 170	75.9	60.6	44.5	70 415	61 402	5 919	71.7	57.5	36.8
2004	75 364	64 923	7 114	75.8	60.3	43.9	71 572	61 773	5 907	71.9	57.4	36.4
2005	76 443	65 714	7 164	75.8	60.4	43.7	73 050	62 702	5 978	72.4	57.6	36.5
2006	77 562	66 585	7 281	75.9	60.5	43.7	74 431	63 834	6 162	72.9	58.0	36.9
2007	78 596	67 516	7 012	75.9	60.6	41.3	75 337	64 799	5 911	72.8	58.2	34.8
2008	79 047	68 382	6 858	75.7	60.9	40.2	74 750	65 039	5 573	71.6	57.9	32.6
2009	78 897	68 856	6 390	74.8	60.8	37.5	71 341	63 699	4 837	67.6	56.2	28.4
2010	78 994	68 990	5 906	74.1	60.3	34.9	71 230	63 456	4 378	66.8	55.5	25.9
2011	79 080	68 810	5 727	73.4	59.8	34.1	72 182	63 360	4 327	67.0	55.0	25.8
2010												
January	78 486	68 986	5 981	74.0	60.6	35.1	70 529	63 542	4 430	66.5	55.8	26.0
February	78 644	69 053	6 007	74.1	60.6	35.3	70 645	63 541	4 479	66.6	55.8	26.3
March	78 918	68 975	6 072	74.3	60.5	35.7	70 929	63 426	4 481	66.8	55.6	26.4
April	79 346	69 128	6 054	74.6	60.6	35.7	71 352	63 453	4 501	67.1	55.6	26.5
May	79 123	69 049	6 044	74.4	60.5	35.7	71 416	63 491	4 432	67.1	55.6	26.2
June	79 047	68 852	5 755	74.2	60.3	34.0	71 338	63 533	4 266	67.0	55.6	25.2
July	79 027	68 866	5 855	74.1	60.2	34.7	71 403	63 399	4 337	67.0	55.4	25.7
August	79 243	68 911	5 919	74.2	60.2	35.1	71 538	63 406	4 394	67.0	55.4	26.1
September	79 175	69 003	5 740	74.1	60.2	34.1	71 545	63 540	4 259	66.9	55.4	25.3
October	78 867	68 934	5 908	73.7	60.1	35.1	71 410	63 352	4 311	66.7	55.2	25.6
November	78 970	69 232	5 839	73.7	60.3	34.8	71 128	63 400	4 409	66.4	55.2	26.2
December	78 884	68 982	5 748	73.6	60.0	34.3	71 494	63 429	4 297	66.7	55.2	25.6
2011												
January	78 594	68 843	5 813	73.3	60.1	34.5	71 593	63 403	4 334	66.8	55.3	25.7
February	78 832	68 818	5 651	73.5	60.0	33.5	71 901	63 351	4 299	67.0	55.2	25.5
March	78 805	68 852	5 735	73.4	60.0	34.1	71 918	63 515	4 332	67.0	55.3	25.7
April	78 895	68 860	5 665	73.4	59.9	33.7	71 942	63 431	4 255	66.9	55.2	25.3
May	79 204	68 878	5 618	73.6	59.9	33.5	72 161	63 385	4 262	67.1	55.1	25.4
June	79 116	68 570	5 724	73.5	59.6	34.1	71 981	63 088	4 316	66.9	54.8	25.7
July	78 977	68 706	5 675	73.3	59.7	33.9	71 930	63 257	4 262	66.7	54.9	25.4
August	79 089	68 784	5 801	73.3	59.7	34.6	72 098	63 322	4 333	66.8	54.9	25.9
September	79 241	68 989	5 774	73.4	59.8	34.5	72 340	63 406	4 362	67.0	55.0	26.1
October	79 291	68 981	5 785	73.3	59.8	34.6	72 379	63 520	4 398	67.0	55.0	26.3
November	79 440	68 711	5 786	73.4	59.5	34.6	72 846	63 352	4 416	67.3	54.8	26.4
December	79 436	68 748	5 704	73.4	59.5	34.2	73 080	63 323	4 387	67.5	54.8	26.3

Table 10-3. Employment by Type of Job

(Thousands of persons, seasonally adjusted, except as noted.)

Year and month	Agricultural	By class of worker								Multiple jobholders		Employed and at work part-time	
		Nonagricultural industries											
		Total	Wage and salary					Self-employed (unincorporated)	Unpaid family workers[1]	Total (thousands)	Percent of total employed	Economic reasons	Non-economic reasons
			Total	Government	Private industries								
					Private households[1]	Other private industries							
1965	4 361	66 726	60 031	9 608	. . .	. . .	6 097	600	. . .	. . .	2 209	8 466
1966	3 979	68 915	62 362	10 323	. . .	. . .	5 991	564	. . .	. . .	1 960	8 112
1967	3 844	70 527	64 848	11 146	. . .	. . .	5 174	505	. . .	. . .	2 163	8 701
1968	3 817	72 103	66 519	11 590	. . .	. . .	5 102	485	. . .	. . .	1 970	9 075
1969	3 606	74 296	68 528	12 025	. . .	. . .	5 252	517	. . .	. . .	2 056	9 652
1970	3 463	75 215	69 491	12 431	. . .	. . .	5 221	502	. . .	. . .	2 446	9 999
1971	3 394	75 972	70 120	12 799	. . .	. . .	5 327	522	. . .	. . .	2 688	10 152
1972	3 484	78 669	72 785	13 393	. . .	. . .	5 365	519	. . .	. . .	2 648	10 612
1973	3 470	81 594	75 580	13 655	. . .	. . .	5 474	540	. . .	. . .	2 554	10 972
1974	3 515	83 279	77 094	14 124	. . .	. . .	5 697	489	. . .	. . .	2 988	11 153
1975	3 408	82 438	76 249	14 675	. . .	. . .	5 705	483	. . .	. . .	3 804	11 228
1976	3 331	85 421	79 175	15 132	. . .	. . .	5 783	464	. . .	. . .	3 607	11 607
1977	3 283	88 734	82 121	15 361	. . .	. . .	6 114	498	. . .	. . .	3 608	12 120
1978	3 387	92 661	85 753	15 525	. . .	. . .	6 429	479	. . .	. . .	3 516	12 650
1979	3 347	95 477	88 222	15 635	. . .	. . .	6 791	463	. . .	. . .	3 577	12 893
1980	3 364	95 938	88 525	15 912	. . .	. . .	7 000	413	. . .	. . .	4 321	13 067
1981	3 368	97 030	89 543	15 689	. . .	. . .	7 097	390	. . .	. . .	4 768	13 025
1982	3 401	96 125	88 462	15 516	. . .	. . .	7 262	401	. . .	. . .	6 170	12 953
1983	3 383	97 450	89 500	15 537	. . .	. . .	7 575	376	. . .	. . .	6 266	12 911
1984	3 321	101 685	93 565	15 770	. . .	. . .	7 785	335	. . .	. . .	5 744	13 169
1985	3 179	103 971	95 871	16 031	. . .	. . .	7 811	289	. . .	. . .	5 590	13 489
1986	3 163	106 434	98 299	16 342	. . .	. . .	7 881	255	. . .	. . .	5 588	13 935
1987	3 208	109 232	100 771	16 800	. . .	. . .	8 201	260	. . .	. . .	5 401	14 395
1988	3 169	111 800	103 021	17 114	. . .	. . .	8 519	260	. . .	. . .	5 206	14 963
1989	3 199	114 142	105 259	17 469	. . .	. . .	8 605	279	. . .	. . .	4 894	15 393
1990	3 223	115 570	106 598	17 769	. . .	. . .	8 719	253	. . .	. . .	5 204	15 341
1991	3 269	114 449	105 373	17 934	. . .	. . .	8 851	226	. . .	. . .	6 161	15 172
1992	3 247	115 245	106 437	18 136	. . .	. . .	8 575	233	. . .	. . .	6 520	14 918
1993	3 115	117 144	107 966	18 579	. . .	. . .	8 959	218	. . .	. . .	6 481	15 240
1994	3 409	119 651	110 517	18 293	. . .	. . .	9 003	131	7 260	5.9	4 625	17 638
1995	3 440	121 460	112 448	18 362	. . .	. . .	8 902	110	7 693	6.2	4 473	17 734
1996	3 443	123 264	114 171	18 217	. . .	. . .	8 971	122	7 832	6.2	4 315	17 770
1997	3 399	126 159	116 983	18 131	. . .	. . .	9 056	120	7 955	6.1	4 068	18 149
1998	3 378	128 085	119 019	18 383	. . .	. . .	8 962	103	7 926	6.0	3 665	18 530
1999	3 281	130 207	121 323	18 903	. . .	. . .	8 790	95	7 802	5.8	3 357	18 758
2000	2 464	134 427	125 114	19 248	718	105 148	9 205	108	7 604	5.6	3 227	18 814
2001	2 299	134 635	125 407	19 335	694	105 378	9 121	107	7 357	5.4	3 715	18 790
2002	2 311	134 174	125 156	19 636	757	104 764	8 923	95	7 291	5.3	4 213	18 843
2003	2 275	135 461	126 015	19 634	764	105 616	9 344	101	7 315	5.3	4 701	19 014
2004	2 232	137 020	127 463	19 983	779	106 701	9 467	90	7 473	5.4	4 567	19 380
2005	2 197	139 532	129 931	20 357	812	108 761	9 509	93	7 546	5.3	4 350	19 491
2006	2 206	142 221	132 449	20 337	803	111 309	9 685	87	7 576	5.2	4 162	19 591
2007	2 095	143 952	134 283	21 003	813	112 467	9 557	112	7 655	5.2	4 401	19 756
2008	2 168	143 194	133 882	21 258	805	111 819	9 219	93	7 620	5.2	5 875	19 343
2009	2 103	137 775	128 713	21 178	783	106 752	8 995	66	7 271	5.2	8 913	18 710
2010	2 206	136 858	127 914	21 003	667	106 244	8 860	84	6 878	4.9	8 874	18 251
2011	2 254	137 615	128 934	20 536	722	107 676	8 603	78	6 880	4.9	8 560	18 334
2010												
January	2 121	136 464	127 410	21 239	688	105 457	8 949	66	6 965	5.0	8 508	18 636
February	2 295	136 459	127 365	21 213	666	105 415	8 993	80	7 055	5.1	8 882	18 323
March	2 202	136 702	127 653	21 189	733	105 752	8 906	74	7 014	5.1	9 064	18 275
April	2 247	137 026	128 007	21 362	711	105 920	8 900	114	7 017	5.0	9 097	18 023
May	2 205	137 074	128 051	21 274	698	106 133	8 926	85	7 119	5.1	8 798	17 918
June	2 120	136 968	127 971	21 217	697	106 179	8 902	110	6 930	5.0	8 652	17 896
July	2 188	136 776	128 043	20 985	692	106 448	8 831	83	6 613	4.8	8 625	18 246
August	2 182	137 080	128 316	20 644	678	107 067	8 705	52	6 810	4.9	8 804	18 688
September	2 184	137 233	128 421	20 827	597	106 778	8 783	69	6 694	4.8	9 383	18 256
October	2 373	136 816	127 839	20 729	562	106 460	8 883	85	6 713	4.8	8 964	18 198
November	2 206	136 686	127 786	20 635	650	106 502	8 791	93	6 732	4.8	8 893	18 305
December	2 173	137 036	128 121	20 724	635	106 767	8 759	97	6 884	4.9	8 869	18 189
2011												
January	2 252	137 156	128 197	20 719	610	106 845	8 818	91	6 835	4.9	8 449	17 923
February	2 247	137 388	128 610	20 874	688	107 003	8 666	87	6 770	4.9	8 383	18 280
March	2 244	137 619	128 706	20 791	695	107 252	8 754	105	6 752	4.8	8 459	18 425
April	2 090	137 505	128 756	20 629	671	107 466	8 645	94	6 798	4.9	8 571	18 326
May	2 244	137 508	128 773	20 348	799	107 722	8 648	79	6 924	5.0	8 541	18 481
June	2 224	137 125	128 529	20 320	766	107 548	8 550	76	6 884	4.9	8 545	18 461
July	2 250	136 993	128 554	20 306	822	107 478	8 532	82	6 777	4.9	8 437	18 280
August	2 373	137 290	128 700	20 309	769	107 678	8 530	66	6 943	5.0	8 787	18 276
September	2 268	137 932	129 595	20 568	756	108 026	8 336	55	6 970	5.0	9 270	18 329
October	2 257	138 167	129 531	20 516	771	108 177	8 553	50	6 903	4.9	8 790	18 401
November	2 262	138 304	129 604	20 434	674	108 485	8 628	57	7 004	5.0	8 469	18 363
December	2 349	138 411	129 662	20 616	640	108 407	8 587	91	7 013	5.0	8 098	18 372

[1]Not seasonally adjusted.
. . . = Not available.

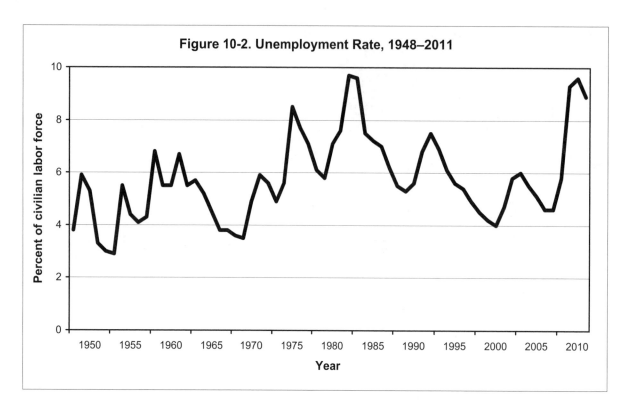

Figure 10-2. Unemployment Rate, 1948–2011

- The unemployment rate peaked at 10.0 percent in October 2009. This was below the postwar record of 10.8 percent, set in November and December 1982. Yet the employment losses of 2008–2009 were proportionately greater than the 2 percent drop in 1981–1982. The difference is in labor force behavior. In 1982, labor force participation actually increased despite job losses, in contrast to the substantial withdrawal from the labor force that occurred in 2008–2009. (Tables 10-1A and B)

- The unemployment rate hovered near 10 percent through November 2010, but has declined significantly since then to 8.2 percent in May and June 2012, reflecting both labor force decline and employment growth, with more of the former. (Table 10-1A and recent data)

- From 2007 to 2010, unemployment rates rose across the board, whether the unemployed were classified by age and sex, by race and ethnicity, or by marital status. The bulk of the rise was accounted for by people who lost jobs or had completed temporary jobs and failed to find new ones, but unemployment rates also rose somewhat for new entrants and reentrants into the labor force. (Tables 10-4 and 10-5)

- In 2010, the median unemployed worker had been out of work 21.4 weeks—double the median length of unemployment in 1983 or 2003. Median duration is more representative of the typical job-seeker than "average duration," which is distorted by the presence of a few extremely long-term unemployed and recently by a technical statistical problem. Nevertheless, the rise in long-term unemployment has been very large and constitutes a very serious problem—and even understates the problem, since it does not include discouraged workers. (Table 10-5)

- Adding discouraged workers, workers marginally attached to the labor force, and persons on involuntary part time to get a comprehensive measure of the jobs gap, BLS calculates an underutilization rate that rose from 8.3 percent in 2007 to 16.7 percent in 2010, but has declined to 14.9 percent in June 2012. (Table 10-5 and recent data)

Table 10-4. Unemployment by Demographic Group

(Unemployment in thousands of persons and as a percent of the civilian labor force in group, seasonally adjusted, except as noted.)

Year and month	Unemployment (thousands of persons)				Unemployment rate (percent)								
					All civilian workers	By age and sex			By race				Hispanic or Latino ethnicity
	Total	Men, 20 years and over	Women, 20 years and over	Both sexes, 16 to 19 years		Men, 20 years and over	Women, 20 years and over	Both sexes, 16 to 19 years	White	Black and other	Black or African American	Asian [1]	
1965	3 366	1 435	1 056	874	4.5	3.2	4.5	14.8	4.1	8.1	. . .	. . .	. . .
1966	2 875	1 120	921	837	3.8	2.5	3.8	12.8	3.4	7.3	. . .	. . .	. . .
1967	2 975	1 060	1 078	839	3.8	2.3	4.2	12.9	3.4	7.4	. . .	. . .	. . .
1968	2 817	993	985	838	3.6	2.2	3.8	12.7	3.2	6.7	. . .	. . .	. . .
1969	2 832	963	1 015	853	3.5	2.1	3.7	12.2	3.1	6.4	. . .	. . .	. . .
1970	4 093	1 638	1 349	1 106	4.9	3.5	4.8	15.3	4.5	8.2	. . .	. . .	. . .
1971	5 016	2 097	1 658	1 262	5.9	4.4	5.7	16.9	5.4	9.9	. . .	. . .	. . .
1972	4 882	1 948	1 625	1 308	5.6	4.0	5.4	16.2	5.1	10.0	10.4	. . .	. . .
1973	4 365	1 624	1 507	1 235	4.9	3.3	4.9	14.5	4.3	9.0	9.4	. . .	7.5
1974	5 156	1 957	1 777	1 422	5.6	3.8	5.5	16.0	5.0	9.9	10.5	. . .	8.1
1975	7 929	3 476	2 684	1 767	8.5	6.8	8.0	19.9	7.8	13.8	14.8	. . .	12.2
1976	7 406	3 098	2 588	1 719	7.7	5.9	7.4	19.0	7.0	13.1	14.0	. . .	11.5
1977	6 991	2 794	2 535	1 663	7.1	5.2	7.0	17.8	6.2	13.1	14.0	. . .	10.1
1978	6 202	2 328	2 292	1 583	6.1	4.3	6.0	16.4	5.2	11.9	12.8	. . .	9.1
1979	6 137	2 308	2 276	1 555	5.8	4.2	5.7	16.1	5.1	11.3	12.3	. . .	8.3
1980	7 637	3 353	2 615	1 669	7.1	5.9	6.4	17.8	6.3	13.1	14.3	. . .	10.1
1981	8 273	3 615	2 895	1 763	7.6	6.3	6.8	19.6	6.7	14.2	15.6	. . .	10.4
1982	10 678	5 089	3 613	1 977	9.7	8.8	8.3	23.2	8.6	17.3	18.9	. . .	13.8
1983	10 717	5 257	3 632	1 829	9.6	8.9	8.1	22.4	8.4	17.8	19.5	. . .	13.7
1984	8 539	3 932	3 107	1 499	7.5	6.6	6.8	18.9	6.5	14.4	15.9	. . .	10.7
1985	8 312	3 715	3 129	1 468	7.2	6.2	6.6	18.6	6.2	13.7	15.1	. . .	10.5
1986	8 237	3 751	3 032	1 454	7.0	6.1	6.2	18.3	6.0	13.1	14.5	. . .	10.6
1987	7 425	3 369	2 709	1 347	6.2	5.4	5.4	16.9	5.3	11.6	13.0	. . .	8.8
1988	6 701	2 987	2 487	1 226	5.5	4.8	4.9	15.3	4.7	10.4	11.7	. . .	8.2
1989	6 528	2 867	2 467	1 194	5.3	4.5	4.7	15.0	4.5	10.0	11.4	. . .	8.0
1990	7 047	3 239	2 596	1 212	5.6	5.0	4.9	15.5	4.8	10.1	11.4	. . .	8.2
1991	8 628	4 195	3 074	1 359	6.8	6.4	5.7	18.7	6.1	11.1	12.5	. . .	10.0
1992	9 613	4 717	3 469	1 427	7.5	7.1	6.3	20.1	6.6	12.7	14.2	. . .	11.6
1993	8 940	4 287	3 288	1 365	6.9	6.4	5.9	19.0	6.1	11.7	13.0	. . .	10.8
1994	7 996	3 627	3 049	1 320	6.1	5.4	5.4	17.6	5.3	10.5	11.5	. . .	9.9
1995	7 404	3 239	2 819	1 346	5.6	4.8	4.9	17.3	4.9	9.6	10.4	. . .	9.3
1996	7 236	3 146	2 783	1 306	5.4	4.6	4.8	16.7	4.7	9.3	10.5	. . .	8.9
1997	6 739	2 882	2 585	1 271	4.9	4.2	4.4	16.0	4.2	8.8	10.0	. . .	7.7
1998	6 210	2 580	2 424	1 205	4.5	3.7	4.1	14.6	3.9	7.8	8.9	. . .	7.2
1999	5 880	2 433	2 285	1 162	4.2	3.5	3.8	13.9	3.7	7.0	8.0	. . .	6.4
2000	5 692	2 376	2 235	1 081	4.0	3.3	3.6	13.1	3.5	6.7	7.6	3.6	5.7
2001	6 801	3 040	2 599	1 162	4.7	4.2	4.1	14.7	4.2	7.7	8.6	4.5	6.6
2002	8 378	3 896	3 228	1 253	5.8	5.3	5.1	16.5	5.1	9.2	10.2	5.9	7.5
2003	8 774	4 209	3 314	1 251	6.0	5.6	5.1	17.5	5.2	. . .	10.8	6.0	7.7
2004	8 149	3 791	3 150	1 208	5.5	5.0	4.9	17.0	4.8	. . .	10.4	4.4	7.0
2005	7 591	3 392	3 013	1 186	5.1	4.4	4.6	16.6	4.4	. . .	10.0	4.0	6.0
2006	7 001	3 131	2 751	1 119	4.6	4.0	4.1	15.4	4.0	. . .	8.9	3.0	5.2
2007	7 078	3 259	2 718	1 101	4.6	4.1	4.0	15.7	4.1	. . .	8.3	3.2	5.6
2008	8 924	4 297	3 342	1 285	5.8	5.4	4.9	18.7	5.2	. . .	10.1	4.0	7.6
2009	14 265	7 555	5 157	1 552	9.3	9.6	7.5	24.3	8.5	. . .	14.8	7.3	12.1
2010	14 825	7 763	5 534	1 528	9.6	9.8	8.0	25.9	8.7	. . .	16.0	7.5	12.5
2011	13 747	6 898	5 450	1 400	8.9	8.7	7.9	24.4	7.9	. . .	15.8	7.0	11.5
2010													
January	14 953	7 958	5 444	1 551	9.7	10.1	7.9	25.9	8.7	. . .	16.5	8.4	12.6
February	15 039	7 999	5 512	1 528	9.8	10.2	8.0	25.4	8.9	. . .	16.0	8.4	12.4
March	15 128	7 989	5 549	1 591	9.8	10.1	8.0	26.2	8.8	. . .	16.7	7.5	12.6
April	15 221	7 994	5 674	1 553	9.9	10.1	8.2	25.7	9.0	. . .	16.4	6.8	12.4
May	14 876	7 707	5 558	1 611	9.6	9.7	8.0	26.7	8.8	. . .	15.4	7.5	12.3
June	14 517	7 709	5 318	1 489	9.4	9.8	7.7	25.9	8.6	. . .	15.2	7.7	12.4
July	14 609	7 624	5 467	1 518	9.5	9.6	7.9	25.9	8.6	. . .	15.7	8.2	12.2
August	14 735	7 705	5 504	1 525	9.6	9.7	8.0	25.8	8.7	. . .	16.1	7.2	12.1
September	14 574	7 629	5 464	1 481	9.5	9.6	7.9	25.8	8.6	. . .	16.0	6.4	12.4
October	14 636	7 457	5 582	1 597	9.5	9.5	8.1	27.0	8.6	. . .	15.9	7.1	12.5
November	15 104	7 842	5 832	1 430	9.8	9.9	8.4	24.5	8.9	. . .	16.1	7.6	13.1
December	14 393	7 390	5 553	1 451	9.4	9.4	8.1	25.2	8.5	. . .	15.8	7.2	12.9
2011													
January	13 919	7 001	5 440	1 479	9.1	8.9	7.9	25.4	8.1	. . .	15.7	6.9	12.0
February	13 751	6 931	5 467	1 352	9.0	8.8	7.9	23.9	8.0	. . .	15.4	6.8	11.6
March	13 628	6 887	5 336	1 404	8.9	8.7	7.8	24.5	7.9	. . .	15.6	7.1	11.3
April	13 792	6 953	5 430	1 410	9.0	8.8	7.9	24.9	8.1	. . .	16.2	6.4	11.8
May	13 892	7 043	5 493	1 356	9.0	8.9	8.0	24.1	8.0	. . .	16.2	7.0	11.8
June	14 024	7 135	5 482	1 408	9.1	9.0	8.0	24.6	8.1	. . .	16.2	6.8	11.6
July	13 908	7 047	5 449	1 412	9.1	8.9	7.9	24.9	8.1	. . .	15.9	7.7	11.3
August	13 920	6 991	5 462	1 467	9.1	8.8	7.9	25.3	7.9	. . .	16.7	7.1	11.3
September	13 897	6 901	5 584	1 412	9.0	8.7	8.1	24.5	7.9	. . .	15.9	7.8	11.3
October	13 759	6 912	5 461	1 386	8.9	8.7	7.9	24.0	8.0	. . .	15.0	7.3	11.4
November	13 323	6 594	5 359	1 370	8.7	8.3	7.8	23.7	7.6	. . .	15.5	6.5	11.4
December	13 097	6 356	5 425	1 316	8.5	8.0	7.9	23.1	7.5	. . .	15.8	6.8	11.0

[1] Not seasonally adjusted.
. . . = Not available.

Table 10-5. Unemployment Rates and Related Data

(Seasonally adjusted, except as noted.)

Year and month	Unemployment rates by marital status (percent of labor force in group)			Unemployment rates by reason for unemployment (percent of total civilian labor force in group.)					Duration of unemployment		Alternative measures of labor under-utilization (percent)		
	Married men, spouse present	Married women, spouse present	Women who maintain families[1]	Total	Job losers and persons who completed temporary jobs	Job leavers	Reentrants	New entrants	Average (mean) weeks unemployed	Median weeks unemployed	Including discouraged workers (U-4)	Including all marginally attached workers (U-5)	Including marginally attached and under-employed (U-6)
1965	2.4	4.5	...	4.5	...	...	...	...	11.8	...	...	...	...
1966	1.9	3.7	...	3.8	...	...	...	...	10.4	...	...	...	...
1967	1.8	4.5	4.9	3.8	1.6	0.6	1.2	0.5	8.7	2.3	...	...	...
1968	1.6	3.9	4.4	3.6	1.4	0.5	1.2	0.5	8.4	4.5	...	...	...
1969	1.5	3.9	4.4	3.5	1.3	0.5	1.2	0.5	7.8	4.4	...	...	...
1970	2.6	4.9	5.4	4.9	2.2	0.7	1.5	0.6	8.6	4.9	...	...	...
1971	3.2	5.7	7.3	5.9	2.8	0.7	1.7	0.7	11.3	6.3	...	...	...
1972	2.8	5.4	7.2	5.6	2.4	0.7	1.7	0.8	12.0	6.2	...	...	...
1973	2.3	4.7	7.1	4.9	1.9	0.8	1.5	0.7	10.0	5.2	...	...	...
1974	2.7	5.3	7.0	5.6	2.4	0.8	1.6	0.7	9.8	5.2	...	...	...
1975	5.1	7.9	10.0	8.5	4.7	0.9	2.0	0.9	14.2	8.4	...	...	...
1976	4.2	7.1	10.1	7.7	3.8	0.9	2.0	0.9	15.8	8.2	...	...	...
1977	3.6	6.5	9.4	7.1	3.2	0.9	2.0	1.0	14.3	7.0	...	...	...
1978	2.8	5.5	8.5	6.1	2.5	0.9	1.8	0.9	11.9	5.9	...	...	...
1979	2.8	5.1	8.3	5.8	2.5	0.8	1.7	0.8	10.8	5.4	...	...	...
1980	4.2	5.8	9.2	7.1	3.7	0.8	1.8	0.8	11.9	6.5	...	...	...
1981	4.3	6.0	10.4	7.6	3.9	0.8	1.9	0.9	13.7	6.9	...	...	...
1982	6.5	7.4	11.7	9.7	5.7	0.8	2.2	1.1	15.6	8.7	...	...	...
1983	6.5	7.0	12.2	9.6	5.6	0.7	2.2	1.1	20.0	10.1	...	...	...
1984	4.6	5.7	10.3	7.5	3.9	0.7	1.9	1.0	18.2	7.9	...	...	...
1985	4.3	5.6	10.4	7.2	3.6	0.8	2.0	0.9	15.6	6.8	...	...	...
1986	4.4	5.2	9.8	7.0	3.4	0.9	1.8	0.9	15.0	6.9	...	...	...
1987	3.9	4.3	9.2	6.2	3.0	0.8	1.6	0.8	14.5	6.5	...	...	...
1988	3.3	3.9	8.1	5.5	2.5	0.8	1.5	0.7	13.5	5.9	...	...	...
1989	3.0	3.7	8.1	5.3	2.4	0.8	1.5	0.5	11.9	4.8	...	...	...
1990	3.4	3.8	8.3	5.6	2.7	0.8	1.5	0.5	12.0	5.3	...	...	...
1991	4.4	4.5	9.3	6.8	3.7	0.8	1.7	0.6	13.7	6.8	...	...	...
1992	5.1	5.0	10.0	7.5	4.2	0.8	1.8	0.7	17.7	8.7	...	...	...
1993	4.4	4.6	9.7	6.9	3.8	0.8	1.7	0.7	18.0	8.3	...	...	...
1994	3.7	4.1	8.9	6.1	2.9	0.6	2.1	0.5	18.8	9.2	6.5	7.4	10.9
1995	3.3	3.9	8.0	5.6	2.6	0.6	1.9	0.4	16.6	8.3	5.9	6.7	10.1
1996	3.0	3.6	8.2	5.4	2.5	0.6	1.9	0.4	16.7	8.3	5.7	6.5	9.7
1997	2.7	3.1	8.1	4.9	2.2	0.6	1.7	0.4	15.8	8.0	5.2	5.9	8.9
1998	2.4	2.9	7.2	4.5	2.1	0.5	1.5	0.4	14.5	6.7	4.7	5.4	8.0
1999	2.2	2.7	6.4	4.2	1.9	0.6	1.4	0.3	13.4	6.4	4.4	5.0	7.4
2000	2.0	2.7	5.9	4.0	1.8	0.5	1.4	0.3	12.6	5.9	4.2	4.8	7.0
2001	2.7	3.1	6.6	4.7	2.4	0.6	1.4	0.3	13.1	6.8	4.9	5.6	8.1
2002	3.6	3.7	8.0	5.8	3.2	0.6	1.6	0.4	16.6	9.1	6.0	6.7	9.6
2003	3.8	3.7	8.5	6.0	3.3	0.6	1.7	0.4	19.2	10.1	6.3	7.0	10.1
2004	3.1	3.5	8.0	5.5	2.8	0.6	1.6	0.5	19.6	9.8	5.8	6.5	9.6
2005	2.8	3.3	7.8	5.1	2.5	0.6	1.6	0.4	18.4	8.9	5.4	6.1	8.9
2006	2.4	2.9	7.1	4.6	2.2	0.5	1.5	0.4	16.8	8.3	4.9	5.5	8.2
2007	2.5	2.8	6.5	4.6	2.3	0.5	1.4	0.4	16.8	8.5	4.9	5.5	8.3
2008	3.4	3.6	8.0	5.8	3.1	0.6	1.6	0.5	17.9	9.4	6.1	6.8	10.5
2009	6.6	5.5	11.5	9.3	5.9	0.6	2.1	0.7	24.4	15.1	9.7	10.5	16.2
2010	6.8	5.9	12.3	9.6	6.0	0.6	2.3	0.8	33.0	21.4	10.3	11.1	16.7
2011	5.8	5.6	12.4	8.9	5.3	0.6	2.2	0.8	39.3	21.4	9.5	10.4	15.9
2010													
January	6.8	5.9	12.3	9.7	6.1	0.6	2.4	0.8	30.3	20.1	10.4	11.2	16.7
February	6.9	6.1	11.6	9.8	6.2	0.6	2.3	0.8	29.8	19.9	10.5	11.2	16.9
March	6.9	6.0	11.3	9.8	6.2	0.6	2.3	0.8	31.4	20.4	10.4	11.1	16.9
April	6.7	6.2	11.0	9.9	6.0	0.6	2.4	0.8	33.1	22.0	10.5	11.2	17.0
May	6.8	6.2	11.6	9.6	6.0	0.6	2.2	0.8	33.9	22.5	10.3	10.9	16.6
June	6.8	5.9	12.1	9.4	5.9	0.6	2.1	0.8	34.5	25.0	10.2	10.9	16.5
July	6.5	5.8	13.4	9.5	5.9	0.6	2.2	0.8	33.7	21.8	10.2	11.0	16.5
August	6.7	5.8	13.4	9.6	6.0	0.6	2.2	0.8	33.6	20.5	10.2	10.9	16.6
September	6.6	5.6	12.9	9.5	6.0	0.5	2.2	0.8	33.5	20.1	10.2	10.9	16.9
October	6.8	5.6	12.4	9.5	5.8	0.6	2.3	0.8	34.3	21.5	10.2	11.0	16.8
November	6.9	5.8	13.0	9.8	6.1	0.6	2.2	0.8	34.2	21.5	10.5	11.3	16.9
December	6.5	5.6	12.0	9.4	5.8	0.6	2.2	0.9	34.9	22.3	10.1	10.9	16.6
2011													
January	5.9	5.6	12.7	9.1	5.5	0.6	2.2	0.9	37.1	21.7	9.7	10.7	16.1
February	5.8	5.4	13.0	9.0	5.4	0.6	2.2	0.9	37.4	21.1	9.6	10.6	15.9
March	6.0	5.7	12.3	8.9	5.4	0.6	2.1	0.9	38.9	21.6	9.4	10.3	15.7
April	6.1	5.7	11.7	9.0	5.3	0.6	2.2	0.9	38.3	20.8	9.6	10.4	15.9
May	6.0	5.8	12.7	9.0	5.4	0.6	2.2	0.8	39.6	21.9	9.5	10.3	15.8
June	6.1	5.6	12.8	9.1	5.4	0.6	2.2	0.8	39.8	22.1	9.7	10.7	16.2
July	6.1	5.6	12.1	9.1	5.3	0.6	2.2	0.8	40.2	21.2	9.7	10.7	16.1
August	5.8	5.7	11.9	9.1	5.3	0.6	2.3	0.8	40.3	21.7	9.6	10.6	16.2
September	5.8	5.8	12.4	9.0	5.2	0.6	2.3	0.9	40.4	21.8	9.6	10.5	16.4
October	5.8	5.7	12.3	8.9	5.1	0.7	2.2	0.8	39.2	20.8	9.5	10.4	16.0
November	5.3	5.3	12.4	8.7	4.9	0.7	2.2	0.8	40.9	21.5	9.3	10.2	15.6
December	5.1	5.4	12.9	8.5	4.9	0.6	2.2	0.8	40.8	21.0	9.1	10.0	15.2

[1]Not seasonally adjusted.
. . . = Not available.

Table 10-6. Labor Force and Employment Estimates Smoothed for Population Adjustments (Unofficial)

(Thousands of persons, seasonally adjusted.)

Year	January	February	March	April	May	June	July	August	September	October	November	December
CIVILIAN LABOR FORCE												
1990	125 845	125 734	125 837	125 697	125 953	125 645	125 816	126 087	126 001	126 116	126 203	126 287
1991	126 112	126 189	126 420	126 742	126 382	126 549	126 384	126 392	126 905	126 909	126 981	126 956
1992	127 566	127 524	127 934	128 184	128 475	128 829	128 945	129 008	128 908	128 444	128 872	128 998
1993	128 856	128 926	129 079	129 077	129 772	129 932	129 931	130 166	129 826	130 145	130 296	130 539
1994	131 210	131 296	131 038	131 272	131 444	131 237	131 341	131 980	132 139	132 477	132 637	132 710
1995	132 811	132 901	132 906	133 404	132 673	132 784	133 193	133 199	133 489	133 607	133 517	133 426
1996	133 545	133 896	134 138	134 381	134 654	134 697	135 302	135 083	135 560	135 982	136 082	136 202
1997	136 560	136 517	137 025	137 164	137 281	137 387	137 668	137 824	137 894	137 865	138 209	138 418
1998	138 370	138 401	138 539	138 465	138 703	138 800	138 947	138 942	139 679	139 685	139 801	140 070
1999	140 456	140 433	140 207	140 452	140 615	140 852	140 977	140 981	141 189	141 353	141 623	141 790
2000	142 269	142 459	142 439	142 758	142 396	142 601	142 290	142 527	142 533	142 639	142 980	143 268
2001	143 822	143 725	143 949	143 596	143 346	143 387	143 686	143 317	144 024	144 123	144 279	144 345
2002	143 925	144 697	144 527	144 772	144 987	144 859	144 855	145 063	145 608	145 372	145 100	145 127
2003	146 000	146 165	146 089	146 542	146 570	147 128	146 559	146 520	146 607	146 795	147 081	146 811
2004	146 926	146 795	147 032	146 939	147 156	147 553	147 787	147 661	147 513	147 893	148 264	148 163
2005	148 134	148 471	148 500	149 037	149 374	149 353	149 549	149 898	150 075	150 124	150 189	150 156
2006	150 342	150 771	150 945	151 015	151 205	151 492	151 517	151 858	151 806	152 187	152 554	152 882
2007	153 296	153 137	153 207	152 592	152 829	153 202	153 217	152 913	153 581	153 351	154 006	154 091
2008	154 250	153 824	154 103	153 941	154 507	154 500	154 666	154 834	154 749	155 067	154 815	154 821
2009	154 432	154 720	154 343	154 652	155 004	154 936	154 746	154 528	153 996	154 034	154 047	153 306
2010	153 671	153 923	154 185	154 752	154 441	153 879	153 976	154 303	154 150	153 942	154 277	153 850
2011	153 488	153 542	153 634	153 664	153 946	153 656	153 607	153 925	154 258	154 313	154 194	154 146
CIVILIAN EMPLOYMENT, TOTAL												
1990	119 093	119 082	119 238	118 898	119 209	119 052	118 891	118 894	118 628	118 651	118 432	118 379
1991	118 089	117 915	117 823	118 293	117 634	117 845	117 785	117 712	118 169	118 052	118 033	117 740
1992	118 265	118 050	118 454	118 748	118 709	118 764	119 071	119 195	119 101	119 020	119 280	119 413
1993	119 503	119 715	119 995	119 938	120 594	120 781	120 970	121 373	121 081	121 363	121 722	122 031
1994	122 547	122 679	122 534	122 908	123 497	123 277	123 362	124 013	124 372	124 811	125 230	125 448
1995	125 402	125 681	125 720	125 722	125 207	125 321	125 629	125 677	125 972	126 241	126 052	125 963
1996	126 013	126 542	126 779	126 924	127 189	127 562	127 922	128 161	128 540	128 909	128 801	128 904
1997	129 358	129 370	129 981	130 247	130 584	130 544	130 970	131 172	131 194	131 368	131 859	131 898
1998	131 958	132 053	132 072	132 484	132 614	132 545	132 643	132 718	133 333	133 359	133 655	133 994
1999	134 436	134 276	134 381	134 402	134 775	134 855	134 905	135 097	135 227	135 529	135 862	136 092
2000	136 560	136 601	136 705	137 276	136 637	136 949	136 541	136 674	136 906	137 103	137 338	137 632
2001	137 797	137 633	137 805	137 322	137 117	136 899	137 099	136 270	136 877	136 424	136 271	136 082
2002	135 737	136 476	136 216	136 167	136 581	136 459	136 458	136 752	137 350	137 058	136 572	136 478
2003	137 471	137 538	137 491	137 692	137 604	137 852	137 537	137 614	137 675	138 052	138 493	138 482
2004	138 544	138 616	138 528	138 757	138 930	139 254	139 638	139 656	139 572	139 818	140 319	140 215
2005	140 336	140 478	140 748	141 350	141 707	141 814	142 127	142 537	142 506	142 654	142 607	142 862
2006	143 261	143 570	143 856	143 877	144 207	144 473	144 323	144 748	144 940	145 441	145 663	146 101
2007	146 160	146 191	146 456	145 723	146 041	146 203	146 047	145 825	146 389	146 092	146 743	146 423
2008	146 548	146 310	146 262	146 286	146 086	145 896	145 690	145 357	145 221	144 956	144 242	143 493
2009	142 352	141 826	140 921	140 822	140 463	140 173	140 063	139 630	138 948	138 575	138 783	138 145
2010	138 679	138 845	139 018	139 490	139 526	139 324	139 327	139 528	139 536	139 265	139 131	139 416
2011	139 528	139 750	139 965	139 830	140 012	139 590	139 657	139 963	140 318	140 509	140 828	141 006

Table 10-7. Insured Unemployment

(Averages of weekly data; thousands of persons, except as noted.)

Year and month	State programs, seasonally adjusted			Federal programs, not seasonally adjusted					
	Initial claims	Insured unemployment	Insured unemployment rate (percent) [1]	Initial claims		Persons claiming benefits			
				Federal employees	Newly discharged veterans	Federal employees	Newly discharged veterans	Railroad retirement	Extended benefits
1970	297	1 848	. . .	. . .	. . .	. . .	. . .	. . .	. . .
1971	296	2 152	4.1	. . .	. . .	. . .	. . .	. . .	. . .
1972	263	1 844	3.5	. . .	. . .	. . .	. . .	. . .	. . .
1973	244	1 629	2.7	. . .	. . .	. . .	. . .	. . .	. . .
1974	352	2 278	3.5	. . .	. . .	. . .	. . .	. . .	. . .
1975	474	3 965	6.0	. . .	. . .	. . .	. . .	. . .	. . .
1976	383	2 978	4.5	. . .	. . .	. . .	. . .	. . .	. . .
1977	374	2 644	3.9	. . .	. . .	. . .	. . .	. . .	. . .
1978	341	2 337	3.3	. . .	. . .	. . .	. . .	. . .	. . .
1979	383	2 428	3.0	. . .	. . .	. . .	. . .	. . .	. . .
1980	488	3 365	3.9	. . .	. . .	. . .	. . .	. . .	. . .
1981	451	3 032	3.5	. . .	. . .	. . .	. . .	. . .	. . .
1982	586	4 094	4.7	. . .	. . .	. . .	. . .	. . .	. . .
1983	441	3 337	3.9	. . .	. . .	. . .	. . .	. . .	. . .
1984	374	2 452	2.8	. . .	. . .	. . .	. . .	. . .	. . .
1985	392	2 584	2.9	. . .	. . .	. . .	. . .	. . .	. . .
1986	378	2 632	2.8	2.13	2.52	20.24	17.11	. . .	. . .
1987	325	2 273	2.4	2.19	2.57	21.29	17.71	. . .	9.51
1988	309	2 075	2.1	2.32	2.74	22.91	18.13	13.28	1.17
1989	330	2 174	2.1	2.14	2.31	22.17	15.09	10.37	0.61
1990	385	2 539	2.4	2.45	2.54	23.89	18.43	10.56	2.36
1991	447	3 338	3.2	2.55	2.93	30.50	22.12	10.73	32.16
1992	409	3 208	3.1	2.75	4.95	32.10	60.25	8.77	4.61
1993	344	2 768	2.6	2.55	3.94	32.06	54.90	7.40	7.59
1994	340	2 667	2.5	2.54	3.02	32.21	37.65	6.21	31.09
1995	359	2 590	2.4	4.57	2.51	31.68	29.78	5.48	14.27
1996	352	2 552	2.3	7.33	2.13	29.84	24.30	5.40	5.53
1997	322	2 300	2.0	2.01	1.75	23.58	19.66	4.00	5.35
1998	317	2 213	1.9	1.64	1.41	19.60	15.68	3.19	6.43
1999	298	2 186	1.8	1.48	1.18	16.85	14.25	3.24	3.05
2000	299	2 112	1.7	1.73	1.05	18.60	12.54	3.92	0.58
2001	406	3 016	2.4	1.47	1.15	18.57	13.98	. . .	0.57
2002	404	3 570	2.8	1.46	1.22	17.54	16.07	. . .	10.79
2003	402	3 532	2.8	1.56	1.46	18.22	19.68	. . .	22.30
2004	342	2 930	2.3	1.50	1.89	18.14	26.90	. . .	4.22
2005	331	2 660	2.1	1.46	2.03	16.92	27.58	. . .	1.69
2006	312	2 456	1.9	1.34	1.96	15.51	26.37	. . .	1.38
2007	321	2 548	1.9	1.30	1.68	14.90	22.80	. . .	0.00
2008	418	3 337	2.5	1.26	1.63	14.53	22.16	. . .	3.43
2009	574	5 808	4.4	1.63	2.05	20.06	30.44	. . .	388.98
2010	459	4 544	3.6	2.72	2.55	28.32	39.22	. . .	571.43
2011	409	3 744	3.0	2.20	2.57	31.18	39.14	. . .	633.43
2009									
January	589	4 927	3.7	1.81	2.17	20.79	27.39	. . .	9.65
February	645	5 306	4.0	1.27	1.91	19.65	28.35	. . .	3.61
March	659	5 763	4.3	1.11	1.85	18.74	28.72	. . .	21.24
April	631	6 171	4.6	1.12	1.75	16.93	28.69	. . .	99.56
May	614	6 506	4.9	1.44	1.68	15.57	28.10	. . .	379.21
June	601	6 524	4.9	1.77	2.01	17.21	28.40	. . .	585.17
July	567	6 148	4.6	1.78	2.07	19.17	29.91	. . .	650.70
August	558	6 055	4.6	1.49	2.17	20.18	30.44	. . .	728.83
September	544	5 978	4.5	1.43	2.25	20.00	30.90	. . .	657.98
October	526	5 761	4.4	2.13	2.52	22.14	33.42	. . .	595.75
November	495	5 462	4.1	2.20	2.06	24.57	35.48	. . .	545.95
December	485	5 148	3.9	1.93	2.09	26.19	36.06	. . .	350.74
2010									
January	481	4 885	3.8	1.87	2.13	26.49	36.89	. . .	239.16
February	486	4 813	3.7	1.29	2.22	23.67	36.31	. . .	174.55
March	468	4 732	3.7	1.29	2.36	22.05	36.18	. . .	153.82
April	472	4 710	3.7	1.29	2.63	19.78	36.98	. . .	238.14
May	460	4 647	3.6	1.56	2.48	17.28	36.35	. . .	385.72
June	464	4 565	3.6	2.07	2.49	18.45	36.76	. . .	467.55
July	458	4 530	3.6	3.12	2.76	22.18	41.71	. . .	612.63
August	473	4 466	3.5	4.13	2.76	25.28	41.12	. . .	913.35
September	449	4 453	3.5	4.19	3.49	29.60	41.56	. . .	945.21
October	448	4 349	3.4	5.72	2.71	40.90	42.55	. . .	963.76
November	430	4 205	3.4	3.06	2.21	46.87	42.11	. . .	898.12
December	422	4 121	3.3	2.75	2.45	48.86	41.96	. . .	886.25
2011									
January	428	3 969	3.2	3.22	2.52	49.25	41.50	. . .	887.49
February	406	3 885	3.1	1.87	2.33	44.18	40.10	. . .	782.46
March	406	3 781	3.0	1.65	2.31	38.55	38.66	. . .	739.79
April	424	3 748	3.0	1.71	2.27	30.86	37.23	. . .	686.68
May	424	3 738	3.0	1.70	2.42	23.60	36.15	. . .	617.15
June	423	3 721	3.0	2.17	2.62	23.21	36.53	. . .	617.40
July	411	3 722	3.0	2.28	2.63	25.15	37.64	. . .	545.14
August	407	3 723	3.0	2.32	2.73	25.48	38.16	. . .	544.98
September	411	3 718	3.0	2.00	2.72	24.35	38.39	. . .	526.36
October	400	3 678	2.9	2.91	2.85	28.37	40.78	. . .	541.28
November	393	3 652	2.9	2.21	2.43	29.18	41.60	. . .	553.12
December	378	3 598	2.9	2.01	2.76	30.71	42.41	. . .	553.75

[1] Insured unemployed as a percent of employment covered by state programs.
. . . = Not available.

Section 10b: Payroll Employment, Hours, and Earnings

Figure 10-3. Total Nonfarm Payroll Employment, 1946–2011

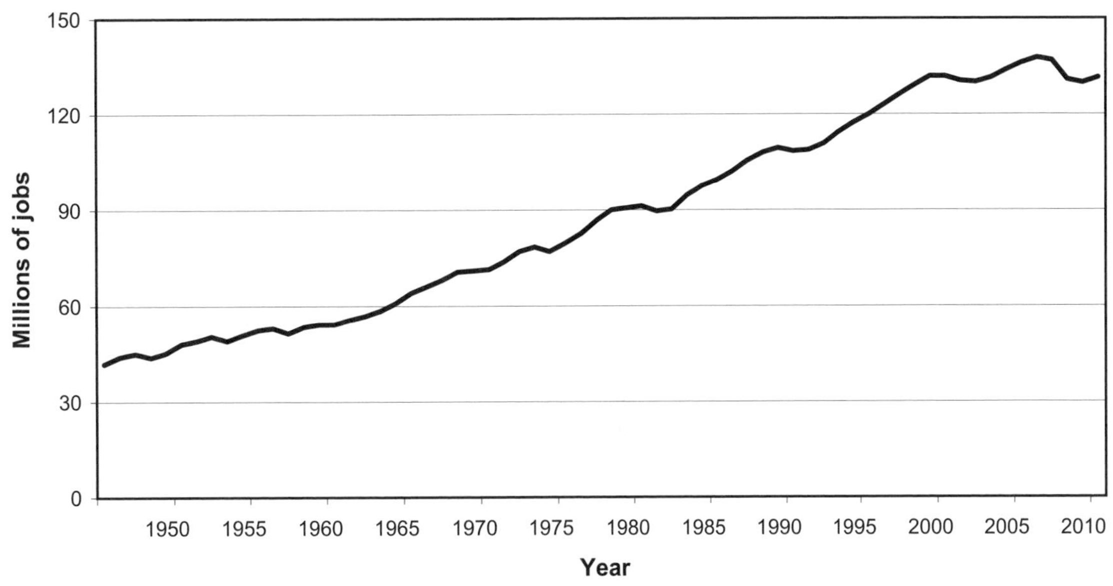

- Nonfarm payroll employment peaked in January 2008 and plunged 6.4 percent, a postwar record, between then and its lowest point in February 2010. The total number of jobs lost by this measure was 8.78 million. (Table 10-8A)

- Preliminary data for June 2012 indicate a nonfarm payroll job gain of 3.8 million since the February 2010 low, roughly comparable to recent gains in the household survey featured in the previous section. The differences in concepts and measurement practice between these two employment surveys are discussed in the Notes and Definitions to this chapter. (Table 10-8A and recent data)

- Based on annual average data, payroll employment grew by 5.8 million jobs between the 2000 and 2007 business cycle high points, an average growth rate of 0.6 percent per year during the latest completed cycle. The previous business cycle lasted 10 years between high points, from 1990 to 2000. During that period, 22.3 million jobs were added to U.S. nonfarm payrolls, for an annual average growth rate of 1.9 percent per year. (Table 10-8B)

- The diffusion index shows the percentage of industries in which employment is higher than six months earlier. Diffusion indexes measure the extent to which expansion and contraction have spread throughout the economy; indexes below 50 percent indicate recession. This index reached a low of 11.8 percent in April 2009—lower than the lowest points reached in any of the previous four recessions (1980, 1981–1982, 1990–1991, and 2001), and thus indicating the most widespread and pervasive decline in 30 years or more. By June 2012, 69.0 percent of industries showed employment gains from six months earlier. (Tables 10-8A and B)

Table 10-8A. Nonfarm Payroll Employment by NAICS Supersector: Recent Data

(Thousands; seasonally adjusted, except as noted.)

Year and month	Total	Private							Service-providing				
		Total	Goods-producing						Total	Private			
			Total	Mining and logging	Construc-tion	Manufacturing				Total	Trade, transportation, and utilities		
						Total	Durable	Nondurable			Total	Wholesale trade	Retail trade
2005	133 703	111 899	22 190	628	7 336	14 227	8 956	5 271	111 513	89 709	25 959	5 764	15 280
2006	136 086	114 113	22 530	684	7 691	14 155	8 981	5 174	113 556	91 582	26 276	5 905	15 353
2007	137 598	115 380	22 233	724	7 630	13 879	8 808	5 071	115 366	93 147	26 630	6 015	15 520
2008	136 790	114 281	21 335	767	7 162	13 406	8 463	4 943	115 456	92 946	26 293	5 943	15 283
2009	130 807	108 252	18 558	694	6 016	11 847	7 284	4 564	112 249	89 695	24 906	5 587	14 522
2010	129 874	107 384	17 751	705	5 518	11 528	7 064	4 464	112 123	89 633	24 636	5 452	14 440
2011	131 359	109 254	18 021	784	5 504	11 733	7 274	4 460	113 338	91 234	25 019	5 529	14 643
2007													
January	137 118	115 023	22 435	706	7 725	14 004	8 885	5 119	114 683	92 588	26 499	5 969	15 451
February	137 211	115 080	22 335	711	7 626	13 998	8 888	5 110	114 876	92 745	26 544	5 987	15 479
March	137 401	115 252	22 395	715	7 706	13 974	8 875	5 099	115 006	92 857	26 596	5 987	15 524
April	137 473	115 298	22 355	719	7 686	13 950	8 865	5 085	115 118	92 943	26 607	6 004	15 515
May	137 612	115 419	22 326	721	7 673	13 932	8 850	5 082	115 286	93 093	26 634	6 010	15 529
June	137 687	115 480	22 324	725	7 687	13 912	8 831	5 081	115 363	93 156	26 627	6 024	15 510
July	137 647	115 476	22 274	728	7 660	13 886	8 812	5 074	115 373	93 202	26 630	6 030	15 506
August	137 629	115 403	22 168	727	7 610	13 831	8 782	5 049	115 461	93 235	26 628	6 031	15 507
September	137 702	115 423	22 093	726	7 577	13 790	8 754	5 036	115 609	93 330	26 657	6 028	15 513
October	137 781	115 484	22 049	727	7 565	13 757	8 721	5 036	115 732	93 435	26 663	6 036	15 516
November	137 893	115 559	22 013	735	7 523	13 755	8 721	5 034	115 880	93 546	26 725	6 042	15 576
December	137 982	115 606	21 973	740	7 490	13 743	8 704	5 039	116 009	93 633	26 714	6 038	15 571
2008													
January	138 023	115 647	21 950	746	7 481	13 723	8 690	5 033	116 073	93 697	26 716	6 037	15 571
February	137 939	115 511	21 878	748	7 435	13 695	8 672	5 023	116 061	93 633	26 662	6 026	15 529
March	137 844	115 399	21 812	755	7 401	13 656	8 644	5 012	116 032	93 587	26 634	6 015	15 505
April	137 636	115 184	21 685	754	7 331	13 600	8 598	5 002	115 951	93 499	26 545	5 993	15 435
May	137 446	114 968	21 612	761	7 282	13 569	8 581	4 988	115 834	93 356	26 465	5 979	15 382
June	137 248	114 737	21 492	766	7 216	13 510	8 548	4 962	115 756	93 245	26 397	5 966	15 336
July	137 038	114 478	21 366	770	7 161	13 435	8 493	4 942	115 672	93 112	26 326	5 946	15 292
August	136 764	114 184	21 249	778	7 115	13 356	8 428	4 928	115 515	92 935	26 231	5 927	15 233
September	136 332	113 759	21 096	782	7 042	13 272	8 370	4 902	115 236	92 663	26 117	5 914	15 164
October	135 843	113 279	20 887	780	6 965	13 142	8 271	4 871	114 956	92 392	26 017	5 877	15 113
November	135 040	112 482	20 614	776	6 810	13 028	8 188	4 840	114 426	91 868	25 798	5 839	14 981
December	134 379	111 824	20 324	770	6 705	12 849	8 063	4 786	114 055	91 500	25 640	5 798	14 882
2009													
January	133 561	110 985	19 874	764	6 558	12 552	7 824	4 728	113 687	91 111	25 483	5 764	14 784
February	132 837	110 260	19 583	749	6 448	12 386	7 706	4 680	113 254	90 677	25 335	5 715	14 713
March	132 038	109 473	19 237	728	6 295	12 214	7 582	4 632	112 801	90 236	25 162	5 671	14 619
April	131 346	108 671	18 898	712	6 151	12 035	7 432	4 603	112 448	89 773	25 013	5 626	14 558
May	130 985	108 359	18 656	694	6 094	11 868	7 294	4 574	112 329	89 703	24 957	5 601	14 550
June	130 503	107 933	18 417	685	6 007	11 725	7 182	4 543	112 086	89 516	24 892	5 577	14 527
July	130 164	107 637	18 266	677	5 925	11 664	7 142	4 522	111 898	89 371	24 797	5 552	14 482
August	129 933	107 418	18 138	669	5 846	11 623	7 108	4 515	111 795	89 280	24 760	5 535	14 471
September	129 734	107 234	18 020	666	5 775	11 579	7 075	4 504	111 714	89 214	24 692	5 520	14 424
October	129 532	107 002	17 907	660	5 717	11 530	7 038	4 492	111 625	89 095	24 628	5 502	14 389
November	129 490	106 960	17 845	662	5 687	11 496	7 010	4 486	111 645	89 115	24 592	5 490	14 379
December	129 319	106 840	17 784	664	5 654	11 466	6 993	4 473	111 535	89 056	24 562	5 475	14 352
2010													
January	129 279	106 800	17 720	669	5 593	11 458	6 990	4 468	111 559	89 080	24 545	5 453	14 384
February	129 244	106 773	17 666	675	5 529	11 462	6 993	4 469	111 578	89 107	24 537	5 444	14 394
March	129 433	106 914	17 704	682	5 552	11 470	7 010	4 460	111 729	89 210	24 568	5 442	14 419
April	129 672	107 107	17 750	689	5 559	11 502	7 034	4 468	111 922	89 357	24 579	5 442	14 421
May	130 188	107 191	17 751	697	5 518	11 536	7 062	4 474	112 437	89 440	24 596	5 439	14 433
June	130 021	107 283	17 754	701	5 507	11 546	7 073	4 473	112 267	89 529	24 604	5 444	14 422
July	129 963	107 375	17 764	707	5 491	11 566	7 095	4 471	112 199	89 611	24 636	5 447	14 436
August	129 912	107 503	17 775	715	5 511	11 549	7 084	4 465	112 137	89 728	24 638	5 448	14 441
September	129 885	107 618	17 764	721	5 492	11 551	7 093	4 458	112 121	89 854	24 676	5 453	14 461
October	130 105	107 814	17 780	730	5 499	11 551	7 096	4 455	112 325	90 034	24 732	5 462	14 498
November	130 226	107 948	17 781	733	5 488	11 560	7 105	4 455	112 445	90 167	24 753	5 469	14 501
December	130 346	108 088	17 785	733	5 477	11 575	7 119	4 456	112 561	90 303	24 775	5 473	14 513
2011													
January	130 456	108 207	17 821	738	5 456	11 627	7 174	4 453	112 635	90 386	24 821	5 483	14 550
February	130 676	108 464	17 894	741	5 489	11 664	7 203	4 461	112 782	90 570	24 866	5 496	14 556
March	130 922	108 725	17 942	756	5 496	11 690	7 226	4 464	112 980	90 783	24 896	5 510	14 563
April	131 173	108 989	17 981	768	5 495	11 718	7 245	4 473	113 192	91 008	24 982	5 518	14 631
May	131 227	109 097	18 001	777	5 498	11 726	7 264	4 462	113 226	91 096	24 993	5 525	14 626
June	131 311	109 199	18 019	786	5 495	11 738	7 281	4 457	113 292	91 180	25 027	5 531	14 642
July	131 407	109 374	18 071	795	5 508	11 768	7 303	4 465	113 336	91 303	25 052	5 533	14 669
August	131 492	109 426	18 067	798	5 498	11 771	7 300	4 471	113 425	91 359	25 060	5 538	14 664
September	131 694	109 642	18 100	804	5 528	11 768	7 304	4 464	113 594	91 542	25 075	5 535	14 679
October	131 806	109 781	18 106	810	5 519	11 777	7 317	4 460	113 700	91 675	25 102	5 547	14 691
November	131 963	109 959	18 114	814	5 520	11 780	7 331	4 449	113 849	91 845	25 154	5 554	14 725
December	132 186	110 193	18 176	822	5 546	11 808	7 361	4 447	114 010	92 017	25 181	5 569	14 732

Table 10-8A. Nonfarm Payroll Employment by NAICS Supersector: Recent Data—Continued

(Thousands; seasonally adjusted, except as noted.)

Year and month	Service-providing—Continued													Diffusion index, 6-month span, private nonfarm [2]
	Private—Continued						Government							
								Federal		State		Local		
	Information	Financial activities	Professional and business services	Education and health services	Leisure and hospitality	Other services	Total	Total	Department of Defense [1]	Total	Education	Total	Education	
2005	3 061	8 153	16 954	17 372	12 816	5 395	21 804	2 732	488	5 032	2 260	14 041	7 856	62.8
2006	3 038	8 328	17 566	17 826	13 110	5 438	21 974	2 732	493	5 075	2 293	14 167	7 913	60.0
2007	3 032	8 301	17 942	18 322	13 427	5 494	22 218	2 734	491	5 122	2 318	14 362	7 987	56.8
2008	2 984	8 145	17 735	18 838	13 436	5 515	22 509	2 762	496	5 177	2 354	14 571	8 084	27.6
2009	2 804	7 769	16 579	19 193	13 077	5 367	22 555	2 832	519	5 169	2 360	14 554	8 079	18.0
2010	2 707	7 652	16 728	19 531	13 049	5 331	22 490	2 977	545	5 137	2 373	14 376	8 013	61.1
2011	2 659	7 681	17 331	19 884	13 320	5 342	22 104	2 858	561	5 082	2 384	14 165	7 893	65.8
2007														
January	3 030	8 347	17 834	18 073	13 338	5 467	22 095	2 731	491	5 087	2 294	14 277	7 960	60.0
February	3 033	8 348	17 877	18 108	13 361	5 474	22 131	2 732	490	5 114	2 316	14 285	7 953	58.6
March	3 030	8 339	17 886	18 159	13 363	5 484	22 149	2 731	491	5 118	2 318	14 300	7 956	63.2
April	3 034	8 315	17 910	18 211	13 375	5 491	22 175	2 732	489	5 121	2 322	14 322	7 965	61.3
May	3 040	8 325	17 938	18 256	13 404	5 496	22 193	2 733	489	5 121	2 319	14 339	7 974	58.6
June	3 038	8 321	17 947	18 311	13 413	5 499	22 207	2 729	493	5 131	2 327	14 347	7 965	59.0
July	3 037	8 323	17 956	18 339	13 417	5 500	22 171	2 727	493	5 119	2 311	14 325	7 946	54.5
August	3 030	8 295	17 970	18 397	13 419	5 496	22 226	2 738	492	5 110	2 301	14 378	7 992	53.2
September	3 030	8 268	17 974	18 448	13 461	5 492	22 279	2 737	490	5 137	2 332	14 405	8 009	56.8
October	3 028	8 255	18 009	18 487	13 499	5 494	22 297	2 734	490	5 132	2 324	14 431	8 023	52.3
November	3 024	8 237	18 012	18 508	13 535	5 505	22 334	2 744	492	5 137	2 325	14 453	8 034	52.6
December	3 024	8 224	18 051	18 554	13 550	5 516	22 376	2 756	492	5 139	2 327	14 481	8 055	52.6
2008														
January	3 024	8 219	18 051	18 605	13 560	5 522	22 376	2 736	488	5 137	2 321	14 503	8 054	52.4
February	3 020	8 208	18 011	18 643	13 557	5 532	22 428	2 747	487	5 150	2 333	14 531	8 071	51.3
March	3 021	8 209	17 948	18 691	13 545	5 539	22 445	2 751	487	5 154	2 336	14 540	8 070	51.9
April	3 012	8 195	17 949	18 746	13 513	5 539	22 452	2 756	488	5 162	2 342	14 534	8 059	49.2
May	3 010	8 191	17 881	18 791	13 482	5 536	22 478	2 756	491	5 168	2 346	14 554	8 071	43.0
June	3 001	8 174	17 840	18 842	13 465	5 526	22 511	2 761	496	5 178	2 354	14 572	8 080	36.8
July	2 987	8 161	17 779	18 884	13 452	5 523	22 560	2 765	500	5 191	2 367	14 604	8 114	32.5
August	2 975	8 145	17 708	18 940	13 425	5 511	22 580	2 768	501	5 207	2 373	14 605	8 106	30.6
September	2 962	8 111	17 638	18 944	13 380	5 511	22 573	2 771	498	5 198	2 377	14 604	8 105	27.6
October	2 952	8 078	17 522	18 956	13 353	5 514	22 564	2 775	503	5 186	2 363	14 603	8 099	27.4
November	2 932	8 033	17 338	18 991	13 300	5 476	22 558	2 780	504	5 190	2 366	14 588	8 085	23.7
December	2 909	7 996	17 218	19 025	13 265	5 447	22 555	2 777	505	5 189	2 367	14 589	8 085	23.3
2009														
January	2 887	7 947	17 074	19 070	13 221	5 429	22 576	2 790	504	5 198	2 375	14 588	8 086	18.4
February	2 876	7 894	16 890	19 084	13 187	5 411	22 577	2 795	504	5 188	2 366	14 594	8 099	13.9
March	2 865	7 854	16 757	19 089	13 126	5 383	22 565	2 797	505	5 182	2 365	14 586	8 098	13.5
April	2 833	7 802	16 609	19 090	13 054	5 372	22 675	2 922	507	5 180	2 364	14 573	8 093	11.8
May	2 808	7 774	16 545	19 143	13 109	5 367	22 626	2 860	512	5 191	2 375	14 575	8 091	12.8
June	2 794	7 749	16 445	19 179	13 084	5 373	22 570	2 815	520	5 174	2 364	14 581	8 098	13.2
July	2 780	7 738	16 414	19 194	13 079	5 369	22 527	2 825	525	5 140	2 332	14 562	8 057	13.0
August	2 768	7 713	16 392	19 237	13 052	5 358	22 515	2 822	526	5 161	2 353	14 532	8 048	15.4
September	2 769	7 704	16 391	19 250	13 058	5 350	22 500	2 829	524	5 155	2 347	14 516	8 050	18.0
October	2 767	7 689	16 399	19 281	13 000	5 331	22 530	2 846	530	5 157	2 358	14 527	8 083	22.0
November	2 752	7 691	16 455	19 316	12 987	5 322	22 530	2 843	533	5 149	2 358	14 538	8 100	22.0
December	2 741	7 679	16 469	19 350	12 933	5 322	22 479	2 830	535	5 148	2 358	14 501	8 074	24.4
2010														
January	2 738	7 668	16 513	19 368	12 923	5 325	22 479	2 865	534	5 132	2 348	14 482	8 068	27.1
February	2 734	7 660	16 542	19 393	12 924	5 317	22 471	2 871	535	5 146	2 365	14 454	8 057	28.8
March	2 720	7 646	16 539	19 458	12 950	5 329	22 519	2 924	535	5 144	2 362	14 451	8 056	34.4
April	2 715	7 654	16 618	19 468	12 988	5 335	22 565	2 987	537	5 138	2 364	14 440	8 049	44.4
May	2 711	7 648	16 650	19 493	13 013	5 329	22 997	3 414	539	5 139	2 372	14 444	8 059	50.9
June	2 696	7 643	16 717	19 517	13 037	5 315	22 738	3 193	546	5 135	2 370	14 410	8 043	53.8
July	2 701	7 639	16 725	19 535	13 049	5 326	22 588	3 051	550	5 153	2 391	14 384	8 028	58.5
August	2 704	7 642	16 770	19 569	13 084	5 321	22 409	2 942	551	5 121	2 365	14 346	7 993	60.5
September	2 696	7 650	16 793	19 567	13 141	5 331	22 267	2 867	549	5 122	2 369	14 278	7 942	61.1
October	2 692	7 655	16 848	19 628	13 123	5 356	22 291	2 863	553	5 139	2 387	14 289	7 962	59.6
November	2 690	7 661	16 927	19 666	13 125	5 345	22 278	2 865	555	5 135	2 386	14 278	7 958	60.3
December	2 687	7 669	17 009	19 678	13 146	5 339	22 258	2 871	558	5 128	2 384	14 259	7 953	63.0
2011														
January	2 678	7 666	17 055	19 696	13 138	5 332	22 249	2 873	557	5 125	2 387	14 251	7 949	65.6
February	2 674	7 669	17 104	19 725	13 195	5 337	22 212	2 877	557	5 107	2 379	14 228	7 931	65.2
March	2 672	7 683	17 192	19 749	13 259	5 332	22 197	2 879	558	5 104	2 383	14 214	7 923	71.2
April	2 671	7 679	17 242	19 804	13 295	5 335	22 184	2 873	557	5 098	2 383	14 213	7 931	68.8
May	2 671	7 693	17 298	19 823	13 280	5 338	22 130	2 869	558	5 087	2 377	14 174	7 899	66.5
June	2 669	7 680	17 303	19 848	13 315	5 338	22 112	2 858	561	5 081	2 377	14 173	7 903	68.2
July	2 665	7 676	17 342	19 898	13 332	5 338	22 033	2 851	563	5 054	2 384	14 128	7 863	70.5
August	2 615	7 681	17 382	19 931	13 344	5 346	22 066	2 847	562	5 075	2 393	14 144	7 881	66.4
September	2 649	7 675	17 441	19 989	13 364	5 349	22 052	2 844	561	5 084	2 395	14 124	7 867	65.8
October	2 646	7 680	17 482	20 026	13 394	5 345	22 025	2 844	566	5 063	2 390	14 118	7 866	63.5
November	2 644	7 691	17 521	20 046	13 436	5 353	22 004	2 839	567	5 056	2 383	14 109	7 858	62.8
December	2 645	7 696	17 593	20 079	13 464	5 359	21 993	2 836	567	5 048	2 378	14 109	7 860	63.5

[1] Not seasonally adjusted.
[2] See notes and definitions for explanation. September value used to represent year.

Table 10-9. Employment, Hours, and Earnings, Total Nonfarm and Manufacturing, Historical Annual and Monthly

(Wage and salary workers on nonfarm payrolls, seasonally adjusted.)

Year and month	All wage and salary workers (thousands)					Production and nonsupervisory workers on private payrolls							
		Private				Number (thousands)		Average hours per week		Average hourly earnings, dollars		Average weekly earnings, dollars	
	Total	Total	Goods-producing		Service-providing	Total private	Manufac-turing	Total private	Manufac-turing	Total private	Manufac-turing	Total private	Manufac-turing
			Total	Manufac-turing									
1939	30 645	26 606	11 511	9 450	19 134	...	8 163	...	37.7	...	0.49	...	18.47
1940	32 407	28 156	12 378	10 099	20 029	...	8 737	...	38.2	...	0.53	...	20.25
1941	36 600	31 874	14 940	12 121	21 660	...	10 641	...	40.7	...	0.61	...	24.83
1942	40 213	34 621	17 275	14 030	22 938	...	12 447	...	43.2	...	0.74	...	31.97
1943	42 574	36 353	18 738	16 153	23 837	...	14 407	...	45.1	...	0.86	...	38.79
1944	42 006	35 819	17 981	15 903	24 026	...	14 031	...	45.4	...	0.91	...	41.31
1945	40 510	34 428	16 308	14 255	24 203	...	12 445	...	43.6	...	0.90	...	39.24
1946	41 759	36 054	16 122	13 513	25 637	...	11 781	...	40.4	...	0.95	...	38.38
1947	43 945	38 379	17 314	14 287	26 631	...	12 453	...	40.5	...	1.10	...	44.55
1948	44 954	39 213	17 579	14 324	27 376	...	12 383	...	40.1	...	1.20	...	48.12
1949	43 843	37 893	16 464	13 281	27 379	...	11 355	...	39.2	...	1.25	...	49.00
1950	45 287	39 167	17 343	14 013	27 945	...	12 032	...	40.6	...	1.32	...	53.59
1951	47 930	41 427	18 703	15 070	29 227	...	12 808	...	40.7	...	1.45	...	59.02
1952	48 909	42 182	18 928	15 291	29 981	...	12 797	...	40.8	...	1.53	...	62.42
1953	50 310	43 552	19 733	16 131	30 577	...	13 437	...	40.6	...	1.63	...	66.18
1954	49 093	42 235	18 515	15 002	30 578	...	12 300	...	39.7	...	1.66	...	65.90
1955	50 744	43 722	19 234	15 524	31 510	...	12 735	...	40.8	...	1.74	...	70.99
1956	52 473	45 087	19 799	15 858	32 674	...	12 869	...	40.5	...	1.84	...	74.52
1957	52 959	45 235	19 669	15 798	33 290	...	12 640	...	39.9	...	1.93	...	77.01
1958	51 426	43 480	18 319	14 656	33 107	...	11 532	...	39.2	...	1.99	...	78.01
1959	53 374	45 182	19 163	15 325	34 211	...	12 089	...	40.3	...	2.08	...	83.82
1960	54 296	45 832	19 182	15 438	35 114	...	12 074	...	39.8	...	2.15	...	85.57
1961	54 105	45 399	18 647	15 011	35 458	...	11 612	...	39.9	...	2.20	...	87.78
1962	55 659	46 655	19 203	15 498	36 455	...	11 986	...	40.5	...	2.27	...	91.94
1963	56 764	47 423	19 385	15 631	37 379	...	12 051	...	40.6	...	2.34	...	95.00
1964	58 391	48 680	19 733	15 888	38 658	40 575	12 298	38.5	40.8	2.53	2.41	97.41	98.33
1946													
January	39 839	34 054	15 031	12 719	24 808	...	10 990	...	40.9	...	0.86	...	35.17
February	39 250	33 472	14 308	11 922	24 942	...	10 292	...	40.4	...	0.85	...	34.34
March	40 192	34 434	15 017	12 545	25 175	...	10 989	...	40.6	...	0.89	...	36.13
April	40 908	35 147	15 439	13 200	25 469	...	11 616	...	40.4	...	0.92	...	37.17
May	41 348	35 616	15 875	13 389	25 473	...	11 758	...	39.8	...	0.93	...	37.01
June	41 732	36 052	16 206	13 598	25 526	...	11 905	...	40.0	...	0.94	...	37.60
July	42 153	36 471	16 461	13 771	25 692	...	12 065	...	40.2	...	0.96	...	38.59
August	42 642	36 961	16 728	13 981	25 914	...	12 241	...	40.6	...	0.98	...	39.79
September	42 908	37 239	16 912	14 135	25 996	...	12 311	...	40.4	...	0.99	...	40.00
October	43 094	37 430	17 002	14 182	26 092	...	12 302	...	40.4	...	1.00	...	40.40
November	43 396	37 757	17 157	14 310	26 239	...	12 421	...	40.3	...	1.02	...	41.11
December	43 379	37 751	17 164	14 301	26 215	...	12 419	...	40.5	...	1.02	...	41.31
1947													
January	43 545	37 926	17 213	14 328	26 332	...	12 445	...	40.5	...	1.03	...	41.72
February	43 563	37 957	17 200	14 278	26 363	...	12 487	...	40.4	...	1.04	...	42.02
March	43 605	38 017	17 196	14 259	26 409	...	12 518	...	40.3	...	1.06	...	42.72
April	43 491	37 933	17 178	14 240	26 313	...	12 531	...	40.5	...	1.06	...	42.93
May	43 637	38 086	17 176	14 189	26 461	...	12 449	...	40.4	...	1.08	...	43.63
June	43 808	38 284	17 253	14 200	26 555	...	12 389	...	40.4	...	1.10	...	44.44
July	43 742	38 218	17 106	14 076	26 636	...	12 265	...	40.4	...	1.10	...	44.44
August	43 958	38 439	17 280	14 200	26 678	...	12 370	...	40.0	...	1.11	...	44.40
September	44 201	38 662	17 398	14 315	26 803	...	12 430	...	40.5	...	1.11	...	44.96
October	44 415	38 849	17 499	14 393	26 916	...	12 464	...	40.5	...	1.13	...	45.77
November	44 486	38 901	17 517	14 414	26 969	...	12 494	...	40.5	...	1.14	...	46.17
December	44 578	38 973	17 563	14 428	27 015	...	12 526	...	40.8	...	1.16	...	47.33
1948													
January	44 686	39 062	17 625	14 438	27 061	...	12 520	...	40.5	...	1.16	...	46.98
February	44 537	38 922	17 447	14 339	27 090	...	12 437	...	40.2	...	1.16	...	46.63
March	44 680	39 057	17 544	14 364	27 136	...	12 489	...	40.4	...	1.16	...	46.86
April	44 369	38 726	17 302	14 183	27 067	...	12 304	...	40.1	...	1.17	...	46.92
May	44 795	39 114	17 508	14 235	27 287	...	12 344	...	40.2	...	1.18	...	47.44
June	45 032	39 296	17 633	14 318	27 399	...	12 402	...	40.3	...	1.19	...	47.96
July	45 160	39 386	17 649	14 359	27 511	...	12 417	...	40.2	...	1.21	...	48.64
August	45 175	39 384	17 655	14 353	27 520	...	12 397	...	40.2	...	1.23	...	49.45
September	45 294	39 489	17 741	14 441	27 553	...	12 450	...	40.1	...	1.24	...	49.72
October	45 250	39 421	17 683	14 390	27 567	...	12 364	...	39.8	...	1.25	...	49.75
November	45 194	39 325	17 599	14 292	27 595	...	12 302	...	39.8	...	1.26	...	50.15
December	45 028	39 140	17 417	14 086	27 611	...	12 127	...	39.6	...	1.26	...	49.90
1949													
January	44 675	38 781	17 170	13 867	27 505	...	11 905	...	39.4	...	1.26	...	49.64
February	44 500	38 607	17 019	13 734	27 481	...	11 792	...	39.4	...	1.26	...	49.64
March	44 238	38 323	16 848	13 581	27 390	...	11 654	...	39.1	...	1.26	...	49.27
April	44 230	38 282	16 685	13 439	27 545	...	11 517	...	38.8	...	1.25	...	48.50
May	43 982	38 020	16 492	13 269	27 490	...	11 352	...	38.9	...	1.25	...	48.63
June	43 739	37 783	16 351	13 178	27 388	...	11 266	...	39.0	...	1.26	...	49.14
July	43 530	37 568	16 222	13 067	27 308	...	11 168	...	39.2	...	1.26	...	49.39
August	43 621	37 636	16 327	13 158	27 294	...	11 251	...	39.2	...	1.25	...	49.00
September	43 784	37 794	16 403	13 225	27 381	...	11 284	...	39.4	...	1.25	...	49.25
October	42 950	36 980	15 739	12 891	27 211	...	10 940	...	39.6	...	1.24	...	49.10
November	43 244	37 294	16 040	12 882	27 204	...	10 964	...	39.1	...	1.24	...	48.48
December	43 516	37 564	16 217	13 062	27 299	...	11 173	...	39.4	...	1.25	...	49.25

. . . = Not available.

Table 10-9. Employment, Hours, and Earnings, Total Nonfarm and Manufacturing, Historical Annual and Monthly—*Continued*

(Wage and salary workers on nonfarm payrolls, seasonally adjusted.)

Year and month	All wage and salary workers (thousands)					Production and nonsupervisory workers on private payrolls							
	Total	Private			Service-providing	Number (thousands)		Average hours per week		Average hourly earnings, dollars		Average weekly earnings, dollars	
		Total	Goods-producing			Total private	Manufac-turing	Total private	Manufac-turing	Total private	Manufac-turing	Total private	Manufac-turing
			Total	Manufac-turing									
1950													
January	43 530	37 596	16 255	13 161	27 275	. . .	11 258	. . .	39.6	. . .	1.27	. . .	50.29
February	43 298	37 372	16 035	13 169	27 263	. . .	11 262	. . .	39.7	. . .	1.26	. . .	50.02
March	43 952	37 874	16 482	13 290	27 470	. . .	11 362	. . .	39.7	. . .	1.28	. . .	50.82
April	44 376	38 282	16 718	13 471	27 658	. . .	11 528	. . .	40.3	. . .	1.29	. . .	51.99
May	44 717	38 674	17 080	13 780	27 637	. . .	11 855	. . .	40.3	. . .	1.30	. . .	52.39
June	45 084	39 062	17 288	13 923	27 796	. . .	11 979	. . .	40.6	. . .	1.30	. . .	52.78
July	45 453	39 363	17 464	14 072	27 989	. . .	12 107	. . .	40.9	. . .	1.31	. . .	53.58
August	46 187	40 000	17 917	14 461	28 270	. . .	12 476	. . .	41.3	. . .	1.33	. . .	54.93
September	46 442	40 214	18 040	14 561	28 402	. . .	12 519	. . .	40.8	. . .	1.33	. . .	54.26
October	46 712	40 463	18 249	14 737	28 463	. . .	12 659	. . .	41.1	. . .	1.36	. . .	55.90
November	46 778	40 516	18 288	14 762	28 490	. . .	12 682	. . .	41.0	. . .	1.37	. . .	56.17
December	46 855	40 541	18 283	14 782	28 572	. . .	12 710	. . .	40.9	. . .	1.39	. . .	56.85
1951													
January	47 289	40 937	18 518	14 950	28 771	. . .	12 816	. . .	41.0	. . .	1.40	. . .	57.40
February	47 577	41 195	18 666	15 076	28 911	. . .	12 929	. . .	40.9	. . .	1.41	. . .	57.67
March	47 871	41 461	18 754	15 125	29 117	. . .	12 936	. . .	41.0	. . .	1.42	. . .	58.22
April	47 856	41 405	18 810	15 166	29 046	. . .	12 960	. . .	41.0	. . .	1.43	. . .	58.63
May	47 952	41 535	18 829	15 164	29 123	. . .	12 941	. . .	41.0	. . .	1.44	. . .	59.04
June	48 067	41 568	18 826	15 176	29 241	. . .	12 934	. . .	40.9	. . .	1.45	. . .	59.31
July	48 061	41 523	18 747	15 110	29 314	. . .	12 848	. . .	40.6	. . .	1.45	. . .	58.87
August	48 008	41 489	18 709	15 061	29 299	. . .	12 772	. . .	40.4	. . .	1.46	. . .	58.98
September	47 955	41 403	18 622	14 996	29 333	. . .	12 659	. . .	40.4	. . .	1.46	. . .	58.98
October	48 009	41 432	18 630	14 973	29 379	. . .	12 615	. . .	40.3	. . .	1.47	. . .	59.24
November	48 149	41 523	18 617	14 999	29 532	. . .	12 628	. . .	40.4	. . .	1.48	. . .	59.79
December	48 308	41 620	18 698	15 045	29 610	. . .	12 667	. . .	40.7	. . .	1.49	. . .	60.64
1952													
January	48 299	41 710	18 719	15 067	29 580	. . .	12 675	. . .	40.8	. . .	1.49	. . .	60.79
February	48 522	41 872	18 813	15 105	29 709	. . .	12 689	. . .	40.8	. . .	1.49	. . .	60.79
March	48 504	41 842	18 775	15 127	29 729	. . .	12 695	. . .	40.6	. . .	1.51	. . .	61.31
April	48 616	41 954	18 806	15 162	29 810	. . .	12 713	. . .	40.3	. . .	1.51	. . .	60.85
May	48 645	41 951	18 784	15 143	29 861	. . .	12 676	. . .	40.5	. . .	1.51	. . .	61.16
June	48 286	41 574	18 419	14 828	29 867	. . .	12 353	. . .	40.6	. . .	1.51	. . .	61.31
July	48 144	41 407	18 268	14 707	29 876	. . .	12 233	. . .	40.2	. . .	1.50	. . .	60.30
August	48 922	42 204	18 928	15 279	29 994	. . .	12 764	. . .	40.7	. . .	1.53	. . .	62.27
September	49 319	42 585	19 206	15 553	30 113	. . .	13 007	. . .	41.1	. . .	1.55	. . .	63.71
October	49 598	42 782	19 312	15 690	30 286	. . .	13 122	. . .	41.2	. . .	1.56	. . .	64.27
November	49 816	43 015	19 473	15 843	30 343	. . .	13 262	. . .	41.2	. . .	1.58	. . .	65.10
December	50 164	43 229	19 610	15 973	30 554	. . .	13 375	. . .	41.2	. . .	1.58	. . .	65.10
1953													
January	50 145	43 351	19 721	16 067	30 424	. . .	13 447	. . .	41.1	. . .	1.59	. . .	65.35
February	50 339	43 542	19 841	16 158	30 498	. . .	13 529	. . .	41.0	. . .	1.61	. . .	66.01
March	50 474	43 690	19 909	16 270	30 565	. . .	13 620	. . .	41.2	. . .	1.61	. . .	66.33
April	50 432	43 662	19 908	16 293	30 524	. . .	13 629	. . .	40.9	. . .	1.62	. . .	66.26
May	50 491	43 774	19 930	16 341	30 561	. . .	13 645	. . .	41.0	. . .	1.62	. . .	66.42
June	50 522	43 788	19 909	16 343	30 613	. . .	13 636	. . .	40.9	. . .	1.63	. . .	66.67
July	50 536	43 813	19 910	16 353	30 626	. . .	13 653	. . .	40.7	. . .	1.64	. . .	66.75
August	50 487	43 733	19 834	16 278	30 653	. . .	13 564	. . .	40.7	. . .	1.64	. . .	66.75
September	50 365	43 616	19 726	16 151	30 639	. . .	13 419	. . .	40.1	. . .	1.65	. . .	66.17
October	50 242	43 478	19 578	15 981	30 664	. . .	13 244	. . .	40.1	. . .	1.65	. . .	66.17
November	49 906	43 157	19 315	15 728	30 591	. . .	12 990	. . .	40.0	. . .	1.65	. . .	66.00
December	49 702	42 959	19 173	15 581	30 529	. . .	12 847	. . .	39.7	. . .	1.65	. . .	65.51
1954													
January	49 467	42 707	18 963	15 440	30 504	. . .	12 706	. . .	39.5	. . .	1.65	. . .	65.18
February	49 381	42 598	18 880	15 307	30 501	. . .	12 593	. . .	39.7	. . .	1.65	. . .	65.51
March	49 158	42 362	18 748	15 197	30 410	. . .	12 493	. . .	39.6	. . .	1.65	. . .	65.34
April	49 177	42 371	18 602	15 065	30 575	. . .	12 361	. . .	39.7	. . .	1.65	. . .	65.51
May	48 965	42 136	18 476	14 974	30 489	. . .	12 282	. . .	39.7	. . .	1.67	. . .	66.30
June	48 896	42 050	18 400	14 910	30 496	. . .	12 220	. . .	39.7	. . .	1.67	. . .	66.30
July	48 834	41 966	18 280	14 799	30 554	. . .	12 121	. . .	39.7	. . .	1.66	. . .	65.90
August	48 825	41 933	18 251	14 772	30 574	. . .	12 089	. . .	39.8	. . .	1.66	. . .	66.07
September	48 881	41 987	18 261	14 805	30 620	. . .	12 104	. . .	39.9	. . .	1.66	. . .	66.23
October	48 944	42 044	18 321	14 841	30 623	. . .	12 142	. . .	39.7	. . .	1.67	. . .	66.30
November	49 179	42 215	18 438	14 913	30 741	. . .	12 206	. . .	40.1	. . .	1.68	. . .	67.37
December	49 331	42 374	18 508	14 967	30 823	. . .	12 254	. . .	40.1	. . .	1.68	. . .	67.37
1955													
January	49 497	42 544	18 609	15 034	30 888	. . .	12 309	. . .	40.4	. . .	1.69	. . .	68.28
February	49 644	42 721	18 726	15 138	30 918	. . .	12 408	. . .	40.6	. . .	1.70	. . .	69.02
March	49 963	43 025	18 910	15 258	31 053	. . .	12 524	. . .	40.7	. . .	1.71	. . .	69.60
April	50 246	43 287	19 067	15 375	31 179	. . .	12 626	. . .	40.8	. . .	1.71	. . .	69.77
May	50 512	43 521	19 223	15 493	31 289	. . .	12 731	. . .	41.1	. . .	1.73	. . .	71.10
June	50 790	43 770	19 331	15 585	31 459	. . .	12 810	. . .	40.8	. . .	1.73	. . .	70.58
July	50 985	43 936	19 376	15 614	31 609	. . .	12 818	. . .	40.7	. . .	1.75	. . .	71.23
August	51 112	44 089	19 432	15 679	31 680	. . .	12 866	. . .	40.7	. . .	1.76	. . .	71.63
September	51 262	44 195	19 427	15 668	31 835	. . .	12 830	. . .	40.7	. . .	1.77	. . .	72.04
October	51 431	44 313	19 482	15 740	31 949	. . .	12 896	. . .	41.0	. . .	1.77	. . .	72.57
November	51 592	44 509	19 554	15 813	32 038	. . .	12 967	. . .	41.1	. . .	1.78	. . .	73.16
December	51 805	44 673	19 608	15 859	32 197	. . .	13 009	. . .	40.9	. . .	1.78	. . .	72.80

. . . = Not available.

Table 10-9. Employment, Hours, and Earnings, Total Nonfarm and Manufacturing, Historical Annual and Monthly—*Continued*

(Wage and salary workers on nonfarm payrolls, seasonally adjusted.)

Year and month	All wage and salary workers (thousands)					Production and nonsupervisory workers on private payrolls							
	Total	Private			Service-providing	Number (thousands)		Average hours per week		Average hourly earnings, dollars		Average weekly earnings, dollars	
		Total	Goods-producing			Total private	Manufac-turing	Total private	Manufac-turing	Total private	Manufac-turing	Total private	Manufac-turing
			Total	Manufac-turing									
1956													
January	51 975	44 808	19 665	15 882	32 310	. . .	13 011	. . .	40.8	. . .	1.78	. . .	72.62
February	52 167	44 955	19 731	15 889	32 436	. . .	12 986	. . .	40.7	. . .	1.79	. . .	72.85
March	52 295	45 043	19 691	15 829	32 604	. . .	12 905	. . .	40.6	. . .	1.80	. . .	73.08
April	52 375	45 099	19 811	15 909	32 564	. . .	12 970	. . .	40.5	. . .	1.82	. . .	73.71
May	52 506	45 139	19 825	15 893	32 681	. . .	12 925	. . .	40.4	. . .	1.83	. . .	73.93
June	52 583	45 216	19 905	15 835	32 678	. . .	12 836	. . .	40.3	. . .	1.83	. . .	73.75
July	51 954	44 549	19 390	15 468	32 564	. . .	12 435	. . .	40.3	. . .	1.82	. . .	73.35
August	52 632	45 181	19 922	15 893	32 710	. . .	12 860	. . .	40.3	. . .	1.85	. . .	74.56
September	52 600	45 119	19 860	15 863	32 740	. . .	12 822	. . .	40.5	. . .	1.87	. . .	75.74
October	52 781	45 262	19 918	15 937	32 863	. . .	12 908	. . .	40.6	. . .	1.88	. . .	76.33
November	52 822	45 269	19 886	15 916	32 936	. . .	12 864	. . .	40.4	. . .	1.88	. . .	75.95
December	52 930	45 346	19 926	15 957	33 004	. . .	12 882	. . .	40.6	. . .	1.91	. . .	77.55
1957													
January	52 888	45 268	19 833	15 970	33 055	. . .	12 881	. . .	40.4	. . .	1.90	. . .	76.76
February	53 098	45 452	19 933	15 998	33 165	. . .	12 885	. . .	40.5	. . .	1.91	. . .	77.36
March	53 156	45 484	19 936	15 994	33 220	. . .	12 855	. . .	40.4	. . .	1.92	. . .	77.57
April	53 238	45 537	19 887	15 970	33 351	. . .	12 811	. . .	40.0	. . .	1.91	. . .	76.40
May	53 149	45 436	19 834	15 931	33 315	. . .	12 762	. . .	40.0	. . .	1.92	. . .	76.80
June	53 066	45 364	19 777	15 873	33 289	. . .	12 697	. . .	40.0	. . .	1.92	. . .	76.80
July	53 122	45 368	19 735	15 854	33 387	. . .	12 669	. . .	40.0	. . .	1.93	. . .	77.20
August	53 128	45 371	19 728	15 867	33 400	. . .	12 673	. . .	40.0	. . .	1.94	. . .	77.60
September	52 932	45 183	19 545	15 710	33 387	. . .	12 528	. . .	39.7	. . .	1.95	. . .	77.42
October	52 765	44 997	19 421	15 599	33 344	. . .	12 437	. . .	39.4	. . .	1.96	. . .	77.22
November	52 557	44 788	19 260	15 466	33 297	. . .	12 301	. . .	39.2	. . .	1.96	. . .	76.83
December	52 385	44 539	19 111	15 332	33 274	. . .	12 170	. . .	39.1	. . .	1.95	. . .	76.25
1958													
January	52 077	44 256	18 902	15 130	33 175	. . .	11 969	. . .	38.9	. . .	1.95	. . .	75.86
February	51 576	43 744	18 529	14 908	33 047	. . .	11 757	. . .	38.7	. . .	1.95	. . .	75.47
March	51 300	43 452	18 335	14 670	32 965	. . .	11 532	. . .	38.8	. . .	1.96	. . .	76.05
April	51 026	43 158	18 120	14 506	32 906	. . .	11 373	. . .	38.9	. . .	1.96	. . .	76.24
May	50 913	43 019	18 008	14 414	32 905	. . .	11 294	. . .	38.9	. . .	1.97	. . .	76.63
June	50 912	42 986	17 984	14 408	32 928	. . .	11 300	. . .	39.1	. . .	1.98	. . .	77.42
July	51 037	43 065	18 038	14 450	32 999	. . .	11 349	. . .	39.3	. . .	1.98	. . .	77.81
August	51 233	43 221	18 147	14 524	33 086	. . .	11 412	. . .	39.5	. . .	2.01	. . .	79.40
September	51 506	43 490	18 331	14 658	33 175	. . .	11 556	. . .	39.5	. . .	2.00	. . .	79.00
October	51 485	43 454	18 218	14 503	33 267	. . .	11 394	. . .	39.6	. . .	2.00	. . .	79.20
November	51 943	43 915	18 610	14 827	33 333	. . .	11 702	. . .	39.9	. . .	2.03	. . .	81.00
December	52 088	43 988	18 592	14 877	33 496	. . .	11 743	. . .	39.9	. . .	2.04	. . .	81.40
1959													
January	52 481	44 376	18 796	14 998	33 685	. . .	11 849	. . .	40.2	. . .	2.04	. . .	82.01
February	52 687	44 571	18 890	15 115	33 797	. . .	11 950	. . .	40.3	. . .	2.05	. . .	82.62
March	53 016	44 884	19 069	15 259	33 947	. . .	12 078	. . .	40.4	. . .	2.07	. . .	83.63
April	53 320	45 178	19 269	15 385	34 051	. . .	12 185	. . .	40.5	. . .	2.08	. . .	84.24
May	53 549	45 396	19 378	15 487	34 171	. . .	12 277	. . .	40.7	. . .	2.08	. . .	84.66
June	53 678	45 535	19 462	15 554	34 216	. . .	12 330	. . .	40.6	. . .	2.09	. . .	84.85
July	53 803	45 630	19 529	15 623	34 274	. . .	12 366	. . .	40.3	. . .	2.09	. . .	84.23
August	53 337	45 156	19 049	15 242	34 288	. . .	11 936	. . .	40.4	. . .	2.07	. . .	83.63
September	53 428	45 189	19 052	15 254	34 376	. . .	11 984	. . .	40.4	. . .	2.08	. . .	84.03
October	53 359	45 094	18 925	15 158	34 434	. . .	11 864	. . .	40.1	. . .	2.07	. . .	83.01
November	53 635	45 351	19 108	15 300	34 527	. . .	11 991	. . .	39.9	. . .	2.07	. . .	82.59
December	54 175	45 807	19 425	15 573	34 750	. . .	12 254	. . .	40.3	. . .	2.11	. . .	85.03
1960													
January	54 274	45 967	19 491	15 687	34 783	. . .	12 362	. . .	40.6	. . .	2.13	. . .	86.48
February	54 513	46 187	19 605	15 765	34 908	. . .	12 434	. . .	40.3	. . .	2.14	. . .	86.24
March	54 458	45 933	19 373	15 707	35 085	. . .	12 362	. . .	40.0	. . .	2.14	. . .	85.60
April	54 812	46 278	19 446	15 654	35 366	. . .	12 299	. . .	40.0	. . .	2.14	. . .	85.60
May	54 472	46 040	19 374	15 575	35 098	. . .	12 218	. . .	40.1	. . .	2.14	. . .	85.81
June	54 347	45 915	19 240	15 466	35 107	. . .	12 102	. . .	39.9	. . .	2.14	. . .	85.39
July	54 303	45 861	19 170	15 413	35 133	. . .	12 047	. . .	39.9	. . .	2.14	. . .	85.39
August	54 272	45 800	19 105	15 360	35 167	. . .	11 986	. . .	39.7	. . .	2.15	. . .	85.36
September	54 228	45 734	19 057	15 330	35 171	. . .	11 956	. . .	39.4	. . .	2.16	. . .	85.10
October	54 144	45 642	18 952	15 231	35 192	. . .	11 846	. . .	39.7	. . .	2.16	. . .	85.75
November	53 962	45 446	18 799	15 112	35 163	. . .	11 726	. . .	39.3	. . .	2.15	. . .	84.50
December	53 743	45 146	18 548	14 947	35 195	. . .	11 556	. . .	38.4	. . .	2.16	. . .	82.94
1961													
January	53 683	45 119	18 508	14 863	35 175	. . .	11 473	. . .	39.3	. . .	2.16	. . .	84.89
February	53 556	44 969	18 418	14 801	35 138	. . .	11 414	. . .	39.4	. . .	2.16	. . .	85.10
March	53 662	45 051	18 438	14 802	35 224	. . .	11 410	. . .	39.5	. . .	2.16	. . .	85.32
April	53 626	44 997	18 432	14 825	35 194	. . .	11 444	. . .	39.5	. . .	2.18	. . .	86.11
May	53 783	45 119	18 523	14 932	35 260	. . .	11 544	. . .	39.7	. . .	2.19	. . .	86.94
June	53 977	45 289	18 618	14 981	35 359	. . .	11 593	. . .	40.0	. . .	2.20	. . .	88.00
July	54 124	45 400	18 640	15 029	35 484	. . .	11 639	. . .	40.0	. . .	2.21	. . .	88.40
August	54 299	45 535	18 725	15 093	35 574	. . .	11 701	. . .	40.1	. . .	2.22	. . .	89.02
September	54 387	45 591	18 730	15 080	35 657	. . .	11 679	. . .	39.5	. . .	2.20	. . .	86.90
October	54 521	45 716	18 805	15 143	35 716	. . .	11 731	. . .	40.3	. . .	2.23	. . .	89.87
November	54 743	45 931	18 927	15 259	35 816	. . .	11 842	. . .	40.7	. . .	2.23	. . .	90.76
December	54 871	46 035	18 981	15 309	35 890	. . .	11 872	. . .	40.4	. . .	2.24	. . .	90.50

. . . = Not available.

Table 10-9. Employment, Hours, and Earnings, Total Nonfarm and Manufacturing, Historical Annual and Monthly—*Continued*

(Wage and salary workers on nonfarm payrolls, seasonally adjusted.)

Year and month	All wage and salary workers (thousands)					Production and nonsupervisory workers on private payrolls							
	Total	Private			Service-providing	Number (thousands)		Average hours per week		Average hourly earnings, dollars		Average weekly earnings, dollars	
		Total	Goods-producing			Total private	Manufac-turing	Total private	Manufac-turing	Total private	Manufac-turing	Total private	Manufac-turing
			Total	Manufac-turing									
1962													
January	54 891	46 040	18 936	15 322	35 955	. . .	11 865	. . .	40.0	. . .	2.25	. . .	90.00
February	55 187	46 309	19 109	15 411	36 078	. . .	11 950	. . .	40.4	. . .	2.26	. . .	91.30
March	55 276	46 375	19 109	15 451	36 167	. . .	11 970	. . .	40.6	. . .	2.26	. . .	91.76
April	55 601	46 679	19 258	15 524	36 343	. . .	12 034	. . .	40.6	. . .	2.26	. . .	91.76
May	55 626	46 668	19 253	15 513	36 373	. . .	12 011	. . .	40.6	. . .	2.27	. . .	92.16
June	55 644	46 644	19 186	15 518	36 458	. . .	12 006	. . .	40.5	. . .	2.26	. . .	91.53
July	55 746	46 720	19 248	15 522	36 498	. . .	12 004	. . .	40.5	. . .	2.27	. . .	91.94
August	55 838	46 775	19 251	15 517	36 587	. . .	11 990	. . .	40.5	. . .	2.28	. . .	92.34
September	55 977	46 888	19 305	15 568	36 672	. . .	12 033	. . .	40.5	. . .	2.28	. . .	92.34
October	56 041	46 927	19 301	15 569	36 740	. . .	12 034	. . .	40.3	. . .	2.29	. . .	92.29
November	56 055	46 910	19 260	15 530	36 795	. . .	11 977	. . .	40.5	. . .	2.29	. . .	92.75
December	56 027	46 901	19 219	15 520	36 808	. . .	11 961	. . .	40.3	. . .	2.29	. . .	92.29
1963													
January	56 116	46 912	19 257	15 545	36 859	. . .	11 974	. . .	40.5	. . .	2.30	. . .	93.15
February	56 231	47 000	19 228	15 542	37 003	. . .	11 965	. . .	40.5	. . .	2.31	. . .	93.56
March	56 322	47 077	19 233	15 564	37 089	. . .	11 990	. . .	40.5	. . .	2.32	. . .	93.96
April	56 580	47 316	19 343	15 602	37 237	. . .	12 029	. . .	40.5	. . .	2.32	. . .	93.96
May	56 616	47 328	19 399	15 641	37 217	. . .	12 066	. . .	40.5	. . .	2.33	. . .	94.37
June	56 658	47 356	19 371	15 624	37 287	. . .	12 050	. . .	40.7	. . .	2.34	. . .	95.24
July	56 795	47 461	19 423	15 646	37 372	. . .	12 080	. . .	40.6	. . .	2.35	. . .	95.41
August	56 910	47 542	19 437	15 644	37 473	. . .	12 060	. . .	40.6	. . .	2.34	. . .	95.00
September	57 078	47 661	19 483	15 674	37 595	. . .	12 088	. . .	40.6	. . .	2.36	. . .	95.82
October	57 284	47 805	19 517	15 714	37 767	. . .	12 131	. . .	40.7	. . .	2.36	. . .	96.05
November	57 255	47 771	19 456	15 675	37 799	. . .	12 072	. . .	40.7	. . .	2.37	. . .	96.46
December	57 360	47 863	19 493	15 712	37 867	. . .	12 108	. . .	40.6	. . .	2.38	. . .	96.63
1964													
January	57 487	47 925	19 406	15 715	38 081	39 914	12 132	38.2	40.1	2.50	2.38	95.50	95.44
February	57 752	48 171	19 570	15 742	38 182	40 123	12 165	38.5	40.7	2.50	2.38	96.25	96.87
March	57 898	48 287	19 587	15 770	38 311	40 171	12 190	38.5	40.6	2.50	2.38	96.25	96.63
April	57 923	48 279	19 593	15 785	38 330	40 208	12 211	38.6	40.7	2.52	2.40	97.27	97.68
May	58 089	48 419	19 630	15 812	38 459	40 332	12 231	38.6	40.8	2.52	2.40	97.27	97.92
June	58 221	48 552	19 682	15 839	38 539	40 448	12 255	38.6	40.8	2.53	2.41	97.66	98.33
July	58 412	48 735	19 740	15 887	38 672	40 624	12 309	38.5	40.8	2.53	2.41	97.41	98.33
August	58 620	48 888	19 810	15 948	38 810	40 770	12 354	38.5	40.9	2.55	2.42	98.18	98.98
September	58 903	49 117	19 943	16 073	38 960	41 026	12 479	38.5	40.9	2.55	2.44	98.18	99.80
October	58 794	48 949	19 723	15 821	39 071	40 827	12 224	38.5	40.7	2.55	2.40	98.18	97.68
November	59 217	49 338	20 026	16 096	39 191	41 157	12 477	38.6	41.0	2.56	2.42	98.82	99.22
December	59 420	49 523	20 111	16 176	39 309	41 308	12 551	38.7	41.2	2.58	2.44	99.85	100.53
1965													
January	59 583	49 646	20 173	16 245	39 410	41 453	12 603	38.7	41.3	2.58	2.45	99.85	101.19
February	59 800	49 826	20 216	16 291	39 584	41 583	12 644	38.7	41.3	2.59	2.46	100.23	101.60
March	60 003	49 993	20 292	16 353	39 711	41 675	12 701	38.7	41.3	2.60	2.47	100.62	102.01
April	60 258	50 207	20 317	16 418	39 941	41 886	12 752	38.7	41.2	2.60	2.47	100.62	101.76
May	60 492	50 398	20 444	16 477	40 048	42 044	12 792	38.8	41.3	2.62	2.49	101.66	102.84
June	60 690	50 562	20 522	16 554	40 168	42 183	12 854	38.6	41.2	2.62	2.49	101.13	102.59
July	60 963	50 762	20 611	16 669	40 352	42 364	12 962	38.6	41.2	2.63	2.49	101.52	102.59
August	61 228	50 957	20 726	16 732	40 502	42 537	12 994	38.5	41.1	2.64	2.50	101.64	102.75
September	61 490	51 152	20 808	16 802	40 682	42 726	13 046	38.6	41.1	2.65	2.51	102.29	103.16
October	61 718	51 340	20 895	16 864	40 823	42 870	13 100	38.5	41.2	2.66	2.52	102.41	103.82
November	61 997	51 561	21 021	16 962	40 976	43 045	13 175	38.6	41.3	2.67	2.52	103.06	104.08
December	62 321	51 822	21 151	17 051	41 170	43 270	13 243	38.6	41.3	2.68	2.53	103.45	104.49
1966													
January	62 528	51 987	21 214	17 143	41 314	43 401	13 301	38.6	41.5	2.68	2.54	103.45	105.41
February	62 796	52 185	21 315	17 288	41 481	43 552	13 426	38.7	41.7	2.69	2.56	104.10	106.75
March	63 191	52 499	21 515	17 400	41 676	43 801	13 508	38.7	41.6	2.70	2.56	104.49	106.50
April	63 436	52 677	21 568	17 517	41 868	43 959	13 598	38.7	41.8	2.71	2.58	104.88	107.84
May	63 711	52 890	21 675	17 625	42 036	44 138	13 678	38.5	41.5	2.72	2.58	104.72	107.07
June	64 110	53 208	21 846	17 733	42 264	44 390	13 753	38.5	41.4	2.72	2.58	104.72	106.81
July	64 301	53 327	21 872	17 760	42 429	44 484	13 758	38.4	41.2	2.74	2.60	105.22	107.12
August	64 507	53 501	21 972	17 882	42 535	44 596	13 843	38.4	41.4	2.75	2.61	105.60	108.05
September	64 645	53 582	21 948	17 886	42 697	44 659	13 841	38.3	41.2	2.76	2.63	105.71	108.36
October	64 854	53 727	21 991	17 956	42 863	44 789	13 906	38.4	41.3	2.77	2.64	106.37	109.03
November	65 019	53 816	21 988	17 981	43 031	44 834	13 918	38.3	41.2	2.78	2.65	106.47	109.18
December	65 199	53 943	22 008	17 998	43 191	44 916	13 906	38.2	40.9	2.78	2.64	106.20	107.98
1967													
January	65 407	54 092	22 057	18 033	43 350	45 050	13 925	38.3	41.1	2.79	2.65	106.86	108.92
February	65 427	54 074	21 987	17 978	43 440	44 967	13 853	37.9	40.4	2.81	2.67	106.50	107.87
March	65 530	54 133	21 919	17 940	43 611	44 991	13 797	37.9	40.5	2.81	2.67	106.50	108.14
April	65 467	54 032	21 842	17 878	43 625	44 871	13 712	37.8	40.4	2.82	2.68	106.60	108.27
May	65 618	54 144	21 779	17 832	43 839	44 961	13 664	37.8	40.4	2.83	2.69	106.97	108.68
June	65 750	54 216	21 761	17 812	43 989	45 004	13 632	37.8	40.4	2.84	2.69	107.35	108.68
July	65 887	54 343	21 772	17 784	44 115	45 105	13 602	37.8	40.5	2.86	2.71	108.11	109.76
August	66 142	54 552	21 887	17 905	44 255	45 267	13 681	37.8	40.6	2.87	2.73	108.49	110.84
September	66 163	54 540	21 775	17 794	44 388	45 236	13 559	37.8	40.6	2.88	2.73	108.86	110.84
October	66 225	54 583	21 779	17 800	44 446	45 278	13 587	37.8	40.6	2.89	2.74	109.24	111.24
November	66 703	55 008	21 996	17 985	44 707	45 701	13 777	37.9	40.6	2.91	2.75	110.29	111.65
December	66 900	55 165	22 037	18 025	44 863	45 800	13 782	37.7	40.7	2.92	2.77	110.08	112.74

. . . = Not available.

Table 10-9. Employment, Hours, and Earnings, Total Nonfarm and Manufacturing, Historical Annual and Monthly—*Continued*

(Wage and salary workers on nonfarm payrolls, seasonally adjusted.)

Year and month	All wage and salary workers (thousands)					Production and nonsupervisory workers on private payrolls							
	Total	Private			Service-providing	Number (thousands)		Average hours per week		Average hourly earnings, dollars		Average weekly earnings, dollars	
		Total	Goods-producing			Total private	Manufac-turing	Total private	Manufac-turing	Total private	Manufac-turing	Total private	Manufac-turing
			Total	Manufac-turing									
1968													
January	66 805	55 011	21 917	18 040	44 888	45 655	13 798	37.6	40.4	2.94	2.81	110.54	113.52
February	67 214	55 395	22 117	18 054	45 097	45 980	13 793	37.8	40.8	2.95	2.82	111.51	115.06
March	67 296	55 454	22 119	18 067	45 177	46 041	13 803	37.7	40.8	2.97	2.84	111.97	115.87
April	67 555	55 677	22 207	18 131	45 348	46 239	13 858	37.6	40.3	2.98	2.85	112.05	114.86
May	67 652	55 747	22 255	18 190	45 397	46 267	13 900	37.7	40.9	3.00	2.87	113.10	117.38
June	67 904	55 917	22 264	18 228	45 640	46 402	13 921	37.8	40.9	3.01	2.88	113.78	117.79
July	68 126	56 108	22 329	18 265	45 797	46 562	13 953	37.7	40.8	3.03	2.89	114.23	117.91
August	68 328	56 286	22 350	18 254	45 978	46 669	13 903	37.7	40.7	3.03	2.89	114.23	117.62
September	68 487	56 420	22 390	18 252	46 097	46 792	13 914	37.7	40.9	3.06	2.92	115.36	119.43
October	68 720	56 619	22 419	18 293	46 301	46 989	13 974	37.7	41.0	3.07	2.94	115.74	120.54
November	68 985	56 878	22 512	18 346	46 473	47 244	14 028	37.5	40.9	3.09	2.96	115.88	121.06
December	69 245	57 100	22 617	18 410	46 628	47 384	14 044	37.5	40.7	3.11	2.97	116.63	120.88
1969													
January	69 438	57 229	22 644	18 432	46 794	47 528	14 086	37.7	40.8	3.12	2.99	117.62	121.99
February	69 698	57 474	22 755	18 502	46 943	47 697	14 134	37.5	40.4	3.14	3.00	117.75	121.20
March	69 906	57 677	22 813	18 558	47 093	47 852	14 169	37.6	40.8	3.15	3.01	118.44	122.81
April	70 072	57 827	22 815	18 554	47 257	47 959	14 144	37.7	41.0	3.17	3.03	119.51	124.23
May	70 328	58 044	22 899	18 588	47 429	48 122	14 161	37.6	40.7	3.19	3.04	119.94	123.73
June	70 636	58 277	22 981	18 640	47 655	48 330	14 206	37.5	40.7	3.20	3.05	120.00	124.14
July	70 730	58 390	22 990	18 642	47 740	48 434	14 194	37.5	40.6	3.22	3.08	120.75	125.05
August	71 005	58 632	23 111	18 767	47 894	48 616	14 287	37.5	40.6	3.24	3.10	121.50	125.86
September	70 918	58 539	22 988	18 620	47 930	48 524	14 159	37.5	40.6	3.26	3.12	122.25	126.67
October	71 119	58 689	22 976	18 613	48 143	48 669	14 174	37.4	40.5	3.28	3.13	122.67	126.77
November	71 088	58 640	22 840	18 467	48 248	48 589	14 035	37.5	40.5	3.29	3.14	123.38	127.17
December	71 240	58 763	22 884	18 485	48 356	48 638	14 013	37.5	40.6	3.30	3.15	123.75	127.89
1970													
January	71 176	58 680	22 726	18 424	48 450	48 564	13 964	37.3	40.4	3.31	3.16	123.46	127.66
February	71 302	58 784	22 747	18 361	48 555	48 600	13 897	37.3	40.2	3.33	3.17	124.21	127.43
March	71 453	58 850	22 738	18 360	48 715	48 690	13 917	37.2	40.1	3.35	3.19	124.62	127.92
April	71 348	58 643	22 552	18 207	48 796	48 479	13 785	37.0	39.8	3.36	3.19	124.32	126.96
May	71 122	58 454	22 336	18 029	48 786	48 287	13 616	37.0	39.8	3.38	3.22	125.06	128.16
June	71 028	58 361	22 241	17 930	48 787	48 226	13 554	36.9	39.8	3.39	3.24	125.09	128.95
July	71 055	58 358	22 195	17 877	48 860	48 242	13 527	37.0	40.0	3.41	3.25	126.17	130.00
August	70 932	58 221	22 105	17 779	48 827	48 089	13 449	37.0	39.8	3.43	3.26	126.91	129.75
September	70 949	58 208	21 988	17 692	48 961	48 101	13 401	36.8	39.6	3.45	3.29	126.96	130.28
October	70 519	57 726	21 477	17 173	49 042	47 619	12 905	36.8	39.5	3.46	3.26	127.33	128.77
November	70 409	57 579	21 345	17 024	49 064	47 466	12 781	36.7	39.5	3.47	3.26	127.35	128.77
December	70 790	57 945	21 673	17 309	49 117	47 778	13 062	36.8	39.5	3.50	3.32	128.80	131.14
1971													
January	70 866	57 988	21 594	17 280	49 272	47 859	13 069	36.8	39.9	3.52	3.36	129.54	134.06
February	70 805	57 928	21 514	17 216	49 291	47 779	13 033	36.7	39.7	3.54	3.39	129.92	134.58
March	70 859	57 951	21 491	17 154	49 368	47 819	12 984	36.7	39.8	3.56	3.39	130.65	134.92
April	71 037	58 092	21 552	17 149	49 485	47 966	12 993	36.8	39.9	3.57	3.41	131.38	136.06
May	71 247	58 277	21 645	17 225	49 602	48 153	13 081	36.7	40.0	3.60	3.43	132.12	137.20
June	71 253	58 245	21 568	17 139	49 685	48 109	13 012	36.8	39.9	3.62	3.45	133.22	137.66
July	71 316	58 305	21 564	17 126	49 752	48 167	13 001	36.7	40.0	3.63	3.46	133.22	138.40
August	71 368	58 327	21 570	17 115	49 798	48 164	12 993	36.7	39.8	3.66	3.48	134.32	138.50
September	71 620	58 552	21 650	17 154	49 970	48 362	13 038	36.7	39.7	3.67	3.48	134.69	138.16
October	71 642	58 527	21 604	17 126	50 038	48 305	13 027	36.8	39.9	3.68	3.50	135.42	139.65
November	71 844	58 696	21 684	17 166	50 160	48 442	13 064	36.9	40.0	3.69	3.49	136.16	139.60
December	72 108	58 918	21 741	17 202	50 367	48 613	13 078	36.9	40.2	3.73	3.55	137.64	142.71
1972													
January	72 445	59 179	21 865	17 283	50 580	49 035	13 173	36.9	40.2	3.80	3.57	140.22	143.51
February	72 652	59 354	21 915	17 361	50 737	49 143	13 235	36.9	40.4	3.82	3.61	140.96	145.84
March	72 945	59 616	22 036	17 447	50 909	49 437	13 316	36.9	40.4	3.84	3.63	141.70	146.65
April	73 163	59 805	22 099	17 508	51 064	49 561	13 373	36.9	40.5	3.86	3.65	142.43	147.83
May	73 467	60 051	22 222	17 602	51 245	49 745	13 451	36.8	40.5	3.87	3.67	142.42	148.64
June	73 760	60 355	22 282	17 641	51 478	49 997	13 475	36.9	40.6	3.88	3.68	143.17	149.41
July	73 709	60 227	22 162	17 556	51 547	49 842	13 387	36.8	40.5	3.90	3.69	143.52	149.45
August	74 137	60 607	22 400	17 741	51 737	50 156	13 562	36.8	40.6	3.92	3.73	144.26	151.44
September	74 268	60 693	22 456	17 774	51 812	50 224	13 572	36.9	40.6	3.94	3.75	145.39	152.25
October	74 672	61 066	22 613	17 893	52 059	50 552	13 681	37.0	40.7	3.97	3.78	146.89	153.85
November	74 965	61 322	22 688	18 005	52 277	50 790	13 783	36.9	40.7	3.98	3.79	146.86	154.25
December	75 270	61 586	22 772	18 158	52 498	51 054	13 902	36.8	40.6	4.01	3.83	147.57	155.50
1973													
January	75 620	61 930	22 955	18 276	52 665	51 349	14 006	36.8	40.4	4.03	3.86	148.30	155.94
February	76 017	62 306	23 160	18 410	52 857	51 686	14 127	36.9	40.9	4.04	3.87	149.08	158.28
March	76 286	62 541	23 262	18 493	53 024	51 901	14 181	37.0	40.9	4.06	3.88	150.22	158.69
April	76 456	62 679	23 316	18 530	53 140	51 982	14 192	36.9	40.8	4.08	3.91	150.55	159.53
May	76 646	62 829	23 382	18 564	53 264	52 082	14 217	36.9	40.7	4.10	3.93	151.29	159.95
June	76 886	63 014	23 485	18 606	53 401	52 234	14 253	36.9	40.7	4.12	3.95	152.03	160.77
July	76 911	63 046	23 522	18 598	53 389	52 238	14 232	36.9	40.7	4.15	3.98	153.14	161.99
August	77 166	63 262	23 559	18 629	53 607	52 393	14 251	36.9	40.6	4.16	4.00	153.50	162.40
September	77 281	63 389	23 548	18 609	53 733	52 410	14 213	36.8	40.7	4.19	4.03	154.19	164.02
October	77 605	63 628	23 641	18 702	53 964	52 655	14 289	36.7	40.6	4.21	4.05	154.51	164.43
November	77 909	63 874	23 719	18 773	54 190	52 847	14 342	36.9	40.6	4.23	4.07	156.09	165.24
December	78 035	63 965	23 779	18 820	54 256	52 954	14 386	36.7	40.6	4.25	4.09	155.98	166.05

Table 10-9. Employment, Hours, and Earnings, Total Nonfarm and Manufacturing, Historical Annual and Monthly—*Continued*

(Wage and salary workers on nonfarm payrolls, seasonally adjusted.)

Year and month	All wage and salary workers (thousands)					Production and nonsupervisory workers on private payrolls							
	Total	Private			Service-providing	Number (thousands)		Average hours per week		Average hourly earnings, dollars		Average weekly earnings, dollars	
		Total	Goods-producing			Total private	Manufac-turing	Total private	Manufac-turing	Total private	Manufac-turing	Total private	Manufac-turing
			Total	Manufac-turing									
1974													
January	78 104	64 014	23 709	18 788	54 395	52 896	14 340	36.6	40.5	4.26	4.10	155.92	166.05
February	78 253	64 118	23 718	18 727	54 535	52 971	14 269	36.6	40.4	4.29	4.13	157.01	166.85
March	78 295	64 143	23 687	18 700	54 608	52 951	14 223	36.6	40.4	4.31	4.15	157.75	167.66
April	78 384	64 193	23 670	18 702	54 714	53 003	14 225	36.4	39.5	4.34	4.16	157.98	164.32
May	78 547	64 326	23 635	18 688	54 912	53 095	14 199	36.5	40.3	4.39	4.25	160.24	171.28
June	78 602	64 363	23 591	18 690	55 011	53 107	14 197	36.5	40.2	4.43	4.30	161.70	172.86
July	78 634	64 346	23 462	18 656	55 172	53 044	14 152	36.5	40.1	4.45	4.33	162.43	173.63
August	78 619	64 291	23 396	18 570	55 223	53 025	14 089	36.5	40.2	4.49	4.38	163.89	176.08
September	78 614	64 192	23 274	18 492	55 340	52 915	14 025	36.4	40.0	4.53	4.42	164.89	176.80
October	78 627	64 143	23 118	18 364	55 509	52 836	13 884	36.3	40.0	4.56	4.48	165.53	179.20
November	78 259	63 727	22 773	18 077	55 486	52 413	13 607	36.1	39.5	4.57	4.49	164.98	177.36
December	77 657	63 098	22 303	17 693	55 354	51 856	13 259	36.1	39.3	4.61	4.52	166.42	177.64
1975													
January	77 297	62 673	21 974	17 344	55 323	51 439	12 933	36.1	39.2	4.61	4.54	166.42	177.97
February	76 919	62 172	21 512	17 004	55 407	50 934	12 622	35.9	38.9	4.63	4.58	166.22	178.16
March	76 649	61 895	21 274	16 853	55 375	50 666	12 483	35.7	38.8	4.66	4.63	166.36	179.64
April	76 463	61 668	21 109	16 759	55 354	50 439	12 407	35.8	39.0	4.66	4.63	166.83	180.57
May	76 623	61 796	21 097	16 746	55 526	50 558	12 406	35.9	39.0	4.68	4.65	168.01	181.35
June	76 519	61 735	21 018	16 690	55 501	50 537	12 371	35.9	39.2	4.72	4.68	169.45	183.46
July	76 768	61 907	20 981	16 678	55 787	50 726	12 374	35.9	39.4	4.73	4.71	169.81	185.57
August	77 154	62 284	21 176	16 824	55 978	51 070	12 538	36.1	39.7	4.77	4.75	172.20	188.58
September	77 232	62 408	21 284	16 904	55 948	51 183	12 617	36.1	39.8	4.79	4.78	172.92	190.24
October	77 535	62 635	21 384	16 984	56 151	51 376	12 687	36.1	39.9	4.81	4.80	173.64	191.52
November	77 679	62 776	21 442	17 025	56 237	51 458	12 700	36.1	39.9	4.85	4.83	175.09	192.72
December	78 017	63 071	21 602	17 140	56 415	51 759	12 811	36.2	40.2	4.87	4.86	176.29	195.37
1976													
January	78 506	63 537	21 799	17 287	56 707	52 182	12 945	36.3	40.3	4.90	4.90	177.87	197.47
February	78 817	63 836	21 893	17 384	56 924	52 430	13 030	36.3	40.4	4.94	4.94	179.32	199.58
March	79 049	64 062	21 980	17 470	57 069	52 615	13 092	36.0	40.2	4.96	4.98	178.56	200.20
April	79 293	64 308	22 050	17 541	57 243	52 810	13 160	36.0	39.6	4.98	4.98	179.28	197.21
May	79 311	64 340	21 988	17 513	57 323	52 802	13 130	36.1	40.3	5.02	5.04	181.22	203.11
June	79 376	64 413	21 982	17 521	57 394	52 830	13 121	36.1	40.2	5.04	5.07	181.94	203.81
July	79 546	64 553	21 988	17 524	57 558	52 973	13 124	36.1	40.3	5.07	5.11	183.03	205.93
August	79 704	64 697	22 038	17 596	57 666	53 072	13 195	36.0	40.2	5.12	5.16	184.32	207.43
September	79 892	64 921	22 142	17 665	57 750	53 268	13 253	36.0	40.2	5.15	5.20	185.40	209.04
October	79 905	64 877	22 037	17 548	57 868	53 165	13 109	35.9	40.0	5.17	5.19	185.60	207.60
November	80 237	65 164	22 207	17 682	58 030	53 362	13 199	35.9	40.1	5.21	5.25	187.04	210.53
December	80 448	65 373	22 261	17 719	58 187	53 543	13 230	35.9	39.9	5.23	5.29	187.76	211.07
1977													
January	80 692	65 636	22 320	17 803	58 372	53 756	13 305	35.6	39.4	5.26	5.35	187.26	210.79
February	80 987	65 931	22 478	17 843	58 509	54 016	13 331	36.0	40.2	5.30	5.36	190.80	215.47
March	81 391	66 341	22 672	17 941	58 719	54 390	13 424	35.9	40.3	5.33	5.40	191.35	217.62
April	81 730	66 655	22 807	18 024	58 923	54 670	13 490	36.0	40.4	5.37	5.45	193.32	220.18
May	82 089	66 957	22 919	18 107	59 170	54 940	13 567	36.0	40.5	5.40	5.49	194.40	222.35
June	82 488	67 281	23 046	18 192	59 442	55 195	13 622	36.0	40.5	5.43	5.54	195.48	224.37
July	82 836	67 537	23 106	18 259	59 730	55 395	13 670	35.9	40.4	5.46	5.58	196.01	225.43
August	83 074	67 746	23 124	18 276	59 950	55 543	13 679	35.9	40.4	5.48	5.61	196.73	226.64
September	83 532	68 129	23 244	18 334	60 288	55 859	13 714	35.9	40.4	5.51	5.65	197.81	228.26
October	83 794	68 331	23 279	18 356	60 515	56 004	13 722	36.0	40.6	5.56	5.69	200.16	231.01
November	84 173	68 658	23 371	18 419	60 802	56 281	13 771	35.9	40.5	5.59	5.72	200.68	231.66
December	84 408	68 870	23 371	18 531	61 037	56 466	13 861	35.8	40.4	5.61	5.75	200.84	232.30
1978													
January	84 595	68 984	23 374	18 593	61 221	56 547	13 917	35.3	39.5	5.66	5.83	199.80	230.29
February	84 948	69 277	23 453	18 639	61 495	56 768	13 950	35.6	39.9	5.69	5.86	202.56	233.81
March	85 461	69 730	23 649	18 699	61 812	57 176	13 992	35.8	40.5	5.73	5.88	205.13	238.14
April	86 163	70 366	24 008	18 772	62 155	57 709	14 037	35.8	40.4	5.79	5.93	207.28	239.57
May	86 509	70 675	24 082	18 848	62 427	57 941	14 096	35.8	40.4	5.82	5.96	208.36	240.78
June	86 951	71 099	24 238	18 919	62 713	58 263	14 129	35.9	40.6	5.87	6.01	210.73	244.01
July	87 205	71 304	24 300	18 951	62 905	58 422	14 152	35.9	40.6	5.90	6.06	211.81	246.04
August	87 481	71 590	24 374	19 006	63 107	58 626	14 187	35.8	40.5	5.93	6.09	212.29	246.65
September	87 618	71 799	24 444	19 068	63 174	58 819	14 241	35.8	40.5	5.97	6.15	213.73	249.08
October	87 954	72 096	24 548	19 142	63 406	59 017	14 291	35.8	40.5	6.03	6.20	215.87	251.10
November	88 391	72 497	24 678	19 257	63 713	59 377	14 388	35.7	40.6	6.06	6.26	216.34	254.16
December	88 674	72 763	24 758	19 334	63 916	59 599	14 459	35.7	40.5	6.10	6.31	217.77	255.56
1979													
January	88 811	72 874	24 740	19 388	64 071	59 659	14 497	35.6	40.4	6.14	6.36	218.58	256.94
February	89 054	73 107	24 784	19 409	64 270	59 840	14 501	35.7	40.5	6.18	6.40	220.63	259.20
March	89 480	73 524	24 998	19 453	64 482	60 216	14 526	35.8	40.6	6.22	6.45	222.68	261.87
April	89 418	73 441	24 958	19 450	64 460	60 067	14 515	35.3	39.3	6.22	6.43	219.57	252.70
May	89 790	73 800	25 071	19 509	64 719	60 368	14 551	35.6	40.2	6.28	6.52	223.57	262.10
June	90 108	74 063	25 161	19 553	64 947	60 583	14 566	35.6	40.2	6.32	6.56	224.99	263.71
July	90 214	74 064	25 163	19 531	65 051	60 558	14 536	35.6	40.2	6.36	6.59	226.42	264.92
August	90 296	74 067	25 059	19 406	65 237	60 516	14 397	35.6	40.1	6.40	6.63	227.84	265.86
September	90 323	74 195	25 088	19 442	65 235	60 629	14 440	35.6	40.1	6.45	6.67	229.62	267.47
October	90 480	74 344	25 038	19 390	65 442	60 746	14 384	35.6	40.2	6.47	6.71	230.33	269.74
November	90 574	74 401	24 947	19 299	65 627	60 778	14 295	35.6	40.1	6.51	6.74	231.76	270.27
December	90 669	74 489	24 970	19 301	65 699	60 860	14 300	35.5	40.1	6.57	6.80	233.24	272.68

Table 10-9. Employment, Hours, and Earnings, Total Nonfarm and Manufacturing, Historical Annual and Monthly—Continued

(Wage and salary workers on nonfarm payrolls, seasonally adjusted.)

Year and month	All wage and salary workers (thousands)					Production and nonsupervisory workers on private payrolls							
	Total	Private			Service-providing	Number (thousands)		Average hours per week		Average hourly earnings, dollars		Average weekly earnings, dollars	
		Total	Goods-producing			Total private	Manufac-turing	Total private	Manufac-turing	Total private	Manufac-turing	Total private	Manufac-turing
			Total	Manufac-turing									
1980													
January	90 800	74 599	24 949	19 282	65 851	60 896	14 241	35.4	40.0	6.57	6.82	232.58	272.80
February	90 879	74 653	24 874	19 219	66 005	60 964	14 170	35.4	40.1	6.63	6.88	234.70	275.89
March	90 991	74 695	24 818	19 217	66 173	60 987	14 165	35.3	39.9	6.70	6.95	236.51	277.31
April	90 846	74 263	24 507	18 973	66 339	60 540	13 914	35.2	39.8	6.72	6.97	236.54	277.41
May	90 415	73 961	24 234	18 726	66 181	60 194	13 632	35.1	39.3	6.76	7.02	237.28	275.89
June	90 095	73 654	23 968	18 490	66 127	59 892	13 405	35.0	39.2	6.82	7.10	238.70	278.32
July	89 832	73 414	23 698	18 276	66 134	59 693	13 227	34.9	39.1	6.86	7.16	239.41	279.96
August	90 092	73 682	23 860	18 414	66 232	59 908	13 349	35.1	39.5	6.91	7.24	242.54	285.98
September	90 205	73 875	23 931	18 445	66 274	60 075	13 396	35.1	39.6	6.95	7.30	243.95	289.08
October	90 485	74 099	24 012	18 506	66 473	60 239	13 437	35.2	39.8	7.02	7.38	247.10	293.72
November	90 741	74 350	24 123	18 601	66 618	60 449	13 528	35.3	39.9	7.09	7.47	250.28	298.05
December	90 936	74 563	24 182	18 640	66 754	60 606	13 550	35.3	40.1	7.13	7.52	251.69	301.55
1981													
January	91 031	74 671	24 152	18 639	66 879	60 710	13 545	35.4	40.1	7.19	7.58	254.53	303.96
February	91 098	74 752	24 118	18 613	66 980	60 736	13 518	35.2	39.8	7.23	7.62	254.50	303.28
March	91 202	74 910	24 203	18 647	66 999	60 875	13 550	35.3	40.0	7.29	7.68	257.34	307.20
April	91 276	75 016	24 151	18 711	67 125	60 973	13 594	35.3	40.1	7.33	7.76	258.75	311.18
May	91 286	75 088	24 148	18 766	67 138	60 973	13 633	35.3	40.2	7.37	7.81	260.16	313.96
June	91 482	75 323	24 290	18 789	67 192	61 134	13 632	35.2	40.0	7.42	7.85	261.18	314.00
July	91 594	75 419	24 302	18 785	67 292	61 222	13 629	35.2	39.9	7.46	7.89	262.59	314.81
August	91 558	75 448	24 258	18 748	67 300	61 216	13 573	35.2	40.0	7.53	7.97	265.06	318.80
September	91 471	75 440	24 210	18 712	67 261	61 235	13 565	35.0	39.6	7.57	8.03	264.95	317.99
October	91 371	75 302	24 051	18 566	67 320	61 066	13 399	35.1	39.6	7.59	8.06	266.41	319.18
November	91 162	75 084	23 875	18 409	67 287	60 817	13 235	35.1	39.4	7.64	8.08	268.16	318.35
December	90 884	74 811	23 656	18 223	67 228	60 511	13 033	34.9	39.2	7.64	8.09	266.64	317.13
1982													
January	90 557	74 516	23 362	18 047	67 195	60 206	12 874	34.1	37.3	7.72	8.26	263.25	308.10
February	90 551	74 540	23 361	17 981	67 190	60 277	12 831	35.1	39.6	7.73	8.21	271.32	325.12
March	90 422	74 398	23 214	17 857	67 208	60 140	12 727	34.9	39.1	7.76	8.24	270.82	322.18
April	90 141	74 131	22 996	17 683	67 145	59 867	12 566	34.8	39.1	7.77	8.28	270.40	323.75
May	90 096	74 093	22 884	17 588	67 212	59 840	12 506	34.8	39.1	7.83	8.33	272.48	325.70
June	89 853	73 837	22 643	17 430	67 210	59 589	12 365	34.8	39.2	7.85	8.37	273.18	328.10
July	89 510	73 620	22 434	17 278	67 076	59 411	12 261	34.8	39.2	7.89	8.40	274.57	329.28
August	89 352	73 422	22 268	17 160	67 084	59 203	12 153	34.7	39.0	7.94	8.43	275.52	328.77
September	89 171	73 248	22 146	17 074	67 025	59 069	12 104	34.8	39.0	7.94	8.45	276.31	329.55
October	88 894	72 938	21 879	16 853	67 015	58 750	11 880	34.6	38.9	7.96	8.44	275.42	328.32
November	88 770	72 793	21 736	16 722	67 034	58 613	11 766	34.6	39.0	7.98	8.46	276.11	329.94
December	88 756	72 775	21 688	16 690	67 068	58 585	11 746	34.7	39.0	8.02	8.49	278.29	331.11
1983													
January	88 981	72 958	21 757	16 705	67 224	58 813	11 783	34.8	39.3	8.06	8.52	280.49	334.84
February	88 903	72 899	21 676	16 706	67 227	58 792	11 794	34.5	39.3	8.10	8.59	279.45	337.59
March	89 076	73 071	21 649	16 711	67 427	58 958	11 817	34.7	39.6	8.10	8.59	281.07	340.16
April	89 352	73 362	21 729	16 794	67 623	59 201	11 894	34.8	39.7	8.13	8.61	282.92	341.82
May	89 629	73 624	21 829	16 885	67 800	59 444	11 987	34.9	40.0	8.17	8.64	285.13	345.60
June	90 007	73 987	21 949	16 960	68 058	59 806	12 054	34.9	40.1	8.19	8.66	285.83	347.27
July	90 425	74 414	22 103	17 059	68 322	60 189	12 155	34.9	40.3	8.23	8.71	287.23	351.01
August	90 117	74 101	22 207	17 118	67 910	59 820	12 200	34.9	40.3	8.20	8.71	286.18	351.01
September	91 231	75 189	22 381	17 255	68 850	60 849	12 318	35.0	40.6	8.26	8.76	289.10	355.66
October	91 502	75 516	22 546	17 367	68 956	61 095	12 408	35.2	40.6	8.31	8.80	292.51	357.28
November	91 854	75 857	22 698	17 479	69 156	61 378	12 503	35.1	40.6	8.32	8.84	292.03	358.90
December	92 210	76 202	22 803	17 551	69 407	61 664	12 553	35.1	40.5	8.33	8.87	292.38	359.24
1984													
January	92 657	76 647	22 942	17 630	69 715	61 906	12 617	35.1	40.6	8.38	8.91	294.14	361.75
February	93 136	77 111	23 146	17 728	69 990	62 329	12 703	35.3	41.1	8.37	8.92	295.46	366.61
March	93 411	77 381	23 209	17 806	70 202	62 516	12 768	35.1	40.7	8.41	8.96	295.19	364.67
April	93 774	77 699	23 305	17 872	70 469	62 801	12 814	35.2	40.8	8.45	8.98	297.44	366.38
May	94 082	77 979	23 389	17 916	70 693	63 012	12 840	35.1	40.7	8.44	8.99	296.24	365.89
June	94 461	78 334	23 497	17 967	70 964	63 296	12 871	35.1	40.6	8.48	9.03	297.65	366.62
July	94 773	78 601	23 571	18 013	71 202	63 517	12 901	35.1	40.6	8.52	9.05	299.05	367.43
August	95 014	78 790	23 608	18 034	71 406	63 654	12 906	35.0	40.5	8.52	9.09	298.20	368.15
September	95 325	79 070	23 617	18 019	71 708	63 874	12 880	35.1	40.5	8.56	9.12	300.46	369.36
October	95 611	79 337	23 626	18 024	71 985	64 083	12 868	34.9	40.5	8.55	9.15	298.40	370.58
November	95 960	79 649	23 639	18 016	72 321	64 325	12 846	35.0	40.4	8.57	9.19	299.95	371.28
December	96 087	79 805	23 673	18 023	72 414	64 441	12 848	35.1	40.5	8.61	9.22	302.21	373.41
1985													
January	96 353	80 017	23 672	18 009	72 681	64 657	12 833	34.9	40.3	8.61	9.27	300.49	373.58
February	96 477	80 128	23 621	17 966	72 856	64 758	12 784	34.8	40.1	8.64	9.29	300.67	372.53
March	96 823	80 428	23 661	17 939	73 162	65 007	12 758	34.9	40.4	8.67	9.32	302.58	376.53
April	97 018	80 588	23 644	17 886	73 374	65 113	12 701	34.9	40.5	8.69	9.35	303.28	378.68
May	97 292	80 818	23 632	17 855	73 660	65 307	12 673	34.9	40.4	8.70	9.37	303.63	378.55
June	97 437	80 939	23 592	17 819	73 845	65 382	12 635	34.9	40.5	8.74	9.39	305.03	380.30
July	97 626	81 006	23 549	17 776	74 077	65 432	12 596	34.8	40.4	8.74	9.42	304.15	380.57
August	97 819	81 200	23 546	17 756	74 273	65 615	12 593	34.8	40.6	8.77	9.43	305.20	382.86
September	98 023	81 385	23 528	17 718	74 495	65 750	12 556	34.8	40.6	8.80	9.44	306.24	383.26
October	98 210	81 556	23 529	17 708	74 681	65 917	12 556	34.8	40.7	8.79	9.46	305.89	385.02
November	98 419	81 745	23 520	17 697	74 899	66 069	12 545	34.8	40.7	8.82	9.49	306.94	386.24
December	98 587	81 893	23 518	17 693	75 069	66 197	12 550	34.9	40.9	8.87	9.55	309.56	390.60

Table 10-9. Employment, Hours, and Earnings, Total Nonfarm and Manufacturing, Historical Annual and Monthly—*Continued*

(Wage and salary workers on nonfarm payrolls, seasonally adjusted.)

Year and month	All wage and salary workers (thousands)					Production and nonsupervisory workers on private payrolls								
	Total	Private			Service-providing	Number (thousands)		Average hours per week		Average hourly earnings, dollars		Average weekly earnings, dollars		
		Total	Goods-producing			Total private	Manufac-turing	Total private	Manufac-turing	Total private	Manufac-turing	Total private	Manufac-turing	
			Total	Manufac-turing										
1986														
January	98 710	81 995	23 530	17 686	75 180	66 293	12 546	35.0	40.7	8.85	9.53	309.75	387.87	
February	98 817	82 058	23 485	17 663	75 332	66 365	12 530	34.8	40.7	8.88	9.56	309.02	389.09	
March	98 910	82 155	23 428	17 624	75 482	66 403	12 498	34.8	40.7	8.89	9.58	309.37	389.91	
April	99 098	82 333	23 427	17 616	75 671	66 531	12 495	34.7	40.5	8.89	9.56	308.48	387.18	
May	99 223	82 433	23 349	17 593	75 874	66 606	12 474	34.8	40.7	8.90	9.59	309.72	390.31	
June	99 130	82 351	23 263	17 530	75 867	66 533	12 424	34.7	40.7	8.91	9.58	309.18	389.91	
July	99 448	82 669	23 235	17 497	76 213	66 810	12 389	34.6	40.6	8.92	9.60	308.63	389.76	
August	99 561	82 761	23 225	17 489	76 336	66 909	12 399	34.7	40.7	8.94	9.61	310.22	391.13	
September	99 907	82 997	23 216	17 498	76 691	67 108	12 411	34.6	40.7	8.94	9.60	309.32	390.72	
October	100 094	83 125	23 208	17 477	76 886	67 206	12 396	34.6	40.6	8.96	9.62	310.02	390.57	
November	100 280	83 275	23 204	17 472	77 076	67 344	12 407	34.7	40.7	9.00	9.64	312.30	392.35	
December	100 484	83 463	23 237	17 478	77 247	67 493	12 425	34.6	40.8	9.01	9.66	311.75	394.13	
1987														
January	100 655	83 610	23 232	17 465	77 423	67 614	12 405	34.7	40.8	9.02	9.67	312.99	394.54	
February	100 887	83 851	23 296	17 499	77 591	67 845	12 438	34.9	41.2	9.05	9.69	315.85	399.23	
March	101 136	84 072	23 307	17 507	77 829	67 991	12 446	34.7	41.0	9.07	9.71	314.73	398.11	
April	101 474	84 365	23 342	17 525	78 132	68 237	12 465	34.7	40.8	9.08	9.71	315.08	396.17	
May	101 701	84 589	23 390	17 542	78 311	68 426	12 481	34.8	41.0	9.11	9.73	317.03	398.93	
June	101 872	84 748	23 390	17 537	78 482	68 552	12 482	34.7	40.9	9.11	9.74	316.12	398.37	
July	102 218	85 058	23 455	17 593	78 763	68 798	12 521	34.7	41.0	9.12	9.74	316.46	399.34	
August	102 388	85 216	23 506	17 630	78 882	68 926	12 560	34.9	40.9	9.18	9.80	320.38	400.82	
September	102 617	85 482	23 566	17 691	79 051	69 139	12 614	34.7	40.8	9.19	9.85	318.89	401.88	
October	103 109	85 840	23 655	17 729	79 454	69 416	12 637	34.8	41.1	9.22	9.84	320.86	404.42	
November	103 340	86 041	23 711	17 775	79 629	69 594	12 678	34.8	41.0	9.27	9.87	322.60	404.67	
December	103 634	86 287	23 772	17 809	79 862	69 826	12 707	34.6	41.0	9.28	9.89	321.09	405.49	
1988														
January	103 728	86 363	23 668	17 790	80 060	69 833	12 684	34.6	41.1	9.29	9.91	321.43	407.30	
February	104 180	86 791	23 769	17 823	80 411	70 228	12 706	34.7	41.1	9.29	9.92	322.36	407.71	
March	104 456	87 009	23 824	17 844	80 632	70 371	12 712	34.5	40.9	9.31	9.94	321.20	406.55	
April	104 701	87 249	23 880	17 874	80 821	70 578	12 733	34.6	41.0	9.36	9.99	323.86	409.59	
May	104 928	87 447	23 896	17 892	81 032	70 693	12 747	34.6	41.0	9.41	10.02	325.59	410.82	
June	105 291	87 776	23 951	17 916	81 340	71 000	12 767	34.6	41.1	9.42	10.04	325.93	412.64	
July	105 514	88 020	23 966	17 926	81 548	71 210	12 774	34.7	41.1	9.45	10.05	327.92	413.06	
August	105 635	88 091	23 926	17 891	81 709	71 273	12 752	34.5	40.9	9.46	10.07	326.37	411.86	
September	105 975	88 341	23 942	17 914	82 033	71 456	12 764	34.5	41.0	9.51	10.12	328.10	414.92	
October	106 243	88 573	23 987	17 966	82 256	71 649	12 812	34.7	41.1	9.56	10.16	331.73	417.58	
November	106 582	88 836	24 030	18 003	82 552	71 872	12 851	34.5	41.1	9.58	10.19	330.51	418.81	
December	106 871	89 135	24 054	18 025	82 817	72 144	12 864	34.6	40.9	9.60	10.20	332.16	417.18	
1989														
January	107 133	89 359	24 097	18 057	83 036	72 361	12 882	34.7	41.1	9.65	10.23	334.86	420.45	
February	107 391	89 579	24 080	18 055	83 311	72 545	12 880	34.5	41.2	9.68	10.26	333.96	422.71	
March	107 583	89 761	24 069	18 060	83 514	72 663	12 878	34.5	41.1	9.70	10.29	334.65	422.92	
April	107 756	89 916	24 100	18 055	83 656	72 788	12 867	34.6	41.1	9.75	10.28	337.35	422.51	
May	107 874	89 998	24 089	18 040	83 785	72 826	12 852	34.4	41.0	9.73	10.30	334.71	422.30	
June	107 991	90 079	24 052	18 013	83 939	72 906	12 822	34.4	40.9	9.77	10.33	336.09	422.50	
July	108 030	90 125	24 027	17 980	84 003	72 943	12 790	34.5	40.9	9.82	10.36	338.79	423.72	
August	108 077	90 088	24 048	17 964	84 029	72 931	12 790	34.5	40.9	9.83	10.39	339.14	424.95	
September	108 326	90 299	24 000	17 922	84 326	73 080	12 745	34.4	40.8	9.87	10.41	339.53	424.73	
October	108 437	90 404	23 997	17 895	84 440	73 176	12 723	34.6	40.8	9.93	10.43	343.58	425.54	
November	108 714	90 657	24 009	17 886	84 705	73 392	12 713	34.4	40.7	9.93	10.44	341.59	424.91	
December	108 809	90 734	23 949	17 881	84 860	73 468	12 705	34.3	40.5	9.98	10.49	342.31	424.85	
1990														
January	109 147	90 996	23 981	17 796	85 166	73 705	12 738	34.5	40.5	10.02	10.51	345.69	425.66	
February	109 396	91 219	24 073	17 895	85 323	73 905	12 851	34.4	40.6	10.08	10.65	346.75	432.39	
March	109 610	91 316	24 024	17 869	85 586	73 962	12 822	34.4	40.7	10.11	10.70	347.78	435.49	
April	109 650	91 273	23 967	17 846	85 683	73 926	12 805	34.3	40.5	10.12	10.68	347.12	432.54	
May	109 800	91 201	23 887	17 796	85 913	73 840	12 755	34.3	40.6	10.16	10.74	348.49	436.04	
June	109 817	91 261	23 848	17 775	85 969	73 823	12 738	34.4	40.7	10.20	10.77	350.88	438.34	
July	109 777	91 217	23 747	17 705	86 030	73 771	12 674	34.2	40.6	10.22	10.80	349.52	438.48	
August	109 569	91 112	23 649	17 650	85 920	73 707	12 625	34.2	40.5	10.24	10.81	350.21	437.81	
September	109 484	91 047	23 571	17 609	85 913	73 601	12 597	34.2	40.5	10.28	10.87	351.58	440.24	
October	109 325	90 882	23 472	17 576	85 853	73 466	12 576	34.1	40.4	10.30	10.92	351.23	441.17	
November	109 179	90 729	23 283	17 428	85 896	73 315	12 438	34.2	40.2	10.32	10.89	352.94	437.78	
December	109 120	90 652	23 203	17 395	85 917	73 248	12 415	34.2	40.3	10.35	10.93	353.97	440.48	
1991														
January	108 998	90 524	23 060	17 329	85 938	73 105	12 349	34.1	40.2	10.38	10.97	353.96	440.99	
February	108 696	90 214	22 903	17 214	85 793	72 820	12 245	34.1	40.1	10.39	10.99	354.30	440.70	
March	108 535	90 047	22 780	17 141	85 755	72 664	12 191	34.0	40.0	10.42	11.01	354.28	440.40	
April	108 323	89 838	22 688	17 094	85 635	72 493	12 157	34.0	40.1	10.46	11.05	355.64	443.11	
May	108 196	89 698	22 617	17 069	85 579	72 400	12 148	34.0	40.1	10.49	11.08	356.66	444.31	
June	108 284	89 723	22 570	17 043	85 714	72 413	12 135	34.1	40.4	10.51	11.13	358.39	449.65	
July	108 236	89 638	22 508	17 016	85 728	72 381	12 131	34.1	40.5	10.54	11.16	359.41	451.98	
August	108 253	89 686	22 494	17 026	85 759	72 439	12 154	34.1	40.6	10.56	11.18	360.10	453.91	
September	108 285	89 742	22 467	17 011	85 818	72 450	12 140	34.1	40.6	10.58	11.23	360.78	455.94	
October	108 297	89 704	22 417	16 998	85 880	72 423	12 138	34.2	40.6	10.59	11.24	362.18	456.34	
November	108 239	89 612	22 315	16 960	85 924	72 349	12 101	34.1	40.7	10.61	11.26	361.80	458.28	
December	108 262	89 621	22 274	16 916	85 988	72 392	12 075	34.1	40.7	10.64	11.27	362.82	458.69	

Table 10-9. Employment, Hours, and Earnings, Total Nonfarm and Manufacturing, Historical Annual and Monthly—Continued

(Wage and salary workers on nonfarm payrolls, seasonally adjusted.)

Year and month	All wage and salary workers (thousands)					Production and nonsupervisory workers on private payrolls							
	Total	Private			Service-providing	Number (thousands)		Average hours per week		Average hourly earnings, dollars		Average weekly earnings, dollars	
		Total	Goods-producing			Total private	Manufac-turing	Total private	Manufac-turing	Total private	Manufac-turing	Total private	Manufac-turing
			Total	Manufac-turing									
1992													
January	108 312	89 624	22 213	16 839	86 099	72 430	12 010	34.1	40.6	10.65	11.24	363.17	456.34
February	108 246	89 557	22 143	16 830	86 103	72 408	12 018	34.1	40.7	10.67	11.30	363.85	459.91
March	108 298	89 583	22 128	16 806	86 170	72 421	12 007	34.1	40.7	10.70	11.33	364.87	461.13
April	108 455	89 716	22 132	16 831	86 323	72 570	12 029	34.3	40.9	10.72	11.36	367.70	464.62
May	108 581	89 828	22 135	16 835	86 446	72 685	12 046	34.3	40.9	10.74	11.39	368.38	465.85
June	108 641	89 879	22 096	16 825	86 545	72 721	12 042	34.2	40.8	10.77	11.41	368.33	465.53
July	108 711	89 894	22 075	16 820	86 636	72 735	12 047	34.2	40.8	10.79	11.44	369.02	466.75
August	108 852	89 969	22 045	16 783	86 807	72 815	12 020	34.2	40.8	10.82	11.46	370.04	467.57
September	108 887	90 058	22 020	16 761	86 867	72 917	12 002	34.3	40.7	10.83	11.47	371.47	466.83
October	109 065	90 237	22 028	16 750	87 037	73 071	12 000	34.2	40.8	10.86	11.47	371.41	467.98
November	109 204	90 363	22 042	16 758	87 162	73 219	12 010	34.2	40.9	10.87	11.49	371.75	469.94
December	109 416	90 538	22 075	16 768	87 341	73 410	12 032	34.2	40.9	10.90	11.51	372.78	470.76
1993													
January	109 726	90 825	22 133	16 791	87 593	73 682	12 057	34.3	41.1	10.93	11.55	374.90	474.71
February	109 968	91 066	22 189	16 806	87 779	73 941	12 075	34.3	41.1	10.95	11.58	375.59	475.94
March	109 917	91 010	22 142	16 795	87 775	73 855	12 074	34.1	40.8	10.99	11.58	374.76	472.46
April	110 225	91 287	22 131	16 772	88 094	74 079	12 056	34.4	41.5	11.00	11.64	378.40	483.06
May	110 490	91 539	22 189	16 766	88 301	74 332	12 055	34.3	41.1	11.02	11.65	377.99	478.82
June	110 664	91 695	22 166	16 743	88 498	74 435	12 039	34.3	40.9	11.03	11.67	378.33	477.30
July	110 959	91 899	22 184	16 740	88 775	74 619	12 041	34.4	41.1	11.05	11.69	380.12	480.46
August	111 119	92 091	22 203	16 741	88 916	74 794	12 049	34.3	41.1	11.08	11.72	380.04	481.69
September	111 358	92 317	22 251	16 768	89 107	74 985	12 080	34.4	41.3	11.10	11.77	381.84	486.10
October	111 636	92 594	22 305	16 777	89 331	75 230	12 093	34.4	41.3	11.13	11.79	382.87	486.93
November	111 897	92 829	22 347	16 800	89 550	75 443	12 118	34.4	41.3	11.15	11.83	383.56	488.58
December	112 204	93 095	22 412	16 814	89 792	75 664	12 140	34.4	41.4	11.18	11.88	384.59	491.83
1994													
January	112 474	93 327	22 464	16 854	90 010	75 872	12 179	34.4	41.4	11.21	11.90	385.62	492.66
February	112 675	93 525	22 452	16 863	90 223	76 076	12 199	34.2	40.9	11.25	11.97	384.75	489.57
March	113 137	93 947	22 549	16 896	90 588	76 437	12 234	34.5	41.7	11.25	11.95	388.13	498.32
April	113 490	94 267	22 641	16 933	90 849	76 735	12 276	34.5	41.8	11.27	11.96	388.82	499.93
May	113 823	94 559	22 704	16 962	91 119	77 013	12 304	34.5	41.8	11.30	11.98	389.85	500.76
June	114 136	94 862	22 765	17 011	91 371	77 265	12 353	34.5	41.8	11.31	12.00	390.20	501.60
July	114 500	95 199	22 807	17 026	91 693	77 566	12 369	34.6	41.8	11.34	12.02	392.36	502.44
August	114 798	95 492	22 876	17 081	91 922	77 802	12 427	34.5	41.7	11.36	12.06	391.92	502.90
September	115 153	95 816	22 946	17 113	92 207	78 071	12 459	34.5	41.6	11.39	12.09	392.96	502.94
October	115 361	96 017	22 974	17 144	92 387	78 255	12 489	34.5	41.8	11.43	12.12	394.34	506.62
November	115 783	96 416	23 051	17 187	92 732	78 600	12 528	34.5	41.8	11.45	12.16	395.03	508.29
December	116 055	96 667	23 095	17 217	92 960	78 842	12 558	34.5	41.8	11.48	12.17	396.06	508.71
1995													
January	116 377	96 980	23 145	17 260	93 232	79 084	12 591	34.5	41.8	11.49	12.19	396.41	509.54
February	116 587	97 180	23 103	17 265	93 484	79 242	12 603	34.4	41.7	11.53	12.25	396.63	510.83
March	116 810	97 383	23 151	17 263	93 659	79 423	12 600	34.3	41.5	11.55	12.24	396.17	507.96
April	116 970	97 536	23 174	17 278	93 796	79 557	12 608	34.3	41.1	11.57	12.26	396.85	503.89
May	116 954	97 536	23 119	17 258	93 835	79 575	12 590	34.2	41.2	11.59	12.28	396.38	505.94
June	117 186	97 741	23 139	17 249	94 047	79 743	12 576	34.3	41.2	11.63	12.31	398.91	507.17
July	117 265	97 828	23 119	17 218	94 146	79 814	12 540	34.3	41.1	11.67	12.37	400.28	508.41
August	117 537	98 108	23 164	17 240	94 373	80 058	12 566	34.3	41.2	11.69	12.39	400.97	510.47
September	117 781	98 351	23 207	17 246	94 574	80 256	12 566	34.3	41.2	11.73	12.41	402.34	511.29
October	117 927	98 463	23 205	17 215	94 722	80 377	12 535	34.3	41.2	11.75	12.43	403.03	512.12
November	118 076	98 613	23 199	17 208	94 877	80 452	12 515	34.3	41.3	11.78	12.45	404.05	514.19
December	118 208	98 742	23 208	17 230	95 000	80 603	12 551	34.2	40.9	11.81	12.49	403.90	510.84
1996													
January	118 187	98 737	23 195	17 207	94 992	80 525	12 516	33.8	39.7	11.86	12.60	400.87	500.22
February	118 621	99 136	23 280	17 229	95 341	80 915	12 533	34.3	41.3	11.87	12.57	407.14	519.14
March	118 885	99 353	23 275	17 192	95 610	81 092	12 489	34.3	41.1	11.89	12.49	407.83	513.34
April	119 045	99 530	23 316	17 204	95 729	81 257	12 505	34.2	41.2	11.96	12.69	409.03	522.83
May	119 368	99 839	23 357	17 221	96 011	81 517	12 518	34.3	41.4	11.98	12.71	410.91	526.19
June	119 647	100 119	23 400	17 227	96 247	81 728	12 523	34.4	41.5	12.03	12.76	413.83	529.54
July	119 879	100 332	23 417	17 222	96 462	81 921	12 517	34.3	41.4	12.06	12.79	413.66	529.51
August	120 076	100 572	23 480	17 256	96 596	82 121	12 546	34.4	41.5	12.09	12.83	415.90	532.45
September	120 295	100 728	23 497	17 252	96 798	82 240	12 544	34.4	41.6	12.14	12.85	417.62	534.56
October	120 538	100 984	23 546	17 268	96 992	82 481	12 558	34.4	41.4	12.16	12.83	418.30	531.16
November	120 834	101 269	23 584	17 277	97 250	82 664	12 559	34.4	41.5	12.21	12.88	420.02	534.52
December	121 002	101 431	23 599	17 285	97 403	82 830	12 571	34.4	41.7	12.25	12.95	421.40	540.02
1997													
January	121 233	101 640	23 620	17 299	97 613	82 973	12 579	34.3	41.4	12.29	12.99	421.55	537.79
February	121 532	101 934	23 686	17 316	97 846	83 251	12 592	34.5	41.6	12.32	12.99	425.04	540.38
March	121 845	102 237	23 738	17 339	98 107	83 478	12 613	34.5	41.8	12.36	13.04	426.42	545.07
April	122 135	102 532	23 767	17 351	98 368	83 725	12 618	34.6	41.8	12.39	13.04	428.69	545.07
May	122 391	102 790	23 810	17 363	98 581	83 946	12 634	34.6	41.7	12.43	13.07	430.08	545.02
June	122 646	102 986	23 836	17 389	98 810	84 079	12 648	34.4	41.5	12.47	13.09	428.97	543.24
July	122 927	103 241	23 861	17 388	99 066	84 318	12 645	34.5	41.6	12.49	13.09	430.91	544.54
August	122 911	103 294	23 952	17 452	98 959	84 266	12 700	34.6	41.7	12.57	13.17	434.92	549.19
September	123 418	103 739	23 996	17 465	99 422	84 658	12 711	34.5	41.7	12.60	13.17	434.70	549.19
October	123 757	104 019	24 053	17 513	99 704	84 864	12 745	34.6	41.8	12.66	13.28	438.04	555.10
November	124 057	104 296	24 111	17 555	99 946	85 053	12 776	34.6	41.9	12.72	13.32	440.11	558.11
December	124 357	104 591	24 183	17 587	100 174	85 286	12 800	34.6	41.9	12.75	13.35	441.15	559.37

Table 10-9. Employment, Hours, and Earnings, Total Nonfarm and Manufacturing, Historical Annual and Monthly—*Continued*

(Wage and salary workers on nonfarm payrolls, seasonally adjusted.)

Year and month	All wage and salary workers (thousands)					Production and nonsupervisory workers on private payrolls							
		Private				Number (thousands)		Average hours per week		Average hourly earnings, dollars		Average weekly earnings, dollars	
	Total	Total	Goods-producing		Service-providing	Total private	Manufac-turing	Total private	Manufac-turing	Total private	Manufac-turing	Total private	Manufac-turing
			Total	Manufac-turing									
1998													
January	124 630	104 860	24 266	17 623	100 364	85 441	12 819	34.6	41.9	12.79	13.35	442.53	559.37
February	124 818	105 032	24 283	17 627	100 535	85 604	12 828	34.6	41.7	12.84	13.39	444.26	558.36
March	124 962	105 170	24 264	17 637	100 698	85 630	12 823	34.5	41.6	12.88	13.43	444.36	558.69
April	125 240	105 424	24 340	17 637	100 900	85 846	12 814	34.4	41.3	12.92	13.41	444.45	553.83
May	125 639	105 764	24 360	17 623	101 279	86 125	12 790	34.5	41.5	12.96	13.45	447.12	558.18
June	125 851	105 972	24 388	17 609	101 463	86 270	12 770	34.4	41.4	12.99	13.43	446.86	556.00
July	125 969	106 039	24 236	17 420	101 733	86 277	12 556	34.5	41.4	13.01	13.35	448.85	552.69
August	126 322	106 363	24 420	17 563	101 902	86 570	12 703	34.5	41.4	13.08	13.47	451.26	557.66
September	126 541	106 556	24 419	17 557	102 122	86 733	12 714	34.3	41.3	13.11	13.53	449.67	558.79
October	126 735	106 734	24 406	17 512	102 329	86 877	12 674	34.5	41.4	13.14	13.52	453.33	559.73
November	127 015	106 971	24 394	17 465	102 621	87 040	12 634	34.4	41.4	13.17	13.54	453.05	560.56
December	127 359	107 280	24 453	17 448	102 906	87 306	12 625	34.5	41.5	13.21	13.56	455.75	562.74
1999													
January	127 486	107 402	24 406	17 432	103 080	87 361	12 607	34.4	41.3	13.27	13.59	456.49	561.27
February	127 890	107 746	24 434	17 395	103 456	87 671	12 575	34.5	41.4	13.30	13.63	458.85	564.28
March	127 996	107 828	24 378	17 368	103 618	87 732	12 562	34.3	41.3	13.33	13.69	457.22	565.40
April	128 370	108 133	24 424	17 343	103 946	87 965	12 540	34.4	41.4	13.38	13.74	460.27	568.84
May	128 584	108 355	24 445	17 333	104 139	88 156	12 534	34.3	41.4	13.43	13.80	460.65	571.32
June	128 850	108 578	24 435	17 296	104 415	88 328	12 503	34.3	41.3	13.47	13.87	462.02	572.83
July	129 140	108 801	24 472	17 306	104 668	88 526	12 525	34.4	41.4	13.52	13.92	465.09	576.29
August	129 333	108 958	24 466	17 286	104 867	88 644	12 502	34.4	41.5	13.54	13.93	465.78	578.10
September	129 537	109 133	24 483	17 279	105 054	88 779	12 494	34.3	41.5	13.61	13.99	466.82	580.59
October	129 942	109 485	24 505	17 272	105 437	89 092	12 483	34.4	41.4	13.64	13.98	469.22	578.77
November	130 235	109 739	24 560	17 281	105 675	89 309	12 488	34.4	41.4	13.66	14.00	469.90	579.60
December	130 533	109 993	24 578	17 276	105 955	89 524	12 489	34.4	41.4	13.70	14.06	471.28	582.08
2000													
January	130 781	110 210	24 406	17 292	106 145	89 691	12 495	34.4	41.5	13.75	14.12	473.00	585.98
February	130 903	110 304	24 434	17 285	106 294	89 763	12 482	34.4	41.5	13.80	14.14	474.72	586.81
March	131 374	110 641	24 378	17 302	106 669	90 034	12 490	34.4	41.4	13.85	14.18	476.44	587.05
April	131 662	110 860	24 424	17 300	106 972	90 263	12 477	34.4	41.6	13.90	14.24	478.16	592.38
May	131 886	110 739	24 445	17 279	107 239	90 168	12 464	34.3	41.3	13.94	14.23	478.14	587.70
June	131 839	110 952	24 435	17 297	107 166	90 336	12 468	34.3	41.3	13.98	14.29	479.51	590.18
July	132 004	111 137	24 472	17 321	107 288	90 473	12 474	34.3	41.5	14.03	14.31	481.23	593.87
August	132 005	111 168	24 466	17 286	107 323	90 500	12 431	34.2	41.1	14.07	14.36	481.19	590.20
September	132 130	111 395	24 483	17 227	107 491	90 654	12 380	34.3	41.1	14.13	14.40	484.66	591.84
October	132 118	111 375	24 505	17 215	107 482	90 632	12 356	34.3	41.1	14.18	14.47	486.37	594.72
November	132 345	111 585	24 560	17 202	107 722	90 761	12 337	34.2	41.1	14.24	14.51	487.01	596.36
December	132 481	111 677	24 578	17 178	107 909	90 803	12 306	34.1	40.4	14.29	14.51	487.29	586.20
2001													
January	132 466	111 631	24 541	17 112	107 925	90 759	12 236	34.2	40.6	14.29	14.48	488.72	587.89
February	132 529	111 623	24 476	17 030	108 053	90 703	12 157	34.1	40.5	14.37	14.56	490.02	589.68
March	132 501	111 556	24 411	16 940	108 090	90 658	12 085	34.0	40.5	14.42	14.59	490.28	590.90
April	132 219	111 227	24 255	16 803	107 964	90 425	11 982	34.0	40.5	14.46	14.65	491.64	593.33
May	132 175	111 146	24 119	16 661	108 056	90 348	11 858	34.0	40.4	14.50	14.70	493.00	593.88
June	132 047	110 910	23 966	16 516	108 081	90 152	11 739	34.0	40.3	14.55	14.74	494.70	594.02
July	131 922	110 737	23 832	16 377	108 090	90 035	11 630	34.0	40.6	14.56	14.81	495.04	601.29
August	131 767	110 549	23 665	16 230	108 102	89 890	11 494	33.9	40.3	14.60	14.85	494.94	598.46
September	131 524	110 282	23 535	16 115	107 989	89 621	11 398	33.8	40.2	14.64	14.90	494.83	598.98
October	131 193	109 918	23 377	15 971	107 816	89 329	11 286	33.7	40.1	14.66	14.88	494.04	596.69
November	130 898	109 572	23 210	15 826	107 688	89 000	11 175	33.8	40.1	14.72	14.96	497.54	599.90
December	130 720	109 365	23 091	15 708	107 629	88 905	11 079	33.9	40.2	14.75	15.01	500.03	603.40
2002													
January	130 591	109 214	22 971	15 597	107 620	88 852	11 002	33.8	40.1	14.76	15.05	498.89	603.51
February	130 445	109 055	22 878	15 517	107 567	88 801	10 953	33.8	40.3	14.79	15.11	499.90	608.93
March	130 421	108 990	22 789	15 446	107 632	88 757	10 901	33.9	40.5	14.82	15.16	502.40	613.98
April	130 337	108 894	22 692	15 395	107 645	88 600	10 860	33.9	40.6	14.84	15.18	503.08	616.31
May	130 328	108 814	22 605	15 338	107 723	88 649	10 823	33.9	40.6	14.88	15.24	504.43	618.74
June	130 375	108 826	22 577	15 297	107 798	88 385	10 796	34.0	40.7	14.94	15.27	507.96	621.49
July	130 275	108 731	22 513	15 248	107 762	88 234	10 759	33.8	40.4	14.98	15.29	506.32	617.72
August	130 264	108 675	22 445	15 167	107 819	88 166	10 697	33.9	40.5	15.02	15.34	509.18	621.27
September	130 209	108 663	22 394	15 116	107 815	88 146	10 666	34.0	40.5	15.07	15.38	512.38	622.89
October	130 330	108 771	22 323	15 058	108 007	88 217	10 630	33.8	40.3	15.12	15.45	511.06	622.64
November	130 338	108 757	22 281	14 991	108 057	88 166	10 580	33.8	40.4	15.16	15.48	512.41	625.39
December	130 175	108 587	22 185	14 908	107 990	87 978	10 521	33.8	40.5	15.21	15.54	514.10	629.37
2003													
January	130 270	108 644	22 149	14 869	108 121	88 025	10 484	33.8	40.3	15.22	15.58	514.44	627.87
February	130 111	108 487	22 022	14 780	108 089	87 875	10 416	33.7	40.3	15.29	15.61	515.27	629.08
March	129 898	108 288	21 946	14 722	107 952	87 583	10 356	33.8	40.4	15.29	15.65	516.80	632.26
April	129 849	108 254	21 863	14 608	107 986	87 536	10 256	33.6	40.1	15.28	15.64	513.41	627.16
May	129 840	108 273	21 830	14 555	108 010	87 499	10 218	33.7	40.2	15.33	15.69	516.62	630.74
June	129 840	108 234	21 788	14 493	108 052	87 476	10 165	33.7	40.3	15.37	15.72	517.97	633.52
July	129 865	108 232	21 708	14 402	108 157	87 463	10 093	33.6	40.1	15.40	15.75	517.44	631.58
August	129 820	108 264	21 706	14 376	108 114	87 529	10 085	33.6	40.2	15.42	15.78	518.11	634.36
September	129 929	108 425	21 700	14 347	108 229	87 644	10 058	33.6	40.5	15.42	15.83	518.11	641.12
October	130 126	108 568	21 691	14 334	108 435	87 727	10 055	33.7	40.6	15.43	15.82	519.99	642.29
November	130 140	108 605	21 687	14 315	108 453	87 775	10 039	33.8	40.9	15.48	15.90	523.22	650.31
December	130 259	108 713	21 703	14 300	108 556	87 837	10 029	33.6	40.7	15.48	15.92	520.13	647.94

Table 10-9. Employment, Hours, and Earnings, Total Nonfarm and Manufacturing, Historical Annual and Monthly—Continued

(Wage and salary workers on nonfarm payrolls, seasonally adjusted.)

Year and month	All wage and salary workers (thousands)					Production and nonsupervisory workers on private payrolls								
	Total	Private			Service-providing	Number (thousands)		Average hours per week		Average hourly earnings, dollars		Average weekly earnings, dollars	
		Total	Goods-producing			Total private	Manufac-turing	Total private	Manufac-turing	Total private	Manufac-turing	Total private	Manufac-turing
			Total	Manufac-turing									
2004													
January	130 421	108 883	21 718	14 293	108 703	87 950	10 030	33.7	40.9	15.51	15.94	522.69	651.95
February	130 465	108 915	21 693	14 279	108 772	87 965	10 014	33.8	41.0	15.55	15.97	525.59	654.77
March	130 802	109 214	21 759	14 288	109 043	88 223	10 025	33.7	40.9	15.56	16.02	524.37	655.22
April	131 051	109 437	21 803	14 316	109 248	88 469	10 059	33.7	40.7	15.60	16.07	525.72	654.05
May	131 361	109 747	21 881	14 342	109 480	88 782	10 091	33.8	41.1	15.64	16.07	528.63	660.48
June	131 442	109 841	21 883	14 330	109 559	88 925	10 085	33.6	40.7	15.68	16.12	526.85	656.08
July	131 488	109 882	21 902	14 332	109 586	89 033	10 099	33.7	40.8	15.71	16.15	529.43	658.92
August	131 610	109 984	21 943	14 344	109 667	89 170	10 115	33.8	40.9	15.75	16.20	532.35	662.58
September	131 771	110 136	21 956	14 330	109 815	89 352	10 103	33.7	40.8	15.79	16.29	532.12	664.63
October	132 119	110 463	22 005	14 333	110 114	89 671	10 104	33.7	40.6	15.82	16.26	533.13	660.16
November	132 182	110 490	21 997	14 307	110 185	89 701	10 078	33.7	40.5	15.85	16.30	534.15	660.15
December	132 316	110 623	22 005	14 287	110 311	89 861	10 063	33.8	40.6	15.87	16.34	536.41	663.40
2005													
January	132 453	110 718	21 962	14 261	110 491	89 966	10 044	33.7	40.6	15.91	16.38	536.17	665.03
February	132 693	110 949	22 038	14 275	110 655	90 191	10 053	33.7	40.6	15.93	16.43	536.84	667.06
March	132 834	111 094	22 067	14 270	110 767	90 372	10 057	33.7	40.4	15.98	16.44	538.53	664.18
April	133 194	111 440	22 138	14 252	111 056	90 713	10 050	33.8	40.4	16.02	16.46	541.48	664.98
May	133 364	111 583	22 173	14 257	111 191	90 832	10 061	33.7	40.4	16.05	16.54	540.89	668.22
June	133 607	111 844	22 184	14 226	111 423	91 094	10 047	33.7	40.4	16.09	16.55	542.23	668.62
July	133 981	112 124	22 203	14 224	111 778	91 327	10 042	33.7	40.5	16.17	16.58	544.93	671.49
August	134 174	112 311	22 227	14 202	111 947	91 509	10 044	33.7	40.5	16.18	16.63	545.27	673.52
September	134 240	112 395	22 225	14 174	112 015	91 594	10 045	33.8	40.7	16.20	16.58	547.56	674.81
October	134 320	112 491	22 290	14 190	112 030	91 694	10 072	33.8	41.1	16.30	16.68	550.94	685.55
November	134 654	112 795	22 354	14 184	112 300	92 035	10 090	33.8	40.9	16.31	16.67	551.28	681.80
December	134 814	112 935	22 375	14 192	112 439	92 206	10 111	33.8	40.8	16.37	16.67	553.31	680.14
2006													
January	135 097	113 250	22 470	14 213	112 627	92 553	10 152	33.9	41.0	16.43	16.70	556.98	684.70
February	135 413	113 535	22 537	14 211	112 876	92 826	10 166	33.8	41.0	16.49	16.70	557.36	684.70
March	135 696	113 793	22 574	14 216	113 122	93 120	10 177	33.8	41.1	16.55	16.72	559.39	687.19
April	135 877	113 958	22 635	14 230	113 242	93 301	10 195	33.9	41.3	16.65	16.76	564.44	692.19
May	135 891	113 965	22 597	14 203	113 294	93 359	10 180	33.7	41.1	16.66	16.78	561.44	689.66
June	135 967	114 045	22 595	14 210	113 372	93 427	10 191	33.9	41.2	16.74	16.80	567.49	692.16
July	136 176	114 203	22 588	14 186	113 588	93 562	10 177	33.9	41.4	16.80	16.79	569.52	695.11
August	136 359	114 348	22 573	14 160	113 786	93 706	10 160	33.9	41.2	16.84	16.83	570.88	693.40
September	136 516	114 434	22 538	14 126	113 978	93 753	10 119	33.8	41.1	16.88	16.82	570.54	691.30
October	136 507	114 439	22 451	14 070	114 056	93 754	10 068	33.9	41.2	16.95	16.89	574.61	695.87
November	136 711	114 628	22 404	14 037	114 307	93 969	10 041	33.8	41.0	16.99	16.92	574.26	693.72
December	136 882	114 794	22 402	14 012	114 480	94 150	10 039	33.9	41.0	17.06	16.98	578.33	696.18
2007													
January	137 118	115 023	22 435	14 004	114 683	94 385	10 032	33.8	41.1	17.11	17.01	578.32	699.11
February	137 211	115 080	22 335	13 998	114 876	94 424	10 036	33.8	41.0	17.16	17.04	580.01	698.64
March	137 401	115 252	22 395	13 974	115 006	94 629	10 016	33.9	41.3	17.24	17.10	584.44	706.23
April	137 473	115 298	22 355	13 950	115 118	94 716	10 013	33.8	41.3	17.29	17.20	584.40	710.36
May	137 612	115 419	22 326	13 932	115 286	94 864	10 009	33.8	41.1	17.35	17.23	586.43	708.15
June	137 687	115 480	22 324	13 912	115 363	94 983	9 998	33.9	41.3	17.44	17.30	591.22	714.49
July	137 647	115 476	22 274	13 886	115 373	95 050	9 988	33.8	41.3	17.47	17.29	590.49	714.08
August	137 629	115 403	22 168	13 831	115 461	94 997	9 946	33.8	41.3	17.52	17.35	592.18	716.56
September	137 702	115 423	22 093	13 790	115 609	95 069	9 932	33.8	41.3	17.57	17.35	593.87	716.56
October	137 781	115 484	22 049	13 757	115 732	95 166	9 906	33.8	41.2	17.60	17.35	594.88	714.82
November	137 893	115 559	22 013	13 755	115 880	95 254	9 915	33.8	41.3	17.65	17.42	596.57	719.45
December	137 982	115 606	21 973	13 743	116 009	95 341	9 921	33.8	41.1	17.70	17.43	598.26	716.37
2008													
January	138 023	115 647	21 950	13 723	116 073	95 388	9 912	33.7	41.2	17.75	17.50	598.18	721.00
February	137 939	115 511	21 878	13 695	116 061	95 297	9 887	33.8	41.2	17.81	17.56	601.98	723.47
March	137 844	115 399	21 812	13 656	116 032	95 236	9 865	33.8	41.3	17.90	17.64	605.02	728.53
April	137 636	115 184	21 685	13 600	115 951	95 057	9 810	33.8	41.2	17.94	17.64	606.37	726.77
May	137 446	114 968	21 612	13 569	115 834	94 878	9 779	33.7	41.1	18.00	17.68	606.60	726.65
June	137 248	114 737	21 492	13 510	115 756	94 671	9 724	33.7	41.0	18.05	17.77	608.29	728.57
July	137 038	114 478	21 366	13 435	115 672	94 453	9 658	33.6	41.0	18.12	17.79	608.83	729.39
August	136 764	114 184	21 249	13 356	115 515	94 219	9 585	33.7	40.8	18.19	17.80	613.00	726.24
September	136 332	113 759	21 096	13 272	115 236	93 856	9 504	33.6	40.5	18.22	17.80	612.19	720.90
October	135 843	113 279	20 887	13 142	114 956	93 443	9 379	33.5	40.4	18.27	17.91	612.05	723.56
November	135 040	112 482	20 614	13 028	114 426	92 749	9 284	33.4	40.1	18.33	17.95	612.22	719.80
December	134 379	111 824	20 324	12 849	114 055	92 169	9 133	33.3	39.8	18.40	17.99	612.72	716.00
2009													
January	133 561	110 985	19 874	12 552	113 687	91 435	8 889	33.3	39.7	18.42	18.01	613.39	715.00
February	132 837	110 260	19 583	12 386	113 254	90 860	8 744	33.3	39.6	18.46	18.07	614.72	715.57
March	132 038	109 473	19 237	12 214	112 801	90 193	8 596	33.1	39.3	18.52	18.14	613.01	712.90
April	131 346	108 671	18 898	12 035	112 448	89 477	8 458	33.1	39.4	18.53	18.15	613.34	715.11
May	130 985	108 359	18 656	11 868	112 329	89 259	8 314	33.1	39.3	18.55	18.12	614.01	712.12
June	130 503	107 933	18 417	11 725	112 086	88 878	8 199	33.0	39.6	18.58	18.20	613.14	720.72
July	130 164	107 637	18 266	11 664	111 898	88 661	8 169	33.1	39.8	18.62	18.29	616.32	727.94
August	129 933	107 418	18 138	11 623	111 795	88 478	8 146	33.1	40.0	18.68	18.33	618.31	733.20
September	129 734	107 234	18 020	11 579	111 714	88 320	8 124	33.1	40.0	18.72	18.41	619.63	736.40
October	129 532	107 002	17 907	11 530	111 625	88 118	8 091	33.0	40.1	18.77	18.39	619.41	737.44
November	129 490	106 960	17 845	11 496	111 645	88 123	8 067	33.2	40.4	18.81	18.41	624.49	743.76
December	129 319	106 840	17 784	11 466	111 535	88 045	8 042	33.2	40.6	18.86	18.40	626.15	747.04

Table 10-9. Employment, Hours, and Earnings, Total Nonfarm and Manufacturing, Historical Annual and Monthly—*Continued*

(Wage and salary workers on nonfarm payrolls, seasonally adjusted.)

Year and month	All wage and salary workers (thousands)					Production and nonsupervisory workers on private payrolls							
	Total	Private			Service-providing	Number (thousands)		Average hours per week		Average hourly earnings, dollars		Average weekly earnings, dollars	
		Total	Goods-producing			Total private	Manufac-turing	Total private	Manufac-turing	Total private	Manufac-turing	Total private	Manufac-turing
			Total	Manufac-turing									
2010													
January	129 279	106 800	17 720	11 458	111 559	88 037	8 042	33.3	40.9	18.91	18.43	629.70	753.79
February	129 244	106 773	17 666	11 462	111 578	88 006	8 039	33.2	40.4	18.93	18.45	628.48	745.38
March	129 433	106 914	17 704	11 470	111 729	88 156	8 039	33.3	41.0	18.95	18.48	631.04	757.68
April	129 672	107 107	17 750	11 502	111 922	88 301	8 061	33.4	41.2	18.99	18.50	634.27	762.20
May	130 188	107 191	17 751	11 536	112 437	88 358	8 086	33.4	41.4	19.02	18.57	635.27	768.80
June	130 021	107 283	17 754	11 546	112 267	88 437	8 098	33.4	41.0	19.05	18.60	636.27	762.60
July	129 963	107 375	17 764	11 566	112 199	88 511	8 110	33.4	41.1	19.08	18.63	637.27	765.69
August	129 912	107 503	17 775	11 549	112 137	88 594	8 092	33.5	41.2	19.12	18.66	640.52	768.79
September	129 885	107 618	17 764	11 551	112 121	88 684	8 090	33.5	41.3	19.15	18.73	641.53	773.55
October	130 105	107 814	17 780	11 551	112 325	88 850	8 086	33.5	41.2	19.24	18.73	644.54	771.68
November	130 226	107 948	17 781	11 560	112 445	88 970	8 085	33.5	41.2	19.23	18.76	644.21	772.91
December	130 346	108 088	17 785	11 575	112 561	89 072	8 099	33.5	41.3	19.23	18.80	644.21	776.44
2011													
January	130 456	108 207	17 821	11 627	112 635	89 170	8 139	33.4	41.1	19.33	18.88	645.62	775.97
February	130 676	108 464	17 894	11 664	112 782	89 397	8 170	33.6	41.4	19.33	18.88	649.49	781.63
March	130 922	108 725	17 942	11 690	112 980	89 636	8 197	33.6	41.5	19.34	18.90	649.82	784.35
April	131 173	108 989	17 981	11 718	113 192	89 854	8 225	33.7	41.4	19.39	18.90	653.44	782.46
May	131 227	109 097	18 001	11 726	113 226	89 933	8 228	33.6	41.5	19.43	18.92	652.85	785.18
June	131 311	109 199	18 019	11 738	113 292	90 023	8 230	33.7	41.4	19.45	18.92	655.47	783.29
July	131 407	109 374	18 071	11 768	113 336	90 173	8 259	33.7	41.4	19.52	18.95	657.82	784.53
August	131 492	109 426	18 067	11 771	113 425	90 223	8 259	33.6	41.3	19.50	18.93	655.20	781.81
September	131 694	109 642	18 100	11 768	113 594	90 430	8 260	33.6	41.3	19.53	18.94	656.21	782.22
October	131 806	109 781	18 106	11 777	113 700	90 546	8 268	33.7	41.5	19.57	19.00	659.51	788.50
November	131 963	109 959	18 114	11 780	113 849	90 745	8 268	33.7	41.5	19.58	18.98	659.85	787.67
December	132 186	110 193	18 176	11 808	114 010	90 956	8 297	33.7	41.6	19.59	19.02	660.18	791.23

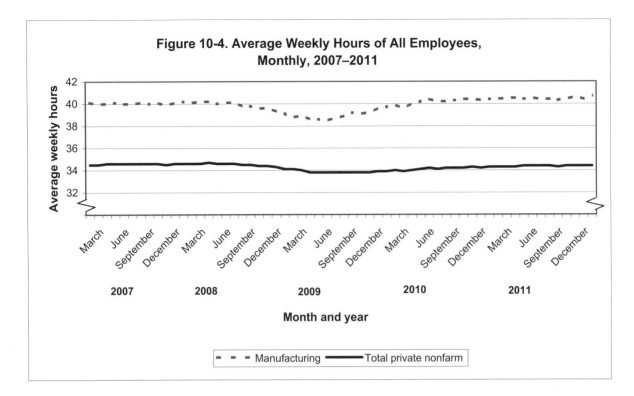

Figure 10-4. Average Weekly Hours of All Employees, Monthly, 2007–2011

- The payroll survey now includes hours and earnings data for all nonfarm jobs, as well as the hours and earnings for production and nonsupervisory worker jobs that have been collected for many years. The newer, more comprehensive series are available beginning with March 2006. The new monthly data on the workweek for all nonfarm jobs and for manufacturing are shown in Figure 10-4. (Table 10-10)

- Firms experiencing increases in demand are likely to meet that demand, at first, by having their existing employees work longer hours. If the demand increase is sustained, they become more likely to hire more people. This is the basis for the long-time reputation of the workweek as a leading indicator for employment. As Figure 10-4 demonstrates, the workweek at manufacturing—the most cyclical sector—has been trending upward, though irregularly, since a low point of 38.5 hours in May 2009. In June 2012, according to preliminary data, it reached 40.7 hours. The workweek for all private nonfarm industry began to edge up in November 2009 and reached 34.4 hours in April 2011, remaining at about that level since then. (Table 10-10 and recent data)

- It is important to note that the "average" all-employee workweek of about 34 1/2 hours reported in the payroll survey is not necessarily an accurate representation of how many hours per week a typical American worker works. This is because it is based on a count of jobs, as reported by employers. Suppose a full-time worker takes a second, "moonlighting" part-time job, newly created in another industry. This <u>reduces</u> the average workweek in the payroll survey, even though the individual is working <u>longer</u> hours than before. If a new labor force entrant takes a half-time job, it reduces the average workweek even if no other workers are working less. For measures of the workweek as reported by persons in the Current Population Survey, see Table 10-19, Figure 10-5, and the discussions of each.

Table 10-10. Average Weekly Hours of All Employees on Private Nonfarm Payrolls by NAICS Supersector

(Hours per week, seasonally adjusted.)

Year and month	Total private	Mining and logging	Construction	Manufacturing		Trade, transportation, and utilities			Information	Financial activities	Professional and business services	Education and health services	Leisure and hospitality	Other services
				Average weekly hours	Overtime hours	Total	Wholesale trade	Retail trade						
2007	34.6	44.0	38.0	40.0	3.3	34.5	38.1	31.7	36.1	36.6	35.4	33.5	26.1	32.9
2008	34.5	43.7	37.8	39.8	3.0	34.4	38.4	31.4	36.5	36.5	35.2	33.7	25.9	32.9
2009	33.9	42.1	37.1	39.0	2.3	34.1	37.9	31.2	36.5	36.6	35.0	33.0	25.6	31.6
2010	34.1	43.4	37.8	40.2	3.0	34.2	38.1	31.4	36.5	36.9	35.4	32.8	25.7	31.6
2011	34.4	44.5	38.3	40.5	3.2	34.6	38.6	31.6	36.6	37.3	35.7	32.8	25.9	31.7
2007														
January	34.5	42.7	38.1	40.1	3.3	34.3	37.6	31.7	36.0	36.5	35.2	33.4	26.2	32.7
February	34.5	43.1	37.8	40.0	3.2	34.4	37.9	31.6	36.1	36.5	35.6	33.4	26.0	32.9
March	34.6	43.3	38.1	40.0	3.3	34.5	38.0	31.7	36.1	36.5	35.4	33.5	26.1	33.0
April	34.6	44.4	38.0	40.1	3.2	34.5	38.0	31.7	36.1	36.5	35.5	33.5	26.1	32.9
May	34.6	44.2	38.1	40.0	3.2	34.5	38.1	31.7	35.9	36.4	35.4	33.6	26.1	33.0
June	34.6	43.9	37.9	40.0	3.3	34.7	38.1	32.0	36.0	36.6	35.4	33.5	26.2	32.9
July	34.6	44.2	37.9	40.1	3.3	34.5	38.1	31.7	36.2	36.5	35.4	33.5	26.0	32.9
August	34.6	44.0	37.9	40.0	3.3	34.5	38.2	31.7	36.1	36.6	35.3	33.6	26.0	32.8
September	34.6	44.5	38.2	40.1	3.3	34.5	38.1	31.7	36.1	36.5	35.4	33.6	26.0	32.8
October	34.5	44.4	38.0	39.9	3.3	34.5	38.1	31.7	36.0	36.5	35.2	33.6	26.0	32.8
November	34.6	44.2	38.2	40.1	3.4	34.6	38.3	31.7	36.2	36.5	35.4	33.5	26.0	32.9
December	34.6	44.2	38.3	40.2	3.3	34.6	38.4	31.7	36.3	36.5	35.3	33.5	26.1	32.8
2008														
January	34.6	43.9	38.4	40.1	3.4	34.6	38.3	31.7	36.5	36.4	35.2	33.6	26.0	32.6
February	34.6	43.9	38.5	40.2	3.3	34.6	38.4	31.7	36.5	36.5	35.2	33.7	25.9	32.9
March	34.6	44.8	38.2	40.2	3.2	34.6	38.4	31.6	36.5	36.5	35.3	33.8	26.0	33.1
April	34.6	42.9	38.2	40.0	3.2	34.5	38.4	31.5	36.6	36.5	35.2	33.8	26.0	33.0
May	34.6	43.6	38.1	40.1	3.2	34.5	38.4	31.5	36.5	36.7	35.2	33.8	26.0	33.0
June	34.6	43.9	38.0	40.1	3.1	34.5	38.5	31.5	36.6	36.6	35.3	33.7	26.0	32.8
July	34.5	43.3	37.8	39.8	3.0	34.4	38.6	31.4	36.6	36.5	35.3	33.7	25.8	32.8
August	34.5	43.6	37.9	39.8	2.9	34.5	38.7	31.4	36.6	36.7	35.3	33.8	25.8	33.0
September	34.4	42.8	37.6	39.6	2.9	34.4	38.5	31.3	36.7	36.5	35.2	33.6	25.8	32.9
October	34.4	44.3	38.3	39.6	2.7	34.4	38.4	31.3	36.7	36.5	35.2	33.7	25.9	32.8
November	34.2	43.8	37.1	39.3	2.5	34.3	38.3	31.2	36.5	36.6	35.1	33.6	25.7	32.8
December	34.1	43.2	37.4	39.1	2.4	34.0	38.3	30.8	36.6	36.5	35.1	33.5	25.6	32.8
2009														
January	34.2	43.0	37.1	38.8	2.3	34.4	38.4	31.3	36.5	36.6	35.1	33.6	25.6	32.6
February	34.0	42.8	37.3	38.9	2.3	34.2	38.1	31.1	36.5	36.5	35.0	33.4	25.5	32.1
March	33.8	42.4	37.2	38.6	2.1	34.1	37.9	31.1	36.4	36.5	34.9	32.9	25.5	31.5
April	33.8	41.9	37.2	38.6	2.2	34.1	37.9	31.2	36.3	36.6	35.0	33.0	25.4	31.3
May	33.8	41.5	37.1	38.5	2.1	34.2	37.9	31.3	36.5	36.5	35.0	32.9	25.5	31.5
June	33.8	41.8	37.2	38.7	2.2	34.0	37.7	31.2	36.4	36.3	35.0	32.8	25.5	31.5
July	33.8	42.0	37.3	38.9	2.3	34.0	37.7	31.2	36.5	36.6	35.0	32.8	25.5	31.4
August	33.8	42.2	37.2	39.2	2.3	34.0	37.7	31.1	36.4	36.5	35.1	32.8	25.5	31.4
September	33.8	42.2	36.9	39.1	2.4	34.1	37.6	31.4	36.4	36.6	35.0	32.9	25.6	31.3
October	33.8	42.0	37.1	39.2	2.5	34.1	37.7	31.3	36.4	36.7	34.8	32.8	25.5	31.4
November	33.9	42.4	37.3	39.6	2.7	34.1	37.8	31.2	36.6	36.6	35.1	32.7	25.5	31.4
December	33.9	42.4	37.2	39.7	2.7	34.0	37.7	31.2	36.4	36.6	35.2	32.8	25.6	31.5
2010														
January	34.0	43.0	37.3	39.9	2.8	34.1	37.8	31.3	36.6	36.7	35.3	33.0	25.6	31.6
February	33.9	42.9	36.4	39.6	2.7	34.0	37.8	31.3	36.5	36.8	35.1	32.8	25.7	31.6
March	34.0	43.2	37.3	40.0	2.9	34.1	37.9	31.3	36.5	36.9	35.4	32.8	25.8	31.6
April	34.1	43.6	37.7	40.2	3.0	34.2	38.0	31.3	36.5	36.9	35.3	32.8	25.7	31.7
May	34.2	43.8	37.6	40.4	3.1	34.2	38.1	31.3	36.5	37.0	35.4	32.8	25.8	31.8
June	34.1	43.3	37.7	40.2	3.0	34.3	38.0	31.4	36.6	37.1	35.2	32.8	25.7	31.7
July	34.2	43.8	37.6	40.2	3.0	34.3	38.2	31.4	36.6	37.0	35.5	32.7	25.8	31.7
August	34.2	43.9	37.8	40.3	3.1	34.4	38.2	31.5	36.7	37.0	35.5	32.7	25.8	31.7
September	34.2	43.5	38.1	40.4	3.2	34.3	38.4	31.3	36.6	37.1	35.6	32.8	25.8	31.8
October	34.3	43.7	38.0	40.4	3.2	34.5	38.4	31.5	36.8	37.1	35.6	32.9	25.9	31.7
November	34.2	42.7	37.9	40.3	3.1	34.4	38.4	31.4	36.7	37.1	35.6	32.8	25.9	31.7
December	34.3	43.9	37.8	40.4	3.1	34.6	38.4	31.7	36.5	37.1	35.7	32.7	25.8	31.7
2011														
January	34.3	44.9	37.7	40.4	3.2	34.6	38.5	31.6	36.6	37.1	35.7	32.7	25.8	31.6
February	34.3	44.1	37.7	40.5	3.2	34.5	38.5	31.5	36.6	37.1	35.7	32.7	25.9	31.7
March	34.3	44.2	38.0	40.5	3.3	34.6	38.6	31.5	36.6	37.1	35.7	32.8	25.8	31.8
April	34.4	44.4	37.8	40.4	3.2	34.7	38.6	31.7	36.6	37.2	35.7	32.9	25.9	31.9
May	34.4	44.7	38.4	40.5	3.1	34.5	38.6	31.5	36.6	37.2	35.7	33.0	25.8	31.8
June	34.4	44.6	38.1	40.4	3.1	34.6	38.7	31.6	36.6	37.2	35.7	32.9	25.9	31.9
July	34.4	44.3	38.3	40.4	3.1	34.5	38.7	31.5	36.7	37.4	35.8	32.9	25.9	31.8
August	34.3	44.0	38.1	40.3	3.2	34.4	38.6	31.4	36.5	37.2	35.7	32.8	25.9	31.6
September	34.4	44.6	38.2	40.4	3.1	34.6	38.8	31.6	36.6	37.6	35.8	32.8	25.9	31.7
October	34.4	45.4	38.1	40.6	3.2	34.6	38.8	31.7	36.7	37.5	35.8	32.8	26.0	31.7
November	34.4	44.3	38.1	40.4	3.3	34.6	38.8	31.7	36.8	37.4	35.8	32.8	26.1	31.7
December	34.5	44.7	38.4	40.7	3.3	34.7	38.8	31.9	36.6	37.3	35.8	32.8	26.1	31.6

Table 10-11. Indexes of Aggregate Weekly Hours of All Employees on Private Nonfarm Payrolls by NAICS Supersector

(2007 =100, seasonally adjusted.)

Year and month	Total private	Mining and logging	Construction	Manufacturing	Trade, transportation, and utilities			Information	Financial activities	Professional and business services	Education and health services	Leisure and hospitality	Other services
					Total	Wholesale trade	Retail trade						
2007	100.0	100.0	100.0	100.0	100.0	100.0	100.0	100.0	100.0	100.0	100.0	100.0	100.0
2008	98.7	105.2	93.3	96.0	98.5	99.6	97.6	99.6	98.0	98.2	103.3	99.1	100.4
2009	92.0	91.9	77.0	83.1	92.5	92.4	92.2	93.5	93.7	91.4	103.1	95.4	94.1
2010	91.8	96.1	71.9	83.4	91.7	90.6	92.0	90.3	93.0	93.1	104.2	95.9	93.4
2011	94.1	109.6	72.7	85.4	94.0	93.2	93.9	88.9	94.3	97.4	106.2	98.4	93.8
2007													
January	99.4	94.7	101.5	101.0	98.9	97.9	99.5	99.6	100.4	98.7	98.3	99.7	99.0
February	99.5	96.3	99.4	100.7	99.3	99.0	99.4	100.0	100.4	100.1	98.5	99.1	99.8
March	99.9	97.3	101.2	100.6	99.8	99.3	100.0	99.9	100.3	99.6	99.0	99.5	100.3
April	100.0	100.3	100.7	100.6	99.8	99.5	99.9	100.0	100.0	100.0	99.3	99.6	100.1
May	100.1	100.1	100.8	100.3	99.9	99.9	100.0	99.7	99.9	99.9	99.9	99.8	100.5
June	100.1	100.0	100.4	100.1	100.5	100.1	100.8	99.9	100.4	99.9	99.9	100.3	100.2
July	100.1	101.1	100.1	100.2	99.9	100.2	99.8	100.4	100.1	100.0	100.0	99.5	100.3
August	100.1	100.5	99.4	99.5	99.9	100.5	99.9	99.9	100.0	99.8	100.6	99.5	99.9
September	100.1	101.5	99.8	99.5	100.0	100.2	99.9	99.9	99.4	100.1	100.9	99.9	99.8
October	99.8	101.4	99.1	98.7	100.0	100.3	99.9	99.6	99.3	99.7	101.1	100.1	99.8
November	100.2	102.1	99.1	99.2	100.6	101.0	100.3	100.0	99.1	100.3	100.9	100.4	100.3
December	100.2	102.8	98.9	99.4	100.5	101.2	100.3	100.3	98.9	100.2	101.2	100.9	100.2
2008													
January	100.3	102.9	99.0	99.0	100.5	100.9	100.3	100.8	98.6	99.9	101.8	100.6	99.7
February	100.2	103.2	98.7	99.0	100.3	101.0	100.0	100.7	98.7	99.7	102.3	100.2	100.8
March	100.1	106.3	97.5	98.8	100.2	100.8	99.5	100.7	98.7	99.6	102.8	100.5	101.6
April	99.9	101.6	96.5	97.9	99.6	100.4	98.8	100.7	98.6	99.4	103.2	100.2	101.3
May	99.7	104.3	95.6	97.9	99.3	100.2	98.4	100.3	99.1	99.0	103.4	100.0	101.2
June	99.5	105.7	94.5	97.5	99.0	100.2	98.1	100.3	98.6	99.0	103.4	99.9	100.4
July	99.0	104.8	93.3	96.2	98.5	100.1	97.5	99.8	98.2	98.7	103.6	99.0	100.4
August	98.7	106.6	93.0	95.6	98.4	100.1	97.2	99.4	98.5	98.3	104.2	98.8	100.8
September	98.1	105.2	91.3	94.6	97.7	99.3	96.4	99.3	97.6	97.6	103.6	98.5	100.5
October	97.7	108.6	92.0	93.6	97.3	98.5	96.1	98.9	97.2	97.0	104.0	98.7	100.2
November	96.4	106.8	87.1	92.1	96.2	97.6	94.9	97.7	96.9	95.7	103.9	97.5	99.5
December	95.6	104.5	86.4	90.4	94.8	96.9	93.1	97.2	96.2	95.1	103.8	96.9	99.0
2009													
January	95.1	103.2	83.9	87.6	95.3	96.6	94.0	96.2	95.8	94.3	104.3	96.6	98.1
February	93.9	100.7	82.9	86.7	94.2	95.0	92.9	95.9	94.9	93.0	103.8	95.9	96.2
March	92.7	97.0	80.7	84.8	93.3	93.8	92.4	95.2	94.5	92.0	102.2	95.5	93.9
April	92.0	93.7	78.9	83.6	92.8	93.0	92.3	93.9	94.1	91.4	102.6	94.6	93.2
May	91.8	90.5	77.9	82.2	92.8	92.6	92.5	93.6	93.5	91.1	102.5	95.4	93.7
June	91.4	90.0	77.0	81.6	92.0	91.7	92.1	92.9	92.7	90.5	102.4	95.2	93.8
July	91.2	89.3	76.2	81.6	91.7	91.3	91.8	92.7	93.3	90.4	102.5	95.2	93.4
August	91.0	88.7	75.0	82.0	91.6	91.0	91.4	92.0	92.8	90.5	102.7	95.0	93.2
September	90.8	88.3	73.5	81.4	91.6	90.6	92.0	92.1	92.9	90.2	103.1	95.4	92.8
October	90.6	87.1	73.1	81.3	91.3	90.5	91.5	92.0	93.0	89.8	103.0	94.6	92.7
November	90.9	88.2	73.1	81.9	91.2	90.5	91.1	92.0	92.8	90.8	102.8	94.5	92.6
December	90.8	88.5	72.5	81.9	90.8	90.1	91.0	91.1	92.6	91.2	103.3	94.5	92.9
2010													
January	91.0	90.4	71.9	82.2	91.0	89.9	91.5	91.5	92.7	91.7	104.1	94.4	93.2
February	90.7	91.0	69.4	81.7	90.7	89.8	91.5	91.1	92.9	91.3	103.6	94.8	93.1
March	91.1	92.6	71.4	82.5	91.1	90.0	91.7	90.7	93.0	92.1	103.9	95.3	93.3
April	91.5	94.4	72.2	83.2	91.4	90.2	91.7	90.5	93.1	92.3	104.0	95.2	93.7
May	91.9	95.9	71.5	83.8	91.5	90.4	91.8	90.4	93.2	92.7	104.1	95.8	93.9
June	91.7	95.4	71.6	83.5	91.8	90.3	92.0	90.1	93.4	92.5	104.2	95.6	93.4
July	92.0	97.3	71.2	83.6	91.9	90.8	92.1	90.3	93.1	93.4	104.0	96.1	93.5
August	92.1	98.6	71.8	83.7	92.2	90.8	92.4	90.6	93.2	93.6	104.2	96.3	93.5
September	92.2	98.6	72.1	84.0	92.1	91.4	91.9	90.1	93.5	94.0	104.5	96.7	93.9
October	92.7	100.2	72.0	84.0	92.8	91.5	92.8	90.5	93.6	94.3	105.1	97.0	94.1
November	92.5	98.4	71.7	83.8	92.6	91.6	92.5	90.2	93.7	94.8	105.0	97.0	93.9
December	92.9	101.1	71.4	84.1	93.2	91.7	93.5	89.6	93.8	95.5	104.8	96.8	93.8
2011													
January	93.0	104.1	70.9	84.5	93.4	92.1	93.4	89.5	93.7	95.8	104.9	96.7	93.4
February	93.2	102.7	71.3	85.0	93.3	92.3	93.1	89.4	93.8	96.0	105.0	97.5	93.7
March	93.5	105.0	72.0	85.2	93.7	92.8	93.2	89.3	93.9	96.5	105.5	97.6	93.9
April	94.0	107.1	71.6	85.2	94.3	92.9	94.2	89.3	94.1	96.8	106.1	98.2	94.3
May	94.0	109.1	72.8	85.4	93.8	93.1	93.6	89.3	94.3	97.1	106.5	97.8	94.1
June	94.1	110.2	72.2	85.3	94.2	93.4	94.0	89.2	94.1	97.2	106.3	98.4	94.3
July	94.3	110.7	72.7	85.5	94.0	93.4	93.9	89.3	94.6	97.6	106.6	98.5	94.1
August	94.1	110.3	72.2	85.3	93.8	93.3	93.5	87.2	94.2	97.6	106.4	98.6	93.6
September	94.5	112.7	72.8	85.5	94.4	93.7	94.2	88.5	95.1	98.2	106.7	98.8	93.9
October	94.6	115.6	72.5	86.0	94.5	93.9	94.6	88.7	94.9	98.4	106.9	99.4	93.9
November	94.8	113.3	72.5	85.6	94.7	94.0	94.8	88.9	94.8	98.7	107.0	100.1	94.0
December	95.3	115.5	73.4	86.5	95.0	94.3	95.5	88.4	94.6	99.1	107.2	100.3	93.8

Table 10-12. Average Hourly Earnings of All Employees on Private Nonfarm Payrolls by NAICS Supersector

(Dollars, seasonally adjusted.)

Year and month	Total private	Mining and logging	Construction	Manu-facturing	Trade, transportation, and utilities			Information	Financial activities	Professional and business services	Education and health services	Leisure and hospitality	Other services
					Total	Wholesale trade	Retail trade						
2007	20.97	24.91	23.02	21.50	18.58	23.96	15.13	28.09	25.62	24.68	21.35	12.39	17.62
2008	21.62	26.20	23.96	22.16	18.93	24.37	15.21	28.66	26.16	25.82	22.12	12.77	18.17
2009	22.21	27.29	24.83	23.04	19.32	25.41	15.39	29.40	26.50	27.03	22.41	12.97	19.54
2010	22.59	27.39	25.19	23.31	19.65	26.13	15.56	30.53	27.20	27.24	22.96	13.08	20.16
2011	23.07	28.13	25.41	23.70	20.04	26.37	15.86	31.58	27.88	27.76	23.64	13.23	20.50
2007													
January	20.60	24.62	22.58	21.20	18.39	23.65	15.11	28.03	25.16	24.24	20.65	12.07	17.54
February	20.71	24.89	22.63	21.30	18.44	23.69	15.12	28.01	25.32	24.29	20.95	12.13	17.52
March	20.79	24.97	22.71	21.28	18.47	23.80	15.11	27.98	25.40	24.41	21.29	12.19	17.35
April	20.81	24.84	22.85	21.43	18.48	23.84	15.09	28.05	25.09	24.43	21.24	12.27	17.47
May	20.90	24.89	22.99	21.44	18.48	23.89	15.06	28.12	25.53	24.61	21.33	12.34	17.42
June	21.00	24.93	23.02	21.54	18.59	24.10	15.14	28.09	25.63	24.76	21.43	12.43	17.55
July	21.02	24.75	23.11	21.57	18.55	23.92	15.09	28.06	25.63	24.78	21.41	12.50	17.65
August	21.05	24.70	23.09	21.61	18.61	24.05	15.10	28.06	25.74	24.81	21.43	12.48	17.72
September	21.11	24.95	23.21	21.69	18.65	24.08	15.13	28.16	25.78	24.86	21.51	12.50	17.77
October	21.11	24.71	23.21	21.54	18.71	24.11	15.20	28.24	25.76	24.91	21.59	12.51	17.78
November	21.19	24.81	23.31	21.67	18.74	24.18	15.18	28.28	25.87	24.98	21.68	12.57	17.81
December	21.25	25.12	23.42	21.80	18.74	24.16	15.15	28.44	25.93	25.04	21.71	12.73	17.83
2008													
January	21.25	25.41	23.39	21.71	18.71	24.11	15.10	28.47	25.98	25.15	21.75	12.62	17.87
February	21.35	24.86	23.48	21.85	18.77	24.15	15.16	28.39	26.05	25.21	22.04	12.67	17.91
March	21.43	26.51	23.58	21.97	18.80	24.22	15.15	28.49	26.11	25.33	22.04	12.75	17.93
April	21.43	24.93	23.66	21.88	18.84	24.21	15.20	28.55	26.13	25.47	21.93	12.75	18.00
May	21.51	25.43	23.80	22.02	18.91	24.28	15.22	28.51	26.16	25.62	21.96	12.76	18.02
June	21.60	25.86	23.91	22.22	18.98	24.39	15.23	28.57	26.18	25.72	22.03	12.78	18.13
July	21.64	26.29	24.00	22.11	18.98	24.43	15.21	28.76	26.25	25.82	22.09	12.79	18.23
August	21.75	26.75	24.16	22.22	19.07	24.61	15.29	28.83	26.27	26.03	22.16	12.82	18.28
September	21.78	26.68	24.24	22.27	19.04	24.44	15.27	28.83	26.39	26.11	22.22	12.84	18.30
October	21.83	26.59	24.29	22.44	19.00	24.43	15.24	28.78	26.29	26.30	22.29	12.82	18.37
November	21.93	27.47	24.41	22.60	19.08	24.62	15.26	28.85	26.25	26.53	22.39	12.83	18.45
December	22.00	27.32	24.55	22.63	19.14	24.71	15.29	29.01	26.27	26.66	22.46	12.84	18.50
2009													
January	22.03	27.46	24.56	22.81	19.15	24.87	15.30	28.94	26.25	26.72	22.47	12.86	18.64
February	22.07	27.50	24.56	22.88	19.20	24.93	15.32	28.79	26.26	26.84	22.42	12.88	18.91
March	22.11	27.73	24.76	23.01	19.24	25.01	15.35	28.67	26.26	26.94	22.22	12.88	19.45
April	22.14	27.67	24.78	23.03	19.23	25.17	15.31	28.81	26.27	27.04	22.32	12.89	19.48
May	22.14	27.52	24.79	23.01	19.26	25.29	15.34	29.19	26.40	27.00	22.30	12.86	19.52
June	22.16	27.43	24.87	23.05	19.24	25.31	15.34	29.40	26.45	27.04	22.31	12.91	19.55
July	22.22	27.28	24.86	23.08	19.28	25.35	15.38	29.62	26.51	27.07	22.42	12.97	19.61
August	22.28	27.38	24.93	23.13	19.45	25.72	15.50	29.63	26.58	27.05	22.46	13.01	19.69
September	22.29	27.24	24.89	23.16	19.42	25.70	15.51	29.62	26.67	27.20	22.33	13.04	19.83
October	22.34	27.30	25.04	23.11	19.42	25.76	15.42	29.87	26.76	27.12	22.55	13.11	19.91
November	22.39	26.95	25.03	23.18	19.47	25.82	15.45	30.01	26.87	27.07	22.56	13.16	19.99
December	22.40	26.98	24.98	23.14	19.51	25.91	15.47	30.05	26.87	27.11	22.59	13.14	20.07
2010													
January	22.46	27.08	25.10	23.18	19.59	26.18	15.50	30.05	26.97	27.15	22.64	13.12	20.07
February	22.46	27.14	25.20	23.19	19.57	26.15	15.49	30.18	26.99	27.20	22.64	13.10	20.09
March	22.49	27.17	25.18	23.18	19.62	26.18	15.55	30.09	27.06	27.17	22.75	13.09	20.09
April	22.54	27.33	25.10	23.20	19.65	26.13	15.63	30.05	27.18	27.16	22.92	13.07	20.07
May	22.57	27.40	25.18	23.31	19.63	26.13	15.53	30.37	27.22	27.24	22.92	13.07	20.09
June	22.56	27.42	25.16	23.25	19.61	26.10	15.54	30.45	27.16	27.26	22.88	13.06	20.16
July	22.63	27.59	25.21	23.35	19.64	26.12	15.54	30.46	27.36	27.29	23.03	13.09	20.09
August	22.67	27.56	25.20	23.44	19.61	26.01	15.52	30.67	27.31	27.38	23.13	13.10	20.11
September	22.71	27.72	25.20	23.43	19.74	26.21	15.61	31.00	27.34	27.39	23.12	13.09	20.17
October	22.75	27.59	25.31	23.44	19.79	26.28	15.67	31.24	27.38	27.44	23.16	13.09	20.28
November	22.76	27.64	25.30	23.40	19.78	26.24	15.67	31.25	27.40	27.41	23.21	13.10	20.39
December	22.78	27.73	25.31	23.48	19.78	26.23	15.68	31.29	27.51	27.32	23.28	13.12	20.36
2011													
January	22.86	27.89	25.39	23.63	19.82	26.24	15.71	31.34	27.56	27.44	23.34	13.17	20.36
February	22.88	28.04	25.38	23.47	19.87	26.25	15.74	31.52	27.63	27.52	23.38	13.17	20.37
March	22.92	28.17	25.34	23.55	19.90	26.22	15.74	31.65	27.68	27.53	23.46	13.18	20.30
April	22.97	28.40	25.38	23.61	19.95	26.30	15.79	31.59	27.72	27.60	23.54	13.21	20.34
May	23.02	28.23	25.38	23.67	20.00	26.30	15.84	31.59	27.73	27.65	23.61	13.24	20.41
June	23.05	27.80	25.39	23.69	20.04	26.39	15.83	31.52	27.80	27.75	23.64	13.23	20.47
July	23.13	27.77	25.42	23.75	20.11	26.44	15.94	31.47	27.86	27.96	23.69	13.23	20.54
August	23.12	28.02	25.48	23.71	20.09	26.39	15.85	31.50	27.91	27.85	23.74	13.22	20.57
September	23.16	28.11	25.51	23.77	20.08	26.38	15.84	31.42	28.05	27.88	23.78	13.27	20.58
October	23.21	28.23	25.47	23.87	20.12	26.43	15.89	31.39	28.21	27.98	23.82	13.29	20.61
November	23.23	28.24	25.43	23.78	20.21	26.53	16.02	31.53	28.27	27.95	23.89	13.31	20.61
December	23.25	28.39	25.44	23.86	20.21	26.49	16.03	31.73	28.30	27.90	23.90	13.33	20.67

Table 10-13. Average Weekly Earnings of All Employees on Private Nonfarm Payrolls by NAICS Supersector

(Dollars, seasonally adjusted.)

Year and month	Total private	Mining and logging	Construc-tion	Manu-facturing	Trade, transportation, and utilities			Information	Financial activities	Profes-sional and business services	Education and health services	Leisure and hospitality	Other services
					Total	Wholesale trade	Retail trade						
2007	725.22	1 094.81	875.06	861.19	641.51	913.03	479.81	1 014.35	936.56	874.68	715.66	323.54	578.84
2008	744.97	1 144.63	905.68	882.19	651.96	936.17	478.00	1 047.50	954.82	909.23	745.03	330.32	597.13
2009	753.18	1 150.12	922.54	898.64	659.78	963.44	481.03	1 073.27	970.00	947.10	739.27	331.64	618.18
2010	770.71	1 189.32	952.78	937.34	672.64	994.71	487.82	1 114.65	1 003.31	963.79	752.26	336.83	637.65
2011	793.10	1 251.83	973.51	959.39	692.54	1 018.88	500.74	1 156.06	1 038.87	991.93	775.50	342.67	649.75
2007													
January	710.70	1 051.27	860.30	850.12	630.78	889.24	478.99	1 009.08	918.34	853.25	689.71	316.23	573.56
February	714.50	1 072.76	855.41	852.00	634.34	897.85	477.79	1 011.16	924.18	864.72	699.73	315.38	576.41
March	719.33	1 081.20	865.25	851.20	637.22	904.40	478.99	1 010.08	927.10	864.11	713.22	318.16	572.55
April	720.03	1 102.90	868.30	859.34	637.56	905.92	478.35	1 012.61	915.79	867.27	711.54	320.25	574.76
May	723.14	1 100.14	875.92	857.60	637.56	910.21	477.40	1 009.51	929.29	871.19	716.69	322.07	574.86
June	726.60	1 094.43	872.46	861.60	645.07	918.21	484.48	1 011.24	938.06	876.50	717.91	325.67	577.40
July	727.29	1 093.95	875.87	864.96	639.98	911.35	478.35	1 015.77	935.50	877.21	717.24	325.00	580.69
August	728.33	1 086.80	875.11	864.40	642.05	918.71	478.67	1 012.97	942.08	875.79	720.05	324.48	581.22
September	730.41	1 110.28	886.62	869.77	643.43	917.45	479.62	1 016.58	940.97	880.04	722.74	325.00	582.86
October	728.30	1 097.12	881.98	859.45	645.50	918.59	481.84	1 016.64	940.24	876.83	725.42	325.26	583.18
November	733.17	1 096.60	890.44	868.97	648.40	926.09	481.21	1 023.74	944.26	884.29	726.28	326.82	585.95
December	735.25	1 110.30	896.99	876.36	648.40	927.74	480.26	1 032.37	946.45	883.91	727.29	332.25	584.82
2008													
January	735.25	1 115.50	898.18	870.57	647.37	923.41	478.67	1 039.16	945.67	885.28	730.80	328.12	582.56
February	738.71	1 091.35	903.98	878.37	649.44	927.36	480.57	1 036.24	950.83	887.39	742.75	328.15	589.24
March	741.48	1 187.65	900.76	883.19	650.48	930.05	478.74	1 039.89	953.02	894.15	744.95	331.50	593.48
April	741.48	1 069.50	903.81	875.20	649.98	929.66	478.80	1 044.93	953.75	896.54	741.23	331.50	594.00
May	744.25	1 108.75	906.78	883.00	652.40	932.35	479.43	1 040.62	960.07	901.82	742.25	331.76	594.66
June	747.36	1 135.25	908.58	891.02	654.81	939.02	479.75	1 045.66	958.19	907.92	742.41	332.28	594.66
July	746.58	1 138.36	907.20	879.98	652.91	943.00	477.59	1 052.62	958.13	911.45	744.43	329.98	597.94
August	750.38	1 166.30	915.66	884.36	657.92	952.41	480.11	1 055.18	964.11	918.86	749.01	330.76	603.24
September	749.23	1 141.90	911.42	881.89	654.98	940.94	477.95	1 058.06	963.24	919.07	746.59	331.27	602.07
October	750.95	1 177.94	930.31	888.62	653.60	938.11	477.01	1 056.23	959.59	925.76	751.17	332.04	602.54
November	750.01	1 203.19	905.61	888.18	654.44	942.95	476.11	1 053.03	960.75	931.20	752.30	329.73	605.16
December	750.20	1 180.22	918.17	884.83	650.76	946.39	470.93	1 061.77	958.86	935.77	752.41	328.70	606.80
2009													
January	753.43	1 180.78	911.18	885.03	658.76	955.01	478.89	1 056.31	960.75	937.87	754.99	329.22	607.66
February	750.38	1 177.00	916.09	890.03	656.64	949.83	476.45	1 050.84	958.49	939.40	748.83	328.44	607.01
March	747.32	1 175.75	921.07	888.19	656.08	947.88	477.39	1 043.59	958.49	940.21	731.04	328.44	612.68
April	748.33	1 159.37	921.82	888.96	655.74	953.94	477.67	1 045.80	961.48	946.40	736.56	327.41	609.72
May	748.33	1 142.08	919.71	885.89	658.69	958.49	480.14	1 065.44	963.60	945.00	733.67	327.93	614.88
June	749.01	1 146.57	925.16	892.04	654.16	954.19	478.61	1 070.16	960.14	946.40	731.77	329.21	615.83
July	751.04	1 145.76	927.28	897.81	655.52	955.70	479.86	1 081.13	970.27	947.45	735.38	330.74	615.75
August	753.06	1 155.44	927.40	906.70	661.30	969.64	482.05	1 078.53	970.17	949.46	736.69	331.76	618.27
September	753.40	1 149.53	918.44	905.56	662.22	966.32	487.01	1 078.17	976.12	952.00	734.66	333.82	620.68
October	755.09	1 146.60	928.98	905.91	662.22	971.15	482.65	1 087.27	982.09	943.78	739.64	334.31	625.17
November	759.02	1 142.68	933.62	917.93	663.93	976.00	482.04	1 098.37	983.44	950.16	737.71	335.58	627.69
December	759.36	1 143.95	929.26	918.66	663.34	976.81	482.66	1 093.82	983.44	954.27	740.95	336.38	632.21
2010													
January	763.64	1 164.44	936.23	924.88	668.02	989.60	485.15	1 099.83	989.80	958.40	747.12	335.87	634.21
February	761.39	1 164.31	917.28	918.32	665.38	988.47	484.84	1 101.57	993.23	954.72	742.59	336.67	634.84
March	764.66	1 173.74	939.21	927.20	669.04	992.22	486.72	1 098.29	998.51	961.82	746.20	337.72	634.84
April	768.61	1 191.59	946.27	932.64	672.03	992.94	489.22	1 096.83	1 002.94	958.75	751.78	335.90	636.22
May	771.89	1 200.12	946.77	941.72	671.35	995.55	486.09	1 108.51	1 007.14	964.30	751.78	337.21	638.86
June	769.30	1 187.29	948.53	934.65	672.62	991.80	487.96	1 114.47	1 007.64	959.55	750.46	335.64	639.07
July	773.95	1 208.44	947.90	938.67	673.65	997.78	487.96	1 114.84	1 012.32	968.80	753.08	337.72	636.85
August	775.31	1 209.88	952.56	944.63	674.58	993.58	488.88	1 125.59	1 010.47	971.99	756.35	337.98	637.49
September	776.68	1 205.82	960.12	946.57	677.08	1 006.46	488.59	1 134.60	1 014.31	975.08	758.34	337.72	641.41
October	780.33	1 205.68	961.78	946.98	682.76	1 009.15	493.61	1 149.63	1 015.80	976.86	761.96	339.03	642.88
November	778.39	1 180.23	958.87	943.02	680.43	1 007.62	492.04	1 146.88	1 016.54	975.80	761.29	339.29	646.36
December	781.35	1 217.35	956.72	948.59	684.39	1 007.23	497.06	1 142.09	1 020.62	975.32	761.26	338.50	645.41
2011													
January	784.10	1 252.26	957.20	954.65	685.77	1 010.24	496.44	1 147.04	1 022.48	979.61	763.22	339.79	643.38
February	784.78	1 236.56	956.83	950.54	685.52	1 010.63	495.81	1 153.63	1 025.07	982.46	764.53	341.10	645.73
March	786.16	1 245.11	962.92	953.78	688.54	1 012.09	495.81	1 158.39	1 026.93	982.82	769.49	340.04	645.54
April	790.17	1 260.96	959.36	953.84	692.27	1 015.18	500.54	1 156.19	1 031.18	985.32	774.47	342.14	648.85
May	791.89	1 261.88	974.59	958.64	690.00	1 015.30	498.96	1 156.19	1 031.56	987.11	779.13	341.59	649.04
June	792.92	1 239.88	967.36	957.08	693.38	1 021.29	500.23	1 153.63	1 034.16	990.68	777.76	342.66	652.99
July	795.67	1 230.21	973.59	959.50	693.80	1 023.23	502.11	1 154.95	1 041.96	1 000.97	779.40	342.66	653.17
August	793.02	1 232.88	970.79	955.51	691.10	1 018.65	497.69	1 149.75	1 038.25	994.25	778.67	342.40	650.01
September	796.70	1 253.71	974.48	960.31	694.77	1 023.54	500.54	1 149.97	1 054.68	998.10	779.98	343.69	652.39
October	798.42	1 281.64	970.41	969.12	696.15	1 025.48	503.71	1 152.01	1 057.88	1 001.68	781.30	345.54	653.34
November	799.11	1 251.03	968.88	960.71	699.27	1 029.36	507.83	1 160.30	1 057.30	1 000.61	783.59	347.39	653.34
December	802.13	1 269.03	976.90	971.10	701.29	1 027.81	511.36	1 161.32	1 055.59	998.82	783.92	347.91	653.17

Table 10-14. Production and Nonsupervisory Workers on Private Nonfarm Payrolls by NAICS Supersector

(Thousands, seasonally adjusted.)

Year and month	Total private	Mining and logging	Construc-tion	Manu-facturing	Trade, transportation, and utilities			Information	Financial activities	Profes-sional and business services	Education and health services	Leisure and hospitality	Other services
					Total	Wholesale trade	Retail trade						
1965	42 302	523	2 906	12 905	10 702	. . .	. . .	1 268	2 434	3 515	3 443	3 443	1 161
1966	44 292	517	2 977	13 703	11 095	. . .	. . .	1 334	2 492	3 715	3 623	3 607	1 230
1967	45 185	501	2 903	13 714	11 369	. . .	. . .	1 365	2 585	3 890	3 818	3 734	1 306
1968	46 519	491	2 986	13 908	11 688	. . .	. . .	1 394	2 700	4 067	4 008	3 898	1 379
1969	48 246	501	3 177	14 147	12 152	. . .	. . .	1 438	2 841	4 252	4 196	4 089	1 452
1970	48 180	496	3 158	13 490	12 388	. . .	. . .	1 422	2 922	4 321	4 305	4 185	1 494
1971	48 151	474	3 238	13 034	12 502	. . .	. . .	1 392	2 978	4 354	4 372	4 286	1 521
1972	49 971	494	3 425	13 497	12 954	2 920	7 257	1 437	3 066	4 518	4 531	4 467	1 583
1973	52 235	502	3 576	14 227	13 437	3 041	7 550	1 504	3 164	4 748	4 747	4 664	1 666
1974	52 846	550	3 469	14 040	13 700	3 148	7 673	1 516	3 217	4 907	4 941	4 766	1 740
1975	51 010	581	2 990	12 576	13 578	3 121	7 714	1 416	3 227	4 939	5 088	4 821	1 795
1976	52 916	606	2 999	13 127	14 038	3 212	8 048	1 459	3 300	5 153	5 309	5 046	1 880
1977	55 207	636	3 209	13 591	14 579	3 323	8 396	1 514	3 452	5 404	5 561	5 284	1 978
1978	58 188	658	3 544	14 150	15 329	3 509	8 861	1 586	3 645	5 717	5 874	5 588	2 099
1979	60 403	737	3 760	14 458	15 843	3 667	9 113	1 650	3 825	5 993	6 157	5 772	2 209
1980	60 372	785	3 623	13 667	15 907	3 708	9 158	1 626	3 957	6 197	6 442	5 850	2 318
1981	60 960	861	3 469	13 492	16 004	3 753	9 238	1 633	4 052	6 396	6 694	5 944	2 414
1982	59 465	834	3 208	12 315	15 821	3 662	9 254	1 564	4 055	6 421	6 812	5 976	2 458
1983	60 005	698	3 240	12 121	15 999	3 639	9 494	1 502	4 128	6 581	7 032	6 161	2 542
1984	63 316	714	3 614	12 821	16 797	3 821	9 964	1 631	4 289	6 918	7 368	6 491	2 672
1985	65 436	686	3 868	12 648	17 427	3 935	10 399	1 660	4 476	7 258	7 770	6 817	2 827
1986	66 802	577	3 984	12 449	17 769	3 941	10 704	1 663	4 698	7 532	8 107	7 066	2 957
1987	68 700	541	4 088	12 537	18 196	3 989	10 986	1 717	4 861	7 859	8 488	7 310	3 104
1988	71 029	545	4 199	12 765	18 771	4 132	11 306	1 775	4 894	8 256	8 956	7 587	3 280
1989	72 927	526	4 257	12 805	19 230	4 235	11 564	1 807	4 931	8 648	9 432	7 833	3 459
1990	73 684	538	4 115	12 669	19 032	4 198	11 308	1 866	4 973	8 889	9 748	8 299	3 555
1991	72 520	515	3 674	12 164	18 640	4 122	11 008	1 871	4 911	8 748	10 212	8 247	3 539
1992	72 786	478	3 546	12 020	18 506	4 071	10 931	1 871	4 908	8 971	10 555	8 406	3 526
1993	74 591	462	3 704	12 070	18 752	4 072	11 104	1 896	5 057	9 451	10 908	8 667	3 623
1994	77 382	461	3 973	12 361	19 392	4 196	11 502	1 928	5 183	10 078	11 338	8 979	3 689
1995	79 845	458	4 113	12 567	19 984	4 361	11 841	2 007	5 165	10 645	11 765	9 330	3 812
1996	81 773	461	4 325	12 532	20 325	4 423	12 057	2 096	5 279	11 161	12 123	9 565	3 907
1997	84 158	479	4 546	12 673	20 698	4 523	12 274	2 181	5 415	11 896	12 478	9 780	4 013
1998	86 316	473	4 807	12 729	21 059	4 605	12 440	2 217	5 605	12 566	12 791	9 947	4 124
1999	88 430	438	5 105	12 524	21 576	4 673	12 772	2 351	5 728	13 184	13 089	10 216	4 219
2000	90 336	446	5 295	12 428	21 965	4 686	13 040	2 502	5 737	13 790	13 362	10 516	4 296
2001	89 983	457	5 332	11 677	21 709	4 555	12 952	2 531	5 810	13 588	13 846	10 662	4 373
2002	88 393	436	5 196	10 768	21 337	4 474	12 774	2 398	5 872	13 049	14 311	10 576	4 449
2003	87 658	420	5 123	10 189	21 078	4 396	12 655	2 347	5 967	12 911	14 532	10 666	4 426
2004	88 937	440	5 309	10 072	21 319	4 444	12 788	2 371	5 989	13 287	14 771	10 955	4 425
2005	91 135	473	5 611	10 060	21 830	4 584	13 030	2 386	6 090	13 854	15 129	11 263	4 438
2006	93 451	519	5 903	10 137	22 166	4 724	13 110	2 399	6 281	14 446	15 539	11 568	4 494
2007	94 902	547	5 883	9 975	22 546	4 851	13 317	2 403	6 326	14 784	15 999	11 861	4 578
2008	94 270	574	5 521	9 629	22 337	4 822	13 134	2 388	6 269	14 585	16 488	11 873	4 606
2009	89 173	510	4 567	8 322	21 116	4 506	12 472	2 240	6 008	13 520	16 841	11 560	4 488
2010	88 512	525	4 172	8 077	20 874	4 378	12 425	2 170	5 906	13 699	17 125	11 507	4 458
2011	90 092	590	4 161	8 231	21 196	4 431	12 627	2 136	5 887	14 253	17 420	11 743	4 475
2010													
January	88 041	491	4 240	8 042	20 806	4 391	12 357	2 183	5 937	13 493	16 981	11 419	4 449
February	88 008	495	4 174	8 039	20 808	4 386	12 369	2 184	5 928	13 530	17 007	11 408	4 435
March	88 152	503	4 203	8 039	20 848	4 382	12 407	2 169	5 909	13 544	17 055	11 430	4 452
April	88 298	508	4 214	8 061	20 848	4 378	12 412	2 175	5 918	13 601	17 066	11 449	4 458
May	88 356	520	4 166	8 086	20 854	4 373	12 420	2 170	5 913	13 627	17 084	11 479	4 457
June	88 434	525	4 157	8 098	20 855	4 373	12 412	2 163	5 902	13 691	17 104	11 492	4 447
July	88 508	532	4 132	8 110	20 882	4 371	12 430	2 167	5 895	13 702	17 128	11 504	4 456
August	88 590	537	4 154	8 092	20 869	4 367	12 435	2 169	5 896	13 732	17 156	11 531	4 454
September	88 682	539	4 149	8 090	20 890	4 367	12 445	2 166	5 898	13 741	17 161	11 592	4 456
October	88 849	549	4 165	8 086	20 925	4 371	12 475	2 162	5 892	13 810	17 213	11 565	4 482
November	88 978	550	4 163	8 085	20 940	4 376	12 475	2 162	5 889	13 888	17 253	11 571	4 477
December	89 075	550	4 143	8 099	20 966	4 381	12 492	2 159	5 892	13 951	17 258	11 587	4 470
2011													
January	89 179	553	4 134	8 139	21 002	4 391	12 525	2 153	5 885	14 003	17 262	11 578	4 470
February	89 401	554	4 157	8 170	21 047	4 401	12 538	2 151	5 885	14 051	17 285	11 629	4 472
March	89 628	568	4 162	8 197	21 067	4 413	12 540	2 149	5 890	14 133	17 309	11 684	4 469
April	89 850	578	4 158	8 225	21 164	4 419	12 615	2 146	5 889	14 162	17 351	11 710	4 467
May	89 929	584	4 155	8 228	21 164	4 428	12 602	2 146	5 895	14 213	17 362	11 713	4 469
June	90 019	591	4 154	8 230	21 202	4 432	12 628	2 144	5 882	14 227	17 380	11 742	4 467
July	90 169	597	4 165	8 259	21 214	4 434	12 638	2 140	5 881	14 267	17 433	11 745	4 468
August	90 219	601	4 148	8 259	21 235	4 438	12 645	2 091	5 882	14 308	17 468	11 762	4 475
September	90 428	606	4 178	8 260	21 258	4 435	12 670	2 126	5 882	14 349	17 507	11 784	4 478
October	90 545	613	4 169	8 268	21 284	4 443	12 685	2 122	5 890	14 382	17 534	11 805	4 478
November	90 742	614	4 165	8 268	21 340	4 459	12 712	2 124	5 896	14 421	17 569	11 857	4 488
December	90 960	621	4 193	8 297	21 365	4 474	12 721	2 128	5 900	14 480	17 607	11 878	4 491

. . . = Not available.

Table 10-15. Average Weekly Hours of Production and Nonsupervisory Workers on Private Nonfarm Payrolls by NAICS Supersector

(Hours per week, seasonally adjusted.)

Year and month	Total private	Mining and logging	Construc-tion	Manufacturing Average weekly hours	Manufacturing Overtime hours	Trade, transportation, and utilities Total	Trade, transportation, and utilities Wholesale trade	Trade, transportation, and utilities Retail trade	Informa-tion	Financial activities	Profes-sional and business services	Education and health services	Leisure and hospitality	Other services
1965	38.6	43.7	37.9	41.2	3.6	39.6	. . .	. . .	38.3	37.1	37.3	35.2	32.5	36.1
1966	38.5	44.1	38.1	41.4	3.9	39.1	. . .	. . .	38.3	37.2	37.0	34.9	31.9	35.8
1967	37.9	43.9	38.1	40.6	3.3	38.5	. . .	. . .	37.6	36.9	36.6	34.5	31.3	35.4
1968	37.7	44.0	37.8	40.7	3.6	38.2	. . .	. . .	37.6	36.8	36.3	34.1	30.8	35.0
1969	37.5	44.3	38.4	40.6	3.6	37.9	. . .	. . .	37.6	36.9	36.3	34.1	30.4	35.0
1970	37.0	43.9	37.8	39.8	2.9	37.6	. . .	. . .	37.2	36.6	35.9	33.8	30.0	34.7
1971	36.7	43.7	37.6	39.9	2.9	37.4	. . .	. . .	37.0	36.4	35.5	33.3	29.9	34.2
1972	36.9	44.1	37.0	40.6	3.4	37.4	39.8	35.1	37.3	36.4	35.5	33.3	29.7	34.2
1973	36.9	43.8	37.2	40.7	3.8	37.2	39.6	34.8	37.3	36.4	35.5	33.3	29.4	34.1
1974	36.4	43.7	37.1	40.0	3.2	36.8	39.2	34.3	37.0	36.3	35.3	33.1	29.1	33.9
1975	36.0	43.7	36.9	39.5	2.6	36.4	39.1	34.0	36.6	36.2	35.1	33.0	28.8	33.8
1976	36.1	44.2	37.3	40.1	3.1	36.3	39.1	33.8	36.7	36.2	34.9	32.7	28.5	33.6
1977	35.9	44.7	37.0	40.3	3.4	36.0	39.2	33.3	36.8	36.2	34.7	32.5	28.1	33.4
1978	35.8	44.9	37.3	40.4	3.6	35.6	39.2	32.7	36.8	36.1	34.6	32.3	27.7	33.2
1979	35.6	44.7	37.5	40.2	3.3	35.4	39.2	32.4	36.6	35.9	34.4	32.2	27.4	33.0
1980	35.2	44.9	37.5	39.6	2.8	35.0	38.8	31.9	36.4	36.0	34.3	32.1	27.0	33.0
1981	35.2	45.1	37.4	39.8	2.8	35.0	38.9	31.9	36.3	36.0	34.3	32.1	26.9	33.0
1982	34.7	44.1	37.2	38.9	2.3	34.6	38.7	31.7	35.8	36.0	34.2	32.1	26.8	33.0
1983	34.9	43.9	37.6	40.1	2.9	34.6	38.8	31.6	36.2	35.9	34.4	32.1	26.8	33.0
1984	35.1	44.6	38.2	40.6	3.4	34.7	38.9	31.6	36.6	36.2	34.3	32.0	26.7	32.9
1985	34.9	44.6	38.2	40.5	3.3	34.4	38.8	31.2	36.5	36.1	34.2	31.9	26.4	32.8
1986	34.7	43.6	37.9	40.7	3.4	34.1	38.7	31.0	36.4	36.1	34.3	32.0	26.2	32.9
1987	34.7	43.5	38.2	40.9	3.7	34.1	38.5	31.0	36.5	36.0	34.3	32.0	26.3	32.8
1988	34.6	43.3	38.2	41.0	3.8	33.8	38.5	30.9	36.1	35.6	34.2	32.0	26.3	32.9
1989	34.5	44.1	38.3	40.9	3.8	33.8	38.4	30.7	36.1	35.6	34.2	32.0	26.1	32.9
1990	34.3	45.0	38.3	40.5	3.9	33.7	38.4	30.6	35.8	35.5	34.2	31.9	26.0	32.8
1991	34.1	45.3	38.1	40.4	3.8	33.7	38.4	30.4	35.6	35.5	34.0	31.9	25.6	32.7
1992	34.2	44.6	38.0	40.7	4.0	33.8	38.5	30.7	35.8	35.6	34.0	32.0	25.7	32.6
1993	34.3	44.9	38.4	41.1	4.4	34.1	38.5	30.7	36.0	35.5	34.0	32.0	25.9	32.6
1994	34.5	45.3	38.8	41.7	5.0	34.3	38.8	30.9	36.0	35.5	34.1	32.0	26.0	32.7
1995	34.3	45.3	38.8	41.3	4.7	34.1	38.6	30.8	36.0	35.5	34.0	32.0	25.9	32.6
1996	34.3	46.0	38.9	41.3	4.8	34.1	38.6	30.7	36.3	35.5	34.1	31.9	25.9	32.5
1997	34.5	46.2	38.9	41.7	5.1	34.3	38.8	30.9	36.3	35.7	34.3	32.2	26.1	32.7
1998	34.5	44.9	38.8	41.4	4.9	34.2	38.6	30.9	36.6	36.0	34.3	32.2	26.2	32.6
1999	34.3	44.2	39.0	41.4	4.9	33.9	38.6	30.8	36.7	35.8	34.4	32.1	26.1	32.5
2000	34.3	44.4	39.2	41.3	4.7	33.8	38.8	30.7	36.8	35.9	34.5	32.2	26.1	32.5
2001	34.0	44.6	38.7	40.3	4.0	33.5	38.4	30.7	36.9	35.8	34.2	32.3	25.8	32.3
2002	33.9	43.2	38.4	40.5	4.2	33.6	38.0	30.9	36.5	35.6	34.2	32.4	25.8	32.1
2003	33.7	43.6	38.4	40.4	4.2	33.6	37.9	30.9	36.2	35.5	34.1	32.3	25.6	31.4
2004	33.7	44.5	38.3	40.8	4.6	33.5	37.8	30.7	36.3	35.5	34.2	32.4	25.7	31.0
2005	33.8	45.6	38.6	40.7	4.6	33.4	37.7	30.6	36.5	35.9	34.2	32.6	25.7	30.9
2006	33.9	45.6	39.0	41.1	4.4	33.4	38.0	30.5	36.6	35.7	34.6	32.5	25.7	30.9
2007	33.9	45.9	39.0	41.2	4.2	33.3	38.2	30.2	36.5	35.9	34.8	32.6	25.5	30.9
2008	33.6	45.1	38.5	40.8	3.7	33.2	38.2	30.0	36.7	35.8	34.8	32.5	25.2	30.8
2009	33.1	43.2	37.6	39.8	2.9	32.9	37.6	29.9	36.6	36.1	34.7	32.2	24.8	30.5
2010	33.4	44.6	38.4	41.1	3.8	33.3	37.9	30.2	36.3	36.2	35.1	32.1	24.8	30.7
2011	33.6	46.7	39.0	41.4	4.1	33.7	38.5	30.5	36.2	36.4	35.2	32.3	24.8	30.7
2010														
January	33.3	44.3	37.8	40.9	3.6	33.0	37.7	30.0	36.6	36.2	35.0	32.3	24.9	30.7
February	33.2	43.6	37.1	40.4	3.4	33.0	37.7	30.1	36.4	35.9	34.9	32.2	24.9	30.6
March	33.3	44.2	37.8	41.0	3.6	33.1	37.8	30.1	36.5	36.2	35.0	32.2	24.9	30.7
April	33.4	44.5	38.8	41.2	3.8	33.2	37.9	30.1	36.4	36.3	35.0	32.2	24.8	30.7
May	33.4	45.2	38.0	41.4	3.9	33.3	38.0	30.2	36.5	36.4	35.1	32.2	24.8	30.8
June	33.4	44.7	38.2	41.0	3.9	33.2	37.8	30.2	36.5	36.3	35.0	32.2	24.7	30.8
July	33.4	44.8	38.1	41.1	3.8	33.4	38.0	30.3	36.2	36.2	35.2	32.1	24.9	30.8
August	33.5	45.6	38.5	41.2	3.9	33.4	38.1	30.3	36.4	36.4	35.2	32.2	24.9	30.8
September	33.5	44.7	39.0	41.3	3.9	33.4	38.2	30.2	36.1	36.4	35.2	32.2	24.8	30.8
October	33.5	44.4	38.8	41.2	3.9	33.4	38.2	30.3	36.3	36.4	35.3	32.3	24.8	30.8
November	33.5	44.7	38.7	41.2	4.0	33.5	38.1	30.3	36.4	36.3	35.1	32.2	24.9	30.6
December	33.5	44.9	38.7	41.3	4.0	33.6	38.2	30.4	36.2	36.4	35.3	32.1	24.8	30.7
2011														
January	33.4	46.1	37.7	41.1	4.1	33.5	38.3	30.4	36.4	36.4	35.2	32.1	24.7	30.7
February	33.6	45.7	38.7	41.4	4.2	33.6	38.4	30.4	36.4	36.4	35.2	32.2	24.8	30.8
March	33.6	45.8	38.6	41.5	4.2	33.7	38.5	30.4	36.3	36.3	35.1	32.2	24.9	30.8
April	33.7	46.6	38.8	41.4	4.1	33.8	38.5	30.6	36.5	36.3	35.3	32.3	24.8	30.8
May	33.6	46.5	39.1	41.5	4.1	33.7	38.6	30.4	36.4	36.4	35.2	32.3	24.8	30.8
June	33.7	47.2	38.9	41.4	4.0	33.7	38.6	30.5	36.3	36.4	35.3	32.3	24.8	30.9
July	33.7	46.4	39.1	41.4	4.1	33.7	38.5	30.6	36.4	36.5	35.2	32.4	24.8	30.7
August	33.6	46.3	39.0	41.3	4.1	33.7	38.4	30.5	36.0	36.4	35.1	32.3	24.7	30.7
September	33.6	46.7	39.0	41.3	4.0	33.7	38.6	30.5	36.1	36.6	35.2	32.4	24.8	30.7
October	33.7	47.5	38.8	41.5	4.1	33.8	38.7	30.7	36.3	36.6	35.3	32.4	24.8	30.9
November	33.7	47.0	38.9	41.5	4.1	33.8	38.6	30.7	36.2	36.5	35.2	32.4	24.8	30.7
December	33.7	47.6	39.2	41.6	4.1	33.8	38.7	30.7	36.0	36.6	35.2	32.3	24.9	30.8

. . . = Not available.

Table 10-16. Indexes of Aggregate Weekly Hours of Production and Nonsupervisory Workers on Private Nonfarm Payrolls by NAICS Supersector

(2002 = 100, seasonally adjusted.)

Year and month	Total private	Mining and logging	Construction	Manufacturing	Trade, transportation, and utilities			Information	Financial activities	Professional and business services	Education and health services	Leisure and hospitality	Other services
					Total	Wholesale trade	Retail trade						
1965	54.6	121.6	55.2	122.1	59.0	. . .	. . .	55.5	43.3	29.4	26.2	41.0	29.4
1966	56.9	121.1	56.8	130.2	60.5	. . .	. . .	58.3	44.3	30.8	27.3	42.2	30.9
1967	57.2	117.0	55.4	127.8	61.1	. . .	. . .	58.6	45.7	31.9	28.4	42.9	32.4
1968	58.5	114.9	56.5	130.1	62.2	. . .	. . .	59.9	47.6	33.1	29.5	44.0	33.9
1969	60.5	118.1	61.0	131.9	64.3	. . .	. . .	61.8	50.2	34.6	30.9	45.6	35.6
1970	59.5	115.7	59.8	123.3	64.9	. . .	. . .	60.4	51.1	34.7	31.3	46.1	36.3
1971	59.1	109.9	61.0	119.3	65.1	. . .	. . .	58.7	51.9	34.7	31.4	46.9	36.5
1972	61.6	115.6	63.4	125.7	67.5	68.4	64.4	61.1	53.4	36.0	32.6	48.5	37.9
1973	64.3	117.0	66.7	132.9	69.6	71.0	66.4	64.1	55.1	37.8	34.1	50.3	39.9
1974	64.3	127.7	64.5	129.0	70.2	72.7	66.7	64.0	55.8	38.8	35.3	50.8	41.4
1975	61.3	134.9	55.2	113.9	68.9	71.8	66.4	59.1	55.9	38.9	36.2	50.9	42.6
1976	63.8	142.4	56.0	120.8	70.9	73.9	68.8	61.2	57.1	40.3	37.5	52.8	44.3
1977	66.3	151.1	59.4	125.8	73.1	76.7	70.7	63.5	59.7	42.1	39.0	54.4	46.3
1978	69.5	156.9	66.2	131.3	76.1	81.0	73.4	66.6	63.0	44.3	40.9	56.6	48.8
1979	71.8	175.2	70.6	133.3	78.3	84.6	74.7	69.0	65.8	46.3	42.7	57.9	51.2
1980	71.0	187.2	68.0	124.4	77.6	84.8	74.0	67.5	68.1	47.7	44.6	57.8	53.6
1981	71.6	206.2	64.9	123.1	78.0	86.0	74.5	67.7	69.8	49.2	46.3	58.7	55.8
1982	69.0	195.5	59.7	109.9	76.4	83.4	74.2	64.0	69.8	49.2	47.1	58.7	56.8
1983	70.0	162.8	61.0	111.6	77.2	83.3	76.0	62.1	70.9	50.7	48.8	60.4	58.9
1984	74.3	169.3	69.1	119.6	81.2	87.5	79.8	68.0	74.2	53.2	50.9	63.6	61.7
1985	76.2	162.7	73.9	117.5	83.5	89.9	82.2	69.1	77.3	55.6	53.5	66.0	65.0
1986	77.5	133.5	75.5	116.3	84.5	89.8	83.9	69.1	81.2	57.8	55.9	67.9	68.1
1987	79.7	125.2	78.1	117.8	86.5	90.5	86.3	71.5	83.7	60.3	58.5	70.5	71.5
1988	82.1	125.6	80.4	120.3	88.6	93.6	88.5	73.1	83.4	63.3	61.8	73.0	75.6
1989	84.1	123.2	81.7	120.3	90.5	95.9	90.0	74.4	83.9	66.3	65.2	74.9	79.7
1990	84.4	128.6	78.8	117.7	89.5	94.9	87.5	76.2	84.5	68.1	67.2	78.9	81.8
1991	82.6	123.8	70.1	112.8	87.4	93.3	84.8	76.1	83.3	66.7	70.2	77.3	81.1
1992	83.1	113.3	67.5	112.4	87.3	92.4	85.1	76.5	83.5	68.4	72.9	79.2	80.6
1993	85.5	110.3	71.3	113.9	89.1	92.4	86.3	78.0	85.9	71.9	75.4	82.1	82.8
1994	89.2	111.0	77.3	118.4	92.7	95.8	89.8	79.2	88.0	77.0	78.3	85.5	84.5
1995	91.6	110.3	79.9	119.0	95.1	99.2	92.3	82.5	87.8	81.2	81.2	88.5	87.0
1996	93.8	112.7	84.3	118.8	96.6	100.7	93.7	86.9	89.8	85.2	83.4	90.7	89.1
1997	97.1	117.6	88.6	121.4	98.9	103.4	95.9	90.4	92.6	91.5	86.7	93.4	91.9
1998	99.4	112.8	93.4	121.1	100.3	104.8	97.2	92.6	96.5	96.7	88.9	95.5	94.3
1999	101.5	102.9	99.7	119.0	101.9	106.2	99.5	98.5	98.0	101.7	90.6	97.8	96.2
2000	103.6	105.1	104.0	117.7	103.5	107.0	101.3	105.0	98.5	106.6	92.8	100.5	97.8
2001	102.1	108.3	103.2	108.1	101.5	102.9	100.5	106.7	99.5	104.0	96.6	100.6	99.0
2002	100.0	100.0	100.0	100.0	100.0	100.0	100.0	100.0	100.0	100.0	100.0	100.0	100.0
2003	98.7	97.4	98.4	94.5	98.6	98.0	98.9	97.0	101.5	98.7	101.4	100.0	97.4
2004	100.2	104.0	101.7	94.3	99.6	98.8	99.4	98.2	101.9	101.8	103.3	103.0	96.1
2005	102.8	114.7	108.3	93.9	101.6	101.8	100.8	99.4	104.8	106.3	106.4	106.2	96.2
2006	105.8	125.8	115.4	95.7	103.3	105.7	101.1	100.2	107.4	112.1	109.0	108.8	97.4
2007	107.3	133.5	114.7	94.4	104.8	109.2	101.8	100.1	108.7	115.2	112.5	110.8	99.3
2008	105.9	137.6	106.5	90.2	103.3	108.6	99.8	100.0	107.5	113.9	115.7	109.7	99.5
2009	98.7	117.2	85.9	76.1	96.8	99.9	94.3	93.5	103.7	105.2	117.2	105.1	96.0
2010	98.8	124.5	80.2	76.2	96.8	97.7	95.0	90.0	102.2	107.6	118.7	104.6	96.0
2011	101.2	146.3	81.2	78.3	99.5	100.4	97.5	88.3	102.6	112.4	121.3	106.6	96.5
2010													
January	98.0	115.6	80.2	75.5	95.7	97.5	93.8	91.2	102.8	105.8	118.3	104.1	95.8
February	97.6	114.7	77.5	74.6	95.7	97.4	94.2	90.7	101.8	105.8	118.1	104.0	95.2
March	98.1	118.1	79.5	75.7	96.2	97.5	94.5	90.4	102.4	106.2	118.5	104.3	95.9
April	98.5	120.1	81.9	76.2	96.5	97.7	94.6	90.4	102.8	106.7	118.5	104.0	96.0
May	98.6	124.9	79.3	76.8	96.8	97.8	94.9	90.4	103.0	107.2	118.7	104.3	96.3
June	98.7	124.7	79.5	76.2	96.5	97.3	94.9	90.1	102.5	107.4	118.8	104.0	96.1
July	98.8	126.7	78.8	76.5	97.2	97.8	95.3	89.5	102.1	108.1	118.6	104.9	96.3
August	99.2	130.1	80.1	76.5	97.2	98.0	95.4	90.1	102.7	108.3	119.2	105.2	96.2
September	99.3	128.0	81.0	76.7	97.3	98.2	95.1	89.2	102.7	108.4	119.2	105.3	96.3
October	99.4	129.5	80.9	76.5	97.4	98.3	95.7	89.6	102.6	109.3	119.9	105.1	96.8
November	99.6	130.6	80.7	76.5	97.8	98.2	95.7	89.8	102.3	109.2	119.8	105.5	96.1
December	99.7	131.2	80.3	76.8	98.2	98.6	96.1	89.2	102.6	110.4	119.5	105.3	96.2
2011													
January	99.5	135.5	78.0	76.8	98.1	99.0	96.4	89.4	102.5	110.5	119.5	104.8	96.2
February	100.4	134.5	80.6	77.6	98.6	99.5	96.5	89.4	102.5	110.8	120.1	105.6	96.6
March	100.6	138.2	80.4	78.1	99.0	100.1	96.5	89.0	102.3	111.2	120.2	106.6	96.5
April	101.2	143.1	80.8	78.2	99.7	100.2	97.7	89.4	102.3	112.0	120.9	106.4	96.5
May	101.0	144.3	81.3	78.4	99.4	100.7	97.0	89.2	102.7	112.1	121.0	106.4	96.5
June	101.4	148.2	80.9	78.2	99.6	100.8	97.5	88.8	102.5	112.6	121.1	106.7	96.8
July	101.5	147.2	81.5	78.5	99.7	100.5	97.9	88.9	102.7	112.6	121.8	106.7	96.2
August	101.3	147.9	81.0	78.3	99.8	100.4	97.6	85.9	102.5	112.6	121.6	106.4	96.3
September	101.5	150.4	81.6	78.3	99.9	100.8	97.8	87.6	103.0	113.2	122.4	106.6	96.7
October	102.0	154.7	81.0	78.8	100.3	101.3	98.6	87.9	103.2	113.8	122.6	107.2	97.0
November	102.2	153.4	81.1	78.8	100.6	101.4	98.8	87.8	103.0	113.8	122.8	107.7	96.6
December	102.4	157.1	82.3	79.2	100.7	102.0	98.9	87.4	103.3	114.2	122.7	108.3	97.0

. . . = Not available.

Table 10-17. Average Hourly Earnings of Production and Nonsupervisory Workers on Private Nonfarm Payrolls by NAICS Supersector

(Dollars, seasonally adjusted.)

| Year and month | Total private | Mining and logging | Construc-tion | Manu-facturing | Trade, transportation, and utilities | | | Information | Financial activities | Profes-sional and business services | Education and health services | Leisure and hospitality | Other services |
					Total	Wholesale trade	Retail trade						
1965	2.63	2.87	3.23	2.49	2.94	. . .	. . .	4.47	2.38	3.28	2.12	1.17	1.25
1966	2.73	3.00	3.41	2.60	3.04	. . .	. . .	4.56	2.47	3.39	2.23	1.26	1.37
1967	2.85	3.14	3.63	2.71	3.15	. . .	. . .	4.68	2.58	3.51	2.36	1.37	1.49
1968	3.02	3.30	3.92	2.89	3.32	. . .	. . .	4.85	2.75	3.65	2.49	1.53	1.62
1969	3.22	3.54	4.30	3.07	3.48	. . .	. . .	5.05	2.92	3.84	2.68	1.69	1.81
1970	3.40	3.77	4.74	3.24	3.65	. . .	. . .	5.25	3.07	4.04	2.88	1.82	2.01
1971	3.63	3.99	5.17	3.45	3.86	. . .	. . .	5.53	3.23	4.26	3.11	1.95	2.24
1972	3.90	4.28	5.55	3.70	4.23	4.58	3.52	5.87	3.37	4.50	3.33	2.08	2.46
1973	4.14	4.59	5.89	3.97	4.46	4.80	3.69	6.17	3.55	4.72	3.54	2.20	2.67
1974	4.43	5.09	6.29	4.31	4.74	5.11	3.92	6.52	3.80	5.01	3.82	2.40	2.95
1975	4.73	5.68	6.78	4.71	5.01	5.45	4.14	6.92	4.08	5.29	4.09	2.58	3.21
1976	5.06	6.19	7.17	5.10	5.31	5.75	4.36	7.37	4.30	5.60	4.39	2.78	3.51
1977	5.44	6.70	7.56	5.55	5.67	6.12	4.65	7.84	4.58	5.95	4.72	3.03	3.84
1978	5.88	7.44	8.11	6.05	6.11	6.61	5.00	8.34	4.93	6.32	5.07	3.33	4.19
1979	6.34	8.20	8.71	6.57	6.56	7.12	5.34	8.86	5.31	6.71	5.44	3.63	4.56
1980	6.85	8.97	9.37	7.15	7.04	7.68	5.71	9.47	5.82	7.22	5.93	3.98	5.05
1981	7.44	9.89	10.24	7.87	7.55	8.28	6.09	10.21	6.34	7.80	6.49	4.36	5.61
1982	7.87	10.64	11.04	8.36	7.91	8.81	6.34	10.76	6.82	8.30	7.00	4.63	6.11
1983	8.20	11.14	11.36	8.70	8.23	9.27	6.60	11.18	7.32	8.70	7.39	4.89	6.51
1984	8.49	11.54	11.56	9.05	8.45	9.61	6.73	11.50	7.65	8.98	7.67	4.99	6.79
1985	8.74	11.87	11.75	9.40	8.60	9.88	6.83	11.81	7.97	9.28	7.98	5.10	7.10
1986	8.93	12.14	11.92	9.60	8.74	10.07	6.93	12.08	8.37	9.55	8.25	5.20	7.38
1987	9.14	12.17	12.15	9.77	8.92	10.32	7.02	12.36	8.73	9.85	8.57	5.30	7.69
1988	9.44	12.45	12.52	10.05	9.15	10.71	7.23	12.63	9.07	10.22	8.96	5.50	8.08
1989	9.80	12.90	12.98	10.35	9.46	11.12	7.46	12.99	9.54	10.69	9.46	5.76	8.58
1990	10.20	13.40	13.42	10.78	9.83	11.58	7.71	13.40	9.99	11.14	10.00	6.02	9.08
1991	10.52	13.82	13.65	11.13	10.08	11.95	7.89	13.90	10.42	11.50	10.49	6.22	9.39
1992	10.77	14.09	13.81	11.40	10.30	12.21	8.12	14.29	10.86	11.78	10.87	6.36	9.66
1993	11.05	14.12	14.04	11.70	10.55	12.57	8.36	14.86	11.36	11.96	11.21	6.48	9.90
1994	11.34	14.41	14.38	12.04	10.80	12.93	8.61	15.32	11.82	12.15	11.50	6.62	10.18
1995	11.65	14.78	14.73	12.34	11.10	13.34	8.85	15.68	12.28	12.53	11.80	6.79	10.51
1996	12.04	15.09	15.11	12.75	11.46	13.80	9.21	16.30	12.71	13.00	12.17	6.99	10.85
1997	12.51	15.57	15.67	13.14	11.90	14.41	9.59	17.14	13.22	13.57	12.56	7.32	11.29
1998	13.01	16.20	16.23	13.45	12.40	15.07	10.05	17.67	13.93	14.27	13.00	7.67	11.79
1999	13.49	16.33	16.80	13.85	12.82	15.62	10.45	18.40	14.47	14.85	13.44	7.96	12.26
2000	14.02	16.55	17.48	14.32	13.31	16.28	10.87	19.07	14.98	15.52	13.95	8.32	12.73
2001	14.54	17.00	18.00	14.76	13.70	16.77	11.29	19.80	15.59	16.33	14.64	8.57	13.27
2002	14.97	17.19	18.52	15.29	14.02	16.98	11.67	20.20	16.17	16.80	15.21	8.81	13.72
2003	15.37	17.56	18.95	15.74	14.34	17.36	11.90	21.01	17.14	17.21	15.64	9.00	13.84
2004	15.69	18.07	19.23	16.14	14.58	17.65	12.08	21.40	17.52	17.48	16.15	9.15	13.98
2005	16.13	18.72	19.46	16.56	14.92	18.16	12.36	22.06	17.94	18.08	16.71	9.38	14.34
2006	16.76	19.90	20.02	16.81	15.39	18.91	12.57	23.23	18.80	19.13	17.38	9.75	14.77
2007	17.43	20.97	20.95	17.26	15.78	19.59	12.75	23.96	19.64	20.15	18.11	10.41	15.42
2008	18.08	22.50	21.87	17.75	16.16	20.13	12.87	24.78	20.28	21.18	18.87	10.84	16.09
2009	18.63	23.29	22.66	18.24	16.48	20.84	13.01	25.45	20.85	22.35	19.49	11.12	16.59
2010	19.07	23.82	23.22	18.61	16.82	21.54	13.24	25.87	21.52	22.78	20.12	11.31	17.06
2011	19.47	24.51	23.64	18.94	17.15	21.97	13.51	26.61	21.91	23.12	20.78	11.45	17.32
2010													
January	18.91	23.36	23.01	18.43	16.74	21.41	13.16	25.59	21.41	22.64	19.79	11.32	16.90
February	18.93	23.69	23.11	18.45	16.75	21.37	13.19	25.63	21.34	22.67	19.86	11.31	16.97
March	18.95	23.84	23.14	18.48	16.72	21.40	13.16	25.61	21.40	22.66	19.93	11.32	17.00
April	18.99	23.93	23.05	18.50	16.76	21.44	13.19	25.58	21.44	22.69	20.01	11.32	17.00
May	19.02	23.78	23.10	18.57	16.79	21.46	13.21	25.74	21.45	22.77	20.04	11.32	17.04
June	19.05	23.87	23.17	18.60	16.80	21.50	13.23	25.81	21.51	22.77	20.08	11.33	17.13
July	19.08	23.89	23.23	18.63	16.80	21.52	13.23	26.12	21.58	22.83	20.13	11.31	17.06
August	19.12	23.88	23.25	18.66	16.83	21.54	13.26	25.97	21.61	22.91	20.18	11.35	17.07
September	19.15	24.15	23.21	18.73	16.90	21.65	13.31	26.05	21.50	22.93	20.24	11.29	17.11
October	19.24	23.86	23.38	18.73	16.98	21.82	13.37	26.24	21.70	22.99	20.34	11.32	17.15
November	19.23	23.99	23.42	18.76	16.97	21.76	13.37	26.19	21.73	22.95	20.36	11.30	17.19
December	19.23	24.00	23.42	18.80	16.97	21.82	13.36	26.15	21.70	22.84	20.42	11.32	17.21
2011													
January	19.33	24.09	23.49	18.88	17.05	21.92	13.40	26.35	21.79	23.03	20.50	11.33	17.23
February	19.33	24.22	23.52	18.88	17.06	21.90	13.41	26.40	21.69	23.02	20.53	11.37	17.22
March	19.34	24.39	23.51	18.90	17.06	21.86	13.42	26.50	21.77	23.01	20.56	11.40	17.22
April	19.39	24.04	23.57	18.90	17.10	21.93	13.46	26.72	21.86	23.08	20.59	11.42	17.27
May	19.43	24.46	23.57	18.92	17.12	21.98	13.43	26.61	21.80	23.10	20.71	11.49	17.28
June	19.45	24.43	23.58	18.92	17.14	22.00	13.46	26.42	21.76	23.17	20.76	11.47	17.34
July	19.52	24.62	23.65	18.95	17.22	22.14	13.54	26.55	21.87	23.24	20.86	11.49	17.36
August	19.50	24.61	23.78	18.93	17.18	22.02	13.49	26.58	21.83	23.14	20.92	11.48	17.36
September	19.53	24.66	23.76	18.94	17.21	22.02	13.51	26.71	21.95	23.11	20.94	11.48	17.38
October	19.57	24.85	23.72	19.00	17.25	22.07	13.59	26.83	21.99	23.15	20.99	11.50	17.41
November	19.58	24.87	23.68	18.98	17.26	22.00	13.69	26.76	22.20	23.21	20.98	11.48	17.39
December	19.59	24.89	23.75	19.02	17.25	21.97	13.67	26.80	22.26	23.12	21.01	11.53	17.42

. . . = Not available.

Table 10-18. Average Weekly Earnings of Production and Nonsupervisory Workers on Private Nonfarm Payrolls by NAICS Supersector

(Dollars, seasonally adjusted.)

Year and month	Total private	Mining and logging	Construc-tion	Manu-facturing	Trade, transportation, and utilities			Information	Financial activities	Profes-sional and business services	Education and health services	Leisure and hospitality	Other services
					Total	Wholesale trade	Retail trade						
1965	101.51	125.48	122.35	102.69	116.36	. . .	. . .	171.24	88.50	122.30	74.84	38.06	45.30
1966	105.23	132.50	130.11	107.47	118.78	. . .	. . .	174.52	91.83	125.53	78.04	40.34	48.94
1967	108.07	137.76	138.55	109.85	121.57	. . .	. . .	176.09	95.35	128.34	81.34	43.06	52.69
1968	113.82	145.26	148.22	117.73	126.69	. . .	. . .	182.65	101.18	132.47	85.02	47.07	56.81
1969	120.70	157.11	164.88	124.74	132.13	. . .	. . .	190.18	107.91	139.37	91.46	51.29	63.44
1970	125.79	165.82	179.11	128.84	137.15	. . .	. . .	195.24	112.32	144.76	97.23	54.57	69.67
1971	133.22	174.18	194.70	137.59	144.11	. . .	. . .	204.50	117.60	151.51	103.57	58.39	76.58
1972	143.87	188.76	205.04	150.23	158.09	181.98	123.57	218.72	122.86	159.88	111.12	61.78	84.14
1973	152.59	201.43	219.32	161.59	165.61	190.33	128.16	230.48	129.32	167.40	117.85	64.92	91.06
1974	161.61	222.24	233.24	172.37	174.18	200.53	134.39	241.07	137.71	176.47	126.50	69.90	99.98
1975	170.29	248.38	249.70	185.69	182.61	212.85	140.99	253.21	147.75	185.81	134.83	74.49	108.67
1976	182.65	273.69	267.00	204.41	192.62	224.66	147.21	270.80	155.54	195.61	143.47	79.47	117.85
1977	195.58	299.46	279.61	224.01	203.87	239.57	154.51	288.29	165.47	206.78	153.38	85.20	128.12
1978	210.29	334.27	302.27	244.49	217.53	258.75	163.74	306.71	177.96	218.42	163.48	92.16	138.74
1979	225.69	366.58	326.55	263.99	232.36	278.74	173.18	324.51	190.72	231.16	174.80	99.47	150.47
1980	241.07	402.51	351.49	283.35	246.60	298.24	182.25	344.38	209.21	247.64	190.16	107.52	166.32
1981	261.53	446.10	382.75	312.74	263.93	322.08	193.97	370.36	228.21	267.46	208.06	117.49	184.77
1982	273.10	469.10	410.39	325.07	274.09	340.84	200.74	385.82	245.16	284.11	224.53	124.14	201.49
1983	286.43	488.89	427.00	348.89	284.76	359.98	208.81	404.89	262.83	298.74	237.50	130.82	214.87
1984	298.26	514.77	441.28	367.77	292.99	373.78	212.82	420.45	276.50	308.24	245.48	133.49	223.33
1985	304.62	529.62	448.35	380.60	295.81	383.22	213.38	430.86	287.66	317.41	254.50	134.71	232.81
1986	309.78	529.20	451.22	390.46	298.07	389.73	214.52	439.84	302.32	327.30	263.73	136.34	242.33
1987	317.39	529.72	463.78	400.00	304.10	397.39	218.05	450.77	314.01	337.57	273.81	139.45	252.58
1988	326.48	539.63	478.74	412.62	309.58	411.71	223.67	455.59	322.87	349.89	286.89	144.51	265.83
1989	338.34	568.55	497.43	423.58	319.40	427.40	229.14	468.77	339.46	365.93	303.02	150.29	282.09
1990	349.72	602.43	513.43	436.13	331.55	444.48	235.56	479.50	354.66	380.61	319.27	156.32	297.88
1991	358.60	625.46	520.41	449.83	339.19	459.17	240.13	495.14	369.54	391.06	334.55	159.20	306.75
1992	368.25	628.94	525.13	464.43	348.60	470.41	249.66	511.95	386.01	400.64	348.29	163.70	315.08
1993	378.91	634.77	539.81	480.93	359.51	484.46	256.89	535.19	403.02	406.20	359.08	167.54	322.69
1994	391.22	653.13	558.53	502.08	370.38	501.14	265.74	551.21	419.20	414.16	368.14	172.27	332.44
1995	400.07	670.40	571.57	509.23	378.79	515.14	272.63	564.92	436.12	426.57	377.73	175.74	342.36
1996	413.28	695.04	588.48	526.59	390.67	533.36	282.76	592.45	451.49	442.81	388.30	181.02	352.68
1997	431.86	720.07	609.48	548.22	407.66	559.39	295.94	622.37	472.37	465.51	404.65	190.66	368.63
1998	448.56	727.19	629.75	557.20	423.33	582.21	310.25	646.52	500.98	490.10	418.82	200.82	384.25
1999	463.15	721.77	655.11	573.14	434.42	602.77	321.69	675.47	517.57	510.99	431.35	208.05	398.77
2000	481.13	734.88	685.78	590.77	449.96	631.24	333.41	700.92	537.37	535.07	449.29	217.20	413.30
2001	493.79	757.96	695.86	595.15	459.53	643.45	346.07	731.18	558.05	557.84	473.39	220.73	428.64
2002	506.75	741.97	711.82	618.62	471.27	644.38	360.87	737.94	575.54	574.60	492.74	227.31	439.87
2003	518.06	765.94	727.00	635.99	481.14	657.29	367.15	760.84	609.08	587.02	505.69	230.49	434.41
2004	529.09	804.01	735.55	658.52	488.51	666.79	371.03	776.72	622.87	597.39	523.78	234.86	433.04
2005	544.33	853.87	750.37	673.34	498.43	685.00	377.58	805.11	645.10	618.66	544.59	241.36	443.40
2006	567.87	907.95	781.59	691.05	514.37	718.50	383.12	850.64	672.21	662.27	564.94	250.34	456.50
2007	590.04	962.63	816.23	711.53	525.91	748.94	385.00	874.45	705.13	700.64	590.09	265.54	477.06
2008	607.95	1 014.69	842.61	724.46	536.11	769.62	386.21	908.78	727.07	737.70	613.79	273.39	495.57
2009	617.18	1 006.67	851.76	726.12	541.88	784.49	388.57	931.08	752.03	775.81	628.45	275.95	506.26
2010	636.92	1 063.11	891.83	765.15	559.63	816.50	400.02	939.85	778.43	798.54	646.65	280.87	523.70
2011	654.87	1 144.04	921.66	784.68	577.84	845.36	412.10	963.99	797.76	813.71	670.83	283.77	532.48
2010													
January	629.70	1 034.85	869.78	753.79	552.42	807.16	394.80	936.59	775.04	792.40	639.22	281.87	518.83
February	628.48	1 032.88	857.38	745.38	552.75	805.65	397.02	932.93	766.11	791.18	639.49	281.62	519.28
March	631.04	1 053.73	874.69	757.68	553.43	808.92	396.12	934.77	774.68	793.10	641.75	281.87	521.90
April	634.27	1 064.89	894.34	762.20	556.43	812.58	397.02	931.11	778.27	794.15	644.32	280.74	521.90
May	635.27	1 074.86	877.80	768.80	559.11	815.48	398.94	939.51	780.78	799.23	645.29	280.74	524.83
June	636.27	1 066.99	885.09	762.60	557.76	812.70	399.55	942.07	780.81	796.95	646.58	279.85	527.60
July	637.27	1 070.27	885.06	765.69	561.12	817.76	400.87	945.54	781.20	803.62	646.17	281.62	525.45
August	640.52	1 088.93	895.13	768.79	562.12	820.67	401.78	945.31	786.60	806.43	649.80	282.62	525.76
September	641.53	1 079.51	905.19	773.55	564.46	827.03	401.96	940.41	782.60	807.14	651.73	279.99	526.99
October	644.54	1 059.38	907.14	771.68	567.13	833.52	405.11	952.51	789.88	811.55	656.98	280.74	528.22
November	644.21	1 072.35	906.35	772.91	568.50	829.06	405.11	953.32	788.80	805.55	655.59	281.37	526.01
December	644.21	1 077.60	906.35	776.44	570.19	833.52	406.14	946.63	789.88	806.25	655.48	280.74	528.35
2011													
January	645.62	1 110.55	885.57	775.97	571.18	839.54	407.36	959.14	793.16	810.66	658.05	279.85	528.96
February	649.49	1 106.85	910.22	781.63	573.22	840.96	407.66	960.96	789.52	810.30	661.07	281.98	530.38
March	649.82	1 117.06	907.49	784.35	574.92	841.61	407.97	961.95	790.25	807.65	662.03	283.86	530.38
April	653.44	1 120.26	914.52	782.46	577.98	844.31	411.88	975.28	793.52	814.72	665.06	283.22	531.92
May	652.85	1 137.39	921.59	785.18	576.94	848.43	408.27	968.60	793.52	813.12	668.93	284.95	532.22
June	655.47	1 153.10	917.26	783.29	577.62	849.20	410.53	959.05	792.06	817.90	670.55	284.46	535.81
July	657.82	1 142.37	924.72	784.53	580.31	852.39	414.32	966.42	798.26	818.05	675.86	284.95	532.95
August	655.20	1 139.44	927.42	781.81	578.97	845.57	411.45	956.88	794.61	812.21	675.72	283.56	532.95
September	656.21	1 151.62	926.64	782.22	579.98	849.97	412.06	964.23	803.37	813.47	678.46	283.56	535.30
October	659.51	1 180.38	920.34	788.50	583.05	854.11	417.21	973.93	804.83	817.20	680.08	285.20	537.97
November	659.85	1 168.89	921.15	787.67	583.39	849.20	420.28	968.71	810.30	816.99	679.75	284.70	533.87
December	660.18	1 184.76	931.00	791.23	583.05	850.24	419.67	964.80	814.72	813.82	678.62	287.10	536.54

. . . = Not available.

Section 10c: Other Significant Labor Market Data

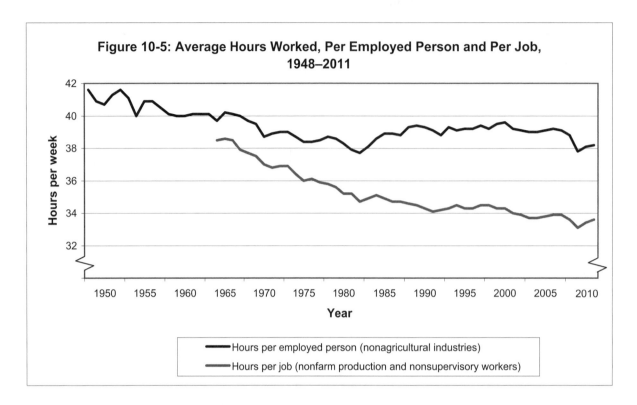

Figure 10-5: Average Hours Worked, Per Employed Person and Per Job, 1948–2011

Legend:
— Hours per employed person (nonagricultural industries)
— Hours per job (nonfarm production and nonsupervisory workers)

- This section of *Business Statistics* includes indicators of hours and earnings from the Current Population Statistics (household) survey that are, for some purposes, more appropriate than similarly-named indicators produced by the payroll survey and shown in the previous section. It also includes annual employment data from the Bureau of Economic Analysis, produced as part of the National Income and Product Accounts (NIPAS), that provide a consistent historical record of U.S. employment going back to 1929.

- Figure 10-5 above shows annual averages of hours worked per week reported by all persons in the household survey employed in nonagricultural industries. (Table 10-19 reports average workweeks for several worker groups; this one was chosen for the graph because it has the longest history.) Along with the recession dips expected in any measure of the average workweek, it displays a clear downward trend through the early 1970s, but no trend since then. The recession low in 2009 is actually higher than the recession low in 1982. The 2000 peak is equal to the 1969 level. (Table 10-19)

- For comparison, average weekly hours for nonfarm production and nonsupervisory workers are also graphed in Figure 10-5. These are the workweeks reported by employers in the Current Employment Statistics (payroll) survey and they pertain to jobs, not to workers. (Table 10-15) This CES measure of "hours per job" represents roughly the same workers as those in the "hours per employed person" measure shown in the graph, and was selected for the graph because it has the longest available history. But it is increasingly pulled downward by the increasing prevalence of part-time work. It is not a good indicator of either the level or the trend of the amount of work being done each week by the typical American worker. (Table 10-19)

- A look at some of the other categories in Table 10-19 confirms the absence of any downtrend in the workers' workweek in recent years. Note, for example, that men reported working an average of 41.7 hours in both 2007 and 1976, and women actually reported working longer—36.1 hours in 2007—against 34.1 hours in 1976. (Table 10-19)

Table 10-19. Hours at Work, Current Population Survey

(Hours per week.)

| Year and month | Hours per person, all industries | | | | Hours per person, nonagricultural industries | | | Memorandum: average weekly hours per job, total private nonfarm, from CES survey | |
| | Total | Men | Women | Persons who usually work full-time | All workers | | Wage and salary workers | All employees | Production and nonsupervisory workers |
					Total	Usually work full-time			
1948	42.8	...	...	...	41.6	...	...	...	...
1949	42.1	...	...	...	40.9	...	...	...	...
1950	41.7	...	...	...	40.7	...	...	...	...
1951	42.2	...	...	...	41.3	...	...	...	...
1952	42.4	...	...	...	41.6	...	...	...	...
1953	41.9	...	...	...	41.1	...	...	...	...
1954	40.9	...	...	...	40.0	...	...	...	...
1955	41.6	...	...	...	40.9	...	...	...	...
1956	41.5	43.8	36.5	...	40.9	...	...	...	...
1957	41.0	43.4	36.1	...	40.5	...	...	...	...
1958	40.6	42.9	35.8	...	40.1	...	...	...	...
1959	40.5	42.8	35.6	...	40.0	...	...	...	...
1960	40.5	43.0	35.4	...	40.0	...	...	...	...
1961	40.5	43.0	35.3	...	40.1	...	...	...	...
1962	40.5	43.2	35.2	...	40.1	...	...	...	...
1963	40.4	43.2	35.1	...	40.1	...	...	...	...
1964	40.0	42.8	34.7	...	39.7	...	...	...	38.5
1965	40.5	43.3	35.1	...	40.2	...	...	...	38.6
1966	40.4	43.2	35.2	...	40.1	...	...	...	38.5
1967	40.4	43.3	35.2	...	40.0	...	...	...	37.9
1968	40.1	43.0	34.9	...	39.7	...	...	...	37.7
1969	39.9	42.9	34.9	...	39.5	...	...	...	37.5
1970	39.1	42.0	34.2	...	38.7	...	...	...	37.0
1971	39.3	42.2	34.3	...	38.9	...	...	...	36.8
1972	39.4	42.3	34.5	...	39.0	...	...	...	36.9
1973	39.3	42.4	34.4	...	39.0	...	...	...	36.9
1974	39.0	42.0	34.3	...	38.7	...	...	...	36.4
1975	38.7	41.6	34.1	...	38.4	...	...	...	36.0
1976	38.7	41.7	34.1	...	38.4	...	38.1	...	36.1
1977	38.8	41.9	34.2	...	38.5	...	38.3	...	35.9
1978	39.0	42.1	34.5	...	38.7	...	38.4	...	35.8
1979	38.9	42.0	34.5	...	38.6	...	38.4	...	35.6
1980	38.5	41.5	34.5	...	38.3	...	38.1	...	35.2
1981	38.1	41.1	34.1	...	37.9	...	37.7	...	35.2
1982	38.0	40.9	34.1	...	37.7	...	37.6	...	34.7
1983	38.3	41.2	34.5	...	38.1	...	37.9	...	34.9
1984	38.8	41.8	34.9	...	38.6	...	38.4	...	35.1
1985	39.0	42.0	35.2	...	38.9	...	38.7	...	34.9
1986	39.1	42.1	35.4	...	38.9	...	38.8	...	34.7
1987	39.0	42.0	35.3	...	38.8	...	38.7	...	34.7
1988	39.4	42.4	35.7	...	39.3	...	39.1	...	34.6
1989	39.6	42.6	35.8	...	39.4	...	39.3	...	34.5
1990	39.4	42.3	35.8	...	39.3	...	39.2	...	34.3
1991	39.2	42.0	35.8	...	39.1	...	39.0	...	34.1
1992	38.9	41.7	35.6	...	38.8	...	38.7	...	34.2
1993	39.4	42.2	36.0	...	39.3	...	39.2	...	34.3
1994	39.2	42.2	35.5	43.4	39.1	43.3	39.1	...	34.5
1995	39.3	42.3	35.6	43.4	39.2	43.2	39.2	...	34.3
1996	39.3	42.3	35.7	43.3	39.2	43.2	39.2	...	34.3
1997	39.5	42.4	36.0	43.4	39.4	43.3	39.4	...	34.5
1998	39.3	42.2	35.8	43.2	39.2	43.1	39.2	...	34.5
1999	39.6	42.4	36.2	43.4	39.5	43.3	39.5	...	34.3
2000	39.7	42.5	36.4	43.4	39.6	43.3	39.6	...	34.3
2001	39.2	41.9	36.1	42.9	39.2	42.8	39.2	...	34.0
2002	39.2	41.8	36.0	42.9	39.1	42.8	39.1	...	33.9
2003	39.0	41.7	35.9	42.9	39.0	42.7	39.0	...	33.7
2004	39.0	41.7	35.9	42.9	39.0	42.8	39.0	...	33.7
2005	39.2	41.8	36.1	42.9	39.1	42.8	39.1	...	33.8
2006	39.2	41.8	36.2	42.9	39.2	42.8	39.2	...	33.9
2007	39.2	41.7	36.1	42.8	39.1	42.7	39.2	34.6	33.9
2008	38.9	41.3	36.1	42.6	38.8	42.5	39.0	34.5	33.6
2009	37.9	40.2	35.3	41.9	37.8	41.8	38.0	33.9	33.1
2010	38.2	40.5	35.5	42.2	38.1	42.2	38.3	34.1	33.4
2011	38.3	40.6	35.6	42.4	38.2	42.3	38.4	34.4	33.6

. . . = Not available.

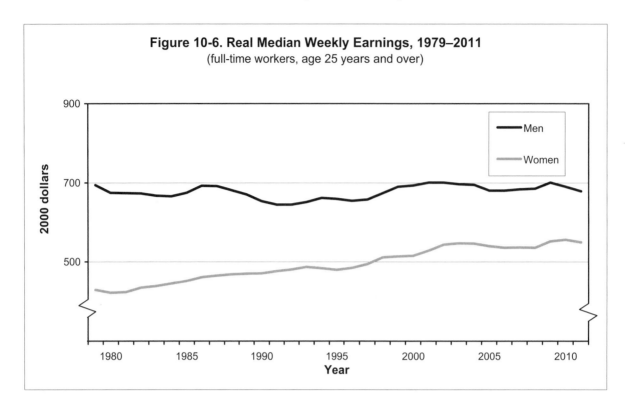

Figure 10-6. Real Median Weekly Earnings, 1979–2011
(full-time workers, age 25 years and over)

- "Median usual weekly earnings of full-time wage and salary workers," as shown in Table 10-20, are derived quarterly from the Current Population Survey, not from the payroll survey that provides the weekly earnings shown in Tables 10-9, 10-13, and 10-18. That is, they are collected from individual households in the CPS sample, providing better approximations of the paychecks of typical bread-winners than the payroll data on average weekly earnings (AWE). (See the Notes and Definitions to this chapter.)

- Focusing on workers 25 and over, women's earnings were moving closer to men's over most of the period covered in this survey, rising from 61.8 percent in 1979 to a new high of 81.0 percent in 2011. (Table 10-20)

- As Figure 10-6 shows, typical workers age 25 and over of both sexes lost ground in real terms in many recent years. The median man's real earnings in 2011 were below those in 2000, and the median woman's only up at a 0.6 percent annual rate since then. (Table 10-20) In contrast, business produc-tivity growth over that 11-year period was 2.3 percent per year. (Table 9-3A)

- Taking a longer look at the entire period shown here, men's real earnings have been essentially stag-nant for the entire 32 years, while women's have increased 0.8 percent per year. For both sexes these earnings fall short of what might have been expected from the 2.0 percent rate of increase in produc-tivity over those 32 years. See the article at the front of this volume, "Business Cycle Perspectives", for analysis of the gap between productivity and real wage growth. (Tables 10-20 and 9-3A)

Table 10-20. Median Usual Weekly Earnings of Full-Time Wage and Salary Workers

(Current dollars, except as noted; not seasonally adjusted.)

| Year and quarter | Total, 16 years and over | Men, 16 years and over | | | | Women, 16 years and over | | | | White | Black or African American | Asian | Hispanic or Latino ethnicity |
| | | Total | 16 to 24 years | 25 years and over | | Total | 16 to 24 years | 25 years and over | | | | | |
				Current dollars	2000 dollars [1]			Current dollars	2000 dollars [1]				
1979	240	291	196	314	694	182	154	194	429	247	198	. . .	. . .
1980	262	313	208	339	675	200	167	212	422	268	212	. . .	. . .
1981	283	339	218	371	674	218	180	233	423	290	234	. . .	. . .
1982	302	364	224	393	673	238	191	254	435	309	245	. . .	. . .
1983	313	378	223	406	667	252	197	267	439	319	261	. . .	. . .
1984	326	391	231	422	666	264	203	282	445	336	269	. . .	. . .
1985	344	406	240	442	675	277	210	296	452	355	277	. . .	. . .
1986	358	419	245	462	693	290	218	308	462	370	291	. . .	277
1987	373	434	257	477	692	303	226	321	465	383	301	. . .	284
1988	385	449	261	487	681	315	235	335	469	394	314	. . .	290
1989	400	469	271	500	670	329	246	351	471	409	319	. . .	298
1990	412	481	282	512	654	346	254	369	471	424	329	. . .	304
1991	427	493	285	523	645	366	266	387	477	442	348	. . .	312
1992	440	501	284	536	645	380	267	400	481	458	357	. . .	322
1993	458	510	288	555	651	394	273	415	487	475	369	. . .	331
1994	467	523	294	576	662	399	276	421	484	484	371	. . .	324
1995	479	538	303	588	660	406	275	428	480	494	383	. . .	329
1996	490	557	307	599	655	418	284	444	485	506	387	. . .	339
1997	503	578	317	615	658	431	292	462	494	519	400	. . .	351
1998	524	598	334	639	674	457	305	485	512	545	426	. . .	370
1999	549	619	356	668	690	473	324	497	514	573	445	. . .	385
2000	576	641	375	693	693	493	344	516	516	590	474	615	399
2001	596	670	391	720	700	512	353	543	528	610	491	639	417
2002	608	679	391	732	701	529	367	568	544	623	498	658	424
2003	620	695	398	744	697	552	371	584	547	636	514	693	440
2004	638	713	400	762	695	573	375	599	546	657	525	708	456
2005	651	722	409	771	680	585	381	612	540	672	520	753	471
2006	671	743	418	797	681	600	395	627	536	690	554	784	486
2007	695	766	443	823	684	614	409	646	537	716	569	830	503
2008	722	798	461	857	685	638	420	670	536	742	589	861	529
2009	739	819	458	873	701	657	424	687	552	757	601	880	541
2010	747	824	443	874	690	669	422	704	556	765	611	855	535
2011	756	832	455	886	678	684	421	718	550	775	615	866	549
2004													
1st quarter	634	711	410	757	700	567	387	592	547	652	521	712	450
2nd quarter	639	714	397	763	696	572	370	601	548	655	536	720	451
3rd quarter	632	704	400	759	689	571	371	602	547	651	531	701	458
4th quarter	647	722	396	768	693	578	371	603	544	671	519	698	467
2005													
1st quarter	653	729	401	775	696	586	380	610	547	677	513	738	470
2nd quarter	643	713	407	762	675	580	374	608	538	663	518	743	473
3rd quarter	649	716	407	768	672	585	379	615	538	667	520	761	462
4th quarter	659	731	418	778	677	588	389	614	534	682	533	767	479
2006													
1st quarter	668	744	417	793	686	600	388	624	540	688	560	766	487
2nd quarter	659	731	421	783	667	593	395	619	527	678	534	765	485
3rd quarter	675	749	409	808	684	599	393	629	532	692	555	798	485
4th quarter	682	749	429	800	683	609	403	638	545	702	569	809	489
2007													
1st quarter	693	759	451	811	686	615	414	646	546	714	561	798	502
2nd quarter	690	763	436	819	679	607	404	635	527	713	562	827	503
3rd quarter	695	767	430	831	687	616	398	654	541	713	578	842	502
4th quarter	700	774	459	831	682	618	421	649	533	722	574	856	507
2008													
1st quarter	719	790	466	848	688	637	419	666	541	742	582	842	520
2nd quarter	719	800	469	862	685	634	415	668	531	738	591	855	537
3rd quarter	720	796	446	857	673	631	406	666	523	739	589	854	529
4th quarter	728	807	462	859	694	650	449	679	549	748	593	889	535
2009													
1st quarter	738	823	461	879	714	649	448	679	552	758	577	869	545
2nd quarter	734	815	450	872	701	652	413	679	546	754	592	909	547
3rd quarter	738	812	448	870	695	657	415	691	552	753	607	877	527
4th quarter	748	825	476	871	694	670	436	700	558	763	629	877	547
2010													
1st quarter	754	844	473	887	704	665	422	698	554	772	610	859	554
2nd quarter	740	810	442	861	680	672	417	704	556	756	607	873	529
3rd quarter	740	813	424	869	686	662	419	702	554	759	611	854	522
4th quarter	752	830	449	878	691	679	436	709	558	772	614	828	539
2011													
1st quarter	755	829	470	880	684	683	426	716	556	774	604	831	549
2nd quarter	753	825	446	884	675	689	417	720	550	770	623	872	565
3rd quarter	753	827	440	888	675	673	422	713	542	772	616	869	545
4th quarter	764	843	466	893	680	688	420	724	551	786	621	880	537

[1]Converted to 2000 dollars by the editor using CPI-U-RS. See notes and definitions.
. . . = Not available.

Table 10-21. Employment by SIC Industry, Historical Annual

(Full-time and part-time employees, thousands.)

NIPA Table 6.4A, B, and C

Year	Total employment	Total domestic	Domestic industries / Private industries / Total private industries	Agriculture, forestry, and fisheries	Mining	Construction	Manufacturing / Total manufacturing	Durable goods	Nondurable goods	Transportation and public utilities	Wholesale trade	Retail trade	Finance, insurance, and real estate	Services
1942 SIC														
1929	37 699	37 699	34 088	3 556	993	1 484	10 428	5 238	5 190	3 989	1 757	4 684	1 520	5 677
1930	35 590	35 590	31 811	3 337	932	1 366	9 309	4 457	4 852	3 742	1 693	4 469	1 491	5 472
1931	32 724	32 723	28 590	3 252	813	1 198	7 895	3 497	4 398	3 282	1 530	4 148	1 423	5 049
1932	29 445	29 444	25 071	3 028	672	907	6 678	2 724	3 954	2 826	1 380	3 688	1 358	4 534
1933	30 940	30 939	25 038	2 995	693	703	7 204	2 893	4 311	2 684	1 377	3 699	1 309	4 374
1934	34 238	34 237	27 417	2 986	822	806	8 364	3 587	4 777	2 774	1 492	4 075	1 332	4 766
1935	35 577	35 576	28 426	3 013	840	866	8 904	3 941	4 963	2 808	1 507	4 200	1 352	4 936
1936	38 599	38 598	30 548	3 106	897	1 104	9 645	4 460	5 185	2 973	1 612	4 543	1 401	5 267
1937	39 701	39 700	32 508	3 083	955	1 082	10 591	5 130	5 461	3 140	1 770	4 904	1 445	5 538
1938	38 322	38 321	30 124	2 949	859	1 055	9 131	4 085	5 046	2 837	1 767	4 780	1 436	5 310
1939	39 633	39 632	31 612	2 859	832	1 219	9 967	4 609	5 358	2 943	1 833	4 992	1 470	5 497
1940	41 437	41 435	33 518	2 809	927	1 285	10 882	5 367	5 515	3 064	1 899	5 321	1 518	5 813
1941	45 785	45 782	37 210	2 779	975	1 774	13 137	6 999	6 138	3 311	2 014	5 754	1 559	5 907
1942	50 219	50 214	39 728	2 692	985	2 131	15 284	8 846	6 438	3 458	1 916	5 623	1 531	6 108
1943	55 996	56 016	40 723	2 563	917	1 566	17 402	10 924	6 478	3 652	1 808	5 570	1 475	5 770
1944	57 221	57 276	39 749	2 372	879	1 110	17 050	10 722	6 328	3 822	1 828	5 529	1 447	5 712
1945	55 548	55 614	38 183	2 259	829	1 135	15 186	8 933	6 253	3 926	1 927	5 717	1 477	5 727
1946	49 643	49 690	40 379	2 343	871	1 739	14 493	7 742	6 751	4 113	2 286	6 769	1 692	6 073
1947	49 936	49 941	42 458	2 427	933	2 062	15 205	8 330	6 875	4 173	2 480	7 061	1 744	6 373
1948	51 332	51 325	43 431	2 498	981	2 278	15 276	8 309	6 967	4 212	2 573	7 223	1 811	6 579
1972 SIC														
1948	51 332	51 325	43 431	2 505	993	2 324	15 521	8 343	7 178	4 212	2 731	6 585	1 776	6 784
1949	50 358	50 373	41 857	2 418	923	2 212	14 429	7 508	6 921	4 026	2 653	6 552	1 805	6 839
1950	52 424	52 428	43 626	2 499	926	2 448	15 241	8 121	7 120	4 064	2 670	6 727	1 883	7 168
1951	56 415	56 470	46 112	2 418	939	2 727	16 453	9 144	7 309	4 267	2 817	7 123	1 970	7 398
1952	57 702	57 770	46 668	2 338	916	2 763	16 752	9 466	7 286	4 279	2 870	7 270	2 044	7 436
1953	58 918	58 996	47 873	2 277	876	2 743	17 587	10 144	7 443	4 326	2 901	7 403	2 125	7 635
1954	57 387	57 514	46 400	2 301	798	2 729	16 395	9 194	7 201	4 120	2 875	7 336	2 199	7 647
1955	59 080	59 218	48 036	2 233	804	2 879	16 965	9 617	7 348	4 182	2 930	7 547	2 302	8 194
1956	60 845	60 987	49 573	2 141	843	3 025	17 327	9 894	7 433	4 290	3 054	7 812	2 406	8 675
1957	61 308	61 441	49 732	2 114	840	2 945	17 245	9 894	7 351	4 276	3 078	7 881	2 459	8 894
1958	59 839	59 967	48 211	2 153	749	2 865	15 919	8 839	7 080	4 011	3 066	7 785	2 513	9 150
1959	61 587	61 721	49 781	2 133	717	3 001	16 656	9 385	7 271	4 015	3 129	8 046	2 578	9 506
1960	62 680	62 823	50 548	2 097	699	2 969	16 779	9 453	7 326	4 024	3 205	8 305	2 660	9 810
1961	62 881	63 006	50 374	2 121	666	2 946	16 333	9 075	7 258	3 920	3 218	8 276	2 719	10 175
1962	64 573	64 664	51 672	2 075	649	3 024	16 901	9 514	7 387	3 920	3 268	8 508	2 781	10 546
1963	65 619	65 691	52 444	2 043	632	3 112	17 028	9 631	7 397	3 919	3 314	8 737	2 857	10 802
1964	67 275	67 338	53 655	1 879	628	3 234	17 330	9 856	7 474	3 972	3 394	9 068	2 939	11 211
1965	69 692	69 713	55 598	1 775	634	3 382	18 120	10 445	7 675	4 050	3 518	9 466	3 047	11 606
1966	73 516	73 531	58 209	1 662	631	3 485	19 319	11 359	7 960	4 192	3 667	9 937	3 136	12 180
1967	75 442	75 457	59 288	1 568	614	3 441	19 544	11 507	8 037	4 289	3 759	10 234	3 245	12 594
1968	77 602	77 618	60 948	1 545	610	3 570	19 898	11 700	8 198	4 352	3 851	10 638	3 412	13 072
1969	79 850	79 872	62 877	1 530	624	3 738	20 306	11 982	8 324	4 472	3 981	11 115	3 564	13 547
1970	79 750	79 770	62 702	1 545	628	3 676	19 442	11 270	8 172	4 525	4 061	11 362	3 696	13 767
1971	79 554	79 573	62 529	1 535	615	3 735	18 611	10 636	7 975	4 488	4 087	11 615	3 777	14 066
1972	81 583	81 604	64 568	1 551	625	3 927	19 080	11 010	8 070	4 538	4 206	11 982	3 917	14 742
1973	85 202	85 226	67 939	1 637	639	4 217	20 139	11 884	8 255	4 689	4 422	12 589	4 138	15 469
1974	86 573	86 594	68 947	1 738	699	4 151	20 121	11 964	8 157	4 746	4 540	12 847	4 270	15 835
1975	85 044	85 069	67 069	1 711	753	3 675	18 379	10 724	7 655	4 581	4 465	12 977	4 319	16 209
1976	87 402	87 427	69 430	1 815	782	3 728	19 082	11 123	7 959	4 600	4 609	13 570	4 443	16 801
1977	90 421	90 444	72 275	1 760	827	4 006	19 801	11 665	8 136	4 734	4 781	14 195	4 641	17 530
1978	94 777	94 805	76 313	1 763	876	4 443	20 668	12 372	8 296	4 955	5 056	15 031	4 947	18 573
1979	98 017	98 039	79 137	1 816	948	4 710	21 182	12 848	8 334	5 167	5 295	15 461	5 198	19 359
1980	98 370	98 394	79 121	1 865	1 032	4 493	20 433	12 270	8 163	5 178	5 346	15 487	5 362	19 924
1981	99 225	99 287	80 139	1 844	1 151	4 338	20 328	12 194	8 134	5 219	5 466	15 659	5 488	20 646
1982	97 305	97 369	78 220	1 718	1 138	4 013	18 923	11 122	7 800	5 131	5 350	15 471	5 528	20 949
1983	98 041	98 111	78 939	1 835	964	4 070	18 527	10 784	7 742	5 027	5 323	15 916	5 667	21 610
1984	102 458	102 531	83 103	1 747	980	4 527	19 473	11 560	7 913	5 192	5 614	16 908	5 894	22 768
1985	104 987	105 059	85 264	1 632	935	4 809	19 348	11 552	7 795	5 269	5 757	17 654	6 132	23 728
1986	106 873	106 940	86 770	1 611	784	4 960	19 035	11 269	7 766	5 283	5 799	18 188	6 435	24 675
1987	109 754	109 820	89 270	1 671	727	5 069	19 091	11 222	7 869	5 412	5 916	18 788	6 707	25 887
1987 SIC														
1987	109 754	109 820	89 270	1 671	727	5 069	19 091	11 193	7 898	5 412	5 937	18 767	6 719	25 875
1988	112 864	112 939	92 033	1 765	729	5 212	19 450	11 437	8 012	5 553	6 085	19 345	6 806	27 089
1989	115 501	115 584	94 300	1 723	704	5 269	19 482	11 435	8 046	5 659	6 319	19 843	6 846	28 456
1990	116 964	117 046	95 233	1 740	721	5 226	19 173	11 153	8 020	5 811	6 251	19 912	6 876	29 522
1991	115 525	115 607	93 763	1 735	700	4 794	18 507	10 618	7 889	5 785	6 097	19 604	6 835	29 705
1992	115 968	116 046	94 151	1 694	644	4 635	18 148	10 310	7 837	5 748	6 090	19 710	6 761	30 721
1993	117 604	118 030	96 106	1 724	617	4 790	18 141	10 268	7 874	5 861	6 018	20 110	6 851	31 993
1994	120 379	120 858	98 853	1 761	608	5 121	18 388	10 485	7 902	6 049	6 197	20 811	6 993	32 924
1995	123 236	123 713	101 636	1 819	590	5 304	18 548	10 698	7 849	6 177	6 437	21 498	6 899	34 365
1996	125 461	125 901	103 832	1 841	583	5 579	18 529	10 815	7 714	6 298	6 522	21 869	7 011	35 601
1997	128 316	128 788	106 698	1 919	599	5 859	18 706	11 030	7 676	6 470	6 711	22 240	7 212	36 983
1998	131 563	132 031	109 709	1 961	591	6 178	18 849	11 231	7 618	6 680	6 876	22 595	7 491	38 488
1999	134 350	134 864	112 253	2 055	537	6 570	18 605	11 141	7 465	6 895	6 951	23 140	7 649	39 850
2000	137 228	137 691	114 597	2 068	537	6 870	18 500	11 142	7 358	7 089	7 058	23 643	7 674	41 157

Table 10-21. Employment by SIC Industry, Historical Annual—*Continued*

(Full-time and part-time employees, thousands.)

NIPA Table 6.4A, B, and C

Year	Total govern-ment	Domestic industries												Rest of the world
		Federal government						State and local government						
		Total federal	General government				Govern-ment enterprises	Total state and local	General government				Govern-ment enterprises	
			General gov't total	Civilian [1]	Military	Work relief			General gov't total	Education	Other [1]	Work relief		
1942 SIC														
1929	3 611	981	644	267	377	. . .	337	2 630	2 509	1 067	1 442	. . .	121	0
1930	3 779	1 034	695	310	385	. . .	339	2 745	2 618	1 095	1 503	20	127	0
1931	4 133	1 019	683	296	387	. . .	336	3 114	2 984	1 105	1 580	299	130	1
1932	4 373	1 006	673	290	383	. . .	333	3 367	3 249	1 093	1 564	592	118	1
1933	5 901	1 470	1 135	294	370	471	335	4 431	4 317	1 069	1 524	1 724	114	1
1934	6 820	2 227	1 868	357	371	1 140	359	4 593	4 473	1 069	1 570	1 834	120	1
1935	7 150	2 209	1 835	449	396	990	374	4 941	4 815	1 097	1 621	2 097	126	1
1936	8 050	4 993	4 612	521	438	3 653	381	3 057	2 922	1 118	1 713	91	135	1
1937	7 192	4 085	3 698	517	474	2 707	387	3 107	2 967	1 149	1 762	56	140	1
1938	8 197	4 987	4 583	507	504	3 572	404	3 210	3 070	1 180	1 871	19	140	1
1939	8 020	4 754	4 342	560	566	3 216	412	3 266	3 123	1 207	1 877	39	143	1
1940	7 917	4 652	4 227	642	793	2 792	425	3 265	3 104	1 194	1 872	38	161	2
1941	8 572	5 281	4 829	944	1 693	2 192	452	3 291	3 119	1 256	1 846	17	172	3
1942	10 486	7 252	6 765	1 702	4 154	909	487	3 234	3 063	1 264	1 794	5	171	5
1943	15 293	12 155	11 611	2 497	9 029	85	544	3 138	2 965	1 256	1 709	. . .	173	-21
1944	17 527	14 405	13 885	2 520	11 365	. . .	520	3 122	2 956	1 256	1 700	. . .	166	-55
1945	17 431	14 258	13 722	2 420	11 302	. . .	536	3 173	3 007	1 273	1 734	. . .	166	-66
1946	9 311	5 902	5 294	1 822	3 472	. . .	608	3 409	3 236	1 347	1 889	. . .	173	-47
1947	7 483	3 808	3 268	1 436	1 832	. . .	540	3 675	3 481	1 445	2 036	. . .	194	-5
1948	7 894	4 007	3 437	1 428	2 009	. . .	570	3 887	3 657	1 504	2 153	. . .	230	7
1972 SIC														
1948	7 894	4 007	3 437	1 428	2 009	. . .	570	3 887	3 657	1 504	2 153	. . .	230	7
1949	8 516	4 462	3 857	1 448	2 409	. . .	605	4 054	3 815	1 581	2 234	. . .	239	-15
1950	8 802	4 603	4 016	1 468	2 548	. . .	587	4 199	3 947	1 636	2 311	. . .	252	-4
1951	10 358	6 131	5 519	1 817	3 702	. . .	612	4 227	3 967	1 684	2 283	. . .	260	-55
1952	11 102	6 737	6 081	1 910	4 171	. . .	656	4 365	4 067	1 762	2 305	. . .	298	-68
1953	11 123	6 611	5 976	1 823	4 153	. . .	635	4 512	4 209	1 851	2 358	. . .	303	-78
1954	11 114	6 394	5 759	1 702	4 057	. . .	635	4 720	4 415	1 946	2 469	. . .	305	-127
1955	11 182	6 234	5 601	1 711	3 890	. . .	633	4 948	4 637	2 076	2 561	. . .	311	-138
1956	11 414	6 202	5 563	1 738	3 825	. . .	639	5 212	4 900	2 199	2 701	. . .	312	-142
1957	11 709	6 277	5 618	1 734	3 884	. . .	659	5 432	5 117	2 310	2 807	. . .	315	-133
1958	11 756	6 044	5 373	1 691	3 682	. . .	671	5 712	5 375	2 430	2 945	. . .	337	-128
1959	11 940	6 030	5 349	1 721	3 628	. . .	681	5 910	5 516	2 559	2 957	. . .	394	-134
1960	12 275	6 090	5 390	1 770	3 620	. . .	700	6 185	5 777	2 732	3 045	. . .	408	-143
1961	12 632	6 200	5 481	1 772	3 709	. . .	719	6 432	6 022	2 863	3 159	. . .	410	-125
1962	12 992	6 349	5 618	1 833	3 785	. . .	731	6 643	6 228	3 012	3 216	. . .	415	-91
1963	13 247	6 302	5 568	1 852	3 716	. . .	734	6 945	6 521	3 214	3 307	. . .	424	-72
1964	13 683	6 382	5 641	1 838	3 803	. . .	741	7 301	6 861	3 431	3 430	. . .	440	-63
1965	14 115	6 387	5 625	1 856	3 769	. . .	762	7 728	7 276	3 705	3 571	. . .	452	-21
1966	15 322	7 057	6 222	1 978	4 244	. . .	835	8 265	7 800	4 049	3 751	. . .	465	-15
1967	16 169	7 497	6 623	2 100	4 523	. . .	874	8 672	8 199	4 321	3 878	. . .	473	-15
1968	16 670	7 551	6 669	2 112	4 557	. . .	882	9 119	8 625	4 582	4 043	. . .	494	-16
1969	16 995	7 492	6 599	2 083	4 516	. . .	893	9 503	8 991	4 828	4 163	. . .	512	-22
1970	17 068	7 129	6 217	2 042	4 175	. . .	912	9 939	9 404	5 060	4 344	. . .	535	-20
1971	17 044	6 717	5 807	2 002	3 805	. . .	910	10 327	9 778	5 298	4 480	. . .	549	-19
1972	17 036	6 308	5 427	2 017	3 410	. . .	881	10 728	10 164	5 467	4 697	. . .	564	-21
1973	17 287	6 174	5 293	2 001	3 292	. . .	881	11 113	10 524	5 641	4 883	. . .	589	-24
1974	17 647	6 146	5 251	2 049	3 202	. . .	895	11 501	10 879	5 858	5 021	. . .	622	-21
1975	18 000	6 060	5 183	2 075	3 108	. . .	877	11 940	11 280	6 052	5 228	. . .	660	-25
1976	17 997	5 934	5 080	2 085	2 995	. . .	854	12 063	11 400	6 124	5 276	. . .	663	-25
1977	18 169	5 871	5 027	2 090	2 937	. . .	844	12 298	11 638	6 251	5 387	. . .	660	-23
1978	18 492	5 881	5 031	2 117	2 914	. . .	850	12 611	11 922	6 292	5 630	. . .	689	-28
1979	18 902	5 881	5 016	2 126	2 890	. . .	865	13 021	12 289	6 361	5 928	. . .	732	-22
1980	19 273	6 010	5 140	2 221	2 919	. . .	870	13 263	12 506	6 481	6 025	. . .	757	-24
1981	19 148	6 006	5 133	2 131	3 002	. . .	873	13 142	12 389	6 466	5 923	. . .	753	-62
1982	19 149	6 084	5 207	2 113	3 094	. . .	877	13 065	12 307	6 421	5 886	. . .	758	-64
1983	19 172	6 095	5 246	2 117	3 129	. . .	849	13 077	12 315	6 478	5 837	. . .	762	-70
1984	19 428	6 196	5 316	2 143	3 173	. . .	880	13 232	12 459	6 581	5 878	. . .	773	-73
1985	19 795	6 311	5 401	2 180	3 221	. . .	910	13 484	12 692	6 759	5 933	. . .	792	-72
1986	20 170	6 384	5 427	2 164	3 263	. . .	957	13 786	12 981	6 940	6 041	. . .	805	-67
1987	20 550	6 475	5 493	2 190	3 303	. . .	982	14 075	13 258	6 992	6 266	. . .	817	-66
1987 SIC														
1987	20 550	6 475	5 493	2 190	3 303	. . .	982	14 075	13 258	6 992	6 266	. . .	817	-66
1988	20 906	6 470	5 465	2 192	3 273	. . .	1 005	14 436	13 608	7 257	6 351	. . .	828	-75
1989	21 284	6 483	5 471	2 207	3 264	. . .	1 012	14 801	13 955	7 458	6 497	. . .	846	-83
1990	21 813	6 532	5 520	2 315	3 205	. . .	1 012	15 281	14 403	7 670	6 733	. . .	878	-82
1991	21 844	6 349	5 356	2 211	3 145	. . .	993	15 495	14 605	7 787	6 818	. . .	890	-82
1992	21 895	6 177	5 211	2 231	2 980	. . .	966	15 718	14 863	7 887	6 976	. . .	855	-78
1993	21 924	5 929	4 976	2 176	2 800	. . .	953	15 995	15 126	8 070	7 056	. . .	869	-426
1994	22 005	5 719	4 749	2 101	2 648	. . .	970	16 286	15 380	8 227	7 153	. . .	906	-479
1995	22 077	5 556	4 571	2 027	2 544	. . .	985	16 521	15 593	8 392	7 201	. . .	928	-477
1996	22 069	5 386	4 398	1 952	2 446	. . .	988	16 683	15 754	8 526	7 228	. . .	929	-440
1997	22 090	5 266	4 276	1 900	2 376	. . .	990	16 824	15 890	8 740	7 150	. . .	934	-472
1998	22 322	5 191	4 200	1 878	2 322	. . .	991	17 131	16 191	8 932	7 259	. . .	940	-468
1999	22 611	5 136	4 146	1 855	2 291	. . .	990	17 475	16 530	9 152	7 378	. . .	945	-514
2000	23 094	5 235	4 260	1 976	2 284	. . .	975	17 859	16 904	9 389	7 515	. . .	955	-463

[1]Excluding work relief 1930–1943.
. . . = Not available.

NOTES AND DEFINITIONS, CHAPTER 10

General note on monthly employment data

This chapter presents data from two different data sets that measure employment monthly. Both are compiled and published by the Bureau of Labor Statistics (BLS), but each set has different characteristics. Users should be aware of these dissimilarities and the consequent differences in the appropriate uses and interpretations of data from the two systems.

One set of monthly employment estimates comes from the Current Population Survey (CPS), a large sample survey of approximately 60,000 U.S. households. The numbers in the sample are expanded to match the latest estimates of the total U.S. population. These are the most comprehensive estimates in their scope—that is, in the universe that they are designed to measure. These estimates represent all civilian workers, including the following groups that are excluded by definition from the other set of estimates: all farm workers; household workers (domestic servants); nonagricultural, nonincorporated self-employed workers; and nonagricultural unpaid family workers.

However, official CPS data are characterized by periodic discontinuities, which occur when new benchmarks for Census measures of the total population are introduced. These updates take place in a single month—usually January—and the official data for previous months are typically <u>not</u> modified to provide a smooth transition. Therefore, shorter-term comparisons (for a year or two or for a business cycle phase) will be misleading if such a discontinuity is included in the period. A recent example will illustrate. Beginning with January 2010, the estimates for civilian non-institutional population, civilian labor force, and employment were all adjusted downward by about 250,000 persons. The reported seasonally adjusted change in employment from December 2009 to January 2010 was an increase of 541,000. If there had been no population control adjustment, the increase in employment would have been 784,000. Such discontinuities occur throughout the history of the series.

For users who would like to examine monthly CPS data in which these discontinuities have been smoothed, BLS now provides unofficial smoothed estimates of total labor force and total employment from January 1990 through December 2011 on its Web site, <http://www.bls.gov>. In this edition of *Business Statistics*, these two series are shown in Table 10-6.

The CPS is a count of persons employed, rather than a count of jobs. A person is counted as employed in this data set only once, no matter how many jobs he or she may hold. The CPS count is limited to persons 16 years of age and over.

The second set of employment estimates—the payroll survey—comes from a very large sample survey of about 141,000 business and government employers at approximately 486,000 worksites, the Current Employment Statistics (CES) survey. It is benchmarked annually to a survey of all employers. Benchmark data are introduced with a smooth adjustment back to the previous benchmark, thus preserving the continuity of the series and making it more appropriate for measurement of employment change over a year or two, a business cycle, or other short- to medium-length periods. This sample is much larger than the CPS sample, including about one-third of all nonfarm payroll employees, and consequently the threshold of statistical significance for changes is lower. The minimum size of the over-the-month change required to be statistically significant is about 100,000 jobs in the payroll survey, versus about 400,000 persons in the household survey.

Over recent years, benchmark revisions to payroll survey employment have ranged in magnitude from an upward revision of 0.6 percent, in 2006, to the March 2009 benchmark, which reduced the seasonally adjusted level of payroll employment in that month by 902,000 persons, or 0.7 percent. The most recent revision increased the level of employment in March 2011 by 162,000, or 0.1 percent. In absolute terms (that is, disregarding the sign), revisions have ranged from 0.1 to 0.7 percentage points over the latest decade and averaged 0.3 percentage points. Within that range, relatively large upward revisions have been seen in strong economies, and relatively large downward revisions in weak ones.

The scope of the CES survey is smaller than that of the CPS survey, as it is limited to wage and salary workers on nonfarm payrolls. There is also a significant definitional difference, because the CES survey is a count of jobs. Thus, a person with more than one nonfarm wage or salary job is counted as employed in each job. In addition, workers are not classified by age; as a result, there may be some workers younger than 16 years old in the job count.

Persons with a job but not at work (absent due to bad weather, work stoppages, personal reasons, and the like) are included in the household survey. However, they are excluded from the payroll survey if on leave without pay for the entire payroll period.

In addition to the differences in definitions and scope between the two series, there are also differences in sample design, collection methodology, and the sampling variability inherent in the surveys.

The payroll survey provides the most reliable and detailed information on the breakdown of employment by industry (for example, the data shown in Table 15-1). In addition, it provides data on weekly hours per job and hourly and weekly earnings per job.

The CPS employment estimates provide information not collected in the CES on the breakdown of employment by demographic characteristics, such as age, race, and Hispanic ethnicity; by education levels; and by occupation. A few of these breakdowns are shown in *Business Statistics*. Many more breakdowns, in richer detail, can be found in the *Handbook of U.S. Labor Statistics*, also published by Bernan Press.

The differences between these two employment measures are discussed in an article on the BLS Web site, "Employment from the BLS household and payroll surveys: summary of recent trends," which is updated monthly along with the release of the monthly data, and can be found at <http://www.bls.gov/web/ces_cps_trends>. Further information can be found in an article by Mary Bowler and Teresa L. Morisi entitled "Understanding the employment measures from the CPS and CES survey" in *Monthly Labor Review*, February 2006, available on the BLS Web site http://www.bls.gov.

Additional annual employment data

In addition to the CPS and CES monthly and annual data series, a third set of historical, annual-only estimates of employment is presented at the end of this chapter. These estimates of "full-time and part-time employees" by industry are compiled by the U.S. Department of Commerce, Bureau of Economic Analysis, as part of the National Income and Product Accounts (NIPAs). These estimates provide the most comprehensive and consistent employment estimates for the years before 1948.

Further detail on the historical and other characteristics of all of these employment series is presented below in the notes associated with specific data tables.

TABLES 10-1 THROUGH 10-5
LABOR FORCE, EMPLOYMENT, AND UNEMPLOYMENT

Source: U.S. Department of Labor, Bureau of Labor Statistics (BLS)

Labor force, employment, and unemployment data are derived from the Current Population Survey (CPS), a sample survey of households conducted each month by the Census Bureau for the Bureau of Labor Statistics (BLS). The data pertain to the U.S. civilian noninstitutional population age 16 years and over.

Due to changes in questionnaire design and survey methodology, data for 1994 and subsequent years are not fully comparable with data for 1993 and earlier years. Additionally, discontinuities in the reported number of persons in the population, and consequently in the estimated numbers of employed and unemployed persons and the number of persons in the labor force, are introduced whenever periodic updates are made to U.S. population estimates.

For example, population controls based on Census 2000 were introduced beginning with the data for January 2000. These data are therefore not comparable with data for December 1999 and earlier. Data for 1990 through 1999 incorporate 1990 census–based population controls and are

not comparable with the preceding years. An additional large population adjustment was introduced in January 2004, making the data from that time forward not comparable with data for December 2003 and earlier; further adjustments have been made in each subsequent January and other discontinuities have been introduced in various earlier years, usually with January data. See "Notes on the Data," below, for information on adjustments in other years, including the incorporation of the 2010 Census count beginning in January 2012.

For the most part, these population adjustments distort comparisons involving the <u>numbers of persons</u> in the population, labor force, and employment. They generally have negligible effects on the <u>percentages</u> that comprise the most important features of the CPS: the unemployment rates, the labor force participation rates, and the employment-population ratios.

BLS now makes available unofficial smoothed data for the total number of persons in the civilian labor force and the number of persons employed for 1990 through 2011, which introduce the population adjustments gradually within the period shown. These data are shown in Table 10-6.

Beginning with the data for January 2000, data classified by industry and occupation use the North American Industry Classification System (NAICS) and the 2000 Standard Occupational Classification System. This creates breaks in the time series between December 1999 and January 2000 for occupational and industry data at all levels of aggregation. Since the recent history is so short, most CPS industry and occupation data have been dropped from *Business Statistics* in favor of other important and economically meaningful data for which a longer consistent history can be supplied. However, detailed employment data by occupation and industry can be found in Bernan Press's *Handbook of U.S. Labor Statistics*.

Pre-1948 data

The Census Bureau began the monthly survey of households that provides labor force data in 1942, and the Census of Population supplied data for 1940. For earlier years, annual data for labor force, employment, and unemployment are retrospective estimates made by BLS.

From 1929 to 1947, the data collected pertained to persons 14 years of age and over. From 1947 to the present the survey pertains to persons 16 years of age and over. Table 10-1B shows summary data for both age definitions in the overlap year, 1947. In that year, the unemployment rates are the same (3.9 percent) for both age definitions. However, the labor force participation rate and the employment/population ratio are higher when the 14- and 15-year-olds are excluded. Naturally, the raw numbers for population, labor force, and employment are smaller when the 14- and 15-year-olds are excluded.

The 1940 Census and the BLS data for 1931 through 1942 did not treat government work relief employment as employment; persons engaged in such work were counted as unemployed. In the labor force survey used today, anyone who worked for pay or profit is counted as employed (see the definitions below). Therefore, today's survey would count work relief as employment and not unemployment, and the BLS figures for the period before 1942 are not consistent with today's unemployment rates. Michael Darby calculated an alternative unemployment rate in which such workers are counted as employed, and this rate is shown in parentheses in Table 10-1B. Work relief employment is included in the BEA total employment figures in Table 10-21.

Race and ethnic origin

Data for two broad racial categories were made available beginning in 1954: *White* and *Black and other*. The latter included Asians and all other "nonwhite" races, and was discontinued after 2002. Data for *Blacks* only are available beginning with 1972; this category is now called *Black or African American*. Data for *Asians* are shown beginning with 2000. Persons in the remaining race categories— American Indian or Alaska Native, Native Hawaiian or Other Pacific Islanders, and persons who selected more than one race category when that became possible, beginning in 2003 (see below)—are included in the estimates of total employment and unemployment, but are not shown separately because their numbers are too small to yield quality estimates.

Hispanic or Latino ethnicity, previously labeled *Hispanic origin*, is not a racial category and is established in a survey question separate from the question about race. Persons of Hispanic or Latino ethnicity may be of any race.

In January 2003, changes that affected classification by race and Hispanic ethnicity were introduced. These changes caused discontinuities in race and ethnic group data between December 2002 and January 2003.

Individuals in the sample are now asked whether they are of Hispanic ethnicity <u>before</u> being asked about their race. Prior to 2003, individuals were asked their ethnic origin <u>after</u> they were asked about their race. Furthermore, respondents are now asked directly if they are Spanish, Hispanic, or Latino. Previously, they were identified based on their or their ancestors' country of origin.

Individuals in the sample are now allowed to choose more than one race category. Before 2003, they were required to select a single primary race. This change had no impact on the size of the overall civilian noninstitutional population and labor force. It did reduce the population and labor force levels of Whites and Blacks beginning in January 2003, as individuals who reported more than one race are now excluded from those groups.

BLS has estimated, based on a special survey, that these changes reduced the population and labor force levels for Whites by about 950,000 and 730,000 persons, respectively,

and for Blacks by about 320,000 and 240,000 persons, respectively, while having little or no impact on either of their unemployment rates. The changes did not affect the size of the Hispanic population or labor force, but they did cause an increase of about half a percentage point in the Hispanic unemployment rate.

Definitions

The employment status of the civilian population is surveyed each month with respect to a specific week in mid-month—not for the entire month. This is known as the "reference week." For a precise definition and explanation of the reference week, see Notes on the Data, which follows these definitions.

The *civilian noninstitutional population* comprises all civilians 16 years of age and over who are not inmates of penal or mental institutions, sanitariums, or homes for the aged, infirm, or needy.

Civilian employment includes those civilians who (1) worked for pay or profit at any time during the Sunday-through-Saturday week that includes the 12th day of the month (the reference week), or who worked for 15 hours or more as an unpaid worker in a family-operated enterprise; or (2) were temporarily absent from regular jobs because of vacation, illness, industrial dispute, bad weather, or similar reasons. Each employed person is counted only once; those who hold more than one job are counted as being in the job at which they worked the greatest number of hours during the reference week.

Unemployed persons are all civilians who were not employed (according to the above definition) during the reference week, but who were available for work—except for temporary illness—and who had made specific efforts to find employment sometime during the previous four weeks. Persons who did not look for work because they were on layoff are also counted as unemployed.

The *civilian labor force* comprises all civilians classified as employed or unemployed.

Civilians 16 years of age and over in the noninstitutional population who are not classified as employed or unemployed are defined as *not in the labor force*. This group includes those engaged in own-home housework; in school; unable to work because of long-term illness, retirement, or age; seasonal workers for whom the reference week fell in an "off" season (if not qualifying as unemployed by looking for a job); persons who became discouraged and gave up the search for work; and the voluntarily idle. Also included are those doing only incidental work (less than 15 hours) in a family-operated business during the reference week.

The civilian *labor force participation rate* represents the percentage of the civilian noninstitutional population (age 16 years and over) that is in the civilian labor force.

The *employment-population ratio* represents the percentage of the civilian noninstitutional population (age 16 years and over) that is employed. This is traditionally called a "ratio," although it is also traditionally expressed as a percent and therefore would be more appropriately called a "rate," as is the case with the labor force participation rate.

Employment is shown by *class of worker*, including a breakdown of total employment into *agricultural* and *nonagricultural* industries. Employment in *nonagricultural industries* includes *wage and salary workers*, the *self-employed*, and *unpaid family workers*.

Wage and salary workers receive wages, salaries, commissions, tips, and/or pay-in-kind. This category includes owners of self-owned incorporated businesses.

Self-employed workers are those who work for profit or for fees in their own business, profession, trade, or farm. This category includes only the unincorporated; a person whose business is incorporated is considered to be a wage and salary worker since he or she is a paid employee of a corporation, even if he or she is the corporation's president and sole employee. These categories are now labeled "Self-employed workers, unincorporated" to clarify this definition.

Wage and salary employment comprises *government* and *private industry* wage and salary workers. Domestic workers and other employees of *private households*, who are not included in the payroll employment series, are shown separately from *all other private industries*. The series for *government* and *other private industries* wage and salary workers are the closest in scope to similar categories in the payroll employment series.

Multiple jobholders are employed persons who, during the reference week, either had two or more jobs as a wage and salary worker, were self-employed and also held a wage and salary job, or worked as an unpaid family worker and also held a wage and salary job. This category does not include self-employed persons with multiple businesses or persons with multiple jobs as unpaid family workers. For purposes of industry and occupational classification, multiple jobholders are counted as being in the job at which they worked the greatest number of hours during the reference week.

Employed and at work part time does not include employed persons who were absent from their jobs during the entire reference week for reasons such as vacation, illness, or industrial dispute.

At work part time for economic reasons ("involuntary" part time) refers to individuals who worked 1 to 34 hours during the reference week because of slack work, unfavorable business conditions, an inability to find full-time work, or seasonal declines in demand. To be included in this category, workers must also indicate that they want and are available for full-time work.

At work part time for noneconomic reasons ("voluntary" part time) refers to persons who usually work part time and were at work for 1 to 34 hours during the reference week for reasons such as illness, other medical limitations, family obligations, education, retirement, Social Security limits on earnings, or working in an industry where the workweek is less than 35 hours. It also includes respondents who gave an economic reason but were not available for, or did not want, full-time work. At work part time for noneconomic reasons excludes persons who usually work full time, but who worked only 1 to 34 hours during the reference week for reasons such as holidays, illnesses, and bad weather.

The *long-term unemployed* are persons currently unemployed (searching or on layoff) who have been unemployed for 15 consecutive weeks or longer. If a person ceases to look for work for two weeks or more, or becomes temporarily employed, the continuity of long-term unemployment is broken. If he or she starts searching for work or is laid off again, the monthly CPS will record the length of his or her unemployment from the time the search recommenced or since the latest layoff.

The civilian *unemployment rate* is the number of unemployed as a percentage of the civilian labor force. The unemployment rates for groups within the civilian population (such as males age 20 years and over) are the number of unemployed in a group as a percent of that group's labor force.

Unemployment rates by reason provides a breakdown of the total unemployment rate. Each unemployed person is classified into one of four groups.

Job losers and persons who completed temporary jobs includes persons on temporary layoff, permanent job losers, and persons who completed temporary jobs and began looking for work after those jobs ended. These three categories are shown separately without seasonal adjustment in the BLS's "Employment Situation" news release and on its Web site. They are combined, under the title shown here, for the purpose of seasonal adjustment. This is the category of unemployment that responds most strongly to the business cycle.

Job leavers terminated their employment voluntarily and immediately began looking for work.

Reentrants are persons who previously worked, but were out of the labor force prior to beginning their current job search.

New entrants are persons searching for a first job who have never worked.

Each of these categories is expressed as a proportion of the entire civilian labor force, so that the sum of the four rates equals the unemployment rate for all civilian workers, except for possible discrepancies due to rounding or separate seasonal adjustment.

Median and average weeks unemployed are summary measures of the length of time that persons classified as unemployed have been looking for work. For persons on layoff, the duration represents the number of full weeks of the layoff. The *average (mean)* number of weeks is computed by aggregating all the weeks of unemployment experienced by all unemployed persons during their current spell of unemployment and dividing by the number of unemployed. The average can be distorted by what is called "top coding" because the length of unemployment is reported in ranges, including a top range of "over __ weeks", rather than exact numbers. See the paragraph below for further explanation. The *median* number of weeks unemployed is the number of weeks of unemployment experienced by the person at the midpoint of the distribution of all unemployed persons, as ranked by duration of unemployment, and is not distorted by top coding. Like medians in other economic time series, it is likely to be a better measure of typical experience.

Beginning with the data for January 2011 and phasing in through April 2011, respondents will be able to report unemployment durations of up to 5 years; before that time, the "top code" was up to 2 years. This change causes a sharp increase in January 2011 and continued rises through April for *average weeks unemployed.* It does not affect total unemployment, total long-term unemployment, or the *median weeks unemployed.* Comparisons of the average weeks statistics on the old and new basis are available on the BLS Web site.

Alternative measures of labor underutilization are calculated by BLS and published in the monthly Employment Situation release. They measure alternative concepts of unused working capacity, and are numbered "U-1" through "U-6" in order of increasing breadth of the definition of underutilization.

"U-1" is persons unemployed 15 weeks or longer, as a percent of the civilian labor force. It is not shown in *Business Statistics.*

"U-2" is job losers and persons who completed temporary jobs, as a percent of the civilian labor force; it is shown in *Business Statistics* in the fifth column of Table 10-5.

"U-3" is the official rate, described above and shown in the final columns of Tables 10-1, the fifth column of Table 10-4, and the fourth column of Table 10-5.

"U-4" through "U-6" are shown in the last three columns of Table 10-5. They are based on additional labor force status questions, now included in the CPS survey, that were introduced beginning in 1994. U-4 and U-5 are increasingly broader rates of unemployment, while U-6 can be described as an "unemployment and underemployment rate."

"U-4" adds discouraged workers to unemployment and the labor force. Discouraged workers are persons not in the officially defined labor force who have given a job-market-related reason for not looking currently for a job—for example, they have not looked for a job because they believed that no jobs were available.

"U-5" adds both discouraged workers and all other "marginally attached" workers to unemployment and the labor force. "Marginally attached" workers are all persons who currently are neither working nor looking for work but indicate that they want and are available for a job and have looked for work some time in the recent past.

"U-6" adds persons employed part time for economic reasons, as shown in Table 10-3, to the number of persons counted as unemployed in "U-5", with the same labor force definition as in "U-5." Recently this statistic, measuring combined unemployment and underemployment, has often been cited in press reports on the employment situation.

For more information, see "BLS introduced new range of alternative unemployment measures" in the October 1995 issue of the *Monthly Labor Review.*

Notes on the data

The CPS data are collected by trained interviewers from about 60,000 sample households selected to represent the U.S. civilian noninstitutional population. The sample size was about 60,000 households from mid-1989 to mid-1995, but was reduced for budgetary reasons in two stages to about 50,000 households, beginning in January 1996. This sample size was maintained from 1996 through 2000. The sample size was increased back to 60,000 households, beginning with the data for July 2001, as part of a plan to meet the requirements of the State Children's Health Insurance Program legislation. The CPS provides data for other data series in addition to the BLS employment status data, such as household income and poverty (see Chapter 3) and health insurance.

The employment status data are based on the activity or status reported for the calendar week, Sunday through Saturday, that includes the 12th day of the month (the reference week). Households are interviewed in the week following the reference week. Sample households are phased in and out of the sample on a rotating basis. Consequently, three-fourths of the sample is the same for any two consecutive months. One-half of the sample is the same as the sample in the same month a year earlier.

Data relating to 1994 and subsequent years are not strictly comparable with data for 1993 and earlier years because of the major 1994 redesign of the survey questionnaire and collection methodology. The redesign included new and revised questions for the classification of individuals as employed or unemployed, the collection of new data on multiple jobholding, a change in the definition of discouraged workers, and the implementation of a more completely automated data collection.

The 1994 redesign of the CPS was the most extensive since 1967. However, there are many other significant periods of year-to-year noncomparability in the labor force data. These typically result from the introduction of new decennial census data into the CPS estimation procedures, expansions of the sample, or other improvements made to increase the reliability of the estimates. Each change introduces a new discontinuity, usually between December of the previous year and January of the newly altered year. The discontinuities are usually minor or negligible with respect to figures expressed as nationwide percentages (such as the unemployment rate or the labor force participation rate), but can be significant with respect to levels (such as labor force and employment in thousands of persons). A list of the dates of the major discontinuities follows, with BLS estimates of their quantitative impact on the national totals. (There are likely to be larger impacts on population subgroups.) The discontinuities occur in January unless otherwise indicated. Note that some of the changes caused adjustments that were carried back to an earlier year.

- 1953: 1950 census data introduced. Labor force and employment were raised by about 350,000.

- 1960: Alaska and Hawaii included. The labor force was increased by about 300,000, mainly in nonagricultural employment.

- 1962: 1960 census data introduced. Labor force and employment were reduced by about 200,000.

- 1972: 1970 census data introduced. Labor force and employment were raised by about 300,000.

- March 1973: Further 1970 census data were introduced, reducing White labor force and employment by about 150,000 and raising Black and other labor force and employment by approximately 210,000.

- July 1975: Adjustment for Vietnamese refugee inflow, raising total and Black and other population by 76,000.

- 1978: Sample expansion and revised estimation procedures increased labor force and employment by about 250,000.

- 1982: Change in estimation procedures introduced. To avoid major breaks, many series were reestimated back to 1970. This did not smooth the breaks occurring between 1972 and 1979.

- 1986, with revisions carried back to 1980: Adjustment for better estimates of immigration, raising labor force by nearly 400,000 and employment by 350,000, mainly among Hispanics.

- 1994: 1990 census data introduced and carried back to 1990, when employment was increased by about 880,000 and the unemployment rate was raised by about 0.1 percentage point.

- 1997: New estimates of immigration and emigration, raising labor force and employment by about 300,000, again mainly among Hispanics.

- 1998: New population estimates and estimation procedures, reducing labor force and employment by around 250,000.

- 1999: New information on immigration, raising labor force and employment by around 60,000, but lowering Hispanic employment by about 200,000.

- 2000: Census 2000 data introduced, using the 2002 NAICS and the 2000 Standard Occupational Classification System. The labor force was increased by about 1.6 million in January 2000, growing to around 2.5 million by December 2002.

- 2003: Further population estimates introduced (based on an annual population update and therefore not carried back to 2000), raising the labor force by 614,000.

- 2004: Population controls updated to reflect revised migration estimates, reducing labor force and employment by around 400,000, mostly among Hispanics.

- 2005: Updated migration and vital statistics data decreased labor force and employment by around 45,000.

- 2006: Updated migration and vital statistics data decreased labor force and employment by about 125,000.

- 2007: Updated migration and vital statistics data increased labor force and employment by about 150,000.

- 2008: Updated migration and vital statistics data decreased labor force by 637,000 and employment by 598,000.

- 2009: Updated migration adjustments, new vital statistics data, and methodological changes decreased labor force by 449,000 and employment by 407,000.

- 2010: Updated information on migration, vital statistics, and other data and methodological changes decreased labor force by 249,000 and employment by 243,000.

- 2011: Updated estimates reduced the labor force by 504,000, employment by 472,000, and unemployment by 32,000; raised the number of persons not in the labor force by 157,000; and had no effect on the unemployment rate.

- 2012: Reflecting the 2010 Census, the civilian noninstitutional population was increased by 1,510,000; the civilian labor force by 258,000; employment by 216,000; and unemployment by 42,000. BLS states, "Although the total unemployment rate was unaffected, the labor force participation rate and the employment-population ratio were each reduced by 0.3 percentage point. This was because the population increase was primarily among persons 55 and older and, to a lesser degree, persons 16 to 24 years of age. Both these age groups have lower levels of labor force participation than the general population."

For further information on these changes, see the BLS online publications *Employment and Earnings* for February of each year. The most recent information is posted on <http://www.bls.gov/cps> under "Publications and Other Documentation."

The monthly labor force, employment, and unemployment data are seasonally adjusted by the X-12-ARIMA method. All seasonally adjusted civilian labor force and unemployment rate statistics, as well as major employment and unemployment estimates, are computed by aggregating independently adjusted series. For example, the seasonally adjusted level of total unemployment is the sum of the seasonally adjusted levels of unemployment for the four age/sex groups (men and women age 16 to 19 years, and men and women age 20 years and over). Seasonally adjusted employment is the sum of the seasonally adjusted levels of employment for the same four groups. The seasonally adjusted civilian labor force is the sum of all eight components. Finally, the seasonally adjusted civilian worker unemployment rate is calculated by taking total seasonally adjusted unemployment as a percent of the total seasonally adjusted civilian labor force.

To minimize subsequent revisions, BLS uses a concurrent technique that estimates factors for the latest month using the most recent data. Then, seasonal adjustment factors are fully revised at the end of each year to reflect recent experience. The revisions also affect the preceding four years. An article describing the seasonal adjustment methodology for the household survey data is available at http://www.bls.gov/cps/cpsrs2010.pdf.

Breakdowns other than the basic age/sex classification described above—such as the employment data by class of worker in Table 10-3—will not necessarily add to totals because of independent seasonal adjustment.

Data availability

Data for each month are usually released on the first Friday of the following month in the "Employment Situation" press release, which also includes data from the establishment survey (Tables 10-8 through 10-18 and Chapter 15). The press release and data are available on the BLS Web site at <http://www.bls.gov>. Data are subsequently published in the BLS monthly periodical *Employment and Earnings*, which contains detailed explanatory notes. The last paper issue of *Employment and Earnings* was for April 2007; subsequent issues are available on the BLS Web site. Selected data are published each month in the *Monthly Labor Review*, also available online at the BLS Web site, which also features frequent articles analyzing developments in the labor force, employment, and unemployment.

Monthly and annual data on the current basis are available beginning with 1948. Historical unadjusted data are published in *Labor Force Statistics Derived from the Current Population Survey* (BLS Bulletin 2307). Historical seasonally adjusted data are available from BLS upon request. Complete historical data are available on the BLS Web site at <http://www.bls.gov/cps>.

Seasonal adjustment factors are revised each year for the five previous years, with the release of December data in early January. New population controls are introduced with the release of January data in early February.

BLS annual data for 1940 through 1947 are published on their Web site at <http://www.bls.gov>. The data for 1929 through 1939 were published in *Employment and Earnings*, May 1972, and in U.S. Commerce Department, Bureau of Economic Analysis, *Long-Term Economic Growth, 1860–1970*, June 1973, p. 163.

The Darby alternative unemployment rate is found in Michael Darby, "Three-and-a-Half Million U.S. Employees Have Been Mislaid," *Journal of Political Economy*, February 1976, v. 84, no. 1. It is also displayed and discussed in Robert A. Margo, "Employment and Unemployment in the 1930s," *Journal of Economic Perspectives*, v. 7, no. 2, Spring 1993.

References

Comprehensive descriptive material can be found at <http://www.bls.gov/cps> under the "Publications and Other Documentation" section. Historical background on the CPS, as well as a description of the 1994 redesign, can be found in three articles from the September 1993 edition of *Monthly Labor Review*: "Why Is It Necessary to Change?"; "Redesigning the Questionnaire"; and "Evaluating Changes in the Estimates." The redesign is also described in the February 1994 issue of *Employment and Earnings*. See also Chapter 1, "Labor Force Data Derived from the Current Population Survey," *BLS Handbook of Methods*, Bulletin 2490 (April 1997).

TABLE 10-6
LABOR FORCE AND EMPLOYMENT ESTIMATES SMOOTHED FOR POPULATION ADJUSTMENTS

SOURCE: U.S. DEPARTMENT OF LABOR, BUREAU OF LABOR STATISTICS

This table presents seasonally adjusted monthly estimates of total civilian labor force and total civilian employment in which discontinuities caused by the introduction of new population controls in the official series—as described above—have been smoothed. They are taken from "Labor Force and Employment Estimates Smoothed for Population Adjustments, 1990-1999 and 2000-2011" <http://www.bls.gov/cps/cpspopsm.pdf>. The method of smoothing is described in Marisa L. Di Natale, "Creating Comparability in CPS Employment Series," on the BLS Web site at <http://www.bls.gov/cps/cpscomp.pdf>. BLS notes that these series do not match the official estimates in BLS publications, which are also the data shown in all other tables in this volume.

TABLE 10-7
INSURED UNEMPLOYMENT

SOURCE: U.S. DEPARTMENT OF LABOR, EMPLOYMENT AND TRAINING ADMINISTRATION

Definitions

State programs of unemployment insurance cover operations of regular programs under state unemployment insurance laws. In 1976, the law was amended to extend coverage to include virtually all state and local government employees, as well as many agricultural and domestic workers. (This took effect on January 1, 1978.) Benefits under state programs are financed by taxes levied by the states on employers.

Federal programs are those directly financed by the federal government. They include unemployment benefits for *federal employees* (Unemployment Compensation for Federal Employees, or UCFE), *newly discharged veterans* (Unemployment Compensation for Ex-Service Members, or UCX), *railroad retirement,* and *extended benefits,* which are sometimes enacted by Congress in times of widespread or protracted unemployment.

UCX pays benefits, based on service, to veterans who were on active duty and honorably separated. In the case of both UCFE and UCX, state laws determine the benefit amounts, number of weeks benefits can be paid, and other eligibility conditions.

An *initial claim* is the first claim in a benefit year filed by a worker after losing his or her job, or the first claim filed at the beginning of a subsequent period of unemployment in the same benefit year. The initial claim establishes the starting date for any insured unemployment that may result if the claimant is unemployed for one week or longer. Transitional claims (filed by claimants as they start a new benefit year in a continuing spell of unemployment) are excluded; therefore, these data more closely represent instances of new unemployment and are widely followed as a leading indicator of job market conditions.

Insured unemployment and *persons claiming benefits* both describe the average number of persons receiving benefits in the indicated month or year.

The *insured unemployment rate* for state programs is the level of insured unemployment as a percentage of employment covered by state programs.

Monthly averages in this book are averages, calculated by the editor, of the weekly data published by the Employment and Training Administration. Annual data are averages of the monthly data.

Data availability

Data are published in weekly press releases from the Employment and Training Administration. These releases are available on their Web site at <http://www.doleta.gov> under "Labor Market Data," as are historical data, under the category "UI/Program Statistics."

TABLES 10-8, 10-9, 10-14, 15-1, AND 15-2
NONFARM PAYROLL EMPLOYMENT

SOURCE: U.S. DEPARTMENT OF LABOR, BUREAU OF LABOR STATISTICS (BLS)

These nonfarm employment data, as well as the hours and earnings data in Tables 10-9 through 10-13, 10-15 through 10-18, and 15-3 through 15-6, are compiled from payroll records. Information is reported monthly on a voluntary basis to BLS and its cooperating state agencies by a large sample of establishments, representing all industries except farming. These data, formally known as the Current Employment Statistics (CES) survey, are often referred to as the "establishment data" or the "payroll data." They are also known as the BLS-790 survey.

The survey, originally based on a stratified quota sample, has been replaced on a phased-in basis by a stratified probability sample. The new sampling procedure went into effect for wholesale trade in June 2000; for mining, construction, and manufacturing in June 2001; and for retail trade, transportation and public utilities, and finance, insurance, and real estate in June 2002. The phase-in was completed in June 2003, upon its extension to the service industries. The phase-in schedule was slightly different for the state and area series.

The sample has always been very large. Currently, it includes approximately 141,000 businesses and government agencies covering about 486,000 individual worksites, which account for about one-third of total benchmark employment of payroll workers. The sample is drawn from a sampling frame of over 8 million unemployment insurance tax accounts.

Data are classified according to the North American Industry Classification System. BLS has reconstructed historical time series to conform with NAICS, to ensure that all published series have a NAICS-based history extending back to at least January 1990. NAICS-based history extends back to January 1939 for total nonfarm and other high-level aggregates. For more detailed series, the starting date for NAICS data varies depending on the extent of the definitional changes between the old Standard Industrial Classification (SIC) and NAICS.

Definitions

An *establishment* is an economic unit, such as a factory, store, or professional office, that produces goods or services at a single location and is engaged in one type of economic activity.

Employment comprises all persons who received pay (including holiday and sick pay) for any part of the payroll period that includes the 12th day of the month. The definition of the payroll period for each reporting respondent is that used by the employer; it could be weekly, biweekly, monthly, or other. Included are all full-time and part-time workers in nonfarm establishments, including salaried officers of corporations. Persons holding more than one job are counted in each establishment that reports them. Not covered are proprietors, the self-employed, unpaid volunteer and family workers, farm workers, domestic workers in households, and military personnel. Employees of the Central Intelligence Agency, the Defense Intelligence Agency, the National Geospatial-Intelligence Agency, and the National Security Agency are not included.

Persons on an establishment payroll who are on paid sick leave (when pay is received directly from the employer), on paid holiday or vacation, or who work during a portion of the pay period despite being unemployed or on strike during the rest of the period, are counted as employed. Not counted as employed are persons who are laid off, on leave without pay, on strike for the entire period, or hired but not paid during the period.

Intermittent workers are counted if they performed any service during the month. BLS considers regular full-time teachers (private and government) to be employed during the summer vacation period, regardless of whether they are specifically paid during those months.

The *government* division includes federal, state, and local activities such as legislative, executive, and judicial functions, as well as the U.S. Postal Service and all government-owned and government-operated business enterprises, establishments, and institutions (arsenals, navy yards, hospitals, state-owned utilities, etc.), and government force account construction. However, as indicated earlier, members of the armed forces and employees of certain national-security-related agencies are not included.

The monthly *diffusion index of employment change*, currently based on 271 private nonfarm NAICS industries, represents the percentage of those industries in which the seasonally adjusted level of employment in that month was higher than six months earlier, plus one-half of the percentage of industries with unchanged employment. Therefore, the diffusion index reported for September represents the change from March to September. *Business Statistics* uses the September value to represent the year as a whole, since it spans the year's midpoint. Diffusion indexes measure the dispersion of economic gains and losses, with values below 50 percent associated with recessions. The current NAICS-based series begins with January 1991. For October 1976 through December 1990, an earlier series is available based on 347 SIC industries (there are more industries using the older classification system because in SIC manufacturing industries were represented in greater detail). September values from this series are used here to represent the years 1977 through 1990.

Production and nonsupervisory workers include all *production and related workers* in mining and manufacturing;

construction workers in construction; and *nonsupervisory workers* in transportation, communication, electric, gas, and sanitary services; wholesale and retail trade; finance, insurance, and real estate; and services. These groups account for about four-fifths of the total employment on private nonagricultural payrolls. Previously, this category was called "production or nonsupervisory workers." The definitions have not changed.

Production and related workers include working supervisors and all nonsupervisory workers (including group leaders and trainees) engaged in fabricating, processing, assembling, inspecting, receiving, storing, handling, packing, warehousing, shipping, trucking, hauling, maintenance, repair, janitorial, guard services, product development, auxiliary production for plant's own use (such as a power plant), record keeping, and other services closely associated with these production operations.

Construction workers include the following employees in the construction division of the NAICS: working supervisors, qualified craft workers, mechanics, apprentices, laborers, and the like, who are engaged in new work, alterations, demolition, repair, maintenance, and other tasks, whether working at the site of construction or working in shops or yards at jobs (such as precutting and preassembling) ordinarily performed by members of the construction trades.

Nonsupervisory employees include employees (not above the working supervisory level) such as office and clerical workers, repairers, salespersons, operators, drivers, physicians, lawyers, accountants, nurses, social workers, research aides, teachers, drafters, photographers, beauticians, musicians, restaurant workers, custodial workers, attendants, line installers and repairers, laborers, janitors, guards, and other employees at similar occupational levels whose services are closely associated with those of the employees listed.

Notes on the data

Benchmark adjustments. The establishment survey data are adjusted annually to comprehensive counts of employment, called "benchmarks." Benchmark information on employment by industry is compiled by state agencies from reports of establishments covered under state unemployment insurance laws; these form an annual compilation of administrative data known as the ES-202. These tabulations cover about 97 percent of all employees on nonfarm payrolls. Benchmark data for the residual are obtained from alternate sources, primarily from Railroad Retirement Board records and the Census Bureau's *County Business Patterns*. The latest benchmark adjustment, which is incorporated into the data in this volume, increased the employment level in the benchmark month March 2011 by 162,000 jobs, which was 0.1 percent.

The estimates for the benchmark month are compared with new benchmark levels for each industry. If revisions are necessary, the monthly series of estimates between benchmark periods are adjusted by graduated amounts between the new benchmark and the preceding one ("wedged back"), and the new benchmark level for each industry is then carried forward month by month based on the sample.

More specifically, the month-to-month changes for each estimation cell are based on changes in a matched sample for that cell, plus an estimate of net business births and deaths. The matched sample for each pair of months consists of establishments that have reported data for both months (which automatically excludes establishments that have gone out of business by the second month). Since new businesses are not immediately incorporated into the sample, a model-based estimate of net business births and deaths in that estimating cell is added. The birth/death adjustment factors are re-estimated quarterly based on the Quarterly Census of Employment and Wages.

Not-seasonally-adjusted data for all months since the last benchmark date are subject to revision.

Beginning in 1959, the data include Alaska and Hawaii. This inclusion resulted in an increase of 212,000 (0.4 percent) in total nonfarm employment for the March 1959 benchmark month.

Seasonal adjustment. The seasonal movements that recur periodically—such as warm and cold weather, holidays, and vacations—are generally the largest single component of month-to-month changes in employment. After adjusting the data to remove such seasonal variation, basic trends become more evident. BLS uses X-12-ARIMA software to produce seasonal factors and perform concurrent seasonal adjustment, using the most recent 10 years of data. New factors are developed each month adding the most current data.

For most series, a special procedure called REGARIMA (regression with autocorrelated errors) is used before calculating the seasonal factors; this adjusts for the length of the interval (which can be either four or five weeks) between the survey weeks. REGARIMA has also been used to isolate extreme weather effects that distort the measurement of seasonal patterns in the construction industry, and to identify variations in local government employment due to the presence or absence of election poll workers.

Seasonal adjustment factors are directly applied to the component levels. Seasonally adjusted totals for employment series are then obtained by aggregating the seasonally adjusted components directly, while hours and earnings series represent weighted averages of the seasonally adjusted component series. Seasonally adjusted data are not published for a small number of series characterized by small seasonal components relative to their trend and/or irregular components. However, these series are used in aggregating to broader seasonally adjusted levels.

Revisions of the seasonally adjusted data, usually for the most recent five-year period, are made once a year coinci-dent with the benchmark revisions. This means that these revisions typically extend back farther than the benchmark revisions.

Data availability

Employment data by industry division are available beginning with 1919. Data for each month usually are released on the first Friday of the following month in a press release that also contains data from the household survey (Tables 10-1 through 10-5). Data are subsequently published in the BLS monthly periodical *Employment and Earnings*, which features detailed explanatory notes. Selected data are published each month in the *Monthly Labor Review*, which frequently contains articles analyzing developments in the labor force, employment, and unemployment. *Employment and Earnings*, the *Monthly Labor Review*, press releases, and complete historical data are available on the BLS Web site at <http://www.bls.gov>.

Benchmark revisions and revised seasonally adjusted data for recent years are made each year with the release of January data in early February. Before 2004, the benchmark revisions were not made until June; the acceleration is due to earlier availability of the benchmark UI (ES-202) data.

References

References can be found at <http://www.bls.gov/ces> under the headings "Special Notices," "Benchmark Information," and "Technical Notes." Extensive changes incorporated in June 2003 are described in "Recent Changes in the National Current Employment Statistics Survey," *Monthly Labor Review*, June 2003; and in the "Explanatory Notes" in any subsequent issue of *Employment and Earnings*. The latest benchmark revision is discussed in an article available on the BLS Web site. See also Chapter 2, "Employment, Hours, and Earnings from the Establishment Survey," *BLS Handbook of Methods*, Bulletin 2490 (April 1997).

TABLES 10-9 THROUGH 10-11, 10-15, 10-16, 15-3, AND 15-6
AVERAGE HOURS PER WEEK; AGGREGATE EMPLOYEE HOURS

SOURCE: U.S. DEPARTMENT OF LABOR, BUREAU OF LABOR STATISTICS (BLS)

See the notes and definitions to Tables 10-8 and related tables, above, for an overall description of the "establishment" or "payroll" survey that is the source of hours data.

Hours and earnings have been reported for production and nonsupervisory workers, as defined above, since the inception of the CES. Beginning with data for March 2006, such data have also been collected for all payroll employees. With sufficient history for calculation of seasonal adjustment factors, BLS began publishing all-employee hours and earnings in February 2010, and these new data are presented in *Business Statistics* Tables 10-10 through 10-13.

Definitions

Average weekly hours represents the average hours paid per worker during the pay period that includes the 12th of the month. Included are hours paid for holidays and vacations, as well as those paid for sick leave when pay is received directly from the firm.

Average weekly hours are different from standard or scheduled hours. Factors such as unpaid absenteeism, labor turnover, part-time work, and work stoppages can cause average weekly hours to be lower than scheduled hours of work for an establishment.

An important characteristic of these data is that average weekly hours pertain to jobs, not to persons; thus, a person with half-time jobs in two different establishments is represented in this series as two jobs that have 20-hour workweeks, not as one person with a 40-hour workweek.

Overtime hours represent the portion of average weekly hours worked in excess of regular hours, for which overtime premiums were paid. Weekend and holiday hours are included only if overtime premiums were paid. Hours for which only shift differential, hazard, incentive, or other similar types of premiums were paid are excluded.

Aggregate hours provide measures of changes over time in labor input to the industry, in index-number form. The indexes are obtained by multiplying seasonally adjusted employment by seasonally adjusted average weekly hours, dividing the resulting series by their monthly averages for a base period, and multiplying the results by 100, so that the annual average for the base period equals 100. For total private, goods-producing, service-providing, and major industry divisions, the indexes are obtained by summing the seasonally adjusted aggregate weekly employee hours for the component industries, dividing by the monthly average for the base period, and multiplying by 100. For the series covering production and nonsupervisory workers, the base period is 2002; for the all-employee series, the base period is 2007.

Notes on the data

Benchmark adjustments. Independent benchmarks are not available for the hours and earnings series. At the time of the annual adjustment of the employment series to new benchmarks, the levels of hours and earnings may be affected by the revised employment weights (which are used in computing the industry averages for hours and earnings), as well as by the changes in seasonal adjustment factors introduced with the benchmark revision.

Method of computing industry series. "Average weekly hours" for individual industries are computed by dividing worker hours (reported by establishments classified in each industry) by the number of workers reported for the same establishments. Estimates for divisions and major industry groups are averages (weighted by employment) of the figures for component industries.

Seasonal adjustment. Hours and earnings series are seasonally adjusted by applying factors directly to the corresponding unadjusted series. Data for some industries are not seasonally adjusted because the seasonal component is small relative to the trend-cycle and/or irregular components. Consequently, they cannot be separated with sufficient precision.

Special adjustments are made to average weekly hours to account for the presence or absence of religious holidays in the April survey reference period and the occasional occurrence of Labor Day in the September reference period. In addition, REGARIMA modeling is used prior to seasonal adjustment to correct for reporting and processing errors associated with the number of weekdays in a month (rather than to correct for the 4- and 5-week effect, which is less significant for hours than it is for employment). This is of particular importance for average weekly hours in the service-providing industries other than retail trade. For this reason, BLS advises that calculations of over-the-year changes (for example, the change for the current month from a year earlier) should use seasonally adjusted data, since the actual not-seasonally-adjusted monthly data may be distorted.

Data availability

See data availability for Tables 10-8 and related, above.

References

See references for Tables 10-8 and related, above.

TABLES 10-9, 10-12, 10-13, 10-17, 10-18, 15-4, AND 15-5
HOURLY AND WEEKLY EARNINGS

SOURCE: U.S. DEPARTMENT OF LABOR, BUREAU OF LABOR STATISTICS (BLS)

See the notes and definitions to Tables 10-8 and related for an overall description of the "establishment" or "payroll" survey that is the source of these earnings data.

Hours and earnings have been reported for production and nonsupervisory workers, as defined above, since the inception of the CES. Beginning with data for March 2006, such data have also been collected for all payroll employees. With sufficient history for calculation of seasonal adjustment factors, BLS began publishing all-employee hours and earnings in February 2010, and these data are presented in new *Business Statistics* Tables 10-10 through 10-13.

Definitions

Earnings are the payments that workers receive during the survey period (before deductions for taxes and other items), including premium pay for overtime or late-shift work but excluding irregular bonuses and other special payments. After being previously excluded, tips were asked to be reported beginning in September 2005. This made little difference in most industries, and BLS asserts that many respondents had already been including tips. In two industries, full-service restaurants and cafeterias, there was a substantial difference, and the historical earnings data for those industries have been reconstructed to reflect the new higher level of earnings. These effects can be seen beginning with the data for 1974.

Notes on the data

The hours and earnings series are based on reports of gross payroll and corresponding paid hours for full- and part-time workers who received pay for any part of the pay period that included the 12th of the month.

Total payrolls are before deductions, such as for the employee share of old-age and unemployment insurance, group insurance, withholding taxes, bonds, and union dues. The payroll figures also include pay for overtime, holidays, vacations, and sick leave (paid directly by the employer for the period reported). Excluded from the payroll figures are fringe benefits (health and other types of insurance and contributions to retirement, paid by the employer, and the employer share of payroll taxes), bonuses (unless earned and paid regularly each pay period), other pay not earned in the pay period reported (retroactive pay), and the value of free rent, fuel, meals, or other payment-in-kind.

Average hourly earnings data reflect not only changes in basic hourly and incentive wage rates, but also such variable factors as premium pay for overtime and late-shift work and changes in output of workers paid on an incentive basis. Shifts in the volume of employment between relatively high-paid and low-paid work also affect the general average of hourly earnings.

Averages of hourly earnings should not be confused with wage rates, which represent the rates stipulated for a given unit of work or time, while earnings refer to the actual return to the worker for a stated period of time. The earnings series do not represent total labor cost to the employer because of the inclusion of tips and the exclusion of irregular bonuses, retroactive items, the cost of employer-provided benefits, and payroll taxes paid by employers.

Average weekly earnings are not the amounts available to workers for spending, since they do not reflect deductions such as income taxes and Social Security taxes. It is also important to understand that average weekly earnings represent earnings per job, not per worker (since a worker may have more than one job) and not per family (since a family may have more than one worker). A person with two half-time jobs will be reflected as two earners with low weekly earnings rather than as one person with the total earnings from his or her two jobs.

Method of computing industry series. Average hourly earnings are obtained by dividing the reported total worker payroll by total worker hours. Estimates for both hours and hourly earnings for nonfarm divisions and major industry groups are employment-weighted averages of the figures for component industries.

Average weekly earnings are computed by multiplying average hourly earnings by average weekly hours. In addition to the factors mentioned above, which exert varying influences upon average hourly earnings, average weekly earnings are affected by changes in the length of the workweek, part-time work, work stoppages, labor turnover, and absenteeism. Persistent long-term uptrends in the proportion of part-time workers in retail trade and many of the service industries have reduced average workweeks (as measured here), and have similarly affected the average weekly earnings series.

Benchmark adjustments. Independent benchmarks are not available for the hours and earnings series. At the time of the annual adjustment of the employment series to new benchmarks, the levels of hours and earnings may be affected by the revised employment weights (which are used in computing the industry averages for hours and earnings), as well as by the changes in seasonal adjustment factors that were also introduced with the benchmark revision.

Seasonal adjustment. Hours and earnings series are seasonally adjusted by applying factors directly to the corresponding unadjusted series; seasonally adjusted average weekly earnings are the product of seasonally adjusted hourly earnings and weekly hours.

REGARIMA modeling is used to correct for reporting and processing errors associated with variations in the number of weekdays in a month (rather than for the 4- and 5-week effect, which is less significant for earnings than for employment). This is of particular importance for average hourly earnings in wholesale trade, financial activities, professional and business services, and other services. For this reason, BLS advises that calculations of over-the-year changes, for example the change for the current month from a year earlier, should use seasonally adjusted data, since the actual not seasonally adjusted monthly data may be distorted.

Data availability

See data availability for Tables 10-8 and related, above.

References

See references for Tables 10-8 and related, above.

TABLE 10-19
HOURS AT WORK, CURRENT POPULATION SURVEY

This table presents annual average measures of hours worked per week reported by workers in the Current Population Survey, in response to questions asking for the hours worked in the survey week by each worker in the household on all his or her jobs combined. These measures are not published in regular BLS reports but are available on request. *Business Statistics* obtained these numbers from BLS staff and presents them here in annual average form.

A study published in the *Monthly Labor Review*, June 2011, indicates that CPS survey respondents may tend to overestimate the length of their workweeks, with greater overestimates the longer the actual workweek. This means that the level of the CPS data series may be overestimated, though not necessarily the time pattern of the series. In the judgment of the editor, the CPS data nevertheless give a more accurate picture of trends in the workweeks of typical American workers.

TABLE 10-20
MEDIAN USUAL WEEKLY EARNINGS OF FULL-TIME WAGE AND SALARY WORKERS

SOURCE: U.S. DEPARTMENT OF LABOR, BUREAU OF LABOR STATISTICS

These data are from the Current Population Survey, which was described in the notes to Tables 10-1 through 10-6. Because they are earnings per worker, not per job, and are limited to full-time workers, the data are not distorted by the increasing proportion of part-time workers, as the CES earnings data are.

Definitions

Full-time wage and salary workers are those workers reported as "employed" in the CPS who receive wages, salaries, commissions, tips, pay in kind, or piece rates, and usually work 35 hours or more per week at their sole or principal job. Both private-sector and public-sector employees are included. All self-employed persons are excluded (even those whose businesses are incorporated). The number of full-time wage and salary workers was 101.3 million, seasonally adjusted, in the fourth quarter of 2011; these workers made up 72 percent of total civilian employment.

Usual weekly earnings are earnings before taxes and other deductions and include any overtime pay, commissions, or tips usually received. In the case of multiple jobholders they refer to the main job. The wording of the question was changed in January 1994 to better deal with persons who found it easier to report earnings on other than a weekly basis. Such reports are then converted to the weekly equivalent. According to BLS, "the term 'usual' is as perceived by the respondent. If the respondent asks for a definition of usual, interviewers are instructed to define the term as more than half the weeks worked during the past 4 or 5 months."

The *median* is the amount that divides a given earnings distribution into two equal groups, one having earnings above the median and the other having earnings below the median.

2000 dollars. For men 25 and older and women 25 and older, median usual weekly earnings are shown on both a current-dollar and a constant-dollar basis. The editor has converted the current-dollar figures to 2000 dollars using the CPI-U-RS, which is shown and described in Chapter 8. The CPI-U-RS was chosen because it is the deflator used by the Census Bureau to convert household income and earnings to constant dollars and by the Bureau of Labor Statistics to convert compensation per hour to constant dollars. It corrects historical values of the CPI to be consistent with current CPI methodology.

Race and ethnicity. See the notes to Tables 10-1 through 10-6 for the definitions of these categories.

Data availability

These data become available about 3 weeks after the end of each quarter in the "Usual Weekly Earnings of Wage and Salary Workers" press release, available on the BLS Web site at <http://www.bls.gov/cps>. Recent data are available at that location. Also available are greater detail by demographic and age groups, by occupation, by union status, and by education; distributional data, by deciles and quartiles; and earnings for part-time workers. Also available are earnings in 1982 dollars using the CPI-U. (In the opinion of the editor, these give a less accurate depiction of longer-term trends, which is why *Business Statistics* provides the CPI-U-RS data explained above.) Historical data are available upon request from BLS by telephone at (202) 691-6378.

TABLE 10-21
FULL-TIME AND PART-TIME EMPLOYEES BY SIC INDUSTRY, HISTORICAL ANNUAL

These estimates, which are made only annually for the full year, are found in Tables 6-4 of the National Income and Product Accounts (NIPAs). They are like the payroll series in counting the number of jobs rather than the number of persons employed. However, they are broader than the payroll series in that they include private household employment (domestic service) in the "service" industry category. They exclude most of the agricultural employment reported in the CPS, but include members of the armed forces and all other government employment including work-relief agencies such as the Works Progress Administration and the Civilian Conservation Corps; these categories are shown separately in Table 10-21. This treatment is consistent with the rest of the NIPAs, in which GDP includes, as output, the work done by relief workers, and the buildings they constructed are included in investment and capital stock. The industry estimates are based on various versions of the Standard Industrial Classification system that were in effect at the time of compilation.

CHAPTER 11: ENERGY

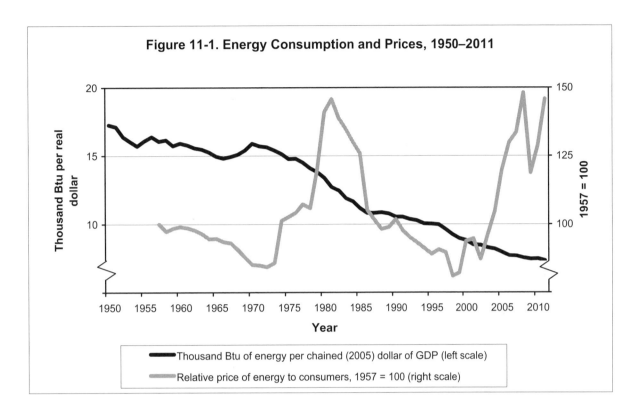

Figure 11-1. Energy Consumption and Prices, 1950–2011

- The downward trend in energy use per dollar of real GDP, which can also be described as an increase in the energy efficiency of national production, may seem surprising in light of long-term trend increases in motor vehicle use, air conditioning, air travel, and other consumer uses of energy. Evidently, these increases are more than offset by factors such as the rising share of services and high-tech goods in GDP and the declining relative importance of energy-intensive materials production processes such as primary metals production. Also, upswings in relative energy prices—measured as the ratio of the CPI for energy to the total CPI—appear to have been associated with somewhat faster declines in the energy/GDP trend. (Figure 11-1 and Tables 8-1 and 11-2)

- Consumption of petroleum and natural gas per dollar of real GDP rose between 1950 and the early 1970s, but has declined 62 percent since then. Use of other forms of energy per real dollar leveled off during the 1970s and 1980s but then resumed its decline, and is down 63 percent over the entire post-war period. (Table 11-2)

- Net imports supplied 30 percent of total energy supply (production plus net imports) in the mid-2000s, compared with 7.4 percent in 1965 and 16.5 percent in 1973. However, the net imports share has declined dramatically since 2005-2006, to 18.9 percent in 2011. This decline reflected a recession-driven decline in imports; a rise in exports; and increases in production of crude oil, natural gas plant liquids, renewable energy, and especially natural gas. (Table 11-1)

- Nuclear power, almost nonexistent in 1965, supplied 10.6 percent of total U.S. energy production in 2011. Renewable energy sources, which provided 6.7 percent in 1965, accounted for 11.8 percent in 2011. The remaining 77.6 percent in 2011 was accounted for by domestic fossil fuel production, compared with 93.2 percent in 1965. (Table 11-1)

Table 11-1. Energy Supply and Consumption

(Quadrillion Btu.)

Year and month	Imports	Exports	Production, by source								Consumption, by end-use sector			
			Total	Fossil fuels					Nuclear electric power	Renew-able energy, total	Total	Residential and commercial	Industrial	Transport-ation
				Total	Coal	Natural gas	Crude oil	Natural gas plant liquids						
1965	5.892	1.829	50.676	47.234	13.055	15.775	16.521	1.883	0.043	3.399	54.017	16.509	25.075	12.434
1966	6.146	1.829	53.534	50.036	13.468	17.011	17.561	1.996	0.064	3.434	57.017	17.517	26.397	13.102
1967	6.159	2.115	56.379	52.596	13.825	17.943	18.651	2.177	0.088	3.695	58.908	18.541	26.616	13.752
1968	6.905	1.998	58.225	54.306	13.609	19.068	19.308	2.321	0.142	3.777	62.419	19.665	27.888	14.866
1969	7.676	2.126	60.541	56.285	13.863	20.446	19.556	2.420	0.154	4.102	65.621	21.000	29.114	15.506
1970	8.342	2.632	63.501	59.186	14.607	21.666	20.401	2.512	0.239	4.076	67.844	22.105	29.641	16.098
1971	9.535	2.151	62.723	58.043	13.186	22.280	20.033	2.544	0.413	4.267	69.289	22.959	29.601	16.729
1972	11.387	2.118	63.920	58.939	14.092	22.208	20.041	2.598	0.584	4.397	72.704	24.036	30.953	17.716
1973	14.613	2.033	63.563	58.241	13.992	22.187	19.493	2.569	0.910	4.411	75.676	24.440	32.623	18.613
1974	14.304	2.203	62.345	56.331	14.074	21.210	18.575	2.471	1.272	4.742	73.955	24.048	31.787	18.120
1975	14.032	2.323	61.320	54.733	14.989	19.640	17.729	2.374	1.900	4.687	71.964	24.306	29.413	18.245
1976	16.760	2.172	61.561	54.723	15.654	19.480	17.262	2.327	2.111	4.727	75.967	25.474	31.393	19.101
1977	19.948	2.052	62.012	55.101	15.755	19.565	17.454	2.327	2.702	4.209	77.954	25.869	32.263	19.822
1978	19.106	1.920	63.104	55.074	14.910	19.485	18.434	2.245	3.024	5.005	79.949	26.644	32.688	20.617
1979	19.460	2.855	65.904	58.006	17.540	20.076	18.104	2.286	2.776	5.123	80.857	26.461	33.925	20.472
1980	15.796	3.695	67.175	59.008	18.598	19.908	18.249	2.254	2.739	5.428	78.068	26.332	32.039	19.697
1981	13.719	4.307	66.951	58.529	18.377	19.699	18.146	2.307	3.008	5.414	76.103	25.877	30.712	19.514
1982	11.861	4.608	66.569	57.458	18.639	18.319	18.309	2.191	3.131	5.980	73.095	26.391	27.614	19.089
1983	11.752	3.693	64.114	54.416	17.247	16.593	18.392	2.184	3.203	6.496	72.968	26.363	27.428	19.177
1984	12.471	3.786	68.840	58.849	19.719	18.008	18.848	2.274	3.553	6.438	76.629	27.403	29.570	19.656
1985	11.781	4.196	67.698	57.539	19.325	16.980	18.992	2.241	4.076	6.084	76.396	27.493	28.816	20.088
1986	14.151	4.021	67.066	56.575	19.509	16.541	18.376	2.149	4.380	6.111	76.644	27.581	28.274	20.789
1987	15.398	3.812	67.542	57.167	20.141	17.136	17.675	2.215	4.754	5.622	79.057	28.209	29.379	21.469
1988	17.296	4.366	68.919	57.875	20.738	17.599	17.279	2.260	5.587	5.457	82.706	29.711	30.677	22.318
1989	18.766	4.661	69.320	57.483	21.360	17.847	16.117	2.158	5.602	6.235	84.777	30.979	31.320	22.478
1990	18.817	4.752	70.705	58.560	22.488	18.326	15.571	2.175	6.104	6.041	84.494	30.265	31.810	22.420
1991	18.335	5.141	70.362	57.872	21.636	18.229	15.701	2.306	6.422	6.069	84.437	30.920	31.399	22.118
1992	19.372	4.937	69.956	57.655	21.694	18.375	15.223	2.363	6.479	5.821	85.783	30.797	32.571	22.415
1993	21.273	4.258	68.315	55.822	20.336	18.584	14.494	2.408	6.410	6.083	87.434	32.037	32.629	22.768
1994	22.390	4.061	70.726	58.044	22.202	19.348	14.103	2.391	6.694	5.988	89.097	32.210	33.521	23.366
1995	22.260	4.511	71.174	57.540	22.130	19.082	13.887	2.442	7.075	6.558	91.026	33.209	33.971	23.846
1996	23.702	4.633	72.486	58.387	22.790	19.344	13.723	2.530	7.087	7.012	94.018	34.676	34.904	24.437
1997	25.215	4.514	72.472	58.857	23.310	19.394	13.658	2.495	6.597	7.018	94.596	34.646	35.200	24.750
1998	26.581	4.299	72.876	59.314	24.045	19.613	13.235	2.420	7.068	6.494	95.021	34.922	34.843	25.256
1999	27.252	3.715	71.742	57.614	23.295	19.341	12.451	2.528	7.610	6.517	96.646	35.933	34.764	25.949
2000	28.973	4.006	71.332	57.366	22.735	19.662	12.358	2.611	7.862	6.104	98.812	37.600	34.664	26.548
2001	30.157	3.771	71.735	58.541	23.547	20.166	12.282	2.547	8.029	5.164	96.174	37.179	32.720	26.275
2002	29.408	3.669	70.716	56.837	22.732	19.382	12.163	2.559	8.145	5.734	97.640	38.136	32.662	26.842
2003	31.061	4.054	70.040	56.099	22.094	19.633	12.026	2.346	7.959	5.982	97.979	38.453	32.532	26.994
2004	33.544	4.434	70.188	55.895	22.852	19.074	11.503	2.466	8.222	6.070	100.160	38.752	33.520	27.895
2005	34.709	4.560	69.428	55.038	23.185	18.556	10.963	2.334	8.161	6.229	100.280	39.483	32.446	28.353
2006	34.679	4.872	70.782	55.968	23.790	19.022	10.801	2.356	8.215	6.599	99.630	38.399	32.401	28.830
2007	34.703	5.482	71.373	56.409	23.493	19.786	10.721	2.409	8.455	6.509	101.290	39.786	32.394	29.117
2008	32.992	7.060	73.111	57.482	23.851	20.703	10.509	2.419	8.427	7.202	99.275	39.977	31.290	28.008
2009	29.706	6.965	72.657	56.685	21.624	21.139	11.348	2.574	8.356	7.616	94.559	38.963	28.525	27.071
2010	29.877	8.234	74.821	58.250	22.038	21.823	11.608	2.781	8.434	8.136	97.656	39.940	30.250	27.466
2011	28.590	10.356	78.123	60.628	22.181	23.506	12.013	2.928	8.259	9.236	97.224	39.635	30.510	27.079
2010														
January	2.516	0.590	6.164	4.733	1.743	1.790	0.970	0.230	0.758	0.672	9.128	4.443	2.487	2.198
February	2.237	0.556	5.738	4.445	1.687	1.648	0.900	0.210	0.682	0.610	8.212	3.835	2.365	2.012
March	2.519	0.654	6.389	5.032	1.969	1.835	0.991	0.236	0.676	0.682	8.206	3.352	2.557	2.297
April	2.580	0.686	6.037	4.774	1.848	1.763	0.936	0.227	0.602	0.661	7.375	2.654	2.435	2.286
May	2.578	0.704	6.192	4.778	1.736	1.832	0.972	0.238	0.697	0.717	7.678	2.795	2.527	2.356
June	2.556	0.684	6.183	4.716	1.802	1.751	0.937	0.226	0.714	0.753	8.005	3.160	2.517	2.328
July	2.705	0.716	6.342	4.889	1.847	1.859	0.956	0.227	0.752	0.701	8.379	3.435	2.532	2.411
August	2.627	0.698	6.397	4.987	1.898	1.874	0.980	0.236	0.748	0.662	8.441	3.402	2.633	2.406
September	2.431	0.675	6.281	4.931	1.897	1.826	0.977	0.232	0.725	0.626	7.694	2.885	2.512	2.298
October	2.390	0.714	6.308	5.006	1.864	1.892	1.008	0.242	0.656	0.646	7.511	2.695	2.482	2.333
November	2.289	0.760	6.235	4.898	1.860	1.833	0.969	0.235	0.655	0.682	7.799	3.048	2.523	2.228
December	2.447	0.797	6.557	5.061	1.886	1.920	1.012	0.242	0.770	0.726	9.230	4.236	2.679	2.314
2011														
January	2.607	0.832	6.514	5.000	1.854	1.922	0.994	0.230	0.760	0.754	9.354	4.456	2.671	2.227
February	2.087	0.751	5.921	4.527	1.736	1.711	0.883	0.198	0.677	0.717	8.136	3.718	2.369	2.049
March	2.501	0.869	6.689	5.181	1.958	1.963	1.013	0.247	0.686	0.822	8.379	3.429	2.646	2.304
April	2.378	0.852	6.311	4.920	1.789	1.925	0.967	0.238	0.570	0.821	7.551	2.836	2.465	2.249
May	2.466	0.832	6.448	5.011	1.755	1.988	1.015	0.253	0.596	0.840	7.615	2.783	2.520	2.313
June	2.407	0.802	6.445	4.934	1.798	1.923	0.974	0.240	0.682	0.828	7.936	3.083	2.537	2.315
July	2.493	0.833	6.506	4.953	1.733	1.987	0.983	0.250	0.756	0.797	8.375	3.494	2.558	2.323
August	2.395	0.893	6.691	5.200	1.933	1.994	1.021	0.251	0.746	0.746	8.386	3.411	2.619	2.356
September	2.288	0.891	6.443	5.065	1.903	1.952	0.973	0.237	0.699	0.680	7.568	2.870	2.460	2.238
October	2.345	0.892	6.658	5.286	1.915	2.052	1.059	0.259	0.662	0.711	7.575	2.776	2.536	2.264
November	2.269	0.900	6.639	5.222	1.904	2.014	1.046	0.258	0.674	0.742	7.754	3.023	2.550	2.181
December	2.354	1.008	6.859	5.330	1.903	2.075	1.084	0.268	0.751	0.779	8.595	3.753	2.581	2.260

Table 11-2. Energy Consumption Per Dollar of Real Gross Domestic Product

Year	Energy consumption (quadrillion Btu)			Gross domestic product (billions of chained [2005] dollars)	Energy consumption per real dollar of GDP (thousand Btu per chained [2005] dollar)		
	Total	Petroleum and natural gas	Other energy		Total	Petroleum and natural gas	Other energy
1950	34.616	19.284	15.332	2 006.0	17.26	9.61	7.64
1951	36.974	21.477	15.497	2 161.1	17.11	9.94	7.17
1952	36.748	22.505	14.243	2 243.9	16.38	10.03	6.35
1953	37.664	23.462	14.202	2 347.2	16.05	10.00	6.05
1954	36.639	24.169	12.470	2 332.4	15.71	10.36	5.35
1955	40.208	26.253	13.955	2 500.3	16.08	10.50	5.58
1956	41.754	27.551	14.203	2 549.7	16.38	10.81	5.57
1957	41.787	28.122	13.665	2 601.1	16.07	10.81	5.25
1958	41.645	29.190	12.455	2 577.6	16.16	11.32	4.83
1959	43.466	31.040	12.426	2 762.5	15.73	11.24	4.50
1960	45.087	32.305	12.782	2 830.9	15.93	11.41	4.52
1961	45.739	33.143	12.596	2 896.9	15.79	11.44	4.35
1962	47.828	34.780	13.048	3 072.4	15.57	11.32	4.25
1963	49.646	36.104	13.542	3 206.7	15.48	11.26	4.22
1964	51.817	37.589	14.228	3 392.3	15.27	11.08	4.19
1965	54.017	39.014	15.003	3 610.1	14.96	10.81	4.16
1966	57.017	41.396	15.621	3 845.3	14.83	10.77	4.06
1967	58.908	43.228	15.680	3 942.5	14.94	10.96	3.98
1968	62.419	46.189	16.230	4 133.4	15.10	11.17	3.93
1969	65.621	49.016	16.605	4 261.8	15.40	11.50	3.90
1970	67.844	51.315	16.529	4 269.9	15.89	12.02	3.87
1971	69.289	53.030	16.259	4 413.3	15.70	12.02	3.68
1972	72.704	55.645	17.059	4 647.7	15.64	11.97	3.67
1973	75.684	57.350	18.334	4 912.8	15.40	11.67	3.73
1974	73.962	55.186	18.776	4 885.7	15.14	11.30	3.84
1975	71.965	52.680	19.284	4 875.4	14.77	10.81	3.96
1976	75.975	55.523	20.452	5 136.9	14.79	10.81	3.98
1977	77.961	57.054	20.907	5 373.1	14.51	10.62	3.89
1978	79.950	57.963	21.987	5 672.8	14.10	10.22	3.88
1979	80.859	57.788	23.070	5 850.1	13.82	9.88	3.94
1980	78.067	54.440	23.627	5 834.0	13.38	9.33	4.05
1981	76.106	51.680	24.426	5 982.1	12.72	8.64	4.08
1982	73.099	48.588	24.511	5 865.9	12.46	8.28	4.18
1983	72.971	47.273	25.698	6 130.9	11.90	7.71	4.19
1984	76.632	49.447	27.185	6 571.5	11.66	7.52	4.14
1985	76.392	48.628	27.764	6 843.4	11.17	7.11	4.06
1986	76.647	48.790	27.857	7 080.5	10.82	6.89	3.93
1987	79.054	50.504	28.551	7 307.0	10.82	6.91	3.91
1988	82.709	52.671	30.038	7 607.4	10.87	6.92	3.95
1989	84.786	53.811	30.975	7 879.2	10.76	6.83	3.93
1990	84.485	53.155	31.330	8 027.1	10.52	6.62	3.90
1991	84.438	52.879	31.559	8 008.3	10.54	6.60	3.94
1992	85.783	54.239	31.544	8 280.0	10.36	6.55	3.81
1993	87.424	54.973	32.450	8 516.2	10.27	6.46	3.81
1994	89.091	56.289	32.803	8 863.1	10.05	6.35	3.70
1995	91.029	57.110	33.920	9 086.0	10.02	6.29	3.73
1996	94.022	58.760	35.262	9 425.8	9.97	6.23	3.74
1997	94.602	59.382	35.221	9 845.9	9.61	6.03	3.58
1998	95.018	59.646	35.372	10 274.7	9.25	5.81	3.44
1999	96.652	60.747	35.905	10 770.7	8.97	5.64	3.33
2000	98.814	62.086	36.729	11 216.4	8.81	5.54	3.27
2001	96.168	60.958	35.210	11 337.5	8.49	5.38	3.11
2002	97.645	61.734	35.911	11 543.1	8.46	5.35	3.11
2003	97.978	61.642	36.336	11 836.4	8.28	5.21	3.07
2004	100.162	63.215	36.947	12 246.9	8.18	5.16	3.02
2005	100.282	62.953	37.328	12 623.0	7.95	4.99	2.96
2006	99.629	62.194	37.435	12 958.5	7.69	4.80	2.89
2007	101.296	63.437	37.859	13 206.4	7.67	4.80	2.87
2008	99.275	61.123	38.152	13 161.9	7.54	4.64	2.90
2009	94.559	58.819	35.740	12 703.1	7.44	4.63	2.81
2010	97.722	60.266	37.456	13 088.0	7.46	4.60	2.86
2011	97.301	60.125	37.176	13 315.1	7.31	4.52	2.79

NOTES AND DEFINITIONS, CHAPTER 11

TABLES 11-1 AND 11-2
ENERGY SUPPLY AND CONSUMPTION

SOURCES: U.S. DEPARTMENT OF ENERGY, ENERGY INFORMATION ADMINISTRATION; U.S. DEPARTMENT OF COMMERCE, BUREAU OF ECONOMIC ANALYSIS

Definitions

The *British thermal unit (Btu)* is a measure used to combine data for different energy sources into a consistent aggregate. It is the amount of energy required to raise the temperature of 1 pound of water 1 degree Fahrenheit when the water is near a temperature of 39.2 degrees Fahrenheit. To illustrate one of the factors used to convert volumes to Btu, conventional motor gasoline has a heat content of 5.253 million Btu per barrel. For further information, see the Energy Information Administration's *Monthly Energy Review*, Appendix A.

Production: Crude oil includes lease condensates.

Renewable energy, total includes conventional hydroelectric power, geothermal, solar thermal and photovoltaic, wind, and biomass. Hydroelectric power includes conventional electrical utility and industrial generation. Biomass includes wood, waste, and alcohol fuels (ethanol blended into motor gasoline).

The sum of domestic energy *production* and net imports of energy (*imports* minus *exports*) does not exactly equal domestic energy *consumption*. The difference is attributed to inventory changes; losses and gains in conversion, transportation, and distribution; the addition of blending compounds; shipments of anthracite to U.S. armed forces in Europe; and adjustments to account for discrepancies between reporting systems.

Consumption by end-use sector is based on total, not net, consumption. Components may not add to totals because of different sector-specific conversion factors.

References and notes on the data

These data are published each month in Tables 1.1, 1.2, 1.7, and 2.1 in the *Monthly Energy Review*. Annual data before 1973 are published in the *Annual Energy Review*. These two publications are no longer published in printed form but are available, along with all current and historical data, on the EIA Web site at <http://www.eia.doe.gov>. The real gross domestic product (GDP) data used to calculate energy consumption per dollar of real GDP are from the Bureau of Economic Analysis; see Table 1-2 and the applicable notes and definitions in this volume of *Business Statistics*.

CHAPTER 12: MONEY, INTEREST, ASSETS, LIABILITIES, AND ASSET PRICES

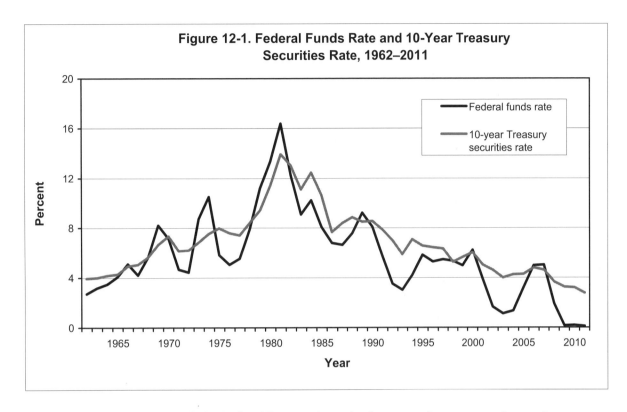

Figure 12-1. Federal Funds Rate and 10-Year Treasury Securities Rate, 1962–2011

- As the recession deepened, the Federal Reserve brought short-term interest rates lower than at any time since the Great Depression, World War II, and its aftermath. The federal funds rate—shown in Figure 12-1—was held at 0.2 percent throughout 2009 and 2010 and 0.1 percent in 2011. "Real" fed funds and other short-term interest rates (subtracting out current underlying inflation rates) have been negative since early 2008. (Tables 12-9A and B)

- Longer-term rates have also declined dramatically. The nominal rate on Treasury 10-year securities, the ultimate in safe longer-term investments, is also shown in Figure 12-1. It reached lows around 2.0 percent by late 2011. Despite the huge volume of federal borrowing (see Tables 6-1, 6-14 and 12-5), this interest rate was lower than at any time in the postwar period. (Tables 12-9A and B)

- The rate spread between Aaa-rated and Baa-rated corporate bonds, representing a market evaluation of risk, was more than 3 percentage points (300 "basis points") in December 2008. This exceeded the previous record postwar spreads seen in 1982. At the end of 2011, the spread had contracted back to 1.32 percentage point. (Table 12-9A and B)

- Looking at the easing in quantitative terms, the Federal Reserve added $1.3 trillion to its balance sheet during 2008 and another $688 billion by the end of 2011. The size of the monetary base has grown at a 33 percent annual rate over the four years since December 2007. (Table 12-3) But with financial institutions reluctant to lend and thereby create deposits, the money supply grew more tamely; M1 grew at a 12 percent annual rate over those years, while M2, the aggregate traditionally most closely associated with the dollar value of GDP and hence with economic activity and inflationary pressure, only increased at a 6.5 percent rate. (Table 12-1)

Table 12-1A. Money Stock Measures and Components of M1: Recent Data

(Billions of dollars, monthly data are averages of daily figures, annual data are for December.)

Year and month	Not seasonally adjusted		Seasonally adjusted					Other checkable deposits		
	M1	M2	M1	M2	Currency	Traveler's checks	Demand deposits	At commercial banks	At thrift institutions	Total
1960	144.5	315.3	140.7	312.4	28.7	0.3	111.6	0.0	0.0	0.0
1961	149.2	338.5	145.2	335.5	29.3	0.4	115.5	0.0	0.0	0.0
1962	151.9	365.8	147.8	362.7	30.3	0.4	117.1	0.0	0.0	0.0
1963	157.5	396.4	153.3	393.2	32.2	0.4	120.6	0.0	0.1	0.1
1964	164.9	428.3	160.3	424.7	33.9	0.5	125.8	0.0	0.1	0.1
1965	172.6	463.1	167.8	459.2	36.0	0.5	131.3	0.0	0.1	0.1
1966	176.9	483.7	172.0	480.2	38.0	0.6	133.4	0.0	0.1	0.1
1967	188.4	528.0	183.3	524.8	40.0	0.6	142.5	0.0	0.1	0.1
1968	202.8	569.7	197.4	566.8	43.0	0.7	153.6	0.0	0.1	0.1
1969	209.3	590.1	203.9	587.9	45.7	0.8	157.3	0.0	0.1	0.1
1970	220.1	627.8	214.4	626.5	48.6	0.9	164.7	0.0	0.1	0.1
1971	234.5	711.2	228.3	710.3	52.0	1.0	175.1	0.0	0.2	0.2
1972	256.1	803.1	249.2	802.3	56.2	1.2	191.6	0.0	0.2	0.2
1973	270.2	856.5	262.9	855.5	60.8	1.4	200.3	0.0	0.3	0.3
1974	281.8	903.5	274.2	902.1	67.0	1.7	205.1	0.2	0.4	0.4
1975	295.3	1 017.8	287.1	1 016.2	72.8	2.1	211.3	0.4	0.5	0.9
1976	314.5	1 153.5	306.2	1 152.0	79.5	2.6	221.5	1.3	1.4	2.7
1977	340.0	1 273.0	330.9	1 270.3	87.4	2.9	236.4	1.8	2.3	4.2
1978	367.9	1 370.8	357.3	1 366.0	96.0	3.3	249.5	5.3	3.1	8.5
1979	393.2	1 479.0	381.8	1 473.7	104.8	3.5	256.6	12.7	4.2	16.8
1980	419.5	1 604.8	408.5	1 599.8	115.3	3.9	261.2	20.8	7.3	28.1
1981	447.0	1 760.3	436.7	1 755.5	122.5	4.1	231.4	63.0	15.6	78.7
1982	485.8	1 917.2	474.8	1 909.3	132.5	4.1	234.1	80.5	23.6	104.1
1983	533.3	2 136.2	521.4	2 125.7	146.2	4.7	238.5	97.3	34.8	132.1
1984	564.6	2 320.9	551.6	2 308.8	156.1	5.0	243.4	104.7	42.4	147.1
1985	633.3	2 506.6	619.8	2 494.6	167.7	5.6	266.9	124.7	54.9	179.5
1986	739.8	2 744.3	724.7	2 731.6	180.4	6.1	302.9	161.0	74.2	235.2
1987	765.4	2 842.9	750.2	2 831.0	196.7	6.6	287.7	178.2	81.0	259.2
1988	803.1	3 005.2	786.7	2 992.8	212.0	7.0	287.1	192.5	88.1	280.6
1989	810.6	3 169.7	792.9	3 156.7	222.3	6.9	278.6	197.4	87.7	285.1
1990	842.7	3 288.2	824.7	3 274.9	246.5	7.7	276.8	208.7	85.0	293.7
1991	915.6	3 389.1	897.0	3 374.8	267.1	7.7	289.6	241.6	90.9	332.5
1992	1 045.6	3 443.8	1 024.9	3 427.1	292.1	8.2	340.0	280.8	103.8	384.6
1993	1 153.3	3 498.0	1 129.8	3 477.4	321.7	8.0	385.4	302.6	112.0	414.6
1994	1 174.5	3 512.9	1 150.8	3 491.5	354.7	8.6	383.6	297.4	106.6	404.0
1995	1 152.7	3 658.1	1 127.5	3 634.2	372.8	9.0	389.0	249.0	107.6	356.6
1996	1 105.8	3 835.6	1 081.4	3 814.3	394.6	8.8	402.2	172.1	103.7	275.8
1997	1 097.5	4 050.4	1 072.5	4 028.5	425.2	8.4	393.7	148.3	96.9	245.2
1998	1 121.2	4 392.3	1 095.7	4 369.6	460.4	8.5	376.8	143.9	106.1	250.0
1999	1 148.2	4 656.6	1 122.4	4 628.9	517.9	8.6	352.8	139.7	103.5	243.2
2000	1 111.7	4 942.9	1 087.8	4 911.6	531.4	8.3	309.9	133.2	105.2	238.3
2001	1 208.3	5 459.4	1 182.8	5 424.9	581.3	8.0	335.9	142.0	115.6	257.6
2002	1 245.6	5 801.4	1 220.6	5 768.7	626.3	7.8	307.1	154.3	125.1	279.4
2003	1 332.3	6 088.8	1 307.0	6 058.6	662.5	7.7	326.6	175.2	134.9	310.2
2004	1 401.3	6 434.4	1 376.7	6 404.4	697.6	7.6	343.6	186.9	141.0	328.0
2005	1 396.8	6 696.8	1 375.0	6 667.9	724.0	7.2	325.1	180.6	138.1	318.7
2006	1 387.3	7 092.9	1 367.2	7 059.7	749.5	6.7	306.0	176.3	128.6	304.9
2007	1 394.5	7 520.7	1 375.4	7 484.5	760.0	6.3	303.8	172.0	133.3	305.3
2008	1 632.0	8 267.8	1 606.9	8 231.7	816.1	5.5	474.9	177.3	133.1	310.4
2009	1 723.7	8 554.2	1 697.8	8 514.2	863.3	5.1	447.4	232.1	149.9	382.0
2010	1 870.7	8 853.2	1 840.3	8 796.4	918.0	4.7	519.4	236.7	161.6	398.3
2011	2 213.1	9 712.6	2 173.9	9 640.1	999.9	4.3	759.2	235.2	175.3	410.5
2010										
January	1 673.7	8 474.4	1 684.1	8 437.6	863.8	5.1	439.3	223.7	152.4	376.1
February	1 685.1	8 517.6	1 704.8	8 489.8	868.0	5.0	447.8	230.6	153.5	384.1
March	1 729.7	8 581.2	1 712.3	8 487.6	871.4	5.0	447.7	235.7	152.6	388.3
April	1 716.2	8 604.0	1 701.6	8 514.2	875.6	4.9	449.8	217.1	154.3	371.3
May	1 708.0	8 584.3	1 705.8	8 562.2	879.4	4.9	446.8	218.7	156.1	374.8
June	1 731.9	8 605.3	1 722.3	8 582.9	882.5	4.8	456.7	224.1	154.3	378.4
July	1 717.8	8 575.8	1 724.5	8 579.4	887.0	4.8	455.2	223.1	154.5	377.6
August	1 739.0	8 605.9	1 743.5	8 606.2	892.6	4.7	466.1	224.5	155.7	380.2
September	1 740.8	8 647.5	1 762.0	8 640.7	899.1	4.7	474.0	228.9	155.4	384.3
October	1 766.8	8 707.4	1 776.8	8 693.5	907.1	4.7	477.4	229.4	158.3	387.7
November	1 828.0	8 771.9	1 822.4	8 724.2	914.0	4.7	506.8	237.5	159.5	397.1
December	1 870.7	8 853.2	1 840.2	8 765.3	918.0	4.7	519.4	236.7	161.6	398.3
2011										
January	1 854.8	8 846.1	1 868.3	8 829.1	922.6	4.7	539.1	237.0	165.1	402.0
February	1 857.9	8 883.3	1 878.8	8 872.6	930.2	4.6	539.7	237.8	166.7	404.5
March	1 908.5	8 995.3	1 891.0	8 920.4	938.6	4.6	542.8	237.6	167.6	405.1
April	1 917.2	9 049.9	1 903.7	8 967.6	947.6	4.6	552.4	231.2	168.1	399.3
May	1 934.5	9 019.5	1 931.5	9 017.6	956.2	4.6	567.4	235.5	168.0	403.4
June	1 954.5	9 106.3	1 945.1	9 094.0	963.0	4.5	575.7	235.7	166.2	401.9
July	1 994.8	9 257.7	2 004.5	9 267.1	969.2	4.5	627.3	236.2	167.6	403.7
August	2 102.0	9 451.6	2 106.2	9 457.0	975.8	4.4	713.6	239.7	172.7	412.4
September	2 097.6	9 488.0	2 122.6	9 476.8	981.7	4.4	727.1	237.4	172.0	409.5
October	2 128.3	9 537.6	2 137.7	9 523.9	986.2	4.4	738.5	235.8	174.1	409.9
November	2 167.6	9 618.1	2 155.0	9 571.6	993.1	4.3	750.0	235.6	175.3	410.8
December	2 213.1	9 712.6	2 168.7	9 616.6	999.9	4.3	759.2	235.2	175.3	410.5

Table 12-1B. Money Stock, Historical: 1929–1946

(Not seasonally adjusted, millions of dollars.)

Classification	1929	1930	1931	1932	1933	1934	1935	1936	1937
June 30									
Currency outside banks	3 639	3 369	3 651	4 616	4 761	4 659	4 783	5 222	5 489
Demand deposits adjusted	22 540	21 706	19 832	15 625	14 411	16 694	20 433	23 780	25 198
M1	26 179	25 075	23 483	20 241	19 172	21 353	25 216	29 002	30 687
Time deposits	28 611	28 992	28 961	24 756	21 656	22 875	23 854	24 908	25 905
M2	54 790	54 067	52 444	44 997	40 828	44 228	49 070	53 910	56 592
December 31									
Currency outside banks	3 557	3 605	4 470	4 669	4 782	4 655	4 917	5 516	5 638
Demand deposits adjusted	22 809	20 967	17 412	15 728	15 035	18 459	22 115	25 483	23 959
M1	26 366	24 572	21 882	20 397	19 817	23 114	27 032	30 999	29 597
Time deposits	28 189	28 676	25 979	24 457	21 715	23 156	24 241	25 361	26 218
M2	54 555	53 248	47 861	44 854	41 532	46 270	51 273	56 360	55 815

Classification	1938	1939	1940	1941	1942	1943	1944	1945	1946
June 30									
Currency outside banks	5 417	6 005	6 699	8 204	10 936	15 814	20 881	25 097	26 516
Demand deposits adjusted	24 313	27 355	31 962	37 317	41 870	56 039	60 065	69 053	79 476
M1	29 730	33 360	38 661	45 521	52 806	71 853	80 946	94 150	105 992
Time deposits	26 236	26 791	27 463	27 879	27 320	30 260	35 720	44 253	51 829
M2	55 966	60 151	66 124	73 400	80 126	102 113	116 666	138 403	157 821
December 31									
Currency outside banks	5 775	6 401	7 325	9 615	13 946	18 837	23 505	26 490	26 730
Demand deposits adjusted	25 986	29 793	34 945	38 992	48 922	60 803	66 930	75 851	83 814
M1	31 761	36 194	42 270	48 607	62 868	79 640	90 435	102 341	110 044
Time deposits	26 305	27 059	27 738	27 729	28 431	32 748	39 790	48 452	53 960
M2	58 066	63 253	70 008	76 336	91 299	112 388	130 225	150 793	164 004

Table 12-1C. Money Stock, Historical: January 1947–January 1959

(Averages of daily figures; seasonally adjusted, billions of dollars.)

Year and month	Money stock (M1)			Time deposits adjusted	M2 (M1 plus time deposits)
	Total	Currency component	Demand deposit component		
1947					
January	109.5	26.7	82.8	33.3	142.8
February	109.7	26.7	83.0	33.5	143.2
March	110.3	26.7	83.7	33.6	143.9
April	111.1	26.6	84.5	33.7	144.8
May	111.7	26.6	85.1	33.8	145.5
June	112.1	26.6	85.5	33.9	146.0
July	112.2	26.5	85.7	34.0	146.2
August	112.6	26.5	86.1	34.4	147.0
September	113.0	26.7	86.3	34.7	147.7
October	112.9	26.5	86.4	35.0	147.9
November	113.3	26.5	86.8	35.2	148.5
December	113.1	26.4	86.7	35.4	148.5
1948					
January	113.4	26.4	87.0	35.5	148.9
February	113.2	26.3	86.8	35.7	148.9
March	112.6	26.2	86.4	35.7	148.3
April	112.3	26.1	86.3	35.7	148.0
May	112.1	26.0	86.0	35.7	147.8
June	112.0	26.0	86.0	35.8	147.8
July	112.2	26.0	86.2	35.8	148.0
August	112.3	26.0	86.2	35.9	148.2
September	112.2	26.0	86.2	35.9	148.1
October	112.1	26.0	86.1	35.9	148.0
November	111.8	26.0	85.9	36.0	147.8
December	111.5	25.8	85.8	36.0	147.5
1949					
January	111.2	25.7	85.5	36.1	147.3
February	111.2	25.7	85.5	36.1	147.3
March	111.2	25.7	85.6	36.1	147.3
April	113.3	25.7	85.6	36.2	149.5
May	111.5	25.7	85.8	36.3	147.8
June	111.3	25.6	85.7	36.4	147.7
July	111.2	25.5	85.7	36.4	147.6
August	111.0	25.5	85.6	36.4	147.4
September	110.9	25.3	85.6	36.4	147.3
October	110.9	25.3	85.6	36.4	147.3
November	111.0	25.2	85.8	36.4	147.4
December	111.2	25.1	86.0	36.4	147.6
1950					
January	111.5	25.1	86.4	36.4	147.9
February	112.1	25.1	86.9	36.6	148.7
March	112.5	25.2	87.3	36.6	149.1
April	113.2	25.3	88.0	36.7	149.9
May	113.7	25.2	88.5	36.9	150.6
June	114.1	25.1	89.0	36.9	151.0
July	114.6	25.0	89.6	36.8	151.4
August	115.0	24.9	90.1	36.7	151.7
September	115.2	24.9	90.3	36.6	151.8
October	115.7	24.9	90.8	36.5	152.2
November	115.9	24.9	90.9	36.6	152.5
December	116.2	25.0	91.2	36.7	152.9
1951					
January	116.7	25.0	91.7	36.7	153.4
February	117.1	25.1	92.0	36.6	153.7
March	117.6	25.2	92.4	36.6	154.2
April	117.8	25.2	92.6	36.7	154.5
May	118.2	25.3	92.8	36.8	155.0
June	118.6	25.4	93.2	36.9	155.5
July	119.1	25.6	93.4	37.2	156.3
August	119.6	25.7	93.8	37.4	157.0
September	120.4	25.8	94.5	37.7	158.1
October	121.0	26.0	95.1	37.8	158.8
November	122.0	26.0	96.0	38.0	160.0
December	122.7	26.1	96.5	38.2	160.9
1952					
January	123.1	26.2	96.9	38.4	161.5
February	123.6	26.3	97.3	38.7	162.3
March	123.8	26.4	97.5	38.9	162.7
April	124.1	26.4	97.6	39.1	163.2
May	124.5	26.5	98.0	39.3	163.8
June	125.0	26.7	98.4	39.5	164.5
July	125.3	26.7	98.6	39.7	165.0
August	125.7	26.8	98.9	40.0	165.7
September	126.4	26.9	99.4	40.3	166.7
October	126.7	27.0	99.7	40.5	167.2
November	127.1	27.2	99.9	40.9	168.0
December	127.4	27.3	100.1	41.1	168.5

Table 12-1C. Money Stock, Historical: January 1947–January 1959—*Continued*

(Averages of daily figures; seasonally adjusted, billions of dollars.)

Year and month	Money stock (M1)			Time deposits adjusted	M2 (M1 plus time deposits)
	Total	Currency component	Demand deposit component		
1953					
January	127.3	27.4	99.9	41.4	168.7
February	127.4	27.5	99.9	41.6	169.0
March	128.0	27.6	100.4	41.9	169.9
April	128.3	27.7	100.7	42.1	170.4
May	128.5	27.7	100.7	42.4	170.9
June	128.5	27.7	100.7	42.6	171.1
July	128.6	27.8	100.8	42.9	171.5
August	128.7	27.8	100.9	43.2	171.9
September	128.6	27.8	100.8	43.5	172.1
October	128.7	27.8	100.9	43.9	172.6
November	128.7	27.8	100.9	44.2	172.9
December	128.8	27.7	101.1	44.5	173.3
1954					
January	129.0	27.7	101.3	44.8	173.8
February	129.1	27.7	101.5	45.2	174.3
March	129.2	27.6	101.6	45.6	174.8
April	128.6	27.6	101.0	46.1	174.7
May	129.7	27.6	102.1	46.5	176.2
June	129.9	27.5	102.3	46.8	176.7
July	130.3	27.5	102.8	47.3	177.6
August	130.7	27.5	103.2	47.8	178.5
September	130.9	27.4	103.5	47.9	178.8
October	131.5	27.4	104.1	48.1	179.6
November	132.1	27.4	104.7	48.2	180.3
December	132.3	27.4	104.9	48.3	180.6
1955					
January	133.0	27.4	105.6	48.5	181.5
February	133.9	27.5	106.4	48.7	182.6
March	133.6	27.5	106.0	48.8	182.4
April	133.9	27.5	106.3	49.0	182.9
May	134.6	27.6	107.0	49.0	183.6
June	134.4	27.6	106.8	49.2	183.6
July	134.8	27.7	107.2	49.3	184.1
August	134.8	27.7	107.0	49.3	184.1
September	135.0	27.7	107.3	49.6	184.6
October	135.2	27.8	107.4	49.7	184.9
November	134.9	27.8	107.1	49.9	184.8
December	135.2	27.8	107.4	50.0	185.2
1956					
January	135.5	27.9	107.7	49.9	185.4
February	135.5	27.9	107.7	49.9	185.4
March	135.7	27.9	107.8	50.1	185.8
April	136.0	27.9	108.1	50.3	186.3
May	135.8	27.9	107.9	50.4	186.2
June	136.0	27.9	108.1	50.7	186.7
July	136.0	28.0	108.0	50.9	186.9
August	135.7	28.0	107.8	51.2	186.9
September	136.2	28.0	108.2	51.5	187.7
October	136.3	28.0	108.2	51.6	187.9
November	136.6	28.1	108.4	51.8	188.4
December	136.9	28.2	108.7	51.9	188.8
1957					
January	136.9	28.2	108.6	52.6	189.5
February	136.8	28.2	108.6	53.1	189.9
March	136.9	28.2	108.7	53.7	190.6
April	136.9	28.2	108.7	54.0	190.9
May	137.0	28.2	108.8	54.5	191.5
June	136.9	28.3	108.6	54.8	191.7
July	137.0	28.3	108.7	55.3	192.3
August	137.1	28.3	108.8	55.7	192.8
September	136.8	28.3	108.4	56.1	192.9
October	136.5	28.3	108.2	56.6	193.1
November	136.3	28.3	108.0	57.0	193.3
December	135.9	28.3	107.6	57.4	193.3
1958					
January	135.5	28.3	107.2	57.6	193.1
February	136.2	28.2	107.9	59.2	195.4
March	136.5	28.2	108.3	60.5	197.0
April	137.0	28.2	108.7	61.5	198.5
May	137.5	28.3	109.2	62.3	199.8
June	138.4	28.3	110.1	63.2	201.6
July	138.4	28.4	110.0	64.0	202.4
August	139.1	28.4	110.7	64.6	203.7
September	139.5	28.5	111.1	64.8	204.3
October	140.1	28.5	111.6	64.9	205.0
November	140.9	28.5	112.4	65.2	206.1
December	141.1	28.6	112.6	65.4	206.5
1959					
January	142.2	28.7	113.5	66.3	208.5

Table 12-1D. Money Stock, Reserves, and Monetary Base: Historical, From January 1959

(Averages of daily figures; seasonally adjusted, except as noted.)

Year and month	Money stock measures, billions of dollars		Reserves and monetary base, adjusted for change in reserve requirements, millions of dollars					
	M1	M2	Total reserves	Nonborrowed reserves	Nonborrowed reserves plus extended credit [1]	Required reserves	Excess reserves, not seasonally adjusted	Monetary base
1959								
January	138.9	286.6	11 112	10 560	10 560	10 614	498	40 425
February	139.4	287.7	11 129	10 624	10 624	10 675	454	40 605
March	139.7	289.2	11 081	10 482	10 482	10 621	460	40 615
April	139.7	290.1	11 116	10 424	10 424	10 684	431	40 694
May	140.7	292.2	11 058	10 317	10 317	10 637	421	40 731
June	141.2	294.1	10 972	10 043	10 043	10 566	407	40 750
July	141.7	295.2	11 109	10 148	10 148	10 693	416	40 896
August	141.9	296.4	11 168	10 177	10 177	10 720	448	40 992
September	141.0	296.7	11 128	10 202	10 202	10 686	443	41 034
October	140.5	296.5	11 057	10 150	10 150	10 616	441	40 903
November	140.4	297.1	11 052	10 194	10 194	10 609	444	40 822
December	140.0	297.8	11 109	10 168	10 168	10 603	506	40 880
1960								
January	140.0	298.2	11 081	10 194	10 194	10 567	514	40 794
February	139.9	298.5	10 884	10 074	10 074	10 430	454	40 666
March	139.8	299.4	10 796	10 155	10 155	10 373	423	40 616
April	139.6	300.1	10 767	10 161	10 161	10 341	426	40 621
May	139.6	300.9	10 840	10 344	10 344	10 396	445	40 639
June	139.6	302.3	10 885	10 451	10 451	10 406	479	40 689
July	140.2	304.1	10 994	10 615	10 615	10 493	501	40 794
August	141.3	306.9	11 078	10 782	10 782	10 536	542	40 895
September	141.2	308.4	11 147	10 932	10 932	10 520	627	41 040
October	140.9	309.5	11 216	11 049	11 049	10 554	662	41 097
November	140.9	310.9	11 299	11 166	11 166	10 556	743	41 130
December	140.7	312.4	11 247	11 172	11 172	10 503	743	40 977
1961								
January	141.1	314.1	11 324	11 259	11 259	10 553	772	40 960
February	141.6	316.5	11 229	11 096	11 096	10 580	649	40 945
March	141.9	318.3	11 108	11 038	11 038	10 563	546	40 851
April	142.1	319.9	11 123	11 066	11 066	10 507	616	40 823
May	142.7	322.2	11 035	10 940	10 940	10 480	556	40 791
June	142.9	324.3	11 087	11 024	11 024	10 497	590	40 902
July	142.9	325.6	11 124	11 070	11 070	10 508	616	40 980
August	143.5	327.6	11 234	11 169	11 169	10 655	579	41 227
September	143.8	329.5	11 289	11 251	11 251	10 709	580	41 417
October	144.1	331.1	11 413	11 342	11 342	10 881	532	41 651
November	144.8	333.4	11 482	11 384	11 384	10 891	591	41 782
December	145.2	335.5	11 499	11 366	11 366	10 915	584	41 853
1962								
January	145.2	337.5	11 490	11 403	11 403	10 867	623	41 864
February	145.7	340.1	11 301	11 233	11 233	10 799	502	41 810
March	146.0	343.1	11 259	11 170	11 170	10 788	472	41 923
April	146.4	345.5	11 330	11 258	11 258	10 838	492	42 096
May	146.8	347.5	11 384	11 323	11 323	10 867	517	42 194
June	146.6	349.3	11 328	11 226	11 226	10 855	473	42 259
July	146.5	350.8	11 394	11 302	11 302	10 860	534	42 398
August	146.6	352.8	11 355	11 231	11 231	10 826	530	42 491
September	146.3	354.9	11 383	11 303	11 303	10 893	490	42 537
October	146.7	357.2	11 450	11 387	11 387	10 972	477	42 700
November	147.3	359.8	11 492	11 372	11 372	10 936	557	42 861
December	147.8	362.7	11 604	11 344	11 344	11 033	572	42 957
1963								
January	148.3	365.2	11 567	11 421	11 421	11 062	505	43 008
February	148.9	367.9	11 456	11 290	11 290	10 995	461	43 155
March	149.2	370.7	11 404	11 255	11 255	10 970	434	43 289
April	149.7	373.3	11 449	11 319	11 319	10 992	457	43 444
May	150.4	376.1	11 426	11 216	11 216	10 996	430	43 586
June	150.4	378.4	11 398	11 139	11 139	10 981	417	43 780
July	151.3	381.1	11 530	11 232	11 232	11 075	454	44 058
August	151.8	383.6	11 484	11 155	11 155	11 039	445	44 149
September	152.0	386.0	11 503	11 184	11 184	11 075	428	44 339
October	152.6	388.3	11 457	11 137	11 137	11 060	397	44 444
November	153.6	391.5	11 547	11 198	11 198	11 106	441	44 744
December	153.3	393.2	11 730	11 397	11 397	11 239	490	45 003
1964								
January	153.7	395.2	11 643	11 369	11 369	11 204	440	45 042
February	154.3	397.6	11 547	11 261	11 261	11 150	397	45 112
March	154.5	399.8	11 563	11 285	11 285	11 177	386	45 371
April	154.8	401.7	11 537	11 326	11 326	11 185	352	45 470
May	155.3	404.2	11 523	11 263	11 263	11 169	354	45 651
June	155.6	407.1	11 595	11 326	11 326	11 220	375	45 959
July	156.8	410.1	11 651	11 387	11 387	11 275	376	46 143
August	157.8	413.4	11 795	11 480	11 480	11 374	421	46 410
September	158.7	416.9	11 863	11 518	11 518	11 432	431	46 714
October	159.2	419.1	11 888	11 567	11 567	11 490	398	46 823
November	160.0	422.0	11 998	11 598	11 598	11 591	408	47 106
December	160.3	424.7	12 011	11 747	11 747	11 605	406	47 161

[1]Extended credit program discontinued January 9, 2003. See notes and definitions for more information.

Table 12-1D. Money Stock, Reserves, and Monetary Base: Historical, From January 1959 —*Continued*

(Averages of daily figures; seasonally adjusted, except as noted.)

Year and month	Money stock measures, billions of dollars		Reserves and monetary base, adjusted for change in reserve requirements, millions of dollars					
	M1	M2	Total reserves	Nonborrowed reserves	Nonborrowed reserves plus extended credit [1]	Required reserves	Excess reserves, not seasonally adjusted	Monetary base
1965								
January	160.7	427.5	11 952	11 653	11 653	11 537	415	47 281
February	160.9	430.4	11 883	11 479	11 479	11 472	412	47 500
March	161.5	433.2	11 884	11 472	11 472	11 518	366	47 584
April	162.0	435.4	12 043	11 571	11 571	11 701	341	47 721
May	161.7	437.1	11 912	11 417	11 417	11 578	334	47 799
June	162.2	440.1	12 005	11 467	11 467	11 643	362	48 061
July	163.0	442.9	12 073	11 544	11 544	11 720	353	48 281
August	163.7	445.8	12 079	11 531	11 531	11 682	396	48 453
September	164.9	449.5	12 071	11 517	11 517	11 662	410	48 712
October	166.0	452.6	12 118	11 630	11 630	11 759	358	49 029
November	166.7	455.7	12 087	11 655	11 655	11 735	352	49 234
December	167.8	459.2	12 316	11 872	11 872	11 892	423	49 620
1966								
January	169.1	462.0	12 295	11 875	11 875	11 916	379	49 850
February	169.6	464.6	12 193	11 711	11 711	11 846	347	50 054
March	170.5	467.2	12 164	11 604	11 604	11 822	342	50 171
April	171.8	469.3	12 258	11 621	11 621	11 903	355	50 439
May	171.3	470.1	12 263	11 575	11 575	11 922	341	50 591
June	171.6	471.2	12 256	11 549	11 549	11 901	356	50 754
July	170.3	470.9	12 371	11 629	11 629	11 993	378	51 019
August	170.8	472.6	12 165	11 430	11 430	11 798	367	50 989
September	172.0	475.4	12 229	11 460	11 460	11 858	371	51 154
October	171.2	475.7	12 199	11 465	11 465	11 867	333	51 200
November	171.4	477.3	12 205	11 598	11 598	11 820	385	51 422
December	172.0	480.2	12 223	11 690	11 690	11 884	339	51 565
1967								
January	171.9	481.6	12 334	11 924	11 924	11 931	403	51 876
February	173.0	485.1	12 280	11 916	11 916	11 911	369	52 173
March	174.8	489.7	12 438	12 237	12 237	12 024	414	52 494
April	174.2	492.1	12 488	12 342	12 342	12 138	350	52 517
May	175.7	497.2	12 418	12 329	12 329	12 053	365	52 682
June	177.0	502.0	12 457	12 351	12 351	12 104	352	52 867
July	178.1	506.3	12 722	12 607	12 607	12 304	418	53 165
August	179.7	510.8	12 678	12 598	12 598	12 313	365	53 347
September	180.7	514.7	12 846	12 758	12 758	12 504	342	53 670
October	181.6	518.2	13 088	12 959	12 959	12 752	335	54 044
November	182.4	521.2	13 131	12 999	12 999	12 773	358	54 241
December	183.3	524.8	13 180	12 952	12 952	12 805	375	54 579
1968								
January	184.3	527.4	13 239	12 993	12 993	12 852	387	54 892
February	184.7	530.4	13 188	12 815	12 815	12 801	386	55 171
March	185.5	533.2	13 186	12 527	12 527	12 849	337	55 436
April	186.6	535.7	13 117	12 432	12 432	12 782	335	55 692
May	188.0	538.9	13 130	12 389	12 389	12 771	360	55 872
June	189.4	542.6	13 251	12 557	12 557	12 923	328	56 323
July	190.5	545.6	13 455	12 928	12 928	13 105	351	56 626
August	191.8	549.4	13 440	12 875	12 875	13 110	329	56 976
September	192.7	553.6	13 435	12 931	12 931	13 074	361	57 160
October	194.0	557.6	13 529	13 086	13 086	13 283	245	57 477
November	196.0	562.4	13 649	13 104	13 104	13 340	308	57 887
December	197.4	566.8	13 767	13 021	13 021	13 341	426	58 357
1969								
January	198.7	569.3	13 629	12 893	12 893	13 383	246	58 597
February	199.3	571.9	13 714	12 879	12 879	13 460	254	58 917
March	200.0	574.4	13 653	12 751	12 751	13 434	219	58 999
April	200.7	575.7	13 471	12 468	12 468	13 304	167	59 062
May	200.8	576.5	13 844	12 470	12 470	13 589	255	59 552
June	201.3	578.5	13 795	12 410	12 410	13 491	304	59 794
July	201.7	579.5	13 491	12 239	12 239	13 266	225	59 713
August	201.7	580.1	13 784	12 565	12 565	13 547	237	60 137
September	202.1	582.1	13 822	12 743	12 743	13 549	274	60 357
October	202.9	583.4	13 904	12 754	12 754	13 741	163	60 633
November	203.6	585.4	14 172	12 969	12 969	13 943	229	61 229
December	203.9	587.9	14 168	13 049	13 049	13 882	286	61 569
1970								
January	206.2	589.6	14 087	13 128	13 128	13 914	174	61 792
February	205.0	586.3	14 099	13 019	13 019	13 891	208	61 931
March	205.7	587.3	14 071	13 173	13 173	13 908	163	62 205
April	206.7	588.4	14 209	13 364	13 364	14 057	152	62 653
May	207.2	591.5	14 007	13 040	13 040	13 850	157	62 977
June	207.6	595.2	14 078	13 197	13 197	13 888	190	63 189
July	208.0	599.1	14 159	12 799	12 799	13 993	166	63 444
August	209.9	604.9	14 282	13 445	13 445	14 108	174	63 725
September	211.8	611.2	14 447	13 847	13 847	14 203	244	64 087
October	212.9	616.4	14 480	14 017	14 017	14 274	205	64 303
November	213.7	621.1	14 470	14 055	14 055	14 236	234	64 574
December	214.4	626.5	14 558	14 225	14 225	14 309	249	65 013

[1]Extended credit program discontinued January 9, 2003. See notes and definitions for more information.

Table 12-1D. Money Stock, Reserves, and Monetary Base: Historical, From January 1959 —*Continued*

(Averages of daily figures; seasonally adjusted, except as noted.)

Year and month	Money stock measures, billions of dollars		Reserves and monetary base, adjusted for change in reserve requirements, millions of dollars					
	M1	M2	Total reserves	Nonborrowed reserves	Nonborrowed reserves plus extended credit [1]	Required reserves	Excess reserves, not seasonally adjusted	Monetary base
1971								
January	215.5	632.9	14 604	14 240	14 240	14 371	234	65 545
February	217.4	641.0	14 819	14 488	14 488	14 565	254	66 037
March	218.8	649.9	14 798	14 479	14 479	14 603	195	66 378
April	220.0	658.4	14 759	14 606	14 606	14 591	168	66 731
May	222.0	666.7	14 982	14 698	14 698	14 763	219	67 315
June	223.5	673.0	15 057	14 564	14 564	14 855	201	67 678
July	224.9	679.6	15 125	14 302	14 302	14 941	184	68 155
August	225.6	685.5	15 190	14 380	14 380	14 994	196	68 413
September	226.5	692.5	15 423	14 928	14 928	15 234	189	68 751
October	227.2	698.4	15 211	14 854	14 854	15 049	163	68 603
November	227.8	704.6	15 247	14 864	14 864	15 010	237	68 894
December	228.3	710.3	15 230	15 104	15 104	15 049	182	69 108
1972								
January	230.1	717.7	15 369	15 347	15 347	15 163	206	69 853
February	232.3	725.7	15 363	15 331	15 331	15 211	152	70 368
March	234.3	733.5	15 480	15 382	15 382	15 291	190	70 820
April	235.6	738.4	15 651	15 534	15 534	15 495	156	71 031
May	235.9	743.3	15 739	15 628	15 628	15 600	139	71 525
June	236.6	749.7	15 909	15 809	15 809	15 706	203	71 817
July	238.8	759.5	15 835	15 597	15 597	15 642	193	72 173
August	240.9	768.7	16 010	15 623	15 623	15 822	188	72 623
September	243.2	778.3	16 000	15 459	15 459	15 788	212	72 984
October	245.0	786.9	16 193	15 637	15 637	15 981	211	73 644
November	246.4	793.9	16 441	15 833	15 833	16 088	354	74 370
December	249.2	802.3	16 645	15 595	15 595	16 361	284	75 167
1973								
January	251.5	810.3	16 708	15 548	15 548	16 450	258	75 925
February	252.2	814.1	16 714	15 120	15 120	16 516	197	76 160
March	251.7	815.3	16 923	15 099	15 099	16 714	209	76 663
April	252.7	819.7	16 731	15 020	15 020	16 508	223	76 962
May	254.9	826.8	16 672	14 829	14 830	16 533	138	77 393
June	256.7	833.3	16 746	14 895	14 903	16 528	217	77 842
July	257.5	836.5	16 988	15 035	15 067	16 705	283	78 531
August	257.7	838.8	16 796	14 631	14 657	16 624	172	78 781
September	257.9	839.3	16 735	14 883	14 909	16 505	231	79 316
October	259.0	842.6	16 924	15 448	15 464	16 672	252	80 173
November	261.0	848.9	16 978	15 585	15 585	16 753	225	80 479
December	262.9	855.5	17 021	15 723	15 723	16 717	304	81 073
1974								
January	263.8	859.7	17 222	16 171	16 174	17 060	162	81 850
February	265.3	864.2	17 125	15 933	15 933	16 941	184	82 341
March	266.7	870.1	17 131	15 817	15 817	16 997	134	82 835
April	267.2	872.9	17 298	15 561	15 561	17 116	182	83 621
May	267.6	874.6	17 423	14 833	15 491	17 263	160	84 432
June	268.5	877.8	17 367	14 361	15 587	17 169	198	84 895
July	269.3	881.4	17 486	14 185	15 615	17 323	162	85 439
August	270.1	884.1	17 391	14 055	15 592	17 203	188	85 974
September	271.0	887.9	17 385	14 102	15 731	17 204	181	86 377
October	272.3	893.3	17 349	15 536	16 021	17 228	120	86 513
November	273.7	898.6	17 453	16 201	16 361	17 248	205	87 043
December	274.2	902.1	17 550	16 823	16 970	17 292	258	87 535
1975								
January	273.9	906.3	17 273	16 874	17 010	17 126	147	87 756
February	275.0	914.1	17 271	17 123	17 176	17 077	194	88 192
March	276.4	925.0	17 439	17 333	17 370	17 239	200	88 916
April	276.2	935.1	17 498	17 387	17 398	17 340	158	89 116
May	279.2	947.9	17 353	17 288	17 291	17 198	155	89 610
June	282.4	963.0	17 715	17 488	17 504	17 513	201	90 817
July	283.7	975.1	17 632	17 331	17 351	17 445	188	91 373
August	284.1	983.1	17 660	17 449	17 461	17 465	195	91 700
September	285.7	991.5	17 834	17 438	17 452	17 643	191	92 119
October	285.4	997.8	17 587	17 397	17 408	17 380	207	92 448
November	286.8	1 006.9	17 849	17 789	17 794	17 566	283	93 373
December	287.1	1 016.2	17 822	17 692	17 704	17 556	266	93 887
1976								
January	288.4	1 026.6	17 616	17 537	17 549	17 376	240	94 281
February	290.8	1 040.3	17 806	17 725	17 734	17 587	219	95 039
March	292.7	1 050.0	17 875	17 821	17 824	17 651	223	95 786
April	294.7	1 060.8	17 719	17 675	17 675	17 564	155	96 479
May	295.9	1 072.1	17 940	17 826	17 826	17 731	210	97 251
June	296.2	1 077.6	17 946	17 820	17 820	17 732	214	97 732
July	297.2	1 086.3	17 846	17 714	17 714	17 612	234	98 234
August	299.0	1 098.7	18 053	17 953	17 953	17 846	207	98 888
September	299.6	1 110.8	18 009	17 948	17 948	17 808	201	99 446
October	302.0	1 125.0	18 077	17 983	17 983	17 858	219	100 066
November	303.6	1 138.2	18 340	18 268	18 268	18 083	257	100 892
December	306.2	1 152.0	18 388	18 335	18 335	18 115	274	101 515

[1]Extended credit program discontinued January 9, 2003. See notes and definitions for more information.

Table 12-1D. Money Stock, Reserves, and Monetary Base: Historical, From January 1959 —*Continued*

(Averages of daily figures; seasonally adjusted, except as noted.)

Year and month	Money stock measures, billions of dollars		Reserves and monetary base, adjusted for change in reserve requirements, millions of dollars					
	M1	M2	Total reserves	Nonborrowed reserves	Nonborrowed reserves plus extended credit [1]	Required reserves	Excess reserves, not seasonally adjusted	Monetary base
1977								
January	308.3	1 165.2	18 421	18 353	18 353	18 156	266	102 237
February	311.5	1 177.6	18 299	18 227	18 227	18 100	198	102 654
March	313.9	1 188.5	18 405	18 301	18 301	18 190	215	103 337
April	316.0	1 199.6	18 479	18 406	18 406	18 287	192	104 076
May	317.2	1 209.0	18 585	18 379	18 379	18 377	208	104 630
June	318.8	1 217.8	18 471	18 208	18 208	18 324	147	105 186
July	320.2	1 226.7	18 748	18 425	18 425	18 473	275	106 394
August	322.3	1 237.0	18 919	17 858	17 858	18 719	200	107 185
September	324.5	1 246.2	18 873	18 247	18 247	18 664	209	107 923
October	326.4	1 254.0	18 963	17 658	17 658	18 753	210	108 750
November	328.6	1 262.4	19 012	18 150	18 150	18 761	251	109 560
December	330.9	1 270.3	18 990	18 420	18 420	18 800	190	110 324
1978								
January	334.4	1 279.7	19 290	18 806	18 806	19 023	267	111 449
February	335.3	1 285.5	19 561	19 155	19 155	19 319	241	112 450
March	337.0	1 292.2	19 286	18 958	18 958	19 087	199	112 778
April	339.9	1 300.4	19 408	18 851	18 851	19 260	148	113 377
May	344.9	1 310.5	19 655	18 443	18 443	19 436	219	114 418
June	346.9	1 318.5	19 868	18 774	18 774	19 691	178	115 376
July	347.6	1 324.1	20 118	18 801	18 801	19 921	197	116 273
August	349.6	1 333.5	19 912	18 772	18 772	19 744	168	116 904
September	352.2	1 345.0	19 994	18 934	18 934	19 801	193	118 112
October	353.3	1 352.3	20 109	18 832	18 832	19 947	162	119 044
November	355.4	1 359.1	19 872	19 169	19 169	19 650	222	119 733
December	357.3	1 366.0	19 753	18 885	18 885	19 521	232	120 445
1979								
January	358.6	1 371.6	19 821	18 818	18 818	19 606	214	121 272
February	359.9	1 377.8	19 396	18 423	18 423	19 187	209	121 504
March	362.5	1 387.8	19 429	18 439	18 439	19 271	158	122 065
April	368.0	1 402.1	19 504	18 587	18 587	19 328	176	122 819
May	369.6	1 410.2	19 553	17 788	17 788	19 412	141	123 487
June	373.4	1 423.0	19 808	18 390	18 390	19 587	221	124 635
July	377.2	1 434.8	19 992	18 822	18 822	19 782	211	125 810
August	378.8	1 446.6	20 008	18 923	18 923	19 786	222	127 079
September	379.3	1 454.1	20 007	18 667	18 667	19 816	191	128 309
October	380.8	1 460.4	20 375	18 353	18 353	20 103	272	129 458
November	380.8	1 465.9	20 398	18 492	18 492	20 153	245	130 369
December	381.8	1 473.7	20 720	19 248	19 248	20 279	442	131 143
1980								
January	385.8	1 482.7	20 693	19 452	19 452	20 442	251	131 998
February	390.1	1 494.6	20 682	19 027	19 027	20 471	211	132 785
March	388.4	1 499.8	20 703	17 879	17 978	20 517	186	133 607
April	383.8	1 502.2	20 629	18 174	18 726	20 432	197	134 740
May	384.8	1 512.3	20 440	19 421	20 164	20 262	178	134 998
June	389.1	1 529.2	20 575	20 196	20 503	20 372	203	135 679
July	394.0	1 545.5	20 796	20 401	20 654	20 511	284	136 637
August	399.2	1 561.5	21 011	20 352	20 594	20 709	302	137 977
September	404.8	1 574.0	21 232	19 921	20 011	20 977	256	139 220
October	409.0	1 584.8	21 147	19 837	19 837	20 941	206	140 150
November	410.7	1 595.8	22 150	20 091	20 091	21 629	521	141 566
December	408.5	1 599.8	22 015	20 325	20 328	21 501	514	142 004
1981								
January	411.3	1 606.9	21 673	20 278	20 348	21 298	374	141 462
February	414.8	1 618.7	21 840	20 536	20 557	21 489	350	142 270
March	419.0	1 636.6	22 072	21 072	21 086	21 791	280	143 029
April	427.4	1 659.2	22 187	20 849	20 857	22 018	169	143 917
May	424.7	1 664.2	22 442	20 219	20 224	22 184	257	144 587
June	425.2	1 670.3	22 326	20 289	20 295	21 988	338	145 001
July	426.9	1 681.9	22 329	20 650	20 653	21 989	340	145 839
August	426.9	1 694.3	22 356	20 936	21 017	22 064	292	146 467
September	427.0	1 706.0	22 487	21 031	21 332	22 073	414	146 941
October	428.4	1 721.8	22 296	21 115	21 553	22 018	278	147 062
November	431.3	1 736.1	22 338	21 675	21 840	21 993	344	147 749
December	436.7	1 755.5	22 443	21 807	21 956	22 124	319	149 021
1982								
January	442.7	1 770.4	22 669	21 152	21 349	22 251	418	149 991
February	441.9	1 774.5	22 551	20 762	20 994	22 248	304	150 459
March	442.7	1 786.5	22 452	20 898	21 206	22 091	361	150 660
April	447.1	1 803.9	22 337	20 769	21 014	22 064	273	151 606
May	446.7	1 815.4	22 402	21 285	21 461	22 043	359	152 868
June	447.5	1 826.0	22 368	21 164	21 268	22 060	308	153 861
July	448.0	1 832.3	22 182	21 490	21 541	21 868	314	154 385
August	451.4	1 846.3	22 348	21 833	21 926	22 036	312	155 470
September	456.9	1 859.5	22 686	21 752	21 871	22 302	384	156 629
October	464.5	1 870.8	22 889	22 412	22 553	22 485	404	157 716
November	471.5	1 884.9	23 354	22 733	22 921	22 952	402	158 667
December	474.8	1 907.1	23 600	22 966	23 152	23 100	500	160 127

[1]Extended credit program discontinued January 9, 2003. See notes and definitions for more information.

Table 12-1D. Money Stock, Reserves, and Monetary Base: Historical, From January 1959 —*Continued*

(Averages of daily figures; seasonally adjusted, except as noted.)

Year and month	Money stock measures, billions of dollars		Reserves and monetary base, adjusted for change in reserve requirements, millions of dollars					
	M1	M2	Total reserves	Nonborrowed reserves	Nonborrowed reserves plus extended credit [1]	Required reserves	Excess reserves, not seasonally adjusted	Monetary base
1983								
January	477.2	1 960.5	23 226	22 697	22 854	22 678	548	161 136
February	484.3	1 997.8	23 901	23 319	23 597	23 466	435	163 170
March	490.6	2 016.0	24 414	23 621	23 939	23 981	433	165 052
April	493.2	2 029.4	24 900	23 890	24 295	24 424	476	166 549
May	500.0	2 043.9	24 860	23 907	24 420	24 411	449	167 842
June	504.0	2 054.3	25 277	23 641	24 599	24 797	480	169 393
July	507.8	2 065.6	25 356	23 903	24 480	24 848	507	170 129
August	510.5	2 074.8	25 376	23 830	24 320	24 929	446	171 208
September	512.8	2 083.9	25 435	23 994	24 509	24 937	498	172 411
October	517.2	2 100.0	25 454	24 610	24 866	24 949	505	173 584
November	519.0	2 113.1	25 396	24 491	24 497	24 867	529	174 605
December	521.4	2 124.2	25 367	24 593	24 595	24 806	561	175 467
1984								
January	525.1	2 139.0	25 451	24 736	24 740	24 838	613	176 896
February	527.5	2 159.1	25 829	25 262	25 266	24 923	906	177 838
March	531.4	2 176.0	25 763	24 811	24 838	25 095	668	178 872
April	535.0	2 192.6	25 691	24 457	24 501	25 218	473	179 898
May	536.7	2 205.0	25 882	22 894	22 931	25 313	569	180 722
June	540.2	2 216.0	26 094	22 793	24 666	25 334	759	181 995
July	540.9	2 224.5	25 980	20 056	25 064	25 351	630	182 991
August	541.0	2 231.2	26 039	18 023	25 066	25 359	680	183 754
September	543.1	2 245.2	26 089	18 847	25 306	25 440	649	184 661
October	543.7	2 259.7	26 259	20 242	25 299	25 641	618	185 219
November	547.5	2 282.2	26 518	21 901	25 738	25 820	698	186 104
December	551.6	2 307.3	26 913	23 727	26 331	26 078	835	187 252
1985								
January	557.0	2 333.2	27 077	25 682	26 732	26 334	742	188 080
February	563.6	2 354.9	27 596	26 307	27 110	26 746	850	189 636
March	566.6	2 367.0	27 590	25 997	27 056	26 916	675	190 320
April	570.4	2 376.2	27 870	26 548	27 416	27 134	736	191 353
May	575.1	2 390.4	28 155	26 821	27 355	27 402	753	192 689
June	582.3	2 413.4	28 848	27 644	28 309	27 926	922	194 762
July	589.1	2 430.4	29 141	28 034	28 541	28 301	840	195 946
August	596.2	2 444.9	29 652	28 580	29 149	28 818	834	198 013
September	603.3	2 457.3	30 030	28 741	29 397	29 333	697	199 306
October	607.8	2 469.0	30 490	29 303	29 932	29 746	744	200 739
November	612.2	2 478.7	30 916	29 175	29 706	29 998	918	202 120
December	619.8	2 493.0	31 569	30 250	30 749	30 505	1 063	203 555
1986								
January	621.4	2 503.1	31 563	30 793	31 290	30 481	1 082	204 221
February	625.2	2 513.8	31 658	30 775	31 267	30 645	1 014	205 314
March	633.5	2 534.1	32 090	31 330	31 848	31 207	883	206 929
April	641.0	2 558.8	32 517	31 625	32 259	31 745	772	208 125
May	652.0	2 586.0	33 265	32 389	32 974	32 387	878	210 154
June	660.6	2 606.2	33 947	33 144	33 674	33 028	919	211 794
July	670.3	2 628.0	34 657	33 916	34 294	33 784	873	213 406
August	678.7	2 647.8	35 191	34 319	34 784	34 451	740	215 273
September	687.4	2 669.4	35 621	34 613	35 183	34 932	690	216 763
October	694.9	2 689.2	36 262	35 420	35 917	35 545	717	218 635
November	705.4	2 702.9	37 270	36 519	36 937	36 369	901	220 714
December	724.7	2 729.6	38 840	38 014	38 317	37 667	1 173	223 416
1987								
January	730.2	2 745.4	39 244	38 664	38 889	38 173	1 070	225 346
February	730.7	2 749.0	39 006	38 450	38 733	37 813	1 193	226 567
March	733.8	2 755.3	38 827	38 300	38 564	37 907	921	227 083
April	743.9	2 769.5	39 533	38 540	38 811	38 677	857	228 964
May	745.8	2 774.9	39 812	38 776	39 064	38 744	1 067	230 521
June	743.2	2 776.6	39 462	38 685	38 958	38 228	1 234	231 302
July	743.0	2 781.1	39 080	38 408	38 602	38 221	859	231 973
August	744.9	2 790.3	39 208	38 561	38 693	38 157	1 051	233 529
September	747.6	2 801.7	39 118	38 178	38 586	38 333	784	234 708
October	756.2	2 817.4	39 826	38 883	39 333	38 737	1 089	237 110
November	753.2	2 822.0	39 334	38 709	39 103	38 394	940	238 807
December	750.2	2 829.4	38 913	38 135	38 618	37 893	1 019	239 829
1988								
January	756.2	2 850.4	39 464	38 383	38 754	38 213	1 252	241 825
February	757.7	2 873.3	39 406	39 010	39 215	38 268	1 138	242 804
March	761.8	2 893.6	39 266	37 514	38 993	38 321	945	243 750
April	768.1	2 913.6	39 622	36 628	39 252	38 737	885	245 760
May	771.7	2 929.1	39 958	37 380	39 487	38 911	1 047	247 434
June	778.3	2 941.2	40 277	37 195	39 748	39 382	895	249 160
July	781.4	2 950.1	40 514	37 075	39 613	39 623	891	251 001
August	783.3	2 955.1	40 470	37 229	39 882	39 500	970	252 064
September	783.7	2 959.9	40 343	37 503	39 562	39 326	1 017	253 358
October	783.3	2 968.3	40 422	38 123	39 904	39 370	1 053	254 579
November	784.9	2 983.2	40 548	37 687	40 009	39 374	1 174	255 675
December	786.7	2 991.1	40 453	38 738	39 982	39 392	1 061	256 897

[1]Extended credit program discontinued January 9, 2003. See notes and definitions for more information.

Table 12-1D. Money Stock, Reserves, and Monetary Base: Historical, From January 1959 —Continued

(Averages of daily figures; seasonally adjusted, except as noted.)

Year and month	Money stock measures, billions of dollars		Reserves and monetary base, adjusted for change in reserve requirements, millions of dollars					
	M1	M2	Total reserves	Nonborrowed reserves	Nonborrowed reserves plus extended credit [1]	Required reserves	Excess reserves, not seasonally adjusted	Monetary base
1989								
January	785.7	2 994.5	40 422	38 773	39 811	39 278	1 144	257 914
February	783.8	2 994.9	40 339	38 852	39 901	39 184	1 154	258 308
March	783.0	3 002.6	39 844	38 032	39 366	38 926	918	259 160
April	779.2	3 008.8	39 533	37 244	38 950	38 719	813	259 559
May	775.0	3 014.4	39 301	37 580	38 778	38 258	1 042	260 264
June	773.5	3 030.7	39 085	37 595	38 512	38 177	908	261 107
July	777.8	3 055.2	39 438	38 744	38 850	38 455	982	262 225
August	779.4	3 077.1	39 397	38 722	38 764	38 505	892	262 843
September	781.0	3 095.3	39 673	38 980	39 002	38 728	945	263 759
October	786.6	3 116.8	40 163	39 607	39 629	39 123	1 040	264 899
November	787.9	3 135.7	40 170	39 820	39 841	39 221	948	265 614
December	792.9	3 154.9	40 486	40 221	40 241	39 545	941	267 761
1990								
January	795.4	3 168.9	40 731	40 291	40 317	39 688	1 042	269 469
February	798.1	3 181.3	40 743	39 295	39 830	39 743	1 000	271 086
March	801.5	3 192.0	40 650	38 526	40 477	39 769	881	272 962
April	806.1	3 203.4	40 845	39 236	40 621	39 974	871	275 129
May	804.2	3 202.4	40 750	39 419	40 291	39 796	954	276 706
June	808.8	3 215.4	40 666	39 785	40 131	39 879	787	278 908
July	810.1	3 226.0	40 575	39 818	40 098	39 707	868	280 972
August	815.7	3 243.5	40 873	39 946	40 074	39 997	876	284 112
September	820.2	3 256.1	41 090	40 466	40 472	40 177	913	287 367
October	819.9	3 260.7	40 808	40 398	40 416	39 968	840	289 273
November	822.1	3 263.8	40 970	40 740	40 765	40 043	928	291 149
December	824.7	3 272.8	41 766	41 440	41 463	40 101	1 665	293 340
1991								
January	827.2	3 288.5	42 293	41 759	41 786	40 153	2 140	297 776
February	832.6	3 305.0	42 071	41 819	41 853	40 267	1 804	300 806
March	838.7	3 322.3	41 804	41 563	41 616	40 623	1 182	302 734
April	843.1	3 332.6	41 862	41 630	41 716	40 833	1 029	302 947
May	848.8	3 343.3	42 411	42 108	42 196	41 376	1 035	304 175
June	856.7	3 352.3	42 712	42 372	42 379	41 716	996	305 483
July	861.6	3 356.2	42 984	42 377	42 423	42 080	904	307 309
August	866.7	3 355.0	43 392	42 628	42 928	42 308	1 085	309 330
September	869.7	3 354.8	43 558	42 912	43 214	42 625	933	310 720
October	878.0	3 359.9	44 007	43 746	43 758	42 950	1 057	312 694
November	887.6	3 365.4	44 614	44 506	44 508	43 722	893	314 971
December	897.0	3 371.9	45 516	45 324	45 325	44 526	990	317 521
1992								
January	910.4	3 380.5	46 373	46 140	46 141	45 381	993	319 617
February	925.2	3 399.3	47 602	47 524	47 526	46 557	1 045	322 452
March	936.7	3 403.3	48 274	48 183	48 185	47 249	1 025	324 382
April	943.8	3 399.1	49 041	48 951	48 953	47 908	1 133	326 734
May	950.6	3 397.9	49 336	49 182	49 182	48 333	1 004	328 827
June	954.3	3 392.9	49 270	49 041	49 041	48 346	924	330 204
July	963.3	3 393.1	49 755	49 471	49 471	48 780	975	333 352
August	973.7	3 398.0	50 479	50 228	50 228	49 540	939	336 941
September	988.0	3 409.4	51 394	51 107	51 107	50 380	1 015	340 655
October	1 003.7	3 422.9	52 767	52 624	52 624	51 704	1 063	344 489
November	1 015.7	3 425.4	53 750	53 646	53 646	52 707	1 043	347 665
December	1 024.9	3 423.5	54 421	54 298	54 298	53 267	1 154	350 884
1993								
January	1 030.4	3 417.6	54 970	54 805	54 806	53 708	1 262	353 715
February	1 033.5	3 413.2	54 686	54 641	54 641	53 593	1 093	355 349
March	1 038.6	3 410.7	54 970	54 879	54 879	53 737	1 233	357 932
April	1 047.1	3 410.0	55 358	55 285	55 285	54 255	1 103	360 952
May	1 065.9	3 435.2	56 655	56 533	56 533	55 656	999	364 923
June	1 075.1	3 441.2	57 086	56 905	56 905	56 191	895	367 897
July	1 084.5	3 440.4	57 729	57 485	57 485	56 662	1 068	371 505
August	1 094.2	3 444.0	58 183	57 831	57 831	57 231	952	374 549
September	1 104.1	3 450.4	58 871	58 443	58 443	57 784	1 086	378 110
October	1 112.9	3 454.8	59 594	59 309	59 309	58 517	1 077	381 505
November	1 124.2	3 468.5	60 304	60 214	60 214	59 184	1 120	384 074
December	1 129.8	3 472.9	60 566	60 484	60 484	59 497	1 069	386 715
1994								
January	1 131.6	3 472.8	60 895	60 822	60 822	59 436	1 459	390 246
February	1 136.3	3 473.8	60 515	60 445	60 445	59 367	1 149	393 242
March	1 140.3	3 479.1	60 299	60 244	60 244	59 315	984	396 073
April	1 141.1	3 481.9	60 503	60 379	60 379	59 361	1 142	398 983
May	1 143.3	3 491.2	59 972	59 772	59 772	59 103	869	401 442
June	1 145.1	3 479.9	60 048	59 715	59 715	58 931	1 117	404 338
July	1 150.6	3 488.2	60 321	59 863	59 863	59 205	1 116	407 873
August	1 150.6	3 485.4	59 959	59 490	59 490	58 949	1 010	409 529
September	1 151.8	3 485.4	59 800	59 313	59 313	58 751	1 048	411 684
October	1 150.1	3 483.7	59 374	58 993	58 993	58 576	797	413 937
November	1 151.0	3 486.8	59 412	59 163	59 163	58 415	996	416 793
December	1 150.8	3 485.8	59 466	59 257	59 257	58 295	1 171	418 468

[1]Extended credit program discontinued January 9, 2003. See notes and definitions for more information.

Table 12-1D. Money Stock, Reserves, and Monetary Base: Historical, From January 1959 —Continued

(Averages of daily figures; seasonally adjusted, except as noted.)

Year and month	Money stock measures, billions of dollars		Reserves and monetary base, adjusted for change in reserve requirements, millions of dollars					
	M1	M2	Total reserves	Nonborrowed reserves	Nonborrowed reserves plus extended credit [1]	Required reserves	Excess reserves, not seasonally adjusted	Monetary base
1995								
January	1 151.5	3 491.0	59 404	59 268	59 272	58 071	1 332	421 133
February	1 147.5	3 488.4	58 652	58 593	58 593	57 683	970	421 671
March	1 146.8	3 489.7	58 209	58 140	58 140	57 386	823	424 816
April	1 149.2	3 497.6	57 973	57 862	57 862	57 216	757	427 834
May	1 145.3	3 522.3	57 641	57 491	57 491	56 768	873	430 477
June	1 144.0	3 547.3	57 376	57 104	57 104	56 393	983	429 986
July	1 145.4	3 565.6	57 817	57 446	57 446	56 711	1 106	430 752
August	1 145.5	3 587.3	57 538	57 256	57 256	56 532	1 006	431 216
September	1 142.0	3 600.4	57 310	57 032	57 032	56 338	971	431 962
October	1 137.3	3 611.6	56 719	56 474	56 474	55 640	1 079	432 636
November	1 134.1	3 618.3	56 305	56 101	56 101	55 360	946	432 969
December	1 127.5	3 628.3	56 483	56 226	56 226	55 193	1 290	434 648
1996								
January	1 123.5	3 646.4	55 884	55 846	55 846	54 417	1 467	434 878
February	1 118.5	3 660.3	54 622	54 587	54 587	53 761	861	432 534
March	1 122.6	3 685.9	55 294	55 273	55 273	54 153	1 142	435 992
April	1 124.8	3 696.4	55 178	55 088	55 088	54 052	1 126	436 888
May	1 116.6	3 707.4	54 041	53 913	53 913	53 130	911	437 511
June	1 115.2	3 720.9	54 145	53 758	53 758	53 031	1 114	440 019
July	1 112.4	3 735.7	53 377	53 009	53 009	52 356	1 021	442 595
August	1 101.5	3 742.6	52 162	51 828	51 828	51 201	961	444 600
September	1 096.1	3 751.0	51 312	50 945	50 945	50 262	1 050	446 078
October	1 086.2	3 767.2	50 037	49 750	49 750	49 030	1 007	446 897
November	1 083.1	3 784.5	49 779	49 565	49 565	48 724	1 055	448 827
December	1 081.4	3 807.0	50 185	50 030	50 030	48 766	1 418	451 941
1997								
January	1 081.3	3 821.3	49 683	49 639	49 639	48 456	1 228	453 568
February	1 078.9	3 833.0	48 715	48 673	48 673	47 681	1 035	454 510
March	1 072.2	3 847.5	47 850	47 694	47 694	46 681	1 169	456 244
April	1 064.3	3 865.4	47 353	47 093	47 093	46 339	1 015	457 939
May	1 063.8	3 875.4	46 657	46 414	46 414	45 374	1 283	459 496
June	1 065.9	3 891.6	46 937	46 570	46 570	45 593	1 344	462 194
July	1 066.2	3 912.7	46 755	46 346	46 346	45 518	1 237	464 739
August	1 074.4	3 942.3	46 913	46 315	46 315	45 653	1 260	467 078
September	1 067.2	3 960.2	46 247	45 809	45 809	44 950	1 297	469 211
October	1 065.4	3 978.0	45 959	45 690	45 690	44 544	1 416	471 907
November	1 070.5	4 000.6	46 411	46 258	46 258	44 742	1 668	475 918
December	1 072.5	4 019.7	46 875	46 551	46 551	45 189	1 687	479 825
1998								
January	1 074.0	4 041.6	46 658	46 448	46 448	44 894	1 764	482 085
February	1 077.9	4 074.2	45 742	45 684	45 684	44 208	1 535	483 155
March	1 077.1	4 101.2	45 854	45 812	45 812	44 503	1 350	484 809
April	1 077.0	4 127.0	46 130	46 058	46 058	44 739	1 391	486 887
May	1 078.6	4 148.5	45 531	45 379	45 379	44 241	1 290	488 929
June	1 076.6	4 171.5	45 417	45 166	45 166	43 798	1 619	491 832
July	1 075.0	4 189.2	44 893	44 635	44 635	43 519	1 374	494 715
August	1 075.3	4 212.4	44 956	44 685	44 685	43 423	1 532	497 986
September	1 080.3	4 254.1	44 850	44 599	44 599	43 152	1 697	502 777
October	1 085.7	4 290.5	44 887	44 714	44 714	43 312	1 575	506 853
November	1 094.6	4 328.0	44 815	44 732	44 732	43 205	1 611	510 284
December	1 095.7	4 359.8	45 170	45 053	45 055	43 658	1 512	513 826
1999								
January	1 097.9	4 381.9	44 925	44 719	44 801	43 436	1 489	516 814
February	1 097.0	4 407.3	44 854	44 738	44 801	43 660	1 194	520 693
March	1 097.5	4 417.1	44 402	44 337	44 474	43 134	1 268	524 881
April	1 101.5	4 444.0	43 600	43 434	43 553	42 445	1 155	528 289
May	1 103.0	4 465.2	43 943	43 815	43 828	42 722	1 221	533 294
June	1 100.0	4 490.4	42 993	42 848	42 843	41 696	1 297	537 012
July	1 098.5	4 514.2	41 937	41 628	41 596	40 974	964	540 293
August	1 098.9	4 533.2	42 263	41 919	41 931	41 102	1 161	544 966
September	1 096.7	4 549.1	41 935	41 597	41 695	40 722	1 213	550 077
October	1 102.4	4 568.7	41 549	41 267	41 329	40 401	1 148	557 345
November	1 111.1	4 590.9	41 740	41 505	41 520	40 412	1 328	570 916
December	1 122.4	4 616.6	42 108	41 787	41 853	40 814	1 294	593 506
2000								
January	1 122.2	4 642.9	42 465	42 092	42 133	40 452	2 013	590 931
February	1 109.0	4 659.0	41 410	41 302	41 326	40 297	1 113	572 935
March	1 108.1	4 689.0	40 694	40 515	40 608	39 486	1 208	571 628
April	1 114.3	4 743.6	40 456	40 152	40 234	39 290	1 166	572 116
May	1 105.6	4 733.6	40 653	40 291	40 267	39 683	970	573 716
June	1 102.9	4 749.9	40 132	39 653	39 608	39 017	1 115	575 787
July	1 103.5	4 765.6	40 066	39 496	39 437	38 923	1 143	577 015
August	1 100.5	4 798.3	39 804	39 225	39 207	38 750	1 054	577 869
September	1 098.7	4 829.0	39 564	39 087	39 149	38 419	1 146	578 325
October	1 098.6	4 847.2	39 375	38 957	38 982	38 227	1 148	580 297
November	1 093.0	4 858.7	39 381	39 098	39 078	38 178	1 203	582 097
December	1 087.8	4 898.0	38 675	38 465	38 493	37 349	1 325	584 997

[1] Extended credit program discontinued January 9, 2003. See notes and definitions for more information.

Table 12-1D. Money Stock, Reserves, and Monetary Base: Historical, From January 1959 —*Continued*

(Averages of daily figures; seasonally adjusted, except as noted.)

Year and month	Money stock measures, billions of dollars		Reserves and monetary base, adjusted for change in reserve requirements, millions of dollars					
	M1	M2	Total reserves	Nonborrowed reserves	Nonborrowed reserves plus extended credit [1]	Required reserves	Excess reserves, not seasonally adjusted	Monetary base
2001								
January	1 097.2	4 951.0	37 852	37 779	37 785	36 589	1 263	587 960
February	1 101.4	4 987.7	38 580	38 529	38 522	37 235	1 345	589 710
March	1 109.6	5 046.1	38 402	38 344	38 405	37 151	1 251	592 244
April	1 115.1	5 109.5	38 376	38 325	38 379	37 119	1 257	595 448
May	1 119.4	5 110.3	38 625	38 412	38 350	37 607	1 019	598 692
June	1 126.4	5 146.7	38 821	38 592	38 519	37 573	1 249	602 070
July	1 139.6	5 179.1	39 476	39 193	39 106	38 075	1 401	607 960
August	1 149.5	5 211.3	39 978	39 795	39 750	38 775	1 203	615 550
September	1 204.3	5 321.0	57 956	54 572	54 609	38 942	19 015	639 481
October	1 165.9	5 309.9	45 497	45 369	45 358	44 170	1 326	630 278
November	1 171.2	5 350.8	40 979	40 895	40 838	39 540	1 439	629 890
December	1 183.0	5 400.3	41 404	41 338	41 336	39 761	1 643	635 646
2002								
January	1 191.2	5 426.1	41 669	41 619	41 600	40 263	1 405	641 240
February	1 191.1	5 453.0	41 831	41 801	41 772	40 458	1 373	646 149
March	1 193.6	5 462.8	41 068	40 989	41 049	39 665	1 403	649 995
April	1 185.8	5 468.1	40 553	40 483	40 543	39 349	1 205	653 767
May	1 189.5	5 490.7	39 511	39 398	39 332	38 252	1 259	657 786
June	1 193.5	5 514.6	39 104	38 962	38 906	37 867	1 238	662 841
July	1 200.3	5 560.9	39 267	39 076	39 019	37 891	1 376	668 542
August	1 186.1	5 598.2	39 867	39 534	39 528	38 261	1 607	670 129
September	1 195.1	5 622.1	38 905	38 676	38 761	37 422	1 484	671 388
October	1 204.4	5 672.8	39 135	38 992	39 025	37 602	1 533	673 828
November	1 209.5	5 716.1	39 792	39 521	39 503	38 155	1 637	677 015
December	1 220.6	5 737.9	40 287	40 207	40 240	38 279	2 008	681 540
2003								
January	1 226.8	5 769.3	40 704	40 677	10 364	38 996	1 707	685 308
February	1 238.7	5 806.7	41 224	41 199	...	39 261	1 964	690 408
March	1 239.8	5 825.6	41 189	41 167	...	39 560	1 629	694 611
April	1 248.7	5 869.8	40 588	40 558	...	39 049	1 539	697 989
May	1 268.2	5 923.9	40 916	40 861	...	39 300	1 617	701 170
June	1 281.0	5 960.7	42 246	42 084	...	40 206	2 039	703 493
July	1 288.6	6 015.5	43 080	42 949	...	41 146	1 934	705 437
August	1 294.6	6 062.8	45 789	45 460	...	42 025	3 764	709 778
September	1 296.5	6 040.4	44 189	44 008	...	42 681	1 508	711 032
October	1 297.1	6 030.3	43 431	43 324	...	41 965	1 466	714 850
November	1 298.7	6 033.5	42 888	42 820	...	41 406	1 482	717 599
December	1 306.9	6 034.6	42 565	42 519	...	41 519	1 046	720 182
2004								
January	1 305.3	6 039.4	42 964	42 858	...	42 076	888	721 815
February	1 321.9	6 079.9	43 019	42 977	...	41 828	1 191	723 660
March	1 329.9	6 120.0	44 893	44 842	...	43 087	1 806	726 382
April	1 331.0	6 159.3	45 639	45 554	...	43 835	1 805	730 135
May	1 332.4	6 231.9	45 435	45 324	...	43 752	1 683	733 591
June	1 342.9	6 241.7	45 863	45 683	...	43 933	1 930	738 440
July	1 340.4	6 251.9	46 127	45 883	...	44 406	1 721	746 178
August	1 353.2	6 276.6	45 555	45 304	...	43 974	1 581	747 820
September	1 361.9	6 314.2	46 537	46 202	...	44 883	1 653	752 482
October	1 361.0	6 337.2	46 332	46 153	...	44 577	1 755	755 200
November	1 374.8	6 369.0	46 054	45 871	...	44 270	1 784	759 112
December	1 376.6	6 385.6	46 462	46 400	...	44 555	1 908	759 106
2005								
January	1 366.4	6 388.5	47 426	47 364	...	45 688	1 738	760 345
February	1 372.3	6 401.4	45 929	45 887	...	44 440	1 489	762 853
March	1 372.3	6 416.2	46 837	46 787	...	45 057	1 780	765 102
April	1 356.6	6 422.5	46 149	46 017	...	44 485	1 664	766 125
May	1 365.0	6 442.8	45 447	45 307	...	43 921	1 525	766 838
June	1 379.5	6 479.0	46 081	45 832	...	44 342	1 739	770 595
July	1 367.5	6 505.9	46 395	45 970	...	44 604	1 791	773 672
August	1 377.1	6 537.6	45 358	44 995	...	43 739	1 619	775 865
September	1 377.1	6 570.9	46 443	46 111	...	44 449	1 994	779 575
October	1 375.5	6 603.1	45 520	45 236	...	43 637	1 883	781 485
November	1 376.4	6 625.2	45 157	45 031	...	43 377	1 780	784 281
December	1 374.8	6 647.5	45 002	44 833	...	43 102	1 900	787 340
2006								
January	1 380.1	6 691.2	44 274	44 164	...	42 698	1 575	791 395
February	1 379.8	6 717.6	44 121	44 068	...	42 572	1 549	795 794
March	1 383.4	6 731.6	43 852	43 683	...	42 346	1 506	798 018
April	1 380.6	6 766.4	44 510	44 262	...	42 686	1 824	800 906
May	1 385.9	6 779.4	44 818	44 643	...	43 021	1 797	804 821
June	1 373.0	6 816.0	45 417	45 165	...	43 636	1 781	804 969
July	1 370.8	6 854.3	44 490	44 139	...	42 937	1 553	804 300
August	1 371.4	6 883.0	43 154	42 785	...	41 635	1 519	804 729
September	1 362.4	6 905.1	43 321	42 918	...	41 561	1 760	805 849
October	1 369.7	6 958.4	42 819	42 590	...	41 126	1 692	806 327
November	1 370.7	6 993.8	42 976	42 816	...	41 287	1 688	808 904
December	1 367.1	7 032.6	43 132	42 941	...	41 270	1 862	812 342

[1]Extended credit program discontinued January 9, 2003. See notes and definitions for more information.
. . . = Not available.

Table 12-1D. Money Stock, Reserves, and Monetary Base: Historical, From January 1959 —*Continued*

(Averages of daily figures; seasonally adjusted, except as noted.)

Year and month	Money stock measures, billions of dollars		Reserves and monetary base, adjusted for change in reserve requirements, millions of dollars					
	M1	M2	Total reserves	Nonborrowed reserves	Nonborrowed reserves plus extended credit [1]	Required reserves	Excess reserves, not seasonally adjusted	Monetary base
2007								
January	1 373.8	7 077.1	41 890	41 679	. . .	40 346	1 544	813 056
February	1 364.9	7 093.3	42 191	42 161	. . .	40 738	1 453	812 202
March	1 366.0	7 125.0	41 938	41 884	. . .	40 321	1 617	812 807
April	1 378.0	7 196.9	42 297	42 218	. . .	40 710	1 587	815 904
May	1 379.9	7 223.2	43 342	43 239	. . .	41 887	1 455	818 316
June	1 364.3	7 248.2	44 089	43 902	. . .	42 337	1 753	819 910
July	1 370.0	7 281.0	42 499	42 237	. . .	40 866	1 634	821 528
August	1 374.3	7 343.5	45 610	44 635	. . .	40 784	4 826	825 260
September	1 373.1	7 364.7	43 343	41 776	. . .	41 610	1 732	823 438
October	1 378.5	7 383.5	43 055	42 801	. . .	41 596	1 459	826 138
November	1 370.9	7 406.2	43 262	42 896	. . .	41 569	1 693	826 714
December	1 375.2	7 438.8	43 156	27 726	. . .	41 372	1 784	824 754
2008								
January	1 381.7	7 483.0	42 385	-3 275	. . .	40 737	1 647	821 086
February	1 382.4	7 562.2	43 571	-16 586	. . .	41 957	1 614	821 305
March	1 387.7	7 626.6	44 961	-49 563	. . .	42 316	2 644	824 358
April	1 392.5	7 679.0	44 701	-90 709	. . .	42 964	1 737	823 266
May	1 391.9	7 689.4	45 917	-109 863	. . .	44 080	1 837	827 228
June	1 399.4	7 703.6	45 953	-125 325	. . .	43 728	2 224	833 104
July	1 420.2	7 754.1	45 746	-119 917	. . .	43 834	1 912	840 014
August	1 404.2	7 742.2	46 592	-121 486	. . .	44 718	1 875	843 613
September	1 459.5	7 823.7	103 366	-186 739	. . .	43 884	59 482	905 167
October	1 471.8	7 932.6	315 475	-332 845	. . .	48 318	267 156	1 130 295
November	1 513.4	7 980.7	609 390	-89 395	. . .	50 582	558 808	1 435 041
December	1 606.7	8 169.0	820 217	166 651	. . .	52 899	767 318	1 654 873
2009								
January	1 589.5	8 252.2	857 131	293 635	. . .	60 297	796 834	1 704 071
February	1 570.6	8 283.4	700 358	117 861	. . .	58 288	642 071	1 555 654
March	1 578.0	8 347.7	779 430	167 319	. . .	56 328	723 103	1 640 143
April	1 612.8	8 353.9	880 837	322 643	. . .	58 239	822 597	1 746 065
May	1 613.9	8 401.4	901 104	375 656	. . .	58 961	842 143	1 768 200
June	1 651.4	8 414.3	809 647	370 924	. . .	60 247	749 400	1 679 701
July	1 661.5	8 411.8	795 969	429 007	. . .	63 724	732 244	1 667 749
August	1 655.5	8 385.2	829 136	497 687	. . .	63 511	765 626	1 704 148
September	1 660.7	8 396.6	922 279	615 452	. . .	62 392	859 887	1 800 497
October	1 674.4	8 424.3	1 056 514	791 456	. . .	62 013	994 501	1 936 099
November	1 679.8	8 455.6	1 140 892	923 585	. . .	63 881	1 077 011	2 018 750
December	1 697.7	8 471.2	1 138 685	968 758	. . .	63 486	1 075 199	2 018 795
2010								
January	1 684.1	8 437.6	1 109 019	966 876	. . .	63 219	1 045 800	1 989 485
February	1 704.8	8 489.8	1 224 805	1 113 578	. . .	62 954	1 161 851	2 110 262
March	1 712.3	8 487.6	1 185 953	1 094 309	. . .	65 584	1 120 369	2 074 581
April	1 701.6	8 514.2	1 116 551	1 036 326	. . .	66 336	1 050 215	2 008 764
May	1 705.8	8 562.2	1 109 769	1 034 144	. . .	64 991	1 044 779	2 005 681
June	1 722.3	8 582.9	1 099 619	1 029 721	. . .	64 693	1 034 926	1 998 540
July	1 724.5	8 579.4	1 087 924	1 022 077	. . .	66 278	1 021 646	1 991 401
August	1 743.5	8 606.2	1 085 946	1 025 862	. . .	66 387	1 019 559	1 994 517
September	1 762.0	8 640.7	1 047 969	995 448	. . .	67 138	980 831	1 962 566
October	1 776.8	8 693.5	1 040 101	991 528	. . .	66 510	973 590	1 962 813
November	1 822.4	8 724.2	1 038 835	992 146	. . .	67 270	971 565	1 968 356
December	1 840.2	8 765.3	1 077 351	1 031 863	. . .	70 716	1 006 636	2 010 240
2011								
January	1 868.3	8 829.1	1 106 507	1 074 261	. . .	70 040	1 036 467	2 044 169
February	1 878.8	8 872.6	1 262 697	1 240 764	. . .	72 686	1 190 012	2 207 724
March	1 891.0	8 920.4	1 436 146	1 416 264	. . .	73 985	1 362 161	2 389 892
April	1 903.7	8 967.6	1 526 480	1 508 637	. . .	74 514	1 451 966	2 489 298
May	1 931.5	9 017.6	1 587 576	1 572 431	. . .	75 072	1 512 505	2 559 321
June	1 945.1	9 094.0	1 666 349	1 653 106	. . .	77 615	1 588 734	2 644 620
July	2 004.5	9 267.1	1 696 473	1 684 077	. . .	78 344	1 618 129	2 680 642
August	2 106.2	9 457.0	1 666 949	1 655 115	. . .	83 585	1 583 364	2 657 378
September	2 122.6	9 476.8	1 642 710	1 631 135	. . .	91 718	1 550 992	2 638 581
October	2 137.7	9 523.9	1 638 605	1 627 395	. . .	93 287	1 545 318	2 639 138
November	2 155.0	9 571.6	1 591 978	1 581 637	. . .	94 060	1 497 919	2 598 948
December	2 168.7	9 616.6	1 597 183	1 587 657	. . .	94 866	1 502 318	2 610 831

[1]Extended credit program discontinued January 9, 2003. See notes and definitions for more information.
. . . = Not available.

Table 12-2. Components of Non-M1 M2

(Billions of dollars, seasonally adjusted; monthly data are averages of daily figures, annual data are for December.)

Year and month	Savings deposits			Small-denomination time deposits			Retail money funds	Total non-M1 M2	Memorandum: Institutional money funds
	At commercial banks	At thrift institutions	Total	At commercial banks	At thrift institutions	Total			
1960	58.3	100.8	159.1	9.7	2.8	12.5	0.0	171.7	0.0
1961	64.2	111.3	175.5	11.1	3.7	14.8	0.0	190.3	0.0
1962	71.3	123.4	194.8	15.5	4.6	20.1	0.0	214.9	0.0
1963	76.8	137.6	214.4	19.9	5.7	25.5	0.0	240.0	0.0
1964	82.9	152.4	235.2	22.4	6.8	29.2	0.0	264.4	0.0
1965	92.4	164.5	256.9	26.7	7.8	34.5	0.0	291.3	0.0
1966	89.9	163.3	253.1	38.7	16.3	55.0	0.0	308.1	0.0
1967	94.1	169.6	263.7	50.7	27.1	77.8	0.0	341.5	0.0
1968	96.1	172.8	268.9	63.5	37.1	100.5	0.0	369.4	0.0
1969	93.8	169.8	263.7	71.6	48.8	120.4	0.0	384.0	0.0
1970	98.6	162.3	261.0	79.3	71.9	151.2	0.0	412.1	0.0
1971	112.8	179.4	292.2	94.7	95.1	189.7	0.0	481.9	0.0
1972	124.8	196.6	321.4	108.2	123.5	231.6	0.0	553.0	0.0
1973	128.0	198.7	326.8	116.8	149.0	265.8	0.1	592.6	0.0
1974	136.8	201.8	338.6	123.1	164.8	287.9	1.4	627.9	0.2
1975	161.2	227.6	388.9	142.3	195.5	337.9	2.4	729.1	0.5
1976	201.8	251.4	453.2	155.5	235.2	390.7	1.8	845.8	0.6
1977	218.8	273.4	492.2	167.5	278.0	445.5	1.8	939.4	1.0
1978	216.5	265.4	481.9	185.1	335.8	521.0	5.8	1 008.7	3.5
1979	195.0	228.8	423.8	235.5	398.7	634.3	33.9	1 092.0	10.4
1980	185.7	214.5	400.3	286.2	442.3	728.5	62.5	1 191.3	16.0
1981	159.0	184.9	343.9	347.7	475.4	823.1	151.7	1 318.8	38.2
1982	190.1	210.0	400.1	379.9	471.0	850.9	181.3	1 432.3	48.8
1983	363.2	321.7	684.9	350.9	433.1	784.1	133.8	1 602.8	40.9
1984	389.3	315.4	704.7	387.9	500.9	888.8	162.2	1 755.7	65.1
1985	456.6	358.6	815.3	386.4	499.3	885.7	172.2	1 873.2	68.2
1986	533.5	407.4	940.9	369.4	489.0	858.4	205.7	2 005.0	89.2
1987	534.8	402.6	937.4	391.7	529.3	921.0	220.7	2 079.2	96.0
1988	542.4	383.9	926.4	451.2	585.9	1 037.1	241.0	2 204.4	97.4
1989	541.1	352.6	893.7	533.8	617.6	1 151.3	316.9	2 362.0	115.9
1990	581.3	341.6	922.9	610.7	562.6	1 173.3	351.9	2 448.1	145.3
1991	664.8	379.6	1 044.5	602.2	463.1	1 065.3	365.2	2 475.0	195.8
1992	754.2	433.1	1 187.2	508.1	359.7	867.7	343.6	2 398.6	222.0
1993	785.3	434.0	1 219.3	467.9	313.6	781.5	342.4	2 343.2	228.1
1994	752.8	398.5	1 151.3	503.6	313.9	817.5	366.2	2 335.0	225.3
1995	774.8	361.0	1 135.9	575.8	356.5	932.4	432.6	2 500.8	279.7
1996	906.1	368.8	1 274.9	594.2	353.7	947.9	502.8	2 725.6	341.6
1997	1 022.8	378.8	1 401.6	625.5	342.2	967.6	577.9	2 947.1	416.7
1998	1 188.6	416.6	1 605.2	626.4	324.9	951.3	707.6	3 264.0	572.1
1999	1 288.6	451.1	1 739.7	636.9	318.3	955.2	799.3	3 494.2	678.5
2000	1 424.3	454.0	1 878.3	700.8	345.2	1 046.0	885.8	3 810.1	834.3
2001	1 739.2	570.9	2 310.1	636.0	338.5	974.5	932.6	4 217.3	1 253.8
2002	2 058.5	713.3	2 771.8	591.2	303.4	894.6	851.0	4 517.3	1 315.7
2003	2 336.5	824.4	3 160.9	541.8	276.1	817.9	748.9	4 727.7	1 164.5
2004	2 631.1	875.6	3 506.7	551.7	276.4	828.1	674.3	5 009.1	1 108.4
2005	2 772.7	828.3	3 601.0	646.5	346.9	993.3	678.3	5 272.6	1 178.8
2006	2 906.6	782.3	3 688.8	780.4	425.2	1 205.7	771.0	5 665.5	1 394.7
2007	3 035.7	825.9	3 861.6	858.7	417.1	1 275.8	926.1	6 063.5	1 963.7
2008	3 318.2	768.0	4 086.2	1 078.2	379.3	1 457.4	1 018.6	6 562.2	2 461.0
2009	3 977.6	835.5	4 813.1	862.7	319.9	1 182.6	777.8	6 773.5	2 256.1
2010	4 409.4	915.3	5 324.7	656.6	271.0	927.6	672.8	6 925.2	1 895.5
2011	5 024.0	997.8	6 021.7	536.4	228.7	765.1	661.0	7 447.9	1 764.7
2010									
January	3 996.1	844.5	4 840.6	838.4	315.8	1 154.2	758.7	6 753.5	2 216.0
February	4 042.2	860.3	4 902.5	822.9	311.4	1 134.3	748.2	6 785.0	2 152.0
March	4 062.0	871.8	4 933.9	805.5	307.2	1 112.8	728.6	6 775.3	2 075.9
April	4 130.1	873.6	5 003.7	790.4	302.2	1 092.6	716.4	6 812.7	1 989.1
May	4 184.1	884.4	5 068.5	774.7	297.7	1 072.4	715.4	6 856.3	1 940.3
June	4 199.9	890.7	5 090.6	759.9	293.2	1 053.1	716.9	6 860.6	1 912.6
July	4 216.8	892.5	5 109.3	746.5	289.5	1 035.9	709.7	6 854.9	1 919.8
August	4 248.9	896.8	5 145.8	732.1	286.4	1 018.4	698.5	6 862.7	1 931.1
September	4 293.0	898.6	5 191.7	713.3	282.5	995.7	691.3	6 878.7	1 938.8
October	4 354.4	906.6	5 261.0	693.5	278.8	972.3	683.4	6 916.7	1 926.6
November	4 365.6	909.9	5 275.5	673.9	274.5	948.5	677.8	6 901.8	1 922.1
December	4 409.4	915.3	5 324.7	656.6	271.0	927.6	672.8	6 925.2	1 895.5
2011									
January	4 453.7	925.9	5 379.6	644.1	265.8	910.0	671.2	6 960.8	1 848.3
February	4 492.9	939.2	5 432.1	634.9	262.8	897.7	664.1	6 993.8	1 824.1
March	4 527.8	955.4	5 483.2	624.0	260.3	884.3	661.9	7 029.4	1 845.9
April	4 573.7	960.1	5 533.8	614.7	257.2	872.0	658.2	7 063.9	1 873.0
May	4 597.9	973.2	5 571.1	604.0	254.3	858.3	656.8	7 086.1	1 893.3
June	4 674.5	972.7	5 647.2	592.7	250.7	843.4	658.4	7 148.9	1 867.8
July	4 799.9	977.1	5 777.0	581.3	246.9	828.2	657.4	7 262.6	1 835.1
August	4 889.3	979.5	5 868.8	569.1	242.6	811.7	670.3	7 350.8	1 746.5
September	4 913.6	979.2	5 892.8	558.0	238.8	796.8	664.5	7 354.1	1 771.2
October	4 948.4	986.5	5 934.9	548.8	234.8	783.7	667.6	7 386.2	1 766.0
November	4 988.1	993.9	5 982.0	540.8	231.1	771.9	662.7	7 416.6	1 756.4
December	5 024.0	997.8	6 021.7	536.4	228.7	765.1	661.0	7 447.9	1 764.7

Table 12-3. Aggregate Reserves, Monetary Base, and FR Balance Sheet

(Millions of dollars; reserves and monetary base adjusted for seasonality and changes in reserve requirements, except as noted; annual data are for December.)

| Year and month | Reserves | | | | | Monetary base | Federal Reserve balance sheet: total assets |
	Total	Nonborrowed	Nonborrowed plus extended credit [1]	Required	Excess reserves, not seasonally adjusted		
1960	11 247	11 172	11 172	10 503	743	40 977	. . .
1961	11 499	11 366	11 366	10 915	584	41 853	. . .
1962	11 604	11 344	11 344	11 033	572	42 957	. . .
1963	11 730	11 397	11 397	11 239	490	45 003	. . .
1964	12 011	11 747	11 747	11 605	406	47 161	. . .
1965	12 316	11 872	11 872	11 892	423	49 620	. . .
1966	12 223	11 690	11 690	11 884	339	51 565	. . .
1967	13 180	12 952	12 952	12 805	375	54 579	. . .
1968	13 767	13 021	13 021	13 341	426	58 357	. . .
1969	14 168	13 049	13 049	13 882	286	61 569	. . .
1970	14 558	14 225	14 225	14 309	249	65 013	. . .
1971	15 230	15 104	15 104	15 049	182	69 108	. . .
1972	16 645	15 595	15 595	16 361	284	75 167	. . .
1973	17 021	15 723	15 723	16 717	304	81 073	. . .
1974	17 550	16 823	16 970	17 292	258	87 535	. . .
1975	17 822	17 692	17 704	17 556	266	93 887	. . .
1976	18 388	18 335	18 335	18 115	274	101 515	. . .
1977	18 990	18 420	18 420	18 800	190	110 324	. . .
1978	19 753	18 885	18 885	19 521	232	120 445	. . .
1979	20 720	19 248	19 248	20 279	442	131 143	. . .
1980	22 015	20 325	20 328	21 501	514	142 004	. . .
1981	22 443	21 807	21 956	22 124	319	149 021	. . .
1982	23 600	22 966	23 152	23 100	500	160 127	. . .
1983	25 367	24 593	24 595	24 806	561	175 467	. . .
1984	26 913	23 727	26 331	26 078	835	187 252	. . .
1985	31 569	30 250	30 749	30 505	1 063	203 555	. . .
1986	38 840	38 014	38 317	37 667	1 173	223 416	. . .
1987	38 913	38 135	38 618	37 893	1 019	239 829	. . .
1988	40 453	38 738	39 982	39 392	1 061	256 897	. . .
1989	40 486	40 221	40 241	39 545	941	267 761	. . .
1990	41 766	41 440	41 463	40 101	1 665	293 340	. . .
1991	45 516	45 324	45 325	44 526	990	317 521	. . .
1992	54 421	54 298	54 298	53 267	1 154	350 884	. . .
1993	60 566	60 484	60 484	59 497	1 069	386 715	. . .
1994	59 466	59 257	59 257	58 295	1 171	418 468	. . .
1995	56 483	56 226	56 226	55 193	1 290	434 648	. . .
1996	50 185	50 030	50 030	48 766	1 418	451 941	. . .
1997	46 875	46 551	46 551	45 189	1 687	479 825	. . .
1998	45 170	45 053	45 053	43 658	1 512	513 826	. . .
1999	42 108	41 787	41 787	40 814	1 294	593 506	. . .
2000	38 675	38 465	38 465	37 349	1 325	584 997	. . .
2001	41 404	41 338	41 338	39 761	1 643	635 646	. . .
2002	40 287	40 207	40 207	38 279	2 008	681 540	. . .
2003	42 565	42 519	. . .	41 519	1 046	720 182	. . .
2004	46 462	46 400	. . .	44 555	1 908	759 106	. . .
2005	45 002	44 833	. . .	43 102	1 900	787 340	. . .
2006	43 132	42 941	. . .	41 270	1 862	812 342	. . .
2007	43 156	27 726	. . .	41 372	1 784	824 754	893 758
2008	820 217	166 651	. . .	52 899	767 318	1 654 873	2 240 946
2009	1 138 685	968 758	. . .	63 486	1 075 199	2 018 795	2 237 258
2010	1 077 351	1 031 863	. . .	70 716	1 006 636	2 010 240	2 423 457
2011	1 597 183	1 587 657	. . .	94 866	1 502 318	2 610 831	2 928 485
2010							
January	1 109 019	966 876	. . .	63 219	1 045 800	1 989 485	2 250 164
February	1 224 805	1 113 578	. . .	62 954	1 161 851	2 110 262	2 289 504
March	1 185 953	1 094 309	. . .	65 584	1 120 369	2 074 581	2 310 533
April	1 116 551	1 036 326	. . .	66 336	1 050 215	2 008 764	2 333 922
May	1 109 769	1 034 144	. . .	64 991	1 044 779	2 005 681	2 337 507
June	1 099 619	1 029 721	. . .	64 693	1 034 926	1 998 540	2 334 296
July	1 087 924	1 022 077	. . .	66 278	1 021 646	1 991 401	2 328 705
August	1 085 946	1 025 862	. . .	66 387	1 019 559	1 994 517	2 304 376
September	1 047 969	995 448	. . .	67 138	980 831	1 962 566	2 301 873
October	1 040 101	991 528	. . .	66 510	973 590	1 962 813	2 298 434
November	1 038 835	992 146	. . .	67 270	971 565	1 968 356	2 348 788
December	1 077 351	1 031 863	. . .	70 716	1 006 636	2 010 240	2 423 457
2011							
January	1 106 507	1 074 261	. . .	70 040	1 036 467	2 044 169	2 446 760
February	1 262 697	1 240 764	. . .	72 686	1 190 012	2 207 724	2 537 175
March	1 436 146	1 416 264	. . .	73 985	1 362 161	2 389 892	2 626 589
April	1 526 480	1 508 637	. . .	74 514	1 451 966	2 489 298	2 695 144
May	1 587 576	1 572 431	. . .	75 072	1 512 505	2 559 321	2 779 103
June	1 666 349	1 653 106	. . .	77 615	1 588 734	2 644 620	2 869 167
July	1 696 473	1 684 077	. . .	78 344	1 618 129	2 680 642	2 867 416
August	1 666 949	1 655 115	. . .	83 585	1 583 364	2 657 378	2 857 394
September	1 642 710	1 631 135	. . .	91 718	1 550 992	2 638 581	2 854 233
October	1 638 605	1 627 395	. . .	93 287	1 545 318	2 639 138	2 848 375
November	1 591 978	1 581 637	. . .	94 060	1 497 919	2 598 948	2 816 773
December	1 597 183	1 587 657	. . .	94 866	1 502 318	2 610 831	2 928 485

[1]Extended credit program discontinued January 9, 2003. See notes and definitions for more information.
. . . = Not available.

Table 12-4A. Commercial Banks: Bank Credit and Selected Liabilities: Recent Data

(All commercial banks in the United States, billions of dollars, seasonally adjusted, annual data are for December.)

Year and month		Bank credit								
	Total	Securities in bank credit			Loans and leases in bank credit					
		Total	U.S. Treasury and agency securities	Other securities	Total	Commercial and industrial	Real estate			
							Total	Revolving home equity	Other residential	Commercial
1960	197.1	78.3	63.1	15.2	118.9	42.1	28.1	. . .	. . .	. . .
1961	213.3	86.8	69.4	17.4	126.4	43.8	29.5	. . .	. . .	. . .
1962	232.0	90.8	69.9	20.9	141.1	47.4	33.3	. . .	. . .	. . .
1963	252.0	91.4	66.8	24.6	160.6	52.2	38.1	. . .	. . .	. . .
1964	272.5	93.7	66.2	27.4	178.9	58.3	42.5	. . .	. . .	. . .
1965	300.5	95.1	63.9	31.2	205.4	69.2	47.8	. . .	. . .	. . .
1966	319.5	96.8	61.5	35.4	222.6	79.0	52.5	. . .	. . .	. . .
1967	352.2	111.1	71.5	39.6	241.1	86.1	56.8	. . .	. . .	. . .
1968	391.8	121.6	74.8	46.8	270.2	96.2	63.3	. . .	. . .	. . .
1969	401.6	112.1	65.1	46.9	289.5	106.6	68.4	. . .	. . .	. . .
1970	435.8	129.3	74.5	54.8	306.5	111.4	71.3	. . .	. . .	. . .
1971	488.9	147.3	81.5	65.8	341.5	117.8	80.0	. . .	. . .	. . .
1972	561.8	159.7	86.9	72.8	402.0	133.1	96.9	. . .	. . .	. . .
1973	643.1	166.9	90.1	76.8	476.2	161.2	117.0	. . .	. . .	. . .
1974	707.5	172.1	88.2	83.9	535.4	191.3	129.8	. . .	. . .	. . .
1975	737.8	204.9	118.1	86.8	532.9	183.4	134.1	. . .	. . .	. . .
1976	798.6	226.7	137.5	89.1	571.9	185.2	148.5	. . .	. . .	. . .
1977	885.6	234.3	137.5	96.8	651.3	204.7	175.1	. . .	. . .	. . .
1978	1 003.7	240.2	138.4	101.9	763.5	237.2	210.5	. . .	. . .	. . .
1979	1 118.1	257.8	146.1	111.7	860.3	279.7	241.7	. . .	. . .	. . .
1980	1 216.9	293.4	171.5	121.9	923.5	312.0	262.3	. . .	. . .	. . .
1981	1 297.7	306.8	179.8	127.0	990.9	350.3	283.6	. . .	. . .	. . .
1982	1 397.6	333.8	202.4	131.4	1 063.8	392.0	299.7	. . .	. . .	. . .
1983	1 549.6	398.1	260.4	137.8	1 151.5	413.9	330.4	. . .	. . .	. . .
1984	1 715.9	401.1	260.0	141.1	1 314.8	473.4	376.2	. . .	. . .	. . .
1985	1 878.2	440.5	263.7	176.7	1 437.7	499.2	422.0	. . .	. . .	. . .
1986	2 073.6	498.9	310.0	189.0	1 574.7	539.5	490.6	. . .	. . .	. . .
1987	2 223.1	526.1	336.1	190.0	1 697.0	565.4	585.7	30.4	. . .	. . .
1988	2 397.1	549.6	360.4	189.3	1 847.5	605.0	663.2	41.1	. . .	. . .
1989	2 561.3	571.0	401.4	169.6	1 990.2	637.4	760.7	51.4	. . .	. . .
1990	2 699.2	619.3	460.0	159.3	2 079.9	640.3	842.6	63.5	. . .	. . .
1991	2 807.6	727.9	564.1	163.8	2 079.6	618.0	868.7	72.0	. . .	. . .
1992	2 908.1	825.1	664.6	160.6	2 082.9	596.9	887.8	75.0	. . .	. . .
1993	3 061.5	896.1	730.0	166.1	2 165.4	583.8	928.7	74.2	. . .	. . .
1994	3 235.6	893.6	721.9	171.7	2 342.1	644.0	987.7	76.0	. . .	. . .
1995	3 463.5	895.1	703.3	191.7	2 568.4	715.2	1 061.9	79.9	. . .	. . .
1996	3 636.9	895.2	698.6	196.6	2 741.7	778.7	1 122.4	86.3	. . .	. . .
1997	3 958.2	987.2	750.2	236.9	2 971.1	845.6	1 220.3	98.9	. . .	. . .
1998	4 369.7	1 097.8	795.2	302.6	3 271.8	939.0	1 311.2	97.3	. . .	. . .
1999	4 628.6	1 144.9	811.0	333.9	3 483.8	1 001.7	1 460.9	101.4	. . .	. . .
2000	5 023.4	1 174.2	787.5	386.7	3 849.2	1 087.1	1 639.4	129.6	. . .	. . .
2001	5 207.8	1 307.2	838.6	468.6	3 900.6	1 024.0	1 758.9	154.1	. . .	. . .
2002	5 640.8	1 490.1	1 003.8	486.3	4 150.7	962.5	2 009.8	212.7	. . .	. . .
2003	6 000.2	1 621.7	1 088.3	533.4	4 378.5	889.6	2 207.3	278.7	. . .	. . .
2004	6 583.3	1 741.0	1 145.4	595.6	4 842.3	913.4	2 552.8	395.3	1 075.7	1 081.8
2005	7 301.8	1 852.2	1 135.2	717.0	5 449.6	1 043.8	2 922.8	443.3	1 207.4	1 272.1
2006	8 088.5	1 984.7	1 187.5	797.2	6 103.8	1 191.9	3 364.7	468.1	1 436.8	1 459.8
2007	8 892.4	2 102.4	1 109.2	993.2	6 790.0	1 431.5	3 590.6	484.7	1 522.2	1 583.7
2008	9 343.5	2 095.9	1 237.1	858.8	7 247.6	1 573.5	3 813.7	588.0	1 498.8	1 727.0
2009	8 986.1	2 326.6	1 447.4	879.2	6 659.5	1 279.5	3 772.5	602.8	1 529.3	1 640.4
2010	9 185.3	2 429.6	1 638.1	791.4	6 755.8	1 209.8	3 607.6	581.6	1 527.6	1 498.4
2011	9 404.2	2 501.1	1 697.7	803.4	6 903.0	1 334.7	3 482.1	548.3	1 517.2	1 416.6
2010										
January	8 918.9	2 325.2	1 448.0	877.2	6 593.7	1 255.0	3 754.9	599.8	1 528.9	1 626.2
February	8 857.9	2 325.8	1 460.7	865.2	6 532.0	1 240.3	3 719.8	598.9	1 502.8	1 618.1
March	8 918.3	2 316.3	1 470.9	845.4	6 602.1	1 226.4	3 703.7	599.2	1 496.5	1 607.9
April	9 237.9	2 315.1	1 505.8	809.3	6 922.8	1 222.5	3 715.0	601.9	1 513.9	1 599.2
May	9 186.6	2 302.3	1 505.1	797.1	6 884.4	1 212.4	3 700.2	599.3	1 514.7	1 586.2
June	9 154.2	2 292.2	1 501.2	791.0	6 862.0	1 208.1	3 682.5	597.3	1 510.8	1 574.4
July	9 187.7	2 352.0	1 555.7	796.2	6 835.8	1 207.9	3 657.4	596.2	1 500.8	1 560.4
August	9 205.4	2 382.0	1 583.0	799.0	6 823.4	1 205.4	3 652.2	594.5	1 507.2	1 550.4
September	9 192.6	2 402.9	1 603.2	799.8	6 789.6	1 200.7	3 639.7	591.7	1 510.1	1 537.9
October	9 210.5	2 431.0	1 631.5	799.5	6 779.5	1 199.0	3 622.4	588.6	1 511.2	1 522.5
November	9 209.1	2 448.3	1 647.4	800.9	6 760.8	1 201.6	3 615.8	585.5	1 519.6	1 510.7
December	9 185.3	2 429.6	1 638.1	791.4	6 755.8	1 209.8	3 607.6	581.6	1 527.6	1 498.4
2011										
January	9 162.3	2 426.8	1 641.1	785.7	6 735.5	1 214.0	3 599.7	577.3	1 534.9	1 487.5
February	9 122.7	2 417.8	1 633.8	783.9	6 704.9	1 217.7	3 568.5	574.3	1 514.4	1 479.8
March	9 119.6	2 430.4	1 645.1	785.4	6 689.2	1 227.4	3 536.8	571.7	1 496.4	1 468.7
April	9 153.3	2 445.7	1 671.9	773.7	6 707.6	1 237.1	3 516.8	568.8	1 487.7	1 460.2
May	9 152.0	2 438.5	1 669.3	769.3	6 713.5	1 251.0	3 503.6	566.2	1 482.8	1 454.7
June	9 153.9	2 429.7	1 659.9	769.8	6 724.2	1 258.8	3 497.2	563.8	1 484.4	1 449.0
July	9 197.9	2 434.8	1 653.8	781.0	6 763.1	1 271.3	3 487.5	560.1	1 487.6	1 439.9
August	9 239.4	2 446.3	1 659.0	787.3	6 793.1	1 291.5	3 482.1	557.8	1 493.3	1 430.9
September	9 254.1	2 454.0	1 665.6	788.4	6 800.1	1 295.8	3 479.1	555.9	1 497.2	1 426.1
October	9 311.9	2 461.9	1 676.8	785.1	6 850.1	1 311.2	3 484.3	552.6	1 513.5	1 418.2
November	9 377.2	2 479.7	1 686.7	793.0	6 897.5	1 320.8	3 489.0	550.6	1 519.6	1 418.8
December	9 404.2	2 501.1	1 697.7	803.4	6 903.0	1 334.7	3 482.1	548.3	1 517.2	1 416.6

. . . = Not available.

Table 12-4A. Commercial Banks: Bank Credit and Selected Liabilities: Recent Data—*Continued*

(All commercial banks in the United States, billions of dollars, seasonally adjusted, annual data are for December.)

Year and month	Bank credit				Selected liabilities			
	Loans and leases in bank credit				Deposits	Borrowings		
		Consumer loans		Other loans and leases		Total	From banks in the United States	From others
	Total	Credit cards and other revolving plans	Other consumer loans					
1960	26.3	...	...	22.4	...	...	...	...
1961	27.6	...	...	25.5	...	...	...	...
1962	30.2	...	...	30.2	...	...	...	...
1963	34.2	...	...	36.2	...	...	...	...
1964	39.5	...	...	38.5	...	...	...	...
1965	45.0	...	...	43.4	...	...	...	...
1966	47.8	...	...	43.4	...	...	...	...
1967	51.2	...	...	46.9	...	...	...	...
1968	57.7	...	...	53.0	...	...	...	...
1969	62.5	...	...	52.0	...	...	...	...
1970	65.2	...	...	58.6	...	...	...	...
1971	73.2	...	...	70.6	...	...	...	...
1972	85.3	...	...	86.8	...	...	...	...
1973	98.4	...	...	99.7	663.7	14.9	...	...
1974	102.1	...	...	112.2	731.4	19.5	...	...
1975	104.3	...	...	111.1	768.0	20.5	...	...
1976	115.8	...	...	122.3	825.9	22.4	...	...
1977	138.0	...	...	133.5	910.9	29.0	...	...
1978	164.4	...	...	151.3	1 004.0	53.3	...	...
1979	183.8	...	...	155.1	1 072.7	176.0	...	...
1980	178.7	...	...	170.5	1 185.1	211.5	...	...
1981	182.1	...	...	174.8	1 248.2	254.8	...	...
1982	187.9	...	...	184.2	1 365.5	280.6	...	...
1983	212.9	...	...	194.3	1 479.1	280.8	...	...
1984	253.8	...	...	211.3	1 612.4	315.2	...	...
1985	291.1	...	...	225.4	1 760.7	344.8	...	...
1986	314.8	...	...	229.8	1 924.1	389.6	...	...
1987	327.1	...	...	218.8	1 985.3	407.7	...	...
1988	355.2	...	...	224.1	2 116.6	456.9	...	...
1989	373.4	...	...	218.8	2 243.1	514.5	...	...
1990	375.2	...	...	221.8	2 337.2	525.0	...	...
1991	363.3	...	...	229.7	2 467.8	464.8	...	...
1992	354.5	...	...	243.8	2 499.1	464.5	...	...
1993	385.9	...	...	267.0	2 534.5	498.1	...	...
1994	443.3	...	...	267.0	2 533.6	583.6	...	...
1995	484.0	...	...	307.3	2 652.0	646.0	...	...
1996	506.9	...	...	333.7	2 832.6	680.2	295.9	384.3
1997	500.0	...	...	405.1	3 078.5	807.5	299.9	507.6
1998	497.7	...	...	524.0	3 292.1	947.7	315.0	632.7
1999	506.7	...	...	514.4	3 473.1	1 083.6	342.8	740.8
2000	556.1	228.7	327.4	566.6	3 720.7	1 169.8	377.0	792.8
2001	574.3	242.1	332.2	543.4	4 075.2	1 168.8	405.6	763.2
2002	610.5	254.8	355.7	567.9	4 349.7	1 319.2	422.4	896.9
2003	665.0	281.4	383.6	616.6	4 628.0	1 366.1	392.1	974.0
2004	691.1	297.6	393.5	684.9	5 151.4	1 479.4	398.8	1 080.6
2005	702.8	304.1	398.7	780.2	5 591.0	1 639.0	370.9	1 268.1
2006	736.8	313.7	423.1	810.4	6 090.2	1 869.8	407.6	1 462.2
2007	798.4	342.2	456.2	969.5	6 659.8	2 134.0	476.2	1 657.8
2008	875.5	385.3	490.3	984.9	7 202.5	2 461.4	382.5	2 078.9
2009	836.0	336.9	499.1	771.5	7 676.9	1 904.5	260.2	1 644.3
2010	1 118.1	606.3	511.8	820.4	7 862.0	1 888.0	228.2	1 659.7
2011	1 097.0	599.8	497.2	989.2	8 420.5	1 605.7	132.3	1 473.4
2010								
January	818.7	323.2	495.5	765.0	7 670.8	1 878.6	254.8	1 623.7
February	810.9	317.2	493.7	761.1	7 699.7	1 861.9	265.2	1 596.7
March	886.6	389.4	497.1	785.5	7 686.7	1 861.6	239.2	1 622.4
April	1 163.0	644.8	518.2	822.2	7 685.6	2 085.9	195.3	1 890.6
May	1 154.8	638.1	516.7	817.0	7 669.5	2 046.9	194.5	1 852.4
June	1 147.8	629.8	518.1	823.5	7 685.3	1 977.7	194.5	1 783.2
July	1 147.0	623.7	523.2	823.5	7 739.1	1 963.3	204.0	1 759.3
August	1 141.6	618.9	522.6	824.3	7 774.3	1 973.3	206.6	1 766.7
September	1 127.4	613.9	513.5	821.8	7 789.4	1 917.8	206.9	1 710.9
October	1 119.9	608.1	511.7	838.3	7 830.2	1 922.1	219.0	1 703.2
November	1 117.0	604.9	512.1	826.4	7 869.3	1 894.3	226.5	1 667.8
December	1 118.1	606.3	511.8	820.4	7 862.0	1 888.0	228.2	1 659.7
2011								
January	1 081.0	600.3	480.7	840.8	7 893.6	1 813.3	204.9	1 608.4
February	1 076.0	597.0	479.1	842.6	7 935.0	1 813.3	192.9	1 620.4
March	1 074.8	594.3	480.6	850.1	7 978.5	1 785.4	184.7	1 600.7
April	1 080.0	593.9	486.1	873.8	8 051.7	1 708.4	157.0	1 551.4
May	1 079.9	594.2	485.7	878.9	8 135.8	1 674.6	154.9	1 519.8
June	1 085.6	597.1	488.5	882.5	8 169.9	1 661.9	172.5	1 489.4
July	1 090.4	596.9	493.4	913.9	8 288.3	1 653.7	145.5	1 508.3
August	1 088.2	596.8	491.3	931.3	8 353.2	1 651.1	152.8	1 498.3
September	1 085.9	596.6	489.3	939.4	8 361.8	1 603.5	145.9	1 457.6
October	1 088.9	596.6	492.3	965.6	8 365.8	1 588.1	138.6	1 449.4
November	1 091.6	597.3	494.3	996.2	8 379.0	1 607.7	138.6	1 469.1
December	1 097.0	599.8	497.2	989.2	8 420.5	1 605.7	132.3	1 473.4

. . . = Not available.

Table 12-4B. Bank Credit and Other Credit Instruments: Historical

(Millions of dollars, year end, not seasonally adjusted.)

Classification	Loans and investments, all commercial banks	Commercial and company finance paper	Commercial paper	Bankers' acceptances
1929	49 467	. . .	334	1 732
1930	46 700	. . .	358	1 556
1931	39 653	. . .	120	974
1932	35 083	. . .	81	710
1933	30 789	. . .	109	764
1934	33 735	. . .	166	543
1935	35 982	. . .	171	397
1936	39 472	. . .	215	373
1937	38 333	. . .	279	343
1938	38 669	. . .	187	270
1939	40 667	. . .	210	233
1940	43 922	. . .	218	209
1941	50 746	. . .	375	194
1942	67 393	. . .	230	118
1943	85 095	. . .	202	117
1944	105 530	. . .	166	129
1945	124 019	. . .	159	154
1946	113 993	. . .	228	227
1947	116 284	. . .	287	261
1948	114 298	674	269	259
1949	120 197	838	257	272
1950	126 675	921	333	394
1951	132 610	1 333	434	490
1952	141 624	1 749	539	492
1953	145 687	1 973	. . .	574
1954	155 916	1 933	. . .	873
1955	160 881	2 035	. . .	642
1956	165 123	2 183	. . .	967
1957	170 068	2 672	. . .	1 307
1958	185 165	2 751	. . .	1 194
1959	190 270	3 202	. . .	1 151
1960	199 509	4 497	. . .	2 027
1961	215 441	4 686	. . .	2 683
1962	235 839	6 000	. . .	2 650
1963	254 162	6 790	. . .	2 890
1964	277 376	8 442	. . .	3 385
1965	306 060	9 300	. . .	3 392
1966	322 661	13 645	. . .	3 604
1967	359 903	17 085	. . .	4 317
1968	401 262	21 173	. . .	4 428

. . . = Not available.

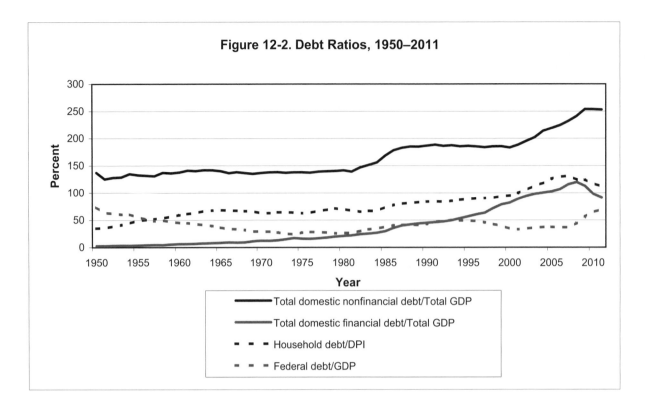

Figure 12-2. Debt Ratios, 1950–2011

- Total domestic nonfinancial debt/Total GDP
- Total domestic financial debt/Total GDP
- Household debt/DPI
- Federal debt/GDP

- Unsustainable debt growth was the source of the credit crisis and economic decline in 2007–2009. Traditionally, analysts have focused on the debt of nonfinancial sectors. Among the major nonfinancial divisions of the economy, the most striking expansion in debt relative to income occurred in the household sector. Household debt in 1984 was no higher, relative to income, than it had been in 1964—but then it began a rapid and uninterrupted expansion. In 2001, debt rose above 100 percent of the annual rate of income, and it reached 131 percent at the end of 2007. Debt and the ratio declined after that, and by the end of 2011, the ratio to DPI was down to 111.5 percent—still higher than anything seen before 2003. (Table 12-5)

- During the expansion period, financial sector debt—much of it reflecting the securitization of nonfinancial sector debt, especially mortgages, in other words debt built upon other debt—grew somewhat more rapidly than nonfinancial sector debt. Between 1985 and 2007, financial sector debt rose from 30 percent to 116 percent of GDP, while total nonfinancial sector debt only grew from 169 to 232 percent.

- Up through 2003, the debt of federal government-related financial entities—government-sponsored enterprises (GSEs) such as "Fannie Mae" and "Freddie Mac" and mortgage pools backed by federal agencies and GSEs—and the debt of private financial sectors both rose rapidly. From 2003 to 2007, there was accelerated growth in the private segment. After 2008, total private financial debt dropped dramatically and total financial debt fell to 91 percent of GDP at the end of 2011. (Tables 1-1 and 12-5)

- Debt of the federal government itself—that is, Treasury securities issued to fund budget deficits—contributed little, on balance, to the rising trend of aggregate debt—until the recession struck in 2008, revenues fell, and spending rose because of both recession-sensitive programs like unemployment insurance and new moves to stabilize credit markets and the economy. (Tables 12-5, 6-1 and 6-15)

Table 12-5. Credit Market Debt Outstanding, by Borrower and Lender

(Billions of dollars, except as noted; end of period; not seasonally adjusted.)

Year and quarter	Total	Domestic financial sectors			Domestic nonfinancial sectors								Nonfinancial business		
					Total		Federal government			Households				Corporate	
		Total	Federal govern-ment-related	Private	Billions of dollars	Percent of GDP	Total	Treasury securities	Budget agency securities and mortgages	Billions of dollars	Percent of DPI	Total	Total	Percent of sector value added
1955	582.0	15.1	3.2	11.9	550.5	132.7	230.0	228.4	1.6	138.4	48.9	136.0	101.1	46.4
1956	611.5	17.8	4.0	13.8	576.5	131.8	224.1	222.8	1.4	153.2	50.6	148.7	110.8	47.6
1957	642.7	20.7	5.1	15.5	603.5	130.9	221.9	220.1	1.7	165.8	51.9	160.8	120.4	49.5
1958	681.6	20.8	5.2	15.6	640.2	137.0	231.1	229.0	1.6	176.5	53.4	171.9	127.7	53.9
1959	738.7	27.4	7.5	20.0	689.9	136.2	238.0	236.2	0.9	198.5	56.7	186.7	136.4	51.3
1960	780.2	32.3	8.1	24.2	724.7	137.7	236.0	234.0	0.7	216.5	59.3	200.1	145.0	52.5
1961	828.5	34.7	8.9	25.8	768.4	141.0	243.2	240.7	1.0	233.9	61.3	213.6	151.9	53.5
1962	888.2	39.3	10.5	28.8	821.4	140.2	250.0	246.8	1.5	255.8	63.2	231.8	162.5	52.4
1963	954.2	46.4	12.0	34.3	877.0	142.0	253.8	250.7	1.4	282.9	66.6	251.0	173.1	52.5
1964	1 028.5	52.7	12.7	40.0	940.9	141.8	259.9	255.9	2.2	312.7	67.6	272.7	186.4	52.4
1965	1 106.9	61.4	15.1	46.4	1 008.0	140.2	261.5	257.0	2.7	340.6	68.4	302.7	207.2	53.0
1966	1 187.3	72.3	20.3	52.0	1 075.5	136.5	265.1	259.3	4.0	363.1	67.6	337.2	232.0	54.1
1967	1 268.0	73.2	20.4	52.8	1 151.5	138.3	278.1	268.2	8.2	386.8	67.3	369.2	253.6	56.2
1968	1 372.9	83.5	24.4	59.1	1 243.3	136.7	290.6	277.6	11.3	415.2	66.5	411.4	284.8	57.2
1969	1 490.6	111.0	33.8	77.2	1 330.4	135.1	287.4	276.8	9.0	445.0	66.0	459.7	317.8	58.8
1970	1 599.6	127.3	43.6	83.7	1 420.2	136.8	299.5	289.9	8.1	460.3	62.6	510.1	361.6	64.8
1971	1 749.5	137.8	49.5	88.2	1 555.2	138.0	324.4	315.9	7.0	503.2	62.8	560.9	389.7	64.6
1972	1 933.5	161.3	57.9	103.3	1 711.2	138.2	339.4	330.1	7.9	558.2	64.2	632.9	430.3	64.3
1973	2 170.8	207.9	77.9	130.0	1 895.5	137.1	346.3	336.7	8.4	628.2	64.2	726.2	496.0	66.1
1974	2 408.0	257.6	98.6	159.0	2 069.1	138.0	358.2	348.8	8.2	684.5	63.9	818.2	550.9	68.0
1975	2 616.3	261.3	108.9	152.4	2 259.8	138.0	443.9	434.9	7.9	741.5	62.5	855.0	567.4	64.7
1976	2 904.1	285.5	123.1	162.3	2 503.0	137.2	513.1	503.7	8.3	828.5	63.6	923.5	606.4	61.3
1977	3 291.7	339.1	145.5	193.6	2 824.0	139.1	569.4	560.9	7.6	956.1	66.6	1 042.3	682.5	61.0
1978	3 776.3	412.7	182.6	230.1	3 207.9	139.9	621.9	614.9	6.2	1 111.2	69.1	1 179.3	761.1	59.8
1979	4 273.7	508.9	231.8	277.1	3 596.3	140.4	657.7	652.1	4.9	1 278.5	71.4	1 337.9	845.9	59.8
1980	4 722.4	584.7	276.6	308.1	3 944.3	141.5	735.0	730.0	4.4	1 396.0	69.7	1 468.9	913.8	59.6
1981	5 255.0	689.2	324.0	365.2	4 351.9	139.2	820.5	815.9	4.1	1 505.9	67.3	1 653.4	1 033.6	59.3
1982	5 766.8	785.5	388.9	396.6	4 773.1	146.7	981.8	978.1	3.4	1 575.8	65.3	1 801.8	1 124.1	62.4
1983	6 462.9	890.1	456.6	433.5	5 348.6	151.3	1 167.0	1 163.4	3.3	1 731.1	66.6	1 989.5	1 240.5	64.3
1984	7 422.5	1 054.9	531.2	523.7	6 134.8	156.1	1 364.2	1 360.8	3.2	1 943.1	67.2	2 313.8	1 451.2	67.1
1985	8 612.0	1 259.0	631.7	627.2	7 110.6	168.6	1 589.9	1 586.6	3.2	2 277.7	74.0	2 565.1	1 632.1	71.1
1986	9 801.5	1 596.6	810.3	786.3	7 953.0	178.3	1 805.9	1 802.2	3.6	2 534.2	77.8	2 860.8	1 860.6	78.1
1987	10 814.8	1 899.7	977.6	922.1	8 656.1	182.8	1 949.8	1 944.6	5.1	2 752.5	80.1	3 111.2	2 053.0	80.5
1988	11 856.3	2 149.5	1 098.4	1 051.2	9 437.0	185.0	2 104.9	2 082.3	22.6	3 039.8	81.6	3 399.3	2 257.3	81.6
1989	12 830.0	2 402.8	1 247.8	1 155.0	10 139.3	185.0	2 251.2	2 227.0	24.2	3 309.2	82.9	3 638.6	2 448.4	84.4
1990	13 757.1	2 613.8	1 418.4	1 195.4	10 825.1	186.6	2 498.1	2 465.8	32.4	3 571.6	84.0	3 767.9	2 577.4	84.9
1991	14 412.3	2 766.8	1 564.2	1 202.6	11 295.2	188.5	2 776.4	2 757.8	18.6	3 758.5	84.6	3 681.7	2 519.7	81.2
1992	15 204.0	3 018.9	1 720.4	1 298.5	11 812.7	186.3	3 080.3	3 061.6	18.8	3 961.7	83.6	3 675.6	2 540.0	78.4
1993	16 280.2	3 317.2	1 885.7	1 431.5	12 494.8	187.4	3 336.5	3 309.9	26.6	4 203.5	85.4	3 801.8	2 686.9	79.1
1994	17 373.9	3 789.7	2 173.4	1 616.3	13 141.1	185.5	3 492.3	3 465.6	26.7	4 527.0	87.3	4 014.3	2 885.0	78.4
1995	18 604.2	4 226.3	2 377.7	1 848.5	13 810.3	186.3	3 636.7	3 608.5	28.2	4 846.1	88.8	4 280.7	3 106.1	79.9
1996	19 922.6	4 749.5	2 609.2	2 140.3	14 515.9	185.2	3 781.7	3 755.1	26.6	5 183.8	90.0	4 524.2	3 279.1	79.6
1997	21 329.9	5 299.7	2 822.8	2 476.9	15 306.5	183.7	3 804.8	3 778.3	26.5	5 489.4	90.4	4 935.4	3 588.3	81.3
1998	23 414.0	6 326.2	3 294.4	3 031.8	16 304.6	185.4	3 752.2	3 723.7	28.5	5 902.9	90.8	5 505.8	3 979.7	85.2
1999	25 476.1	7 376.5	3 887.7	3 488.8	17 351.4	185.5	3 681.0	3 652.7	28.3	6 377.6	93.7	6 111.8	4 391.9	88.6
2000	27 208.1	8 168.4	4 319.7	3 848.7	18 225.2	183.1	3 385.1	3 357.8	27.3	6 963.5	95.0	6 678.7	4 766.4	90.3
2001	29 388.6	9 156.8	4 962.3	4 194.5	19 366.4	188.3	3 379.5	3 352.7	26.8	7 627.8	99.7	7 055.7	4 979.9	94.8
2002	31 900.1	10 038.2	5 509.0	4 529.2	20 789.1	195.3	3 637.0	3 609.8	27.3	8 439.1	105.4	7 265.1	5 037.5	94.9
2003	34 702.6	10 944.5	5 944.5	5 000.0	22 504.8	202.0	4 033.1	4 008.2	24.9	9 462.9	113.0	7 440.4	5 139.0	93.4
2004	38 681.8	11 898.3	6 060.3	5 838.0	25 344.7	213.8	4 395.0	4 370.7	24.3	10 531.5	118.5	7 932.8	5 376.7	91.5
2005	42 136.2	12 956.9	6 140.7	6 816.2	27 665.4	219.2	4 701.9	4 678.0	23.8	11 701.4	126.1	8 639.5	5 741.8	91.1
2006	46 173.8	14 278.6	6 468.9	7 809.7	30 012.6	224.4	4 885.3	4 861.7	23.5	12 834.6	129.4	9 571.8	6 258.8	92.9
2007	50 897.6	16 223.8	7 374.6	8 849.2	32 547.5	232.0	5 122.3	5 099.2	23.1	13 680.9	131.2	10 876.5	7 101.9	102.2
2008	53 284.9	17 122.7	8 143.4	8 979.3	34 453.4	241.1	6 361.5	6 338.2	23.3	13 665.5	124.0	11 538.6	7 445.2	106.5
2009	53 188.7	15 708.3	8 083.3	7 625.0	35 390.1	253.9	7 805.4	7 781.9	23.5	13 394.5	124.2	11 190.9	7 231.8	109.7
2010	53 396.7	14 261.8	7 574.0	6 687.8	36 861.8	253.8	9 385.6	9 361.5	24.2	13 115.6	117.3	11 295.1	7 533.3	109.1
2011	54 243.0	13 793.8	7 552.1	6 241.7	38 195.4	253.1	10 453.6	10 428.3	25.3	12 930.0	111.5	11 804.9	8 031.6	110.8
2009														
1st quarter	53 596.5	17 080.0	8 160.3	8 919.7	34 773.0	250.3	6 826.9	6 804.4	22.5	13 511.0	125.5	11 527.2	7 470.6	112.3
2nd quarter	53 387.4	16 524.0	8 118.8	8 405.2	35 057.4	253.0	7 165.3	7 143.1	22.3	13 473.4	124.5	11 483.8	7 458.8	114.1
3rd quarter	53 267.2	16 099.9	8 098.1	8 001.8	35 289.0	253.5	7 544.0	7 520.8	23.2	13 434.7	124.9	11 359.9	7 368.5	112.8
4th quarter	53 188.7	15 708.3	8 083.3	7 625.0	35 390.1	251.2	7 805.4	7 781.9	23.5	13 394.5	123.9	11 190.9	7 231.8	108.8
2010														
1st quarter	52 695.5	14 843.7	7 633.4	7 210.3	35 738.8	250.3	8 283.2	8 259.6	23.6	13 249.1	120.5	11 184.3	7 316.1	107.4
2nd quarter	52 663.5	14 594.2	7 637.6	6 956.6	35 962.5	248.6	8 627.7	8 603.8	23.9	13 187.6	118.3	11 133.2	7 328.3	106.6
3rd quarter	52 973.4	14 439.4	7 594.1	6 845.4	36 398.0	249.2	9 017.8	8 993.8	24.0	13 147.0	117.0	11 215.8	7 445.8	107.1
4th quarter	53 396.7	14 261.8	7 574.0	6 687.8	36 861.8	249.8	9 385.6	9 361.5	24.2	13 115.6	115.7	11 295.1	7 533.3	108.1
2011														
1st quarter	53 606.1	14 193.9	7 624.3	6 569.6	37 086.4	249.4	9 645.9	9 621.4	24.5	12 994.7	113.2	11 400.2	7 647.0	108.0
2nd quarter	53 544.2	14 014.9	7 553.3	6 461.6	37 208.0	247.8	9 738.6	9 714.1	24.5	12 916.9	111.7	11 539.5	7 788.4	107.9
3rd quarter	53 890.1	13 898.4	7 560.0	6 338.4	37 707.2	248.5	10 127.6	10 102.6	25.0	12 913.8	110.9	11 663.7	7 911.5	108.1
4th quarter	54 243.0	13 793.8	7 552.1	6 241.7	38 195.4	249.3	10 453.6	10 428.3	25.3	12 930.0	110.6	11 804.9	8 031.6	108.8

Table 12-5. Credit Market Debt Outstanding, by Borrower and Lender—*Continued*

(Billions of dollars, except as noted; end of period; not seasonally adjusted.)

| Year and quarter | Credit market debt outstanding owed by: —Continued | | | Credit market assets held by: | | | | | | | | | | |
| | Domestic nonfinancial sectors —Continued | | Foreign credit market debt held in United States | Total | Selected government-related sectors | | | | | | | Selected domestic financial sectors | |
	Nonfinancial business —Continued / Non-corporate	State and local governments			Total	Federal government	Government-sponsored enterprises	Federally related mortgage pools	State and local governments	State and local retirement funds	Federal government retirement funds	Total, selected sectors	Monetary authority
1955	34.8	46.1	16.4	582.0	51.3	21.0	5.0	0.1	14.7	10.5	0.0	367.9	24.4
1956	37.9	50.4	17.3	611.5	55.4	21.6	6.0	0.1	15.9	11.7	0.0	389.4	24.7
1957	40.4	55.0	18.5	642.7	58.9	22.2	7.3	0.2	15.9	13.3	0.0	409.8	23.8
1958	44.2	60.7	20.5	681.6	62.6	23.6	7.7	0.2	16.1	15.0	0.0	443.4	26.3
1959	50.2	66.7	21.4	738.7	70.1	25.7	9.9	0.2	17.5	16.8	0.0	470.8	26.7
1960	55.0	72.2	23.2	780.2	76.0	26.7	11.1	0.2	19.1	18.9	0.0	502.2	27.0
1961	61.7	77.8	25.4	828.5	82.0	28.4	12.1	0.3	20.1	21.1	0.0	540.7	28.8
1962	69.3	83.8	27.5	888.2	89.4	30.3	13.7	0.4	21.7	23.2	0.0	586.9	30.5
1963	78.0	89.2	30.8	954.2	96.6	31.9	15.3	0.5	23.3	25.6	0.0	638.6	33.7
1964	86.3	95.6	35.0	1 028.5	104.7	34.7	16.0	0.6	25.0	28.3	0.0	695.6	36.6
1965	95.6	103.2	37.4	1 106.9	115.5	37.6	18.3	0.9	27.5	31.3	0.0	758.4	40.6
1966	105.3	110.0	39.4	1 187.3	129.8	42.7	23.3	1.3	27.5	34.9	0.0	804.0	43.7
1967	115.6	117.4	43.3	1 268.0	138.5	47.3	23.3	2.0	27.6	38.3	0.0	868.9	49.1
1968	126.6	126.1	46.0	1 372.9	154.4	52.2	26.5	2.5	31.4	41.6	0.0	941.8	53.0
1969	141.9	138.3	49.2	1 490.6	175.6	55.4	35.1	3.2	36.4	45.5	0.0	993.0	57.2
1970	148.6	150.3	52.0	1 599.6	191.5	58.2	43.9	4.8	35.1	49.6	0.0	1 064.6	62.2
1971	171.2	166.7	56.5	1 749.5	201.1	60.3	45.0	9.5	33.4	52.9	0.0	1 175.4	69.6
1972	202.6	180.7	61.1	1 933.5	223.0	62.1	49.0	14.4	40.1	57.4	0.0	1 317.7	71.2
1973	230.1	194.8	67.4	2 170.8	260.2	64.8	64.4	18.0	49.8	63.1	0.0	1 478.2	80.5
1974	267.3	208.2	81.2	2 408.0	304.6	72.1	85.3	21.5	56.4	69.4	0.0	1 606.2	85.3
1975	287.6	219.4	95.3	2 616.3	345.9	85.5	89.8	28.5	63.8	78.3	0.0	1 736.6	93.5
1976	317.1	237.8	115.7	2 904.1	398.6	93.7	94.5	40.7	82.0	87.7	0.0	1 925.7	100.3
1977	359.8	256.2	128.6	3 291.7	471.6	103.6	101.4	56.8	110.6	99.2	0.0	2 177.2	108.9
1978	418.2	295.6	155.7	3 776.3	582.6	120.6	128.1	70.4	147.5	116.0	0.0	2 454.5	117.4
1979	492.0	322.2	168.5	4 273.7	696.0	141.4	158.1	94.8	175.2	126.6	0.0	2 752.3	124.5
1980	555.1	344.4	193.4	4 722.4	804.5	165.5	184.5	114.0	193.4	147.2	0.0	2 999.2	128.0
1981	619.8	372.1	214.0	5 255.0	931.1	189.9	217.7	129.0	225.6	169.0	0.0	3 292.5	136.9
1982	677.6	413.8	208.1	5 766.8	1 058.9	205.8	233.7	178.5	250.1	190.7	0.0	3 561.8	144.5
1983	749.0	461.1	224.1	6 462.9	1 177.7	215.3	236.4	244.8	282.4	198.8	0.0	3 968.1	159.2
1984	862.6	513.6	232.8	7 422.5	1 339.7	232.6	265.9	289.0	319.0	233.2	0.0	4 522.1	167.6
1985	933.0	677.9	242.5	8 612.0	1 618.0	251.2	291.0	367.9	455.6	252.4	0.0	5 081.7	186.0
1986	1 000.2	752.1	251.9	9 801.5	1 920.0	258.0	307.6	531.6	525.8	297.1	0.0	5 766.6	205.5
1987	1 058.2	842.6	259.0	10 814.8	2 156.6	242.8	330.9	669.4	583.6	328.8	1.1	6 279.7	226.5
1988	1 142.0	893.0	269.8	11 856.3	2 298.7	217.4	364.2	745.3	618.6	350.5	2.7	6 797.2	240.6
1989	1 190.2	940.4	287.9	12 830.0	2 489.2	209.4	359.9	869.5	664.1	381.5	4.9	7 212.1	233.3
1990	1 190.5	987.4	318.2	13 757.1	2 749.6	243.1	373.9	1 019.9	703.4	402.0	7.4	7 551.1	241.4
1991	1 162.0	1 078.6	350.4	14 412.3	2 961.6	251.0	388.9	1 156.5	750.6	404.6	10.0	7 777.6	272.5
1992	1 135.5	1 095.1	372.4	15 204.0	3 176.3	239.0	458.1	1 272.0	752.3	441.8	13.1	8 136.3	300.4
1993	1 114.9	1 153.0	468.2	16 280.2	3 400.7	227.5	546.7	1 356.8	784.9	468.6	16.2	8 749.1	336.7
1994	1 129.3	1 107.5	443.1	17 373.9	3 590.9	222.1	667.9	1 472.4	729.9	478.7	19.9	9 214.5	368.2
1995	1 174.6	1 046.7	567.6	18 604.2	3 702.7	197.6	762.8	1 570.7	638.6	509.8	23.3	9 871.1	380.8
1996	1 245.1	1 026.2	657.2	19 922.6	3 916.0	201.6	833.8	1 711.7	604.8	538.4	25.6	10 412.0	393.1
1997	1 347.1	1 076.9	723.6	21 329.9	4 204.3	213.1	934.2	1 826.3	605.0	598.3	27.5	11 202.9	431.4
1998	1 526.1	1 143.8	783.2	23 414.0	4 895.5	218.8	1 251.5	2 019.0	714.6	661.5	30.2	12 380.9	452.5
1999	1 719.9	1 181.0	748.2	25 476.1	5 645.2	256.3	1 538.8	2 293.5	816.5	707.0	33.1	13 529.9	478.1
2000	1 912.3	1 197.9	814.5	27 208.1	6 216.5	263.1	1 794.4	2 493.2	887.3	743.2	35.1	14 414.6	511.8
2001	2 075.7	1 303.4	865.4	29 388.6	6 913.3	267.0	2 099.1	2 831.8	981.2	689.4	44.8	15 536.6	551.7
2002	2 227.6	1 447.9	1 072.8	31 900.1	7 520.3	275.0	2 323.1	3 158.6	1 067.4	638.7	57.6	16 831.1	629.4
2003	2 301.4	1 568.4	1 253.3	34 702.6	8 026.5	272.4	2 564.1	3 343.3	1 125.6	657.5	63.6	18 189.9	666.7
2004	2 556.1	2 485.4	1 438.8	38 681.8	8 213.4	274.7	2 613.0	3 384.0	1 198.1	675.3	68.2	19 830.5	717.8
2005	2 897.7	2 622.6	1 513.9	42 136.2	8 458.6	273.8	2 543.9	3 548.5	1 323.0	693.4	76.0	21 739.2	744.2
2006	3 313.0	2 720.9	1 882.6	46 173.8	8 988.2	275.2	2 590.5	3 841.1	1 389.0	808.0	84.3	23 809.0	778.9
2007	3 774.6	2 867.8	2 126.3	50 897.6	9 958.4	281.1	2 829.5	4 464.4	1 466.9	820.3	96.1	25 576.0	740.6
2008	4 093.4	2 887.8	1 708.8	53 284.9	10 654.2	366.4	3 037.5	4 961.4	1 335.2	833.5	120.3	26 525.2	986.0
2009	3 959.1	2 999.3	2 090.3	53 188.7	10 989.1	661.8	2 699.7	5 376.7	1 298.5	824.7	127.7	26 271.5	1 987.7
2010	3 761.8	3 065.5	2 273.1	53 396.7	10 514.0	746.9	6 333.1	1 139.5	1 339.3	816.5	138.7	25 959.7	2 259.2
2011	3 773.3	3 006.8	2 253.8	54 243.0	10 430.6	744.7	6 133.4	1 304.8	1 254.9	834.8	158.1	26 843.3	2 635.6
2009													
1st quarter	4 056.6	2 907.9	1 743.5	53 596.5	10 775.1	445.9	2 980.1	5 042.0	1 355.7	827.0	124.5	26 438.0	1 168.1
2nd quarter	4 025.1	2 935.3	1 805.9	53 387.4	10 886.2	532.0	2 909.0	5 170.7	1 325.9	823.8	124.7	26 535.6	1 469.5
3rd quarter	3 991.5	2 950.4	1 878.3	53 267.2	10 968.9	608.4	2 812.7	5 297.5	1 302.8	821.7	125.8	26 370.4	1 776.6
4th quarter	3 959.1	2 999.3	2 090.3	53 188.7	10 989.1	661.8	2 699.7	5 376.7	1 298.5	824.7	127.7	26 271.5	1 987.7
2010													
1st quarter	3 868.2	3 022.3	2 113.0	52 695.5	10 512.1	677.7	6 577.4	980.2	1 323.7	823.7	129.4	26 066.4	2 151.8
2nd quarter	3 805.0	3 014.0	2 106.8	52 663.5	10 486.6	680.3	6 494.1	1 046.5	1 312.9	819.3	133.6	25 817.5	2 187.3
3rd quarter	3 770.0	3 017.4	2 136.0	52 973.4	10 479.3	726.3	6 385.1	1 096.0	1 317.9	815.8	138.3	25 780.3	2 150.3
4th quarter	3 761.8	3 065.5	2 273.1	53 396.7	10 514.0	746.9	6 333.1	1 139.5	1 339.3	816.5	138.7	25 959.7	2 259.2
2011													
1st quarter	3 753.1	3 045.7	2 325.9	53 606.1	10 587.5	778.2	6 327.9	1 187.0	1 327.2	825.0	142.2	26 096.6	2 479.2
2nd quarter	3 751.1	3 013.0	2 321.4	53 544.2	10 514.4	757.0	6 252.4	1 236.0	1 302.4	820.5	146.1	26 295.5	2 700.4
3rd quarter	3 752.2	3 002.2	2 284.4	53 890.1	10 475.1	761.4	6 176.5	1 277.3	1 270.0	835.6	154.2	26 462.5	2 686.1
4th quarter	3 773.3	3 006.8	2 253.8	54 243.0	10 430.6	744.7	6 133.4	1 304.8	1 254.9	834.8	158.1	26 843.3	2 635.6

Table 12-5. Credit Market Debt Outstanding, by Borrower and Lender—*Continued*

(Billions of dollars, except as noted; end of period; not seasonally adjusted.)

Year and quarter	Credit market assets held by:—*Continued*											
	Selected domestic financial sectors—*Continued*									House-holds	Foreign holdings in United States	All other financial and non-financial sectors
	U.S. chartered depository institutions	Credit unions	Life insurance companies	Property-c-asualty insurance companies	Private pension funds	Money market mutual funds	Mutual funds	Asset-backed security issuers	Finance companies			
1955	220.5	2.0	80.5	11.5	11.2	0.0	0.8	0.0	17.0	117.6	6.7	38.6
1956	233.0	2.4	85.6	11.9	12.7	0.0	1.1	0.0	18.0	124.9	7.3	34.5
1957	245.2	2.9	90.5	12.6	14.5	0.0	1.2	0.0	19.3	131.9	7.5	34.6
1958	268.4	3.1	95.5	13.4	16.2	0.0	1.5	0.0	19.0	132.7	7.5	35.4
1959	283.2	3.8	100.5	14.6	17.9	0.0	1.8	0.0	22.4	142.8	11.7	43.3
1960	302.0	4.5	105.6	15.5	19.7	0.0	2.0	0.0	25.9	150.9	12.6	38.5
1961	329.0	4.9	110.9	16.5	21.2	0.0	2.4	0.0	27.0	154.9	13.1	37.9
1962	361.2	5.6	116.9	18.0	22.9	0.0	2.6	0.0	29.2	158.2	14.8	38.9
1963	395.2	6.3	123.3	18.7	24.8	0.0	2.8	0.0	33.7	159.8	15.9	43.3
1964	433.8	7.2	130.3	19.5	27.2	0.0	3.2	0.0	37.9	166.2	16.9	45.1
1965	475.6	8.2	137.8	20.6	29.1	0.0	3.9	0.0	42.7	170.0	17.4	45.5
1966	501.1	9.4	145.9	22.0	31.9	0.0	5.1	0.0	44.9	190.0	17.3	46.1
1967	550.3	10.2	153.3	23.5	32.8	0.0	4.3	0.0	45.5	195.2	20.0	45.4
1968	602.4	11.7	160.7	25.4	33.8	0.0	4.1	0.0	50.6	203.5	22.6	50.6
1969	628.4	13.8	167.6	27.0	34.6	0.0	5.1	0.0	59.2	241.4	23.2	57.5
1970	677.9	15.2	174.6	30.9	36.6	0.0	5.7	0.0	61.5	242.4	35.0	66.1
1971	763.1	17.2	182.8	34.6	35.0	0.0	5.5	0.0	67.6	233.2	62.8	77.0
1972	871.6	20.1	192.5	38.3	40.5	0.0	6.0	0.0	77.5	230.0	73.2	89.7
1973	984.7	23.7	204.8	41.8	46.8	0.0	6.6	0.0	89.4	254.7	74.7	103.0
1974	1 071.8	26.4	217.7	46.4	55.6	0.8	7.4	0.0	94.8	299.5	79.8	117.8
1975	1 147.2	31.7	234.6	53.7	71.2	1.5	8.0	0.0	95.0	320.7	88.3	124.8
1976	1 267.7	38.4	258.3	66.2	77.8	2.1	8.4	0.0	106.6	331.3	99.4	149.1
1977	1 422.1	45.6	285.8	83.7	88.2	1.9	12.3	0.0	128.6	358.4	135.4	149.1
1978	1 595.4	52.0	318.9	100.2	98.7	5.1	12.5	0.0	154.2	406.7	161.3	171.2
1979	1 764.8	53.8	352.0	113.7	120.8	24.9	14.5	0.0	183.4	486.1	149.7	189.6
1980	1 903.2	53.0	385.1	123.5	151.4	42.0	17.1	0.0	195.8	521.0	169.7	228.0
1981	2 023.9	55.0	419.8	132.0	178.6	107.5	20.2	0.0	218.6	546.6	197.0	287.9
1982	2 140.0	57.3	463.2	139.6	225.4	137.6	25.4	0.0	228.9	612.2	240.0	294.0
1983	2 399.0	69.4	513.8	147.6	267.5	119.7	34.9	3.0	254.0	703.8	263.3	349.9
1984	2 691.1	85.0	570.1	162.0	305.9	164.1	53.9	19.8	302.5	808.7	340.4	411.7
1985	2 933.7	98.4	646.6	191.8	329.0	178.2	129.9	34.8	353.2	967.4	419.9	525.1
1986	3 190.3	113.9	734.5	234.6	333.6	213.1	259.9	71.4	409.9	1 001.0	536.4	577.5
1987	3 409.2	131.3	823.1	274.6	347.2	215.0	291.1	113.2	448.3	1 176.4	586.5	615.6
1988	3 634.5	148.8	927.2	306.0	369.2	225.5	304.5	147.6	493.3	1 382.4	689.1	689.0
1989	3 678.8	156.0	1 028.3	335.6	420.8	293.7	327.2	201.1	537.3	1 479.6	815.8	833.3
1990	3 633.6	166.6	1 134.5	364.2	464.3	371.3	360.1	250.3	564.8	1 741.2	881.7	833.4
1991	3 506.8	179.4	1 218.9	394.1	489.7	403.9	440.2	299.5	572.5	1 824.9	909.6	938.7
1992	3 500.4	197.1	1 304.4	410.6	515.7	408.6	566.4	357.9	575.0	1 886.5	983.1	1 021.7
1993	3 627.4	218.7	1 415.5	443.3	551.9	429.0	725.9	437.8	563.1	1 995.5	1 095.0	1 039.9
1994	3 781.1	246.8	1 487.5	465.6	591.5	459.0	718.8	501.0	595.1	2 377.7	1 162.8	1 028.1
1995	3 954.9	263.0	1 587.5	493.1	608.4	545.5	771.3	612.0	654.6	2 379.7	1 464.8	1 185.9
1996	4 093.0	288.5	1 657.0	514.2	602.3	634.3	820.2	712.2	697.1	2 545.0	1 795.6	1 254.1
1997	4 359.8	305.3	1 751.1	538.2	646.8	721.9	901.1	826.5	720.8	2 501.4	2 035.6	1 385.7
1998	4 697.2	324.2	1 828.0	548.9	639.7	970.5	1 028.4	1 078.8	812.8	2 554.6	2 202.0	1 381.0
1999	5 098.5	351.7	1 886.0	536.5	746.9	1 155.3	1 076.8	1 253.3	946.6	2 670.9	2 196.1	1 433.9
2000	5 486.8	379.7	1 943.9	534.3	621.9	1 317.5	1 103.1	1 413.6	1 101.9	2 563.6	2 451.1	1 562.4
2001	5 720.7	421.2	2 071.5	536.6	587.0	1 584.9	1 229.7	1 662.6	1 170.7	2 460.1	2 850.2	1 628.4
2002	6 143.7	465.4	2 300.3	584.7	581.7	1 567.1	1 368.4	1 897.8	1 292.5	2 596.5	3 303.0	1 649.3
2003	6 642.5	516.6	2 478.8	660.5	653.5	1 471.3	1 506.4	2 125.1	1 468.7	2 837.4	3 836.1	1 812.6
2004	7 311.0	556.4	2 643.9	746.5	654.6	1 346.3	1 623.0	2 555.1	1 675.9	3 949.7	4 634.7	2 053.6
2005	8 011.3	592.5	2 753.9	819.3	699.9	1 340.8	1 747.1	3 289.6	1 740.6	4 298.4	5 191.3	2 448.7
2006	8 628.6	622.6	2 786.4	864.1	758.3	1 560.8	1 932.0	4 068.1	1 809.2	4 434.2	6 199.7	2 742.7
2007	9 201.0	657.9	2 871.2	869.3	860.8	1 936.4	2 203.1	4 419.3	1 816.3	5 047.8	7 272.6	3 042.9
2008	9 442.9	697.8	2 882.8	853.4	951.4	2 675.0	2 276.4	4 024.9	1 734.4	4 973.7	7 504.6	3 627.0
2009	9 131.1	731.0	3 022.6	886.7	1 063.0	2 031.0	2 657.2	3 244.4	1 516.7	5 243.8	7 724.2	2 960.1
2010	9 341.5	755.6	3 174.2	890.6	1 122.4	1 621.0	3 031.4	2 224.6	1 539.2	5 423.1	8 374.4	3 125.6
2011	9 468.4	790.8	3 323.9	918.1	1 161.2	1 628.2	3 458.9	1 970.1	1 488.1	5 147.7	8 575.7	3 245.8
2009												
1st quarter	9 387.5	698.6	2 924.2	855.8	987.9	2 575.2	2 319.9	3 836.1	1 684.6	5 418.0	7 576.8	3 388.6
2nd quarter	9 368.7	717.0	2 954.3	861.8	1 005.1	2 412.1	2 436.0	3 670.0	1 641.1	5 142.5	7 610.6	3 212.4
3rd quarter	9 188.6	725.8	2 985.3	870.7	1 037.7	2 163.8	2 540.0	3 487.5	1 594.4	5 276.4	7 595.0	3 056.5
4th quarter	9 131.1	731.0	3 022.6	886.7	1 063.0	2 031.0	2 657.2	3 244.4	1 516.7	5 243.8	7 724.2	2 960.1
2010												
1st quarter	9 373.2	737.2	3 042.6	886.8	1 090.0	1 828.5	2 784.9	2 560.2	1 611.1	5 253.0	7 852.0	3 012.0
2nd quarter	9 265.2	750.2	3 083.7	887.2	1 097.5	1 703.3	2 834.3	2 431.2	1 577.6	5 390.4	7 939.5	3 029.5
3rd quarter	9 308.9	741.2	3 134.3	892.2	1 102.3	1 599.5	2 971.0	2 322.2	1 558.6	5 358.8	8 161.2	3 193.8
4th quarter	9 341.5	755.6	3 174.2	890.6	1 122.4	1 621.0	3 031.4	2 224.6	1 539.2	5 423.1	8 374.4	3 125.6
2011												
1st quarter	9 211.3	765.4	3 215.5	895.2	1 130.9	1 582.4	3 160.9	2 136.1	1 519.6	5 417.0	8 397.6	3 107.4
2nd quarter	9 185.9	774.3	3 244.5	890.3	1 133.8	1 521.0	3 267.8	2 086.3	1 491.2	5 215.0	8 393.5	3 125.8
3rd quarter	9 299.0	781.6	3 296.9	890.6	1 153.0	1 527.2	3 317.9	2 019.7	1 490.4	5 188.0	8 558.2	3 206.3
4th quarter	9 468.4	790.8	3 323.9	918.1	1 161.2	1 628.2	3 458.9	1 970.1	1 488.1	5 147.7	8 575.7	3 245.8

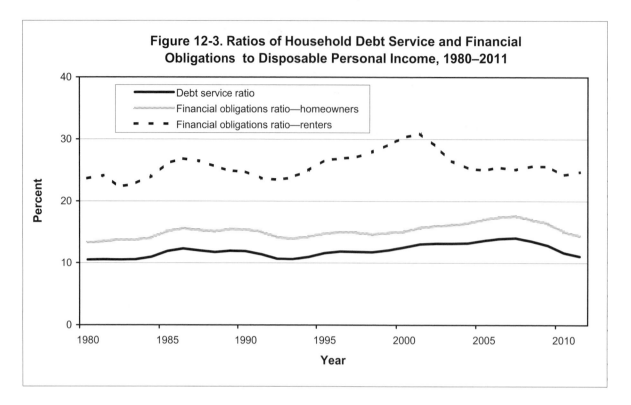

Figure 12-3. Ratios of Household Debt Service and Financial Obligations to Disposable Personal Income, 1980–2011

- The Federal Reserve calculates aggregate household debt service (payments of principal and interest) and total financial obligations as a percentage of aggregate disposable personal income (DPI) for the period 1980 to the present. These measures provide supplements to the ratio of the total level of household debt to DPI (shown in Figure 12-2 and Table 12-5), and are important because lengthening maturities and lower interest rates can mitigate much of the burden of a high level of debt. Unlike the debt/income ratio, the debt service ratio leveled off between 2002 and 2004, reflecting the decline in interest rates. However, the debt service ratio rose to a new record high of 14.0 percent in 2006 and 2007. Since then it has dropped back to 11.1 percent at the end of 2011, the lowest since 1994. (Table 12-6)

- Financial obligations ratios are higher than the debt service ratio. They are calculated separately for homeowners and renters and include all debt service, rental payments on primary residences, property taxes, homeowners' insurance, and automobile lease payments. The financial obligations ratio for homeowners stood at a record 17.6 percent of income at the end of 2007, but has dropped back to 14.4 percent since then, also the lowest since 1994. (Table 12-6)

- Reflecting the lower average incomes of the renters' group, the financial obligations ratio for renters is about double the ratio for homeowners. But the renters' ratio peaked in 2001. It then declined rapidly in the early 2000s. At the end of 2010 the ratio was about the same as in 1990. (Table 12-6)

- Additional evidence on debt trends is seen in the ratio of aggregate household debt to aggregate household financial and tangible assets, which rose from around 10 percent in 1960 to over 20 percent in 2008, and was 17.6 percent at the end of 2011. (Table 12-6) Narrowing the comparison to mortgage debt alone, home mortgage debt as a percent of the value of real estate has increased from a range of 30 to 35 percent that prevailed from 1960 through 1987 to 66 percent in the first quarter of 2009, and remains around 64 percent through the end of 2011. In other words, homeowners as a group now have only 36 percent equity in their homes, compared with the nearly 70 percent that they had as recently as 1982. (Table 12-7)

Table 12-6. Household Assets, Liabilities, Net Worth, Financial Obligations, and Delinquency Rates

(Billions of dollars, except as noted; end of period; not seasonally adjusted, except as noted.)

Year and quarter	Financial assets of the household sector [1]													
	Total [2]	Checkable deposits and currency	Time and savings deposits	Money market fund shares	U.S. savings bonds	Other Treasury securities	Agency- and GSE-backed securities	Municipal securities	Corporate and foreign bonds	Mortgages	Corporate equities	Mutual fund shares	Security credit	Life insurance reserves
1950	737.8	58.9	67.2	0.0	49.6	16.9	0.1	5.5	6.0	17.6	129.8	3.3	1.0	55.0
1951	803.3	63.3	72.2	0.0	49.1	16.3	0.1	5.7	6.3	18.6	152.1	3.5	0.9	57.8
1952	832.4	65.5	79.7	0.0	49.2	18.2	0.0	11.0	6.0	19.2	151.0	3.9	0.7	60.7
1953	850.3	66.8	87.9	0.0	49.4	18.7	0.2	13.9	6.0	20.2	145.8	4.1	0.7	63.6
1954	929.1	68.9	97.2	0.0	50.0	16.1	0.1	16.0	4.9	21.4	198.8	6.1	1.0	66.3
1955	1 018.6	70.0	105.8	0.0	50.2	18.6	0.6	19.2	5.0	22.7	248.2	7.8	0.9	69.3
1956	1 087.4	71.9	115.2	0.0	50.1	20.1	1.0	21.9	6.1	24.3	271.0	9.0	0.9	72.7
1957	1 100.1	71.0	127.2	0.0	48.2	23.3	1.5	23.9	7.2	26.2	244.5	8.7	0.9	75.5
1958	1 228.8	73.7	141.3	0.0	47.7	20.9	0.8	24.6	7.9	28.8	322.3	13.2	1.2	78.5
1959	1 304.2	75.6	152.5	0.0	45.9	25.7	2.3	28.4	8.2	30.7	357.3	15.8	1.0	82.0
1960	1 352.7	77.6	164.5	0.0	45.6	26.6	1.0	31.0	10.6	33.5	359.8	17.0	1.1	85.2
1961	1 497.8	77.0	182.8	0.0	46.4	25.5	0.6	32.5	10.8	36.8	443.2	22.9	1.2	88.6
1962	1 540.6	77.2	208.8	0.0	47.0	26.8	0.2	32.1	10.2	39.0	431.2	20.9	1.2	92.4
1963	1 639.3	82.1	234.9	0.0	48.1	24.7	0.0	32.1	10.1	40.5	469.9	24.8	1.2	96.6
1964	1 794.0	84.9	261.0	0.0	49.1	24.5	0.2	34.9	10.3	42.0	544.1	28.4	1.7	101.1
1965	1 960.4	91.6	288.5	0.0	49.7	25.1	1.1	36.5	9.0	42.6	616.1	34.4	2.5	105.9
1966	1 982.4	93.5	307.1	0.0	50.2	28.8	5.9	41.2	11.1	44.6	548.3	33.9	2.7	110.6
1967	2 232.6	103.8	342.3	0.0	51.2	27.8	6.3	38.2	15.1	46.5	682.1	43.0	4.9	115.5
1968	2 496.0	112.7	372.5	0.0	51.9	29.9	6.1	36.5	18.0	49.0	815.3	49.5	7.0	120.3
1969	2 440.1	110.9	381.3	0.0	51.8	41.4	11.3	47.2	22.0	49.1	667.4	45.6	5.2	125.4
1970	2 532.9	118.6	423.5	0.0	52.1	31.0	15.9	47.1	29.7	50.0	650.2	44.5	4.4	130.7
1971	2 821.5	132.1	491.0	0.0	54.4	19.8	14.6	46.0	37.4	47.3	743.7	53.0	4.9	137.1
1972	3 231.1	144.4	564.2	0.0	57.7	19.7	8.9	47.7	38.5	48.2	921.4	56.4	5.0	143.9
1973	3 238.3	152.5	624.9	0.0	60.4	28.1	8.3	55.1	41.5	47.2	693.9	43.7	4.9	151.3
1974	3 213.8	157.4	681.0	2.4	63.3	32.9	13.7	62.2	54.4	50.5	445.0	31.8	3.9	158.4
1975	3 678.8	158.7	762.2	3.7	67.4	44.4	7.6	66.8	64.3	50.4	584.6	38.7	4.5	168.6
1976	4 161.2	169.2	860.8	3.4	72.0	30.7	11.7	72.9	74.3	52.8	731.6	41.4	5.7	177.8
1977	4 439.3	184.2	963.0	3.2	76.8	27.8	8.4	78.8	79.8	55.3	631.3	40.4	5.7	187.8
1978	4 967.8	200.7	1 058.3	8.9	80.7	29.6	9.9	104.2	73.6	62.4	640.0	41.1	8.5	199.4
1979	5 692.6	220.5	1 126.1	39.5	79.9	76.0	12.5	123.6	66.6	71.6	768.1	44.8	10.4	210.3
1980	6 574.1	238.1	1 248.0	64.4	72.5	101.3	18.6	130.1	59.0	87.2	1 010.4	52.1	16.2	220.6
1981	6 970.9	284.4	1 319.5	154.6	68.2	100.6	14.2	160.3	60.0	101.4	905.2	52.6	14.7	230.1
1982	7 582.9	303.9	1 447.8	186.7	68.3	116.8	13.4	201.1	53.0	110.9	966.3	65.1	17.8	238.0
1983	8 342.5	313.6	1 644.7	149.9	71.5	159.2	14.5	246.7	57.0	111.2	1 088.6	98.0	20.6	246.7
1984	8 848.3	327.0	1 864.2	193.0	74.5	203.2	27.7	290.4	44.7	102.5	1 008.7	117.5	21.6	252.8
1985	9 994.9	344.8	2 001.9	196.3	79.8	202.5	23.4	395.1	94.7	115.5	1 229.5	213.8	35.1	264.3
1986	11 129.9	461.9	2 102.5	235.1	93.3	177.6	23.3	410.9	127.8	111.9	1 494.0	378.7	44.0	282.6
1987	11 775.2	460.8	2 217.4	256.0	101.1	207.1	32.1	516.6	144.6	119.5	1 462.6	424.5	39.1	309.5
1988	12 909.5	460.5	2 392.7	273.0	109.6	283.9	52.4	586.0	135.1	121.8	1 757.1	439.1	40.9	335.7
1989	14 236.9	462.2	2 466.9	351.1	117.7	277.2	74.8	613.3	178.1	130.7	2 147.5	513.0	53.2	365.3
1990	14 695.0	450.8	2 512.1	389.4	126.2	377.8	117.3	647.7	237.6	140.9	1 961.4	511.5	62.4	391.7
1991	16 249.0	505.0	2 440.8	407.7	138.1	397.4	115.5	701.8	270.9	142.7	2 759.2	645.0	87.0	418.6
1992	17 084.2	616.4	2 333.0	365.5	157.3	470.1	114.4	672.2	283.2	136.8	3 094.2	799.4	76.2	447.7
1993	18 467.0	667.5	2 218.3	363.5	171.9	501.3	58.3	640.8	428.8	129.4	3 437.0	1 098.0	102.3	484.8
1994	19 201.9	636.3	2 181.4	373.1	179.9	691.1	187.6	594.1	534.8	120.5	3 294.2	1 096.6	109.0	520.3
1995	21 780.3	586.5	2 317.2	472.4	185.0	643.0	216.4	533.4	616.7	113.3	4 434.2	1 253.0	127.6	566.2
1996	23 545.1	544.8	2 457.9	500.9	187.0	701.9	332.8	493.0	648.7	105.8	4 712.2	1 561.9	162.9	610.6
1997	27 026.6	503.8	2 594.9	571.3	186.5	611.4	389.7	497.6	640.2	98.7	6 144.1	1 949.3	215.5	665.0
1998	30 351.8	528.6	2 696.9	671.3	186.6	546.4	441.7	498.7	706.5	94.3	7 506.8	2 352.2	276.7	718.3
1999	34 827.6	508.9	2 792.3	774.2	186.4	623.7	541.8	528.1	603.9	101.6	9 763.0	2 894.6	323.9	783.9
2000	33 766.6	405.1	3 049.3	937.3	184.8	394.3	594.0	531.2	656.7	103.4	8 140.2	2 708.0	412.4	819.1
2001	32 692.9	400.0	3 331.1	1 101.1	190.3	243.7	407.3	580.7	838.6	108.7	6 825.9	2 618.2	454.3	880.0
2002	30 879.5	464.1	3 642.6	1 087.7	194.9	68.8	247.6	678.3	1 205.2	116.6	5 163.3	2 223.3	412.7	920.9
2003	35 991.3	458.2	3 965.9	969.2	203.8	204.2	384.0	703.7	1 140.4	120.9	6 784.2	2 915.3	475.4	1 013.2
2004	41 062.1	400.0	4 454.6	916.1	204.4	288.2	406.0	1 561.8	1 268.3	131.3	7 475.5	3 432.3	578.3	1 060.4
2005	44 888.8	285.8	4 937.1	949.2	205.1	265.6	513.5	1 639.1	1 428.6	139.5	8 083.5	3 675.5	575.3	1 082.6
2006	49 417.6	245.8	5 422.4	1 114.5	202.4	197.2	443.1	1 681.4	1 661.4	122.2	9 632.9	4 198.1	655.7	1 055.2
2007	52 156.8	160.2	5 914.6	1 346.7	196.4	68.3	693.3	1 725.4	2 129.8	109.8	9 614.8	4 610.9	866.4	1 076.8
2008	42 861.1	349.6	6 118.8	1 581.8	194.0	62.6	736.9	1 767.2	2 066.2	111.2	5 742.5	3 346.8	742.7	1 049.8
2009	45 727.0	373.6	6 231.9	1 313.1	191.2	624.3	141.9	1 896.5	2 227.0	101.5	7 397.6	4 164.9	668.6	1 109.2
2010	49 404.5	348.3	6 433.6	1 129.7	187.9	1 019.1	126.0	1 954.6	1 955.7	90.2	8 579.2	4 613.4	694.3	1 137.2
2011	50 229.4	660.2	6 832.8	1 107.2	185.2	930.1	93.1	1 891.8	1 887.1	78.8	8 356.8	4 652.2	752.3	1 200.8
2009														
1st quarter	41 395.7	33.5	6 145.6	1 555.3	193.9	293.8	519.2	1 794.1	2 475.0	109.1	5 038.9	3 145.6	666.3	1 051.5
2nd quarter	42 741.2	40.2	6 088.9	1 484.0	193.5	292.4	227.3	1 828.2	2 453.7	106.9	6 104.4	3 581.2	657.3	1 072.7
3rd quarter	44 917.9	37.5	6 084.5	1 358.6	192.4	455.2	248.1	1 845.4	2 382.5	104.2	7 223.5	3 976.5	671.7	1 095.5
4th quarter	45 727.0	37.4	6 231.9	1 313.1	191.2	624.3	141.9	1 896.5	2 227.0	101.5	7 397.6	4 164.9	668.6	1 109.2
2010														
1st quarter	46 562.3	28.9	6 356.7	1 198.7	190.2	789.8	109.3	1 929.1	2 064.5	99.9	7 639.0	4 327.3	680.0	1 115.4
2nd quarter	45 027.3	26.1	6 371.9	1 140.0	189.6	1 022.2	105.3	1 932.4	1 964.4	96.5	6 887.4	4 011.5	686.0	1 098.5
3rd quarter	47 268.3	26.1	6 418.5	1 125.9	188.7	1 092.5	100.7	1 914.0	1 880.1	93.4	7 820.7	4 336.3	696.8	1 122.8
4th quarter	49 404.5	34.8	6 433.6	1 129.7	187.9	1 019.1	126.0	1 954.6	1 955.7	90.2	8 579.2	4 613.4	694.3	1 137.2
2011														
1st quarter	51 124.8	35.1	6 533.9	1 098.6	186.8	940.2	208.8	1 966.0	1 934.6	87.6	9 303.2	4 965.0	703.3	1 155.3
2nd quarter	50 968.2	43.2	6 665.9	1 086.8	186.0	788.1	186.2	1 941.4	1 938.6	84.3	9 174.1	5 021.6	757.7	1 167.8
3rd quarter	48 211.7	53.7	6 740.5	1 101.0	185.1	871.8	139.5	1 920.5	1 902.9	82.4	7 629.8	4 408.1	804.9	1 172.6
4th quarter	50 229.4	66.0	6 832.8	1 107.2	185.2	930.1	93.1	1 891.8	1 887.1	78.8	8 356.8	4 652.2	752.3	1 200.8

[1]Includes nonprofit organizations.
[2]Includes components not shown separately.

Table 12-6. Household Assets, Liabilities, Net Worth, Financial Obligations, and Delinquency Rates —Continued

(Billions of dollars, except as noted; end of period; not seasonally adjusted, except as noted.)

Year and quarter	Financial assets of the household sector[1] —Continued		Tangible assets of the household sector		Debt as a percent of total assets[1]	Total liabilities[1]	Net worth[1]	Ratios to disposable personal income (percent, seasonally adjusted)				Consumer credit card accounts held at banks (percent, seasonally adjusted)	
	Pension fund reserves	Equity in non-corporate business	Total[1]	House-hold real estate[3]				House-hold debt service	Household financial obligations			Delinquency rate	Charge-off rate
									Total	Home-owners	Renters		
1950	23.2	294.4	387.2	243.3	6.5	76.8	1 048.1	...	...	...	...	...	...
1951	26.8	320.5	430.7	270.9	6.6	85.5	1 148.5	...	...	...	...	...	...
1952	33.5	322.2	463.8	294.8	7.3	97.8	1 198.4	...	...	...	...	...	...
1953	38.5	321.9	493.2	315.1	7.9	110.5	1 233.0	...	...	...	...	...	...
1954	43.9	325.7	520.7	337.6	8.1	122.9	1 326.8	...	...	...	...	...	...
1955	52.0	334.8	565.3	367.4	8.7	144.3	1 439.6	...	...	...	...	...	...
1956	58.2	351.0	607.8	394.3	9.0	159.5	1 535.7	...	...	...	...	...	...
1957	64.6	362.9	643.4	417.2	9.5	172.0	1 571.5	...	...	...	...	...	...
1958	74.9	377.8	669.9	438.4	9.3	184.0	1 714.7	...	...	...	...	...	...
1959	85.0	378.4	705.4	463.6	9.9	206.6	1 803.0	...	...	...	...	...	...
1960	93.9	388.4	737.1	486.9	10.4	224.7	1 865.0	...	...	...	...	...	...
1961	107.2	405.0	769.1	511.1	10.3	243.5	2 023.3	...	...	...	...	...	...
1962	113.7	421.3	802.9	533.2	10.9	265.6	2 077.8	...	...	...	...	...	...
1963	128.0	425.8	838.3	553.2	11.4	294.7	2 182.9	...	...	...	...	...	...
1964	144.8	444.7	883.1	579.8	11.7	324.4	2 352.7	...	...	...	...	...	...
1965	162.0	470.8	929.7	605.6	11.8	353.4	2 536.7	...	...	...	...	...	...
1966	172.5	504.0	1 004.5	649.0	12.2	376.6	2 610.4	...	...	...	...	...	...
1967	195.6	528.5	1 072.7	685.7	11.7	404.2	2 901.1	...	...	...	...	...	...
1968	218.7	572.8	1 198.8	768.2	11.2	436.2	3 258.7	...	...	...	...	...	...
1969	230.9	606.3	1 306.2	832.4	11.9	463.7	3 282.6	...	...	...	...	...	...
1970	253.7	636.3	1 387.9	874.5	11.7	478.7	3 442.0	...	...	...	...	...	...
1971	293.5	701.9	1 514.8	957.2	11.6	525.5	3 810.8	...	...	...	...	...	...
1972	349.3	782.5	1 710.9	1 098.6	11.3	585.5	4 356.6	...	...	...	...	...	...
1973	358.5	917.0	1 939.3	1 251.4	12.1	652.4	4 525.1	...	...	...	...	...	...
1974	367.5	1 026.8	2 059.7	1 261.1	13.0	709.1	4 564.4	...	...	...	...	...	...
1975	467.0	1 126.1	2 281.5	1 413.7	12.4	768.1	5 192.2	...	...	...	...	...	...
1976	534.5	1 255.5	2 537.6	1 590.0	12.4	860.1	5 838.6	...	...	...	...	...	...
1977	589.9	1 418.2	2 941.3	1 886.8	13.0	991.0	6 389.5	...	...	...	...	...	...
1978	691.4	1 648.5	3 401.6	2 210.9	13.3	1 150.6	7 218.9	...	...	...	...	...	...
1979	801.1	1 913.5	3 954.1	2 603.3	13.3	1 320.3	8 326.4	...	...	...	...	...	...
1980	969.7	2 154.3	4 441.6	2 943.2	12.7	1 447.4	9 568.2	10.5	15.4	13.3	23.6	...	...
1981	1 063.5	2 312.2	4 906.0	3 293.0	12.7	1 558.5	10 318.4	10.6	15.6	13.5	24.2	...	...
1982	1 289.1	2 357.4	5 136.2	3 447.4	12.4	1 632.7	11 086.4	10.5	15.6	13.8	22.3	...	...
1983	1 535.8	2 421.3	5 397.4	3 605.9	12.6	1 799.4	11 940.5	10.6	15.6	13.7	22.8	...	...
1984	1 707.5	2 425.1	6 052.5	4 126.3	13.0	2 011.3	12 889.5	11.0	16.1	14.1	24.0	...	...
1985	2 088.6	2 498.8	6 768.1	4 698.8	13.6	2 367.9	14 395.2	11.9	17.3	15.1	26.0	...	2.98
1986	2 326.8	2 627.0	7 403.1	5 147.5	13.7	2 632.1	15 900.9	12.3	17.9	15.6	26.8	...	3.42
1987	2 504.8	2 718.5	8 021.2	5 597.2	13.9	2 840.7	16 955.7	12.0	17.5	15.3	26.5	...	3.26
1988	2 738.3	2 862.4	8 741.5	6 118.1	14.0	3 140.2	18 510.9	11.8	17.2	15.1	25.6	...	3.22
1989	3 169.0	2 983.5	9 439.4	6 641.1	14.0	3 425.5	20 250.9	12.0	17.3	15.5	24.9	...	3.27
1990	3 310.3	3 096.8	9 729.6	6 807.8	14.6	3 693.6	20 731.0	11.9	17.3	15.4	24.8	...	3.84
1991	3 830.6	3 051.1	9 929.9	6 969.7	14.4	3 905.5	22 273.4	11.4	16.9	15.0	23.7	5.30	4.66
1992	4 139.4	3 027.3	10 250.4	7 257.5	14.5	4 113.0	23 221.6	10.7	16.0	14.1	23.4	4.69	4.54
1993	4 617.5	3 170.8	10 605.7	7 498.1	14.5	4 383.9	24 688.8	10.6	16.0	13.9	23.9	3.90	3.35
1994	4 898.3	3 385.4	11 047.5	7 770.8	15.0	4 712.1	25 537.3	11.0	16.4	14.2	25.0	3.27	3.07
1995	5 725.1	3 566.8	11 472.1	8 055.3	14.6	5 043.3	28 209.2	11.6	17.1	14.8	26.6	3.93	3.94
1996	6 386.7	3 687.9	11 963.8	8 431.7	14.6	5 405.7	30 103.3	11.9	17.2	15.0	26.9	4.59	4.65
1997	7 360.7	4 131.9	12 692.9	8 864.8	13.8	5 757.2	33 962.4	11.8	17.2	14.9	27.1	4.79	5.39
1998	8 265.4	4 382.5	13 760.2	9 694.3	13.4	6 199.6	37 912.4	11.8	17.0	14.6	28.0	4.71	5.17
1999	9 264.1	4 638.5	14 945.6	10 645.3	12.8	6 755.9	43 017.3	12.1	17.3	14.9	29.1	4.52	4.49
2000	9 171.3	5 133.3	16 867.3	12 197.6	13.8	7 352.9	43 281.0	12.5	17.6	15.1	30.3	4.61	4.53
2001	8 764.3	5 331.4	18 416.8	13 571.7	14.9	7 976.2	43 133.5	13.1	18.2	15.7	30.9	4.77	6.27
2002	8 189.6	5 684.0	19 979.2	14 854.5	16.6	8 759.2	42 099.5	13.2	18.1	16.0	28.8	4.97	5.48
2003	9 718.9	6 300.2	21 853.6	16 458.5	16.4	9 823.1	48 021.9	13.1	17.9	16.1	26.5	4.56	5.95
2004	10 635.5	7 548.6	24 891.6	18 959.3	16.0	10 991.2	54 962.5	13.2	17.9	16.4	25.3	4.15	4.62
2005	11 460.1	8 872.6	28 477.9	22 049.3	15.9	12 142.5	61 224.3	13.7	18.3	17.0	25.0	3.62	6.03
2006	12 750.6	9 197.0	29 579.9	22 730.7	16.2	13 349.4	65 648.1	14.0	18.7	17.4	25.4	4.01	3.67
2007	13 390.7	9 335.2	28 254.0	20 860.7	17.0	14 244.8	66 166.0	14.0	18.9	17.6	25.1	4.63	4.27
2008	10 408.5	7 723.8	24 787.4	17 545.2	20.2	14 094.1	53 554.5	13.5	18.5	17.0	25.6	5.66	6.42
2009	11 914.5	6 472.1	23 740.2	17 137.9	19.3	13 872.3	55 594.9	12.8	18.0	16.4	25.6	6.34	10.26
2010	13 090.7	7 069.7	23 448.2	16 560.9	18.0	13 692.7	59 159.9	11.7	16.6	15.1	24.2	4.15	7.85
2011	13 147.1	7 444.3	23 288.9	16 049.5	17.6	13 481.0	60 037.3	11.1	16.2	14.4	24.7	3.27	4.68
2009													
1st quarter	9 885.9	7 337.2	23 788.3	16 736.7	20.7	13 912.5	51 271.5	13.5	18.6	17.1	25.9	6.53	7.47
2nd quarter	10 656.1	6 735.7	23 551.6	16 815.3	20.3	13 890.2	52 402.6	13.2	18.3	16.8	25.6	6.74	9.73
3rd quarter	11 535.3	6 497.7	23 593.4	17 013.5	19.6	13 881.7	54 629.5	13.1	18.3	16.7	25.7	6.49	10.16
4th quarter	11 914.5	6 472.1	23 740.2	17 137.9	19.3	13 872.3	55 594.9	12.8	18.0	16.4	25.6	6.34	10.26
2010													
1st quarter	12 291.0	6 573.7	23 810.7	17 219.8	18.8	13 728.1	56 645.0	12.4	17.5	15.9	25.2	5.80	10.01
2nd quarter	11 606.7	6 722.5	23 861.9	17 137.1	19.1	13 693.5	55 195.7	12.1	17.2	15.6	24.9	5.07	10.94
3rd quarter	12 332.1	6 930.5	23 483.8	16 719.2	18.6	13 672.0	57 080.2	11.9	16.9	15.3	24.5	4.57	8.57
4th quarter	13 090.7	7 069.7	23 448.2	16 560.9	18.0	13 692.7	59 159.9	11.7	16.6	15.1	24.2	4.15	7.85
2011													
1st quarter	13 487.7	7 219.9	23 346.4	16 338.1	17.4	13 614.7	60 856.5	11.4	16.4	14.8	24.2	3.84	6.82
2nd quarter	13 405.8	7 151.1	23 292.2	16 260.2	17.4	13 538.0	60 722.4	11.3	16.3	14.6	24.3	3.62	5.56
3rd quarter	12 438.6	7 283.2	23 352.5	16 233.4	18.0	13 476.1	58 088.1	11.2	16.2	14.5	24.4	3.45	5.64
4th quarter	13 147.1	7 444.3	23 288.9	16 049.5	17.6	13 481.0	60 037.3	11.1	16.2	14.4	24.7	3.27	4.68

[1]Includes nonprofit organizations.
[3]Excludes nonprofit organizations.
. . . = Not available.

Table 12-7. Mortgage Debt Outstanding

(Billions of dollars, except as noted; end of period; not seasonally adjusted.)

Year and quarter	Total	By type of property					By type of holder						
		Home		Multi-family residences	Commercial	Farm	U.S.-chartered depository institutions	Life insurance companies	Federal and related agencies	Mortgage pools or trusts			Other
		Billions of dollars	Percent of value of real estate							Total [1]	Federally related agencies	ABS issuers	
1950	73	45	19	9	12	6	35	16	3	0	0	0	19
1951	83	52	19	11	13	7	40	19	3	0	0	0	20
1952	92	58	20	11	14	7	45	21	4	0	0	0	21
1953	101	66	21	12	16	8	51	23	5	0	0	0	22
1954	114	75	22	13	17	8	59	26	5	0	0	0	24
1955	130	88	24	13	19	9	69	29	5	0	0	0	26
1956	144	99	25	14	22	10	77	33	6	0	0	0	28
1957	157	107	26	15	24	10	83	35	7	0	0	0	30
1958	172	117	27	17	27	11	93	37	8	0	0	0	34
1959	191	130	28	19	30	12	105	39	10	0	0	0	37
1960	208	141	29	21	33	13	115	42	11	0	0	0	41
1961	229	154	30	24	37	14	127	44	12	0	0	0	46
1962	252	168	32	27	42	15	143	47	12	0	0	0	49
1963	279	185	33	30	47	17	164	51	11	1	1	0	53
1964	307	202	35	35	51	19	183	55	12	1	1	0	56
1965	334	219	36	38	56	21	202	60	13	1	1	0	59
1966	358	233	36	41	61	23	214	65	16	1	1	0	62
1967	382	246	36	45	66	25	228	68	19	2	2	0	65
1968	411	263	34	48	73	27	247	70	23	3	3	0	69
1969	440	279	33	53	79	29	264	72	28	3	3	0	73
1970	469	292	33	60	87	30	278	74	34	5	5	0	79
1971	518	318	33	70	97	32	313	75	37	10	10	0	83
1972	590	357	33	83	114	35	366	77	40	14	14	0	92
1973	666	400	32	93	134	40	418	81	47	18	18	0	102
1974	728	435	35	100	148	45	451	86	61	21	21	0	108
1975	786	474	34	101	161	50	485	89	73	29	29	0	110
1976	870	535	34	106	174	55	547	92	76	41	41	0	115
1977	999	628	33	114	193	64	637	97	84	57	57	0	125
1978	1 151	738	33	125	215	73	730	106	100	70	70	0	144
1979	1 317	856	33	135	239	87	808	118	121	95	95	0	175
1980	1 458	958	33	143	260	97	853	131	143	114	114	0	217
1981	1 579	1 030	31	142	300	107	890	138	160	129	129	0	262
1982	1 661	1 070	31	146	334	111	871	142	177	179	179	0	293
1983	1 850	1 186	33	161	389	114	950	151	188	245	245	0	316
1984	2 092	1 321	32	186	472	112	1 084	157	202	300	289	11	349
1985	2 368	1 526	32	206	542	94	1 189	172	213	392	368	25	401
1986	2 655	1 729	34	239	602	84	1 279	194	202	549	532	18	431
1987	2 956	1 928	34	258	694	76	1 403	212	189	701	669	31	451
1988	3 273	2 162	35	275	766	71	1 540	233	192	786	745	40	522
1989	3 526	2 369	36	287	801	69	1 609	254	198	922	870	53	542
1990	3 781	2 606	38	287	820	68	1 601	268	239	1 086	1 020	66	587
1991	3 932	2 774	40	284	806	67	1 527	260	266	1 270	1 156	113	610
1992	4 043	2 942	41	271	763	68	1 471	242	286	1 440	1 272	168	604
1993	4 175	3 101	41	268	738	68	1 494	224	326	1 561	1 357	204	570
1994	4 339	3 278	42	268	723	70	1 560	216	316	1 697	1 472	225	551
1995	4 525	3 445	43	274	734	72	1 642	213	308	1 812	1 571	242	550
1996	4 806	3 682	44	286	764	74	1 731	208	294	1 989	1 712	278	583
1997	5 118	3 916	44	298	826	79	1 840	207	285	2 166	1 826	339	620
1998	5 603	4 272	44	331	916	83	1 948	214	292	2 487	2 019	468	663
1999	6 210	4 698	44	372	1 053	87	2 133	231	320	2 832	2 294	539	694
2000	6 769	5 122	42	402	1 160	85	2 350	236	340	3 098	2 493	604	745
2001	7 476	5 674	42	444	1 269	89	2 511	243	372	3 557	2 832	725	793
2002	8 377	6 429	43	483	1 370	95	2 799	250	432	3 995	3 159	836	901
2003	9 391	7 253	44	557	1 497	83	3 084	261	694	4 353	3 343	1 010	999
2004	10 654	8 285	44	605	1 668	96	3 605	273	703	4 834	3 384	1 450	1 239
2005	12 085	9 399	43	665	1 916	105	4 055	285	665	5 688	3 548	2 140	1 391
2006	13 461	10 465	46	702	2 186	108	4 416	304	687	6 608	3 841	2 767	1 445
2007	14 521	11 176	54	785	2 448	113	4 659	326	725	7 411	4 464	2 946	1 400
2008	14 610	11 071	63	838	2 566	135	4 615	342	801	7 555	4 961	2 594	1 296
2009	14 329	10 873	63	847	2 478	131	4 372	326	816	7 604	5 377	2 228	1 211
2010	13 815	10 527	64	838	2 314	136	4 195	317	5 128	3 041	1 139	1 901	1 134
2011	13 477	10 268	64	844	2 232	132	4 050	333	5 035	2 984	1 305	1 679	1 076
2009													
1st quarter	14 603	11 064	66	843	2 562	134	4 616	339	823	7 548	5 042	2 506	1 277
2nd quarter	14 546	11 011	65	851	2 551	133	4 564	335	815	7 577	5 171	2 406	1 255
3rd quarter	14 440	10 929	64	853	2 526	132	4 438	332	820	7 612	5 298	2 315	1 237
4th quarter	14 329	10 873	63	847	2 478	131	4 372	326	816	7 604	5 377	2 228	1 211
2010													
1st quarter	14 152	10 731	62	842	2 446	133	4 311	321	5 211	3 106	980	2 126	1 202
2nd quarter	14 037	10 664	62	839	2 400	134	4 253	318	5 193	3 098	1 046	2 051	1 175
3rd quarter	13 913	10 583	63	840	2 356	135	4 221	318	5 142	3 074	1 096	1 978	1 159
4th quarter	13 815	10 527	64	838	2 314	136	4 195	317	5 128	3 041	1 139	1 901	1 134
2011													
1st quarter	13 714	10 450	64	837	2 291	135	4 082	318	5 162	3 035	1 187	1 848	1 115
2nd quarter	13 620	10 382	64	837	2 266	134	4 046	323	5 128	3 023	1 236	1 787	1 101
3rd quarter	13 536	10 324	64	838	2 241	133	4 038	329	5 074	3 009	1 277	1 732	1 086
4th quarter	13 477	10 268	64	844	2 232	132	4 050	333	5 035	2 984	1 305	1 679	1 076

[1]Outstanding principal balances of mortgage-backed securities issued or guaranteed by the holder indicated.

Table 12-8. Consumer Credit

(Outstanding at end of period, billions of dollars.)

	Seasonally adjusted			Not seasonally adjusted						
Year and month	Total	By major credit type		Total	By major holder					
		Revolving	Non-revolving		Depository institutions	Finance companies [1]	Credit unions	Federal government [1]	Nonfinancial businesses	Securitized pools [2]
1960	60.0	...	60.0	61.2	28.9	15.4	3.4	0.0	13.5	0.0
1961	62.2	...	62.2	63.4	30.7	15.5	3.6	0.0	13.6	0.0
1962	68.1	...	68.1	69.3	33.6	17.3	4.1	0.0	14.3	0.0
1963	76.6	...	76.6	77.9	38.3	19.6	4.5	0.0	15.5	0.0
1964	86.0	...	86.0	87.4	43.4	21.6	5.4	0.0	16.8	0.0
1965	96.0	...	96.0	97.5	49.1	23.9	6.5	0.0	18.1	0.0
1966	101.8	...	101.8	103.4	52.2	24.8	7.5	0.0	19.0	0.0
1967	106.8	...	106.8	108.6	55.8	24.6	8.3	0.0	19.9	0.0
1968	117.4	2.0	115.4	119.3	62.7	26.1	9.7	0.0	20.8	0.0
1969	127.2	3.6	123.6	129.2	67.8	27.8	11.7	0.0	21.9	0.0
1970	131.6	5.0	126.6	133.7	70.1	27.6	13.0	0.0	23.0	0.0
1971	146.9	8.2	138.7	149.2	79.0	29.2	14.8	0.0	26.2	0.0
1972	166.2	9.4	156.8	168.8	92.1	31.9	17.0	0.0	27.8	0.0
1973	190.1	11.3	178.7	193.0	108.1	35.4	19.6	0.0	29.8	0.0
1974	198.9	13.2	185.7	201.9	112.1	36.1	21.9	0.0	31.8	0.0
1975	204.0	14.5	189.5	207.0	116.2	32.6	25.7	0.0	32.6	0.0
1976	225.7	16.5	209.2	229.0	128.9	33.7	31.2	0.0	35.2	0.0
1977	260.6	37.4	223.1	264.9	152.1	37.3	37.6	0.5	37.4	0.0
1978	306.1	45.7	260.4	311.3	179.6	44.4	45.2	0.9	41.2	0.0
1979	348.6	53.6	295.0	354.6	205.7	55.4	47.4	1.5	44.6	0.0
1980	351.9	55.0	297.0	358.0	202.9	62.2	44.1	2.6	46.2	0.0
1981	371.3	60.9	310.4	377.9	208.2	70.1	46.7	4.8	48.1	0.0
1982	389.8	66.3	323.5	396.7	217.5	75.3	48.8	6.4	48.7	0.0
1983	437.1	79.0	358.0	444.9	245.2	83.3	56.1	4.6	55.7	0.0
1984	517.3	100.4	416.9	526.6	303.1	89.9	67.9	5.6	60.2	0.0
1985	599.7	124.5	475.2	610.6	354.8	111.7	74.0	6.8	63.3	0.0
1986	654.8	141.1	513.7	666.4	383.1	134.0	77.1	8.2	64.0	0.0
1987	686.3	160.9	525.5	698.6	399.4	140.0	81.0	10.0	68.1	0.0
1988	731.9	184.6	547.3	745.2	427.6	144.7	88.3	13.2	71.4	0.0
1989	794.6	211.2	583.4	809.3	445.8	138.9	91.7	16.0	69.6	47.3
1990	808.2	238.6	569.6	824.4	431.6	133.4	91.6	19.2	71.9	76.7
1991	798.0	263.8	534.3	815.6	412.3	121.6	90.3	21.1	67.3	103.0
1992	806.1	278.4	527.7	824.8	400.3	118.1	91.7	24.2	70.3	120.3
1993	865.7	309.9	555.7	886.2	433.6	116.1	101.6	27.2	77.2	130.5
1994	997.3	365.6	631.7	1 021.2	497.2	134.4	119.6	37.2	86.6	146.1
1995	1 140.7	443.9	696.8	1 168.2	542.4	152.1	131.9	43.5	85.1	213.1
1996	1 253.4	507.5	745.9	1 273.9	572.2	154.9	144.1	51.4	77.7	273.5
1997	1 324.8	540.0	784.8	1 344.2	562.2	167.5	152.4	57.2	84.4	320.5
1998	1 421.0	581.4	839.6	1 441.3	564.4	183.3	155.4	64.9	79.3	393.9
1999	1 531.1	610.7	920.4	1 553.6	569.5	201.6	167.9	81.8	76.1	456.7
2000	1 717.0	682.6	1 034.3	1 741.3	615.8	234.4	184.4	96.7	81.5	528.4
2001	1 867.9	714.8	1 153.0	1 891.8	639.5	280.0	189.6	111.9	73.1	597.8
2002	1 972.1	750.9	1 221.2	1 997.0	671.3	307.5	195.7	117.3	74.8	630.4
2003	2 077.4	768.3	1 309.1	2 102.9	747.3	393.0	205.9	102.9	59.1	594.8
2004	2 192.2	799.6	1 392.7	2 220.1	795.6	492.3	215.4	86.1	59.2	571.5
2005	2 290.9	829.5	1 461.4	2 320.6	816.1	516.5	228.6	89.8	59.6	609.9
2006	2 384.6	871.0	1 455.2	2 384.6	836.4	531.9	236.1	86.9	57.0	636.3
2007	2 528.5	941.9	1 520.4	2 528.5	894.6	572.1	236.6	93.0	59.3	673.0
2008	2 548.6	957.5	1 538.3	2 548.6	964.7	554.3	236.2	104.3	56.3	632.9
2009	2 438.5	865.5	1 516.7	2 438.5	906.0	471.9	237.1	178.6	51.7	593.3
2010	2 411.6	800.2	1 554.2	2 411.6	1 185.2	575.0	226.5	308.8	53.1	63.0
2011	2 508.2	864.9	1 643.3	2 508.2	1 192.3	567.3	223.0	417.4	53.1	55.0
2010										
January	2 430.5	914.6	1 516.0	2 424.2	892.9	476.2	232.6	192.7	50.7	579.1
February	2 419.0	907.4	1 511.6	2 383.9	869.9	469.4	230.3	196.9	49.7	567.7
March	2 423.2	906.7	1 516.5	2 373.3	1 226.9	591.1	228.0	202.2	53.0	72.1
April	2 415.3	900.9	1 514.5	2 368.5	1 226.4	586.7	227.8	203.9	52.9	70.8
May	2 406.6	894.8	1 511.7	2 359.4	1 216.7	582.2	227.4	209.5	52.8	70.8
June	2 401.9	887.2	1 514.7	2 354.5	1 214.1	578.6	225.8	214.9	52.7	68.4
July	2 395.3	880.2	1 515.1	2 354.5	1 212.8	577.5	225.7	219.3	52.7	66.5
August	2 394.8	873.9	1 520.9	2 376.3	1 210.2	575.4	226.5	245.7	52.9	65.6
September	2 398.5	867.8	1 530.7	2 383.4	1 197.1	570.0	224.9	272.6	52.7	66.0
October	2 404.7	862.4	1 542.3	2 385.7	1 187.6	548.7	227.4	304.5	52.4	65.0
November	2 407.7	858.1	1 549.6	2 391.1	1 192.7	547.0	227.5	308.1	52.5	63.3
December	2 411.6	857.4	1 554.2	2 411.6	1 185.2	575.0	226.5	308.8	53.1	63.0
2011										
January	2 413.4	853.4	1 560.0	2 407.0	1 164.6	572.0	224.2	333.1	52.6	60.6
February	2 423.9	851.8	1 572.1	2 388.8	1 146.9	567.0	221.9	341.3	51.9	59.7
March	2 432.5	857.0	1 575.5	2 382.6	1 143.3	564.8	218.1	347.5	51.5	57.5
April	2 435.0	850.9	1 584.0	2 388.1	1 150.4	557.7	220.3	351.8	51.6	56.4
May	2 443.4	857.1	1 586.3	2 396.2	1 154.1	557.3	221.4	357.3	51.5	54.6
June	2 452.9	858.9	1 594.0	2 405.4	1 159.5	557.7	220.9	362.4	51.7	53.3
July	2 463.3	856.2	1 607.0	2 422.5	1 159.0	558.3	222.5	378.1	51.8	52.7
August	2 455.4	857.1	1 598.3	2 436.9	1 165.2	559.3	224.6	384.2	52.2	51.5
September	2 467.0	858.1	1 608.9	2 451.8	1 162.8	560.6	223.9	398.5	52.2	53.8
October	2 471.9	859.7	1 612.3	2 452.9	1 160.4	560.1	224.6	402.2	52.1	53.5
November	2 491.0	864.6	1 626.4	2 474.3	1 171.0	563.5	225.1	408.7	52.3	53.7
December	2 508.2	864.9	1 643.3	2 508.2	1 192.3	567.3	223.0	417.4	53.1	55.0

[1]Student Loan Marketing Association (Sallie Mae) included in federal government sector until end of 2004, and in finance companies since then.
[2]Outstanding balances of pools upon which securities have been issued; these balances are no longer carried on the balance sheets of the loan originators.
. . . = Not available.

Table 12-9A. Summary Interest Rates, Bond Yields, and Stock Prices: Recent Data

(Percent per annum, except as noted.)

Year and month	Federal funds interest rate	Federal Reserve discount rate[1]	U.S. Treasury bills, secondary market, 3-month	Inflation: percent change from year earlier in PCE chain-type price index excluding food and energy	Real 3-month Treasury bill rate	Comm-ercial paper, 3-month[2]	Bank prime rate	Treasury 10-year nominal yields	Bond yields Domestic corporate (Moody's) Aaa	Baa	State and local bonds (Bond Buyer)	Standard and Poor's composite (500 stocks) Index, 1941-1943 = 10	Dividend-price ratio	Earnings-price ratio
1970	7.17	5.87	6.39	4.69	1.70	. . .	7.91	7.35	8.04	9.11	6.33	83.22	3.83	6.45
1971	4.67	5.95	4.33	4.71	-0.38	5.25	5.73	6.16	7.39	8.56	5.47	98.29	3.14	5.41
1972	4.44	4.88	4.06	3.23	0.83	4.66	5.25	6.21	7.21	8.16	5.26	109.20	2.84	5.50
1973	8.74	4.50	7.04	3.82	3.22	8.21	8.03	6.85	7.44	8.24	5.19	107.43	3.06	7.12
1974	10.51	6.45	7.85	7.93	-0.08	10.05	10.81	7.56	8.57	9.50	6.17	82.85	4.47	11.59
1975	5.82	7.83	5.79	8.38	-2.59	6.26	7.86	7.99	8.83	10.61	7.05	86.16	4.31	9.15
1976	5.05	6.25	4.98	6.08	-1.10	5.24	6.84	7.61	8.43	9.75	6.64	102.01	3.77	8.90
1977	5.54	5.50	5.26	6.42	-1.16	5.54	6.83	7.42	8.02	8.97	5.68	98.20	4.62	10.79
1978	7.94	5.46	7.18	6.69	0.49	7.93	9.06	8.41	8.73	9.49	6.02	96.02	5.28	12.03
1979	11.20	7.46	10.05	7.28	2.77	10.95	12.67	9.43	9.63	10.69	6.52	103.01	5.47	13.46
1980	13.35	10.29	11.39	9.16	2.23	12.61	15.26	11.43	11.94	13.67	8.59	118.78	5.26	12.66
1981	16.39	11.77	14.04	8.74	5.30	15.34	18.87	13.92	14.17	16.04	11.33	128.05	5.20	11.96
1982	12.24	13.42	10.60	6.45	4.15	11.90	14.85	13.01	13.79	16.11	11.66	119.71	5.81	11.60
1983	9.09	11.01	8.62	5.18	3.44	8.88	10.79	11.10	12.04	13.55	9.51	160.41	4.40	8.03
1984	10.23	8.50	9.54	4.15	5.39	10.12	12.04	12.46	12.71	14.19	10.10	160.46	4.64	10.02
1985	8.10	8.80	7.47	3.79	3.68	7.95	9.93	10.62	11.37	12.72	9.10	186.84	4.25	8.12
1986	6.80	7.69	5.97	3.77	2.20	6.49	8.33	7.67	9.02	10.39	7.32	236.34	3.49	6.09
1987	6.66	6.32	5.78	3.80	1.98	6.82	8.21	8.39	9.38	10.58	7.64	286.83	3.08	5.48
1988	7.57	5.66	6.67	4.34	2.33	7.66	9.32	8.85	9.71	10.83	7.68	265.79	3.64	8.01
1989	9.21	6.20	8.11	4.13	3.98	8.99	10.87	8.49	9.26	10.18	7.23	322.84	3.45	7.42
1990	8.10	6.93	7.50	4.27	3.23	8.06	10.01	8.55	9.32	10.36	7.27	334.59	3.61	6.47
1991	5.69	6.98	5.38	3.89	1.49	5.87	8.46	7.86	8.77	9.80	6.92	376.18	3.24	4.79
1992	3.52	5.45	3.43	3.36	0.07	3.75	6.25	7.01	8.14	8.98	6.44	415.74	2.99	4.22
1993	3.02	3.25	3.00	2.37	0.63	3.22	6.00	5.87	7.22	7.93	5.60	451.41	2.78	4.46
1994	4.21	3.00	4.25	2.21	2.04	4.66	7.15	7.09	7.97	8.63	6.18	460.42	2.82	5.83
1995	5.83	3.60	5.49	2.30	3.19	5.93	8.83	6.57	7.59	8.20	5.95	541.72	2.56	6.09
1996	5.30	5.21	5.01	1.94	3.07	5.41	8.27	6.44	7.37	8.05	5.76	670.50	2.19	5.24
1997	5.46	5.02	5.06	1.92	3.14	5.52	8.44	6.35	7.27	7.87	5.52	873.43	1.77	4.57
1998	5.35	5.00	4.78	1.45	3.33	5.37	8.35	5.26	6.53	7.22	5.09	1 085.50	1.49	3.46
1999	4.97	4.92	4.64	1.49	3.15	5.21	8.00	5.65	7.05	7.88	5.43	1 327.33	1.25	3.17
2000	6.24	4.62	5.82	1.74	4.08	6.33	9.23	6.03	7.62	8.37	5.71	1 427.22	1.15	3.63
2001	3.88	5.73	3.40	1.79	1.61	3.65	6.91	5.02	7.08	7.95	5.15	1 194.18	1.32	2.95
2002	1.67	3.40	1.61	1.73	-0.12	1.70	4.67	4.61	6.49	7.80	5.04	993.94	1.61	2.92
2003	1.13	. . .	1.01	1.53	-0.52	1.13	4.12	4.01	5.66	6.76	4.75	965.23	1.77	3.84
2004	1.35	2.34	1.37	2.09	-0.72	1.52	4.34	4.27	5.63	6.39	4.68	1 130.65	1.72	4.89
2005	3.22	4.19	3.15	2.26	0.89	3.44	6.19	4.29	5.23	6.06	4.40	1 207.23	1.83	5.36
2006	4.97	5.96	4.73	2.29	2.44	5.07	7.96	4.80	5.59	6.48	4.40	1 310.46	1.87	5.78
2007	5.02	5.86	4.36	2.35	2.01	5.13	8.05	4.63	5.56	6.48	4.40	1 477.19	1.86	5.29
2008	1.92	2.39	1.37	2.34	-0.97	2.83	5.09	3.66	5.63	7.44	4.86	1 220.04	2.37	3.54
2009	0.16	0.50	0.15	1.51	-1.36	0.40	3.25	3.26	5.31	7.29	4.62	948.05	2.40	1.86
2010	0.18	0.72	0.14	1.31	-1.17	0.29	3.25	3.22	4.94	6.04	4.29	1 139.97	1.98	6.04
2011	0.10	0.75	0.05	1.31	-1.26	0.21	3.25	2.78	4.64	5.66	4.51	1 268.89	2.05	6.77
2010														
January	0.11	0.50	0.06	1.75	-1.69	0.18	3.25	3.73	5.26	6.25	4.33	1 123.58	1.92	. . .
February	0.13	0.59	0.11	1.71	-1.60	0.20	3.25	3.69	5.35	6.34	4.36	1 089.16	2.00	. . .
March	0.16	0.75	0.15	1.78	-1.63	0.24	3.25	3.73	5.27	6.27	4.36	1 152.05	1.90	5.21
April	0.20	0.75	0.16	1.58	-1.42	0.30	3.25	3.85	5.29	6.25	4.41	1 197.32	1.84	. . .
May	0.20	0.75	0.16	1.58	-1.42	0.44	3.25	3.42	4.96	6.05	4.29	1 125.06	1.98	. . .
June	0.18	0.75	0.12	1.47	-1.35	0.46	3.25	3.20	4.88	6.23	4.36	1 083.36	2.09	6.51
July	0.18	0.75	0.16	1.44	-1.28	0.37	3.25	3.01	4.72	6.01	4.32	1 079.80	2.10	. . .
August	0.19	0.75	0.16	1.37	-1.21	0.27	3.25	2.70	4.49	5.66	4.03	1 087.28	2.10	. . .
September ...	0.19	0.75	0.15	1.23	-1.08	0.25	3.25	2.65	4.53	5.66	3.87	1 122.08	2.06	6.30
October	0.19	0.75	0.13	0.97	-0.84	0.25	3.25	2.54	4.68	5.72	3.87	1 171.58	1.97	. . .
November	0.19	0.75	0.14	0.97	-0.83	0.25	3.25	2.76	4.87	5.92	4.40	1 198.89	1.94	. . .
December	0.18	0.75	0.14	0.93	-0.79	0.27	3.25	3.29	5.02	6.10	4.92	1 241.53	1.90	6.15
2011														
January	0.17	0.75	0.15	1.04	-0.89	0.26	3.25	3.39	5.04	6.09	5.28	1 282.62	1.84	. . .
February	0.16	0.75	0.13	1.10	-0.97	0.25	3.25	3.58	5.22	6.15	5.15	1 321.12	1.80	. . .
March	0.14	0.75	0.10	1.04	-0.94	0.23	3.25	3.41	5.13	6.03	4.92	1 304.49	1.90	6.13
April	0.10	0.75	0.06	1.18	-1.12	0.22	3.25	3.46	5.16	6.02	4.99	1 331.51	1.92	. . .
May	0.09	0.75	0.04	1.31	-1.27	0.18	3.25	3.17	4.96	5.78	4.59	1 338.31	1.95	. . .
June	0.09	0.75	0.04	1.42	-1.38	0.17	3.25	3.00	4.99	5.75	4.51	1 287.29	2.04	6.35
July	0.07	0.75	0.04	1.57	-1.53	0.17	3.25	3.00	4.93	5.76	4.52	1 325.18	1.99	. . .
August	0.10	0.75	0.02	1.68	-1.66	0.21	3.25	2.30	4.37	5.36	4.02	1 185.31	2.20	. . .
September ...	0.08	0.75	0.01	1.65	-1.64	0.22	3.25	1.98	4.09	5.27	4.01	1 173.88	2.25	7.69
October	0.07	0.75	0.02	1.70	-1.68	0.24	3.25	2.15	3.98	5.37	4.13	1 207.22	2.28	. . .
November	0.08	0.75	0.01	1.77	-1.76	0.21	3.25	2.01	3.87	5.14	4.05	1 226.41	2.22	. . .
December	0.07	0.75	0.01	1.91	-1.90	0.18	3.25	1.98	3.93	5.25	3.95	1 243.32	2.24	6.91

[1]Federal Reserve Bank of New York. Through 2002, represents the rate for adjustment credit. Beginning in 2003, represents the rate for primary credit. See notes and definitions for more information.
[2]Prior to September 1997, this series represents both nonfinancial and financial commercial paper rates. Beginning September 1997, rates for financial companies only are shown. See notes and definitions for more information.
. . . = Not available.

Table 12-9B. Summary Interest Rates, Bond Yields, and Stock Prices: Historical Data

(Percent per annum, except as noted.)

Year and month	Federal funds interest rate	Federal Reserve discount rate[1]	U.S. Treasury bills, secondary market, 3-month	Inflation: percent change from year earlier in PCE chain-type price index excluding food and energy	Real 3-month Treasury bill rate	Commercial paper, 3-month[2]	Bank prime rate	Treasury 10-year nominal yields	Bond yields Domestic corporate (Moody's) Aaa	Bond yields Domestic corporate (Moody's) Baa	State and local bonds (Bond Buyer)	S&P composite Index, 1941-1943 = 10	Dividend-price ratio	Earnings-price ratio
1929	...	5.17	4.42	...	...	5.85	5.5–6	3.60	4.73	5.90	4.27	26.02	3.47	7.51
1930	...	3.04	2.23	...	...	3.59	3.5–6	3.29	4.55	5.90	4.07	21.03	4.51	6.33
1931	...	2.11	1.40	...	...	2.64	2.75–5	3.34	4.58	7.62	4.01	13.66	6.15	7.51
1932	...	2.82	0.88	...	...	2.73	3.25–4	3.68	5.01	9.30	4.65	6.93	7.43	5.95
1933	...	2.56	0.52	...	...	1.73	1.5–4	3.31	4.49	7.76	4.71	8.96	4.21	4.36
1934	...	1.54	0.28	...	...	1.02	1.50	3.12	4.00	6.32	4.03	9.84	3.72	5.16
1935	...	1.50	0.17	...	...	0.76	1.50	2.79	3.60	5.75	3.41	10.60	3.82	7.23
1936	...	1.50	0.17	...	...	0.75	1.50	2.65	3.24	4.77	3.07	15.47	3.44	6.57
1937	...	1.33	0.28	...	...	0.94	1.50	2.68	3.26	5.03	3.10	15.41	4.86	8.25
1938	...	1.00	0.07	...	...	0.81	1.50	2.56	3.19	5.80	2.91	11.49	5.18	5.55
1939	...	1.00	0.05	...	...	0.59	1.50	2.36	3.01	4.96	2.76	12.06	4.05	7.34
1940	...	1.00	0.04	...	...	0.56	1.50	2.21	2.84	4.75	2.50	11.02	5.59	9.80
1941	...	1.00	0.13	...	...	0.53	1.50	2.12	2.77	4.33	2.10	9.82	6.82	12.14
1942	...	1.00	0.34	...	...	0.66	1.50	2.46	2.83	4.28	2.36	8.67	7.24	11.42
1943	...	1.00	0.38	...	...	0.69	1.50	2.47	2.73	3.91	2.06	11.50	4.93	7.82
1944	...	1.00	0.38	...	...	0.73	1.50	2.48	2.72	3.61	1.86	12.47	4.86	7.34
1945	...	1.00	0.38	...	...	0.75	1.50	2.37	2.62	3.29	1.67	15.16	4.17	6.39
1946	...	1.00	0.38	...	...	0.81	1.50	2.19	2.53	3.05	1.64	17.08	3.85	6.31
1947	...	1.00	0.61	...	...	1.03	1.63	2.25	2.61	3.24	2.01	15.17	4.93	10.69
1948	...	1.34	1.05	...	...	1.44	1.88	2.44	2.82	3.47	2.40	15.53	5.54	14.60
1949	...	1.50	1.10	...	...	1.49	2.00	2.31	2.66	3.42	2.21	15.23	6.59	15.48
1950	...	1.59	1.22	...	...	1.45	2.07	2.32	2.62	3.24	1.98	18.40	6.57	13.99
1951	...	1.75	1.55	...	...	2.16	2.56	2.57	2.86	3.41	2.00	22.34	6.13	11.82
1952	...	1.75	1.77	...	...	2.33	3.00	2.68	2.96	3.52	2.19	24.50	5.80	9.47
1953	...	1.99	1.94	...	...	2.52	3.17	2.94	3.20	3.73	2.74	24.73	5.80	10.26
1954	...	1.60	0.94	...	...	1.58	3.05	2.55	2.90	3.51	2.39	29.69	4.95	8.57
1955	1.79	1.89	1.72	...	...	2.18	3.16	2.84	3.05	3.53	2.48	40.49	4.08	7.95
1956	2.73	2.77	2.62	...	...	3.31	3.77	3.08	3.36	3.88	2.76	46.62	4.09	7.55
1957	3.11	3.12	3.22	...	...	3.81	4.20	3.47	3.89	4.71	3.28	44.38	4.35	7.89
1958	1.57	2.15	1.77	...	...	2.46	3.83	3.43	3.79	4.73	3.16	46.24	3.97	6.23
1959	3.31	3.36	3.39	...	...	3.97	4.48	4.07	4.38	5.05	3.56	57.38	3.23	5.78
1960	3.21	3.53	2.87	1.79	1.08	3.85	4.82	4.01	4.41	5.19	3.52	55.85	3.47	5.90
1961	1.95	3.00	2.35	1.25	1.10	2.97	4.50	3.90	4.35	5.08	3.45	66.27	2.98	4.62
1962	2.71	3.00	2.77	1.37	1.40	3.26	4.50	3.95	4.33	5.02	3.15	62.38	3.37	5.82
1963	3.18	3.23	3.16	1.30	1.86	3.55	4.50	4.00	4.26	4.86	3.17	69.87	3.17	5.50
1964	3.50	3.55	3.55	1.53	2.02	3.97	4.50	4.19	4.41	4.83	3.21	81.37	3.01	5.32
1965	4.07	3.55	3.95	1.26	2.69	...	4.54	4.28	4.49	4.87	3.26	88.17	3.00	5.59
1966	5.11	4.04	4.86	2.26	2.60	...	5.63	4.93	5.13	5.67	3.81	85.26	3.40	6.63
1967	4.22	4.50	4.29	3.06	1.23	...	5.63	5.07	5.51	6.23	3.94	91.93	3.20	5.73
1968	5.66	4.19	5.34	4.29	1.05	...	6.31	5.64	6.18	6.94	4.45	98.70	3.07	5.67
1969	8.21	5.17	6.67	4.69	1.98	...	7.96	6.67	7.03	7.81	5.72	97.84	3.24	6.08
1945														
January	...	1.00	0.38	...	...	...	1.50	...	2.69	3.46	...	13.49	...	...
February	...	1.00	0.38	...	...	...	1.50	...	2.65	3.41	...	13.94	...	...
March	...	1.00	0.38	...	...	...	1.50	...	2.62	3.38	...	13.93	...	...
April	...	1.00	0.38	...	...	...	1.50	...	2.61	3.36	...	14.28	...	...
May	...	1.00	0.38	...	...	...	1.50	...	2.62	3.32	...	14.82	...	...
June	...	1.00	0.38	...	...	...	1.50	...	2.61	3.29	...	15.09	...	...
July	...	1.00	0.38	...	...	...	1.50	...	2.60	3.26	...	14.78	...	...
August	...	1.00	0.38	...	...	...	1.50	...	2.61	3.26	...	14.83	...	...
September	...	1.00	0.38	...	...	...	1.50	...	2.62	3.24	...	15.84	...	...
October	...	1.00	0.38	...	...	...	1.50	...	2.62	3.20	...	16.50	...	...
November	...	1.00	0.38	...	...	...	1.50	...	2.62	3.15	...	17.04	...	...
December	...	1.00	0.38	...	...	...	1.50	...	2.61	3.10	...	17.33	...	...
1946														
January	...	1.00	0.38	...	...	...	1.50	...	2.54	3.01	...	18.02	...	...
February	...	1.00	0.38	...	...	...	1.50	...	2.48	2.95	...	18.07	...	...
March	...	1.00	0.38	...	...	...	1.50	...	2.47	2.94	...	17.53	...	...
April	...	1.00	0.38	...	...	...	1.50	...	2.46	2.96	...	18.66	...	...
May	...	1.00	0.38	...	...	...	1.50	...	2.51	3.02	...	18.70	...	...
June	...	1.00	0.38	...	...	...	1.50	...	2.49	3.03	...	18.58	...	...
July	...	1.00	0.38	...	...	...	1.50	...	2.48	3.03	...	18.05	...	...
August	...	1.00	0.38	...	...	...	1.50	...	2.51	3.03	...	17.70	...	...
September	...	1.00	0.38	...	...	...	1.50	...	2.58	3.10	...	15.09	...	...
October	...	1.00	0.38	...	...	...	1.50	...	2.60	3.15	...	14.75	...	...
November	...	1.00	0.38	...	...	...	1.50	...	2.59	3.17	...	14.69	...	...
December	...	1.00	0.38	...	...	...	1.50	...	2.61	3.17	...	15.13	...	...

[1]Federal Reserve Bank of New York. Through 2002, represents the rate for adjustment credit. Beginning in 2003, represents the rate for primary credit. See notes and definitions for more information.
[2]Prior to September 1997, this series represents both nonfinancial and financial commercial paper rates. Beginning September 1997, rates for financial companies only are shown. See notes and definitions for more information.
. . . = Not available.

Table 12-9B. Summary Interest Rates, Bond Yields, and Stock Prices: Historical Data—*Continued*

(Percent per annum, except as noted.)

Year and month	Federal funds interest rate	Federal Reserve discount rate[1]	U.S. Treasury bills, secondary market, 3-month	Inflation: percent change from year earlier in PCE chain-type price index excluding food and energy	Real 3-month Treasury bill rate	Commercial paper, 3-month [2]	Bank prime rate	Treasury 10-year nominal yields	Bond yields Domestic corporate (Moody's) Aaa	Bond yields Domestic corporate (Moody's) Baa	State and local bonds (Bond Buyer)	Standard and Poor's composite (500 stocks) Index, 1941-1943 = 10	Standard and Poor's composite (500 stocks) Dividend-price ratio	Standard and Poor's composite (500 stocks) Earnings-price ratio
1947														
January	...	1.00	0.38	...	...	...	1.50	...	2.57	3.13	...	15.21	...	...
February	...	1.00	0.38	...	...	...	1.50	...	2.55	3.12	...	15.80	...	...
March	...	1.00	0.38	...	...	...	1.50	...	2.55	3.15	...	15.16	...	...
April	...	1.00	0.38	...	...	...	1.50	...	2.53	3.16	...	14.60	...	...
May	...	1.00	0.38	...	...	...	1.50	...	2.53	3.17	...	14.34	...	...
June	...	1.00	0.38	...	...	...	1.50	...	2.55	3.21	...	14.84	...	...
July	...	1.00	0.66	...	...	...	1.50	...	2.55	3.18	...	15.77	...	...
August	...	1.00	0.75	...	...	...	1.50	...	2.56	3.17	...	15.46	...	...
September	...	1.00	0.80	...	...	...	1.50	...	2.61	3.23	...	15.06	...	...
October	...	1.00	0.85	...	...	...	1.50	...	2.70	3.35	...	15.45	...	...
November	...	1.00	0.92	...	...	...	1.50	...	2.77	3.44	...	15.27	...	...
December	...	1.00	0.95	...	...	...	1.75	...	2.86	3.52	...	15.03	...	...
1948														
January	...	1.25	0.97	...	...	...	1.75	...	2.86	3.52	...	14.83	...	...
February	...	1.25	1.00	...	...	...	1.75	...	2.85	3.53	...	14.10	...	...
March	...	1.25	1.00	...	...	...	1.75	...	2.83	3.53	...	14.30	...	...
April	...	1.25	1.00	...	...	...	1.75	...	2.78	3.47	...	15.40	...	...
May	...	1.25	1.00	...	...	...	1.75	...	2.76	3.38	...	16.15	...	...
June	...	1.25	1.00	...	...	...	1.75	...	2.76	3.34	...	16.82	...	...
July	...	1.25	1.00	...	...	...	1.75	...	2.81	3.37	...	16.42	...	...
August	...	1.50	1.06	...	...	...	2.00	...	2.84	3.44	...	15.94	...	...
September	...	1.50	1.09	...	...	...	2.00	...	2.84	3.45	...	15.76	...	...
October	...	1.50	1.12	...	...	...	2.00	...	2.84	3.50	...	16.19	...	...
November	...	1.50	1.14	...	...	...	2.00	...	2.84	3.53	...	15.29	...	...
December	...	1.50	1.16	...	...	...	2.00	...	2.79	3.53	...	15.19	...	...
1949														
January	...	1.50	1.17	...	...	...	2.00	...	2.71	3.46	...	15.36	...	...
February	...	1.50	1.17	...	...	...	2.00	...	2.71	3.45	...	14.77	...	...
March	...	1.50	1.17	...	...	...	2.00	...	2.70	3.47	...	14.91	...	...
April	...	1.50	1.17	...	...	...	2.00	...	2.70	3.45	...	14.89	...	...
May	...	1.50	1.17	...	...	...	2.00	...	2.71	3.45	...	14.78	...	...
June	...	1.50	1.17	...	...	...	2.00	...	2.71	3.47	...	13.97	...	...
July	...	1.50	1.02	...	...	...	2.00	...	2.67	3.46	...	14.76	...	...
August	...	1.50	1.04	...	...	...	2.00	...	2.62	3.40	...	15.29	...	...
September	...	1.50	1.07	...	...	...	2.00	...	2.60	3.37	...	15.49	...	...
October	...	1.50	1.05	...	...	...	2.00	...	2.61	3.36	...	15.89	...	...
November	...	1.50	1.08	...	...	...	2.00	...	2.60	3.35	...	16.11	...	...
December	...	1.50	1.10	...	...	...	2.00	...	2.58	3.31	...	16.54	...	...
1950														
January	...	1.50	1.07	...	...	...	2.00	...	2.57	3.24	...	16.88	...	...
February	...	1.50	1.12	...	...	...	2.00	...	2.58	3.24	...	17.21	...	...
March	...	1.50	1.12	...	...	...	2.00	...	2.58	3.24	...	17.35	...	...
April	...	1.50	1.15	...	...	...	2.00	...	2.60	3.23	...	17.84	...	...
May	...	1.50	1.16	...	...	...	2.00	...	2.61	3.25	...	18.44	...	...
June	...	1.50	1.15	...	...	...	2.00	...	2.62	3.28	...	18.74	...	...
July	...	1.50	1.16	...	...	...	2.00	...	2.65	3.32	...	17.38	...	...
August	...	1.59	1.20	...	...	...	2.00	...	2.61	3.23	...	18.43	...	...
September	...	1.75	1.30	...	...	...	2.08	...	2.64	3.21	...	19.08	...	...
October	...	1.75	1.31	...	...	...	2.25	...	2.67	3.22	...	19.87	...	...
November	...	1.75	1.36	...	...	...	2.25	...	2.67	3.22	...	19.83	...	...
December	...	1.75	1.34	...	...	...	2.25	...	2.67	3.20	...	19.75	...	...
1951														
January	...	1.75	1.34	...	...	...	2.44	...	2.66	3.17	...	21.21	...	...
February	...	1.75	1.36	...	...	...	2.50	...	2.66	3.16	...	22.00	...	...
March	...	1.75	1.40	...	...	...	2.50	...	2.78	3.23	...	21.63	...	...
April	...	1.75	1.47	...	...	...	2.50	...	2.87	3.35	...	21.92	...	...
May	...	1.75	1.55	...	...	...	2.50	...	2.89	3.40	...	21.93	...	...
June	...	1.75	1.45	...	...	...	2.50	...	2.94	3.49	...	21.55	...	...
July	...	1.75	1.56	...	...	...	2.50	...	2.94	3.53	...	21.93	...	...
August	...	1.75	1.62	...	...	...	2.50	...	2.88	3.50	...	22.89	...	...
September	...	1.75	1.63	...	...	...	2.50	...	2.84	3.46	...	23.48	...	...
October	...	1.75	1.54	...	...	...	2.62	...	2.89	3.50	...	23.36	...	...
November	...	1.75	1.56	...	...	...	2.75	...	2.96	3.56	...	22.71	...	...
December	...	1.75	1.73	...	...	...	2.85	...	3.01	3.61	...	23.41	...	...

[1]Federal Reserve Bank of New York. Through 2002, represents the rate for adjustment credit. Beginning in 2003, represents the rate for primary credit. See notes and definitions for more information.
[2]Prior to September 1997, this series represents both nonfinancial and financial commercial paper rates. Beginning September 1997, rates for financial companies only are shown. See notes and definitions for more information.
. . . = Not available.

Table 12-9B. Summary Interest Rates, Bond Yields, and Stock Prices: Historical Data—*Continued*

(Percent per annum, except as noted.)

Year and month	Federal funds interest rate	Federal Reserve discount rate[1]	U.S. Treasury bills, secondary market, 3-month	Inflation: percent change from year earlier in PCE chain-type price index excluding food and energy	Real 3-month Treasury bill rate	Commercial paper, 3-month[2]	Bank prime rate	Treasury 10-year nominal yields	Bond yields — Domestic corporate (Moody's) Aaa	Baa	State and local bonds (Bond Buyer)	Standard and Poor's composite (500 stocks) Index, 1941-1943 = 10	Dividend-price ratio	Earnings-price ratio
1952														
January	...	1.75	1.57	...	...	...	3.00	...	2.98	3.59	...	24.19	...	...
February	...	1.75	1.54	...	...	...	3.00	...	2.93	3.53	...	23.75	...	...
March	...	1.75	1.59	...	...	...	3.00	...	2.96	3.51	...	23.81	...	...
April	...	1.75	1.57	...	...	...	3.00	...	2.93	3.50	...	23.74	...	...
May	...	1.75	1.67	...	...	...	3.00	...	2.93	3.49	...	23.73	...	...
June	...	1.75	1.70	...	...	...	3.00	...	2.94	3.50	...	24.38	...	...
July	...	1.75	1.81	...	...	...	3.00	...	2.95	3.50	...	25.08	...	...
August	...	1.75	1.83	...	...	...	3.00	...	2.94	3.51	...	25.18	...	...
September ...	...	1.75	1.71	...	...	...	3.00	...	2.95	3.52	...	24.78	...	...
October	...	1.75	1.74	...	...	...	3.00	...	3.01	3.54	...	24.26	...	...
November	...	1.75	1.85	...	...	...	3.00	...	2.98	3.53	...	25.03	...	...
December	...	1.75	2.09	...	...	...	3.00	...	2.97	3.51	...	26.04	...	...
1953														
January	...	1.88	1.96	...	...	...	3.00	...	3.02	3.51	2.44	26.18	...	...
February	...	2.00	1.97	...	...	...	3.00	...	3.07	3.53	2.59	25.86	...	...
March	...	2.00	2.01	...	...	...	3.00	...	3.12	3.57	2.65	25.99	...	...
April	...	2.00	2.19	...	...	...	3.03	2.83	3.23	3.65	2.67	24.71	...	...
May	...	2.00	2.16	...	...	...	3.25	3.05	3.34	3.78	2.82	24.84	...	...
June	...	2.00	2.11	...	...	...	3.25	3.11	3.40	3.86	3.03	23.95	...	...
July	...	2.00	2.04	...	...	...	3.25	2.93	3.28	3.86	2.95	24.29	...	...
August	...	2.00	2.04	...	...	...	3.25	2.95	3.24	3.85	2.90	24.39	...	...
September ...	...	2.00	1.79	...	...	...	3.25	2.87	3.29	3.88	2.87	23.27	...	...
October	...	2.00	1.38	...	...	...	3.25	2.66	3.16	3.82	2.71	23.97	...	...
November	...	2.00	1.44	...	...	...	3.25	2.68	3.11	3.75	2.60	24.50	...	...
December	...	2.00	1.60	...	...	...	3.25	2.59	3.13	3.74	2.59	24.83	...	...
1954														
January	...	2.00	1.18	...	...	...	3.25	2.48	3.06	3.71	2.50	25.46	...	...
February	...	1.79	0.97	...	...	...	3.25	2.47	2.95	3.61	2.42	26.02	...	...
March	...	1.75	1.03	...	...	...	3.13	2.37	2.86	3.51	2.39	26.57	...	...
April	...	1.63	0.97	...	...	...	3.00	2.29	2.85	3.47	2.47	27.63	...	...
May	...	1.50	0.76	...	...	...	3.00	2.37	2.88	3.47	2.49	28.73	...	...
June	...	1.50	0.64	...	...	...	3.00	2.38	2.90	3.49	2.47	28.96	...	...
July	0.80	1.50	0.72	...	...	...	3.00	2.30	2.89	3.50	2.32	30.13	...	...
August	1.22	1.50	0.92	...	...	...	3.00	2.36	2.87	3.49	2.26	30.73	...	...
September ...	1.06	1.50	1.01	...	...	...	3.00	2.38	2.89	3.47	2.31	31.45	...	...
October	0.85	1.50	0.98	...	...	...	3.00	2.43	2.87	3.46	2.34	32.18	...	...
November	0.83	1.50	0.93	...	...	...	3.00	2.48	2.89	3.45	2.32	33.44	...	...
December	1.28	1.50	1.15	...	...	...	3.00	2.51	2.90	3.45	2.36	34.97	...	...
1955														
January	1.39	1.50	1.22	...	...	...	3.00	2.61	2.93	3.45	2.40	35.60	...	...
February	1.29	1.50	1.17	...	...	...	3.00	2.65	2.93	3.47	2.43	36.79	...	...
March	1.35	1.50	1.28	...	...	...	3.00	2.68	3.02	3.48	2.44	36.50	...	...
April	1.43	1.63	1.59	...	...	...	3.00	2.75	3.01	3.49	2.41	37.76	...	...
May	1.43	1.75	1.45	...	...	...	3.00	2.76	3.04	3.50	2.38	37.60	...	...
June	1.64	1.75	1.41	...	...	...	3.00	2.78	3.05	3.51	2.41	39.78	...	...
July	1.68	1.75	1.60	...	...	...	3.00	2.90	3.06	3.52	2.54	42.69	...	...
August	1.96	1.97	1.90	...	...	...	3.23	2.97	3.11	3.56	2.60	42.43	...	...
September ...	2.18	2.18	2.07	...	...	...	3.25	2.97	3.13	3.59	2.58	44.34	...	...
October	2.24	2.25	2.23	...	...	...	3.40	2.88	3.10	3.59	2.51	42.11	...	...
November	2.35	2.36	2.24	...	...	...	3.50	2.89	3.10	3.58	2.45	44.95	...	...
December	2.48	2.50	2.54	...	...	...	3.50	2.96	3.15	3.62	2.57	45.37	...	...
1956														
January	2.45	2.50	2.41	...	...	...	3.50	2.90	3.11	3.60	2.50	44.15	...	...
February	2.50	2.50	2.32	...	...	...	3.50	2.84	3.08	3.58	2.44	44.43	...	...
March	2.50	2.50	2.25	...	...	...	3.50	2.96	3.10	3.60	2.57	47.49	...	...
April	2.62	2.65	2.60	...	...	...	3.65	3.18	3.24	3.68	2.70	48.05	...	...
May	2.75	2.75	2.61	...	...	...	3.75	3.07	3.28	3.73	2.68	46.54	...	...
June	2.71	2.75	2.49	...	...	...	3.75	3.00	3.26	3.76	2.54	46.27	...	...
July	2.75	2.75	2.31	...	...	...	3.75	3.11	3.28	3.80	2.65	48.78	...	...
August	2.73	2.81	2.60	...	...	...	3.84	3.33	3.43	3.93	2.80	48.49	...	...
September ...	2.95	3.00	2.84	...	...	...	4.00	3.38	3.56	4.07	2.93	46.84	...	...
October	2.96	3.00	2.90	...	...	...	4.00	3.34	3.59	4.17	2.95	46.24	...	...
November	2.88	3.00	2.99	...	...	...	4.00	3.49	3.69	4.24	3.16	45.76	...	...
December	2.94	3.00	3.21	...	...	...	4.00	3.59	3.75	4.37	3.22	46.44	...	...

[1]Federal Reserve Bank of New York. Through 2002, represents the rate for adjustment credit. Beginning in 2003, represents the rate for primary credit. See notes and definitions for more information.
[2]Prior to September 1997, this series represents both nonfinancial and financial commercial paper rates. Beginning September 1997, rates for financial companies only are shown. See notes and definitions for more information.
. . . = Not available.

Table 12-9B. Summary Interest Rates, Bond Yields, and Stock Prices: Historical Data—*Continued*

(Percent per annum, except as noted.)

Year and month	Federal funds interest rate	Federal Reserve discount rate[1]	U.S. Treasury bills, secondary market, 3-month	Inflation: percent change from year earlier in PCE chain-type price index excluding food and energy	Real 3-month Treasury bill rate	Commercial paper, 3-month[2]	Bank prime rate	Treasury 10-year nominal yields	Bond yields Domestic corporate (Moody's) Aaa	Baa	State and local bonds (Bond Buyer)	Standard and Poor's composite (500 stocks) Index, 1941-1943 = 10	Dividend-price ratio	Earnings-price ratio
1957														
January	2.84	3.00	3.11	...	...	...	4.00	3.46	3.77	4.49	3.18	45.43	...	...
February	3.00	3.00	3.10	...	...	...	4.00	3.34	3.67	4.47	3.00	43.47	...	...
March	2.96	3.00	3.08	...	...	...	4.00	3.41	3.66	4.43	3.09	44.03	...	...
April	3.00	3.00	3.07	...	...	...	4.00	3.48	3.67	4.44	3.13	45.05	...	...
May	3.00	3.00	3.06	...	...	...	4.00	3.60	3.74	4.52	3.27	46.78	...	...
June	3.00	3.00	3.29	...	...	...	4.00	3.80	3.91	4.63	3.41	47.55	...	...
July	2.99	3.00	3.16	...	...	...	4.00	3.93	3.99	4.73	3.39	48.51	...	...
August	3.24	3.15	3.37	...	...	...	4.42	3.93	4.10	4.82	3.54	45.84	...	...
September	3.47	3.50	3.53	...	...	...	4.50	3.92	4.12	4.93	3.53	43.98	...	...
October	3.50	3.50	3.58	...	...	...	4.50	3.97	4.10	4.99	3.42	41.24	...	...
November	3.28	3.23	3.31	...	...	...	4.50	3.72	4.08	5.09	3.37	40.35	...	...
December	2.98	3.00	3.04	...	...	...	4.50	3.21	3.81	5.03	3.04	40.33	...	...
1958														
January	2.72	2.94	2.44	...	...	...	4.34	3.09	3.60	4.83	2.91	41.12	...	...
February	1.67	2.75	1.53	...	...	...	4.00	3.05	3.59	4.66	3.02	41.26	...	...
March	1.20	2.35	1.30	...	...	...	4.00	2.98	3.63	4.68	3.06	42.11	...	...
April	1.26	2.03	1.13	...	...	...	3.83	2.88	3.60	4.67	2.96	42.34	...	...
May	0.63	1.75	0.91	...	...	...	3.50	2.92	3.57	4.62	2.92	43.70	...	...
June	0.93	1.75	0.83	...	...	...	3.50	2.97	3.57	4.55	2.97	44.75	...	...
July	0.68	1.75	0.91	...	...	...	3.50	3.20	3.67	4.53	3.09	45.98	...	...
August	1.53	1.75	1.69	...	...	...	3.50	3.54	3.85	4.67	3.35	47.70	...	...
September	1.76	1.91	2.44	...	...	...	3.83	3.76	4.09	4.87	3.54	48.96	...	...
October	1.80	2.00	2.63	...	...	...	4.00	3.80	4.11	4.92	3.45	50.95	...	...
November	2.27	2.40	2.67	...	...	...	4.00	3.74	4.09	4.87	3.32	52.50	...	...
December	2.42	2.50	2.77	...	...	...	4.00	3.86	4.08	4.85	3.33	53.49	...	...
1959														
January	2.48	2.50	2.82	...	...	...	4.00	4.02	4.12	4.87	3.42	55.62	...	...
February	2.43	2.50	2.70	...	...	...	4.00	3.96	4.14	4.89	3.36	54.77	...	...
March	2.80	2.92	2.80	...	...	...	4.00	3.99	4.13	4.85	3.30	56.15	...	...
April	2.96	3.00	2.95	...	...	...	4.00	4.12	4.23	4.86	3.39	57.10	...	...
May	2.90	3.05	2.84	...	...	...	4.23	4.31	4.37	4.96	3.57	57.96	...	...
June	3.39	3.50	3.21	...	...	...	4.50	4.34	4.46	5.04	3.71	57.46	...	...
July	3.47	3.50	3.20	...	...	...	4.50	4.40	4.47	5.08	3.71	59.74	...	...
August	3.50	3.50	3.38	...	...	...	4.50	4.43	4.43	5.09	3.58	59.40	...	...
September	3.76	3.83	4.04	...	...	...	5.00	4.68	4.52	5.18	3.78	57.05	...	...
October	3.98	4.00	4.05	...	...	...	5.00	4.53	4.57	5.28	3.62	57.00	...	...
November	4.00	4.00	4.15	...	...	...	5.00	4.53	4.56	5.26	3.55	57.23	...	...
December	3.99	4.00	4.49	...	...	...	5.00	4.69	4.58	5.28	3.70	59.06	...	...
1960														
January	3.99	4.00	4.35	2.02	2.33	...	5.00	4.72	4.61	5.34	3.72	58.03	...	...
February	3.97	4.00	3.96	2.14	1.82	...	5.00	4.49	4.56	5.34	3.60	55.78	...	...
March	3.84	4.00	3.31	2.05	1.26	...	5.00	4.25	4.49	5.25	3.57	55.02	...	...
April	3.92	4.00	3.23	1.99	1.24	...	5.00	4.28	4.45	5.20	3.56	55.73	...	...
May	3.85	4.00	3.29	2.04	1.25	...	5.00	4.35	4.46	5.28	3.60	55.22	...	...
June	3.32	3.65	2.46	1.82	0.64	...	5.00	4.15	4.45	5.26	3.55	57.26	...	...
July	3.23	3.50	2.30	1.76	0.54	...	5.00	3.90	4.41	5.22	3.50	55.84	...	...
August	2.98	3.18	2.30	1.75	0.55	...	4.85	3.80	4.28	5.08	3.33	56.51	...	...
September	2.60	3.00	2.48	1.57	0.91	...	4.50	3.80	4.25	5.01	3.42	54.81	...	...
October	2.47	3.00	2.30	1.46	0.84	...	4.50	3.89	4.30	5.11	3.53	53.73	...	...
November	2.44	3.00	2.37	1.54	0.83	...	4.50	3.93	4.31	5.08	3.40	55.47	...	...
December	1.98	3.00	2.25	1.35	0.90	...	4.50	3.84	4.35	5.10	3.40	56.80	...	...
1961														
January	1.45	3.00	2.24	1.34	0.90	...	4.50	3.84	4.32	5.10	3.39	59.72	...	...
February	2.54	3.00	2.42	1.26	1.16	...	4.50	3.78	4.27	5.07	3.31	62.17	...	...
March	2.02	3.00	2.39	1.28	1.11	...	4.50	3.74	4.22	5.02	3.45	64.12	...	...
April	1.49	3.00	2.29	1.24	1.05	...	4.50	3.78	4.25	5.01	3.48	65.83	...	...
May	1.98	3.00	2.29	1.21	1.08	...	4.50	3.71	4.27	5.01	3.43	66.50	...	...
June	1.73	3.00	2.33	1.29	1.04	...	4.50	3.88	4.33	5.03	3.52	65.62	...	...
July	1.17	3.00	2.24	1.27	0.97	...	4.50	3.92	4.41	5.09	3.51	65.44	...	...
August	2.00	3.00	2.39	1.23	1.16	...	4.50	4.04	4.45	5.11	3.52	67.79	...	...
September	1.88	3.00	2.28	1.35	0.93	...	4.50	3.98	4.45	5.12	3.53	67.26	...	...
October	2.26	3.00	2.30	1.32	0.98	...	4.50	3.92	4.42	5.13	3.42	68.00	...	...
November	2.61	3.00	2.48	1.07	1.41	...	4.50	3.94	4.39	5.11	3.41	71.08	...	...
December	2.33	3.00	2.60	1.19	1.41	...	4.50	4.06	4.42	5.10	3.47	71.74	...	...

[1]Federal Reserve Bank of New York. Through 2002, represents the rate for adjustment credit. Beginning in 2003, represents the rate for primary credit. See notes and definitions for more information.
[2]Prior to September 1997, this series represents both nonfinancial and financial commercial paper rates. Beginning September 1997, rates for financial companies only are shown. See notes and definitions for more information.
. . . = Not available.

Table 12-9B. Summary Interest Rates, Bond Yields, and Stock Prices: Historical Data—*Continued*

(Percent per annum, except as noted.)

Year and month	Federal funds interest rate	Federal Reserve discount rate[1]	U.S. Treasury bills, secondary market, 3-month	Inflation: percent change from year earlier in PCE chain-type price index excluding food and energy	Real 3-month Treasury bill rate	Commercial paper, 3-month [2]	Bank prime rate	Treasury 10-year nominal yields	Bond yields Domestic corporate (Moody's) Aaa	Bond yields Domestic corporate (Moody's) Baa	State and local bonds (Bond Buyer)	Standard and Poor's composite (500 stocks) Index, 1941-1943 = 10	Dividend-price ratio	Earnings-price ratio
1962														
January	2.15	3.00	2.72	1.29	1.43	. . .	4.50	4.08	4.42	5.08	3.34	69.07	. . .	. . .
February	2.37	3.00	2.73	1.36	1.37	. . .	4.50	4.04	4.42	5.07	3.21	70.22	. . .	. . .
March	2.85	3.00	2.72	1.56	1.16	. . .	4.50	3.93	4.39	5.04	3.14	70.29	. . .	. . .
April	2.78	3.00	2.73	1.44	1.29	. . .	4.50	3.84	4.33	5.02	3.06	68.05	. . .	. . .
May	2.36	3.00	2.69	1.45	1.24	. . .	4.50	3.87	4.28	5.00	3.11	62.99	. . .	. . .
June	2.68	3.00	2.73	1.48	1.25	. . .	4.50	3.91	4.28	5.02	3.25	55.63	. . .	. . .
July	2.71	3.00	2.92	1.40	1.52	. . .	4.50	4.01	4.34	5.05	3.27	56.97	. . .	. . .
August	2.93	3.00	2.82	1.30	1.52	. . .	4.50	3.98	4.35	5.06	3.23	58.52	. . .	. . .
September ...	2.90	3.00	2.78	1.29	1.49	. . .	4.50	3.98	4.32	5.03	3.11	58.00	. . .	. . .
October	2.90	3.00	2.74	1.25	1.49	. . .	4.50	3.93	4.28	4.99	3.02	56.17	. . .	. . .
November	2.94	3.00	2.83	1.30	1.53	. . .	4.50	3.92	4.25	4.96	3.04	60.04	. . .	. . .
December	2.93	3.00	2.87	1.24	1.63	. . .	4.50	3.86	4.24	4.92	3.07	62.64	. . .	. . .
1963														
January	2.92	3.00	2.91	1.31	1.60	. . .	4.50	3.83	4.21	4.91	3.10	65.06	. . .	. . .
February	3.00	3.00	2.92	1.25	1.67	. . .	4.50	3.92	4.19	4.89	3.15	65.92	. . .	. . .
March	2.98	3.00	2.89	1.06	1.83	. . .	4.50	3.93	4.19	4.88	3.05	65.67	. . .	. . .
April	2.90	3.00	2.90	1.16	1.74	. . .	4.50	3.97	4.21	4.87	3.10	68.76	. . .	. . .
May	3.00	3.00	2.93	1.20	1.73	. . .	4.50	3.93	4.22	4.85	3.11	70.14	. . .	. . .
June	2.99	3.00	2.99	1.19	1.80	. . .	4.50	3.99	4.23	4.84	3.21	70.11	. . .	. . .
July	3.02	3.24	3.18	1.19	1.99	. . .	4.50	4.02	4.26	4.84	3.22	69.07	. . .	. . .
August	3.49	3.50	3.32	1.27	2.05	. . .	4.50	4.00	4.29	4.83	3.13	70.98	. . .	. . .
September ...	3.48	3.50	3.38	1.26	2.12	. . .	4.50	4.08	4.31	4.84	3.20	72.85	. . .	. . .
October	3.50	3.50	3.45	1.51	1.94	. . .	4.50	4.11	4.32	4.83	3.20	73.03	. . .	. . .
November	3.48	3.50	3.52	1.52	2.00	. . .	4.50	4.12	4.33	4.84	3.30	72.62	. . .	. . .
December	3.38	3.50	3.52	1.64	1.88	. . .	4.50	4.13	4.35	4.85	3.27	74.17	. . .	. . .
1964														
January	3.48	3.50	3.52	1.59	1.93	. . .	4.50	4.17	4.39	4.83	3.22	76.45	. . .	. . .
February	3.48	3.50	3.53	1.68	1.85	. . .	4.50	4.15	4.36	4.83	3.14	77.39	. . .	. . .
March	3.43	3.50	3.54	1.73	1.81	. . .	4.50	4.22	4.38	4.83	3.28	78.80	. . .	. . .
April	3.47	3.50	3.47	1.71	1.76	. . .	4.50	4.23	4.40	4.85	3.28	79.94	. . .	. . .
May	3.50	3.50	3.48	1.62	1.86	. . .	4.50	4.20	4.41	4.85	3.20	80.72	. . .	. . .
June	3.50	3.50	3.48	1.53	1.95	. . .	4.50	4.17	4.41	4.85	3.20	80.24	. . .	. . .
July	3.42	3.50	3.46	1.55	1.91	. . .	4.50	4.19	4.40	4.83	3.18	83.22	. . .	. . .
August	3.50	3.50	3.50	1.59	1.91	. . .	4.50	4.19	4.41	4.82	3.19	82.00	. . .	. . .
September ...	3.45	3.50	3.53	1.46	2.07	. . .	4.50	4.20	4.42	4.82	3.23	83.41	. . .	. . .
October	3.36	3.50	3.57	1.27	2.30	. . .	4.50	4.19	4.42	4.81	3.25	84.85	. . .	. . .
November	3.52	3.62	3.64	1.33	2.31	. . .	4.50	4.15	4.43	4.81	3.18	85.44	. . .	. . .
December	3.85	4.00	3.84	1.32	2.52	. . .	4.50	4.18	4.44	4.81	3.13	83.96	. . .	. . .
1965														
January	3.90	4.00	3.81	1.31	2.50	. . .	4.50	4.19	4.43	4.80	3.06	86.12	. . .	. . .
February	3.98	4.00	3.93	1.23	2.70	. . .	4.50	4.21	4.41	4.78	3.09	86.75	. . .	. . .
March	4.04	4.00	3.93	1.19	2.74	. . .	4.50	4.21	4.42	4.78	3.17	86.83	. . .	. . .
April	4.09	4.00	3.93	1.21	2.72	. . .	4.50	4.20	4.43	4.80	3.15	87.97	. . .	. . .
May	4.10	4.00	3.89	1.31	2.58	. . .	4.50	4.21	4.44	4.81	3.17	89.28	. . .	. . .
June	4.04	4.00	3.80	1.20	2.60	. . .	4.50	4.21	4.46	4.85	3.24	85.04	. . .	. . .
July	4.09	4.00	3.84	1.19	2.65	. . .	4.50	4.20	4.48	4.88	3.27	84.91	. . .	. . .
August	4.12	4.00	3.84	1.25	2.59	. . .	4.50	4.25	4.49	4.88	3.24	86.49	. . .	. . .
September ...	4.01	4.00	3.92	1.32	2.60	. . .	4.50	4.29	4.52	4.91	3.35	89.38	. . .	. . .
October	4.08	4.00	4.03	1.25	2.78	. . .	4.50	4.35	4.56	4.93	3.40	91.39	. . .	. . .
November	4.10	4.00	4.09	1.29	2.80	. . .	4.50	4.45	4.60	4.95	3.45	92.15	. . .	. . .
December	4.32	4.42	4.38	1.45	2.93	. . .	4.92	4.62	4.68	5.02	3.54	91.73	. . .	. . .
1966														
January	4.42	4.50	4.59	1.35	3.24	. . .	5.00	4.61	4.74	5.06	3.52	93.32	. . .	. . .
February	4.60	4.50	4.65	1.49	3.16	. . .	5.00	4.83	4.78	5.12	3.64	92.69	. . .	. . .
March	4.65	4.50	4.59	1.56	3.03	. . .	5.35	4.87	4.92	5.32	3.72	88.88	. . .	. . .
April	4.67	4.50	4.62	1.80	2.82	. . .	5.50	4.75	4.96	5.41	3.56	91.60	. . .	. . .
May	4.90	4.50	4.64	1.89	2.75	. . .	5.50	4.78	4.98	5.48	3.65	86.78	. . .	. . .
June	5.17	4.50	4.50	2.25	2.25	. . .	5.52	4.81	5.07	5.58	3.77	86.06	. . .	. . .
July	5.30	4.50	4.80	2.45	2.35	. . .	5.75	5.02	5.16	5.68	3.95	85.84	. . .	. . .
August	5.53	4.50	4.96	2.45	2.51	. . .	5.88	5.22	5.31	5.83	4.12	80.65	. . .	. . .
September ...	5.40	4.50	5.37	2.64	2.73	. . .	6.00	5.18	5.49	6.09	4.12	77.81	. . .	. . .
October	5.53	4.50	5.35	3.02	2.33	. . .	6.00	5.01	5.41	6.10	3.93	77.13	. . .	. . .
November	5.76	4.50	5.32	3.09	2.23	. . .	6.00	5.16	5.35	6.13	3.86	80.99	. . .	. . .
December	5.40	4.50	4.96	3.09	1.87	. . .	6.00	4.84	5.39	6.18	3.86	81.33	. . .	. . .

[1]Federal Reserve Bank of New York. Through 2002, represents the rate for adjustment credit. Beginning in 2003, represents the rate for primary credit. See notes and definitions for more information.
[2]Prior to September 1997, this series represents both nonfinancial and financial commercial paper rates. Beginning September 1997, rates for financial companies only are shown. See notes and definitions for more information.
. . . = Not available.

Table 12-9B. Summary Interest Rates, Bond Yields, and Stock Prices: Historical Data—*Continued*

(Percent per annum, except as noted.)

Year and month	Federal funds interest rate	Federal Reserve discount rate[1]	U.S. Treasury bills, secondary market, 3-month	Inflation: percent change from year earlier in PCE chain-type price index excluding food and energy	Real 3-month Treasury bill rate	Commercial paper, 3-month[2]	Bank prime rate	Treasury 10-year nominal yields	Bond yields Domestic corporate (Moody's) Aaa	Bond yields Domestic corporate (Moody's) Baa	State and local bonds (Bond Buyer)	Standard and Poor's composite (500 stocks) Index, 1941-1943 = 10	Standard and Poor's composite (500 stocks) Dividend-price ratio	Standard and Poor's composite (500 stocks) Earnings-price ratio
1967														
January	4.94	4.50	4.72	3.15	1.57	...	5.96	4.58	5.20	5.97	3.54	84.45	...	...
February	5.00	4.50	4.56	3.08	1.48	...	5.75	4.63	5.03	5.82	3.52	87.36	...	...
March	4.53	4.50	4.26	3.10	1.16	...	5.71	4.54	5.13	5.85	3.55	89.42	...	...
April	4.05	4.10	3.84	3.02	0.82	...	5.50	4.59	5.11	5.83	3.60	90.96	...	...
May	3.94	4.00	3.60	2.96	0.64	...	5.50	4.85	5.24	5.96	3.89	92.59	...	...
June	3.98	4.00	3.54	2.89	0.65	...	5.50	5.02	5.44	6.15	3.96	91.43	...	...
July	3.79	4.00	4.21	2.93	1.28	...	5.50	5.16	5.58	6.26	4.02	93.01	...	...
August	3.90	4.00	4.27	3.06	1.21	...	5.50	5.28	5.62	6.33	3.99	94.49	...	...
September ...	3.99	4.00	4.42	3.10	1.32	...	5.50	5.30	5.65	6.40	4.12	95.81	...	...
October	3.88	4.00	4.56	3.14	1.42	...	5.50	5.48	5.82	6.52	4.29	95.66	...	...
November	4.13	4.18	4.73	3.20	1.53	...	5.68	5.75	6.07	6.72	4.34	92.66	...	...
December	4.51	4.50	4.97	3.14	1.83	...	6.00	5.70	6.19	6.93	4.43	95.30	...	...
1968														
January	4.60	4.50	5.00	3.49	1.51	...	6.00	5.53	6.17	6.84	4.29	95.04	...	...
February	4.71	4.50	4.98	3.75	1.23	...	6.00	5.56	6.10	6.80	4.31	90.75	...	...
March	5.05	4.66	5.17	4.01	1.16	...	6.00	5.74	6.11	6.85	4.54	89.09	...	...
April	5.76	5.20	5.38	4.10	1.28	...	6.20	5.64	6.21	6.97	4.34	95.67	...	...
May	6.11	5.50	5.66	4.26	1.40	...	6.50	5.87	6.27	7.03	4.54	97.87	...	...
June	6.07	5.50	5.52	4.41	1.11	...	6.50	5.72	6.28	7.07	4.49	100.53	...	...
July	6.02	5.50	5.31	4.40	0.91	...	6.50	5.50	6.24	6.98	4.33	100.30	...	...
August	6.03	5.48	5.09	4.49	0.60	...	6.50	5.42	6.02	6.82	4.21	98.11	...	...
September ...	5.78	5.25	5.19	4.55	0.64	...	6.45	5.46	5.97	6.79	4.38	101.34	...	...
October	5.91	5.25	5.35	4.58	0.77	...	6.25	5.58	6.09	6.84	4.49	103.76	...	...
November	5.82	5.25	5.45	4.65	0.80	...	6.25	5.70	6.19	7.01	4.60	105.40	...	...
December	6.02	5.36	5.96	4.72	1.24	...	6.60	6.03	6.45	7.23	4.82	106.48	...	...
1969														
January	6.30	5.50	6.14	4.66	1.48	...	6.95	6.04	6.59	7.32	4.85	102.04	...	...
February	6.61	5.50	6.12	4.58	1.54	...	7.00	6.19	6.66	7.30	4.98	101.46	...	...
March	6.79	5.50	6.02	4.66	1.36	...	7.24	6.30	6.85	7.51	5.26	99.30	...	...
April	7.41	5.95	6.11	4.69	1.42	...	7.50	6.17	6.89	7.54	5.19	101.26	...	...
May	8.67	6.00	6.04	4.71	1.33	...	7.50	6.32	6.79	7.52	5.33	104.62	...	...
June	8.90	6.00	6.44	4.66	1.78	...	8.23	6.57	6.98	7.70	5.75	99.14	...	...
July	8.61	6.00	7.00	4.80	2.20	...	8.50	6.72	7.08	7.84	5.75	94.71	...	...
August	9.19	6.00	6.98	4.69	2.29	...	8.50	6.69	6.97	7.86	6.00	94.18	...	...
September ...	9.15	6.00	7.09	4.69	2.40	...	8.50	7.16	7.14	8.05	6.26	94.51	...	...
October	9.00	6.00	7.00	4.71	2.29	...	8.50	7.10	7.33	8.22	6.09	95.52	...	...
November	8.85	6.00	7.24	4.72	2.52	...	8.50	7.14	7.35	8.25	6.30	96.21	...	...
December	8.97	6.00	7.82	4.78	3.04	...	8.50	7.65	7.72	8.65	6.82	91.11	...	...
1970														
January	8.98	6.00	7.87	4.73	3.14	...	8.50	7.79	7.91	8.86	6.63	90.31	...	...
February	8.98	6.00	7.13	4.76	2.37	...	8.50	7.24	7.93	8.78	6.22	87.16	...	...
March	7.76	6.00	6.63	4.66	1.97	...	8.39	7.07	7.84	8.63	6.05	88.65	...	...
April	8.10	6.00	6.51	4.66	1.85	...	8.00	7.39	7.83	8.70	6.65	85.95	...	...
May	7.94	6.00	6.84	4.61	2.23	...	8.00	7.91	8.11	8.98	7.00	76.06	...	...
June	7.60	6.00	6.68	4.63	2.05	...	8.00	7.84	8.48	9.25	6.93	75.59	...	...
July	7.21	6.00	6.45	4.54	1.91	...	8.00	7.46	8.44	9.40	6.42	75.72	...	...
August	6.61	6.00	6.41	4.61	1.80	...	8.00	7.53	8.13	9.44	6.17	77.92	...	...
September ...	6.29	6.00	6.12	4.62	1.50	...	7.83	7.39	8.09	9.39	6.31	82.58	...	...
October	6.20	6.00	5.91	4.69	1.22	...	7.50	7.33	8.03	9.33	6.37	84.37	...	...
November	5.60	5.85	5.28	4.82	0.46	...	7.28	6.84	8.05	9.38	5.71	84.28	...	...
December	4.90	5.52	4.87	4.96	-0.09	...	6.92	6.39	7.64	9.12	5.47	90.05	...	...
1971														
January	4.14	5.23	4.44	5.02	-0.58	...	6.29	6.24	7.36	8.74	5.35	93.49	...	...
February	3.72	4.91	3.70	5.03	-1.33	...	5.88	6.11	7.08	8.39	5.23	97.11	...	...
March	3.71	4.75	3.38	4.97	-1.59	...	5.44	5.70	7.21	8.46	5.17	99.60	...	...
April	4.15	4.75	3.86	4.95	-1.09	4.57	5.28	5.83	7.25	8.45	5.37	103.04	...	...
May	4.63	4.75	4.14	5.03	-0.89	5.06	5.46	6.39	7.53	8.62	5.90	101.64	...	...
June	4.91	4.75	4.75	5.07	-0.32	5.38	5.50	6.52	7.64	8.75	5.95	99.72	...	...
July	5.31	4.88	5.40	5.07	0.33	5.75	5.91	6.73	7.64	8.76	6.06	99.00	...	...
August	5.56	5.00	4.94	4.86	0.08	5.74	6.00	6.58	7.59	8.76	5.82	97.24	...	...
September ...	5.55	5.00	4.69	4.59	0.10	5.69	6.00	6.14	7.44	8.59	5.37	99.40	...	...
October	5.20	5.00	4.46	4.25	0.21	5.42	5.90	5.93	7.39	8.48	5.06	97.29	...	...
November	4.91	4.90	4.22	3.95	0.27	4.84	5.53	5.81	7.26	8.38	5.20	92.78	...	...
December	4.14	4.63	4.01	3.75	0.26	4.66	5.49	5.93	7.25	8.38	5.21	99.17	...	...

[1]Federal Reserve Bank of New York. Through 2002, represents the rate for adjustment credit. Beginning in 2003, represents the rate for primary credit. See notes and definitions for more information.
[2]Prior to September 1997, this series represents both nonfinancial and financial commercial paper rates. Beginning September 1997, rates for financial companies only are shown. See notes and definitions for more information.
... = Not available.

Table 12-9B. Summary Interest Rates, Bond Yields, and Stock Prices: Historical Data—*Continued*

(Percent per annum, except as noted.)

Year and month	Federal funds interest rate	Federal Reserve discount rate[1]	U.S. Treasury bills, secondary market, 3-month	Inflation: percent change from year earlier in PCE chain-type price index excluding food and energy	Real 3-month Treasury bill rate	Commercial paper, 3-month [2]	Bank prime rate	Treasury 10-year nominal yields	Bond yields Domestic corporate (Moody's) Aaa	Baa	State and local bonds (Bond Buyer)	Standard and Poor's composite (500 stocks) Index, 1941-1943 = 10	Dividend-price ratio	Earnings-price ratio
1972														
January	3.50	4.50	3.38	3.79	-0.41	4.03	5.18	5.95	7.19	8.23	5.12	103.30	. . .	. . .
February	3.29	4.50	3.20	3.67	-0.47	3.81	4.75	6.08	7.27	8.23	5.28	105.24	. . .	. . .
March	3.83	4.50	3.73	3.55	0.18	4.10	4.75	6.07	7.24	8.24	5.31	107.69	. . .	. . .
April	4.17	4.50	3.71	3.40	0.31	4.55	4.97	6.19	7.30	8.24	5.43	108.81	. . .	. . .
May	4.27	4.50	3.69	3.19	0.50	4.45	5.00	6.13	7.30	8.23	5.30	107.65	. . .	. . .
June	4.46	4.50	3.91	2.99	0.92	4.60	5.04	6.11	7.23	8.20	5.33	108.01	. . .	. . .
July	4.55	4.50	3.98	2.90	1.08	4.83	5.25	6.11	7.21	8.23	5.41	107.21	. . .	. . .
August	4.80	4.50	4.02	2.97	1.05	4.75	5.27	6.21	7.19	8.19	5.30	111.01	. . .	. . .
September ...	4.87	4.50	4.66	3.14	1.52	5.07	5.50	6.55	7.22	8.09	5.36	109.39	. . .	. . .
October	5.04	4.50	4.74	3.04	1.70	5.21	5.73	6.48	7.21	8.06	5.18	109.56	. . .	. . .
November	5.06	4.50	4.78	3.08	1.70	5.18	5.75	6.28	7.12	7.99	5.02	115.05	. . .	. . .
December	5.33	4.50	5.07	3.07	2.00	5.40	5.79	6.36	7.08	7.93	5.05	117.50	. . .	. . .
1973														
January	5.94	4.77	5.41	2.70	2.71	5.77	6.00	6.46	7.15	7.90	5.05	118.42	. . .	. . .
February	6.58	5.05	5.60	2.73	2.87	6.17	6.02	6.64	7.22	7.97	5.13	114.16	. . .	. . .
March	7.09	5.50	6.09	2.94	3.15	6.76	6.30	6.71	7.29	8.03	5.29	112.42	. . .	. . .
April	7.12	5.50	6.26	3.31	2.95	7.13	6.61	6.67	7.26	8.09	5.15	110.27	. . .	. . .
May	7.84	5.90	6.36	3.47	2.89	7.26	7.01	6.85	7.29	8.06	5.15	107.22	. . .	. . .
June	8.49	6.33	7.19	3.72	3.47	8.00	7.49	6.90	7.37	8.13	5.17	104.75	. . .	. . .
July	10.40	6.98	8.01	3.86	4.15	9.26	8.30	7.13	7.45	8.24	5.40	105.83	. . .	. . .
August	10.50	7.29	8.67	4.12	4.55	10.26	9.23	7.40	7.68	8.53	5.48	103.80	. . .	. . .
September ...	10.78	7.50	8.29	4.29	4.00	10.31	9.86	7.09	7.63	8.63	5.10	105.61	. . .	. . .
October	10.01	7.50	7.22	4.64	2.58	9.14	9.94	6.79	7.60	8.41	5.05	109.84	. . .	. . .
November	10.03	7.50	7.83	4.87	2.96	9.11	9.75	6.73	7.67	8.42	5.18	102.03	. . .	. . .
December	9.95	7.50	7.45	5.13	2.32	9.28	9.75	6.74	7.68	8.48	5.12	94.78	. . .	. . .
1974														
January	9.65	7.50	7.77	5.59	2.18	8.86	9.73	6.99	7.83	8.48	5.22	96.11	. . .	. . .
February	8.97	7.50	7.12	5.93	1.19	8.00	9.21	6.96	7.85	8.53	5.20	93.45	. . .	. . .
March	9.35	7.50	7.96	6.33	1.63	8.64	8.85	7.21	8.01	8.62	5.40	97.44	. . .	. . .
April	10.51	7.60	8.33	6.49	1.84	9.92	10.02	7.51	8.25	8.87	5.73	92.46	. . .	. . .
May	11.31	8.00	8.23	7.10	1.13	10.82	11.25	7.58	8.37	9.05	6.02	89.67	. . .	. . .
June	11.93	8.00	7.90	7.73	0.17	11.18	11.54	7.54	8.47	9.27	6.13	89.79	. . .	. . .
July	12.92	8.00	7.55	8.23	-0.68	11.93	11.97	7.81	8.72	9.48	6.68	82.82	. . .	. . .
August	12.01	8.00	8.96	8.76	0.20	11.79	12.00	8.04	9.00	9.77	6.71	76.03	. . .	. . .
September ...	11.34	8.00	8.06	9.20	-1.14	11.36	12.00	8.04	9.24	10.18	6.76	68.12	. . .	. . .
October	10.06	8.00	7.46	9.62	-2.16	9.55	11.68	7.90	9.27	10.48	6.57	69.44	. . .	. . .
November	9.45	8.00	7.47	9.89	-2.42	8.95	10.83	7.68	8.89	10.60	6.61	71.74	. . .	. . .
December	8.53	7.81	7.15	10.06	-2.91	9.18	10.50	7.43	8.89	10.63	7.05	67.07	. . .	. . .
1975														
January	7.13	7.40	6.26	10.16	-3.90	7.39	10.05	7.50	8.83	10.81	6.82	72.56	. . .	. . .
February	6.24	6.82	5.50	10.24	-4.74	6.36	8.96	7.39	8.62	10.65	6.39	80.10	. . .	. . .
March	5.54	6.40	5.49	9.95	-4.46	6.06	7.93	7.73	8.67	10.48	6.73	83.78	. . .	. . .
April	5.49	6.25	5.61	9.67	-4.06	6.11	7.50	8.23	8.95	10.58	6.95	84.72	. . .	. . .
May	5.22	6.12	5.23	9.10	-3.87	5.70	7.40	8.06	8.90	10.69	6.97	90.10	. . .	. . .
June	5.55	6.00	5.34	8.51	-3.17	5.67	7.07	7.86	8.77	10.62	6.94	92.40	. . .	. . .
July	6.10	6.00	6.13	8.22	-2.09	6.32	7.15	8.06	8.84	10.55	7.07	92.49	. . .	. . .
August	6.14	6.00	6.44	7.56	-1.12	6.59	7.66	8.40	8.95	10.59	7.17	85.71	. . .	. . .
September ...	6.24	6.00	6.42	7.18	-0.76	6.79	7.88	8.43	8.95	10.61	7.44	84.67	. . .	. . .
October	5.82	6.00	5.96	6.88	-0.92	6.35	7.96	8.14	8.86	10.62	7.39	88.57	. . .	. . .
November	5.22	6.00	5.48	6.80	-1.32	5.78	7.53	8.05	8.78	10.56	7.43	90.07	. . .	. . .
December	5.20	6.00	5.44	6.70	-1.26	5.88	7.26	8.00	8.79	10.56	7.31	88.70	. . .	. . .
1976														
January	4.87	5.79	4.87	6.62	-1.75	5.16	7.00	7.74	8.60	10.41	7.07	96.86	. . .	. . .
February	4.77	5.50	4.88	6.29	-1.41	5.13	6.75	7.79	8.55	10.24	6.94	100.64	. . .	. . .
March	4.84	5.50	5.00	6.09	-1.09	5.25	6.75	7.73	8.52	10.12	6.91	101.08	. . .	. . .
April	4.82	5.50	4.86	5.98	-1.12	5.09	6.75	7.56	8.40	9.94	6.60	101.93	. . .	. . .
May	5.29	5.50	5.20	6.02	-0.82	5.44	6.75	7.90	8.58	9.86	6.87	101.16	. . .	. . .
June	5.48	5.50	5.41	5.94	-0.53	5.83	7.20	7.86	8.62	9.89	6.87	101.77	. . .	. . .
July	5.31	5.50	5.23	5.87	-0.64	5.54	7.25	7.83	8.56	9.82	6.79	104.20	. . .	. . .
August	5.29	5.50	5.14	6.11	-0.97	5.36	7.01	7.77	8.45	9.64	6.61	103.29	. . .	. . .
September ...	5.25	5.50	5.08	6.15	-1.07	5.33	7.00	7.59	8.38	9.40	6.51	105.45	. . .	. . .
October	5.02	5.50	4.92	6.14	-1.22	5.10	6.77	7.41	8.32	9.29	6.30	101.89	. . .	. . .
November	4.95	5.43	4.75	5.92	-1.17	4.98	6.50	7.29	8.25	9.23	6.29	101.19	. . .	. . .
December	4.65	5.25	4.35	5.85	-1.50	4.66	6.35	6.87	7.98	9.12	5.94	104.66	. . .	. . .

[1] Federal Reserve Bank of New York. Through 2002, represents the rate for adjustment credit. Beginning in 2003, represents the rate for primary credit. See notes and definitions for more information.
[2] Prior to September 1997, this series represents both nonfinancial and financial commercial paper rates. Beginning September 1997, rates for financial companies only are shown. See notes and definitions for more information.
. . . = Not available.

Table 12-9B. Summary Interest Rates, Bond Yields, and Stock Prices: Historical Data—*Continued*

(Percent per annum, except as noted.)

Year and month	Federal funds interest rate	Federal Reserve discount rate[1]	U.S. Treasury bills, secondary market, 3-month	Inflation: percent change from year earlier in PCE chain-type price index excluding food and energy	Real 3-month Treasury bill rate	Commercial paper, 3-month[2]	Bank prime rate	Treasury 10-year nominal yields	Bond yields Domestic corporate (Moody's) Aaa	Baa	State and local bonds (Bond Buyer)	Standard and Poor's composite (500 stocks) Index, 1941-1943 = 10	Dividend-price ratio	Earnings-price ratio
1977														
January	4.61	5.25	4.62	5.94	-1.32	4.72	6.25	7.21	7.96	9.08	5.87	103.81	. . .	. . .
February	4.68	5.25	4.67	6.17	-1.50	4.76	6.25	7.39	8.04	9.12	5.88	100.96	. . .	. . .
March	4.69	5.25	4.60	6.26	-1.66	4.75	6.25	7.46	8.10	9.12	5.89	100.57	. . .	. . .
April	4.73	5.25	4.54	6.37	-1.83	4.75	6.25	7.37	8.04	9.07	5.72	99.05	. . .	. . .
May	5.35	5.25	4.96	6.42	-1.46	5.26	6.41	7.46	8.05	9.01	5.75	98.76	. . .	. . .
June	5.39	5.25	5.02	6.62	-1.60	5.42	6.75	7.28	7.95	8.91	5.62	99.29	. . .	. . .
July	5.42	5.25	5.19	6.70	-1.51	5.39	6.75	7.33	7.94	8.87	5.63	100.18	. . .	. . .
August	5.90	5.27	5.49	6.61	-1.12	5.76	6.83	7.40	7.98	8.82	5.62	97.75	. . .	. . .
September	6.14	5.75	5.81	6.44	-0.63	6.10	7.13	7.34	7.92	8.80	5.51	96.23	. . .	. . .
October	6.47	5.80	6.16	6.44	-0.28	6.51	7.52	7.52	8.04	8.89	5.64	93.74	. . .	. . .
November	6.51	6.00	6.10	6.51	-0.41	6.54	7.75	7.58	8.08	8.95	5.49	94.28	. . .	. . .
December	6.56	6.00	6.07	6.50	-0.43	6.61	7.75	7.69	8.19	8.99	5.57	93.82	. . .	. . .
1978														
January	6.70	6.37	6.44	6.52	-0.08	6.75	7.93	7.96	8.41	9.17	5.71	90.25	. . .	. . .
February	6.78	6.50	6.45	6.29	0.16	6.76	8.00	8.03	8.47	9.20	5.62	88.98	. . .	. . .
March	6.79	6.50	6.29	6.42	-0.13	6.75	8.00	8.04	8.47	9.22	5.61	88.82	. . .	. . .
April	6.89	6.50	6.29	6.58	-0.29	6.82	8.00	8.15	8.56	9.32	5.79	92.71	. . .	. . .
May	7.36	6.84	6.41	6.66	-0.25	7.06	8.27	8.35	8.69	9.49	6.03	97.41	. . .	. . .
June	7.60	7.00	6.73	6.63	0.10	7.59	8.63	8.46	8.76	9.60	6.22	97.66	. . .	. . .
July	7.81	7.23	7.01	6.59	0.42	7.85	9.00	8.64	8.88	9.60	6.28	97.19	. . .	. . .
August	8.04	7.43	7.08	6.64	0.44	7.83	9.01	8.41	8.69	9.48	6.12	103.92	. . .	. . .
September	8.45	7.83	7.85	6.80	1.05	8.39	9.41	8.42	8.69	9.42	6.09	103.86	. . .	. . .
October	8.96	8.26	7.99	7.06	0.93	8.98	9.94	8.64	8.89	9.59	6.13	100.58	. . .	. . .
November	9.76	9.50	8.64	7.08	1.56	10.14	10.94	8.81	9.03	9.83	6.19	94.71	. . .	. . .
December	10.03	9.50	9.08	6.93	2.15	10.37	11.55	9.01	9.16	9.94	6.50	96.11	. . .	. . .
1979														
January	10.07	9.50	9.35	6.82	2.53	10.25	11.75	9.10	9.25	10.13	6.46	99.71	. . .	. . .
February	10.06	9.50	9.32	6.74	2.58	9.95	11.75	9.10	9.26	10.08	6.31	98.23	. . .	. . .
March	10.09	9.50	9.48	6.77	2.71	9.90	11.75	9.12	9.37	10.26	6.33	100.11	. . .	. . .
April	10.01	9.50	9.46	7.06	2.40	9.85	11.75	9.18	9.38	10.33	6.28	102.07	. . .	. . .
May	10.24	9.50	9.61	7.35	2.26	9.95	11.75	9.25	9.50	10.47	6.25	99.73	. . .	. . .
June	10.29	9.50	9.06	7.35	1.71	9.76	11.65	8.91	9.29	10.38	6.12	101.73	. . .	. . .
July	10.47	9.69	9.24	7.25	1.99	9.87	11.54	8.95	9.20	10.29	6.13	102.71	. . .	. . .
August	10.94	10.24	9.52	7.39	2.13	10.42	11.91	9.03	9.23	10.35	6.20	107.36	. . .	. . .
September	11.43	10.70	10.26	7.50	2.76	11.63	12.90	9.33	9.44	10.54	6.52	108.60	. . .	. . .
October	13.77	11.77	11.70	7.49	4.21	13.23	14.39	10.30	10.13	11.40	7.08	104.47	. . .	. . .
November	13.18	12.00	11.79	7.60	4.19	13.57	15.55	10.65	10.76	11.99	7.30	103.66	. . .	. . .
December	13.78	12.00	12.04	7.95	4.09	13.24	15.30	10.39	10.74	12.06	7.22	107.78	. . .	. . .
1980														
January	13.82	12.00	12.00	8.21	3.79	13.04	15.25	10.80	11.09	12.42	7.35	110.87	. . .	. . .
February	14.13	12.52	12.86	8.94	3.92	13.78	15.63	12.41	12.38	13.57	8.16	115.34	. . .	. . .
March	17.19	13.00	15.20	9.31	5.89	16.81	18.31	12.75	12.96	14.45	9.16	104.69	. . .	. . .
April	17.61	13.00	13.20	8.88	4.32	15.78	19.77	11.47	12.04	14.19	8.63	102.97	. . .	. . .
May	10.98	12.94	8.58	8.81	-0.23	9.49	16.57	10.18	10.99	13.17	7.59	107.69	. . .	. . .
June	9.47	11.40	7.07	8.92	-1.85	8.27	12.63	9.78	10.58	12.71	7.63	114.55	. . .	. . .
July	9.03	10.87	8.06	9.14	-1.08	8.41	11.48	10.25	11.07	12.65	8.13	119.83	. . .	. . .
August	9.61	10.00	9.13	9.20	-0.07	9.57	11.12	11.10	11.64	13.15	8.67	123.50	. . .	. . .
September	10.87	10.17	10.27	9.48	0.79	10.97	12.23	11.51	12.02	13.70	8.94	126.51	. . .	. . .
October	12.81	11.00	11.62	9.58	2.04	12.52	13.79	11.75	12.31	14.23	9.11	130.22	. . .	. . .
November	15.85	11.47	13.73	9.74	3.99	15.18	16.06	12.68	12.97	14.64	9.56	135.65	. . .	. . .
December	18.90	12.87	15.49	9.62	5.87	18.07	20.35	12.84	13.21	15.14	10.20	133.48	. . .	. . .
1981														
January	19.08	13.00	15.02	9.75	5.27	16.58	20.16	12.57	12.81	15.03	9.66	132.97	. . .	. . .
February	15.93	13.00	14.79	9.46	5.33	15.49	19.43	13.19	13.35	15.37	10.09	128.40	. . .	. . .
March	14.70	13.00	13.36	9.06	4.30	13.94	18.05	13.12	13.33	15.34	10.16	133.19	. . .	. . .
April	15.72	13.00	13.69	9.18	4.51	14.56	17.15	13.68	13.88	15.56	10.62	134.43	. . .	. . .
May	18.52	13.87	16.30	9.06	7.24	17.56	19.61	14.10	14.32	15.95	10.77	131.73	. . .	. . .
June	19.10	14.00	14.73	8.88	5.85	16.32	20.03	13.47	13.75	15.80	10.67	132.28	. . .	. . .
July	19.04	14.00	14.95	8.77	6.18	17.00	20.39	14.28	14.38	16.17	11.14	129.13	. . .	. . .
August	17.82	14.00	15.51	8.71	6.80	17.23	20.50	14.94	14.89	16.34	12.26	129.63	. . .	. . .
September	15.87	14.00	14.70	8.40	6.30	16.09	20.08	15.32	15.49	16.92	12.92	118.27	. . .	. . .
October	15.08	14.00	13.54	8.16	5.38	14.85	18.45	15.15	15.40	17.11	12.83	119.80	. . .	. . .
November	13.31	13.03	10.86	7.93	2.93	12.16	16.84	13.39	14.22	16.39	11.89	122.92	. . .	. . .
December	12.37	12.10	10.85	7.68	3.17	12.12	15.75	13.72	14.23	16.55	12.91	123.79	. . .	. . .

[1]Federal Reserve Bank of New York. Through 2002, represents the rate for adjustment credit. Beginning in 2003, represents the rate for primary credit. See notes and definitions for more information.
[2]Prior to September 1997, this series represents both nonfinancial and financial commercial paper rates. Beginning September 1997, rates for financial companies only are shown. See notes and definitions for more information.
. . . = Not available.

Table 12-9B. Summary Interest Rates, Bond Yields, and Stock Prices: Historical Data—Continued

(Percent per annum, except as noted.)

Year and month	Federal funds interest rate	Federal Reserve discount rate[1]	U.S. Treasury bills, secondary market, 3-month	Inflation: percent change from year earlier in PCE chain-type price index excluding food and energy	Real 3-month Treasury bill rate	Commercial paper, 3-month[2]	Bank prime rate	Treasury 10-year nominal yields	Bond yields Domestic corporate (Moody's) Aaa	Bond yields Domestic corporate (Moody's) Baa	State and local bonds (Bond Buyer)	Standard and Poor's composite (500 stocks) Index, 1941-1943 = 10	Dividend-price ratio	Earnings-price ratio
1982														
January	13.22	12.00	12.28	7.40	4.88	13.09	15.75	14.59	15.18	17.10	13.28	117.28	...	...
February	14.78	12.00	13.48	7.02	6.46	14.53	16.56	14.43	15.27	17.18	12.97	114.50	...	...
March	14.68	12.00	12.68	6.89	5.79	13.80	16.50	13.86	14.58	16.82	12.82	110.84	...	...
April	14.94	12.00	12.70	6.64	6.06	14.06	16.50	13.87	14.46	16.78	12.58	116.31	...	...
May	14.45	12.00	12.09	6.49	5.60	13.42	16.50	13.62	14.26	16.64	11.95	116.35	...	...
June	14.15	12.00	12.47	6.49	5.98	13.96	16.50	14.30	14.81	16.92	12.44	109.70	...	...
July	12.59	11.81	11.35	6.54	4.81	12.94	16.26	13.95	14.61	16.80	12.28	109.38	...	...
August	10.12	10.68	8.68	6.32	2.36	10.15	14.39	13.06	13.71	16.32	11.23	109.65	...	...
September ...	10.31	10.00	7.92	6.02	1.90	10.36	13.50	12.34	12.94	15.63	10.66	122.43	...	...
October	9.71	9.68	7.71	6.07	1.64	9.20	12.52	10.91	12.12	14.73	9.68	132.66	...	...
November	9.20	9.35	8.07	5.85	2.22	8.69	11.85	10.55	11.68	14.30	10.06	138.10	...	...
December	8.95	8.73	7.94	5.82	2.12	8.51	11.50	10.54	11.83	14.14	9.96	139.37	...	...
1983														
January	8.68	8.50	7.86	5.93	1.93	8.17	11.16	10.46	11.79	13.94	9.50	144.27	...	...
February	8.51	8.50	8.11	5.93	2.18	8.34	10.98	10.72	12.01	13.95	9.58	146.80	...	...
March	8.77	8.50	8.35	5.61	2.74	8.52	10.50	10.51	11.73	13.61	9.20	151.88	...	...
April	8.80	8.50	8.21	5.52	2.69	8.53	10.50	10.40	11.51	13.29	9.04	157.71	...	...
May	8.63	8.50	8.19	5.11	3.08	8.33	10.50	10.38	11.46	13.09	9.11	164.10	...	...
June	8.98	8.50	8.79	5.07	3.72	9.00	10.50	10.85	11.74	13.37	9.52	166.39	...	...
July	9.37	8.50	9.08	5.11	3.97	9.25	10.50	11.38	12.15	13.39	9.53	166.96	...	...
August	9.56	8.50	9.34	5.16	4.18	9.54	10.89	11.85	12.51	13.64	9.72	162.42	...	...
September ...	9.45	8.50	9.00	5.20	3.80	9.24	11.00	11.65	12.37	13.55	9.58	167.16	...	...
October	9.48	8.50	8.64	4.73	3.91	8.99	11.00	11.54	12.25	13.46	9.66	167.65	...	...
November	9.34	8.50	8.76	4.58	4.18	9.10	11.00	11.69	12.41	13.61	9.74	165.23	...	...
December	9.47	8.50	9.00	4.31	4.69	9.53	11.00	11.83	12.57	13.75	9.89	164.36	...	...
1984														
January	9.56	8.50	8.90	3.91	4.99	9.20	11.00	11.67	12.20	13.65	9.63	166.39	...	...
February	9.59	8.50	9.09	4.17	4.92	9.32	11.00	11.84	12.08	13.59	9.64	157.25	...	...
March	9.91	8.50	9.52	4.42	5.10	9.83	11.21	12.32	12.57	13.99	9.94	157.44	...	...
April	10.29	8.87	9.69	4.60	5.09	10.18	11.93	12.63	12.81	14.31	9.96	157.60	...	...
May	10.32	9.00	9.83	4.69	5.14	10.65	12.39	13.41	13.28	14.74	10.49	156.55	...	...
June	11.06	9.00	9.87	4.45	5.42	10.98	12.60	13.56	13.55	15.05	10.67	153.12	...	...
July	11.23	9.00	10.12	4.19	5.93	11.19	13.00	13.36	13.44	15.15	10.42	151.08	...	...
August	11.64	9.00	10.47	4.00	6.47	11.18	13.00	12.72	12.87	14.63	9.99	164.42	...	...
September ...	11.30	9.00	10.37	3.75	6.62	11.04	12.97	12.52	12.66	14.35	10.10	166.11	...	...
October	9.99	9.00	9.74	3.79	5.95	10.12	12.58	12.16	12.63	13.94	10.25	164.82	...	...
November	9.43	8.83	8.61	3.77	4.84	9.03	11.77	11.57	12.29	13.48	10.17	166.27	...	...
December	8.38	8.37	8.06	4.11	3.95	8.44	11.06	11.50	12.13	13.40	9.95	164.48	...	...
1985														
January	8.35	8.00	7.76	4.26	3.50	8.03	10.61	11.38	12.08	13.26	9.51	171.61	...	...
February	8.50	8.00	8.27	4.07	4.20	8.54	10.50	11.51	12.13	13.23	9.65	180.88	...	...
March	8.58	8.00	8.52	4.01	4.51	8.90	10.50	11.86	12.56	13.69	9.77	179.42	...	...
April	8.27	8.00	7.95	3.66	4.29	8.37	10.50	11.43	12.23	13.51	9.42	180.62	...	...
May	7.97	7.81	7.48	3.74	3.74	7.83	10.31	10.85	11.72	13.15	9.01	184.90	...	...
June	7.53	7.50	6.95	3.75	3.20	7.35	9.78	10.16	10.94	12.40	8.69	188.89	...	...
July	7.88	7.50	7.08	3.51	3.57	7.56	9.50	10.31	10.97	12.43	8.81	192.54	...	...
August	7.90	7.50	7.14	3.63	3.51	7.72	9.50	10.33	11.05	12.50	9.08	188.31	...	...
September ...	7.92	7.50	7.10	3.71	3.39	7.83	9.50	10.37	11.07	12.48	9.27	184.06	...	...
October	7.99	7.50	7.16	3.71	3.45	7.80	9.50	10.24	11.02	12.36	9.08	186.18	...	...
November	8.05	7.50	7.24	3.80	3.44	7.77	9.50	9.78	10.55	11.99	8.54	197.45	...	...
December	8.27	7.50	7.10	3.68	3.42	7.75	9.50	9.26	10.16	11.58	8.42	207.26	...	...
1986														
January	8.14	7.50	7.07	3.72	3.35	7.71	9.50	9.19	10.05	11.44	8.08	208.19	...	...
February	7.86	7.50	7.06	3.54	3.52	7.63	9.50	8.70	9.67	11.11	7.44	219.37	...	...
March	7.48	7.10	6.56	3.57	2.99	7.20	9.10	7.78	9.00	10.50	7.08	232.33	...	...
April	6.99	6.83	6.06	3.70	2.36	6.60	8.83	7.30	8.79	10.19	7.19	237.98	...	...
May	6.85	6.50	6.15	3.64	2.51	6.62	8.50	7.71	9.09	10.29	7.54	238.46	...	...
June	6.92	6.50	6.21	3.79	2.42	6.71	8.50	7.80	9.13	10.34	7.87	245.30	...	...
July	6.56	6.16	5.83	3.88	1.95	6.33	8.16	7.30	8.88	10.16	7.51	240.18	...	...
August	6.17	5.82	5.53	3.70	1.83	5.92	7.90	7.17	8.72	10.18	7.21	245.00	...	...
September ...	5.89	5.50	5.21	3.85	1.36	5.68	7.50	7.45	8.89	10.20	7.11	238.27	...	...
October	5.85	5.50	5.18	3.98	1.20	5.68	7.50	7.43	8.86	10.24	7.08	237.36	...	...
November	6.04	5.50	5.35	3.95	1.40	5.76	7.50	7.25	8.68	10.07	6.84	245.09	...	...
December	6.91	5.50	5.53	3.90	1.63	6.10	7.50	7.11	8.49	9.97	6.87	248.61	...	...

[1]Federal Reserve Bank of New York. Through 2002, represents the rate for adjustment credit. Beginning in 2003, represents the rate for primary credit. See notes and definitions for more information.
[2]Prior to September 1997, this series represents both nonfinancial and financial commercial paper rates. Beginning September 1997, rates for financial companies only are shown. See notes and definitions for more information.
. . . = Not available.

Table 12-9B. Summary Interest Rates, Bond Yields, and Stock Prices: Historical Data—*Continued*

(Percent per annum, except as noted.)

Year and month	Federal funds interest rate	Federal Reserve discount rate[1]	U.S. Treasury bills, secondary market, 3-month	Inflation: percent change from year earlier in PCE chain-type price index excluding food and energy	Real 3-month Treasury bill rate	Commercial paper, 3-month[2]	Bank prime rate	Treasury 10-year nominal yields	Bond yields Domestic corporate (Moody's) Aaa	Bond yields Domestic corporate (Moody's) Baa	State and local bonds (Bond Buyer)	Standard and Poor's composite (500 stocks) Index, 1941-1943 = 10	Standard and Poor's composite (500 stocks) Dividend-price ratio	Standard and Poor's composite (500 stocks) Earnings-price ratio
1987														
January	6.43	5.50	5.43	3.83	1.60	5.84	7.50	7.08	8.36	9.72	6.66	264.51	. . .	. . .
February	6.10	5.50	5.59	3.79	1.80	6.05	7.50	7.25	8.38	9.65	6.61	280.93	. . .	. . .
March	6.13	5.50	5.59	3.70	1.89	6.16	7.50	7.25	8.36	9.61	6.65	292.47	. . .	. . .
April	6.37	5.50	5.64	3.79	1.85	6.45	7.75	8.02	8.85	10.04	7.55	289.32	. . .	. . .
May	6.85	5.50	5.66	3.78	1.88	6.93	8.14	8.61	9.33	10.51	8.00	289.12	. . .	. . .
June	6.73	5.50	5.67	3.69	1.98	6.92	8.25	8.40	9.32	10.52	7.79	301.38	. . .	. . .
July	6.58	5.50	5.69	3.74	1.95	6.65	8.25	8.45	9.42	10.61	7.72	310.09	. . .	. . .
August	6.73	5.50	6.04	3.84	2.20	6.71	8.25	8.76	9.67	10.80	7.82	329.36	. . .	. . .
September ...	7.22	5.95	6.40	3.87	2.53	7.37	8.70	9.42	10.18	11.31	8.26	318.66	. . .	. . .
October	7.29	6.00	6.13	3.91	2.22	7.89	9.07	9.52	10.52	11.62	8.70	280.16	. . .	. . .
November	6.69	6.00	5.69	3.84	1.85	7.17	8.78	8.86	10.01	11.23	7.95	245.01	. . .	. . .
December	6.77	6.00	5.77	3.85	1.92	7.61	8.75	8.99	10.11	11.29	7.96	240.96	. . .	. . .
1988														
January	6.83	6.00	5.81	3.93	1.88	6.87	8.75	8.67	9.88	11.07	7.69	250.48	. . .	. . .
February	6.58	6.00	5.66	3.93	1.73	6.58	8.51	8.21	9.40	10.62	7.49	258.13	. . .	. . .
March	6.58	6.00	5.70	4.09	1.61	6.62	8.50	8.37	9.39	10.57	7.74	265.74	. . .	. . .
April	6.87	6.00	5.91	4.22	1.69	6.86	8.50	8.72	9.67	10.90	7.81	262.61	. . .	. . .
May	7.09	6.00	6.26	4.31	1.95	7.19	8.84	9.09	9.90	11.04	7.91	256.12	. . .	. . .
June	7.51	6.00	6.46	4.44	2.02	7.49	9.00	8.92	9.86	11.00	7.78	270.68	. . .	. . .
July	7.75	6.00	6.73	4.54	2.19	7.82	9.29	9.06	9.96	11.11	7.76	269.05	. . .	. . .
August	8.01	6.37	7.06	4.40	2.66	8.26	9.84	9.26	10.11	11.21	7.79	263.73	. . .	. . .
September ...	8.19	6.50	7.24	4.52	2.72	8.17	10.00	8.98	9.82	10.90	7.66	267.97	. . .	. . .
October	8.30	6.50	7.35	4.46	2.89	8.24	10.00	8.80	9.51	10.41	7.46	277.40	. . .	. . .
November	8.35	6.50	7.76	4.52	3.24	8.66	10.05	8.96	9.45	10.48	7.46	271.02	. . .	. . .
December	8.76	6.50	8.07	4.64	3.43	9.11	10.50	9.11	9.57	10.65	7.61	276.51	. . .	. . .
1989														
January	9.12	6.50	8.27	4.67	3.60	9.04	10.50	9.09	9.62	10.65	7.35	285.41	. . .	. . .
February	9.36	6.59	8.53	4.72	3.81	9.37	10.93	9.17	9.64	10.61	7.44	294.01	. . .	. . .
March	9.85	7.00	8.82	4.59	4.23	9.95	11.50	9.36	9.80	10.67	7.59	292.71	. . .	. . .
April	9.84	7.00	8.65	4.43	4.22	9.81	11.50	9.18	9.79	10.61	7.49	302.25	. . .	. . .
May	9.81	7.00	8.43	4.37	4.06	9.47	11.50	8.86	9.57	10.46	7.25	313.93	. . .	. . .
June	9.53	7.00	8.15	4.18	3.97	9.11	11.07	8.28	9.10	10.03	7.02	323.73	. . .	. . .
July	9.24	7.00	7.88	3.99	3.89	8.68	10.98	8.02	8.93	9.87	6.96	331.93	. . .	. . .
August	8.99	7.00	7.90	3.86	4.04	8.57	10.50	8.11	8.96	9.88	7.06	346.61	. . .	. . .
September ...	9.02	7.00	7.75	3.69	4.06	8.70	10.50	8.19	9.01	9.91	7.26	347.33	. . .	. . .
October	8.84	7.00	7.64	3.71	3.93	8.53	10.50	8.01	8.92	9.81	7.22	347.40	. . .	. . .
November	8.55	7.00	7.69	3.72	3.97	8.35	10.50	7.87	8.89	9.81	7.14	340.22	. . .	. . .
December	8.45	7.00	7.63	3.67	3.96	8.29	10.50	7.84	8.86	9.82	6.98	348.57	. . .	. . .
1990														
January	8.23	7.00	7.64	3.52	4.12	8.10	10.11	8.21	8.99	9.94	7.10	339.97	. . .	. . .
February	8.24	7.00	7.74	3.77	3.97	8.14	10.00	8.47	9.22	10.14	7.22	330.45	. . .	. . .
March	8.28	7.00	7.90	4.03	3.87	8.28	10.00	8.59	9.37	10.21	7.29	338.47	. . .	. . .
April	8.26	7.00	7.77	4.10	3.67	8.30	10.00	8.79	9.46	10.30	7.39	338.18	. . .	. . .
May	8.18	7.00	7.74	4.20	3.54	8.25	10.00	8.76	9.47	10.41	7.35	350.25	. . .	. . .
June	8.29	7.00	7.73	4.38	3.35	8.14	10.00	8.48	9.26	10.22	7.24	360.39	. . .	. . .
July	8.15	7.00	7.62	4.38	3.24	7.99	10.00	8.47	9.24	10.20	7.19	360.03	. . .	. . .
August	8.13	7.00	7.45	4.67	2.78	7.88	10.00	8.75	9.41	10.41	7.32	330.75	. . .	. . .
September ...	8.20	7.00	7.36	4.66	2.70	7.96	10.00	8.89	9.56	10.64	7.43	315.41	. . .	. . .
October	8.11	7.00	7.17	4.63	2.54	7.98	10.00	8.72	9.53	10.74	7.49	307.12	. . .	. . .
November	7.81	7.00	7.06	4.49	2.57	7.91	10.00	8.39	9.30	10.62	7.18	315.29	. . .	. . .
December	7.31	6.79	6.74	4.36	2.38	7.80	10.00	8.08	9.05	10.43	7.09	328.75	. . .	. . .
1991														
January	6.91	6.50	6.22	4.52	1.70	7.10	9.52	8.09	9.04	10.45	7.08	325.49	. . .	. . .
February	6.25	6.00	5.94	4.31	1.63	6.49	9.05	7.85	8.83	10.07	6.91	362.26	. . .	. . .
March	6.12	6.00	5.91	3.99	1.92	6.41	9.00	8.11	8.93	10.09	7.10	372.28	. . .	. . .
April	5.91	5.98	5.65	3.81	1.84	6.07	9.00	8.04	8.86	9.94	7.02	379.68	. . .	. . .
May	5.78	5.50	5.46	3.85	1.61	5.92	8.50	8.07	8.86	9.86	6.95	377.99	. . .	. . .
June	5.90	5.50	5.57	3.68	1.89	6.11	8.50	8.28	9.01	9.96	7.13	378.29	. . .	. . .
July	5.82	5.50	5.58	3.79	1.79	6.05	8.50	8.27	9.00	9.89	7.05	380.23	. . .	. . .
August	5.66	5.50	5.33	3.69	1.64	5.72	8.50	7.90	8.75	9.65	6.90	389.40	. . .	. . .
September ...	5.45	5.20	5.22	3.78	1.44	5.57	8.20	7.65	8.61	9.51	6.80	387.20	. . .	. . .
October	5.21	5.00	4.99	3.67	1.32	5.35	8.00	7.53	8.55	9.49	6.68	386.88	. . .	. . .
November	4.81	4.58	4.56	3.76	0.80	4.98	7.58	7.42	8.48	9.45	6.73	385.92	. . .	. . .
December	4.43	4.11	4.07	3.89	0.18	4.61	7.21	7.09	8.31	9.26	6.69	388.51	. . .	. . .

[1]Federal Reserve Bank of New York. Through 2002, represents the rate for adjustment credit. Beginning in 2003, represents the rate for primary credit. See notes and definitions for more information.
[2]Prior to September 1997, this series represents both nonfinancial and financial commercial paper rates. Beginning September 1997, rates for financial companies only are shown. See notes and definitions for more information.
. . . = Not available.

Table 12-9B. Summary Interest Rates, Bond Yields, and Stock Prices: Historical Data—*Continued*

(Percent per annum, except as noted.)

Year and month	Federal funds interest rate	Federal Reserve discount rate[1]	U.S. Treasury bills, secondary market, 3-month	Inflation: percent change from year earlier in PCE chain-type price index excluding food and energy	Real 3-month Treasury bill rate	Commercial paper, 3-month [2]	Bank prime rate	Treasury 10-year nominal yields	Bond yields Domestic corporate (Moody's) Aaa	Baa	State and local bonds (Bond Buyer)	Standard and Poor's composite (500 stocks) Index, 1941-1943 = 10	Dividend-price ratio	Earnings-price ratio
1992														
January	4.03	3.50	3.80	3.69	0.11	4.07	6.50	7.03	8.20	9.13	6.54	416.08	. . .	. . .
February	4.06	3.50	3.84	3.69	0.15	4.11	6.50	7.34	8.29	9.23	6.74	412.56	. . .	. . .
March	3.98	3.50	4.04	3.72	0.32	4.30	6.50	7.54	8.35	9.25	6.76	407.36	. . .	. . .
April	3.73	3.50	3.75	3.84	-0.09	4.04	6.50	7.48	8.33	9.21	6.67	407.41	. . .	. . .
May	3.82	3.50	3.63	3.56	0.07	3.88	6.50	7.39	8.28	9.13	6.57	414.81	. . .	. . .
June	3.76	3.50	3.66	3.39	0.27	3.92	6.50	7.26	8.22	9.05	6.49	408.27	. . .	. . .
July	3.25	3.02	3.21	3.45	-0.24	3.44	6.02	6.84	8.07	8.84	6.13	415.05	. . .	. . .
August	3.30	3.00	3.13	3.23	-0.10	3.38	6.00	6.59	7.95	8.65	6.16	417.93	. . .	. . .
September ...	3.22	3.00	2.91	2.94	-0.03	3.24	6.00	6.42	7.92	8.62	6.25	418.48	. . .	. . .
October	3.10	3.00	2.86	3.06	-0.20	3.33	6.00	6.59	7.99	8.84	6.41	412.50	. . .	. . .
November	3.09	3.00	3.13	3.00	0.13	3.66	6.00	6.87	8.10	8.96	6.36	422.84	. . .	. . .
December	2.92	3.00	3.22	2.84	0.38	3.67	6.00	6.77	7.98	8.81	6.22	435.64	. . .	. . .
1993														
January	3.02	3.00	3.00	2.72	0.28	3.25	6.00	6.60	7.91	8.67	6.16	435.23	. . .	. . .
February	3.03	3.00	2.93	2.54	0.39	3.18	6.00	6.26	7.71	8.39	5.87	441.70	. . .	. . .
March	3.07	3.00	2.95	2.44	0.51	3.17	6.00	5.98	7.58	8.15	5.64	450.16	. . .	. . .
April	2.96	3.00	2.87	2.37	0.50	3.14	6.00	5.97	7.46	8.14	5.76	443.08	. . .	. . .
May	3.00	3.00	2.96	2.52	0.44	3.14	6.00	6.04	7.43	8.21	5.73	445.25	. . .	. . .
June	3.04	3.00	3.07	2.49	0.58	3.25	6.00	5.96	7.33	8.07	5.63	448.06	. . .	. . .
July	3.06	3.00	3.04	2.26	0.78	3.20	6.00	5.81	7.17	7.93	5.57	447.29	. . .	. . .
August	3.03	3.00	3.02	2.33	0.69	3.18	6.00	5.68	6.85	7.60	5.45	454.13	. . .	. . .
September ...	3.09	3.00	2.95	2.32	0.63	3.16	6.00	5.36	6.66	7.34	5.29	459.24	. . .	. . .
October	2.99	3.00	3.02	2.11	0.91	3.26	6.00	5.33	6.67	7.31	5.25	463.90	. . .	. . .
November	3.02	3.00	3.10	2.20	0.90	3.40	6.00	5.72	6.93	7.66	5.47	462.89	. . .	. . .
December	2.96	3.00	3.06	2.11	0.95	3.36	6.00	5.77	6.93	7.69	5.35	465.95	. . .	. . .
1994														
January	3.05	3.00	2.98	1.98	1.00	3.19	6.00	5.75	6.92	7.65	5.31	472.99	. . .	. . .
February	3.25	3.00	3.25	2.06	1.19	3.49	6.00	5.97	7.08	7.76	5.40	471.58	. . .	. . .
March	3.34	3.00	3.50	2.21	1.29	3.85	6.06	6.48	7.48	8.13	5.91	463.81	. . .	. . .
April	3.56	3.00	3.68	2.07	1.61	4.05	6.45	6.97	7.88	8.52	6.23	447.23	. . .	. . .
May	4.01	3.24	4.14	2.00	2.14	4.57	6.99	7.18	7.99	8.62	6.19	450.90	. . .	. . .
June	4.25	3.50	4.14	2.20	1.94	4.57	7.25	7.10	7.97	8.65	6.11	454.83	. . .	. . .
July	4.26	3.50	4.33	2.30	2.03	4.75	7.25	7.30	8.11	8.80	6.23	451.40	. . .	. . .
August	4.47	3.76	4.48	2.29	2.19	4.84	7.51	7.24	8.07	8.74	6.21	464.24	. . .	. . .
September ...	4.73	4.00	4.62	2.33	2.29	5.02	7.75	7.46	8.34	8.98	6.28	466.96	. . .	. . .
October	4.76	4.00	4.95	2.40	2.55	5.51	7.75	7.74	8.57	9.20	6.52	463.81	. . .	. . .
November	5.29	4.40	5.29	2.33	2.96	5.81	8.15	7.96	8.68	9.32	6.97	461.01	. . .	. . .
December	5.45	4.75	5.60	2.32	3.28	6.26	8.50	7.81	8.46	9.10	6.80	455.19	. . .	. . .
1995														
January	5.53	4.75	5.71	2.49	3.22	6.22	8.50	7.78	8.46	9.08	6.53	465.25	. . .	. . .
February	5.92	5.25	5.77	2.45	3.32	6.15	9.00	7.47	8.26	8.85	6.22	481.92	. . .	. . .
March	5.98	5.25	5.73	2.37	3.36	6.15	9.00	7.20	8.12	8.70	6.10	493.15	. . .	. . .
April	6.05	5.25	5.65	2.48	3.17	6.12	9.00	7.06	8.03	8.60	6.02	507.91	. . .	. . .
May	6.01	5.25	5.67	2.43	3.24	6.06	9.00	6.63	7.65	8.20	5.95	523.81	. . .	. . .
June	6.00	5.25	5.47	2.26	3.21	5.94	9.00	6.17	7.30	7.90	5.84	539.35	. . .	. . .
July	5.85	5.25	5.42	2.15	3.27	5.79	8.80	6.28	7.41	8.04	5.92	557.37	. . .	. . .
August	5.74	5.25	5.40	2.25	3.15	5.82	8.75	6.49	7.57	8.19	6.06	559.11	. . .	. . .
September ...	5.80	5.25	5.28	2.21	3.07	5.74	8.75	6.20	7.32	7.93	5.91	578.77	. . .	. . .
October	5.76	5.25	5.28	2.23	3.05	5.82	8.75	6.04	7.12	7.75	5.80	582.92	. . .	. . .
November	5.80	5.25	5.36	2.11	3.25	5.74	8.75	5.93	7.02	7.68	5.64	595.53	. . .	. . .
December	5.60	5.25	5.14	2.21	2.93	5.64	8.65	5.71	6.82	7.49	5.45	614.57	. . .	. . .
1996														
January	5.56	5.24	5.00	2.06	2.94	5.40	8.50	5.65	6.81	7.47	5.43	614.42	. . .	. . .
February	5.22	5.00	4.83	2.02	2.81	5.15	8.25	5.81	6.99	7.63	5.43	649.54	. . .	. . .
March	5.31	5.00	4.96	1.99	2.97	5.31	8.25	6.27	7.35	8.03	5.79	647.07	. . .	. . .
April	5.22	5.00	4.95	1.88	3.07	5.39	8.25	6.51	7.50	8.19	5.94	647.17	. . .	. . .
May	5.24	5.00	5.02	1.88	3.14	5.39	8.25	6.74	7.62	8.30	5.98	661.23	. . .	. . .
June	5.27	5.00	5.09	1.88	3.21	5.49	8.25	6.91	7.71	8.40	6.02	668.50	. . .	. . .
July	5.40	5.00	5.15	1.92	3.23	5.53	8.25	6.87	7.65	8.35	5.92	644.07	. . .	. . .
August	5.22	5.00	5.05	1.78	3.27	5.42	8.25	6.64	7.46	8.18	5.76	662.68	. . .	. . .
September ...	5.30	5.00	5.09	1.95	3.14	5.52	8.25	6.83	7.66	8.35	5.87	674.88	. . .	. . .
October	5.24	5.00	4.99	1.95	3.04	5.43	8.25	6.53	7.39	8.07	5.72	701.45	. . .	. . .
November	5.31	5.00	5.03	2.03	3.00	5.41	8.25	6.20	7.10	7.79	5.59	735.67	. . .	. . .
December	5.29	5.00	4.91	1.94	2.97	5.51	8.25	6.30	7.20	7.89	5.64	743.25	. . .	. . .

[1]Federal Reserve Bank of New York. Through 2002, represents the rate for adjustment credit. Beginning in 2003, represents the rate for primary credit. See notes and definitions for more information.
[2]Prior to September 1997, this series represents both nonfinancial and financial commercial paper rates. Beginning September 1997, rates for financial companies only are shown. See notes and definitions for more information.
. . . = Not available.

Table 12-9B. Summary Interest Rates, Bond Yields, and Stock Prices: Historical Data—*Continued*

(Percent per annum, except as noted.)

Year and month	Federal funds interest rate	Federal Reserve discount rate[1]	U.S. Treasury bills, secondary market, 3-month	Inflation: percent change from year earlier in PCE chain-type price index excluding food and energy	Real 3-month Treasury bill rate	Commercial paper, 3-month[2]	Bank prime rate	Treasury 10-year nominal yields	Bond yields Domestic corporate (Moody's) Aaa	Bond yields Domestic corporate (Moody's) Baa	State and local bonds (Bond Buyer)	Standard and Poor's composite (500 stocks) Index, 1941-1943 = 10	Dividend-price ratio	Earnings-price ratio
1997														
January	5.25	5.00	5.03	1.95	3.08	5.32	8.25	6.58	7.42	8.09	5.72	766.22	. . .	. . .
February	5.19	5.00	5.01	2.05	2.96	5.28	8.25	6.42	7.31	7.94	5.63	798.39	. . .	. . .
March	5.39	5.00	5.14	2.08	3.06	5.42	8.30	6.69	7.55	8.18	5.76	792.16	. . .	. . .
April	5.51	5.00	5.16	2.15	3.01	5.60	8.50	6.89	7.73	8.34	5.88	763.93	. . .	. . .
May	5.50	5.00	5.05	2.07	2.98	5.60	8.50	6.71	7.58	8.20	5.70	833.09	. . .	. . .
June	5.56	5.00	4.93	2.13	2.80	5.56	8.50	6.49	7.41	8.02	5.53	876.29	. . .	. . .
July	5.52	5.00	5.05	1.99	3.06	5.51	8.50	6.22	7.14	7.75	5.35	925.29	. . .	. . .
August	5.54	5.00	5.14	1.86	3.28	5.50	8.50	6.30	7.22	7.82	5.41	927.74	. . .	. . .
September ...	5.54	5.00	4.95	1.77	3.18	5.51	8.50	6.21	7.15	7.70	5.39	937.02	. . .	. . .
October	5.50	5.00	4.97	1.71	3.26	5.55	8.50	6.03	7.00	7.57	5.38	951.16	. . .	. . .
November	5.52	5.00	5.14	1.62	3.52	5.64	8.50	5.88	6.87	7.42	5.33	938.92	. . .	. . .
December	5.50	5.00	5.16	1.64	3.52	5.70	8.50	5.81	6.76	7.32	5.19	962.37	. . .	. . .
1998														
January	5.56	5.00	5.04	1.65	3.39	5.44	8.50	5.54	6.61	7.19	5.06	963.36	. . .	. . .
February	5.51	5.00	5.09	1.51	3.58	5.45	8.50	5.57	6.67	7.25	5.10	1 023.74	. . .	. . .
March	5.49	5.00	5.03	1.38	3.65	5.49	8.50	5.65	6.72	7.32	5.21	1 076.83	. . .	. . .
April	5.45	5.00	4.95	1.40	3.55	5.48	8.50	5.64	6.69	7.33	5.23	1 112.20	. . .	. . .
May	5.49	5.00	5.00	1.44	3.56	5.50	8.50	5.65	6.69	7.30	5.20	1 108.42	. . .	. . .
June	5.56	5.00	4.98	1.18	3.80	5.50	8.50	5.50	6.53	7.13	5.12	1 108.39	. . .	. . .
July	5.54	5.00	4.96	1.39	3.57	5.50	8.50	5.46	6.55	7.15	5.14	1 156.58	. . .	. . .
August	5.55	5.00	4.90	1.62	3.28	5.50	8.50	5.34	6.52	7.14	5.10	1 074.63	. . .	. . .
September ...	5.51	5.00	4.61	1.40	3.21	5.32	8.49	4.81	6.40	7.09	4.99	1 020.64	. . .	. . .
October	5.07	4.86	3.96	1.45	2.51	5.09	8.12	4.53	6.37	7.18	4.93	1 032.47	. . .	. . .
November	4.83	4.63	4.41	1.42	2.99	5.15	7.89	4.83	6.41	7.34	5.03	1 144.43	. . .	. . .
December	4.68	4.50	4.39	1.55	2.84	5.04	7.75	4.65	6.22	7.23	4.98	1 190.05	. . .	. . .
1999														
January	4.63	4.50	4.34	1.59	2.75	4.81	7.75	4.72	6.24	7.29	5.01	1 248.77	. . .	. . .
February	4.76	4.50	4.44	1.52	2.92	4.82	7.75	5.00	6.40	7.39	5.03	1 246.58	. . .	. . .
March	4.81	4.50	4.44	1.44	3.00	4.84	7.75	5.23	6.62	7.53	5.10	1 281.66	. . .	. . .
April	4.74	4.50	4.29	1.47	2.82	4.80	7.75	5.18	6.64	7.48	5.08	1 334.76	. . .	. . .
May	4.74	4.50	4.50	1.43	3.07	4.83	7.75	5.54	6.93	7.72	5.18	1 332.07	. . .	. . .
June	4.76	4.50	4.57	1.59	2.98	5.04	7.75	5.90	7.23	8.02	5.37	1 322.55	. . .	. . .
July	4.99	4.50	4.55	1.49	3.06	5.14	8.00	5.79	7.19	7.95	5.36	1 380.99	. . .	. . .
August	5.07	4.56	4.72	1.31	3.41	5.28	8.06	5.94	7.40	8.15	5.58	1 327.49	. . .	. . .
September ...	5.22	4.75	4.68	1.55	3.13	5.32	8.25	5.92	7.39	8.20	5.69	1 318.17	. . .	. . .
October	5.20	4.75	4.86	1.47	3.39	5.93	8.25	6.11	7.55	8.38	5.92	1 300.01	. . .	. . .
November	5.42	4.86	5.07	1.51	3.56	5.85	8.37	6.03	7.36	8.15	5.86	1 391.00	. . .	. . .
December	5.30	5.00	5.20	1.47	3.73	5.93	8.50	6.28	7.55	8.19	5.95	1 428.68	. . .	. . .
2000														
January	5.45	5.00	5.32	1.55	3.77	5.81	8.50	6.66	7.78	8.33	6.08	1 425.59	. . .	. . .
February	5.73	5.24	5.55	1.71	3.84	5.90	8.73	6.52	7.68	8.29	6.00	1 388.87	. . .	. . .
March	5.85	5.34	5.69	1.88	3.81	6.03	8.83	6.26	7.68	8.37	5.83	1 442.21	. . .	. . .
April	6.02	5.50	5.66	1.67	3.99	6.15	9.00	5.99	7.64	8.40	5.75	1 461.36	. . .	. . .
May	6.27	5.71	5.79	1.67	4.12	6.57	9.24	6.44	7.99	8.90	6.00	1 418.48	. . .	. . .
June	6.53	6.00	5.69	1.67	4.02	6.59	9.50	6.10	7.67	8.48	5.80	1 461.96	. . .	. . .
July	6.54	6.00	5.96	1.69	4.27	6.54	9.50	6.05	7.65	8.35	5.63	1 473.00	. . .	. . .
August	6.50	6.00	6.09	1.76	4.33	6.49	9.50	5.83	7.55	8.26	5.51	1 485.46	. . .	. . .
September ...	6.52	6.00	6.00	1.77	4.23	6.47	9.50	5.80	7.62	8.35	5.56	1 468.05	. . .	. . .
October	6.51	6.00	6.11	1.79	4.32	6.52	9.50	5.74	7.55	8.34	5.59	1 390.14	. . .	. . .
November	6.51	6.00	6.17	1.88	4.29	6.52	9.50	5.72	7.45	8.28	5.54	1 375.04	. . .	. . .
December	6.40	6.00	5.77	1.80	3.97	6.33	9.50	5.24	7.21	8.02	5.22	1 330.93	. . .	. . .
2001														
January	5.98	5.52	5.15	1.86	3.29	5.51	9.05	5.16	7.15	7.93	5.10	1 335.63	. . .	. . .
February	5.49	5.00	4.88	1.85	3.03	5.19	8.50	5.10	7.10	7.87	5.18	1 305.75	. . .	. . .
March	5.31	4.81	4.42	1.74	2.68	4.81	8.32	4.89	6.98	7.84	5.13	1 185.85	. . .	. . .
April	4.80	4.28	3.87	1.87	2.00	4.47	7.80	5.14	7.20	8.07	5.27	1 189.84	. . .	. . .
May	4.21	3.73	3.62	1.82	1.80	3.96	7.24	5.39	7.29	8.07	5.29	1 270.37	. . .	. . .
June	3.97	3.47	3.49	1.99	1.50	3.69	6.98	5.28	7.18	7.97	5.20	1 238.71	. . .	. . .
July	3.77	3.25	3.51	2.02	1.49	3.62	6.75	5.24	7.13	7.97	5.20	1 204.45	. . .	. . .
August	3.65	3.16	3.36	1.96	1.40	3.44	6.67	4.97	7.02	7.85	5.03	1 178.50	. . .	. . .
September ...	3.07	2.77	2.64	1.15	1.49	2.84	6.28	4.73	7.17	8.03	5.09	1 044.64	. . .	. . .
October	2.49	2.02	2.16	1.72	0.44	2.29	5.53	4.57	7.03	7.91	5.05	1 076.59	. . .	. . .
November	2.09	1.58	1.87	1.76	0.11	2.00	5.10	4.65	6.97	7.81	5.04	1 129.68	. . .	. . .
December	1.82	1.33	1.69	1.72	-0.03	1.81	4.84	5.09	6.77	8.05	5.25	1 144.93	. . .	. . .

[1]Federal Reserve Bank of New York. Through 2002, represents the rate for adjustment credit. Beginning in 2003, represents the rate for primary credit. See notes and definitions for more information.
[2]Prior to September 1997, this series represents both nonfinancial and financial commercial paper rates. Beginning September 1997, rates for financial companies only are shown. See notes and definitions for more information.
. . . = Not available.

Table 12-9B. Summary Interest Rates, Bond Yields, and Stock Prices: Historical Data—*Continued*

(Percent per annum, except as noted.)

Year and month	Federal funds interest rate	Federal Reserve discount rate[1]	U.S. Treasury bills, secondary market, 3-month	Inflation: percent change from year earlier in PCE chain-type price index excluding food and energy	Real 3-month Treasury bill rate	Commercial paper, 3-month[2]	Bank prime rate	Treasury 10-year nominal yields	Bond yields Domestic corporate (Moody's) Aaa	Baa	State and local bonds (Bond Buyer)	Standard and Poor's composite (500 stocks) Index, 1941-1943 = 10	Dividend-price ratio	Earnings-price ratio
2002														
January	1.73	1.25	1.65	1.44	0.21	1.72	4.75	5.04	6.55	7.87	5.16	1 140.21	. . .	. . .
February	1.74	1.25	1.73	1.46	0.27	1.80	4.75	4.91	6.51	7.89	5.11	1 100.67	. . .	. . .
March	1.73	1.25	1.79	1.50	0.29	1.87	4.75	5.28	6.81	8.11	5.29	1 153.79	. . .	. . .
April	1.75	1.25	1.72	1.63	0.09	1.83	4.75	5.21	6.76	8.03	5.22	1 112.03	. . .	. . .
May	1.75	1.25	1.73	1.73	0.00	1.80	4.75	5.16	6.75	8.09	5.19	1 079.27	. . .	. . .
June	1.75	1.25	1.70	1.67	0.03	1.78	4.75	4.93	6.63	7.95	5.09	1 014.05	. . .	. . .
July	1.73	1.25	1.68	1.63	0.05	1.76	4.75	4.65	6.53	7.90	5.02	903.59	. . .	. . .
August	1.74	1.25	1.62	1.78	-0.16	1.71	4.75	4.26	6.37	7.58	4.95	912.55	. . .	. . .
September ...	1.75	1.25	1.63	2.51	-0.88	1.74	4.75	3.87	6.15	7.40	4.74	867.81	. . .	. . .
October	1.75	1.25	1.58	1.87	-0.29	1.71	4.75	3.94	6.32	7.73	4.88	854.63	. . .	. . .
November	1.34	0.83	1.23	1.77	-0.54	1.37	4.35	4.05	6.31	7.62	4.95	909.93	. . .	. . .
December	1.24	0.75	1.19	1.80	-0.61	1.32	4.25	4.03	6.21	7.45	4.85	899.18	. . .	. . .
2003														
January	1.24	. . .	1.17	1.75	-0.58	1.27	4.25	4.05	6.17	7.35	4.90	895.84	. . .	. . .
February	1.26	2.25	1.17	1.68	-0.51	1.25	4.25	3.90	5.95	7.06	4.81	837.62	. . .	. . .
March	1.25	2.25	1.13	1.69	-0.56	1.21	4.25	3.81	5.89	6.95	4.76	846.62	. . .	. . .
April	1.26	2.25	1.13	1.51	-0.38	1.23	4.25	3.96	5.74	6.85	4.74	890.03	. . .	. . .
May	1.26	2.25	1.07	1.53	-0.46	1.20	4.25	3.57	5.22	6.38	4.41	935.96	. . .	. . .
June	1.22	2.20	0.92	1.44	-0.52	1.02	4.22	3.33	4.97	6.19	4.33	988.00	. . .	. . .
July	1.01	2.00	0.90	1.47	-0.57	1.03	4.00	3.98	5.49	6.62	4.74	992.54	. . .	. . .
August	1.03	2.00	0.95	1.39	-0.44	1.06	4.00	4.45	5.88	7.01	5.10	989.53	. . .	. . .
September ...	1.01	2.00	0.94	1.36	-0.42	1.06	4.00	4.27	5.72	6.79	4.92	1 019.44	. . .	. . .
October	1.01	2.00	0.92	1.44	-0.52	1.06	4.00	4.29	5.70	6.73	4.89	1 038.73	. . .	. . .
November	1.00	2.00	0.93	1.45	-0.52	1.08	4.00	4.30	5.65	6.66	4.73	1 049.90	. . .	. . .
December	0.98	2.00	0.90	1.51	-0.61	1.07	4.00	4.27	5.62	6.60	4.65	1 080.64	. . .	. . .
2004														
January	1.00	2.00	0.88	1.75	-0.87	1.04	4.00	4.15	5.54	6.44	4.61	1 132.52	. . .	. . .
February	1.01	2.00	0.93	1.84	-0.91	1.03	4.00	4.08	5.50	6.27	4.55	1 143.36	. . .	. . .
March	1.00	2.00	0.94	1.90	-0.96	1.03	4.00	3.83	5.33	6.11	4.41	1 123.98	. . .	. . .
April	1.00	2.00	0.94	2.02	-1.08	1.06	4.00	4.35	5.73	6.46	4.82	1 133.08	. . .	. . .
May	1.00	2.00	1.02	2.07	-1.05	1.16	4.00	4.72	6.04	6.75	5.07	1 102.78	. . .	. . .
June	1.03	2.01	1.27	2.22	-0.95	1.39	4.01	4.73	6.01	6.78	5.05	1 132.76	. . .	. . .
July	1.26	2.25	1.33	2.19	-0.86	1.51	4.25	4.50	5.82	6.62	4.87	1 105.85	. . .	. . .
August	1.43	2.43	1.48	2.15	-0.67	1.65	4.43	4.28	5.65	6.46	4.70	1 088.94	. . .	. . .
September ...	1.61	2.58	1.65	2.17	-0.52	1.81	4.58	4.13	5.46	6.27	4.56	1 117.66	. . .	. . .
October	1.76	2.75	1.76	2.18	-0.42	1.97	4.75	4.10	5.47	6.21	4.49	1 118.07	. . .	. . .
November	1.93	2.93	2.07	2.23	-0.16	2.20	4.93	4.19	5.52	6.20	4.52	1 168.94	. . .	. . .
December	2.16	3.15	2.19	2.23	-0.04	2.38	5.15	4.23	5.47	6.15	4.48	1 199.21	. . .	. . .
2005														
January	2.28	3.25	2.33	2.28	0.05	2.56	5.25	4.22	5.36	6.02	4.41	1 181.41	. . .	. . .
February	2.50	3.49	2.54	2.32	0.22	2.71	5.49	4.17	5.20	5.82	4.35	1 199.63	. . .	. . .
March	2.63	3.58	2.74	2.37	0.37	2.91	5.58	4.50	5.40	6.06	4.57	1 194.90	. . .	. . .
April	2.79	3.75	2.78	2.24	0.54	3.02	5.75	4.34	5.33	6.05	4.46	1 164.42	. . .	. . .
May	3.00	3.98	2.84	2.25	0.59	3.15	5.98	4.14	5.15	6.01	4.31	1 178.28	. . .	. . .
June	3.04	4.01	2.97	2.10	0.87	3.30	6.01	4.00	4.96	5.86	4.23	1 202.26	. . .	. . .
July	3.26	4.25	3.22	2.04	1.18	3.49	6.25	4.18	5.06	5.95	4.31	1 222.24	. . .	. . .
August	3.50	4.44	3.44	2.07	1.37	3.69	6.44	4.26	5.09	5.96	4.32	1 224.27	. . .	. . .
September ...	3.62	4.59	3.42	2.21	1.21	3.79	6.59	4.20	5.13	6.03	4.29	1 225.91	. . .	. . .
October	3.78	4.75	3.71	2.32	1.39	4.05	6.75	4.46	5.35	6.30	4.49	1 191.96	. . .	. . .
November	4.00	5.00	3.88	2.32	1.56	4.23	7.00	4.54	5.42	6.39	4.57	1 237.37	. . .	. . .
December	4.16	5.15	3.89	2.30	1.59	4.37	7.15	4.47	5.37	6.32	4.46	1 262.07	. . .	. . .
2006														
January	4.29	5.26	4.24	2.15	2.09	4.48	7.26	4.42	5.29	6.24	4.37	1 278.72	. . .	. . .
February	4.49	5.50	4.43	2.06	2.37	4.63	7.50	4.57	5.35	6.27	4.41	1 276.65	. . .	. . .
March	4.59	5.53	4.51	2.06	2.45	4.79	7.53	4.72	5.53	6.41	4.44	1 293.74	. . .	. . .
April	4.79	5.75	4.60	2.21	2.39	4.94	7.75	4.99	5.84	6.68	4.58	1 302.18	. . .	. . .
May	4.94	5.93	4.72	2.24	2.48	5.05	7.93	5.11	5.95	6.75	4.59	1 290.00	. . .	. . .
June	4.99	6.02	4.79	2.37	2.42	5.25	8.02	5.11	5.89	6.78	4.60	1 253.12	. . .	. . .
July	5.24	6.25	4.95	2.36	2.59	5.37	8.25	5.09	5.85	6.76	4.61	1 260.24	. . .	. . .
August	5.25	6.25	4.96	2.51	2.45	5.29	8.25	4.88	5.68	6.59	4.39	1 287.15	. . .	. . .
September ...	5.25	6.25	4.81	2.40	2.41	5.25	8.25	4.72	5.51	6.43	4.27	1 317.81	. . .	. . .
October	5.25	6.25	4.92	2.33	2.59	5.24	8.25	4.73	5.51	6.42	4.30	1 363.38	. . .	. . .
November	5.25	6.25	4.94	2.21	2.73	5.24	8.25	4.60	5.33	6.20	4.14	1 388.63	. . .	. . .
December	5.24	6.25	4.85	2.27	2.58	5.24	8.25	4.56	5.32	6.22	4.11	1 416.42	. . .	. . .

[1]Federal Reserve Bank of New York. Through 2002, represents the rate for adjustment credit. Beginning in 2003, represents the rate for primary credit. See notes and definitions for more information.
[2]Prior to September 1997, this series represents both nonfinancial and financial commercial paper rates. Beginning September 1997, rates for financial companies only are shown. See notes and definitions for more information.
. . . = Not available.

Table 12-9B. Summary Interest Rates, Bond Yields, and Stock Prices: Historical Data—*Continued*

(Percent per annum, except as noted.)

Year and month	Federal funds interest rate	Federal Reserve discount rate[1]	U.S. Treasury bills, secondary market, 3-month	Inflation: percent change from year earlier in PCE chain-type price index excluding food and energy	Real 3-month Treasury bill rate	Commercial paper, 3-month[2]	Bank prime rate	Treasury 10-year nominal yields	Bond yields Domestic corporate (Moody's) Aaa	Bond yields Domestic corporate (Moody's) Baa	State and local bonds (Bond Buyer)	Standard and Poor's composite (500 stocks) Index, 1941-1943 = 10	Dividend-price ratio	Earnings-price ratio
2007														
January	5.25	6.25	4.98	2.50	2.48	5.24	8.25	4.76	5.40	6.34	4.23	1 424.16	1.81	. . .
February	5.26	6.25	5.03	2.58	2.45	5.23	8.25	4.72	5.39	6.28	4.22	1 444.79	1.82	. . .
March	5.26	6.25	4.94	2.44	2.50	5.22	8.25	4.56	5.30	6.27	4.15	1 406.95	1.89	5.85
April	5.25	6.25	4.87	2.30	2.57	5.23	8.25	4.69	5.47	6.39	4.26	1 463.65	1.84	. . .
May	5.25	6.25	4.73	2.19	2.54	5.23	8.25	4.75	5.47	6.39	4.31	1 511.14	1.81	. . .
June	5.25	6.25	4.61	2.14	2.47	5.25	8.25	5.10	5.79	6.70	4.60	1 514.49	1.81	5.65
July	5.26	6.25	4.82	2.20	2.62	5.25	8.25	5.00	5.73	6.65	4.56	1 520.70	1.80	. . .
August	5.02	6.01	4.20	2.12	2.08	5.30	8.25	4.67	5.79	6.65	4.64	1 454.62	1.92	. . .
September	4.94	5.53	3.89	2.21	1.68	5.19	8.03	4.52	5.74	6.59	4.51	1 497.12	1.88	5.15
October	4.76	5.24	3.90	2.25	1.65	4.91	7.74	4.53	5.66	6.48	4.39	1 539.66	1.84	. . .
November	4.49	5.00	3.27	2.38	0.89	4.75	7.50	4.15	5.44	6.40	4.46	1 463.39	1.95	. . .
December	4.24	4.83	3.00	2.46	0.54	4.76	7.33	4.10	5.49	6.65	4.42	1 479.23	1.93	4.51
2008														
January	3.94	4.48	2.75	2.29	0.46	3.70	6.98	3.74	5.33	6.54	4.27	1 378.76	2.06	. . .
February	2.98	3.50	2.12	2.18	-0.06	3.03	6.00	3.74	5.53	6.82	4.64	1 354.87	2.10	. . .
March	2.61	3.04	1.26	2.32	-1.06	2.70	5.66	3.51	5.51	6.89	4.93	1 316.94	2.17	4.57
April	2.28	2.49	1.29	2.37	-1.08	2.72	5.24	3.68	5.55	6.97	4.70	1 370.47	2.09	. . .
May	1.98	2.25	1.73	2.47	-0.74	2.61	5.00	3.88	5.57	6.93	4.58	1 403.22	2.07	. . .
June	2.00	2.25	1.86	2.52	-0.66	2.70	5.00	4.10	5.68	7.07	4.69	1 341.25	2.15	4.01
July	2.01	2.25	1.63	2.50	-0.87	2.72	5.00	4.01	5.67	7.16	4.68	1 257.33	2.27	. . .
August	2.00	2.25	1.72	2.46	-0.74	2.76	5.00	3.89	5.64	7.15	4.69	1 281.47	2.23	. . .
September	1.81	2.25	1.13	2.35	-1.22	2.91	5.00	3.69	5.65	7.31	4.86	1 217.01	2.36	3.94
October	0.97	1.81	0.67	2.16	-1.49	3.19	4.56	3.81	6.28	8.88	5.50	968.80	2.83	. . .
November	0.39	1.25	0.19	2.01	-1.82	1.54	4.00	3.53	6.12	9.21	5.23	883.04	3.11	. . .
December	0.16	0.86	0.03	1.77	-1.74	1.09	3.61	2.42	5.05	8.43	5.56	877.56	3.00	1.65
2009														
January	0.15	0.50	0.13	1.65	-1.52	1.10	3.25	2.52	5.05	8.14	5.07	865.58	3.01	. . .
February	0.22	0.50	0.30	1.65	-1.35	0.67	3.25	2.87	5.27	8.08	4.90	805.23	3.07	. . .
March	0.18	0.50	0.21	1.52	-1.31	0.62	3.25	2.82	5.50	8.42	4.99	757.13	2.92	0.86
April	0.15	0.50	0.16	1.59	-1.43	0.48	3.25	2.93	5.39	8.39	4.78	848.15	2.60	. . .
May	0.18	0.50	0.18	1.52	-1.34	0.37	3.25	3.29	5.54	8.06	4.56	902.41	2.41	. . .
June	0.21	0.50	0.18	1.47	-1.29	0.36	3.25	3.72	5.61	7.50	4.81	926.12	2.35	0.82
July	0.16	0.50	0.18	1.39	-1.21	0.33	3.25	3.56	5.41	7.09	4.72	935.82	2.31	. . .
August	0.16	0.50	0.17	1.40	-1.23	0.29	3.25	3.59	5.26	6.58	4.60	1 009.72	2.12	. . .
September	0.15	0.50	0.12	1.41	-1.29	0.23	3.25	3.40	5.13	6.31	4.24	1 044.55	2.06	1.19
October	0.12	0.50	0.07	1.67	-1.60	0.22	3.25	3.39	5.15	6.29	4.20	1 067.66	2.02	. . .
November	0.12	0.50	0.05	1.72	-1.67	0.19	3.25	3.40	5.19	6.32	4.37	1 088.07	1.99	. . .
December	0.12	0.50	0.05	1.75	-1.70	0.20	3.25	3.59	5.26	6.37	4.21	1 110.38	1.95	4.57
2010														
January	0.11	0.50	0.06	1.75	-1.69	0.18	3.25	3.73	5.26	6.25	4.33	1 123.58	1.92	. . .
February	0.13	0.59	0.11	1.71	-1.60	0.20	3.25	3.69	5.35	6.34	4.36	1 089.16	2.00	. . .
March	0.16	0.75	0.15	1.78	-1.63	0.24	3.25	3.73	5.27	6.27	4.36	1 152.05	1.90	5.21
April	0.20	0.75	0.16	1.58	-1.42	0.30	3.25	3.85	5.29	6.25	4.41	1 197.32	1.84	. . .
May	0.20	0.75	0.16	1.58	-1.42	0.44	3.25	3.42	4.96	6.05	4.29	1 125.06	1.98	. . .
June	0.18	0.75	0.12	1.47	-1.35	0.46	3.25	3.20	4.88	6.23	4.36	1 083.36	2.09	6.51
July	0.18	0.75	0.16	1.44	-1.28	0.37	3.25	3.01	4.72	6.01	4.32	1 079.80	2.10	. . .
August	0.19	0.75	0.16	1.37	-1.21	0.27	3.25	2.70	4.49	5.66	4.03	1 087.28	2.10	. . .
September	0.19	0.75	0.15	1.23	-1.08	0.25	3.25	2.65	4.53	5.66	3.87	1 122.08	2.06	6.30
October	0.19	0.75	0.13	0.97	-0.84	0.25	3.25	2.54	4.68	5.72	3.87	1 171.58	1.97	. . .
November	0.19	0.75	0.14	0.97	-0.83	0.25	3.25	2.76	4.87	5.92	4.40	1 198.89	1.94	. . .
December	0.18	0.75	0.14	0.93	-0.79	0.27	3.25	3.29	5.02	6.10	4.92	1 241.53	1.90	6.15
2011														
January	0.17	0.75	0.15	1.04	-0.89	0.26	3.25	3.39	5.04	6.09	5.28	1 282.62	1.84	. . .
February	0.16	0.75	0.13	1.10	-0.97	0.25	3.25	3.58	5.22	6.15	5.15	1 321.12	1.80	. . .
March	0.14	0.75	0.10	1.04	-0.94	0.23	3.25	3.41	5.13	6.03	4.92	1 304.49	1.90	6.13
April	0.10	0.75	0.06	1.18	-1.12	0.22	3.25	3.46	5.16	6.02	4.99	1 331.51	1.92	. . .
May	0.09	0.75	0.04	1.31	-1.27	0.18	3.25	3.17	4.96	5.78	4.59	1 338.31	1.95	. . .
June	0.09	0.75	0.04	1.42	-1.38	0.17	3.25	3.00	4.99	5.75	4.51	1 287.29	2.04	6.35
July	0.07	0.75	0.04	1.57	-1.53	0.17	3.25	3.00	4.93	5.76	4.52	1 325.18	1.99	. . .
August	0.10	0.75	0.02	1.68	-1.66	0.21	3.25	2.30	4.37	5.36	4.02	1 185.31	2.20	. . .
September	0.08	0.75	0.01	1.65	-1.64	0.22	3.25	1.98	4.09	5.27	4.01	1 173.88	2.25	7.69
October	0.07	0.75	0.02	1.70	-1.68	0.24	3.25	2.15	3.98	5.37	4.13	1 207.22	2.28	. . .
November	0.08	0.75	0.01	1.77	-1.76	0.21	3.25	2.01	3.87	5.14	4.05	1 226.41	2.22	. . .
December	0.07	0.75	0.01	1.91	-1.90	0.18	3.25	1.98	3.93	5.25	3.95	1 243.32	2.24	6.91

[1]Federal Reserve Bank of New York. Through 2002, represents the rate for adjustment credit. Beginning in 2003, represents the rate for primary credit. See notes and definitions for more information.
[2]Prior to September 1997, this series represents both nonfinancial and financial commercial paper rates. Beginning September 1997, rates for financial companies only are shown. See notes and definitions for more information.
. . . = Not available.

Table 12-10. Selected Interest Rates

(Percent per annum; interest rates are nominal [not adjusted for inflation], except as noted.)

Year and month	Eurodollar deposits, 1-month	U.S. Treasury bills, secondary market, 6-month[1]	CDs (secondary market) 3-month	Interest rate swaps 1-year	Interest rate swaps 30-year	U.S. Treasury securities, constant maturities — Nominal yields 1-year[2]	5-year	10-year	20-year	30-year	Inflation-indexed yields 5-year	20-year	Long-term average
1960	...	3.20	...	...	...	...	...	...	...	...	...	...	...
1961	...	2.59	...	...	...	...	...	...	...	...	...	...	...
1962	...	2.90	...	...	...	3.10	3.70	3.95	...	...	...	...	...
1963	...	3.26	...	...	...	3.36	3.83	4.00	...	...	...	...	...
1964	...	3.68	3.92	...	...	3.85	4.07	4.19	...	...	...	...	...
1965	...	4.05	4.36	...	...	4.15	4.25	4.28	...	...	...	...	...
1966	...	5.06	5.45	...	...	5.20	5.11	4.93	...	...	...	...	...
1967	...	4.61	4.99	...	...	4.88	5.10	5.07	...	...	...	...	...
1968	...	5.47	5.82	...	...	5.69	5.70	5.64	...	...	...	...	...
1969	...	6.86	7.23	...	...	7.12	6.93	6.67	...	...	...	...	...
1970	...	6.51	7.55	...	...	6.90	7.38	7.35	...	...	...	...	...
1971	6.40	4.52	5.00	...	...	4.89	5.99	6.16	...	...	...	...	...
1972	5.00	4.47	4.66	...	...	4.95	5.98	6.21	...	...	...	...	...
1973	9.19	7.20	9.30	...	...	7.32	6.87	6.85	...	...	...	...	...
1974	10.79	7.95	10.29	...	...	8.20	7.82	7.56	...	...	...	...	...
1975	6.35	6.10	6.44	...	...	6.78	7.78	7.99	...	...	...	...	...
1976	5.26	5.26	5.27	...	...	5.88	7.18	7.61	...	...	...	...	...
1977	5.75	5.52	5.63	...	...	6.08	6.99	7.42	...	7.75	...	...	...
1978	8.33	7.58	8.21	...	...	8.34	8.32	8.41	...	8.49	...	...	...
1979	11.66	10.04	11.20	...	...	10.65	9.51	9.43	...	9.28	...	...	...
1980	13.77	11.32	13.02	...	...	12.00	11.45	11.43	...	11.27	...	...	...
1981	16.72	13.81	15.93	...	...	14.80	14.25	13.92	...	13.45	...	...	...
1982	12.74	11.06	12.27	...	...	12.27	13.01	13.01	...	12.76	...	...	...
1983	9.38	8.74	9.07	...	...	9.58	10.79	11.10	...	11.18	...	...	...
1984	10.45	9.78	10.39	...	...	10.91	12.26	12.46	...	12.41	...	...	...
1985	8.12	7.65	8.04	...	...	8.42	10.12	10.62	...	10.79	...	...	...
1986	6.78	6.02	6.51	...	...	6.45	7.30	7.67	...	7.78	...	...	...
1987	6.88	6.03	6.87	...	...	6.77	7.94	8.39	...	8.59	...	...	...
1988	7.69	6.91	7.73	...	...	7.65	8.48	8.85	...	8.96	...	...	...
1989	9.16	8.03	9.09	...	...	8.53	8.50	8.49	...	8.45	...	...	...
1990	8.15	7.46	8.15	...	...	7.89	8.37	8.55	...	8.61	...	...	...
1991	5.81	5.44	5.83	...	...	5.86	7.37	7.86	...	8.14	...	...	...
1992	3.62	3.54	3.68	...	...	3.89	6.19	7.01	...	7.67	...	...	...
1993	3.07	3.12	3.17	...	...	3.43	5.14	5.87	6.29	6.59	...	...	...
1994	4.34	4.64	4.63	...	...	5.32	6.69	7.09	7.49	7.37	...	...	...
1995	5.86	5.56	5.92	...	...	5.94	6.38	6.57	6.95	6.88	...	...	...
1996	5.32	5.08	5.39	...	...	5.52	6.18	6.44	6.83	6.71	...	...	...
1997	5.52	5.18	5.62	...	...	5.63	6.22	6.35	6.69	6.61	...	...	...
1998	5.45	4.83	5.47	...	...	5.05	5.15	5.26	5.72	5.58	...	...	...
1999	5.15	4.75	5.33	...	...	5.08	5.55	5.65	6.20	5.87	...	...	...
2000	6.33	5.90	6.46	6.73	6.93	6.11	6.16	6.03	6.23	5.94	...	...	...
2001	3.81	3.34	3.71	3.87	6.20	3.49	4.56	5.02	5.63	5.49	...	...	...
2002	1.71	1.68	1.73	2.21	5.80	2.00	3.82	4.61	5.43	5.43	...	...	...
2003	1.14	1.05	1.15	1.36	5.24	1.24	2.97	4.01	4.96	...	1.27	...	2.54
2004	1.43	1.58	1.57	2.13	5.38	1.89	3.43	4.27	5.04	...	1.04	2.14	2.21
2005	3.33	3.39	3.51	4.04	5.03	3.62	4.05	4.29	4.64	...	1.50	1.97	1.94
2006	5.09	4.81	5.16	5.33	5.44	4.94	4.75	4.80	5.00	4.91	2.28	2.31	2.27
2007	5.28	4.44	5.27	5.09	5.45	4.53	4.43	4.63	4.91	4.84	2.15	2.36	2.34
2008	3.03	1.62	2.97	2.75	4.57	1.83	2.80	3.66	4.36	4.28	1.30	2.18	2.20
2009	0.61	0.28	0.55	0.90	3.87	0.47	2.20	3.26	4.11	4.08	1.06	2.21	2.24
2010	0.34	0.20	0.31	0.55	4.00	0.32	1.93	3.22	4.03	4.25	0.26	1.73	1.72
2011	0.30	0.10	0.30	0.48	3.65	0.18	1.52	2.78	3.62	3.91	-0.41	1.19	1.19
2010													
January	0.30	0.15	0.20	0.53	4.48	0.35	2.48	3.73	4.50	4.60	0.42	2.00	1.98
February	0.28	0.18	0.19	0.51	4.48	0.35	2.36	3.69	4.48	4.62	0.42	2.03	2.03
March	0.28	0.22	0.23	0.53	4.48	0.40	2.43	3.73	4.49	4.64	0.56	1.98	2.10
April	0.30	0.24	0.30	0.59	4.50	0.45	2.58	3.85	4.53	4.69	0.62	1.90	1.99
May	0.38	0.22	0.45	0.78	4.09	0.37	2.18	3.42	4.11	4.29	0.41	1.72	1.76
June	0.44	0.19	0.52	0.78	3.95	0.32	2.00	3.20	3.95	4.13	0.34	1.69	1.72
July	0.44	0.20	0.41	0.60	3.76	0.29	1.76	3.01	3.80	3.99	0.34	1.80	1.79
August	0.37	0.19	0.32	0.46	3.45	0.26	1.47	2.70	3.52	3.80	0.13	1.65	1.59
September	0.34	0.19	0.28	0.44	3.41	0.26	1.41	2.65	3.47	3.77	0.13	1.58	1.44
October	0.34	0.18	0.27	0.38	3.49	0.23	1.18	2.54	3.52	3.87	-0.32	1.32	1.19
November	0.33	0.18	0.27	0.44	3.84	0.25	1.35	2.76	3.82	4.19	-0.21	1.44	1.31
December	0.32	0.19	0.30	0.50	4.14	0.29	1.93	3.29	4.17	4.42	0.21	1.67	1.67
2011													
January	0.32	0.18	0.29	0.46	4.26	0.27	1.99	3.39	4.28	4.52	0.06	1.70	1.73
February	0.32	0.17	0.28	0.47	4.42	0.29	2.26	3.58	4.42	4.65	0.25	1.85	1.90
March	0.30	0.16	0.28	0.44	4.29	0.26	2.11	3.41	4.27	4.51	-0.09	1.58	1.65
April	0.26	0.12	0.23	0.41	4.27	0.25	2.17	3.46	4.28	4.50	-0.14	1.48	1.56
May	0.26	0.09	0.21	0.37	4.05	0.19	1.84	3.17	4.01	4.29	-0.34	1.47	1.49
June	0.24	0.10	0.22	0.39	3.96	0.18	1.58	3.00	3.91	4.23	-0.38	1.53	1.48
July	0.22	0.08	0.24	0.43	3.96	0.19	1.54	3.00	3.95	4.27	-0.49	1.36	1.31
August	0.25	0.06	0.29	0.44	3.31	0.11	1.02	2.30	3.24	3.65	-0.75	0.81	0.76
September	0.33	0.04	0.33	0.49	2.93	0.10	0.90	1.98	2.83	3.18	-0.72	0.69	0.71
October	0.35	0.05	0.37	0.57	2.90	0.11	1.06	2.15	2.87	3.13	-0.63	0.72	0.74
November	0.35	0.05	0.41	0.66	2.77	0.11	0.91	2.01	2.72	3.02	-0.85	0.55	0.52
December	0.35	0.05	0.49	0.67	2.70	0.12	0.89	1.98	2.67	2.98	-0.78	0.56	0.51

[1]Federal Reserve Bank of New York. Through 2002, represents the rate for adjustment credit. Beginning in 2003, represents the rate for primary credit. See notes and definitions for more information.
[2]Prior to September 1997, this series represents both nonfinancial and financial commercial paper rates. Beginning September 1997, rates for financial companies only are shown. See notes and definitions for more information.
. . . = Not available.

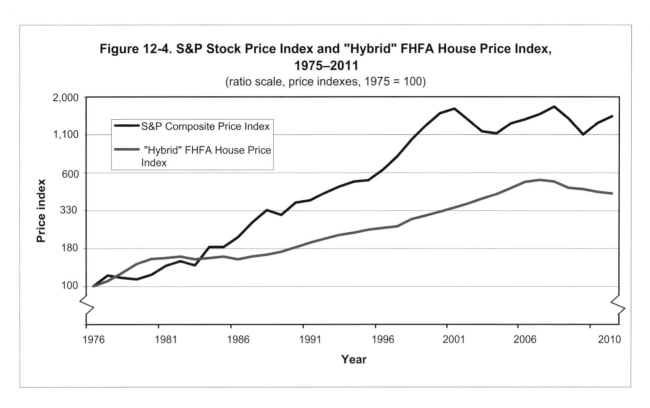

Figure 12-4. S&P Stock Price Index and "Hybrid" FHFA House Price Index, 1975–2011

(ratio scale, price indexes, 1975 = 100)

- The rise in prices of existing homes sold, as measured by the Federal Housing Finance Agency (FHFA) Purchase-Only House Price Index, ended in 2006, after annual rates of appreciation of 10 percent in 2004 and 2005. From the end of 2006 through the end of 2011, these prices declined 19 percent. (A different, privately compiled index, the Standard & Poor's Case-Shiller Home Price Index, is the measure most frequently quoted in the press. See the Notes and Definitions for a discussion of the characteristics of these different indexes.) (Table 12-11)

- In Figure 12-4 we show national average changes in the prices of purchased houses for the years 1992 through 2011. Such a purchase-only measure is not available for earlier years, so for the purpose of longer-term comparisons this index has been extended back to 1975 using changes in a similar FHFA index for houses purchased or refinanced. The two FHFA indexes shown in Table 12-11 have been linked to each other, to make a "hybrid" index, and rebased to 1975 = 100.

- The long-terms gains in national average housing prices have been no match for those in the prices of common stocks. This is demonstrated in Figure 12-4 above, where our "hybrid" FHFA house price index is compared with the S&P 500 stock index, both rebased to 1975=100 so that their growth since then can be directly compared. Over the 36 years, house prices rose at an average 4.2 percent annual rate, while the index of stock prices, though more volatile than home prices, rose at a 7.8 percent rate. (This price increase comparison does not take account of tax considerations, stock dividends, or the value of shelter provided by the owner-occupied home. Past history is no guarantee of future results.) (Table 12-11)

Table 12-11. Selected Stock and Housing Market Data

Year and month	Stock price indexes			Interest rate on fixed-rate first mortgages	FHFA House Price Indexes			
					House Price Index (purchases and refinance)		Purchase-Only Index	
	Dow Jones industrials (30 stocks)	Standard and Poor's composite (500 stocks) (1941–1943 = 10)	Nasdaq composite (Feb. 5, 1971 = 100)		Level at end of period (1980:I = 100)	Appreciation from same quarter one year earlier (percent)	Level at end of period (1991:I = 100)	Appreciation from same quarter one year earlier (percent)
1960	618.04	55.85	...	...	...	...	...	...
1961	691.55	66.27	...	...	...	...	...	...
1962	639.76	62.38	...	...	...	...	...	...
1963	714.81	69.87	...	...	...	...	...	...
1964	834.05	81.37	...	...	...	...	...	...
1965	910.88	88.17	...	...	...	...	...	...
1966	873.60	85.26	...	...	...	...	...	...
1967	879.12	91.93	...	...	...	...	...	...
1968	906.00	98.70	...	...	...	...	...	...
1969	876.72	97.84	...	...	...	...	...	...
1970	753.19	83.22	...	...	...	...	...	...
1971	884.76	98.29	107.44	...	...	...	...	...
1972	950.71	109.20	128.52	7.38	...	...	...	...
1973	923.88	107.43	109.90	8.04	...	...	...	...
1974	759.37	82.85	76.29	9.19	...	...	...	...
1975	802.49	86.16	77.20	9.04	64.82	...	...	...
1976	974.92	102.01	89.90	8.86	70.22	8.33	...	...
1977	894.63	98.20	98.71	8.84	79.94	13.84	...	...
1978	820.23	96.02	117.53	9.63	91.97	15.05	...	...
1979	844.40	103.01	136.57	11.19	99.75	8.46	...	...
1980	891.41	118.78	168.61	13.77	101.35	1.60	...	...
1981	932.92	128.05	203.18	16.63	103.59	2.21	...	...
1982	884.36	119.71	188.97	16.08	99.26	-4.18	...	...
1983	1 190.34	160.41	285.43	13.23	103.79	4.56	...	...
1984	1 178.48	160.46	248.88	13.87	106.74	2.84	...	...
1985	1 328.23	186.84	290.19	12.42	111.87	4.81	...	...
1986	1 792.76	236.34	366.96	10.18	119.89	7.17	...	...
1987	2 275.99	286.83	402.57	10.20	129.02	7.62	...	...
1988	2 060.82	265.79	374.43	10.34	137.32	6.43	...	...
1989	2 508.91	322.84	437.81	10.32	145.48	5.94	...	...
1990	2 678.94	334.59	409.17	10.13	150.98	3.78	...	...
1991	2 929.33	376.18	491.69	9.25	158.11	4.72	101.46	...
1992	3 284.29	415.74	599.26	8.40	164.23	3.87	104.25	2.75
1993	3 522.06	451.41	715.16	7.33	170.38	3.74	107.09	2.72
1994	3 793.77	460.42	751.65	8.35	179.04	5.08	110.17	2.88
1995	4 493.76	541.72	925.19	7.95	189.65	5.93	112.92	2.50
1996	5 742.89	670.50	1 164.96	7.80	198.67	4.76	116.06	2.78
1997	7 441.15	873.43	1 469.49	7.60	208.74	5.07	119.93	3.33
1998	8 625.52	1 085.50	1 794.91	6.94	217.71	4.30	126.71	5.65
1999	10 464.88	1 327.33	2 728.15	7.43	227.26	4.39	134.56	6.20
2000	10 734.90	1 427.22	3 783.67	8.06	240.62	5.88	143.90	6.94
2001	10 189.13	1 194.18	2 035.00	6.97	253.36	5.29	153.67	6.79
2002	9 226.43	993.94	1 539.73	6.54	263.97	4.19	165.50	7.70
2003	8 993.59	965.23	1 647.17	5.82	276.19	4.63	178.37	7.78
2004	10 317.39	1 130.65	1 986.53	5.84	290.66	5.24	196.41	10.11
2005	10 547.67	1 207.23	2 099.32	5.86	303.85	4.54	216.36	10.16
2006	11 408.67	1 310.46	2 263.41	6.41	306.89	1.00	223.10	3.12
2007	13 169.98	1 477.19	2 578.47	6.34	302.47	-1.44	217.85	-2.35
2008	11 252.62	1 220.04	2 161.65	6.04	289.74	-4.21	197.03	-9.56
2009	8 876.15	948.05	1 845.38	5.04	277.19	-4.33	193.08	-2.00
2010	10 662.80	1 139.97	2 349.89	4.69	274.56	-0.95	185.05	-4.16
2011	11 966.36	1 268.89	2 680.42	4.46	267.39	-2.61	180.40	-2.51
2010								
January	10 471.24	1 123.58	2 267.77	5.03	...	...	...	...
February	10 214.51	1 089.16	2 194.44	4.99	...	...	...	...
March	10 677.52	1 152.05	2 362.24	4.97	273.06	-7.00	189.17	-3.12
April	11 052.15	1 197.32	2 475.72	5.10	...	...	...	...
May	10 500.19	1 125.06	2 319.24	4.89	...	...	...	...
June	10 159.27	1 083.36	2 235.23	4.74	271.16	-5.34	192.37	-1.93
July	10 222.24	1 079.80	2 210.27	4.56	...	...	...	...
August	10 350.40	1 087.28	2 205.28	4.43	...	...	...	...
September	10 598.07	1 122.08	2 298.35	4.35	275.37	-1.17	189.56	-2.94
October	11 044.49	1 171.58	2 441.30	4.23	...	...	...	...
November	11 198.31	1 198.89	2 530.99	4.30	...	...	...	...
December	11 465.26	1 241.53	2 631.56	4.71	274.56	-0.95	185.05	-4.16
2011								
January	11 802.37	1 282.62	2 717.21	4.76	...	...	...	...
February	12 190.00	1 321.12	2 783.54	4.95	...	...	...	...
March	12 081.48	1 304.49	2 722.29	4.84	265.36	-2.82	178.66	-5.56
April	12 434.88	1 331.51	2 797.07	4.84	...	...	...	...
May	12 579.99	1 338.31	2 815.08	4.64	...	...	...	...
June	12 097.31	1 287.29	2 687.76	4.51	262.08	-3.35	181.69	-5.55
July	12 512.33	1 325.18	2 810.58	4.55	...	...	...	...
August	11 326.62	1 185.31	2 504.62	4.27	...	...	...	...
September	11 175.45	1 173.88	2 524.14	4.11	266.27	-3.30	182.78	-3.58
October	11 515.93	1 207.22	2 594.78	4.07	...	...	...	...
November	11 804.33	1 226.41	2 606.29	3.99	...	...	...	...
December	12 075.68	1 243.32	2 601.67	3.96	267.39	-2.61	180.40	-2.51

. . . = Not available.

NOTES AND DEFINITIONS, CHAPTER 12

Most of the data in this chapter are found on the Federal Reserve Board Web site, <http://www.federalreserve.gov>. Current releases and most historical data are found at that site by selecting Economic Research & Data/Statistical Releases and Historical Data and then selecting the appropriate report. This is the location for all data not otherwise specified.

Historical data not found online are taken from two volumes of statistical data that were published by the Board of Governors of the Federal Reserve System: *Banking and Monetary Statistics,* 1943, and *Banking and Monetary Statistics, 1941–1970,* 1976. These will be referred to as *B&MS* 1943 and *B&MS* 1976.

TABLES 12-1 AND 12-2
MONEY STOCK MEASURES AND COMPONENTS

SOURCE: BOARD OF GOVERNORS OF THE FEDERAL RESERVE SYSTEM

Estimates of two monetary aggregates (M1 and M2) and the components of these measures are published weekly. The monthly data are averages of daily figures.

The Federal Reserve Board ceased publication of the M3 aggregate on March 23, 2006. Weekly publication was also discontinued for the following components of M3: large-denomination time deposits, repurchase agreements (RPs), and Eurodollars. The Board continues to publish institutional money market mutual funds as a memorandum item in this release. Measures of large-denomination time deposits continue to be published in the flow of funds accounts (Z.1 release) and in the H.8 release weekly for commercial banks.

The Board stated that "M3 does not appear to convey any additional information about economic activity that is not already embodied in M2 and has not played a role in the monetary policy process for many years. Consequently, the Board judged that the costs of collecting the underlying data and publishing M3 outweigh the benefits." ("Discontinuance of M3," H.6, Money Stock Measures [November 10, 2005, revised March 9, 2006]. [Accessed November 6, 2006.]

Definitions

M1 consists of (1) currency, (2) traveler's checks of nonbank issuers, (3) demand deposits, and (4) other checkable deposits.

M2 consists of M1 plus savings deposits (including money market deposit accounts), small-denomination time deposits, and balances in retail money market mutual funds.

Currency consists of currency outside the U.S. Treasury, the Federal Reserve Banks, and the vaults of depository institutions.

Traveler's checks is the outstanding amount of U.S. dollar-denominated traveler's checks of nonbank issuers. Traveler's checks issued by depository institutions are included in demand deposits.

Demand deposits consists of demand deposits at domestically chartered commercial banks, U.S. branches and agencies of foreign banks, and Edge Act corporations (excluding those amounts held by depository institutions, the U.S. government, and foreign banks and official institutions) less cash items in the process of collection and Federal Reserve float. A "demand deposit" is a deposit that the depositor has a right to withdraw at any time without prior notice to the depository institution—most commonly, a checking account. "Federal Reserve float" is Federal Reserve credit that appears on the books of the depository institution of both the check writer and the check receiver while a check is being processed. This amount and cash items in the process of collection are subtracted to avoid double counting of deposits, so that they will not be counted both at the bank in which the check is deposited and at the bank on which the check is drawn.

Other checkable deposits at commercial banks consists of negotiable order of withdrawal (NOW) and automatic transfer service (ATS) balances at domestically chartered commercial banks, U.S. branches and agencies of foreign banks, and Edge Act corporations.

Other checkable deposits at thrift institutions consists of NOW and ATS balances at thrift institutions, credit union share draft balances, and demand deposits at thrift institutions.

Savings deposits includes money market deposit accounts and other savings deposits at *commercial banks* and *thrift institutions*.

Small time deposits are deposits issued at *commercial banks* and *thrift institutions* in amounts less than $100,000. All Individual Retirement Account (IRA) and Keogh account balances at commercial banks and thrift institutions are subtracted from small time deposits.

Retail money funds exclude IRA and Keogh account balances at money market mutual funds.

Institutional money funds are included in the money stock report for informational purposes. They are not part of M1 or M2.

Notes on the data

Seasonal adjustment. Seasonally adjusted M1 is calculated by summing currency, traveler's checks, demand deposits, and other checkable deposits (each seasonally adjusted separately). Seasonally adjusted M2 is computed by adjusting each of its non-M1 components and then adding this result to seasonally adjusted M1.

Revisions. Money stock measures are revised frequently and have a benchmark and seasonal factor review in the middle of the year; this review typically extends back a number of years. The monetary aggregates were redefined in major revisions introduced in 1980.

Historical: January 1947–January 1959. These data are not currently maintained online and are found in *B&MS* 1976. They are not continuous with the current data series; for that reason the values for January 1959 are shown so that users can link to the current data. The *demand deposit component* includes demand deposits held in commercial banks by individuals, partnerships, and corporations both domestic and foreign, and demand deposits held by nonbank financial institutions and foreign banks. Note that this includes demand deposit liabilities to foreign governments, central banks, and international institutions—said to be "relatively small" in the source document. *Time deposits adjusted* is time and savings deposits at commercial banks, other than large negotiable certificates of deposit (CDs), and excluding all deposits due to the U.S. government and domestic commercial banks. The editor has added this to the *Money stock (M1)* to approximate *M2*, which is not shown as such in the source document.

Historical: 1929–1946. These data are also taken from *B&MS* 1976. They pertain only to the last day of June and the last day of December, the "call dates" on which banks reported to the federal government. For more data and analysis concerning monetary developments in this period, including monthly money supply estimates, see Milton Friedman and Anna Jacobson Schwartz, *A Monetary History of the United States, 1867–1960,* Princeton, Princeton University Press, 1963. In Table 12-1B, *Demand deposits adjusted* refers to the elimination of interbank and U.S. government deposits and cash items in process of collection, not to seasonal adjustment, which is not applicable to call report data. The editor has retitled as *M1* the "Total" money stock shown in the source document, and has added time deposits to it in order to approximate *M2*, which is not shown in the source document.

Data availability

Estimates are released weekly in Federal Reserve Statistical Release H.6, "Money Stock Measures." Current and historical data are available on the Federal Reserve Web site.

References

Board of Governors of the Federal Reserve System, *The Federal Reserve System: Purposes and Functions,* available online at <http://www.federalreserve.gov> in the category "About the Fed/Features," includes a chapter discussing monetary policy and the monetary aggregates and a glossary of terms as an appendix.

An explanation of the 1980 redefinition of the monetary aggregates is found in the *Federal Reserve Bulletin* for February 1980.

TABLES 12-3 AND 12-1D
AGGREGATE RESERVES, MONETARY BASE, AND FR BALANCE SHEET

SOURCE: BOARD OF GOVERNORS OF THE FEDERAL RESERVE SYSTEM

The data on reserves and the monetary base presented here are in millions of dollars, seasonally adjusted (with one exception), and adjusted for changes in reserve requirements ("break-adjusted") in order to provide a consistent gauge of the effect of Federal Reserve open-market operations. Break adjustment is required because an observed increase in reserves will not represent an easing in monetary conditions if it is simply equal to the increase in reserves required by the Federal Reserve. Therefore, the mandated increases and decreases are deducted to provide the break-adjusted series. Monthly data are averages of daily figures. Annual data are for December.

The series "Federal Reserve balance sheet: total assets" was introduced in the 14th edition of *Business Statistics*. It demonstrates the extent to which the Federal Reserve has, beginning in 2007, undertaken "quantitative easing"—direct purchases of financial assets—in addition to conventional easing, which has consisted of reducing short-term interest rates to near zero and supporting that rate level with purchases and sales of short-term securities on the open market. The balance sheet data are accessed on a different part of the Federal Reserve Web site—"Monetary Policy" instead of "Economic Research and Data"—which features an extensive explanation and discussion of the meaning and importance of this indicator. The balance sheet is reported in millions of dollars for each Wednesday, and is shown here with the last Wednesday of the month representing the month and the last Wednesday of December representing the year. These values are not adjusted for seasonal variation.

Definitions

Total reserves consists of reserve balances with the Federal Reserve Banks plus vault cash used to satisfy reserve requirements. Seasonally adjusted, break-adjusted total reserves equal seasonally adjusted, break-adjusted required reserves plus unadjusted excess reserves.

Seasonally adjusted, break-adjusted *nonborrowed reserves* equal seasonally adjusted, break-adjusted total reserves less unadjusted total borrowings of depository institutions from the Federal Reserve.

Extended credit consisted of borrowing at the discount window under the terms and conditions established for the extended credit program to help depository institutions deal with sustained liquidity pressures. Since there was not the same need to repay such borrowing promptly as there was with traditional short-term adjustment credit, the money market impact of extended credit was similar to that of nonborrowed reserves. The extended credit program was significant in the 1980s but used infrequently in subsequent years.

It ended with the 2002 revision of the discount window program, effective January 9, 2003. See the explanation of the discount rate in the notes and definitions for Table 12-9A.

To adjust *required reserves* for discontinuities due to regulatory changes in reserve requirements, a multiplicative procedure is used to estimate what required reserves would have been in past periods, had current reserve requirements been in effect. Break-adjusted required reserves include required reserves against transactions deposits and personal time and savings deposits (but not reservable nondeposit liabilities).

Excess reserves, not seasonally adjusted equals unadjusted total reserves less unadjusted required reserves.

The seasonally adjusted, break-adjusted *monetary base* consists of (1) seasonally adjusted, break-adjusted total reserves; plus (2) the seasonally adjusted currency component of the money stock; plus (3) the seasonally adjusted, break-adjusted difference between current vault cash and the amount applied to satisfy current reserve requirements for all quarterly reporters on the "Report of Transaction Accounts, Other Deposits and Vault Cash" and for all weekly reporters whose vault cash exceeds their required reserves.

Federal Reserve balance sheet: total assets is total assets from the Consolidated Statement of Condition of All Federal Reserve Banks, which is reported each Wednesday. The last Wednesday of the month is used to represent the month, and the last Wednesday in December is used to represent the year. Currently, the principal components of total assets are Treasury, federal agency, and mortgage-backed securities. Other types of assets representing Federal Reserve credit extension, some of which have varied during the course of the crisis, have been repurchase agreements; term auction credit; portfolio holdings of various limited liability companies (LLCs) set up to manage assets taken over from other institutions; liquidity swaps with foreign central banks; and other loans, including traditional loans to member commercial banks made at the discount rate (see the definitions for Table 12-9). Total assets are equal to the sum of Federal Reserve liabilities and capital. The principal components of liabilities are Federal Reserve notes and the deposits of member banks representing their reserves.

Revisions

The data on reserves and the monetary base are revised annually around midyear to reflect the result of annual reviews of seasonal factors and break factors. The Federal Reserve balance sheet is not subject to revision.

Data availability

Reserve and monetary base data are released weekly in Federal Reserve Release H.3, "Aggregate Reserves of Depository Institutions and the Monetary Base." Current and historical data are available on the Federal Reserve Web site.

The Federal Reserve balance sheet appears each week in the H.4.1 release, Factors Affecting Reserve Balances, released each Thursday at 4:30 p.m., and available on the Federal Reserve Web site under Economic Research and Data/Statistical Releases and Historical Data. However, to obtain the full historical data for total assets, the user must go to Monetary policy/Credit and liquidity programs and the balance sheet/Recent balance sheet trends/Total assets/View as table/All/Copy data. Other explanatory material, including a monthly report on changes in these programs, is available at the Monetary policy location.

TABLE 12-4A
COMMERCIAL BANKS: BANK CREDIT AND SELECTED LIABILITIES

SOURCE: BOARD OF GOVERNORS OF THE FEDERAL RESERVE SYSTEM.

Definitions and notes on the data

This table presents selected balance sheet items (not a complete balance sheet with total assets and liabilities) for all commercial banks in the United States. This category covers the following types of institutions in the 50 states and the District of Columbia: domestically chartered commercial banks that report weekly (large domestic), other domestically chartered commercial banks (small domestic), branches and agencies of foreign banks, and Edge Act and Agreement corporations (foreign related institutions). International Banking Facilities are excluded.

Data are collected weekly for Wednesday values, and monthly data are pro rata averages of Wednesday values. Annual data represent December figures.

Data are complete for large domestic banks. Data for other institutions are estimated on the basis of weekly samples and end-of-quarter condition reports. Data are adjusted for breaks caused by the reclassifications of assets and liabilities.

Data before 1988 are based on previous versions of this survey—the G.7 release, "Loans and Securities at Commercial Banks," and the G.10 release, "Major Nondeposit Funds of Commercial Banks."

Most of the categories of credit and liabilities are self-explanatory.

U.S. Treasury and agency securities includes liabilities of the U.S. Treasury, liabilities of U.S. government agencies, and liabilities of U.S. government-sponsored enterprises.

Loans and leases in bank credit excludes various forms of credit extended to other commercial banks in the United States.

Security loans, previously shown as a separate category under "Loans and leases in bank credit", are now included in "*Other loans and leases.*"

Allowances for loan and lease losses, interbank loans, cash assets, trading assets including derivatives, and other assets are not components of bank credit and are omitted from Table 12-4. Interbank loans include loans made to commercial banks, reverse RPs with commercial banks, and federal funds sold to commercial banks.

Selected liabilities show *deposits* and *borrowings*. Other components of total liabilities, "trading liabilities" and "other liabilities," are omitted.

Revisions

Data are revised annually around midyear to reflect new benchmark information and revised seasonal factors.

Data availability

Federal Reserve Statistical Release H.8, "Assets and Liabilities of Commercial Banks in the United States," is issued each Friday around 4:30 p.m. (EST). Current and historical data are available on the Federal Reserve Web site.

TABLE 12-4B
BANK CREDIT AND OTHER CREDIT INSTRUMENTS: HISTORICAL

December data are taken from *B&MS* 1976 and *B&MS* 1943.

Loans and investments, all commercial banks is the sum of these items from commercial bank balance sheets, including total loans, holdings of U.S. Government securities, and holdings of other securities, which according to the 1976 source book "consist mainly of State and municipal issues."

Commercial paper reflects outstanding values of these short-term securities.

Bankers' acceptances reflects amounts of these short-term borrowing instruments reported by banks and dealers in the United States as well as by agencies of foreign banks located in the United States. From 1929 through 1934, acceptances includes acceptances held by Federal Reserve Banks, both for their own account ($391 million in December 1929) and for account of foreign correspondent banks ($548 million in December 1929). These Federal Reserve holdings declined rapidly after 1931 and amounted to zero by December 1934. By then, most of the outstanding acceptances were held by banks.

TABLE 12-5
CREDIT MARKET DEBT OUTSTANDING, BY BORROWER AND LENDER

SOURCE: BOARD OF GOVERNORS OF THE FEDERAL RESERVE SYSTEM

The flow of funds accounts, compiled quarterly by the Federal Reserve Board, supplement the national income and product accounts (NIPAs) by providing a comprehensive and detailed accounting of financial transactions with a balance sheet for each financial and nonfinancial sector of the economy. Table 12-5 is taken from these accounts. It shows the *credit market debt outstanding owed* by the major sectors in the economy, and it shows the major lending sectors in the credit markets under *credit market assets held*. One purpose of these statistics is to show the comparative growth of the various lending sectors.

Aggregates of these data can include multiple layers of financial intermediation, such as banks making advances to finance companies that subsequently lend to households. Adding bank data to finance company data involves duplication of such debt. In macroeconomic analysis, the most widely used flow of funds measure is the total debt of domestic nonfinancial sectors. By eliminating the financial sectors, this measure has little duplication due to financial intermediation. The Federal Reserve uses this along with the monetary aggregates as an indicator of monetary conditions.

Definitions and notes on the data

Quarterly data on debt outstanding are shown on an end-of-period basis, not adjusted for seasonal variation or for "breaks" or discontinuities in the series. Due to these discontinuities, caution should be used in interpreting changes in debt levels. Break-adjusted values of changes, representing best estimates of actual fund flows, can be found in the quarterly flow of funds report, along with a suggested method for calculating percentage changes.

The data on credit market debt exclude corporate equities and mutual fund shares. However, these values of these instruments held by households and nonprofits appear as assets in the household sector accounts in Table 12-6.

Data for the current and several preceding years are revised each year to reflect revisions in source data, including the NIPAs; the revisions are issued about a month after the release of the annual NIPA revisions.

Sectors owing debt

Domestic financial sectors

Federal government-related sectors include government-sponsored enterprises (GSEs) such as Fannie Mae (originally the Federal National Mortgage Association), Freddie Mac (originally the Federal Home Loan Mortgage Corporation), and Ginnie Mae (originally the Government National Mortgage Association); agency and GSE-backed mortgage pools; and the monetary authority (Federal Reserve). However, the Federal Reserve usually owes no credit market debt.

The *private* sector includes a broad category introduced recently into the Flow of Funds accounts, "U.S.-chartered depository institutions", which replaces and comprises two earlier categories, commercial banks and bank holding companies and savings institutions; it also includes credit unions, life insurance companies, asset-backed securities (ABS) issuers, brokers and dealers, finance and mortgage companies, REITs (real estate investment trusts), and funding corporations.

Domestic nonfinancial sectors

Federal government consists of all federal government agencies and funds included in the unified budget. However, the District of Columbia government is included in the state and local sector.

Treasury securities as shown here <u>excludes</u> securities issued by the Treasury but held by agencies within the U.S. government (e.g., in the Social Security trust funds). In this respect, it corresponds to the "Federal debt" shown in Table 6-15, except that the latter table uses a fiscal-year basis rather than a calendar-year basis. Federal government debt as shown here is smaller than the official total public debt and the "debt subject to limit." Both of those <u>include</u> the securities held by U.S. government agencies. The value shown here is considered to be a more accurate measure of the effect of government borrowing in relation to the economy and credit markets than those obtained from the larger aggregates.

Budget agency securities and mortgages are those issued by government-owned corporations and agencies, such as the Export-Import Bank, that issue securities individually. There are no mortgages currently included in the debt of agencies.

Households also includes personal trusts, nonprofit organizations, and domestic hedge funds.

Nonfinancial noncorporate business now includes noncorporate farm business, formerly shown separately.

State and local governments represent operating funds only. State and local government retirement funds are included in the financial sector.

Foreign credit market debt held in the United States shows the foreign credit market debt owed to U.S. residents. This debt is included along with the debt of domestic financial and nonfinancial sectors in total credit market debt outstanding.

Percentage measures

Table 12-5 includes three measures of relative debt burdens, calculated by the editor.

Domestic nonfinancial debt as a percent of GDP is the total debt owed by domestic nonfinancial sectors as a percent of the current-dollar value of total Gross Domestic Product. (Table 1-1)

Household debt as a percent of DPI is the value of debt owed by households as a percent of the current-dollar value of disposable personal income. (Table 4-1)

Corporate nonfinancial business debt as a percent of sector value added is the total debt owed by domestic corporate nonfinancial business as a percent of the current-dollar gross value added of domestic corporate nonfinancial business. (Table 1-15)

For the annual ratios, debt outstanding at the end of the year is taken as a percent of the product or income data for the full preceding year. For the quarterly ratios, the debt outstanding at the end of the quarter is taken as a percent of the annual rate of the product or income flow for that quarter. This means that the end-year ratios will almost inevitably be higher than the corresponding end-quarter ratios and should therefore not be compared with them.

Credit market assets held by sector

Selected government-related sectors

This grouping includes two nonfinancial and four financial sectors. The nonfinancial sectors are the *federal government*, as reflected in the U.S. Budget accounts, and the operations of *state and local governments*, including the District of Columbia. *State and local employee retirement funds* and *federal government retirement funds* are shown separately and considered to be financial sectors. The other two government-related financial sectors are *government-sponsored enterprises (GSEs)* and *federally related mortgage pools*.

Government-sponsored enterprises (GSEs) are financial institutions that provide credit to housing, agriculture, and other specific areas of the economy, such as Federal Home Loan Banks, Fannie Mae, and Freddie Mac (see above for explanation of the latter two terms).

Federally related mortgage pools are entities established for bookkeeping purposes that record the issuance of pooled securities representing an interest in mortgages backed by federal agencies and GSEs. Rather than being composed of a group of institutions, the sector is made up of a set of contractual arrangements in regard to pooled mortgages.

Selected domestic financial sectors

The former categories "commercial banks" and "savings institutions" are now combined in the category *U.S.-chartered depository institutions*. The *monetary authority* (the Federal Reserve) has been put in this group because it is sometimes included in banking sector totals. Other important financial sectors are *credit unions, life insurance companies, property-casualty insurance companies,* and *private pension funds*. Additional private financial sectors are *money market mutual funds*, which issue shares and invest in short-term liquid assets; *mutual funds*, whose investments are not restricted to the short-term area; *asset-backed security (ABS) issuers*, which issue debt obligations that are backed by pooled assets, a financial procedure similar to that of federally related mortgage pools; and *finance companies*, which provide credit to businesses and individuals.

Private domestic nonfinancial sectors

Households were the dominant private domestic nonfinancial lenders in earlier years, but lending by domestic households has now been surpassed by *foreign holdings* of assets representing claims on U.S. entities.

A number of lending sectors of smaller importance are included in the category "*All other financial and nonfinancial.*" One of those is nonfinancial business, a sector that is important on the borrowing side but not on the lending side. The financial sectors included in this total are closed-end funds, exchange-traded funds, real estate investment trusts (REITs), brokers and dealers, and funding corporations.

Data availability

Debt estimates are released quarterly, about nine weeks following the end of the quarter. The data can be found in Federal Reserve Statistical Release Z.1, "Flow of Funds of the United States," available on the Federal Reserve Web site. The data in Table 12-5 are found in Tables L.1 and L.2 of that release. Current and historical data are also available on the same Federal Reserve Web site.

References

A *Guide to the Flow of Funds Accounts* can be ordered; ordering information is available on the Federal Reserve Web site along with the Z.1 release. Individual table descriptions can be accessed at the same location. The *Federal Reserve Bulletin* for July 2001 includes an article entitled "The U.S. Flow of Funds Accounts and Their Uses." To access *Bulletin* articles on the Federal Reserve Web site, select Economic Research & Data/ Federal Reserve Bulletin and select the year.

TABLE 12-6
HOUSEHOLD ASSETS, LIABILITIES, NET WORTH, FINANCIAL OBLIGATIONS, AND DELINQUENCY RATES

SOURCE: BOARD OF GOVERNORS OF THE FEDERAL RESERVE SYSTEM

The quarterly data on household sector assets, liabilities, and net worth are also obtained from the Federal Reserve Board's flow of funds accounts, which are described above. These data appear in Table B.100 of the Z.1 statistical release, also cited above.

The household credit ratios and rates are also compiled by the Federal Reserve. The household debt service ratio relates required debt service (interest and principal) payments to disposable personal income (DPI). The financial obligations ratios include not only required debt payments, but also rental payments, automobile lease payments, homeowners' insurance, and property taxes. They are also expressed as a percentage of DPI. Unlike the debt service ratio, the financial obligations ratios are not distorted by the trend toward debt-financed homeownership in prefer-

ence to rental or the trend toward auto leasing in preference to loan financing.

The delinquency and charge-off rates relate delinquent (past due 30 days or more) and charged-off consumer credit card credit at commercial banks to total bank holdings of that type of credit.

Definitions and notes on the data

Quarterly data on holdings of *financial assets* are shown on an end-of-period basis, not adjusted for seasonal variations. Data for the current and preceding years are revised annually to reflect revisions in source data.

It is important to note that for most categories in this reporting system, the values for the household sector are calculated as residuals. That is, starting with a known total (such as total Treasury securities outstanding), the amounts in that category reported or estimated to be held by other sectors are subtracted and the remainder is assigned to the household sector. This means that any error in estimating one of the other sectors causes an equal and opposite error in the household sector.

It should also be noted that the Flow of Funds "household" balance sheet includes nonprofit organizations, personal trusts, farm households, and domestic hedge funds. Household sector assets exclude holdings by unincorporated businesses.

The table shows total household ownership of *checkable deposits and currency, time and savings deposits, money market fund shares, U.S. savings bonds, other Treasury securities, agency- and GSE-backed securities, municipal securities, corporate and foreign bonds, mortgages, corporate equities* (at market value), *mutual fund shares* (with equities at market value and other assets at book value), *security credit, life insurance reserves, pension fund reserves,* and *equity in noncorporate business*. Note that the reserves of life insurance companies and pension funds, though held by institutions, are counted here as assets of the household sector. *Pension fund reserves* includes insurance and pension fund reserves of federal, state, and local government employee funds—but not the Social Security system—as well as private industry funds. Bank personal trusts were formerly included as a type of household financial asset. However, in a recent revision of the flow of funds accounts, the various assets in these trusts were instead included in the appropriate categories, such as bonds, equities, and so forth. Included in total *financial assets,* but not shown separately, are foreign deposits, open market paper, and claims on insurance companies, such as unearned premium reserves of other insurance companies and health insurance reserves of life insurance companies.

Tangible assets complete the asset side of the household balance sheet. Tangible assets comprise equipment and software owned by nonprofit organizations, real estate, and consumer durable goods. *Household real estate* includes farm homes, mobile homes, second homes not rented, vacant homes for sale, vacant land, and owner-occupied housing. It is valued at market value, while equipment, software, and consumer durables are valued at replacement (current) cost.

Debt as a percent of total assets is calculated by the editor as household credit market debt outstanding, from Table 12-5, as a percent of the total of tangible and financial assets in this table. It covers both households and nonprofit organizations, as defined above.

Total liabilities consists of household credit market debt, as shown in Table 12-5, plus security credit, trade payables of nonprofit organizations, and deferred and unpaid life insurance premiums.

Net worth is the sum of the value of financial and tangible assets minus total liabilities.

The *household debt-service* and *financial obligations ratios* are estimated on a quarterly basis by the Federal Reserve based on aggregate and consumer survey data. They are seasonally adjusted, unlike almost all of the other data in Table 12-6. Fourth-quarter values are shown to represent the calendar year. The denominator for the aggregate ratio is disposable personal income (DPI) from the NIPAs. (See Chapter 4.) The allocation of the NIPA data between *renters* and *homeowners* is estimated by the Federal Reserve based on data from its triennial Survey of Consumer Finances and the Census Bureau's Current Population Survey (CPS). (For more information on the CPS, see the notes and definitions to Chapters 3 and 10.)

Debt service payments are the minimum required monthly payments of principal and interest on mortgage debt (including home equity loans), revolving credit (credit card debt), and auto, student, mobile home, recreational vehicle, marine, and personal loans.

The *financial obligations ratios* include, in addition to debt service, rental payments on primary residences, property taxes, homeowners' insurance, and automobile lease payments.

Delinquency and *charge-off rates of credit card accounts held at banks* are compiled from the quarterly FFIEC (Federal Financial Institutions Examination Council) Consolidated Reports of Condition and Income (FFIEC 031 through 034) and pertain to all insured U.S.-chartered commercial banks. The *delinquency rate* concerns loans past due 30 days or more and still accruing interest as well as those in nonaccrual status, measured as a percentage of end-of-period loans. The *charge-off rate* is the value of net charge-offs (loans removed from the books and charged against loss reserves, minus recoveries) as a percentage of average loans outstanding over the quarter, annualized.

Data availability

Household balance sheet estimates are released quarterly, about nine weeks following the end of a quarter, in the Federal Reserve Statistical Release Z.1, "Flow of Funds Accounts of the United States." Further information on data availability is given in the notes to Table 12-5, a table which is also based on the flow of funds accounts.

The revised debt service ratio and the new financial obligations ratios are described in "Recent Changes to a Measure of U.S. Household Debt Service," *Federal Reserve Bulletin,* October 2003. The data are estimated by the Federal Reserve about three months after the end of each quarter. Current and historical data and articles from the *Bulletin* are available on the Federal Reserve Web site by selecting Economic Research and Data and either Statistical Releases and Historical Data or Federal Reserve Bulletin, then selecting the year.

Delinquency and charge-off rates of credit card accounts held at banks are also available on the Federal Reserve Web site, listed under "Charge-off and Delinquency Rates on Loans at Commercial Banks." Rates are posted approximately 60 days after the end of the quarter.

TABLE 12-7
MORTGAGE DEBT OUTSTANDING

SOURCE: BOARD OF GOVERNORS OF THE FEDERAL RESERVE SYSTEM

These data are also published in the Federal Reserve's Statistical Release Z.1, "Flow of Funds Accounts," Table L.217. They are based on reports from various government and private organizations.

Definitions and notes on the data

By type of property

Home mortgages includes home equity loans; these are also shown separately in the flow of funds accounts.

Multifamily residences refers to mortgages on structures of five or more units.

By type of holder

Federal and related agencies shows mortgages held directly by the federal government and GSEs (see notes and definitions for Table 12-5 above).

Mortgage pools or trusts show mortgages that were refinanced by their holders through the issuance of mortgage-backed securities. They are shown in two columns: refinancings by *federally related agencies*—mainly the GSEs Fannie Mae, Freddie Mac, and Ginnie Mae (see above)—and refinancings by private conduits (these are referred to as *ABS issuers* in the flow of funds accounts, which stands for issuers of asset-backed securities).

Other holders encompasses a variety of groups, including finance companies, individuals, state and local governments, credit unions, and others.

Home mortgage debt as a percentage of the value of real estate is calculated by the editor, using total home mortgage debt as a percentage of the value of household real estate, which is shown in Table 12-6.

Data availability

Mortgage debt data are compiled quarterly about nine weeks following the end of the quarter in Federal Reserve Statistical Release Z.1, "Flow of Funds Accounts of the United States." The release and current and historical data are available on the Federal Reserve Web site.

TABLE 12-8
CONSUMER CREDIT

SOURCE: BOARD OF GOVERNORS OF THE FEDERAL RESERVE SYSTEM

The consumer credit series cover most short- and intermediate-term credit extended to individuals through regular business channels, excluding loans secured by real estate (such as first and second mortgages and home equity credit). In October 2003, the scope of this survey was expanded to incorporate student loans extended by the federal government and by SLM Holding Corporation (SLM), the parent company of Sallie Mae (Student Loan Marketing Association). The historical data have been revised back to 1977 to reflect this inclusion.

The failure to include home equity credit is an important limitation of this data set. The household debt series presented in Table 12-5 are more comprehensive, comprising both mortgage and consumer debt.

Consumer credit is categorized by major types of credit and by major holders.

Definitions and notes on the data

The major types of consumer credit are *revolving* and *nonrevolving*. *Revolving credit* includes credit arising from purchases on credit card plans of retail stores and banks, cash advances and check credit plans of banks, and some overdraft credit arrangements. *Nonrevolving credit* includes automobile loans, mobile home loans, and all other loans not included in revolving credit, such as loans for education, boats, trailers, or vacations. These loans may be secured or unsecured.

Debt secured by real estate (including first liens, junior liens, and home equity loans) is excluded. Credit extended to governmental agencies and nonprofit or charitable organizations, as well as credit extended to business or to individuals exclusively for business purposes, is excluded.

Categories of *holders* include *U.S.-chartered depository institutions* (comprising commercial banks and savings institutions), *finance companies, credit unions, federal government, nonfinancial businesses*, and *pools of securitized assets*. The Student Loan Marketing Association (Sallie Mae) is included in "Federal government" until the end of 2004, at which time it became fully privatized. Beginning with the end of 2004, Sallie Mae is included in "Finance companies." Retailers and gasoline companies are included in the nonfinancial businesses category. *Pools of securitized assets* comprises the outstanding balances of pools upon which securities have been issued; these balances are no longer carried on the balance sheets of the loan originators.

The consumer credit series are benchmarked to comprehensive data that periodically become available. Current monthly estimates are brought forward from the latest benchmarks in accordance with weighted changes indicated by sample data. Classifications are made on a "holder" basis. Thus, installment paper sold by retail outlets is included in the figures for the banks and finance companies that purchased the paper.

The amount of outstanding credit represents the sum of the balances in the installment receivable accounts of financial institutions and retail outlets at the end of each month.

The estimates of the amount of credit outstanding include any finance and insurance charges included as part of the installment contract. Unearned income on loans is included in some cases when lenders cannot separate the components.

The seasonally-adjusted data are adjusted for differences in the number of trading days and for seasonal influences.

Data availability

Current data are available monthly in the Federal Reserve Statistical Release G.19, "Consumer Credit," available along with all current and historical data on the Federal Reserve Web site. In the autumn of each year there is a revision of several years of past data reflecting benchmarking and seasonal factor review.

TABLES 12-9, 12-10 AND 12-11
INTEREST RATES, BOND YIELDS, STOCK PRICES, AND HOUSING MARKET DATA

SOURCES: BOARD OF GOVERNORS OF THE FEDERAL RESERVE SYSTEM; BUREAU OF ECONOMIC ANALYSIS; MOODY'S INVESTORS SERVICE; THE BOND BUYER; DOW JONES, INC.; STANDARD AND POOR'S CORPORATION; NEW YORK STOCK EXCHANGE; FEDERAL HOUSING FINANCE AGENCY (FHFA), PREVIOUSLY OFHEO (OFFICE OF FEDERAL HOUSING ENTERPRISE OVERSIGHT)

Definitions and notes on the data

Interest rates and bond yields are percents per year and are averages of business day figures, except as noted. With a few exceptions, they are nominal rates or yields not adjusted for inflation.

The daily effective *federal funds rate*—the rate that currently serves as the principal marker for Federal Reserve monetary policy—is a weighted average of rates on trades through New York brokers. Monthly figures include each calendar day in the month. Annualized figures use a 360-day year.

The *Federal Reserve discount rate* is the rate for discount window borrowing at the Federal Reserve Bank of New York. Monthly figures include each calendar day in the month. Annualized figures use a 360-day year. Before 1945, annual averages calculated by editor.

Beginning in January 2003, the rules governing the discount window programs were revised. "Adjustment credit," which had been extended at a below-market rate (as can be seen in the average discount rates from 1978 through 2002 shown in Table 12-9, which are below the federal funds rate), was replaced by a new type of credit called "primary credit." Primary credit is available for very short terms as a backup source of liquidity to depository institutions in generally sound financial condition, as judged by the lending Federal Reserve Bank. Primary credit is extended at a rate <u>above</u> the federal funds rate, eliminating the incentive for institutions to exploit the spread of money market rates over the discount rate.

Through December 2002, Table 12-9 displays the adjustment credit rate. Beginning in February 2003, the new primary credit rate is shown. The rule change, and the change in discount rates shown, did not entail a change in the stance of monetary policy at that time. The overall stance of monetary policy is consistently measured by the level of the federal funds rate.

The *U.S. Treasury bills, 3-month rate* and the *U.S. Treasury bills, 6-month rate* are the yields on these securities based on their prices as traded in the secondary market. The rates are quoted on a discount basis. Annualized figures use a 360-day year. From 1934 to 1944, the 3-month rate is based on dealers' quotations. From 1931 through 1933, it is the average rate on new issues. For 1929 and 1930, it is the rate on 3- to 6-month Treasury notes and certificates.

The *inflation* column shown here, calculated by the editor, is the rate of change in the PCE chain-type price index, excluding food and energy. For monthly entries, it is the change from the same month a year earlier. This price index is calculated by the Bureau of Economic Analysis (BEA) and shown in Table 8-3. This inflation rate is shown along with other rates in Table 8-4; see the notes and definitions for that table.

The *real 3-month Treasury bill rate* is calculated by the editor by subtracting the inflation estimate from the nominal interest rate. Note that subtraction means changing the sign and adding; hence negative inflation (that is, price decline or deflation), as experienced in the 1930s, contributes to large positive real interest rates.

Commercial paper, 3-month rates are interpolated from data on certain commercial paper trades settled by the Depository Trust Company. This company is a clearinghouse and custodian for nearly all domestic commercial paper activity. The trades, which are on a discount basis, represent sales of commercial paper by dealers or direct issuers. Annualized figures use a 360-day year. From 1971 through September 1997, the series represented both nonfinancial and financial commercial paper. Since September 1997, rates have been reported separately for nonfinancial and financial companies; only rates for financial companies are shown here. This introduces a slight discontinuity in this series between August and September 1997. Before 1971, the prevailing rate in New York City for 4- to 6-month commercial paper; hence, this series is also discontinuous between December 1970 and January 1971, and is obtained from *B&MS* 1943 and 1976.

The *bank prime rate* is one of several base rates used by banks to price short-term business loans. It is the rate posted by a majority of the top 25 (by amount of assets in domestic offices) insured U.S.-chartered commercial banks. Monthly figures include each calendar day in the month. Annualized figures use a 360-day year. Before 1949, the data are not on the Federal Reserve Web site but have been reproduced from *B&MS* 1976. In that volume, the prime rate is described as "the rate that banks charge their most creditworthy business customers on short-term loans", as posted by the largest banks. The same source goes on to write, "A nationally publicized and uniform prime rate did not emerge until the depression of the 1930s. The rate in that period—1 ½ percent—represented a floor below which banks were said to regard lending as unprofitable. The date shown [for the beginning of a changed rate] is that on which the new rate was put into effect by the first bank to make the change. The table shows a range of rates for 1929-1933 because no information is available to indicate when the rate changed in that period." For further information, the source document cites "The Prime Rate," *Monthly Review,* Federal Reserve Bank of New York, April and May 1962, pp. 54-59 and 70-73, respectively.

U.S. Treasury securities, constant maturities.[1] The rates shown for 1-year, 5-year, 10-year, 20-year, and 30-year securities are yields on actively traded issues adjusted to constant maturities. Yields on Treasury securities at "constant maturity" are interpolated by the Treasury Department from the daily yield curve. This curve, which relates the yield on a security to its time to maturity, is based on the closing market bid yields on actively traded Treasury securities in the over-the-counter market. These market yields are calculated from composites of quotations reported by

---

[1] From February 18, 2002, to February 9, 2006, the U.S. Treasury published a factor for adjusting the daily nominal 20-year constant maturity in order to estimate a 30-year nominal rate. The historical adjustment factor can be found at www.treas.gov/offices/domestic-finance/debt-management/interest-rate/ltcompositeindex_historical.shtml.

U.S. Government securities dealers to the Federal Reserve Bank of New York. The constant maturity yield values are read from the yield curve at fixed maturities. For example, this method provides a yield for a 10-year maturity, even if no outstanding security has exactly 10 years remaining to maturity. The 30-year series was discontinued as of February 2002, because the Treasury Department was no longer issuing such bonds at that time. However, issuance of 30-year bonds was resumed in 2005 as an additional means of financing rising deficits, and the 30-year interest rate series resumes in 2006. The current 20-year series begins with 1993 and is not comparable with an earlier 20-year series. For further information, see the historical data series on the Federal Reserve Web site.

Before 1962, the *Treasury 10-year* is not available on the constant-maturity basis. The entries in that column are from *B&MS* 1943 and 1976 where they are labeled "United States government bonds (long-term)." Before 1941, they represent yields on bonds that were partly tax exempt. In 1941, the yield for the partly tax-exempt series was 1.95 percent—comparable with the entries for previous years—while the entry comparable with subsequent years was 2.12 percent.

Domestic corporate bond yields, Aaa and Baa. The rates shown are for general obligation bonds based on Thursday figures, and are provided by Moody's Investors Service and republished by the Federal Reserve. The Aaa rates through December 6, 2001 are averages of Aaa utility and Aaa industrial bond rates. As of December 7, 2001, these rates are averages of Aaa industrial bonds only.

The *state and local bond yields* are the Bond Buyer index as republished by the Federal Reserve. The index is based on 20 state and local government general obligation bonds of mixed quality maturing in 20 years or less. Quotes are as of the Thursday of each week. These rates have typically in the past been lower than those on U.S. Treasury or private long-term bonds because the interest on them is exempt from U.S. income taxes, but some recent data display different patterns because of changing assessments of credit risks relative to Treasury securities. Before 1953, the source is Standard and Poor's yields on high-grade municipal bonds as republished in *B&MS* 1943 and 1976.

Stock price indexes and yields. The *Dow Jones industrial* average is an average price of 30 stocks compiled by Dow Jones, Inc. The *Standard and Poor's composite* is an index of the prices of 500 stocks that are weighted by the volume of shares outstanding, accounting for about 90 percent of New York Stock Exchange value, with a base of 1941–1943 = 10, compiled by Standard and Poor's Corporation. (Before February 1957, these data are based on a conversion of an earlier 90-stock index, and are obtained from *B&MS* 1943 and 1976.) The *dividend-price ratio* is compiled by Standard and Poor's, covering the 500 stocks in the S&P index. It represents aggregate cash dividends (based on the latest known annual rate) divided by aggregate market value based on Wednesday closing prices. The *earnings/price ratio* measures

earnings (after taxes) for four quarters, ending with the indicated quarter, as a ratio to stock prices for the last day of that quarter. Monthly data are averages of weekly figures; annual data are averages of monthly or quarterly figures. The *Nasdaq composite index* is an average price of over 5,000 stocks traded on the Nasdaq exchange.

The *Eurodollar deposits* rate shown is the bid rate at about 9:30 a.m. (EST) for 1-month Eurodollar deposits. Annualized figures use a 360-day year.

CDs (secondary market), 3-month rates are averages of dealer offering rates on nationally traded certificates of deposit. Annualized figures use a 360-day year.

Interest rate swaps. An interest rate swap is a type of financial market derivative in which two parties, known as "counterparties," exchange two streams of cash flows. The rates shown here are the results of transactions in which streams of fixed-rate interest flows are exchanged for streams of floating-rate interest flows. The rates shown are the fixed interest rates which are exchanged for floating-rate flows paying the three-month LIBOR (London Interbank Offered Rate, a rate at which highly-rated banks can borrow short-term). They are International Swaps and Derivatives Association (ISDA ®) mid-market par swap rates, collected at 11 a.m. EST by Garban Intercapital plc and published on Reuters Page ISDAFIX ®1. ISDAFIX is a registered service mark of ISDA. Reprinted by the Federal Reserve from Reuters Limited.

Inflation-indexed yields. In recent years, the Treasury Department has issued Treasury Inflation-Protected Securities (TIPS), which are marketable long-term bonds whose redemption value is increased by the change in the CPI-U from the date of purchase. (See notes and definitions to Chapter 8.) The purchaser of these bonds, unlike with ordinary securities, is guaranteed that the real value of his or her principal will remain intact. He or she need not make his or her own estimate of future inflation in order to make a rational bid. Therefore, the observed purchase price represents a real rate of interest that purchasers and sellers are mutually willing to accept. Inflation-indexed yields are shown here for 5 and 20 years (adjusted to constant maturities by the Treasury) and for the long-term average, which is the unweighted average of the bid yields for all TIPS with remaining terms to maturity over 10 years.

The *fixed-rate first mortgage* rates are primary market contract interest rates on commitments for fixed-rate conventional 30-year first mortgages. The rates are obtained by the Federal Reserve from the Federal Home Loan Mortgage Corporation (FHLMC, or Freddie Mac).

FHFA (formerly OFHEO) House Price Indexes. The value of single-family owner-occupied houses has been an increasingly important element in household wealth and credit expansion and the subsequent collapse. The Federal Housing Finance Agency (FHFA), a government agency charged with regulation of the government-sponsored mortgage finance institutions Fannie Mae and Freddie Mac and the 12 Federal Home Loan Banks, uses data from those institutions to compile quarterly House Price Indexes of the value of existing single-family homes. Not included are condominiums, cooperatives, multi-unit properties, and planned unit developments. These indexes were developed by the predecessor agency, the Office of Federal Housing Enterprise Oversight (OFHEO), and has been published since the fourth quarter of 1995.

The data come from all properties for which a conventional, "conforming" mortgage has been purchased or securitized by Fannie Mae or Freddie Mac since January 1975. (Conventional mortgages are those not insured or guaranteed by the FHA, VA, or other federal government entities. A conforming mortgage is one no larger than the maximum that the insuring institution will insure. The limit has increased over time and has been $417,000 since the beginning of 2006. Loan limits for mortgages originated in the latter half of 2007 through Dec. 31, 2008, were raised to as much as $729,750 in high-cost areas in the continental United States. Legislation generally extended those limits for 2009-originated mortgages, and the limits for 2010 originations were further extended for certain places.) Every new mortgage transaction that can be matched against a previous transaction for that property yields a rate of price change over the period between the two transactions, which enters into the calculation of the index. This data set is very large, with about 32 million repeat transactions over the 32-year span. The index is computed using a modified version of the Case-Shiller geometric weighted repeat-sales procedure.

Due to the size of this data set, indexes so defined can be calculated, and are published, not only for the United States as a whole but also for regions, states, metropolitan statistical areas (MSAs) and metropolitan divisions (subdivisions of MSAs). Obviously, the national average price trend shown here is not representative of price behavior in some "hot" local markets.

In addition, FHFA now publishes Purchase-Only Indexes for the house purchase subgroup of new mortgage transactions, excluding refinancing transactions. Nation-wide, this index is based on 4.7 million transactions over the latest 16 years. While this is still a very large statistical base, it is subject to somewhat greater revision and is less reliable for smaller geographical areas.

The FHFA price indexes are subject to revision for preceding quarters and years, because each new transaction, when reported, affects the rate of price change for all periods since the last time that the property involved in the new transaction changed hands or was refinanced. Indeed, last year's indexes indicated that prices peaked in 2007, but this year's revised data show a 2006 peak.

Seasonally adjusted data are also available for the purchase-only indexes. Seasonal price patterns appear to have some significance, especially for regional indexes. The seasonally adjusted indexes are not shown here because the year-over-change, calculated from not-seasonally-adjusted data, is the main focus of attention in these data.

The FHFA indexes do not come from a random sample of house prices, and users need to consider possible sources of bias. Expensive houses are under-represented in general because the transactions are limited to conforming mortgages. This is important if the price trends for expensive houses are different.

It has also been suspected that prices of houses that are refinanced may behave differently than the prices of houses sold. It does appear that the latter are more volatile. Between the end of 1991 and the end of 2006, total house prices rose 94 percent while purchased houses rose 120 percent. Since then the total index declined 13 percent while the prices of purchased houses fell 19 percent.

New privately-developed house price indexes are now receiving regular media attention, and even provide the basis for a futures contract trading on the Chicago Mercantile Exchange. Standard & Poor's now issues S&P/Case-Shiller® Home Price Indexes each month. They cover resales only for houses at all price ranges, based on information obtained from county assessor and recorder offices. They are value-weighted, meaning that price trends for more expensive homes have greater influence on changes in the index. The FHFA index weights price trends equally for all properties. S&P/Case-Shiller data are only collected for 20 major metropolitan statistical areas. Series description and data can be found at <http://www.homeprice.standardandpoors.com>.

Data availability and references

Interest rates and bond yields are published weekly in the Federal Reserve's H.15 release, "Selected Interest Rates"; the release and current and historical data are available on the Federal Reserve Web site and in *B&MS* 1943 and 1976. The starting dates for individual interest rate series vary; some date back to 1911, and many begin in the 1950s and 1960s.

Stock market data are published monthly in *Economic Indicators,* and annually in *Economic Report of the President,* available online at <http://www.gpo.gov/fdsys>. Some historical interest rate data that are not available on the Federal Reserve Web site were also taken from the *Economic Report of the President.*

The FHFA house price indexes for the United States as a whole, regions, states, and metropolitan and sub-metropolitan groups are published every 3 months, approximately 2 months after the end of the previous quarter. The release and supporting data and explanatory material are available at <http://www.fhfa.gov>.

The OFHEO (now FHFA) and other price indexes for houses are discussed and compared in Jordan Rappaport, "Comparing Aggregate Housing Price Measures," *Business Economics,* October 2007, pp. 55-65.

CHAPTER 13: INTERNATIONAL COMPARISONS

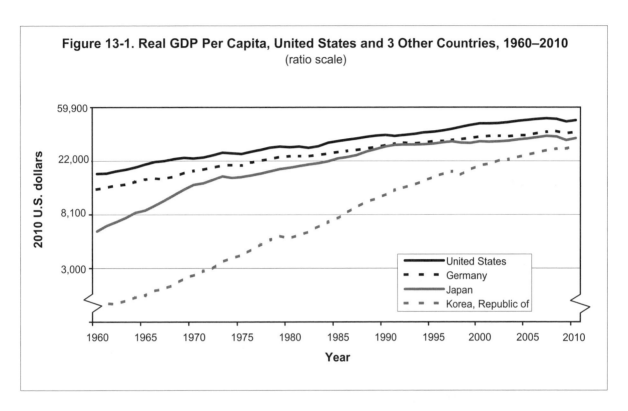

Figure 13-1. Real GDP Per Capita, United States and 3 Other Countries, 1960–2010
(ratio scale)

- In the United States, gross domestic product (GDP) per capita grew at an annual rate of 2.2 percent between 1960 and 2007. Canada, Australia, and the United Kingdom had similar growth rates. Growth was somewhat faster and more variable in continental Europe, ranging from 2.3 percent in Germany to 2.7 percent in Italy and Spain, and higher still in industrial Asia—3.8 percent in Japan and 6.4 percent in the Republic of Korea. The growth paths of the United States, Germany, Japan, and Korea are compared in Figure 13-1. (Table 13-2)

- The recession after 2007 affected all the countries shown. In Korea, growth slowed to a 2.6 percent annual rate after 2007. The other countries had one or two years of decline, and Spain had three. Relative strength in Asia kept the decline small in Australia, but elsewhere, per capita output dropped between 3.9 percent (France) and 7.7 percent (Italy). All the countries except Spain saw increasing output in 2010, but only Australia and Korea were above their pre-recession peaks. (Table 13-2)

- In 2011, consumer price change in the 10 countries shown in Table 13-4A ranged from a decline of 0.3 percent in Japan to an increase of 5.2 percent in the United Kingdom. (Table 13-4A)

- The countries shown employ different percentages of their working-age population, even in prosperous years like 2007. In that year, Canada was highest with 64.0 percent of its population at work; Australia, the United States, and the Netherlands were close behind. Italy and France were lowest, at 45.6 and 51.6 percent respectively, and Germany, Japan, and the United Kingdom in between at 53.2, 57.6, and 60.0 percent respectively. (Table 13-6)

461

Table 13-1. International Comparisons: Growth Rates in Real Gross Domestic Product (GDP)

(Percent change at annual rate.)

Area and country	1993–2002 annual average	2003	2004	2005	2006	2007	2008	2009	2010 [1]	2011 [1]	2012 [1]
World	3.3	3.6	4.9	4.6	5.3	5.4	2.8	-0.7	5.2	3.8	3.3
Advanced economies	2.8	1.9	3.1	2.7	3.1	2.8	0.1	-3.7	3.2	1.6	1.2
Of which:											
United States	3.4	2.5	3.5	3.1	2.7	1.9	-0.3	-3.5	3.0	1.8	1.8
Euro area [2]	2.1	0.7	2.2	1.7	3.2	3.0	0.4	-4.3	1.9	1.6	-0.5
Germany	1.4	-0.4	0.7	0.8	3.9	3.4	0.8	-5.1	3.6	3.0	0.3
France	2.0	0.9	2.3	1.9	2.7	2.2	-0.2	-2.6	1.4	1.6	0.2
Italy	1.6	0.0	1.5	0.7	2.0	1.5	-1.3	-5.2	1.5	0.4	-2.2
Spain	3.2	3.1	3.3	3.6	4.0	3.6	0.9	-3.7	-0.1	0.7	-1.7
Japan	0.8	1.4	2.7	1.9	2.0	2.4	-1.2	-6.3	4.4	-0.9	1.7
United Kingdom	3.1	2.8	3.0	2.2	2.8	2.7	-0.1	-4.9	2.1	0.9	0.6
Canada	3.5	1.9	3.1	3.0	2.8	2.2	0.7	-2.8	3.2	2.3	1.7
Memorandum:											
Newly industrialized Asian economies [3]	5.4	3.2	5.9	4.8	5.8	5.9	1.8	-0.7	8.4	4.2	3.3
Emerging and developing economies	4.1	6.2	7.5	7.3	8.2	8.9	6.0	2.8	7.3	6.2	5.4
Regional groups:											
Central and eastern Europe	3.2	4.8	7.3	5.8	6.4	5.5	3.1	-3.6	4.5	5.1	1.1
Commonwealth of Independent States [4]	-1.2	7.7	8.1	6.7	8.9	8.9	5.3	-6.4	4.6	4.5	3.7
Russia	-0.9	7.3	7.2	6.4	8.2	8.5	5.2	-7.8	4.0	4.1	3.3
Developing Asia	7.1	8.1	8.5	9.5	10.3	11.5	7.7	7.2	9.5	7.9	7.3
China	9.8	10.0	10.1	11.3	12.7	14.2	9.6	9.2	10.4	9.2	8.2
India	5.8	6.9	7.6	9.0	9.5	10.0	6.2	6.8	9.9	7.4	7.0
Latin America and the Caribbean	2.7	2.1	6.0	4.6	5.6	5.8	4.3	-1.7	6.1	4.6	3.6
Brazil	2.9	1.1	5.7	3.2	4.0	6.1	5.2	-0.6	7.5	2.9	3.0
Mexico	2.7	1.4	4.0	3.2	5.2	3.2	1.2	-6.2	5.4	4.1	3.5
Middle East and North Africa	3.3	7.3	5.9	5.4	6.0	6.7	4.6	2.6	4.3	3.1	3.2
Sub-Saharan Africa	3.7	4.9	7.1	6.2	6.4	7.1	5.6	2.8	5.3	4.9	5.5

[1] All figures are forecasts as published by the International Monetary Fund as of early 2012.
[2] Euro area consists of: Austria, Belgium, Cyprus, Finland, France, Germany, Greece, Ireland, Italy, Luxembourg, Malta, Netherlands, Portugal, Slovak Republic, Slovenia, and Spain.
[3] Consists of Hong Kong SAR (Special Adminsitrative Region of China), Korea (Republic of), Singapore, and Taiwan Province of China.
[4] Includes Georgia and Mongolia, which are not members of the Commonwealth of Independent States, but are included for reasons of geography and similarities in economic structure.

Table 13-2. International Comparisons: Real Gross Domestic Product (GDP) Per Capita

(2010 U.S. dollars.)

Year	United States	Australia	Canada	France	Germany [1]	Italy	Japan	Korea, Republic of	Netherlands	Spain	United Kingdom
1960	17 368	14 893	14 436	11 062	13 003	10 320	5 938	1 510	13 850	. . .	13 610
1961	17 484	14 417	14 593	11 470	13 425	11 092	6 582	1 552	14 063	. . .	13 813
1962	18 260	14 968	15 326	12 040	13 887	11 701	7 081	1 540	14 464	. . .	13 835
1963	18 786	15 554	15 842	12 566	14 141	12 268	7 627	1 635	14 737	. . .	14 340
1964	19 601	16 254	16 552	13 234	14 931	12 508	8 391	1 747	15 792	10 834	15 024
1965	20 599	16 707	17 291	13 739	15 557	12 808	8 769	1 801	16 402	11 389	15 257
1966	21 691	16 899	18 099	14 331	15 848	13 469	9 586	1 970	16 642	12 084	15 467
1967	21 998	17 742	18 295	14 912	15 762	14 332	10 537	2 038	17 327	12 459	15 758
1968	22 834	18 396	18 894	15 459	16 562	15 174	11 659	2 217	18 300	13 148	16 344
1969	23 312	19 271	19 563	16 424	17 630	16 009	12 902	2 468	19 321	14 152	16 608
1970	23 089	20 125	19 876	17 284	18 339	16 770	14 097	2 626	20 257	14 575	16 929
1971	23 564	19 975	20 093	18 034	18 713	16 995	14 492	2 843	20 872	15 052	17 192
1972	24 553	20 081	20 943	18 686	19 400	17 523	15 495	2 972	21 390	16 083	17 766
1973	25 728	20 684	22 129	19 763	20 228	18 644	16 507	3 352	22 373	17 145	19 002
1974	25 352	20 682	22 628	20 556	20 382	19 542	16 086	3 604	22 963	17 947	18 748
1975	25 054	20 880	22 707	20 231	20 279	19 019	16 377	3 804	22 767	17 882	18 635
1976	26 143	21 436	23 574	21 034	21 386	20 273	16 845	4 247	23 586	18 258	19 130
1977	27 072	21 558	24 106	21 688	22 149	20 704	17 416	4 676	24 036	18 518	19 595
1978	28 282	21 791	24 811	22 435	22 842	21 299	18 169	5 080	24 537	18 543	20 233
1979	28 845	22 388	25 501	23 109	23 778	22 503	19 004	5 423	24 861	18 415	20 753
1980	28 434	22 785	25 719	23 367	24 032	23 227	19 385	5 238	24 992	18 555	20 298
1981	28 867	23 370	26 294	23 464	24 113	23 395	20 048	5 539	24 624	18 425	20 042
1982	28 037	22 983	25 240	23 888	24 035	23 474	20 580	5 906	24 208	18 555	20 507
1983	29 039	22 572	25 670	24 054	24 499	23 740	21 065	6 529	24 613	18 794	21 255
1984	30 854	23 665	26 907	24 295	25 292	24 500	21 863	7 084	25 270	19 052	21 791
1985	31 846	24 654	27 937	24 565	25 945	25 179	23 103	7 539	25 805	19 423	22 523
1986	32 652	24 868	28 331	24 993	26 520	25 897	23 631	8 378	26 381	19 994	23 373
1987	33 397	25 695	29 147	25 453	26 887	26 721	24 484	9 314	26 712	21 051	24 388
1988	34 455	26 424	30 202	26 489	27 715	27 829	26 121	10 298	27 452	22 075	25 565
1989	35 350	27 129	30 440	27 437	28 510	28 750	27 418	10 885	28 499	23 095	26 074
1990	35 612	27 150	30 040	28 004	29 444	29 315	28 848	11 781	29 491	23 933	26 204
1991	35 059	26 580	29 062	28 156	30 434	29 736	29 694	12 798	29 967	24 486	25 748
1992	35 770	26 952	28 969	28 433	30 876	29 954	29 824	13 396	30 250	24 632	25 720
1993	36 315	27 753	29 321	28 124	30 408	29 670	29 780	14 100	30 414	24 303	26 233
1994	37 339	28 740	30 394	28 651	31 122	30 302	29 957	15 183	31 129	24 814	27 286
1995	37 829	29 376	30 925	29 135	31 618	31 158	30 445	16 373	31 935	25 439	28 040
1996	38 788	30 181	31 097	29 345	31 841	31 491	31 175	17 383	32 883	25 994	28 780
1997	40 036	31 157	32 091	29 882	32 354	32 063	31 588	18 214	34 111	26 929	29 655
1998	41 296	32 383	33 129	30 780	33 020	32 503	30 865	17 050	35 233	28 033	30 640
1999	42 797	33 390	34 677	31 652	33 660	32 974	30 766	18 746	36 636	29 213	31 592
2000	44 081	34 101	36 153	32 596	34 698	34 176	31 586	20 225	37 810	30 432	32 716
2001	44 101	34 499	36 404	32 956	35 063	34 776	31 555	20 874	38 247	31 188	33 392
2002	44 465	35 453	37 048	33 024	35 003	34 824	31 582	22 242	38 030	31 571	33 974
2003	45 170	36 203	37 384	33 088	34 911	34 547	31 979	22 752	37 979	32 014	34 792
2004	46 313	37 118	38 173	33 684	35 340	34 733	32 825	23 714	38 702	32 527	35 645
2005	47 296	37 760	38 955	34 045	35 622	34 703	33 457	24 601	39 395	33 154	36 182
2006	48 095	38 220	39 647	34 645	36 866	35 208	34 141	25 790	40 659	33 962	36 976
2007	48 532	39 222	40 084	35 221	37 893	35 469	34 947	27 018	42 161	34 545	37 719
2008	47 923	39 459	39 893	34 995	38 334	34 733	34 556	27 553	42 754	34 292	37 441
2009	45 854	39 137	38 323	33 853	36 635	32 723	32 424	27 562	41 033	32 774	35 389
2010	46 844	39 497	39 104	34 168	38 021	32 997	33 612	29 184	41 512	32 625	35 621

[1]Before 1991, data are based on growth in West Germany alone.

. . . = Not available.

Table 13-3. International Comparisons: Real Gross Domestic Product (GDP) Per Employed Person

(2010 U.S. dollars.)

Year	United States	Australia	Canada	France	Germany [1]	Italy	Japan	Korea, Republic of	Netherlands	Spain	United Kingdom
1960	45 970	36 820	41 576	25 810	27 625	24 758	11 787	. . .	37 637	. . .	29 861
1961	47 023	36 485	42 240	27 043	28 507	26 620	13 002	. . .	38 171	. . .	30 208
1962	49 004	37 675	43 950	28 906	29 733	28 354	13 940	. . .	39 031	. . .	30 366
1963	50 443	38 798	45 233	30 443	30 497	30 450	15 037	5 894	39 777	. . .	31 591
1964	52 218	39 979	46 514	32 029	32 500	31 411	16 503	6 351	42 452	. . .	32 879
1965	54 240	40 601	47 727	33 458	34 047	33 249	17 163	6 372	44 325	. . .	33 274
1966	56 098	40 062	48 905	34 918	35 104	35 823	18 542	6 966	45 215	. . .	33 838
1967	56 184	41 775	48 803	36 513	36 175	37 923	20 207	7 121	47 758	. . .	35 079
1968	57 691	42 997	50 164	38 229	38 115	40 425	22 243	7 546	50 489	. . .	36 715
1969	58 056	44 869	51 082	40 304	40 331	43 201	24 714	8 383	53 040	. . .	37 461
1970	57 841	45 933	52 008	42 202	41 833	45 284	26 966	8 803	55 637	. . .	38 402
1971	59 552	46 610	52 848	44 217	42 948	46 093	27 953	9 400	57 695	35 668	39 233
1972	60 923	46 936	54 095	45 912	44 549	47 918	30 148	9 595	60 257	38 104	40 549
1973	62 396	47 699	55 060	48 249	46 121	50 616	31 850	10 447	63 510	40 048	42 794
1974	60 913	47 924	54 756	50 028	46 976	52 583	31 593	10 948	65 064	42 144	42 124
1975	61 473	49 085	54 744	49 841	47 768	51 444	32 649	11 480	65 568	43 229	42 024
1976	62 725	50 414	56 461	51 591	50 342	54 558	33 672	12 268	68 317	45 152	43 388
1977	63 342	50 446	57 422	52 957	51 909	55 783	34 733	13 289	69 368	46 735	44 380
1978	64 140	51 507	57 928	54 712	52 948	57 400	36 211	14 002	70 388	48 622	45 574
1979	64 344	52 581	57 628	56 234	54 100	60 152	37 808	14 965	70 815	49 768	46 324
1980	63 855	52 678	57 200	56 902	53 958	61 329	38 609	14 595	69 645	51 633	45 580
1981	64 752	53 758	57 529	57 539	54 178	61 897	39 918	15 295	67 725	52 831	46 234
1982	64 015	53 805	57 711	58 799	54 384	62 026	40 931	16 153	67 682	53 952	48 197
1983	66 044	54 535	58 856	59 563	55 747	62 549	41 555	17 964	69 958	55 099	50 346
1984	68 024	56 169	60 753	60 787	56 830	64 571	43 263	19 839	71 688	57 365	50 616
1985	69 439	57 525	61 875	61 911	57 349	65 755	45 755	20 550	72 203	59 305	51 795
1986	70 267	56 555	61 485	62 972	57 555	67 173	46 811	22 270	73 086	59 848	53 539
1987	70 709	58 068	62 301	63 931	57 559	69 160	48 541	23 704	66 799	60 280	54 888
1988	72 049	58 502	63 479	66 282	58 855	71 295	51 413	25 659	67 173	61 206	55 812
1989	73 151	58 565	63 709	67 894	60 022	73 211	53 387	26 314	68 740	61 918	55 637
1990	73 655	58 449	63 395	69 062	61 246	73 542	55 437	27 926	69 351	61 907	55 816
1991	74 172	59 327	63 172	69 693	63 029	73 298	56 138	29 711	69 235	62 730	56 530
1992	76 293	61 204	64 364	71 216	65 383	74 405	55 967	30 829	69 008	64 207	57 992
1993	77 429	63 327	65 558	71 579	65 729	75 779	55 851	32 397	69 960	65 400	59 836
1994	78 839	64 299	67 326	72 884	67 546	78 706	56 270	34 149	71 548	67 275	61 905
1995	79 708	64 017	68 006	73 692	68 667	81 093	57 146	36 167	71 688	67 840	63 019
1996	81 565	65 813	68 492	74 070	69 540	81 516	58 609	37 950	72 653	68 496	64 235
1997	83 376	67 985	69 926	75 190	70 861	82 783	59 114	39 455	73 431	69 129	65 194
1998	85 775	69 855	71 040	76 424	71 446	83 121	58 593	39 582	74 154	69 507	66 867
1999	88 587	71 685	73 102	77 169	71 909	83 433	59 327	43 067	75 591	70 259	68 239
2000	90 001	72 254	75 075	77 971	72 852	84 869	61 405	44 940	76 492	71 320	70 096
2001	90 919	73 293	75 482	78 214	73 433	84 702	61 988	45 824	76 047	71 642	71 235
2002	92 812	74 741	75 836	78 516	73 846	83 656	63 139	47 779	75 180	71 996	72 182
2003	94 234	75 539	75 484	79 120	74 390	82 407	64 241	49 184	75 865	71 963	73 519
2004	96 449	76 911	76 506	81 053	74 990	83 302	65 862	50 503	77 711	71 824	74 897
2005	97 720	76 639	77 731	81 968	75 642	83 368	66 882	51 814	79 251	71 531	75 753
2006	98 503	76 745	78 398	83 078	77 710	83 430	67 948	53 803	80 453	71 487	77 181
2007	99 293	77 767	78 241	83 788	78 472	83 612	69 296	55 870	81 607	71 816	78 702
2008	99 404	77 640	77 480	83 296	78 161	82 282	68 728	56 805	81 830	72 737	78 085
2009	99 624	78 061	76 545	81 974	74 482	79 299	65 364	57 158	78 904	74 976	75 509
2010	103 229	78 047	77 948	83 050	76 769	80 917	68 233	59 858	82 403	76 670	76 334

[1] Before 1991, data are based on growth in West Germany alone.
. . . = Not available.

Table 13-4A. International Comparisons: Consumer Price Indexes

(1982–1984 = 100.)

Year	United States Index	Percent change	Australia Index	Percent change	Canada Index	Percent change	France Index	Percent change	Germany [1] Index	Percent change	Italy Index	Percent change	Japan Index	Percent change	Netherlands Index	Percent change	Spain Index	Percent change	United Kingdom Index	Percent change
1950	24.1	. . .	12.6	. . .	21.6	. . .	11.2	. . .	34.0	. . .	. . .	. . .	. . .	. . .	21.0	. . .	5.5	. . .	9.8	. . .
1951	26.0	7.9	15.1	19.7	23.8	10.4	13.1	16.9	36.6	7.6	. . .	. . .	. . .	. . .	23.1	9.6	6.0	9.4	10.7	9.1
1952	26.5	1.9	17.7	17.3	24.5	2.9	14.7	11.8	37.3	2.1	. . .	. . .	. . .	. . .	23.1	0.0	5.9	-2.0	11.7	9.2
1953	26.7	0.8	18.4	4.3	24.2	-1.4	14.5	-1.2	36.7	-1.7	10.3	. . .	. . .	. . .	23.1	0.0	6.0	1.6	12.1	3.1
1954	26.9	0.7	18.6	0.9	24.4	0.7	14.4	-0.4	36.8	0.4	10.6	2.8	. . .	. . .	24.0	4.0	6.1	1.2	12.3	2.0
1955	26.8	-0.4	19.0	2.2	24.4	0.0	14.6	1.2	37.3	1.4	10.9	2.3	. . .	. . .	24.5	1.9	6.3	4.0	12.8	4.4
1956	27.2	1.5	20.1	5.9	24.7	1.4	14.9	2.0	38.4	2.8	11.2	3.4	. . .	. . .	24.9	1.9	6.7	5.9	13.5	5.1
1957	28.1	3.3	20.6	2.6	25.6	3.5	15.3	2.7	39.1	2.0	11.4	1.3	. . .	. . .	26.5	6.5	7.4	10.8	14.0	3.5
1958	28.9	2.8	20.9	1.2	26.3	2.7	17.6	15.0	40.0	2.3	11.7	2.8	. . .	. . .	27.0	1.7	8.4	13.4	14.4	3.2
1959	29.1	0.7	21.3	1.9	26.4	0.7	18.7	6.2	40.3	0.6	11.7	-0.4	. . .	. . .	27.2	0.8	9.0	7.3	14.5	0.4
1960	29.6	1.7	22.1	3.8	26.8	1.3	19.4	3.7	40.9	1.6	11.9	2.3	. . .	. . .	27.9	2.5	9.1	1.2	14.6	1.0
1961	29.9	1.0	22.6	2.5	27.1	1.3	20.0	3.3	42.0	2.5	12.2	2.1	. . .	. . .	28.4	1.7	9.2	0.8	15.1	3.5
1962	30.2	1.0	22.6	-0.2	27.5	1.3	21.0	4.7	43.1	2.8	12.7	4.7	. . .	. . .	28.9	1.9	9.7	5.7	15.8	4.3
1963	30.6	1.3	22.7	0.4	27.8	1.3	22.0	4.8	44.4	3.0	13.7	7.5	. . .	. . .	30.0	3.8	10.6	8.7	16.1	1.9
1964	31.0	1.3	23.2	2.5	28.3	1.9	22.7	3.4	45.5	2.4	14.5	5.9	. . .	. . .	31.7	5.5	11.3	7.0	16.6	3.3
1965	31.5	1.6	24.1	3.8	29.0	2.4	23.3	2.5	46.9	3.2	15.2	4.6	. . .	. . .	33.3	5.2	12.8	13.2	17.4	4.7
1966	32.4	2.9	24.9	3.2	30.2	4.2	23.9	2.7	48.5	3.3	15.5	2.3	. . .	. . .	35.3	5.8	13.6	6.2	18.1	3.9
1967	33.4	3.1	25.7	3.2	31.3	3.4	24.6	2.6	49.4	1.9	16.1	3.7	. . .	. . .	36.4	3.1	14.5	6.4	18.6	2.6
1968	34.8	4.2	26.4	2.7	32.5	3.9	25.7	4.6	50.2	1.6	16.3	1.4	. . .	. . .	37.7	3.7	15.2	5.0	19.4	4.7
1969	36.7	5.5	27.2	3.0	34.0	4.8	27.3	6.5	51.1	1.8	16.7	2.7	. . .	. . .	40.5	7.4	15.5	2.2	20.5	5.4
1970	38.8	5.7	28.2	3.7	35.1	3.0	28.8	5.2	52.9	3.6	17.5	4.9	38.4	. . .	42.3	4.4	16.4	5.7	21.8	6.4
1971	40.5	4.4	29.8	6.0	36.1	3.0	30.3	5.5	55.7	5.2	18.4	4.8	41.0	6.7	45.5	7.5	17.7	8.2	23.8	9.4
1972	41.8	3.2	31.7	6.0	37.8	4.8	32.2	6.2	58.7	5.4	19.4	5.7	42.9	4.6	49.1	7.8	19.2	8.3	25.5	7.1
1973	44.4	6.2	34.6	9.2	40.8	7.8	34.6	7.3	62.8	7.1	21.6	10.8	48.0	11.8	53.0	8.0	21.4	11.4	27.8	9.1
1974	49.3	11.0	39.9	15.3	45.3	11.0	39.3	13.7	67.2	6.9	25.7	19.1	59.0	23.1	58.1	9.6	24.8	15.7	32.3	16.0
1975	53.8	9.1	45.9	15.2	50.1	10.7	43.9	11.8	71.2	6.0	30.0	17.0	66.0	11.8	64.0	10.2	29.0	17.0	40.1	24.2
1976	56.9	5.8	52.0	13.4	53.7	7.2	48.2	9.6	74.2	4.2	35.1	16.8	72.2	9.5	69.6	8.8	34.1	17.6	46.8	16.5
1977	60.6	6.5	58.5	12.3	58.1	8.0	52.7	9.4	77.0	3.7	41.0	17.0	78.0	8.0	74.3	6.7	42.4	24.5	54.2	15.8
1978	65.2	7.6	63.1	8.0	63.2	8.9	57.5	9.1	79.1	2.7	46.0	12.1	81.4	4.4	77.3	4.1	50.8	19.8	58.7	8.3
1979	72.6	11.3	68.8	9.1	69.1	9.3	63.6	10.8	82.3	4.1	52.8	14.8	84.4	3.6	80.6	4.2	58.8	15.7	66.6	13.4
1980	82.4	13.5	75.8	10.2	76.0	10.0	72.3	13.6	86.8	5.4	64.0	21.2	91.0	7.8	85.8	6.5	67.9	15.6	78.5	18.0
1981	90.9	10.3	83.1	9.6	85.5	12.5	82.0	13.4	92.2	6.3	75.4	17.8	95.3	4.8	91.6	6.7	77.8	14.5	87.9	11.9
1982	96.5	6.2	92.5	11.2	94.9	10.9	91.6	11.8	97.1	5.2	87.8	16.5	98.0	2.8	97.1	6.0	89.0	14.4	95.4	8.6
1983	99.6	3.2	101.8	10.1	100.4	5.8	100.5	9.6	100.2	3.2	100.7	14.7	99.8	1.8	99.8	2.8	99.9	12.2	99.8	4.6
1984	103.9	4.3	105.8	3.9	104.7	4.3	107.9	7.4	102.7	2.5	111.5	10.8	102.2	2.4	103.1	3.3	111.1	11.3	104.8	5.0
1985	107.6	3.6	112.9	6.7	108.9	4.0	114.2	5.8	104.8	2.0	121.8	9.2	104.2	2.0	105.4	2.2	120.9	8.8	111.1	6.1
1986	109.6	1.9	123.2	9.1	113.4	4.1	117.2	2.7	104.7	-0.1	129.0	5.9	104.9	0.7	105.6	0.2	131.6	8.8	114.9	3.4
1987	113.6	3.6	133.6	8.5	118.4	4.4	120.9	3.1	104.9	0.2	135.1	4.7	104.9	0.0	105.1	-0.5	138.5	5.2	119.7	4.2
1988	118.3	4.1	143.3	7.3	123.0	3.9	124.2	2.7	106.2	1.2	141.9	5.0	105.7	0.8	105.8	0.7	145.2	4.8	125.6	4.9
1989	124.0	4.8	154.1	7.5	129.3	5.1	128.6	3.6	109.2	2.8	150.8	6.3	108.1	2.2	107.0	1.1	155.0	6.8	135.4	7.8
1990	130.7	5.4	165.3	7.3	135.5	4.8	133.0	3.4	112.1	2.6	160.5	6.5	111.4	3.1	109.6	2.5	165.4	6.7	148.2	9.5
1991	136.2	4.2	170.7	3.2	143.1	5.6	137.3	3.2	116.3	3.7	170.6	6.3	115.0	3.3	113.8	3.9	175.2	5.9	156.9	5.9
1992	140.3	3.0	172.4	1.0	145.2	1.4	140.5	2.4	122.3	5.1	179.6	5.3	117.0	1.7	118.1	3.7	185.6	5.9	162.7	3.7
1993	144.5	3.0	175.5	1.8	147.9	1.9	143.5	2.1	127.6	4.4	187.8	4.6	118.5	1.3	120.5	2.1	194.1	4.6	165.3	1.6
1994	148.2	2.6	178.8	1.9	148.1	0.1	145.8	1.6	131.2	2.8	195.5	4.1	119.2	0.6	123.8	2.8	203.3	4.7	169.3	2.4
1995	152.4	2.8	187.1	4.6	151.4	2.2	148.4	1.8	133.4	1.8	205.8	5.3	119.1	-0.1	126.0	1.8	212.8	4.7	175.2	3.5
1996	156.9	3.0	192.0	2.6	153.6	1.5	151.3	2.0	135.3	1.4	214.0	4.0	119.2	0.1	128.7	2.1	220.3	3.6	179.4	2.4
1997	160.5	2.3	192.5	0.3	156.2	1.7	153.2	1.2	137.9	1.9	218.3	2.0	121.5	1.9	131.5	2.2	224.7	2.0	185.1	3.1
1998	163.0	1.6	194.1	0.9	157.8	1.0	154.3	0.7	139.3	1.0	222.6	2.0	122.2	0.6	134.1	2.0	228.8	1.8	191.4	3.4
1999	166.6	2.2	197.0	1.5	160.5	1.8	155.0	0.5	140.0	0.6	226.3	1.7	121.8	-0.3	137.0	2.2	234.1	2.3	194.3	1.5
2000	172.2	3.4	205.8	4.5	164.9	2.7	157.7	1.7	142.0	1.4	232.1	2.5	121.0	-0.7	140.2	2.3	242.1	3.4	200.1	3.0
2001	177.1	2.8	214.8	4.4	169.0	2.5	160.3	1.7	144.8	1.9	238.5	2.7	120.1	-0.8	146.1	4.2	250.8	3.6	203.6	1.8
2002	179.9	1.6	221.2	3.0	172.8	2.2	163.4	1.9	146.9	1.5	244.5	2.5	119.0	-0.9	150.9	3.3	259.6	3.5	207.0	1.7
2003	184.0	2.3	227.4	2.8	177.6	2.8	166.8	2.1	148.5	1.0	251.0	2.7	118.7	-0.3	154.0	2.1	267.5	3.0	213.0	2.9
2004	188.9	2.7	232.7	2.3	180.9	1.8	170.3	2.1	150.9	1.7	256.6	2.2	118.7	0.0	156.0	1.2	275.6	3.0	219.4	3.0
2005	195.3	3.4	238.9	2.7	184.9	2.2	173.4	1.8	153.2	1.5	261.5	1.9	118.3	-0.3	158.6	1.7	284.9	3.4	225.6	2.8
2006	201.6	3.2	247.4	3.5	188.5	2.0	176.2	1.6	155.7	1.6	267.1	2.1	118.7	0.3	160.4	1.2	294.9	3.5	232.8	3.2
2007	207.3	2.8	253.1	2.3	192.7	2.2	178.9	1.5	159.2	2.3	272.0	1.8	118.7	0.0	163.0	1.6	303.1	2.8	242.7	4.3
2008	215.3	3.8	264.1	4.4	197.2	2.3	183.9	2.8	163.3	2.6	281.1	3.3	120.3	1.4	167.1	2.5	315.5	4.1	252.4	4.0
2009	214.5	-0.4	269.0	1.8	197.7	0.3	184.1	0.1	163.9	0.4	283.3	0.8	118.7	-1.4	169.0	1.2	314.6	-0.3	251.1	-0.5
2010	218.1	1.6	276.6	2.8	201.3	1.8	186.9	1.5	165.8	1.1	287.7	1.5	117.8	-0.7	171.2	1.3	320.2	1.8	262.7	4.6
2011	224.9	3.2	286.0	3.4	207.2	2.9	190.8	2.1	169.6	2.3	295.7	2.8	117.5	-0.3	175.2	2.3	330.5	3.2	276.3	5.2

[1]Data prior to 1991 are for West Germany only.
. . . = Not available.

Table 13-4B. International Comparisons: Harmonized Indexes of Consumer Prices

(2005 = 100.)

Year	United States		Japan		European Union		Euro Area		Austria		Belgium		Denmark		France	
	Index	Percent change	Index	Percent change	Index	Percent change	Index	Percent change	Index	Percent change	Index	Percent change	Index	Percent change	Index	Percent change
1996	. . .	. . .	101.8	. . .	84.9	. . .	84.6	. . .	87.2	. . .	85.3	. . .	84.3	. . .	86.6	. . .
1997	. . .	. . .	103.4	1.6	86.4	1.7	85.9	1.6	88.2	1.2	86.5	1.5	85.9	1.9	87.8	1.3
1998	84.1	. . .	104.1	0.7	87.5	1.3	86.9	1.1	89.0	0.8	87.3	0.9	87.0	1.3	88.3	0.7
1999	85.8	2.0	103.7	-0.4	88.5	1.2	87.9	1.1	89.4	0.5	88.3	1.1	88.8	2.1	88.8	0.6
2000	88.7	3.4	102.8	-0.9	90.2	1.9	89.7	2.1	91.2	2.0	90.7	2.7	91.2	2.7	90.5	1.8
2001	90.8	2.3	101.8	-1.0	92.2	2.2	91.8	2.4	93.3	2.3	92.9	2.4	93.3	2.3	92.1	1.8
2002	91.6	0.9	100.7	-1.1	94.1	2.1	93.9	2.2	94.8	1.7	94.3	1.6	95.6	2.5	93.9	1.9
2003	93.7	2.3	100.4	-0.3	96.0	2.0	95.8	2.1	96.1	1.3	95.8	1.5	97.5	2.0	95.9	2.2
2004	96.3	2.8	100.4	0.0	97.9	2.0	97.9	2.1	97.9	2.0	97.5	1.9	98.3	0.8	98.1	2.3
2005	100.0	3.9	100.0	-0.4	100.0	2.2	100.0	2.2	100.0	2.1	100.0	2.5	100.0	1.7	100.0	1.9
2006	103.2	3.2	100.3	0.3	102.2	2.2	102.2	2.2	101.7	1.7	102.3	2.3	101.8	1.8	101.9	1.9
2007	105.9	2.6	100.4	0.1	104.6	2.3	104.4	2.1	103.9	2.2	104.2	1.8	103.5	1.7	103.6	1.6
2008	110.6	4.4	102.0	1.6	108.4	3.7	107.8	3.3	107.3	3.2	108.9	4.5	107.3	3.7	106.8	3.2
2009	109.7	-0.9	100.5	-1.5	109.5	1.0	108.1	0.3	107.7	0.4	108.9	0.0	108.4	1.0	106.9	0.1
2010	112.4	2.5	99.7	-0.8	111.8	2.1	109.8	1.6	109.5	1.7	111.4	2.3	110.8	2.2	108.8	1.7
2011	116.8	3.9	99.4	-0.3	115.2	3.1	112.8	2.7	113.4	3.6	115.3	3.5	113.8	2.7	111.3	2.3

Year	Germany		Italy		Netherlands		Norway		Spain		Sweden		Switzerland		United Kingdom	
	Index	Percent change	Index	Percent change	Index	Percent change	Index	Percent change	Index	Percent change	Index	Percent change	Index	Percent change	Index	Percent change
1996	88.6	. . .	81.8	. . .	80.4	. . .	84.3	. . .	77.9	. . .	87.5	. . .	. . .	. . .	88.1	. . .
1997	90.0	1.6	83.3	1.8	81.9	1.9	86.5	2.6	79.4	1.9	89.1	1.8	. . .	. . .	89.7	1.8
1998	90.5	0.6	85.0	2.0	83.4	1.8	88.2	2.0	80.8	1.8	90.0	1.0	. . .	. . .	91.1	1.6
1999	91.1	0.7	86.4	1.6	85.1	2.0	90.0	2.0	82.6	2.2	90.5	0.6	. . .	. . .	92.3	1.3
2000	92.4	1.4	88.6	2.5	87.1	2.3	92.8	3.1	85.5	3.5	91.7	1.3	. . .	. . .	93.1	0.9
2001	94.1	1.8	90.7	2.4	91.5	5.1	95.3	2.7	87.9	2.8	94.1	2.7	. . .	. . .	94.2	1.2
2002	95.4	1.4	93.1	2.6	95.1	3.9	96.1	0.8	91.0	3.6	95.9	1.9	. . .	. . .	95.4	1.3
2003	96.4	1.0	95.7	2.8	97.2	2.2	97.9	1.9	93.9	3.1	98.2	2.3	. . .	. . .	96.7	1.4
2004	98.1	1.8	97.8	2.2	98.5	1.4	98.5	0.6	96.7	3.1	99.2	1.0	. . .	. . .	98.0	1.3
2005	100.0	1.9	100.0	2.2	100.0	1.5	100.0	1.5	100.0	3.4	100.0	0.8	100.0	. . .	100.0	2.0
2006	101.8	1.8	102.2	2.2	101.7	1.7	102.5	2.5	103.6	3.6	101.5	1.5	101.0	1.0	102.3	2.3
2007	104.1	2.3	104.3	2.1	103.3	1.6	103.2	0.7	106.5	2.8	103.2	1.7	101.8	0.8	104.7	2.3
2008	107.0	2.8	108.0	3.5	105.5	2.2	106.7	3.4	110.9	4.1	106.7	3.3	104.2	2.4	108.5	3.6
2009	107.2	0.2	108.8	0.7	106.6	1.0	109.2	2.3	110.6	-0.2	108.7	1.9	103.4	-0.8	110.8	2.1
2010	108.4	1.1	110.6	1.7	107.6	0.9	111.8	2.4	112.9	2.0	110.8	1.9	104.1	0.7	114.5	3.3
2011	111.1	2.5	113.8	2.9	110.2	2.5	113.1	1.2	116.4	3.1	112.3	1.4	104.2	0.1	119.6	4.5

. . . = Not available.

Table 13-5. International Comparisons: Civilian Working Age Population

(Approximating U.S. concepts, thousands of persons.)

Year	United States	Australia	Canada	France	Germany [1]	Italy	Japan	Netherlands	United Kingdom
1960	117 245	. . .	11 494	31 369	43 436	37 130	64 990	. . .	38 952
1961	118 771	. . .	11 708	31 596	43 647	37 358	65 820	. . .	39 287
1962	120 153	. . .	11 940	32 319	43 972	37 815	67 330	. . .	39 804
1963	122 416	. . .	12 179	33 166	44 232	38 083	69 170	. . .	40 036
1964	124 485	7 668	12 453	33 717	44 525	38 515	71 000	. . .	40 281
1965	126 513	7 830	12 755	34 219	44 909	38 724	72 650	. . .	40 481
1966	128 058	8 023	13 083	34 606	45 174	39 276	74 090	. . .	40 631
1967	129 874	8 208	13 444	34 995	45 111	39 456	75 340	. . .	40 779
1968	132 028	8 403	13 805	35 362	45 163	39 833	76 550	. . .	40 874
1969	134 335	8 612	14 162	35 742	45 570	39 781	77 580	. . .	41 006
1970	137 085	8 819	14 528	36 151	46 094	40 279	78 616	. . .	41 101
1971	140 216	9 036	14 872	36 578	46 688	40 385	79 556	. . .	40 397
1972	144 126	9 238	15 186	36 965	47 101	40 780	80 467	. . .	40 564
1973	147 096	9 425	15 526	37 352	47 594	41 186	82 147	9 750	40 741
1974	150 120	9 614	15 924	37 711	47 904	41 745	83 173	9 885	40 913
1975	153 153	9 763	16 323	38 020	48 018	42 131	84 192	9 803	41 103
1976	156 150	9 957	16 582	38 330	48 128	42 312	85 164	9 960	41 332
1977	159 033	10 136	16 964	38 679	48 419	42 529	86 070	10 103	41 608
1978	161 910	10 406	17 302	39 008	48 789	43 000	87 021	10 256	41 904
1979	164 863	10 575	17 663	39 371	49 254	43 436	88 000	10 415	42 228
1980	167 745	10 778	18 032	39 750	49 848	43 860	89 078	10 588	42 570
1981	170 130	10 994	18 398	40 125	50 344	44 184	89 927	10 744	42 869
1982	172 271	11 204	18 716	40 476	50 714	44 847	90 918	10 871	43 083
1983	174 215	11 401	18 981	40 828	50 928	45 457	92 075	10 996	43 328
1984	176 383	11 602	19 220	41 165	51 084	45 853	93 226	11 131	43 596
1985	178 206	11 826	19 460	41 500	51 252	46 174	94 405	11 271	43 864
1986	180 587	12 074	19 715	41 846	51 448	46 628	95 626	11 403	44 087
1987	182 753	12 323	19 985	42 217	51 645	46 986	96 955	11 561	44 297
1988	184 613	12 593	20 257	42 605	51 894	47 778	98 243	11 667	44 456
1989	186 393	12 823	20 540	43 008	52 283	47 660	99 493	11 766	44 601
1990	189 164	13 051	20 852	43 344	53 438	48 016	100 656	11 865	44 706
1991	190 925	13 227	21 176	43 617	66 487	48 044	101 750	11 979	44 793
1992	192 805	13 391	21 459	43 879	67 083	48 203	102 592	12 077	44 859
1993	194 838	13 561	21 731	44 146	67 709	47 375	103 466	12 162	44 899
1994	196 814	13 729	21 994	44 388	68 022	47 520	104 200	12 246	44 973
1995	198 584	13 936	22 274	44 616	68 240	47 646	104 857	12 319	45 091
1996	200 591	14 117	22 567	44 855	68 498	47 748	105 467	12 387	45 249
1997	203 133	14 321	22 858	45 144	68 797	47 820	106 367	12 455	45 423
1998	205 220	14 525	23 124	45 439	68 914	47 904	107 044	12 538	45 609
1999	207 753	14 698	23 385	45 766	69 187	47 960	107 594	12 614	45 818
2000	212 577	14 902	23 687	46 113	69 365	48 029	108 120	12 703	46 085
2001	215 092	15 140	24 028	46 508	69 600	48 107	108 620	12 803	46 413
2002	217 570	15 390	24 383	46 909	69 900	48 232	109 030	12 892	46 707
2003	221 168	15 611	24 703	47 295	70 160	48 562	109 381	12 962	47 007
2004	223 357	15 802	25 028	47 698	70 432	49 080	109 661	13 019	47 364
2005	226 082	16 099	25 345	48 124	70 752	49 606	109 828	13 075	47 792
2006	228 815	16 371	25 711	48 502	70 892	49 913	109 959	13 128	48 197
2007	231 867	16 701	26 094	48 827	70 968	50 301	110 189	13 190	48 611
2008	233 788	17 015	26 486	49 119	71 021	50 711	110 270	13 271	48 998
2009	235 801	17 401	26 883	49 390	70 943	51 064	110 271	13 368	49 363
2010	237 830	17 854	27 250	49 653	70 858	51 311	110 261	13 459	49 741
2011	239 618	18 121	27 578	49 918	70 991	51 579	110 882	13 533	50 112

[1] Data prior to 1991 are for West Germany only.
. . . = Not available.

Table 13-6. International Comparisons: Civilian Employment-Population Ratios

(Approximating U.S. concepts. Civilian employment as a percent of civilian working-age population.)

Year	United States	Australia	Canada	France	Germany [1]	Italy	Japan	Netherlands	United Kingdom
1960	56.1	. . .	52.6	58.6	59.2	54.0	66.7	. . .	60.6
1961	55.4	. . .	52.4	58.2	59.6	54.0	66.8	. . .	60.8
1962	55.5	. . .	52.8	57.1	59.3	53.2	66.0	. . .	60.4
1963	55.4	. . .	53.0	56.6	59.2	51.9	64.9	. . .	60.2
1964	55.7	58.6	53.7	56.9	58.8	51.1	64.1	. . .	60.7
1965	56.2	59.1	54.4	56.4	58.5	49.6	63.6	. . .	61.0
1966	56.9	59.6	55.4	56.4	58.0	48.1	63.7	. . .	60.9
1967	57.3	60.0	55.4	56.2	56.3	48.5	64.0	. . .	60.0
1968	57.5	60.1	55.0	55.5	56.2	47.9	64.1	. . .	59.6
1969	58.0	60.2	55.3	55.9	56.6	47.6	63.9	. . .	59.5
1970	57.4	61.1	54.5	56.1	56.6	47.4	63.8	. . .	59.2
1971	56.6	61.1	54.5	55.8	56.2	47.1	63.4	. . .	60.2
1972	57.0	60.6	54.9	55.6	55.8	45.9	62.9	. . .	60.1
1973	57.8	61.2	56.4	55.8	55.9	45.8	63.2	51.8	60.8
1974	57.8	61.3	57.3	55.8	54.8	46.2	62.2	51.6	60.7
1975	56.1	60.1	56.9	54.9	53.2	46.0	61.2	51.7	60.2
1976	56.8	59.7	58.2	54.9	52.8	46.1	61.1	51.2	59.5
1977	57.9	59.2	57.9	54.9	52.5	46.2	61.3	51.6	59.2
1978	59.3	58.0	58.5	54.7	52.6	45.9	61.3	51.3	59.1
1979	59.9	57.8	59.8	54.3	52.9	45.9	61.4	51.4	59.3
1980	59.2	58.3	60.3	53.9	53.1	46.0	61.3	52.1	58.5
1981	59.0	58.4	60.8	53.2	52.5	45.9	61.2	51.7	56.6
1982	57.8	57.3	58.0	54.8	51.6	45.1	61.2	50.8	55.2
1983	57.9	55.3	57.6	54.2	50.6	44.7	61.4	49.3	54.5
1984	59.5	56.0	58.3	53.3	50.6	44.5	61.0	49.3	55.3
1985	60.1	56.6	59.4	52.9	50.8	44.4	60.6	50.1	55.7
1986	60.7	57.8	60.3	53.0	51.3	44.2	60.4	50.3	55.7
1987	61.5	57.9	61.2	52.5	51.5	43.8	60.1	49.8	56.6
1988	62.3	58.7	62.2	52.2	51.6	43.7	60.4	50.7	58.3
1989	63.0	60.2	62.7	52.4	52.0	43.6	60.8	51.4	59.6
1990	62.8	60.2	62.2	52.2	52.3	43.9	61.3	52.7	59.8
1991	61.7	58.0	60.2	51.7	55.5	44.5	61.8	53.7	58.1
1992	61.5	57.0	58.9	51.3	54.2	44.0	62.0	54.3	56.6
1993	61.7	56.6	58.5	50.6	53.2	44.5	61.7	53.9	56.1
1994	62.5	57.7	59.0	50.1	52.6	43.6	61.3	54.0	56.4
1995	62.9	59.1	59.3	50.5	52.4	43.1	60.9	55.4	57.0
1996	63.2	59.1	59.1	50.5	52.0	43.2	60.9	56.2	57.3
1997	63.8	58.9	59.7	50.0	51.6	43.2	61.0	57.7	58.1
1998	64.1	59.3	60.4	50.2	52.3	43.5	60.2	59.1	58.5
1999	64.3	59.6	61.3	50.5	52.1	43.9	59.4	60.3	59.0
2000	64.4	60.3	62.0	51.5	52.2	44.5	59.0	61.1	59.4
2001	63.7	60.0	61.8	51.7	52.2	45.1	58.4	62.1	59.5
2002	62.7	60.2	62.4	51.9	51.5	45.6	57.5	62.3	59.6
2003	62.3	60.8	63.1	51.5	50.8	45.3	57.1	61.6	59.8
2004	62.3	61.1	63.3	51.2	50.6	45.1	57.1	61.1	59.9
2005	62.7	62.1	63.3	51.1	51.1	44.9	57.3	60.9	60.0
2006	63.1	62.7	63.5	51.1	52.1	45.5	57.5	61.7	60.0
2007	63.0	63.3	64.0	51.6	53.2	45.6	57.6	62.9	60.0
2008	62.2	63.9	64.1	52.1	54.0	45.6	57.4	63.4	59.9
2009	59.3	62.9	62.2	51.3	54.0	44.6	56.4	62.8	58.5
2010	58.5	63.0	62.3	51.2	54.4	44.0	56.2	60.8	58.2
2011	58.4	63.1	62.5	51.0	55.7	44.0	56.2	60.5	58.0

[1]Data prior to 1991 are for West Germany only.
. . . = Not available.

Table 13-7. International Comparisons: Civilian Unemployment Rates

(Approximating U.S. concepts. Civilian unemployment as a percent of civilian labor force.)

Year	United States	Australia	Canada	France	Germany [1]	Italy	Japan	Netherlands	United Kingdom
1960	5.5	1.6	6.5	1.5	1.1	3.7	1.7	. . .	2.2
1961	6.7	3.0	6.7	1.2	0.6	3.2	1.5	. . .	2.0
1962	5.5	2.9	5.5	1.4	0.6	2.8	1.3	. . .	2.7
1963	5.7	2.3	5.2	1.6	0.5	2.4	1.3	. . .	3.3
1964	5.2	1.4	4.4	1.2	0.4	2.7	1.2	. . .	2.5
1965	4.5	1.3	3.6	1.6	0.3	3.5	1.2	. . .	2.1
1966	3.8	1.6	3.3	1.6	0.3	3.7	1.4	. . .	2.3
1967	3.8	1.9	3.8	2.1	1.3	3.4	1.3	. . .	3.3
1968	3.6	1.8	4.5	2.7	1.1	3.5	1.2	. . .	3.2
1969	3.5	1.8	4.4	2.3	0.6	3.5	1.1	. . .	3.1
1970	4.9	1.7	5.7	2.5	0.5	3.2	1.2	. . .	3.1
1971	5.9	1.9	6.2	2.8	0.6	3.3	1.3	. . .	4.2
1972	5.6	2.6	6.2	2.9	0.7	3.8	1.4	. . .	4.4
1973	4.9	2.3	5.6	2.8	0.7	3.7	1.3	3.1	3.7
1974	5.6	2.7	5.3	2.9	1.6	3.1	1.4	3.6	3.7
1975	8.5	4.9	6.9	3.6	3.4	3.4	1.9	5.1	4.5
1976	7.7	4.8	6.9	4.0	3.4	3.9	2.0	5.4	5.4
1977	7.1	5.6	7.8	4.5	3.4	4.1	2.0	4.9	5.6
1978	6.1	6.3	8.1	4.6	3.3	4.1	2.3	5.1	5.5
1979	5.8	6.3	7.3	5.2	2.9	4.4	2.1	5.1	5.4
1980	7.1	6.1	7.3	5.6	2.8	4.4	2.0	6.0	6.9
1981	7.6	5.8	7.3	6.6	4.0	4.9	2.2	8.9	9.7
1982	9.7	7.2	10.7	6.9	5.6	5.4	2.4	10.2	10.8
1983	9.6	10.0	11.6	7.2	6.9	5.9	2.7	11.4	11.5
1984	7.5	9.0	10.9	8.5	7.1	5.9	2.8	11.5	11.8
1985	7.2	8.3	10.1	9.0	7.2	6.0	2.5	9.6	11.4
1986	7.0	8.1	9.2	9.0	6.6	7.5	2.7	10.0	11.4
1987	6.2	8.1	8.4	9.2	6.3	7.9	2.6	9.8	10.5
1988	5.5	7.2	7.4	8.9	6.3	7.9	2.4	9.3	8.6
1989	5.3	6.2	7.1	8.3	5.7	7.8	2.2	8.4	7.3
1990	5.6	6.9	7.7	8.0	5.0	7.0	2.0	7.6	7.1
1991	6.8	9.6	9.8	8.2	5.6	6.9	2.0	7.1	8.9
1992	7.5	10.8	10.7	9.1	6.7	7.3	2.1	6.8	10.0
1993	6.9	10.9	10.8	10.2	8.0	9.8	2.4	6.3	10.4
1994	6.1	9.8	9.6	10.8	8.5	10.8	2.6	6.9	9.5
1995	5.6	8.5	8.6	10.2	8.2	11.3	2.9	7.1	8.7
1996	5.4	8.5	8.8	10.7	9.0	11.3	3.1	6.6	8.1
1997	4.9	8.5	8.4	10.8	9.9	11.3	3.1	5.6	7.0
1998	4.5	7.7	7.7	10.4	9.3	11.4	3.8	4.4	6.3
1999	4.2	6.9	7.0	10.1	8.5	11.0	4.2	3.5	6.0
2000	4.0	6.3	6.1	8.6	7.8	10.1	4.4	3.1	5.5
2001	4.7	6.8	6.5	7.8	7.9	9.1	4.5	2.5	5.1
2002	5.8	6.4	7.0	8.0	8.6	8.6	4.9	3.1	5.2
2003	6.0	5.9	6.9	8.6	9.3	8.5	4.6	4.1	5.0
2004	5.5	5.4	6.4	9.0	10.3	8.1	4.2	5.0	4.8
2005	5.1	5.0	6.0	9.0	11.2	7.8	3.8	5.3	4.9
2006	4.6	4.8	5.5	8.9	10.3	6.9	3.6	4.3	5.5
2007	4.6	4.4	5.2	8.1	8.7	6.2	3.6	3.6	5.4
2008	5.8	4.3	5.3	7.5	7.6	6.8	3.7	3.1	5.7
2009	9.3	5.6	7.3	9.2	7.8	7.9	4.8	3.8	7.7
2010	9.6	5.2	7.1	9.5	7.1	8.5	4.8	4.6	7.9
2011	8.9	5.1	6.5	9.4	6.0	8.5	4.2	4.5	8.1

[1]Data prior to 1991 are for West Germany only.
. . . = Not available.

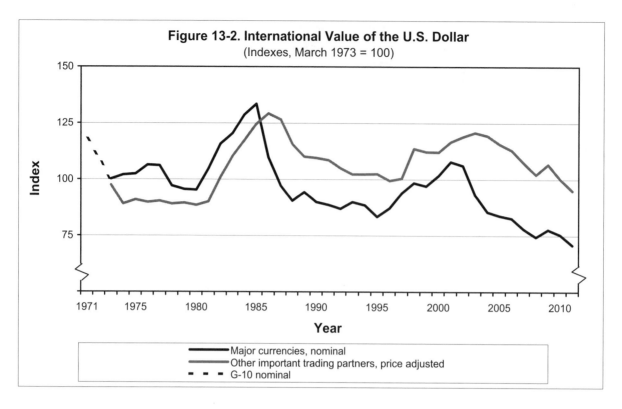

Figure 13-2. International Value of the U.S. Dollar
(Indexes, March 1973 = 100)

- Figure 13-2 above displays two indexes of the dollar's value. One is relative to a weighted average of seven "major" currencies—the euro, the British pound, the Canadian dollar, the Japanese yen, the Swiss franc, the Australian dollar, and the Swedish krona. These are all major industrial countries whose currencies are freely traded on world markets. Measured against these major currencies in terms of annual averages, the dollar has depreciated 34 percent from 2001 to 2011, roughly comparable to the 32 percent drop from 1985 to 1988. The dollar depreciation trend seems unsurprising in light of the large current-account deficits detailed in Chapter 7. (Table 13-8 and Chapter 7)

- However, the major-currency index does not well represent U.S. competitiveness relative to the emerging-market currencies ("Other important trading partners" or OITP) that account for much of the U.S. trade deficit. Many emerging-market countries, especially China, are able to control the international values of their currencies (through, for example, direct capital controls) and keep their currencies from appreciating relative to the dollar to maintain their competitiveness in the U.S. market. Recently the Chinese have allowed some yuan appreciation, as can be seen in Table 13-8, and inflation in China has also affected its real exchange rate. An index of the value of the dollar relative to OITP (including China) that adjusts exchange rates for inflation is also shown in Figure 13-2. Overall, there has been a 16 percent decline in the price-adjusted OITP index from 2001 to December 2011. (Table 13-8)

Table 13-8. Foreign Exchange Rates

(Not seasonally adjusted.)

Year and month	Foreign currency per U.S. dollar							Trade-weighted exchange indexes of value of U.S. dollar					
								Nominal				Price-adjusted	
	Canada, dollar	China (P.R.), yuan (renminbi)	EMU members, euro	Germany, mark	Japan, yen	Switzerland, franc	United Kingdom, pound	G-10 countries (March 1973 = 100)	Broad (January 1997 = 100)	Major currencies (March 1973 = 100)	Other important trading partners (January 1997 = 100)	Broad (March 1973 = 100)	Other important trading partners (March 1973 = 100)
1971	1.0099	. . .	. . .	3.4673	348.05	4.1158	0.4091	117.81	. . .	. . .	. . .	. . .	. . .
1972	0.9908	. . .	. . .	3.1889	303.11	3.8181	0.3995	109.07	. . .	. . .	. . .	. . .	. . .
1973	1.0002	. . .	. . .	2.6719	271.40	3.1698	0.4077	99.14	31.70	100.17	2.03	98.97	97.47
1974	0.9781	. . .	. . .	2.5873	291.94	2.9791	0.4273	101.41	32.58	102.03	2.14	95.63	89.11
1975	1.0173	. . .	. . .	2.4614	296.77	2.5834	0.4501	98.50	33.68	102.39	2.39	94.45	90.88
1976	0.9861	. . .	. . .	2.5184	296.48	2.5003	0.5541	105.63	35.83	106.44	2.71	94.51	89.84
1977	1.0635	. . .	. . .	2.3225	268.38	2.4038	0.5731	103.35	36.88	106.10	3.02	92.88	90.38
1978	1.1408	. . .	. . .	2.0089	210.46	1.7899	0.5213	92.39	35.09	97.13	3.18	87.30	89.04
1979	1.1716	. . .	. . .	1.8331	219.21	1.6635	0.4712	88.07	35.36	95.59	3.41	88.41	89.43
1980	1.1694	. . .	. . .	1.8183	226.58	1.6776	0.4302	87.39	36.35	95.35	3.75	89.75	88.43
1981	1.1989	1.7100	. . .	2.2606	220.45	1.9647	0.4940	103.26	40.34	104.76	4.27	96.58	90.03
1982	1.2339	1.8979	. . .	2.4281	249.05	2.0318	0.5721	116.50	46.83	115.75	5.52	106.10	101.03
1983	1.2326	1.9810	. . .	2.5545	237.45	2.1004	0.6597	125.32	52.81	120.46	7.44	110.57	110.30
1984	1.2952	2.3303	. . .	2.8483	237.59	2.3517	0.7481	138.34	60.11	128.69	9.78	117.91	117.12
1985	1.3659	2.9434	. . .	2.9443	238.47	2.4576	0.7708	143.24	67.16	133.55	13.14	122.73	124.63
1986	1.3898	3.4616	. . .	2.1711	168.50	1.7988	0.6813	112.27	62.35	109.77	16.49	107.40	129.33
1987	1.3262	3.7314	. . .	1.7976	144.62	1.4916	0.6098	96.95	60.42	97.16	19.92	98.66	126.62
1988	1.2309	3.7314	. . .	1.7561	128.14	1.4633	0.5614	92.75	60.92	90.43	24.07	92.07	115.57
1989	1.1841	3.7673	. . .	1.8792	137.99	1.6354	0.6104	98.52	66.90	94.29	29.61	93.80	110.04
1990	1.1670	4.7921	. . .	1.6159	144.82	1.3898	0.5605	89.05	71.41	89.91	40.10	91.22	109.56
1991	1.1460	5.3337	. . .	1.6585	134.51	1.4338	0.5658	89.73	74.35	88.59	46.69	89.68	108.58
1992	1.2088	5.5206	. . .	1.5624	126.75	1.4069	0.5662	86.64	76.91	87.00	53.13	87.79	104.96
1993	1.2902	5.7795	. . .	1.6537	111.23	1.4780	0.6660	93.17	83.78	89.90	63.37	89.13	102.33
1994	1.3659	8.6397	. . .	1.6219	102.20	1.3668	0.6528	91.32	90.87	88.43	80.54	88.96	102.34
1995	1.3727	8.3700	. . .	1.4331	94.11	1.1822	0.6335	84.30	92.65	83.41	92.51	86.51	102.40
1996	1.3637	8.3389	. . .	1.5049	108.80	1.2364	0.6407	87.34	97.46	87.25	98.24	88.52	99.40
1997	1.3849	8.3193	. . .	1.7339	121.09	1.4508	0.6106	96.35	104.43	93.93	104.64	93.23	100.45
1998	1.4836	8.3008	. . .	1.7593	130.82	1.4497	0.6034	98.82	115.89	98.45	125.89	101.20	113.61
1999	1.4858	8.2783	0.9375	1.8359	113.71	1.5027	0.6184	. . .	116.16	97.06	129.20	100.34	112.18
2000	1.4855	8.2784	1.0830	. . .	107.82	1.6899	0.6598	. . .	119.55	101.76	129.81	104.11	112.13
2001	1.5490	8.2770	1.1167	. . .	121.52	1.6880	0.6946	. . .	126.06	107.87	135.92	110.11	116.69
2002	1.5706	8.2771	1.0579	. . .	125.27	1.5571	0.6656	. . .	126.82	106.18	140.41	110.27	118.94
2003	1.4012	8.2772	0.8836	. . .	115.92	1.3452	0.6117	. . .	119.26	93.15	143.57	103.61	120.75
2004	1.3016	8.2768	0.8039	. . .	108.16	1.2428	0.5456	. . .	113.76	85.51	143.38	98.98	119.34
2005	1.2115	8.1936	0.8034	. . .	110.14	1.2462	0.5493	. . .	110.84	83.86	138.87	97.32	115.68
2006	1.1344	7.9723	0.7962	. . .	116.35	1.2535	0.5425	. . .	108.70	82.60	135.40	96.21	112.99
2007	1.0742	7.6058	0.7294	. . .	117.77	1.1999	0.4995	. . .	103.58	77.96	130.23	91.63	107.41
2008	1.0668	6.9477	0.6801	. . .	103.38	1.0829	0.5392	. . .	99.90	74.42	126.80	87.78	102.19
2009	1.1414	6.8307	0.7177	. . .	93.60	1.0861	0.6385	. . .	105.69	77.69	135.91	91.38	106.68
2010	1.0301	6.7696	0.7532	. . .	87.75	1.0426	0.6472	. . .	101.86	75.39	130.38	87.12	100.13
2011	0.9890	6.4630	0.7184	. . .	79.71	0.8876	0.6233	. . .	97.17	70.88	125.76	82.65	94.96
2010													
January	1.0438	6.8269	0.7010	. . .	91.10	1.0345	0.6189	. . .	101.43	73.86	131.48	87.60	102.55
February	1.0572	6.8285	0.7310	. . .	90.14	1.0722	0.6403	. . .	102.95	75.54	132.66	88.65	103.00
March	1.0229	6.8262	0.7369	. . .	90.72	1.0666	0.6641	. . .	102.05	75.23	131.00	87.72	101.43
April	1.0052	6.8256	0.7453	. . .	93.45	1.0690	0.6522	. . .	101.53	75.41	129.52	87.09	99.97
May	1.0403	6.8275	0.7960	. . .	91.97	1.1295	0.6817	. . .	104.36	78.50	131.79	89.27	101.33
June	1.0376	6.8184	0.8181	. . .	90.81	1.1255	0.6771	. . .	104.93	79.06	132.33	89.69	101.62
July	1.0422	6.7762	0.7806	. . .	87.50	1.0530	0.6534	. . .	103.30	76.77	131.73	88.30	101.09
August	1.0404	6.7873	0.7750	. . .	85.37	1.0388	0.6385	. . .	102.49	75.95	131.00	87.53	100.33
September	1.0330	6.7396	0.7632	. . .	84.36	1.0002	0.6414	. . .	101.48	74.99	130.03	86.53	99.32
October	1.0179	6.6678	0.7194	. . .	81.73	0.9686	0.6302	. . .	98.84	72.30	127.67	84.11	97.21
November	1.0129	6.6538	0.7324	. . .	82.52	0.9847	0.6265	. . .	99.12	72.83	127.59	84.12	96.70
December	1.0081	6.6497	0.7564	. . .	83.34	0.9689	0.6412	. . .	99.78	73.79	127.76	84.79	96.95
2011													
January	0.9939	6.5964	0.7479	. . .	82.63	0.9565	0.6336	. . .	98.62	72.93	126.28	83.71	95.61
February	0.9876	6.5761	0.7323	. . .	82.54	0.9500	0.6202	. . .	97.88	72.00	125.87	83.22	95.35
March	0.9766	6.5645	0.7133	. . .	81.65	0.9185	0.6189	. . .	96.94	70.81	125.37	82.53	95.11
April	0.9580	6.5267	0.6916	. . .	83.18	0.8972	0.6105	. . .	95.36	69.59	123.42	81.26	93.68
May	0.9680	6.4957	0.6976	. . .	81.13	0.8740	0.6123	. . .	95.31	69.66	123.18	81.22	93.39
June	0.9766	6.4746	0.6943	. . .	80.43	0.8401	0.6166	. . .	95.29	69.58	123.27	81.10	93.08
July	0.9553	6.4575	0.7005	. . .	79.24	0.8214	0.6189	. . .	94.62	69.12	122.36	80.57	92.31
August	0.9817	6.4036	0.6977	. . .	76.97	0.7800	0.6114	. . .	95.15	69.07	123.68	81.12	93.38
September	1.0025	6.3885	0.7274	. . .	76.80	0.8767	0.6341	. . .	97.99	71.17	127.31	83.48	96.12
October	1.0198	6.3710	0.7282	. . .	76.64	0.8958	0.6342	. . .	98.90	71.61	128.83	83.98	96.89
November	1.0248	6.3564	0.7376	. . .	77.56	0.9079	0.6327	. . .	99.54	72.24	129.41	84.44	97.15
December	1.0235	6.3482	0.7602	. . .	77.80	0.9334	0.6416	. . .	100.46	73.23	130.13	85.12	97.50

. . . = Not available.

NOTES AND DEFINITIONS, CHAPTER 13

TABLE 13-1
INTERNATIONAL COMPARISONS: GROWTH RATES IN REAL GROSS DOMESTIC PRODUCT

SOURCE: ECONOMIC REPORT OF THE PRESIDENT, ANNUAL REPORT OF THE COUNCIL OF ECONOMIC ADVISERS, FEBRUARY 2012

Table 13-1 is reprinted from the February 2012 *Annual Report of the U.S. Council of Economic Advisers*, where it appears as Table B-112. It is based on data from the Department of Commerce's Bureau of Economic Analysis (BEA) and the International Monetary Fund. The report is found at <www.whitehouse.gov/administration/eop/cea/economic-report-of-the-President>. Note that all of the 2011 data are based on forecasts, and the U.S. data are now superseded by later BEA estimates shown elsewhere in the volume and expected subsequently as well.

TABLES 13-2 AND 13-3
INTERNATIONAL COMPARISONS: REAL GROSS DOMESTIC PRODUCT PER CAPITA, REAL GROSS DOMESTIC PRODUCT PER EMPLOYED PERSON

SOURCE: U.S. DEPARTMENT OF LABOR, BUREAU OF LABOR STATISTICS (BLS)

Definitions and notes on the data

Real gross domestic product (GDP) per capita can be taken as a rough measure of potential economic welfare; that is, the potential standard of living available to each of a country's residents. Because income distributions are typically skewed, GDP per capita (which is an average or "mean") should not be taken as a representation of the value of the standard of living actually enjoyed by a typical ("median") individual. See the subsection entitled "Whose standard of living?" in the article at the beginning of this volume.

Real gross domestic product per employed person is a rough measure of productivity (ignoring any differences in hours worked by employees).

The GDP, population, and employment measures for each country come from the country's own national accounts and population sources. Not all countries use annual chain-weighted methods such as those incorporated in U.S. GDP. (See notes and definitions to Chapter 1.) Some of the employment and population figures have been recalculated for greater comparability by BLS. GDP figures are converted from national currency values to U.S. 2010-dollar equivalents using 2010 purchasing power parities (PPPs) published by the OECD (Organisation for Economic Co-operation and Development) in the OECD-Eurostat PPP Program.

PPPs are currency conversion rates that allow output in different currency units to be expressed in a common unit of value (in this case, U.S. dollars). They are preferable to international market exchange rates for this purpose.

According to BLS, "At best, market exchange rates represent only the relative prices of goods and services that are traded internationally, not the relative value of total domestic output, which also consists of goods, and particularly services, that are not traded internationally, or which are isolated from the effects of foreign trade. Market exchange rates also are affected by... currency traders' views of the stability of governments in various countries, relative interest rates among countries, and other incentives for holding financial assets in one currency rather than another."

Measuring PPPs is difficult and subject to error, and BLS emphasizes that statistics using PPPs should be used with caution: "The per capita GDPs of most OECD countries fall within a relatively narrow range, and changes in rankings can occur as a result of relatively minor adjustments to PPP estimates."

In addition to the 11 countries shown here, BLS also calculates and publishes similar data for Austria, Belgium, Czech Republic, Denmark, Finland, Ireland, Norway, Sweden, and Singapore. In the latest report, referenced below, there are also data, graphs, and discussion on hours worked, GDP per hour worked and gross national income per capita.

References

These data and related information are contained in Department of Labor, Bureau of Labor Statistics, Division of International Labor Comparisons, "International comparisons of gross domestic product per capita and per hour, 1960–2010" (August 15, 2011), available online at <http://www.bls.gov/ilc>.

TABLES 13-4A AND 13-4B
INTERNATIONAL COMPARISONS: CONSUMER PRICE INDEXES

SOURCE: U.S. DEPARTMENT OF LABOR, BUREAU OF LABOR STATISTICS

Notes on the data

These data are prepared by the BLS Division of International Labor Comparisons.

In Table 13-4A, the indexes are not adjusted for comparability across countries (except insofar as they are rebased to the common base 1982-1984 =100, which preserves the year-to-year changes in the original index). National differences exist with respect to population coverage, frequency of market basket weight changes, and treatment of homeowner costs. For some countries, BLS publishes indexes for all households and for workers' households; in such cases, *Business Statistics* shows the all-households index.

BLS links published indexes together to form historical series and rebases the foreign indexes to the U.S. base 1982–1984 = 100. Percent changes may differ from changes published elsewhere due to rounding differences.

Table 13-4B shows Harmonized Indexes of Consumer Prices (HICP), internationally comparable measures covering all households and excluding owner-occupied housing costs, conforming to the conceptual basis of the European Union's Harmonized Index of Consumer Prices. This is the index that EU member states must produce for comparisons across countries, and that is used by the European Central Bank for the conduct of monetary policy. The U.S. entry is an "experimental" BLS series, expanded to cover the entire non-institutional population and narrowed to remove owner-occupied housing costs. As can be seen, these changes do alter year-to-year comparisons. These data are produced outside of regular BLS production systems, so the BLS points out that they may have "less than full production quality." These indexes have all been rebased to 2005 = 100.

The European Union index covers the following 27 countries: Austria, Belgium, Bulgaria, Cyprus, the Czech Republic, Denmark, Estonia, Finland, France, Germany, Greece, Hungary, Ireland, Italy, Latvia, Lithuania, Luxembourg, Malta, the Netherlands, Poland, Portugal, Romania, Slovakia, Slovenia, Spain, Sweden, and the United Kingdom. Its geographic coverage has expanded as the EU membership expands; data for new member countries are linked in to the earlier series.

The Euro area index covers the following 16 countries: Austria, Belgium, Cyprus, Finland, France, Germany, Greece, Ireland, Italy, Luxembourg, Malta, the Netherlands, Portugal, Slovakia, Slovenia, and Spain. As with the EU index, the newer countries have been linked in as membership has expanded.

References

For a description of the official U.S. index, see the notes and definitions for Table 8-1.

The indexes for the other countries and the harmonized indexes are presented and described in "International Indexes of Consumer Prices, 18 countries and areas, 1996-2009" (August 3, 2010), available at <http://www.bls.gov/ilc>. They were updated in July 2012.

For more information on the HICP, see "International comparisons of Harmonized Indexes of Consumer Prices," at <http://www.bls.gov/opub/mlr/2007/02/ressum.pdf>. For more information on the United States HICP, see "Comparing U.S. and European inflation: the CPI and the HICP," at <http://www.bls.gov/opub/mlr/2006/05/art3full.pdf>.

TABLES 13-5 THROUGH 13-7
INTERNATIONAL COMPARISONS: WORKING-AGE POPULATION, EMPLOYMENT-POPULATION RATIOS, AND UNEMPLOYMENT RATES

SOURCE: U.S. DEPARTMENT OF LABOR, BUREAU OF LABOR STATISTICS

Notes on the data

Current and historical data on working-age population, labor force, employment, and unemployment for 10 industrial countries are collected and adjusted by BLS to approximate U.S. concepts and definitions. (For the U.S. concepts and definitions, see the notes and definitions for Tables 10-1 through 10-6.) Nine of those countries are shown in Tables 13-5 through 13-7; the tenth is Sweden. The German data are for the former West Germany through 1990, and for unified Germany from 1991 to the present. Adding the former East Germany raised the 1991 unemployment rate from 4.3 percent (for West Germany alone) to 5.6 percent for unified Germany.

It should be noted that there is also a set of employment-population ratios, quite different from the ones shown here, published by BLS in the report for "International comparisons of gross domestic product per capita and per hour" that is referenced above in the notes for Tables 13-2 and 13-3. The ratios in that report are for employment divided by the total resident population (including children). The ratios shown and described here are for employment divided by the working-age population.

Historically, there were large differences between published and BLS-adjusted unemployment rates; however, in recent years, the two unemployment rate series have nearly converged for most countries. Major differences between the country's own official unemployment rates and those adjusted by BLS remain for Canada, Germany, the Netherlands, and Sweden.

There are many qualifications to the adjustments for comparability. Many of the adjusted measures still use a lower age limit than the U.S. limit of 16 years, if the age at which compulsory schooling ends in that country is lower than 16. Currently, however, no country's age limit is lower than 15 years. In Japan and Germany, the institutional population is included. In some countries where the customary significance of layoffs is different, workers on layoff are counted as employed, although in the United States they are considered unemployed. In addition, each country except Japan has some break in historical continuity because of methodological change. The source document includes documentation of each country's series breaks and deviations from exact comparability.

Data availability and references

In addition to the series shown here, BLS calculates and publishes comparative labor force participation rates, employment-population ratios, and unemployment rates by sex; employment by sex and by economic sector; and unemployment rates by age. Data for 1960 through 1969 are from the BLS report "International comparisons of annual labor force statistics: 10 countries, 1960–2007" (October 21, 2008). The data for 1970 through 2010 are from BLS, Division of International Labor Comparisons, "International comparisons of annual labor force statistics: 10 countries, 1970-2010" (March 30, 2011) and recent updates in June 2012. This report and monthly updates to unemployment rates are available on the International Labor Comparisons Web site at <http://www.bls.gov/ilc>.

TABLE 13-8
FOREIGN EXCHANGE RATES

SOURCE: BOARD OF GOVERNORS OF THE FEDERAL RESERVE SYSTEM

Definitions and notes on the data

This table shows measures of the U.S. dollar relative to the currencies of some important individual countries and also relative to average values for major groups of countries. In *Business Statistics*, all of these measures are defined as the foreign currency price of the U.S. dollar. When the measure is relatively high, the dollar is relatively strong—but less competitive (in the sense of price competition)—and the other currency or group of currencies named in the measure is relatively weak and more competitive.

For consistency, this definition is used in *Business Statistics* even in the case of currencies that are commonly quoted in the financial press and elsewhere as dollars per foreign currency unit instead of foreign currency units per dollar. Notably, this is the case for the euro and for the British pound. Where *Business Statistics* shows the average 2010 value of the dollar as 0.7540 euros, the more usual statement—and the one found on the Federal Reserve release used as a source for this information—is that in 2010, the euro was worth on average $1.3261. (The value shown in the table is 1 divided by 1.3261, with slight rounding differences.) Where *Business Statistics* shows the 2010 value of the dollar as 0.6472 British pounds, the more usual statement is that the pound was worth $1.5452. The Canadian dollar is also sometimes quoted relative to the U.S. dollar, rather than as shown here and in documents from the Federal Reserve.

The definition of the dollar's value used in *Business Statistics* is the most useful for economic analysis from the U.S. point of view and for foreign tourists in the United States. For American tourists overseas, it is easier to use the inverse of this measure, the value of the other currency; for example, the traveler in Paris can more easily translate prices into dollars by multiplying by the dollar value of the euro than by dividing by the euro value of the dollar.

The foreign exchange rates shown are averages of the daily noon buying rates for cable transfers in New York City certified for customs purposes by the Federal Reserve Bank of New York.

The introduction of the euro in January 1999 as the common currency for 11 European countries—Austria, Belgium, Finland, France, Germany, Ireland, Italy, Luxembourg, Netherlands, Portugal, and Spain—marked a major change in the international currency system, and the use of the euro subsequently spread to five more countries. Greece entered the European Monetary Union (EMU) in January 2001 and Slovenia entered in January 2007. Cyprus and Malta joined in January 2008 and the Slovak Republic in January 2009. The euro is also the national currency in Monaco, the Vatican City and San Marino, and is the de

facto currency in Andorra, Kosovo, and Montenegro. The values of the currencies of these countries no longer fluctuate relative to each other, but the value of the euro still fluctuates relative to the dollar and to currencies for countries outside the EMU. The currency and coins of the individual countries continued to circulate from 1999 through the end of 2001, but in January 2002, new euro currency and coins were introduced, replacing the currency and coins of the individual countries. Once a country has entered the monetary union, its values relative to the dollar will continue to fluctuate—but only due to fluctuations in the value of the euro relative to the dollar.

There is no fully satisfactory historical equivalent to the euro. For comparisons over time, the Federal Reserve Board uses a "restated German mark," derived simply by dividing each historical value of the mark by the euro conversion factor, 1.95583. The G-10 dollar index described below includes five of the currencies that later merged into the euro, but also includes the currencies of Canada, Japan, the United Kingdom, Switzerland, and Sweden.

Trade-weighted indexes of the value of the dollar against groups of foreign currencies also appear in this table. In each case, weighted averages of the individual currency values of the dollar are set at 100 in a base period. The weights are based on goods trade only and exclude trade in services. Base periods differ for different indexes.

The first four columns show the more familiar type of foreign exchange indexes, which use *nominal* values of each currency. The last two columns are *price-adjusted* (indexes of "real" exchange rates), aggregating values of the dollar in terms of each currency that have been adjusted for inflation, using each country's consumer price index.

Where any currency has had an episode of hyperinflation with consequent huge depreciation in terms of the dollar, the nominal index will not reflect the actual competitiveness of the dollar in terms of that currency over the longer term. As there have been hyperinflations in some of the countries making up the broad index and its "other important trading partners" component (see below), price-adjusted indexes are also shown for those two groupings in the final two columns.

The *G-10 Index (March 1973 = 100)*. This measure is an index of the exchange value of the U.S. dollar in terms of the weighted average currencies of the G-10 ("Other industrialized") countries, which are Belgium, Canada, France, Germany, Italy, Japan, the Netherlands, Sweden, Switzerland, and the United Kingdom. Unlike the three indexes that follow, the weights in this index—which represented "multilateral" (world market) trade shares—were fixed. The Federal Reserve stopped calculating this index as of December 1998.

The three newer indexes, introduced in December 1998, use weights that focus more directly on U.S. competitiveness and that change as trade flows shift. Each country's weight is based on an average of the country's share of U.S. imports, the country's share of U.S. exports, and the country's share of exports that go to other countries that are large importers of U.S. goods. The weights are updated each year; the latest weights were introduced on August 15, 2011. The index formula uses geometric averaging.

The *broad index (January 1997 = 100)*. The new overall index includes currencies of all economies that have a share of U.S. non-oil goods imports or goods exports of at least 0.5 percent. These economies encompass the euro area and 25 other countries. The list of currencies is updated each year, though no changes have been made in the list of included countries. These countries are then classified in either the major currency index or the other important trading partners as outlined below.

The *major currency index (March 1973 = 100)*. This index serves purposes similar to those of the discontinued G-10 index, and its level and movements are similar. It is a measure of the competitiveness of U.S. products in the major industrial countries and a gauge of financial pressure on the dollar. The index includes countries whose currencies are traded in deep and relatively liquid financial markets and circulate widely outside the country of issue. These are also countries for which information on short and long-term interest rates is readily available. This index includes the euro, Canada, Japan, the United Kingdom, Switzerland, Australia, and Sweden. This list has not changed since the introduction of the new indexes in 1998.

The *other important trading partners (OITP) index (January 1997 = 100)*. This index captures the competitiveness of U.S. products in key emerging markets in Latin America, Asia, the Middle East, and Eastern Europe, whose currencies do not circulate widely outside the country of issue. Hyperinflations and large depreciations for some of these countries have led to a persistent upward trend in the nominal version of this index. Hence, the nominal OITP index is mainly useful for analysis of short-term developments, and the price-adjusted index is shown to give a more appropriate measure of longer-term competitiveness. This index includes Mexico, China, Taiwan, South Korea, Singapore, Hong Kong, Malaysia, Brazil, Thailand, Philippines, Indonesia, India, Israel, Saudi Arabia, Russia, Argentina, Venezuela, Chile, and Colombia.

Data availability and references

Current press releases, historical data, and information on weights and methods for exchange rates and exchange rate indexes are available on the Federal Reserve Web site at <http://www.federalreserve.gov/>; go to "Economic Research and Data", then "Statistical Releases and Historical Data," and select the G.5 release. The dollar value indexes are described in the article "Indexes of the Foreign Exchange Value of the Dollar," *Federal Reserve Bulletin* (Winter 2005), also available on the Federal Reserve Web site.

Additional information on exchange rates can be found on the Federal Reserve Bank of St. Louis Web site at <http://www.stls.frb.org/fred/data/exchange.html>.

PART B

INDUSTRY PROFILES

CHAPTER 14: PRODUCT AND INCOME BY INDUSTRY

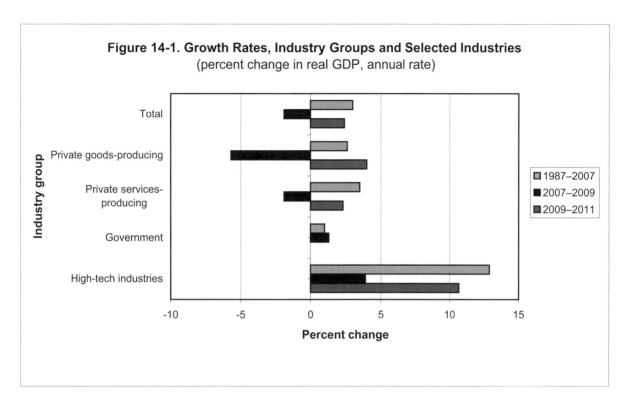

Figure 14-1. Growth Rates, Industry Groups and Selected Industries
(percent change in real GDP, annual rate)

- Between 1987 and 2007 (the peak of the most recent business cycle), total real gross domestic product (GDP) rose at an average annual rate of 3.0 percent. The goods-producing sector grew at a 2.6 percent rate, while private service-producing industries grew at a 3.5 percent rate. The high-tech sector (information-communications-technology-producing industries), which accounted for just 3.4 percent of total GDP in 1987—the first year in which they can be identified separately—grew at a 12.9 percent annual rate over the subsequent 20 years, but still only accounted for 4.2 percent of total GDP. (Tables 14-1 and 14-2; Figure 14-1)

- The latest recession began in December 2007 and ended in June 2009. From 2007 to 2009, using annual figures, total real GDP fell at a 1.9 percent per year rate, with goods output down at a sharp 5.7 percent rate and private services, a 1.9 percent rate. The high-tech subgroup still grew during the recession, though more slowly. In the first two years of recovery, goods rebounded at a 4.0 percent rate according to preliminary 2011 data, and private services 2.3 percent; high-tech speeded up to 10.7 percent. (Table 14-2, Figure 14-1)

- Table 14-3 can be used to assess the share of each industry group in total domestic factor income and the shares paid to employees and accruing to land and capital in each private industry. Factor income is a better measure for such purposes than the BEA definition of GDP (value added) because GDP includes, but factor income excludes, taxes on production and imports. In the U.S. accounts these are assigned to industries that do not bear the ultimate burden (see the Notes to this chapter).

- In private goods-producing industries in 2010, employee compensation received 53.4 percent of value added, while in private services-producing industries excluding real estate and rental and leasing, compensation received 65.0 percent of total value. ("Real estate and rental and leasing" is reported to be a highly capital-intensive industry, especially because it includes the value of owner-occupied housing, which has no paid labor counterpart.) (Table 14-3)

Table 14-1. Gross Domestic Product (Value Added) by NAICS Industry Group

(Billions of dollars.)

Year	Total gross domestic product	Private industries Total	Agriculture, forestry, fishing, and hunting	Mining	Utilities	Construc-tion	Manufacturing Durable goods	Manufacturing Nondurable goods	Wholesale trade	Retail trade	Transportation and ware-housing	Information	Finance and insurance	Real estate and rental and leasing
1947	244.1	213.7	19.9	5.8	3.5	8.9	32.0	30.5	15.5	23.1	14.1	6.8	5.9	19.7
1948	269.1	239.2	23.2	7.7	3.9	11.1	36.2	33.8	17.1	24.5	15.5	7.5	6.7	21.6
1949	267.2	235.9	18.6	6.6	4.4	11.2	35.7	32.7	16.7	24.9	15.1	8.1	7.6	23.1
1950	293.7	262.2	19.9	7.7	4.9	12.8	43.8	35.5	18.7	26.0	16.8	8.7	8.2	25.5
1951	339.3	300.4	23.0	8.5	5.6	15.3	53.7	41.0	21.3	28.5	19.0	9.6	9.3	28.3
1952	358.3	313.8	22.1	8.3	6.1	16.4	56.9	41.5	21.5	29.9	19.8	10.3	10.4	30.9
1953	379.3	332.8	20.0	8.8	6.8	17.1	64.0	43.5	22.1	30.8	20.6	11.3	11.5	33.9
1954	380.4	332.1	19.6	8.9	7.5	17.2	58.9	42.8	22.3	31.4	19.2	11.5	12.3	36.8
1955	414.7	363.8	18.8	10.1	8.1	18.4	68.0	47.1	25.1	33.4	21.0	12.4	13.4	39.7
1956	437.4	383.1	18.6	10.9	8.6	20.3	70.3	49.1	27.0	34.6	22.0	13.2	14.5	42.2
1957	461.1	403.0	18.4	11.0	9.3	21.3	74.7	49.7	28.5	36.6	22.9	14.1	15.6	45.2
1958	467.2	405.4	20.6	10.1	10.0	21.0	67.1	50.3	29.2	37.3	21.8	14.8	16.8	48.3
1959	506.6	441.4	19.0	9.9	11.0	22.7	77.8	54.3	33.4	40.6	22.9	16.2	18.1	51.7
1960	526.4	457.1	19.9	10.1	12.0	23.1	78.4	55.1	34.9	41.5	23.2	17.1	19.5	55.2
1961	544.8	471.2	20.1	10.2	12.7	24.1	77.6	56.4	35.9	42.6	23.5	18.0	20.6	58.7
1962	585.7	506.9	20.3	10.4	13.4	25.9	87.6	59.7	38.3	45.7	25.0	19.3	21.1	63.4
1963	617.8	533.2	20.5	10.6	14.0	27.7	93.3	62.4	39.9	47.7	25.9	20.8	22.0	67.4
1964	663.6	572.9	19.6	11.0	15.0	30.3	101.0	66.3	43.0	52.4	27.5	22.6	24.1	71.6
1965	719.1	622.2	22.4	11.2	15.6	33.3	113.4	71.5	46.5	56.2	29.7	24.4	26.4	76.3
1966	787.7	680.3	23.4	11.8	16.7	36.6	126.5	78.4	51.0	60.5	32.4	26.7	29.0	81.4
1967	832.4	714.2	22.9	12.0	17.6	38.2	129.1	80.4	53.9	64.9	33.1	28.7	32.3	86.4
1968	909.8	778.2	23.6	12.9	19.0	41.8	140.4	87.8	59.2	71.6	35.9	31.1	36.3	93.1
1969	984.4	840.7	26.3	13.5	20.4	46.7	147.4	91.7	63.8	77.6	38.1	34.3	40.9	101.2
1970	1 038.3	880.0	27.3	15.1	21.7	49.5	140.4	95.1	67.7	83.0	40.2	37.4	44.1	108.7
1971	1 126.8	954.5	29.4	15.2	24.7	54.5	148.3	100.6	73.4	90.7	44.3	40.6	48.7	121.0
1972	1 237.9	1 050.6	34.3	16.0	27.0	60.2	165.7	108.3	81.7	98.3	48.8	45.4	53.1	132.1
1973	1 382.3	1 180.1	52.2	19.2	29.0	68.2	187.0	115.8	91.8	108.2	53.8	50.2	57.0	146.9
1974	1 499.5	1 276.8	50.0	29.6	30.3	73.0	194.2	124.2	104.2	113.6	59.1	54.3	64.6	159.4
1975	1 637.7	1 390.9	51.4	34.2	38.5	73.7	200.4	136.9	113.9	127.5	60.0	60.3	73.6	175.3
1976	1 824.6	1 555.5	50.1	37.9	42.9	84.2	232.2	154.8	122.0	144.1	69.4	67.8	80.5	192.7
1977	2 030.1	1 738.7	51.2	43.9	47.5	92.8	267.6	171.6	134.1	158.7	77.0	75.8	95.0	210.1
1978	2 293.8	1 976.4	59.5	50.3	52.1	109.7	306.0	184.4	152.2	177.4	87.5	87.5	112.7	237.1
1979	2 562.2	2 216.8	70.2	59.1	53.8	124.8	334.6	210.3	174.4	193.0	97.5	96.9	125.0	268.5
1980	2 788.1	2 404.8	62.1	90.8	61.0	131.5	339.2	219.2	186.3	198.3	102.6	108.3	137.7	309.2
1981	3 126.8	2 701.6	75.6	121.5	72.0	133.1	376.2	243.4	206.2	218.0	110.1	123.5	155.0	347.8
1982	3 253.2	2 791.4	71.6	118.5	83.2	131.0	359.2	247.3	206.6	226.9	106.3	135.3	168.0	376.8
1983	3 534.6	3 041.7	57.2	102.8	94.4	139.6	385.5	272.0	222.4	255.3	118.0	152.5	193.9	417.7
1984	3 930.9	3 393.0	77.0	107.2	105.7	160.7	451.0	280.7	249.8	286.8	131.4	160.0	213.4	464.1
1985	4 217.5	3 634.6	76.6	106.2	113.0	177.0	458.6	292.8	269.2	309.1	137.1	176.4	233.1	506.3
1986	4 460.1	3 840.4	73.7	70.3	117.5	197.2	468.4	308.9	279.3	331.4	147.0	185.6	262.2	541.9
1987	4 736.4	4 077.9	78.8	73.1	125.8	210.1	492.5	330.6	285.6	345.7	152.6	197.4	282.4	567.8
1988	5 100.4	4 395.3	78.1	74.1	125.1	226.5	537.9	362.2	314.3	366.8	161.4	205.4	301.5	614.2
1989	5 482.1	4 729.7	91.6	78.6	138.2	238.6	562.4	387.7	335.7	390.7	166.3	222.4	322.0	658.9
1990	5 800.5	4 994.3	95.7	88.4	145.5	243.6	558.9	410.1	347.7	400.4	172.8	235.6	346.5	702.6
1991	5 992.1	5 133.2	88.3	79.5	153.8	228.8	554.2	422.5	362.6	407.9	182.3	244.3	382.0	727.8
1992	6 342.3	5 442.0	99.3	73.6	159.7	233.2	574.5	442.2	380.1	430.0	192.0	260.5	414.3	777.8
1993	6 667.4	5 735.9	90.6	74.4	164.3	250.4	603.0	456.0	402.5	462.9	206.4	279.6	441.3	818.0
1994	7 085.2	6 119.9	105.6	75.9	171.2	277.2	650.2	477.1	444.5	500.5	223.7	299.4	456.3	865.3
1995	7 414.7	6 420.0	91.3	76.7	175.3	294.2	675.4	505.5	460.2	525.0	231.7	311.5	489.6	916.2
1996	7 838.5	6 812.6	114.2	90.0	173.4	320.9	705.0	503.5	492.5	556.8	241.3	338.6	527.1	963.2
1997	8 332.4	7 271.0	108.4	94.8	169.9	346.7	748.9	528.3	524.9	589.9	261.8	349.4	582.4	1 028.2
1998	8 793.5	7 694.4	100.3	81.0	165.1	383.7	781.2	545.6	557.3	626.9	275.6	386.1	634.7	1 062.1
1999	9 353.5	8 199.6	92.8	82.0	172.7	428.4	802.4	565.6	579.1	653.4	287.1	438.5	681.7	1 152.3
2000	9 951.5	8 736.1	95.6	108.9	173.9	467.3	839.1	576.5	617.7	686.2	301.4	417.8	762.0	1 235.7
2001	10 286.2	9 010.8	98.6	119.3	177.6	490.5	758.8	585.2	613.3	703.9	302.6	451.1	838.7	1 316.1
2002	10 642.3	9 289.3	94.4	109.5	181.0	494.3	767.8	587.8	614.9	731.2	302.4	499.7	863.5	1 358.7
2003	11 142.2	9 706.9	115.5	134.9	192.0	516.1	766.4	607.9	638.1	769.5	319.8	506.6	902.4	1 414.1
2004	11 853.3	10 345.6	142.7	159.3	208.0	554.2	822.0	660.6	684.2	795.1	347.0	558.8	919.0	1 481.4
2005	12 623.0	11 037.1	127.1	192.3	205.9	612.5	878.3	691.0	725.5	837.6	369.5	586.5	1 019.4	1 579.4
2006	13 377.2	11 709.4	122.5	229.8	236.0	651.0	921.3	727.1	769.7	875.8	394.0	590.6	1 092.7	1 672.6
2007	14 028.7	12 268.8	144.5	254.5	248.6	653.8	939.9	758.1	816.7	887.9	404.9	635.5	1 080.0	1 777.0
2008	14 291.5	12 437.1	159.4	319.2	257.7	614.2	904.1	724.4	824.1	848.6	415.0	636.8	1 041.5	1 875.2
2009	13 939.0	12 018.1	140.0	213.4	258.3	541.9	800.4	739.8	768.5	837.2	391.7	615.4	1 099.0	1 865.6
2010	14 526.5	12 558.0	157.0	239.5	264.9	511.6	914.5	787.4	797.3	884.9	402.5	623.5	1 241.9	1 765.2
2011	15 094.0	13 097.4	177.8	287.6	250.8	520.3	989.3	847.8	844.9	917.0	418.8	662.3	1 256.2	1 751.7

Table 14-1. Gross Domestic Product (Value Added) by NAICS Industry Group—*Continued*

(Billions of dollars.)

Year	Profes-sional, scientific, and technical services	Manage-ment of companies and enterprises	Adminis-trative and waste manage-ment services	Educational services	Health care and social assistance	Arts, entertain-ment, and recreation	Accom-modation and food services	Other services except govern-ment	Total govern-ment	Federal	State and local	Private goods-producing industries	Private services-producing industries	Information-communi-cations-technology-producing industries[1]
1947	3.2	3.6	1.3	0.8	3.8	1.6	6.4	7.4	30.4	20.3	10.1	97.0	116.7	. . .
1948	3.6	4.0	1.4	1.0	4.2	1.6	6.8	7.8	30.0	18.4	11.5	112.0	127.2	. . .
1949	3.8	4.0	1.5	1.0	4.4	1.7	7.0	8.0	31.3	18.7	12.6	104.7	131.2	. . .
1950	4.1	4.4	1.7	1.1	4.8	1.7	7.2	8.6	31.6	18.2	13.4	119.7	142.4	. . .
1951	4.8	5.1	2.0	1.2	5.4	1.8	7.8	9.3	38.9	23.9	15.0	141.4	159.0	. . .
1952	5.3	5.4	2.2	1.2	5.9	2.0	8.2	9.6	44.5	28.0	16.5	145.3	168.5	. . .
1953	5.8	5.7	2.4	1.3	6.5	2.1	8.5	10.2	46.5	28.8	17.8	153.4	179.4	. . .
1954	6.2	5.7	2.6	1.4	6.7	2.2	8.7	10.4	48.2	28.9	19.3	147.3	184.8	. . .
1955	6.9	6.3	2.8	1.5	7.9	2.3	9.2	11.4	50.9	30.0	20.9	162.4	201.4	. . .
1956	7.6	6.6	3.1	1.7	8.4	2.5	9.5	12.4	54.3	31.1	23.2	169.1	214.0	. . .
1957	8.5	7.0	3.4	1.8	9.2	2.6	10.1	13.2	58.1	32.6	25.5	175.0	228.0	. . .
1958	8.9	6.8	3.7	2.0	10.1	2.7	10.3	13.7	61.8	34.0	27.8	169.1	236.3	. . .
1959	10.0	7.6	4.0	2.2	11.3	3.1	11.2	14.5	65.2	35.1	30.1	183.7	257.8	. . .
1960	10.5	7.8	4.3	2.4	11.8	3.3	11.4	15.6	69.3	36.4	32.9	186.6	270.5	. . .
1961	11.4	8.0	4.7	2.6	12.6	3.5	11.8	16.3	73.5	37.8	35.7	188.4	282.8	. . .
1962	12.5	8.7	5.1	3.0	13.7	3.7	12.6	17.3	78.8	40.1	38.6	204.0	302.9	. . .
1963	13.4	9.1	5.5	3.2	14.7	4.0	13.3	18.0	84.5	42.6	42.0	214.5	318.8	. . .
1964	14.8	9.8	6.0	3.6	16.3	4.3	14.5	19.2	90.7	45.1	45.6	228.2	344.7	. . .
1965	16.3	10.6	6.6	4.0	17.6	4.5	15.7	20.1	96.9	47.1	49.7	251.7	370.5	. . .
1966	18.6	11.7	7.4	4.6	19.8	4.8	17.0	21.9	107.4	52.1	55.3	276.8	403.4	. . .
1967	20.3	12.2	7.9	5.0	22.6	5.0	18.4	23.2	118.3	56.7	61.5	282.6	431.6	. . .
1968	21.9	13.4	8.6	5.6	25.5	5.4	20.3	24.8	131.6	62.5	69.1	306.5	471.8	. . .
1969	24.5	14.3	9.7	6.6	29.1	5.6	22.1	26.7	143.8	66.7	77.1	325.7	515.0	. . .
1970	26.9	14.7	10.4	7.5	32.9	6.1	23.7	27.8	158.3	71.1	87.2	327.4	552.7	. . .
1971	29.2	15.7	11.3	8.4	36.4	6.5	25.8	29.7	172.3	75.4	96.9	348.0	606.5	. . .
1972	32.7	17.2	12.7	9.6	40.9	6.9	28.1	31.7	187.3	80.5	106.8	384.4	666.2	. . .
1973	37.7	19.0	14.5	10.4	46.0	8.0	31.0	34.3	202.2	83.0	119.2	442.4	737.7	. . .
1974	41.6	20.6	16.3	11.1	52.4	8.8	32.6	37.0	222.6	90.4	132.2	471.0	805.8	. . .
1975	45.9	22.7	17.7	12.0	61.1	9.7	36.6	39.6	246.8	98.2	148.7	496.5	894.4	. . .
1976	51.4	25.7	20.4	12.5	70.2	11.0	41.6	44.1	269.0	107.4	161.7	559.2	996.3	. . .
1977	61.0	28.9	24.1	13.0	79.4	13.1	46.4	47.6	291.4	116.1	175.4	627.1	1 111.6	. . .
1978	70.4	32.9	28.3	14.2	90.2	14.6	54.0	55.3	317.3	125.5	191.8	709.9	1 266.5	. . .
1979	82.7	36.1	33.3	15.7	102.5	16.4	61.5	60.6	345.4	135.3	210.1	799.0	1 417.8	. . .
1980	95.8	39.8	37.5	17.6	116.5	17.7	65.2	68.5	383.3	150.4	233.0	842.8	1 562.0	. . .
1981	109.3	45.3	42.7	19.3	133.6	20.0	72.9	76.0	425.2	170.7	254.5	949.9	1 751.7	. . .
1982	120.4	47.2	45.5	20.9	148.3	21.2	78.9	78.3	461.8	185.6	276.2	927.7	1 863.7	. . .
1983	137.4	53.4	51.6	23.8	165.8	23.3	88.1	86.8	492.9	197.4	295.6	957.1	2 084.6	. . .
1984	158.5	61.3	61.2	26.3	180.8	24.8	96.0	96.3	537.9	219.8	318.1	1 076.7	2 316.3	. . .
1985	179.6	67.9	68.8	28.4	197.0	27.6	104.4	105.3	582.9	235.8	347.1	1 111.2	2 523.4	. . .
1986	201.5	74.1	76.9	30.2	215.1	29.9	114.1	115.3	619.7	244.6	375.1	1 118.6	2 721.8	. . .
1987	221.1	76.9	86.4	33.3	244.4	32.6	119.7	121.1	658.4	256.6	401.8	1 185.0	2 892.9	161.3
1988	254.5	73.2	96.6	35.6	265.9	35.2	133.6	133.0	705.1	272.1	433.1	1 278.8	3 116.5	176.1
1989	284.6	77.5	108.3	38.7	298.7	41.0	143.0	144.8	752.4	285.9	466.5	1 358.9	3 370.8	188.4
1990	315.1	80.3	121.2	41.2	335.4	47.6	152.0	153.9	806.2	298.9	507.3	1 396.5	3 597.7	197.3
1991	320.6	81.4	122.0	45.4	368.0	49.3	156.6	155.9	858.9	320.8	538.0	1 373.2	3 760.0	203.8
1992	347.4	84.7	134.5	48.9	404.0	56.2	162.7	166.3	900.3	333.0	567.4	1 422.8	4 019.2	215.9
1993	365.5	92.4	143.1	51.7	424.7	58.0	172.9	178.3	931.4	334.7	596.7	1 474.3	4 261.6	227.4
1994	386.5	96.4	156.7	55.5	444.7	60.6	181.7	190.7	965.3	337.2	628.1	1 586.1	4 533.8	253.4
1995	411.9	103.2	172.3	58.9	465.1	65.9	189.5	200.7	994.6	337.0	657.6	1 643.1	4 776.9	275.9
1996	454.3	111.3	191.0	62.5	482.9	70.8	202.0	211.2	1 025.9	341.6	684.3	1 733.6	5 079.0	304.0
1997	504.0	124.1	214.0	66.9	504.5	79.7	220.5	223.8	1 061.3	347.1	714.2	1 827.2	5 443.8	343.2
1998	555.0	138.0	234.0	73.0	528.3	81.2	239.8	245.6	1 099.1	351.9	747.2	1 891.7	5 802.7	372.0
1999	607.0	148.1	255.1	79.5	559.0	91.0	264.4	259.3	1 153.9	361.5	792.4	1 971.5	6 228.3	405.6
2000	662.4	171.1	283.3	85.9	592.1	98.6	283.0	277.6	1 215.4	378.4	837.0	2 087.4	6 648.7	409.9
2001	701.1	174.6	295.0	88.7	640.5	94.8	296.4	264.2	1 275.4	385.1	890.3	2 052.3	6 958.5	380.8
2002	718.9	178.3	301.0	98.9	690.9	102.1	309.0	285.0	1 353.0	416.6	936.4	2 053.7	7 235.6	422.6
2003	744.6	192.4	322.9	106.1	741.0	106.1	321.7	288.8	1 435.3	447.3	988.0	2 140.8	7 566.1	437.9
2004	808.7	203.3	335.6	116.0	790.1	114.7	344.0	300.8	1 507.7	478.4	1 029.3	2 338.9	8 006.6	494.4
2005	870.3	218.4	371.4	120.2	833.3	118.9	366.5	313.0	1 585.9	501.8	1 084.1	2 501.2	8 535.8	535.0
2006	947.5	234.5	385.1	129.1	886.2	127.7	384.7	331.6	1 667.8	526.5	1 141.3	2 651.6	9 057.8	560.0
2007	1 024.7	257.7	415.2	137.9	939.0	137.2	411.7	343.8	1 759.9	552.3	1 207.6	2 750.9	9 517.9	587.4
2008	1 100.2	263.2	419.8	147.6	1 006.3	132.4	404.9	342.7	1 854.4	580.9	1 273.5	2 721.2	9 715.9	599.1
2009	1 033.3	249.0	395.8	156.7	1 053.7	130.0	387.6	340.8	1 920.9	613.2	1 307.7	2 435.5	9 582.6	601.9
2010	1 095.8	263.7	423.4	163.1	1 109.2	139.1	416.7	356.8	1 968.5	649.6	1 319.0	2 610.1	9 948.0	666.9
2011	1 171.1	282.5	444.3	169.3	1 151.2	144.1	441.6	368.7	1 996.7	667.6	1 329.1	2 822.7	10 274.0	697.1

[1]Consists of computer and electronic products manufacturing; publishing, including software; information and data processing services; and computer systems design and related services.
. . . = Not available.

Table 14-2. Chain-Type Quantity Indexes for Value Added by NAICS Industry Group

(2005 = 100.)

Year	Total gross domestic product	Private industries												
		Total	Agriculture, forestry, fishing, and hunting	Mining	Utilities	Construction	Manufacturing		Wholesale trade	Retail trade	Transportation and warehousing	Information	Finance and insurance	Real estate and rental and leasing
							Durable goods	Nondurable goods						
1947	14.1	13.2	20.2	65.2	10.2	34.8	10.6	19.0	6.4	12.7	19.5	4.9	10.1	10.5
1948	14.7	13.9	23.2	66.7	11.5	40.4	11.2	20.3	6.6	12.9	18.9	5.2	10.2	10.8
1949	14.6	13.7	22.2	58.4	12.9	40.5	10.5	20.1	6.7	13.6	17.0	5.4	10.5	11.4
1950	15.9	15.0	23.4	65.5	14.0	45.1	12.5	22.0	7.4	14.8	18.5	5.5	10.9	12.1
1951	17.1	16.0	22.2	71.7	16.3	50.3	14.3	23.6	7.6	14.9	20.7	5.9	11.8	12.8
1952	17.8	16.5	23.3	69.9	17.4	52.4	15.1	23.7	7.9	15.3	20.0	6.1	12.3	13.7
1953	18.6	17.3	24.4	72.2	18.9	54.4	16.5	24.6	8.1	15.9	20.2	6.5	12.8	14.5
1954	18.5	17.1	25.1	69.6	20.7	56.3	14.8	24.2	8.2	16.0	18.9	6.5	13.2	15.3
1955	19.8	18.5	25.8	78.3	21.7	60.0	16.7	26.0	9.0	17.3	20.8	6.9	14.4	16.3
1956	20.2	18.9	25.8	81.1	23.0	63.3	16.3	26.5	9.4	17.4	21.3	7.1	15.3	17.0
1957	20.6	19.3	24.8	80.5	24.7	63.5	16.5	26.8	9.6	17.7	21.3	7.4	16.1	17.9
1958	20.4	18.9	25.5	74.0	25.8	65.9	14.3	26.8	9.7	17.7	19.7	7.6	15.8	18.7
1959	21.9	20.4	25.5	76.7	28.2	71.4	16.2	29.2	11.0	18.8	20.8	8.1	16.0	20.0
1960	22.4	20.9	26.8	78.5	30.2	72.2	16.2	29.3	11.5	19.0	21.1	8.4	16.8	21.1
1961	22.9	21.3	27.0	79.0	31.8	73.3	16.0	29.9	11.8	19.0	21.1	8.7	17.7	22.1
1962	24.3	22.7	26.5	81.4	33.5	76.8	17.8	31.8	12.6	20.3	22.2	9.3	18.2	23.6
1963	25.4	23.9	27.5	84.9	35.1	78.9	19.4	34.3	13.1	20.9	23.4	9.9	18.6	24.6
1964	26.9	25.3	27.0	88.0	37.7	82.9	21.0	36.0	13.9	22.3	24.3	10.6	19.6	25.8
1965	28.6	27.1	28.7	91.7	39.3	86.5	23.6	38.3	15.0	23.6	26.4	11.4	20.1	27.3
1966	30.4	28.8	27.9	97.2	42.1	87.3	25.9	41.1	16.0	24.9	28.8	12.4	20.8	28.6
1967	31.2	29.3	29.8	98.6	44.2	85.4	25.7	40.7	16.7	25.2	28.6	13.1	22.0	29.4
1968	32.7	30.6	29.0	101.4	48.2	84.9	27.0	43.3	17.8	26.4	30.0	13.9	23.1	30.9
1969	33.7	31.7	29.9	104.6	51.1	82.0	27.6	44.7	18.5	26.6	31.1	15.0	25.3	32.7
1970	33.8	31.6	30.7	108.4	52.7	75.2	25.2	44.4	19.0	27.0	30.8	16.0	26.0	33.4
1971	34.9	32.7	32.2	106.1	56.8	73.0	25.6	46.5	20.1	28.2	31.4	16.7	26.4	35.6
1972	36.8	34.7	32.6	105.4	58.0	74.1	28.1	50.1	21.6	30.0	34.0	17.9	27.8	37.5
1973	38.9	37.0	32.4	108.8	65.0	76.8	31.5	53.8	22.4	31.8	36.2	19.2	29.6	39.4
1974	38.7	36.6	31.7	104.0	66.1	74.0	30.4	50.4	22.1	30.4	36.5	19.8	31.8	41.0
1975	38.6	36.5	36.8	105.7	70.4	67.0	27.4	49.2	22.6	30.6	34.0	20.5	34.0	42.7
1976	40.7	38.6	35.7	105.5	69.7	71.9	30.3	54.8	23.4	33.0	36.9	21.6	34.1	44.4
1977	42.6	40.5	37.1	113.5	69.3	72.8	32.7	58.9	24.6	34.3	38.5	23.2	34.5	44.9
1978	44.9	42.9	35.9	117.4	68.9	77.0	34.8	60.8	27.1	36.3	40.5	25.9	37.7	47.3
1979	46.3	44.5	38.9	104.7	63.3	79.6	35.4	64.7	29.2	36.3	42.8	28.0	39.2	50.5
1980	46.2	44.2	38.4	115.6	59.1	75.1	33.5	61.4	29.0	34.3	41.8	30.4	41.6	52.7
1981	47.4	45.4	48.4	114.9	59.0	68.5	34.4	66.3	30.7	35.3	40.8	32.0	42.6	53.2
1982	46.5	44.3	51.0	109.8	57.7	60.5	31.0	64.2	30.9	35.2	38.8	32.0	43.8	53.3
1983	48.6	46.3	36.4	104.3	60.8	62.8	33.1	70.5	32.2	38.5	43.8	34.2	43.6	55.3
1984	52.1	49.8	47.1	114.5	66.3	70.7	38.4	70.8	34.8	42.2	45.9	33.9	45.3	57.3
1985	54.2	52.0	55.8	121.1	70.5	75.8	39.5	73.2	36.7	44.5	46.6	34.8	45.7	59.3
1986	56.1	53.5	54.9	116.8	74.0	77.5	39.8	72.3	40.3	47.8	46.7	35.0	47.2	59.6
1987	57.9	55.5	56.8	122.4	82.7	79.1	42.6	78.0	39.2	46.1	49.0	37.4	51.0	60.5
1988	60.3	58.1	50.7	136.9	82.0	83.0	46.9	80.1	41.3	50.7	50.4	38.6	52.4	62.9
1989	62.4	60.2	56.7	132.3	90.4	85.3	47.6	80.5	43.3	53.0	52.4	41.3	53.2	64.8
1990	63.6	61.3	60.1	130.8	95.6	84.8	46.7	80.1	42.7	53.8	55.1	42.6	54.8	66.1
1991	63.4	61.2	60.8	133.1	96.8	78.6	45.2	80.7	44.4	53.7	57.7	43.1	56.5	66.6
1992	65.6	63.5	68.0	129.0	97.7	80.4	46.2	84.7	48.5	56.5	61.3	45.4	56.4	69.8
1993	67.5	65.3	59.0	131.2	96.4	82.6	48.1	87.9	50.0	59.2	64.0	47.8	58.5	71.6
1994	70.2	68.4	70.4	142.4	99.4	87.3	51.8	92.4	53.1	63.5	69.2	50.3	58.8	74.0
1995	72.0	70.1	59.6	143.5	102.6	88.2	55.8	91.8	52.9	66.7	71.2	52.0	59.8	76.4
1996	74.7	73.1	66.3	133.7	101.7	93.0	59.3	91.2	57.8	72.9	75.1	55.3	61.1	78.2
1997	78.0	76.8	71.6	138.1	97.1	95.2	64.2	93.7	64.1	79.2	79.0	56.4	64.4	81.3
1998	81.4	80.5	69.8	148.8	95.0	98.3	70.6	92.1	74.2	84.2	78.1	62.1	68.6	82.1
1999	85.3	84.8	73.0	137.8	104.7	103.6	76.0	94.1	78.1	86.6	80.8	70.5	74.1	86.7
2000	88.9	88.7	81.6	121.0	108.3	107.0	84.4	94.0	83.5	89.9	86.2	67.8	82.5	90.0
2001	89.8	89.8	78.9	136.8	93.9	104.5	79.3	91.6	87.7	92.7	83.1	72.9	92.0	92.6
2002	91.4	91.3	82.1	138.4	97.4	100.9	82.2	92.4	88.5	95.8	81.9	81.0	91.8	92.4
2003	93.8	93.5	90.6	120.5	100.9	101.2	85.1	95.1	93.9	98.0	86.1	82.5	92.9	93.9
2004	97.0	96.9	96.5	119.2	104.8	101.1	93.0	101.5	98.9	98.0	93.9	92.7	92.0	96.2
2005	100.0	100.0	100.0	100.0	100.0	100.0	100.0	100.0	100.0	100.0	100.0	100.0	100.0	100.0
2006	102.7	103.0	100.8	108.4	100.5	97.0	106.7	101.1	103.0	102.2	104.0	101.5	106.4	102.5
2007	104.6	105.0	93.1	111.4	104.0	91.6	110.7	104.4	108.6	102.5	105.2	109.3	102.6	106.7
2008	104.3	103.9	101.3	107.2	108.8	85.5	108.9	93.0	107.4	96.6	106.2	111.2	95.9	109.7
2009	100.6	99.3	112.2	129.6	96.4	74.5	92.7	90.5	92.9	94.3	93.5	107.2	102.4	107.6
2010	103.7	102.9	108.8	121.7	99.6	72.1	108.5	95.1	96.5	103.8	96.7	110.3	109.1	102.9
2011	105.5	104.7	95.3	129.4	93.4	71.9	117.1	95.4	99.7	105.8	96.9	116.0	111.0	100.2

Table 14-2. Chain-Type Quantity Indexes for Value Added by NAICS Industry Group—*Continued*

(2005 = 100.)

Year	Professional, scientific, and technical services	Management of companies and enterprises	Administrative and waste management services	Educational services	Health care and social assistance	Arts, entertainment, and recreation	Accommodation and food services	Other services except government	Total government	Federal	State and local	Private goods-producing industries	Private services-producing industries	Information-communications-technology-producing industries[1]
1947	7.7	17.7	4.9	18.1	9.2	14.2	17.3	40.5	33.4	64.4	19.5	18.5	11.1	. . .
1948	7.8	18.4	5.0	20.9	9.6	13.9	17.3	41.4	32.2	60.4	19.8	20.0	11.3	. . .
1949	7.9	18.2	5.1	21.5	9.9	13.7	17.9	41.2	32.1	58.2	20.8	19.2	11.5	. . .
1950	8.2	19.6	5.5	21.7	10.5	13.8	19.0	41.9	32.5	58.3	21.4	21.6	12.3	. . .
1951	8.6	21.0	5.8	21.7	10.9	14.6	19.2	42.3	38.3	75.8	21.8	23.4	13.0	. . .
1952	8.8	21.9	6.1	21.6	11.5	14.5	19.7	42.4	41.4	84.5	22.3	24.2	13.3	. . .
1953	9.1	23.1	6.4	22.1	12.1	14.8	20.4	42.9	42.1	84.9	23.2	25.6	13.9	. . .
1954	9.3	22.5	6.4	22.3	12.9	14.8	20.5	42.6	42.0	82.8	24.0	24.5	14.0	. . .
1955	9.7	24.3	6.8	23.2	13.2	15.3	21.9	45.3	42.2	81.2	25.0	26.8	15.1	. . .
1956	10.0	24.6	7.2	23.5	13.7	16.0	22.1	46.8	42.9	80.4	26.3	26.9	15.6	. . .
1957	10.9	25.2	7.7	25.3	14.5	16.2	22.9	48.3	43.8	80.3	27.7	27.0	16.2	. . .
1958	11.2	24.5	8.1	26.5	15.6	16.5	22.7	49.8	44.2	78.5	29.1	25.5	16.3	. . .
1959	12.0	26.6	8.7	27.1	16.6	17.7	23.9	51.1	45.0	78.0	30.4	27.9	17.5	. . .
1960	12.2	27.1	9.0	28.3	17.3	18.6	24.3	53.1	46.6	79.8	32.0	28.2	18.1	. . .
1961	13.0	27.6	9.5	29.7	18.0	19.1	24.3	54.3	48.2	81.5	33.5	28.3	18.6	. . .
1962	13.6	29.3	10.0	31.5	19.5	19.6	25.9	55.4	50.0	84.7	34.7	30.3	19.7	. . .
1963	14.3	31.1	10.5	32.8	20.7	20.4	26.9	56.6	51.6	85.6	36.5	32.4	20.6	. . .
1964	15.0	32.8	11.1	33.8	23.1	21.4	28.5	58.5	53.4	86.9	38.6	34.3	21.7	. . .
1965	15.9	35.6	11.9	36.2	24.0	21.8	30.4	60.4	55.4	88.1	40.9	37.2	23.0	. . .
1966	17.4	38.5	12.9	38.5	25.4	22.2	31.9	63.6	58.8	94.3	43.1	39.6	24.4	. . .
1967	18.4	38.8	13.3	40.6	26.4	22.4	32.7	65.0	61.7	100.1	44.8	39.6	25.2	. . .
1968	19.1	41.1	14.0	42.2	28.2	23.0	33.9	65.9	64.3	102.6	47.4	41.1	26.5	. . .
1969	20.1	42.5	15.0	43.8	30.3	22.7	34.3	67.2	65.9	103.0	49.4	41.8	27.7	. . .
1970	20.8	42.1	15.3	45.8	32.2	23.4	35.1	66.6	66.0	98.6	51.4	39.8	28.4	. . .
1971	21.2	43.7	15.5	48.4	34.3	23.8	36.3	67.3	66.2	94.7	53.4	40.5	29.7	. . .
1972	22.5	46.9	16.9	49.1	36.3	24.6	38.5	69.8	66.5	91.5	55.3	43.2	31.4	. . .
1973	24.3	51.1	18.1	50.0	38.9	27.2	40.7	72.2	66.7	87.8	57.2	46.5	33.3	. . .
1974	25.0	47.4	19.0	51.8	40.5	27.6	39.3	68.6	68.5	88.6	59.4	44.6	33.6	. . .
1975	24.6	46.6	18.2	53.0	43.3	28.2	39.5	68.0	69.3	87.2	61.3	42.5	34.3	. . .
1976	25.6	50.8	19.2	53.5	45.6	30.2	42.5	71.0	70.4	88.9	62.1	45.9	35.9	. . .
1977	28.0	54.3	20.8	54.0	49.0	34.1	44.7	71.3	71.0	88.8	63.1	48.9	37.3	. . .
1978	30.2	57.0	22.7	56.2	51.3	36.0	47.9	74.7	72.7	90.8	64.6	51.1	39.8	. . .
1979	32.7	57.7	24.9	56.5	53.8	38.0	48.9	75.3	73.6	90.8	66.0	52.5	41.6	. . .
1980	34.1	56.6	25.9	57.7	55.8	38.8	46.4	76.0	74.9	92.5	67.0	50.6	42.0	. . .
1981	35.2	56.9	26.6	56.8	57.2	41.4	47.7	73.7	75.2	93.5	67.0	52.4	43.0	. . .
1982	35.1	57.8	26.0	56.9	57.0	41.8	49.1	70.9	75.3	93.0	67.4	48.9	42.9	. . .
1983	37.1	62.8	28.1	61.1	58.9	43.7	53.3	74.1	76.0	95.3	67.3	50.2	45.2	. . .
1984	40.6	70.3	32.0	64.3	60.4	44.2	56.0	78.1	76.8	96.8	67.8	55.9	47.8	. . .
1985	43.9	74.9	34.8	66.3	61.8	47.9	58.3	80.6	78.8	99.1	69.7	58.7	49.8	. . .
1986	47.4	80.5	37.7	66.7	63.1	49.7	62.6	82.4	80.7	100.5	71.8	58.7	51.9	. . .
1987	49.5	82.9	41.4	70.1	67.2	52.2	61.2	83.9	82.2	102.8	73.0	62.2	53.3	10.6
1988	54.0	76.2	43.8	70.4	67.8	54.4	64.9	88.0	84.3	104.1	75.5	65.7	55.7	11.9
1989	57.7	78.4	47.4	72.4	70.5	60.4	66.0	92.0	86.4	105.6	77.9	66.9	58.2	12.9
1990	60.5	78.8	50.1	72.7	73.4	66.5	66.7	94.0	88.5	107.5	80.0	66.4	59.7	13.6
1991	58.6	75.2	48.4	75.8	74.9	65.7	64.5	91.2	89.0	107.6	80.7	65.0	60.1	13.9
1992	60.6	73.8	50.8	78.4	77.2	73.0	65.2	93.3	89.5	107.0	81.7	67.2	62.5	15.1
1993	61.7	76.3	52.8	80.6	77.2	73.5	67.8	96.6	89.5	104.7	82.7	68.8	64.3	16.4
1994	63.4	76.7	56.7	83.3	77.3	74.6	70.2	101.1	89.8	102.6	84.0	73.8	66.8	19.1
1995	64.7	78.8	61.1	86.2	78.3	78.8	72.0	103.0	89.7	98.3	85.9	75.4	68.6	23.1
1996	68.8	84.0	66.1	87.7	79.2	81.4	75.2	103.9	90.1	96.3	87.4	78.1	71.7	27.6
1997	73.1	91.4	71.1	90.4	80.4	88.8	77.5	102.7	91.1	95.6	89.1	82.2	75.3	33.4
1998	78.2	93.0	74.6	92.3	81.4	88.2	80.7	108.4	92.3	95.4	90.9	85.8	79.0	41.6
1999	82.1	93.1	78.8	94.6	83.4	93.5	85.7	109.3	93.4	94.8	92.8	89.9	83.3	50.7
2000	85.6	98.4	83.8	96.5	85.4	96.6	89.3	111.0	95.1	96.1	94.7	94.4	87.0	56.9
2001	88.3	102.6	83.5	95.0	88.0	89.8	89.7	99.3	95.9	94.7	96.5	91.4	89.3	58.1
2002	89.4	103.1	83.1	99.6	91.5	94.2	90.4	102.4	97.8	96.7	98.3	92.4	91.0	67.1
2003	90.7	103.5	89.5	100.1	94.8	94.4	93.4	100.4	98.7	98.5	98.9	94.0	93.3	74.0
2004	96.0	101.3	90.8	102.7	97.7	99.5	97.2	100.7	99.4	99.9	99.3	99.2	96.3	89.0
2005	100.0	100.0	100.0	100.0	100.0	100.0	100.0	100.0	100.0	100.0	100.0	100.0	100.0	100.0
2006	104.7	100.9	101.1	101.0	103.6	104.5	101.9	101.7	100.4	99.7	100.8	102.5	103.1	108.3
2007	108.2	99.5	105.5	102.0	105.4	108.6	104.7	101.7	101.2	99.9	101.8	103.2	105.5	119.4
2008	113.9	101.5	107.3	104.3	110.7	102.3	99.6	97.4	103.0	102.6	103.2	98.0	105.7	126.7
2009	105.9	99.1	97.1	105.1	111.8	98.4	90.8	92.4	103.9	106.4	102.8	91.7	101.6	128.9
2010	111.1	94.7	103.3	105.3	115.4	104.8	98.3	94.3	104.5	109.8	102.1	96.8	104.7	147.9
2011	116.6	96.6	107.1	104.3	118.3	108.2	101.6	94.2	104.0	110.5	101.1	99.2	106.3	158.0

[1]Consists of computer and electronic products manufacturing; publishing, including software; information and data processing services; and computer systems design and related services.
. . . = Not available.

Table 14-3. Gross Domestic Factor Income by NAICS Industry Group

(Billions of current dollars.)

NAICS industry	2000	2001	2002	2003	2004	2005	2006	2007	2008	2009	2010
Gross domestic factor income, total	9 288.7	9 617.2	9 920.9	10 384.5	11 036.3	11 753.7	12 441.8	13 056.1	13 305.8	12 980.8	13 529.8
Compensation of employees	5 793.5	5 984.5	6 116.4	6 388.3	6 699.6	7 071.5	7 483.6	7 863.0	8 079.1	7 815.4	7 980.6
Gross operating surplus	3 495.2	3 632.7	3 804.5	3 996.2	4 336.7	4 682.2	4 958.2	5 193.1	5 226.7	5 165.4	5 549.2
Private industries	8 061.9	8 329.2	8 553.2	8 933.5	9 511.9	10 150.8	10 756.5	11 277.5	11 431.1	11 037.6	11 540.4
Compensation of employees	4 773.3	4 905.2	4 966.0	5 162.4	5 408.4	5 715.6	6 063.4	6 364.0	6 499.5	6 181.1	6 309.5
Gross operating surplus	3 288.6	3 424.0	3 587.2	3 771.1	4 103.5	4 435.2	4 693.1	4 913.5	4 931.6	4 856.5	5 230.9
Agriculture, forestry, fishing, and hunting	110.0	113.1	99.6	123.7	147.6	141.8	129.1	146.8	161.5	142.3	158.8
Compensation of employees	30.2	31.6	31.9	31.9	35.4	35.6	39.7	42.4	43.0	42.9	44.0
Gross operating surplus	79.8	81.5	67.7	91.8	112.2	106.2	89.4	104.4	118.5	99.4	114.8
Mining	95.2	103.9	94.3	117.6	139.5	167.2	201.2	222.0	277.2	184.0	207.6
Compensation of employees	35.6	38.1	35.9	37.9	42.6	47.6	57.5	62.6	73.5	65.2	69.2
Gross operating surplus	59.6	65.8	58.4	79.7	96.9	119.6	143.7	159.4	203.7	118.8	138.4
Utilities	139.5	148.0	142.5	150.8	164.4	159.7	185.6	194.9	201.9	200.9	206.3
Compensation of employees	47.5	51.6	54.3	53.6	56.4	56.5	60.4	61.5	66.9	68.0	68.3
Gross operating surplus	92.0	96.4	88.2	97.2	108.0	103.2	125.2	133.4	135.0	132.9	138.0
Construction	462.3	485.3	488.6	510.1	547.6	605.3	643.4	646.0	606.8	534.7	504.2
Compensation of employees	307.3	325.5	327.8	339.9	357.4	390.7	425.8	441.8	440.3	377.4	354.4
Gross operating surplus	155.0	159.8	160.8	170.2	190.2	214.6	217.6	204.2	166.5	157.3	149.8
Durable goods manufacturing	821.4	740.4	748.7	746.8	801.8	857.3	899.5	917.2	880.8	776.4	890.7
Compensation of employees	605.8	577.0	556.1	574.2	575.5	591.9	611.8	622.1	615.2	547.7	559.2
Gross operating surplus	215.6	163.4	192.6	172.6	226.3	265.4	287.7	295.1	265.6	228.7	331.5
Nondurable goods manufacturing	548.1	556.3	557.0	577.1	628.6	657.0	691.2	721.7	687.3	693.7	739.3
Compensation of employees	297.3	297.1	301.4	305.1	306.4	308.6	313.6	316.5	325.9	304.5	308.0
Gross operating surplus	250.8	259.2	255.6	272.0	322.2	348.4	377.6	405.2	361.4	389.2	431.3
Wholesale trade	479.8	476.4	474.9	491.0	527.2	559.1	594.6	640.7	649.9	603.5	624.3
Compensation of employees	327.8	330.1	330.1	338.8	358.8	381.7	407.1	431.1	438.5	410.7	416.7
Gross operating surplus	152.0	146.3	144.8	152.2	168.4	177.4	187.5	209.6	211.4	192.8	207.6
Retail trade	550.9	568.0	591.0	621.4	636.2	665.4	692.5	704.7	669.1	671.1	709.4
Compensation of employees	404.2	415.9	428.1	445.1	459.3	477.6	493.0	506.5	501.0	477.3	484.5
Gross operating surplus	146.7	152.1	162.9	176.3	176.9	187.8	199.5	198.2	168.1	193.8	224.9
Transportation and warehousing	283.9	290.4	285.3	304.4	328.5	349.2	372.5	381.9	390.3	367.1	378.1
Compensation of employees	202.3	206.6	204.0	209.7	222.7	233.8	243.4	255.1	257.9	244.5	249.4
Gross operating surplus	81.6	83.8	81.3	94.7	105.8	115.4	129.1	126.8	132.4	122.6	128.7
Information	381.7	413.3	461.2	467.7	518.9	544.6	548.4	591.9	597.5	577.9	585.3
Compensation of employees	242.2	240.8	224.3	228.5	235.5	237.5	245.8	258.4	259.9	246.7	247.9
Gross operating surplus	139.5	172.5	236.9	239.2	283.4	307.1	302.6	333.5	337.6	331.2	337.4
Finance and insurance	734.3	809.9	832.9	868.9	882.1	980.2	1 051.5	1 035.8	996.0	1 053.0	1 195.3
Compensation of employees	407.1	442.3	447.3	467.3	497.4	541.8	584.4	610.3	610.4	568.0	584.7
Gross operating surplus	327.2	367.6	385.6	401.6	384.7	438.4	467.1	425.5	385.6	485.0	610.6
Real estate and rental and leasing	1 104.1	1 176.1	1 206.9	1 254.0	1 311.2	1 401.9	1 478.6	1 574.3	1 662.8	1 648.0	1 541.9
Compensation of employees	78.9	81.1	86.2	87.6	95.3	101.7	108.4	112.5	110.7	103.1	104.4
Gross operating surplus	1 025.2	1 095.0	1 120.7	1 166.4	1 215.9	1 300.2	1 370.2	1 461.8	1 552.1	1 544.9	1 437.5
Professional, scientific, and technical services	645.9	683.2	699.1	721.3	781.6	836.6	914.4	993.3	1 074.0	1 011.1	1 073.0
Compensation of employees	462.3	476.4	469.4	479.8	508.3	555.8	607.5	654.0	694.2	671.2	691.7
Gross operating surplus	183.6	206.8	229.7	241.5	273.3	280.8	306.9	339.3	379.8	339.9	381.3
Management of companies and enterprises	165.6	168.9	172.3	185.8	195.9	210.7	226.1	248.5	252.0	238.3	252.7
Compensation of employees	146.2	149.5	152.1	164.0	173.0	185.8	200.6	219.4	222.5	209.6	222.9
Gross operating surplus	19.4	19.4	20.2	21.8	22.9	24.9	25.5	29.1	29.5	28.7	29.8
Administrative and waste management services	277.2	288.8	294.6	316.2	328.4	363.9	377.0	406.2	410.6	387.0	414.1
Compensation of employees	218.9	224.0	227.5	239.7	248.3	274.7	292.4	310.2	314.6	291.3	306.9
Gross operating surplus	58.3	64.8	67.1	76.5	80.1	89.2	84.6	96.0	96.0	95.7	107.2
Educational services	82.3	84.7	94.5	101.3	110.8	114.6	123.0	131.3	140.5	149.2	155.3
Compensation of employees	74.3	79.7	88.8	94.6	102.5	106.1	113.4	121.2	128.9	135.7	140.7
Gross operating surplus	8.0	5.0	5.7	6.7	8.3	8.5	9.6	10.1	11.6	13.5	14.6
Health care and social assistance	577.9	625.6	674.7	723.4	771.0	812.4	863.7	914.3	981.0	1 027.2	1 081.6
Compensation of employees	485.2	521.3	564.2	608.5	649.1	687.4	733.2	773.8	825.0	862.2	884.8
Gross operating surplus	92.7	104.3	110.5	114.9	121.9	125.0	130.5	140.5	156.0	165.0	196.8
Arts, entertainment, and recreation	89.9	85.7	92.5	95.8	103.6	107.1	115.0	122.6	117.9	116.1	124.5
Compensation of employees	55.1	57.8	61.4	64.1	67.5	69.2	75.9	80.6	80.9	80.4	82.0
Gross operating surplus	34.8	27.9	31.1	31.7	36.1	37.9	39.1	42.0	37.0	35.7	42.5
Accommodation and food services	246.5	259.4	270.9	281.1	300.8	319.5	334.3	357.0	348.4	331.9	358.7
Compensation of employees	175.0	183.0	188.2	197.8	211.8	222.0	231.4	253.7	251.0	240.6	253.4
Gross operating surplus	71.5	76.4	82.7	83.3	89.0	97.5	102.9	103.3	97.4	91.3	105.3
Other services, except government	265.5	251.5	271.8	275.0	286.0	297.2	314.6	326.7	325.6	324.0	339.4
Compensation of employees	170.1	175.7	187.0	194.2	205.0	209.5	217.8	230.4	239.0	234.0	236.4
Gross operating surplus	95.4	75.8	84.8	80.8	81.0	87.7	96.8	96.3	86.6	90.0	103.0
Government	1 226.9	1 288.0	1 367.7	1 451.0	1 524.2	1 603.0	1 685.4	1 778.5	1 874.7	1 943.2	1 989.5
Compensation of employees	1 020.3	1 079.3	1 150.4	1 225.9	1 291.1	1 355.9	1 420.3	1 499.0	1 579.5	1 634.4	1 671.1
Gross operating surplus	206.6	208.7	217.3	225.1	233.1	247.1	265.1	279.5	295.2	308.8	318.4
Addenda:											
Private goods-producing industries	2 036.9	1 999.1	1 988.3	2 075.3	2 265.2	2 428.6	2 564.6	2 653.5	2 613.5	2 331.1	2 500.6
Compensation of employees	1 276.1	1 269.3	1 253.2	1 289.0	1 317.3	1 374.4	1 448.5	1 485.3	1 497.9	1 337.7	1 334.8
Gross operating surplus	760.8	729.8	735.1	786.3	947.9	1 054.2	1 116.1	1 168.2	1 115.6	993.4	1 165.8
Private services-producing industries	6 025.0	6 330.1	6 564.9	6 858.2	7 246.8	7 722.2	8 191.8	8 624.0	8 817.6	8 706.4	9 039.8
Compensation of employees	3 497.2	3 635.9	3 712.8	3 873.4	4 091.1	4 341.2	4 614.8	4 878.7	5 001.6	4 843.4	4 974.7
Gross operating surplus	2 527.8	2 694.2	2 852.1	2 984.8	3 155.7	3 381.0	3 577.0	3 745.3	3 816.0	3 863.0	4 065.1
Information-communications-technology-producing industries [1]	400.7	371.2	412.8	427.9	484.0	524.0	548.4	574.7	586.2	588.9	653.6
Compensation of employees	378.0	359.9	321.7	315.9	329.0	348.1	370.1	389.0	394.5	377.3	395.7
Gross operating surplus	22.7	11.3	91.1	112.0	155.0	175.9	178.3	185.7	191.7	211.6	257.9

[1]Consists of computer and electronic products manufacturing; publishing, including software; information and data processing services; and computer systems design and related services.

NOTES AND DEFINITIONS, CHAPTER 14

TABLES 14-1 THROUGH 14-3
GROSS DOMESTIC PRODUCT (VALUE ADDED) AND GROSS FACTOR INCOME BY INDUSTRY

SOURCE: U.S. DEPARTMENT OF COMMERCE, BUREAU OF ECONOMIC ANALYSIS (BEA)

In the introduction to the notes and definitions for Chapter 1, it was observed that gross domestic product (GDP), while primarily measured as the sum of final demands for goods and services, is also the sum of the values created by each industry in the economy. In this chapter, selected data are presented from the industry accounts in the national income and product accounts (NIPAs). The industry accounts measure the contribution of each major industry to GDP. Currently these are only calculated on an annual basis. However, BEA is working on quarterly GDP by industry statistics, which they plan to make available within 30 days of BEA's third release of quarterly GDP, that is, within 120 days after the end of the reference quarter. These plans, with "prototype" estimates for 2007 through 2011, are described in "Prototype Quarterly Statistics on U.S. GDP by Industry, 2007–2011", June 2012, a "BEA Briefing," available on the BEA Web site, <http://www.bea.gov>.

In recent years, estimates of GDP by industry have been prepared using a methodology integrated with annual input-output accounts in order to produce estimates of gross industry output, industry input, and the difference between the two—industry value added—with greater consistency and timeliness than was previously possible. The current integrated industry accounts also include a wealth of related information too extensive for inclusion here, such as quantity and price indexes for gross output and intermediate inputs, cost per unit of real value added allocated to the three components of value added, and components of domestic supply (domestic output, imports, exports, and inventory change).

The estimates of GDP by NAICS industry have been extended back to 1947, using approximations of current methods in earlier years when the source data were less comprehensive. Table 14-1 presents current-dollar GDP for NAICS industry groups. Table 14-2 presents indexes of real value added for each industry group.

In Table 14-3, the editor presents a measure derived from the components of current-dollar value added as published by BEA. This measure, "gross domestic factor income," enables users to obtain a clearer picture of the quantitative impact of each industry on the economy and of the shares of capital and labor in each industry.

The 2004 revision incorporated a change in terminology. An industry's contribution to total GDP, formerly referred to as "gross product originating" (GPO) or "gross product by industry," is now called "value added." This is consistent with the use of the term "value added" in most economic writing. However, it should not be confused with a concept known as "Census value added," which is used in U.S. censuses and surveys of manufactures. Census value added is calculated at the individual establishment level and does not exclude purchased business services. This means that census value added is not a true measure of economic value added.

Definitions and notes on the data

An industry's *gross domestic product (value added)*, formerly *GPO*, is equal to the market value of its gross output (which consists of the value, including taxes, of sales or receipts and other operating income plus the value of inventory change) minus the value of its intermediate inputs (energy, raw materials, semifinished goods, and services that are purchased from domestic industries or from foreign sources).

In concept, this is also equal to the sum of *compensation of employees, taxes on production and imports less subsidies,* and *gross operating surplus.* (See Chapter 1 and its notes and definitions for more information.)

Compensation of employees consists of wage and salary accruals and supplements to wages and salaries. This approximates the labor share of production, subject to the note below about proprietors' income.

Taxes on production and imports less subsidies. Although this is shown in BEA source data as a single net line item, it represents two separate components.

Taxes on production and imports are included in the market value of the goods and services sold to final consumers and therefore in the consumer valuation of those goods. Since they are not part of the payments to the labor and capital inputs in the producing industries, they must be added to the sum of the returns to those inputs in order to account for the total value to consumers. Taxes that fall into this classification include property taxes, sales and excise taxes, and Customs duties.

BEA allocates these taxes to the industry level at which they are assessed by law. Most sales taxes are considered by BEA to be part of the value added by retail trade. Some sales taxes, most fuel taxes, and all customs duties are allocated by BEA to wholesale trade. Residential real property taxes, including those on owner-occupied dwellings, are allocated by BEA to the real estate industry.

Subsidies to business by government are included in the labor and/or capital payments made by that industry. Since they are payments to the industry in addition to the market values paid by consumers, they are *subtracted* from the values of the labor and capital inputs to make them consistent with the market values as defined in value added. The role of subsidies is obvious in the source data for the agricultural sector, where the net "taxes on production and imports less subsidies" has a negative sign: farm subsidies more than offset this industry's taxes on production and imports, which mainly consist of property taxes, since sales, excise, and import taxes are not levied on farms.

For private sector businesses, *gross operating surplus* consists of business income (corporate profits before tax, proprietors' income, and rental income of persons), net interest and miscellaneous payments, business current transfer payments (net), and capital consumption allowances. For government, households, and institutions, it consists of consumption of fixed capital and (for government) government enterprises' current surplus. This approximates the share of the value of production ascribable to capital and land as measured in the NIPAs accounts; however, as BEA notes, "an unknown portion [of proprietors' income] reflects the labor contribution of proprietors." (*Survey of Current Business*, June 2004, p. 27, footnote 7.) Another aspect to be noted is that gross operating surplus includes the return to owner-occupied housing in the real estate sector. Because there is in the NIPAs no employee compensation attributed to owner-occupied housing, the capital share in that industry as measured by gross operating surplus is very large.

Quantity indexes for value added. Measures of the constant-dollar change in each industry's gross output minus its intermediate input use are calculated by BEA, using a Fisher index-number formula which incorporates weights from two adjacent years. The changes for successive years are chained together in indexes, with the value for the year 2005 set at 100. The indexes are multiplied by 2005 current-dollar value added to provide estimates of value added in "chained 2005 dollars," but because the actual weights used change from year to year, components in chained 2005 dollars typically do not add up to total GDP in 2005 dollars—and do not contain any information not already summarized in the indexes. For that reason, only the indexes are published here.

Gross domestic factor income (not a category published as such in the NIPAs) is calculated by the editor as value added minus "taxes on production and imports less subsidies." The effect of this procedure is to take out the specified taxes, and to leave in the subsidies embedded in the employee compensation and gross operating surplus components. The editor believes that this provides a valuable alternative basis for assessing the importance of different industries in the economy and the shares of labor and capital in each industry's output.

The editor's reasoning is based on the facts that more than half of these taxes are sales, excise, and import taxes, and the assignment of these taxes to industries is economically arbitrary. BEA assigns them to the industry with the legal liability to pay, not to the entity bearing the major incidence of the tax. Yet economists have demonstrated that most of the burdens of sales and excise taxes and import duties are not borne by the factors in the legally liable industry; instead, they are passed on to consumers. In addition, because the wholesale and retail trade industries are classified as "services-producing," BEA's allocation of those taxes has a very peculiar result: taxes on goods are represented as paid by "service" industries. The process adopted instead by the editor in Table 14-3, which excludes these taxes and focuses on "gross domestic factor income," has the effect (for example) of keeping the wholesale trade industry from appearing to be both larger and more heavily taxed than it really is.

Private goods-producing industries consists of agriculture, forestry, fishing, and hunting; mining; construction; and manufacturing.

Private services-producing industries consists of utilities; wholesale trade; retail trade; transportation and warehousing; information; finance, insurance, real estate, rental, and leasing; professional and business services; educational services, health care, and social assistance; arts, entertainment, recreation, accommodation, and food services; and other services, except government.

Information-communications-technology-producing industries is a category that cuts across the goods and services framework, consisting of computer and electronic products manufacturing; publishing industries (which includes software) from the information sector; information and data processing services; and computer systems design and related services.

Data availability and references

The GDP by industry data shown here have been recalculated back to 1947 consistent with the 2009 comprehensive revision of the NIPAs. The data for 2011 in Tables 14-1 and 14-2 are advance estimates, with considerably less detail and using approximations of the detailed methods, released on April 26, 2012. All data and *Survey of Current Business* articles are available on the BEA Web site at <http://www.bea.gov>. Click on "Annual Industry Accounts." For the tables, click on "Interactive Tables" under "Gross Domestic Product (GDP) by Industry."

CHAPTER 15: EMPLOYMENT, HOURS, AND EARNINGS BY NAICS INDUSTRY

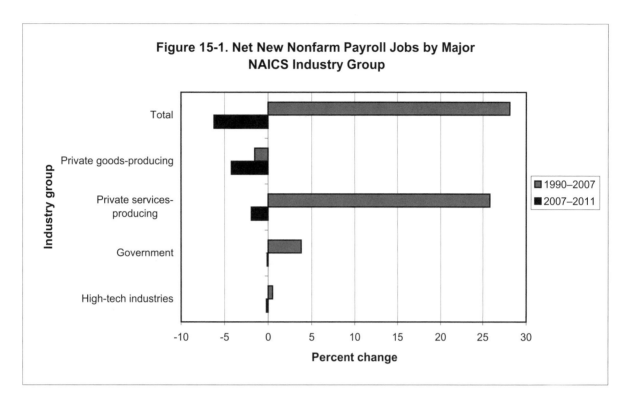

Figure 15-1. Net New Nonfarm Payroll Jobs by Major NAICS Industry Group

- From 1990 to the year of the business cycle peak in 2007, U.S. nonfarm employers added a net total of 28.1 million jobs, based on the annual averages displayed in this chapter. Employment began to decline in February 2008 and didn't begin to increase until March 2010, despite the judgment by the National Bureau of Economic Research Business Cycle Dating Committee that the recession ended in June 2009. In 2011, average payroll employment averaged 6.2 million jobs less than the 2007 average, with losses in government employment as well as in the private sectors, and in the smaller high-technology subgroup as well. (See "Business Cycle Perspectives" at the beginning of this volume, Tables 10-8 and 10-9, and Table 15-1)

- Based on the annual averages, some industries have showed indications of employment turnaround since 2009, including mining, motor vehicle manufacturing, management and consulting services, and temporary help agencies. Some other industries have displayed continued growth even during recession, such as internet publishing, computer systems design, and private education, health care, and social assistance. (Table 15-1)

- The average workweek for production and nonsupervisory workers is up since 2009 in nearly all industries and industry groups. (Table 15-3)

- Average hourly earnings for production and nonsupervisory workers in 2011 ranged from just over $11 in the leisure and hospitality sector to over $30 in petroleum and coal products manufacturing and utilities. (Table 15-4)

Table 15-1. Nonfarm Employment by NAICS Sector and Industry

(Wage and salary workers on nonfarm payrolls, thousands.)

Industry	1990	1991	1992	1993	1994	1995	1996	1997	1998	1999
TOTAL NONFARM	109 487	108 374	108 726	110 844	114 291	117 298	119 708	122 776	125 930	128 993
Total Private	91 072	89 829	89 940	91 855	95 016	97 866	100 169	103 113	106 021	108 686
Goods-Producing	23 723	22 588	22 095	22 219	22 774	23 156	23 409	23 886	24 354	24 465
Mining and logging	765	739	689	666	659	641	637	654	645	598
Logging	84.6	78.7	78.7	81.0	82.0	82.5	80.7	82.1	80.0	80.8
Mining	680.1	660.5	609.8	584.9	576.5	558.1	556.4	571.3	564.7	517.4
Oil and gas extraction	190.2	191.0	182.2	170.9	162.4	151.7	146.9	144.1	140.8	131.2
Mining, except oil and gas [1]	302.2	285.1	271.8	250.9	255.2	252.4	249.4	249.5	243.1	234.5
Coal mining	136.0	125.6	117.5	100.2	103.5	96.7	90.5	89.4	85.3	78.6
Support activities for mining	187.6	184.5	155.7	163.1	158.8	154.0	160.1	177.7	180.8	151.7
Construction	5 263	4 780	4 608	4 779	5 095	5 274	5 536	5 813	6 149	6 545
Construction of buildings	1 413.0	1 252.9	1 187.3	1 227.4	1 300.8	1 325.4	1 380.2	1 435.4	1 508.8	1 586.3
Heavy and civil engineering	813.0	759.1	734.2	738.4	761.7	774.7	800.1	824.9	865.3	908.7
Specialty trade contractors	3 037.3	2 768.4	2 686.0	2 813.6	3 032.5	3 174.1	3 355.1	3 552.6	3 775.1	4 049.6
Manufacturing	17 695	17 068	16 799	16 774	17 020	17 241	17 237	17 419	17 560	17 322
Durable goods	10 737	10 220	9 946	9 901	10 132	10 373	10 486	10 705	10 911	10 831
Wood products	543.0	500.7	504.1	526.4	562.9	576.1	585.2	597.8	611.6	622.7
Nonmetallic mineral products	528.4	494.7	487.3	491.0	505.3	513.1	517.3	525.7	535.3	540.8
Primary metals	688.6	656.1	630.3	618.4	630.4	641.7	639.3	638.8	641.5	625.0
Fabricated metal products	1 610.0	1 541.3	1 497.2	1 509.5	1 565.3	1 623.4	1 647.5	1 695.8	1 739.5	1 728.4
Machinery	1 409.8	1 347.9	1 311.2	1 330.9	1 381.4	1 442.3	1 468.9	1 495.9	1 514.1	1 468.3
Computer and electronic products [1]	1 902.5	1 809.3	1 707.3	1 655.9	1 651.1	1 688.4	1 746.6	1 803.3	1 830.9	1 780.5
Computer and peripheral equipment	367.4	348.6	328.5	305.7	297.7	295.6	304.6	316.7	322.1	310.1
Communications equipment	223.0	212.5	202.0	202.6	210.0	224.3	228.9	235.0	237.4	228.7
Semiconductors and electronic components	574.0	546.6	519.4	519.4	535.4	571.0	606.6	639.8	649.8	630.5
Electronic instruments	634.8	598.0	556.2	525.3	501.4	490.5	497.8	502.8	509.2	498.3
Electrical equipment and appliances	633.1	597.7	579.4	575.8	588.5	592.8	591.0	586.3	591.6	588.0
Transportation equipment [1]	2 134.5	2 029.3	1 978.1	1 915.0	1 937.4	1 978.5	1 975.1	2 027.6	2 078.4	2 088.6
Motor vehicles and parts	1 054.2	1 017.6	1 047.0	1 077.8	1 168.5	1 241.5	1 240.3	1 253.9	1 271.5	1 312.5
Furniture and related products	601.7	561.5	563.2	575.7	600.4	607.0	604.2	615.5	641.6	665.2
Miscellaneous manufacturing	685.7	681.8	687.7	702.5	709.0	709.7	710.7	718.2	726.8	724.0
Nondurable goods	6 958	6 848	6 853	6 872	6 889	6 868	6 751	6 714	6 649	6 491
Food manufacturing	1 507.3	1 515.2	1 518.3	1 534.6	1 539.2	1 560.0	1 562.0	1 557.9	1 554.9	1 549.8
Beverage and tobacco products	217.7	214.7	208.5	207.1	204.6	202.6	204.4	206.3	208.9	208.3
Textile mills	491.8	479.9	479.0	478.7	477.6	468.5	443.2	436.2	424.5	397.1
Textile product mills	235.6	225.1	228.0	232.6	242.9	242.1	237.1	236.4	234.7	232.4
Apparel	902.8	876.9	879.3	857.3	831.9	791.1	722.3	680.8	621.4	540.5
Leather and allied products	133.2	124.4	120.8	118.1	113.9	104.9	94.2	89.5	82.9	74.9
Paper and paper products	647.2	638.5	639.6	639.7	639.4	639.5	631.4	630.6	624.9	615.6
Printing and related support activities	808.5	792.3	780.3	785.2	802.3	817.3	815.8	821.1	827.9	814.6
Petroleum and coal products	152.8	154.8	152.3	146.2	144.0	140.4	137.3	136.0	134.5	127.8
Chemicals	1 035.7	1 024.1	1 028.9	1 024.9	1 004.7	987.9	984.5	986.8	992.6	982.5
Plastics and rubber products	824.8	802.1	817.9	847.8	888.1	913.7	918.7	932.7	941.4	947.0
Service-Providing	85 764	85 787	86 631	88 625	91 517	94 142	96 299	98 890	101 576	104 528
Private Service-Providing	67 349	67 241	67 845	69 636	72 242	74 710	76 760	79 227	81 667	84 221
Trade, transportation, and utilities	22 666	22 281	22 125	22 378	23 128	23 834	24 239	24 700	25 186	25 771
Wholesale trade	5 268.4	5 185.3	5 109.7	5 093.2	5 247.3	5 433.1	5 522.0	5 663.9	5 795.2	5 892.5
Durable goods	2 833.7	2 766.6	2 698.8	2 687.0	2 786.0	2 908.8	2 977.8	3 071.9	3 162.4	3 219.6
Nondurable goods	1 900.2	1 891.3	1 891.5	1 888.3	1 927.0	1 969.3	1 977.5	2 007.9	2 032.7	2 061.1
Electronic markets, agents, and brokers	534.5	527.4	519.4	517.9	534.4	555.0	566.7	584.1	600.1	611.8

[1] Includes other industries, not shown separately.

Table 15-1. Nonfarm Employment by NAICS Sector and Industry—*Continued*

(Wage and salary workers on nonfarm payrolls, thousands.)

Industry	2000	2001	2002	2003	2004	2005	2006	2007	2008	2009	2010	2011
TOTAL NONFARM	131 785	131 826	130 341	129 999	131 435	133 703	136 086	137 598	136 790	130 807	129 874	131 359
Total Private	110 995	110 708	108 828	108 416	109 814	111 899	114 113	115 380	114 281	108 252	107 384	109 254
Goods-Producing	24 649	23 873	22 557	21 816	21 882	22 190	22 530	22 233	21 335	18 558	17 751	18 021
Mining and logging	599	606	583	572	591	628	684	724	767	694	705	784
Logging	79.0	73.5	70.4	69.4	67.6	65.2	64.4	60.1	56.6	50.4	49.7	48.3
Mining	520.2	532.5	512.2	502.7	523.0	562.2	619.7	663.8	709.8	643.3	654.8	735.4
Oil and gas extraction	124.9	123.7	121.9	120.2	123.4	125.7	134.5	146.2	160.5	159.8	158.7	174.4
Mining, except oil and gas [1]	224.8	218.7	210.6	202.7	205.1	212.8	220.3	223.4	226.0	208.3	204.5	217.0
Coal mining	72.2	74.3	74.4	70.0	70.6	73.9	78.0	77.2	81.2	81.5	80.8	86.2
Support activities for mining	170.6	190.1	179.8	179.8	194.6	223.7	264.9	294.3	323.4	275.2	291.6	344.0
Construction	6 787	6 826	6 716	6 735	6 976	7 336	7 691	7 630	7 162	6 016	5 518	5 504
Construction of buildings	1 632.5	1 588.9	1 574.8	1 575.8	1 630.0	1 711.9	1 804.9	1 774.2	1 641.7	1 357.2	1 229.7	1 219.0
Heavy and civil engineering	937.0	953.0	930.6	903.1	907.4	951.2	985.1	1 005.4	964.5	851.3	825.1	829.0
Specialty trade contractors	4 217.0	4 283.9	4 210.4	4 255.7	4 438.6	4 673.1	4 901.1	4 850.2	4 555.8	3 807.9	3 463.4	3 455.4
Manufacturing	17 263	16 441	15 259	14 509	14 315	14 227	14 155	13 879	13 406	11 847	11 528	11 733
Durable goods	10 877	10 336	9 485	8 964	8 925	8 956	8 981	8 808	8 463	7 284	7 064	7 274
Wood products	615.4	576.3	557.0	539.5	551.6	561.0	560.6	517.1	457.7	360.2	342.1	335.2
Nonmetallic mineral products	554.2	544.5	516.0	494.2	505.5	505.3	509.6	500.5	465.0	394.3	370.9	366.6
Primary metals	621.8	570.9	509.4	477.4	466.8	466.0	464.0	455.8	442.0	362.1	362.3	389.5
Fabricated metal products	1 752.6	1 676.4	1 548.5	1 478.9	1 497.1	1 522.0	1 553.1	1 562.8	1 527.5	1 311.6	1 281.7	1 344.2
Machinery	1 457.0	1 370.6	1 231.8	1 151.6	1 145.2	1 165.5	1 183.2	1 187.1	1 187.6	1 028.6	996.1	1 056.7
Computer and electronic products [1]	1 820.0	1 748.8	1 507.2	1 355.2	1 322.8	1 316.4	1 307.5	1 272.5	1 244.2	1 136.9	1 094.6	1 107.0
Computer and peripheral equipment	301.9	286.2	250.0	224.0	210.0	205.1	196.2	186.2	183.2	166.4	157.6	159.2
Communications equipment	238.6	225.4	179.0	149.2	143.0	141.4	136.2	128.1	127.3	120.5	117.4	115.1
Semiconductors and electronic components	676.3	645.4	524.5	461.1	454.1	452.0	457.9	447.5	431.8	378.1	369.4	384.0
Electronic instruments	487.7	483.6	456.8	435.4	436.9	441.0	444.5	443.2	441.0	421.6	406.4	404.2
Electrical equipment and appliances	590.9	556.9	496.5	459.6	445.1	433.5	432.7	429.4	424.3	373.6	359.5	366.8
Transportation equipment [1]	2 057.1	1 939.1	1 830.0	1 775.1	1 766.7	1 772.3	1 768.9	1 711.9	1 608.0	1 347.9	1 333.1	1 381.7
Motor vehicles and parts	1 313.6	1 212.9	1 151.2	1 125.3	1 112.8	1 096.7	1 070.0	994.2	875.5	664.1	678.5	716.9
Furniture and related products	680.1	642.9	604.7	573.7	574.1	566.3	558.3	529.4	478.0	384.3	357.2	352.8
Miscellaneous manufacturing	728.0	709.5	683.3	658.3	650.6	647.2	643.7	641.7	628.9	584.4	566.8	573.4
Nondurable goods	6 386	6 105	5 774	5 546	5 390	5 271	5 174	5 071	4 943	4 564	4 464	4 460
Food manufacturing	1 553.1	1 551.2	1 525.7	1 517.5	1 493.7	1 477.6	1 479.4	1 484.1	1 480.9	1 456.4	1 450.6	1 456.3
Beverage and tobacco products	207.0	209.0	207.4	199.6	194.6	191.9	194.2	198.2	198.4	187.4	183.4	188.2
Textile mills	378.2	332.9	290.9	261.3	236.9	217.6	195.0	169.7	151.2	124.4	119.0	120.5
Textile product mills	229.6	217.0	204.2	187.7	183.2	176.4	166.7	157.7	147.2	125.7	119.0	116.8
Apparel	483.5	415.2	350.0	303.9	278.0	250.5	232.4	214.6	199.0	167.5	156.6	151.8
Leather and allied products	68.8	58.0	50.2	44.5	41.8	39.6	36.8	33.8	33.1	29.0	27.8	29.3
Paper and paper products	604.7	577.6	546.6	516.2	495.5	484.2	470.5	458.2	444.9	407.0	394.7	391.3
Printing and related support activities	806.8	768.3	706.6	680.4	662.6	646.3	634.4	622.0	594.1	521.9	487.6	469.3
Petroleum and coal products	123.2	121.1	118.1	114.3	111.7	112.1	113.2	114.5	117.4	115.3	113.9	112.2
Chemicals	980.4	959.0	927.5	906.1	887.0	872.1	865.9	860.9	847.1	804.1	786.5	788.3
Plastics and rubber products	950.9	896.2	846.8	814.3	804.7	802.3	785.5	757.2	729.4	624.9	624.8	635.6
Service-Providing	107 136	107 952	107 784	108 183	109 553	111 513	113 556	115 366	115 456	112 249	112 123	113 338
Private Service-Providing	86 346	86 834	86 271	86 600	87 932	89 709	91 582	93 147	92 946	89 695	89 633	91 234
Trade, transportation, and utilities	26 225	25 983	25 497	25 287	25 533	25 959	26 276	26 630	26 293	24 906	24 636	25 019
Wholesale trade	5 933.2	5 772.7	5 652.3	5 607.5	5 662.9	5 764.4	5 904.5	6 015.2	5 942.7	5 586.6	5 452.1	5 528.8
Durable goods	3 250.7	3 130.4	3 007.9	2 940.6	2 950.5	2 999.2	3 074.8	3 121.5	3 052.0	2 809.9	2 713.5	2 752.8
Nondurable goods	2 064.8	2 031.3	2 015.0	2 004.6	2 010.0	2 022.4	2 041.3	2 062.2	2 047.7	1 966.1	1 928.1	1 940.4
Electronic markets, agents, and brokers	617.7	611.1	629.4	662.2	702.4	742.8	788.5	831.5	842.9	810.7	810.5	835.6

[1]Includes other industries, not shown separately.

Table 15-1. Nonfarm Employment by NAICS Sector and Industry—*Continued*

(Wage and salary workers on nonfarm payrolls, thousands.)

Industry	1990	1991	1992	1993	1994	1995	1996	1997	1998	1999
Retail trade	13 182	12 896	12 828	13 021	13 491	13 897	14 143	14 389	14 609	14 970
Motor vehicle and parts dealers [1]	1 494.4	1 435.1	1 428.1	1 475.3	1 564.7	1 627.1	1 685.6	1 723.4	1 740.9	1 796.6
Automobile dealers	983.3	938.3	934.8	970.4	1 031.8	1 071.6	1 113.0	1 134.5	1 142.0	1 179.7
Furniture and home furnishings stores	431.5	412.8	410.3	418.6	441.6	461.2	474.2	484.7	499.1	524.4
Electronics and appliance stores	450.7	449.4	446.3	459.4	495.7	534.7	555.5	575.2	590.6	623.8
Building material and garden supply stores	890.9	863.0	872.1	891.9	946.2	981.8	1 007.2	1 043.1	1 062.3	1 101.0
Food and beverage stores	2 778.8	2 767.9	2 743.9	2 774.8	2 825.0	2 879.8	2 927.8	2 956.9	2 965.7	2 984.5
Health and personal care stores	792.0	788.5	780.2	778.6	797.0	811.9	826.4	853.3	876.0	898.2
Gasoline stations	910.2	889.3	876.4	881.2	902.3	922.3	946.4	956.2	961.3	943.5
Clothing and clothing accessories stores	1 313.0	1 275.8	1 249.1	1 259.9	1 261.7	1 246.3	1 220.6	1 235.9	1 268.6	1 306.6
Sporting goods, hobby, book, and music stores	463.6	459.5	466.2	472.8	498.9	519.8	528.8	545.1	555.1	582.7
General merchandise stores [1]	2 499.8	2 416.7	2 414.2	2 450.2	2 541.0	2 635.4	2 657.3	2 657.6	2 686.5	2 751.8
Department stores	1 493.9	1 440.8	1 445.2	1 486.8	1 560.4	1 629.8	1 645.0	1 653.5	1 679.2	1 709.2
Miscellaneous store retailers	738.2	734.7	736.8	752.9	795.7	841.1	874.3	913.2	950.3	985.5
Nonstore retailers	419.2	403.7	404.5	404.9	421.2	435.4	438.5	444.5	453.0	471.6
Transportation and warehousing	3 475.6	3 462.8	3 461.8	3 553.8	3 701.0	3 837.8	3 935.3	4 026.5	4 168.0	4 300.3
Air transportation	529.2	525.4	519.6	516.6	511.2	510.9	525.7	542.0	562.7	586.3
Rail transportation	271.8	255.6	248.1	242.2	234.6	232.5	225.2	221.0	225.0	228.8
Water transportation	56.8	57.4	56.7	52.8	52.3	50.8	51.0	50.7	50.5	51.7
Truck transportation	1 122.4	1 104.6	1 107.4	1 154.8	1 206.2	1 249.1	1 282.4	1 308.2	1 354.4	1 391.5
Transit and ground passenger transportation	274.2	283.9	287.9	299.9	316.6	327.9	339.1	349.6	362.7	371.0
Pipeline transportation	59.8	60.7	60.1	58.7	57.0	53.6	51.4	49.7	48.1	46.9
Scenic and sightseeing transportation	15.7	16.5	17.7	19.3	21.3	22.0	23.2	24.5	25.4	26.1
Support activities for transportation	364.1	376.6	369.9	381.8	404.7	430.4	445.8	473.4	496.8	518.1
Couriers and messengers	375.0	378.9	388.8	414.3	466.2	516.8	539.9	546.0	568.2	585.9
Warehousing and storage	406.6	403.2	405.6	413.4	431.0	443.8	451.8	461.5	474.2	494.1
Utilities	740.0	736.1	726.0	710.7	689.3	666.2	639.6	620.9	613.4	608.5
Information	2 688	2 677	2 641	2 668	2 738	2 843	2 940	3 084	3 218	3 419
Publishing industries, except Internet	870.6	863.4	854.2	873.1	891.0	910.7	927.2	955.5	982.3	1 004.8
Motion picture and sound recording industries	254.6	258.9	254.3	259.6	278.4	311.1	334.7	353.0	369.5	384.4
Broadcasting, except Internet	283.8	281.2	279.7	284.0	290.1	298.1	309.1	313.0	321.2	329.4
Telecommunications	1 008.5	999.9	972.9	969.5	989.5	1 009.3	1 038.1	1 108.0	1 167.4	1 270.8
Data processing, hosting, and related services	211.4	212.8	219.6	223.4	226.9	242.6	252.0	268.4	282.8	307.1
Other information services [1]	59.3	61.2	60.5	58.1	62.5	71.8	79.0	85.5	95.3	121.9
Internet publishing and broadcasting	29.4	28.3	28.2	28.7	29.7	33.7	39.6	45.4	53.9	78.1
Financial activities	6 614	6 558	6 540	6 709	6 867	6 827	6 969	7 178	7 462	7 648
Finance and insurance	4 976.4	4 935.1	4 912.4	5 033.0	5 132.5	5 069.0	5 151.4	5 302.1	5 528.6	5 664.9
Monetary authorities–central bank	24.0	24.2	23.7	23.4	23.4	23.0	22.8	22.1	21.7	22.6
Credit intermediation and related activities [1]	2 424.8	2 352.4	2 317.3	2 360.7	2 375.7	2 314.4	2 368.2	2 433.6	2 531.9	2 591.0
Depository credit intermediation [1]	1 908.5	1 830.7	1 769.0	1 760.5	1 736.7	1 700.2	1 691.4	1 696.6	1 708.9	1 709.7
Commercial banking	1 361.8	1 333.7	1 302.8	1 308.7	1 297.4	1 281.7	1 275.1	1 277.9	1 286.0	1 281.2
Securities, commodity contracts, investments	457.9	455.0	475.7	507.9	553.4	562.2	589.6	636.1	692.2	737.3
Insurance carriers and related activities	2 016.1	2 048.2	2 039.5	2 082.5	2 118.8	2 108.2	2 108.0	2 143.6	2 209.4	2 236.1
Funds, trusts, and other financial vehicles	53.5	55.3	56.2	58.5	61.2	61.2	62.8	66.8	73.4	78.0
Real estate and rental and leasing	1 637.1	1 623.0	1 627.7	1 676.3	1 734.2	1 758.1	1 817.1	1 875.9	1 933.7	1 982.5
Real estate	1 109.0	1 109.8	1 116.7	1 148.6	1 185.9	1 181.7	1 208.6	1 243.8	1 277.7	1 302.6
Rental and leasing services	514.2	499.4	496.4	511.0	529.9	557.4	587.7	609.5	630.8	653.1
Lessors of nonfinancial intangible assets	13.9	13.9	14.6	16.7	18.4	19.0	20.8	22.6	25.3	26.8

[1]Includes other industries, not shown separately.

Table 15-1. Nonfarm Employment by NAICS Sector and Industry—*Continued*

(Wage and salary workers on nonfarm payrolls, thousands.)

Industry	2000	2001	2002	2003	2004	2005	2006	2007	2008	2009	2010	2011
Retail trade	15 280	15 239	15 025	14 917	15 058	15 280	15 353	15 520	15 283	14 522	14 440	14 643
Motor vehicle and parts dealers [1]	1 846.9	1 854.6	1 879.4	1 882.9	1 902.3	1 918.6	1 909.7	1 908.3	1 831.2	1 637.5	1 629.2	1 687.9
Automobile dealers	1 216.5	1 225.1	1 252.8	1 254.4	1 257.3	1 261.4	1 246.7	1 242.2	1 176.7	1 018.2	1 011.5	1 055.4
Furniture and home furnishings stores	543.5	541.2	538.7	547.3	563.4	576.1	586.9	574.6	531.1	449.2	437.9	442.2
Electronics and appliance stores	647.3	632.6	594.8	573.9	571.5	585.0	580.5	582.5	569.6	515.7	522.3	525.5
Building material and garden supply stores	1 142.1	1 151.8	1 176.5	1 185.0	1 227.1	1 276.1	1 324.1	1 309.3	1 248.0	1 155.6	1 131.8	1 140.7
Food and beverage stores	2 993.0	2 950.5	2 881.6	2 838.4	2 821.6	2 817.8	2 821.1	2 843.6	2 862.0	2 830.0	2 808.2	2 829.1
Health and personal care stores	927.6	951.5	938.8	938.1	941.1	953.7	961.1	993.1	1 002.8	986.0	980.5	980.5
Gasoline stations	935.7	925.3	895.9	882.0	875.6	871.1	864.1	861.5	842.4	825.5	819.3	828.0
Clothing and clothing accessories stores	1 321.6	1 321.1	1 312.5	1 304.5	1 364.3	1 414.6	1 450.9	1 500.0	1 468.0	1 363.9	1 352.5	1 356.0
Sporting goods, hobby, book, and music stores	602.7	601.1	591.8	584.7	585.9	597.9	606.0	623.3	621.9	589.2	579.1	574.3
General merchandise stores [1]	2 819.8	2 842.2	2 812.0	2 822.4	2 863.1	2 934.3	2 935.0	3 020.6	3 025.6	2 966.2	2 997.7	3 080.1
Department stores	1 755.0	1 768.3	1 684.0	1 620.6	1 605.3	1 595.1	1 557.2	1 591.5	1 540.5	1 472.9	1 501.6	1 546.7
Miscellaneous store retailers	1 007.1	993.3	959.5	930.7	913.5	899.9	881.0	865.4	842.5	782.4	761.5	766.9
Nonstore retailers	492.4	473.5	443.7	427.3	428.8	434.6	432.8	437.9	438.0	421.1	420.6	431.7
Transportation and warehousing	4 410.3	4 372.0	4 223.6	4 185.4	4 248.6	4 360.9	4 469.6	4 540.9	4 508.3	4 236.4	4 190.7	4 292.2
Air transportation	614.4	615.3	563.5	528.3	514.5	500.8	487.0	491.8	490.7	462.8	458.3	456.0
Rail transportation	231.7	226.7	217.8	217.7	225.7	227.8	227.5	233.7	231.0	218.2	216.4	228.8
Water transportation	56.0	54.0	52.6	54.5	56.4	60.6	62.7	65.5	67.1	63.4	62.3	62.5
Truck transportation	1 405.8	1 386.8	1 339.3	1 325.6	1 351.7	1 397.6	1 435.8	1 439.2	1 389.0	1 268.2	1 250.4	1 298.9
Transit and ground passenger transportation	372.1	374.8	380.8	382.2	384.9	389.2	399.3	412.1	423.3	421.7	429.7	436.1
Pipeline transportation	46.0	45.4	41.7	40.2	38.4	37.8	38.7	39.9	41.7	42.6	42.3	42.9
Scenic and sightseeing transportation	27.5	29.1	25.6	26.6	27.2	28.8	27.5	28.6	28.0	27.6	27.3	28.6
Support activities for transportation	537.4	539.2	524.7	520.3	535.1	552.2	570.6	584.2	592.0	548.5	542.5	563.9
Couriers and messengers	605.0	587.0	560.9	561.7	556.6	571.4	582.4	580.7	573.4	546.3	528.1	528.5
Warehousing and storage	514.4	513.8	516.7	528.3	558.1	594.7	638.1	665.2	672.1	637.1	633.4	645.8
Utilities	601.3	599.4	596.2	577.0	563.8	554.0	548.5	553.4	558.9	560.0	552.8	555.2
Information	3 630	3 629	3 395	3 188	3 118	3 061	3 038	3 032	2 984	2 804	2 707	2 659
Publishing industries, except Internet	1 035.0	1 020.7	964.1	924.8	909.1	904.1	902.4	901.2	880.4	796.4	759.0	749.0
Motion picture and sound recording industries	382.6	376.8	387.9	376.2	385.0	377.5	375.7	380.6	371.3	357.6	370.2	361.3
Broadcasting, except Internet	343.5	344.6	334.1	324.3	325.0	327.7	328.3	325.2	318.7	300.5	290.3	281.5
Telecommunications	1 396.6	1 423.9	1 280.9	1 166.8	1 115.1	1 071.3	1 047.6	1 030.6	1 019.4	965.7	902.9	865.3
Data processing, hosting, and related services	315.7	316.8	303.9	280.0	267.1	262.5	263.2	267.8	260.3	248.5	243.0	243.0
Other information services [1]	157.1	146.5	123.6	115.9	116.9	117.7	120.8	126.3	133.5	135.0	141.7	158.7
Internet publishing and broadcasting	110.8	100.4	76.3	67.2	66.1	67.2	69.1	72.9	80.6	83.3	92.0	108.0
Financial activities	7 687	7 808	7 847	7 977	8 031	8 153	8 328	8 301	8 145	7 769	7 652	7 681
Finance and insurance	5 676.7	5 769.2	5 813.6	5 919.1	5 945.3	6 018.9	6 156.0	6 132.0	6 014.9	5 774.9	5 718.3	5 751.8
Monetary authorities–central bank	22.8	23.0	23.4	22.6	21.8	20.8	21.2	21.6	22.4	21.0	20.0	18.9
Credit intermediation and related activities [1]	2 547.8	2 597.7	2 686.0	2 792.4	2 817.0	2 869.0	2 924.9	2 866.3	2 732.7	2 590.2	2 550.0	2 558.9
Depository credit intermediation [1]	1 681.2	1 701.2	1 733.0	1 748.5	1 751.5	1 769.2	1 802.0	1 823.5	1 815.2	1 753.8	1 728.8	1 738.4
Commercial banking	1 250.5	1 258.4	1 278.1	1 280.1	1 280.8	1 296.0	1 322.9	1 351.4	1 357.5	1 316.9	1 305.9	1 314.6
Securities, commodity contracts, investments	804.5	830.5	789.4	757.7	766.1	786.1	818.3	848.6	864.2	811.3	800.5	807.0
Insurance carriers and related activities	2 220.6	2 233.7	2 233.2	2 266.0	2 258.6	2 259.3	2 303.7	2 306.8	2 305.2	2 264.1	2 261.1	2 281.6
Funds, trusts, and other financial vehicles	81.1	84.4	81.7	80.4	81.7	83.7	87.9	88.7	90.5	88.4	86.8	85.3
Real estate and rental and leasing	2 010.6	2 038.4	2 033.3	2 057.5	2 085.5	2 133.5	2 172.5	2 169.1	2 129.6	1 994.0	1 933.8	1 928.7
Real estate	1 316.0	1 343.4	1 356.6	1 387.1	1 418.7	1 460.8	1 499.0	1 500.4	1 485.0	1 420.2	1 395.7	1 401.6
Rental and leasing services	666.8	666.3	649.1	643.1	641.1	645.8	645.5	640.3	616.9	547.3	513.5	503.0
Lessors of nonfinancial intangible assets	27.8	28.7	27.6	27.3	25.7	26.9	28.1	28.4	27.7	26.5	24.6	24.1

[1]Includes other industries, not shown separately.

Table 15-1. Nonfarm Employment by NAICS Sector and Industry—*Continued*

(Wage and salary workers on nonfarm payrolls, thousands.)

Industry	1990	1991	1992	1993	1994	1995	1996	1997	1998	1999
Professional and business services	10 848	10 714	10 970	11 495	12 174	12 844	13 462	14 335	15 147	15 957
Professional and technical services [1]	4 538.2	4 509.2	4 575.6	4 689.1	4 823.3	5 078.4	5 312.7	5 628.8	5 992.3	6 345.4
Legal services	943.6	946.0	949.8	963.9	965.6	959.2	968.4	987.5	1 021.1	1 051.4
Accounting and bookkeeping services	664.1	655.4	657.8	654.2	670.1	706.3	729.8	761.2	802.0	837.6
Architectural and engineering services	941.5	906.2	901.8	922.7	952.0	997.1	1 024.5	1 063.4	1 114.8	1 168.1
Computer systems design and related services	409.7	419.9	444.9	484.8	531.4	611.2	701.4	826.7	974.9	1 132.9
Management and technical consulting services	305.1	314.3	340.2	366.2	396.5	451.8	492.7	541.7	590.4	619.0
Management of companies and enterprises	1 667.4	1 638.1	1 623.4	1 640.1	1 665.9	1 685.8	1 702.7	1 729.7	1 756.1	1 773.8
Administrative and waste services	4 642.8	4 566.6	4 770.5	5 165.6	5 684.4	6 079.7	6 446.5	6 976.6	7 398.0	7 837.5
Administrative and support services [1]	4 413.3	4 334.3	4 533.8	4 917.0	5 423.7	5 806.4	6 164.5	6 686.0	7 098.7	7 527.0
Employment services [1]	1 512.1	1 466.0	1 610.4	1 884.3	2 246.8	2 448.1	2 625.3	2 953.9	3 245.8	3 581.6
Temporary help services	1 155.8	1 123.3	1 212.5	1 388.8	1 632.2	1 743.8	1 849.0	2 059.7	2 245.2	2 469.6
Business support services	504.6	503.3	524.5	549.0	574.4	629.8	678.3	733.9	772.2	780.5
Services to buildings and dwellings	1 174.6	1 150.9	1 159.7	1 197.9	1 267.2	1 302.4	1 361.5	1 424.1	1 460.0	1 534.7
Waste management and remediation services	229.4	232.4	236.7	248.6	260.7	273.3	282.0	290.5	299.3	310.5
Education and health services	10 984	11 506	11 891	12 303	12 807	13 289	13 683	14 087	14 446	14 798
Educational services	1 688.0	1 737.0	1 713.0	1 755.0	1 895.0	2 010.0	2 078.0	2 155.0	2 233.0	2 320.0
Health care and social assistance	9 295.8	9 769.8	10 178.0	10 548.1	10 911.7	11 278.4	11 604.9	11 932.2	12 213.5	12 477.1
Health care	8 210.7	8 617.7	8 954.8	9 253.6	9 529.7	9 808.9	10 092.6	10 358.0	10 540.9	10 690.9
Ambulatory health care services [1]	2 841.6	3 028.4	3 199.9	3 385.5	3 578.8	3 767.5	3 939.9	4 093.0	4 161.2	4 226.6
Offices of physicians	1 278.0	1 345.2	1 401.1	1 442.0	1 480.9	1 540.4	1 603.8	1 660.5	1 723.6	1 786.6
Outpatient care centers	260.5	271.4	286.5	303.1	314.5	328.8	340.2	352.1	363.3	375.4
Home health care services	287.5	340.7	393.4	463.8	553.2	621.8	667.2	702.8	659.5	629.6
Hospitals	3 512.6	3 617.3	3 711.4	3 740.0	3 724.0	3 733.7	3 772.8	3 821.6	3 892.4	3 935.5
Nursing and residential care facilities [1]	1 856.4	1 972.0	2 043.5	2 128.1	2 227.0	2 307.7	2 379.9	2 443.4	2 487.3	2 528.8
Nursing care facilities	1 169.8	1 240.2	1 273.4	1 319.3	1 377.1	1 413.0	1 448.4	1 474.6	1 489.3	1 501.0
Social assistance [1]	1 085.1	1 152.2	1 223.3	1 294.4	1 381.9	1 469.5	1 512.3	1 574.2	1 672.6	1 786.2
Child day care services	387.8	413.2	446.5	468.9	510.0	557.1	559.2	570.4	615.1	673.7
Leisure and hospitality	9 288	9 256	9 437	9 732	10 100	10 501	10 777	11 018	11 232	11 543
Arts, entertainment, and recreation	1 132.0	1 177.0	1 236.3	1 301.9	1 375.6	1 459.4	1 522.1	1 599.9	1 645.2	1 709.1
Performing arts and spectator sports	272.7	282.7	289.5	286.8	296.1	307.7	328.6	349.6	350.0	361.1
Museums, historical sites, zoos, and parks	68.0	71.0	75.0	78.3	81.8	83.9	88.9	93.8	97.4	103.1
Amusements, gambling, and recreation	791.3	823.4	871.8	936.8	997.7	1 067.8	1 104.5	1 156.5	1 197.9	1 244.9
Accommodation and food services	8 155.6	8 078.9	8 200.5	8 430.4	8 724.1	9 041.6	9 254.3	9 417.9	9 586.2	9 833.7
Accommodation	1 616.0	1 574.3	1 561.5	1 580.5	1 615.3	1 652.5	1 698.9	1 729.5	1 773.5	1 831.7
Food services and drinking places	6 539.6	6 504.6	6 639.0	6 849.9	7 108.7	7 389.1	7 555.4	7 688.5	7 812.7	8 002.0
Other services	4 261	4 249	4 240	4 350	4 428	4 572	4 690	4 825	4 976	5 087
Repair and maintenance	1 009.0	960.0	964.0	998.0	1 023.5	1 078.9	1 135.5	1 169.3	1 189.2	1 222.0
Personal and laundry services	1 119.9	1 109.2	1 098.9	1 116.0	1 120.3	1 143.9	1 165.7	1 180.4	1 205.6	1 220.3
Membership associations and organizations	2 132.2	2 179.5	2 177.1	2 236.4	2 284.5	2 348.9	2 389.1	2 474.9	2 581.3	2 644.4
Government	18 415	18 545	18 787	18 989	19 275	19 432	19 539	19 664	19 909	20 307
Federal	3 196	3 110	3 111	3 063	3 018	2 949	2 877	2 806	2 772	2 769
Federal, except U.S. Postal Service	2 370.5	2 296.2	2 310.7	2 269.4	2 197.2	2 098.8	2 009.8	1 940.2	1 891.3	1 879.5
U.S. Postal Service	825.1	813.2	800.0	793.2	820.6	849.9	867.2	866.0	880.5	889.7
State government	4 305	4 355	4 408	4 488	4 576	4 635	4 606	4 582	4 612	4 709
State government education	1 729.9	1 767.6	1 798.6	1 834.1	1 881.9	1 919.0	1 910.7	1 904.0	1 922.2	1 983.2
State government, excluding education	2 574.6	2 587.3	2 609.7	2 653.8	2 693.6	2 715.5	2 695.1	2 677.9	2 690.2	2 725.6
Local government	10 914	11 081	11 267	11 438	11 682	11 849	12 056	12 276	12 525	12 829
Local government education	5 902.1	5 994.1	6 075.9	6 206.3	6 329.4	6 453.1	6 592.3	6 758.5	6 920.9	7 120.4
Local government, excluding education	5 012.4	5 086.9	5 191.6	5 231.9	5 352.2	5 396.0	5 464.1	5 516.9	5 603.9	5 708.6

[1]Includes other industries, not shown separately.

Table 15-1. Nonfarm Employment by NAICS Sector and Industry—*Continued*

(Wage and salary workers on nonfarm payrolls, thousands.)

Industry	2000	2001	2002	2003	2004	2005	2006	2007	2008	2009	2010	2011
Professional and business services	16 666	16 476	15 976	15 987	16 394	16 954	17 566	17 942	17 735	16 579	16 728	17 331
Professional and technical services [1]	6 701.7	6 871.1	6 648.8	6 602.7	6 747.1	7 024.6	7 356.7	7 659.5	7 799.4	7 508.5	7 441.3	7 691.3
Legal services	1 065.7	1 091.3	1 115.3	1 142.1	1 163.1	1 168.0	1 173.2	1 175.4	1 161.5	1 124.9	1 114.2	1 115.1
Accounting and bookkeeping services	866.4	872.2	837.3	815.3	805.9	849.3	889.0	935.9	951.0	914.2	886.5	920.5
Architectural and engineering services	1 237.9	1 274.7	1 246.1	1 226.9	1 258.2	1 310.9	1 385.7	1 432.2	1 439.4	1 324.7	1 275.4	1 293.8
Computer systems design and related services	1 254.3	1 297.8	1 152.8	1 116.6	1 148.6	1 195.2	1 284.6	1 372.1	1 439.6	1 422.6	1 449.0	1 530.1
Management and technical consulting services	672.7	715.1	707.7	718.0	763.0	824.2	886.4	952.7	1 002.0	994.9	999.4	1 070.2
Management of companies and enterprises	1 796.0	1 779.0	1 705.4	1 687.2	1 724.4	1 758.9	1 810.9	1 866.4	1 904.5	1 866.9	1 872.3	1 914.8
Administrative and waste services	8 168.3	7 826.0	7 621.9	7 696.8	7 922.9	8 170.2	8 398.3	8 416.3	8 031.5	7 203.3	7 414.0	7 724.4
Administrative and support services [1]	7 855.4	7 508.7	7 303.6	7 374.7	7 594.4	7 832.5	8 050.2	8 061.3	7 674.7	6 851.6	7 056.7	7 359.2
Employment services [1]	3 849.3	3 468.2	3 273.2	3 326.4	3 455.5	3 606.9	3 680.9	3 545.9	3 133.0	2 480.8	2 722.5	2 952.1
Temporary help services	2 635.6	2 337.7	2 193.7	2 224.2	2 387.2	2 549.4	2 637.4	2 597.4	2 348.4	1 823.3	2 093.6	2 316.2
Business support services	786.7	779.7	756.6	749.7	757.8	766.4	792.9	817.4	832.3	820.0	808.6	812.3
Services to buildings and dwellings	1 570.5	1 606.2	1 606.1	1 636.1	1 693.7	1 737.5	1 801.4	1 849.5	1 839.8	1 753.3	1 745.0	1 777.0
Waste management and remediation services	312.9	317.3	318.3	322.1	328.6	337.6	348.1	355.0	356.8	351.7	357.3	365.2
Education and health services	15 109	15 645	16 199	16 588	16 953	17 372	17 826	18 322	18 838	19 193	19 531	19 884
Educational services	2 390.0	2 511.0	2 643.0	2 695.0	2 763.0	2 836.0	2 901.0	2 941.0	3 040.0	3 090.0	3 155.0	3 240.7
Health care and social assistance	12 718.0	13 134.0	13 555.7	13 892.6	14 190.2	14 536.3	14 925.3	15 380.2	15 798.3	16 102.7	16 375.4	16 642.8
Health care	10 857.8	11 188.1	11 536.0	11 817.1	12 055.3	12 313.9	12 601.8	12 946.8	13 289.9	13 543.0	13 776.9	14 045.7
Ambulatory health care services [1]	4 320.3	4 461.5	4 633.2	4 786.4	4 952.3	5 113.5	5 285.8	5 473.5	5 646.6	5 793.4	5 974.7	6 145.5
Offices of physicians	1 839.9	1 911.2	1 967.8	2 002.5	2 047.8	2 093.5	2 147.8	2 201.6	2 252.6	2 279.1	2 312.7	2 355.4
Outpatient care centers	386.4	399.7	413.0	426.8	450.5	473.2	492.6	512.0	533.3	557.5	599.9	623.7
Home health care services	633.3	638.6	679.8	732.6	776.6	821.0	865.6	913.8	961.4	1 027.1	1 084.6	1 139.1
Hospitals	3 954.3	4 050.9	4 159.6	4 244.6	4 284.7	4 345.4	4 423.4	4 515.0	4 627.3	4 667.4	4 678.5	4 731.0
Nursing and residential care facilities [1]	2 583.2	2 675.8	2 743.3	2 786.2	2 818.4	2 855.0	2 892.5	2 958.3	3 016.1	3 082.2	3 123.7	3 169.2
Nursing care facilities	1 513.6	1 546.8	1 573.2	1 579.8	1 576.9	1 577.4	1 581.4	1 602.6	1 618.7	1 644.9	1 657.1	1 668.4
Social assistance [1]	1 860.2	1 945.9	2 019.7	2 075.4	2 134.8	2 222.3	2 323.5	2 433.4	2 508.4	2 559.8	2 598.5	2 597.2
Child day care services	695.8	714.6	744.1	755.3	764.7	789.7	818.3	850.4	859.4	852.8	848.0	844.2
Leisure and hospitality	11 862	12 036	11 986	12 173	12 493	12 816	13 110	13 427	13 436	13 077	13 049	13 320
Arts, entertainment, and recreation	1 787.9	1 824.4	1 782.6	1 812.9	1 849.6	1 892.3	1 928.5	1 969.2	1 970.1	1 915.5	1 913.3	1 909.5
Performing arts and spectator sports	381.8	382.3	363.7	371.7	367.5	376.3	398.5	405.0	405.7	396.8	406.2	394.3
Museums, historical sites, zoos, and parks	110.4	115.0	114.0	114.7	118.3	120.7	123.8	130.3	131.6	129.4	127.7	132.3
Amusements, gambling, and recreation	1 295.7	1 327.1	1 305.0	1 326.5	1 363.8	1 395.3	1 406.3	1 433.9	1 432.8	1 389.2	1 379.4	1 383.0
Accommodation and food services	10 073.5	10 211.3	10 203.2	10 359.8	10 643.2	10 923.0	11 181.1	11 457.4	11 466.3	11 161.9	11 135.4	11 410.3
Accommodation	1 884.4	1 852.2	1 778.6	1 775.4	1 789.5	1 818.6	1 832.1	1 866.9	1 868.7	1 763.0	1 759.6	1 797.2
Food services and drinking places	8 189.1	8 359.1	8 424.6	8 584.4	8 853.7	9 104.4	9 349.0	9 590.4	9 597.5	9 398.9	9 375.8	9 613.1
Other services	5 168	5 258	5 372	5 401	5 409	5 395	5 438	5 494	5 515	5 367	5 331	5 342
Repair and maintenance	1 241.5	1 256.5	1 246.9	1 233.6	1 228.8	1 236.0	1 248.5	1 253.4	1 227.0	1 150.4	1 138.8	1 160.1
Personal and laundry services	1 242.9	1 255.0	1 257.2	1 263.5	1 272.9	1 276.6	1 288.4	1 309.7	1 322.6	1 280.6	1 265.3	1 284.6
Membership associations and organizations	2 683.3	2 746.4	2 867.8	2 903.6	2 907.5	2 882.2	2 901.2	2 931.1	2 965.7	2 936.0	2 926.4	2 896.8
Government	20 790	21 118	21 513	21 583	21 621	21 804	21 974	22 218	22 509	22 555	22 490	22 104
Federal	2 865	2 764	2 766	2 761	2 730	2 732	2 732	2 734	2 762	2 832	2 977	2 858
Federal, except U.S. Postal Service	1 984.8	1 891.0	1 923.8	1 952.4	1 947.5	1 957.3	1 962.6	1 964.7	2 014.4	2 128.5	2 318.1	2 226.4
U.S. Postal Service	879.7	873.0	842.4	808.6	782.1	774.2	769.7	769.1	747.4	703.4	658.5	630.9
State government	4 786	4 905	5 029	5 002	4 982	5 032	5 075	5 122	5 177	5 169	5 137	5 082
State government education	2 030.6	2 112.9	2 242.8	2 254.7	2 238.1	2 259.9	2 292.5	2 317.5	2 354.4	2 360.2	2 373.1	2 383.7
State government, excluding education	2 755.9	2 791.8	2 786.3	2 747.6	2 743.9	2 771.6	2 782.0	2 804.3	2 822.5	2 808.8	2 764.1	2 698.0
Local government	13 139	13 449	13 718	13 820	13 909	14 041	14 167	14 362	14 571	14 554	14 376	14 165
Local government education	7 293.9	7 479.3	7 654.4	7 709.4	7 765.2	7 856.1	7 913.0	7 986.8	8 083.9	8 078.8	8 013.4	7 892.9
Local government, excluding education	5 844.6	5 970.0	6 063.2	6 110.2	6 144.1	6 184.6	6 253.8	6 375.5	6 486.5	6 474.9	6 362.9	6 272.0

[1]Includes other industries, not shown separately.

Table 15-2. Production and Nonsupervisory Workers on Private Nonfarm Payrolls by NAICS Industry

(Wage and salary workers on nonfarm payrolls, thousands.)

Industry	1990	1991	1992	1993	1994	1995	1996	1997	1998	1999
Total Private	73 684	72 520	72 786	74 591	77 382	79 845	81 773	84 158	86 316	88 430
Goods-Producing	17 322	16 352	16 044	16 236	16 795	17 137	17 318	17 698	18 008	18 067
Mining and logging	538	515	478	462	461	458	461	479	473	438
Construction	4 115	3 674	3 546	3 704	3 973	4 113	4 325	4 546	4 807	5 105
Manufacturing	12 669	12 164	12 020	12 070	12 361	12 567	12 532	12 673	12 729	12 524
Durable goods	7 397	7 001	6 853	6 880	7 134	7 352	7 426	7 599	7 721	7 651
Wood products	451.5	414.3	418.6	438.5	470.4	479.3	486.6	498.3	509.6	516.2
Nonmetallic mineral products	413.2	384.1	378.4	380.7	392.3	399.7	404.8	412.5	420.6	426.0
Primary metals	525.1	496.9	478.7	473.0	487.4	500.3	500.3	501.6	505.3	491.9
Fabricated metal products	1 190.1	1 131.6	1 101.0	1 116.9	1 172.0	1 223.0	1 241.6	1 285.3	1 319.6	1 304.9
Machinery	938.9	884.9	857.7	875.5	922.5	969.9	984.5	1 006.9	1 016.1	978.4
Computer and electronic products	980.2	925.6	876.3	856.0	864.0	890.3	915.3	951.1	964.7	932.9
Electrical equipment and appliances	465.2	435.6	425.0	422.0	434.7	438.4	433.9	427.7	431.8	433.2
Transportation equipment [1]	1 473.4	1 406.4	1 388.6	1 367.0	1 415.6	1 472.2	1 481.0	1 521.9	1 530.2	1 526.5
Motor vehicles and parts	869.5	840.1	868.0	896.0	978.4	1 048.9	1 052.4	1 062.4	1 050.2	1 075.8
Furniture and related products	475.2	440.1	442.9	454.0	475.7	480.0	477.9	489.8	512.2	532.4
Miscellaneous manufacturing	484.2	481.2	486.0	495.0	499.0	499.1	500.1	503.4	511.0	508.9
Nondurable goods	5 272	5 163	5 167	5 191	5 227	5 214	5 106	5 075	5 008	4 872
Food manufacturing	1 165.0	1 174.2	1 182.0	1 195.3	1 200.4	1 221.0	1 227.7	1 227.7	1 227.6	1 228.7
Beverage and tobacco products	117.2	116.9	116.2	117.6	118.2	117.3	120.1	121.4	122.5	120.1
Textile mills	417.9	407.2	406.0	404.0	403.3	393.2	371.7	367.1	357.2	333.7
Textile product mills	194.9	185.0	187.4	191.0	199.0	197.9	192.5	192.6	189.7	186.8
Apparel	805.2	781.0	785.3	764.2	740.1	697.9	631.1	593.7	534.0	458.3
Leather and allied products	116.6	107.5	104.4	101.4	97.2	88.5	78.5	73.6	67.0	59.9
Paper and paper products	493.2	488.4	489.9	490.9	492.8	493.8	487.5	488.7	484.1	474.0
Printing and related support activities	597.6	581.7	573.6	579.7	591.4	599.1	594.0	597.0	598.4	585.1
Petroleum and coal products	97.5	97.4	96.8	93.0	90.9	88.8	87.2	87.8	87.1	84.6
Chemicals	620.3	599.7	586.2	590.1	595.6	598.4	595.1	593.3	600.6	595.2
Plastics and rubber products	646.7	623.9	638.9	663.8	698.5	718.7	720.3	731.7	739.3	746.0
Private Service-Providing	56 362	56 168	56 743	58 355	60 587	62 708	64 455	66 460	68 308	70 363
Trade, transportation, and utilities	19 032	18 640	18 506	18 752	19 392	19 984	20 325	20 698	21 059	21 576
Wholesale trade	4 198.3	4 122.0	4 071.0	4 072.2	4 196.4	4 360.8	4 423.2	4 523.2	4 605.0	4 673.1
Retail trade	11 308.4	11 007.9	10 931.4	11 104.0	11 502.1	11 841.0	12 056.7	12 273.6	12 439.8	12 771.5
Transportation and warehousing	2 940.8	2 928.4	2 934.3	3 019.4	3 152.8	3 260.2	3 339.3	3 406.8	3 521.6	3 641.9
Utilities	584.9	581.5	569.5	556.5	540.9	521.8	505.5	493.8	492.2	489.2
Information	1 866	1 871	1 871	1 896	1 928	2 007	2 096	2 181	2 217	2 351
Financial activities	4 973	4 911	4 908	5 057	5 183	5 165	5 279	5 415	5 605	5 728
Professional and business services	8 889	8 748	8 971	9 451	10 078	10 645	11 161	11 896	12 566	13 184
Education and health services	9 748	10 212	10 555	10 908	11 338	11 765	12 123	12 478	12 791	13 089
Leisure and hospitality	8 299	8 247	8 406	8 667	8 979	9 330	9 565	9 780	9 947	10 216
Other services	3 555	3 539	3 526	3 623	3 689	3 812	3 907	4 013	4 124	4 219

[1]Includes other industries, not shown separately.

Table 15-2. Production and Nonsupervisory Workers on Private Nonfarm Payrolls by NAICS Industry —Continued

(Wage and salary workers on nonfarm payrolls, thousands.)

Industry	2000	2001	2002	2003	2004	2005	2006	2007	2008	2009	2010	2011
Total Private	90 336	89 983	88 393	87 658	88 937	91 135	93 451	94 902	94 270	89 173	88 512	90 092
Goods-Producing	18 169	17 466	16 400	15 732	15 821	16 145	16 559	16 405	15 724	13 399	12 774	12 981
Mining and logging	446	457	436	420	440	473	519	547	574	510	525	590
Construction	5 295	5 332	5 196	5 123	5 309	5 611	5 903	5 883	5 521	4 567	4 172	4 161
Manufacturing	12 428	11 677	10 768	10 189	10 072	10 060	10 137	9 975	9 629	8 322	8 077	8 231
Durable goods	7 659	7 164	6 530	6 152	6 140	6 220	6 355	6 250	5 975	4 990	4 829	4 986
Wood products	507.4	470.0	450.3	434.4	445.4	454.4	451.2	407.0	357.5	277.8	269.0	267.3
Nonmetallic mineral products	439.5	427.1	398.8	374.7	387.8	387.0	391.2	383.6	363.4	302.7	283.5	277.7
Primary metals	490.0	446.9	396.2	370.3	363.7	362.7	362.6	357.5	347.7	272.5	275.3	302.2
Fabricated metal products	1 325.8	1 253.5	1 147.0	1 092.5	1 108.6	1 129.3	1 161.8	1 170.9	1 142.9	960.5	935.3	991.1
Machinery	961.4	890.7	786.9	732.3	729.7	748.9	769.8	774.0	771.7	641.0	615.9	662.9
Computer and electronic products	949.3	875.8	744.1	672.7	655.8	700.1	755.6	743.8	730.0	654.3	629.3	632.0
Electrical equipment and appliances	433.1	402.2	351.9	319.5	307.2	300.1	302.9	305.2	305.3	266.1	251.1	248.3
Transportation equipment [1]	1 497.8	1 398.7	1 310.2	1 269.3	1 265.2	1 276.8	1 303.7	1 274.5	1 177.2	948.1	937.0	972.1
Motor vehicles and parts	1 073.0	986.8	931.0	906.3	902.9	893.7	872.7	804.2	695.5	510.0	524.9	555.7
Furniture and related products	544.4	509.2	475.1	444.5	443.3	435.7	432.8	409.0	364.2	284.3	263.0	259.8
Miscellaneous manufacturing	509.8	489.8	469.2	442.1	432.2	424.4	423.4	424.6	415.6	382.2	370.2	372.6
Nondurable goods	4 769	4 513	4 238	4 037	3 932	3 841	3 782	3 725	3 653	3 332	3 248	3 245
Food manufacturing	1 227.9	1 221.3	1 202.3	1 192.5	1 177.8	1 170.0	1 172.2	1 183.5	1 183.9	1 161.1	1 152.2	1 155.9
Beverage and tobacco products	116.9	115.6	119.5	106.4	106.5	111.5	114.6	118.1	111.8	111.5	106.1	108.4
Textile mills	315.2	275.8	242.2	216.9	193.9	174.2	157.8	137.3	122.0	98.6	95.9	98.6
Textile product mills	183.4	173.7	162.0	148.3	147.1	143.0	134.9	123.2	115.3	97.7	91.7	88.6
Apparel	403.8	341.4	286.0	241.5	218.6	192.7	182.0	173.4	163.3	132.3	120.4	111.7
Leather and allied products	55.4	46.8	40.0	34.9	32.7	30.9	28.6	27.3	27.5	23.9	22.3	23.4
Paper and paper products	467.5	446.3	421.4	392.7	373.7	365.2	357.4	350.5	343.7	313.0	302.2	298.2
Printing and related support activities	575.7	544.4	492.6	471.2	459.5	447.3	446.6	442.6	424.5	369.3	341.7	325.4
Petroleum and coal products	83.1	80.9	78.0	74.4	76.7	75.4	72.2	72.6	77.1	69.7	69.5	70.2
Chemicals	587.7	562.2	531.9	524.9	520.2	510.0	507.7	504.4	512.5	478.7	473.8	482.7
Plastics and rubber products	752.6	704.4	661.9	633.4	625.6	620.4	607.6	592.3	571.5	476.5	472.0	482.0
Private Service-Providing	72 167	72 517	71 993	71 926	73 116	74 990	76 893	78 498	78 546	75 774	75 738	77 111
Trade, transportation, and utilities	21 965	21 709	21 337	21 078	21 319	21 830	22 166	22 546	22 337	21 116	20 874	21 196
Wholesale trade	4 686.4	4 555.1	4 473.5	4 395.9	4 443.5	4 583.6	4 724.3	4 850.9	4 822.1	4 505.6	4 377.5	4 431.4
Retail trade	13 039.9	12 952.3	12 774.0	12 654.9	12 788.0	13 029.6	13 110.2	13 317.1	13 134.0	12 471.8	12 425.4	12 626.8
Transportation and warehousing	3 753.2	3 718.2	3 611.3	3 563.1	3 637.1	3 774.0	3 889.1	3 934.6	3 930.7	3 688.1	3 627.1	3 695.1
Utilities	485.1	482.8	478.4	463.7	449.9	443.0	442.6	443.5	450.4	451.0	443.5	442.9
Information	2 502	2 531	2 398	2 347	2 371	2 386	2 399	2 403	2 388	2 240	2 170	2 136
Financial activities	5 737	5 810	5 872	5 967	5 989	6 090	6 281	6 326	6 269	6 008	5 906	5 887
Professional and business services	13 790	13 588	13 049	12 911	13 287	13 854	14 446	14 784	14 585	13 520	13 699	14 253
Education and health services	13 362	13 846	14 311	14 532	14 771	15 129	15 539	15 999	16 488	16 841	17 125	17 420
Leisure and hospitality	10 516	10 662	10 576	10 666	10 955	11 263	11 568	11 861	11 873	11 560	11 507	11 743
Other services	4 296	4 373	4 449	4 426	4 425	4 438	4 494	4 578	4 606	4 488	4 458	4 475

[1]Includes other industries, not shown separately.

Table 15-3. Average Weekly Hours of Production and Nonsupervisory Workers on Private Nonfarm Payrolls by NAICS Industry

(Hours.)

Industry	1990	1991	1992	1993	1994	1995	1996	1997	1998	1999
Total Private	34.3	34.1	34.2	34.3	34.5	34.3	34.3	34.5	34.5	34.3
Goods-Producing	40.1	40.1	40.2	40.6	41.1	40.8	40.8	41.1	40.8	40.8
Mining and logging	45.0	45.3	44.6	44.9	45.3	45.3	46.0	46.2	44.9	44.2
Construction	38.3	38.1	38.0	38.4	38.8	38.8	38.9	38.9	38.8	39.0
Manufacturing	40.5	40.4	40.7	41.1	41.7	41.3	41.3	41.7	41.4	41.4
Overtime hours	3.9	3.8	4.0	4.4	5.0	4.7	4.8	5.1	4.9	4.9
Durable goods	41.1	40.9	41.3	41.9	42.6	42.1	42.1	42.6	42.1	41.9
Overtime hours	3.9	3.7	3.9	4.5	5.3	5.0	5.0	5.4	5.0	5.0
Wood products	40.4	40.2	40.9	41.2	41.7	41.0	41.2	41.4	41.4	41.3
Nonmetallic mineral products	40.9	40.5	41.0	41.5	42.2	41.8	42.0	41.9	42.2	42.1
Primary metals	42.1	41.5	42.4	43.1	44.1	43.4	43.6	44.3	43.5	43.8
Fabricated metal products	41.0	40.8	41.2	41.6	42.3	41.9	41.9	42.3	41.9	41.7
Machinery	42.1	41.9	42.4	43.2	43.9	43.5	43.3	44.0	43.1	42.3
Computer and electronic products	41.3	40.9	41.4	41.7	42.2	42.2	41.9	42.5	41.9	41.5
Electrical equipment and appliances	41.2	41.4	41.8	42.4	43.0	41.9	42.1	42.1	41.8	41.8
Transportation equipment [1]	42.0	41.9	41.9	43.0	44.3	43.7	43.8	44.2	43.3	43.6
Motor vehicles and parts	41.4	41.5	41.6	43.3	44.8	43.8	43.8	43.9	42.6	43.8
Furniture and related products	38.0	37.8	38.6	39.0	39.3	38.5	38.2	39.1	39.4	39.3
Miscellaneous manufacturing	39.0	39.2	39.3	39.2	39.4	39.2	39.1	39.7	39.2	39.3
Nondurable goods	39.6	39.7	40.0	40.1	40.5	40.1	40.1	40.5	40.5	40.5
Overtime hours	3.9	4.0	4.2	4.3	4.6	4.3	4.4	4.7	4.6	4.6
Food manufacturing	39.3	39.2	39.2	39.3	39.8	39.6	39.5	39.8	40.1	40.2
Beverage and tobacco products	38.9	38.8	38.7	38.3	39.3	39.3	39.7	40.0	40.3	41.0
Textile mills	40.2	40.7	41.3	41.6	41.9	40.9	40.8	41.6	41.0	41.0
Textile product mills	38.5	38.6	38.7	39.3	39.4	38.6	38.7	39.2	39.2	39.1
Apparel	34.7	35.4	35.6	35.6	35.7	35.3	35.2	35.6	35.5	35.4
Leather and allied products	37.4	37.6	37.9	38.4	38.2	37.7	37.8	38.2	37.4	37.2
Paper and paper products	43.6	43.6	43.8	43.8	44.2	43.4	43.5	43.9	43.6	43.6
Printing and related support activities	38.7	38.6	39.0	39.2	39.6	39.1	39.1	39.5	39.3	39.1
Petroleum and coal products	44.4	43.9	43.6	44.0	44.3	43.7	43.7	43.1	43.6	42.6
Chemicals	42.8	43.1	43.3	43.2	43.4	43.4	43.3	43.4	43.2	42.8
Plastics and rubber products	40.6	40.5	41.2	41.4	41.8	41.1	41.0	41.4	41.3	41.3
Private Service-Providing	32.5	32.4	32.5	32.5	32.7	32.6	32.6	32.8	32.8	32.7
Trade, transportation, and utilities	33.7	33.7	33.8	34.1	34.3	34.1	34.1	34.3	34.2	33.9
Wholesale trade	38.4	38.4	38.5	38.5	38.8	38.6	38.6	38.8	38.6	38.6
Retail trade	30.6	30.4	30.7	30.7	30.9	30.8	30.7	30.9	30.9	30.8
Transportation and warehousing	37.7	37.3	37.4	38.9	39.5	38.9	39.1	39.4	38.7	37.6
Utilities	41.6	41.5	41.7	42.1	42.3	42.3	42.0	42.0	42.0	42.0
Information	35.8	35.6	35.8	36.0	36.0	36.0	36.3	36.3	36.6	36.7
Financial activities	35.5	35.5	35.6	35.5	35.5	35.5	35.5	35.7	36.0	35.8
Professional and business services	34.2	34.0	34.0	34.0	34.1	34.0	34.1	34.3	34.3	34.4
Education and health services	31.9	31.9	32.0	32.0	32.0	32.0	31.9	32.2	32.2	32.1
Leisure and hospitality	26.0	25.6	25.7	25.9	26.0	25.9	25.9	26.1	26.2	26.1
Other services	32.8	32.7	32.6	32.6	32.7	32.6	32.5	32.7	32.6	32.5

[1]Includes other industries, not shown separately.

Table 15-3. Average Weekly Hours of Production and Nonsupervisory Workers on Private Nonfarm Payrolls by NAICS Industry—*Continued*

(Hours.)

Industry	2000	2001	2002	2003	2004	2005	2006	2007	2008	2009	2010	2011
Total Private	34.3	34.0	33.9	33.7	33.7	33.8	33.9	33.9	33.6	33.1	33.4	33.6
Goods-Producing	40.7	39.9	39.9	39.8	40.0	40.1	40.5	40.6	40.2	39.2	40.4	40.9
Mining and logging	44.4	44.6	43.2	43.6	44.5	45.6	45.6	45.9	45.1	43.2	44.6	46.7
Construction	39.2	38.7	38.4	38.4	38.3	38.6	39.0	39.0	38.5	37.6	38.4	39.0
Manufacturing	41.3	40.3	40.5	40.4	40.8	40.7	41.1	41.2	40.8	39.8	41.1	41.4
Overtime hours	4.7	4.0	4.2	4.2	4.6	4.6	4.4	4.2	3.7	2.9	3.8	4.1
Durable goods	41.8	40.6	40.7	40.8	41.3	41.1	41.4	41.5	41.1	39.8	41.4	41.9
Overtime hours	4.8	3.9	4.2	4.3	4.7	4.6	4.4	4.2	3.7	2.7	3.8	4.2
Wood products	41.0	40.2	39.9	40.4	40.7	40.0	39.8	39.4	38.6	37.4	39.1	39.7
Nonmetallic mineral products	41.6	41.6	42.0	42.2	42.4	42.2	43.0	42.3	42.1	40.8	41.7	42.3
Primary metals	44.2	42.4	42.4	42.3	43.1	43.1	43.6	42.9	42.2	40.7	43.7	44.6
Fabricated metal products	41.9	40.7	40.6	40.7	41.1	41.0	41.4	41.6	41.3	39.4	41.4	42.0
Machinery	42.3	40.9	40.5	40.8	41.9	42.1	42.4	42.6	42.3	40.1	42.1	43.1
Computer and electronic products	41.4	39.8	39.7	40.4	40.4	40.0	40.5	40.6	41.0	40.4	40.9	40.5
Electrical equipment and appliances	41.6	39.8	40.1	40.6	40.7	40.6	41.0	41.2	40.9	39.3	41.1	40.8
Transportation equipment [1]	43.3	41.9	42.5	41.9	42.5	42.4	42.7	42.8	41.9	41.2	42.9	43.2
Motor vehicles and parts	43.4	41.6	42.6	42.0	42.6	42.3	42.2	42.3	41.4	40.1	43.4	43.4
Furniture and related products	39.2	38.3	39.1	38.9	39.5	39.2	38.8	39.2	38.1	37.7	38.5	39.9
Miscellaneous manufacturing	39.0	38.8	38.7	38.4	38.5	38.7	38.7	38.9	38.9	38.5	38.7	38.9
Nondurable goods	40.3	39.9	40.0	39.8	40.0	39.9	40.6	40.8	40.4	39.8	40.8	40.8
Overtime hours	4.5	4.1	4.2	4.1	4.4	4.4	4.4	4.2	3.7	3.2	3.8	4.0
Food manufacturing	40.1	39.6	39.6	39.3	39.3	39.0	40.1	40.7	40.5	40.0	40.7	40.2
Beverage and tobacco products	42.0	40.9	39.4	39.1	39.2	40.1	40.8	40.7	38.8	35.7	37.5	39.2
Textile mills	41.4	40.0	40.6	39.1	40.1	40.3	40.6	40.3	38.7	37.7	41.2	41.7
Textile product mills	38.7	38.4	39.0	39.4	38.7	38.9	39.8	39.7	38.6	37.9	39.0	39.1
Apparel	35.7	36.0	36.7	35.6	36.1	35.8	36.5	37.2	36.4	36.0	36.6	38.2
Leather and allied products	37.5	36.4	37.5	39.3	38.4	38.4	38.9	38.2	37.6	33.6	39.1	39.8
Paper and paper products	42.8	42.1	41.8	41.5	42.1	42.5	42.9	43.1	42.9	41.8	42.9	42.9
Printing and related support activities	39.2	38.7	38.4	38.2	38.4	38.4	39.2	39.1	38.3	38.0	38.2	38.0
Petroleum and coal products	42.7	43.8	43.0	44.5	44.9	45.5	45.0	44.1	44.6	43.4	43.0	43.8
Chemicals	42.2	41.9	42.3	42.4	42.8	42.3	42.5	41.9	41.5	41.4	42.2	42.5
Plastics and rubber products	40.8	40.0	40.6	40.4	40.4	40.0	40.6	41.3	41.0	40.2	41.9	42.0
Private Service-Providing	32.7	32.5	32.5	32.3	32.3	32.4	32.4	32.4	32.3	32.1	32.2	32.4
Trade, transportation, and utilities	33.8	33.5	33.6	33.6	33.5	33.4	33.4	33.3	33.2	32.9	33.3	33.7
Wholesale trade	38.8	38.4	38.0	37.9	37.8	37.7	38.0	38.2	38.2	37.6	37.9	38.5
Retail trade	30.7	30.7	30.9	30.9	30.7	30.6	30.5	30.2	30.0	29.9	30.2	30.5
Transportation and warehousing	37.4	36.7	36.8	36.8	37.2	37.0	36.9	37.0	36.4	36.0	37.1	37.8
Utilities	42.0	41.4	40.9	41.1	40.9	41.1	41.4	42.4	42.7	42.0	42.0	42.1
Information	36.8	36.9	36.5	36.2	36.3	36.5	36.6	36.5	36.7	36.6	36.3	36.2
Financial activities	35.9	35.8	35.6	35.5	35.5	35.9	35.7	35.9	35.8	36.1	36.2	36.4
Professional and business services	34.5	34.2	34.2	34.1	34.2	34.2	34.6	34.8	34.8	34.7	35.1	35.2
Education and health services	32.2	32.3	32.4	32.3	32.4	32.6	32.5	32.6	32.5	32.2	32.1	32.3
Leisure and hospitality	26.1	25.8	25.8	25.6	25.7	25.7	25.7	25.5	25.2	24.8	24.8	24.8
Other services	32.5	32.3	32.1	31.4	31.0	30.9	30.9	30.9	30.8	30.5	30.7	30.7

[1]Includes other industries, not shown separately.

Table 15-4. Average Hourly Earnings of Production and Nonsupervisory Workers on Private Nonfarm Payrolls by NAICS Industry

(Dollars.)

Industry	1990	1991	1992	1993	1994	1995	1996	1997	1998	1999
Total Private	10.20	10.52	10.77	11.05	11.34	11.65	12.04	12.51	13.01	13.49
Goods-Producing	11.46	11.76	11.99	12.28	12.63	12.96	13.38	13.82	14.23	14.71
Mining and logging	13.40	13.82	14.09	14.12	14.41	14.78	15.09	15.57	16.20	16.33
Construction	13.42	13.65	13.81	14.04	14.38	14.73	15.11	15.67	16.23	16.80
Manufacturing	10.78	11.13	11.40	11.70	12.04	12.34	12.75	13.14	13.45	13.85
Excluding overtime [1]	10.28	10.63	10.86	11.10	11.36	11.68	12.05	12.37	12.70	13.08
Durable goods	11.40	11.81	12.09	12.41	12.78	13.05	13.45	13.83	14.07	14.46
Wood products	8.82	9.02	9.24	9.40	9.66	9.92	10.24	10.52	10.85	11.18
Nonmetallic mineral products	11.11	11.34	11.57	11.83	12.11	12.39	12.80	13.17	13.59	13.97
Primary metals	12.97	13.37	13.72	14.08	14.47	14.75	15.12	15.39	15.66	16.00
Fabricated metal products	10.64	10.97	11.17	11.40	11.64	11.91	12.26	12.64	12.97	13.34
Machinery	11.73	12.12	12.40	12.72	12.94	13.13	13.49	13.94	14.23	14.77
Computer and electronic products	10.89	11.35	11.64	11.95	12.19	12.29	12.75	13.24	13.85	14.37
Electrical equipment and appliances	10.00	10.30	10.50	10.65	10.94	11.25	11.80	12.24	12.51	12.90
Transportation equipment [2]	14.44	15.12	15.59	16.21	16.93	17.21	17.66	17.99	17.91	18.24
Motor vehicles and parts	15.00	15.67	15.92	16.56	17.38	17.72	18.14	18.43	18.21	18.49
Furniture and related products	8.53	8.75	9.01	9.25	9.52	9.76	10.09	10.50	10.89	11.28
Miscellaneous manufacturing	8.87	9.15	9.43	9.64	9.90	10.23	10.59	10.89	11.18	11.55
Nondurable goods	9.87	10.18	10.45	10.70	10.96	11.30	11.68	12.04	12.45	12.85
Food manufacturing	9.04	9.32	9.59	9.82	10.00	10.27	10.50	10.77	11.09	11.40
Beverage and tobacco products	13.24	13.65	14.07	14.30	14.97	15.40	15.73	16.00	16.03	16.54
Textile mills	8.17	8.49	8.82	9.12	9.35	9.63	9.88	10.22	10.58	10.90
Textile product mills	7.37	7.60	7.85	8.09	8.29	8.60	8.95	9.30	9.61	10.04
Apparel	6.22	6.43	6.60	6.75	6.96	7.22	7.45	7.76	8.05	8.35
Leather and allied products	7.18	7.43	7.68	7.88	8.23	8.50	8.94	9.31	9.68	9.93
Paper and paper products	12.06	12.45	12.78	13.13	13.49	13.94	14.38	14.76	15.20	15.58
Printing and related support activities	11.11	11.32	11.53	11.67	11.89	12.08	12.41	12.78	13.20	13.67
Petroleum and coal products	17.00	17.90	18.83	19.43	19.96	20.24	20.18	21.10	21.75	22.22
Chemicals	12.85	13.30	13.70	13.97	14.33	14.86	15.37	15.78	16.23	16.40
Plastics and rubber products	9.76	10.07	10.35	10.56	10.66	10.86	11.17	11.48	11.79	12.25
Private Service-Providing	9.72	10.06	10.35	10.62	10.89	11.21	11.59	12.07	12.61	13.09
Trade, transportation, and utilities	9.83	10.08	10.30	10.55	10.80	11.10	11.46	11.90	12.40	12.82
Wholesale trade	11.58	11.95	12.21	12.57	12.93	13.34	13.80	14.41	15.07	15.62
Retail trade	7.71	7.89	8.12	8.36	8.61	8.85	9.21	9.59	10.05	10.45
Transportation and warehousing	12.50	12.61	12.77	12.71	12.84	13.18	13.45	13.78	14.12	14.56
Utilities	16.14	16.70	17.17	17.95	18.66	19.19	19.78	20.59	21.48	22.03
Information	13.40	13.90	14.29	14.86	15.32	15.68	16.30	17.14	17.67	18.40
Financial activities	9.99	10.42	10.86	11.36	11.82	12.28	12.71	13.22	13.93	14.47
Professional and business services	11.14	11.50	11.78	11.96	12.15	12.53	13.00	13.57	14.27	14.85
Education and health services	10.00	10.49	10.87	11.21	11.50	11.80	12.17	12.56	13.00	13.44
Leisure and hospitality	6.02	6.22	6.36	6.48	6.62	6.79	6.99	7.32	7.67	7.96
Other services	9.08	9.39	9.66	9.90	10.18	10.51	10.85	11.29	11.79	12.26

[1] Derived by assuming that overtime hours are paid at the rate of time and one-half.
[2] Includes other industries, not shown separately.

Table 15-4. Average Hourly Earnings of Production and Nonsupervisory Workers on Private Nonfarm Payrolls by NAICS Industry—*Continued*

(Dollars.)

Industry	2000	2001	2002	2003	2004	2005	2006	2007	2008	2009	2010	2011
Total Private	14.02	14.54	14.97	15.37	15.69	16.13	16.76	17.43	18.08	18.63	19.07	19.47
Goods-Producing	15.27	15.78	16.33	16.80	17.19	17.60	18.02	18.67	19.33	19.90	20.28	20.66
Mining and logging	16.55	17.00	17.19	17.56	18.07	18.72	19.90	20.97	22.50	23.29	23.82	24.51
Construction	17.48	18.00	18.52	18.95	19.23	19.46	20.02	20.95	21.87	22.66	23.22	23.64
Manufacturing	14.32	14.76	15.29	15.74	16.14	16.56	16.81	17.26	17.75	18.24	18.61	18.94
Excluding overtime [1]	13.55	14.06	14.54	14.96	15.29	15.68	15.96	16.43	16.97	17.59	17.78	18.04
Durable goods	14.92	15.38	16.02	16.45	16.82	17.33	17.68	18.20	18.71	19.36	19.81	20.12
Wood products	11.63	11.99	12.33	12.71	13.03	13.16	13.39	13.68	14.19	14.92	14.85	14.81
Nonmetallic mineral products	14.53	14.86	15.39	15.76	16.25	16.61	16.59	16.93	16.90	17.28	17.48	18.16
Primary metals	16.64	17.06	17.68	18.13	18.57	18.94	19.36	19.66	20.19	20.10	20.13	19.96
Fabricated metal products	13.77	14.19	14.68	15.01	15.31	15.80	16.17	16.53	16.99	17.48	17.94	18.13
Machinery	15.21	15.48	15.92	16.29	16.67	17.02	17.20	17.72	17.97	18.39	18.96	19.53
Computer and electronic products	14.73	15.42	16.20	16.68	17.27	18.39	18.94	19.94	21.04	21.87	22.78	23.32
Electrical equipment and appliances	13.23	13.78	13.98	14.36	14.90	15.24	15.53	15.93	15.78	16.27	16.87	17.96
Transportation equipment [2]	18.89	19.47	20.63	21.22	21.48	22.09	22.41	23.04	23.86	24.98	25.23	25.36
Motor vehicles and parts	19.11	19.66	21.09	21.68	21.71	22.26	22.14	22.00	22.21	21.86	22.02	21.97
Furniture and related products	11.73	12.14	12.62	12.99	13.16	13.45	13.80	14.32	14.54	15.04	15.06	15.24
Miscellaneous manufacturing	11.93	12.45	12.91	13.30	13.84	14.07	14.36	14.66	15.20	16.13	16.56	16.83
Nondurable goods	13.31	13.75	14.15	14.63	15.05	15.26	15.33	15.67	16.15	16.56	16.80	17.07
Food manufacturing	11.77	12.18	12.55	12.80	12.98	13.04	13.13	13.55	14.01	14.39	14.41	14.63
Beverage and tobacco products	17.40	17.67	17.73	17.96	19.14	18.76	18.18	18.54	19.35	20.49	21.78	20.02
Textile mills	11.23	11.40	11.73	11.99	12.13	12.38	12.55	13.00	13.58	13.71	13.56	13.79
Textile product mills	10.31	10.49	10.85	11.15	11.31	11.61	11.86	11.78	11.73	11.44	11.79	12.21
Apparel	8.61	8.83	9.11	9.58	9.77	10.26	10.65	11.05	11.40	11.37	11.43	11.96
Leather and allied products	10.35	10.69	11.00	11.66	11.63	11.50	11.44	12.04	12.96	13.90	13.03	13.48
Paper and paper products	15.91	16.38	16.85	17.33	17.91	17.99	18.01	18.44	18.89	19.29	20.04	20.26
Printing and related support activities	14.09	14.48	14.93	15.37	15.71	15.74	15.80	16.15	16.75	16.75	16.91	17.28
Petroleum and coal products	22.80	22.90	23.04	23.63	24.39	24.47	24.11	25.21	27.41	29.61	31.31	31.71
Chemicals	17.09	17.57	17.97	18.50	19.17	19.67	19.60	19.55	19.50	20.30	21.07	21.46
Plastics and rubber products	12.70	13.21	13.55	14.18	14.59	14.80	14.97	15.39	15.85	16.01	15.71	15.95
Private Service-Providing	13.62	14.18	14.59	14.99	15.29	15.73	16.42	17.11	17.77	18.35	18.81	19.21
Trade, transportation, and utilities	13.31	13.70	14.02	14.34	14.58	14.92	15.39	15.78	16.16	16.48	16.82	17.15
Wholesale trade	16.28	16.77	16.98	17.36	17.65	18.16	18.91	19.59	20.13	20.84	21.54	21.97
Retail trade	10.87	11.29	11.67	11.90	12.08	12.36	12.57	12.75	12.87	13.01	13.24	13.51
Transportation and warehousing	15.05	15.33	15.76	16.25	16.52	16.70	17.27	17.72	18.41	18.81	19.16	19.50
Utilities	22.75	23.58	23.96	24.77	25.61	26.68	27.40	27.88	28.83	29.48	30.04	30.82
Information	19.07	19.80	20.20	21.01	21.40	22.06	23.23	23.96	24.78	25.45	25.87	26.61
Financial activities	14.98	15.59	16.17	17.14	17.52	17.94	18.80	19.64	20.28	20.85	21.52	21.91
Professional and business services	15.52	16.33	16.80	17.21	17.48	18.08	19.13	20.15	21.18	22.35	22.78	23.12
Education and health services	13.95	14.64	15.21	15.64	16.15	16.71	17.38	18.11	18.87	19.49	20.12	20.78
Leisure and hospitality	8.32	8.57	8.81	9.00	9.15	9.38	9.75	10.41	10.84	11.12	11.31	11.45
Other services	12.73	13.27	13.72	13.84	13.98	14.34	14.77	15.42	16.09	16.59	17.06	17.32

[1]Derived by assuming that overtime hours are paid at the rate of time and one-half.
[2]Includes other industries, not shown separately.

Table 15-5. Average Weekly Earnings of Production and Nonsupervisory Workers on Private Nonfarm Payrolls by NAICS Industry

(Dollars.)

Industry	1990	1991	1992	1993	1994	1995	1996	1997	1998	1999
Total Private	349.72	358.60	368.25	378.91	391.22	400.07	413.28	431.86	448.56	463.15
Goods-Producing	459.42	471.32	482.58	498.82	519.58	528.55	546.41	568.43	580.96	599.99
Mining and logging	602.43	625.46	628.94	634.77	653.13	670.40	695.04	720.07	727.19	721.77
Construction	513.43	520.41	525.13	539.81	558.53	571.57	588.48	609.48	629.75	655.11
Manufacturing	436.13	449.83	464.43	480.93	502.08	509.23	526.59	548.22	557.20	573.14
Durable goods	468.46	483.28	499.60	519.99	544.63	549.45	566.53	589.06	591.80	606.55
Wood products	356.42	362.46	377.73	387.33	402.83	406.53	422.29	435.74	449.87	461.39
Nonmetallic mineral products	453.91	459.17	474.45	490.67	510.95	517.75	538.10	551.65	573.04	587.42
Primary metals	545.36	555.34	581.45	606.49	637.73	639.70	658.81	681.52	681.68	700.93
Fabricated metal products	436.00	448.01	459.67	474.21	492.07	498.48	513.47	534.38	543.20	555.86
Machinery	493.25	507.79	525.32	549.76	567.93	571.19	584.62	613.19	613.77	625.07
Computer and electronic products	450.06	464.31	482.05	498.95	514.98	518.19	534.39	562.68	579.85	596.37
Electrical equipment and appliances	412.42	426.81	439.04	451.44	470.24	471.72	496.69	515.77	522.54	538.98
Transportation equipment [1]	606.68	633.96	652.75	697.14	750.29	751.45	773.73	795.74	774.77	795.57
Motor vehicles and parts	621.68	650.36	662.82	717.68	779.29	776.41	794.09	808.28	775.56	809.31
Furniture and related products	324.37	330.64	348.07	360.81	373.90	375.18	385.82	410.48	428.67	443.68
Miscellaneous manufacturing	345.82	358.54	370.67	378.21	389.64	400.88	413.94	431.72	437.95	454.14
Nondurable goods	390.65	404.29	417.95	429.15	443.76	452.74	467.91	487.04	503.99	520.06
Food manufacturing	355.65	364.90	375.69	386.07	398.53	406.75	414.74	428.58	444.72	458.73
Beverage and tobacco products	515.73	530.09	544.25	547.60	588.39	605.00	624.82	639.69	646.26	679.06
Textile mills	328.11	345.48	364.45	379.74	391.64	394.17	403.08	425.53	434.15	447.38
Textile product mills	283.60	293.54	303.69	317.69	326.44	332.33	346.91	364.16	376.21	392.41
Apparel	215.89	227.82	235.13	239.88	248.51	254.91	261.99	276.01	286.17	295.62
Leather and allied products	268.32	279.41	291.11	302.85	314.18	319.98	337.86	355.63	361.87	369.80
Paper and paper products	525.58	542.08	559.98	575.60	595.85	604.66	625.38	647.64	662.27	679.05
Printing and related support activities	429.93	437.00	450.02	457.91	470.74	472.37	484.99	504.46	518.32	534.15
Petroleum and coal products	754.13	786.05	821.72	855.36	883.81	883.68	881.24	908.50	949.28	947.60
Chemicals	550.25	573.27	593.24	603.75	622.53	644.46	666.28	685.43	700.53	701.06
Plastics and rubber products	396.26	408.25	426.65	436.85	445.99	446.01	458.29	475.04	487.04	505.45
Private Service-Providing	316.03	325.87	336.08	345.65	355.63	364.80	377.37	395.51	413.50	427.98
Trade, transportation, and utilities	331.55	339.19	348.60	359.51	370.38	378.79	390.67	407.66	423.33	434.42
Wholesale trade	444.48	459.17	470.41	484.46	501.14	515.14	533.36	559.39	582.21	602.77
Retail trade	235.56	240.13	249.66	256.89	265.74	272.63	282.76	295.94	310.25	321.69
Transportation and warehousing	471.82	471.02	477.81	494.54	507.13	513.40	525.72	542.51	546.89	548.00
Utilities	670.80	693.61	716.65	756.50	790.13	811.72	831.24	865.02	902.44	924.40
Information	479.50	495.14	511.95	535.19	551.21	564.92	592.45	622.37	646.52	675.47
Financial activities	354.66	369.54	386.01	403.02	419.20	436.12	451.49	472.37	500.98	517.57
Professional and business services	380.61	391.06	400.64	406.20	414.16	426.57	442.81	465.51	490.10	510.99
Education and health services	319.27	334.55	348.29	359.08	368.14	377.73	388.30	404.65	418.82	431.35
Leisure and hospitality	156.32	159.20	163.70	167.54	172.27	175.74	181.02	190.66	200.82	208.05
Other services	297.88	306.75	315.08	322.69	332.44	342.36	352.68	368.63	384.25	398.77

[1] Includes other industries, not shown separately.

Table 15-5. Average Weekly Earnings of Production and Nonsupervisory Workers on Private Nonfarm Payrolls by NAICS Industry—*Continued*

(Dollars.)

Industry	2000	2001	2002	2003	2004	2005	2006	2007	2008	2009	2010	2011
Total Private	481.13	493.79	506.75	518.06	529.09	544.33	567.87	590.04	607.95	617.18	636.92	654.87
Goods-Producing	621.86	630.04	651.55	669.13	688.17	705.31	730.16	757.50	776.63	779.68	818.96	844.90
Mining and logging	734.88	757.96	741.97	765.94	804.01	853.87	907.95	962.63	1 014.69	1 006.67	1 063.11	1 144.04
Construction	685.78	695.86	711.82	727.00	735.55	750.37	781.59	816.23	842.61	851.76	891.83	921.66
Manufacturing	590.77	595.15	618.62	635.99	658.52	673.34	691.05	711.53	724.46	726.12	765.15	784.68
Durable goods	624.35	624.51	652.67	671.35	694.06	712.88	731.97	754.77	767.99	771.39	819.06	842.21
Wood products	477.03	481.33	492.07	514.10	530.04	526.65	533.15	539.41	547.53	557.65	580.70	587.77
Nonmetallic mineral products	604.76	618.91	647.00	664.96	688.33	700.63	712.67	716.78	711.11	705.54	728.22	768.38
Primary metals	734.79	723.82	749.32	767.45	799.77	815.90	843.63	843.26	851.29	817.67	880.50	890.25
Fabricated metal products	576.71	576.71	596.42	610.40	628.80	647.21	668.94	687.16	701.57	689.06	742.76	762.16
Machinery	643.81	632.81	645.38	664.51	699.31	716.13	728.84	754.34	759.94	737.97	797.62	842.74
Computer and electronic products	609.97	613.18	642.77	674.69	697.97	735.59	766.75	809.10	861.58	883.02	932.26	943.90
Electrical equipment and appliances	550.48	548.03	560.33	583.27	607.00	618.88	637.04	656.46	645.60	639.34	693.49	732.16
Transportation equipment [1]	817.48	816.58	877.46	889.42	912.63	937.75	957.69	986.79	1 000.71	1 028.37	1 081.53	1 095.49
Motor vehicles and parts	828.73	818.68	898.54	910.02	924.72	940.64	934.41	930.51	920.57	876.45	956.36	953.99
Furniture and related products	459.95	464.87	493.95	505.26	519.61	527.49	535.90	561.08	553.90	566.75	579.66	608.00
Miscellaneous manufacturing	464.80	483.07	499.01	510.54	533.27	545.01	555.87	570.12	591.95	620.74	640.85	655.15
Nondurable goods	536.85	548.30	566.75	582.48	602.72	608.92	621.97	639.96	652.26	658.68	685.21	696.35
Food manufacturing	472.09	481.81	497.25	503.03	509.55	508.66	526.02	551.32	566.91	575.51	586.41	587.93
Beverage and tobacco products	730.35	721.68	698.39	702.45	751.20	751.54	741.34	755.22	750.25	731.37	816.53	784.87
Textile mills	464.51	456.64	476.52	469.33	486.68	498.47	509.39	524.40	525.00	516.86	559.13	574.60
Textile product mills	398.99	402.47	423.05	438.77	437.79	451.14	472.28	467.74	453.10	433.13	459.40	477.49
Apparel	307.51	317.63	334.24	340.73	352.04	366.93	389.05	411.57	415.10	408.86	418.28	457.05
Leather and allied products	388.46	388.83	412.99	457.83	446.66	441.96	445.47	459.50	486.58	466.62	509.20	536.85
Paper and paper products	681.38	689.76	705.20	719.55	754.17	764.15	772.57	795.58	809.57	806.19	858.65	869.32
Printing and related support activities	552.15	560.89	573.05	587.58	603.97	604.73	618.92	632.02	642.50	635.68	646.11	655.78
Petroleum and coal products	973.53	1 003.34	990.88	1 052.32	1 095.00	1 114.51	1 085.50	1 112.73	1 222.07	1 284.44	1 345.72	1 389.09
Chemicals	721.41	735.57	759.56	784.26	819.93	831.79	833.84	819.51	809.29	841.18	888.25	910.88
Plastics and rubber products	517.56	528.62	550.14	572.53	589.99	591.59	608.37	635.63	649.02	643.91	658.55	669.47
Private Service-Providing	445.74	461.08	473.80	484.71	494.22	509.56	532.60	554.89	574.20	588.20	606.12	622.42
Trade, transportation, and utilities	449.96	459.53	471.27	481.14	488.51	498.43	514.37	525.91	536.11	541.88	559.63	577.84
Wholesale trade	631.24	643.45	644.38	657.29	666.79	685.00	718.50	748.94	769.62	784.49	816.50	845.36
Retail trade	333.41	346.07	360.87	367.15	371.03	377.58	383.12	385.00	386.21	388.57	400.02	412.10
Transportation and warehousing	562.56	562.57	579.91	598.41	614.89	618.55	636.80	654.95	670.22	677.56	710.85	737.37
Utilities	955.09	977.25	979.26	1 017.44	1 048.01	1 095.91	1 135.57	1 182.65	1 230.65	1 239.34	1 262.89	1 296.85
Information	700.92	731.18	737.94	760.84	776.72	805.11	850.64	874.45	908.78	931.08	939.85	963.99
Financial activities	537.37	558.05	575.54	609.08	622.87	645.10	672.21	705.13	727.07	752.03	778.43	797.76
Professional and business services	535.07	557.84	574.60	587.02	597.39	618.66	662.27	700.64	737.70	775.81	798.54	813.71
Education and health services	449.29	473.39	492.74	505.69	523.78	544.59	564.94	590.09	613.73	628.45	646.65	670.83
Leisure and hospitality	217.20	220.73	227.31	230.49	234.86	241.36	250.34	265.54	273.39	275.95	280.87	283.77
Other services	413.30	428.64	439.87	434.41	433.04	443.40	456.50	477.06	495.57	506.26	523.70	532.48

[1]Includes other industries, not shown separately.

Table 15-6. Indexes of Aggregate Weekly Hours of Production and Nonsupervisory Workers on Private Nonfarm Payrolls by NAICS Industry

(2002 = 100.)

Industry	1990	1991	1992	1993	1994	1995	1996	1997	1998	1999
Total Private	84.4	82.6	83.1	85.5	89.2	91.6	93.8	97.1	99.4	101.5
Goods-Producing	106.1	100.1	98.7	100.8	105.6	106.8	108.1	111.2	112.3	112.6
Mining and logging	128.6	123.8	113.3	110.3	111.0	110.3	112.7	117.6	112.8	102.9
Construction	78.8	70.1	67.5	71.3	77.3	79.9	84.3	88.6	93.4	99.7
Manufacturing	117.7	112.8	112.4	113.9	118.4	119.0	118.8	121.4	121.1	119.0
Durable goods	114.3	107.6	106.4	108.3	114.2	116.4	117.6	121.6	122.0	120.6
Wood products	101.6	92.6	95.2	100.5	109.1	109.3	111.6	114.8	117.5	118.5
Nonmetallic mineral products	100.7	92.8	92.6	94.2	98.8	99.7	101.5	103.1	105.8	106.9
Primary metals	131.5	122.9	120.8	121.5	128.0	129.3	129.9	132.3	131.1	128.4
Fabricated metal products	104.6	99.1	97.3	99.7	106.3	109.9	111.6	116.6	118.6	116.7
Machinery	123.8	116.2	113.9	118.6	126.9	132.2	133.7	138.9	137.4	129.8
Computer and electronic products	137.2	128.2	122.9	121.1	123.6	127.1	130.0	136.8	136.7	131.1
Electrical equipment and appliances	136.0	127.9	125.9	126.8	132.4	130.3	129.4	127.7	127.8	128.3
Transportation equipment [1]	111.1	105.8	104.4	105.5	112.6	115.4	116.5	120.8	118.8	119.5
Motor vehicles and parts	90.9	87.9	91.1	97.9	110.6	115.9	116.1	117.5	112.8	118.7
Furniture and related products	97.1	89.4	92.0	95.3	100.5	99.2	98.3	102.9	108.4	112.6
Miscellaneous manufacturing	104.1	103.9	105.3	107.0	108.3	107.8	107.7	110.1	110.4	110.3
Nondurable goods	123.0	120.8	121.7	122.7	124.7	123.1	120.5	120.9	119.4	116.1
Food manufacturing	96.2	96.5	97.2	98.6	100.4	101.6	101.8	102.6	103.3	103.7
Beverage and tobacco products	96.9	96.4	95.4	95.6	98.7	97.9	101.4	103.1	104.9	104.7
Textile mills	170.4	168.4	170.3	170.8	171.6	163.5	154.1	155.2	148.9	139.1
Textile product mills	118.7	113.1	114.8	118.7	124.0	121.0	118.0	119.4	117.6	115.5
Apparel	266.5	263.6	266.6	259.0	252.1	234.8	211.6	201.3	180.9	154.6
Leather and allied products	290.0	268.9	263.5	259.1	246.9	221.8	197.5	187.1	166.6	148.3
Paper and paper products	121.9	120.6	121.7	122.0	123.5	121.5	120.2	121.6	119.6	117.2
Printing and related support activities	122.3	118.7	118.4	120.3	123.8	123.9	122.8	124.6	124.3	120.9
Petroleum and coal products	128.9	127.5	126.0	122.0	120.0	115.5	113.5	112.7	113.4	107.6
Chemicals	118.2	115.0	112.9	113.5	115.1	115.4	114.8	114.7	115.4	113.2
Plastics and rubber products	97.7	94.1	98.0	102.3	108.7	109.8	110.0	112.7	113.7	114.6
Private Service-Providing	78.3	77.8	78.8	81.2	84.6	87.3	89.7	93.1	95.8	98.4
Trade, transportation, and utilities	89.5	87.4	87.3	89.1	92.7	95.1	96.6	98.9	100.3	101.9
Wholesale trade	94.9	93.3	92.4	92.4	95.8	99.2	100.7	103.4	104.8	106.2
Retail trade	87.5	84.8	85.1	86.3	89.8	92.3	93.7	95.9	97.2	99.5
Transportation and warehousing	83.5	82.3	82.6	88.4	93.7	95.6	98.3	101.0	102.6	103.2
Utilities	124.3	123.5	121.6	119.9	117.1	112.9	108.6	106.1	105.7	105.0
Information	76.2	76.1	76.5	78.0	79.2	82.5	86.9	90.4	92.6	98.5
Financial activities	84.5	83.3	83.5	85.9	88.0	87.8	89.8	92.6	96.5	98.0
Professional and business services	68.1	66.7	68.4	71.9	77.0	81.2	85.2	91.5	96.7	101.7
Education and health services	67.2	70.2	72.9	75.4	78.3	81.2	83.4	86.7	88.9	90.6
Leisure and hospitality	78.9	77.3	79.2	82.1	85.5	88.5	90.7	93.4	95.5	97.8
Other services	81.8	81.1	80.6	82.8	84.5	87.0	89.1	91.9	94.3	96.2

[1]Includes other industries, not shown separately.

Table 15-6. Indexes of Aggregate Weekly Hours of Production and Nonsupervisory Workers on Private Nonfarm Payrolls by NAICS Industry—*Continued*

(2002 = 100.)

Industry	2000	2001	2002	2003	2004	2005	2006	2007	2008	2009	2010	2011
Total Private	103.6	102.1	100.0	98.7	100.2	102.8	105.8	107.3	105.9	98.7	98.8	101.2
Goods-Producing	113.1	106.6	100.0	95.7	96.8	98.9	102.5	101.7	96.5	80.2	78.8	81.1
Mining and logging	105.1	108.3	100.0	97.4	104.0	114.7	125.8	133.5	137.6	117.2	124.5	146.3
Construction	104.0	103.2	100.0	98.4	101.7	108.3	115.4	114.7	106.5	85.9	80.2	81.2
Manufacturing	117.7	108.1	100.0	94.5	94.3	93.9	95.7	94.4	90.2	76.1	76.2	78.3
Durable goods	120.4	109.4	100.0	94.4	95.2	96.2	98.9	97.4	92.2	74.7	75.1	78.4
Wood products	115.8	105.0	100.0	97.8	100.8	101.2	99.9	89.3	76.7	57.8	58.5	59.0
Nonmetallic mineral products	109.1	106.1	100.0	94.3	98.0	97.4	100.3	96.9	91.2	73.8	70.5	70.1
Primary metals	128.9	113.0	100.0	93.4	93.3	93.1	94.1	91.4	87.4	66.0	71.7	80.3
Fabricated metal products	119.1	109.3	100.0	95.3	97.7	99.2	103.1	104.5	101.3	81.2	83.1	89.4
Machinery	127.5	114.1	100.0	93.6	95.9	98.8	102.2	103.3	102.3	80.6	81.2	89.6
Computer and electronic products	133.1	117.9	100.0	92.1	89.8	94.8	103.6	102.2	101.2	89.4	87.2	86.6
Electrical equipment and appliances	127.7	113.4	100.0	92.0	88.7	86.4	88.0	89.1	88.5	74.1	73.2	71.8
Transportation equipment [1]	116.3	105.3	100.0	95.5	96.5	97.3	100.0	98.0	88.6	70.1	72.1	75.4
Motor vehicles and parts	117.3	103.6	100.0	95.9	97.0	95.2	92.9	85.8	72.7	51.6	57.5	60.8
Furniture and related products	114.7	104.8	100.0	93.0	94.3	91.9	90.4	86.1	74.6	57.6	54.4	55.7
Miscellaneous manufacturing	109.5	104.7	100.0	93.6	91.8	90.6	90.4	91.0	89.2	81.1	79.0	80.0
Nondurable goods	113.3	106.0	100.0	94.7	92.8	90.3	90.4	89.6	86.9	78.1	78.0	78.0
Food manufacturing	103.4	101.4	100.0	98.4	97.1	95.8	98.6	101.1	100.6	97.5	98.4	97.5
Beverage and tobacco products	104.2	100.3	100.0	88.4	88.8	94.8	99.3	102.2	92.0	84.5	84.5	90.3
Textile mills	132.4	112.2	100.0	86.3	79.0	71.3	65.1	56.3	47.9	37.8	40.2	41.7
Textile product mills	112.3	105.5	100.0	92.4	90.1	88.0	85.0	77.5	70.5	58.5	56.5	54.9
Apparel	137.5	117.1	100.0	81.9	75.1	65.7	63.4	61.5	56.7	45.4	42.0	40.7
Leather and allied products	138.4	113.3	100.0	91.3	83.6	79.0	74.1	69.3	68.8	53.5	57.9	61.9
Paper and paper products	113.5	106.6	100.0	92.5	89.2	88.0	86.9	85.8	83.5	74.2	73.5	72.6
Printing and related support activities	119.4	111.5	100.0	95.3	93.4	90.9	92.5	91.6	86.1	74.1	69.0	65.3
Petroleum and coal products	105.8	105.6	100.0	98.7	102.6	102.4	96.9	95.6	102.4	90.2	89.1	91.6
Chemicals	110.4	104.7	100.0	99.0	99.0	95.9	96.1	94.1	94.6	88.3	88.9	91.2
Plastics and rubber products	114.2	104.9	100.0	95.2	94.2	92.3	91.9	91.1	87.1	71.3	73.6	75.3
Private Service-Providing	101.0	100.8	100.0	99.5	101.1	103.8	106.7	108.9	108.5	103.8	104.3	106.8
Trade, transportation, and utilities	103.5	101.5	100.0	98.6	99.6	101.6	103.3	104.8	103.3	96.8	96.8	99.5
Wholesale trade	107.0	102.9	100.0	98.0	98.8	101.8	105.7	109.2	108.6	99.9	97.7	100.4
Retail trade	101.3	100.5	100.0	98.9	99.4	100.8	101.1	101.8	99.8	94.3	95.0	97.5
Transportation and warehousing	105.6	102.7	100.0	98.8	101.9	105.2	107.9	109.4	107.7	100.0	101.3	105.2
Utilities	104.1	102.3	100.0	97.4	94.2	93.1	93.8	96.2	98.3	97.0	95.4	95.3
Information	105.0	106.7	100.0	97.0	98.2	99.4	100.2	100.1	100.0	93.5	90.0	88.3
Financial activities	98.5	99.5	100.0	101.5	101.9	104.8	107.4	108.7	107.5	103.7	102.2	102.6
Professional and business services	106.6	104.0	100.0	98.7	101.8	106.3	112.1	115.2	113.9	105.2	107.6	112.4
Education and health services	92.8	96.6	100.0	101.4	103.3	106.4	109.0	112.5	115.7	117.2	118.7	121.3
Leisure and hospitality	100.5	100.6	100.0	100.0	103.0	106.2	108.8	110.8	109.7	105.1	104.6	106.6
Other services	97.8	99.0	100.0	97.4	96.1	96.2	97.4	99.3	99.5	96.0	96.0	96.5

[1]Includes other industries, not shown separately.

NOTES AND DEFINITIONS, CHAPTER 15

TABLES 15-1 THROUGH 15-6
EMPLOYMENT, HOURS, AND EARNINGS BY NAICS INDUSTRY

SOURCE: U.S. DEPARTMENT OF LABOR, BUREAU OF LABOR STATISTICS

See the notes and definitions for Tables 10-8 through 10-18 regarding definitions of *employment, production and nonsupervisory workers, average weekly hours, overtime hours, average hourly earnings, average weekly earnings,* and the *indexes of aggregate weekly hours.* Availability and reference information is also provided in those notes and definitions.

CHAPTER 16: KEY SECTOR STATISTICS

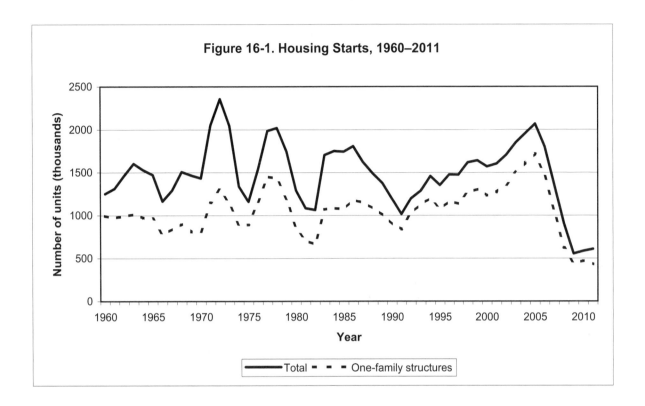

Figure 16-1. Housing Starts, 1960–2011

- The housing sector was the source of the boom and bust cycle of 2001–2009. In 2005, as shown in Figure 16-1, 2.1 million housing units were started, the highest since 1972. Of those, 1.7 million were one-family homes, an all-time record. By 2009, both total and single-family starts had plunged to the lowest levels of their 50-year history; total starts recovered slightly in 2010 and 2011, but single-family fell back to a new low in 2011. (Table 16-3)

- New orders for nondefense capital goods at U.S. manufacturing firms plunged 52 percent between January 2008 and their lowest point in April 2009. Even excluding the volatile aircraft sector, they were down 33 percent. In December 2011, however, the value of nondefense capital goods orders was back at its January 2008 level. (Table 16-6)

- Sales of cars and light trucks were 10.4 million in 2009, down 39 percent from their recent high in 2005; they recovered 22 percent from 2009 to 2011. (Table 16-8)

- Service industries were affected later and less. Revenues of the information industry continued to increase through the third quarter of 2008, and fell back only modestly in the following two quarters before resuming growth. Professional, scientific, and technical services declined through the second quarter of 2009 but were back at previous highs by the second quarter of 2011. The administrative services total and its employment services component, which includes temporary help, were back at previous highs by the third quarter of 2010. The increase in hospital revenues was uninterrupted. (Table 16-15)

- As a percentage of the total supply of petroleum and products (domestic crude oil and natural gas liquids production plus net imports), net imports increased from 17 percent in 1955 to 65 percent in 2005, but were reduced to 52 percent in 2011. (Table 16-1)

- Sales by electronic shopping and mail order grew from 1.9 percent of total retail sales in 1992 to 7.3 percent in 2011. (Table 16-9) E-commerce alone grew from 0.6 percent of total retail sales at the end of 1999 to 4.8 percent at the end of 2011. (Table 16-10)

Table 16-1. Petroleum and Petroleum Products—Prices, Imports, Domestic Production, and Stocks

(Not seasonally adjusted.)

Year and month	Crude oil futures price (dollars per barrel) Current dollars	Crude oil futures price (dollars per barrel) 2005 dollars	Imports Total energy-related petroleum products (thousands of barrels)	Imports Crude petroleum Total	Imports Crude petroleum Average per day	Imports Crude petroleum Unit price (dollars per barrel)	Supply Petroleum and products Exports	Supply Petroleum and products Imports	Supply Petroleum and products Net imports	Supply Domestic production Crude oil	Supply Domestic production Natural gas plant liquids	Stocks Crude oil and petroleum products	Stocks Crude petroleum Non-SPR	Stocks Crude petroleum Strategic petroleum reserve
1955	...	...	...	...	...	...	368	1 248	880	6 807	771	715	266	...
1956	...	...	...	...	...	...	430	1 436	1 006	7 151	800	780	266	...
1957	...	...	...	...	...	...	568	1 574	1 006	7 170	808	841	282	...
1958	...	...	...	...	...	...	276	1 700	1 424	6 710	808	789	263	...
1959	...	...	...	...	...	...	211	1 780	1 569	7 054	879	809	257	...
1960	...	...	...	...	...	...	202	1 815	1 613	7 035	929	785	240	...
1961	...	...	...	...	...	...	174	1 917	1 743	7 183	991	825	245	...
1962	...	...	...	...	...	...	168	2 082	1 914	7 332	1 021	834	252	...
1963	...	...	...	...	...	...	208	2 123	1 915	7 542	1 098	836	237	...
1964	...	...	...	...	...	...	202	2 259	2 057	7 614	1 154	839	230	...
1965	...	...	...	...	...	...	187	2 468	2 281	7 804	1 210	836	220	...
1966	...	...	...	...	...	...	198	2 573	2 375	8 295	1 284	874	238	...
1967	...	...	...	...	...	...	307	2 537	2 230	8 810	1 409	944	249	...
1968	...	...	...	...	...	...	231	2 840	2 609	9 096	1 504	1 000	272	...
1969	...	...	...	...	...	...	233	3 166	2 933	9 238	1 590	980	265	...
1970	...	...	...	...	...	...	259	3 419	3 160	9 637	1 660	1 018	276	...
1971	...	...	...	...	...	...	224	3 926	3 702	9 463	1 693	1 044	260	...
1972	...	...	...	...	...	...	222	4 741	4 519	9 441	1 744	959	246	...
1973	...	...	...	1 392 970	3 816	3.30	231	6 256	6 025	9 208	1 738	1 008	242	...
1974	...	...	...	1 367 081	3 745	11.17	221	6 112	5 892	8 774	1 688	1 074	265	...
1975	...	...	...	1 584 730	4 342	11.59	209	6 056	5 846	8 375	1 633	1 133	271	...
1976	...	...	...	2 050 424	5 618	12.43	223	7 313	7 090	8 132	1 604	1 112	285	...
1977	...	...	...	2 519 806	6 904	13.33	243	8 807	8 565	8 245	1 618	1 312	340	7
1978	...	...	...	2 392 350	6 554	13.43	362	8 363	8 002	8 707	1 567	1 278	309	67
1979	...	...	...	2 467 315	6 760	18.68	471	8 456	7 985	8 552	1 584	1 341	339	91
1980	...	...	...	1 977 247	5 417	31.36	544	6 909	6 365	8 597	1 573	1 392	358	108
1981	...	...	...	1 763 072	4 830	35.13	595	5 996	5 401	8 572	1 609	1 484	363	230
1982	...	...	...	1 420 753	3 892	33.39	815	5 113	4 298	8 649	1 550	1 430	350	294
1983	30.66	54.80	...	1 293 819	3 545	29.51	739	5 051	4 312	8 688	1 559	1 454	344	379
1984	29.44	50.70	...	1 319 683	3 616	27.68	722	5 437	4 715	8 879	1 630	1 556	345	451
1985	27.89	46.51	...	1 260 856	3 454	26.20	781	5 067	4 286	8 971	1 609	1 519	321	493
1986	15.05	24.50	...	1 634 567	4 478	13.90	785	6 224	5 439	8 680	1 551	1 593	331	512
1987	19.15	30.10	...	1 744 977	4 781	16.80	764	6 678	5 914	8 349	1 595	1 607	349	541
1988	15.96	24.13	...	1 887 860	5 172	13.69	815	7 402	6 587	8 140	1 625	1 597	330	560
1989	19.58	28.37	...	2 146 552	5 881	16.49	859	8 061	7 202	7 613	1 546	1 581	341	580
1990	24.50	33.94	...	2 216 604	6 073	19.75	857	8 018	7 161	7 355	1 559	1 621	323	586
1991	21.50	28.75	2 828 953	2 146 064	5 880	17.46	1 001	7 627	6 626	7 417	1 659	1 617	325	569
1992	20.58	26.73	2 947 582	2 294 570	6 269	16.80	950	7 888	6 938	7 171	1 697	1 592	318	575
1993	18.48	23.49	3 257 008	2 543 374	6 968	15.13	1 003	8 620	7 618	6 847	1 736	1 647	335	587
1994	17.19	21.41	3 416 045	2 704 196	7 409	14.23	942	8 996	8 054	6 662	1 727	1 653	337	592
1995	18.40	22.42	3 361 882	2 767 312	7 582	15.81	949	8 835	7 886	6 560	1 762	1 563	303	592
1996	22.03	26.27	3 622 385	2 893 647	7 906	18.98	981	9 478	8 498	6 465	1 830	1 507	284	566
1997	20.61	24.12	3 802 574	3 069 430	8 409	17.67	1 003	10 162	9 158	6 452	1 817	1 560	305	563
1998	14.40	16.70	4 088 027	3 242 711	8 884	11.49	945	10 708	9 764	6 252	1 759	1 647	324	571
1999	19.30	22.02	4 081 181	3 228 092	8 844	15.76	940	10 852	9 912	5 881	1 850	1 493	284	567
2000	30.26	33.69	4 314 825	3 399 239	9 288	26.44	1 040	11 459	10 419	5 822	1 911	1 468	286	541
2001	25.95	28.35	4 475 026	3 471 067	9 510	21.40	971	11 871	10 900	5 801	1 868	1 586	312	550
2002	26.15	28.19	4 337 075	3 418 022	9 364	22.61	984	11 530	10 546	5 746	1 880	1 548	278	599
2003	30.99	32.74	4 654 638	3 676 005	10 071	26.98	1 027	12 264	11 238	5 681	1 719	1 568	269	638
2004	41.47	42.70	4 917 591	3 820 979	10 440	34.48	1 048	13 145	12 097	5 419	1 809	1 645	286	676
2005	56.70	56.70	5 004 339	3 754 671	10 287	46.81	1 165	13 714	12 549	5 178	1 717	1 698	324	685
2006	66.25	64.49	4 880 734	3 734 246	10 231	58.01	1 317	13 707	12 390	5 102	1 739	1 720	312	689
2007	72.41	68.64	4 807 811	3 690 568	10 111	64.28	1 433	13 468	12 036	5 064	1 783	1 665	286	697
2008	99.75	91.56	4 613 444	3 590 628	9 810	95.22	1 802	12 915	11 114	4 950	1 784	1 737	326	702
2009	62.09	56.88	4 266 007	3 314 787	9 082	56.93	2 024	11 691	9 667	5 361	1 910	1 776	325	727
2010	79.61	71.65	4 279 526	3 377 077	9 252	74.67	2 353	11 793	9 441	5 483	2 074	1 794	333	727
2011	95.11	84.33	4 164 178	3 321 918	9 101	99.82	2 924	11 360	8 436	5 675	2 183	1 751	331	696
2011														
January	89.58	79.77	375 278	289 719	9 346	84.50	2 687	11 954	9 266	5 526	2 022	1 803	347	727
February	89.74	79.59	303 752	240 735	8 598	87.17	2 575	10 503	7 929	5 436	1 920	1 773	350	727
March	102.98	90.98	371 233	294 379	9 496	93.81	2 660	11 593	8 933	5 635	2 168	1 770	363	727
April	110.04	96.88	332 758	252 246	8 408	103.19	2 903	11 592	8 689	5 560	2 157	1 776	369	727
May	101.36	89.08	352 560	277 006	8 936	108.74	2 642	11 669	9 028	5 647	2 222	1 805	370	727
June	96.29	84.73	363 869	294 372	9 812	105.93	2 607	11 794	9 187	5 598	2 176	1 808	358	727
July	97.34	85.35	350 802	282 360	9 108	104.27	2 919	11 667	8 748	5 468	2 193	1 820	348	718
August	86.34	75.50	364 355	300 919	9 707	102.65	3 071	11 145	8 074	5 680	2 201	1 801	349	696
September	85.61	74.73	345 778	282 699	9 423	101.00	3 158	11 209	8 051	5 592	2 145	1 781	332	696
October	86.43	75.44	324 353	261 785	8 445	98.87	3 104	10 994	7 890	5 892	2 274	1 770	339	696
November	97.16	84.73	335 329	264 770	8 826	102.48	3 182	11 166	7 985	6 012	2 342	1 772	338	696
December	98.58	85.91	344 110	280 927	9 062	104.16	3 549	10 957	7 407	6 028	2 351	1 751	331	696

... = Not available.

Table 16-2. New Construction Put in Place

(Billions of dollars, monthly data are at seasonally adjusted annual rates.)

Year and month	Total	Private											
		Total [1]	Residential	Office	Commercial		Health care	Educational	Amuse-ment and recreation	Transpor-tation	Commu-nication	Power	Manu-facturing
					Total [1]	Multi-retail							
1975	152.6	109.3	51.6	...	...	...	...	...	...	...	...	...	...
1976	172.1	128.2	68.3	...	...	...	...	...	...	...	...	...	...
1977	200.5	157.4	92.0	...	...	...	...	...	...	...	...	...	...
1978	239.9	189.7	109.8	...	...	...	...	...	...	...	...	...	...
1979	272.9	216.2	116.4	...	...	...	...	...	...	...	...	...	...
1980	273.9	210.3	100.4	...	...	...	...	...	...	...	...	...	...
1981	289.1	224.4	99.2	...	...	...	...	...	...	...	...	...	...
1982	279.3	216.3	84.7	...	...	...	...	...	...	...	...	...	...
1983	311.9	248.4	125.8	...	...	...	...	...	...	...	...	...	...
1984	370.2	300.0	155.0	...	...	...	...	...	...	...	...	...	...
1985	403.4	325.6	160.5	...	...	...	...	...	...	...	...	...	...
1986	433.5	348.9	190.7	...	...	...	...	...	...	...	...	...	...
1987	446.6	356.0	199.7	...	...	...	...	...	...	...	...	...	...
1988	462.0	367.3	204.5	...	...	...	...	...	...	...	...	...	...
1989	477.5	379.3	204.3	...	...	...	...	...	...	...	...	...	...
1990	476.8	369.3	191.1	...	...	...	...	...	...	...	...	...	...
1991	432.6	322.5	166.3	...	...	...	...	...	...	...	...	...	...
1992	463.7	347.8	199.4	...	...	...	...	...	...	...	...	...	...
1993	485.5	358.2	208.2	20.0	34.4	11.5	14.9	4.8	4.6	4.7	9.8	23.6	23.4
1994	531.9	401.5	241.0	20.4	39.6	12.2	15.4	5.0	5.1	4.7	10.1	21.0	28.8
1995	548.7	408.7	228.1	23.0	44.1	12.0	15.3	5.7	5.9	4.8	11.1	22.0	35.4
1996	599.7	453.0	257.5	26.5	49.4	13.3	15.4	7.0	7.0	5.8	11.8	17.4	38.1
1997	631.9	478.4	264.7	32.8	53.1	12.2	17.4	8.8	8.5	6.2	12.5	16.4	37.6
1998	688.5	533.7	296.3	40.4	55.7	13.3	17.7	9.8	8.6	7.3	12.5	21.7	40.5
1999	744.6	575.5	326.3	45.1	59.4	15.2	18.4	9.8	9.6	6.5	18.4	22.0	35.1
2000	802.8	621.4	346.1	52.4	64.1	14.9	19.5	11.7	8.8	6.9	18.8	29.3	37.6
2001	840.2	634.4	396.7	35.3	59.0	15.6	22.4	13.1	7.5	6.8	18.4	32.6	22.7
2002	847.9	634.4	396.7	35.3	59.0	15.6	22.4	13.1	7.5	6.8	18.4	32.6	22.7
2003	891.5	675.4	446.0	30.6	57.5	15.4	24.2	13.4	7.8	6.6	14.5	33.6	21.4
2004	991.4	771.2	532.9	32.9	63.2	18.8	26.3	12.7	8.4	6.8	15.5	27.6	23.2
2005	1 104.1	870.0	611.9	37.3	66.6	22.8	28.5	12.8	7.5	7.1	18.8	29.2	28.4
2006	1 167.2	911.8	613.7	45.7	73.4	29.2	32.0	13.8	9.3	8.7	22.2	33.7	32.3
2007	1 152.4	863.3	493.2	53.8	85.9	34.8	35.6	16.7	10.2	9.0	27.5	54.1	40.2
2008	1 067.6	758.8	350.3	55.5	82.7	32.0	38.4	18.6	10.5	9.9	26.3	69.2	52.8
2009	903.2	588.3	245.9	37.3	50.5	18.4	35.3	16.9	8.4	9.1	19.7	76.1	56.3
2010	804.6	500.6	238.8	24.4	36.5	12.5	29.6	13.4	6.5	9.9	17.7	66.1	39.8
2011	778.2	495.0	237.0	22.5	40.0	13.4	28.6	14.2	7.0	9.8	17.4	63.9	40.6
2009													
January	962.7	653.2	274.6	47.8	64.3	24.1	38.2	18.6	9.0	8.8	20.5	70.4	62.0
February	959.9	638.5	258.8	44.8	62.7	23.9	38.7	18.2	9.4	9.0	18.4	74.2	65.0
March	955.0	629.5	246.8	42.7	60.3	22.0	38.6	18.1	9.5	9.2	19.3	82.1	63.8
April	929.6	610.7	242.9	41.1	57.6	21.3	37.9	17.6	9.3	9.5	20.3	72.6	62.8
May	911.2	594.2	230.9	40.8	54.0	19.4	36.5	18.0	9.3	9.6	19.9	77.0	61.5
June	902.0	581.0	228.5	38.9	49.7	18.4	36.5	17.9	8.9	9.5	19.7	78.6	58.3
July	899.6	577.0	234.3	37.2	47.8	17.2	34.5	16.8	9.2	9.3	19.5	79.6	56.3
August	889.6	575.2	242.6	35.6	44.9	16.3	34.3	16.9	8.0	9.1	19.8	79.9	54.0
September	880.3	569.4	248.1	31.7	44.9	15.8	33.4	16.0	7.5	9.1	20.0	77.7	51.8
October	869.4	561.5	254.3	31.0	41.5	15.2	33.1	15.0	7.5	8.6	19.2	73.4	51.1
November	850.7	548.1	251.0	29.1	41.4	14.5	31.5	14.6	6.7	8.5	19.6	71.8	48.4
December	832.6	532.2	245.5	28.4	41.5	14.1	30.8	14.2	6.7	8.5	19.9	69.5	43.3
2010													
January	816.1	520.3	255.0	27.4	40.0	13.8	30.2	14.2	5.9	9.2	17.4	56.9	43.3
February	795.8	505.5	240.9	28.2	38.6	13.5	29.2	14.3	6.1	9.5	18.3	56.4	43.8
March	806.0	508.2	242.8	25.5	38.1	13.3	29.1	14.5	7.1	9.5	16.5	57.0	48.6
April	824.0	517.6	251.8	24.8	37.5	13.1	29.5	13.9	7.3	9.4	17.7	61.7	45.0
May	816.3	507.0	244.2	24.2	36.2	12.3	29.7	13.7	6.7	9.6	18.0	63.8	42.4
June	816.3	504.2	241.4	23.9	37.0	12.6	29.1	13.6	6.6	10.1	17.2	65.7	42.0
July	788.5	484.2	233.8	22.4	34.5	12.3	29.0	12.9	6.2	10.2	17.7	60.8	39.4
August	791.7	483.3	229.4	23.3	36.1	12.2	29.6	13.2	6.4	10.1	18.4	61.6	37.9
September	798.9	483.9	231.2	24.3	35.4	12.5	30.2	12.9	6.9	9.7	17.4	62.3	36.7
October	800.3	493.7	236.6	23.7	35.2	11.3	29.5	12.4	6.1	10.5	17.6	70.6	35.3
November	798.3	499.5	235.7	22.4	35.1	11.6	29.8	12.9	6.4	10.2	18.1	79.3	33.3
December	779.9	488.4	229.3	23.2	34.6	11.2	29.8	13.0	6.2	10.1	17.5	77.4	31.4
2011													
January	752.6	464.6	237.7	22.0	35.4	11.9	27.1	12.5	6.0	9.4	17.2	53.5	29.5
February	746.1	461.5	231.2	21.5	36.1	12.2	28.1	12.6	5.9	9.3	17.5	54.1	31.9
March	753.4	467.1	226.8	21.6	36.9	12.6	28.3	13.3	5.8	9.2	17.4	58.6	35.1
April	755.4	475.3	236.0	21.6	38.6	13.1	27.6	13.2	7.0	9.0	17.8	57.5	33.3
May	775.8	495.3	243.1	22.9	39.9	13.2	27.4	13.5	7.4	9.2	17.4	62.7	38.3
June	786.8	502.1	236.9	23.4	40.9	13.4	28.8	14.8	7.3	9.6	17.8	64.9	43.8
July	763.5	485.8	222.4	23.0	41.7	13.4	29.1	14.8	7.3	9.6	17.9	64.9	41.5
August	786.3	501.5	232.2	23.2	42.5	14.0	29.0	14.3	7.3	10.0	17.3	67.5	44.2
September	790.3	507.2	236.5	22.6	40.9	13.8	29.5	15.0	7.7	10.3	17.7	66.5	46.5
October	795.7	512.8	243.7	23.0	41.1	14.0	28.6	14.8	7.4	10.3	17.0	67.8	45.4
November	804.0	520.4	248.2	22.6	41.9	14.0	29.5	15.6	7.4	10.6	16.3	69.1	44.9
December	820.6	534.6	249.4	23.0	41.9	15.0	29.9	15.6	7.3	11.2	17.6	73.8	50.0

[1]Includes categories not shown separately.
. . . = Not available.

Table 16-2. New Construction Put in Place—*Continued*

(Billions of dollars, monthly data are at seasonally adjusted annual rates.)

Year and month	Total	Public													Federal
		State and local													
		Total [1]	Residential	Office	Health care	Educa-tional	Public safety	Amuse-ment and recreation	Transpor-tation	Power	Highway and street	Sewage and waste disposal	Water supply		
1975	43.3	37.2	...	...	...	...	...	...	...	...	...	...	...		6.1
1976	44.0	37.2	...	...	...	...	...	...	...	...	...	...	...		6.8
1977	43.1	36.0	...	...	...	...	...	...	...	...	...	...	...		7.1
1978	50.1	42.0	...	...	...	...	...	...	...	...	...	...	...		8.1
1979	56.6	48.1	...	...	...	...	...	...	...	...	...	...	...		8.6
1980	63.6	54.0	...	...	...	...	...	...	...	...	...	...	...		9.6
1981	64.7	54.3	...	...	...	...	...	...	...	...	...	...	...		10.4
1982	63.1	53.1	...	...	...	...	...	...	...	...	...	...	...		10.0
1983	63.5	52.9	...	...	...	...	...	...	...	...	...	...	...		10.6
1984	70.2	59.0	...	...	...	...	...	...	...	...	...	...	...		11.2
1985	77.8	65.8	...	...	...	...	...	...	...	...	...	...	...		12.0
1986	84.6	72.2	...	...	...	...	...	...	...	...	...	...	...		12.4
1987	90.6	76.6	...	...	...	...	...	...	...	...	...	...	...		14.1
1988	94.7	82.5	...	...	...	...	...	...	...	...	...	...	...		12.3
1989	98.2	86.0	...	...	...	...	...	...	...	...	...	...	...		12.2
1990	107.5	95.4	...	...	...	...	...	...	...	...	...	...	...		12.1
1991	110.1	97.3	...	...	...	...	...	...	...	...	...	...	...		12.8
1992	115.8	101.5	...	...	...	...	...	...	...	...	...	...	...		14.4
1993	127.4	112.9	3.4	2.8	2.3	24.2	4.6	4.3	9.8	7.4	34.5	11.2	6.4		14.4
1994	130.4	116.0	4.2	3.0	2.4	25.3	4.5	4.7	9.2	5.1	37.3	12.0	6.4		14.4
1995	140.0	124.3	4.5	3.3	2.6	27.5	5.0	5.1	9.6	5.7	38.6	13.0	7.3		15.8
1996	146.7	131.4	3.7	3.6	2.8	31.0	5.5	5.0	10.4	4.8	40.6	13.6	7.7		15.3
1997	153.4	139.4	3.3	3.8	2.9	34.3	5.6	5.7	10.3	4.4	44.4	13.1	8.1		14.1
1998	154.8	140.5	3.2	3.7	2.3	35.1	6.1	6.2	10.5	2.8	45.4	13.2	8.9		14.3
1999	169.1	155.1	3.2	3.6	2.5	39.8	6.2	7.2	11.4	2.9	51.0	14.5	9.6		14.0
2000	181.3	167.2	3.0	4.5	2.8	46.8	5.9	7.6	13.0	5.5	51.6	14.0	9.5		14.2
2001	213.4	196.9	3.8	6.3	3.5	59.5	6.0	9.2	17.3	3.8	56.7	15.3	11.7		16.6
2002	213.4	196.9	3.8	6.3	3.5	59.5	6.0	9.2	17.3	3.8	56.7	15.3	11.7		16.6
2003	216.1	198.2	3.7	6.1	4.0	59.3	5.8	8.4	16.5	6.8	56.3	15.6	11.7		17.9
2004	220.2	201.8	4.1	6.0	5.0	59.7	5.5	7.8	16.4	7.0	57.4	17.1	12.0		18.3
2005	234.2	216.9	4.0	5.2	5.1	65.8	6.0	7.3	16.3	8.3	63.2	18.3	13.5		17.3
2006	255.4	237.8	4.3	5.6	5.6	69.8	6.6	9.4	17.7	7.8	71.0	21.5	14.3		17.6
2007	289.1	268.5	5.1	7.2	7.0	78.4	8.4	10.7	21.1	11.4	75.5	23.3	15.0		20.6
2008	308.7	285.0	4.9	8.5	7.0	84.5	9.7	10.9	23.2	11.0	80.4	24.1	16.0		23.7
2009	314.9	286.5	5.8	9.2	6.8	83.7	9.4	10.6	25.5	11.8	81.3	23.5	14.8		28.4
2010	304.0	272.8	7.6	8.3	6.2	71.9	7.6	9.7	26.5	10.8	81.3	24.6	14.4		31.1
2011	283.3	252.9	6.2	7.4	6.9	67.4	7.3	8.5	23.2	8.6	78.0	21.0	13.4		30.4
2009															
January	309.6	281.0	5.2	9.0	6.9	85.5	9.2	10.1	23.6	9.6	79.8	23.4	15.0		28.6
February	321.4	291.7	5.5	9.0	7.1	88.0	9.8	10.7	25.4	11.9	80.9	23.3	15.8		29.6
March	325.5	296.0	5.4	9.1	7.0	90.3	9.6	10.6	23.3	16.3	79.4	25.1	15.5		29.4
April	318.9	292.7	5.3	9.5	6.8	88.6	10.1	10.6	23.4	15.4	79.5	23.9	15.7		26.2
May	317.1	290.9	5.3	9.2	7.2	88.4	10.1	10.9	24.2	12.8	79.7	23.8	14.7		26.2
June	321.0	293.0	5.9	9.4	7.2	87.6	10.0	11.2	24.9	12.5	82.1	23.1	14.9		27.9
July	322.6	293.7	6.5	9.2	6.9	86.5	9.6	10.9	26.8	12.1	83.0	22.9	14.9		28.9
August	314.0	286.0	6.0	8.8	6.6	82.4	9.1	10.6	27.1	11.6	82.5	22.6	14.4		28.5
September	310.9	282.5	6.1	8.9	6.9	78.8	9.0	10.8	27.1	11.0	82.5	22.9	14.3		28.4
October	307.9	278.9	5.8	9.1	6.7	78.1	9.0	10.9	26.1	9.2	82.9	22.7	14.3		29.0
November	302.6	273.8	5.7	9.5	6.3	76.3	8.8	9.8	25.7	9.3	79.1	24.4	14.7		28.9
December	300.3	270.2	6.2	9.3	6.5	75.0	9.1	9.7	25.0	9.2	77.7	23.9	14.7		30.1
2010															
January	295.9	268.1	6.0	8.6	6.2	76.0	8.3	10.2	24.5	9.3	76.6	26.2	12.3		27.7
February	290.3	261.0	5.8	8.2	6.1	74.2	8.3	9.4	25.6	8.4	76.8	22.1	12.8		29.3
March	297.8	268.2	6.6	8.4	6.4	72.4	7.9	9.1	27.7	10.1	78.5	23.8	13.7		29.6
April	306.4	273.6	7.2	8.6	6.0	72.0	7.8	9.6	28.2	10.7	80.4	25.2	14.4		32.8
May	309.3	277.1	7.6	8.1	5.9	72.8	7.8	9.3	28.1	9.0	85.1	24.5	15.2		32.2
June	312.1	278.5	8.2	8.1	5.7	74.2	7.5	9.5	27.2	11.4	82.7	24.6	15.5		33.5
July	304.3	273.5	7.9	8.2	6.3	74.7	7.3	9.8	26.6	11.2	77.2	25.3	15.0		30.8
August	308.4	278.6	8.2	8.6	6.5	73.1	7.2	10.3	25.6	11.2	82.4	26.2	15.2		29.8
September	315.0	281.8	8.1	8.8	6.5	72.5	7.4	10.2	29.3	11.5	83.3	25.1	14.9		33.3
October	306.6	274.0	8.8	8.1	6.4	67.6	7.3	9.9	25.3	12.3	84.3	24.8	14.7		32.5
November	298.9	267.0	8.5	8.1	6.1	66.6	7.4	9.3	24.7	11.5	82.3	23.5	14.5		31.9
December	291.5	263.1	7.4	8.1	6.4	65.7	7.1	9.2	25.9	12.0	80.0	22.9	14.2		28.4
2011															
January	288.1	256.7	6.9	8.0	6.6	66.0	6.9	8.8	24.7	9.8	79.2	21.6	14.1		31.4
February	284.5	253.1	6.5	8.0	6.7	64.9	7.0	9.4	24.2	9.8	77.9	20.8	14.0		31.4
March	286.3	254.9	6.4	7.8	7.0	66.5	7.0	9.5	24.9	9.3	77.3	21.9	13.1		31.4
April	280.2	249.8	6.7	7.9	7.3	66.5	7.1	8.6	24.4	8.9	74.3	20.4	13.4		30.4
May	280.5	248.8	6.4	7.5	7.0	66.9	7.3	8.7	23.7	7.7	75.8	20.8	12.4		31.7
June	284.6	253.8	6.4	7.8	7.2	66.8	7.7	8.3	23.9	9.8	76.5	21.6	12.7		30.8
July	277.7	247.4	5.6	6.9	7.4	66.7	7.0	8.4	22.1	7.6	76.4	20.6	13.9		30.2
August	284.8	253.0	6.3	6.9	7.0	69.3	7.4	7.9	23.8	7.5	77.2	20.4	13.9		31.8
September	283.1	253.8	6.4	7.6	7.2	69.3	7.2	7.7	22.5	7.5	79.4	20.5	13.4		29.3
October	282.9	253.7	6.0	7.0	6.5	69.1	7.2	8.1	22.1	8.1	79.6	20.8	13.8		29.2
November	283.6	255.5	5.7	7.2	6.7	66.8	7.5	8.7	21.6	9.3	82.0	21.2	13.5		28.1
December	286.1	256.1	5.8	6.7	6.9	67.7	7.7	8.8	22.5	9.1	81.4	22.0	12.6		29.9

[1]Includes categories not shown separately.
. . . = Not available.

Table 16-3. Housing Starts and Building Permits; New House Sales and Prices

Year and month	Housing starts and building permits									Shipments of manufactured homes (thousands, seasonally adjusted annual rate)	New house sales and prices			
	New private housing units (thousands)										Seasonally adjusted			
	Started (not seasonally adjusted)			Seasonally adjusted annual rate							Sold (thousands, annual rate)	For sale, end-of-period (thousands)	Median sales price (dollars)	Price index (2005 = 100)
				Started			Authorized by building permits							
	Total [1]	One-family structures	Five units or more	Total [1]	One-family structures	Five units or more	Total [1]	One-family structures	Five units or more					
1975	1 160	892	204	1 160	892	204	939	675	200	213	549	316	39 300	22.1
1976	1 538	1 162	289	1 538	1 162	289	1 296	894	309	246	646	358	44 200	24.0
1977	1 987	1 451	414	1 987	1 451	414	1 690	1 126	443	266	819	408	48 800	27.0
1978	2 020	1 433	462	2 020	1 433	462	1 801	1 183	487	276	817	419	55 700	30.9
1979	1 745	1 194	429	1 745	1 194	429	1 552	982	445	277	709	402	62 900	35.3
1980	1 292	852	331	1 292	852	331	1 191	710	366	222	545	342	64 600	38.9
1981	1 084	705	288	1 084	705	288	986	564	319	241	436	278	68 900	42.0
1982	1 062	663	320	1 062	663	320	1 000	546	366	240	412	255	69 300	43.0
1983	1 703	1 068	522	1 703	1 068	522	1 605	901	570	296	623	304	75 300	43.9
1984	1 750	1 084	544	1 750	1 084	544	1 682	922	617	295	639	358	79 900	45.7
1985	1 742	1 072	576	1 742	1 072	576	1 733	957	657	284	688	350	84 300	46.2
1986	1 805	1 179	542	1 805	1 179	542	1 769	1 078	583	244	750	361	92 000	48.0
1987	1 621	1 146	409	1 621	1 146	409	1 535	1 024	421	233	671	370	104 500	50.6
1988	1 488	1 081	348	1 488	1 081	348	1 456	994	386	218	676	371	112 500	52.5
1989	1 376	1 003	318	1 376	1 003	318	1 338	932	340	198	650	366	120 000	54.6
1990	1 193	895	260	1 193	895	260	1 111	794	263	188	534	321	122 900	55.7
1991	1 014	840	138	1 014	840	138	949	754	152	171	509	284	120 000	56.4
1992	1 200	1 030	139	1 200	1 030	139	1 095	911	138	211	610	267	121 500	57.2
1993	1 288	1 126	133	1 288	1 126	133	1 199	987	160	254	666	295	126 500	59.4
1994	1 457	1 198	224	1 457	1 198	224	1 372	1 068	241	304	670	340	130 000	62.9
1995	1 354	1 076	244	1 354	1 076	244	1 333	997	272	340	667	374	133 900	64.3
1996	1 477	1 161	271	1 477	1 161	271	1 426	1 069	290	363	757	326	140 000	66.0
1997	1 474	1 134	296	1 474	1 134	296	1 441	1 062	310	354	804	287	146 000	67.5
1998	1 617	1 271	303	1 617	1 271	303	1 612	1 188	355	373	886	300	152 500	69.2
1999	1 641	1 302	307	1 641	1 302	307	1 664	1 247	351	348	880	315	161 000	72.8
2000	1 569	1 231	299	1 569	1 231	299	1 592	1 198	329	250	877	301	169 000	75.6
2001	1 603	1 273	293	1 603	1 273	293	1 637	1 236	335	193	908	310	175 200	77.9
2002	1 705	1 359	308	1 705	1 359	308	1 748	1 333	341	169	973	344	187 600	81.4
2003	1 848	1 499	315	1 848	1 499	315	1 889	1 461	346	131	1 086	377	195 000	86.0
2004	1 956	1 611	303	1 956	1 611	303	2 070	1 613	366	131	1 203	431	221 000	92.8
2005	2 068	1 716	311	2 068	1 716	311	2 155	1 682	389	147	1 283	515	240 900	100.0
2006	1 801	1 465	293	1 801	1 465	293	1 839	1 378	384	117	1 051	537	246 500	104.8
2007	1 355	1 046	277	1 355	1 046	277	1 398	980	359	96	776	496	247 900	104.9
2008	906	622	266	906	622	266	905	576	295	82	485	352	232 100	99.5
2009	554	445	97	554	445	97	583	441	121	50	375	234	216 700	95.1
2010	587	471	104	587	471	104	605	447	135	50	323	190	221 800	95.0
2011	609	431	167	609	431	167	624	418	184	52	306	152	227 200	94.3
2009														
January	32	23	8	490	358	119	545	337	185	57	336	341	208 600	. . .
February	40	25	14	582	358	210	558	377	161	54	372	326	209 700	. . .
March	43	31	10	505	353	122	513	361	131	50	339	311	205 100	92.7
April	43	35	7	478	387	80	521	391	109	48	337	300	219 200	. . .
May	52	40	12	540	408	124	556	431	104	48	376	291	222 300	. . .
June	59	49	9	585	482	93	601	458	118	46	393	280	214 700	96.2
July	57	49	6	594	509	70	595	489	87	50	411	270	214 200	. . .
August	53	43	9	586	487	93	616	491	105	48	418	261	207 100	. . .
September	53	46	6	585	510	66	609	477	113	48	386	252	216 600	94.3
October	45	39	5	534	476	53	583	472	95	49	396	243	215 100	. . .
November	42	35	6	588	497	81	623	483	114	51	375	237	218 800	. . .
December	37	30	6	581	484	84	664	508	138	51	352	234	222 600	96.2
2010														
January	39	32	7	614	510	97	636	504	111	51	345	233	218 200	. . .
February	41	35	4	604	526	62	650	510	120	53	336	231	221 900	. . .
March	55	47	7	636	542	86	687	536	128	54	381	227	224 800	94.8
April	62	52	9	687	566	108	637	476	143	54	422	217	208 300	. . .
May	56	45	11	583	457	114	575	435	120	56	280	216	230 500	. . .
June	54	46	8	536	445	86	587	425	139	55	305	212	219 500	95.2
July	52	41	9	546	426	101	579	411	147	51	283	209	212 100	. . .
August	56	39	16	599	417	168	580	402	156	50	282	206	226 600	. . .
September	53	39	13	594	449	139	563	404	131	47	317	201	228 000	94.2
October	45	36	8	543	438	93	558	408	129	44	291	199	204 200	. . .
November	41	33	6	545	452	79	560	418	122	44	287	195	219 600	. . .
December	34	27	7	539	429	101	632	447	160	40	326	190	241 200	96.3
2011														
January	40	27	13	632	433	187	566	417	128	45	308	187	240 100	. . .
February	35	27	8	518	393	108	536	379	141	44	273	183	220 100	. . .
March	50	36	13	600	428	161	590	398	176	47	301	179	220 500	93.7
April	49	38	10	552	414	124	578	401	155	47	312	174	224 700	. . .
May	54	41	13	551	409	136	624	412	191	47	308	169	222 000	. . .
June	61	45	15	615	443	165	633	412	198	49	304	166	240 200	94.5
July	58	41	16	614	429	176	627	417	186	47	297	165	229 900	. . .
August	55	39	15	581	422	152	645	429	189	51	292	161	219 600	. . .
September	59	37	21	647	422	219	616	428	167	55	306	160	217 000	93.0
October	53	36	16	630	439	175	667	444	199	61	314	159	224 800	. . .
November	53	33	20	708	460	239	709	451	235	63	327	155	214 300	. . .
December	43	31	10	697	520	153	701	454	223	58	339	152	218 600	94.0

[1] Includes structures with 2 to 4 units, not shown separately.
. . . = Not available.

Table 16-4. Manufacturers' Shipments

(Millions of dollars, seasonally adjusted.)

Year and month	Total	Total durable goods¹	Total nondurable goods¹	Construction materials and supplies	Information technology industries	Capital goods Total	Nondefense Total	Nondefense Excluding aircraft and parts	Defense	Consumer goods Total	Consumer goods Durable	Consumer goods Nondurable
1992	2 904 024	1 518 862	1 385 162	281 232	236 015	566 268	471 485	435 696	94 783	1 098 480	253 111	845 369
1993	3 020 497	1 604 544	1 415 953	303 391	241 680	580 859	493 875	463 753	86 984	1 127 629	274 813	852 816
1994	3 238 112	1 764 061	1 474 051	332 734	264 092	616 435	538 203	512 327	78 232	1 192 098	314 931	877 167
1995	3 479 677	1 902 815	1 576 862	353 198	291 885	666 167	590 578	565 729	75 589	1 256 611	324 036	932 575
1996	3 597 188	1 978 597	1 618 591	371 401	311 028	704 635	630 932	605 295	73 703	1 292 955	328 402	964 553
1997	3 834 699	2 147 384	1 687 315	399 880	349 846	779 232	702 971	665 074	76 261	1 358 516	360 193	998 323
1998	3 899 813	2 231 588	1 668 225	418 756	362 564	821 736	747 046	695 717	74 690	1 351 812	373 404	978 408
1999	4 031 887	2 326 736	1 705 151	434 138	374 384	839 754	768 799	713 042	70 955	1 424 828	412 646	1 012 182
2000	4 208 584	2 373 688	1 834 896	444 812	399 751	875 396	808 345	757 617	67 051	1 500 532	391 463	1 109 069
2001	3 970 499	2 174 406	1 796 093	424 517	353 237	801 999	728 495	678 288	73 504	1 480 495	367 522	1 112 973
2002	3 914 723	2 123 621	1 791 102	424 008	284 799	728 585	652 342	609 595	76 243	1 494 575	395 953	1 098 622
2003	4 015 388	2 142 589	1 872 799	429 183	274 829	719 602	634 273	600 616	85 329	1 584 329	418 821	1 165 508
2004	4 308 970	2 264 667	2 044 303	463 148	287 837	752 905	661 740	629 146	91 165	1 700 835	419 182	1 281 653
2005	4 742 077	2 424 844	2 317 233	509 865	295 447	821 906	730 368	686 939	91 538	1 895 119	422 555	1 472 564
2006	5 015 552	2 562 194	2 453 358	546 866	319 890	884 199	794 638	744 282	89 561	1 980 031	421 860	1 558 171
2007	5 319 457	2 687 028	2 632 429	560 208	322 846	936 404	836 426	768 662	99 978	2 106 081	421 822	1 684 259
2008	5 468 095	2 619 931	2 848 164	543 769	315 383	953 501	838 116	772 231	115 385	2 252 714	359 362	1 893 352
2009	4 419 501	2 062 631	2 356 870	426 353	264 405	815 857	692 374	636 669	123 483	1 846 487	271 838	1 574 649
2010	4 916 649	2 298 907	2 617 742	445 505	267 451	850 197	722 769	671 685	127 428	2 058 769	329 811	1 728 958
2011	5 491 351	2 515 078	2 976 273	469 764	265 676	892 865	786 619	729 178	106 246	2 372 325	374 938	1 997 387
2008												
January	467 843	229 709	238 134	46 885	27 554	82 029	72 649	64 924	9 380	190 484	34 464	156 020
February	463 395	227 515	235 880	47 198	26 668	79 308	70 168	64 159	9 140	189 630	34 030	155 600
March	459 910	221 554	238 356	45 872	26 473	79 491	70 085	64 619	9 406	188 701	30 723	157 978
April	474 455	227 724	246 731	46 887	26 948	82 094	71 994	65 780	10 100	196 581	31 569	165 012
May	476 550	225 589	250 961	46 404	28 159	82 156	72 287	66 113	9 869	199 559	30 784	168 775
June	482 730	225 490	257 240	46 846	27 374	81 930	72 147	66 047	9 783	203 789	30 500	173 289
July	485 887	227 080	258 807	46 712	26 560	81 223	71 329	64 794	9 894	204 519	30 078	174 441
August	469 089	218 160	250 929	45 828	26 062	79 163	69 370	64 061	9 793	197 059	29 059	168 000
September	454 759	217 519	237 240	44 898	26 340	80 233	70 571	65 548	9 662	187 952	29 304	158 648
October	432 779	205 980	226 799	43 843	24 115	75 232	65 426	61 400	9 806	176 273	27 598	148 675
November	398 533	196 236	202 297	41 031	24 426	74 272	64 733	61 498	9 539	158 255	26 411	131 844
December	380 830	191 035	189 795	38 720	24 566	75 421	66 518	61 339	8 903	148 326	24 742	123 584
2009												
January	366 663	176 110	190 553	37 236	21 960	70 049	61 535	55 258	8 514	149 492	22 830	126 662
February	368 417	175 697	192 720	37 694	22 987	70 338	60 271	55 864	10 067	149 301	22 446	126 855
March	357 372	171 927	185 445	35 860	22 731	69 162	59 549	54 813	9 613	144 250	22 191	122 059
April	353 327	167 039	186 288	35 032	21 308	66 501	56 584	51 932	9 917	145 733	22 271	123 462
May	353 068	163 970	189 098	34 699	21 413	66 453	56 338	51 934	10 115	147 357	21 286	126 071
June	361 620	163 464	198 156	34 618	21 952	67 189	56 706	52 588	10 483	153 950	19 742	134 208
July	365 603	170 788	194 815	35 349	22 491	66 983	56 787	52 640	10 196	152 275	22 325	129 950
August	368 104	169 237	198 867	35 149	22 025	65 509	54 939	51 295	10 570	156 396	22 882	133 514
September	375 344	174 105	201 239	35 373	21 708	68 410	57 465	52 035	10 945	158 439	23 286	135 153
October	380 038	174 603	205 435	35 285	22 381	67 514	56 562	52 329	10 952	162 317	23 499	138 818
November	385 014	177 080	207 934	35 424	22 346	68 339	57 190	52 902	11 149	163 928	24 562	139 366
December	390 895	181 884	209 011	35 172	21 488	69 817	59 206	53 673	10 611	165 561	25 154	140 407
2010												
January	394 974	184 239	210 735	35 696	22 132	68 845	56 982	53 106	11 863	167 614	26 225	141 389
February	393 326	180 423	212 903	36 036	22 067	69 373	57 950	54 165	11 423	165 352	24 279	141 073
March	400 474	182 346	218 128	36 492	22 390	70 444	59 122	55 037	11 322	169 807	24 813	144 994
April	405 218	188 719	216 499	37 768	22 148	69 968	58 908	54 823	11 060	168 352	25 892	142 460
May	403 646	189 553	214 093	38 126	22 103	69 724	59 096	55 588	10 628	167 484	26 537	140 947
June	401 895	188 561	213 334	37 404	22 068	70 778	60 320	56 288	10 458	167 108	26 787	140 321
July	414 400	199 953	214 447	37 113	22 619	72 473	61 833	55 982	10 640	170 588	29 843	140 745
August	412 079	195 461	216 618	37 154	22 180	70 952	60 983	56 389	9 969	170 909	29 035	141 874
September	417 727	197 358	220 369	37 051	22 368	71 958	61 317	57 299	10 641	174 030	29 626	144 404
October	419 567	196 166	223 401	37 344	22 485	71 173	61 175	56 777	9 998	176 739	29 149	147 590
November	424 232	196 502	227 730	37 658	22 791	71 247	61 452	57 538	9 795	179 525	28 558	150 967
December	434 269	201 117	233 152	37 420	22 544	73 582	63 699	58 855	9 883	184 976	29 734	155 242
2011												
January	440 892	201 174	239 718	38 191	22 331	71 319	62 022	58 207	9 297	190 435	30 176	160 259
February	441 022	201 176	239 846	38 023	22 047	71 455	61 866	57 611	9 589	190 647	30 608	160 039
March	454 480	208 781	245 699	38 889	22 174	73 946	64 048	59 651	9 898	196 616	32 196	164 420
April	453 257	204 541	248 716	38 415	22 196	72 896	63 645	59 318	9 251	197 757	30 536	167 221
May	453 933	206 082	247 851	38 789	22 252	73 442	64 329	60 169	9 113	195 981	30 315	165 666
June	456 833	207 567	249 266	39 146	22 343	74 135	65 294	60 988	8 841	197 432	30 488	166 944
July	467 495	217 802	249 693	39 370	22 059	74 787	66 350	61 156	8 437	202 612	35 255	167 357
August	464 589	213 170	251 419	39 698	22 204	76 905	68 212	62 928	8 693	199 680	31 005	168 675
September	463 879	211 477	252 402	39 323	22 226	76 013	67 436	62 276	8 577	200 813	30 451	170 362
October	466 604	215 099	251 505	39 884	21 901	76 113	68 156	62 021	7 957	201 729	32 310	169 419
November	466 392	214 251	252 141	39 902	21 668	74 749	66 837	61 720	7 912	202 049	31 812	170 237
December	470 761	219 924	250 837	40 362	22 296	77 107	68 444	63 371	8 663	200 409	31 827	168 582

¹Includes categories not shown separately.

Table 16-5. Manufacturers' Inventories

(Current cost basis, end of period; seasonally adjusted, millions of dollars.)

Year and month	Total	Total durable goods [1]	Durables total by stage of fabrication			Total nondurable goods[1]	Nondurables total by stage of fabrication		
			Materials and supplies	Work in process	Finished goods		Materials and supplies	Work in process	Finished goods
1992	378 710	237 914	69 658	104 185	64 071	140 796	53 148	23 420	64 228
1993	379 778	238 766	72 637	102 034	64 095	141 012	54 206	23 404	63 402
1994	399 924	253 104	78 574	106 556	67 974	146 820	57 087	24 448	65 285
1995	424 761	267 382	85 529	106 655	75 198	157 379	60 753	25 772	70 854
1996	430 430	272 466	86 288	110 616	75 562	157 964	59 151	26 472	72 341
1997	443 435	280 961	92 290	109 906	78 765	162 474	60 157	28 516	73 801
1998	448 853	290 472	93 529	115 151	81 792	158 381	58 229	27 077	73 075
1999	463 465	296 464	97 856	114 037	84 571	167 001	61 038	28 763	77 200
2000	481 184	306 394	106 039	111 025	89 330	174 790	61 496	29 996	83 298
2001	427 751	267 633	91 261	93 845	82 527	160 118	55 754	27 053	77 311
2002	422 924	260 394	88 494	92 367	79 533	162 530	56 597	27 826	78 107
2003	408 216	246 854	82 283	88 644	75 927	161 362	56 894	27 017	77 451
2004	440 760	265 005	92 089	91 109	81 807	175 755	61 830	29 877	84 048
2005	473 921	283 742	98 470	98 738	86 534	190 179	66 948	32 828	90 403
2006	522 568	317 506	111 543	106 643	99 320	205 062	70 375	36 989	97 698
2007	561 835	334 621	116 406	117 720	100 495	227 214	75 217	44 954	107 043
2008	541 561	330 298	117 583	111 993	100 722	211 263	72 087	41 112	98 064
2009	504 636	296 449	100 596	107 264	88 589	208 187	71 403	41 928	94 856
2010	549 239	324 525	106 977	123 470	94 078	224 714	76 207	44 292	104 215
2011	600 825	358 105	116 916	138 328	102 861	242 720	81 580	46 781	114 359
2008									
January	569 627	334 518	116 592	117 832	100 094	235 109	78 387	47 924	108 798
February	570 970	334 814	116 993	117 717	100 104	236 156	78 228	49 142	108 786
March	574 271	336 884	117 698	118 446	100 740	237 387	78 985	48 782	109 620
April	573 835	336 791	117 613	118 162	101 016	237 044	79 737	48 102	109 205
May	574 080	336 897	117 866	117 752	101 279	237 183	80 387	49 552	107 244
June	580 972	336 712	118 405	116 680	101 627	244 260	82 844	49 203	112 213
July	581 283	337 687	119 935	115 912	101 840	243 596	82 262	50 715	110 619
August	582 649	338 302	120 182	115 222	102 898	244 347	82 912	50 632	110 803
September	576 303	336 506	120 488	113 423	102 595	239 797	82 528	49 655	107 614
October	568 302	335 680	120 126	113 212	102 342	232 622	80 022	46 104	106 496
November	559 309	333 784	120 184	112 329	101 271	225 525	76 819	44 169	104 537
December	541 561	330 298	117 583	111 993	100 722	211 263	72 087	41 112	98 064
2009									
January	537 293	328 389	117 712	111 716	98 961	208 904	70 525	41 891	96 488
February	529 681	324 642	116 974	110 524	97 144	205 039	68 892	41 024	95 123
March	523 394	318 254	113 914	108 964	95 376	205 140	68 338	41 712	95 090
April	516 779	314 336	111 798	108 063	94 475	202 443	67 037	41 435	93 971
May	512 755	310 128	109 486	107 848	92 794	202 627	67 436	41 351	93 840
June	507 311	304 059	105 389	107 392	91 278	203 252	67 922	41 149	94 181
July	503 694	301 295	103 400	107 607	90 288	202 399	68 299	40 683	93 417
August	501 140	297 346	102 055	105 836	89 455	203 794	68 293	41 209	94 292
September	498 038	295 437	101 887	105 357	88 193	202 601	67 786	41 264	93 551
October	501 053	295 866	101 121	106 606	88 139	205 187	68 297	41 612	95 278
November	503 995	296 857	100 728	107 729	88 400	207 138	69 698	41 737	95 703
December	504 636	296 449	100 596	107 264	88 589	208 187	71 403	41 928	94 856
2010									
January	505 664	297 440	100 122	108 327	88 991	208 224	70 612	41 066	96 546
February	510 388	299 657	100 984	109 669	89 004	210 731	71 878	41 744	97 109
March	512 931	300 962	101 397	110 120	89 445	211 969	72 359	42 298	97 312
April	515 165	302 986	101 567	111 568	89 851	212 179	71 510	42 180	98 489
May	513 891	305 430	102 259	112 433	90 738	208 461	69 534	40 920	98 007
June	517 860	309 371	103 831	113 936	91 604	208 489	69 887	40 644	97 958
July	520 554	310 912	103 670	114 702	92 540	209 642	70 619	40 535	98 488
August	523 491	312 865	103 790	115 958	93 117	210 626	70 099	41 162	99 365
September	528 945	315 847	104 182	118 005	93 660	213 098	71 324	41 035	100 739
October	535 081	318 654	105 114	119 248	94 292	216 427	72 104	42 015	102 308
November	541 292	322 047	106 143	121 036	94 868	219 245	73 423	42 459	103 363
December	549 239	324 525	106 977	123 470	94 078	224 714	76 207	44 292	104 215
2011									
January	556 808	328 196	108 104	124 972	95 120	228 612	76 961	44 685	106 966
February	563 565	332 227	108 985	126 409	96 833	231 338	78 736	45 179	107 423
March	571 115	337 907	109 979	129 883	98 045	233 208	79 073	45 160	108 975
April	579 290	341 067	111 504	130 952	98 611	238 223	79 729	46 639	111 855
May	584 012	345 619	112 791	133 202	99 626	238 393	79 942	46 284	112 167
June	585 643	347 267	113 086	134 049	100 132	238 376	79 313	46 569	112 494
July	588 875	350 260	113 724	135 423	101 113	238 615	79 131	46 129	113 355
August	591 799	353 297	114 651	136 327	102 319	238 502	80 239	45 060	113 203
September	591 168	353 185	114 948	135 576	102 661	237 983	79 086	45 286	113 611
October	597 571	355 393	115 382	136 802	103 209	242 178	81 853	46 270	114 055
November	600 646	357 659	116 001	138 270	103 388	242 987	81 579	46 476	114 932
December	600 825	358 105	116 916	138 328	102 861	242 720	81 580	46 781	114 359

[1]Includes categories not shown separately.

Table 16-5. Manufacturers' Inventories—*Continued*

(Current cost basis, end of period; seasonally adjusted, millions of dollars.)

Year and month	Construction materials and supplies	Information technology industries	By topical categories Capital goods Total	Capital goods Nondefense Total	Capital goods Nondefense Excluding aircraft and parts	Defense	Consumer goods Total	Consumer goods Durable	Consumer goods Nondurable
1992	36 719	40 172	120 465	97 321	78 884	23 144	103 377	20 854	82 523
1993	38 311	39 185	118 465	97 148	79 591	21 317	104 824	21 855	82 969
1994	40 909	41 560	123 402	103 385	85 747	20 017	109 539	23 964	85 575
1995	43 441	46 940	129 746	111 625	94 695	18 121	116 374	25 307	91 067
1996	44 142	43 568	132 832	115 307	93 488	17 525	116 366	24 762	91 604
1997	45 691	48 117	137 644	122 662	98 874	14 982	119 662	24 932	94 730
1998	46 446	45 313	145 126	127 147	97 371	17 979	117 486	24 946	92 540
1999	48 479	46 187	146 387	126 348	99 658	20 039	124 284	26 138	98 146
2000	50 454	52 744	149 182	131 768	110 196	17 414	130 880	27 289	103 591
2001	46 312	42 986	128 787	114 985	93 341	13 802	121 543	25 403	96 140
2002	46 590	39 028	122 515	108 066	88 563	14 449	124 750	25 662	99 088
2003	45 350	35 244	115 066	99 229	81 784	15 837	124 944	24 983	99 961
2004	51 243	33 172	117 838	99 064	83 822	18 774	133 858	26 227	107 631
2005	55 102	39 226	127 343	110 763	92 992	16 580	144 824	28 091	116 733
2006	60 874	39 951	139 658	122 611	101 907	17 047	153 508	27 775	125 733
2007	62 533	38 765	150 371	131 514	104 763	18 857	171 777	27 731	144 046
2008	61 699	37 480	150 834	134 281	107 290	16 553	154 388	24 524	129 864
2009	51 518	36 920	145 411	126 061	97 710	19 350	158 924	21 912	137 012
2010	54 715	37 185	160 573	140 190	103 926	20 383	169 061	23 364	145 697
2011	58 719	38 395	181 505	160 837	114 891	20 668	181 679	24 944	156 735
2008									
January	62 662	38 539	150 800	132 298	104 940	18 502	178 427	27 357	151 070
February	62 344	38 524	150 973	132 388	105 447	18 585	178 485	27 182	151 303
March	62 042	38 996	152 399	134 023	106 677	18 376	179 534	27 105	152 429
April	62 218	38 983	152 178	133 598	106 922	18 580	178 233	26 455	151 778
May	62 483	38 641	151 565	133 280	106 644	18 285	177 882	26 129	151 753
June	62 584	38 353	150 725	132 815	106 693	17 910	185 044	26 053	158 991
July	63 190	38 110	151 264	133 589	107 321	17 675	182 785	25 773	157 012
August	63 463	38 143	151 073	133 783	107 574	17 290	182 271	25 580	156 691
September	63 536	37 940	149 855	132 994	107 433	16 861	179 095	25 661	153 434
October	63 151	37 631	150 011	133 175	107 445	16 836	171 812	25 613	146 199
November	62 435	37 218	150 128	133 243	107 067	16 885	164 772	25 186	139 586
December	61 699	37 480	150 834	134 281	107 290	16 553	154 388	24 524	129 864
2009									
January	61 020	37 097	151 271	133 936	107 016	17 335	153 853	24 348	129 505
February	59 195	37 122	151 314	133 975	106 309	17 339	151 128	23 901	127 227
March	57 632	36 821	149 652	132 057	104 551	17 595	152 090	23 683	128 407
April	56 061	37 281	149 811	131 864	103 963	17 947	151 344	23 487	127 857
May	54 695	37 121	148 917	130 723	102 574	18 194	152 433	23 065	129 368
June	53 498	36 174	147 517	129 442	100 691	18 075	152 776	22 297	130 479
July	52 791	36 125	146 751	128 374	99 052	18 377	152 515	21 985	130 530
August	52 058	36 092	145 119	126 656	98 273	18 463	154 274	21 890	132 384
September	51 800	36 265	143 776	125 281	97 791	18 495	152 769	21 640	131 129
October	51 634	36 368	145 235	126 166	97 468	19 069	155 177	21 438	133 739
November	51 587	36 625	146 560	127 158	97 566	19 402	156 736	21 502	135 234
December	51 518	36 920	145 411	126 061	97 710	19 350	158 924	21 912	137 012
2010									
January	51 709	37 139	146 815	126 912	97 779	19 903	158 281	22 090	136 191
February	51 371	37 304	147 842	127 718	97 895	20 124	160 722	22 431	138 291
March	52 243	36 548	147 224	127 068	97 174	20 156	160 603	22 539	138 064
April	52 529	36 504	148 159	128 291	97 506	19 868	160 274	22 673	137 601
May	52 750	36 590	149 154	129 403	98 213	19 751	155 680	22 977	132 703
June	53 577	37 230	151 233	131 336	99 469	19 897	155 506	23 152	132 354
July	53 800	37 072	152 217	132 237	100 293	19 980	156 560	23 255	133 305
August	53 921	37 111	153 357	133 466	100 936	19 891	157 364	23 417	133 947
September	54 233	37 097	155 728	136 005	101 679	19 723	159 402	23 282	136 120
October	54 153	37 353	157 603	137 706	102 824	19 897	162 204	23 281	138 923
November	54 428	37 364	159 540	139 065	103 512	20 475	164 362	23 529	140 833
December	54 715	37 185	160 573	140 190	103 926	20 383	169 061	23 364	145 697
2011									
January	55 212	37 310	163 025	142 580	105 004	20 445	170 943	23 639	147 304
February	55 712	37 702	164 925	144 474	106 329	20 451	173 091	23 936	149 155
March	56 380	38 442	168 924	147 546	107 917	21 378	174 565	23 943	150 622
April	57 089	38 888	170 847	149 747	109 299	21 100	178 686	24 017	154 669
May	57 823	39 236	173 615	152 138	110 729	21 477	177 885	24 193	153 692
June	57 694	39 399	175 053	154 049	111 616	21 004	176 859	24 146	152 713
July	57 802	39 565	176 793	155 709	112 598	21 084	176 882	24 473	152 409
August	58 046	39 662	178 785	157 580	113 670	21 205	176 319	24 609	151 710
September	58 096	39 403	178 334	157 729	113 878	20 605	175 627	24 822	150 805
October	58 242	39 423	180 265	159 423	115 005	20 842	179 599	24 930	154 669
November	58 697	39 363	181 879	160 775	115 725	21 104	181 015	24 782	156 233
December	58 719	38 395	181 505	160 837	114 891	20 668	181 679	24 944	156 735

Table 16-6. Manufacturers' New Orders

(Net, millions of dollars, seasonally adjusted.)

Year and month	Total [1]	Total durable goods [1]	By topical categories								
					Capital goods				Consumer goods		
			Construction materials and supplies	Information technology industries	Total	Nondefense		Defense	Total	Durable	Nondurable
						Total	Excluding aircraft and parts				
1993	2 960 015	1 544 062	304 264	239 387	561 097	488 166	466 433	72 931	1 128 447	275 631	852 816
1994	3 199 686	1 725 635	335 962	265 010	616 252	542 094	523 461	74 158	1 192 584	315 417	877 167
1995	3 426 503	1 849 641	355 161	297 605	680 857	612 132	576 769	68 725	1 256 721	324 146	932 575
1996	3 567 384	1 948 793	373 536	310 074	737 268	648 797	607 174	88 471	1 293 537	328 984	964 553
1997	3 779 835	2 092 520	403 860	352 700	792 859	728 362	676 119	64 497	1 360 010	361 687	998 323
1998	3 808 143	2 139 918	419 330	365 723	809 727	745 600	698 279	64 127	1 352 708	374 300	978 408
1999	3 957 242	2 252 091	435 034	389 160	840 603	772 703	728 089	67 900	1 425 617	413 435	1 012 182
2000	4 161 472	2 326 576	446 792	409 500	910 933	831 335	767 754	79 598	1 501 810	392 741	1 109 069
2001	3 868 319	2 072 226	421 030	337 677	776 306	693 270	658 261	83 036	1 477 155	364 182	1 112 973
2002	3 822 414	2 031 312	423 691	274 230	699 862	624 023	590 461	75 839	1 494 103	395 481	1 098 622
2003	3 974 420	2 101 621	431 662	282 645	737 515	638 000	609 074	99 515	1 585 016	419 508	1 165 508
2004	4 288 486	2 244 183	468 865	294 216	789 019	690 780	645 550	98 239	1 701 561	419 908	1 281 653
2005	4 765 683	2 448 450	517 054	300 650	899 669	817 810	706 089	81 859	1 894 055	421 491	1 472 564
2006	5 089 847	2 636 489	549 724	333 013	996 741	894 384	778 580	102 357	1 979 173	421 002	1 558 171
2007	5 398 585	2 766 156	565 293	324 465	1 066 490	963 308	789 746	103 182	2 105 788	421 529	1 684 259
2008	5 447 159	2 598 995	543 568	315 076	1 009 928	883 378	783 332	126 550	2 251 442	358 090	1 893 352
2009	4 167 256	1 810 386	414 152	255 862	658 757	554 497	590 323	104 260	1 846 046	271 397	1 574 649
2010	4 919 387	2 301 645	453 151	281 563	901 543	758 092	690 773	143 451	2 058 555	329 597	1 728 958
2011	5 501 484	2 525 211	472 718	266 764	968 096	858 049	761 475	110 047	2 372 435	375 048	1 997 387
2008											
January	474 714	236 580	47 893	27 345	94 017	84 512	68 292	9 505	190 162	34 142	156 020
February	468 431	232 551	46 640	26 822	89 805	79 803	66 064	10 002	189 514	33 914	155 600
March	469 586	231 230	46 652	26 054	90 919	81 274	67 515	9 645	188 739	30 761	157 978
April	476 987	230 256	47 701	26 985	89 104	80 031	69 822	9 073	196 680	31 668	165 012
May	481 301	230 340	46 785	28 507	90 702	80 597	68 916	10 105	199 335	30 560	168 775
June	486 971	229 731	47 699	28 365	88 835	77 250	68 723	11 585	203 966	30 677	173 289
July	485 579	226 772	46 940	26 586	87 082	77 250	68 369	9 832	204 318	29 877	174 441
August	466 613	215 684	45 652	26 111	82 086	71 932	66 885	10 154	196 889	28 889	168 000
September	449 972	212 732	43 801	25 596	83 360	70 063	63 744	13 297	187 956	29 308	158 648
October	418 190	191 391	43 236	23 464	72 920	63 979	58 441	8 941	175 762	27 087	148 675
November	385 557	183 260	39 757	25 305	71 480	61 759	60 285	9 721	158 129	26 285	131 844
December	362 089	172 294	38 069	23 809	69 470	54 302	54 472	15 168	148 213	24 629	123 584
2009											
January	338 175	147 622	34 319	20 662	52 203	46 170	46 781	6 033	149 386	22 724	126 662
February	335 807	143 087	35 553	22 034	50 389	41 871	48 016	8 518	149 063	22 208	126 855
March	326 804	141 359	33 417	22 455	50 521	42 866	47 905	7 655	144 148	22 089	122 059
April	328 058	141 770	33 423	20 565	50 505	40 737	45 543	9 768	145 621	22 159	123 462
May	336 330	147 232	33 472	21 241	57 486	46 503	47 324	10 983	147 237	21 166	126 071
June	343 157	145 001	33 067	21 262	54 706	47 143	49 729	7 563	153 858	19 650	134 208
July	352 660	157 845	34 329	21 582	60 313	51 334	49 678	8 979	152 346	22 396	129 950
August	353 017	154 150	34 636	20 870	54 971	46 114	48 577	8 857	156 451	22 937	133 514
September	359 083	157 844	35 211	21 143	58 654	49 152	51 691	9 502	158 466	23 313	135 153
October	366 248	160 813	36 107	21 773	59 029	50 494	50 719	8 535	162 297	23 479	138 818
November	366 793	158 859	35 685	21 492	56 763	48 278	51 301	8 485	163 967	24 601	139 366
December	367 949	158 938	35 126	21 108	55 043	46 041	52 885	9 002	165 679	25 272	140 407
2010											
January	391 779	181 044	35 765	22 075	70 353	57 381	51 465	12 972	167 837	26 448	141 389
February	391 599	178 696	36 502	21 764	72 639	60 503	53 039	12 136	165 207	24 134	141 073
March	399 940	181 812	37 419	23 698	71 076	58 325	56 585	12 751	169 734	24 740	144 994
April	406 199	189 700	38 525	23 503	76 268	63 868	55 101	12 400	168 554	26 094	142 460
May	403 774	189 681	38 173	23 094	74 787	62 335	57 944	12 452	167 425	26 478	140 947
June	404 208	190 874	38 236	23 718	77 550	66 043	60 870	11 507	166 996	26 675	140 321
July	413 338	198 891	37 916	23 678	75 508	63 656	56 931	11 852	170 408	29 663	140 745
August	409 411	192 793	38 188	24 306	73 336	61 887	58 999	11 449	170 730	28 856	141 874
September	426 038	205 669	38 050	24 850	84 182	71 531	60 212	12 651	174 000	29 596	144 404
October	420 480	197 079	37 215	22 346	78 435	68 273	57 552	10 162	176 722	29 132	147 590
November	428 538	200 808	38 568	24 347	76 369	64 403	60 838	11 966	179 550	28 583	150 967
December	431 583	198 431	38 547	24 659	72 189	60 642	61 750	11 547	185 062	29 820	155 242
2011											
January	442 260	202 542	39 386	22 121	77 677	64 640	60 254	13 037	190 316	30 057	160 259
February	435 486	195 640	38 698	22 622	73 365	64 742	59 452	8 623	190 688	30 649	160 039
March	457 096	211 397	39 120	21 543	82 216	71 772	62 508	10 444	196 669	32 249	164 420
April	450 343	201 627	38 742	21 439	76 774	66 598	62 196	10 176	197 752	30 531	167 221
May	455 513	207 662	39 101	22 227	80 133	70 328	64 086	9 805	195 918	30 252	165 666
June	454 563	205 297	39 348	23 085	79 902	69 875	64 782	10 027	197 438	30 494	166 944
July	469 642	219 949	39 620	21 921	81 999	72 842	65 197	9 157	202 619	35 262	167 357
August	464 209	212 790	39 397	22 543	82 468	73 477	62 998	8 991	199 547	30 872	168 675
September	465 368	212 966	39 212	22 794	82 902	73 056	65 082	9 846	200 827	30 465	170 362
October	463 563	212 058	39 862	22 923	78 545	71 497	66 435	7 048	201 802	32 383	169 419
November	471 400	219 259	40 368	21 617	83 190	75 804	62 767	7 386	202 192	31 955	170 237
December	481 229	230 392	40 231	22 035	89 578	84 115	66 710	5 463	200 505	31 923	168 582

[1]Includes categories not shown separately.

Table 16-7. Manufacturers' Unfilled Orders, Durable Goods Industries

(End of period, millions of dollars, seasonally adjusted.)

Year and month	Total [1]	Transportation equipment		By topical categories							
		Nondefense aircraft and parts	Defense aircraft and parts	Construction materials and supplies	Information technology industries	Capital goods					Consumer durable goods
						Total	Nondefense			Defense	
							Total	Excluding aircraft and parts			
1992	451 312	127 664	49 635	20 916	80 268	319 074	179 591	92 512	139 483	3 861
1993	425 915	110 999	46 671	21 797	77 956	299 256	173 870	95 274	125 386	4 696
1994	435 131	101 161	44 710	25 122	79 033	299 287	177 994	106 764	121 293	5 249
1995	447 570	109 448	42 350	27 177	84 894	313 990	199 632	118 022	114 358	5 348
1996	488 988	130 498	45 178	29 449	84 151	346 496	217 502	120 167	128 994	5 876
1997	513 023	143 321	40 812	33 607	87 271	360 280	243 018	131 640	117 262	7 353
1998	496 233	137 352	37 716	34 264	90 599	348 147	241 245	134 063	106 902	8 315
1999	505 514	126 352	35 608	35 239	105 573	349 252	245 298	149 343	103 954	9 159
2000	549 389	138 172	42 458	37 372	115 549	384 735	268 186	159 672	116 549	10 494
2001	509 702	123 876	51 523	33 797	99 869	358 752	232 505	139 154	126 247	7 119
2002	478 699	112 851	57 050	33 504	89 319	330 114	204 159	119 977	125 955	6 655
2003	504 274	107 365	62 684	36 066	97 261	348 085	207 941	128 580	140 144	7 321
2004	556 110	119 898	55 228	41 971	103 545	383 846	236 716	145 117	147 130	8 163
2005	653 400	185 328	52 247	49 314	108 818	460 249	322 786	164 408	137 463	7 225
2006	797 129	260 687	55 760	52 118	121 957	571 832	421 368	198 967	150 464	6 429
2007	947 570	371 510	58 034	57 227	123 288	700 456	546 560	220 168	153 896	6 120
2008	996 797	410 475	65 759	56 928	122 992	757 684	592 035	231 414	165 649	4 655
2009	802 460	321 858	54 859	44 382	114 389	602 003	455 606	184 300	146 397	4 175
2010	879 247	337 787	56 568	52 224	128 532	654 178	491 616	203 739	162 562	3 916
2011	969 434	381 953	59 891	55 317	129 705	730 060	563 723	236 790	166 337	4 029
2008										
January	961 369	380 839	58 442	58 235	123 079	712 444	558 423	223 536	154 021	5 798
February	973 123	389 303	58 382	57 677	123 233	722 941	568 058	225 441	154 883	5 682
March	989 322	398 185	59 242	58 457	122 814	734 369	579 247	228 337	155 122	5 720
April	997 865	402 064	59 385	59 271	122 851	741 379	587 284	232 379	154 095	5 819
May	1 008 106	408 200	60 527	59 652	123 199	749 925	595 594	235 182	154 331	5 595
June	1 017 206	411 112	60 566	60 505	124 190	756 830	600 697	237 858	156 133	5 772
July	1 023 153	413 870	61 240	60 733	124 216	762 689	606 618	241 433	156 071	5 571
August	1 026 144	413 543	61 979	60 557	124 265	765 612	609 180	244 257	156 432	5 401
September	1 026 698	415 993	62 720	59 460	123 521	768 739	608 672	242 453	160 067	5 405
October	1 017 535	417 873	63 572	58 853	122 870	766 427	607 225	239 494	159 202	4 894
November	1 009 451	416 768	64 384	57 579	123 749	763 635	604 251	238 281	159 384	4 768
December	996 797	410 475	65 759	56 928	122 992	757 684	592 035	231 414	165 649	4 655
2009										
January	972 844	406 439	64 010	54 011	121 694	739 838	576 670	222 937	163 168	4 549
February	944 416	395 268	63 330	51 870	120 741	719 889	558 270	215 089	161 619	4 311
March	918 399	385 380	62 938	49 427	120 465	701 248	541 587	208 181	159 661	4 209
April	898 111	375 777	62 563	47 818	119 722	685 252	525 740	201 792	159 512	4 097
May	886 162	370 647	61 307	46 591	119 550	676 285	515 905	197 182	160 380	3 977
June	871 579	363 944	61 789	45 040	118 860	663 802	506 342	194 323	157 460	3 885
July	863 794	361 065	61 449	44 020	117 951	657 132	500 889	191 361	156 243	3 956
August	853 571	355 258	60 249	43 507	116 796	646 594	492 064	188 643	154 530	4 011
September	842 104	346 785	58 022	43 345	116 231	636 838	483 751	188 299	153 087	4 038
October	833 359	342 273	57 132	44 167	115 623	628 353	477 683	186 689	150 670	4 018
November	819 968	335 516	55 347	44 428	114 769	616 777	468 771	185 088	148 006	4 057
December	802 460	321 858	54 859	44 382	114 389	602 003	455 606	184 300	146 397	4 175
2010										
January	806 633	323 247	56 304	44 451	114 332	603 511	456 005	182 659	147 506	4 398
February	810 229	326 284	56 110	44 917	114 029	606 777	458 558	181 533	148 219	4 253
March	813 569	323 460	55 881	45 844	115 337	607 409	457 761	183 081	149 648	4 180
April	821 267	328 099	55 239	46 601	116 692	613 709	462 721	183 359	150 988	4 382
May	827 101	328 918	55 019	46 648	117 683	618 772	465 960	185 715	152 812	4 323
June	833 191	329 627	55 198	47 480	119 333	625 544	471 683	190 297	153 861	4 211
July	838 729	330 932	55 102	48 283	120 392	628 579	473 506	191 246	155 073	4 031
August	842 588	328 956	54 720	49 317	122 518	630 963	474 410	193 856	156 553	3 852
September	857 422	336 445	56 064	50 316	125 000	643 187	484 624	196 769	158 563	3 822
October	864 630	342 967	55 968	50 187	124 861	650 449	491 722	197 544	158 727	3 805
November	875 342	343 054	56 432	51 097	126 417	655 571	494 673	200 844	160 898	3 830
December	879 247	337 787	56 568	52 224	128 532	654 178	491 616	203 739	162 562	3 916
2011										
January	887 116	338 808	57 339	53 419	128 322	660 536	494 234	205 786	166 302	3 797
February	888 337	339 916	57 341	54 094	128 897	662 446	497 110	207 627	165 336	3 838
March	897 489	344 691	57 496	54 325	128 266	670 716	504 834	210 484	165 882	3 891
April	901 244	345 438	57 491	54 652	127 509	674 594	507 787	213 362	166 807	3 886
May	909 446	347 926	58 460	54 964	127 484	681 285	513 786	217 279	167 499	3 823
June	913 890	349 022	58 429	55 166	128 226	687 052	518 367	221 073	168 685	3 829
July	922 570	352 376	58 392	55 416	128 088	694 264	524 859	225 114	169 405	3 836
August	928 914	357 798	59 722	55 115	128 427	699 827	530 124	225 184	169 703	3 703
September	937 149	360 522	59 281	55 004	128 995	706 716	535 744	227 990	170 972	3 717
October	940 858	360 108	59 454	54 982	130 017	709 148	539 085	232 404	170 063	3 790
November	952 624	368 511	59 897	55 448	129 966	717 589	548 052	233 451	169 537	3 933
December	969 434	381 953	59 891	55 317	129 705	730 060	563 723	236 790	166 337	4 029

[1]Includes categories not shown separately.

Table 16-8. Motor Vehicle Sales and Inventories

(Units.)

Year and month	Retail sales of new passenger cars						Retail inventories of new domestic passenger cars (thousands of units, end of period)		
	Thousands of units, not seasonally adjusted			Millions of units, seasonally adjusted annual rate			Not seasonally adjusted	Seasonally adjusted	Inventory to sales ratio
	Total	Domestic	Foreign	Total	Domestic	Foreign			
1970	8 402.6	7 119.4	1 283.2	8.403	7.119	1.283	. . .	. . .	. . .
1971	10 227.9	8 661.8	1 566.0	10.228	8.662	1.566	. . .	. . .	. . .
1972	10 873.4	9 252.6	1 620.7	10.873	9.253	1.621	1 311.0	1 379.0	1.700
1973	11 350.2	9 588.6	1 761.5	11.350	9.589	1.762	1 600.0	1 654.0	2.500
1974	8 773.7	7 361.8	1 411.9	8.774	7.362	1.412	1 672.0	1 730.0	3.400
1975	8 537.9	6 950.9	1 586.9	8.538	6.951	1.587	1 419.0	1 468.0	2.200
1976	9 994.0	8 492.0	1 502.0	9.994	8.492	1.502	1 465.0	1 494.0	1.900
1977	11 046.0	8 971.2	2 074.8	11.046	8.971	2.075	1 731.0	1 743.0	2.300
1978	11 164.0	9 163.9	2 000.1	11.164	9.164	2.000	1 729.0	1 731.0	2.300
1979	10 558.8	8 230.1	2 328.7	10.559	8.230	2.329	1 691.0	1 667.0	2.400
1980	8 981.8	6 581.4	2 400.4	8.982	6.581	2.401	1 448.0	1 440.0	2.600
1981	8 534.3	6 208.8	2 325.5	8.534	6.209	2.326	1 471.0	1 495.0	3.600
1982	7 979.4	5 758.2	2 221.2	7.980	5.758	2.221	1 126.0	1 127.0	2.200
1983	9 178.6	6 793.0	2 385.6	9.179	6.793	2.386	1 352.0	1 350.0	2.000
1984	10 390.2	7 951.7	2 438.5	10.390	7.952	2.439	1 415.0	1 411.0	2.100
1985	10 978.4	8 204.7	2 773.7	10.978	8.205	2.774	1 630.0	1 619.0	2.500
1986	10 418.3	8 215.0	3 190.7	11.406	8.215	3.191	1 499.0	1 515.0	2.000
1987	10 170.9	7 080.9	3 090.0	10.171	7.081	3.090	1 680.0	1 716.0	2.800
1988	10 545.6	7 539.4	3 006.2	10.546	7.539	3.006	1 601.0	1 601.0	2.300
1989	9 776.8	7 078.1	2 698.7	9.777	7.078	2.699	1 669.0	1 687.0	3.100
1990	9 300.2	6 896.9	2 403.3	9.300	6.897	2.403	1 408.0	1 418.0	2.600
1991	8 175.0	6 136.9	2 038.1	8.175	6.137	2.038	1 283.0	1 296.0	2.600
1992	8 214.4	6 276.6	1 937.8	8.214	6.277	1.938	1 276.0	1 288.0	2.300
1993	8 517.7	6 734.0	1 783.7	8.518	6.734	1.784	1 364.9	1 377.3	2.359
1994	8 990.4	7 255.2	1 735.2	8.990	7.255	1.735	1 436.6	1 449.3	2.325
1995	8 636.2	7 128.8	1 507.4	8.637	7.129	1.508	1 618.5	1 631.2	2.550
1996	8 526.8	7 253.7	1 273.1	8.527	7.254	1.273	1 363.4	1 375.9	2.378
1997	8 272.5	6 906.2	1 366.3	8.273	6.907	1.366	1 329.9	1 342.4	2.249
1998	8 142.1	6 763.9	1 378.2	8.143	6.764	1.378	1 324.4	1 383.0	2.214
1999	8 696.5	6 981.7	1 714.8	8.697	6.982	1.715	1 367.6	1 421.9	2.366
2000	8 852.1	6 832.8	2 019.3	8.852	6.833	2.019	1 377.0	1 408.7	2.815
2001	8 422.1	6 322.7	2 099.4	8.422	6.323	2.099	955.7	993.4	2.284
2002	8 108.7	5 877.6	2 231.1	8.102	5.871	2.231	1 132.0	1 245.3	2.538
2003	7 610.5	5 527.5	2 083.0	7.615	5.527	2.087	1 115.8	1 234.1	2.702
2004	7 545.1	5 396.2	2 148.9	7.545	5.396	2.149	1 034.2	1 152.0	2.385
2005	7 719.8	5 533.0	2 186.8	7.720	5.533	2.187	930.6	1 032.3	2.304
2006	7 820.7	5 476.1	2 344.6	7.821	5.476	2.345	1 031.7	1 109.5	2.468
2007	7 618.4	5 253.4	2 365.0	7.618	5.253	2.365	906.8	978.2	2.226
2008	6 813.5	4 535.3	2 278.2	6.813	4.535	2.278	1 144.1	1 217.4	4.146
2009	5 456.2	3 619.1	1 837.1	5.456	3.619	1.837	686.4	751.9	2.201
2010	5 728.7	3 880.9	1 847.8	5.729	3.881	1.848	757.8	816.1	2.450
2011	6 193.6	4 261.0	1 933.0	6.194	4.261	1.933	814.5	825.5	2.253
2009									
January	315.2	202.4	112.8	4.735	3.039	1.696	1 074.9	1 121.0	4.427
February	340.8	219.9	120.9	4.694	2.952	1.742	1 019.0	1 046.1	4.252
March	445.6	286.8	158.8	4.996	3.188	1.808	994.1	1 019.8	3.838
April	429.7	282.8	146.9	4.825	3.150	1.675	932.9	992.9	3.782
May	484.1	319.4	164.7	4.930	3.211	1.719	836.8	950.6	3.552
June	456.2	300.1	156.1	5.095	3.347	1.748	779.5	905.7	3.248
July	550.3	360.4	189.9	6.186	4.165	2.021	631.2	827.3	2.384
August	721.5	477.6	243.9	8.021	5.339	2.682	463.2	678.9	1.526
September	398.2	267.7	130.5	5.039	3.355	1.684	558.8	730.5	2.612
October	427.3	288.0	139.3	5.430	3.684	1.746	663.0	757.3	2.467
November	374.7	255.2	119.5	5.657	3.899	1.758	725.4	756.6	2.328
December	512.6	358.8	153.8	5.865	4.099	1.766	686.4	751.9	2.201
2010									
January	361.7	245.5	116.2	5.695	3.876	1.819	719.4	754.2	2.335
February	399.2	278.8	120.4	5.442	3.729	1.713	768.1	789.1	2.539
March	541.1	382.8	158.3	5.865	4.135	1.730	755.2	767.2	2.227
April	501.3	351.2	150.1	5.595	3.897	1.698	729.4	780.0	2.402
May	562.7	397.3	165.4	5.621	3.925	1.696	682.4	811.3	2.480
June	500.0	341.8	158.2	5.554	3.798	1.756	698.5	829.0	2.619
July	524.0	345.8	178.2	5.656	3.846	1.810	620.9	852.1	2.659
August	498.9	327.1	171.8	5.692	3.773	1.919	640.4	869.7	2.766
September	471.3	313.7	157.6	5.836	3.848	1.988	690.6	874.5	2.727
October	445.1	288.4	156.7	5.834	3.820	2.014	767.2	863.5	2.713
November	403.5	264.1	139.4	5.902	3.927	1.975	822.6	860.1	2.628
December	519.9	344.4	175.5	6.050	3.997	2.053	757.8	816.1	2.450
2011									
January	387.6	261.1	126.5	6.128	4.139	1.989	774.3	808.0	2.343
February	490.5	343.1	147.4	6.699	4.598	2.101	758.6	769.1	2.007
March	652.8	446.5	206.3	6.774	4.610	2.164	708.8	727.0	1.892
April	608.1	417.1	191.0	6.692	4.550	2.142	630.4	697.7	1.840
May	543.5	373.1	170.4	5.742	3.883	1.859	581.0	702.9	2.172
June	524.3	361.7	162.6	5.604	3.862	1.742	593.2	734.9	2.283
July	504.0	342.9	161.1	5.682	3.973	1.709	531.3	757.4	2.288
August	505.7	351.1	154.6	5.674	3.985	1.689	558.8	770.5	2.320
September	483.2	337.8	145.4	6.012	4.168	1.844	597.5	763.6	2.198
October	477.4	332.1	145.3	6.377	4.467	1.910	698.4	770.6	2.070
November	459.8	314.2	145.6	6.621	4.597	2.024	788.4	772.2	2.015
December	557.1	380.3	176.8	6.500	4.400	2.100	814.5	825.5	2.253

. . . = Not available.

Table 16-8. Motor Vehicle Sales and Inventories—Continued

(Units.)

Year and month	Retail sales of new trucks and buses								Unit sales of cars and light trucks (millions of units, seasonally adjusted annual rate)		
	Thousands of units, not seasonally adjusted				Millions of units, seasonally adjusted annual rate						
	Total	0–14,000 pounds		14,001 pounds and over	Total	0–14,000 pounds		14,001 pounds and over	Total	Domestic	Foreign
		Domestic	Foreign			Domestic	Foreign				
1970	. . .	1 408.5	. . .	337.3	. . .	1.408	. . .	0.335	. . .	8.527	. . .
1971	. . .	1 693.0	. . .	338.9	. . .	1.700	. . .	0.339	. . .	10.362	. . .
1972	. . .	2 122.5	. . .	437.4	. . .	2.116	. . .	0.437	. . .	11.369	. . .
1973	. . .	2 509.4	. . .	495.7	. . .	2.513	. . .	0.495	. . .	12.102	. . .
1974	. . .	2 180.1	. . .	423.9	. . .	2.176	. . .	0.424	. . .	9.538	. . .
1975	. . .	2 052.6	. . .	298.3	. . .	2.055	. . .	0.298	. . .	9.006	. . .
1976	3 300.5	2 738.3	237.5	324.7	3.307	2.733	0.239	0.324	12.966	11.225	1.741
1977	3 813.0	3 112.8	323.1	377.1	3.778	3.116	0.324	0.378	14.486	12.088	2.399
1978	4 256.8	3 481.1	335.9	439.8	4.246	3.469	0.340	0.440	14.973	12.633	2.340
1979	3 589.7	2 730.2	469.4	390.1	3.704	2.740	0.469	0.390	13.768	10.970	2.798
1980	2 487.4	1 731.1	484.6	271.7	2.635	1.731	0.480	0.271	11.192	8.312	2.881
1981	2 255.6	1 581.7	447.6	226.3	2.328	1.585	0.444	0.226	10.564	7.794	2.770
1982	2 562.8	1 967.5	410.4	184.9	2.708	1.971	0.413	0.185	10.363	7.729	2.634
1983	3 117.3	2 465.2	463.3	188.8	3.319	2.480	0.461	0.189	12.120	9.273	2.846
1984	4 093.1	3 207.2	607.7	278.2	4.247	3.199	0.609	0.278	14.197	11.150	3.047
1985	4 741.7	3 618.4	828.3	295.0	4.855	3.634	0.831	0.295	15.443	11.838	3.604
1986	4 912.1	3 671.4	967.2	273.5	4.916	3.676	0.969	0.273	16.051	11.891	4.160
1987	4 991.5	3 792.0	912.2	287.3	4.916	3.783	0.907	0.288	14.861	10.864	3.997
1988	5 231.9	4 199.7	697.9	334.3	5.076	4.194	0.697	0.334	15.436	11.733	3.703
1989	5 055.9	4 113.6	630.3	312.0	4.942	4.123	0.629	0.313	14.529	11.201	3.328
1990	4 837.0	3 956.8	602.7	277.5	4.841	3.960	0.602	0.278	13.863	10.857	3.006
1991	4 355.4	3 605.6	528.8	221.0	4.434	3.612	0.528	0.221	12.314	9.748	2.566
1992	4 892.2	4 247.0	395.9	249.3	4.918	4.247	0.398	0.248	12.860	10.524	2.336
1993	5 667.8	5 000.5	364.5	302.8	5.643	4.991	0.365	0.302	13.874	11.725	2.148
1994	6 407.3	5 658.2	396.3	352.8	6.388	5.659	0.395	0.354	15.044	12.914	2.130
1995	6 469.8	5 690.9	390.5	388.4	6.409	5.703	0.393	0.390	14.732	12.832	1.900
1996	6 921.8	6 131.8	430.9	359.1	6.834	6.127	0.429	0.357	15.083	13.381	1.702
1997	7 217.8	6 270.4	571.2	376.2	7.074	6.283	0.570	0.376	15.126	13.190	1.936
1998	7 815.8	6 745.3	646.2	424.3	7.612	6.720	0.644	0.425	15.506	13.484	2.022
1999	8 704.2	7 420.0	762.9	521.3	8.494	7.429	0.763	0.521	16.888	14.411	2.478
2000	8 953.5	7 650.8	840.8	461.9	8.844	7.649	0.841	0.461	17.342	14.481	2.861
2001	9 046.3	7 718.4	977.8	350.1	9.083	7.715	0.978	0.350	17.115	14.038	3.078
2002	9 035.6	7 646.9	1 066.3	322.4	9.070	7.647	1.066	0.322	16.816	13.518	3.298
2003	9 357.0	7 801.4	1 227.2	328.4	9.405	7.802	1.227	0.328	16.643	13.329	3.315
2004	9 753.3	8 075.5	1 246.2	431.6	9.747	8.076	1.246	0.429	16.867	13.472	3.395
2005	9 724.9	8 012.9	1 215.6	496.5	9.748	8.012	1.215	0.497	16.948	13.545	3.402
2006	9 227.8	7 336.8	1 346.6	544.4	9.145	7.337	1.347	0.545	16.504	12.813	3.691
2007	8 841.8	7 082.6	1 388.1	371.1	8.821	7.083	1.388	0.373	16.089	12.336	3.753
2008	6 680.0	5 285.0	1 096.5	298.5	6.703	5.285	1.097	0.298	13.195	9.820	3.375
2009	5 145.1	4 061.1	884.2	199.8	5.273	4.061	0.884	0.199	10.402	7.680	2.721
2010	6 043.6	4 927.3	898.7	217.6	6.255	4.927	0.899	0.217	11.554	8.808	2.746
2011	6 846.8	5 558.2	982.5	306.1	7.033	5.555	0.981	0.306	12.729	9.816	2.914
2009											
January	355.1	266.6	72.9	15.6	5.466	3.946	0.975	0.210	9.656	6.985	2.671
February	360.8	271.3	75.0	14.5	4.926	3.566	0.987	0.199	9.247	6.518	2.729
March	427.2	327.0	82.5	17.7	4.994	3.770	0.926	0.198	9.692	6.958	2.734
April	402.9	322.5	65.1	15.3	4.743	3.756	0.788	0.175	9.369	6.906	2.463
May	454.3	364.7	75.1	14.5	5.137	4.060	0.860	0.183	9.850	7.271	2.579
June	418.6	337.3	63.9	17.4	5.083	3.964	0.813	0.194	9.872	7.311	2.561
July	461.5	366.0	79.4	16.1	5.306	4.207	0.904	0.195	11.297	8.372	2.925
August	553.1	432.5	106.0	14.6	6.362	4.979	1.193	0.190	14.193	10.318	3.875
September	361.3	287.6	58.3	15.4	4.545	3.599	0.754	0.192	9.392	6.954	2.438
October	426.6	343.8	64.5	18.3	5.124	4.148	0.769	0.207	10.347	7.832	2.515
November	387.0	310.1	59.5	17.4	5.410	4.379	0.808	0.223	10.844	8.278	2.566
December	536.7	431.7	82.0	23.0	5.422	4.360	0.835	0.227	11.060	8.459	2.601
2010											
January	350.8	279.6	55.3	15.9	5.337	4.337	0.778	0.222	10.810	8.213	2.597
February	394.0	321.5	57.6	14.9	5.180	4.218	0.756	0.206	10.416	7.947	2.469
March	542.8	434.4	88.1	20.3	6.035	4.865	0.956	0.214	11.686	9.000	2.686
April	496.1	408.8	70.4	16.9	5.885	4.847	0.842	0.196	11.284	8.744	2.540
May	554.8	464.9	73.1	16.8	6.137	5.082	0.842	0.213	11.545	9.007	2.538
June	500.5	415.0	66.3	19.2	5.909	4.844	0.853	0.212	11.251	8.642	2.609
July	541.7	441.3	81.7	18.7	6.110	4.973	0.904	0.233	11.533	8.819	2.714
August	512.6	413.7	81.7	17.2	6.043	4.882	0.941	0.220	11.515	8.655	2.860
September	502.6	410.1	74.5	18.0	6.167	4.993	0.948	0.226	11.777	8.841	2.936
October	520.1	424.0	77.6	18.5	6.523	5.345	0.959	0.219	12.138	9.165	2.973
November	484.5	389.0	77.1	18.4	6.560	5.330	1.006	0.224	12.238	9.257	2.981
December	643.1	525.0	95.3	22.8	6.630	5.410	0.997	0.223	12.457	9.407	3.050
2011											
January	447.3	357.8	71.5	18.0	6.767	5.515	1.002	0.250	12.645	9.654	2.991
February	518.8	418.9	80.5	19.4	6.809	5.492	1.049	0.268	13.240	10.090	3.150
March	614.9	489.4	100.0	25.5	6.518	5.213	1.035	0.270	13.022	9.823	3.199
April	569.1	464.3	81.8	23.0	6.712	5.475	0.965	0.272	13.132	10.025	3.107
May	539.9	443.3	71.5	25.1	6.257	5.074	0.871	0.312	11.687	8.957	2.730
June	552.1	452.9	71.7	27.5	6.215	5.019	0.889	0.307	11.512	8.881	2.631
July	576.2	472.2	80.3	23.7	6.822	5.592	0.925	0.305	12.199	9.565	2.634
August	591.0	478.5	84.9	27.6	6.752	5.465	0.951	0.336	12.090	9.450	2.640
September	594.5	482.1	85.1	27.3	5.975	5.975	1.065	0.345	13.052	10.143	2.909
October	569.6	462.8	77.8	29.0	7.186	5.842	0.999	0.345	13.218	10.309	2.909
November	558.2	453.1	78.4	26.7	7.298	5.984	0.992	0.322	13.597	10.581	3.016
December	715.2	582.9	99.0	33.3	7.372	6.012	1.023	0.337	13.499	10.408	3.091

. . . = Not available.

Table 16-9. Retail and Food Services Sales

(All retail establishments and food services; millions of dollars; not seasonally adjusted.)

Year and month	Retail and food services, total [1]	Retail (NAICS industry categories)											Food services and drinking places
		GAFO (department store type goods), total [2]	Motor vehicles and parts	Furniture and home furnishings	Electronics and appliances	Building materials and garden	Food and beverages	Health and personal care	Gasoline	Clothing and accessories	General merchandise	Nonstore retailers	
1992	2 014 096	533 388	418 393	52 336	42 631	130 989	370 513	89 699	156 324	120 103	247 876	78 501	202 865
1993	2 153 090	570 782	472 916	55 456	48 614	140 964	374 516	92 589	162 376	124 749	265 996	85 811	215 467
1994	2 330 231	616 347	541 141	60 416	57 266	157 228	384 340	96 359	171 222	129 083	285 190	96 280	225 000
1995	2 450 625	650 040	579 715	63 470	64 770	164 561	390 386	101 632	181 113	131 333	300 498	103 516	233 012
1996	2 603 791	682 613	627 507	67 707	68 363	176 683	401 073	109 554	194 425	136 581	315 305	117 761	242 245
1997	2 726 129	713 387	653 817	72 715	70 061	191 063	409 373	118 670	199 700	140 293	331 363	126 190	257 364
1998	2 852 955	757 936	688 415	77 412	74 527	202 423	416 525	129 582	191 727	149 151	351 081	133 904	271 194
1999	3 086 988	815 665	764 204	84 294	78 977	218 290	433 699	142 697	212 524	159 751	380 179	151 797	283 900
2000	3 287 536	862 739	796 210	91 170	82 206	228 994	444 764	155 233	249 816	167 674	404 228	180 453	304 261
2001	3 378 905	882 700	815 579	91 484	80 240	239 379	462 429	166 532	251 383	167 287	427 468	180 563	316 638
2002	3 459 077	912 707	818 811	94 438	83 740	248 539	464 856	179 983	250 619	172 304	446 520	189 279	330 525
2003	3 612 704	946 361	841 588	96 736	86 689	263 463	474 385	192 426	275 187	178 694	468 771	206 359	349 726
2004	3 847 125	1 004 411	866 372	103 757	94 416	295 274	490 380	199 290	324 006	190 253	497 382	228 977	373 557
2005	4 086 625	1 060 478	888 307	109 120	101 340	320 802	508 484	210 085	378 923	200 969	528 385	255 579	396 463
2006	4 296 871	1 112 667	899 997	112 795	107 989	334 130	525 232	223 336	421 976	213 189	554 256	284 343	422 786
2007	4 443 807	1 147 500	910 139	111 144	110 673	320 854	547 837	237 164	451 822	221 205	578 582	308 767	444 551
2008	4 402 508	1 143 031	787 079	99 560	108 663	304 556	569 735	246 787	502 983	215 776	596 358	319 283	456 102
2009	4 078 698	1 096 628	673 531	86 111	97 963	266 871	568 841	253 150	389 690	204 626	591 613	311 416	451 070
2010	4 307 531	1 125 458	746 924	87 216	99 152	267 900	581 972	261 190	446 150	213 735	607 968	341 189	466 001
2011	4 647 648	1 165 978	826 299	88 821	99 996	278 902	613 908	272 286	526 196	226 748	629 123	393 745	493 501
2009													
January	311 330	81 969	50 225	6 878	8 370	17 875	47 124	20 694	26 461	13 392	43 620	26 082	36 137
February	300 545	81 018	50 126	6 674	8 151	17 362	42 628	19 858	25 524	14 690	43 442	24 004	34 890
March	329 718	85 323	57 303	6 995	7 576	21 886	45 765	21 573	28 331	15 561	46 515	25 504	38 393
April	331 023	85 308	56 096	6 697	6 907	25 449	46 479	21 105	29 307	16 341	46 784	23 839	37 738
May	348 944	91 038	57 930	7 072	7 337	27 454	49 183	21 120	32 796	17 270	50 268	23 181	40 148
June	345 650	86 434	59 710	7 026	7 576	26 879	47 000	21 031	35 786	15 444	47 293	24 314	38 251
July	349 260	87 273	62 490	7 308	7 526	24 488	48 957	20 874	36 182	16 019	47 315	24 102	39 130
August	354 597	92 771	66 410	7 277	7 852	21 980	47 903	20 605	36 822	17 652	49 063	23 998	38 798
September	325 769	83 846	52 267	7 091	7 236	21 761	46 264	20 657	34 219	15 636	44 423	24 770	36 493
October	339 734	88 823	54 972	6 982	7 059	21 746	47 937	21 389	34 905	17 069	48 764	26 116	38 165
November	340 543	98 692	50 110	7 525	9 510	20 366	47 446	20 639	34 220	18 359	53 779	28 245	35 453
December	401 585	134 133	55 892	8 586	12 863	19 625	52 155	23 605	35 137	27 193	70 347	37 261	37 474
2010													
January	315 998	80 711	49 940	6 467	7 598	15 716	47 113	20 807	34 040	13 245	44 149	27 566	35 476
February	312 327	82 247	51 956	6 621	7 852	15 855	44 306	20 186	31 802	14 857	45 060	25 806	35 323
March	362 217	90 711	67 645	7 453	7 752	22 249	48 178	22 559	37 115	17 435	48 988	28 613	39 342
April	358 067	87 762	64 593	6 903	7 131	27 459	47 122	21 575	38 162	17 092	48 803	26 308	39 356
May	367 321	92 219	65 484	7 108	7 592	26 946	49 743	21 419	39 001	17 783	50 842	25 323	40 739
June	360 372	89 088	64 950	7 083	7 948	26 174	47 921	21 565	38 062	16 185	48 645	26 532	39 358
July	363 830	90 342	67 343	7 425	7 915	23 749	49 851	21 424	38 883	16 883	48 979	25 123	40 956
August	364 525	94 128	66 437	7 512	8 093	22 326	48 524	21 660	38 355	17 941	49 678	27 108	40 227
September	347 945	86 532	62 087	7 262	7 614	21 885	47 645	21 368	36 945	16 248	45 999	27 219	38 279
October	357 404	90 095	61 883	6 938	7 293	22 577	48 774	21 841	38 224	17 435	49 378	27 750	40 031
November	368 182	103 621	59 390	7 787	9 447	22 084	49 035	21 891	36 796	20 026	55 959	32 171	37 323
December	429 343	138 002	65 216	8 657	12 917	20 880	53 760	24 895	38 765	28 605	72 208	41 670	39 591
2011													
January	338 500	81 186	58 718	6 329	7 469	16 476	48 674	22 242	37 659	13 633	44 578	31 746	36 768
February	340 500	84 462	63 669	6 559	7 686	16 460	45 856	21 290	36 290	15 820	46 044	29 717	37 177
March	390 622	93 171	76 556	7 605	8 092	22 643	50 069	23 625	43 860	18 117	49 927	32 831	41 786
April	384 506	92 521	70 852	6 960	7 214	25 222	50 985	22 250	45 268	18 498	50 733	29 669	41 510
May	396 066	94 310	70 618	7 148	7 516	28 694	51 905	22 783	47 615	18 618	51 708	30 462	42 748
June	392 888	93 161	71 537	7 101	7 752	28 007	51 506	22 413	46 880	17 637	51 193	30 491	41 806
July	388 749	93 214	70 503	7 316	7 882	24 256	53 005	21 909	47 493	17 776	50 990	28 531	43 088
August	398 950	98 373	72 557	7 772	8 293	24 540	52 054	23 032	47 602	19 056	51 642	31 844	42 232
September	379 330	91 623	68 024	7 556	7 578	23 299	50 360	22 265	44 738	17 818	48 615	31 139	41 271
October	384 345	93 453	66 851	7 098	7 695	24 018	51 298	22 622	44 421	18 095	51 324	32 712	42 350
November	395 724	107 147	64 740	8 110	9 969	23 222	51 730	22 468	42 312	20 787	57 735	37 937	39 755
December	457 468	143 357	71 674	9 267	12 850	22 065	56 466	25 387	42 058	30 893	74 634	46 666	43 010

[1]Includes store categories not shown separately.
[2]Includes furniture, home furnishings, electronics, appliances, clothing, sporting goods, hobby, book, music, general merchandise, office supplies, stationery, and gifts.

Table 16-9. Retail and Food Services Sales—*Continued*

(All retail establishments and food services; millions of dollars; seasonally adjusted.)

Year and month	Total	Retail and food services / Retail (NAICS industry categories) Total	GAFO (department store type goods) [2]	Motor vehicles and parts	Furniture and home furnishings	Electronics and appliances	Building materials and garden	Food and beverages Total [1]	Groceries	Beer, wine, and liquor	Health and personal care	Gasoline
1992	2 014 096	1 811 231	533 388	418 393	52 336	42 631	130 989	370 513	337 370	21 687	89 699	156 324
1993	2 153 090	1 937 623	570 782	472 916	55 456	48 614	140 964	374 516	341 318	21 538	92 589	162 376
1994	2 330 231	2 105 231	616 347	541 141	60 416	57 266	157 228	384 340	350 523	22 101	96 359	171 222
1995	2 450 625	2 217 613	650 040	579 715	63 470	64 770	164 561	390 386	356 409	22 007	101 632	181 113
1996	2 603 791	2 361 546	682 613	627 507	67 707	68 363	176 683	401 073	365 547	23 157	109 554	194 425
1997	2 726 129	2 468 765	713 387	653 817	72 715	70 061	191 063	409 373	372 570	24 081	118 670	199 700
1998	2 852 955	2 581 761	757 936	688 415	77 412	74 527	202 423	416 525	378 188	25 382	129 582	191 727
1999	3 086 988	2 803 088	815 665	764 204	84 294	78 977	218 290	433 699	394 250	26 476	142 697	212 524
2000	3 287 536	2 983 275	862 739	796 210	91 170	82 206	228 994	444 764	402 515	28 507	155 233	249 816
2001	3 378 905	3 062 267	882 700	815 579	91 484	80 240	239 379	462 429	418 127	29 621	166 532	251 383
2002	3 459 077	3 128 552	912 707	818 811	94 438	83 740	248 539	464 856	419 813	29 894	179 983	250 619
2003	3 612 704	3 262 978	946 361	841 588	96 736	86 689	263 463	474 385	427 987	30 469	192 426	275 187
2004	3 847 125	3 473 568	1 004 411	866 372	103 757	94 416	295 274	490 380	441 136	32 189	199 290	324 006
2005	4 086 625	3 690 162	1 060 478	888 307	109 120	101 340	320 802	508 484	457 667	33 567	210 085	378 923
2006	4 296 871	3 874 085	1 112 667	899 997	112 795	107 989	334 130	525 232	471 699	36 016	223 336	421 976
2007	4 443 807	3 999 256	1 147 500	910 139	111 144	110 673	320 854	547 837	491 360	38 128	237 164	451 822
2008	4 402 508	3 946 406	1 143 031	787 079	99 560	108 663	304 556	569 735	511 388	39 522	246 787	502 983
2009	4 078 698	3 627 628	1 096 628	673 531	86 111	97 963	266 871	568 841	510 132	40 139	253 150	389 690
2010	4 307 531	3 841 530	1 125 458	746 924	87 216	99 152	267 900	581 972	521 412	41 387	261 190	446 150
2011	4 647 648	4 154 147	1 165 978	826 299	88 821	99 996	278 902	613 908	551 173	43 266	272 286	526 196
2009												
January	338 246	300 207	92 928	56 382	7 452	8 894	23 165	47 433	42 559	3 356	20 735	28 731
February	337 081	299 198	92 906	54 221	7 391	8 834	23 010	46 966	42 109	3 315	20 925	29 958
March	331 380	293 813	90 476	53 083	7 094	8 159	22 501	47 103	42 210	3 329	21 026	28 792
April	332 258	294 595	90 812	53 251	7 163	8 064	22 543	47 083	42 212	3 323	21 169	28 817
May	335 557	297 930	91 264	54 496	7 194	7 990	22 667	47 372	42 434	3 359	21 078	30 311
June	339 659	302 121	90 719	56 254	7 184	8 047	22 570	47 360	42 506	3 301	21 137	32 892
July	340 600	303 011	90 658	57 543	7 165	7 891	22 255	47 233	42 371	3 314	21 042	32 744
August	348 621	311 135	91 457	63 065	7 100	7 919	21 991	47 423	42 499	3 369	21 004	34 575
September	339 523	302 171	91 454	53 727	7 112	7 962	21 843	47 557	42 658	3 357	21 274	34 740
October	342 223	304 880	91 917	56 639	7 074	7 907	21 125	47 526	42 685	3 353	21 261	34 491
November	346 812	309 096	91 399	57 889	7 126	8 333	21 546	47 820	42 895	3 350	21 343	36 677
December	348 184	310 446	92 134	57 291	7 197	8 124	21 487	48 173	43 185	3 427	21 247	37 143
2010												
January	348 585	311 124	92 634	57 833	7 170	8 227	21 201	47 958	43 070	3 367	21 210	37 284
February	348 794	310 524	93 666	55 922	7 316	8 469	21 159	48 749	43 730	3 447	21 293	37 065
March	355 695	317 124	93 918	60 382	7 350	8 188	22 322	48 447	43 397	3 447	21 444	37 227
April	358 023	319 325	93 458	61 408	7 297	8 258	24 126	48 189	43 114	3 466	21 705	37 159
May	355 693	317 041	93 326	61 914	7 290	8 328	22 229	48 246	43 242	3 420	21 440	36 280
June	354 404	315 704	93 290	61 314	7 257	8 394	21 977	48 017	43 001	3 429	21 717	35 308
July	355 436	316 615	93 307	62 556	7 287	8 263	21 926	47 768	42 807	3 368	21 795	35 477
August	358 715	319 584	93 657	63 179	7 315	8 157	21 898	48 515	43 432	3 471	21 901	35 980
September	361 756	322 495	93 618	63 811	7 284	8 331	22 168	48 696	43 604	3 465	22 006	37 243
October	366 507	327 184	94 147	65 847	7 235	8 218	22 746	48 937	43 822	3 505	22 084	38 301
November	370 165	330 586	95 708	66 204	7 244	8 194	22 622	49 329	44 193	3 501	22 224	39 103
December	372 587	332 956	94 719	66 406	7 214	8 236	22 967	49 388	44 314	3 474	22 327	40 720
2011												
January	375 739	336 373	94 201	67 961	7 087	8 181	22 380	49 933	44 849	3 499	22 673	41 384
February	378 934	338 743	95 791	68 351	7 232	8 273	22 147	50 433	45 230	3 586	22 458	42 051
March	382 094	341 367	96 544	67 969	7 420	8 438	22 502	50 499	45 372	3 553	22 651	43 642
April	383 507	343 049	96 582	67 758	7 334	8 313	22 711	51 184	46 026	3 546	22 407	44 121
May	383 447	342 618	96 450	66 774	7 301	8 260	22 920	50 943	45 762	3 574	22 647	44 376
June	385 266	344 159	97 025	67 638	7 306	8 199	23 295	51 208	45 980	3 604	22 617	43 569
July	386 928	345 892	97 219	67 871	7 353	8 299	23 269	51 449	46 229	3 605	22 704	44 057
August	387 838	346 636	97 365	67 141	7 423	8 280	23 550	51 548	46 331	3 607	22 849	44 446
September	392 354	350 582	98 389	70 039	7 511	8 253	23 612	51 448	46 199	3 641	22 836	44 649
October	395 995	353 856	98 503	71 116	7 511	8 674	24 075	51 831	46 522	3 648	22 920	44 644
November	397 868	355 620	98 684	71 800	7 558	8 645	23 936	51 838	46 524	3 670	22 857	45 157
December	398 012	355 554	98 444	73 057	7 716	8 248	24 581	51 488	46 160	3 645	22 933	44 179

[1] Includes store categories not shown separately.
[2] Includes furniture, home furnishings, electronics, appliances, clothing, sporting goods, hobby, book, music, general merchandise, office supplies, stationery, and gifts.

Table 16-9. Retail and Food Services Sales—*Continued*

(All retail establishments and food services; millions of dollars; seasonally adjusted, except as noted.)

	Retail and food services—*Continued*												Food services and drinking places
	Retail (NAICS industry categories)—*Continued*												
Classification basis, year, and month	Clothing and accessories					Sporting goods, hobby, book, and music	General merchandise			Miscellaneous store retailers	Nonstore retailers		
	Total [1]	Men's clothing [3]	Women's clothing	Family clothing [3]	Shoes		Total	Department stores [4]	Other general merchandise		Total [1]	Electronic shopping and mail order	
1992	120 103	10 179	31 815	33 146	18 616	49 026	247 876	177 089	70 787	54 840	78 501	35 210	202 865
1993	124 749	9 962	32 350	35 297	19 028	52 091	265 996	187 685	78 311	61 545	85 811	40 677	215 467
1994	129 083	10 032	30 585	38 103	19 907	57 249	285 190	198 945	86 245	69 457	96 280	47 037	225 000
1995	131 333	9 315	28 696	39 999	20 341	60 642	300 498	205 920	94 578	75 977	103 516	52 680	233 012
1996	136 581	9 546	28 238	42 259	21 235	63 768	315 305	212 203	103 102	82 819	117 761	61 106	242 245
1997	140 293	10 069	27 822	45 243	21 450	65 288	331 363	220 108	111 255	90 232	126 190	70 067	257 364
1998	149 151	10 196	28 332	50 154	22 238	68 645	351 081	223 290	127 791	98 369	133 904	80 297	271 194
1999	159 751	9 667	29 549	55 318	22 690	72 458	380 179	230 304	149 875	104 218	151 797	94 282	283 900
2000	167 674	9 507	31 447	58 913	22 875	75 808	404 228	232 475	171 753	106 719	180 453	113 790	304 261
2001	167 287	8 625	31 453	60 150	22 884	76 836	427 468	228 377	199 091	103 087	180 563	114 749	316 638
2002	172 304	8 112	31 246	64 289	23 201	76 680	446 520	220 743	225 777	102 783	189 279	122 214	330 525
2003	178 694	8 249	32 565	67 494	23 167	76 767	468 771	214 470	254 301	101 913	206 359	134 304	349 726
2004	190 253	8 566	34 954	72 444	23 685	79 284	497 382	215 691	281 691	104 177	228 977	154 157	373 557
2005	200 969	8 737	37 075	77 292	25 263	80 889	528 385	215 266	313 119	107 279	255 579	175 900	396 463
2006	213 189	8 844	38 809	81 712	26 682	83 148	554 256	213 155	341 101	113 694	284 343	202 251	422 786
2007	221 205	8 772	40 294	84 592	26 811	84 651	578 582	209 392	369 190	116 418	308 767	223 681	444 551
2008	215 776	8 538	38 315	83 059	26 688	84 037	596 358	198 740	397 618	111 589	319 283	228 203	456 102
2009	204 626	7 707	35 860	81 420	25 060	80 890	591 613	187 576	404 037	102 926	311 416	233 530	451 070
2010	213 735	7 803	37 431	85 282	26 359	81 620	607 968	186 218	421 750	106 514	341 189	260 557	466 001
2011	226 748	8 530	38 609	88 723	27 412	84 671	629 123	184 936	444 187	113 452	393 745	301 883	493 501
2009													
January	17 143	544	2 928	5 357	2 075	6 936	49 404	15 878	33 526	8 629	25 303	18 740	38 039
February	17 421	516	2 959	5 650	2 120	6 816	49 430	15 736	33 694	8 783	25 443	18 802	37 883
March	16 565	565	2 917	6 123	2 055	6 654	49 075	15 658	33 417	8 731	25 030	18 609	37 567
April	16 832	698	2 996	6 280	2 048	6 843	48 919	15 653	33 266	8 766	25 145	18 791	37 663
May	17 038	680	3 007	6 563	2 064	6 724	49 306	15 775	33 531	8 549	25 205	18 930	37 627
June	16 808	635	2 968	6 026	2 054	6 732	48 990	15 497	33 493	8 495	25 652	19 171	37 538
July	16 979	603	2 961	6 626	2 079	6 758	48 913	15 519	33 394	8 460	26 028	19 545	37 589
August	17 334	579	3 118	7 229	2 138	6 850	49 296	15 663	33 633	8 459	26 119	19 741	37 486
September	17 240	609	3 045	6 107	2 114	6 746	49 454	15 590	33 864	8 432	26 084	19 794	37 352
October	17 311	643	3 053	7 080	2 091	6 651	50 011	15 764	34 247	8 478	26 406	19 824	37 343
November	17 107	654	2 999	7 724	2 081	6 592	49 358	15 562	33 796	8 581	26 724	20 201	37 716
December	17 173	981	2 967	10 655	2 138	6 785	49 988	15 606	34 382	8 702	27 136	20 504	37 738
2010													
January	17 378	506	3 024	5 014	2 150	6 746	50 185	15 678	34 507	8 508	27 424	20 649	37 461
February	17 392	501	3 010	5 643	2 174	6 642	50 961	15 625	35 336	8 308	27 248	20 499	38 270
March	17 891	605	3 136	6 938	2 214	6 742	50 783	15 889	34 894	8 808	27 540	21 071	38 571
April	17 711	672	3 103	6 787	2 195	6 710	50 506	15 517	34 989	8 765	27 491	21 000	38 698
May	17 667	670	3 079	6 940	2 176	6 760	50 337	15 450	34 887	8 870	27 680	21 153	38 652
June	17 583	640	3 073	6 395	2 168	6 802	50 293	15 458	34 835	8 923	28 119	21 505	38 700
July	17 641	583	3 088	7 014	2 175	6 809	50 356	15 371	34 985	8 797	27 940	21 435	38 821
August	17 828	555	3 167	7 349	2 224	6 761	50 626	15 435	35 191	8 843	28 581	21 997	39 131
September	17 704	605	3 139	6 442	2 185	6 745	50 549	15 334	35 215	9 023	28 935	22 261	39 261
October	18 069	682	3 195	7 007	2 224	6 821	50 793	15 351	35 442	9 192	28 941	22 291	39 323
November	18 507	720	3 202	8 411	2 244	7 008	51 647	15 840	35 807	9 139	29 365	22 554	39 579
December	18 149	1 064	3 171	11 342	2 223	6 964	51 174	15 419	35 755	9 167	30 244	22 894	39 631
2011													
January	18 215	528	3 043	5 214	2 226	6 856	50 900	15 264	35 636	9 082	31 721	24 174	39 366
February	18 360	539	3 197	5 932	2 232	7 006	51 871	15 541	36 330	9 258	31 303	23 797	40 191
March	18 652	650	3 187	7 060	2 227	7 061	51 926	15 464	36 462	9 144	31 463	23 936	40 727
April	18 676	749	3 135	7 117	2 216	7 065	52 166	15 499	36 667	9 341	31 973	24 320	40 458
May	18 705	736	3 174	7 011	2 252	7 053	52 074	15 386	36 688	9 351	32 214	24 654	40 829
June	18 951	718	3 226	6 833	2 295	7 076	52 439	15 544	36 895	9 404	32 457	24 889	41 110
July	18 931	639	3 243	7 249	2 289	6 993	52 603	15 418	37 185	9 600	32 763	25 200	41 036
August	18 877	596	3 128	7 685	2 287	7 127	52 621	15 324	37 297	9 705	33 069	25 371	41 202
September	19 245	698	3 255	6 854	2 328	7 179	53 126	15 494	37 632	9 680	33 004	25 355	41 772
October	19 012	740	3 248	7 209	2 297	7 161	53 052	15 353	37 699	9 673	34 187	26 255	42 139
November	19 193	766	3 300	8 587	2 340	7 116	53 082	15 389	37 693	9 704	34 734	26 576	42 248
December	19 371	1 171	3 367	11 972	2 361	6 997	53 020	15 351	37 669	9 496	34 468	26 767	42 458

[1] Includes store categories not shown separately.
[3] Not seasonally adjusted.
[4] Excluding leased departments.

Table 16-10. Quarterly U.S. Retail Sales: Total and E-Commerce

Year and quarter	Retail sales (millions of dollars)		E-commerce as a percent of total sales	Percent change from prior quarter		Percent change from same quarter a year ago	
	Total	E-commerce		Total sales	E-commerce sales	Total sales	E-commerce sales
NOT SEASONALLY ADJUSTED							
2008							
1st quarter	953 577	34 595	3.6	-10.3	-18.3	3.2	11.5
2nd quarter	1 032 233	34 550	3.3	8.2	-0.1	1.6	7.2
3rd quarter	1 004 489	33 541	3.3	-2.7	-2.9	0.2	3.1
4rd quarter	962 634	39 595	4.1	-4.2	18.0	-9.5	-6.5
2009							
1st quarter	833 805	32 475	3.9	-13.4	-18.0	-12.6	-6.1
2nd quarter	911 223	32 902	3.6	9.3	1.3	-11.7	-4.8
3rd quarter	917 856	34 153	3.7	0.7	3.8	-8.6	1.8
4rd quarter	975 587	45 684	4.7	6.3	33.8	1.3	15.4
2010							
1st quarter	888 667	37 166	4.2	-8.9	-18.6	6.6	14.4
2nd quarter	978 726	37 718	3.9	10.1	1.5	7.4	14.6
3rd quarter	970 155	39 230	4.0	-0.9	4.0	5.7	14.9
4rd quarter	1 051 917	53 225	5.1	8.4	35.7	7.8	16.5
2011							
1st quarter	965 068	43 713	4.5	-8.3	-17.9	8.6	17.6
2nd quarter	1 061 124	44 224	4.2	10.0	1.2	8.4	17.2
3rd quarter	1 049 523	44 550	4.2	-1.1	0.7	8.2	13.6
4rd quarter	1 120 468	61 789	5.5	6.8	38.7	6.5	16.1
SEASONALLY ADJUSTED							
1999							
4th quarter	724 737	4 571	0.6	2.2	. . .	9.0	. . .
2000							
1st quarter	742 333	5 824	0.8	2.4	27.4	9.3	. . .
2nd quarter	741 582	6 504	0.9	-0.1	11.7	7.0	. . .
3rd quarter	747 819	7 388	1.0	0.8	13.6	5.4	. . .
4th quarter	753 245	7 858	1.0	0.7	6.4	3.9	71.9
2001							
1st quarter	756 957	8 253	1.1	0.5	5.0	2.0	41.7
2nd quarter	764 827	8 418	1.1	1.0	2.0	3.1	29.4
3rd quarter	759 081	8 355	1.1	-0.8	-0.7	1.5	13.1
4th quarter	787 100	9 422	1.2	3.7	12.8	4.5	19.9
2002							
1st quarter	772 932	10 097	1.3	-1.8	7.2	2.1	22.3
2nd quarter	779 542	10 870	1.4	0.9	7.7	1.9	29.1
3rd quarter	789 978	11 631	1.5	1.3	7.0	4.1	39.2
4th quarter	792 817	12 409	1.6	0.4	6.7	0.7	31.7
2003							
1st quarter	799 504	13 003	1.6	0.8	4.8	3.4	28.8
2nd quarter	806 000	14 011	1.7	0.8	7.8	3.4	28.9
3rd quarter	829 025	15 062	1.8	2.9	7.5	4.9	29.5
4th quarter	832 261	15 855	1.9	0.4	5.3	5.0	27.8
2004							
1st quarter	847 868	17 097	2.0	1.9	7.8	6.0	31.5
2nd quarter	857 215	17 872	2.1	1.1	4.5	6.4	27.6
3rd quarter	870 400	18 926	2.2	1.5	5.9	5.0	25.7
4th quarter	892 367	20 025	2.2	2.5	5.8	7.2	26.3
2005							
1st quarter	900 378	21 227	2.4	0.9	6.0	6.2	24.2
2nd quarter	918 660	22 523	2.5	2.0	6.1	7.2	26.0
3rd quarter	935 577	24 043	2.6	1.8	6.7	7.5	27.0
4rd quarter	939 298	24 712	2.6	0.4	2.8	5.3	23.4
2006							
1st quarter	966 148	26 770	2.8	2.9	8.3	7.3	26.1
2nd quarter	968 895	27 717	2.9	0.3	3.5	5.5	23.1
3rd quarter	975 174	29 184	3.0	0.6	5.3	4.2	21.4
4rd quarter	975 660	30 670	3.1	0.0	5.1	3.9	24.1
2007							
1st quarter	989 144	32 350	3.3	1.4	5.5	2.4	20.8
2nd quarter	997 157	34 032	3.4	0.8	5.2	2.9	22.8
3rd quarter	1 005 154	34 975	3.5	0.8	2.8	3.1	19.8
4rd quarter	1 016 641	36 207	3.6	1.1	3.5	4.2	18.1
2008							
1st quarter	1 010 490	36 244	3.6	-0.6	0.1	2.2	12.0
2nd quarter	1 016 290	36 691	3.6	0.6	1.2	1.9	7.8
3rd quarter	1 002 911	36 180	3.6	-1.3	-1.4	-0.2	3.4
4rd quarter	915 673	33 393	3.6	-8.7	-7.7	-9.9	-7.8
2009							
1st quarter	895 260	34 151	3.8	-2.2	2.3	-11.4	-5.8
2nd quarter	896 957	35 133	3.9	0.2	2.9	-11.7	-4.2
3rd quarter	918 917	36 909	4.0	2.4	5.1	-8.4	2.0
4rd quarter	928 333	38 269	4.1	1.0	3.7	1.4	14.6
2010							
1st quarter	948 172	39 159	4.1	2.1	2.3	5.9	14.7
2nd quarter	963 389	40 472	4.2	1.6	3.4	7.4	15.2
3rd quarter	972 440	42 381	4.4	0.9	4.7	5.8	14.8
4rd quarter	1 003 118	44 485	4.4	3.1	4.9	8.1	16.2
2011							
1st quarter	1 029 862	46 131	4.5	2.7	3.7	8.6	17.8
2nd quarter	1 041 406	47 352	4.5	1.1	2.6	8.1	17.2
3rd quarter	1 053 190	48 567	4.6	1.1	2.6	8.3	14.5
4rd quarter	1 071 649	51 381	4.8	1.8	5.8	6.8	15.5

. . . = Not available.

Table 16-11. Retail Inventories

(All retail stores; end of period, millions of dollars.)

Year and month	Not seasonally adjusted			Seasonally adjusted								
											General merchandise	
	Total	Excluding motor vehicles and parts	Motor vehicles and parts	Total	Excluding motor vehicles and parts	Motor vehicles and parts	Furniture, home furnishings, electronics, and appliances	Building materials and garden	Food and beverages	Clothing and accessories	Total	Department stores [1]
1992	256 166	184 700	71 466	260 276	191 118	69 158	16 183	21 099	27 408	27 390	49 306	37 878
1993	274 071	196 418	77 653	278 444	203 310	75 134	18 113	22 621	27 498	28 080	53 283	40 458
1994	299 812	211 223	88 589	304 519	218 757	85 762	20 397	24 857	28 112	29 518	56 581	41 908
1995	317 304	220 921	96 383	322 216	228 842	93 374	21 817	26 337	28 718	29 298	59 530	43 455
1996	328 160	227 888	100 272	333 255	236 015	97 240	22 253	27 447	29 658	29 778	60 591	44 124
1997	338 789	234 269	104 520	343 824	242 517	101 307	22 109	28 897	29 891	31 079	60 715	44 309
1998	351 252	245 397	105 855	356 515	253 885	102 630	22 662	30 921	30 837	32 308	61 542	43 438
1999	378 809	259 875	118 934	384 074	268 563	115 511	24 093	33 005	32 635	33 735	64 297	43 835
2000	400 391	268 979	131 412	405 928	277 826	128 102	25 620	34 269	32 108	36 753	64 929	42 667
2001	387 858	266 369	121 489	393 637	274 795	118 842	24 496	34 235	33 165	35 627	64 790	40 464
2002	409 314	271 757	137 557	415 018	280 121	134 897	25 853	36 086	32 907	37 361	65 978	38 750
2003	425 790	277 513	148 277	431 201	285 670	145 531	27 195	37 398	32 504	38 462	66 655	36 823
2004	454 938	297 651	157 287	460 364	305 970	154 394	30 164	41 593	33 433	41 372	70 969	37 230
2005	465 752	310 004	155 748	471 514	318 568	152 946	30 760	44 980	33 761	43 086	74 177	38 012
2006	480 191	323 497	156 694	486 218	332 433	153 785	31 247	46 828	34 658	47 548	75 586	37 092
2007	494 026	333 666	160 360	500 034	342 620	157 414	32 020	48 822	36 419	47 812	75 893	36 441
2008	471 552	322 698	148 854	477 444	331 095	146 349	28 506	46 530	37 201	46 657	72 992	33 183
2009	423 584	307 783	115 801	429 287	315 195	114 092	26 387	43 129	37 093	41 673	69 860	30 895
2010	449 779	320 063	129 716	455 295	327 409	127 886	28 061	43 614	38 409	42 938	73 558	30 876
2011	466 025	331 853	134 172	471 683	339 385	132 298	27 251	43 967	40 583	46 249	76 698	31 032
2008												
January	492 482	331 841	160 641	502 378	343 896	158 482	31 925	48 890	36 403	47 791	76 719	36 160
February	495 974	333 295	162 679	502 405	343 491	158 914	31 880	48 292	36 590	47 670	76 871	36 412
March	498 764	335 580	163 184	497 424	340 221	157 203	31 476	47 503	36 604	47 226	75 265	35 847
April	501 402	337 520	163 882	498 567	341 674	156 893	31 693	47 722	36 859	47 405	75 912	35 623
May	493 635	334 511	159 124	497 388	341 021	156 367	31 239	47 670	36 909	46 960	75 739	35 576
June	490 010	333 316	156 694	496 497	340 831	155 666	31 271	47 754	37 035	46 942	75 237	35 094
July	487 400	336 122	151 278	500 738	342 774	157 964	31 684	47 993	37 106	47 307	75 271	34 972
August	482 900	338 043	144 857	495 593	341 705	153 888	31 490	48 255	37 200	47 202	74 610	34 498
September	495 165	350 332	144 833	495 203	341 816	153 387	31 448	48 264	37 347	47 407	74 912	34 639
October	518 087	367 596	150 491	494 295	341 745	152 550	31 376	47 989	37 595	47 438	74 967	34 692
November	516 243	365 131	151 112	484 856	336 236	148 620	29 253	47 714	37 432	47 147	74 284	33 838
December	471 552	322 698	148 854	477 444	331 095	146 349	28 506	46 530	37 201	46 657	72 992	33 183
2009												
January	458 970	317 598	141 372	468 727	328 960	139 767	28 142	46 011	37 560	46 165	72 400	32 523
February	456 179	317 911	138 268	463 001	327 943	135 058	27 765	45 853	37 590	46 305	71 960	32 474
March	457 906	321 220	136 686	457 535	325 513	132 022	27 437	45 681	37 656	45 313	72 094	32 623
April	453 442	319 737	133 705	452 199	323 540	128 659	27 297	45 049	37 641	44 638	71 542	32 365
May	439 652	315 077	124 575	444 019	321 147	122 872	26 962	44 518	37 726	44 169	71 180	32 118
June	432 945	313 200	119 745	439 253	320 057	119 196	26 781	43 845	37 534	43 781	71 249	32 275
July	423 579	312 989	110 590	434 443	319 166	115 277	26 594	43 481	37 668	43 362	70 824	31 855
August	414 049	314 022	100 027	422 929	317 410	105 519	26 528	43 185	37 469	42 883	70 263	31 782
September	427 976	323 078	104 898	425 579	315 108	110 471	26 591	43 054	37 557	42 195	69 794	31 641
October	450 618	339 342	111 276	428 150	315 835	112 315	27 032	42 847	37 668	41 920	70 184	31 552
November	456 740	341 161	115 579	428 262	314 602	113 660	26 472	42 212	37 768	41 850	69 948	31 090
December	423 584	307 783	115 801	429 287	315 195	114 092	26 387	43 129	37 093	41 673	69 860	30 895
2010												
January	420 122	304 466	115 656	429 656	315 085	114 571	26 427	42 887	37 646	41 514	69 406	31 053
February	423 843	304 983	118 860	431 080	314 937	116 143	26 334	42 847	37 683	41 394	69 239	30 911
March	433 483	312 827	120 656	433 611	317 018	116 593	26 652	42 926	37 943	41 457	70 238	30 563
April	435 941	315 290	120 651	435 345	318 941	116 404	26 808	43 223	37 723	41 657	70 931	30 743
May	431 205	313 586	117 619	435 702	319 500	116 202	27 270	43 654	37 687	41 884	70 941	30 558
June	434 446	313 418	121 028	440 585	319 993	120 592	27 369	43 193	37 754	42 082	71 327	30 537
July	433 247	314 738	118 509	444 748	321 036	123 712	27 383	43 015	37 743	42 176	72 043	30 768
August	438 652	318 660	119 992	448 625	321 958	126 667	27 503	42 934	37 761	42 220	72 283	30 632
September	454 995	331 571	123 424	453 323	323 409	129 914	27 672	43 066	37 980	42 247	72 504	30 203
October	474 899	347 127	127 772	452 350	323 546	128 804	27 571	43 103	38 054	42 297	72 666	30 538
November	482 047	351 428	130 619	452 905	324 580	128 325	27 841	43 421	38 190	42 098	72 988	30 839
December	449 779	320 063	129 716	455 295	327 409	127 886	28 061	43 614	38 409	42 938	73 558	30 876
2011												
January	446 491	317 807	128 684	456 213	328 746	127 467	27 937	43 984	38 821	43 261	73 425	30 813
February	446 269	318 520	127 749	453 918	329 084	124 834	27 530	44 039	38 830	43 529	73 727	30 808
March	459 056	328 058	130 998	458 807	332 223	126 584	27 823	44 294	38 953	43 918	74 818	31 117
April	460 229	329 060	131 169	459 373	332 745	126 628	27 730	44 392	39 467	44 100	74 598	30 939
May	457 121	328 155	128 966	461 685	334 181	127 504	27 567	44 242	39 565	44 603	75 080	31 154
June	456 090	328 391	127 699	462 447	335 079	127 368	27 685	44 132	39 705	44 874	75 134	30 928
July	450 037	327 874	122 163	462 206	334 605	127 601	27 507	44 039	39 992	45 012	74 906	30 815
August	457 151	333 846	123 305	466 991	337 019	129 972	27 485	44 129	40 217	45 597	75 588	30 915
September	470 346	345 796	124 550	468 199	337 302	130 897	27 108	44 415	40 378	45 869	75 523	30 862
October	491 558	361 553	130 005	468 273	337 328	130 945	27 164	44 379	40 351	46 174	75 676	30 863
November	500 523	365 870	134 653	470 650	338 325	132 325	27 193	44 238	40 490	46 283	75 691	30 688
December	466 025	331 853	134 172	471 683	339 385	132 298	27 251	43 967	40 583	46 249	76 698	31 032

[1]Excluding leased departments.

Table 16-12. Merchant Wholesalers—Sales and Inventories

(Millions of dollars.)

Classification basis, year, and month	Not seasonally adjusted						Seasonally adjusted					
	Sales			Inventories (current cost, end of period)			Sales			Inventories (current cost, end of period)		
	Total	Durable goods establish-ments	Nondurable goods establish-ments	Total	Durable goods establish-ments	Nondurable goods establish-ments	Total	Durable goods establish-ments	Nondurable goods establish-ments	Total	Durable goods establish-ments	Nondurable goods establish-ments
1992	1 767 130	861 182	905 948	197 793	121 809	75 984	1 767 130	861 182	905 948	196 914	123 435	73 479
1993	1 848 215	939 945	908 270	205 815	127 094	78 721	1 848 215	939 945	908 270	204 842	128 851	75 991
1994	1 974 899	1 037 638	937 261	222 826	139 941	82 885	1 974 899	1 037 638	937 261	221 978	141 975	80 003
1995	2 158 980	1 141 701	1 017 279	239 275	151 709	87 566	2 158 980	1 141 701	1 017 279	238 392	154 089	84 303
1996	2 284 343	1 190 342	1 094 001	241 396	154 207	87 189	2 284 343	1 190 342	1 094 001	241 058	156 683	84 375
1997	2 377 845	1 256 384	1 121 461	258 900	165 371	93 529	2 377 845	1 256 384	1 121 461	258 454	168 089	90 365
1998	2 427 120	1 306 545	1 120 575	272 575	175 994	96 581	2 427 120	1 306 545	1 120 575	272 297	178 918	93 379
1999	2 599 159	1 406 371	1 192 788	290 407	187 763	102 644	2 599 159	1 406 371	1 192 788	290 207	190 924	99 283
2000	2 814 554	1 486 673	1 327 881	309 764	198 579	111 185	2 814 554	1 486 673	1 327 881	309 246	201 852	107 394
2001	2 785 152	1 422 195	1 362 957	298 651	182 595	116 056	2 785 152	1 422 195	1 362 957	297 588	185 592	111 996
2002	2 835 528	1 421 503	1 414 025	302 807	182 242	120 565	2 835 528	1 421 503	1 414 025	301 436	185 168	116 268
2003	2 971 816	1 461 729	1 510 087	309 856	186 248	123 608	2 971 816	1 461 729	1 510 087	308 055	189 163	118 892
2004	3 316 403	1 680 871	1 635 532	340 823	212 937	127 886	3 316 403	1 680 871	1 635 532	339 431	215 994	123 437
2005	3 613 381	1 814 405	1 798 976	368 842	232 362	136 480	3 613 381	1 814 405	1 798 976	367 505	235 515	131 990
2006	3 904 209	1 982 844	1 921 365	399 872	255 356	144 516	3 904 209	1 982 844	1 921 365	398 586	258 709	139 877
2007	4 174 286	2 074 466	2 099 820	426 664	261 895	164 769	4 174 286	2 074 466	2 099 820	424 806	265 317	159 489
2008	4 431 775	2 076 292	2 355 483	442 903	276 183	166 720	4 431 775	2 076 292	2 355 483	442 249	279 821	162 428
2009	3 699 214	1 669 710	2 029 504	391 532	225 794	165 738	3 699 214	1 669 710	2 029 504	389 908	229 047	160 861
2010	4 132 327	1 875 793	2 256 534	432 070	245 126	186 944	4 132 327	1 875 793	2 256 534	429 260	248 656	180 604
2011	4 677 337	2 093 773	2 583 564	473 737	270 277	203 460	4 677 337	2 093 773	2 583 564	471 549	273 932	197 617
2008												
January	357 227	167 143	190 084	434 151	267 364	166 787	369 644	176 866	192 778	430 273	268 697	161 576
February	345 074	160 742	184 332	438 643	270 835	167 808	368 136	173 474	194 662	434 215	270 442	163 773
March	374 686	179 184	195 502	436 363	270 233	166 130	371 594	176 394	195 200	434 969	271 448	163 521
April	387 143	184 432	202 711	440 582	274 830	165 752	379 319	180 781	198 538	441 809	275 366	166 443
May	393 339	181 842	211 497	438 815	276 223	162 592	385 407	180 651	204 756	444 309	276 979	167 330
June	403 469	188 417	215 052	446 450	278 335	168 115	394 556	182 138	212 418	449 433	278 052	171 381
July	400 657	184 351	216 306	453 718	283 375	170 343	391 100	180 647	210 453	455 627	281 224	174 403
August	384 054	176 497	207 557	453 994	284 941	169 053	384 078	176 904	207 174	459 241	284 623	174 618
September	383 198	180 889	202 309	456 922	288 183	168 739	373 618	173 089	200 529	457 554	286 381	171 173
October	379 314	178 808	200 506	453 728	286 952	166 776	355 947	165 298	190 649	450 644	284 479	166 165
November	305 731	142 965	162 766	449 662	284 289	165 373	326 711	154 037	172 674	447 351	283 237	164 114
December	317 883	151 022	166 861	442 903	276 183	166 720	313 546	148 148	165 398	442 249	279 821	162 428
2009												
January	285 273	127 460	157 813	439 622	274 541	165 081	303 793	138 908	164 885	437 149	276 170	160 979
February	275 290	125 387	149 903	431 101	268 267	162 834	307 019	142 104	164 915	428 205	268 074	160 131
March	307 718	142 345	165 373	420 549	258 941	161 608	295 975	135 547	160 428	419 310	260 086	159 224
April	302 964	135 168	167 796	412 284	253 287	158 997	297 636	133 612	164 024	413 387	254 063	159 324
May	297 782	129 668	168 114	403 261	247 658	155 603	300 286	133 753	166 533	407 902	248 490	159 412
June	320 293	145 101	175 192	398 392	243 903	154 489	303 299	135 353	167 946	400 549	243 690	156 859
July	312 954	140 291	172 663	393 589	240 947	152 642	306 855	137 693	169 162	394 516	239 148	155 368
August	308 908	139 060	169 848	385 665	235 306	150 359	309 842	139 226	170 616	389 443	234 872	154 571
September	319 451	146 586	172 865	384 720	234 068	150 652	311 756	140 577	171 179	384 913	232 481	152 432
October	326 959	149 679	177 280	388 990	234 617	154 373	314 528	142 102	172 426	386 270	232 216	154 054
November	312 021	138 971	173 050	394 236	232 363	161 873	323 648	144 375	179 273	391 806	231 271	160 535
December	329 601	149 994	179 607	391 532	225 794	165 738	324 983	146 015	178 968	389 908	229 047	160 861
2010												
January	299 417	130 256	169 161	393 383	227 679	165 704	327 364	146 690	180 674	390 649	229 174	161 475
February	297 448	131 058	166 390	394 687	230 408	164 279	331 658	148 602	183 056	391 435	230 238	161 197
March	359 964	162 949	197 015	395 175	231 526	163 649	336 103	150 520	185 583	393 490	232 864	160 626
April	348 835	157 124	191 711	393 721	232 513	161 208	341 364	154 373	186 991	394 596	233 543	161 053
May	337 917	150 849	187 068	392 039	233 863	158 176	340 153	155 679	184 474	395 833	234 779	161 054
June	357 010	166 453	190 557	394 079	235 291	158 788	338 780	156 095	182 685	396 106	235 086	161 020
July	340 666	155 952	184 714	400 334	239 055	161 279	342 513	157 213	185 300	401 395	237 148	164 247
August	354 056	163 489	190 567	401 437	239 947	161 490	344 468	158 028	186 440	406 020	239 350	166 670
September	352 836	165 060	187 776	410 725	243 088	167 637	346 293	158 842	187 451	412 226	241 354	170 872
October	357 257	163 104	194 153	424 846	247 043	177 803	354 528	160 381	194 147	421 311	244 266	177 045
November	358 994	161 624	197 370	426 159	247 069	179 090	361 015	162 670	198 345	423 206	245 833	177 373
December	367 927	167 875	200 052	432 070	245 126	186 944	363 906	163 732	200 174	429 260	248 656	180 604
2011												
January	345 734	149 369	196 365	438 921	249 071	189 850	376 856	168 122	208 734	434 085	250 761	183 324
February	336 398	146 728	189 670	443 425	252 437	190 988	374 427	166 312	208 115	437 988	252 397	185 591
March	413 865	185 368	228 497	446 738	252 144	194 594	385 965	171 199	214 766	443 400	253 561	189 839
April	387 872	167 507	220 365	446 154	254 378	191 776	388 422	170 447	217 975	446 698	255 169	191 529
May	396 558	169 324	227 234	450 017	259 192	190 825	387 051	169 033	218 018	454 942	260 177	194 765
June	407 610	182 970	224 640	452 861	263 133	189 728	389 296	172 277	217 019	456 715	262 845	193 870
July	376 195	168 341	207 854	457 918	267 569	190 349	390 187	175 474	214 713	460 271	265 391	194 880
August	417 221	192 248	224 973	455 522	268 534	186 988	395 149	180 298	214 851	462 065	268 062	194 003
September	402 955	187 199	215 756	457 333	270 679	186 654	395 783	179 550	216 233	459 278	268 974	190 304
October	400 006	181 802	218 204	469 385	274 449	194 896	398 145	179 270	218 875	465 787	271 336	194 451
November	394 417	178 051	216 366	468 732	272 654	196 078	398 316	180 097	218 219	466 121	271 164	194 957
December	398 506	184 866	213 640	473 737	270 277	203 460	404 636	185 285	219 351	471 549	273 932	197 617

. . . = Not available.

Table 16-13. Manufacturing and Trade Sales and Inventories

Year and month	Sales, billions of dollars					Inventories, billions of dollars, end of period, seasonally adjusted				Ratios, inventories to sales, seasonally adjusted [1]			
	Not seasonally adjusted, total	Seasonally adjusted				Total	Manufacturing	Retail trade	Merchant wholesalers	Total	Manufacturing	Retail trade	Merchant wholesalers
		Total	Manufacturing	Retail trade	Merchant wholesalers								
1992	6 482.4	6 462.7	2 896.7	1 805.1	1 760.9	823.6	369.7	256.2	197.8	1.52	1.57	1.68	1.31
1993	6 806.3	6 804.6	3 020.4	1 936.4	1 847.8	850.7	370.8	274.1	205.8	1.50	1.51	1.69	1.31
1994	7 318.2	7 322.4	3 242.2	2 103.3	1 976.9	913.2	390.5	299.8	222.8	1.47	1.45	1.67	1.29
1995	7 856.3	7 865.7	3 481.8	2 220.2	2 163.7	971.5	415.0	317.3	239.3	1.48	1.44	1.73	1.30
1996	8 243.1	8 218.3	3 586.7	2 355.6	2 276.0	990.2	420.7	328.2	241.4	1.45	1.43	1.68	1.27
1997	8 681.3	8 684.4	3 836.6	2 470.8	2 377.1	1 031.1	433.5	338.8	258.9	1.42	1.37	1.65	1.26
1998	8 908.7	8 907.6	3 898.6	2 582.7	2 426.3	1 062.7	438.8	351.3	272.6	1.44	1.39	1.63	1.32
1999	9 434.1	9 431.7	4 033.4	2 801.4	2 597.0	1 122.0	452.8	378.8	290.4	1.41	1.35	1.60	1.30
2000	10 006.4	9 999.1	4 202.3	2 979.4	2 817.4	1 180.2	470.1	400.4	309.8	1.41	1.36	1.60	1.29
2001	9 817.9	9 820.5	3 972.3	3 062.3	2 785.9	1 104.0	417.5	387.9	298.7	1.43	1.38	1.59	1.32
2002	9 878.8	9 881.4	3 917.3	3 129.7	2 834.4	1 124.4	412.3	409.3	302.8	1.36	1.29	1.56	1.26
2003	10 250.2	10 249.8	4 017.0	3 261.9	2 970.9	1 133.3	397.6	425.8	309.9	1.34	1.25	1.57	1.23
2004	11 098.9	11 057.5	4 294.3	3 461.4	3 301.8	1 224.7	429.0	454.9	340.8	1.30	1.18	1.56	1.18
2005	12 045.6	12 049.5	4 743.2	3 687.6	3 618.6	1 295.7	461.1	465.8	368.8	1.28	1.17	1.52	1.18
2006	12 793.8	12 806.3	5 016.3	3 880.3	3 909.7	1 388.8	508.7	480.2	399.9	1.29	1.21	1.50	1.19
2007	13 493.0	13 495.7	5 322.2	4 001.3	4 172.1	1 467.7	547.0	494.0	426.7	1.29	1.23	1.49	1.18
2008	13 846.3	13 798.9	5 446.8	3 938.5	4 413.7	1 442.6	528.2	471.6	442.9	1.32	1.26	1.51	1.22
2009	11 746.3	11 753.7	4 425.5	3 628.6	3 699.6	1 306.3	491.2	423.6	391.5	1.39	1.39	1.47	1.32
2010	12 890.5	12 890.0	4 921.8	3 840.3	4 128.1	1 416.0	534.1	449.8	432.1	1.28	1.28	1.39	1.18
2011	14 322.8	14 340.0	5 500.1	4 155.7	4 684.2	1 523.7	583.9	466.0	473.7	1.26	1.28	1.35	1.17
2007													
January	1 001.1	1 076.6	419.7	327.0	330.0	1 412.4	525.0	487.6	399.8	1.31	1.25	1.49	1.21
February	989.3	1 092.1	428.2	328.4	335.5	1 418.5	527.7	489.2	401.5	1.30	1.23	1.49	1.20
March	1 143.8	1 103.6	433.6	331.3	338.8	1 420.7	529.8	486.9	404.0	1.29	1.22	1.47	1.19
April	1 093.4	1 110.5	436.6	329.9	344.0	1 427.6	533.9	488.6	405.2	1.29	1.22	1.48	1.18
May	1 176.7	1 125.0	443.7	334.3	347.0	1 437.8	538.5	492.5	406.8	1.28	1.21	1.47	1.17
June	1 164.3	1 120.7	442.6	330.7	347.4	1 444.9	541.1	495.6	408.1	1.29	1.22	1.50	1.17
July	1 101.4	1 122.9	445.2	332.3	345.4	1 447.2	541.6	496.7	408.9	1.29	1.22	1.49	1.18
August	1 185.4	1 129.1	446.5	333.9	348.7	1 452.5	542.9	499.5	410.1	1.29	1.22	1.50	1.18
September	1 115.0	1 137.4	447.2	337.2	353.0	1 461.0	548.5	498.9	413.6	1.28	1.23	1.48	1.17
October	1 184.1	1 148.0	454.6	336.8	356.6	1 465.4	551.0	499.9	414.4	1.28	1.21	1.48	1.16
November	1 158.8	1 168.6	463.0	341.4	364.3	1 475.2	556.2	499.5	419.5	1.26	1.20	1.46	1.15
December	1 179.7	1 161.0	461.3	338.2	361.5	1 486.7	561.8	500.0	424.8	1.28	1.22	1.48	1.18
2008													
January	1 097.5	1 175.8	467.8	338.3	369.6	1 502.3	569.6	502.4	430.3	1.28	1.22	1.49	1.16
February	1 097.2	1 166.4	463.4	334.9	368.1	1 507.6	571.0	502.4	434.2	1.29	1.23	1.50	1.18
March	1 184.8	1 166.9	459.9	335.4	371.6	1 506.7	574.3	497.4	435.0	1.29	1.25	1.48	1.17
April	1 194.6	1 190.7	474.5	336.9	379.3	1 514.2	573.8	498.6	441.8	1.27	1.21	1.48	1.16
May	1 242.3	1 200.1	476.6	338.1	385.4	1 515.8	574.1	497.4	444.3	1.26	1.20	1.47	1.15
June	1 255.4	1 216.4	482.7	339.2	394.6	1 526.9	581.0	496.5	449.4	1.26	1.20	1.46	1.14
July	1 222.9	1 213.9	485.9	337.0	391.1	1 537.6	581.3	500.7	455.6	1.27	1.20	1.49	1.16
August	1 211.0	1 188.7	469.1	335.6	384.1	1 537.5	582.6	495.6	459.2	1.29	1.24	1.48	1.20
September	1 168.1	1 156.9	454.8	328.6	373.6	1 529.1	576.3	495.2	457.6	1.32	1.27	1.51	1.22
October	1 140.1	1 103.8	432.8	315.1	355.9	1 513.2	568.3	494.3	450.6	1.37	1.31	1.57	1.27
November	989.3	1 029.5	398.5	304.2	326.7	1 491.5	559.3	484.9	447.4	1.45	1.40	1.59	1.37
December	1 043.0	989.7	380.8	295.3	313.5	1 461.3	541.6	477.4	442.2	1.48	1.42	1.62	1.41
2009													
January	896.3	970.7	366.7	300.2	303.8	1 443.2	537.3	468.7	437.1	1.49	1.47	1.56	1.44
February	881.0	974.6	368.4	299.2	307.0	1 420.9	529.7	463.0	428.2	1.46	1.44	1.55	1.39
March	973.9	947.2	357.4	293.8	296.0	1 400.2	523.4	457.5	419.3	1.48	1.46	1.56	1.42
April	950.2	945.6	353.3	294.6	297.6	1 382.4	516.8	452.2	413.4	1.46	1.46	1.53	1.39
May	964.5	951.3	353.1	297.9	300.3	1 364.7	512.8	444.0	407.9	1.43	1.45	1.49	1.36
June	1 012.5	967.0	361.6	302.1	303.3	1 347.1	507.3	439.3	400.5	1.39	1.40	1.45	1.32
July	980.5	975.5	365.6	303.0	306.9	1 332.7	503.7	434.4	394.5	1.37	1.38	1.43	1.29
August	1 001.7	989.1	368.1	311.1	309.8	1 313.5	501.1	422.9	389.4	1.33	1.36	1.36	1.26
September	998.0	989.3	375.3	302.2	311.8	1 308.5	498.0	425.6	384.9	1.32	1.33	1.41	1.23
October	1 017.7	999.4	380.0	304.9	314.5	1 315.5	501.1	428.2	386.3	1.32	1.32	1.40	1.23
November	989.9	1 017.8	385.0	309.1	323.6	1 324.1	504.0	428.3	391.8	1.30	1.31	1.39	1.21
December	1 080.1	1 026.3	390.9	310.4	325.0	1 323.8	504.6	429.3	389.9	1.29	1.29	1.38	1.20
2010													
January	940.1	1 033.5	395.0	311.1	327.4	1 326.0	505.7	429.7	390.6	1.28	1.28	1.38	1.19
February	937.2	1 035.5	393.3	310.5	331.7	1 332.9	510.4	431.1	391.4	1.29	1.30	1.39	1.18
March	1 107.2	1 053.7	400.5	317.1	336.1	1 340.0	512.9	433.6	393.5	1.27	1.28	1.37	1.17
April	1 077.0	1 065.9	405.2	319.3	341.4	1 345.1	515.2	435.3	394.6	1.26	1.27	1.36	1.16
May	1 073.6	1 060.8	403.6	317.0	340.2	1 345.4	513.9	435.7	395.8	1.27	1.27	1.37	1.16
June	1 106.6	1 056.4	401.9	315.7	338.8	1 354.6	517.9	440.6	396.1	1.28	1.29	1.40	1.17
July	1 062.1	1 073.5	414.4	316.6	342.5	1 366.7	520.6	444.7	401.4	1.27	1.26	1.40	1.17
August	1 104.2	1 076.1	412.1	319.6	344.5	1 378.1	523.5	448.6	406.0	1.28	1.27	1.40	1.18
September	1 094.7	1 086.5	417.7	322.5	346.3	1 394.5	528.9	453.3	412.2	1.28	1.27	1.41	1.19
October	1 099.9	1 101.3	419.6	327.2	354.5	1 408.7	535.1	452.4	421.3	1.28	1.28	1.38	1.19
November	1 103.2	1 115.8	424.2	330.6	361.0	1 417.4	541.3	452.9	423.2	1.27	1.28	1.37	1.17
December	1 184.8	1 131.1	434.3	333.0	363.9	1 433.8	549.2	455.3	429.3	1.27	1.26	1.37	1.18
2011													
January	1 050.1	1 154.1	440.9	336.4	376.9	1 447.1	556.8	456.2	434.1	1.25	1.26	1.36	1.15
February	1 047.0	1 154.2	441.0	338.7	374.4	1 455.5	563.6	453.9	438.0	1.26	1.28	1.34	1.17
March	1 247.5	1 181.9	454.5	341.4	386.0	1 473.4	571.1	458.9	443.4	1.25	1.26	1.34	1.15
April	1 186.3	1 185.1	453.3	343.4	388.4	1 485.3	579.3	459.3	446.7	1.25	1.28	1.34	1.15
May	1 215.5	1 184.4	453.9	343.4	387.1	1 500.6	584.0	461.7	454.9	1.27	1.29	1.34	1.18
June	1 243.6	1 190.3	456.8	344.2	389.3	1 504.8	585.6	462.4	456.7	1.26	1.28	1.34	1.17
July	1 167.4	1 203.6	467.5	345.9	390.2	1 511.4	588.9	462.2	460.3	1.26	1.26	1.34	1.18
August	1 258.7	1 206.4	464.6	346.6	395.1	1 520.9	591.8	467.0	462.1	1.26	1.27	1.35	1.17
September	1 219.0	1 210.2	463.9	350.6	395.8	1 518.6	591.2	468.2	459.3	1.25	1.27	1.34	1.16
October	1 213.1	1 218.6	466.6	353.9	398.1	1 531.6	597.6	468.3	465.8	1.26	1.28	1.32	1.17
November	1 204.6	1 220.3	466.4	355.6	398.3	1 537.4	600.6	470.7	466.1	1.26	1.29	1.32	1.17
December	1 270.0	1 231.0	470.8	355.6	404.6	1 544.1	600.8	471.7	471.5	1.25	1.28	1.33	1.17

[1] Annual data are averages of monthly ratios.

Table 16-14. Real Manufacturing and Trade Sales and Inventories

(Billions of chained [2005] dollars, ratios; seasonally adjusted; annual sales figures are averages of seasonally adjusted monthly data.)

NIPA Tables 1BU, 2BU, 3BU

Year and month	Sales, monthly average				Inventories, end of period				Ratios, end-of-period inventories to monthly average sales			
	Total	Manufac-turing	Retail trade	Merchant wholesalers	Total	Manufac-turing	Retail trade	Merchant wholesalers	Total	Manufac-turing	Retail trade	Merchant wholesalers
1997	807.5	365.1	228.0	209.8	1 110.9	490.0	349.5	276.0	1.38	1.34	1.53	1.32
1998	846.7	377.1	241.6	224.7	1 165.0	507.6	364.7	297.3	1.38	1.35	1.51	1.32
1999	893.8	389.1	259.4	242.8	1 225.8	523.8	390.5	315.3	1.37	1.35	1.51	1.30
2000	920.3	393.8	269.3	255.7	1 271.2	531.9	411.1	331.4	1.38	1.35	1.53	1.30
2001	907.2	371.9	275.6	256.4	1 226.2	505.7	400.5	322.6	1.35	1.36	1.45	1.26
2002	919.9	369.8	283.9	263.5	1 246.7	500.5	424.2	323.2	1.36	1.35	1.49	1.23
2003	937.2	370.6	295.6	268.8	1 256.5	492.0	441.5	323.3	1.34	1.33	1.49	1.20
2004	972.0	378.4	307.9	284.7	1 304.9	498.0	465.2	341.7	1.34	1.32	1.51	1.20
2005	1 014.3	395.2	320.7	298.4	1 344.9	519.0	469.8	356.0	1.33	1.31	1.47	1.19
2006	1 043.7	400.0	332.6	311.6	1 387.5	536.0	480.6	370.8	1.33	1.34	1.45	1.19
2007	1 056.7	400.4	337.9	319.3	1 413.2	551.4	484.8	376.6	1.34	1.38	1.44	1.18
2008	1 012.2	377.0	323.8	311.3	1 376.2	537.3	458.3	379.3	1.36	1.43	1.42	1.22
2009	921.4	327.2	307.8	284.3	1 258.3	505.9	412.5	338.4	1.37	1.55	1.34	1.19
2010	959.1	336.5	322.0	299.8	1 317.2	526.1	428.8	360.4	1.37	1.56	1.33	1.20
2011	992.0	345.4	334.8	311.9	1 350.3	551.6	415.9	378.4	1.36	1.60	1.24	1.21
2007												
January	1 046.1	393.4	338.2	314.7	1 386.3	537.2	478.5	370.4	1.33	1.37	1.42	1.18
February	1 051.4	398.4	337.8	315.6	1 389.3	538.0	480.2	370.9	1.32	1.35	1.42	1.18
March	1 056.4	400.7	338.1	318.6	1 388.1	537.9	478.5	371.5	1.31	1.34	1.42	1.17
April	1 056.1	399.5	336.0	321.5	1 392.4	540.3	480.1	371.6	1.32	1.35	1.43	1.16
May	1 062.6	401.6	339.0	323.2	1 395.8	543.0	480.2	372.3	1.31	1.35	1.42	1.15
June	1 055.2	398.4	335.6	322.0	1 397.4	543.3	480.9	372.9	1.32	1.36	1.43	1.16
July	1 052.0	398.0	336.1	318.5	1 399.5	542.6	482.9	373.8	1.33	1.36	1.44	1.17
August	1 059.0	401.5	338.5	320.2	1 402.0	541.6	485.9	374.3	1.32	1.35	1.44	1.17
September	1 060.6	399.7	341.3	321.0	1 407.7	546.4	484.2	376.8	1.33	1.37	1.42	1.17
October	1 061.3	403.4	339.1	319.8	1 408.9	547.0	486.5	375.2	1.33	1.36	1.44	1.17
November	1 062.4	404.2	338.7	320.5	1 408.9	548.5	484.7	375.3	1.33	1.36	1.43	1.17
December	1 057.2	405.6	335.8	316.4	1 413.2	551.4	484.8	376.6	1.34	1.36	1.44	1.19
2008												
January	1 060.0	406.2	335.3	319.4	1 418.2	557.4	483.5	376.7	1.34	1.37	1.44	1.18
February	1 044.9	398.4	331.3	315.7	1 415.1	557.3	480.6	376.4	1.35	1.40	1.45	1.19
March	1 035.5	388.8	331.3	315.6	1 409.2	558.0	476.5	373.6	1.36	1.44	1.44	1.18
April	1 046.2	395.7	332.3	318.8	1 406.6	554.8	474.0	376.6	1.34	1.40	1.43	1.18
May	1 036.6	387.0	331.6	318.7	1 401.2	551.2	472.8	376.2	1.35	1.42	1.43	1.18
June	1 036.1	386.2	329.1	320.9	1 403.3	552.9	471.8	377.4	1.35	1.43	1.43	1.18
July	1 018.4	380.9	323.7	313.7	1 406.4	549.8	476.2	379.8	1.38	1.44	1.47	1.21
August	1 007.7	372.0	323.4	312.2	1 400.7	548.5	470.0	380.9	1.39	1.48	1.45	1.22
September	983.5	361.6	317.7	303.8	1 393.9	544.5	467.8	380.5	1.42	1.51	1.47	1.25
October	974.3	358.8	309.6	304.6	1 390.5	544.0	466.6	378.8	1.43	1.52	1.51	1.24
November	954.1	345.8	311.1	295.7	1 388.1	544.6	462.4	379.8	1.46	1.58	1.49	1.28
December	949.1	343.1	309.0	296.1	1 376.2	537.3	458.3	379.3	1.45	1.57	1.48	1.28
2009												
January	929.3	331.0	312.3	284.4	1 367.6	536.8	451.1	378.2	1.47	1.62	1.44	1.33
February	932.5	334.4	308.4	288.4	1 354.5	532.1	447.7	373.2	1.45	1.59	1.45	1.29
March	917.8	328.0	304.6	283.1	1 341.7	528.1	444.8	367.4	1.46	1.61	1.46	1.30
April	910.9	322.1	304.5	281.9	1 331.8	524.0	442.6	363.8	1.46	1.63	1.45	1.29
May	908.8	317.9	306.5	281.7	1 318.1	521.7	435.2	359.7	1.45	1.64	1.42	1.28
June	906.9	318.8	306.2	279.2	1 302.2	517.6	429.9	353.3	1.44	1.62	1.40	1.27
July	920.4	325.0	306.4	286.7	1 288.6	514.7	424.1	348.4	1.40	1.58	1.38	1.22
August	918.8	321.6	312.9	282.3	1 271.2	511.4	415.2	343.0	1.38	1.59	1.33	1.22
September	920.4	328.3	304.8	284.5	1 265.0	507.1	417.6	338.9	1.37	1.55	1.37	1.19
October	922.8	331.0	306.6	282.7	1 266.2	508.6	416.0	340.2	1.37	1.54	1.36	1.20
November	932.1	331.8	309.2	288.7	1 265.2	508.3	412.6	342.6	1.36	1.53	1.34	1.19
December	936.5	336.1	310.8	287.6	1 258.3	505.9	412.5	338.4	1.34	1.51	1.33	1.18
2010												
January	929.8	333.0	310.5	284.2	1 258.8	505.4	414.4	337.6	1.35	1.52	1.34	1.19
February	936.5	333.4	311.1	289.6	1 264.0	509.0	415.1	338.4	1.35	1.53	1.33	1.17
March	949.1	336.6	318.5	292.6	1 267.8	509.0	417.0	340.4	1.34	1.51	1.31	1.16
April	954.0	336.2	320.6	296.4	1 273.2	509.8	420.0	342.1	1.34	1.52	1.31	1.15
May	952.7	331.1	320.1	300.7	1 276.7	507.8	422.2	345.4	1.34	1.53	1.32	1.15
June	958.2	331.1	321.4	305.0	1 283.1	510.2	425.1	346.6	1.34	1.54	1.32	1.14
July	967.1	338.3	320.9	307.4	1 291.3	512.0	426.2	351.7	1.34	1.51	1.33	1.14
August	966.7	336.5	323.2	306.1	1 297.8	512.8	430.0	353.7	1.34	1.52	1.33	1.16
September	968.7	339.2	326.0	303.0	1 306.7	516.2	432.2	357.0	1.35	1.52	1.33	1.18
October	970.9	337.3	329.0	304.3	1 315.2	520.1	429.9	363.5	1.36	1.54	1.31	1.19
November	976.4	339.0	331.4	305.6	1 311.4	522.7	427.1	359.6	1.34	1.54	1.29	1.18
December	979.0	345.8	331.2	302.2	1 317.2	526.1	428.8	360.4	1.35	1.52	1.30	1.19
2011												
January	987.7	347.8	331.6	307.9	1 321.9	529.8	429.0	361.0	1.34	1.52	1.29	1.17
February	977.3	343.7	333.1	300.5	1 322.1	531.9	426.8	361.1	1.35	1.55	1.28	1.20
March	988.3	347.0	332.8	308.5	1 328.2	534.5	428.6	362.9	1.34	1.54	1.29	1.18
April	979.7	340.2	332.0	307.2	1 333.2	538.4	428.2	364.1	1.36	1.58	1.29	1.19
May	979.4	337.7	331.3	310.0	1 338.3	540.2	425.3	369.7	1.37	1.60	1.28	1.19
June	987.6	340.6	333.6	313.1	1 338.5	540.5	423.5	371.2	1.36	1.59	1.27	1.19
July	989.8	343.4	333.1	313.0	1 342.0	542.2	422.8	373.5	1.36	1.58	1.27	1.19
August	995.4	345.6	332.6	316.8	1 343.1	543.2	422.3	373.9	1.35	1.57	1.27	1.18
September	993.9	345.8	336.0	312.7	1 338.2	543.3	420.3	371.0	1.35	1.57	1.25	1.19
October	1 005.5	349.7	338.9	317.6	1 344.6	548.2	417.5	374.8	1.34	1.57	1.23	1.18
November	1 004.8	349.7	340.3	315.8	1 347.1	550.9	417.3	374.8	1.34	1.58	1.23	1.19
December	1 014.7	354.2	341.8	320.1	1 350.3	551.6	415.9	378.4	1.33	1.56	1.22	1.18

Table 16-15. Selected Services—Quarterly Estimated Revenue for Employer Firms

(Millions of dollars.)

2002 NAICS code	Kind of business	2006				2007			
		1st quarter	2nd quarter	3rd quarter	4th quarter	1st quarter	2nd quarter	3rd quarter	4th quarter
SEASONALLY ADJUSTED									
51	**Information**	250 937	254 950	258 346	262 769	263 855	266 293	270 033	272 215
5112	Software publishers	30 247	30 927	31 922	32 136	34 481	33 470	33 207	34 131
512	Motion picture and sound recording industries	22 245	23 202	23 459	24 301	23 922	23 621	24 146	23 429
54 pt	**Professional, Scientific, and Technical Services (Except Landscape Architectural Services and Veterinary Services)**	274 014	277 544	283 074	289 736	298 257	304 484	310 272	315 925
5411	Legal services	54 325	56 030	57 478	59 283	61 658	58 569	58 821	60 449
5412	Accounting, tax preparation, bookkeeping, and payroll services	26 040	25 013	25 763	26 561	26 864	28 389	29 148	30 181
56 pt	**Administrative and Support and Waste Management and Remediation Services (Except Landscaping Services)**	130 874	132 679	134 415	136 959	139 069	142 961	144 153	143 697
5613	Employment services	46 089	46 470	47 438	48 803	49 659	50 981	50 549	51 443
5615	Travel arrangement and reservation services	7 719	8 024	8 471	9 162	9 323	9 300	9 240	9 248
562	Waste management and remediation services	17 696	18 134	17 962	18 077	18 874	18 725	18 746	18 922
622	**Hospitals**	159 968	162 804	165 613	169 594	172 065	174 331	177 024	179 809
NOT SEASONALLY ADJUSTED									
51	**Information**	245 165	254 695	255 763	271 440	258 050	265 760	267 333	281 198
511	Publishing industries (except Internet)	. . .	. . .	67 614	72 562	67 376	69 318	70 108	75 421
51111	Newspaper publishers	. . .	. . .	11 589	13 075	11 252	12 089	11 757	12 465
51112	Periodical publishers	. . .	. . .	11 536	11 908	10 642	11 613	11 731	12 017
5111 pt	Book, directory and mailing list, and other publishers	. . .	. . .	13 972	13 001	11 725	12 380	15 073	14 078
5112	Software publishers	29 521	30 587	30 517	34 578	33 757	33 236	31 547	36 861
512	Motion picture and sound recording industries	21 511	23 016	21 958	26 780	23 204	23 408	22 649	25 725
515	Broadcasting (except Internet)	. . .	. . .	22 994	25 825	23 530	25 117	24 662	26 610
5151	Radio and television broadcasting	13 563	13 973	12 917	14 951	13 376	13 970	13 146	14 501
5152	Cable and other subscription programming	. . .	. . .	10 077	10 874	10 154	11 147	11 516	12 109
516, 5181, 519	Internet publishing and broadcasting, Internet service providers and web search portals, and other information services	. . .	. . .	10 465	11 318	11 440	11 548	12 065	13 478
517	Telecommunications [1]	. . .	. . .	115 810	117 558	116 446	119 344	121 215	123 025
5171	Wired telecommunications carriers	48 950	48 327	48 232	47 925	46 045	46 496	46 910	46 609
5172	Wireless telecommunications carriers (except satellite)	37 242	38 408	39 832	40 531	41 131	41 927	43 327	44 198
5175	Cable and other program distribution	. . .	. . .	22 278	23 551	23 632	25 162	25 172	26 450
5182	Data processing, hosting, and related services	15 391	16 313	16 922	17 397	16 054	17 025	16 634	16 939
54	**Professional, Scientific, and Technical Services** [1]	. . .	. . .	282 492	303 575	303 671	314 751	309 660	329 932
54 pt	Professional, scientific, and technical services (except landscape architectural services and veterinary services)	272 370	280 875	274 865	296 400	296 467	307 224	302 515	322 875
5411	Legal services	50 088	55 918	55 409	66 160	56 849	58 335	57 115	67 098
5412	Accounting, tax preparation, bookkeeping, and payroll services	31 561	26 189	21 641	24 091	32 183	29 922	24 601	27 404
5413	Architectural, engineering, and related services	. . .	. . .	59 152	60 649	61 203	62 235	64 468	66 295
5415	Computer systems design and related services	51 129	52 927	52 801	56 502	57 194	61 083	62 114	63 998
5416	Management, scientific, and technical consulting services	34 594	34 358	33 640	33 373	35 066	37 478	36 787	37 483
5417	Scientific research and development services	. . .	. . .	. . .	. . .	22 433	23 492	23 602	24 991
5418	Advertising and related services	18 528	19 476	19 484	21 619	20 353	22 032	21 915	23 134
56	**Administrative and Support and Waste Management and Remediation Services** [1]	. . .	. . .	150 240	153 054	147 949	158 144	158 754	158 914
56 pt	Administrative and support and waste management and remediation services (except landscaping services)	128 505	133 016	134 891	138 577	136 506	143 344	144 674	145 327
561	Administrative and support services	. . .	. . .	131 721	134 615	130 151	139 232	139 464	139 727
5613	Employment services	44 891	46 191	47 391	50 462	48 368	50 573	50 498	53 243
5615	Travel arrangement and reservation services	7 557	8 586	8 437	8 759	9 127	9 904	9 268	8 813
562	Waste management and remediation services	16 687	18 188	18 519	18 439	17 798	18 912	19 290	19 187
62 pt	**Selected Health Care Services**	200 757	203 093	203 422	207 979	215 018	217 267	217 928	221 808
622	Hospitals	161 728	163 781	163 957	168 237	173 958	175 377	175 254	178 371
623	Nursing and residential care facilities	39 029	39 312	39 465	39 742	41 060	41 890	42 674	43 437

. . . = Not available.

[1] Includes components not shown separately.

Table 16-15. Selected Services—Quarterly Estimated Revenue for Employer Firms—*Continued*

(Millions of dollars.)

2002 NAICS code	Kind of business	2008				2009			
		1st quarter	2nd quarter	3rd quarter	4th quarter	1st quarter	2nd quarter	3rd quarter	4th quarter
SEASONALLY ADJUSTED									
51	**Information**	276 106	278 271	280 742	273 378	267 444	267 420	268 457	271 511
5112	Software publishers	35 874	36 223	36 102	34 441	33 543	34 072	34 502	36 504
512	Motion picture and sound recording industries	23 869	24 592	24 123	22 875	22 562	22 536	22 538	22 785
54 pt	**Professional, Scientific, and Technical Services (Except Landscape Architectural Services and Veterinary Services)**	317 939	325 862	328 345	321 365	308 292	305 996	307 468	307 262
5411	Legal services	60 578	62 579	61 622	60 004	59 381	59 338	59 769	58 934
5412	Accounting, tax preparation, bookkeeping, and payroll services	30 099	30 084	29 913	29 986	29 348	29 846	29 615	29 380
56 pt	**Administrative and Support and Waste Management and Remediation Services (Except Landscaping Services)**	148 542	148 908	146 518	143 814	136 703	134 519	136 816	139 552
5613	Employment services	52 405	52 397	51 113	49 072	45 913	44 492	46 063	47 549
5615	Travel arrangement and reservation services	9 695	9 748	9 510	8 998	8 541	8 206	8 419	8 702
562	Waste management and remediation services	20 063	20 163	19 261	19 473	18 067	17 694	18 132	18 969
622	**Hospitals**	182 931	183 852	184 749	186 710	190 923	196 132	199 011	200 986
NOT SEASONALLY ADJUSTED									
51	**Information**	270 308	277 714	277 654	282 673	261 828	266 885	265 504	280 742
511	Publishing industries (except Internet)	69 295	70 940	71 486	72 892	62 612	65 091	64 996	71 495
51111	Newspaper publishers	11 021	11 167	10 844	10 887	8 784	9 234	8 979	9 361
51112	Periodical publishers	10 970	11 104	11 624	11 287	9 685	9 599	9 468	10 347
5111 pt	Book, directory and mailing list, and other publishers	12 291	12 591	14 829	13 281	11 707	12 220	14 014	11 815
5112	Software publishers	35 013	36 078	34 189	37 437	32 436	34 038	32 535	39 972
512	Motion picture and sound recording industries	23 248	24 297	22 724	25 002	22 066	22 243	21 231	24 858
515	Broadcasting (except Internet)	25 325	26 450	26 077	26 732	23 670	24 565	24 249	26 450
5151	Radio and television broadcasting	13 965	14 199	13 655	13 196	11 233	11 800	11 306	13 164
5152	Cable and other subscription programming	11 360	12 251	12 422	13 536	12 437	12 765	12 943	13 286
516, 5181, 519	Internet publishing and broadcasting, Internet service providers and web search portals, and other information services	13 290	13 421	13 605	13 809	13 187	13 311	13 519	14 740
517	Telecommunications [1]	122 177	124 346	125 921	125 614	122 311	123 665	123 814	125 272
5171	Wired telecommunications carriers	46 059	46 258	46 525	45 355	43 353	43 585	42 831	42 906
5172	Wireless telecommunications carriers (except satellite)	44 209	44 968	46 008	46 290	45 503	46 005	46 861	47 315
5175	Cable and other program distribution	26 383	27 210	27 496	28 262	27 818	28 492	28 536	29 481
5182	Data processing, hosting, and related services	16 973	18 260	17 841	18 624	17 982	18 010	17 695	17 927
54	**Professional, Scientific, and Technical Services** [1]	323 112	336 025	329 244	335 516	313 259	315 259	309 435	320 092
54 pt	Professional, scientific, and technical services (except landscape architectural services and veterinary services)	316 031	328 143	321 450	328 114	306 134	307 220	302 241	313 407
5411	Legal services	55 853	62 141	60 513	66 004	54 809	58 863	59 231	64 297
5412	Accounting, tax preparation, bookkeeping, and payroll services	35 758	31 829	25 456	27 017	34 836	31 607	25 469	26 119
5413	Architectural, engineering, and related services	63 823	67 139	68 374	68 579	61 113	59 249	58 164	56 434
5415	Computer systems design and related services	65 511	66 851	66 583	66 774	63 220	64 782	64 450	68 014
5416	Management, scientific, and technical consulting services	37 134	39 022	38 919	39 085	34 787	35 007	35 989	36 189
5417	Scientific research and development services	24 155	26 076	26 516	25 156	24 771	25 747	26 929	28 309
5418	Advertising and related services	21 756	22 121	22 638	22 685	20 332	19 976	20 017	22 193
56	**Administrative and Support and Waste Management and Remediation Services** [1]	157 186	163 242	162 033	158 348	145 361	147 780	149 688	152 791
56 pt	Administrative and support and waste management and remediation services (except landscaping services)	145 832	149 300	147 220	145 257	134 294	134 909	137 622	140 866
561	Administrative and support services	138 247	142 777	142 175	138 758	128 270	129 768	130 939	133 841
5613	Employment services	51 042	51 873	51 113	50 839	44 719	44 047	46 109	49 308
5615	Travel arrangement and reservation services	9 472	10 362	9 615	8 557	8 302	8 723	8 562	8 276
562	Waste management and remediation services	18 939	20 465	19 858	19 590	17 091	18 012	18 749	18 950
62 pt	**Selected Health Care Services**	229 170	229 713	227 277	229 543	237 812	243 435	243 552	246 238
622	Hospitals	185 126	184 955	183 086	185 030	193 214	197 309	197 220	199 378
623	Nursing and residential care facilities	44 044	44 758	44 191	44 513	44 598	46 126	46 332	46 860

[1]Includes components not shown separately.

Table 16-15. Selected Services—Quarterly Estimated Revenue for Employer Firms—*Continued*

(Millions of dollars.)

2002 NAICS code	Kind of business	2010				2011			
		1st quarter	2nd quarter	3rd quarter	4th quarter	1st quarter	2nd quarter	3rd quarter	4th quarter
SEASONALLY ADJUSTED									
51	**Information**	273 565	275 643	279 074	281 730	282 046	287 475	288 959	290 745
5112	Software publishers	35 591	36 171	36 503	37 036	37 153	37 728	38 172	38 459
512	Motion picture and sound recording industries	23 655	23 642	24 017	23 854	21 166	23 258	24 142	23 525
54 pt	**Professional, Scientific, and Technical Services (Except Landscape Architectural Services and Veterinary Services)**	313 327	315 501	321 596	324 331	327 043	335 017	340 739	346 594
5411	Legal services	60 710	59 234	60 383	60 142	60 745	61 428	61 507	62 432
5412	Accounting, tax preparation, bookkeeping, and payroll services	30 070	28 958	28 638	28 250	29 388	30 318	31 693	32 222
56 pt	**Administrative and Support and Waste Management and Remediation Services (Except Landscaping Services)**	141 748	146 999	148 299	149 885	151 899	155 374	157 756	156 031
5613	Employment services	49 264	51 336	52 160	53 725	55 806	55 337	56 093	55 709
5615	Travel arrangement and reservation services	8 991	9 413	9 394	9 164	8 935	9 233	9 446	9 753
562	Waste management and remediation services	19 543	20 828	20 807	20 730	21 890	21 668	22 292	21 628
622	**Hospitals**	198 354	203 991	207 853	212 348	212 114	215 685	212 388	219 874
NOT SEASONALLY ADJUSTED									
51	**Information**	267 820	275 092	276 004	291 309	276 123	286 900	285 780	300 630
511	Publishing industries (except Internet)	62 463	65 505	66 086	71 664	63 936	67 421	67 482	72 342
51111	Newspaper publishers	8 231	8 690	8 597	9 177	8 097	8 589	8 251	8 832
51112	Periodical publishers	9 338	9 371	9 658	10 028	9 319	9 554	9 739	10 107
5111 pt	Book, directory and mailing list, and other publishers	10 727	11 273	13 409	11 794	10 890	11 588	13 458	11 214
5112	Software publishers	34 167	36 171	34 422	40 665	35 630	37 690	36 034	42 189
512	Motion picture and sound recording industries	23 229	23 264	22 696	25 929	20 849	22 839	22 838	25 548
515	Broadcasting (except Internet)	25 916	27 008	25 698	28 898	26 894	28 244	26 704	29 236
5151	Radio and television broadcasting	12 950	12 647	12 206	14 549	12 616	12 537	11 729	13 747
5152	Cable and other subscription programming	12 966	14 361	13 492	14 349	14 278	15 707	14 975	15 489
516, 5181, 519	Internet publishing and broadcasting, Internet service providers and web search portals, and other information services	14 014	14 306	14 396	15 464	15 656	16 666	16 583	18 893
517	Telecommunications [1]	124 516	126 086	127 858	129 073	129 075	131 236	131 732	134 011
5171	Wired telecommunications carriers	42 007	42 297	42 282	42 173	41 526	41 776	41 470	41 505
5172	Wireless telecommunications carriers (except satellite)	47 671	48 071	49 696	50 087	51 043	51 974	52 713	54 143
5175	Cable and other program distribution	29 378	30 275	30 405	31 242	30 920	31 822	31 851	32 541
5182	Data processing, hosting, and related services	17 682	18 923	19 270	20 281	19 713	20 494	20 441	20 600
54	**Professional, Scientific, and Technical Services** [1]	317 712	324 310	324 834	338 016	331 050	344 124	344 334	361 568
54 pt	Professional, scientific, and technical services (except landscape architectural services and veterinary services)	310 820	316 448	317 094	330 818	324 100	336 022	336 309	353 526
5411	Legal services	56 157	58 701	60 081	65 374	56 250	60 875	61 138	67 926
5412	Accounting, tax preparation, bookkeeping, and payroll services	35 874	30 551	24 829	24 888	35 177	31 955	27 573	28 323
5413	Architectural, engineering, and related services	53 324	55 558	57 697	59 620	56 779	59 863	61 276	60 880
5415	Computer systems design and related services	68 426	68 820	71 168	75 376	74 253	76 598	78 438	84 484
5416	Management, scientific, and technical consulting services	36 275	38 858	38 423	39 076	38 611	41 050	41 256	42 913
5417	Scientific research and development services	28 180	29 000	30 569	29 624	29 322	30 819	30 913	30 785
5418	Advertising and related services	20 655	21 950	21 945	24 294	21 362	22 548	23 369	25 537
56	**Administrative and Support and Waste Management and Remediation Services** [1]	150 254	159 933	162 363	163 838	160 493	168 615	172 064	170 151
56 pt	Administrative and support and waste management and remediation services (except landscaping services)	139 067	147 451	149 383	151 180	148 870	155 848	159 044	157 216
561	Administrative and support services	131 747	138 709	140 745	143 253	139 785	146 492	148 813	148 783
5613	Employment services	47 934	50 771	52 264	55 605	54 299	54 728	56 261	57 603
5615	Travel arrangement and reservation services	8 676	10 034	9 563	8 724	8 595	9 861	9 607	9 304
562	Waste management and remediation services	18 507	21 224	21 618	20 585	20 708	22 123	23 251	21 368
62 pt	**Selected Health Care Services**	247 540	253 183	253 891	260 011	263 189	266 616	260 497	267 972
622	Hospitals	200 536	205 215	206 190	210 649	214 235	216 763	210 689	218 335
623	Nursing and residential care facilities	47 004	47 968	47 701	49 362	48 954	49 853	49 808	49 637

[1]Includes components not shown separately.

NOTES AND DEFINITIONS

TABLE 16-1
PETROLEUM AND PETROLEUM PRODUCTS—PRICES, IMPORTS, DOMESTIC PRODUCTION, AND STOCKS

SOURCES: FUTURES PRICES—U.S. DEPARTMENT OF ENERGY, ENERGY INFORMATION ADMINISTRATION (EIA), AND U.S. DEPARTMENT OF COMMERCE, BUREAU OF ECONOMIC ANALYSIS; IMPORTS—U.S. DEPARTMENT OF COMMERCE, CENSUS BUREAU (SEE NOTES AND DEFINITIONS FOR TABLES 7-9 THROUGH 7-14); SUPPLY (NET IMPORTS AND DOMESTIC PRODUCTION) AND STOCKS—EIA.

Definitions and notes on the data

The *crude oil futures price* in *current dollars per barrel* is the price for next-month delivery in Cushing, Oklahoma (a pipeline hub), of light, sweet crude oil, as determined by trading on the New York Mercantile Exchange (NYMEX). Official daily closing prices are reported each day at 2:30 p.m., and are tabulated weekly in Table 13 of *EIA's Weekly Petroleum Status Report*. The monthly averages shown in this volume are the average prices for the nearest future from each trading day of the month. For example, for most days in January, the futures contract priced will be for February; for the last few days in January, the February contract will have expired and the March contract will be quoted. The annual averages are averages of the monthly averages.

The *crude oil futures price* in *2005 dollars* is calculated by the editor, by dividing each month's current-dollar price by that month's chain price index for total personal consumption expenditures (PCE), with the price index average for the year 2005 set at 1.0000. The PCE chain price index is compiled by the Bureau of Economic Analysis (BEA). It is described in the notes and definitions for Chapter 1 and is also presented in Chapter 8, Table 8-2, and discussed in its notes and definitions.

The import data in Columns 3 through 6 of this table are those published as Exhibit 16, "Imports of Energy-related Petroleum Products, including Crude Petroleum," in the monthly Census-BEA foreign trade press release, FT900. *Total energy-related petroleum products* includes the following Standard International Trade Classification (SITC) commodity groupings: crude oil, petroleum preparations, and liquefied propane and butane gas.

The data in Columns 7 through 11, on exports, imports, and net imports (imports minus exports) of petroleum and products and domestic production of crude oil and natural gas plant liquids (all expressed as thousands of barrels per day), and in Columns 12 through 14, depicting stocks of crude oil in millions of barrels, are derived from the Department of Energy's weekly petroleum supply reporting system. They are published in EIA's *Monthly Energy Review*, which is classified under Reports and Products/Multifuel Energy Overview on the Web site, and can be found there in Tables 3.1 and 3.4. Stock totals are as

of the end of the period. Geographic coverage includes the 50 states and the District of Columbia.

Data availability

Data on futures prices, petroleum supply and stocks are available from the EIA Web site at <http://www.eia.doe .gov>, under the categories "Publications and Reports/ Monthly Energy Review" and "Petroleum/Weekly Petroleum Status Report." The *Monthly Energy Review* is no longer published in printed form.

The import data are available in the FT900 report from the Census Bureau at www.census.gov. See the notes and definitions for Tables 7-9 through 7-14 for further information.

TABLE 16-2
CONSTRUCTION PUT IN PLACE

SOURCE: U.S. DEPARTMENT OF COMMERCE, CENSUS BUREAU

The Census Bureau's estimates of the value of new construction put in place are intended to provide monthly estimates of the total dollar value of construction work done in the United States.

Definitions and notes on the data

The estimates cover all construction work done each month on new private residential and nonresidential buildings and structures, public construction, and improvements to existing buildings and structures. Included are the cost of labor, materials, and equipment rental; cost of architectural and engineering work; overhead costs assigned to the project; interest and taxes paid during construction; and contractor's profits.

The total value put in place for a given period is the sum of the value of work done on all projects underway during this period, regardless of when work on each individual project was started or when payment was made to the contractors. For some categories, estimates are derived by distributing the total construction cost of the project by means of historic construction progress patterns. Published estimates represent payments made during a period for some categories.

The statistics on the value of construction put in place result from direct measurement and indirect estimation. A series results from direct measurement when it is based on reports of the actual value of construction progress or construction expenditures obtained in a complete census or a sample survey. All other series are developed by indirect estimation using related construction statistics. On an annual basis, estimates for series directly measured monthly, quarterly, or annually accounted for about 71 percent of total construction in 1998 (private multifamily residential, private residential improvements, private nonresidential buildings, farm nonresidential construction, public utility construction, all other private construction, and virtually all of public construction). On a monthly basis, directly measured data are available for about 55 percent of the value in place estimates.

Beginning in 1993, the Construction Expenditures Branch of the Census Bureau's Manufacturing and Construction Division began collecting these data using a new classification system, which bases project types on their end usage instead of on building/nonbuilding types. Data collection on this system for federal construction began in January 2002.

With the changes in project classifications, data presented in these tables for 1993 to date are not directly comparable with data for previous years, except at aggregate levels. For that reason, *Business Statistics* shows earlier historical data only at these aggregate levels. Although some categories, such as lodging, office, education, and religion, have the same names as categories in previously published data, there have been changes within the classifications that make these values noncomparable. For example, private medical office buildings were classified as "office" buildings previously, but are categorized as "health care" under the new classification.

The seasonally adjusted data are obtained by removing normal seasonal movement from the unadjusted data to bring out underlying trends and business cycles, which is accomplished by using the Census X-12-ARIMA method. Seasonal adjustment accounts for month-to-month variations resulting from normal or average changes in any phenomena affecting the data, such as weather conditions, the differing lengths of months, and the varying number of holidays, weekdays, and weekends within each month. It does not adjust for abnormal conditions within each month or for year-to-year variations in weather. The seasonally adjusted annual rate is the seasonally adjusted monthly rate multiplied by 12.

Residential consists of new houses, town houses, apartments, and condominiums for sale or rent; these dwellings are built by the owner or for the owner on contract. It includes improvements inside and outside residential structures, such as remodeling, additions, major replacements, and additions of swimming pools and garages. Manufactured housing, houseboats, and maintenance and repair work are not included.

Office includes general office buildings, administration buildings, professional buildings, and financial institution buildings. Office buildings at manufacturing sites are classified as *manufacturing,* but office buildings owned by manufacturing companies but not at such a site are included in the *office* category. In the state and local government category, *office* includes capitols, city halls, courthouses, and similar buildings.

Commercial includes buildings and structures used by the retail, wholesale, farm, and selected service industries. One of the subgroups of this category is *multi-retail,* which consists of department and variety stores, shopping centers and malls, and warehouse-type retail stores.

Health care includes hospitals, medical buildings, nursing homes, adult day-care centers, and similar institutions.

Educational includes schools at all levels, higher education facilities, trade schools, libraries, museums, and similar institutions.

Amusement and recreation includes theme and amusement parks, sports structures not located at educational institutions, fitness centers and health clubs, neighborhood centers, camps, movie theaters, and similar establishments.

Transportation includes airport facilities; rail facilities, track, and bridges; bus, rail, maritime, and air terminals; and docks, marinas, and similar structures.

Communication includes telephone, television, and radio distribution and maintenance structures.

Power includes electricity production and distribution and gas and crude oil transmission, storage, and distribution.

Manufacturing includes all buildings and structures at manufacturing sites but not the installation of production machinery or special-purpose equipment.

Included in *total private construction*, but not shown separately in these pages, are lodging facilities (hotels and motels), religious structures, and private public safety, sewage and waste disposal, water supply, highway and street, and conservation and development spending.

Included in *total state and local construction,* but not shown separately in these pages, are state and local construction of commercial buildings, conservation and development (dams, levees, jetties, and dredging), lodging, religious facilities, and communication structures.

Public safety includes correctional facilities, police and sheriffs' stations, fire stations, and similar establishments.

Highway and street includes pavement, lighting, retaining walls, bridges, tunnels, toll facilities, and maintenance and rest facilities.

Sewage and waste disposal includes sewage systems, solid waste disposal, and recycling.

Water supply includes water supply, transmission, and storage facilities.

Among the data sources for construction expenditures are the Census Bureau's Survey of Construction, Building Permits Survey, Consumer Expenditure Survey (conducted for the Bureau of Labor Statistics), Annual Capital Expenditures Survey, and Construction Progress Reporting Survey;

also included are data from the F.W. Dodge Division of the McGraw-Hill Information Systems Company, the U.S. Department of Agriculture, and utility regulatory agencies.

Data availability

Each month's "Construction Spending" press release is released on the last workday of the following month. The release, more detailed data, and a discussion of methodologies can be found on the Census Bureau's Web site at <http://www.census.gov/constructionspending>.

TABLE 16-3
HOUSING STARTS AND BUILDING PERMITS; NEW HOUSE SALES AND PRICES

SOURCES: U.S. DEPARTMENT OF COMMERCE, CENSUS BUREAU

These data are mainly found in two major Census Bureau reports, "New Residential Construction" and "New Residential Sales." They cover new housing units intended for occupancy and maintained by the occupants, excluding hotels, motels, and group residential structures. Manufactured home units are reported in a separate survey.

Definitions

A *housing unit* is a house, an apartment, or a group of rooms or single room intended for occupancy as separate living quarters. Occupants must live separately from other individuals in the building and have direct access to the housing unit from the outside of the building or through a common hall. Each apartment unit in an apartment building is counted as one housing unit. As of January 2000, a previous requirement for residents to have the capability to eat separately has been eliminated. (Based on the old definition, some senior housing projects were excluded from the multifamily housing statistics because individual units did not have their own eating facilities.) Housing starts exclude group quarters such as dormitories or rooming houses, transient accommodations such as motels, and manufactured homes. Publicly owned housing units are excluded, but units in structures built by private developers with subsidies or for sale to local public housing authorities are both classified as private housing.

The *start* of construction of a privately owned housing unit is when excavation begins for the footings or foundation of a building primarily intended as a housekeeping residential structure and designed for nontransient occupancy. All housing units in a multifamily building are defined as being started when excavation for the building begins.

One-family structures includes fully detached, semi-detached, row houses, and townhouses. In the case of attached units, each must be separated from the adjacent unit by a ground-to-roof wall to be classified as a one-unit structure and must not share facilities such as heating or water supply. Units built one on top of another and those built side-by-side without a ground-to-roof wall and/or with common facilities are classified by the number of units in the structure.

Apartment buildings are defined as buildings containing *five units or more*. The type of ownership is not the criterion—a condominium apartment building is not classified as one-family structures but as a multifamily structure.

A *manufactured* home is a moveable dwelling, 8 feet or more wide and 40 feet or more long, designed to be towed on its own chassis with transportation gear integral to the unit when it leaves the factory, and without need of a permanent foundation. Multiwides and expandable manufactured homes are included. Excluded are travel trailers, motor homes, and modular housing. The shipments figures are based on reports submitted by manufacturers on the number of homes actually shipped during the survey month. Shipments to dealers may not necessarily be placed for residential use in the same month as they are shipped. The number of manufactured "homes" used for nonresidential purposes (for example, those used for offices) is not known.

Units authorized by building permits represents the approximately 97 percent of housing in permit-requiring areas.

The *start* occurs when excavation begins for the footing or foundation. Starts are estimated for all areas, regardless of whether permits are required.

New house *sales* are reported only for new single-family residential structures. The sales transaction must intend to include both house and land. Excluded are houses built for rent, houses built by the owner, and houses built by a contractor on the owner's land. A sale is reported when a deposit is taken or a sales agreement is signed; this can occur prior to a permit being issued.

Once the sale is reported, the sold housing unit drops out of the survey. Consequently the Census Bureau does not find out if the sales contract is cancelled or if the house is ever resold. As a result, if conditions are worsening and cancellations are high, sales are temporarily overestimated. When conditions improve and the cancelled sales materialize as actual sales, the Census sales estimates are then underestimated because the case did not re-enter the survey. In the long run, cancellations do not cause the survey to overestimate or underestimate sales; but in the short run, cancellations and ultimate resales are not reflected in this survey, and fluctuations can appear less severe than in reality.

A house is *for sale* when a permit to build has been issued (or work begun in non-permit areas) and a sales contract has not been signed nor a deposit accepted.

The *sales price* used in this survey is the price agreed upon between the purchaser and the seller at the time the first sales contract is signed or deposit made. It includes the price of the improved lot. The *median sales price* is the sales price of the house that falls on the middle point of a distribution by price of the total number of houses sold. Half of the houses sold have a price lower than the median; half have a price higher than the median. Changes in the *sales price* data reflect changes in the distribution of houses by region, size, and the like, as well as changes in the prices of houses with identical characteristics.

The *price index* measures the change in price of a new single-family house of constant physical characteristics, using the characteristics of houses built in 1996. Characteristics held constant include floor area, whether inside or outside a metropolitan area, number of bedrooms, number of bathrooms, number of fireplaces, type of parking facility, type of foundation, presence of a deck, construction method, exterior wall material, type of heating, and presence of air-conditioning. The indexes are calculated separately for attached and detached houses and combined with base period weights. The price measured includes the value of the lot.

See the notes and definitions to Table 12-11 for a discussion of the characteristics of other price indexes for single-family houses.

Notes on the data

Monthly permit authorizations are based on data collected by a mail survey from a sample of about 9,000 permit-issuing places, selected from and representing a universe of 20,000 such places in the United States. The remaining places are surveyed annually. Data for 1994 through 2003 represented 19,000 places; data for 1984 through 1993 represented 17,000 places; data for 1978 through 1983 represented 16,000 places; data for 1972 through 1977 represented 14,000 places; data for 1967 through 1971 represented 13,000 places; data for 1963 through 1966 represented 12,000 places; and data for 1959 through 1962 represented 10,000 places.

Housing starts and sales data are obtained from the Survey of Construction, for which Census Bureau field representatives sample both permit-issuing and non-permit-issuing places.

Effective with the January 2005 data release, the Survey of Construction implemented a new sample of building permit offices, replacing a previous sample selected in 1985. As a result, writes the Census Bureau, "Data users should uses caution when analyzing year over year changes in housing prices and characteristics between 2004 and 2005." In the newer sample, land may be more abundant, lot sizes larger, and sales prices lower.

For 2004, the permit data were compiled for both the new 20,000 place universe and the old 19,000 place universe. Ratios of the new estimates to the old were calculated by state for total housing units, structures by number of units, and valuation. For the United States as a whole, the new

estimate was 100.9 percent of the old estimate. The complete table of ratios can be found on the Census Bureau Web site at <http://www.census.gov/const/www/permitsindex>.

Effective with the data for April 2001, the Census Bureau made changes to the methodology used for new house sales, including discontinuing an adjustment for construction in areas in which building permits are required without a permit being issued. It was believed that such unauthorized construction has virtually ceased. The upward adjustment was not phased out but dropped completely in revised estimates as of January 1999. The total effect of these changes was to lower the number of sales by about 2.9 percent relative to those published for earlier years.

The data used in the price index are collected in the Survey of Construction, through monthly interviews with the builders or owners. The size of the sample is currently about 20,000 observations per year.

Data availability and references

Housing starts and building permit data have been collected monthly by the Bureau of the Census since 1959.

The monthly report for "New Residential Construction" (permits, starts, and completions) is issued in the middle of the following month. The monthly report and associated descriptions and historical data can be found at <http://www.census.gov/construction/nrc>.

The monthly report for "New Residential Sales" (sales, houses for sale, and prices) is issued toward the end of the following month. The monthly report and associated descriptions and historical data can be found at <http://www.census.gov/construction/nrs>.

The manufactured housing data (not seasonally adjusted) and background information can be found at <http://www.manufacturedhousing.org/statistics>. Data with and without seasonal adjustment can be found at <http://www.census.gov/construction/mhs>.

Data and background on the price index for new one-family houses can be found at <http://www.census/gov>, in the alphabetical index under the category "Construction price indexes."

TABLES 16-4 THROUGH 16-7
MANUFACTURERS' SHIPMENTS, INVENTORIES, AND ORDERS

SOURCE: U.S. DEPARTMENT OF COMMERCE, CENSUS BUREAU

These data are from the Census Bureau's monthly M3 survey, a sample-based survey that provides measures of changes in the value of domestic manufacturing activity and indications of future production commitments. The sample is not a probability sample. It includes approximately 4,300 reporting units, including most companies with $500 million or more in annual shipments and a selection of smaller companies. Currently, reported monthly data represent approximately 60 percent of shipments at the total manufacturing level.

One important technology industry, semiconductors, is represented in the shipments and inventories data in this report but not in new or unfilled orders. This affects the new and unfilled orders totals for computers and electronic products, durable goods industries, and total manufacturing. Based on shipments data, semiconductors accounted for about 15 percent of computers and electronic products, 3 percent of durable goods industries, and 1.5 percent of total manufacturing. Since semiconductors are intermediate materials and components rather than finished final products, the absence of these data does not distort new and unfilled orders data for important final demand categories, such as capital goods and information technology.

Definitions and notes on the data

Shipments. The value of shipments data represent net selling values, f.o.b. (free on board) plant, after discounts and allowances and excluding freight charges and excise taxes. For multi-establishment companies, the M3 reports are typically company- or division-level reports that encompass groups of plants or products. The data reported are usually net sales and receipts from customers and do not include the value of interplant transfers. The reported sales are used to calculate month-to-month changes that bring forward the estimates for the entire industry (that is, estimates of the statistical "universe") that have been developed from the Annual Survey of Manufactures (ASM). The value of products made elsewhere under contract from materials owned by the plant is also included in shipments, along with receipts for contract work performed for others, resales, miscellaneous activities such as the sale of scrap and refuse, and installation and repair work performed by employees of the plant.

Inventories. Inventories in the M3 survey are collected on a current cost or pre-LIFO (last in, first out) basis. As different inventory valuation methods are reflected in the reported data, the estimates differ slightly from replacement cost estimates. Companies using the LIFO method for valuing inventories report their pre-LIFO value; the adjustment to their base-period prices is excluded. In the ASM, inventories are collected according to this same definition. However, there are discontinuities in the historical data in both surveys. Inventory data prior to 1982 are not comparable to later years because of changes in valuation methods. Until 1982, respondents were asked in the ASM to report their inventories at book values—that is, according to whatever method they used for tax purposes (LIFO, FIFO [first in, first out], and so forth). Because of this, the value of aggregate inventories for an industry was not precise. The change in instructions for reporting current cost inventories was carried to the monthly survey beginning in January 1987. The data for 1982 to 1987 were redefined (but not re-collected by survey) on a pre-LIFO, or current cost, basis.

Inventory data are requested from respondents by three stages of fabrication: finished goods, work in process, and raw materials and supplies. Response to the stage of fabrication inquiries is lower than for total inventories; not all companies keep their monthly data at this level of detail. It should be noted that a product considered to be a finished good in one industry, such as steel mill shapes, may be reported as a raw material in another industry, such as stamping plants. For some purposes, this difference in definitions is an advantage. When a factory accumulates inventory that it considers to be raw materials, it can be expected that that accumulation is intentional. But when a factory—whether a materials-making or a final-product producer—has a buildup of finished goods inventories, it may indicate involuntary accumulation as a result of sales falling short of expectations. Hence, the two types of accumulation can have different economic interpretations, even if they represent identical types of goods.

Like total inventories, stage of fabrication inventories are benchmarked to the ASM data. Stage of fabrication data are benchmarked at the major group level, as opposed to the level of total inventories, which is benchmarked at the individual industry level.

New orders, as reported in the monthly survey, are net of order cancellations and include orders received and filled during the month as well as orders received for future delivery. They also include the value of contract changes that increase or decrease the value of the unfilled orders to which they relate. Orders are defined to include those supported by binding legal documents such as signed contracts, letters of award, or letters of intent, although this definition may not be strictly applicable in some industries.

Unfilled orders includes new orders (as defined above) that have not been reflected as shipments. Generally, unfilled orders at the end of the reporting period are equal to unfilled orders at the beginning of the period plus net new orders received less net shipments.

Series are adjusted for seasonal variation and variation in the number of trading days in the month using the X-12-ARIMA version of the Census Bureau's seasonal adjustment program.

Benchmarking and revisions

The data shown in the volume have been benchmarked to the 2007 Economic Census and the 2008 ASM. In each benchmark revision, new and unfilled orders are adjusted to be consistent with the benchmarked shipments and inventory data, seasonal adjustment factors are revised and updated, and other corrections are made.

Data availability and references

Data have been collected monthly since 1958.

The "Advance Report on Durable Goods Manufacturers' Shipments, Inventories and Orders" is available as a press release about 18 working days after the end of each month. It includes seasonally adjusted and not seasonally adjusted estimates of shipments, new orders, unfilled orders, and inventories for durable goods industries.

The monthly "Manufacturers' Shipments, Inventories, and Orders" report is released on the 23rd working day after the end of the month. Content includes revisions to the advance durable goods data, estimates for nondurable goods industries, tabulations by market category, and ratios of shipments to inventories and to unfilled orders. Revisions may affect selected data for the two previous months.

Press releases, historical data, descriptions of the survey, and documentation are available on the Census Bureau Web site at <http://www.census.gov>, under the category "Manufacturing" in the alphabetic listing there.

TABLE 16-8
MOTOR VEHICLE SALES AND INVENTORIES

SOURCE: U.S. DEPARTMENT OF COMMERCE, BUREAU OF ECONOMIC ANALYSIS

Retail sales and *inventories of cars, trucks, and buses.* These estimates are prepared by the Bureau of Economic Analysis (BEA), based on data from the American Automobile Manufacturers Association, Ward's Automotive Reports, and other sources. Seasonal adjustments are recalculated annually. Data are available on the BEA Web site at <http://www.bea.gov> as a part of the national income and product accounts data set; they are found under the "Supplemental Estimates" heading. They are also available on the STAT-USA subscription Web site at <http://www.stat-usa.gov>.

In this table, unlike in most other tables that include inventories in *Business Statistics,* the yearly values shown for inventories and the inventory to sales ratio are annual averages of monthly figures, not year-end values.

TABLES 16-9 AND 16-11
RETAIL AND FOOD SERVICES SALES; RETAIL INVENTORIES

SOURCE: U.S. DEPARTMENT OF COMMERCE, CENSUS BUREAU

Every month, the Census Bureau prepares estimates of retail sales and inventories by kind of business, based on a mail-out/mail-back survey of about 12,500 retail businesses with paid employees.

Retail sales and inventories are now compiled using the new NAICS classification system, which replaced the old SIC system. Historical data have been restated on the NAICS basis back to January 1992. In NAICS, Eating and drinking places and Mobile food services have been reclassified out of retail trade and into sector 72, Accommodation and food services, which also includes Hotels. The retail sales survey still collects and publishes sales data for Food services and drinking places. It no longer includes them in

the Retail total, but they are included in a new Retail and food services total.

Subtotals of durable and nondurable goods are no longer published. They were always imprecise for retail sales, since general merchandise stores (including department stores) were included in nondurable goods, yet obviously sold substantial quantities of durable goods.

Definitions

Sales is the value of merchandise sold for cash or credit at retail or wholesale. Services that are incidental to the sale of merchandise, and excise taxes that are paid by the manufacturer or wholesaler and passed along to the retailer, are also included. Sales are net, after deductions for refunds and merchandise returns. They exclude sales taxes collected directly from customers and paid directly to a local, state, or federal tax agency. The sales estimates include only sales by establishments primarily engaged in retail trade, and are not intended to measure the total sales for a given commodity or merchandise line.

Inventories is the value of stocks of goods held for sale through retail stores, valued at cost, as of the last day of the report period. Stocks may be held either at the store or at warehouses that maintain supplies primarily intended for distribution to retail stores within the organization.

Inventory data prior to 1980 are not comparable to later years, due to changes in valuation methods. Prior to 1980, inventories are the book values of merchandise on hand at the end of the period. They are valued according to the valuation method used by each respondent. Thus the aggregates are a mixture of LIFO (last in, first out) and non-LIFO values. Beginning with 1980, inventories are valued using methods other than LIFO in order to better reflect the current costs of goods held as inventory.

Leased departments consists of the operations of one company conducted within the establishment of another company, such as jewelry counters or optical centers within department stores. The values for sales and inventories at department stores in Tables 16-9 and 16-10 exclude sales of leased departments.

GAFO (department store type goods) is a special aggregate grouping of sales at general merchandise stores and at other stores that sell merchandise normally sold in department stores—clothing and accessories, furniture and home furnishings, electronics, appliances, sporting goods, hobby, book, music, office supplies, stationery, and gifts.

Notes on the data

The data published here have been benchmarked to the 2007, 2002, 1997, and 1992 Economic Censuses and the Annual Retail Trade Surveys for 2009 and previous years. Each year, the monthly series are benchmarked to the latest annual survey and new factors are incorporated to adjust for seasonal, trading-day, and holiday variations, using the Census Bureau's X-12-ARIMA program.

The survey sample is stratified by kind of business and estimated sales. All firms with sales above applicable size cut-offs are included. Firms are selected randomly from the remaining strata. The sample used for the end-of-month inventory estimates is a sub-sample of the monthly sales sample, about one-third of the size of the whole sample.

New samples, designed to produce NAICS estimates, were introduced with the 1999 Annual Retail Trade Survey and the March 2001 Monthly Retail Trade Survey. On November 30, 2006, another new sample was introduced, affecting the data for September 2006 and the following months. The sample is updated quarterly to take account of business births and deaths.

Data availability and references

An "Advance Monthly Retail Sales" report is released about nine working days after the close of the reference month, based on responses from a sub-sample of the complete retail sample.

The revised and more complete monthly "Retail Trade, Sales, and Inventories" reports are released six weeks after the close of the reference month. They contain preliminary figures for the current month and final figures for the prior 12 months. Statistics include retail sales, inventories, and ratios of inventories to sales. Data are both seasonally adjusted and unadjusted.

The "Annual Benchmark Report for Retail Trade" is released each spring. It includes updated seasonal adjustment factors; revised and benchmarked monthly estimates of sales and inventories; monthly data for the most recent 10 or more years; detailed annual estimates and ratios for the United States by kind of business; and comparable prior-year statistics and year-to-year changes. The latest such report available when *Business Statistics* was compiled was U.S. Census Bureau, *Annual Revision of Monthly Retail and Food Services: Sales and inventories—January 1992 through March 2012,* available on the Census Bureau Web site at <http://www.census.gov/retail/mrts>, along with the latest data releases and complete historical data.

TABLE 16-10
QUARTERLY RETAIL SALES: TOTAL AND E-COMMERCE

Source: U.S. Department of Commerce, Census Bureau

Beginning with the fourth quarter of 1999, the Census Bureau has conducted a quarterly survey of retail e-commerce sales from the Monthly Retail Trade Survey sample. (The monthly survey does not report electronic shopping separately; it is combined with mail order.) E-commerce sales are the sales of goods and services in which an order

is placed by the buyer or the price and terms of sale are negotiated over the Internet or an extranet, Electronic Data Interchange (EDI) network, electronic mail, or other online system. Payment may or may not be made online. The quarterly release is issued around the 20th of February, May, August, and November, and is available along with full historical data on the Census Bureau Web site at <http://www.census.gov>. It can be located under the heading "Retail" in the alphabetical Web site index, under "E" for "Economic data and information."

These estimates reflect the NAICS definition of retail sales, which excludes food service. Online travel services, financial brokers and dealers, and ticket sales agencies are not classified as retail and are not included in these estimates; they are, however, included in the annual survey of selected services.

TABLE 16-12
MERCHANT WHOLESALERS—SALES AND INVENTORIES

Source: U.S. Department of Commerce, Census Bureau

These data are based on a monthly mail-out/mail-back sample survey conducted by the Census Bureau. The sample consists of about 4,500 establishments, with a response rate of about 75 percent; missing reports are imputed based on reports of similar reporters.

These data are now based on the new NAICS classification system, which replaced the old SIC system. Historical data have been restated on the NAICS basis back to January 1992.

Classification changes in NAICS

NAICS shifts a significant number of businesses from the Wholesale to the Retail sector. An important new criterion for classification concerns whether or not the establishment is intended to solicit walk-in traffic. If it is, and if it uses mass-media advertising, it is now classified as Retail, even if it also serves business and institutional clients.

Definitions

Merchant wholesalers includes merchant wholesalers that take title of the goods they sell, as well as jobbers, industrial distributors, exporters, and importers. The survey does not cover marketing sales offices and branches of manufacturing, refining, and mining firms, nor does it include NAICS 4251: Wholesale Electronic Markets and Agents and Brokers.

Notes on the data

Inventories are valued using methods other than LIFO (last in, first out) in order to better reflect the current costs of goods held as inventory.

A survey has been conducted monthly since 1946. New samples are drawn every 5 years, most recently in 2006. The samples are updated every quarter to add new businesses and to drop companies that are no longer active.

Data availability and references

"Monthly Wholesale Trade, Sales and Inventories" reports are released six weeks after the close of the reference month. They contain preliminary current-month figures and final figures for the previous month. Statistics include sales, inventories, and stock/sale ratios, along with standard errors. Data are both seasonally adjusted and unadjusted.

The "Annual Benchmark Report for Wholesale Trade" is released each spring. It contains estimated annual sales, monthly and year-end inventories, inventory/sales ratios, purchases, gross margins, and gross margin/sales ratios by kind of business. Annual estimates are benchmarked to annual surveys and the most recent census of wholesale trade. Monthly sales and inventories estimates are revised consistent with the annual data, seasonal adjustment factors are updated, and revised data for both seasonally adjusted and unadjusted values are published.

Data and documentation are available on the Census Bureau Web site at <http://www.census.gov>, under "Economic Indicators" and in the alphabetic index under "E" for economic data.

TABLES 16-13 AND 16-14
MANUFACTURING AND TRADE SALES AND INVENTORIES

SOURCES: U.S. DEPARTMENT OF COMMERCE, CENSUS BUREAU (CURRENT-DOLLAR SERIES) AND U.S. DEPARTMENT OF COMMERCE, BUREAU OF ECONOMIC ANALYSIS (BEA; CONSTANT-DOLLAR SERIES)

The current-dollar data on which these tables are based bring together summary data from the separate series on manufacturers' shipments, inventories, and orders; merchant wholesalers' sales and inventories; and retail sales and inventories, all of which are included in this chapter. Generally, current-dollar inventories are collected on a current cost (or pre-LIFO [last in, first out]) basis. See the notes and definitions for Tables 16-4, 16-5, 16-9, 16-11, and 16-12 for further information about these data.

Based on these current-dollar values and relevant price data, BEA makes estimates of real sales, inventories, and inventory-sales ratios. Note, however, that annual figures for sales are shown as annual totals in Table 16-13 but as averages of the monthly data in Table 16-14, reflecting the practices of the respective source agencies. Also note that constant-dollar detail may not add to constant-dollar totals because of the chain-weighting formula; see the discussion of chain-weighted measures in the notes and definitions for Chapter 1.

Inventory values are as of the end of the month or year. In Table 16-13, annual values for monthly current-dollar inventory-sales ratios are averages of seasonally adjusted monthly ratios. However, for the real ratios in Table 16-14, annual figures for inventory-sales ratios are calculated by BEA as year-end (December) inventories divided by the monthly average of sales for the entire year. In all cases, the ratios in these two tables (like those in Table 1-8) represent the number of months' sales on hand as inventory at the end of the reporting period.

Data availability

Sales, inventories, and inventory-sales ratios for manufacturers, merchant wholesalers, and retailers are published monthly by the Census Bureau in a press release entitled "Manufacturing and Trade Inventories and Sales." Recent and historical data are available on the Census Bureau Web site at <http://www.census.gov/mtis/www/mtis.html>. They can also be found by going to the general Census website, <http://www.census.gov>, going to the alphabetical index, finding "Economic Indicators" under "E" and then finding "Manufacturing and trade."

Sales and inventories in constant dollars are available on the BEA Web site at <http://www.bea.gov>. To locate these data on that site, click on "National Economic Accounts." Scroll down to "Supplemental Estimates," click "Underlying Detail Tables," and then click on "List of Underlying Detail Tables." For the most recent data, if there is more than one table with the same title, select the last table listed.

References

For information about the 1996 historical revisions to sales and inventories in constant dollars, see "Real Inventories, Sales, and Inventory-Sales Ratios for Manufacturing and Trade, 1977–95," *Survey of Current Business* (May 1996).

TABLE 16-15
SELECTED SERVICES, QUARTERLY: ESTIMATED REVENUE FOR EMPLOYER FIRMS

SOURCE: U.S. DEPARTMENT OF COMMERCE, CENSUS BUREAU

Census data on quarterly revenue for selected service industries are based on information collected from a probability sample of approximately 13,000 employer firms (firms with employees) chosen from the sample for the larger Service Annual Survey and expanded to represent totals—for employer firms only—for the selected industries. Industries are defined according to the 2002 NAICS. The scope of the survey and the size of the sample have increased several times since the inception of this survey in 2004, and more industries are available than are shown here in Table 16-15, which focuses on industries with a longer statistical history.

Data for selected industry groups are adjusted for seasonal variation using the X-12 ARIMA program.

Data availability and references

The quarterly release "U.S. Government Estimates of Quarterly Revenue for Selected Services" is available on the Census Web site at <http://www.census.gov/>, under the general category of "Economic Indicators", around the middle of the third month following the end of the quarter. In the alphabetic index it appears under "Q". Information about the survey and its reliability is included in this release. Also available on the Web site are historical data benchmarked to the results of the latest Service Annual Survey.

PART C

REGIONAL AND STATE DATA

CHAPTER 17: REGIONAL AND STATE DATA

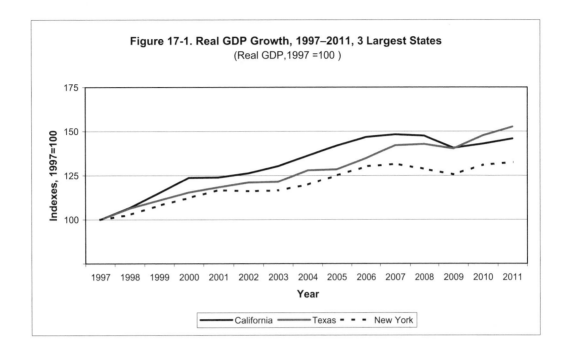

Figure 17-1. Real GDP Growth, 1997–2011, 3 Largest States
(Real GDP, 1997 = 100)

- Some of the diversity of recent economic experience among states is illustrated in Figure 17-1. The path of real GDP since 1997, when the current data series begin, is shown for the three states that had trillion-dollar economies in 2011, based on the current-dollar value of their GDP: California, Texas, and New York. (Table 17-1)

- Over most of the last 14 years California grew fastest of the three, reflecting its leadership in high-tech. Output dropped sharply from 2007 to 2009 in both California and New York, reflecting troubles in the financial and housing markets. Texas was still growing in 2008 and declined modestly in 2009. Texas did not share in the nationwide housing bubble, having regulated mortgage markets more tightly following its own boom and bust in the 1980s and early 1990s; the state also benefited from high oil prices. All three states recovered during the following two years, according to BEA's revised data for 2010 and preliminary estimates for 2011. Texas and New York, but not California, are estimated to have surpassed their previous highs. (Table 17-1)

- Personal income per capita is a useful measure for comparing the fiscal and economic capacity of different states. (As per capita income is a "mean", it is less useful for comparing the incomes of typical residents than median income; state median household incomes are shown in Table 3-6.) Of the three states shown in Figure 17-1, New York had the highest level of per capita income in 2011—$50,545. California was next with $44,481, and Texas third with $39,593. The 1997–2011 current-dollar income growth rates were similar—3.8 percent per year for New York, 3.7 percent for Texas, and 3.6 percent for California. (Table 17-2) The chain price index for personal consumption expenditures rose at an average annual rate of 2.1 percent over this period, indicating that all three states averaged real growth in personal income per capita of 1½ percent per year or better. (Table 1-6A)

Table 17-1. Gross Domestic Product by Region and State

(Billions of dollars; index numbers.)

Year	United States (sum of states)[1]	New England							Mideast						
		Total	Connect-icut	Maine	Massa-chusetts	New Hamp-shire	Rhode Island	Vermont	Total	Delaware	District of Columbia	Maryland	New Jersey	New York	Pennsyl-vania
VALUE															
1977	1 986.4	104.9	29.6	7.6	50.7	6.3	7.2	3.3	401.9	6.1	15.6	35.6	65.8	179.9	99.0
1978	2 243.2	117.9	33.2	8.4	56.9	7.4	8.0	3.9	446.3	6.7	17.0	39.5	72.9	200.1	110.1
1979	2 489.4	130.7	36.9	9.3	63.0	8.4	8.8	4.4	488.7	7.3	18.4	43.6	81.1	217.7	120.5
1980	2 713.9	144.5	40.8	10.3	69.7	9.3	9.6	4.9	526.5	7.9	19.9	47.5	88.3	235.7	127.2
1981	3 057.3	161.4	45.6	11.3	77.8	10.5	10.7	5.4	582.9	8.8	21.7	53.1	98.8	261.8	138.6
1982	3 211.4	174.7	50.2	12.1	83.8	11.4	11.4	5.8	618.9	9.5	23.0	56.3	105.8	282.2	142.1
1983	3 445.4	193.0	55.5	13.2	93.1	12.6	12.3	6.3	672.7	10.6	24.6	62.2	118.0	305.3	152.0
1984	3 853.7	220.4	63.6	14.9	106.4	14.8	13.8	6.9	748.8	11.9	26.6	69.9	133.6	339.4	167.4
1985	4 126.7	241.2	69.2	16.0	116.6	16.6	15.2	7.5	805.6	13.1	28.5	76.9	145.9	364.3	176.9
1986	4 340.8	263.0	75.3	17.4	127.2	18.4	16.6	8.2	864.3	14.1	30.1	83.7	158.8	390.1	187.4
1987	4 649.0	289.1	83.0	19.2	138.9	21.0	17.9	9.2	934.9	15.6	32.1	91.4	174.6	418.3	202.9
1988	5 053.0	316.6	90.7	21.4	151.6	22.9	19.7	10.3	1 025.2	16.9	35.2	101.3	194.7	456.6	220.6
1989	5 366.1	332.7	95.8	22.7	158.2	23.8	21.1	11.1	1 075.3	18.9	37.5	107.4	205.1	473.3	233.2
1990	5 651.7	340.0	100.2	23.3	159.5	23.8	21.7	11.7	1 125.3	19.9	39.7	112.8	214.4	493.2	245.3
1991	5 842.7	343.8	101.5	23.4	160.7	24.8	21.7	11.7	1 153.0	21.7	41.4	115.4	221.9	497.3	255.2
1992	6 167.6	359.1	105.8	24.3	167.4	26.3	22.7	12.5	1 206.0	22.9	43.2	119.5	230.8	519.7	269.8
1993	6 467.7	370.4	107.7	25.2	173.5	27.4	23.6	13.0	1 254.0	23.5	45.4	125.5	240.4	537.5	281.7
1994	6 912.8	392.6	113.1	26.5	185.7	29.2	24.4	13.7	1 309.1	25.6	46.7	133.3	251.6	555.3	296.6
1995	7 299.4	419.1	123.2	28.2	196.4	31.9	25.6	13.9	1 373.0	27.7	47.1	139.1	263.5	582.7	313.0
1996	7 750.0	444.7	129.1	29.3	210.6	34.6	26.5	14.7	1 445.3	29.2	47.8	145.0	278.2	620.2	325.0
1997	8 284.4	479.1	140.3	30.8	226.9	36.9	28.7	15.5	1 535.9	31.5	49.7	154.8	292.7	664.7	342.7
1997 [2]	8 270.5	470.9	137.1	30.4	223.7	36.3	28.2	15.2	1 543.4	34.0	50.2	152.9	301.0	661.3	344.1
1998 [2]	8 727.0	495.8	143.7	32.1	235.8	38.7	29.4	16.0	1 613.1	35.8	51.7	161.8	312.0	687.9	364.1
1999 [2]	9 286.9	523.0	149.4	34.2	251.0	40.5	31.0	16.9	1 704.2	37.7	56.0	172.3	327.1	731.1	380.0
2000 [2]	9 884.2	568.7	163.5	36.4	273.0	44.2	33.6	18.0	1 796.8	40.6	58.3	182.9	350.1	769.3	395.6
2001 [2]	10 218.0	588.1	168.2	38.2	282.5	44.7	35.7	18.8	1 883.6	43.6	63.5	195.6	364.9	809.0	406.9
2002 [2]	10 572.4	601.7	168.9	40.0	288.4	46.7	38.1	19.6	1 941.7	43.7	67.9	206.6	376.9	822.4	424.1
2003 [2]	11 067.8	623.1	173.9	41.5	297.7	48.8	40.7	20.5	2 012.5	47.3	71.9	216.6	392.5	842.7	441.5
2004 [2]	11 774.4	658.4	187.5	44.4	310.3	51.3	42.9	21.9	2 124.2	50.6	77.7	232.0	410.8	891.5	461.7
2005 [2]	12 539.1	685.8	196.3	45.5	323.3	53.7	44.2	22.7	2 256.5	54.4	82.5	247.2	430.2	959.9	482.2
2006 [2]	13 289.2	720.7	209.5	47.6	337.5	56.1	46.5	23.6	2 394.2	56.3	86.7	259.8	454.7	1 030.4	506.4
2007 [2]	13 936.2	751.8	221.1	49.1	352.4	57.9	47.3	24.0	2 502.2	59.6	91.9	272.0	471.4	1 076.3	531.1
2008 [2]	14 193.1	760.8	219.4	49.5	361.7	58.5	47.2	24.4	2 542.4	58.0	96.8	281.1	482.1	1 079.7	544.7
2009 [2]	13 834.7	755.2	213.5	50.2	360.6	59.0	47.7	24.2	2 522.0	60.1	98.3	283.6	470.4	1 072.3	537.2
2010 [2]	14 416.6	785.6	221.3	50.7	377.8	61.6	48.8	25.3	2 629.1	64.0	103.5	293.3	480.4	1 128.8	558.9
2011 [2]	14 981.0	813.0	230.1	51.6	391.8	63.6	50.1	25.9	2 698.2	65.8	107.6	301.1	487.0	1 158.0	578.8
QUANTITY INDEX 1997 =100															
1977	54.6	50.7	50.2	58.1	51.5	36.7	59.7	46.6	62.2	49.7	89.5	56.0	52.1	65.1	65.5
1978	57.5	53.5	52.9	59.8	54.4	40.5	61.5	51.3	64.8	51.9	91.6	58.4	54.3	68.0	68.0
1979	59.3	55.6	55.0	61.4	56.4	42.8	63.6	53.6	66.3	52.2	92.7	60.2	56.4	69.4	69.3
1980	59.3	56.6	56.1	62.6	57.5	44.0	63.3	55.0	65.9	51.3	91.9	60.4	56.4	69.4	67.6
1981	60.9	58.0	57.4	63.0	58.9	45.8	64.8	56.8	66.9	52.3	90.3	61.6	57.9	70.7	67.9
1982	60.1	58.6	58.8	63.7	59.2	46.7	64.6	56.6	66.5	52.9	87.6	61.0	58.0	71.2	65.3
1983	61.8	61.7	61.8	66.5	62.6	49.7	66.5	58.8	68.7	57.1	88.5	64.0	62.1	72.7	67.1
1984	66.2	67.3	67.5	71.2	68.5	55.7	71.1	61.8	73.0	61.3	90.3	68.3	67.0	77.1	70.8
1985	68.9	71.2	71.1	74.3	72.5	60.7	75.8	65.4	75.4	65.2	91.7	72.2	70.5	79.2	72.5
1986	70.3	74.7	74.3	77.6	76.1	64.8	79.6	68.3	77.6	67.0	92.2	75.6	73.9	81.2	73.9
1987	73.4	80.0	80.0	82.6	81.0	72.2	83.1	74.2	81.6	71.7	94.9	79.6	78.9	84.7	77.9
1988	77.2	85.0	84.9	88.9	85.8	76.7	88.9	80.7	86.4	75.0	99.0	85.1	84.7	89.6	81.7
1989	78.9	85.9	86.0	90.6	86.2	76.6	91.3	84.3	87.3	80.5	100.9	87.0	85.9	89.4	83.1
1990	80.1	84.5	86.4	89.8	83.6	73.8	90.3	85.8	88.0	82.3	103.0	88.0	86.6	89.7	84.3
1991	80.0	82.3	84.3	87.2	81.1	74.2	87.1	83.5	86.6	85.6	101.1	86.4	86.3	86.9	84.5
1992	82.4	83.7	85.4	88.3	82.2	77.1	88.3	87.4	88.1	86.4	101.8	87.1	87.8	88.1	87.1
1993	84.1	83.8	84.3	88.8	82.8	78.1	89.3	88.6	89.0	85.7	103.2	88.5	88.8	88.5	88.4
1994	88.0	86.8	86.3	91.2	86.6	81.5	90.1	91.3	90.9	91.4	103.2	91.8	90.7	89.7	90.9
1995	91.0	90.5	91.6	93.5	89.6	87.7	92.5	91.6	92.9	95.2	100.4	93.3	92.9	91.6	93.9
1996	95.0	94.4	94.0	96.3	94.5	94.4	94.0	95.6	96.1	97.0	99.1	95.5	96.9	95.4	96.4
1997	100.0	100.0	100.0	100.0	100.0	100.0	100.0	100.0	100.0	100.0	100.0	100.0	100.0	100.0	100.0
1997 [2]	100.0	100.0	100.0	100.0	100.0	100.0	100.0	100.0	100.0	100.0	100.0	100.0	100.0	100.0	100.0
1998 [2]	104.3	104.1	102.9	103.4	104.6	107.6	102.2	104.5	102.9	102.6	100.1	104.1	102.0	102.8	103.8
1999 [2]	109.3	108.4	105.0	107.7	110.2	112.6	105.5	109.3	107.0	106.1	105.1	108.5	105.3	108.0	106.4
2000 [2]	113.9	116.2	112.7	112.1	118.7	121.7	111.5	115.3	110.9	110.8	105.4	112.5	110.4	112.3	108.5
2001 [2]	115.3	118.2	113.6	114.4	121.5	121.5	115.6	118.2	114.0	112.6	111.3	117.3	112.8	116.6	108.9
2002 [2]	117.3	118.6	111.8	117.2	121.7	124.8	120.4	121.1	115.1	113.3	114.6	120.9	114.4	116.1	111.3
2003 [2]	119.8	120.5	112.5	118.8	123.5	128.3	125.4	124.9	116.6	119.4	117.1	123.8	116.6	116.4	113.3
2004 [2]	123.8	124.1	118.0	123.0	125.8	131.8	128.7	129.7	119.5	124.2	121.5	128.5	118.9	119.7	114.9
2005 [2]	127.2	125.4	119.7	122.3	127.2	133.8	128.1	131.5	122.9	129.8	124.4	132.6	120.5	125.0	115.7
2006 [2]	130.6	128.0	124.0	123.8	129.0	135.8	130.4	133.0	126.2	130.9	126.1	134.8	123.3	130.1	117.2
2007 [2]	133.0	129.9	127.3	124.0	131.1	136.6	128.9	131.9	127.9	134.9	128.6	137.0	124.2	131.5	119.3
2008 [2]	132.1	128.8	123.4	122.4	132.1	135.7	125.9	131.6	126.9	128.0	132.4	138.8	124.3	128.6	119.5
2009 [2]	127.1	124.7	116.9	120.4	128.7	133.2	124.4	126.9	123.2	130.5	131.4	136.5	118.3	125.5	114.9
2010 [2]	131.1	129.0	120.4	120.8	134.2	138.9	125.7	132.1	127.3	134.5	135.6	140.6	120.1	130.9	118.6
2011 [2]	133.0	131.3	122.8	120.4	137.2	141.0	126.6	132.8	128.4	136.6	138.2	141.8	119.5	132.4	120.1

[1] See notes and definitions for explanation.
[2] NAICS basis, not continuous with previous years, which are based on the SIC.

Table 17-1. Gross Domestic Product by Region and State—*Continued*

(Billions of dollars; index numbers.)

Year	Great Lakes						Plains							
	Total	Illinois	Indiana	Michigan	Ohio	Wisconsin	Total	Iowa	Kansas	Minnesota	Missouri	Nebraska	North Dakota	South Dakota
VALUE														
1977	390.0	115.1	47.9	89.3	97.0	40.7	149.8	27.0	20.5	36.8	41.2	13.9	5.2	5.1
1978	434.2	128.1	53.7	99.3	107.6	45.4	169.6	30.8	22.8	41.6	46.2	15.9	6.4	6.0
1979	469.8	139.3	57.9	105.4	117.1	50.1	188.6	33.5	26.3	46.9	50.6	17.4	7.2	6.7
1980	482.4	145.3	58.9	104.1	121.2	52.9	198.2	34.6	28.3	50.2	52.4	18.3	7.6	6.8
1981	529.3	159.6	64.7	114.7	132.8	57.5	221.9	38.3	32.0	55.4	57.8	20.9	10.0	7.7
1982	538.5	164.3	65.0	115.2	134.6	59.5	227.9	37.3	33.5	57.5	60.7	21.3	10.0	7.7
1983	578.3	173.1	69.3	127.8	144.9	63.2	240.2	37.5	35.3	62.0	65.5	21.8	10.0	8.1
1984	650.6	194.2	78.9	143.7	163.9	70.0	270.1	41.3	38.4	71.4	74.5	24.6	10.6	9.2
1985	689.9	206.3	82.0	153.6	174.2	73.8	282.8	42.4	40.7	75.8	77.9	25.7	10.7	9.6
1986	729.1	218.7	86.4	163.5	182.6	77.8	293.7	43.2	41.8	79.5	83.3	26.0	9.8	10.1
1987	765.9	231.2	91.7	169.2	191.8	82.0	311.5	45.3	44.2	85.4	88.9	26.8	10.3	10.7
1988	827.2	252.2	99.5	180.6	205.3	89.6	333.6	49.1	46.7	91.9	95.8	29.3	9.7	11.2
1989	877.5	266.6	107.2	190.6	217.8	95.2	355.3	52.9	48.8	98.3	101.4	31.3	10.7	11.8
1990	910.6	279.0	110.9	193.1	227.4	100.2	372.3	56.1	51.9	102.8	103.6	33.7	11.5	12.8
1991	939.6	288.5	114.6	197.7	234.0	104.8	388.2	57.9	54.0	106.1	109.2	35.6	11.7	13.7
1992	1 006.6	306.2	124.7	212.1	250.7	113.0	414.6	61.9	56.9	114.5	115.3	38.2	12.9	14.9
1993	1 058.2	320.1	132.1	226.4	259.6	120.0	427.7	63.4	59.0	117.9	118.9	39.4	13.0	16.1
1994	1 154.2	348.0	143.3	251.5	281.9	129.4	467.3	70.2	63.3	128.2	130.6	43.5	14.3	17.3
1995	1 204.3	364.5	150.4	256.6	297.5	135.3	491.6	73.1	65.3	135.1	140.1	45.1	14.8	18.1
1996	1 266.7	383.5	158.4	270.3	311.1	143.4	527.5	78.8	69.6	145.9	148.3	49.0	16.5	19.4
1997	1 345.3	408.0	167.4	286.4	332.5	151.0	558.8	83.1	74.1	156.7	158.3	50.3	16.5	19.8
1997 [2]	1 353.2	408.7	168.2	291.7	333.3	151.3	553.2	81.8	73.5	154.0	157.5	50.8	16.0	19.6
1998 [2]	1 423.4	428.3	180.0	304.5	350.3	160.3	580.2	83.8	77.4	164.3	164.7	51.9	17.1	21.0
1999 [2]	1 494.2	449.4	187.8	323.6	363.7	169.8	608.5	87.3	81.0	174.1	172.6	54.0	17.2	22.2
2000 [2]	1 568.5	474.5	198.2	337.5	380.9	177.4	648.5	93.3	85.7	188.8	181.0	57.3	18.3	24.0
2001 [2]	1 590.7	487.0	200.0	337.4	382.7	183.5	666.8	94.1	89.4	194.0	185.3	59.7	19.1	25.2
2002 [2]	1 646.5	497.8	208.7	351.8	398.0	190.2	693.4	98.6	91.7	201.6	192.2	61.4	20.4	27.6
2003 [2]	1 709.2	518.6	220.2	362.7	409.7	198.1	731.2	104.6	96.6	212.5	199.9	66.3	22.3	28.9
2004 [2]	1 780.0	545.6	231.8	365.6	428.2	208.9	774.3	115.6	99.7	227.1	208.4	69.6	23.3	30.6
2005 [2]	1 846.0	568.1	239.3	375.8	444.1	218.7	807.7	120.0	104.9	237.8	216.3	72.5	24.7	31.5
2006 [2]	1 907.1	600.7	248.6	376.2	452.9	228.7	839.4	124.1	111.7	245.0	223.7	76.5	26.1	32.3
2007 [2]	1 978.6	626.6	261.8	386.6	467.1	236.5	886.6	134.1	120.6	253.4	233.0	82.1	28.5	34.9
2008 [2]	1 963.5	632.0	261.0	369.0	465.5	236.1	916.0	133.9	124.3	262.1	241.4	85.2	31.8	37.3
2009 [2]	1 911.2	623.1	250.6	350.8	451.0	235.7	904.5	133.1	121.6	257.5	237.4	85.9	32.0	37.0
2010 [2]	1 995.1	646.8	267.3	368.4	466.9	245.7	945.1	140.9	126.1	270.8	243.4	90.1	35.7	38.2
2011 [2]	2 072.9	670.7	278.1	385.2	484.0	254.8	985.8	149.0	130.9	281.7	249.5	94.2	40.3	40.1
QUANTITY INDEX **1997 =100**														
1977	63.5	62.0	61.3	70.9	63.2	56.7	57.8	64.6	62.2	50.9	58.5	57.5	66.9	54.6
1978	66.1	64.7	64.2	73.8	65.5	59.3	60.8	68.2	63.8	53.5	61.3	60.9	74.9	58.3
1979	66.8	65.7	64.5	73.1	66.5	61.3	63.0	69.7	67.8	56.0	62.8	62.6	77.2	61.0
1980	63.5	63.4	61.1	66.6	63.7	60.4	61.6	67.8	67.0	55.8	60.3	61.9	74.2	58.2
1981	64.0	64.3	61.8	66.5	64.4	60.6	63.7	69.9	68.9	57.3	61.1	65.5	85.4	61.7
1982	61.1	62.0	58.4	62.4	61.1	59.4	62.1	65.3	68.3	56.5	60.3	63.9	82.1	60.0
1983	63.1	62.7	59.8	66.6	63.6	60.5	62.6	62.6	68.7	58.4	62.3	62.3	80.5	59.6
1984	68.1	67.2	65.3	72.1	69.1	64.2	67.3	66.0	71.8	64.4	67.6	67.0	82.3	64.2
1985	70.4	69.2	66.5	75.1	71.6	66.3	69.2	67.4	74.5	67.0	68.6	69.3	82.8	66.7
1986	71.5	70.7	67.6	76.4	72.3	67.4	69.5	66.5	74.8	67.5	70.5	68.1	77.2	67.5
1987	73.5	73.0	70.1	77.3	74.4	69.4	71.9	68.0	77.3	70.8	73.3	68.3	79.2	68.9
1988	77.0	77.1	73.6	80.5	77.2	73.6	74.6	71.6	79.4	73.7	76.5	72.2	72.9	69.5
1989	78.6	78.6	76.3	81.8	78.9	75.1	76.5	74.2	80.0	75.9	78.1	74.3	77.2	70.6
1990	79.0	79.4	76.6	80.1	79.7	76.6	77.6	76.4	81.8	76.7	77.2	77.5	79.8	74.4
1991	78.6	79.3	76.6	78.8	79.1	77.6	78.4	76.8	82.6	76.6	78.4	80.0	79.5	78.0
1992	82.3	82.4	81.5	82.1	82.8	81.8	81.8	80.4	85.1	80.9	80.8	84.0	85.9	82.4
1993	84.3	84.2	84.0	84.6	83.5	85.0	82.2	80.5	85.7	81.1	81.0	84.3	84.8	87.1
1994	89.7	89.4	89.1	92.0	88.5	89.5	87.8	87.2	90.0	86.0	86.8	91.1	91.2	91.8
1995	91.8	91.9	91.9	92.2	91.7	91.4	90.5	89.7	91.1	88.6	91.2	92.5	92.9	93.7
1996	95.4	95.5	95.6	95.5	94.8	95.7	95.3	94.9	94.9	94.3	94.9	97.9	100.0	98.2
1997	100.0	100.0	100.0	100.0	100.0	100.0	100.0	100.0	100.0	100.0	100.0	100.0	100.0	100.0
1997 [2]	100.0	100.0	100.0	100.0	100.0	100.0	100.0	100.0	100.0	100.0	100.0	100.0	100.0	100.0
1998 [2]	103.3	103.1	105.1	102.4	103.3	103.9	103.3	100.8	103.9	105.3	102.5	100.6	105.7	106.4
1999 [2]	106.5	106.3	108.0	106.3	105.3	108.0	106.6	103.4	106.8	110.0	105.1	103.3	105.6	112.2
2000 [2]	109.6	110.1	112.1	108.5	108.1	110.8	111.5	108.8	110.4	117.5	107.9	108.1	109.7	120.2
2001 [2]	108.5	110.5	110.2	105.9	106.0	111.8	111.9	106.6	111.9	118.4	107.7	109.4	111.3	123.5
2002 [2]	110.4	110.8	113.3	109.0	108.3	113.9	114.3	109.7	112.8	121.0	109.5	110.3	116.9	133.0
2003 [2]	112.5	113.1	117.5	110.4	109.3	116.5	117.8	113.8	115.7	125.1	111.5	116.2	123.6	136.0
2004 [2]	114.2	115.6	120.3	109.2	111.2	119.6	120.9	121.8	115.7	130.0	112.9	117.5	123.9	138.5
2005 [2]	115.0	116.4	120.7	109.6	111.9	121.8	122.9	124.0	118.2	132.1	113.9	120.0	127.2	141.1
2006 [2]	115.4	119.2	121.9	107.2	110.7	123.9	124.1	125.2	122.1	132.2	114.3	123.2	130.2	141.5
2007 [2]	116.4	120.6	125.1	107.2	111.1	124.7	126.8	131.0	127.6	132.4	115.4	127.2	136.2	146.8
2008 [2]	113.2	119.0	122.0	100.8	108.4	121.9	128.2	127.8	128.6	134.5	116.9	128.6	147.6	153.4
2009 [2]	106.6	114.3	113.5	91.7	101.7	117.4	123.9	124.1	123.8	129.3	111.4	127.5	150.7	152.5
2010 [2]	110.6	117.7	120.1	96.2	104.4	122.1	128.2	130.4	127.1	134.4	113.7	132.0	164.2	152.9
2011 [2]	112.2	119.3	121.5	98.4	105.5	123.5	129.5	132.9	127.8	136.0	113.7	132.2	176.7	154.1

[2]NAICS basis, not continuous with previous years, which are based on the SIC.

Table 17-1. Gross Domestic Product by Region and State—*Continued*

(Billions of dollars; index numbers.)

Year		Southeast											
	Total	Alabama	Arkansas	Florida	Georgia	Kentucky	Louisiana	Mississippi	North Carolina	South Carolina	Tennessee	Virginia	West Virginia
VALUE													
1977	388.0	26.7	15.2	65.3	40.8	29.2	39.7	16.0	43.8	20.1	33.6	43.2	14.4
1978	440.9	30.5	17.5	75.7	46.2	32.7	45.2	17.8	49.9	23.0	38.2	48.4	16.0
1979	491.2	33.7	19.1	86.3	51.6	35.8	51.7	20.0	54.5	25.5	42.2	53.4	17.4
1980	541.3	36.1	20.3	97.9	56.2	37.0	63.9	21.4	58.8	27.6	45.0	58.7	18.4
1981	614.6	40.3	22.9	112.2	63.8	41.1	77.2	24.0	65.9	31.0	50.3	66.2	19.8
1982	646.2	41.8	23.5	122.3	68.5	42.2	78.1	24.6	69.0	32.4	52.0	71.5	20.5
1983	701.7	45.7	25.3	136.8	76.7	44.1	76.9	26.0	77.5	35.9	57.1	79.4	20.4
1984	788.9	50.0	28.5	156.0	88.5	49.3	82.6	28.7	88.2	41.2	64.0	89.8	22.2
1985	848.5	53.8	29.3	170.9	98.2	51.9	84.4	30.1	96.5	44.0	68.4	98.0	22.9
1986	898.2	56.1	30.8	185.9	108.1	53.2	77.1	31.0	104.8	47.7	73.3	107.3	22.9
1987	971.3	60.8	32.7	204.8	117.0	56.3	78.5	33.5	113.3	52.7	80.7	117.6	23.4
1988	1 056.0	66.0	35.0	224.8	126.6	61.9	83.2	35.5	124.3	57.3	87.4	128.1	25.9
1989	1 122.4	68.4	37.1	241.6	133.8	65.5	87.6	37.2	133.9	61.3	91.6	137.7	26.7
1990	1 181.5	71.6	38.7	256.6	140.6	68.4	95.2	38.8	139.7	65.2	94.1	145.0	27.8
1991	1 237.4	76.0	41.6	267.7	147.8	71.7	96.0	40.9	146.4	68.0	101.2	151.1	29.1
1992	1 315.7	81.3	45.0	284.7	160.1	77.5	90.9	44.0	159.3	71.8	111.7	159.0	30.4
1993	1 396.3	84.6	47.6	304.4	171.7	81.6	95.9	47.3	168.0	76.2	119.6	167.7	31.9
1994	1 505.9	90.1	51.4	327.2	188.0	87.6	105.1	51.6	181.3	82.1	129.9	177.1	34.6
1995	1 600.7	95.8	54.6	347.0	203.4	91.9	112.9	55.0	193.5	87.2	137.1	186.2	36.1
1996	1 694.6	100.1	58.0	370.9	220.0	96.6	118.8	57.5	203.8	90.8	143.2	197.8	37.2
1997	1 802.3	104.8	60.3	393.1	235.2	103.6	126.0	59.9	221.3	96.5	152.7	210.4	38.6
1997 2	1 799.0	101.9	59.9	395.0	237.1	103.4	115.9	58.0	228.7	97.2	153.1	211.0	37.8
1998 2	1 905.8	106.5	61.9	420.6	254.3	108.0	120.6	60.7	242.8	103.3	162.5	225.5	39.1
1999 2	2 041.3	112.1	66.2	450.6	277.5	113.6	124.6	63.7	266.0	110.1	172.2	243.8	41.0
2000 2	2 147.4	116.0	68.3	481.2	294.0	113.2	131.3	65.6	281.5	115.4	177.5	261.8	41.4
2001 2	2 243.2	120.1	71.1	506.5	305.0	116.4	137.8	67.6	292.0	120.0	183.7	280.1	43.0
2002 2	2 334.6	125.2	74.2	536.1	314.0	121.4	139.2	69.5	302.2	124.4	193.1	290.9	44.5
2003 2	2 458.7	130.9	78.0	574.4	324.8	125.4	156.0	73.8	311.1	130.5	200.5	307.4	45.9
2004 2	2 624.7	142.0	83.8	621.4	342.9	131.7	171.5	77.5	327.3	134.8	213.5	329.6	48.7
2005 2	2 830.0	151.0	88.5	681.2	363.2	138.8	196.9	81.4	354.7	141.9	224.3	356.4	51.9
2006 2	2 995.0	159.1	93.8	731.5	380.5	146.4	204.4	85.9	378.2	149.1	236.3	374.6	55.2
2007 2	3 116.7	165.7	97.5	760.9	399.6	150.5	207.3	92.1	396.7	157.7	242.2	389.6	56.9
2008 2	3 156.7	170.2	100.4	748.1	404.3	153.6	214.0	95.5	407.4	159.2	248.0	397.9	58.2
2009 2	3 105.5	164.8	98.9	726.2	391.5	152.0	202.3	92.2	411.5	156.6	245.0	405.0	59.6
2010 2	3 221.4	170.2	102.2	736.1	403.2	159.4	232.4	95.5	424.6	160.4	256.2	419.4	61.9
2011 2	3 330.4	173.1	105.8	754.3	418.9	164.8	247.7	97.8	439.9	165.8	266.5	428.9	66.8
QUANTITY INDEX 1997 =100													
1977	54.6	50.7	50.2	58.1	51.5	36.7	59.7	46.6	62.2	49.7	89.5	56.0	52.1
1978	57.5	53.5	52.9	59.8	54.4	40.5	61.5	51.3	64.8	51.9	91.6	58.4	54.3
1979	59.3	55.6	55.0	61.4	56.4	42.8	63.6	53.6	66.3	52.2	92.7	60.2	56.4
1980	59.3	56.6	56.1	62.6	57.5	44.0	63.3	55.0	65.9	51.3	91.9	60.4	56.4
1981	60.9	58.0	57.4	63.0	58.9	45.8	64.8	56.8	66.9	52.3	90.3	61.6	57.9
1982	60.1	58.6	58.8	63.7	59.2	46.7	64.6	56.6	66.5	52.9	87.6	61.0	58.0
1983	61.8	61.7	61.8	66.5	62.6	49.7	66.5	58.8	68.7	57.1	88.5	64.0	62.1
1984	66.2	67.3	67.5	71.2	68.5	55.7	71.1	61.8	73.0	61.3	90.3	68.3	67.0
1985	68.9	71.2	71.1	74.3	72.5	60.7	75.8	65.4	75.4	65.2	91.7	72.2	70.5
1986	70.3	74.7	74.3	77.6	76.1	64.8	79.6	68.3	77.6	67.0	92.2	75.6	73.9
1987	73.4	80.0	80.0	82.6	81.0	72.2	83.1	74.2	81.6	71.7	94.9	79.6	78.9
1988	77.2	85.0	84.9	88.9	85.8	76.7	88.9	80.7	86.4	75.0	99.0	85.1	84.7
1989	78.9	85.9	86.0	90.6	86.2	76.6	91.3	84.3	87.3	80.5	100.9	87.0	85.9
1990	80.1	84.5	86.4	89.8	83.6	73.8	90.3	85.8	88.0	82.3	103.0	88.0	86.6
1991	80.0	82.3	84.3	87.2	81.1	74.2	87.1	83.5	86.6	85.6	101.1	86.4	86.3
1992	82.4	83.7	85.4	88.3	82.2	77.1	88.3	87.4	88.1	86.4	101.8	87.1	87.8
1993	84.1	83.8	84.3	88.8	82.8	78.1	89.3	88.6	89.0	85.7	103.2	88.5	88.8
1994	88.0	86.8	86.3	91.2	86.6	81.5	90.1	91.3	90.9	91.4	103.2	91.8	90.7
1995	91.0	90.5	91.6	93.5	89.6	87.7	92.5	91.6	92.9	95.2	100.4	93.3	92.9
1996	95.0	94.4	94.0	96.3	94.5	94.4	94.0	95.6	96.1	97.0	99.1	95.5	96.9
1997	100.0	100.0	100.0	100.0	100.0	100.0	100.0	100.0	100.0	100.0	100.0	100.0	100.0
1997 2	100.0	100.0	100.0	100.0	100.0	100.0	100.0	100.0	100.0	100.0	100.0	100.0	100.0
1998 2	104.2	103.1	101.5	104.7	105.3	102.7	104.4	102.9	104.3	104.0	104.1	104.7	102.1
1999 2	109.4	106.8	107.1	110.0	112.7	105.9	105.2	105.9	112.4	108.5	107.9	110.5	105.9
2000 2	112.3	108.3	108.4	114.9	117.2	103.8	101.5	106.5	117.3	111.5	108.9	115.8	104.6
2001 2	114.4	109.3	109.6	117.8	118.9	103.9	103.7	106.5	118.7	112.6	110.0	120.9	105.4
2002 2	116.8	111.9	112.6	122.0	120.2	106.6	104.9	107.4	120.1	114.4	113.5	122.6	106.7
2003 2	120.1	114.3	116.1	127.7	122.2	107.9	109.6	110.9	121.5	117.9	115.9	126.7	106.7
2004 2	124.4	119.9	120.3	134.2	125.4	109.8	115.0	112.6	124.4	118.6	120.6	132.0	108.5
2005 2	129.5	123.2	123.7	142.5	129.2	112.0	119.0	114.0	131.4	120.8	123.3	138.4	109.4
2006 2	132.6	125.4	127.0	148.1	131.4	114.5	116.3	116.1	136.9	122.5	126.6	141.0	111.0
2007 2	134.0	126.8	127.6	149.5	134.3	114.0	112.8	120.4	140.3	126.0	126.6	142.5	110.2
2008 2	132.4	127.2	128.1	144.2	133.0	113.6	111.2	122.0	140.0	124.5	126.9	142.3	108.9
2009 2	127.6	120.8	124.3	136.4	124.8	108.8	113.1	116.4	136.7	118.0	120.9	141.3	109.5
2010 2	131.2	123.6	127.5	137.6	128.0	113.4	123.7	119.0	140.1	120.6	126.2	145.5	112.6
2011 2	132.4	122.7	127.9	138.3	130.2	114.1	124.4	118.0	142.6	122.0	128.7	145.9	117.7

2NAICS basis, not continuous with previous years, which are based on the SIC.

Table 17-1. Gross Domestic Product by Region and State—*Continued*

(Billions of dollars; index numbers.)

Year	Southwest					Rocky Mountain					
	Total	Arizona	New Mexico	Oklahoma	Texas	Total	Colorado	Idaho	Montana	Utah	Wyoming
VALUE											
1977	184.1	19.6	10.1	24.0	130.4	54.9	25.4	7.2	6.4	10.4	5.5
1978	211.0	23.3	11.5	27.1	149.1	64.0	29.4	8.5	7.4	12.0	6.7
1979	243.8	27.5	13.1	31.5	171.6	73.0	33.8	9.3	8.2	13.7	8.1
1980	287.2	30.8	15.7	37.6	203.1	82.9	38.3	9.9	8.9	15.3	10.4
1981	343.4	34.3	18.5	45.4	245.2	94.9	44.0	10.7	10.2	17.3	12.7
1982	364.4	35.8	19.2	49.3	260.1	99.3	47.7	10.7	10.2	18.4	12.4
1983	372.2	39.8	19.9	47.7	264.9	104.5	50.7	11.8	10.6	19.8	11.6
1984	407.5	46.1	21.4	51.3	288.6	114.1	56.2	12.6	11.0	22.1	12.2
1985	433.2	50.7	22.5	52.8	307.2	119.9	59.6	13.0	10.9	24.1	12.2
1986	422.4	55.9	21.8	49.0	295.7	120.0	61.0	13.2	11.0	24.3	10.5
1987	432.2	60.0	22.4	49.1	300.7	124.8	63.9	14.0	11.4	25.1	10.4
1988	468.4	64.9	23.5	52.7	327.4	133.1	67.8	15.3	11.7	27.3	11.0
1989	497.8	67.9	24.9	55.0	350.0	140.8	71.2	16.9	12.6	28.7	11.4
1990	534.0	70.6	26.6	57.8	378.9	150.8	75.6	18.0	13.2	31.2	12.7
1991	556.9	73.4	30.3	59.6	393.6	159.0	79.8	18.9	13.9	33.5	13.0
1992	593.9	82.7	32.6	62.2	416.4	171.7	87.3	20.6	14.9	35.6	13.2
1993	635.5	89.3	36.9	65.6	443.8	187.2	95.7	23.1	16.1	38.6	13.8
1994	686.3	100.4	41.7	68.3	476.0	203.7	104.5	25.5	17.1	42.6	14.1
1995	730.6	109.9	42.1	70.9	507.7	219.3	112.7	27.8	17.5	46.7	14.6
1996	791.9	119.5	44.5	76.3	551.5	235.9	121.1	28.9	18.1	52.0	15.8
1997	866.1	129.3	48.7	81.1	607.0	253.7	133.2	30.3	18.9	55.2	16.1
1997 [2]	856.4	128.0	47.6	78.7	602.2	251.4	132.9	28.2	19.2	56.5	14.6
1998 [2]	900.8	139.3	46.5	80.7	634.3	267.7	142.1	29.6	20.1	61.2	14.7
1999 [2]	955.3	150.9	48.8	85.0	670.6	289.2	155.4	32.8	20.8	64.6	15.7
2000 [2]	1 034.4	161.8	50.3	91.3	731.1	316.4	172.0	36.1	21.6	69.5	17.1
2001 [2]	1 082.1	170.0	52.1	97.1	762.9	331.6	181.0	36.4	23.1	72.4	18.7
2002 [2]	1 112.3	177.1	53.7	98.8	782.8	341.9	186.5	37.7	23.8	74.6	19.3
2003 [2]	1 176.2	189.1	57.9	104.7	824.5	356.1	192.0	39.5	25.7	77.8	21.1
2004 [2]	1 281.2	201.0	64.2	112.3	903.7	379.2	201.6	44.1	27.8	82.5	23.3
2005 [2]	1 379.4	222.6	67.8	120.5	968.6	412.9	217.3	48.7	30.1	90.6	26.3
2006 [2]	1 504.1	246.1	71.4	132.2	1 054.4	444.0	230.2	50.5	32.2	100.2	30.8
2007 [2]	1 621.3	259.2	74.4	140.4	1 147.4	474.2	242.6	54.3	35.1	108.5	33.7
2008 [2]	1 700.7	261.1	77.1	153.2	1 209.3	496.1	252.5	55.1	35.8	113.8	38.9
2009 [2]	1 590.6	245.7	74.7	140.7	1 129.5	479.4	244.4	53.7	34.9	112.3	34.2
2010 [2]	1 697.4	249.8	77.1	147.6	1 222.9	500.8	253.1	56.0	36.5	119.2	35.8
2011 [2]	1 801.0	258.4	79.4	155.0	1 308.1	522.3	264.3	57.9	38.0	124.5	37.6
QUANTITY INDEX 1997 =100											
1977	65.1	65.5	63.5	62.0	61.3	70.9	63.2	56.7	57.8	64.6	62.2
1978	68.0	68.0	66.1	64.7	64.2	73.8	65.5	59.3	60.8	68.2	63.8
1979	69.4	69.3	66.8	65.7	64.5	73.1	66.5	61.3	63.0	69.7	67.8
1980	69.4	67.6	63.5	63.4	61.1	66.6	63.7	60.4	61.6	67.8	67.0
1981	70.7	67.9	64.0	64.3	61.8	66.5	64.4	60.6	63.7	69.9	68.9
1982	71.2	65.3	61.1	62.0	58.4	62.4	61.1	59.4	62.1	65.3	68.3
1983	72.7	67.1	63.1	62.7	59.8	66.6	63.6	60.5	62.6	62.6	68.7
1984	77.1	70.8	68.1	67.2	65.3	72.1	69.1	64.2	67.3	66.0	71.8
1985	79.2	72.5	70.4	69.2	66.5	75.1	71.6	66.3	69.2	67.4	74.5
1986	81.2	73.9	71.5	70.7	67.6	76.4	72.3	67.4	69.5	66.5	74.8
1987	84.7	77.9	73.5	73.0	70.1	77.3	74.4	69.4	71.9	68.0	77.3
1988	89.6	81.7	77.0	77.1	73.6	80.5	77.2	71.9	74.6	71.6	79.4
1989	89.4	83.1	78.6	78.6	76.3	81.8	78.9	73.6	76.5	74.2	80.0
1990	89.7	84.3	79.0	79.4	76.6	80.1	79.7	76.6	77.6	76.4	81.8
1991	86.9	84.5	78.6	79.3	76.6	78.8	79.1	77.6	78.4	76.8	82.6
1992	88.1	87.1	82.3	82.4	81.5	82.1	82.8	81.8	81.8	80.4	85.1
1993	88.5	88.4	84.3	84.2	84.0	84.6	83.5	85.0	82.2	80.5	85.7
1994	89.7	90.9	89.7	89.4	89.1	92.0	88.5	89.5	87.8	87.2	90.0
1995	91.6	93.9	91.8	91.9	91.9	92.2	91.7	91.4	90.5	89.7	91.1
1996	95.4	96.4	95.4	95.5	95.6	95.5	94.8	95.7	95.3	94.9	94.9
1997	100.0	100.0	100.0	100.0	100.0	100.0	100.0	100.0	100.0	100.0	100.0
1997 [2]	100.0	100.0	100.0	100.0	100.0	100.0	100.0	100.0	100.0	100.0	100.0
1998 [2]	106.1	109.4	101.8	102.3	106.3	105.6	106.1	104.3	103.3	106.4	102.6
1999 [2]	111.4	118.5	108.5	105.6	110.8	112.4	114.3	114.9	105.4	110.4	108.1
2000 [2]	116.1	126.4	109.8	108.9	115.4	120.5	124.1	127.2	107.3	115.8	110.3
2001 [2]	119.4	131.1	112.8	113.1	118.2	123.8	128.3	126.8	110.8	117.8	118.0
2002 [2]	122.0	134.3	115.5	113.8	121.0	125.5	130.0	129.8	111.9	119.0	120.1
2003 [2]	123.5	141.3	118.8	114.9	121.3	127.1	130.5	133.2	116.7	119.0	122.1
2004 [2]	129.7	146.5	127.1	118.2	127.9	131.0	133.1	144.4	121.2	124.5	125.9
2005 [2]	131.6	157.3	127.3	118.9	128.4	136.9	138.1	157.1	124.9	131.7	124.9
2006 [2]	138.4	168.5	130.0	125.2	134.8	142.1	141.8	159.6	128.3	140.3	136.7
2007 [2]	144.5	172.4	130.8	128.1	142.1	146.8	145.0	166.0	133.7	147.2	141.9
2008 [2]	145.2	170.4	129.7	132.6	142.8	149.1	146.8	165.8	132.8	151.0	149.3
2009 [2]	141.1	156.4	130.6	128.5	140.2	145.6	142.7	159.1	129.1	148.0	152.7
2010 [2]	146.9	158.1	132.2	131.0	147.6	149.7	146.1	165.1	133.0	154.3	151.9
2011 [2]	150.9	160.5	132.4	132.4	152.5	151.8	148.9	166.1	132.9	157.5	150.1

[2]NAICS basis, not continuous with previous years, which are based on the SIC.

Table 17-1. Gross Domestic Product by Region and State—*Continued*

(Billions of dollars; index numbers.)

Year	Far West						
	Total	Alaska	California	Hawaii	Nevada	Oregon	Washington
VALUE							
1977	312.9	7.5	229.6	9.4	7.4	22.0	36.8
1978	359.4	9.1	262.8	10.5	8.9	25.4	42.7
1979	403.6	10.9	293.5	11.9	10.3	28.4	48.7
1980	450.9	15.3	328.0	13.4	11.6	30.0	52.7
1981	509.0	21.8	368.8	14.6	13.2	31.6	58.9
1982	541.4	23.5	393.8	15.7	13.9	31.6	62.9
1983	582.7	22.6	426.1	17.3	15.1	33.7	67.9
1984	653.2	23.8	482.2	19.1	16.5	37.4	74.2
1985	705.5	26.1	523.9	20.7	17.9	39.4	77.3
1986	750.2	19.2	563.1	22.4	19.7	41.7	84.0
1987	819.4	22.9	615.4	24.3	22.0	44.6	90.3
1988	892.8	21.3	671.6	26.8	25.0	49.1	99.1
1989	964.4	23.5	723.0	29.4	27.8	52.6	108.1
1990	1 037.2	25.0	773.5	32.5	31.0	56.6	118.6
1991	1 064.8	22.3	790.0	34.4	32.8	59.4	125.9
1992	1 100.2	22.8	807.4	36.1	36.1	63.4	134.5
1993	1 138.4	23.3	826.4	36.7	40.0	69.4	142.5
1994	1 193.7	23.6	861.4	37.4	45.2	75.4	150.8
1995	1 260.7	25.4	911.6	37.8	49.2	81.6	155.1
1996	1 343.3	26.7	964.2	38.1	54.4	93.3	166.5
1997	1 443.2	27.6	1 037.1	39.1	59.5	100.4	179.6
1997 [2]	1 442.9	25.2	1 039.2	38.0	58.7	96.9	185.0
1998 [2]	1 540.2	23.3	1 114.0	38.0	64.0	101.2	199.7
1999 [2]	1 671.1	23.9	1 211.9	39.3	70.6	104.6	220.9
2000 [2]	1 803.6	25.9	1 319.5	41.5	75.9	113.2	227.7
2001 [2]	1 832.1	27.7	1 340.0	42.5	79.1	112.5	230.3
2002 [2]	1 900.3	28.9	1 387.2	44.8	82.8	119.6	237.1
2003 [2]	2 000.9	30.9	1 461.1	48.1	89.2	124.6	247.1
2004 [2]	2 152.4	34.4	1 569.8	52.3	100.7	137.3	258.0
2005 [2]	2 320.9	37.8	1 688.9	56.9	114.5	143.4	279.3
2006 [2]	2 484.8	41.8	1 798.2	61.0	123.8	159.9	300.1
2007 [2]	2 604.9	44.5	1 870.9	64.1	133.2	167.1	325.1
2008 [2]	2 656.9	49.8	1 900.5	66.0	132.0	175.0	333.7
2009 [2]	2 566.3	45.3	1 828.8	64.3	124.5	171.6	331.9
2010 [2]	2 642.1	47.7	1 877.6	65.6	126.2	185.2	339.8
2011 [2]	2 757.5	51.4	1 958.9	67.0	130.4	194.7	355.1
QUANTITY INDEX 1997 =100							
1977	50.9	58.5	57.5	66.9	54.6	49.1	56.8
1978	53.5	61.3	60.9	74.9	58.3	52.0	60.4
1979	56.0	62.8	62.6	77.2	61.0	53.7	62.0
1980	55.8	60.3	61.9	74.2	58.2	54.2	61.6
1981	57.3	61.1	65.5	85.4	61.7	56.0	62.8
1982	56.5	60.3	63.9	82.1	60.0	55.4	61.2
1983	58.4	62.3	62.3	80.5	59.6	57.6	64.2
1984	64.4	67.6	67.0	82.3	64.2	61.9	67.3
1985	67.0	68.6	69.3	82.8	66.7	64.8	70.4
1986	67.5	70.5	68.1	77.2	67.5	66.8	71.1
1987	70.8	73.3	68.3	79.2	68.9	70.2	75.1
1988	73.7	76.5	72.2	72.9	69.5	73.9	78.7
1989	75.9	78.1	74.3	77.2	70.6	75.6	78.6
1990	76.7	77.2	77.5	79.8	74.4	76.7	79.9
1991	76.6	78.4	80.0	79.5	78.0	77.5	82.2
1992	80.9	80.8	84.0	85.9	82.4	80.4	85.7
1993	81.1	81.0	84.3	84.8	87.1	83.2	87.0
1994	86.0	86.8	91.1	91.2	91.8	88.1	90.5
1995	88.6	91.2	92.5	92.9	93.7	91.7	93.5
1996	94.3	94.9	97.9	100.0	98.2	95.5	96.7
1997	100.0	100.0	100.0	100.0	100.0	100.0	100.0
1997 [2]	100.0	100.0	100.0	100.0	100.0	100.0	100.0
1998 [2]	106.1	94.9	106.7	97.4	106.4	105.4	106.1
1999 [2]	113.8	93.9	115.1	98.2	114.3	109.3	114.9
2000 [2]	121.0	91.8	123.7	100.9	119.7	118.4	115.8
2001 [2]	120.9	95.9	123.8	100.1	120.9	116.9	114.1
2002 [2]	123.4	99.6	126.3	102.5	123.7	122.6	115.2
2003 [2]	127.0	97.4	130.2	106.8	130.4	126.2	117.1
2004 [2]	132.9	102.5	136.2	112.2	142.5	136.3	118.9
2005 [2]	138.7	101.4	141.9	117.6	155.6	140.1	124.8
2006 [2]	144.2	107.0	146.7	121.4	162.0	154.1	129.9
2007 [2]	146.8	109.3	148.2	123.1	168.2	159.2	136.6
2008 [2]	146.8	110.2	147.6	124.2	162.9	166.3	137.7
2009 [2]	140.5	118.2	140.6	118.4	150.6	160.8	133.9
2010 [2]	143.3	117.0	143.0	120.1	151.1	173.7	136.3
2011 [2]	146.3	120.0	145.8	119.8	152.9	182.0	138.9

[2]NAICS basis, not continuous with previous years, which are based on the SIC.

Table 17-2. Personal Income and Employment by Region and State

(Millions of dollars, except as noted.)

Region or state and year	Personal income, total	Earnings by place of work			Less: Contributions for government social insurance	Plus: Adjustment for residence	Equals: Net earnings by place of residence	Plus: Dividends, interest, and rent	Plus: Personal current transfer receipts	Per capita (dollars)		Population (thousands)	Total employment (thousands)
		Nonfarm	Farm	Total						Personal income	Disposable personal income		
UNITED STATES (sum of states)													
1958	367 150	292 553	15 359	307 912	11 371	-182	296 359	47 261	23 529	2 108	1 887	174 153	. . .
1959	390 821	316 664	13 068	329 732	13 824	-192	315 716	50 798	24 306	2 206	1 967	177 136	. . .
1960	408 128	330 420	13 741	344 161	16 349	-260	327 552	54 836	25 740	2 268	2 013	179 972	. . .
1961	425 625	341 001	14 474	355 475	16 905	-250	338 320	57 855	29 450	2 326	2 069	182 976	. . .
1962	453 003	364 608	14 534	379 142	19 011	-202	359 929	62 682	30 392	2 439	2 162	185 739	. . .
1963	475 971	383 849	14 420	398 269	21 548	-173	376 548	67 214	32 209	2 526	2 237	188 434	. . .
1964	510 348	412 855	13 233	426 088	22 247	-170	403 671	73 173	33 504	2 671	2 399	191 085	. . .
1965	551 193	443 495	15 582	459 077	23 268	-111	435 698	79 317	36 178	2 849	2 552	193 460	. . .
1966	598 480	488 870	16 637	505 507	31 127	-99	474 281	84 582	39 617	3 061	2 723	195 499	. . .
1967	641 974	523 424	15 266	538 690	34 558	-96	504 036	89 924	48 014	3 253	2 884	197 375	. . .
1968	704 759	575 918	15 432	591 350	38 338	-119	552 893	95 772	56 094	3 536	3 103	199 312	. . .
1969	772 084	631 215	17 433	648 648	43 792	-107	604 749	105 013	62 322	3 836	3 320	201 298	91 053
1970	832 238	671 411	17 660	689 071	46 012	-112	642 947	114 558	74 733	4 084	3 581	203 799	91 278
1971	897 559	719 019	18 141	737 160	50 859	-122	686 179	123 132	88 248	4 340	3 851	206 818	91 581
1972	987 073	793 307	21 949	815 256	58 897	-145	756 214	132 729	98 130	4 717	4 128	209 275	94 312
1973	1 105 426	884 499	34 874	919 373	75 183	-153	844 037	148 541	112 848	5 230	4 606	211 349	98 428
1974	1 217 673	968 581	30 099	998 680	84 873	-163	913 644	170 390	133 639	5 708	5 002	213 334	100 112
1975	1 329 714	1 033 803	29 152	1 062 955	88 975	-199	973 781	185 509	170 424	6 172	5 489	215 457	98 901
1976	1 469 355	1 160 337	25 236	1 185 573	100 987	-211	1 084 375	200 498	184 482	6 754	5 964	217 554	101 591
1977	1 626 621	1 295 401	24 510	1 319 911	112 699	-235	1 206 977	224 893	194 751	7 402	6 506	219 761	105 042
1978	1 830 836	1 467 571	28 424	1 495 995	130 827	-257	1 364 911	255 616	210 309	8 243	7 213	222 098	109 687
1979	2 052 037	1 640 850	30 233	1 671 083	152 274	-231	1 518 578	297 330	236 129	9 138	7 944	224 569	113 147
1980	2 292 903	1 790 748	20 755	1 811 503	165 669	-255	1 645 579	367 107	280 217	10 091	8 779	227 225	113 983
1981	2 572 070	1 962 327	27 547	1 989 874	195 066	-208	1 794 600	458 323	319 147	11 209	9 709	229 466	114 914
1982	2 757 048	2 058 870	24 786	2 083 656	208 173	-255	1 875 228	526 312	355 508	11 901	10 377	231 664	114 163
1983	2 941 857	2 198 024	17 432	2 215 456	225 147	-212	1 990 097	567 643	384 117	12 583	11 080	233 792	115 646
1984	3 256 048	2 432 295	32 118	2 464 413	256 554	-254	2 207 605	647 715	400 728	13 807	12 211	235 825	120 528
1985	3 482 520	2 610 934	32 182	2 643 116	280 384	-257	2 362 475	694 758	425 287	14 637	12 887	237 924	123 797
1986	3 683 091	2 772 954	33 350	2 806 304	302 394	228	2 504 138	727 831	451 122	15 338	13 521	240 133	126 232
1987	3 909 771	2 974 891	39 704	3 014 595	322 011	259	2 692 843	749 363	467 565	16 137	14 123	242 289	129 548
1988	4 216 123	3 233 770	39 454	3 273 224	360 256	226	2 913 194	806 520	496 409	17 244	15 184	244 499	133 564
1989	4 541 996	3 420 658	46 164	3 466 822	383 937	236	3 083 121	916 328	542 547	18 402	16 114	246 819	136 178
1990	4 831 282	3 627 230	47 623	3 674 853	408 655	313	3 266 511	969 500	595 271	19 354	16 985	249 623	138 331
1991	5 013 484	3 744 437	42 500	3 786 937	428 559	367	3 358 745	988 967	665 772	19 818	17 504	252 981	137 613
1992	5 335 268	3 998 738	50 774	4 049 512	453 762	478	3 596 228	993 372	745 668	20 799	18 423	256 514	138 166
1993	5 558 374	4 182 270	47 658	4 229 928	476 378	493	3 754 043	1 013 647	790 684	21 385	18 901	259 919	140 774
1994	5 866 796	4 406 376	51 053	4 457 429	507 203	533	3 950 759	1 089 725	826 312	22 297	19 676	263 126	144 197
1995	6 194 245	4 647 549	39 899	4 687 448	531 890	703	4 156 261	1 159 118	878 866	23 262	20 472	266 278	147 916
1996	6 584 404	4 908 173	55 382	4 963 555	554 164	675	4 410 066	1 250 337	924 001	24 442	21 357	269 394	151 056
1997	6 994 388	5 238 319	51 440	5 289 759	586 311	672	4 704 120	1 341 139	949 129	25 654	22 260	272 647	154 541
1998	7 519 327	5 655 589	49 079	5 704 668	623 701	755	5 081 722	1 459 720	977 885	27 258	23 541	275 854	158 481
1999	7 906 131	6 040 317	49 572	6 089 889	660 324	1 017	5 430 582	1 453 995	1 021 554	28 333	24 368	279 040	161 531
2000	8 554 866	6 548 165	52 468	6 600 633	704 861	1 122	5 896 894	1 574 990	1 082 982	30 319	25 956	282 162	165 371
2001	8 878 830	6 789 672	54 779	6 844 451	732 130	1 058	6 113 379	1 577 379	1 188 072	31 157	26 828	284 969	165 510
2002	9 054 702	6 951 836	42 784	6 994 620	750 231	898	6 245 287	1 527 299	1 282 116	31 481	27 833	287 625	165 063
2003	9 369 072	7 228 400	59 770	7 288 170	777 575	819	6 511 414	1 515 977	1 341 681	32 295	28 851	290 108	166 020
2004	9 928 790	7 656 172	76 295	7 732 467	825 892	762	6 907 337	1 605 771	1 415 682	33 909	30 334	292 805	169 027
2005	10 476 669	8 048 405	71 394	8 119 799	871 241	738	7 249 296	1 718 902	1 508 471	35 452	31 367	295 517	172 551
2006	11 256 516	8 539 008	57 333	8 596 341	920 430	646	7 676 557	1 975 147	1 604 812	37 725	33 197	298 380	176 125
2007	11 900 562	8 872 550	67 955	8 940 505	958 097	537	7 982 945	2 199 709	1 717 908	39 506	34 569	301 231	179 900
2008	12 451 660	9 079 314	82 304	9 161 618	985 847	588	8 176 359	2 396 098	1 879 203	40 947	36 230	304 094	179 645
2009	11 916 773	8 657 917	69 121	8 727 038	962 537	845	7 765 346	2 012 915	2 138 512	38 846	35 129	306 772	174 209
2010	12 353 577	8 909 014	77 215	8 986 229	985 182	845	8 001 892	2 070 501	2 281 184	39 937	36 081	309 330	173 767
2011	12 981 741	9 287 880	90 089	9 377 968	924 951	736	8 453 753	2 192 735	2 335 253	41 663	37 167	311 592	. . .

. . . = Not available.

Table 17-2. Personal Income and Employment by Region and State—*Continued*

(Millions of dollars, except as noted.)

Region or state and year	Personal income, total	Derivation of personal income									Per capita (dollars)		Population (thousands)	Total employment (thousands)
		Earnings by place of work			Less: Contributions for government social insurance	Plus: Adjustment for residence	Equals: Net earnings by place of residence	Plus: Dividends, interest, and rent	Plus: Personal current transfer receipts		Personal income	Disposable personal income		
		Nonfarm	Farm	Total										
NEW ENGLAND														
1958	23 256	18 681	319	19 001	722	18	18 296	3 270	1 690		2 276	2 021	10 219	. . .
1959	24 805	20 228	249	20 477	872	20	19 625	3 494	1 686		2 377	2 103	10 437	. . .
1960	25 866	21 079	318	21 397	1 025	27	20 399	3 706	1 761		2 456	2 155	10 532	. . .
1961	27 122	21 986	269	22 255	1 073	28	21 210	3 935	1 977		2 543	2 242	10 666	. . .
1962	28 790	23 385	259	23 644	1 215	31	22 460	4 323	2 007		2 666	2 344	10 800	. . .
1963	30 053	24 314	252	24 566	1 357	36	23 245	4 682	2 126		2 736	2 401	10 986	. . .
1964	32 182	25 867	289	26 157	1 400	42	24 799	5 177	2 207		2 877	2 567	11 186	. . .
1965	34 512	27 595	340	27 936	1 450	44	26 529	5 653	2 330		3 046	2 710	11 329	. . .
1966	37 527	30 463	345	30 807	1 937	51	28 921	6 094	2 512		3 283	2 897	11 430	. . .
1967	40 817	32 894	240	33 133	2 133	58	31 059	6 676	3 082		3 530	3 104	11 562	. . .
1968	44 278	35 767	267	36 034	2 367	71	33 737	6 859	3 682		3 805	3 295	11 637	. . .
1969	48 997	38 949	294	39 243	2 634	850	37 458	7 428	4 111		4 175	3 570	11 735	5 516
1970	52 711	41 501	306	41 807	2 769	856	39 894	7 914	4 903		4 438	3 860	11 878	5 518
1971	56 072	43 667	283	43 950	3 008	884	41 825	8 371	5 876		4 674	4 124	11 996	5 454
1972	60 743	47 661	288	47 949	3 449	941	45 440	8 896	6 408		5 025	4 367	12 088	5 573
1973	66 530	52 615	398	53 013	4 355	997	49 656	9 678	7 196		5 477	4 790	12 148	5 783
1974	72 384	56 318	430	56 748	4 823	1 084	53 008	10 846	8 531		5 954	5 200	12 157	5 843
1975	77 634	58 557	313	58 871	4 913	1 171	55 128	11 370	11 136		6 376	5 653	12 176	5 685
1976	84 888	64 835	428	65 264	5 515	1 300	61 048	12 171	11 669		6 954	6 116	12 207	5 811
1977	92 982	71 653	384	72 037	6 127	1 453	67 363	13 509	12 110		7 586	6 656	12 257	6 007
1978	103 424	80 707	397	81 104	7 097	1 638	75 645	14 973	12 806		8 407	7 327	12 303	6 276
1979	115 808	90 538	380	90 917	8 287	1 867	84 497	17 046	14 265		9 381	8 111	12 345	6 503
1980	131 114	100 302	368	100 671	9 186	2 180	93 665	21 043	16 406		10 598	9 133	12 372	6 623
1981	146 743	109 612	472	110 084	10 785	2 347	101 646	26 323	18 773		11 800	10 105	12 436	6 666
1982	159 995	117 383	513	117 896	11 773	2 523	108 646	30 826	20 523		12 833	11 057	12 468	6 667
1983	172 736	128 327	479	128 806	13 048	2 654	118 413	32 403	21 920		13 770	11 991	12 544	6 799
1984	193 957	144 853	567	145 420	15 177	2 830	133 073	37 913	22 972		15 342	13 427	12 642	7 159
1985	209 448	158 528	556	159 084	16 771	2 984	145 297	39 984	24 167		16 440	14 290	12 741	7 400
1986	225 755	172 283	574	172 857	18 496	3 153	157 514	42 867	25 374		17 592	15 207	12 833	7 638
1987	245 535	190 119	641	190 760	20 167	3 311	173 904	45 538	26 094		18 958	16 271	12 951	7 771
1988	269 692	209 695	658	210 353	22 618	3 512	191 247	50 400	28 045		20 612	17 891	13 085	8 018
1989	287 995	219 275	608	219 883	23 601	3 437	199 718	56 965	31 311		21 848	18 923	13 182	8 005
1990	297 157	223 120	701	223 820	24 072	3 445	203 193	58 954	35 010		22 462	19 499	13 230	7 853
1991	302 930	224 009	645	224 654	24 508	3 444	203 589	58 866	40 475		22 867	19 966	13 248	7 526
1992	319 527	236 653	794	237 447	25 687	4 665	216 425	59 212	43 889		24 077	20 997	13 271	7 566
1993	330 333	246 297	731	247 028	26 867	4 104	224 265	60 599	45 469		24 773	21 531	13 334	7 689
1994	345 678	258 129	678	258 808	28 422	3 915	234 300	63 608	47 769		25 804	22 396	13 396	7 782
1995	364 408	271 573	603	272 176	29 927	4 705	246 953	66 694	50 761		27 048	23 352	13 473	7 875
1996	386 599	286 953	688	287 641	31 309	5 527	261 859	72 516	52 225		28 521	24 353	13 555	8 004
1997	410 458	307 252	594	307 846	33 366	5 156	279 636	76 652	54 170		30 087	25 408	13 642	8 165
1998	441 242	330 873	657	331 530	35 427	6 615	302 717	83 637	54 887		32 128	26 906	13 734	8 336
1999	464 677	354 940	702	355 641	37 624	6 507	324 525	83 425	56 727		33 581	27 964	13 838	8 481
2000	510 702	391 907	775	392 682	40 848	6 816	358 650	92 155	59 896		36 610	30 029	13 950	8 697
2001	533 501	408 792	710	409 502	42 131	6 260	373 631	94 883	64 987		37 996	31 491	14 041	8 770
2002	538 505	412 971	653	413 625	42 834	5 670	376 460	92 022	70 023		38 131	32 933	14 122	8 710
2003	550 256	423 962	704	424 667	43 762	5 409	386 313	90 790	73 152		38 798	33 844	14 182	8 697
2004	580 159	449 405	816	450 221	46 778	6 034	409 477	93 653	77 028		40 837	35 642	14 207	8 789
2005	602 449	466 629	788	467 417	48 776	6 141	424 782	95 837	81 830		42 376	36 517	14 217	8 885
2006	649 981	491 345	662	492 007	50 753	6 626	447 880	116 167	85 934		45 627	39 177	14 246	9 004
2007	688 585	512 158	824	512 982	53 003	7 029	467 008	130 559	91 018		48 223	40 901	14 279	9 161
2008	713 073	518 381	796	519 177	54 733	6 696	471 139	141 716	100 218		49 726	42 900	14 340	9 171
2009	684 352	499 064	630	499 694	54 099	4 745	450 341	119 784	114 228		47 513	41 984	14 404	8 940
2010	705 913	514 232	764	514 996	55 145	4 684	464 535	122 734	118 644		48 840	43 095	14 454	8 936
2011	740 177	536 157	787	536 944	51 546	4 912	490 310	129 693	120 174		51 074	44 290	14 492	. . .

. . . = Not available.

Table 17-2. Personal Income and Employment by Region and State—*Continued*

(Millions of dollars, except as noted.)

Region or state and year	Personal income, total	Derivation of personal income								Per capita (dollars)		Population (thousands)	Total employment (thousands)
		Earnings by place of work			Less: Contributions for government social insurance	Plus: Adjustment for residence	Equals: Net earnings by place of residence	Plus: Dividends, interest, and rent	Plus: Personal current transfer receipts	Personal income	Disposable personal income		
		Nonfarm	Farm	Total									
MIDEAST													
1958	90 914	75 869	992	76 861	3 047	-561	73 252	11 946	5 715	2 410	2 126	14 445	. . .
1959	96 281	81 067	789	81 856	3 679	-600	77 577	12 769	5 935	2 520	2 212	38 202	. . .
1960	100 510	84 839	902	85 741	4 353	-726	80 662	13 728	6 119	2 604	2 280	38 597	. . .
1961	104 517	87 593	906	88 499	4 580	-754	83 166	14 358	6 994	2 671	2 338	39 133	. . .
1962	110 532	92 869	734	93 602	5 116	-763	87 724	15 658	7 150	2 795	2 440	39 552	. . .
1963	115 407	96 572	799	97 371	5 641	-795	90 934	16 880	7 593	2 879	2 513	40 083	. . .
1964	123 661	103 037	803	103 840	5 691	-853	97 296	18 504	7 861	3 049	2 700	40 555	. . .
1965	132 238	109 770	897	110 667	5 938	-888	103 841	19 992	8 405	3 223	2 843	41 025	. . .
1966	142 526	119 941	917	120 858	7 889	-963	112 006	21 119	9 401	3 446	3 021	41 360	. . .
1967	153 589	128 354	972	129 326	8 607	-1 127	119 592	22 395	11 602	3 691	3 219	41 617	. . .
1968	168 444	140 302	921	141 223	9 391	-1 244	130 587	23 985	13 872	4 018	3 472	41 924	. . .
1969	181 420	152 275	1 105	153 379	11 063	-1 711	140 606	25 557	15 257	4 308	3 670	42 111	19 432
1970	195 852	162 604	1 063	163 667	11 648	-1 618	150 402	27 345	18 105	4 606	3 981	42 517	19 465
1971	209 590	172 466	970	173 436	12 763	-1 687	158 986	28 866	21 738	4 889	4 281	42 870	19 299
1972	226 658	187 087	966	188 053	14 524	-1 850	171 679	30 560	24 419	5 272	4 551	42 992	19 521
1973	245 956	204 116	1 387	205 503	18 181	-1 983	185 339	33 316	27 301	5 742	4 986	42 837	19 968
1974	267 917	219 698	1 293	220 991	20 147	-2 211	198 633	37 477	31 808	6 273	5 426	42 709	19 954
1975	289 318	231 247	1 199	232 446	20 828	-2 527	209 092	39 760	40 467	6 771	5 946	42 728	19 480
1976	313 453	251 669	1 280	252 948	22 884	-2 869	227 195	42 574	43 684	7 346	6 421	42 667	19 563
1977	341 482	275 126	1 099	276 225	24 856	-3 266	248 103	47 364	46 014	8 026	6 976	42 547	19 848
1978	375 220	304 691	1 314	306 005	28 197	-3 788	274 021	52 383	48 816	8 845	7 660	42 421	20 411
1979	413 320	335 407	1 524	336 931	32 242	-4 438	300 251	59 494	53 575	9 758	8 389	42 358	20 871
1980	459 655	365 079	1 141	366 220	35 077	-5 273	325 870	72 162	61 623	10 874	9 340	42 272	20 911
1981	511 332	397 747	1 504	399 251	40 961	-5 833	352 457	89 386	69 509	12 081	10 295	42 329	20 978
1982	552 995	420 856	1 459	422 315	43 975	-6 062	372 278	103 523	77 194	13 048	11 150	42 382	20 858
1983	591 398	450 302	1 090	451 412	47 845	-6 163	397 404	110 517	83 477	13 901	12 048	42 544	21 045
1984	650 569	494 561	1 901	496 462	54 377	-6 474	435 611	128 083	86 875	15 241	13 236	42 687	21 766
1985	695 700	531 785	2 010	533 795	59 560	-6 760	467 476	136 914	91 310	16 257	14 053	42 794	22 333
1986	739 831	569 596	2 196	571 791	64 792	-6 744	500 255	143 097	96 478	17 209	14 870	42 991	22 837
1987	790 486	617 843	2 295	620 139	69 475	-7 161	543 503	147 850	99 134	18 303	15 672	43 190	23 321
1988	863 253	680 069	2 205	682 274	77 994	-7 846	596 433	161 608	105 212	19 874	17 181	43 435	23 927
1989	928 403	717 061	2 578	719 639	82 250	-8 087	629 302	185 350	113 751	21 301	18 330	43 585	24 201
1990	986 464	758 301	2 519	760 820	85 066	-8 768	666 986	194 855	124 623	22 542	19 511	43 762	24 260
1991	1 009 194	763 739	2 053	765 792	87 865	-9 240	668 687	199 485	141 022	22 899	19 947	44 071	23 703
1992	1 062 717	810 248	2 650	812 899	92 357	-10 887	709 655	196 623	156 439	23 939	20 871	44 392	23 597
1993	1 093 766	836 997	2 520	839 517	95 837	-10 788	732 892	195 665	165 209	24 460	21 266	44 717	23 714
1994	1 133 990	866 167	2 308	868 476	100 829	-10 523	757 124	205 767	171 100	25 217	21 884	44 970	23 879
1995	1 190 946	906 695	1 765	908 460	104 512	-11 482	792 466	217 816	180 664	26 357	22 834	45 186	24 157
1996	1 256 732	951 858	2 698	954 556	107 626	-11 977	834 952	232 104	189 676	27 691	23 820	45 384	24 387
1997	1 327 517	1 009 331	1 852	1 011 183	112 202	-12 347	886 635	248 915	191 967	29 125	24 847	45 580	24 763
1998	1 410 199	1 075 279	2 318	1 077 598	117 980	-13 491	946 127	265 990	198 082	30 776	26 096	45 822	25 194
1999	1 472 262	1 138 405	2 304	1 140 708	123 962	-14 699	1 002 048	264 313	205 901	31 932	26 913	46 106	25 631
2000	1 585 504	1 225 157	2 772	1 227 929	132 242	-13 374	1 082 313	285 899	217 292	34 181	28 693	46 386	26 277
2001	1 637 375	1 269 388	2 828	1 272 215	138 230	-13 112	1 120 873	282 783	233 719	35 122	29 431	46 619	26 446
2002	1 662 681	1 294 151	1 934	1 296 085	141 971	-14 015	1 140 100	270 424	252 156	35 496	30 693	46 841	26 423
2003	1 707 492	1 335 820	2 859	1 338 679	145 566	-14 204	1 178 909	266 371	262 212	36 303	31 729	47 035	26 529
2004	1 808 114	1 417 790	3 600	1 421 391	153 264	-15 414	1 252 712	278 989	276 413	38 338	33 510	47 162	26 916
2005	1 898 598	1 487 030	3 453	1 490 483	160 827	-15 853	1 313 803	299 397	285 398	40 191	34 721	47 239	27 334
2006	2 046 137	1 582 511	2 884	1 585 395	169 143	-17 356	1 398 896	344 900	302 341	43 227	37 081	47 334	27 733
2007	2 177 747	1 656 728	3 423	1 660 151	178 042	-18 308	1 463 801	395 043	318 904	45 873	38 937	47 474	28 228
2008	2 271 110	1 701 715	3 471	1 705 186	184 545	-18 944	1 501 698	426 269	343 143	47 627	41 001	47 685	28 371
2009	2 185 633	1 636 880	2 669	1 639 549	181 719	-17 416	1 440 414	356 837	388 382	45 587	40 214	47 944	27 775
2010	2 271 403	1 697 730	3 289	1 701 018	186 970	-18 409	1 495 640	364 691	411 073	47 122	41 487	48 203	27 791
2011	2 374 692	1 760 421	4 067	1 764 487	174 558	-19 355	1 570 574	385 081	419 036	49 081	42 561	48 383	. . .

. . . = Not available.

Table 17-2. Personal Income and Employment by Region and State—*Continued*

(Millions of dollars, except as noted.)

Region or state and year	Personal income, total	Earnings by place of work			Less: Contributions for government social insurance	Plus: Adjustment for residence	Equals: Net earnings by place of residence	Plus: Dividends, interest, and rent	Plus: Personal current transfer receipts	Per capita (dollars)		Population (thousands)	Total employment (thousands)
		Nonfarm	Farm	Total						Personal income	Disposable personal income		
GREAT LAKES													
1958	79 772	64 976	2 424	67 401	2 492	-112	64 797	9 916	5 059	2 242	2 008	35 578	. . .
1959	85 064	70 743	1 911	72 654	3 045	-126	69 483	10 639	4 943	2 368	2 113	35 928	. . .
1960	88 440	73 378	2 016	75 394	3 656	-123	71 615	11 568	5 257	2 437	2 159	36 290	. . .
1961	90 561	73 505	2 448	75 953	3 617	-111	72 225	12 206	6 130	2 473	2 204	36 616	. . .
1962	96 106	78 544	2 354	80 898	4 043	-116	76 740	13 212	6 154	2 603	2 308	36 927	. . .
1963	100 657	82 491	2 366	84 857	4 561	-114	80 182	14 132	6 343	2 694	2 386	37 357	. . .
1964	108 259	89 221	2 046	91 267	4 762	-122	86 384	15 401	6 474	2 859	2 565	37 868	. . .
1965	118 280	97 046	2 633	99 679	4 946	-133	94 600	16 746	6 935	3 080	2 752	38 405	. . .
1966	128 714	107 139	2 973	110 112	6 742	-146	103 224	17 960	7 529	3 305	2 933	38 951	. . .
1967	135 587	112 457	2 537	114 994	7 271	-135	107 588	18 990	9 009	3 446	3 050	39 347	. . .
1968	148 010	123 117	2 433	125 550	7 985	-145	117 420	20 177	10 413	3 733	3 266	39 645	. . .
1969	160 960	134 751	2 871	137 622	9 310	288	128 599	21 027	11 334	4 034	3 469	39 904	17 785
1970	169 128	139 807	2 518	142 325	9 504	263	133 085	22 495	13 548	4 195	3 649	40 320	17 630
1971	181 688	149 025	2 900	151 925	10 425	335	141 835	23 752	16 102	4 473	3 943	40 622	17 549
1972	198 678	163 784	3 169	166 954	12 096	384	155 242	25 463	17 972	4 867	4 230	40 824	17 933
1973	223 058	183 715	5 214	188 930	15 629	436	173 736	28 384	20 938	5 447	4 761	40 947	18 710
1974	242 856	197 752	4 663	202 415	17 400	537	185 552	32 373	24 932	5 918	5 155	41 037	18 911
1975	261 450	205 382	5 824	211 206	17 671	630	194 165	35 254	32 031	6 360	5 614	41 105	18 399
1976	289 369	232 028	4 821	236 849	20 243	778	217 384	37 792	34 193	7 026	6 144	41 187	18 891
1977	321 738	260 962	4 823	265 785	22 759	962	243 989	42 032	35 717	7 780	6 769	41 353	19 508
1978	357 351	292 740	4 516	297 256	26 310	1 188	272 133	46 813	38 405	8 609	7 452	41 510	20 190
1979	394 609	321 099	5 227	326 327	29 955	1 406	297 778	53 403	43 429	9 483	8 176	41 611	20 491
1980	427 919	334 101	3 321	337 423	30 983	1 680	308 120	65 287	54 512	10 263	8 910	41 694	19 978
1981	467 100	356 142	3 697	359 839	35 398	1 438	325 880	80 610	60 610	11 215	9 696	41 648	19 795
1982	488 502	360 110	2 933	363 042	36 329	1 338	328 051	92 433	68 017	11 773	10 313	41 492	19 248
1983	512 689	379 282	-121	379 161	38 845	1 323	341 639	98 367	72 683	12 394	10 894	41 366	19 265
1984	565 479	418 399	4 404	422 803	44 261	1 426	379 968	111 055	74 456	13 661	12 061	41 393	20 028
1985	599 673	446 337	4 953	451 290	48 194	1 465	404 561	116 927	78 186	14 479	12 732	41 418	20 492
1986	630 428	471 888	4 486	476 373	51 649	1 538	426 263	122 313	81 851	15 208	13 391	41 455	20 934
1987	662 129	500 824	5 030	505 855	54 321	1 605	453 139	124 877	84 112	15 921	13 922	41 590	21 516
1988	707 371	542 892	3 394	546 286	60 500	1 728	487 514	132 106	87 750	16 955	14 887	41 721	22 070
1989	758 613	572 979	7 031	580 010	64 370	1 764	517 404	147 135	94 074	18 117	15 824	41 873	22 556
1990	800 635	603 474	6 007	609 481	68 628	1 961	542 815	155 036	102 784	19 021	16 641	42 091	22 928
1991	824 736	622 072	3 611	625 683	71 893	2 008	555 799	156 986	111 951	19 407	17 063	42 496	22 845
1992	883 129	667 538	6 137	673 675	76 360	2 236	599 552	159 902	123 675	20 585	18 176	42 903	22 971
1993	920 576	700 555	5 218	705 772	80 852	2 319	627 240	163 325	130 011	21 273	18 696	43 275	23 359
1994	980 371	747 541	6 094	753 635	87 256	2 523	668 902	177 448	134 021	22 491	19 714	43 590	24 060
1995	1 027 993	785 247	3 358	788 606	91 794	2 662	699 474	187 456	141 063	23 404	20 448	43 924	24 713
1996	1 082 802	818 105	6 939	825 045	94 889	2 963	733 118	202 226	147 458	24 476	21 247	44 239	25 105
1997	1 143 441	863 648	6 619	870 267	99 402	3 310	774 175	216 981	152 284	25 699	22 193	44 494	25 513
1998	1 220 815	925 461	5 589	931 050	104 514	3 441	829 977	236 091	154 747	27 294	23 479	44 728	25 957
1999	1 267 538	976 031	4 540	980 571	109 871	3 870	874 570	231 895	161 073	28 187	24 232	44 969	26 329
2000	1 348 478	1 033 685	5 339	1 039 024	114 327	4 211	928 908	248 859	170 710	29 823	25 669	45 216	26 775
2001	1 382 884	1 059 180	5 562	1 064 742	115 982	4 133	952 893	242 672	187 320	30 459	26 373	45 402	26 493
2002	1 409 899	1 087 294	3 620	1 090 914	117 466	4 147	977 595	233 202	199 103	30 953	27 338	45 550	26 257
2003	1 456 861	1 132 890	6 343	1 139 233	121 024	4 300	1 022 509	226 566	207 786	31 873	28 492	45 708	26 221
2004	1 506 978	1 171 944	10 282	1 182 226	127 254	4 584	1 059 556	230 682	216 740	32 872	29 460	45 844	26 437
2005	1 551 823	1 204 650	7 093	1 211 743	132 564	4 901	1 084 080	235 074	232 669	33 773	30 034	45 949	26 675
2006	1 635 232	1 249 381	6 897	1 256 278	138 498	5 151	1 122 932	267 598	244 702	35 493	31 417	46 072	26 897
2007	1 702 732	1 275 034	9 178	1 284 212	142 802	5 323	1 146 733	291 333	264 666	36 865	32 445	46 188	27 141
2008	1 764 222	1 288 858	13 725	1 302 583	146 159	5 734	1 162 158	315 739	286 325	38 125	33 809	46 275	26 884
2009	1 687 402	1 218 600	10 486	1 229 086	140 203	5 451	1 094 333	261 288	331 781	36 401	33 028	46 356	25 806
2010	1 738 106	1 246 766	11 023	1 257 789	142 660	5 328	1 120 457	268 073	349 576	37 427	33 962	46 439	25 749
2011	1 825 714	1 299 108	16 502	1 315 610	134 176	5 691	1 187 125	283 882	354 707	39 247	35 121	46 519	. . .

. . . = Not available.

Table 17-2. Personal Income and Employment by Region and State—*Continued*

(Millions of dollars, except as noted.)

Region or state and year	Personal income, total	Earnings by place of work			Less: Contributions for government social insurance	Plus: Adjustment for residence	Equals: Net earnings by place of residence	Plus: Dividends, interest, and rent	Plus: Personal current transfer receipts	Per capita (dollars)		Population (thousands)	Total employment (thousands)
		Nonfarm	Farm	Total						Personal income	Disposable personal income		
PLAINS													
1958	30 348	21 260	3 862	25 122	826	7	24 303	4 088	1 957	2 024	1 829	14 994	. . .
1959	31 096	22 960	2 674	25 634	1 000	8	24 642	4 356	2 097	2 046	1 846	15 195	. . .
1960	32 698	23 878	3 124	27 002	1 156	7	25 853	4 628	2 218	2 120	1 900	15 424	. . .
1961	33 897	24 764	3 045	27 809	1 211	6	26 604	4 829	2 464	2 177	1 951	15 570	. . .
1962	36 209	26 284	3 544	29 828	1 317	7	28 518	5 131	2 560	2 313	2 071	15 657	. . .
1963	37 682	27 526	3 489	31 015	1 493	3	29 526	5 460	2 696	2 398	2 145	15 715	. . .
1964	39 265	29 431	2 797	32 228	1 554	5	30 678	5 798	2 788	2 487	2 254	15 787	. . .
1965	43 108	31 374	4 111	35 485	1 632	4	33 857	6 230	3 021	2 725	2 463	15 819	. . .
1966	46 386	34 457	4 312	38 769	2 197	0	36 572	6 551	3 263	2 920	2 619	15 888	. . .
1967	48 685	36 945	3 680	40 625	2 549	-5	38 072	6 719	3 894	3 054	2 731	15 942	. . .
1968	53 056	40 496	3 672	44 168	2 837	-14	41 318	7 234	4 505	3 306	2 935	16 047	. . .
1969	58 190	44 462	4 221	48 683	3 164	-414	45 105	8 144	4 940	3 592	3 140	16 202	7 506
1970	62 923	47 457	4 444	51 901	3 342	-358	48 201	8 930	5 792	3 849	3 403	16 350	7 516
1971	67 617	50 789	4 611	55 400	3 697	-355	51 348	9 617	6 653	4 104	3 672	16 475	7 544
1972	74 763	55 475	6 163	61 638	4 228	-361	57 050	10 460	7 252	4 514	3 987	16 563	7 731
1973	87 540	61 766	11 295	73 061	5 405	-399	67 257	11 833	8 450	5 265	4 687	16 628	8 065
1974	92 793	68 202	7 689	75 891	6 194	-432	69 265	13 677	9 850	5 566	4 874	16 672	8 219
1975	101 673	73 756	7 507	81 263	6 600	-423	74 239	15 311	12 122	6 073	5 387	16 743	8 181
1976	109 482	83 432	4 415	87 847	7 518	-521	79 808	16 507	13 167	6 492	5 724	16 864	8 438
1977	121 261	92 407	5 201	97 607	8 276	-659	88 671	18 673	13 916	7 154	6 296	16 950	8 657
1978	137 489	104 033	7 851	111 884	9 619	-818	101 447	20 884	15 158	8 074	7 085	17 028	8 953
1979	151 931	116 631	6 621	123 251	11 228	-986	111 037	23 916	16 978	8 886	7 732	17 097	9 232
1980	164 154	125 656	1 886	127 541	12 066	-1 142	114 333	29 543	20 277	9 540	8 296	17 208	9 227
1981	185 705	135 419	5 464	140 883	13 959	-1 335	125 589	37 001	23 115	10 757	9 334	17 264	9 180
1982	198 011	140 443	4 013	144 456	14 744	-1 341	128 371	43 885	25 755	11 451	9 957	17 292	9 050
1983	207 462	149 060	1 575	150 635	15 669	-1 432	133 533	46 222	27 707	11 975	10 566	17 325	9 163
1984	230 818	163 945	6 540	170 485	17 709	-1 601	151 176	50 771	28 872	13 279	11 824	17 382	9 470
1985	243 340	173 151	7 454	180 605	19 110	-1 709	159 786	52 975	30 578	13 984	12 426	17 402	9 612
1986	254 419	181 808	8 063	189 871	20 471	-1 826	167 574	54 797	32 048	14 628	13 034	17 393	9 701
1987	267 958	193 695	9 793	203 488	21 693	-1 935	179 859	55 126	32 973	15 375	13 612	17 428	9 949
1988	280 290	207 116	7 413	214 528	24 098	-2 100	188 330	57 375	34 585	15 986	14 158	17 533	10 156
1989	301 245	219 611	9 208	228 819	25 708	-2 181	200 931	62 866	37 448	17 121	15 100	17 595	10 357
1990	319 413	232 056	10 549	242 605	27 940	-2 419	212 246	66 680	40 487	18 048	15 906	17 698	10 544
1991	331 694	241 854	8 125	249 979	29 494	-2 474	218 010	69 039	44 645	18 589	16 470	17 843	10 597
1992	354 655	259 682	10 656	270 338	31 356	-2 714	236 268	70 016	48 372	19 674	17 444	18 026	10 708
1993	365 479	272 335	6 256	278 591	33 015	-2 800	242 776	71 371	51 331	20 071	17 760	18 210	10 934
1994	391 974	289 744	10 497	300 241	35 465	-3 019	261 758	76 608	53 608	21 325	18 868	18 381	11 230
1995	410 298	306 779	5 768	312 547	37 359	-3 162	272 026	81 519	56 753	22 119	19 484	18 550	11 537
1996	442 590	324 116	13 578	337 694	38 964	-3 382	295 348	87 880	59 362	23 661	20 752	18 705	11 761
1997	465 474	344 711	9 926	354 637	41 483	-3 794	309 361	94 865	61 249	24 692	21 527	18 851	11 980
1998	499 369	371 987	9 215	381 202	44 126	-4 056	333 021	103 135	63 213	26 299	22 893	18 988	12 238
1999	520 948	395 534	7 917	403 451	46 513	-4 387	352 551	102 154	66 243	27 231	23 744	19 131	12 411
2000	559 195	422 645	9 532	432 177	49 047	-4 681	378 449	109 822	70 924	29 011	25 259	19 275	12 601
2001	579 129	438 441	8 939	447 380	50 770	-4 709	391 901	109 253	77 975	29 891	26 111	19 375	12 589
2002	593 412	453 497	6 046	459 543	51 949	-4 783	402 811	106 663	83 938	30 481	27 158	19 468	12 502
2003	618 856	471 677	12 741	484 418	53 863	-4 909	425 646	106 255	86 955	31 624	28 493	19 569	12 515
2004	651 446	495 879	16 950	512 829	56 461	-5 069	451 299	108 983	91 164	33 089	29 902	19 688	12 664
2005	673 520	515 134	16 299	531 433	59 190	-5 377	466 866	110 099	96 555	34 011	30 432	19 803	12 861
2006	714 501	540 898	11 510	552 408	62 659	-5 551	484 198	126 066	104 236	35 802	31 846	19 957	13 058
2007	758 810	562 753	15 832	578 585	65 506	-5 746	507 333	139 523	111 954	37 741	33 363	20 106	13 279
2008	812 501	585 768	24 986	610 754	68 344	-6 182	536 229	154 831	121 440	40 126	35 699	20 249	13 299
2009	781 340	565 538	19 732	585 270	66 999	-5 727	512 544	131 403	137 392	38 315	34 826	20 393	13 000
2010	808 950	581 644	21 551	603 195	68 616	-5 543	529 036	135 448	144 466	39 390	35 801	20 537	12 953
2011	851 014	603 506	26 894	630 400	64 224	-5 876	560 300	143 184	147 531	41 232	37 052	20 640	. . .

. . . = Not available.

Table 17-2. Personal Income and Employment by Region and State—*Continued*

(Millions of dollars, except as noted.)

Region or state and year	Personal income, total	Earnings by place of work			Less: Contributions for government social insurance	Plus: Adjustment for residence	Equals: Net earnings by place of residence	Plus: Dividends, interest, and rent	Plus: Personal current transfer receipts	Personal income	Disposable personal income	Population (thousands)	Total employment (thousands)
		Nonfarm	Farm	Total						Per capita (dollars)			

										Personal income	Disposable personal income		
SOUTHEAST													
1958	58 225	45 290	3 589	48 878	1 738	466	47 606	6 556	4 063	1 555	1 422	37 435	...
1959	62 320	49 022	3 466	52 488	2 106	505	50 887	7 086	4 347	1 635	1 487	38 115	...
1960	64 662	50 874	3 352	54 226	2 445	553	52 334	7 725	4 603	1 663	1 507	38 885	...
1961	68 099	52 671	3 774	56 445	2 510	578	54 514	8 290	5 295	1 722	1 563	39 544	...
1962	72 693	56 746	3 535	60 280	2 803	634	58 112	9 025	5 556	1 809	1 633	40 179	...
1963	77 534	60 725	3 766	64 491	3 284	691	61 898	9 735	5 901	1 903	1 716	40 742	...
1964	83 819	66 170	3 627	69 796	3 441	752	67 108	10 553	6 158	2 027	1 847	41 349	...
1965	91 082	72 171	3 506	75 676	3 675	855	72 856	11 503	6 723	2 176	1 975	41 857	...
1966	99 910	80 477	3 715	84 192	4 912	952	80 232	12 337	7 340	2 364	2 130	42 257	...
1967	108 421	87 222	3 701	90 923	5 655	1 105	86 372	13 303	8 746	2 544	2 291	42 611	...
1968	120 195	97 286	3 574	100 860	6 394	1 202	95 668	14 427	10 100	2 793	2 488	43 042	...
1969	133 687	107 855	4 061	111 916	7 217	1 135	105 834	16 464	11 390	3 078	2 705	43 440	19 085
1970	146 233	116 480	4 050	120 529	7 781	1 015	113 763	18 691	13 778	3 325	2 952	43 974	19 254
1971	161 167	127 757	4 261	132 018	8 838	989	124 169	20 718	16 279	3 580	3 202	45 013	19 635
1972	181 372	144 512	4 964	149 476	10 454	1 050	140 072	22 880	18 420	3 941	3 484	46 019	20 523
1973	207 034	164 053	7 277	171 330	13 505	1 120	158 945	26 259	21 829	4 406	3 915	46 992	21 636
1974	231 390	181 855	6 661	188 516	15 476	1 238	174 278	30 721	26 391	4 825	4 271	47 955	22 069
1975	252 983	193 662	5 997	199 660	16 283	1 480	184 856	33 874	34 253	5 185	4 674	48 788	21 642
1976	282 893	219 111	6 366	225 477	18 670	1 669	208 476	37 082	37 335	5 713	5 111	49 514	22 351
1977	314 718	246 148	5 766	251 914	20 907	1 902	232 910	42 048	39 761	6 255	5 578	50 312	23 208
1978	358 233	281 116	6 935	288 051	24 367	2 208	265 892	48 772	43 570	7 009	6 218	51 113	24 305
1979	404 260	315 265	6 843	322 108	28 409	2 571	296 270	57 733	50 256	7 778	6 859	51 977	24 987
1980	456 292	348 102	4 174	352 277	31 472	3 114	323 919	72 487	59 886	8 629	7 603	52 881	25 324
1981	516 878	384 200	6 648	390 849	37 410	3 533	356 972	91 371	68 536	9 638	8 462	53 627	25 594
1982	554 972	404 263	6 758	411 021	40 103	3 746	374 664	104 253	76 055	10 230	9 028	54 249	25 499
1983	598 916	436 431	4 892	441 324	43 702	3 811	401 433	114 607	82 876	10 918	9 714	54 856	26 030
1984	667 490	486 815	8 386	495 201	49 939	3 992	449 254	130 885	87 351	12 024	10 768	55 515	27 280
1985	719 023	525 299	7 425	532 724	54 905	4 187	482 005	143 747	93 270	12 794	11 391	56 199	28 090
1986	764 145	560 657	6 939	567 596	60 004	4 412	512 003	152 720	99 421	13 439	11 971	56 861	28 826
1987	816 018	604 764	8 319	613 083	64 257	4 702	553 528	158 940	103 550	14 183	12 574	57 536	29 529
1988	885 115	656 505	10 926	667 431	72 111	5 146	600 466	173 649	111 000	15 229	13 569	58 120	30 527
1989	960 489	696 013	11 410	707 423	77 506	5 494	635 411	201 853	123 225	16 353	14 507	58 733	31 251
1990	1 022 843	739 128	10 880	750 008	83 412	6 263	672 859	214 764	135 220	17 186	15 284	59 516	31 840
1991	1 074 282	770 520	12 426	782 947	87 924	6 804	701 826	219 553	152 902	17 757	15 887	60 501	31 724
1992	1 150 752	830 362	13 222	843 585	93 957	7 262	756 889	221 200	172 664	18 709	16 767	61 508	32 180
1993	1 213 303	879 265	12 820	892 085	100 011	7 649	799 723	228 547	185 034	19 403	17 356	62 531	33 186
1994	1 290 878	933 787	14 017	947 805	107 423	7 577	847 959	246 410	196 508	20 305	18 121	63 574	34 135
1995	1 371 695	991 028	12 448	1 003 476	113 622	7 910	897 765	262 560	211 370	21 233	18 908	64 602	35 254
1996	1 458 514	1 047 906	14 189	1 062 094	119 023	7 469	950 540	284 364	223 610	22 230	19 679	65 611	36 087
1997	1 547 392	1 113 691	13 888	1 127 579	126 536	8 282	1 009 325	305 983	232 084	23 215	20 432	66 655	37 050
1998	1 660 978	1 200 512	12 954	1 213 465	135 291	8 159	1 086 334	335 754	238 890	24 561	21 520	67 627	38 044
1999	1 747 241	1 283 773	13 084	1 296 856	143 524	9 562	1 162 894	334 510	249 838	25 481	22 302	68 569	38 847
2000	1 879 680	1 381 140	14 372	1 395 512	151 979	7 960	1 251 493	361 127	267 059	27 047	23 663	69 497	39 656
2001	1 968 292	1 441 106	16 199	1 457 305	158 756	8 230	1 306 779	366 794	294 719	27 991	24 586	70 318	39 545
2002	2 025 058	1 491 170	10 238	1 501 408	163 625	9 617	1 347 401	358 131	319 526	28 461	25 492	71 152	39 737
2003	2 103 566	1 562 505	13 764	1 576 269	170 222	9 934	1 415 982	353 246	334 338	29 232	26 455	71 962	40 167
2004	2 249 054	1 663 383	16 849	1 680 233	181 261	10 357	1 509 329	382 186	357 539	30 801	27 889	73 019	41 219
2005	2 403 753	1 765 407	17 866	1 783 273	192 609	10 726	1 601 389	415 267	387 096	32 418	29 054	74 148	42 308
2006	2 580 723	1 874 373	13 232	1 887 605	205 828	11 682	1 693 459	477 100	410 164	34 379	30 674	75 066	43 341
2007	2 728 855	1 946 019	12 254	1 958 273	213 713	12 339	1 756 900	533 181	438 775	35 848	31 918	76 123	44 337
2008	2 843 864	1 977 079	14 897	1 991 977	218 912	13 456	1 786 520	572 713	484 631	36 906	33 208	77 058	44 028
2009	2 743 072	1 906 696	13 633	1 920 329	214 672	13 781	1 719 438	478 383	545 250	35 251	32 317	77 815	42 568
2010	2 836 417	1 953 003	12 529	1 965 532	219 272	14 745	1 761 005	492 807	582 605	36 108	33 110	78 553	42 434
2011	2 968 814	2 024 112	12 342	2 036 454	204 202	15 471	1 847 723	520 931	600 160	37 472	33 989	79 227	...

. . . = Not available.

Table 17-2. Personal Income and Employment by Region and State—*Continued*

(Millions of dollars, except as noted.)

Region or state and year	Personal income, total	Earnings by place of work			Less: Contributions for government social insurance	Plus: Adjustment for residence	Equals: Net earnings by place of residence	Plus: Dividends, interest, and rent	Plus: Personal current transfer receipts	Per capita (dollars)		Population (thousands)	Total employment (thousands)
		Nonfarm	Farm	Total						Personal income	Disposable personal income		
SOUTHWEST													
1958	25 294	19 740	1 637	21 376	708	3	20 671	3 185	1 438	1 860	1 681	13 598	. . .
1959	26 799	21 103	1 480	22 582	847	4	21 740	3 503	1 556	1 932	1 741	13 874	. . .
1960	27 820	21 917	1 474	23 391	1 005	5	22 391	3 784	1 645	1 954	1 756	14 235	. . .
1961	29 344	22 911	1 629	24 540	1 039	7	23 507	3 986	1 851	2 014	1 808	14 572	. . .
1962	30 843	24 350	1 411	25 761	1 131	9	24 640	4 208	1 995	2 066	1 850	14 930	. . .
1963	32 201	25 651	1 198	26 849	1 276	12	25 585	4 464	2 152	2 131	1 908	15 108	. . .
1964	34 482	27 645	1 133	28 777	1 329	14	27 462	4 773	2 247	2 257	2 051	15 278	. . .
1965	36 981	29 471	1 349	30 820	1 399	17	29 438	5 091	2 451	2 399	2 176	15 414	. . .
1966	40 167	32 555	1 410	33 965	1 881	17	32 102	5 390	2 674	2 580	2 321	15 567	. . .
1967	43 716	35 678	1 294	36 973	2 180	19	34 812	5 662	3 242	2 778	2 493	15 734	. . .
1968	48 717	39 865	1 424	41 289	2 450	25	38 863	6 042	3 812	3 045	2 704	15 998	. . .
1969	54 295	44 498	1 513	46 011	2 889	-70	43 052	6 992	4 252	3 325	2 917	16 328	7 219
1970	59 826	48 234	1 837	50 071	3 105	-83	46 883	7 904	5 039	3 599	3 193	16 621	7 311
1971	65 344	52 645	1 680	54 325	3 502	-87	50 736	8 723	5 886	3 826	3 436	17 077	7 457
1972	72 786	58 798	2 017	60 814	4 087	-105	56 622	9 569	6 595	4 159	3 692	17 503	7 807
1973	83 134	66 437	3 298	69 734	5 309	-118	64 307	10 987	7 840	4 633	4 133	17 943	8 215
1974	93 954	75 797	2 139	77 936	6 216	-79	71 641	12 956	9 358	5 119	4 523	18 354	8 511
1975	105 874	84 516	2 113	86 629	6 833	-46	79 750	14 292	11 832	5 635	5 052	18 789	8 633
1976	119 588	96 937	2 084	99 021	7 905	26	91 141	15 500	12 947	6 206	5 529	19 270	9 001
1977	133 904	110 118	1 865	111 983	9 030	-220	102 733	17 424	13 747	6 794	6 007	19 710	9 466
1978	154 903	128 445	1 693	130 138	10 769	-358	119 012	20 651	15 241	7 676	6 774	20 180	10 046
1979	179 695	147 993	2 983	150 975	12 999	-349	137 627	24 656	17 412	8 649	7 560	20 777	10 528
1980	207 235	169 458	1 543	171 001	14 993	-454	155 555	31 265	20 416	9 672	8 428	21 426	10 923
1981	242 928	195 600	2 843	198 443	18 576	-188	179 678	39 922	23 327	11 050	9 525	21 985	11 449
1982	266 303	210 968	2 354	213 322	20 466	-249	192 606	47 317	26 380	11 684	10 146	22 791	11 682
1983	282 202	220 036	2 408	222 444	21 391	-177	200 877	51 863	29 462	12 057	10 678	23 405	11 712
1984	310 770	241 779	2 673	244 452	24 041	-177	220 234	59 283	31 253	13 070	11 642	23 776	12 259
1985	333 306	257 948	2 575	260 523	26 112	-144	234 267	65 559	33 480	13 792	12 275	24 166	12 617
1986	343 473	264 028	2 582	266 610	26 716	-24	239 869	67 120	36 484	13 971	12 550	24 585	12 483
1987	353 317	271 004	3 531	274 535	27 117	67	247 486	67 294	38 537	14 277	12 782	24 748	12 785
1988	373 756	287 487	4 177	291 664	29 853	166	261 976	70 923	40 856	15 035	13 521	24 860	13 055
1989	399 573	303 394	4 119	307 513	31 824	247	275 936	78 518	45 119	15 930	14 248	25 083	13 241
1990	429 496	325 832	4 970	330 802	34 104	346	297 044	82 435	50 017	16 902	15 097	25 411	13 553
1991	450 815	343 145	4 539	347 684	36 671	308	311 321	84 032	55 462	17 394	15 622	25 917	13 759
1992	484 363	368 911	5 379	374 290	39 031	351	335 611	84 259	64 493	18 284	16 492	26 491	13 885
1993	512 943	393 111	6 187	399 298	41 542	401	358 157	85 777	69 009	18 917	17 042	27 116	14 332
1994	546 930	418 610	5 310	423 920	44 685	424	379 659	93 302	73 969	19 693	17 725	27 772	14 845
1995	583 637	446 897	4 289	451 186	47 393	406	404 199	99 568	79 870	20 536	18 458	28 420	15 396
1996	627 956	481 649	3 911	485 560	50 616	407	435 351	107 441	85 164	21 639	19 321	29 020	15 883
1997	681 302	526 884	5 014	531 899	54 693	398	477 604	115 018	88 680	22 997	20 407	29 625	16 482
1998	739 859	577 172	4 817	581 990	59 237	408	523 161	125 724	90 975	24 467	21 626	30 240	17 066
1999	783 243	617 856	6 646	624 502	62 760	504	562 245	126 242	94 755	25 407	22 466	30 827	17 402
2000	859 138	681 392	5 510	686 902	67 507	570	619 965	138 756	100 418	27 378	24 138	31 381	17 915
2001	901 256	716 156	6 305	722 461	71 081	442	651 822	138 450	110 984	28 260	25 025	31 892	18 013
2002	914 153	725 100	6 223	731 323	72 422	453	659 354	132 595	122 203	28 188	25 511	32 431	18 064
2003	950 504	753 255	7 294	760 549	75 633	536	685 452	134 291	130 762	28 870	26 377	32 924	18 238
2004	1 019 582	810 133	8 419	818 552	79 947	584	739 190	141 505	138 888	30 458	27 919	33 475	18 668
2005	1 107 818	869 625	8 127	877 752	85 653	554	792 653	162 595	152 570	32 489	29 430	34 098	19 299
2006	1 209 262	947 462	5 240	952 702	92 073	472	861 101	183 946	164 215	34 605	31 128	34 945	20 037
2007	1 290 504	997 150	6 020	1 003 170	97 782	326	905 714	205 406	179 385	36 226	32 522	35 624	20 735
2008	1 395 093	1 063 128	4 933	1 068 062	102 120	205	966 147	229 957	198 988	38 465	34 711	36 269	21 086
2009	1 312 988	984 679	2 834	987 513	99 540	270	888 243	198 960	225 785	35 583	32 851	36 899	20 676
2010	1 376 709	1 023 501	6 750	1 030 251	103 359	319	927 211	204 992	244 506	36 719	33 899	37 493	20 687
2011	1 462 417	1 086 207	5 776	1 091 984	99 200	217	993 001	216 226	253 190	38 453	35 088	38 031	. . .

. . . = Not available.

Table 17-2. Personal Income and Employment by Region and State—*Continued*

(Millions of dollars, except as noted.)

Region or state and year	Personal income, total	Earnings by place of work			Less: Contributions for government social insurance	Plus: Adjustment for residence	Equals: Net earnings by place of residence	Plus: Dividends, interest, and rent	Plus: Personal current transfer receipts	Per capita (dollars)		Population (thousands)	Total employment (thousands)
		Nonfarm	Farm	Total						Personal income	Disposable personal income		
ROCKY MOUNTAIN													
1958	8 400	6 290	710	7 000	252	-3	6 745	1 123	531	2 029	1 827	4 139	. . .
1959	8 867	6 784	580	7 364	291	-3	7 070	1 203	594	2 098	1 880	4 226	. . .
1960	9 381	7 240	590	7 830	354	-3	7 473	1 283	624	2 156	1 920	4 350	. . .
1961	9 931	7 737	537	8 274	382	-3	7 889	1 352	690	2 208	1 966	4 497	. . .
1962	10 711	8 216	722	8 937	412	-3	8 523	1 467	721	2 339	2 090	4 580	. . .
1963	11 048	8 599	636	9 235	478	-2	8 756	1 535	758	2 385	2 126	4 632	. . .
1964	11 547	9 102	520	9 621	491	-2	9 129	1 641	777	2 471	2 242	4 673	. . .
1965	12 415	9 578	737	10 315	499	-2	9 814	1 761	840	2 640	2 392	4 703	. . .
1966	13 170	10 324	706	11 031	646	-1	10 384	1 885	902	2 781	2 505	4 735	. . .
1967	14 000	10 938	717	11 655	720	-1	10 934	1 997	1 069	2 927	2 626	4 783	. . .
1968	15 217	11 973	755	12 728	803	-1	11 924	2 078	1 215	3 126	2 781	4 868	. . .
1969	17 010	13 222	889	14 111	884	15	13 242	2 423	1 345	3 441	3 016	4 943	2 216
1970	18 966	14 577	1 003	15 580	965	16	14 631	2 733	1 601	3 765	3 338	5 038	2 271
1971	21 054	16 284	966	17 250	1 105	19	16 165	3 018	1 871	4 053	3 617	5 194	2 343
1972	23 895	18 533	1 269	19 802	1 323	22	18 500	3 305	2 090	4 451	3 943	5 368	2 482
1973	27 437	21 161	1 751	22 913	1 732	22	21 203	3 792	2 442	4 964	4 395	5 527	2 646
1974	31 039	23 921	1 837	25 757	2 006	25	23 776	4 425	2 838	5 494	4 839	5 650	2 740
1975	34 283	26 563	1 386	27 949	2 181	37	25 804	4 949	3 530	5 930	5 290	5 782	2 778
1976	38 222	30 304	1 027	31 330	2 515	42	28 858	5 484	3 880	6 461	5 729	5 916	2 912
1977	42 852	34 586	686	35 272	2 873	44	32 442	6 264	4 146	7 049	6 221	6 079	3 060
1978	49 745	40 305	958	41 263	3 414	54	37 904	7 305	4 536	7 950	7 005	6 257	3 257
1979	56 593	46 011	749	46 759	4 095	54	42 718	8 724	5 151	8 789	7 691	6 439	3 402
1980	64 520	51 189	965	52 153	4 581	78	47 650	10 829	6 041	9 787	8 579	6 592	3 474
1981	73 555	57 455	1 057	58 511	5 550	49	53 010	13 486	7 059	10 909	9 513	6 743	3 559
1982	79 688	61 086	826	61 911	6 016	51	55 946	15 710	8 032	11 542	10 096	6 904	3 596
1983	84 804	64 328	1 143	65 471	6 398	53	59 126	16 847	8 831	12 055	10 727	7 035	3 642
1984	92 144	70 204	1 041	71 245	7 176	72	64 141	18 785	9 218	12 962	11 584	7 109	3 801
1985	96 745	73 807	841	74 647	7 732	89	67 004	19 963	9 777	13 497	12 030	7 168	3 861
1986	100 127	75 835	1 240	77 074	8 020	111	69 165	20 469	10 493	13 907	12 446	7 200	3 854
1987	103 466	78 239	1 584	79 823	8 211	135	71 748	20 587	11 132	14 359	12 798	7 206	3 885
1988	108 663	82 921	1 637	84 558	9 072	171	75 657	21 292	11 714	15 087	13 452	7 203	4 021
1989	117 760	87 996	2 217	90 213	9 762	206	80 657	24 185	12 918	16 278	14 431	7 234	4 114
1990	125 998	94 567	2 515	97 083	10 828	241	86 496	25 533	13 969	17 248	15 230	7 305	4 230
1991	134 080	101 365	2 467	103 832	11 850	272	92 253	26 420	15 406	17 932	15 892	7 477	4 335
1992	144 634	110 354	2 547	112 901	12 836	303	100 368	27 112	17 154	18 792	16 637	7 696	4 434
1993	156 627	119 846	3 224	123 069	14 026	334	109 378	28 779	18 470	19 729	17 440	8 171	4 626
1994	168 444	129 383	2 097	131 480	15 217	384	116 647	32 382	19 415	20 614	18 176	8 171	4 886
1995	181 605	138 693	2 000	140 692	16 206	449	124 935	35 343	21 327	21 672	19 091	8 380	5 046
1996	195 544	148 806	2 191	150 997	17 085	520	134 432	38 808	22 305	22 829	19 987	8 565	5 249
1997	209 840	160 612	2 059	162 671	18 215	591	145 047	41 941	22 853	23 993	20 881	8 746	5 440
1998	227 665	174 045	2 398	176 443	19 145	686	157 984	46 108	23 572	25 528	22 128	8 918	5 625
1999	244 060	189 563	2 741	192 303	20 458	788	172 634	46 597	24 828	26 836	23 192	9 094	5 767
2000	269 821	211 101	2 372	213 473	22 307	855	192 020	51 143	26 657	29 110	25 069	9 269	5 966
2001	287 222	224 761	3 038	227 799	23 435	917	205 280	52 745	29 196	30 455	26 511	9 431	5 999
2002	291 847	229 293	2 284	231 576	24 214	915	208 278	51 471	32 098	30 505	27 209	9 567	5 993
2003	299 153	235 239	2 345	237 583	25 042	957	213 498	51 932	33 722	30 919	27 849	9 675	6 021
2004	318 318	250 215	3 361	253 576	26 709	1 027	227 894	54 849	35 574	32 457	29 284	9 808	6 167
2005	341 570	266 481	3 467	269 948	28 671	1 060	242 337	60 975	38 259	34 253	30 515	9 972	6 368
2006	372 380	288 564	2 432	290 996	31 267	1 115	260 843	70 274	41 263	36 544	32 273	10 190	6 597
2007	396 108	301 692	3 289	304 982	33 086	1 184	273 079	78 544	44 485	38 064	33 391	10 406	6 850
2008	418 744	312 311	3 713	316 023	34 173	1 256	283 106	86 430	49 208	39 469	35 102	10 610	6 903
2009	398 479	297 666	2 753	300 418	33 103	1 235	268 551	72 815	57 113	36 917	33 558	10 794	6 699
2010	413 978	305 434	3 412	308 846	33 938	1 237	276 145	75 735	62 098	37 807	34 397	10 950	6 676
2011	436 989	318 825	4 537	323 362	32 141	1 324	292 545	80 512	63 932	39 420	35 459	11 085	. . .

. . . = Not available.

Table 17-2. Personal Income and Employment by Region and State—*Continued*

(Millions of dollars, except as noted.)

Region or state and year	Personal income, total	Earnings by place of work			Less: Contributions for government social insurance	Plus: Adjustment for residence	Equals: Net earnings by place of residence	Plus: Dividends, interest, and rent	Plus: Personal current transfer receipts	Per capita (dollars)		Population (thousands)	Total employment (thousands)
		Nonfarm	Farm	Total						Personal income	Disposable personal income		
FAR WEST													
1958	50 941	40 446	1 827	42 272	1 584	0	40 688	7 177	3 076	2 489	2 227	20 469	. . .
1959	55 590	44 757	1 919	46 677	1 984	0	44 693	7 749	3 148	2 627	2 345	21 159	. . .
1960	58 751	47 215	1 965	49 180	2 356	-1	46 824	8 414	3 513	2 713	2 397	21 659	. . .
1961	62 154	49 834	1 867	51 700	2 494	-1	49 205	8 899	4 049	2 777	2 457	22 378	. . .
1962	67 119	54 216	1 975	56 191	2 976	-3	53 212	9 657	4 250	2 904	2 567	23 114	. . .
1963	71 388	57 970	1 914	59 885	3 458	-5	56 422	10 326	4 640	2 998	2 648	23 811	. . .
1964	77 133	62 382	2 019	64 401	3 580	-6	60 815	11 325	4 992	3 163	2 842	24 389	. . .
1965	82 577	66 490	2 009	68 499	3 730	-7	64 763	12 341	5 474	3 315	2 979	24 908	. . .
1966	90 081	73 513	2 259	75 772	4 925	-8	70 840	13 246	5 996	3 559	3 178	25 311	. . .
1967	97 160	78 936	2 125	81 061	5 443	-10	75 608	14 182	7 370	3 769	3 353	25 779	. . .
1968	106 841	87 113	2 385	89 499	6 111	-12	83 376	14 970	8 496	4 086	3 595	26 151	. . .
1969	117 525	95 203	2 480	97 683	6 630	-199	90 854	16 978	9 694	4 412	3 848	26 635	12 295
1970	126 599	100 751	2 439	103 190	6 899	-203	96 088	18 544	11 967	4 671	4 143	27 101	12 313
1971	135 027	106 387	2 469	108 856	7 521	-220	101 115	20 068	13 844	4 898	4 393	27 570	12 300
1972	148 178	117 457	3 113	120 570	8 736	-225	111 609	21 596	14 972	5 308	4 683	27 918	12 742
1973	164 737	130 637	4 253	134 890	11 068	-228	123 594	24 291	16 852	5 815	5 170	28 328	13 405
1974	185 339	145 038	5 388	150 427	12 611	-324	137 491	27 915	19 933	6 435	5 703	28 801	13 865
1975	206 499	160 120	4 812	164 933	13 666	-521	150 747	30 698	25 054	7 037	6 311	29 346	14 103
1976	231 461	182 022	4 815	186 836	15 736	-635	170 465	33 389	27 607	7 734	6 877	29 929	14 625
1977	257 684	204 402	4 685	209 087	17 871	-449	190 767	37 579	29 339	8 434	7 455	30 553	15 287
1978	294 470	235 533	4 760	240 293	21 055	-381	218 858	43 836	31 776	9 412	8 266	31 285	16 248
1979	335 820	267 907	5 907	273 814	25 059	-355	248 401	52 358	35 061	10 506	9 167	31 965	17 133
1980	382 014	296 861	7 356	304 217	27 313	-437	276 467	64 491	41 056	11 654	10 176	32 780	17 523
1981	427 810	326 152	5 862	332 014	32 427	-219	299 368	80 225	48 217	12 796	11 186	33 434	17 693
1982	456 582	343 762	5 930	349 692	34 767	-261	314 665	88 365	53 553	13 395	11 814	34 086	17 564
1983	491 650	370 238	5 966	376 204	38 250	-281	337 673	96 816	57 162	14 162	12 544	34 716	17 989
1984	544 820	411 739	6 605	418 345	43 874	-322	374 149	110 939	59 732	15 425	13 678	35 321	18 767
1985	585 286	444 079	6 368	450 447	48 001	-368	402 078	118 689	64 519	16 241	14 324	36 037	19 392
1986	624 913	476 861	7 271	484 132	52 245	-392	431 494	124 448	68 972	16 974	14 978	36 815	19 959
1987	670 862	518 402	8 511	526 913	56 770	-466	469 676	129 152	72 033	17 823	15 571	37 641	20 793
1988	727 983	567 087	9 045	576 131	64 009	-552	511 570	139 167	77 246	18 888	16 631	38 542	21 790
1989	787 918	604 330	8 993	613 323	68 917	-643	543 762	159 455	84 700	19 930	17 370	39 534	22 453
1990	849 277	650 752	9 482	660 234	74 606	-757	584 871	171 243	93 162	20 913	18 263	40 610	23 122
1991	885 753	677 733	8 634	686 368	78 354	-754	607 259	174 585	103 908	21 381	18 848	41 428	23 124
1992	935 491	714 989	9 389	724 378	82 179	-738	641 460	175 048	118 982	22 154	19 652	42 226	22 825
1993	965 348	733 865	10 703	744 568	84 229	-726	659 613	179 584	126 151	22 556	20 011	42 798	22 934
1994	1 008 531	763 013	10 052	773 065	87 907	-749	684 410	194 200	129 922	23 307	20 661	43 271	23 380
1995	1 063 662	800 637	9 668	810 305	91 077	-785	718 443	208 161	137 058	24 315	21 470	43 745	23 938
1996	1 133 666	848 781	11 188	859 969	94 652	-852	764 466	224 998	144 202	25 582	22 363	44 314	24 580
1997	1 208 963	912 189	11 487	923 677	100 414	-925	822 337	240 784	145 842	26 834	23 254	45 054	25 149
1998	1 319 200	1 000 260	11 130	1 011 390	107 982	-1 007	902 401	263 280	153 519	28 805	24 829	45 798	26 021
1999	1 406 162	1 084 216	11 640	1 095 855	115 613	-1 128	979 115	264 859	162 189	30 236	25 699	46 506	26 663
2000	1 542 349	1 201 138	11 796	1 212 934	126 603	-1 235	1 085 095	287 229	170 024	32 685	27 379	47 188	27 484
2001	1 589 171	1 231 849	11 197	1 243 046	131 744	-1 103	1 110 198	289 800	189 173	33 183	28 204	47 891	27 656
2002	1 619 148	1 258 360	11 786	1 270 146	135 751	-1 106	1 133 288	282 792	203 068	33 389	29 429	48 493	27 378
2003	1 682 385	1 313 051	13 721	1 326 772	142 462	-1 203	1 183 106	286 524	212 754	34 297	30 496	49 053	27 632
2004	1 795 140	1 397 422	16 017	1 413 439	154 218	-1 342	1 257 880	314 924	222 336	36 191	32 213	49 602	28 167
2005	1 897 138	1 473 450	14 301	1 487 751	162 951	-1 415	1 323 386	339 658	234 095	37 874	33 245	50 090	28 822
2006	2 048 299	1 564 474	14 475	1 578 950	170 209	-1 494	1 407 247	389 095	251 957	40 504	35 395	50 571	29 458
2007	2 157 219	1 621 016	17 134	1 638 150	174 163	-1 610	1 462 377	426 121	268 721	42 272	36 754	51 031	30 168
2008	2 233 054	1 632 073	15 783	1 647 856	176 861	-1 632	1 469 362	468 442	295 250	43 269	38 159	51 609	29 903
2009	2 123 507	1 548 794	16 385	1 565 179	172 202	-1 495	1 391 482	393 445	338 580	40 706	36 680	52 168	28 744
2010	2 202 101	1 586 704	17 896	1 604 600	175 222	-1 516	1 427 863	406 022	368 216	41 785	37 518	52 701	28 541
2011	2 321 924	1 659 543	19 184	1 678 727	164 904	-1 648	1 512 175	433 227	376 523	43 633	38 729	53 215	. . .

. . . = Not available.

Table 17-2. Personal Income and Employment by Region and State—*Continued*

(Millions of dollars, except as noted.)

Region or state and year	Personal income, total	Derivation of personal income								Per capita (dollars)		Population (thousands)	Total employment (thousands)
		Earnings by place of work			Less: Contributions for government social insurance	Plus: Adjustment for residence	Equals: Net earnings by place of residence	Plus: Dividends, interest, and rent	Plus: Personal current transfer receipts	Personal income	Disposable personal income		
		Nonfarm	Farm	Total									
ALABAMA													
1958	4 595	3 669	305	3 974	135	1	3 839	411	344	1 453	1 331	3 163	. . .
1959	4 832	3 929	248	4 177	159	1	4 019	450	363	1 508	1 380	3 204	. . .
1960	5 040	4 088	257	4 345	187	2	4 160	495	385	1 539	1 403	3 274	. . .
1961	5 197	4 190	247	4 437	194	2	4 246	522	429	1 567	1 435	3 316	. . .
1962	5 464	4 421	227	4 648	219	4	4 433	563	468	1 644	1 494	3 323	. . .
1963	5 822	4 692	275	4 967	259	6	4 714	613	496	1 734	1 577	3 358	. . .
1964	6 327	5 156	248	5 404	265	8	5 146	668	513	1 864	1 705	3 395	. . .
1965	6 884	5 622	257	5 879	273	10	5 616	718	551	2 000	1 825	3 443	. . .
1966	7 386	6 155	245	6 400	376	15	6 039	748	599	2 132	1 929	3 464	. . .
1967	7 802	6 522	209	6 731	429	21	6 323	788	690	2 256	2 041	3 458	. . .
1968	8 526	7 100	229	7 329	472	24	6 881	844	801	2 474	2 221	3 446	. . .
1969	9 405	7 733	280	8 013	551	137	7 599	914	892	2 734	2 418	3 440	1 411
1970	10 219	8 282	250	8 533	590	136	8 078	1 044	1 097	2 962	2 662	3 450	1 413
1971	11 212	9 010	279	9 289	655	144	8 778	1 150	1 285	3 206	2 892	3 497	1 423
1972	12 483	10 050	348	10 398	765	171	9 804	1 249	1 431	3 526	3 157	3 540	1 471
1973	14 118	11 284	535	11 818	983	188	11 024	1 413	1 681	3 943	3 531	3 581	1 526
1974	15 731	12 657	340	12 997	1 136	198	12 059	1 661	2 011	4 336	3 878	3 628	1 552
1975	17 543	13 667	414	14 081	1 221	204	13 063	1 879	2 600	4 766	4 308	3 681	1 543
1976	19 857	15 670	479	16 149	1 421	218	14 946	2 071	2 840	5 313	4 774	3 737	1 594
1977	21 918	17 572	383	17 955	1 595	247	16 607	2 315	2 996	5 794	5 201	3 783	1 651
1978	24 783	19 940	509	20 449	1 840	270	18 880	2 640	3 263	6 464	5 785	3 834	1 713
1979	27 625	22 021	521	22 542	2 102	297	20 737	3 086	3 802	7 139	6 357	3 869	1 736
1980	30 522	23 890	211	24 101	2 281	327	22 147	3 913	4 461	7 825	6 955	3 900	1 732
1981	33 931	25 739	491	26 229	2 655	426	24 000	4 922	5 009	8 669	7 679	3 919	1 719
1982	35 926	26 641	411	27 052	2 795	447	24 705	5 684	5 537	9 152	8 200	3 925	1 687
1983	38 443	28 668	292	28 960	3 053	440	26 347	6 098	5 997	9 772	8 754	3 934	1 717
1984	42 488	31 580	481	32 061	3 428	491	29 123	7 026	6 339	10 752	9 679	3 952	1 780
1985	45 699	34 049	466	34 515	3 740	501	31 276	7 729	6 695	11 504	10 291	3 973	1 822
1986	48 219	36 094	458	36 552	3 973	525	33 104	8 151	6 964	12 080	10 806	3 992	1 858
1987	51 136	38 517	542	39 059	4 195	534	35 397	8 618	7 120	12 735	11 328	4 015	1 912
1988	54 881	41 352	806	42 158	4 680	531	38 009	9 446	7 426	13 639	12 228	4 024	1 970
1989	59 549	43 676	941	44 617	5 001	551	40 167	10 992	8 390	14 776	13 176	4 030	2 006
1990	63 254	46 554	849	47 403	5 410	529	42 523	11 496	9 235	15 618	13 943	4 050	2 048
1991	66 969	48 990	1 124	50 114	5 766	562	44 910	11 855	10 204	16 337	14 645	4 099	2 060
1992	71 714	52 675	1 004	53 679	6 163	620	48 135	11 977	11 602	17 264	15 514	4 154	2 097
1993	74 871	55 130	1 019	56 149	6 541	671	50 278	12 274	12 318	17 766	15 943	4 214	2 159
1994	79 481	58 121	1 070	59 190	7 010	766	52 946	13 469	13 065	18 656	16 688	4 260	2 180
1995	84 005	61 095	790	61 885	7 396	844	55 332	14 579	14 094	19 551	17 454	4 297	2 242
1996	87 682	63 569	918	64 487	7 649	854	57 692	15 124	14 865	20 245	18 006	4 331	2 275
1997	92 243	66 520	956	67 476	8 024	956	60 408	16 295	15 540	21 118	18 717	4 368	2 321
1998	97 858	70 428	1 078	71 506	8 426	1 069	64 148	17 854	15 857	22 217	19 693	4 405	2 371
1999	101 719	73 932	1 244	75 176	8 808	1 136	67 505	17 653	16 562	22 961	20 333	4 430	2 388
2000	107 151	77 199	957	78 156	9 084	1 264	70 337	19 140	17 674	24 067	21 355	4 452	2 400
2001	112 013	80 508	1 385	81 893	9 422	1 292	73 763	19 128	19 123	25 072	22 353	4 468	2 370
2002	115 414	83 837	977	84 814	9 713	1 315	76 416	18 439	20 559	25 762	23 285	4 480	2 369
2003	120 061	87 294	1 364	88 658	10 070	1 375	79 963	18 341	21 757	26 660	24 305	4 503	2 380
2004	128 020	92 380	1 794	94 175	10 525	1 425	85 074	19 878	23 067	28 256	25 815	4 531	2 441
2005	135 636	97 687	1 775	99 463	11 191	1 492	89 765	20 997	24 875	29 681	26 885	4 570	2 505
2006	144 463	103 836	1 079	104 916	11 879	1 560	94 597	23 075	26 791	31 208	28 054	4 629	2 565
2007	151 999	107 702	875	108 577	12 411	1 630	97 796	25 348	28 854	32 528	29 180	4 673	2 633
2008	160 179	110 438	1 166	111 604	12 811	1 752	100 544	28 051	31 584	33 949	30 738	4 718	2 611
2009	155 409	106 966	1 073	108 039	12 558	1 703	97 183	23 204	35 022	32 663	30 106	4 758	2 511
2010	160 332	108 822	880	109 702	12 936	1 739	98 504	23 927	37 901	33 504	30 905	4 785	2 496
2011	166 414	111 093	564	111 657	11 924	1 863	101 596	25 344	39 474	34 650	31 655	4 803	. . .

. . . = Not available.

Table 17-2. Personal Income and Employment by Region and State—*Continued*

(Millions of dollars, except as noted.)

Region or state and year	Personal income, total	Earnings by place of work			Less: Contributions for government social insurance	Plus: Adjustment for residence	Equals: Net earnings by place of residence	Plus: Dividends, interest, and rent	Plus: Personal current transfer receipts	Per capita (dollars)		Population (thousands)	Total employment (thousands)
		Nonfarm	Farm	Total						Personal income	Disposable personal income		
ALASKA													
1958	559	533	2	535	22	0	513	25	21	2 495	. . .	224	. . .
1959	593	566	1	567	24	0	544	28	21	2 646	. . .	224	. . .
1960	701	673	2	675	28	-2	645	34	22	3 062	2 703	229	. . .
1961	698	664	2	666	28	-3	634	36	27	2 932	2 611	238	. . .
1962	731	697	1	698	29	-5	664	40	26	2 970	2 622	246	. . .
1963	790	757	1	758	33	-8	717	46	27	3 087	2 714	256	. . .
1964	890	854	1	855	37	-13	805	55	29	3 382	3 045	263	. . .
1965	962	926	1	927	41	-18	868	63	31	3 549	3 144	271	. . .
1966	1 032	995	1	997	48	-23	926	72	34	3 807	3 385	271	. . .
1967	1 130	1 094	1	1 096	53	-30	1 012	79	39	4 065	3 610	278	. . .
1968	1 227	1 199	2	1 201	67	-38	1 095	84	48	4 305	3 808	285	. . .
1969	1 412	1 376	1	1 378	94	-26	1 258	100	54	4 769	4 071	296	144
1970	1 597	1 564	2	1 566	105	-47	1 414	111	72	5 248	4 559	304	149
1971	1 767	1 728	2	1 730	118	-61	1 551	125	91	5 583	4 883	316	153
1972	1 939	1 903	2	1 905	134	-76	1 695	141	103	5 940	5 125	326	158
1973	2 268	2 113	2	2 115	165	-94	1 856	165	246	6 805	5 960	333	167
1974	2 802	2 840	2	2 842	241	-210	2 391	203	208	8 130	6 946	345	189
1975	3 957	4 478	4	4 482	407	-614	3 461	258	237	10 666	9 038	371	227
1976	4 760	5 630	4	5 634	526	-885	4 224	303	233	12 109	10 263	393	243
1977	4 922	5 213	5	5 218	463	-454	4 302	343	278	12 388	10 536	397	237
1978	5 025	5 083	5	5 088	434	-326	4 328	399	299	12 495	10 812	402	238
1979	5 327	5 316	4	5 319	467	-289	4 563	471	293	13 199	11 271	404	241
1980	6 070	6 013	3	6 016	527	-329	5 161	566	343	14 975	13 057	405	244
1981	6 917	6 970	2	6 972	686	-470	5 816	694	406	16 528	14 086	418	252
1982	8 461	8 069	3	8 071	798	-562	6 712	886	864	18 819	16 331	450	277
1983	9 203	8 984	2	8 986	852	-622	7 512	1 058	633	18 843	16 537	488	297
1984	9 963	9 623	2	9 625	948	-637	8 040	1 241	682	19 395	17 267	514	309
1985	10 705	10 023	2	10 025	970	-629	8 426	1 393	886	20 104	17 966	532	316
1986	10 707	9 757	7	9 764	916	-569	8 279	1 432	997	19 673	17 805	544	310
1987	10 379	9 233	9	9 242	858	-532	7 853	1 487	1 039	19 244	17 260	539	310
1988	10 757	9 553	11	9 564	929	-556	8 079	1 560	1 117	19 848	17 913	542	317
1989	11 778	10 395	6	10 400	1 026	-618	8 756	1 784	1 238	21 525	19 129	547	329
1990	12 501	10 977	8	10 986	1 145	-652	9 189	1 943	1 369	22 594	19 937	553	339
1991	13 167	11 589	9	11 598	1 214	-699	9 686	2 012	1 469	23 092	20 597	570	347
1992	13 957	12 228	9	12 237	1 283	-735	10 220	2 106	1 631	23 706	21 240	589	351
1993	14 673	12 683	11	12 695	1 364	-753	10 578	2 278	1 817	24 478	21 963	599	358
1994	15 195	12 985	12	12 997	1 418	-772	10 808	2 526	1 861	25 186	22 538	603	363
1995	15 580	13 166	13	13 179	1 428	-778	10 974	2 659	1 948	25 778	23 096	604	365
1996	15 931	13 262	14	13 276	1 430	-791	11 055	2 781	2 096	26 179	23 377	609	369
1997	16 671	13 656	16	13 673	1 471	-781	11 421	2 987	2 263	27 197	24 204	613	374
1998	17 323	14 103	17	14 120	1 522	-832	11 766	3 096	2 460	27 943	24 786	620	381
1999	17 830	14 421	20	14 441	1 543	-834	12 064	3 059	2 707	28 538	25 368	625	381
2000	19 158	15 298	21	15 319	1 616	-887	12 815	3 273	3 069	30 508	27 081	628	392
2001	20 438	16 658	20	16 677	1 724	-936	14 017	3 212	3 209	32 251	28 711	634	401
2002	21 309	17 705	19	17 724	1 802	-993	14 929	3 072	3 308	33 174	30 008	642	405
2003	21 824	18 454	12	18 466	1 873	-1 015	15 578	3 017	3 229	33 657	30 704	648	409
2004	23 070	19 756	15	19 770	1 993	-1 074	16 704	3 179	3 188	34 993	32 146	659	417
2005	24 617	21 056	14	21 070	2 131	-1 139	17 800	3 442	3 375	36 911	33 701	667	425
2006	26 304	22 464	10	22 474	2 298	-1 268	18 908	3 796	3 600	38 951	35 380	675	434
2007	28 108	23 271	8	23 279	2 374	*	19 532	4 484	4 091	41 316	37 220	680	442
2008	30 809	24 540	5	24 545	2 460	-1 509	20 576	4 947	5 286	44 816	40 461	687	446
2009	30 233	25 486	7	25 493	2 517	-1 584	21 392	4 169	4 672	43 259	39 745	699	445
2010	31 589	26 426	10	26 436	2 623	-1 609	22 204	4 365	5 020	44 233	40 597	714	448
2011	32 905	27 369	10	27 379	2 483	-1 719	23 177	4 640	5 089	45 529	41 258	723	. . .

. . . = Not available.

Table 17-2. Personal Income and Employment by Region and State—Continued

(Millions of dollars, except as noted.)

| Region or state and year | Personal income, total | Earnings by place of work | | | Less: Contributions for government social insurance | Plus: Adjustment for residence | Equals: Net earnings by place of residence | Plus: Dividends, interest, and rent | Plus: Personal current transfer receipts | Per capita (dollars) | | Population (thousands) | Total employment (thousands) |
		Nonfarm	Farm	Total						Personal income	Disposable personal income		
ARIZONA													
1958	2 257	1 771	130	1 901	79	-2	1 820	302	135	1 892	1 709	1 193	...
1959	2 492	1 972	124	2 096	95	-2	1 999	340	153	1 976	1 773	1 261	...
1960	2 725	2 164	128	2 292	117	-2	2 172	387	166	2 063	1 841	1 321	...
1961	2 967	2 327	135	2 462	125	-2	2 335	438	194	2 109	1 893	1 407	...
1962	3 196	2 525	138	2 663	139	-2	2 522	462	212	2 173	1 942	1 471	...
1963	3 358	2 678	113	2 791	162	0	2 629	498	231	2 208	1 974	1 521	...
1964	3 600	2 851	130	2 981	167	*	2 814	536	250	2 314	2 105	1 556	...
1965	3 816	3 006	128	3 134	174	1	2 961	573	282	2 409	2 192	1 584	...
1966	4 162	3 368	121	3 490	232	0	3 257	600	305	2 579	2 333	1 614	...
1967	4 525	3 619	149	3 768	265	0	3 503	645	377	2 749	2 473	1 646	...
1968	5 188	4 099	192	4 292	312	2	3 982	771	435	3 085	2 754	1 682	...
1969	6 071	4 714	203	4 918	322	-26	4 570	1 009	492	3 495	3 071	1 737	711
1970	6 873	5 319	180	5 499	362	-29	5 108	1 173	593	3 829	3 379	1 795	747
1971	7 832	6 067	201	6 268	430	-28	5 809	1 312	711	4 131	3 689	1 896	786
1972	8 986	7 060	205	7 265	525	-32	6 708	1 461	817	4 473	3 953	2 009	850
1973	10 423	8 236	240	8 476	695	-31	7 750	1 689	984	4 904	4 384	2 125	925
1974	11 791	9 077	384	9 461	791	-41	8 629	1 973	1 189	5 301	4 711	2 224	955
1975	12 654	9 472	218	9 690	816	-47	8 827	2 166	1 662	5 535	5 034	2 286	935
1976	14 231	10 662	330	10 992	916	-47	10 029	2 377	1 825	6 061	5 478	2 348	976
1977	16 055	12 261	267	12 527	1 061	-56	11 410	2 721	1 925	6 615	5 935	2 427	1 048
1978	18 963	14 565	318	14 884	1 292	-69	13 523	3 269	2 171	7 532	6 700	2 518	1 150
1979	22 451	17 290	399	17 689	1 606	-71	16 012	3 968	2 471	8 509	7 521	2 639	1 240
1980	25 964	19 374	477	19 851	1 810	-80	17 962	5 033	2 970	9 484	8 418	2 738	1 283
1981	29 737	21 649	415	22 064	2 177	-14	19 873	6 374	3 490	10 582	9 311	2 810	1 313
1982	31 447	22 444	396	22 841	2 299	-6	20 535	7 018	3 894	10 882	9 616	2 890	1 315
1983	34 529	24 631	327	24 958	2 580	4	22 382	7 883	4 264	11 630	10 371	2 969	1 379
1984	39 268	28 111	526	28 637	3 018	8	25 626	9 070	4 571	12 803	11 442	3 067	1 504
1985	43 410	31 296	491	31 787	3 435	20	28 372	10 076	4 962	13 636	12 117	3 184	1 622
1986	47 424	34 332	471	34 803	3 805	40	31 038	10 944	5 443	14 335	12 759	3 308	1 701
1987	51 201	37 040	635	37 675	4 075	66	33 665	11 588	5 947	14 896	13 235	3 437	1 765
1988	55 088	40 051	762	40 813	4 557	107	36 363	12 203	6 522	15 583	13 926	3 535	1 833
1989	58 971	41 429	690	42 119	4 852	164	37 432	13 984	7 555	16 281	14 476	3 622	1 865
1990	61 916	43 483	642	44 125	5 222	225	39 129	14 420	8 367	16 806	14 932	3 684	1 894
1991	65 364	46 156	739	46 895	5 566	222	41 551	14 462	9 351	17 253	15 372	3 789	1 903
1992	69 550	49 626	673	50 299	5 940	248	44 607	14 290	10 653	17 762	15 891	3 916	1 925
1993	74 686	53 432	789	54 221	6 408	266	48 080	15 111	11 496	18 371	16 403	4 065	2 011
1994	82 292	59 086	577	59 663	7 093	277	52 847	17 173	12 272	19 385	17 277	4 245	2 141
1995	89 378	64 438	824	65 262	7 404	296	58 154	18 178	13 046	20 164	17 953	4 432	2 258
1996	97 054	70 679	737	71 416	8 317	324	63 423	19 743	13 888	21 159	18 642	4 587	2 388
1997	105 307	76 875	740	77 616	8 945	358	69 029	21 800	14 477	22 231	19 527	4 737	2 497
1998	115 841	85 315	872	86 187	9 699	404	76 892	23 920	15 030	23 722	20 758	4 883	2 611
1999	123 500	92 501	849	93 350	10 418	462	83 394	24 066	16 040	24 583	21 492	5 024	2 697
2000	135 687	102 646	807	103 453	11 338	516	92 631	26 098	16 958	26 293	22 966	5 161	2 796
2001	142 864	108 173	747	108 920	11 880	563	97 604	26 026	19 235	27 091	23 815	5 273	2 823
2002	148 175	111 705	764	112 469	12 262	549	100 755	25 968	21 452	27 459	24 708	5 396	2 842
2003	155 607	117 206	732	117 937	12 731	577	105 783	26 521	23 303	28 239	25 601	5 510	2 914
2004	170 026	127 372	1 006	128 378	13 774	631	115 235	29 288	25 503	30 080	27 233	5 652	3 040
2005	188 152	139 700	967	140 666	15 127	655	126 194	33 608	28 350	32 223	28 814	5 839	3 208
2006	206 958	153 362	692	154 054	16 613	678	138 119	37 951	30 888	34 326	30 557	6 029	3 370
2007	218 588	159 709	819	160 528	17 407	732	143 853	41 254	33 481	35 441	31 564	6 168	3 466
2008	226 465	160 239	625	160 864	17 607	748	144 005	44 690	37 770	36 059	32 661	6 280	3 408
2009	215 361	150 290	507	150 797	16 770	708	134 735	36 811	43 816	33 952	31 409	6 343	3 235
2010	221 503	152 102	720	152 823	17 075	724	136 472	37 878	47 154	34 539	31 946	6 413	3 201
2011	232 560	158 263	910	159 172	16 082	781	143 871	40 283	48 405	35 875	32 828	6 483	...

. . . = Not available.
* = Less than $50,000, but the estimates for this item are included in the total.

Table 17-2. Personal Income and Employment by Region and State—*Continued*

(Millions of dollars, except as noted.)

Region or state and year	Personal income, total	Earnings by place of work			Less: Contributions for government social insurance	Plus: Adjustment for residence	Equals: Net earnings by place of residence	Plus: Dividends, interest, and rent	Plus: Personal current transfer receipts	Per capita (dollars)		Population (thousands)	Total employment (thousands)
		Nonfarm	Farm	Total						Personal income	Disposable personal income		
ARKANSAS													
1958	2 251	1 605	285	1 890	66	-1	1 824	218	209	1 304	1 207	1 726	. . .
1959	2 469	1 724	364	2 089	79	-1	2 009	235	225	1 406	1 299	1 756	. . .
1960	2 500	1 783	313	2 096	92	-2	2 002	257	240	1 397	1 287	1 789	. . .
1961	2 712	1 892	368	2 260	95	-2	2 163	280	269	1 502	1 385	1 806	. . .
1962	2 889	2 080	324	2 404	109	-3	2 292	309	288	1 559	1 422	1 853	. . .
1963	3 069	2 226	323	2 549	126	-4	2 418	341	310	1 637	1 494	1 875	. . .
1964	3 333	2 414	361	2 774	137	-5	2 633	374	326	1 757	1 626	1 897	. . .
1965	3 521	2 596	288	2 883	147	-6	2 731	433	357	1 859	1 712	1 894	. . .
1966	3 917	2 848	393	3 242	191	-5	3 046	480	391	2 063	1 879	1 899	. . .
1967	4 155	3 096	301	3 397	221	-5	3 170	516	468	2 185	1 990	1 901	. . .
1968	4 508	3 411	337	3 748	251	-7	3 489	493	525	2 370	2 135	1 902	. . .
1969	5 005	3 744	346	4 090	279	30	3 840	581	584	2 616	2 334	1 913	800
1970	5 482	3 997	415	4 412	297	20	4 135	664	684	2 840	2 548	1 930	805
1971	6 090	4 468	407	4 875	341	19	4 553	735	802	3 088	2 805	1 972	831
1972	6 881	5 089	482	5 571	406	18	5 183	804	893	3 409	3 083	2 018	867
1973	8 189	5 769	913	6 683	526	14	6 171	935	1 083	3 978	3 585	2 058	902
1974	9 174	6 493	833	7 326	610	7	6 723	1 136	1 315	4 368	3 908	2 100	927
1975	10 075	6 942	795	7 737	640	6	7 103	1 302	1 669	4 668	4 254	2 158	905
1976	11 185	8 050	641	8 691	746	-4	7 941	1 421	1 823	5 157	4 640	2 169	941
1977	12 486	9 058	725	9 784	849	-8	8 927	1 624	1 936	5 657	5 106	2 207	981
1978	14 496	10 329	1 176	11 506	990	-13	10 502	1 866	2 128	6 469	5 837	2 241	1 021
1979	15 930	11 467	995	12 462	1 137	-15	11 310	2 180	2 440	7 020	6 287	2 269	1 031
1980	17 214	12 454	372	12 826	1 227	-3	11 597	2 728	2 889	7 521	6 701	2 289	1 032
1981	19 510	13 388	852	14 240	1 428	-21	12 791	3 448	3 271	8 508	7 589	2 293	1 026
1982	20 526	13 853	642	14 495	1 504	-18	12 973	3 996	3 557	8 947	7 933	2 294	1 011
1983	21 819	15 022	417	15 438	1 639	-48	13 752	4 216	3 850	9 463	8 491	2 306	1 039
1984	24 325	16 655	882	17 537	1 869	-67	15 601	4 689	4 036	10 486	9 479	2 320	1 079
1985	25 896	17 646	863	18 509	2 006	-72	16 431	5 191	4 274	11 128	10 031	2 327	1 098
1986	27 108	18 686	804	19 490	2 141	-95	17 253	5 352	4 503	11 625	10 508	2 332	1 110
1987	28 161	19 714	937	20 651	2 252	-114	18 285	5 241	4 635	12 023	10 819	2 342	1 137
1988	30 114	20 981	1 349	22 331	2 508	-148	19 675	5 576	4 863	12 855	11 592	2 343	1 170
1989	32 208	22 192	1 238	23 431	2 678	-149	20 604	6 233	5 370	13 727	12 341	2 346	1 189
1990	33 939	23 708	1 048	24 756	2 977	-211	21 568	6 557	5 814	14 402	12 928	2 357	1 204
1991	35 994	25 242	1 129	26 370	3 182	-239	22 949	6 593	6 452	15 103	13 605	2 383	1 230
1992	39 149	27 511	1 432	28 943	3 467	-264	25 212	6 778	7 158	16 204	14 616	2 416	1 255
1993	41 002	29 063	1 338	30 401	3 688	-295	26 418	7 028	7 555	16 692	15 050	2 456	1 301
1994	43 634	31 042	1 467	32 510	3 993	-320	28 197	7 509	7 928	17 496	15 708	2 494	1 329
1995	46 297	32 894	1 484	34 378	4 210	-291	29 877	7 889	8 531	18 260	16 355	2 535	1 382
1996	49 309	34 338	1 924	36 262	4 369	-281	31 612	8 671	9 025	19 170	17 165	2 572	1 405
1997	51 621	36 015	1 814	37 829	4 583	-280	32 965	9 235	9 421	19 846	17 680	2 601	1 427
1998	54 623	38 414	1 597	40 012	4 863	-284	34 865	10 019	9 739	20 798	18 456	2 626	1 453
1999	57 164	40 755	1 807	42 562	5 090	-316	37 156	9 943	10 066	21 556	19 168	2 652	1 471
2000	60 468	43 185	1 699	44 884	5 321	-362	39 201	10 574	10 693	22 574	20 031	2 679	1 493
2001	64 233	45 530	2 001	47 531	5 498	-363	41 669	10 706	11 858	23 864	21 291	2 692	1 483
2002	65 647	47 292	1 260	48 552	5 660	-394	42 497	10 336	12 813	24 260	21 931	2 706	1 478
2003	69 231	49 499	2 512	52 011	5 834	-402	45 775	10 124	13 332	25 407	23 218	2 725	1 480
2004	73 720	52 571	2 757	55 328	6 135	-412	48 781	10 660	14 278	26 810	24 540	2 750	1 501
2005	77 475	55 292	1 883	57 175	6 492	-399	50 283	11 845	15 347	27 858	25 299	2 781	1 531
2006	82 918	58 571	1 508	60 079	6 964	-400	52 715	13 445	16 759	29 385	26 627	2 822	1 565
2007	89 312	60 341	1 927	62 268	7 175	-360	54 734	16 492	18 086	31 353	28 247	2 849	1 582
2008	94 461	61 837	2 386	64 223	7 480	-354	56 390	18 318	19 753	32 861	29 724	2 875	1 581
2009	92 871	61 010	1 490	62 500	7 491	-282	54 727	16 063	22 081	32 059	29 497	2 897	1 546
2010	95 844	62 558	1 318	63 876	7 713	-294	55 869	16 633	23 342	32 805	30 202	2 922	1 547
2011	99 933	64 551	1 319	65 870	7 174	-296	58 400	17 478	24 054	34 014	31 020	2 938	. . .

. . . = Not available.

Table 17-2. Personal Income and Employment by Region and State—*Continued*

(Millions of dollars, except as noted.)

Region or state and year	Personal income, total	Earnings by place of work — Nonfarm	Earnings by place of work — Farm	Earnings by place of work — Total	Less: Contributions for government social insurance	Plus: Adjustment for residence	Equals: Net earnings by place of residence	Plus: Dividends, interest, and rent	Plus: Personal current transfer receipts	Per capita — Personal income	Per capita — Disposable personal income	Population (thousands)	Total employment (thousands)
CALIFORNIA													
1958	38 644	30 505	1 340	31 845	1 112	-3	30 729	5 692	2 223	2 597	2 310	14 880	...
1959	42 364	33 965	1 415	35 379	1 423	-4	33 952	6 140	2 273	2 739	2 427	15 467	...
1960	44 790	35 845	1 437	37 283	1 719	-5	35 559	6 647	2 584	2 822	2 493	15 870	...
1961	47 485	37 934	1 370	39 303	1 830	-5	37 468	7 018	2 999	2 878	2 546	16 497	...
1962	51 257	41 284	1 433	42 717	2 247	-6	40 464	7 613	3 179	3 002	2 652	17 072	...
1963	54 775	44 351	1 368	45 719	2 623	-6	43 090	8 168	3 517	3 100	2 739	17 668	...
1964	59 405	47 803	1 517	49 320	2 729	-7	46 584	9 009	3 812	3 273	2 943	18 151	...
1965	63 378	50 761	1 464	52 226	2 845	-8	49 372	9 793	4 213	3 410	3 066	18 585	...
1966	68 879	55 923	1 583	57 506	3 739	-11	53 757	10 469	4 653	3 653	3 265	18 858	...
1967	74 208	59 919	1 496	61 414	4 094	-12	57 309	11 145	5 755	3 870	3 446	19 176	...
1968	81 373	65 934	1 722	67 657	4 579	-14	63 064	11 666	6 643	4 196	3 694	19 394	...
1969	89 337	71 809	1 704	73 513	4 830	-130	68 553	13 168	7 616	4 532	3 962	19 711	9 033
1970	96 133	75 949	1 708	77 657	5 020	-114	72 523	14 309	9 301	4 801	4 266	20 023	9 057
1971	102 282	80 005	1 707	81 711	5 452	-124	76 135	15 451	10 695	5 027	4 519	20 346	9 036
1972	112 207	88 379	2 172	90 550	6 337	-127	84 087	16 599	11 522	5 451	4 812	20 585	9 368
1973	124 033	97 799	2 930	100 730	7 979	-113	92 638	18 638	12 758	5 944	5 298	20 868	9 844
1974	138 832	107 860	3 644	111 504	9 020	-127	102 357	21 358	15 117	6 557	5 825	21 173	10 163
1975	153 687	117 666	3 273	120 939	9 606	-17	111 316	23 377	18 994	7 136	6 419	21 537	10 286
1976	171 862	132 964	3 478	136 442	10 984	86	125 544	25 332	20 986	7 835	6 982	21 935	10 633
1977	191 580	149 944	3 544	153 488	12 566	-65	140 857	28 442	22 280	8 572	7 591	22 350	11 119
1978	218 613	172 805	3 491	176 296	14 800	-76	161 421	33 103	24 089	9 572	8 421	22 839	11 816
1979	249 280	196 439	4 572	201 011	17 658	-52	183 301	39 510	26 469	10 719	9 372	23 255	12 461
1980	283 904	218 286	5 583	223 868	19 245	-85	204 539	48 634	30 731	11 928	10 420	23 801	12 762
1981	319 204	240 879	4 362	245 240	23 003	247	222 484	60 558	36 162	13 144	11 506	24 286	12 935
1982	341 069	255 162	4 600	259 761	24 901	253	235 113	66 322	39 634	13 742	12 116	24 820	12 863
1983	368 163	276 298	4 233	280 531	27 639	266	253 158	72 676	42 329	14 517	12 833	25 360	13 182
1984	411 268	310 260	4 904	315 164	32 061	240	283 344	83 751	44 174	15 913	14 066	25 844	13 797
1985	443 596	336 304	4 939	341 243	35 322	187	306 108	89 728	47 760	16 777	14 738	26 441	14 285
1986	474 995	362 877	5 376	368 253	38 689	143	329 707	93 989	51 299	17 526	15 407	27 102	14 710
1987	512 411	396 911	6 608	403 519	42 356	63	361 226	97 660	53 524	18 447	16 040	27 777	15 300
1988	555 467	433 471	6 968	440 439	47 655	23	392 807	105 399	57 260	19 515	17 118	28 464	16 022
1989	597 464	458 611	6 829	465 440	50 960	8	414 488	120 359	62 617	20 448	17 763	29 218	16 426
1990	640 548	489 727	7 206	496 933	54 185	-50	442 699	128 969	68 880	21 380	18 614	29 960	16 835
1991	662 252	505 684	6 309	511 993	56 329	-37	455 627	130 151	76 473	21 734	19 139	30 471	16 750
1992	695 028	528 831	6 815	535 646	58 392	-37	477 270	129 349	88 408	22 439	19 904	30 975	16 391
1993	711 327	537 929	7 760	545 689	59 105	31	486 615	131 356	93 356	22 744	20 176	31 275	16 367
1994	738 250	555 748	7 541	563 289	61 142	47	502 194	140 544	95 511	23 448	20 790	31 484	16 541
1995	776 490	582 427	7 226	589 652	62 901	37	526 788	149 931	99 771	24 498	21 600	31 697	16 940
1996	825 689	615 673	8 124	623 797	64 880	25	558 942	161 860	104 887	25 788	22 487	32 019	17 342
1997	879 160	661 589	8 685	670 274	69 059	-70	601 145	172 947	105 068	27 063	23 367	32 486	17 667
1998	963 067	728 714	8 205	736 920	74 352	-76	662 492	189 612	110 964	29 195	25 081	32 988	18 371
1999	1 027 715	791 305	8 966	800 271	80 470	-128	719 674	191 287	116 754	30 679	25 937	33 499	18 860
2000	1 135 342	887 048	8 872	895 920	89 266	-296	806 358	207 463	121 521	33 404	27 669	33 988	19 466
2001	1 168 723	908 405	8 428	916 833	94 003	-313	822 517	211 202	135 003	33 896	28 526	34 479	19 610
2002	1 187 348	925 832	8 956	934 788	97 031	-269	837 489	204 840	145 019	34 049	29 856	34 872	19 374
2003	1 232 981	966 250	10 150	976 401	102 270	-284	873 847	206 644	152 490	34 975	30 938	35 253	19 506
2004	1 312 227	1 029 164	12 281	1 041 445	111 248	*	929 892	222 128	160 207	36 887	32 652	35 575	19 795
2005	1 387 661	1 082 552	10 768	1 093 320	117 096	-260	975 963	243 777	167 921	38 731	33 779	35 828	20 161
2006	1 495 533	1 144 440	10 718	1 155 158	120 647	-238	1 034 273	280 234	181 026	41 518	36 042	36 021	20 514
2007	1 566 400	1 178 406	12 957	1 191 362	122 372	-188	1 068 802	306 004	191 594	43 211	37 270	36 250	20 966
2008	1 610 698	1 180 382	11 304	1 191 685	124 630	-101	1 066 954	334 878	208 866	44 003	38 513	36 604	20 706
2009	1 526 531	1 114 307	12 730	1 127 037	120 718	-34	1 006 285	282 003	238 243	41 301	36 969	36 961	19 912
2010	1 587 404	1 145 047	13 582	1 158 629	122 248	-112	1 036 269	291 114	260 021	42 514	37 883	37 338	19 771
2011	1 676 565	1 199 139	14 705	1 213 843	114 467	-167	1 099 209	311 016	266 340	44 481	39 186	37 692	...

. . . = Not available.

Table 17-2. Personal Income and Employment by Region and State—*Continued*

(Millions of dollars, except as noted.)

Region or state and year	Personal income, total	Earnings by place of work — Nonfarm	Earnings by place of work — Farm	Earnings by place of work — Total	Less: Contributions for government social insurance	Plus: Adjustment for residence	Equals: Net earnings by place of residence	Plus: Dividends, interest, and rent	Plus: Personal current transfer receipts	Per capita — Personal income	Per capita — Disposable personal income	Population (thousands)	Total employment (thousands)
COLORADO													
1958	3 578	2 755	178	2 933	95	1	2 840	518	220	2 147	1 914	1 667	. . .
1959	3 848	2 988	157	3 144	109	1	3 037	552	259	2 250	2 010	1 710	. . .
1960	4 124	3 222	174	3 397	133	1	3 265	583	275	2 331	2 055	1 769	. . .
1961	4 441	3 489	176	3 665	150	1	3 516	623	302	2 408	2 123	1 844	. . .
1962	4 673	3 682	156	3 838	163	1	3 675	679	319	2 461	2 172	1 899	. . .
1963	4 894	3 883	140	4 023	191	0	3 833	722	339	2 528	2 232	1 936	. . .
1964	5 178	4 126	138	4 263	197	*	4 066	768	343	2 628	2 370	1 970	. . .
1965	5 532	4 320	213	4 534	197	0	4 336	820	375	2 787	2 508	1 985	. . .
1966	5 951	4 734	192	4 925	263	-1	4 662	882	407	2 965	2 650	2 007	. . .
1967	6 418	5 087	186	5 273	294	-1	4 978	957	483	3 126	2 783	2 053	. . .
1968	7 132	5 655	244	5 899	333	-2	5 565	1 019	549	3 364	2 962	2 120	. . .
1969	7 985	6 339	251	6 590	388	2	6 204	1 176	605	3 687	3 199	2 166	1 001
1970	8 985	7 072	289	7 361	427	2	6 935	1 319	730	4 040	3 550	2 224	1 032
1971	10 133	8 027	301	8 328	499	3	7 833	1 450	850	4 399	3 888	2 304	1 072
1972	11 481	9 225	333	9 558	606	4	8 957	1 581	943	4 774	4 162	2 405	1 149
1973	13 186	10 612	440	11 052	797	3	10 257	1 821	1 108	5 283	4 628	2 496	1 243
1974	14 835	11 794	535	12 330	905	4	11 429	2 122	1 283	5 837	5 091	2 541	1 276
1975	16 350	12 904	464	13 368	966	8	12 410	2 329	1 610	6 322	5 591	2 586	1 285
1976	18 111	14 574	336	14 911	1 104	9	13 816	2 537	1 758	6 880	6 056	2 632	1 340
1977	20 314	16 563	266	16 829	1 260	12	15 581	2 868	1 865	7 535	6 587	2 696	1 411
1978	23 476	19 376	209	19 585	1 505	20	18 101	3 344	2 031	8 485	7 395	2 767	1 506
1979	27 073	22 418	218	22 636	1 837	20	20 819	3 971	2 282	9 502	8 232	2 849	1 593
1980	31 165	25 327	290	25 617	2 101	28	23 544	4 975	2 646	10 714	9 288	2 909	1 651
1981	35 968	28 868	307	29 175	2 586	5	26 594	6 266	3 108	12 078	10 409	2 978	1 717
1982	39 505	31 556	185	31 741	2 895	2	28 848	7 135	3 522	12 904	11 105	3 062	1 760
1983	42 423	33 487	360	33 848	3 130	0	30 717	7 808	3 898	13 538	11 950	3 134	1 788
1984	46 499	36 746	425	37 171	3 539	8	33 640	8 751	4 108	14 669	13 002	3 170	1 883
1985	48 988	38 716	394	39 111	3 835	17	35 292	9 394	4 301	15 267	13 490	3 209	1 915
1986	50 869	40 118	397	40 515	4 021	22	36 516	9 739	4 615	15 713	13 936	3 237	1 914
1987	52 836	41 516	479	41 995	4 122	34	37 907	9 954	4 975	16 205	14 323	3 260	1 903
1988	55 695	43 829	581	44 411	4 501	49	39 959	10 505	5 231	17 072	15 127	3 262	1 968
1989	60 269	46 338	621	46 959	4 829	66	42 196	12 244	5 829	18 398	16 190	3 276	2 003
1990	64 093	49 416	713	50 129	5 245	91	44 975	12 872	6 247	19 377	17 003	3 308	2 040
1991	68 160	52 971	640	53 610	5 748	102	47 965	13 260	6 935	20 123	17 704	3 387	2 087
1992	73 772	57 785	679	58 465	6 233	117	52 348	13 634	7 790	21 102	18 563	3 496	2 135
1993	80 051	62 965	815	63 781	6 841	129	57 069	14 631	8 352	22 152	19 443	3 614	2 234
1994	86 537	67 700	584	68 285	7 392	146	61 039	16 640	8 858	23 237	20 353	3 724	2 345
1995	94 039	73 040	545	73 585	7 897	167	65 855	18 269	9 915	24 575	21 524	3 827	2 425
1996	101 777	78 993	671	79 664	8 437	185	71 413	20 102	10 262	25 964	22 569	3 920	2 519
1997	110 110	86 220	677	86 897	9 118	206	77 985	21 704	10 421	27 402	23 625	4 018	2 629
1998	120 100	93 981	807	94 788	9 529	232	85 491	23 970	10 639	29 174	24 958	4 117	2 732
1999	130 663	104 224	938	105 162	10 384	262	95 040	24 283	11 340	30 919	26 374	4 226	2 816
2000	147 056	118 625	775	119 401	11 536	289	108 154	26 914	11 988	33 986	28 865	4 327	2 926
2001	156 468	126 234	1 069	127 304	12 146	339	115 497	27 881	13 091	35 355	30 455	4 426	2 941
2002	157 752	127 678	705	128 384	12 560	346	116 170	26 793	14 789	35 131	31 054	4 490	2 910
2003	159 918	129 770	749	130 518	12 848	362	118 032	26 465	15 421	35 312	31 573	4 529	2 906
2004	168 587	137 268	951	138 219	13 669	383	124 933	27 554	16 100	36 849	33 007	4 575	2 954
2005	179 695	145 296	1 140	146 437	14 536	397	132 298	30 072	17 326	38 795	34 373	4 632	3 031
2006	194 390	155 073	845	155 918	15 430	417	140 905	34 887	18 598	41 181	36 194	4 720	3 101
2007	205 242	160 312	1 043	161 355	16 213	446	145 588	39 663	19 991	42 724	37 236	4 804	3 212
2008	216 030	166 328	987	167 315	16 897	458	150 876	42 956	22 197	44 180	39 044	4 890	3 251
2009	205 787	157 887	832	158 720	16 233	442	142 929	36 890	25 968	41 388	37 384	4 972	3 166
2010	213 494	161 554	938	162 492	16 420	456	146 527	38 366	28 600	42 295	38 210	5 048	3 155
2011	225 591	169 272	1 138	170 410	15 520	487	155 377	40 684	29 531	44 088	39 336	5 117	. . .

. . . = Not available.
* = Less than $50,000, but the estimates for this item are included in the total.

Table 17-2. Personal Income and Employment by Region and State—*Continued*

(Millions of dollars, except as noted.)

Region or state and year	Personal income, total	Earnings by place of work			Less: Contributions for government social insurance	Plus: Adjustment for residence	Equals: Net earnings by place of residence	Plus: Dividends, interest, and rent	Plus: Personal current transfer receipts	Per capita (dollars)		Population (thousands)	Total employment (thousands)
		Nonfarm	Farm	Total						Personal income	Disposable personal income		
CONNECTICUT													
1958	6 401	5 120	67	5 188	184	-2	5 002	1 009	390	2 617	2 304	2 446	. . .
1959	6 840	5 546	58	5 604	230	-2	5 372	1 092	376	2 711	2 382	2 523	. . .
1960	7 121	5 782	63	5 845	278	3	5 571	1 162	389	2 799	2 438	2 544	. . .
1961	7 528	6 045	58	6 103	290	3	5 816	1 264	448	2 911	2 545	2 586	. . .
1962	8 044	6 474	60	6 534	320	3	6 216	1 387	441	3 039	2 653	2 647	. . .
1963	8 488	6 822	64	6 885	369	4	6 520	1 499	469	3 113	2 703	2 727	. . .
1964	9 114	7 294	62	7 356	379	5	6 982	1 638	495	3 258	2 884	2 798	. . .
1965	9 793	7 811	71	7 882	395	2	7 488	1 782	523	3 428	3 014	2 857	. . .
1966	10 757	8 744	73	8 818	553	0	8 265	1 928	564	3 705	3 231	2 903	. . .
1967	11 793	9 461	58	9 519	602	2	8 918	2 173	701	4 018	3 475	2 935	. . .
1968	12 577	10 192	68	10 260	671	7	9 596	2 127	854	4 243	3 604	2 964	. . .
1969	14 464	11 125	67	11 192	752	728	11 168	2 348	947	4 821	4 068	3 000	1 417
1970	15 410	11 724	72	11 795	783	722	11 733	2 531	1 146	5 071	4 398	3 039	1 414
1971	16 211	12 140	69	12 209	840	746	12 115	2 672	1 424	5 295	4 665	3 061	1 388
1972	17 474	13 231	68	13 299	968	785	13 115	2 854	1 505	5 692	4 942	3 070	1 416
1973	19 109	14 721	81	14 802	1 234	808	14 376	3 103	1 630	6 226	5 444	3 069	1 480
1974	20 896	15 987	84	16 071	1 395	841	15 517	3 461	1 918	6 794	5 939	3 076	1 511
1975	22 371	16 627	75	16 703	1 423	916	16 196	3 629	2 546	7 252	6 432	3 085	1 468
1976	24 311	18 204	83	18 287	1 577	1 011	17 721	3 881	2 709	7 878	6 903	3 086	1 493
1977	26 824	20 257	84	20 340	1 778	1 121	19 684	4 308	2 832	8 684	7 612	3 089	1 546
1978	29 884	22 837	80	22 917	2 062	1 275	22 130	4 834	2 920	9 656	8 379	3 095	1 615
1979	33 650	25 742	79	25 821	2 421	1 448	24 848	5 551	3 251	10 855	9 345	3 100	1 673
1980	38 357	28 675	84	28 759	2 682	1 691	27 768	6 852	3 738	12 321	10 551	3 113	1 705
1981	43 117	31 424	82	31 506	3 140	1 865	30 231	8 572	4 314	13 780	11 749	3 129	1 727
1982	46 612	33 554	108	33 662	3 413	2 020	32 269	9 546	4 796	14 849	12 645	3 139	1 726
1983	49 765	36 170	105	36 275	3 737	2 140	34 679	9 906	5 181	15 737	13 740	3 162	1 743
1984	55 639	40 603	129	40 732	4 306	2 288	38 714	11 509	5 416	17 496	15 361	3 180	1 823
1985	59 652	44 243	127	44 370	4 742	2 424	42 052	11 856	5 745	18 635	16 211	3 201	1 879
1986	64 135	47 887	140	48 027	5 166	2 576	45 437	12 622	6 076	19 895	17 206	3 224	1 937
1987	70 053	53 184	143	53 327	5 654	2 696	50 369	13 404	6 281	21 573	18 474	3 247	1 984
1988	77 079	58 784	157	58 941	6 347	2 884	55 477	14 827	6 775	23 557	20 434	3 272	2 039
1989	83 387	61 842	140	61 982	6 655	2 777	58 104	17 694	7 590	25 397	22 041	3 283	2 032
1990	86 244	63 468	185	63 653	6 748	2 757	59 662	18 094	8 487	26 198	22 815	3 292	2 003
1991	87 296	64 315	165	64 480	6 940	2 724	60 265	17 528	9 504	26 430	23 046	3 303	1 923
1992	93 367	67 452	188	67 640	7 155	3 924	64 408	17 777	11 182	28 287	24 396	3 301	1 904
1993	96 134	70 092	210	70 302	7 415	3 342	66 229	18 238	11 666	29 051	24 935	3 309	1 925
1994	99 121	72 643	186	72 829	7 766	3 116	68 178	18 863	12 080	29 891	25 666	3 316	1 906
1995	104 266	76 184	173	76 357	8 131	3 869	72 095	19 249	12 923	31 366	26 740	3 324	1 944
1996	109 560	79 620	161	79 780	8 472	4 648	75 957	20 345	13 259	32 835	27 517	3 337	1 975
1997	116 817	86 129	158	86 287	8 991	4 192	81 487	21 703	13 626	34 877	28 852	3 349	2 000
1998	125 278	91 735	180	91 915	9 435	5 578	88 058	23 422	13 798	37 226	30 476	3 365	2 028
1999	131 113	97 667	193	97 859	9 885	5 403	93 377	23 597	14 140	38 718	31 533	3 386	2 057
2000	143 021	106 837	226	107 063	10 515	5 631	102 178	25 953	14 890	41 920	33 837	3 412	2 096
2001	149 537	112 830	200	113 030	10 818	5 016	107 228	26 506	15 802	43 561	35 266	3 433	2 108
2002	149 567	113 681	189	113 870	11 324	4 427	106 974	25 629	16 964	43 243	36 552	3 459	2 117
2003	151 832	116 568	195	116 763	11 583	4 128	109 308	25 263	17 261	43 576	37 241	3 484	2 113
2004	161 428	123 216	209	123 425	12 198	4 664	115 891	27 233	18 304	46 174	39 419	3 496	2 139
2005	168 804	128 726	200	128 926	12 617	4 684	120 993	28 830	18 981	48 134	40 346	3 507	2 169
2006	184 049	135 634	180	135 814	13 102	5 105	127 818	35 988	20 243	52 324	43 728	3 517	2 200
2007	197 029	142 214	220	142 434	13 679	5 401	134 155	41 396	21 478	55 859	46 034	3 527	2 243
2008	201 954	142 733	200	142 933	14 148	5 070	133 855	44 369	23 731	56 959	47 969	3 546	2 255
2009	188 819	135 492	179	135 671	13 873	3 228	125 027	36 366	27 425	53 012	45 725	3 562	2 194
2010	193 932	138 709	170	138 879	14 002	3 142	128 019	37 087	28 826	54 239	46 813	3 575	2 181
2011	203 703	144 961	166	145 128	13 074	3 280	135 334	39 109	29 260	56 889	47 992	3 581	. . .

. . . = Not available.

Table 17-2. Personal Income and Employment by Region and State—*Continued*

(Millions of dollars, except as noted.)

Region or state and year	Personal income, total	Earnings by place of work			Less: Contributions for government social insurance	Plus: Adjustment for residence	Equals: Net earnings by place of residence	Plus: Dividends, interest, and rent	Plus: Personal current transfer receipts	Per capita (dollars)		Population (thousands)	Total employment (thousands)
		Nonfarm	Farm	Total						Personal income	Disposable personal income		
DELAWARE													
1958	1 157	917	35	952	32	-49	871	235	52	2 672	2 249	433	. . .
1959	1 207	974	30	1 004	42	-50	912	244	52	2 738	2 288	441	. . .
1960	1 265	1 022	34	1 056	53	-51	953	258	54	2 817	2 358	449	. . .
1961	1 301	1 049	30	1 078	51	-51	976	260	65	2 823	2 377	461	. . .
1962	1 378	1 113	33	1 146	58	-52	1 036	274	67	2 937	2 442	469	. . .
1963	1 475	1 208	26	1 234	69	-56	1 109	297	70	3 055	2 562	483	. . .
1964	1 599	1 307	26	1 333	68	-58	1 206	318	74	3 216	2 703	497	. . .
1965	1 763	1 443	35	1 478	69	-65	1 344	339	80	3 477	2 919	507	. . .
1966	1 861	1 583	26	1 609	99	-69	1 441	332	88	3 607	3 041	516	. . .
1967	1 984	1 683	32	1 715	117	-69	1 530	346	108	3 780	3 201	525	. . .
1968	2 174	1 848	29	1 877	119	-71	1 687	360	127	4 072	3 426	534	. . .
1969	2 379	1 992	55	2 048	139	-43	1 865	376	139	4 406	3 638	540	271
1970	2 528	2 132	35	2 167	147	-48	1 971	392	165	4 594	3 819	550	275
1971	2 763	2 348	38	2 387	168	-60	2 158	410	194	4 888	4 104	565	280
1972	3 040	2 606	49	2 655	196	-68	2 392	433	215	5 297	4 435	574	293
1973	3 392	2 927	96	3 023	253	-97	2 674	470	248	5 858	4 899	579	305
1974	3 695	3 171	82	3 253	282	-108	2 864	528	303	6 336	5 322	583	302
1975	3 968	3 340	92	3 432	293	-110	3 029	532	408	6 740	5 745	589	292
1976	4 354	3 692	84	3 776	325	-121	3 330	586	438	7 345	6 175	593	296
1977	4 694	3 990	56	4 046	352	-133	3 561	657	477	7 892	6 644	595	296
1978	5 159	4 436	61	4 497	402	-163	3 933	727	499	8 624	7 265	598	304
1979	5 678	4 876	54	4 931	460	-184	4 286	819	572	9 482	7 919	599	312
1980	6 399	5 418	13	5 430	512	-231	4 688	1 017	694	10 756	8 977	595	312
1981	7 049	5 816	43	5 859	594	-249	5 015	1 253	781	11 827	9 795	596	314
1982	7 599	6 242	66	6 308	651	-270	5 387	1 384	829	12 684	10 655	599	317
1983	8 154	6 707	78	6 786	704	-317	5 765	1 505	884	13 468	11 470	605	325
1984	9 019	7 375	96	7 471	780	-357	6 335	1 737	948	14 748	12 648	612	340
1985	9 831	8 049	104	8 153	865	-399	6 889	1 945	997	15 900	13 648	618	357
1986	10 411	8 463	144	8 606	934	-398	7 275	2 057	1 078	16 589	14 201	628	370
1987	11 213	9 277	114	9 392	1 017	-452	7 923	2 166	1 124	17 604	15 137	637	387
1988	12 187	10 100	182	10 282	1 154	-496	8 632	2 317	1 238	18 819	16 256	648	403
1989	13 533	11 046	192	11 238	1 267	-604	9 367	2 826	1 340	20 559	17 727	658	415
1990	14 201	11 681	141	11 822	1 318	-678	9 826	2 935	1 440	21 209	18 262	670	420
1991	15 077	12 249	133	12 382	1 388	-688	10 307	3 102	1 669	22 073	19 208	683	414
1992	15 636	13 003	117	13 120	1 428	-969	10 723	3 097	1 817	22 500	19 598	695	413
1993	16 165	13 344	108	13 453	1 488	-916	11 049	3 174	1 942	22 885	19 890	706	421
1994	16 853	14 064	122	14 186	1 588	-1 072	11 526	3 263	2 064	23 487	20 300	718	424
1995	17 812	14 594	87	14 682	1 677	-912	12 092	3 468	2 251	24 409	21 107	730	442
1996	19 123	15 392	121	15 512	1 763	-936	12 813	3 818	2 492	25 808	22 153	741	453
1997	19 970	16 415	95	16 510	1 868	-1 209	13 433	4 017	2 519	26 574	22 527	751	464
1998	21 676	17 744	142	17 886	1 986	-1 383	14 517	4 475	2 684	28 397	24 080	763	481
1999	22 530	19 048	140	19 187	2 131	-1 650	15 406	4 320	2 804	29 072	24 665	775	493
2000	24 384	20 292	148	20 440	2 232	-1 707	16 500	4 823	3 061	31 009	26 428	786	504
2001	25 741	21 696	212	21 908	2 331	-1 845	17 732	4 651	3 358	32 350	27 520	796	500
2002	26 709	22 490	87	22 577	2 394	-1 858	18 325	4 763	3 621	33 130	28 983	806	501
2003	27 616	23 324	174	23 498	2 485	-1 956	19 057	4 680	3 879	33 760	29 838	818	506
2004	29 522	24 830	257	25 086	2 668	-2 044	20 374	4 973	4 174	35 534	31 398	831	520
2005	31 077	26 391	292	26 683	2 797	-2 227	21 659	4 889	4 529	36 771	32 052	845	530
2006	33 350	27 814	207	28 021	3 019	-2 356	22 646	5 778	4 925	38 812	33 875	859	540
2007	34 702	28 272	208	28 480	3 074	-2 254	23 152	6 229	5 321	39 808	34 692	872	549
2008	35 854	28 550	151	28 701	3 185	-2 331	23 185	6 804	5 866	40 565	35 757	884	549
2009	34 761	27 318	164	27 482	3 111	-2 001	22 370	5 787	6 603	38 981	35 056	892	530
2010	36 079	28 039	150	28 189	3 148	-1 948	23 093	5 941	7 045	40 097	35 883	900	529
2011	37 769	29 127	98	29 225	2 941	-2 097	24 187	6 288	7 294	41 635	36 750	907	. . .

. . . = Not available.

Table 17-2. Personal Income and Employment by Region and State—*Continued*

(Millions of dollars, except as noted.)

| Region or state and year | Personal income, total | Derivation of personal income | | | | | | | | Per capita (dollars) | | Population (thousands) | Total employment (thousands) |
| | | Earnings by place of work | | | Less: Contributions for government social insurance | Plus: Adjustment for residence | Equals: Net earnings by place of residence | Plus: Dividends, interest, and rent | Plus: Personal current transfer receipts | Personal income | Disposable personal income | | |
		Nonfarm	Farm	Total									
DISTRICT OF COLUMBIA													
1958	2 054	2 740	0	2 740	79	-1 038	1 623	325	106	2 714	2 357	757	...
1959	2 119	2 888	0	2 888	89	-1 127	1 672	338	109	2 784	2 378	761	...
1960	2 144	3 075	0	3 075	101	-1 309	1 665	367	112	2 802	2 379	765	...
1961	2 261	3 266	0	3 266	107	-1 395	1 764	374	123	2 906	2 509	778	...
1962	2 442	3 519	0	3 519	114	-1 481	1 925	390	127	3 099	2 663	788	...
1963	2 597	3 787	0	3 787	138	-1 595	2 054	409	135	3 254	2 823	798	...
1964	2 762	4 067	0	4 067	135	-1 731	2 201	422	140	3 462	3 052	798	...
1965	2 993	4 421	0	4 421	140	-1 883	2 398	445	150	3 756	3 333	797	...
1966	3 125	4 770	0	4 770	186	-2 068	2 516	449	160	3 951	3 466	791	...
1967	3 349	5 394	0	5 394	213	-2 475	2 706	451	192	4 234	3 738	791	...
1968	3 524	5 814	0	5 814	234	-2 742	2 838	457	230	4 530	3 991	778	...
1969	3 416	6 140	0	6 140	252	-3 181	2 708	474	234	4 483	3 833	762	676
1970	3 753	6 688	0	6 688	274	-3 481	2 933	518	302	4 970	4 273	755	672
1971	4 126	7 270	0	7 270	299	-3 791	3 180	571	375	5 497	4 788	751	666
1972	4 482	7 877	0	7 877	343	-4 120	3 414	621	447	6 026	5 218	744	668
1973	4 747	8 396	0	8 396	414	-4 404	3 578	657	512	6 470	5 586	734	662
1974	5 227	9 236	0	9 236	472	-4 861	3 904	728	595	7 252	6 289	721	673
1975	5 707	10 213	0	10 213	521	-5 468	4 224	741	741	8 034	7 003	710	677
1976	6 077	11 123	0	11 123	573	-6 033	4 518	792	768	8 728	7 489	696	674
1977	6 572	12 200	0	12 200	609	-6 672	4 919	865	787	9 639	8 363	682	680
1978	6 946	13 296	0	13 296	668	-7 451	5 177	959	810	10 367	8 899	670	693
1979	7 358	14 532	0	14 532	770	-8 391	5 371	1 083	904	11 224	9 500	656	704
1980	7 799	15 962	0	15 962	859	-9 605	5 497	1 276	1 026	12 218	10 378	638	701
1981	8 522	17 308	0	17 308	1 040	-10 485	5 783	1 606	1 133	13 381	11 210	637	689
1982	9 240	18 366	0	18 366	1 115	-11 111	6 140	1 832	1 267	14 570	12 275	634	673
1983	9 726	19 308	0	19 308	1 294	-11 492	6 521	1 879	1 326	15 379	13 094	632	667
1984	10 759	21 017	0	21 017	1 465	-12 388	7 164	2 181	1 414	16 986	14 485	633	689
1985	11 454	22 476	0	22 476	1 681	-13 157	7 638	2 401	1 416	18 051	15 378	635	703
1986	12 084	23 736	0	23 736	1 859	-13 760	8 118	2 497	1 470	18 932	16 165	638	721
1987	12 768	25 497	0	25 497	2 023	-14 750	8 723	2 530	1 515	20 046	16 972	637	733
1988	13 969	28 129	0	28 129	2 318	-16 248	9 562	2 780	1 627	22 157	18 945	630	756
1989	14 882	29 739	0	29 739	2 556	-17 320	9 862	3 395	1 625	23 843	20 378	624	763
1990	15 748	31 850	0	31 850	2 758	-18 457	10 634	3 379	1 734	26 015	22 400	605	773
1991	16 423	33 666	0	33 666	2 938	-19 611	11 117	3 369	1 938	27 333	23 792	601	759
1992	17 147	35 604	0	35 604	3 124	-20 914	11 566	3 404	2 177	28 694	25 092	598	752
1993	17 789	37 045	0	37 045	3 273	-21 773	11 999	3 400	2 391	29 883	26 243	595	750
1994	18 151	37 940	0	37 940	3 419	-22 284	12 237	3 483	2 431	30 804	26 843	589	730
1995	18 165	38 367	0	38 367	3 475	-22 512	12 379	3 429	2 357	31 291	27 268	581	718
1996	18 878	38 817	0	38 817	3 509	-22 411	12 897	3 420	2 561	32 981	28 467	572	704
1997	19 761	40 093	0	40 093	3 626	-23 091	13 375	3 830	2 556	34 807	29 697	568	699
1998	20 633	41 682	0	41 682	3 759	-24 089	13 833	4 075	2 724	36 503	30 732	565	702
1999	21 151	44 918	0	44 918	4 104	-26 344	14 471	3 954	2 726	37 093	30 783	570	715
2000	23 146	47 411	0	47 411	4 336	-26 939	16 135	4 204	2 807	40 462	33 441	572	737
2001	26 094	51 203	0	51 203	4 944	-27 228	19 032	4 161	2 901	45 421	38 342	575	748
2002	26 564	54 116	0	54 116	5 261	-29 527	19 328	4 026	3 211	46 347	40 234	573	759
2003	27 544	56 570	0	56 570	5 496	-30 815	20 260	4 019	3 266	48 451	42 389	569	763
2004	29 729	61 331	0	61 331	5 920	-33 184	22 227	4 190	3 312	52 362	45 717	568	774
2005	31 965	64 853	0	64 853	6 252	-34 683	23 919	4 449	3 597	56 362	48 727	567	782
2006	34 787	68 636	0	68 636	6 586	-36 229	25 822	5 262	3 703	60 957	52 769	571	791
2007	37 525	72 196	0	72 196	6 948	-37 641	27 608	5 922	3 995	65 329	56 017	574	803
2008	41 015	76 321	0	76 321	7 481	-38 970	29 870	6 849	4 296	70 686	61 973	580	810
2009	40 483	77 185	0	77 185	7 764	-39 465	29 956	5 667	4 859	68 357	60 628	592	813
2010	42 773	81 445	0	81 445	8 125	-41 744	31 576	5 755	5 442	70 710	62 782	605	825
2011	45 178	84 535	0	84 535	7 634	-43 486	33 415	6 097	5 667	73 105	63 938	618	...

. . . = Not available.

Table 17-2. Personal Income and Employment by Region and State—*Continued*

(Millions of dollars, except as noted.)

Region or state and year	Personal income, total	Earnings by place of work — Nonfarm	Farm	Total	Less: Contributions for government social insurance	Plus: Adjustment for residence	Equals: Net earnings by place of residence	Plus: Dividends, interest, and rent	Plus: Personal current transfer receipts	Per capita — Personal income	Disposable personal income	Population (thousands)	Total employment (thousands)
FLORIDA													
1958	8 711	6 447	369	6 817	216	-1	6 599	1 532	580	1 881	1 708	4 630	. . .
1959	9 621	7 134	442	7 576	282	-1	7 293	1 673	655	2 001	1 810	4 808	. . .
1960	10 087	7 499	381	7 880	329	-1	7 551	1 821	715	2 016	1 822	5 004	. . .
1961	10 665	7 778	440	8 218	343	-1	7 873	1 963	829	2 034	1 839	5 243	. . .
1962	11 519	8 404	454	8 857	389	-1	8 468	2 123	928	2 110	1 906	5 458	. . .
1963	12 367	9 066	436	9 502	449	-1	9 053	2 304	1 011	2 197	1 985	5 628	. . .
1964	13 565	9 993	493	10 485	481	-1	10 004	2 506	1 055	2 346	2 136	5 781	. . .
1965	14 845	10 941	466	11 407	516	-1	10 891	2 783	1 171	2 493	2 263	5 954	. . .
1966	16 335	12 171	476	12 647	679	-1	11 966	3 063	1 306	2 676	2 425	6 104	. . .
1967	18 115	13 371	515	13 886	808	-2	13 076	3 411	1 628	2 902	2 605	6 242	. . .
1968	20 831	15 260	529	15 788	963	-4	14 821	4 074	1 936	3 238	2 872	6 433	. . .
1969	24 290	17 585	636	18 221	1 132	-22	17 067	5 028	2 195	3 658	3 218	6 641	2 857
1970	27 368	19 645	546	20 191	1 272	-19	18 899	5 824	2 646	3 998	3 559	6 845	2 966
1971	30 669	21 796	639	22 435	1 472	-13	20 949	6 532	3 188	4 282	3 835	7 163	3 082
1972	35 315	25 327	738	26 066	1 796	-11	24 259	7 302	3 755	4 696	4 138	7 520	3 338
1973	41 353	29 860	836	30 696	2 420	-9	28 267	8 525	4 561	5 217	4 623	7 927	3 666
1974	46 502	32 992	908	33 900	2 780	0	31 119	9 885	5 497	5 591	4 973	8 317	3 766
1975	50 408	34 390	998	35 388	2 859	-9	32 520	10 706	7 183	5 901	5 352	8 542	3 676
1976	55 303	37 736	1 035	38 771	3 168	11	35 613	11 728	7 962	6 360	5 730	8 695	3 730
1977	61 970	42 322	1 033	43 355	3 570	23	39 807	13 450	8 713	6 972	6 263	8 889	3 929
1978	71 600	49 054	1 234	50 288	4 245	26	46 069	15 845	9 686	7 841	6 995	9 132	4 239
1979	82 686	56 196	1 311	57 507	5 105	22	52 424	19 037	11 225	8 731	7 735	9 471	4 454
1980	97 624	64 477	1 667	66 144	5 915	16	60 246	24 032	13 346	9 921	8 752	9 840	4 688
1981	113 148	72 762	1 403	74 166	7 230	114	67 049	30 500	15 599	11 101	9 773	10 193	4 865
1982	122 328	77 618	1 776	79 394	7 942	137	71 589	33 082	17 657	11 682	10 204	10 471	4 954
1983	135 879	85 793	2 465	88 258	8 777	160	79 641	36 925	19 313	12 640	11 317	10 750	5 167
1984	151 446	96 825	1 826	98 651	10 141	210	88 720	42 154	20 571	13 718	12 391	11 040	5 502
1985	166 214	106 444	1 831	108 276	11 348	255	97 182	46 833	22 198	14 643	13 075	11 351	5 772
1986	179 572	115 679	1 967	117 646	12 681	315	105 279	50 381	23 912	15 391	13 693	11 668	6 015
1987	194 277	127 280	2 140	129 420	13 790	376	116 005	52 916	25 355	16 193	14 380	11 997	6 094
1988	212 795	139 638	2 699	142 336	15 642	452	127 147	57 894	27 755	17 291	15 420	12 306	6 390
1989	236 759	148 959	2 482	151 441	16 954	531	135 018	70 482	31 260	18 734	16 690	12 638	6 596
1990	253 324	159 096	2 082	161 178	17 989	638	143 827	75 257	34 240	19 437	17 398	13 033	6 740
1991	264 396	165 659	2 457	168 116	18 866	684	149 935	75 967	38 494	19 776	17 838	13 370	6 718
1992	279 479	177 448	2 458	179 906	20 059	750	160 596	74 679	44 203	20 474	18 468	13 651	6 763
1993	295 218	189 387	2 534	191 921	21 342	803	171 382	76 493	47 343	21 197	19 089	13 927	7 002
1994	312 116	200 468	2 164	202 632	22 867	864	180 629	81 032	50 455	21 919	19 703	14 239	7 234
1995	334 574	214 448	2 209	216 656	24 231	932	193 357	86 836	54 381	23 014	20 644	14 538	7 494
1996	357 219	228 904	1 951	230 855	25 535	1 003	206 323	93 434	57 462	24 050	21 357	14 853	7 740
1997	378 429	242 337	2 163	244 500	27 120	1 098	218 478	100 351	59 600	24 919	21 931	15 186	8 005
1998	409 670	263 112	2 648	265 760	29 065	1 221	237 915	110 701	61 055	26 453	23 196	15 487	8 298
1999	430 694	284 057	2 710	286 767	30 988	1 344	257 123	110 085	63 486	27 329	23 944	15 759	8 567
2000	466 644	309 556	2 589	312 145	33 237	1 505	280 413	118 514	67 717	29 079	25 392	16 048	8 842
2001	487 499	322 437	2 582	325 019	35 611	1 573	290 981	122 703	73 815	29 804	26 158	16 357	8 917
2002	508 400	337 843	2 517	340 361	37 165	1 537	304 733	123 831	79 836	30 462	27 346	16 689	9 056
2003	531 218	358 925	2 167	361 092	39 039	1 537	323 589	122 754	84 875	31 241	28 451	17 004	9 286
2004	582 766	387 219	2 283	389 503	42 313	1 592	348 782	142 663	91 320	33 463	30 297	17 415	9 662
2005	633 193	420 631	2 701	423 332	46 199	1 636	378 768	156 369	98 055	35 489	31 622	17 842	10 088
2006	690 268	449 676	2 678	452 354	49 909	1 720	404 165	181 692	104 412	37 996	33 847	18 167	10 407
2007	721 052	460 073	2 270	462 343	50 944	1 883	413 281	196 531	111 239	39 256	34 977	18 368	10 577
2008	740 676	453 732	2 119	455 851	50 810	1 951	406 991	211 211	122 473	39 978	36 289	18 527	10 325
2009	697 274	432 229	2 227	434 456	49 177	1 838	387 117	172 003	138 154	37 382	34 519	18 653	9 908
2010	719 828	440 057	2 350	442 407	50 073	1 903	394 237	176 504	149 088	38 210	35 284	18 839	9 866
2011	753 983	456 145	2 263	458 409	46 645	2 029	413 793	186 650	153 539	39 563	36 124	19 058	. . .

. . . = Not available.

Table 17-2. Personal Income and Employment by Region and State—*Continued*

(Millions of dollars, except as noted.)

Region or state and year	Personal income, total	Derivation of personal income								Per capita (dollars)		Population (thousands)	Total employment (thousands)
		Earnings by place of work			Less: Contributions for government social insurance	Plus: Adjustment for residence	Equals: Net earnings by place of residence	Plus: Dividends, interest, and rent	Plus: Personal current transfer receipts	Personal income	Disposable personal income		
		Nonfarm	Farm	Total									
GEORGIA													
1958	5 973	4 844	361	5 205	186	-11	5 008	587	379	1 570	1 436	3 804	. . .
1959	6 372	5 255	310	5 565	224	-13	5 328	643	401	1 647	1 502	3 868	. . .
1960	6 666	5 481	326	5 807	261	-15	5 531	718	417	1 685	1 523	3 956	. . .
1961	6 949	5 637	347	5 984	266	-16	5 703	773	473	1 731	1 568	4 015	. . .
1962	7 471	6 145	312	6 457	297	-20	6 140	843	488	1 828	1 646	4 086	. . .
1963	8 121	6 652	400	7 052	349	-24	6 679	920	522	1 946	1 751	4 172	. . .
1964	8 803	7 312	334	7 646	376	-29	7 241	1 015	547	2 067	1 874	4 258	. . .
1965	9 708	8 047	377	8 424	407	-35	7 982	1 125	601	2 241	2 026	4 332	. . .
1966	10 691	9 021	389	9 410	545	-43	8 821	1 214	656	2 442	2 193	4 379	. . .
1967	11 619	9 826	386	10 212	624	-52	9 536	1 303	781	2 636	2 377	4 408	. . .
1968	12 865	11 007	343	11 350	682	-62	10 607	1 328	930	2 870	2 556	4 482	. . .
1969	14 332	12 273	420	12 692	786	-76	11 830	1 439	1 063	3 149	2 746	4 551	2 119
1970	15 560	13 138	398	13 536	836	-69	12 631	1 630	1 299	3 379	2 990	4 605	2 121
1971	17 193	14 392	456	14 849	951	-65	13 833	1 814	1 546	3 650	3 265	4 710	2 167
1972	19 341	16 304	471	16 775	1 127	-57	15 591	2 009	1 741	4 023	3 550	4 807	2 253
1973	21 986	18 368	788	19 156	1 444	-55	17 657	2 319	2 010	4 481	3 983	4 907	2 356
1974	24 245	20 006	672	20 678	1 626	-55	18 997	2 736	2 511	4 854	4 314	4 995	2 374
1975	26 089	20 920	638	21 558	1 679	-45	19 834	2 928	3 327	5 157	4 673	5 059	2 313
1976	29 154	23 885	630	24 514	1 945	-77	22 493	3 112	3 548	5 687	5 107	5 126	2 400
1977	32 313	27 069	365	27 434	2 188	-97	25 149	3 483	3 681	6 200	5 534	5 212	2 503
1978	36 742	30 785	568	31 353	2 550	-79	28 724	4 014	4 004	6 951	6 163	5 286	2 621
1979	41 273	34 501	597	35 099	2 972	-96	32 031	4 681	4 562	7 656	6 707	5 391	2 700
1980	46 128	38 164	40	38 204	3 309	-113	34 781	5 891	5 456	8 408	7 397	5 486	2 741
1981	52 303	42 101	524	42 625	3 928	-29	38 668	7 415	6 220	9 393	8 229	5 568	2 776
1982	56 729	44 992	683	45 674	4 282	-69	41 323	8 611	6 794	10 041	8 854	5 650	2 793
1983	62 193	49 613	475	50 088	4 793	-111	45 184	9 631	7 378	10 857	9 558	5 728	2 877
1984	70 880	56 593	955	57 548	5 612	-176	51 761	11 237	7 883	12 148	10 753	5 835	3 068
1985	77 822	62 656	785	63 441	6 362	-192	56 887	12 480	8 455	13 052	11 475	5 963	3 207
1986	84 680	68 697	826	69 524	7 086	-241	62 197	13 477	9 005	13 917	12 252	6 085	3 335
1987	91 137	74 328	897	75 225	7 618	-242	67 365	14 322	9 449	14 679	12 853	6 208	3 433
1988	99 295	80 753	1 158	81 911	8 517	-237	73 156	15 942	10 197	15 721	13 844	6 316	3 545
1989	106 798	84 971	1 358	86 328	9 063	-198	77 067	18 420	11 311	16 658	14 606	6 411	3 608
1990	114 382	90 510	1 262	91 772	9 680	-121	81 971	19 837	12 574	17 563	15 424	6 513	3 664
1991	120 488	94 149	1 566	95 716	10 145	-139	85 432	20 509	14 547	18 110	16 025	6 653	3 622
1992	130 474	102 442	1 642	104 084	10 866	-191	93 027	21 201	16 245	19 139	16 973	6 817	3 698
1993	138 629	109 317	1 477	110 793	11 615	-180	98 998	22 242	17 388	19 866	17 548	6 978	3 866
1994	149 907	117 330	1 942	119 272	12 568	-234	106 470	24 698	18 739	20 945	18 486	7 157	4 020
1995	161 393	126 724	1 766	128 490	13 504	-321	114 664	26 534	20 195	22 023	19 389	7 328	4 188
1996	175 077	137 075	1 858	138 934	14 432	-375	124 127	29 499	21 451	23 340	20 425	7 501	4 333
1997	186 651	146 827	1 816	148 643	15 463	-462	132 719	31 988	21 944	24 287	21 123	7 685	4 449
1998	201 938	159 603	1 806	161 409	16 779	-583	144 047	35 442	22 449	25 680	22 195	7 864	4 610
1999	215 405	173 098	1 945	175 043	18 118	-613	156 312	35 336	23 757	26 772	23 108	8 046	4 739
2000	234 814	188 577	1 842	190 419	19 381	-766	170 272	38 750	25 792	28 541	24 614	8 227	4 854
2001	245 829	196 185	2 212	198 397	20 098	-850	177 450	39 914	28 465	29 346	25 438	8 377	4 856
2002	251 217	200 462	1 636	202 098	20 457	-895	180 746	38 129	32 341	29 526	26 185	8 508	4 879
2003	259 167	208 171	2 147	210 318	21 081	-917	188 319	38 079	32 769	30 056	26 933	8 623	4 918
2004	272 953	220 124	2 163	222 287	22 805	-982	198 500	39 328	35 125	31 126	27 962	8 769	5 058
2005	292 544	232 786	2 478	235 264	23 920	-1 006	210 337	43 856	38 351	32 775	29 203	8 926	5 234
2006	311 855	245 700	1 589	247 289	25 322	-1 016	220 951	50 072	40 832	34 061	30 144	9 156	5 393
2007	330 702	256 692	1 872	258 564	26 354	-1 072	231 138	55 498	44 066	35 369	31 242	9 350	5 532
2008	340 819	258 020	2 642	260 662	27 032	-1 098	232 532	58 752	49 535	35 857	32 126	9 505	5 512
2009	327 555	246 718	2 021	248 739	26 325	-1 155	221 260	50 267	56 028	34 046	31 043	9 621	5 310
2010	337 468	251 383	1 829	253 212	26 836	-1 177	225 199	52 086	60 183	34 747	31 682	9 712	5 274
2011	354 372	261 928	1 725	263 653	25 181	-1 241	237 231	55 131	62 010	36 104	32 514	9 815	. . .

. . . = Not available.

Table 17-2. Personal Income and Employment by Region and State—*Continued*

(Millions of dollars, except as noted.)

Region or state and year	Personal income, total	Derivation of personal income								Per capita (dollars)		Population (thousands)	Total employment (thousands)
		Earnings by place of work			Less: Contributions for government social insurance	Plus: Adjustment for residence	Equals: Net earnings by place of residence	Plus: Dividends, interest, and rent	Plus: Personal current transfer receipts	Personal income	Disposable personal income		
		Nonfarm	Farm	Total									
HAWAII													
1958	1 167	963	64	1 027	40	0	987	138	42	1 929	. . .	605	. . .
1959	1 305	1 077	73	1 151	45	0	1 106	154	46	2 098	. . .	622	. . .
1960	1 493	1 215	82	1 296	52	0	1 244	201	48	2 326	2 002	642	. . .
1961	1 616	1 316	75	1 391	57	0	1 334	223	59	2 452	2 107	659	. . .
1962	1 731	1 402	79	1 481	61	0	1 420	244	67	2 530	2 214	684	. . .
1963	1 846	1 504	88	1 592	76	0	1 516	260	70	2 706	2 372	682	. . .
1964	2 008	1 646	89	1 735	82	0	1 653	285	70	2 868	2 548	700	. . .
1965	2 199	1 794	91	1 885	85	0	1 800	317	81	3 123	2 787	704	. . .
1966	2 403	1 982	95	2 078	113	0	1 964	344	95	3 385	2 973	710	. . .
1967	2 612	2 144	98	2 243	130	0	2 112	379	121	3 612	3 165	723	. . .
1968	2 940	2 441	118	2 559	152	0	2 407	393	140	4 005	3 482	734	. . .
1969	3 367	2 826	119	2 945	183	0	2 763	445	160	4 532	3 882	743	416
1970	3 873	3 238	133	3 371	212	0	3 159	507	207	5 077	4 372	763	434
1971	4 210	3 475	131	3 605	236	0	3 369	571	270	5 319	4 658	792	437
1972	4 640	3 839	131	3 971	274	0	3 697	621	323	5 671	4 902	818	453
1973	5 159	4 297	138	4 435	349	0	4 086	703	370	6 128	5 312	842	473
1974	5 931	4 741	340	5 081	401	0	4 680	806	444	6 911	6 024	858	485
1975	6 472	5 251	202	5 453	443	0	5 010	885	577	7 396	6 600	875	499
1976	7 032	5 735	173	5 909	485	0	5 424	934	674	7 880	6 981	892	505
1977	7 636	6 244	185	6 428	523	0	5 905	1 024	707	8 338	7 352	916	509
1978	8 462	6 943	168	7 111	597	0	6 514	1 188	760	9 111	7 973	929	528
1979	9 594	7 839	194	8 033	701	0	7 332	1 423	839	10 098	8 810	950	556
1980	11 026	8 750	374	9 124	781	0	8 343	1 720	963	11 394	9 959	968	575
1981	11 968	9 450	199	9 650	902	0	8 747	2 089	1 132	12 235	10 701	978	568
1982	12 700	10 058	235	10 292	954	0	9 338	2 135	1 227	12 780	11 394	994	567
1983	14 059	10 839	338	11 177	1 037	0	10 140	2 569	1 350	13 883	12 384	1 013	577
1984	15 325	11 873	239	12 112	1 136	0	10 976	2 925	1 424	14 909	13 348	1 028	582
1985	16 210	12 653	221	12 875	1 238	0	11 637	3 064	1 509	15 591	13 893	1 040	598
1986	17 131	13 457	255	13 712	1 352	0	12 361	3 198	1 572	16 288	14 479	1 052	612
1987	18 281	14 582	240	14 822	1 477	0	13 345	3 309	1 628	17 118	15 007	1 068	643
1988	19 972	16 069	263	16 332	1 700	0	14 632	3 600	1 739	18 496	16 183	1 080	669
1989	22 203	17 715	247	17 962	1 894	0	16 068	4 209	1 926	20 285	17 553	1 095	696
1990	24 294	19 653	260	19 913	2 188	0	17 725	4 481	2 088	21 818	18 901	1 113	724
1991	25 876	21 006	231	21 237	2 358	0	18 879	4 701	2 296	22 763	19 636	1 137	745
1992	27 823	22 489	218	22 707	2 513	0	20 195	4 961	2 667	24 014	21 148	1 159	746
1993	28 811	23 071	215	23 287	2 556	0	20 730	5 159	2 922	24 566	21 665	1 173	742
1994	29 507	23 240	209	23 449	2 588	0	20 861	5 484	3 163	24 847	21 939	1 188	737
1995	30 112	23 295	199	23 494	2 566	0	20 928	5 612	3 572	25 160	22 346	1 197	734
1996	30 399	23 402	195	23 597	2 545	0	21 051	5 687	3 661	25 253	22 316	1 204	733
1997	31 372	23 955	205	24 160	2 550	0	21 610	6 088	3 674	25 892	22 871	1 212	734
1998	32 259	24 464	218	24 681	2 575	0	22 107	6 405	3 747	26 546	23 382	1 215	736
1999	33 244	25 232	245	25 477	2 651	0	22 826	6 511	3 907	27 467	24 145	1 210	735
2000	35 222	26 765	241	27 005	2 785	0	24 221	6 885	4 116	29 024	25 454	1 214	757
2001	35 937	27 357	237	27 594	2 937	0	24 657	6 869	4 411	29 313	25 706	1 226	766
2002	37 475	29 184	250	29 434	3 136	0	26 298	6 412	4 765	30 232	26 960	1 240	758
2003	39 032	31 043	248	31 291	3 363	0	27 928	6 195	4 909	31 197	28 000	1 251	775
2004	42 285	33 560	249	33 809	3 529	0	30 280	6 738	5 267	33 202	29 807	1 274	797
2005	45 332	35 914	259	36 173	3 782	0	32 391	7 243	5 698	35 067	31 110	1 293	822
2006	49 124	38 324	256	38 580	4 055	0	34 525	8 586	6 013	37 507	33 249	1 310	843
2007	52 555	40 224	236	40 460	4 205	0	36 255	9 694	6 606	39 946	35 441	1 316	868
2008	55 314	40 977	249	41 226	4 286	0	36 940	11 050	7 324	41 520	37 173	1 332	863
2009	54 639	40 094	276	40 370	4 235	0	36 135	10 243	8 261	40 572	37 046	1 347	836
2010	56 647	41 199	273	41 471	4 494	0	36 977	10 606	9 064	41 550	37 908	1 363	833
2011	59 190	42 483	274	42 757	4 252	0	38 505	11 243	9 442	43 053	38 904	1 375	. . .

. . . = Not available.

Table 17-2. Personal Income and Employment by Region and State—*Continued*

(Millions of dollars, except as noted.)

Region or state and year	Personal income, total	Derivation of personal income									Per capita (dollars)		Population (thousands)	Total employment (thousands)
		Earnings by place of work			Less: Contributions for government social insurance	Plus: Adjustment for residence	Equals: Net earnings by place of residence	Plus: Dividends, interest, and rent	Plus: Personal current transfer receipts		Personal income	Disposable personal income		
		Nonfarm	Farm	Total										
IDAHO														
1958	1 166	824	165	990	37	-3	949	139	78		1 805	1 628	646	. . .
1959	1 234	883	164	1 047	43	-3	1 001	148	85		1 878	1 690	657	. . .
1960	1 263	912	159	1 071	50	-3	1 018	155	90		1 882	1 683	671	. . .
1961	1 337	970	159	1 129	56	-3	1 070	165	102		1 955	1 761	684	. . .
1962	1 431	1 045	168	1 212	62	-3	1 147	178	106		2 068	1 867	692	. . .
1963	1 461	1 061	175	1 236	69	-2	1 165	188	109		2 140	1 923	683	. . .
1964	1 508	1 140	135	1 275	70	-2	1 203	193	112		2 218	2 019	680	. . .
1965	1 730	1 246	233	1 479	76	-2	1 401	209	120		2 522	2 299	686	. . .
1966	1 756	1 321	180	1 502	93	-1	1 408	219	129		2 549	2 313	689	. . .
1967	1 868	1 386	207	1 593	107	-1	1 486	227	155		2 715	2 454	688	. . .
1968	1 992	1 514	186	1 700	121	-1	1 578	240	174		2 866	2 577	695	. . .
1969	2 307	1 675	253	1 927	127	12	1 812	301	194		3 264	2 912	707	315
1970	2 538	1 828	267	2 094	137	14	1 971	338	229		3 539	3 183	717	324
1971	2 762	1 999	249	2 249	154	15	2 109	384	269		3 739	3 363	739	332
1972	3 154	2 278	321	2 599	183	16	2 432	416	306		4 133	3 741	763	347
1973	3 664	2 588	453	3 041	240	18	2 819	495	351		4 686	4 208	782	365
1974	4 325	2 964	628	3 592	282	22	3 332	572	421		5 353	4 770	808	381
1975	4 636	3 366	387	3 754	316	28	3 466	647	524		5 573	5 011	832	393
1976	5 228	3 916	343	4 259	370	35	3 924	712	591		6 100	5 478	857	419
1977	5 724	4 417	240	4 658	418	35	4 275	822	627		6 479	5 803	883	435
1978	6 607	5 123	309	5 431	487	42	4 986	951	669		7 253	6 478	911	460
1979	7 271	5 658	233	5 891	567	48	5 372	1 118	782		7 796	6 950	933	469
1980	8 187	6 022	408	6 430	605	61	5 886	1 367	935		8 637	7 708	948	464
1981	9 023	6 480	428	6 908	700	52	6 260	1 692	1 071		9 378	8 288	962	462
1982	9 369	6 471	394	6 865	717	62	6 210	1 929	1 230		9 622	8 591	974	452
1983	10 144	6 993	583	7 576	779	63	6 861	1 983	1 301		10 331	9 294	982	463
1984	10 887	7 614	500	8 115	870	77	7 321	2 220	1 346		10 988	9 916	991	472
1985	11 428	8 012	457	8 470	930	83	7 623	2 362	1 443		11 497	10 346	994	474
1986	11 659	8 122	479	8 601	955	99	7 745	2 392	1 522		11 774	10 651	990	474
1987	12 241	8 564	596	9 160	988	108	8 279	2 395	1 567		12 428	11 221	985	487
1988	13 245	9 375	674	10 049	1 121	123	9 051	2 512	1 682		13 437	12 116	986	508
1989	14 550	10 090	881	10 971	1 229	138	9 880	2 845	1 824		14 632	13 045	994	525
1990	15 796	11 028	1 001	12 029	1 417	151	10 764	3 065	1 968		15 603	13 868	1 012	548
1991	16 676	11 819	829	12 648	1 548	173	11 273	3 199	2 204		16 015	14 264	1 041	566
1992	18 286	13 092	876	13 969	1 686	190	12 472	3 346	2 467		17 063	15 106	1 072	586
1993	20 080	14 350	1 086	15 435	1 844	208	13 799	3 625	2 656		18 110	16 073	1 109	612
1994	21 603	15 780	780	16 560	2 032	235	14 764	4 023	2 817		18 865	16 751	1 145	647
1995	23 152	16 673	845	17 518	2 163	279	15 634	4 425	3 093		19 665	17 446	1 177	667
1996	24 693	17 509	953	18 462	2 228	324	16 558	4 829	3 306		20 525	18 175	1 203	689
1997	25 751	18 339	758	19 097	2 324	368	17 141	5 183	3 426		20 961	18 486	1 229	708
1998	27 844	19 655	958	20 613	2 464	436	18 585	5 689	3 570		22 234	19 638	1 252	734
1999	29 684	21 264	1 006	22 271	2 594	503	20 180	5 704	3 800		23 269	20 470	1 276	752
2000	32 076	23 167	1 012	24 179	2 819	525	21 885	6 070	4 122		24 685	21 577	1 299	781
2001	33 877	24 213	1 122	25 334	2 869	522	22 988	6 280	4 609		25 665	22 558	1 320	786
2002	34 906	25 048	1 094	26 142	2 947	524	23 719	6 194	4 993		26 042	23 557	1 340	791
2003	36 065	26 046	853	26 900	3 065	549	24 385	6 387	5 293		26 452	24 097	1 363	802
2004	39 544	27 965	1 370	29 335	3 266	587	26 655	7 217	5 672		28 412	25 920	1 392	826
2005	42 197	29 853	1 209	31 062	3 548	597	28 111	7 971	6 115		29 544	26 528	1 428	862
2006	46 253	32 832	1 130	33 962	3 955	628	30 635	9 002	6 616		31 493	28 045	1 469	905
2007	49 077	34 058	1 611	35 670	4 130	673	32 213	9 663	7 201		32 607	29 004	1 505	933
2008	50 801	34 055	1 848	35 903	4 149	740	32 495	10 293	8 014		33 110	29 800	1 534	924
2009	48 183	32 328	1 342	33 670	4 070	758	30 359	8 588	9 236		30 997	28 554	1 554	884
2010	50 114	33 205	1 566	34 771	4 311	750	31 210	8 911	9 993		31 897	29 446	1 571	877
2011	52 821	34 075	2 220	36 294	4 077	804	33 021	9 461	10 338		33 326	30 510	1 585	. . .

. . . = Not available.

Table 17-2. Personal Income and Employment by Region and State—*Continued*

(Millions of dollars, except as noted.)

Region or state and year	Personal income, total	Earnings by place of work			Less: Contributions for government social insurance	Plus: Adjustment for residence	Equals: Net earnings by place of residence	Plus: Dividends, interest, and rent	Plus: Personal current transfer receipts	Per capita (dollars)		Population (thousands)	Total employment (thousands)
		Nonfarm	Farm	Total						Personal income	Disposable personal income		
ILLINOIS													
1958	24 589	20 153	862	21 015	704	-110	20 201	3 038	1 350	2 487	2 207	9 886	. . .
1959	26 096	21 755	659	22 414	852	-127	21 435	3 254	1 407	2 613	2 318	9 986	. . .
1960	26 933	22 490	648	23 137	1 073	-132	21 932	3 529	1 472	2 670	2 350	10 086	. . .
1961	27 956	22 907	814	23 721	1 088	-138	22 495	3 761	1 699	2 760	2 437	10 130	. . .
1962	29 508	24 201	798	24 999	1 195	-153	23 651	4 094	1 763	2 870	2 526	10 280	. . .
1963	30 668	25 114	822	25 935	1 329	-158	24 448	4 405	1 815	2 948	2 601	10 402	. . .
1964	32 760	26 966	666	27 631	1 337	-174	26 120	4 793	1 847	3 096	2 771	10 580	. . .
1965	35 514	28 954	903	29 857	1 356	-194	28 308	5 225	1 981	3 321	2 964	10 693	. . .
1966	38 472	31 879	977	32 856	1 820	-222	30 814	5 514	2 145	3 550	3 142	10 836	. . .
1967	40 914	33 873	936	34 809	1 986	-238	32 585	5 774	2 555	3 737	3 295	10 947	. . .
1968	43 842	36 610	692	37 302	2 192	-264	34 846	6 003	2 993	3 987	3 475	10 995	. . .
1969	47 837	39 953	913	40 866	2 717	94	38 243	6 357	3 236	4 333	3 706	11 039	5 179
1970	50 816	42 169	723	42 892	2 811	19	40 100	6 879	3 837	4 568	3 928	11 125	5 144
1971	54 544	44 867	885	45 752	3 075	-22	42 655	7 298	4 590	4 867	4 252	11 206	5 104
1972	59 242	48 790	1 000	49 790	3 518	-41	46 231	7 844	5 167	5 262	4 538	11 258	5 155
1973	66 343	54 066	1 842	55 907	4 491	-58	51 359	8 837	6 147	5 892	5 117	11 260	5 351
1974	72 735	59 106	1 674	60 780	5 079	-69	55 632	10 095	7 008	6 452	5 579	11 274	5 441
1975	79 233	62 176	2 465	64 641	5 196	-95	59 350	10 899	8 984	7 008	6 146	11 306	5 342
1976	86 566	69 296	1 715	71 011	5 882	-74	65 054	11 598	9 914	7 620	6 620	11 360	5 458
1977	95 351	76 899	1 718	78 617	6 516	-8	72 094	12 886	10 371	8 359	7 243	11 406	5 587
1978	105 450	85 878	1 514	87 392	7 467	80	80 005	14 407	11 038	9 222	7 968	11 434	5 748
1979	115 824	93 867	1 839	95 707	8 483	165	87 388	16 413	12 023	10 140	8 697	11 423	5 803
1980	125 551	99 252	383	99 635	8 955	266	90 946	20 021	14 584	10 980	9 439	11 435	5 675
1981	139 036	106 001	1 526	107 528	10 260	204	97 471	24 808	16 756	12 150	10 424	11 443	5 664
1982	147 000	108 791	917	109 707	10 701	133	99 139	29 460	18 400	12 868	11 231	11 423	5 563
1983	153 106	113 692	-486	113 206	11 259	99	102 046	31 357	19 702	13 420	11 790	11 409	5 520
1984	168 437	124 773	1 226	126 000	12 810	-6	113 184	35 183	20 071	14 760	13 036	11 412	5 718
1985	176 973	131 686	1 716	133 402	13 763	-74	119 565	36 463	20 946	15 524	13 665	11 400	5 780
1986	185 656	139 605	1 426	141 031	14 681	-125	126 224	37 728	21 703	16 304	14 367	11 387	5 892
1987	196 340	150 002	1 435	151 437	15 563	-212	135 662	38 522	22 156	17 236	15 034	11 391	6 031
1988	211 302	164 263	862	165 125	17 350	-340	147 435	40 956	22 912	18 551	16 284	11 390	6 187
1989	224 449	172 359	2 173	174 532	18 409	-354	155 769	44 347	24 333	19 672	17 149	11 410	6 294
1990	238 635	182 888	1 764	184 652	19 126	-272	165 253	46 826	26 556	20 835	18 180	11 453	6 390
1991	244 660	187 235	978	188 214	20 062	-285	167 867	48 199	28 594	21 148	18 568	11 569	6 369
1992	263 740	200 813	2 060	202 872	21 162	-331	181 379	49 624	32 737	22 553	19 908	11 694	6 351
1993	272 422	209 273	1 715	210 988	22 340	-492	188 156	49 923	34 344	23 068	20 269	11 810	6 441
1994	288 060	220 653	2 309	222 962	23 829	-513	198 620	53 856	35 583	24 181	21 176	11 913	6 611
1995	304 796	233 873	610	234 482	25 100	-772	208 610	58 300	37 887	25 382	22 179	12 008	6 773
1996	324 408	245 850	2 501	248 351	26 167	-823	221 361	63 219	39 827	26 806	23 282	12 102	6 875
1997	342 789	261 285	2 144	263 428	27 611	-868	234 948	67 300	40 541	28 130	24 251	12 186	6 981
1998	365 040	278 941	1 539	280 480	29 288	-847	250 345	73 364	41 331	29 746	25 509	12 272	7 133
1999	378 415	295 252	1 078	296 330	30 701	-1 045	264 584	71 795	42 037	30 619	26 170	12 359	7 218
2000	405 919	314 541	1 794	316 335	32 402	-1 344	282 590	78 603	44 726	32 645	27 885	12 434	7 355
2001	415 020	322 460	1 662	324 122	33 177	-1 652	289 294	77 482	48 244	33 232	28 564	12 488	7 317
2002	423 278	330 799	956	331 755	33 600	-1 619	296 536	74 798	51 945	33 793	29 734	12 526	7 220
2003	435 901	343 833	1 949	345 782	34 500	-1 573	309 709	72 032	54 160	34 717	30 969	12 556	7 198
2004	455 291	359 386	3 740	363 127	36 705	-1 729	324 692	74 416	56 182	36 164	32 360	12 590	7 250
2005	472 073	371 380	1 830	373 210	38 861	-1 701	332 648	77 896	61 528	37 437	33 141	12 610	7 336
2006	504 493	391 781	2 078	393 859	40 815	-1 894	351 151	90 967	62 375	39 900	35 081	12 644	7 448
2007	532 587	405 072	3 190	408 262	42 674	-2 246	363 342	100 169	69 076	41 950	36 583	12 696	7 572
2008	554 521	411 802	5 651	417 453	43 534	-1 880	372 039	109 373	73 110	43 502	38 376	12 747	7 554
2009	525 247	389 863	4 045	393 908	41 653	-1 786	350 469	89 253	85 524	41 045	37 044	12 797	7 310
2010	539 880	396 866	3 590	400 456	42 263	-1 844	356 348	91 764	91 767	42 040	37 981	12 842	7 276
2011	568 049	413 222	5 710	418 932	39 664	-1 914	377 355	97 427	93 268	44 140	39 206	12 869	. . .

. . . = Not available.

Table 17-2. Personal Income and Employment by Region and State—*Continued*

(Millions of dollars, except as noted.)

Region or state and year	Personal income, total	Derivation of personal income								Per capita (dollars)		Population (thou-sands)	Total employ-ment (thou-sands)
		Earnings by place of work			Less: Contribu-tions for govern-ment social insurance	Plus: Adjust-ment for residence	Equals: Net earnings by place of residence	Plus: Dividends, interest, and rent	Plus: Personal current transfer receipts	Personal income	Disposable personal income		
		Nonfarm	Farm	Total									
INDIANA													
1958	9 198	7 479	424	7 903	295	35	7 643	985	570	2 007	1 816	4 583	. . .
1959	9 784	8 178	295	8 473	356	41	8 157	1 056	571	2 121	1 907	4 613	. . .
1960	10 289	8 528	366	8 894	415	40	8 519	1 166	604	2 201	1 964	4 674	. . .
1961	10 595	8 579	464	9 042	411	43	8 674	1 228	692	2 240	2 011	4 730	. . .
1962	11 345	9 282	452	9 734	461	48	9 322	1 327	697	2 396	2 138	4 736	. . .
1963	11 916	9 771	470	10 241	526	48	9 763	1 429	724	2 483	2 203	4 799	. . .
1964	12 690	10 598	301	10 899	545	46	10 400	1 541	749	2 613	2 342	4 856	. . .
1965	14 038	11 553	553	12 106	581	49	11 574	1 658	806	2 852	2 553	4 922	. . .
1966	15 151	12 804	480	13 284	818	55	12 521	1 764	866	3 031	2 687	4 999	. . .
1967	15 873	13 422	431	13 853	916	59	12 996	1 866	1 011	3 141	2 777	5 053	. . .
1968	17 258	14 659	379	15 038	992	69	14 114	1 964	1 180	3 389	2 971	5 093	. . .
1969	18 990	16 012	550	16 563	1 097	25	15 491	2 220	1 279	3 692	3 193	5 143	2 327
1970	19 730	16 470	381	16 850	1 116	58	15 792	2 437	1 501	3 791	3 319	5 204	2 291
1971	21 453	17 524	596	18 120	1 229	118	17 009	2 653	1 790	4 086	3 616	5 250	2 290
1972	23 510	19 483	507	19 990	1 442	151	18 698	2 841	1 970	4 439	3 887	5 296	2 367
1973	27 088	21 953	1 228	23 182	1 865	195	21 512	3 241	2 335	5 083	4 494	5 329	2 483
1974	29 014	23 617	735	24 352	2 091	256	22 516	3 741	2 757	5 423	4 720	5 350	2 493
1975	31 235	24 288	1 098	25 386	2 122	301	23 565	4 159	3 512	5 837	5 175	5 351	2 405
1976	34 939	27 777	1 077	28 854	2 440	351	26 765	4 509	3 665	6 504	5 709	5 372	2 489
1977	38 740	31 431	725	32 156	2 757	413	29 812	5 079	3 849	7 167	6 267	5 405	2 578
1978	43 299	35 399	732	36 132	3 196	467	33 403	5 661	4 236	7 950	6 921	5 446	2 670
1979	47 774	38 892	673	39 565	3 636	543	36 472	6 435	4 867	8 726	7 563	5 475	2 708
1980	51 357	40 023	380	40 403	3 725	666	37 344	7 928	6 085	9 353	8 168	5 491	2 626
1981	56 380	42 996	309	43 305	4 286	712	39 730	9 849	6 801	10 287	8 941	5 480	2 603
1982	58 360	43 033	309	43 342	4 378	776	39 739	11 043	7 578	10 673	9 360	5 468	2 522
1983	60 957	45 301	-260	45 041	4 660	827	41 208	11 590	8 159	11 184	9 872	5 450	2 542
1984	67 695	49 743	752	50 495	5 258	989	46 227	12 910	8 558	12 402	10 994	5 458	2 642
1985	71 327	52 601	680	53 281	5 686	1 075	48 669	13 649	9 008	13 065	11 538	5 459	2 695
1986	74 932	55 494	578	56 071	6 056	1 169	51 184	14 235	9 512	13 739	12 161	5 454	2 755
1987	79 482	59 691	766	60 457	6 435	1 238	55 260	14 523	9 698	14 522	12 805	5 473	2 849
1988	84 704	64 611	289	64 900	7 220	1 362	59 043	15 390	10 271	15 424	13 606	5 492	2 935
1989	92 067	68 799	965	69 764	7 738	1 428	63 454	17 465	11 148	16 668	14 629	5 524	3 010
1990	97 005	72 470	864	73 334	8 410	1 503	66 427	18 463	12 114	17 454	15 331	5 558	3 070
1991	100 334	75 774	243	76 018	8 899	1 527	68 646	18 357	13 331	17 865	15 747	5 616	3 072
1992	108 377	81 376	853	82 228	9 475	1 740	74 493	18 646	15 238	19 099	16 906	5 675	3 121
1993	114 121	86 101	869	86 970	10 081	1 927	78 815	19 212	16 094	19 885	17 552	5 739	3 197
1994	121 510	91 945	831	92 776	10 920	2 076	83 932	20 790	16 788	20 973	18 438	5 794	3 287
1995	126 651	96 177	353	96 531	11 441	2 329	87 419	22 167	17 065	21 644	18 994	5 851	3 379
1996	133 798	100 178	1 197	101 375	11 831	2 470	92 014	23 784	18 001	22 655	19 815	5 906	3 418
1997	140 588	105 447	1 167	106 614	12 429	2 633	96 819	25 295	18 474	23 607	20 548	5 955	3 476
1998	150 987	113 416	771	114 188	13 214	2 665	103 639	28 158	19 191	25 169	21 848	5 999	3 546
1999	156 559	119 284	471	119 756	13 857	3 017	108 916	27 522	20 121	25 899	22 490	6 045	3 599
2000	167 276	126 035	864	126 899	14 435	3 356	115 820	29 788	21 668	27 459	23 983	6 092	3 647
2001	171 750	128 731	1 051	129 782	14 624	3 418	118 576	29 220	23 953	28 028	24 560	6 128	3 588
2002	175 300	133 050	451	133 501	15 007	3 329	121 823	28 048	25 429	28 476	25 314	6 156	3 547
2003	182 704	140 127	1 297	141 424	15 544	3 367	129 247	27 009	26 448	29 484	26 518	6 197	3 548
2004	190 283	145 308	2 062	147 370	16 284	3 617	134 703	27 540	28 040	30 528	27 543	6 233	3 586
2005	195 526	149 729	1 386	151 115	17 029	3 786	137 872	27 158	30 495	31 141	27 902	6 279	3 626
2006	206 868	155 673	1 228	156 901	17 931	4 048	143 018	30 964	32 886	32 667	29 146	6 333	3 666
2007	214 641	159 227	1 523	160 750	18 463	4 391	146 678	33 414	34 548	33 645	29 843	6 380	3 716
2008	224 188	161 495	2 759	164 254	18 920	4 399	149 734	36 165	38 290	34 894	31 170	6 425	3 680
2009	215 243	152 564	2 156	154 720	18 102	4 201	140 820	30 638	43 785	33 323	30 366	6 459	3 522
2010	220 555	155 684	2 049	157 733	18 475	3 937	143 195	31 622	45 739	33 981	30 900	6 491	3 535
2011	231 674	161 955	2 812	164 767	17 236	4 166	151 697	33 443	46 534	35 550	31 970	6 517	. . .

. . . = Not available.

Table 17-2. Personal Income and Employment by Region and State—*Continued*

(Millions of dollars, except as noted.)

Region or state and year	Personal income, total	Earnings by place of work			Less: Contributions for government social insurance	Plus: Adjustment for residence	Equals: Net earnings by place of residence	Plus: Dividends, interest, and rent	Plus: Personal current transfer receipts	Per capita (dollars)		Population (thousands)	Total employment (thousands)
		Nonfarm	Farm	Total						Personal income	Disposable personal income		
IOWA													
1958	5 394	3 436	1 012	4 448	135	27	4 340	722	331	1 992	1 802	2 708	. . .
1959	5 527	3 768	743	4 511	166	29	4 375	790	362	2 025	1 837	2 729	. . .
1960	5 673	3 884	732	4 616	186	33	4 464	824	385	2 058	1 850	2 756	. . .
1961	6 009	3 996	853	4 848	189	36	4 695	890	424	2 180	1 969	2 756	. . .
1962	6 271	4 179	884	5 063	203	39	4 898	929	444	2 280	2 060	2 750	. . .
1963	6 670	4 403	1 001	5 405	233	41	5 213	993	464	2 428	2 195	2 747	. . .
1964	6 985	4 722	922	5 644	247	44	5 441	1 064	479	2 544	2 319	2 746	. . .
1965	7 747	5 055	1 248	6 303	261	48	6 091	1 134	522	2 825	2 570	2 742	. . .
1966	8 436	5 623	1 347	6 970	352	52	6 670	1 200	566	3 054	2 749	2 762	. . .
1967	8 595	6 017	1 081	7 098	418	56	6 736	1 184	675	3 077	2 763	2 793	. . .
1968	9 231	6 487	1 021	7 508	457	60	7 111	1 338	782	3 293	2 933	2 803	. . .
1969	10 280	7 108	1 239	8 347	544	82	7 885	1 540	856	3 665	3 233	2 805	1 289
1970	10 968	7 539	1 216	8 754	568	89	8 275	1 701	992	3 878	3 448	2 829	1 295
1971	11 480	8 041	1 013	9 054	627	88	8 515	1 838	1 127	4 025	3 620	2 852	1 297
1972	12 867	8 773	1 485	10 258	720	94	9 632	2 019	1 216	4 498	3 979	2 861	1 316
1973	15 492	9 873	2 732	12 605	931	88	11 761	2 327	1 404	5 409	4 824	2 864	1 374
1974	16 069	11 080	1 722	12 801	1 094	84	11 792	2 652	1 626	5 603	4 865	2 868	1 407
1975	17 954	12 049	1 972	14 021	1 169	100	12 952	2 986	2 017	6 231	5 500	2 881	1 407
1976	19 152	13 715	1 229	14 944	1 324	92	13 712	3 225	2 215	6 596	5 772	2 904	1 455
1977	21 177	15 320	1 228	16 548	1 461	65	15 152	3 684	2 341	7 267	6 363	2 914	1 488
1978	24 460	16 943	2 444	19 387	1 675	62	17 774	4 105	2 581	8 379	7 361	2 919	1 513
1979	26 233	18 970	1 577	20 547	1 960	71	18 659	4 682	2 892	8 994	7 820	2 917	1 554
1980	27 894	20 091	719	20 811	2 067	92	18 836	5 653	3 405	9 573	8 307	2 914	1 537
1981	31 521	21 234	1 643	22 878	2 329	117	20 666	6 980	3 876	10 840	9 413	2 908	1 507
1982	32 452	21 253	818	22 071	2 357	190	19 904	8 129	4 419	11 236	9 861	2 888	1 471
1983	33 094	22 096	6	22 101	2 426	205	19 880	8 477	4 736	11 529	10 205	2 871	1 474
1984	36 633	23 715	1 462	25 177	2 684	238	22 731	9 050	4 852	12 815	11 508	2 859	1 499
1985	37 832	24 338	1 750	26 088	2 810	278	23 555	9 127	5 150	13 370	12 002	2 830	1 495
1986	39 067	25 059	2 129	27 188	2 967	271	24 492	9 231	5 344	13 993	12 591	2 792	1 494
1987	40 912	26 871	2 463	29 333	3 174	268	26 427	9 025	5 459	14 786	13 178	2 767	1 514
1988	42 096	28 858	1 653	30 511	3 544	310	27 277	9 125	5 694	15 206	13 519	2 768	1 557
1989	45 670	30 720	2 400	33 120	3 789	319	29 650	9 949	6 071	16 484	14 595	2 771	1 600
1990	48 250	32 468	2 505	34 973	4 105	328	31 196	10 456	6 598	17 350	15 330	2 781	1 635
1991	49 518	33 932	1 782	35 714	4 325	381	31 770	10 643	7 105	17 700	15 681	2 798	1 654
1992	52 954	36 156	2 705	38 861	4 578	407	34 691	10 590	7 674	18 789	16 723	2 818	1 669
1993	53 053	37 989	893	38 882	4 831	391	34 442	10 576	8 034	18 700	16 573	2 837	1 692
1994	58 062	40 511	2 865	43 375	5 204	404	38 575	11 137	8 349	20 367	18 108	2 851	1 725
1995	60 232	42 641	1 824	44 465	5 473	467	39 459	11 992	8 781	21 006	18 636	2 867	1 785
1996	65 627	44 647	3 725	48 372	5 468	521	43 425	12 981	9 221	22 787	20 228	2 880	1 815
1997	68 655	47 210	3 407	50 618	5 996	604	45 226	13 951	9 478	23 747	20 918	2 891	1 841
1998	72 276	50 985	2 164	53 149	6 369	692	47 472	15 086	9 718	24 898	21 923	2 903	1 883
1999	74 512	54 093	1 595	55 688	6 639	768	49 817	14 602	10 093	25 539	22 497	2 918	1 899
2000	79 920	57 007	2 443	59 449	6 886	873	53 436	15 667	10 816	27 285	24 129	2 929	1 921
2001	81 827	58 325	2 238	60 564	7 097	939	54 405	15 721	11 701	27 908	24 736	2 932	1 901
2002	84 573	60 264	2 098	62 362	7 223	992	56 131	15 555	12 887	28 823	26 020	2 934	1 878
2003	86 489	62 968	2 396	65 364	7 560	1 037	58 842	14 824	12 824	29 398	26 741	2 942	1 874
2004	93 316	66 705	4 847	71 552	7 943	1 070	64 680	15 337	13 299	31 594	28 849	2 954	1 904
2005	95 467	69 695	3 982	73 677	8 360	1 018	66 335	15 012	14 119	32 204	29 150	2 964	1 937
2006	100 573	73 126	3 064	76 190	8 824	1 038	68 404	16 654	15 514	33 719	30 320	2 983	1 966
2007	107 500	76 125	4 037	80 162	9 264	1 218	72 117	18 871	16 513	35 843	31 967	2 999	1 991
2008	115 583	78 812	6 039	84 851	9 703	1 264	76 412	21 142	18 029	38 314	34 374	3 017	1 997
2009	112 537	77 229	4 933	82 162	9 614	1 252	73 800	18 374	20 363	37 106	33 929	3 033	1 958
2010	116 027	79 616	4 873	84 489	9 946	1 343	75 886	18 765	21 376	38 039	34 772	3 050	1 953
2011	123 933	82 812	7 565	90 377	9 356	1 375	82 395	19 745	21 793	40 470	36 688	3 062	. . .

. . . = Not available.

Table 17-2. Personal Income and Employment by Region and State—*Continued*

(Millions of dollars, except as noted.)

Region or state and year	Personal income, total	Earnings by place of work Nonfarm	Earnings by place of work Farm	Earnings by place of work Total	Less: Contributions for government social insurance	Plus: Adjustment for residence	Equals: Net earnings by place of residence	Plus: Dividends, interest, and rent	Plus: Personal current transfer receipts	Per capita (dollars) Personal income	Per capita (dollars) Disposable personal income	Population (thousands)	Total employment (thousands)
KANSAS													
1958	4 453	3 024	528	3 552	121	147	3 578	617	258	2 079	1 882	2 142	. . .
1959	4 487	3 176	366	3 542	142	163	3 563	644	280	2 078	1 880	2 160	. . .
1960	4 674	3 237	443	3 680	161	173	3 693	680	302	2 141	1 921	2 183	. . .
1961	4 877	3 391	451	3 842	177	176	3 841	701	335	2 202	1 978	2 215	. . .
1962	5 081	3 575	423	3 997	183	192	4 006	730	345	2 278	2 037	2 231	. . .
1963	5 211	3 681	404	4 085	206	212	4 091	754	366	2 350	2 093	2 217	. . .
1964	5 480	3 925	369	4 293	213	234	4 314	787	379	2 481	2 253	2 209	. . .
1965	5 845	4 097	463	4 559	222	257	4 595	838	413	2 650	2 405	2 206	. . .
1966	6 272	4 494	479	4 973	293	292	4 972	857	444	2 851	2 552	2 200	. . .
1967	6 569	4 788	407	5 196	339	322	5 179	859	532	2 990	2 670	2 197	. . .
1968	7 141	5 254	401	5 654	376	353	5 631	893	616	3 222	2 849	2 216	. . .
1969	7 950	5 720	465	6 185	423	441	6 203	1 058	689	3 555	3 117	2 236	1 029
1970	8 596	6 033	606	6 639	444	439	6 634	1 158	803	3 824	3 377	2 248	1 017
1971	9 326	6 506	706	7 212	494	430	7 148	1 261	916	4 152	3 720	2 246	1 022
1972	10 418	7 207	963	8 170	575	453	8 047	1 386	985	4 619	4 099	2 256	1 048
1973	11 944	8 099	1 386	9 485	737	468	9 216	1 577	1 151	5 275	4 672	2 264	1 090
1974	12 949	9 080	1 060	10 140	856	483	9 767	1 858	1 324	5 710	5 000	2 268	1 122
1975	14 140	10 057	807	10 865	938	497	10 423	2 104	1 613	6 206	5 503	2 279	1 133
1976	15 438	11 386	585	11 971	1 070	514	11 414	2 243	1 781	6 716	5 950	2 299	1 169
1977	16 871	12 552	499	13 050	1 176	559	12 434	2 511	1 927	7 279	6 404	2 318	1 208
1978	18 709	14 255	287	14 542	1 375	604	13 771	2 836	2 102	8 020	7 032	2 333	1 252
1979	21 406	16 088	706	16 794	1 617	651	15 829	3 258	2 319	9 119	7 917	2 347	1 296
1980	23 546	17 644	101	17 744	1 760	727	16 711	4 078	2 756	9 939	8 616	2 369	1 309
1981	26 704	19 307	347	19 654	2 066	752	18 341	5 187	3 177	11 197	9 613	2 385	1 322
1982	28 948	20 021	577	20 598	2 191	775	19 182	6 201	3 564	12 056	10 397	2 401	1 306
1983	30 134	21 024	383	21 407	2 288	749	19 869	6 465	3 800	12 475	10 983	2 416	1 323
1984	33 037	23 055	750	23 805	2 567	792	22 030	7 089	3 918	13 629	12 118	2 424	1 365
1985	34 742	24 138	809	24 948	2 733	837	23 052	7 558	4 132	14 312	12 672	2 427	1 368
1986	36 385	25 451	938	26 389	2 885	821	24 324	7 726	4 335	14 957	13 352	2 433	1 368
1987	38 068	26 764	1 175	27 939	3 003	894	25 829	7 782	4 457	15 567	13 787	2 445	1 421
1988	39 901	28 250	1 145	29 396	3 310	905	26 990	8 234	4 676	16 207	14 353	2 462	1 432
1989	42 059	29 956	831	30 787	3 497	954	28 244	8 685	5 130	17 008	14 949	2 473	1 454
1990	44 750	31 531	1 383	32 915	3 858	972	30 029	9 152	5 569	18 034	15 921	2 481	1 474
1991	46 489	32 913	1 036	33 949	4 087	951	30 814	9 632	6 044	18 605	16 497	2 499	1 489
1992	49 914	35 530	1 410	36 941	4 349	962	33 554	9 657	6 702	19 710	17 573	2 532	1 502
1993	52 079	37 327	1 348	38 676	4 559	1 056	35 173	9 804	7 101	20 371	18 109	2 557	1 525
1994	54 796	39 435	1 437	40 872	4 859	929	36 942	10 520	7 334	21 235	18 854	2 581	1 551
1995	56 883	41 438	797	42 235	5 049	1 096	38 282	10 887	7 714	21 870	19 307	2 601	1 600
1996	60 802	43 666	1 509	45 175	5 279	1 150	41 046	11 787	7 969	23 255	20 446	2 615	1 632
1997	64 576	46 718	1 425	48 143	5 630	1 057	43 570	12 646	8 360	24 504	21 387	2 635	1 677
1998	69 261	50 498	1 312	51 810	6 024	1 082	46 868	13 897	8 496	26 032	22 722	2 661	1 724
1999	71 848	53 356	1 402	54 758	6 294	971	49 435	13 548	8 865	26 826	23 406	2 678	1 739
2000	76 684	56 935	1 007	57 942	6 599	1 078	52 420	14 647	9 617	28 468	24 833	2 694	1 758
2001	80 151	59 866	1 151	61 017	6 849	978	55 145	14 501	10 505	29 662	26 012	2 702	1 771
2002	80 705	61 007	476	61 483	6 972	1 002	55 513	14 007	11 184	29 742	26 593	2 714	1 748
2003	83 901	63 523	1 649	65 173	7 146	884	58 911	13 341	11 649	30 812	27 869	2 723	1 737
2004	87 177	66 652	1 608	68 261	7 495	822	61 587	13 611	11 978	31 882	28 899	2 734	1 747
2005	90 876	69 275	1 943	71 219	7 844	913	64 288	13 952	12 636	33 102	29 676	2 745	1 761
2006	98 577	74 081	1 170	75 252	8 350	889	67 791	17 170	13 617	35 678	31 761	2 763	1 794
2007	104 847	77 288	1 569	78 857	8 734	780	70 903	19 333	14 611	37 663	33 248	2 784	1 844
2008	113 633	81 038	2 494	83 532	9 128	883	75 287	22 551	15 795	40 466	36 015	2 808	1 860
2009	108 496	77 398	2 231	79 629	8 847	1 047	71 829	18 657	18 011	38 301	34 820	2 833	1 816
2010	111 441	79 324	2 219	81 543	9 128	881	73 295	19 304	18 842	38 977	35 383	2 859	1 805
2011	116 230	82 041	2 264	84 305	8 556	871	76 620	20 475	19 135	40 481	36 410	2 871	. . .

. . . = Not available.

Table 17-2. Personal Income and Employment by Region and State—*Continued*

(Millions of dollars, except as noted.)

Region or state and year	Personal income, total	Earnings by place of work			Less: Contributions for government social insurance	Plus: Adjustment for residence	Equals: Net earnings by place of residence	Plus: Dividends, interest, and rent	Plus: Personal current transfer receipts	Per capita (dollars)		Population (thousands)	Total employment (thousands)
		Nonfarm	Farm	Total						Personal income	Disposable personal income		
KENTUCKY													
1958	4 531	3 343	363	3 706	142	83	3 648	504	379	1 530	1 384	2 961	. . .
1959	4 762	3 570	336	3 906	169	97	3 835	534	393	1 588	1 436	2 999	. . .
1960	4 917	3 671	323	3 994	184	97	3 907	581	429	1 617	1 459	3 041	. . .
1961	5 235	3 767	397	4 163	184	89	4 067	613	555	1 714	1 557	3 054	. . .
1962	5 558	4 104	396	4 500	209	92	4 383	671	504	1 805	1 627	3 079	. . .
1963	5 846	4 371	405	4 776	240	92	4 628	713	504	1 888	1 705	3 096	. . .
1964	6 109	4 666	298	4 964	245	99	4 818	762	530	1 953	1 774	3 129	. . .
1965	6 631	5 041	366	5 407	258	107	5 256	797	579	2 112	1 915	3 140	. . .
1966	7 247	5 618	382	6 001	339	116	5 778	842	627	2 303	2 065	3 147	. . .
1967	7 844	6 114	383	6 497	399	95	6 193	905	746	2 473	2 229	3 172	. . .
1968	8 580	6 774	372	7 146	445	104	6 805	932	843	2 686	2 397	3 195	. . .
1969	9 478	7 416	428	7 843	511	174	7 507	1 027	944	2 964	2 596	3 198	1 332
1970	10 260	7 991	393	8 385	549	164	8 000	1 155	1 105	3 176	2 811	3 231	1 336
1971	11 157	8 704	408	9 111	616	107	8 602	1 257	1 298	3 383	3 022	3 298	1 360
1972	12 360	9 651	507	10 158	716	101	9 543	1 376	1 441	3 705	3 266	3 336	1 392
1973	13 931	10 964	579	11 543	922	59	10 680	1 532	1 720	4 132	3 685	3 372	1 461
1974	15 700	12 265	665	12 931	1 063	26	11 893	1 756	2 051	4 595	4 018	3 417	1 496
1975	17 137	13 216	483	13 699	1 124	11	12 586	1 968	2 584	4 940	4 419	3 469	1 465
1976	19 266	15 043	557	15 600	1 293	-23	14 284	2 160	2 823	5 457	4 862	3 530	1 523
1977	21 718	17 052	683	17 736	1 454	1	16 282	2 477	2 959	6 075	5 367	3 575	1 579
1978	24 406	19 343	605	19 948	1 690	13	18 271	2 963	3 172	6 758	5 953	3 611	1 645
1979	27 703	21 619	679	22 299	1 950	4	20 353	3 652	3 698	7 603	6 701	3 644	1 665
1980	29 727	22 679	561	23 241	2 064	28	21 205	4 067	4 454	8 113	7 173	3 664	1 642
1981	33 005	24 426	941	25 366	2 407	-7	22 952	5 027	5 026	8 992	7 901	3 670	1 634
1982	35 183	25 327	903	26 230	2 539	-16	23 675	6 022	5 486	9 552	8 419	3 683	1 616
1983	36 432	26 505	232	26 737	2 654	11	24 094	6 397	5 942	9 861	8 743	3 694	1 624
1984	40 781	29 267	1 120	30 388	3 000	-66	27 322	7 242	6 218	11 035	9 881	3 695	1 676
1985	42 503	30 693	875	31 568	3 218	-77	28 272	7 723	6 507	11 503	10 252	3 695	1 698
1986	43 584	31 576	648	32 224	3 453	-47	28 723	8 049	6 812	11 819	10 529	3 688	1 733
1987	45 987	33 793	734	34 527	3 682	-76	30 768	8 173	7 045	12 485	11 066	3 683	1 765
1988	49 877	37 036	783	37 819	4 089	-88	33 642	8 766	7 469	13 553	12 062	3 680	1 816
1989	53 430	38 953	1 142	40 095	4 383	-133	35 579	9 657	8 193	14 530	12 838	3 677	1 865
1990	56 741	41 191	1 124	42 315	4 789	-94	37 432	10 342	8 967	15 360	13 544	3 694	1 906
1991	60 088	43 165	1 125	44 290	5 079	-131	39 080	10 802	10 205	16 142	14 328	3 722	1 903
1992	64 578	46 972	1 312	48 283	5 513	-398	42 372	10 998	11 208	17 150	15 226	3 765	1 949
1993	66 918	49 241	1 118	50 359	5 866	-406	44 087	11 166	11 666	17 554	15 560	3 812	1 993
1994	70 469	51 923	1 168	53 092	6 306	-511	46 275	11 961	12 233	18 308	16 193	3 849	2 035
1995	73 774	54 326	712	55 038	6 619	-542	47 877	12 766	13 132	18 978	16 724	3 887	2 110
1996	78 319	56 888	1 139	58 026	6 887	-602	50 537	13 886	13 896	19 982	17 571	3 920	2 141
1997	83 089	60 404	1 146	61 550	7 290	-616	53 644	14 760	14 684	21 021	18 383	3 953	2 189
1998	88 652	64 647	1 014	65 661	7 736	-552	57 373	16 199	15 080	22 244	19 420	3 985	2 228
1999	92 545	69 034	783	69 817	8 252	-641	60 923	15 953	15 668	23 032	20 103	4 018	2 271
2000	100 354	73 684	1 485	75 169	8 517	-655	65 998	17 508	16 849	24 785	21 725	4 049	2 314
2001	103 181	75 720	1 067	76 787	8 748	-744	67 295	17 500	18 386	25 363	22 221	4 068	2 282
2002	105 747	78 504	655	79 159	9 031	-823	69 306	16 704	19 738	25 856	23 025	4 090	2 270
2003	108 477	82 009	699	82 708	9 253	-1 044	72 411	15 787	20 279	26 347	23 641	4 117	2 281
2004	113 984	85 808	1 248	87 057	9 665	-1 196	76 195	15 988	21 800	27 492	24 792	4 146	2 310
2005	119 151	89 815	1 580	91 395	10 150	-1 591	79 653	16 439	23 059	28 486	25 509	4 183	2 343
2006	126 719	94 178	1 248	95 426	10 670	-1 860	82 897	19 001	24 821	30 034	26 894	4 219	2 381
2007	132 703	97 545	765	98 310	11 137	-2 017	85 156	20 871	26 676	31 175	27 780	4 257	2 420
2008	139 491	100 362	1 158	101 520	11 619	-2 296	87 604	22 789	29 098	32 516	29 046	4 290	2 410
2009	137 757	97 863	1 109	98 972	11 478	-2 494	85 000	19 394	33 363	31 910	29 111	4 317	2 336
2010	140 483	99 286	591	99 877	11 643	-2 615	85 619	19 976	34 887	32 316	29 442	4 347	2 342
2011	147 103	103 175	811	103 986	10 855	-2 805	90 327	21 093	35 684	33 667	30 371	4 369	. . .

. . . = Not available.

Table 17-2. Personal Income and Employment by Region and State—*Continued*

(Millions of dollars, except as noted.)

| Region or state and year | Personal income, total | Earnings by place of work | | | Less: Contributions for government social insurance | Plus: Adjustment for residence | Equals: Net earnings by place of residence | Plus: Dividends, interest, and rent | Plus: Personal current transfer receipts | Per capita (dollars) | | Population (thousands) | Total employment (thousands) |
		Nonfarm	Farm	Total						Personal income	Disposable personal income		
LOUISIANA													
1958	5 146	4 113	188	4 301	140	-3	4 159	609	378	1 631	1 491	3 155	...
1959	5 386	4 273	204	4 477	159	-2	4 317	659	411	1 679	1 517	3 208	...
1960	5 486	4 352	186	4 538	185	-1	4 351	699	436	1 683	1 534	3 260	...
1961	5 699	4 460	218	4 678	187	-1	4 490	723	486	1 734	1 579	3 287	...
1962	6 012	4 742	205	4 947	208	0	4 739	769	504	1 797	1 633	3 345	...
1963	6 416	5 039	261	5 300	246	0	5 055	826	535	1 900	1 719	3 377	...
1964	6 870	5 490	226	5 716	262	0	5 454	861	554	1 993	1 823	3 446	...
1965	7 435	6 003	198	6 201	285	0	5 915	922	598	2 127	1 946	3 496	...
1966	8 225	6 761	240	7 000	389	3	6 615	968	642	2 317	2 088	3 550	...
1967	9 008	7 402	268	7 669	432	5	7 242	1 013	752	2 516	2 273	3 581	...
1968	9 864	8 155	299	8 454	489	4	7 969	1 045	850	2 738	2 454	3 603	...
1969	10 446	8 654	241	8 895	568	4	8 330	1 154	961	2 886	2 567	3 619	1 440
1970	11 276	9 158	283	9 441	591	4	8 854	1 268	1 154	3 089	2 787	3 650	1 429
1971	12 284	9 926	320	10 246	657	-9	9 580	1 385	1 318	3 310	2 991	3 711	1 445
1972	13 453	10 933	349	11 281	756	-21	10 504	1 499	1 450	3 576	3 208	3 762	1 488
1973	15 067	12 123	579	12 702	960	-37	11 705	1 676	1 686	3 977	3 580	3 789	1 550
1974	17 166	13 723	614	14 336	1 117	-54	13 165	2 026	1 975	4 493	4 008	3 821	1 598
1975	19 271	15 502	419	15 921	1 242	-83	14 596	2 234	2 440	4 958	4 471	3 887	1 641
1976	21 926	17 916	455	18 371	1 453	-113	16 806	2 430	2 690	5 549	4 955	3 952	1 702
1977	24 525	20 222	454	20 676	1 625	-139	18 911	2 719	2 895	6 107	5 439	4 016	1 756
1978	28 155	23 568	374	23 942	1 929	-187	21 826	3 177	3 152	6 912	6 111	4 073	1 849
1979	32 055	26 737	503	27 240	2 273	-233	24 734	3 735	3 587	7 744	6 795	4 139	1 897
1980	37 022	30 688	175	30 863	2 595	-337	27 931	4 814	4 277	8 767	7 669	4 223	1 964
1981	42 794	35 084	267	35 351	3 173	-363	31 815	6 202	4 777	9 991	8 671	4 283	2 030
1982	45 970	36 670	263	36 934	3 374	-342	33 217	7 241	5 511	10 561	9 309	4 353	2 023
1983	47 781	37 059	231	37 290	3 378	-321	33 591	7 917	6 273	10 871	9 691	4 395	1 984
1984	51 025	39 234	322	39 556	3 664	-313	35 579	8 915	6 532	11 595	10 393	4 400	2 023
1985	53 004	40 068	230	40 298	3 775	-282	36 241	9 728	7 036	12 024	10 763	4 408	2 009
1986	52 874	39 159	235	39 394	3 647	-224	35 523	9 629	7 721	11 998	10 880	4 407	1 928
1987	53 080	39 256	397	39 654	3 609	-188	35 857	9 403	7 820	12 219	11 058	4 344	1 904
1988	55 880	41 414	632	42 045	3 983	-169	37 894	9 792	8 194	13 029	11 838	4 289	1 935
1989	59 385	43 487	468	43 955	4 214	-136	39 606	10 817	8 962	13 963	12 608	4 253	1 953
1990	64 046	47 141	404	47 545	4 674	-111	42 760	11 415	9 871	15 171	13 687	4 222	2 005
1991	67 759	49 636	469	50 106	5 028	-129	44 949	11 537	11 274	15 931	14 412	4 253	2 030
1992	72 366	52 631	578	53 209	5 256	-128	47 824	11 593	12 948	16 857	15 319	4 293	2 038
1993	75 792	54 691	590	55 281	5 493	-132	49 656	11 872	14 264	17 559	15 935	4 316	2 086
1994	81 042	57 975	679	58 654	5 925	-157	52 573	12 696	15 773	18 641	16 897	4 347	2 126
1995	84 804	60 908	674	61 581	6 213	-183	55 185	13 712	15 907	19 367	17 518	4 379	2 194
1996	88 662	63 616	884	64 501	6 507	-206	57 788	14 714	16 160	20 155	18 059	4 399	2 239
1997	93 229	67 548	644	68 193	6 906	-221	61 066	15 712	16 451	21 088	18 780	4 421	2 290
1998	98 217	71 582	466	72 047	7 336	-241	64 470	17 064	16 683	22 119	19 733	4 440	2 339
1999	100 180	73 380	636	74 016	7 437	-233	66 345	16 667	17 168	22 458	20 094	4 461	2 355
2000	105 332	76 921	619	77 540	7 683	-245	69 613	18 102	17 617	23 554	21 059	4 472	2 385
2001	113 178	82 655	654	83 309	8 145	-121	75 044	17 746	20 388	25 275	22 635	4 478	2 382
2002	115 865	85 576	424	86 000	8 397	-120	77 483	16 806	21 575	25 763	23 410	4 497	2 404
2003	119 488	89 718	861	90 579	8 699	-165	81 714	16 161	21 613	26 429	24 276	4 521	2 427
2004	125 957	94 189	822	95 011	8 961	-168	85 882	16 486	23 589	27 669	25 450	4 552	2 443
2005	135 318	97 967	714	98 681	9 185	-145	89 351	18 529	27 439	29 567	27 082	4 577	2 415
2006	143 223	104 161	721	104 882	9 904	-162	94 816	22 674	25 733	33 287	30 118	4 303	2 432
2007	156 618	110 833	829	111 662	10 571	-161	100 930	28 849	26 839	35 794	32 455	4 376	2 529
2008	167 935	120 199	788	120 987	11 246	-177	109 564	28 305	30 067	37 861	33 948	4 436	2 576
2009	162 494	115 754	888	116 642	11 127	-204	105 311	24 524	32 658	36 177	33 290	4 492	2 556
2010	168 356	118 995	804	119 799	11 433	-233	108 133	25 514	34 709	37 039	34 245	4 545	2 549
2011	176 489	123 873	986	124 859	10 721	-228	113 910	26 623	35 957	38 578	35 307	4 575	...

. . . = Not available.

Table 17-2. Personal Income and Employment by Region and State—*Continued*

(Millions of dollars, except as noted.)

Region or state and year	Personal income, total	Earnings by place of work			Less: Contributions for government social insurance	Plus: Adjustment for residence	Equals: Net earnings by place of residence	Plus: Dividends, interest, and rent	Plus: Personal current transfer receipts	Per capita (dollars)		Population (thousands)	Total employment (thousands)
		Nonfarm	Farm	Total						Personal income	Disposable personal income		
MAINE													
1958	1 679	1 294	101	1 395	52	-20	1 323	215	141	1 778	1 626	944	. . .
1959	1 748	1 408	59	1 466	60	-24	1 382	219	148	1 827	1 673	957	. . .
1960	1 854	1 472	103	1 575	70	-28	1 477	225	152	1 901	1 724	975	. . .
1961	1 873	1 512	67	1 579	73	-29	1 477	230	167	1 883	1 708	995	. . .
1962	1 952	1 575	66	1 641	78	-30	1 533	247	172	1 963	1 774	994	. . .
1963	2 016	1 625	59	1 685	87	-30	1 567	268	181	2 030	1 845	993	. . .
1964	2 180	1 733	90	1 823	92	-31	1 700	297	184	2 196	2 012	993	. . .
1965	2 358	1 831	126	1 957	92	-30	1 834	331	192	2 365	2 169	997	. . .
1966	2 511	1 997	107	2 105	118	-33	1 953	348	210	2 513	2 301	999	. . .
1967	2 641	2 145	55	2 199	137	-35	2 027	365	248	2 630	2 396	1 004	. . .
1968	2 823	2 325	55	2 380	157	-38	2 185	360	279	2 840	2 556	994	. . .
1969	3 113	2 504	74	2 579	181	-23	2 375	425	312	3 138	2 789	992	443
1970	3 402	2 704	78	2 782	193	-18	2 571	460	371	3 413	3 069	997	446
1971	3 646	2 870	66	2 937	211	-17	2 709	499	438	3 590	3 276	1 016	443
1972	3 993	3 159	65	3 224	241	-20	2 963	539	490	3 858	3 502	1 035	453
1973	4 508	3 497	148	3 645	301	-11	3 333	591	584	4 308	3 874	1 046	470
1974	5 032	3 799	195	3 995	337	-6	3 651	678	703	4 747	4 276	1 060	478
1975	5 394	4 062	82	4 144	357	-19	3 767	728	899	5 026	4 575	1 073	475
1976	6 211	4 722	163	4 885	422	-23	4 440	796	975	5 698	5 167	1 090	498
1977	6 761	5 178	129	5 306	461	-25	4 820	903	1 038	6 116	5 552	1 105	513
1978	7 474	5 814	90	5 904	531	-23	5 350	1 010	1 115	6 700	6 045	1 115	531
1979	8 338	6 466	76	6 542	607	-16	5 919	1 159	1 260	7 412	6 647	1 125	545
1980	9 391	7 130	49	7 179	670	-14	6 494	1 426	1 471	8 333	7 450	1 127	553
1981	10 384	7 637	118	7 755	773	-51	6 931	1 776	1 677	9 164	8 125	1 133	551
1982	11 254	8 113	104	8 217	834	-50	7 332	2 083	1 839	9 901	8 715	1 137	553
1983	12 075	8 808	72	8 881	910	-41	7 930	2 156	1 989	10 548	9 403	1 145	565
1984	13 438	9 764	118	9 882	1 043	-31	8 808	2 532	2 098	11 628	10 421	1 156	587
1985	14 492	10 624	102	10 726	1 132	-11	9 584	2 688	2 220	12 462	11 114	1 163	606
1986	15 687	11 555	93	11 648	1 239	28	10 437	2 947	2 303	13 406	11 889	1 170	630
1987	17 098	12 713	136	12 848	1 356	46	11 538	3 203	2 357	14 434	12 677	1 185	653
1988	18 772	14 138	118	14 256	1 543	59	12 772	3 500	2 500	15 593	13 735	1 204	686
1989	20 352	15 164	125	15 289	1 651	57	13 695	3 966	2 691	16 683	14 707	1 220	702
1990	21 199	15 641	173	15 814	1 791	56	14 079	4 116	3 005	17 211	15 222	1 232	701
1991	21 596	15 607	127	15 734	1 808	73	13 999	4 139	3 459	17 457	15 558	1 237	678
1992	22 558	16 245	178	16 423	1 910	116	14 629	4 110	3 819	18 214	16 305	1 239	681
1993	23 218	16 755	156	16 911	2 018	175	15 068	4 121	4 029	18 690	16 738	1 242	692
1994	24 297	17 457	148	17 606	2 132	235	15 708	4 373	4 215	19 552	17 457	1 243	703
1995	25 332	17 991	123	18 114	2 214	305	16 206	4 688	4 439	20 372	18 197	1 243	705
1996	26 864	18 793	151	18 943	2 280	358	17 022	5 096	4 746	21 507	19 105	1 249	714
1997	28 315	19 839	104	19 943	2 406	431	17 969	5 382	4 964	22 566	19 896	1 255	727
1998	30 434	21 322	178	21 500	2 557	505	19 448	5 874	5 112	24 171	21 153	1 259	747
1999	31 862	22 776	194	22 970	2 705	573	20 839	5 755	5 268	25 151	22 010	1 267	763
2000	34 097	24 140	207	24 347	2 839	692	22 200	6 295	5 601	26 699	23 230	1 277	785
2001	36 232	25 802	193	25 995	2 972	723	23 747	6 452	6 034	28 181	24 610	1 286	790
2002	37 383	26 827	156	26 982	3 004	700	24 679	6 261	6 443	28 846	25 753	1 296	789
2003	39 001	28 040	159	28 199	3 115	692	25 775	6 230	6 995	29 851	26 929	1 307	794
2004	41 164	29 680	187	29 866	3 255	730	27 341	6 372	7 451	31 335	28 337	1 314	808
2005	41 982	30 269	187	30 457	3 363	759	27 853	6 026	8 104	31 834	28 520	1 319	810
2006	44 307	31 696	168	31 864	3 593	809	29 081	6 962	8 265	33 474	29 915	1 324	819
2007	46 354	32 590	183	32 774	3 753	840	29 860	7 677	8 816	34 930	31 132	1 327	830
2008	48 469	33 155	179	33 334	3 865	867	30 335	8 308	9 826	36 429	32 562	1 331	827
2009	47 990	32 568	156	32 724	3 844	825	29 705	7 222	11 063	36 093	32 944	1 330	805
2010	48 799	33 286	196	33 482	3 935	852	30 399	7 425	10 974	36 763	33 566	1 327	801
2011	50 435	34 021	195	34 216	3 606	921	31 532	7 848	11 056	37 973	34 326	1 328	. . .

. . . = Not available.

Table 17-2. Personal Income and Employment by Region and State—*Continued*

(Millions of dollars, except as noted.)

Region or state and year	Personal income, total	Earnings by place of work			Less: Contributions for government social insurance	Plus: Adjustment for residence	Equals: Net earnings by place of residence	Plus: Dividends, interest, and rent	Plus: Personal current transfer receipts	Per capita (dollars)		Population (thousands)	Total employment (thousands)
		Nonfarm	Farm	Total						Personal income	Disposable personal income		
MARYLAND													
1958	6 581	5 039	104	5 143	188	466	5 422	849	311	2 207	1 940	2 982	. . .
1959	6 950	5 359	85	5 444	239	516	5 721	902	327	2 267	1 975	3 066	. . .
1960	7 311	5 618	94	5 712	289	582	6 005	966	340	2 349	2 041	3 113	. . .
1961	7 770	5 938	90	6 027	312	641	6 357	1 022	391	2 447	2 141	3 176	. . .
1962	8 400	6 412	85	6 497	350	720	6 867	1 117	416	2 574	2 225	3 263	. . .
1963	8 996	6 844	67	6 912	380	804	7 335	1 225	436	2 657	2 287	3 386	. . .
1964	9 820	7 431	86	7 517	396	886	8 007	1 353	460	2 812	2 460	3 492	. . .
1965	10 727	8 031	98	8 128	398	1 003	8 733	1 491	504	2 980	2 598	3 600	. . .
1966	11 845	9 013	79	9 092	526	1 117	9 683	1 605	557	3 206	2 755	3 695	. . .
1967	12 917	9 598	95	9 693	585	1 366	10 474	1 751	691	3 438	2 949	3 757	. . .
1968	14 309	10 664	87	10 751	641	1 528	11 638	1 845	826	3 751	3 129	3 815	. . .
1969	16 243	11 865	133	11 997	750	2 154	13 401	1 897	944	4 199	3 486	3 868	1 679
1970	17 951	12 942	122	13 064	815	2 512	14 761	2 063	1 126	4 558	3 857	3 938	1 702
1971	19 633	14 074	94	14 168	916	2 764	16 016	2 245	1 373	4 881	4 188	4 023	1 729
1972	21 552	15 480	128	15 608	1 059	3 000	17 550	2 429	1 574	5 281	4 456	4 081	1 781
1973	23 853	17 259	209	17 468	1 353	3 203	19 319	2 718	1 816	5 805	4 927	4 109	1 846
1974	26 322	18 951	165	19 116	1 531	3 478	21 063	3 155	2 105	6 368	5 367	4 133	1 868
1975	28 641	20 107	204	20 311	1 622	3 864	22 553	3 442	2 647	6 890	5 914	4 157	1 846
1976	31 431	22 278	175	22 453	1 806	4 179	24 826	3 754	2 851	7 534	6 470	4 172	1 866
1977	34 287	24 339	130	24 468	1 972	4 586	27 083	4 167	3 037	8 174	6 960	4 195	1 919
1978	38 033	27 095	184	27 279	2 258	4 952	29 973	4 709	3 351	9 030	7 674	4 212	2 004
1979	42 112	29 929	160	30 089	2 607	5 381	32 863	5 448	3 802	9 971	8 424	4 223	2 059
1980	47 197	32 775	58	32 833	2 861	5 947	35 919	6 751	4 527	11 164	9 488	4 228	2 070
1981	52 571	35 975	130	36 105	3 381	6 395	39 120	8 264	5 187	12 335	10 362	4 262	2 095
1982	57 107	37 856	145	38 001	3 617	6 964	41 347	9 987	5 774	13 334	11 284	4 283	2 084
1983	61 600	41 324	90	41 414	4 072	7 347	44 690	10 614	6 295	14 281	12 257	4 313	2 151
1984	68 537	46 014	266	46 280	4 673	8 033	49 640	12 261	6 636	15 701	13 456	4 365	2 243
1985	74 736	50 418	277	50 695	5 285	8 674	54 084	13 636	7 015	16 935	14 587	4 413	2 342
1986	80 460	54 752	287	55 039	5 838	9 291	58 491	14 484	7 485	17 932	15 457	4 487	2 428
1987	87 052	60 047	301	60 347	6 332	10 049	64 064	15 216	7 772	19 067	16 239	4 566	2 553
1988	95 337	66 080	367	66 446	7 259	11 132	70 319	16 732	8 286	20 468	17 651	4 658	2 647
1989	102 738	70 445	366	70 810	7 847	11 964	74 927	18 789	9 022	21 733	18 557	4 727	2 704
1990	108 865	74 709	357	75 066	8 522	12 450	78 993	19 988	9 883	22 681	19 420	4 800	2 737
1991	113 329	76 672	310	76 982	8 828	13 122	81 276	20 931	11 122	23 282	20 114	4 868	2 662
1992	118 713	79 991	343	80 334	9 136	13 957	85 155	21 086	12 472	24 112	20 923	4 923	2 636
1993	123 328	83 217	321	83 538	9 479	14 351	88 410	21 902	13 016	24 805	21 490	4 972	2 659
1994	129 493	87 434	309	87 743	10 046	14 822	92 519	23 378	13 597	25 780	22 278	5 023	2 706
1995	134 952	91 432	215	91 647	10 443	14 863	96 067	24 659	14 226	26 618	22 900	5 070	2 765
1996	141 548	95 144	395	95 539	10 805	15 225	99 959	26 404	15 185	27 689	23 692	5 112	2 806
1997	149 563	101 576	281	101 858	11 464	15 201	105 594	28 467	15 501	29 000	24 424	5 157	2 870
1998	159 994	108 459	326	108 785	12 142	16 522	113 166	30 646	16 183	30 742	26 036	5 204	2 925
1999	169 278	115 873	350	116 223	12 884	17 414	120 754	31 339	17 186	32 216	27 232	5 255	2 990
2000	184 174	125 534	415	125 949	13 768	19 706	131 888	34 111	18 175	34 678	29 229	5 311	3 065
2001	194 581	134 592	416	135 008	14 840	19 695	139 863	34 904	19 813	36 203	30 640	5 375	3 106
2002	201 793	140 919	223	141 142	15 548	20 436	146 030	34 473	21 290	37 092	32 053	5 440	3 142
2003	209 701	147 586	321	147 907	16 221	21 222	152 908	33 964	22 828	38 153	33 281	5 496	3 181
2004	224 646	158 520	452	158 972	17 427	22 999	164 544	36 235	23 866	40 499	35 402	5 547	3 240
2005	237 146	167 442	408	167 850	18 354	24 147	173 643	37 730	25 773	42 405	36 722	5 592	3 309
2006	252 431	176 743	320	177 063	19 584	24 745	182 223	43 240	26 967	44 858	38 686	5 627	3 368
2007	264 798	182 918	305	183 224	20 375	25 716	188 564	46 995	29 238	46 839	40 143	5 653	3 439
2008	277 793	188 673	323	188 996	21 176	26 142	193 961	51 864	31 968	48 864	42 528	5 685	3 435
2009	272 829	187 206	283	187 489	21 167	26 089	192 411	44 282	36 136	47 611	42 155	5 730	3 366
2010	283 634	193 362	246	193 608	22 024	27 367	198 951	46 022	38 661	49 023	43 451	5 786	3 365
2011	297 465	200 562	193	200 755	20 756	28 416	208 415	49 089	39 961	51 038	44 699	5 828	. . .

. . . = Not available.

Table 17-2. Personal Income and Employment by Region and State—*Continued*

(Millions of dollars, except as noted.)

Region or state and year	Personal income, total	Derivation of personal income								Per capita (dollars)		Population (thousands)	Total employment (thousands)
		Earnings by place of work			Less: Contributions for government social insurance	Plus: Adjustment for residence	Equals: Net earnings by place of residence	Plus: Dividends, interest, and rent	Plus: Personal current transfer receipts	Personal income	Disposable personal income		
		Nonfarm	Farm	Total									
MASSACHUSETTS													
1958	11 565	9 445	68	9 512	353	-56	9 103	1 587	874	2 308	2 043	5 010	. . .
1959	12 356	10 216	59	10 275	427	-69	9 779	1 702	874	2 415	2 125	5 117	. . .
1960	12 877	10 650	68	10 719	499	-75	10 144	1 812	921	2 496	2 177	5 160	. . .
1961	13 517	11 145	60	11 205	528	-83	10 595	1 895	1 027	2 590	2 278	5 219	. . .
1962	14 306	11 822	61	11 882	617	-93	11 173	2 082	1 051	2 718	2 380	5 263	. . .
1963	14 872	12 224	61	12 284	679	-99	11 506	2 255	1 110	2 783	2 435	5 344	. . .
1964	15 884	12 946	63	13 008	697	-109	12 202	2 531	1 151	2 916	2 594	5 448	. . .
1965	16 951	13 744	69	13 812	714	-122	12 977	2 762	1 212	3 081	2 737	5 502	. . .
1966	18 293	15 024	72	15 096	942	-141	14 012	2 980	1 300	3 305	2 910	5 535	. . .
1967	19 897	16 192	56	16 248	1 032	-158	15 058	3 234	1 605	3 557	3 125	5 594	. . .
1968	21 751	17 664	65	17 729	1 138	-176	16 415	3 400	1 936	3 872	3 349	5 618	. . .
1969	23 646	19 260	66	19 327	1 259	-126	17 942	3 548	2 157	4 185	3 557	5 650	2 679
1970	25 505	20 587	69	20 656	1 323	-108	19 225	3 729	2 550	4 472	3 861	5 704	2 679
1971	27 218	21 775	63	21 839	1 443	-111	20 284	3 914	3 020	4 743	4 152	5 739	2 644
1972	29 397	23 665	63	23 728	1 647	-110	21 971	4 111	3 314	5 102	4 391	5 762	2 697
1973	32 047	26 016	71	26 087	2 069	-134	23 884	4 447	3 716	5 541	4 805	5 784	2 787
1974	34 725	27 703	70	27 772	2 269	-150	25 353	4 967	4 405	6 011	5 200	5 777	2 811
1975	37 186	28 665	69	28 734	2 290	-155	26 289	5 165	5 732	6 453	5 672	5 762	2 728
1976	40 201	31 437	76	31 513	2 550	-182	28 781	5 483	5 937	6 993	6 102	5 749	2 756
1977	43 720	34 559	79	34 638	2 811	-224	31 602	6 019	6 099	7 611	6 611	5 744	2 833
1978	48 369	38 734	104	38 837	3 242	-287	35 308	6 591	6 469	8 422	7 290	5 743	2 958
1979	53 849	43 324	90	43 414	3 788	-360	39 266	7 421	7 163	9 371	8 037	5 746	3 074
1980	60 736	48 049	106	48 155	4 217	-482	43 456	9 106	8 173	10 570	9 021	5 746	3 134
1981	67 749	52 583	116	52 700	4 993	-596	47 110	11 348	9 291	11 744	9 933	5 769	3 142
1982	74 405	56 618	131	56 749	5 497	-725	50 527	13 835	10 043	12 892	11 034	5 771	3 143
1983	80 858	62 388	164	62 552	6 141	-902	55 509	14 705	10 644	13 942	11 990	5 799	3 215
1984	91 342	71 082	182	71 264	7 225	-1 175	62 863	17 284	11 195	15 639	13 519	5 841	3 402
1985	98 786	77 860	160	78 020	8 002	-1 360	68 658	18 413	11 714	16 798	14 432	5 881	3 510
1986	106 265	84 478	175	84 653	8 883	-1 489	74 281	19 661	12 323	18 003	15 387	5 903	3 605
1987	115 125	92 812	154	92 966	9 651	-1 665	81 651	20 803	12 672	19 397	16 483	5 935	3 632
1988	126 339	102 171	174	102 345	10 771	-1 898	89 675	23 021	13 643	21 127	18 198	5 980	3 739
1989	132 913	105 859	153	106 012	11 133	-2 019	92 860	24 675	15 379	22 095	18 931	6 015	3 710
1990	137 300	107 176	153	107 330	11 135	-2 076	94 119	25 950	17 231	22 797	19 549	6 023	3 615
1991	140 313	107 427	172	107 599	11 310	-2 280	94 010	26 542	19 761	23 314	20 154	6 018	3 451
1992	147 235	113 898	171	114 070	11 893	-2 383	99 793	26 822	20 620	24 422	21 166	6 029	3 482
1993	152 619	118 702	165	118 867	12 487	-2 592	103 788	27 610	21 221	25 182	21 752	6 061	3 548
1994	160 869	125 228	150	125 378	13 273	-2 799	109 306	29 117	22 446	26 393	22 729	6 095	3 616
1995	169 886	132 266	146	132 412	14 054	-2 865	115 493	30 635	23 758	27 662	23 664	6 141	3 649
1996	180 938	141 071	166	141 238	14 818	-3 126	123 294	33 159	24 485	29 279	24 786	6 180	3 713
1997	192 455	150 627	168	150 795	15 892	-3 406	131 497	35 617	25 341	30 911	25 914	6 226	3 802
1998	207 008	162 903	108	163 010	16 937	-3 636	142 438	39 106	25 464	33 006	27 400	6 272	3 885
1999	219 031	175 908	109	176 018	18 170	-4 209	153 639	39 000	26 391	34 671	28 570	6 317	3 949
2000	243 132	196 896	131	197 027	20 076	-5 082	171 869	43 440	27 823	38 222	30 795	6 361	4 058
2001	253 007	203 068	110	203 177	20 591	-5 103	177 484	45 151	30 373	39 547	32 414	6 398	4 096
2002	254 103	202 848	131	202 979	20 488	-4 855	177 637	43 469	32 997	39 597	34 050	6 417	4 026
2003	258 600	206 242	132	206 374	20 714	-4 763	180 897	42 840	34 863	40 264	34 924	6 423	3 993
2004	271 086	218 974	146	219 120	22 496	-4 925	191 699	43 161	36 225	42 276	36 683	6 412	4 016
2005	282 367	227 030	126	227 157	23 564	-4 904	198 688	44 749	38 931	44 097	37 838	6 403	4 056
2006	304 855	239 339	131	239 470	24 383	-5 084	210 003	54 193	40 659	47 559	40 663	6 410	4 117
2007	322 543	250 878	135	251 014	25 538	-5 469	220 006	60 092	42 445	50 150	42 235	6 432	4 195
2008	335 753	255 154	180	255 334	26 403	-5 695	223 236	65 584	46 933	51 902	44 564	6 469	4 210
2009	324 496	246 234	137	246 371	26 130	-5 409	214 832	56 192	53 472	49 788	43 818	6 518	4 114
2010	336 320	255 149	180	255 329	26 695	-5 652	222 981	57 704	55 634	51 304	45 013	6 555	4 130
2011	353 228	266 977	155	267 132	25 101	-6 024	236 007	61 028	56 194	53 621	46 235	6 588	. . .

. . . = Not available.

Table 17-2. Personal Income and Employment by Region and State—*Continued*

(Millions of dollars, except as noted.)

Region or state and year	Personal income, total	Earnings by place of work			Less: Contributions for government social insurance	Plus: Adjustment for residence	Equals: Net earnings by place of residence	Plus: Dividends, interest, and rent	Plus: Personal current transfer receipts	Per capita (dollars)		Population (thousands)	Total employment (thousands)
		Nonfarm	Farm	Total						Personal income	Disposable personal income		
MICHIGAN													
1958	17 198	13 951	299	14 250	560	30	13 720	2 294	1 183	2 243	2 026	7 667	. . .
1959	18 277	15 142	221	15 363	695	34	14 703	2 501	1 073	2 353	2 114	7 767	. . .
1960	19 094	15 789	240	16 029	824	37	15 241	2 741	1 112	2 437	2 175	7 834	. . .
1961	19 167	15 401	300	15 701	786	38	14 953	2 882	1 332	2 428	2 184	7 893	. . .
1962	20 590	16 712	276	16 988	888	41	16 141	3 145	1 304	2 596	2 315	7 933	. . .
1963	22 037	18 010	300	18 310	1 038	44	17 316	3 393	1 327	2 735	2 431	8 058	. . .
1964	24 222	19 802	295	20 097	1 077	49	19 070	3 787	1 366	2 959	2 663	8 187	. . .
1965	26 948	22 093	274	22 367	1 122	54	21 300	4 173	1 476	3 225	2 892	8 357	. . .
1966	29 435	24 412	349	24 761	1 571	63	23 253	4 565	1 617	3 458	3 085	8 512	. . .
1967	30 778	25 198	276	25 474	1 652	68	23 891	4 886	2 002	3 566	3 177	8 630	. . .
1968	34 080	28 052	304	28 357	1 853	76	26 580	5 188	2 312	3 919	3 430	8 696	. . .
1969	36 414	30 767	351	31 118	2 203	107	29 023	4 832	2 559	4 147	3 559	8 781	3 640
1970	37 347	31 035	341	31 376	2 193	112	29 295	4 837	3 216	4 198	3 654	8 897	3 558
1971	40 385	33 733	310	34 043	2 446	104	31 700	4 846	3 838	4 501	3 953	8 972	3 571
1972	44 849	37 703	427	38 129	2 901	112	35 341	5 191	4 318	4 970	4 288	9 025	3 687
1973	50 370	42 827	561	43 389	3 794	138	39 733	5 712	4 925	5 552	4 826	9 072	3 858
1974	53 986	44 633	649	45 283	4 077	140	41 346	6 487	6 153	5 926	5 178	9 109	3 854
1975	57 440	45 629	578	46 207	4 087	154	42 274	7 090	8 075	6 307	5 595	9 108	3 695
1976	64 657	52 801	478	53 279	4 789	197	48 687	7 659	8 311	7 092	6 200	9 117	3 844
1977	72 803	60 451	560	61 011	5 485	223	55 748	8 521	8 534	7 950	6 886	9 157	4 016
1978	80 979	68 216	511	68 728	6 394	270	62 603	9 300	9 076	8 800	7 550	9 202	4 186
1979	89 056	74 423	546	74 968	7 197	310	68 081	10 509	10 466	9 629	8 263	9 249	4 228
1980	95 248	75 135	537	75 672	7 181	354	68 845	12 595	13 808	10 291	8 961	9 256	4 030
1981	101 992	79 184	517	79 701	8 141	382	71 942	15 424	14 626	11 075	9 611	9 209	3 978
1982	105 030	78 429	410	78 840	8 195	391	71 036	17 665	16 329	11 522	10 130	9 115	3 823
1983	111 142	83 354	221	83 575	8 954	426	75 047	18 813	17 282	12 284	10 761	9 048	3 866
1984	122 968	92 827	550	93 377	10 357	489	83 509	21 983	17 476	13 588	11 937	9 049	4 040
1985	133 283	101 881	661	102 542	11 666	509	91 385	23 861	18 038	14 685	12 807	9 076	4 233
1986	141 659	108 700	492	109 192	12 551	492	97 133	25 612	18 914	15 520	13 555	9 128	4 349
1987	146 669	112 768	669	113 437	12 897	511	101 050	26 169	19 450	15 964	13 895	9 187	4 483
1988	155 728	121 107	592	121 699	14 304	522	107 917	27 546	20 264	16 894	14 768	9 218	4 582
1989	167 227	128 111	980	129 092	15 164	517	114 445	30 874	21 908	18 072	15 726	9 253	4 709
1990	174 296	133 015	777	133 792	16 100	459	118 150	32 408	23 738	18 719	16 368	9 311	4 791
1991	179 824	136 499	667	137 166	16 638	476	121 004	32 400	26 420	19 129	16 833	9 400	4 721
1992	191 274	146 728	758	147 487	17 675	605	130 416	32 869	27 988	20 179	17 880	9 479	4 751
1993	200 784	154 530	738	155 268	18 756	671	137 183	33 674	29 926	21 046	18 484	9 540	4 812
1994	216 842	167 972	564	168 537	20 565	775	148 747	37 883	30 212	22 593	19 787	9 598	4 985
1995	226 693	176 339	698	177 036	21 663	751	156 125	38 729	31 839	23 428	20 407	9 676	5 142
1996	236 927	182 461	618	183 078	22 197	776	161 658	41 854	33 415	24 279	21 013	9 759	5 247
1997	248 650	190 515	612	191 127	23 286	870	168 710	44 615	35 325	25 349	21 840	9 809	5 330
1998	264 936	204 615	631	205 246	24 457	917	181 706	48 141	35 089	26 903	23 062	9 848	5 381
1999	275 718	214 540	820	215 360	25 873	1 033	190 520	47 544	37 655	27 858	23 861	9 897	5 475
2000	292 606	228 046	602	228 648	27 085	1 048	202 611	51 054	38 941	29 400	25 293	9 952	5 587
2001	299 973	232 778	556	233 334	26 864	1 170	207 640	48 984	43 349	30 024	26 080	9 991	5 490
2002	303 099	236 506	589	237 095	27 194	1 203	211 104	47 085	44 911	30 262	26 845	10 016	5 454
2003	314 285	245 978	704	246 682	27 688	1 273	220 267	46 894	47 125	31 300	28 094	10 041	5 430
2004	319 434	248 478	1 141	249 619	28 493	1 361	222 487	47 793	49 154	31 768	28 620	10 055	5 454
2005	325 749	252 992	1 060	254 052	29 404	1 439	226 087	47 456	52 206	32 409	29 038	10 051	5 480
2006	334 858	254 780	1 165	255 945	30 177	1 546	227 314	51 644	55 900	33 365	29 830	10 036	5 468
2007	344 234	255 502	1 196	256 698	30 694	1 602	227 606	55 702	60 926	34 419	30 595	10 001	5 456
2008	351 009	251 069	1 806	252 875	30 797	1 531	223 608	60 484	66 917	35 288	31 516	9 947	5 328
2009	332 079	231 300	1 304	232 604	28 778	1 502	205 327	49 484	77 268	33 538	30 705	9 902	5 041
2010	342 874	237 438	1 630	239 069	29 225	1 582	211 426	50 317	81 131	34 714	31 779	9 877	5 040
2011	360 806	249 211	2 227	251 438	27 645	1 652	225 445	53 132	82 230	36 533	32 970	9 876	. . .

. . . = Not available.

Table 17-2. Personal Income and Employment by Region and State—*Continued*

(Millions of dollars, except as noted.)

| Region or state and year | Personal income, total | Derivation of personal income | | | | | | | | Per capita (dollars) | | Population (thousands) | Total employment (thousands) |
| | | Earnings by place of work | | | Less: Contributions for government social insurance | Plus: Adjustment for residence | Equals: Net earnings by place of residence | Plus: Dividends, interest, and rent | Plus: Personal current transfer receipts | Personal income | Disposable personal income | | |
		Nonfarm	Farm	Total									
MINNESOTA													
1958	6 650	4 885	600	5 485	179	1	5 307	880	464	2 007	1 802	3 313	. . .
1959	6 903	5 280	411	5 691	220	0	5 471	945	488	2 051	1 835	3 366	. . .
1960	7 340	5 570	515	6 085	260	-1	5 824	1 009	507	2 143	1 909	3 425	. . .
1961	7 717	5 813	541	6 354	269	-3	6 082	1 064	571	2 224	1 983	3 470	. . .
1962	8 138	6 258	467	6 725	303	-3	6 419	1 129	590	2 316	2 056	3 513	. . .
1963	8 635	6 517	622	7 139	339	-4	6 795	1 215	625	2 446	2 179	3 531	. . .
1964	8 979	6 974	402	7 377	348	-4	7 025	1 303	651	2 524	2 275	3 558	. . .
1965	9 926	7 526	653	8 179	372	-7	7 800	1 418	708	2 763	2 481	3 592	. . .
1966	10 765	8 305	734	9 039	522	-13	8 504	1 501	761	2 976	2 655	3 617	. . .
1967	11 575	9 032	644	9 675	601	-17	9 057	1 593	925	3 163	2 811	3 659	. . .
1968	12 743	9 997	680	10 677	683	-24	9 970	1 715	1 058	3 441	3 041	3 703	. . .
1969	14 186	11 176	721	11 897	782	-33	11 082	1 943	1 162	3 775	3 277	3 758	1 691
1970	15 451	11 946	876	12 822	826	-29	11 967	2 111	1 373	4 050	3 565	3 815	1 699
1971	16 447	12 731	796	13 527	911	-28	12 588	2 265	1 594	4 270	3 797	3 852	1 706
1972	17 887	13 820	960	14 779	1 038	-30	13 711	2 414	1 762	4 626	4 051	3 867	1 780
1973	21 061	15 461	2 179	17 640	1 336	-38	16 267	2 729	2 066	5 421	4 812	3 885	1 878
1974	22 705	17 047	1 644	18 691	1 528	-34	17 130	3 152	2 423	5 824	5 067	3 898	1 921
1975	24 462	18 410	1 266	19 676	1 615	-34	18 027	3 512	2 924	6 231	5 462	3 926	1 920
1976	26 609	20 694	784	21 477	1 847	-43	19 588	3 813	3 209	6 725	5 861	3 957	1 977
1977	30 000	22 915	1 503	24 418	2 045	-55	22 318	4 307	3 375	7 538	6 557	3 980	2 034
1978	33 720	26 150	1 627	27 777	2 412	-70	25 295	4 801	3 623	8 420	7 288	4 005	2 122
1979	37 603	29 736	1 247	30 983	2 858	-88	28 037	5 514	4 052	9 312	7 983	4 038	2 218
1980	41 786	32 353	960	33 313	3 111	-92	30 110	6 818	4 857	10 229	8 810	4 085	2 248
1981	46 288	34 956	1 044	36 000	3 620	-130	32 250	8 464	5 575	11 258	9 663	4 112	2 233
1982	49 639	36 508	821	37 329	3 853	-153	33 323	10 047	6 268	12 015	10 380	4 131	2 192
1983	52 385	39 025	119	39 143	4 161	-182	34 800	10 827	6 758	12 649	10 975	4 141	2 219
1984	59 249	43 734	1 444	45 178	4 796	-238	40 144	12 015	7 090	14 250	12 487	4 158	2 324
1985	62 859	46 810	1 340	48 150	5 234	-286	42 630	12 695	7 534	15 023	13 164	4 184	2 385
1986	66 483	49 586	1 641	51 227	5 702	-325	45 201	13 411	7 871	15 810	13 900	4 205	2 417
1987	70 885	53 362	2 142	55 504	6 107	-375	49 022	13 742	8 121	16 737	14 590	4 235	2 509
1988	74 544	57 667	1 259	58 926	6 854	-455	51 617	14 356	8 571	17 351	15 151	4 296	2 580
1989	81 313	61 472	2 051	63 523	7 339	-438	55 746	16 251	9 316	18 744	16 341	4 338	2 634
1990	86 524	65 450	1 956	67 406	7 901	-467	59 039	17 472	10 014	19 710	17 123	4 390	2 692
1991	89 389	68 391	1 208	69 599	8 381	-474	60 744	17 869	10 776	20 129	17 591	4 441	2 717
1992	95 784	74 215	1 404	75 620	9 019	-509	66 091	17 978	11 714	21 306	18 570	4 496	2 762
1993	98 414	77 496	190	77 685	9 497	-514	67 674	18 377	12 363	21 601	18 755	4 556	2 817
1994	106 052	82 161	1 342	83 503	10 218	-559	72 726	20 326	13 001	23 003	19 982	4 610	2 904
1995	112 515	87 062	524	87 586	10 799	-604	76 183	22 575	13 757	24 144	20 880	4 660	2 995
1996	121 927	92 960	1 922	94 882	11 455	-672	82 755	24 776	14 397	25 871	22 141	4 713	3 056
1997	129 062	99 293	907	100 200	12 128	-764	87 307	27 138	14 617	27 095	23 136	4 763	3 109
1998	140 904	108 495	1 399	109 894	13 052	-822	96 021	29 750	15 133	29 273	24 932	4 813	3 181
1999	148 942	116 497	1 257	117 753	13 933	-930	102 890	30 123	15 930	30 562	26 239	4 873	3 248
2000	160 833	126 083	1 437	127 520	14 914	-1 023	111 583	32 175	17 075	32 599	27 781	4 934	3 317
2001	166 167	130 838	1 004	131 842	15 459	-1 086	115 297	31 717	19 153	33 348	28 570	4 983	3 333
2002	170 998	135 443	981	136 423	15 844	-1 099	119 480	30 741	20 777	34 071	29 748	5 019	3 327
2003	178 147	140 495	1 891	142 386	16 489	-1 138	124 760	31 602	21 785	35 252	31 138	5 054	3 340
2004	188 330	148 515	2 467	150 981	17 410	-1 201	132 370	33 034	22 925	37 017	32 826	5 088	3 384
2005	193 990	152 742	3 089	155 831	18 172	-1 208	136 452	33 623	23 915	37 892	33 217	5 120	3 446
2006	205 857	159 137	2 680	161 817	19 003	-1 188	141 626	37 923	26 308	39 867	34 831	5 164	3 492
2007	216 840	165 790	2 612	168 402	19 806	-1 275	147 321	40 718	28 802	41 642	36 174	5 207	3 536
2008	228 069	170 757	4 535	175 292	20 448	-1 285	153 559	43 295	31 214	43 466	37 993	5 247	3 524
2009	217 609	162 535	3 161	165 695	19 805	-1 179	144 711	37 013	35 885	41 204	36 901	5 281	3 425
2010	227 288	168 133	4 374	172 507	20 222	-1 212	151 073	38 327	37 888	42 798	38 334	5 311	3 420
2011	238 768	174 556	5 059	179 615	18 881	-1 129	159 605	40 544	38 618	44 672	39 404	5 345	. . .

. . . = Not available.

Table 17-2. Personal Income and Employment by Region and State—*Continued*

(Millions of dollars, except as noted.)

Region or state and year	Personal income, total	Earnings by place of work Nonfarm	Earnings by place of work Farm	Earnings by place of work Total	Less: Contributions for government social insurance	Plus: Adjustment for residence	Equals: Net earnings by place of residence	Plus: Dividends, interest, and rent	Plus: Personal current transfer receipts	Per capita Personal income	Per capita Disposable personal income	Population (thousands)	Total employment (thousands)
MISSISSIPPI													
1958	2 393	1 757	273	2 030	72	9	1 967	222	204	1 147	1 075	2 086	. . .
1959	2 645	1 919	334	2 253	87	10	2 176	249	219	1 237	1 151	2 138	. . .
1960	2 678	1 988	281	2 269	101	12	2 180	265	233	1 227	1 135	2 182	. . .
1961	2 894	2 072	353	2 425	104	13	2 334	298	262	1 312	1 223	2 206	. . .
1962	3 021	2 226	297	2 524	115	15	2 424	324	273	1 347	1 244	2 243	. . .
1963	3 330	2 372	432	2 804	136	17	2 685	355	290	1 484	1 369	2 244	. . .
1964	3 453	2 541	370	2 911	143	20	2 787	363	303	1 541	1 433	2 241	. . .
1965	3 749	2 822	352	3 173	152	22	3 043	378	328	1 669	1 547	2 246	. . .
1966	4 080	3 157	347	3 504	197	23	3 330	390	360	1 817	1 671	2 245	. . .
1967	4 420	3 383	386	3 769	226	25	3 567	421	431	1 984	1 826	2 228	. . .
1968	4 836	3 766	364	4 130	252	32	3 909	438	489	2 179	1 994	2 219	. . .
1969	5 334	4 159	349	4 508	291	35	4 251	531	552	2 403	2 186	2 220	909
1970	5 838	4 431	394	4 826	311	36	4 551	598	689	2 628	2 381	2 221	917
1971	6 467	4 858	436	5 293	351	58	5 000	654	814	2 855	2 627	2 266	939
1972	7 370	5 594	494	6 087	422	73	5 738	713	918	3 194	2 896	2 307	979
1973	8 453	6 321	692	7 013	539	93	6 567	821	1 065	3 597	3 282	2 350	1 019
1974	9 323	7 014	515	7 528	616	123	7 035	976	1 312	3 920	3 541	2 379	1 031
1975	10 096	7 508	377	7 885	654	150	7 381	1 083	1 631	4 207	3 862	2 400	1 001
1976	11 535	8 586	576	9 162	757	182	8 586	1 171	1 778	4 746	4 323	2 430	1 039
1977	12 873	9 679	610	10 288	851	223	9 660	1 311	1 902	5 233	4 781	2 460	1 071
1978	14 352	10 989	455	11 445	984	279	10 740	1 518	2 094	5 768	5 209	2 488	1 101
1979	16 280	12 190	704	12 895	1 131	337	12 101	1 789	2 391	6 491	5 841	2 508	1 114
1980	17 690	13 153	186	13 339	1 216	425	12 547	2 278	2 864	7 005	6 303	2 525	1 111
1981	19 911	14 387	335	14 722	1 425	454	13 751	2 911	3 250	7 842	7 004	2 539	1 107
1982	21 046	14 775	425	15 200	1 500	472	14 171	3 301	3 574	8 231	7 487	2 557	1 079
1983	22 006	15 526	101	15 627	1 594	529	14 562	3 506	3 938	8 570	7 762	2 568	1 088
1984	24 174	16 860	479	17 339	1 774	592	16 157	3 943	4 074	9 377	8 540	2 578	1 117
1985	25 512	17 802	437	18 239	1 914	621	16 946	4 298	4 268	9 857	8 975	2 588	1 124
1986	26 388	18 684	203	18 887	2 032	606	17 460	4 407	4 521	10 174	9 303	2 594	1 131
1987	27 953	19 637	589	20 225	2 125	643	18 743	4 500	4 710	10 799	9 841	2 589	1 141
1988	29 844	20 972	737	21 709	2 379	683	20 013	4 812	5 019	11 566	10 581	2 580	1 169
1989	32 176	22 284	569	22 853	2 558	725	21 020	5 659	5 496	12 499	11 379	2 574	1 189
1990	33 826	23 691	494	24 184	2 812	749	22 122	5 746	5 958	13 117	11 938	2 579	1 203
1991	35 731	24 794	589	25 383	2 990	809	23 202	5 859	6 669	13 749	12 573	2 599	1 211
1992	38 441	26 712	672	27 385	3 189	827	25 023	5 938	7 480	14 651	13 411	2 624	1 234
1993	40 957	28 853	586	29 439	3 452	846	26 832	6 147	7 979	15 426	14 077	2 655	1 287
1994	44 399	31 349	845	32 195	3 797	843	29 241	6 698	8 460	16 512	15 022	2 689	1 335
1995	46 764	32 913	680	33 594	3 985	930	30 539	7 010	9 216	17 176	15 605	2 723	1 365
1996	49 683	34 317	1 079	35 396	4 115	972	32 254	7 571	9 858	18 079	16 381	2 748	1 389
1997	52 429	36 254	994	37 247	4 333	1 110	34 024	8 174	10 230	18 880	17 063	2 777	1 415
1998	55 949	39 010	968	39 978	4 617	1 188	36 549	9 082	10 318	19 947	17 997	2 805	1 453
1999	58 137	41 065	946	42 011	4 827	1 285	38 469	9 002	10 666	20 555	18 539	2 828	1 477
2000	61 396	42 857	788	43 644	4 963	1 479	40 160	9 765	11 472	21 555	19 491	2 848	1 482
2001	65 090	44 151	1 577	45 728	5 054	1 620	42 293	9 961	12 836	22 815	20 699	2 853	1 449
2002	66 124	45 928	633	46 562	5 251	1 644	42 955	9 349	13 821	23 131	21 233	2 859	1 455
2003	68 755	47 949	1 350	49 299	5 419	1 720	45 601	8 721	14 433	23 970	22 150	2 868	1 453
2004	72 579	50 393	1 810	52 204	5 719	1 878	48 363	8 670	15 545	25 122	23 325	2 889	1 471
2005	77 748	52 622	1 785	54 408	5 937	2 022	50 493	9 828	17 426	26 755	24 746	2 906	1 485
2006	81 098	55 485	848	56 333	6 429	2 210	52 114	11 307	17 676	27 917	25 681	2 905	1 512
2007	86 585	57 624	1 169	58 793	6 686	2 360	54 467	13 671	18 447	29 568	27 163	2 928	1 545
2008	91 220	59 873	1 228	61 101	6 912	2 504	56 692	13 943	20 584	30 945	28 466	2 948	1 542
2009	88 896	57 810	1 266	59 075	6 825	2 522	54 771	11 770	22 355	30 045	28 037	2 959	1 497
2010	92 284	59 021	1 345	60 366	6 930	2 680	56 116	12 113	24 056	31 071	29 035	2 970	1 493
2011	95 835	60 276	1 330	61 606	6 313	2 885	58 179	12 638	25 019	32 176	29 863	2 979	. . .

. . . = Not available.

Table 17-2. Personal Income and Employment by Region and State—*Continued*

(Millions of dollars, except as noted.)

| Region or state and year | Personal income, total | Earnings by place of work | | | Less: Contributions for government social insurance | Plus: Adjustment for residence | Equals: Net earnings by place of residence | Plus: Dividends, interest, and rent | Plus: Personal current transfer receipts | Per capita (dollars) | | Population (thousands) | Total employment (thousands) |
		Nonfarm	Farm	Total						Personal income	Disposable personal income		
MISSOURI													
1958	8 684	6 821	562	7 383	260	-149	6 974	1 113	598	2 075	1 863	4 186	. . .
1959	9 195	7 364	469	7 833	311	-165	7 356	1 206	633	2 159	1 934	4 258	. . .
1960	9 476	7 616	444	8 060	358	-176	7 526	1 279	671	2 190	1 948	4 326	. . .
1961	9 792	7 787	484	8 271	375	-182	7 715	1 332	745	2 252	2 003	4 349	. . .
1962	10 320	8 258	486	8 744	408	-198	8 138	1 411	771	2 369	2 099	4 357	. . .
1963	10 839	8 767	441	9 207	469	-222	8 516	1 514	808	2 468	2 182	4 392	. . .
1964	11 449	9 397	335	9 732	491	-246	8 996	1 623	830	2 578	2 315	4 442	. . .
1965	12 449	10 078	534	10 612	517	-271	9 824	1 737	888	2 787	2 486	4 467	. . .
1966	13 319	11 090	418	11 508	695	-310	10 503	1 856	960	2 945	2 619	4 523	. . .
1967	14 175	11 848	404	12 253	796	-346	11 111	1 944	1 120	3 123	2 774	4 539	. . .
1968	15 687	13 046	479	13 525	898	-382	12 245	2 130	1 313	3 434	3 029	4 568	. . .
1969	16 561	14 160	450	14 611	954	-758	12 899	2 233	1 428	3 569	3 087	4 640	2 216
1970	18 059	15 082	525	15 607	1 004	-702	13 902	2 465	1 692	3 855	3 381	4 685	2 203
1971	19 448	16 079	571	16 651	1 108	-683	14 860	2 638	1 951	4 118	3 646	4 723	2 200
1972	21 167	17 455	714	18 170	1 261	-703	16 206	2 849	2 112	4 453	3 895	4 753	2 242
1973	23 565	19 088	1 216	20 303	1 584	-737	17 983	3 132	2 450	4 935	4 363	4 775	2 325
1974	25 266	20 653	640	21 293	1 766	-763	18 764	3 610	2 892	5 280	4 631	4 785	2 341
1975	27 619	21 917	699	22 616	1 841	-773	20 002	3 962	3 655	5 759	5 124	4 795	2 291
1976	30 450	24 744	472	25 216	2 095	-850	22 271	4 285	3 895	6 313	5 574	4 824	2 365
1977	33 848	27 559	718	28 277	2 330	-990	24 957	4 825	4 066	6 986	6 169	4 845	2 424
1978	37 767	30 824	922	31 746	2 695	-1 142	27 909	5 436	4 422	7 753	6 796	4 871	2 512
1979	42 203	34 163	1 180	35 343	3 087	-1 305	30 951	6 250	5 002	8 632	7 530	4 889	2 576
1980	45 802	36 497	243	36 741	3 284	-1 520	31 936	7 782	6 084	9 306	8 124	4 922	2 549
1981	51 211	39 306	775	40 081	3 793	-1 660	34 628	9 746	6 838	10 383	9 024	4 932	2 540
1982	54 769	41 164	348	41 512	4 049	-1 727	35 736	11 577	7 456	11 110	9 611	4 929	2 516
1983	58 376	44 268	-104	44 164	4 389	-1 752	38 022	12 344	8 010	11 808	10 436	4 944	2 562
1984	64 732	48 883	425	49 307	4 997	-1 878	42 433	13 938	8 361	13 011	11 556	4 975	2 667
1985	69 181	52 299	796	53 096	5 479	-1 994	45 623	14 738	8 820	13 836	12 238	5 000	2 738
1986	72 691	55 328	584	55 913	5 879	-2 048	47 986	15 420	9 285	14 471	12 814	5 023	2 801
1987	76 552	59 172	741	59 606	6 196	-2 171	51 259	15 732	9 562	15 139	13 366	5 057	2 836
1988	80 930	62 768	662	63 430	6 824	-2 262	54 344	16 498	10 088	15 926	14 099	5 082	2 885
1989	86 263	66 177	913	67 090	7 268	-2 391	57 430	17 904	10 929	16 928	14 915	5 096	2 938
1990	90 177	69 116	709	69 825	7 828	-2 622	59 375	18 960	11 842	17 582	15 492	5 129	2 972
1991	94 731	71 261	591	71 852	8 163	-2 641	61 049	19 836	13 846	18 320	16 280	5 171	2 942
1992	100 829	76 005	865	76 870	8 603	-2 809	65 458	20 583	14 787	19 327	17 218	5 217	2 957
1993	105 164	79 538	503	80 042	9 024	-2 918	68 100	21 185	15 879	19 951	17 742	5 271	3 041
1994	112 001	84 782	728	85 510	9 707	-2 922	72 881	22 472	16 648	21 035	18 653	5 324	3 113
1995	117 418	89 978	222	90 201	10 299	-3 155	76 746	22 960	17 712	21 832	19 287	5 378	3 196
1996	124 385	94 591	1 054	95 645	10 737	-3 283	81 625	24 271	18 490	22 901	20 130	5 432	3 255
1997	132 117	100 544	1 065	101 610	11 378	-3 493	86 739	26 195	19 183	24 104	21 089	5 481	3 328
1998	140 360	107 607	548	108 155	11 938	-3 699	92 519	28 023	19 818	25 419	22 181	5 522	3 383
1999	145 826	113 714	239	113 953	12 574	-3 758	97 620	27 418	20 788	26 218	22 866	5 562	3 423
2000	156 359	121 114	778	121 893	13 233	-4 054	104 606	29 535	22 219	27 885	24 330	5 607	3 470
2001	161 545	124 629	818	125 448	13 645	-3 913	107 890	29 148	24 507	28 637	25 010	5 641	3 454
2002	166 195	129 239	378	129 617	13 952	-4 006	111 659	28 314	26 222	29 286	26 152	5 675	3 429
2003	172 529	133 985	1 094	135 079	14 396	-3 943	116 740	28 411	27 378	30 218	27 299	5 709	3 438
2004	180 547	139 409	2 250	141 659	14 922	-3 935	122 801	28 793	28 953	31 412	28 487	5 748	3 473
2005	186 753	145 608	1 419	147 027	15 689	-4 227	127 112	28 642	30 999	32 253	28 965	5 790	3 526
2006	198 727	152 529	1 276	153 805	16 706	-4 393	132 706	33 172	32 849	34 013	30 394	5 843	3 579
2007	209 131	157 979	1 375	159 354	17 461	-4 395	137 497	36 590	35 043	35 521	31 551	5 888	3 642
2008	223 554	165 531	2 377	167 908	18 276	-4 866	144 767	40 689	38 098	37 738	33 704	5 924	3 625
2009	215 242	159 046	1 735	160 781	17 829	-4 765	138 188	34 056	42 999	36 108	32 961	5 961	3 525
2010	220 635	161 348	1 636	162 984	17 881	-4,423	140 680	34 831	45 124	36 799	33 608	5 996	3 490
2011	229 898	165 770	2 289	168 059	16 472	-4 560	147 026	36 753	46 119	38 248	34 593	6 011	. . .

. . . = Not available.

Table 17-2. Personal Income and Employment by Region and State—*Continued*

(Millions of dollars, except as noted.)

| Region or state and year | Personal income, total | Earnings by place of work | | | Less: Contributions for government social insurance | Plus: Adjustment for residence | Equals: Net earnings by place of residence | Plus: Dividends, interest, and rent | Plus: Personal current transfer receipts | Per capita (dollars) | | Population (thousands) | Total employment (thousands) |
		Nonfarm	Farm	Total						Personal income	Disposable personal income		
MONTANA													
1958	1 377	906	237	1 143	44	0	1 099	178	100	2 068	1 887	666	...
1959	1 347	955	147	1 101	51	0	1 051	189	107	2 014	1 799	669	...
1960	1 403	995	162	1 158	62	0	1 096	199	108	2 066	1 861	679	...
1961	1 400	1 040	110	1 150	62	*	1 088	195	117	2 012	1 800	696	...
1962	1 645	1 103	277	1 380	64	0	1 316	210	119	2 357	2 143	698	...
1963	1 631	1 152	213	1 365	72	0	1 292	217	121	2 320	2 095	703	...
1964	1 662	1 205	169	1 374	74	0	1 300	236	126	2 354	2 152	706	...
1965	1 787	1 281	190	1 472	76	0	1 396	257	134	2 531	2 299	706	...
1966	1 916	1 366	227	1 593	99	0	1 494	280	143	2 710	2 452	707	...
1967	1 952	1 407	191	1 598	108	0	1 489	294	169	2 785	2 510	701	...
1968	2 052	1 486	196	1 682	115	-1	1 566	295	191	2 932	2 641	700	...
1969	2 286	1 613	242	1 855	127	-1	1 726	350	210	3 294	2 888	694	298
1970	2 527	1 736	291	2 027	137	-1	1 888	397	241	3 624	3 228	697	301
1971	2 695	1 895	251	2 146	152	-1	1 993	421	280	3 790	3 419	711	307
1972	3 128	2 132	401	2 534	179	0	2 355	464	310	4 350	3 880	719	319
1973	3 637	2 389	575	2 964	229	0	2 736	541	360	5 000	4 444	727	333
1974	3 957	2 701	466	3 166	264	1	2 903	631	423	5 367	4 756	737	344
1975	4 356	3 011	401	3 412	285	3	3 130	712	514	5 814	5 202	749	344
1976	4 704	3 446	226	3 671	326	3	3 349	786	569	6 202	5 506	759	359
1977	5 108	3 886	71	3 957	371	4	3 591	904	613	6 622	5 841	771	372
1978	6 002	4 427	303	4 731	435	3	4 299	1 029	674	7 655	6 795	784	390
1979	6 465	4 881	119	5 000	500	6	4 507	1 199	759	8 192	7 170	789	396
1980	7 129	5 187	121	5 308	537	14	4 785	1 452	893	9 038	7 936	789	393
1981	8 102	5 639	228	5 867	631	25	5 262	1 808	1 032	10 187	8 980	795	395
1982	8 545	5 791	172	5 964	661	18	5 320	2 069	1 155	10 628	9 476	804	391
1983	8 998	6 119	127	6 246	700	9	5 555	2 177	1 266	11 054	9 899	814	398
1984	9 537	6 488	44	6 532	758	6	5 779	2 407	1 351	11 617	10 440	821	408
1985	9 672	6 621	-85	6 536	790	3	5 749	2 494	1 429	11 762	10 571	822	406
1986	10 049	6 597	238	6 835	805	-2	6 028	2 496	1 525	12 350	11 211	814	402
1987	10 343	6 789	318	7 107	828	-3	6 277	2 468	1 598	12 848	11 570	805	406
1988	10 595	7 207	112	7 319	926	-1	6 392	2 517	1 686	13 241	11 862	800	416
1989	11 650	7 582	420	8 002	992	-3	7 008	2 795	1 847	14 569	12 972	800	424
1990	12 280	8 042	396	8 438	1 114	-4	7 321	2 935	2 024	15 346	13 693	800	433
1991	13 157	8 666	552	9 218	1 222	-12	7 984	3 042	2 132	16 250	14 588	810	444
1992	13 922	9 360	490	9 849	1 335	-2	8 513	3 096	2 312	16 859	15 107	826	456
1993	15 025	10 088	774	10 862	1 477	1	9 386	3 155	2 484	17 787	15 955	845	470
1994	15 494	10 695	390	11 085	1 566	6	9 525	3 391	2 578	17 989	16 068	861	494
1995	16 256	11 091	340	11 431	1 586	9	9 854	3 647	2 756	18 546	16 599	877	504
1996	17 070	11 584	310	11 894	1 595	13	10 311	3 900	2 859	19 261	17 198	886	519
1997	17 826	12 042	240	12 282	1 617	14	10 679	4 229	2 918	20 033	17 815	890	526
1998	19 151	12 910	301	13 210	1 670	19	11 559	4 562	3 031	21 459	19 069	892	537
1999	19 786	13 582	389	13 971	1 722	22	12 271	4 502	3 013	22 045	19 547	898	544
2000	21 200	14 546	256	14 802	1 820	27	13 009	4 818	3 374	23 457	20 770	904	555
2001	22 931	15 839	342	16 181	1 956	34	14 260	5 019	3 653	25 284	22 509	907	560
2002	23 370	16 395	187	16 582	2 054	33	14 561	5 014	3 795	25 635	23 174	912	568
2003	24 752	17 247	337	17 583	2 175	32	15 440	5 367	3 945	26 915	24 530	920	575
2004	26 495	18 491	544	19 035	2 296	35	16 775	5 494	4 226	28 489	25 988	930	589
2005	28 179	19 733	599	20 332	2 490	35	17 877	5 797	4 506	29 975	27 039	940	603
2006	30 447	21 267	190	21 457	2 694	34	18 797	6 753	4 897	31 959	28 655	953	623
2007	32 464	22 222	408	22 629	2 900	37	19 766	7 470	5 228	33 651	29 898	965	641
2008	34 490	22 799	541	23 340	2 969	39	20 410	8 365	5 716	35 323	31 630	976	642
2009	33 187	22 076	400	22 476	2 936	33	19 572	7 118	6 497	33 727	30 766	984	626
2010	34 736	22 806	584	23 390	3 046	37	20 381	7 382	6 973	35 053	32 024	991	624
2011	36 507	23 603	720	24 323	2 876	39	21 487	7 824	7 197	36 573	33 069	998	...

. . . = Not available.
* = Less than $50,000, but the estimates for this item are included in the total.

Table 17-2. Personal Income and Employment by Region and State—*Continued*

(Millions of dollars, except as noted.)

| Region or state and year | Personal income, total | Earnings by place of work | | | Less: Contributions for government social insurance | Plus: Adjustment for residence | Equals: Net earnings by place of residence | Plus: Dividends, interest, and rent | Plus: Personal current transfer receipts | Per capita (dollars) | | Population (thousands) | Total employment (thousands) |
		Nonfarm	Farm	Total						Personal income	Disposable personal income		
NEBRASKA													
1958	2 855	1 823	525	2 348	75	-9	2 265	431	160	2 064	1 886	1 383	. . .
1959	2 875	1 988	358	2 347	93	-9	2 245	456	174	2 058	1 873	1 397	. . .
1960	3 062	2 127	392	2 519	116	-11	2 392	484	185	2 161	1 950	1 417	. . .
1961	3 129	2 233	320	2 553	119	-11	2 423	501	205	2 164	1 936	1 446	. . .
1962	3 401	2 357	438	2 794	128	-10	2 657	529	216	2 323	2 103	1 464	. . .
1963	3 494	2 439	394	2 833	140	-9	2 684	581	229	2 367	2 135	1 476	. . .
1964	3 583	2 584	312	2 896	146	-8	2 742	604	236	2 417	2 208	1 482	. . .
1965	3 944	2 699	498	3 197	148	-8	3 041	646	258	2 681	2 458	1 471	. . .
1966	4 249	2 907	593	3 499	196	-8	3 295	674	280	2 918	2 653	1 456	. . .
1967	4 399	3 139	489	3 628	228	-8	3 392	666	341	3 019	2 731	1 457	. . .
1968	4 688	3 431	444	3 875	245	-8	3 622	672	394	3 196	2 866	1 467	. . .
1969	5 264	3 800	604	4 404	269	-100	4 035	799	429	3 571	3 142	1 474	704
1970	5 644	4 120	542	4 662	289	-107	4 266	880	498	3 793	3 364	1 488	715
1971	6 196	4 436	688	5 124	320	-110	4 693	941	562	4 119	3 718	1 504	728
1972	6 870	4 878	809	5 687	364	-119	5 204	1 046	620	4 525	4 011	1 518	748
1973	8 039	5 466	1 227	6 693	467	-123	6 103	1 196	741	5 259	4 676	1 529	775
1974	8 384	6 079	771	6 850	541	-133	6 177	1 361	847	5 452	4 788	1 538	793
1975	9 529	6 577	1 110	7 687	579	-140	6 969	1 524	1 036	6 182	5 539	1 541	790
1976	9 982	7 476	589	8 066	661	-147	7 257	1 622	1 103	6 445	5 751	1 549	811
1977	10 820	8 152	533	8 685	723	-146	7 817	1 830	1 174	6 961	6 130	1 554	831
1978	12 533	9 126	1 087	10 212	832	-169	9 211	2 019	1 303	8 030	7 111	1 561	854
1979	13 526	10 191	755	10 947	970	-197	9 779	2 294	1 452	8 646	7 554	1 564	876
1980	14 395	11 041	107	11 148	1 051	-214	9 883	2 818	1 694	9 155	8 010	1 572	877
1981	16 699	11 866	836	12 702	1 228	-253	11 221	3 526	1 952	10 579	9 337	1 579	871
1982	17 970	12 342	768	13 110	1 307	-260	11 542	4 277	2 151	11 361	9 880	1 582	861
1983	18 614	12 949	549	13 498	1 351	-276	11 871	4 416	2 328	11 749	10 489	1 584	867
1984	20 716	14 198	1 160	15 358	1 520	-327	13 511	4 764	2 441	13 040	11 777	1 589	886
1985	21 799	14 903	1 449	16 352	1 646	-352	14 354	4 852	2 593	13 756	12 414	1 585	898
1986	22 406	15 459	1 414	16 873	1 766	-350	14 757	4 938	2 711	14 232	12 841	1 574	898
1987	23 415	16 325	1 638	17 963	1 867	-347	15 749	4 894	2 773	14 947	13 436	1 567	925
1988	25 011	17 404	2 035	19 440	2 080	-381	16 979	5 139	2 893	15 915	14 302	1 571	947
1989	26 443	18 493	1 847	20 340	2 222	-390	17 727	5 613	3 103	16 790	14 987	1 575	965
1990	28 388	19 761	2 200	21 961	2 460	-383	19 118	5 905	3 365	17 948	15 996	1 582	988
1991	29 562	20 752	1 998	22 749	2 605	-422	19 722	6 214	3 626	18 523	16 565	1 596	992
1992	31 272	22 084	2 119	24 203	2 735	-462	21 006	6 329	3 937	19 403	17 384	1 612	999
1993	32 246	23 219	1 748	24 968	2 876	-477	21 615	6 426	4 205	19 836	17 742	1 626	1 021
1994	34 459	24 920	1 852	26 772	3 079	-489	23 204	6 869	4 386	21 024	18 788	1 639	1 061
1995	36 468	26 788	1 327	28 115	3 230	-536	24 349	7 457	4 661	22 008	19 569	1 657	1 071
1996	39 923	28 408	2 596	31 004	3 404	-591	27 009	7 956	4 958	23 853	21 203	1 674	1 097
1997	41 080	30 068	1 762	31 830	3 615	-667	27 548	8 394	5 138	24 359	21 430	1 686	1 111
1998	43 852	32 018	1 649	33 667	3 848	-701	29 118	9 255	5 479	25 859	22 711	1 696	1 138
1999	46 057	34 219	1 573	35 792	4 043	-783	30 967	9 288	5 802	27 017	23 727	1 705	1 158
2000	48 998	36 439	1 441	37 880	4 225	-854	32 801	10 108	6 088	28 590	25 063	1 714	1 176
2001	51 336	38 072	1 801	39 874	4 411	-905	34 557	10 086	6 693	29 849	26 293	1 720	1 175
2002	52 249	39 480	1 047	40 527	4 553	-947	35 026	10 095	7 127	30 231	27 189	1 728	1 167
2003	55 652	41 218	2 625	43 843	4 716	-1 000	38 127	10 101	7 424	32 009	29 143	1 739	1 171
2004	57 905	43 254	2 885	46 139	4 924	-1 019	40 196	9 926	7 783	33 100	30 135	1 749	1 184
2005	60 064	44 981	2 926	47 907	5 187	-1 043	41 677	10 177	8 210	34 098	30 795	1 761	1 198
2006	62 810	47 376	1 745	49 121	5 595	-1 021	42 505	11 471	8 833	35 432	31 715	1 773	1 213
2007	67 569	49 356	2 766	52 122	5 812	-1 113	45 197	13 029	9 343	37 887	33 740	1 783	1 234
2008	72 567	51 324	3 746	55 070	6 015	-1 167	47 888	14 639	10 040	40 396	36 283	1 796	1 241
2009	70 085	50 768	3 280	54 048	6 026	-1 128	46 893	12 191	11 001	38 664	35 383	1 813	1 227
2010	72 353	52 088	3 440	55 528	6 268	-1 132	48 128	12 653	11 572	39 534	36 189	1 830	1 226
2011	76 624	53 849	4 573	58 423	5 888	-1 208	51 326	13 429	11 869	41 584	37 664	1 843	. . .

. . . = Not available.

Table 17-2. Personal Income and Employment by Region and State—*Continued*

(Millions of dollars, except as noted.)

Region or state and year	Personal income, total	Earnings by place of work			Less: Contributions for government social insurance	Plus: Adjustment for residence	Equals: Net earnings by place of residence	Plus: Dividends, interest, and rent	Plus: Personal current transfer receipts	Per capita (dollars)		Population (thousands)	Total employment (thousands)
		Nonfarm	Farm	Total						Personal income	Disposable personal income		
NEVADA													
1958	705	595	22	617	26	-2	589	79	37	2 622	2 310	269	. . .
1959	775	662	19	681	30	-2	649	88	38	2 779	2 468	279	. . .
1960	850	729	15	744	36	-2	705	104	41	2 922	2 572	291	. . .
1961	941	804	13	817	40	-3	775	118	49	2 988	2 606	315	. . .
1962	1 134	985	19	1 003	50	-4	949	133	51	3 222	2 828	352	. . .
1963	1 276	1 127	20	1 147	66	-6	1 075	143	58	3 214	2 805	397	. . .
1964	1 388	1 221	12	1 233	67	-5	1 161	162	65	3 257	2 909	426	. . .
1965	1 487	1 285	14	1 298	66	-5	1 228	187	72	3 349	2 999	444	. . .
1966	1 571	1 359	18	1 377	80	-4	1 294	199	78	3 522	3 145	446	. . .
1967	1 668	1 429	17	1 446	86	-3	1 356	217	95	3 715	3 309	449	. . .
1968	1 935	1 641	20	1 661	100	-4	1 556	265	113	4 169	3 631	464	. . .
1969	2 174	1 888	32	1 921	132	-34	1 754	295	125	4 530	3 851	480	244
1970	2 432	2 096	34	2 130	144	-39	1 947	338	148	4 932	4 356	493	256
1971	2 713	2 322	35	2 356	165	-42	2 150	379	184	5 218	4 662	520	267
1972	3 036	2 589	42	2 631	194	-45	2 393	425	218	5 553	4 931	547	280
1973	3 466	2 976	56	3 032	256	-55	2 721	491	254	6 093	5 415	569	304
1974	3 866	3 277	35	3 312	287	-57	2 968	583	315	6 479	5 740	597	317
1975	4 357	3 621	33	3 654	312	-58	3 284	636	438	7 029	6 390	620	326
1976	5 000	4 190	36	4 226	367	-68	3 791	721	489	7 731	6 924	647	349
1977	5 777	4 919	27	4 946	438	-84	4 425	819	534	8 519	7 580	678	384
1978	6 990	6 032	23	6 055	552	-117	5 386	1 001	603	9 718	8 558	719	432
1979	8 140	6 995	9	7 004	678	-132	6 194	1 235	712	10 639	9 292	765	468
1980	9 463	7 957	57	8 014	775	-159	7 080	1 519	863	11 679	10 279	810	489
1981	10 774	8 909	28	8 937	940	-165	7 831	1 890	1 053	12 711	11 151	848	500
1982	11 551	9 199	33	9 232	964	-166	8 102	2 276	1 173	13 104	11 603	882	494
1983	12 267	9 727	26	9 753	1 049	-177	8 528	2 456	1 283	13 600	12 137	902	499
1984	13 413	10 606	36	10 641	1 191	-187	9 263	2 775	1 375	14 501	12 963	925	523
1985	14 561	11 442	29	11 471	1 313	-195	9 963	3 087	1 510	15 310	13 605	951	545
1986	15 682	12 350	28	12 378	1 452	-212	10 713	3 286	1 683	15 992	14 169	981	570
1987	17 103	13 645	49	13 694	1 615	-236	11 843	3 464	1 796	16 713	14 728	1 023	616
1988	19 406	15 676	65	15 742	1 872	-276	13 593	3 838	1 975	18 052	15 850	1 075	662
1989	21 798	17 420	79	17 499	2 118	-321	15 060	4 457	2 281	19 165	16 818	1 137	710
1990	24 465	19 576	83	19 659	2 494	-374	16 792	5 065	2 608	20 042	17 562	1 221	756
1991	26 930	21 047	76	21 123	2 662	-346	18 115	5 606	3 209	20 777	18 399	1 296	769
1992	29 864	23 170	73	23 243	2 895	-308	20 041	6 191	3 633	22 099	19 541	1 351	776
1993	32 222	25 145	119	25 264	3 170	-347	21 747	6 636	3 838	22 833	20 109	1 411	819
1994	35 821	27 885	82	27 967	3 543	-358	24 067	7 731	4 024	23 892	21 136	1 499	898
1995	39 403	30 728	70	30 798	3 893	-354	26 552	8 497	4 355	24 914	22 038	1 582	953
1996	43 722	33 996	70	34 067	4 217	-374	29 476	9 565	4 681	26 239	22 957	1 666	1 024
1997	47 838	37 108	71	37 179	4 501	-329	32 349	10 502	4 988	27 118	23 787	1 764	1 089
1998	53 046	41 020	93	41 113	4 809	-339	35 965	11 768	5 313	28 624	24 943	1 853	1 131
1999	57 363	45 130	85	45 216	5 109	-373	39 734	12 074	5 555	29 650	25 814	1 935	1 196
2000	62 535	48 550	104	48 654	5 010	-333	43 311	13 250	5 974	30 977	26 875	2 019	1 251
2001	65 313	50 539	118	50 657	5 306	-295	45 056	13 476	6 780	31 125	27 199	2 098	1 270
2002	67 834	52 154	90	52 244	5 555	-302	46 387	13 791	7 656	31 205	27 791	2 174	1 296
2003	73 078	55 980	90	56 071	5 633	-357	50 082	14 810	8 187	32 496	29 221	2 249	1 350
2004	82 161	62 161	124	62 285	6 178	-434	55 674	17 673	8 815	35 019	31 349	2 346	1 438
2005	91 837	68 563	135	68 698	6 785	-517	61 396	20 925	9 515	37 760	33 419	2 432	1 530
2006	97 844	73 985	131	74 116	7 825	-526	65 764	21 745	10 335	38 786	34 314	2 523	1 606
2007	103 710	78 192	95	78 287	8 205	-609	69 473	22 950	11 288	39 872	35 373	2 601	1 650
2008	105 824	76 966	145	77 110	7 743	-585	68 783	24 332	12 709	39 879	36 162	2 654	1 622
2009	98 080	70 436	131	70 567	7 506	-410	62 651	20 284	15 145	36 533	33 522	2 685	1 519
2010	99 892	70 286	139	70 425	7 432	-353	62 640	20 893	16 359	36 938	33 947	2 704	1 495
2011	103 957	72 402	147	72 549	6 878	-351	65 320	22 101	16 536	38 173	34 667	2 723	. . .

. . . = Not available.

Table 17-2. Personal Income and Employment by Region and State—*Continued*

(Millions of dollars, except as noted.)

| Region or state and year | Personal income, total | Derivation of personal income | | | | | | | | Per capita (dollars) | | Population (thousands) | Total employment (thousands) |
| | | Earnings by place of work | | | Less: Contributions for government social insurance | Plus: Adjustment for residence | Equals: Net earnings by place of residence | Plus: Dividends, interest, and rent | Plus: Personal current transfer receipts | Personal income | Disposable personal income | | |
		Nonfarm	Farm	Total									
NEW HAMPSHIRE													
1958	1 164	887	21	908	39	57	926	155	83	2 003	1 808	581	. . .
1959	1 264	975	16	991	46	70	1 015	164	86	2 122	1 912	596	. . .
1960	1 336	1 024	20	1 044	55	79	1 067	179	90	2 193	1 958	609	. . .
1961	1 406	1 068	21	1 088	56	85	1 117	188	102	2 276	2 039	618	. . .
1962	1 508	1 141	19	1 160	62	94	1 192	211	105	2 385	2 132	632	. . .
1963	1 569	1 185	18	1 202	68	100	1 234	223	113	2 418	2 149	649	. . .
1964	1 685	1 270	18	1 288	71	108	1 326	244	116	2 542	2 307	663	. . .
1965	1 820	1 364	21	1 385	75	119	1 430	267	123	2 693	2 433	676	. . .
1966	2 004	1 518	24	1 542	103	139	1 579	292	132	2 942	2 628	681	. . .
1967	2 188	1 668	17	1 685	116	154	1 723	311	155	3 140	2 802	697	. . .
1968	2 420	1 837	20	1 857	128	173	1 902	339	180	3 414	3 024	709	. . .
1969	2 712	1 991	21	2 012	129	232	2 116	393	203	3 745	3 305	724	334
1970	2 881	2 113	17	2 130	135	220	2 215	424	241	3 883	3 406	742	334
1971	3 118	2 269	15	2 283	150	230	2 363	463	292	4 091	3 655	762	336
1972	3 448	2 525	16	2 541	176	252	2 617	508	322	4 411	3 880	782	350
1973	3 899	2 882	21	2 903	229	284	2 957	562	380	4 863	4 333	802	374
1974	4 299	3 119	14	3 133	257	329	3 205	639	455	5 262	4 667	817	381
1975	4 649	3 265	17	3 283	266	359	3 375	688	586	5 602	5 043	830	370
1976	5 293	3 786	19	3 805	310	411	3 906	763	624	6 249	5 582	847	394
1977	5 986	4 304	18	4 322	353	480	4 449	876	660	6 866	6 102	872	418
1978	6 910	5 029	19	5 048	420	572	5 200	987	723	7 730	6 807	894	446
1979	7 921	5 754	22	5 775	503	680	5 952	1 141	828	8 686	7 639	912	468
1980	9 072	6 374	14	6 388	560	847	6 675	1 428	969	9 816	8 664	924	482
1981	10 289	7 036	23	7 059	665	956	7 350	1 803	1 136	10 985	9 667	937	492
1982	11 353	7 605	19	7 624	737	1 047	7 934	2 172	1 246	11 979	10 667	948	498
1983	12 470	8 521	17	8 538	841	1 171	8 869	2 270	1 331	13 015	11 582	958	518
1984	14 121	9 613	22	9 635	977	1 386	10 043	2 669	1 408	14 455	12 906	977	553
1985	15 612	10 794	24	10 818	1 126	1 508	11 201	2 937	1 474	15 663	13 867	997	586
1986	17 240	12 093	25	12 117	1 276	1 589	12 431	3 263	1 546	16 819	14 795	1 025	617
1987	19 070	13 650	43	13 693	1 420	1 712	13 985	3 505	1 579	18 088	15 894	1 054	635
1988	20 960	15 053	46	15 099	1 611	1 865	15 353	3 893	1 714	19 361	17 133	1 083	660
1989	22 350	15 643	35	15 678	1 689	1 955	15 944	4 489	1 917	20 235	17 917	1 105	660
1990	22 510	15 505	44	15 549	1 723	1 995	15 821	4 542	2 147	20 236	18 016	1 112	643
1991	23 370	15 474	45	15 519	1 746	2 181	15 955	4 542	2 874	21 056	18 898	1 110	616
1992	24 435	16 534	51	16 586	1 854	2 238	16 969	4 405	3 061	21 861	19 636	1 118	629
1993	25 200	17 285	42	17 328	1 931	2 358	17 754	4 481	2 964	22 311	19 951	1 129	642
1994	27 012	18 434	40	18 474	2 087	2 457	18 843	4 802	3 367	23 642	21 176	1 143	666
1995	28 760	19 643	35	19 679	2 232	2 446	19 893	5 242	3 626	24 845	22 192	1 158	679
1996	31 305	20 977	41	21 017	2 355	2 613	21 276	6 450	3 580	26 649	23 656	1 175	696
1997	32 764	22 739	38	22 777	2 531	2 821	23 068	5 976	3 720	27 546	24 059	1 189	717
1998	35 773	25 134	40	25 174	2 745	2 942	25 370	6 543	3 860	29 664	25 923	1 206	739
1999	37 926	27 014	44	27 059	2 914	3 400	27 545	6 439	3 942	31 036	26 934	1 222	756
2000	42 283	30 008	44	30 052	3 203	4 037	30 886	7 151	4 246	34 102	29 286	1 240	778
2001	43 699	31 097	42	31 139	3 326	4 087	31 900	7 164	4 634	34 805	30 157	1 256	789
2002	44 711	32 099	42	32 141	3 416	3 910	32 634	7 026	5 051	35 231	31 547	1 269	787
2003	45 828	33 513	49	33 562	3 562	3 863	33 863	6 795	5 170	35 808	32 414	1 280	796
2004	48 661	35 801	58	35 859	3 820	3 976	36 015	6 997	5 650	37 718	34 277	1 290	811
2005	50 028	37 369	51	37 420	3 993	3 973	37 399	6 747	5 882	38 528	34 669	1 298	825
2006	53 765	39 451	41	39 492	4 173	4 081	39 400	8 099	6 266	41 092	36 822	1 308	835
2007	56 418	40 275	43	40 318	4 339	4 407	40 385	9 244	6 788	42 984	38 293	1 313	848
2008	58 162	40 536	39	40 576	4 486	4 532	40 622	10 169	7 371	44 199	39 728	1 316	844
2009	55 983	39 279	26	39 305	4 482	4 287	39 110	8 549	8 324	42 537	39 023	1 316	821
2010	57 542	40 324	31	40 355	4 609	4 508	40 253	8 657	8 632	43 698	40 057	1 317	817
2011	60 356	41 977	23	42 000	4 311	4 762	42 452	9 141	8 763	45 787	41 473	1 318	. . .

. . . = Not available.

Table 17-2. Personal Income and Employment by Region and State—*Continued*

(Millions of dollars, except as noted.)

Region or state and year	Personal income, total	Derivation of personal income								Per capita (dollars)		Population (thou-sands)	Total employ-ment (thou-sands)
		Earnings by place of work			Less: Contribu-tions for govern-ment social insurance	Plus: Adjust-ment for residence	Equals: Net earnings by place of residence	Plus: Dividends, interest, and rent	Plus: Personal current transfer receipts	Personal income	Disposable personal income		
		Nonfarm	Farm	Total									
NEW JERSEY													
1958	14 384	11 475	134	11 609	469	684	11 824	1 714	847	2 442	2 163	5 890	. . .
1959	15 463	12 461	106	12 567	557	769	12 780	1 828	855	2 571	2 280	6 015	. . .
1960	16 296	13 077	121	13 199	660	855	13 394	2 006	896	2 670	2 358	6 103	. . .
1961	17 121	13 624	120	13 745	694	912	13 962	2 134	1 024	2 733	2 413	6 265	. . .
1962	18 416	14 581	110	14 691	771	1 013	14 933	2 404	1 079	2 888	2 546	6 376	. . .
1963	19 331	15 220	108	15 328	869	1 088	15 546	2 625	1 159	2 960	2 607	6 531	. . .
1964	20 736	16 165	103	16 269	881	1 205	16 593	2 939	1 205	3 114	2 793	6 660	. . .
1965	22 285	17 295	119	17 414	934	1 317	17 797	3 203	1 285	3 293	2 932	6 767	. . .
1966	24 139	18 884	120	19 004	1 212	1 514	19 306	3 448	1 385	3 523	3 135	6 851	. . .
1967	26 020	20 244	105	20 349	1 345	1 680	20 684	3 694	1 642	3 756	3 319	6 928	. . .
1968	28 589	22 142	103	22 245	1 533	1 888	22 600	4 025	1 964	4 081	3 574	7 005	. . .
1969	31 930	24 079	105	24 184	1 827	3 117	25 474	4 243	2 212	4 500	3 901	7 095	3 061
1970	34 610	26 046	100	26 146	1 957	3 071	27 260	4 660	2 689	4 813	4 218	7 190	3 125
1971	37 230	27 819	93	27 912	2 168	3 155	28 899	5 054	3 277	5 113	4 542	7 282	3 119
1972	40 446	30 382	89	30 471	2 482	3 354	31 343	5 440	3 663	5 513	4 829	7 337	3 184
1973	44 208	33 597	127	33 724	3 128	3 511	34 108	5 969	4 131	6 027	5 325	7 335	3 288
1974	48 130	36 187	138	36 325	3 458	3 701	36 569	6 713	4 847	6 561	5 775	7 335	3 301
1975	51 776	37 719	97	37 816	3 541	3 983	38 258	7 180	6 338	7 053	6 295	7 341	3 191
1976	56 546	41 563	102	41 665	3 930	4 326	42 061	7 642	6 842	7 699	6 805	7 344	3 248
1977	61 957	45 750	112	45 862	4 313	4 720	46 269	8 471	7 217	8 439	7 376	7 342	3 325
1978	68 849	51 327	127	51 454	4 985	5 305	51 774	9 394	7 681	9 359	8 159	7 356	3 465
1979	76 470	56 830	127	56 957	5 744	6 052	57 265	10 663	8 542	10 372	8 948	7 373	3 552
1980	86 123	62 265	116	62 381	6 325	7 144	63 200	13 162	9 761	11 676	10 053	7 376	3 601
1981	96 195	68 068	150	68 218	7 346	7 755	68 628	16 606	10 961	12 986	11 149	7 407	3 631
1982	104 010	72 797	166	72 962	7 972	8 290	73 281	18 713	12 016	13 997	12 029	7 431	3 639
1983	112 222	79 397	191	79 589	8 983	8 519	79 125	20 121	12 976	15 027	13 059	7 468	3 739
1984	124 048	88 235	200	88 435	10 427	8 903	86 911	23 604	13 533	16 506	14 408	7 515	3 914
1985	132 934	95 574	226	95 800	11 396	9 266	93 670	25 079	14 186	17 571	15 192	7 566	4 026
1986	141 913	103 145	228	103 373	12 409	9 833	100 797	26 264	14 851	18 618	16 067	7 622	4 122
1987	153 050	113 016	259	113 275	13 525	10 350	110 100	27 602	15 347	19 952	17 056	7 671	4 220
1988	167 840	125 244	255	125 498	15 240	10 689	120 947	30 554	16 339	21 763	18 816	7 712	4 317
1989	179 512	131 690	246	131 937	15 883	10 198	126 251	35 765	17 496	23 235	20 102	7 726	4 351
1990	189 061	137 643	243	137 886	16 036	10 440	132 290	37 465	19 305	24 354	21 163	7 763	4 310
1991	193 443	139 420	228	139 649	16 560	10 535	133 623	37 630	22 190	24 754	21 607	7 815	4 172
1992	207 020	148 454	237	148 691	17 565	12 510	143 636	37 680	25 704	26 270	22 974	7 881	4 170
1993	213 023	154 252	265	154 517	18 224	12 918	149 211	36 943	26 869	26 799	23 335	7 949	4 197
1994	221 140	160 825	283	161 107	19 274	13 028	154 862	39 040	27 238	27 593	23 935	8 014	4 232
1995	234 591	169 382	277	169 659	20 033	14 090	163 717	41 817	29 058	29 022	25 242	8 083	4 296
1996	249 483	179 232	297	179 529	20 869	15 513	174 173	45 346	29 963	30 613	26 445	8 150	4 352
1997	265 679	189 423	247	189 670	21 590	18 319	186 400	48 559	30 720	32 326	27 690	8 219	4 412
1998	283 528	201 239	264	201 503	22 796	20 648	199 355	52 598	31 574	34 212	29 017	8 287	4 489
1999	295 592	211 813	232	212 044	23 866	22 283	210 461	52 196	32 935	35 360	29 748	8 360	4 551
2000	325 986	232 754	338	233 092	25 647	25 447	232 892	57 929	35 165	38 667	32 334	8 431	4 713
2001	336 606	239 093	284	239 376	26 615	26 756	239 517	58 064	39 025	39 635	33 318	8 493	4 741
2002	341 558	246 188	303	246 491	27 390	23 864	242 965	56 350	42 242	39 936	34 609	8 553	4 777
2003	347 692	253 799	307	254 106	27 764	23 750	250 092	54 549	43 051	40 423	35 405	8 601	4 815
2004	365 260	266 819	336	267 155	29 017	26 600	264 737	56 817	43 706	42 302	37 142	8 635	4 894
2005	379 650	277 551	346	277 896	30 577	29 324	276 643	57 097	45 910	43 880	37 994	8 652	4 980
2006	411 429	293 143	384	293 527	31 695	33 244	295 076	66 687	49 666	47 500	41 046	8 662	5 059
2007	436 120	304 024	398	304 422	33 374	37 663	308 711	75 685	51 723	50 256	42 889	8 678	5 121
2008	454 206	310 199	403	310 602	34 414	37 759	313 947	83 795	56 464	52 141	45 152	8 711	5 120
2009	433 835	297 918	388	298 306	33 647	32 259	296 917	71 905	65 013	49 549	43 931	8 756	4 992
2010	450 004	305 057	361	305 418	34 312	36 052	307 158	73 548	69 299	51 139	45 391	8 800	4 962
2011	469 115	313 719	343	314 063	31 764	38 587	320 886	77 916	70 313	53 181	46 562	8 821	. . .

. . . = Not available.

Table 17-2. Personal Income and Employment by Region and State—*Continued*

(Millions of dollars, except as noted.)

| Region or state and year | Personal income, total | Derivation of personal income | | | | | | | | Per capita (dollars) | | Population (thou-sands) | Total employ-ment (thou-sands) |
| | | Earnings by place of work | | | Less: Contribu-tions for govern-ment social insurance | Plus: Adjust-ment for residence | Equals: Net earnings by place of residence | Plus: Dividends, interest, and rent | Plus: Personal current transfer receipts | Personal income | Disposable personal income | | |
		Nonfarm	Farm	Total									
NEW MEXICO													
1958	1 627	1 321	114	1 435	45	-13	1 378	165	84	1 836	1 669	886	...
1959	1 750	1 446	99	1 545	54	-14	1 477	181	93	1 904	1 723	919	...
1960	1 803	1 493	86	1 579	61	-14	1 505	196	102	1 890	1 715	954	...
1961	1 887	1 532	102	1 634	61	-14	1 559	210	118	1 955	1 775	965	...
1962	1 960	1 620	83	1 703	66	-15	1 622	218	120	2 002	1 811	979	...
1963	2 025	1 671	87	1 758	74	-16	1 668	229	129	2 048	1 853	989	...
1964	2 139	1 784	66	1 850	78	-17	1 755	250	135	2 127	1 950	1 006	...
1965	2 267	1 876	78	1 954	81	-19	1 855	267	145	2 240	2 037	1 012	...
1966	2 389	1 966	100	2 066	104	-19	1 944	289	156	2 372	2 157	1 007	...
1967	2 477	2 039	90	2 129	121	-20	1 989	293	195	2 477	2 253	1 000	...
1968	2 678	2 181	102	2 284	124	-21	2 138	312	228	2 695	2 438	994	...
1969	2 952	2 399	107	2 506	152	-22	2 332	359	261	2 920	2 598	1 011	395
1970	3 263	2 592	131	2 723	163	-22	2 538	399	325	3 189	2 849	1 023	399
1971	3 598	2 855	130	2 985	188	-22	2 774	446	378	3 416	3 103	1 053	416
1972	4 040	3 225	137	3 362	221	-20	3 121	496	422	3 748	3 376	1 078	440
1973	4 548	3 610	180	3 790	283	-17	3 490	559	500	4 119	3 714	1 104	461
1974	5 141	4 079	147	4 226	328	-15	3 882	658	601	4 551	4 084	1 130	478
1975	5 872	4 595	177	4 772	367	-13	4 393	741	738	5 050	4 614	1 163	491
1976	6 597	5 262	124	5 386	421	-12	4 953	818	826	5 520	4 999	1 195	512
1977	7 423	5 981	135	6 116	481	-11	5 624	930	870	6 059	5 481	1 225	539
1978	8 516	6 878	168	7 046	565	-11	6 470	1 091	954	6 802	6 092	1 252	568
1979	9 662	7 744	207	7 951	667	-9	7 274	1 287	1 101	7 545	6 747	1 281	592
1980	10 908	8 545	180	8 725	740	-4	7 982	1 617	1 310	8 331	7 467	1 309	597
1981	12 376	9 603	130	9 733	895	-14	8 824	2 055	1 497	9 286	8 226	1 333	611
1982	13 524	10 250	116	10 366	973	-17	9 376	2 502	1 647	9 916	8 764	1 364	619
1983	14 549	10 872	127	10 998	1 035	-14	9 950	2 799	1 800	10 434	9 443	1 394	631
1984	15 914	11 912	146	12 058	1 165	-6	10 888	3 103	1 923	11 233	10 204	1 417	655
1985	17 201	12 760	208	12 968	1 272	1	11 697	3 443	2 061	11 959	10 837	1 438	674
1986	17 870	13 143	194	13 337	1 328	8	12 017	3 635	2 218	12 217	11 128	1 463	680
1987	18 685	13 708	241	13 949	1 371	23	12 601	3 738	2 346	12 638	11 386	1 479	699
1988	19 713	14 441	321	14 761	1 510	35	13 286	3 916	2 512	13 227	11 926	1 490	733
1989	21 069	15 237	383	15 620	1 611	42	14 051	4 223	2 795	14 009	12 568	1 504	749
1990	22 555	16 354	417	16 771	1 823	51	14 999	4 511	3 045	14 823	13 313	1 522	761
1991	24 228	17 577	403	17 980	1 976	64	16 068	4 761	3 399	15 577	14 040	1 555	784
1992	25 942	18 854	485	19 339	2 102	80	17 318	4 843	3 781	16 260	14 674	1 595	797
1993	27 883	20 381	531	20 912	2 270	99	18 741	5 041	4 101	17 039	15 334	1 636	825
1994	29 900	21 807	458	22 264	2 470	116	19 910	5 580	4 410	17 772	15 973	1 682	857
1995	32 029	23 306	391	23 697	2 646	128	21 179	6 008	4 841	18 617	16 757	1 720	898
1996	33 801	24 105	402	24 508	2 726	148	21 930	6 596	5 275	19 289	17 294	1 752	909
1997	35 440	25 264	544	25 808	2 859	171	23 121	6 933	5 387	19 968	17 799	1 775	923
1998	37 769	26 893	586	27 479	2 999	193	24 673	7 427	5 669	21 059	18 786	1 793	939
1999	38 803	27 766	680	28 446	3 112	221	25 555	7 234	6 015	21 461	19 100	1 808	943
2000	41 425	29 817	541	30 358	3 287	246	27 318	7 718	6 390	22 746	20 196	1 821	965
2001	45 336	32 465	787	33 251	3 531	249	29 969	8 237	7 129	24 751	22 162	1 832	969
2002	46 341	33 905	545	34 451	3 693	251	31 009	7 483	7 849	24 977	22 634	1 855	980
2003	48 139	35 653	562	36 215	3 862	257	32 610	7 155	8 374	25 639	23 426	1 878	999
2004	51 579	37 939	864	38 802	4 069	262	34 995	7 646	8 938	27 092	24 825	1 904	1 023
2005	55 342	40 367	834	41 201	4 320	274	37 155	8 563	9 624	28 641	26 028	1 932	1 047
2006	59 274	43 297	602	43 899	4 727	293	39 465	9 328	10 482	30 209	27 241	1 962	1 076
2007	63 036	45 011	845	45 856	5 012	327	41 171	10 494	11 371	31 675	28 482	1 990	1 101
2008	67 338	47 019	803	47 822	5 287	329	42 864	11 734	12 740	33 490	30 502	2 011	1 103
2009	65 970	45 517	550	46 066	5 205	355	41 216	10 199	14 555	32 389	29 804	2 037	1 071
2010	68 882	46 653	1 033	47 686	5 334	385	42 736	10 589	15 557	33 342	30 672	2 066	1 064
2011	71 993	47 870	1 338	49 209	4 937	416	44 687	11 280	16 025	34 575	31 520	2 082	...

. . . = Not available.

Table 17-2. Personal Income and Employment by Region and State—*Continued*

(Millions of dollars, except as noted.)

Region or state and year	Personal income, total	Derivation of personal income								Per capita (dollars)		Population (thousands)	Total employment (thousands)
		Earnings by place of work			Less: Contributions for government social insurance	Plus: Adjustment for residence	Equals: Net earnings by place of residence	Plus: Dividends, interest, and rent	Plus: Personal current transfer receipts	Personal income	Disposable personal income		
		Nonfarm	Farm	Total									
NEW YORK													
1958	42 869	35 955	377	36 332	1 434	-580	34 318	5 953	2 597	2 582	2 265	16 601	. . .
1959	45 476	38 384	315	38 699	1 711	-652	36 337	6 419	2 721	2 726	2 373	16 685	. . .
1960	47 513	40 221	353	40 574	2 040	-727	37 807	6 913	2 794	2 822	2 452	16 838	. . .
1961	49 540	41 710	364	42 074	2 191	-780	39 104	7 230	3 207	2 904	2 511	17 061	. . .
1962	52 264	44 138	287	44 425	2 489	-866	41 070	7 898	3 295	3 021	2 615	17 301	. . .
1963	54 369	45 627	337	45 964	2 712	-930	42 322	8 498	3 549	3 114	2 696	17 461	. . .
1964	58 101	48 426	318	48 744	2 681	-1 026	45 037	9 341	3 723	3 303	2 901	17 589	. . .
1965	61 623	51 083	366	51 450	2 803	-1 111	47 536	10 072	4 016	3 475	3 040	17 734	. . .
1966	66 170	55 487	427	55 914	3 719	-1 265	50 929	10 605	4 636	3 708	3 224	17 843	. . .
1967	71 436	59 427	380	59 807	4 031	-1 408	54 368	11 168	5 900	3 983	3 434	17 935	. . .
1968	78 713	65 173	388	65 561	4 444	-1 589	59 528	11 971	7 213	4 361	3 733	18 051	. . .
1969	82 789	70 343	440	70 783	5 283	-3 346	62 154	12 900	7 735	4 573	3 850	18 105	8 494
1970	88 953	74 832	420	75 252	5 525	-3 292	66 434	13 610	8 909	4 868	4 177	18 272	8 466
1971	94 869	79 029	410	79 438	6 021	-3 394	70 023	14 102	10 744	5 166	4 495	18 365	8 345
1972	101 448	84 811	353	85 164	6 786	-3 646	74 732	14 722	11 993	5 528	4 757	18 352	8 348
1973	108 487	91 136	470	91 606	8 402	-3 861	79 343	15 855	13 288	5 963	5 157	18 195	8 465
1974	117 010	96 729	444	97 173	9 177	-4 081	83 916	17 677	15 418	6 474	5 582	18 073	8 392
1975	125 678	101 166	380	101 546	9 443	-4 422	87 681	18 492	19 506	6 970	6 098	18 032	8 172
1976	134 260	108 567	402	108 969	10 240	-4 860	93 870	19 619	20 772	7 469	6 511	17 975	8 125
1977	145 174	117 731	332	118 063	11 004	-5 407	101 652	21 792	21 730	8 132	7 063	17 852	8 199
1978	158 209	129 508	434	129 942	12 359	-6 062	111 521	23 923	22 765	8 928	7 721	17 720	8 384
1979	173 149	142 215	540	142 755	14 064	-6 902	121 788	27 046	24 315	9 819	8 430	17 634	8 581
1980	192 979	155 974	531	156 504	15 326	-8 101	133 078	31 968	27 933	10 985	9 395	17 567	8 602
1981	215 380	171 059	544	171 604	18 051	-8 838	144 715	39 130	31 536	12 260	10 385	17 568	8 666
1982	234 315	183 691	519	184 210	19 659	-9 692	154 859	44 953	34 503	13 321	11 264	17 590	8 673
1983	252 337	197 670	370	198 040	21 222	-10 140	166 679	48 327	37 332	14 267	12 272	17 687	8 730
1984	279 079	217 192	493	217 685	23 937	-10 775	182 974	56 587	39 518	15 727	13 566	17 746	9 003
1985	298 210	234 166	559	234 725	26 271	-11 401	197 053	59 442	41 715	16 761	14 357	17 792	9 227
1986	318 024	252 356	653	253 009	28 844	-12 068	212 096	61 728	44 200	17 833	15 258	17 833	9 424
1987	339 123	272 932	735	273 667	30 681	-12 814	230 173	63 599	45 351	18 978	16 076	17 869	9 472
1988	371 746	300 828	652	301 480	34 313	-13 610	253 557	69 967	48 222	20 720	17 762	17 941	9 684
1989	399 258	314 933	777	315 710	36 040	-13 203	266 466	79 904	52 887	22 202	18 903	17 983	9 752
1990	427 268	334 411	775	335 186	36 559	-13 503	285 124	84 128	58 015	23 710	20 371	18 021	9 727
1991	429 233	328 531	647	329 179	37 425	-13 531	278 222	86 423	64 588	23 685	20 471	18 123	9 483
1992	450 562	349 488	750	350 238	39 094	-16 710	294 433	83 919	72 209	24 693	21 351	18 247	9 410
1993	461 006	358 069	795	358 864	40 118	-16 624	302 122	82 180	76 705	25 089	21 595	18 375	9 431
1994	476 377	367 512	673	368 185	41 885	-16 637	309 663	86 283	80 431	25 807	22 218	18 459	9 465
1995	502 113	386 451	541	386 991	43 395	-18 905	324 691	91 942	85 480	27 106	23 292	18 524	9 511
1996	529 721	408 631	767	409 398	44 681	-21 642	343 075	97 365	89 281	28 497	24 285	18 588	9 595
1997	559 927	435 613	459	436 072	46 509	-24 148	365 415	105 128	89 384	30 012	25 401	18 657	9 732
1998	589 236	461 474	690	462 164	48 905	-27 694	385 565	110 775	92 896	31 416	26 324	18 756	9 923
1999	616 057	489 836	768	490 603	51 340	-29 301	409 962	110 278	95 816	32 625	27 104	18 883	10 109
2000	657 894	527 931	774	528 705	55 178	-33 281	440 245	117 346	100 304	34 623	28 618	19 002	10 346
2001	676 980	545 924	919	546 843	57 401	-34 163	455 280	114 776	106 923	35 476	29 031	19 083	10 422
2002	678 393	544 557	699	545 256	58 458	-30 603	456 195	105 929	116 269	35 448	30 194	19 138	10 334
2003	695 392	557 819	845	558 664	59 804	-30 213	468 646	105 714	121 031	36 264	31 262	19 176	10 361
2004	741 167	593 956	1 071	595 027	62 802	-33 938	498 287	112 434	130 446	38 660	33 239	19 172	10 509
2005	786 512	626 401	1 066	627 467	65 613	-36 985	524 869	132 054	129 589	41 108	34 957	19 133	10 649
2006	851 437	675 261	920	676 181	69 240	-41 829	565 112	148 932	137 392	44 567	37 417	19 105	10 788
2007	915 526	716 243	1 281	717 524	73 526	-47 434	596 563	175 493	143 470	47 852	39 673	19 132	11 045
2008	949 250	734 135	1 395	735 530	76 273	-47 489	611 768	184 490	152 992	49 408	41 633	19 212	11 167
2009	904 026	694 399	923	695 323	74 523	-39 521	581 278	150 517	172 230	46 824	40 627	19 307	10 954
2010	942 523	726 885	1 334	728 218	76 566	-43 574	608 078	153 468	180 977	48 596	41 971	19 395	10 973
2011	983 868	754 162	1 694	755 856	71 181	-46 364	638 311	161 500	184 057	50 545	42 835	19 465	. . .

. . . = Not available.

Table 17-2. Personal Income and Employment by Region and State—*Continued*

(Millions of dollars, except as noted.)

Region or state and year	Personal income, total	Earnings by place of work Nonfarm	Earnings by place of work Farm	Earnings by place of work Total	Less: Contributions for government social insurance	Plus: Adjustment for residence	Equals: Net earnings by place of residence	Plus: Dividends, interest, and rent	Plus: Personal current transfer receipts	Per capita Personal income	Per capita Disposable personal income	Population (thousands)	Total employment (thousands)
NORTH CAROLINA													
1958	6 549	5 064	628	5 692	214	9	5 487	662	400	1 497	1 382	4 376	. . .
1959	7 004	5 602	519	6 121	257	9	5 873	701	430	1 571	1 433	4 458	. . .
1960	7 410	5 873	605	6 478	306	9	6 181	772	457	1 620	1 472	4 573	. . .
1961	7 832	6 135	645	6 780	314	10	6 476	832	524	1 680	1 526	4 663	. . .
1962	8 412	6 648	627	7 275	346	10	6 939	920	552	1 787	1 615	4 707	. . .
1963	8 850	7 068	606	7 674	412	11	7 273	982	595	1 866	1 682	4 742	. . .
1964	9 596	7 683	635	8 317	435	11	7 893	1 080	623	1 998	1 823	4 802	. . .
1965	10 352	8 436	532	8 968	467	11	8 512	1 161	679	2 129	1 923	4 863	. . .
1966	11 492	9 496	618	10 115	617	10	9 508	1 246	738	2 347	2 108	4 896	. . .
1967	12 436	10 359	607	10 966	714	10	10 261	1 316	859	2 511	2 258	4 952	. . .
1968	13 708	11 637	518	12 156	825	12	11 343	1 384	981	2 740	2 430	5 004	. . .
1969	15 322	12 884	673	13 557	899	16	12 674	1 540	1 107	3 046	2 665	5 031	2 458
1970	16 688	13 879	672	14 551	971	13	13 594	1 757	1 338	3 273	2 884	5 099	2 469
1971	18 205	15 178	627	15 805	1 101	10	14 714	1 922	1 569	3 500	3 113	5 201	2 490
1972	20 600	17 279	750	18 029	1 308	4	16 725	2 118	1 757	3 890	3 414	5 296	2 602
1973	23 428	19 491	1 161	20 652	1 677	2	18 977	2 412	2 038	4 353	3 848	5 382	2 720
1974	25 851	21 306	1 109	22 416	1 900	8	20 524	2 793	2 533	4 734	4 159	5 461	2 743
1975	27 942	22 236	1 066	23 302	1 977	14	21 339	3 080	3 522	5 048	4 542	5 535	2 647
1976	31 216	25 128	1 147	26 275	2 271	15	24 019	3 414	3 783	5 581	4 968	5 593	2 754
1977	34 242	28 007	856	28 863	2 512	22	26 373	3 876	3 993	6 041	5 353	5 668	2 851
1978	38 713	31 742	1 142	32 885	2 922	21	29 984	4 425	4 304	6 744	5 949	5 740	2 946
1979	42 937	35 473	756	36 229	3 390	19	32 858	5 157	4 923	7 401	6 473	5 802	3 046
1980	48 272	38 859	651	39 509	3 727	23	35 805	6 595	5 872	8 183	7 160	5 899	3 052
1981	54 457	42 716	1 051	43 767	4 390	-20	39 356	8 327	6 774	9 142	7 984	5 957	3 072
1982	58 450	44 828	1 063	45 892	4 645	-30	41 217	9 690	7 544	9 711	8 605	6 019	3 042
1983	63 810	49 482	633	50 115	5 173	-48	44 894	10 781	8 134	10 500	9 277	6 077	3 129
1984	72 559	56 063	1 290	57 353	5 970	-82	51 301	12 661	8 597	11 771	10 446	6 164	3 292
1985	78 747	61 043	1 157	62 200	6 590	-145	55 465	14 062	9 220	12 592	11 138	6 254	3 392
1986	84 667	65 994	1 143	67 137	7 295	-209	59 633	15 229	9 805	13 393	11 840	6 322	3 494
1987	91 198	72 061	1 144	73 205	7 871	-290	65 044	15 953	10 201	14 241	12 488	6 404	3 610
1988	99 420	78 418	1 486	79 904	8 850	-350	70 704	17 687	11 029	15 341	13 533	6 481	3 751
1989	108 027	83 763	1 723	85 485	9 515	-402	75 568	20 183	12 277	16 454	14 417	6 565	3 838
1990	114 583	88 092	2 136	90 228	10 306	-446	79 476	21 536	13 571	17 194	15 145	6 664	3 902
1991	120 020	91 023	2 396	93 418	10 794	-431	82 193	22 189	15 638	17 691	15 662	6 784	3 866
1992	130 259	99 974	2 343	102 317	11 701	-454	90 162	22 773	17 324	18 886	16 764	6 897	3 964
1993	138 771	106 118	2 615	108 733	12 502	-470	95 761	23 956	19 054	19 704	17 454	7 043	4 087
1994	148 277	113 284	2 827	116 111	13 461	-528	102 122	26 341	19 814	20 630	18 213	7 187	4 201
1995	158 756	120 613	2 711	123 324	14 300	-602	108 422	28 184	22 150	21 615	19 036	7 345	4 355
1996	170 369	127 575	2 998	130 573	14 999	-659	114 914	31 439	24 015	22 714	19 941	7 501	4 459
1997	183 344	137 045	3 067	140 111	16 118	-727	123 267	34 867	25 210	23 945	20 924	7 657	4 603
1998	197 581	148 572	2 412	150 984	17 264	-717	133 003	38 357	26 222	25 301	21 960	7 809	4 716
1999	209 278	159 714	2 242	161 956	18 411	-786	142 759	38 597	27 923	26 326	22 902	7 949	4 812
2000	225 528	172 451	2 965	175 416	19 521	-904	154 991	40 635	29 902	27 906	24 246	8 082	4 887
2001	232 831	177 386	3 118	180 504	20 226	-811	159 468	40 022	33 340	28 359	24 715	8 210	4 841
2002	236 698	182 100	1 505	183 605	20 511	-809	162 285	38 215	36 198	28 428	25 258	8 326	4 834
2003	243 696	188 388	1 597	189 985	21 417	-752	167 816	38 000	37 880	28 934	25 952	8 423	4 849
2004	260 698	199 305	2 372	201 677	22 472	-788	178 418	41 561	40 719	30 480	27 429	8 553	4 963
2005	277 743	210 438	3 148	213 586	23 978	-894	188 714	44 981	44 049	31 905	28 428	8 705	5 093
2006	297 596	224 941	2 550	227 491	25 756	-1 052	200 684	49 208	47 705	33 373	29 553	8 917	5 251
2007	316 956	236 645	2 218	238 863	27 364	-1 295	210 204	55 446	51 306	34 761	30 583	9 118	5 437
2008	332 733	242 626	2 360	244 986	28 171	-1 375	215 440	60 488	56 805	35 741	31 819	9 309	5 425
2009	322 675	232 744	2 511	235 254	27 401	-1 175	206 679	50 395	65 601	34 147	31 053	9 450	5 229
2010	334 677	240 412	2 542	242 954	27 868	-1 230	213 856	52 250	68 571	35 007	31 850	9 560	5 202
2011	349 212	249 549	2 163	251 712	25 967	-1 337	224 408	55 465	69 338	36 164	32 568	9 656	. . .

. . . = Not available.

Table 17-2. Personal Income and Employment by Region and State—*Continued*

(Millions of dollars, except as noted.)

Region or state and year	Personal income, total	Earnings by place of work			Less: Contributions for government social insurance	Plus: Adjustment for residence	Equals: Net earnings by place of residence	Plus: Dividends, interest, and rent	Plus: Personal current transfer receipts	Per capita (dollars)		Population (thousands)	Total employment (thousands)
		Nonfarm	Farm	Total						Personal income	Disposable personal income		
NORTH DAKOTA													
1958	1 156	624	324	948	31	-10	907	176	73	1 907	1 765	606	...
1959	1 064	679	186	865	34	-11	820	166	78	1 722	1 587	618	...
1960	1 185	705	274	978	41	-11	926	176	83	1 869	1 724	634	...
1961	1 076	734	145	879	43	-11	824	162	90	1 679	1 542	641	...
1962	1 517	795	479	1 273	47	-14	1 212	210	94	2 381	2 208	637	...
1963	1 403	846	328	1 174	56	-14	1 103	202	98	2 179	2 002	644	...
1964	1 393	912	241	1 153	59	-17	1 077	211	104	2 146	1 977	649	...
1965	1 622	970	382	1 352	62	-17	1 274	234	114	2 499	2 317	649	...
1966	1 640	1 022	349	1 372	74	-16	1 282	235	123	2 535	2 334	647	...
1967	1 642	1 051	311	1 362	89	-16	1 257	238	147	2 623	2 398	626	...
1968	1 710	1 121	285	1 406	95	-16	1 295	251	164	2 754	2 514	621	...
1969	1 924	1 226	385	1 611	103	-52	1 456	286	183	3 099	2 783	621	274
1970	2 016	1 367	306	1 673	115	-55	1 502	302	212	3 257	2 948	619	281
1971	2 328	1 499	434	1 933	130	-58	1 745	335	248	3 715	3 420	627	284
1972	2 784	1 680	668	2 348	148	-62	2 139	369	276	4 412	4 051	631	288
1973	3 925	1 901	1 529	3 430	190	-65	3 174	441	310	6 207	5 704	632	300
1974	3 891	2 155	1 164	3 319	225	-78	3 016	520	356	6 136	5 466	634	308
1975	4 080	2 442	946	3 388	257	-84	3 048	612	420	6 390	5 721	638	314
1976	4 005	2 796	479	3 274	295	-99	2 881	660	464	6 206	5 554	645	326
1977	4 168	3 038	275	3 313	304	-106	2 903	759	506	6 421	5 776	649	331
1978	5 267	3 470	867	4 337	355	-118	3 864	851	553	8 095	7 260	651	345
1979	5 407	3 885	503	4 388	414	-136	3 838	956	613	8 290	7 412	652	353
1980	5 166	4 215	-383	3 832	448	-153	3 231	1 211	723	7 894	6 920	654	355
1981	6 793	4 705	374	5 079	531	-175	4 372	1 591	830	10 300	9 058	660	359
1982	7 365	4 985	307	5 292	575	-178	4 539	1 896	930	11 009	9 902	669	360
1983	7 726	5 232	366	5 599	613	-182	4 804	1 888	1 035	11 417	10 349	677	365
1984	8 349	5 476	612	6 088	652	-187	5 248	1 991	1 109	12 268	11 163	680	366
1985	8 616	5 577	698	6 275	678	-187	5 410	2 027	1 179	12 728	11 592	677	364
1986	8 720	5 611	694	6 305	698	-184	5 423	2 012	1 285	13 025	11 920	670	357
1987	8 984	6 078	790	6 634	727	-185	5 722	1 918	1 344	13 589	12 379	661	363
1988	8 292	6 078	-59	6 020	794	-191	5 035	1 909	1 348	12 653	11 407	655	366
1989	9 289	6 307	442	6 749	842	-197	5 710	2 110	1 468	14 371	12 999	646	370
1990	10 117	6 670	773	7 444	936	-192	6 316	2 229	1 573	15 866	14 380	638	374
1991	10 278	7 029	615	7 644	1 009	-201	6 434	2 245	1 599	16 167	14 632	636	382
1992	11 258	7 492	1 076	8 569	1 079	-220	7 270	2 222	1 765	17 639	16 055	638	388
1993	11 347	7 993	627	8 620	1 166	-240	7 214	2 272	1 861	17 696	15 999	641	397
1994	12 352	8 499	1 061	9 560	1 246	-256	8 059	2 398	1 895	19 156	17 394	645	411
1995	12 311	8 945	432	9 377	1 298	-281	7 798	2 514	1 999	19 004	17 147	648	418
1996	13 840	9 458	1 309	10 767	1 360	-316	9 091	2 669	2 081	21 279	19 296	650	426
1997	13 549	9 928	310	10 238	1 409	-341	8 487	2 893	2 169	20 854	18 728	650	430
1998	15 008	10 574	973	11 548	1 475	-368	9 705	3 106	2 197	23 177	20 925	648	436
1999	15 141	11 044	688	11 732	1 513	-399	9 820	3 027	2 295	23 502	21 185	644	439
2000	16 430	11 618	1 090	12 708	1 584	-424	10 701	3 266	2 464	25 592	23 092	642	443
2001	16 982	12 374	785	13 158	1 638	-463	11 058	3 371	2 553	26 574	23 915	639	445
2002	17 333	12 957	579	13 536	1 681	-485	11 370	3 280	2 684	27 161	24 851	638	443
2003	18 825	13 683	1 492	15 175	1 770	-516	12 889	3 184	2 752	29 468	27 224	639	444
2004	19 293	14 638	953	15 591	1 876	-571	13 144	3 235	2 913	29 925	27 631	645	454
2005	20 542	15 439	1 208	16 646	1 957	-622	14 067	3 349	3 127	31 795	29 174	646	463
2006	21 375	16 371	787	17 157	2 055	-680	14 422	3 676	3 277	32 914	29 891	649	472
2007	23 637	17 119	1 622	18 741	2 166	-749	15 827	4 267	3 543	36 208	32 685	653	482
2008	26 880	18 476	2 819	21 295	2 402	-815	18 077	4 997	3 805	40 877	36 869	658	491
2009	26 459	18 854	2 035	20 890	2 493	-797	17 600	4 638	4 221	39 790	36 511	665	493
2010	28 935	20 577	2 600	23 177	2 676	-831	19 670	4 799	4 465	42 890	39 427	675	503
2011	31 288	23 204	2 182	25 386	2 745	-1 042	21 599	5 074	4 615	45 747	41 213	684	...

. . . = Not available.

Table 17-2. Personal Income and Employment by Region and State—*Continued*

(Millions of dollars, except as noted.)

Region or state and year	Personal income, total	Derivation of personal income								Per capita (dollars)		Population (thousands)	Total employment (thousands)
		Earnings by place of work			Less: Contributions for government social insurance	Plus: Adjustment for residence	Equals: Net earnings by place of residence	Plus: Dividends, interest, and rent	Plus: Personal current transfer receipts	Personal income	Disposable personal income		
		Nonfarm	Farm	Total									
OHIO													
1958	20 847	17 269	382	17 651	700	-119	16 832	2 569	1 446	2 172	1 945	9 599	. . .
1959	22 299	18 943	262	19 205	860	-133	18 212	2 719	1 368	2 306	2 058	9 671	. . .
1960	23 214	19 566	334	19 900	1 002	-131	18 767	2 936	1 512	2 385	2 115	9 734	. . .
1961	23 644	19 537	374	19 910	984	-121	18 805	3 078	1 760	2 399	2 140	9 854	. . .
1962	24 926	20 796	336	21 132	1 125	-126	19 882	3 314	1 731	2 510	2 230	9 929	. . .
1963	25 960	21 717	335	22 051	1 236	-129	20 687	3 491	1 782	2 600	2 306	9 986	. . .
1964	27 718	23 356	306	23 662	1 354	-134	22 174	3 755	1 789	2 750	2 475	10 080	. . .
1965	30 015	25 305	358	25 663	1 408	-147	24 108	4 013	1 893	2 942	2 631	10 201	. . .
1966	32 773	27 964	496	28 461	1 864	-166	26 431	4 303	2 038	3 173	2 823	10 330	. . .
1967	34 374	29 259	329	29 588	1 957	-161	27 470	4 525	2 379	3 301	2 934	10 414	. . .
1968	37 924	32 226	413	32 639	2 133	-184	30 322	4 912	2 690	3 606	3 167	10 516	. . .
1969	41 316	35 344	418	35 762	2 360	-187	33 215	5 201	2 900	3 911	3 386	10 563	4 695
1970	43 614	36 737	435	37 171	2 409	-178	34 584	5 634	3 395	4 088	3 591	10 669	4 683
1971	46 395	38 655	415	39 070	2 605	-128	36 337	6 044	4 014	4 322	3 857	10 735	4 627
1972	50 378	42 093	506	42 599	2 987	-125	39 487	6 453	4 438	4 688	4 118	10 747	4 710
1973	56 089	47 153	667	47 820	3 865	-153	43 802	7 121	5 166	5 209	4 583	10 767	4 902
1974	61 623	50 973	798	51 771	4 312	-129	47 330	8 090	6 203	5 724	5 023	10 766	4 964
1975	65 713	52 659	815	53 474	4 338	-75	49 062	8 719	7 933	6 101	5 402	10 770	4 809
1976	72 586	58 959	789	59 747	4 944	-85	54 718	9 383	8 486	6 751	5 946	10 753	4 889
1977	80 693	66 241	676	66 917	5 557	-98	61 262	10 516	8 915	7 492	6 560	10 771	5 034
1978	89 424	73 907	630	74 536	6 407	-116	68 014	11 826	9 584	8 283	7 234	10 795	5 206
1979	99 044	81 237	763	82 000	7 332	-137	74 531	13 569	10 943	9 172	7 956	10 799	5 291
1980	108 244	84 953	576	85 528	7 615	-153	77 761	16 697	13 786	10 022	8 746	10 801	5 204
1981	117 830	90 936	169	91 105	8 719	-460	81 927	20 582	15 320	10 922	9 476	10 788	5 135
1982	123 385	91 776	271	92 047	8 904	-582	82 560	23 042	17 783	11 470	10 075	10 757	4 967
1983	130 705	96 885	-69	96 816	9 613	-704	86 499	25 185	19 021	12 173	10 709	10 738	4 960
1984	144 285	107 136	874	108 010	10 933	-838	96 239	28 417	19 628	13 437	11 891	10 738	5 160
1985	152 957	114 033	868	114 902	11 870	-925	102 107	29 925	20 926	14 249	12 567	10 735	5 287
1986	159 588	119 415	684	120 099	12 856	-957	106 285	31 140	22 162	14 873	13 138	10 730	5 401
1987	167 097	126 210	737	126 947	13 615	-996	112 337	31 728	23 033	15 529	13 606	10 760	5 548
1988	178 707	136 353	789	137 142	15 095	-1 049	120 998	33 533	24 177	16 549	14 563	10 799	5 682
1989	191 375	143 753	1 172	144 925	16 102	-1 091	127 732	37 869	25 774	17 672	15 469	10 829	5 803
1990	202 486	151 020	1 206	152 226	17 256	-1 081	133 889	39 922	28 676	18 638	16 341	10 864	5 863
1991	208 109	155 467	704	156 171	18 100	-1 088	136 983	40 222	30 904	19 013	16 737	10 946	5 842
1992	220 866	165 836	1 188	167 023	19 214	-1 290	146 519	40 400	33 948	20 025	17 672	11 029	5 854
1993	229 527	173 338	937	174 275	20 295	-1 357	152 623	41 603	35 301	20 676	18 191	11 101	5 960
1994	243 329	184 483	1 164	185 647	21 829	-1 504	162 313	44 368	36 647	21 818	19 173	11 152	6 136
1995	253 778	192 242	895	193 138	22 967	-1 433	168 738	46 425	38 615	22 653	19 833	11 203	6 300
1996	264 716	199 030	1 251	200 281	23 637	-1 396	175 248	49 459	40 009	23 545	20 441	11 243	6 395
1997	280 936	209 992	1 691	211 683	24 347	-1 481	185 855	53 870	41 211	24 912	21 564	11 277	6 500
1998	298 833	224 563	1 274	225 836	25 112	-1 596	199 128	57 734	41 971	26 418	22 808	11 312	6 616
1999	309 384	236 268	849	237 117	26 243	-1 621	209 253	56 763	43 368	27 293	23 597	11 335	6 691
2000	326 075	248 042	1 199	249 241	26 568	-1 569	221 103	58 836	46 135	28 695	24 758	11 364	6 782
2001	333 369	253 621	1 121	254 742	27 174	-1 642	225 926	57 136	50 306	29 275	25 361	11 387	6 711
2002	340 514	260 530	559	261 088	27 160	-1 668	232 261	54 539	53 715	29 849	26 289	11 408	6 641
2003	350 723	270 964	850	271 814	28 296	-1 722	241 795	52 651	56 277	30 672	27 333	11 435	6 630
2004	361 666	280 832	1 457	282 289	29 969	-1 764	250 557	52 238	58 872	31 580	28 162	11 452	6 678
2005	371 931	287 846	1 145	288 990	30 816	-1 854	256 321	53 374	62 236	32 445	28 751	11 463	6 723
2006	390 457	297 803	1 041	298 844	32 209	-1 942	264 693	59 978	65 786	34 008	30 027	11 481	6 762
2007	404 623	302 899	1 202	304 102	32 960	-2 098	269 044	65 425	70 154	35 183	30 947	11 500	6 811
2008	419 173	308 605	1 531	310 136	34 327	-2 098	273 712	69 419	76 043	36 401	32 270	11 515	6 746
2009	405 238	294 814	1 936	296 750	33 545	-2 049	261 156	57 923	86 159	35 150	31 901	11 529	6 479
2010	417 235	302 363	1 837	304 200	34 064	-2 074	268 062	59 380	89 792	36 162	32 815	11 538	6 451
2011	436 297	314 024	2 726	316 750	32 094	-2 149	282 507	62 745	91 045	37 791	33 869	11 545	. . .

. . . = Not available.

Table 17-2. Personal Income and Employment by Region and State—*Continued*

(Millions of dollars, except as noted.)

Region or state and year	Personal income, total	Earnings by place of work Nonfarm	Earnings by place of work Farm	Earnings by place of work Total	Less: Contributions for government social insurance	Plus: Adjustment for residence	Equals: Net earnings by place of residence	Plus: Dividends, interest, and rent	Plus: Personal current transfer receipts	Per capita Personal income	Per capita Disposable personal income	Population (thousands)	Total employment (thousands)
OKLAHOMA													
1958	4 072	3 022	328	3 350	113	4	3 241	499	331	1 796	1 631	2 267	. . .
1959	4 244	3 203	262	3 465	130	5	3 341	545	359	1 854	1 676	2 289	. . .
1960	4 469	3 300	335	3 635	150	7	3 492	600	378	1 913	1 728	2 336	. . .
1961	4 619	3 429	301	3 730	159	8	3 579	624	416	1 941	1 746	2 380	. . .
1962	4 815	3 655	240	3 895	178	11	3 728	647	441	1 984	1 783	2 427	. . .
1963	4 979	3 823	214	4 037	208	12	3 841	667	471	2 042	1 837	2 439	. . .
1964	5 336	4 113	208	4 321	207	14	4 128	717	491	2 181	1 981	2 446	. . .
1965	5 718	4 344	278	4 621	216	17	4 423	770	526	2 344	2 129	2 440	. . .
1966	6 127	4 732	267	4 999	286	21	4 734	809	584	2 497	2 255	2 454	. . .
1967	6 680	5 186	276	5 462	336	25	5 151	829	700	2 684	2 419	2 489	. . .
1968	7 326	5 774	219	5 993	384	31	5 640	897	789	2 927	2 620	2 503	. . .
1969	8 121	6 304	276	6 579	402	63	6 240	1 026	855	3 204	2 822	2 535	1 107
1970	8 919	6 801	359	7 159	431	65	6 793	1 145	981	3 475	3 098	2 566	1 120
1971	9 712	7 387	335	7 721	484	64	7 302	1 280	1 131	3 710	3 349	2 618	1 132
1972	10 672	8 154	417	8 572	558	73	8 087	1 344	1 240	4 016	3 573	2 657	1 183
1973	12 164	9 095	734	9 828	720	83	9 191	1 567	1 406	4 515	4 056	2 694	1 221
1974	13 597	10 389	452	10 841	846	107	10 102	1 831	1 664	4 976	4 399	2 732	1 256
1975	15 227	11 527	404	11 931	928	142	11 145	2 030	2 052	5 493	4 932	2 772	1 269
1976	16 868	12 957	338	13 295	1 054	177	12 418	2 204	2 245	5 974	5 335	2 823	1 305
1977	18 829	14 809	183	14 992	1 198	153	13 947	2 494	2 388	6 570	5 833	2 866	1 359
1978	21 391	17 019	175	17 194	1 417	149	15 926	2 893	2 571	7 343	6 451	2 913	1 428
1979	24 933	19 478	635	20 113	1 687	163	18 589	3 391	2 952	8 395	7 356	2 970	1 481
1980	28 847	22 612	265	22 877	1 964	171	21 084	4 353	3 410	9 487	8 260	3 041	1 547
1981	33 881	26 295	332	26 627	2 444	195	24 378	5 629	3 874	10 943	9 391	3 096	1 625
1982	37 885	28 841	487	29 329	2 743	200	26 786	6 731	4 368	11 816	10 070	3 206	1 673
1983	38 619	28 855	214	29 069	2 740	238	26 567	7 258	4 794	11 737	10 333	3 290	1 638
1984	41 456	30 716	376	31 092	2 969	287	28 409	8 072	4 975	12 618	11 213	3 286	1 665
1985	43 085	31 516	381	31 897	3 109	328	29 115	8 655	5 315	13 171	11 713	3 271	1 648
1986	43 301	31 404	645	32 049	3 162	378	29 265	8 388	5 649	13 312	12 103	3 253	1 588
1987	43 194	31 410	566	31 976	3 182	425	29 219	8 099	5 877	13 455	12 070	3 210	1 599
1988	44 864	32 511	767	33 278	3 500	473	30 251	8 400	6 213	14 166	12 702	3 167	1 608
1989	47 860	34 380	802	35 181	3 742	497	31 937	9 305	6 619	15 192	13 552	3 150	1 623
1990	50 623	36 419	862	37 281	4 086	559	33 755	9 747	7 122	16 077	14 170	3 149	1 655
1991	52 187	37 741	624	38 365	4 369	590	34 587	9 830	7 770	16 434	14 630	3 175	1 668
1992	55 614	40 172	846	41 017	4 607	611	37 021	9 897	8 696	17 269	15 447	3 221	1 680
1993	57 801	42 097	869	42 966	4 865	647	38 747	9 907	9 147	17 772	15 905	3 252	1 716
1994	60 458	43 736	827	44 563	5 139	703	40 127	10 616	9 715	18 427	16 463	3 281	1 748
1995	62 768	45 362	289	45 651	5 363	741	41 028	11 273	10 467	18 973	16 939	3 308	1 800
1996	66 590	47 970	360	48 330	5 564	768	43 534	12 088	10 968	19 936	17 717	3 340	1 850
1997	70 491	50 955	665	51 620	5 810	841	46 652	12 570	11 269	20 899	18 442	3 373	1 897
1998	74 741	54 274	519	54 794	6 116	875	49 553	13 687	11 501	21 949	19 345	3 405	1 947
1999	78 220	56 865	838	57 703	6 302	928	52 329	13 852	12 038	22 757	20 077	3 437	1 962
2000	84 985	61 556	827	62 383	6 684	1 011	56 710	15 538	12 737	24 602	21 721	3 454	2 003
2001	90 839	66 383	807	67 190	7 141	1 015	61 064	15 698	14 077	26 200	23 198	3 467	2 010
2002	91 363	66 444	968	67 412	7 346	1 037	61 103	15 104	15 155	26 185	23 584	3 489	1 979
2003	94 147	69 112	954	70 066	7 578	1 073	63 562	14 696	15 890	26 862	24 400	3 505	1 966
2004	101 182	74 312	1 234	75 546	8 056	1 119	68 609	15 682	16 892	28 702	26 137	3 525	1 989
2005	107 640	78 350	1 322	79 672	8 534	1 159	72 297	17 126	18 217	30 333	27 312	3 549	2 032
2006	118 749	86 343	690	87 033	9 200	1 214	79 046	19 859	19 843	33 040	29 555	3 594	2 091
2007	124 762	89 058	638	89 696	9 631	1 241	81 305	22 130	21 327	34 329	30 581	3 634	2 144
2008	138 298	98 558	883	99 440	10 087	1 247	90 600	24 398	23 300	37 694	33 871	3 669	2 187
2009	126 401	88 437	100	88 537	9 761	1 136	79 913	20 440	26 048	34 001	31 188	3 718	2 141
2010	133 070	92 216	913	93 128	10 057	1 166	84 238	21 319	27 513	35 389	32 504	3 760	2 135
2011	141 335	97 857	975	98 832	9 593	1 232	90 471	22 636	28 228	37 277	33 857	3 792	. . .

. . . = Not available.

Table 17-2. Personal Income and Employment by Region and State—*Continued*

(Millions of dollars, except as noted.)

Region or state and year	Personal income, total	Earnings by place of work			Less: Contributions for government social insurance	Plus: Adjustment for residence	Equals: Net earnings by place of residence	Plus: Dividends, interest, and rent	Plus: Personal current transfer receipts	Per capita (dollars)		Population (thousands)	Total employment (thousands)
		Nonfarm	Farm	Total						Personal income	Disposable personal income		
OREGON													
1958	3 595	2 826	176	3 002	145	-11	2 847	465	283	2 092	1 834	1 718	. . .
1959	3 891	3 115	178	3 293	180	-14	3 099	506	286	2 228	1 954	1 746	. . .
1960	4 019	3 235	174	3 409	207	-17	3 184	531	304	2 268	1 986	1 772	. . .
1961	4 167	3 318	161	3 479	211	-19	3 249	566	352	2 332	2 060	1 787	. . .
1962	4 438	3 550	172	3 723	232	-22	3 468	610	359	2 441	2 148	1 818	. . .
1963	4 676	3 790	163	3 953	266	-27	3 660	645	371	2 524	2 201	1 853	. . .
1964	5 038	4 119	150	4 269	271	-32	3 966	687	384	2 668	2 346	1 888	. . .
1965	5 488	4 481	168	4 650	276	-38	4 336	737	414	2 833	2 510	1 937	. . .
1966	5 925	4 881	195	5 076	352	-42	4 682	796	447	3 009	2 648	1 969	. . .
1967	6 290	5 139	185	5 324	392	-46	4 886	871	533	3 178	2 799	1 979	. . .
1968	6 856	5 629	183	5 812	444	-54	5 314	942	600	3 421	2 982	2 004	. . .
1969	7 578	6 144	226	6 370	483	-91	5 796	1 120	662	3 675	3 149	2 062	920
1970	8 248	6 541	216	6 757	506	-67	6 184	1 259	805	3 927	3 427	2 100	926
1971	9 023	7 139	204	7 343	569	-56	6 717	1 374	932	4 197	3 694	2 150	951
1972	10 109	8 062	259	8 321	680	-50	7 591	1 496	1 022	4 605	4 014	2 195	1 001
1973	11 437	9 111	371	9 482	881	-56	8 546	1 679	1 213	5 109	4 471	2 239	1 058
1974	13 003	10 142	477	10 619	1 004	-63	9 553	1 955	1 496	5 701	4 956	2 281	1 089
1975	14 378	10 973	394	11 367	1 057	-31	10 278	2 199	1 901	6 185	5 466	2 325	1 105
1976	16 364	12 733	370	13 102	1 235	-16	11 852	2 445	2 067	6 898	6 042	2 372	1 156
1977	18 358	14 488	320	14 808	1 421	-74	13 314	2 809	2 235	7 526	6 499	2 439	1 223
1978	21 103	16 867	318	17 184	1 694	-131	15 359	3 303	2 441	8 409	7 236	2 510	1 296
1979	23 966	19 075	390	19 465	1 989	-203	17 273	3 956	2 738	9 295	7 971	2 578	1 350
1980	26 640	20 385	477	20 863	2 125	-252	18 486	4 905	3 249	10 086	8 705	2 641	1 350
1981	28 820	21 218	407	21 625	2 365	-262	18 997	6 062	3 761	10 802	9 365	2 668	1 319
1982	29 623	21 094	294	21 388	2 398	-249	18 741	6 642	4 240	11 116	9 668	2 665	1 270
1983	31 437	22 210	301	22 511	2 558	-232	19 720	7 159	4 558	11 849	10 411	2 653	1 295
1984	34 161	24 271	402	24 673	2 890	-278	21 504	7 949	4 707	12 811	11 310	2 667	1 342
1985	35 890	25 624	426	26 050	3 070	-315	22 665	8 299	4 926	13 429	11 808	2 673	1 370
1986	37 728	27 012	548	27 560	3 251	-361	23 949	8 766	5 014	14 059	12 298	2 684	1 406
1987	39 770	28 937	517	29 455	3 438	-420	25 596	8 983	5 191	14 724	12 882	2 701	1 455
1988	43 248	31 887	708	32 594	3 924	-493	28 178	9 548	5 522	15 776	13 972	2 741	1 522
1989	47 318	34 424	674	35 099	4 254	-546	30 298	10 959	6 060	16 956	14 739	2 791	1 574
1990	51 187	37 640	713	38 352	4 766	-608	32 979	11 617	6 591	17 895	15 709	2 860	1 626
1991	54 088	39 671	727	40 398	5 091	-666	34 641	12 145	7 302	18 469	16 157	2 929	1 636
1992	57 446	42 507	730	43 238	5 457	-753	37 028	12 292	8 126	19 201	16 780	2 992	1 654
1993	61 444	45 435	851	46 286	5 833	-844	39 609	13 156	8 680	20 077	17 502	3 060	1 698
1994	66 231	49 051	776	49 827	6 318	-898	42 611	14 609	9 010	21 219	18 443	3 121	1 781
1995	71 747	52 510	689	53 199	6 793	-1 072	45 334	16 448	9 965	22 531	19 631	3 184	1 845
1996	77 121	56 949	841	57 790	7 469	-1 294	49 026	17 495	10 600	23 751	20 585	3 247	1 920
1997	82 127	61 139	958	62 097	7 940	-1 478	52 678	18 548	10 900	24 854	21 372	3 304	1 986
1998	87 218	65 187	862	66 049	8 386	-1 600	56 062	19 820	11 336	26 016	22 427	3 352	2 024
1999	91 691	69 539	823	70 362	8 746	-1 749	59 867	19 470	12 355	27 016	23 192	3 394	2 049
2000	98 530	75 260	822	76 082	9 426	-1 918	64 737	20 789	13 003	28 728	24 544	3 430	2 095
2001	101 438	77 047	828	77 875	9 474	-1 962	66 438	20 305	14 695	29 250	25 252	3 468	2 089
2002	104 690	79 786	829	80 615	9 619	-1 999	68 997	19 999	15 694	29 797	26 366	3 513	2 065
2003	108 487	82 796	1 133	83 929	9 913	-2 065	71 952	20 386	16 149	30 582	27 263	3 547	2 084
2004	112 974	86 132	1 267	87 399	10 604	-2 086	74 710	21 634	16 630	31 650	28 173	3 569	2 137
2005	117 634	89 988	1 251	91 239	11 193	-2 184	77 863	21 989	17 782	32 557	28 530	3 613	2 200
2006	127 403	96 033	1 396	97 429	12 059	-2 326	83 045	25 406	18 953	34 706	30 299	3 671	2 264
2007	133 821	99 746	1 447	101 193	12 531	-2 466	86 196	27 217	20 408	35 950	31 570	3 722	2 318
2008	140 976	101 801	1 375	103 176	12 687	-2 495	87 994	30 226	22 756	37 407	32 926	3 769	2 307
2009	135 079	96 065	1 125	97 190	12 238	-2 248	82 705	25 308	27 066	35 467	31 997	3 809	2 206
2010	139 395	98 506	1 185	99 691	12 704	-2 378	84 609	26 031	28 754	36 317	32 688	3 838	2 201
2011	146 778	103 182	1 315	104 497	12 143	-2 575	89 779	27 672	29 327	37 909	33 720	3 872	. . .

. . . = Not available.

Table 17-2. Personal Income and Employment by Region and State—*Continued*

(Millions of dollars, except as noted.)

Region or state and year	Personal income, total	Earnings by place of work			Less: Contributions for government social insurance	Plus: Adjustment for residence	Equals: Net earnings by place of residence	Plus: Dividends, interest, and rent	Plus: Personal current transfer receipts	Per capita (dollars)		Population (thousands)	Total employment (thousands)
		Nonfarm	Farm	Total						Personal income	Disposable personal income		
PENNSYLVANIA													
1958	23 868	19 743	342	20 085	846	-45	19 194	2 871	1 803	2 158	1 926	11 058	. . .
1959	25 066	21 001	253	21 254	1 042	-57	20 156	3 039	1 871	2 231	1 986	11 234	. . .
1960	25 981	21 827	299	22 125	1 211	-75	20 839	3 220	1 922	2 293	2 037	11 329	. . .
1961	26 524	22 006	302	22 309	1 225	-80	21 003	3 337	2 183	2 328	2 081	11 392	. . .
1962	27 633	23 105	219	23 324	1 334	-97	21 893	3 573	2 167	2 434	2 161	11 355	. . .
1963	28 639	23 885	261	24 147	1 473	-106	22 568	3 826	2 245	2 507	2 223	11 424	. . .
1964	30 643	25 642	269	25 911	1 530	-128	24 253	4 131	2 259	2 660	2 388	11 519	. . .
1965	32 847	27 497	278	27 775	1 593	-148	26 034	4 444	2 370	2 827	2 529	11 620	. . .
1966	35 386	30 204	266	30 470	2 147	-193	28 130	4 681	2 575	3 034	2 694	11 664	. . .
1967	37 882	32 009	360	32 368	2 316	-222	29 830	4 984	3 068	3 243	2 883	11 681	. . .
1968	41 134	34 660	314	34 974	2 420	-258	32 296	5 326	3 512	3 503	3 089	11 741	. . .
1969	44 663	37 856	372	38 227	2 810	-413	35 004	5 667	3 992	3 804	3 306	11 741	5 250
1970	48 058	39 964	387	40 351	2 930	-379	37 042	6 101	4 914	4 069	3 563	11 812	5 226
1971	50 968	41 926	335	42 261	3 190	-361	38 709	6 484	5 775	4 289	3 799	11 884	5 159
1972	55 691	45 931	347	46 278	3 658	-371	42 249	6 915	6 527	4 678	4 057	11 905	5 247
1973	61 269	50 800	485	51 284	4 632	-335	46 317	7 647	7 305	5 155	4 501	11 885	5 402
1974	67 533	55 423	463	55 886	5 228	-341	50 317	8 677	8 539	5 692	4 946	11 864	5 419
1975	73 548	58 703	426	59 128	5 407	-374	53 347	9 373	10 827	6 182	5 457	11 898	5 302
1976	80 786	64 444	517	64 962	6 010	-362	58 590	10 182	12 013	6 796	5 981	11 887	5 353
1977	88 798	71 116	469	71 586	6 607	-360	64 618	11 414	12 766	7 473	6 541	11 882	5 429
1978	98 024	79 030	508	79 537	7 526	-369	71 642	12 672	13 710	8 262	7 204	11 865	5 562
1979	108 552	87 024	642	87 666	8 596	-393	78 677	14 435	15 440	9 142	7 930	11 874	5 664
1980	119 159	92 686	424	93 110	9 194	-428	83 488	17 988	17 683	10 040	8 725	11 868	5 624
1981	131 635	99 520	637	100 157	10 550	-411	89 196	22 528	19 911	11 100	9 581	11 859	5 584
1982	140 723	101 904	564	102 469	10 962	-243	91 264	26 655	22 804	11 880	10 346	11 845	5 474
1983	147 359	105 915	360	106 275	11 571	-80	94 624	28 071	24 664	12 448	10 973	11 838	5 433
1984	159 128	114 728	847	115 575	13 095	109	102 589	31 714	24 825	13 468	11 876	11 815	5 577
1985	168 534	121 102	844	121 947	14 061	257	108 142	34 411	25 981	14 318	12 610	11 771	5 679
1986	176 939	127 144	884	128 028	14 908	358	113 478	36 067	27 395	15 017	13 248	11 783	5 772
1987	187 282	137 075	887	137 961	15 897	456	122 520	36 737	28 025	15 857	13 902	11 811	5 957
1988	202 175	149 689	749	150 438	17 710	686	133 415	39 258	29 502	17 067	15 009	11 846	6 120
1989	218 480	159 209	997	160 205	18 656	879	142 429	44 671	31 381	18 412	16 143	11 866	6 216
1990	231 322	168 008	1 002	169 010	19 872	980	150 118	46 959	34 245	19 433	17 091	11 903	6 293
1991	241 689	173 201	734	173 935	20 727	934	154 142	48 031	39 516	20 171	17 854	11 982	6 212
1992	253 640	183 710	1 203	184 913	22 009	1 239	164 143	47 437	42 060	21 050	18 611	12 049	6 216
1993	262 454	191 070	1 031	192 101	23 255	1 256	170 102	48 066	44 286	21 655	19 152	12 120	6 256
1994	271 976	198 393	922	199 316	24 618	1 619	176 317	50 320	45 339	22 355	19 717	12 166	6 323
1995	283 314	206 470	645	207 114	25 489	1 895	183 520	52 501	47 292	23 226	20 406	12 198	6 423
1996	297 979	214 642	1 118	215 760	25 998	2 274	192 035	55 750	50 194	24 384	21 298	12 220	6 477
1997	312 618	226 210	770	226 980	27 144	2 581	202 417	58 913	51 287	25 566	22 187	12 228	6 585
1998	335 132	244 681	896	245 577	28 392	2 504	219 690	63 421	52 021	27 367	23 709	12 246	6 674
1999	347 654	256 918	814	257 732	29 637	2 899	230 994	62 226	54 434	28 348	24 511	12 264	6 774
2000	369 919	271 236	1 097	272 333	31 081	3 401	244 652	67 486	57 781	30 113	26 002	12 284	6 912
2001	377 374	276 879	997	277 877	32 099	3 671	249 449	66 226	61 698	30 683	26 546	12 299	6 927
2002	387 664	285 881	622	286 503	32 919	3 673	257 257	64 883	65 524	31 438	27 821	12 331	6 909
2003	399 547	296 721	1 213	297 933	33 796	3 808	267 946	63 445	68 157	32 288	28 844	12 375	6 904
2004	417 790	312 334	1 484	313 819	35 428	4 152	282 543	64 339	70 909	33 664	30 136	12 411	6 979
2005	432 248	324 392	1 342	325 734	37 234	4 572	293 071	63 177	76 000	34 719	30 730	12 450	7 084
2006	462 704	340 914	1 053	341 967	39 020	5 069	308 017	74 999	79 688	36 984	32 603	12 511	7 186
2007	489 076	353 075	1 230	354 305	40 745	5 642	319 202	84 718	85 156	38 927	34 060	12 564	7 271
2008	512 992	363 836	1 200	365 036	42 015	5 947	328 967	92 467	91 558	40 674	35 883	12 612	7 289
2009	499 700	352 853	911	353 764	41 508	5 223	317 480	78 680	103 541	39 449	35 544	12 667	7 120
2010	516 390	362 942	1 198	364 140	42 794	5 438	326 783	79 957	109 649	40 604	36 538	12 718	7 137
2011	541 297	378 317	1 738	380 054	40 283	5 589	345 361	84 192	111 744	42 478	37 773	12 743	. . .

. . . = Not available.

Table 17-2. Personal Income and Employment by Region and State—*Continued*

(Millions of dollars, except as noted.)

Region or state and year	Personal income, total	Earnings by place of work			Less: Contributions for government social insurance	Plus: Adjustment for residence	Equals: Net earnings by place of residence	Plus: Dividends, interest, and rent	Plus: Personal current transfer receipts	Per capita (dollars)		Population (thousands)	Total employment (thousands)
		Nonfarm	Farm	Total						Personal income	Disposable personal income		
RHODE ISLAND													
1958	1 794	1 442	8	1 450	75	44	1 418	226	149	2 090	1 866	858	. . .
1959	1 893	1 542	6	1 548	86	51	1 513	233	146	2 208	1 977	857	. . .
1960	1 934	1 580	8	1 588	96	54	1 546	237	150	2 262	2 011	855	. . .
1961	2 023	1 634	7	1 641	98	57	1 600	257	166	2 358	2 090	858	. . .
1962	2 168	1 750	7	1 757	108	63	1 712	288	169	2 489	2 215	871	. . .
1963	2 265	1 806	7	1 813	117	67	1 763	323	179	2 586	2 298	876	. . .
1964	2 414	1 932	8	1 940	122	73	1 891	340	184	2 728	2 458	885	. . .
1965	2 599	2 077	8	2 085	133	82	2 035	366	198	2 910	2 616	893	. . .
1966	2 838	2 296	9	2 305	162	96	2 238	382	218	3 157	2 816	899	. . .
1967	3 080	2 467	7	2 474	174	105	2 405	410	265	3 388	3 035	909	. . .
1968	3 364	2 699	8	2 707	200	116	2 624	432	308	3 649	3 231	922	. . .
1969	3 586	2 901	8	2 909	230	65	2 744	495	347	3 847	3 386	932	440
1970	3 895	3 117	9	3 126	245	66	2 948	525	423	4 098	3 647	951	440
1971	4 131	3 277	8	3 285	267	61	3 079	555	497	4 285	3 817	964	436
1972	4 504	3 614	8	3 621	306	56	3 371	588	546	4 613	4 060	976	447
1973	4 846	3 873	6	3 879	381	71	3 569	652	625	4 955	4 366	978	452
1974	5 135	3 973	9	3 982	410	88	3 660	741	734	5 385	4 737	954	439
1975	5 537	4 112	9	4 121	415	82	3 788	778	972	5 851	5 251	946	424
1976	6 084	4 631	9	4 640	472	89	4 256	835	993	6 402	5 693	950	442
1977	6 662	5 096	8	5 104	520	103	4 688	935	1 040	6 975	6 216	955	459
1978	7 309	5 659	9	5 668	597	102	5 174	1 025	1 111	7 636	6 706	957	474
1979	8 128	6 297	8	6 304	684	110	5 730	1 164	1 235	8 497	7 388	957	483
1980	9 151	6 861	8	6 868	746	124	6 247	1 476	1 428	9 645	8 445	949	484
1981	10 229	7 405	9	7 414	849	155	6 720	1 875	1 634	10 733	9 405	953	484
1982	11 011	7 785	27	7 812	900	209	7 121	2 097	1 793	11 540	10 170	954	475
1983	11 849	8 389	37	8 426	988	265	7 703	2 234	1 912	12 389	10 956	956	480
1984	13 110	9 315	32	9 348	1 136	335	8 547	2 598	1 965	13 629	12 107	962	504
1985	14 086	10 087	42	10 129	1 220	394	9 302	2 698	2 086	14 538	12 891	969	519
1986	15 095	10 914	43	10 957	1 330	417	10 043	2 881	2 170	15 445	13 616	977	537
1987	16 217	11 835	41	11 875	1 430	483	10 928	3 053	2 236	16 387	14 299	990	546
1988	17 845	13 042	42	13 084	1 599	558	12 043	3 412	2 390	17 909	15 729	996	560
1989	19 402	13 747	32	13 780	1 664	619	12 734	4 058	2 609	19 389	17 028	1 001	560
1990	19 940	14 054	31	14 085	1 792	664	12 957	4 098	2 884	19 821	17 453	1 006	550
1991	20 194	13 822	32	13 853	1 798	691	12 746	3 945	3 504	19 981	17 674	1 011	524
1992	21 082	14 681	29	14 710	1 916	708	13 502	3 926	3 654	20 820	18 495	1 013	529
1993	21 927	15 217	30	15 247	2 007	748	13 989	3 972	3 965	21 600	19 155	1 015	533
1994	22 553	15 756	25	15 782	2 098	820	14 504	4 106	3 943	22 199	19 655	1 016	533
1995	23 761	16 541	25	16 566	2 172	850	15 244	4 360	4 157	23 364	20 683	1 017	536
1996	24 807	17 080	23	17 103	2 213	917	15 808	4 765	4 235	24 299	21 407	1 021	540
1997	26 271	18 017	16	18 032	2 321	978	16 690	5 083	4 499	25 621	22 361	1 025	546
1998	27 784	19 133	15	19 148	2 458	1 060	17 750	5 486	4 548	26 945	23 388	1 031	554
1999	28 861	20 126	15	20 142	2 575	1 154	18 720	5 410	4 731	27 741	24 038	1 040	565
2000	30 980	21 609	17	21 626	2 745	1 319	20 200	5 873	4 908	29 498	25 351	1 050	578
2001	32 980	22 949	18	22 966	2 865	1 306	21 407	6 089	5 483	31 197	26 918	1 057	581
2002	34 282	24 023	22	24 045	2 993	1 248	22 299	6 260	5 722	32 160	28 423	1 066	585
2003	35 866	25 580	24	25 604	3 132	1 218	23 690	6 292	5 883	33 477	29 861	1 071	591
2004	37 585	26 867	25	26 893	3 268	1 295	24 919	6 384	6 282	34 976	31 228	1 075	600
2005	38 570	27 830	23	27 853	3 409	1 306	25 750	6 284	6 536	36 117	32 052	1 068	604
2006	40 664	29 134	23	29 157	3 592	1 357	26 921	6 988	6 755	38 251	33 819	1 063	610
2007	42 661	29 784	23	29 807	3 683	1 464	27 587	7 701	7 373	40 349	35 528	1 057	616
2008	44 122	30 058	18	30 075	3 756	1 512	27 831	8 355	7 936	41 822	37 224	1 055	607
2009	42 773	29 051	18	29 069	3 703	1 413	26 779	7 083	8 911	40 595	36 888	1 054	587
2010	44 200	29 854	18	29 872	3 788	1 425	27 509	7 350	9 341	41 995	38 115	1 053	587
2011	46 248	30 865	17	30 882	3 505	1 534	28 912	7 811	9 526	43 992	39 454	1 051	. . .

. . . = Not available.

Table 17-2. Personal Income and Employment by Region and State—*Continued*

(Millions of dollars, except as noted.)

Region or state and year	Personal income, total	Derivation of personal income								Per capita (dollars)		Population (thousands)	Total employment (thousands)
		Earnings by place of work			Less: Contributions for government social insurance	Plus: Adjustment for residence	Equals: Net earnings by place of residence	Plus: Dividends, interest, and rent	Plus: Personal current transfer receipts	Personal income	Disposable personal income		
		Nonfarm	Farm	Total									
SOUTH CAROLINA													
1958	3 013	2 437	183	2 620	95	13	2 539	286	189	1 308	1 211	2 304	. . .
1959	3 245	2 675	165	2 840	113	15	2 742	304	199	1 382	1 265	2 348	. . .
1960	3 415	2 821	170	2 991	135	17	2 873	332	210	1 427	1 306	2 392	. . .
1961	3 585	2 911	196	3 107	138	19	2 988	358	238	1 488	1 359	2 409	. . .
1962	3 852	3 150	185	3 336	153	22	3 205	394	253	1 590	1 443	2 423	. . .
1963	4 074	3 353	189	3 542	189	25	3 378	423	272	1 656	1 505	2 460	. . .
1964	4 389	3 643	180	3 823	202	30	3 650	454	284	1 773	1 625	2 475	. . .
1965	4 840	4 028	182	4 210	221	35	4 024	506	310	1 941	1 770	2 494	. . .
1966	5 436	4 609	196	4 806	290	43	4 559	535	342	2 157	1 949	2 520	. . .
1967	5 879	4 993	197	5 190	341	49	4 898	579	401	2 321	2 097	2 533	. . .
1968	6 522	5 616	155	5 772	386	57	5 442	608	471	2 549	2 284	2 559	. . .
1969	7 249	6 158	188	6 346	416	115	6 045	667	537	2 821	2 503	2 570	1 170
1970	7 937	6 656	189	6 845	448	116	6 513	755	669	3 055	2 741	2 598	1 196
1971	8 692	7 251	204	7 455	509	128	7 074	839	779	3 265	2 936	2 662	1 215
1972	9 769	8 205	214	8 419	599	145	7 965	928	876	3 594	3 170	2 718	1 262
1973	11 147	9 348	302	9 650	773	159	9 037	1 066	1 044	4 016	3 562	2 775	1 328
1974	12 656	10 493	342	10 835	897	174	10 111	1 228	1 318	4 451	3 940	2 843	1 365
1975	13 719	10 991	277	11 268	927	185	10 526	1 379	1 814	4 730	4 296	2 900	1 326
1976	15 457	12 647	234	12 881	1 088	220	12 014	1 524	1 919	5 255	4 712	2 941	1 376
1977	16 941	13 977	188	14 165	1 198	243	13 210	1 724	2 006	5 668	5 065	2 989	1 411
1978	19 162	15 864	247	16 111	1 389	261	14 982	1 975	2 205	6 301	5 614	3 041	1 466
1979	21 572	17 785	260	18 044	1 607	285	16 722	2 306	2 544	6 988	6 158	3 087	1 507
1980	24 250	19 648	36	19 684	1 777	319	18 226	2 935	3 089	7 736	6 840	3 135	1 523
1981	27 360	21 649	173	21 822	2 097	349	20 073	3 714	3 572	8 606	7 571	3 179	1 536
1982	29 120	22 427	195	22 622	2 201	381	20 802	4 396	3 923	9 078	8 071	3 208	1 514
1983	31 662	24 534	50	24 584	2 470	394	22 508	4 969	4 185	9 701	8 701	3 234	1 547
1984	35 663	27 621	269	27 890	2 850	441	25 480	5 768	4 415	10 900	9 744	3 272	1 625
1985	38 284	29 471	196	29 667	3 097	496	27 067	6 432	4 785	11 590	10 332	3 303	1 655
1986	40 761	31 573	91	31 664	3 426	562	28 800	6 914	5 046	12 194	10 874	3 343	1 697
1987	43 740	34 081	251	34 332	3 666	605	31 271	7 280	5 189	12 939	11 489	3 381	1 738
1988	47 448	37 148	350	37 498	4 149	626	33 976	7 937	5 535	13 906	12 421	3 412	1 809
1989	51 613	39 674	367	40 041	4 506	581	36 115	9 119	6 379	14 931	13 239	3 457	1 858
1990	55 471	42 743	301	43 044	4 957	507	38 594	9 812	7 065	15 844	14 044	3 501	1 913
1991	58 039	44 035	399	44 434	5 176	494	39 753	10 172	8 114	16 256	14 537	3 570	1 886
1992	61 583	46 640	378	47 018	5 458	505	42 065	10 384	9 134	17 010	15 243	3 620	1 897
1993	64 662	48 997	338	49 336	5 799	510	44 047	10 823	9 791	17 651	15 801	3 663	1 931
1994	68 841	51 349	491	51 840	6 152	620	46 308	11 892	10 641	18 579	16 598	3 705	1 979
1995	72 664	54 227	385	54 612	6 510	744	48 846	12 472	11 346	19 384	17 241	3 749	2 038
1996	77 285	56 899	464	57 363	6 736	864	51 491	13 605	12 189	20 359	18 025	3 796	2 080
1997	82 160	60 278	474	60 751	7 162	1 014	54 603	14 784	12 772	21 287	18 772	3 860	2 141
1998	88 470	65 015	335	65 350	7 700	1 091	58 741	16 296	13 433	22 573	19 853	3 919	2 195
1999	93 605	69 642	403	70 046	8 114	1 184	63 116	16 191	14 298	23 550	20 712	3 975	2 240
2000	100 913	74 443	525	74 968	8 559	1 419	67 828	17 702	15 383	25 076	22 161	4 024	2 275
2001	104 215	76 219	647	76 865	8 827	1 423	69 462	17 598	17 155	25 637	22 722	4 065	2 244
2002	107 002	78 716	226	78 942	9 118	1 438	71 262	17 015	18 726	26 049	23 489	4 108	2 290
2003	110 660	82 382	540	82 921	9 447	1 463	74 938	16 141	19 582	26 663	24 241	4 150	2 317
2004	117 248	86 644	639	87 282	9 907	1 569	78 944	17 166	21 138	27 844	25 353	4 211	2 384
2005	124 392	91 206	649	91 855	10 375	1 729	83 209	18 454	22 729	29 131	26 282	4 270	2 428
2006	134 197	97 021	461	97 482	11 320	1 921	88 084	21 617	24 496	30 794	27 646	4 358	2 491
2007	142 167	101 130	287	101 417	11 776	2 223	91 864	24 172	26 130	31 990	28 616	4 444	2 567
2008	149 325	103 465	496	103 961	12 099	2 360	94 222	25 730	29 373	32 971	29 857	4 529	2 557
2009	145 285	99 544	506	100 051	11 751	2 206	90 505	21 449	33 331	31 653	29 194	4 590	2 458
2010	150 528	102 047	428	102 475	11 973	2 310	92 812	22 073	35 642	32 462	29 950	4 637	2 452
2011	157 565	105 784	340	106 124	11 159	2 466	97 431	23 360	36 774	33 673	30 771	4 679	. . .

. . . = Not available.

Table 17-2. Personal Income and Employment by Region and State—*Continued*

(Millions of dollars, except as noted.)

Region or state and year	Personal income, total	Derivation of personal income								Per capita (dollars)		Population (thousands)	Total employment (thousands)
		Earnings by place of work			Less: Contributions for government social insurance	Plus: Adjustment for residence	Equals: Net earnings by place of residence	Plus: Dividends, interest, and rent	Plus: Personal current transfer receipts	Personal income	Disposable personal income		
		Nonfarm	Farm	Total									
SOUTH DAKOTA													
1958	1 156	648	311	958	26	0	933	150	73	1 762	1 620	656	. . .
1959	1 044	706	141	847	34	0	813	149	82	1 565	1 448	667	. . .
1960	1 290	739	324	1 063	35	0	1 029	175	86	1 888	1 751	683	. . .
1961	1 297	810	251	1 061	39	0	1 022	180	94	1 872	1 722	693	. . .
1962	1 481	864	369	1 232	45	1	1 188	194	100	2 101	1 940	705	. . .
1963	1 430	874	299	1 173	51	1	1 123	201	106	2 020	1 855	708	. . .
1964	1 397	917	216	1 132	50	1	1 083	205	109	1 993	1 854	701	. . .
1965	1 575	949	334	1 283	51	2	1 234	223	119	2 277	2 126	692	. . .
1966	1 704	1 015	394	1 409	64	2	1 346	228	129	2 495	2 315	683	. . .
1967	1 729	1 070	344	1 414	77	3	1 340	235	154	2 577	2 387	671	. . .
1968	1 856	1 161	363	1 523	83	3	1 443	235	177	2 774	2 545	669	. . .
1969	2 024	1 272	357	1 629	90	6	1 546	284	194	3 030	2 760	668	303
1970	2 190	1 371	373	1 744	96	6	1 654	314	222	3 286	3 025	667	305
1971	2 393	1 496	404	1 900	107	6	1 799	338	255	3 564	3 322	671	306
1972	2 770	1 662	564	2 226	121	7	2 111	376	282	4 089	3 813	677	309
1973	3 514	1 878	1 027	2 905	159	7	2 753	433	327	5 175	4 794	679	323
1974	3 527	2 108	688	2 795	184	8	2 620	524	383	5 187	4 735	680	326
1975	3 888	2 302	708	3 010	201	10	2 819	612	456	5 706	5 288	681	326
1976	3 846	2 621	278	2 899	225	12	2 686	659	501	5 600	5 122	687	336
1977	4 376	2 871	445	3 316	238	13	3 091	757	529	6 352	5 887	689	342
1978	5 033	3 266	617	3 883	275	15	3 623	836	574	7 302	6 722	689	355
1979	5 553	3 598	652	4 251	323	16	3 944	961	648	8 059	7 398	689	359
1980	5 564	3 814	137	3 951	344	18	3 625	1 181	758	8 054	7 298	691	353
1981	6 489	4 044	445	4 489	392	14	4 111	1 508	869	9 410	8 556	690	348
1982	6 869	4 171	374	4 545	412	12	4 144	1 758	966	9 946	8 996	691	344
1983	7 133	4 467	255	4 723	441	5	4 287	1 806	1 040	10 293	9 473	693	353
1984	8 103	4 884	689	5 572	491	-2	5 079	1 924	1 100	11 621	10 807	697	362
1985	8 309	5 085	611	5 697	530	-5	5 162	1 978	1 170	11 898	11 040	698	365
1986	8 667	5 312	663	5 976	574	-11	5 390	2 060	1 217	12 452	11 566	696	366
1987	9 141	5 644	844	6 488	618	-19	5 851	2 033	1 257	13 133	12 133	696	381
1988	9 517	6 090	716	6 807	692	-26	6 089	2 114	1 314	13 631	12 583	698	388
1989	10 209	6 486	724	7 210	751	-36	6 423	2 355	1 431	14 653	13 465	697	396
1990	11 206	7 060	1 022	8 082	852	-55	7 175	2 506	1 525	16 075	14 725	697	409
1991	11 727	7 576	895	8 471	924	-68	7 478	2 600	1 649	16 666	15 288	704	420
1992	12 645	8 199	1 076	9 275	994	-84	8 197	2 656	1 792	17 740	16 270	713	431
1993	13 178	8 772	947	9 719	1 062	-98	8 559	2 732	1 887	18 248	16 641	722	442
1994	14 252	9 437	1 212	10 649	1 152	-127	9 371	2 885	1 996	19 503	17 886	731	464
1995	14 471	9 927	642	10 569	1 210	-150	9 209	3 134	2 128	19 610	17 886	738	472
1996	16 085	10 387	1 462	11 849	1 261	-190	10 397	3 441	2 247	21 672	19 845	742	479
1997	16 436	10 950	1 050	12 000	1 327	-189	10 484	3 648	2 305	22 085	19 984	744	485
1998	17 708	11 809	1 169	12 978	1 420	-240	11 318	4 018	2 373	23 736	21 501	746	494
1999	18 622	12 612	1 164	13 775	1 518	-256	12 002	4 149	2 471	24 816	22 359	750	505
2000	19 970	13 449	1 336	14 785	1 606	-277	12 902	4 422	2 646	26 421	23 876	756	516
2001	21 121	14 337	1 141	15 478	1 671	-258	13 549	4 710	2 862	27 865	25 253	758	512
2002	21 359	15 107	487	15 594	1 723	-239	13 632	4 670	3 057	28 103	25 849	760	510
2003	23 313	15 804	1 595	17 399	1 786	-234	15 378	4 793	3 142	30 526	28 475	764	510
2004	24 879	16 706	1 941	18 646	1 891	-235	16 521	5 046	3 312	32 294	30 111	770	519
2005	25 829	17 394	1 731	19 125	1 981	-207	16 937	5 344	3 548	33 306	30 793	775	529
2006	26 582	18 278	788	19 065	2 125	-197	16 744	6 000	3 838	33 948	31 024	783	540
2007	29 285	19 096	1 851	20 947	2 264	-213	18 471	6 716	4 098	36 993	33 741	792	551
2008	32 215	19 830	2 976	22 807	2 372	-196	20 239	7 517	4 459	40 313	37 033	799	560
2009	30 912	19 707	2 358	22 065	2 384	-157	19 524	6 475	4 913	38 302	35 774	807	555
2010	32 271	20 560	2 408	22 968	2 494	-170	20 304	6 769	5 199	39 519	36 875	817	556
2011	34 274	21 274	2 962	24 235	2 326	-182	21 728	7 164	5 382	41 590	38 493	824	. . .

. . . = Not available.

Table 17-2. Personal Income and Employment by Region and State—*Continued*

(Millions of dollars, except as noted.)

Region or state and year	Personal income, total	Earnings by place of work			Less: Contributions for government social insurance	Plus: Adjustment for residence	Equals: Net earnings by place of residence	Plus: Dividends, interest, and rent	Plus: Personal current transfer receipts	Per capita (dollars)		Population (thousands)	Total employment (thousands)
		Nonfarm	Farm	Total						Personal income	Disposable personal income		
TENNESSEE													
1958	5 271	4 206	315	4 521	175	27	4 373	528	370	1 518	1 392	3 471	. . .
1959	5 650	4 582	305	4 888	207	23	4 704	560	386	1 604	1 469	3 522	. . .
1960	5 805	4 766	246	5 012	242	23	4 793	608	404	1 624	1 477	3 575	. . .
1961	6 142	4 961	294	5 256	247	22	5 031	652	459	1 696	1 547	3 622	. . .
1962	6 521	5 330	254	5 585	273	22	5 334	711	477	1 776	1 594	3 673	. . .
1963	6 910	5 683	278	5 961	323	22	5 659	748	502	1 859	1 687	3 718	. . .
1964	7 434	6 183	238	6 421	339	21	6 104	805	525	1 971	1 808	3 771	. . .
1965	8 108	6 752	254	7 006	363	21	6 663	866	578	2 135	1 949	3 798	. . .
1966	8 938	7 602	258	7 860	502	21	7 379	923	636	2 338	2 116	3 822	. . .
1967	9 579	8 147	219	8 366	564	35	7 837	980	763	2 482	2 252	3 859	. . .
1968	10 677	9 072	225	9 297	634	33	8 696	1 106	875	2 753	2 467	3 878	. . .
1969	11 524	9 904	256	10 160	659	-155	9 345	1 201	978	2 957	2 617	3 897	1 789
1970	12 505	10 537	269	10 806	695	-155	9 956	1 352	1 197	3 176	2 833	3 937	1 785
1971	13 791	11 586	267	11 853	789	-165	10 899	1 496	1 397	3 439	3 091	4 010	1 817
1972	15 538	13 152	326	13 478	937	-192	12 349	1 650	1 539	3 800	3 412	4 088	1 924
1973	17 731	14 915	493	15 407	1 211	-181	14 015	1 899	1 817	4 284	3 846	4 138	2 025
1974	19 685	16 479	318	16 797	1 383	-191	15 222	2 242	2 221	4 685	4 207	4 202	2 055
1975	21 414	17 341	251	17 591	1 430	-190	15 971	2 509	2 934	5 026	4 559	4 261	1 983
1976	24 115	19 652	372	20 023	1 639	-184	18 199	2 721	3 195	5 570	5 033	4 329	2 052
1977	26 805	22 170	300	22 470	1 846	-241	20 383	3 067	3 355	6 089	5 505	4 402	2 135
1978	30 615	25 574	320	25 893	2 151	-308	23 435	3 515	3 665	6 826	6 169	4 462	2 227
1979	34 248	28 369	342	28 711	2 480	-358	25 874	4 106	4 268	7 555	6 780	4 533	2 279
1980	37 847	30 453	197	30 650	2 675	-424	27 551	5 158	5 138	8 227	7 374	4 600	2 259
1981	42 205	33 181	361	33 542	3 155	-457	29 930	6 448	5 827	9 120	8 173	4 628	2 255
1982	45 048	34 472	303	34 775	3 352	-414	31 009	7 645	6 395	9 696	8 736	4 646	2 217
1983	47 964	37 162	-34	37 129	3 652	-428	33 049	8 044	6 871	10 293	9 296	4 660	2 239
1984	53 490	41 276	412	41 688	4 190	-427	37 070	9 223	7 197	11 413	10 367	4 687	2 344
1985	57 302	44 415	334	44 750	4 590	-444	39 716	9 936	7 650	12 152	10 995	4 715	2 399
1986	61 105	47 717	241	47 958	5 066	-481	42 410	10 484	8 211	12 895	11 679	4 739	2 477
1987	65 786	51 953	307	52 259	5 474	-512	46 273	10 860	8 652	13 754	12 400	4 783	2 578
1988	71 289	56 326	392	56 719	6 097	-525	50 097	11 898	9 295	14 783	13 391	4 822	2 663
1989	76 300	59 467	443	59 911	6 543	-549	52 819	13 257	10 224	15 718	14 183	4 854	2 735
1990	81 121	62 784	444	63 228	6 958	-585	55 685	14 119	11 317	16 574	15 004	4 894	2 777
1991	85 632	65 893	511	66 404	7 394	-582	58 428	14 352	12 853	17 242	15 671	4 967	2 778
1992	93 558	72 238	668	72 906	7 997	-423	64 486	14 605	14 467	18 527	16 844	5 050	2 837
1993	99 315	77 327	595	77 923	8 604	-549	68 770	15 024	15 521	19 331	17 551	5 138	2 943
1994	106 112	83 038	657	83 695	9 380	-644	73 670	16 163	16 278	20 283	18 369	5 231	3 061
1995	113 671	88 794	444	89 238	10 006	-733	78 500	17 360	17 812	21 339	19 297	5 327	3 145
1996	119 901	93 153	394	93 548	10 369	-708	82 471	18 704	18 726	22 136	19 910	5 417	3 195
1997	126 654	98 877	385	99 262	11 016	-912	87 334	19 853	19 467	23 031	20 646	5 499	3 269
1998	136 253	106 829	207	107 036	11 710	-1 067	94 260	21 657	20 337	24 462	21 927	5 570	3 353
1999	143 053	113 453	56	113 509	12 358	-1 247	99 904	21 884	21 265	25 370	22 764	5 639	3 409
2000	152 224	119 802	321	120 123	12 918	-1 416	105 789	23 342	23 093	26 689	24 009	5 704	3 471
2001	158 443	124 317	448	124 765	13 323	-1 451	109 992	23 279	25 172	27 551	24 845	5 751	3 434
2002	163 227	129 802	74	129 876	13 872	-1 421	114 583	21 578	27 066	28 162	25 817	5 796	3 425
2003	169 829	135 537	255	135 793	14 433	-1 366	119 994	21 164	28 672	29 041	26 830	5 848	3 450
2004	179 012	143 788	385	144 173	15 198	-1 443	127 532	21 010	30 469	30 285	28 054	5 911	3 530
2005	187 679	149 716	546	150 262	15 842	-1 195	133 226	21 879	32 575	31 327	28 832	5 991	3 597
2006	200 227	158 423	275	158 697	16 684	-1 080	140 934	25 249	34 043	32 885	30 026	6 089	3 666
2007	211 342	163 533	-147	163 386	17 434	-1 092	144 860	28 987	37 495	34 221	31 175	6 176	3 727
2008	219 359	164 446	251	164 697	17 913	-878	145 906	32 402	41 051	35 112	32 323	6 247	3 693
2009	212 980	157 968	326	158 293	17 641	-540	140 113	27 181	45 686	33 774	31 633	6 306	3 544
2010	222 007	163 626	176	163 802	17 979	-602	145 221	27 310	49 476	34 921	32 684	6 357	3 541
2011	233 933	170 726	451	171 177	16 700	-667	153 811	28 720	51 403	36 533	33 879	6 403	. . .

. . . = Not available.

Table 17-2. Personal Income and Employment by Region and State—*Continued*

(Millions of dollars, except as noted.)

Region or state and year	Personal income, total	Earnings by place of work			Less: Contributions for government social insurance	Plus: Adjustment for residence	Equals: Net earnings by place of residence	Plus: Dividends, interest, and rent	Plus: Personal current transfer receipts	Per capita (dollars)		Population (thousands)	Total employment (thousands)
		Nonfarm	Farm	Total						Personal income	Disposable personal income		
TEXAS													
1958	17 339	13 626	1 064	14 690	472	14	14 232	2 219	888	1 874	1 691	9 252	. . .
1959	18 313	14 482	994	15 476	567	15	14 924	2 438	951	1 947	1 754	9 405	. . .
1960	18 823	14 960	925	15 885	677	15	15 223	2 602	998	1 956	1 755	9 624	. . .
1961	19 871	15 624	1 090	16 714	695	15	16 034	2 715	1 122	2 024	1 815	9 820	. . .
1962	20 871	16 549	950	17 500	748	16	16 767	2 882	1 222	2 076	1 857	10 053	. . .
1963	21 838	17 479	784	18 262	831	16	17 447	3 070	1 321	2 150	1 921	10 159	. . .
1964	23 407	18 897	728	19 626	877	17	18 766	3 270	1 371	2 279	2 070	10 270	. . .
1965	25 179	20 246	865	21 111	929	18	20 199	3 482	1 498	2 426	2 198	10 378	. . .
1966	27 489	22 490	921	23 410	1 259	15	22 167	3 692	1 630	2 620	2 351	10 492	. . .
1967	30 034	24 835	779	25 614	1 458	13	24 169	3 896	1 969	2 834	2 536	10 599	. . .
1968	33 525	27 810	910	28 720	1 630	13	27 103	4 062	2 360	3 099	2 740	10 819	. . .
1969	37 151	31 081	927	32 008	2 013	-85	29 910	4 597	2 644	3 364	2 944	11 045	5 005
1970	40 772	33 523	1 168	34 690	2 150	-96	32 445	5 187	3 139	3 628	3 216	11 237	5 045
1971	44 202	36 336	1 015	37 351	2 400	-101	34 850	5 685	3 667	3 840	3 444	11 510	5 123
1972	49 088	40 359	1 257	41 616	2 784	-127	38 705	6 267	4 116	4 175	3 703	11 759	5 334
1973	55 998	45 496	2 144	47 641	3 610	-154	43 876	7 172	4 950	4 659	4 144	12 019	5 608
1974	63 426	52 252	1 156	53 408	4 251	-131	49 027	8 494	5 904	5 170	4 556	12 268	5 822
1975	72 121	58 921	1 314	60 236	4 722	-128	55 385	9 356	7 380	5 738	5 123	12 568	5 938
1976	81 892	68 055	1 292	69 347	5 514	-93	63 741	10 100	8 051	6 347	5 630	12 903	6 207
1977	91 596	77 067	1 280	78 347	6 290	-306	71 751	11 279	8 565	6 943	6 107	13 192	6 521
1978	106 034	89 983	1 032	91 015	7 495	-427	83 093	13 396	9 545	7 856	6 920	13 498	6 900
1979	122 649	103 481	1 741	105 222	9 039	-432	95 751	16 010	10 888	8 832	7 686	13 887	7 215
1980	141 516	118 927	621	119 548	10 479	-541	108 527	20 263	12 726	9 870	8 553	14 338	7 496
1981	166 934	138 053	1 966	140 019	13 060	-355	126 604	25 864	14 466	11 320	9 712	14 746	7 900
1982	183 447	149 432	1 354	150 786	14 451	-426	131 065	31 065	16 472	11 965	10 384	15 331	8 074
1983	194 505	155 679	1 740	157 418	15 035	-406	141 977	33 923	18 604	12 348	10 917	15 752	8 064
1984	214 133	171 040	1 625	172 665	16 889	-466	155 311	39 038	19 784	13 377	11 896	16 007	8 434
1985	229 610	182 376	1 495	183 871	18 296	-493	165 082	43 384	21 143	14 110	12 546	16 273	8 674
1986	234 878	185 148	1 272	186 421	18 421	-450	167 550	44 154	23 174	14 182	12 752	16 561	8 514
1987	240 237	188 846	2 089	190 935	18 488	-446	172 001	43 868	24 368	14 453	12 950	16 622	8 723
1988	254 091	200 484	2 327	202 811	20 286	-449	182 076	46 405	25 609	15 245	13 733	16 667	8 880
1989	271 673	212 348	2 244	214 592	21 619	-457	192 517	51 006	28 150	16 165	14 479	16 807	9 005
1990	294 401	229 576	3 049	232 625	22 974	-490	209 162	53 757	31 482	17 260	15 463	17 057	9 243
1991	309 037	241 671	2 773	244 444	24 760	-568	219 116	54 978	34 943	17 763	15 999	17 398	9 404
1992	333 257	260 259	3 376	263 635	26 382	-588	236 665	55 229	41 363	18 765	16 977	17 760	9 483
1993	352 573	277 201	3 999	281 200	28 000	-610	252 590	55 718	44 265	19 413	17 542	18 162	9 781
1994	374 279	293 981	3 448	297 429	29 983	-671	266 775	59 933	47 572	20 161	18 209	18 564	10 098
1995	399 463	313 792	2 784	316 576	31 979	-759	283 838	64 109	51 516	21 070	18 995	18 959	10 440
1996	430 511	338 895	2 412	341 307	34 009	-833	306 465	69 014	55 032	22 260	19 942	19 340	10 738
1997	470 065	373 789	3 065	376 855	37 080	-972	338 803	73 715	57 547	23 812	21 188	19 740	11 165
1998	511 509	410 690	2 840	413 531	40 424	-1 064	372 043	80 691	58 775	25 376	22 474	20 158	11 570
1999	542 720	440 724	4 279	445 002	42 928	-1 107	400 968	81 090	60 662	26 399	23 400	20 558	11 800
2000	597 041	487 373	3 335	490 708	46 198	-1 203	443 307	89 401	64 333	28 506	25 168	20 944	12 151
2001	622 217	509 134	3 965	513 100	48 530	-1 385	463 185	88 489	70 543	29 185	25 867	21 320	12 211
2002	628 274	513 046	3 945	516 991	49 122	-1 383	466 487	84 040	77 747	28 966	26 268	21 690	12 263
2003	652 610	531 284	5 046	536 331	51 463	-1 371	483 497	85 919	83 194	29 622	27 137	22 031	12 358
2004	696 796	570 510	5 316	575 826	54 048	-1 428	520 350	88 889	87 556	31 115	28 635	22 394	12 617
2005	756 683	611 207	5 005	616 212	57 671	-1 535	557 006	103 299	96 378	33 220	30 207	22 778	13 012
2006	824 281	664 459	3 256	667 715	61 533	-1 712	604 470	116 808	103 002	35 287	31 844	23 360	13 500
2007	884 119	703 372	3 718	707 090	65 731	-1 974	639 385	131 528	113 206	37 098	33 404	23 832	14 025
2008	962 992	757 312	2 623	759 935	69 138	-2 119	688 678	149 135	125 179	39 615	35 715	24 309	14 388
2009	905 256	700 435	1 677	702 113	67 804	-1 929	632 379	131 510	141 367	36 500	33 719	24 802	14 229
2010	953 254	732 530	4 084	736 614	70 894	-1 955	663 766	135 207	154 282	37 747	34 867	25 253	14 286
2011	1 016 529	782 217	2 553	784 770	68 588	-2 212	713 971	142 026	160 532	39 593	36 130	25 675	. . .

. . . = Not available.

Table 17-2. Personal Income and Employment by Region and State—*Continued*

(Millions of dollars, except as noted.)

Region or state and year	Personal income, total	Earnings by place of work			Less: Contributions for government social insurance	Plus: Adjustment for residence	Equals: Net earnings by place of residence	Plus: Dividends, interest, and rent	Plus: Personal current transfer receipts	Per capita (dollars)		Population (thousands)	Total employment (thousands)
		Nonfarm	Farm	Total						Personal income	Disposable personal income		
UTAH													
1958	1 592	1 307	53	1 361	54	0	1 308	190	95	1 885	1 709	845	. . .
1959	1 710	1 413	49	1 462	62	1	1 401	209	101	1 965	1 770	870	. . .
1960	1 827	1 513	44	1 557	75	1	1 483	239	105	2 030	1 826	900	. . .
1961	1 952	1 627	35	1 662	79	1	1 583	251	117	2 085	1 870	936	. . .
1962	2 132	1 768	54	1 822	87	1	1 735	274	122	2 225	2 003	958	. . .
1963	2 215	1 866	41	1 907	105	1	1 803	281	132	2 274	2 043	974	. . .
1964	2 327	1 951	30	1 981	106	1	1 876	310	141	2 380	2 168	978	. . .
1965	2 464	2 042	47	2 089	109	1	1 981	330	152	2 479	2 261	994	. . .
1966	2 617	2 199	49	2 248	144	1	2 105	351	162	2 594	2 355	1 009	. . .
1967	2 764	2 310	63	2 373	159	1	2 216	358	191	2 713	2 455	1 019	. . .
1968	2 975	2 496	67	2 563	175	1	2 390	366	220	2 892	2 588	1 029	. . .
1969	3 251	2 693	74	2 767	176	2	2 594	410	248	3 105	2 746	1 047	444
1970	3 611	2 959	78	3 037	191	2	2 848	465	299	3 389	3 032	1 066	455
1971	4 016	3 279	77	3 356	218	3	3 140	523	352	3 649	3 289	1 101	467
1972	4 505	3 682	88	3 770	260	5	3 515	588	402	3 971	3 560	1 135	494
1973	5 045	4 137	130	4 267	339	8	3 936	637	472	4 316	3 866	1 169	523
1974	5 680	4 688	96	4 784	396	11	4 400	743	538	4 738	4 238	1 199	545
1975	6 384	5 210	67	5 278	433	14	4 859	851	673	5 173	4 686	1 234	553
1976	7 322	6 012	74	6 086	502	17	5 601	990	730	5 755	5 152	1 272	580
1977	8 351	6 910	64	6 974	575	22	6 420	1 144	787	6 344	5 667	1 316	613
1978	9 625	7 973	72	8 045	678	27	7 395	1 354	876	7 055	6 292	1 364	651
1979	11 034	9 041	82	9 124	810	36	8 349	1 686	998	7 792	6 922	1 416	678
1980	12 506	9 997	60	10 057	897	52	9 212	2 118	1 176	8 492	7 575	1 473	687
1981	14 165	11 196	42	11 238	1 087	53	10 204	2 583	1 377	9 347	8 298	1 515	697
1982	15 510	11 898	46	11 944	1 175	53	10 822	3 104	1 584	9 953	8 832	1 558	707
1983	16 756	12 647	36	12 684	1 267	42	11 459	3 571	1 726	10 506	9 440	1 595	719
1984	18 448	14 056	57	14 112	1 448	38	12 702	3 966	1 779	11 371	10 264	1 622	761
1985	19 593	14 929	57	14 985	1 578	39	13 446	4 213	1 933	11 926	10 726	1 643	789
1986	20 490	15 558	87	15 645	1 658	34	14 021	4 378	2 091	12 322	11 072	1 663	801
1987	21 231	16 243	131	16 374	1 723	24	14 675	4 315	2 241	12 652	11 315	1 678	830
1988	22 236	17 339	210	17 549	1 926	23	15 646	4 256	2 334	13 162	11 772	1 689	865
1989	23 782	18 481	205	18 686	2 092	21	16 615	4 592	2 575	13 941	12 482	1 706	897
1990	25 704	20 190	253	20 443	2 363	16	18 096	4 783	2 825	14 847	13 131	1 731	938
1991	27 549	21 841	233	22 074	2 595	11	19 489	4 936	3 124	15 479	13 772	1 780	961
1992	29 636	23 697	280	23 976	2 812	6	21 170	4 999	3 466	16 135	14 350	1 837	979
1993	31 978	25 634	301	25 935	3 056	7	22 886	5 333	3 759	16 845	14 945	1 898	1 026
1994	34 848	28 027	220	28 247	3 371	6	24 883	6 092	3 873	17 775	15 691	1 960	1 102
1995	37 795	30 504	166	30 670	3 680	0	26 991	6 614	4 191	18 765	16 497	2 014	1 150
1996	41 151	33 089	173	33 263	3 926	0	29 337	7 381	4 433	19 899	17 455	2 068	1 218
1997	44 518	35 950	198	36 148	4 222	0	31 926	7 986	4 606	21 001	18 379	2 120	1 270
1998	48 057	38 877	233	39 110	4 491	-6	34 613	8 635	4 810	22 188	19 418	2 166	1 309
1999	50 555	41 301	240	41 541	4 719	-2	36 820	8 648	5 087	22 943	20 038	2 203	1 338
2000	55 025	44 774	205	44 980	5 031	2	39 950	9 610	5 465	24 515	21 453	2 245	1 378
2001	58 504	47 623	315	47 938	5 285	14	42 667	9 837	6 000	25 618	22 576	2 284	1 380
2002	59 873	48 842	197	49 039	5 419	8	43 628	9 708	6 537	25 754	23 156	2 325	1 390
2003	61 485	50 325	226	50 551	5 661	13	44 903	9 649	6 933	26 051	23 580	2 360	1 401
2004	65 453	53 760	317	54 077	6 100	22	47 999	10 130	7 323	27 254	24 703	2 402	1 453
2005	71 530	57 905	287	58 192	6 609	31	51 614	11 979	7 937	29 104	25 990	2 458	1 517
2006	78 378	63 581	167	63 748	7 271	43	56 520	13 227	8 631	31 035	27 468	2 526	1 597
2007	85 106	68 121	197	68 318	7 778	37	60 577	15 156	9 373	32 761	28 851	2 598	1 675
2008	90 610	70 627	217	70 844	7 967	38	62 915	17 392	10 304	34 025	30 437	2 663	1 686
2009	86 930	68 184	106	68 290	7 728	11	60 573	14 317	12 040	31 920	29 116	2 723	1 635
2010	90 250	70 075	203	70 278	7 931	3	62 351	14 912	12 988	32 517	29 715	2 775	1 634
2011	95 194	73 218	267	73 485	7 525	2	65 961	15 972	13 261	33 790	30 541	2 817	. . .

. . . = Not available.

Table 17-2. Personal Income and Employment by Region and State—*Continued*

(Millions of dollars, except as noted.)

Region or state and year	Personal income, total	Earnings by place of work			Less: Contributions for government social insurance	Plus: Adjustment for residence	Equals: Net earnings by place of residence	Plus: Dividends, interest, and rent	Plus: Personal current transfer receipts	Per capita (dollars)		Population (thousands)	Total employment (thousands)
		Nonfarm	Farm	Total						Personal income	Disposable personal income		
VERMONT													
1958	654	492	55	547	19	-5	523	78	52	1 720	1 555	380	. . .
1959	703	541	51	591	22	-5	564	84	55	1 816	1 634	387	. . .
1960	744	570	56	626	27	-5	594	91	59	1 913	1 719	389	. . .
1961	774	583	56	639	28	-5	606	101	67	1 986	1 787	390	. . .
1962	813	624	46	670	31	-5	634	109	70	2 068	1 862	393	. . .
1963	844	653	43	696	36	-5	655	114	74	2 125	1 894	397	. . .
1964	903	692	49	742	38	-5	698	128	77	2 264	2 034	399	. . .
1965	990	769	45	814	41	-7	765	144	81	2 452	2 218	404	. . .
1966	1 124	883	59	942	58	-10	874	164	87	2 722	2 427	413	. . .
1967	1 217	962	46	1 008	71	-10	927	183	107	2 878	2 562	423	. . .
1968	1 342	1 049	51	1 100	74	-11	1 015	201	126	3 121	2 750	430	. . .
1969	1 477	1 167	58	1 224	83	-27	1 114	219	144	3 380	2 931	437	203
1970	1 618	1 256	62	1 318	89	-27	1 202	244	172	3 625	3 162	446	205
1971	1 748	1 336	61	1 397	98	-24	1 275	268	205	3 848	3 451	454	206
1972	1 928	1 467	68	1 535	111	-21	1 403	295	230	4 163	3 666	463	211
1973	2 122	1 626	72	1 697	141	-20	1 537	323	262	4 528	4 035	469	220
1974	2 297	1 736	59	1 795	155	-17	1 623	359	315	4 855	4 327	473	222
1975	2 497	1 825	61	1 887	162	-11	1 713	383	401	5 203	4 659	480	220
1976	2 788	2 055	78	2 133	184	-6	1 944	413	431	5 747	5 176	485	228
1977	3 028	2 259	66	2 326	203	-2	2 120	467	441	6 153	5 495	492	236
1978	3 478	2 635	95	2 730	244	-2	2 484	527	467	6 979	6 227	498	252
1979	3 922	2 955	105	3 060	284	5	2 782	610	530	7 756	6 874	506	261
1980	4 407	3 213	108	3 321	310	14	3 025	755	627	8 599	7 593	513	266
1981	4 975	3 527	124	3 651	365	17	3 303	949	723	9 650	8 491	516	270
1982	5 359	3 708	123	3 831	392	23	3 462	1 092	805	10 324	9 175	519	271
1983	5 719	4 050	83	4 133	431	21	3 724	1 132	863	10 930	9 734	523	277
1984	6 308	4 476	84	4 560	490	27	4 098	1 321	889	11 977	10 697	527	289
1985	6 820	4 920	101	5 020	548	29	4 500	1 392	927	12 867	11 426	530	300
1986	7 333	5 356	99	5 455	602	32	4 886	1 493	955	13 731	12 135	534	311
1987	7 972	5 925	124	6 049	656	39	5 433	1 569	970	14 755	12 933	540	320
1988	8 698	6 507	122	6 629	747	45	5 927	1 747	1 024	15 822	13 939	550	334
1989	9 590	7 019	123	7 141	808	48	6 381	2 083	1 125	17 195	15 097	558	341
1990	9 965	7 275	115	7 390	883	48	6 555	2 155	1 255	17 643	15 527	565	341
1991	10 161	7 363	104	7 467	907	55	6 615	2 172	1 373	17 869	15 835	569	334
1992	10 849	7 842	177	8 019	959	63	7 123	2 172	1 554	18 941	16 841	573	342
1993	11 235	8 245	128	8 373	1 008	72	7 437	2 175	1 623	19 446	17 272	578	349
1994	11 826	8 611	129	8 740	1 066	86	7 760	2 347	1 718	20 255	18 028	584	359
1995	12 403	8 948	100	9 048	1 125	100	8 023	2 520	1 859	21 057	18 752	589	362
1996	13 124	9 412	147	9 559	1 171	116	8 503	2 701	1 920	22 106	19 561	594	367
1997	13 837	9 902	110	10 012	1 225	139	8 926	2 891	2 021	23 168	20 326	597	373
1998	14 963	10 646	136	10 782	1 294	165	9 653	3 206	2 104	24 921	21 808	600	383
1999	15 884	11 448	146	11 594	1 375	186	10 405	3 225	2 253	26 268	22 964	605	391
2000	17 189	12 417	150	12 567	1 469	219	11 317	3 445	2 427	28 196	24 535	610	401
2001	18 046	13 047	148	13 194	1 561	231	11 865	3 520	2 661	29 477	25 754	612	405
2002	18 460	13 494	113	13 607	1 610	240	12 237	3 377	2 846	29 994	26 726	615	407
2003	19 129	14 019	145	14 164	1 657	272	12 780	3 370	2 979	30 960	27 961	618	409
2004	20 234	14 868	190	15 058	1 741	295	13 612	3 505	3 117	32 640	29 543	620	415
2005	20 697	15 404	200	15 604	1 829	324	14 099	3 201	3 396	33 317	29 798	621	420
2006	22 341	16 091	119	16 210	1 910	358	14 658	3 937	3 746	35 867	31 946	623	424
2007	23 580	16 416	220	16 636	2 009	387	15 014	4 449	4 118	37 820	33 496	623	429
2008	24 612	16 746	180	16 925	2 075	409	15 260	4 931	4 422	39 433	35 169	624	428
2009	24 293	16 440	115	16 554	2 067	401	14 889	4 373	5 031	38 879	35 592	625	419
2010	25 120	16 910	169	17 079	2 116	410	15 373	4 511	5 237	40 134	36 731	626	420
2011	26 205	17 355	231	17 586	1 950	438	16 074	4 756	5 375	41 832	37 848	626	. . .

. . . = Not available.

Table 17-2. Personal Income and Employment by Region and State—*Continued*

(Millions of dollars, except as noted.)

Region or state and year	Personal income, total	Earnings by place of work — Nonfarm	Earnings by place of work — Farm	Earnings by place of work — Total	Less: Contributions for government social insurance	Plus: Adjustment for residence	Equals: Net earnings by place of residence	Plus: Dividends, interest, and rent	Plus: Personal current transfer receipts	Per capita — Personal income	Per capita — Disposable personal income	Population (thousands)	Total employment (thousands)
VIRGINIA													
1958	6 871	5 382	260	5 642	184	361	5 819	722	331	1 756	1 555	3 914	. . .
1959	7 322	5 834	193	6 027	234	386	6 179	782	361	1 853	1 634	3 951	. . .
1960	7 597	5 987	215	6 202	268	432	6 366	859	373	1 906	1 719	3 986	. . .
1961	8 089	6 313	225	6 538	284	463	6 717	945	428	1 975	1 787	4 095	. . .
1962	8 740	6 824	222	7 046	317	512	7 241	1 047	452	2 091	1 862	4 180	. . .
1963	9 354	7 406	137	7 542	369	565	7 738	1 131	485	2 188	1 894	4 276	. . .
1964	10 339	8 114	222	8 336	383	615	8 568	1 260	512	2 373	2 034	4 357	. . .
1965	11 159	8 706	208	8 914	402	704	9 216	1 383	560	2 530	2 218	4 411	. . .
1966	12 082	9 590	156	9 746	544	779	9 982	1 490	610	2 711	2 427	4 456	. . .
1967	13 234	10 377	202	10 579	630	933	10 882	1 618	734	2 936	2 562	4 508	. . .
1968	14 686	11 635	178	11 814	696	1 008	12 126	1 706	855	3 222	2 750	4 558	. . .
1969	16 428	13 208	213	13 421	800	956	13 577	1 872	979	3 560	2 931	4 614	2 148
1970	17 669	14 218	213	14 431	871	851	14 412	2 078	1 180	3 792	3 162	4 660	2 158
1971	19 443	15 646	193	15 839	1 000	877	15 716	2 314	1 413	4 091	3 451	4 753	2 196
1972	21 661	17 463	254	17 717	1 167	933	17 483	2 556	1 622	4 486	3 666	4 828	2 263
1973	24 393	19 682	355	20 037	1 484	1 005	19 557	2 898	1 938	4 971	4 035	4 907	2 384
1974	27 306	21 865	316	22 181	1 701	1 134	21 615	3 390	2 301	5 485	4 327	4 978	2 451
1975	30 136	23 552	266	23 818	1 821	1 394	23 391	3 797	2 948	5 960	4 659	5 056	2 425
1976	33 614	26 391	237	26 628	2 071	1 617	26 174	4 220	3 220	6 549	5 176	5 133	2 501
1977	37 443	29 522	169	29 691	2 302	1 857	29 246	4 744	3 454	7 193	5 495	5 206	2 585
1978	42 408	33 303	291	33 594	2 621	2 189	33 162	5 428	3 817	8 025	6 227	5 284	2 698
1979	47 654	37 198	157	37 355	3 050	2 582	36 887	6 385	4 382	8 950	6 874	5 325	2 767
1980	54 258	41 172	69	41 241	3 388	3 154	41 007	8 041	5 209	10 107	7 593	5 368	2 797
1981	61 121	45 598	272	45 870	4 045	3 367	45 192	9 915	6 014	11 227	8 491	5 444	2 812
1982	66 437	49 082	122	49 204	4 406	3 431	48 229	11 636	6 572	12 095	9 175	5 493	2 824
1983	72 304	53 697	44	53 742	4 947	3 424	52 219	12 976	7 109	12 993	9 734	5 565	2 897
1984	80 697	60 541	327	60 868	5 704	3 529	58 694	14 483	7 521	14 298	10 697	5 644	3 041
1985	87 350	66 282	229	66 511	6 438	3 645	63 718	15 594	8 038	15 284	11 426	5 715	3 181
1986	94 082	71 980	276	72 256	7 281	3 792	68 768	16 796	8 519	16 188	12 135	5 812	3 316
1987	101 980	78 939	373	79 312	7 982	3 993	75 323	17 809	8 848	17 191	12 933	5 932	3 480
1988	111 336	86 190	527	86 717	9 038	4 364	82 044	19 843	9 448	18 442	13 939	6 037	3 558
1989	120 041	91 757	644	92 400	9 809	4 587	87 178	22 523	10 339	19 614	15 097	6 120	3 655
1990	126 278	95 518	688	96 206	10 388	5 338	91 156	23 901	11 221	20 312	17 735	6 217	3 700
1991	132 030	99 083	623	99 706	10 867	5 859	94 698	24 942	12 390	20 953	18 403	6 301	3 642
1992	140 101	105 197	674	105 871	11 472	6 308	100 707	25 454	13 940	21 842	19 232	6 414	3 657
1993	147 091	110 419	546	110 965	12 070	6 737	105 632	26 708	14 751	22 596	19 852	6 510	3 730
1994	155 163	116 047	645	116 692	12 781	6 719	110 629	28 918	15 616	23 534	20 618	6 593	3 813
1995	162 498	121 488	569	122 057	13 319	6 926	115 665	29 958	16 876	24 360	21 312	6 671	3 903
1996	171 165	128 368	571	128 939	13 998	6 386	121 327	32 022	17 816	25 354	22 081	6 751	3 983
1997	182 303	137 508	429	137 937	14 999	6 947	129 885	33 982	18 435	26 695	23 134	6 829	4 082
1998	194 597	147 961	422	148 383	16 087	6 618	138 914	36 599	19 084	28 199	24 083	6 901	4 156
1999	207 326	159 334	326	159 659	17 312	7 986	150 334	36 839	20 153	29 617	25 054	7 000	4 247
2000	224 788	174 946	564	175 510	18 671	6 050	162 888	40 295	21 604	31 634	26 775	7 106	4 374
2001	239 315	187 091	480	187 572	19 703	5 970	173 839	41 440	24 036	33 246	28 302	7 198	4 410
2002	245 841	191 552	366	191 918	20 326	7 409	179 001	41 227	25 613	33 737	29 445	7 287	4 403
2003	258 087	202 136	288	202 424	21 273	7 663	188 814	41 965	27 308	35 033	30 842	7 367	4 453
2004	275 618	218 707	545	219 252	23 184	8 002	204 069	42 742	28 807	36 869	32 537	7 476	4 575
2005	294 734	233 538	594	234 131	24 771	8 092	217 452	46 016	31 266	38 898	33 980	7 577	4 693
2006	316 298	246 380	298	246 679	26 362	8 844	229 161	53 067	34 069	41 218	35 857	7 674	4 772
2007	335 319	257 274	248	257 522	27 347	9 100	239 275	59 825	36 220	43 261	37 556	7 751	4 866
2008	350 091	263 620	348	263 968	28 264	9 944	245 648	64 477	39 965	44 691	39 139	7 833	4 872
2009	342 340	260 338	274	260 612	28 315	10 306	242 603	54 756	44 981	43 192	38 576	7 926	4 766
2010	355 193	267 893	324	268 218	29 181	11 112	250 149	56 925	48 119	44 267	39 497	8 024	4 765
2011	371 796	276 290	481	276 771	27 137	11 625	261 260	60 587	49 950	45 920	40 417	8 097	. . .

. . . = Not available.

Table 17-2. Personal Income and Employment by Region and State—*Continued*

(Millions of dollars, except as noted.)

Region or state and year	Personal income, total	Earnings by place of work			Less: Contributions for government social insurance	Plus: Adjustment for residence	Equals: Net earnings by place of residence	Plus: Dividends, interest, and rent	Plus: Personal current transfer receipts	Per capita (dollars)		Population (thousands)	Total employment (thousands)
		Nonfarm	Farm	Total						Personal income	Disposable personal income		
WASHINGTON													
1958	6 271	5 025	223	5 247	239	16	5 024	778	469	2 261	2 019	2 773	. . .
1959	6 662	5 373	232	5 605	281	21	5 344	833	484	2 362	2 120	2 821	. . .
1960	6 898	5 518	256	5 774	313	25	5 486	898	514	2 416	2 163	2 855	. . .
1961	7 247	5 798	247	6 044	327	29	5 746	938	563	2 514	2 248	2 882	. . .
1962	7 829	6 298	271	6 569	357	34	6 246	1 017	567	2 661	2 374	2 942	. . .
1963	8 024	6 441	275	6 716	395	42	6 363	1 063	598	2 716	2 419	2 955	. . .
1964	8 404	6 737	251	6 988	394	51	6 645	1 128	631	2 838	2 582	2 961	. . .
1965	9 064	7 242	271	7 513	417	62	7 158	1 243	663	3 055	2 769	2 967	. . .
1966	10 272	8 373	366	8 739	593	71	8 217	1 366	689	3 360	3 011	3 057	. . .
1967	11 253	9 211	327	9 539	687	82	8 934	1 490	829	3 545	3 163	3 174	. . .
1968	12 511	10 269	341	10 610	769	99	9 939	1 620	951	3 826	3 389	3 270	. . .
1969	13 657	11 159	398	11 557	910	83	10 730	1 850	1 077	4 085	3 582	3 343	1 539
1970	14 316	11 363	346	11 709	913	65	10 861	2 020	1 435	4 189	3 746	3 417	1 491
1971	15 031	11 719	391	12 110	981	63	11 193	2 167	1 671	4 361	3 937	3 447	1 457
1972	16 246	12 684	506	13 191	1 117	73	12 147	2 315	1 784	4 713	4 210	3 447	1 481
1973	18 374	14 340	756	15 095	1 438	90	13 747	2 616	2 011	5 284	4 705	3 477	1 558
1974	20 905	16 179	890	17 069	1 659	133	15 543	3 010	2 352	5 892	5 253	3 548	1 622
1975	23 648	18 131	906	19 037	1 840	200	17 397	3 343	2 907	6 535	5 849	3 619	1 659
1976	26 441	20 770	754	21 523	2 140	247	19 631	3 654	3 157	7 165	6 397	3 691	1 739
1977	29 412	23 593	605	24 197	2 459	227	21 965	4 143	3 304	7 797	6 943	3 772	1 815
1978	34 276	27 805	754	28 559	2 977	269	25 851	4 841	3 584	8 820	7 772	3 886	1 939
1979	39 514	32 244	739	32 983	3 567	322	29 738	5 764	4 011	9 847	8 601	4 013	2 058
1980	44 912	35 472	861	36 333	3 862	387	32 858	7 147	4 907	10 810	9 464	4 155	2 105
1981	50 126	38 727	864	39 591	4 531	431	35 491	8 932	5 703	11 834	10 333	4 236	2 119
1982	53 177	40 181	766	40 947	4 752	463	36 658	10 103	6 416	12 435	11 071	4 277	2 094
1983	56 522	42 181	1 065	43 246	5 114	484	38 615	10 897	7 010	13 144	11 826	4 300	2 140
1984	60 690	45 107	1 023	46 129	5 648	541	41 022	12 298	7 370	13 972	12 629	4 344	2 214
1985	64 324	48 033	750	48 783	6 088	584	43 279	13 118	7 927	14 619	13 180	4 400	2 277
1986	68 669	51 408	1 057	52 465	6 586	607	46 486	13 777	8 407	15 422	13 933	4 453	2 351
1987	72 918	55 094	1 088	56 182	7 026	658	49 814	14 249	8 855	16 090	14 426	4 532	2 470
1988	79 133	60 430	1 030	61 460	7 929	749	54 280	15 220	9 633	17 055	15 351	4 640	2 600
1989	87 357	65 765	1 157	66 922	8 665	834	59 091	17 687	10 579	18 405	16 389	4 746	2 718
1990	96 282	73 179	1 211	74 390	9 829	927	65 488	19 167	11 626	19 637	17 449	4 903	2 842
1991	103 441	78 736	1 283	80 019	10 701	994	70 312	19 970	13 159	20 583	18 396	5 026	2 877
1992	111 373	85 762	1 544	87 306	11 692	1 093	76 707	20 149	14 517	21 581	19 313	5 161	2 907
1993	116 871	89 601	1 746	91 347	12 200	1 187	80 334	20 998	15 538	22 139	19 871	5 279	2 951
1994	123 528	94 104	1 431	95 535	12 897	1 232	83 869	23 306	16 353	22 981	20 572	5 375	3 060
1995	130 328	98 512	1 470	99 982	13 497	1 382	87 867	25 013	17 448	23 778	21 252	5 481	3 101
1996	140 803	105 499	1 945	107 444	14 110	1 582	94 916	27 611	18 277	25 280	22 410	5 570	3 192
1997	151 795	114 742	1 553	116 295	14 894	1 734	103 134	29 713	18 948	26 749	23 519	5 675	3 298
1998	166 287	126 773	1 734	128 507	16 338	1 840	114 009	32 579	19 699	28 821	25 055	5 770	3 379
1999	178 319	138 589	1 501	140 089	17 094	1 955	124 950	32 459	20 911	30 521	26 111	5 843	3 442
2000	191 562	148 218	1 736	149 954	18 500	2 199	133 653	35 568	22 341	32 410	27 954	5 911	3 523
2001	197 324	151 843	1 566	153 410	18 301	2 404	137 512	34 737	25 075	32 966	28 868	5 986	3 520
2002	200 493	153 700	1 642	155 342	18 609	2 456	139 189	34 678	26 626	33 126	29 780	6 052	3 479
2003	206 983	158 527	2 087	160 615	19 411	2 517	143 721	35 473	27 790	33 909	30 782	6 104	3 509
2004	222 422	166 648	2 082	168 730	20 666	2 555	150 620	43 572	28 230	35 998	32 848	6 179	3 582
2005	230 057	175 377	1 875	177 252	21 963	2 685	157 973	42 281	29 803	36 766	33 237	6 257	3 684
2006	252 091	189 228	1 965	191 194	23 325	2 864	170 732	49 329	32 030	39 570	35 545	6 371	3 796
2007	272 625	201 177	2 392	203 569	24 476	3 027	182 120	55 770	34 735	42 192	37 626	6 462	3 925
2008	289 434	207 408	2 705	210 114	25 055	3 057	188 116	63 010	38 308	44 106	39 956	6 562	3 960
2009	278 944	202 407	2 115	204 522	24 988	2 781	182 314	51 437	45 193	41 837	38 625	6 667	3 827
2010	287 175	205 241	2 708	207 948	25 721	2 936	185 163	53 013	48 999	42 589	39 273	6 743	3 794
2011	302 529	214 968	2 733	217 701	24 681	3 164	196 184	56 556	49 790	44 294	40 364	6 830	. . .

. . . = Not available.

Table 17-2. Personal Income and Employment by Region and State—*Continued*

(Millions of dollars, except as noted.)

Region or state and year	Personal income, total	Earnings by place of work			Less: Contributions for government social insurance	Plus: Adjustment for residence	Equals: Net earnings by place of residence	Plus: Dividends, interest, and rent	Plus: Personal current transfer receipts	Per capita (dollars)		Population (thousands)	Total employment (thousands)
		Nonfarm	Farm	Total						Personal income	Disposable personal income		
WEST VIRGINIA													
1958	2 920	2 421	58	2 479	114	-21	2 345	275	301	1 583	1 444	1 845	. . .
1959	3 011	2 523	46	2 569	135	-20	2 413	295	303	1 623	1 468	1 855	. . .
1960	3 060	2 565	50	2 614	155	-20	2 439	317	304	1 652	1 483	1 853	. . .
1961	3 100	2 556	43	2 599	153	-20	2 426	330	344	1 696	1 524	1 828	. . .
1962	3 235	2 671	32	2 703	168	-19	2 516	351	367	1 788	1 608	1 809	. . .
1963	3 375	2 796	25	2 821	186	-18	2 618	379	379	1 879	1 683	1 796	. . .
1964	3 600	2 975	23	2 999	173	-17	2 809	406	385	2 003	1 815	1 797	. . .
1965	3 849	3 179	25	3 204	184	-13	3 007	431	411	2 155	1 957	1 786	. . .
1966	4 081	3 449	15	3 463	244	-10	3 209	438	434	2 299	2 073	1 775	. . .
1967	4 331	3 633	29	3 662	268	-8	3 386	453	492	2 448	2 210	1 769	. . .
1968	4 591	3 852	23	3 875	298	2	3 578	469	544	2 604	2 326	1 763	. . .
1969	4 875	4 138	31	4 169	324	-79	3 766	510	599	2 792	2 447	1 746	652
1970	5 430	4 547	26	4 573	350	-82	4 141	568	722	3 109	2 753	1 747	660
1971	5 963	4 943	26	4 969	395	-100	4 473	620	871	3 369	2 999	1 770	670
1972	6 601	5 464	31	5 496	455	-114	4 927	676	997	3 673	3 256	1 797	684
1973	7 238	5 929	45	5 973	567	-117	5 289	763	1 186	4 009	3 579	1 805	700
1974	8 051	6 563	29	6 592	647	-131	5 814	894	1 344	4 438	3 916	1 814	711
1975	9 153	7 398	15	7 412	709	-158	6 545	1 008	1 601	4 973	4 405	1 841	717
1976	10 265	8 407	4	8 411	817	-195	7 400	1 111	1 754	5 468	4 820	1 877	739
1977	11 484	9 498	-1	9 497	915	-226	8 355	1 257	1 872	6 026	5 322	1 906	758
1978	12 803	10 624	13	10 637	1 056	-263	9 317	1 406	2 080	6 667	5 907	1 920	781
1979	14 297	11 708	18	11 726	1 211	-273	10 242	1 620	2 435	7 373	6 490	1 939	790
1980	15 739	12 464	9	12 474	1 297	-301	10 876	2 033	2 830	8 066	7 077	1 951	782
1981	17 132	13 171	-22	13 149	1 477	-279	11 394	2 542	3 197	8 767	7 705	1 954	762
1982	18 209	13 578	-28	13 550	1 563	-233	11 754	2 949	3 506	9 340	8 259	1 950	740
1983	18 625	13 370	-15	13 355	1 571	-192	11 592	3 147	3 886	9 575	8 516	1 945	722
1984	19 961	14 300	24	14 324	1 737	-140	12 447	3 546	3 969	10 355	9 250	1 928	732
1985	20 690	14 730	22	14 752	1 828	-119	12 805	3 742	4 143	10 851	9 684	1 907	732
1986	21 105	14 818	48	14 866	1 922	-92	12 852	3 852	4 401	11 212	10 041	1 882	731
1987	21 584	15 206	8	15 214	1 992	-26	13 195	3 865	4 524	11 619	10 395	1 858	738
1988	22 935	16 277	6	16 283	2 180	6	14 109	4 056	4 770	12 532	11 290	1 830	751
1989	24 204	16 831	34	16 866	2 282	86	14 670	4 511	5 024	13 398	11 978	1 807	757
1990	25 878	18 101	47	18 148	2 472	71	15 747	4 744	5 387	14 436	12 908	1 793	778
1991	27 135	18 851	38	18 889	2 637	45	16 297	4 775	6 063	15 086	13 544	1 799	779
1992	29 050	19 922	63	19 985	2 817	110	17 278	4 819	6 953	16 081	14 513	1 806	789
1993	30 078	20 721	65	20 786	3 039	114	17 862	4 812	7 405	16 549	14 937	1 818	801
1994	31 436	21 861	61	21 922	3 184	161	18 899	5 031	7 507	17 269	15 538	1 820	822
1995	32 493	22 598	24	22 622	3 328	207	19 501	5 262	7 730	17 817	16 015	1 824	838
1996	33 845	23 203	9	23 212	3 428	221	20 005	5 695	8 145	18 567	16 662	1 823	847
1997	35 242	24 079	0	24 080	3 522	374	20 931	5 981	8 329	19 373	17 330	1 819	858
1998	37 168	25 337	1	25 339	3 707	416	22 048	6 486	8 635	20 472	18 315	1 816	873
1999	38 136	26 309	-14	26 295	3 810	465	22 950	6 361	8 826	21 049	18 829	1 812	872
2000	40 067	27 519	18	27 537	4 124	591	24 004	6 801	9 263	22 173	19 815	1 807	880
2001	42 466	28 908	28	28 936	4 102	691	25 525	6 796	10 145	23 573	21 093	1 801	878
2002	43 876	29 557	-35	29 522	4 125	736	26 133	6 502	11 241	24 302	22 051	1 805	873
2003	44 897	30 497	-16	30 481	4 255	822	27 048	6 011	11 838	24 773	22 656	1 812	871
2004	46 500	32 255	29	32 284	4 377	880	28 787	6 033	11 680	25 599	23 497	1 816	881
2005	48 139	33 708	13	33 722	4 567	984	30 138	6 076	11 924	26 443	24 028	1 820	894
2006	51 862	36 001	-23	35 977	4 630	994	32 342	6 692	12 828	28 372	25 747	1 828	907
2007	54 100	36 629	-60	36 569	4 514	1 139	33 193	7 489	13 417	29 497	26 639	1 834	921
2008	57 576	38 463	-46	38 416	4 554	1 123	34 986	8 247	14 343	31 286	28 116	1 840	924
2009	57 535	37 753	-57	37 696	4 584	1 056	34 168	7 377	15 990	31 137	28 519	1 848	906
2010	59 417	38 904	-58	38 846	4 706	1 150	35 289	7 496	16 632	32 042	29 357	1 854	907
2011	62 178	40 720	-91	40 629	4 427	1 176	37 379	7 842	16 958	33 513	30 362	1 855	. . .

. . . = Not available.

Table 17-2. Personal Income and Employment by Region and State—*Continued*

(Millions of dollars, except as noted.)

| Region or state and year | Personal income, total | Earnings by place of work | | | Less: Contributions for government social insurance | Plus: Adjustment for residence | Equals: Net earnings by place of residence | Plus: Dividends, interest, and rent | Plus: Personal current transfer receipts | Per capita (dollars) | | Population (thousands) | Total employment (thousands) |
		Nonfarm	Farm	Total						Personal income	Disposable personal income		
WISCONSIN													
1958	7 940	6 125	456	6 582	233	52	6 400	1 029	510	2 066	1 843	3 843	. . .
1959	8 609	6 725	474	7 198	282	59	6 975	1 109	524	2 212	1 967	3 891	. . .
1960	8 910	7 005	428	7 434	341	63	7 156	1 196	557	2 249	1 982	3 962	. . .
1961	9 200	7 082	496	7 578	348	67	7 297	1 257	646	2 295	2 040	4 009	. . .
1962	9 735	7 553	492	8 045	374	74	7 745	1 332	658	2 404	2 127	4 049	. . .
1963	10 075	7 880	439	8 319	433	81	7 967	1 413	695	2 450	2 159	4 112	. . .
1964	10 869	8 500	478	8 978	449	91	8 620	1 524	724	2 610	2 326	4 165	. . .
1965	11 766	9 140	545	9 685	479	104	9 310	1 677	779	2 780	2 470	4 232	. . .
1966	12 883	10 081	670	10 751	668	123	10 206	1 814	862	3 014	2 653	4 274	. . .
1967	13 648	10 706	564	11 269	759	137	10 647	1 939	1 063	3 172	2 770	4 303	. . .
1968	14 906	11 570	645	12 215	815	158	11 558	2 111	1 237	3 431	2 993	4 345	. . .
1969	16 404	12 675	638	13 313	934	249	12 628	2 417	1 359	3 747	3 213	4 378	1 944
1970	17 621	13 396	639	14 036	974	253	13 314	2 708	1 599	3 981	3 463	4 426	1 954
1971	18 913	14 246	693	14 939	1 070	264	14 133	2 910	1 870	4 241	3 738	4 460	1 957
1972	20 698	15 716	729	16 445	1 248	287	15 485	3 134	2 079	4 601	4 011	4 498	2 014
1973	23 168	17 716	916	18 632	1 615	313	17 330	3 473	2 365	5 127	4 480	4 518	2 116
1974	25 499	19 423	806	20 229	1 841	339	18 728	3 960	2 811	5 619	4 884	4 538	2 159
1975	27 830	20 630	867	21 497	1 928	345	19 914	4 388	3 528	6 090	5 349	4 570	2 148
1976	30 620	23 196	763	23 958	2 188	390	22 161	4 643	3 817	6 679	5 832	4 585	2 211
1977	34 151	25 940	1 145	27 085	2 444	432	25 073	5 029	4 048	7 403	6 440	4 613	2 293
1978	38 199	29 340	1 129	30 469	2 847	487	28 109	5 619	4 471	8 247	7 115	4 632	2 380
1979	42 911	32 680	1 407	34 087	3 307	525	31 305	6 476	5 130	9 197	7 956	4 666	2 460
1980	47 519	34 738	1 446	36 184	3 507	548	33 225	8 045	6 248	10 085	8 764	4 712	2 443
1981	51 862	37 025	1 175	38 201	3 992	601	34 810	9 946	7 106	10 973	9 478	4 726	2 415
1982	54 727	38 081	1 025	39 106	4 150	620	35 576	11 223	7 927	11 573	10 092	4 729	2 373
1983	56 779	40 051	472	40 523	4 360	675	36 839	11 421	8 519	12 026	10 584	4 721	2 376
1984	62 094	43 919	1 002	44 921	4 905	792	40 808	12 561	8 724	13 112	11 567	4 736	2 467
1985	65 132	46 135	1 028	47 163	5 209	880	42 835	13 030	9 268	13 719	12 098	4 748	2 495
1986	68 594	48 674	1 306	49 980	5 504	961	45 437	13 598	9 560	14 424	12 718	4 756	2 537
1987	72 541	52 154	1 423	53 577	5 811	1 065	48 830	13 935	9 776	15 182	13 309	4 778	2 605
1988	76 929	56 557	863	57 420	6 531	1 233	52 121	14 682	10 126	15 953	13 998	4 822	2 684
1989	83 494	59 956	1 740	61 697	6 956	1 264	56 004	16 580	10 911	17 192	15 049	4 857	2 740
1990	88 213	64 081	1 397	65 479	7 735	1 352	59 095	17 418	11 700	17 986	15 716	4 905	2 814
1991	91 809	67 096	1 019	68 115	8 194	1 378	61 299	17 809	12 702	18 494	16 197	4 964	2 840
1992	98 872	72 786	1 279	74 065	8 832	1 513	66 745	18 363	13 765	19 674	17 244	5 025	2 894
1993	103 722	77 314	959	78 272	9 381	1 571	70 462	18 914	14 346	20 398	17 836	5 085	2 950
1994	110 630	82 488	1 226	83 714	10 113	1 689	75 289	20 550	14 791	21 550	18 803	5 134	3 040
1995	116 074	86 616	802	87 418	10 623	1 787	78 582	21 835	15 657	22 387	19 483	5 185	3 120
1996	122 953	90 586	1 372	91 958	11 058	1 936	82 837	23 911	16 206	23 509	20 327	5 230	3 171
1997	130 478	96 410	1 005	97 415	11 729	2 157	87 843	25 902	16 734	24 777	21 296	5 266	3 226
1998	141 019	103 926	1 374	105 300	12 443	2 303	95 159	28 696	17 165	26 619	22 827	5 298	3 282
1999	147 462	110 686	1 322	112 008	13 196	2 486	101 298	28 271	17 893	27 652	23 753	5 333	3 346
2000	156 603	117 022	880	117 901	13 837	2 720	106 784	30 579	19 240	29 141	25 079	5 374	3 405
2001	162 773	121 590	1 171	122 761	14 143	2 839	111 457	29 849	21 467	30 105	26 038	5 407	3 387
2002	167 708	126 410	1 066	127 475	14 504	2 900	115 872	28 732	23 104	30 799	27 218	5 445	3 395
2003	173 248	131 989	1 542	133 531	14 996	2 955	121 490	27 981	23 777	31 619	28 194	5 479	3 415
2004	180 303	137 939	1 881	139 821	15 803	3 099	127 117	28 695	24 491	32 699	29 236	5 514	3 469
2005	186 545	142 703	1 671	144 375	16 455	3 231	131 151	29 190	26 204	33 635	29 839	5 546	3 510
2006	198 556	149 342	1 386	150 728	17 366	3 393	136 755	34 046	27 755	35 598	31 404	5 578	3 552
2007	206 648	152 333	2 067	154 400	18 010	3 673	140 063	36 623	29 961	36 831	32 408	5 611	3 587
2008	215 330	155 887	1 978	157 865	18 581	3 781	143 065	40 299	31 965	38 172	33 676	5 641	3 578
2009	209 595	150 059	1 046	151 105	18 125	3 582	136 561	33 989	39 046	36 970	33 342	5 669	3 454
2010	217 562	154 415	1 917	156 332	18 634	3 727	141 426	34 990	41 147	38 225	34 503	5 692	3 446
2011	228 888	160 696	3 027	163 724	17 537	3 935	150 122	37 137	41 629	40 073	35 763	5 712	. . .

. . . = Not available.

Table 17-2. Personal Income and Employment by Region and State—*Continued*

(Millions of dollars, except as noted.)

Region or state and year	Personal income, total	Earnings by place of work			Less: Contributions for government social insurance	Plus: Adjustment for residence	Equals: Net earnings by place of residence	Plus: Dividends, interest, and rent	Plus: Personal current transfer receipts	Per capita (dollars)		Population (thousands)	Total employment (thousands)
		Nonfarm	Farm	Total						Personal income	Disposable personal income		
WYOMING													
1958	686	498	75	573	23	-1	549	98	38	2 177	1 968	315	...
1959	728	545	64	610	27	-1	581	105	42	2 274	2 045	320	...
1960	763	597	51	647	34	-1	612	107	45	2 306	2 062	331	...
1961	801	611	57	667	34	-1	632	117	53	2 377	2 139	337	...
1962	829	618	67	685	35	-1	649	125	54	2 490	2 230	333	...
1963	847	637	67	704	40	-1	663	128	56	2 520	2 231	336	...
1964	872	680	47	727	43	-1	684	133	55	2 572	2 343	339	...
1965	903	688	53	741	41	-1	700	145	58	2 719	2 475	332	...
1966	930	705	58	763	48	0	715	153	61	2 878	2 603	323	...
1967	997	748	70	818	53	0	765	161	71	3 098	2 784	322	...
1968	1 065	822	62	884	59	0	825	159	81	3 288	2 942	324	...
1969	1 180	901	70	971	66	*	905	186	89	3 587	3 169	329	158
1970	1 305	982	79	1 061	72	0	989	213	103	3 910	3 472	334	159
1971	1 447	1 084	88	1 172	81	-1	1 090	239	119	4 257	3 807	340	165
1972	1 628	1 215	126	1 341	96	-3	1 242	256	129	4 692	4 243	347	172
1973	1 904	1 436	153	1 589	128	-7	1 454	298	152	5 389	4 806	353	182
1974	2 242	1 774	111	1 885	159	-14	1 712	358	172	6 150	5 387	365	194
1975	2 557	2 071	67	2 138	182	-16	1 940	410	208	6 721	5 986	380	203
1976	2 857	2 355	48	2 403	213	-23	2 167	458	232	7 224	6 382	395	214
1977	3 355	2 809	45	2 854	249	-30	2 575	526	254	8 152	7 205	412	231
1978	4 036	3 405	65	3 471	309	-39	3 123	627	286	9 366	8 259	431	250
1979	4 751	4 012	96	4 108	381	-56	3 671	749	330	10 515	9 133	452	266
1980	5 533	4 656	86	4 742	442	-77	4 224	917	392	11 668	10 167	474	279
1981	6 298	5 272	52	5 324	546	-87	4 691	1 136	471	12 808	11 085	492	289
1982	6 760	5 369	29	5 398	569	-84	4 745	1 473	541	13 349	11 763	506	287
1983	6 483	5 082	36	5 118	522	-62	4 534	1 309	640	12 703	11 321	510	274
1984	6 773	5 301	14	5 315	560	-56	4 699	1 442	633	13 416	12 048	505	276
1985	7 064	5 529	17	5 546	599	-54	4 893	1 500	672	14 137	12 691	500	277
1986	7 060	5 440	39	5 479	581	-43	4 856	1 465	740	14 244	12 935	496	264
1987	6 814	5 128	60	5 188	550	-28	4 610	1 454	750	14 287	12 911	477	258
1988	6 893	5 171	60	5 231	598	-23	4 609	1 503	781	14 821	13 367	465	264
1989	7 509	5 504	90	5 594	621	-16	4 958	1 709	842	16 382	14 671	458	265
1990	8 125	5 890	153	6 043	690	-12	5 341	1 879	905	17 910	16 056	454	271
1991	8 537	6 068	213	6 281	737	-2	5 542	1 984	1 011	18 589	16 725	459	277
1992	9 019	6 420	222	6 642	770	-8	5 864	2 036	1 119	19 344	17 428	466	280
1993	9 492	6 809	248	7 057	809	-10	6 238	2 035	1 219	20 065	18 013	473	285
1994	9 962	7 180	122	7 302	857	-9	6 436	2 237	1 288	20 741	18 607	480	298
1995	10 362	7 386	103	7 488	880	-7	6 601	2 389	1 372	21 358	19 167	485	301
1996	10 853	7 631	83	7 714	899	-2	6 813	2 596	1 444	22 233	19 517	488	304
1997	11 636	8 062	185	8 247	935	3	7 316	2 839	1 482	23 774	20 776	489	307
1998	12 513	8 623	99	8 722	991	5	7 737	3 253	1 524	25 496	22 275	491	313
1999	13 372	9 191	168	9 359	1 039	4	8 324	3 460	1 588	27 192	23 700	492	316
2000	14 463	9 989	123	10 112	1 101	12	9 022	3 732	1 709	29 261	25 312	494	326
2001	15 441	10 851	190	11 041	1 180	8	9 869	3 728	1 844	31 216	27 278	495	331
2002	15 946	11 330	100	11 429	1 233	4	10 200	3 762	1 984	31 890	28 670	500	334
2003	16 933	11 851	180	12 031	1 294	1	10 738	4 065	2 129	33 634	30 594	503	337
2004	18 239	12 732	179	12 910	1 378	0	11 532	4 454	2 253	35 825	32 662	509	344
2005	19 969	13 694	232	13 925	1 488	-1	12 437	5 157	2 376	38 839	34 826	514	355
2006	22 912	15 810	100	15 910	1 917	-6	13 987	6 405	2 520	43 836	38 553	523	371
2007	24 220	16 979	30	17 009	2 065	-9	14 935	6 592	2 693	45 281	39 560	535	390
2008	26 813	18 502	120	18 621	2 191	-20	16 410	7 425	2 978	49 104	43 670	546	400
2009	24 392	17 190	73	17 263	2 135	-10	15 118	5 902	3 372	43 568	39 986	560	388
2010	25 383	17 793	120	17 914	2 229	-9	15 675	6 164	3 544	44 961	41 265	565	386
2011	26 875	18 657	193	18 850	2 143	-8	16 699	6 570	3 606	47 301	42 929	568	...

. . . = Not available.
* = Less than $50,000, but the estimates for this item are included in the total.

NOTES AND DEFINITIONS, CHAPTER 17

TABLE 17-1
GROSS DOMESTIC PRODUCT BY REGION AND STATE

SOURCE: U.S. DEPARTMENT OF COMMERCE, BUREAU OF ECONOMIC ANALYSIS (BEA)

A state's gross domestic product (GDP) is the sum of the value added or GDP originating in all the industries in a state. For explanation of GDP, see the notes and definitions to Tables 1-1 through 1-15. In concept, the sum of state GDPs, including the District of Columbia, is identical with national GDP except for Federal military and civilian activity located overseas, which cannot be attributed to a particular state. But because of that definitional difference, the "sum of states" GDP will differ from the national values shown in Chapter 1. GDP by state is only calculated on an annual basis.

Definitions and notes on the data

The value of an industry's GDP is equal to the market value of its gross output (which consists of sales or receipts and other operating income, taxes on production and imports, and inventory change) minus the value of its intermediate inputs (which consist of energy, raw materials, semifinished goods, and services that are purchased from domestic industries or foreign sources). In concept, this definition is equal to the sum of labor and property-type income earned in that industry in the production of GDP, plus commodity taxes. Property-type income is the sum of corporate profits, proprietors' income, rental income of persons, net interest, capital consumption allowances, business transfer payments, and the current surplus of government enterprises less subsidies.

In practice, GDP by state, like GDP by industry, is measured using the incomes data rather than data on gross output and intermediate inputs, which are not available on a sufficiently detailed and timely basis.

Therefore, the *value* of *GDP by state* is defined as the sum of labor and property-type incomes originating in each of 63 industries in that state, plus commodity taxes, and plus the allocated value of the statistical discrepancy between national GDP and national gross national income. Starting with the 2004 comprehensive revision of the data from 1997 forward, the annual industry accounts and the GDP-by-state accounts allocate the statistical discrepancy across all private-sector industries, making the GDP by state estimates more similar to GDP estimates than they had been in the past. In the SIC-based measures for 1977 through 1997, the statistical discrepancy has not been allocated to industries and states.

The *quantity indexes* of state GDP are aggregates of the real output of each industry in the state, net of intermedi-ate inputs, based on chained constant-dollar estimates and expressed as index numbers. The quantity indexes are derived by applying national implicit deflators calculated for each industry group to the current-dollar GDP estimates for that industry group in each state, and then applying the chain-type index formula used in the national accounts to aggregate the industry groups to the state total.

To the extent that a state's output is produced and sold in national markets at relatively uniform output and input prices, or sold locally at national prices, GDP by state captures the differences across states that reflect the relative differences in the mix of goods and services produced by the states. However, real GDP by state does not capture the effects on real output of geographic differences in the output and input <u>prices</u> of goods and services produced and sold locally.

Estimates for the latest year (2011) are made using more limited source data and an abbreviated estimation methodology.

GDP by state is now calculated on a North American Industry Classification System (NAICS) basis back through 1997. Data for earlier years, beginning with 1977, were calculated on the Standard Industrial Classification (SIC) basis. According to BEA (in a "Cautionary note" on the Web site, dated June 7, 2007), "There is a discontinuity in the GDP by state time series at 1997, where the data change from SIC industry definitions to NAICS industry definitions. This discontinuity results from many sources, including differences in source data and different estimation methodologies. In addition, the NAICS-based GDP by state estimates are consistent with U.S. gross domestic product (GDP) while the SIC-based GDP by state estimates are consistent with U.S. gross domestic income (GDI). This data discontinuity may affect both the levels and the growth rates of the GDP by state estimates. Users of the GDP by state estimates are strongly cautioned against appending the two data series in an attempt to construct a single time series of GDP by state estimates for 1963 to 2006."

Business Statistics nevertheless provides SIC-based data (as published last year; no longer available on the BEA website) for 1977 to 1997 for those who require information about economic growth before 1997 by state.

Data availability and references

The estimates published here were released on June 5, 2012, and will be further described and explained in the July 2012 *Survey of Current Business*. In addition to the data reproduced here, this article includes per capita real GDP by state and the contributions of the major industry sectors to economic growth in each state. The June press release, this article, and all historical data can be found on the Bureau of Economic Analysis (BEA) Web site <http://www.bea.gov>.

TABLE 17-2
PERSONAL INCOME AND EMPLOYMENT BY REGION AND STATE

SOURCE: U.S. DEPARTMENT OF COMMERCE, BUREAU OF ECONOMIC ANALYSIS (BEA)

This table presents annual time-series data on personal income and employment for the United States as a whole, each individual state, the District of Columbia, and eight geographic regions for 1958 through 2011. In almost all respects, the data are consistent with the national personal income data as defined and presented in Chapters 1 and 4. BEA also publishes quarterly estimates of state personal income, which are not shown here.

The sum of state personal incomes for the United States shown in this table (which includes the District of Columbia) is somewhat smaller than U.S. personal income as shown in the national income and product accounts (NIPAs) in Chapters 1 and 4, due to slightly different definitions. The national total of the state estimates consists only of the income earned by persons who live in the United States and of foreign residents who work in the United States. The measure of personal income in the NIPAs is broader. It includes the earnings of federal civilian and military personnel stationed abroad (see below for a change in the definition of "stationed abroad") and of U.S. residents on foreign assignment for less than a year. It also includes the investment income received by federal retirement plans for federal workers stationed abroad. NIPA personal income includes all income earned by U.S. citizens living abroad for less than a year; state personal income excludes the portion earned while the individual lives abroad. Earnings of foreign residents are included in the NIPAs only if they live and work in the United States for a year or more; state personal income, on the other hand, includes income paid to foreign nationals working in the United States regardless of length of residency. There are also statistical differences that reflect different timing of the availability of source data.

In an article entitled "State Personal Income: Second Quarter of 2005 and Revised Estimates for 2002–2005:I" in the October 2005 *Survey of Current Business,* BEA announced "New Treatment of State Estimates of Military Compensation." This announcement says, "BEA's state estimates of military compensation are based on troop data by base and national estimates of average pay from the Department of Defense (DOD). For 2001–2004, the DOD estimates of troops stationed at U.S. bases do not show a large decrease for troops sent to Afghanistan and Iraq. Those estimates reflect the DOD's new method of reporting active duty military personnel for the Army and the Air Force. The DOD now reports active duty regular military personnel according to the troops' home bases and reserve personnel according to the state of the reservists' bases. However, for the Marines, DOD continues to use an approach that reduces domestic base personnel figures when troops are sent overseas. Since BEA's state estimates of military earnings reflect the geographic distribution of military personnel as reported by the DOD, the surge in military earnings due to the activation of reservists and the special pay associated with the war is recorded in the states from which the forces were deployed. This practice is consistent with the pay being received by family members at home and with news reports of strong retail sales at affected military bases.... Since the Persian Gulf war, the demographics of the armed forces have evolved, and BEA has changed its military residency definition accordingly. The current Army has a larger proportion of mature troops with families to support, in contrast to the typical young, single soldiers of the past."

Definitions

A state's *personal income* is the sum of earnings, dividends, interest, rental income, and current transfer receipts, net of government contributions for social insurance, of persons resident in that state—not persons working in that state. Its derivation from source data on earnings by place of work is shown in Table 17-2 and is further explained below.

Earnings by place of work consists of payments to persons working in the state of wage and salary disbursements, all supplements to wages and salaries (including employer contributions for government social insurance and all other benefits), and farm and nonfarm proprietors' income.

Contributions for government social insurance, which is subtracted from total earnings, includes both the employer and the employee contributions for persons working in the state. Personal income is defined as net of all contributions for government social insurance, though not net of other taxes on wages or other income.

Adjustment for residence. BEA adjusts earnings by place of work to a place-of-residence basis, to account for interstate and international commuting. The difference between earnings by place of residence and earnings by place of work is shown in the "Adjustment for residence" column. This adjustment is a net figure, equaling income received by state (or area) residents from employment outside the state minus income paid to persons residing outside the state but working in the state. The treatment of wages earned by U.S. residents from employment at international organizations and foreign embassies and consulates was changed in the 2009 comprehensive revision, shifting those wages from state wages and salaries to the adjustment for residence category.

The effect of interstate commuting can be seen in its most extreme form in the District of Columbia, with its adjustment for residence of negative $43 billion: this says that more than half of total earnings by people working there are paid to persons living outside D.C. Compare with Maryland, which has an adjustment for residence of positive $28 billion net, and Virginia with positive $12 billion, from the District of Columbia and other employment sources outside the state. There is also a large negative adjustment for New York, associated with positive adjustments for New Jersey and Connecticut.

Dividends, interest, and rent are aggregates for state residents of these categories as defined in U.S. personal income. The rental income component of personal income, which includes the imputed rent on owner-occupied homes, is net of capital consumption with capital consumption adjustment. The revised treatment of disaster losses in the NIPAs (see notes and definitions to Chapter 1, Tables 1-11 through 1-13) means that the estimates of state rental incomes are no longer offset by extreme events such as Hurricane Katrina, which had been the case in the pre-2009 estimates; now, only normal depreciation enters into rental income calculations.

Personal current transfer receipts are aggregates for state residents of such receipts as defined in U.S. personal income.

Population is the U.S. Census Bureau estimate for the <u>middle</u> of the year. Note that because Hurricane Katrina occurred in August 2005, the population decline in Louisiana caused by that event does not appear until the entry for 2006.

Total employment is the total number of jobs, full-time plus part-time; each job that any person holds is counted at full weight. The employment estimates are on a place-of-work basis. Both wage and salary employment and self-employment are included. The main source for the wage and salary employment estimates is the Bureau of Labor Statistics estimates from unemployment insurance data (the ES-202 data), which also provides benchmarks for the payroll employment measures (see Table 10-7 and its notes and definitions). Self-employment is estimated mainly from individual and partnership federal income tax returns. Therefore, this definition of employment is broader than the BLS "total nonfarm payroll employment."

This concept of employment also differs from the concept of employment in the Current Population Survey (CPS), which is derived from a monthly count of persons employed; any individual will appear only once in the CPS in a given month, no matter how many different jobs he or she might hold. (See the notes and definitions to Tables 10-1 through 10-5.) In addition, a self-employed individual who files more than one Schedule C income-tax filing will be counted more than once in the state figures. Finally, the state figures include members of the armed forces, who are not covered in the CPS. Due to these differences and other possible reporting inconsistencies, the BEA employment estimates are different from, and usually larger than, state employment estimates from the CPS.

The employment estimates correspond closely in coverage to the earnings estimates by place of work. However, the earnings estimates include the income of limited partnerships and of tax-exempt cooperatives, for which there are no corresponding employment estimates.

Per capita income is total income divided by the state's midyear population. In this year's edition of *Business Sta-*tistics, per capita incomes have been revised back to 2000, as a result of adjustment to the intercensal years to make them consistent with the 2010 Census.

Per capita incomes are averages—"means" in the technical language of statistics—subject to the qualifications discussed in the article at the beginning of this volume, under the "Whose Standard of Living?" heading. They provide useful measures of the fiscal capacity and economic strength of the state as a whole, but may not reflect the income of typical state residents. For recent data on <u>median</u> household income by state, which give a better idea of the cash income received by a typical resident of the state, see Table 3-6 in Chapter 3.

The states and the District of Columbia are divided into regions by BEA as follows:

- **New England:** Connecticut, Maine, Massachusetts, New Hampshire, Rhode Island, and Vermont

- **Mideast:** Delaware, District of Columbia, Maryland, New Jersey, New York, and Pennsylvania

- **Great Lakes:** Illinois, Indiana, Michigan, Ohio, and Wisconsin

- **Plains:** Iowa, Kansas, Minnesota, Missouri, Nebraska, North Dakota, and South Dakota

- **Southeast:** Alabama, Arkansas, Florida, Georgia, Kentucky, Louisiana, Mississippi, North Carolina, South Carolina, Tennessee, Virginia, and West Virginia

- **Southwest:** Arizona, New Mexico, Oklahoma, and Texas

- **Rocky Mountain:** Colorado, Idaho, Montana, Utah, and Wyoming

- **Far West:** Alaska, California, Hawaii, Nevada, Oregon, and Washington

These BEA regional groupings differ from the region and division definitions used by the Census Bureau.

Data availability and references

The 2009 comprehensive revision of state personal incomes is presented and described in the November 2009 *Survey of Current Business*, which can be found in the publications section of the general BEA web site. Detailed data on the revised basis back to 1929 are available at <http://www.bea.gov/bea/regional/spi>. The estimates for 2011 and revisions of the data for 2008 through 2010 were released March 28, 2012, and are presented and discussed in "Regional Quarterly Report," *Survey of Current Business,* April 2012, pp. 58-64, available on the general BEA website.

INDEX